Why We Love Australia

By Charles Rawlings-Way & Meg Worby, Lonely Planet Writers

We've both been living in this great southern land for 30-something years, and there are still places here that we haven't explored. This isn't to say that we've been sitting at home eating popcorn and watching David Attenborough – we're travel writers! It's just that Australia is so damn big. Even if we spent the next 30-something years on an endless round-Australia road trip, there'd still be surprises out there. And that, for a couple of restless road-addicts, is a very comforting reality.

For more about our writers, see page 1112

Above: Twelve Apostles (p543)

Australia

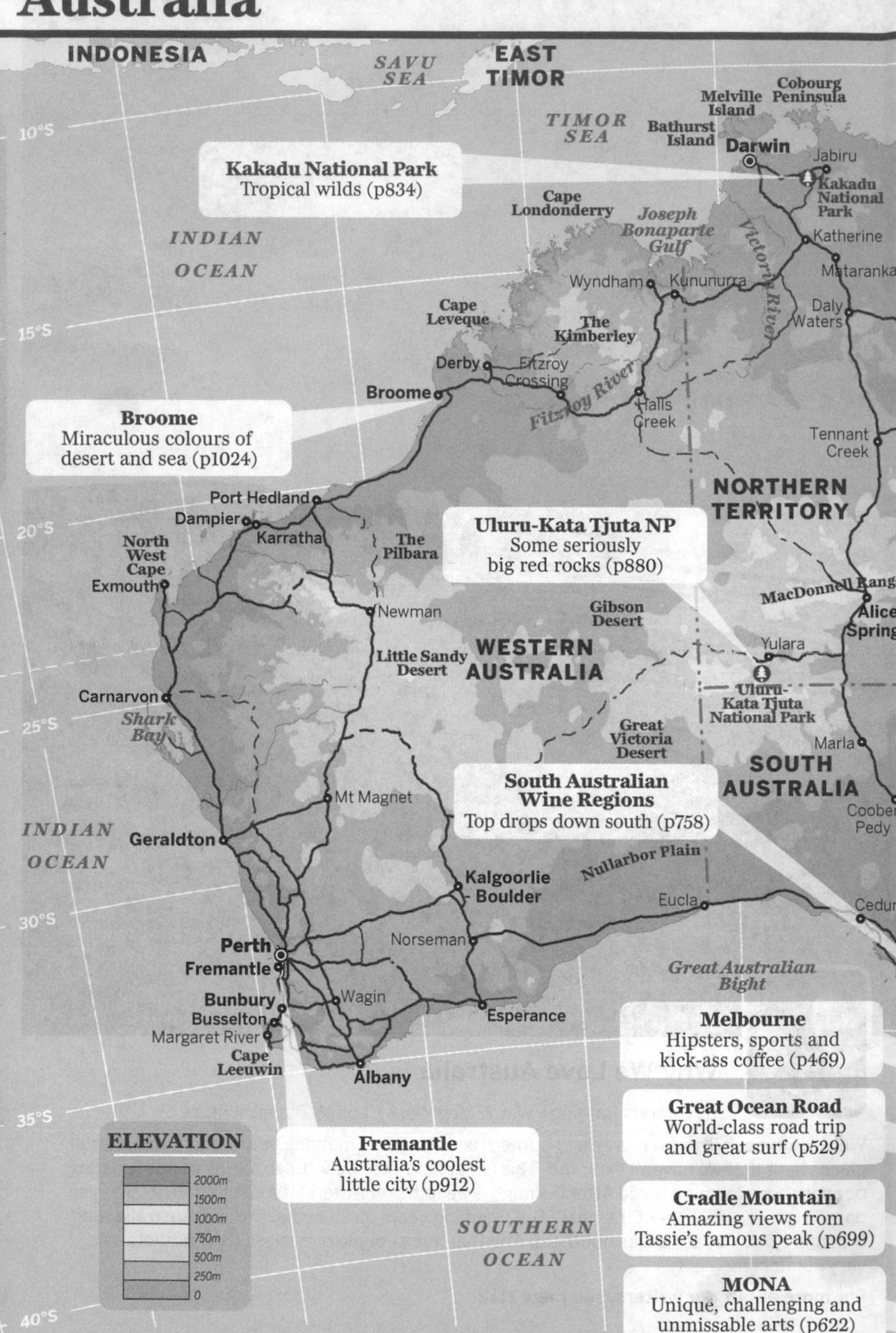

INDONESIA
SAVU SEA
EAST TIMOR
TIMOR SEA
Melville Island
Cobourg Peninsula
Bathurst Island
Darwin
Jabiru
Kakadu National Park
Kakadu National Park
Tropical wilds (p834)
Cape Londonderry
Joseph Bonaparte Gulf
Victoria River
Katherine
Mataranka
INDIAN OCEAN
Wyndham
Kununurra
Daly Waters
Cape Leveque
The Kimberley
Derby
Fitzroy Crossing
Fitzroy River
Broome
Halls Creek
Broome
Miraculous colours of desert and sea (p1024)
Tennant Creek
Port Hedland
Dampier
Karratha
The Pilbara
NORTHERN TERRITORY
Uluru-Kata Tjuta NP
Some seriously big red rocks (p880)
North West Cape
Exmouth
Newman
Gibson Desert
MacDonnell Ranges
Alice Springs
WESTERN AUSTRALIA
Little Sandy Desert
Yulara
Uluru-Kata Tjuta National Park
Carnarvon
Shark Bay
Great Victoria Desert
Marla
SOUTH AUSTRALIA
South Australian Wine Regions
Top drops down south (p758)
Mt Magnet
Coober Pedy
INDIAN OCEAN
Geraldton
Nullarbor Plain
Kalgoorlie-Boulder
Eucla
Ceduna
Norseman
Perth
Fremantle
Great Australian Bight
Bunbury
Wagin
Busselton
Esperance
Margaret River
Cape Leeuwin
Albany
Melbourne
Hipsters, sports and kick-ass coffee (p469)
Great Ocean Road
World-class road trip and great surf (p529)
ELEVATION
2000m
1500m
1000m
750m
500m
250m
0
Fremantle
Australia's coolest little city (p912)
Cradle Mountain
Amazing views from Tassie's famous peak (p699)
SOUTHERN OCEAN
MONA
Unique, challenging and unmissable arts (p622)
10°S
15°S
20°S
25°S
30°S
35°S
40°S
110°E
115°E
120°E
125°E
130°E
135°E

Australia

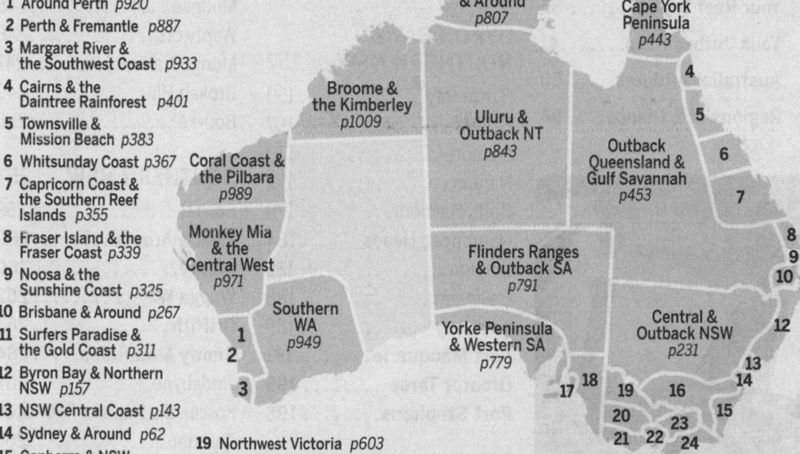

THIS EDITION WRITTEN AND RESEARCHED BY

Charles Rawlings-Way, Meg Worby

Kate Armstrong, Brett Atkinson, Carolyn Bain, Celeste Brash, Peter Dragicevich, Anthony Ham, Paul Harding, Alan Murphy, Miriam Raphael, Benedict Walker, Steve Waters

PLAN YOUR TRIP

SYDNEY P66

KIMBERLEY COOLE / GETTY IMAGES ©

WILDLIFE P1056

JOHN WHITE PHOTOS / GETTY IMAGES ©

ON THE ROAD

Contents

ON THE ROAD

Contents

Welcome to Australia

Is the grass always greener on the other side of the fence? Peek over the pickets and find out. This vast country is affluent, multicultural and laced with natural splendour.

Hip Cities

Most Australians live along the coast, and most of these folks live in cities – 89% of Australians, in fact. It follows that cities here are a lot of fun. Sydney is a glamorous collusion of beaches, boutiques and bars. Melbourne is all arts, alleyways and Aussie Rules football. Brisbane is a subtropical town on the way up; Adelaide has festive grace and pubby poise. Boomtown Perth breathes west coast optimism; Canberra transcends political agendas. While the tropical northern frontier town of Darwin, and the chilly southern sandstone city of Hobart, couldn't be more different.

The Wide Open Road

There's a heckuva lot of tarmac across this wide brown land. From Margaret River to Cooktown, Jabiru to Dover, the best way to appreciate Australia is to hit the road. Car hire is relatively affordable, paved road conditions are generally good, and beyond the big cities traffic fades away. If you're driving a campervan, you'll find well-appointed caravan parks in most sizable towns. If you're feeling adventurous, hire a 4WD and go off-road: Australia's national parks and secluded corners are custom-made for camping trips down the dirt road.

Food & Drink

Australia plates up a multicultural fusion of European techniques and fresh Pacific-rim ingredients – aka 'Mod Oz' (Modern Australian). Seafood plays a starring role – from succulent Moreton Bay bugs to delicate King George whiting. Of course, beer in hand, you'll still find beef, lamb and chicken at Aussie barbecues. Don't drink beer? Australian wines are world-beaters: punchy Barossa Valley shiraz, Hunter Valley semillon and cool-climate Tasmanian sauvignon blanc. Tasmania produces outstanding whisky too. Need a caffeine hit? You'll find cafes everywhere, coffee machines in petrol stations, and baristas in downtown coffee carts.

Arts & Culture

No matter which city you're wheeling into, you'll never go wanting for an offbeat theatre production, a rockin' live band, lofty art-gallery opening, movie launch or music festival mosh. This was once a country where 'cultural cringe' held sway – the notion that anything locally produced simply wasn't up to scratch. But these days the tables have turned. Aboriginal arts – particularly painting and dance – seem immune to such fluctuations and remain timelessly captivating.

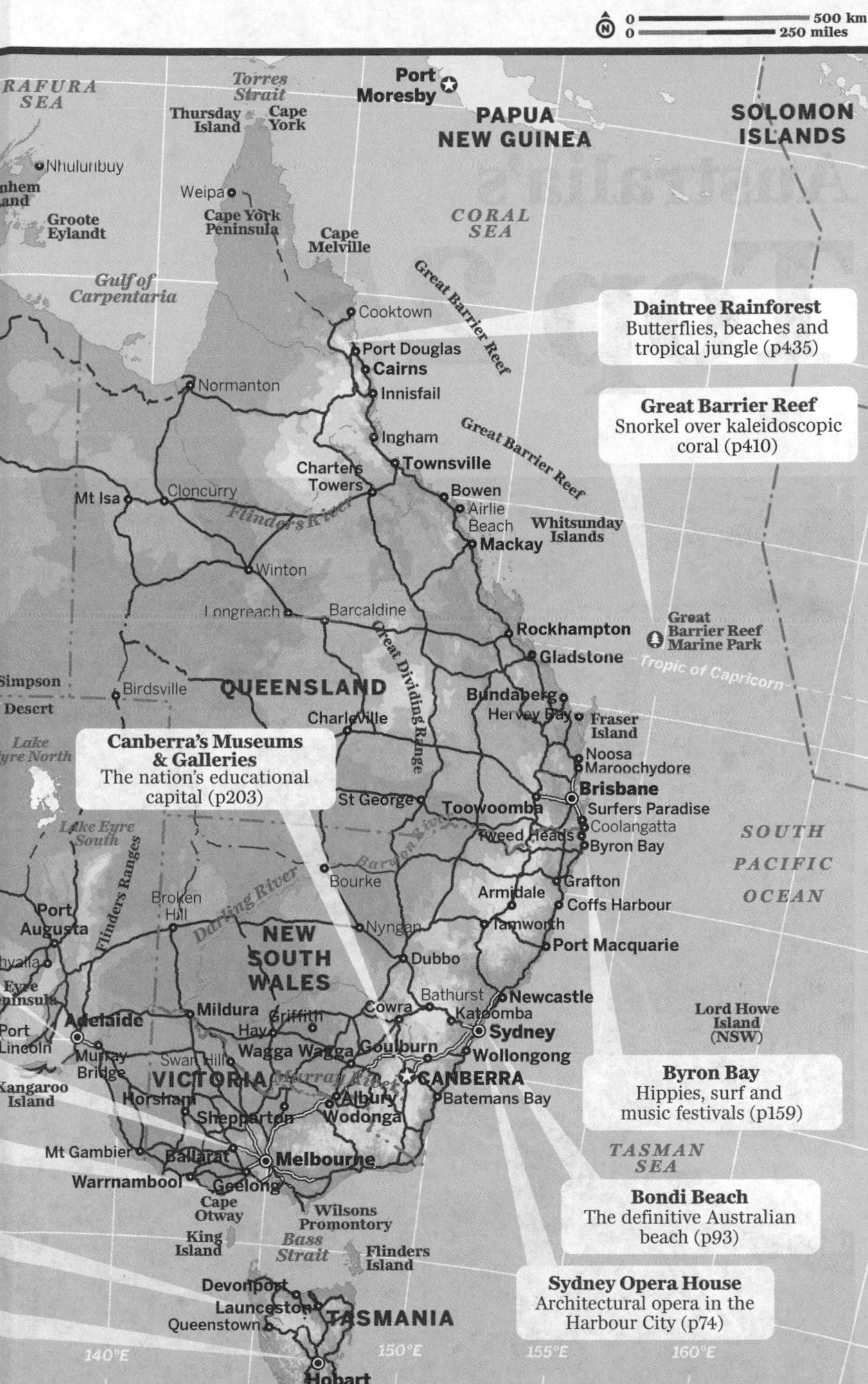

0 500 km
0 250 miles
Torres Strait
Port Moresby
ARAFURA SEA
Thursday Island
Cape York
PAPUA NEW GUINEA
SOLOMON ISLANDS
Nhulunbuy
Arnhem Land
Weipa
Groote Eylandt
Cape York Peninsula
CORAL SEA
Cape Melville
Gulf of Carpentaria
Great Barrier Reef
Cooktown
Daintree Rainforest
Butterflies, beaches and tropical jungle (p435)
Port Douglas
Cairns
Normanton
Innisfail
Great Barrier Reef
Snorkel over kaleidoscopic coral (p410)
Ingham
Great Barrier Reef
Townsville
Charters Towers
Mt Isa
Cloncurry
Bowen
Airlie Beach
Flinders River
Whitsunday Islands
Mackay
Winton
Longreach
Barcaldine
Rockhampton
Great Barrier Reef Marine Park
Great Dividing Range
Gladstone
Tropic of Capricorn
Simpson Desert
Birdsville
QUEENSLAND
Bundaberg
Hervey Bay
Fraser Island
Charleville
Lake Eyre North
Canberra's Museums & Galleries
The nation's educational capital (p203)
Noosa
Maroochydore
Brisbane
St George
Toowoomba
Surfers Paradise
Coolangatta
Lake Eyre South
Tweed Heads
Byron Bay
SOUTH PACIFIC OCEAN
Barwon River
Bourke
Grafton
Flinders Ranges
Darling River
Armidale
Coffs Harbour
Broken Hill
Port Augusta
Nyngan
Tamworth
NEW SOUTH WALES
Port Macquarie
Whyalla
Dubbo
Eyre Peninsula
Bathurst
Newcastle
Mildura
Cowra
Katoomba
Lord Howe Island (NSW)
Adelaide
Griffith
Sydney
Port Lincoln
Hay
Murray Bridge
Swan Hill
Wagga Wagga
Goulburn
Wollongong
VICTORIA
Murray River
CANBERRA
Byron Bay
Hippies, surf and music festivals (p159)
Kangaroo Island
Horsham
Albury
Batemans Bay
Wodonga
Shepparton
Mt Gambier
Ballarat
Melbourne
TASMAN SEA
Warrnambool
Geelong
Bondi Beach
The definitive Australian beach (p93)
Cape Otway
Wilsons Promontory
King Island
Bass Strait
Flinders Island
Sydney Opera House
Architectural opera in the Harbour City (p74)
Devonport
Launceston
TASMANIA
Queenstown
140°E
150°E
155°E
160°E
Hobart

Australia's Top 25

1

Native Wildlife

1 Furry, cuddly, or ferocious – you can find all this and more on a wildlife-spotting (p1060) journey around Australia. Head to Hervey Bay for whale watching; see nesting sea turtles (and later, hatchlings) on Queensland beaches; and adorable little penguins and fur seals on Victoria's Phillip Island. Queensland, Western Australia and the Northern Territory shelter dinosaur-like crocodiles, and everywhere Australia's birds make themselves known (you can't miss the cackle of the kookaburra). In between, you'll discover a panoply of extraordinary animals found nowhere else on earth: koalas, kangaroos, quokkas, wombats and platypuses.

Below: Blue-winged kookaburra, Queensland

Great Barrier Reef

2 Unesco World Heritage–listed? Check. Oprah Winfrey–endorsed? Check. The Great Barrier Reef (p410) is as fragile as it is beautiful. Stretching more than 2000km along the Queensland coastline, it's a complex ecosystem populated with dazzling coral, languid sea turtles, gliding rays, timid reef sharks and tropical fish of every colour and size. Whether you dive on it, snorkel over it or explore it via scenic flight or glass-bottomed boat, this vivid undersea kingdom and its coral-fringed islands is unforgettable.

MARTIN WILLIS / GETTY IMAGES ©

2

JEFF HUNTER / GETTY IMAGES ©

Uluru-Kata Tjuta National Park

3 No matter how many times you've seen it on postcards, nothing prepares you for the burnished grandeur of Uluru as it first appears on the outback horizon. With its desert location, deep cultural significance and dazzling beauty, Uluru is well worth the many hundreds of kilometres it takes to get there. But Uluru-Kata Tjuta National Park (p880) offers even more – along with the equally captivating Kata Tjuta (the Olgas), there are mystical walks, sublime sunsets and ancient cultures to encounter.

Sydney Opera House

4 The instantly recognisable Sydney Opera House (p74) on Sydney Harbour is Australia's headline act. An exercise in architectural lyricism like no other, Jørn Utzon's building on Bennelong Point more than holds its own amid the visual feast of the harbour's attention-grabbing bridge, shimmering blue waters and jaunty green ferries. Everyone can experience the magic on offer here – a stunningly sited waterside bar, acclaimed French restaurant, guided tours and star-studded performance schedule make sure of that.

3

4

WALTER BIBIKOW / GETTY IMAGES ©

MARK MAWSON / GETTY IMAGES ©

Daintree Rainforest

5 Lush rainforest replete with fan palms, prehistoric-looking ferns and twisted mangroves head towards a brilliant white-sand coastline in the World Heritage–listed Daintree (p435) rainforest. Upon entering the forest, you'll be greeted by birdsong, frog croaking and the buzz of insects. Explore the area via wildlife-spotting night tours, mountain treks, canopy walks, self-guided trails, 4WD trips, horse riding, kayaking, croc-spotting cruises, tropical-fruit orchard tours and tastings...Whew! If you're lucky, you might even spot a cassowary.

Above: Aerial walkway, Daintree Discovery Centre (p435)

Fremantle

6 Fremantle – Western Australia's major port 22km south of Perth – is a raffish, artsy, student-filled harbour town, defined by a classic cache of Victorian architecture. It's an isolated place – closer to Singapore than Sydney. But like any port, the world washes in on the tide and washes out again, leaving the locals buzzing with global zeitgeist. Funky Fremantle (p912) has sea-salty soul to burn: expect craft-beer breweries, live-music rooms, hipster bars, late-night coffee joints, Indian Ocean seafood shacks, buskers, beaches, markets and students on the run from the books.

Bondi Beach

7 Definitively Sydney and irresistibly hip, Bondi (p93) is one of the world's great beaches. Surfers, models, skate punks and backpackers surf a hedonistic wave through the pubs, bars and restaurants along Campbell Pde, but the beach is a timeless constant. It's the closest ocean beach to the city, has consistently good (though crowded) waves and is great for a rough 'n' tumble swim. Don't miss a jaunt along the Bondi to Coogee Clifftop Walk, kicking off at the southern end of the beach.

TRAVJES23 / GETTY IMAGES ©

Gourmet Food & Wine

8 Right across Australia you'll find gourmet offerings for all budgets: oysters and seafood in Sydney (p83); wines, whisky and cheeses in Tasmania; coffee and fabulous Greek and Italian in Melbourne; punchy red wines and riesling in South Australia; marron in Western Australia (WA), and native meats and bush tucker in the Northern Territory. The nation's many wine regions have spawned a culture of fine cuisine using regional ingredients – if you're touring the cellar doors, you'll never be far from a romantic lunch.

The Whitsundays

9 You can hop around a whole stack of tropical islands in this seafaring life and never find anywhere with the sheer beauty of the Whitsundays (p377). Travellers of all monetary persuasions launch yachts from party town Airlie Beach and drift between these lush green isles in a slow search for paradise (you'll probably find it in more than one place). Don't miss Whitehaven Beach – one of Australia's best. Wish you were here?

Top Right: Airlie Beach (p372)

Hobart & MONA

10 Occupying an improbable riverside location a ferry ride from Hobart's harbourfront, the Museum of Old & New Art – aka MONA (p622) – is an innovative, world-class institution. Described by its owner, Hobart philanthropist David Walsh, as a 'subversive adult Disneyland', three levels of astounding underground galleries showcase more than 400 challenging and controversial artworks. You might not like everything you see, but a visit here is a sure-fire conversation starter and one of Australia's unique arts experiences.

MONA

Byron Bay

11 Up there with kangaroos and Akubra hats, big-hearted Byron Bay (p159; just Byron to its mates) is one of the enduring icons of Australian culture. Families on school holidays, surfers and sun-seekers from across the globe gather by the foreshore at sunset, drawn to this spot on the world map by fabulous restaurants, a chilled pace of life and an astonishing range of activities on offer. But mostly they're here because this is one of the most beautiful stretches of coast in the country.

Melbourne

12 Why the queue? Oh, that's just the line to get into the latest hot 'no bookings' restaurant (p469). The next best restaurant/chef/cafe/barista/food truck may be the talk of the town, but there are things locals would never change: the leafy parks and gardens in the inner-city 'burbs; the crowded trams that whisk folk to sea-breezy southern St Kilda; and the allegiances that living in such a sports-mad city brings. The city's world-renowned street-art scene expresses Melbourne's fears, frustrations and joys. Bottom: Centre Place (p475), Melbourne

11

12

Broome & Northwest WA

13 Harsh, remote and beautiful, Australia's final frontier boasts three World Heritage sites: Shark Bay, Ningaloo and Purnululu. Distances here are immense and towns scarce. Broome (p1024) is one of the world's great travellers' crossroads, where every evening a searing crimson sun slips into the turquoise Indian Ocean. The far-flung Dampier Peninsula is a top experience in its own right, not only for the drive here, but for extraordinary cliffs, red soils, seafood, Indigenous cultural experiences, and luxury camping. Top: Dampier Peninsula (p1032)

Great Ocean Road

14 The Twelve Apostles – craggy rock formations jutting out of wild waters – are one of Victoria's most vivid sights, but it's the 'getting there' road trip that doubles their impact. Drive slowly along roads that curl beside spectacular Bass Strait beaches, then whip inland through rainforest studded with small towns. The secrets of the Great Ocean Road (p530) don't stop there; further along is maritime treasure Port Fairy and hidden Cape Bridgewater. For the ultimate in slow travel, walk the Great Ocean Walk from Apollo Bay to the Apostles. Bottom: The Twelve Apostles (p543)

Canberra's Museums & Galleries

15 Though Canberra is only a century old, Australia's purpose-built capital has always been preoccupied with history. The drawcard here is a portfolio of museums and galleries focused on interpreting the national narrative. Institutions such as the National Gallery of Australia (p203), National Museum of Australia, National Portrait Gallery and Australian War Memorial offer visitors a fascinating insight into the country's history and culture – both ancient and modern.

Top: National Museum of Australia (p205), Canberra

Margaret River Region

16 The decadent joy of drifting from winery to winery along eucalypt-shaded country roads is just one of the delights of Western Australia's southwest. There are caves to explore, historic towns to visit and spring wild flowers to ogle. Surfers bob around in the world-class breaks near Margaret River (p942), but it's not unusual to find yourself on a white-sand beach where the only footprints are your own. In late winter and early spring, spot whales migrating along the 'Hump-back Highway'.

Cradle Mountain

17 A precipitous comb of rock carved out by millenniums of ice and wind, crescent-shaped Cradle Mountain (p699) is Tasmania's most recognisable – and spectacular – mountain peak. It's an all-day walk (and boulder scramble) to the summit and back, for unbelievable panoramas over Tasmania's alpine heart. Or you can stand in awe below and fill your camera with the perfect views across Dove Lake to the mountain. If the peak has disappeared in clouds or snow, warm yourself by the fire in one of the nearby lodges...and come back tomorrow.

The Outback & Broken Hill

18 Whether you're belting along South Australia's Oodnadatta Track (p805) or on the Birdsville Track in southwest Queensland, you'll know you're not just visiting the outback, you've become part of it. Out here, the sky is bluer and the dust redder than anywhere else. Days are measured in hundreds of kilometres, spinifex mounds and tyre blowouts. Nights are spent in the five-zillion-star hotel, waiting for one to fall... If time is not on your side, a road trip to the outback mining town of Broken Hill may be as far from the coast as you get.

17

18

DARRELL GULIN / GETTY IMAGES ©

BENGOODE / GETTY IMAGES ©

Darwin & Kakadu National Park

19 Levelled by WWII bombs and Cyclone Tracy, Darwin (p812) knows a thing or two about reinvention. This frontier city has emerged from the tropical steam to become a multicultural, hedonistic hotspot: the launch pad for trips into some of Australia's most remarkable wilderness. Two hours southeast, Kakadu National Park is the place to see Indigenous rock art under jagged escarpments and idyllic waterholes at the base of plummeting waterfalls. Raucous bird life and saltwater crocodiles are guaranteed highlights.

Above: Maguk (Barramundi Gorge; p841)

Fraser Island

20 The world's largest patch of sand, Fraser Island (p349) is home to dingos, shipwrecks and all manner of bird life. Four-wheel drive vehicles (regular cars aren't allowed) fan out around epic camp spots and long white beaches. The wild coastline curbs any thoughts of doing much more than wandering between pristine creeks and freshwater lakes. Beach camping under the stars will bring you back to nature. A short ferry trip away is Hervey Bay, where humpback whales shoot along the coast in winter and spring.

Top right: Maheno shipwreck (p351)

South Australian Wine Regions

21 Adelaide is drunk on the success of its three world-famous wine regions, all within two hours' (designated) drive: the Barossa Valley (p758) to the north, with its gutsy reds, old vines and German know-how; McLaren Vale to the south, a Mediterranean palette of sea, vines and shiraz; and the Clare Valley, known for riesling and wobbly bike rides (in that order). Better-kept secrets are the cool-climate stunners from the Adelaide Hills and the country cabernet sauvignon from the Coonawarra.

Bottom right: Vineyard, Barossa Valley

AUSCAPE / UIG / GETTY IMAGES ©

Ningaloo Marine Park

22 Swim beside 'gentle giant' whale sharks, snorkel among pristine coral, surf off seldom-visited reefs and dive at one of the world's premier locations at this World Heritage–listed marine park, which sits off the North West Cape on the Coral Coast in Western Australia. Rivalling the Great Barrier Reef for beauty, Ningaloo (p999) has much more accessible wonders: shallow lagoons are entered straight from the beach for excellent snorkelling. Development is very low-key, so be prepared to camp, or take day trips from Exmouth or Coral Bay.

Above: Whale shark

Indigenous Art

23 Immersed in 'The Dreaming' – a vast unchanging network of life tracing back to spiritual ancestors – Indigenous art is a conduit between past and present, supernatural and earthly, people and land. Central Australian dot paintings (p1050) are exquisite, as are Tiwi Island carvings and fabrics, Arnhem Land bark paintings, Torres Strait Islander prints and carvings, and works from Aboriginal-owned art cooperatives. You can make an informed purchase at commercial galleries or (even better) direct from Aboriginal communities.

Above right: Injalak Arts tour guide Garry Djorlom, Injalak Hill (p841)

The Gold Coast

24 Brash, hedonistic, over-hyped... Queensland's Gold Coast (p311) is all of these things, but if you're looking for a party, bring it on! Beyond the fray is the beach – an improbably gorgeous coastline of clean sand, warm water and peeling surf breaks. The bronzed gods of the surf, Australia's surf life-savers, patrol the sand and pit their skills against one another in surf carnivals – gruelling events involving ocean swimming, beach sprints and surf boat racing. Also here are Australia's biggest theme parks – rollercoaster nirvana!

Sporting Obsessions

25 Australian Rules football is a religion here: the pinnacle of the Australian Football League (AFL) season is the Grand Final (p492) in Melbourne. Melbourne also hosts the Australian Open tennis, the Australian Formula One Grand Prix, the Melbourne Cup horse race, and the annual Boxing Day test cricket match. In Queensland and New South Wales, catch a National Rugby League (NRL) match during winter. Watching big-screen sport in a pub is an essential experience – grab a beer and yell along with the locals.

Right: Melbourne Cricket Ground (p513)

RICHARD I'ANSON / GETTY IMAGES ©

Need to Know

For more information, see Survival Guide (p1069)

Currency
Australian dollar ($)

Language
English

Visas
All visitors to Australia need a visa, except New Zealanders. Apply online for an ETA or eVisitor visa, each allowing a three-month stay: www.immi.gov.au.

Money
ATMs widely available in cities and larger towns. Credit cards accepted for hotels, restaurants, transport and activity bookings.

Mobile Phones
European phones will work on Australia's network, but most American and Japanese phones will not. Use global roaming or a local SIM card and pre-paid account.

Time
Australia has three main time zones: Australian Eastern, Central and Western Standard Time. Sydney is on AEST, which is GMT/UCT + 10 hours.

When to Go

High Season (Dec–Feb)

➡ Summertime: local holidays, busy beaches and cricket.

➡ Prices rise 25% for big-city accommodation.

➡ Outdoor rock concerts, film screenings and food festivals abound.

Shoulder Season (Mar–May & Sep–Nov)

➡ Warm sun, clear skies, shorter queues.

➡ Easter (late March or early April) is busy with Aussie families on the loose.

➡ Autumn leaves are atmospheric in Victoria, Tasmania and South Australia.

Low Season (Jun–Aug)

➡ Cool rainy days down south; mild days and sunny skies up north.

➡ Low tourist numbers; attractions keep slightly shorter hours.

➡ Head for the desert, the tropical north or the snow.

Useful Websites

Lonely Planet (www.lonelyplanet.com/australia) Destination information, hotel bookings, traveller forum and more.

Tourism Australia (www.australia.com) Main government tourism site with visitor info.

Bureau of Meteorology (www.bom.gov.au) Nationwide weather forecasts.

The Australian (www.theaustralian.com.au) National broadsheet newspaper online.

Parks Australia (www.environment.gov.au/parks) Info on national parks and reserves.

Coastalwatch (www.coastalwatch.com) Surf reports and surf-cams.

Important Numbers

Regular Australian phone numbers have a two-digit area code followed by an eight-digit number. Drop the initial 0 if calling from abroad.

Country code	☎61
International access code	☎0011
Emergency (ambulance, fire, police)	☎000

Exchange Rates

Canada	C$1	$1.02
China	Y1	$0.21
Euro	€1	$1.42
Japan	¥100	$1.09
New Zealand	NZ$1	$0.94
South Korea	W100	$0.09
UK	UK£1	$1.90
US	US$1	$1.26

For current exchange rates see www.xe.com

Daily Costs

Budget: Less than $100

- Hostel dorm bed: $25–35 a night
- Double room in a hostel: from $80
- Simple pizza or pasta meal: $10–15
- Short bus or tram ride: $4

Midrange: $100–280

- Double room in a motel, B&B or hotel: $100–200
- Breakfast or lunch in a cafe: $20–40
- Short taxi ride: $25
- Car hire per day: from $35

Top End: More than $280

- Double room in a top-end hotel: from $200
- Three-course meal in a classy restaurant: $80
- Nightclub cover charge: $10–20
- Domestic flight Sydney to Melbourne: from $100

Opening Hours

Opening hours vary from state to state, but use the following as a general guide.

Banks 9.30am to 4pm Monday to Thursday; until 5pm Friday

Bars 4pm until late

Cafes 7am to 5pm

Pubs 11am to midnight

Restaurants noon to 2.30pm and 6pm to 9pm

Shops 9am to 5pm Monday to Friday, until noon or 5pm Saturday

Supermarkets 7am to 8pm; some 24 hours.

Arriving in Australia

Sydney Airport (p1086) AirportLink trains run to the city centre every 10 minutes from around 5am to 1am (20 minutes). Pre-booked shuttle buses service city hotels. A taxi into the city costs $40 to $50 (30 minutes).

Melbourne Airport (p1086) SkyBus services (24-hour) run to the city (20 minutes), leaving every 10 to 30 minutes. A taxi into the city costs around $40 (25 minutes).

Brisbane Airport (p1086) Airtrain trains run into the city centre (20 minutes) every 15 to 30 minutes from 5am (6am weekends) to 10pm. Pre-booked shuttle buses service city hotels. A taxi into the city costs $35 to $45 (25 minutes).

Getting Around

Australia is the sixth-largest country in the world: how you get from A to B requires some thought.

Car Travel at your own tempo, explore remote areas and visit regions with no public transport. Hire cars in major towns; drive on the left.

Plane Fast-track your holiday with affordable, frequent, fast flights between major centres. Carbon offset your flights if you're feeling guilty.

Bus Reliable, frequent long-haul services around the country. Not always cheaper than flying.

Train Slow, expensive and infrequent…but the scenery is great! Opt for a sleeper carriage rather than an 'overnighter' seat.

For much more on **getting around**, see p1086.

What's New

Darling Harbour & Barangaroo, Sydney

Darling Harbour is re-imagining itself: out go the '80s edifices, in come a giant new convention centre and new Barangaroo complex of offices, parks and entertainment venues.

Australian Age of Dinosaurs Museum, Winton

This new museum and research facility has a fab reception centre and plans for a new natural history section. The not-for-profit research centre organises dinosaur digs every May and June. (p458)

Spirit of Queensland, Queensland

This new high-speed train makes the 1681km Brisbane-to-Cairns dash in a pinch under 25 hours. Carriages feature airline-style seats with entertainment consoles and 'Rail Bed' lie-flat seating.

Mawson's Huts Replica Museum, Hobart

What's that little timber shack on the Hobart waterfront? With super-knowledgeable staff, this new museum is an authentic reproduction of Sir Douglas Mawson's 1911 Antarctic base. (p621)

Adelaide Oval, Adelaide

The Adelaide Oval is looking good after a $610-million upgrade. The grassy hill, fig trees and old scoreboard have survived – it's still one of the world's prettiest cricket grounds. (p712)

Trevillian Quay, Canberra

In Kingston on the southern shores of Lake Burley Griffin, Trevillian Quay is a new canal-side strip of cafes, restaurants and bars. (p211)

MANY6160, Fremantle

A boho mash-up of local artists' studios, pop-up galleries and shops occupying the spacious ground floor of the former Myer department store. (p919)

Godinymayin Yijard Rivers Arts & Culture Centre, Katherine

Katherine's new social and cultural hub is this terrific new arts centre. The jaunty building has fast become the town's architectural icon. (p846)

Kayaking in Ningaloo Marine Park, WA

Ningaloo Reef has a new kayak trail, with moorings at selected snorkelling sites. An overnight trail is being developed, with camping on remote GPS-located beaches.

Broken Hill, NSW

In 2015 Broken Hill became the first entire Australian city or town to be included on the National Heritage List of 102 'exceptional' sites that contribute to the national identity. (p249)

Drinking in Double Bay, Sydney

Sydney's tough new liquor licensing laws have pushed late-night booze hounds out of Kings Cross and into formerly staid Double Bay. New bars and restaurants are shaking up the scene.

For more recommendations and reviews, see lonelyplanet.com/australia

If You Like...

Beaches

Bondi Beach An essential Sydney experience: carve up the surf or just laze around and people-watch. (p93)

Wineglass Bay It's worth the scramble up and over the saddle to visit this gorgeous goblet of Tasmanian sand. (p660)

Whitehaven Beach The jewel of the Whitsundays in Queensland, with powdery white sand and crystal-clear waters. (p381)

Bells Beach Australia's best-known surf beach is near Torquay on Victoria's Great Ocean Road. (p538)

Hellfire Bay Talcum powder sand in the middle of Western Australia's Cape Le Grand National Park, which is precisely in the middle of nowhere. (p964)

Carrickalinga Beach Southeast of Adelaide near the McLaren Vale Wine Region: good fishing, aquamarine swimming and very few people. (p740)

Avalon The most photogenic of Sydney's gorgeous Northern Beaches. (p99)

Crowdy Head Untrammelled golden-sand New South Wales (NSW) beaches set against a backdrop of rugged rock formations. (p196)

Islands

Kangaroo Island A great spot in South Australia (SA) for wildlife-watching and super-fresh seafood. (p745)

Bruny Island A windswept, sparsely populated retreat south of Hobart, with magical coastal scenery. (p639)

Fraser Island The world's largest sand island has giant dunes, freshwater lakes and abundant wildlife. (p349)

The Whitsundays Check yourself into a resort or go sailing around this pristine Queensland archipelago. (p377)

North Stradbroke Island Brisbane's holiday playground, with surf beaches and passing whales. (p301)

Rottnest Island A ferry ride from Fremantle in Western Australia (WA) is this atmospheric atoll with a chequered history. (p922)

Lizard Island A real get-away-from-it-all isle in Far North Queensland: splash out on a resort or rough it with some camping. (p440)

Lady Elliot Island Ringed by the Great Barrier Reef, this remote Queensland island is the place to play castaway. (p359)

Wilderness

Blue Mountains National Park The closest true wilderness to Sydney: spectacular canyons, cliffs and dense eucalypt forests. (p136)

Flinders Ranges National Park Treading a line between desolation and beauty, the ancient outcrops of SA's Ikara (Wilpena Pound) are mesmerising. (p798)

Nitmiluk (Katherine Gorge) National Park Tackle the epic five-day Jatbula Trail in this rugged Northern Territory (NT) wilderness, with plenty of cooling swim-spots on the way. (p849)

Cradle Mountain-Lake St Clair National Park Immerse yourself in Tasmania's sometimes forbidding, ever-photogenic landscape. (p699)

The Kimberley In northern WA you'll find pounding waterfalls, spectacular gorges, barren peaks and an empty coastline. (p1012)

Daintree Rainforest Explore Far North Queensland's ancient forest with abundant activities and few tourists. (p435)

Sturt National Park Rich in wildlife and deliciously remote, NSW's far northwest is an accessible slice of the outback. (p255)

Wine Regions

Barossa Valley Home to Australia's greatest reds, with 80-plus cellar doors around historic German-settled villages, in SA. (p758)

McLaren Vale An hour south of Adelaide, this is Mediterranean-feeling shiraz heaven. (p737)

Tamar Valley Tasmania's key cool-climate wine area, a short hop from Launceston. (p673)

Clare Valley SA's Clare Valley makes riesling that rocks – enough said. (p763)

Yarra Valley An hour from Melbourne, the Yarra Valley is the place for syrupy whites and complex cabernets. (p522)

Hunter Valley Dating back to the 1820s, the Hunter Valley is Australia's oldest wine region – super semillon. (p151)

Granite Belt Queensland's high-altitude wine region produces some surprisingly good wines. (p306)

Pubs & Live Music

Northcote Social Club One of Melbourne's best live-music spots, with a buzzing front bar and a big deck out the back. (p512)

Newtown Social Club Sydney's old Sandringham Hotel features great live music that ranges from local bands to indie giants. (p128)

Governor Hindmarsh Hotel A sprawling old Adelaide rocker with decent pub grub and all kinds of live tunes. (p729)

Knopwood's Retreat There's no sight more welcoming than the fire in 'Knoppie's' grate on a chilly Hobart evening. (p633)

Sail & Anchor A Fremantle craft-beer pub sporting the tag line, 'In fermentation, there is truth'. (p918)

Top: View of the Three Sisters (p138) from Echo Point, Blue Mountains National Park

Bottom: National Gallery of Australia (p203) with George Baldessin's *Pear - version number 2* (1973) in the foreground and Thanakupi's *Eran* (2010) in the background.

Bills On The Ningaloo Reef This new gastropub at Coral Bay (WA) has immediately upped the culinary ante. (p993)

Corner Hotel Legendary rock room in Richmond, Melbourne. (p512)

Breakfast Creek Hotel So enduringly popular this Brisbane hotel is almost kitsch. (p292)

Palace Hotel An extravagantly muralled old Broken Hill pub enjoying a revival. (p253)

Art Galleries

National Gallery of Australia This superb Canberra museum houses 7500-plus works by Aboriginal and Torres Strait Islander artists. (p203)

MONA Australia's most thematically challenging art museum is the talk of Hobart town. (p622)

National Gallery of Victoria International home to travelling exhibitions par excellence (Monet, Dalí, Caravaggio): queue up with the rest of Melbourne to get in. (p480)

Art Gallery of NSW This old-stager keeps things hip with ever-changing exhibitions, including the always-controversial Archibald Prize for portraiture. (p76)

Art Gallery of South Australia On Adelaide's North Tce, this art house does things with progressive style. (p710)

Art Gallery of Ballarat Australia's oldest and largest regional gallery, crammed with works by noted Australian artists. (p566)

Museum & Art Gallery of the Northern Territory Darwin's classy art gallery is packed full of superb Indigenous art. (p814)

Pro Hart Gallery In Broken Hill, NSW there is a collection of works by this miner-turned-world-renowned painter. (p251)

Indigenous Culture

Kakadu National Park Extraordinary rock-art galleries dapple the cliffs at Nourlangie and Ubirr in the NT. (p834)

Koorie Heritage Trust In Melbourne: a great place to discover southeastern Aboriginal culture, with tours, and contemporary and traditional art. (p480)

Kuku-Yalanji Dreamtime Walks Guided walks through Mossman Gorge in Queensland with Indigenous guides. (p434)

Uluru-Kata Tjuta Cultural Centre Understand local Aboriginal law, custom and religion on Uluru's doorstep. (p880)

Bookabee Tours Indigenous-run tours of Adelaide and the Flinders Ranges in SA. (p718)

Godinymayin Yijard Rivers Arts & Culture Centre Katherine's new social and architectural high-water mark (NT). (p846)

Ngurrangga Tours Cultural expeditions from Karratha (WA) to nearby petroglyphs and waterholes. (p1002)

Carnarvon Gorge Get a close-up view of stunning rock art inside these twisted gorges in Queensland. (p366)

Dampier Peninsula Interact with remote WA communities and learn how to spear fish and catch mudcrabs. (p1032)

Outback Adventure

4WD to Cape York One of the country's great wilderness adventures is the off-road journey to mainland Australia's northern tip: take a tour or go it alone. (p443)

The Red Centre Explore Uluru and Kata Tjuta in Australia's desert heart on a tour from Alice Springs. (p880)

Karijini National Park Scramble, abseil, slide and dive through gorges on an adventure tour in this remote WA park. (p1004)

Oodnadatta Track Tackle this historic former rail route in SA, passing Kati Thanda (Lake Eyre), remote pubs and skittery emus and lizards. (p805)

Nullarbor Plain The ultimate outback road trip: 2700km from Adelaide to Perth across the long, wide, empty Nullarbor Plain. (p965)

Mungo National Park A wonderful outback destination in NSW, with amazing land formations, wildlife and Aboriginal cultural tours. (p247)

Arnhem Land Take a day tour of remote Arnhem Land from Jabiru in Kakadu National Park, NT. (p841)

Purnululu National Park Wander through these ancient eroded beehive domes in WA. (p1022)

Month by Month

TOP EVENTS

Adelaide Fringe, February

Sydney Gay & Lesbian Mardi Gras, March

Byron Bay Bluesfest, April

AFL Grand Final, September

Tropfest, December

January

January yawns into action as Australia recovers from its Christmas hangover, but then everyone realises: 'Hey, this is summer!' The festival season kicks in with sun-stroked outdoor music festivals; Melbourne hosts the Australian Open tennis.

Sydney Festival

'It's big' says the promo material. Indeed, sprawling over three summer weeks, this fab affiliation of music, dance, talks, theatre and visual arts – much of it free and family-focussed – is an artistic behemoth (www.sydneyfestival.org.au).

MONA FOMA

In Hobart, MONA FOMA (MOFO; www.mofo.net.au) is MONA's Festival of Music & Art. Under the auspices of Brian Ritchie, the bass player from the Violent Femmes, it's as edgy, progressive and unexpected as the museum itself.

Australia Day

26 January is Australia's 'birthday' (www.australia-day.com) – the date when the First Fleet landed in 1788. Australians celebrate with picnics, barbecues, fireworks and, increasingly, nationalistic flag-waving, drunkenness and chest-beating. In less mood to celebrate are the Indigenous Australians, who refer to it as Invasion Day or Survival Day.

Tamworth Country Music Festival

This late-January hoedown (www.tamworthcountrymusicfestival.com.au) in northern New South Wales is all about big hats, golden guitars and some of the finest country music you'll hear this side of Nashville, Tennessee (mostly Australian acts, with a few world-class internationals).

February

February is usually Australia's warmest month: hot and sticky up north as the wet season continues, but divine in Tasmania and Victoria. Everywhere else, locals go back to work, to the beach or to the cricket.

Adelaide Fringe

All the acts that don't make the cut (or don't want to) for the more highbrow Adelaide Festival end up in the month-long Fringe (www.adelaidefringe.com.au), second only to Edinburgh's version. Hyperactive comedy, music and circus acts spill from the Garden of Unearthly Delights in the parklands.

March

March is harvest time in Australia's vineyards and in recent years it has been just as hot as January and February, despite its autumnal status. Melbourne's streets jam up with the Formula One Grand Prix.

Sydney Gay & Lesbian Mardi Gras

A month-long arts festival (www.mardigras.org.au) culminating in a flamboyant parade along Sydney's Oxford St on the first Saturday in March attracts 300,000 spectators. Gyms empty out, solariums darken, waxing emporiums tally their profits. After-party tickets are gold.

WOMADelaide

This annual festival of world music, arts, food and dance (www.womadelaide.com.au) is held over four days in Adelaide's luscious Botanic Park, attracting crowds from around Australia. Eight stages host hundreds of acts. It's very family friendly and you can get a cold beer, too.

April

Melbourne and the Adelaide Hills are atmospheric as European trees turn golden then maroon. Up north the rain is abating and the desert temperatures are becoming manageable. Easter means pricey accommodation everywhere.

Byron Bay Bluesfest

Every Easter, Byron Bay on the NSW north coast swells to breaking point with rock, folk and blues fans, here for a five-day extravaganza of rootsy tunes (www.bluesfest.com.au). Tickets are pricey, but the line-up is invariably awesome (Lenny Kravitz, Ben Harper, Bonnie Raitt, Buddy Guy, Paul Kelly...).

May

The dry season begins in the Northern Territory, northern Western Australia (WA) and Far North Queensland: relief from humidity. A great time to visit Uluru (Ayers Rock), before the tour buses arrive in droves.

Whale Watching

Between May and October along the southeastern Australian coast, migrating southern right and humpback whales come close to shore to feed, breed and calf. See them at Hervey Bay (NSW), Warrnambool (Victoria), Victor Harbor (South Australia), Albany (WA) and North Stradbroke Island (Queensland).

June

Winter begins: snow falls across the Southern Alps ski resorts and football season fills grandstands across the country. Peak season in the tropical north: waterfalls and outback tracks are accessible (accommodation prices less so).

Laura Aboriginal Dance Festival

Sleepy Laura, 330km north of Cairns on the Cape York Peninsula in Far North Queensland, hosts the largest traditional Indigenous gathering in Australia (www.lauradancefestival.com). Communities from the region come together for dance, song and ceremony. The Laura Races and Rodeo happen the following weekend.

Ski Season

When winter blows in, snow bunnies and powder hounds dust off their skis and snowboards and make for the mountains (www.ski.com.au). Victoria and NSW have the key resorts; there are a couple of small runs in Tasmania too.

July

Pubs with open fires, cosy coffee shops and empty beaches down south; packed markets, tours and accommodation up north. Bring warm clothes for anywhere south of Alice Springs. Don't miss 'MIFF'.

Melbourne International Film Festival

Right up there with Toronto and Cannes, MIFF (www.miff.com.au) has been running since 1952 and has grown into a wildly popular event; tickets sell like piping-hot chestnuts in the inner city. Myriad short films, feature-length spectaculars and documentaries flicker across city screens from late July to early August.

Beer Can Regatta

The NT festival calendar is studded with quirky gems like this one at Darwin's Mindil Beach, where hundreds of 'boats' constructed from empty beer cans race across the shallows (www.beercanregatta.org.au). Much drinking and laughter: staying afloat is a secondary concern.

August

August is when southerners, sick of winter's grey-sky drear, head to Queensland for some sun. Last chance to head to the tropical Top End and outback before things get too hot and wet.

Cairns Festival

Running for three weeks from late August to early September, this massive art-and-culture fest (www.cairns.qld.gov.au/festival) brings a stellar program of music, theatre, dance, comedy, film, Indigenous art and public exhibitions. Outdoor events held in public plazas, parks and gardens make good use of Cairns' tropical setting.

September

Spring heralds a rampant bloom of wild flowers across outback WA and Sout Australia (SA), with flower festivals happening in places such as Canberra and Toowoomba. Football finishes and the spring horse-racing carnival begins.

Brisbane Festival

One of Australia's largest and most diverse arts festivals runs for 22 days in September and features an impressive line-up of concerts, plays, dance performances and fringe events around the city (www.brisbanefestival.com.au). It finishes off with 'Riverfire', an elaborate fireworks show over the river.

Australian Rules Grand Final

The pinnacle of the Australian Football League (AFL; www.afl.com.au) season is this high-flying spectacle in Melbourne, watched (on TV) by millions of impassioned Aussies. Tickets to the game are scarce, but at half-time everyone's neighbourhood BBQ moves into the local park for a little amateur kick-to-kick.

October

The weather avoids extremes everywhere: a good time to go camping or to hang out at some vineyards. After the football and before the cricket, sports fans twiddle their thumbs.

Jazz in the Vines

There are lots of food-and-wine festivals like this across Australia's wine regions (Barossa, McLaren Vale, Yarra Valley...). The Hunter Valley's proximity to the Sydney jazz scene ensures a top line-up at Tyrrell's Vineyard (www.jazzinthevines.com.au).

November

Northern beaches may close due to 'stingers' – jellyfish in the shallow waters off north Queensland, the NT and WA. Outdoor events ramp up; the surf life-saving season flexes its muscles on beaches everywhere.

Melbourne Cup

On the first Tuesday in November, Australia's (if not the world's) premier horse race chews up the turf in Melbourne (www.melbournecup.com). Country towns schedule racing events to coincide with the day and the country does actually pause to watch the 'race that stops a nation'.

Margaret River Gourmet Escape

Western Australia's contribution to the national circuit of fine food-and-wine fests (www.gourmetescape.com.au). The line-up of celebrity chefs is impressive: dozens of culinary doyens plating up seriously good food. But it's the Margaret River wines that really steal the show.

Sculpture by the Sea

In mid-November, the cliff-top trail from Bondi Beach to Tamarama in Sydney transforms into an exquisite sculpture garden (www.sculpturebythesea.com). Serious prize money is on offer for the most creative offerings from international and local sculptors. Happens on Perth's Cottesloe Beach in March.

December

Ring the bell, school's out! Holidays begin two weeks before Christmas. Cities are packed with shoppers and the weather is desirably hot. Up north, monsoon season is under way: afternoon thunderstorms bring rain.

Tropfest

The world's largest short-film festival (www.tropfest.com.au) happens on Sydney's grassy Centennial Park one Sunday in early December. To discourage cheating and inspire creativity, a compulsory prop appears in each entry (eg kiss, sneeze, balloon). And it's free!

Sydney to Hobart Yacht Race

The world's most arduous open-ocean yacht race is the 628-nautical-mile Sydney to Hobart (www.rolexsydneyhobart.com) departing Sydney Harbour on Boxing Day. The winners sail into Hobart around December 29.

Itineraries

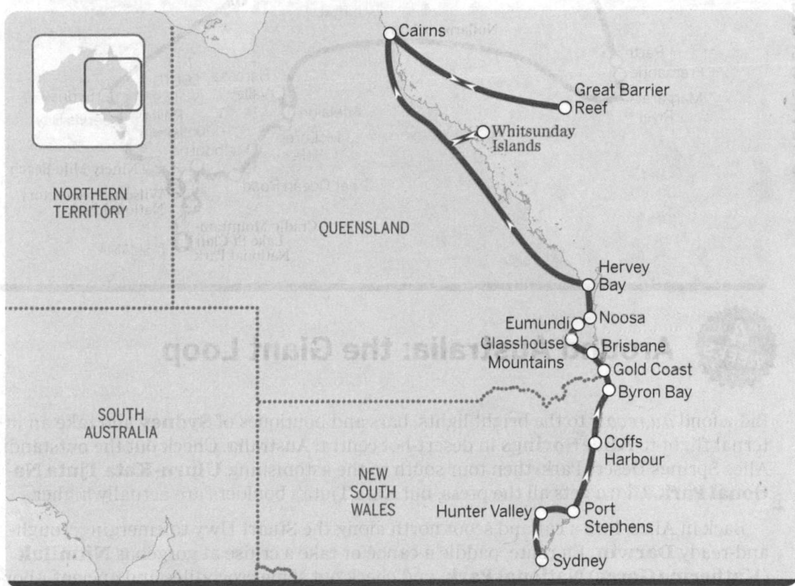

4 WEEKS Sydney to Cairns

Hugging the east coast between Sydney and Cairns for 2864km, this is the most well-trodden path in Australia. You could do it in two weeks, but why not take four and really chill out.

Start with a few days immersed in the bright lights and glitz of **Sydney**, then meander north along the Pacific Hwy through central and northern New South Wales (NSW). Hang out in the **Hunter Valley** for some fine vino-quaffing, and stop to splash in the sea at family-friendly **Port Stephens** and **Coffs Harbour**, home of the iconic/kitsch 'Big Banana'. Skip up to **Byron Bay** for New Age awakenings and superb beaches, then head over the Queensland border to the party-prone, surf-addled **Gold Coast**. Pause in hip **Brisbane** then amble up through the **Glasshouse Mountains** and hippie **Eumundi** to affluent **Noosa** on the Sunshine Coast.

The Bruce Hwy traces the stunning coast into Far North Queensland. Spot some passing whales off the coast of **Hervey Bay** and track further north to the blissful **Whitsundays** archipelago, the coral charms of the **Great Barrier Reef** and the scuba-diving nexus of **Cairns**.

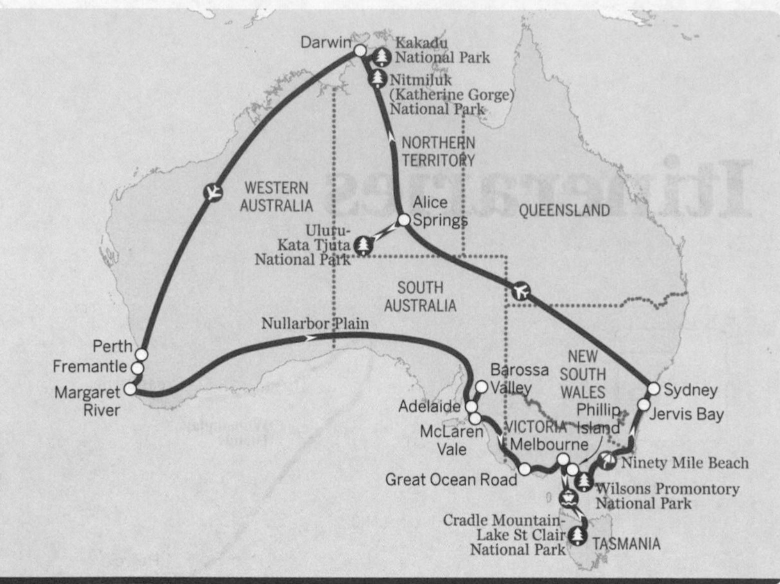

Around Australia: the Giant Loop

Bid a fond *au revoir* to the bright lights, bars and boutiques of **Sydney** and take an internal flight to **Alice Springs** in desert-hot central Australia. Check out the outstanding Alice Springs Desert Park, then tour south to the astonishing **Uluru-Kata Tjuta National Park**. Uluru gets all the press, but Kata Tjuta's boulders are actually higher.

Back in Alice, hire a car and scoot north along the Stuart Hwy to emerging, rough-and-ready **Darwin**. En route, paddle a canoe or take a cruise at gorgeous **Nitmiluk (Katherine Gorge) National Park**, and check out some crocodiles and ancient Aboriginal rock-art galleries at **Kakadu National Park**.

From Darwin, hop another flight to **Perth** – a confident city that sets its own agenda – and the soulful old port town of **Fremantle** nearby. Continuing south, wine away some hours around **Margaret River** until you're ready to tackle the flat immensity of the **Nullarbor Plain** – if you're not up for the epic drive to festival-frenzied **Adelaide**, the Indian Pacific train ride is unforgettable.

Check out the world-class wine regions around Adelaide (the **Barossa Valley** and **McLaren Vale** are both an hour away), or head east along the impossibly scenic **Great Ocean Road** to sports-mad **Melbourne**. Don't miss a game of Australian Rules football or cricket at the cauldron-like Melbourne Cricket Ground.

If you have a few extra days, take the car ferry across to **Tasmania**. Australia's divine island state preserves some of the country's oldest forests and World Heritage–listed mountain ranges: **Cradle Mountain–Lake St Clair National Park** is accessible and absolutely beautiful.

From Melbourne, continue along the Victorian coast to the penguins and koalas on **Phillip Island** and white-sand seclusion of **Wilsons Promontory National Park**. Spend a couple of days somewhere along **Ninety Mile Beach** then cruise up the southern NSW coast to idyllic **Jervis Bay** (spot any whales?). Back in **Sydney**, there are so many beaches you're sure to find a patch of sand with your name on it.

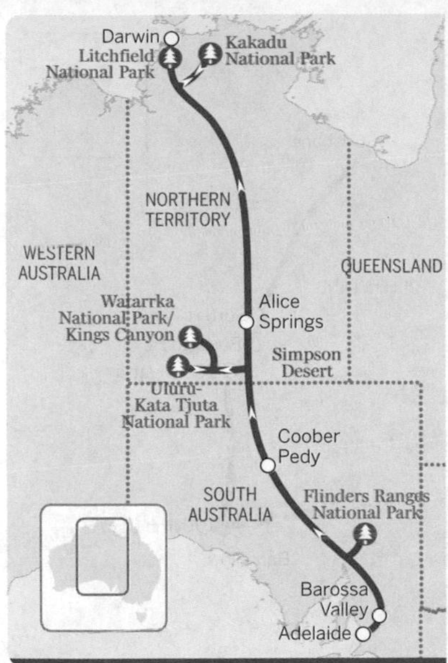

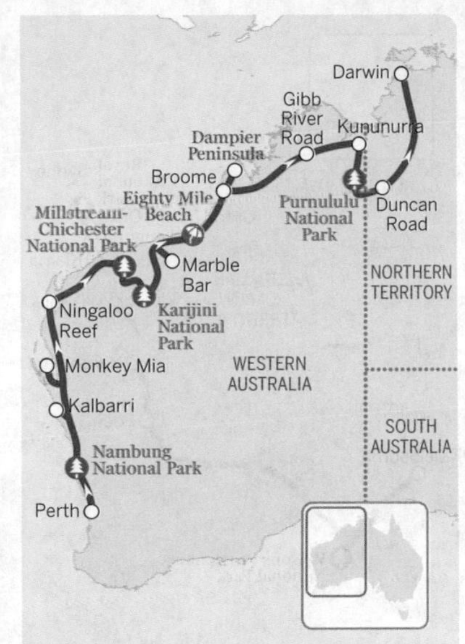

Adelaide to Darwin

This classic 3000km dash up the Stuart Hwy takes you into Australia's desert heart.

From the eat-streets and old stone pubs of **Adelaide**, head north to the **Barossa Valley** for world-beating red wines. Next stop is rust-coloured **Flinders Ranges National Park**: Ikara (Wilpena Pound) jags up from the semidesert.

Just off the Stuart Hwy are the dugouts of unique **Coober Pedy**. Continuing north, the Lasseter Hwy delivers you to weighty, iconic **Uluru-Kata Tjuta National Park**. The chasm of **Watarrka (Kings Canyon) National Park** is 300km further north.

Overnight in the desert oasis of **Alice Springs**, then continue north to the wetlands and rock-scapes of World Heritage-listed **Kakadu National Park** and the waterfalls and swimming holes of **Litchfield National Park**.

Gone are the days when **Darwin** was just a redneck outpost: these days the city is very multicultural, as a visit to the fabulous Mindil Beach Sunset Market will confirm. Don't miss the quirky Deckchair Cinema and excellent Museum & Art Gallery of the Northern Territory.

Perth, the Pilbara & the Kimberley

Feeling adventurous? Steer your 4WD north from **Perth**...all the way to Darwin!

First stop is otherworldly **Nambung National Park**, followed by **Kalbarri** with its soaring sea cliffs and incredible gorges. Commune with dolphins at Shark Bay's **Monkey Mia**, then hug the coast for superb snorkelling at **Ningaloo Reef**.

Inland are the ironstone hues of the Pilbara. Cool-off at tranquil **Millstream-Chichester National Park** then plunge into the gorges at **Karijini National Park**. Down a beer at **Marble Bar**, Australia's hottest town, before spying turtles at **Eighty Mile Beach**.

The Big Empty stretches northeast to **Broome**: watch the camels on Cable Beach at sunset. Nearby **Dampier Peninsula** beckons with pristine beaches and camping in Indigenous communities. From here, veer east into the Kimberley along legendary **Gibb River Road**.

Restock in **Kununurra** before heading to the sandstone domes of **Purnululu National Park**. Take the exquisitely lonely **Duncan Road** into the NT: once you're on the asphalt, **Darwin** isn't far away.

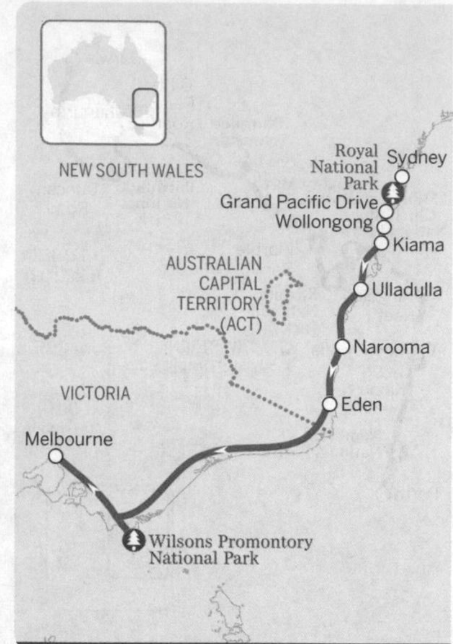

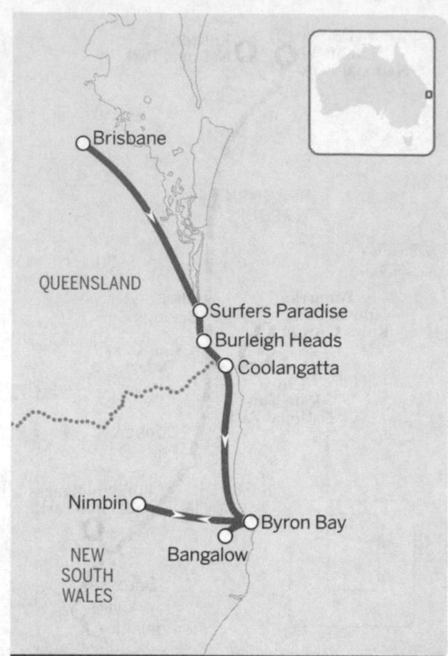

1 WEEK Sydney to Melbourne

Most people fly into Sydney, Australia's biggest city. But don't miss Melbourne, Sydney's arty rival, some 1000km to the south.

Check out **Sydney** from its sparkling harbour: the gorgeous Sydney Opera House and colossal Sydney Harbour Bridge are unmissable. For a bird's-eye view, tackle the Bridge Climb over the great grey arch. Feel like a swim? Bondi Beach is a quintessential Australian experience.

Heading south, zip through **Royal National Park** to the elevated **Grand Pacific Drive**, continuing to **Wollongong** and the lovely coastal town of **Kiama**. Nearby, the Illawarra Fly Tree Top Walk and Zipline traverse the rainforest canopy.

Continuing south, meander through **Ulladulla**, **Narooma** and the aptly named **Eden** near the Victorian border. The road from here to Melbourne is low-key: spice things up with some blissful bushwalks at **Wilsons Promontory National Park**.

Melbourne is a bayside city famous for the arts, Australian Rules football and coffee. Wander the laneways, mooch around the galleries, grab a pub dinner and catch a live band.

1 WEEK Brisbane to Byron Bay

Strap a surfboard to the roof rack and cruise into your very own *Endless Summer*: this stretch of Australia's east coast is famous for its surf.

Once a sleepy river town, **Brisbane** is booming, growing so fast that it can be difficult to navigate. Its urban charms (great restaurants, arts scene, coffee and bars) meld seamlessly with the natural environment (cliffs, parklands and the serpentine Brisbane River).

Heading south to the Gold Coast, the cityscape of **Surfers Paradise** rises on the horizon. There are as many apartment towers here as shades of fake tan: check it out if you like casinos, theme parks and boozy backpackers. More low-key are the surfie town of **Burleigh Heads** and the surf life-saving mecca **Coolangatta**.

Despite big summer (and Easter) crowds and big development money, **Byron Bay** in northern NSW remains a hippie haven with great pubs, restaurants, beaches and the famous Pass point break. Don't miss inland day-trips to pretty **Bangalow** and Australia's near-mythical alternative-lifestyle hangout, **Nimbin**.

Plan Your Trip

Your Reef Trip

The World Heritage–listed Great Barrier Reef, stretching over 2000km from just south of the Tropic of Capricorn (near Gladstone in Queensland) to just south of Papua New Guinea, is the most extensive reef system in the world, and made entirely by living organisms.

When to Go

High season on the Reef is from June to December. For the best underwater visibility, visit between August and January.

➡ From December to March **northern Queensland** (north of Townsville) is working its way through the wet season, bringing oppressive heat and monsoonal rainfall. From July to September things are much drier and cooler.

➡ Anytime is a good time to visit the **Whitsundays**. Winter (June to August) can be pleasantly warm, but you will occasionally need a jumper. As per the rest of Quuensland, summers here (December to March) are hot and humid.

➡ **Southern** and **central Queensland** experience mild winters – cool enough for diving or snorkelling in a wetsuit.

Picking Your Spot

The GBR is enormous! It follows that there are myriad popular spots from which to access it – but bear in mind that the qualities of individual areas do change over time, depending on the weather, tidal changes or any recent cyclone damage.

Best Reef Experiences

Watching Wildlife

Watching sea turtles hatching on Lady Elliot Island or Heron Island; spying reef sharks, turtles and rays on a kayaking trip off Green Island; spotting koalas on Magnetic Island and dingoes on Fraser Island.

Best Snorkelling

Pack your mask, your fins and your snorkel and head to Knuckle, Hardy and Fitzroy Reefs, Magnetic Island or the Whitsunday Islands.

Best View from Above

Take a scenic chopper or plane ride from Cairns, Hamilton and the Whitsunday Islands. Skydiving over Airlie Beach is fun, too.

Best Sailing Experience

Sailing from Airlie Beach through the Whitsunday Islands, or exploring Agincourt Reef from Port Douglas.

Essential Websites

Dive Queensland (www.dive-queensland.com.au)

Great Barrier Reef Marine Park Authority (www.gbrmpa.gov.au)

Queensland Department of National Parks, Sport & Racing (www.nprsr.qld.gov.au)

Reef Highlights

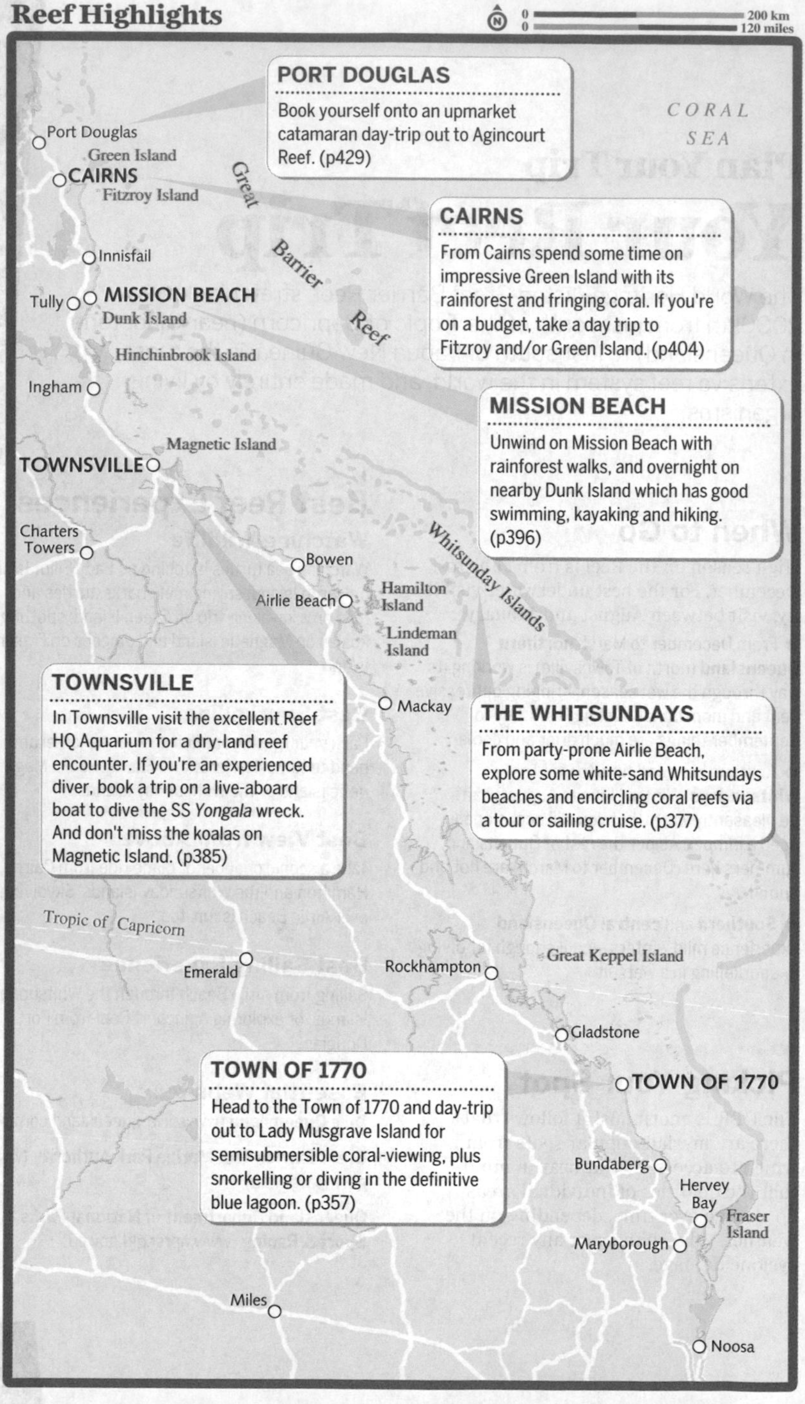

PORT DOUGLAS

Book yourself onto an upmarket catamaran day-trip out to Agincourt Reef. (p429)

CAIRNS

From Cairns spend some time on impressive Green Island with its rainforest and fringing coral. If you're on a budget, take a day trip to Fitzroy and/or Green Island. (p404)

MISSION BEACH

Unwind on Mission Beach with rainforest walks, and overnight on nearby Dunk Island which has good swimming, kayaking and hiking. (p396)

TOWNSVILLE

In Townsville visit the excellent Reef HQ Aquarium for a dry-land reef encounter. If you're an experienced diver, book a trip on a live-aboard boat to dive the SS *Yongala* wreck. And don't miss the koalas on Magnetic Island. (p385)

THE WHITSUNDAYS

From party-prone Airlie Beach, explore some white-sand Whitsundays beaches and encircling coral reefs via a tour or sailing cruise. (p377)

TOWN OF 1770

Head to the Town of 1770 and day-trip out to Lady Musgrave Island for semisubmersible coral-viewing, plus snorkelling or diving in the definitive blue lagoon. (p357)

Mainland Gateways

The major mainland Reef access points all offer slightly different experiences or activities. Here's a brief overview, ordered from south to north.

Agnes Water & Town of 1770 Small towns and good choices if you want to beat the crowds. Tours head to Fitzroy Reef Lagoon, one of the most pristine sections of the Reef, where visitor numbers are still limited. The still-water lagoon is excellent for snorkelling and almost as impressive when viewed from a boat.

Gladstone A slightly bigger town but still a relatively small gateway. It's an exceptional choice for divers and snorkellers, being the closest access point to the Southern Reef Islands and innumerable cays, including Lady Elliot Island.

Airlie Beach A small town with a big party scene and a flotilla of sailing outfits. The major lure here is spending a few days aboard a boat and seeing some of the Whitsunday Islands' fringing coral reefs. Whether you're travelling five-star or no-star, there'll be a tour to match your budget.

Townsville A top gateway for divers. A four- or five-night live-aboard tour around numerous islands and pockets of the Reef is a great choice. In particular, Kelso Reef and the wreck of the SS *Yongala* are teeming with marine life. There are also a couple of day-trip options on glass-bottomed boats. Reef HQ Aquarium, which is basically a version of the Reef in an aquarium, is also here.

Mission Beach Closer to the Reef than any other gateway destination. It's a small, quiet town with a few boat and diving tours to sections of the outer reef. The choice isn't huge, but neither are the crowds.

Cairns The main launching pad for Reef tours with a bewildering number of operators offering inexpensive day trips on large boats to intimate five-day luxury charters. Trips cover a wide section of the Reef, with some operators travelling as far north as Lizard Island. Inexpensive tours are likely to travel to inner, less pristine reefs. Scenic flights are also an option.

Port Douglas A swanky resort town and a gateway to the Low Isles and Agincourt Reef, an outer ribbon reef featuring crystal-clear water and hyper-coloured corals. Diving, snorkelling and cruising trips tend to be classier, pricier and less crowded than in Cairns. You can also take a scenic flight from here.

Cooktown Close to Lizard Island, but tour operators (and much of the town) shut down between November and May for the wet season.

Islands

Rising above the waterline throughout the Reef are hundreds of islands and cays offering instant access to the undersea marvels. Here is a list of some of our favourite islands, travelling from south to north.

Lady Elliot Island A coral cay that's popular with birdwatchers: there are around 57 bird species living here. Sea turtles also nest here and it's possibly the best location on the Reef to see manta rays. It's also a famed diving spot. There's a resort here, or you can visit Lady Elliot on a day trip from Bundaberg.

Heron Island A tiny coral cay sitting in the middle of a huge spread of reef. It's a diving mecca, but the snorkelling is also good and it's possible to do a reef walk from here. Heron is a nesting ground for green and loggerhead turtles and home to some 30 species of birds. The sole resort on the island charges accordingly.

Hamilton Island The big daddy of the Whitsunday resort islands, Hamilton is a sprawling family-friendly development laden with infrastructure. The atmosphere isn't exactly intimate, but there's a wealth of tours heading from here to outer-reef spots that can't be explored from the mainland.

Hook Island An outer Whitsunday isle fringed with reefs. There's excellent swimming and snorkelling here, and the island's sizable bulk offers good bushwalking. There's affordable accommodation and camping on Hook and it's easily accessed from Airlie Beach – a top choice if you're working with modest funds.

Orpheus Island A national park and one of the Reef's most exclusive and romantic hideaways. This island is great for snorkelling – you can step right off the beach and be surrounded by the Reef's colourful marine life. Clusters of fringing reefs also provide plenty of diving opportunities.

Green Island Another of the Reef's true coral cays. The fringing reefs here are considered to be among the most beautiful surrounding any island, and the diving and snorkelling are first rate. Cloaked in dense rainforest, the entire island is a national park. Bird life abounds.

Lizard Island Remote, rugged and the perfect place to beat a retreat from civilisation. Expect talcum-white beaches, remarkably blue water and very few visitors. The Reef's best-known dive site is at Cod Hole, where you can paddle up next to docile potato cod, which weigh as much as 60kg each. Pixie Bommie is another highly regarded dive site here.

Diving & Snorkelling

Much of the diving and snorkelling on the Reef is boat-based, although on some islands you can walk straight off the beach and dip into the coral kingdom just offshore. Free use of snorkelling gear is usually part of any cruise to the Reef; cruises generally involve around three hours of underwater wandering. Overnight or live-aboard trips provide a more in-depth experience and greater coverage of the reefs.

If you're keen to experience scuba diving but don't have a diving certificate, many operators provide introductory dives – a guided dive where an experienced diver conducts an underwater tour. A lesson in safety and procedure is given beforehand and you don't require a five-day Professional Association of Diving Instructors (PADI) course or a buddy.

Diving Essentials

In order to minimise the risk of residual nitrogen in the blood that can cause decompression injury, your last dive should be completed at least 24 hours before flying anywhere – even in a balloon or for a parachute jump. It's fine to dive soon after arriving by air.

TOP SNORKELLING SITES

Some non-divers may wonder if it's really worth going to the Great Barrier Reef 'just to snorkel'. The answer is a resounding 'Yes!'. Much of the rich, colourful coral lies just underneath the surface (as coral needs bright sunlight to flourish) and is easily accessible. Here's a round-up of what we think are the top snorkelling sites:

➡ Fitzroy Reef Lagoon (Town of 1770)

➡ Heron Island, Great Keppel Island, Lady Elliot Island, Lady Musgrave Island (Capricorn Coast)

➡ Hook Island, Hayman Island, Border Island, Hardy Reef, Knuckle Reef (Whitsundays)

➡ Lizard Island, Michaelmas Reef, Hastings Reef, Norman Reef, Saxon Reef, Green Island (Cairns)

➡ Opal Reef, Agincourt Reef, Mackay Reef (Port Douglas)

Find out whether your insurance policy classifies diving as a 'dangerous sport' exclusion. For a nominal annual fee, the **Divers Alert Network** (www.diversalertnetwork.org) provides insurance for medical or evacuation services required in the event of a diving accident. DAN's international hotline for emergencies is ☎919-684-9111.

Underwater visibility around coastal areas is 1m to 3m, whereas several kilometres offshore visibility can extend out to 15m. The outer edge of the reef has visibility of 20m to 35m; the Coral Sea has visibility of 50m and beyond.

In northern Queensland, the water is warm all year, from around 24°C to 30°C. Heading south the water gradually gets cooler, dropping to a low of 20°C in winter.

Top Reef Dive Spots

The Great Barrier Reef is home to some of the planet's best reef-diving sites. Here are a few top spots to get you started:

SS Yongala A sunken shipwreck that has been home to a vivid marine community for more than 90 years.

Cod Hole Go nose-to-nose with a potato cod.

Heron Island Join a crowd of colourful fish, straight off the beach.

Lady Elliot Island Has 19 highly regarded dive sites.

Pixie Bommie Delve into the Reef's after-five world on a night dive.

Boat Excursions

Unless you're staying on a coral atoll in the middle of the Great Barrier Reef, you'll need to join a boat excursion to experience the Reef's real beauty. Day trips set sail from many places along the coast, as well as from island resorts. Trips typically include the use of snorkelling gear, snacks and a buffet lunch, with scuba diving an optional extra. On some boats a naturalist or marine biologist presents a talk on Reef ecology.

Boat trips vary dramatically in passenger numbers, type of vessel and quality – which is reflected in the price – so it's worth getting all the details before committing. When selecting a tour, consider the vessel (motorised catamaran or sailing ship), the number of passengers (anywhere from six to 400), and what kind of extras are offered (food, talks, hotel transfers etc). The destination is also key: outer reefs are

TREADING LIGHTLY ON THE REEF

The Great Barrier Reef is incredibly fragile: it's worth taking some time to educate yourself on responsible practices to minimise the impact of your visit.

- It is an offence to damage or remove coral in the marine park.
- If you touch or walk on coral you'll damage it (and probably get some nasty cuts).
- Don't touch or harass marine animals, and don't enter the water near a dugong.
- If you have a boat, be aware of the rules in relation to anchoring around the reef, including 'no anchoring areas' to avoid coral damage.
- If you're diving, check that you are weighted correctly before entering the water and keep your buoyancy control well away from the reef. Ensure that equipment such as secondary regulators and gauges aren't dragging over the reef.
- If you're snorkelling (especially if you're a beginner) practice your technique away from coral until you've mastered control in the water.
- Hire a wetsuit or a 'rashie' rather than slathering on sunscreen, which can damage the reef.
- Watch where your fins are – try not to stir up sediment or disturb coral.
- Note that there are limits on the amount and types of shells that you can collect.
- Take all litter away with you – even biodegradable materials like apple cores – and dispose of it back on the mainland.

usually more pristine; inner reefs often show signs of damage from humans, coral bleaching and the coral-eating crown-of-thorns starfish. Some operators offer the option of a trip in a glass-bottomed boat or semisubmersible.

Many boats have underwater cameras for hire – although you'll save money by hiring these back on the mainland (or using your own waterproof camera or underwater housing). Some boats also have professional photographers on board who will dive with you and take high-quality shots of you as you bubble away underneath the surface.

Live-Aboards

If you're keen to do as much diving as possible, a live-aboard Reef experience is an excellent option. Trips generally involve three dives per day, plus some night dives, all in more remote parts of the Great Barrier Reef. Trip lengths generally range from one to six nights. Three-day/three-night voyages, which allow up to 11 dives (nine day and two night dives), are the most common.

It's worth checking out the various options as some boats offer specialist itineraries following marine life and events such as whale migrations or coral spawning, or offer trips to more remote spots like the far northern reefs, Pompey Complex, Coral Sea Reefs or Swain Reefs.

It's recommended to go with operators who are Dive Queensland members: see www.dive-queensland.com.au for a full list. Membership ensures that operators follow a minimum set of guidelines. Ideally, they are also accredited by **Ecotourism Australia** (www.ecotourism.org.au).

Popular departure points for live-aboard dive vessels, along with the locales they visit include:

Bundaberg Access to the Bunker Island group, including Lady Musgrave and Lady Elliot Islands. Some trips visit the Fitzroy, Llewellyn and rarely visited Boult Reefs, or Hoskyn and Fairfax Islands.

Town of 1770 Bunker Island group.

Gladstone Swains and Bunker Island group.

Mackay Lihou Reef and the Coral Sea.

Airlie Beach The Whitsundays, Knuckle Reef and Hardy Reef.

Townsville SS *Yongala* wreck, plus canyons of Wheeler Reef and Keeper Reef.

Cairns Cod Hole, Ribbon Reefs, the Coral Sea and the far northern reefs.

Port Douglas Osprey Reef, Cod Hole, Ribbon Reefs, Coral Sea and the far northern reefs.

Dive Courses

In Queensland there are numerous places where you can learn to dive, take a refresher course or improve your submarine skills. Dive courses here are generally of a high standard, and all schools teach either PADI or Scuba Schools International (SSI) qualifications. Which certification you choose isn't as important as choosing a good instructor, so be sure to seek local recommendations and meet with the instructor before committing to a program.

A popular place to learn is Cairns, where you can choose between courses for the budget-minded (four-day courses from around $500) that combine pool training and reef dives; and longer, more intensive courses that include reef diving on a live-aboard boat (five-day courses including three-day/two-night live-aboard from $750).

Other places where you can learn to dive and then head out on the Reef include Airlie Beach, Bundaberg, Hamilton Island, Magnetic Island, Mission Beach, Port Douglas and Townsville.

Camping on the Great Barrier Reef

Pitching a tent on a tropical island is a unique and affordable way to experience the Great Barrier Reef. Campers can enjoy idyllic tropical settings at a fraction of the cost of the five-star resorts that may be just down the track. Camp-site facilities range from virtually nothing (a sandy patch in the shade) to well-established grounds with showers, flushing toilets, interpretive signs and picnic tables.

Most island camp sites are remote, so ensure you're adequately prepared for medical and general emergencies. Wherever you stay, you'll need to bring your own food and drinking water (5L per day per person is recommended). Inclement weather can often prevent planned pick-ups, so bring enough supplies to last an extra three or four days in case you get stranded. Camp only in designated areas, keep to marked trails and take out everything that you bring in with you. Fires are banned – you'll need a gas stove or similar.

National park camping permits need to be booked in advance, either online or by phone through the **Queensland Department of National Parks, Sport & Racing** (13 74 68; www.nprsr.qld.gov.au).

Here are a few of our fave camping spots to start you dreaming:

Whitsunday Islands Nearly a dozen beautifully sited camping areas, scattered across the islands of Hook, Whitsunday and Henning.

Capricornia Cays Camping available on Masthead Island, North West Island and Lady Musgrave Island – the latter a fantastic, uninhabited isle with boat-access camping, limited to a maximum of 40 people. Off Town of 1770.

Dunk Island Equal parts resort and national park with good swimming, kayaking and hiking. Off Mission Beach.

Fitzroy Island Resort and national park with short bushwalking trails and coral just off the sand. Off Cairns.

Frankland Islands Coral-fringed island with white-sand beaches. Off Cairns.

Lizard Island Amazing beaches, magnificent coral and abundant wildlife. Visitors mostly arrive by plane from Cairns.

Orpheus Island Secluded island (accessible by air from Townsville or Cairns) with lush tropical forest and superb fringing reef.

Plan Your Trip

Your Outback Trip

Exactly where Australia's outback starts and ends is hard to pin down on a map. But you'll know you're there when the sky yawns enormously wide, the horizon is unnervingly empty, and the sparse inhabitants you encounter are incomparably resilient and distinctively Australian. Enduring Indigenous culture, unique wildlife and intriguing landscapes await the modern-day adventurer.

About the Outback

The Australian outback is a vast, imprecise region radiating out from the centre of the continent. While most Australians live on the coast, that thin green fringe of the continent is hardly typical of this enormous land mass. Inland is the desert soul of Australia.

Weather patterns vary from region to region – from sandy arid desert to semiarid scrubland to tropical savannah – but you can generally rely on hot sunny days, starry nights and mile after mile of unbroken horizon.

When to Go

Best Months

Winter June through August is when southeastern Australia (where most of the population lives) is sniffling through rainy and cloudy winter days, and the outback comes into its own. Rain isn't unheard of in central Australia – in fact there's been a hell of a lot of it over recent years – but clear skies, moderate daytime temperatures, cold nights and good driving conditions are the norm. Winter is also the best time to visit the tropical Top End, with low humidity, dry days and mild temperatures.

Spring September and October is springtime – and prime time to head into the outback, especially

Best Outback Experiences

Things to Pack

Sunscreen, sunglasses, a hat, insect repellent, plenty of water and some good tunes for the car stereo.

Best Outback Track

The Oodnadatta Track is 620km of red dust, emus, lizards, salt lakes and historic railroad remnants.

Indigenous Culture

Kakadu National Park in the tropical Top End wilderness offers ancient rock art and cultural tours run by Indigenous guides.

Best National Park

In Uluru-Kata Tjuta National Park, iconic Uluru is simply unmissable, while nearby Kata Tjuta is less well known but just as impressive.

Best Outback Highway

Cross the country's outback heartland from Adelaide to Darwin on the Stuart Hwy.

Off the Beaten Outback Track

TIWI ISLANDS

Leave the car far behind and venture across the waters to Bathurst Island to experience Tiwi Island culture with its fascinating history and unique art. (p828)

KEEP RIVER NATIONAL PARK

A little-visited yet rewarding detour on the way to northern WA. Keep River National Park features Aboriginal art, wildlife, short walks and stunning sandstone formations. (p852)

VICTORIA RIVER REGION

The Victoria Hwy travels through legendary cattle country, much of it returning to nature as national park. Detours lead off the highway and onto 4WD tracks boasting remote camps under big skies. (p852)

KAKADU & ARNHEM LAND

You can drive into Kakadu in a conventional 2WD car, but you'll need a 4WD to fully explore the area's hidden treasures. 4WD tour operators can also get you into Arnhem Land. (p834)

THE GULF COAST & LIMMEN NATIONAL PARK

Venture into little-known Limmen National Park, which can be accessed via Roper Bar or Borroloola. The big attractions here are the fishing, scenery and rough-and-ready camp sites. (p853)

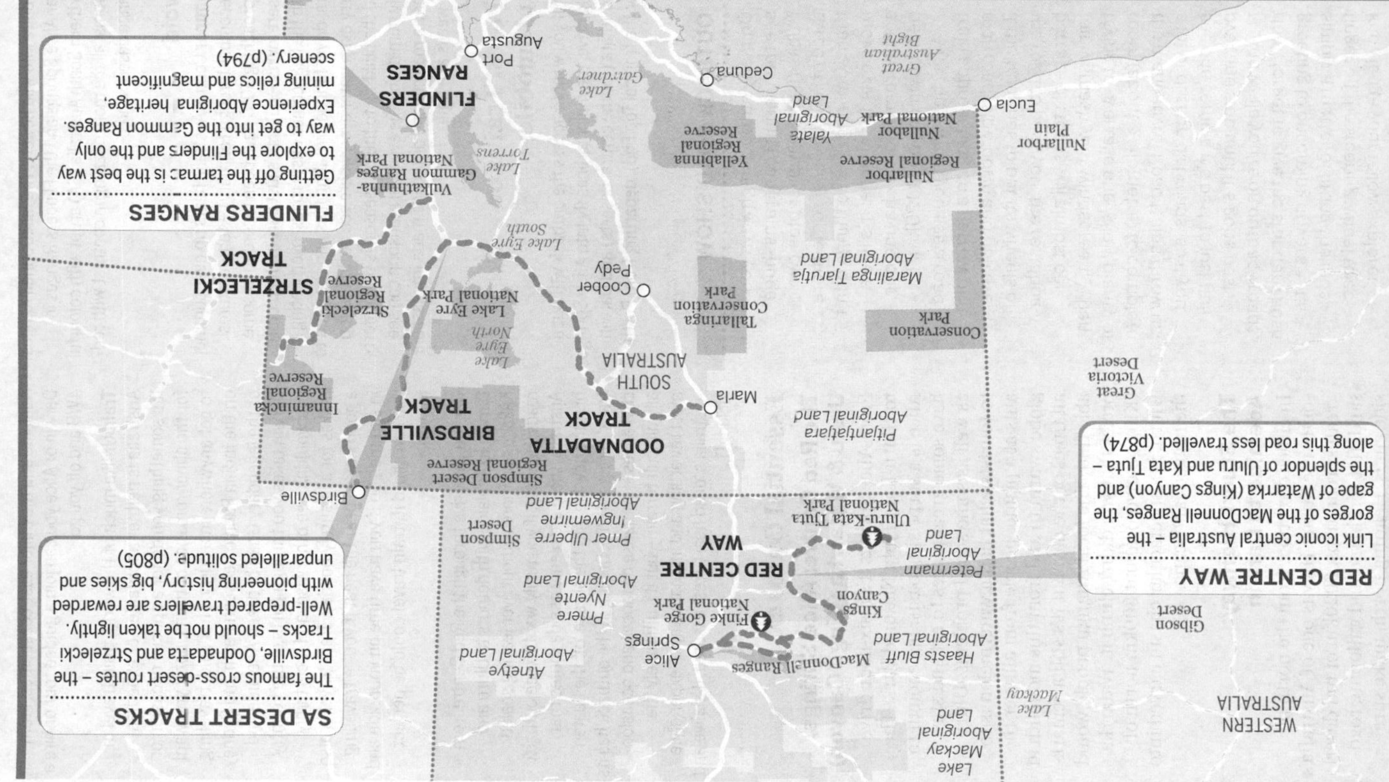
SA DESERT TRACKS
The famous cross-desert routes – the Birdsville, Oodnadatta and Strzelecki Tracks – should not be taken lightly. Well-prepared travellers are rewarded with pioneering history, big skies and unparalleled solitude. (p805)
FLINDERS RANGES
Getting off the tarmac is the best way to explore the Flinders and the only way to get into the Gammon Ranges. Experience Aborigina heritage, mining relics and magnificent scenery. (p794)
RED CENTRE WAY
Link iconic central Australia – the gorges of the MacDonnell Ranges, the gape of Watarrka (Kings Canyon) and the splendor of Uluru and Kata Tjuta – along this road less travelled. (p874)
WESTERN AUSTRALIA
Gibson Desert
Great Victoria Desert
Lake Mackay
Lake Mackay Aboriginal Land
Haasts Bluff Aboriginal Land
MacDonnell Ranges
Kings Canyon
Peterman Aboriginal Land
Uluru-Kata Tjuta National Park
Finke Gorge National Park
Alice Springs
RED CENTRE WAY
Atnetye Aboriginal Land
Pmere Nyente Aboriginal Land
Pmer Ulperre Ingwemirne Aboriginal Land
Simpson Desert
Simpson Desert Regional Reserve
Birdsville
BIRDSVILLE TRACK
OODNADATTA TRACK
Innamincka Regional Reserve
Strzelecki Regional Reserve
STRZELECKI TRACK
Lake Eyre North
Lake Eyre National Park
Lake Eyre South
Vulkathunha-Gammon Ranges National Park
Lake Torrens
FLINDERS RANGES
Port Augusta
Pitjantjatjara Aboriginal Land
Marla
SOUTH AUSTRALIA
Coober Pedy
Tallaringa Conservation Park
Maralinga Tjarutja Aboriginal Land
Conservation Park
Lake Gairdner
Yellabinna Regional Reserve
Nullarbor Regional Reserve
Nullarbor National Park
Yalata Aboriginal Land
Ceduna
Nullarbor Plain
Eucla
Great Australian Bight

if you're into wild flowers. The MacDonnell Ranges near Alice Springs and the Flinders Ranges in northern South Australia (SA) erupt with colourful blooms, all the more dazzling in contrast with red-orange desert sands.

Avoid

Summer Central Australia heats up over summer (December through February) – temperatures approaching 50°C have been recorded in some desert towns – but that's just part of the picture. With the heat comes dusty roads, overheating cars, driver fatigue, irritating flies and the need to carry extra water everywhere you go. In the Top End the build-up to the Wet season is uncomfortably humid, and the eventual monsoon can see many a road cut and dirt roads made impassable for weeks at a time.

Planes, Trains or Automobiles?

Air If you want to access the outback without a long drive, the major airlines fly into Alice Springs and Yulara (for the central deserts) and Darwin (for the tropical Top End), departing from Perth, Adelaide and the major east-coast cities. From Darwin or Alice you can join a guided tour or hire a 4WD and off you go.

Train Unlike much of the world, train travel in Australia is neither affordable nor expedient. It's something you do for a special occasion or for the sheer romance of trains, not if you want to get anywhere in a hurry. That said, travelling on the Indian Pacific between Perth and Sydney or the legendary Ghan between Adelaide and Darwin takes you through parts of the country you wouldn't see otherwise, and it certainly makes for a leisurely holiday. Train travel is also a good way to beat the heat if you're travelling in summer. So if you have time on your side and you can afford it, train travel could be perfect for you.

Car You can drive through the Red Centre from Darwin to Adelaide with detours to Uluru and Kakadu and more without ever leaving sealed roads. However, if you really want to see outback Australia, there are plenty of side routes that breathe new life into the phrase 'off the beaten track' (bring a 4WD). Driving in the outback has its challenges – immense distances and occasionally difficult terrain – but it's ultimately the most rewarding and intimate way to experience Australia's 'dead heart' (rest assured, it's alive and kicking!).

OUTBACK ROAD SHOW

On many outback highways you'll see thundering road trains: huge trucks (a prime mover plus two, three or four trailers) some more than 50m long. These things don't move over for anyone: it's like a scene from *Mad Max* having one bear down on you at 120km/h.

A few tips: when you see a road train approaching on a narrow bitumen road, slow down and pull over – if the truck has to put its wheels off the road to pass you, the resulting barrage of stones will almost certainly smash your windscreen. When trying to overtake one, allow plenty of room (about a kilometre) to complete the manoeuvre. Road trains throw up a lot of dust on dirt roads, so if you see one coming it's best to just pull over and stop until it's gone past.

And while you're on outback roads, don't forget to give the standard bush greeting to oncoming drivers – it's simply a matter of lifting the index finger off the steering wheel to acknowledge your fellow explorer.

Essential Outback

The Red Centre: Alice Springs, Uluru & Watarrka (Kings Canyon)

From Alice Springs it's a six-hour drive to Uluru-Kata Tjuta National Park. The Alice is a surprising oasis: big enough to have some great places to eat and stay, as well as some social problems. Uluru is to tourists what half a watermelon is to ants at a picnic: people from all over the globe swarm to and from this monolith at all times of the day. But it's still a remarkable find. The local Anangu people would prefer that you didn't climb it. Watarrka (Kings Canyon), about 300km north of Uluru, is a spectacular chasm carved into the rugged landscape.

The Stuart Highway: Adelaide to Darwin

In either direction, from the north or south, the Stuart Hwy is one of Australia's greatest road trips: 3020km of red desert sand, flat scrubland and galloping roadside emus. Heading north, make sure

OUTBACK CYCLING

Pedalling your way through the outback is certainly not something to tackle lightly, and certainly not something you'd even consider in summer. But you do see the odd wiry, suntanned soul pushing their panniers along the Stuart Hwy between Adelaide and Darwin. Availability of drinking water is the main concern: isolated water sources (bores, tanks, creeks etc) shown on maps may be dry or undrinkable. Make sure you've got the necessary spare parts and bike-repair knowledge. Check with locals if you're heading into remote areas, and always tell someone where you're headed. And if you make it through, try for a book deal – this is intrepid travel defined.

you stop at spookily pock-marked Coober Pedy – the opal-mining capital of the world – and detour to Uluru on your way to the Alice. Nitmiluk (Katherine Gorge) National Park is also en route, a photogenic series of sheer rocky gorges and waterholes. Kakadu National Park is next, with World Heritage–listed tropical wetlands. When you get to Darwin, reward yourself with a cold beer and some nocturnal high jinks on Mitchell St.

The Tropics: Darwin, Kakadu & Katherine

The outback in the tropical Top End is a different experience to the deserts further south. Here, the wet and dry seasons determine how easy it is to get from A to B. In the Wet, roads become impassable and crocodiles move freely through the wetlands. But before you cancel your plans, this is also a time of abundance and great natural beauty in the national parks – plus Kakadu resorts approach half-price! Darwin isn't technically in the outback, but it still feels like a frontier town, especially in the Dry when backpackers from around the world fill the bars and Mindil Beach market. Katherine, three hours to the south, is much more 'country', and the jumping-off point for the astonishing Nitmiluk (Katherine Gorge) National Park.

The Victoria Highway: Katherine to the Kimberley

The Victoria Hwy is a significant section of the epic Savannah Way from Cairns to Broome, the classic 'across-the-top' route. Leaving Katherine it winds through cattle country, where farms can be as big as small European countries. There are 4WD and hiking opportunities aplenty, plus outback camp sites, rock art galleries, national parks, red gorges and crocodiles. This region also boasts some of the Top End's best barramundi fishing. The immense Gregory National Park, a former cattle station is best explored with 4WD, although in the Dry a 2WD will get you into most of the historic sites, camp sites and Keep River National Park near the border with Western Australia.

Cape York

Another remote part of Australia's outback that few people visit is Cape York in Queensland – as far north as you can go without bumping into the Torres Strait Islands (the archipelago between Australia and Papua New Guinea). Heading north from Cairns, the landscape changes to tropical savannah: vast grasslands threaded with river systems, flowing into the Gulf of Carpentaria. Like in the Top End, the Wet and the Dry transform the scenery here. Most travellers find their way to Cairns and Port Douglas further south, but venture north along the Mulligan Hwy to explore remote national parks, Indigenous communities and mining towns.

Facilities

Outback roadhouses emerge from the desert heat haze with surprising regularity. It always pays to calculate the distance to the next fuel stop, but even on the remote Oodnadatta Track you'll find petrol and cold beer every few hundred kilometres. Most roadhouses (many of them open 24 hours) sell fuel and have attached restaurants where you can get a decent steak and a fry-up feed. Just don't expect an epicurean experience. There's often accommodation for road-weary drivers out the back – including camp sites, air-conditioned motel-style rooms, and basic cabins.

OUTBACK DRIVING & SAFETY CHECKLIST

Due to the lack of water, long distances between fuel stops and isolation, you need to be particularly organised and vigilant when travelling in the outback, especially on remote sandy tracks. Here are a few tips:

Communication

➡ Report your route and schedule to the police, a friend or relative.

➡ Mobile phones are pretty useless if you venture off the highway. Consider hiring a satellite phone, high-frequency (HF) radio transceiver equipped to pick up the Royal Flying Doctor Service bases, or emergency position-indicating radio beacon (EPIRB).

➡ In an emergency, stay with your vehicle; it's easier to spot than you are, and you won't be able to carry a heavy load of water very far.

➡ If you do become stranded, consider setting fire to a spare tyre (let the air out first). The pall of smoke will be visible for miles.

Your Vehicle

➡ Have your vehicle serviced and checked before you leave.

➡ Load your vehicle evenly, with heavy items inside and light items on the roof rack.

➡ Consider carrying spare fuel in an appropriate container.

➡ Carry essential tools: a spare tyre (two is preferable), fan belt, radiator hose, tyre-pressure gauge and air pump, and a shovel.

➡ An off-road jack might come in handy, as will a snatchem strap or tow rope for quick extraction when you're stuck (useful if there's another vehicle to pull you out).

Supplies & Equipment

➡ Carry plenty of water: in warm weather allow 5L per person per day and an extra amount for the radiator, carried in several containers.

➡ Bring plenty of food in case of a breakdown.

➡ Carry a first-aid kit, a good set of maps, a torch with spare batteries, a compass and a GPS.

➡ For updates on road conditions, see Resources on p1094.

Weather & Road Conditions

➡ Check road conditions before travelling: roads that are passable in the Dry (March to October) can disappear beneath water during the Wet.

➡ Don't attempt to cross flooded bridges or causeways unless you're sure of the depth, and of any road damage hidden underwater.

Dirt-road Driving

➡ Inflate your tyres to the recommended levels for the terrain you're travelling on; on desert sand, deflate your tyres to 20-25psi to avoid getting bogged. Don't forget to re-inflate them when you leave the sand.

➡ Reduce speed on unsealed roads, as traction is decreased and braking distances increase.

➡ Dirt roads are often corrugated: keeping an even speed is the best approach.

➡ Dust on outback roads can obscure your vision, so always stop and wait for it to settle.

➡ Choose a low gear for steep inclines and the lowest gear for steep declines. Use the brake sparingly and don't turn sideways on a hill.

Road Hazards

➡ Take a rest every few hours: driver fatigue is an all-too-common problem.

➡ Wandering cattle, sheep, emus, kangaroos, camels etc make driving fast a dangerous prospect. Take care and avoid nocturnal driving, as this is often when native animals come out. Many car-hire companies prohibit night-time driving.

➡ Road trains are an ever-present menace on the main highways. Give them a wide berth, they're much bigger than you!

Resources

Australian Bureau of Meteorology (www.bom.gov.au) Weather information.

Department of Environment, Water & Natural Resources (www.environment.sa.gov.au) Advice, maps and camping permits for SA's national parks.

Department of Planning, Transport & Infrastructure (☎1300 361 033; www.transport.sa.gov.au) SA road conditions.

Department of the Environment (www.environment.gov.au/parks) Extensive information about the federally administered Kakadu and Uluru-Kata Tjuta National Parks.

Live Traffic NSW (☎1300 131 122; www.livetraffic.com) NSW road conditions.

Main Roads Western Australia (☎13 81 38; www.mainroads.wa.gov.au) WA road conditions.

Road Report (☎1800 246 199; www.roadreport.nt.gov.au) NT road conditions.

Tourism NT (www.travelnt.com) Bountiful info on the Northern Territory outback. Also produces *The Essential NT Drive Guide*, a great booklet with driving distances, national parks, and outback info and advice for 2WD and 4WD travellers.

Tourism Western Australia (www.westernaustralia.com) Comprehensive website for general statewide information.

Traffic & Travel Information (☎13 19 40; http://highload.131940.qld.gov.au) Queensland road conditions.

Parks & Wildlife Commission NT (www.parksandwildlife.nt.gov.au) General advice on the NT's national parks: access, walking tracks, camping etc.

South Australian Tourism Commission (www.southaustralia.com) The lowdown on the South Australian outback, from the Flinders Ranges to Coober Pedy.

Organised Tours

If you don't feel like doing all the planning and driving, a guided tour is a great way to experience the Aussie outback. These range from beery backpacker jaunts between outback pubs, to Indigenous cultural tours and multiday bushwalking treks into remote wilderness.

PERMITS FOR ABORIGINAL LAND

➡ In the outback, if you plan on driving through pastoral stations and Aboriginal communities you may need to get permission first. This is for your safety; many travellers have tackled this rugged landscape on their own and required complicated rescues after getting lost or breaking down.

➡ Permits are issued by various Aboriginal land-management authorities; see destination chapters for details. Processing applications can take anywhere from a few minutes to a few days.

Outback Tracks

The Australian outback is criss-crossed by sealed highways, but one of the more interesting ways to get from A to B is by taking a detour along historic cattle and rail routes. While you may not necessarily need a 4WD to tackle some of these roads, the rugged construction of these vehicles makes for a much more comfortable drive. But whatever your wheels of choice, you will need to be prepared for the isolation and lack of facilities.

Don't attempt the tougher routes during the hottest part of the year (December to February, inclusive); apart from the risk of heat exhaustion, simple mishaps can lead to tragedy in these conditions. There's also no point going anywhere on outback dirt roads if there's been recent flooding.

Birdsville Track

Spanning 517km from Marree in SA to Birdsville just across the border of Queensland, this old droving trail is one of Australia's best-known outback routes – although it's not known for spectacular and varying scenery. It's often feasible to travel it in a well-prepared, conventional vehicle but not recommended. Don't miss a beer at the Birdsville Hotel!

FAST FACTS: ULURU & KATA TJUTA

- Uluru is composed of arkose, a course-grained sandstone laced with feldspar.
- Kata Tjuta rock is a conglomerate: gravel, pebbles and rocks bound in sand and mud.
- Uluru is 3.6km long, 348m high, 1.9km wide and 9.4km around the base. Kata Tjuta is higher at 546m.

Canning Stock Route

This old 2006km cattle-droving trail runs southwest from Halls Creek to Wiluna in WA. The route crosses the Great Sandy Desert and Gibson Desert and, since the track is entirely unmaintained, it's a route to be taken very seriously. You should travel only in a well-equipped 4WD party of at least three vehicles, equipped with high-frequency (HF) radio or emergency position-indicating radio beacon (EPIRB). Nobody does this trip in summer.

From Wiluna, the 1000km Gunbarrel Hwy runs to Warakurna near the NT border (where it joins the Outback Way). Again, 4WDs only, with water and fuel for the entire journey.

Finke & Old Andado Tracks

The Finke Track (the first part of which is the Old South Rd) follows the route of the old Ghan railway (long since dismantled) between Alice Springs and the Aboriginal settlement of Finke (Aputula). Along the way you can call into Chambers Pillar Historical Reserve to view the colourful sandstone tower. From Finke the road heads east along the Goyder Creek, a tributary of the Finke River, before turning north towards Andado Station and, 18km further, the homestead. At Old Andado the track swings north for the 321km trip to Alice. The Old Andado Track winds its way through the Simpson Desert to link the Old Andado Homestead with Alice Springs. On the way you pass the Mac Clark Conservation Reserve, which protects a stand of rare waddy trees. A high-clearance 4WD is definitely recommended and you should be equipped with high-frequency (HF) radio or emergency position-indicating radio beacon (EPIRB).

Gibb River Road

This short cut between Derby and Kununurra runs through the heart of the spectacular Kimberley in northern WA – it's approximately 660km, compared with about 920km via Hwy 1. The going is much slower, but the surroundings are so beautiful you'll probably find yourself lingering anyway. Although badly corrugated in places, it can usually be negotiated by conventional vehicles in the Dry (May to October) without too much difficulty; it's impassable in the Wet.

Nathan River Road

This road, which resembles a farm track in parts, is a scenic section of the Savannah Way, a cobbled-together route which winds all the way from Cairns to Broome. This particular section traverses some remote country along the western edge of the Gulf of Carpentaria between Roper Bar and Borroloola, much of it protected within Limmen National Park. A high-clearance vehicle is a must and carrying two spare tyres is recommended because of the frequent sharp rocks. Excellent camping beside barramundi- and crocodile-filled streams and waterholes is the main attraction here.

Oodnadatta Track

Mostly running parallel to the old Ghan railway line through outback SA, this iconic track is fully bypassed by the sealed Stuart Hwy to the west. Using this track, it's 429km from Marree to Oodnadatta, then another 216km to the Stuart Hwy at Marla. As long as there is no rain, any well-prepared conventional vehicle should be able to manage this fascinating route, but a 4WD will do it in style.

Outback Way

This route runs west from Uluru to Laverton in WA, from where you can drive down to Kalgoorlie and on to Perth. The road is well maintained and is normally OK for conventional vehicles, but it's pretty remote. It passes through Aboriginal land, for which travel permits must be obtained in advance; contact the WA Department of Aborignal Affairs for details (www.daa.wa.gov.au). It's almost 1500km from Yulara (the town nearest Uluru) to Kalgoorlie. For 300km, from near the Giles Meteorological Station, this road and the Gunbarrel

Hwy run on the same route. Taking the old Gunbarrel (to the north of Warburton) to Wiluna in WA is a much rougher trip, requiring a 4WD.

Plenty & Sandover Highways

These remote routes run east from the Stuart Hwy, north of Alice Springs, to Boulia or Mt Isa in Queensland. The Plenty Highway skirts the northern fringe of the Simpson Desert and offers the chance of gem fossicking in the Harts Range. The Sandover Hwy offers a memorable if monotonous experience in remote touring. It is a novelty to see another vehicle. Both roads are not to be taken lightly; they are often very rough going with little water and with sections that are very infrequently used. Signs of human habitation are rare and facilities are few and far between.

Red Centre Way & Mereenie Loop Road

Starting in Alice Springs this well-used track is an alternative route to the big attractions of the Red Centre. The route initially follows the sealed Larapinta and Namatjira Drives skirting the magnificent MacDonnell Ranges to Glen Helen Gorge. Beyond Glen Helen the route meets the Mereenie Loop Rd. This is where things get interesting. The Mereenie Loop Rd requires a permit ($5) and is usually so heavily corrugated that it will rattle a conventional 2WD until it finds its weak spot. This is the rugged short cut to Watarrka (Kings Canyon) National Park; from Watarrka the sealed Luritja Rd connects to the Lasseter Highway and Uluru-Kata Tjuta National Park.

Simpson Desert

The route crossing the Simpson Desert from Mt Dare, near Finke, to Birdsville is a real test of both driver and vehicle. A 4WD is definitely required on the unmaintained tracks and you should be in a party of at least three vehicles equipped with sat phones, HF radio and/or EPIRB.

Strzelecki Track

This track covers much of the same territory through SA as the Birdsville Track. Starting south of Marree at Lyndhurst, it reaches Innamincka 460km northeast and close to the Queensland border. It was at Innamincka that the hapless explorers Burke and Wills died. A 4WD is a safe bet, even though this route has been much improved due to work on the Moomba gas fields.

Tanami Track

Turning off the Stuart Hwy just north of Alice Springs, this 1000km route runs northwest across the Tanami Desert to Halls Creek in WA. The road has received extensive work so conventional vehicles are often OK, although there are sandy stretches on the WA side and it can be very corrugated if it hasn't been graded recently. Get advice on road conditions in Alice Springs.

Plan Your Trip
Australia Outdoors

Australia serves up plenty of excuses to just sit back and roll your eyes across the landscape, but that same landscape lends itself to boundless outdoor pursuits – whether it's getting active on the trails and mountains on dry land, or on the swells and reefs offshore.

When to Go

September & October

Spring brings the climax of football season, which means a lot of yelling from the grandstands. The more actively inclined rejoice in sunnier weather and warmer days, perfect for bushwalking, wildlife watching and rock climbing.

December–February

Australians hit the beach in summer: prime time for surfing, sailing, swimming, fishing, snorkelling, skydiving, paragliding...

March–May

Autumn is a nostalgic time in Australia, with cool nights and wood smoke: perfect weather for a bushwalk or perhaps a cycling trip – not too hot, not too cold.

June–August

When winter hits, make a beeline for the outback, the tropical Top End or the snow. Pack up your 4WD and head into the desert for a hike or scenic flight, or grab your snowboard and head into the mountains for some powdery fun.

On the Land

Bushwalking is a major pastime in all Australian states and territories. Cycling is a great way to get around, despite the mammoth distances sometimes involved. There's also skiing in the mountains and wildlife-watching pretty much everywhere.

Bushwalking

Bushwalking is supremely popular in Australia, with vast swathes of untouched scrub and forest providing ample opportunity. Hikes vary from 20-minute jaunts off the roadside to week-long wilderness epics. The best time to head into the bush varies from state to state, but as a general rule the further north you go the more tropical and humid the climate gets: June to August are the best walking months up north; down south, summer and early autumn (December to March) are better.

Notable walks include the Overland Track and the South Coast Track in Tasmania, and the Australian Alps Walking Track, Great Ocean Walk and Great South West Walk in Victoria. The Bibbulmun Track in Western Australia (WA) is epic, as is the Thorsborne Trail across Hinchinbrook Island and the Gold Coast Hinterland Great Walk in Queensland.

In New South Wales (NSW) you can trek between Sydney and Newcastle on the

Great North Walk, tackle Royal National Park's Coast Track, the Six Foot Track in the Blue Mountains, or scale Mt Kosciuszko, Australia's highest peak. In South Australia (SA) you can bite off a chunk of the 1200km Heysen Trail, while in the Northern Territory (NT) there's the majestic 233.5km Larapinta Trail and remote tracks in Nitmiluk (Katherine Gorge) National Park.

Bushwalking Safety

Before you lace up your boots, make sure you're walking in a region – and on tracks – within your realm of experience, and that you feel healthy and comfortable walking for a sustained period. Check with local authorities for weather and track updates: be aware that weather conditions and terrain can vary significantly within regions, and that seasonal changes can considerably alter any track.

Responsible Bushwalking

To help preserve the ecology and beauty of Australia, consider the following tips when bushwalking:

➡ Carry out all your rubbish, including sanitary napkins, tampons, condoms and toilet paper. Never bury your rubbish: digging disturbs soil and ground cover and encourages erosion. Buried rubbish will likely be dug up by animals, who may be injured or poisoned by it.

➡ Where there is a toilet, use it. Where there is none, bury your waste. Dig a small hole 15cm (6in) deep and at least 100m (320ft) from any watercourse. Cover the waste with soil and a rock. In snow, dig down to the soil.

➡ For personal washing, use biodegradable soap and a water container at least 50m (160ft) away from the watercourse. Disperse the waste water widely to allow the soil to filter it fully.

➡ Wash cooking utensils 50m (160ft) from watercourses using a scourer, sand or snow instead of detergent.

➡ Stick to existing tracks and avoid short cuts. Walking around a muddy bog only makes it bigger – plough straight through.

➡ Don't depend on open fires for cooking. Cook on a lightweight kerosene, alcohol or Shellite (white gas) stove and avoid those powered by disposable butane gas canisters.

➡ If you light a fire, use an existing fireplace. Don't surround fires with rocks. Use only dead, fallen wood. In huts, leave wood for the next person.

➡ Do not feed the wildlife as this can lead to animals becoming dependent on hand-outs, to unbalanced populations and to diseases.

BEST BUSHWALKS

➡ Thorsborne Trail, Queensland

➡ Great South West Walk, Victoria

➡ Overland Track, Tasmania

➡ Heysen Trail, Deep Creek Conservation Park, South Australia

➡ Larapinta Trail, Northern Territory

➡ Seek advice from environmental organisations such as the **Wilderness Society** (www.wilderness.org.au), the **Australian Conservation Foundation** (www.acfonline.org.au) and **Planet Ark** (www.planetark.org).

Cycling

Cyclists in Australia have access to plenty of cycling routes and can tour the country for days, weekends or even multiweek trips. Or you can just rent a bike for a few hours and wheel around a city.

Standout longer routes include the Murray to the Mountains Rail Trail and the East Gippsland Rail Trail in Victoria. In WA the Munda Biddi Trail offers 900km of mountain biking, or you can rampage along the same distance on the Mawson Trail in SA. The 480km Tasmania Trail is a north–south mountain-bike route across the length of the island state.

Rental rates charged by most outfits for road or mountain bikes start at around $20/40 per hour/day. Deposits range from $50 to $200, depending on the rental period. Most states have bicycle organisations that can provide maps and advice.

Wildlife Watching

The local wildlife is one of Australia's top selling points, and justifiably so. National parks are the best places to meet the residents, although many species are nocturnal so you may need to hone your torch (flashlight) skills to spot them.

Australia is a twitcher's (committed birdwatcher) haven, with a wide variety of habitats and **bird life**, particularly water birds. Canberra has the richest bird life of any Australian capital city. Birds are also big business in the tropical north, particularly in Kakadu National Park in NT where the bird life is astonishing (...not to mention the **crocodiles**).

In NSW there are **platypuses** and **gliders** in New England National Park, and

120 bird species in Dorrigo National Park. Border Ranges National Park is home to a quarter of all of Australia's bird species. Willandra National Park is World Heritage-listed and encompasses dense temperate wetlands and wildlife, and **koalas** are a dime a dozen around Port Macquarie. WA is also rife with bird-watching hotspots.

In Victoria, Wilsons Promontory teems with wildlife – in fact, **wombats** sometimes seem to outnumber people.

In SA make a beeline for Flinders Chase National Park on Kangaroo Island (KI) to see **koalas**, **kangaroos** and platypuses; and Flinders National Park in the north for **emus**. In Queensland, head to Malanda for bird life, **turtles** and **pademelons**; Cape Tribulation for even better bird life; Magnetic Island for koala spotting; Fraser Island for **dingoes**; and the Daintree Rainforest for **cassowaries**. In Tasmania, Maria Island is another twitcher's paradise, while Mt William and Mt Field National Parks teem with native fauna, including **Tasmanian devils** (...though probably not Tasmanian tigers).

Skiing & Snowboarding

Australia has a small but enthusiastic skiing industry, with snowfields straddling the NSW–Victoria border. The season is relatively short, however, running from about mid-June to early September, and snowfalls can be unpredictable. In NSW the top places to ski are within Kosciuszko National Park in the Snowy Mountains; in Victoria head for Mt Buller, Falls Creek or Mt Hotham in the High Country. Tasmania also has a few small ski fields.

On the Water

As Australia's national anthem will inform you, this land is 'girt by sea'. Surfing, fishing, sailing, diving and snorkelling are what people do here – national pastimes one and all. Marine-mammal-watching trips have also become popular in recent years. Inland there are vast lakes and meandering rivers, offering rafting, canoeing, kayaking and (yet more) fishing opportunities.

Where to Surf in Australia

Bells Beach, Cactus, Margaret River, the Superbank...mention any of them in the right company and stories of surfing legend will undoubtedly emerge. The Superbank hosts the first event on the Association of Surfing Professionals (ASP) World Tour calendar each year, and Bells Beach the second, with Bells the longest-serving host of an ASP event. Cactus dangles the lure of remote mystique, while Margaret River is a haunt for surfers chasing bigger waves.

While the aforementioned might be jewels, they're dot points in the sea of stars that Australia has to offer. Little wonder – the coastline is vast, touching the Indian, Southern and South Pacific Oceans. With that much potential swell, you'll find anything from innocent breaks to gnarly reefs not far from all six Australian state capitals.

New South Wales

➡ Manly through Avalon, otherwise known as Sydney's Northern Beaches.

➡ Byron Bay, Lennox Head and Angourie Point on the far north coast.

➡ Nambucca Heads and Crescent Head on the mid-north coast.

➡ The areas around Jervis Bay and Ulladulla on the south coast.

Queensland

➡ The Superbank (a 2km-long sandbar stretching from Snapper Rocks to Kirra Point).

➡ Burleigh Heads through to Surfers Paradise on the Gold Coast.

➡ North Stradbroke Island in Moreton Bay.

➡ Caloundra, Alexandra Heads near Maroochydore and Noosa on the Sunshine Coast.

Victoria

➡ Bells Beach, the spiritual home of Australian surfing (...when the wave is on, few would argue, but the break is notoriously inconsistent).

➡ Smiths Beach on Phillip Island.

➡ Point Leo, Flinders, Gunnamatta, Rye and Portsea on the Mornington Peninsula.

➡ On the southwest coast, Barwon Heads, Point Lonsdale, Torquay and numerous spots along the Great Ocean Road.

Tasmania

➡ Marrawah on the exposed northwest coast – can offer huge waves.

➡ St Helens and Bicheno on the east coast.

➡ Eaglehawk Neck on the Tasman Peninsula. Legendary Shipstern Bluff isn't far from here – Australia's heaviest wave.

➡ Closer to Hobart, Cremorne Point and Clifton Beach.

South Australia

➡ Cactus Beach, west of Ceduna on remote Point Sinclair – internationally recognised for quality and consistency.

➡ Greenly Beach on the western side of the Eyre Peninsula.

➡ Pennington Bay – the most consistent surf on Kangaroo Island.

➡ Pondalowie Bay and Stenhouse Bay on the Yorke Peninsula in Innes National Park.

➡ Victor Harbor, Port Elliot and Middleton Beach south of Adelaide.

Western Australia

➡ Margaret River, Gracetown and Yallingup in the southwest.

➡ Trigg Point and Scarborough Beach, just north of Perth.

➡ Further north at Geraldton and Kalbarri.

➡ Down south at Denmark on the Southern Ocean.

Diving & Snorkelling

The Great Barrier Reef has more dazzling diving and snorkelling sites than you can poke a fin at.

In WA, Ningaloo Reef is every bit as interesting as the east-coast reefs, without the tourist numbers. There are spectacular artificial reefs here, too, created by sunken ships at Albany and Dunsborough.

The Rapid Bay jetty off the Gulf St Vincent coast in SA is renowned for its abundant marine life, and in Tasmania the Bay of Fires and Eaglehawk Neck are popular spots. In NSW head for Jervis Bay and Fish Rock Cave off South West Rocks.

Fishing

Barramundi fishing is hugely popular across the Top End, particularly around Borroloola in the NT, and Karumba and Lake Tinaroo in Queensland.

Ocean fishing is possible right around the country, from pier or beach, or you can organise a deep-sea charter. There are magnificent glacial lakes and clear highland streams for trout fishing in Tasmania.

Before casting a line, be warned that strict limits to catches and sizes apply in Australia, and many species are threatened and therefore protected. Check local guidelines via fishing equipment stores or through individual state's government fishing bodies for information.

TOP FIVE WILDLIFE ENCOUNTERS

➡ Whales, Hervey Bay, Queensland.

➡ Grey kangaroos, Namadgi National Park, Australian Capital Territory.

➡ Penguins, Phillip Island, Victoria.

➡ Tasmanian devils, Maria Island, Tasmania.

➡ Dolphins, Monkey Mia, WA

Whale, Dolphin & Marine-life Watching

Southern right and humpback **whales** pass close to Australia's coast on their migratory route between the Antarctic and warmer waters. The best spots for whale-watching cruises are Hervey Bay in Queensland, Eden in southern NSW, the mid-north coast of NSW, Warrnambool in Victoria, Albany on WA's southwest cape, and numerous places in SA. Whale-watching season is roughly May to October. For **whale sharks** and **manta rays** try WA's Ningaloo Marine Park.

Dolphins can be seen year-round along the east coast at Jervis Bay, Port Stephens and Byron Bay in NSW; off the coast of WA at Bunbury and Rockingham; off North Stradbroke Island in Queensland; and you can swim with them off Sorrento in Victoria. You can also see **fairy penguins** in Victoria on Phillip Island. In WA, **fur seals** and **sea lions** can variously be seen at Rottnest Island, Esperance, Rockingham and Green Head, and all manner of beautiful sea creatures inhabit Monkey Mia (including **dugongs**). Sea lions also visit the aptly named (though not technically correct) Seal Bay on SA's Kangaroo Island.

Resources

Bicycles Network Australia (www.bicycles.net.au) Information, news and links.

Bushwalking Australia (www.bushwalkingaustralia.org) Website for the national body, with links to state/territory bushwalking clubs and federations.

Coastalwatch (www.coastalwatch.com) Surf-cams, reports and weather charts for all the best breaks.

Dive-Oz (www.diveoz.com.au) Diving resource.

Fishnet (www.fishnet.com.au) Devoted to all aspects of Australian fishing (nothing to do with stockings...).

Ski Online (www.ski.com.au) Commercial site with holiday offers plus snow-cams, forecasts and reports.

Regions at a Glance

It's easy to divide Australia into six neat states and two mainland territories. But when you're travelling around in a country this massive, political boundaries sometimes lose their significance. Rainforests and deserts don't pay much attention to state lines – and often exist side by side within the same state! So we've dug a bit deeper to describe 38 distinct regions within Australia's states and territories, defined as much by climate, landscape and culture as they are by governmental jurisdiction.

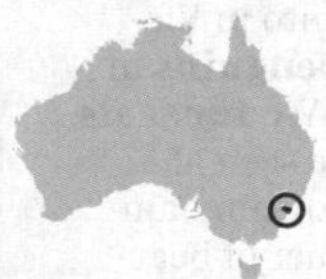

Sydney & Around

Beaches
Food & Drink
Nightlife

Sydney is Australia's financial 'big smoke', but most travellers come here for the gorgeous beaches, multicultural restaurants, hip bars and nightlife. The Sydney creed: eat, drink and party, then sleep it off on the sand the next day.

p62

NSW Central Coast

Surf Beaches
Lakes
Wineries

Truck north out of Sydney and you'll soon hit the Central Coast, a landscape of brilliant beaches, huge lakes and laid-back surf towns. Inland is the Hunter Valley, Australia's oldest wine region.

p143

Byron Bay & Northern NSW

Surf Beaches
Festivals
Hinterland Towns

Byron Bay: be in it, be around it...or just be! The 1970s hippie mantras still echo, but these days Byron is as much about surfing and music festivals as it is stoner vibes (for that, head into the hinterland).

p157

Canberra & NSW South Coast

History & Culture
Politics
Coastal Towns

Long derided as dull, new Canberra bristles with urban energy. Canberra's museums and galleries are superb, while the goings-on at Parliament House keep everyone entertained. Tracking southeast is a string of laid-back beach towns.

p201

Central & Outback NSW

Food & Drink
History
Outback Landscapes

The inland agricultural towns and remote outback landscapes of central and outback NSW are quintessentially Australian. Look forward to stylish eating and drinking in Orange and Mudgee, and amazing mining heritage in Broken Hill.

p231

Southern NSW

Small Towns
Rivers
Mountains

Leaving Sydney can be deflating...but not if you head south! Be charmed by historic Southern Highlands towns, the lush landscapes around the Murray and Murrumbidgee rivers, and Mt Kosciuszko, Australia's highest peak.

p257

Brisbane & Around

Urban Culture
Arts
Islands

Watch out Sydney and Melbourne, Brisbane is rising! Sassy bars, classy restaurants, vibrant arts and good coffee: Brisbane is ambitious, edgy and progressive. Beyond the city are laid-back island escapes and an unexpected wine region.

p267

Surfers Paradise & the Gold Coast

Surf Beaches
Nightlife
Theme Parks

Queensland's splashy Gold Coast is the place to learn to surf or party all night (or one after the other). The massive Gold Coast theme parks are a hit with families.

p311

Noosa & the Sunshine Coast

Beaches
National Parks
Surfing

The Sunshine Coast sounds kitsch, but once you splash in here that cliched name is soon forgotten. Local beaches are superb, some of the best of which are isolated sandy pockets within Noosa National Park.

p325

Fraser Island & the Fraser Coast

Wilderness
Wildlife
4WD Tracks

Fraser Island is the world's biggest sand island – an otherworldly atoll dappled with dunes, rainforests and freshwater lakes. Spotting dingoes and humpback whales heads the agenda, with fishing, swimming and boating next on the list.

p339

Capricorn Coast & the Southern Reef Islands

Beaches
Islands
Indigenous Culture

The Capricorn Coast doesn't receive as much traffic as other parts of Queensland – more beach, island, cave and snorkel space for you! Don't miss a steak dinner in Rockhampton and the Aboriginal rock art at Carnarvon Gorge.

p355

Whitsunday Coast

Islands
Beaches
Sailing

Queensland's Whitsunday islands have been much photographed, written-about and touted: now it's time to visit! Exclusive resorts, brilliant white-sand beaches, island-hopper sailing trips and memorable nights in Airlie Beach await.

p367

Townsville & Mission Beach

Beaches
Islands
Wildlife

As far a small cities go, Townsville has its urban charms. But what you're really here for are beaches and island retreats nearby. Don't miss Mission Beach, a chilled-out beach town with cassowaries roaming through the undergrowth.

p383

Cairns & the Daintree Rainforest

Tropical Reefs
Rainforest
Activities

Cairns and Port Douglas are prime launchpads for your Great Barrier Reef snorkelling trip. Cairns is activities central: ballooning, fishing, rafting, bungee jumping... The Daintree Rainforest ecosystem is astoundingly rich.

p401

Cape York Peninsula

Tropical Wilderness
4WD Tracks
Indigenous Culture

Queensland's far northern tip is a long way from anywhere, especially when the summer monsoons arrive. Take a 4WD to get the most out of these tropical wilds. There are enriching Aboriginal cultural experiences to be had here, too.

p443

Outback Queensland & Gulf Savannah

Country Culture
Outback Landscapes
Fishing

Sidestep the tourists and head into Queensland's outback heart, a land of rodeos, country music, remote pubs, dinosaur bones and endless skies. Things get tropical in the Gulf Savannah – barramundi fishing is the game.

p453

Melbourne & Around

Arts
Spectator Sports
Eating & Drinking

Melbourne is downright arty, with more galleries, band rooms, bookshops and theatres than hours in your holiday. Don't miss the cricket or Australian Rules football at the MCG, bar-hopping, coffee drinking or restaurant dining.

p469

Great Ocean Road

Coastal Scenery
Surfing
Small Towns

Wow, what a showstopper! A few days spent touring along the Great Ocean Road is one of the world's great road trips. Pack your surfboard, your camera and your appetite for fish-and-chips and cruise between sleepy coastal towns.

p529

Gippsland & Wilsons Promontory

Coastal Scenery
Bushwalking
Wildlife

Gippsland's divine, untrammelled coastline makes it hard to believe there's a city of 4.4-million people just down the highway. Walking, camping and wildlife watching in Wilsons Promontory National Park is a highlight.

p549

Grampians & the Goldfields

History
Small Towns
Wilderness

In the 1850s, Victoria's goldfields were the place to be. Gold-rush history defines the photogenic towns in the state's central-west, while the majestic Grampians National Park offers accessible wilderness and rich Aboriginal heritage.

p563

Victorian High Country

Mountains
Snow Sports
Food & Wine

Strap on your skis and head to Mt Buller or Falls Creek for a dose of winter magic. But in spring and summer the Victorian Alps are divine, with historic towns, wineries and gourmet food offerings dappling neighbouring valleys.

p583

Northwest Victoria

Rivers
Small Towns
History

The Murray River defines this area of Victoria, snaking its way into South Australia. Irrigation has turned the Mallee green – a patchwork of orchards and vineyards. Riverside towns like Echuca and Swan Hill are rich in paddleboat history.

p603

Hobart & Southeast Tasmania

Urban Culture
History
Gourmet Food

Infused with colonial history and graced with natural beauty, Hobart is the perfect small city. Superb eating and drinking, year-round festivals and marvellous MONA make it an essential detour.

p617

Launceston & Eastern Tasmania

Urban Culture
Beaches
Wine Regions

Launceston has long played second-fiddle to Hobart's cultural cello, but 'Lonnie' has hipster bars, cool cafes and restaurants, too. The East Coast is beachy heaven (don't miss Wineglass Bay). Tamar Valley Wine Region offers a different path to nirvana.

p651

North & Western Tasmania

Wilderness
Bushwalking
Wildlife

Tasmania's World Heritage-listed wilderness area is seriously beautiful. Hike the epic Overland Track to get amongst it, or scramble up Cradle Mountain for a good look. Down at ground level marsupials and reptiles are rampant.

p679

Adelaide & Around

Festivals
Wine Regions
Wildlife

Adelaide has outstanding festivals, including the high-arts Adelaide Festival and its errant offspring the Fringe Festival. The McLaren Vale Wine Region produces luscious shiraz, while Kangaroo Island's beaches and wildlife await offshore.

p707

Barossa Valley & Southeastern SA

Wine Regions
Rivers
Caves

The Barossa is the heartland of the Australian wine industry, bottling up big-name reds, while the Clare Valley does a refined riesling. Further afield, the mighty Murray River curls towards a limestone coastline riddled with amazing caves.

p755

Yorke Peninsula & Western SA

Coastal Scenery
National Parks
Seafood

Spend a few days exploring Yorke Peninsula, with its wheat-coloured fields rolling down to empty beaches. Further west, Lincoln and Coffin Bay national parks are glorious enclaves. Fresh seafood is ever-tempting across the Eyre Peninsula.

p779

Flinders Ranges & Outback SA

Mountains
Bushwalking
4WD Tracks

The photogenic Flinders Ranges rise from the semi-desert in a jagged spine. There's brilliant bushwalking and camping here. Further north, legendary 4WD tracks rattle across the bone-dry desert to quirky outback towns.

p791

Darwin & Around

Nightlife
National Parks
Indigenous Culture

Darwin after dark is a delirious experience, with backpackers cutting loose in the Mitchell St bars. Just down the highway are three of Australia's best national parks – Kakadu, Litchfield and Nitmiluk – with waterholes, Aboriginal cultural experiences and astonishing tropical wildlife.

p807

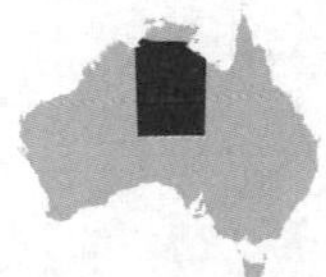

Uluru & Outback NT

Desert Scenery
Indigenous Culture
Wildlife

Uluru and Kata Tjuta are truly enormous red rocks. Watarrka is the inverse – a dazzlingly deep desert canyon. Join an Aboriginal cultural tour for a deeper insight, and encounter outback wildlife at the excellent Alice Springs Desert Park.

p843

Perth & Fremantle

Drinking
Eating
Museums

Perth and bohemian 'Freo' bake beneath the Western Australian sun: cool off with craft beers in hip bars and sunset-soaked pubs. The foodie scene here is booming too – but before you get too relaxed, spend some hours in WA's best museums.

p887

Around Perth

National Parks
Water Sports
History

A day-trip from Perth delivers you to the amazing Pinnacles in Nambung National Park, or into some beautiful historic towns. Down by the seaside there's fishing, surfing, snorkelling, windsurfing, sandboarding, diving and swimming with dolphins on offer.

p920

Margaret River & the Southwest Coast

Wineries
Surfing
Wilderness

WA is hot and dry, but this corner catches enough rain to sustain some brilliant vineyards and tall-tree forests. Sassy Margaret River is the regional hub, with amazing caves and some of Australia's best surf nearby.

p933

Southern WA

Coastal Scenery
Wilderness
Small Towns

Unlike WA's southwestern corner, the south coast is too far from Perth to attract day-trippers. Give yourself a good week to explore the region's tall forests, empty beaches, cliffs, wineries and endearing small towns.

p949

Monkey Mia & the Central West

Marine Life
Wilderness
Wild Flowers

Shark Bay's Monkey Mia is famous for its dolphins, but these waters also sustain dugongs, sea turtles, humpback whales, stingrays and (as you'd expect) sharks. Back on dry land are amazing gorges and a carpet of wild flowers in spring.

p971

Coral Coast & the Pilbara

Marine Life
National Parks
Seafood

Don't miss the absurdly fertile waters of World Heritage–listed Ningaloo Marine Park – one of the few places on Earth you can swim with whale sharks. Super seafood and the oasislike national parks are further Pilbara enticements.

p989

Broome & the Kimberley

Wilderness
Indigenous Culture
Luxury Accommodation

Australia's wild western frontier is the Kimberley – a gigantic wilderness area laced with gorges, spinifex, desert sands and waterfalls. Aboriginal culture is at the fore: check out some Indigenous art or take a tour.

p1009

On the Road

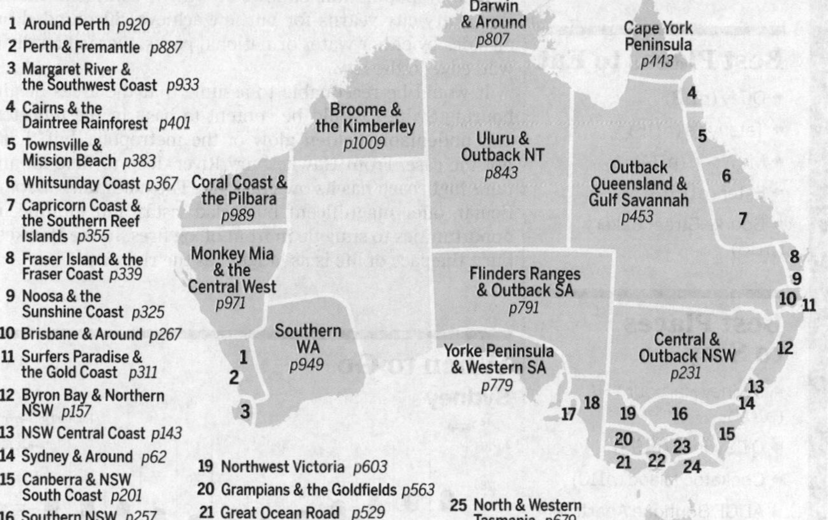
Darwin & Around p807
Cape York Peninsula p143
Broome & the Kimberley p1009
Uluru & Outback NT p843
Outback Queensland & Gulf Savannah p453
Coral Coast & the Pilbara p989
Monkey Mia & the Central West p971
Flinders Ranges & Outback SA p791
Southern WA p949
Yorke Peninsula & Western SA p779
Central & Outback NSW p231
1
2
3
4
5
6
7
8
9
10
11
12
13
14
15
16
17
18
19
20
21
22
23
24
25
26
27

Sydney & Around

Includes ➡

Best Places to Eat

- ➡ Quay (p113)
- ➡ Tetsuya's (p115)
- ➡ Mr Wong (p114)
- ➡ Ester (p116)
- ➡ Bourke Street Bakery (p116)

Best Places to Stay

- ➡ Sydney Harbour YHA (p107)
- ➡ QT Sydney (p108)
- ➡ Cockatoo Island (p110)
- ➡ ADGE Boutique Apartment Hotel (p110)
- ➡ Park Hyatt (p107)

Why Go?

Chances are Sydney will be your introduction to the island continent and, quite simply, there isn't a better one. The city's spectacular harbour setting, sun-kissed beaches and sophisticated sheen make it unique in Australia, while it's outdoorsy population endows it with a confident charm that every city yearns for but few achieve. Surrounded on all sides by either water or national parks, there's literally a wild edge to the city.

It would be reasonable to assume that the areas neighbouring Sydney would be content to bask in the reflected and undeniably golden glow of the metropolis, but that's not the case. From Hawkesbury River deep to Blue Mountains high, each has its own delights. The mountains, in particular, offer magnificent bush-clad vistas and munificent opportunities to snuggle in front of log fires. In the Hawkesbury, the pace of life is as languid as the river itself.

When to Go

Sydney

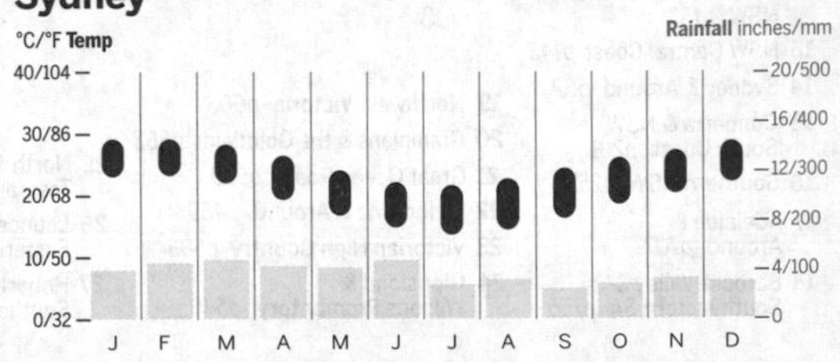

Jan The year kicks off with a spectacular fireworks display over Sydney Harbour.

Mar Sydney's summer party season culminates with the Gay & Lesbian Mardi Gras.

Jul Enjoy wood fires, wine and winter menus in the Blue Mountains.

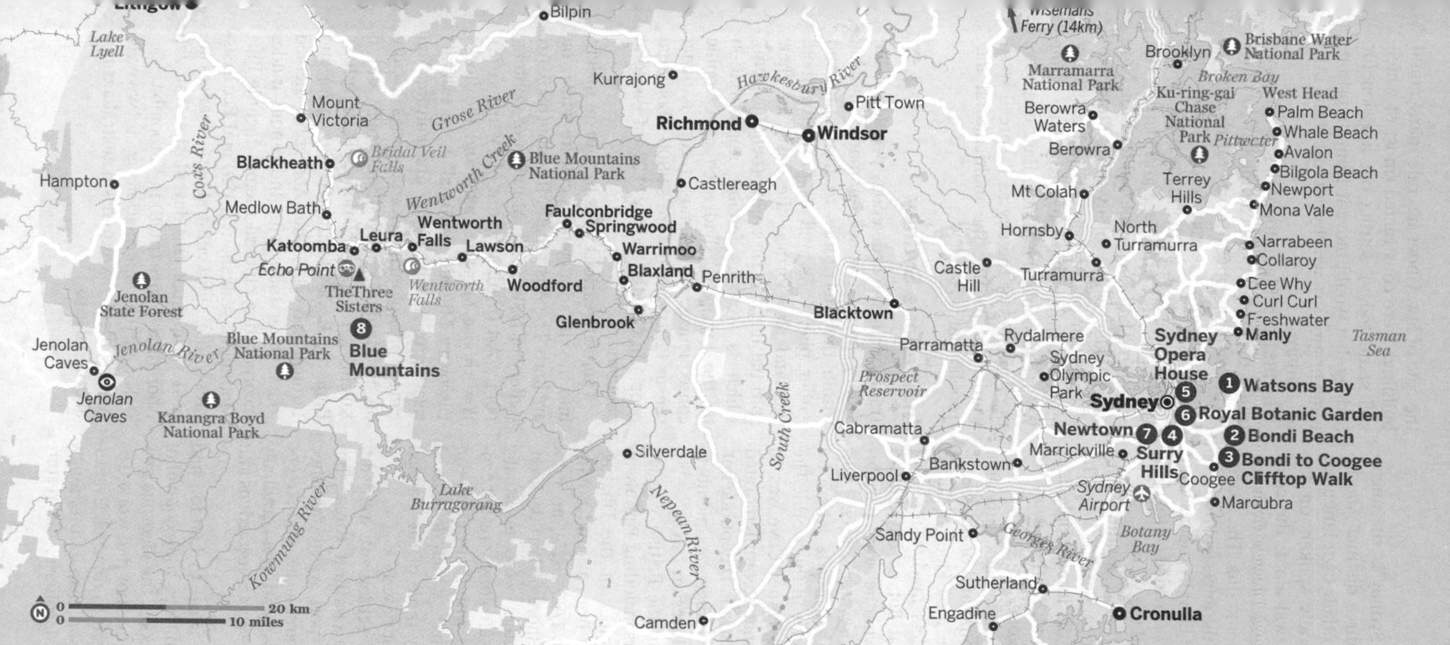

Sydney & Around Highlights

1. Hopping on one of Sydney's harbour ferries and heading to **Watsons Bay** (p93).
2. Whiling away the day on the golden sands of **Bondi Beach** (p93).
3. Enjoying the dramatic coastal scenery of the **Bondi to Coogee clifftop walk** (p96).
4. Eating and drinking your way through hip **Surry Hills** (p116).
5. Attending a performance at the **Sydney Opera House** (p127).
6. Strolling the leafy paths of the **Royal Botanic Garden** (p74) with Sydney Harbour sparkling below.
7. Rummaging through the secondhand stores and eclectic boutiques of bohemian **Newtown** (p131).
8. Following a bush trail under dense and ancient forest canopies in the **Blue Mountains** (p139).

History

What is now Greater Sydney is the ancestral home of at least three distinct Aboriginal peoples, each with their own language. Ku-ring-gai was generally spoken on the northern shore, Dharawal along the coast south of Botany Bay, and Dharug from the harbour to the Blue Mountains. The coastal area around Sydney is the ancestral home of the Eora people (which literally means 'from this place'), who were divided into clans such as the Gadigal and the Wangal.

In 1770 Lieutenant (later Captain) James Cook dropped anchor at Botany Bay. The ship's arrival alarmed the local people, and Cook noted in his journal: 'All they seem'd to want was for us to be gone.'

In 1788 the British came back, this time for good. Under the command of naval captain Arthur Phillip, the 'First Fleet' included a motley crew of convicts, marines and livestock. Upon arriving at Botany Bay, Phillip was disappointed by what he saw – particularly the lack of a fresh water source – and ordered the ships to sail north, where he found 'the finest harbour in the world'. The date of the landing at Sydney Cove was 26 January, an occasion that is commemorated each year with the Australia Day public holiday (known to many Indigenous members of the community as 'Invasion Day').

Armed resistance to the British was led by Indigenous warriors including Pemulwuy (c 1750–1802), a member of the Dharug-speaking Bidjigal clan from around Botany Bay, and Musquito (c 1780–1825), an Eora man from the north shore of Port Jackson. The Indigenous fighters were eventually crushed and the British colony wrested control. The fleet brought with them European diseases such as smallpox, which devastated the Eora people (only three of the Gadigal clan are said to have survived).

The early days of settlement were difficult, with famine a constant threat, but gradually a bustling port was established with stone houses, warehouses and streets. The surrounding bushland was gradually converted into farms, vegetable gardens and orchards.

In 1793 Phillip returned to London and self-serving military officers took control of Government House. Soon, the vigorous new society that the first governor had worked so hard to establish began to unravel. Eventually London took action, dispatching a new governor, Lachlan Macquarie, to restore the rule of law. Under his rule many grand buildings were constructed (most of which still stand today), setting out a vision for Sydney that would move it from its prison-camp origins to a worthy outpost of the British Empire.

In 1813 the Blue Mountains were penetrated by explorers Blaxland, Lawson and Wentworth, opening the way for the colony to expand onto the vast fertile slopes and plains of the west. By the 1830s the Lachlan, Macquarie, Murrumbidgee and Darling river systems had been explored and the New South Wales (NSW) colony started to thrive.

The 20th century saw an influx of new migrants from Europe (especially after WWII), Asia and the Middle East, changing the dynamics of the city as it spread westwards and became the multicultural metropolis that it is today.

Indigenous Sydney

Traditionally the Indigenous peoples of the Sydney area were semi-nomadic, moving within their territories to fish, hunt and gather plants. As well as providing food, the land also formed the basis for their spiritual life and Dreaming (belief system), which is why its forcible appropriation by the Europeans had such catastrophic consequences. At the most recent national census (2011) there were 54,800 Aboriginal people in Greater Sydney (1.2% of the total population).

There are various ways to gain an insight into the city's Indigenous culture while you are here. The Australian Museum (p86), Art Gallery of NSW (p76), Museum of Contemporary Art (p70), Museum of Sydney (p78), Powerhouse Museum (p85) and the Rocks Discovery Museum (p70) all have exhibits relating to Aboriginal life and culture. You can see pre-colonial rock engravings up close on the Manly Scenic Walkway (p99) and in Ku-ring-gai Chase National Park (p102). Both the Royal Botanic Garden (p74) and Taronga Zoo (p97) offer Aboriginal-themed tours. Other tours with Indigenous guides incorporating cultural themes include Blue Mountains Walkabout (p139) and EcoTreasures (p105). Short cultural performances are held throughout the day at the Waradah Aboriginal Centre (p138) in Katoomba.

For further information, go to www.visitnsw.com or www.tourism.australia.com//aboriginal.aspx.

National Parks

Sydney is ringed by national parks, with Ku-ring-gai Chase (p102) and Marramarra to the north, Wollemi and Blue Mountains (p135) to the west, Royal National Park to the south and Sydney Harbour National Park (p66), clinging to the edges of the harbour to the east. Other parks are ringed by the city itself, the most accessible of which is Lane Cove National Park (p97).

Check the website of the **NSW National Parks & Wildlife Service** (NPWS; www.nationalparks.nsw.gov.au) for details of visitor centres, walking tracks and camping options. Some parks charge a daily entry fee, which is generally $7 per vehicle. If you plan on visiting a number of parks, consider purchasing an annual multi-park pass ($65), which gives unlimited entry to all the state's parks and reserves except Kosciuszko National Park.

Many parks have camp sites with varying levels of facilities; some are free, others cost between $5 and $10 a night per person. Popular sites are often booked out during holidays. Bush camping is allowed in some parks.

Activities

Sydney and the surrounding national parks offer a huge array of activities suiting every level of fitness and fearlessness.

Bushwalking

Almost every national park has marked trails or wilderness-walking opportunities; these range from gentle wanders to longer, more challenging treks.

Near Sydney, the wilderness areas of Royal National Park hide dramatic clifftop walks including a 28km coastal walking trail. There are smaller bushwalks around the inlets of Broken Bay in Ku-ring-gai Chase National Park. West of Sydney, the sandstone bluffs, eucalyptus forests and wild flowers of the Blue Mountains offer a breathtaking experience. Keen walkers should try the 45km Six Foot Track from Katoomba to the Jenolan Caves.

The **NPWS website** (www.nationalparks.nsw.gov.au) offers loads of information about walks within its parks and reserves, and the **National Parks Association of NSW** (www.npansw.org.au) publishes the highly regarded *Bushwalks in the Sydney Region Volumes 1 & 2* by S Lord and G Daniel. Also look out for *Sydney's Best Bush, Park & City Walks*, which includes 50 walks and covers most of the major national parks, and the highly regarded *Blue Mountains: Best Bushwalks* (both by Veechi Stuart). Another useful resource is the online bushwalking and camping resource **Wildwalks** (www.wildwalks.com), which provides free maps and track notes for over 900 walks.

Cycling

Sydney's ever-growing network of cycling paths is a pivotal component of Sydney City Council's praiseworthy Sydney 2030 sustainability initiative. See www.sydneycycleways.net/for details. Other popular cycling destinations include the Blue Mountains and the Great North Rd around the Hawkesbury River.

You can access cycling guides and maps, a handy bike-shop finder and safety tips on the **Bicycle NSW website** (www.bicyclensw.org.au). Lonely Planet's *Cycling Australia* is another useful resource.

Scenic Drives

Spectacular scenic drives include the Greater Blue Mountains Drive and the Bells Line of Road between Richmond and Lithgow.

Surfing

You can fine-tune your surfing skills (or indeed learn some) at Bondi, Manly and dozens of other Sydney beaches. For surf forecasts and other information, go to www.coastalwatch.com.

Whale & Dolphin Watching

Every year between late May and late November, southern right and humpback whales migrate along the coast. You can view these magnificent creatures on a whale-watching cruise or grab a perch on any of the coastal cliffs and play spot-the-spouts.

Dolphins are very occasionally seen off Sydney's Eastern Beaches.

Getting There & Around

- Sydney Airport is the main gateway for most visitors to Australia and is also the country's major domestic hub.
- Sydney is NSW's major bus hub, with services extending as far afield as Brisbane in the north, Melbourne in the south and Adelaide in the west.
- Trains also head to Brisbane, Melbourne and Adelaide, with the luxurious Indian Pacific continuing all the way to Perth.
- By car and motorcycle, you'll probably reach Sydney via the Hume Hwy (Rte 31) if you're coming from the south, or via the Pacific Hwy (Rte 1) if you're coming from the north. The Princes Hwy heads south from Sydney along NSW's southern coast.
- For more information on getting to/from Sydney, see p132.

SYDNEY

POP 4.4 MILLION

Sunny, sophisticated and supremely self-confident, Sydney is the show pony of Australian cities. Built around one of the most beautiful harbours in the world, its myriad attractions include three of Australia's most emblematic sights – Sydney Harbour Bridge, Sydney Opera House and Bondi Beach. This is the country's oldest, largest and most diverse city, home to magnificent galleries, even more magnificent beaches and an edgy multiculturalism that injects colour and vitality into the inner neighbourhoods and outer suburbs.

 Sights

Sydney Harbour

Stretching 20km inland from the ocean to the mouth of the Parramatta River, this magnificent natural harbour is the city's shimmering soul. Providing a serene and picture-perfect backdrop to Sydney's fast-paced urban lifestyle, the harbour's beaches, coves, islands and wildlife-filled pockets of national park offer innumerable options for recreation, relaxation and rejuvenation. Exploring this vast and visually arresting area by ferry is one of Sydney's great joys.

Forming the gateway to the harbour from the ocean are North Head and South Head. The former fishing village of Watsons Bay nestles on South Head's harbour side, and the city's favourite day-trip destination, Manly, occupies a promontory straddling harbour and ocean near North Head.

The focal point of the inner harbour and the city's major ferry hub is Circular Quay. From here, you are able to catch ferries to destinations along both shores of the harbour, as well as up the river and to some of the harbour islands.

★Sydney Harbour Bridge BRIDGE

(Map p72; Circular Quay) Sydneysiders adore their giant 'coathanger'. Opened in 1932, this majestic structure spans the harbour at one of its narrowest points. The best way to experience the bridge is on foot – don't expect much of a view crossing by car or train. Stairs climb up the bridge from both shores, leading to a footpath running the length of the eastern side. You can climb the southeastern pylon to the Pylon Lookout or ascend the great arc on the wildly popular BridgeClimb (p105).

The harbour bridge is a spookily big object – moving around town you'll catch sight of it in the corner of your eye, sometimes in the most surprising of places. At 134m high, 1149m long, 49m wide and weighing 52,800 tonnes, it's the largest and heaviest (but not the longest) steel arch in the world.

The two halves of chief engineer JJC Bradfield's mighty arch were built outwards from each shore. In 1930, after nine years of merciless toil by 1400 workers, the two arches were only centimetres apart when 100km/h winds set them swaying. The coathanger hung tough and the arch was finally bolted together.

Perhaps Sydney poet Kenneth Slessor said it best: 'Day and night, the bridge trembles and echoes like a living thing.'

Sydney Harbour National Park NATIONAL PARK

(www.nationalparks.nsw.gov.au) Sydney Harbour National Park protects large swathes of bushland around the harbour shoreline, plus several **harbour islands**. In among the greenery you'll find walking tracks, scenic lookouts, Aboriginal carvings, beaches and a handful of historic sites. The park incorporates **South Head** (Map p68; www.nationalparks.nsw.gov.au; Cliff St; 5am-10pm; Watsons Bay) and Nielsen Park (p91) on the south side of the harbour, but most of the park is on the North Shore – including **Bradleys Head**, **Middle Head**, **Dobroyd Head** and North Head (p98).

Pylon Lookout VIEWPOINT

(Map p72; 02-9240 1100; www.pylonlookout.com.au; adult/child $13/6.50; 10am-5pm; Circular Quay) The views from the top of the Harbour Bridge's southeast pylon are awesome, and museum exhibits here explain how the bridge was built. The pylons may look as though they're shouldering all the weight, but they're largely decorative – right down to their granite facing. Enter via the bridge stairs on Cumberland St.

Cockatoo Island ISLAND

(Map p68; 02-8969 2100; www.cockatooisland.gov.au; Cockatoo Island) Studded with photogenic industrial relics, convict architecture and art installations, fascinating Cockatoo Island (Wareamah) opened to the public in 2007 and now has regular ferry services, a campground, rental accommodation, a cafe and a bar. Information boards and audio guides ($5) explain the island's time as a prison, shipyard and naval base.

A spooky tunnel passes clear through the middle of the island and you can also explore the remains of the prison. During WWII most of the old sandstone buildings were stripped of their roofs and converted into bomb shelters. Solitary confinement cells were unearthed here recently after being filled in and forgotten in the 1890s.

Goat Island ISLAND

(Map p68; ☎02-9253 0888; www.nationalparks.nsw.gov.au; tour adult/child $38/29) Goat Island, west of the Harbour Bridge, has been a shipyard, quarantine station and gunpowder depot in its previous lives. Heritage tours are offered for groups of 20 or more (see the national parks website for details).

Fort Denison FORTRESS

(Map p68; www.fortdenison.com.au; tour $16/14; ⏲tours 11am, 12.15pm, 1.45pm & 2.45pm) Called Mat-te-wan-ye (rocky island) by the Gadigal people, in colonial times the small fortified island off Mrs Macquaries Point was a sorry site of suffering, used to isolate recalcitrant convicts. It was nicknamed 'Pinchgut' for its meagre rations. Fears of a Russian invasion during the mid-19th-century Crimean War led to its fortification. The NPWS offers tours of the Martello tower (cheaper if prebooked with your ferry ticket), although plenty of people just pop over to visit the cafe.

Both Captain Cook Cruises (p105) and Manly Fast Ferry (p134) have several services per day heading to the island from Darling Harbour and Circular Quay.

Shark Island ISLAND

(Map p68; www.nationalparks.nsw.gov.au; ferry adult/child $20/17) Little Shark Island, off Rose Bay, makes a great picnic getaway. There's not a lot here except for toilets and drinking water – and at 250m by 100m, you'll soon have explored every inch of it. Captain Cook Cruises (p105) runs four ferries per day to the island from Circular Quay (jetty 6) and Darling Harbour (pier 26).

The Rocks & Circular Quay

Sydney Cove carries the weight of Sydney iconography, with the Harbour Bridge and the Opera House abutting each point of its horseshoe. The site of Australia's first European settlement is unrecognisable from the squalid place it once was, where ex-convicts, sailors and whalers boozed and brawled in countless harbourside pubs and nearly as many brothels and opium dens. The open sewers and foul alleys of **the Rocks** have been transformed into an 'olde worlde' tourist trap, while the Circular Quay promenade serves as a backdrop for buskers of mixed merit and locals disgorging from harbour ferries.

The Rocks remained a commercial and maritime hub until shipping services left Circular Quay in the late 1800s. A bubonic

SYDNEY IN...

Two Days

Start your first day with our walking tour through **the Rocks**. Visit the **Museum of Contemporary Art** (p70) and then follow the harbour past the **Opera House** (p74) to the **Royal Botanic Garden** (p74) and on to the **Art Gallery of NSW** (p76). That night, enjoy a performance at the **Opera House** (p127) or check out the action in **Kings Cross** or **Darlinghurst**.

Next day, it's time to spend the day soaking up the sun and scene at **Bondi** – be sure to take the **clifftop walk** to Coogee and then make your way back to Bondi for a sunset dinner at **Icebergs Dining Room** (p120).

Four Days

On day three, board a ferry and sail through the harbour to **Manly**, where you can swim at the beach or follow the **Manly Scenic Walkway** (p99). That night, head to **Surry Hills** for drinks and dinner.

On day four, learn about Sydney's convict heritage at the **Hyde Park Barracks Museum** (p77) and then spend the afternoon shopping in **Paddington** or **Newtown**.

One Week

With a week, you can spare a couple of days to visit the majestic **Blue Mountains**, fitting in a full day of bushwalking before rewarding yourself with a gourmet dinner. Back in Sydney, explore **Watsons Bay**, **Darling Harbour** and **Taronga Zoo**.

Sydney

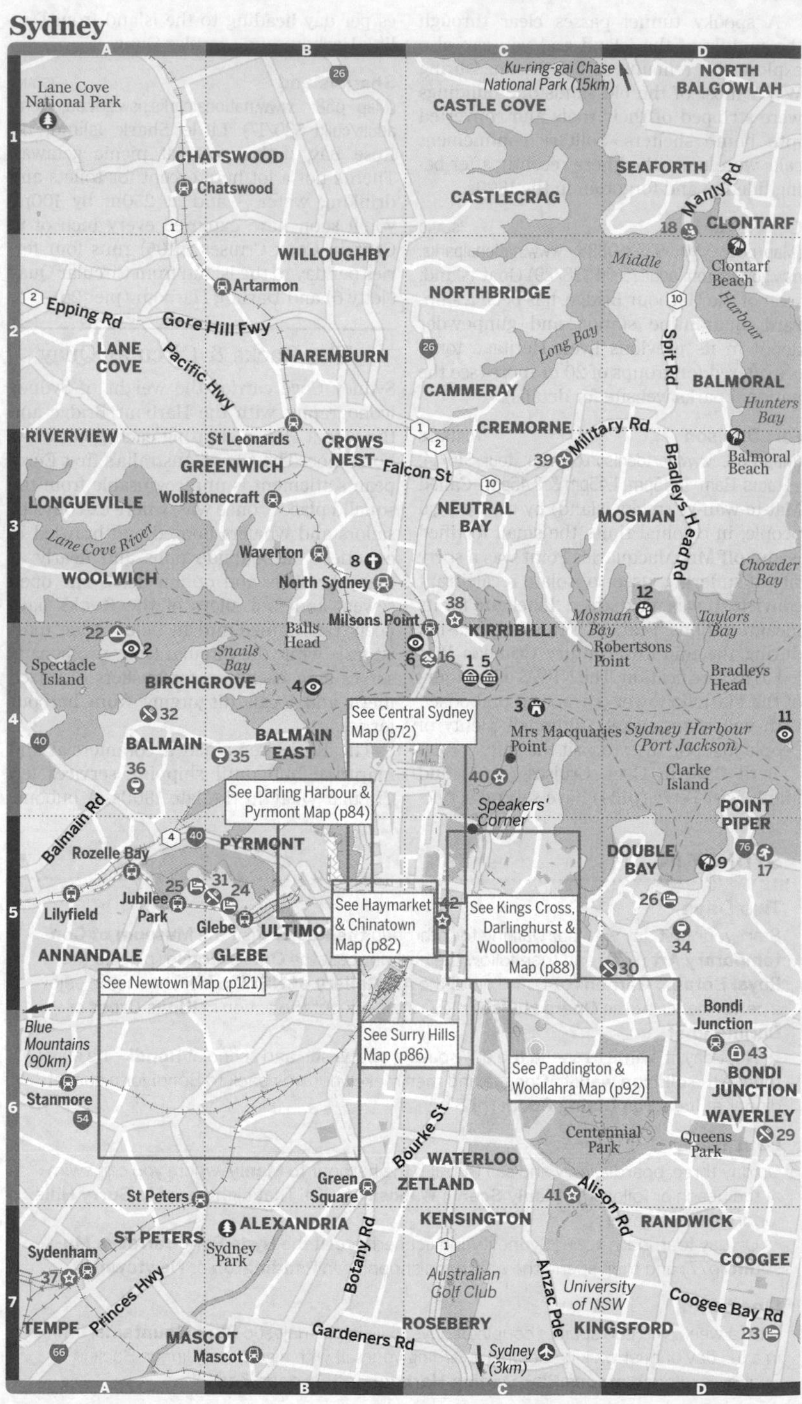
Lane Cove National Park
Ku-ring-gai Chase National Park (15km)
NORTH BALGOWLAH
CASTLE COVE
CHATSWOOD
Chatswood
SEAFORTH
Manly Rd
CASTLECRAG
CLONTARF
WILLOUGHBY
Middle Harbour
Clontarf Beach
Artarmon
NORTHBRIDGE
Epping Rd
Gore Hill Fwy
LANE COVE
Pacific Hwy
NAREMBURN
Long Bay
Spit Rd
BALMORAL
CAMMERAY
Hunters Bay
RIVERVIEW
St Leonards
CROWS NEST
CREMORNE
Military Rd
GREENWICH
Falcon St
Balmoral Beach
Bradleys Head Rd
LONGUEVILLE
Wollstonecraft
NEUTRAL BAY
MOSMAN
Lane Cove River
Waverton
WOOLWICH
North Sydney
Chowder Bay
Milsons Point
KIRRIBILLI
Mosman Bay
Taylors Bay
Balls Head
Snails Bay
Robertsons Point
Spectacle Island
BIRCHGROVE
Bradleys Head
See Central Sydney Map (p72)
BALMAIN
BALMAIN EAST
Mrs Macquaries Point
Sydney Harbour (Port Jackson)
Clarke Island
See Darling Harbour & Pyrmont Map (p84)
Speakers' Corner
POINT PIPER
Balmain Rd
Rozelle Bay
PYRMONT
DOUBLE BAY
Jubilee Park
Lilyfield
Glebe
ULTIMO
See Haymarket & Chinatown Map (p82)
See Kings Cross, Darlinghurst & Woolloomooloo Map (p88)
ANNANDALE
GLEBE
See Newtown Map (p121)
Blue Mountains (90km)
See Surry Hills Map (p86)
Bondi Junction
See Paddington & Woollahra Map (p92)
BONDI JUNCTION
Stanmore
WAVERLEY
Centennial Park
Queens Park
Bourke St
WATERLOO
Green Square
ZETLAND
St Peters
Alison Rd
KENSINGTON
RANDWICK
ALEXANDRIA
ST PETERS
Sydney Park
Sydenham
Botany Rd
Princes Hwy
Australian Golf Club
Anzac Pde
University of NSW
COOGEE
Coogee Bay Rd
TEMPE
MASCOT
Gardeners Rd
ROSEBERY
KINGSFORD
Mascot
Sydney (3km)

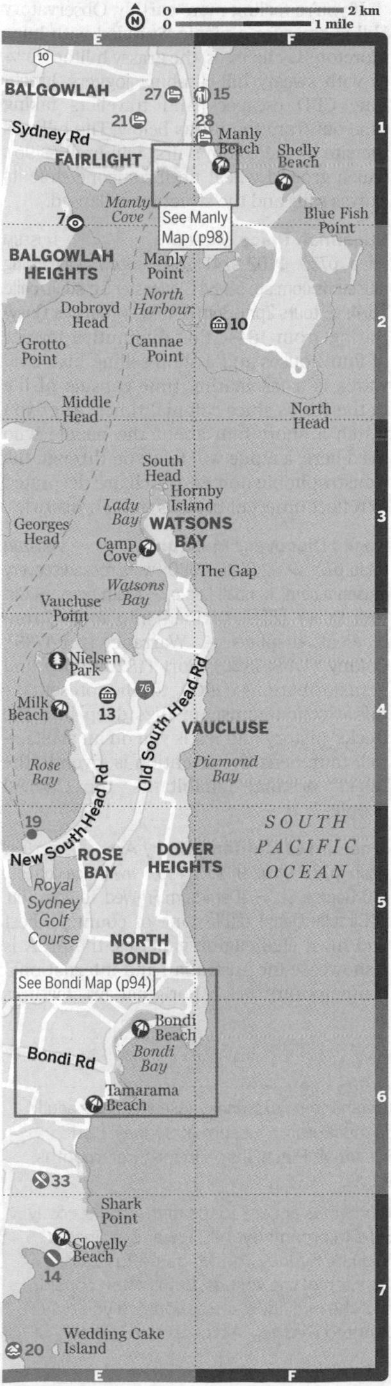

Sydney

Sights
1 Admiralty House C4
2 Cockatoo Island A4
3 Fort Denison C4
4 Goat Island B4
5 Kirribilli House C4
6 Luna Park C4
7 Manly Scenic Walkway E1
8 Mary MacKillop Place B3
9 Murray Rose Pool D5
10 Quarantine Station F2
11 Shark Island D4
12 Taronga Zoo D3
13 Vaucluse House E4

Activities, Courses & Tours
14 Gordons Bay Underwater Nature Trail E7
15 Manly Surf School F1
16 North Sydney Olympic Pool C4
17 Sydney by Seaplane D5
18 Sydney Harbour Kayaks D1
19 Sydney Seaplanes E5
20 Wylie's Baths E7

Sleeping
21 Cecil Street B&B E1
22 Cockatoo Island A4
23 Dive Hotel D7
24 Forsyth Bed & Breakfast B5
25 Glebe Point YHA A5
26 InterContinental Sydney Double Bay D5
27 Manly Bunkhouse E1
28 Novotel Sydney Manly Pacific F1

Eating
29 Bronte Road Bistro D6
30 Four in Hand D5
31 Glebe Point Diner B5
32 Riverview Hotel & Dining A4
33 Three Blue Ducks E6

Drinking & Nightlife
34 Golden Sheaf Hotel D5
35 London Hotel B4
36 Welcome Hotel A4

Entertainment
37 Camelot Lounge A7
38 Ensemble Theatre C3
39 Hayden Orpheum Picture Palace C3
40 OpenAir Cinema C4
41 Royal Randwick Racecourse C6
42 Slide C5

Shopping
43 Westfield Bondi Junction D6

plague outbreak in 1900 continued the decline. Construction of the Harbour Bridge in the 1920s brought further demolition and entire streets disappeared under the bridge's southern approach. It wasn't until the 1970s that the Rocks' cultural and architectural heritage was recognised and the ensuing tourism-driven redevelopment saved many old buildings.

Beyond the **Argyle Cut** (Map p72; Argyle St; Circular Quay), an impressive tunnel excavated by convicts, is **Millers Point**, a charming district of early colonial homes.

SH Ervin Gallery GALLERY

(Map p72; 02-9258 0173; www.shervingallery.com.au; Watson Rd; adult/concession/under 12 $7/5/free; 11am-5pm Tue-Sun; Wynyard) High on the hill inside the old Fort St School (1856), the SH Ervin Gallery exhibits invariably rewarding historical and contemporary Australian art. Annual mainstays include the Salon des Refusés (alternative Archibald Prize entries) and the Portia Geach Memorial Award. There's a cafe here, too.

Sydney Observatory OBSERVATORY

(Map p72; 02-9921 3485; www.sydneyobservatory.com.au; 1003 Upper Fort St; 10am-5pm; Circular Quay) FREE Built in the 1850s, Sydney's copper-domed, Italianate observatory squats atop pretty **Observatory Hill**, overlooking the harbour. Inside is a collection of vintage apparatus, including Australia's oldest working telescope (1874). Also on offer are audiovisual displays, including Aboriginal sky stories and a virtual reality **3D Theatre** (www.sydneyobservatory.com.au; adult/child $10/8; 2.30pm & 3.30pm daily, plus 11am & noon Sat & Sun; Circular Quay). Bookings are essential for night-time stargazing sessions (adult/child $18/12).

If you're feeling more earthly, Observatory Hill is great for a picnic. Studded with huge Moreton Bay fig trees, the grassy hilltop buzzes with sweaty hill-climbing joggers, lunchtime CBD escapees and travellers taking time out from the Rocks below. The hill was the site of the colony's first windmill (1796), which ground wheat until someone stole its canvas sails and the structure collapsed.

Susannah Place Museum MUSEUM

(Map p72; 02-9241 1893; www.sydneylivingmuseums.com.au; 58-64 Gloucester St; adult/child $8/4; tours 2pm, 3pm & 4pm; Circular Quay) Dating from 1844, this diminutive terrace of four houses and a shop selling historical wares is a fascinating time capsule of life in the Rocks since colonial times. After you watch a short film about the people who lived here, a guide will take you through the claustrophobic homes, which are decorated to reflect different periods in their histories.

Rocks Discovery Museum MUSEUM

(Map p72; 02-9240 8680; www.rocksdiscoverymuseum.com; Kendall Lane; 10am-5pm; Circular Quay) FREE Divided into four chronological displays – Warrane (pre-1788), Colony (1788–1820), Port (1820–1900) and Transformations (1900 to the present) – this excellent museum digs deep into the Rocks' history and leads you on an artefact-rich tour. Sensitive attention is given to the Rocks' original inhabitants, the Gadigal people.

Museum of Contemporary Art GALLERY

(Map p72; 02-9245 2400; www.mca.com.au; 140 George St; 10am-5pm Fri-Wed, to 9pm Thu; Circular Quay) FREE One of country's best and most challenging galleries, the MCA is a showcase for Australian and international contemporary art. Aboriginal art features

DISCOUNT PASSES

Sydney Museums Pass (www.sydneylivingmuseums.com.au/sydney-museums-pass; adult/child $18/9) allows a single visit to four boutique museums: Museum of Sydney, Hyde Park Barracks, Justice & Police Museum and Susannah Place. It's valid for three months and available at each of the participating museums.

Ultimate Sydney Pass (adult/child $99/70) provides access to the high-profile, costly attractions operated by British-based Merlin Entertainment: Sydney Tower Eye (including the Skywalk), Sydney Sea Life Aquarium, Wild Life Sydney Zoo, Madame Tussauds and Manly Sea Life Sanctuary. It's available from each of the venues, but is often considerably cheaper online (visit any of the websites of the individual attractions). If you only plan on visiting some of these attractions, discounted **Sydney Attractions Passes** are available in any combination you desire.

WORTH A TRIP

PARRAMATTA RIVER

Sydney Harbour gets all the attention but a jaunt upriver to the geographical centre of the metropolis is just as interesting. As you pass old industrial sites and gaze into millionaires' back yards, a window opens onto a watery world in the heart of Sydney where school rowing crews get put through their paces, groups of mates glide pasts on yachts, solo kayakers work up a sweat and Mediterranean men fish off the wharves at night.

In geological terms the harbour is actually a drowned river valley, which makes it very hard to distinguish what's harbour and what's river, but as you glide past Cockatoo Island, where the Parramatta and Lane Cove Rivers meet, it's river all the way.

The ferry from Circular Quay to Parramatta takes about 1¼ hours (adult/child $7.60/3.80), although on some low tides the boats stop at Rydalmere, one wharf earlier, and a bus continues from there. If you feel like making a day of it, Sydney Olympic Park and Parramatta both have a smattering of interesting sights. And if you want to speed up your return trip, both are connected to the train network.

In Parramatta, make your first stop the **Parramatta Heritage & Visitor Information Centre** (1300 889 714; www.discoverparramatta.com; 346a Church St; 9am-5pm; Parramatta) and grab a map of key sights. The centre is a museum in its own right, with temporary exhibits by local artists, as well as a permanent exhibition on Parramatta's history and culture.

The second European settlement in Australia, Parramatta was founded by First Fleet convict labour when Sydney Cove proved to be lousy for growing vegetables. Although Sydney's reserves of glamour are running dry by the time you get this far west, there are some interesting historic sights to visit, including:

Old Government House (02-9635 8149; www.nationaltrust.org.au; Parramatta Park; adult/child $10/8; 10am-4pm Tue-Sun; Parramatta) The country residence of the early governors, this elegant Georgian Palladian building is now a preciously maintained museum furnished with original colonial furniture. It dates from 1799, making it the oldest remaining public building in Australia. Phone for details of monthly ghost nights.

Elizabeth Farm (02-9635 9488; www.sydneylivingmuseums.com.au; 70 Alice St; adult/child $8/4; 10.30am-3.30pm Sat & Sun; Rosehill) Elizabeth Farm contains part of Australia's oldest surviving European home (1793), built by renegade pastoralist and rum trader John Macarthur. Heralded as the founder of Australia's wool industry, Macarthur was a ruthless capitalist whose politicking made him immensely wealthy and a thorn in the side of successive governors. The pretty homestead is now a hands-on museum where you can recline on the reproduction furniture and thumb voyeuristically through Elizabeth Macarthur's letters.

prominently. The fab Gotham City–style art deco building bears the wounds of a redevelopment that has grafted on additional gallery space and a rooftop cafe/sculpture terrace – and ruined the George St facade in the process.

Volunteer-led guided tours are offered at 11am and 1pm daily, and at 7pm Thursdays and 3pm on weekends.

St Patrick's Church CHURCH
(Map p72; 02-9254 9855; www.stpatschurchhill.org; 20 Grosvenor St; 9am-4.30pm; Wynyard) This attractive sandstone church (1844) was built on land donated by William Davis, an Irishman transported for his role in the 1798 uprisings. Inside it's incredibly quiet, which makes the brass altar, the stained-glass windows and the colourful statues of St Patrick, St Joan of Arc and St Michael (complete with dragon) seem even more striking. Guided tours are infrequent but worthwhile; visit the website for details.

Davis' home (on the site of the chapel-turned-cafe) was arguably the first Catholic chapel in Australia; it was used for clandestine devotions and secretly housed a consecrated host after the colony's only Catholic priest was deported in 1818.

Customs House HISTORIC BUILDING
(Map p72; 02-9242 8555; www.sydneycustomshouse.com.au; 31 Alfred St; 10am-7pm Mon-Fri, 11am-4pm Sat & Sun; Circular Quay) FREE This elegant harbourside edifice (1885) houses a bar, **Cafe**

Central Sydney, The Rocks & Circular Quay

0 200 m
0 0.1 miles

A B C D

1 2 3 4 5 6 7

2 Sydney Harbour Bridge
20
Walsh Bay
Dawes Point Park
Hickson Rd Reserve
Sydney Harbour (Port Jackson)
Bennelong Point
Sydney Harbour Tunnel
42
83
Hickson Rd
Lower Fort St
Bradfield Hwy
Campbells Cove
Clyne Reserve
Towns Pl
Dalgety Rd
Cumberland St
Hickson Rd
3 Sydney Opera House
75
THE ROCKS
Circular Quay West
Sydney Cove
Windmill St
71
Trinity Ave
34
57
41
Munn Street Reserve
Playfair St
88
Mrs Macquaries Point; Open-Air Cinema (800m)
Argyle St
6 61
22
60
50
High La
High St
Observatory Hill
Sydney Visitor Centre
MILLERS POINT
39
37 33 86
29
63
George St
80
11
40
48
28
67
17
Circular Quay East
Kent St
47
Harrington St
First Fleet Park
45
Circular Quay
35
43
Gloucester St
46
44
Cahill Exp
Circular Quay
23
65
70
84
City Host Information Kiosk
Alfred St
Albert St
Royal Botanic Garden 1
Hickson Rd
Jenkins St
Essex St
Rugby Pl
9
15
Loftus St
Young St
26
78
Grosvenor St
Lang Park
Bridge Ln
Macquarie Pl
Bridge St
82
53 58 38
Pitt St
18
66
56
Phillip St
Phillip La
Jamison St
Bond St
Spring St
O'Connell St
Bent St
Western Dstr
74
Margaret St
Wynyard Park
Curtin Pl
George St
Wynyard La
Bligh St
68
Macquarie St
Wynyard
Hunter St
59
27
Shelley St
Lime St
72
Pitt St
Erskine St
York La
Clarence St
51 79
Castlereagh St
King Street Wharf
52
Sussex St
Kent St
Angel Pl
16
Martin Pl
8
Elizabeth St
Martin Place
19
Hospital Rd
York St
12
49
4
77
Phillip St
10
The Mint
King St
King St
14
Art Gallery Rd
24
Sussex St
Kent St
64
89
76
Pitt St Mall
54
St James Rd
The Domain
Darling Harbour
30
85
St James
5
Market St
81
St Marys Rd
55
21
25
73
College St
Cockle Bay
69
13
Hyde Park
Cook + Phillip Park
62
Druitt Pl
32
87
Pitt St
Parkway
Druitt St
Riley St
31
Park St
Town Hall
36
Druitt La
William St
Bathurst St
7
George St
Elizabeth St

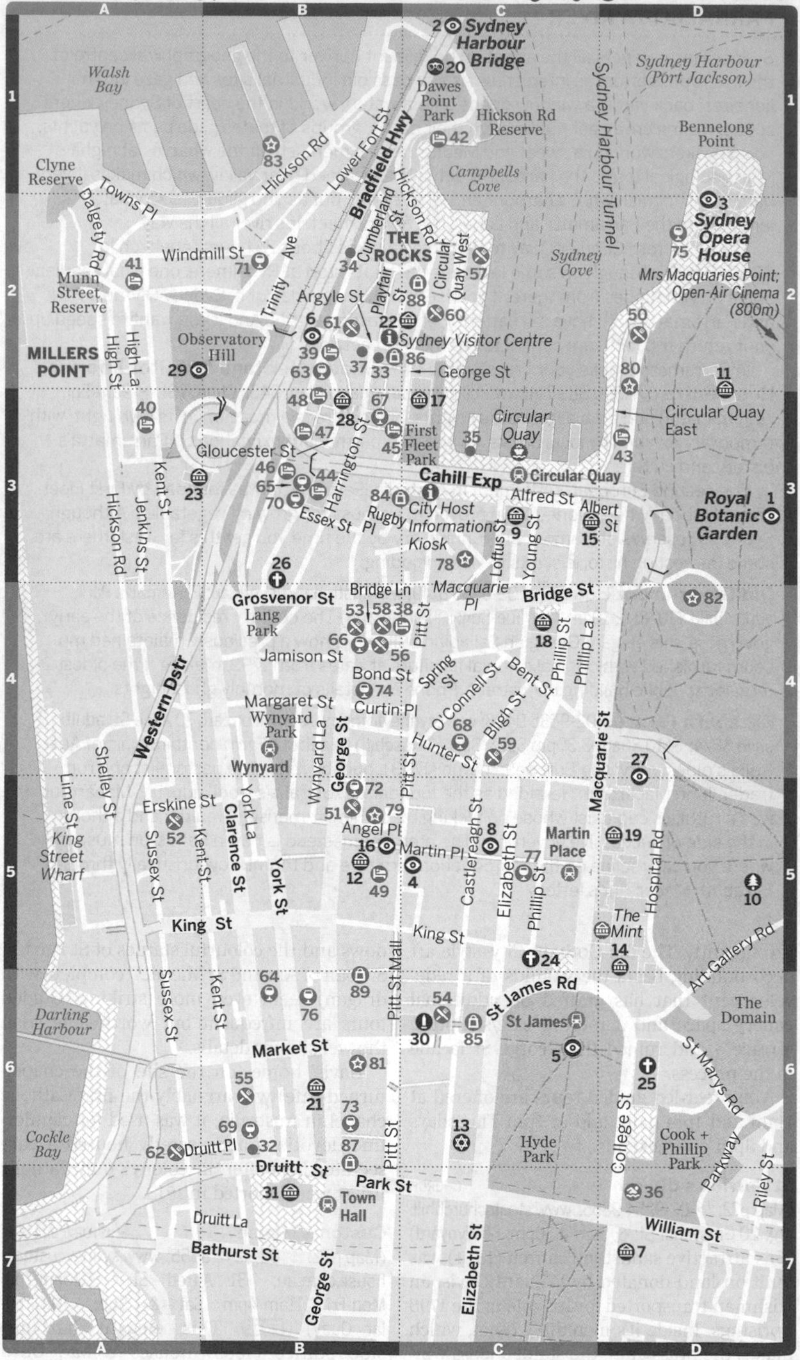

Central Sydney, The Rocks & Circular Quay

Top Sights
1 Royal Botanic Garden ... D3
2 Sydney Harbour Bridge ... C1
3 Sydney Opera House ... D2

Sights
4 5 Martin Place ... C5
5 Archibald Memorial Fountain ... C6
6 Argyle Cut ... B2
7 Australian Museum ... D7
8 Commonwealth Bank branch ... C5
9 Customs House ... C3
Customs House Library ... (see 9)
10 Domain ... D5
11 Government House ... D2
12 GPO Sydney ... B5
13 Great Synagogue ... C6
14 Hyde Park Barracks Museum ... D5
15 Justice & Police Museum ... C3
16 Martin Place ... B5
17 Museum of Contemporary Art ... C3
18 Museum of Sydney ... C4
19 Parliament House ... D5
20 Pylon Lookout ... C1
21 Queen Victoria Building ... B6
22 Rocks Discovery Museum ... C2
23 SH Ervin Gallery ... A3
24 St James' Church ... C5
25 St Mary's Cathedral ... D6
26 St Patrick's Church ... B3
27 State Library of NSW ... D4
28 Susannah Place Museum ... B3
29 Sydney Observatory ... A2
30 Sydney Tower Eye ... C6
31 Sydney Town Hall ... B7

Activities, Courses & Tours
32 BlueBananas ... B6
33 Bonza Bike Tours ... B2
34 BridgeClimb ... B2
35 Captain Cook Cruises ... C3
36 Cook & Phillip Park ... D7
37 The Rocks Walking Tours ... B2

Sleeping
38 Establishment Hotel ... C4
39 Harbour Rocks ... B2
40 Langham ... A3
41 Lord Nelson Brewery Hotel ... A2
42 Park Hyatt ... C1
43 Pullman Quay Grand Sydney Harbour D3
QT Sydney ... (see 81)
44 Quay West Suites ... B3
45 Russell ... B3
46 Shangri-La ... B3
47 Sydney Harbour Bed & Breakfast ... B3
48 Sydney Harbour YHA ... B3
49 Westin Sydney ... B5

Eating
50 Aria ... D2
51 Ash St Cellar ... B5
Cafe Sydney ... (see 9)
52 Central Baking Depot ... A5
53 Est ... B4
54 Ippudo Sydney ... C6
55 Le Grand Café ... B6
56 Mr Wong ... B4
57 Quay ... C2
58 Rockpool ... B4
59 Rockpool Bar & Grill ... C4
60 Sailors Thai Canteen ... C2
61 Saké ... B2
62 Sepia ... A6
Spice Temple ... (see 59)

Drinking & Nightlife
63 Australian Hotel ... B2
64 Baxter Inn ... B6
65 Blu Bar on 36 ... B3
66 Establishment ... B4
67 Fortune of War ... B3
68 Frankie's Pizza ... C4
69 Grandma's ... B6
70 Harts Pub ... B3
71 Hero of Waterloo ... B2
72 Ivy ... B5
Lord Nelson Brewery Hotel ... (see 41)
73 Marble Bar ... B6
74 O Bar ... B4
75 Opera Bar ... D2
76 Rook ... B6
77 Spice Cellar ... C5

Entertainment
Bangarra Dance Theatre ... (see 83)
78 Basement ... C3
79 City Recital Hall ... B5
80 Dendy Opera Quays ... D2
81 State Theatre ... B6
82 Sydney Conservatorium of Music ... D4
Sydney Dance Company ... (see 83)
Sydney Opera House ... (see 3)
83 Sydney Theatre Company ... B1

Shopping
84 Australian Wine Centre ... B3
85 David Jones ... C6
86 Gannon House ... B2
87 Kinokuniya ... B6
88 Opal Minded ... C2
Queen Victoria Building ... (see 21)
89 Strand Arcade ... B6
Westfield Sydney ... (see 30)

Sydney (Map p72; ☎02-9251 8683; www.cafesydney.com; L5, Customs House, 31 Alfred St; mains $38-39; ⊙noon-11pm Mon-Fri, 5-11pm Sat, noon-3.30pm Sun; Circular Quay), on the top floor, and the three-level **Customs House Library** (Map p72; ☎02-9242 8555; 31 Alfred St; ⊙10am-7pm Mon-Fri, 11am-4pm Sat & Sun; Circular Quay), which has a great selection of international newspapers and magazines, internet access and interesting temporary exhibitions. In the lobby, look for the swastikas in the tiling (and the plaque explaining their symbolism), and a fascinating 1:500 model of the inner city under the glass floor.

Justice & Police Museum MUSEUM
(Map p72; ☎02-9252 1144; www.sydneylivingmuseums.com.au; cnr Albert & Phillip Sts; adult/child $10/5; ⊙10am-5pm Sat & Sun; Circular Quay) Occupying the old Water Police Station (1858), this mildly unnerving museum documents the city's dark and disreputable past through old police photographs and an often macabre collection of exhibits.

★**Sydney Opera House** BUILDING
(Map p72; ☎02-9250 7250; www.sydneyoperahouse.com; Bennelong Point; tours adult/child $37/20; ⊙tours 9am-5pm; Circular Quay) Designed by Danish architect Jørn Utzon, this World Heritage–listed building is Australia's most recognisable landmark. Visually referencing the billowing white sails of a seagoing yacht (but described by some local wags as more accurately resembling the sexual congress of turtles), it's a commanding presence on Circular Quay. The complex comprises five performance spaces where dance, concerts, opera and theatre are staged.

The best way to experience the building is to attend a performance, but you can also take a one-hour guided tour, conducted in a variety of languages. There's also a two-hour 'access all areas' backstage tour ($165), which departs at 7am and includes breakfast in the Green Room.

Royal Botanic Garden & the Domain

★**Royal Botanic Garden** GARDENS
(Map p72; ☎02-9231 8111; www.rbgsyd.nsw.gov.au; Mrs Macquaries Rd; ⊙7am-8pm Oct-Feb, to 5.30pm Mar-Sep; Circular Quay) FREE These expansive gardens are the city's favourite picnic destination, jogging route and snuggling spot. Bordering Farm Cove,

City Walk
The Rocks

START THE ROCKS DISCOVERY MUSEUM
FINISH CADMAN'S COTTAGE
LENGTH 880M
DURATION ONE HOUR

The area where British convicts landed on 26 January 1788 remains the first port of call for most visitors to Sydney. Start this walk at the ❶**Rocks Discovery Museum** (p70), where the exhibits offer an excellent overview of the area's rich and often disreputable history. From the museum, walk north up Kendall Lane to its junction with ❷**Mill Lane**, named after a steam-powered flour mill that was once located here. The mill was demolished around 1920, one of many 18th- and 19th-century buildings in the Rocks to suffer the same fate during the 20th century.

Turn left (west) into Mill Lane and walk up to ❸**The Rocks Square** on the corner of Playfair St where, in 1973, local residents, conservationists, social activists and members of trade unions clashed with police and put themselves in the path of bulldozers that were demolishing structures on this site. The protesters were intent on preserving the streets and buildings that had been home to local families for generations, and their fight became known in the national media as the 'Battle for the Rocks'. In 1975 the NSW State Government, which had initially backed the developers, bowed to popular opinion and declared that all remaining historic buildings north of the Cahill Expressway were to be retained, conserved and restored.

Turn left (south) into Playfair St and walk past ❹**Argyle Terrace** (1877) and ❺**Argyle Stores** (1828–1913) on your right. Then turn right and walk west up Argyle St to ❻**Argyle Cut** (p70), a road cut through a sandstone ridge of rock to allow access between Circular Quay and the port at Millers Point. It was created between the 1830s and 1860s, initially by convicts and later by qualified stonemasons.

Turn left into Cumberland St until you see the ❼**Australian Hotel** on the corner of Gloucester St. The ❽**King George V Recreation Centre** opposite the hotel was designed by Lippmann Associates and

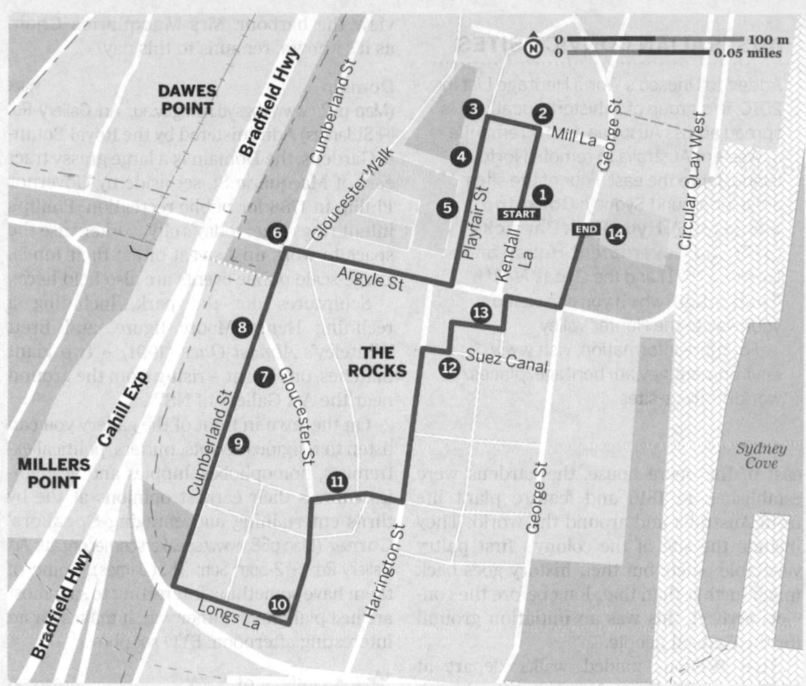

opened in 1998; wedged between the historic street and the boundary wall of the elevated freeway, it's an interesting contemporary architectural intervention in this historic precinct.

Continue along Cumberland St. On the left-hand side of the road is ❾ **Sydney Harbour YHA** (p107), an unusual building which straddles an archaeological dig site. In 1994 the remains of over 30 houses, two laneways, shops and pubs were excavated here, along with over 750,000 artefacts.

Turn left into narrow Longs Lane, which will take you through to Gloucester St. On the northwest corner of the lane is handsome ❿ **Jobbins Terrace**, constructed between 1855 and 1857. Further along Gloucester St, the modest 1844 terrace now functioning as the ⓫ **Susannah Place Museum** (p70) presents an interesting contrast.

From the museum's shop, which sells a quirky range of Australiana souvenirs, walk down the stairs in Cumberland Pl to Harrington St, then turn left and walk north down to ⓬ **Suez Canal**, a narrow laneway on the right-hand side. In the 19th century this was one of the most infamous locations in Sydney, frequented by prostitutes and members of the 'Rocks Push' larrikin gang that ruled the area from the 1870s to the end of the 1890s. Members were known for assault and battery against police and pedestrians; one of their tried and trusted techniques was to have female members of the gang entice drunks and seamen into dark areas to be assaulted and robbed.

Turn into Suez Canal and then left into the Well Courtyard, once used for dog baiting and cock fighting. Then walk down the steps to stone-paved Greenway Lane, named after famous convict architect Francis Greenway, who lived nearby on the corner of Argyle and George Sts.

Exit onto Argyle St; the building at No 45–47 is ⓭ **Gannon House**, built in 1839 as a residence and carpentry store by former convict Michael Gannon; he was known for the quality of his coffins.

Turn right, towards the harbour, and walk down to George St. In the park opposite is diminutive ⓮ **Cadman's Cottage**, built in 1815–16 for John Cadman, the Government Coxswain. It's Sydney's oldest house and the only remaining element of the city's original dockyard precinct.

AUSTRALIAN CONVICT SITES

Added to Unesco's World Heritage List in 2010, this group of 11 historic locations is spread across Australia, from Fremantle in Western Australia to remote Norfolk Island, far to the east. Four of the sites are in or around Sydney: **Cockatoo Island** (p66), **Hyde Park Barracks** (p77), **Old Government House and Domain** (p71) and the **Great North Road** (p135), which you can visit on your way to the Hunter Valley.

For more information, visit www.environment.gov.au/heritage/places/world/convict-sites.

east of the opera house, the gardens were established in 1816 and feature plant life from Australia and around the world. They include the site of the colony's first paltry vegetable patch, but their history goes back much further than that; long before the convicts arrived, this was an initiation ground for the Gadigal people.

Free 1½-hour guided walks depart at 10.30am daily. From November to March there's an additional hour-long tour at 1pm on weekdays. Book ahead for an **Aboriginal Heritage Tour** (☎02-9231 8134; adult/child $37/17; ⊙10am Fri), which covers local history, traditional plant uses and bush-food tastings.

Government House HISTORIC BUILDING
(Map p72; ☎02-9931 5222; www.sydneylivingmuseums.com.au; Macquarie St; ⊙grounds 10am-4pm, tours 10.30am-3pm Fri-Sun; 🚉Circular Quay) FREE Encased in English-style grounds within the Royal Botanic Gardens, this Gothic sandstone mansion (built 1837–43) is the official residence of the Governor of NSW. It's also used for hosting visiting heads of state and royalty. The interior can only be accessed on a free guided tour; collect your ticket from the gatehouse.

Mrs Macquaries Point PARK
(Map p68; Mrs Macquaries Rd; 🚉Circular Quay) Adjoining the Royal Botanic Garden but officially part of the Domain, Mrs Macquaries Point forms the northeastern tip of Farm Cove and provides beautiful views over the bay to the Opera House and city skyline. It was named in 1810 after Elizabeth, Governor Macquarie's wife, who ordered a seat chiselled into the rock from which she could view the harbour. **Mrs Macquaries Chair**, as it's known, remains to this day.

Domain PARK
(Map p72; www.rbgsyd.nsw.gov.au; Art Gallery Rd; 🚉St James) Administered by the Royal Botanic Gardens, the Domain is a large grassy tract east of Macquarie St, set aside by Governor Phillip in 1788 for public recreation. Phillip's intent rings true: today's city workers use the space to work up a sweat or eat their lunch. Large-scale public events are also held here.

Sculptures dot the park, including a reclining Henry Moore figure, and Brett Whiteley's *Almost Once* (1991) – two giant matches, one burnt – rising from the ground near the Art Gallery of NSW.

On the lawn in front of the gallery you can listen to religious zealots, nutters, political extremists, homophobes, hippies and academics express their earnest opinions at the by turns entertaining and enraging **Speakers' Corner** (Map p68; www.speakerscorner.org.au; Art Gallery Rd; ⊙2-5pm Sun; 🚉St James). Some of them have something interesting to say; most are just plain mad. Either way, it makes for an interesting afternoon. BYO soapbox.

★**Art Gallery of NSW** GALLERY
(Map p88; ☎1800 679 278; www.artgallery.nsw.gov.au; Art Gallery Rd; ⊙10am-5pm Thu-Tue, to 10pm Wed; 🚉St James) FREE With its classical Greek frontage and modern rear end, this much-loved institution plays a prominent and gregarious role in Sydney society. Blockbuster international touring exhibitions arrive regularly and there's an outstanding permanent collection of Australian art, including a substantial Indigenous section. The gallery also plays host to lectures, concerts, screenings, celebrity talks and children's activities. A range of free guided tours is offered on different themes and in various languages; enquire at the desk or check the website.

Macquarie St

Splendid sandstone colonial buildings grace this historic street, which defines the central city's eastern edge. Many of these buildings were commissioned by Lachlan Macquarie, the first NSW governor with a vision for Sydney beyond its convict origins. He enlisted convict architect Francis Greenway to help realise his plans, and together they set a gold standard for town planning and architectural excellence that the city has – alas – never since managed to replicate.

State Library of NSW LIBRARY
(Map p72; ☎02-9273 1414; www.sl.nsw.gov.au; Macquarie St; ⏰9am-8pm Mon-Thu, 10am-5pm Fri-Sun; 🚇Martin Pl) FREE Among the State Library's over five million tomes are James Cook's and Joseph Banks' journals and William Bligh's log from the mutinous HMAV *Bounty*. It's worth dropping in to peruse the temporary exhibitions in the galleries, and the elaborately sculpted bronze doors and grand atrium of the neoclassical Mitchell Wing (1910); note the map of Abel Tasman's journeys in the mosaic floor. The main reading room is an elegant temple of knowledge clad in milky marble.

Outside, on the Macquarie St side of the building, is a sculpture of explorer Matthew Flinders; look for his intrepid cat Trim on the windowsill behind.

Parliament House HISTORIC BUILDING
(Map p72; ☎02-9230 2111; www.parliament.nsw.gov.au; 6 Macquarie St; ⏰9am-5pm Mon-Fri; 🚇Martin Pl) FREE Twin of the nearby Mint, the venerable Parliament House (1816) has been home to the Parliament of New South Wales since 1829, making it the world's oldest continually operating parliament building. And like the Mint, its front section (which now blends into a modern addition on the eastern side) was part of the Rum Hospital (built in exchange for a monopoly on the rum trade).

You need to pass through a metal detector to access the inner sanctum, where you can check out art exhibitions in the lobby and the historical display in the wood-panelled Jubilee Room. On nonsitting days both assembly chambers are open, but when Parliament is sitting, you're restricted to the Public Gallery.

Hyde Park Barracks Museum MUSEUM
(Map p72; ☎02-8239 2311; www.sydneylivingmuseums.com.au; Queens Sq, Macquarie St; adult/child $10/5; ⏰10am-5pm; 🚇St James) Convict architect Francis Greenway designed this squarish, decorously Georgian structure (1819) as convict quarters. Between 1819 and 1848, 50,000 men and boys did time here, most of whom had been sentenced by British courts to transportation to Australia for property crime. It later became an immigration depot, a women's asylum and a law court. These days it's a fascinating (if not entirely cheerful) museum, focusing on the barracks' history and the archaeological efforts that helped reveal it.

St James' Church CHURCH
(Map p72; ☎02-8227 1300; www.sjks.org.au; 173 King St; ⏰10am-4pm Mon-Fri, 9am-1pm Sat, 7am-4pm Sun; 🚇St James) Built from convict-made bricks, Sydney's oldest church (1819) is widely considered to be architect Francis Greenway's masterpiece. It was originally designed as a courthouse, but the brief changed and the cells became the crypt. Check out the dark-wood choir loft, the sparkling copper dome, the crypt and the 1950s stained-glass 'Creation Window'.

Hyde Park

★Hyde Park PARK
(Map p82; Elizabeth St; 🚇St James & Museum) Formal but much-loved Hyde Park has manicured gardens and a tree-formed tunnel running down its spine which looks particularly pretty at night, illuminated by fairy lights. The park's northern end is crowned by the richly symbolic art deco **Archibald Memorial**

SYDNEY FOR CHILDREN

Organised kids' activities ramp up during school holidays (December/January, April, July and September); check www.sydneyforkids.com.au, www.au.timeout.com/sydney/kids and www.childmags.com.au for listings.

Darling Harbour is home to **Sea Life** (p82), **Wild Life** (p83) and the **Maritime Museum** (p83), as well as the kid-focused **Monkey Baa Theatre Company** (p129) and a great playground at **Tumbalong Park** (p83). The hands-on **Powerhouse Museum** (p85) in neighbouring Ultimo is also worth investigating, as are the children's events run by the **Art Gallery of NSW** (p76). Elsewhere, **Taronga Zoo** (p97) and **Luna Park** (p97) are sure to please.

Otherwise, if the weather's fine, head to the beach. The harbour beaches have less wave action, but most of the surf beaches have enclosed ocean pools suitable even for toddlers and babies. Great options include **Nielsen Park** (p91), **Balmoral Beach** (p97) and **Clovelly Beach** (p93). Gnarly seven-year-olds can learn to surf with **Let's Go Surfing** (p103) at North Bondi.

Fountain (Map p72; St James), featuring Greek mythological figures, while at the other end is the Anzac Memorial (p78).

St Mary's Cathedral CHURCH

(Map p72; 02-9220 0400; www.stmaryscathedral.org.au; St Marys Rd; crypt $5; 6.30am-6.30pm; St James) Built to last, this 106m-long Gothic Revival–style cathedral was begun in 1868, consecrated in 1905 and substantially finished in 1928, but the massive, 75m-high spires weren't added until 2000. The crypt has an impressive terrazzo mosaic floor depicting the Creation, inspired by the Celtic-style illuminations of the *Book of Kells*.

Anzac Memorial MEMORIAL

(Map p82; www.anzacmemorial.nsw.gov.au; Hyde Park; 9am-5pm; Museum) FREE Fronted by the Pool of Remembrance, this dignified art deco memorial (1934) commemorates the soldiers of the Australia and New Zealand Army Corps (Anzacs) who served in WWI. The interior dome is studded with 120,000 stars – one for each New South Welsh man and woman who served. These twinkle above Rayner Hoff's poignant sculpture *Sacrifice,* featuring a naked soldier draped over a shield and sword. There's also a small museum downstairs where a 13-minute film screens every 30 minutes.

City Centre

Museum of Sydney MUSEUM

(MoS; Map p72; 02-9251 5988; www.sydneylivingmuseums.com.au; cnr Phillip & Bridge Sts; adult/child $10/5; 9.30am-5pm; Circular Quay) Built on the site of Sydney's first (and infamously pungent) Government House, the MoS is a fragmented, storytelling museum, which uses state-of-the-art installations to explore the city's people, places, cultures and evolution. The history of the Indigenous Eora people is highlighted – touching on the millenniums of continuous occupation of this place. Be sure to open some of the many stainless-steel and glass drawers (they close themselves).

Martin Place SQUARE

(Map p72; Martin Place) Studded with imposing edifices, long, lean Martin Place was closed to traffic in 1971, forming a terraced pedestrian mall complete with fountains and areas for public gatherings. It's the closest thing to a main civic square that Sydney has. In 2014 the Lindt cafe at 53 Martin Place was the site of a 16-hour siege, ending in the death of two hostages and the gunman. At the time of writing, a permanent memorial to the victims was being planned.

As iconic in its time as the Opera House, **GPO Sydney** (Map p72; www.gposydney.com; 1 Martin Pl; Martin Place), built in 1874, is a beautiful colonnaded Victorian palazzo that was once Sydney's General Post Office. It has since been gutted, stabbed with office towers and transformed into the Westin Sydney hotel, swanky shops, restaurants and bars. Inspired by Italian Renaissance palaces, architect James Barnet caused a minor fracas by basing the faces carved on the sandstone facade on local identities. Queen Victoria dominates the central white-marble statuary, surrounded by allegorical figures. Under a staircase in the basement there is a small historical display and a pipe housing the dribbling remnants of the Tank Stream.

Built in 1916, 12-storey **5 Martin Place** (Map p72; www.5martinplace.com.au; 5 Martin Pl; Martin Place) was Australia's first steel-framed 'skyscraper'. At the time of writing, it was in the process of a major redevelopment, with a glass tower being grafted on to it.

A **Commonwealth Bank branch** (Map p72; 48 Martin Pl; Martin Place) has taken over the old State Savings Bank building: it's a beaut example of interwar beaux-arts architecture, featuring green-marble Ionian columns and an enclosed brass-and-marble teller area.

Near the George St end of Martin Place you'll find the **Cenotaph**, commemorating Australia's war dead. Abutting Martin Place on George St is the former **Commercial Banking Corporation of Sydney** – an impressive marbled edifice, worth a look if you're passing by.

Sydney Tower Eye TOWER

(Map p72; 1800 258 693; www.sydneytowereye.com.au; 100 Market St; adult/child $27/16, Skywalk adult/child $70/49; 9am-9.30pm; St James) The 309m-tall Sydney Tower (built 1970–81) offers unbeatable 360-degree views from the observation level 250m up – and even better ones for the daredevils braving the Skywalk on its roof. The visit starts with the 4D Experience – a short 3D film giving you a bird's-eye view (a parakeet's to be exact) of city, surf, harbour and what lies beneath the water, accompanied by mist sprays and bubbles; it's actually pretty darn cool.

Great Synagogue SYNAGOGUE
(Map p72; 02-9267 2477; www.greatsynagogue.org.au; 187a Elizabeth St; tours adult/child $10/5; tours noon Thu & 1st & 3rd Tue; St James) The heritage-listed Great Synagogue (1878) is the spiritual home of Sydney's oldest Jewish congregation, established in 1831. It's considered the Mother Synagogue of Australia and is architecturally the most important in the southern hemisphere, combining Romanesque, Gothic, Moorish and Byzantine elements. Tours include the AM Rosenblum Museum's artefacts and a video presentation on Jewish beliefs, traditions and history in Australia.

Queen Victoria Building HISTORIC BUILDING
(QVB; Map p72; 02-9264 9209; www.qvb.com.au; 455 George St; tours $15; 11am-5pm Sun, 9am-6pm Mon-Wed, Fri & Sat, 9am-9pm Thu; Town Hall) Unbelievably, this High Victorian masterpiece (1898) was repeatedly slated for demolition before it was restored in the mid-1980s. Occupying an entire city block on the site of the city's first markets, the QVB is a Venetian Romanesque temple to the gods of retail.

Sure, the 200 speciality shops are great, but check out the wrought-iron balconies, the Byzantine copper domes, the stained-glass shopfronts, the mosaic floors, the replica crown jewels, the ballroom, the tinkling baby grand and the hyperkitsch animated Royal Clock (featuring the Battle of Hastings and an hourly beheading of Charles I). Informative 45-minute tours (11.30am Tuesday, Thursday and Saturday) depart from the concierge desk on the ground floor.

Outside there's an imposing statue of Queen Vic herself. Nearby is a wishing well featuring a bronze replica of her beloved pooch, Islay, which disconcertingly speaks in the baritone voice of former radio rabble-rouser John Laws.

Sydney Town Hall HISTORIC BUILDING
(Map p72; www.sydneytownhall.com.au; 483 George St; 8am-6pm Mon-Fri; Town Hall) Mansard roofs, sandstone turrets, wrought-iron trimmings and over-the-top balustrades: the French Second Empire wedding-cake exterior of the Town Hall (built 1868–89) is something to behold. Unless there's something on, you can explore the halls off the main entrance. The wood-lined concert hall has a humongous pipe organ with nearly 9000 pipes; it was once the largest in the world. It's used regularly for recitals, some of which are free.

Haymarket

Chinatown AREA
(Map p82; www.sydney-chinatown.info; Town Hall) With a discordant soundtrack of blaring Canto pop, Dixon St is the heart and soul of Chinatown: a narrow, shady pedestrian mall with a string of restaurants and their urgently attendant spruikers. The ornate dragon gates *(paifang)* at either end of the street are topped with fake bamboo tiles, golden Chinese calligraphy (with English translations), ornamental lions to keep evil spirits at bay and a fair amount of pigeon poo.

This is actually Sydney's third Chinatown: the first was in the Rocks in the late 19th century before it moved to the Darling Harbour end of Market St. Dixon St's Chinatown dates from the 1920s. Look for the fake-bamboo awnings guarded by dragons, dogs and lions, and kooky upturned-wok lighting fixtures.

On Hay St, the surreal **Golden Water Mouth** (Map p82; Hay St; Town Hall) sculpture drips with gilt and water. Formed from a eucalyptus trunk from Condobolin, the destination of many gold-rush-era Chinese, its feng shui is supposed to promote positive energy and good luck. A little further down Hay St, **Paddy's Markets** (Map p82; www.paddysmarkets.com.au; 9-13 Hay St; 10am-6pm Wed-Sun; Central) fills the lower level of a hefty brick building. It started out in the mid-19th century with mainly European traders, but the tightly packed market stalls are more evocative of present-day Vietnam these days.

Darling Harbour & Pyrmont

Dotted between the flyovers and fountains of Sydney's purpose-built tourist hub (opened for the bicentennial in 1988) are some of the city's highest-profile paid attractions. Every other inch of this former dockland is given over to visitor amusements, bars and restaurants.

Darling Harbour is currently in the grip of a major redevelopment involving the demolition of many of its '80s edifices and the building of a giant convention centre. At the same time, the precinct is spreading north along its eastern shore with the rapid construction of the Barangaroo complex of office towers, waterside parks and entertainment venues. When it's finished, Sydney's second mega-casino will glare across the water at its competitor, the Star, which has also recently been redeveloped.

Sydney Harbour

Taronga Zoo
Even if you've hired a car, the best way to reach this excellent zoo is by ferry. Zip to the top in a cable car then wind your way back down to the wharf.

Manly
Catch a ferry to Manly to explore the outer harbour. Stroll to the beach, drink at the wharf and make sure you're well positioned on your return journey for any photos you missed.

Kirribilli
Unless the prime minister and governor-general invite you into their homes for tea, the best views you'll get of Kirribilli House and Admiralty House are from the water. Keep your eyes peeled.

Sydney Harbour Bridge
As you pass by the bridge, keep an eye out for the hardy souls trudging along the top on their bridge climb. Head here at sunrise or sunset for golden harbour views.

TOP TIP
Don't forget that the harbour continues west of the bridge. Back up a Manly trip with a river ferry service.

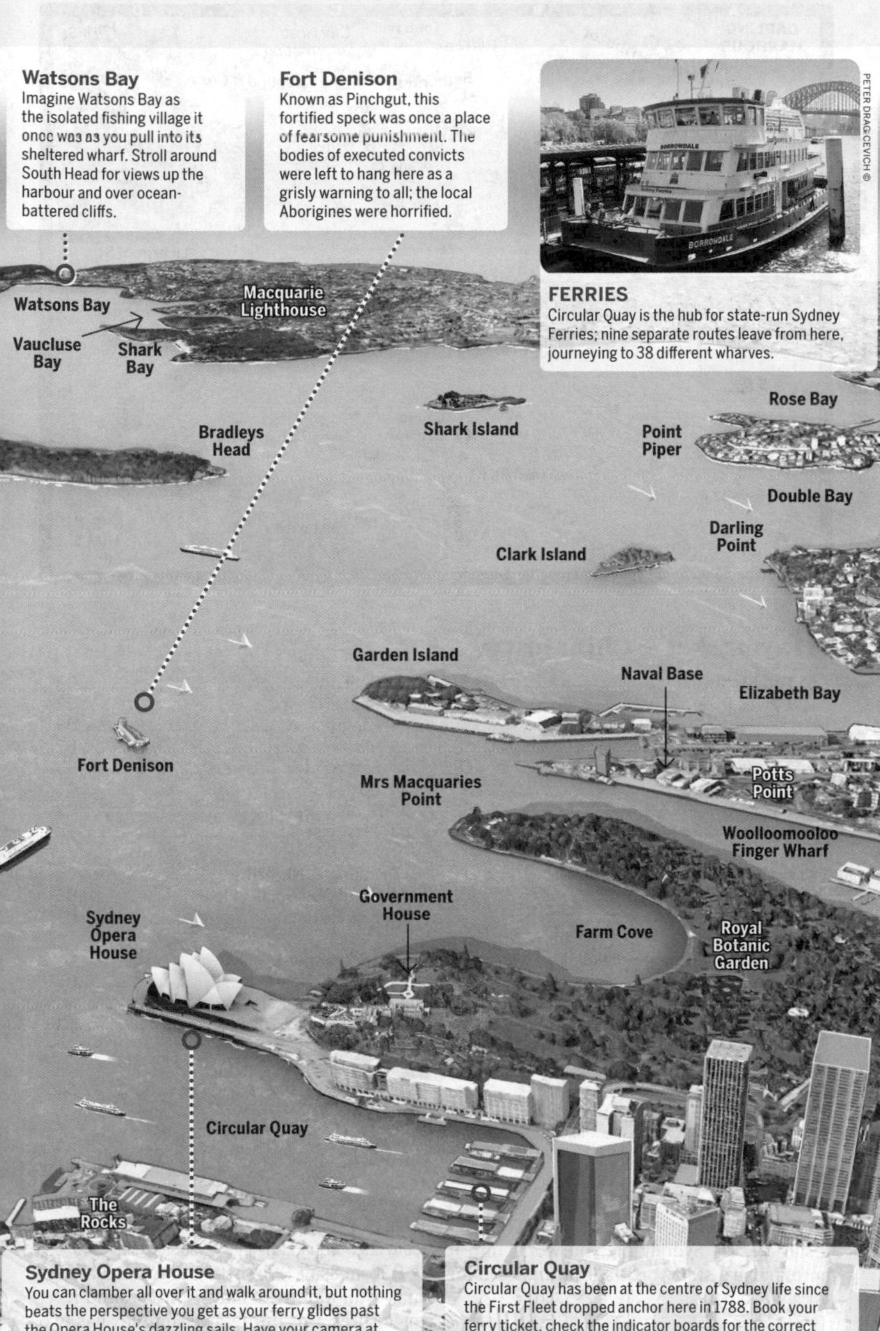
Watsons Bay
Imagine Watsons Bay as the isolated fishing village it once was as you pull into its sheltered wharf. Stroll around South Head for views up the harbour and over ocean-battered cliffs.
Fort Denison
Known as Pinchgut, this fortified speck was once a place of fearsome punishment. The bodies of executed convicts were left to hang here as a grisly warning to all; the local Aborigines were horrified.
PETER DRAG CEVICH ©
BORROWDALE
FERRIES
Circular Quay is the hub for state-run Sydney Ferries; nine separate routes leave from here, journeying to 38 different wharves.
Watsons Bay
Macquarie Lighthouse
Vaucluse Bay
Shark Bay
Bradleys Head
Shark Island
Rose Bay
Point Piper
Double Bay
Darling Point
Clark Island
Garden Island
Naval Base
Elizabeth Bay
Fort Denison
Mrs Macquaries Point
Potts Point
Woolloomooloo Finger Wharf
Government House
Sydney Opera House
Farm Cove
Royal Botanic Garden
Circular Quay
The Rocks
Sydney Opera House
You can clamber all over it and walk around it, but nothing beats the perspective you get as your ferry glides past the Opera House's dazzling sails. Have your camera at the ready.
Circular Quay
Circular Quay has been at the centre of Sydney life since the First Fleet dropped anchor here in 1788. Book your ferry ticket, check the indicator boards for the correct pier and get onboard.

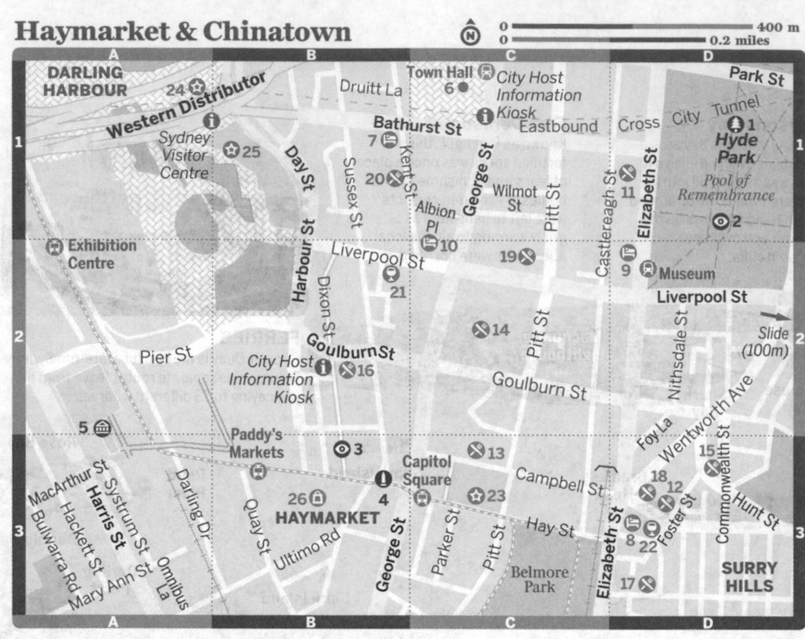

Haymarket & Chinatown

Top Sights
1 Hyde Park D1

Sights
2 Anzac Memorial D1
3 Chinatown B3
4 Golden Water Mouth B3
5 Powerhouse Museum A2

Activities, Courses & Tours
6 I'm Free C1

Sleeping
7 Adina Apartment Hotel Sydney B1
8 Big Hostel D3
9 Hyde Park Inn D2
10 Meriton Serviced Apartments Kent Street C2

Eating
11 Alpha D1
12 Bar H D3
13 Chat Thai C3
14 Din Tai Fung C2
15 Longrain D3
16 Mamak B2
17 Single Origin Roasters D3
18 Spice I Am D3
19 Sydney Madang C2
20 Tetsuya's B1

Drinking & Nightlife
21 Good God Small Club B2
22 Wild Rover D3

Entertainment
23 Capitol Theatre C3
24 IMAX A1
25 Monkey Baa Theatre Company B1

Shopping
26 Paddy's Markets B3

In the meantime, it's business as usual for all of the other operators. If you're after a slice of real Sydney life you won't find it here, but it's still worth allocating an hour for a walkabout.

Sydney Sea Life Aquarium AQUARIUM
(Map p84; 02-8251 7800; www.sydneyaquarium.com.au; Aquarium Pier; adult/child $40/28; 9.30am-8pm; Town Hall) As well as regular wall-mounted tanks and ground-level enclosures, this impressive complex has two large pools that you can walk through, safely

enclosed in Perspex tunnels, as an intimidating array of sharks and rays pass overhead. Other highlights include clownfish (howdy Nemo), platypuses, moon jellyfish (in a disco-lit tube), sea dragons and the swoon-worthy finale: the two-million-litre Great Barrier Reef tank.

The aquarium's two dugongs were rescued after washing up on Queensland beaches. Attempts to return them to the wild failed, so the Dugong Island enclosure was built to house them. As sad as it is to see such large marine mammals in captivity, it offers a fascinating and rare opportunity to get close to them.

Needless to say, kids love this place; arrive early to beat the crowds. It's cheaper to book online.

Wild Life Sydney Zoo ZOO

(Map p84; 02-9333 9245; www.wildlifesydney.com.au; Aquarium Pier; adult/child $40/28; 9.30am-7pm; Town Hall) Complementing its sister and neighbour, Sea Life, this large complex houses an impressive collection of Australian native reptiles, butterflies, spiders, snakes and mammals (including kangaroos and koalas). The nocturnal section is particularly good, bringing out the extrovert in the quolls, potoroos, echidnas and possums. As interesting as Wild Life is, it's not a patch on Taronga Zoo. Still, it's worth considering as part of a combo with Sea Life, or if you're short on time. Tickets are cheaper online.

Madame Tussauds MUSEUM

(Map p84; www.madametussauds.com/sydney; Aquarium Pier; adult/child $40/28; 9.30am-8pm; Town Hall) In this celebrity-obsessed age, it's hardly surprising that Madame Tussauds' hyperrealistic waxwork dummies are just as popular now as when the eponymous madame lugged her macabre haul of French revolution death masks to London in 1803. Where else do mere mortals get to strike a pose with Hugh Jackman and cosy up to Kylie?

Cockle Bay Wharf BUILDING

(Map p84; www.cocklebaywharf.com; Town Hall) The first vaguely tasteful development in Darling Harbour, Cockle Bay Wharf occupies the harbour's cityside frontage as far as Pyrmont Bridge. Its sharp, contemporary angles are softened by the use of timber and whimsical sculptures (we particularly like the jaunty dancing storks).

Tumbalong Park PARK

(Map p84; Town Hall) Flanked by the new Darling Walk development, this grassy circle on Darling Harbour's southern rump is set up for family fun. Sunbakers and frisbee throwers occupy the lawns; tourists dunk their feet in fountains on hot summer afternoons; and there's an excellent children's playground with a 21m flying fox.

★Chinese Garden of Friendship GARDENS

(Map p84; 02-9240 8888; www.chinesegarden.com.au; Harbour St; adult/child $6/3; 9.30am-5pm; Town Hall) Built according to Taoist principles, the Chinese Garden of Friendship is usually an oasis of tranquillity – although construction noise from Darling Harbour's redevelopment can intrude from time to time. Designed by architects from Guangzhou (Sydney's sister city) for Australia's bicentenary in 1988, the garden interweaves pavilions, waterfalls, lakes, paths and lush plant life.

Australian National Maritime Museum MUSEUM

(Map p84; 02-9298 3777; www.anmm.gov.au; 2 Murray St; adult/child $7/3.50; 9.30am-5pm; Pyrmont Bay) Beneath an Utzon-like roof (a low-rent Opera House?), the Maritime Museum sails through Australia's inextricable relationship with the sea. Exhibitions range from Indigenous canoes to surf culture, to the navy. Entry includes free tours and there are kids' activities on Sundays. The 'big ticket' (adult/child $27/16) includes entry to the vessels moored outside, including the submarine HMAS *Onslow*, the destroyer HMAS *Vampire* and an 1874 square rigger, the *James Craig*, which periodically offers sailing trips (p103). Normally a replica of Cook's *Endeavour* also drops anchor.

Sydney Fish Market MARKET

(Map p84; 02-9004 1108; www.sydneyfishmarket.com.au; Bank St; 7am-4pm; Fish Market) This piscatorial precinct on Blackwattle Bay shifts over 15 million kilograms of seafood annually, and has retail outlets, restaurants, a sushi bar, an oyster bar and a highly regarded cooking school. Chefs, locals and overfed seagulls haggle over mud crabs, Balmain bugs, lobsters and slabs of salmon at the daily fish auction, which kicks off at 5.30am weekdays. Check it out on a behind-the-scenes tour (adult/child $30/10).

Darling Harbour & Pyrmont

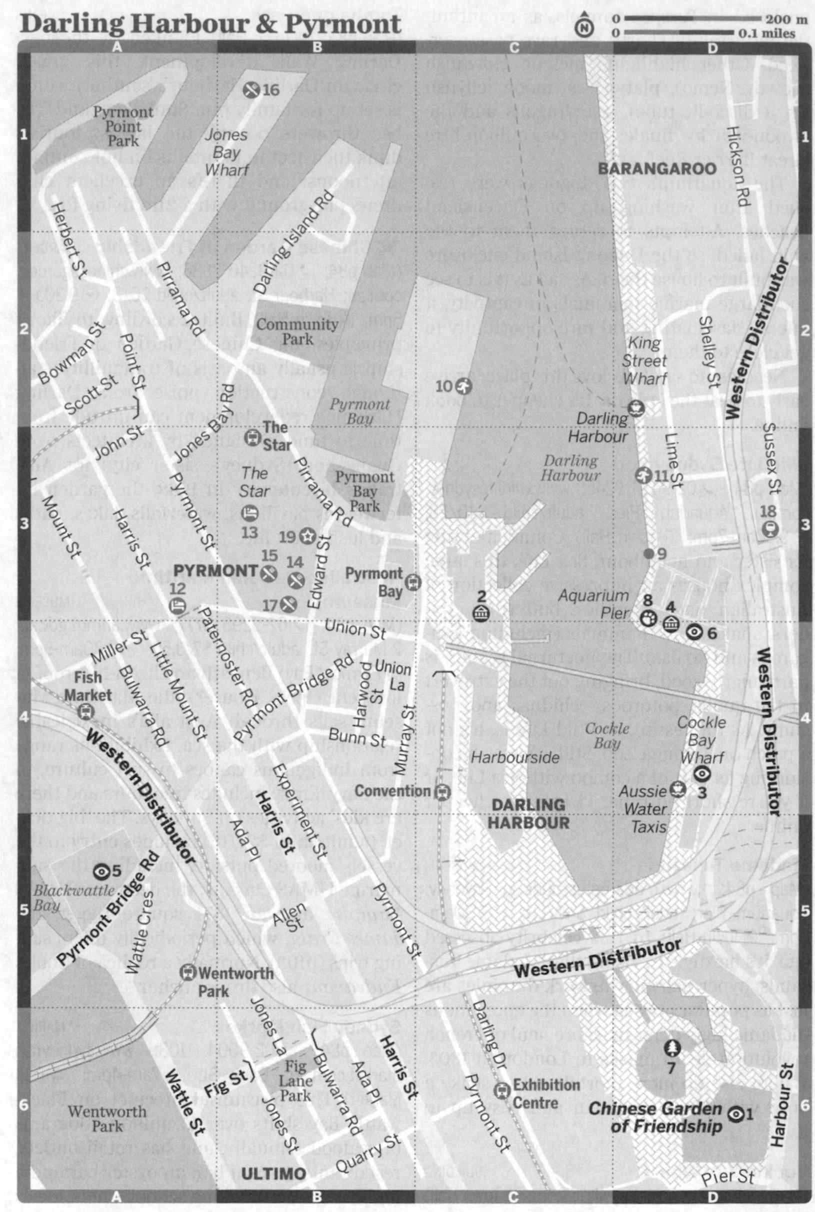

Ultimo, Glebe & Chippendale

Clinging to the city's southern edge and crisscrossed by fume-belching arterial routes, Ultimo and Chippendale have never been the prettiest parts of central Sydney. However, in recent years world-famous architects have been working their magic on major developments on either side of Broadway, the main route dividing the two neighbourhoods. Chippendale, in particular, has started to sprout hip eateries, bars and

Darling Harbour & Pyrmont

Top Sights
1 Chinese Garden of Friendship D6

Sights
2 Australian National Maritime Museum C3
3 Cockle Bay Wharf D4
4 Madame Tussauds D4
5 Sydney Fish Market A5
6 Sydney Sea Life Aquarium D4
7 Tumbalong Park D6
8 Wild Life Sydney Zoo D3

Activities, Courses & Tours
9 Harbour Jet D3
10 James Craig C2
Sailing Sydney .... (see 9)
11 Sydney Showboats D3

Sleeping
12 1888 Hotel A3
13 The Darling B3

Eating
14 Adriano Zumbo B3
15 Café Court B3
16 Flying Fish B1
17 Sokyo B3

Drinking & Nightlife
18 Slip Inn & Chinese Laundry D3

Entertainment
19 Sydney Lyric B3

galleries and is quickly moving from up-and-coming to up-and-come.

To the west of Ultimo, Glebe has a more leafy and residential feel, its rows of Victorian terraces housing blue-collar families, students, urban hippies, gays and lesbians, and one of the largest Aboriginal communities in the inner city.

Powerhouse Museum MUSEUM
(Map p82; 02-9217 0111; www.powerhousemuseum.com; 500 Harris St; adult/child $15/8; 9.30am-5pm; Paddy's Markets) A short walk from Darling Harbour, this science and design museum whirs away inside the former power station for Sydney's defunct, original tram network. High-voltage interactive demonstrations wow school groups with the low-down on how lightning strikes, magnets grab and engines growl. It's a huge hit with kids but equally popular with adults, touching on subjects such as fashion and furniture design.

Central Park AREA
(Map p121; www.centralparksydney.com; Broadway; Central Station) Occupying the site of an old brewery, this work-in-progress residential and shopping development will eventually cover 6500 sq metres, and is already revitalising the central fringe suburb of Chippendale. Most impressive is Jean Nouvel's award-winning, vertical garden-covered tower, **One Central Park** (2013; 117m). The cantilevered roof has been designed to reflect sunlight onto the greenery below. A striking new Frank Gehry building is being built on the University of Technology campus across Broadway.

White Rabbit GALLERY
(Map p121; www.whiterabbitcollection.org; 30 Balfour St; 10am-5pm Wed-Sun, closed Feb & Aug; Redfern) FREE If you're an art lover or a bit of a Mad Hatter, this particular rabbit hole will leave you grinning like a Cheshire Cat. There are so many works in this private collection of cutting-edge, contemporary Chinese art, that only a fraction can be displayed at one time. Who knew that the People's Republic was turning out work that was so edgy, funny, sexy and idiosyncratic?

Surry Hills

Sydney's hippest neighbourhood bears absolutely no resemblance to the beautiful hills of Surrey, England, from which it takes its name. And these days it also bears little resemblance to the tightly knit, working-class community so evocatively documented in Ruth Park's classic Depression-era novels.

The rows of Victorian terrace houses remain, but they're now home to a mishmash of inner-city hipsters, foodies and gay guys, all of whom keep the many excellent neighbourhood restaurants and bars in business.

Brett Whiteley Studio GALLERY
(Map p86; 1800 679 278; www.brettwhiteley.org; 2 Raper St; 10am-4pm Fri-Sun; Central) FREE Acclaimed local artist Brett Whiteley (1939–92) lived fast and without restraint. His hard-to-find studio (look for the signs on Devonshire St) has been preserved as a gallery for some of his best work. At the door is a miniature of his famous sculpture *Almost Once,* which you can see in all its glory in the Domain.

Surry Hills

Darlinghurst

Immediately east of the city, Darlinghurst is synonymous with Sydney's vibrant and visible gay community. The shabby lower end of Oxford St has traditionally been Sydney's sequinned mile, and while it's seen better days, it's still home to most of the city's gay venues and the Mardi Gras parade.

Australian Museum MUSEUM

(Map p72; ☎02-9320 6000; www.australianmuseum.net.au; 6 College St; adult/child $15/8; ⏲9.30am-5pm; 🚆Museum) This natural-history museum, established just 40 years after the First Fleet dropped anchor, has endeavoured to shrug off its museum-that-should-be-in-a-museum feel by jazzing things up a little. Hence dusty taxidermy has been interspersed with video projections and a terrarium with live snakes, while dinosaur skeletons cosy up to life-size recreations. Yet it's the more old-fashioned sections that are arguably the most interesting – the large collection of crystals and precious stones, and the hall of skeletons.

Sydney Jewish Museum MUSEUM

(Map p88; ☎02-9360 7999; www.sydneyjewishmuseum.com.au; 148 Darlinghurst Rd; adult/child $10/7; ⏲10am-4pm Sun-Thu, to 2pm Fri; 🚆Kings Cross) Created largely as a Holocaust memorial, this museum examines Australian Jewish history, culture and tradition, from the time of the First Fleet (which included 16 known Jews), to the immediate aftermath of WWII (when Australia became home to the greatest number of Holocaust survivors per capita, after Israel), to the present day. Allow at least two hours to take it all in. Free 45-minute tours leave at noon on Monday, Wednesday, Friday and Sunday.

Surry Hills

Sights
1 Brett Whiteley Studio D3

Sleeping
2 Bounce B2
3 Railway Square YHA A1
4 Sydney Central YHA A1
5 Wake Up! A1

Eating
6 4Fourteen D2
7 Bodega C1
8 Bourke Street Bakery D3
9 Devon B2
10 Devonshire C3
11 El Loco C2
12 Le Monde C2
13 MoVida C2
14 Porteño C4
15 Reuben Hills C1
16 Sample Coffee C2

Drinking & Nightlife
17 121BC C2
18 Vasco D4

Entertainment
19 Belvoir B3
20 Venue 505 .... B3

Woolloomooloo

Possibly the only word in the world with eight 'o's, the suburb of Woolloomooloo, down **McElhone Stairs** (Map p88; Victoria St; Kings Cross) from Kings Cross, was once a slum full of drunks and sailors (a fair few of whom were drunken sailors). Things are more genteel these days – the pubs are relaxed and Woolloomooloo Wharf is now home to a boutique hotel and a row of upmarket restaurants. Outside the wharf is the famous Harry's Cafe de Wheels (p118), where generations of Sydneysiders have stopped to sober up over a late-night 'Tiger' (beef pie served with mushy peas, mashed potato and gravy) on the way home from a big night at the Cross.

Woolloomooloo Finger Wharf HISTORIC BUILDING
(Map p88; Cowper Wharf Rdwy; Kings Cross) A former wool and cargo dock, this beautiful Edwardian wharf faced oblivion for decades before a 2½-year demolition-workers' green ban on the site in the late 1980s saved it. It received a huge sprucing up in the late 1990s and has emerged as one of Sydney's most exclusive eating, drinking, sleeping and marina addresses.

Kings Cross & Potts Point

Crowned by a huge illuminated **Coca-Cola sign** – Sydney's equivalent of LA's iconic Hollywood sign – 'the Cross' has long been the home of Sydney's vice industry. In the 19th and early 20th centuries the suburb was home to grand estates and stylish apartments, but it underwent a radical change in the 1930s when wine-soaked intellectuals, artists, musicians, pleasure-seekers and ne'er-do-wells rowdily claimed the streets for their own. The neighbourhood's reputation was sealed during WWII and the Vietnam War, when American sailors based at the nearby Garden Island naval base flooded the Cross with a tide of shore-leave debauchery.

Although the streets retain an air of seedy hedonism, the neighbourhood has recently undergone something of a cultural renaissance. Sleazy one minute and sophisticated the next, it's well worth a visit.

The gracious, tree-lined enclaves of neighbouring **Potts Point** and **Elizabeth Bay** have been popular residential areas ever since Alexander Macleay, Colonial Secretary of New South Wales, commissioned architect John Verge to design a mansion overlooking the water here in the 1830s.

Handsome **Rushcutters Bay** is a five-minute walk east of Kings Cross; its harbourside park is a lovely spot for a walk or jog.

Elizabeth Bay House HISTORIC BUILDING
(Map p88; 02-9356 3022; www.sydneylivingmuseums.com.au; 7 Onslow Ave; adult/child $8/4; 11am-4pm Fri-Sun; Kings Cross) Now dwarfed by 20th-century apartments, Colonial Secretary Alexander Macleay's elegant Greek Revival mansion was one of the finest houses in the colony when it was completed in 1839. The architectural highlight is an exquisite oval entrance saloon with a curved and cantilevered staircase.

Paddington & Woollahra

Paddington is an elegant area of beautifully restored terrace houses and steep

Kings Cross, Darlinghurst & Woolloomooloo

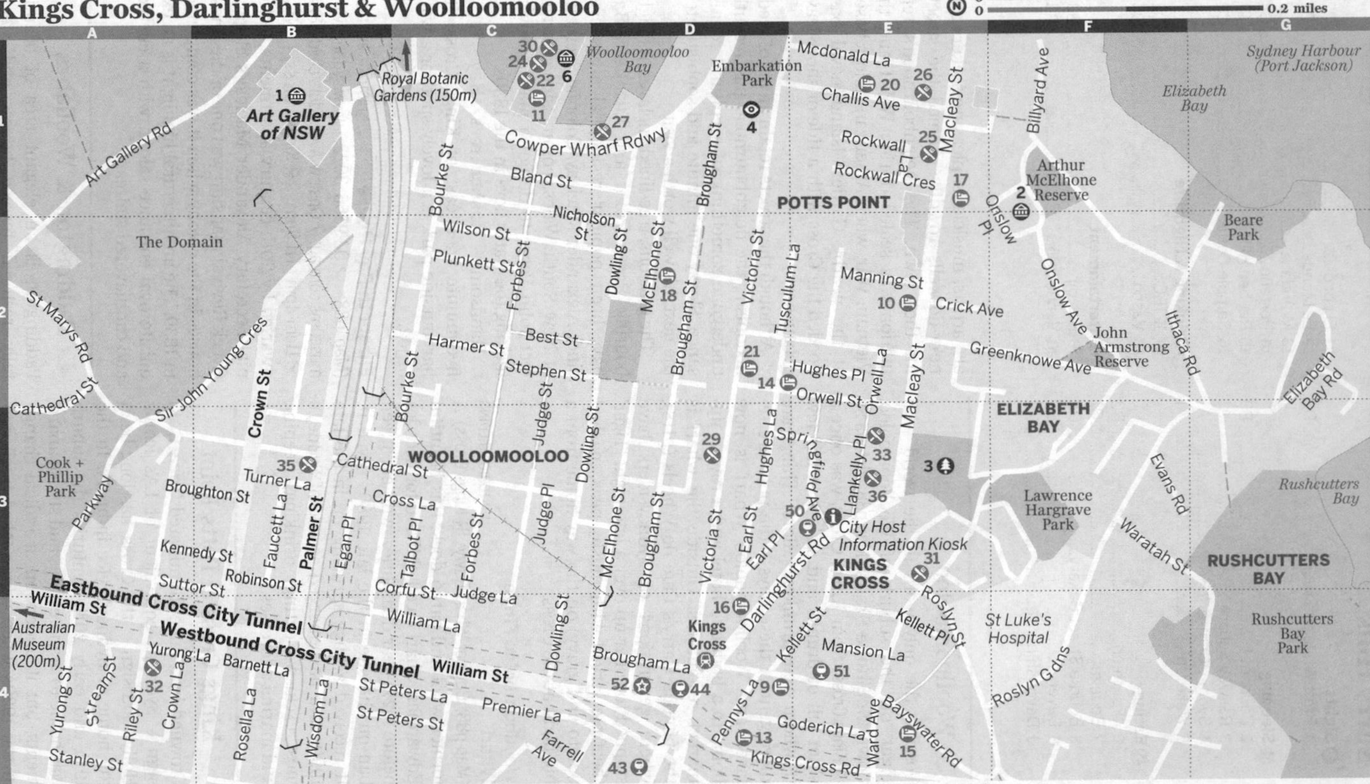

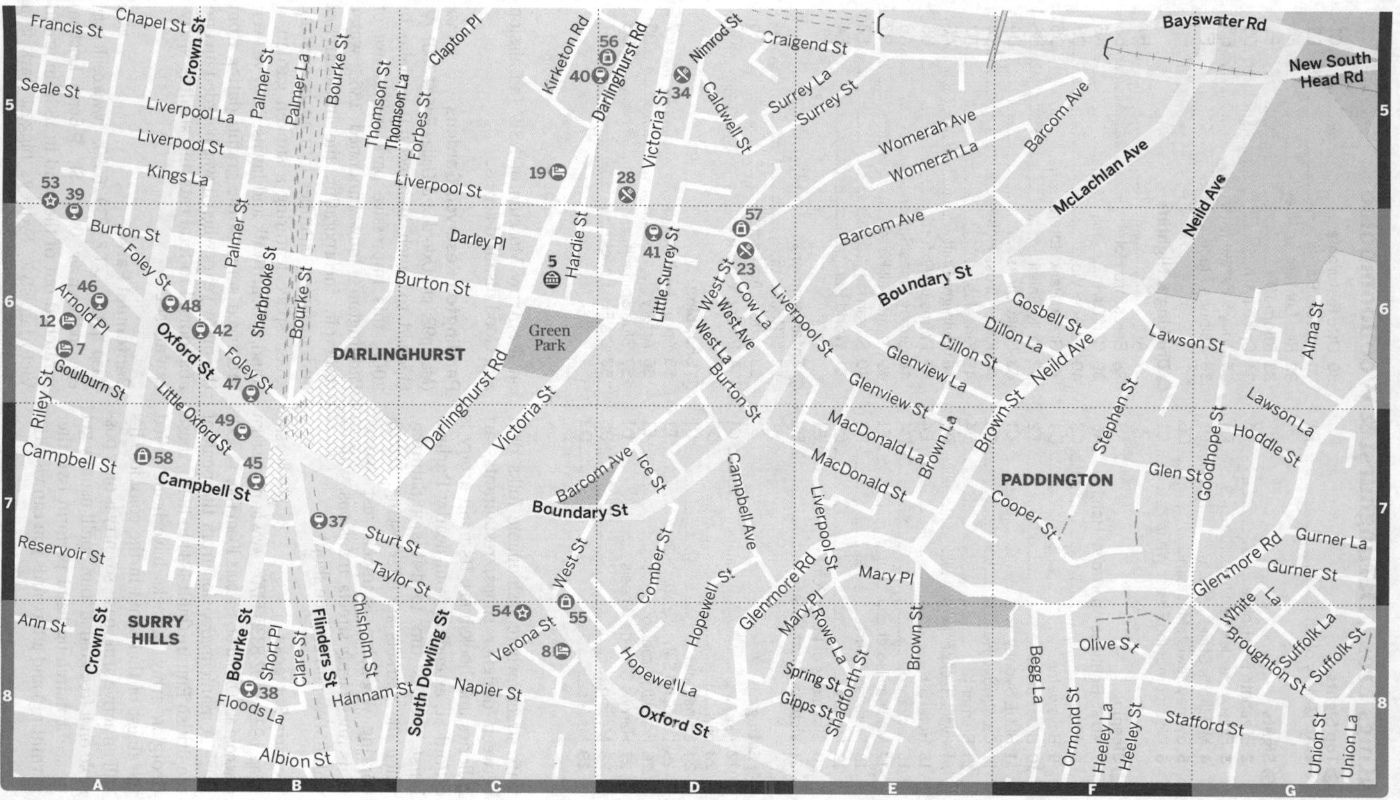

DARLINGHURST
PADDINGTON
SURRY HILLS
Green Park
Bayswater Rd
New South Head Rd
Francis St
Chapel St
Crown St
Palmer St
Palmer La
Bourke St
Thomson St
Thomson La
Forbes St
Clapton Pl
Kirketon Rd
Darlinghurst Rd
Victoria St
Nimrod St
Craigend St
Caldwell St
Surrey La
Surrey St
Seale St
Liverpool La
Liverpool St
Kings La
Womerah Ave
Womerah La
Barcom Ave
McLachlan Ave
Neild Ave
Darley Pl
Hardie St
Little Surrey St
Burton St
Foley St
Arnold Pl
Sherbrooke St
West St
Cow La
West Ave
West La
Boundary St
Gosbell St
Dillon La
Dillon St
Lawson St
Alma St
Oxford St
Goulburn St
Riley St
Little Oxford St
Glenview La
Glenview St
Brown St
Stephen St
Lawson La
Hoddle St
Goodhope St
Campbell St
MacDonald La
MacDonald St
Brown La
Glen St
Ice St
Cooper St
Sturt St
Reservoir St
Taylor St
Comber St
Campbell Ave
Glenmore Rd
Gurner La
Gurner St
Mary Pl
Ann St
Short Pl
Clare St
Flinders St
Chisholm St
South Dowling St
Verona St
Hopewell St
Rowe La
Shadforth St
White La
Suffolk La
Suffolk St
Broughton St
Olive St
Begg La
Floods La
Hannam St
Napier St
Hopewell La
Spring St
Gipps St
Ormond St
Heeley La
Heeley St
Stafford St
Union St
Union La
Albion St
A
B
C
D
E
F
G
5
6
7
8

Kings Cross, Darlinghurst & Woolloomooloo

Top Sights
1 Art Gallery of NSW B1

Sights
2 Elizabeth Bay House F2
3 Fitzroy Gardens E3
4 McElhone Stairs D1
5 Sydney Jewish Museum C6
6 Woolloomooloo Finger Wharf C1

Sleeping
7 ADGE Boutique Apartment Hotel A6
8 Arts C8
9 Bayswater D4
10 Blue Parrot E2
11 BLUE Sydney C1
12 Cambridge Hotel A6
13 Diamant D4
14 Eva's Backpackers D2
15 Hotel 59 .... E4
16 Jackaroo D4
17 Macleay Hotel E1
18 Mariners Court D2
19 Medusa C5
20 Simpsons of Potts Point E1
21 Victoria Court Hotel D2

Eating
22 Aki's C1
23 bills D6
24 China Doll C1
25 Cho Cho San E1
26 Fratelli Paradiso E1
27 Harry's Cafe de Wheels D1
28 Messina D5
29 Ms G's D3
30 Otto Ristorante C1
31 Piccolo Bar E3
32 Red Lantern on Riley A4
33 Room 10 .... E3
34 Spice I Am D5
35 Toby's Estate B3
36 Wilbur's Place E3

Drinking & Nightlife
37 Arq B7
38 Beresford Hotel B8
39 Cliff Dive A6
40 Eau-de-Vie D5
41 Green Park Hotel D6
42 Hello Sailor B6
43 Hinky Dinks D4
44 Kings Cross Hotel D4
45 Kinselas B7
46 Midnight Shift A6
47 Palms on Oxford B6
48 Shady Pines Saloon A6
49 Stonewall Hotel B7
50 Sugarmill E3
51 World Bar E4

Entertainment
52 El Rocco D4
53 Oxford Art Factory A5
54 Palace Verona C8

Shopping
55 Ariel C7
56 Artery D5
57 Blue Spinach D6
58 C's Flashback A7

leafy streets where fashionable folks drift between designer shops, restaurants, art galleries and bookshops. Its main artery is Oxford St, extending from nearby Darlinghurst. The best time to visit is on Saturday, when the markets are effervescing. Neighbouring Woollahra is upper-crust Sydney at its finest: leafy streets, mansions, wall-to-wall BMWs and antique shops.

Victoria Barracks HISTORIC SITE
(Map p92; ☎02-8335 5170; www.armymuseumnsw.com.au; Oxford St; ⏰tours 10am Thu; 🚌380) **FREE** A manicured vision from the peak of the British Empire (built 1841 to 1848), these Georgian army barracks have been called the finest of their kind in the colonies. It's still an active army base, so entry is only possible on a free guided tour. You'll usually get to see a marching band perform (weather permitting) and afterwards you can visit the on-site Army Museum of NSW (admission $2). Good disabled access.

Paddington Reservoir Gardens PARK
(Map p92; cnr Oxford St & Oatley Rd; 🚌380) Opened to much architectural acclaim in 2008, this impressive park makes use of Paddington's long-abandoned 1866 water reservoir, incorporating the brick arches and surviving chamber into an interesting green space featuring a sunken garden, a pond, a boardwalk and lawns. They've even preserved some of the graffiti dating from the many years when it was boarded up and abandoned to feral cats and stealthy spray-can artists.

Centennial Park PARK
(Map p92; ☎02-9339 6699; www.centennialparklands.com.au; Oxford St; 🚆Bondi Junction) Scratched out of the sand in 1888 in grand Victorian style, Sydney's biggest park is a

rambling 189-hectare expanse full of horse riders, joggers, cyclists and in-line skaters. During summer Moonlight Cinema (p127) attracts the crowds.

Double Bay

Once a bastion of the blue-rinse, a strange thing has been happening in Double Bay lately. With the introduction of lockout laws in the inner city in 2014, a section of the Kings Cross party crowd started seeking late-night sustenance in the nearest unaffected town centre – which just happened to be the staid streets of Double Bay.

It's a suburb in transition, with the reopening of the InterContinental hotel (where Michael Hutchence met his untimely demise) adding a bit of razzle-dazzle, new restaurants shaking up what was a tired eating scene, and a whole lot of new bars and clubs attracting a young and up-for-it crowd.

Murray Rose Pool BEACH

(Redleaf Pool; Map p68; 536 New South Head Rd; Double Bay) FREE Not really a pool at all, family-friendly Murray Rose (named after a champion Olympic swimmer) is the closest swimming spot to the city – as such, it attracts an urbane cross-section of inner-eastern locals. A boardwalk runs around the top of the shark net, and there are two sought-after floating pontoons.

Vaucluse

Pretty Vaucluse is one of a seriously well-heeled set of suburbs clinging to the harbour's southern shore. Together they form a conservative conglomeration of elite private schools, European sedans, overpriced boutiques and heavily mortgaged waterside mansions.

Nielsen Park PARK, BEACH

(Shark Beach; Map p68; Vaucluse Rd; 325) Something of a hidden gem, this gorgeous harbourside park with a sandy beach was once part of the then 206-hectare Vaucluse House estate. Secluded beneath the trees is Greycliffe House, a gracious 1851 Gothic sandstone pile (not open to visitors), which

REINVENTING THE CROSS

In the early years of the colony, Kings Cross was home to the city's wealthy citizens, who were attracted by its harbour views and handy distance from the smells and noise of the central city. Its grand villas, farming estates and genteel atmosphere were worlds away from the rough-and-tumble scene around Circular Quay and the Rocks.

This bucolic idyll lasted until the early 20th century, when the estates were subdivided and most of the villas were demolished (Tusculum on Manning St and Elizabeth Bay House on Onslow Ave were exceptions). Blocks of apartments took their place and the city's bohemian set moved in, attracted by cheap rents and a modernist vibe. These bohemians were closely followed by Sydney's criminal underclass, who set up businesses selling sly grog (untaxed alcohol), running illegal betting shops and operating brothels. The streets were home to writers, actors, poets, journalists, artists, petty crims and infamous brothel owners such as Tilly Devine and Kate Leigh – it was a neighbourhood where the louche charm of this convict-established city was pronounced, and where creativity flourished alongside crime.

The local scene changed during the Vietnam War, when heroin was imported from Southeast Asia and drug lords took over the streets, distributing drugs, running prostitution rings and opening sleazy nightclubs where strippers and dealers plied their trades. The bohemians moved out and addicts, street prostitutes, petty crims and enforcers moved in, joined by Sydneysiders who came to walk on the wild side every Friday and Saturday night.

But as the adage says, 'what goes around, comes around'. In recent years bohemians have returned, joined by upwardly mobile young professionals lured by the hip cafes, bars, restaurants and live-music venues that are mushrooming in the streets and laneways off Darlinghurst Rd. To experience the renaissance, head to Llankelly Pl (a laneway where drug deals once took place and where arty cafes such as **Room 10** (p118) now preside), eat in the restaurants on Macleay St, sit by the recently restored and much-loved dandelion-shaped El Alamein fountain in **Fitzroy Gardens** (Map p88; cnr Macleay St & Darlinghurst Rd; Kings Cross) or party at the **Kings Cross Hotel** (p125).

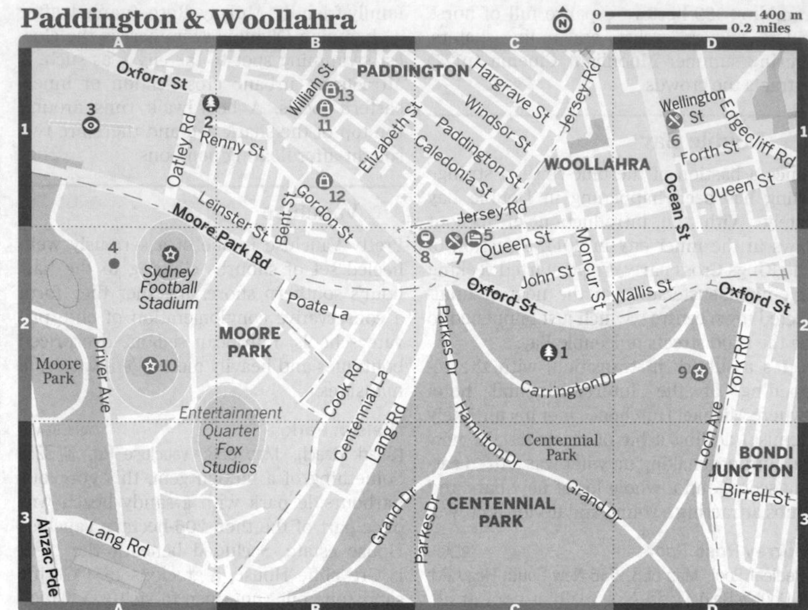

Paddington & Woollahra

Sights
1 Centennial Park.......C2
2 Paddington Reservoir Gardens.......A1
3 Victoria Barracks.......A1

Activities, Courses & Tours
4 SCG Tour Experience.......A2

Sleeping
5 Kathryn's on Queen.......C2

Eating
6 Chiswick Restaurant.......D1
7 Vincent.......C2

Drinking & Nightlife
8 Wine Library.......C2

Entertainment
9 Moonlight Cinema.......D2
10 Sydney Cricket Ground.......A2

Shopping
11 Corner Shop.......B1
12 Paddington Markets.......B1
13 Poepke.......B1

serves as the headquarters of Sydney Harbour National Park.

Vaucluse House HISTORIC BUILDING
(Map p68; ☎02-9388 7922; www.sydneylivingmuseums.com.au; Wentworth Rd; adult/child $8/4; ⏰11am-4pm Fri-Sun; 🚌325) Construction of this imposing, turreted specimen of Gothic Australiana, set amid 10 hectares of lush gardens, commenced in 1805, but the house was tinkered with into the 1860s. Decorated with beautiful European period pieces including Bohemian glass, heavy oak Jacobethan furniture and Meissen china, the house offers visitors a rare glimpse into early Sydney colonial life, as lived by the well-to-do.

Milk Beach BEACH
(Map p68; 52 Vaucluse Rd; 🚌325) The only things to distract you from serious beach time at divine Milk Beach are seaplanes and the glistening Sydney skyline. With wow-worthy harbour views and limited access down a steep bush path, this isolated stretch of sand at the base of Hermit Bay is still one of the city's best kept secrets. Heritage-listed Strickland House is out back, and clear, warm waters are in front, at this tiny parcel of paradise.

Watsons Bay

The narrow peninsula ending in South Head is one of Sydney's most sublime spots and it's easily reached by ferry from Circular Quay. Watsons Bay was once a small fishing village, as evidenced by the tiny heritage cottages that pepper the suburb's narrow streets (and now cost a fortune). On the ocean side is **the Gap**, a dramatic clifftop lookout gazing over the crashing surf.

At the northern end of Camp Cove beach, the **South Head Heritage Trail** kicks off, leading into a section of Sydney Harbour National Park. It passes old battlements and a path heading down to **Lady Bay** (popular with nudists and gay men), before continuing on to the candy-striped **Hornby Lighthouse** and the sandstone **Lightkeepers' Cottages** (1858) on South Head itself.

Before you get back on the ferry, tradition demands that you sit in the beer garden at the **Watsons Bay Hotel** at sunset and watch the sun fall behind the disembodied Harbour Bridge, jutting up above Bradleys Head.

Camp Cove BEACH

(Map p68; Cliff St; Watsons Bay) Immediately north of Watsons Bay, this small swimming beach is popular with both families and topless sunbathers. When Governor Phillip realised Botany Bay didn't cut it as a site for a convict colony, he sailed north into Sydney Harbour, dropped anchor and sank his boots into Camp Cove's gorgeous golden sand on 21 January 1788.

Eastern Beaches

Improbably good-looking arcs of sand framed by jagged cliffs, the Eastern Beaches are a big part of the Sydney experience. Most famous of all is the broad sweep of Bondi Beach, where the distracting scenery and constant procession of beautiful bods never fails to take your mind off whatever it was you were just thinking about...

★**Bondi Beach** BEACH

(Map p94; Campbell Pde; 380) Definitively Sydney, Bondi is one of the world's great beaches: ocean and land collide, the Pacific arrives in great foaming swells, and all people are equal, as democratic as sand. It's the closest ocean beach to the city centre (8km away), has consistently good (though crowded) waves, and is great for a rough-and-tumble swim (the average water temperature is a considerate 21°C). If the sea's angry, try the child-friendly saltwater sea baths at either end of the beach.

Two surf clubs – Bondi and North Bondi – patrol the beach between sets of red-and-yellow flags, positioned to avoid the worst rips and holes. Thousands of unfortunates have to be rescued from the surf each year (enough to make a TV show about it), so don't become a statistic – swim between the flags.

Surfers carve up sandbar breaks at either end of the beach; it's a good place for learners, too. Prefer wheels to fins? There's a **skate ramp** (Map p94; Queen Elizabeth Dr; 380) at the beach's southern end. If posing in your budgie smugglers (Speedos) isn't having enough impact, there's an outdoor **workout area** (Map p94; Queen Elizabeth Dr; 380) near the North Bondi Surf Club. Coincidentally (or perhaps not), this is the part of the beach where the gay guys hang out.

Bondi Pavilion has changing rooms, lockers, cafes and a gelato shop. Ice-cream vendors also strut the sand in summer. At the beach's northern end there's a grassy spot with coin-operated barbecues. Booze is banned on the beach.

Tamarama Beach BEACH

(Map p94; Pacific Ave; 361) Surrounded by high cliffs, Tamarama has a deep tongue of sand with just 80m of shoreline. Diminutive, yes, but ever-present rips make Tamarama the most dangerous patrolled beach in New South Wales; it's often closed to swimmers. It's hard to picture now, but between 1887 and 1911 a roller coaster looped out over the water as part of an amusement park.

Bronte Beach BEACH

(Bronte Rd; 378) A winning family-oriented beach hemmed in by sandstone cliffs and a grassy park, Bronte lays claims to the title of the oldest surf lifesaving club in the world (1903). Contrary to popular belief, the beach is named after Lord Nelson, who doubled as the Duke of Bronte (a place in Sicily), and not the famous literary sorority. There's a kiosk and a changing room attached to the surf club, and covered picnic tables near the public barbecues.

Clovelly Beach BEACH

(Map p68; Clovelly Rd; 339) It might seem odd, but this concrete-edged ocean channel is a great place to swim, sunbathe and snorkel. It's safe for the kids, and despite

Bondi

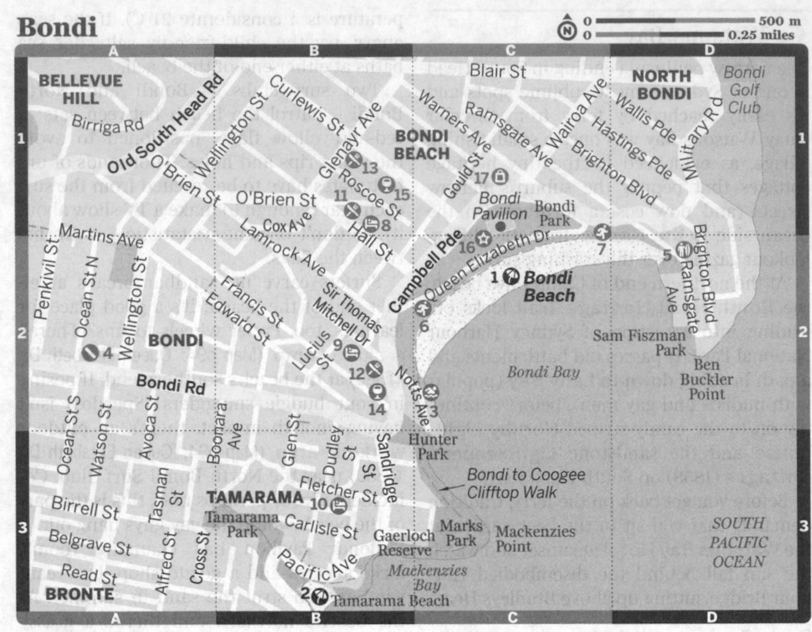

Bondi

Top Sights

1 Bondi Beach C2

Sights

2 Tamarama Beach B3

Activities, Courses & Tours

3 Bondi Icebergs Swimming Club C2
4 Dive Centre Bondi A2
5 Let's Go Surfing D2
6 Skate Ramp C2
7 Workout Area C1

Sleeping

8 Adina Apartments Bondi Beach B1
9 Bondi Beach House B2
10 Bondi Beachouse YHA B3

Eating

11 A Tavola B1
12 Bondi Trattoria B2
Icebergs Dining Room .... (see 3)
13 Lox, Stock & Barrel B1

Drinking & Nightlife

14 Anchor B2
15 Neighbourhood B1

Entertainment

16 Bondi Openair Cinema C2

Shopping

17 Bondi Markets C1

the swell surging into the inlet, underwater visibility is great. A beloved friendly grouper fish lived here for many years until he was speared by a tourist. Bring your goggles, but don't go killing anything...

On the other side of the car park is the entrance to the Gordons Bay Underwater Nature Trail, a 500m underwater chain guiding divers past reefs, sand flats and kelp forests.

Coogee Beach BEACH

(Arden St; 372-373) Bondi without the glitz and the posers, Coogee (locals pronounce the double *o* as in the word 'took') has a deep sweep of sand, historic ocean baths and plenty of green space for barbecues and frisbee hurling. Between the world wars, Coogee had an English-style pier, with a 1400-seat theatre and a 600-seat ballroom... until the surf took it.

Newtown & Around

The inner west is a sociological stew of students, goths, urban hippies, artists, Mediterranean immigrants and sexual subculturists. At its heart is Sydney University, a bastion of old-world architecture that dominates the surrounding suburbs. Southwest of the university, Newtown shadows sinuous King St, lined with interesting boutiques, secondhand clothes stores, bookshops, yoga studios, pubs, cafes and Thai restaurants. It's definitely climbing the social rungs, but Newtown is still freethinking and idiosyncratic.

University of Sydney UNIVERSITY
(Map p121; 02-9351 2222; www.sydney.edu.au; Parramatta Rd; 422-440) Australia's oldest tertiary institution (1850) has over 49,000 students and even boasts its own postcode. You don't need to have a PhD to grab a free campus map and wander around. Flanked by two grand halls that wouldn't be out of place in Harry Potter's beloved Hogwarts, the **Quadrangle** has a Gothic Revival design that tips its mortarboard towards the stately colleges of Oxford. It's well worth seeking out the august collections of the Nicholson Museum, **University Art Gallery** (Map p121; www.sydney.edu.au/museums; Science Rd; 10am-4.30pm Mon-Fri, noon-4pm 1st Sat of month; 422-440) FREE and Macleay Museum.

Nicholson Museum MUSEUM
(Map p121; www.sydney.edu.au/museums; University Pl; 10am-4.30pm Mon-Fri, noon-4pm 1st Sat of month; 422-440) FREE Within the University of Sydney's quadrangle, this museum is a must-see for ancient-history geeks. Inside is an amazing accumulation of Greek, Roman, Cypriot, Egyptian and Near Eastern antiquities, including Padiashaikhet the mummy. It was founded in 1860 by orphan-made-good Sir Charles Nicholson, a key figure in the establishment of both the university and the Australian Museum (p86).

Macleay Museum MUSEUM
(Map p121; www.sydney.edu.au/museums; Science Rd; 10am-4.30pm Mon-Fri, noon-4pm 1st Sat of month; 422-440) FREE The University of Sydney's natural history museum is the oldest of its kind in Australia, having its roots in the collection of the Macleay family (of Elizabeth Bay House (p87) fame). There's also a historic photographic collection and an early assemblage of Aboriginal, Torres Strait and Pacific Island cultural material.

Carriageworks ARTS CENTRE
(Map p121; www.carriageworks.com.au; 245 Wilson St; 10am-6pm; Redfern) FREE Built between 1880 and 1889, this intriguing group of huge Victorian-era workshops was part of the Eveleigh Railyards. The rail workers chugged out in 1988 and in 2007 the artists pranced in. It's now home to various avant-garde arts and performance projects, and there's usually something interesting to check out.

Sydney Park PARK
(Map p68; Sydney Park Rd; St Peters) Full of dog walkers, kite flyers and stragglers from last night's party, 40-hectare Sydney Park is a great place to chill out. From the bald hilltop you can see the city rising like a volcanic island from a sea of suburbia, while to the south there are views over the airport to Botany Bay. Much of the land has been reclaimed from swamps, clay pits and brickworks.

Balmain

Jutting out into the harbour, the pretty peninsula suburb of Balmain was once a notoriously rough neighbourhood of dockyard workers but is now an arty enclave flush with beautifully restored Victorian houses, welcoming pubs, cafes and trendy shops. It's easily reached by ferry.

Lower North Shore

At the northern end of the Harbour Bridge are the unexpectedly tranquil waterside suburbs of **Milsons Point** and **McMahons Point**. Both command astonishing city views. Just east of the bridge is the stately suburb of **Kirribilli**, home to **Admiralty House** (Map p68) and **Kirribilli House** (Map p68), the Sydney residences of the governor general and prime minister respectively.

East of here are the upmarket residential suburbs of **Neutral Bay**, **Cremorne** and **Mosman**, known for their pretty coves, harbourside parks and 'ladies who lunch'. An excellent coastal walk stretches from Cremorne Point, past Mosman Bay and into a section of Sydney Harbour National Park hugging **Bradleys Head**. A less built-up alternative is the track tracing the **Middle Head** section of the national park, from **Chowder Bay** to **Balmoral**.

City Walk
Bondi to Coogee

START BONDI BEACH
FINISH COOGEE BEACH
LENGTH 6KM
DURATION TWO TO THREE HOURS

Arguably Sydney's most famous, most popular and best walk, this coastal path shouldn't be missed. Both ends are well connected to bus routes, as are most points in between should you feel too hot and bothered to continue – although a cooling dip at any of the beaches en route should cure that. There's little shade on this track, so make sure you apply sunscreen and don a hat before setting out.

Starting at ❶ **Bondi Beach** (p93), take the stairs up the south end to Notts Ave, passing above the glistening ❷ **Icebergs swimming pool** (p104). Step onto the cliff-top trail at the end of Notts Ave. Walking south, the blustery sandstone cliffs and grinding Pacific Ocean couldn't be more spectacular (watch for dolphins, whales and surfers). Small but perfectly formed ❸ **Tamarama** (p93) has a deep reach of sand that is totally disproportionate to its width.

Descend from the cliff tops onto ❹ **Bronte Beach** (p93). Take a dip, lay out a picnic under the Norfolk Island pines or head to a cafe for a caffeine hit. After your break, pick up the path on the southern side of the beach.

Some famous Australians are among the subterranean denizens of the amazing cliff-edge ❺ **Waverley Cemetery**. On a clear day this is a prime vantage point for whale watchers.

Pass the locals enjoying a beer or a game of bowls at the Clovelly Bowling Club, then breeze past the cockatoos and canoodling lovers in ❻ **Burrows Park** to sheltered ❼ **Clovelly Beach** (p93). Follow the footpath up through the car park, along Cliffbrook Pde, then down the steps to the upturned dinghies lining ❽ **Gordons Bay**, one of Sydney's best shore-dive spots.

The trail continues past ❾ **Dolphin Point** then lands you smack-bang on glorious ❿ **Coogee Beach** (p94). Swagger into the Coogee Bay Hotel and toast your efforts with a cold drink or two.

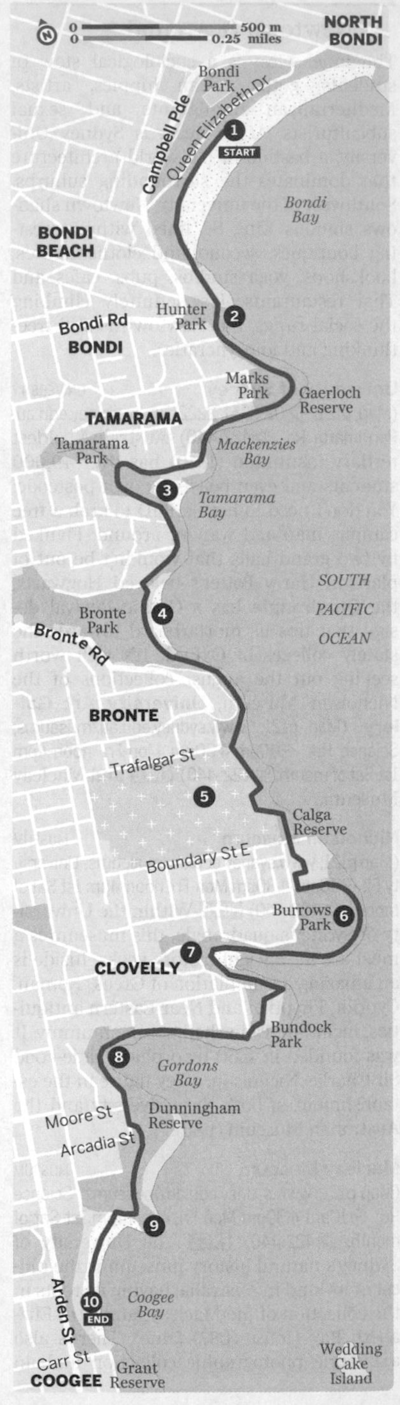

Luna Park AMUSEMENT PARK

(Map p68; ☎02-9922 6644; www.lunaparksydney.com; 1 Olympic Dr; ⏰11am-10pm Fri & Sat, 2-6pm Sun, 11am-4pm Mon; ⛴Milsons Point) FREE A sinister chip-toothed clown face forms the entrance to this old-fashioned amusement park overlooking Sydney Harbour. It's one of several 1930s features, including the Coney Island funhouse, a pretty carousel and the nausea-inducing rotor. You can purchase a two-ride pass ($16), or buy a height-based unlimited-ride pass (from $30, cheaper if purchased online). Hours are extended during school and public holidays.

Mary MacKillop Place CHURCH, MUSEUM

(Map p68; ☎02-8912 4878; www.marymackillopplace.org.au; 7 Mount St; adult/child $9/6; ⏰10am-4pm; 🚉North Sydney) This museum tells the life story of St Mary of the Cross (aka Mary MacKillop), Australia's only Catholic saint. Born in Melbourne in 1842, she was a dedicated and outspoken educator, and a pioneer who prevailed over conservative hierarchical ideals, despite being excommunicated for six months. You'll find her tomb inside the chapel.

Taronga Zoo ZOO

(Map p68; ☎02-9969 2777; www.taronga.org.au; Bradleys Head Rd; adult/child $46/23; ⏰9.30am-5pm; ⛴Taronga Zoo) 🍃 A 12-minute ferry ride from Circular Quay, Taronga Zoo has 75 hectares of bushy harbour hillside full of kangaroos, koalas and similarly hirsute Australians, and imported guests. The zoo's 4000 critters have million-dollar harbour views, but seem blissfully unaware of the privilege.

Highlights include the nocturnal platypus habitat, the Great Southern Oceans section and the Asian elephant display. Feedings and encounters happen throughout the day, while in summer, twilight concerts jazz things up.

Tours include **Nura Diya** (90min tour adult/child $99/69; ⏰9.45am Mon, Wed & Fri), where Indigenous guides introduce you to native animals and share Dreaming stories about them, giving an insight into traditional Aboriginal life; advance bookings essential. **Roar & Snore** (☎02-9978 4791; adult/child $320/205) is an overnight family experience that includes a night-time safari, a buffet dinner, breakfast and tents under the stars.

Catching the ferry is part of the fun, and given that parking is expensive (per day $17), it's well worth considering. From the wharf, the Sky Safari cable car or a bus will whisk you to the main entrance, from which you can traverse the zoo downhill back to the ferry. A Zoo Pass (adult/child/family $53/27/148) from Circular Quay includes return ferry rides, the bus or cable-car ride to the top and zoo admission. Disabled access is good, even when arriving by ferry.

Balmoral Beach BEACH

(Map p68; The Esplanade; 🚌245) The beachy enclave of Balmoral faces off with Manly across Middle Harbour, and has some good restaurants and a beaut swimming beach. Split in two by an unfeasibly picturesque rocky outcrop, Balmoral attracts picnicking North Shore families. Swimmers migrate to the shark-netted southern end.

WORTH A TRIP

GO WILD IN THE SUBURBS

Lane Cove National Park (www.nationalparks.nsw.gov.au; Lady Game Dr; per car $7; ⏰9am-6pm; 🚉North Ryde) This 601-hectare park, surrounded by North Shore suburbia, is a great place to stretch out on some middle-sized bushwalks. It's home to dozens of critters, including some endangered owls and toads. If you visit in spring, the water dragons will be getting horny and the native orchids and lilies will be flowering.

There's a boat shed on Lane Cove River that rents out rowboats and kayaks, but swimming isn't a good idea. You can also cycle and camp, and some sections are wheelchair accessible.

👁 Manly

Laid-back Manly clings to a narrow isthmus abutting North Head, Sydney Harbour's northern gatepost. The suburb's unusual name comes from Governor Phillip's description of the physique of the native people he met here; his Excellency was clearly indulging in an early example of the very Sydney habit of body-scrutinising.

The Corso connects Manly's ocean and harbour beaches; here surf shops, burger joints, juice bars and pubs are plentiful. The refurbished Manly Wharf has classier pubs and restaurants, and there are some good cafes scattered around the back streets.

In summer, allocate a day to walking and splashing about. In winter, it's worth heading over for a quick look around, if only for

Manly

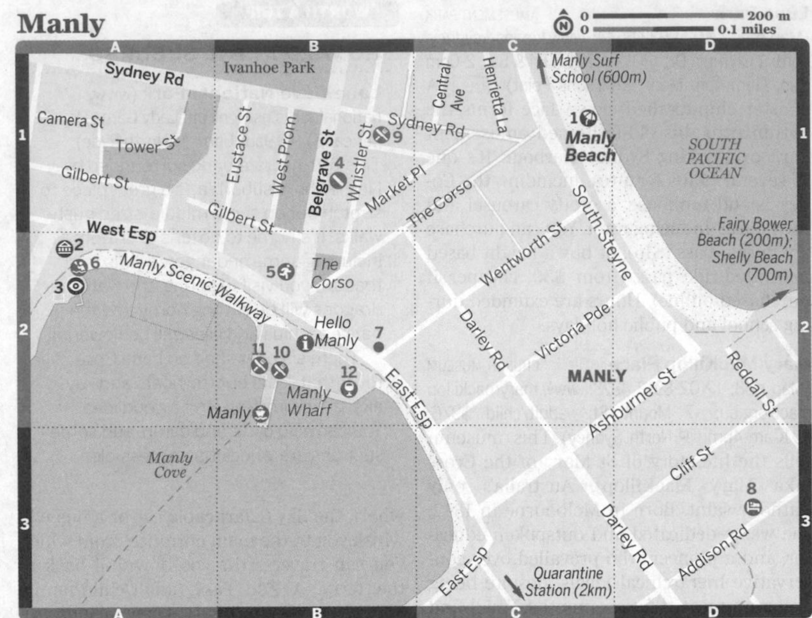

Sydney's best ferry journey. Don't bother staying after dark – there are much better eateries and bars elsewhere.

Manly Sea Life Sanctuary AQUARIUM
(Map p98; ☎1800 199 742; www.manlysealifesanctuary.com.au; West Esplanade; adult/child $25/15; ⏰9.30am-5pm; ⛴Manly) This ain't the place to come if you're on your way to Manly Beach for a surf. Underwater glass tubes enable you to become alarmingly intimate with 3m grey nurse sharks. Reckon they're not hungry? **Shark Dive Xtreme** (introductory/certified dives $280/205) enables you to enter their world.

Upstairs, the residents of the penguin enclosure have lawless amounts of fun. Manly has one of the last mainland colonies of little penguins in Australia, and this display aims to educate people about these cute-as-a-button critters (don't fret, none of these little guys were taken from the wild).

Manly Art Gallery & Museum MUSEUM
(Map p98; www.manly.nsw.gov.au; West Esplanade; ⏰10am-5pm Tue-Sun; ⛴Manly) FREE A short stroll from Manly Wharf, this passionately managed community gallery maintains a local focus, with exhibits of surfcraft, camp swimwear and beachy bits and pieces. There's also a ceramics gallery, and lots of old Manly photos to peer at.

★**Manly Beach** BEACH
(Map p98; ⛴Manly) Sydney's second-most famous beach stretches for nearly two golden kilometres, lined by Norfolk Island pines and scrappy midrise apartment blocks. The southern end of the beach, nearest the Corso, is known as South Steyne, with North Steyne in the centre and Queenscliff at the northern end; each has its own surf lifesaving club.

Shelly Beach BEACH
(Map p68; ⛴Manly) This sheltered north-facing ocean cove is just a short 1km walk from the busy Manly beach strip. The tranquil waters are a protected haven for marine life, so it offers wonderful snorkelling.

North Head NATIONAL PARK
(Map p68; North Head Scenic Dr; 🚌135) About 3km south of Manly, spectacular, chunky North Head offers dramatic cliffs, lookouts and sweeping views of the ocean, the harbour and the city; hire a bike and go exploring.

North Head is believed to have been used as a ceremonial site by the native Camaraigal people. These days, most of the headland is part of Sydney Harbour National Park.

Manly

Top Sights
1 Manly Beach C1

Sights
2 Manly Art Gallery & Museum A2
3 Manly Sea Life Sanctuary A2

Activities, Courses & Tours
4 Dive Centre Manly B1
5 Manly Bike Tours B2
6 Manly Kayak Centre A2
7 Manly Ocean Adventures B2

Sleeping
8 101 Addison Road D3

Eating
9 Barefoot Coffee Traders B1
10 Chat Thai B2
11 Hugos Manly B2

Drinking & Nightlife
12 Manly Wharf Hotel B2

The 9km, four-hour Manly Scenic Walkway loops around the park; pick up a brochure from the visitor centre. Also here is the historic Quarantine Station.

Manly Scenic Walkway OUTDOORS
(Map p68; www.manly.nsw.gov.au; Manly) This epic walk has two major components: the 10km western stretch between Manly and Spit Bridge, and the 9.5km eastern loop around North Head. Either download a map or pick one up from the information centre near the wharf.

The western section traces the coast past million-dollar harbour-view properties and then through a rugged 2.5km section of Sydney Harbour National Park, which remains much as it was when the First Fleet sailed in. After crossing the Spit Bridge you can take a bus either back to Manly (bus 140, 143 or 144) or into the city (176 to 180).

The eastern loop is known as the North Head Circuit Track and takes between three and four hours. From the wharf, follow Eastern Esplanade and Stuart St to Spring Cove, head into the North Head section of Sydney Harbour National Park, and make your way through the bush to the spectacular Fairfax Lookout on North Head (approximately 45 minutes in total). From the lookout, walk the Fairfax Loop (1km, 30 minutes) and then head back via the Cabbage Tree Bay Walk, which follows the sea-sprayed shoreline back to Manly Beach via picturesque Shelly Beach and tiny Fairy Bower Beach.

Quarantine Station HISTORIC BUILDING
(Map p68; 02-9466 1551; www.quarantinestation.com.au; 1 North Head Scenic Dr; museum 10am-4pm Sun-Thu, to 8pm Fri & Sat; 135) FREE From 1835 to 1983 this eerie-but-elegant complex was used to isolate new arrivals suspected of carrying disease, in an attempt to limit the spread of cholera, smallpox and bubonic plague. These days the 'Q Station' has been reborn as a tourist destination with a museum, accommodation, restaurants and a whole swathe of tour options.

Northern Beaches

The 20km stretch of coast between Manly and Palm Beach has been called the most impressive urban surfing landscape in the world, and the sun-bronzed locals who swim and catch the waves at Freshwater, Curl Curl, Dee Why, Collaroy, Narrabeen, Mona Vale, Newport, Bilgola, Avalon, Whale and Palm Beaches are uniformly proud to agree. Each of these beaches has a markedly different atmosphere.

Driving is by far the best way to explore, but if that's not an option and you still feel the need to make a *Home & Away* pilgrimage, bus L90 will get you from Railway Sq to Palm Beach in just under two hours.

Dee Why BEACH
(The Strand; 176) A no-fuss family beach fronted by chunky apartments, some good cafes and ubiquitous surf shops. Grommets hit the waves and mums hit the rock pool.

Narrabeen BEACH
(Ocean St; L88, L90) Immortalised by the Beach Boys in *Surfin' USA,* Narrabeen is hard-core surf turf – get some experience before hitting the breaks. Not the best swimming, but there is a pool and a lagoon too.

Bilgola BEACH
(Bilgola Ave; L88, L90) With its saltwater pool, Bilgola feels like a bit of a secret gem. Good swimming.

Avalon BEACH
(Barrenjoey Rd; L88, L90) Caught in a sandy '70s time warp, Avalon is the mythical Australian beach you always dreamt of but could never find. Challenging surf and tangerine sand.

Sydney's Beaches

In Sydney, nothing beats a day at the beach. Sun, sand and surf dominate the culture for six months of every year...at least. There are no privatised beaches here: lay down a towel and you've claimed your personal patch of paradise for as long as you want it.

Ocean Beaches

The city's magnificent run of ocean beaches stretches from Royal National Park in the south to Palm Beach in the the north. Surfers, scenesters, swimmers and sunbathers are lured onto the golden sand and into the powerful swells of the Tasman Sea. Serious surfers head to Cronulla in the south; Maroubra, Bronte, Tamarama and Bondi in the east; and Curl Curl, Narrabeen, Queenscliff, Freshwater and Manly in the north. Of these, Bronte and Manly are also popular with swimmers, joining Coogee, Clovelly, Bondi, Bilgola, Whale and Palm as regular entries on 'Best Beaches' lists. Each of these beaches has a devoted crew of regulars – families flock to Clovelly, Bronte and Whale Beach, while bronzed, body-enhanced singles strut their stuff at Bondi, Coogee and Palm Beach.

Sydney's best-known beaches – Bondi and Manly – host an incongruous mix of pasty-skinned foreigners, weather-wizened surf gurus, grommets and geriatric locals who've been perfecting their body-surfing techniques for decades. Always crowded, these two beaches showcase the most endearing and eclectic aspects of Sydney's character, and shouldn't be missed.

OLIVER STREWE / GETTY IMAGES ©

KOKKAI NG / GETTY IMAGES ©

1. Bondi Icebergs Swimming Club (p104) **2.** Surfers, Bondi Beach (p93)

Ocean Pools

If you find Sydney's ocean surf a little intimidating or if you just want to soothe your jetlag with a few slow laps, take advantage of the city's famous ocean pools. There are 40 seawater pools up and down the coast, most of which are free. The most popular are Wylie's Baths, Giles Baths and the Ross Jones Memorial Pool in Coogee; the Bondi Icebergs Swimming Club; and the pool at Fairy Bower Beach in Manly. Our favourite is rugged little Mahon Pool near Maroubra.

Harbour Beaches & Pools

The pick of Sydney's harbour beaches include Camp Cove and Lady Bay near South Head (the latter of which is mainly a gay nude beach). Shark Beach at Nielsen Park in Vaucluse and Balmoral Beach on the north shore. Also popular are the netted swimming enclosures at Cremorne Point on the North Shore and Murray Rose Pool near Double Bay. There are plenty of little sandy gems scattered about that even Sydneysiders would be hard pressed to find, including Parsley Bay and Milk Beach right in the heart of residential Vaucluse.

BEACHES BY NEIGHBOURHOOD

Sydney Harbour Lots of hidden coves; the best are out near the Heads.

Bondi to Coogee High cliffs frame a string of surf beaches, with excellent coffee and cold beer just a stumble away.

Northern Beaches A steady succession of magical surf beaches stretching 30km north from Manly to Palm Beach.

Whale Beach BEACH

(Whale Beach Rd; L90) Sleepy Whale Beach, 3km south of Palm Beach, is well worth seeking out – a paradisiacal slice of deep, orange sand flanked by steep cliffs; good for surfers and families.

Palm Beach BEACH

(Ocean Rd; L90) Long, lovely Palm Beach is a meniscus of bliss, famous as the setting for cheesy TV soap *Home & Away*. The 1881 **Barrenjoey Lighthouse** (L90) punctuates the northern tip of the headland in an annexe of Ku-ring-gai Chase National Park. You'll need some decent shoes for the steep 20-minute hike (no toilets!), but the views across Pittwater are worth the effort. On Sundays short tours run every half-hour from 11am to 3pm; no need to book ahead.

Ku-ring-gai Chase National Park PARK

(02-9472 8949; www.nationalparks.nsw.gov.au; Bobbin Head Rd, Mount Colah; per car per day $11, landing fee by boat adult/child $3/2) This spectacular 14,928-hectare park, 24km from the city centre, forms Sydney's northern boundary. It's a classic mix of sandstone, bushland and water vistas, taking in over 100km of coastline along the southern edge of Broken Bay, where it heads into the Hawkesbury River.

Ku-ring-gai takes its name from its original inhabitants, the Guringai people, who were all but wiped out just after colonisation through violence at the hands of British settlers and introduced disease. It's well worth reading Kate Grenville's Booker-nominated *The Secret River* for an engrossing but harrowing telling of this story.

Remnants of Aboriginal life are visible today thanks to the preservation of more than 800 sites, including rock paintings, middens and cave art. To learn more, enter the park through the Mt Colah entrance and visit the **Kalkari Discovery Centre** (02-9472 9300; Ku-ring-gai Chase Rd; 9am-5pm) FREE, which has displays and videos on Australian fauna and Aboriginal culture. There is a self-guided walk on which you can see swamp wallabies, bush turkeys, native ducks and goannas.

From the Resolute picnic area at West Head you can amble 100m to Red Hands Cave, where there are some very faint ochre handprints. About another 500m along Resolute Track (after a short steep section) is an Aboriginal engraving site. You can turn around and head back now, or continue to one more site and make a 3.5km loop that takes in Resolute Beach. The view from the West Head Lookout is truly spectacular – don't miss it.

Less than 3km west of the picnic area along West Head Rd is the Basin Track, which offers an easy stroll to a good set of engravings. Approximately 2.5km further along the track is the Basin, a shallow round inlet where there is a camping area with barbecues, showers and toilets. Access is via the Basin Track or by ferry or water taxi from Palm Beach. For information about the park, stop at the **Bobbin Head Information Centre** (02-9472 8949; Bobbin Head; 10am-4pm), operated by the NSW National Parks & Wildlife Service. Also here are a marina, picnic areas, a cafe and a boardwalk leading through mangroves.

Access to the park is by car or the Palm Beach Ferry that is run by Fantasea. This runs hourly from Palm Beach to Mackerel Beach, via the Basin. To get to Palm Beach from the CBD, catch bus L90 from Railway Sq or bus 156 or 169 from Manly Wharf.

If you are arriving by car, enter Ku-ring-gai Chase Rd off Pacific Hwy, Mt Colah; Bobbin Head Rd, North Turramurra; or McCarrs Creek Rd, Terrey Hills.

Activities

Diving

Sydney's best shore dives are at Gordons Bay, north of Coogee; Shark Point, Clovelly; and Ship Rock, Cronulla. Other destinations include North Bondi, Camp Cove and Bare Island. Popular boat-dive sites are the grey nurse shark colony at Magic Point, off Maroubra; Wedding Cake Island off Coogee; Sydney Heads; and off Royal National Park.

Dive Centre Bondi DIVING

(Map p94; 02-9369 3855; www.divebondi.com.au; 198 Bondi Rd; 9am-6pm Mon-Fri, 7.30am-6pm Sat & Sun; 380) This Professional Association of Diving Instructors (PADI) centre offers learn-to-dive courses (three days $395), plus various boat and shore dives around Sydney.

Dive Centre Manly DIVING

(Map p98; 02-9977 4355; www.divesydney.com.au; 10 Belgrave St; 8.30am-6pm; Manly) Offers snorkel safaris ($50), two-day learn-to-dive PADI courses (from $445), guided shore dives (one/two dives $95/125) and boat dives (two dives $175).

Kayaking

Sydney Harbour Kayaks KAYAKING
(Map p68; ☎02-9960 4389; www.sydneyharbourkayaks.com.au; Smiths Boat Shed, 81 Parriwi Rd, Mosman; ⌚9am-5pm Mon-Fri, 7.30am-5pm Sat & Sun; 🚌173-180) Rents kayaks (from $20 per hour) and stand-up paddle boards (from $25), and leads four-hour ecotours ($99) from near the Spit Bridge.

Manly Kayak Centre KAYAKING
(Map p98; ☎1300 529 257; www.manlykayakcentre.com.au; West Esplanade; 1/2/8hr from $25/40/70; ⌚9am-5pm; ⛴Manly) As long as you can swim, you can hire a kayak or paddle board from this stand near Manly Sea Life Sanctuary; with additional stands near **Manly Wharf Hotel** (Map p98; www.manlywharfhotel.com.au; Manly Wharf; ⌚11.30am-midnight; ⛴Manly) and the Quarantine Station (p99). You'll be provided with a life jacket, paddling instruction and tips on secluded beaches to visit. Three-hour kayak tours cost $89.

Sailing

James Craig SAILING
(Map p84; ☎02-9298 3888; www.shf.org.au; Wharf 7, Pyrmont; adult/child $150/50; ⛴Pyrmont Bay) The *James Craig* is a hulking three-masted iron barque built in England in 1874 that's normally moored outside the Maritime Museum. It sails out beyond the heads roughly twice-monthly (bookings essential). Trips include morning tea, lunch, afternoon tea and a sea shanty or three.

Champagne Sailing SAILING
(☎02-9948 1578; www.champagnesailing.com.au; 4hr charters $1200) If you've got champagne tastes or ever fancied recreating Duran Duran's *Rio* video, charter a 10m catamaran and muster your 20 best friends to split the bill.

Sailing Sydney SAILING
(Map p84; ☎1300 670 008; www.sailingsydney.net; King St Wharf 9; adult/child $129/99; ⛴Darling Harbour) Learn the ropes on a 2½-hour cruise on an actual America's Cup yacht.

Surfing

On the South Shore, get tubed at Bondi, Tamarama, Coogee, Maroubra and Cronulla. The North Shore is home to a dozen surf beaches between Manly and Palm Beach, including Curl Curl, Dee Why, Narrabeen, Mona Vale and Newport.

WORTH A TRIP

SOUTHSIDE SURFING

Cronulla (🚆Cronulla) is a beachy surf suburb south of Botany Bay, its long surf beach stretching beyond the dunes to the Botany Bay refineries. It can be an edgy place (captured brilliantly in the 1970s cult teen novel *Puberty Blues*), with dingy fish-and-chip shops, insomniac teens and a ragged sense of impending 'something', which in 2005 erupted into racial violence. That said, the beach is beautiful, with a pleasant promenade, and it's easy to reach by train from Bondi Junction.

Let's Go Surfing SURFING
(Map p94; ☎02-9365 1800; www.letsgosurfing.com.au; 128 Ramsgate Ave; board & wetsuit hire 1hr/2hr/day/week $25/30/50/150; ⌚9am-5pm) North Bondi is a great place to learn to surf, and this well-established surf school offers lessons catering to practically everyone. There are classes for grommets aged seven to 16 (1½ hours, $49) and adults (two hours, $99; women-only classes available), or you can book a private tutor (1½ hours, $175). There's a second shop in Bondi Pavilion.

Manly Surf School SURFING
(Map p68; ☎02-9932 7000; www.manlysurfschool.com; North Steyne Surf Club; ⛴Manly) Offers two-hour surf lessons year-round (adult/child $70/55), as well as private tuition. Also runs surf safaris up to the Northern Beaches, including two lessons, lunch, gear and city pick-ups ($120).

Swimming

There are 100-plus public swimming pools in Sydney, and many beaches have protected rock pools. Harbour beaches offer sheltered and shark-netted swimming, but nothing beats Pacific Ocean waves. Always swim within the flagged lifeguard-patrolled areas, and never underestimate the surf.

Cook & Phillip Park SWIMMING
(Map p72; www.cookandphillip.org.au; 4 College St; adult/child $7/5.20; ⌚6am-10pm Mon-Fri, 7am-8pm Sat & Sun; 🚆St James) This Olympic-sized indoor pool has a hydrotherapy area and a gym ($20 including pool use), plus yoga, pilates, a basketball court, swimming lessons and a wave pool for cooling off the kids.

Bondi Icebergs Swimming Club SWIMMING
(Map p94; ☎02-9130 4804; www.icebergs.com.au; 1 Notts Ave; adult/child $6/4; ⊙6.30am-6.30pm Fri-Wed) Sydney's most famous pool commands the best view in Bondi and has a cute little cafe.

Wylie's Baths SWIMMING
(Map p68; ☎02-9665 2838; www.wylies.com.au; 4B Neptune St; adult/child $4.80/1; ⊙7am-7pm Oct-Mar, to 5pm Apr-Sep; 🚌372-374) On the rocky coast south of Coogee Beach, this superb seawater pool (1907) is targeted at swimmers more than splashabouts. After your swim, take a yoga class ($18), enjoy a massage, or have a coffee at the kiosk, which has magnificent ocean views.

Mahon Pool SWIMMING
(Marine Pde; 🚌376-377) FREE Hidden within the cliffs, 500m north of Maroubra Beach, Mahon Pool is an idyllic rock pool, where the surf crashes over the edges at high tide. It's quite possibly Sydney's most beautiful bogey hole (sea bath).

North Sydney Olympic Pool SWIMMING
(Map p68; ☎02-9955 2309; www.northsydney.nsw.gov.au; 4 Alfred St South; adult/child $7.10/3.50; ⊙5.30am-9pm Mon-Fri, 7am-7pm Sat & Sun; 🚆Milsons Point/Luna Park) Next to Luna Park is this art deco Olympic-sized outdoor pool, plus a 25m indoor pool, kids' splash zones, a gym ($18.50 with pool access), a crèche and a cafe, all with unbelievable harbour views.

Aquatic Centre SWIMMING
(☎02-9752 3666; www.aquaticcentre.com.au; Olympic Blvd; adult/child $7/6; ⊙5am-9pm Mon-Fri, 6am-7pm Sat & Sun; 🚆Olympic Park) Indulge your Ian Thorpe or Misty Hyman fantasies in the actual record-shattering pool which was used in the 2000 Olympics. There's also a leisure pool with a whirlpool in one corner, a state-of-the-art gym, a cafe and a swim shop. Wheelchair accessible.

Tours

Bike Tours

BlueBananas CYCLING
(Map p72; ☎02-9114 8488; www.bluebananas.com.au; 281 Clarence St; 🚆Town Hall) Take some of the puff out of a guided cycling tour on an electric bike. Options include the 1½-hour Bike the Bridge tour ($59) and the 2½-hour Sydney City Tour ($99).

Bike Buffs CYCLING
(☎0414 960 332; www.bikebuffs.com.au; adult/child $95/70; 🚆Circular Quay) Offers daily four-hour, two-wheeled tours around the harbourside sights (including jaunts over the Harbour Bridge), departing from Argyle Place. They also hire bikes (per half day/day/week $35/60/295).

Bonza Bike Tours CYCLING
(Map p72; ☎02-9247 8800; www.bonzabiketours.com; 30 Harrington St; adult/child $119/99; 🚆Circular Quay) These bike boffins run a 2½-hour Sydney Highlights tour (adult/child $66/79) and a four-hour Sydney Classic tour ($119/99). Other tours tackle the Harbour Bridge and Manly. They also hire bikes (per hour/half day/day $15/35/50).

Manly Bike Tours CYCLING
(Map p98; ☎02-8005 7368; www.manlybiketours.com.au; 54 West Promenade; hire per hr/day from $15/31; ⊙9am-6pm; ⛴Manly) Hires bikes and runs daily two-hour bike tours around Manly (10.30am, $89, bookings essential).

Boat Tours

Manly Ocean Adventures BOAT TOUR
(Map p98; ☎1300 062 659; www.manlyoceanadventures.com.au; 1/40 East Esplanade; from $85; ⛴Manly) Blast out to sea in a speedboat, following the coastline from Manly all the way to Bondi. From May to December they also offer whale-watching excursions.

Harbour Jet BOAT TOUR
(Map p84; ☎1300 887 373; www.harbourjet.com; King St Wharf 9; adult/child from $85/50; ⛴Darling Harbour) One of several jet-boat operators (Sydney Jet, Oz Jet Boating, Thunder Jet – take your pick), these guys run a 35-minute white-knuckle ride with 270-degree spins, fishtails and 75km/h power stops that'll test how long it's been since you had breakfast.

Whale Watching Sydney CRUISE
(☎02-9583 1199; www.whalewatchingsydney.net) Humpback and southern right whales habitually shunt up and down the Sydney coastline, sometimes venturing into the harbour. Between mid-May and December, WWS runs three-hour tours (adult/child $94/59) beyond the heads. For a faster, more thrilling ride, they also offer two-hour jet-boat expeditions ($60/40). Boats depart from Jetty 6, Circular Quay or from Cockle Bay Wharf, Darling Harbour.

Captain Cook Cruises CRUISE
(Map p72; 02-9206 1111; www.captaincook.com.au; Wharf 6, Circular Quay; Circular Quay) As well as ritzy lunch and dinner cruises, this crew offers the aquatic version of a hop-on/hop-off bus tour, stopping at Watsons Bay, Taronga Zoo, Garden Island, Circular Quay, Luna Park and Darling Harbour.

Sydney Showboats CRUISE
(Map p84; 02-8296 7388; www.sydneyshowboats.com.au; King St Wharf 5; from $125; Darling Harbour) Settle in for a three-hour, three-course dinner cruise on this paddle steamer, complete with cabaret singers, showgirls flashing their knickers, and a personal magician for your table. Very, very camp.

Private Tours

Bailey's Sydney TOUR
(0409 008 767; www.baileys-sydney.com; full day from $395) Offers highly personalised private tours of Sydney 'for people who don't like tours'.

Real Sydney Tours BUS TOUR
(0402 049 426; www.realsydneytours.com.au; 1-3 passengers from $465, additional passengers from $135) Private minibus tours around Sydney or to further-flung locations such as the Blue Mountains and the Hunter Valley.

Scenic Flights

Blue Sky Helicopters SCENIC FLIGHTS
(02-9700 7888; www.blueskyhelicopters.com) Departing from the airport, this experienced crew offers scenic flights, ranging from a 15-minute Bridge & Back trip ($330) to a five-hour Blue Mountains Helitour (from $2500).

Sydney by Seaplane SCENIC FLIGHTS
(Map p68; 1300 720 995; www.sydneybyseaplane.com; Rose Bay Marina, 594 New South Head Rd, Rose Bay; 15min/30min/45min/1hr flights per person $190/260/445/525; Rose Bay) Scenic flights over Sydney Harbour and the Northern Beaches. Fly-and-dine packages are available for picnics in obscure places. Departs from Rose Bay and Palm Beach.

Sydney Seaplanes SCENIC FLIGHTS
(Map p68; 1300 732 752; www.seaplanes.com.au; Seaplane Base, Lyne Park, Rose Bay; 15min/30min flights per person $200/265; Rose Bay) Aerial excitement meets epicurean delight when you take a seaplane flight from Rose Bay to remote Berowra Waters Inn (p135) on the Hawkesbury (per person $585) or **Jonah's** (02-9974 5599; www.jonahs.com.au; 69 Bynya Rd, Whale Beach; breakfast $50, mains $49; 7.30-9am, noon-2.30pm & 6.30-11pm; L90) at Whale Beach ($535). Also offers scenic flights around Sydney Harbour.

Walking Tours

I'm Free WALKING TOUR
(Map p82; 0405 515 654; www.imfree.com.au; 483 George St; 10.30am, 2.30pm & 6pm; Town Hall) FREE Departing thrice daily from the square off George St between the Town Hall and St Andrew's Cathedral (no bookings taken – just show up), these highly rated three-hour tours are nominally free but are run by enthusiastic young guides for tips. The route takes in the Rocks, Circular Quay, Martin Place, Pitt St and Hyde Park.

Peek Tours WALKING TOUR
(0420 244 756; www.peektours.com.au; Circular Quay) If you find that a cool beverage makes local history easier to digest, this crew will lead you on a two-hour tour of the Rocks, stopping in historic pubs ($60, including a drink at each). They also offer a 90-minute walking tour of Bondi Beach ($40) and other guided walks on request.

Sydney Architecture Walks WALKING TOUR
(0403 888 390; www.sydneyarchitecture.org; adult/student walk $49/35, cycle incl bike $120/110) These bright young archi-buffs run two 3½-hour cycling tours and five themed two-hour walking tours (The City; Utzon and the Sydney Opera House; Harbourings; Art, Place and Landscape; and Modern Sydney).

The Rocks Walking Tours WALKING TOUR
(Map p72; 02-9247 6678; www.rockswalkingtours.com.au; cnr Argyle & Harrington Sts; adult/child/family $25/12/62; 10.30am & 1.30pm; Circular Quay) Regular 90-minute tours through the historic Rocks, with plenty of not-so-tall tales and interesting minutiae.

Other Tours

BridgeClimb WALKING TOUR
(Map p72; 02-8274 7777; www.bridgeclimb.com; 3 Cumberland St; adult $218-348, child $148-228; Circular Quay) Don a headset, a safety cord and a dandy grey jumpsuit and you'll be ready to embark on an exhilarating climb to the top of Sydney's famous harbour bridge. The priciest climbs are at dawn and sunset. A cheaper, 90-minute 'sampler' climb (heading only halfway up) is also available.

EcoTreasures CULTURAL TOUR
(0415 121 648; www.ecotreasures.com.au) Small group tours include Manly Snorkel Walk & Talk (90 minutes, adult/child

$65/40) and longer excursions to the Northern Beaches and Ku-ring-gai Chase National Park, including Aboriginal Heritage Tours led by Indigenous guides.

SCG Tour Experience TOUR
(Map p92; ☎1300 724 737; www.sydneycricketground.com.au; Venue Services Office, Allianz Stadium, Driver Ave; adult/child/family $30/20/78; ⊙11am & 2pm Mon-Fri, 11am Sat; 373-377) Run up the players' race from the dressing rooms in your own sporting fantasy during this behind-the-scenes guided tour of the facilities at the Sydney Cricket Ground.

Festivals & Events

Field Day MUSIC
(www.fielddaynyd.com.au) Groove New Year's Day away in the Domain with well-known international and local acts (2015 headliners: SBTRKT, Alt-J, Danny Brown, Jamie XX, Salt-n-Pepa).

Sydney Festival CULTURAL
(www.sydneyfestival.org.au) Sydney's premier arts and culture festival showcases three weeks of music, theatre and visual art every January.

Flickerfest FILM
(☎02-9365 6888; www.flickerfest.com.au; Bondi Pavilion, Queen Elizabeth Dr; 380) Bondi's international short-film festival stages shorts, docos, animation and workshops over 10 days in mid-January.

Australia Day NATIONAL DAY
(www.australiaday.gov.au) On 26 January, Sydneysiders celebrate with picnics, barbecues, fireworks, ferry races and, increasingly, much flag-waving and drunkenness.

Chinese New Year CULTURAL
(www.sydneychinesenewyear.com) Seventeen-day, Chinatown-based festival featuring food, fireworks, dragon dancers and dragon-boat races to see in the lunar new year. Actual dates vary, but it's always in January or February.

St Jerome's Laneway Festival MUSIC
(www.lanewayfestival.com.au) A one-day music festival held in early February at the Sydney College of the Arts, Rozelle, which reliably and presciently schedules the world's hippest new indie acts, just as they're breaking (past headliners have included Florence + The Machine, Lorde and St Vincent).

Sydney Gay & Lesbian Mardi Gras GAY & LESBIAN
(www.mardigras.org.au) A two-week festival culminating in the world-famous massive parade and party on the first Saturday in March.

Sydney Royal Easter Show FAIR
(www.eastershow.com.au) Ostensibly an agricultural show, this wonderful Sydney tradition is a two-week fiesta of carnival rides, kiddie-centric show bags and sugary horrors. Crowds are massive.

Biennale of Sydney CULTURAL
(www.biennaleofsydney.com.au) High-profile festival of art and ideas held between March and June in even-numbered years.

Fashion Week FASHION
(www.mbffsydney.com.au) Each April, local designer duds are on display on the catwalk in Carriageworks. Expect plenty of skin, gossip…oh, and some beautiful clothes.

Vivid Sydney CULTURAL
(www.vividsydney.com) Immersive light installations and projections in the city, performances from local and international musicians, and public talks and debates with leading global creative thinkers; held over 18 days from late May.

State of Origin Series SPORTS
(www.nrl.com) Rugby league fanatics consider this series of three matches between Queensland and New South Wales (held in May, June and July) to be the pinnacle of the game.

City2Surf SPORT
(www.city2surf.com.au) Over 80,000 people run the 14km from Hyde Park to Bondi Beach on the second Sunday in August.

Festival of the Winds CARNIVAL
(www.waverley.nsw.gov.au) Held on the second Sunday in September, this festival brings spectacular kites shaped like animals and aliens to Bondi Beach. The kids will love it, and with the wind doing all the work it's very ecofriendly.

National Rugby League Grand Final SPORTS
(www.nrl.com.au) The two teams left standing at the end of the National Rugby League (NRL) season head to Sydney Olympic Park to decide who's the best. On the Sunday of the October long weekend.

Sculpture by the Sea ART
(www.sculpturebythesea.com) For 17 days from late October, the clifftop trail from Bondi Beach to Tamarama transforms into a sculpture garden. Serious prize money is on offer for the most creative, curious or quizzical offerings from international and local sculptors.

Tropfest FILM
(www.tropfest.com) The world's largest short-film festival is enjoyed from picnic blankets in Centennial Park on one day in early December.

Sydney Hobart Yacht Race SPORTS
(www.rolexsydneyhobart.com) On 26 December Sydney Harbour is a sight to behold as hundreds of boats crowd its waters to farewell the yachts competing in this gruelling race.

New Year's Eve FIREWORKS
(www.sydneynewyearseve.com) The biggest party of the year, with flamboyant firework displays on the harbour.

Sleeping

Sydney offers a huge quantity and variety of accommodation, with solid options in every price range. Even so, the supply shrivels up under the summer sun, particularly around weekends and big events. All but the smallest hotels vary their prices from day to day, depending on occupancy. Fridays and Saturdays tend to be the most expensive nights, while Sundays are usually the cheapest. Rates skyrocket over the busy Christmas/New Year period.

The Rocks & Circular Quay

★**Sydney Harbour YHA** HOSTEL $
(Map p72; 02-8272 0900; www.yha.com.au; 110 Cumberland St; dm/r from $52/192; ; Circular Quay) Any qualms about the unhostel-like prices will be shelved the moment you head up to the rooftop of this sprawling, modern YHA and see the million-dollar views of Circular Quay. All of the spacious rooms, including the dorms, have private bathrooms and there are a host of sustainability initiatives in place.

Lord Nelson Brewery Hotel PUB $$
(Map p72; 02-9251 4044; www.lordnelsonbrewery.com; 19 Kent St; r from $180; ; Circular Quay) Built in 1836, this atmospheric sandstone pub has a tidy set of upstairs rooms, with exposed stone walls and dormer windows with harbour glimpses. Most of the nine, light-filled rooms have en suites; there are also cheaper rooms with shared facilities. The downstairs microbrewery is a welcoming place for a pint. Rates include breakfast.

Sydney Harbour Bed & Breakfast B&B $$
(Map p72; 02-9247 1130; www.bbsydneyharbour.com.au; 142 Cumberland St; r with/without bathroom $240/165; ; Circular Quay) This quaint 100-year-old guesthouse offers lovely rooms which have an Australian flavour without straying into twee territory. Rooms come in a variety of configurations, have tea-and-coffee making facilities and feature hand-crafted furnishings and polished floors. Rates include a cooked breakfast.

Russell HOTEL $$
(Map p72; 02-9241 3543; www.therussell.com.au; 143A George St; s without bathroom $159, d without bathroom $169-209, d $259-299; ; Circular Quay) Old-world charm meets gentle contemporary styling at this long-standing favourite. The rooftop garden, downstairs wine bar and Circular Quay location are major drawcards. Next door to the historic Fortune of War pub, front rooms can be noisy on weekends.

★**Park Hyatt** HOTEL $$$
(Map p72; 02-9256 1234; www.sydney.park.hyatt.com; 7 Hickson Rd; r from $860; ; Circular Quay) At Sydney's most expensive hotel the impeccable service levels and facilities are second to none. With full frontal views across Circular Quay, you can catch all the action from your bed, balcony or bathtub. From the rooftop pool you feel you can almost touch the Harbour Bridge. And with 24-hour personal butler service for all guests, it's not like you need to be anywhere else.

Pullman Quay Grand Sydney Harbour APARTMENTS $$$
(Map p72; 02-9256 4000; www.pullmanhotels.com; 61 Macquarie St; apt from $472; ; Circular Quay) With the Opera House as its neighbour, the building known locally as 'the toaster' has a scorching-hot location. These well-designed contemporary apartments set you in the glitzy heart of Sydney, encircled by top restaurants, cocktail bars and that attention-seeking harbour.

Langham HOTEL $$$
(Map p72; ☎02-8248 5200; www.sydney.langhamhotels.com; 89-113 Kent St; r from $635; P⊖❄@☎≋🐾; 🚇Wynyard) Recently reopened after a $30 million revamp, this opulent hotel eschews excessive glitz in favour of an elegant antique ambience. This is where you head for a true five-star stay featuring afternoon turn-down service, in-house pastry kitchen, page-long pillow menu and an extravagant pool and day spa experience, where guests can swim under a star-dazzled ceiling.

Shangri-La HOTEL $$$
(Map p72; ☎02-9250 6000; www.shangri-la.com; 176 Cumberland St; r from $350; ❄☎≋; 🚇Circular Quay) The Hong Kong–based chain's Sydney offering is a suitably sleek tower with palatial rooms and seriously spectacular views. As expected, service is efficient and discreet, whatever the request. The acclaimed Altitude Restaurant on the 36th floor offers a well-edited menu focusing on seasonal produce.

Quay West Suites APARTMENTS $$$
(Map p72; ☎02-9240 6000; www.quaywestsuitessydney.com.au; 98 Gloucester St; apt from $387; ⊖❄@☎≋; 🚇Circular Quay) One of the older high-rise hotels, Quay West's early 1990s decor could just about qualify as retro. The roomy apartments are a home away from home, each with a full kitchen, lounge and laundry room. The views are extraordinary and the cheesy 'Roman-style' pool on level 24 is a lot of fun.

Harbour Rocks BOUTIQUE HOTEL $$$
(Map p72; ☎02-8220 9999; www.harbourrocks.com.au; 34 Harrington St; r from $350; ⊖❄@☎; 🚇Circular Quay) This deluxe boutique hotel on the site of Sydney's first hospital has undergone a chic and sympathetic transformation from colonial warehouse to a series of New York loft-style rooms, with high ceilings, charcoal brick walls and elegant furnishings.

City Centre

Meriton Serviced Apartments Kent Street APARTMENTS $$
(Map p82; ☎02-8263 5500; www.staymsa.com/kent; 528 Kent St; apt from $195; ⊖❄☎≋; 🚇Town Hall) There's a lot to be said for staying in a serviced apartment, not least the ability to be able to wash your smalls whenever the need arises. Each of the one- to three-bedroom apartments in this modern tower has laundry facilities and a full kitchen complete with a dishwasher. Not that you'll want to cook, with Chinatown at your feet.

Adina Apartment Hotel Sydney APARTMENT $$
(Map p82; ☎02-9274 0000; www.adinahotels.com.au; 511 Kent St; studio from $180, 1-/2-bedroom apt from $240/280; ⊖❄☎≋; 🚇Town Hall) Near both Chinatown and Darling Harbour but with double-glazed windows to ensure a good night's sleep, Adina offers spacious, fully equipped apartments and smaller studio rooms with kitchenettes. The larger apartments offer the best value.

Hyde Park Inn HOTEL $$
(Map p82; ☎02-9264 6001; www.hydeparkinn.com.au; 271 Elizabeth St; s/d from $165/176; P⊖❄@☎; 🚇Museum) Right on the park, this relaxed place offers studio rooms with kitchenettes, deluxe rooms with balconies and full kitchens, and some two-bedroom apartments. All have flat-screen TVs with cable access. Breakfast and parking is included in the rate.

★**QT Sydney** BOUTIQUE HOTEL $$$
(Map p72; ☎02-8262 0000; www.qtsydney.com.au; 49 Market St; r from $380; P⊖❄☎; 🚇St James) Fun, sexy and completely OTT, this ultra-theatrical hotel is located in the historic State Theatre. Art deco eccentricity is complemented by retro games and DIY martini kits in all the rooms, which have 12 madcap styles. There's also a spa complete with hammam and old-school barber, plus a bar and grill operated by one of the city's most fashionable restaurateurs.

Westin Sydney HOTEL $$$
(Map p72; ☎02-8223 1111; www.westinsydney.com; 1 Martin Pl; r from $310; P⊖❄@☎≋; 🚇Martin Place) This luxury address is popular with business travellers who choose between elegant heritage rooms in the grand General Post Office building or bedding down in a modern high-rise. Thoughtful extras like lending guests exercise gear (including running shoes!) are impressive.

Establishment Hotel BOUTIQUE HOTEL $$$
(Map p72; ☎02-9240 3100; www.merivale.com.au; 5 Bridge Lane; r from $350; ⊖❄@☎; 🚇Wynyard) A room at this so-hip-it-hurts hotel is your VIP pass to the city's most decadent nights out. What Establishment lacks in facilities it makes up for with its fabulous clutch of acclaimed bars and restaurants,

not to mention designer good looks that wander from Japanese-style rooms to muted, tranquil abodes both with massive bathrooms stocked with Bulgari toiletries.

Haymarket

Railway Square YHA HOSTEL $
(Map p86; 02-9281 9666; www.yha.com.au; 8-10 Lee St; dm from $39, d with/without bathroom from $130/116; ; Central) This hostel's not just central, it's actually *in* Central station. A nouveau-industrial renovation has turned a former parcel shed (complete with platform) into a hip hostel. You can even sleep in dorms in converted train carriages. The kids will love it (but bring earplugs). Private en suite rooms also available.

Wake Up! HOSTEL $
(Map p86; 02-9288 7888; www.wakeup.com.au; 509 Pitt St; dm $38-44, s $98, d with/without bathroom $148/118; ; Central) Flashpackers sleep soundly in this converted 1900 department store on top of Sydney's busiest intersection. It's a convivial, colourful, professionally run hostel with 520 beds, lots of activities, a tour desk, 24-hour check-in, a sunny cafe, a bar and no excuse for neglecting your inner party animal.

Sydney Central YHA HOSTEL $
(Map p86; 02-9218 9000; www.yha.com.au; 11 Rawson Pl; dm from $39, d with/without bathroom from $125/115; P; Central) Near Central station, this 1913 heritage-listed monolith is the mother of all Sydney YHA properties. The renovated hostel includes everything from a travel agency to an in-house cinema. The rooms are brightly painted and the kitchens are great but the highlight is sweating it out in the sauna, then cooling off in the rooftop pool.

Darling Harbour & Pyrmont

1888 Hotel BOUTIQUE HOTEL $$
(Map p84; 02-8586 1888; www.1888hotel.com.au; 139 Murray St; d from $169, ste from $249; ; Town Hall) In a heritage-listed wool store, this stylish gem combines stark industrial minimalism with the warmth of ironbark wood beams and luxury appointments. Rooms range from the aptly named shoebox to the airy lofts and attic suites with harbour views. The cool but casual staff point out the hip hotel must-have's: lobby space set up for Instagram selfies, bikes for hire and an iPad in every room.

The Darling CASINO HOTEL $$$
(Map p84; 02-9777 9000; www.thedarling.com.au; 80 Pyrmont St, Pyrmont ; r from $430; P; Pyrmont Bay) Beyond the bling of Star City Casino lies the sumptuous Darling. Sink into beds laid with 400-thread-count Egyptian cotton sheets and choose from a menu of 12 pillows. Hard to get up? No problem. Guests can adjust the lighting, air temperature and select a time for the blinds to open in the morning via remote control. The sweets and alcoholic treats in the well-stocked mini bar make for a great midnight feast.

Ultimo, Glebe & Chippendale

Glebe Point YHA HOSTEL $
(Map p68; 02-9692 8418; www.yha.com.au; 262-264 Glebe Point Rd, Glebe; dm $28-45, s without bathroom $70, d without bathroom $84-105; ; 431) A great choice for working travellers, this chilled-out hostel has decent facilities, plenty of organised activities and simple rooms with sinks. Less uptight than some YHAs, there's a convivial vibe particularly on the rooftop terrace which is popular on barbecue nights. A real plus are the surrounding cafes and easy access to public transport into town.

Forsyth Bed & Breakfast B&B $$
(Map p68; 02-9552 2110; www.forsythbnb.com; 3 Forsyth St, Glebe; d $195-225; ; 431) Count yourself lucky if you nab one of the two guest rooms at this bijou escape in Glebe's leafy back streets. Forsyth B&B has light, art-filled rooms, one with a balcony overlooking the city. The accommodating owners provide personalised itineraries, airport transfers and help with public transport. Breakfast is served in the Japanese-inspired garden. Minimum three-night stay.

Surry Hills

Bounce HOSTEL $
(Map p86; 02-9281 2222; www.bouncehotel.com.au; 28 Chalmers St, Surry Hills; dm/r from $40/149; ; Central) This popular hostel has scooped up a pile of awards for its boutique take on budget accommodation. Beyond the standard dorms there are double rooms with sleek en suites, luxury hotel quality beds and TVs. Soak up those skyline views on the rooftop terrace. Guests are provided with extra-large lockers with a power supply to safely charge electronics.

CITY CAMPING

Cockatoo Island (Map p68; 02-8898 9774; www.cockatooisland.gov.au; camp sites from $45, 2-bed tents from $150, apt from $225, houses from $595; Cockatoo Island) Waking up on an island in the middle of the harbour is an extraordinary Sydney experience. Bring your own tent or 'glamp' in a two-person tent complete with a double bed on the water's edge. Noncampers will enjoy the elegant garden apartments. For self-caterers, there's a well-equipped camp kitchen; for everyone else, there are three cafes and bars.

Lane Cove River Tourist Park (02-9888 9133; www.lcrtp.com.au; Plassey Rd, Macquarie Park; unpowered/powered camp sites per 2 people $37/39, cabins from $135, luxury tents $200; ; North Ryde) Have a back-to-nature experience in the heart of suburbia, staying in this national park camp site 14km northwest of the CBD. There are caravan and camping sites, cabins and a pool to cool off in when the city swelters. For a romantic bush getaway, the Tandara luxury glamping option is worth the price. Park admission is included in the rates.

Big Hostel HOSTEL $
(Map p82; 02-9281 6030; www.bighostel.com; 212 Elizabeth St, Surry Hills; dm $32-36, s/d $89/110; ; Central) A great, no-frills hostel experience with a cool rooftop terrace and a snazzy communal area. A definite plus is the free breakfast and free wi-fi on the ground floor.

Darlinghurst

Cambridge Hotel HOTEL $$
(Map p88; 02-9212 1111; www.cambridgehotel.com.au; 212 Riley St, Surry Hills; r from $170; ; 380) You couldn't wish for a more conveniently situated hotel than this urban bolt-hole. Most of the spacious, contemporary rooms have private balconies with city skyline vistas. Downstairs the happening Baccomatto Osteria serves brilliant Italian food, including the hotel breakfast.

★ADGE Boutique Apartment Hotel APARTMENTS $$$
(Map p88; 02-8093 9888; www.adgehotel.com.au; 222 Riley St, Surry Hills; apt from $374; ; 380) As soon as you spot the bold wall murals, it's clear the ADGE is all about putting a clever twist on the ubiquitous serviced apartment experience. The 12 idiosyncratic but extremely comfortable two-bedroom apartments are bedecked with garishly striped carpets, smart TVs and colourful retro fridges. Free wi-fi, a welcome drink and a nightly turn-down service make this hotel one of Sydney's best boutique options.

Medusa BOUTIQUE HOTEL $$$
(Map p88; 02-9331 1000; www.medusa.com.au; 267 Darlinghurst Rd, Darlinghurst; r from $310; ; Kings Cross) Medusa's shocking pink exterior and witty, luscious decor was once the height of hotel hipsterdom. Today the small colour-saturated suites with large beds and regal furnishings (the best face the courtyard) are looking less decadent. Thankfully the staff are as energetic as ever and small touches like the Aesop toiletries go a long way. So does the tremendous location.

Woolloomooloo

Mariners Court HOTEL $$
(Map p88; 02-9320 3888; www.marinerscourt.com.au; 44-50 McElhone St, Woolloomooloo; r $110-160; ; Kings Cross) This won't be the flashest place you'll stay in Sydney (the vibe is kinda 1994), but it offers that rare combination of location, price and a bit of elbow room. Not to mention a complimentary hot breakfast buffet. All rooms have courtyards or balconies, some with leafy outlooks. Good wheelchair access.

BLUE Sydney HOTEL $$$
(Map p88; 02-9331 9000; www.bluehotel.com.au; 6 Cowper Wharf Rdwy, Woolloomooloo; r from $250; ; 311) Carved out of the historic Woolloomooloo finger wharf, now home to some top restaurants, much of the industrial machinery has been left exposed, to be admired over cocktails in the Water Bar. Rooms are mostly split-level, with king-size beds perched above living areas. Standard rooms are lit by skylight, giving the feel of staying on a luxury liner.

Kings Cross & Potts Point

Blue Parrot HOSTEL $
(Map p88; 02-9356 4888; www.blueparrot.com.au; 87 Macleay St, Potts Point; dm $35-42; ; Kings Cross) If Polly wanted a cracker of a hostel she might head to this well-maintained, secure little place which feels more like a share house (albeit a rather clean one!) run by sisters Effie and Sasha, rather than a backpackers. The courtyard is strung with hammocks. There are no private rooms, just dorms – and as a 'genuine' youth hostel, Blue Parrot only accepts 18- to 35-year-olds.

Eva's Backpackers HOSTEL $
(Map p88; 02-9358 2185; www.evasbackpackers.com.au; 6-8 Orwell St, Kings Cross; dm from $34-36, r from $89; ; Kings Cross) Far enough from the Kings Cross fray, Eva's is a longtime favourite offering free breakfast and wi-fi, plus an ace rooftop barbecue area and a sociable kitchen-dining room. Clean and secure.

Jackaroo HOSTEL $
(Map p88; 02-9332 2244; www.jackaroohostel.com; 107-109 Darlinghurst Rd, Kings Cross; dm $34-36, r with/without bathroom $90/80; ; Kings Cross) There's no accommodation positioned closer to the heart of the action than this hostel directly above Kings Cross station. Ordinarily that wouldn't be a good thing, but Jackaroo passes muster. While communal spaces are lacklustre and rooms cramped, they are very clean. Try to nab a rear-facing one but pack earplugs regardless. The vibe is bustling and (extremely) youthful. A no-frills breakfast is included.

Hotel 59 B&B $$
(Map p88; 02-9360 5900; www.hotel59.com.au; 59 Bayswater Rd, Rushcutters Bay; s $99, d $130-140; ; Kings Cross) In the style of a simple European pensione, Hotel 59 offers good bang for your buck on the quiet part of Bayswater Road close to Rushcutters Bay Park. The cafe downstairs does whopping cooked breakfasts (included in the price) for those barbarous Kings Cross hangovers. Two-night minimum.

Diamant HOTEL $$
(Map p88; 02-9295 8888; www.diamant.com.au; 14 Kings Cross Rd, Kings Cross; r $159-375, ste $315-425, apt $500-3200; P; Kings Cross) Presiding over William St this swish high-rise bridges the junction between Kings Cross and Darlinghurst. Space-age corridors open onto slick, spacious black-and-white rooms – all have king-size beds, quality linen, huge plasma screens and iPads. Courtyard suites offer roomy private balconies equipped with stylish outdoor furniture. Guests have free 24-hour access to a large public gym in the building.

Victoria Court Hotel B&B $$
(Map p88; 02-9357 3200; www.victoriacourt.com.au; 122 Victoria St; r from $169; P; Kings Cross) Chintzy charm reigns supreme at this faded but well-run B&B, which has 25 rooms in a pair of three-storey 1881 terrace houses. The larger more expensive rooms have balconies. The continental breakfast is served in the courtyard.

Macleay Hotel HOTEL $$
(Map p88; 02-9357 7755; www.themacleay.com; 28 Macleay St, Elizabeth Bay; r from $165; ; Kings Cross) At the posh end of Potts Point, surrounded by fabulous restaurants, is this understated hotel. The studios are a little faded but all have small kitchenettes and there's a laundry on each floor. An added plus is the rooftop pool and gym. Ask for a room on a higher floor for city and harbour views.

Bayswater BOUTIQUE HOTEL $$
(Map p88; 02-8070 0100; www.sydneylodges.com; 17 Bayswater Rd, Kings Cross; r from $120; ; Kings Cross) This smart hotel tries for the boutique experience but unfortunately misses the mark when it comes to the small details. What it does offer is attractive and affordable lodgings with a great address. Cheaper rooms are compact so upsize to a King Deluxe for more space and larger windows. Given the location, it can get noisy on weekend nights.

Simpsons of Potts Point BOUTIQUE HOTEL $$$
(Map p88; 02-9356 2199; www.simpsonshotel.com; 8 Challis Ave; r from $255; P; Kings Cross) At the quiet end of a busy cafe strip this 1892 villa has been affectionately restored with decorative flourishes of yesteryear. The perennially popular Simpsons is widely loved for its charming service and the cosy luxury of the 12 guest rooms. The downstairs lounge is perfect for a game of chess and a complimentary sherry.

Paddington & Woollahra

Kathryn's on Queen B&B $$
(Map p92; 02-9327 4535; www.kathryns.com.au; 20 Queen St, Woollahra; r $180-260; ; 380) Deftly run by the ever-smiley Kathryn, this grandiose 1888 Victorian terrace opposite Centennial Park has two tastefully decorated rooms dotted with antiques; choose between the en suite attic room or the 1st-floor room with a balcony. Great location for chichi shopping and dining.

Arts HOTEL $$
(Map p88; 02-9361 0211; www.artshotel.com.au; 21 Oxford St, Paddington; r from $174; ; 380) A well-managed 64-room hotel with simple but comfortable rooms in a handy location on the Paddington-Darlinghurst border. There's heavy-duty triple-glazing on the Oxford St frontage, while the rear rooms face a quiet lane. The central courtyard has a small solar-heated pool and there are free bikes for guests.

Double Bay

InterContinental Sydney Double Bay HOTEL $$$
(Map p68; 02-8388 8388; www.ihg.com; 30 Cross St, Double Bay; d from $570, ste from $850; ; Double Bay) Following a lavish renovation, this resort has been restored to the grandeur that first made it a celebrity hotspot back in the day. Swathed in Italian marble and twinkling chandeliers, it's all class from the Stillery gin bar to the slick rooftop pool overlooking the bay. Many of the light and airy guest rooms have superb harbour views.

Eastern Beaches

Bondi Beachouse YHA HOSTEL $
(Map p94; 02-9365 2088; www.yha.com.au; 63 Fletcher St, Bondi; dm $26-37, tw & d without bathroom $65-90, tw & d with bathroom $90-110, f with bathroom $162-180; ; 361 from Bondi Junction) Perched on a hillside between Bondi and Tamarama Beaches, this 95-bed art deco hostel is the best in Bondi. Dorms sleep four to eight, and some of the private rooms have ocean views – all are clean and well maintained. Facilities include a cinema room, games room, courtyard barbecue, free bodyboard and snorkel use, and a stunning rooftop deck.

Adina Apartments Bondi Beach APARTMENTS $$
(Map p94; 02-9300 4800; adinahotels.com.au; 69-73 Hall St; ; 389) Bondi's newest hotel is super modern, smartly appointed and just a barefoot dash to the surf. The apartments all have balconies and there's a fabulous retail and restaurant precinct downstairs. The hotel offers small conveniences such as grocery delivery to the rooms, a lap-pool, gym and in-house movies making it perfect for longer stays.

Bondi Beach House GUESTHOUSE $$
(Map p94; 0417 336 444; www.bondibeachhouse.com.au; 28 Sir Thomas Mitchell Rd, Bondi; s $100-125, d $135-230, ste $270-300; ; 380) In a tranquil pocket behind Campbell Pde, this charming place offers a homely atmosphere with rustic-chic furnishings and a well-equipped communal kitchen. Though only a two-minute walk from the beach, you may well be tempted to stay in all day – the courtyard and terrace are great spots for relaxing, and the rooms are conducive to long sleep-ins.

Dive Hotel BOUTIQUE HOTEL $$
(Map p68; 02-9665 5538; www.divehotel.com.au; 234 Arden St, Coogee; r from $190; ; 372-374) Plenty of hotels don't live up to their name and thankfully neither does this one. Right across the road from the beach, the 17 contemporary rooms at this relaxed, family-run affair are well designed. They come with kitchenettes and small stylish bathrooms fitted out with mosaic tiles and stainless steel sinks. Breakfast included.

Newtown & Around

Tara Guest House B&B $$
(Map p121; 02-9519 4809; www.taraguesthouse.com.au; 13 Edgeware Rd, Enmore; d with/without bathroom $215/185; ; Newtown) When you stay at a guesthouse run by designers with a passion for cooking and gardening, you know you're in for a good time. Brom and Julian have created a peaceful retreat with four graceful spaces with soaring ceilings and French doors opening onto large verandahs. The communal breakfast is a highlight. Rates include airport transfers.

Urban Hotel BOUTIQUE HOTEL $$
(Map p121; 02-8960 7800; www.theurbanhotel.com.au; 52-60 Enmore Rd, Newtown; r from $148; ; Newtown) A minute's walk from Newtown station and a bunch of great bars

and eats, this brand-new hotel in a former RSL Club offers industrial-sleek studio accommodation. The Urban stands out from the crowd with a slew of extras like free wi-fi, free landline calls Australia-wide and relaxed check-in/-out options. Kitchens include mini bars stocked with local craft beers.

Manly

Manly Bunkhouse HOSTEL $

(Map p68; ☎02-9976 0472; www.bunkhouse.com.au; 35 Pine St; dm $38, tw & d $90 ; @ wifi; Manly) Backpackers (mainly Dutch) mix it up with international students and holiday workers at this laid-back hostel minutes from Manly Beach. The bright and clean four-person dorms with en suite are the way to go, as the overpriced private rooms are in need of sprucing up.

Cecil Street B&B B&B $$

(Map p68; ☎02-9977 8036; www.cecilstreetbb.com.au; 18 Cecil St, Manly; s/d $110/$130; P wifi; Manly) This low-key bed and breakfast is in a handsome Federation-style home on a hill above Manly. The two simple but tastefully decorated rooms make the most of high ceilings, lead-light windows and polished timber floors. The only downside is the steep hike back from the beach.

101 Addison Road B&B $$

(Map p98; ☎02-9977 6216; www.bb-manly.com; 101 Addison Rd; s/d $165/185; P wifi; Manly) This sumptuously decorated 1880s cottage is perched on a quiet street close to the beach and ferry wharf. Two rooms are available but the delightful host only takes single bookings (from one to four people) – meaning you'll have free rein of the antique-strewn accommodation, including a private lounge with a grand piano and open fire.

Novotel Sydney Manly Pacific HOTEL $$$

(Map p68; ☎02-9977 7666; www.novotelmanlypacific.com.au; 55 North Steyne; r from $279; P @ wifi pool; Manly) Right on Manly's ocean beach, this midriser has a dated corporate vibe but is a million miles from the city's business hustle. Check the surf from oceanfront balconies, or hit the rooftop pool if you don't want sand in your laptop.

Eating

Sydney's cuisine celebrates the city's place on the Pacific Rim, marrying the freshest local ingredients with the flavours of Asia, the Americas and, of course, the colonial past. The top restaurants are properly pricey, but eating out needn't be expensive. There's a top-notch cafe scene and plenty of reasonably priced ethnic eateries where you can grab a cheap and tasty pizza or bowl of noodles.

The Rocks & Circular Quay

Sailors Thai Canteen THAI $$

(Map p72; ☎02-9251 2466; www.sailorsthai.com.au; 106 George St; mains $24-29; noon-3pm Mon-Fri & 5-10pm daily; Circular Quay) Wedge yourself into a gap between arts-community operators, politicians and media manoeuvrers at Sailors' long communal table and order from the fragrant menu of Thai street-food classics. The balcony tables fill up fast, but fortune might be smiling on you. Downstairs the vibe's more formal and the prices higher.

★Quay MODERN AUSTRALIAN $$$

(Map p72; ☎02-9251 5600; www.quay.com.au; L3, Overseas Passenger Terminal; 3/4 courses $130/150; noon-2.30pm Tue-Fri, 6-10pm daily; Circular Quay) Quay is shamelessly guilty of breaking the rule that good views make for bad food. Chef Peter Gilmore never rests on his laurels, consistently delivering the exquisitely crafted, adventurous cuisine which has landed Quay on the prestigious World's Best Restaurants list. And the view? Like dining in a postcard.

Saké JAPANESE $$$

(Map p72; ☎02-9259 5656; www.sakerestaurant.com.au; 12 Argyle St; mains $25-45; noon-3pm & 5.30-10.30pm; Circular Quay) Colourful sake barrels and lots of dark wood contribute to the louche Oriental glamour of this large, buzzy restaurant. Solo travellers can prop themselves around the open kitchen and snack on delectable Wagyu dumplings and maki rolls, while couples tuck into multi-course banquets of contemporary Japanese cuisine (from $88).

City Centre

Central Baking Depot BAKERY $

(Map p72; www.centralbakingdepot.com.au; 37-39 Erskine St; items $5-13; 7am-4pm Mon-Sat; Wynyard) CBD produces quality baked goods right in the heart of the CBD (Central Business District). Drop by for a savoury snack (pies, sausage rolls, croissants, pizza slices, sandwiches), or a sweet treat with coffee. Seating is limited to a modest scattering of tables and a window bench.

THE CULT OF THE CELEBRITY CHEF

Many Sydneysiders consider a sprinkling of celebrity to be an essential ingredient when it comes to dining out. There is a veritable constellation of chefs cooking around town who have attained local and international stardom courtesy of television cooking programs or cookbooks. These include the following:

Colin Fassnidge (**Four In Hand**, p119; **4Fourteen**, p117) Irish-born chef famous for his nose-to-tail cooking and withering assessments of *My Kitchen Rules* contestants.

Bill Granger (**bills**, p118) Lifestyle chef and author of 10 cookbooks whose food and style are thought by many to be quintessentially Sydney.

Luke Nguyen (**Red Lantern on Riley**, p118) Presents his own television programs (*Luke Nguyen's Vietnam, The Songs of Sapa, Luke Nguyen's Greater Mekong*) and has written several cookbooks.

Matt Moran (**Aria**, Map p72; ☎02-9240 2255; www.ariarestaurant.com; 1 Macquarie St; lunch & pretheatre mains $46, 2-/3-/4-course dinner $105/130/155; ⊙noon-2.30pm Mon-Fri, 5.30-11pm daily; Circular Quay; **Chiswick Restaurant**, p119; **Opera Bar**, p122) Matt's portrait is on show at the National Portrait Gallery in Canberra and he is known to millions of Australians through regular TV appearances.

Neil Perry (**Rockpool,** p115; **Rockpool Bar & Grill**, p115; **Spice Temple**) The city's original rock-star chef (with ponytail to match) has a long list of cookbooks and appearances on television cooking programs to his credit.

Sydney Madang
KOREAN $

(Map p82; 371a Pitt St; mains $13-20; ⊙11.30am-midnight; Museum) Down a teensy Little Korea lane is this backdoor gem – an authentic barbecue joint that's low on interior charisma but high on quality and quantity. Noisy, cramped and chaotic, yes, but the chilli seafood soup will have you coming back tomorrow.

Le Grand Café
FRENCH, CAFE $

(Map p72; www.afsydney.com.au/about/le-grand-cafe; 257 Clarence St; mains $10-15; ⊙8am-6.15pm Mon-Thu, to 4.30pm Fri, to 2pm Sat; Town Hall) All we can say about this cafe in the foyer of the Harry Seidler–designed Alliance Française building is *ooh la la*. The classic French snacks (think pastries, baguettes and croque-monsieur) are delicious, and the surrounds are extremely smart.

★Mr Wong
CHINESE $$

(Map p72; ☎02-9240 3000; www.merivale.com.au/mrwong; 3 Bridge Lane; mains $25-38; ⊙noon-3pm & 5.30-11pm; Wynyard) Dumpling junkies shuffle down a dirty lane and into the bowels of an old warehouse for a taste of Mr Wong's deliciously addictive Cantonese fare. There's a dark-edged glamour to the cavernous basement dining room. Despite seating 240, there are often queues out the door.

Spice Temple
CHINESE $$

(Map p72; ☎02-8078 1888; www.rockpool.com; 10 Bligh St; dishes $14-45; ⊙noon-3pm Mon-Fri, 6-10.30pm Mon-Sat; ; Martin Place) Tucked away in the basement of his Rockpool Bar & Grill is Neil Perry's darkly atmospheric temple to the cuisine of China's western provinces, especially Sichuan, Yunnan, Hunan, Jiangxi, Guangxi and Xingjiang. Expect plenty of heat and lots of thrills.

Ippudo Sydney
JAPANESE $$

(Map p72; ☎02-8078 7020; www.ippudo.com.au; L5 Westfield Sydney, 188 Pitt St; mains $15-25; ⊙11am-10pm; St James) An exuberant chorus of welcome greets guests on arrival at this wonderful ramen house, tucked away near the Westfield food court. Founded in Fukuoka in 1985 and now in 11 countries, the Sydney branch serves all the soupy, noodley favourites.

Alpha
GREEK $$

(Map p82; ☎02-9098 1111; www.alpharestaurant.com.au; 238 Castlereagh St; mains $19-35; ⊙noon-3pm & 6-10pm; Museum) Located directly across from the Greek consulate in the grand dining room of the Hellenic Club, this wonderful restaurant brings all the zing and drama of the Mediterranean to the heart of the city. Chef Peter Conistis' menu covers the classics, with his own unique tweaks.

Din Tai Fung CHINESE $$

(Map p82; www.dintaifung.com.au; L1, World Sq, 644 George St; dishes $11-19; ⏲11.30am-2.30pm & 5.30-9pm; 🚇Museum) The noodles and buns are great, but it's the dumplings that made this Taiwanese chain famous, delivering an explosion of fabulously flavoursome broth as you bite into their delicate casings. Come early, come hungry, come prepared to share your table. They also have stalls in The Star (p115) and Westfield Sydney (p130) food courts.

Ash St Cellar MODERN AUSTRALIAN $$

(Map p72; ☎02-9240 3000; www.merivale.com.au/ashstcellar; 1 Ash St; large plates $18-26; ⏲8.30am-11pm Mon-Fri; 🚇Wynyard) Part of the so-hot-right-now Ivy complex, Ash St Cellar is an urbane lane-side wine bar that does excellent cheese, charcuterie and shared plates. Sit outside if it's not too gusty and agonise over the 200-plus wines on the list. Despite the suits sweeping through, the vibe is relaxed and unhurried.

★Tetsuya's FRENCH, JAPANESE $$$

(Map p82; ☎02-9267 2900; www.tetsuyas.com; 529 Kent St; degustation $220; ⏲noon-3pm Sat, 6-10pm Tue-Sat; 🚇Town Hall) Down a clandestine security driveway, this extraordinary restaurant is for those seeking a culinary journey rather than a simple stuffed belly. Settle in for 10-plus courses of French- and Japanese-inflected food from the creative genius of Japanese-born Tetsuya Wakuda. Book way ahead.

Rockpool MODERN AUSTRALIAN $$$

(Map p72; ☎02-9252 1888; www.rockpool.com; 11 Bridge St; lunch mains $35-55, 9-/10-course dinner $145/165; ⏲noon-3pm Mon-Fri, 6-11pm Mon-Sat; 🚇Circular Quay) The Neil Perry empire now stretches to eight acclaimed restaurants in three cities, and this grand dining room is the mothership. After 25 years, Rockpool's creations still manage to wow diners. Expect crafty, contemporary cuisine with Asian influences, faultless service and an alluring wine list.

Est. MODERN AUSTRALIAN $$$

(Map p72; ☎02-9240 3000; www.merivale.com.au/est; L1, 252 George St; 4-course lunch/dinner $118/155, degustation $180; ⏲noon-2.30pm Fri, 6-10pm Mon-Sat; 🚇Wynyard) Pressed-tin ceilings, huge columns, oversized windows and modern furniture make the interior design almost as interesting as the food. This is Sydney fine dining at its best; thick wallet and fancy threads a must. Seafood fills around half of the slots on the menu.

Sepia JAPANESE, FUSION $$$

(Map p72; ☎02-9283 1990; www.sepiarestaurant.com.au; 201 Sussex St; 4 courses/degustation $160/190; ⏲noon-3pm Fri & Sat, 6-10pm Tue-Sat; 🚇Town Hall) There's nothing washed out or brown-tinged about Sepia's food: Martin Benn's picture-perfect creations are presented in glorious technicolour, with each taste worth a thousand words. A Japanese sensibility permeates the boundary-pushing menu, earning Sepia the city's top dining gong.

Rockpool Bar & Grill STEAK $$$

(Map p72; ☎02-8078 1900; www.rockpool.com; 66 Hunter St; mains $26-115; ⏲noon-3pm Mon-Fri, 6-11pm Mon-Sat; 🚇Martin Place) You'll feel like a 1930s Manhattan stockbroker when you dine at this sleek operation in the art deco City Mutual Building. The bar is famous for its dry-aged, full-blood Wagyu burger (make sure you order a side of the hand-cut fat chips), but carnivores will be equally enamoured with the succulent steaks, stews and fish dishes served in the grill.

Haymarket

Mamak MALAYSIAN $

(Map p82; www.mamak.com.au; 15 Goulburn St; mains $6-17; ⏲11.30am-2.30pm & 5.30-10pm Mon-Thu, to 2am Fri & Sat; 🚇Town Hall) Get here early (from 5.30pm) if you want to score a table without queuing, because this eat-and-run Malaysian joint is one of the most popular cheapies in the city. The satays are cooked over charcoal and are particularly delicious when accompanied by a flaky golden roti.

Chat Thai THAI $$

(Map p82; ☎02-9211 1808; www.chatthai.com.au; 20 Campbell St; mains $10-20; ⏲10am-2am; 🚇Central) Cooler than your average Thai joint, this Thaitown linchpin is so popular that a list is posted outside for you to affix your name to should you want a table. Expat Thais flock here for the dishes that don't make it onto your average suburban Thai restaurant menu – particularly the more unusual sweets.

Darling Harbour & Pyrmont

Café Court FOOD COURT $

(Map p84; www.star.com.au; ground fl, The Star; mains $10-18; ⏲11am-9pm Sun & Mon, to 11pm Tue-Sat; 🚇The Star) The Star has done a great job of filling its ground-floor food court with some of the best operators of their kind, such as Din Tai Fung for dumplings,

Messina (p118) for gelato and Adriano Zumbo for sweet delights.

Adriano Zumbo BAKERY $
(Map p84; www.adrianozumbo.com; Café Court, The Star, 80 Pyrmont St; sweets $2.50-10; 11am-9pm Sun, to 11pm Mon-Sat; The Star) The man who introduced Sydney to the macaron has indulged his Willy Wonka fantasies in this concept shop, where baked treats are artfully displayed amid pink neon. The macarons (or zumbarons, as they're known here), tarts, pastries and cakes are as astonishing to look at as they are to eat.

Sokyo JAPANESE $$$
(Map p84; 02-9657 9161; www.star.com.au/sokyo; The Star, 80 Pyrmont St; breakfast $23-38, set lunch $45, mains $30-58; 7-10.30am & 5.30-11pm daily, noon-3pm Thu-Sat; The Star) Bringing an injection of Toyko glam to the edge of the casino complex, Sokyo serves well-crafted sushi and sashimi, delicate tempura, tasty robata grills and sophisticated mains. It also dishes up Sydney's best Japanese-style breakfast. Solo travellers should grab a counter seat by the sushi kitchen to watch all the action unfurl.

Flying Fish SEAFOOD $$$
(Map p84; 02-9518 6677; www.flyingfish.com.au; Jones Bay Wharf; mains $47-49; noon-2.30pm daily, 6-10.30pm Mon-Sat; The Star) Beyond the architects and investment groups along Jones Bay Wharf is this romantic seafood restaurant. The city lights work their magic all too easily here, aided by excellent food and an indulgent cocktail list. Aside from all that romance stuff, it has the coolest toilets in town – the clear-glass stalls frost over when you close the door.

Ultimo, Glebe & Chippendale

★Ester MODERN AUSTRALIAN $$
(Map p121; 02-8068 8279; www.ester-restaurant.com.au; 46 Meagher St; mains $26-36; noon-5pm Sun, noon-3pm Fri, 6pm-late Tue-Sat; Redfern) Ester breaks the trend for hip new eateries by accepting bookings, but in other respects it exemplifies Sydney's contemporary dining scene: informal but not sloppy; innovative without being overly gimmicky; hip, but never try-hard. Influences straddle continents and dishes are made to be shared. If humanly possible, make room for dessert.

Glebe Point Diner MODERN AUSTRALIAN $$$
(Map p68; 02-9660 2646; www.glebepointdiner.com.au; 407 Glebe Point Rd; mains $29-39; noon-3pm Thu-Sun, 6-11pm Mon-Sat; Jubilee Park) A sensational neighbourhood diner, where only the best local produce is used and everything – from the home-baked bread and hand-churned butter to the nougat finale – is made from scratch. The food is creative and comforting at the same time; a rare combination.

Surry Hills

★Bourke Street Bakery BAKERY $
(Map p86; www.bourkestreetbakery.com.au; 633 Bourke St; items $5-14; 8am-5pm; Central) Queuing outside this teensy bakery is an essential Surry Hills experience. It sells a tempting selection of pastries, cakes, bread and sandwiches, along with sausage rolls which are near legendary in these parts. There are a few tables inside but on a fine day you're better off on the street.

Reuben Hills CAFE $
(Map p86; www.reubenhills.com.au; 61 Albion St; mains $12-18; 7am-4pm; ; Central) An industrial fitout and Latin American menu await here at Reuben Hills (aka hipster central). Fantastic single-origin coffee and fried chicken, but the eggs, tacos and *baleadas* (Honduran tortillas) are no slouches, either.

Sample Coffee CAFE $
(Map p86; www.samplecoffee.com.au; 118 Devonshire St; items $3-5; 6.30am-4pm Mon-Fri; Central) If the alpine scene on the wall induces the urge to yodel, quickly shove one of Sample's deliciously moist muffins in your mouth. The food is limited to some lovely sweet things to go with coffee, which is the real star of the show here. Enter from Holt St.

Le Monde CAFE $
(Map p86; www.lemondecafe.com.au; 83 Foveaux St; mains $9-18; 6.30am-4pm Mon-Fri, 7.30am-2pm Sat; Central) Some of Sydney's best breakfasts are served between the demure dark wooden walls of this small streetside cafe. Top-notch coffee and a terrific selection of tea will gear you up to face the world.

Spice I Am THAI $
(Map p82; www.spiceiam.com; 90 Wentworth Ave; mains $12-19; 11.30am-3.30pm & 5.45-10pm Tue-Sun; ; Central) Once the preserve of expat Thais, this little red-hot chilli pepper

now has queues out the door. No wonder, as everything we've tried from the 70-plus dishes on the menu is superfragrant and superspicy. It's been so successful that they've opened an upmarket version in **Darlinghurst** (Map p88; ☎02-9332 2445; 296-300 Victoria St; mains $18-30; ⊙11.30am-3.30pm Thu-Sun, 5.45-10.30pm daily; 🖉; 🚆Kings Cross).

Devon CAFE **$$**

(Map p86; www.devoncafe.com.au; 76 Devonshire St; mains $14-21; ⊙7am-4.30pm daily, 6-10pm Thu-Sat) If it's boring old bacon and eggs you're after, look elsewhere. Devon shamelessly plunders the cuisines of 'multicultural Australia' to deliver an extremely creative menu, with plenty of twists on old favourites. There's even an 'Ogre's Happy Meal' (oxtongue, apparently – we weren't tempted).

Porteño ARGENTINE **$$**

(Map p86; ☎02-8399 1440; www.porteno.com.au; 358 Cleveland St; sharing plates $15-48; ⊙6pm-midnight Tue-Sat; 🚆Central) Lamb and suckling pig are spit-roasted for eight hours before the doors even open at this acclaimed and extremely hip restaurant, devoted to the robust meatiness of Argentinian cuisine. Arrive early to avoid a lengthy wait, although there's no hardship in hanging out upstairs at the very cool Gardel's Bar until a table comes free.

Longrain THAI **$$**

(Map p82; ☎02-9280 2888; www.longrain.com; 85 Commonwealth St; mains $18-38; ⊙noon-2.30pm Fri, 6-11pm daily; 🚆Central) Devotees flock to this century-old, wedge-shaped printing-press building to feast on fragrant modern Thai dishes, and to sip delicately flavoured and utterly delicious cocktails. Sit at shared tables or at the bar.

Bodega TAPAS **$$**

(Map p86; ☎02-9212 7766; www.bodegatapas.com; 216 Commonwealth St; tapas $12-28; ⊙noon-2pm Fri, 6-10pm Tue-Sat; 🚆Central) The coolest progeny of Sydney's tapas explosion, Bodega has a casual vibe, good-lookin' staff and a funky matador mural. Dishes vary widely in size and price. Wash 'em down with Spanish and South American wine, sherry, port or beer, and plenty of Latin gusto.

Bar H ASIAN **$$**

(Map p82; ☎02-9280 1980; www.barhsurryhills.com; 80 Campbell St; dishes $10-34; ⊙10am-3pm Sun, 6-10.30pm Mon-Sat; 🚆Museum) Marrying Chinese and Japanese dishes with native Australian bush ingredients, this sexy, shiny, black-walled corner eatery is completely unique and extremely impressive. Dishes range considerably in size and are designed to be shared; confer with your waiter about quantities.

MoVida SPANISH **$$**

(Map p86; ☎02-8964 7642; www.movida.com.au; 50 Holt St; tapas $5-13, raciones $17-26, mains $29; ⊙noon-late Mon-Sat; 🚆Central) A Sydney incarnation of a Melbourne legend, MoVida serves top-notch tapas and *raciones* (larger shared plates), and a great selection of Spanish wines. Book well ahead for a table or get in early for a seat by the bar.

Single Origin Roasters CAFE **$$**

(Map p82; ☎02-9211 0665; www.singleorigin.com.au; 60-64 Reservoir St; mains $13-17; ⊙6.30am-4pm Mon-Fri; 🚆Central) Unshaven graphic artists roll cigarettes at little outdoor tables in the bricky hollows of deepest Surry Hills, while inside impassioned, bouncing-off-the-walls caffeine fiends prepare their beloved brews, along with a tasty selection of cafe fare.

El Loco MEXICAN **$$**

(Map p86; www.merivale.com.au/elloco; 64 Foveaux St; mains $10-18; ⊙noon-midnight Mon-Thu, to 3am Fri & Sat, to 10pm Sun; 🚆Central) As much as we lament the passing of live rock at the Excelsior Hotel, we have to admit that the hip Mexican cantina that's taken over the band room is pretty darn cool. The food's tasty, inventive and, at $5 per taco, fantastic value.

Devonshire MODERN EUROPEAN **$$$**

(Map p86; ☎02-9698 9427; www.thedevonshire.com.au; 204 Devonshire St; mains $37; ⊙noon-2.30pm Fri, 6-10pm Tue-Sat; 🚆Central) It's a long way from a two-Michelin-starred Mayfair restaurant to grungy old Devonshire St for chef Jeremy Bentley, although cuisinewise, perhaps not as far as you'd think. His food is simply extraordinary – complex, precisely presented and full of flavour. And while there's white linen on the tables, the atmosphere isn't the least bit starchy.

4Fourteen MODERN AUSTRALIAN **$$$**

(Map p86; ☎02-9331 5399; www.4fourteen.com.au; 414 Bourke St; mains $30-42; ⊙noon-3pm Tue-Sun, 6-11pm Tue-Sat; 🚆Central) When he's not busy terrorising contestants on TV cooking shows, Irish-born chef Colin Fassnidge can be found cranking out hearty, meaty dishes at one of his Sydney eateries, the newest of which is this big, fun buzzy place. Solo diners should grab a seat by the kitchen for dinner with a show.

Darlinghurst

Messina ICE CREAM $

(Map p88; www.gelatomessina.com; 241 Victoria St; 2 scoops $6; noon-11pm; Kings Cross) Join the queues of people who look like they never eat ice cream at the counter of Sydney's most popular gelato shop. Clearly even the beautiful people can't resist quirky flavours such as figs in Marsala and salted caramel. The attached dessert bar serves sundaes.

bills CAFE $$

(Map p88; www.bills.com.au; 433 Liverpool St; mains $14-25; 7.30am-2.30pm; Kings Cross) Bill Granger almost single-handedly started the Sydney craze for stylish brunching. This sunny corner cafe with its newspaper-strewn communal table was the original; there are other branches in Surry Hills and Bondi Beach.

Red Lantern on Riley VIETNAMESE $$$

(Map p88; 02-9698 4355; www.redlantern.com.au; 60 Riley St; mains $36-39; noon-3pm Thu & Fri, 6-10pm daily; Museum) This atmospheric eatery is run by television presenters Luke Nguyen *(Luke Nguyen's Vietnam)*, Mark Jensen *(Ready Steady Cook)* and Pauline Nguyen (author of the excellent *Secrets of the Red Lantern* cookbook-cum-autobiography). It serves modern takes on classic Vietnamese dishes.

Woolloomooloo

Toby's Estate CAFE $

(Map p88; 02-9358 1196; www.tobysestate.com.au; 129 Cathedral St; meals $10-15; 7am-4pm; ; St James) Coffee is undoubtedly the main event at this cool little charcoal-coloured roastery, but Toby's is also a great place for a quick sandwich, a vegie wrap or a fat muffin. And the caffeine? Strong, perfectly brewed and usually fair trade.

Aki's INDIAN $$

(Map p88; 02-9332 4600; www.akisindian.com.au; 1/6 Cowper Wharf Rdwy; mains $22-36; noon-10pm Sun-Fri, 6-10.30pm Sat; ; Kings Cross) The first cab off the rank as you walk onto Woolloomooloo's wharf is Aki's. And you need walk no further: this is beautifully presented, intuitively constructed high-Indian cuisine, supplemented by a six-page wine list showcasing local and international drops.

Otto Ristorante ITALIAN $$$

(Map p88; 02-9368 7488; www.ottoristorante.com.au; 8/6 Cowper Wharf Rdwy; mains $41-59; noon-3pm & 6-11pm; Kings Cross) Forget the glamorous waterfront location and the A-list crowd – Otto will be remembered for single-handedly dragging Sydney's Italian cooking into the new century with dishes such as *strozzapreti con gamberi* (artisan pasta with fresh Yamba prawns, tomato, chilli and black olives). Bookings essential.

China Doll ASIAN $$$

(Map p88; 02-9380 6744; www.chinadoll.com.au; 4/6 Cowper Wharf Rdwy; mains $34-46; noon-2.30pm & 6pm-late; Kings Cross) Gaze over the Woolloomooloo marina and city skyline as you tuck into deliciously inventive dishes drawing inspiration from all over Asia. Plates are designed to be shared, although waiters can arrange half serves for solo diners.

Kings Cross & Potts Point

Room 10 CAFE $

(Map p88; 10 Llankelly Pl; mains $9-14; 7am-4pm; Kings Cross) If you're wearing a flat cap, sprouting a beard and obsessed by coffee, chances are you'll recognise this tiny room as your spiritual home in the Cross. The food's limited to sandwiches, salads and such – tasty and uncomplicated.

Harry's Cafe de Wheels FAST FOOD $

(Map p88; www.harryscafedewheels.com.au; Cowper Wharf Rdwy; pies $5-7; 9am-1am Sun, 8.30am-3am Mon-Sat; Kings Cross) Open since 1938 (except for a few years when founder Harry 'Tiger' Edwards was on active service), Harry's served meat pies to everyone from Pamela Anderson to Frank Sinatra and Colonel Sanders. You can't leave without trying a Tiger: a hot meat pie with sloppy peas, mashed potato, gravy and tomato sauce.

Piccolo Bar CAFE $

(Map p88; www.piccolobar.com.au; 6 Roslyn St; mains $6-16; 8am-4pm; ; Kings Cross) A surviving slice of the old bohemian Cross, this tiny cafe hasn't changed much in over 60 years. The walls are covered in movie-star memorabilia, and Vittorio Bianchi still serves up strong coffee, omelettes and abrasive charm, as he's done for over 40 years.

Ms G's ASIAN $$
(Map p88; ☎02-9240 3000; www.merivale.com/msgs; 155 Victoria St; mains $25-38; ⏰1-9pm Sun, noon-3pm Fri, 6-11pm Mon-Sat; 🚉Kings Cross) Offering a cheeky, irreverent take on Asian cooking (hence the name – geddit?), Ms G's is nothing if not an experience. It can be loud, frantic and painfully hip, but the adventurous combinations of pan-Asian and European flavours have certainly got Sydney talking.

Cho Cho San JAPANESE $$
(Map p88; ☎02-9331 6601; www.chochosan.com.au; 73 Macleay St; mains $14-36; ⏰noon-3pm Fri-Sun, 6-11pm daily; 🚉Kings Cross) Glide through the shiny brass sliding door and take a seat at the polished concrete communal table which runs the length of this stylish Japanese restaurant. The food is just as artful as the surrounds, with tasty *izakaya*-style bites emanating from both the raw bar and the *hibachi* grill.

Fratelli Paradiso ITALIAN $$
(Map p88; www.fratelliparadiso.com; 12-16 Challis Ave; breakfast $12-14, mains $22-31; ⏰7am-11pm; 🚉Kings Cross) This underlit trattoria has them queuing at the door (especially on weekends). The intimate room showcases seasonal Italian dishes cooked with Mediterranean zing. Lots of busy black-clad waiters, lots of Italian chatter, lots of oversized sunglasses. No bookings.

Wilbur's Place CAFE, BISTRO $$
(Map p88; www.wilbursplace.com; 36 Llankelly Pl; brunch $9-19, dinner $28; ⏰8am-3pm Sat, 5-9.30pm Tue-Sat; 🚉Kings Cross) With limited bench seating inside and a few tables on the lane, tiny Wilbur's is an informal spot for a quick bite on what's become the Cross' coolest cafe strip. Expect simple, straightforward food that is expertly assembled.

Paddington & Woollahra

Vincent FRENCH $$
(Map p92; ☎02-8039 1500; www.vincentfrench.com.au; 14 Queen St; mains $26-36; ⏰noon-3pm Fri-Sun, 6-11pm Tue-Sun; 🚌380) The glassed-in terrace of the Hughenden Hotel is the charmingly informal setting for this zippy bistro. The menu is excellent, revelling in classics such as cheesy souffles, rich terrines, steak *frites* topped with butter, and fall-apart slow-roasted lamb shoulder.

Four in Hand MODERN AUSTRALIAN $$$
(Map p68; ☎02-9362 1999; www.fourinhand.com.au; 105 Sutherland St; mains $34-42; ⏰noon-2.30pm & 6pm-late Tue-Sun; 🚉Edgecliff) You can't go far in Paddington without tripping over a beautiful old pub with amazing food. This is the best of them, famous for its slow-cooked and nose-to-tail meat dishes, although it also offers fabulously fresh seafood dishes and a delectable array of desserts. The bar menu (mains $19 to $29) is a more affordable option.

Chiswick Restaurant MODERN AUSTRALIAN $$$
(Map p92; ☎02-8388 8633; www.chiswickrestaurant.com.au; 65 Ocean St; mains $31-38; ⏰noon-2.30pm & 6-10pm; 🚌389) There may be a celebrity at centre stage (TV regular Matt Moran) but the real star of this show is the pretty kitchen garden, which wraps around the dining room and dictates what's on the menu. Meat from the Moran family farm and local seafood feature prominently too.

Eastern Beaches

Three Blue Ducks CAFE $$
(Map p68; ☎02-9389 0010; www.threeblueducks.com; 141-143 Macpherson St, Bronte; breakfast $16-25, lunch $24-31, dinner $28-32; ⏰7am-2.30pm Sun-Tue, 7am-2.30pm & 6-11pm Wed-Sat; 🚌378) These ducks are a fair waddle from the water, but that doesn't stop queues forming outside the graffiti-covered walls for weekend breakfasts. The adventurous chefs have a strong commitment to using local, organic and fair-trade food whenever possible.

A Tavola ITALIAN $$
(Map p94; ☎02-9130 1246; www.atavola.com.au; 75 Hall St, Bondi; mains $22-38; ⏰noon-3pm Wed-Sun, 5.30-11pm daily) Carrying on the tradition of its Darlinghurst sister, Bondi's A Tavola gathers around a big communal marble table where, before the doors open, the pasta-making action happens. Expect robust flavours, sexy waiters and delicious home-made pasta.

Lox, Stock & Barrel DINER, DELI $$
(Map p94; ☎02-9300 0368; www.loxstockandbarrel.com.au; 140 Glenayr Ave, Bondi; breakfast & lunch $11-18, dinner $29; ⏰7am-3.30pm daily, 6pm-late Wed-Sun) Stare down the barrel of a smoking hot bagel and ask yourself one question: Wagyu corned beef Reuben, or homemade pastrami and Russian coleslaw? In the evening the menu sets its sights on steak, lamb shoulder and slow-roasted eggplant.

Bondi Trattoria ITALIAN $$
(Map p94; ☎02-9365 4303; www.bonditrattoria.com.au; 34 Campbell Pde, Bondi; breakfast $9-19, lunch $17-29, dinner $19-36; ⊙8am-late; 380) For a Bondi brunch, you can't go past the trusty 'Trat', as it's known in these parts. Tables spill out onto Campbell Pde for those hungry for beach views, while inside there's a trad trat feel: wooden tables, and the obligatory Tuscan mural and black-and-white photography. As the day progresses, pizza, pasta and risotto dominate the menu.

Icebergs Dining Room ITALIAN $$$
(Map p94; ☎02-9365 9000; www.idrb.com; 1 Notts Ave; mains $40-48; ⊙noon-3pm & 6.30-11pm Tue-Sun; 380) Poised above the famous Icebergs swimming pool, Icebergs' views sweep across the Bondi Beach arc to the sea. Inside, bow-tied waiters deliver fresh, sustainably sourced seafood and steaks cooked with elan. To limit the hip-pocket impact, call in at lunchtime for a pasta and salad.

Bronte Road Bistro FRENCH $$$
(Map p68; ☎02-9389 3028; www.bronteroadbistro.com; 282 Bronte Rd, Waverley; mains $34; ⊙noon-2.30pm Sat & Sun, 5.30-9.30pm Tue-Sat; 314-317) This friendly neighbourhood bistro offers a crowd-pleasing menu of French favourites.

Newtown & Around

Mary's BURGERS $
(Map p121; 6 Mary St; mains $14; ⊙4pm-midnight Mon-Sat, noon-10pm Sun; Newtown) Not put off by the grungy aesthetics, the ear-splitting heavy metal or the fact that the building was previously a sexual health clinic and a Masonic Temple? Then head up to the mezzanine of this dimly lit hipster bar for some of the best burgers and fried chicken in town.

Black Star Pastry BAKERY $
(Map p121; www.blackstarpastry.com.au; 277 Australia St; mains $7-10; ⊙7am-5pm; Newtown) Wise folks follow the black star to pay homage to excellent coffee, a large selection of sweet things and a few very good savoury things (gourmet pies and the like). There are only a couple of tables; it's more a snack-and-run or picnic-in-the-park kind of place.

Fleetwood Macchiato CAFE $
(Map p121; 43 Erskineville Rd; mains $9-18; ⊙7am-3pm; ; Erskineville) The best name for a cafe ever? We think so. Luckily Fleetwood Macchiato backs it up with excellent coffee, delicious cooked breakfasts, tasty sandwiches and homemade cakes, preserves, pickles, yoghurt and mayonnaise.

Luxe CAFE $$
(Map p121; www.luxesydney.com.au; 191 Missenden Rd; breakfast $8-20, lunch $11-22; ⊙8am-4pm; Macdonaldtown) Campos, next door, might be the pinnacle of Sydney's caffeine culture, but if you want to sit down, read the paper and eat something more substantial, Luxe is the dux. The menu stretches to cooked brekkies, pasta and burgers, and the counter of this industrial-chic bakery-cafe is chocka with chunky sandwiches, moist cakes and delicate tarts.

Bloodwood MODERN AUSTRALIAN $$
(Map p121; ☎02-9557 7699; www.bloodwoodnewtown.com; 416 King St; dishes $9-30; ⊙5-11pm Mon-Fri, noon-11pm Sat & Sun; Newtown) Relax over a few drinks and a progression of small plates (we love those polenta chips!) in the front bar, or make your way to the rear to enjoy soundly conceived and expertly cooked dishes from across the globe. The decor is industrial-chic and the vibe is alternative – very Newtown.

Balmain

Riverview Hotel & Dining MODERN BRITISH $$
(Map p68; ☎02-9810 1151; www.theriverviewhotel.com.au; 29 Birchgrove Rd, Balmain; pizzas $20-22, mains $28-33; ⊙noon-11pm; Balmain) The Riv's head chef, Brad Sloane, worked under the legendary Marco Pierre White in London. British expats flock here to try his nose-to-tail dishes in the elegant upstairs dining room, while locals are equally keen on the pizzas served in the downstairs bar.

Manly

Barefoot Coffee Traders CAFE $
(Map p98; 18 Whistler St; items $3-6; ⊙6.30am-5.30pm; Manly) Run by surfer lads serving fair-trade organic coffee from a bathroom-sized shop, Barefoot heralds a new wave of Manly cool. Food is limited but the Belgian chocolate waffles go magically well with a macchiato.

Chat Thai THAI $
(Map p98; ☎02-9976 2939; www.chatthai.com.au; Manly Wharf; mains $10-18; ⊙11am-9.30pm; Manly) Set inside Manly Wharf, this branch of the Thaitown favourite (p115) misses out on the harbour views but delivers on flavour.

Newtown

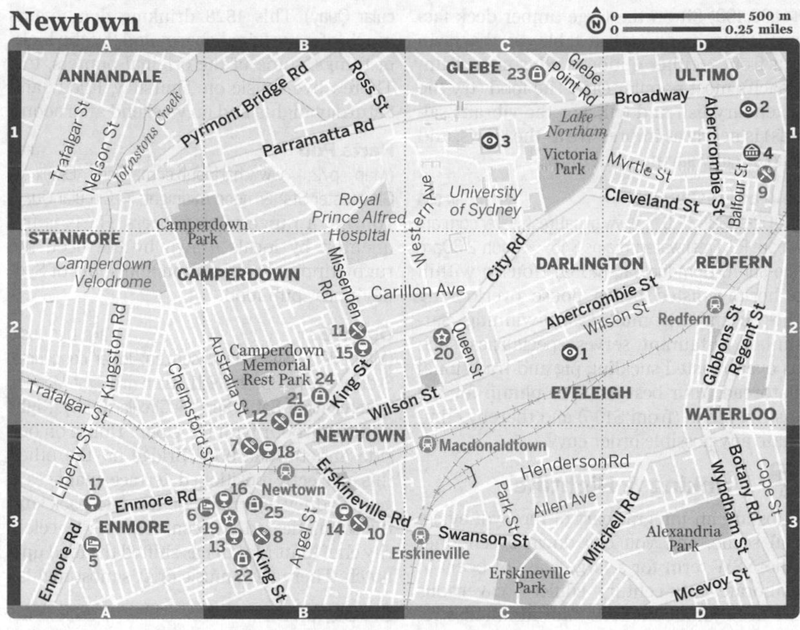

Newtown

Sights

1 Carriageworks C2
2 Central Park D1
Macleay Museum .... (see 3)
Nicholson Museum .... (see 3)
University Art Gallery .... (see 3)
3 University of Sydney C1
4 White Rabbit D1

Sleeping

5 Tara Guest House A3
6 Urban Hotel B3

Eating

7 Black Star Pastry B3
8 Bloodwood B3
9 Ester D1
Eveleigh Farmers' Market .... (see 1)
10 Fleetwood Macchiato B3
11 Luxe B2
12 Mary's B2

Drinking & Nightlife

13 Earl's Juke Joint B3
14 Imperial Hotel B3
15 Marlborough Hotel B2
16 Midnight Special B3
17 Sly Fox A3
18 Zanzibar B3

Entertainment

19 Newtown Social Club B3
20 Vanguard C2

Shopping

21 Better Read Than Dead B2
22 Faster Pussycat B3
23 Glebe Markets C1
24 Quick Brown Fox B2
25 Reclaim B3

Hugos Manly ITALIAN $$
(Map p98; 02-8116 8555; www.hugos.com.au; Manly Wharf; pizzas $20-28, mains $32-38; noon-midnight; Manly) Occupying an altogether more glamorous location than its Kings Cross parent, Hugos Manly serves the same acclaimed pizzas but tops them with harbour views and an expanded Italian menu. A dedicated crew concocts cocktails, or you can just slide in for a cold beer.

Northern Beaches

Boathouse CAFE $$
(www.theboathousepb.com.au; Governor Phillip Park, Palm Beach; mains $25; 7.30am-4pm;

L90, 190) Sit on the large timber deck facing Pittwater or grab a table on the lawn out front – either option is alluring at Palm Beach's most popular cafe. The food (try the legendary fish and chips or the vibrant salads) is nearly as impressive as the views, and that's really saying something.

Pilu at Freshwater ITALIAN **$$$**
(02-9938 3331; www.piluatfreshwater.com.au; Moore Rd, Freshwater; mains $45; noon-2.30pm Tue-Sun, 6-11pm Tue-Sat; 139) Housed within a heritage-listed beach house overlooking the ocean, this multi-award-winning Sardinian restaurant serves specialities such as oven-roasted suckling pig and traditional flatbread. Your best bet is to plump for the tasting menu (from $105) and thereby eliminate any possible order envy.

Drinking & Nightlife

Pubs are an integral part of the Sydney social scene, and you can down a schooner (the NSW term for a large glass of beer) in elaborate 19th-century edifices, cavernous art deco joints, modern and minimalist recesses, and everything in between. Bars are generally more stylish and urbane, sometimes with a dress code.

There's a thriving live-music scene, but good dance clubs are strangely thin on the ground.

The Rocks & Circular Quay

Lord Nelson Brewery Hotel PUB, BREWERY
(Map p72; 02-9251 4044; 19 Kent St; 11am-11pm; Circular Quay) Built in 1836 and converted into a pub in 1841, this atmospheric sandstone boozer is one of three claiming to be Sydney's oldest (all using slightly different criteria). The on-site brewery cooks up its own natural ales (try the Old Admiral).

Hero of Waterloo PUB
(Map p72; www.heroofwaterloo.com.au; 81 Lower Fort St; 10am-11pm; Circular Quay) Enter this rough-hewn 1843 sandstone pub to meet some locals, chat up the Irish bar staff and grab an earful of the swing, folk and Celtic bands (Friday to Sunday). Downstairs is a dungeon where, in days gone by, drinkers would sleep off a heavy night before being shanghaied to the high seas via a tunnel leading straight to the harbour.

Fortune of War PUB
(Map p72; www.fortuneofwar.com.au; 137 George St; 9am-midnight Sun-Thu, to 3am Fri & Sat; Circular Quay) This 1828 drinking den retains much of its original charm and, by the looks of things, some of the original punters, too. There's live music on Thursday, Friday and Saturday nights and on weekend afternoons.

Harts Pub PUB
(Map p72; www.hartspub.com; cnr Essex & Gloucester Sts; noon-midnight; Circular Quay) Pouring a range of craft beers, Harts is frequented by locals drawn by the beer, the rugby tipping competition and some of Sydney's best pub food.

Opera Bar BAR, LIVE MUSIC
(Map p72; www.operabar.com.au; lower concourse, Sydney Opera House; 11.30am-midnight Mon-Fri, 9am-midnight Sat & Sun; Circular Quay) Right on the harbour with the Opera House on one side and the Harbour Bridge on the other, this perfectly positioned terrace manages a very Sydney marriage of the laid-back and the sophisticated. A recent takeover by celebrity chef Matt Moran has shifted the food up a notch. There's live music or DJs most nights.

Blu Bar on 36 COCKTAIL BAR
(Map p72; www.shangri-la.com; Level 36, 176 Cumberland St; 5pm-midnight; Circular Quay) The drinks may be pricey, but it's well worth heading up to the top of the Shangri-La hotel for the views, which seem to stretch all the way to New Zealand. The dress code is officially 'smart casual', but err on the side of smart if you can't handle rejection.

City Centre

Baxter Inn BAR
(Map p72; www.thebaxterinn.com; 152-156 Clarence St; 4pm-1am Mon-Sat; Town Hall) Yes, it really is down that dark lane and through that unmarked door (it's easier to find if there's a queue; otherwise look for the bouncer lurking nearby). Whisky's the main poison and the friendly bar staff really know their stuff.

Frankie's Pizza BAR
(Map p72; www.frankiespizzabytheslice.com; 50 Hunter St; 4pm-3am Sun-Thu, noon-3am Fri & Sat; Martin Place) Descend the stairs and you'll think you're in a 1970s pizzeria, complete with plastic grapevines, snapshots covering the walls and tasty $6 pizza slices. But open the nondescript door in the corner and an indie wonderland reveals itself. Bands play here at least four nights a week (join them on Tuesdays for live karaoke) and there's another bar hidden below.

Establishment BAR
(Map p72; www.merivale.com/establishmentbar; 252 George St; ⏲11am-late Mon-Sat, noon-10pm Sun; 🚉Wynyard) Establishment's cashed-up crush proves that the art of swilling cocktails after a hard city day is not lost. Sit at the majestic marble bar or in the swish courtyard, or be absorbed by a leather lounge as stockbrokers scribble their phone numbers on the backs of coasters for flirty new aquaintances.

Marble Bar BAR
(Map p72; www.marblebarsydney.com.au; basement, 488 George St; ⏲4pm-midnight Sun-Thu, to 2am Fri & Sat; 🚉Town Hall) Built for a staggering £32,000 in 1893 as part of the Adams Hotel on Pitt St, this ornate underground bar is one of the best places in town for putting on the ritz (even if this is the Hilton). Musos play anything from jazz to funk, Wednesday to Saturday.

When the Adams was demolished in 1968, every marble slab, wood carving and bronze capital was dismantled, restored, then reassembled here.

Grandma's COCKTAIL BAR
(Map p72; www.grandmasbarsydney.com; basement, 275 Clarence St; ⏲3pm-midnight Mon-Fri, 5pm-1am Sat; 🚉Town Hall) Billing itself as a 'retrosexual haven of cosmopolitan kitsch and faded granny glamour', Grandma's hits the mark. A stag's head greets you on the stairs and ushers you into a tiny subterranean world of parrot wallpaper and tiki cocktails. Someone's suprisingly cool granny must be very proud.

O Bar COCKTAIL BAR
(Map p72; www.obardining.com.au; Level 47, Australia Sq, 264 George St; ⏲5pm-late; 🚉Wynyard) At around $20, the cocktails at this 47th-floor revolving bar aren't cheap, but they're still cheaper than admission to Sydney Tower – and it's considerably more glamorous. The views are truly wonderful.

Rook COCKTAIL BAR
(Map p72; www.therook.com.au; L7, 56-58 York St; ⏲noon-midnight Mon-Fri, 4pm-midnight Sat; 🚉St James) Seemingly designed for one-time grungsters turned stockbrokers, this covered rooftop bar has an artfully dishevelled look and serves a mean cocktail. It's not cheap though. Is spending $50 on lobster thermidor and then following it up with a deep-fried Mars Bar the ultimate ironic statement?

ℹ LOCKOUTS & LAST DRINKS

In an effort to cut down on alcohol-fuelled violence, tough new licensing laws have been introduced to a large area of the central city bounded by The Rocks, Circular Quay, Woolloomooloo, Kings Cross, Darlinghurst, Haymarket and the eastern side of Darling Harbour.

Within this zone, licensed venues are not permitted to admit people after 1.30am. However, if you arrive before then, the venue is permitted to continue serving you alcohol until 3am.

This has had a major impact on the city's previous party hub, Kings Cross. Although some clubs remain open serving nonalcoholic drinks after 3am, much of the late-night action has drifted to the surrounding neighbourhoods, such as Newtown and Double Bay.

Good God Small Club BAR, CLUB
(Map p82; www.goodgodgoodgod.com; 55 Liverpool St; front bar free, club varies; ⏲5-11pm Wed, to 1am Thu, to 3am Fri & Sat; 🚉Town Hall) In a defunct underground taverna near Chinatown, Good God's rear dancetaria hosts everything from live indie bands to Jamaican reggae, '50s soul, rockabilly and tropical house music. Its success lies in the focus on great music rather than glamorous surrounds.

Slip Inn & Chinese Laundry PUB, CLUB
(Map p84; www.merivale.com.au/chineselaundry; 111 Sussex St; club $20-30; ⏲11am-late Mon-Fri, 4pm-late Sat; 🚉Wynyard) Slip in to this warren of moody rooms on the edge of Darling Harbour and bump hips with the kids. There are bars, pool tables, a beer garden and Mexican food, courtesy of El Loco. On Friday and Saturday nights the bass cranks up at the attached Chinese Laundry nightclub.

Spice Cellar BAR, CLUB
(Map p72; www.thespicecellar.com.au; 58 Elizabeth St; ⏲bar 4pm-late Wed-Fri & 7pm-late Sat, club 9pm-late Thu-Sun; 🚉Martin Place) Saunter down to this stylish underground bunker for cocktails in the lounge bar. The attached club has one of Sydney's hottest little dance floors, which despite its size attracts the occasional turntable legend to its decks.

Ivy BAR, CLUB
(Map p72; ☎02-9254 8100; www.merivale.com/ivy; L1, 330 George St; ⏲noon-late Mon-Fri, 6.30pm-late Sat; 🚉Wynyard) Hidden down a

GAY & LESBIAN SYDNEY

Gays and lesbians have migrated to Oz's Emerald City from all over Australia, New Zealand and the world, adding to a community that is visible, vocal and an integral part of the city's social fabric. Locals will assure you that things aren't as exciting as they once were, but Sydney is still indisputably one of the world's great queer cities.

Darlinghurst and Newtown have traditionally been the gayest neighbourhoods, although all of the inner suburbs have a higher than average proportion of gay and lesbian residents. Most of the gay venues are on the Darlinghurst section of Oxford St. However, some of the best events are held at mixed pubs, such as the Wednesday lesbian nights at **Zanzibar** (Map p121; 02-9519 1511; www.zanzibarnewtown.com.au; 323 King St; 10am-4am Mon-Sat, 11am-midnight Sun; Newtown) and the **Sly Fox** (Map p121; www.theslyfoxhotel.com; 199 Enmore Rd; 10am-3am Mon-Thu, to 6am Fri & Sat; Newtown), and the legendary Sunday afternoon session at the **Beresford** (Map p88; www.merivale.com.au/theberesfordhotel; 354 Bourke St; noon-midnight; Central).

The biggest event on the calendar is the famous **Mardi Gras** (p106), which includes a two-week festival, a parade which attracts up to half a million spectators, and a vast dance party.

Free gay and lesbian media includes LOTL (www.lotl.com), the Star Observer (www.starobserver.com.au) and SX (www.gaynewsnetwork.com.au).

Venues include:

Imperial Hotel (Map p121; www.theimperialhotel.com.au; 35 Erskineville Rd; admission free-$15; 3pm-midnight Sun-Thu, to 5am Fri & Sat; Erskineville) The art deco Imperial is legendary as the setting for *The Adventures of Priscilla, Queen of the Desert*. The front bar is a lively place for pool-shooting and cruising, with the action shifting to the cellar club late on a Saturday night. But it's in the cabaret bar that the legacy of Priscilla is kept alive.

Arq (Map p88; www.arqsydney.com.au; 16 Flinders St; 9pm-5am Thu & Sun, 9pm-noon Fri & Sat; Museum) If Noah had to fill his Arq with groovy gay clubbers, he'd head here with a big net and some tranquillisers. This flash megaclub has a cocktail bar, a recovery room and two dance floors with high-energy house, drag shows and a hyperactive smoke machine.

Midnight Shift (Map p88; 02-9358 3848; www.themidnightshift.com.au; 85 Oxford St; admission free-$10; 4pm-late Thu-Sun; Museum) The grand dame of the Oxford St gay scene, known for its lavish drag productions, was in the midst of a thorough renovation when we last visited. When the dust has settled expect a much improved downstairs bar to complement the serious tits-to-the-wind club upstairs.

Palms on Oxford (Map p88; 02-9357 4166; 124 Oxford St; 8pm-1am Thu & Sun, to 3am Fri & Sat; Museum) No one admits to coming here, but the lengthy queues prove they are lying. In this underground dance bar, the heyday of Stock Aitken Waterman never ended. It may be uncool, but if you don't scream when Kylie hits the turntables, you'll be the only one.

Stonewall Hotel (Map p88; 02-9360 1963; www.stonewallhotel.com; 175 Oxford St; noon-3am; Museum) Nicknamed 'Stonehenge' by those who think it's archaic, Stonewall has three levels of bars and dance floors, and attracts a younger crowd. Cabaret, karaoke and quiz nights spice things up; Wednesday's Malebox is an inventive way to bag yourself a boy.

lane off George St, Ivy is a scarily fashionable complex of bars, restaurants, discreet lounges…even a swimming pool. It's also Sydney's most hyped venue; expect lengthy queues of suburban kids teetering on unfeasibly high heels, waiting to shed up to $40 on a Saturday for entry to Sydney's hottest club night, Pacha.

Surry Hills

Wild Rover BAR

(Map p82; www.thewildrover.com.au; 75 Campbell St; 4pm-midnight Mon-Sat, to 10pm Sun; Central) Look for the old sign on the window reading 'Gestetner's Surry Hills Shirt Warehouse' and enter this supremely cool brick-lined speakeasy, where a big range of craft beer is served in chrome steins. Live bands play upstairs a couple of nights a week.

121BC WINE BAR

(Map p86; www.121bc.com.au; 4/50 Holt St; ⏲5pm-midnight Tue-Sat; 🚉Central) The first challenge is finding it (enter from Gladstone St) and the second is scoring a table. After that, it's easy – seat yourself at the communal table under the bubbly light fixture and ask the waitstaff to suggest delicious drops and snacks to suit your inclinations. Everything's good, so you can't really go wrong.

Vasco COCKTAIL BAR

(Map p86; www.vascobar.com; 421 Cleveland St; ⏲5pm-midnight Tue-Sat; 🚌372) Like the much, much hipper and better-looking Italian cousin of a Hard Rock Cafe, Vasco serves beer, wine and rock-themed cocktails in a room lined with band photos and guitars. Order a plate of *salumi* or pasta to snack on as you sip your Monkey Gone to Heaven, while Jagger sneers on the screen.

Darlinghurst

Green Park Hotel PUB

(Map p88; www.greenparkhotel.com.au; 360 Victoria St; ⏲11am-midnight Sun-Wed, to 2am Thu-Sat; 🚉Kings Cross) The ever-rockin' Green Park has pool tables, rolled-arm leather couches, a beer garden with funky Dr Seuss–inspired lighting, and a huge tiled central bar teeming with travellers, gay guys and pierced locals.

Hinky Dinks COCKTAIL BAR

(Map p88; www.hinkydinks.com.au; 185 Darlinghurst Rd; ⏲1-10pm Sun, 4pm-midnight Mon-Sat; 🚉Kings Cross) Everything's just hunky dory in this little cocktail bar styled after a 1950s milkshake parlour. Try the Hinky Fizz, an alcohol-soaked strawberry sorbet served in a waxed paper sundae cup.

Eau-de-Vie COCKTAIL BAR

(Map p88; www.eaudevie.com.au; 229 Darlinghurst Rd; ⏲6pm-1am; 🚉Kings Cross) Take the door marked 'restrooms' at the back of the Kirketon Hotel's main bar and enter this sophisticated black-walled speakeasy, where a team of dedicated shirt-and-tie-wearing mixologists concoct the sort of beverages that win best-cocktail gongs.

Cliff Dive COCKTAIL BAR

(Map p88; www.thecliffdive.com.au; basement, 16 Oxford Sq; ⏲6pm-3am Thu-Sat; 🚉Museum) Head down the stairs and throw yourself into a world of rough-hewn stone walls, glowing tropical fish lanterns, Polynesian knick-knacks and cocktails served in tiki glasses. There are plenty of nooks to hunker down in after you've worked up a tropical sweat on the dance floor.

Hello Sailor COCKTAIL BAR

(Map p88; www.hellosailor.com.au; 96 Oxford St; ⏲5pm-3am Tue-Sun; 📶; 🚉Museum) Entered from lanelike Foley St, this 'seafood shack and cocktail bar' gets filled to the gills on the weekends. A diverse but hip crowd drops anchor until the wee hours, partying under maritime flags, navigation maps and sepia pictures of tall ships.

Shady Pines Saloon BAR

(Map p88; www.shadypinessaloon.com; shop 4, 256 Crown St; ⏲4pm-midnight; 🚉Museum) With no sign or street number on the door and entry via a shady back lane (look for the white door before Bikram Yoga on Foley St), this subterranean honky-tonk bar caters to the urban boho. Sip whisky and rye with the good ole hipster boys amid Western memorabilia and taxidermy.

Kinselas BAR

(Map p88; ☎02-9331 3100; www.kinselas.com.au; 383 Bourke St; ⏲10am-4am; 🚉Museum) A Taylor Sq institution, this converted funeral parlour has come back from the dead more times than we care to recall. The downstairs is all art deco stylings (spot the chapel), while Lo-Fi upstairs is a chic cocktail bar with the best balcony for posing and people-watching. Continue up to The Standard Bowl for 'Bands! Booze! Bowling!'.

Kings Cross & Potts Point

World Bar BAR, CLUB

(Map p88; ☎02-9357 7700; www.theworldbar.com; 24 Bayswater Rd; ⏲3pm-3am; 🚉Kings Cross) World Bar (a reformed bordello) is an unpretentious grungy club with three floors to lure in the backpackers and cheap drinks to loosen things up. DJs play indie, hip hop, power pop and house nightly. There are live bands on Fridays, but Wednesday (The Wall) and Saturday (Cakes) are the big nights.

Kings Cross Hotel PUB, CLUB

(Map p88; www.kingscrosshotel.com.au; 244-248 William St; ⏲noon-1am Sun-Thu, to 3am Fri & Sat; 🚉Kings Cross) With five floors above ground and one below, this grand old pub is a hive of boozy entertainment which positively swarms on weekends. Head up to the roof bar for awesome city views, or drop by the 2nd-floor band room for a blast of live music.

Sugarmill BAR

(Map p88; www.sugarmill.com.au; 33 Darlinghurst Rd; 10am-5am; Kings Cross) For a bloated, late-night, Kings Cross bar, Sugarmill is actually pretty cool. Columns and high pressed-tin ceilings hint at its banking past, while the band posters plastered everywhere do their best to dispel any lingering capitalist vibes. Ten-dollar meals and drag queen–hosted bingo nights pull in the locals. For barbecue with a view, head to Sweethearts (www.sweetheartsbbq.com.au) on the rooftop.

Paddington & Woollahra

Wine Library WINE BAR

(Map p92; www.wine-library.com.au; 18 Oxford St; noon-11.30pm Mon-Sat, to 10pm Sun; 380) An impressive range of wines by the glass, a smart-casual ambience and a Mediterranean-inclined menu make this the most desirable library in town.

Double Bay

Golden Sheaf Hotel PUB

(Map p68; 02-9327 5877; www.goldensheaf.com.au; 429 New South Head Rd, Double Bay; 10am-1am; Double Bay) This noble, rambling old brick pub has a shady beer garden, a sports bar with pool tables, a bistro, a cocktail bar, a rooftop terrace and a dance floor. The musical mandate includes lots of live music and DJs. An impressive memorabilia wall includes autographed photos and albums from the likes of the Beatles and Bowie.

Eastern Beaches

Anchor BAR

(Map p94; www.anchorbarbondi.com; 8 Campbell Pde; 4.30pm-midnight Tue-Fri, 12.30pm-midnight Sat & Sun; 380-382) Surfers, backpackers and the local cool kids slurp down icy margaritas at this bustling bar at the south end of the strip. It's also a great spot for a late snack.

Neighbourhood BAR

(Map p94; www.neighbourhoodbondi.com.au; 143 Curlewis St; 5.30-11pm Mon-Thu, noon-11pm Fri, 9am-11pm Sat & Sun; 380-382) The natural habitat for the curious species known as the Bondi Hipster, this smart food and wine bar has a brick-lined interior giving way to a wood-lined courtyard. Bondi Radio broadcasts live from a booth near the kitchen.

Newtown & Around

Earl's Juke Joint BAR

(Map p121; 407 King St; 4pm-midnight Mon-Sat, to 10pm Sun; Newtown) The current it-bar of the minute, swinging Earl's serves craft beers and killer cocktails to the Newtown hiperati.

Midnight Special BAR

(Map p121; www.themidnightspecial.com.au; 44 Enmore Rd; 5pm-midnight Tue-Sat, to 10pm Sun; Newtown) Band posters and paper lanterns decorate the black walls of this groovy little bar. Musicians take to the tiny stage a couple of nights a week.

Marlborough Hotel PUB, CLUB

(Map p121; 02-9519 1222; www.marlboroughhotel.com.au; 145 King St; 10am-4am Mon-Sat, noon-midnight Sun; Macdonaldtown) One of many great old art deco pubs in Newtown, the Marly has a front sports bar with live bands on weekends and a shady beer garden. Head upstairs for soul food and rockabilly bands at Miss Peaches, or downstairs for all sorts of kooky happenings at the Tokyo Sing Song nightclub.

Balmain

Welcome Hotel PUB

(Map p68; 02-9810 1323; www.thewelcomehotel.com.au; 91 Evans St, Rozelle; 11.30am-11.30pm Mon-Sat, noon-10pm Sun; 441-445) If you get lost in the back streets of Rozelle, you might find yourself chowing down in the Welcome Hotel's acclaimed Italian restaurant, or working your way through the craft beer selection in the palm-shaded courtyard. You might even get to commune with Winston, the resident foxhound ghost.

London Hotel PUB

(Map p68; 02-9555 1377; www.londonhotel.com.au; 234 Darling St, Balmain; 11am-midnight Mon-Sat, noon-10pm Sun; Balmain) The Harbour Bridge views from the London's long balcony are quintessentially Sydney – about as far from London as you can get. There's a great range of Oz beers on tap, plus a few quality overseas interlopers.

✪ Entertainment

Sydney has an eclectic and innovative arts, entertainment and music scene. Pick up the *Shortlist* section in Friday's *Sydney Morning Herald* for comprehensive entertainment details. Tickets for most shows can be purchased directly from venues or through the **Moshtix** (www.moshtix.com.au), **Ticketmaster** (www.ticketmaster.com.au) or **Ticketek** (www.ticketek.com.au) ticketing agencies.

Cinema

First-run cinemas abound and most have discounted tickets on a Tuesday. If you're in town over summer, try to attend one of the open-air cinemas – they're great fun.

Dendy Opera Quays CINEMA
(Map p72; ☎02-9247 3800; www.dendy.com.au; 2 Circular Quay East; adult/child $20/14; ⊙sessions 9.30am-9.30pm; 🚉Circular Quay) When the harbour glare and squawking seagulls get too much, follow the scent of popcorn into the dark folds of this plush cinema. Screening first-run, independent world films, it's augmented by friendly attendants and a cafe/bar.

OpenAir Cinema CINEMA
(Map p68; www.stgeorgeopenair.com.au; Mrs Macquaries Rd; tickets $37; ⊙Jan & Feb; 🚉Circular Quay) Right on the harbour, the outdoor three-storey screen here comes with surround sound, sunsets, skyline and swanky food and wine. Most tickets are purchased in advance, but a limited number of tickets go on sale at the door each night at 6.30pm; check the website for details.

IMAX CINEMA
(Map p82; ☎02-9281 3300; www.imax.com.au; 31 Wheat Rd; adult/child short $23/17, feature $34/24; ⊙sessions 10am-10pm; 🚉Town Hall) It's big bucks for a 45-minute movie, but everything about IMAX is big, and this is reputedly the biggest IMAX in the world. The eight-storey screen shimmers with kid-friendly documentaries (sharks, interstellar etc) as well as blockbuster features, many in 3D.

Palace Verona CINEMA
(Map p88; ☎02-9360 6099; www.palacecinemas.com.au; 17 Oxford St; adult/child $19/14; ⊙sessions 10am-9pm; 📶; 🚌380) This urbane four-screen cinema has a cool cafe and bar, useful for discussing the merits of the arty flick you've just seen.

Moonlight Cinema CINEMA
(Map p92; www.moonlight.com.au; Belvedere Amphitheatre, cnr Loch & Broome Aves; adult/child $19/15; ⊙sunset Dec-Mar; 🚉Bondi Junction) Take a picnic and join the bats under the stars in magnificent Centennial Park; enter via the Woollahra Gate on Oxford St. A mix of new-release blockbuster, art-house and classic films is screened.

Bondi Openair Cinema CINEMA
(Map p94; www.openaircinemas.com.au; Dolphin Lawn, next to Bondi Pavilion; tickets $15-45; ⊙Jan & Feb) Enjoy open-air screenings by the sea, with live bands providing prescreening entertainment. Online bookings recommended.

Hayden Orpheum Picture Palace CINEMA
(Map p68; ☎02-9908 4344; www.orpheum.com.au; 380 Military Rd, Cremorne; adult/child $20/15; ⊙sessions 10.30am-8.50pm; 🚌244) Return to cinema's golden age at this fab art deco gem (1935). It still has its original Wurlitzer organ, which gets a workout at special events.

Classical Music

★Sydney Opera House PERFORMING ARTS
(Map p72; ☎02-9250 7777; www.sydneyoperahouse.com; Bennelong Point; 🚉Circular Quay) The glamorous jewel at the heart of Australian performance, Sydney's famous opera house has five main stages. Opera may have star billing, but theatre, comedy, music and dance are all performed here.

City Recital Hall CLASSICAL MUSIC
(Map p72; ☎02-8256 2222; www.cityrecitalhall.com; 2 Angel Pl; ⊙box office 9am-5pm Mon-Fri; 🚉Martin Place) Based on the classic configuration of the 19th-century European concert hall, this custom-built 1200-seat venue boasts near-perfect acoustics. Catch top-flight companies such as Musica Viva, the Australian Brandenburg Orchestra and the Australian Chamber Orchestra here.

Sydney Conservatorium of Music CLASSICAL MUSIC
(Map p72; ☎02-9351 1222; www.music.usyd.edu.au; Conservatorium Rd; 🚉Circular Quay) This historic venue showcases the talents of its students and their teachers. Choral, jazz, operatic and chamber concerts happen from March to November, along with free lunchtime recitals on Wednesday at 1.10pm.

Dance

Sydney Dance Company DANCE
(SDC; Map p72; ☎02-9221 4811; www.sydneydancecompany.com; Pier 4/5, 15 Hickson Rd;

Wynyard) Australia's number-one contemporary-dance company has been staging wildly modern, sexy, sometimes shocking works for nearly 40 years. Performances are usually held across the street at the Roslyn Packer Theatre, or at Carriageworks.

Bangarra Dance Theatre DANCE
(Map p72; 02-9251 5333; www.bangarra.com.au; Pier 4/5, 15 Hickson Rd; tickets $30-93; Wynyard) Bangarra is hailed as Australia's finest Aboriginal performance company. Artistic director Stephen Page conjures a fusion of contemporary themes, Indigenous traditions and Western technique. When not touring internationally, the company performs at the Opera House or at their own small theatre in Walsh Bay.

Live Music, Cabaret & Comedy

Oxford Art Factory LIVE MUSIC
(Map p88; www.oxfordartfactory.com; 38-46 Oxford St; Museum) Indie kids party against an arty backdrop at this two-room multipurpose venue modelled on Andy Warhol's NYC creative base. There's a gallery, a bar and a performance space that often hosts international acts and DJs. Check the website for what's on.

Newtown Social Club LIVE MUSIC
(Map p121; 1300 724 867; www.newtownsocialclub.com; 387 King St; 7pm-midnight Tue-Thu, noon-2am Fri & Sat, noon-10pm Sun; ; Newtown) The legendary Sandringham Hotel (aka the 'Sando', where God used to drink, according to local band The Whitlams) may have changed names but if anything it has heightened its commitment to live music. Gigs range from local bands on the make to indie luminaries such as Gruff Rhys and Stephen Malkmus.

Vanguard LIVE MUSIC
(Map p121; 02-9557 7992; www.thevanguard.com.au; 42 King St; Macdonaldtown) Intimate 1920s-themed Vanguard stages live music most nights (including some well-known names), as well as burlesque, comedy and classic-movie screenings. Most seats are reserved for dinner-and-show diners.

Basement LIVE MUSIC
(Map p72; 02-9251 2797; www.thebasement.com.au; 7 Macquarie Pl; admission $8-60; Circular Quay) Once solely a jazz venue, the Basement now hosts international and local musicians working in many disciplines and genres. Dinner-and-show tickets net you a table by the stage, guaranteeing a better view than the standing-only area by the bar.

El Rocco JAZZ, COMEDY
(Map p88; www.elrocco.com.au; 154 Brougham St; 5pm-midnight Mon-Sat, 5-10pm Sun; Kings Cross) Between 1955 and 1969 this was the city's premier finger-snappin', beret-wearing boho cellar bar, hosting performances by Frank Sinatra and Sarah Vaughan. Those heady days are long gone but live jazz is back on the agenda, along with the Happy Endings Comedy Club (www.happyendingscomedyclub.com.au) on Saturdays.

Camelot Lounge LIVE MUSIC
(Map p68; www.camelotlounge.wordpress.com; 19 Marrickville Rd; Sydenham) In ever-increasingly hip Marrickville, this eclectic little venue hosts jazz, world music, blues, folk, comedy, cabaret and all manner of other weird stuff.

Slide CABARET
(Map p68; 02-8915 1899; www.slide.com.au; 41 Oxford St; 7pm-late Wed-Sat; Museum) Slide inside a gorgeously converted banking chamber for dinner and a sexy show: cabaret, circus, burlesque etc.

Spectator Sports

On any given Sydney weekend there'll be all manner of balls being hurled, kicked and batted around. Sydneysiders are passionate about the **National Rugby League** (www.nrl.com), the season kicking off in March and culminating in the grand final in early October.

Over the same period, hometown favourites the Sydney Swans and Greater Western Sydney Giants play in the **Australian Football League** (www.afl.com.au).

Sydney Cricket Ground SPECTATOR SPORT
(SCG; Map p92; 02-9360 6601; www.sydneycricketground.com.au; Driver Ave; 373-377) During the cricket season (October to March), the stately SCG is the venue for sparsely attended interstate cricket matches (featuring the NSW Blues), and sell-out international five-day test, one-day and 20/20 limited-over matches. As the cricket season ends the Australian Rules (AFL) season starts and the stadium becomes a blur of red-and-white-clad Sydney Swans (www.sydneyswans.com.au) fans.

Sydney Football Stadium SPECTATOR SPORT
(Allianz Stadium; Map p92; www.allianzstadium.com.au; Moore Park Rd; 373-377) It's now officially named after an insurance com-

pany, but these naming rights change periodically, so we'll stick with the untainted-by-sponsorship moniker for this elegant 45,500-capacity stadium. It's home to local heroes the Sydney Roosters rugby league team (www.roosters.com.au), the NSW Waratahs rugby union team (www.waratahs.com.au) and the Sydney FC A-league football (soccer) team (www.sydneyfc.com).

All of these teams have passionate fans (possibly the most vocal are the crazies in the Roosters' 'chook pen'), so a home game can be a lot of fun. Book through **Ticketek** (☎132 849; www.ticketek.com.au).

Royal Randwick Racecourse HORSE RACING
(Map p68; www.australianturfclub.com.au; Alison Rd; 339) The action at Sydney's most famous racecourse peaks in April with the $4 million Queen Elizabeth Stakes; check the online calendar for race days.

Theatre

Sydney Theatre Company THEATRE
(STC; Map p72; ☎02-9250 1777; www.sydneytheatre.com.au; Pier 4/5, 15 Hickson Rd; box office 9am-8.30pm Mon-Fri, 11am-8.30pm Sat, 2hr before show Sun; Wynyard) Established in 1978, the STC is Sydney theatre's top dog and has played an important part in the careers of many famous Australian actors (especially Cate Blanchett, who was co-artistic director from 2008 to 2013). Tours of the company's Wharf and Roslyn Packer theatres are held at 10.30am every Tuesday ($10). Performances are also staged at the Opera House.

Belvoir THEATRE
(Map p86; ☎02-9699 3444; www.belvoir.com.au; 25 Belvoir St; Central) In a quiet corner of Surry Hills, this intimate venue is the home of an often-experimental and consistently excellent theatre company. Shows sometimes feature big stars.

State Theatre THEATRE
(Map p72; ☎02-9373 6655; www.statetheatre.com.au; 49 Market St; St James) The beautiful 2000-seat State Theatre is a lavish, gilt-ridden, chandelier-dangling palace. It hosts the Sydney Film Festival, concerts, comedy, opera, musicals and the odd celebrity chef.

Capitol Theatre THEATRE
(Map p82; ☎1300 558 878; www.capitoltheatre.com.au; 13 Campbell St; Central) Lavishly restored, this large city theatre is home to long-running musicals *(Wicked, Les Miserables, Matilda)* and the occasional ballet or big-name concert.

Sydney Lyric THEATRE
(Map p84; ☎02-9509 3600; www.sydneylyric.com.au; The Star, Pirrama Rd; The Star) This 2000-seat theatre within the casino stages big-name musicals and the occasional concert.

Ensemble Theatre THEATRE
(Map p68; ☎02-9929 0644; www.ensemble.com.au; 78 McDougall St, Kirribilli; North Sydney) The long-running Ensemble presents mainstream theatre by overseas and Australian playwrights (think David Williamson and David Hare), generally with well-known Australian actors.

Monkey Baa Theatre Company THEATRE
(Map p82; ☎02-8624 9340; www.monkeybaa.com.au; 1 Harbour St; tickets $25; Town Hall) If you can drag them away from the neighbouring playground, bring your budding culture vultures here to watch Australian children's books come to life. This energetic company devises and stages their own adaptations.

Shopping

Sydneysiders head cityward – particularly to Pitt St Mall – if they have something special to buy or when serious retail therapy is required. Paddington has traditionally been Sydney's premier fashion enclave, although it's now facing stiff competition from the giant Westfield malls in Pitt St and Bondi Junction. Newtown's King St has come into its own as one of the city's most interesting strips, especially for vintage boutiques and bookshops.

Serious shoppers should consider downloading the suburb-by-suburb shopping guides produced by **Urban Walkabout** (www.urbanwalkabout.com/sydney); free printed versions of the maps are also available at tourist information offices and booths across the city.

The Rocks & Circular Quay

Australian Wine Centre WINE
(Map p72; www.australianwinecentre.com; Goldfields House, 1 Alfred St; 10am-8pm Mon-Sat, to 6.30pm Sun; Circular Quay) This multilingual basement store is packed with quality Australian wine, beer and spirits. Smaller producers are well represented, along with a staggering range of prestigious Penfolds Grange wines. International shipping can be arranged.

Opal Minded JEWELLERY
(Map p72; www.opalminded.com; 55 George St; 9am-6.30pm; Circular Quay) As good a place as any to stock up on that quintessential piece of Aussie bling.

Gannon House ART
(Map p72; 02-9251 4474; www.gannonhousegallery.com; 45 Argyle St; Circular Quay) Specialising in contemporary Australian and Aboriginal art, Gannon House purchases works directly from artists and Aboriginal communities. You'll find the work of prominent artists such as Gloria Petyarre here, alongside lesser-known names.

City Centre

Westfield Sydney MALL
(Map p72; www.westfield.com.au/sydney; 188 Pitt St Mall; 9.30am-6.30pm Fri-Wed, to 9pm Thu; St James) The city's most glamorous shopping mall is a bafflingly large complex gobbling up Sydney Tower and a fair chunk of Pitt St Mall. The 5th-floor food court is excellent.

David Jones DEPARTMENT STORE
(Map p72; www.davidjones.com.au; 86-108 Castlereagh St; 9.30am-7pm Sat-Wed, to 9pm Thu & Fri; St James) DJs is Sydney's premier department store, occupying two enormous city buildings. The Castlereagh St store has women's and children's clothing; Market St has menswear, electrical goods and a highbrow food court. David Jones also takes up a sizeable chunk of **Westfield Bondi Junction** (Map p68; 02-9947 8000; www.westfield.com.au; 500 Oxford St; 9.30am-6pm Fri-Wed, to 9pm Thu; Bondi Junction).

Strand Arcade SHOPPING CENTRE
(Map p72; www.strandarcade.com.au; 412 George St; 9am-5.30pm Mon-Wed & Fri, to 8pm Thu, 9am-4pm Sat, 11am-4pm Sun; St James) Constructed in 1891, the Strand rivals the QVB in the ornateness stakes. The three floors of designer fashions, Australiana and old-world coffee shops will make your short-cut through here considerably longer.

Queen Victoria Building SHOPPING CENTRE
(QVB; Map p72; www.qvb.com.au; 455 George St; 11am-5pm Sun, 9am-6pm Mon-Wed, Fri & Sat, 9am-9pm Thu; Town Hall) The magnificent QVB takes up a whole block and boasts nearly 200 shops on five levels. It's a High Victorian masterpiece – without doubt Sydney's most beautiful shopping centre.

Kinokuniya BOOKS
(Map p72; 02-9262 7996; www.kinokuniya.com; L2, The Galeries, 500 George St; 10am-7pm Fri-Wed, 10am-9pm Thu; Town Hall) This outpost of the Japanese chain is the largest bookshop in Sydney, with over 300,000 titles. The comics section is a magnet for geeky teens – the imported Chinese, Japanese and European magazine section isn't. There's a cool little cafe here, too.

Darlinghurst

Artery ARTS
(Map p88; 02-9380 8234; www.artery.com.au; 221 Darlinghurst Rd; 10am-6pm Mon-Fri, to 4pm Sat & Sun; Kings Cross) Step into a world of mesmerising dots and swirls at this small gallery devoted to Aboriginal art. Artery's motto is 'ethical, contemporary, affordable', and while large canvases by more established artists cost in the thousands, small, unstretched canvases start at around $35.

Blue Spinach FASHION
(Map p88; 02-9331 3904; www.bluespinach.com.au; 348 Liverpool St; Kings Cross) High-end consignment clothing for penny-pinching label lovers of all genders. If you can make it beyond the shocking blue facade (shocking doesn't really do it justice), you'll find Paul Smith and Gucci at (relatively) bargain prices.

C's Flashback VINTAGE
(Map p88; 02-9331 7833; www.csflashback.com.au; 316 Crown St; 10am-6pm Fri-Wed, to 8pm Thu; Museum) Looking for a second-hand Hawaiian shirt, some beat-up cowboy boots or a little sequinned 1940s hat like the Queen wears? We're not sure exactly what C was on, but her flashback men's and women's threads are pretty trippy.

Paddington & Woollahra

Poepke FASHION
(Map p92; www.poepke.com; 47 William St; 10am-6pm Mon-Sat, noon-5pm Sun; 380) One of Paddington's more interesting women's boutiques, stocking a curated range from Australian and international designers.

Corner Shop FASHION
(Map p92; 02-9380 9828; www.thecornershop.com.au; 43 William St; 10am-6pm Mon-Sat, noon-5pm Sun; 380) This treasure trove of a boutique is stocked with a healthy mix of casual and high-end women's clothing from Australian and international designers, with some jewellery for good measure.

SYDNEY'S WEEKEND MARKETS

Sydneysiders enjoy going to local markets nearly as much as going to the beach (and that's really saying something). Many inner-city suburbs host weekend markets in the grounds of local schools and churches, and these sell everything from organic food to original designer clothing. You'll inevitably encounter some tragic hippy paraphernalia, appalling art and overpriced tourist tat, but there are often exciting purchases to be made, too.

Glebe Markets (Map p121; www.glebemarkets.com.au; Glebe Public School, cnr Glebe Point Rd & Derby Pl; ⏲10am-4pm Sat; Glebe) The best of the west; Sydney's dreadlocked, shoeless, inner-city contingent beats a course to this crowded hippy-ish market.

Paddington Markets (Map p92; www.paddingtonmarkets.com.au; 395 Oxford St; ⏲10am-4pm Sat; 380) Originating in the 1970s, when they were drenched in the scent of patchouli oil, these markets are considerably more mainstream these days. They're still worth exploring for their new and vintage clothing, crafts and jewellery. Expect a crush.

Bondi Markets (Map p94; www.bondimarkets.com.au; Bondi Beach Public School, Campbell Pde; ⏲9am-1pm Sat, 10am-4pm Sun; 380-382) On Sundays, when the kids are at the beach, their school fills up with Bondi characters rummaging through tie-dyed second-hand clothes, original fashion, books, beads, earrings, aromatherapy oils, candles, old records and more. There's a farmers' market here on Saturdays.

Eveleigh Farmers' Market (Map p121; www.eveleighmarket.com.au; Carriageworks, 245 Wilson St; ⏲8am-1pm Sat; Redfern) Over 70 regular stallholders sell their goodies at Sydney's best farmers' market, held in a heritage-listed railway workshop. Food and coffee stands do a brisk business; celebrity chef Kylie Kwong can often be spotted cooking up a storm.

Ariel BOOKS
(Map p88; ☎02-9332 4581; www.arielbooks.com.au; 42 Oxford St; ⏲9am-10.30pm; 380) Furtive artists, architects and students roam Ariel's aisles late into the evening. 'Underculture' is the thrust here – glossy art, film, fashion and design books, along with kids' books, travel guides and a queer-lit section.

Newtown & Around

Quick Brown Fox CLOTHING, ACCESSORIES
(Map p121; ☎02-9519 6622; www.quickbrownfox.com.au; 231 King St; ⏲10.30am-6.30pm; Newtown) No lazy dogs here – just plenty of fast-looking, tanned vixens snapping up funky vintage fashions that veer from 'hello, boys!' cuteness to indecent-exposure sexiness. Catchy patterns and fabrics, chic boots and bags.

Better Read Than Dead BOOKS
(Map p121; ☎02-9557 8700; www.betterread.com.au; 265 King St; ⏲9.30am-9pm; Newtown) This just might be our favourite Sydney bookshop, and not just because of the pithy name and the great selection of Lonely Planet titles. Nobody seems to mind if you waste hours perusing the beautifully presented aisles, stacked with high-, middle- and deliciously low-brow reading materials.

Reclaim HOMEWARES, GIFTS
(Map p121; www.reclaim.net.au; 356 King St; ⏲10am-6pm; Newtown) Absolutely the place to shop for Iggy Pop throw cushions, antique tea sets, quirky homewares and funky gifts. It's all put together by local singer Monica Trapaga (of Monica and the Moochers).

Faster Pussycat CLOTHING, ACCESSORIES
(Map p121; ☎02-9519 1744; www.fasterpussycatonline.com; 431a King St; ⏲11am-6pm; Newtown) Inspired by 'trash pop culture, hot rods and rock and roll', this cool cat coughs up clothing and accessories for all genders and ages (including baby punkwear) in several shades of Newtown black.

Information

EMERGENCY

In the event of an emergency, call ☎000 to contact the police, ambulance and fire service. For a searchable list of all police stations in NSW, go to www.police.nsw.gov.au.

Lifeline (☎13 11 14; www.lifelinesydney.org; ⏲24hr) Round-the-clock phone counselling services, including suicide prevention.

NSW Rape Crisis (☎1800 424 017; www.nswrapecrisis.com.au; ⏲24hr) Offers counselling, 24 hours a day.

INTERNET ACCESS

The vast majority of hotels and hostels offer their guests internet access, although you'll still have to pay for it in many hostels and top hotels. Libraries are a good bet for free wi-fi and bookable terminals.

MEDICAL SERVICES

Kings Cross Clinic (02-9358 3066; www.kingscrossclinic.com.au; 13 Springfield Ave; 9am-6pm Mon-Fri, 10am-1pm Sat; Kings Cross) General and travel-related medical services.

Royal Prince Alfred Hospital (RPA; 02-9515 6111; www.sswahs.nsw.gov.au/rpa; Missenden Rd, Camperdown; Macdonaldtown)

St Vincent's Hospital (02-8382 1111; www.stvincents.com.au; 390 Victoria St; Kings Cross)

Sydney Hospital (02-9382 7111; www.seslhd.health.nsw.gov.au/SHSEH; 8 Macquarie St; Martin Place)

MONEY

There are plenty of ATMs throughout Sydney. Foreign-exchange offices are found in Kings Cross and around Chinatown, Circular Quay and Central Station.

TOURIST INFORMATION

City Host Information Kiosks (www.cityofsydney.nsw.gov.au) Branches in Circular Quay (Map p72; cnr Pitt & Alfred Sts; 9am-5pm; Circular Quay), Haymarket (Map p82; Dixon St; 11am-7pm; Town Hall), Kings Cross (Map p88; cnr Darlinghurst Rd & Springfield Ave; 9am-5pm; Kings Cross) and Town Hall (Map p82; George St; 9am-5pm; Town Hall).

Hello Manly (Map p98; 02-9976 1430; www.hellomanly.com.au; Manly Wharf; 9am-5pm; Manly) This helpful visitors centre, just outside the ferry wharf and alongside the bus interchange, has free pamphlets covering the Manly Scenic Walkway (p99) and other Manly attractions, plus loads of local bus information.

Sydney Visitor Centres (www.bestof.com.au) Have a wide range of brochures, and staff can book accommodation, tours and attractions. Branches in The Rocks (Map p72; 02-8273 0000; cnr Argyle & Playfair Sts; Circular Quay) and Darling Harbour (Map p82; 02-8273 0000; Palm Grove, behind IMAX; 9.30am-5.30pm; Town Hall).

Getting There & Away

AIR

Also known as Kingsford Smith Airport, Sydney Airport (p1086) has separate international (T1) and domestic (T2 and T3) sections, 4km apart on either side of the runway. Each has left-luggage services, ATMs, currency exchange bureaux and rental-car counters.

Airlines flying to other Australian destinations include:

Jetstar (www.jetstar.com.au) Flies to Ballina Byron Bay, Gold Coast, Brisbane, Sunshine Coast, Hamilton Island, Townsville, Cairns, Melbourne, Hobart, Launceston, Adelaide, Uluru, Darwin and Perth.

Qantas (www.qantas.com.au) Flies to Canberra, Wagga Wagga, Albury, Dubbo, Tamworth, Moree, Port Macquarie, Armidale, Coffs Harbour, Lord Howe Island, Gold Coast, Brisbane, Toowoomba, Fraser Coast, Hamilton Island, Cairns, Darwin, Alice Springs, Broome, Karratha, Perth, Adelaide, Melbourne and Hobart.

Regional Express (www.rex.com.au) Flies to Newcastle, Taree, Ballina Byron Bay, Grafton, Lismore, Armidale, Dubbo, Parkes, Orange, Bathurst, Griffith, Wagga Wagga, Albury, Merimbula, Broken Hill and Mildura.

Tigerair (www.tigerair.com/au/en) Flies to Coffs Harbour, Gold Coast, Brisbane, Mackay, Whitsunday Coast, Cairns, Perth, Adelaide and Melbourne.

Virgin Australia (www.virginaustralia.com) Flies to Canberra, Albury, Port Macquarie, Coffs Harbour, Ballina Byron Bay, Gold Coast, Brisbane, Sunshine Coast, Hervey Bay, Mackay, Hamilton Island, Townsville, Cairns, Darwin, Uluru, Perth, Adelaide, Melbourne, Launceston and Hobart.

BUS

Long-distance bus services arrive at **Sydney Coach Terminal** (Map p86; 02-9281 9366; www.sydneycoachterminal.com.au; Eddy Ave; 6am-6pm; Central), underneath Central Station. The major operators are:

Australia Wide (02-9516 1300; www.austwidecoaches.com.au) Services to Orange and Bathurst.

Firefly (1300 730 740; www.fireflyexpress.com.au) Runs Adelaide to Sydney via Melbourne and Canberra.

Greyhound (1300 473 946; www.greyhound.com.au) Has the most extensive nationwide network.

Murrays (13 22 51; www.murrays.com.au) Runs from Canberra and the South Coast to Sydney.

Port Stephens Coaches (02-4982 2940; www.pscoaches.com.au) Coaches to Newcastle and Nelson Bay.

Premier Motor Service (133 410; www.premierms.com.au) Runs Cairns to Melbourne, via Brisbane, Gold Coast and Sydney.

TRAIN

NSW TrainLink (13 22 32; www.nswtrainlink.info) connects Sydney's Central station with destinations including Melbourne (from $70, 11 hours), Broken Hill (from $70, 13½ hours), Canberra (from $40, 4¼ hours), Coffs Harbour (from $67, nine hours) and Brisbane (from $70, 14¼ hours).

Sydney's local train network, run by **Sydney Trains** (☎13 15 00; www.sydneytrains.info) includes regular direct services to NSW destinations such as Kiama (2¼ hours), Wollongong (1½ hours), Katoomba (two hours), Gosford (1½ hours) and Newcastle's Hamilton station (1½ hours). For all of these services, peak/off-peak fares are $8.30/5.81.

The famous **Indian Pacific** (☎1800 703 357; www.greatsouthernrail.com.au) heads clear across the continent from Sydney to Perth.

ℹ Getting Around

TO/FROM THE AIRPORT

Bus Services from the airport are limited but there is a direct bus to Bondi Junction (routes 400 and 410, $4.50, 1¼ hours) which departs roughly every 20 minutes.

Shuttle Airport shuttles head to hotels and hostels in the city centre, and some reach surrounding suburbs and beach destinations. Operators include **Sydney Airporter** (☎02-9666 9988; www.kst.com.au), **Super Shuttle** (☎1300 018 460; www.signaturelimousinessydney.com.au), **Airport Shuttle North** (☎1300 505 100; www.airportshuttlenorth.com) and **Manly Express** (☎02-8068 8473; www.manlyexpress.com.au).

Taxi Fares from the airport are approximately $45 to $55 to the city centre, $55 to $65 to North Sydney and $90 to $100 to Manly.

Train Trains from both the domestic and international terminals, connecting into the main train network, are run by **Airport Link** (www.airportlink.com.au; adult/child $18/14; ⏲4.30am-12.30am). They're frequent (every 10 minutes), quick (13 minutes to Central) and easy to use, but airport tickets are charged at a hefty premium. If there are a few of you it's cheaper to catch a cab. Another alternative is to catch the bus to Rockdale station (routes 400 & 410, $3.50, 12 minutes) and then catch the regular train to Central ($3, 15 minutes).

CAR & MOTORCYCLE

➡ Avoid driving in central Sydney if you can: there's a confusing one-way street system, parking's elusive and expensive (even at hotels), and parking inspectors, tolls and tow-away zones proliferate. Conversely, a car is handy for accessing Sydney's outer reaches (particularly the beaches) and for day trips.

➡ All of the major international car rental companies have offices at Sydney Airport and other locations. The main city hub for rental cars is William St, Darlinghurst. Reliable local operators include **Bayswater Car Rental** (☎02-9360 3622; www.bayswatercarrental.com.au), cut-price **Ace Rentals** (☎02-8338 1055; www.acerentalcars.com.au) and, for campervans, **Jucy Rentals** (☎1800 150 850; www.jucy.com.au).

➡ There are hefty **tolls** on most of Sydney's motorways and major links (including the Harbour Bridge, Harbour Tunnel, Cross City Tunnel and Eastern Distributor). The tolling system is electronic, meaning that it's up to you to organise an electronic tag or visitors' pass through any of the following websites: www.roam.com.au, www.roamexpress.com.au or www.myetoll.com.au. Note that some car-hire companies now supply etags.

➡ The Sydney Travellers Car Market (p1090) is based in the Kings Cross Car Park off Ward Ave. This provides useful information about the paperwork needed to buy, sell and register vehicles. Sellers can leave their vehicles in the market for one week for free (after which it's $60 per week). Vehicles are only permitted to be left overnight between Monday and Thursday at no cost; usual car-park charges apply from Friday to Sunday. Note that you're not permitted to sleep in the vehicle while it is in the car park. It is also illegal to sell vehicles on the street anywhere in central Sydney.

PUBLIC TRANSPORT

Transport NSW (☎13 15 00; www.transportnsw.info) is the body that coordinates all of the state-run bus, ferry, train and light rail services. You'll find a useful journey planner on their website.

Sydneysiders love to complain about their public transport system, but visitors should find it surprisingly easy to navigate. The train system is the linchpin, with lines radiating out from Central station. Ferries head all around the harbour and up the river to Parramatta; light rail is useful for Pyrmont and Glebe; and buses are particularly useful for getting to the beaches.

Bus

Sydney Buses (☎13 15 00; www.sydneybuses.info) has an extensive network, operating from around 5am to midnight when less frequent NightRide services commence. Bus routes starting with an X indicate limited-stop express routes; those with an L have limited stops.

You can buy a ticket from the driver on most services ($2.40 to $4.70, depending on the length of the journey), but you'll need an Opal card or prepaid paper ticket (available at newsagents, convenience stores and supermarkets) for prepay-only services. Fares are based on 'sections', which are roughly 1.6km in length. Prepaid tickets need to be dunked into the green ticket machines as you enter the bus. If you'll be catching buses a lot (but not trains or ferries), consider a prepaid 10-ride TravelTen ticket (sections 1-2/3-5/6+ $20/31/38).

INTEGRATED TICKETS & PASSES

Although you can still buy individual tickets for most public transport services, a smartcard system called **Opal** (www.opal.com.au) also operates.

The card can be obtained (for free) and loaded with credit at numerous newsagencies and convenience stores across Sydney. When commencing a journey you'll need to touch the card to an electronic reader, located at train station gates, near the doors of buses and light rail carriages, and at the ferry wharves. You then need to touch a reader when you complete your journey so that the system can deduct the correct fare. Advantages include cheaper single journeys, daily charges capped at $15 ($2.50 on Sundays) and free travel after taking any eight journeys in a week (it resets itself every Monday). You can use the Opal card at the airport train stations, but none of the aforementioned bonuses apply.

Paper-based **MyMulti passes** can be purchased at ferry and train ticket offices and many newsagencies and convenience stores, but you're much better off getting an Opal card instead. For instance, the MyMulti Day Pass costs $24 as opposed to the $15 Opal cap.

Route 555 is a free service which heads up and down George St, from Circular Quay to Central Station.

Ferry

➡ Most **Sydney Ferries** (☎13 15 00; www.transportnsw.info) operate between 6am and midnight. The standard single fare for most harbour destinations is $6.20; boats to Manly, Sydney Olympic Park and Parramatta cost $7.60. If you're heading to Taronga Zoo by ferry, consider the all-inclusive ZooPass (adult/child $53/27).

➡ Private companies **Manly Fast Ferry** (☎02-9583 1199; www.manlyfastferry.com.au; adult/child $9/6) and **Sydney Fast Ferries** (☎02-9818 6000; www.sydneyfastferries.com.au; adult/child $9.75/7.50; 📶) both offer boats that blast from Circular Quay to Manly in 18 minutes.

Light Rail

➡ Trams run between Central Station and Dulwich Hill, stopping in Chinatown, Darling Harbour, The Star casino, Sydney Fish Market and Glebe en route.

➡ Tickets cost $3.80 for a short journey and $4.80 for a longer one, and can be purchased from the conductor.

Train

➡ **Sydney Trains** (☎13 15 00; www.sydneytrains.info) has a large suburban railway web with relatively frequent services, although there are no lines to the northern or eastern beaches.

➡ Trains run from around 5am to 1am – check timetables for your line.

➡ A short inner-city one-way trip costs $4.

➡ If you don't have an Opal card, purchase your ticket in advance from an automated machine or a counter at the bigger stations.

TAXI

➡ Metered taxis are easy to flag down in the central city and inner suburbs, except for at changeover times (3pm and 3am).

➡ Fares are regulated, so all companies charge the same. Flagfall is $3.50, with a $2.50 'night owl surcharge' after 10pm on a Friday and Saturday until 6am the following morning. The fare thereafter is $2.14 per kilometre, with an additional surcharge of 20% between 10pm and 6am nightly. There's also a $2.40 fee for bookings.

➡ The **UberX** ride-sharing app operates in Sydney but the state government maintains that it is illegal for drivers to offer the service.

Major taxi companies include:

Legion Cabs (☎13 14 51; www.legioncabs.com.au)

Premier Cabs (☎13 10 17; www.premiercabs.com.au)

RSL Cabs (☎02-9581 1111; www.rslcabs.com.au)

Taxis Combined (☎13 33 00; www.taxiscombined.com.au)

WATER TAXI

Water taxis are a fast way to shunt around the harbour (Circular Quay to Watsons Bay in as little as 15 minutes). Companies will quote on any pick-up point within the harbour and the river, including private jetties, islands and other boats.

Aussie Water Taxis (Map p84; ☎02-9211 7730; www.aussiewatertaxis.com; Cockle Bay Wharf) The smallest seats 16 passengers and can be rented per hour or point to point.

H2O Maxi Taxis (☎1300 420 829; www.h2owatertaxis.com.au) Smallest seats 21 people. Harbour Islands a speciality: Fort Denison/Cockatoo Island/Shark Island costs

$110/125/150 for up to 10 people from Circular Quay. Has a handy quote calculator on its website.

Water Taxis Combined (☎02-9555 8888; www.watertaxis.com.au) Fares based on up to four passengers: Circular Quay to Watsons Bay $110; to Rose Bay $110; to Woolloomooloo $70. It also offers harbour cruise packages.

Yellow Water Taxis (☎02-9299 0199; www.yellowwatertaxis.com.au) Set price for up to four passengers, then $10 per person for additional people. Sample fares from King St Wharf: Circular Quay and Fort Denison $83; Taronga Zoo $95; Cockatoo Island and Shark Island $121; Watsons Bay $127.

HAWKESBURY RIVER

Less than an hour from Sydney, the tranquil Hawkesbury River flows past honeycomb-coloured cliffs, historic townships and riverside hamlets into bays and inlets and between a series of national parks, including Ku-ring-gai Chase (p102) and **Brisbane Water**.

Further upstream, a narrow forested waterway diverts from the Hawkesbury and peters down to the chilled-out river town of **Berowra Waters**, where a handful of businesses, boat sheds and residences cluster around the free, 24-hour ferry across Berowra Creek.

The riverside hamlet of **Wisemans Ferry** spills over a bow of the Hawkesbury River where it slides east towards **Brooklyn**. The surrounding area retains remnants of the convict-built **Great North Road**, originally constructed to link Sydney with the Hunter Valley and now part of the Australian Convict Sites listing on Unesco's World Heritage list. To download a self-guided tour brochure, go to www.rms.nsw.gov.au and type 'convict trail' into the search box.

Activities

Riverboat Postman CRUISE

(☎0400 600 111; www.riverboatpostman.com.au; Brooklyn Public Wharf, Dangar Rd; adult/child/senior $50/15/44; ⏰10am Mon-Fri; 🚉Hawkesbury River) Departing Brooklyn, the Riverboat Postman is Australia's last operating mail boat and a decidedly old-school way to get a feel for the river. It chugs 40km up the Hawkesbury from Brooklyn to as far as Marlow, returning to Brooklyn at 1.15pm. The fare includes morning tea and a ploughman's lunch.

Sleeping

The best way to experience the Hawkesbury is on a fully equipped houseboat. Rates skyrocket during summer and school holidays, but most outfits offer affordable low-season, midweek and long-term rental specials. To give a very rough guide, a two-/six-berth boat for three nights costs from $950/1050 from September to early December, with prices doubling during the Christmas–New Year period and on weekends and holidays throughout the year. Options include **Hawkesbury Afloat** (☎02-9985 7722; www.hawkesburyafloat.com.au; 45 Brooklyn Rd, Brooklyn), **Holidays Afloat** (☎02-9985 5555; www.holidaysafloat.com.au; 87 Brooklyn Rd, Brooklyn) and **Ripples on the Hawkesbury** (☎02-9985 5555; www.ripples.com.au; 87 Brooklyn Rd, Brooklyn).

Eating

Berowra Waters Inn MODERN AUSTRALIAN $$$

(☎02-9456 1027; www.berowrawatersinn.com; East or West public wharves; per person $175; ⏰noon-2pm Fri-Sun, 6-10pm Fri & Sat) Wow! On the riverbank upstream from Berowra Waters township and only accessible by boat or seaplane, this Glenn Murcutt–designed restaurant is a real show-stopper. The restaurant has a sensational Mod Oz degustation menu and brilliant river views – perfect for a special occasion (like your holiday!). Call for bookings and to arrange a ferry.

Getting There & Away

Trains run from Sydney's Central Station to Berowra and on to Brooklyn's Hawkesbury River station ($7/3.50, one hour, roughly hourly). Note that the Berowra train station is a solid 6km trudge from Berowra Waters.

Wisemans Ferry is most easily accessed by river but can be reached by a pretty road which winds along the north bank of the river from the Central Coast, through Dharug National Park. Largely unsealed but photogenic roads run north from Wisemans Ferry to tiny St Albans.

BLUE MOUNTAINS

POP 78,500

A region with more than its fair share of natural beauty, the Blue Mountains was an obvious choice for Unesco World Heritage status. The slate-coloured haze that gives the mountains their name comes from a fine mist of oil exuded by the huge eucalypts that

Blue Mountains

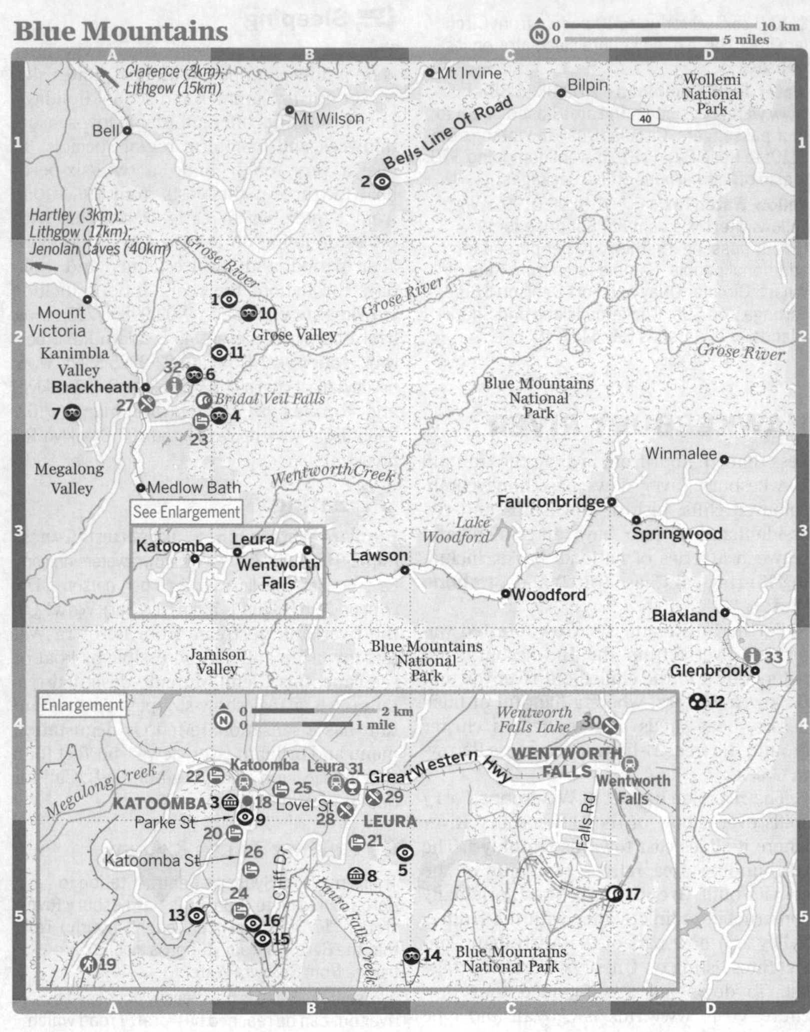

form a dense canopy across the landscape of deep, often inaccessible valleys and chiselled sandstone outcrops.

The foothills begin 65km inland from Sydney, rising to an 1100m-high sandstone plateau riddled with valleys eroded into the stone over thousands of years. There are eight connected conservation areas in the region, including the **Blue Mountains National Park** (www.nationalparks.nsw.gov.au/Blue-Mountains-National-Park), which has some truly fantastic scenery, excellent bushwalks (hikes), Aboriginal engravings and all the canyons and cliffs you could ask for. **Wollemi National Park** (www.nationalparks.nsw.gov.au/Wollemi-National-Park), north of the Bells Line of Road, is NSW's largest forested wilderness area, stretching all the way to the Hunter Valley.

Although it's possible to visit on a day trip from Sydney, we strongly recommend that you stay at least one night so that you can explore a few of the towns, do at least one bushwalk and eat at some of the excellent restaurants. The hills can be surprisingly cool throughout the year, so bring warm clothes.

Blue Mountains

Sights

1 Anvil Rock ... B2
2 Blue Mountains Botanic Garden Mount Tomah ... B1
3 Blue Mountains Cultural Centre ... B4
Echo Point ... (see 15)
4 Evans Lookout ... B2
5 Everglades Historic House & Gardens ... B5
6 Govetts Leap Lookout ... A2
7 Hargraves Lookout ... A2
8 Leuralla NSW Toy & Railway Museum ... B5
9 Paragon ... B4
10 Perrys Lookdown ... B2
11 Pulpit Rock ... B2
12 Red Hands Cave ... D4
13 Scenic World ... A5
14 Sublime Point ... C5
15 Three Sisters ... B5
16 Waradah Aboriginal Centre ... B5
17 Wentworth Falls Reserve ... D5

Activities, Courses & Tours

Australian School of Mountaineering ... (see 9)
18 Blue Mountains Adventure Company ... B4
19 Golden Stairs Walk ... A5
High 'n' Wild Australian Adventures ... (see 20)

Sleeping

20 Blue Mountains YHA ... B5
21 Broomelea ... B5
22 Flying Fox ... B4
Greens of Leura ... (see 29)
23 Jemby-Rinjah Eco Lodge ... A2
24 Lilianfels ... B5
25 No 14 ... B4
26 Shelton-Lea ... B5

Eating

27 Ashcrofts ... A2
Bistro Niagara ... (see 18)
28 Cafe Madeleine ... B4
29 Leura Garage ... B4
Leura Gourmet Cafe & Deli ... (see 28)
30 Nineteen23 ... C4
Sanwiye Korean Cafe ... (see 9)
Silk's Brasserie ... (see 28)
True to the Bean ... (see 9)
Vesta ... (see 27)

Drinking & Nightlife

31 Alexandra Hotel ... B4

Information

32 Blue Mountains Heritage Centre ... A2
Echo Point Visitors Centre ... (see 15)
33 Glenbrook Information Centre ... D4

Transport

Blue Mountains Explorer Bus ... (see 18)
Trolley Tours ... (see 9)

Sights

Glenbrook

Arriving from Sydney, the first of the Blue Mountains towns you will encounter is unassuming Glenbrook. From here, you can drive or walk into the lower reaches of the national park; this is the only part of the park where vehicle entry fees apply ($7). Six kilometres from the park entrance gate is the Mt Portal Lookout with panoramic views into the Glenbrook Gorge, over the Nepean River and back to Sydney.

Red Hands Cave ARCHAEOLOGICAL SITE

Less a cave than an alcove, this Aboriginal shelter is decorated with hand stencils dating from between 500 and 1600 years ago. It's an easy, 7km return walk southwest of the Glenbrook Visitor Centre (p142).

Wentworth Falls

As you head into the town of Wentworth Falls, you'll get your first real taste of Blue Mountains scenery: views to the south open out across the majestic Jamison Valley.

Wentworth Falls Reserve WATERFALL, PARK

(Falls Rd; Wentworth Falls) The falls that lend the town its name launch a plume of droplets over a 300m drop. This is the starting point of a network of walking tracks, which delve into the sublime Valley of the Waters, with waterfalls, gorges, woodlands and rainforests. Be sure to stretch your legs along the 1km return to Princes Rock which offers excellent views of Wentworth Falls and the Jamison Valley.

Leura

Leura is the Blue Mountains' prettiest town, fashioned around undulating streets, well-tended gardens and sweeping Victorian verandahs. Leura Mall, the tree-lined main street, offers rows of country craft stores and cafes for the daily tourist influx.

Sublime Point LOOKOUT

(Sublime Point Rd, Leura; P) South of Leura, this sharp, triangular outcrop narrows to a dramatic lookout with sheer cliffs on each side. We prefer it to Katoomba's more famous Echo Point, mainly because it's much, much quieter. On sunny days cloud shadows dance across the vast blue valley below.

Everglades Historic House & Gardens GARDENS

(☎ 02-4784 1938; www.everglades.org.au; 37 Everglades Ave, Leura; adult/child $10/4; ⏰10am-5pm) National Trust–owned Everglades was built in the 1930s. While the house is moderately interesting, the magnificent 5 hectares of garden created by Danish 'master gardener' Paul Sorenson are the real drawcard.

Leuralla NSW Toy & Railway Museum MUSEUM, GARDENS

(☎ 02-4784 1169; www.toyandrailwaymuseum.com.au; 36 Olympian Pde; adult/child $14/6, gardens only $10/5; ⏰10am-5pm) The art deco mansion that was once home to HV 'Doc' Evatt, the first UN president, is jam-packed with an incredible array of collectables – from grumpy Edwardian baby dolls to *Dr Who* figurines, to a rare set of Nazi propaganda toys. Railway memorabilia is scattered throughout the handsome gardens.

Katoomba

Swirling, otherworldly mists, steep streets lined with art deco buildings, astonishing valley views and a quirky miscellany of restaurants, buskers, artists, homeless people, bawdy pubs and classy hotels – Katoomba, the biggest town in the mountains, manages to be bohemian and bourgeois, embracing and menacing all at once.

Echo Point LOOKOUT

(Three Sisters; Echo Point Rd, Katoomba) Echo Point's clifftop viewing platform is the busiest spot in the Blue Mountains thanks to the views it offers of the area's most essential sight: a rocky trio called the **Three Sisters** (Echo Point, Echo Point Rd, Katoomba). The story goes that the sisters were turned to stone by a sorcerer to protect them from the unwanted advances of three young men, but the sorcerer died before he could turn them back into humans.

Warning: Echo Point draws vast, serenity-spoiling tourist gaggles, their idling buses farting fumes into the mountain air – arrive early or late to avoid them. The surrounding parking is expensive ($4.40 per hour), so park a few streets back and walk.

Waradah Aboriginal Centre CULTURAL CENTRE

(www.waradahaboriginalcentre.com.au; 33-37 Echo Point Rd; show adult/child $12/7; ⏰9am-5pm) Located in the World Heritage Plaza, this gallery and shop displays some exceptional examples of Aboriginal art alongside tourist tat like painted boomerangs and didgeridoos. However, the main reason to visit is to catch one of the 15-minute shows. Held throughout the day, they provide an interesting and good-humoured introduction to Indigenous culture.

Scenic World CABLE CAR

(☎ 02-4780 0200; www.scenicworld.com.au; cnr Violet St & Cliff Dr, Katoomba; adult/child $35/18; ⏰9am-5pm) Take the glass-floored Skyway gondola across the gorge and then ride what's billed as the steepest railway in the world down the 52-degree incline to the Jamison Valley floor. From here you can wander a 2.5km forest boardwalk (or hike the 12km, six-hour return track to the Ruined Castle rock formation) before catching a cable car back up the slope.

Blue Mountains Cultural Centre GALLERY

(www.bluemountainsculturalcentre.com.au; 30 Parke St; adult/child $5/free; ⏰10am-5pm) It's a captivating experience to walk through the World Heritage display, with a satellite image of the Blue Mountains beneath your feet, mountain scenery projected on the walls and ceiling, and bush sounds surrounding you. The neighbouring gallery hosts interesting exhibitions and there's a great view from the roof terrace. Drop into the library for free internet access.

Paragon NOTABLE BUILDING

(www.facebook.com/TheParagonCafe; 65 Katoomba St; ⏰10am-4pm Sun-Fri, to 10.30pm Sat) It's not one of Katoomba's better eateries, but it's well worth dropping into this heritage-listed 1916 cafe for its fabulous period decor. The handmade chocolates are pretty good too. Make sure you wander through to the *Great Gatsby*–esque mirrored cocktail bar at the rear.

Blackheath

The crowds and commercial frenzy fizzle considerably 10km north of Katoomba in neat, petite Blackheath. The town measures up in the scenery stakes, and it's an excellent base for visiting the Grose and Megalong Valleys. East of town are **Evans Lookout** (Evans Lookout Rd) and **Govetts Leap Lookout** (Govetts Leap Rd), offering views of the highest falls in the Blue Mountains. To the northeast, via Hat Hill Rd, are **Pulpit Rock**, **Perrys Lookdown** and **Anvil Rock**. To the west and southwest lie the Kanimbla and Megalong Valleys, with spectacular views from **Hargraves Lookout** (Shipley Rd).

Bushwalking

For tips on walks to suit your level of experience and fitness call the National Parks' Blue Mountains Heritage Centre in Blackheath, or the information centres in Glenbrook or Katoomba. All three sell a variety of walk pamphlets, maps and books.

Note that the bush here is dense and that it can be easy to become lost – there have been deaths as a consequence. Always leave your name and walk plan with the Katoomba police or at the National Parks centre. The police, National Parks and information centres all offer free personal locator beacons and it's strongly suggested you take one with you, especially for longer hikes. Remember to carry clean drinking water and plenty of food.

The two most popular bushwalking areas are the Jamison Valley, south of Katoomba, and the Grose Valley, northeast of Katoomba and east of Blackheath. The **Golden Stairs Walk** (Glenraphael Dr, Katoomba) is a less-congested route to the Ruined Castle than the track leading from Scenic World (p138). To get there, continue along Cliff Dr from Scenic World for 1km and look for Glenraphael Dr on your left. It quickly becomes rough and unsealed. Watch out for the signs to the Golden Stairs on the left after a couple of kilometres. It is a steep, exhilarating trail down into the valley (about 8km, five hours return).

One of the most rewarding long-distance walks is the 45km, three-day **Six Foot Track** from Katoomba along the Megalong Valley to Cox's River and on to the Jenolan Caves. It has camp sites along the way.

Cycling

The mountains are also a popular cycling destination, with many people taking their bikes on the train to Woodford and then cycling downhill to Glenbrook, a ride of two to three hours. Cycling maps are available from the visitor centres.

Adventure Activities & Tours

Blue Mountains Adventure Company ADVENTURE SPORTS
(☎02-4782 1271; www.bmac.com.au; 84a Bathurst Rd, Katoomba; ⏲8am-7pm) Abseiling from $150, abseiling and canyoning combo from $195, canyoning from $150, bushwalking from $30 and rock climbing from $195.

High 'n' Wild Australian Adventures ADVENTURE SPORTS
(☎02-4782 6224; www.highandwild.com.au; Blue Mountains YHA, 207 Katoomba St, Katoomba) Guided abseiling/rock climbing/canyoning from $135/169/190.

Australian School of Mountaineering ADVENTURE SPORTS
(☎02-4782 2014; www.asmguides.com; 166 Katoomba St, Katoomba) Abseiling/canyoning/bushcraft/rock climbing from $165/180/195/195.

River Deep Mountain High ADVENTURE SPORTS
(☎02-4782 6109; www.rdmh.com.au) Offers abseiling (from $150), canyoning (from $150) and canyoning and abseiling packages ($195), plus a range of hiking and mountain-biking tours.

Tread Lightly Eco Tours ECOTOUR
(☎0414 976 752; www.treadlightly.com.au) Has a wide range of day and night walks ($65 to $135) and 4WD tours that emphasise the region's ecology.

Aboriginal Blue Mountains Walkabout CULTURAL TOUR
(☎0408 443 822; www.bluemountainswalkabout.com; tour $95) Full-day Indigenous-owned and -guided adventurous trek with a spiritual theme; starts at Faulconbridge train station and ends at Springwood station.

Festivals & Events

Yulefest FESTIVAL
(www.yulefest.com) Out-of-kilter Christmas-style celebrations between June and August.

WORTH A TRIP

BELLS LINE OF ROAD

This stretch of road between North Richmond and Lithgow is the most scenic route across the Blue Mountains and is highly recommended if you have your own transport. It's far quieter than the highway and offers bountiful views.

Bilpin, at the base of the mountains, is known for its apple orchards. The Bilpin Markets are held at the district hall every Saturday from 10am to noon.

Midway between Bilpin and Bell, the **Blue Mountains Botanic Garden Mount Tomah** (02-4567 3000; www.rbgsyd.nsw.gov.au; 9.30am-5.30pm) FREE is a cool-climate annexe of Sydney's Royal Botanic Garden where native plants cuddle up to exotic species, including some magnificent rhododendrons.

To access Bells Line from central Sydney, head over the Harbour Bridge and take the M2 and then the M7 (both have tolls). Exit at Richmond Rd, which becomes Blacktown Rd, then Lennox Rd, then (after a short dog-leg) Kurrajong Rd and finally Bells Line of Road.

Winter Magic Festival FESTIVAL
(www.wintermagic.com.au) This one-day festival, held at the winter solstice in June, sees Katoomba's main street taken over by market stalls, costumed locals and performances.

Leura Gardens Festival GARDENS
(www.leuragardensfestival.com; all gardens $20, single garden $5) Green-thumbed tourists flock to Leura during October, when 10 private gardens are open to the public.

Sleeping

There's a good range of accommodation in the Blue Mountains, but you'll need to book ahead during winter and for Friday and Saturday nights (Sydneysiders love coming here for romantic weekends away). Leafy Leura is your best bet for romance, while Blackheath is a good base for hikers; both are better choices than built-up Katoomba, although it does have excellent hostels.

Leura

★**Broomelea** B&B $$
(02-4784 2940; www.broomelea.com.au; 273 Leura Mall; r $180-200; @) The consummate romantic Blue Mountains B&B, this Edwardian house offers four-poster beds, manicured gardens, cane furniture on the verandah, an open fire and a snug lounge. There's also a self-contained cottage for families.

Greens of Leura B&B $$
(02-4784 3241; www.thegreensleura.com.au; 24-26 Grose St; r $175-220; @) On a quiet street parallel to the Mall, this pretty timber house set in a lovely garden offers five rooms named after English writers (Browning, Austen etc). All are individually decorated; some have four-poster beds and spas.

Katoomba

★**Blue Mountains YHA** HOSTEL $
(02-4782 1416; www.yha.com.au; 207 Katoomba St; dm $30, d with/without bathroom $112/99; @) Behind the austere brick exterior of this popular 200-bed hostel are dorms and family rooms that are comfortable, light-filled and spotlessly clean. Facilities include a lounge (with an open fire), a pool table, an excellent communal kitchen and an outdoor space with barbecues.

No 14 HOSTEL $
(02-4782 7104; www.no14.com.au; 14 Lovel St; dm $28, r with/without bathroom $89/79; @) Resembling a cheery share house, this small hostel has a friendly vibe and helpful managers. There's no TV, so guests actually tend to talk to each other. A basic breakfast and internet access is included in the rates.

Flying Fox HOSTEL $
(02-4782 4226; www.theflyingfox.com.au; 190 Bathurst Rd; camp sites per person $20, dm $28-30, r $80-85;) The owners are travellers at heart and have endowed this unassuming hostel with an endearing home-away-from-home feel. There's no party scene here – just mulled wine and Tim Tams in the lounge, free breakfasts and a weekly pasta night.

Shelton-Lea B&B $$
(02-4782 9883; www.sheltonlea.com; 159 Lurline St; r $130-210;) This homely mountain cottage has been tweaked to create four suites, each with its own sitting area and kitchenette. There's a hint of art deco in the decor and lots of frilly furnishings.

Lilianfels HOTEL **$$$**
(☎02-4780 1200; www.lilianfels.com.au; 5-19 Lilianfels Ave; r from $229;) Right next to Echo Point and enjoying spectacular views, this luxury resort has 85 guest rooms, the region's top-rated restaurant (Darley's; three courses $125) and an indulgent array of facilities including spa, heated indoor and outdoor pools, tennis court, billiards/games room, library and gym.

Blackheath

Jemby-Rinjah Eco Lodge CABINS **$$$**
(☎02-4787 7622; www.jemby.com.au; 336 Evans Lookout Rd; from $215) These eco-cabins are lodged so deeply in the bottlebrush you'll have to bump into one to find it. All of the one- and two-bedroom weatherboard cabins are self-equipped; the deluxe model also has a Japanese hot tub.

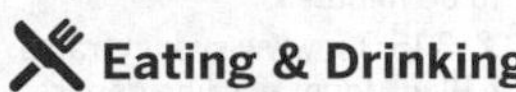

Eating & Drinking

Wentworth Falls

Nineteen23 MODERN AUSTRALIAN **$$$**
(☎0488 361 923; www.nineteen23.com.au; 1 Lake St; 2/3 courses $60/75; ⊙noon-3pm Sat & Sun, 6-10pm Thu-Sun) Wearing its 1920s ambience with aplomb, this elegant dining room is a particular favourite with loved-up couples happy to gaze into each other's eyes over a lengthy degustation. While the food isn't particularly experimental, it's beautifully cooked and bursting with flavour.

Leura

Leura Gourmet Cafe & Deli DELI **$**
(☎02-4784 1438; 159 Leura Mall; ⊙8am-5pm Mon-Fri; Leura) Perfect picnic prep with gourmet salads, pies and quiches to go. Local food enthusiasts will want to shop up on local jams, olive oils and vinegars. The great gelato selection is brilliant for bribing kids on a bushwalk and the attached cafe has impressive views.

Leura Garage MEDITERRANEAN **$$**
(☎02-4784 3391; www.leuragarage.com.au; 84 Railway Pde; lunch $17-28, shared plates $13-33; ⊙noon-late Thu-Mon) If you were in any doubt that this hip cafe-bar was once a garage, the suspended mufflers and stacks of old tyres press the point. At dinner the menu shifts gears to rustic shared plates served on wooden slabs, including deli treat–laden pizza.

Cafe Madeleine CAFE **$$**
(www.josophans.com.au; 187a Leura Mall; mains $12-18; ⊙9am-5pm) The sister to a chocolate shop, Madeleine excels in sweet treats such as chocolate-drenched waffles, cakes and hot chocolates. Mind you, the eggy breakfasts and French-influenced savoury dishes are also excellent.

Silk's Brasserie MODERN AUSTRALIAN **$$$**
(☎02-4784 2534; www.silksleura.com; 128 Leura Mall; mains lunch $24-39, dinner $35-39; ⊙noon-3pm & 6-10pm) A warm welcome awaits at Leura's long-standing fine diner. Despite its contemporary approach, it's a brasserie at heart, so the serves are generous and flavoursome. Save room for the decadent desserts.

Alexandra Hotel PUB
(www.alexandrahotel.com.au; 62 Great Western Hwy) The Alex is a gem of an old pub. Join the locals competing at the pool table or listening to DJs and live bands on the weekend.

Katoomba

Sanwiye Korean Cafe KOREAN **$**
(☎0405 402 130; www.facebook.com/sanwiyekoreancafe; 177 Katoomba St; mains $10-16; ⊙11am-9.30pm Tue-Sun) In the sea of overpriced mediocrity that is the Katoomba dining scene, this tiny place distinguishes itself with fresh and tasty food made with love by the Korean owners.

True to the Bean CAFE **$**
(www.facebook.com/truetothebean; 123 Katoomba St; waffles $3-6; ⊙7am-5pm Mon-Sat, 8am-2pm Sun;) The Sydney obsession with single-estate coffee has made its way to Katoomba's main drag in the form of this tiny espresso bar. Food is limited to the likes of bircher muesli and waffles.

Bistro Niagara BISTRO **$$**
(☎02-4782 9530; www.facebook.com/BistroNiagara; 92 Bathurst Rd; mains $26; ⊙5.30pm-9.30pm Wed-Sun, 11am-10.30pm Sat & Sun; Katoomba) Serving up classics like bubbling double cheese souffle and banoffe pies this cosy mountain bistro is a hit with locals and travellers who are both given a cheery welcome by the staff. At the heart of the restaurant is the wood-fire oven which might be cooking up a suckling pig or a sticky apple and pear tarte tatin depending on the night. On weekends a casual lunch menu runs all afternoon which is perfect for hungry bushwalkers.

Blackheath

Vesta BISTRO **$$**
(www.vestablackheath.com.au; 33 Govetts Leap Rd, Blackheath; mains $30; ⏲4-10pm Wed & Thu, noon-10pm Fri-Sun) Feeling the sting of a Blue Mountain's cold snap? It's easy to warm up with Vesta's century-old wood-fired bakery oven roaring in the background serving up hearty plates of roasted meats (all free range, grass fed and local) and bottles of Aussie wines to a boisterous crowd of locals.

Ashcrofts EUROPEAN **$$$**
(☎02-4787 8297; www.ashcrofts.com; 18 Govetts Leap Rd, Blackheath; mains $40; ⏲6-10pm Thu-Sun, noon-3pm & 6-10pm Sun) This acclaimed restaurant may have new owners but it still retains its excellent reputation as a longtime mountains favourite. The snug dining room is a charming spot to dip into the short, but polished menu which changes seasonally and favours creative pairings such as venison with beetroot, parsnip and dark chocolate.

Information

Blue Mountains Heritage Centre (☎02-4787 8877; www.nationalparks.nsw.gov.au/Blue-Mountains-National-Park; end of Govetts Leap Rd, Blackheath; ⏲9am-4.30pm) The extremely helpful, official NPWS visitor centre.

Echo Point Visitors Centre (☎1300 653 408; www.bluemountainscitytourism.com.au; Echo Point, Katoomba; ⏲9am-5pm) A sizeable centre with can-do staff.

Glenbrook Information Centre (☎1300 653 408; www.bluemountainscitytourism.com.au; Great Western Hwy; ⏲8.30am-4pm; 📶)

Getting There & Around

To reach the Blue Mountains by road, leave Sydney via Parramatta Rd. At Strathfield detour onto the toll-free M4, which becomes the Great Western Hwy west of Penrith and takes you to all of the Blue Mountains towns. It takes approximately 1½ hours to drive from central Sydney to Katoomba. A scenic alternative is the Bells Line of Road (p140).

Blue Mountains Bus (☎02-4751 1077; www.bmbc.com.au; fares $2.40-4.70) Connects the main towns.

Blue Mountains Explorer Bus (☎1300 300 915; www.explorerbus.com.au; 283 Bathurst Rd, Katoomba; adult/child $40/20; ⏲9.45am-5pm) Offers hop-on, hop-off service on a Katoomba–Leura loop. Leaves from Katoomba station every 30 to 60 minutes.

Sydney Trains (☎13 15 00; www.sydneytrains.info) Trains on the Blue Mountains line depart Sydney's Central Station approximately hourly for Glenbrook, Springwood, Faulconbridge, Wentworth Falls, Leura, Katoomba and Blackheath; allow two hours for Katoomba (adult/child $8.80/4.40).

Trolley Tours (☎1800 801 577; www.trolleytours.com.au; 76 Bathurst St, Katoomba; adult/child $25/15; ⏲9.45am-4.45pm) Runs a hop-on, hop-off bus barely disguised as a trolley, looping around 29 stops in Katoomba and Leura.

NSW Central Coast

Includes ➡

Best Places to Eat

- ➡ Pearls on the Beach (p145)
- ➡ Edwards (p150)
- ➡ Subo (p150)
- ➡ Muse Kitchen (p155)

Best Places to Stay

- ➡ Longhouse (p155)
- ➡ Thistle Hill (p154)
- ➡ Junction Hotel (p149)

Why Go?

After limping through the traffic of Sydney's northern suburbs it would be forgivable to make a break for the freeway as soon as it begins. Truth be told, much of the heavily populated Central Coast is a family-orientated suburbia-on-sea. But if you only have a couple of days to escape the big smoke, you will find some delightful diversions along this 100km stretch of coast. There are golden surf beaches, hidden hamlets and languid inland lakes, the largest of which, Lake Macquarie, covers four times the area of Sydney Harbour. And what it lacks in culture and gourmet goodies can be found in rollicking Newcastle and the hedonistic wine country of the Hunter Valley.

When to Go

Newcastle

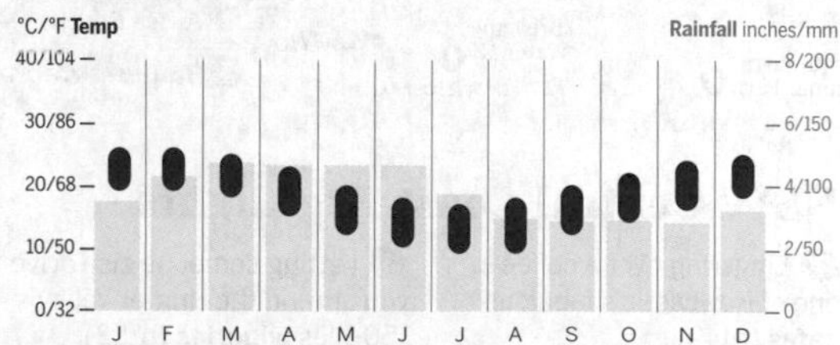

Jan–Mar Late summer brings Surfest and craft beer to Newcastle and music to the Hunter Valley.

May–Jul Migrating whales and a whole month of wine and food celebrations in the Hunter.

Oct–Dec Wine and jazz, spectacular Christmas lights and one of Australia's biggest emerging arts festivals.

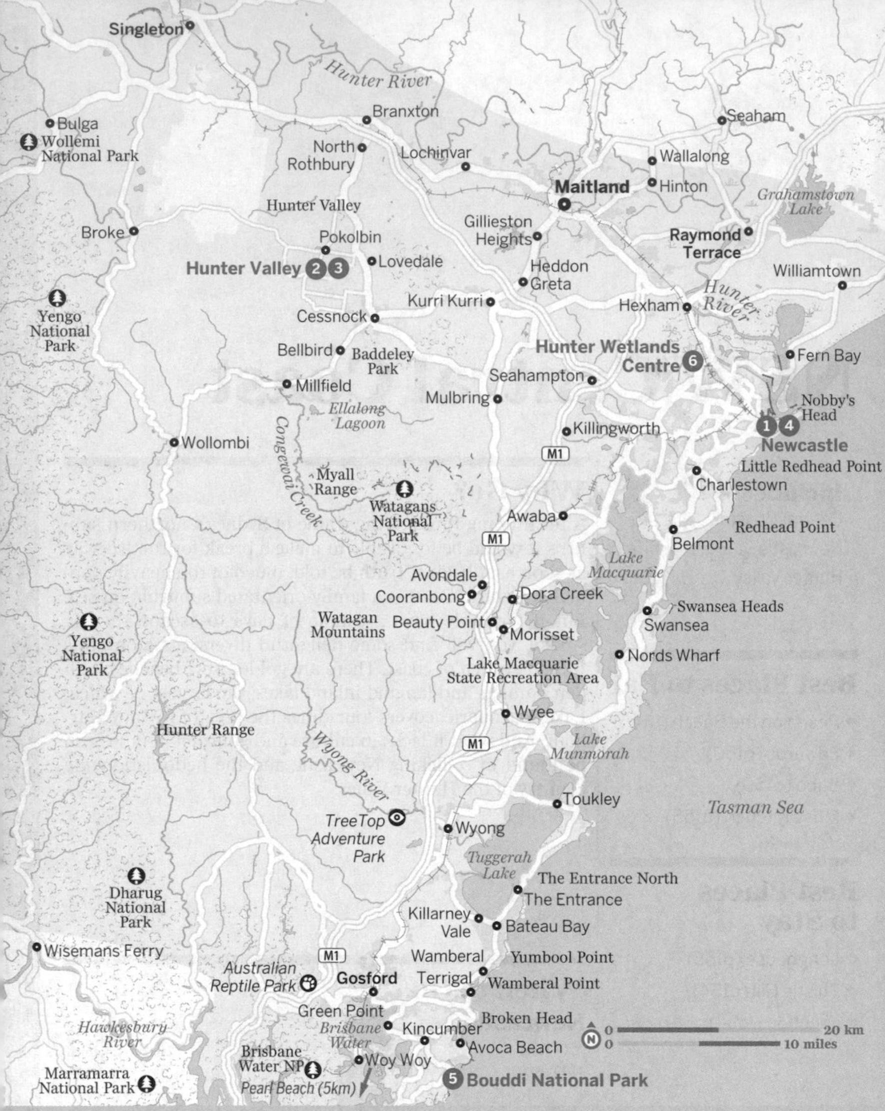

NSW Central Coast Highlights

❶ Lingering over a coffee in one of Newcastle's fabulous **cafes** (p149).

❷ Enjoying some old rockers, old wine and (smelly) old cheese at a big event in the **Hunter Valley** (p154).

❸ Letting someone else drive you around the Hunter Valley's 150-plus **wineries** (p152).

❹ Diving into the icy waters of the art deco **Newcastle Ocean Baths** (p147).

❺ Watching migrating whales from your tent in the **Bouddi National Park** (p145).

❻ Cruising the **Hunter Wetlands Centre** (p147) by canoe, bike or Segway.

CENTRAL COAST

You can choose to head straight up the M1 Pacific Motorway freeway to Newcastle (via various Central Coast exits) or meander along the coast. The largest town in the area is the transport and services hub of **Gosford**. Relaxed **Avoca** has a lovely beach and an old cinema, while **Terrigal** has a beautiful crescent-shaped beach with good surf, a bustling town centre and a variety of top spots to refuel. A series of saltwater 'lakes' spreads north up the coast between Bateau Bay and Newcastle, including the deep, placid waters of **Lake Macquarie**.

Sights

Australian Reptile Park ZOO
(☎02-4340 1022; www.reptilepark.com.au; Pacific Hwy, Somersby; adult/child $33/17; ⊙9am-5pm) Get up close to koalas and pythons, watch funnel-web spiders being milked (for the production of antivenin) and a Galapagos tortoise being fed. There are wonderful tours for kids.

Brisbane Water National Park NATIONAL PARK
(☎02-4320 4200; www.nationalparks.nsw.gov.au/brisbane-water-national-park; Woy Woy Rd, Kariong; vehicle access at Girrakool & Somersby Falls picnic areas $7) Bordering the Hawkesbury River southwest of Gosford, this park is known for its spring wild flowers and rambling cycling and walking trails. The Bulgandry Aboriginal Engraving Site is situated 3km south of the Central Coast Hwy on Woy Woy Rd. A favourite retreat for Sydneysiders is the pretty village of **Pearl Beach**, on the southeastern edge of the park.

Bouddi National Park NATIONAL PARK
(☎02-4320 4200; www.nationalparks.nsw.gov.au/bouddi-national-park; vehicle access $7) A spectacular park where short walking trails lead to isolated beaches and dramatic lookouts from where you can experience the annual whale migration between June and November. There are camp sites (per two people $20 to $28) at Little Beach, Putty Beach and Tallow Beach; book ahead. Only the Putty Beach site has drinkable water and flush toilets.

TreeTop Adventure Park AMUSEMENT PARK
(☎02-4025 1008; www.treetopadventurepark.com.au; 1 Red Hill Rd, Wyong Creek; adult/child from $45/35; ⊙9am-6pm Mon-Fri, to 4.30pm Sat & Sun Sep-Apr, 9am-6pm Oct-Mar) Zip fast and furious through the canopy of the Ourimbah State Forest at this high-thrills adventure park which features over 100 challenging courses including the world's longest roller-coaster zip line.

Sleeping & Eating

Tiarri MOTEL $$
(☎02-4384 1423; www.tiarriterrigal.com.au; 16 Tiarri Cres, Terrigal; r/ste $145/190;) This boutique motel in a quiet street on the slopes above Terrigal has clean, modern and comfortable rooms; the upstairs ones open onto a little bush-shaded terrace. Adults only.

Crowne Plaza Terrigal HOTEL $$
(☎02-4384 9111, 1800 007 697; www.crowneplaza.com.au; Pine Tree Lane; d from $180) The hub of Terrigal's tourist trade, this monolith has some plush rooms with great views over the beach. There are a couple of restaurants, a gym, a spa and a sauna, too. Rates fluctuate radically with season and availability.

Woy Woy Fishermen's Wharf SEAFOOD $$
(☎02-4341 1171; www.woywoyfishermenswharf.com.au; The Boulevarde, Woy Woy; mains $27; ⊙takeaway 11am-4pm Sun-Wed, to 7pm Thu-Sat, restaurant noon-3pm Sun-Wed, to late Thu-Sat) The Cregan family have been serving their outstanding fish and chips since 1974. Munch in the park (like the pelicans who are fed daily at 3pm), or take a table at their smart restaurant which dangles out over the water.

Pearls on the Beach MODERN AUSTRALIAN $$$
(☎02-4342 4400; www.pearlsonthebeach.com.au; 1 Tourmaline Ave, Pearl Beach; mains $39; ⊙noon-2.30pm & 6-10pm Thu-Sun) The comfortable whitewashed cottage right on the sand at Pearl Beach is an idyllic place to share simple, flavourful dishes at this highly rated restaurant. Save room for the very tempting dessert menu.

Information

Central Coast Visitor Centre (☎02-4343 4444; www.visitcentralcoast.com.au; 52 The Avenue, Kariong; ⊙9am-5pm Mon-Fri, 9.30am-3.30pm Sat & Sun)

Gosford Visitor Centre (☎02-4343 4444; 200 Mann St; ⊙9.30am-4pm Mon-Fri, to 1.30pm Sat)

Lake Macquarie Visitor Centre (☎02-4921 0740; www.visitlakemac.com.au; 228 Pacific Hwy, Swansea; ⊙9am-5pm Mon-Fri, to 4pm Sat & Sun)

The Entrance Visitor Centre (☎02-4333 1966; Marine Pde; ⊙9am-5pm)

Getting There & Around

➡ Gosford is a stop on the Newcastle & Central Coast line, with frequent trains from Sydney and Newcastle (both adults $8.10, children $4.05, 1½ hours). Trains also stop at Wondabyne within Brisbane Water National Park upon request (rear carriage only).

➡ Local buses connecting the various towns and beaches are operated by **Busways** (☎02-4368 2277; www.busways.com.au) and **Redbus** (☎02-4332 8655; www.redbus.com.au).

Newcastle

POP 546,788

For many years the port city of Newcastle has been on the brink of big things. Coal, steel and timber were its lifeblood but the cultural, the gastronomical and the creatively entrepreneurial have been on the rise for a long while, and now Newcastle's time has finally come.

Newcastle may be one-tenth the size of Sydney, but Australia's second-oldest city is punching well above its weight. Superb surf beaches, historical architecture and a sun-drenched climate are only part of the city's charms. There is fine dining, hip bars, quirky boutiques, and a diverse arts scene. And did we mention the laid-back attitude? Yes, Newcastle is definitely worth a day or two of your time.

Sights

City Centre

Christ Church Cathedral CHURCH
(☎02-4929 2052; www.newcastlecathedral.org.au; 52 Church St; ⏰7am-6pm) Dominating the city skyline, Newcastle's Anglican cathedral (built 1892) is filled with treasures like a gold chalice and remembrance book set with precious stones, made from jewellery donated by locals who lost loved ones in WWI. The self-guided tour brochure offers an insight into special features such as the stained-glass window by Edward Burne-Jones and William Morris.

Lock Up ARTS CENTRE
(☎02-4925 2265; www.thelockup.org.au; 90 Hunter St; ⏰10am-4pm Wed-Sat, 11am-3pm Sun) FREE These days artists in residence, rather than prisoners, are incarcerated in this former police station (1861). There's a dynamic contemporary art program, artists studios and creepy jail-house relics like the well-preserved padded cell, where the leather walls are stuffed with horsehair.

Newcastle Art Gallery GALLERY
(☎02-4974 5100; www.nag.org.au; 1 Laman St; ⏰10am-5pm Tue-Sun) FREE Ignore the brutalist exterior as inside this remarkable regional gallery are more than 5000 wonderful works; highlights include art by Newcastle-born William Dobell and John Olsen as well as Brett Whiteley and modernist Grace Cossington Smith.

Newcastle East

★**Fort Scratchley** HISTORIC SITE
(☎02-4974 5033; www.fortscratchley.com.au; Nobbys Rd; tours adult/child $15/7.50; ⏰10am-4pm Wed-Mon, last tour 2.30pm) FREE Perched above Newcastle Harbour, this fascinating military site was constructed during the Crimean War to protect the city against a feared Russian invasion. During WWII the fort returned fire on a Japanese submarine, making it the only Australian fort to have engaged in a maritime attack. Learn all about it on a guided tour of the fort and its labyrinth of underground tunnels.

Nobby's Head WATERFRONT
Originally an island, this headland at the entrance to Newcastle's harbour was joined to the mainland by a stone breakwater built by convicts between 1818 and 1846; many of those poor souls were lost to the wild seas during its construction. The walk along the spit towards the lighthouse and meteorological station is exhilarating.

Bathers Way WATERFRONT
(www.visitnewcastle.com.au/pages/bathers-way) This scenic coastal path from Nobby's Beach to Glenrock Reserve winds past swathes of beach and fascinating historical sites including Fort Scratchley and the Convict Lumber Yard. Interpretative signs describing Indigenous, convict and natural history dot the 5km trail. Look out for the **Merewether 'Aquarium'**, a pedestrian tunnel which has been transformed into a pop art underwater world by local artist Trevor Dixon.

Honeysuckle Precinct

Newcastle Museum MUSEUM
(☎02-4974 1400; www.newcastlemuseum.com.au; 6 Workshop Way; ⏰10am-5pm Tue-Sun) FREE This attractive museum in the restored Honeysuckle rail workshops tells a tale of

WORTH A TRIP

NEWCASTLE NATURE RESERVES

Hunter Wetlands Centre (02-4951 6466; www.wetlands.org.au; 412 Sandgate Rd, Shortland; adult/child $5/2; 9am-4pm) Transformed from a dump and abandoned sporting fields into a magnificent conservation sanctuary, this swampy centre is home to over 200 species of birds, including magpie geese, freckled ducks and egrets, and a huge diversity of animal residents. To get here, take the Pacific Hwy towards Maitland and turn left at the cemetery, or catch the train to Sandgate and walk (10 minutes).

Extensive walking and bike trails criss-cross the site, or you can hire a canoe ($10 for two hours) and paddle along picturesque Ironbank Creek. The popular Segway tours are also a fun way to quietly view the animals.

Blackbutt Reserve (02-4904 3344; www.newcastle.nsw.gov.au/recreation/blackbutt_reserve; Carnley Ave, Kotara; park 7am-7pm, wildlife exhibits 10am-5pm) Sitting in a tract of bushland with plenty of walking trails and picnic areas, this council-run reserve has enclosures of native critters: koalas, wallabies, wombats and a cacophonic chorus of native birds. It's a short walk from Kotara train station.

the city from its Indigenous Awabakal origins to its rough-and-tumble social history, shaped by a cast of convicts, coal miners and steelworkers. Exhibitions are interactive and engaging. If you're travelling with kids check out Supernova, the hands-on science centre.

Maritime Centre MUSEUM
(02-4929 2588; www.maritimecentrenewcastle.org.au; Lee Wharf, 3 Honeysuckle Dr; adult/child $10/5; 10am-4pm Tue-Sun) Newcastle's nautical heritage is on show at the visitor centre.

Activities

Swimming & Surfing

At the east end of town, surfers and swimmers adore **Newcastle Beach**, but if you're irrationally paranoid about sharks, the **ocean baths** (Shortland Esplanade; 6am-9pm summer, 6am-4.30pm winter) FREE are a mellow alternative, encased in wonderful multicoloured art deco architecture. There's a shallow pool for toddlers and a backdrop of heaving ocean and chugging cargo ships. Surfers should goofy-foot it to **Nobby's Beach**, just north of the baths – the fast left-hander known as the Wedge is at its northern end.

South of Newcastle Beach, below King Edward Park, is Australia's oldest ocean bath, the convict-carved **Bogey Hole**. It's an atmospheric place to splash about when the surf's crashing over its edge. The most popular surfing breaks are at **Bar Beach** and **Merewether Beach**, further south.

The city's famous surfing festival, **Surfest** (www.surfest.com; Merewether Beach), takes place in February each year.

Walking & Cycling

The visitor centre has plenty of brochures outlining self-guided themed tours of the city. These include the *Bather's Way,* and the *Newcastle East Heritage Walk,* which heads past colonial highlights in the city centre. The *Newcastle by Design* brochure outlines a short stroll down and around Hunter St, covering some of the inner city's interesting architecture.

Festivals & Events

Craft Beer Week FOOD
(www.newcastlecraftbeerweek.com; Mar) There's an active local brewing scene in Newcastle and this annual celebration of all things craft beer features events in venues around Newcastle, Maitland and Lake Macquarie.

This is Not Art Festival ART
(TiNA; 02-4927 0675; octapod.org/tina; early Oct) In early October, an independent arts and new media festival for emerging and established writers, artists and music makers.

Sleeping

Newcastle Beach YHA HOSTEL $
(02-4925 3544; www.yha.com.au; 30 Pacific St; dm/s/d $33/55/80;) It may have the look of a grand English mansion but this heritage-listed YHA has the ambience of a laid-back beach bungalow. Just a bikini strap away from the surf, there's complimentary bodyboard use, surfboard hire, plus several free pub meals each week.

Stockton Beach Holiday Park CAMPGROUND $
(02-4928 1393; www.stocktonbeach.com; 3 Pitt St; sites/cabins from $55/174;)

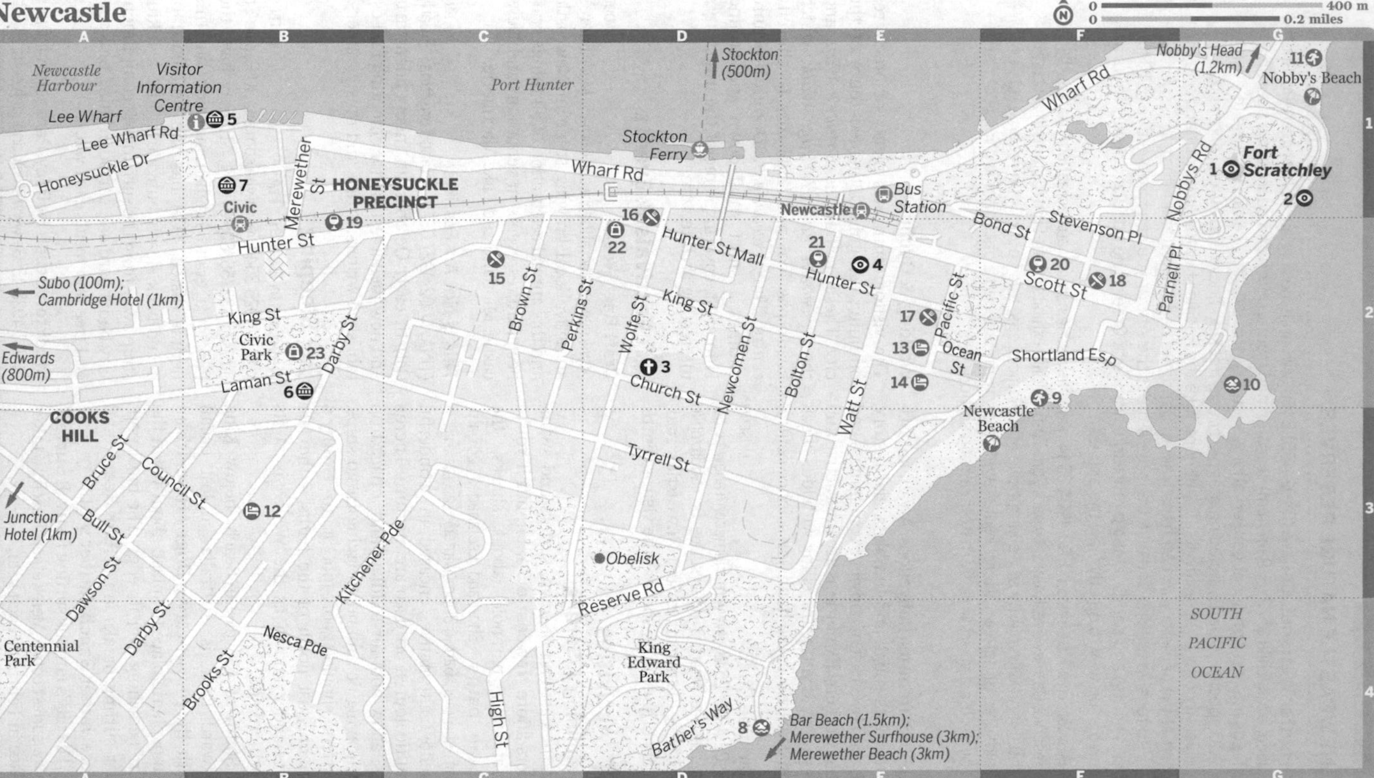
Newcastle
400 m
0.2 miles
Newcastle Harbour
Visitor Information Centre
Lee Wharf
Lee Wharf Rd
Honeysuckle Dr
Merewether St
HONEYSUCKLE PRECINCT
Civic
Hunter St
Port Hunter
Stockton (500m)
Stockton Ferry
Wharf Rd
Bus Station
Newcastle
Nobby's Head (1.2km)
Nobby's Beach
Fort Scratchley
Nobbys Rd
Bond St
Stevenson Pl
Parnell Pl
Hunter St Mall
Scott St
King St
Pacific St
Ocean St
Shortland Esp
Newcastle Beach
Subo (100m); Cambridge Hotel (1km)
Edwards (800m)
Civic Park
Laman St
Darby St
Brown St
Perkins St
Wolfe St
Newcomen St
Bolton St
Watt St
Church St
Tyrrell St
COOKS HILL
Bruce St
Council St
Bull St
Junction Hotel (1km)
Dawson St
Darby St
Centennial Park
Brooks St
Nesca Pde
Kitchener Pde
Obelisk
Reserve Rd
High St
King Edward Park
Bather's Way
Bar Beach (1.5km); Merewether Surfhouse (3km); Merewether Beach (3km)
SOUTH PACIFIC OCEAN

Newcastle

The beach is at your doorstep (or should that be tent flap?) at this tourist park behind the dunes in Stockton, a short ferry ride across from Newcastle. With large, grassy camp sites, en suites for vans and smart, newly built two- and three bed villas, it's a flash place to park yourself for a couple of days.

Junction Hotel BOUTIQUE HOTEL $$
(☎02-4962 8888; www.junctionhotel.com.au; 204 Corlette St; r from $129;) The upstairs of this suburban pub has been transformed with nine flamboyantly appointed rooms featuring African animal themes and wacky colours. All have generous-sized beds and flashy bathrooms with disco lights and little privacy. Well located among the Junction's boutiques and cafes, it's just a 10-minute walk to the beach.

Crown on Darby APARTMENTS $$
(☎02-4941 6777; www.crownondarby.com.au; 101 Darby St; apt from $140;) If giant TV screens, comfy beds and proximity to good coffee are your accommodation yardstick, consider this modern complex of 38 apartments on Newcastle's coolest street. The studios are bigger than your average hotel room and have kitchenettes, while the one- to four-bedroom apartments have full kitchens and generous living rooms.

Novotel Newcastle Beach HOTEL $$$
(☎02-4032 3700; novotelnewcastlebeach.com.au; 5 King St; r from $287;) What the Novotel's studio rooms lack in size they make up for in style. There's no pool, but the beach is just across the road, and there is a small gym. Accommodation and breakfast are free for kids under 16.

Eating

Darby and Beaumont are the main eat streets and there are also plenty of restaurants along the waterfront. The **Newcastle City Farmers Market** (www.newcastlecityfarmersmarket.com.au; Newcastle Showground, Griffiths Rd; 8am-1pm Sun, 2.30-9pm Wed) is held twice a week.

One Penny Black Espresso CAFE $
(☎02-4929 3169; www.onepennyblack.com.au; 196 Hunter St; mains $12; 7am-4.30pm) Perpetually popular for a reason, you'll probably have to queue for an excellent espresso or filter coffee served by staff who know their stuff. Devotees also rave about the toasties and fabulous breakfast platters.

Napoli Centrale Pizza Bar PIZZA $$
(☎02-4023 2339; www.napolicentrale.com.au; 173 King St; mains $20; 11am-10pm Tue-Sat) This understated pizza and pasta joint is the new hotspot for locals craving wood-fired pizza. The sparsely topped, crisply based pies are so authentic they feature imported Neapolitan flour and San Marzano tomatoes. Bookings are essential, or you can grab a takeaway from the window and eat on the beach.

Scottie's Fish Cafe SEAFOOD $$
(☎02-4926 3780; www.scottiescafe.com.au; 36 Scott St; mains $28; 11am-9pm Mon-Fri, 8am-9pm Sat & Sun) Pull up a seat under palm trees laced with colourful festoon lighting and settle in for a classy take on the classic fish and chippery.

Merewether Surfhouse CAFE, RESTAURANT **$$**
(☎02-4918 0000; www.surfhouse.com.au; Henderson Pde; mains cafe $15-20, bar $19, restaurant $35; ⊙cafe & pizza shop 7am-late, restaurant 11.30am-late Wed-Sat, to 4pm Sun) Watch the action on Merewether Beach from one of the many spaces in this architecturally notable complex. The swanky promenade cafe offers coffee and lazy breakfasts. Later in the day there's $10 pizza and gelato, or head to the top floor where the restaurant, with its floor-to-ceiling windows, nails surf and turf at fine dining prices.

★**Edwards** MODERN AUSTRALIAN **$$$**
(☎02-4965 3845; www.theedwards.com.au; 148 Parry St; mains $35; ⊙10am-midnight Tue-Sat, to 10pm Sun) If new Newcastle had a beating heart, it would be found at this happening bar-cafe-diner. It's the place to be at all hours for delicious egg breakfasts, share plates from the wood-fired oven and late-night bar snacks.

Co-owned by Silverchair bass player Chris Joannou, this fabulous industrial space used to be a drive-through dry cleaners (you can still throw your dirty clothes in the coin laundry).

★**Subo** MODERN AUSTRALIAN **$$$**
(☎02-4023 4048; www.subo.com.au; 551d Hunter St; 5 courses $85; ⊙6-10pm Wed-Sun) Book in advance for a table at tiny Subo, an innovative, highly lauded restaurant serving light, exquisite food with a contemporary French influence. The restaurant exclusively serves a five-course menu that changes seasonally.

Restaurant Mason FRENCH **$$$**
(☎02-4926 1014; www.restaurantmason.com; 3/35 Hunter St; mains breakfast $18-21, lunch $20-36, dinner $35-42; ⊙noon-3.30pm & 6pm-late Tue-Fri, 8am-3pm & 6pm-late Sat; ✎) There's a summery feel to this modern French fine-dining restaurant, with tables placed under the plane trees outside and a main dining space that opens to the elements. Dishes make the most of fresh local produce.

Drinking & Entertainment

★**Coal & Cedar** BAR
(coalandcedar.com; 380-382 Hunter St; ⊙4pm-late Tue-Sun) Pull up a stool at the long wooden bar in this Prohibition-era styled speakeasy; in the early days it was so underground they didn't even publish the address. Now the secret is out, you'll find Newcastle's finest drinking potent whiskies to a blues soundtrack.

Reserve Wine Bar WINE BAR
(☎02-4929 3393; reservewinebar.com.au; 102 Hunter St; ⊙noon-8pm Tue, to late Wed-Fri, 3pm-late Sat) Calling itself a 'grape emporium', this bar in a former bank has over 350 different wines in the vault, with many a drop from Newcastle's Hunter Valley backyard. Enjoy your tipple with a bite from the decadent grazing menu.

Grain Store BREWERY
(☎02-4023 2707; www.grainstorenewcastle.com.au; 64 Scott St; ⊙11.30am-11pm Tue-Sat, to 9pm Sun) Once the grain and keg store for the old Tooheys beer factory, this rustic brewery cafe is an atmospheric place to refresh with one of the 21 eclectic Australian brewed craft beers on tap.

Cambridge Hotel LIVE MUSIC
(www.yourcambridge.com; 789 Hunter St) A backpacker favourite that launched Silverchair, Newcastle's most famous cultural export, and continues to showcase touring bands and local acts.

Shopping

The city's cultural renaissance has been fuelled in part by the **Renew Newcastle** initiative that lends vacant spaces to artists. Wander down **Hunter Street Mall** to check out some of the boutiques and studios revitalising Newcastle.

Emporium ARTS, FASHION
(renewnewcastle.org/projects/project/the-emporium/; 185 Hunter St Mall; ⊙10am-4pm Wed & Sat, to 5pm Thu-Fri) On the ground floor of the former David Jones department store are boutiques and galleries filled with a treasure trove of locally made art, fashion, furniture and design.

Olive Tree Markets MARKET
(www.theolivetreemarket.com.au; Civic Park; ⊙9am-3pm 1st Sat of the month) FREE A contemporary handmade market with over 120 stalls run by an eclectic mix of local artists and designers.

Information

As well as at the public libraries, you can access free wi-fi in Hunter Street Mall, the Honeysuckle Precinct, Hamilton's Beaumont St and Newcastle Airport.

John Hunter Hospital (☎02-4921 3000; www.health.nsw.gov.au; Lookout Rd, New Lambton Heights) Has 24-hour emergency care.

Visitor Information Centre (☎02-4929 2588; www.visitnewcastle.com.au; Lee Wharf, 3 Honeysuckle Dr; ⊙10am-4pm Tue-Sun)

Getting There & Away

AIR

Newcastle Airport (02-4928 9800; www.newcastleairport.com.au) At Williamtown, 23km north of the city.

Jetstar (13 15 38; www.jetstar.com.au) Flies to/from Melbourne, the Gold Coast and Brisbane.

QantasLink (13 13 13; www.qantas.com.au) Flies to/from Brisbane.

Regional Express (Rex; 13 17 13; www.rex.com.au) Flies to/from Sydney and Ballina.

Virgin (13 67 89; www.virginaustralia.com) Flies to/from Brisbane and Melbourne.

BUS

Nearly all long-distance buses stop behind Newcastle train station.

Busways (02-4983 1560; www.busways.com.au) At least two buses daily to Tea Gardens ($20.10, 1½ hours), Hawks Nest ($20.50, 1¾ hours), Bluey's Beach ($28, two hours), Forster ($32, 3¼ hours) and Taree ($35, four hours).

Greyhound (1300 473 946; www.greyhound.com.au) Two daily coaches to/from Sydney ($31, 2¾ hours), Port Macquarie ($56, 4¾ hours), Coffs Harbour ($78, seven hours), Byron Bay ($127, 11½ hours) and Brisbane ($157, 14½ hours).

Port Stephens Coaches (02-4982 2940; www.pscoaches.com.au; adult/child $4.60/2.30) Regular buses to Anna Bay (1¼ hours), Nelson Bay (1½ hours), Shoal Bay (1½ hours) and Fingal Bay (two hours).

Premier Motor Service (13 34 10; www.premierms.com.au) Daily coaches to/from Sydney ($34, three hours), Port Macquarie ($47, 3¾ hours), Coffs Harbour ($58, six hours), Byron Bay ($71, 11 hours) and Brisbane ($76, 14½ hours).

Rover Coaches (02-4990 1699; www.rovercoaches.com.au) Four buses to/from Cessnock ($4.70, 1¼ hours) on weekdays and two on Saturday; no Sunday service.

TRAIN

Sydney Trains (13 15 00; www.sydneytrains.info) has regular services to Gosford ($8.10, 1½ hours) and Sydney ($8.10, three hours). A line also heads to the Hunter Valley; Branxton ($6.30, 50 minutes) is the closest stop to wine country.

Getting Around

TO/FROM THE AIRPORT

- Port Stephens Coaches has frequent buses stopping at the airport en route between Newcastle ($4.60, 40 minutes) and Nelson Bay ($4.60, one hour).
- A taxi to Newcastle city centre costs about $60.

Hunter Valley Day Tours (02-4951 4574; www.huntervalleydaytours.com.au) Provides shuttles to Newcastle ($35 for one person, $45 for two), the Hunter Valley ($125 for one or two people), Lake Macquarie and Port Stephens.

BUS

Newcastle has an extensive network of **local buses** (13 15 00; www.newcastlebuses.info). There's a fare-free bus zone in the inner city between 7.30am and 6pm. Otherwise you need to purchase a one-hour fare ($3.70) from the driver. The main depot is next to Newcastle train station.

FERRY

Stockton Ferry (adult/child $2.60/1.30) Leaves every half-hour from Queens Wharf from 5.15am to about 11pm.

TRAIN

Services leaving Newcastle station stop at Hamilton, Wickham and Civic before branching out to either Sydney or the Hunter Valley. Travel between these stations costs $3.30.

Hunter Valley

A filigree of narrow lanes criss-crosses this verdant valley, but a pleasant country drive isn't the main motivator for visitors – sheer decadence is. The Hunter is one big gorge fest: fine wine, boutique beer, chocolate, cheese, olives, you name it. Bacchus would surely approve.

Home to some of the oldest vines (1860s) and biggest names in Australian wine, the Hunter is known for its semillon, shiraz and, increasingly, chardonnay. If it's no longer the crowning jewel of the Australian wine industry, it still turns in some excellent vintages.

There is a new generation of winemakers exerting greater influence over the local styles and doing much to reinvigorate the local scene. These wineries are refreshingly attitude free and welcoming of novices. Staff will rarely give you the evil eye if you swirl your glass once too often, or don't conspicuously savour the bouquet.

While some vignerons deride the Disneyland aspect of the Hunter Valley, the region also offers everything from hot-air balloons and horse riding to open-air concerts. Accordingly, it is a hugely popular weekender for Sydney couples, wedding parties and groups of mates wanting to drink hard while someone else drives. Every Friday they descend and prices leap up accordingly.

Hunter Valley

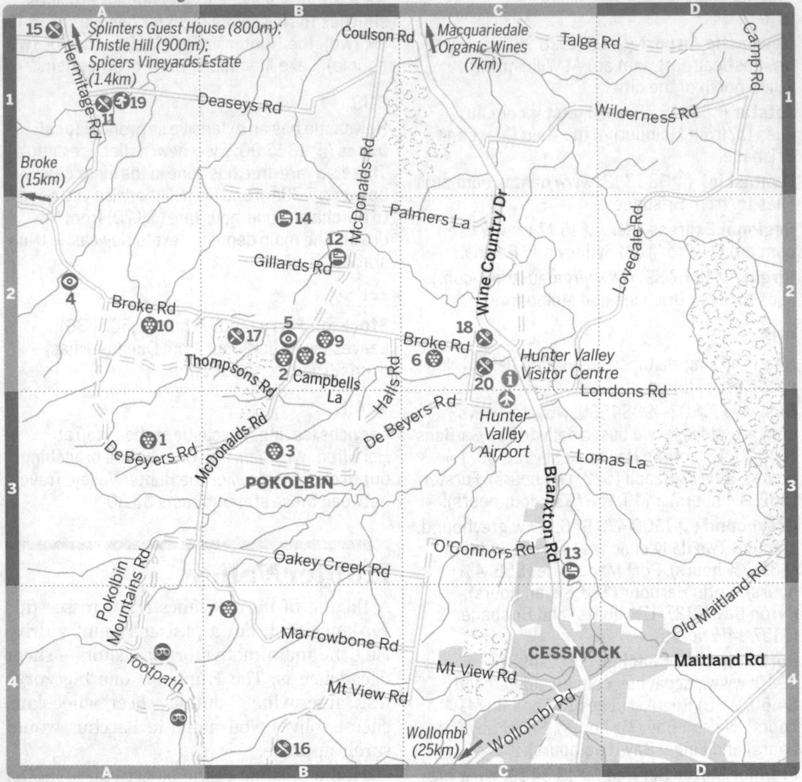

The Hunter Valley is exceedingly hot during summer so, like its shiraz, it's best enjoyed in the cooler months.

Sights & Activities

Most attractions lie in an area bordered to the north by the New England Hwy and to the south by Wollombi/Maitland Rd, with the main cluster of wineries and restaurants in Pokolbin (population 694). For spectacular views and a more chilled-out pace head to the vineyards northwest around Broke and Singleton.

The valley's 150-plus wineries range from small-scale, family-run affairs to massive commercial operations. Most offer free tastings, although some charge a small fee.

Grab a copy of the free *Hunter Valley Official Guide* from the visitor centre at Pokolbin and use its handy map to plot your course, or just follow your nose, hunting out the tucked-away small producers.

Tyrrell's Wines WINERY
(02-4993 7000; www.tyrrells.com.au; 1838 Broke Rd, Pokolbin; tours $5; 9am-5pm Mon-Sat, 10am-4pm Sun, winery tours 10.30am) Check out the Tyrrell's winemakers wall and it reads like a who's who of Australian viticulture. Having pioneered chardonnay growing in the valley, Tyrrell's is a fiercely independent, old-school vineyard (since 1858) with engaging wine tours.

James Estate WINERY
(02-6547 5168; www.jamesestatewines.com.au; 951 Bylong Valley Way, Baerami; 10am-4.30pm) Bordered by the Wollemi National Park and with sweeping panoramas of the Goulburn River, James Estate has a 4km ridge walk and purpose-built mountain bike tracks to enjoy before a tasting. The winery is at the very top of the Hunter Valley, a one hour drive northwest of Pokolbin.

Hunter Valley

Sights

1 Audrey Wilkinson Vineyard........ A3
2 Brokenwood........ B2
3 Cockfighter's Ghost........ B3
4 Hunter Distillery........ A2
5 Hunter Valley Gardens........ B2
6 Lake's Folly........ C2
7 Mount Pleasant........ B4
8 Small Winemakers Centre........ B2
9 Tempus Two........ B2
10 Tyrrell's Wines........ A2

Activities, Courses & Tours

11 Keith Tulloch Winery........ A1

Sleeping

12 Hermitage Lodge........ B2
13 Hunter Valley YHA........ C3
14 Longhouse........ B2

Eating

15 Binnorie Dairy........ A1
16 Bistro Molines........ B4
17 Enzo........ B2
Hunter Valley Cheese Company........ (see 5)
18 Hunter Valley Chocolate Company........ C2
Hunter Valley Smelly Cheese Shop........ (see 9)
19 Muse Kitchen........ A1
20 Muse Restaurant........ C2

Drinking & Nightlife

Goldfish Bar & Kitchen........ (see 9)

Audrey Wilkinson Vineyard WINERY

(02-4998 7411; www.audreywilkinson.com.au; 750 DeBeyers Rd, Pokolbin; 10am-5pm) Enjoy the expansive views with a picnic at this hilltop cellar door. It's a sublime setting for one of the oldest vineyards (first planted in 1866) and there's an interesting historic display.

Brokenwood WINERY

(02-4998 7559; www.brokenwood.com.au; 401-427 McDonalds Rd, Pokolbin; tours $30; 9.30am-5pm Mon-Sat, 10am-5pm Sun) Known for its single-vineyard semillon and shiraz, this acclaimed winery offers a fascinating behind-the-scenes tour where you can try wines in various stages of development.

Macquariedale Organic Wines WINERY

(02-6574 7012; www.macquariedale.com.au; 170 Sweetwater Rd, Belford; 10am-5pm) A boutique winemaker that's certified organic and biodynamic. The estate also grows garlic and olives.

Mount Pleasant WINERY

(02-4998 7505; www.mountpleasantwines.com.au; 401 Marrowbone Rd, Pokolbin; 10am-5pm, winery tour 11am) There is plenty to taste at one of the great historic estates of the Hunter. If you are looking to buy, Mt Pleasant offers well-priced introductions to the local styles.

Lake's Folly WINERY

(02-4998 7507; www.lakesfolly.com.au; 2416 Broke Rd, Pokolbin; 10am-4pm) Try the highly acclaimed cabernet blend and chardonnay which are both grown, vintaged and bottled on the estate. These small production wines tend to sell out so the cellar door is closed for around four months of the year. Call ahead.

Cockfighter's Ghost WINERY

(02-4993 3688; www.cockfightersghost.com.au; DeBeyers Rd, Pokolbin; 10am-5pm) A big player, producing the midpriced Cockfighter's Ghost range which you can taste at their contemporary cellar door.

Small Winemakers Centre WINERY

(02-4998 7668; www.smallwinemakerscentre.com.au; 426 McDonalds Rd, Pokolbin; 10am-5pm) Showcases more than 30 varieties of wines from great little estates which don't have their own cellar doors.

Tempus Two WINERY

(02-4993 3999; www.tempustwo.com.au; 2144 Broke Rd, Pokolbin; 10am-5pm) This sprawling complex is a favourite with tour buses which descend upon the cellar door, Japanese restaurant and Smelly Cheese Shop (p155). Meerea Park has a tasting room here, which is worth seeking out.

Hunter Distillery DISTILLERY

(02-4998 6737; www.hunterdistillery.com.au; 1686 Broke Rd, Polkolbin; tastings $5; 10am-5pm) Like wandering into a science lab; this distillery offers flavoured vodka tastings in test tube shots.

Hunter Valley Gardens GARDENS
(www.hvg.com.au; Broke Rd, Pokolbin; adult/child $2/15; 9am-5pm) A fairy tale of mazes and floral displays. Popular annual events include Snow Time in July and the Christmas Lights Spectacular.

Balloon Aloft BALLOONING
(02-4991 1955; www.balloonaloft.com; $279) Take to the skies for a sunrise hot-air balloon ride over the vineyards. Follow up with bubbles and breakfast at Peterson House Winery.

Tours

If no one's volunteering to stay sober enough to drive, don't worry; there are plenty of winery tours available. Some operators will collect you in Sydney or Newcastle for a lengthy day trip.

Hunter Valley Boutique Wine Tours WINERY TOUR
(0419 419 931; www.huntervalleytours.com.au) Small-group tours from $65 per person for a half-day (three cellars) and from $99 for a full day including lunch.

Aussie Wine Tours WINERY TOUR
(0402 909 090; www.aussiewinetours.com.au) Determine your own itinerary on one of these private, chauffeur-driven tours.

Kangarrific Tours WINERY TOUR
(0431 894 471; www.kangarrifictours.com; $115) This small-group tour departs from Sydney and promises the Hunter's most diverse itinerary. Taste everything from wine to gelato and have morning tea with the eponymous roos.

SENSIBLE SUPPING

DrinkWise Australia recommends that in order to comply with the breath-alcohol limit of 0.05, men who are driving should drink no more than two standard drinks in the first hour and then no more than one per hour after that (women, who tend to reach a higher blood-alcohol concentration faster than men, should drink only one standard drink in the first hour). Wineries usually offer 20mL tastes of wine – five of these equal one standard drink.

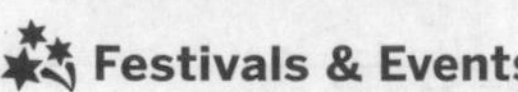

Festivals & Events

Superstars regularly drop by for weekend concerts at the bigger vineyards. If there's something special on, accommodation books up well in advance. Check what's on at www.winecountry.com.au.

A Day on the Green MUSIC
(www.adayonthegreen.com.au) Concert series at Bimbadgen Estate during summer.

Lovedale Long Lunch FOOD
(www.lovedalelonglunch.com.au) Seven wineries and chefs team up to serve huge lunches accompanied by music and art; third weekend of May.

Hunter Valley Wine & Food Month WINE, FOOD
(www.winecountry.com.au) In June.

Jazz in the Vines MUSIC
(www.jazzinthevines.com.au) Party in a paddock at Tyrrell's vineyard each October.

Sleeping

Prices shoot up savagely on Friday and Saturday nights and two-night minimum stays are common. Many places don't accept children.

Hunter Valley YHA HOSTEL $
(02-4991 3278; www.yha.com.au; 100 Wine Country Dr, Nulkaba; dm $32, r with/without bathroom $88/77;) At the end of a long day of wine tasting or grape picking (it's often busy during February with workers) there's plenty of bonhomie around the barbecue and pool at this recently refurbished hostel. There are bikes for hire and a brewery pub within walking distance. The rooms can get stiflingly hot, though.

Thistle Hill B&B $$
(02-6574 7217; www.thill.com.au; 591 Hermitage Rd, Pokolbin; r/cottages from $200/350;) This idyllic 10-hectare property features rose gardens, a lime orchard, a vineyard, a self-contained cottage sleeping up to five and a luxurious guesthouse with six double rooms. Rooms and common areas have an elegant French provincial sensibility.

Hermitage Lodge CABINS $$
(02-4998 7639; www.hermitagelodge.com.au; 609 McDonalds Rd, Polkolbin; r from $160;) Ideally located within walking distance of a variety of cellar doors, these bright, spacious studios and suites have

sunny decks overlooking a shiraz vineyard. There's a good northern Italian restaurant on-site. The entry level rooms are only a small step up from motel accommodation, but offer good value.

Splinters Guest House B&B $$
(☎ 02-6574 7118; www.splinters.com.au; 617 Hermitage Rd, Pokolbin; r/cottages from $200/240;) Gregarious owner Bobby Jory runs this tranquil B&B with great elan, spoiling guests with treats such as gourmet breakfasts, port and chocolates in rooms, and wine and cheese on the terrace. There are three smart doubles with comfortable beds, and two rustic self-catering cottages.

★ **Longhouse** APARTMENTS $$$
(☎ 0402 101 551; www.thelonghouse.net.au; 385 Palmers Lane, Pokolbin; apt from $299;) More than 50 architecture students designed this stylish pad, based on a traditional Australian wool shed. Made from concrete, corrugated iron and reclaimed timber, it is divided into three two-bed apartments with an incredible 48m deck. Feel good about your outlay knowing that 100% of the profits go towards architectural community aid projects.

Spicers Vineyards Estate RESORT $$$
(☎ 02-6574 7229; www.spicersgroup.com.au; 555 Hermitage Rd, Pokolbin; ste $395-495;) Surrounded by bushland these 12 luxury spa suites have king-size beds, complimentary minibar, and cosy lounge areas with open fireplace; a perfect spot for sipping shiraz in the winter. Unwind at the day spa or in the pool before a meal at the top-notch **Restaurant Botanica** (☎ 02-6574 7229; spicers retreats.com; 555 Hermitage Rd, Polkolbin; 2 courses $65, 3 courses $79; ⏲ 6-10pm daily, 11am-3pm Sat & Sun).

Eating

Many Hunter restaurants don't open midweek, so it's worth planning a weekend visit. Bookings are essential. Many wineries have on-site restaurants.

★ **Muse Kitchen** EUROPEAN $$
(☎ 02-4998 7899; www.musedining.com.au; Keith Tulloch Winery, cnr Hermitage & Deasys Rds, Pokolbin; mains $30-36; ⏲ noon-3pm Wed-Sun, 6-9pm Sat) For a fabulous lunch, head to this relaxed incarnation of the Hunter's top restaurant, Muse. Dine outside on a seasonal menu of European bistro food inspired by the vegetables, fruits and herbs grown up the road. Save room for the exquisite dessert selection and wine tasting at the **Keith Tulloch** (☎ 02-4998 7500; keithtullochwine.com.au; cnr Hermitage & Deasys Rds, Pokolbin; tastings $5; ⏲ 10am-5pm) cellar door.

Enzo CAFE $$
(www.enzohuntervalley.com.au; cnr Broke & Ekerts Rds, Pokolbin; mains breakfast $15-29, lunch $22-30; ⏲ 9am-4pm) Claim a table by the fireside in winter or in the garden in summer to enjoy the rustic dishes served at this popular Italian-inflected cafe. Combine your visit with a tasting at neighbouring David Hook Wines.

Muse Restaurant MODERN AUSTRALIAN $$$
(☎ 02-4998 6777; www.musedining.com.au; 1 Broke Rd, Pokolbin; 2-/3-course meals $75/95; ⏲ 6.30-10pm Wed-Fri, noon-3pm & 6.30-10pm Sat, noon-3pm Sun;) Inside the dramatic Hungerford Hill winery complex is the area's highest rated restaurant, offering sensational contemporary fare and stellar service. Vegetarians get their own menu (two courses $60, three for $80).

Bistro Molines FRENCH $$$
(☎ 02-4990 9553; www.bistromolines.com.au; 749 Mt View Rd, Mt View; mains $38-42; ⏲ noon-3pm Thu-Mon, 7-9pm Fri & Sat) Set in the Tallavera Grove winery, this French restaurant has a carefully crafted, seasonally driven menu that is nearly as impressive as the vineyard views.

Margan MODERN AUSTRALIAN $$$
(☎ 02-6579 1102; www.margan.com.au; 1238 Milbrodale Rd, Broke; mains breakfast $18, lunch $38, 3-/4-/5-course tasting menus $65/80/100; ⏲ noon-3pm & 6-9.30pm Fri & Sat, 9-10.30am & noon-3pm Sun) There's a tempting array of dishes at this rammed-earth restaurant where much of the produce is sourced from the kitchen garden; the rest comes from local providores whenever possible. Views stretch across the vines to the Brokenback Range.

Providores

Binnorie Dairy CHEESE SHOP $
(☎ 02-4998 6660; www.binnorie.com.au; 1 Mistletoe Lane, Pokolbin; ⏲ 10am-5pm Tue-Sat, to 4pm Sun) Offers an exceptional range of handcrafted creamy soft cheeses from a stylish shopfront. The goat's cheese log, labne and marinated feta are particularly moreish.

Hunter Valley Smelly Cheese Shop DELI $
(www.smellycheese.net.au; Tempus Two Winery, 2144 Broke Rd, Pokolbin; mains $9-16;

⌚10am-5pm) Along with the stinky desirables filling the cheese room, there are deli platters, pizzas, burgers and baguettes to go, as well as a freezer of superb gelati. There's another branch at Pokolbin Village.

Hunter Valley Cheese Company CHEESE SHOP $
(www.huntervalleycheese.com.au; McGuigans Winery, 447 McDonalds Rd, Pokolbin; ⌚9am-5.30pm) Staff will chew your ear about cheesy comestibles all day long, especially during the daily 11am and 3pm cheese talk. There's a bewildering variety of styles available for purchase.

Hunter Valley Chocolate Company CHOCOLATE SHOP $
(www.hvchocolate.com.au; Peterson House, Broke Rd, Pokolbin; ⌚9am-5pm) Sells a tempting array of locally made chocolate, truffles, fudge and other treats. Next door is Peterson House – the only producer of sparkling wine in the Hunter.

Drinking & Nightlife

Goldfish Bar & Kitchen BAR
(www.thegoldfish.com.au; Tempus Two Winery, cnr Broke & McDonalds Rds, Pokolbin; ⌚noon-late) All wined out? Try a classic cocktail on the balcony or in the lounge of this popular bar. A courtesy bus can run you home on a Saturday night.

Wollombi Tavern PUB
(www.wollombitavern.com.au; Great North Rd, Wollombi; ⌚10am-late) This fabulous little pub is the home of Dr Jurd's Jungle Juice, a dangerous brew of port, brandy and wine. On weekends, the tavern is a favourite pit stop for motorbike clubs (the nonscary sort).

Information

Hunter Valley Visitor Centre (☎02-4993 6700; www.huntervalleyvisitorcentre.com.au; 455 Wine Country Dr, Polkolbin; ⌚9am-5pm Mon-Sat, to 4pm Sun) Has a huge stock of leaflets and info on valley accommodation, attractions and dining.

Getting There & Away

BUS

Rover Coaches (☎02-4990 1699; www.rovercoaches.com.au) Has four buses heading between Newcastle and Cessnock ($4.70, 1¼ hours) on weekdays and two on Saturday; no Sunday service. Other buses head to Cessnock from the train stations at Morisset ($4.70, one hour, two daily) and Maitland ($4.70, 50 minutes, frequent).

TRAIN

Sydney Trains has a line heading through the Hunter Valley from Newcastle ($6.30, 50 minutes). Branxton is the closest station to the vineyards, although only Maitland has bus services to Cessnock.

Getting Around

Exploring without a car can be challenging. The YHA hostel (p154) hires bikes, as do **Grapemobile** (☎02-4998 7660; www.grapemobile.com.au; 307 Palmers Lane, Pokolbin; hire per 8hr $35; ⌚10am-6pm) and **Hunter Valley Cycling** (☎0418 281 480; www.huntervalleycycling.com.au; 266 DeBeyers Rd, Pokolbin; hire per 1/2 days $35/45).

Vineyard Shuttle (☎02-4991 3655; www.vineyardshuttle.com.au; per person $15; ⌚6pm-midnight Tue-Sat) Offers a door-to-door service between Pokolbin accommodation and restaurants.

Byron Bay & Northern NSW

Includes ➡

Best Places to Eat

- ➡ Town Restaurant & Cafe (p170)
- ➡ Beachwood Cafe (p178)
- ➡ Stunned Mullet (p195)
- ➡ The Roadhouse (p163)
- ➡ Hearthfire Bakery (p187)

Best Places to Stay

- ➡ Byron Bay Cottages (p163)
- ➡ Atlantic (p163)
- ➡ Sugarloaf Point Lighthouse (p198)
- ➡ Lily Pily (p187)
- ➡ Nimbin Rox YHA (p173)

Why Go?

Beach towns and national parks leapfrog each other all the way up this stupendous stretch of coast. Inland, lush farmland and ancient tracts of World Heritage–listed rainforest do the same.

Providing a buffer between New South Wales' big cities to the south and Queensland's built-up Gold Coast to the north, the North Coast offers an altogether quieter and simpler way of life. In cute little towns throughout the region dyed-in-the-wool country types rub shoulders with big-city escapees and posthippie alternative lifestylers – if you're looking for fresh local produce, a top-notch meal or a psychic reading, you shouldn't be disappointed. And if you're searching for a surf break, rest assured that there will be an awesome one around the next corner.

When to Go

Byron Bay

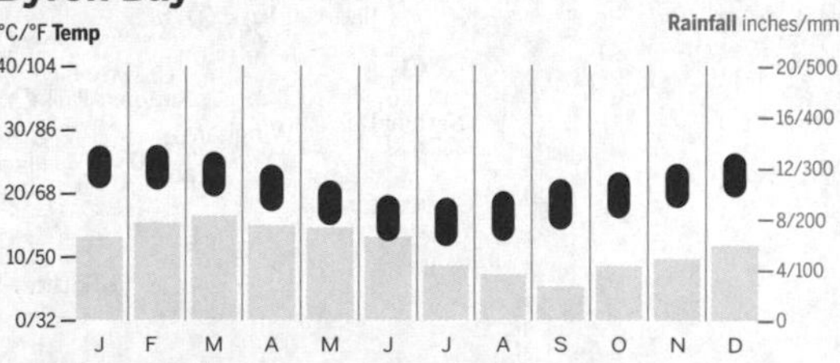

Jun & Jul Winter brings migrating whales to the coast, lanterns to Lismore and rockers to Byron Bay.

Sep–Nov Returning whales, blooming jacarandas and Byron Bay's Surf Fest.

Dec–Apr Life's a beach; there are 'Tropical Fruits' in Lismore and Byron gets the blues.

Byron Bay & Northern NSW Highlights

1. Laying claim to your own stretch of empty beach in coastal wilderness such as **Myall Lakes National Park** (p197).
2. Delving into the ancient World Heritage–listed Gondwana rainforest of **Dorrigo National Park** (p186).
3. Getting closely acquainted with whales and dolphins in a cruise from **Port Stephens** (p198).
4. Enjoying the charm of pretty hinterland villages such as **Bellingen** (p186).
5. Learning to surf amid spouting whales in **Byron Bay** (p159).
6. Cruising the bucolic back roads along the Macleay River in **Kempsey Shire** (p189).
7. Witnessing the weird blend of farmers, hippies and foodies at local markets such as the one held in **Bangalow** (p170).

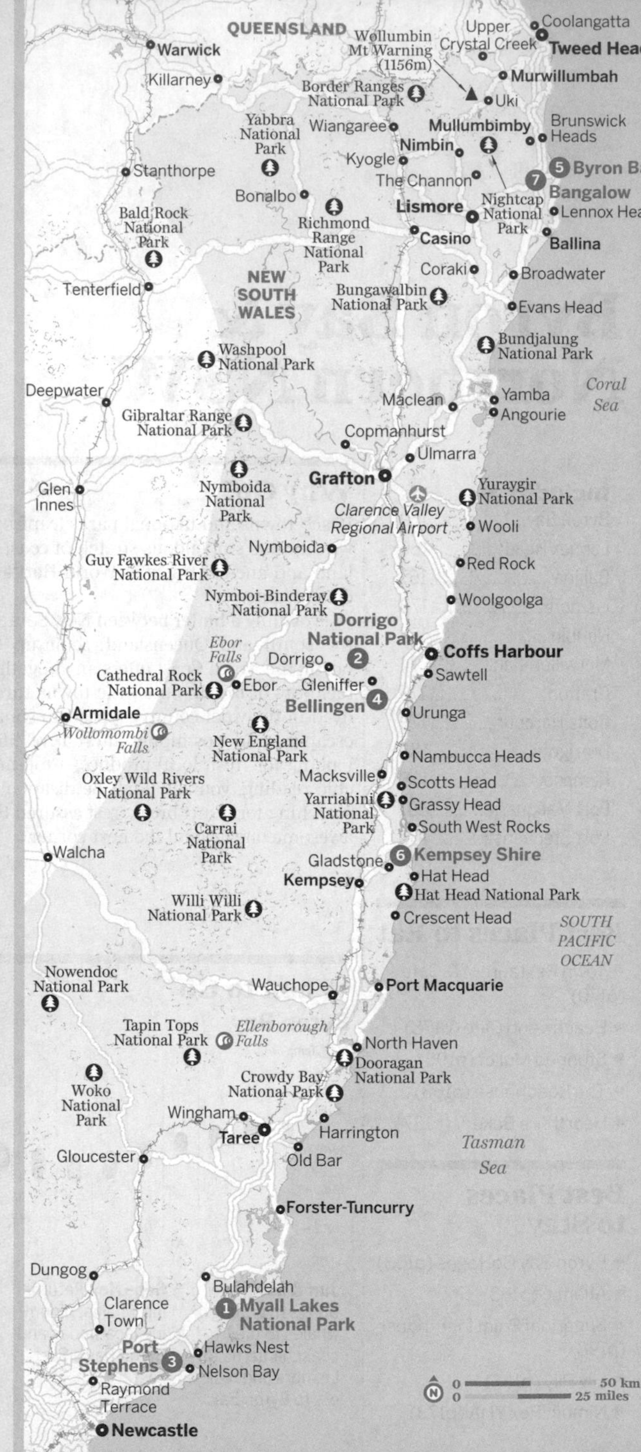

Getting There & Around

AIR

There are domestic airports at Taree, Port Macquarie, Coffs Harbour (great for Bellingen), Grafton, Ballina (Byron Bay) and Lismore. Additionally, Newcastle Airport is handy for Port Stephens, and Gold Coast Airport is only 4km from Tweed Heads.

BUS

Greyhound (www.greyhound.com.au) and **Premier** (www.premierms.com.au) both have coach services linking Sydney and Brisbane via the Pacific Hwy. Other companies cover smaller stretches along the way.

TRAIN

NSW TrainLink (www.nswtrainlink.info) services between Sydney and Brisbane stop at Wingham, Taree, Nambucca Heads, Coffs Harbour and Grafton.

BALLINA & BYRON SHIRES

Where back-to-nature meets life's-a-beach, this stretch of coast offers a mix of family-friendly and party-hearty destinations. The beachy towns of Ballina and Lennox Heads are less buzzy options than the tourist Babylon of Byron Bay to the north.

Byron Bay

POP 4960

The reputation of this famous beach town precedes it to such an extent that first impressions may leave you wondering what all the fuss is about. The beaches are great, but there are spectacular beaches all along this coast. What makes Byron special is the singular vibe of the town itself. It's here that coastal surf culture flows into the hippie tide washing down from the hinterland, creating one great barefooted, alternative-lifestyle mash-up.

The town centre is low-rise and relaxed, and the locals are dedicated to preserving its essential small-town soul. Of course Byron does get crowded and it also attracts its fair share of off-the-leash teens. Yet its unique atmosphere has a way of converting even the most cynical with its long, balmy days, endless beaches, reliable surf breaks, fine food, raucous nightlife and ambling milieu.

James Cook named Cape Byron, mainland Australia's most easterly point, after renowned navigator John Byron, grandfather of the poet Lord Byron. Later bureaucrats mistakenly planned out streets named after fellow poets such as Jonson, Burns and Shelley.

Sights

★Cape Byron State Conservation Park

STATE PARK

(www.nationalparks.nsw.gov.au/cape-byron-state-conservation-area) The views from the summit are spectacular, rewarding those who have climbed up from the **Captain Cook Lookout** (Lighthouse Rd; 🚗) on the **Cape Byron Walking Track**. Ribboning around the headland, the track dips and (mostly) soars its way to the **lighthouse** (Lighthouse Rd; ⏲10am-4pm) FREE. Along the way, look out for dolphins (year-round) and migrating whales during their northern (June to July) and southern (September to November) migrations. You're also likely to encounter brush turkeys and wallabies. Allow about two hours for the entire 3.7km loop.

Inside the 1901 lighthouse there are maritime and nature displays. If you want to venture to the top you'll need to take one of the volunteer run tours, which operate from around 10am to 3pm (gold-coin donation). There's also a cafe here and self-contained accommodation in the lighthouse-keeper's cottages.

You can drive right up to the lighthouse and pay $7 for the privilege of parking (or nothing at all if you chance upon a park in the small lot 300m below).

Beaches

West of the town centre, wild **Belongil Beach** with its high dunes avoids the worst of the crowds and is clothing optional in parts. At its eastern end is the **Wreck**, a powerful right-hand surf break.

Immediately in front of town, lifesaver-patrolled **Main Beach** is busy from sunrise to sunset with yoga classes, buskers and fire dancers. As it stretches east it merges into **Clarkes Beach**. The most popular surf break is at the **Pass** near the eastern headland.

Around the rocks is gorgeous **Watego's Beach**, a wide crescent of white sand surrounded by rainforest. A further 400m walk brings you to secluded **Little Watego's** (inaccessible by car) another lovely patch of sand directly under rocky Cape Byron. Head here at sunset for an impressive moon rise. Tucked under the south side of the Cape (entry via Tallow Beach Rd) is **Cosy Corner** which offers a decent-size wave and sheltered beach when the northerlies are blowing elsewhere.

Tallow Beach is a deserted sandy stretch that extends for 7km south from Cape Byron. This is the place to flee the crowds. Much of the beach is backed by **Arakwal National Park**, but the suburb of **Suffolk Park** sprawls along the sand near its southern end. **Kings Beach** is a popular gay beach, just off Seven Mile Beach Rd past the Broken Head Holiday Park.

Activities

Adventure sports abound in Byron Bay and most operators offer a free pick-up service from local accommodation. Surfing and diving are the biggest draws.

Surfing

Most hostels provide free boards to guests, or you can rent equipment.

Black Dog Surfing SURFING
(02-6680 9828; www.blackdogsurfing.com; 11 Byron St; 3½hr lessons $60) Intimate group lessons including women's and kids' courses. Highly rated.

Surfing Byron Bay SURFING
(02-6685 7099; www.gosurfingbyronbay.com; 84 Jonson St; 2½hr lessons $60) Surfing lessons for adults and kids, plus a 'surf yoga' combo.

Byron Bay Surf School SURFING
(1800 707 274; www.byronbaysurfschool.com; 29 Shirley St; 3½hr lessons $65) Lessons and surf camps.

Mojosurf SURFING
(1800 113 044; www.mojosurf.com; 9 Marvell St; 1/2 lessons $69/119) Lessons and epic surf safaris.

Soul Surf School SURFING
(1800 089 699; www.soulsurfschool.com.au; 4hr lessons $59) Half-day to five-day courses for beginners.

Diving

About 3km offshore, **Julian Rocks Marine Reserve** is a meeting point for cold southerly and warm northerly currents, attracting a profusion of marine species including three types of turtle. You might spot leopard sharks and manta rays in summer, and grey nurse sharks in winter.

Sundive DIVING, SNORKELLING
(02-6685 7755; www.sundive.com.au; 8/9-11 Byron St; dives from $95, snorkelling tours $65) Two to three expeditions to Julian Rocks daily, plus various courses.

Dive Byron Bay DIVING
(02-6685 8333; www.byronbaydivecentre.com.au; 9 Marvell St; dives from $99, snorkelling tours $65; 9am-5pm) Freediving course $495 and Professional Association of Diving Instructors (PADI) courses from $325.

Flying & Other Airborne Pursuits

Byron Bay Ballooning BALLOONING
(1300 889 660; www.byronbayballooning.com.au; Tyagarah Airfield; adult/child $325/175) Sunrise flights including champagne breakfast.

Skydive Byron Bay SKYDIVING
(02-6684 1323; www.skydivebyronbay.com; Tyagarah Airfield; tandem flights from $334) Hurtle to earth from 4267m.

Byron Airwaves HANG-GLIDING
(02-6629 0354; www.byronair.com) Tandem hang-gliding ($145) and courses ($1500).

Byron Bay Microlights MICROLIGHTING
(0407 281 687; www.byronbaymicrolights.com.au; Tyagarah Airfield; 15-/30-/45min flights $100/180/245) Whale watching ($180) and scenic flights ($100).

Byron Gliding GLIDING
(02-6684 7627; www.byrongliding.com; Tyagarah Airfield; flights from $120) Scenic flights over the coast and hinterland.

Alternative Therapies

Byron is an alternative-therapy heartland, offering a diverse range of treatments claiming to heal the body and mind.

Byron at Byron Spa SPA
(02-6639 2110; www.thebyronatbyron.com.au/spa; 77-97 Broken Head Rd; 1hr massages from $145) Six ultraluxurious treatment rooms nestled among the rainforest. Includes use of the resort swimming pool.

Be Salon & Spa SPA
(0413 432 584; www.besalonspa.com.au; 14 Middleton St; 30min massages $60) Manicures, pedicures, facials and waxing are offered alongside psychic readings, massage, rebalancing and naturopathy.

Relax Haven MASSAGE
(02-6685 8304; www.relaxhaven.com.au; 107 Jonson St; 10am-6.30pm) Flotation tanks (one hour $79), massage (one hour $89), kinesiology, quantum hypnotherapy and theta energy healing.

Other

Go Sea Kayaks KAYAKING
(☎0416 222 344; www.goseakayakbyronbay.com.au; adult/child $69/59) If you don't see a whale, turtle or dolphin, you can go again for free.

Surf & Bike Hire BICYCLE RENTAL
(☎02-6680 7066; www.byronbaysurfandbikehire.com.au; 31 Lawson St; ⊙9am-5pm) Rents bikes and surfboards (from $10 per day) plus other active gear.

Tours

Mountain Bike Tours MOUNTAIN BIKING
(☎0429 122 504; www.mountainbiketours.com.au; half/full day $59/99) Environmentally aware bike tours into the rainforest and along the coast.

Vision Walks WILDLIFE TOUR
(☎02-6685 0059; www.visionwalks.com; night tours adult/child $99/75, other tours from $45/28) See all manner of creatures in their natural habitat, including nocturnal animals (on the Night Vision Walk) and hippies (on the Hippie Trail Hinterland Tour).

Byron Bay Adventure Tours HIKING
(☎1300 120 028; www.byronbayadventuretours.com.au; day tours $119) Day walks and overnight tours to Mt Warning and the hinterland.

Festivals & Events

Byron Bay Bluesfest MUSIC
(www.bluesfest.com.au; Tyagarah Tea Tree Farm;) Held over Easter, this jam attracts high-calibre international performers and local heavyweights.

Splendour in the Grass MUSIC
(www.splendourinthegrass.com; North Byron Parklands) Three-day festival featuring big-name indie artists in late July.

Byron Bay Writers' Festival LITERATURE
(www.byronbaywritersfestival.com.au) In early August, this festival gathers together top-shelf writers and literary followers from across Australia.

Byron Bay Surf Festival SURFING
(www.byronbaysurffestival.com) Three-day late-October celebration of surf culture.

Sleeping

Book well in advance for January or during any of the annual music festivals. If you're not 17, Schoolies Week, which actually runs for about a month from mid-November, is one to avoid. During these periods, places taking one-night-only bookings are rare.

Booking services include **Byron Bay Accom** (☎02-6680 8666; www.byronbayaccom.net; 6/73-75 Jonson St; ⊙9am-5pm Mon-Fri, 10am-5pm Sat & Sun).

Byron Beach Resort HOSTEL $
(☎02-6685 7868; byronbeachresort.com.au; 25 Childe St; dm $18-30, d from $90, 2-bed apt from $150) This fabulous, well-managed resort opposite Belongil Beach is a terrific and affordable alternative to staying in central Byron. Attractive dorms, cottages and self-contained apartments are scattered through the hammock-filled gardens. There's daily yoga, free bikes and the fun Treehouse (p165) pub next door. It's a 15-minute walk (or free shuttle ride) down the Belongil Beach into town.

Cape Byron YHA HOSTEL $
(☎02-6685 8788; www.yha.com.au; cnr Middleton & Byron Sts; dm $38-40, d with/without bathroom $140/100;) Gathered around an attractive palm-lined heated pool this modern, tidy complex is in the centre of town and only a short walk away from the beach. Friendly and knowledgeable staff run free walking tours and other activities. There are substantial discounts in the low season.

Nomads Arts Factory Lodge HOSTEL $
(☎02-6685 7709; www.nomadsworld.com/arts-factory; Skinners Shoot Rd; camp sites/dm/d from $17/34/90;) For an archetypal Byron experience, try this ramshackle hostel by a picturesque swamp, 15-minutes walk from town. Choose from colourful six- to 10-bed dorms, a female-only lakeside cottage, or tepees. Couples can opt for aptly titled 'cube' rooms, island-retreat canvas huts or the pricier 'love shack' with bathroom. There's yoga, didge lessons and regular bush-tucker walks.

Aquarius HOSTEL $
(☎02-6685 7663; www.aquarius-backpackers.com.au; 16 Lawson St; dm/motel r from $35/120;) This motel-style hostel across the road from the beach has balconies off each room and plenty of communal space – including a bar with a pool table and ping pong. Motel rooms have kitchenettes and some have spa baths. Dorms are for international guests only.

Nomads HOSTEL $
(☎02-6680 7966; www.nomadsworld.com; 1 Lawson Lane; dm $48-52, d $150-190;) Byron's biggest (and priciest) backpackers packs a punch with its glossy designer-led decor. The

Byron Bay

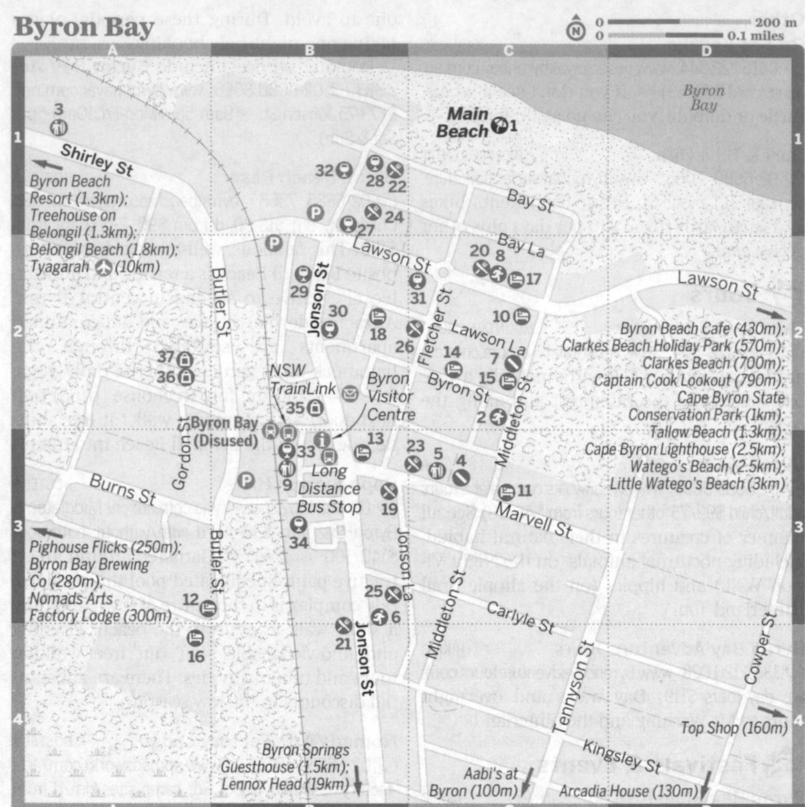

dorm rooms are comfortable, but they're not half as good as the king rooms, which have a bathroom, fridge and plasma television.

Clarkes Beach Holiday Park CAMPGROUND $
(☎02-6685 6496; www.northcoastparks.com.au/clarkes; off Lighthouse Rd; camp sites/cabins from $46/175;) The tightly packed cabins and shady tent sites at this holiday park sit within an attractive bush setting, close to the beach and the lighthouse.

Arcadia House B&B $$
(☎02-6680 8699; www.arcadiahousebyron.com.au; 48 Cowper St; r from $155;) Amid a large garden on a quiet street is this delightful old Queenslander with airy verandahs and six elegant rooms with four-poster beds. It's about a 10-minute walk to the beach, or jump on a complimentary bike.

Aabi's at Byron GUESTHOUSE $$
(☎02-6680 9519; www.guesthousesbyronbay.com.au; 17 Ruskin St; r from $180;) Statues of Hindu deities watch over the pool at this gorgeous contemporary complex. Rooms are luxurious, plus there's a shared kitchen, lounge, BBQ and large pool and spa.

Bamboo Cottage GUESTHOUSE $$
(☎0414 187 088; www.byron-bay.com/bamboocottage; 76 Butler St; s/d without bathroom $129/149, d with bathroom $169, apt $240;) Featuring global charm and a tropical setting, Bamboo Cottage treats guests to Asian- and Pacific Island–inflected rooms in a home-away-from-home atmosphere. It's on the quiet side of the tracks.

Byron Springs Guesthouse GUESTHOUSE $$
(☎0457 808 101; www.byronsprings.com.au; 2 Oodgeroo Garden; s/d without bathroom from $75/110, d with bathroom $150;) Polished floorboards, white linen and a leafy setting a couple of kilometres south of town make this a good choice if you like to be removed from the throng. A continental breakfast is included and there are complimentary bikes.

Byron Bay

Byron Central Apartments APARTMENTS $$
(02-6685 8800; www.byroncentral.com; 5-7 Byron St; apt $136-210;) Hidden within a town-centre commercial building a couple of blocks from the beach, this complex has a pleasant set of apartments grouped around a swimming pool. The deluxe units have loft bedrooms, new furnishings and full kitchens.

Glen-Villa Resort RESORT $$
(02-6685 7382; www.glenvillaresort.com.au; 80-86 Butler St; cabins from $110;) Targeting couples via a strict two-person-per-booking rule (groups and families should look elsewhere), this holiday park is clean, comfortable and secure. It's tucked away in the backstreets and blissfully quiet.

Hibiscus Motel MOTEL $$
(02-6685 6195; www.hibiscusmotel.com.au; 33 Lawson St; d from $155;) Ignore the highway motel exterior and you'll discover spacious and sparkling rooms, not to mention welcoming staff. Less than a minute to the surf.

★ **Atlantic** HOTEL $$$
(02-6685 5118; www.atlanticbyronbay.com.au; 13 Marvell St; r from $180;) There are three fabulously decorated Caribbean-style plantation cottages at this chic enclave in the centre of town, all with private decks opening on to tropical gardens. If this isn't cool enough, there's also the option of sleeping in a polished-aluminium Airstream caravan parked on the back lawn.

★ **Byron Bay Cottages** COTTAGES $$$
(02-6620 9300; www.byronbaylighthouse.com; cottages from $350) Byron's best-kept secret requires booking well in advance. It's worth it for the experience of staying in one of these four restored 1920s cottages (sleeping four to seven) metres from the sand of Clarkes Beach, or in the heritage-listed Assistant Lighthouse Keepers' Cottages.

Byron at Byron RESORT $$$
(02-6639 2000; www.thebyronatbyron.com.au; 77-97 Broken Head Rd; ste from $390;) About 4km south of town, these luxe one-bedroom villas are spread through the resort's junglelike greenery. When you're not drinking cocktails by the infinity pool, taking complimentary yoga classes or indulging in the spa (p160), follow the boardwalks down to Tallow Beach.

Eating

★ **The Roadhouse** CAFE $
(0403 355 498; byronbaycafebar.com.au; 6/142 Bangalow Rd; mains $14; 6am-3pm Mon, to 10pm Tue-Sun) A short trip out of town will find you at Byron's most atmospheric night spot. Rocking incredible, locally sourced wholefoods and elixirs by day, Roadhouse transforms into a dimly lit, blues-infused bar at

night with more than 500 types of whisky on the menu. Book ahead.

Top Shop CAFE $
(65 Carlyle St; mains $10-14; ⏲6.30am-5pm) On the hill east of town, Top Shop has long been the choice of local surfers. Today it's an upmarket version of the old-school takeaway, with diners ripping into breakfast burgers, sausage rolls and quinoa kale salads on the lawn while chugging back homemade ice coffees.

Three Blue Ducks at the Farm FARM RESTAURANT
(☎02-6684 7888; http://thefarmbyronbay.com.au; 11 Ewingsdale Rd, Ewingsdale) After the success of its first Sydney cafe, the team from the Three Blue Ducks decided to move up north and showcase its paddock-to-plate food philosophy on the grounds of this lovely cattle and chicken farm just out of Byron.

Naked Treaties CAFE $
(www.nakedtreaties.com.au; 2/3 Marvell S; items $8-15; ⏲8am-4pm; ✎) This raw bar celebrates everything vegan, organic, and gluten, dairy and sugar free. There's an encyclopedia of superfood smoothies, plus a rotating menu of savoury goods including raw pad thai. Cold-pressed organic coffee is made with fresh almond milk and sweetened with coconut nectar.

Bay Leaf Café CAFE $
(www.facebook.com/bayleafcoffee; 2 Marvell St; mains $9-17; ⏲6.30am-5pm) Green-juice-sipping diners spill down the front steps of this hip, wedge-shaped cafe where breakfast is the star. The excellent menu is prepared in a busy open kitchen and might feature vanilla wild-rice risotto or house-made crumpets with rum-and-raisin caramelised banana.

Blue Olive DELI $
(27 Lawson St; mains $10-13; ⏲10am-5.30pm Tue-Sat, to 4pm Sun) Fine cheeses, deli items and light meals; enjoy the beautifully prepared foods at shady pavement tables or decamp to the beach.

Italian at the Pacific ITALIAN $$
(☎02-6680 7055; www.italianatthepacific.com.au; 2 Bay St; mains $28-36; ⏲6-10pm) Adjoining the Beach Hotel, this lively Italian offers only a limited selection of pasta and larger dishes, but what it does do, it does well. Try the slow-cooked lamb-shank lasagne – it might just be the best you've ever tasted.

Byron Beach Cafe CAFE $$
(☎02-6685 8400; www.byronbeachcafe.com.au; Lawson St; mains breakfast $15-22, lunch & dinner $25-33; ⏲7.30am-5pm Sun-Wed, to 9pm Thu-Sat) Step out of the surf and straight into this iconic cafe right on Clarkes Beach, the ideal spot for a lazy brunch. There are loads of interesting breakfast options and the menu gets more restaurant-like as the day progresses.

St Elmo SPANISH $$
(☎02-6680 7426; www.stelmodining.com; cnr Fletcher St & Lawson Lane; dishes $14-26; ⏲4-11pm Mon-Sat, to 10pm Sun) Perch on a designer stool at this buzzing tapas restaurant, where good-looking staff create magical cocktails and the wine list extends to over 100 different drops. The sharp, Iberian-inspired menu has some fantastic seafood plates.

Orgasmic Food MIDDLE EASTERN $$
(☎02-6680 7778; 11 Bay Lane; mains $15-25; ⏲10am-10pm; ✎) This alley eatery is one giant step above a falafel stall. Its hearty meze plates are ideal for picnics.

Cicchetti Byron Bay ITALIAN $$
(☎02-6685 6677; www.cicchetti.com.au; 108 Jonson St; shared plates $16-22, mains $38, 5-course degustation $75; ⏲5.30-11pm Mon-Thu, noon-11pm Fri-Sun) This glamorous restaurant, with an all-Italian staff, is hugely popular. The crowds love the on-trend dining featuring an extensive list of Venetian antipasto dishes and generous mains (for a minimum of two). Solo diners can perch at the bar with a cocktail and a board of goodies.

Byron at Byron Restaurant MODERN AUSTRALIAN $$$
(☎02-6639 2111; www.thebyronatbyron.com.au; 77-97 Broken Head Rd; mains $37-40; ⏲8am-9pm) With flickering candles and a rainforest backdrop this intimate resort restaurant offers light, Mediterranean-style dishes created around the best of Northern Rivers produce, such as sweet Bangalow pork and Yamba prawns. On Thursday night there's a good-value two-course Farmers' Market dinner ($49).

Petit Snail FRENCH $$$
(☎02-6685 8526; www.thepetitsnail.com.au; 5 Carlyle St; mains $31-45; ⏲6.30-9.30pm Wed-Sat; ✎) Get stuck into traditional Gallic fare such as steak tartare, duck confit and lots of *fromage*. There's outdoor dining on the verandah. Vegetarians get their own menu (mains $21 to $25).

Drinking & Nightlife

For entertainment listings, check out the gig guide in Thursday's *Byron Shire News* (www.byronnews.com.au) or tune into Bay 99.9 FM.

Byron Bay Brewing Co BREWERY
(www.byronbaybrewery.com.au; 1 Skinners Shoot Rd; ⊙noon-late Mon-Sat, to 10pm Sun) At this old piggery turned booze barn you can drink frosty glasses of house pale lager amid the brewing vats or sit outside in the tropical courtyard under the shade of a giant fig tree. Entertainment includes live music, DJs and trivia nights. Brewery tours are held at 4pm.

Balcony Bar BAR
(☎02-6680 9666; www.balcony.com.au; Level 1, 3 Lawson St; ⊙8am-11pm) With its verandah poking out amid the palm trees overlooking the centre of town, this tapas and cocktail bar is a fine place to park yourself, particularly during the sunset happy hour.

Miss Margarita BAR
(☎02-6685 6828; missmargarita.com.au; 2 Jonson St; ⊙noon-3pm & 5pm-1am Mon-Fri, 11.30am-1am Sat & Sun) A beach cantina offering seven versions of the classic margarita and an array of colourful, fruity cocktails. Soak up the tequila with enchiladas, salsa and creamy guacamole.

Railway Friendly Bar PUB
(The Rails; ☎02-6685 7662; www.therailsbyronbay.com; 86 Jonson St; ⊙11am-late) This indoor-outdoor pub draws everyone from lobster-red British tourists to high-on-life earth mothers. The front beer garden, conducive to boozy afternoons, has live music and excellent food.

Woody's Surf Shack BAR
(www.woodysbyronbay.com; The Plaza, 90-96 Jonson St; ⊙8pm-3am Mon-Sat) Traditionally the last stop of the night, there's now a lockout for this clubby bar, so if you fancy shooting pool until 3am you'll need to get in before 1.30am.

Great Northern PUB
(☎02-6685 6454; www.thenorthern.com.au; 35-43 Jonson St; ⊙noon-late) This grungy live-music stalwart is brash and boisterous and plays host to everyone from Billy Bragg to Dizzee Rascal.

Beach Hotel PUB
(www.beachhotel.com.au; cnr Jonson & Bay Sts; ⊙11am-late) Soak up the atmosphere and the views in the iconic beachfront beer garden. Out the back they screen surf movies, and the original *Crocodile Dundee* hat adorns the bar.

Treehouse on Belongil PUB
(☎02-6680 9452; www.treehouseonbelongil.com; 25 Childe St; ⊙7.30am-11pm) A homespun beach bar where wooden decks spill out among the trees and live, original music is played all weekend. Most of the food comes from the wood-fired oven and there's a great menu of icy beverages.

Cocomangas CLUB
(www.cocomangas.com.au; 32 Jonson St; ⊙9pm-late Wed-Sat) Byron's longest-standing nightclub, with regular backpacker nights. No entry after 1.30am.

LaLaLand CLUB
(☎02-6680 7070; www.lalalandbyronbay.com.au; 6 Lawson St; ⊙5pm-3am) Stylishly renovated, this is one of Byron's better clubs.

Entertainment

Pighouse Flicks CINEMA
(☎02-6685 5828; www.pighouseflicks.com.au; 1 Skinners Shoot Rd; tickets $10-14) Attached to Byron Bay Brewing Co, this lounge cinema shows classic reruns and art-house flicks.

Shopping

Byron has surprisingly good shopping, from upmarket boutiques to hippie stores draped in dreamcatchers.

Markets include a weekly **Farmers' Market** (www.byronfarmersmarket.com.au; Butler Street Reserve; ⊙8-11am Thu) and **Artisan Market** (www.byronmarkets.com.au; Railway Park, Jonson St; ⊙4-9pm Sat Nov-Mar), and the **Byron Community Market** (www.byronmarkets.com.au; Butler Street Reserve; ⊙8am-2pm 1st Sun of the month).

Information

Bay Centre Medical (☎02-6685 6206; www.byronmed.com.au; 6 Lawson St; ⊙8am-5pm Mon-Fri, to noon Sat)

Byron District Hospital (☎02-6685 6200; www.ncahs.nsw.gov.au; cnr Wordsworth & Shirley Sts; ⊙24hr)

Byron Visitor Centre (☎02-6680 8558; www.visitbyronbay.com; Stationmaster's Cottage, 80 Jonson St; admission by donation; ⊙9am-5pm) Ground zero for tourist information, and last-minute accommodation and bus bookings.

Getting There & Away

BUS

Coaches stop on Jonson St near the tourist office.

Blanch's (☎02-6686 2144; www.blanchs.com.au) Regular buses to/from Ballina Byron Gateway Airport ($9.60, one hour), Ballina ($9.60, 55 minutes), Lennox Head ($7.60, 35 minutes), Bangalow ($6.40, 20 minutes) and Mullumbimby ($6.40, 25 minutes).

Brisbane Byron Express (☎1800 626 222; www.brisbane2byron.com) Two daily buses to/from Brisbane ($38, two hours) and Brisbane Airport ($54, three hours); only one on Sunday.

Byron Bay Express (www.byronbayexpress.com.au) Five buses a day to/from Gold Coast Airport (1¾ hours) and Surfers Paradise (2¼ hours) for $30/55 one way/return.

Byron Easy Bus (☎02-6685 7447; www.byronbayshuttle.com.au) Minibus service to Ballina Byron Gateway Airport ($20, 40 minutes), Gold Coast Airport ($39, two hours), Brisbane ($40, 3½ hours) and Brisbane Airport ($54, four hours).

Greyhound (☎1300 473 946; www.greyhound.com.au) Coaches to/from Sydney (from $95, 12 to 14 hours, three daily), Port Macquarie ($75, six hours, two daily), Nambucca Heads ($59, 4½ hours, two daily), Coffs Harbour ($46, 3½ hours, four daily) and Brisbane ($38, four hours, five daily).

Northern Rivers Buslines (☎02-6626 1499; www.nrbuslines.com.au) Weekday buses to/from Lismore (1½ hours), Bangalow (30 minutes) and Mullumbimby (20 minutes); all $9.70.

NSW TrainLink (☎13 22 32; www.nswtrainlink.info; Jonson St) TrainLink coaches can be booked at the old train station. Destinations include Grafton ($25, 3¾ hours), Yamba ($13.70, three hours), Ballina ($7, 41 minutes), Lismore ($9.22, one hour) and Murwillumbah ($9.22, one hour).

Premier (☎13 34 10; www.premierms.com.au) Daily coach to/from Sydney ($92, 14 hours), Port Macquarie ($66, 7½ hours), Nambucca Heads ($58, 5¾ hours), Coffs Harbour ($50, five hours) and Brisbane ($30, 3½ hours).

CAR

Earth Car Rentals (☎02-6685 7472; www.earthcar.com.au; 1 Byron St)

Hertz (☎02-6680 7925; www.hertz.com.au; 5 Marvell St)

Getting Around

Byron Bay Taxis (☎02-6685 5008; www.byronbaytaxis.com.au; ⊙24hr)

Lennox Head

POP 7000

A protected National Surfing Reserve, Lennox Head's picturesque coastline has some of the best surf on the coast, with a world-class point break. Its village atmosphere makes it a mellow alternative to its boisterous well-touristed neighbour, Byron, 17km north.

Sights

Seven Mile Beach BEACH

Long, lovely Seven Mile Beach starts at the township and stretches north. There's 4WD access though you will need a permit from the Caltex Service Station. The best place for a dip is near the surf club, at the northern end of town.

Lake Ainsworth LAKE

Lying just inshore from the beach, this freshwater lake is tinged brown by tannins leeching from the tea trees along its banks. Don't fret: they're supposedly beneficial to the skin. The **Lennox Head Community Market** (Lennox Head Community Centre; ⊙8am-2pm 2nd & 5th Sun of month) is held on the foreshore.

Activities

Wind & Water WINDSURFING, SURFING

(☎0419 686 188; www.windnwater.net; 1hr lesson from $80) Windsurfing, kitesurfing and board surfing lessons on Lake Ainsworth and Seven Mile Beach.

Seabreeze Hang Gliding ADVENTURE SPORTS

(☎0428 560 248; www.seabreezehanggliding.com; from $145) Leap off Lennox Head or Cape Byron on a tandem flight, or learn how to go it solo.

Sleeping & Eating

Real-estate agency **Professionals** (☎02-6687 7579; www.lennoxheadaccom.net.au; 72 Ballina St) has a large range of holiday rentals.

Lennox Head Beach House YHA HOSTEL $

(☎02-6687 7636; www.yha.com.au; 3 Ross St; dm/s/d $34/55/82; @) Only 100m from the beach, this place has immaculate rooms and a great vibe. For $5 you can use the surfboards, sailboards and bikes.

Lake Ainsworth Holiday Park CAMPGROUND $

(☎02-6687 7249; www.northcoastholidayparks.com.au; Pacific Pde; camp sites/cabins from $33/95; ᯤ) By the lake and near the beach, this family-friendly holiday park has a wide range of units, from rustic cabins without bathrooms to a deluxe villa sleeping six. There's new amenities and a kitchen for campers.

Lennox Point Holiday Apartments APARTMENTS $$

(☎02-6687 5900; www.lennoxholidayapartments.com; 20-21 Pacific Pde; apt from $180; ❄ᯤ≋) Gaze at the surf from your modern apartment or take a splash with a borrowed board from reception. The one-bedroom apartments are the same size as the two-bedrooms, so they feel more spacious.

Cafe Marius LATIN AMERICAN $$
(☎02-6687 5897; www.cafemarius.com.au; 90-92 Ballina St; mains $15-22; ⏰7am-3.30pm Mon-Thu, to 9pm Fri & Sat, 8am-3.30pm Sun) Hip kids serve a delicious selection of Latin American and Spanish treats from morning to late in this cool little licensed cafe.

Foam MODERN AUSTRALIAN $$
(☎02-6687 7757; www.foamlennox.com; 41 Pacific Pde; breakfast mains $10-17, lunch mains $26-36) With the atmosphere of a luxury beach house, the deck at Foam is the ultimate spot to share a bottle of cold white wine and a long lunch as you gape at the beauty of Seven Mile Beach.

Getting There & Away

Blanch's (☎02-6686 2144; www.blanchs.com.au) Regular buses to/from Ballina Byron Gateway Airport ($6.40, 30 minutes), Ballina ($6.40, 15 minutes), Byron Bay ($7.60, 35 minutes) and Mullumbimby ($10, one hour).

Northern Rivers Buslines (☎02-6626 1499; www.nrbuslines.com.au) One or two buses to/from Lismore on weekdays ($9.70, one hour).

Ballina

POP 19,000

At the mouth of the Richmond River, Ballina is spoilt for white sandy beaches and crystal-clear waters. In the late 19th century it was a rich lumber town; a scattering of gracious historic buildings can still be found on its backstreets. These days Ballina is popular with family holidaymakers and retirees, and home to the region's airport.

Sights

Just across the bridge at the east of the main strip is calm **Shaws Bay Lagoon**, a popular place for family splashes. Nearby **Shelly Beach** is white, sandy and patrolled. **South Ballina Beach** is a good excursion option via the car ferry on Burns Point Ferry Rd.

Ballina Naval & Maritime Museum MUSEUM
(☎02-6681 1002; www.ballinamaritimemuseum.org.au; 8 Regatta Ave; adult/child $5/2; ⏰9am-4pm) In the 19th century Ballina was the third-biggest port in NSW, and following WWII many ex-navy personnel took jobs in the shipyards here. The most interesting display is the actual balsa-wood raft that sailed across the Pacific from Ecuador as part of Las Balsas expedition, which docked in Ballina in 1973.

Big Prawn LANDMARK
(Ballina Bunnings, 507 River St) Ballina's big prawn was nearly thrown on the BBQ in 2009, but no one had the stomach to dispatch it. After a 5000-signature proprawn petition and a $400,000 restoration in 2013, the 9m, 35-tonne, 14-year-old crustacean is looking as tasty as ever.

Activities

Ballina Boat Hire BOATING
(☎0402 028 767; www.ballinaboathire.com.au; rear 268 River St; per half day $90) Has tinnies for fishing, barbecue boats and catamarans.

Summerland Surf School SURFING
(☎0428 824 393; www.summerlandsurfschool.com.au; 2hr lesson $69) Based south of Ballina in Evans Head.

Kool Katz SURFING
(☎02-6685 5169; www.koolkatzsurf.com; 4hr lesson $49) Surf lessons at Shaws Bay, Shelly Beach or Lennox Head.

Tours

Kayak Ballina KAYAKING
(☎02-6681 4000; kayakballina.com; $85) Kayak Ballina's beautiful dolphin-filled waterways on these three-hour guided tours; you can spot dolphins and migratory birds.

Richmond River Cruises CRUISE
(☎02-6687 5688; www.rrcruises.com.au; Regatta Ave; adult/child $30/15) Chugs up the Richmond River on two-hour morning- and afternoon-tea cruises most Sundays and Wednesdays.

Aboriginal Cultural Concepts CULTURAL TOUR
(☎0405 654 280; www.aboriginalculturalconcepts.com; half-/full-day tours per person $100/180; ⏰Wed-Sat) Get an Indigenous insight into the local area on heritage tours exploring mythological sites along the Bundjalung coast.

Sleeping

Shaws Bay Holiday Park CARAVAN PARK $
(☎02-6686 2326; www.northcoastholidayparks.com.au; 1 Brighton St; camp sites/cabins from $38/134; ❄@📶) Manicured and well positioned, this park is on the lagoon and an easy walk from the centre. In addition to usual camping and caravan spots there's also a range of self-contained units, including three flash villas.

Ballina Palms Motor Inn MOTEL $$
(☎02-6686 4477; www.ballinapalms.com; cnr Bentinck & Owen Sts; s/d $115/125; ❄📶🏊) With its lush garden setting and tidy rooms, this well-kept place is our pick. The rooms aren't overly large, but they all have kitchenettes and snazzy furnishings.

Ballina Manor HOTEL $$$
(☎02-6681 5888; www.ballinamanor.com.au; 25 Norton St; r $165-290; ❄📶) This former school has been converted into a luxurious guesthouse, filled with restored 1920s furnishings. All rooms are indulgent: the most grand has a four-poster bed and spa bath.

Eating

Beanz FAST FOOD $
(222 River St; mains $8-11; ⏲11am-4pm; 🌿) For healthy fast food go to this salad bar on the main strip. Its predominately vegie options include falafel wraps, burgers and salads.

Ballina Gallery Cafe CAFE $$
(☎02-6681 3888; www.ballinagallerycafe.com.au; 46 Cherry St; mains breakfast $12-18, lunch $14-26; ⏲7.30am-3pm Wed-Sun) Ballina's 1920s former council chambers are home to the town's best cafe. Interesting breakfasts such as saganaki baked eggs and green fritters are offered with a side serve of contemporary art inside, or dine outside on the verandah.

Lighthouse Beach Cafe CAFE $$
(☎02-6686 4380; lighthousebeachcafe.com.au; 65 Lighthouse Pde; breakfast mains $13-20, lunch mains $18, dinner $18-27; ⏲7am-3pm Mon-Wed, to 9pm Thu-Sat, to 6pm Sun) With terrific views of East Ballina's Lighthouse Beach, this family-friendly cafe at the surf club turns out hearty breakfast platters and some tasty pasta and seafood dishes.

Shopping

During the daylight-saving months there's a weekly **Twilight Market** (Fawcett Park; ⏲4-8pm Thu Oct-Mar), while the **Ballina Missingham Farmers' Market** (Kingsford Smith Dr; ⏲6am-noon Sun) takes place year-round. The big one is **Ballina Markets** (Canal Rd; ⏲7am-1pm 3rd Sun of the month), held by the river.

Information

Ballina Airport Services Desk (Ballina Airport; ⏲10.15am-noon & 3.15-5pm Tue, Thu & Sat, 3.15-5pm Mon, Wed, Fri & Sun) An outpost of the information centre in town; opening hours are synced with flights.

Ballina visitor information centre (☎02-6686 3484; www.discoverballina.com; 6 River St; ⏲9am-5pm)

Getting There & Away

AIR

Ballina Byron Gateway Airport (BNK; ☎02-6681 1858; www.ballinabyronairport.com.au; Southern Cross Dr) Ballina Airport is 5km north of the centre of town. A taxi to the centre of Ballina should cost roughly $12 to $15 and there are regular Blanch's buses and shuttle services.

Jetstar (☎13 15 38; www.jetstar.com.au) Flies to/from Sydney and Melbourne.

Regional Express (Rex; ☎13 17 13; www.regionalexpress.com.au) Flies to/from Sydney.

Virgin (☎13 67 89; www.virginaustralia.com) Flies to/from Sydney.

AIRPORT SHUTTLES

Byron Easy Bus (☎02-6685 7447; www.byronbayshuttle.com.au) Scheduled door-to-door service from the airport to Lennox Head ($15, 15 minutes), Byron Bay ($20, 40 minutes) and Bangalow ($25, 50 minutes). Also shuttles from town to Gold Coast Airport ($39, 1¾ hours) and Brisbane Airport ($54, four hours).

BUS

Blanch's (☎02-6686 2144; www.blanchs.com.au) Local buses, including services to Lennox Head ($6.40, 15 minutes), Bangalow ($7.60, 30 minutes), Byron Bay ($9.60, 55 minutes) and Mullumbimby ($10, 1½ hours).

Greyhound (☎1300 473 946; www.greyhound.com.au) Has at least two coaches daily to/from Sydney ($147, 12½ hours), Nambucca Heads ($52, four hours), Coffs Harbour ($38, three hours), Byron Bay ($6, 45 minutes) and Brisbane ($40, 4½ hours).

Northern Rivers Buslines (☎02-6626 1499; www.nrbuslines.com.au) Eight buses to Lismore on weekdays and three on weekends ($9.70, 1¼ hours).

NSW TrainLink (☎13 22 32; www.nswtrainlink.info) Daily coaches to/from Grafton ($21, three hours), Yamba ($17, 2¼ hours), Lismore ($7, 45 minutes), Murwillumbah ($15, 1½ hours) and Tweed Heads ($20, two hours).

Premier (☎13 34 10; www.premierms.com.au) Daily coach to/from Sydney ($92, 13¼ hours), Port Macquarie ($66, seven hours), Nambucca Heads ($52, 5¼ hours), Coffs Harbour ($47, 4½ hours) and Brisbane ($36, 4½ hours).

CAR & MOTORCYCLE

The airport has plenty of car-hire desks. If you're driving to Byron Bay, take the prettier coast road through Lennox Head.

Mullumbimby & Brunswick Heads

POP 3173 & 1636

These two intriguing towns straddle the Pacific Hwy 18km north of Byron Bay.

A pyramid-shaped mountain acts as a backdrop for inland Mullumbimby (aka Mullum), an attractive country town lined with lazy palms, tropical architecture and a cosmopolitan spread of cafes, boutiques and pubs. The four-day **Mullum Music Festival** (www.mullummusicfestival.com) at the end of November is the prime time to visit. There's also a weekly **farmers' market** (www.mullumfarmersmarket.org.au; Mullumbimby Showground, 51 Main Arm Rd; ⏲7-11am Fri), and community markets on the third Saturday of the month.

Across the highway, beautiful Brunswick Heads (aka Bruns) reaps a bounty of fresh oysters and mud crabs from its peaceful Brunswick River inlets and beaches.

Sights

Crystal Castle & Shambhala Gardens GARDENS
(☎02-6684 3111; www.crystalcastle.com.au; 81 Monet Dr, Mullumbimby; adult/child $22/18) These magical gardens are dotted with monolithic crystal pieces, a huge gold Buddha and mystical statues. Wander across the terraced lawns and through the bamboo forest or take a guided tour on Monday afternoons (1.30pm). There's an open-air cafe for a casual bite plus tarot readings and aura photos.

Sleeping

Hotel Brunswick HOTEL $
(☎02-6685 1236; www.hotelbrunswick.com.au; 4 Mullumbimbi St, Brunswick Heads; s/d without bathroom $55/85) The 1940s Hotel Brunswick is a sight to behold. It has decent pub rooms and the **restaurant** (mains $20; ⏲10am-9pm) serves great nosh. There's live music Thursday to Sunday.

Brunswick River Inn MOTEL $$
(☎02-6685 1010; www.brunswickriverinn.com.au; 2 The Terrace, Brunswick Heads; r from $159; P❄📶) This recently renovated motel has bright, spacious rooms with Brunswick River views from the balconies, and is just a quick walk to the surf beach.

Eating

★ **Milk & Honey** PIZZA $$
(☎02-6684 1422; milkandhoneymullumbimby.com.au; 59a Station St, Mullumbimby; mains $24; ⏲5-9pm Tue-Sat) The wood-fire oven here turns out the best pizza in the region. Delicious combos such as pancetta, pineapple and pickled chilli or field mushroom, Parmesan and parsley are made with Byron market produce. Book ahead or be prepared to takeaway.

Rock & Roll Coffee Company THAI $$
(☎02-6684 4224; rockandrollcoffee.com.au; 3/55 Burringbar St, Mullumbimby; mains $15-20; ⏲7.30am-3pm Mon-Fri, to 2pm Sat, 5-9pm Wed-Fri) Outstanding Thai-Vietnamese street food is the mainstay at this laneside diner. You can also kick back with a terrific coffee or dandelion tea.

Getting There & Away

Blanch's (☎02-6686 2144; www.blanchs.com.au) Runs regular buses to/from Byron Bay ($6.40 25 minutes), Lennox Head ($10, one hour) and Ballina ($10, 1½ hours).

Northern Rivers Buselines (☎02-6626 1499; www.nrbuslines.com.au) Runs weekday buses to/from Byron Bay ($9.70, 20 minutes) and Bangalow ($9.70, 40 minutes).

NSW TrainLink (☎13 22 32; www.nswtrainlink.info) Services to Lismore ($8, one hour).

LISMORE & THE TWEED RIVER REGION

Away from the coast, the lush scenery, organic markets and alternative lifestyles make this one of Australia's most alluring regions – for locals and visitors alike. In fact the post-hippie rural lifestyle out here has become so mainstream that the epicentre of Nimbin is almost a theme park.

Twenty-three million years ago, a giant shield volcano burst forth here, gifting the landscape its mysterious contours. Erosion has taken its toll and all that remains is the lava plug (the peculiarly shaped Wollumbin Mt Warning) and the giant ring of jagged ridges that outlines the caldera.

Bangalow

POP 1520

Surrounded by subtropical forest and rolling green farmland, sophisticated Bangalow is home to a small, creative community, a dynamic, sustainable food scene and a range of urbane boutiques. The town is heaving during the monthly **Bangalow Market** (www.bangalowmarket.com.au; Bangalow Showgrounds; 9am-3pm 4th Sun of month), but it's well worth making the 14km trip from Byron at any time.

Sleeping

Bungalow 3 GUESTHOUSE $$
(0401 441 582; messengerproperty.com.au/bungalow3; 3 Campbell St; studio from $130, house from $230;) This pretty, weatherboard cottage in central Bangalow has two simply decorated white rooms, and French doors opening on to the deck and edible garden. There is an additional one-bedroom studio. Larger groups can hire out the whole place.

Possum Creek Eco Lodge BUNGALOWS $$$
(02-6687 1188; www.possumcreeklodge.com.au; Cedarvale Rd; bungalows from $198-235;) Set within grassy hills about 4km north of Bangalow, this complex has three well-spaced self-contained houses with views across the lush valleys. The 'eco' in the name includes water-conservation technologies and solar power.

Summer Hills Retreat CABINS $$$
(02-6687 2288; www.summerhills.com; 100 Binna Burra Rd; cabins from $349;) Amid hilly farmland are these four luxury cabins with well-stocked kitchens and spa baths (outdoors in the cabana suite). It's a wonderfully private place to stay and guests have access to nature trails, a yoga room and a beautiful salt-water pool.

Eating & Drinking

Sparrow Coffee CAFE $
(02-6687 2726; 8/36 Bangalow Rd; mains $12; 6am-3pm Mon-Sat) The folk from the acclaimed Harvest restaurant and bakery in nearby Newrybar have opened this tiny joint which delivers excellent Allpress coffee, indulgent sweet treats and ready-made lunchboxes.

Utopia CAFE $$
(02-6687 2088; www.utopiacafe.com.au; 13 Byron St; mains $14-26; 8.30am-4pm;) Open, airy and hung with interesting art, this long cafe has a good selection of magazines to divert you while you wait for your morning coffee and cooked brekky. The sweets are to die for.

Italian Diner ITALIAN $$
(www.theitaliandiner.com.au; 37-39 Byron St; mains $30; 7.30am-2.30pm & 5.30-9pm Mon-Fri, 8am-3pm & 5.30-9pm Sat & Sun) Sitting on the verandah of this buzzy bistro with a Campari and a bowl of *spaghetti ai gamberi* made with sweet local prawns, it's hard not to imagine that you're enjoying a long lunch somewhere in Italy. There's fabulous wood-fired pizzas and luscious desserts.

Town Restaurant & Cafe MODERN AUSTRALIAN $$$
(02-6687 2555; townbangalow.com.au; 33 Byron St; cafe mains $15-22, restaurant degustation $85; Downtown 8am-3pm Mon-Sat, 9am-3pm Sun, Uptown 7-9.30pm Thu-Sat) Upstairs (Uptown, if you will) is one of northern NSW's best restaurants, serving a six-course set menu artfully constructed from seasonal local produce. Head Downtown for perfect breakfasts, light lunches and a counter heavy with sweet creations.

Bangalow Hotel PUB
(www.bangalowhotel.com.au; 1 Byron St; 10am-midnight Mon-Sat, noon-10pm Sun) Sit on the deck of this much-loved pub, listen to live music, and order gourmet burgers or reserve a table at the classy but cool **Bangalow Dining Rooms** (02-6687 1144; www.bangalowdining.com; The Bangalow Hotel, 1 Byron St; mains $32; noon-3pm & 5.30-9pm).

Getting There & Away

Byron Easy Bus (p168) operates shuttles to/from Ballina Byron Gateway Airport.

Blanch's (02-6686 2144; www.blanchs.com.au) Weekday buses to/from Ballina ($7.60, 30 minutes) and Byron Bay ($6.40, 20 minutes).

Northern Rivers Buslines (02-6626 1499; www.nrbuslines.com.au;) Weekday buses to/from Lismore (1¼ hours), Byron Bay (30 minutes), Brunswick Heads (30 minutes) and Mullumbimby (40 minutes); all $9.70.

NSW TrainLink (13 22 32; www.nswtrainlink.info) Daily coaches to/from Murwillumbah ($9.70, 1¼ hours), Tweed Heads ($11.30, two hours), Burleigh Heads ($13.70, 1½ hours) and Surfers Paradise ($15.30, two hours).

Lismore

POP 27,500

With its heritage buildings and country town saunter, Lismore is the unassuming commercial centre of the Northern Rivers region. A vibrant community of creatives, a thriving Southern Cross University student population and a larger than average gay and lesbian presence add to the town's eclecticism.

It's an interesting place to visit, though most travellers prefer to stay on the coast or venture further into the hinterland.

Sights & Activities

Lismore Regional Gallery GALLERY
(www.lismoregallery.org; 131 Molesworth St; 10am-4pm Tue, Wed & Fri, to 6pm Thu, to 2pm Sat & Sun) FREE Lismore's diminutive gallery has just enough space for two temporary exhibitions; they're usually excellent.

Koala Care Centre WILDLIFE REFUGE
(www.friendsofthekoala.org; Rifle Range Rd; adult/family $5/10; tours 10am & 2pm Mon-Fri, 10am Sat) This centre takes in sick, injured and orphaned koalas; visits are only possible by guided tour at the designated times. To see koalas in the wild, head to **Robinson's Lookout** (Robinson Ave, Girard's Hill), immediately south of the town centre.

Wilson River Experience Walk WALKING
Starts in the city centre and skirts the river for 3km. Along the way you'll pass a bush-tucker garden, nurturing plants which once formed the daily diet of the local Widjabal clan.

Birdwing Butterfly Walk WALKING
In the suburb of Goonellabah, 6km east of the centre, the Birdwing Butterfly Walk has been planted with vines to attract the rare insect. You might also spot platypuses in the Tucki Tucki Creek, especially at dawn or sunset. To get here, take the Bruxner Hwy and turn right on Kadina St.

Festivals & Events

Lismore Lantern Parade PARADE
(www.lanternparade.com) Over 30,000 people line the streets to watch giant illuminated creatures glide past on the Saturday closest to the winter solstice (June).

Tropical Fruits GAY & LESBIAN
(www.tropicalfruits.org.au) This legendary New Year's bash is country NSW's biggest gay and lesbian event. There are also parties at Easter and on the Queen's Birthday holiday (June).

Sleeping

Melville House B&B $$
(02-6621 5778; www.melvillehouselismore.com; 267 Ballina St; s/d without bathroom $60/80, s with bathroom $90-110, d with bathroom $120-140;) This grand family home was built in 1942 by the owner's grandfather and features the area's largest private swimming pool. The six rooms offer superb value and are decorated with local art, cut glass and antiques.

Elindale House B&B $$
(02-6622 2533; www.elindale.com.au; 34 Second Ave; s/d $135/150;) Any chintziness is tempered with modern art at this excellent B&B in a characterful wooden house. The four rooms all have their own bathroom and some have hefty four-poster beds.

Eating

Goanna Bakery & Cafe BAKERY, CAFE $
(www.goannabakery.com.au; 171 Keen St; mains $11-17; 8am-5.30pm Mon-Fri, to 3pm Sat & Sun;) As well as baking organic sourdough bread and a delectable array of sweet things, this cavernous bakery-cafe serves a good selection of vegetarian and vegan meals.

Lismore Pie Cart FAST FOOD $
(cnr Magellan & Molesworth Sts; pies $4.80; 6am-5pm Mon-Fri, to 2pm Sat) A local institution serving homemade meat pies, mash, mushy peas and gravy.

Palate at the Gallery MODERN AUSTRALIAN $$
(02-6622 8830; www.palateatthegallery.com; 133 Molesworth St; mains breakfast $10-20, lunch $16-29, dinner $26-32; 10am-2.30pm Tue & Wed, 10am-2.30pm & 6-9pm Thu & Fri, 8am-2pm & 6-9pm Sat, 8am-2pm Sun;) This slick pavilion has French doors that open onto a sunny, shrub-lined terrace. It morphs seamlessly from swish daytime cafe to Lismore's top restaurant, offering delicious dishes throughout.

Shopping

Lismore has more markets than anywhere else in the region, with a weekly **organic market** (www.tropo.org.au; Lismore Showground; 7.30-11am Tue), **produce market** (www.farmersmarkets.org.au; Magellan St; 3.30-6.30pm Thu) and **farmers' market** (8-11am Sat), and a **car boot market** (Lismore Shopping Sq, Uralba St; 8am-2pm Sun) every first and third Sunday.

Information

Lismore visitor information centre (02-6626 0100; www.visitlismore.com.au; cnr Molesworth & Ballina Sts; 9.30am-4pm)

Getting There & Away

AIR

Lismore Regional Airport (LSY; 02-6622 8296; www.lismore.nsw.gov.au; Bruxner Hwy) Three kilometres south of the city.

Regional Express (Rex; ☎13 17 13; www.regionalexpress.com.au) Flies to/from Sydney.

BUS

Buses stop at the **Lismore City Transit Centre** (cnr Molesworth & Magellan Sts).

Northern Rivers Buslines (☎02-6622 1499; www.nrbuslines.com.au) Local buses plus services to/from Grafton (three hours), Ballina (1¼ hours), Lennox Head (one hour), Bangalow (1¼ hours) and Byron Bay (1½ hours); all $9.70.

NSW TrainLink (☎13 22 32; www.nswtrainlink.info) Coaches to/from Byron Bay ($6.45, one hour), Ballina ($7, 45 minutes), Mullumbimby ($8, one hour), Brunswick Heads ($9.60, 1½ hours) and Brisbane ($28.25, three hours).

Waller's (☎02-6622 6266; www.wallersbus.com) At least three buses on weekdays to/from Nimbin ($9, 30 minutes).

Nimbin

POP 1668

Welcome to Australia's alternative lifestyle capital, an intriguing little town that struggles under the weight of its own cliches. Nimbin was once an unremarkable Northern Rivers dairy village but that changed forever in May 1973. Thousands of students, hippies and devotees of the back-to-earth movement descended on the town for the Aquarius Festival with many staying on and creating new communities in the beautiful valleys in an attempt to live out the ideals expressed during the 10-day celebration.

Another landmark in Nimbin's history came in 1979 with the Terania Creek Battle, the first major conservation victory of its kind in Australia, which is often credited with ensuring the survival of NSW's vast tracts of rainforest. **Protestor Falls**, in what is now Nightcap National Park, is named in the conservationists' honour.

Today the old psychedelic murals of the rainbow serpent Dreaming and marijuana bliss that line Nimbin's main street are fading and the dreadlocked, beaded locals are weathered. While genuine remnants of the peace-and-love generation remain, the town has changed a lot since the '80s. The brazen pot dealers who make a living from the bus tours that barrel up from Byron peddle harder drugs as well, and alcohol-fueled violence is on the rise.

Sadly the **Rainbow Cafe**, bought by the hippies when they first arrived, and which served as the town lounge room (and star tourist attraction) for some 40 years, was burnt down in 2014, taking with it the Nimbin Museum.

Sights

Hemp Embassy CULTURAL CENTRE

(☎02-6689 1842; www.hempembassy.net; 51 Cullen St; ⏲9am-5pm) Part shop, part stronghold for minor political group the Hemp Party, this colourful place raises consciousness about marijuana legalisation, and provides all the tools and fashion items you'll need to attract police attention. The embassy organises the **MardiGrass festival** (www.nimbinmardigrass.com) each May.

Djanbung Gardens GARDEN

(☎02-6689 1755; www.permaculture.com.au; 74 Cecil St; tours $5; ⏲10.30am-3pm Wed-Sat, tours 11am Sat) FREE Nimbin was at the forefront of the organic gardening movement and this world-renowned permaculture education centre, created out of a degraded cow pasture, is home to food forests, vegetable gardens, a drought-proof system of dams, ponds and furry farm animals. There's a range of short-courses available.

Nightcap National Park NATIONAL PARK

(www.nationalparks.nsw.gov.au/nightcap-national-park) The spectacular waterfalls, sheer cliff of solidified lava and dense rainforest of 80-sq-km Nightcap National Park are perhaps to be expected from somewhere with the highest annual rainfall in NSW. It's part of the Gondwana Rainforests World Heritage Area and home to many native birds and protected creatures. From Nimbin, a 10km drive via Tuntable Falls Rd and Newton Dr leads to the edge of the park and then on to Mt Nardi (800m).

The **Historic Nightcap Track** (16km, 1½ days), which was stomped out by postal workers in the late 19th century, runs from Mt Nardi to **Rummery Park**, a picnic spot and camping ground. **Peate's Mountain Lookout**, just on from Rummery Park, offers a panoramic view all the way to Byron. The **Minyon Loop** (7.5km, four hours) is a terrific half-day hike around the spectacular Minyon Falls, which are good for an icy splash. A largely unsealed but very scenic road leads from the Channon to the Terania Creek Picnic Area, where an easy track heads to **Protestor Falls** (1.4km return).

Sleeping

There are dozens of local farms happy to host volunteers; contact **Willing Workers**

OFF THE BEATEN TRACK

BORDER RANGES NATIONAL PARK

Border Ranges National Park (www.nationalparks.nsw.gov.au/border-ranges-national-park; vehicle entry $7) The vast Border Ranges National Park covers 317 sq km on the NSW side of the McPherson Range, which runs along the NSW–Queensland border. It's part of the Gondwana Rainforests World Heritage Area and it's estimated that representatives of a quarter of all bird species in Australia can be found here.

The eastern section of the park can be explored on the 44km **Tweed Range Scenic Drive** (gravel and usable in dry weather), which loops through the park from Lillian Rock (midway between Uki and Kyogle) to Wiangaree (north of Kyogle on Summerland Way). The signposting on access roads isn't good (when in doubt take roads signposted to the national park), but it's well worth the effort.

The road runs through mountain rainforest, with steep hills and lookouts over the Tweed Valley to Wollumbin Mt Warning and the coast. The short walk out to the **Pinnacle Lookout** is a highlight and one of the best places to see the silhouette of Wollumbin against a rising sun. At **Antarctic Beech** there is a forest of 2000-year-old beech trees. From here, a walking track (about 5km) leads down to lush rainforest, swimming holes and a picnic area at **Brindle Creek**.

on Organic Farms (www.wwoof.com.au) for more information.

★ **Nimbin Rox YHA** HOSTEL $
(☎02-6689 0022; www.nimbinrox.com; 74 Thornburn St; camping/teepees/dm/d from $14/28/38/72; @🛜🏊) Escape the coastal crowds at this hostel and camping ground perched on a lush hill at the edge of town. There are plenty of spots to unwind with hammocks strung among the trees, a lovely heated pool and nearby swimming creek. Friendly managers go out of their way to please with free pancake breakfasts and a regular shuttle run into town.

Grey Gum Lodge GUESTHOUSE $
(☎02-6689 1713; www.greygumlodge.com; 2 High St; r $75-120; @🛜) The valley views from the front verandah of this palm-draped wooden Queenslander-style house are gorgeous. All the rooms are comfortable, tastefully furnished and have their own bathrooms.

Rainbow Retreat Backpackers HOSTEL $
(☎02-6689 1262; www.rainbowretreatnimbin.com; 75 Thorburn St; camp sites/dm/s/d $15/25/40/60, cabins from $120) Very basic, but totally in the age-of-Aquarius spirit, this back-to-the-bush retreat has a set of brightly coloured cabins, a small guesthouse enveloped by banana palms and shady camp sites.

Eating

Nimbin Pizza & Trattoria ITALIAN $
(☎02-6689 1427; 70 Cullen St; mains $12-15; ⏰5.30-9pm) Tasty pizza and pasta, and live music most Thursdays.

Nimbin Hotel PUB FOOD $
(☎02-6689 1246; www.nimbinhotel.com.au; Cullen St; mains $11-18; ⏰11am-10pm) This classic boozer has a vast back porch overlooking a verdant valley. The surprisingly good Hummingbird Bistro serves up everything from a 'treehugger's salad' to curries and grilled barramundi. There's live music most weekends and backpacker rooms upstairs.

Shopping

Nimbin Markets MARKET
(www.facebook.com/NimbinMarkets; Nimbin Community Centre) Nimbin's rainbow tribe comes out in force on market days, the fourth and fifth Sundays of the month (⏰8am to 3pm).

Blue Knob Farmers' Market MARKET
(719 Blue Knob Rd, Lillian Rock; ⏰9am-1pm Sat) A real-deal farmers' markets in the garden of the Blue Knob Hall Gallery.

Nimbin Candle Factory CRAFTS
(☎02-6689 1010; www.nimbincandles.com.au; ⏰9am-5pm Mon-Fri) Sells hand-dipped paraffin candles shaped like marijuana leaves, pyramids, wizards and unicorns in the Old Butter Factory by the bridge on the Murwillumbah side of town.

Nimbin Artists Gallery ARTS, CRAFTS
(www.nimbinartistsgallery.org; 49 Cullen St; ⏰10am-5pm) Local artists and craftspeople display and sell their wares here.

WORTH A TRIP

UKI & WOLLUMBIN NATIONAL PARK

Uki (pronounced 'uke-eye', population 250) is a sleepy village tucked alongside the surging Tweed River, under the numinous peak of Wollumbin Mt Warning. Although not as self-consciously hippyish as nearby Nimbin, it does have more than its fair share of holistic health and organics shops. Alternative lifestylers can be spotted at the weekly **farmers' market** (Uki Hall; 8am-12.30pm Sat) and the **Uki Buttery Bazaar** (Uki Village Buttery; 8am-2pm 3rd Sun of month).

Northwest of Uki, 41-sq-km **Wollumbin National Park** (www.nationalparks.nsw.gov.au/wollumbin-national-park) surrounds Wollumbin Mt Warning (1156m), the most dramatic feature of the hinterland, towering over the valley. The summit is the first part of mainland Australia to see sunlight each day, a drawcard that encourages many to trek to the top. You should be aware that, under the law of the local Bundjalung people, only certain people are allowed to climb the sacred mountain; they ask you not to climb it, out of respect for this. Instead, you can get an artist's impression of the view from the 360-degree mural at the Murwillumbah Visitor Information Centre .

A great place to stay is **Mavis's Kitchen and Cabins** (02-6679 5664; www.maviseskitchen.com.au; 64 Mt Warning Rd; mains $24-28; 11am-3pm Wed, Thu & Sun, 11am-3pm & 5.30-9pm Fri & Sat), a sublime slice of North Coast life with gorgeous gardens and a country-style menu offering slow-cooked organic fare.

Information

Nimbin visitor information centre (02-6689 1388; www.visitnimbin.com.au; 46 Cullen St; 10am-4pm)

Getting There & Away

BUS

Gosel's (02-6677 9394) Two buses on weekdays to Uki ($12.70, 40 minutes) and Murwillumbah ($14.70, one hour).

Waller's (02-6622 6266; www.wallersbus.com) At least three buses on weekdays to/from Lismore ($9, 30 minutes).

SHUTTLES & TOURS

Various operators offer day tours and shuttles to Nimbin from Byron Bay, sometimes with stops at surrounding sights. Most leave at 10am and return around 6pm.

Grasshoppers (0438 269 076; www.grasshoppers.com.au; return incl BBQ lunch $49)

Happy Coach (02-6685 3996; return $25)

Jim's Alternative Tours (0401 592 247; www.jimsalternativetours.com; tours $40)

Murwillumbah

POP 8530

Sitting pretty on the banks of the wide Tweed River, this old-fashioned country town is surrounded by a lush green coat of sugar cane and banana palms, while the ancient volcanic caldera of Wollumbin Mt Warning looms in the distance.

Sights

Tweed Regional Gallery & Margaret Olley Art Centre GALLERY
(artgallery.tweed.nsw.gov.au; 2 Mistral Rd; 10am-5pm Wed-Sun) FREE This exceptional gallery overlooking the river is an architectural delight and home to some of Australia's finest, including a new extension devoted to acclaimed Lismore-born painter Margaret Olley (1923–2011) which features a re-creation of her famous home studio.

Tropical Fruit World GARDENS
(02-6677 7222; www.tropicalfruitworld.com.au; Duranbah Rd; adult/child $45/25; 10am-4pm) North of town under the Big Avocado, this fruity theme park–plantation claims to have the world's largest collection of rare and tropical fruit – 500 varieties in total. It offers guided tractor tours, tastings, boat rides, native critters, a petting zoo and a miniature train.

Sleeping

Mount Warning-Murwillumbah YHA HOSTEL $
(02-6672 3763; www.yha.com.au; 1 Tumbulgum Rd; dm/d from $33/72) This former river-captain's home now houses a colourful waterfront hostel with eight-bed dorms. There's free ice cream at night plus canoe and bike hire.

Eating

Sugar Beat CAFE $
(02-6672 2330; www.sugarbeatcafe.com.au; 6-8 Commercial Rd; mains $7-17; 7.30am-5pm Mon-Fri,

to 2pm Sat; ☑) Park yourself by the sunny window or take in the scene from one of the pavement tables. Food choices include tasty cafe-style fusion fare and locally famous baked goods.

Modern Grocer CAFE, DELI $
(☎02-6672 5007; www.themoderngrocer.com; 3 Wollumbin St; mains $8-11; ⌚8.30am-5pm Mon-Fri, to 2pm Sat) The deli counter has goodies fit to turn picnics into gluttonous feasts. Sit yourself at the communal table and tuck into a cooked breakfast, sandwich or wrap.

Shopping

The weekly **Caldera Farmers' Market** (www.murwillumbahfarmersmarket.com.au; Murwillumbah Showground, 37 Queensland Rd; ⌚7-11am Wed) has produce, food stalls and live music. The **Cottage Market** (Knox Park) is held on the first and third Saturday of the month (⌚8am-1pm), and the **Showground Market** (www.murwillumbahshowground.com; Murwillumbah Showground) fills up the fourth Sunday (⌚8am-1pm).

Information

Murwillumbah visitor information centre (☎02-6672 1340; www.tweedtourism.com.au; cnr Alma St & Tweed Valley Way; ⌚9am-4.30pm) Worth a stop. Has national-park information and passes, plus a really great rainforest display and gallery.

Getting There & Away

Gosel's (☎02-6677 9394) Two buses on weekdays to Nimbin ($14.70, one hour) via Uki.

NSW TrainLink (☎13 22 32; www.nswtrainlink.info) Coaches to/from Lismore ($12.90, two hours), Ballina ($10.40, 1½ hours), Bangalow ($9.70, 1¼ hours), Byron Bay ($6.45, one hour) and Brisbane ($15.30, 1½ hours).

Premier (☎13 34 10; www.premierms.com.au) Daily coaches to/from Sydney ($92, 14¾ hours), Port Macquarie ($66, 7½ hours), Coffs Harbour ($52, 6¼ hours), Byron Bay ($12, one hour) and Brisbane ($25, 1¾ hours).

CLARENCE COAST

Grafton

POP 19,000

Don't be fooled by the franchises along the highway – Grafton's grid of gracious streets has grand pubs and some splendid old houses. In late October the town is awash with the soft lilac rain of jacaranda flowers. Susan Island, in the middle of the river, is home to a large colony of fruit bats; their evening flight is an impressive sight.

Sights

Victoria Street AREA
Victoria St is the city's main heritage precinct, with some fine examples of 19th-century architecture, including the **courthouse** (1862) at No 47, the **Anglican Cathedral** (commenced 1884) on the corner of Duke St, and **Roches Family Hotel** (1871) at No 85.

Grafton Regional Gallery GALLERY
(☎02-6642 3177; www.graftongallery.nsw.gov.au; 158 Fitzroy St; admission by donation; ⌚10am-4pm Tue-Sun) Occupying an impressive 1880 house, this small gallery has an interesting collection of NSW landscape paintings and regularly displays special exhibitions.

Clarence River Historical Society MUSEUM
(www.clarencehistory.org.au; 190 Fitzroy St; adult/child $3/1; ⌚1-4pm Tue-Thu & Sun) Based in pretty Schaeffer House (1903) this little museum displays treasures liberated from attics across town.

Festivals & Events

July Racing Carnival SPORTS
(www.crjc.com.au) A week-long carnival culminating in the Grafton Cup, the richest horse-racing event in country Australia.

Jacaranda Festival CULTURAL
(www.jacarandafestival.org.au) For two weeks from late October, Australia's longest-running floral festival paints the town mauve.

Sleeping

Gateway Village CAMPGROUND $
(☎02-6642 4225; www.thegatewayvillage.com.au; 598 Summerland Way; camp sites/cabins from $22/120; ❄@📶🏊) Putting the 'park' back into holiday park, this attractive complex has manicured gardens and an ornamental lake filled with waterlilies.

Annies B&B B&B $$
(☎0421 914 295; www.anniesbnbgrafton.com; 13 Mary St; s/d $145/160; ❄📶🏊) This beautiful Victorian house on a leafy corner has private rooms with an old-fashioned ambience, set apart from the rest of the family home. A continental breakfast is provided.

ABORIGINAL MID & NORTH COAST NEW SOUTH WALES

The area from the Tomaree Peninsula to Forster and as far west as Gloucester is the land of the **Worimi** people. Very little of it is now in their possession, but in 2001 the sand dunes of the Stockton Bight were returned to them, creating the Worimi Conservation Lands (p199). Dark Point Aboriginal Place in Myall Lakes National Park (p197) has been significant to the Worimi for around 4000 years. Local lore has it that in the late 19th century it was the site of one of many massacres at the hands of white settlers, when a community was herded onto the rocks and pushed off.

Heading north from Worimi land, you enter **Birpai** country, which includes Taree and Port Macquarie. The Sea Acres Rainforest Centre (p191) has a section devoted to the local people, and Birpai guides lead bush-tucker tours from here.

After travelling through the lands of the **Dainggatti** people (roughly equivalent to Kempsey Shire) you then enter **Gumbainggir** country, which stretches up to the Clarence River. Places such as Nambucca Heads still have a sizeable Aboriginal community. Nearby, Red Rock is the site of another 19th-century massacre.

The northern part of the NSW coast and much of the Gold Coast is the domain of the **Bundjalung** nation, including their sacred mountain Wollumbin Mt Warning (p174). Tours run by Aboriginal Cultural Concepts (p167) offer an introduction to Bundjalung life. The **Minjungbal Aboriginal Cultural Centre** (07-5524 2109; www.facebook.com/MinjungbalMuseum; Kirkwood Rd, South Tweed Heads ; adult/child $15/7.50; 10am-4pm Mon-Fri) at Tweed Heads is also worth visiting.

Eating

Heart & Soul Wholefood Cafe CAFE $
(02-6642 2166; cafeheartandsoul.com.au; 124a Prince St; $8-15; 7.30am-3pm, to 2pm Sat, 8am-noon Sun;) This beautifully styled cafe is the work of two couples who love plant-based foods. Expect ceramic bowls filled with warming Asian numbers and bright salad dishes. Sweet treats such as the choc mint 'cheesefake' are worth sampling.

Vines at 139 CAFE $$
(02-6642 5500; 139 Fitzroy St; mains $18-25; 7.30am-10pm) A lovely heritage house full of floral prints and jam jars. It's a popular place with a menu that strays all over the world, from Thai curries to Mediterranean salads.

Information

Clarence River visitor information centre (02-6642 4677; www.clarencetourism.com; cnr Spring St & Pacific Hwy; 9am-5pm;) South of the river.

National Parks and Wildlife Service office (NPWS; 02-6641 1500; Level 4, 49 Victoria St; 8.30am-4.30pm Mon-Fri)

Getting There & Away

AIR

Clarence Valley Regional Airport (GFN; 02-6643 0200; www.clarence.nsw.gov.au) Twelve kilometres southeast of town.

Regional Express (Rex; 13 17 13; www.rex.com.au) Flies to/from Sydney and Taree.

TRAIN & BUS

Busways (02-6642 2954; www.busways.com.au) Runs local services including four to eight buses to Maclean (one hour), Yamba (1¼ hours) and Angourie (1½ hours) daily; all $12.

Greyhound (1300 473 946; www.greyhound.com.au) Coaches to/from Sydney ($132, 10½ hours, three daily), Nambucca Heads ($31, 2½ hours, two daily), Coffs Harbour ($17, one hour, three daily), Byron Bay ($28, three hours, three daily) and Brisbane ($61, 6½ hours, three daily).

Northern Rivers Buslines (02-6626 1499; www.nrbuslines.com.au) One bus to/from Maclean ($9.70, 43 minutes) and Lismore ($9.70, three hours) on weekdays.

NSW TrainLink (13 22 32; www.nswtrainlink.info) Three trains head to/from Sydney ($71, 10 hours), Kempsey ($25, three hours), Nambucca Heads ($19, two hours) and Coffs Harbour ($12, 1¼ hours) daily, and one continues to Brisbane ($47, 4¼ hours). There's also a daily coach to Maclean ($6.50, 35 minutes), Yamba ($9.60, 1¼ hours), Ballina ($21, three hours), Lennox Head ($23.40, 3½ hours) and Byron Bay ($25, 3½ hours).

Premier (13 34 10; www.premierms.com.au) Daily coach to/from Sydney ($67, 9½ hours), Nambucca Heads ($34, 1¾ hours), Coffs Harbour ($34, one hour), Byron Bay ($47, 4¼ hours) and Brisbane ($52, 7½ hours).

Ryans Bus Service (02-6652 3201; www.ryansbusservice.com.au) Weekday buses to/

from Woolgoolga ($21, 1½ hours), Red Rock ($20, 50 minutes) and Coffs Harbour ($21.80, two hours).

Yuraygir National Park

The 535-sq-km **Yuraygir National Park** (vehicle entry $7) covers a 60km stretch of coast north from Red Rock, and is an important habitat for the endangered coastal emu. The isolated beaches are best discovered on the **Yuraygir Coastal Walk**, a 65km waymarked walk from Angourie to Red Rock following a series of tracks, trails, beaches and rock platforms, and passing through the villages of Brooms Head, Minnie Water and Wooli. It's best walked north to south with the sun at your back. Walkers can bush-camp at basic **camping grounds** (www.nationalparks.nsw.gov.au/Yuraygir-National-Park; adult/child $10/5) along the route; only some have drinking water available. The visitor centres stock fold-out walk guides ($2).

Wooli (population 493) occupies a long isthmus within the southern half of the park, with a river estuary on one side and the ocean on the other; this only adds to its isolated charm. In early October it hosts the **Australian National Goanna Pulling Championships** (www.goannapulling.com.au), where participants squat on all fours, attach leather harnesses to their heads and engage in a cranial tug-of-war.

If you fancy settling in for a few days' fishing, kayaking and lazing on the beach, **Solitary Islands Marine Park Resort** (☎02-6649 7519; www.solitaryislandsresort.com.au; 383 North St; camp sites/cabins from $31/140; ❄📶) 🍃 has a range of cabins in a scrubby riverside setting.

Grafton to Yamba

The delta between Grafton and the coast is a patchwork of farmland in which the now sinuous and spreading Clarence River forms more than 100 islands, some very large. Here you'll see the southernmost sugar-cane plantations and Queenslander-style houses – wooden structures perched on stilts and with high-pitched roofs to allow air circulation in the hot summers. The burning of the cane fields (May to December) adds a smoky tang to the air.

It's worth taking a small detour from the Pacific Hwy to **Ulmarra** (population 435), a heritage-listed town with a river port. The **Ulmarra Hotel** (www.ulmarrahotel.com.au; 2 Coldstream St, Ulmarra) is a quaint old corner pub with a wrought-iron verandah and a greener-than-green beer garden that stretches down to the river.

Maclean (population 2600) is a picturesque little riverside town (with no less than three pubs) that takes its Scottish heritage seriously, even wrapping its lamp posts in tartan. Stroll the riverfront, check out the shops and have a meal at the unexpectedly hip **On the Bite** (215 River St, Maclean; mains $12-18; ⏲7am-4.30pm Mon-Sat).

Yamba & Angourie

POP 6040 & 184

At the mouth of the Clarence River, the fishing town of Yamba is rapidly growing in popularity thanks to its quasi-bohemian lifestyle, top beaches and excellent eateries. Oft heard statements such as 'Byron Bay 20 years ago' are not unfounded. Its neighbour Angourie, 5km to the south, is a tiny, chilled-out place that has long been a draw for experienced surfers who were thrilled when it became one of Australia's first surf reserves.

Sights & Activities

Surfing for the big boys and girls is at **Angourie Point**, but Yamba's beaches have something for everyone else. **Main Beach** is the busiest, with an ocean pool, banana palms and a grassy slope for those who don't want to get sandy. **Convent Beach** is a sunbaker's haven and **Turner's**, protected by the breakwater, is ideal for surf lessons. You can sometimes spot dolphins along the long stretch of **Pippi Beach**.

A walking and cycling track winds along Yamba's coastline. The prettiest bit is from Pippi Beach around Lovers Point to Convent Beach. The Yuraygir Coastal Walk begins in Angourie.

Angourie Blue Pools SPRING

(The Crescent) These springwater-fed waterholes are the remains of the quarry used for the breakwater. The daring climb the cliff faces and plunge to the depths. The saner can slip silently into the water, surrounded by bush, only metres from the surf.

Bundjalung National Park NATIONAL PARK

(www.nationalparks.nsw.gov.au/bundjalung-national park; vehicle entry $7) Stretching for 25km along the coast north of the Clarence River to South Evans Head, this national park is largely untouched. Most of it is best explored with a 4WD. However, the southern reaches can be easily reached from Yamba via the passenger-only Clarence River Ferries to Iluka (at least four daily). This section of the park includes Iluka Nature Reserve, a stand of rainforest facing Iluka Beach, part of the Gondwana Rainforests World Heritage Area. On the other side of Iluka Bluff the literally named Ten Mile Beach unfurls.

Yamba Kayak KAYAKING
(☎02-6646 0065; www.yambakayak.com; 3/5hr $70/90) Half- and full-day adventures are the speciality, with forays into nearby wilderness areas.

Yamba-Angourie Surf School SURFING
(☎02-6646 1496; www.yambaangouriesurfschool.com.au; 2hr/3-day lessons $50/120) Lessons are run by former Australian surfing champion Jeremy Walters.

Clarence River Ferries CRUISE
(☎0408 664 556; www.clarenceriverferries.com; 11am-3pm) As well as regular ferries to Iluka (adults $7.20, children $3.60), it runs a live-music cruise on Sunday (adult/child $30/15) and a Harwood Island cruise twice a week (adult/child $20/10).

GONDWANA RAINFORESTS OF AUSTRALIA

Spread between 41 distinct sites (including 16 national parks) in the north of NSW and the southernmost parts of Queensland, this Unesco World Heritage List–inscribed area is the world's largest expanse of subtropical rainforest. In evolutionary terms it's a time capsule, representing ecosystems that have existed since before the breakup of Gondwana, the ancient supercontinent that once included Australia, New Zealand, Antarctica, South America, Africa and India. It's thought that Gondwana started to break up around 80 million years ago, with Australia separating from Antarctica around 45 million years ago.

To journey into the Jurassic, visit Iluka Nature Reserve (p177), Dorrigo National Park (p186), New England National Park (p188), Nightcap National Park (p172), Wollumbin National Park (p174) or Border Ranges National Park (p173).

Sleeping

Yamba YHA HOSTEL $
(☎02-6646 3997; www.yha.com.au; 26 Coldstream St, Yamba; dm $30-34, r $80; @ 🛜 🏊) This welcoming, family-run hostel has a popular bar and restaurant downstairs, and a barbecue area with a tiny pool on the roof.

Blue Dolphin Holiday Resort CAMPGROUND $
(☎02-6646 2194; www.bluedolphin.com.au; Yamba Rd, Yamba; camp sites/cabins from $37/105; ❄ @ 🛜 🏊) Right on the river the units at this sprawling holiday park range from simple cabins to luxurious houses. There's plenty to keep the kids happy with two pool complexes and a playground.

Yamba Beach Motel MOTEL $$
(☎02-6646 9411; www.yambabeachmotel.com.au; 30 Clarence St, Yamba; r $139-199; ❄ 🛜 🏊) At this boutique-style motel, rooms have large flat-screen TVs, extremely comfy beds and quality toiletries. There's also an excellent cafe that will deliver meals to your room, and a beach just down the hill.

Clubyamba APARTMENTS $$
(☎0427 461 981; www.clubyamba.com.au; 14 Henson Lane, Yamba; apt from $145; 🛜) At the top of the hill are four brightly painted contemporary apartments and two sea-view suites. There's also an architecturally designed one-bedroom town house near the river. All are luxurious options.

Surf Motel MOTEL $$
(☎02-6646 2200; www.yambasurfmotel.com.au; 2 Queen St, Yamba; r $120-180; ❄ 🛜) On a bluff overlooking Yamba's main beach, this modern place has eight spacious studios with kitchenettes. Some have balconies, too. Aside from the surf, it's blissfully quiet.

Eating & Drinking

★**Beachwood Cafe** TURKISH $$
(☎02-6646 9781; www.beachwoodcafe.com.au; 22 High St, Yamba; mains breakfast $13-16, lunch $18-22; 7am-2pm Tue-Sun) Cookbook author Sevtap Yüce steps out of the pages to deliver her bold *Turkish Flavours* to the plate at this wonderful little cafe. Most of the tables are outside, where the grass verge has been commandeered for a kitchen garden.

Leche Cafe CAFE $$
(☎0401 471 202; www.facebook.com/LecheCafe; 27 Coldstream St, Yamba; $14-25; 6am-2pm) After some backyard yoga at Leche Cafe you might

want to tuck into coconut bread and a Byron Bay–based Marvell coffee. The lunch menu is just as wholesome with beetroot burgers, cauliflower curries and fish tacos.

Irons & Craig CAFE $$
(☎02-6646 1258; ironsandcraig.com; 29 Coldstream St, Yamba; $12 16; ⏲7am 3pm Thu Tue, to 11am Wed) At this 1930s beach house there is pitch-perfect coffee, and kids fizz for the milkshakes (with homemade ice cream) in a jar. There's a five-course degustation dinner at least once a month.

Pacific Hotel PUB
(☎02-6646 2466; www.pacifichotelyamba.com.au; 18 Pilot St, Yamba) Perched on the the cliffs overlooking Yamba Beach, this hotel has some of the best pub views in Australia. There's regular live music and DJ nights, and the food's good, too.

Getting There & Away

Busways (☎02-6645 8941; www.busways.com.au) There are four to eight buses from Yamba to Angourie ($3.30, nine minutes), Maclean ($8.90, 19 minutes) and Grafton ($12, 1¼ hours) daily.

Greyhound (☎1300 473 946; www.greyhound.com.au) Has a daily coach to/from Sydney ($139, 11½ hours), Coffs Harbour ($28, two hours), Byron Bay ($15, 2¼ hours), Surfers Paradise ($41, five hours) and Brisbane ($46, 6¼ hours).

NSW TrainLink (☎13 22 32; www.nswtrainlink.info) Has a daily coach to Maclean ($7, 30 minutes), Grafton ($9.60, 1¼ hours), Lennox Head ($19, 2½ hours), Ballina ($17, 2¼ hours) and Byron Bay ($13.70, three hours).

COFFS HARBOUR REGION

Coffs Harbour

POP 71,798

Despite its inland city centre, Coffs has a string of fabulous beaches. Equally popular with families and backpackers, the town offers plenty of water-based activities, action sports and wildlife encounters, not to mention the cultural beacon that is the Big Banana.

Originally called Korff's Harbour, the town was settled by Europeans in the 1860s. The jetty was built in 1892 to load cedar and other logs. Bananas were first grown in the area in the 1880s, and the industry reached its peak in the 1960s. These days tourism is the mainstay of the local economy.

The town is split into three areas: the jetty area, the commercial centre and the beaches.

Sights

Park Beach is a long, lovely stretch of sand backed by dense shrubbery and sand dunes, which conceal the buildings beyond. **Jetty Beach** is somewhat more sheltered. **Diggers Beach**, reached by turning off the highway near the Big Banana, is popular with surfers, with swells averaging 1m to 1.5m. Naturists let it all hang out at **Little Diggers Beach**, just inside the northern headland.

★Muttonbird Island ISLAND
(www.nationalparks.nsw.gov.au/Muttonbird-Island-Nature-Reserve) The Gumbainggir people knew this island as Giidany Miirlarl, meaning Place of the Moon. It was joined to Coffs Harbour by the northern breakwater in 1935. The walk to the top (quite steep at the end) provides sweeping vistas. From late August to early April this eco treasure is occupied by some 12,000 pairs of wedge-tailed shearwaters, with their cute offspring visible in December and January.

North Coast Regional Botanic Garden GARDENS
(www.ncrbg.com.au; Hardacre St; admission by donation; ⏲9am-5pm) Immerse yourself in the subtropical surrounds of the greenhouses, sensory gardens and lush rainforest of these botanic gardens. The 8km **Coffs Creek Walk** passes by, starting at the pool on Coff St and finishing near the ocean.

Bunker Cartoon Gallery GALLERY
(www.coffsharbour.nsw.gov.au; John Champion Way; adult/child $2/1; ⏲10am-4pm Mon-Sat) Displays rotating selections from its permanent collection of 18,000 cartoons in a WWII bunker.

Coffs Harbour Regional Gallery GALLERY
(www.coffsharbour.nsw.gov.au; Rigby House, cnr Coff & Duke Sts; ⏲10am-4pm Tue-Sat) FREE Exhibits regional art and touring exhibitions.

Big Banana AMUSEMENT PARK
(www.bigbanana.com; 351 Pacific Hwy; combo pass adult/child $57/49; ⏲9am-5pm) FREE Built in 1964, the Big Banana started the craze for 'Big Things' in Australia. Admission is free, with charges for associated attractions such as ice skating, toboggan rides, minigolf, the waterpark, plantation tours and the irresistibly named 'World of Bananas Experience'.

Coffs Harbour

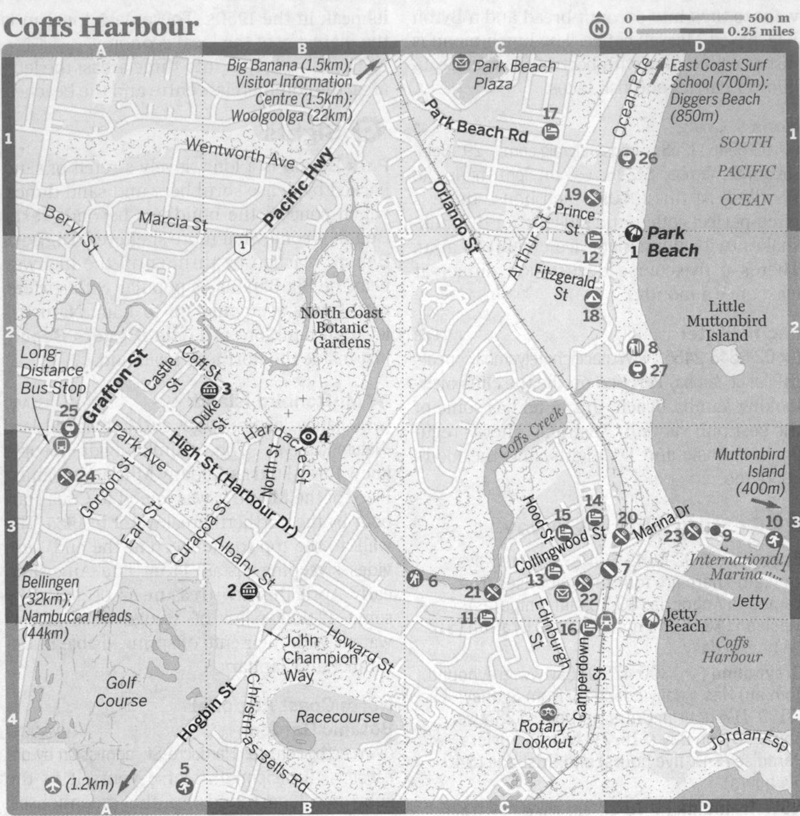

Coffs Harbour

Top Sights
1 Park Beach D2

Sights
2 Bunker Cartoon Gallery B3
3 Coffs Harbour Regional Gallery B2
4 North Coast Regional Botanic Garden B3

Activities, Courses & Tours
5 Coffs City Skydivers A4
6 Coffs Creek Walk & Cycleway C3
7 Jetty Dive D3
8 Lee Winkler's Surf School D2
9 Liquid Assets D3
10 Spirit of Coffs Harbour D3

Sleeping
11 Aussitel Backpackers C3
12 Bosuns Inn Motel C2
13 Caribbean Motel C3
14 Coffs Harbour YHA C3
15 Coffs Jetty BnB C3
16 Observatory Apartments C4
17 Pacific Property Management C1
18 Park Beach Holiday Park C2

Eating
19 Cafe Aqua C1
20 Fiasco D3
21 Mangrove Jack's C3
22 Old John's C3
23 Yknot Bistro D3
24 Zulus A3

Drinking & Nightlife
25 Coast Hotel A2
26 Hoey Moey D1
27 Surf Club Park Beach D2

Solitary Islands Aquarium AQUARIUM
(www.solitaryislandsaquarium.com; Bay Dr, Charlesworth Bay; adult/child $10/6; ⌚10am-4pm Sat & Sun, daily during school holidays) On weekends this small aquarium belonging to Southern Cross University's Marine Science Centre is open to the public. Touch tanks and enthusiastic guides provide close encounters with fish, coral and an octopus (try catching him at feeding time) that frequent the waters of the Solitary Islands Marine Park.

Activities

Canoes, kayaks and stand-up paddleboards can be hired from Mangrove Jack's cafe (p182). Keen hikers should pick up a copy of the *Solitary Islands Coastal Walk* brochure from the visitor centre ($2).

Jetty Dive DIVING
(☎02-6651 1611; www.jettydive.com.au; 398 Harbour Dr) The Solitary Islands Marine Park is a meeting place of tropical waters and southern currents, making for a wonderful combination of corals, reef fish and seaweeds. This dive shop offers spectacular diving and snorkelling trips (double boat dives $170), PADI certification ($495), and, from June to October, whale watching (adult/child $59/49).

Spirit of Coffs Harbour WHALE WATCHING
(☎02-6650 0155; www.gowhalewatching.com.au; Coffs Harbour Marina; per person $45; ⌚9.30am May-Nov) Whale watching on an 18.3m catamaran.

Coffs City Skydivers SKYDIVING
(☎02-6651 1167; www.coffsskydivers.com.au; Coffs Harbour Airport; tandem jumps $229-399) Throw yourself out of a plane from 4572m in the highest beach skydive in Australia.

East Coast Surf School SURFING
(☎02-6651 5515; www.eastcoastsurfschool.com.au; Diggers Beach; lessons from $55) A particularly female-friendly outfit run by former pro surfer Helene Enevoldson.

Lee Winkler's Surf School SURFING
(☎02-6650 0050; www.leewinklerssurfschool.com.au; Park Beach; from $55) One of the oldest surf schools in Coffs.

Tours

Liquid Assets ADVENTURE TOUR
(☎02-6658 0850; www.surfrafting.com; 38 Marina Dr; half-day tours from $50) Offers a suite of watery tours and activities, including kayaking, white-water rafting, surfing and platypus spotting.

Festivals & Events

Pittwater to Coffs Harbour Regatta SPORTS
(www.pittwatertocoffs.com.au) A mini Sydney to Hobart–style celebration which starts in Sydney on 2 January and finishes here.

Coffs Harbour International Buskers & Comedy Festival MUSIC
(www.coffsharbourbuskers.com) Held in late September.

Sleeping

One of many holiday-apartment agents is **Pacific Property Management** (☎02-6652 1466; www.coffsaccommodation.com.au; 101 Park Beach Rd).

Coffs Harbour YHA HOSTEL $
(☎02-6652 6462; www.yha.com.au; 51 Collingwood St; dm $27-33, r $70-140; ⊝@≋) With hostels offering service and amenities such as these, it's a wonder hotels don't go out of business. The dorms are spacious, the private rooms have bathrooms, and the TV lounge and kitchen are immaculate. You can hire surfboards and bikes.

Aussitel Backpackers HOSTEL $
(☎02-6651 1871; www.aussitel.com; 312 Harbour Dr; dm/d from $27/65; @≋) Don't be put off by the bright orange exterior. This capacious brick house has homely dorms and a shady courtyard. Surfboards, stand-up paddleboards, kayaks, canoes and snorkelling gear are free to borrow. Car rental is cheap.

Park Beach Holiday Park CAMPGROUND $
(☎02-6648 4888; www.coffsholidays.com.au; Ocean Pde; camp sites/cabins from $35/87; ≋) This place is massive and ideally located at the beach. Kids are well catered for with a jumping pillow and an exceptionally fun pool featuring slides and fountains.

Bosuns Inn Motel MOTEL $
(☎02-6651 2251; www.motelcoffsharbour.com; 37 Ocean Pde; r $95; ❄≋) The friendly owners keep everything shipshape at this well-priced, nautical-style motel across the road from Park Beach. There's a nice pool at the rear.

Coffs Jetty BnB B&B $$
(☎02-6651 4587; www.coffsjetty.com.au; 41a Collingwood St; d from $125;) A cut above your average B&B, this suburban town house has tastefully appointed rooms and terrific

bathrooms. It's an easy walk to the beach and restaurants.

Caribbean Motel MOTEL $$
(02-6652 1500; www.caribbeanmotel.com.au; 353 Harbour Dr; r/apt from $132/165) Close to the jetty, this 24-unit motel has been tastefully renovated. The best rooms have balconies, views and spa baths, and there are great-value one-bedroom suites with kitchenettes.

Observatory Apartments APARTMENTS $$
(02-6650 0462; www.theobservatory.com.au; 30-36 Camperdown St; apt from $170) The studio, two- and three-bedroom apartments in this attractive modern complex are bright and airy, with chef-friendly kitchens. They all have balconies with ocean views and some have spa baths.

Eating

Old John's CAFE $
(www.facebook.com/oldjohns; 358 Harbour Dr; mains $10-17; 7am-4pm Sun-Tue, to 11pm Wed-Sat) Cheery young staff prepare top brews and excellent food at this hip cafe, which is decked out with mismatched furniture and great art. Evenings see live music, cocktails and $15 pasta and wine deals.

Cafe Aqua CAFE $
(02-6652 5566; www.cafeaqua.com.au; 57 Ocean Pde; mains $10-19; 7am-3pm) This excellent cafe near Park Beach whips up substantial cooked breakfasts and an impressive range of bagels and burgers for lunch. The coffee's good, too.

Yknot Bistro PUB FOOD $$
(02-6651 1741; www.yknotbistro.com.au; Coffs Harbour Yacht Club, 30 Marina Dr; mains breakfast $13-18, lunch $17-30, dinner $21-33; 7am-2.30pm & 6-8.30pm) This busy eatery serves pub-style seafood, steaks and pasta. Best of all, it has an ocean view – rare in Coffs – and plenty of outdoor seating.

Mangrove Jack's CAFE $$
(02-6652 5517; www.mangrovejackscafe.com.au; Promenade Centre, Harbour Dr; mains breakfast $9-16, lunch $17-25, dinner $24-30; 7.30am-3pm Sun-Thu, 7.30am-3pm & 5-9pm Fri & Sat) The attraction here is the wonderful location on a quiet bend of Coffs Creek. Enjoy a cold beer or a coffee on the balcony and catch up on some emails using the free wi-fi.

★ **Fiasco** ITALIAN $$$
(02-6651 2006; www.fiascorestaurant.com.au; 22 Orlando St; mains $38; 5-9pm Tue-Sat) Classic Italian fare is prepared in an open kitchen using produce from the best local suppliers and herbs from its own garden. Expect earthy delights such as bean soup, wood-fired pizza and homemade pasta. If you're not overly hungry, grab some antipasti at the bar.

Zulus ETHIOPIAN $$$
(02-6652 1588; www.zuluscoffs.com; Best Western Zebra Motel, 27 Grafton St; mains $35; 6-8.30pm Tue-Sat) This jungle-print African restaurant loves to surprise; just take a look at the menu. It may not be truly authentic, but it is certainly high on flavour and finger-licking fun.

Drinking & Nightlife

See Thursday's edition of the *Coffs Harbour Advocate* (www.coffscoastadvocate.com.au) for listings.

Surf Club Park Beach PUB
(02-6652 9870; www.surfclubparkbeach.com; 23 Surf Club Rd, Park Beach; 7am-11pm) A Sunday afternoon session on the beach deck listening to local musicians is one of the top Coffs experiences. Drinks can move into a seafood or tapas dinner.

Hoey Moey PUB
(www.hoeymoey.com.au; 84 Ocean Pde; 10am-late) The massive inner beer garden gives a good indication of how much this place kicks off in summer. Pool competitions, live music, quiz nights and crab racing fill up the week.

Coast Hotel PUB
(www.coasthotel.com.au; 2 Moonee St; 11am-late) Lovers of a lazy afternoon in the beer garden will enjoy the landscaped decking and couch-filled breakaway areas.

Information

Visitor information centre (02-6648 4990; www.coffscoast.com.au; Big Banana, 351 Pacific Hwy; 9am-5pm)

Getting There & Away

AIR

Coffs Harbour Airport (CFS; 02-6648 4767; www.coffscoast.com.au/airport; Airport Dr) Three kilometres southwest of town.

QantasLink (13 13 13; www.qantas.com.au) Flies to/from Sydney.

Tigerair (☎02-8073 3421; www.tigerair.com.au) Flies to/from Sydney.

Virgin (☎13 67 89; www.virginaustralia.com) Flies to/from Sydney and Melbourne.

BUS

Long-distance and regional buses leave from a shelter adjacent to the visitor centre.

Busways (☎02-6652 2744; www.busways.com.au) Runs at least five buses to/from Nambucca Heads and Bellingen on weekdays (both $11.90, 1¼ hours), and at least one on Saturday.

Greyhound (☎1300 473 946; www.greyhound.com.au) Coaches to/from Sydney ($66, 8½ hours, daily), Port Macquarie ($37, 2½ hours, two daily), Nambucca Heads ($13, 45 minutes, two daily), Byron Bay ($45, 3½ hours, four daily) and Brisbane ($81, seven hours, three daily).

New England Coaches (☎02-6732 1051; www.newenglandcoaches.com.au) At least two coaches per week to/from Dorrigo ($45, 1½ hours) and Bellingen ($35, 50 minutes).

Premier (☎13 34 10; www.premierms.com.au) Daily coach to Sydney ($66, 8½ hours), Port Macquarie ($47, 2¼ hours), Nambucca Heads ($34, 40 minutes), Byron Bay ($50, five hours) and Brisbane ($59, 8½ hours).

Ryans Bus Service (☎02-6652 3201; www.ryansbusservice.com.au) Buses to/from Woolgoolga ($13, one hour, six on weekdays and two on Saturday) and Grafton ($21.80, two hours, two on weekdays).

TRAIN

NSW TrainLink (☎13 22 32; www.nswtrainlink.info) Three trains head to/from Sydney ($67, nine hours), Kempsey ($13, 1¾ hours), Nambucca Heads ($5, 40 minutes) and Grafton ($11.30, 1¼ hours) daily, and one continues to Brisbane ($59, 5½ hours).

Getting Around

Busways, Ryans and **Sawtell** (☎02-6653 3344; www.sawtellcoaches.com.au) run local bus routes; Sawtell has regular services to the airport.

Coffs District Taxis (☎13 10 08; www.coffstaxis.com.au) operates a 24-hour service.

Woolgoolga

POP 4720

Two superb beaches lie about 20km north of Coffs. First up is surfing hotspot **Emerald Beach** with its winning southern left-hand reef break and appropriately named Look at Me Now headland. About 12km north Woolgoolga (locally known as 'Woopi') is famous for its surf-and-Sikh community. If you're driving by on the highway you're sure to notice the impressive Guru Nanak Temple, a Sikh *gurdwara* (place of worship). There is a twice-monthly Saturday **Bollywood Bazaar** here, while in September the town goes all out with the annual **Curryfest** (www.facebook.com/WoolgoolgaCurryfest) celebration.

Sleeping

Woolgoolga Beach Caravan Park CAMPGROUND $
(☎02-6648 4711; www.coffscoastholidayparks.com.au; 55 Beach St; camp sites/cabins from $36/78; 📶) Right on the beach; surprisingly quiet at night.

Solitary Islands Lodge B&B $$
(☎02-6654 1335; www.solitaryislandslodge.com.au; 3 Arthur St; r $160; 📶) The three immaculate guest rooms in this modern hilltop house have impressive sea views. The charming hosts stock the rooms with ingredients for a continental breakfast.

Waterside Cabins CABIN $$
(☎02-6654 1644; www.watersidecabins.com.au; Hearnes Lake Rd; cabins from $113; ❄🏊) These stylish two- and three-bedroom units are part of a large complex of cabin-style residences. The four rental cabins are in a leafy spot near the lake; there's a walkway to the beach.

Eating

White Salt FISH & CHIPS $
(☎02-6654 8832; 70 Beach St; $10-18; ⏰11.30am-2pm daily & 5-8pm Wed-Mon) Fresh ingredients and a quality catch to match. Check out the salads, featuring Tahitian raw fish, or for something more old-school design your own box of battered whiting and chips.

Bluebottles Brasserie CAFE $$
(☎02-6654 1962; www.bluebottlesbrasserie.com.au; 53 Beach St; mains breakfast $12-17, lunch $14-23, dinner $24-30; ⏰6.15am-4pm Mon-Thu, to 9pm Fri & Sat, 7am-3pm Sun) Starting with strong, early-morning presurf coffees and stacks of corn fritters, the all-day breakfast menu rolls on to generous salads and afternoon cakes.

Getting There & Away

Ryans has infrequent buses to/from Coffs Harbour ($13, one hour), Red Rock ($11, 15 minutes) and Grafton ($21, 1½ hours). Coaches on the Pacific Hwy route stop here.

Sawtell

POP 3451

The beach community of Sawtell is spiritually closer to glamorous Noosa than to its inland neighbour, Coffs Harbour, just 10 minutes away. Heritage-listed fig trees shade the main street and a range of upmarket cafes and boutiques. It's also the home of the **Sawtell Chilli Festival** (www.sawtellchillifestival.com.au; Jul).

Sleeping

Sawtell Motor Inn MOTEL **$$**
(02-6658 9872; www.sawtellmotorinn.com.au; 57 Boronia St; r from $150;) Just off the main street and a five-minute walk to the beach, this quiet and clean motel has bright, spacious units decked out in cane furniture. Some have kitchenettes and spa baths.

Eating

Sea Salt FISH & CHIPS **$**
(02-6658 9199; www.seasaltsawtell.com.au; 29 First Ave; $8-12; 11am-7.30pm) Gourmet snapper burgers, fish tacos and prawn rolls as well as fabulous gelato.

Split Espresso CAFE **$$**
(02-6658 3026; www.splitcafe.com.au; 3-4 First Ave; breakfast mains $13-17, lunch mains $16; 7am-5pm) Rolls out great coffee and rib-sticking brekkies such as plump hot cakes dripping with maple syrup, while doubling as a bike showroom. Staff will happily advise on local rides.

Hello Sawtell MODERN AUSTRALIAN **$$**
(0417 933 107; www.facebook.com/hellosawtell; 20 First Ave; share plates $16, mains $26; 6-10pm Tue-Sun) Lively crowds spill out into the passageway as they feast on smart, delicious shared plates at this impeccably styled restaurant. Book ahead.

Getting There & Away

Sawtell Coaches (www.sawtellcoaches.com.au) run between Coffs Harbour and Sawtell.

Nambucca Heads

POP 19,530

Nambucca Heads is languidly strewn over a dramatically curling headland interlaced with the estuaries of the glorious Nambucca River. It's a relatively quiet and unspoilt place, evoking sun-soaked holidays of the '70s and '80s, when a fishing rod and zinc cream was all you needed.

Nambucca (pronounced 'nam-*buk*-a') means 'many bends', and the river valley was ruled by the Gumbainggir people until European timber cutters arrived in the 1840s. There are still strong Aboriginal communities in Nambucca Heads and up the valley in Bowraville.

Sights

Of the numerous viewpoints, **Captain Cook Lookout**, set on a high bluff, is the place to ponder the swath of beaches. A road here leads down to the tide pools of **Shelly Beach**. Going north, Shelly Beach blends into **Beilbys Beach** and then **Main Beach**, which is the only one that's patrolled.

★**V-Wall** BREAKWATER
For decades residents and holidaymakers have decorated the rocks of Nambucca's breakwater with vivacious multicoloured artwork, and with notes to lovers, families and new-found friends. Visitors are encouraged to paint their own message, if they can find some space on the boulders.

Sleeping

White Albatross Holiday Park CAMPGROUND **$**
(02-6568 6468; www.whitealbatross.com.au; 52 Wellington Dr; camp sites from $41, cabins $87-180;) Located near the river mouth, this large holiday park is laid out around a sheltered lagoon. The cabins are kept fastidiously clean and have full kitchens. There is a jolly on-site tavern with a great deck.

Marcel Towers APARTMENT **$$**
(02-6568 7041; www.marceltowers.com.au; 12-14 Wellington Dr; d from $130;) All units in this tidy but dated block of holiday apartments have views over the estuary. If the views lead to inspiration, the complex has row boats and kayaks for you to borrow.

Riverview Boutique Hotel GUESTHOUSE **$$**
(02-6568 6386; www.riverviewlodgenambucca.com.au; 4 Wellington Dr; s/d from $139/179;) Built in 1887, this former pub is now a wooden, two-storey charmer with eight stylish rooms; some rooms have views.

Eating

Bookshop Café CAFE **$**
(02-6568 5855; cnr Ridge & Bowra Sts; meals $9-14; 8am-5pm;) The verandah tables here are *the* place in town for breakfast. As the

WORTH A TRIP

RED ROCK

The village of Red Rock (population 310) is set between a beautiful beach and a glorious fish-filled river inlet. It takes its name from the red-tinged rock stack at the headland. The local Gumbainggir people know it by a more sombre name: Blood Rock. In the 1880s a detachment of armed police slaughtered the inhabitants of an Aboriginal camp, chasing the survivors to the headland, where they were driven off. The Blood Rock Massacres are commemorated by a simple plaque, and the area is considered sacred.

The **Yarrawarra Aboriginal Cultural Centre** (02-6640 7100; www.yarrawarra.org; 170 Red Rock Rd, Corindi Beach; 9am-4pm Wed-Sun) has an interesting art gallery and a bush-tucker cafe, where you can try kangaroo and lemon-myrtle damper. It also holds bush-medicine tours and art classes; call ahead if you're interested in joining one.

Accommodation (including some flash permanently pitched tents) is available at **Red Rock caravan park** (02-6649 2730; www.redrock.org.au; 1 Lawson St; camp sites/cabins from $23/105;).

On weekdays Ryans has occasional buses to/from Woolgoolga ($11, 15 minutes) and Grafton ($20, 50 minutes).

day progresses, there are cakes, slices, sandwiches and salads to sample.

Lom Talay THAI $$
(02-6568 8877; 58 Ridge St; mains $15; 5.30-9pm Tue-Sat) There's a great ambience at this modest Thai restaurant. Locals and tourists dig into lime-scented curries loaded with vegies and hearty staples such as pad thai. Summer nights are busy, so book ahead. BYO.

Nambucca Boatshed & Cafe CAFE $$
(02-6568 6511; nambuccaboatshed.com.au; Riverside Dr; mains $12-18; 7.30am-4pm Mon-Sat, 8am-3pm Sun) Right on the river's edge, the highlight of this low-key verandah cafe is the sublime view. Work off a plentiful burger lunch with a frolic in a kayak, on a paddleboard or in a tinny hired from the **tackle shop** (02-6568 6432; www.nambuccacbd.com.au/beachcomber.html; Riverside Dr; 7am-5pm) next door.

Information

Nambucca Heads Visitor Information (02-6568 6954; www.nambuccatourism.com.au; cnr Riverside Dr & Pacific Hwy; 9am-5pm)

Getting There & Away

BUS

Long-distance buses stop at the visitor centre.

Busways (02-6568 3012; www.busways.com.au) Six buses to/from Bellingen ($9.70, 1¼ hours) and Coffs Harbour ($11.90, 1¼ hours) on weekdays, and one or two on Saturday.

Greyhound (1300 473 946; www.greyhound.com.au) Two coaches daily to/from Sydney ($100, eight hours), Port Macquarie ($22, 1¾ hours), Coffs Harbour ($13, 45 minutes), Byron Bay ($60, 4½ hours) and Brisbane ($106, 8¼ hours).

Premier (13 34 10; www.premierms.com.au) Daily coach to/from Sydney ($63, eight hours), Port Macquarie ($38, 1¾ hours), Coffs Harbour ($34, 40 minutes), Byron Bay ($58, 5¾ hours) and Brisbane ($63, 9¼ hours).

TRAIN

NSW TrainLink (13 22 32; www.nswtrainlink.info) Three daily trains to/from Sydney ($66, eight hours), Wingham ($25, three hours), Kempsey ($8, one hour) and Coffs Harbour ($5, 40 minutes), and two to Brisbane ($62, 6¼ hours).

Dorrigo

POP 1080

Dorrigo is a pretty little place arrayed around the T-junction of two wider-than-wide streets.

The town's main attraction is the **Dangar Falls**, 1.2km north of town, which cascades over a series of rocky shelves before plummeting into a basin. You can swim here if you have a yen for glacial bathing.

Sleeping

Heritage Hotel Motel Dorrigo HOTEL $$
(02-6657 2016; www.hotelmoteldorrigo.com.au; cnr Cudgery & Hickory Sts; r from $105;) The charm of this pub's exterior is not echoed in the bar or the dining room. Upstairs, the renovated bedrooms are adequate, especially for the price. Motel units face the rear car park.

WORTH A TRIP

SCOTTS HEAD

For a scenic 17km detour from the Pacific Hwy, heading north towards Nambucca Heads, take Tourist Drive 14 towards Stuarts Point and drive through the eucalyptus forest to **Grassy Head**. From here the road continues through **Yarriabini National Park** (www.nationalparks.nsw.gov.au/yarriabini-national-park) to **Scotts Head** (population 820), a small, popular beach settlement. While you're here, it's worth stopping at **Taverna Six** (☎02-6569 7191; www.tavernasix.com; 6 Short St; mains breakfast $13-16, dinner $26-28; ⌚8.30am-1pm daily, 6.30-9pm Wed-Sat), a cosy Greek eatery with wonderful food. Continuing on, the road follows a stream lined by tall trees on its way back to the highway.

Mossgrove B&B **$$**
(☎02-6657 5388; www.mossgrove.com.au; 589 Old Coast Rd; r $195) Set on 2.5 hectares, 8km from Dorrigo, this lovely federation-era home has two upmarket rooms, a guest lounge and a bathroom, all tastefully renovated to suit the era. A continental breakfast is included.

Eating & Drinking

Dorrigo Wholefoods CAFE **$**
(☎02-6657 1002; www.dorrigowholefoods.com.au; 28 Hickory St; mains $12; ⌚7.30am-3pm Mon-Fri, 8am-2pm Sat) Head past the bulk legumes and make up a plate from a cabinet of salads, cakes and savory morsels such as lobster pot pie and ricotta fritters. Staff whip up super juice combinations.

Thirty Three on Hickory EUROPEAN **$$**
(☎02-6657 1882; www.thirtythreeonhickory.com.au; 33 Hickory St; mains $17-23; ⌚5-9pm Wed-Sun) This 1920s weatherboard cottage has stained-glass windows and a blossoming garden. The speciality is sourdough pizza, and there is also hearty bistro fare, served with white tablecloths, sparkling silverware and a cosy wood fire.

Red Dirt Distillery DISTILLERY
(☎02-6657 1373; www.reddirtdistillery.com.au; 51-53 Hickory St; ⌚10am-4pm Mon-Fri, to 2pm Sat & Sun) Sample the creative range of vodkas and liqueur made from local fruits and Dorrigo red-dirt potatoes.

Information

Dorrigo Information Centre (☎02-6657 2486; www.dorrigo.com; 36 Hickory St; ⌚10am-3pm)

Getting There & Away

Three New England Coaches (p189) per week head to Coffs Harbour ($45, 1½ hours)

Dorrigo National Park

From Bellingen the Waterfall Way climbs up the escarpment to Dorrigo. The drive passes several plunging torrents and provides a teaser for the lush vistas of Dorrigo National Park.

Stretching for 119 sq km, this park is part of the Gondwana Rainforests World Heritage Area. It's home to a huge diversity of vegetation and over 120 species of bird. The **Rainforest Centre** (☎02-9513 6617; www.nationalparks.nsw.gov.au/Dorrigo-National-Park; Dome Rd; adult/child $2/1; ⌚9am-4.30pm; 📶), at the park entrance, has displays and a film about the park's ecosystems, and can advise you on which walk to tackle. It even provides free wi-fi and a charging station for phones and cameras. It's also home to the excellent **Canopy Cafe** (www.canopycafedorrigo.com; mains $14-19; ⌚9am-4.30pm) and the **Skywalk**, a viewing platform that juts out over the rainforest and provides vistas over the valleys below.

Starting from the Rainforest Centre, the **Wonga Walk** is a two-hour, 6.6km-return walk on a bitumen track through the depths of the rainforest. Along the way it passes a couple of very beautiful waterfalls, one of which you can walk behind.

Bellingen

POP 12,854

Buried in foliage on a hillside above the Bellinger River, this gorgeous town dances to the beat of its own bongo drum. Thick with gourmet, organic cuisine and accommodation, 'Bello' is hippie without the dippy. Located between the spectacular rainforest of Dorrigo National Park and a spoiled-for-choice selection of beaches, it is a definite jewel on the East Coast route.

The wide river valley here was part of the extensive territory of the Gumbainggir people until cedar cutters arrived in the 1840s. River craft were able to reach here until the 1940s, when dredging was discontinued. In 1988 it found a new claim to fame as the setting of Peter Carey's Booker Prize-winning novel *Oscar and Lucinda*.

Sights

Bellingen Island WILDLIFE RESERVE
(www.bellingen.com/flyingfoxes) This little semi-attached island on the Bellinger River (it's only completely cut off when the river is in flood) is home to a huge colony of grey-headed flying foxes. At dusk they fly out in their thousands to feed; it's an impressive sight, best viewed from the bridge in the centre of town. For a closer look take the steep path onto the island from Red Ledge Lane, on the northern bank.

The best months to visit are from October to January, when the babies are being born and nursed.

Activities

Bellingen Canoe Adventures CANOEING
(☎02-6655 9955; www.canoeadventures.com.au; 4 Tyson St, Fernmount; hire per hour/day $15/55) Guided day trips on the Bellinger River (adult/child $90/60), and full-moon tours (adult/child $25/20).

Valery Trails HORSE RIDING
(☎02-6653 4301; www.valerytrails.com.au; 758 Valery Rd, Valery; 2hr ride adult/child $65/55) A stable of over 75 horses and plenty of acreage to explore; located 15km northeast of town.

Festivals & Events

Camp Creative ART
(www.campcreative.com.au) Five days of arts workshops for adults and kids in mid-January.

Bellingen Readers & Writers Festival LITERATURE
(bellingenwritersfestival.com.au) Established and emerging writers appear at talks, panels, readings and workshops over the Queen's Birthday long weekend in June.

Bellingen Jazz Festival JAZZ
(www.bellingenjazzfestival.com.au) A strong line-up of jazz names performs over a long weekend in mid-August.

Sleeping

Bellingen YHA HOSTEL $
(☎02-6655 1116; www.yha.com.au; 2 Short St; dm $33, r without/with bathroom $80/105; @ wi-fi) A tranquil, engaging atmosphere pervades this renovated weatherboard house, with impressive views from the broad verandah. Staff will pick you up from the bus stop and train station in Urunga if you call ahead.

Federal Hotel HOTEL $
(☎02-6655 1003; www.federalhotel.com.au; 77 Hyde St; s/d with shared bathroom $80/100; wi-fi) This beautiful old pub has renovated weatherboard rooms, some of which open onto a balcony facing the main street. Downstairs there's a lively pub scene that includes food and live music.

Bellingen Riverside Cottages CABINS $$
(☎02-6655 9866; www.bellingenriversidecottages.com.au; 224 North Bank Rd; cottages from $150; air-con, wi-fi, pets) These polished mountain cabins have cosy interiors with country furnishings and big, sun-sucking windows. Timber balconies overlook the river, which you can tackle on a complimentary kayak. Your first night includes a sizeable brekky hamper.

Bellingen River Family Cabins CABINS $$
(☎02-6655 0499; www.bellingencabins.com.au; 850 Waterfall Way; cabins $150; air-con) Two large two-bedroom cabins overlook the wide river valley on this family farm 4km east of Bellingen. The units are well equipped and sleep up to six; extras include complimentary use of kayaks and breakfast supplies. One cabin is wheelchair accessible.

★ **Lily Pily** B&B $$$
(☎02-6655 0522; www.lilypily.com.au; 54 Sunny Corner Rd; r from $260; air-con, wi-fi) Set on a knoll, this beautiful architect-designed complex has three bedrooms overlooking the river. It's a high-end place designed to pamper, with champagne on arrival, lavish breakfasts served until noon, luxurious furnishings and more. It's 3km south of the centre.

Eating & Drinking

★ **Hearthfire Bakery** BAKERY $
(☎02-6655 0767, www.hearthfire.com.au; 73 Hyde St; items $9-14; ⏰7am-5pm Mon-Fri, 7.30am-2pm Sat, 9am-2pm Sun) Follow the smell of hot-from-the-woodfire organic sourdough and you'll find this outstanding country bakery and cafe. Try the famous macadamia fruit loaf or settle in with a coffee and an incredibly indulgent pie. There is a full breakfast menu.

Bellingen Green Grocers HEALTH FOOD $
(☎02-6655 0846; 58-60 Hyde St; ⏰7.30am-6pm Mon-Fri, to 5pm Sat, to 4pm Sun) Everything here is supplied by growers within 150km of town. The mouth-watering produce is perfect for a riverside picnic, while in the

THE WATERFALL WAY

Once you've travelled the 40km from the Pacific Hwy through Bellingen to Dorrigo, there's still another 125km of the Waterfall Way to go before you reach Armidale. Should you press on, the route offers a number of highlights.

➡ Fifty kilometres past Dorrigo (2km west of Ebor) there's a right turn for Ebor Falls in **Guy Fawkes River National Park** (www.nationalparks.nsw.gov.au/guy-fawkes-river-national-park).

➡ The Waterfall Way then edges **Cathedral Rock National Park** (www.nationalparks.nsw.gov.au/cathedral-rock-national-park). On the left after 8km is Point Lookout Rd, which leads to **New England National Park** (www.nationalparks.nsw.gov.au/new-england-national-park), another section of the Gondwana Rainforests World Heritage Area.

➡ After another 28km, look for the left turn to the 260m-high Wollomombi Falls, a highlight of **Oxley Wild Rivers National Park** (www.nationalparks.nsw.gov.au/oxley-wild-rivers-national-park).

attached **cafe** (11am-2.30pm Mon-Sat) they serve up wraps, salads and smoothies.

Hyde CAFE $
(62 Hyde St; snacks $6; 7.30am-4.30pm Mon-Fri, 9am-1.30pm Sat;) Sip excellent coffee inside this vintage furniture shop. Thankfully, the muffins and cakes are not preloved.

Bellingen Gelato Bar ICE CREAM $
(www.bellingengelato.com.au; 101 Hyde St; 10am-6pm Wed-Sun) A 1950s American-styled cafe with sensational homemade ice cream.

Purple Carrot CAFE $$
(02-6655 1847; 105 Hyde St; mains $13-16; 8am-3pm) The brekky-biased menu offers eggs galore alongside dishes such as brioche French toast, smoked trout on a potato rösti and creamy pesto mushrooms. Get in early for Sunday brunch.

Oak Street Food & Wine MODERN AUSTRALIAN $$$
(02-6655 9000; www.oakstreetfoodandwine.com.au; 2 Oak St; lunch $12-18, dinner mains $34; noon-9.30pm Wed-Sat, 10am-3pm Sun) This much-loved restaurant continues to turn out sophisticated, accessible dishes that make the most of the Bellinger Valley bounty. There is a fabulous Sunday brunch menu.

★ **No 5 Church St** BAR
(www.5churchstreet.com; 5 Church St; mains $16; 11am-10pm Wed-Fri, 8am-10pm Sat, 8am-4pm Sun;) Morphing effortlessly from cafe to bar, Bellingen's coolest venue stages an eclectic roster of live music, movie nights and community gatherings. The menu comes with a directory of local growers who have produced the ingredients for all the tasty dishes.

Shopping

The **community market** (www.bellingenmarkets.com.au; Bellingen Park, Church St; 9am-3pm 3rd Sat of the month) is a regional sensation, with more than 250 stalls. There's also a **growers' market** (www.bellingengrowersmarket.com; Bellingen Showgrounds, cnr Hammond & Black Sts; 8am-1pm 2nd & 4th Sat of the month).

Old Butter Factory ARTS, CRAFTS
(www.theoldbutterfactory.com.au; 1 Doepel St; 9am-5pm) Houses craft, gift and homeware shops, plus a gallery, opal dealers and a cafe.

Emporium Bellingen CLOTHING
(02-6655 2204; www.emporiumbellingen.com.au; 73-75 Hyde St; 9am-5pm Mon-Sat, 10am-5pm Sun) Located in the historic Hammond and Wheatley building (1909) this beautifully presented boutique has a good range of homeware and clothes. Upstairs is a treasure trove of colourful market imports.

Heartland Didgeridoos MUSIC, CLOTHING
(02-6655 9881; www.heartlanddidgeridoos.com.au; 2/25 Hyde St; 10am-4.30pm Mon-Sat) Has a stellar reputation for producing high-quality instruments.

Bellingen Book Nook BOOKS
(02-6655 9372; 25 Hyde St; 10am-4pm Tue-Sat) Secondhand books are stacked to the ceiling in this tiny bookworm cave.

Information

Waterfall Way information centre (02-6655 1522; www.coffscoast.com.au; 29-31 Hyde St; 9am-5pm) Stocks brochures on scenic drives, walks and an arts trail.

Getting There & Away

From Bellingen the spectacular Waterfall Way climbs steeply for 29km to Dorrigo.

Busways (☎02-6655 7410; www.busways.com.au) Five or six buses run to/from Nambucca Heads and Coffs Harbour on weekdays (both $11.90, 1¼ hours); two run on Saturday.

New England Coaches (☎02-6732 1051; www.newenglandcoaches.com.au) Three coaches per week to Urunga ($40) and Coffs Harbour ($35).

KEMPSEY SHIRE

Kempsey Shire takes in the large agricultural town of Kempsey, the farms of the Macleay Valley and a line-up of gorgeous surf beaches.

If you've got the time for a scenic detour, leave the highway at Kempsey and take Crescent Head Rd to the coast. From here the road to Gladstone edges leafy Hat Head National Park before following the Belmore River to its junction with the Macleay River. The drive to South West Rocks follows the Macleay, its banks lined with dense reeds, old farmhouses and vintage shacks built on stilts.

Kempsey

POP 29,361

Two icons of Australiana came from Kempsey – the Akubra hat and late country-music legend Slim Dusty – but the town certainly couldn't be accused of cashing in on them. The Akubra factory is closed to the public and the sleek **Slim Dusty Centre** (☎02-6562 6533; www.slimdustycentre.com.au; 490 Pacific Hwy , South Kempsey) remains empty until an additional couple of million dollars is found to install a permanent display about his life, and to build a road to the centre. Until then, the only moderately interesting attraction on offer is the **Kempsey Museum** (www.kempseymuseum.org; 62 Lachlan St; adult/child $4/2; ⏲10am-4pm).

Getting There & Away

Local bus services are run by Busways (p195). Services extend to Port Macquarie, Crescent Head and South West Rocks.

NSW Trainlink (p196), Greyhound (p195) and Premier (p195) all run services along the Pacific Hwy, stopping in Kempsey.

South West Rocks

POP 4820

One of many pretty seaside towns on this stretch of coast, South West Rocks has spectacular beaches and enough interesting diversions for a night or two.

The lovely curve of **Trial Bay**, stretching east from the township, takes its name from the *Trial*, a boat which sunk here during a storm in 1816 after being stolen by convicts fleeing Sydney. The eastern half of the bay is now protected by **Arakoon National Park**, centred on a headland that's popular with kangaroos, kookaburras and campers. The hamlet of **Arakoon** has some lovely camping options as well as a flock of beach-house rentals. On its eastern flank, **Little Bay Beach** is a small grin of sand sheltered from the surf by a rocky barricade. A great place for a swim, it's also the starting point for some good walks.

Sights & Activities

The South West Rocks area is great for divers, especially Fish Rock Cave, south of Smoky Cape. **South West Rocks** (☎02-6566 6474; www.southwestrocksdive.com.au; 5/98 Gregory St) and **Fish Rock** (☎02-6566 6614; www.fishrock.com.au; 134 Gregory St) dive centres both offer dives (one-/two-day double boat dives $130/250) and accommodation.

Trial Bay Gaol MUSEUM

(☎02-6566 6168; www.nationalparks.nsw.gov.au/arakoon-national-park/; Cardwell St; adult/child $10/7; ⏲9am-4.30pm) Occupying Trial Bay's eastern headland, this imposing structure was built between 1877 and 1886 to house convicts brought in to build a breakwater. Nature had other ideas and the breakwater washed away. The prison subsequently fell into disuse, aside from a brief interlude in WWII when men of German and Austrian heritage were interned here. Today it contains an interesting museum devoted to its chequered history.

It's a pleasant 4km dawdle along the beach from South West Rocks.

Sleeping

Horseshoe Bay Holiday Park CAMPGROUND $

(☎02-6566 6370; www.mvcholidayparks.com.au; 1 Livingstone St; camp sites/cabins from $49/99) Planted a hop and a skip from both the main street and the beach, this caravan park gets extremely busy during the summer holidays.

Trial Bay Gaol Campground CAMPGROUND $

(☎02-6566 6168; www.nationalparks.nsw.gov.au/arakoon-national-park/; Cardwell St; camp sites from $28) Behind the gaol, this stunning NPWS camping ground affords generous beach views from most sites and hosts ever-present

WORTH A TRIP

GLADSTONE

It's worth stopping at riverside Gladstone (population 387) for a zip around the **Macleay Valley Community Art Gallery** (www.kempsey.nsw.gov.au/gallery/; 5 Kinchela St; 10.30am-4pm Thu-Sun) FREE and a drink at the **Heritage Hotel** (www.heritagehotel.net.au; 21 Kinchela St; mains from $16; ⏲10am-midnight Mon-Sat, to 9pm Sun), an excellent old pub with an oasislike beer garden.

kangaroos. Amenities include drinking water and flush toilets, and coin-slot hot showers and gas BBQs.

Smoky Cape Retreat B&B $$
(☎02-6566 7740; smokycaperetreat.com.au; 1 Cockatoo Pl, Arakoon; r $160;) This cosy retreat in bushland near Arakoon has three private spa suites and rambling gardens that house a saltwater pool and a tennis court. The owners run a charming cafe on their deck where they serve a complimentary hot breakfast.

Heritage Guesthouse B&B $$
(☎02-6566 6625; www.heritageguesthouse.com.au; 21-23 Livingstone St; d $120-175;) This renovated 1880s house has lovely, old-fashioned rooms, some with spa baths. Choose from the simpler rooms downstairs or the more lavish versions, with ocean views, upstairs. Rates include continental breakfast.

Rockpool Motor Inn MOTEL $$
(☎02-6566 7755; www.rockpoolmotorinn.com.au; 45 McIntyre St; r from $140;) This modern block just a few streets from the beach has smartly furnished rooms and superhelpful staff. The on-site restaurant isn't bad either.

Eating

Chillati Gelati GELATERIA $
(31 Livingstone St; ⏲10am-5pm Sun-Thu, to 8.30pm Fri & Sat) Every beach town needs a good ice cream shop, and South West Rocks has a real winner. The colourful range of 30 gelato flavours is made on the premises with local milk. It also makes good coffee.

Malt & Honey CAFE $
(☎02-6566 5200; 5-7 Livingstone St; mains $10-16; ⏲7.30am-4pm Tue-Sun) This cafe across from the beach leans towards more clever dishes than its neighbours, including robust salads and moist homemade cakes.

Trial Bay Kiosk CAFE $$
(☎02-6566 7100; www.trialbaykiosk.com.au; Cardwell St; mains breakfast $10-16, lunch & dinner $18-28; ⏲8am-2pm & 5.30-9.30pm Fri & Sat) Sit on the terrace and soak up the views from this cafe near the gaol. At lunchtime the menu wanders into bistro territory, traversing the likes of steak and mash, risotto, and fish and chips.

Information

Visitor information centre (☎02-6566 7099; www.macleayvalleycoast.com.au; 1 Ocean Ave; ⏲9am-4pm)

Getting There & Away

Busways (☎02-6562 4724; www.busways.com.au) Runs buses to/from Kempsey two or three times daily Monday to Saturday ($13.60, 46 minutes).

Hat Head National Park

Covering almost the entire coast from Crescent Head to South West Rocks, this 74-sq-km **national park** (vehicle entry $7) protects scrubland, swamps and some amazing beaches, backed by one of the largest dune systems in NSW.

The isolated beachside village of **Hat Head** (population 326) sits at its centre. At the far end of town, behind the holiday park, a picturesque wooden footbridge crosses the Korogoro Creek estuary. The water is so clear you can see fish darting around.

The best views can be had from **Smoky Cape Lighthouse**, at the northern end of the park. During the annual whale migration it's a prime place from which to spot them.

Sleeping

Hat Head Holiday Park CAMPGROUND $
(☎02-6567 7501; www.mvcholidayparks.com.au; Straight St; sites/cabins from $35/121) An old-fashioned family-orientated holiday park close to the beach and footbridge.

NPWS Camp Sites CAMPGROUND $
(www.nationalparks.nsw.gov.au/hat-head-national-park; camp sites per adult/child $5/3) You can camp at Hungry Gate, 5km south of Hat Head, or at secluded Smoky Cape, just below Smoky Cape Lighthouse. Both operate on a first-in basis; neither takes bookings. Non-

flush toilets and a barcecue area are provided; you'll need to bring water with you.

Smoky Cape Lighthouse B&B, COTTAGES $$$
(☎02-6566 6301; www.smokycapelighthouse.com; Lighthouse Rd; s/d from $150/220, cottages per 2 nights from $500) Romantic evenings can be spent gazing out to sea and hearing the wind whip around the historic lighthouse-keeper's residence high up on the headland.

Crescent Head

POP 979

This beachside hideaway has one of the best right-hand surf breaks in the country. Today many come just to watch the longboard riders surf the epic waves of **Little Nobby's Junction**. There's also good shortboard riding off Plomer Rd. Untrammelled **Killick Beach** stretches 14km north.

Sleeping & Eating

Local agency **Point Break Realty** (☎02-6566 0306; www.crescentheadholidayaccommodation.com.au; 4 Rankine St) specialises in holiday rentals.

Surfari HOSTEL, MOTEL $
(☎02-6566 0009; www.surfaris.com; 353 Loftus Rd; dm/r from $40/150;) These guys started the original Sydney–Byron surf tours and now base themselves in Crescent Head because 'the surf is guaranteed every day'. The rooms are clean and comfortable and surf-and-stay packages are a speciality. It's located 3.5km along the road to Gladstone.

Sun Worship Eco Apartments APARTMENTS $$$
(☎1300 664 757; www.sunworship.com.au; 9 Belmore St; apt from $220;) Stay in guilt-mitigated luxury in one of five spacious, rammed-earth villas featuring sustainable design, including flow-through ventilation, solar orientation and solar hot water.

Crescent Head Tavern PUB FOOD $$
(www.crescentheadtavern.com; 2 Main St; mains $15-30; noon-2pm & 5.30-7.30pm) The local pub has cold beer, a sun-soaked deck and a massive menu of burgers, seafood, pizza and salads.

Getting There & Away

Busways (☎02-6562 4724; www.busways.com.au) Busways buses run between Crescent Head and Kempsey ($10.10, 25 minutes) two to three times a day; no Sunday services.

PORT MACQUARIE

POP 76,500

Making the most of its position at the entrance to the subtropical coast, Port, as it's commonly known, is overwhelmingly holiday focused, with a string of beautiful beaches.

Sights

Port's awesome beaches are all within short driving distance from the centre of town. Most of them are great for swimming and surfing, and they seldom get crowded. Surfing is particularly good at **Town**, **Flynn's** and **Lighthouse** beaches, all of which are patrolled in summer. The rainforest runs down to the sand at **Shelly** and **Miners** beaches, the latter of which is an unofficial nudist beach.

Whale season is May to November; there are numerous vantage points around town, or you can get a closer look on a whale-watching cruise.

It's possible to walk all the way from the **Town Wharf** to Lighthouse Beach. Along the way, the **breakwater** has been transformed into a work of community guerrilla art. The elaborately painted rocks range from beautiful memorials to 'party hard'-type inanities.

Koala Hospital WILDLIFE RESERVE
(www.koalahospital.org.au; Lord St; admission by donation; 8am-4.30pm) Chlamydia, traffic accidents and dog attacks are the biggest causes of injury for koalas living near urban areas; about 250 end up in this shelter each year. You can walk around the open-air enclosures any time of the day, but you'll learn more during the tours (3pm). Some of the longer-term patients have signs detailing their stories. Check the website for volunteer opportunities.

Roto House HISTORIC BUILDING
(www.nationalparks.nsw.gov.au/macquarie-nature-reserve; Lord St; admission by gold-coin donation; 10am-4.30pm) This beautifully preserved late Victorian weatherboard villa was built by surveyor John Flynn in 1891 and was occupied by his family right up until 1979. The enthusiastic volunteers will happily give you a guided tour.

Sea Acres National Park NATIONAL PARK
(www.nationalparks.nsw.gov.au/sea-acres-national-park; Pacific Dr; adult/child $8/4; 9am-4.30pm) This 72-hectare pocket of national park protects the state's largest and most diverse strand of coastal rainforest. It's alive with

Port Macquarie

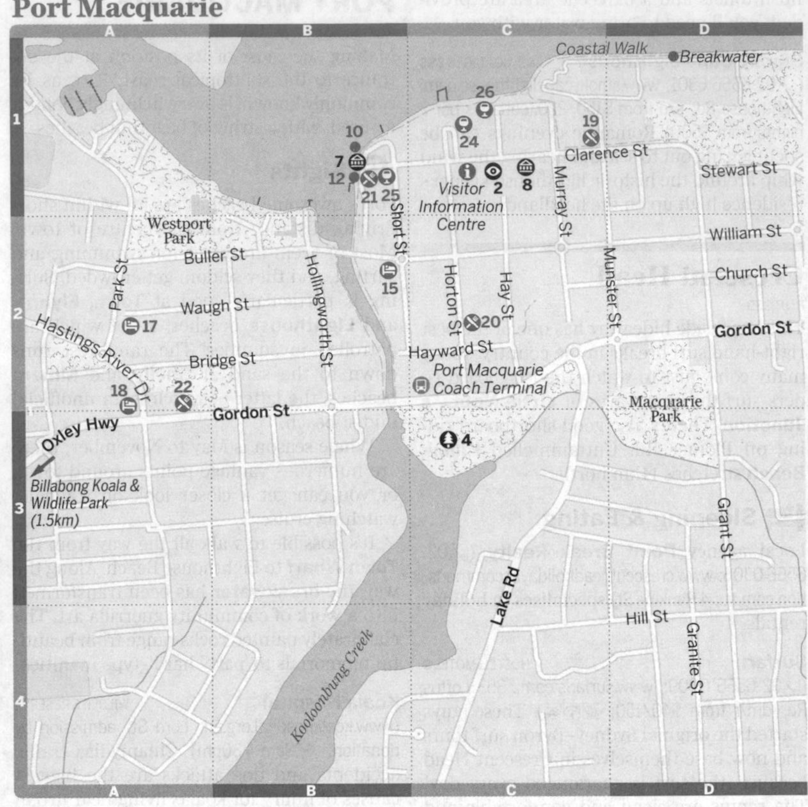

Port Macquarie

Top Sights

1 Flynn's Beach F4

Sights

2 Glasshouse C1
Glasshouse Regional Gallery .... (see 2)
3 Koala Hospital E4
4 Kooloonbung Creek Nature Park C3
5 Maritime Museum E2
6 Observatory E2
7 Pilot's Boatshed B1
8 Port Macquarie Historical Museum C1
9 Roto House E4

Activities, Courses & Tours

10 Port Macquarie Cruise Adventures B1
11 Port Macquarie Surf School F4
12 Port Venture Cruises B1

Sleeping

13 Eastport Motor Inn E3
14 Flynns on Surf F4
15 Mantra Quayside B2
16 Observatory E2
17 Ozzie Pozzie YHA A2
18 Port Macquarie Backpackers A2

Eating

19 Corner Restaurant C1
20 Fusion 7 .... C2
21 LV's on Clarence B1
Milkbar Town Beach .... (see 16)
22 Social Grounds A2
23 Stunned Mullet E2

Drinking & Nightlife

24 Beach House C1
25 Grape & Petal B1
26 Zebu Bar & Grill C1

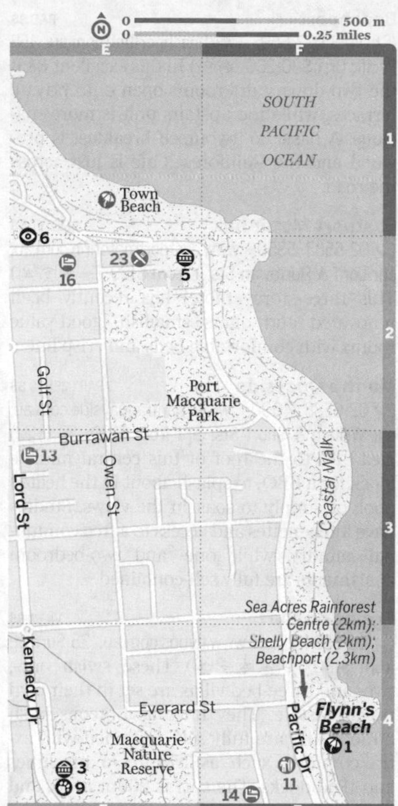

birds, goannas, brush turkeys and diamond pythons.

The Rainforest Centre has an excellent cafe (p194) and audiovisual displays about the local Birpai people. The highlight is the wheelchair-accessible 1.3km-long boardwalk through the forest. Fascinating one-hour guided tours by knowledgeable volunteers are run during the high season.

Kooloonbung Creek Nature Park PARK
(Gordon St) FREE Encompassing 50 hectares of bush and wetland, this park is home to many bird species. A series of walking trails and wheelchair-accessible boardwalks heads through mangroves and casuarina forest.

Billabong Koala & Wildlife Park ZOO
(☎02-6585 1060; www.billabongkoala.com.au; 61 Billabong Dr; adult/child $24.50/14; ⏰9am-5pm) Time your visit for the 'koala patting' (10.30am, 1.30pm and 3.30pm) at the park's koala-breeding centre. There are heaps of other Australian critters as well as monkeys, meerkats and endangered snow leopards.

Port Macquarie Historical Museum MUSEUM
(www.port-macquarie-historical-museum.org.au; 22 Clarence St; adult/child $5/2; ⏰9.30am-4.30pm Mon-Sat) An 1836 house has been transformed into this surprisingly interesting little museum. Aboriginal and convict history are given due regard before more eclectic displays take over, including a 'street of shops' and a display of beautiful old clothes (including a whole section on underwear).

Glasshouse ARTS CENTRE
(☎02-6581 8888; www.glasshouse.org.au; cnr Clarence & Hay Sts) This civic and architectural showpiece was built on the site of convict overseers' cottages; archaeological artefacts are on display in the foyer and basement. It houses the **regional art gallery** (⏰10am-4pm Tue-Sun) FREE, a 600-seat theatre and the tourist information centre.

Maritime Museum MUSEUM
(www.maritimemuseumcottages.org.au; 6 William St; adult/child $5/2; ⏰10am-4pm) The old pilot station (1882) above Town Beach has been converted into a small maritime museum. There's an even smaller extension of the museum in the 1890s **Pilot's Boatshed** (www.maritimemuseumboatshed.org.au; admission by donation; ⏰10am-2pm) at the Town Wharf.

Observatory OBSERVATORY
(www.pmobs.org.au; William St; adult/child $8/5; ⏰7.30pm Wed & Sun, 8.15pm Oct-Apr) Sneak a peek through the telescope at the astronomical observatory on one of its public viewing and presentation nights.

Activities

Port Macquarie Coastal Walk WALKING
FREE This wonderful coastal walk begins at Town Green foreshore and winds for about 9km along the coast to **Tracking Point Lighthouse** (Lighthouse Rd) in Sea Acres National Park (p191). There are plenty of opportunities for swimming (it takes in eight beaches) and between May and November you can often view the whale migration. The walk can also be divided into shorter 2km sections.

Port Macquarie Surf School SURFING
(☎02-6584 7733; www.portmacquariesurfschool.com.au; 46 Pacific Dr; lessons from $40) Offers a wide range of lessons for all ability levels.

Soul Surfing SURFING
(☎02-6582 0114; www.soulsurfing.com.au; classes from $50) Particularly good for beginners.

Tours

Port Venture Cruises CRUISE
(☎1300 795 577; www.portventure.com.au; Town Wharf; adult/child from $17/10) Offers twilight, lunch and 'eco-history' cruises with dolphin watching included. Whale-watching cruises from mid-May to mid-November ($50).

Port Macquarie Cruise Adventures CRUISE
(☎0414 897 444; www.cruiseadventures.com.au; Town Wharf; cruises from $15) Dolphin-watching, whale-spotting, lunch, sunset and everglades cruises.

Port Macquarie Hastings Heritage WALKING TOUR
(☎0447 429 016; www.pmheritage.com.au; per person $29; 9.30am Wed-Sat) Two-and-a-half-hour walking tours through Port's history, leaving from the Glasshouse. There's an additional 90-minute cemetery tour ($19) at 2pm Wednesday to Saturday.

Sleeping

Ozzie Pozzie YHA HOSTEL $
(☎02-6583 8133; www.ozziepozzie.com; 36 Waugh St; dm/s/d from $31/66/88;) In an unusual compound fashioned from three converted suburban houses, this hostel has clean rooms and a relaxed atmosphere. There's a range of activities on offer, along with pool and table-tennis tables, free bodyboards, and bike hire ($5 per day).

Port Macquarie Backpackers HOSTEL $
(☎02-6583 1791; www.portmacquariebackpackers.com.au; 2 Hastings River Dr; dm/s/d from $31/65/80;) This heritage-listed house has pressed-tin walls, colourful murals and a leafy backyard with a small pool. Traffic can be noisy, but the freebies (including wi-fi, bikes, beach shuttles and bodyboards) compensate.

Observatory HOTEL $$
(☎02-6586 8000; www.observatory.net.au; 40 William St; r/apt from $165/179;) Rooms and apartments are attractive and well equipped at this upmarket hotel opposite Town Beach; many have balconies overlooking the water. Downstairs is the casually chic **Milkbar** (mains $9-16; 7.30am-3pm Mon-Fri, to noon Sat & Sun) cafe.

Beachport B&B $$
(☎0423 072 669; www.beachportbnb.com.au; 155 Pacific Dr; r $80-200;) In this excellent B&B the two downstairs rooms open onto private terraces, while the upstairs unit is more spacious. A basic do-it-yourself breakfast is provided and the Rainforest Cafe is just across the road.

Eastport Motor Inn MOTEL $$
(☎02-6583 5850; www.eastportmotorinn.com.au; cnr Lord & Burrawan Sts; r from $129;) This three-storey motel has recently been renovated and offers smallish, good-value rooms with comfortable beds and crisp linen.

Mantra Quayside APARTMENTS $$
(☎02-6588 4000; www.mantraquayside.com.au; cnr William & Short Sts; apt from $180;) Head up to the roof of this central midrise block for a BBQ, to splash about in the heated pool, or simply to soak in the views. Studios have kitchenettes and access to a free communal laundry, while one- and two-bedroom apartments are fully self-contained.

Flynns on Surf VILLA $$
(☎02-6584 2244; www.flynns.com.au; 25 Surf St; from $180;) These swish one-, two- and three-bed villas are set in their own private estate. They have a gorgeous bush outlook and are fully self-contained with extra comforts such as Nespresso machines and iPod docks. The surf is 200m away, and it's a three-minute walk into town.

Eating

Social Grounds CAFE $
(151 Gordon St; mains $7-14; 6am-3pm Mon-Sat) Pull up a chair at the shared tables on the deck of this hip local hang-out. The wall menu wanders from eggs and bagels to towering Reuben sandwiches and gutsy salads. The coffee is dependably good.

Rainforest Cafe CAFE $
(☎02-6582 4444; www.rainforestcafe.com.au; Sea Acres Rainfmorest Centre, Pacific Dr; mains breakfast $10-15, lunch $12-22; 9am-4pm;) You may be surrounded by lush foliage, but don't expect bush tucker: the talented chef is as French as they come. The focus is on healthy sandwiches and salads, and heavenly cakes and pastries.

LV's on Clarence CAFE $$
(☎02-6583 9210; 74 Clarence St; mains $14-23; 7am-3pm Mon-Sat, to 11.30am Sun) Whether you're dropping by for a lunchtime slider or

lingering over a coffee and homemade sweet, this down-to-earth cafe is a great option any time of day.

★ Stunned Mullet MODERN AUSTRALIAN $$$
(☎02-6584 7757; www.thestunnedmullet.com.au; 24 William St; mains $36-39; ⌚noon-2.30pm & 6-10pm) This fresh, seaside spot is one serious dining destination. The inspired contemporary menu features classic dishes such as pork belly with seared scallops, alongside exotic listings such as Patagonian toothfish. The extensive international wine list befits Port's best restaurant.

Fusion 7 FUSION $$$
(☎02-6584 1171; www.fusion7.com.au; 124 Horton St; mains $35; ⌚6-9pm Tue-Sat) Chef-owner Lindsey Schwab worked in London with the father of fusion cuisine, Peter Gordon. He now oversees a short but innovative menu where local produce features prominently and desserts are particularly delicious.

Corner Restaurant MODERN AUSTRALIAN $$$
(☎02-6583 3300; cornerrestaurant.com.au; 11 Clarence St; breakfast mains $12-19, lunch $15-24, dinner $36; ⌚7am-9pm Mon-Sat, to 5pm Sun) This sleek operation has a definite Sydney-ish sheen, starting with the excellent daytime cafe fare such as house-cured salmon and inventive risottos. Dinner heads into fine-dining territory with a modern menu and attentive staff.

Drinking & Nightlife

Grape & Petal WINE BAR
(☎02-6584 6880; www.tameeka.com.au; 72 Clarence St; ⌚3-10pm Tue, 7.30am-10pm Wed-Sat, 7.30am-3pm Sun) There's something a bit naughty about the waterside Grape & Petal. You should be at the beach but instead you're in an eclectically decorated salon drinking rosé and feasting on a cheese plate. Or you're whiling away the evening with some tapas and a drop from the chunky wine list.

Zebu Bar & Grill COCKTAIL BAR
(☎02-6589 2888; www.zebu.com.au; 1 Hay St; ⌚noon-midnight) Muddled, shaken and infused are overused words at this popular cocktail lounge at the Rydges Hotel. Live music, pizzas and the river-view eye candy all add to the good time.

Beach House BAR
(www.thebeachhouse.net.au; 1 Horton St; ⌚7.30am-10pm Sun, to midnight Mon-Thu, to late Fri & Sat) An enviable position right on the grassy water's edge makes this place perfect for lazy afternoon drinks. DJs and live bands happen on weekends.

Information

Port Macquarie Base Hospital (☎02-5524 2000; www.mnclhd.health.nsw.gov.au; Wrights Rd)

Visitor information centre (☎02-6581 8000; www.portmacquarieinfo.com.au; Glasshouse, cnr Hay & Clarence Sts; ⌚9am-5.30pm Mon-Fri, to 4pm Sat & Sun)

Getting There & Away

AIR

Port Macquarie Airport (PQQ; ☎02-6581 8111; www.portmacquarieairport.com.au; Oliver Dr) Port Macquarie Airport is 5km from the centre of town; a taxi will cost $20 and there are regular local bus services.

QantasLink (☎13 13 13; www.qantas.com.au) Flies to/from Sydney.

Virgin (☎13 67 89; www.virginaustralia.com) Flies to/from Sydney and Brisbane.

BUS

Port Macquarie Coach Terminal (Gordon St) Regional buses depart from Port Macquarie Coach Terminal.

Busways (☎02-6583 2499; www.busways.com.au) Runs local bus services and heads as far afield as North Haven ($13.30, one hour), Port Macquarie Airport ($5, 28 minutes) and Kempsey ($16.50, one hour).

Greyhound (☎1300 473 946; www.greyhound.com.au) Two daily buses head to/from Sydney ($74, 6½ hours), Newcastle ($56, four hours), Coffs Harbour ($37, 2½ hours), Byron Bay ($76, six hours) and Brisbane ($119, 10 hours).

Premier (☎13 34 10; www.premierms.com.au) Daily coach to/from Sydney ($60, 6½ hours), Newcastle ($47, 3¾ hours), Coffs Harbour ($47, 2¼ hours), Byron Bay ($66, 7½ hours) and Brisbane ($67, 11 hours).

GREATER TAREE

Taree (population 17,800) is a large town, conveniently sited on the Pacific Hwy, which serves the fertile Manning Valley. Heading up the valley, the nearby town of **Wingham** (population 4520) combines English county cuteness with a rugged lumberjack history.

In the other direction, at the mouth of the Manning River, is the sprawling beach town of **Harrington** (population 2260), sheltered by a spectacular rocky breakwater and watched over by pelicans. It's a leisure-orientated place, popular with both holidaymakers and retirees – 48% of the population is over the age of 60.

Crowdy Head (population 221) is a small fishing village 6km northeast of Harrington at the edge of Crowdy Bay National Park. It was named when Captain Cook witnessed a gathering of Aboriginal people on the headland in 1770. The views of deserted beaches and wilderness from the 1878 **lighthouse** are superb. Even if you don't drive through the national park it's worth leaving the Pacific Hwy at Kew and taking the coastal route to Port Macquarie via Ocean Dr. After stopping at the North Brother lookout you'll pass through **Laurieton** (population 1930). Turn left here and cross the bridge to **North Haven** (population 1600), an absolute blinder of a surf beach. Continuing north the road passes Lake Cathie (pronounced 'cat-eye'), a shallow body of water that's perfect for kids to have a paddle in.

Sights

Wingham Brush Nature Reserve FOREST
(Isabella St, Wingham) A boardwalk traverses this idyllic patch of rainforest, home to giant Moreton Bay figs and flocks of flying foxes. You might even spot an osprey or a diamond python.

Crowdy Bay National Park NATIONAL PARK
(www.nationalparks.nsw.gov.au/crowdy-bay-national-park; vehicle admission $7) Known for its rock formations and rugged cliffs, this park backs onto a long and beautiful beach. There's a 4.8km (two-hour) loop track over the Diamond headland. The roads running through the park are unsealed and full of potholes, but the dappled light through the gum trees makes it a lovely drive.

Dooragan National Park NATIONAL PARK
(www.nationalparks.nsw.gov.au/dooragan-national-park) Immediately north of Crowdy Bay National Park, on the shores of Watson Taylor Lake, this little park is dominated by North Brother Mountain. A sealed road leads to the lookout at the top, which offers incredible views of the coast.

Sleeping

NPWS Campgrounds CAMPGROUND $
(☎02-6588 5555; camp sites per adult/child $10/5) Of the Crowdy Bay National Park camping grounds, **Diamond Head** is the most popular and best equipped (flush toilets and gas barbecues), while **Kylie's Hut** is the most rudimentary. **Crowdy Gap** (adult/child $5/3), by the beach in the southern part of the park, is cheaper. You'll need to bring your own drinking water to all of them.

Bank Guest House B&B $$
(☎02-6553 5068; www.thebankandtellers.com.au; 48 Bent St, Wingham; s/d from $165/175; ❄📶🐾) A friendly place offering stylishly decorated rooms in a 1920s bank manager's residence. Has a pet-friendly room in the rear garden.

Eating

Bent on Food CAFE $$
(☎02-6557 0727; www.bentonfood.com.au; 95 Isabella St, Wingham; mains $10-25; ⏰8am-5pm Mon-Fri, to 3pm Sat & Sun) This excellent cafe serves sophisticated cooked meals and baked goods. The associated cookery school offers classes in everything from cheese-making to game meats.

Harrington Hotel PUB FOOD $$
(☎02-6556 1205; www.harringtonhotel.com.au; 30 Beach St, Harrington; mains $15-26) Locals hang out at this spacious pub, sipping beer on the large waterside terrace. The expansive bistro has glorious views and excellent food.

Information

Manning Valley visitor information centre (☎02-6592 5444; www.manningvalley.info; 21 Manning River Dr, Taree; ⏰9am-4.30pm)

Getting There & Away

Taree Airport (TRO; ☎02-6553 9863; 1 Lansdowne Rd, Cundletown) is 5km northeast of central Taree.

Regional Express (Rex; ☎13 17 13; www.regionalexpress.com.au) has flights to/from Sydney and Grafton.

NSW TrainLink (☎13 22 32; www.nswtrainlink.info) trains stop at Wingham and Taree, heading to/from Sydney ($57, 5½ hours, four daily), Nambucca Heads ($23.40, three hours, three daily), Coffs Harbour ($28.25, 3½ hours, three daily), Grafton ($39.60, five hours, three daily) and Brisbane ($72, nine hours, two daily).

GREAT LAKES REGION

Despite its somewhat grand name, this compact area is an unassuming kind of place reflecting the series of lakes that hug the coast all the way from Port Stephens to the regional centre of Forster-Tuncurry. The joy here is forsaking the highway for leafy roads through national parks.

Booti Booti National Park

This 15.67-sq-km national park stretches along a skinny peninsula with **Seven Mile Beach** on its eastern side and **Wallis Lake** on its west. The park's $7 vehicle-entry charge doesn't apply to the Lakes Way, which passes straight through its heart. The northern section of the park is swathed in coastal rainforest and topped by 224m **Cape Hawke**. At the Cape Hawke headland there's a **viewing platform**, well worth the sweat of climbing the 420-something steps. **Green Cathedral** (consecrated in 1940) is an interesting place to explore, with its wooden pews under palm trees, looking out to the lake.

There's self-registration camping at the **Ruins** (camp sites per adult/child $14/7), at the southern end of Seven Mile Beach.

Information

NPWS office (02-6591 0300; www.nationalparks.nsw.gov.au/booti-booti-national-park; The Ruins; 8.30am-4.30pm Mon-Fri)

Pacific Palms

POP 664

Nestled between Myall Lakes and Booti Booti National Parks, Pacific Palms is one of those places that well-heeled city dwellers slink off to on weekends, so expect to find a couple of excellent cafes for your espresso craving.

Most of the houses cling to **Blueys Beach** or **Boomerang Beach**, both long stretches of golden sand that are popular with surfers. The most popular swimming beach is the patrolled **Elizabeth Beach**.

Sleeping & Eating

Mobys Beachside Retreat RESORT $$

(02-6591 0000; www.mobysretreat.com.au; 4 Red Gum Rd, Boomerang Beach; apt from $180;) Directly opposite Boomerang Beach, Mobys fits 75 self-contained holiday apartments with sleek decor and excellent amenities into a relatively small area. A tennis court and a children's playground are on site, as well as a popular restaurant.

Twenty by Twelve CAFE $

(02-6554 0452; 207 Boomerang Dr; mains $7-17; 7.30am-3pm;) Light meals, local organic produce and delicious deli treats.

Information

Pacific Palms visitor centre (02-6554 0123; www.greatlakes.org.au; Boomerang Dr; 10am-4pm;)

Getting There & Away

Busways (02-4997 4788; www.busways.com.au) At least two Busways buses stop at Blueys Beach daily, en route to Newcastle ($28, two hours) and Taree ($17, one hour).

Myall Lakes National Park

On an extravagantly pretty section of the coast, this large **national park** (www.nationalparks.nsw.gov.au/myall-lakes-national-park; vehicle admission $7) incorporates a patchwork of lakes, islands, dense littoral rainforest and beaches. The lakes support an incredible quantity and variety of bird life, including bowerbirds, white-bellied sea eagles and tawny frogmouths. There are paths through coastal rainforest and past beach dunes at **Mungo Brush** in the south, perfect for spotting wild flowers and dingoes.

The best beaches and surf are in the north around **Seal Rocks**, a hamlet hugging Sugarloaf Bay. The beach has emerald-green rock pools and golden sand. Take the short walk to the **Sugarloaf Point Lighthouse** for epic ocean views. There's a detour to lonely **Lighthouse Beach**, a popular surfing spot. By the lighthouse is a lookout over the actual Seal Rocks – islets where Australian fur seals can sometimes be spotted. **Humpback whales** swim past during their annual migration.

Offshore, **Broughton Island** is uninhabited except for muttonbirds, little penguins and an enormous diversity of fish. The diving is tops and the beaches are incredibly secluded. **Moonshadow** (02-4984 9388; www.moonshadow.com.au; 35 Stockton St, Nelson Bay) runs full-day trips to the island from Nelson Bay on Sundays between October and Easter (more frequently over the summer school holidays), which include snorkelling and boom-net rides (adult/child $85/45).

Sleeping

Seal Rocks Holiday Park CAMPGROUND $

(02-4997 6164; www.sealrocksholidaypark.com.au; Kinka Rd, Seal Rocks; camp sites/cabins from $33/89;) Offers a range of budget accommodation, including grassed camping and caravan sites that are right on the water.

NPWS Campgrounds CAMPGROUND $
(☎1300 072 757; www.nationalparks.nsw.gov.au/Myall-Lakes-National-Park; Broughton Island per 2 people $30, others per adult/child $10/5) There are 19 basic camping grounds dotted around the park; only some have drinking water and flush toilets. At the time of writing, the only one requiring advance bookings was Broughton Island, although there are plans to change this; check the website for details.

★ **Sugarloaf Point Lighthouse** COTTAGE $$$
(☎02-4997 6590; www.sealrockslighthouseaccommodation.com.au; cottages from $340;) Watch the crashing waves and wildlife from one of three fully renovated, heritage lighthouse-keeper's cottages. Each is self-contained and has two or three bedrooms and a barbecue.

Bombah Point Eco Cottages COTTAGE $$$
(☎02-4997 4401; www.bombah.com.au; 969 Bombah Point Rd; d $220-275;) In the heart of the national park, these architect-designed glass-fronted cottages sleep up to six guests. The 'Eco' in the name is well deserved: sewage is treated on site using a bioreactor system, electricity comes courtesy of solar panels, and filtered rainwater tanks provide water.

Getting There & Away

From Hawks Nest scenic Mungo Brush Rd heads through the park to Bombah Broadwater, where the **Bombah Point ferry** (per car $6) makes the five-minute crossing every half-hour from 8am to 6pm. Continuing north, a 10km section of Bombah Point Rd heading to the Pacific Hwy at Bulahdelah is unsealed.

The Lakes Way leaves the Pacific Hwy 5km north of Buladelah and shadows the northern edge of Myall Lake and Smiths Lake before continuing on to Pacific Palms and Forster-Tuncurry. Seal Rocks Rd branches off the Lakes Way at Bungwahl.

Tea Gardens & Hawks Nest

POP 2430 & 1120

This tranquil pair of towns straddles the mouth of the Myall River, linked by the graceful Singing Bridge. Tea Gardens' charm is its river culture; it's older and more genteel. At Hawks Nest it's all about the beaches. **Jimmy's Beach** fronts a glasslike stretch of water facing Nelson Bay, while **Bennett's Beach** looks to the ocean and Broughton Island.

A great way to explore the Myall River and surrounding waterways is by kayak or house boat. **Lazy Paddles** (☎0412 832 220; www.lazypaddles.com.au; tours adult/child $50/35, hire per 2/4/10hr $40/55/65) offers two-hour historical and nature tours, as well as kayak hire.

Sleeping & Eating

Hawks Nest Motel MOTEL $$
(☎02-4997 1166; www.hawksnestmotel.com.au; 5 Yamba St, Hawks Nest; r from $140;) Updated with new carpets, new furniture and bright photographic prints, this older-style two-storey brick motel is an appealing option.

Boatshed CAFE, RESTAURANT $$
(☎02-4997 0307; www.teagardensboatshed.com.au; 110 Marine Dr, Tea Gardens; mains breakfast $17, lunch $18-30, dinner $34-40; ⌚8.30am-2.30pm daily, 6-9pm Wed-Sat) Good coffee, delicious food and a lovely deck for enjoying a sunset drink.

Benchmark on Booner INTERNATIONAL $$
(☎02-4997 2980; www.benchmarkrestaurant.com.au; 100 Booner St, Hawks Nest; mains $16-32; ⌚noon-3pm & 5.30-9pm Mon-Sat) More adventurous than you'd expect for a restaurant attached to a small-town motel. Choose between a casual wood-fired pizza dinner or an upmarket meal in the dining room.

Information

Tea Gardens visitor centre (☎02-4997 0111; www.teagardens.nsw.au; 245 Myall St, Tea Gardens; ⌚10am-4pm)

Getting There & Away

While only 5km by water from Nelson Bay, the drive here necessitates returning to the Pacific Hwy via Medowie and then doubling back – a distance of 81km. An alternative for foot passengers and cyclists are the ferries (p200) from Nelson Bay.

Busways (☎02-4983 1560; www.busways.com.au) Has at least two buses to/from Newcastle daily ($21, 90 minutes).

PORT STEPHENS

POP 68,935

An hour's drive north of Newcastle, the sheltered harbour of Port Stephens is blessed with near-deserted beaches, national parks and an extraordinary sand-dune system. The main centre, **Nelson Bay**, is home to both a fishing fleet and an armada of tourist vessels, the latter trading on the town's status as the 'dolphin capital of Australia'.

Just east of Nelson Bay is slightly smaller **Shoal Bay**, with a long swimming beach that's best in the morning, as winds come up in the afternoon. The road ends a short drive south at **Fingal Bay**, with another lovely beach on the fringes of Tomaree National Park. The park stretches west around the clothing-optional **Samurai Beach**, a popular surfing spot, and **One Mile Beach**, a gorgeous semicircle of the softest sand and bluest water favoured by those in the know: surfers, beachcombers, idle romantics.

The park ends at the surfside village of **Anna Bay**, which has the incredible Worimi Conservation Lands as a backdrop. Gan Gan Rd connects Anna Bay, One Mile Beach and Samurai Beach with Nelson Bay Rd.

Sights

Worimi Conservation Lands NATURE RESERVE

(www.worimiconservationlands.com; 3-day entry permits $10) Located at Stockton Bight, these are the longest moving sand dunes in the southern hemisphere, stretching over 35km. Thanks to the generosity of the Worimi people, you're able to roam around (provided you don't disturb any Aboriginal sites) and drive along the beach (4WD only; permit required). Get your permits from the visitor centre or NPWS office in Nelson Bay, the Anna Bay BP and IGA, or the 24-hour Metro service station near the Lavis Lane entry.

It's possible to become so surrounded by shimmering sand that you'll lose sight of the ocean or any sign of life. At the far western end of the beach, the wreck of the *Sygna* founders in the water.

Tomaree National Park NATIONAL PARK

(www.nationalparks.nsw.gov.au/tomaree-national-park) This wonderfully wild expanse harbours several threatened species, including the spotted-tailed quoll and powerful owl.

At the eastern end of Shoal Bay there's a short walk to the surf at unpatrolled **Zenith Beach**, or you can tackle the **Tomaree Head Summit Walk** (one hour return, 1km) and be rewarded by stunning ocean views. For picnics and snorkelling try **Fishermans Bay** with its rock pools. Ask at the NPWS about longer treks, including the coastal walk from Tomaree Head to Big Rocky.

Nelson Head Lighthouse Cottage HISTORIC BUILDING

(www.innerlighttearooms.com; Lighthouse Rd, Nelson Bay; ⏲10am-4pm) FREE Built in 1875 this restored building has a tearoom with inspiring views and a small museum with displays on the area's history.

Murray's Craft Brewing Co. BREWERY

(☎02-4982 6411; www.murraysbrewingco.com.au; , Bob's Farm, 3443 Nelson Bay Rd; ⏲tours at 2.15pm) This brewery is the creator of cult recipes such as the award winning Murray's Grand Cru, a hybrid of Belgian Trippel and Golden Strong Ale styles. Also on site is the Port Stephens Winery with an expansive cellar door.

Activities

Port Stephens Surf School SURFING

(☎0411 419 576; www.portstephenssurfschool.com.au; 2hr/2-/3-day lessons $60/110/165) Surf lessons, stand-up paddleboarding and board hire (one hour/two hours $17/28).

Oakfield Ranch CAMEL RIDES

(☎0429 664 172; www.oakfieldranch.com.au; Birubi Pt car park, James Patterson St, Anna Bay) Twenty-minute camel rides along the beach on weekends and public holidays.

Tours

Imagine Cruises CRUISE

(☎02-4984 9000; www.imaginecruises.com.au; Dock C, d'Albora Marinas, Nelson Bay) Trips include 3½-hour Sail, Swim, Snorkel & Dolphin Watch trips (adult/child $63/30, December to March), 90-minute Dolphin Watch cruises ($28/15, November to May), three-hour Whale Watch cruises ($63/30, May to mid-November) and two-hour Seafood Dinner cruises ($45/25, December to April).

Dolphin Swim Australia DOLPHIN SWIM

(☎1300 721 358; www.dolphinswimaustralia.com.au; 5hr trips $289; ⏲Sat & Sun Sep-May) Experience moving through a wild dolphin pod as you hang on to a rope and get towed through the water behind a catamaran.

Port Stephens Paddlesports KAYAKING

(☎0405 033 518; www.portstephensecosports.com.au; kayak/paddleboard hire per hour $25/30; ⏲Sep-May) Offers a range of kayak and stand-up paddle excursions, including 1½-hour sunset tours ($35/25) and 2½-hour discovery tours ($40/30).

Port Stephens 4WD Tours DRIVING TOUR

(☎02-4984 4760; www.portstephens4wd.com.au; James Paterson St, Anna Bay) Offers a 1½-hour Beach & Dune tour (adult/child $52/31), a three-hour Sygna Shipwreck tour (adult/child $90/50) and a sandboarding experience ($28/20).

Sleeping

Samurai Port Stephens YHA HOSTEL $
(02-4982 1921; www.samuraiportstephens.com; Frost Rd, Anna Bay; dm $35, d $91-123;) These attractively furnished, wooden-floored bungalows are arranged around a swimming pool and set in koala-populated bushland dotted with Asian sculpture. There's a bush kitchen with BBQs and a ramshackle games shed with pool table.

Melaleuca Surfside Backpackers HOSTEL $
(02-4981 9422; www.melaleucabackpackers.com.au; 2 Koala Pl, One Mile Beach; camp sites/dm/d from $20/32/100;) Architect-designed cabins are set amid peaceful scrub inhabited by koalas and kookaburras at this friendly, well-run place. There's a welcoming lounge area and kitchen, and the owners offer sandboarding and other excursions.

Marty's at Little Beach HOTEL $$
(02-4984 9100; http://martys.net.au; cnr Gowrie Ave & Intrepid Close, Nelson Bay; r from $130, apt from $240;) This low-key motel is an easy stroll to Little Beach and Shoal Bay, and has simple beach-house-inspired rooms and modern, self-contained apartments.

Beaches Serviced Apartments APARTMENTS $$
(02-4984 3255; www.beachesportstephens.com.au; 12 Gowrie Ave, Nelson Bay; apt from $190;) You'll find all the comforts of home in these beautifully kept apartments, ranging from studio to three bedrooms. There's a pretty palm-lined pool, and a putting green, too.

Eating

Nice at Nelson Bay CAFE $$
(02-4981 3001; www.niceatnelsonbay.com.au; Nelson Towers Arcade, 71a Victoria Pde; mains $18; 8am-2pm) The best breakfast in town is hidden in an arcade near the waterfront where it serves up no less than six variations of eggs Benedict and artfully plated pancakes.

Little Beach Boathouse SEAFOOD $$
(02-4984 9420; littlebeachboathouse.com.au; Little Beach Marina, 4 Victoria Pde; lunch mains $20, dinner mains $32; noon-3pm & 5.30-9pm Tue-Sat) In a cosy dining room right on the water you can order fabulously fresh salads and local seafood share plates. It's hard to concentrate on the food with views of diving dolphins and majestic pelicans coming in to land.

Sandpipers MODERN AUSTRALIAN $$
(02-4984 9990; www.sandpipersrestaurant.com.au; 81 Magnus St, Nelson Bay; mains $30; 5.30-10pm Mon-Sat) This upmarket but informal restaurant in the Nelson Bay shopping strip offers a great-value midweek special which might include slow-cooked pork belly or freshly caught fish-of-the-day. The Port Stephens oysters are a must.

Information

NPWS office (02-4984 8200; www.nationalparks.nsw.gov.au; 12b Teramby Rd, Nelson Bay; 8.30am-4.30pm Mon-Fri)

Visitor information centre (02-4980 6900; www.portstephens.org.au; 60 Victoria Pde, Nelson Bay; 9am-5pm) Has interesting displays on the marine park.

Getting There & Away

Port Stephens Coaches (02-4982 2940; www.pscoaches.com.au) zip around Port Stephens' townships heading to Newcastle and Newcastle Airport ($4.60, 1½ hours). There's also a daily service to/from Sydney ($39, four hours) stopping at Anna Bay, Nelson Bay and Shoal Bay.

Both **Port Stephens Ferry Service** (0412 682 117; www.portstephensferryservice.com.au) and the **MV Wallamba** (0408 494 262) chug from Nelson Bay to Tea Gardens (stopping at Hawks Nest) and back two to three times a day (adult/child/bicycle return $20/10/2).

Canberra & NSW South Coast

Includes ➡

Best Places to Eat

- Temporada (p210)
- Močan & Green Grout (p210)
- Tallwood (p222)
- Hungry Duck (p219)
- Gunyah Restaurant (p221)

Best Places to Stay

- Hotel Hotel (p207)
- East Hotel (p209)
- Paperbark Camp (p221)
- Kiama Harbour Cabins (p218)

Why Go?

Journey south from Sydney through the raw beauty of stunning Royal National Park to emerge at laid-back Wollongong, a friendly city framed by excellent beaches and featuring good restaurants and an unpretentious but energetic after-dark scene.

Further south is a roll-call of relaxed coastal towns with a menu of easygoing activities. Go kayaking around Huskisson and Jervis Bay, spy on seals and penguins around Narooma, or learn to surf at Batemans Bay. Migrating whales are the attraction at pretty Eden near the New South Wales (NSW) and Victoria border, and NSW's colonial heritage is celebrated in food-obsessed Berry and sleepy Central Tilba.

Inland from coastal NSW, the stellar museums, galleries and public buildings of the modern city of Canberra tell the story of Australia with poignancy and passion. Emerging neighbourhoods in the national capital like New Acton, Braddon and the Kingston Foreshore are introducing a hip sheen with excellent cafes, bars and restaurants.

When to Go

Canberra

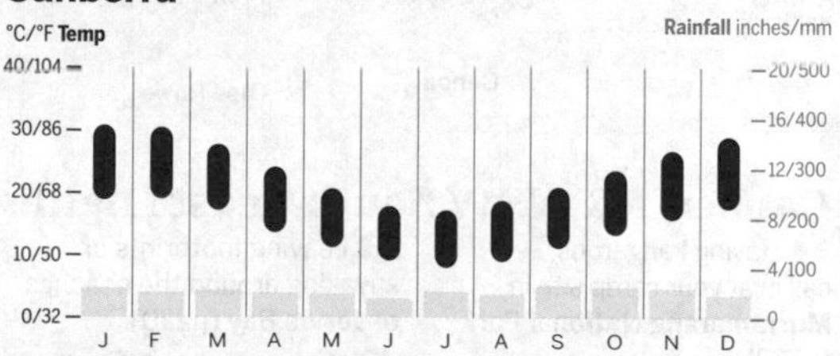

Feb–May (except Easter) Sun's still shining and kids are back at school.

May–Nov Spot whales along the coast.

Dec Enjoy an Aussie-style Christmas on the coast – seafood for lunch and beach cricket.

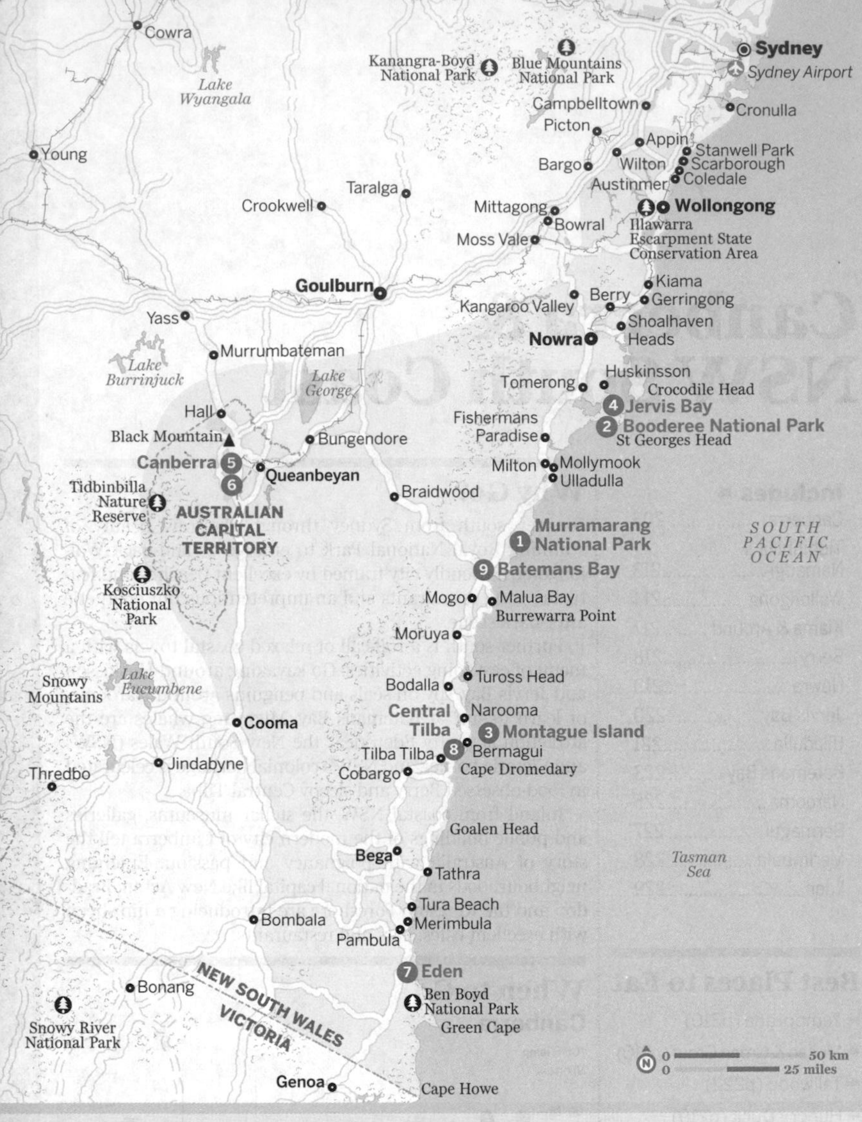

Canberra & NSW South Coast Highlights

1 Having kangaroos call in at your camp site in **Murramarang National Park** (p223).

2 Exploring **Booderee National Park** (p222).

3 Hanging out with the seals and penguins at **Montague Island** (p225).

4 Leaving footprints or kayaking around the beaches of **Jervis Bay** (p220).

5 Understanding Australia's military heritage at Canberra's **Australian War Memorial** (p203).

6 Tapping into Canberra's urban scene in **Braddon**, **New Acton** and the **Kingston Foreshore** (p209).

7 Watching whales pass by the postcard-pretty coastline around **Eden** (p229).

8 Returning to the charming, wood-panelled past at **Central Tilba** (p226).

9 Learning to surf like an Aussie at **Batemans Bay** (p223).

Getting There & Around

AIR

The region's main airport is in Canberra and smaller airports are at Moruya and Merimbula.

BUS

Buses run between Canberra and the capital cities, and from the capital cities along the coast.

CAR & MOTORCYCLE

The quickest route between Canberra and the coast is the Kings Hwy. The Princes Hwy from Wollongong to Eden in the south is the main route for exploring the coast.

TRAIN

Trains run between Canberra and Sydney. There are no direct trains between Canberra and Melbourne.

CANBERRA

POP 381,488

Designed by visionary American architect Walter Burley Griffin, who was assisted by his wife Marion Mahony Griffin, Canberra features expansive open spaces, aesthetics influenced by the 19th-century arts and crafts movement and a seamless alignment of built and natural elements. Unfortunately, the city is totally geared towards the car – it's difficult to explore by public transport and almost impossible to do so on foot. You really need wheels (two or four) to do it justice, and the city's scenic hinterland also warrants exploration.

Though Canberra seems big on architectural symbolism and low on spontaneity, the city's cultural institutions have lively visitor and social programs, and there's a cool urban energy emerging in Braddon, New Acton and the Kingston Foreshore.

During parliamentary-sitting weeks the town hums with the buzz of national politics, but it can be a tad sleepy during university holidays, especially around Christmas and New Year.

History

The Ngunnawal people called this place Kanberra, believed to mean 'meeting place'. The name was probably derived from huge intertribal gatherings that happened annually when large numbers of Bogong moths appeared in the city.

The Ngunnawal's way of life was violently disrupted following European settlement around 1820, but they survived and have increased their profile and numbers.

In 1901 Australia's separate colonies were federated and became states. The rivalry between Sydney and Melbourne meant neither could become the new nation's capital, so a location between the two cities was carved out of the Limestone Plains in NSW as a compromise. This new city was officially named Canberra in 1913, and replaced Melbourne as the national capital in 1927.

Sights

Most sights are around Lake Burley Griffin.

★ Australian War Memorial — MUSEUM

(Map p208; ☎02-6243 4211; www.awm.gov.au; Treloar Cres, Campbell; ⏰10am-5pm) **FREE** Canberra's most rewarding museum experience includes halls dedicated to WWI, WWII and conflicts from 1945 to the present day. A spectacular aircraft hall segues to sound-and-light shows staged in the massive Anzac Hall. Most exciting are Striking by Night, re-creating a WWII night operation over Berlin (staged on the hour), and Over the Front: the Great War in the Air (at a quarter past the hour).

Entry to the museum is via a Commemorative Courtyard with a roll of honour of the nation's war dead. Family members have attached bright-red paper poppies to the names of their fallen relatives. These poppies of remembrance reflect those that flowered on the battlegrounds of Belgium, France and Gallipoli in the spring of 1915.

Behind the courtyard is the mosaic-encrusted Hall of Memory. This is home to the Tomb of the Unknown Australian Soldier, representing all Australians who have given their lives during wartime.

Free guided tours leave from the main entrance's Orientation Gallery regularly. Alternatively, purchase the Self-Guided Tour leaflet with map ($5).

★ National Gallery of Australia — GALLERY

(Map p208; ☎02-6240 6502; www.nga.gov.au; Parkes Pl, Parkes; admission costs for special exhibitions; ⏰10am-5pm) **FREE** Includes an extraordinary Aboriginal Memorial from Central Arnhem Land created for Australia's 1988 bicentenary. The work of 43 artists, this 'forest of souls' presents 200 hollow log coffins (one for every year of European settlement) and is part of an excellent collection of Aboriginal and Torres Strait Islander art. Also exhibited is Australian art from the colonial to contemporary period, and Australia's

Canberra

finest collection of Asian art. Notable Pacific art and standout European and American works complete an impressive collection. Check the website for free guided tours.

★ Parliament House NOTABLE BUILDING

(Map p208; 02-6277 5399; www.aph.gov.au; from 9am Mon & Tue, from 8.30am Wed & Thu sitting days, 9am-5pm non-sitting days) FREE Opened in 1988, Australia's national parliament building is dug into Capital Hill, and has a grass-topped roof topped by an 81m-high flagpole. The rooftop lawns encompass 23 hectares of gardens and provide superb 360-degree views. Underneath incorporates 17 courtyards, an entrance foyer, the Great Hall, the House of Representatives, the Senate and seemingly endless corridors. Visit on a free guided tour (30 minutes on sitting days, 45 minutes on non-sitting days); these leave at 9.30am, 11am, 1pm, 2pm and 3.30pm.

Visitors can also self-navigate and watch parliamentary proceedings from the public galleries. Tickets for Question Time (2pm on sitting days) in the House of Representatives are free but must be booked through the Sergeant at Arms; tickets aren't required for the Senate chamber. See the website for a calendar of sitting days.

★**National Portrait Gallery** GALLERY
(Map p208; ☎02-6102 7000; www.portrait.gov.au; King Edward Tce, Parkes; ⊙10am-5pm) FREE This gallery tells the story of Australia through its faces – from wax cameos of Aboriginal tribespeople to colonial portraits of the nation's founding families and contemporary works such as Howard Arkley's Day-Glo portrait of musician Nick Cave. There is a good cafe for post-exhibition coffee and reflection.

★**National Arboretum** GARDENS, VIEWPOINT
(Map p204; www.nationalarboretum.act.gov.au; Forest Dr, off Tuggeranong Parkway; ⊙6am-8.30pm) FREE Located on land previously impacted by bushfires, Canberra's National Arboretum is an ever-developing showcase of trees from around the world. It is early days for many of the plantings, but it's still worth visiting the spectacular visitor centre, and for excellent views over the city. Regular guided tours are informative, and there is a brilliant adventure playground for kids.

Catch bus 81 (weekdays) or bus 981 (weekends) from the Civic bus interchange.

Museum of Australian Democracy MUSEUM
(Map p208; ☎02-6270 8222; www.moadoph.gov.au; Old Parliament House, 18 King George Tce, Parkes; adult/concession/family $2/1/5; ⊙9am-5pm) The seat of government from 1927 to 1988, this building offers visitors a whiff of bygone parliamentary activity. It's most meaningful for those who have studied Australian history or closely followed political high jinks in Canberra, but still rewarding for other visitors. Displays cover Australian prime ministers, the roots of global and local democracy, and the history of local protest movements. You can also visit the old Senate and House of Representative chambers, the parliamentary library and the prime minister's office.

Aboriginal Tent Embassy HISTORIC SITE
(Map p208) The lawn in front of Old Parliament House is home to the Aboriginal Tent Embassy – an important site in the struggle for equality and representation for Indigenous Australians.

Lake Burley Griffin LANDMARK
(Map p208) The 35km shore of this lake is home to most of the city's cultural institutions. It was filled by damming the Molonglo River in 1963 with the 33m-high Scrivener Dam, and was named after American architect Walter Burley Griffin, who won an international competition with his wife – and fellow architect – to design Australia's new capital city in 1911. Highlights include the **National Carillon** (Map p208; ☎02-6257 1068) and the **Captain Cook Memorial Water Jet** (Map p208; ⊙10am-noon & 2-4pm, plus 7-9pm daylight-saving months).

Reconciliation Place PARK
(Map p208) On the shore of Lake Burley Griffin, the artwork of Reconciliation Pl represents the nation's commitment to the cause of reconciliation between Indigenous and non-Indigenous Australians.

National Museum of Australia MUSEUM
(Map p208; ☎02-6208 5000; www.nma.gov.au; Lawson Cres, Acton Peninsula; admission to permanent collection free, guided tours adult/child/family $10/5/25; ⊙9am-5pm) FREE With exhibits organised chronologically, some visitors find this museum exhilarating while others find it annoying. Exhibits focus on environmental change, Indigenous culture, national Australian icons and much more. Don't miss the introductory film, shown in the small rotating **Circa Theatre**. Bus 7 (weekdays) and bus 934 (weekends) run here from Civic, and the museum is also on the route of the Canberra City Explorer (p206).

National Film & Sound Archive MUSEUM
(Map p208; ☎02-6248 2000; www.nfsa.gov.au; McCoy Circuit, Acton; ⊙9am-5pm Mon-Fri) FREE Set in a delightful art deco building, this archive preserves Australian moving-picture and sound recordings. There are also temporary exhibitions, talks and film screenings in the **Arc Cinema** (Map p208; adult/concession $10/8).

Australian National Botanic Gardens GARDENS
(Map p204; ☎02-6250 9540; www.anbg.gov.au; Clunies Ross St, Acton; ⊙8.30am-5pm Feb-Dec, 8.30am-5pm Mon-Fri, to 8pm Sat & Sun Jan, visitor centre 9.30am-4.30pm) FREE On Black Mountain's lower slopes, these 90-hectare gardens showcase Australian floral diversity. Self-guided trails include the Joseph Banks Walk, and there's a 90-minute return trail from near the eucalypt lawn leading into the garden's higher areas before continuing into the Black Mountain Nature Park and on to the summit.

The visitor centre is the departure point for **free guided walks** at 11am and 2pm. On weekends, an electric bus negotiates the **Flora Explorer Tour** (adult/child $6/3; ⌚10.30am & 1.30pm Sat & Sun).

Telstra Tower VIEWPOINT
(Map p204; ☎02-6219 6111; www.telstratower.com.au; Black Mountain Dr; adult/child & concession $7.50/3; ⌚9am-10pm) Black Mountain (812m), northwest of the city, is topped by the 195m-high Telstra Tower, which has a great vista from 66m up its shaft.

National Library of Australia LIBRARY
(Map p208; ☎02-6262 1111; www.nla.gov.au; Parkes Pl, Parkes; ⌚Treasures Gallery 10am-5pm, reading room 10am-8pm Mon-Thu, 10am-5pm Fri, 1.30-5pm Sun) FREE This library has accumulated over six million items since being established in 1901; most can be accessed in the reading rooms. Don't miss the **Treasures Gallery**, where artefacts such as Captain Cook's *Endeavour* journal and Captain Bligh's list of mutineers are among the regularly refreshed display – free 40-minute tours are held at 10.30am daily and at 11.30am on Monday, Wednesday and Friday.

National Capital Exhibition MUSEUM
(Map p208; ☎02-6272 2902; www.nationalcapital.gov.au; Barrine Dr, Commonwealth Park; ⌚9am-5pm Mon-Fri, 10am-4pm Sat & Sun) FREE Learn about the Indigenous peoples of the Canberra area and see copies of exquisite Burley Griffin drawings of the city at this modest museum near Regatta Point.

Questacon MUSEUM
(Map p208; ☎02-6270 2800; www.questacon.edu.au; King Edward Tce, Parkes; adult/child $20.50/15; ⌚9am-5pm) This kid-friendly science centre has educational and fun interactive exhibits. Explore the physics of sport, athletics and fun parks, cause tsunamis, and take shelter from cyclones and earthquakes. Exciting science shows, presentations and puppet shows are all included.

National Zoo & Aquarium ZOO, AQUARIUM
(Map p204; ☎02-6287 8400; www.nationalzoo.com.au; 999 Lady Denman Dr, Yarralumla; adult/child/family $38/21.50/105; ⌚10am-5pm) Book ahead to cuddle a cheetah ($175), get close to a red panda, white lion or giraffe (from $50), or take a tour behind the scenes to hand feed lions, tigers and bears (from $120). Bus 81 from the Civic interchange stops close by on weekends only.

Mt Ainslie VIEWPOINT
(Map p204) Northeast of the city, 843m-high Mt Ainslie has fine views day and night. Walking tracks start behind the War Memorial, climb Mt Ainslie and end at **Mt Majura** (888m).

Activities

Canberra's lakes and mountains offer bushwalking, swimming, cycling and other activities.

Lake Burley Griffin BOATING
(Map p208; ☎02-6249 6861; www.actboathire.com; Acton Jetty, Civic; ⌚9am-5pm Mon-Fri, 8.30am-6pm Sat & Sun) Canoe, kayak and paddleboat hire ($15 to $30 per hour).

Bushwalking

Tidbinbilla Nature Reserve (p213), southwest of the city, has walking and bicycle tracks, a eucalypt forest and a platypus habitat. Also good for bushwalking is Namadgi National Park (p213), 30 minutes south of Canberra.

Cycling

Canberra has an extensive network of dedicated cycle-paths. The Canberra & Region Visitors Centre stocks the *Lake Burley Griffin Cycle Routes* brochure and the *Walking & Cycling Map* published by **Pedal Power ACT** (http://pedalpower.org.au).

Mr Spokes Bike Hire BICYCLE RENTAL
(Map p208; ☎02-6257 1188; www.mrspokes.com.au; Barrine Dr, Acton; per hr/half day/full day $20/30/40; ⌚9am-5pm Wed-Sun, daily during school holidays) Near the Acton Park ferry terminal.

Real Fun BICYCLE RENTAL
(☎0410 547 838; www.realfun.com.au) Delivers bicycles (per day/week $45/95) to your door.

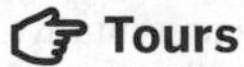

Tours

Balloon Aloft BALLOONING
(☎02-6249 8660; www.canberraballoons.com.au; Kallaroo Rd, Pialligo; rides adult/child from $290/210) Aerial views over Canberra – the ideal way to understand the city's unique design.

Canberra City Explorer BUS TOUR
(Map p208; ☎02-9567 8400; www.canberracityexplorer.com.au; departs Melbourne Bldg, Northbourne Ave; 24hr adult/child $35/20, 48hr $60/30; ⌚9am-6pm) Handy hop-on, hop-off service with 13 stops.

Southern Cross Yacht Club CRUISE
(Map p208; ☎02-6273 1784; www.cscc.com.au; 1 Mariner Pl, Yarralumla; from $15) Lake cruises, including lunch and dinner options.

Lake Burley Griffin Cruises CRUISE
(Map p208; ☎0419 418 846; www.lakecruises.com.au; adult/child $18/9; ⏲mid-Oct–mid-May) Informative lake cruises.

Festivals & Events

See www.events.act.gov.au.

National Multicultural Festival CULTURAL
(www.multiculturalfestival.com.au) Three days of art, culture and food in February.

Royal Canberra Show AGRICULTURAL SHOW
(www.canberrashow.org.au) The country comes to town in late February.

Enlighten CULTURAL
(www.enlightencanberra.com.au) Events and experiences showcasing 'Canberra in a whole new light'. Held in early March.

Canberra Festival ART, CULTURAL
(www.events.act.gov.au) Canberra's annual birthday party, in March.

Canberra Balloon Spectacular BALLOONING
(www.balloonspectacular.com.au) Hot-air balloons fill the lawns in front of Old Parliament House in March.

National Folk Festival ART, CULTURAL
(www.folkfestival.asn.au) One of Australia's largest folk festivals, held over Easter.

Canberra District Wine Harvest Festival WINE
(www.canberrawines.com.au) Wine, food and music, in April.

Canberra International Music Festival MUSIC
(www.cimf.org.au) Classical music in iconic Canberra locations and buildings during May.

Floriade FLOWER SHOW
(www.floriadeaustralia.com) Celebrating the city's spectacular spring flowers from September to October.

Sleeping

Canberra's accommodation is busiest during parliamentary sitting days. Hotels charge peak rates mid-week, but drop rates at weekends. Peak rates also apply during the Floriade festival.

North of Lake Burley Griffin

Canberra City YHA HOSTEL $
(Map p208; ☎02-6248 9155; www.yha.com.au; 7 Akuna St, Civic; dm $36-45, d & tw $118, f $144-200; ❄@🛜🏊) School groups often stay at this hostel. Most rooms and dorms use shared bathrooms, although family rooms have private facilities. Amenities include bike hire ($25 per day), a small indoor pool, sauna, kitchen, an outdoor terrace and a cafe.

QT Canberra BOUTIQUE HOTEL $$
(Map p208; ☎02-6247 6244; www.qtcanberra.com.au; 1 London Circuit, New Acton; d $155-255) A playful irreverence towards politics underscores the spectacular lobby, and very comfortable rooms are trimmed with cool design touches like retro postcards of past Aussie prime ministers. Downstairs the country's political movers and shakers do their finest *House of Cards* impressions in the Capitol Bar & Grill.

★**Hotel Hotel** BOUTIQUE HOTEL $$$
(Map p208; ☎02-6287 6287; www.hotel-hotel.com.au; 25 Edinburgh Ave, New Acton; r $228-340) Hotel Hotel's spectacular exterior translates to an equally hip interior. Rooms are quirkily decorated, and while the (very) subdued lighting isn't to everyone's taste, we're big fans of the hotel's audacious and dramatic ambience. Reception is filled with nooks, crannies and mini-libraries, and Hotel Hotel's Monster Kitchen & Bar (p210) is equally interesting.

South of Lake Burley Griffin

Victor Lodge GUESTHOUSE $
(Map p208; ☎02-6295 7777; www.victorlodge.com.au; 29 Dawes St, Kingston; with shared bathroom s from $89, d & tw $116; ❄🛜) Adjacent to good cafes and restaurants in Kingston, Victor Lodge features simply furnished and compact rooms. There's a kitchen, a barbecue area, continental breakfasts and bicycle hire.

Blue & White Lodge B&B $$
(Map p204; ☎02-6248 0498; www.blueandwhitelodge.com.au; 524 Northbourne Ave, Downer; s/d from $90/100; ❄🛜) This Mediterranean-style B&B has spotless and comfortable rooms, some with shared bathrooms, and a cooked breakfast is just $10. The owners also manage neighbouring Canberran Lodge. Buses to the city are nearby.

Central Canberra

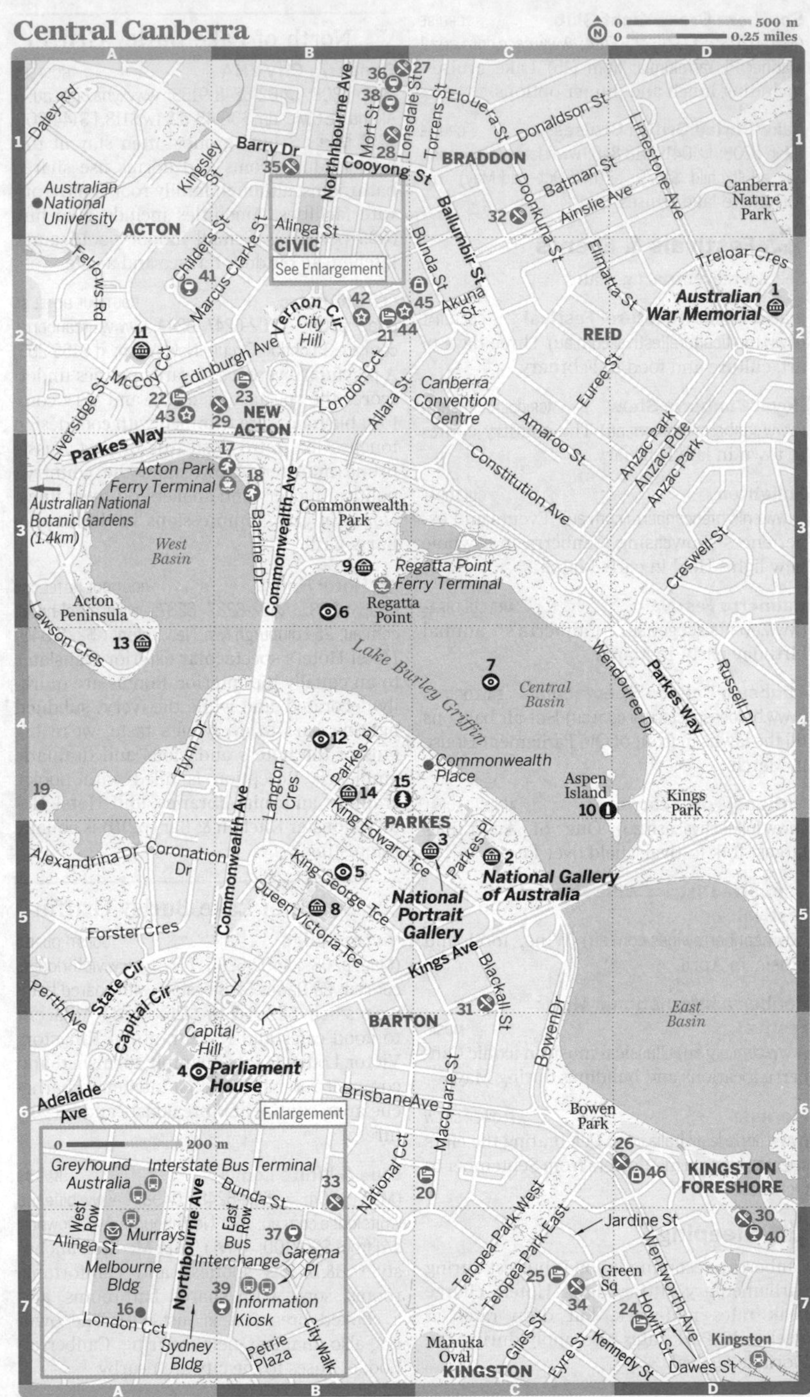

Central Canberra

Top Sights		
1	Australian War Memorial	D2
2	National Gallery of Australia	C5
3	National Portrait Gallery	C5
4	Parliament House	A6
Sights		
5	Aboriginal Tent Embassy	B5
6	Captain Cook Memorial Water Jet	B3
7	Lake Burley Griffin	C4
8	Museum of Australian Democracy	B5
9	National Capital Exhibition	B3
10	National Carillon	C4
11	National Film & Sound Archive	A2
12	National Library of Australia	B4
13	National Museum of Australia	A4
14	Questacon	B4
15	Reconciliation Place	B4
Activities, Courses & Tours		
16	Canberra City Explorer	A7
17	Lake Burley Griffin	B3
	Lake Burley Griffin Cruises	(see 17)
18	Mr Spokes Bike Hire	B3
19	Southern Cross Yacht Club	A4
Sleeping		
20	Burbury Hotel	C6
21	Canberra City YHA	B2
22	Hotel Hotel	A2
23	QT Canberra	B2
24	Victor Lodge	D7
25	York Canberra	C7
Eating		
26	Brodburger	D6
	Elk & Pea	(see 27)
27	Lonsdale Street Eatery	B1
28	Lonsdale Street Roasters	B1
	Malamay	(see 20)
29	Močan & Green Grout	B2
	Monster Kitchen & Bar	(see 22)
30	Morks	D7
31	Ottoman	C5
32	Sage Dining Room	C1
33	Sammy's Kitchen	B6
34	Silo Bakery	C7
35	Temporada	B1
Drinking & Nightlife		
36	BentSpoke Brewing Co	B1
37	Honky Tonks	B7
38	Knightsbridge Penthouse	B1
39	Phoenix	B7
40	Rum Bar	D7
41	Wig & Pen	A2
Entertainment		
	Arc Cinema	(see 11)
42	Canberra Theatre Centre	B2
43	Palace Electric Cinema	A2
44	Ticketek	B2
Shopping		
45	Canberra Centre	C2
	Craft ACT	(see 42)
	National Library Bookshop	(see 12)
46	Old Bus Depot Markets	D6

★ **East Hotel** HOTEL $$$

(Map p204; ☎02-6295 6925, 1800 816 469; www.easthotel.com.au; 69 Canberra Ave, Kingston; studio r $265-320, apt $315-270; P ❄ @ 📶) Straddling the divide between boutique and business, East Hotel offers stylishly executed spaces. Rooms feature a work desk, iPod dock, espresso machine and fully equipped kitchenette, and family rooms come complete with Xbox and beanbags. Next door is the chic Ox Eatery and a bar.

Burbury Hotel HOTEL $$$

(Map p208; ☎02-6173 2700; www.burburyhotel.com.au; 1 Burbury Close, Barton; r $200-285, apt $300-380; P ❄ @ 📶) This business hotel offers rooms and one- and two-bedroom suites. The decor is neutral and relaxing, and rooms are pleasantly light. Adjacent, recently completed apartments are excellent for families, and the complex also includes two impressive Asian restaurants.

York Canberra APARTMENT $$$

(Map p208; ☎02-6295 2333; www.yorkcanberra.com.au; 31 Giles St, Kingston; r $250, 1-bed apt $275, 2-bed apt $350; P ❄ 📶) Located near Kingston's cafes and restaurants, the York is an excellent choice for families. It offers well-sized suites and apartments, some with fully equipped kitchens and washing machine/dryer, and the rest with kitchenettes.

Eating

Established dining hubs include Civic, Kingston, Manuka and Griffith, and there are good Asian eateries in Dickson. New Acton, the Kingston Foreshore development south of the lake, and Lonsdale St in Braddon, are emerging areas. Note many restaurants close on Sunday and Monday.

WINERIES OF THE ACT

Canberra's wine region produces high-country cool-climate wines with riesling and shiraz the star varietals.

See www.canberrawines.com.au or the *Canberra District Wineries Guide* map.

Brindabella Hills Winery (☎02-6230 2583; www.brindabellahills.com.au; 156 Woodgrove Close, via Wallaroo Rd, Hall; ⏱10am-5pm Sat & Sun) This sizeable vineyard near Hall has been operating for more than 20 years. Set on a beautiful ridge, it has won awards for its shiraz, cabernet sauvignon and riesling. Excellent tapas plates are also available.

Clonakilla Wines (☎02-6277 5877; www.clonakilla.com.au; 3 Crisps Lane, Murrumbateman; ⏱cellar door 10am-5pm) Boutique winery producing a handful of highly sought varieties, including an award-winning shiraz viognier.

Eden Road Wines (☎02-6226 8800; www.edenroadwines.com.au; 3182 Barton Hwy, Murrumbateman; ⏱cellar door 11am-4pm Wed-Sun) New winery producing fantastic shiraz.

Helm Wines (☎02-6227 5953; www.helmwines.com.au; 19 Butts Rd, Murrumbateman; ⏱10am-5pm Thu-Mon) The best rieslings produced in the region can be tasted in the pretty tasting room, a former schoolhouse built in 1888.

Lark Hill (☎02-6238 1393; www.larkhillwinery.com.au; 521 Bungendore Rd, Bungendore; ⏱11am-4pm Wed-Mon) Set high in the hills on the Lake George Escarpment overlooking Bungendore village, Lark Hill sells biodynamic wines and operates a vineyard restaurant for weekend lunches.

Wily Trout Vineyard (☎02-6230 2487; www.wilytrout.com.au; 431 Nanima Rd, Hall; ⏱10am-5pm) Home to the popular **Poachers Pantry** (p213) with its smokehouse cafe.

North of Lake Burley Griffin

Lonsdale Street Roasters CAFE $

(Map p208; http://lonsdalestreetroasters.com; Shop 3, 7 Lonsdale St, Braddon; ⏱6.30am-4pm Mon-Fri, to 3pm Sat, 8am-2pm Sun) In hip Braddon, this grungy-chic cafe serves up damn fine coffee. There's another bigger **branch** (Map p208; 23 Lonsdale St; mains $9-22; ⏱6am-4pm Mon-Wed, to 9.30pm Thu-Sat, 7am-7pm Sun) just up the road with a big terrace and a great menu of cafe favourites.

Elk & Pea MEXICAN $

(Map p208; www.elkandpea.com.au; 21 Lonsdale St, Braddon; tacos $7.50, shared plates $15-20; ⏱8am-10pm Tue-Sun, to 3pm Mon) Say *hola* to another new opening along ever-evolving Lonsdale St. Mexican influences include spicy huevos rancheros eggs for brekkie, burgers and burritos for lunch, and Canberra's best tacos for dinner. Breakfast martinis and gazpacho Bloody Marys will give you a morning pick-me-up, and live music bubbles away from 3pm on Saturdays.

★Temporada SPANISH $$

(Map p208; www.temporada.com.au; 15 Moore St, Civic; small plates $8-15, large plates $20-36; ⏱noon-late Mon-Sat) Spanish flavours dominate at our favourite new Canberra restaurant, and the chefs are keen to demonstrate their skill with wood-fired food. Oysters come out deliciously smoky, marinated lamb partners with grilled sausage and flatbread, and barbecued octopus is subtly refreshed with watermelon. Excellent cocktails, wines and Australian craft beers seal the deal.

★Močan & Green Grout CAFE $$

(Map p208; www.mocanandgreengrout.com; 1/19 Marcus Clarke St, New Acton; breakfast & lunch mains $9-16, dinner shared plates $16-25; ⏱7am-6pm Mon, to 9pm Tue-Sat, 8am-4pm Sun; 📶) Often awash with morning sunshine, this New Acton cafe with an open kitchen is one of Canberra's best places to start the day. Free-range-this and local-that feature on the concise seasonal menu, and an espresso and the baked Tripoli eggs will really kickstart your morning. Dinner is served from Tuesday to Saturday with small-plate highlights including Japanese-influenced soft-shell crab.

Monster Kitchen & Bar MODERN AUSTRALIAN, CAFE $$

(Map p208; www.hotelhotel.com.au; Hotel Hotel, 25 Edinburgh Ave, New Acton; breakfast $11-24, bar snacks & shared plates $10-33; ⏱6.30am-1am) Concealed in the cool Hotel Hotel is one of Canberra's more versatile eateries. Hotel guests, New Acton trendies and politicians check their Twitter feeds over breakfast, before bar snacks and shared plates with a subtle Middle Eastern influence get everyone talking during lunch and dinner. At night it morphs into a bar (and a good place to overhear political gossip).

Lanterne Rooms MALAYSIAN **$$**
(Map p204; ☎02-6249 6889; www.lanternerooms.chairmangroup.com.au; Shop 3, Blamey Pl, Campbell; lunch banquet $33.50, dinner mains $30-35; ⏲noon-2.30pm & 6-10.30pm Tue-Fri, 6-10.30pm Sat) Serving expertly cooked Nyonya dishes in a colourful interior referencing Penang farmhouses from the colonial era, Lanterne Rooms is sophisticated and welcoming.

Sammy's Kitchen MALAYSIAN **$$**
(Map p208; ☎02-6247 1464; www.sammyskitchen.com.au; 9 Bunda St, Civic; mains $10-25; ⏲11.30am-10pm) Sammy's is a long-standing local favourite serving up cheap and plentiful Chinese and Malay dishes. No frills, but lots of fun.

Malaysian Chapter MALAYSIAN **$$**
(Map p204; ☎02-6251 5670; www.malaysianchapter.com.au; 6 Weedon Close, Bencoolen; mains $15-20, set menu per person $26; ⏲noon-2pm & 5.30-9pm Tue-Sat, 5.30-9pm Mon) Fans of home-style Malaysian food should definitely make the trek – around 10km northwest from Civic – to this unassuming, family-run spot in Bencoolen Mall. Highlights include a zingy tamarind-based fish and excellent satay that conjures up memories of lazy nights in Penang's hawker centres. Leave room for dessert including cooling sago incorporating pandan, coconut and palm sugar.

Sage Dining Room FRENCH **$$$**
(Map p208; ☎02-6249 6050; www.sagerestaurant.net.au; Batman St, Braddon; 3-/5-course meals $75/95; ⏲noon-2pm & 5.30-10pm Tue-Sat) In the Gorman House Arts Centre, Sage is the home kitchen of French chef Clement Chauvin who once graced the kitchen at London's Claridges, and Maison Pic in France. Subtle French plays on local ingredients make for exquisite tastes.

South of Lake Burley Griffin

Brodburger BURGERS **$**
(Map p208; ☎02-6162 0793; www.brodburger.com.au; Glassworks Bldg, 11 Wentworth Ave, Kingston; burgers $13-20; ⏲11.30am-3pm & 5.30pm-late Tue-Sat, noon-4pm Sun) Brodburger started as a lakeside caravan takeaway joint. Now it's got a permanent location, but the flame-grilled burgers are as good as ever. Salmon, chicken and lamb ones all go well with Aussie beer and wine, but we can't go past the all-encompassing flavour-packed Brodeluxe.

Silo Bakery BAKERY, CAFE **$$**
(Map p208; ☎02-6260 6060; http://silobakery.com.au; 36 Giles St, Kingston; breakfast $9-22, lunch $20-22; ⏲7am-4pm Tue-Sat) Sourghdough bread, pastries and tarts are perfect breakfast temptations, and filled baguettes, rustic mains and cheese platters keep diners happy at lunch. Good coffee and wines by the glass complete the package. Book for lunch.

Morks THAI **$$**
(Map p208; ☎02-6295 0112; www.morks.com.au; Trevillian Quay, Kingston Foreshore; mains $24-28; ⏲noon-2pm & 6-10pm Tue-Sat, noon-2pm Sun) Our favourite of the restaurants along the new Trevillian Quay development on the Kingston Foreshore, Morks offers a contemporary spin on Thai cuisine. Ask for a table outside, watch the punters shuffling to adjacent wholefood cafes, specialist coffee roasters and bustling bars, and enjoy the authentic Thai zip and zing of red duck curry or pork crackling with chilli jam.

Ottoman TURKISH **$$$**
(Map p208; ☎02-6273 6111; www.ottomancuisine.com.au; cnr Broughton & Blackall Sts, Barton; mains $29-33, 7-course degustation menu $75; ⏲noon-2.30pm & 6-10pm Tue-Fri, 6-10pm Sat) This splendid Turkish restaurant in a sprawling villa is a favourite destination for Canberra's power brokers. Traditional dishes (mezze, dolma, kebabs) are given a cunning mod Oz twist. Look forward to exemplary service and an expansive wine list.

Aubergine MODERN AUSTRALIAN **$$$**
(Map p204; ☎02-6260 8666; www.aubergine.com.au; 18 Barker St, Griffith; 4-course set menu $90; ⏲6-10pm Mon-Sat) Award-winning Aubergine's menu is exciting and perfectly balanced. Service and food presentation are assured, with the spacious and dramatic dining room showcasing innovative and seasonal dishes like roast duck with confit egg yolk.

Malamay CHINESE **$$$**
(Map p208; ☎02-6162 1220; http://malamay.chairmangroup.com.au; Burbury Hotel, 1 Burbury Close, Barton; mains $33-38, lunch banquet $42, dinner banquet $65.50; ⏲noon-2.30pm & 6-10.30pm Tue-Fri, 6-10.30pm Sat) The spicy flavours of Sichuan cuisine entice at this restaurant. A glamorous interior fit out channels Shanghai

circa 1930, and is a perfect setting for a leisurely set banquet or zesty mains, including lamb with cumin and chilli salt.

Drinking & Nightlife

Pubs and bars are concentrated in Civic and nearby around Lonsdale and Mort Sts in Braddon. The Kingston Foreshore area south of the lake is emerging.

★BentSpoke Brewing Co CRAFT BEER
(Map p208; www.bentspokebrewing.com.au; 38 Mort St, Braddon; ⏲11am-midnight) With 18 excellent beers and ciders on tap, BentSpoke is one of Australia's best craft brewers. Sit at the biking-themed bar or relax outside and kick things off with a tasting tray of four beers ($16). Our favourite is the Barley Griffin Ale, subtly tinged with a spicy Belgian yeast. Good pub food, too.

Rum Bar BAR
(Map p208; www.facebook.com/therumbarcanberra; Trevillian Quay, Kingston Foreshore; ⏲5-10pm Tue, from 3pm Wed-Fri, from noon Sat & Sun) The city's biggest selection of rum combines with a cosmopolitan canal-front spot along the Trevillian Quay strip on the Kingston Foreshore. Cocktails, tapas and craft beer are additional drawcards, and other bars and pubs make the area a worthwhile after-dark or lazy afternoon destination.

Honky Tonks BAR
(Map p208; www.drinkhonkytonks.com.au; 17 Garema Pl, Civic; ⏲4pm-late Mon-Thu, 2pm-late Fri-Sun) Canberra's compadres meet up here to eat tacos, drink margaritas and listen to eclectic sets from the DJ. It's loads of fun.

Knightsbridge Penthouse COCKTAIL BAR
(Map p208; ☎02-6262 6221; www.knightsbridgepenthouse.com.au; 34 Mort St, Braddon; ⏲5pm-midnight Tue & Wed, 5pm-late Thu-Sat) Arty and gay-friendly, with good DJs, excellent cocktails and a mellow ambience.

Wig & Pen CRAFT BEER
(Map p208; www.facebook.com/wigandpen.canberra; 100 Childers St, Llewellyn Hall; ⏲11.30am-midnight Mon-Fri, 2pm-midnight Sat, 2-8pm Sun) Long-standing Canberra brewpub now relocated on campus to the ANU's School of Music. Those lucky, lucky students...

Phoenix PUB
(Map p208; ☎02-6247 1606; www.lovethephoenix.com; 23 East Row, Civic; ⏲noon-1am Mon-Wed, to 3am Thu-Sat) The Phoenix is a staunch supporter of local music and has a laid-back and hip vibe.

★ Entertainment

Entertainment listings are in Thursday's *Canberra Times* and on the BMA website (www.bmamag.com). **Ticketek** (Map p208; ☎02-6219 6666; www.ticketek.com.au; Akuna St, Civic) sells tickets.

Palace Electric Cinema CINEMA
(Map p208; ☎02-6222 4900; www.palacecinemas.com.au/cinemas/electric/; 2 Phillip Law St, NewActon Nishi) Arthouse and independent movies with cheaper Monday tickets.

Canberra Theatre Centre THEATRE
(Map p208; ☎box office 02-6275 2700; www.canberratheatre.org.au; London Circuit, Civic Sq, Civic; ⏲box office 9am-5pm Mon-Fri, 10am-2pm Sat) Canberra's live theatre hub.

Shopping

Canberra Centre MALL
(Map p208; ☎02-6247 5611; www.canberracentre.com.au; Bunda St, Civic; ⏲9am-5.30pm Mon-Thu, 9am-9pm Fri, 9am-5pm Sat, 10am-4pm Sun) Canberra's premier shopping centre. Includes a multiscreen cinema.

Craft ACT HOMEWARES, JEWELLERY
(Map p208; ☎02-6262 9993; www.craftact.org.au; 1st fl, North Bldg, 180 London Circuit, Civic; ⏲10am-5pm Tue-Fri, noon-4pm Sat) Contemporary design store and exhibitions.

Old Bus Depot Markets MARKET
(Map p208; ☎02-6292 8391; www.obdm.com.au; 21 Wentworth Ave, Kingston; ⏲10am-4pm Sun) Arts, crafts, local artisan produce and regional wines.

National Library Bookshop BOOKS
(Map p208; ☎02-6262 1424; http://bookshop.nla.gov.au; Parkes Pl, Parkes; ⏲9am-5pm) Exclusively Australian books.

Information

Canberra & Region Visitors Centre (Map p204; ☎1300 554 114, 02-6205 0044; www.visitcanberra.com.au; 330 Northbourne Ave, Dickson; ⏲9am-4pm) Around 3km north of Civic.

Getting There & Away

AIR

Qantas (☎13 13 13, TTY 1800 652 660; www.qantas.com.au; Jolimont Centre, Northbourne

Ave, Civic) and **Virgin Australia** (www.virginaustralia.com.au) flights connect **Canberra Airport** (Map p204; ☎02-6275 2226; www.canberraairport.com.au) with all Australian state capitals.

BUS

The interstate bus terminal is at the Jolimont Centre.

Greyhound Australia (Map p208; ☎1300 4739 46863, 1300 GREYHOUND; www.greyhound.com.au; ⊙Jolimont Centre branch 6am-9.30pm) Frequent services to Sydney ($42, 3½ hours) and Melbourne ($91, nine hours).

Murrays (Map p208; ☎13 22 51; www.murrays.com.au; ⊙Jolimont Centre branch 7am-7pm) Daily express services to Sydney ($42, 3½ hours), Batemans Bay ($30, 2½ hours), Narooma ($37, 4½ hours) and Wollongong ($47, 3½ hours) as well as the ski fields.

CAR & MOTORCYCLE

The Hume Hwy connects Sydney and Melbourne, passing 50km north of Canberra. The Federal Hwy runs north to connect with the Hume near Goulburn, and the Barton Hwy (Rte 25) meets the Hume near Yass. To the south, the Monaro Hwy connects Canberra with Cooma.

TRAIN

Kingston train station (Wentworth Ave) is the city's rail terminus. Book trains and connecting buses inside the station.

NSWTrainLink (p264) trains run to/from Sydney ($40, 4½ hours, two to three daily). For Melbourne, a NSWTrainLink coach to Cootamundra ($14, 2½ hours) links with the Sydney-to-Melbourne train service ($75, six hours). A daily **V/Line** (☎13 61 96; www.vline.com.au) Canberra Link service combines a train from Melbourne to Albury Wodonga with a bus to Canberra ($55, 8½ hours).

ℹ Getting Around

TO/FROM THE AIRPORT

Canberra Airport is 8km southeast of the city. A taxi to the city centre costs around $50 to $55. **Airport Express** (☎1300 368 897; www.royalecoach.com.au; one way/return $12/20) runs between the airport and the city.

PUBLIC TRANSPORT

Canberra's public transport provider is the **ACT Internal Omnibus Network** (Action; ☎13 17 10; www.action.act.gov.au; single trip adult/concession $4.60/2.30, daily pass $8.80/4.40) The main bus interchange is along Alinga St, East Row and Mort St. See the **information kiosk** (Map p208; East Row, Civic; ⊙7.30am-5.30pm Mon-Fri) for route maps and timetables.

Purchase tickets from Action agents (including the visitors centre and newsagents), or on board from drivers.

TAXI

Canberra Elite Taxis (☎13 22 27; www.canberracabs.com.au) Canberra taxi service.

Cabxpress (☎02-6260 6011; www.cabxpress.com.au) Canberra taxi service.

AROUND CANBERRA

The Canberra & Region Visitors Centre has maps and information.

Tidbinbilla & Namadgi

Tidbinbilla Nature Reserve NATURE RESERVE
(☎02-6205 1233; www.tidbinbilla.act.gov.au; per car $11; ⊙visitor centre 9am-5pm) Located 45km southwest of Canberra, with bushwalking and wildlife including kangaroos and emus, and platypuses and lyrebirds at dusk. Check online for ranger-guided activities.

Namadgi National Park NATIONAL PARK
(www.tams.act.gov.au) Namadgi is the Aboriginal word for the mountains southwest of Canberra, and this park includes eight peaks higher than 1700m. There's good bushwalking, mountain biking, fishing, horse riding and viewing of Aboriginal rock art. Make camping bookings online or at the **Namadgi Visitor Centre** (☎02-6207 2900; Naas Rd, Tharwa; ⊙9am-4pm Mon-Fri, to 4.30pm Sat & Sun), 2km south of Tharwa.

Surrounding Towns & Villages

A number of NSW towns lie across the border. Around 15 minutes from Canberra along the Barton Hwy is **Hall**, where the **Poachers Pantry** (☎02-6230 2487; www.poacherspantry.com.au; Nanima Rd, Hall; ⊙pantry 10am-5pm daily, smokehouse cafe noon-3pm Fri, 10-11.30am Sat & Sun) is renowned for cured meats and a smokehouse cafe.

Excellent wineries feature at **Murrumbateman** (30 minutes' drive from Canberra). **Bungendore** is 35km east of Canberra and bustles with visitors to its galleries and antique stores at weekends. The **Bungendore Wood Works Gallery** (☎02-6238 1682; http://bungendorewoodworks.com.au; cnr Malbon & Ellendon Sts, Bungendore; ⊙9am-5pm) showcases

Australian timber and has a fine cafe, and there's good accommodation at the **Old Stone House** (☎02-6238 1888; www.theoldstonehouse.com.au; 41 Molonglo St, Bungendore; r $220; ❄).

WOLLONGONG

POP 292,190

The 'Gong', 80km south of Sydney, is the envy of many cities. Restaurants, bars, arts, culture and entertainment all combine with a laid-back beachy lifestyle, and the bright lights of Sydney are easily accessible by local rail.

There are 17 patrolled beaches and a spectacular sandstone escarpment running from the Royal National Park south past Wollongong and Port Kembla.

Grand Pacific Dr showcases excellent surf, safe beaches, bushwalking and sky-high adventures.

Sights

Belmore Basin HARBOUR, PORT

Wollongong's fishing fleet is based at the harbour's southern end. The basin was cut from solid rock in 1868. There's a fishing cooperative and an **old lighthouse** (built in 1872) on the point. Nearby, on the headland, is the newer **Breakwater Lighthouse**.

Science Centre & Planetarium MUSEUM

(☎02-4283 6665; http://sciencecentre.uow.edu.au; Squires Way, Fairy Meadow; adult/child $13/9; ⏲10am-4pm) Quizzical kids of all ages can indulge their senses here. It's operated by the University of Wollongong and covers everything from dinosaurs to electronics. Planetarium shows run throughout the day.

Wollongong Botanic Gardens GARDENS

(61 Northfields Ave, Keiraville) FREE Habitats include tropical, temperate and woodland. A top spot for a picnic lunch.

Wollongong City Gallery GALLERY

(www.wollongongcitygallery.com; cnr Kembla & Burelli Sts; ⏲10am-5pm Tue-Fri, noon-4pm Sat & Sun) FREE Modern Australian, Indigenous and Asian art, and diverse temporary exhibits.

Beaches

North Beach generally has better surf than **Wollongong City Beach**. The harbour's beaches are safer for children. North are the surfer magnets of **Bulli**, **Sandon Point**, **Thirroul** (where DH Lawrence lived during his time in Australia) and pretty **Austinmer**.

Activities

Pines Surfing Academy SURFING

(☎0410 645 981; www.pinessurfingacademy.com.au; North Beach; 3-day course $120, board hire 1/3hr $20/30; ⏲mid-Dec–late Jan) Summer-only surf lessons and paddleboarding.

Sydney Hang Gliding Centre ADVENTURE SPORTS

(☎0400 258 258; www.hanggliding.com.au; tandem flights from $245; ⏲7am-7pm) Tandem flights above the spectacular coastline from breathtaking Bald Hill at Stanwell Park.

Cockatoo Run SCENIC RAILWAY

(☎1300 653 801; www.3801limited.com.au; adult/child/family $60/50/175; ⏲10.50am selected Sun, Wed & Thu) Heritage tourist train traversing the escarpment and rainforest across the Southern Highlands to Moss Vale.

Sleeping

Coledale Beach Camping Reserve CAMPGROUND $

(☎02-4267 4302; www.coledalebeach.com.au; Beach Rd; unpowered/powered sites from $25/30) About 20 minutes north of Wollongong, wake up to great surf and the occasional company of dolphins and whales.

Keiraleagh HOSTEL $

(☎02-4228 6765; www.backpack.net.au; 60 Kembla St; dm/s/d from $24/55/75; @ 📶) This welcoming and rambling heritage house has basic dorms, a sizeable patio and a barbecue.

Beach Park Motor Inn MOTEL $$

(☎02-4226 1577; www.beachparkmotorinn.com.au; 16 Pleasant Ave; r $88-185; ❄ 📶) The friendly owners keep the slightly twee rooms in this white-brick establishment spick and span. It's a short walk from the beach.

Chifley HOTEL $$

(☎02-4201 2111; www.silverneedlehotels.com; 60-62 Harbour St; r from $152) Wollongong's newest hotel has ocean and golf-course views, tastefully designed rooms and shared public areas. Good beaches, pubs and restaurants are a short walk away.

Eating

North of the Crown St mall, Keira St is Wollongong's main dining precinct. New cafes and restaurants have also opened around the Wollongong Central shopping centre on the corner of Crown and Keira Sts.

Wollongong

Wollongong

Sights
1 Belmore Basin ... D3
2 Breakwater Lighthouse ... D3
3 North Beach ... C1
4 Old Lighthouse ... D3
5 Wollongong City Beach ... C4
6 Wollongong City Gallery ... B4

Activities, Courses & Tours
7 Pines Surfing Academy ... C1

Sleeping
8 Beach Park Motor Inn ... B1
9 Keiraleagh ... B3

Eating
10 Balinese Spice Magic ... A3
11 Caveau ... A3
12 Diggies ... C1
13 Lee & Me ... B4

Drinking & Nightlife
14 His Boy Elroy ... A4
15 Howlin' Wolf ... B4
16 Illawarra Brewery ... C4

Balinese Spice Magic INDONESIAN $
(www.balinesespicemagic.com.au; 130 Keira St; lunch $10-13, dinner $16-20; ⌚11.30am-2.30pm Wed-Fri, 5.30-10pm Tue-Sat) Look forward to excellent Indonesian food and welcoming service from the friendly family owners. Thai and Vietnamese eateries also line Keira St, but this is our pick of the best flavours to remind you of your time drifting aimlessly around Southeast Asia.

Lee & Me CAFE $
(www.leeandme.com.au; 87 Crown St; breakfast or lunch $11-16; ⏱7am-4pm Mon-Fri, 8am-4pm Sat & Sun) A cafe and art-and-clothing store in a two-storey, late-19th-century heritage building. Standout dishes include buttermilk-malt hotcakes or the classic beef burger.

Diggies CAFE $$
(☎02-4226 2688; www.diggies.com.au; 1 Cliff Rd; lunch $16-26, dinner $21-32; ⏱6.30am-4pm Sun-Thu, to 10pm Fri & Sat) With a view to the rolling waves, this is the perfect spot for feasting any time of the day. From 4pm Sunday afternoon during summer, cocktails and tunes are let loose on the deck.

Caveau MODERN AUSTRALIAN $$$
(☎02-4226 4855; www.caveau.com.au; 122-124 Keira St; 7-course degustation menu $99, with wine $145; ⏱6-11pm Tue-Sat) This lauded restaurant serves gourmet treats such as kingfish tartare and poached scampi. The menu changes seasonally and there's a three-course menu ($79) available from Tuesday to Thursday.

Drinking & Entertainment

His Boy Elroy BAR
(www.hisboyelroy.com.au; Globe Lane; breakfast $11-16, snacks & burgers $6-19; ⏱9am-10pm Sun, Wed & Thu, 8am-midnight Fri & Sat) His Boy Elroy combines Asian and South American street food – think burgers, tacos and Vietnamese *banh mi* – with Australian craft beers, robust cocktails and a good wine list. Breakfasts are also very tasty. Check out the surrounding lane for more new bars and cafes.

Illawarra Brewery BAR
(www.thebrewery.net.au; cnr Crown & Harbour Sts; ⏱11am-late) This slick bar with ocean views has six craft beers on tap, plus occasional seasonal brews. Guest beers from around Australia complete a happy and hoppy picture, and there's decent food on tap as well.

Howlin' Wolf BAR
(3/53-61 Crown St; ⏱5-10pm Sun-Wed, to midnight Thu-Sat) Live music, whisky and cider, tapas and a rockin' vibe. What more do you want?

Information

Visitor Centre (☎1800 240 737; www.visitwollongong.com.au; 93 Crown St; ⏱9am-5pm Mon-Sat, 10am-4pm Sun) Bookings and information.

Getting There & Away

All long-distance buses leave from the eastern side of the railway station. **Trains** (☎13 15 00; www.sydneytrains.info) on the South Coast Line run to Sydney's Central Station ($8.10, 90 minutes).

Murrays (☎13 22 51; www.murrays.com.au) Buses travelling to Canberra ($47.40, 3½ hours).

Premier (☎13 34 10; www.premierms.com.au) Buses to Sydney ($18, two hours) and Eden ($69, eight hours).

Getting Around

Bringing a bike on the train from Sydney is a great way to get around. A cycle path runs north to Bulli and south to Port Kembla.

For taxis, call ☎02-4229 9311.

AROUND WOLLONGONG

South of the City

Just south of Wollongong, **Lake Illawarra** is popular for water sports, including windsurfing. There are good ocean beaches on the Windang Peninsula to the east of the lake. Further south is **Shellharbour**, a popular holiday resort, and one of the coast's oldest towns. Its name derives from the shell middens (remnants of Aboriginal occupation) that the European colonists found here.

Illawarra Escarpment State Conservation Area

Rainforest hugs the edge of the ever-eroding sandstone cliffs of the escarpment, which rises to 534m at **Mt Kembla**. For wonderful coastal views, drive up to the **Mt Keira lookout** (464m); take the freeway north and follow the signs.

North of the City

On the road north to Royal National Park, the **Lawrence Hargrave Lookout** at Bald Hill above Stanwell Park is a cliff-top viewing point. Hargrave, a pioneer aviator, made his first attempts at flying early in the 20th century. Modern hang-gliders keep his obsession alive, and **HangglideOz** (☎0417 939 200; www.hangglideoz.com.au; from $245) and

DON'T MISS

HERE'S TO THE VIEW

Built in 1886 and heritage listed, **Scarborough Hotel** (☎02-4267 5444; www.scarboroughhotel.com.au; 383 Lawrence Hargrave Dr, Scarborough; mains $25-30; ⊙9am-4pm Mon-Fri, to 5pm Sat & Sun) boasts one of Australia's finest beer gardens. The ocean view is truly spectacular and the excellent food is definitely worth the trek. Share the massive seafood platter ($98) with a travelling companion and you won't be disappointed. Downstairs is the **Matthew Gillett Gallery** (www.matthewgillettgallery.com; ⊙9am-4pm), with always-interesting contemporary exhibitions from Australian artists.

Sydney Hang Gliding Centre (p214) both offer tandem flights.

Symbio Wildlife Gardens (☎02-4294 1244; www.symbiozoo.com.au; 7-11 Lawrence Hargrave Dr, Stanwell Tops; adult/child $27/15; ⊙9.30am-5pm) has more than 1000 cute and furry critters, including indigenous Australian and exotic overseas species.

Royal National Park

The 15,091-hectare **Royal National Park** (☎02-9542 0648; www.environment.nsw.gov.au; cars $11, pedestrians & cyclists free; ⊙park gates locked at 8.30pm) was established in 1879, making it the oldest national park in the world after Yellowstone in the USA. Stretching inland from 32km of beautiful coast, it encompasses pockets of subtropical rainforest, windblown coastal scrub, sandstone gullies dominated by gum trees, fresh- and saltwater wetlands, secluded beaches and dramatic cliffs. Traditionally the home of the Dharawal people, there are also numerous **Aboriginal sites** and artefacts.

Walking tracks include the spectacular 26km (two-day) **Coast Track**. Most beaches are unpatrolled and rips can make them dangerous. **Garie**, **Era**, **South Era** and **Burning Palms** are popular surf beaches, and **Werrong Beach** is clothing optional.

On the southern shore of Port Hacking, **Bundeena** is surrounded by the park. Walk 30 minutes to Jibbon Head for a good beach and interesting Aboriginal rock art. Bundeena is also the starting point of the coastal walk.

Sleeping

Bush camping is allowed in some areas, but you must obtain a permit (adult/child $5/3) from the visitor centre.

Bonnie Vale Campground CAMPGROUND $
(http://www.nationalparks.nsw.gov.au/Royal-National-Park/bonnie-vale/camping; Sea Breeze Lane; adult/child $14/7) This 74-space site near Bundeena is equipped with toilets, hot showers and picnic tables.

Beachhaven B&B B&B $$$
(☎02-9544 1333; www.beachhavenbnb.com.au; Hordens Beach, Bundeena; r from $300; ❄📶) Shaded by palms and with direct access to gorgeous Hordens Beach, this place has two swank rooms. Amenities include a spa overlooking the sand.

Information

Visitor Centre (☎02-9542 0648; www.environment.nsw.gov.au/nationalparks; Farnell Ave; ⊙8.30am-4.30pm) Entrance fees, camping permits, maps and bushwalking information. The centre is at Audley, 2km inside the park's northeastern entrance, off the Princes Hwy.

Getting There & Away

Cronulla National Park Ferries (☎02-9523 2990; www.cronullaferries.com.au; adult/child $6.40/3.20; ⊙hourly 5.30am-6.30pm) travel to Bundeena from Cronulla, accessible by train from Sydney.

KIAMA & AROUND

POP 12,817

Kiama's a large town with fine old buildings, magnificent mature trees, numerous beaches and crazy rock formations, but it's the blowhole that's the clincher.

Sights & Activities

There's a compact surf beach right in town, and **Bombo Beach**, 3km north of the centre, has a CityRail stop right near the sand.

Blowhole Point LANDMARK
Most dramatic when the surf's up, with water exploding out of a fissure in the headland. Floodlit at night.

Little Blowhole LANDMARK
(off Tingira Cres, Marsden Head) Just half a metre wide, but definitely challenging its big brother.

Saddleback Mountain NATURE RESERVE
Great views of the Illawarra Escarpment. From Manning St, turn right onto Saddleback Mountain Rd.

Illawarra Fly NATURE RESERVE
(1300 362 881; www.illawarrafly.com.au; 182 Knights Hill Rd, Knights Hill; adult/child/family $25/10/64; 9am-5pm, last entry 4.15pm) There are spectacular views from this 500m viewing tower and Treetop Walk amid the rainforest canopy at the top of the escarpment, 25km west of town. Recently added is an exciting zipline (adult/child $75/45); the cost of the zipline includes entry to the viewing tower and Treetop Walk. Allow around 2½ hours for the whole adventure and note the zipline must be prebooked online.

Minnamurra Rainforest Centre NATURE RESERVE
(02-4236 0469; www.environment.nsw.gov.au/contact/MinnamurraRainforest.htm; car $11; 9am-5pm, last entry 4pm) On the eastern edge of **Budderoo National Park**, about 14km inland from Kiama. A 1.6km loop walk transits through the rainforest following a cascading stream. Look out for water dragons and lyrebirds. A secondary 2.6km walk on a steepish track leads to the **Minnamurra Falls**.

Coastal Walk WALKING
This pretty 6km trail stretches from Love's Bay in Kiama Heights to the northern end of Werri Beach.

Sleeping & Eating

★**Kiama Harbour Cabins** CABIN $$$
(02-4232 2707; www.kiamacoast.com.au; Blowhole Point; cottages from $220;) In the best position in town, these cottages are neat as a pin and well equipped with barbecues on front verandahs overlooking the beach and the ocean pool.

Chachi's ITALIAN $$
(02-4233 1144; www.chachisrestaurant.com.au; 32 Collins St; mains $22-35; 11.30am-2.30pm Tue-Fri, 5.30-9pm Tue-Sat) Located in a historic strip of terraced houses, Chachi's is well loved among locals for its casual alfresco dining.

Information

Visitor Centre (1300 654 262, 02-4232 3322; www.kiama.com.au; Blowhole Point Rd; 9am-5pm) On Blowhole Point.

Getting There & Around

Premier (13 34 10; www.premierms.com.au) buses run twice daily to Berry ($18, 30 minutes), Eden ($69, 7½ hours) and Sydney ($25, 2½ hours). **Kiama Coaches** (02-4232 3466; www.kiamacoaches.com.au) runs to Gerroa, Gerringong and Minnamurra (via Jamberoo).

Frequent **Sydney Trains** (13 15 00; www.sydneytrains.info) departures run to Wollongong, Sydney and Nowra (Bomaderry).

If you're driving, take the beach detour via Gerringong and Gerroa and rejoin the highway either in Berry or just north of Nowra.

SHOALHAVEN COAST

This region's coastal beauty includes great beaches, state forests and national parks, including the huge (190,751-hectare) Morton National Park. Accommodation prices increase on weekends and during school holidays.

Berry

POP 1690

Berry is a popular inland stop on the South Coast. Look forward to a smattering of antique and design stores, and an emerging foodie scene with good cafes and restaurants. Wonderfully scenic **Kangaroo Valley** is a short drive away.

Sights & Activities

The town's short main street features National Trust–classified buildings and there are good-quality vineyards in the rolling countryside around Berry.

Berry Museum MUSEUM
(135 Queen St; 11am-2pm Sat, to 3pm Sun) FREE In an interesting 1884 bank building.

Jasper Valley Wines WINERY
(www.jaspervalleywines.com; 152 Croziers Rd; 10am-5pm Fri-Sun) Located 5km south of Berry, and offering tastings and lunches.

Silos Estate WINERY
(02-4448 6082; www.thesilos.com; B640 Princes Hwy, Jaspers Brush; mains $34; lunch & dinner Thu-Sun) Tastings, an acclaimed restaurant, and boutique accommodation ($175 to $245).

Festivals & Events

Berry Country Fair FAIR
Market with arts, crafts and local produce. Held on the first Sunday of the month.

Berry Celtic Festival CULTURAL
(www.berryrotary.com.au; Berry Showgrounds; adult/child $10/5) Caber tossers, haggis hurlers and bagpipes. Held on the last Saturday in May.

Sleeping

Village Boutique MOTEL $$
(02-4464 3570; www.berrymotel.com.au; 72 Queen St; r $165-240;) Large, comfortable rooms feature at this upmarket place at the edge of the main strip.

Bellawongarah at Berry B&B $$$
(02-4464 1999; www.accommodation-berry.com.au; 869 Kangaroo Valley Rd, Bellawongarah; r from $250;) Rainforest surrounds this wonderful place, 8km from Berry on the mountain road to Kangaroo Valley. Asian art features in the main house, while an 1868 Wesleyan church with a French provincial ambience is rented as a self-contained cottage.

Eating

Berry Woodfired Sourdough BAKERY $$
(www.berrysourdoughcafe.com.au; Prince Alfred St; mains $10-26; 8am-3pm Wed-Sun) Stock up on bread or dine in at this bakery that's beloved by foodies. The owners also run **Milkwood Bakery** (109 Queen St; 7am-6pm) on Berry's main drag. Try the delicious gourmet pies.

★ **Hungry Duck** ASIAN $$
(02-4464 2323; www.hungryduck.com.au; 85 Queen St; mains $17-34, 5-/9-course banquet $50/80; 6-9.30pm Wed-Mon) A contemporary Asian menu is served tapas-style, although larger mains are also available. There's a rear courtyard and kitchen garden where herbs are plucked direct to the plate. Fresh fish, meat and eggs are all sourced locally.

Getting There & Away

Frequent trains go to Wollongong ($6.30, 75 minutes) with connections to other South Coast towns and Sydney.

Premier (13 34 10; www.premierms.com.au) has buses to Kiama ($18, 30 minutes), Nowra ($18, 20 minutes) and Sydney ($25, three hours, twice daily).

WORTH A TRIP

KANGAROO VALLEY

From either Nowra or Berry, a shaded forested road meanders to pretty Kangaroo Valley. This lovely historic town is cradled by mountains, and the sleepy main street has cafes, craft shops and a great pub. Activities in the surrounding area include biking, hiking, canoeing and camping. See www.kangaroovalley-tourist.asn.au for operators and B&B accommodation.

Nowra

POP 9257

Nowra, around 17km from the coast, is the largest town in the Shoalhaven area. Although there are prettier beach towns, it can be a handy regional base for Berry, 17km northeast, or the beaches of Jervis Bay, 25km southeast.

Sights & Activities

The visitor centre can advise on local walks. **Ben's Walk** starts at the bridge near Scenic Dr and follows the south bank of the Shoalhaven River. North of the river, the circular 5.5km **Bomaderry Creek Walking Track** runs through sandstone gorges.

Shoalhaven Zoo WILDLIFE RESERVE
(02-4421 3949; http://shoalhavenzoo.com.au; Rock Hill Rd, North Nowra; adult/child/family $22/12/58; 9am-5pm) Meet native animals at this 6.5-hectare park on the north bank of the Shoalhaven River. It also has a camp site (adult/child from $10/6).

Shoalhaven River Cruises CRUISE
(0429 981 007; www.shoalhavenrivercruise.com; 2/3hr cruise $29/49) Interesting cruises leave from the wharf just east of the bridge.

Sleeping & Eating

Whitehouse GUESTHOUSE $$
(02-4421 2084; www.whitehouseguesthouse.com; 30 Junction St; r $104-168;) A friendly family runs this beautifully restored guesthouse with a verandah and comfortable en suite rooms.

George Bass Motor Inn MOTEL $$
(02-4421 6388; www.georgebass.com.au; 65 Bridge Rd; r from $124;) An unpretentious but well-appointed single-storey motor inn, the George Bass has clean and sunny rooms.

Deli on Kinghorne CAFE $
(www.thedeli.net.au; 84 Kinghorne St; meals $5-15; ⏲6.30am-5pm Mon-Fri, to 3pm Sat & Sun) The best coffee in town, hearty breakfasts and lunches, and lots of sunny outdoor seating.

Wharf Rd MODERN AUSTRALIAN $$
(☎02-4422 6651; www.wharfrd.com.au; 10 Wharf Rd; small/large plates $16/32; ⏲noon-late Tue-Sat, 11.30am-3pm Sun) Right on the river, Wharf Rd is Nowra's most cosmopolitan dining experience. Shared plates include alpaca sirloin, blue-eye trevalla with chilli, or avocado and squid tacos. Check the website for weekday lunch specials.

Drinking

Hop Dog Beerworks CRAFT BEER
(www.hopdog.com.au; Unit 2, 175 Princes Hwy; ⏲tastings & sales 10am-4pm Wed-Thu, to 5pm Fri, to 3pm Sat) In an industrial estate south of town, Hop Dog's uber-hoppy brews include a Belgian IPA and an India Black Ale. Bottles and growlers are available to take away.

Information

NPWS Office (☎02-4423 2170; www.nationalparks.nsw.gov.au; 55 Graham St) National parks information.

Visitor Centre (☎02-4421 0778; www.shoalhaven.nsw.gov.au; cnr Princes Hwy & Pleasant Way) Across the bridge north of town.

WORTH A TRIP

DAY TRIPS FROM NOWRA

East of Nowra, the Shoalhaven River meanders through estuaries and wetlands to good surf at **Crookhaven Heads**, aka 'Crooky'. **Greenwell Point**, about 15km east of Nowra, specialises in fresh oysters.

On the estuary's north side are **Shoalhaven Heads** and the **Seven Mile Beach National Park** stretching up to Gerroa.

Just before Shoalhaven Heads, Coolangatta is the site of the earliest European settlement on NSW's South Coast. **Coolangatta Estate** (☎02-4448 7131; www.coolangattaestate.com.au; r from $140; ⏲winery 10am-5pm) offers a golf course, winery and restaurant, and accommodation in convict-built lodgings.

Getting There & Away

Premier (☎13 34 10; www.premierms.com.au) has buses to Sydney ($25, three hours) via Berry ($18, 20 minutes), and Eden ($57, five hours) via Ulladulla ($19, one hour).

CityRail (☎13 15 00; www.sydneytrains.info) trains run from Sydney's Central or Bondi Junction stations to Kiama, from where there are connections to Nowra (Bomaderry).

Jervis Bay

This large, sheltered bay combines snow-white sand, crystalline waters, national parks and frolicking dolphins. Seasonal visitors include Sydney holidaymakers (summer and most weekends), and migrating whales (May to November).

In 1995 the Aboriginal community won a land claim in the Wreck Bay area and now jointly administers Booderee National Park at the southern end of the bay. By a strange quirk this area is actually part of the Australian Capital Territory, not NSW.

Most development is around Huskisson and Vincentia, and the northern shore has less tourist infrastructure. Beecroft Peninsula forms the northeastern side of Jervis Bay, ending in the dramatic sheer cliffs of Point Perpendicular. Most of the peninsula is navy land but is usually open to the public.

Sights & Activities

Huskisson is the centre for most activities. South of Huskisson, the sand of **Hyams Beach** is reputedly the world's whitest.

Jervis Bay National Park NATIONAL PARK
(www.nationalparks.nsw.gov.au) Reaching Callala Bay, you transit Jervis Bay National Park, 4854 hectares of low scrub and woodland. The bay is a marine park.

Lady Denman Heritage Complex MUSEUM
(☎02-4441 5675; www.ladydenman.asn.au; Dent St; adult/child $10/5; ⏲10am-4pm) With a historic collection, the 1912 *Lady Denman* ferry and **Timbery's Aboriginal Arts & Crafts** gallery and shop. There's a growers' market on the first Saturday of the month, and a visitor information centre.

Dive Jervis Bay DIVING, SNORKELLING
(☎02-4441 5255; www.divejervisbay.com; 64 Owen St) The marine park is popular with divers

and snorkellers who can visit a nearby seal colony (May to October).

Jervis Bay Kayaks KAYAKING
(02-4441 7157; www.jervisbaykayaks.com; 13 Hawke St; kayak hire 3hr/day $49/69, tours $55-165) Rentals, guided sea-kayaking trips, and self-guided camping and kayaking expeditions.

Huskisson Sea Pool SWIMMING
(6am-8pm Fri-Wed Nov-Apr) FREE Saltwater pool that's almost Olympic-sized.

Hire Au Go-Go CYCLING
(02-4441 5241; http://hireaugogo.com; 1 Tomerong St; 1hr/day $19/60) Explore the water's edge on an electric bike.

Dolphin Watch Cruises BOAT TOUR
(02-4441 6311; www.dolphinwatch.com.au; 50 Owen St; dolphin-/whale-/seal-watching tour $35/65/80) Dolphin-, seal- and whale-watching trips.

Sleeping

Prices increase on weekends. Hyams Beach offers private rentals with **Hyams Beach Real Estate** (02-4443 0242; www.hyamsbeachre.com.au; 76 Cyrus St).

Huskisson Beach Tourist Resort CAMPGROUND $
(02-4441 5142; www.holidayhaven.com.au; Beach St; sites per 2 people $40-85, cabins $105-205;) Flash cabins and a beachfront location.

Jervis Bay Motel MOTEL $$
(02-4441 5781; www.jervisbaymotel.com.au; 41 Owen St; r $119-189;) Pleasant decor and lovely views from the (more expensive) upstairs rooms.

Huskisson B&B B&B $$$
(02-4441 7551; www.huskissonbnb.com.au; 12 Tomerong St; r $225;) Bright, airy and colourful rooms containing comfy beds and fluffy towels.

★ **Paperbark Camp** CAMPGROUND $$$
(1300 668 167; www.paperbarkcamp.com.au; 571 Woollamia Rd; d from $395; Sep-Jun) Camp in ecofriendly style in 12 luxurious solar-powered safari tents with en suites and wraparound decks. It's set in dense bush 3.5km from Huskisson; borrow kayaks to paddle up the creek to the bay.

Eating

Supply CAFE $
(02-4441 5815; www.supplyjervisbay.com.au; Shop 1, 54 Owen St; mains $12-18; 7.30am-5pm Mon-Sat, to 3pm Sun) Huskisson's best coffee and satisfying breakfasts feature at this cafe and deli.

Wild Ginger ASIAN $$
(02-4441 5577; www.wild-ginger.com.au; 42 Owen St; mains $31.50; 4.30pm-late Tue-Sun) A relaxed showcase of flavours from across Southeast Asia and Japan. Look forward to tasty local seafood.

Gunyah Restaurant MODERN AUSTRALIAN $$$
(02-4441 7299; 3-course meals $70; 6.30-9pm Sep-Jun) Sit under the canopy on the forested balcony of this acclaimed restaurant at Paperbark Camp. The focus is on local ingredients, and booking is essential for outside guests.

Drinking & Entertainment

Huskisson PUB
(02-4441 5001; www.thehuskisson.com.au; Owen St) Fabulous bay views and excellent food see the outside deck here packed over summer. There's live music most weekends. Recently refurbished and stylish rooms (from $150) are decent value.

Getting There & Around

Jervis Bay Territory (02-4423 5244) runs buses from Huskisson to Nowra.

Nowra Coaches (02-4423 5244; www.nowracoaches.com.au) runs buses around Jervis Bay and on to Nowra.

Ulladulla

POP 12,137

This fishing-focused town celebrates Easter's Blessing of the Fleet ceremony, and there are beautiful beaches nearby.

Sights & Activities

North of the centre, gorgeous **Mollymook Beach** stretches for over 2km. Adjacent **Narrawallee Beach** ends at a pretty kayak-friendly inlet. Both have beach breaks, although serious surfers head to **Collers Beach**.

Coomee Nulunga Cultural Trail WALKING
This 700m walking trail begins near Lighthouse Oval (take Deering St east of the highway) and follows a path from the headland through native bush to the beach.

DON'T MISS

BOODEREE NATIONAL PARK

Booderee National Park (02-4443 097702-4443 0977; www.booderee.gov.au; 2-day car or motorcycle entry $11) Occupying Jervis Bay's southeastern spit, this sublime national park offers good swimming, surfing and diving on both bay and ocean beaches. Much of it is heathland, with some forest, including small pockets of rainforest.

Surfing is good at **Caves Beach** and **Pipeline**.

Walking-trail maps and camping information are available at the **visitor centre** (02-4443 0977; www.booderee.gov.au; 9am-4pm). While walking, look out for 206 species of bird, 27 species of land mammal and 23 species of reptile.

Booderee Botanic Gardens (8.30am-4pm) within the national park features enormous rhododendrons and coastal plants once used for food and medicine by local Indigenous groups.

There's **camping** (camp sites $12-22) at Green Patch and Bristol Point, and the secluded Caves Beach. Book online through the visitor centre at peak times.

Sleeping

Ulladulla Headland Tourist Park CAMPGROUND $
(02-4455 2457; www.holidayhaven.com.au; South St; camp site $26-45, cabin $95-210;) This headland property has a leafy setting with ocean views. Facilities are well kept.

Ulladulla Lodge HOSTEL $
(02-4454 0500; www.ulladullalodge.com.au; 63 Pacific Hwy; dm/d from $35/80) This guesthouse-style place is clean and comfy and guests have access to bikes, surfboards and bodyboards.

Bannisters HOTEL $$$
(02-4455 3044; www.bannisters.com.au; 191 Mitchell Pde, Mollymook; r $295-400, ste $470-1475;) The bones of this 1970s concrete-block motel provide the basis of this hip, unassumingly luxurious place. Splash to the lip of the infinity pool for sublime views up the coast, or enjoy them from your balcony.

Eating

Hayden's Pies BAKERY $
(03-4455 7798; 166 Princes Hwy; pies $4-7; 7am-5pm) With traditional and gourmet pies, this little bakery is awash with crusty goodness and delicious aromas.

★**Tallwood** MODERN AUSTRALIAN, CAFE $$
(02-4455 5192; www.tallwoodeat.com.au; 2/85 Tallwood Ave, Mollymook; breakfast $9-24, dinner $20-36; 7.30am-late Wed-Sun;) Tallwood kicks off the day with excellent coffee and delicious breakfasts like ricotta hotcakes, before segueing into more innovative dishes at lunch and dinner. Highlights to be enjoyed in the colourful and modern surroundings include Portuguese fish cakes with saffron mayo, Balinese-spiced duck, and *dukkah*-spiced eggplant. There are good vegetarian options, and Australian craft beers and wines are proudly featured.

Ulladulla Oyster Bar SEAFOOD $$
(www.ulladullaoysterbar.com.au; Shop 5, The Plaza, 107 Princes Hwy; oysters & tapas $10-20; 10am-8pm Tue-Wed, to 10pm Thu-Sat) Sydney rock oysters are served natural – try the lime and wasabi version – or grilled with ginger, soy and mirin. Wash them down with Hop Dog craft beer from Nowra or local wine.

Cupitt's Winery & Restaurant MODERN AUSTRALIAN $$$
(02-4455 7888; www.cupitt.com.au; 60 Washburton Rd; mains $32-37; noon-2.30pm Wed-Sun, 6-8.30pm Fri & Sat) Enjoy respected cuisine and wine tasting in this restored 1851 creamery. There's boutique vineyard accommodation (one/two nights $330/550) and plans for a new craft brewery.

Bannisters Restaurant SEAFOOD $$$
(02-4455 3044; www.bannisters.com.au; 191 Mitchell Pde, Mollymook; breakfast $15, dinner mains $30-50; 8-11am & 6pm-late) Elegantly situated on Bannister's Point, 1km north of town. Famed UK chef Rick Stein's seafood fare matches the fine views.

Information

Visitor Centre (02-4444 8819; www.shoalhavenholidays.com.au; Princes Hwy; 9am-5pm) Bookings and information.

Getting There & Away

Premier (☎13 34 10; www.premierms.com.au) runs between Sydney ($35, five hours) and Eden ($50, four hours), via Batemans Bay ($16, 45 minutes) and Nowra ($19, one hour).

Murramarang National Park

Murramarang National Park NATIONAL PARK
(www.nationalparks.nsw.gov.au; per car per day $7) This beautiful 12,386-hectare coastal park is home to wild kangaroos, rich bird-life and the protected **Murramarang Aboriginal Area**, which contains ancient middens and Indigenous cultural treasures.

Wasp Head, **Depot**, **Pebbly** and **Merry Beaches** are popular with surfers. Walking trails snake off from these beaches, and a steep but enjoyable walk is up **Durras Mountain** (283m).

Sleeping

NPWS has **camp sites** (www.environment.nsw.gov.au/NationalParks/; unpowered/powered sites $20/28) at **Depot Beach** (☎02-4478 6582), **Pebbly Beach** (☎02-4478 6023) and **Pretty Beach** (☎02-4457 2019). Book ahead during school holidays. Also available are self-contained **cabins** (forest/beach from $115/140) at Depot Beach and Pretty Beach.

Durras Lake North Holiday Park CAMPGROUND $
(☎02 4478 6072; www.durrasnorthpark.com.au; 57 Durras Rd, Durras North; camp sites per 2 people $35-85, cabins $90-120) Shaded camp sites, cute cabins and it's very popular with kangaroos.

EcoPoint Murramarang Resort CAMPGROUND $$
(☎02-4478 6355; www.murramarangresort.com.au; Mill Beach, Banyandah St, South Durras; camp sites per 2 people $30-51, villas $149-253; 🏊) A favourite hang-out of the marsupial mob, this big, modern place has Norfolk pines dividing it from the beach. Posh extras include en suite camp sites and cabins with spa tubs.

Getting There & Away

The Princes Hwy forms the park's western edge, but it's 10km from the beaches. Many of the roads are pretty rough, but those to Durras, Durras Lake, Depot Beach and Durras North are all sealed, as is Mt Agony Rd to Pebbly Beach (but not Pebbly Beach Rd).

EUROBODALLA COAST

Meaning 'Land of Many Waters', this southern coastline celebrates all things blue. Swathes of green also punctuate the area's sprawling Eurobodalla National Park.

Townships, lakes and inlets backed by spotted-gum forests rich in native wildlife all feature, and the area is part of the homelands of the Yuin people and includes their sacred mountain, Gulaga.

Batemans Bay

POP 11,334

Good beaches and a sparkling estuary make this fishing port one of the South Coast's most popular holiday centres.

Sights

Beaches

Closest to town is **Corrigans Beach**, and longer beaches north of the bridge lead into Murramarang National Park. Surfers flock to **Pink Rocks**, **Surf Beach**, **Malua Bay**, **McKenzies Beach** and **Bengello Beach**. **Broulee** has a wide crescent of sand, but there's a strong rip at the northern end.

Activities

Merinda Cruises CRUISE
(☎02-4472 4052; Boatshed, Clyde St; 3hr cruise adult/child $30/15; ⏲11.30am) Cruises up the Clyde River Estuary from the ferry wharf just east of the bridge.

Region X KAYAKING
(☎0400 184 034; http://regionx.com.au; kayak rental 1hr $30, tours $50-90) Rent a kayak to explore nearby waterways or take a paddling tour.

Bay & Beyond KAYAKING
(☎02-4478 7777; www.bayandbeyond.com.au; kayak tours per person $60-120) Guided kayak trips along the coast and into nearby estuaries.

Broulee Surf School SURFING
(☎02-4471 7370; www.brouleesurfschool.com.au; adult/child from $45/40) Learn to surf at nearby Broulee.

Soulrider Surf School SURFING
(☎02-4478 6297; www.soulrider.com.au; 1hr adult/child $45/40) At various locations along the coast.

Surf the Bay Surf School SURFING
(☎0432 144 220; www.surfthebay.com.au; group/private lesson $40/90) Surfing and paddle-boarding school.

Total Eco Adventures WATER SPORTS
(☎02-4471 6969; www.totalecoadventures.com.au; 7/77 Coronation Dr, Broulee) Kayaking, snorkelling, stand-up paddling and surfing.

Sleeping

Accommodation rates increase in summer. **Bay River Houseboats** (☎02-4472 5649; www.bayriverhouseboats.com.au; Wray St; 4 nights from $840) and **Clyde River Houseboats** (☎02-4472 6369; www.clyderiverhouseboats.com.au; 3 nights $700-1350) lease 6-/10-berth boats.

Shady Willow Holiday Park HOSTEL, CAMPGROUND $
(☎02-4472 6111; www.shadywillows.com.au; cnr South St & Old Princes Hwy; powered sites $26, dm/d $28/58, cabins from $71;) Set amid shady palms near town, this YHA has a rather boho ambience. Doubles sleep in a caravan and a cabin accommodates groups of four.

Clyde River Motor Inn MOTEL $$
(☎02-4472 6444; www.clydemotel.com.au; 3 Clyde St; r/apt from $110/145, townhouses from $179;) Rooms are centrally located at this very comfortable motel, and at another location there are spacious townhouses and three-bedroom apartments.

Lincoln Downs HOTEL $$
(☎1800 789 250; www.lincolndowns.com.au; Princes Hwy; r from $149;) Excellent motel-style rooms, many of which overlook a private lake. There's also a resident peacock.

Eating

Innes Boatshed FISH & CHIPS $
(1 Clyde St; fish & chips $14, 6 oysters $9; 9am-2.30pm Sun-Thu, to 8pm Fri & Sat) Since the 1950s, this has been one of the South Coast's best-loved fish-and-chip and oyster joints. Head out to the spacious deck but mind the pelicans. Cash only.

Little Restaurant & Bar BISTRO $$
(1 Orient St; mains $27; 5-10pm Tue-Sat) Look for the bright-orange exterior of this bustling combo of bar and restaurant. Seafood and steaks are the stars – try the seared scallops – and it's all well-priced and good value.

On the Pier SEAFOOD $$$
(☎02-4472 6405; www.onthepier.com.au; 2 Old Punt Rd; mains $30-34; 9-11am, noon-2pm & 6-10pm Sun, 6-10pm Mon & Thu, noon-2pm & 6-10pm Fri & Sat) Batemans Bay's most celebrated restaurant, with dishes such as crispy-skin pork belly and grilled scallops. The seafood platter ($69 per person) is excellent.

Drinking & Entertainment

Bayview Hotel PUB
(☎02-4472 4522; www.bayviewhotel.com.au; 20 Orient St; 10am-midnight) Cold brews, live bands, DJs and trivia nights.

Information

Visitor Centre (☎1800 802 528; www.eurobodalla.com.au; Princes Hwy; 9am-5pm) Covering town and the wider Eurobodalla area.

Getting There & Away

The scenic Kings Hwy climbs the escarpment and heads to Canberra from just north of Batemans Bay.

Murrays (☎13 22 51; www.murrays.com.au) Buses to Canberra ($36.60, 2½ hours), Moruya ($13.30, one hour) and Narooma ($20.50, two hours).

Premier (☎13 34 10; www.premierms.com.au) Buses to Sydney ($45, six hours) and Eden ($46, three hours) via Ulladulla ($16, 45 minutes) and Moruya ($11, 30 minutes).

Mogo

POP 263

Mogo is a historic strip of wooden houses with cafes and souvenir shops.

The nearby **Gold Rush Colony** (☎02-4474 2123; www.goldrushcolony.com.au; 26 James St; adult/child $20/12; 10am-5pm) is a rambling re-creation of a pioneer village, complete with free gold panning and **miners' cabins** (www.goldrushcolony.com.au; dm/d $26/130;) for accommodation.

Mogo Zoo (☎02-4474 4855; www.mogozoo.com.au; 222 Tomakin Rd; adult/child $29.50/16; 9am-5pm), 2km east off the highway, is a small but interesting zoo with rare white lions and an enthralling troop of gorillas.

Moruya

POP 2531

Moruya (black swan) has Victorian buildings gathered around a broad river. There's a popular Saturday **market** (www.moruyacountrymarkets.com.au; 7.30am-12.30pm) and the best place to stay is the **Post & Telegraph B&B** (02-4474 5745; www.southcoast.com.au/postandtel; cnr Page & Campbell Sts; s/d $125/150).

River (02-4474 5505; www.therivermoruya.com.au; 16b Church St; mains $30-36; noon-2.30pm Wed-Sun, 6-9.30pm Wed-Sat;) combines local and seasonal ingredients with international flavours. Book ahead.

Moruya Airport (02-4474 2095; George Bass Dr) is 7km from town, near North Head. **Rex** (13 17 13; www.rex.com.au) flies from Merimbula and Sydney. **Murrays** (13 22 51; www.murrays.com.au) buses head to Canberra ($40, 3½ hours) and Sydney ($34.70, nine hours).

Narooma

POP 2409

At the mouth of a tree-lined inlet and flanked by surf beaches, Narooma is a pretty seaside town. This is also the jumping-off point for Montague Island, a very rewarding offshore excursion.

Sights

★Montague Island (Baranguba) NATURE RESERVE

Nine kilometres offshore from Narooma, this small, pest-free island is home to seabirds and fur seals. Little penguins nest here, especially from September to February.

Three-hour **guided tours** (1800 240 003; www.montagueisland.com.au; per person $120-155) conducted by NPWS rangers are dependent on numbers and weather conditions, so book ahead through the visitor centre. Take the afternoon tour for a better chance of seeing penguins.

You can stay in renovated **lighthouse keepers' cottages** (www.conservationvolunteers.com.au/project/info?projectId=52086; 2 nights s/d per person from $595/720) if you also sign up for conservation work. Meals are included, but you'll be expected to help with the preparation. Rates are slightly cheaper out of whale season. Book well ahead.

Bar Rock Lookout VIEWPOINT

Walk from Riverside Dr along the inlet to the ocean. Just below the lookout is **Australia Rock**, a boulder that vaguely resembles a certain country.

Beaches

The best place for swimming is over the bridge in the **netted swimming area** at the south end of Bar Beach. There's a surf club at **Narooma Beach**, but better surf at **Bar Beach** when a southeasterly blows.

Activities

Island Charters Narooma DIVING, SNORKELLING

(02-4476 1047; www.islandchartersnarooma.com; Bluewater Dr; diving from $95, snorkelling from $75) Offers diving, snorkelling and whale watching. Local attractions include grey nurse sharks, fur seals and the wreck of the SS *Lady Darling*. For the cheapest deal, book at the visitor centre.

Wagonga Princess CRUISE

(02-4476 2665; www,wagongainletcruises.com; adult/child $35/25; 1pm Sun, Wed & Fri Feb-Dec, daily Jan) Three-hour cruise up the Wagonga inlet on a heritage ferry.

Festivals & Events

Oyster Festival FOOD

Held in May, it's a shucking good time.

Great Southern Blues Festival MUSIC

(www.bluesfestival.tv) Local and international performers convene in October.

Sleeping

Narooma YHA HOSTEL $

(02-4476 3287; www.yha.com.au; 243 Princes Hwy; dm/d from $26/70; @) This friendly establishment has compact doubles and clean dorms, all with en suite bathrooms. Laid-back garden areas and free bikes and bodyboards seal the deal.

Easts Narooma Shores Holiday Park CAMPGROUND $

(02-4476 2046; www.eastsnarooma.com.au; Princes Hwy; sites $44, cabins $95-185; @) This well-maintained and friendly spot by the inlet has a big pool and palm trees.

Whale Motor Inn MOTEL $$

(02-4476 2411; www.whalemotorinn.com; 104 Wagonga St; d $168-210;) Spot whales from your balcony (binoculars are available) at this motel with great views and nicely renovated rooms.

Horizon Holiday Apartments APARTMENT $$

(02-4476 5200; www.horizonapartmentsnarooma.com.au; 147 Princes Hwy; apt from $129) These modern apartments are well priced and some have partial ocean views.

Eating

Quarterdeck Marina SEAFOOD $$
(13 Riverside Dr; mains $13-28; ⏲8am-4pm Thu-Mon) Enjoy excellent breakfasts and seafood lunches under the gaze of dozens of tikis and autographed photos of 1950s TV stars. Great inlet views, too, and occasional live music. Try the tasty Mexican corn cakes for brunch.

Inlet FISH & CHIPS $$
(www.facebook.com/theinletnarooma; Riverside Dr; mains $18-26; ⏲11.30am-2.30pm Tue-Sun, 5-10pm Tue-Sat) Formerly Taylor's Seafood, and now gussied up as the Inlet. Don't worry: the fresh seafood, fish and chips, and glorious inlet views are all intact.

Whale Restaurant MODERN AUSTRALIAN $$$
(☎02-4476 2411; www.whalemotorinn.com; 104 Wagonga St; mains $29-36; ⏲6-9pm Tue-Sat) Treat yourself to flathead, eye-fillet steak or rack of lamb while enjoying views of the coast. BYO wine.

Information

NPWS Office (☎02-4476 0800; www.nationalparks.nsw.gov.au; cnr Graham & Burrawang Sts) Information for Deua, Gulaga and Wadbilliga national parks.

Visitor Centre (☎1800 240 003, 02-4476 2881; www.eurobodalla.com.au; Princes Hwy; ⏲9am-5pm) Includes a small museum.

Getting There & Away

Murrays (☎13 22 51; www.murrays.com.au) Buses to Moruya ($14.50, one hour), Batemans Bay ($20.50, two hours) and Canberra ($47.40, 4½ hours).

Premier (☎13 34 10; www.premierms.com.au) Buses to Eden ($41, 2½ hours) and Sydney ($58, seven hours) via Wollongong ($56, five hours).

Tilba Tilba & Central Tilba

POP 391

The coastal road from Bermagui rejoins the Princes Hwy just before the loop road to these National Trust villages in the shadow of Gulaga.

Tilba Tilba is half the size of its singularly named neighbour, 2km down the road.

Central Tilba has remained virtually unchanged since it was a 19th-century goldmining boomtown. Cafes and craft shops fill the heritage buildings along Bate St. Behind the pub, walk up to the water tower for terrific views of Gulaga. There's information and maps at **Bates Emporium** (Bate St; ⏲8am-5pm; wi-fi).

Sights & Activities

Tilba Valley Wines WINERY
(☎02-4473 7308; www.tilbavalleywines.com; 947 Old Hwy; ⏲10am-5pm Oct-Apr, 11am-4pm Wed-Sun May-Jul & Sep) On the shores of Corunna Lake.

ABC Cheese Factory DAIRY FACTORY
(www.southcoastcheese.com.au; ⏲9am-5pm) Excellent cheeses and a good cafe.

Festivals & Events

Cobargo Folk Festival MUSIC
(www.cobargofolkfestival.com) Held in late February in historic Cobargo, 20km south towards Bega.

Tilba Easter Festival ART
(http://www.tilba.com.au/tilbafestival.html) Music and entertainment during Easter.

Sleeping

See www.tilba.com.au.

Green Gables B&B $$
(☎02-4473 7435; www.greengables.com.au; 269 Corkhill Dr; r from $170) This 1879 cottage offers three attractive rooms with rural views.

Bryn at Tilba B&B $$
(www.thebrynattilba.com.au; 91 Punkalla-Tilba Rd; r $180-220) Beautiful rooms with dark wood and white linen.

Getting There & Away

Premier (☎13 34 10; www.premierms.com.au) Buses to Sydney ($59, eight hours) via Narooma ($8, 25 minutes), and Eden ($36, two hours) via Merimbula ($28, 90 minutes).

SAPPHIRE COAST

Not to be outdone by Queensland's Gold Coast, the southernmost part of NSW considers itself precious too. Take virtually any road east of the Princes Hwy for mainly unblemished coast set amid rugged spectacular surroundings.

Bermagui

POP 1473

South of bird-filled Wallaga Lake, Bermagui (Bermie) is a laid-back fishing port with fisherfolk, surfers, alternative lifestylers and Indigenous Australians.

The town's flash **Fishermen's Wharf** (Lamont St) complex was designed by renowned architect and Bermagui resident Philip Cox.

Sights & Activities

Local walks include a 6km trail north along the coast to **Camel Rock** and a further 2km to **Wallaga Lake**. The route follows **Haywards Beach**, a good surfing spot.

There's also good surfing at Camel Rock and **Cuttagee**, and **Shelly Beach** is safe for kids. Around 1km round the point is **Blue Pool**, a cliff-side ocean pool.

Sleeping

For holiday rentals, see **Julie Rutherford Real Estate** (☎02-6493 3444; www.julierutherford.com.au).

Zane Grey Park CAMPGROUND $
(Bermagui Tourist Park; ☎02-6493 4382; www.zanegreytouristpark.com.au; Lamont St; unpowered/powered sites $28/39, cabins $100-286) From its prime position on Dickson's Point, you could throw a frisbee into Horseshoe Bay.

Bermagui Beach Hotel HOTEL $$
(☎02-6493 4206; www.bermaguibeachhotel.com.au; 10 Lamont St; dm from $35, d/ste from $100/120; ❄) This gorgeous 1895 pub has nine suites, four of them with balcony views towards the beach and Gulaga. Cheaper motel rooms and dorms are good value.

Bermagui Motor Inn MOTEL $$
(☎02-6493 4311; www.bermaguimotorinn.com.au; 38 Lamont St; s/d $110/125; ❄) This centrally located motel has flash new decor, comfy beds and friendly owners.

Eating & Drinking

Bluewave Seafoods FISH & CHIPS $
(www.bluewaveseafood.com.au; Fishermen's Wharf; fish & chips $15; ⏲10am-8pm) Overlooking the marina, this smart takeaway joint is the reincarnation of the original fishermen's co-op. Watch the pesky seagulls!

Bermagui Oyster Room SEAFOOD $$
(1/14 Lamont St; oysters 4/8/12 from $8/14/20, tapas $6-12; ⏲10am-6pm Wed-Thu, to 9pm Fri, to 4pm Sat & Sun) Enjoy super-fresh, organic Wapengo Bay oysters and tasty tapas at this stylish and airy spot on Bermagui's main street.

Il Passaggio ITALIAN $$
(☎02-6493 5753; www.ilpassaggio.com.au; Fishermen's Wharf; pizzas $20, mains $27-35; ⏲noon-2pm Fri-Sun, 6pm-late Thu-Sun) An authentic Italian menu includes pizza, antipasti, and linguini with prawns and chilli.

Mimosa Dry Stone MODERN AUSTRALIAN $$$
(☎02-6494 0164; www.mimosawines.com.au; 2845 Bermagui-Tathra Rd; mains $30-36, pizza $20-28; ⏲noon-3pm Thu-Sun) Midway between Bermagui and Tathra, this winery has a respected restaurant. It's often booked for weddings, so phone ahead.

Horse & Camel Wine Bar WINE BAR
(www.horseandcamel.com.au; Fishermen's Wharf; ⏲3-10pm Wed-Sun) Celebrate fishing harbour views with a vino or craft beer.

Mister Jones CAFE
(www.misterjones.com.au; 1/4 Bunga St; ⏲7am-noon Mon-Sat) This humble art-studio cafe would go unnoticed if it weren't for the loyal coffee lovers sitting outside.

Getting There & Away

Premier (☎13 34 10; www.premierms.com.au) Runs daily buses between Sydney ($60, 10 hours) and Eden ($31, 1¾ hours).

WILDLIFE AROUND MERIMBULA

You can see whales off the coast near Merimbula from September to November, but there are other possibilities for land-based wildlife watching as well.

Kangaroos and wallabies Pambula-Merimbula Golf Course and Pambula Beach. Dusk (from 4.30pm) is the best time.

Potoroo Palace (☎02-6494 9225; www.potoroopalace.com; 2372 Princes Hwy; adult/child $20/12; ⏲10am-4pm) has echidnas, kangaroos, dingoes, koalas, potoroos and native birds. It's 9km north of Merimbula on the road to Bega.

Panboola (www.panboola.com; Pambula) incorporates walking trails through the Pambula wetlands; great for spotting water birds.

Bermagui to Merimbula

Mimosa Rocks National Park (www.nationalparks.nsw.gov.au) FREE is a wonderful 5802-hectare coastal park with dense bush, sea caves, lagoons and beachside camp sites.

Dating from 1862, **Tathra Wharf** (adult/child $2/free; ⏲10am-5pm) is NSW's last remaining coastal steamship wharf. Inside is an interesting local museum and a cafe with views of Tathra's gracefully arcing bay.

The 2654-hectare **Bournda National Park** (www.nationalparks.nsw.gov.au; per car $7) has empty surf beaches, rugged headlands and forested walking trails. **Hobart Beach** (☎02-6495 5000; per site $20) has 63 bush camp sites.

Merimbula

POP 6873

Arrayed along a long, golden beach and an appealing inlet, Merimbula hosts both holidaymakers and retirees. In summer, this is one of the few places on the far South Coast that really gets crowded.

Sights

Nature Boardwalk NATURE RESERVE

Follows the estuary 1.75km southwest of the causeway around mangroves, oyster farms and melaleucas. Birds, mammals and crustaceans are all visible.

Merimbula Aquarium AQUARIUM

(Lake St; adult/child $15/10; ⏲10am-5pm) With 27 tanks and an Oceanarium for sharks and other larger predators.

Activities

Merimbula Marina CRUISE

(☎02-6495 1686; www.merimbulamarina.com; Merimbula jetty; cruises $40-69) Whale-watching cruises from mid-August to November and other scenic and dolphin trips during the year. Also boat hire.

Coastlife Adventures SURFING, KAYAKING

(☎02-6494 1122; www.coastlife.com.au; group/private surf lessons $65/120, kayak tours from $65) Surf and stand-up paddle lessons, marine kayak tours and kayak hire.

Cycle n' Surf CYCLING, SURFING

(☎02-6495 2171; www.cyclensurf.com.au; 1b Marine Pde; bicycle hire per half-/full-day $30/45) Hires out bikes, bodyboards and surfboards.

Merimbula Divers Lodge DIVING

(☎02-6495 3611; www.merimbuladiverslodge.com.au; 15 Park St; 1/2 shore dives $69/120, equipment $55/99) Basic instruction and snorkelling trips – good for beginners. Nearby wrecks include the *Empire Gladstone*, which sank in 1950.

Sleeping

Self-contained apartments are let on a weekly basis. See **Getaway Merimbula & Eden** (☎02-6495 2000; www.getawaymerimbula.com.au; Promenade, Market St).

Wandarrah YHA Lodge HOSTEL $

(☎02-6495 3503; www.yha.com.au; 8 Marine Pde; dm/s/d/f from $28/55/69/135; @) This clean place, with friendly owners, a good kitchen and spacious shared areas, is near the surf beach and the bus stop. Pick-ups by arrangement, or let the staff know if you're arriving late.

Merimbula Beach Holiday Park CAMPGROUND $

(☎02-6495 3381; www.merimbulabeachholidaypark.com.au; 2 Short Point Rd; camp sites $32-54, cabins & villas $110-280; 📶🏊) Away from the town centre but close to the surf action and vistas of Short Point Beach.

Merimbula Lakeview Hotel MOTEL $$

(☎02-6495 1202; www.merimbulalakeview.com.au; Market St; r from $99; ❄📶) This waterfront establishment has a good location and moderately stylish rooms. The rooms are close to the hotel's beer garden...which may be good or bad come summertime.

Eating & Drinking

Wheelers Oyster Farm SEAFOOD $$

(www.wheelersoysters.com.au; 162 Arthur Kaine Dr, Pambula; mains $22-36; ⏲shop 10am-5pm daily, restaurant noon-2.30pm daily, 6pm-late Mon-Sat) Delicious fresh oysters – either takeaway or from the shop or enjoyed in Wheelers spectacular restaurant. The menu features oysters prepared loads of ways and other great seafood and steak dishes. Tours showcasing some people's favourite bivalve depart at 11am daily.

Waterfront Cafe CAFE, SEAFOOD $$

(☎02-6495 7684; www.thewaterfrontcafe.net.au; Shop 1, Promenade; mains $19-30; ⏲8am-10pm) A great lakeside location. Good cafe fare; excellent seafood dominates the menu.

WORTH A TRIP

BEN BOYD NATIONAL PARK

The wilderness barely pauses for breath before starting again at 10,485-hectare Ben Boyd National Park. Boyd was an entrepreneur who failed spectacularly in his efforts to build an empire around Eden in 1850. This park protects some of his follies, along with a dramatic coastline peppered with isolated beaches.

The southern section is accessed by mainly gravel roads (per vehicle $7) leading off sealed Edrom Rd, which leaves the Princes Hwy 19km south of Eden. At its southern tip, the elegant 1883 **Green Cape Lightstation** (☎02-6495 5555; www.nationalparks.nsw.gov.au; Green Cape Rd; cottage midweek/weekend from $200/280) offers awesome views. There are **tours** (adult/child $7/5; ⏰3pm Thu-Mon) and a lavishly restored keepers' cottage (sleeps six).

Eleven kilometres along Edrom Rd there's a turn-off to the historic **Davidson Whaling Station** on Twofold Bay, where you can have a picnic in the rustic gardens of **Loch Gaira Cottage** (1896).

Further along is the turn-off for **Boyd's Tower**, built in the late 1840s with Sydney sandstone. It was intended to be a lighthouse, but the government wouldn't give Boyd permission to operate it.

The 31km **Light to Light Walk** links Boyd's wannabe lighthouse to the real one at Green Cape. There are **camp sites** (☎02-6495 5000; per site $20) along the route at **Saltwater Creek** and **Bittangabee Bay**.

The northern section of the park can be accessed from the Princes Hwy north of Eden.

Ritzy TAPAS **$$**
(☎02-6495 1085; 56 Market St; tapas $10-24; ⏰4pm-midnight Mon-Sat) This atmospheric little hidey-hole in the centre of town dishes up shared tapas plates, and has a good selection of wine and beer.

Zanzibar MODERN AUSTRALIAN **$$$**
(☎02-6495 3636; http://zanzibarmerimbula.com.au; cnr Main & Market Sts; 2/3/5 courses $65/75/85; ⏰noon-2pm Thu & Fri, 6pm-late Tue-Sat) This culinary gem prides itself on locally caught seafood and hand-picked South Coast produce. Intriguing menu options include marinated yellowfin tuna, beetroot and crème fraiche. The five-course 'Locavore' menu is a well-spent $85.

ℹ Information

NPWS Office (☎02-6495 5000; www.environment.nsw.gov.au; cnr Merimbula & Sapphire Coast Drs; ⏰9am-4pm Mon-Fri) Bushwalking information.

Visitor Centre (☎02-6495 1129; www.sapphirecoast.com.au; cnr Market & Beach Sts; ⏰9am-5pm) Bookings and accommodation.

ℹ Getting There & Around

AIR

Merimbula Airport (MIM; ☎02-6495 4211; www.merimbulaairport.com.au; Arthur Kaine Dr) is 1km out of town on the road to Pambula. **Rex** (☎13 17 13; www.rex.com.au) flies daily to Melbourne (from $165, 90 minutes), Sydney (from $165, 1¼ hours) and Moruya (from $74, 30 minutes).

BUS

Premier (☎13 34 10; www.premierms.com.au) has two daily buses to Sydney ($69, 8½ hours). **NSW TrainLink** (☎13 22 32; www.nswtrainlink.info) runs a daily bus to Canberra ($33, four hours).

Eden

POP 3043

Eden's a sleepy place where often the only bustle is down at the wharf when the fishing boats come in. Around the surrounding area are stirring beaches, national parks and wilderness areas.

Migrating humpback whales and southern right whales pass so close to the coast that experts consider this to be one of Australia's best whale-watching locations. Often the whales can be seen feeding or resting in Twofold Bay during their southern migration back to Antarctic waters during October and November.

Sights & Activities

Killer Whale Museum MUSEUM
(www.killerwhalemuseum.com.au; 94 Imlay St; adult/child $9/2.50; ⏰9.15am-3.45pm Mon-Sat, 11.15am-3.45pm Sun) Established in 1931, the museum's

main purpose is to preserve the skeleton of Old Tom, a killer whale and local legend.

Whale Lookout VIEWPOINT
A good spot to look for whales is at the base of Bass St. When whales are spotted, the Killer Whale Museum sounds a siren.

Sapphire Coast Marine Discovery Centre AQUARIUM
(02-6496 1699; www.sapphirecoastdiscovery.com.au; Main Wharf; adult/child $10/5; 11am-2pm Tue-Fri) Learn about the sea at the rocky reef aquarium or take a snorkelling trip (per person $25, minimum four people).

Cat Balou Cruises CRUISE
(0427 962 027; www.catbalou.com.au; Main Wharf; adult/child $75/60) This crew operates 3½-hour whale-spotting voyages in October and November. At other times of the year, dolphins and seals can usually be seen during the two-hour bay cruise (adult/child $35/20).

Ocean Wilderness KAYAKING
(0405 529 214; www.oceanwilderness.com.au; 4/6hr tours from $85/130) Sea-kayaking trips through Twofold Bay and to Ben Boyd National Park, and a full-day excursion to Davidson Whaling Station.

Festivals & Events

Whale Festival WHALES
(www.edenwhalefestival.com.au) Carnival, street parade and market stalls, all with a proud cetacean spin. Held in November.

Sleeping

Eden Tourist Park CAMPGROUND $
(02-6496 1139; www.edentouristpark.com.au; Aslings Beach Rd; unpowered/powered sites $28/34, cabins & units $85-130) Situated on the spit separating Aslings Beach from Lake Curalo, this park echoes with birdsong from sheltering trees.

Twofold Bay Motor Inn MOTEL $$
(02-6496 3111; www.twofoldbaymotorinn.com.au; 164-166 Imlay St; r $130-175;) Substantial rooms, some with water views, are the norm at this centrally located motel. There's also a tiny indoor pool.

Seahorse Inn BOUTIQUE HOTEL $$
(02-6496 1361; www.seahorseinnhotel.com.au; Boydtown; d $175-349;) At Boydtown, 6km south of Eden, the Seahorse Inn overlooks Twofold Bay. It's a lavish boutique hotel with all the trimmings, and there's a good restaurant and garden bar open to nonguests.

Eating

Sprout CAFE $
(www.sprouteden.com.au; 134 Imlay St; mains $10-18; 7.30am-4.30pm Mon-Fri, 8am-3pm Sat & Sun;) Lots of organic and sustainable produce, top-notch burgers and the best coffee in town.

Wharfside Café CAFE $$
(Main Wharf; mains $15-28; 8am-3pm daily, 6-10pm Fri & Sat) Decent breakfasts, strong coffee and harbour views make this a good way to start the day. Try the Asian prawn salad with a glass of wine for lunch, or ask if local oysters and mussels are available. The Main Wharf is downhill from town.

Information

Visitor Centre (02-6496 1953; www.visiteden.com.au; Mitchell St; 9am-5pm Mon-Sat, 10am-4pm Sun) Bookings and information.

Getting There & Away

Premier (13 34 10; www.premierms.com.au) runs north to Wollongong ($69, eight hours) and Sydney ($71, nine hours). **NSW TrainLink** (13 22 32; www.nswtrainlink.info) runs a daily bus service to Canberra ($35, 4½ hours). For Melbourne, V/Line runs a bus and train combination ($46, nine hours) via Bairnsdale.

Central & Outback NSW

Includes ➡

Best Places to Eat

- Palace Hotel (p253)
- Agrestic Grocer (p241)
- Lowe Wines (p245)
- Poetry on a Plate (p256)
- Goldfish Bowl (p236)

Best Places to Stay

- Perry Street Hotel (p246)
- De Russie Suites (p241)
- Opal Caravan Park (p238)
- Warrawong on the Darling (p255)
- Red Earth Motel (p252)

Why Go?

Trust us, there is life beyond Sydney and the New South Wales coast – and it's worthy of attention. Epicurean retreats like Mudgee and Orange send a siren call to city slickers, Broken Hill's mining heritage is rich and nation-defining, and national parks offer sand dunes, ancient rock art, wildlife-filled forests and glorious walking trails.

From the rolling green hills of New England to the red-dirt glow of the outback, there are some beautifully Australian moments to savour: stargazing into pristine skies, sharing a yarn with eccentrics in mining communities, marvelling over art in the most unlikely places (on pub walls, down opal mines, in a remote paddock). Festivals mark the regions' calendars with excuses to party – from the quirky (Elvis, country music) to the brawny (motor sport), to celebrations of season (harvests, autumn foliage, spring cherry blossoms). Who needs the beach, anyway?

When to Go

Tamworth

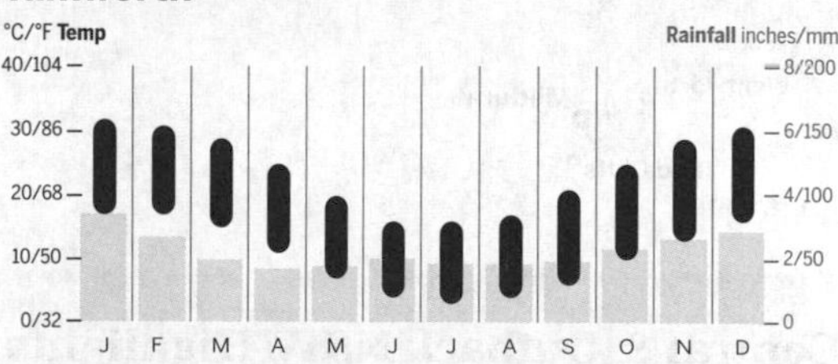

Jan School holidays see locals head for national parks. Big music festivals in Parkes and Tamworth.

Easter-Oct High season in the outback, with cooler temperatures (and cold nights).

Sep-Oct Food and wine celebrations in Mudgee and Orange; Cherry Blossom Festival in Cowra.

Central & Outback NSW Highlights

1. Visiting underground opal mines then taking a hot soak at **Lightning Ridge** (p237).
2. Wining and dining exceedingly well in **Mudgee** (p245) and **Orange** (p240).
3. Cycling from rhinos to meerkats in Dubbo's **Western Plains Zoo** (p244).
4. Exploring unexpected art in unlikely places in and around **Broken Hill** (p249).
5. Taking a sunset tour of the Walls of China in **Mungo National Park** (p247).
6. Finding peace and tranquillity in Cowra's **Japanese Garden** (p242).

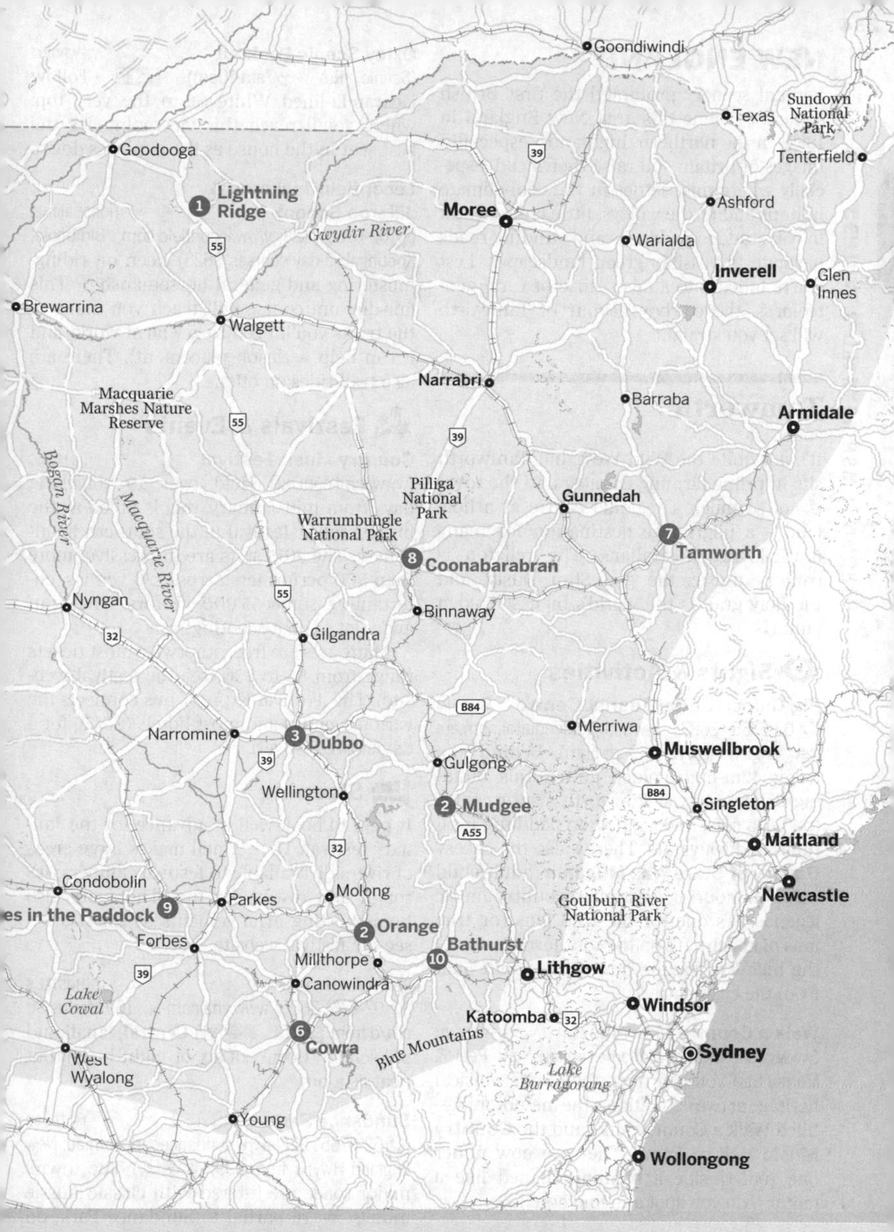

7 Hearing live music and tall tales of country music legends in **Tamworth** (p234).

8 Stargazing into clear night skies in **Coonabarabran** (p238) or **Broken Hill** (p249).

9 Appreciating the fair-dinkum humour of **Utes in the Paddock** (p244).

10 Being bowled over by Bathurst's first-rate **Fossil & Mineral Museum** (p239).

NEW ENGLAND

Verdant scenery prompted the first British settlers to name this area New England in 1839. In the northern 'highlands' especially, images of Britain still raise their head, especially where mist settles in the cool-climate hilltops and fertile valleys, little churches sit in oak-studded paddocks and winding roads navigate impossibly green landscapes. Lest you're lulled into a false sense of rural genteelness, the cowboy flavour of Tamworth will set you straight.

Tamworth

POP 36,130

It's not quite the Wild West, but Tamworth sits in prime farming country and the town is not so much a regional centre as a holy land – a pilgrimage destination for many music-loving Australians. The religion is country music, the god Slim Dusty, and the holy grail is the world's biggest golden guitar.

Sights & Activities

Big Golden Guitar Tourist Centre MUSEUM
(02-6765 2688; www.biggoldenguitar.com.au; New England Hwy; 9am-5pm) Behind the iconic 12m-high golden guitar, this building is home to the Tamworth visitor centre (p235), a cafe, and a gift shop peddling local tunes and souvenirs. There's also the cheesy **Gallery of Stars Wax Museum** (adult/child $10/5) honouring Australian country music legends. It's one for the true fans (or true fans of kitsch). It's on the southern stretch of the highway leading into town, about 5km from the city centre.

Walk a Country Mile Museum MUSEUM
(www.countrymusichalloffame.com.au; cnr Peel & Murray Sts) You can track the town's musical heritage at two exhibitions: the memorabilia-filled Walk a Country Mile, and the **Country Music Hall of Fame**. They are now under one roof (inside a building shaped like a guitar – do you spot a theme here…?).

★ **Tamworth Marsupial Park** PARK
(Endeavour Dr; 8am-4.45pm;) FREE Over-friendly cockatoos, showy peacocks and a mob of native animals live here alongside a playground, barbecues and picnic shelters. There are lovely short walks to the neighbouring botanic gardens. Take Brisbane St east.

Oxley Scenic Lookout VIEWPOINT
(Scenic Rd; 7am-10pm) FREE Follow jacaranda-lined White St to the very top, where you'll reach this viewpoint. It's the best seat in the house as the sun goes down.

Leconfield Jackaroo & Jillaroo School HORSE RIDING
(02-6769 4328; www.leconfield.com; 'Bimboola', Kootingal; 5-day courses $625) Keen on riding, mustering and general horsemanship? This fair-dinkum course will teach you many of the tricks you'll need to get farm work (and it can help with job placement). There are also trail rides on offer.

Festivals & Events

Country Music Festival MUSIC
(www.tcmf.com.au) Held over 10 rollicking days from mid-January, this is billed as the biggest music festival in the southern hemisphere. The 2015 stats are impressive: more than 800 performers across 120 venues, entertaining some 55,000 visitors. That's an awful lot of boot-scooting!

Many acts are free, otherwise most tickets range from $5 to $50 (see the festival website). The 'Festival Express' bus connects the various venues and most hotels ($5/20 for a day/entire festival).

Sleeping

It pays to book well in advance for the January festival. The council makes large areas of riverside available to festival campers; it's rough and rowdy but fun. There are also home-hosting arrangements at this time – see the festival website.

Tamworth YHA HOSTEL $
(02-6761 2600; www.yha.com.au; 169 Marius St; dm/d from $27/61;) Central, small and old-school (dorms of six or eight beds), but neat as a pin.

Sundance Park MOTEL $$
(02-6765 7922; www.sundancepark.com.au; New England Hwy; r from $99;) The town's major roads are littered with classic Aussie motels. We're partial to Sundance Park, on the southern outskirts of town, for its crackerjack swimming pool (in the shape of a guitar, tiled in the Australian flag). Rooms are decent value.

Quality Hotel Powerhouse HOTEL $$
(02-6766 7000; www.powerhousetamworth.com.au; New England Hwy; r/apt from $185/205;) Home to classy, well-equipped hotel

rooms, suites and serviced apartments, and a host of on-site amenities. It's on the highway towards Armidale.

Retreat at Frog-Moore Park B&B $$$
(☎02-6766 3353; www.frogmoorepark.com.au; 78 Bligh St; r incl breakfast from $225;) Five individually styled suites (with names like Moroccan Fantasy and The Dungeon) make this avant-garde B&B one of Tamworth's quirkier and more luxurious options. Rooms are large, the gardens are delightful, and the breakfasts could just be the best in town.

Eating & Drinking

The visitor centre compiles a flyer outlining the week's live-music options, found at a handful of the pubs and clubs around town; Friday and Saturday nights are your best bet.

Addimi CAFE, BISTRO $$
(☎02-6766 7802; www.addimi.com.au; 306 Peel St; dinner mains $21-38; ⊙7am-4pm Mon & Tue, to 10pm Wed-Sat, 7.30am-3pm Sun) A stylish, central, all-day option, with a menu running from popular breakfast dishes through to tapas and cocktails. Dinner-time offerings are crowd-pleasing Mod-Oz fare.

★**Le Pruneau** FRENCH $$
(☎02-6765 3666; www.lepruneau.com.au; 67 Denison St; lunch mains $10-22, dinner mains $32-36; ⊙7.30am-10pm Tue-Sat, to 3pm Sun) You'll need a map to find this French-owned cottage-style cafe and restaurant in West Tamworth, but it's worth seeking out for its creatively delicious cooking. There's a local organic market behind the cottage on Saturday mornings. Dinner bookings advised.

Longyard PUB $$
(www.thelongyard.com.au; The Ringers Rd; meals $16-33; ⊙10am-late) The Longyard, directly behind the visitor centre, is a big, rowdy, popular watering hole with a decent menu of pub-grub classics (bumper portions of burgers, steaks etc) plus weekend live music.

Information

Visitor Centre (☎02-6767 5300; www.destinationtamworth.com.au; New England Hwy; ⊙9am-5pm) South of town centre, at the Big Golden Guitar.

Getting There & Away

Long-distance buses leave from the train station on Marius St.

Greyhound (☎1300 473 946; www.greyhound.com.au) Has nightly services along the New England Hwy between Sydney and Brisbane – these stop at Tamworth, Armidale, Tenterfield and Toowoomba en route. Tamworth to Brisbane is 9½ hours ($125), to Sydney is 6½ hours ($75).

New England Coaches (☎02-6732 1051; www.newenglandcoaches.com.au) Runs a couple of useful services: Tamworth to Coffs Harbour ($90); and Tamworth to Brisbane ($115). Both services run three times a week.

NSW TrainLink (☎13 22 32; www.nswtrainlink.info) Runs trains daily to Armidale ($20, two hours) and Sydney ($59, 6¼ hours).

Armidale

POP 25,400

Armidale's heritage buildings, gardens and moss-covered churches look like the stage set for a period drama. This old-world scenery coupled with spectacular autumn foliage (March to May) plays a big part in attracting people to this regional centre, which sits at an elevation of 980m and is surrounded by some of Australia's best grazing country. Mild summers, crisp winters and quality educational institutions win admirers.

Sights

The visitor centre has handouts offering oodles of suggestions for all audiences. There's good heritage info, plus booklets outlining the region's natural attractions and the Waterfall Way (p188) – the spectacular route down to the coast at Coffs Harbour.

New England Regional Art Museum MUSEUM
(NERAM; www.neram.com.au; 106-114 Kentucky St; ⊙10am-4pm Tue-Sun) FREE At the southern edge of town, NERAM has a sizeable permanent collection and good contemporary exhibitions. The *Yellow Room Triptych* by Margaret Olley is a highlight.

Aboriginal Cultural Centre & Keeping Place GALLERY
(www.acckp.com.au; 128 Kentucky St; ⊙9am-4pm Mon-Fri, 10am-2pm Sat) FREE Down the road from the Regional Art Museum, this centre will broaden your perception of Indigenous art. There's a small sweet cafe here serving up some imaginative examples of bush tucker.

Tours

Heritage Bus Tours BUS TOUR
(☎02-6770 3888; ⊙10am) FREE A generous gesture from the local council: free (and

detail-rich) 2½-hour tours of Armidale depart from the visitor centre daily at 10am; bookings required.

Sleeping & Eating

Armidale Tourist Park CAMPGROUND, HOSTEL $
(02-6772 6470; www.armidaletouristpark.com.au; 39 Waterfall Way; sites $22-46, dm $38, cabins $82-160;) Friendly and leafy, with a budget bunkhouse and a range of cabins.

Armidale Pines Motel MOTEL $$
(02-6772 0625; www.armidalepinesmotel.com; 141 Marsh St; r from $135;) In the heart of town, this spick-and-span motel has generous rooms and fresh decor.

★ **Petersons Guesthouse** GUESTHOUSE $$$
(02-6772 0422; www.petersonsguesthouse.com.au; Dangarsleigh Rd; r from $200;) Beautifully restored to its former opulence, this 1911 estate has seven large, characterful suites and magnificent grounds (popular for wedding parties). Dinner is possible, and the estate offers cool-climate wine tastings and Sunday picnic lunches (call ahead for hours, as the estate is closed to visitors when functions are held).

Goldfish Bowl BAKERY, CAFE $
(160 Rusden St; lunch $8-19; 7am-4pm Mon-Fri, to 1pm Sat) First-rate coffee and delectable baked goods pulled from the wood-fired oven make this a worthy pit stop. Load up on pastries, sourdough bread or gourmet pizza for carb-loaded heaven.

Bistro on Cinders BISTRO $$
(www.bistrooncinders.com; 14 Cinders Lane; mains $12-25; 8.30am-3pm Mon-Sat) Behind the post office is this cool contemporary eatery with a small courtyard. Grab a quick morning coffee, pause for salmon scrambled eggs, or linger over a lunch of homemade ricotta gnocchi.

Information

Visitor Centre (02-6770 3888; www.armidaletourism.com.au; 82 Marsh St; 9am-5pm)

Getting There & Around

Long-distance buses leave from the visitor centre.

Greyhound (1300 473 946; www.greyhound.com.au) Has nightly services along the New England Hwy between Sydney and Brisbane – these stop at Tamworth, Armidale, Tenterfield and Toowoomba en route. Armidale to Sydney is eight hours ($113).

New England Coaches (02-6732 1051; www.newenglandcoaches.com.au) Runs some useful services: Armidale to Coffs Harbour ($70); and Armidale to Brisbane ($105). Both services run three times a week.

NSW TrainLink (13 22 32; www.nswtrainlink.info) Runs trains daily to Tamworth ($20, two hours) and Sydney ($66, eight hours). It also has bus services to Tenterfield ($25, 2½ hours).

Tenterfield & Around

POP 2997

Tenterfield is the hub of a region boasting a smattering of villages and 10 national parks. In the town itself are dozens of charming heritage buildings, including the train station from 1886 (no longer in service, but home to a museum). The town is the birthplace of entertainer Peter Allen (the 'Boy from Oz').

Sights

Tenterfield Saddler LANDMARK
(www.tenterfieldsaddler.com; 123 High St; 10am-3pm Thu-Sun) This bluestone building opened as a saddlery in 1870 and was celebrated by Peter Allen in his well-known song (written for his grandfather who was a saddler here for 50 years). It's still open for business.

Bald Rock National Park NATIONAL PARK
(www.nationalparks.nsw.gov.au; per car per day $7) About 35km northeast of Tenterfield (take Naas Rd, signposted 'Woodenbong' – really), you can hike to the top of Australia's largest exposed granite monolith (which looks like a stripy little Uluru). There are lovely walks in the area (including two routes up the rock for great views), plus picnic sites and a camping area (adult/child $10/5) near the base. Kangaroos and birdsong are highlights.

Sir Henry Parkes Memorial School of Arts HISTORIC BUILDING
(www.henryparkestenterfield.com; Rouse St; museum 10am-4pm) Australian history boffins will enjoy the museum (adult/child $5/2) in this beautifully restored old hall. It's notable as the place where Sir Henry Parkes, the 'Father of Federation', delivered the 1889 Tenterfield Oration, a speech proposing that the six separate British colonies in Australia should unite. Others may simply appreciate the library, cinema and courtyard cafe.

Sleeping & Eating

The main street is dotted with dining options, including decent pubs.

★Commercial Boutique Hotel BOUTIQUE HOTEL $$
(☎02-6736 4870; www.thecommercialboutiquehotel.com; 288 Rouse St; r $160-260) A glorious 1940s art deco pub has found a new lease of life, reinvented as a glamorous boutique hotel (with eight monochrome rooms). The dining area has had a makeover too, and is now a handsome bar showcasing local wine and craft beers. The restaurant is open from 10am weekdays; brunch from 9am weekends. Dinner isn't served Monday or Tuesday night, but you're welcome to bring takeaway and enjoy a drink!

Peter Allen Motor Inn MOTEL $$
(☎02-6736 2499; www.peterallenmotorinn.com.au; 177 Rouse St; r from $105; ❄📶) Who can resist the name?! One of a dozen motels lining the main road, this not-remotely-flamboyant place has friendly new owners sprucing things up. Facilities are good; the price is right.

Information

Visitor Centre (☎02-6736 1082; www.tenterfieldtourism.com.au; 157 Rouse St; ⏰9.30am-5pm Mon-Sat, to 4pm Sun)

Getting There & Away

Greyhound (☎1300 473 946; www.greyhound.com.au) Has nightly services along the New England Hwy between Sydney and Brisbane – these stop at Tamworth, Armidale, Tenterfield and Toowoomba. Tenterfield to Brisbane is 5½ hours ($96).

New England Coaches (☎02-6372 1051; www.newenglandcoaches.com.au) Runs a useful service three times a week between Armidale, Tamworth and Brisbane, stopping at Tenterfield.

Northern Rivers Buslines (☎02-6626 1499; www.nrbuslines.com.au) Has three weekly buses to/from Lismore ($6, two hours), with connections to Byron Bay.

NSW TrainLink (☎13 22 32; www.nswtrainlink.info) Runs buses daily to Armidale ($25, 2½ hours), where you can change to a train for Sydney.

NORTHWEST

People tend to race through this flat archetypal Australian landscape, possibly with Queensland beaches on their minds. If Queensland isn't on the itinerary, chances are Lightning Ridge is. Like other outback mining communities, the town throws up as many characters as it does gems.

Castlereagh Highway

The Castlereagh Hwy (Rte 55, part of the 'Great Inland Way' linking Sydney and Cairns) forks off the Oxley Hwy at Gilgandra then runs to the Queensland border through Coonamble, Walgett and the rugged opal country of Lightning Ridge.

Lightning Ridge

POP 2600

This strikingly imaginative outback mining town (one of the world's few sources of valuable black opals) has real frontier spirit, and is home to eccentric artisans, true-blue bushies and a generally unconventional collective. It's an entertaining place to spend a few days.

Sights & Activities

Several underground mines and opal showrooms are open to the public.

★Chambers of the Black Hand GALLERY, MINE
(☎02-6829 0221; www.chambersoftheblackhand.com.au; 3 Mile Rd (Yellow Car Door 5); adult/child $35/10; ⏰tours from 9.30am & 3pm Apr-Oct, 10.30am Nov-Mar) This place is remarkable, and symbolises the crazy and creative sides of the Ridge. Artist and miner Ron Canlin has turned a 12m-deep mining claim into a cavernous gallery of carvings and paintings: superheroes, celebrities, pharaohs, Buddhas, animals, you name it. Call to confirm tour times; courtesy-bus pick-up from your accommodation is offered.

Walk-In Mine MINE
(☎02-6829 0473; www.walkinmine.com.au; Bald Hill; adult/child $15/6; ⏰9am-5pm Apr-Oct, 8.30am-12.30pm Nov-Mar) Visit this mine to get a feel for the type of environment encountered by the average opal miner, and for life in the Ridge.

★Hot Artesian Bore Baths SWIMMING
(Pandora St; ⏰24hr) FREE Enjoy scenic vistas while soaking in these unique open-air baths. The hot (41.5°C), mineral-rich water is drawn from 1200m below ground. Sunrise or sunset here can be magnificent, and

chatting with the locals is a treat. Note: it's usually closed from 10am to noon for cleaning, and the high temperatures aren't suitable for small kids.

Sport & Aquatic Complex SWIMMING
(Gem St; pool/water park $4/7; ⏲11am-6pm Oct-Apr) When the sun's cranking, the artesian baths won't cool you down. So head here instead – a 50m pool built by community-raised funds. There's a fun water park area for kids.

☞ Tours

Car Door Tours DRIVING TOUR
The local community demonstrates its wit with four self-drive car-door tours, which explore different areas of interest around town. Each of the tours is marked by coloured car doors (green, blue, yellow and red) and can be followed using the excellent handout ($1) from the visitor centre.

Black Opal Tours TOUR
(☎02-6829 0368; www.blackopaltours.com.au; adult/child $35/15; ⏲tours 8.30am & 12.30pm Apr-Oct, 8.15am Nov-Mar) Do some exploring (and fossicking) with this outfit on its daily three-hour tours, which take in some quirky local sights and give context to them. You can also do a 4½-hour package that includes the Chambers of the Black Hand (p237) ($70/15).

Sleeping & Eating

★**Opal Caravan Park** CAMPGROUND, CABINS $
(☎02-6829 1446; www.opalcaravanpark.com.au; 142 Pandora St; camp sites $27-45, cabins from $110;) This new, well-planned bushland park opposite the artesian baths offers excellent modern facilities: self-contained cabins, a swimming pool, wi-fi, camp sites with en suite, and a camp kitchen with pizza oven. There's even a small area for fossicking.

Bruno's ITALIAN $$
(☎02-6829 4157; www.brunosrestaurant.com.au; 38b Morilla St; lunch $12.50-14.50, dinner mains $15-21; ⏲7.30am-10pm Tue-Sun) A genuine Italian chef, a wood-fired oven and some seriously tasty desserts (panna cotta, tiramisu) are the surprise package here. There's a good range of pasta, pizza and meaty mains (eg veal scaloppine, steak) on offer.

ℹ Information

Visitor Centre (☎02-6829 1670; www.lightningridgeinfo.com.au; Morilla St; ⏲9am-5pm)

ℹ Getting There & Away

NSW TrainLink (☎13 22 32; www.nswtrainlink.info) Runs daily buses connecting the Ridge and Dubbo ($67, 4½ hours).

Newell Highway

The Newell Hwy (Rte 39), the through-route from Victoria, passes through stargazing Coonabarabran and the burgeoning Aboriginal art hub of Moree, before hitting the border at Goondiwindi.

Coonabarabran

POP 3200

Coonabarabran ('Coona' to locals) is widely recognised as an ideal place for stargazing thanks to its pristine air, high altitude (505m) and low humidity. The **visitor centre** (☎1800 242 881; www.warrumbungleregion.com.au; Newell Hwy; ⏲9am-5pm) is south of the clock tower (with megafauna exhibits). Motels dot the highway, and buses run to Lithgow (via Mudgee).

Sights & Activities

Coona has a few private observatories offering affordable, family-friendly night-sky shows (note that you'll need to phone first, as weather conditions need to be agreeable, and start times vary according to sunset).

Siding Spring Observatory OBSERVATORY
(rsaa.anu.edu.au/observatories/siding-spring-observatory; adult/child $5.50/3.50; ⏲9.30am-4pm Mon-Fri, 10am-4pm Sat & Sun) Coonabarabran's skies are so clear, the Australian National University chose to set up this research facility some 27km west of the town, on the edge of Warrumbungle National Park. The site is home to telescopes belonging to national and international institutions and includes the 3.9m Anglo-Australian Telescope, the largest optical (visible light) telescope in Australia.

There are no public stargazing facilities here, but there's a **visitor centre** where you can boggle your mind with solar system facts and figures.

Milroy Observatory OBSERVATORY
(☎0448 129 119; www.milroyobservatory.com.au; adult/child $30/15) Milroy Observatory offers the largest public-access telescope in the southern hemisphere (it's a 1m device that sits on a hilltop about 10km outside Coona). The astronomer-in-charge, Cam Wylie, runs regular 90-minute stargazing sessions.

Warrumbungle Observatory OBSERVATORY
(☎0488 425 112; www.tenbyobservatory.com; adult/child $20/10) A private observatory offering 90-minute night-sky viewing, run by an astronomer with the delightful name of Peter Starr. It's about 9km from town, en route to Siding Spring.

Warrumbungle National Park NATIONAL PARK
(☎02-6825 4364; www.nationalparks.nsw.gov.au; per car per day $7) Sitting 35km west of Coonabarabran, this 232-sq-km park has spectacular granite domes, ample bushwalking trails, plentiful wildlife and explosive wild flower displays during spring. It's one of NSW's most beautiful parks, although a bushfire swept through in 2013; some areas will take years to fully recover.

Park fees are payable at the NPWS visitor centre; there are excellent camp sites nearby at Camp Blackman (adult/child from $5/3). Walking tracks include the peerless 12.5km Breadknife and Grand High Tops Walk.

Pilliga National Park NATIONAL PARK
(☎02-6843 4011; www.nationalparks.nsw.gov.au) Between Coonabarabran and Narrabri, the Pilliga Forest springs either side of the highway. For a closer look at this semiarid landscape, begin at the Discovery Centre in Baradine (46km north of Coona). Here you can pick up maps and directions to the **Sandstone Caves** with Aboriginal rock art, or to a striking new forest highlight: **Sculptures in the Scrub**.

Moree

POP 9350

Motels line the highways, and are also found along Warialda St (close to the aquatic centre).

Sights & Activities

★Yaama Ganu Centre GALLERY
(www.yaamaganu.com.au; 211 Balo St; 9am-4pm Mon-Fri, to 1pm Sat, to noon Sun) FREE For a lively local take on the art scene, check out the wonderful centre, home to a gallery of Indigenous art and a bright, friendly cafe.

Moree Plains Gallery GALLERY
(www.moreeplainsgallery.org.au; cnr Frome & Heber Sts; 10am-5pm Mon-Fri, to 1pm Sat) FREE In one of the town's historic buildings, Moree gallery has an inspiring collection of contemporary Aboriginal art.

Moree Artesian Aquatic Centre SWIMMING
(www.maacltd.com; 20 Anne St; adult/child $8/6; 6am-8pm Mon-Fri, 7am-7pm Sat & Sun) Locals frolic at this smart complex of swimming pools, and soak in its mineral-rich artesian pools (around 40°C). Some town motels also have artesian pools on-site for guests.

Information

Visitor Centre (☎02-6757 3350; www.moreetourism.com.au; cnr Gwydir & Newell Hwys; 9am-5pm Mon-Fri, to 1pm Sat & Sun)

CENTRAL WEST

The Central West's relative proximity to Sydney and its population of eager city escapees, weekend-awayers and holiday-homers have no doubt given many of the agricultural towns just beyond the Blue Mountains a leg-up. Drive further west and the red outback soil takes over.

Bathurst

POP 31,294

Bathurst is Australia's oldest inland settlement, boasting a cool climate and a beautiful manicured central square where formidable Victorian buildings transport you to the past. And then, in a dramatic change of pace, it's also the bastion of Australian motor sport.

Sights

Ask at the visitor centre for information about wineries, hiking trails and scenic drives in the region.

★Australian Fossil & Mineral Museum MUSEUM
(www.somervillecollection.com.au; 224 Howick St; adult/child $12/6; 10am-4pm Mon-Sat, to 2pm Sun) Don't let the dry name fool you – this place is a treasure chest full of wonder. It's home to the internationally renowned Somerville Collection: rare fossils, plus gemstones and minerals in every colour of the rainbow (amethysts, diamonds, rubies, ancient insects frozen in amber). The museum also houses Australia's only complete Tyrannosaurus rex skeleton.

Courthouse HISTORIC BUILDING, MUSEUM
(www.bathursthistory.org.au; Russell St; museum adult/child $4/2.50; museum 10am-4pm

Tue-Sat, 11am-2pm Sun) This 1880 building is the most impressive of Bathurst's historical structures. Its east wing houses the small **Historical Museum**.

Mt Panorama LANDMARK
(www.mount-panorama.com.au) FREE Rev-heads will enjoy the 6.2km **Mt Panorama Motor Racing Circuit**, venue for the epic Bathurst 1000 V8 race each October (which sees crowds of up to 200,000). It's a public road, so you can drive around the circuit – but only up to an unthrilling 60km/h. There's a lookout and racing-themed children's playground at the top.

All roads lead to the track, including southwest along William St.

National Motor Racing Museum MUSEUM
(www.nmrm.com.au; Murrays Corner, Mt Panorama; adult/child $12.50/5.50; ⌚9am-4.30pm) Sits at the base of Mt Panorama and celebrates all things motor sports.

Festivals & Events

Bathurst 1000 MOTOR RACING
(www.v8supercars.com.au; ⌚Oct) Petrolheads throng to Bathurst for this 1000km touring-car race, considered the pinnacle of Australian motor sport. It's completed over 161 laps of Mt Panorama.

Sleeping

Jack Duggans Irish Pub PUB $
(☎02-6331 2712; www.jackduggans.com.au; 135 George St; dm/s/d with shared bathroom $30/50/65) This lively spot in the heart of town has a good restaurant and bar downstairs (run by a real Irishman, with live music on weekends and good *craic*). Upstairs are small, high-quality budget rooms.

Accommodation Warehouse APARTMENTS $$
(☎02-6332 2801; www.accomwarehouse.com.au; 121a Keppel St; s/d $100/130; ❄📶) A three-level woollen mill dating from the 1870s has been cleverly converted into five self-contained apartments. They're not slick; they're sweet and cosy and have considerably more character than a modern motel room. It's down a lane, arrowed off Keppel St.

Rydges Mount Panorama HOTEL $$
(☎02-6338 1888; www.rydges.com/bathurst; 1 Conrod Straight; r from $150; 📶🏊) Large (129 studios and apartments) and smartly furnished, with loads of facilities. Every room has a view over the racetrack, but you'll need to book well ahead for the Bathurst 1000.

Eating & Drinking

Church Bar PIZZA $$
(1 Ribbon Gang Lane; pizzas $17-25; ⌚noon-midnight) This restored 1850s church now attracts punters praying to a different deity: the god of wood-fired pizza. The soaring ceilings and verdant courtyard off William St make it one of the town's best eating and socialising venues.

Hub CAFE $$
(52 Keppel St; mains $13-25; ⌚7am-5pm Mon-Sat, to 3pm Sun) On a strip with a few cool cafe options, the courtyard canopy of red umbrellas and green leaves makes this popular spot the perfect place for an alfresco meal.

Webb & Co BAR
(www.webbandco.com.au; off George St; ⌚3pm-late Mon-Sat, noon-10pm Sun) Tucked down a central arcade (next to Crema coffee bar), this classy 'beverage emporium' proffers great craft beer, cocktails and local wine, plus a most excellent menu of share plates, mains ($26) and grazing feasts.

Information

Visitor Centre (☎02-6332 1444; www.visitbathurst.com.au; Kendall Ave; ⌚9am-5pm)

Getting There & Away

Australia Wide Coaches (☎02-6362 7963; www.austwidecoaches.com.au) Has a daily link between Sydney and Orange that stops at Katoomba and Bathurst (Sydney–Bathurst $40, 3½ hours).

NSW TrainLink (☎13 22 32; www.nswtrainlink.info) Trains go frequently to Sydney ($9, 4¼ hours) and Orange ($12, one hour).

Orange

POP 38,000

There might be pears, apples and stone fruit aplenty in the surrounding orchards, but it just so happens the town was named after Prince William of Orange. It's become a convivial, fast-growing regional centre with a booming food and wine scene.

Sights

★**Mt Canobolas** NATURE RESERVE
Southwest of Orange, this conservation area encompasses waterfalls, views, walking trails and bike paths. Swimmer-friendly **Lake Canobolas** is a great place to start with plenty of picnic areas and a lakeside children's playground – the turn-off to

the lake is on the extension of Coronation Rd, 8km west of town.

Orange Regional Gallery GALLERY
(www.org.nsw.gov.au; cnr Byng & Peisley Sts; 9am-5pm) FREE Next to the visitor centre, the gallery has an ambitious, varied program of exhibitions and some Australian masters.

Festivals & Events

Orange has four seasonal festivals, where the region's producers make star appearances.

Slow Summer FOOD
In early February, which coincides with the Banjo Paterson Poetry Festival.

F.O.O.D Week FOOD & WINE
(Food of Orange District; www.orangefoodweek.com.au) In mid-April.

Orange Apple Festival FOOD
At the height of the harvest in May.

Orange Wine Festival WINE
In October.

Sleeping

Orange is a popular weekend-break destination, and there are numerous cottages and B&Bs. The website www.orangeaccommodationgroup.com.au lists most options in and around town.

★ **De Russie Suites** BOUTIQUE HOTEL $$
(02-6360 0973; www.derussiehotels.com.au; 72 Hill St; d $155-260;) As good as anything in Sydney, this little slice of hotel heaven has boutique written all over it. It has luxe mod cons, including kitchenettes in every studio (a hamper of breakfast supplies is included).

Templers Mill Motel MOTEL $$
(02-6362 5611; www.oesc.com.au; 94 Byng St; r from $130;) Part of the enormous Ex-Services Club, this large and well-run motel has brand-new rooms, plus renovated older options. It's a short walk to restaurants and the main street; the club's facilities (pool, gym etc) are free for guests.

Eating & Drinking

Byng Street Local Store CAFE $
(www.byngstreet.com.au; 47 Byng St; mains $7-15; 7am-6pm Mon-Fri, to 3pm Sat & Sun) This cute corner cafe is a big hit with locals. The bread, muffins and pastries are freshly baked on-site, the coffee is excellent, and the hunger-busters (fresh salads and sandwiches) are damn tasty.

★ **Agrestic Grocer** CAFE $$
(426 Molong Rd; lunch $16-28; 8.30am-5.30pm Mon-Fri, to 4pm Sat & Sun) 'This is what happens when shopkeepers and farmers unite', says the flyer. The results are pretty wonderful. This rustic cafe-grocer celebrates local produce a few kilometres north of town (on the Mitchell Hwy). Breakfast on house-made crumpets, lunch on Italian panzanella salad or Korean barbecue burger. It's all delicious.

Lolli Redini MODERN AUSTRALIAN $$$
(02-6361 7748; www.lolliredini.com.au; 48 Sale St; 2/3 courses $68/85; 6-9pm Tue-Sat & noon-2pm Sat) See Orange's finest produce wrapped in all its glory at this much-lauded restaurant (bookings essential). The matching of food with wines is well-thought-out, the setting and service are exemplary, and the kitchen creations (including many for vegetarians) sing with flavour.

★ **Ferment** WINE BAR
(www.orangewinecentre.com.au; 87 Hill St; 11am-8pm) Inside a gorgeous heritage building, Ferment shines a spotlight on local wines (it's the cellar door for a handful of small producers). You can talk wine, graze on platters

FOOD & WINE IN ORANGE

Orange is a delicious destination for wine and food tourism. The region has a reputation for distinctive cool-climate wines (see www.winesoforange.com.au). Orchard fruits, berries and nuts are also grown here, and quality lamb and beef are raised.

Dozens of **cellar doors and farm gates** are open to the public – a good place to begin exploration is the visitor centre. Pick up the *Orange & District Wine & Food Guide*, with a map outlining six routes in town and beyond. It also highlights cellar doors, farm gates (berry farms, orchards) and local-produce outlets (providores, microbrewers), plus picnic areas along the way.

It's great to explore with your own transport, and there are also companies that can take you touring: **Orange Wine Tours** (02-5310 6818; www.orangewinetours.com.au) has options starting from three hours ($75).

or just admire the stylish fit-out. Ferment's clever offer: half-day bike hire and lunchtime picnic for two for $55.

Union Bank WINE BAR
(☎02-6361 4441; www.unionbank.com.au; cnr Sale & Byng Sts; mains $16-32; ⏲noon-late Mon-Sat, to 9pm Sun) This polished wine bar has a menu for everyone (grazers, sharers, hungry folks) and a wine list to match – 20 by-the-glass offerings make it easy to sample the region. The courtyard is perfect for Saturday afternoon live music.

Information

Orange Visitor Centre (☎02-6393 8000; www.visitorange.com.au; cnr Byng & Peisley Sts; ⏲9am-5pm)

Verto (☎1300 483 786; www.verto.org.au) Can help you find fruit-picking work in the Orange and Young region.

Getting There & Away

Australia Wide Coaches (☎02-6362 7963; www.austwidecoaches.com.au) Has a daily link between Sydney and Orange ($40, four hours), via Bathurst.

NSW TrainLink (☎13 22 32; www.nswtrainlink.info) Runs frequent trains to Sydney ($27, five hours) and Dubbo ($19, two hours).

Cowra

POP 10,000

Cowra is a surprising town with a unique story. In August 1944 more than 1000 Japanese prisoners attempted to break out of a prisoner-of-war camp here (231 of them died, along with four Australians). Since the war Cowra has aligned itself with Japan and the causes of reconciliation and world peace.

Start your explorations at the visitor centre, which shows an excellent nine-minute holographic film about the breakout scene (it has been praised by Bill Bryson, no less).

Sights

★ **Japanese Garden** GARDENS
(www.cowragarden.com.au; Binni Creek Rd; adult/child $15/8; ⏲8.30am-5pm) Built as a token of Cowra's connection with Japanese POWs (but with no overt mention of the war or the breakout), this tranquil 5-hectare garden and attached cultural centre are superbly presented and well worth visiting (albeit with a steep entry fee). Audio guides ($2) explain the plants, history and design of the garden.

You can buy food for the koi (carp), or feed yourself at the on-site cafe (which serves mostly Australian fare, with a small nod to Japanese cuisine).

Cowra & Japanese War Cemeteries CEMETERY
(Doncaster Rd) These moving, well-maintained cemeteries are signposted off the road to Canowindra, around 5km north of town.

POW Campsite & Guard Tower MEMORIAL
(Evans St) From the war cemeteries north of town, signs lead to the site of the Japanese

VILLAGE CHARM

The stately buildings, wide streets, parks and well-tended English gardens align the larger towns of the Central West with a past built on gold-mining and bushranger folklore. The towns have their charms, but the history is often best explored in the small villages, where photogenic main streets feature wide verandahs and old pubs, plus urbane attractions to appeal to weekend visitors: cafes and restaurants, wineries and galleries, and B&Bs and cottages to rent.

Following are some of our favourite small-town escapes:

Gulgong This time-warped hamlet (www.gulgong.net), 29km north of Mudgee, once featured alongside author Henry Lawson on the $10 note. Its eccentric local pioneer museum is a cracker.

Millthorpe Only 22km southeast of Orange, this pioneering village (www.millthorpevillage.com.au) is a cute slice of the mid-1800s. There are some wine-tasting venues and renowned local eateries, including Gerry's @ The Commercial for pub food, and Tonic for fancy-pants dining.

Canowindra Pronounced 'ca-noun-dra', this village (www.canowindra.org.au) 32km north of Cowra has hot-air balloon flights and a couple of cellar doors, plus a museum dedicated to an intriguing local fossil find.

breakout. A voice-over from the watchtower recounts the story. You can still see the camp foundations, and info panels explain the military and migrant camps of wartime Cowra.

World Peace Bell MONUMENT
(cnr Darling & Kendal Sts) Audio at this outdoor site explains the background and significance of the World Peace Bell. It's a replica of the bell that stands outside the United Nations, and the only one of its kind in Australia.

Festivals & Events

Cherry Blossom Festival CULTURAL
Cowra's pretty *sakura matsuri* (cherry blossom festival) is held over a week in late September, with Japanese food and culture on show.

Sleeping

Decent pubs and cafes line the main (Kendal) street.

Vineyard Motel MOTEL $$
(02-6342 3641; www.vineyardmotel.com.au; 42 Chardonnay Rd; s/d from $120/140;) The views from the verandah of this quiet, old-school motel, 4km from town, are quite mesmerising, and the welcome is warm. There are only six rooms, and it's walking distance from the Quarry vineyard restaurant.

Breakout Motor Inn MOTEL $$
(02-6342 6111; www.breakoutmotel.com.au; 181 Kendal St; r from $130;) Among a handful of options at the eastern end of the main street, this modern motel stands out.

Eating & Drinking

Quarry MODERN AUSTRALIAN $$
(02-6342 3650; www.thequarryrestaurant.com.au; 7191 Boorowa Rd; lunch mains $20-30, dinner mains $33; noon-2.30pm Thu-Sun, 6.30-10pm Fri & Sat) Four kilometres out of town, the Quarry restaurant is handsomely set amid the vineyards, and the kitchen output wins regular praise (especially the puddings!). There's a sizeable wine list, too – the Quarry is the cellar door for a number of local vineyards.

Oxley Wine Bar WINE BAR
(9-11 Kendal St; noon-9pm Wed-Thu, 8am-midnight Fri & Sat, 8am-3pm Sun) A great new main-street addition, where there's live music, Saturday DJs and retro stylings to accompany your craft beers, local wines and pizzas.

Information

Visitor Centre (02-6342 4333; www.cowratourism.com.au; Olympic Park, Mid Western Hwy)

Getting There & Away

NSW TrainLink (13 22 32; www.nswtrainlink.info) Has buses to Lithgow (via Bathurst), where you take a train on to Sydney ($42, six hours). There are also bus services to Orange ($19, 1½ hours).

Parkes

POP 10,000

Parkes has two wildly different claims to fame. First: it's home to an enormous radio telescope. Second: hundreds of Elvis impersonators descend in January. Otherwise, it's a fairly sleepy inland rural town.

Sights

Henry Parkes Centre MUSEUM
(1800 623 465; www.henryparkescentre.com.au; Newell Hwy; adult/child $12/6; 9am-5pm Mon-Fri, 10am-4pm Sat & Sun) North of town, this complex is home to Parkes' **visitor centre** (www.visitparkes.com.au) plus a handful of exhibitions. The King's Castle is a fun private collection of Elvis memorabilia – many items were once owned by the King (including his iconic peacock belt). There are also impressive collections dedicated to vintage cars, antique machinery and local history.

Parkes Radio Telescope TELESCOPE
(02-6861 1777; www.csiro.au/parkes; Newell Hwy; visitor centre 8.30am-4.15pm) Built by the Commonwealth Scientific & Industrial Research Organisation (CSIRO) in 1961, this telescope is 6km east of the Newell Hwy, 19km north of Parkes.

It became famous thanks to the film *The Dish* (2000), which told a (somewhat fictionalised) account of the telescope's role in relaying live footage of the Apollo 11 moon landing in 1969. There's a visitor centre with space info, a 3D theatre and information on radio astronomy (the study of radio waves that come from celestial objects).

Festivals & Events

Elvis Festival MUSIC
(www.parkeselvisfestival.com.au) In the second week of January, Parkes' population doubles as visitors flock to celebrate Elvis' birthday and spend five days whooping it up with

WORTH A TRIP

UTES IN THE PADDOCK

About 70km from Parkes on the Condobolin road (well signposted), **Utes in the Paddock** (www.utesinthepaddock.com.au) is a one-of-a-kind art installation, and a quirky and fun tribute to outback life. Here, 20 iconic vehicles (only Holdens!) have been given a creative makeover. Admire Utezilla, the Emute, the TribUte, and Dame Edna on the 'loo'.

impersonators, concerts, busking competitions, a street parade (Elvis-themed floats, vintage cars, the works), karaoke and outdoor cinema.

Sleeping & Eating

Hotel Gracelands HOTEL $$
(☎02-6862 3459; www.gracelandsparkes.com.au; 7-9 Bushman St; s/d from $89/119; ❄📶) Most Parkes motels are along the highway, but this is a backstreet option, freshly renovated and home to compact, spotless rooms. There's a good restaurant, Ikon, attached.

Old Parkes Convent B&B $$
(☎02-6862 5385; www.parkesconvent.com.au; 33 Currajong St; s/d $150/190; ❄) This charming heritage building has two impeccably attired apartments filled with antiques.

Bellas ITALIAN $$
(☎02-6862 4212; ww.bellascafe.com.au; 245 Clarinda St; dinner mains $18-33; ⏲8am-10pm Mon-Sat, to 2pm Sun) Breakfast at this quality all-day option treads familiar ground (with some fun tempters like Sicilian doughnuts). From lunchtime, the menu skews heavily to Italy: crowd-pleasing panini, pizzas, pasta and risottos.

Dish Cafe CAFE $$
(Parkes Radio Telescope; lunch $9-20; ⏲8.30am-3.30pm) In the shadow of the telescope, this cafe has a range of brekky and lunch options (full marks for 'eggs benedish' on the menu).

Getting There & Away

NSW TrainLink (☎13 22 32; www.nswtrainlink.info) Runs up to three daily connections with Sydney (from $56, seven to 10 hours), involving train and bus services connecting at Orange or Lithgow.

Dubbo

POP 32,300

The important rural centre of Dubbo is on one of the main inland north–south driving routes and is a gateway of sorts to the outback.

Sights

★**Taronga Western Plains Zoo** ZOO
(☎02-6881 1400; www.taronga.org.au; Obley Rd; 2-day passes adult/child $47/24; ⏲9am-4pm) This is Dubbo's star attraction, not to mention one of the best zoos in regional Australia. You can walk the 6km circuit, hire a bike ($15) or drive your car, getting out at enclosures along the way. Guided walks (adult/child $15/7.50) start at 6.45am on weekends (additional days in school holidays). There are free barbecues and picnic grounds at the zoo, as well as cafes and kiosks.

Book ahead for special animal encounters, or for the glorious accommodation packages – spend a night at a bush camp, in family-sized cabins or safari-style lodges, overlooking savannah.

Western Plains Cultural Centre MUSEUM
(www.wpccdubbo.org.au; 76 Wingewarra St; ⏲10am-4pm Wed-Sun) FREE Incorporating Dubbo's regional **museum** and **gallery** plus a lovely cafe, the cultural centre is housed in a swanky architectural space cleverly incorporating the main hall of Dubbo's former high school. The combination befits the centre's exhibitions, both contemporary and historic.

Old Dubbo Gaol MUSEUM
(www.olddubbogaol.com.au; 90 Macquarie St; adult/child $15/5; ⏲9am-4pm) This is a museum where 'animatronic' characters tell their stories. There are also characters in costume and guided tours on weekends (daily in school holidays); twilight tours are possible too. Creepy but authentic.

Sleeping

There are plenty of hotels on Cobra St, and two large, family friendly camping grounds with cabins. Although they're not cheap, the accommodation packages at Taronga Western Plains Zoo make for a night to remember.

Ibis Budget Dubbo HOTEL $
(☎02-6882 9211; www.ibisbudget.com; cnr Mitchell & Newell Hwys; tw/d/f $59/69/89; ❄@📶🏊)

If you're simply after value for money, this is a good bet. Rooms are no-frills and compact, but come with TV, air-con and en suite. Breakfast is cheap at $7.

No 95 Dubbo MOTEL $$
(☎02-6882 7888; www.no95.com.au; 95 Cobra St; r $135;) Don't be put off by the uninspiring facade: inside, the rooms are equipped with top-notch furniture, linen and appliances. Facilities are first rate.

Westbury Guesthouse GUESTHOUSE $$
(☎02-6881 6105; www.westburydubbo.com.au; cnr Brisbane & Wingewarra Sts; s/d $125/150;) This lovely old heritage home (1915) has six spacious, elegant rooms, and a delightful Thai restaurant attached.

Eating

Village Bakery Cafe CAFE $
(www.villagebakerycafe.com.au; 113a Darling St; 6am-5.30pm;) Award-winning meat pies, sandwiches and a kids' playground make this an easy choice, helped along by cabinets full of old school cakes and desserts.

Two Doors Tapas & Wine Bar TAPAS $$
(☎02-6885 2333; www.twodoors.com.au; 215 Macquarie St; dishes $7-20; 4pm-late Tue-Fri, from 10am Sat) Kick back in a leafy courtyard below street level, while munching on flavour-packed plates of halloumi skewers, soft-shell crab or slow-roasted pork belly.

Information

Visitor Centre (☎02-6801 4450; www.dubbo.com.au; cnr Macquarie St & Newell Hwy; 9am-5pm) At the northern end of town. Good info, bikes for hire.

Getting There & Around

Rex (www.rex.com.au) and **Qantas** (www.qantas.com.au) have flights to Sydney; Rex also has flights to Broken Hill.

Dubbo is a regional hub for transport, with major highways meeting here:

- A32 Mitchell Hwy between Sydney and Adelaide
- A39 Newell Hwy between Melbourne and Brisbane
- B84 Golden Hwy from Newcastle

NSW TrainLink (☎13 22 32; www.nswtrainlink.info) Runs frequent trains to/from Sydney (from $55, 6½ hours), plus buses to most regional centres and major NSW outback towns, including Lightning Ridge, Bourke and Broken Hill.

Mudgee

POP 9830

Mudgee is an Aboriginal word for 'nest in the hills', a fitting name for this pretty town surrounded by vineyards and rolling hills. The wineries come hand-in-hand with excellent food, making Mudgee a stellar weekend getaway.

Sights

Mudgee's 35 cellar doors (all family-owned operations) are primarily clustered north-east of town. Get details from the visitor centre: some vineyards have outstanding restaurants, some have accommodation, some open weekends only.

★**Lowe Wines** WINERY
(☎03-6372 0800; www.lowewine.com.au; Tinja Lane; 10am-5pm) You can follow a walking/cycling trail through the orchards and vines of this idyllic organic farm, past donkeys and chickens to picnic grounds. The cellar door has tastings and a superb grazing platter ($30) of local flavours, and Zin House (p246) is on the grounds. Check the website for events, too.

Logan Wines WINERY
(www.loganwines.com.au; 33 Castlereagh Hwy; 10am-5pm) An impressive and modern cellar-door experience 15km east of Mudgee.

Pieter van Gent Winery & Vineyard WINERY
(www.pvgwinery.com.au; 141 Black Springs Rd; 9am-5pm Mon-Sat, 10.30am-4pm Sun) Heavenly white port and muscat, and tastings in a photogenic oak-barrel room.

MUDGEE WINES AT A GLANCE

- Best sources of information: **visitor centre** (p246; the *Mudgee Region* booklet has a great map); the website www.mudgeewine.com.au
- Best winery tours: **Mudgee Wine & Country Tours** (☎02-6372 2367; www.mudgeewinetours.com.au; half-/full-day wine tours $50/80) and **Mudgee Tourist Bus** (☎02-6372 4475; www.mudgeetouristbus.com.au; half-/full-day wine tours $45/70)
- Best wine bar: **Roth's** (p246)
- Best time to visit: September for the Mudgee Wine & Food Festival

Robert Stein Winery & Vineyard WINERY
(www.robertstein.com.au; Pipeclay Lane; ⌚10am-4.30pm) A small, rustic cellar door plus a vintage motorcycle museum (free). There's also an excellent paddock-to-plate restaurant, Pipeclay Pumphouse.

di Lusso Estate WINERY
(www.dilusso.com.au; 162 Eurunderee Lane; ⌚10am-5pm Mon-Sat, to 4pm Sun) Play bocce, taste-test home-grown olives and figs, eat pizza and sample Italian wine varietals (nebbiolo, sangiovese etc) at this sweet slice of Italy.

Sleeping

Mudgee Riverside Tourist Park CAMPGROUND, CABINS $
(☎02-6372 2531; www.mudgeeriverside.com.au; 22 Short St; sites $24-31, cabins from $90; ❄) Super-central, leafy and well run.

★**Perry Street Hotel** BOUTIQUE HOTEL $$
(☎02-6372 7650; www.perrystreethotel.com.au; cnr Perry & Gladstone Sts; ste from $165; ❄📶) Stunning apartment suites make a sophisticated choice in town. The attention to detail is outstanding, right down to the kimono bathrobes, Nespresso machine and free gourmet snacks.

Cobb & Co Boutique Hotel BOUTIQUE HOTEL $$
(☎02-6372 7245; www.cobbandcocourt.com.au; 97 Market St; r from $160; ❄📶) In the centre of town, this place has mod cons elegantly suited to its heritage style. Two-night minimum stay on weekends.

Eating & Drinking

Alby & Esthers CAFE $$
(www.albyandesthers.com.au; 61 Market St; mains $10-18; ⌚8am-5pm Mon-Thu, to late Fri & Sat) Down an alleyway is this supremely pretty courtyard cafe, serving up fine local produce and good coffee. It morphs into a wine bar on Friday and Saturday nights.

★**Zin House** MODERN AUSTRALIAN $$$
(☎02-6372 1660; www.zinhouse.com.au; 329 Tinja Lane; lunch $75; ⌚from 5.30pm Fri, from noon Sat & Sun) The glorious Lowe (p245) vineyard is home to this weekend highlight: long, leisurely six-course lunches of simply prepared local produce (either home-grown or impeccably sourced). Diners share farmhouse tables in a beautifully designed home. You can also enjoy Friday night tapas here ($45). Gather your friends; book ahead.

★**Roth's** WINE BAR
(www.rothswinebar.com.au; 30 Market St; ⌚5pm-midnight Wed-Sat) The oldest wine bar (1923) in NSW sits behind a small heritage facade, and serves up great local wines (by the glass from $6), fine bar food and excellent live music. Bliss.

Information

Visitor Centre (☎02-6372 1020; www.visitmudgeeregion.com.au; 84 Market St; ⌚9am-5pm)

Getting There & Around

Countryfit (☎02-6372 3955; 6-42 Short St) Rents bicycles.

NSW TrainLink (☎13 22 32; www.nswtrainlink.info) Buses to Lithgow connect with Sydney trains ($37, five hours).

OUTBACK

NSW is rarely credited for its far-west outback corner, but it should be. Out here, grey saltbush and red sand make it easy to imagine yourself superimposed onto the world's biggest Aboriginal dot painting, a canvas reaching as far as the eye can see.

Wentworth

POP 1248

The colonial river-port of Wentworth, at the confluence of the Murray and Darling Rivers, is a smaller, quieter sibling to the regional centre of Mildura, 30km away across the border in Victoria. It's a sweetly subdued place with scenic riverbanks and a handful of historic buildings.

Wentworth is considered a gateway to Outback NSW, and serves as one of the jumping-off points for Mungo National Park.

Sights

Murray-Darling River Junction RIVER
The point where the Darling River flows into the Murray lies in the town's southwestern corner. The riverside park, accessible from Cadell St, has enormous red river gums shading the banks, plus an elevated lookout from where you can observe the two colours of the merging rivers.

Perry Sand Hills OUTDOORS
Around 6km north of town (signposted off the Broken Hill and then Renmark roads),

these low orange sand dunes date back 40,000 years. They are at their best (and most photogenic) at sunset or sunrise.

Historic Buildings

By the Darling River, there's a replica of the modest, colonial-era **wharf**. Along Darling St, the **Old Post Office** (1899), **Wentworth Court House** (1880) and **St John the Evangelist Anglican Church** (1871) are handsome relics. At the northwestern end of town, **Old Wentworth Gaol** (03-5027 3337; Beverley St; adult/child $8/6; 10am-5pm) is a fascinating step back in time, while the nearby **Wentworth Pioneer Museum** (03-5027 3160; 117 Beverley St; adult/child $5/2; 10am-4pm) has an eclectic collection: riverboat photos, megafauna displays and more.

Tours

Some tour operators from Mildura (p606) may offer pick-up in Wentworth.

Wentworth River Cruises BOAT TOUR

(0408 647 097; www.wentworthcruises.com.au; adult/child from $25/15) Three different weekly cruises: the 2pm Wednesday cruise includes afternoon tea; the twilight cruise (6.30pm Wednesday September to March) includes fish and chips and live music; or enjoy a barbecue buffet on board the Sunday cruise at 12.30pm.

Sleeping & Eating

River-cruising **houseboats** are an interesting option, and plenty of companies operate out of the Mildura–Wentworth area. **Murray Darling Houseboats** (www.murraydarlinghouseboats.com.au) gives loads of information and lists operators and their fleets.

Wentworth Grande Resort HOTEL $$

(03-5027 2225; www.wentworthgranderesort.com.au; 61-79 Darling St; d/f from $99/160;) Easily the smartest option in the town centre, this large place has a range of decent, well-maintained rooms next to the Darling River.

★ **Avoca-On-Darling** GUESTHOUSE $$$

(03-5027 3020; sites.google.com/site/avocaondarling/; homestead per person incl meals $160) Ian and Barb run a true homestay guesthouse at Avoca, an 1870s heritage homestead 26km from Wentworth on gum-laden riverbanks. Homestead rooms share bathrooms and include all meals; there's also a self-contained cook's cottage ($160), jackaroo's quarters ($25 per person) and simple camp sites.

Travel 6km north of Wentworth along the Broken Hill road, then take the Lower Darling Rd, then turn off at the sign after a further 18.5km.

Even if you're not staying, call ahead to arrange a property tour and Devonshire tea ($15).

★ **Artback Gallery & Cafe** CAFE $

(03-5027 2298; www.artbackaustralia.com.au; cnr Darling & Adelaide Sts; meals $8-20; 10am-4pm Thu-Sat, 8.30am-4pm Sun;) Main-street offerings of pub grub and takeaway are outshone by this creative corner venue, a stylish two-level conversion of an 1882 bluestone building.

Information

Visitor Centre (03-5027 5080; www.visitwentworth.com.au; 66 Darling St; 9am-5pm Mon-Fri, to 1pm Sat & Sun)

Getting There & Away

There are no bus connections north. **Sunraysia Bus Lines** (03-5023 0274; www.sunbus.net.au) operates between Mildura and Wentworth (35 minutes) on weekdays only.

Mungo National Park

This remote, beautiful and important place covers 278.5 sq km of the Willandra Lakes Region World Heritage Area. It is one of Australia's most accessible slices of the outback.

Lake Mungo is a dry lake and site of the oldest archaeological finds in Australia. It also has the longest continual record of Aboriginal life (the world's oldest recorded cremation site has been found here).

Sights & Activities

Visitor Centre MUSEUM

(www.visitmungo.com.au) The visitor centre has displays on the park's cultural and natural history, and it's here you can pick up maps, pay park and camping fees, and enquire about tours. Next door is the Shearers' Quarters accommodation and the **Historic Woolshed**, dating from 1869 and well worth a look.

Behind the visitor centre is a re-creation of the 20,000-year-old human footprints discovered in the park in 2003. These lead to the outdoor **Meeting Place**, of significance to the region's Indigenous groups.

MUNGO NATIONAL PARK AT A GLANCE

When to Visit Year-round, but best April to October (summer temperatures are scorching)

Gateway Towns Mildura, Wentworth, Balranald, Broken Hill

Main Attractions Walls of China land formations; outback isolation; wildlife; Aboriginal sites

Transport Unsealed roads into the park are accessible in 2WD vehicles except after rains

★ Walls of China OUTDOORS

A 33km semicircle ('lunette') of sand dunes, the fabulous Walls of China has been created by the unceasing westerly wind. From the visitor centre a road leads across the dry lakebed to a car park, then it's a short walk to the **viewing platform**. Getting up close to the formations is the preserve of guided tours.

★ Mungo Track SCENIC DRIVE

The Mungo Track is a 70km signposted loop road around the heart of Mungo, linking the park's main attractions – you'll pass diverse landscapes, lookouts, short walks and plenty of emus and kangaroos.

Although it's unsealed, in dry weather the road is generally fine for 2WD cars; in good weather (ie not too hot), mountain-bikers may be tempted.

Beyond the Walls of China parking area, the road continues to the pretty **Red Top Lookout**, which boasts fine views over the deeply eroded ravines of the lunette sand dunes. After that point, the Mungo Track is a one-way road that loops all the way back to the visitor centre.

Pick up a map from the visitor centre before setting out, and come equipped with enough petrol, a spare tyre and plenty of drinking water. You can break the journey with an overnight stay at Belah Camp.

Walking Trails

From Main Camp camping ground, there are short walks such as the Grasslands Nature Stroll and a path to Mungo Lookout.

From the visitor centre, the 2.5km **Foreshore Walk** follows the ancient shoreline of Lake Mungo, or you can walk or cycle the 10km **Pastoral Heritage Trail**, linking the old Mungo Woolshed with the remnants of the Zanci Homestead precinct built in the 1920s.

Tours

Day tours to the park are offered from the main gateway towns of Mildura, Wentworth and Balranald, plus Broken Hill. These all include food, and a walk to the Walls of China (off-limits without a guide).

Companies based in Wentworth will often pick up in Mildura, and vice versa. If you prefer, operators will usually allow you to meet them in Mungo to join their tour.

Aboriginal Discovery Tours CULTURAL TOUR

(☎03-5021 8900; www.visitmungo.com.au/discovery-tours; adult/child $35/20) For those who visit the park independently, the NPWS conducts tours from the visitor centre led by Indigenous rangers, with the most popular option being the walk to the Walls of China. Check online for schedules: tours generally run daily in school holidays, weekends the rest of the year. Departure times depend on weather forecast, sunset time etc.

Harry Nanya Tours CULTURAL TOUR

(☎03-5027 2076; www.harrynanyatours.com.au; adult/child $180/110) Indigenous-owned company based in Wentworth, specialising in highly regarded tours of the park. Tours run during the day (April to October), or at sunset (November to March). Pick-ups are available from Mildura or Wentworth (adult/child $180/110, duration eight hours), or join the tour at Mungo ($90/45, five hours). Overnight options available.

Outback Geo Adventures TOUR

(☎0407 267 087; www.outbackgeoadventures.com.au; per person $150) Operates from Balranald. The eight-hour day tour to Mungo includes all the park's highlights; there's a two-person minimum.

MurrayTrek Tours TOUR

(☎1800 797 530; www.murraytrek.com.au; per person $145-175) Sunset and day tours from Mildura.

Discover Mildura TOUR

(☎03-5024 7448; www.discovermildura.com; per person $165) Day trips from Mildura.

Sleeping & Eating

Camping or accommodation prices quoted do not include park visitor fees.

Barbecues and shaded picnic tables are available by the visitor centre. Unless you plan to eat all meals at Mungo Lodge, you need to be entirely self-sufficient and bring supplies from gateway towns.

Main Camp CAMPGROUND $
(adult/child $5/3) Located 2km from the visitor centre (where you self-register and pay). Free gas barbecues and pit toilets are available; flush toilets and showers are at the visitor centre. BYO drinking water.

Belah Camp CAMPGROUND $
(adult/child $5/3) Remote Belah Camp is on the eastern side of the dunes. No wood fires are allowed – BYO cooking appliances.

Shearers' Quarters HOSTEL $
(☎1300 072 757; www.visitmungo.com.au/accommodation; adult/child $30/10; ❄) The former shearers' quarters comprises five neat, good-value rooms (each sleeping up to six in various configurations; BYO bedding). Rooms share a communal kitchen and bathroom, and a barbecue area.

Mungo Lodge LODGE $$$
(☎1300 663 748; www.mungolodge.com.au; ste $199-269; ❄📶) Mungo's plushest option is an attractive (and pricey) deluxe cabin at Mungo Lodge, on the Mildura road about 4km from the park visitor centre. There are cheaper self-catering budget cabins that are quite scruffy but scheduled for an upgrade. There are also a handful of unadvertised budget beds ($20) in very basic quarters.

The lodge houses an inviting bar, lounge and restaurant area open for breakfast, lunch and dinner (mains $22 to $32). Bookings advised for meals.

ℹ Information

There's a park entry fee of $7 per vehicle per day, payable at the visitor centre.

Note: there is no mobile-phone coverage in the area.

NPWS Office (☎03-5021 8900; ⏲8.30am-4.30pm Mon-Fri) On the corner of the Sturt Hwy at Buronga, near Mildura.

Visitor Centre (☎03-5021 8900; www.visitmungo.com.au; ⏲approximately 8am-4pm)

ℹ Getting There & Away

Mungo is 110km from Mildura and 150km from Balranald on good, unsealed roads that become instantly impassable after rain – a 2WD vehicle is generally fine in dry weather. From Wentworth the route is about 150km, and the road is sealed for 100km.

The closest places selling fuel are Balranald, Mildura, Wentworth, Pooncarie and Menindee.

Ask at the tourist offices in the gateway towns to see if the roads into Mungo are open *and* accessible by 2WD. You can also phone ☎132 701 or 03-5027 5090, or check online at www.visitwentworth.com.au/Mungo-Road.aspx.

Broken Hill

POP 18,500

The massive mullock heap (of mine residue) that forms a backdrop for Broken Hill's town centre accentuates the unique character of this desert frontier town. For all its remoteness, the fine facilities and high-quality attractions can feel like an oasis somewhere close to the end of the earth. Some of the state's most impressive national parks are nearby, as is an intriguing near-ghost town, and everywhere there is an impressive spirit of community and creativity.

Broken Hill's unique historic value was recognised in 2015, when it becamc the first Australian city to be included on the National Heritage List. It joins 102 other sites (including the Sydney Opera House and the Great Barrier Reef) as examples of exceptional places that contribute to the national identity.

History

A boundary rider, Charles Rasp, laid the foundations in Broken Hill that took Australia from an agricultural country to an industrial nation. In 1883 he discovered a silver lode and formed the Broken Hill Proprietary Company (which now goes by the name of BHP Billiton). It ultimately became Australia's largest company and an international giant.

Early conditions in the mine were appalling. Hundreds of miners died and many more suffered from lead poisoning and lung disease. This gave rise to the other great force in Broken Hill: the unions. Many miners were immigrants, but all were united in their efforts to improve conditions. The Big Strike of 1919–20 lasted for over 18 months, when the miners finally achieved a 35-hour week and the end of dry drilling.

Today the world's richest deposits of silver, lead and zinc are still being worked here, although mining operations are winding down, leading to a declining population.

Broken Hill

Top Sights

1 Broken Hill Regional Art Gallery D2
2 Line of Lode Miners Memorial C4
3 Palace Hotel C3

Sights

4 Albert Kersten Mining & Minerals Museum C3
5 Silver City Mint & Art Centre C2

Activities, Courses & Tours

6 Silver City Tours D2
7 Tri State Safaris C1

Sleeping

8 Caledonian B&B C2
9 Imperial C2
Palace Hotel .... (see 3)
10 Red Earth Motel D2
11 Royal Exchange Hotel C3

Eating

12 Café Alfresco D2
13 Silly Goat D2
14 Thom, Dick & Harry's D3

Drinking & Nightlife

Palace Hotel .... (see 3)

Sights & Activities

★Line of Lode Miners Memorial

MEMORIAL, VIEWPOINT

(Federation Way; 6am-9pm) FREE Teetering atop the silver skimp dump is this moving memorial with memorable views. It houses the impressively stark Cor-Ten steel memorial to the 900 miners who have died since Broken Hill first became a mining town; it's an appalling litany of gruesome deaths. To get here, travel south along Iodide St, cross the railway tracks then follow the signs.

At the time of research, the restaurant here had closed, but another may open in its place.

★ **Broken Hill Regional Art Gallery** GALLERY
(www.bhartgallery.com.au; 404-408 Argent St; admission by gold-coin donation; ⏲10am-5pm Mon-Fri, to 4pm Sat & Sun) This impressive gallery is housed in the beautifully restored Sully's Emporium from 1885. It's the oldest regional gallery in NSW and holds 1800 works in its permanent collection. Artists featured include Australian masters such as John Olsen, Sidney Nolan and Arthur Streeton, plus there is strong Indigenous representation.

★ **Royal Flying Doctor Service** MUSEUM
(☎08-8080 3714; www.flyingdoctor.org.au/Broken-Hill-Base.html; Airport Rd; adult/child $8.50/4; ⏲9am-5pm Mon-Fri, 10am-3pm Sat & Sun) This iconic Australian institution has a visitor centre at the airport. There are stirring displays and stories of health innovation and derring-do in the service of those who live and work in remote places (note: this base serves a staggeringly vast area of 640,000 sq km). It's a real eye-opener, and the video is guaranteed to stir emotions.

★ **Palace Hotel** HISTORIC BUILDING
(☎08-8088 1699; thepalacehotelbrokenhill.com.au; cnr Argent & Sulphide Sts) Star of the hit Australian movie *The Adventures of Priscilla, Queen of the Desert,* this impressive three-storey pub (1889) has an elaborate cast-iron verandah, plus wonderfully kitsch landscape murals covering almost every inch of the public areas. They're described as 'Italian Renaissance meets Outback' and were painted in the 1970s by Indigenous artist Gordon Waye. There's also a quality restaurant, accommodation and the outback essential: cold beer.

★ **Pro Hart Gallery** GALLERY
(www.prohart.com.au; 108 Wyman St; adult/child $5/3; ⏲10am-5pm Mar-Nov, to 4pm Dec-Feb) Kevin 'Pro' Hart (1928–2006) was a former miner and is widely considered one of outback Australia's premier painters. His iconic work is spread over three storeys, his studio has been re-created, and there's a fascinating video presentation about his life and work. You can also admire his Rolls-Royce collection.

Albert Kersten Mining & Minerals Museum MUSEUM
(Geomuseum; cnr Bromide & Crystal Sts; adult/child $7/5; ⏲10am-4.45pm Mon-Fri, 1-4.45pm Sat & Sun) Fascinating displays (and a mind-bending video) explain how the richest lode of silver, lead and zinc in the world was formed through the aeons. Rare minerals and crystals are displayed, as well as a 42kg silver nugget and the celebrated Silver Tree, an epergne (table centrepiece) crafted from 8.5kg of pure silver in 1879.

Jack Absalom's Gallery GALLERY
(www.jackabsalom.com.au; 638 Chapple St; ⏲10am-5pm Mar-Dec) FREE Octogenarian Jack Absalom was one of the celebrated 'Brushmen of the Bush', a group of five artists that hailed from Broken Hill (Pro Hart was another member). Absalom's oil paintings (and opal collection) are on show in a purpose-built space attached to his home; his works beautifully capture the light and colour of outback landscapes.

Day Dream Mine MINE
(☎08-8088 5682; www.daydreammine.com.au; underground & surface tours adult/child $30/10; ⏲tours 10am & 11.30am) The first mines were walk-in, pick-and-shovel horrors. For an eye-opening experience, tour this historic mine (dating from the 1880s) where you squeeze down the steps with your helmet light quivering on your head. Sturdy footwear is essential. It's a scenic 13km dirt drive off the Silverton road – a total of 33km from Broken Hill.

There are additional tours during school holidays, and claustrophobes can tour the surface area only for $8. Cash only.

Silver City Mint & Art Centre GALLERY
(www.silvercitymint.com.au; 66 Chloride St; adult/child $7.50/3; ⏲10am-4pm) This is home to the Big Picture, an amazing 100m-by-12m diorama of the Broken Hill outback – the work of one painter, over two years. It's certainly impressive, but also pricey, and the $2.50 charge to simply enter the gallery (really an elaborate souvenir shop) is cheeky.

★ **Outback Astronomy** ASTRONOMY
(☎0427 055 225; www.outbackastronomy.com.au; Racecourse Rd) Broken Hill is surrounded by desert, making it a great place to experience inky black skies and celestial splendour. This new company runs one-hour night-sky-viewing shows. The presenter points out constellations and various features visible to the naked eye, and through powerful binoculars (provided).

Viewing is from a lounge chair in the great outdoors (dress appropriately, especially in winter), at the racecourse on the northeast edge of town.

The website lists a calendar of forthcoming shows.

School of the Air SCHOOL LESSONS
(www.schoolair-p.schools.nsw.edu.au; 586 Lane St; admission $4.40; ⏲8.15am school days) For a back-to-school experience and a lesson in the outback's vastness, sit in on a class that broadcasts to kids in isolated homesteads. Bookings must be made at least a day in advance at the visitor centre. The school is closed during school holidays.

Tours

Broken Hill City Sights Tours TOUR
(☎08-8087 2484; www.bhoutbacktours.com.au; half-/full-day tours from $60/125) Day and half-day tours of Broken Hill, Silverton, Menindee Lakes and White Cliffs. Can transport you to Day Dream Mine. Minimum two passengers.

Silver City Tours TOUR
(☎08-8087 6956; www.silvercitytours.com.au; 380 Argent St) Half- and full-day tours that include Broken Hill city sights, Menindee Lakes and Kinchega National Park, White Cliffs and Silverton. Multiday packages available.

Tri State Safaris 4WD TOUR
(☎08-8088 2389; www.tristate.com.au; day tours $220) Well-regarded Broken Hill operator offering one- to 15-day tours to remote outback places like Mutawintji, Kinchega or Mungo National Parks, Corner Country, Birdsville and the Simpson Desert. Travellers can opt to tag-along on tours in their own 4WD vehicles.

PHONES, TIMES & FOOTBALL

When the NSW government refused to give Broken Hill the services it needed, saying the town was just a pinprick on the map, the council replied that Sydney was also a pinprick from where it was, and Broken Hill would henceforth be part of South Australia (SA). Since the town was responsible for much of NSW's wealth, Broken Hill was told it was to remain part of NSW. In protest, the town adopted SA time, phone area code and football, playing Australian Rules from then on.

Tourists beware: time in Broken Hill is Central Standard Time (CST), 30 minutes later than the surrounding area on Eastern Standard Time (EST); you're in the ☎08 phone code region; and don't talk about rugby in the pub.

Festivals & Events

St Pat's Day Races SPORTS
(www.stpatricks.org.au) These horse races in March are the biggest party on the Broken Hill calendar.

Sleeping

★Caledonian B&B B&B $
(☎08-8087 1945; www.caledonianbnb.com.au; 140 Chloride St; s/d with shared bathroom incl breakfast $79/89, cottages from $130; ❄📶) This fine B&B is in a refurbished pub (1898) known as 'the Cally' – it also has three self-contained cottages, each sleeping up to six. Hugh and Barb are welcoming hosts and the rooms are lovingly maintained. Wake up and smell Hugh's espresso coffee and you'll be hooked.

Palace Hotel HISTORIC HOTEL $
(☎08-8088 1699; www.thepalacehotelbrokenhill.com.au; 227 Argent St; dm/s/d with shared bathroom from $30/45/65, d $115-135; ❄) This huge and ageing icon won't be to everyone's taste, but a stay here is one of the outback's most unique sleeping experiences. There are newer rooms with balcony access and en suite, but most rooms are proudly retro and the murals in the public areas are extraordinary. For the full experience, try the Priscilla Suite ($135).

★Red Earth Motel MOTEL $$
(☎08-8088 5694; www.redearthmotel.com.au; 469 Argent St; studio apt $160, 2-/3-bedroom apt $220/260; ❄📶🏊) One of the best motels in rural NSW, this outstanding family-run place has large, stylish rooms – each has a separate sitting area and kitchen facilities, making them ideal for longer stays. There's a guest laundry, plus pool and barbecue area.

Imperial GUESTHOUSE $$
(☎08-8087 7444; www.imperialfineaccommodation.com; 88 Oxide St; r/apt incl breakfast from $170/270; ❄📶🏊) One of Broken Hill's best, this converted heritage pub, with a spectacular wrought-iron verandah, has been graciously renovated and doesn't skimp on creature comforts.

OUTBACK SUNSET IN THE LIVING DESERT

Living Desert Reserve (adult/child $5/2) One of the most memorable experiences of Broken Hill is viewing the sunset from the **Sculpture Symposium** on the highest hilltop 12km from town. The sculptures are the work of 12 international artists who carved the huge sandstone blocks on-site.

This spectacular outdoor gallery is part of the 24-sq-km Living Desert reserve, which is home to a **flora and fauna sanctuary** featuring a 2.2km Cultural Walk Trail and a 1km Flora Trail.

You can drive up to the sculpture summit, or walk up from the sanctuary (around 20 minutes). The lower car park is close to a nice barbecue and picnic area.

The reserve gates close about 30 minutes after sunset. The sanctuary's walks are accessible 9am to 5pm March to November, and 6am to 2pm December to February. Sunset times and opening hours are posted at the visitor centre.

Royal Exchange Hotel HOTEL $$
(☎08-8087 2308; www.royalexchangehotel.com; 320 Argent St; r $135-180; ❄📶) This restored 1930s hotel with an art deco bent is an accommodation oasis in the heart of town.

Eating & Drinking

★Silly Goat CAFE $
(360 Argent St; dishes $8-16; ⏰7.30am-5pm Tue-Fri, 8am-2pm Sat, 8am-1pm Sun) What's this? Pour-overs and single-origin coffee in the outback? Nice work, Silly Goat. The menu here would be at home in any big-city cafe, the array of cakes is tempting, the coffee is great, and the vibe is busy and cheerful.

Bells Milk Bar MILK BAR $
(www.bellsmilkbar.com.au; 160 Patton St; snacks $4-7; ⏰10am-5.30pm; 📶) In South Broken Hill (follow Crystal St west from the train station), this glorious old milk bar is a slice of 1950s nostalgia. Sip on a 'soda spider' or milkshake and soak up the memorabilia from one of the Formica tables.

Thom, Dick & Harry's CAFE $
(thomdickharrys.com.au; 354 Argent St; baguettes $8.50; ⏰8am-5.30pm Mon-Thu, to 6pm Fri, 9am-2pm Sat) A narrow shop cluttered with stylish kitchenware and gourmet produce. Sit in among it (or out on the street) for a decent coffee and delicious baguette.

Silvers Restaurant INTERNATIONAL $$
(☎08-8088 4380; cnr Argent & Silver Sts; mains $25-37; ⏰from 6pm Mon-Sat) It's not cheap, but the unassuming restaurant at the Junction Hotel offers a surprise: tucked among the traditional classics is a selection of tasty curry dishes (vegie, goat, lamb kofta, Sri Lankan chicken). Service is good, and the dessert trolley is a fine retro touch.

Café Alfresco MODERN AUSTRALIAN $$
(397 Argent St; dinner mains $15-29; ⏰7am-late) The service ticks along at an outback pace but this all-day place pulls an unfussy local crowd pining for its bumper portions of meat dishes (classics like steak and chicken parma) or crowd-pleasing pizza and pasta.

★Palace Hotel PUB
(☎08 8088 1699; thepalacehotelbrokenhill.com.au; 227 Argent St; ⏰from 3pm Mon-Wed, from noon Thu-Sat) In a town with *dozens* of pubs, it's hard to go past the storied Palace for true-blue outback entertainment. There's good food in the **Sidebar restaurant** (mains $17 to $36), drinks and snacks on the 1st-floor balcony, occasional live music, and on Fridays you can play 'two-up' (gambling on the fall of two coins) from 9pm.

Information

NPWS Office (☎08-8080 3200; 183 Argent St; ⏰8.30am-4.30pm Mon-Fri) National park information, road-closure updates and park accommodation bookings.

Visitor Centre (☎08-8088 3560; www.visitbrokenhill.com.au; cnr Blende & Bromide Sts; ⏰8.30am-5pm Mar-Nov, to 3pm Dec-Feb)

Getting There & Away

Buses R Us (☎08-8285 6900; www.busesrus.com.au) Provides two or three weekly bus connections with Adelaide ($120, seven hours). Buses arrive at and depart from the visitor centre.

Indian Pacific (☎1800 703 357; www.greatsouthernrail.com.au) For an epic overland rail journey (4352km over four days), the Indian Pacific travels once or twice weekly between Sydney, Adelaide and Perth. The train stops for roughly two hours in Broken Hill – time enough for a whistle-stop tour.

NSW TrainLink (13 22 32; www.nswtrainlink.info) Runs the weekly Outback Explorer train to Sydney ($138, 13¼ hours). Also operates daily buses to Dubbo that link with the Dubbo–Sydney rail service ($138, 16½ hours total journey).

Rex (13 17 13; www.rex.com.au) Flies daily to Adelaide and Sydney. There are flights to Mildura five times a week, with onward connections to Melbourne.

Around Broken Hill

Silverton

POP ABOUT 60 PEOPLE & 4 DONKEYS

Quirkiness overflows at Silverton, an old silver-mining town and now an almost-ghost town. Visiting is like walking into a Russell Drysdale painting.

Silverton's fortunes peaked in 1885, when it had a population of 3000, but in 1889 the mines closed and the people (and some houses) moved to Broken Hill.

Sights & Activities

Silverton is the setting of films such as *Mad Max II* and *A Town Like Alice*. The town's heart and soul is the **Silverton Hotel**, which displays film memorabilia and walls covered with miscellany typifying Australia's peculiar brand of larrikin humour.

The 1889 **Silverton Gaol** (adult/child $4/1; 9.30am-4pm) once housed 14 cells. Today the museum is a treasure trove: room after room is crammed full of a century of local life (wedding dresses, typewriters, mining equipment, photos). The **School Museum** (adult/child $2.50/1; 9.30am-3.30pm Mon, Wed & Fri-Sun) is another history pit stop, tracing the local school from its earliest incarnation, in a tent in 1884.

Considerably more offbeat is the **Mad Max 2 Museum** (Stirling St; adult/child $7.50/5; 10am-4pm). It's probably the last thing you expect to find out here, on the edge of nowhere – and it's the culmination of Englishman Adrian Bennett's lifetime obsession with the theme.

There's also a number of excellent **art galleries** dotting the settlement. Who would expect such arid landscapes to inspire such amazing creativity?

The road beyond Silverton becomes isolated and the horizons vast, but it's worth driving 5km to **Mundi Mundi Lookout** where the view over the plain is so extensive it reveals the curvature of the Earth.

Sleeping & Eating

★ Silverton Hotel PUB $$
(08-8088 5313; silvertonhotel@bigpond.com; Layard St; d $120, extra person $25) In an area off the pub's beer garden you'll find seven suprisingly modern and comfy motel units that can each sleep up to five. The pub itself is a rough diamond: full of character (and characters), and with a menu of basic, inexpensive fare (hot dogs, burgers, fish and chips).

Silverton Tea Rooms CAFE $
(Stirling St; mains $7-20; 8am-5.30pm) Silverton Tea Rooms, with 'cafe' sprawled across the corrugated-iron roof, has a menu offering bushman's burger, damper (campfire bread) and pie or ice cream made with quandong (a local native fruit).

Getting There & Away

Silverton is 25km west of Broken Hill along a sealed road.

Mutawintji National Park

This exceptional 690-sq-km park lies in the Byngnano Range – the eroded and sculptured remains of a 400-million-year-old seabed. Its gorges and rock pools teem with wildlife, and the mulga plains here stretch to the horizon.

The Malyangapa and Bandjigali peoples have lived in the area for thousands of years, and there are important rock engravings, stencils, paintings and scattered remains of their day-to-day life. Many of these are protected within the **Mutawintji Historic Site**, only accessible with a guide – for instance the popular one-day tour ($220) from Broken Hill run by Tri State Safaris (p252). You can also tag-along in your own 4WD on this tour, from Broken Hill ($110) or by joining the group at the park ($40).

The park brochure from the NPWS Office (p253) in Broken Hill includes a simple map and eight walks or drives through the park. You can camp at Homestead Creek (adult/child $5/3); bring all supplies.

The park is 130km northeast of Broken Hill. In dry weather it's generally accessible to 2WD vehicles, but always come prepared and tell someone where you're travelling. Check road-closure info on 08-8082 6660 or 08-8091 5155.

Corner Country

Out here, it's a different world; both harsh and peaceful, stretching forever to the endless sky. This far-western corner of NSW is a semidesert of red plains, heat, dust and flies – the perfect place to fall off the map.

Tibooburra

Tiny Tibooburra, the hottest town in the state, is a quintessential outback frontier town with two rough-around-the-edges sandstone pubs and a landscape of large red rock formations known as 'gibbers'. It's the gateway to Sturt National Park – be sure to visit the **NPWS office** (☎08-8091 3308; www.nationalparks.nsw.gov.au; Briscoe St; ⏰8.30am-4.30pm Mon-Fri) and park visitor centre in Tibooburra before setting out.

Both pubs offer accommodation, meals and quirkiness. Visit the **Tibooburra Hotel** (☎08-8091 3310; www.tibooburrahotel.com.au; Briscoe St), known as 'the Two-Storey', for its wall of hats. At **Toole's Family Hotel** (☎08-8091 3314; www.tibooburra.com.au; Briscoe St), known as 'the Family', check out the bar adorned with paintings by one-time resident artist Clifton Pugh.

Tibooburra Beds Motel (☎08-8091 3333; www.tibooburrabeds.com.au; cnr Briscoe & Brown Sts; d $130) is a newer option offering an unexpected touch of luxury in its three modern motel-style units.

Getting There & Away

The Silver City Hwy connects Tibooburra with Broken Hill (332km) via Milparinka. The road is a mixture of tarmac and unsealed – it can be hazardous (and even closed) after (rare) rains. Ask about road conditions at the visitor centre in Broken Hill, at NPWS offices in Broken Hill or Tibooburra, or call ☎08-8082 6660.

Sturt National Park

North and northwest of Tibooburra, vast Sturt National Park encompasses over 3400 sq km of classic outback terrain. There are camping grounds and picnic areas in four locations; note that only untreated water is available in the park, so come prepared with fuel, food and water to ensure you travel safely in this hot, remote terrain.

About 27km from Tibooburra, **Mt Wood Historic Homestead** (☎08-8091 3308; Tibooburra; d from $100, shearers' quarters bunks $15) provides the impetus for a real outback stay. It's operated by the NPWS and offers comfy homestead rooms (communal kitchen and bathroom facilities) or budget bunks in shearers' quarters.

Most tracks through the park are negotiable in a 2WD vehicle (in dry weather only). The only exception is Middle Rd, which is 4WD-only.

The park stretches northwest to **Cameron Corner**, reached by a well-signposted 140km dirt road from Tibooburra. A post marks the spot where Queensland, South Australia and NSW meet. In the Queensland corner, **Cameron Corner Store** (☎08-8091 3872; Cameron Corner) has fuel, meals, basic accommodation and camping, and advice on road conditions.

Along the borders you'll see the 5600km **Dingo Fence**, built in the 1880s to keep dingoes out of the relatively fertile southeast part of the continent.

Wilcannia

In the past, Wilcannia hasn't had a lot of love from travellers, but a couple of new businesses are happily changing opinions.

The town has a large Indigenous population, and a fine collection of old sandstone buildings dating from its heyday as a prosperous Darling River port in the 1880s.

Sleeping & Eating

★Warrawong on the Darling CAMPGROUND, MOTEL **$$**
(☎1300 688 225; www.warrawongonthedarling.com.au; Barrier Hwy; camp sites $20-35, d $120-140) Just east of town, this new riverside property has lush green camp sites by a billabong, plus the opportunity for bush camping. The self-contained motel units are excellent value, each with kitchenette and barbecue. Amenities are large and spotless. Cheerful managers make the place sparkle – plus there's a friendly emu named Rissole. Still to come: a restaurant-bar and waterfront cabins.

Courthouse Cafe & Gallery CAFE **$**
(☎08-8091 5910; www.courthouse.net.au; cnr Reid & Cleaton Sts; lunch $6-13; ⏰10am-4pm Wed-Mon) On a street lined with heritage buildings, this sweet cafe offers pit stop-worthy coffee and food (including a fine ploughman's lunch), homemade cakes and an arty bent.

Getting There & Away

Wilcannia lies about halfway between Broken Hill and Cobar, on the Barrier Hwy. The sealed road to White Cliffs is signposted just west of town.

White Cliffs

There are few stranger places in Australia than the tiny pock-marked opal-mining town of White Cliffs, 93km northwest of Wilcannia on a sealed road. Surrounded by pretty hostile country and enduring temperatures that soar well past 40°C, many residents have moved underground.

You can visit **opal showrooms** where local miners sell their finds (these are well signed), or try fossicking around the old diggings, where you'll see interpretative signs. Watch your step.

You can stay underground at the **White Cliffs Underground Motel** (☎08-8091 6677; www.undergroundmotel.com.au; s/d with shared bathroom incl breakfast $115/145; ❄) that is custom-built with a tunnelling machine. It has a pool, a lively dining room and simple, cool, silent rooms. The motel's **museum** on local life is very good – it's free for guests, a pricey $10 for nonguests.

Bourke

POP 2047

Australian poet Henry Lawson once said, 'If you know Bourke, you know Australia.' Immortalised for Australians in the expression 'back of Bourke' (in the middle of nowhere), this town sits on the edge of the outback, miles from anywhere and sprawled along the Darling River.

Sights & Activities

Back O' Bourke Exhibition Centre MUSEUM

(☎02-6872 1321; www.visitbourke.com.au; Kidman Way; adult/child $22/10; ⊙9am-5pm Apr-Oct, to 4pm Mon-Fri Nov-Mar) This highly worthwhile exhibition space follows the legends of the back country (both Indigenous and settler) through interactive displays. It also houses the **Bourke visitor centre** and sells packages that include one or all of the town's major attractions – a river cruise on the *Jandra*, an entertaining outback show (staged at 11am) and a bus tour of the town and surrounds (note that the cruise and show operate April to October only).

For self-exploration, ask for the leaflet called *Back O' Bourke Mud Map Tours*, detailing walks, drives, attractions and businesses in the area, including station stays.

Bourke's Historic Cemetery CEMETERY

(Kidman Way) Bourke's fascinating cemetery is peppered with epitaphs such as 'perished in the bush'. Professor Fred Hollows, the renowned eye surgeon, is buried here.

PV Jandra BOATING

(☎02-6872 1321; departs Kidman's Camp; adult/child $16/10; ⊙9am & 3pm Mon-Sat, 2.30pm Sun Apr-Oct) River trade was once Bourke's lifeline. The three-tiered **wharf** at the northern end of Sturt St is a reconstruction of the original built in 1897 and, on the river, the *PV Jandra* is a replica of an 1895 paddle steamer. Hear local history and view river bird life on its one-hour cruises.

Sleeping & Eating

Kidman's Camp CAMPGROUND, CABINS $$

(☎02-6872 1612; www.kidmanscamp.com.au/bourke/; Cunnamulla Rd, North Bourke; camp sites $30-34, cabins $99-139; 📶❄) An excellent place to base yourself, on river frontage about 8km out of Bourke. The *Jandra* cruise departs from here, and 'Poetry on a Plate' is staged in the grounds. Plus there are gardens, swimming pools and cabins – family-sized with shared bathrooms, or comfy log cabins with bathroom, kitchenette and verandah.

Bourke Riverside Motel MOTEL $$

(☎02-6872 2539; www.bourkeriversidemotel.com.au; 3-13 Mitchell St; s/d from $110/125; ❄📶❄) This rambling motel has riverside gardens and a range of well-appointed rooms and suites: some have heritage overtones and antique furniture, some have kitchen, some are family-sized. A fine choice.

★ **Poetry on a Plate** AUSTRALIAN $$

(www.poetryonaplate.com.au; Kidman's Camp; adult/child $25/10; ⊙6.30pm Tue, Thu & Sun Apr-Oct) A heart-warmingly unique offering: a well-priced night of bush ballads and storytelling around a campfire under the stars, with a simple, slow-cooked meal and dessert to boot. Dress warmly and bring your own drinks, as well as your own camp chair and eating utensils (plate, cutlery and mug) – or pay an extra $5 to hire these.

Getting There & Away

NSW TrainLink (☎13 22 32; www.nswtrainlink.info) Buses run daily to/from Dubbo ($67, 4½ hours), where there are train connections to Sydney.

Southern NSW

Includes ➡

Best Places to Eat

- Biota Dining (p259)
- Raw & Wild (p259)
- Eschalot (p260)
- Wild Brumby Mountain Schnapps (p265)
- Café Darya (p265)

Best Places to Stay

- Links Manor (p259)
- Bundanoon YHA (p259)
- Globe Inn (p260)
- Briardale B&B (p261)
- Lake Crackenback Resort (p266)

Why Go?

Between Sydney and Albury, atmospheric old towns straddle the Hume Hwy, each of them with a claim to fame, be it bushrangers, rich grazing land or old money.

Highlights include the Southern Highlands town of Bowral, and the sleepy heritage settlements of Yass and Gundagai. Right on the New South Wales (NSW)–Victoria border, Albury combines an emerging arts scene with a fine museum and good cafes and bars, and to the north, riverside Wagga Wagga is NSW's biggest inland city.

Northwest of the highway, the land flattens out, becoming redder and drier. The Murray and Murrumbidgee Rivers provide much-needed irrigation in the Riverina district fuelling a food tourism scene around Griffith.

Between Albury and the NSW coast, the Snowy Mountains are defined by the massive hulk of Mt Kosciuszko, Australia's highest summit. Visit in winter for good skiing and alpine sports, or mountain biking, hiking and fishing in summer.

When to Go

Bowral

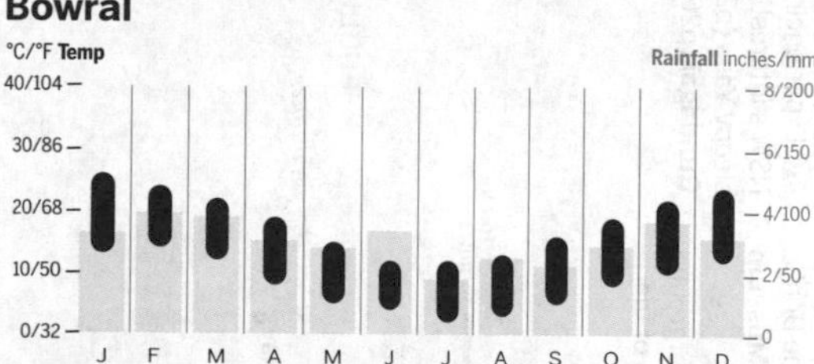

Easter Head to the riverside town of Deniliquin for the Big Sky Blues & Roots Festival.

Jun–Aug Enjoy Australia's best skiing and snowboarding in the Snowy Mountains.

Oct Experience the culinary highlights of the Riverina's annual Taste festival.

Southern NSW Highlights

1. Learning about 'The Don' at Bowral's **Bradman Museum of Cricket** (p259).
2. Exploring the underground **cave systems** (p260) of the Southern Highlands.
3. Experiencing regional NSW's interesting heritage in sleepy **Yass** (p260) and quirky **Gundagai** (p261).
4. Combining art with local cuisine, wine and beer in **Albury** (p260) and **Wagga Wagga** (p262).
5. Discovering your inner Italian in Griffith's main street **eateries** (p264).
6. Mountain biking around the hills of lakeside **Jindabyne** (p264).
7. Skiing and snowboarding in bustling wintertime **Thredbo** (p266).

THE SOUTHERN HIGHLANDS

Bowral

POP 12,154

Just off the Hume Hwy, Bowral is one of the Southern Highlands' main towns, a pretty area revelling in its Englishness. Other towns to explore include Moss Vale.

Sights

★International Cricket Hall of Fame MUSEUM

(☎02-4862 1247; www.internationalcrickethall.com.au; St Jude St, Bowral; adult/child $20/11; ⏲10am-5pm) Bowral is where the late great cricketer Sir Donald Bradman, Australia's most legendary sporting hero, spent his boyhood. Within the Hall of Fame complex, there's a pretty cricket oval, and fans pay homage to Bradman at the **Bradman Museum of Cricket** (www.bradman.com.au), which has an engrossing collection of Ashes and Don-centric memorabilia. The ever-expanding collection showcasing the international game is a must for all sports fans, not just cricket buffs.

Festivals & Events

Bowral Tulip Time Festival CULTURAL

(www.tuliptime.net.au) Spring flower festival. held in September.

Sleeping & Eating

This area is popular with Sydney day trippers and overnighters, and has a good dining and B&B scene. Top spots for lunch include **Centennial Vineyards** (☎02-4861 8700; www.centennialrestaurant.com.au; Centennial Rd; mains $28-39; ⏲noon-3pm Wed-Mon), **Southern Highland Wines** (☎02-4686 2300; www.shw.com.au; Oldbury Rd; mains $27-34; ⏲noon-3pm Thu-Mon) and **McVitty Grove Estate** (☎02-4878 5044; www.feastatmcvitty.com.au; Wombeyan Caves Rd; tapas $18-20, mains $28-34; ⏲10am-4pm Thu-Sun).

★Links Manor GUESTHOUSE $$$

(☎02-4861 1977; www.linkshouse.com.au; 17 Links Rd; r $190-340; ❄📶) This boutique guesthouse has a drawing room and garden courtyard straight out of *Remains of the Day*. Prices are highest on Friday and Saturday.

★Raw & Wild CAFE $$

(250 Bong Bong St; mains $14-24; ⏲8am-5.30pm Sun-Thu, to 9pm Fri & Sat; 🖉) 🌿 Enter through the health food shop to Bowral's best cafe, with a focus on all things organic, local, wild and sustainable. Did we mention it's all very tasty as well? Good beers and wines mean you don't need to be *too* virtuous. On weekends, tapas nights are very popular.

> **THE MIGHTY HUME**
>
> The four-lane Hume Hwy, running nearly 900km from Sydney to Melbourne, has many scenic routes and heritage towns just off it. Note the highway's speed limit of 110km/h is rigorously enforced, and speeding fines are hefty.

★Biota Dining MODERN AUSTRALIAN $$$

(☎02-4862 2005; http://biotadining.com; 18 Kangaloon Rd, Bowral; brunch mains $19, degustation $105-165; ⏲9-11am Sat & Sun, noon-2.30pm Fri-Mon, 6-9.30pm daily) Innovative seasonal menus include interesting dishes like salted cucumber with oysters and beach plants, and the wine list is as good as the weekend brunch. Try the crab and creamed egg sliders with a restorative pepperberry Bloody Mary.

Information

Southern Highlands Visitors Centre (☎02-4871 2888; www.southern-highlands.com.au; 62-70 Main St, Mittagong; ⏲9am-5pm Mon-Fri, to 4pm Sat & Sun) In Mittagong, near Bowral.

Berrima & Bundanoon

POP 246 (BERRIMA), 2419 (BUNDANOON)

South along the Hume Hwy is heritage-classified Berrima, founded in 1829, and featuring galleries, antique shops, and good food and wine. South of Berrima is sleepy Bundanoon, a gateway to Morton National Park.

Sights

Morton National Park NATIONAL PARK

(www.nationalparks.nsw.gov.au; per vehicle $3) Morton National Park features the deep gorges and high sandstone plateaus of the Budawang Range and includes the 81m-high Fitzroy Falls. The **NPWS visitor centre** (☎02-4887 7270; www.nationalparks.nsw.gov.au; Nowra Rd, Fitzroy Falls) has information on walking and hiking.

Sleeping & Eating

★Bundanoon YHA HOSTEL $

(☎02-4883 6010; www.yha.com.au; 115 Railway Ave; dm/d/tr $34/78/102) Occupies a restored

CAVES OF THE SOUTHERN HIGHLANDS

The spectacular limestone **Wombeyan Caves** (☎02-4843 5976; www.nationalparks.nsw.gov.au; Wombeyan Caves Rd; Figtree Cave adult/child $18/12, 2 caves & tour Discovery Pass $30/23; ⊙9am-4pm) lie up an unsealed mountain road 65km northwest of Mittagong. Nearby are walking trails, and a campground with cabins and cottage accommodation.

The **Abercrombie Caves** (☎02-6368 8603; http://abercrombiecaves.com; self-guided/guided tours $18/30; ⊙9am-4pm Thu-Mon) are reached via a turn-off 72km south of Bathurst. The complex has one of the world's largest natural tunnels, the Grand Arch.

About 57km southeast of Yass, along some partly dirt roads, the limestone **Careys Cave** (☎02-6227 9622; www.weejaspercaves.com; adult/child $15.40/9.90; ⊙tours noon, 1.30pm & 3pm Sat & Sun, noon & 1.30pm Fri & Mon) is at Wee Jasper. Phone ahead for tours.

The **Jenolan Caves** (☎1300 763 311; www.jenolancaves.org.au; Jenolan Caves Rd; adult/child from $32/22; ⊙tours 9am-5pm) are also in the region.

Edwardian guesthouse wrapped in a shady verandah.

Bendooley Bar & Grill BISTRO **$$**
(☎02-4877 2235; www.bendooleyestate.com.au; pizza $22-25, mains $27-34; ⊙10am-3pm) A top spot for a leisurely lunch showcasing local and seasonal produce. Try the prawn and chilli pizza with an Aussie craft beer. Attached to Berkelouw's Book Barn & Café.

Josh's Café CAFE **$$**
(☎02-4877 2200; 9 Old Hume Hwy, Berrima; mains $25-32; ⊙noon-3pm Wed-Sat, 6-9pm Thu-Sat, 9am-3pm Sun) An eclectic cafe with a focus on Turkish flavours.

★**Eschalot** MODERN AUSTRALIAN **$$$**
(☎02-4877 1977; www.eschalot.com.au; 24 Old Hume Hwy, Berrima; mains $36-40, 7-course degustation $110; ⊙noon-2.30pm Thu-Sun, 6-9pm Wed-Sat) This heritage sandstone cottage showcases superb modern Australian cooking. Flavours could include sesame-crusted alpaca *tataki* (seared and thinly sliced meat) with watermelon, kaffir cream and wild rice, and desserts are heavenly.

Shopping

Berkelouw's Book Barn & Café BOOKS
(☎02-4877 1370; www.berkelouw.com.au; Old Hume Hwy, Bendooley; ⊙9am-5pm) Three kilometres north of Berrima, Berkelouw's Book Barn & Café stocks secondhand and antiquated tomes.

Getting There & Away

NSW TrainLink (☎13 22 32; www.nswtrainlink.info) trains runs from Bundanoon to Wollongong ($8.60, two hours) and Sydney Central ($21, two hours).

YASS & AROUND

POP 5591

Laced with heritage buildings and sleepy corner pubs, Yass is atmospheric and quiet (thanks to the highway bypass).

Yass Valley Visitor Centre (☎1300 886 014; www.yassvalley.com.au; 259 Comur St; ⊙9.30am-4.30pm Mon-Fri, 10am-4pm Sat & Sun) is in Coronation Park. The adjacent **Yass & District Museum** (☎02-6226 2577; www.yass-history.org.au; adult/child $5/free; ⊙10am-4pm Sat & Sun) has a model of the town in the 1890s. The 1835 **Cooma Cottage** (☎02-6226 1470; www.nationaltrust.org.au/nsw/CoomaCottage; adult/child $5/3; ⊙10am-4pm Fri-Sun) is on the Yass Valley Way on the Sydney side of town. Walking maps from the visitor centre include coverage of the **Hume & Hovell Walking Track**.

In early November, the **Wine, Roses & All That Jazz Festival** features music, gourmet food and wine tasting. The best place to stay is the graceful **Globe Inn** (☎02-6226 3680; www.theglobeinn.com.au; 70 Rossi St; s/d from $130/160).

ALBURY

POP 45,627

This major regional centre on the Murray River sits on the state border opposite its Victorian twin, Wodonga. It's a good launchpad for trips to the snowfields and high country of both Victoria and NSW and for exploring the upper Murray River. It's also a good spot to break the journey between Sydney and Melbourne.

Sights

Library Museum MUSEUM
(☎02-6023 8333; www.alburycity.nsw.gov.au; cnr Kiewa & Swift Sts; ⊙10am-7pm Mon, Wed & Thu, to

5pm Tue & Fri, to 4pm Sat, noon-4pm Sun) FREE Exhibitions and local history, including Indigenous culture and 20th-century migration into the area.

Albury Regional Art Gallery GALLERY
(☎02-6043 5800; www.alburycity.nsw.gov.au; 546 Dean St; ⏲10am-5pm Mon-Fri, to 4pm Sat, noon-4pm Sun) FREE After a $10.5 million makeover, Albury's art gallery reopened in mid-2015 as probably the finest NSW gallery outside of Sydney. Highlights include the Indigenous and contemporary galleries.

Activities

Noreuil Park SWIMMING
Just before the Lincoln Causeway with beautiful shady plane trees and a **river swimming pool**. Try the loop, a magical 20-minute float on your back.

Wonga Wetlands BIRDWATCHING
(Riverina Hwy, Splitters Creek) See up to 154 bird species and an Indigenous camp site established by local Wiradjuri people at this innovative project to restore local wetlands.

Sleeping

Albury Motor Village YHA HOSTEL $
(☎02-6040 2999; www.yha.com.au; 372 Wagga Rd; dm/d/f $30/70/90; @≋) About 4.5km north of central Albury with cabins, vans and backpacker dorms.

★**Briardale B&B** B&B $$
(☎02-6025 5131; www.briardalebnb.com.au; 396 Poplar Dr; r $155-190; ❄) This elegant North Albury B&B has beautiful rooms with an understated antique style. The property adjoins a spacious park.

Quest Albury APARTMENT $$
(☎02-6058 0900; www.questalbury.com.au; 550 Kiewa St; r from $149; ❄📶) Studio suites and apartments feature contemporary decor with soothing dark-wood furniture.

Eating & Drinking

Green Zebra CAFE $
(☎02-6023 1100; www.greenzebra.com.au; 484 Dean St; mains $11.50-17.50; ⏲8am-6.30pm Mon-Fri, 7.30am-3pm Sat & Sun; ✎) 🍃 Homemade pasta, salads and other organic dishes are all winners at this excellent main street cafe.

Mr Benedict CAFE $$
(www.mrbenedict.com.au; 664 Dean St; mains $12-21; ⏲7.30am-3pm Wed-Sun) Our favourite Albury cafe combines the best coffee in town, a well-chosen beer and wine list, and interesting breakfast and lunch blackboard specials.

Kinross Woolshed PUB FOOD $$
(☎02-6043 1155; www.kinrosswoolshed.com.au; Old Sydney Rd, Thurgoona; mains $12-32; ⏲9am-late Mon-Fri, from 7am Sat, from 8am Sun) Drive (or get the shuttle bus) to this country pub in an 1890s woolshed. Country music kicks off on Saturday nights after $2 bacon-and-egg rolls.

Border Wine Room MODERN AUSTRALIAN $$
(www.borderwineroom.com.au; 492a Dean St; mains $28-37; ⏲4pm-midnight Tue-Sat) This classy bar and restaurant delivers innovative food often imbued with subtle hints of Middle Eastern and Asian cuisine.

Bamboo CRAFT BEER
(www.bamboolbury.com.au; 498 Dean St; ⏲noon-3pm Wed-Sun, 5.30pm-late Tue-Sun) Craft beer, Asian street food and occasional live music in the garden courtyard.

YOU'RE HALFWAY THERE...

On the Murrumbidgee River, **Gundagai** is around halfway between Sydney and Melbourne. There's a good riverside campground and motels, but the best place to stay is **Hillview Farmstay** (☎02-6944 7535; www.hillviewfarmstay.com.au; Hume Hwy; 1-/2-/4-bedroom cottage $145/175/450; ❄) on a 1000-acre farm around 34km to the south.

Gold rushes and bushrangers were part of Gundagai's colourful early history. The notorious bushranger Captain Moonlite was tried in Gundagai's 1859 courthouse and is buried in the town's northern **cemetery**. Also in the cemetery is the grave of Yarri, an Indigenous man who saved almost 50 locals during a flood in the early 1800s.

The evocative **Prince Alfred Bridge** – closed to traffic and pedestrians – crosses the flood plain of the river. Alongside is a stretch of the longest wooden railway track in New South Wales.

The **Mt Parnassus Lookout** has 360-degree views. Ask at the visitor centre about the equally scenic **Rotary Lookout**.

About 8km east of town, the famous **Dog on the Tuckerbox** is a poignant sculpture of a dog from a 19th-century bush ballad.

Information

Albury Visitor Information Centre (☎1300 252 879; www.visitalburywodonga.com.au; Railway Pl; ⏰9am-5pm) Opposite the railway station.

Getting There & Away

The **airport** (Borella Rd) is 4km out of town. **Rex** (☎13 17 13; www.rex.com.au), **Virgin Australia** (www.virginaustralia.com.au) and **Qantas** (☎13 13 13; www.qantas.com.au) share routes to Sydney (from $130, 1¼ hours) and Melbourne (from $109, one hour).

Greyhound (☎1300 473 946; www.greyhound.com.au) Buses to Melbourne ($52, 3¾ hours), Wagga Wagga ($35, 2½ hours) and Sydney (from $82, 10 hours).

NSW TrainLink (☎13 22 32; www.nswtrainlink.inf) XPT trains to Wagga Wagga ($19, 1¼ hours) and Sydney ($72, eight hours), and to Melbourne ($46, 3½ hours). NSW TrainLink buses also run to Echuca ($32, 4¼ hours) and **V/Line trains** (☎13 61 96; www.vline.com.au) run to Melbourne ($33, 3¾ hours).

WAGGA WAGGA

POP 46,913

The Murrumbidgee River squiggles around Wagga Wagga's northern end, and riverside eucalypts complement tree-lined streets and lovely gardens. Known as 'place of many crows' to the Wiradjuri people, 'Wagga' is NSW's largest inland city.

Sights & Activities

Botanic Gardens GARDENS
(Macleay St; ⏰sunrise-sunset) Featuring a small **zoo** with kangaroos, wombats and emus, and a free-flight aviary. Nearby Baden Powell Dr leads to a good lookout and scenic **Captain Cook Drive**.

Museum of the Riverina MUSEUM
(www.wagga.nsw.gov.au/museum; Baden Powell Dr; ⏰10am-4pm Tue-Sat, to 2pm Sun) FREE Two sites at the Civic Centre and the Botanic Gardens; the latter site focuses on Wagga's people, places and events.

Wagga Wagga Art Gallery GALLERY
(☎02-6926 9660; www.wagga.nsw.gov.au/gallery; Civic Centre, Morrow St; ⏰10am-4pm Tue-Sat, to 2pm Sun) FREE Local and national artists, and the wonderful **National Art Glass Gallery**.

Wiradjuri Walking Track WALKING
A 12km and a 30km circuit each begin at the visitor centre; the circuits include lookouts and places of Aboriginal significance.

Wagga Beach SWIMMING
At the end of Tarcutta St, this is a good swimming option by the river.

WAGGA WINES & OILS

Harefield Ridge (www.cottontailwines.com.au; 562 Pattersons Rd; ⏰11.30am-late Wed-Sun) Cellar-door tastings and meals.

Wagga Wagga Winery (☎02-6922 1221; www.waggawaggawinery.com.au; Oura Rd; ⏰11am-10pm Thu-Sun) Cellar-door tastings and meals.

Charles Sturt University Winery (www.winery.csu.edu.au; McKeown Dr; ⏰11am-4pm Fri-Sun) Wine, olive oil and cheese tastings.

Wollundry Grove Olives (☎02-6924 6494; www.wollundrygroveolives.com.au; 15 Mary Gilmore Rd; ⏰11am-4pm) Award-winning olive oil and table olives.

Festivals & Events

Taste FOOD, WINE
(www.tasteriverina.com.au) October is a month of tasty culinary events across the Riverina area.

Sleeping

Wagga Wagga Beach Caravan Park CAMPGROUND $
(☎02-6931 0603; www.wwbcp.com.au; 2 Johnston St; sites per adult $25, cabins $115-170; ❄📶) Includes a swimming beach fashioned from the riverbank.

Townhouse Hotel HOTEL $$
(☎02-6921 4337; http://townhousewagga.com.au; 70 Morgan St; r $119-189; ❄📶🏊) Centrally located with excellent service and stylish rooms, although not all have exterior windows.

Dunns B&B B&B $$
(☎02-6925 7771; www.dunnsbedandbreakfast.com.au; 63 Mitchelmore St; s/d $130/140; ❄📶) A pristinely decorated Federation home with a private balcony and sitting room. It's out near the Botanic Gardens.

Eating & Drinking

Mates Gully Organics CAFE $$
(www.matesgully.com.au; 32 Fitzmaurice St; mains $14-33; ⏰8am-4pm Sun-Wed, to 9.30pm Thu-Sat; 📶) 🌿 Shared tables and wall art create a cool vibe, and much of the produce is home-grown. There's also occasional live music.

Oak Room Kitchen & Bar BISTRO $$

(www.townhousewagga.com/the-oakroom/; Townhouse Hotel, 70 Morgan St; bar snacks $7-17, mains $28-39; ⊙6pm-late Mon-Sat) The bustling Oak Room combines small plates, like seared Queensland scallops, with larger meals, including house-made gnocchi and roast lamb from the nearby Riverina region. The bar is open for drinks and snacks from 5pm.

Magpies Nest BISTRO $$$

(☎02-6933 1523; www.magpiesnestwagga.com; 20 Pine Gully Rd; set menu $55; ⊙5.30pm-late Tue-Sat) A delightfully informal restaurant set in a restored 1860s stone stable overlooking the Murrumbidgee River flats and surrounded by olive groves and vineyards.

Thirsty Crow Brewing Co CRAFT BEER

(www.thirstycrow.com.au; 31 Kincaid St; pizzas $19-25; ⊙4-10pm Mon & Tue, 11am-11.30pm Wed-Sat, noon-9.30pm Sun) Come for the tasty beer – our favourite is the hoppy Dark Alleyway IPA – and stay for the wood-fired pizzas.

Information

Visitor Centre (☎1300 100 122; www.visitwagga.com; 183 Tarcutta St; ⊙9am-5pm) Bookings and information.

Getting There & Away

Qantas (☎13 13 13; www.qantas.com.au) flies to Sydney (from $129, one hour) and **Rex** (☎13 17 13; www.rex.com.au) flies to Melbourne (from $129, 1¼ hours) and Sydney (from $126, 1¼ hours).

NSW TrainLink (☎13 22 32; www.nswtrainlink.info) buses leave from **Wagga train station** (☎02-6939 5488, 13 22 32), where you can make bookings. Trains run to Albury ($25, 1¼ hours), Melbourne ($88, five hours) and Sydney Central ($88, 6¾ hours).

GRIFFITH

POP 17,616

You're likely to see Indians, Fijians and Italians in Griffith, a tribute to the cultural diversity of this small agricultural town. The local culinary scene makes Griffith the wine-and-food capital of the Riverina.

Sights & Activities

Pioneer Park Museum MUSEUM

(☎02-6962 4196; cnr Remembrance & Scenic Drs; adult/child $10/6; ⊙9.30am-4pm) North of town with a re-creation of an early Riverina village, and a recently added wine exhibition.

DENILIQUIN: FESTIVAL TOWN

On the NSW Labour Day long weekend in October, sleepy Deniliquin celebrates the **Ute Muster** (www.deniutemuster.com.au; ⊙Oct), attracting thousands for an action-packed weekend in their utes. Events include rodeos, chainsaw sculpturing, woodchopping, and kids' activities. The muster also draws big names in Australian music.

Across the Easter weekend, the **Big Sky Blues & Roots Festival** (www.bigskybluesfestival.com; ⊙Easter weekend) presents an international and eclectic range of artists. Recent events have featured Elvis Costello and the ever-funky George Clinton.

Sir Dudley de Chair Lookout VIEWPOINT

This panoramic lookout is near the **Hermit's Cave**, which was inhabited by an Italian-born man for decades in the early 20th century; watch out for snakes.

McWilliam's Hanwood Estate WINERY

(www.mcwilliamswine.com; Jack McWilliam Rd, Hanwood; ⊙tastings 10am-4pm Tue-Sat) The region's oldest winery (1913).

De Bortoli WINERY

(www.debortoli.com.au; De Bortoli Rd; ⊙9am-5pm Mon-Sat, to 4pm Sun) Try the astounding Black Noble dessert wine.

Catania Fruit Salad Farm FARM

(☎02-6963 0219; www.cataniafruitsaladfarm.com.au; Farm 43, Cox Rd, Handwood; ⊙tours 1.30pm Feb-Nov) Farm tours include a session tasting pickles, relishes, fruits and jams.

Festivals & Events

UnWINEd FOOD, WINE

(www.unwined-riverina.com; ⊙Jun) Wine tastings, lunches and live music.

Sleeping

Myalbangera Outstation HOSTEL $

(☎0428 130 093; Farm 1646, Rankin Springs Rd, Yenda; dm $19-25, d $40-45; ❄) Backpacker option 12km out of town. The owners can assist with finding seasonal work.

Banna Suites APARTMENT $$

(☎02-6962 4278; www.bannasuites.com; 470 Banna Ave; 1-/2-bedroom apt from $150/260) Chic and cosmopolitan apartments right on Griffith's main street.

DON'T MISS

ITALIAN GREATS IN GRIFFITH

➡ Best cannoli: **Bertoldo's Bakery** (324 & 150 Banna Ave; ⏲8.30am-5pm)

➡ Best focaccia: **La Piccola Italian Deli** (444a Banna Ave; ⏲8.30am-5.30pm Mon-Fri, 8.30am-1pm Sat, 9am-noon Sun)

➡ Best pizza: **Belvedere**

Grand Motel MOTEL $$
(☎02-6969 4400; www.grandmotelgriffith.com.au; 454 Banna Ave; r $135-175; ❄📶🏊) Lofty ceilings and bright modern rooms, but avoid the ones without windows.

Eating

Banna Ave is lined with Italian eateries.

Roastery CAFE $$
(www.facebook.com/TheRoasteryGriffith; 232 Banna Ave; mains $12-24; ⏲7am-5pm Mon-Fri, 8am-3pm Sat & Sun) The Roastery sources its own beans from around the world and combines Griffith's best coffee and local Riverina wines with cafe favourites and counter food.

Belvedere ITALIAN, PIZZA $$
(www.facebook.com/Belvedereristorante; 494 Banna Ave; pizzas $14-30, mains $18-30; ⏲noon-late Tue-Sun) Our favourite pizza spot in town, plus the surprise of its very own Tresetti craft lager.

La Scala ITALIAN $$
(☎02-6962 4322; 455b Banna Ave; mains $26-30; ⏲6-9.30pm Tue-Sat) Expect old-school recipes, mural-covered walls and cheap house white by the glass. Just brilliant.

Shopping

Riverina Grove FOOD
(☎02-6962 7988; www.riverinagrove.com.au; 4 Whybrow St) From marinated feta and olive oils to homemade jams and chutney. Lots of free tastings, too.

Information

Various farms and vineyards provide year-round harvest jobs. Ask at the visitor centre.

Visitor Centre (☎02-6962 4145; www.visitgriffith.com.au; cnr Banna & Jondaryan Aves) Bookings and information.

Getting There & Around

Rex (☎13 17 13; www.rex.com.au) flies to Sydney (from $173, 1¼ hours).

All buses stop at the visitor centre, except NSW TrainLink ones, which stop at the train station. Services run to Melbourne ($80, 9½ hours) and Sydney ($70, 10¼ hours) via Mildura ($59, six hours) and Cootamundra ($28, 2¾ hours).

SNOWY MOUNTAINS

The 'Snowies' form part of the Great Dividing Range where it straddles the NSW–Victorian border. They include the highest mountain on the Australian mainland, Mt Kosciuszko (koz-zy-*os*-ko), at 2228m. This is Australia's only true alpine area; snow falls from early June to late August. Summer is also a very pleasant time to visit.

Getting There & Around

Cooma is the Snowy Mountains' eastern gateway, but to best experience the region, base yourself in Jindabyne – especially in summer – or in Thredbo and the ski fields.

If you're only going to ski, public transport is an option, but in summer you'll need a car to fully explore.

At the time of writing, there were no flights to the Snowy Mountains.

Greyhound (☎1300 4739 46863; www.greyhound.com.au) Regular skiing packages from Sydney and Canberra in winter.

Murrays (☎13 22 51; www.murrays.com.au) Daily winter bus services including skiing packages from Sydney and Canberra.

NSW TrainLink (☎13 22 32; www.nswtrainlink.info) Links Cooma year-round to Canberra ($14, 1¼ hours) and Sydney Central ($53, seven hours). At the time of writing, buses linking Jindabyne with Canberra and Cooma were being trialled.

Snowliner Coaches (☎02-6452 1584; www.snowliner.com.au) Offers a public-accessible school run from Cooma to Jindabyne (adult/child $15/8) during NSW school terms.

V/Line (☎13 61 96; www.vline.com.au) Buses from Canberra to Cooma ($13, 1¼ hours).

Jindabyne

Jindabyne is the closest town to Kosciuszko National Park's major ski resorts, and more than 20,000 visitors pack in over winter. In summer, the town assumes a more peaceful vibe, and fishing in the rivers and lake – and increasingly excellent mountain biking – are the mainstay activities.

Activities

Sacred Ride ADVENTURE SPORTS
(☎02-6456 1988, 1300 736 581; www.sacredride.com.au; 6 Thredbo Tce) Gear hire and activities

including wake boarding, mountain biking, white-water rafting, abseiling, canoeing and kayaking. These are the guys to see regarding mountain biking.

Mountain Adventure Centre SPORTS
(☎1800 623 459; www.mountainadventurecentre.com.au; Shop 5, Snowline Centre, cnr Kosciuszko & Thredbo Rds; ⏲9am-4pm Nov-May, 8am-6pm Jun-Oct) Outdoor gear for sale and hire, and adventure activities can be arranged. In summer, try mountain biking, canoeing or hiking, and winter offers cross-country skiing, telemarking and snowshoeing.

Discovery Holiday Parks BOATING
(☎02-6456 2099; www.discoveryholidayparks.com.au; cnr Kosciuszko Rd & Alpine Way) Motorboats, canoes and paddleboats for hire.

Sleeping

Winter prices increase greatly, so book ahead. See **Jindabyne & Snowy Mountains Accommodation Centre** (☎1800 527 622; www.snowaccommodation.com.au) and **Visit Snowy Mountains** (☎02-6457 7132; www.visitsnowymountains.com.au) for holiday rentals.

Snowy Mountains Backpackers HOSTEL $
(☎1800 333 468; www.snowybackpackers.com.au; 7-8 Gippsland St; summer dm/d $25/60, winter dm $30-50, d $90-140; @) This good-value place in the village has clean dorms, en suite rooms, sunny public spaces, and advice on transport and activities.

Banjo Paterson Inn HOTEL $$
(☎02-6456 2372; www.banjopatersoninn.com.au; 1 Kosciuszko Rd; r summer $100-130, winter $150-230) The best rooms have balconies and lake views. Other facilities include a rowdy bar and microbrewery. In winter it's extremely popular.

Eating

In winter, Italian, Indian, Japanese and Mexican flavours are all available, but fewer restaurants open during summer.

Red Door Roastery CAFE $
(www.facebook.com/TheRedDoorRoastery; Town Centre Mall; mains $9-16; ⏲7.30am-3pm) Grab an outdoor table with lake views and plan your day's adventure over 'Jindy's' best coffee and an all-day menu with a terrific breakfast wrap.

★**Wild Brumby Mountain Schnapps** BISTRO $$
(www.wildbrumby.com; Alpine Way; mains $12-30; ⏲10am-5pm) Located between Jindabyne and Thredbo, this is the place to go for punchy schnapps. Sit on the verandah and team a beer with a cheese and charcuterie platter.

★**Café Darya** MIDDLE EASTERN $$
(☎02-6457 1867; www.cafedarya.com.au; Snowy Mountains Plaza; mezze $14, mains $29-32; ⏲6-9pm Tue-Sat) Fill up on slow-cooked lamb shank in Persian spices and rose petals or a rustic trio of dips. BYO beer and wine. Cash only.

Drinking & Nightlife

Banjo Patterson Inn MICROBREWERY, BAR
(www.banjopatersoninn.com.au; 1 Kosciuszko Rd) Kosciuszko Pale Ale is brewed on site, and there's decent food at Clancy's Bistro. Hitting the dance floor at the winter-only Banjo's Nightclub completes a big night out.

Information

Snowy Region Visitor Centre (☎02-6450 5600; www.environment.nsw.gov.au; Kosciuszko Rd; ⏲9am-4pm) Operated by the NPWS with display areas, a cinema and cafe. Ask about fishing, and winery and brewery visits.

Kosciuszko National Park

Covering 673,492 hectares and stretching for 150km, this is the jewel in NSW's national-park crown.

In spring and summer, walking trails and camp sites are framed by alpine flowers. Caves, limestone gorges, historic huts and homesteads also feature, and cycling and mountain biking are very popular.

If you're driving straight through the park, no park fees are payable, but if you're

SKIING THE SNOWYS

The ski season at **Thredbo** (☎1300 020 589; www.thredbo.com.au) and the Snowy's other ski areas of **Perisher Blue** (☎02-6459 4495, 1300 369 909; www.perisherblue.com.au) and **Charlotte Pass** (www.charlottepass.com.au) is usually from early June to late August.

Thredbo's terrains suit skiers of all experiences. Options include the Supertrail (3.7km), the easy Village Trail (5km), or the challenging Karels T-Bar (5.9km).

Perisher Valley, Smiggin Holes, Mt Blue Cow and Guthega make up Perisher Blue.

At the base of Mt Kosciuszko, Charlotte Pass is one of the highest, oldest and most isolated ski resorts in Australia. It's also a good base for summer activities.

CLIMBING AUSTRALIA'S HIGHEST MOUNTAIN

Australia's highest mountain is relatively easy to climb, although getting to the top can still be strenuous. Hiking is possible when there's no snow, but weather conditions can be changeable throughout the year.

Guided options include the **Mt Kosciuszko Day Walk** (www.thredbo.com.au; adult/child/family $44/30/88; ⏲10am-3.30pm Tue, Thu & Sat late Oct-late Apr) or the **Sunset Tour** (www.thredbo.com.au; adult $93; ⏲specific days around Christmas & New Year).

Solo options are as follows:

Mt Kosciuszko Track From Thredbo, take the **Kosciuszko Express Chairlift**. From the top of the lift it's a steep 13km-return climb to the summit and back.

Summit Walk Drive to the end of the paved road above Charlotte Pass, then follow a wide gravel track. It's a 9km climb to the summit (18km return), including a steep final climb.

Main Range Track Also beginning above Charlotte Pass, this strenuous 20km loop includes minor creeks en route.

overnighting or driving beyond Jindabyne towards Charlotte Pass, the fee is $16 per vehicle per 24 hours.

Thredbo

At 1370m, Thredbo is oft lauded as Australia's number-one ski resort. A smattering of worthwhile summer activities also feature.

Sights & Activities

Thredbo Landslide Memorial MEMORIAL

(Bobuck Lane) This memorial can be seen along Bobuck Lane where the two lodges, Carinya and Bimbadeen, were destroyed in a 1997 landslide. The 18 posts supporting the platform signify the 18 lives tragically lost.

Bobsled ADVENTURE SPORTS

(1/6/10 rides $7/36/50; ⏲10am-4.30pm year-round) Seven-hundred-metre, luge-style track down the mountain.

Kosciuszko Express Chairlift CHAIRLIFT

(day pass adult/child return $34/18; ⏲year-round) Ascends 560m. Climbing Mt Kosciuszko is possible from the top station.

Thredbo Snow Sports Outdoor Adventures ADVENTURE SPORTS

(☎02-6459 4100; www.thredbo.com.au) Winter alpine adventures.

K7 Kosciuszko Adventures ADVENTURE SPORTS

(☎0421 862 354; www.k7adventures.com) Summer and winter adventures.

Sleeping

Thredbo YHA Lodge HOSTEL $

(☎02-6457 6376; www.yha.com.au; 8 Jack Adams Path; summer tw $99, dm/tw without bathroom $35/85; @) Thredbo's best budget option with great common areas. Rates surge in winter and adults must be YHA members.

Candlelight Lodge LODGE $$

(☎1800 020 900, 02-6457 6318; www.candlelightlodge.com.au; 32 Diggings Tce; s/d winter from $210/250, summer from $135/180; ☏) This Tyrolean lodge has great rooms, all with views. The restaurant's fondue (winter only) is fabulous.

★ **Lake Crackenback Resort** RESORT $$$

(☎1800 020 524; www.lakecrackenback.com.au; 1650 Alpine Way; r from $255; ❄@☏≋) Apartments and chalets are classy at this lakeside spa resort, the restaurants are excellent, and plenty of activities are on offer throughout winter and summer.

Eating & Drinking

Gourmet 42 CAFE $

(100 Mowamba Pl, Village Sq; mains $12-19; ⏲7.30am-3pm) Hungover snowboarders and sleepy bar staff rock up for coffee, soup and pasta.

Knickerbocker MODERN AUSTRALIAN $$

(☎02-6457 6844; www.jeanmichelknickerbocker.com.au; Diggings Tce; mains $32-33; ⏲noon-2pm Sat & Sun, 6pm-late Wed-Sun) Sit indoors for alpine cosiness, or rug up on the deck with brilliant views. Seriously gourmet meals go down well after drinks in the bar (from 4pm).

Information

Thredbo Visitor Centre (☎02-6459 4294; www.thredbo.com.au; Friday Dr; ⏲9am-5pm summer, 8am-6pm winter) Bookings and information.

Brisbane & Around

Includes ➡

Best Places to Eat

- ➡ Brew (p286)
- ➡ Kwan Brothers (p289)
- ➡ Baker's Arms (p286)
- ➡ Varias (p308)
- ➡ Island Fruit Barn (p303)

Best Places to Stay

- ➡ Latrobe Apartment (p286)
- ➡ Limes (p282)
- ➡ Bowen Terrace (p282)
- ➡ Casabella Apartment (p286)
- ➡ Vacy Hall (p310)

Why Go?

Australia's most underrated city? Booming Brisbane is an energetic river town on the way up, with an edgy arts scene, pumping nightlife, and great coffee and restaurants. Lush parks and historic buildings complete the picture, all folded into the elbows of the meandering Brisbane River.

Brisbanites are out on the streets: the weather is brilliant and so are the bodies. Fit-looking locals get up early to go jogging, swimming, cycling, kayaking or rock climbing, or just to walk the dog. And when it's too hot outside, Brisbane's subcultural undercurrents run cool and deep, with bookshops, globally inspired restaurants, cafes, bars and band rooms aplenty.

East of 'Brizzy' is Moreton Bay, with its low-lying sandy isles, beaches and passing parade of whales, turtles and dolphins. To the west is the rural inland hub of Toowoomba (also underrated) and the surprising Granite Belt Wine Region, which bottles up some impressive drops.

When to Go

Brisbane

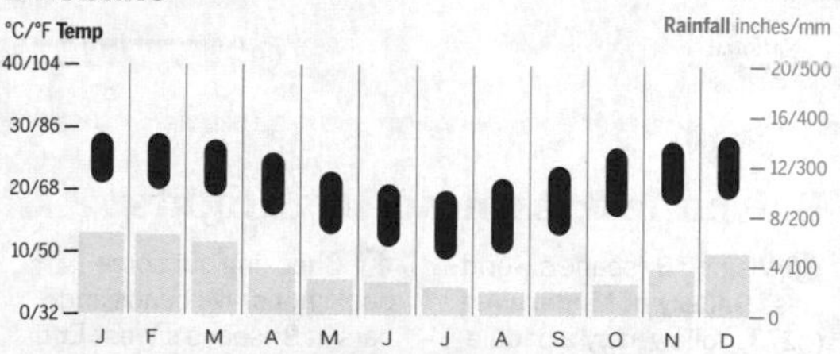

Jan Brisbane swelters during summer, making it the perfect time to head to North Stradbroke Island.

May–Aug Cool, mild temperatures (bring a jacket) and clear skies – Brisbane is at its best!

Sep Spring has sprung. Warm temperatures and the very arty Brisbane Festival.

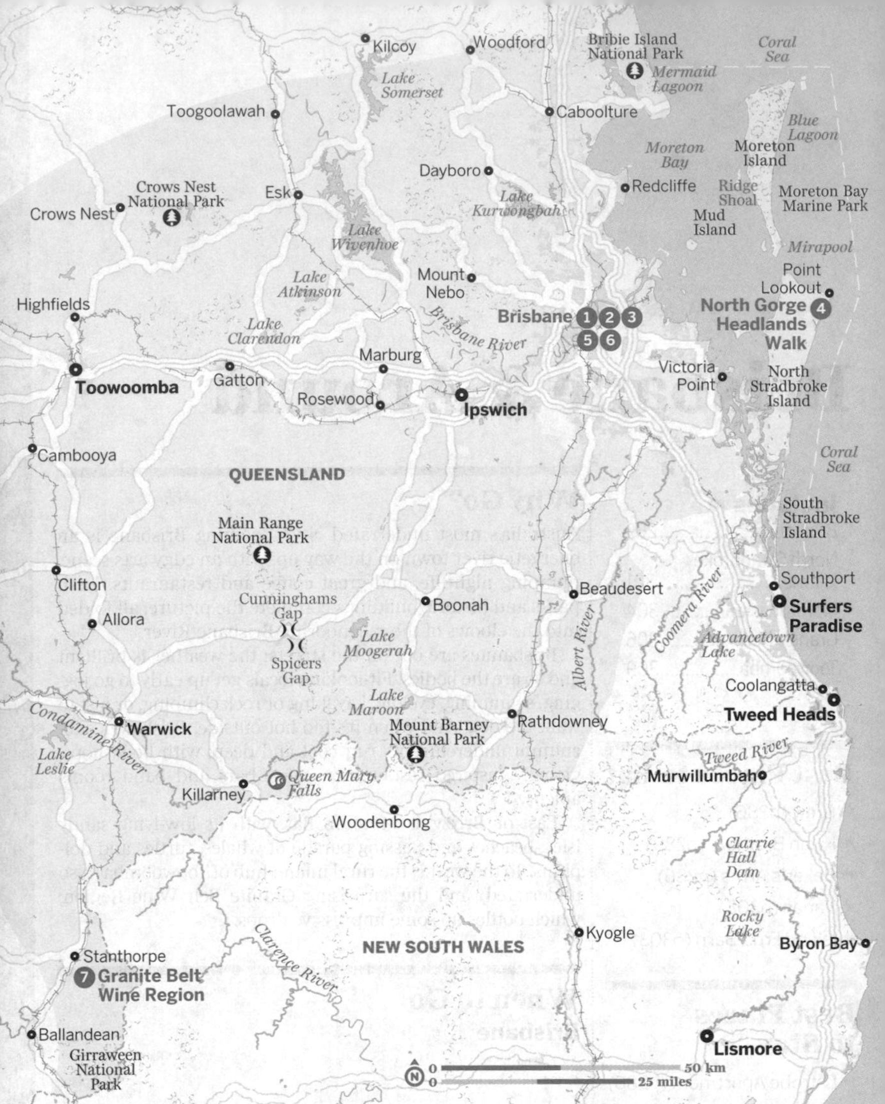

Brisbane & Around Highlights

1. Visiting Brisbane's world-class **Gallery of Modern Art** (p273), followed by a paddle at Streets Beach in the **South Bank Parklands** (p274).

2. Catching some live comedy at the **Brisbane Powerhouse** (p296), before a night on the tiles in **Fortitude Valley** (p293).

3. Checking out some bookshops, live bands and bars in Brisbane's **West End** (p294).

4. Roaming along the **North Gorge Headlands Walk** (p302) on North Stradbroke Island, spotting turtles, rays and dolphins offshore.

5. Going bush in the city: hiking up bushy slopes to the **Mt Coot-tha Lookout** (p272).

6. Chugging up, down or across the **Brisbane River** (p277) on a ferry.

7. Meandering between cellar doors in the **Granite Belt Wine Region** (p307).

BRISBANE IN...

Two Days

Start with breakfast in Brisbane's boho West End – we like **Gunshop Café** (p291) and the **Burrow** (p290) – then saunter across to the **South Bank Parklands** (p274). Spend a few hours swanning around at the **Gallery of Modern Art** (p273), then grab some lunch at a riverside eatery and cool off with a swim at **Streets Beach** (p275). As the evening rolls in, jump on a ferry to the **Brisbane Powerhouse** (p275) in New Farm for a bite, a drink or perhaps a show.

On day two head downtown for a gander at the mix of old and new architecture, visiting the newly renovated **City Hall** (p273) – don't miss the **Museum of Brisbane** (p273) on the 3rd floor – and the **Treasury Building** (p273), before ambling through the lush **City Botanic Gardens** (p273). Finish the day in **Fortitude Valley**: a brew at **Alfred & Constance** (p293), a noodle soup in **Chinatown** (p274), and a night of indulgences in the bars and clubs.

Four Days

On day three check out the rather French cafes in New Farm – **Chouquette** (p289) is hard to beat – then scoot over to Paddington to check out the retro shops. Take a drive up to the lookout on top of **Mt Coot-tha Reserve** (p269) then meander away an hour or two in the **Brisbane Botanic Gardens** (p272). Dress up for dinner and drinks in the city: slake your thirst at **Super Whatnot** (p293) then eat in style at **E'cco** (p287).

On day four take a river cruise to **Lone Pine Koala Sanctuary** (p272). Recount the day's wildlife encounters over a beer and a steak at the **Breakfast Creek Hotel** (p292) then head back to the West End for beers at the **Archive Beer Boutique** (p294) and a live band at **Lock 'n' Load** (p295).

BRISBANE

POP 2.2 MILLION

Brisbane's charms are evident: the arts, the cafes, the bars, the weather, the old Queenslander houses, the go-get-'em attitude. But perhaps it's the Brisbane River itself – which broke so many hearts when it flooded in 2011 and 2013 – that gives the city its edge. The river's organic convolutions carve the city into a patchwork of urban villages, each with a distinct style and topography: bohemian, low-lying West End; hip, hilltop Paddington; exclusive, peninsular New Farm; prim, pointy Kangaroo Point. Move from village to village and experience Queensland's diverse, eccentric, happening capital.

History

The first settlement in the Brisbane area was established at Redcliffe on Moreton Bay in 1824 as a penal colony for Sydney's more recalcitrant convicts. After struggling with inadequate water supplies and hostility from the displaced local Aboriginal population, the colony was relocated to the banks of the Brisbane River, the site of the city centre today. The new site suffered at the hands of numerous crooked warders and was abandoned in 1839. Subsequently, the Moreton Bay area was thrown open to free settlers in 1842, marking the beginning of Brisbane's rise to prominence.

By the time of Queensland's separation from New South Wales in 1859, Brisbane had a population of around 6000. Huge wealth flowed into the city from the new pastoral and gold-mining enterprises in the Darling Downs, and grandiose buildings were erected to reflect this new-found affluence. The frontier-town image was hard to shake off, however, and it wasn't until the 1982 Commonwealth Games and Expo '88 that Brisbane's reputation as a cultural centre came into being.

Sights

Greater Brisbane

Mt Coot-tha Reserve NATURE RESERVE

(Map p270; www.brisbane.qld.gov.au; Mt Coot-tha Rd, Mt Coot-tha; 24hr) FREE A 15-minute drive or bus ride from the city, this huge bush reserve is topped by 287m Mt Coot-tha (more of a hill, really). On the hillsides you'll find the Brisbane Botanic Gardens, the Sir Thomas Brisbane Planetarium, walking trails and

Greater Brisbane

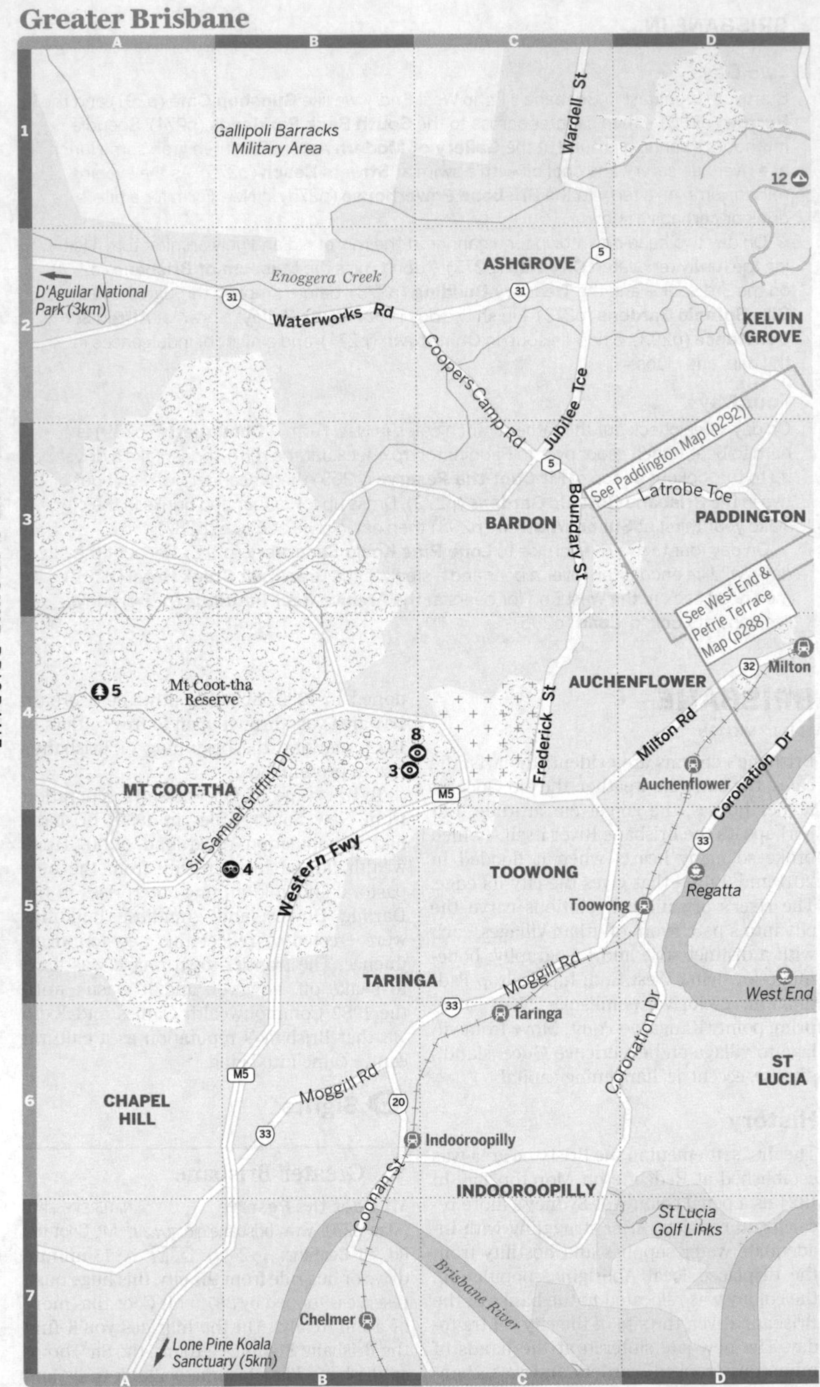

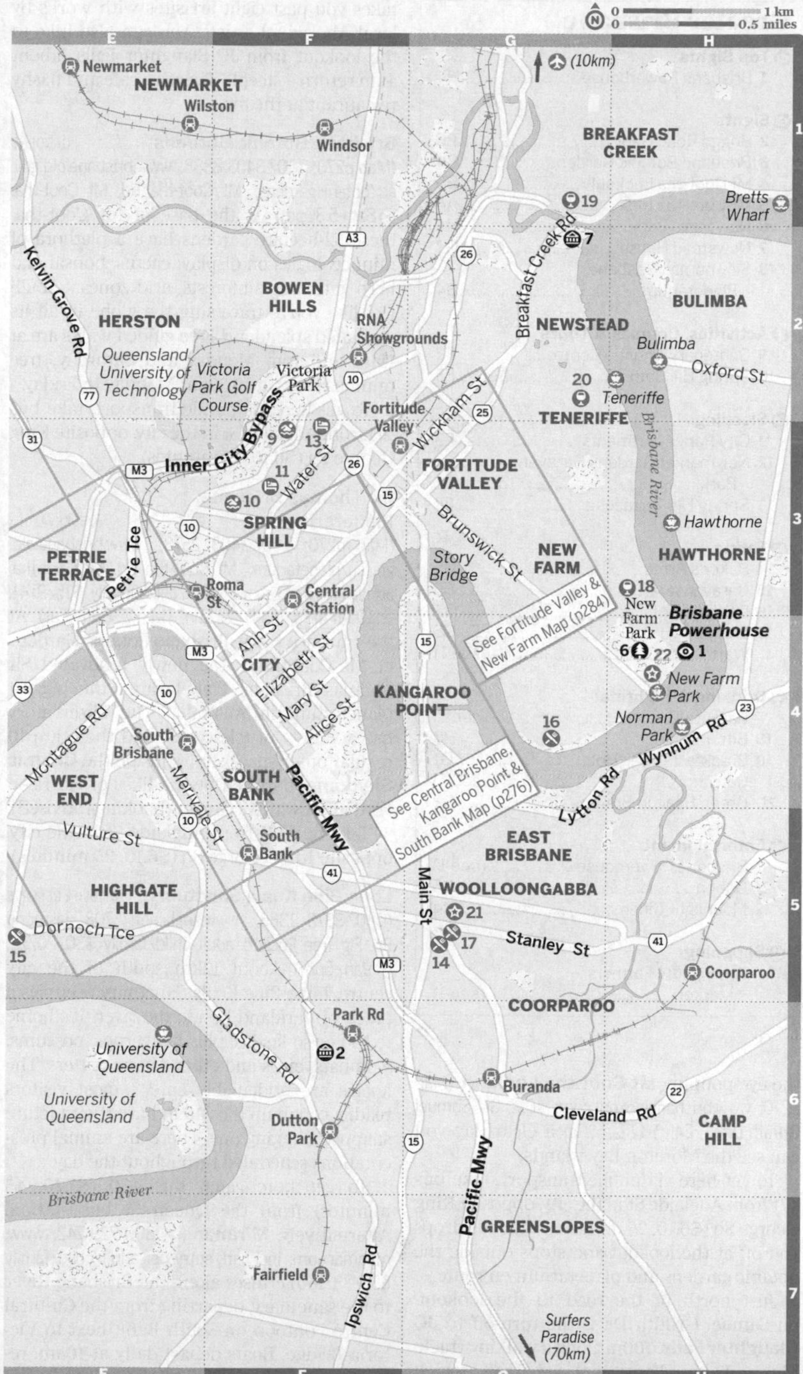
0 1 km
0 0.5 miles
E
F
G
H
(10km)
Newmarket
NEWMARKET
Wilston
Windsor
BREAKFAST CREEK
Bretts Wharf
19
Breakfast Creek Rd
7
A3
26
Kelvin Grove Rd
BOWEN HILLS
BULIMBA
HERSTON
RNA Showgrounds
NEWSTEAD
Bulimba
Oxford St
Queensland University of Technology
Victoria Park Golf Course
Victoria Park
10
20
Teneriffe
77
Inner City Bypass
Fortitude Valley
Wickham St
25
TENERIFFE
Brisbane River
9
13
31
M3
11
Water St
26
FORTITUDE VALLEY
10
15
SPRING HILL
Brunswick St
Hawthorne
10
HAWTHORNE
PETRIE TERRACE
Petrie Tce
Story Bridge
NEW FARM
Roma St
Central Station
18
New Farm Park
See Fortitude Valley & New Farm Map (p284)
Brisbane Powerhouse
Ann St
M3
15
6
22
1
CITY
Elizabeth St
33
10
Mary St
KANGAROO POINT
New Farm Park
Alice St
Norman Park
23
Montague Rd
South Brisbane
16
Wynnum Rd
WEST END
Merivale St
SOUTH BANK
Pacific Mwy
See Central Brisbane, Kangaroo Point & South Bank Map (p276)
Lytton Rd
10
Vulture St
South Bank
EAST BRISBANE
Main St
41
HIGHGATE HILL
WOOLLOONGABBA
21
Dornoch Tce
17
Stanley St
15
14
41
M3
Coorparoo
COORPAROO
Park Rd
Gladstone Rd
University of Queensland
2
Buranda
University of Queensland
22
Cleveland Rd
CAMP HILL
Dutton Park
15
Pacific Mwy
Brisbane River
GREENSLOPES
Fairfield
Ipswich Rd
Surfers Paradise (70km)
1
2
3
4
5
6
7

Greater Brisbane

Top Sights
1 Brisbane Powerhouse H4

Sights
2 Boggo Road Gaol F6
3 Brisbane Botanic Gardens B4
4 Mt Coot-tha Lookout B5
5 Mt Coot-tha Reserve A4
6 New Farm Park H4
7 Newstead House G2
8 Sir Thomas Brisbane Planetarium B4

Activities, Courses & Tours
9 Centenary Aquatic Centre F3
10 Spring Hill Baths F3

Sleeping
11 City Park Apartments F3
12 Newmarket Gardens Caravan Park D1
13 Spring Hill Terraces F3

Eating
14 Baker's Arms G5
15 Caravanserai E5
16 Double Shot G4
17 Enoteca G5
Watt .... (see 1)

Drinking & Nightlife
Bar Alto .... (see 1)
18 Bitter Suite H3
19 Breakfast Creek Hotel G1
Canvas .... (see 14)
20 Green Beacon Brewing Co G2

Entertainment
Brisbane Powerhouse .... (see 1)
21 Gabba G5
22 Moonlight Cinema H4

Shopping
Jan Powers Farmers Market .... (see 1)

the eye-popping **Mt Coot-tha Lookout** (Map p270; www.brisbanelookout.com; 1012 Sir Samuel Griffith Dr; 24hr) FREE. On a clear day you can see the Moreton Bay islands.

To get here via public transport, take bus 471 from Adelaide St in the city, opposite King George Sq ($6.10, 25 minutes). The bus drops you off at the lookout and stops outside the botanic gardens and planetarium en route.

Just north of the road to the lookout, on Samuel Griffith Dr, is the turn-off to **JC Slaughter Falls**, 700m along a walking track; plus a 1.5km **Aboriginal Art Trail**, which takes you past eight art sites with works by local Aboriginal artists. You can also hike to the lookout from JC Slaughter Falls (about 4km return – steep!). There's a cafe and flashy restaurant at the top.

Brisbane Botanic Gardens GARDENS
(Map p270; 07-3403 8888; www.brisbane.qld.gov.au/botanicgardens; Mt Coot-tha Rd, Mt Coot-tha; 8am-5.30pm) At the base of Mt Coot-tha, these 52-hectare gardens have a plethora of mini ecologies on display: cactus, bonsai and herb gardens, rainforests, arid zones… You'll feel like you're traversing the globe in all its vegetated splendour! Free guided walks are at 11am and 1pm Monday and Saturday; free minibus tours at 10.30am Monday to Friday.

To get here via public transport, take bus 471 from Adelaide St in the city, opposite King George Sq ($6.10, 25 minutes).

Sir Thomas Brisbane Planetarium OBSERVATORY
(Map p270; 07-3403 2578; www.brisbane.qld.gov.au/planetarium; Mt Coot-tha Rd, Mt Coot-tha; admission free, shows adult/child/family $15/9/41; 10am-4pm Tue-Fri & Sun, 11am-7.30pm Sat) At the entrance to the Brisbane Botanic Gardens at Mt Coot-tha is the newly renovated Sir Thomas Brisbane Planetarium, the biggest planetarium in Australia. The observatory has a variety of telescopes, and there are 10 regular outer-space shows inside the **Cosmic Skydome**, narrated by the likes of Harrison Ford and Ewan McGregor (bookings advised).

Take bus 471 from Adelaide St in the city, opposite King George Sq ($6.10, 25 minutes).

Lone Pine Koala Sanctuary WILDLIFE RESERVE
(07-3378 1366; www.koala.net; 708 Jesmond Rd, Fig Tree Pocket; adult/child/family $30/20/72; 9am-5pm) About 12km south of the city centre, Lone Pine Koala Sanctuary occupies a patch of parkland beside the river. It's home to 130 or so koalas, plus kangaroos, possums, wombats, birds and other Aussie critters. The koalas are undeniably cute – most visitors readily cough up the $16 to have their picture snapped hugging one. There are animal presentations scheduled throughout the day.

To get here catch bus 430 ($7.20, 45 minutes) from the Queen St bus station. Alternatively, **Mirimar** (1300 729 742; www.miramar.com; incl park entry per adult/child/family $55/33/160) cruises along the Brisbane River to the sanctuary, departing from the Cultural Centre Pontoon on South Bank next to Victoria Bridge. Boats depart daily at 10am, returning from Lone Pine at 1.45pm.

Newstead House HISTORIC BUILDING
(Map p270; www.newsteadhouse.com.au; cnr Breakfast Creek Rd & Newstead Ave, Newstead; adult/child/family $9/6/20; ⏲10am-4pm Mon-Thu, 2-5pm Sun) On a breezy hill overlooking the river, Brisbane's oldest house dates from 1846 and is beautifully fitted out with Victorian furnishings, antiques, clothing and period displays. It's a modest, peach-coloured L-shaped affair, surrounded by manicured lawns with lovely river views. Wedding photographers do their best to avoid the big brick electrical substation in the gardens. Free Sunday afternoon concerts.

Central Brisbane

★City Hall LANDMARK
(Map p276; ☎07-3403 8463; www.brisbane.qld.gov.au; King George Sq; ⏲9am-5pm) FREE Overlooking King George Sq, this fine 1930s sandstone edifice is fronted by a row of sequoia-sized Corinthian columns. It has an 85m-high clock tower with a fabulous lookout, from which bells peal across the city rooftops. In 2013 the hall opened up again after a three-year renovation. Free guided tours run hourly from 10.15am to 3.30pm; free clock tower tours run every 15 minutes from 10.45am to 4.45pm. Phone for guided-tour bookings; clock tower tours are on a first-come, first-served basis. Also here is the excellent Museum of Brisbane.

★Museum of Brisbane MUSEUM
(Map p276; ☎07-3339 0800; www.museumofbrisbane.com.au; Level 3, Brisbane City Hall, King George Sq; ⏲10am-5pm) FREE Inside Brisbane's renovated City Hall, this excellent little museum illuminates the city from a variety of viewpoints, with interactive exhibits exploring both social history and the current cultural landscape. When we visited, the three long-term exhibits were a fabulous display on the islands and history of Moreton Bay, with excellent Aboriginal content; an exhibit on the history of the Brisbane River; and an exhibition on iconic Queensland novelist David Malouf, featuring work from five artists he's inspired.

Commissariat Store Museum MUSEUM
(Map p276; www.queenslandhistory.org; 115 William St; adult/child/family $6/3/12; ⏲10am-4pm Tue-Fri) Built by convicts in 1829, this former government storehouse is the oldest occupied building in Brisbane. Inside is an immaculate little museum devoted to convict and colonial history. Don't miss the convict 'fingers' and the exhibit on Italians in Queensland.

City Botanic Gardens PARK
(Map p276; www.brisbane.qld.gov.au; Alice St; ⏲24hr; 📶) Brisbane's favourite green space descends gently from the Queensland University of Technology campus to the river: a mass of lawns, tangled Moreton Bay figs, bunya pines, macadamia trees and Tai Chi troupes. Free guided tours leave the rotunda at 11am and 1pm daily.

Old Government House HISTORIC BUILDING
(Map p276; ☎07-3138 8005; www.ogh.qut.edu.au; 2 George St; ⏲10am-4pm Sun-Fri) FREE Hailed as Queensland's most important historic building, this 1862 gem was designed by estimable government architect Charles Tiffin as an appropriately plush residence for Sir George Bowen, Queensland's first governor. The lavish innards were restored in 2009. Free morning guided tours Tuesday to Thursday: phone for bookings.

Treasury Building HISTORIC BUILDING
(Map p276; www.treasurybrisbane.com.au; cnr Queen & William Sts; ⏲24hr) FREE At the western end of the Queen St Mall is the magnificent Italian Renaissance–style Treasury Building, dating from 1889. No tax collectors inside – just Brisbane's casino.

Opposite the casino fronting a grassy plaza stands the equally gorgeous former **Land Administration Building**, which has been converted into a five-star hotel called Treasury (p282).

South Bank

On South Bank, just over Victoria Bridge from the Central Business District (CBD), the **Queensland Cultural Centre** is the epicentre of Brisbane's cultural life. It's a huge compound that includes concert and theatre venues, four museums and the Queensland State Library.

★Gallery of Modern Art GALLERY
(GOMA; Map p276; www.qagoma.qld.gov.au; Stanley Pl; ⏲10am-5pm; 📶) FREE All angular glass, concrete and black metal, must-see GOMA focuses on Australian art from the 1970s to today. Continually changing and often confronting, exhibits range from painting, sculpture and photography to video, installation and film. There's also an arty bookshop, kids' activity rooms, a cafe and free guided tours at 11am, 1pm and 2pm. Brilliant!

OFF THE BEATEN TRACK

D'AGUILAR NATIONAL PARK

Suburban malaise? Slake your wilderness cravings at this 500-sq-km **national park** (www.nprsr.qld.gov.au/parks/daguilar; 60 Mount Nebo Rd, The Gap), just 10km northwest of the city centre but worlds away (it's pronounced 'dee-ag-lar'). At the park's entrance the **Walkabout Creek visitor information centre** (07-3512 2300; www.walkaboutcreek.com.au; wildlife centre adult/child/family $6.80/3.30/17.10; 9am-4.15pm) has maps. Also here is the **South East Queensland Wildlife Centre** where you can see a resident platypus, plus turtles, lizards, pythons and gliders. There's also a small walk-through aviary, and a cafe. A new multi-million-dollar redevelopment is slated: come back in 2020 and see if it's finished.

Walking trails in the park range from a few hundred metres to 13km, and include the 6km Morelia Track at Manorina day-use area and the 4.3km Greene's Falls Track at Mt Glorious. Mountain biking and horse riding are also options. You can camp in the park too, in remote, walk-in bush **camp sites** (13 74 68; http://parks.nprsr.qld.gov.au/permits; per person $5.75). There are a couple of walks (1.5km and 5km) kicking off from the visitor centre, but other walks are a fair distance away (so you'll need your own wheels).

To get here catch bus 385 ($7.20, 30 minutes) from Roma St Station to the Gap Park 'n' Ride, then walk a few hundred metres up the road.

South Bank Parklands PARK

(Map p276; www.visitsouthbank.com.au; Grey St; dawn-dusk) This beautiful green strip is home to performance spaces, sculptures, buskers, eateries, bars, pockets of rainforest, barbecue areas, bougainvillea-draped pergolas and hidden lawns. The big-ticket attractions here are Streets Beach, a kitsch artificial swimming beach resembling a tropical lagoon (packed on weekends); and the London Eye-style **Wheel of Brisbane** (Map p276; 07-3844 3464; www.thewheelofbrisbane.com.au; Grey St; adult/child/family $17.50/12/50; 11am-9.30pm Mon-Thu, 10am-11pm Fri & Sat, 10am-10pm Sun), which offers 360-degree views from its 60m heights. Rides last around 10 minutes and include audio commentary (and air-con!).

Queensland Art Gallery GALLERY

(QAG; Map p276; www.qagoma.qld.gov.au; Melbourne St; 10am-5pm) FREE Duck into the QAG to see the fine permanent collection. Australian art dates from the 1840s to the 1970s: check out works by celebrated masters including Sir Sydney Nolan, Arthur Boyd, William Dobell and George Lambert. Free guided tours at 11am, 1pm and 2pm.

Queensland Museum & Sciencentre MUSEUM

(Map p276; www.southbank.qm.qld.gov.au; cnr Grey & Melbourne Sts; Queensland museum admission free, Sciencentre adult/child/family $14.50/11.50/44.50; 9.30am-5pm) Queensland's history is given the once-over here, with interesting exhibits including a skeleton of the state's own dinosaur *Muttaburrasaurus* (aka 'Mutt'), and the *Avian Cirrus*, the tiny plane in which Queenslander Bert Hinkler made the first England-to-Australia solo flight in 1928. Have a snack to a whale soundtrack in the outdoor 'Whale Mall'.

Also here is the Sciencentre, an educational fun house with over 100 hands-on, interactive exhibits that delve into life science and technology. Expect long queues during school holidays.

Fortitude Valley

Chinatown AREA

(Map p284; Duncan St, Fortitude Valley; 24hr) Brisbane's Chinatown occupies just one street (check out the replica Tang dynasty archway and the lions at the Ann St end), but it's just as flamboyant and flavour-filled as its Sydney and Melbourne counterparts. Glazed flat ducks hang behind steamy windows; aromas of Thai, Chinese, Vietnamese, Laotian and Japanese cooking fill the air. There are free outdoor movies during summer, and the whole place goes nuts during Chinese New Year festivities.

Institute of Modern Art GALLERY

(IMA; Map p284; www.ima.org.au; 420 Brunswick St, Fortitude Valley; noon-6pm Tue-Sat, to 8pm Thu) FREE The Institute of Modern Art in the Judith Wright Centre of Contemporary Arts (p296) is an excellent noncommercial gallery with an industrial vibe, and has regular showings by local names. With risqué, emerging and experimental art for grown-ups, it's GOMA's naughty little cousin.

New Farm

★ Brisbane Powerhouse ARTS CENTRE
(Map p270; www.brisbanepowerhouse.org; 119 Lamington St, New Farm; 9am-5pm Mon-Fri, 10am-4pm Sat & Sun) FREE On the eastern flank of New Farm Park stands the Powerhouse, a once-derelict power station that's been superbly transformed into a contemporary arts centre. Inside the brick husk are graffiti remnants, pieces of industrial machinery and lights made from old electrical transformers. The Powerhouse hosts a range of visual arts, food-and-wine events, and comedy and musical performances (many free). There are also two riverside restaurants. Download the free Generator app for an audio tour of the amazing old building.

New Farm Park PARK
(Map p270; www.newfarmpark.com.au; Brunswick St, New Farm; 24hr;) New Farm Park, on the tail end of Brunswick St by the river, is a large, open parkland with picnic areas and gas barbecues, jacaranda trees, rose gardens and free wif-fi. The amazing playground here – a Crusoe-esque series of platforms among some vast Moreton Bay figs trees – is a real hit with the kids. Jan Powers Farmers Market (p298) and Moonlight Cinema (p296) happen here, too.

Activities

Walking

Feel like stretching your legs? Check out www.brisbane.qld.gov.au/facilities-recreation/sports-leisure/walking/walking-trails for a series of excellent art and heritage trails around town.

Sadly the city's excellent Riverwalk pathway was destroyed in the 2011 floods, but a stroll along the riverbanks remains rewarding. The new, more flood-resistant Riverwalk – including a section linking New Farm with the CBD – is being built at a cost of $72 million, and at the time of writing was expected to be open in 2015.

Cycling

Brisbane is hilly but it's still one of Australia's most bike-friendly cities, with over 900km of bike paths, including tracks along the Brisbane River. A good starter takes you from the City Botanic Gardens, across the Goodwill Bridge and out to the University of Queensland. It's about 7km one way, and you can stop for a beer at the Regatta pub in Toowong en route.

Bicycles are allowed on Brisbane's trains, except on weekdays during peak hours. You can also take bikes on CityCats and ferries for free.

CityCycle BICYCLE RENTAL
(1300 229 253; www.citycycle.com.au; hire per hour/day $2.20/165, first 30min free; hire 5am-10pm, return 24hr) Brisbane's public bike-share is great! Subscribe via the website (per day/week/three months $2/11/27.50), then hire a bike (additional fee) from any of the 150 stations around the city. It's very pricey to hire for more than an hour, so make use of the free first 30 minutes per bike and ride from station to station, swapping bikes as you go. Sometimes a helmet and lock come with the bike, but often not: the website lists bike shops where you can buy them.

Bicycle Revolution BICYCLE RENTAL
(Map p288; www.bicyclerevolution.org.au; 294 Montague Rd, West End; per day/week $35/150; 9am-5pm Mon, to 6pm Tue-Fri, 8am-2pm Sat) Friendly community shop with a handsome range of recycled bikes assembled by staff with reconditioned parts. Very hipster.

Swimming

Streets Beach SWIMMING
(Map p276; www.visitbrisbane.com.au/south-bank; daylight hours) FREE A central spot for a quick (and free) dip is the artificial, riverside Streets Beach at South Bank. Lifeguards, hollering kids, beach babes, strutting gym-junkies, ice-cream carts – they're all here.

Centenary Aquatic Centre SWIMMING
(Map p270; 1300 332 583; www.cityaquatics.com.au; 400 Gregory Tce, Spring Hill; adult/child/family $5.10/3.70/15.60; 5am-8pm Mon-Thu, to 6pm Fri, 7am-6pm Sat & Sun) This is the best pool in town and has been recently refurbished, with an Olympic-sized lap pool, a kids' pool and a diving pool with a high tower.

Spring Hill Baths SWIMMING
(Map p270; 1300 733 053; www.cityaquatics.com.au; 14 Torrington St, Spring Hill; adult/child/family $5.10/3.70/15.60; 6.30am-7pm Mon-Thu, to 6pm Fri, 8am-5pm Sat & Sun) Opened in 1886, this quaint heated 25m pool is encircled by cute timber change rooms. It's one of the oldest public baths in the southern hemisphere.

Climbing & Abseiling

Story Bridge Adventure Climb ADVENTURE TOUR
(Map p276; 1300 254 627; www.sbac.net.au; 170 Main St, Kangaroo Point; adult/child from $99/85)

Central Brisbane, Kangaroo Point & South Bank

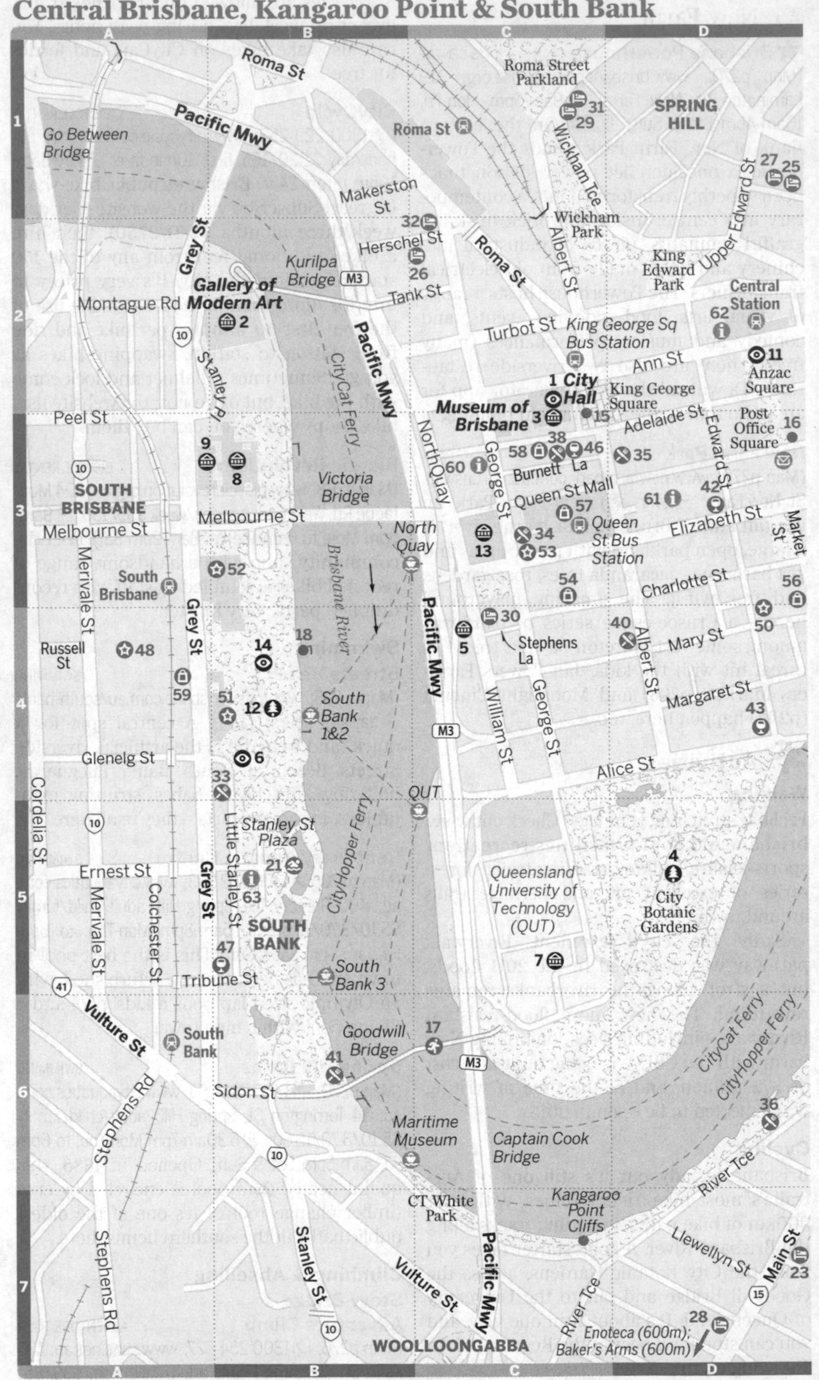

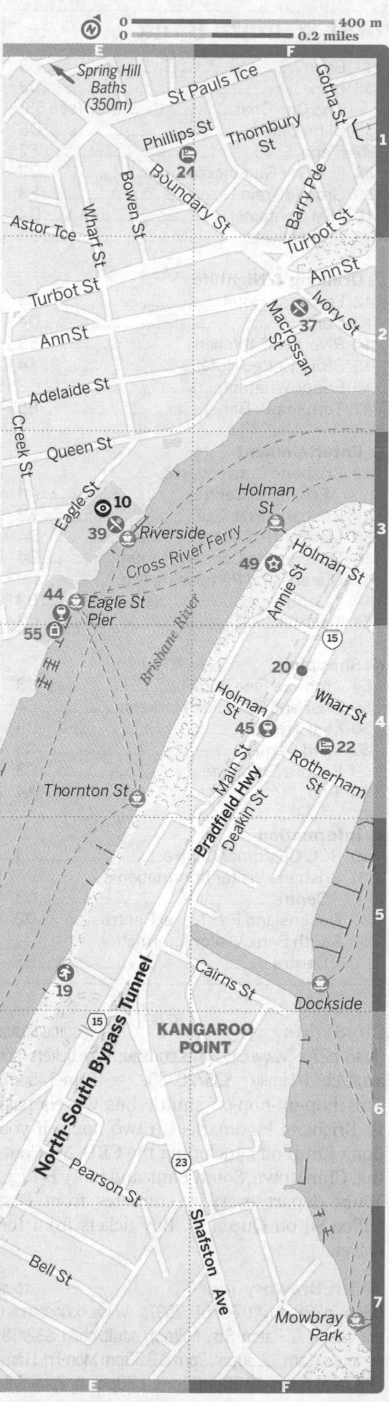

A Brisbane must-do, the bridge climb offers unbeatable views of the city – at dawn, day, twilight or night. The 2½-hour climb scales the southern half of the bridge, taking you 80m above the twisting, muddy Brisbane River below. Minimum age 10. Abseiling expeditions also available.

Riverlife Adventure Centre ROCK CLIMBING
(Map p276; ☎07-3891 5766; www.riverlife.com.au; Naval Stores, Kangaroo Point Bikeway, Kangaroo Point; ⊙9am-5pm) Near the 20m Kangaroo Point Cliffs, Riverlife runs rock-climbing sessions (from $55) and abseiling exploits ($45). It also offers kayaking river trips (from $45) and hires out bikes (per four hours $35), kayaks (per two hours $35) and in-line skates (per four hours $40).

Urban Climb ROCK CLIMBING
(Map p288; ☎07-3844 2544; www.urbanclimb.com.au; 2/220 Montague Rd, West End; adult/child $20/18; ⊙noon-10pm Mon-Fri, 10am-6pm Sat & Sun) A large indoor climbing wall with 200-plus routes.

In-Line Skating

You can hire skates and equipment from Riverlife Adventure Centre.

Planet Inline SKATING
(Map p276; ☎0413 099 333; www.planetinline.com; Goodwill Bridge; tours $15) Skaters reclaim the streets on Wednesday night with Planet Inline skate tours starting at 7.15pm from the top of the Goodwill Bridge. It also runs a Saturday-morning breakfast-club tour, and Sunday-afternoon tours that differ each week and last about three hours.

Skydiving & Ballooning

Jump the Beach Brisbane SKYDIVING
(☎1300 800 840; www.jumpthebeachbrisbane.com.au; skydives from $279) Picks up from the CBD and offers tandem skydives over Brisbane, landing on the sand in Redcliffe.

Fly Me to the Moon BALLOONING
(☎07-3423 0400; www.brisbanehotairballooning.com.au; adult/child from $299/230) One-hour hot-air balloon trips over Brisbane. Pick-up and breakfast included.

Tours

CityCat BOAT
(☎13 12 30; www.translink.com.au; 1 way $6.10; ⊙5.25am-11.50pm) Ditching the car or bus and catching a sleek CityCat ferry along the Brisbane river is sightseeing with style. Stand

Central Brisbane, Kangaroo Point & South Bank

Top Sights
1 City Hall ... C2
2 Gallery of Modern Art ... B2
3 Museum of Brisbane ... C3

Sights
4 City Botanic Gardens ... D5
5 Commissariat Store Museum ... C4
6 Courier-Mail Piazza ... B4
7 Old Government House ... C5
8 Queensland Art Gallery ... B3
9 Queensland Museum & Sciencentre ... A3
10 Riverside Centre ... E3
11 Shrine of Remembrance ... D2
12 South Bank Parklands ... B4
13 Treasury Building ... C3
14 Wheel of Brisbane ... B4

Activities, Courses & Tours
15 Brisbane Greeters ... C3
16 CitySights ... D3
17 Planet Inline ... C6
18 River City Cruises ... B4
19 Riverlife Adventure Centre ... E5
20 Story Bridge Adventure Climb ... F4
21 Streets Beach ... B5

Sleeping
22 Bridgewater Apartments ... F4
23 EconoLodge City Star Brisbane ... D7
24 Kookaburra Inn ... E1
25 Mantra Terrace ... D1
26 Meriton Serviced Apartments ... C2
27 Punthill Brisbane ... D1
28 Queensland Motel ... D7
29 Soho Motel ... C1
30 Treasury ... C4
31 Urban Brisbane ... C1
32 X-Base Brisbane Uptown ... C2

Eating
33 Ahmet's ... B4
34 Bean ... C3
35 Brew ... D3
Cha Cha Char ... (see 55)
36 Cliffs Cafe ... D6
37 E'cco ... F2
38 Felix for Goodness ... C3
39 Groove Train ... E3
40 Miel Container ... D4
41 Stokehouse ... B6

Drinking & Nightlife
42 Embassy Hotel ... D3
43 Nant ... D4
44 Riverbar & Kitchen ... E3
45 Story Bridge Hotel ... F4
46 Super Whatnot ... C3
47 Tomahawk Bar ... B5

Entertainment
48 Brisbane Convention & Exhibition Centre ... A4
49 Brisbane Jazz Club ... F3
50 Metro Arts Centre ... D4
51 Queensland Conservatorium ... B4
52 Queensland Performing Arts Centre ... B3
53 Ticketek ... C3

Shopping
54 Archives Fine Books ... C3
55 Brisbane Riverside Markets ... E4
56 Malt Traders ... D3
57 Mind Games ... C3
58 Record Exchange ... C3
59 Title ... A4

Information
60 BCC Customer Centre ... C3
61 Brisbane Visitor Information Centre ... D3
62 Queensland Rail Travel Centre ... D2
63 South Bank Visitor Information Centre ... B5

on an open-air deck and glide under the Story Bridge to South Bank and the city centre. Ferries run every 15 to 30 minutes between the University of Queensland in the southwest to the Apollo Road terminal north of the city, stopping at 14 terminals in between, including New Farm Park, North Quay (for the CBD), South Bank and West End.

Brisbane Bicycle Tours BICYCLE TOUR
(☎0417 462 875; www.brisbanebicycletours.com.au; 2/4hr tours from $50/75) Check out the River City on two wheels, exploring the city centre or along riverside pathways. Easy-going pace (if you haven't been on a bike for a while), with lots of rest stops.

CitySights GUIDED TOUR
(Map p276; www.citysights.com.au; day tickets per adult/child/family $35/20/80; ⏰9am-3.45pm) This hop-on-hop-off shuttle bus wheels past 19 Brisbane landmarks (in two hours if you don't jump off), including the CBD, Mt Coot-tha, Chinatown, South Bank and Story Bridge. Tours depart every 45 minutes from Post Office Sq on Queen St. Buy tickets from the driver.

XXXX Brewery Tour TOUR
(Map p288; ☎07-3361 7597; www.xxxx.com.au; cnr Black & Paten Sts, Milton; adult/child $32/18; ⏰tours 11am, 12.30pm, 2pm & 3.30pm Mon-Fri, 11am, 11.30am, noon, 12.30pm, 1pm, 1.30pm & 2pm Sat)

Feel a XXXX coming on? This brewery tour includes a few humidity-beating ales (leave the car at home). Also on offer are combined brewery and Suncorp Stadium tours (adult/child $48/28) at 10.30am Monday to Thursday. Book all tours in advance, and wear enclosed shoes. There's also an alehouse here if you feel like kicking on.

Brisbane Greeters GUIDED TOUR
(Map p276; ☎07-3156 6364; www.brisbanegreeters.com.au; Brisbane City Hall, King George Sq; ⏰10am) FREE Free, small-group, hand-held introductory tours of Brizzy with affable volunteers. Call to see what's running, or to organise a customised tour. Bookings essential.

Brisbane Lights Tours GUIDED TOUR
(☎07-3822 6028; www.brisbanelightstours.com; adult/child/family from $69/30/160) Three-hour nocturnal tours departing at 6.30pm nightly (hotel pick-ups included), covering a dozen city landmarks, with dinner (or a snack) at Mt Coot-tha Lookout and a 20-minute CityCat cruise.

Lucy Boots Bushwalking Tours HIKING
(☎0499 117 199; www.lucybootsbushtours.com.au; tours from $99) Take a guided hike through some easily accessible wilderness on a day trip from Brisbane: Lamington National Park, Tamborine Mountain, the Glasshouse Mountains, Bribie Island or Springbrook National Park. Prices include lunch and Brisbane pick-up and drop-off.

River City Cruises CRUISE
(Map p276; ☎0428 278 473; www.rivercitycruises.com.au; South Bank Parklands Jetty A; adult/child/family $29/15/65) River City runs 1½-hour cruises with commentary from South Bank to New Farm and back. They depart from South Bank at 10.30am and 12.30pm (plus 2.30pm during summer).

Ghost Tours TOUR
(☎07-3344 7265; www.ghost-tours.com.au; walking/coach tours from $20/50) 'Get creeped' on these 90-minute guided walking tours or 2½-hour bus tours of Brisbane's haunted heritage: murder scenes, cemeteries, eerie arcades and the infamous **Boggo Road Gaol** (Map p270; ☎07-3844 0059, 0411 111 903; www.boggoroadgaol.com; Annerley Rd, Dutton Park; historical tours adult/child/family $25/12.50/50, ghost tours adult/child over 12 yr $40/25; ⏰historical tours 11am & 1pm Tue-Sat, 9am, 10am, 11am, noon & 1pm Sun, ghost tours 7.30pm Wed & Sun, 7pm & 8pm Fri). Offers several tours a week; bookings essential.

Festivals & Events

Check out www.visitbrisbane.com.au for full listings of what's happening around town.

Brisbane International TENNIS
(www.brisbaneinternational.com.au) Pro tennis tournament attracting the world's best. Held at the Queensland Tennis Centre in January, just prior to the Australian Open (in Melbourne).

Chinese New Year CULTURAL
(www.chinesenewyear.com.au) Held in Fortitude Valley's Chinatown Mall (Duncan St) in January/February. Firecrackers, whirling dragons and fantastic food.

Brisbane Comedy Festival COMEDY
(www.briscomfest.com) Four-week festival in March featuring local and international laugh-mongers; held at the Brisbane Powerhouse (p296).

Brisbane Winter Carnival SPORTS
(www.racingqueensland.com.au) The state's major horse-racing carnival, held in May and June. The biggest day is the **Stradbroke Handicap** (www.stradbrokehandicap.com.au) in early June.

BRISBANE FESTIVAL

In September, Brisbane's streets become a hurly-burly of colour, flair, flavour and fireworks during the city's biggest annual arts event – the **Brisbane Festival** (www.brisbanefestival.com.au). Running over three weeks, the festival involves more than 300 performances and 60-odd events, enticing 2000-plus artists from across the planet. Art exhibitions, dance, theatre, opera, symphonies, circus performers, buskers and vaudeville acts generate an eclectic scene, with many free street events and concerts around town.

Each year the festival opens with a bang – literally. Staged over the Brisbane River, with vantage points at South Bank, the city and West End, **Riverfire** is a massive fireworks show with dazzling visual choreography and a synchronised soundtrack.

Brisbane Pride Festival GAY & LESBIAN
(www.brisbanepridefestival.com.au) Brisbane's annual gay and lesbian celebration is held over four weeks in September (some events in June, including the fab Queen's Ball).

'Ekka' Royal Queensland Show CULTURAL
(www.ekka.com.au) Country and city collide in August for Queensland's largest annual event, the Ekka (formerly the Brisbane Exhibition, which was shortened to 'Ekka'). Baby animals, showbags, spooky carnies, shearing demonstrations, rides and over-sugared kids ahoy!

Brisbane Writers Festival LITERATURE
(BWF; www.brisbanewritersfestival.com.au) Queensland's premier literary event has been running for 50 years: words, books, and people who put words in books. Held in September.

Brisbane Festival PERFORMING ARTS
(www.brisbanefestival.com.au) Brisbane's major festival (p279) of the arts, held over three weeks in September.

Valley Fiesta MUSIC
(www.valleyfiesta.com.au) Rock bands and DJs take over Fortitude Valley's Brunswick St and Chinatown malls for three days in October: Brisbane's biggest free music fest.

Brisbane International Film Festival FILM
(BIFF; www.biff.com.au) Twelve days of quality films flicker across Brisbane screens in November.

Sleeping

Brisbane has an excellent selection of accommodation options that will suit any budget. Many are beyond the business beds of the city centre, but they're usually within walking distance or have good public-transport connections.

Head for Spring Hill for peace and quiet; Fortitude Valley for party nights; Paddington for cafes and boutiques; Petrie Terrace for hostels; gay-friendly New Farm for restaurants; and West End for bars and bookshops.

Greater Brisbane

Newmarket Gardens Caravan Park CAMPGROUND $
(Map p270; ☎07-3356 1458; www.newmarketgardens.com.au; 199 Ashgrove Ave, Newmarket; unpowered/powered sites $40/42, on-site vans $56, budget r $66, cabins $130-155; P ❄ @ wifi) Some of the trees at this suburban caravan park are mangoes – beware falling fruit! It's just 4km north of the city, accessible by bus and train. There's a row of six simple budget rooms (no air-con), five tidy cabins (with air-con) and a sea of van and tent sites. Not much in the way of distractions for kids.

Central Brisbane

X-Base Brisbane Uptown HOSTEL $
(Map p276; ☎07-3238 5888; www.stayatbase.com; 466 George St; dm/d from $21/85; ❄ @ wifi) This purpose-built hostel near Roma St Station flaunts its youth with mod interiors, decent facilities and overall cleanliness. Each room has air-con, a bathroom and individual lockers, and it's wheelchair-accessible. The bar downstairs is a party palace, with big-screen sports, DJs and open-mic nights.

Kookaburra Inn GUESTHOUSE $
(Map p276; ☎1800 733 533, 07-3832 1303; www.kookaburra-inn.com.au; 41 Phillips St, Spring Hill; s/tw & d without bathroom from $67/84; ❄ wifi) This small, simple two-level guesthouse has basic rooms with washbasin and fridge, and clean shared bathrooms. The building itself is unremarkable, but there's a lounge, kitchen and outdoor patio. A decent budget option if you've done dorms to death. Air-con in some doubles only. Free wi-fi.

Spring Hill Terraces MOTEL $$
(Map p270; ☎07-3854 1048; www.springhillterraces.com; 260 Water St, Spring Hill; d $95-145, unit $175; P ❄ wifi pool) Offering good old-fashioned service, security and a tiny pool (a pond?), Spring Hill Terraces has inoffensive motel-style rooms and roomier terrace units with balconies and leafy courtyards. A 10-minute walk from Fortitude Valley.

Punthill Brisbane HOTEL $$
(Map p276; ☎07-3055 5777, 1300 731 299; www.punthill.com.au; 40 Astor Tce; 1-/3-bedroom apt from $150/180; P ❄ wifi pool) The lobby here is full of retro bicycles (for hire) and every balcony has a bird cage with a faux-feathered friend in it…but aside from these quirks, what you can expect is stylish suites (all taupe, charcoal, ivory and nice art) in a central location for competitive prices. A good option all-round. Parking $25.

Meriton Serviced Apartments APARTMENTS $$
(Map p276; ☎13 16 72, 07-3999 8000; www.staymsa.com; 43 Herschel St; d from $120, 1-/2-/3-bedroom apt from $150/315/365; P ❄ wifi pool) Want a room with a view? Shiny and black, the 249m Infinity Tower is Brisbane's tallest

BRISBANE FOR CHILDREN

From toddlers to teenagers, there's no shortage of options to keep kids busy (and parents happy) in Brisbane. For info on current happenings pick up the free monthly magazine *Brisbane's Child* (www.brisbaneschild.com.au). During school holidays the Brisbane City Council runs the 'Chill Out' activities program for 10- to 17-year-olds: see www.brisbane.qld.gov.au/whats-on/type/recreation-programs/chill-out.

Out and about, swing by the **South Bank Parklands** (p274), which has lawns, barbecues, playgrounds and the slow-spinning **Wheel of Brisbane** (p274) – a real mind-blower for anyone under 15. The lifeguard-patrolled **Streets Beach** (p275) is here too, with a shallow section for really small swimmers. **New Farm Park** (p275) is another beaut spot by the river, with a series of treehouselike platforms interlinking huge (and shady) Moreton Bay fig trees.

The Brisbane River is a big plus. Take a ferry ride around the bends of central Brisbane, or chug further afield to the **Lone Pine Koala Sanctuary** (p272), where the kids can cuddle up to a critter. If you're heading out Mt Coot-tha way, catch a starry show at the **Sir Thomas Brisbane Planetarium** (p272).

Too humid to be outside? Head for the air-con at the Queensland Cultural Centre on South Bank. Here the **Queensland Museum** (p274) runs some fab, hands-on programs for little tackers during school holidays. The incorporated **Sciencentre** has plenty of push-this-button-and-see-what-happens action. The **Queensland Art Gallery** (p274) has a Children's Art Centre which runs regular programs throughout the year, as does the **State Library of Queensland** (p299) and the **Gallery of Modern Art** (p273). Over in Fortitude Valley at the Judith Wright Centre of Contemporary Arts, **C!RCA** (Map p284; ☎07-3852 3110; www.circa.org.au; Level 3, 420 Brunswick St, Fortitude Valley) offers action-packed 'circus classes' (tumbling, balancing, jumping, trapeze work) for budding young carnies.

Day-care or babysitting options include **Dial an Angel** (☎07-3878 1077, 1300 721 111; www.dialanangel.com) and **Care4Kidz** (www.careforkidz.com.au).

building. It houses some 80 levels of stylish Meriton apartments of various sizes and configurations, all with views. The studio and one-bedroom options are great bang for your buck. Parking $35.

Urban Brisbane HOTEL $$
(Map p276; ☎07-3831 6177; www.hotelurban.com.au; 345 Wickham Tce; d/1-/2-bedroom from $180/225/270; P❄@📶🏊) Still looking sexy after a recent $10-million makeover, the Urban has stylish rooms with masculine hues, balconies and high-end fittings (supercomfy beds, big TVs, fuzzy bathrobes). There's also a heated outdoor pool, a bar, and lots of uniformed flight attendants checking in and out. Good value for money. Parking $15.

Mantra Terrace BOUTIQUE HOTEL $$
(Map p276; ☎1300 737 111, 07-3009 3400; www.8hotels.com; 52 Astor Tce; d from $179; P❄📶) Behind an ultramod black-and-white facade, the seven-storey Mantra Terrace has compact, contemporary rooms with natty wallpaper and thoughtful touches (original artwork, free wi-fi). The bigger suites have kitchenettes and lounge areas, and there's a bar-restaurant on the ground floor. Parking is $28.

Soho Motel MOTEL $$
(Map p276; ☎07-3831 7722; www.sohobrisbane.com.au; 333 Wickham Tce; r $100-160; P❄@📶) This bricky 50-room joint a short hop from Roma St Station is better inside than it looks from the street, with smart, compact rooms with little balconies. The owners are friendly and savvy, and pay attention to the little things: free wi-fi, 11am check-out, free parking, custom-made furniture and plush linen. Good value for money.

City Park Apartments APARTMENTS $$
(Map p270; ☎07-3839 8683; www.cityparkapts.com.au; 251 Gregory Tce, Spring Hill; d from $140, 1-/2-bedroom apt from $180/230; P❄📶🏊) Despite tropical palms and postmodern trimmings, this neatly maintained, three-tier complex of units manages to look a tad Tuscan. Reasonable prices, a shady kidney-shaped pool and easy CBD access. Cheaper for longer stays.

Treasury LUXURY HOTEL $$$

(Map p276; 07-3306 8888; www.treasurybrisbane.com.au; 130 William St; r from $260;) Brisbane's most lavish hotel is behind the equally lavish exterior of the former Land Administration Building. Each room is unique and awash with heritage features; high ceilings, framed artwork, polished wood furniture and elegant furnishings. Perfect if plush and a little bit showy floats your boat. The best rooms have river views. Superefficient staff; parking $30.

Kangaroo Point

Bridgewater Apartments APARTMENTS $$

(Map p276; 07-3391 5300; www.bridgewaterapartments.com.au; 55 Baildon St, Kangaroo Point; studio apts from $160, 1-/2-/3-bedroom apt from $180/230/320;) Wobbling distance from the Story Bridge Hotel (and Story Bridge itself), this slick, secure apartment complex comprises a three-storey maze of units and a 13-storey tower with beaut views. A charcoal-and-cream colour scheme prevails. Nightly, weekly and monthly rates available.

EconoLodge City Star Brisbane MOTEL $$

(Map p276; 07-3391 6222; www.citystar.com.au; 650 Main St, Kangaroo Point; d/tw/f from $119/134/154;) Visiting Brisbane for business or pleasure? There's an even split in guest motives here, but either way, they're comfortably accommodated in this superclean, superefficient motel (new beds!) on the main road through Kangaroo Point. The free ferry to Eagle St Pier in the CBD is a short walk away.

Queensland Motel MOTEL $$

(Map p276; 07-3391 1061; www.queenslandmotel.id.au; 777 Main St, Kangaroo Point; d/tr/f $120/155/270;) A no-frills, affable, old-school motel near 'the Gabba' cricket ground; 20 minutes' walk to the city. Shoot for a room on the top floor, with palm trees rustling outside your window.

Fortitude Valley

Bunk Backpackers HOSTEL $

(Map p284; 07-3257 3644, 1800 682 865; www.bunkbrisbane.com.au; 21 Gipps St, Fortitude Valley; dm $23-33, s $60, d/apt from $80/170;) This old arts college was reborn as a backpackers 10 years ago – and the party hasn't stopped! It's a huge, five-level place with dozens of rooms (mostly eight-bed dorms), just staggering distance from the Valley nightlife. There's also an in-house bar (Birdees), a Mexican cantina, and a few awesome apartments on the top floor. Not for bed-by-10pm slumberers.

Central Brunswick Apartments APARTMENTS $$

(Map p284; 07-3852 1411; www.centralbrunswickhotel.com.au; 455 Brunswick St; r $130-150;) Emerging from the husk of an old brick brewery building, these 60 mod studio apartments are a hit with business bods. All have fully equipped kitchens, and there's an on-site gym, free wi-fi and rooftop BBQ. Parking $10.

★ **Limes** BOUTIQUE HOTEL $$$

(Map p284; 07-3852 9000; www.limeshotel.com.au; 142 Constance St, Fortitude Valley; d from $229;) A slick slice of style in the Valley, Limes has 21 handsome rooms that make good use of tight space – each has plush furniture, a kitchenette and thoughtful extras (iPod docks, free wi-fi, free gym pass). The rooftop bar, hot tub and cinema (!) are magic. Parking nearby for $18.

Alpha Mosaic Brisbane HOTEL $$$

(Map p284; 07-3332 8888; www.alphamosaichotelbrisbane.com.au; 12 Church St, Fortitude Valley; 1-/2-bedrom apt from $229/459;) Brand-spankin' new in 2014, the Alpha Mosaic is a ritzy 18-level number, continuing the evolution of Fortitude Valley from brassy to classy. Nice art, nice views, nice staff... Damn, this place is nice! The bar and restaurant set-ups are breezy and easy-going. Close to James St, too. Parking $25.

New Farm

★ **Bowen Terrace** GUESTHOUSE $

(Map p284; 07-3254 0458; www.bowenterrace.com.au; 365 Bowen Tce, New Farm; dm/s/d without bathroom $35/42/72, d/f with bathroom $119/145;) A beautifully restored, 100-year-old Queenslander, this quiet guesthouse offers rooms with TVs, bar fridges, quality linen and lofty ceilings with fans. Out the back there's a deck overlooking the enticing pool. No air-con but real value for money, with far more class than your average hostel. Walls between rooms are a bit thin (built before TV was invented).

Spicers Balfour Hotel BOUTIQUE HOTEL $$$

(Map p284; 1300 597 540; www.spicersretreats.com/spicers-balfour-hotel; 37 Balfour St, New Farm; r from $329;) The nine fancy rooms here score highly in the style and comfort stakes,

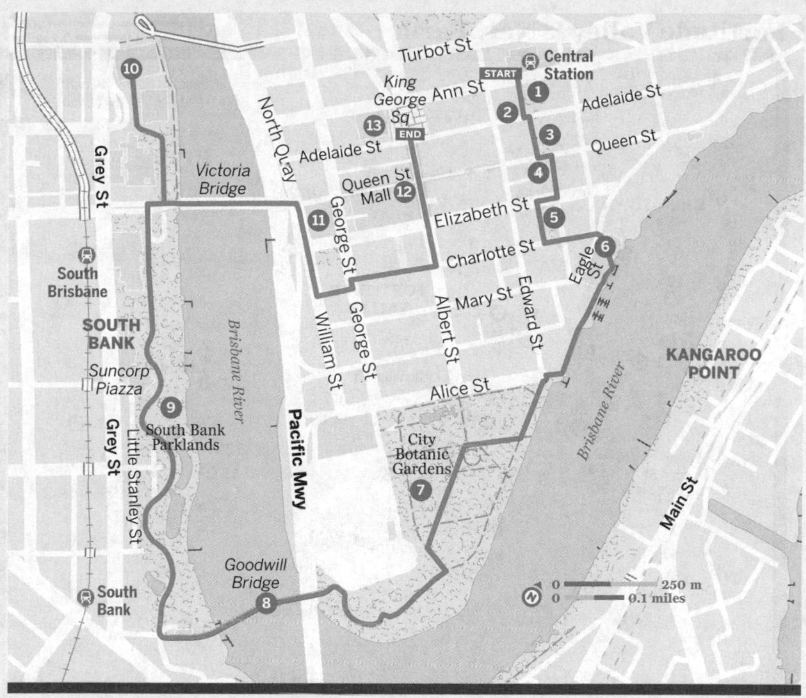

City Walk
CBD & South Bank Circuit

START CENTRAL STATION
END KING GEORGE SQ
LENGTH 5KM; TWO HOURS

Cross Ann St south of Central Station to the sobering 1 **Shrine of Remembrance** above the northern edge of 2 **Anzac Square**, with its bulbous boab trees and wandering ibises. At the southern side of the square, scale one of the pedestrian bridges over Adelaide St, which lead to the elevated, manicured 3 **Post Office Square**. The square is fronted at its southern end by Brisbane's stately stone 4 **GPO**. Take the alley between the wings of the post office through to Elizabeth St. Cross the road and stick your head into beautiful white-stone 5 **St Stephen's Cathedral**.

Walk through the grassy courtyard behind the cathedral until reaching Charlotte St. Take a left, cross Eagle St and duck through 6 **Eagle Street Pier** on the river. Check the Story Bridge views to your left, then go down the steps to the riverside boardwalk and truck south.

At Edward and Alice Sts, detour through the 7 **City Botanic Gardens** (p273). Cast an eye across the river to the Kangaroo Point cliffs, then skirt around the back of the Brisbane Riverstage to the pedestrian-only 8 **Goodwill Bridge**: check out HMAS *Diamantina* in the Queensland Maritime Museum to your left. From here, jag north into the 9 **South Bank Parklands** (p274).

If time is your friend, duck into the outstanding 10 **Gallery of Modern Art** (p273). Otherwise, cross Victoria Bridge back into central Brisbane. Just south of the gorgeous 11 **Treasury Building** (p273) on William St, an unnamed alley cuts through to George St. Dogleg across George into Charlotte St, continue along Charlotte then turn left into Albert St in Brisbane's modern CBD.

Continue along Albert St, cross 12 **Queen Street Mall** and then Adelaide St into King George Sq, with towering 13 **City Hall** (p273) anchoring the southwest side. After taking in the scene, back-track to the mall for a much-deserved pick-me-up.

Fortitude Valley & New Farm

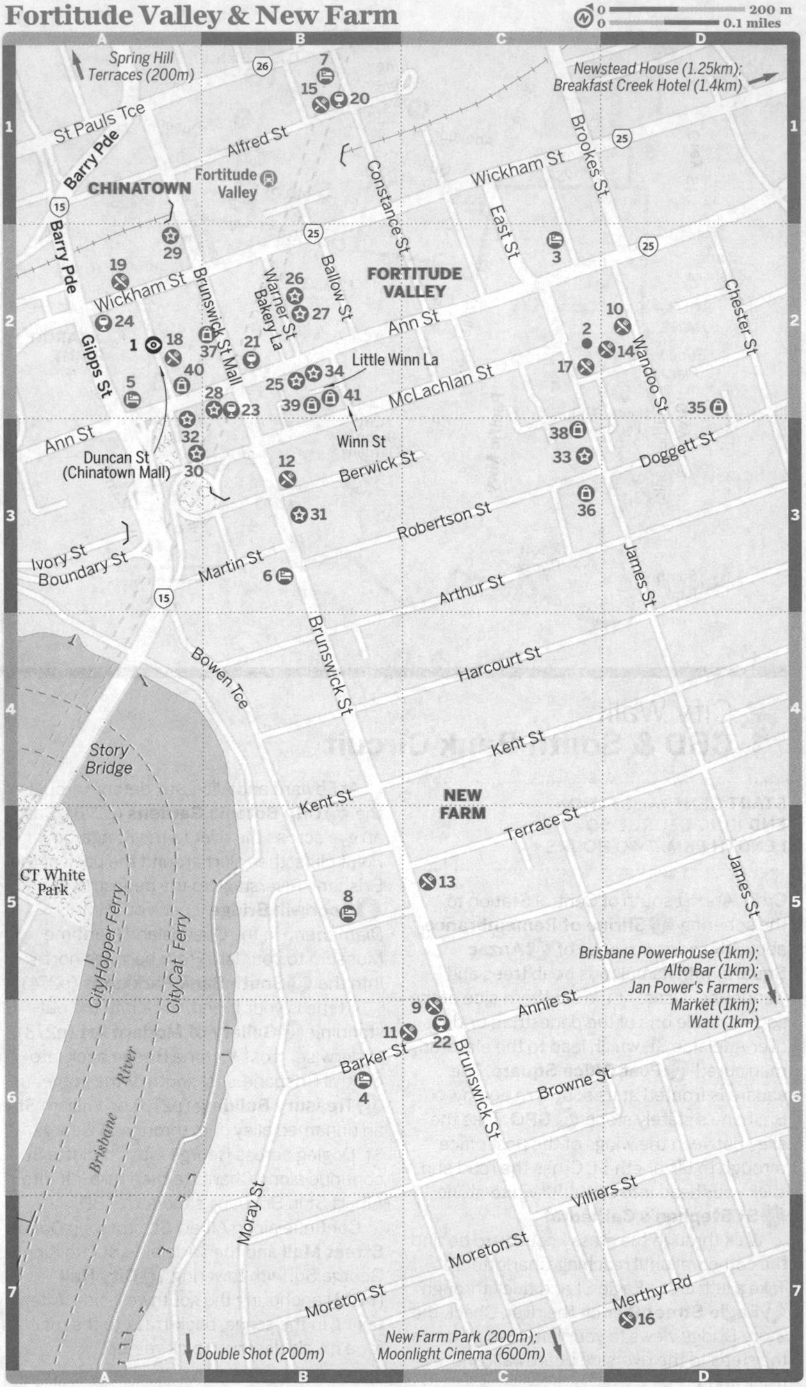

0 200 m
0 0.1 miles

Spring Hill Terraces (200m)
Newstead House (1.25km); Breakfast Creek Hotel (1.4km)
St Pauls Tce
Barry Pde
Alfred St
CHINATOWN
Fortitude Valley
Constance St
Wickham St
Brookes St
East St
Ballow St
FORTITUDE VALLEY
Brunswick St Mall
Warner St
Bakery La
Wickham St
Gipps St
Ann St
Little Winn La
McLachlan St
Chester St
Wandoo St
Winn St
Duncan St (Chinatown Mall)
Berwick St
Doggett St
Robertson St
Ivory St
Boundary St
Martin St
Arthur St
James St
Bowen Tce
Brunswick St
Harcourt St
Story Bridge
Kent St
NEW FARM
Terrace St
CT White Park
CityHopper Ferry
CityCat Ferry
Brisbane River
Brisbane Powerhouse (1km); Alto Bar (1km); Jan Power's Farmers Market (1km); Watt (1km)
Annie St
Barker St
Brunswick St
Browne St
Moray St
Villiers St
Moreton St
Merthyr Rd
New Farm Park (200m); Moonlight Cinema (600m)
Double Shot (200m)

Fortitude Valley & New Farm

Sights

1 Chinatown ... A2
Institute of Modern Art ... (see 31)

Activities, Courses & Tours

C!RCA ... (see 31)
2 James St Cooking School ... C2

Sleeping

3 Alpha Mosaic Brisbane ... C2
4 Bowen Terrace ... B6
5 Bunk Backpackers ... A2
6 Central Brunswick Apartments ... B3
7 Limes ... B1
8 Spicers Balfour Hotel ... B5

Eating

9 Anise ... C6
10 Campos ... D2
11 Chouquette ... C6
12 Harajuku Gyoza ... B3
13 Himalayan Cafe ... C5
14 James St Market ... D2
15 Kwan Brothers ... B1
16 Smoke BBQ ... D7
17 Spoon Deli Cafe ... C2
18 Thai Wi-Rat ... A2
19 Vietnamese ... A2

Drinking & Nightlife

20 Alfred & Constance ... B1
21 Bowery ... B2
22 Gertie's Bar & Lounge ... C6
23 Press Club ... B2
24 Sabotage Social ... A2

Entertainment

25 Beat MegaClub ... B2
26 Brightside ... B2
27 Church ... B2
28 Cloudland ... B2
29 Crowbar ... A2
30 Family ... A3
31 Judith Wright Centre of Contemporary Arts ... B3
32 Oh Hello ... A3
33 Palace Centro ... C3
34 Zoo ... B2

Shopping

35 Angelo's Fresh Pasta ... D2
36 Blonde Venus ... C3
37 Brisbane Valley Markets ... B2
38 James Street ... C3
39 Künstler ... B2
40 Trash Monkey ... A2
41 Winn Lane ... B2

spread over two levels in a lavishly renovated old Queenslander (not a floral print or a doily in sight). There is a slight snootiness to proceedings ('high tea' is taken in the restaurant): just drop the pretensions and enjoy the rooftop bar and hip neighbourhood.

West End

Gonow Family Backpacker HOSTEL $
(Map p288; ☎07-3846 3473; www.gonowfamily.com.au; 147 Vulture St; dm $18-30, d $69; P Wi-Fi) These have to be the cheapest beds in Brisbane, and Gonow is doing a decent job of delivering a clean, respectful, secure hostel experience despite the bargain-basement pricing. It's not a party place: you'll be better off elsewhere if you're looking to launch drunken forays into the night. The upstairs rooms have more ceiling height.

Brisbane Backpackers HOSTEL $
(Map p288; ☎07-3844 9956, 1800 626 452; www.brisbanebackpackers.com.au; 110 Vulture St; dm $21-34, d/tw/tr from $99/110/135; P ❄ @ Wi-Fi pool) Is there such a thing as 'backpacker kitsch'? If so, this hulking hostel probably qualifies, with staff in too-tight T-shirts and dubious marketing suggesting that travellers 'only sleep with the best'. But if you're looking to party, you're in the right place. There's a great pool and bar area, and rooms are basic but generally well maintained.

Petrie Terrace

Aussie Way Backpackers HOSTEL $
(Map p288; ☎07-3369 0711; www.aussiewaybackpackers.com; 34 Cricket St, Petrie Terrace; dm/s/tw/d $26/55/69/69, f $81-135; ❄ Wi-Fi pool) Set in a photogenic, two-storey timber Queenslander on the appealingly named Cricket St, Aussie Way feels more like a cosy guesthouse than a hostel, with spacious, tastefully furnished rooms and a fab pool for sticky Brisbane afternoons. The doubles in the second building out the back are just lovely. All quiet after 10.30pm.

Brisbane City YHA HOSTEL $
(Map p288; ☎07-3236 1004; www.yha.com.au; 392 Upper Roma St; dm from $33, tw & d with/without bathroom from $113/99, f from $133; P ❄ @ Wi-Fi pool) This immaculate, well-run hostel has a rooftop pool and a sundeck with eye-popping river views. The maximum dorm size is six beds (not too big); most have bathrooms. Big on security, activities, tours and kitchen space

(lots of fridges). The cafe-bar has trivia nights and happy hours, but this is a YHA, not party central. Parking $10.

Banana Benders Backpackers HOSTEL **$**
(Map p288; ☎1800 241 157, 07-3367 1157; www.bananabenders.com; 118 Petrie Tce, Petrie Terrace; dm $27-30, tr $32, d & tw $70-76; ❄📶) This friendly, banana-coloured backpackers has basic rooms and a great little deck out the back. It's a bit out of the way (a good thing), a 10-minute walk uphill from Roma St Station. The crowd here could be classed as 'mature': it's not really a party pad.

Chill Backpackers HOSTEL **$**
(Map p288; ☎07-3236 0088, 1800 851 875; www.chillbackpackers.com; 328 Upper Roma St; dm/d/tr from $30/89/105; P❄@📶) This bright aqua building on the CBD fringe has small, clean, modern rooms, and there's a roof deck with fab river views (just like the YHA up the road, but from a slightly reduced altitude). In terms of vibe, it's in the middle between party and puritan. Has 24-hour check-in.

Paddington

★**Casabella Apartment** APARTMENT **$$**
(Map p292; ☎07-3217 6507; www.casabella-apartment.com; 211 Latrobe Tce, Paddington; apt $175; P📶) The understorey of this fuchsia-coloured house at the quiet end of Paddo's main drag has been converted into a very comfortable self-contained unit. There are two bedrooms (sleeping three), warm Mediterranean colour schemes, recycled timber floors and lots of louvres to let the cross-breeze through (no air-con). Lovely! Free street parking; two-night minimum stay.

★**Latrobe Apartment** APARTMENT **$$$**
(Map p292; ☎0448 944 026; www.stayz.com.au/77109; 183a Latrobe Tce, Paddington; apt from $200; P❄📶) Underneath a chiropractor in affluent Paddington is this excellent two-bedroom apartment, sleeping four, with two bathrooms, polished floorboards, sexy lighting and a fabulous barbecue deck. It's a sleek, contemporary design, with quality everything: linen, toiletries, kitchenware, TV, iPod dock, leather lounge... Cafes and free parking up at street level.

Eating

Like most things in Brisbane, dining experiences can be broadly defined by which neighbourhood you're in. The city centre is the place for fine dining and coffee nooks. In Fortitude Valley you'll find cheap cafes and Chinatown. Nearby, New Farm has plenty of multicultural eateries, French-styled cafes and award winners. Eclectic West End is littered with bohemian cafes and cheap multicultural diners. South Bank swings between mainstream and pricey eats. But no matter where you are, you'll always be able to eat outside! (Is 'Brisbane' actually Latin for 'al fresco'?)

Greater Brisbane

★**Baker's Arms** BAKERY **$**
(Map p270; ☎07-3391 6599; www.thebakersarms.com.au; 29 Logan Rd, Woolloongabba; mains $8-10; ⏲7am-3pm) There's no fixed menu at this busy Logan Rd bakehouse: instead, a deliciously varied selection of cakes, tarts, frittatas, salads, pies, soups and saucer-sized biscuits is prepared daily, subject to ingredients and bakerly whim. Check what's on offer in the cabinet, then place your order to the clatter-and-bash coffee machine soundtrack. Sunny footpath tables to boot.

Enoteca ITALIAN **$$$**
(Map p270; ☎07-3392 4315; www.1889enoteca.com.au; 10-12 Logan Rd, Woolloongabba; mains lunch $21-38, dinner $35-42; ⏲noon-2.30pm Tue-Fri & Sun, 6pm-late Tue-Sat) Simple and simply wonderful traditional Roman pasta, fish and meat dishes served in a gorgeous 1889 shopfront south of the city centre in Woolloongabba. Even if you're not here for a meal (there's a little wine store here too) check out the lavish lead-lighting, marvellous marble bar, and walk-around glass display cabinet filled with Italian vino vessels.

Central Brisbane

★**Brew** CAFE **$**
(Map p276; ☎07-3211 4242; www.brewgroup.com.au; Lower Burnett Lane; mains $9-30; ⏲7am-4pm Mon, to 10pm Tue & Wed, to 11.30pm Thu & Fri, 9am-11.30pm Sat, 9am-3pm Sun) You'd expect to find this kind of subcultural underground cafe in Seattle or Berlin...but Brisbane? Breaking new coffee-cultural ground in Queensland, Brew takes the caffeine into the alleyways, serving simple food (tapas, pastas, sliders) to go with the black stuff. Wines, cocktails and bottled beers also available, for when you feel like a different kind of brew.

Felix for Goodness CAFE $

(Map p276; www.felixforgoodness.com; 50 Burnett Lane; mains $6-17; ⏲7am-3pm Mon-Fri; ✎) Yet another winning destination in Burnett Lane, hard-working Felix does things properly: proper homemade salads, tarts, baguettes, pies and cakes, proper coffee and proper fresh-fruit smoothies. Local and organic wholefoods all the way, made fresh every day. Night-time savoury platters and all-Australian beers and wines were about to commence when we visited.

Miel Container BURGERS $

(Map p276; ☎0423 466 503; www.facebook.com/mielcontainer; cnr Mary & Albert Sts; mains $12-24; ⏲11am-10pm Mon-Thu, to midnight Fri & Sat) This rude-red shipping container has planted itself in a nook below the downtown Brisbane skyscrapers. Beaut homemade burgers are the mainstay: choose your bun, your burger, your vegies, cheese and sauces, then search for a spare seat by the footpath. A real hit with the lunchtime city suits.

Bean CAFE $

(Map p276; www.facebook.com/beanbrisbane; rear 181 George St; mains $9-15; ⏲7am-6pm Mon & Tue, to 10pm Wed-Sat) Another of Brisbane's new breed of hip laneway coffee shops, Bean is down a grungy, graffiti-spangled driveway off George St, surrounded by fire escapes, aircon units and cigarette-smoking office workers. You can grab a biscuit, a beer or an eggy breakfast here, but coffee is the main game. Live acoustic tunes Thursday evenings.

Groove Train CAFE $$

(Map p276; www.groovetrain.com.au; Riverside Centre, 123 Eagle St; mains $19-34; ⏲7am-late) An orange and dark-wood bunker hunkered down by the Riverside ferry terminal, Groove Train is long, low, lean and groovy. Watch the boats chug to-and-fro as you tuck into wood-fired pizzas, wok fry-ups, burgers, calzoni, risottos and big salads. Gets moody and barlike at night.

★E'cco MODERN AUSTRALIAN $$$

(Map p276; ☎07-3831 8344; www.eccobistro.com; 100 Boundary St; mains $40-43; ⏲noon-2.30pm Tue-Fri, 6-10pm Tue-Sat; ✎) One of the finest restaurants in the state, award-winning E'cco is a culinary must! Menu masterpieces from chef Philip Johnson include liquorice-spiced pork belly with caramelised peach, onion jam and kipfler potatoes. The interior is suitably swish: all black, white and stainless steel.

Cha Cha Char STEAK $$$

(Map p276; ☎07-3211 9944; www.chachachar.com.au; Shop 5, 1 Eagle St Pier; mains $36-56; ⏲noon-11pm Mon-Fri, 6-11pm Sat & Sun) Wallowing in awards, this long-running favourite serves Brisbane's best steaks, along with first-rate seafood and roast game meats. The classy semicircular dining room in the Eagle St Pier complex has floor-to-ceiling windows and river views.

Kangaroo Point

Cliffs Cafe CAFE $

(Map p276; www.cliffscafe.com.au; 29 River Tce, Kangaroo Point; mains $7-22; ⏲7am-5pm Mon-Sat) A steep climb up from the riverside (or an easy drive to the door), this clifftop cafe has superb river and city-skyline views. It's a casual, open-air pavilion: big breakfasts, burgers, battered barramundi and chips, salads, desserts and good coffee are the standouts.

South Bank

Ahmet's TURKISH $$

(Map p276; ☎07-3846 6699; www.ahmets.com; Shop 10, 168 Grey St; mains $21-34, banquets per person $38-46; ⏲11.30am-3pm & 6pm-late; ✎) On restaurant-lined Grey St, Ahmet's serves delectable Turkish fare amid a riot of colours and Grand Bazaar and Bosphorus murals. Try a Sucuk pide (oven-baked Turkish bread with Turkish salami, egg, tomato and mozzarella). Deep street-side terrace and regular live music.

Stokehouse MODERN AUSTRALIAN $$$

(Map p276; ☎07-3020 0600; www.stokehouse.com.au; River Quay, Sidon St; mains $34-40; ⏲noon-late) Looking for a classy restaurant in which to pop the question? This angular, concrete-and-dark-timber bunker by the river is for you! Start with the Moreton Bay bugs with braised leeks, then move on to the salt-crusted Yorkshire pork with sherry-glazed prunes and cauliflower. Flashy Stoke Bar is next door (for champagne after she/he says 'Yes!').

Fortitude Valley

James Street Market MARKET $

(Map p284; www.jamesstmarket.com.au; 22 James St, Fortitude Valley; ⏲8.30am-7pm Mon-Fri, 8am-6pm Sat & Sun) Paradise for gourmands, this small but lavishly stocked market has gourmet cheeses, a bakery-patisserie, fruit and veg,

West End & Petrie Terrace

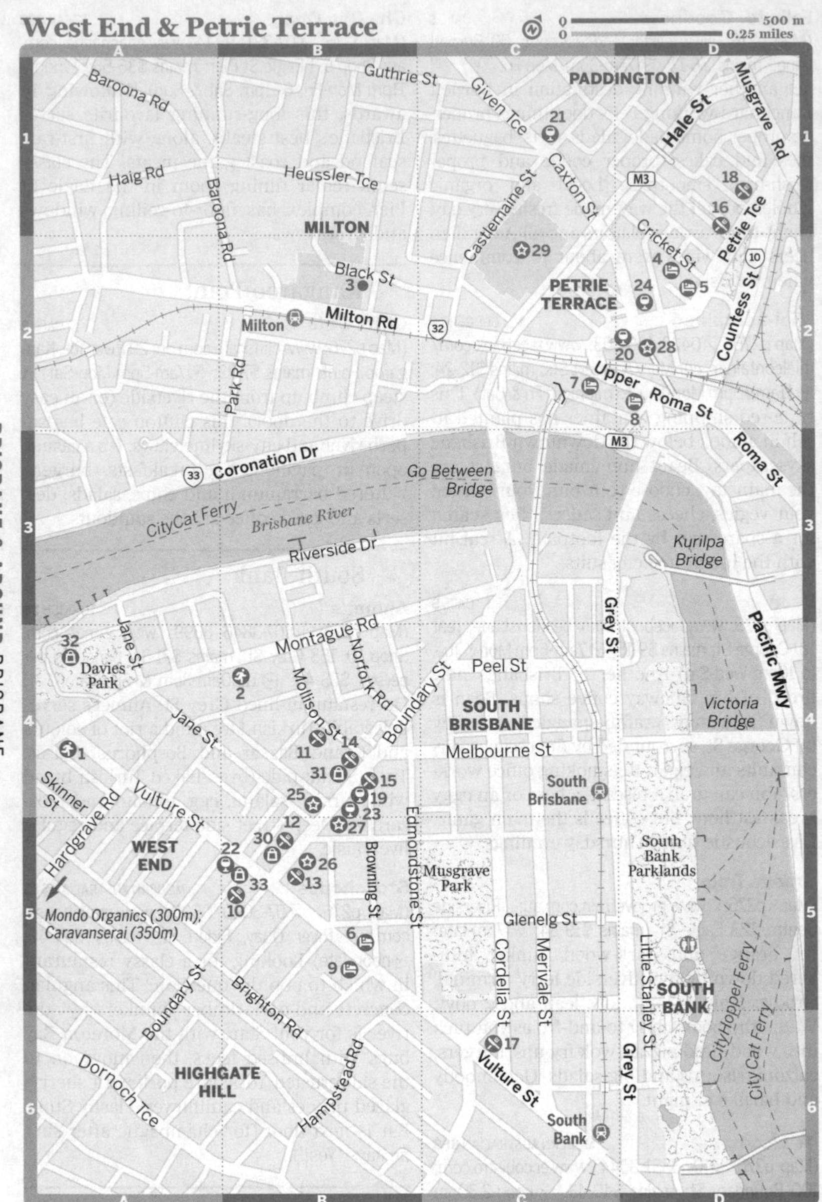

flowers, and lots of quality goodies. The fresh seafood counter serves excellent sushi and sashimi. The **James St Cooking School** (Map p284; ☎07-3252 8850; www.jamesstcookingschool.com.au; 3hr class $135-155) is upstairs.

Harajuku Gyoza JAPANESE $
(Map p284; ☎07-3852 4624; www.harajukugyoza.com; 394 Brunswick St, Fortitude Valley; mains $8-12; ⊙noon-late) Swing into this darkened, main-street Japanese joint for a quick-fire feed of gyoza (dumplings) or a ramen soup, best

West End & Petrie Terrace

shared with a boozy bunch of buddies. Good fun, good prices, cold Kirin on tap and Koshihikari rice beer in the fridge. No bookings.

Vietnamese VIETNAMESE $
(Map p284; ☎07-3252 4112; www.thevietnameserestaurant.com.au; 194 Wickham St, Fortitude Valley; mains $10-20; ⊙11am-3pm & 5-10pm) Aptly if unimaginatively named, this is indeed the place in town to eat Vietnamese, with exquisitely prepared dishes served to an always crowded house. Go for something from the 'Chef's Recommendation' list: crispy beef strips with honey and chilli, or clay-pot prawns with oyster sauce. Great value for money.

Campos CAFE $
(Map p284; www.camposcoffee.com; 11 Wandoo St, Fortitude Valley; mains $9-17; ⊙6.30am-4pm) Caffeine fiends sidestep milk crates and stacks of cardboard boxes down a little black-walled alley behind the James St Market for some of the best coffee in town. Food-wise it's substantial cafe fare (baked eggs, bagels, buttermilk pancakes). Takeaway bags of beans, too.

Thai Wi-Rat THAI, LAOTIAN $
(Map p284; ☎07-3257 0884; 20 Duncan St, Fortitude Valley; mains $10-18; ⊙10am-4pm & 5-9.30pm) This modest, brightly illuminated hole-in-the-wall on the Chinatown mall cooks up solid, chilli-heavy Thai and Laotian, including *pla dook yang* (grilled whole catfish). It also does a mean curry laksa (nectar of the gods). Takeaway available.

★ **Kwan Brothers** ASIAN $$
(Map p284; ☎07-3251 6588; www.kwanbros.com.au; 43 Alfred St, Fortitude Valley; small plates $10-15, mains $15-27; ⊙noon-3pm & 5-11pm Mon-Thu, noon-late Fri-Sun;) The Brothers Kwan like to stay up late, sitting around their moody, renovated warehouse beneath disco balls and Chinese umbrellas, sharing plates of crispy tofu with lemongrass and chilli, Korean fried cauliflower and BBQ pork-belly sliders. Wash it down with a draught Kirin beer then head for bed before the sun comes up.

Spoon Deli Cafe CAFE $$
(Map p284; ☎07-3257 1750; www.spoondeli.com.au; Shop B3, 22 James St, Fortitude Valley; breakfast $7-21, mains $10-29; ⊙6.30am-6pm Mon-Fri, 7am-5pm Sat & Sun;) Inside James St Market, this upscale deli serves gloriously rich pastas, burgers, salads and soups, plus colossal panini and lasagne slabs. The fresh juices are a liquid meal unto themselves. Walls are lined with deli produce: vinegars, oils, herbs and hampers. You'll feel hungry as soon as you walk in!

New Farm

Chouquette CAFE $
(Map p284; ☎07-3358 6336; www.chouquette.com.au; 19 Barker St, New Farm; items $3-11, 10 chouquettes $3.50; ⊙6.30am-5pm Wed-Sat, to 12.30pm Sun;) The best patisserie this side of Toulouse? Something to think about as you grab a nutty coffee and a bag of the

namesake *chouquettes* (small choux pastries topped with granulated sugar), a shiny slice of *tarte au citron,* or a filled baguette. French-speaking staff.

Double Shot CAFE $

(Map p270; ☎07-3358 6556; 125 Oxlade Dr, New Farm; mains $11-19; ⏲6am-3pm Tue-Sun) This hyperactive little neighbourhood cafe has woken up the slumbering lowlanders of New Farm. Brunching mums and dog-walkers cram into the tight shopfront for Spanish sardines on toast, breakfast burritos and terrific pastries, cakes and tarts. Staff are on the ball, and will do their best to squeeze you in.

Anise FRENCH $$

(Map p284; ☎07-3358 1558; www.anise.com.au; 697 Brunswick St, New Farm; mains $24-34, 7-course degustation with/without wine $155/100; ⏲noon-2.30pm Thu-Sat, 6-9.30pm Mon-Sat) This uber-stylish 22-seat restaurant–wine bar features seasonally inspired Gallic fare. Patrons sit at the narrow bar and enjoy *amuse-bouches* (hors d'oeuvres) such as oysters and Alsace foie gras, followed by the likes of pork cutlets with mustard mash or duck breast with pumpkin, gingerbread and licorice jus. Great for a special occasion.

Watt MODERN AUSTRALIAN $$

(Map p270; ☎07-3358 5464; www.wattrestaurant.com.au; Brisbane Powerhouse, 119 Lamington St, New Farm; mains bar $9-22, restaurant $27-39; ⏲9am-late Mon-Fri, 8am-late Sat & Sun) On the riverbank level of the Brisbane Powerhouse is casual, breezy Watt. Order up some duck salad with sweet chilli, rocket and orange, or a smoked ham-hock terrine with lentils and cornichons. Wines by the glass; DJ tunes on Sunday afternoons. Eat in the bar or the pricier restaurant.

Smoke BBQ BARBECUE $$

(Map p284; ☎07-3358 1922; www.thesmokebbq.com.au; 85 Merthyr Rd, New Farm; mains $15-38; ⏲11.30am-2pm Tue-Sun, 6-9pm Mon-Sun) The smell of hickory hangs heavy in the air of this American-style BBQ joint. The menu includes tender short ribs, pulled pork and charcoal chicken (with vodka barbecue sauce), along with requisite sides such as coleslaw, mac-and-cheese and fries. In-house joke: 'The trouble with barbecue is two or three days later you're hungry again'.

Himalayan Cafe NEPALESE $$

(Map p284; ☎07-3358 4015; 640 Brunswick St, New Farm; mains $15-25; ⏲5.30-10pm Tue-Sun; ✎) Awash with prayer flags and colourful cushions, this karmically positive, unfussy restaurant serves authentic Tibetan and Nepalese fare such as tender *fhaiya darkau* (lamb with vegies, coconut milk and spices). Repeat the house mantra: 'May positive forces be with every single living thing that exists'.

West End

★George's Seafood FISH & CHIPS $

(Map p288; ☎07-3844 4100; 150 Boundary St, West End; mains $7-16; ⏲11am-8pm Mon, 9.30am-8pm Tue-Sat, 10.30am-8pm Sun) With a counter full of fresh mud crabs, Moreton Bay rock oysters, banana prawns and whole snapper, this old-time fish-and-chipper has had a facelift but is still the real deal. The $9.50 cod-and-chips dinner is unbeatable.

Swampdog SEAFOOD $

(Map p288; ☎07-3255 3715; www.swampdog.com.au; 186 Vulture St, West End; mains $10-15; ⏲noon-8.30pm) 🍃 'Change the way you eat fish and chips' is the motto here, a busy seafood shack on an unforgiving stretch of Vulture St (hell for parking). Sourced from sustainable fisheries, the product here is fresh and filling (try the sardines on sourdough). 'This is restaurant quality at less than cafe prices!' says one happy customer.

Burrow CAFE $

(Map p288; ☎07-3846 0030; www.theburrowwestend.com.au; 37 Mollison St, West End; mains $10-17; ⏲7am-late Tue-Sun; 📶) In the open-sided understorey of a shambling old Queenslander, Burrow is a Baja California cantina crossed with a student share-house: laid-back and beachy with surf murals and wafting Pink Floyd. Try the hangover-removing Bill Murray cheeseburger (heavy on the Jarlsberg); or a Big Voodoo Daddy pizza with jerk chicken, Cajun sausage and bourbon BBQ glaze. Craft beer, too.

Blackstar Coffee Roasters CAFE $

(Map p288; www.blackstarcoffee.com.au; 44 Thomas St, West End; mains $7-13; ⏲7am-5pm) A neighbourhood fave, West End's own bean roaster has top coffee, a simple breakfast menu (wraps, spanakopita, eggs Benedict), wailing Roy Orbison and regular spoken-word and ukulele nights (not at the same time...). Grab a cold-pressed coffee on a hot day.

Chop Chop Chang's ASIAN $

(Map p288; ☎07-3846 7746; www.chopchopchangs.com.au; 185 Boundary St, West End; mains $12-22;

11.30am-3pm & 5.30-9.30pm) 'Happiness never decreases by being shared.' So said the Buddha. And the hungry hordes at Chop Chop Chang's seem to concur, passing around bowls of pan-Asian street food and bottles of *sriracha* chilli sauce with smiles on their faces. Try the caramelised pork with tamarind. Open later on Friday and Saturday nights.

★Gunshop Café CAFE, MODERN AUSTRALIAN **$$**
(Map p288; 07-3844 2241; www.thegunshopcafe.com; 53 Mollison St, West End; mains $16-29; 6.30am-2pm Mon, to late Tue-Sat, to 2.30pm Sun) With cool tunes, quirky lighting and happy staff, this peaceably repurposed gun shop has exposed-brick walls, sculptural ceiling lamps and an inviting back garden. The locally sourced menu changes daily, but regulars include Hervey Bay scallops with crab, zucchini fritters and saffron yogurt; and excellent brioche French toast for breakfast. Craft beers, Australian wines and afternoon pick-me-ups available.

Little Greek Taverna GREEK **$$**
(Map p288; 07-3255 2215; www.littlegreektaverna.com.au; Shop 5, 1 Browning St, West End; mains $15-17, banquets per person $35-43; 11am-9pm) Up-tempo, eternally busy and in a prime West End location, the LGT is a great spot for a big Greek feast and some people watching. Launch into a prawn and saganaki salad or a classic lamb gyros (souvlaki), washed down with a sleep-defeating Greek coffee. It's kid-friendly, too.

Caravanserai TURKISH **$$**
(Map p270; 07-3217 2617; www.caravanserairestaurant.com.au; 1 Dornoch Tce, West End; mains $24-34; noon-2.30pm Fri & Sat, 6pm-late Tue-Sun) Woven tablecloths, red walls and candlelit tables create a snug atmosphere at this standout Turkish restaurant. Share an 'Istanbul Sublime' meze platter (grilled halloumi, kofta meatballs, garlic prawns and more good stuff), or tuck into the excellent lamb ribs.

Petrie Terrace

Scout CAFE **$**
(Map p288; www.scoutcafe.com.au; 190 Petrie Tce, Petrie Terrace; mains $6-18; 7am-4pm) This old-timey neighbourhood shopfront was vacant for 17 years before Scout showed up and started selling bagels. The vibe is downbeat, affable and arty. If the breakfast bagel doesn't tempt, order some Macedonian beans with feta and roasted cherry tomatoes and watch the kids scribble chalk drawings on the footpath in the sun.

Tibetan Kitchen TIBETAN **$$**
(Map p288; 07-3367 0955; www.tibetankitchen.com.au/springhill; 216 Petrie Tce, Petrie Terrace; mains $14-19; 5.30pm-late;) Tasty Tibetan fare beneath paper lanterns and a massive pair of Tibetan Buddhist horns suspended from the ceiling. Try the *bakra ko tihun* (goat curry on the bone with pumpkin and squash). And if you've never tasted Nepalese rice beer, here's your chance.

Paddington

Gelateria Cremona GELATERIA **$**
(Map p292; 07-3367 0212; 5/151 Baroona Rd, Rosalie; gelato from $4.80; 5-10pm Mon, 2-10pm Tue-Fri, 1-10pm Sat & Sun;) Authentic Italian gelato in dinky little tubs or cones, perfect for a promenade on a humid Brisbane evening. Try the classic salted caramel or Dutch chocolate, or a lighter seasonal fruit sorbet (terrific feijoa!). It's down the hill from the main Paddington strip in the cute Rosalie shopping enclave.

Merlo Torrefazione CAFE **$**
(Map p292; 07-3368 2099; www.merlo.com.au; 1/78 Latrobe Tce, Paddington; items $3-6; 6am-5.30pm Mon-Fri, to 5pm Sat & Sun) Keeping Paddington awake, this roaster-cafe is one of several Merlos around town (a local success story). Bite a biscuit or sniff at some slice, but what you're really here for is the coffee: a bag of beans to go or a quick-fire cup, strong enough to get you through until the next one.

Il Posto ITALIAN **$$**
(Map p292; 07-3367 3111; www.ilposto.com.au; 107 Latrobe Tce, Paddington; mains $20-29; noon-4pm Wed-Sun & 5.30pm-late daily) Pizza and pasta just like they make in Rome, served on an outdoor piazza (or inside if it's too humid). Pizzas come either *rosse* or *bianche* (with or without tomato base), and are thin and crispy. Great staff, Peroni beer on tap, and kid-friendly too (also just like Rome).

Drinking & Nightlife

The prime drinking destination in Brisbane is Fortitude Valley, with its lounges, live-music bars and nightclubs (both straight and gay). Most clubs here are open Wednesday to Sunday nights; some are free, others charge up to $20. Dress nicely and bring your ID. In the CBD there's a bottoms-up after-work crowd, while the West End has cool bars full

Paddington

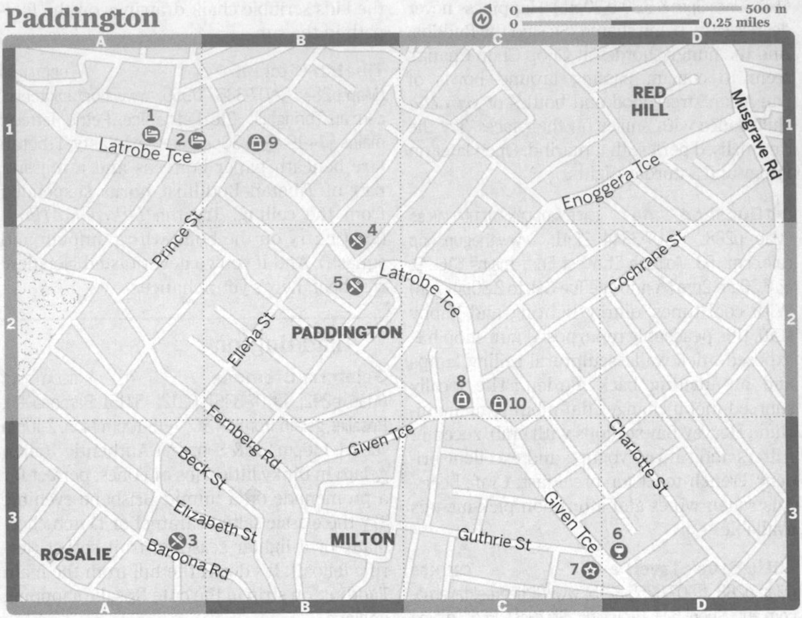

Paddington

Sleeping
1 Casabella Apartment A1
2 Latrobe Apartment A1

Eating
3 Gelateria Cremona A3
4 Il Posto B2
5 Merlo Torrefazione B2

Drinking & Nightlife
6 Kettle & Tin D3

Entertainment
7 Paddo Tavern C3

Shopping
8 Dogstar C2
9 Paddington Antique Centre B1
10 Retro Metro C2

of inner-city funksters. New Farm has some hip bars, attracting a mostly neighbourhood crowd.

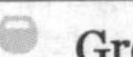

Greater Brisbane

★**Green Beacon Brewing Co** BREWERY
(Map p270; www.greenbeacon.com.au; 26 Helen St, Teneriffe; ⊙5pm-late Mon & Tue, noon-late Wed & Thu, 11am-late Fri-Sun) In the photogenic red-brick backstreets of Teneriffe, this excellent new brewery is packing them in. Behind the long bar is a row of vast stainless-steel vats, where the good stuff ferments before flowing through the taps and into your glass: hand-crafted pale ale, wheat beer, amber ale, IPA and porter, plus seasonal specials and moreish bar food. Winner!

Canvas WINE BAR
(Map p270; www.canvasclub.com.au; 16b Logan Rd, Woolloongabba; ⊙noon-midnight Tue-Fri, 8am-midnight Sat & Sun) In the shadow of the Gabba cricket ground, Canvas is hip, compact and arty. Step down off Logan St – an emerging eating/drinking/antiques hub – pause to ogle the kooky mural, then order a 'Guerrilla Warfare' cocktail from the moustached bartender.

Breakfast Creek Hotel PUB
(Map p270; www.breakfastcreekhotel.com; 2 Kingsford Smith Dr, Albion; ⊙10am-late) This historic 1889 pub is a Brisbane classic. Built in lavish French Renaissance style, it has various bars and dining areas, including a beer garden and an art deco 'private bar' where you can drink beer tapped from a wooden keg. The stylish Substation No 41 bar serves cocktails and legendary steaks.

Central Brisbane

★ Super Whatnot
BAR

(Map p276; www.superwhatnot.com; 48 Burnett Lane; ⊙3-11pm Mon-Thu, noon-1am Fri, 3pm-1am Sat, 3-8pm Sun) Trailblazing Super Whatnot is a funky, industrial lane space, with a mezzanine floor and sunken lounge. Drinks: bottled boutique Australian beers and cocktails (try the authoritarian Border Control). Food: American-inspired bar snacks (hot dogs, mini burritos, nachos). Tunes: vinyl DJs Thursday to Saturday spinning funk, soul and hip hop; regular live acoustic acts. Winning combo!

Riverbar & Kitchen
BAR

(Map p276; www.riverbarandkitchen.com.au; 71 Eagle St; ⊙7am-11.30pm) A chilled-out spot for an afternoon ale, down by the brown Brisbane River at the base of the Eagle St Pier complex. Decked-out like a boat shed, with coiled ropes, white-painted timber and woody booths, the vibe is casual, breezy and free-flowing (like the river itself). Good food, too.

Nant
BAR

(Map p276; www.nant.com.au; 2 Edward St; ⊙3pm-late Tue-Sat) A stylish new speakeasy showcasing Nant whisky – super-duper single malt from Tasmania's central highlands. Also on offer are bourbons, ryes and Prohibition-style gins: taste a few too many, then wobble into the City Botanic Gardens to look for bats. Leather couches, high ceilings, affable bar staff and regular live music.

Embassy Hotel
PUB

(Map p276; www.embassybar.com.au; 214 Elizabeth St; ⊙11am-10pm Mon-Wed, 11am-late Fri, noon-late Sat) This 1928-built boozer has experienced a lot of reincarnations over the years, the latest one involving craft beer, pressed-tin wall panels, exposed red brickwork and killer steak sandwiches. Expect plenty of backpackers on the loose from the hostel upstairs.

Kangaroo Point

Story Bridge Hotel
PUB

(Map p276; www.storybridgehotel.com.au; 200 Main St, Kangaroo Point; ⊙9am-late) Beneath the bridge at Kangaroo Point, this beautiful 1886 pub and beer garden is perfect for a pint after a long day exploring. Live jazz on Sundays (from 3pm); lots of different drinking and eating areas.

South Bank

Tomahawk Bar
BAR

(Map p276; www.tomahawkbar.com.au; 5/182 Grey St; ⊙11am-10pm Sun, Tue & Wed, to 11pm Thu, to midnight Fri & Sat) The coolest place for a beer in South Bank, hands down. Laid-back, beardy bar staff pour craft beers and organic ciders, with lots of Danish, American and a single Kiwi offering in the taps. Bar snacks are a hit too: pork-belly burgers, baked discs of Camembert and fish-stick butties.

Fortitude Valley

★ Alfred & Constance
BAR

(Map p284; www.alfredandconstance.com.au; 130 Constance St, Fortitude Valley; ⊙7am-late Mon-Fri, 8am-late Sat & Sun) Wow! Fabulously eccentric A&C occupies two old weatherboard houses away from the main Valley action. Inside, fluoro-clad ditch diggers, tattooed lesbians, suits and surfies roam between the tiki bar, rooftop terrace, cafe area and lounge rooms checking out the interior design: chandeliers, skeletons, surfboards, old hi-fi equipment... It's weird, and very wonderful.

Sabotage Social
BAR

(Map p284; www.sabotagesocial.com.au; cnr Gipps & Wickham Sts, Fortitude Valley) Whisky is the flavour of the month in Brisbane (or maybe the year), with a crop of whisky-wizened bars popping up around town. This one is a good 'un, with cherry-red chesterfields, gilded walls, a '90s-heavy playlist and an ace beer (or rather, whisky) garden.

Bowery
COCKTAIL BAR

(Map p284; www.facebook.com/thebowerybar; 676 Ann St, Fortitude Valley; ⊙5pm-late Tue-Sun) The exposed-brick walls, gilded mirrors, booths and foot-worn floorboards at this long, narrow bar bring a touch of substance to the Valley fray. The cocktails and wine list are top-notch (and priced accordingly), and there's live jazz/dub Tuesday to Thursday. DJs spin on weekends.

Press Club
COCKTAIL BAR

(Map p284; www.pressclub.net.au; 339 Brunswick St, Fortitude Valley; ⊙7pm-late Tue-Thu, 6pm-late Fri-Sun) Amber hues, leather sofas, ottomans, glowing chandeliers, fabric-covered lanterns... It's all rather glamorously Moroccan here (with a touch of that kooky cantina from *Star Wars*). Live music on Thursdays (jazz, funk, rockabilly) and DJs on weekends.

Cloudland CLUB

(Map p284; www.katarzyna.com.au/venues/cloudland; 641 Ann St, Fortitude Valley; ⌚5pm-late Mon & Tue, 11.30am-late Wed-Sun) Like stepping into a surreal cloud forest, this multilevel club has a huge plant-filled lobby with a retractable glass roof, vast chandeliers and wrought-iron birdcagelike nooks. Even if you're not a clubber, peek through the windows during the day: the interior design is astonishing!

Oh Hello CLUB

(Map p284; www.ohhello.com.au; 621 Ann St, Fortitude Valley; ⌚9pm-5am Thu-Sun) Oh hello! Fancy seeing you here. This convivial club is perfect if you like the idea of clubbing but find the reality a bit deflating. It's unpretentious (you can wear a T-shirt), there's a great selection of craft beers, and the cool kids here don't think too highly of themselves.

Family CLUB

(Map p284; www.thefamily.com.au; 8 McLachlan St, Fortitude Valley; ⌚9pm-5am Fri-Sun) Queue up for one of Brisbane's biggest and best clubs. The music here is phenomenal, pumping through four levels with myriad dance floors, bars, funky themed booths and elite DJs from home and away. The 'Fluffy' gay dance party happens on Sundays.

Church CLUB

(Map p284; www.thechurchnightclub.com.au; 25 Warner St, Fortitude Valley; ⌚9pm-5am Fri & Sat) Feel like swinging a hip? This bedeviled, black-painted holy house on a Valley side-street is home to the Magic City Superclub, an unfettered dance fest held on Friday and Saturday nights.

Beat MegaClub CLUB

(Map p284; www.thebeatmegaclub.com.au; 677 Ann St, Fortitude Valley; ⌚9pm-5am Mon & Tue, 8pm-5am Wed-Sun) Five rooms plus seven bars plus three chill-out areas plus hard house/electro/retro/techno beats equals the perfect storm for dance junkies. It's big with the gay and lesbian crowd, with regular drag performances.

New Farm

Bar Alto BAR

(Map p270; www.baralto.com.au; Brisbane Powerhouse, 119 Lamington St, New Farm; ⌚11am-late Tue-Sun) At the arts-loving Brisbane Powerhouse, this snappy upstairs bar-restaurant has an enormous balcony with chunky timber tables overlooking the river – a mighty fine vantage point any time of day. There's a devastatingly good wine list and marvellous food.

Gertie's Bar & Lounge WINE BAR

(Map p284; 699 Brunswick St, New Farm; ⌚4pm-midnight Tue-Fri, 3pm-midnight Sat, 2pm-midnight Sun) A sophisticated affair, Gertie's always seems to have groups of good-looking city girls sipping cocktails inside the fold-back windows. Even without the eye-candy, Gertie's – moodily lit, with old soul on the stereo and retro photos on the walls – is a great place for a low-key drink, or a bowl of pasta and a glass of wine.

Bitter Suite BAR

(Map p270; www.bittersuite.com.au; 75 Welsby St, New Farm; ⌚11.30am-11pm Tue-Thu, to 11.30pm Fri, 8am-11.30pm Sat, 8am-10pm Sun) This lofty old red-brick warehouse on a quiet New Farm backstreet has been reborn as an effervescent beer barn, with 60-plus craft beers available, a daily selection of which flows through eight taps. Super bar food (Peking duck pancakes) and weekend breakfasts.

West End

★ **Archive Beer Boutique** BAR

(Map p288; www.archivebeerboutique.com.au; ⌚11am-late) Interesting beer, interesting people, interesting place: welcome to Archive, a temple of beer with many a fine frothy on tap (try the Holgate Cowboy Sour Porter). Check the bar made of books! Oh, and the food's good, too (steaks, mussels, pasta). Upstairs is **Loft West End** (Map p288; www.loftwestend.com; ⌚4pm-late Wed-Sat), a sassy cocktail bar and food room.

End BAR

(Map p288; www.73vulture.com; 1/73 Vulture St, West End; ⌚3pm-midnight) This mod-industrial shopfront conversion is a real locals' hang-out, with hipsters, cheese boards, Morrissey on the turntable, DJs and live acoustic troubadours. The Blackstar mocha stout (caffeine courtesy of the local roaster) will cheer up your rainy river afternoon.

Lychee Lounge COCKTAIL BAR

(Map p288; www.lycheelounge.com.au; 94 Boundary St, West End; ⌚3pm-midnight Sun-Thu, to 1am Fri & Sat) Sink into the lush furniture and stare up at the macabre doll-head chandeliers at this exotic Asian lounge bar, with mellow beats, mood lighting and an open frontage to Boundary St. Is this what a *real* opium den looks like?

Petrie Terrace

Statler & Waldorf BAR
(Map p288; www.statlerandwaldorf.co; 25 Caxton St, Petrie Terrace; ⌚11am-midnight Wed-Sun) Remember those two cynical old critics from *The Muppet Show*? They leer down from a painting above the fireplace at this atmospheric booze room, which has given the otherwise trashy Caxton St a much-needed lift. Expect old floorboards, craft beers, cocktails, Scotch appreciation sessions and good conversation.

Cabiria BAR
(Map p288; www.cabiria.com.au; 6 The Barracks, 61 Petrie Tce, Petrie Terrace; ⌚7am-3pm Mon, 7am-late Tue-Fri, 4pm-late Sat) Brisbane's old police barracks have been converted into a complex of quality bars and eateries, the pick of which is cool Cabiria. It's a skinny, dimly lit, moody room with big mirrors and shimmering racks of booze (35 different tequilas!). Awesome New York–style sandwiches, too.

Paddington

Kettle & Tin BAR
(Map p292; www.kettleandtin.com.au; 215 Given Tce, Paddington; ⌚7am-5pm Mon, to late Tue-Sun) The chalkboard out the front of this cool cafe-bar grabbed our attention: 'We serve beer and whiskey, because no great story ever started with a salad'. The food here is terrific too (and terrifically calorific: try the confit duck nachos or pork-belly fries). Live acoustic music Sunday afternoons.

Dowse Bar BAR
(Map p288; www.facebook.com/dowsebar; cnr Given Tce & Dowse St, Paddington; ⌚4pm-late Thu-Sun) Tucked underneath the bigger, flashier Iceworks bar, Dowse Bar is an intimate, retro-quirky booze room that brings a bit of bearded student/hipster vibe to Paddington. Live acoustic acts croon to the crowd, who sit on old couches among wacky lamps and murals.

☆ Entertainment

Most big-ticket international bands have Brisbane on their radar, and the city's nightclubs regularly attract top-class DJs. Theatres, cinemas and other performing-arts venues are among Australia's biggest and best.

Free entertainment street-press includes the *Music* (www.themusic.com.au) and *Scene* (www.scenemagazine.com.au). *Q News* (www.qnews.com.au) covers the gay and lesbian scene. The *Courier-Mail* (www.news.com.au/couriermail) newspaper has arts and entertainment listings (and too much rugby), or check the *Brisbane Times* (www.brisbanetimes.com.au).

Ticketek (Map p276; ☎13 28 49; www.ticketek.com.au; cnr Elizabeth & George Sts; ⌚9am-5pm Mon-Fri) is a central booking agency that handles major events, sports and performances. Try **Qtix** (☎13 62 46; www.qtix.com.au) for loftier arts performances.

Brightside LIVE MUSIC
(Map p284; www.thebrightsidebrisbane.com.au; 27 Warner St, Fortitude Valley; ⌚8pm-late Thu-Sat) The foundation stone of this 1906 church says 'To the glory of God'. But it's the god of live alternative rock the faithful are here to worship these days: heavy, impassioned, unhinged and unfailingly loud. Just like 1991, minus the cigarettes.

Lock 'n' Load LIVE MUSIC
(Map p288; www.locknloadbistro.com.au; 142 Boundary St, West End; ⌚10am-late Mon-Fri, 7am-late Sat & Sun; 📶) This ebullient, woody, two-storey gastropub lures an upbeat crowd of music fans. Bands play the small front stage (jazz and originals). Catch a gig, then show up for breakfast the next morning (the potato and ham-hock hash-cakes go well with hangovers).

Hi-Fi LIVE MUSIC
(Map p288; www.thehifi.com.au; 125 Boundary St, West End; ⌚ gig nights 8pm-late) This mod, minimalist rock room has unobstructed sight lines and a great line-up of local and international talent (Sepultura, Kingswood, Violent Soho...). Retro Vinyl bar is out the front.

Crowbar LIVE MUSIC
(Map p284; www.facebook.com/crowbarbrisbane; 243 Brunswick St, Fortitude Valley; ⌚gig nights 8pm-late) A haven of metal, hardcore and punk: black-clad musos of menace from around Australia, the US and UK, in-your-face and unrelenting.

Zoo LIVE MUSIC
(Map p284; www.thezoo.com.au; 711 Ann St, Fortitude Valley; ⌚7pm-late Wed-Sun) 🍃 Going strong since 1992, the Zoo has surrendered a bit of musical territory to the Hi-Fi and Brightside, but is still a grungy spot for indie rock, hip hop, acoustic, reggae and electronic acts (lots of raw local talent).

Brisbane Jazz Club JAZZ

(Map p276; ☎07-3391 2006; www.brisbanejazzclub.com.au; 1 Annie St, Kangaroo Point; $15-25; ⏰6.30-11pm Thu-Sat, 5-10pm Sun) Straight out of the bayou, this tiny riverside jazz shack has been Brisbane's jazz beacon since 1972. Anyone who's anyone in the scene plays here when they're in town.

Brisbane Convention & Exhibition Centre LIVE MUSIC

(Map p276; www.bcec.com.au; cnr Merivale & Glenelg Sts, South Bank) When the big guns are in town (Nick Cave, Bob Dylan) they rock this 8000-seat auditorium in South Bank.

Palace Barracks CINEMA

(Map p288; www.palacecinemas.com.au; 61 Petrie Tce, Petrie Terrace; adult/child $18.50/13; ⏰9am-late) Near Roma St Station in the Barracks Centre, the plush, six-screen Palace Barracks shows Hollywood and alternative fare, and has a bar.

Moonlight Cinema CINEMA

(Map p270; www.moonlight.com.au; Brisbane Powerhouse, 119 Lamington Rd, New Farm; adult/child $16/12; ⏰7pm Wed-Sun) Next to the Brisbane Powerhouse, New Farm Park hosts al fresco cinema between December and February at the Moonlight Cinema. Arrive early to get a spot.

Palace Centro CINEMA

(Map p284; www.palacecinemas.com.au; 39 James St, Fortitude Valley; adult/child $17.50/13; ⏰10am-late) Screens art-house films and hosts a French film festival in March/April, and a Scandinavian film fest in July.

Brisbane Powerhouse PERFORMING ARTS

(Map p270; www.brisbanepowerhouse.org; 119 Lamington St, New Farm) Nationally and internationally acclaimed theatre, music, comedy, dance… There are loads of happenings at the Powerhouse – many free – and the venue, with its cool bars and restaurants, enjoys a charismatic setting overlooking the Brisbane River.

Judith Wright Centre of Contemporary Arts PERFORMING ARTS

(Map p284; www.judithwrightcentre.com; 420 Brunswick St, Fortitude Valley; ⏰box office 9am-4pm Mon-Fri; 📶) A medium-sized creative space (300 seats max) for cutting-edge performances: contemporary dance and world music, Indigenous theatre, circus and visual arts.

Metro Arts Centre THEATRE

(Map p276; www.metroarts.com.au; Level 2, 109 Edward St; ⏰performances vary, gallery 10am-4.30pm Mon-Fri, 2-4.30pm Sat) This arty downtown venue hosts community theatre, local dramatic pieces, dance and art shows. It's an effervescent spot for a taste of Brisbane's creative talent, be it offbeat, quirky, fringe, progressive or just downright weird. Artists and performers give free evening talks on the first Friday of every month.

Queensland Performing Arts Centre PERFORMING ARTS

(QPAC; Map p276; www.qpac.com.au; Queensland Cultural Centre, cnr Grey & Melbourne Sts, South Bank; ⏰box office 9am-8.30pm Mon-Sat) Brisbane's main high-arts performance centre comprises three venues and features concerts, plays, dance and performances of all genres: anything from flamenco to Broadway musicals and the American Ballet Theatre.

Queensland Conservatorium OPERA, LIVE MUSIC

(Map p276; www.griffith.edu.au/music/queensland-conservatorium; 140 Grey St, South Bank; ⏰box office 7am-10pm Mon-Fri, 8am-6pm Sat & Sun) Part of Griffith University, the conservatorium hosts opera, as well as touring artists playing classical, jazz, rock and world music. Many concerts are free.

Paddo Tavern COMEDY

(Map p292; www.standup.com.au; 186 Given Tce, Paddington; ⏰10am-late) If a car wash married its supermarket cousin, their firstborn would probably look like this ugly Paddington pub, which has incongruously adopted a Wild West theme inside (Stetsons, saddle seats, old rifles on the wall). But it's one of the best places in Brisbane to see stand-up comedy: check the website for listings.

Sport

Like most other Australians, Brisbanites are sports-mad. You can catch interstate and international cricket at the **Gabba** (Brisbane Cricket Ground; Map p270; www.thegabba.com.au; 411 Vulture St, Woolloongabba), south of Kangaroo Point. The cricket season runs from October to March: if you're new to the game, try and get along to a Twenty20 match – cricket at its most explosive.

The Gabba is also the home ground for the Brisbane Lions, an **Australian Football League** (AFL; www.afl.com.au) team which dominated the league in the early 2000s (lately, not so much). Watch them in action, often at night under lights, between April and September.

Rugby league is also a massive spectator sport in Brizzy. The Brisbane Broncos, part of the **National Rugby League** (NRL; www.nrl.com.au) competition, play home games over winter at **Suncorp Stadium** (Map p288; www.suncorpstadium.com.au; 40 Castlemaine St, Milton) in Milton (between Petrie Terrace and Paddington). In rugby union, the Queensland Reds in the Super Rugby comp and the national Wallabies team also play at Suncorp and have strong followings.

Also calling Suncorp home are the Queensland Roar football (soccer) team, part of the **A-League** (www.aleague.com.au). The domestic football season lasts from August to February, and has been attracting fat crowds in recent years.

Shopping

Brisbane is home to some fabulous riverside markets, eye-catching boutiques and galleries, plus one-of-a-kind shops – particularly around Fortitude Valley and Paddington – selling everything from indie fashions to Indigenous artwork, vintage apparel, new and used books and rare vinyl. **Queen St Mall** and the **Myer Centre** in the CBD house big chain stores, upmarket outlets and the obligatory touristy trash.

Central Brisbane

Archives Fine Books BOOKS
(Map p276; www.archivesfinebooks.com.au; 40 Charlotte St; ⌚9am-6pm Mon-Thu, to 7pm Fri, to 5pm Sat) You could get lost in here for hours: rickety bookshelves, squeaky floorboards and (allegedly) a million second-hand books.

Mind Games GAMES
(Map p276; www.mindgamesbrisbane.com; Level 2, Myer Centre, Queen St Mall; ⌚ 9am-5.30pm Mon-Thu, to 9pm Fri, to 4pm Sat, 10am-4pm Sun) Intellectual, rainy-day gaming the old-fashioned way: chess, crosswords, Rubik's cubes, mahjong, Scrabble, 1000-piece jigsaws of the Arc de Triomphe...

Malt Traders WINE
(Map p276; www.malttraders.com.au; 10 Market St; ⌚10am-7pm Mon & Tue, to 8pm Wed, to 9pm Fri, noon-7pm Sat) The best little bottleshop in the CBD, these guys zoom-in on single-malt whiskys, organic cider, single-vineyard wines and craft beers. 'Explore, indulge, entertain.'

Record Exchange MUSIC
(Map p276; www.therecordexchange.com.au; Level 1, 65 Adelaide St; ⌚9am-5pm) This warrenlike, upstairs shop is home to an astounding collection of vinyl, CDs, DVDs, posters and other rock memorabilia. 'Brisbane's most interesting shop' (self-professed).

South Bank

Title BOOKS
(Map p276; www.titlestore.com.au; 1/133 Grey St; ⌚10am-6pm) Offbeat and alternative art, music, photography and cinema books, plus vinyl, CDs and DVDs – a quality dose of subversive rebelliousness (just what South Bank needs!). Pick up that Woody Guthrie 100th-birthday Centennial Collection you've had your eye on.

Fortitude Valley

Trash Monkey CLOTHING, ACCESSORIES
(Map p284; www.trashmonkey.com.au; 9/8 Duncan St, Fortitude Valley; ⌚10am-7pm Mon-Wed, to 9pm Thu-Sat, to 5pm Sun) Countercultural mayhem in the Valley! Goths, skaters, punks, alt-rockers and rockabilly rebels head here for their shoes, T-shirts, caps, nylon stockings, dress-up gear, socks, belts and beanies, much of which is spangled with tattoo-centric designs. You've been hankering after some leopard-skin brothel creepers, right?

Angelo's Fresh Pasta FOOD
(Map p284; www.angelospasta.com.au; 22 Doggett St, Fortitude Valley; pasta around $5; ⌚8am-5pm Mon-Fri, to noon Sat) This local company has been making pasta since 1968, and sells the stringy stuff from a little red shed in a back-street car park. Tomato tagliatelle, duck-egg linguine, pumpkin-and-spinach cannelloni... brilliant! Look for the pallets of crushed tomato tins by the street.

Winn Lane CLOTHING, BOOKS
(Map p284; www.winnlane.com.au; Winn Lane) Duck behind Ann St (off Winn St) and discover this arty congregation of boutiques, bookshops, jewellers and casual eats. Spangled with street art, the vibe is emerging and quirky. Don't miss **Künstler** (Map p284; www.kunstler.com.au; 5 Winn Lane; ⌚10am-5pm Tue-Sat, to 3pm Sun), probably Brisbane's smallest shop, selling art and architecture books.

James Street CLOTHING, FOOD
(Map p284; www.jamesst.com.au; James St, Fortitude Valley) Fortitude Valley's fashion-fuelled

TO MARKET, TO MARKET

Jan Powers Farmers Market (Map p270; www.janpowersfarmersmarkets.com.au; Brisbane Powerhouse, 119 Lamington St, New Farm; ⌚6am-noon 2nd & 4th Sat of month) Fancy some purple heirloom carrots or blue bananas? This fab farmers market, with around 120 stalls, coughs up some unusual produce. Also great for more predictably coloured flowers, cheeses, coffee and fish. The CityCat ferry takes you straight there.

Davies Park Market (Map p288; www.daviesparkmarket.com.au; Davies Park, West End; ⌚6am-2pm Sat) Under a grove of huge Moreton Bay fig trees in the West End, this hippie riverside market features organic foods, gourmet breakfasts, herbs and flowers, bric-a-brac and buskers.

Brisbane Valley Markets (Map p284; www.brisbane-markets.com.au/brisbane-valley-markets.html; Brunswick St & Duncan St Malls, Fortitude Valley; ⌚8am-4pm Sat, 9am-4pm Sun) These colourful markets fill the Brunswick St Mall and the Duncan St (Chinatown) Mall in Fortitude Valley with eclectic crafts, clothes, books, records, food stalls and works by budding designers.

Brisbane Riverside Markets (Map p276; www.brisbane-markets.com.au/brisbane-riverside-markets.html; Eagle St Pier; ⌚7am-4pm Sun) Hugging the river, the Sunday Riverside Markets have dozens of stalls selling glassware, handicrafts, art, juices and snacks, and there are live tunes. The CityCat ferry stop is just a couple of inches away.

Boundary Street Markets (Map p288; www.boundarystreetmarkets.com.au; cnr Boundary & Mollison Sts, West End; ⌚4-10pm Fri, 9am-3pm Sat & Sun) Set in and around a former ice-cream factory, these bohemian markets feature pop-up shops, buskers, food vans, vintage gear and quirky folks (West End at its best), plus live bands at the Motor Room.

underbelly (or maybe its toned six-pack) lives along a few blocks of James St under a colonnade of fig trees. High-end boutiques (Scanlan Theodore, Mimco, Kookai, Blonde Venus) bump hips with cafes and the excellent James St Market (p287).

Blonde Venus CLOTHING
(Map p284; www.blondevenus.com.au; Shop 3, 181 Robertson St, Fortitude Valley; ⌚10am-6pm Mon-Sat, 11am-4.30pm Sun) One of the top boutiques in Brisbane, Blonde Venus has been around for 20-plus years, stocking a well-curated selection of both indie and couture labels.

West End

★Egg Records MUSIC
(Map p288; www.eggrecords.com.au; 79 Vulture St, West End; ⌚9.30am-5.30pm Mon-Fri, to 4pm Sat & Sun) This well-organised collection of LPs, CDs and fantastically kitsch memorabilia is a must-see for anyone with even the slightest hint of 'collector' in their DNA. Loads of second-hand vinyl and CDs, plus heavy-metal T-shirts and a cavalcade of plasticky treasures featuring Doctor Who, Star Wars characters, Evel Knievel…awesome!

Avid Reader BOOKS
(Map p288; www.avidreader.com.au; 193 Boundary St, West End; ⌚8.30am-8.30pm Mon-Fri, to 6pm Sat, to 5pm Sun) Diverse pages, a little cafe in the corner and frequent readings and bookish events: a real West End cultural hub.

Paddington

Retro Metro CLOTHING
(Map p292; ☎07-3876 3854; www.mustdobrisbane.com; 297 Given Tce, Paddington; ⌚10am-5pm Tue-Sat, 11am-4pm Sun) A highlight of Paddington's boutique-lined main street, Retro Metro stocks a brilliant selection of vintage gear: cowboy boots, suits, cocktail dresses, handbags, jewellery, vinyl, '80s rock T-shirts, sunglasses, vases, ashtrays and other interesting knick-knackery. Look for the shabby old white Queenslander with vinyl records nailed to the facade.

Dogstar CLOTHING
(Map p292; www.dogstar.com.au; 2 Latrobe Tce, Paddington; ⌚10am-5pm Mon-Fri, to 4pm Sat, to 3pm Sun) There's more than a touch of Japanese style evident at this hip boutique. Beautiful fabrics and fine details feature prominently in skirts, jackets, wraps, tunics, jewellery and retro winter knits.

Paddington Antique Centre ANTIQUES (Map p292; ☎07-3369 8088; www.paddingtonantiquecentre.com.au; 167 Latrobe Tce, Paddington; ⊙10am-5pm) The city's biggest antique emporium is inside a 1929 theatre, with over 50 dealers selling all manner of historic treasure/trash: clothes, jewellery, dolls, books, '60s Hawaiian shirts, lamps, musical instruments, toys, German WWII helmets... There's a cafe here, too.

Information

EMERGENCY

Police (☎000; 200 Roma St) Brisbane's police HQ.

RACQ (☎13 11 11; www.racq.com.au) Automotive roadside assistance.

INTERNET ACCESS

Brisbane Square Library (www.brisbane.qld.gov.au; 266 George St; ⊙9am-6pm Mon-Thu, to 7pm Fri, 10am-3pm Sat & Sun;) Free wi-fi access.

Hispeed Internet (61 Petrie Tce, Petrie Terrace; ⊙8am-late;) Inside the Barracks shopping centre.

State Library of Queensland (www.slq.qld.gov.au; Stanley Pl, South Bank; ⊙10am-8pm Mon-Thu, to 5pm Fri-Sun;) Quick 30-minute terminals and free wi-fi.

MEDICAL SERVICES

CBD Medical Centre (☎07-3211 3611; www.cbdmedical.com.au; Level 1, 245 Albert St; ⊙7am-7pm Mon-Fri, 8.30am-5pm Sat, 9.30am-5pm Sun) General medical services and vaccinations.

Pharmacy on the Mall (☎07-3221 4585; www.pharmacies.com.au/pharmacy-on-the-mall; 141 Queen St; ⊙7am-9pm Mon-Thu, to 9.30pm Fri, 8am-9pm Sat, 8.30am-6pm Sun)

Royal Brisbane & Women's Hospital (☎07-3646 8111; www.health.qld.gov.au/rbwh; Butterfield St, Herston) Has a 24-hour casualty ward.

MONEY

American Express (☎1300 139 060; www.americanexpress.com; 260 Queen St; ⊙8.30am-4.30pm Mon-Thu, to 5pm Fri) Inside the Westpac bank.

Travelex (☎07-3174 1018; www.travelex.com.au; 300 Queen St; ⊙9.30am-4pm Mon-Thu, to 5pm Fri) Money exchange.

POST

Main post office (GPO; Map p276; www.auspost.com.au; 261 Queen St; ⊙7am-6pm Mon-Fri, 10am-1.30pm Sat)

TOURIST INFORMATION

BCC Customer Centre (Map p276; ☎07-3407 2861; www.brisbane.qld.gov.au; 266 George St; ⊙9am-5pm Mon-Fri) This Brisbane City Council centre provides info on disabled access around Brisbane. In the same building as the Brisbane Square Library.

Brisbane visitor information centre (Map p276; ☎07-3006 6290; www.visitbrisbane.com.au; Queen St Mall; ⊙9am-5.30pm Mon-Thu, to 7pm Fri, to 5pm Sat, 10am-5pm Sun) Terrific one-stop info counter for all things Brisbane.

South Bank visitor information centre (Map p276; www.visitsouthbank.com.au; Stanley St Plaza, South Bank; ⊙9am-5pm) The low-down on South Bank, plus tours, accommodation and transport bookings, and tickets to entertainment events.

Getting There & Away

The Brisbane Transit Centre – which incorporates Roma St Station – is about 500m northwest of the city centre, and is the main terminus and booking point for all long-distance buses and trains, as well as Citytrain services. Central Station is also an important hub for trains.

AIR

Brisbane Airport (www.bne.au, Airport Drive) is about 16km northeast of the city centre at Eagle Farm. It has separate international and domestic terminals about 2km apart, linked by the Airtrain (p300), which runs every 15 to 30 minutes from 5.40am to 10pm (between terminals per adult/child $5/free). It's a busy international arrival and departure point with frequent flights to Asia, Europe, the Pacific islands, North America and New Zealand.

Several airlines link Brisbane with the rest of the country. The main players:

Jetstar (www.jetstar.com)

Qantas (www.qantas.com.au)

Tigerair (www.tigerair.com)

Virgin Australia (www.virginaustralia.com)

Qantas, Virgin Australia and Jetstar all fly to towns and cities within Queensland, especially the more popular coastal destinations and the Whitsunday Islands. Tiger Airways flies between Brisbane and Melbourne, Sydney, Adelaide, Darwin and Cairns.

Skytrans (www.skytrans.com.au) is a smaller airline flying between Brisbane and regional hubs including Toowoomba, Charleville and Mt Isa.

BUS

Brisbane's main bus terminus and booking office for long-distance buses is the **Brisbane Transit Centre** (Roma St Station; www.brisbanetransitcentre.com.au; Roma St). Booking desks for

Greyhound (p309) and **Premier Motor Service** (www.premierms.com.au) are here.

Approximate fares and journey times for long-haul routes include the following (although it's probably going to be just as affordable to fly, and a *lot* quicker!):

DESTINATION	DURATION (HR)	ONE-WAY FARE ($)
Adelaide	62	396
Cairns	30	205
Darwin	49	418
Melbourne	36	298
Sydney	18	105
Townsville	24	285

Airport to the Gold Coast & Byron Bay

Con-x-ion (www.con-x-ion.com) operates direct shuttle bus services from Brisbane Airport to the Gold Coast ($49). Services meet every major flight and will drop you anywhere on the Gold Coast. **AA Express** (www.aaexpress.com.au) buses also connect the Brisbane Transit Centre and the Gold Coast ($45).

Further south to Byron Bay, there are multiple daily buses from Brisbane airport ($54, three hours) and the Brisbane Transit Centre ($40) with **Byron Easy Bus** (www.byroneasybus.com.au). The **Brisbane 2 Byron** (www.brisbane2byron.com) bus plies the same routes for similar fares.

Airport to the Sunshine Coast

Sun-Air Bus Service (www.sunair.com.au) One of several operators with direct services from Brisbane Airport to the Sunshine Coast.

Con-x-ion (www.con-x-ion.com) Plies the same route as Sun-Air. One-way fares start at around $40 (to the southern Sunshine Coast areas; more expensive the further north you go).

CAR & MOTORCYCLE

Brisbane has a 70km network of motorways, tunnels and bridges (some of them tolled) run by **Queensland Motorways** (☎13 33 31; www.qldmotorways.com.au). If you're just passing through from north to south or south to north, take the Gateway Motorway (M1), which bypasses the city centre ($4.25 toll at the time of writing; see www.govia.com.au for payment options, in advance or retrospectively).

Car Rental

The major car-rental companies – **Avis** (www.avis.com.au), **Budget** (www.budget.com.au), **Europcar** (www.europcar.com.au), **Hertz** (www.hertz.com.au) and **Thrifty** (www.thrifty.com.au) – have offices at Brisbane Airport and in the city.

Smaller rental companies with branches near the airport (and shuttles to get you to/from there) include **Ace Rental Cars** (☎1800 049 225; www.acerentalcars.com.au; 330 Nudgee Rd, Hendra), **Apex Car Rentals** (☎1800 121 029; www.apexrentacar.com.au; 400 Nudgee Rd, Hendra), and **East Coast Car Rentals** (☎3839 9111, 1800 028 881; www.eastcoastcarrentals.com.au; 76 Wickham St, Fortitude Valley).

TRAIN

Brisbane's main station for long-distance trains is Roma St Station (essentially the same complex as the Brisbane Transit Centre). For reservations and information contact the **Queensland Rail Travel Centre** (Map p276; ☎1800 872 467, 07-3235 1323; www.queenslandrail.com.au; Concourse Level, 305 Edward St; ⏲8am-5pm Mon-Fri) at Central Station.

NSW TrainLink Brisbane to Sydney

Spirit of Queensland Brisbane to Cairns

Spirit of the Outback Brisbane to Longreach via Rockhampton

Sunlander Brisbane to Cairns via Townsville

Tilt Train Brisbane to Cairns

Westlander Brisbane to Charleville

ℹ Getting Around

TO/FROM THE AIRPORT

Airtrain (☎07-3215 5000; www.airtrain.com.au) trains runs every 15 to 30 minutes, 5.40am to 10pm, from Brisbane Airport to Fortitude Valley, Central Station, Roma St Station (Brisbane Transit Centre) and other key destinations (one way/return $16.50/31). There are also half-hourly services between the airport and Gold Coast Citytrain stops (one way $37).

If you prefer door-to-door service, **Con-x-ion** (www.con-x-ion.com) runs regular shuttle buses between the airport and CBD hotels (one way/return $20/36); it also connects Brisbane Airport to Gold Coast hotels (one way/return $49/92).

A taxi into the centre from the airport will cost $40 to $50.

CAR & MOTORCYCLE

There is ticketed two-hour parking on many streets in the CBD and the inner suburbs. Heed the signs: Brisbane's parking inspectors are pretty ruthless. During the day, parking is cheaper around South Bank and the West End than in the city centre, but it's free in the CBD during the evening.

A GPS unit could be your best friend: Brisbane's streets are organically laid-out and convoluted.

PUBLIC TRANSPORT

Brisbane's excellent public-transport network – bus, train and ferry – is run by **TransLink** (☎13 12 30; www.translink.com.au), which runs a Transit

Information Centre at Roma St Station (Brisbane Transit Centre). The Brisbane Visitor Information Centre (p299) can also help with public transport info.

Fares Buses, trains and ferries operate on a zone system: most of the inner-city suburbs are in Zone 1, which translates into a single fare of $5.20/2.60 per adult/child. If travelling into Zone 2, tickets are $6.10/3.10. A Go Card will save you some money.

NightLink In addition to the services described in the following sections, there are also dedicated nocturnal NightLink bus, train and fixed-rate taxi services from the city and Fortitude Valley: see www.translink.com.au for details.

See CityCycle (p275) for details on Brisbane's public bike-hire network.

Bus

Translink runs Brisbane's bus services, including the free City Loop and Spring Hill Loop bus services that circle the CBD and Spring Hill, stopping at key spots such as QUT, Queen Street Mall, City Botanic Gardens, Central Station and Roma Street Parkland. The loop buses run every 10 minutes on weekdays between 7am and 6pm.

The main stops for local buses are the underground **Queen Street Bus Station** (Map p276) and **King George Square Bus Station** (Map p276). You can also pick up many buses from the stops along Adelaide St, between George and Edward Sts.

Buses generally run every 10 to 30 minutes Monday to Friday, from 5am until about 11pm, and with the same frequency on Saturday morning (starting at 6am). Services are less frequent at other times, and cease at 9pm Sunday and at midnight on other days. CityGlider and BUZ services are high-frequency services along busy routes.

Ferry

In addition to the fast CityCat (p277) services, Translink runs Cross River Ferries, connecting Kangaroo Point with the CBD, and New Farm Park with Norman Park on the adjacent shore (and also Teneriffe and Bulimba further north). Fares/zones apply as per all other Brisbane transport.

Free (yes free!) CityHopper ferries zigzag back and forth across the water between North Quay, South Bank, the CBD, Kangaroo Point and Sydney St in New Farm. These additional services start around 6am and run until about 11pm.

Train

TransLink's fast Citytrain network has six main lines, which run as far north as Gympie on the Sunshine Coast and as far south as Varsity Lakes on the Gold Coast. All trains go through Roma St Station, Central Station and Fortitude Valley Station; there's also a handy South Bank Station.

GO CARD

If you plan to use public transport for more than a few trips, you'll save money by purchasing a **Go Card** (starting balance adult/child $10/5). Purchase the card, add credit and then use it on city buses, trains and ferries, and you'll save more than 30% off individual fares. Go Cards are sold (and can be recharged) at transit stations and newsagents, by phone or online. See www.translink.com.au/tickets-and-fares/go-card for details.

The Airtrain service integrates with the Citytrain network in the CBD and along the Gold Coast line.

Trains run from around 4.30am, with the last train on each line leaving Central Station between 11.30pm and midnight. On Sunday the last trains run at around 10pm.

TAXI

In the city there are taxi ranks at Roma St Station and at the top end of Edward St, by the junction with Adelaide St. You might have a tough time hailing one late at night in Fortitude Valley: there's a rank near the corner of Brunswick St and Ann St, but expect long queues.

Black & White (☎13 32 22; www.blackandwhitecabs.com.au)

Yellow Cab Co (☎13 19 24; www.yellowcab.com.au)

AROUND BRISBANE

North Stradbroke Island

POP 2000

An easy 30-minute ferry chug from the Brisbane suburb of Cleveland, this unpretentious holiday isle is like Noosa and Byron Bay rolled into one. There's a string of glorious powdery white beaches, great surf and some quality places to stay and eat (catering to Brisbane's naughty-weekend-away set). It's also a hot-spot for spying dolphins, turtles, manta rays and, between June and November, hundreds of humpback whales. 'Straddie' also boasts freshwater lakes and 4WD tracks.

There are only a few small settlements on the island, with a handful of accommodation and eating options – mostly near **Point Lookout** in the northeast. On the west coast, **Dunwich** is where the ferries dock. **Amity** is a small village on the northwestern corner. Much of the island's southern section is closed to visitors due to sand mining.

Interestingly, North and South Stradbroke Islands used to be one single island, but a savage storm blew through the sand spit between the two in 1896.

Sights

At Point Lookout, the eye-popping **North Gorge Headlands Walk** is an absolute highlight. It's an easy 20-minute loop around the headland along boardwalks, with the thrum of cicadas as your soundtrack. Keep an eye out for turtles, dolphins and manta rays offshore. The view from the headland down Main Beach is a showstopper.

There are several gorgeous **beaches** around Point Lookout. A patrolled swimming area, Cylinder Beach is popular with families and is flanked by Home Beach and the ominously named Deadman's Beach. Further around the point, Frenchman's Beach is another peaceful, secluded spot if you're not fussed by the odd nudist wandering past. Most of these spots have surf breaks, too. Near the Headlands Walk, surfers and bodyboarders descend on Main Beach in search of the ultimate wave.

Fisherfolk take their 4WDs further down Main Beach (4WD permit required; $39.55 from Straddie Camping) towards **Eighteen Mile Swamp**, continuing all the way down the east coast to Jumpinpin, the channel that separates North and South Stradbroke, a legendary **fishing** spot.

About 4km east of Dunwich, the tannin-stained **Brown Lake** is the colour of stewed tea, but is completely OK for swimming. There are picnic tables, barbecues and a toilet at the lake. About 4km further along this road, take the 2.6km (40-minute) bush track to Straddie's glittering centrepiece, **Blue Lake**, part of **Naree Budjong Djara National Park** (www.nprsr.qld.gov.au/parks/naree-budjong-djara): keep an eye out for forest birds, skittish lizards and swamp wallabies along the way. There's a wooden viewing platform at the lake, which is encircled by a forest of paperbarks, eucalypts and banksias. You can cool off in the water, if you don't mind the spooky unseen depths. Further north towards Point Lookout, the Keyholes is a freshwater lake and lagoon system. There's 4WD access via the beach (permit required). Another happy diversion is a visit to **Myora Springs** – swimming holes surrounded by lush vegetation and walking tracks – near the coast about 4km north of Dunwich.

North Stradbroke Island Historical Museum MUSEUM
(☎07-3409 9699; www.stradbrokemuseum.com.au; 15-17 Welsby St, Dunwich; adult/child $3.50/1; ⊙10am-2pm Tue-Sat, 11am-3pm Sun) Once the 'Dunwich Benevolent Asylum' – a home for the destitute – this small but impressive museum describes shipwrecks and harrowing voyages, and gives an introduction to the island's rich Aboriginal history (the Quandamooka people are the traditional owners of Minjerribah, aka Straddie). Island artefacts include the skull of a sperm whale washed up on Main Beach in 2004, and the old Point Lookout lighthouse lens.

Activities

North Stradbroke Island Surf School SURFING
(☎07-3409 8342; www.northstradbrokeislandsurfschool.com.au; lessons from $50; ⊙daily) Small-group, 90-minute surf lessons in the warm Straddie waves. Solo lessons available if you're feeling bashful.

Straddie Adventures KAYAKING, SAND BOARDING
(☎0433 171 477; www.straddieadventures.com.au; ⊙daily) Hires out surfboards, snorkelling equipment and bicycles. Also runs sea-kayaking trips (adult/child $60/45) and sand-boarding sessions ($30/25).

Straddie Super Sports BICYCLE RENTAL
(☎07-3409 9252; 18 Bingle Rd, Dunwich; ⊙8am-4.30pm Mon-Fri, 8am-3pm Sat, 9am-2pm Sun) Hires out mountain bikes (per hour/day $6.50/30), kayaks (per half/full day $30/50) and has fishing gear for sale. Possibly the friendliest shop in Queensland!

Manta Lodge & Scuba Centre DIVING
(☎07-3409 8888; www.mantalodge.com.au; 1 East Coast Rd, Point Lookout) Based at the YHA, Manta Scuba Centre offers a broad range of options. You can simply hire a wetsuit ($20), snorkel gear ($25), or a surfboard ($50). Or take the plunge with a scuba course, starting at $499. Snorkelling trips (from $60) include a boat trip and all gear.

Tours

North Stradbroke Island 4WD Tours & Camping Holidays DRIVING
(☎07-3409 8051; www.stradbroke4wdtours.com; adult/child half day $35/20, full day $85/55) Offers 4WD tours around the Point Lookout area, with lots of bush, beaches and wildlife. Beach fishing is $45/30 per adult/child.

Straddie Kingfisher Tours ADVENTURE TOUR
(☎07-3409 9502; www.straddiekingfishertours.com.au; adult/child island pick-up $80/40, from Brisbane or Gold Coast $195/145) Operates six-hour 4WD and fishing tours; also has whale-watching tours in season. Ask about kayaking and sand-boarding options.

Sleeping

Straddie Camping CAMPGROUND $
(☎07-3409 9668; www.straddiecamping.com.au; 1 Junner St, Dunwich; 4WD camp site from $16.55, unpowered/powered sites from $39/46, cabins from $120; ⊙booking office 8am-4pm) There are eight island campgrounds operated by this outfit, including two 4WD-only foreshore camps (permits required – $39.55). The best of the bunch are grouped around Point Lookout: **Cylinder Beach**, **Adder Rock** and **Home Beach** all overlook the sand. **Amity Point** campground has new eco cabins. Good weekly rates; book well in advance.

Manta Lodge YHA HOSTEL $
(☎07-3409 8888; www.mantalodge.com.au; 1 East Coast Rd, Point Lookout; dm/d/tw/f from $34/86/86/113; @ 🛜) This three-storey, lemon-yellow hostel has clean (if unremarkable) rooms and a great beachside location (who wants to sit around in a dorm anyway?). There are jungly hammocks and a communal firepit out the back, plus a dive school downstairs. New showers; new beds. Surfboards, bodyboards and snorkelling gear for hire.

Straddie Views B&B $$
(☎07-3409 8875; www.northstradbrokeisland.com/straddiebb; 26 Cumming Pde, Point Lookout; s/d from $125/150) There are two spacious downstairs suites in this B&B, run by a friendly Straddie local. Cooked breakfast is served on the upstairs deck with fab sea views.

Straddie Bungalows BUNGALOWS $$
(☎07-3409 7017; www.straddiebungalows.com.au; 33 Ballow St, Amity; 1-/2-/3-bedroom bungalows from $179/189/229; ❄🛜🏊) These elevated, beachy bungalows with Thai design touches are on the waterfront in chilled-out Amity: a good choice if you want to stay away from the Point Lookout fray. Terrific pool; terrific for families. And you can spot dolphins from the jetty!

Stradbroke Island Beach Hotel HOTEL $$$
(☎07-3409 8188; www.stradbrokehotel.com.au; East Coast Rd, Point Lookout; d from $235; ❄🛜🏊) Straddie's only pub has 13 cool, inviting rooms with shell-coloured tiles, blonde timbers, high-end gadgets and balconies. Walk to the beach, or get distracted by the open-walled bar downstairs en route (serves breakfast, lunch and dinner; mains $18 to $40). Flashy three- and four-bed apartments also available for multinight stays.

Allure APARTMENTS $$$
(☎07-3415 0000, 1800 555 200; www.allurestradbroke.com.au; 43 East Coast Rd, Point Lookout; apt from $249; ❄🛜🏊) These large, ultramodern apartments are set in a leafy compound. Each villa (or 'shack', as the one-bedroom apartments are called) features lots of beachy colours, original artwork and an outdoor deck with barbecue. There isn't much space between villas, but they're cleverly designed with privacy in mind. Much cheaper rates for stays of more than one night.

Eating

★**Island Fruit Barn** CAFE $
(☎07-3409 9125; www.stradbrokeholidays.com.au; 16 Bingle Rd, Dunwich; mains $10-12; ⊙7am-5pm Mon-Fri, to 4pm Sat & Sun; 🌿) On the main road in Dunwich, Island Fruit Barn is a casual little congregation of tables with excellent breakfasts, smoothies, salads, soups, cakes and sandwiches, all made using top-quality ingredients. Order a spinach-and-feta roll, then stock up in the gourmet grocery section.

Oceanic Gelati GELATERIA $
(☎07-3415 3222; www.stradbrokeholidays.com.au; 19 Mooloomba Rd, Point Lookout; gelati from $4; ⊙9.30am-5pm) 'OMG! This is the best gelati ever.' So says one satisfied customer, and we're in complete agreement. Try the dairy-free tropical, cooling lemon or classic vanilla.

Seashells Cafe CAFE $$
(☎07-3409 7886; www.stradbrokeholidays.com.au; 21 Ballow St, Amity; mains $13-28; ⊙9am-8pm Mon-Sat, to 2pm Sun) The best eating option in Amity is this breezy, open-sided cafe-bar. There's cold XXXX beer on tap and mainstay mains such as seafood basket, veg fettuccine and lamb shanks, plus coffee and cake throughout the day. Bare feet welcome! The chef is from France – could he be any further from home?

Look MODERN AUSTRALIAN $$
(☎07-3415 3390; www.beachbarcafe.com; 1/29 Mooloomba Rd; mains $22-38; ⊙8am-3pm daily, 6-9pm Thu-Sat) Look! Pizzas, fishy mains, pastas, salads, funky tunes and breezy outdoor seating with water views. Lots of wines by the glass and smokin' chilli prawns.

Information

Although it's quiet most of the year, the island population swells significantly at Christmas, Easter and during school holidays: book accommodation or camping permits well in advance.

If you plan to go off-road, get info and a 4WD permit ($39.55) from Straddie Camping (p303).

Getting There & Away

The hub for ferries to North Stradbroke Island is the Brisbane seaside suburb of Cleveland. Regular **Citytrain** (www.translink.com.au) services run from Brisbane's Central and Roma St stations to Cleveland station ($10.30, one hour); buses to the ferry terminal meet the trains at Cleveland station ($5.20, 10 minutes).

Stradbroke Ferries & Fast Ferries (☎07-3488 5300; www.stradbrokeferries.com.au; return per vehicle incl passengers $149, walk-on adult/child $10/5, fast ferry return adult/child $20/10; ⏲5am-8pm) Teaming up with Big Red Cat, Stradbroke Ferries' passenger/vehicle services run to Dunwich and back eight times daily (45 minutes). Fast passenger ferries run 15 times daily (25 minutes). Cheaper online fares for vehicles.

Big Red Cat (☎07-3488 9777, 1800 733 228; www.bigredcat.com.au; return per vehicle incl passengers $149, walk-on adult/child $10/5; ⏲5.15am-7pm) In a tandem operation with Stradbroke Ferries, the feline-looking Big Red Cat vehicle/passenger ferry does the Cleveland–Dunwich run around eight times daily (45 minutes). Save a few dollars by booking online.

Gold Cats Stradbroke Flyer (☎07-3286 1964; www.flyer.com.au; Middle St, Cleveland; return adult/child/family $19/10/50; ⏲5am-7.30pm) Gold Cats Stradbroke Flyer runs around a dozen return, passenger-only trips daily between Cleveland and One Mile Jetty at Dunwich (30 minutes).

Amity Trader (☎07-3820 6557; www.amitytrader.com; 4WD/walk-on passengers return $270/40) Ferries for 4WD vehicles and walk-on passengers from Amity to Kooringal on Moreton Island return several times weekly. Call for current timetable.

Getting Around

Straddie is big: it's best to have your own wheels to explore it properly. If you plan to go off-road, you can get information and buy a 4WD permit ($39.55) from Straddie Camping (p303).

Alternatively, **Stradbroke Island Buses** (☎07-3415 2417; www.stradbrokebuses.com) meet the ferries at Dunwich and run to Amity and Point Lookout (one way/return $5/10). The last bus to Dunwich leaves Point Lookout at 6.20pm. There's also the **Stradbroke Cab Service** (☎0408 193 685), which charges around $60 from Dunwich to Point Lookout.

Straddie Super Sports (p302) in Dunwich hires out mountain bikes (per hour/day $6.50/30).

Moreton Island

POP 250

If you're not going further north in Queensland than Brisbane but want a slice of tropical paradise, slip over to blissful Moreton Island. You'll be reassured to learn that Moreton's cache of sandy shores, bushland, bird life, dunes and glorious lagoons are protected – 95% of the isle comprises **Moreton Island National Park & Recreation Area** (www.nprsr.qld.gov.au/parks/moreton-island). Apart from a few rocky headlands, it's all sand, with Mt Tempest, the highest coastal sand hill in the world, towering high at a lofty 280m. Off the west coast are the rusty, hulking Tangalooma Wrecks, which provide excellent snorkelling and diving.

The island has a rich history, from early Aboriginal settlements to the site of Queensland's first and only whaling station at **Tangalooma**, which operated between 1952 and 1962. These days, swimming, snorkelling and 4WD trails keep visitors occupied (in fact, the island is a 4WD-only domain).

Tangalooma now hosts the island's sole resort, and there are three other small settlements on the west coast: **Bulwer** near the northwestern tip, **Cowan Cowan** between Bulwer and Tangalooma, and **Kooringal** near the southern tip.

Sights & Activities

Check out the dolphin feeding which happens each evening around sunset at Tangalooma, halfway down the western side of the island. Around half a dozen dolphins swim in from the ocean and take fish from the hands of volunteer feeders. You have to be a guest of the Tangalooma Island Resort to participate, but onlookers are welcome. Also at the resort is the **Tangalooma Marine Education & Conservation Centre** (www.tangalooma.com/info/dolphin_feeding/tmecc; Tangalooma Island Resort; ⏲10am-noon & 1-5pm), which has a display on the diverse marine and bird life of Moreton Bay. You can pick up a map of island walking trails here. The centre also runs pelican-, kookaburra- and fish-feeding tours, plus nature walks.

Just north of the resort, off the coast, are the famous **Tangalooma Wrecks** – 15 sunken ships forming a sheltered boat mooring and a brilliant snorkelling spot. You can hire **snorkelling** gear from the resort, or Tangatours runs two-hour kayaking and snorkelling trips around the wrecks ($79) as well as guided **paddle-boarding** ($49) and dusk **kayaking** tours ($59).

Island **bushwalks** include a desert trail (two hours) leaving from the resort, as well as the strenuous trek up Mt Tempest, 3km inland from Eagers Creek – worthwhile, but you'll need transport to reach the start.

Built in 1857 at the island's northern tip, **Cape Moreton Lighthouse** is the oldest operating lighthouse in Queensland, and is the place to come for great views when the whales are passing by.

Tours

Most island tours depart from Brisbane or the Gold Coast. **Dolphin Wild** (☎07-3880 4444; www.dolphinwild.com.au; adult/child/family incl lunch $125/75/325, snorkelling tour per adult/child additional $20/10) runs dolphin-spotting tours from the Redcliffe Peninsula north of Brisbane. **Tangatours** (☎07-3410 6927; www.tangatours.com.au), operating from Tangalooma Island Resort, offers activity-based tours.

Adventure Moreton Island ADVENTURE TOUR
(☎1300 022 878; www.adventuremoretonisland.com; 1-day tours from $144) Operating in cahoots with Tangatours at Tangalooma Island Resort, these tours offer a range of activities (paddleboarding, snorkelling, sailing, kayaking, fishing etc), ex-Brisbane. Overnight resort accommodation packages also available (including tour from $323).

Moreton Bay Escapes ADVENTURE TOUR
(☎1300 559 355; www.moretonbayescapes.com.au; 1-day tours adult/child from $189/139, 2-day camping tours $309/179) A certified ecotour, this one day 4WD tour includes snorkelling or kayaking, sand boarding, marine wildlife watching and a picnic lunch. Camp overnight to see more of the isle.

Moreton Island Adventures DRIVING TOUR
(☎07-3909 3333; www.moretonislandadventures.com.au; 14 Howard Smith Dr, Port of Brisbane; 1-day tours adult/child from $170/140) Guided 4WD trips with either an eco or adventure bent, departing Port of Brisbane on the flashy Micat vehicle ferry. Accommodation also available in dorm-style units and upmarket en-suite tents (two-/four-bed tents from $80/110; units from $130).

Sleeping & Eating

Aside from the resort, there are a few holiday flats and houses for rent at Kooringal, Cowan Cowan and Bulwer: see listings at www.moretonisland.com.au. Moreton Island Adventures also offers camping and unit accommodation.

There are also 10 national-park **camping grounds** (☎13 74 68; www.nprsr.qld.gov.au/experiences/camping; sites per person/family $5.75/23) on Moreton Island, all with water, toilets and cold showers; five of these are right on the beach. Book online or by phone before you get to the island.

There's a small convenience store plus cafes, restaurants and bars at the resort; plus (expensive) shops at Kooringal and Bulwer: otherwise, bring food and drink supplies with you from the mainland.

Tangalooma Island Resort HOTEL, APARTMENTS $$$
(☎07-3637 2000, 1300 652 250; www.tangalooma.com; d from $250, 2-/3-/4-bedroom apt from $630/730/830;) This beautifully sited place has the island accommodation market cornered. There are abundant sleeping options, starting with simple hotel rooms. Units and suites are a step up, with beachside access and more contemporary decor. The apartments – a step up again – range from two- to four-bedroom configurations. The resort also has several eating options. Accommodation packages sometimes include return ferry fares and transfers.

Information

There are no paved roads on Moreton Island, but 4WDs can travel along the beaches and cross-island tracks (regular cars not permitted) – seek local advice about tides and creek crossings before venturing out. You can pick up maps from the ferry operators. Permits for 4WDs cost $45.10, valid for one month, and are available through ferry operators, online or via phone from the Department of National Parks, Recreation, Sport and Racing. Ferry bookings are mandatory if you want to take a vehicle across.

Online, see www.visitmoretonisland.com.

Getting There & Around

Several ferries operate from the mainland. To explore once you get to the island, bring a 4WD or take a tour. Most tours are ex-Brisbane, and include ferry transfers.

Amity Trader (p304) Vehicle ferry from North Stradbroke Island to Kooringal.

Micat (www.micat.com.au; 14 Howard Smith Dr, Port of Brisbane; return adult/child $50/35, vehicle incl 2 people $195-230) Vehicle ferries from Port of Brisbane to Tangalooma around eight times weekly (75 minutes); see the website for directions to the ferry terminal.

Moreton Island Tourist Services (☎07-3408 2661; www.moretonisland.net.au) Four-wheel drive taxi transfers around the island; one-way trips range from $50 to $220.

Tangalooma Flyer (☎07-3637 2000; www.tangalooma.com; return adult/child $80/45) Fast passenger catamaran operated by Tangalooma Island Resort. It makes the 75-minute trip to the resort three times daily from Holt St Wharf in Brisbane (see the website for directions). A shuttle bus (adult/child one way $21/10.50) scoots to the wharf from the CBD or airport; bookings essential.

Granite Belt

Dappling the western flanks of the Great Dividing Range about 210km southwest of Brisbane, the Granite Belt region features rolling hillsides lined with vine rows and orchards (apples, pears, plums, peaches) that thrive in the cool, crisp air here (Stanthorpe, the regional hub, sits at an altitude of 915m). This is Queensland's only real wine region of any size – the only place in the state where it's cool enough to grow commercial quantities of grapes. Further south, on the New South Wales (NSW) border, balancing boulders and spring wild flowers attract bushwalkers to the photogenic Girraween National Park.

Stanthorpe & Ballandean

Queensland's coolest town (literally), **Stanthorpe** (population 4300) is one of the state's lesser-known tourist hotspots. With a distinct four-season climate, the town is a winter retreat where normally sweltering Queenslanders can cosy up in front of an open fire with a bottle of vino rosso from one of the 50-plus local wineries. In 1860 an Italian priest planted the first grapevines here, but it wasn't until the influx of Italian immigrants in the 1940s (who brought with them a lifetime of viticultural nous) that the wine industry really took off. Today, functional Stanthorpe and the tiny village of **Ballandean** (population 470), about 20km to the south, boast a flourishing wine industry, with cellar-door sales, onsite dining, vineyard events and boutique accommodation.

But it's not all wine and song: the Granite Belt's changing seasons also make it a prime fruit-growing area and there's plenty of fruit picking available for backpackers who don't mind chilly mornings.

Sights & Activities

Wine-tasting is a must-do in this neck of the woods, as is a drive through the boulder-strewn, vine-lined Granite Belt landscape. If you plan on swilling one too many, opt for a tour.

Weekenders come not only for the wine but also the food: across the Granite Belt region you'll find some brilliant boutique foodie businesses offering delectible edibles (and drinkables).

The Stanthorpe visitor information centre (p309) stocks the *Stanthorpe to Ballandean Bike Trail* brochure, detailing a 34km trail between the two hubs.

Stanthorpe Regional Art Gallery GALLERY
(☎07-4681 1874; www.srag.org.au; cnr Lock & Marsh Sts, Stanthorpe; ⏰10am-4pm Tue-Fri, to 1pm Sat & Sun) FREE One of Queensland's better regional art galleries, housing a small but surprisingly engaging collection of works by local artists – mostly canvases and ceramics. It makes a beaut rainy-day detour. Check the website or call for info on Sunday afternoon live music.

Granite Belt Brewery BREWERY
(☎07-4681 1370; www.granitebeltbrewery.com.au; 146 Glenlyon Dr, Stanthorpe; ⏰10am-5pm) It's not just about the wine around here – there's a local brewery too! Swing into the bar at the Happy Valley accommodation/restaurant to sample a few brews. A $12 tasting paddle (or the smaller, driver-friendly $7 version) gives you a sample of four current offerings, which might include the Granite Pilsner, Poziers Porter or Irish Red Ale.

Granite Belt Dairy CHEESE
(☎07-4685 2277; www.granitebeltdairy.com.au; cnr Amiens Rd & Duncan Lane, Thulimbah; ⏰10am-4pm) What's wine without cheese? The Granite Belt's leading cheesemaker delivers a tasty array of the good stuff, all available for sampling. Also on offer at the adjoining **Jersey Girls Cafe** are fantastic milkshakes and cheesecakes, Devonshire teas and light lunches, plus fresh-baked bread, chutneys and other picnic hamper-fillers. Don't leave without trying the whiffy Bastard Tail washed-rind soft cheese.

GRANITE BELT WINERIES

With dozens of Granite Belt wineries offering free tastings, you could easily spend a week wading through the wines of the region and still only make a ripple on the surface (see www.granitebeltwinecountry.com.au/wine/cellar-doors). Or you could spend a day or two visiting a select few. It's usually worth an advance phone call to the smaller cellar doors to make sure they're open.

Ballandean Estate (07-4684 1226; www.ballandeanestate.com; 354 Sundown Rd, Ballandean; 9am-5pm) One of Queensland's oldest and biggest wineries, with many award-winning vintages and an impressive cafe-restaurant called the Barrel Room Cafe (p308). Free winery tours at 11am.

Boireann Wines (07-4683 2194; www.boireannwinery.com.au; 26 Donnellys Castle Rd, The Summit; 10am-4pm Fri-Mon) Boireann's hand-made premium reds rank among the finest in the region (and have been awarded five stars by Aussie wine guru James Halliday). Small cellar door about 10km north of Stanthorpe.

Golden Grove Estate (07-4684 1291; www.goldengroveestate.com.au; 337 Sundown Rd, Ballandean; 10am-3pm) Established family-run estate with many unique varieties, including an excellent nero d'avola red, a Sicilian native grape. Another James Halliday five-star winery.

Ravens Croft Wines (07-4683 3252; www.ravenscroftwines.com.au; 274 Spring Creek Rd, Stanthorpe; 10.30am-4.30pm Fri-Sun) Highly respected winemaker producing superb reds (petit verdot, cabernet sauvignon and South African pinotage) and whites (including a top-notch verdelho). It's a modest cellar door in the backcountry west of Stanthorpe.

Robert Channon Wines (07-4683 3260; www.robertchannonwines.com.au; 32 Bradley Lane, Stanthorpe; 11am-4pm Mon, Tue & Fri, 10am-5pm Sat & Sun) Lots of trophy-winning wines (it was the first winery in Queensland to be awarded five stars by James Halliday), and a buzzy weekend cafe with views over a pretty lake. Try the verdelho.

Bramble Patch STRAWBERRIES
(07-4683 4205; www.bramblepatch.com.au; 381 Townsend Rd, Glen Aplin; 10am-4pm) Follow the strawberry signs along Townsend Rd to this berry patch with a sense of humour. Stock-up or eat on site: ice cream with home-made berry compote, waffles with berries, jams, relishes, fortified berry wines, and of course fresh fruits (November to April). Love the chilli plum sauce.

Sleeping

Top of the Town Tourist Park CARAVAN PARK $
(07-4681 4888; www.topoftown.com.au; 10 High St, Stanthorpe; powered sites $40, cabins/motel d from $110/125;) A bushy site on the northern side of Stanthorpe, this is a serviceable option if you're here for seasonal work in the vineyards and orchards. A snug six-person cottage costs $230 per night.

Backpackers of Queensland HOSTEL $
(0429 810 998; www.backpackersofqueensland.com.au; 80 High St, Stanthorpe; per week $195;) The management here helps young fruit pickers find work, and accommodates them in utilitarian comfort. There's a minimum one-week stay in five-bed dorms with en-suite bathrooms. No booze, drugs, smoking or monkey business.

Diamondvale B&B Cottages COTTAGE $$
(07-4681 3367; www.diamondvalecottages.com.au; 26 Diamondvale Rd, Stanthorpe; 1-/2-/4-bedroom from $195/350/750;) In bucolic bushland outside of Stanthorpe, Diamondvale is a friendly place with five private cottages and a four-bedroom lodge, each with old-fashioned details, and a wood-burning fireplace, kitchen and verandah. The communal barbecue hut is a winner, and you can walk 2km along the creek into town (or jump in for a swim).

Stannum Lodge Motor Inn MOTEL $$
(07-4681 2000; www.stannumlodge.com.au; 12 Wallangarra Rd, Stanthorpe; d/tw from $125/135;) Streaking ahead of the rest of Stanthorpe's motels, Stannum Lodge is a low, bricky 1985 number, but it's quite possibly the cleanest motel we've ever seen! Brand new TVs and linen, a neat little pool, free wi-fi and affable hosts seal the deal. There's also a cute gazebo out the back for wine and cheese indulgences.

WORTH A TRIP

GIRRAWEEN NATIONAL PARK

A short drive east of Ballandean, **Girraween National Park** (www.nprsr.qld.gov.au/parks/girraween) is home to some astonishing granite boulders, pristine forests and brilliant blooms of springtime wild flowers (Girraween means 'place of flowers'), all of which make a marvellous setting for a stroll. Wildlife is abundant and there are 17km of trails to take you around and to the top of some of the surreal granite outcrops. Short walks include the 1.6km return walk to the Granite Arch and a 3.6km return scramble up the Pyramid (1080m). The granddaddy of Girraween walks is the 11km return trek to the top of Mt Norman (1267m).

Ballandean and Stanthorpe are a short drive away, and there are a couple of excellent places to stay in the area.

Girraween Environmental Lodge (07-4684 5138; www.girraweenlodge.com.au; Pyramids Rd, Ballandean; d $250, extra adult/child $40/20;) is an eco-friendly bushland retreat set on 160 wildlife-rich hectares adjacent to the national park. Made largely of recycled timber, the 10 simply elegant, self-contained timber cabins here sleep up to six people, are ultracomfy and have wood heaters, DVD players and private decks with barbecues. There's also an outdoor spa and plunge pool. No restaurant: BYO food.

In a large paddock with grazing cattle, **Wisteria Cottage** (07-4684 5121; www.wisteriacottage.com.au; 2117 Pyramids Rd, Wyberba; d incl breakfast from $190) has three simple, tasteful and private timber cottages: one two-bedroom cottage (sleeping six), and two one-bedroom cottages (sleeping two and four). The cabins have wide verandahs and cosy wood fires. Breakfast comes in a big hamper, or there's the **Heavenly Chocolate** (07-4684 5121; www.heavenlychocolate.com.au; 2117 Pyramids Rd, Wyberba; 10am-4pm Fri-Mon) shop on site!

There are also two good drive-in **camping grounds** (13 74 68; http://parks.nprsr.qld.gov.au/permits; per person/family $5.75/23) in the park – **Castle Rock** and **Bald Rock Creek** – which teem with wildlife and have drinking water, barbecues and hot showers. Book online or via phone before you arrive.

The **visitor centre** at the end of Pyramids Rd has information on the park and walking tracks (opening hours vary, but map brochures should be available even if there's no one present). Although winter nights here can be cold, it's hot work scaling the boulders, so take plenty of water.

To reach the park, head 8km south of Ballandean, turn left on Pyramids Rd, and continue another 7km to the park entrance.

Azjure Studio Retreat BOUTIQUE HOTEL **$$$**
(0405 127 070; www.azjure.com.au; 165 Sundown Rd, Ballandean; 1-/2-bedroom studios from $300/430;) This much-awarded retreat features three snappily designed, ultramod free-standing studios for two people (plus a villa for four) with sweeping views across the vines. Each has a roomy open-plan layout, huge windows, a verandah with barbecue and high-end fittings (including a spa tub with views). Kangaroos hop past in the twilight.

Eating

★**Varias** MODERN AUSTRALIAN **$$**
(07-4685 5050; www.varias.com.au; Queensland College of Wine Tourism, 22 Caves Rd, Stanthorpe; mains $25-34; lunch 11am-3pm daily, breakfast 9-11.30am Sat & Sun, wine & tapas 4-7pm Fri) This chic bistro features the delectable handiwork of student chefs at the adjunct Queensland College of Wine Tourism, a low-slung, angular, steel-and-stone construction fronting the New England Hwy. Courses are paired with the college's excellent Bianca Ridge wines. With a flickering fire and floor-to-ceiling windows overlooking the vines, it's Stanthorpe's classiest restaurant by a country mile.

Barrel Room Cafe MODERN AUSTRALIAN **$$**
(07-4684 1326; www.thebarrel-room.com; Ballandean Estate, 354 Sundown Rd, Ballandean; mains $27-35; 11.30am-2.30pm Wed-Mon, 6pm-late Thu-Sun) This snug cafe-restaurant at Ballandean Estate (p307) winery, framed by massive 140-year-old wine barrels, is a beaut spot for a decadent meal and a bottle or two. Organic lamb shoulder with Israeli couscous and whipped feta, and duck breast with truffled gnocchi and mushroom ragu, are a couple of recent hits from the seasonal menu.

Patty's on McGregor MODERN AUSTRALIAN $$$
(☎07-4681 3463; www.pattysonmcgregor.com.au; 2 McGregor Tce, Stanthorpe; mains $30-38; ⏲6.30pm-late Thu-Sat) A long-running Stanthorpe favourite, Patty's quirky backstreet shopfront serves a changing selection of beautifully prepared dishes with Eastern accents – perhaps a rogan josh curry with local organic lamb, or a za'atar-crusted pork loin with pear and garden honey, and always a vegetarian dish of the day. Expect black-and-white tile floors, candlelit tables, local artwork and BYO with no corkage!

Information

Most of the Granite Belt wineries are located south of Stanthorpe around Ballandean. Pick up the *Granite Belt Wine Country* booklet from the **Stanthorpe visitor information centre** (☎1800 762 665, 07-4681 2057; www.granitebeltwinecountry.com.au; 28 Leslie Pde, Stanthorpe; ⏲9am-5pm).

Getting There & Around

Greyhound Australia (☎13 14 99; www.greyhound.com.au) and **Crisps Coaches** (www.crisps.com.au) service Stanthorpe. There are buses to Warwick ($16, 45 minutes), Toowoomba ($47, 2½ hours), Brisbane ($58, 4½ hours) and Tenterfield in NSW ($20, 45 minutes), with connections to Byron Bay through Northern Rivers Buslines (p237).

To tour the Granite Belt wineries, either take a guided tour or bring your own set of wheels (plus a sober friend to do the driving).

Toowoomba

POP 157,700

Squatting on the edge of the Great Dividing Range, 700m above sea level, Toowoomba is a sprawling country hub with wide tree-lined streets, stately homes and down-to-earth locals. There's not a whole lot going on here from the travellers' perspective (in fact, when we asked a local friend 'What should we do when we get to Toowoomba?', his reply was 'Leave.'...): but if you've been darting across the state from end to end and need a break, it's not a bad spot to stop and chill out for a day or two.

The air is distinctly crisper up here on the range, and in spring the town's gardens blaze with colour. Not only is the 'Garden City' Queensland's largest and oldest inland city, it is also the birthplace of two national icons: the archetypal Aussie cake, the lamington, and Oscar-winner Geoffrey Rush.

Sights & Activities

Cobb & Co Museum MUSEUM
(☎07-4659 4900; www.cobbandco.qm.qld.gov.au; 27 Lindsay St; adult/child/family $12.50/6.50/32; ⏲10am-4pm) Immediately north of Queens Park, the rather good Cobb & Co Museum houses an impressive carriage collection with hands-on displays depicting town life and outback travel back in horse-powered days. The museum also has a blacksmith forge, photographic displays of early Toowoomba and an Aboriginal collection – shields, axe heads, boomerangs – plus animated films relating Dreaming stories. Look for the half-dozen spinning windmills out the front.

Picnic Point PARK
(www.picnic-point.com.au; Tourist Rd; ⏲24hr) FREE Riding high on the rim of the Great Dividing Range and strung along the eastern edge of town are Toowoomba's Escarpment Parks, the pick of which is Picnic Point. There are walking trails here, plenty of the namesake picnic spots and a **cafe-restaurant** (mains $14-27; ⏲8.30am-5pm Mon-Thu, to 9pm Fri, 8am-9pm Sat, 8am-5pm Sun), but what everyone really comes for are the eye-popping views over the Lockyer Valley (Toowoomba is really lofty!).

Ju Raku En Japanese Garden GARDENS
(www.toowoombarc.qld.gov.au; West St; ⏲7am-dusk) FREE Ju Raku En is a beautiful, Zen-like spot about 4km south of the centre at the University of Southern Queensland. Designed by a Japanese professor in Kyoto, the 5-hectare garden has a rippling lake, carefully aligned boulders, conifers, bamboo stands, cherry blossom trees, lovely bridges and wiggly paths.

Toowoomba Regional Art Gallery GALLERY
(☎07-4688 6652; www.toowoombarc.qld.gov.au/trag; 531 Ruthven St; ⏲10am-4pm Tue-Sat, 1-4pm Sun) FREE The small Toowoomba Regional Art Gallery houses an interesting collection of paintings, ceramics and drawings, plus rare books, maps and manuscripts in the library section. Regular touring exhibitions attract a few more visitors than usual.

Sleeping

Big4 Toowoomba Garden City CARAVAN PARK $
(☎07-46351747, 1800333667; www.big4toowoombagchp.com.au; 34a Eiser St, Harristown; powered sites from $39, 1-/2-/3-bedroom cabins from $103/135/170; ❄📶🏊) It's a bit of journey into town, but this quiet backstreet caravan

park is the best bet for campers visiting Toowoomba. Expect grassy sites, tidy cabins, flower beds, two swimming pools and a beaut outdoor BBQ area ('Drunk and loutish behaviour wil not be tolerated!').

★ Vacy Hall GUESTHOUSE **$$**
(07-4639 2055; www.vacyhall.com.au; 135 Russell St; d $125-245;) Uphill from the town centre, this magnificent 1873 mansion (originally a wedding gift from a cashed-up squatter to his daughter) offers 12 heritage-style rooms with loads of authentic charm. A wide verandah wraps around the house, all rooms have en suites or private bathrooms; most have working fireplaces. Superhigh ceilings make some rooms taller than they are wide. Free wi-fi.

Ecoridge Hideaway CHALET **$$**
(07-4630 9636; www.ecoridgehideaway.com.au; 712 Rockmount Rd, Preston; r from $140) Ecoridge is an excellent alternative to the often unremarkable accommodation in central Toowoomba. Around 15km from the city on a back road to Gatton, the three self-contained cabins here are simple and elegant, with wood heaters, gas cooking and eye-popping sunrise views across the Great Dividing Range. Cheaper for longer stays.

Central Plaza Hotel HOTEL, APARTMENTS **$$**
(1300 300 402, 07-4688 5333; www.toowoombacentralplaza.com.au; 523 Ruthven St; 1-/2-/3-bedroom apt from $180/380/415;) Flashy, corporate and an impressive nine floors high, the Central Plaza offers a modicum of urbane poshness in this big country town, where motels are many and most hotels are places you go to drink beer. Inside you'll find nice art, mod furniture and colourful, well-designed apartments with rooftop views.

Eating

Phatburgers BURGERS **$**
(07-4638 4738; www.phatburgers.com.au; 520 Ruthven St; burgers $6-20; 10am-9pm) Chipper Phat plates up brilliant burgers, lurid orange napkins and live DJs spinning retro rock. Top of the calorie charts is the Burghoffer, which is big enough to stop traffic (if you manage to eat one at a single sitting, drop us a line). Love the homemade ground chilli paste.

Artisan PIZZA **$**
(07-4638 0727; www.facebook.com/artisanpizzaandsandwich; 41a Russell St; mains $8-18; 11am-3pm Tue-Fri, 5-9pm Tue-Sat) Artisan is a hip, semi-industrial space with long, chunky-timber communal tables, stainless-steel chairs, old floorboards and art deco ceilings. The busy open kitchen in the corner serves up simple pizzas, salads and flat-bread sandwiches. Good coffee too.

Ortem CAFE **$$**
(07-4632 0090; www.ortem.com.au; 15 Railway St; mains $17-22; 7am-4pm) Opposite the train station, this hip industrial cafe offers a small-but-arty menu of salads, risottos, burgers and big breakfasts, plus superior coffee. Outdoor seating in front, cool contemporary art and happy staff (always a good sign) round out the experience. There's also an events space upstairs: check the website for happenings (trivia nights, film screenings etc).

Chutney Mary's INDIAN **$$**
(07-4638 0822; www.chutneymary.com.au; 335 Ruthven St; mains $17-23; noon-3pm Mon-Sat, 5pm-late daily) Spice up your Toowoomba tenure with a visit to Chutney Mary's, where reliable curries, naans, tandoor and rice dishes accompany colourful Indian trinkets.

Drinking

Spotted Cow PUB
(www.spottedcow.com.au; cnr Ruthven & Campbell Sts; 11am-late) A mustard-coloured pub with old blues on the stereo and regular live bands (Aussie acts such as Dan Sultan and Steve Kilbey), the Spotted Cow is a Toowoomba institution. There are 70 different beers on offer if you've worked up a thirst, and tasty bistro meals (mains $11 to $40: go for the 1kg pot of mussels for $27). Trivia on Wednesday nights.

Information

Toowoomba visitor information centre (1800 331 155, 07-4639 3797; www.southernqueenslandcountry.com.au; 86 James St; 9am-5pm;) Located southeast of the centre, at the junction with Kitchener St. Peel yourself off a vast map of town. Also has self-guided *Toowoomba Tourist Drive* maps.

Getting There & Away

Toowoomba is 126km west of Brisbane on the Warrego Hwy. Greyhound (p309) provides regular daily services between Brisbane and Toowoomba ($36, two hours), and runs south to Stanthorpe less frequently ($47, 2½ hours).

If you're coming straight from Brisbane Airport, the **Airport Flyer** (1300 304 350, 07-4630 1444; www.theairportflyer.com.au; one way/return $86/155) runs door-to-door services to/from Toowoomba (cheaper for more than one passenger).

Surfers Paradise & the Gold Coast

Includes ➡

Best Places to Eat

- BSKT Cafe (p317)
- Borough Barista (p320)
- Cafe dbar (p322)

Best Places to Stay

- La Costa Motel (p321)
- Binna Burra Mountain Lodge (p323)
- Olympus Apartments (p315)

Why Go?

Boasting 52km of golden beaches, 300 sunny days and millions of visitors each year, the Gold Coast serves up a steamy cocktail of sun, surf, sand and activity. This is one of the best places to learn to surf in Australia, so grab a longboard while you're here. Behind Surfers Paradise's famous beach is a shimmering strip of high-rise apartments, restaurants, bars, clubs and theme parks, where the fun can suck you into a dizzying vortex and spit you back out, happy but exhausted. Thc hypc settles as you head south: Broadbeach is sandy and chic; Burleigh Heads has seaside charms; and Coolangatta is known for its laid-back surfer vibe. Don't miss the Gold Coast's lush subtropical hinterland – including Lamington and Springbrook National Parks – whose delights include rainforest walks, spectacular waterfalls, sweeping views and private mountain retreats.

When to Go

Surfers Paradise

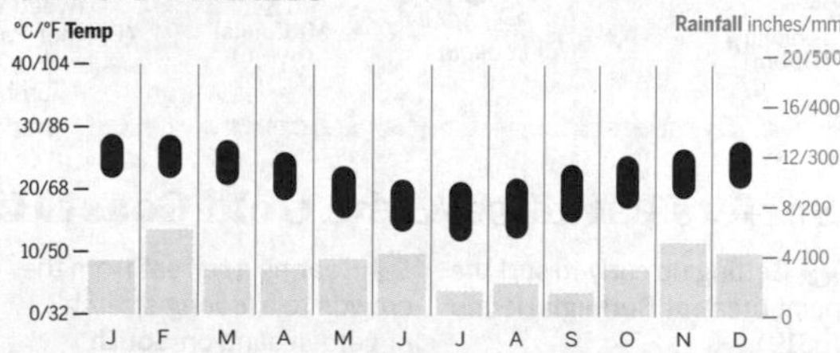

Dec–Feb Sunshine, higher temperatures, and busy beaches.

Jun–Aug The Australian winter brings tourists from chillier climes chasing the sun.

Nov–Dec School-leavers (schoolies) swarm into Surfers Paradise to party. (You've been warned.)

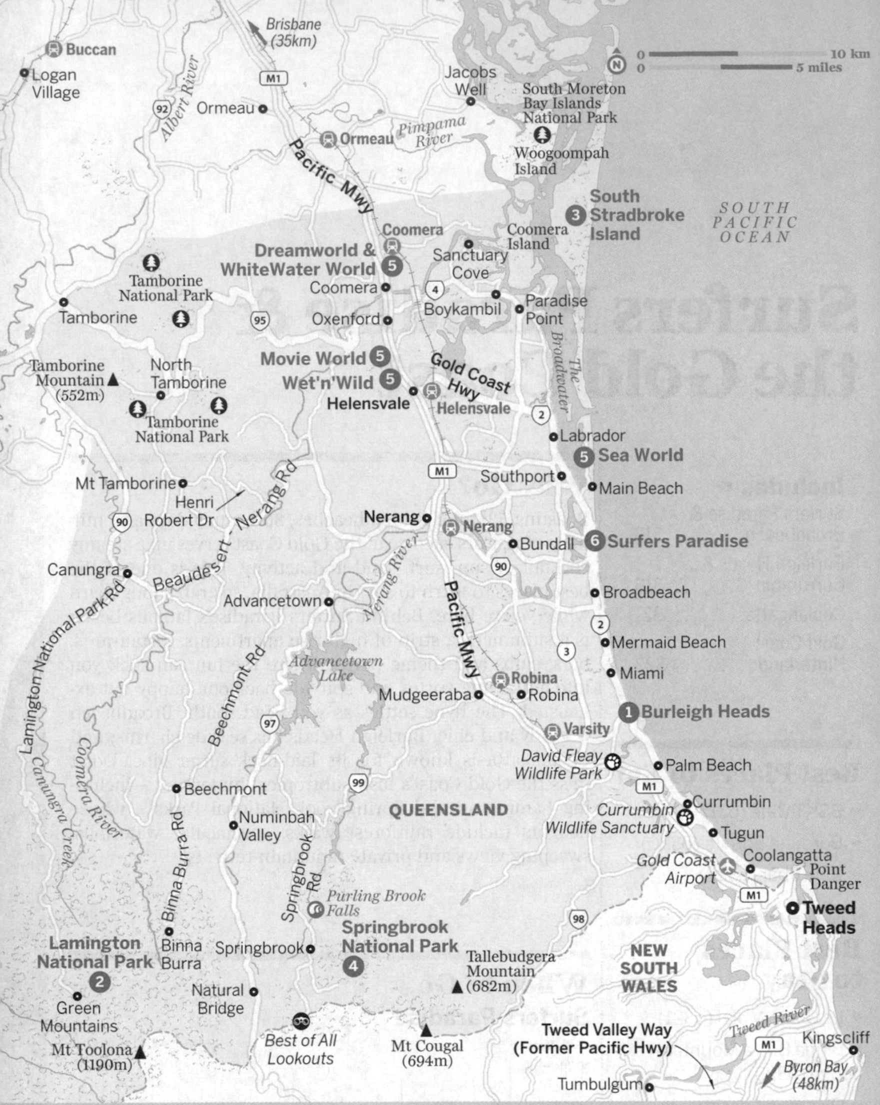

Surfers Paradise & the Gold Coast Highlights

1. Getting up early to surf the point break at **Burleigh Heads** (p319).
2. Bushwalking through craggy gorges and rainforests in **Lamington National Park** (p323).
3. Beating a retreat from the crowds to a *looong* stretch of golden sand on **South Stradbroke Island** (p320).
4. Taking in the view at the aptly named Best of All Lookout in **Springbrook National Park** (p324).
5. Testing your nerve (and your digestive system) on the roller coasters at the Gold Coast's **theme parks** (p316).
6. Drinking, dancing and watching the sun come up over the beach at **Surfers Paradise** (p313).

Getting There & Away

AIR

Gold Coast Airport (www.goldcoastairport.com.au; Longa Ave, Bilinga) is in Coolangatta, 25km south of Surfers Paradise. All the main Australian domestic airlines fly here. **Scoot** (www.flyscoot.com), **Air Asia** (1300 760 330; www.airasia.com) and **Air New Zealand** (13 24 76; www.airnewzealand.co.nz) fly in from overseas.

Brisbane Airport (www.bne.com.au) is 16km northeast of Brisbane city centre. It is a useful arrival point for the Gold Coast, especially for international visitors.

BUS

Greyhound (www.greyhound.com.au) Has frequent services to/from Brisbane ($21, 1½ hours), Byron Bay ($30, 2½ hours) and beyond.

Premier Motor Service (13 34 10; www.premierms.com.au) A couple of daily services head to Brisbane (from $21, 1½ hours), Byron Bay (from $29, 2½ hours) and other coastal areas.

CAR & MOTORCYCLE

The Gold Coast is an easy one-hour drive south of Brisbane. Coming from the south, you'll cross the New South Wales (NSW)–Queensland state border (a suburban road!) at Tweed Heads: Coolangatta (the southernmost town on the Gold Coast) is immediately across the border.

TRAIN

TransLink (13 12 30; translink.com.au) Citytrain services connect Brisbane with Nerang, Robina and Varsity Lakes stations on the Gold Coast (75 minutes) roughly every half-hour. The same line extends north of Brisbane to Brisbane Airport.

Getting Around

TO/FROM THE AIRPORT

Con-X-ion Airport Transfers (1300 266 946; www.con-x-ion.com; one way adult/child from $20/12) Transfers to/from Gold Coast Airport (one way adult/child from $20/12), Brisbane airport (one way adult/child from $49/25) and Gold Coast theme parks.

Gold Coast Tourist Shuttle (1300 655 655, 07-5574 5111; www.gcshuttle.com.au; one way per adult/child $21/13) Meets flights into Gold Coast Airport and transfers to most Gold Coast accommodation. Also runs to Gold Coast theme parks.

BUS

Surfside Buslines (13 12 30; www.surfside.com.au) A subsidiary of Brisbane's main TransLink operation, Surfside runs regular buses up and down the Gold Coast, plus shuttles from the Gold Coast train stations into Surfers Paradise and beyond (including the theme parks).

Surfside (in conjunction with Gold Coast Tourist Shuttle) also offers a Freedom Pass including return Gold Coast Airport transfers and unlimited theme park transfers plus local bus travel for $78/39 per adult/child, valid for three days (five-, seven- and 10-day passes also available).

SCHOOLIES ON THE LOOSE

Every year in November, thousands of teenagers flock to Surfers Paradise to celebrate the end of their high-school education in a three-week party known as 'Schoolies Week'. Although local authorities have stepped in to regulate excesses, boozed-up and drug-addled teens are still the norm.

For more info see www.schoolies.com.

TAXI

Gold Coast Cabs (13 10 08; www.gccabs.com.au)

TRAM

G:link (Gold Coast Light Rail; 13 12 30; translink.com.au; tickets from $4.80, multiday use Goexplore cards adult/child $15/7.50) Launched in 2014 the G:link, a handy light rail/tram service, connects Southport and Broadbeach, with stops along the way. Buy tickets at the G:link stops, 7-Eleven shops, and some newsagents.

Surfers Paradise & Broadbeach

POP 24,300

Some say the surfers prefer beaches elsewhere and that (except for the beautiful beach) paradise has been tragically lost, but there's no denying that this wild and trashy party zone attracts a phenomenal number of visitors – 20,000 per day! Party people come here for a heady dose of clubs, bars, malls and maybe a bit of beach-time when the hangover kicks in. It's a sexy place: lots of shirtless, tattooed backpackers and more cleavage than the Grand Canyon.

The decibel level tails off markedly directly south of Surfers Paradise in Broadbeach, which ups the area's chic element with good cafes, stylish shops and restaurants, and a gorgeous stretch of golden shore.

Surfers Paradise

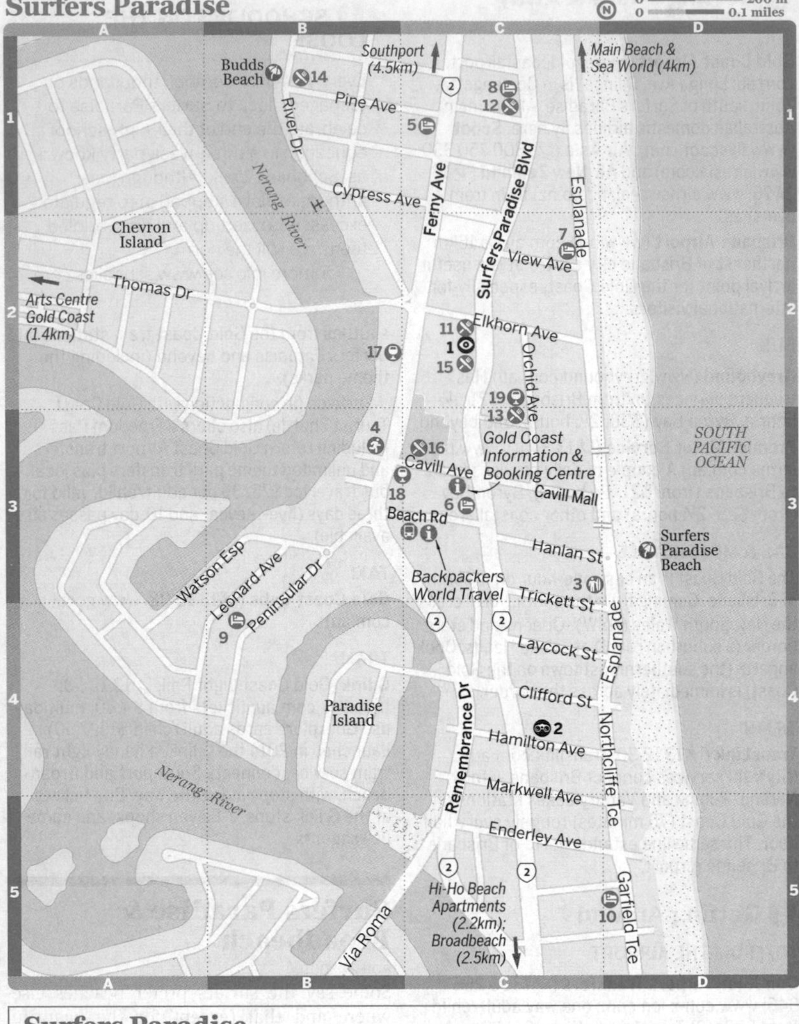

Surfers Paradise

Sights

1 Infinity C2
2 SkyPoint Observation Deck C4

Activities, Courses & Tours

3 Cheyne Horan School of Surf C3
4 Whales in Paradise B3

Sleeping

5 Budds in Surfers C1
6 Gold Coast Accommodation Service C3
7 Olympus Apartments C2
8 QT C1
9 Sleeping Inn Surfers B4
10 Surfers Beachside Holiday Apartments D5

Eating

11 Baritalia C2
12 Bazaar C1
13 Black Coffee Lyrics C3
14 Bumbles Café B1
15 Coles C2
16 Woolworths C3

Drinking & Nightlife

17 Helm Bar & Bistro B2
18 Melbas on the Park B3
19 Sin City C2

Sights

SkyPoint Observation Deck VIEWPOINT
(www.skypoint.com.au; Level 77, Q1 Bldg, Hamilton Ave, Surfers Paradise; adult/child/family $22/13/57; ⏲7.30am-8.30pm Sun-Thu, to 11.30pm Fri & Sat) Surfers Paradise's sights are generally spread across beach towels, but for an eagle-eye view, zip up to this 230m-high observation deck near the top of Q1, one of the world's notably tall buildings. You can also tackle the **SkyPoint Climb** up the spire to a height of 270m (adult/child from $69/49).

A helpful tour desk that sells tickets to the region's other activities is also located here.

Infinity MAZE
(www.infinitygc.com.au; Chevron Renaissance, cnr Surfers Paradise Blvd & Elkhorn Ave, Surfers Paradise; adult/child/family $27/18/73; ⏲10am-10pm) Lose the kids for an hour (literally) in this walk-through maze, cunningly disguised with elaborate audiovisual displays.

Activities

Balloon Down Under BALLOONING
(☎07-5500 4797; www.balloondownunder.com; 1hr flights adult/child $299/240) Up, up and away on sunrise flights over the Gold Coast, ending with a champagne breakfast.

Whales in Paradise WHALE WATCHING
(☎07-5538 2111; www.whalesinparadise.com.au; cnr Cavill & Ferny Aves, Surfers Paradise; adult/child/family $95/60/250; ⏲Jun-Nov) Leaves central Surfers three times a day for 3½ hours of whale-watching action.

SURFING SCHOOLS

This region is a great spot to learn how to surf. Hang 10 at one of the many great surf schools along the Gold Coast.

Surfing Services Australia (☎07-5535 5557; www.surfingservices.com.au; Currumbin; adult/child $35/25)

Cooly Surf (☎07-5536 1470; www.surfshopaustralia.com.au; cnr Marine Pde & Dutton St, Coolangatta; 2hr surfing lessons $45; ⏲9am-5pm)

Cheyne Horan (☎1800 227 873; www.cheynehoran.com.au; 2hr lessons $49, 3/5 lessons $129/189; ⏲10am & 2pm)

Brad Holmes (☎07-5539 4068, 0418 757 539; www.bradholmessurfcoaching.com; Broadbeach; 90min lessons $75)

Walkin' on Water (☎07-5534 1886, 0418 780 311; www.walkinonwater.com; Greenmount Beach, Coolangatta; 2hr lessons $50)

Festivals & Events

Quicksilver Pro Surfing Competition SURFING
(www.aspworldtour.com) The world's best surfers hit the waves around March in the first comp of the annual world tour.

Surfers Paradise Festival FOOD, ARTS
(www.surfersparadisefestival.com) Food, wine and live music for four weeks in April.

Gold Coast Film Festival FILM
(www.gcfilmfestival.com) Mainstream and left-of-centre flicks from all over the world on outdoor screens, in April.

Gold Coast Marathon SPORTS
(www.goldcoastmarathon.com.au) Sweaty people running a really long way; in July.

Gold Coast 600 SPORTS
(www.v8supercars.com.au) For three days in October the streets of Surfers are transformed into a temporary race circuit for high-speed V8 Supercars.

Sleeping

The **Gold Coast Accommodation Service** (☎07-5592 0067; www.goldcoastaccommodationservice.com) can arrange and book accommodation and tours.

Budds in Surfers HOSTEL $
(☎07-5538 9661; www.buddsinsurfers.com.au; 6 Pine Ave, Surfers Paradise; dm/tw/d/f from $28/80/80/120; @📶🏊) Laid-back Budds features tidy bathrooms, clean tiles, free wi-fi, a sociable bar and a beaut pool, all just a short hop from calm-water Budds Beach. Bike hire available.

Sleeping Inn Surfers HOSTEL $
(☎1800 817 832, 07-5592 4455; www.sleepinginn.com.au; 26 Peninsular Dr, Surfers Paradise; dm $28-32, d $78-88; @📶🏊) This backpackers occupies an old apartment block away from the centre, so, as the name suggests, there's a chance you may get to sleep in. There are pizza and barbecue nights, a kitchen, and free pick-ups from the transit centre. An adjoining apartment block offers some great renovated private rooms, too.

★**Olympus Apartments** APARTMENT $$
(☎07-5538 7288; www.olympusapartments.com.au; 62 Esplanade, Surfers Paradise; 1-bedroom apt $100-160, 2-bedroom apt $150-300; P📶🏊)

DON'T MISS

GOLD COAST THEME PARKS

The gravity-defying roller coasters and water slides at the Gold Coast's American-style parks offer some seriously dizzy action – keeping your lunch down is a constant battle. Discount tickets are sold in most of the tourist offices on the Gold Coast; the VIP Pass (per person $110) grants unlimited entry to Sea World, Movie World and Wet'n'Wild (all owned by Warner Brothers).

A couple of tips: the parks can get insanely crowded, so arrive early or face a long walk from the far side of the car park. Also note that the parks don't let you bring your own food and drinks.

Dreamworld (1800 073 300, 07-5588 1111; www.dreamworld.com.au; Dreamworld Pkwy, Coomera; adult/child $95/75; 10am-5pm) Touts itself as Australia's 'biggest' theme park. There are the 'Big 9 Thrill Rides', plus the Wiggles World and the DreamWorks experience, both for younger kids. Other attractions include Tiger Island, plus a range of interactive animal encounters. A one-day World Pass (adult/child online $95/85, gate $105/95) ensures entry to both Dreamworld and WhiteWater World.

Sea World Sea World continues to attract controversy for its marine shows, where dolphins and sea lions perform tricks for the crowd. While Sea World claims the animals lead a good life, welfare groups argue that keeping such sensitive sea mammals in captivity is harmful, and is especially exacerbated when mixed with human interaction. The park also displays penguins and polar bears, and has water slides and roller coasters.

Movie World (13 33 86, 07-5573 3999; www.movieworld.com.au; Pacific Hwy, Oxenford; adult/child $83/50; 9.30am-5pm) Movie-themed shows, rides and attractions, including the Batwing Spaceshot, Justice League 3D Ride and Scooby-Doo Spooky Coaster. Batman, Austin Powers, Porky Pig et al roam through the crowds.

Wet'n'Wild (13 33 86, 07-5556 1660; www.wetnwild.com.au; Pacific Hwy, Oxenford; adult/child $63/48; 10am-5pm) The ultimate water slide here is the Kamikaze, where you plunge down an 11m drop in a two-person tube at 50km/h. This vast water park also has pitch-black slides, white-water rapids and wave pools.

WhiteWater World (1800 073 300, 07-5588 1111; www.whitewaterworld.com.au; Dreamworld Pkwy, Coomera; adult/child $60/40; 10am-4pm Mon-Fri, to 5pm Sat & Sun) This park features the Cave of Waves, Pipeline Plunge and more than 140 water activities and slides. A one-day World Pass (adult/child online $95/85, gate $105/95) ensures entry to both Dreamworld and WhiteWater World.

Great value for money and directly opposite the beach, this friendly, smallish high-rise has well-kept, spacious apartments with one or two bedrooms: mod furnishings, nice art, super clean, and all facing the sea.

Hi-Ho Beach Apartments APARTMENT $$
(07-5538 2777; www.hihobeach.com.au; 2 Queensland Ave, Broadbeach; 1-/2-bedroom apt from $100/130;) A top choice for location, close to the beach and cafes. You're not paying for glitzy lobbies here: it's standard, value-for-money, no-frills accommodation (a bit '90s decor-wise), but well managed, clean and quiet. Dig the Vegas-esque sign!

Surfers Beachside Holiday Apartments APARTMENT $$
(07-5570 3000; www.surfersbeachside.com.au; 10 Vista St, Surfers Paradise; 1-/2-bedroom apt, 3 nights $600/700) Delightful management is a huge plus at this unpretentious, family-friendly spot. Each apartment is individually owned and therefore decorated, but interiors are to a clean and comfortable standard. Minimum three-night stay in high season, but speak to management if you want fewer sleeps.

QT HOTEL $$
(07-5584 1200; www.qtgoldcoast.com.au; 7 Staghorn Ave, Surfers Paradise; r from $165) This funky-cool-meets-retro-hip high-rise is as eclectic as a great aunt's yard sale: Acapulco chairs, retro bikes and ubersized '80s-style lampshades in the foyer. The wow-inducing decor is meant to reflect Surfers Paradise-meets-Miami circa '50s and '60s, and the fun-in-the-sun theme succeeds. Room interiors

are less nostalgic (though fabrics are quirky); rooms are light, comfortable and modern.

In keeping with the fun and casual vibe, each room provides (on loan) a couple of pairs of rubber thongs (err, that's flip-flops in Oz-speak, folks) in a cotton bag.

Eating

Self-caterers will find supermarkets in the **Chevron Renaissance Centre** (cnr Elkhorn Ave & Surfers Paradise Blvd, Surfers Paradise; 7am-10pm Mon-Sat, 8am-8pm Sun) and **Circle on Cavill** (cnr Cavill & Ferny Aves, Surfers Paradise; 7am-10pm Mon-Sat, 8am-8pm Sun) shopping centres.

★BSKT Cafe CAFE $
(07-5526 6565; www.bskt.com.au; 4 Lavarack Ave, Mermaid Beach; mains $10-27; 7am-4pm Mon-Thu, to 10pm Fri & Sat, to 5pm Sun) This hip corner cafe is 100m from Mermaid Beach, a quick jaunt south of Broadbeach. The brainchild of four buddies whose focus is organic ingredients, it's a mod-industrial affair with chunky timber tables, super staff and adventurous mains. Vegans will be right at home here too, as will kids – there's a fenced play area.

Bumbles Café CAFE $
(07-5538 6668; www.bumblescafe.com; 21 River Dr, Budds Beach, Surfers Paradise; mains $12-22; 7.30am-4pm) This gorgeous spot – a converted house-cum-shop (and at one stage, a brothel) – is *the* place for breakfast, sweet treats and coffee. It comprises a series of rooms, from the pink Princess Room, perfect for afternoon tea, to a library. Oh, and it serves up the region's tastiest range of cakes.

Cardamom Pod VEGETARIAN $
(www.cardamompod.com.au; Lot 1, 70 Surf Pde, Broadbeach; 11.30am-9pm Mon-Fri, 7.30am-9pm Sat & Sun) Vegetarians rejoice! This magical Krishna-inspired, vegan-friendly eatery conjurs up some of the best vegetarian cuisine around. The vegan lasagne is worth coming for alone, but you can choose any two curries and two salads, all served with rice for $26. Finish off with a trademark dessert: raw, and gluten and sugar free (and delicious). Everything is made from scratch on the premises.

Black Coffee Lyrics CAFE $$
(0402 189 437; www.blackcoffeelyrics.com.au; 40/3131 Surfers Paradise Blvd, Surfers Paradise; mains $12-21; noon-2:30pm & 5pm-late Tue-Fri, from 8am Sat & Sun) This trendy spot hidden in an unexpected location – within an arcade – oozes cool. An antithesis to the bright Surfers sun, it's a dark locale, where American bourbon-style bar meets industrial funk. It delivers. Simple gourmet sandwiches and egg dishes are the choice to soak up boutique brews and cocktails, including espresso martinis.

Baritalia ITALIAN $$
(07-5592 4700; www.baritaliagoldcoast.com.au; Shop 15, Chevron Renaissance Centre, cnr Elkhorn Ave & Surfers Paradise Blvd, Surfers Paradise; mains $25-35; 7.30am-late) This Italian bar and restaurant has a fab outdoor terrace and hip international staff. Go for the chilli mussels with white wine in a tomato broth, or excellent pastas, pizzas and risotto (there are gluten free choices, too). Decent wines by the glass and good coffee.

Bazaar INTERNATIONAL $$$
(07-5584 1238; 7 Staghorn Ave, Surfers Paradise; breakfast/dinner $32/72; 6.30am-10.30am & 5.30-9pm Mon-Sat, noon-3pm Sun) In sophisticated PR-speak, 'you can eat your way around the globe at the funky 21st century-style QT extravaganza'. In crude terms, this means you can stuff yourself silly by selecting from various food stations – Spanish charcuterie, Italian pizzas, Asian woks and an Australian seafood bar. It's the ultimate see-food-and-eat-it experience, in fun, stylish surrounds.

Children under 12 pay half.

Drinking & Nightlife

Helm Bar & Bistro BAR
(www.helmbarsurfers.com.au; 30-34 Ferny Ave, Surfers Paradise; 10am-9pm) Unless you like Irish pubs, this nautical-themed bar is the best drinking spot in town, perfect for a beer or six as the sun sets over the Nerang River. Good pizzas and steaks, too.

Sin City CLUB
(www.sincitynightclub.com.au; 22 Orchid Ave, Surfers Paradise; 9pm-late) This flashy Vegas-style sin pit is the place for wrongdoings: sexy staff, big-name DJs and a strange melange of high rollers and university students.

Melbas on the Park CLUB
(www.melbas.com.au; 46 Cavill Ave, Surfers Paradise) Long-standing Melba's is a party palace, with a large lounge and nightclub plus restaurant. Attracts a slightly older crowd than the regular backpacker booze joints.

WORTH A TRIP

MAIN BEACH & THE SPIT

North of Surfers Paradise, the Southport Spit separates Southport (an otherwise dull residential and business district) from the Pacific Ocean. Main Beach is home to one of the big theme parks, Sea World (p316), and Mariner's Cove, which has the useful **Mariner's Cove Tourism Information & Booking Centre** (07-5571 1711; Main Beach; 9am-3pm). Here you can book any number of water-based activities:

Australian Kayaking Adventures (0412 940 135; www.australiankayakingadventures.com.au; half-day tours adult/child $95/75, sunset tours $55/45)

Jet Ski Safaris (07-5526 3111, 0409 754 538; www.jetskisafaris.com.au; Mariner's Cove, 60-70 Sea World Dr, Main Beach; tours per jet ski 1/2½hr from $190/395)

Island Adventures (07-5532 2444; goldcoastadventures.com.au; Mariner's Cove, 60-70 Sea World Dr, Main Beach; 3hr tours adult/child $99/69, full-day tours adult/child $129/79) Whale watching.

Broadwater Canal Cruises (0410 403 020; www.broadwatercanalcruises.com.au; Mariner's Cove, 60-70 Sea World Dr, Main Beach; 2hr cruises adult/child $23/15; 10am & noon)

For land lubbers, **Federation Walk** is a pretty 3.7km trail running through patches of littoral rainforest and connecting to the Gold Coast Oceanway, a 36km walking/cycling trail running to Coolangatta. Starts opposite the entrance to Sea World, in the Phillip Park carpark.

Southeast of here, apartment blocks begin their inexorable rise towards Surfers Paradise. Here, you'll find the lovely, Spanish Mission–style 1934 **Main Beach Pavilion** (Macarthur Pde, Main Beach; 9am-5pm). Inside are some fabulous old photos of the Gold Coast in preskyscraper days.

Sleeping & Eating

Main Beach and the Spit have some good places to eat and sleep for those who'd prefer to be out of the hustle and bustle of nearby Surfers Paradise.

Surfers Paradise YHA at Main Beach (07-5571 1776; www.yha.com.au; 70 Sea World Dr, Main Beach; dm $32, d & tw $81; @) has a great 1st-floor position overlooking the marina, plus a free shuttle service. Can also arrange tours and activities.

For good nosh, try **Providore** (07-5532 9390; www.facebook.com/miragemarket; Shop 37, Marina Mirage, 74 Sea World Dr, Main Beach; mains $16-29; 7am-6pm), a trendy Italian deli-cafe selling wines by the glass, breads, cheeses and picnic produce. If you want a no-nonsense approach, **Peter's Fish Market** (07-5591 7747; www.petersfish.com.au; 120 Sea World Dr, Main Beach; meals $9-16; 9am-7.30pm) serves fresh and cooked seafood in all shapes and sizes, at great prices. Alternatively, the **Fisherman's Wharf Tavern** (07-5571 0566; Mariner's Cove, Main Beach; mains $22-32; 10am-midnight) is a beers-from-10am kinda joint, but whips up reliable burgers and other decent pub meals.

Getting There & Away

Regular local bus 705 runs between Surfers Paradise and Main Beach/The Spit.

Entertainment

Arts Centre Gold Coast THEATRE, CINEMA

(07-5588 4000; www.theartscentregc.com.au; 135 Bundall Rd, Surfers Paradise; box office 8am-9pm Mon-Fri, 9am-9pm Sat, 11am-7pm Sun) A bastion of culture and civility beside the Nerang River, the Arts Centre has two cinemas, a restaurant, a bar, the Gold Coast City Gallery and a 1200-seat theatre, which regularly hosts impressive productions (comedy, jazz, opera, kids' concerts etc).

Information

Backpackers World Travel (07-5561 0634; www.backpackerworldtravel.com; 6 Beach Rd, Surfers Paradise; 10am-4pm;) Accommodation, tour and transport bookings and internet access ($4.50 per hour; wi-fi $5 per 24 hours).

Gold Coast Information & Booking Centre (1300 309 440; www.visitgoldcoast.com; Cavill Ave, Surfers Paradise; 8.30am-5pm Mon-Sat, 9am-4pm Sun) The main Gold Coast tourist information booth; also sells theme-park tickets and has public transport info.

Surfers Paradise Day & Night Medical Centre (☎07-5592 2299; www.goldcoast7daymedicalcentres.com.au; 3221 Surfers Paradise Blvd, Surfers Paradise; ⏰6am-11pm) General medical centre and pharmacy. Make an appointment or just walk in.

Getting There & Away

Long-distance buses stop at the **Surfers Paradise Transit Centre** (10 Beach Rd, Surfers Paradise), including those run by Greyhound (p313) and Premier Motor Service (p313).

Getting Around

To get you to locations around Surfers Paradise, useful Surfside (p313) bus numbers include route 705 between Broadbeach and Seaworld (Main Beach) via Surfers Paradise, and route 731 between Southport and Broadbeach, also via Surfers Paradise.

The newly launched G:link (p313) tram is another handy alternative to driving.

CAR

Car hire costs around $40 to $50 per day.

East Coast Car Rentals (☎07-5592 0444, 1800 028 881; www.eastcoastcarrentals.com.au; 80 Ferny Ave; ⏰7am-6pm Mon-Fri, 8am-5pm Sat, 8am-4pm Sun)

Red Back Rentals (☎07-5592 1655; www.redbackrentals.com.au; Surfers Paradise Transit Centre, 10 Beach Rd; ⏰7.30am-4pm Mon-Sat)

Scooter Hire Gold Coast (☎07-5511 0398; www.scooterhiregoldcoast.com.au; 3269 Surfers Paradise Blvd; ⏰8am-5.30pm) Scooter hire (50cc) from around $75 per day.

Burleigh Heads & Currumbin

POP 9200 & 2785

The true, sandy essence of the Gold Coast permeates the chilled-out surfie town of Burleigh Heads. With its cheery cafes and beachfront restaurants, famous break, beautiful beach and little national park on the rocky headland, Burleigh charms everyone.

Slightly south, Currumbin is a sleepy little family-focused town, with safe swimming in Currumbin Creek.

Sights

Burleigh Head National Park PARK
(www.nprsr.qld.gov.au/parks/burleigh-head; Goodwin Tce, Burleigh Heads) FREE A walk around the headland through Burleigh Head National Park is a must for any visitor – it's a 27-hectare rainforest reserve with plenty of bird life and several walking trails. Great views of the Burleigh surf en route.

David Fleay Wildlife Park WILDLIFE RESERVE
(☎07-5576 2411; www.nprsr.qld.gov.au/parks/david-fleay; cnr Loman Lane & West Burleigh Rd, West Burleigh; adult/child/family $20.10/9.25/51.30; ⏰9am-5pm) Opened by the doctor who first succeeded in breeding platypuses, this wildlife park has 4km of walking tracks through mangroves and rainforest, and plenty of native wildlife shows throughout the day. It's around 3km inland from Burleigh Heads.

Currumbin Wildlife Sanctuary WILDLIFE RESERVE
(☎1300 886 511, 07-5534 1266; www.cws.org.au; 28 Tomewin St, Currumbin; adult/child/family $49/35/133; ⏰8am-5pm) Currumbin Wildlife Sanctuary has Australia's biggest rainforest aviary, where you can hand-feed a technicolour blur of rainbow lorikeets. There's also kangaroo feeding, photo ops with koalas and crocodiles, reptile shows and Aboriginal dance displays. It's cheaper after 3pm. Coach transfers available (return $18).

Activities

Currumbin Rock Pools SWIMMING
(www.gcparks.com.au; Currumbin Creek Rd, Currumbin Valley) FREE These natural swimming holes are a cool spot during the hot summer months, with grassy banks, barbecues and rocky ledges from which teenagers plummet. It's 14km up Currumbin Creek Rd from the coast.

Burleigh Heads Bowls Club BOWLING
(☎07-5535 1023; www.burleighbowls.org.au; cnr Connor & James Sts, Burleigh Heads; per person $5; ⏰noon-5pm Sun) If the surf is flat on a Sunday afternoon, kick off your shoes for some 'Barefoot Bowls' at the local lawn bowls club. Bookings essential.

Burleigh Brewing Company TOUR
(☎07-5593 6000; www.burleighbrewing.com.au; 17a Ern Harley Dr, Burleigh Heads; tours $20) Tours of Burleigh's local boutique brewery on the first Saturday of every month; drinks at the brewery bar every Friday from 5.30pm to 8pm.

Sleeping

Burleigh Beach Tourist Park CARAVAN PARK $
(☎07-5667 2750; www.goldcoasttouristparks.com.au; 36 Goodwin Tce, Burleigh Heads; unpowered/powered sites from $31/41, cabins $145-210; ❄@🛜🏊) This council-owned park is snug,

OFF THE BEATEN TRACK

SOUTH STRADBROKE ISLAND

This narrow, 21km-long sand island is largely undeveloped – the perfect antidote to the chaotic Gold Coast strip. At the northern end, the narrow channel separating it from North Stradbroke Island is a top fishing spot; at the southern end, the Spit is only 200m away. South Stradbroke was actually attached to North Stradbroke until a huge storm in 1896 blasted through the isthmus joining them. There's the luxury **Ramada Couran Cove Island Resort** (07-5597 9999; www.courancove.com.au; d/ste from $350/450;) here, plus three campgrounds, lots of wallabies and plenty of bush, sand and sea. And no cars!

For details on camping on the island – at Tipplers, North Currigee and South Currigee campgrounds – including transport info, see www.mystraddie.com.au.

but it's well run and in a great spot near the beach. Aim for one of the three blue cabins at the front of the park. Cabin prices are based on a seven-night stay.

Burleigh Palms Holiday Apartments APARTMENT $$
(07-5576 3955; www.burleighpalms.com; 1849 Gold Coast Hwy, Burleigh Heads; 1-bedroom apt per night/week from $170/620;) Even though they're on the highway, these large and comfortable self-contained units – it's a quick dash to the beach through the back alley – are solid value. The owners have a wealth of local info, and do the cleaning themselves to keep the accommodation costs down.

Hillhaven Holiday Apartments APARTMENT $$
(07-5535 1055; www.hillhaven.com.au; 2 Goodwin Tce, Burleigh Heads; 2-bedroom apt from $170;) Right on the headland adjacent to the national park, these 22 apartments have awesome views of Burleigh Heads and the surf. It's ultra quiet and only 150m to the beach. Quality ranges from 'standard' to 'gold deluxe'.

Eating

★ **Borough Barista** CAFE $
(14 Esplanade, Burleigh Heads; mains $5-19; 5.30am-2pm) It's cool tunes and friendly vibes at this little open-walled caffeine shack. There's a simple menu of burgers and salads and an unmistakable panache when it comes to coffee (served from 5.30am.) The grilled magic mushroom burger ($13.50) will turn you vegetarian. It's worth the journey to nearby Palm Beach to the larger sister cafe, **Barefoot Barista** (www.barefootbarista.com.au; 10 Palm Beach Ave, Palm Beach; mains $11-18; 5am-4pm Mon-Fri, to 3pm Sat & Sun).

Fishmonger SEAFOOD $
(07-5535 2927; 9 James St, Burleigh Heads; dishes $7-16; 10am-7.30pm) This low-key fish-and-chip shop has been here since 1948 – enough time to perfect its recipe! Grab some takeaway and head for the beach.

Justin Lane Pizzeria & Bar PIZZA $$
(07-5576 8517; www.justinlane.com.au; 1708 Gold Coast Hwy, Burleigh Heads; pizzas $19-24; 5pm-late) One of several cool eateries to hit Burleigh Heads, Justin Lane is located in a rehabilitated arcade. This pizzeria and bar is a fun and vibrant place with heaps of buzz energy, hustle and bustle. Oh, plus great pizzas.

Elephant Rock Café MODERN AUSTRALIAN, CAFE $$
(07-5598 2133; www.elephantrock.com.au; 776 Pacific Pde, Currumbin; mains $28-35; 7am-late Tue-Sat, to 5pm Sun & Mon) On the refreshingly under-developed Currumbin beachfront you'll find this breezy, two-tier cafe, which morphs from beach-chic by day into chic at night. Great ocean views and even better Indonesian seafood curry.

★ **Fish House** SEAFOOD $$$
(07-5535 7725; www.thefishhouse.com.au; 50 Goodwin Tce, Burleigh Heads; mains $36-56; noon-3pm & 6-9pm Wed-Sun) This stylish red-brick box across the road from the beach is famous for its underwater stuff: whiting, swordfish, trevally, John Dory…all locally caught or imported fresh from interstate. Dress nicely, and get ready to speak loudly (lots of hard surfaces) and people watch (folk fly from interstate to eat here). Eating here is an experience worth taking your time over.

Drinking & Nightlife

Currumbin Beach Vikings SLSC PUB
(07-5534 2932; www.currumbinslsc.com.au; 741 Pacific Pde, Currumbin; 7am-10.30pm) In an incredible position on Currumbin beach below craggy Elephant Rock, this surf pavilion is perfect for an afternoon beer. The menu (mains $20 to $30) is predictable, but the view will knock your socks off.

Getting There & Away

Premier Motor Service (www.premierms.com.au) links Burleigh Heads to various points north and south, including Byron Bay (from $29). Surfside Buslines' (p313) local bus 702 (which links Gold Coast Airport to Southport, stopping along the way) stops at Burleigh Heads.

Coolangatta

POP 5200

A down-to-earth seaside town on Queensland's southern border, Coolangatta has quality surf beaches (including the legendary Superbank break) and a tight-knit community. The legendary Coolangatta Gold surf-lifesaving comp happens here every October. Follow the boardwalk north around Kirra Point to the suburb of Kirra itself, with a beautiful stretch of beach and challenging surf.

Activities & Tours

Gold Coast Skydive ADVENTURE SPORTS
(07-5599 1920; www.goldcoastskydive.com.au; 1/78 Musgrave St, Kirra Beach; tandem jumps from $365) Plummet out of the sky from 3660m up? Go on – you know you want to! Incredibly for some, this is a very popular activity. This crew is the only tandem skydiving operation on the Gold Coast.

Tweed Endeavour Cruises CRUISE
(07-5536 8800; www.goldcoastcruising.com; 2hr cruises from adult/child $40/20) These guys have cruise options ranging from crab-catching to surf 'n' turf lunches on rainforest cruises along the Tweed River.

Sleeping

Coolangatta YHA HOSTEL $
(07-5536 7644; www.coolangattayha.com; 230 Coolangatta Rd, Bilinga; dm $29-34, s/d/f from $45/68/90;) Next to the airport, a 4km haul from the action, this friendly YHA is redeemed by free transfers to Coolangatta and its proximity to Kirra Beach, across the highway. You can also hires surfboards ($20 per day) and bikes ($25). Breakfast costs $5.

★ **La Costa Motel** MOTEL $$
(07-5599 2149; www.lacostamotel.com.au; 127 Golden Four Dr, Bilinga; d $150) One of the few motels of the 1950s 'highway heritage', this weatherboard mint-green motel, located just off the Gold Coast Hwy, has stayed true to its retro roots on the outside, while the interiors are neat and modern and include kitchenettes. A lovely apartment suits longer stays. Prices lower significantly outside high season.

★ **Hotel Komune** HOTEL, HOSTEL $$
(07-5536 6764; www.komuneresorts.com; 146 Marine Pde, Coolangatta; dm from $35, 1-/2-bedroom apt from $105/145;) This spot offers a different take on the hostel concept. With beach-funk decor, a palm-laden pool area and an ultra laid-back vibe, this 10-storey converted apartment tower is the ultimate surf retreat. There are budget dorms, apartments and a hip penthouse begging for a party.

The on-site bar–night club picks up around 9pm, with music Friday to Sunday.

Nirvana APARTMENT $$$
(07-5506 5555; www.nirvanabythesea.com.au; 1 Douglas St, Kirra; 2-/3-bedroom apt from

LOCAL KNOWLEDGE

LUKE EGAN: FORMER PRO SURFER

The Gold Coast is one of the top five surfing destinations in the world. The most unique thing about the Goldy is that the waves break mostly on sand, so for sandy bottoms we get some of the most perfect waves in the world.

Best Surf Beaches

The length of ride on the famous points of Burleigh Heads, Kirra Beach, Rainbow Bay and Snapper Rocks make the Goldy a must for every passionate surfer.

Where to Learn

The waves at Greenmount Point and Currumbin allow first-timers plenty of time to get to their feet and still enjoy a long ride. Learning to surf at these two places would be close to the best place to learn anywhere in Australia, and probably the world.

Best Experience

There isn't a better feeling than being 'surfed out' – the feeling you have after a day of surfing. Even though I no longer compete on the world surfing tour I still surf every day like it's my last.

$210/380; P) Attaining some sort of salty nirvana across from Kirra Beach, this sleek apartment tower (actually more appropriate to the city than a beach) comes with all the whistles and bells: lap pool, gym, cinema room, ocean views and sundry salons.

Eating

Burger Lounge BURGERS $
(07-5599 5762; www.burgerlounge.com.au; cnr Musgrave & Douglas Sts, Kirra; mains $13-17; 11am-9pm) Awesome bun-fest at the base of the Nirvana apartment tower (fast-food nirvana?). The chicken-and-mango-chilli burger is a winner! Lots of good beers, cocktails and wines, too, and sangria by the jug.

★**Cafe dbar** MODERN AUSTRALIAN $$
(07-5599 2031; www.cafedbar.com.au; 275 Boundary St, Coolangatta; mains $14-26; 11.15am-3pm Mon-Thu, to 8pm Fri-Sun) This lovely spot is perched above the cliffs of Point Danger, on the easternmost point of two states, almost on top of the NSW and Queensland border. You can munch on any number of fabulous breakfast options (our favourite meal here), fresh salads or tapas, and sip on good coffee.

Bread 'n' Butter TAPAS $$
(07-5599 4666; www.breadnbutter.com.au; 76 Musgrave St, Coolangatta; tapas $15-27, pizzas $20-25; 5.30pm-late) Head upstairs to the Bread 'n' Butter balcony, where moody lighting and chilled tunes make this tapas bar perfect for a drink, some woodfired pizza or some tapas (or all three). DJs spin on Friday and Saturday nights.

Bellakai MODERN AUSTRALIAN $$$
(07-5599 5116; www.facebook.com/bellakai.coolangatta; 82 Marine Pde, Coolangatta; mains $30-37; 5am-9.30pm) From 5am (yes, 5am) until late, Bellakai plates up some mighty fine morsels. The menu changes seasonally, but it will go something like this: spiced soft-shell crab with eggplant and chilli jam, or fresh calamari. Pricey, but not snobby. Good coffee, too.

Getting There & Away

Greyhound (1300 473 946; www.greyhound.com.au) links Brisbane and Coolangatta and beyond (coaches stop on Warner St; tickets from $21), while **Premier Motor Service** (13 34 10; www.premierms.com.au) heads as far north as Cairns. Coaches stop on Wharf St.

Gold Coast Hinterland

Inland from the surf, sand and half-naked bods on the Gold Coast, the densely forested mountains of the McPherson Range feel a million miles away. There are some brilliant national parks here, with subtropical jungle, waterfalls, lookouts and rampant wildlife. Springbrook National Park is arguably the wettest place in southeast Queensland, with cool air and a dense sea of forest. Lamington National Park attracts birdwatchers and hikers; kitschy Tamborine Mountain lures the craft/cottage weekend set.

Tours

Bushwacker Ecotours ECO-TOUR
(07-3848 8806, 1300 559 355; www.bushwacker-ecotours.com.au; tours adult/child from $129/99) Eco-tours to the hinterland with rainforest walks in Springbrook National Park and around. Departing Gold Coast or Brisbane.

JPT Tour Group TOUR
(07-56301602; www.daytours.com.au; tours from adult/child $102/63) A variety of day tours ex-Brisbane or Gold Coast, including Lamington National Park via Tamborine Mountain, and nocturnal glow-worm tours to Natural Bridge.

Mountain Coach Company TOUR
(1300 762 665, 07-5524 4249; www.mountaincoach.com.au) Daily tours from the Gold Coast to Tamborine Mountain (adult/child $59/49), Lamington National Park ($89/57) and Springbrook National Park ($89/57). Transfer-only prices also available ex-Gold Coast (Tamborine Mountain adult/child $30/20; Lamington National Park $50/40).

Tamborine Mountain

This squat, mountaintop rainforest community – comprising Eagle Heights, North Tamborine and Mt Tamborine – is 45km inland from the Gold Coast beaches, and has cornered the artsy-craftsy, Germanic-kitsch, package-tour, chocolate/fudge/liqueur market in a big way. If this is your bag, **Gallery Walk** in Eagle Heights is the place to stock up.

For a good choice of funky cafes and eateries, head to Main St, North Tamborine, a favourite among the locals. Or head further afield for some excellent wineries (with good restaurants and views).

WORTH A TRIP

LAMINGTON NATIONAL PARK

Australia's largest remnant of subtropical rainforest cloaks the deep valleys and steep cliffs of the McPherson Range, reaching elevations of 1100m on the Lamington Plateau. Here, the 200-sq-km **Lamington National Park** (www.nprsr.qld.gov.au/parks/lamington) is a Unesco World Heritage Site and has over 160km of walking trails.

The two most accessible sections of the park are the **Binna Burra** and **Green Mountains** sections, both reached via long, narrow, winding roads from Canungra (not great for big campervans). Binna Burra can also be accessed from Nerang.

Bushwalks within the park include everything from short jaunts to multiday epics. For experienced hikers, the Gold Coast Hinterland Great Walk is a three-day trip along a 54km path from the Green Mountains section to the Springbrook Plateau. Other favourites include the excellent Tree Top Canopy Walk along a series of rope-and-plank suspension bridges at Green Mountains, and the 21km Border Track that follows the dividing range between New South Wales and Queensland and links Binna Burra to Green Mountains.

Walking guides are available from the Binna Burra and Green Mountains **ranger stations** (⏲7.30am-4pm Mon-Fri, 9am-3.30pm Sat&Sun).

Sleeping

Green Mountains Campground (☎13 74 68; www.nprsr.qld.gov.au/parks/lamington/camping.html; Green Mountains; site per person/family $5.75/23) There's a tiered, national parks camping ground at the end of Lamington National Park Rd, adjacent to the day-use visitor car park. There are plenty of spots for tents and caravans (and a toilet/shower block); book in advance.

Binna Burra Mountain Lodge (☎1300 246 622, 07-5533 3622; www.binnaburralodge.com.au; 1069 Binna Burra Rd, Beechmont; unpowered/powered sites $28/35, d incl breakfast with/without bathroom $300/190) This wonderful spot is the nearest thing to a ski lodge in the bush. You can stay in rustic log cabins, superb flashy apartments (sky lodges), or in a tent surrounded by forest in this atmospheric mountain retreat. The central restaurant serves a dinner buffet ($45) and breakfast ($28).

There's also the cafe-style Teahouse (mains $14 to $18) by the campground, open 10am to 4pm. Transport is available. Nature walks and other activities are included for those in huts and lodges.

O'Reilly's Rainforest Retreat (☎1800 688 722, 07-5502 4911; www.oreillys.com.au; Lamington National Park Rd, Green Mountains; r from $179, 1-/2-bedroom villa from $330/360; @📶🏊) This famous 1926 guesthouse has lost its original grandeur but retains a rustic charm – and sensational views! Newer luxury villas and doubles add a contemporary sheen. There are plenty of organised activities, plus a day spa, cafe, bar and restaurant (mains $26 to $40), open for breakfast, lunch and dinner.

Sights & Activities

Tamborine National Park NATIONAL PARK
(www.nprsr.qld.gov.au/parks/tamborine) Queensland's oldest national park has 13 sections stretching across the 8km plateau, offering waterfalls and super views of the Gold Coast. Accessed via easy-to-moderate walking trails are **Witches Falls**, **Curtis Falls**, **Cedar Creek Falls** and **Cameron Falls**. Pick up a map at the visitor centre in North Tamborine.

Skywalk WALKING
(☎07-5545 2333, 07-5545 2222; www.rainforestskywalk.com.au; 333 Geissman Dr, North Tamborine; adult/child/family $19.50/9.50/49; ⏲9.30am-4pm) Take a walk through the rainforest canopy at Skywalk, 30m above the ground. The 1.5km-long path descends to the forest floor and leads to Cedar Creek; there are high (and slightly swaying) views from a cantilevered viewpoint (you'll see). Look out for rare Richmond Birdwing butterflies en route.

Sleeping & Eating

Songbirds Rainforest Retreat HOTEL $$$
(☎07-5545 2563; www.songbirds.com.au; Lot 10, Tamborine Mountain Rd, North Tamborine; villas from $298) By far the classiest outfit on the hill. Each of the six very plush Southeast Asian-inspired villas has a double spa with rainforest views. The award-winning restaurant, also on site, is worth visiting for a *looong* lunch.

St Bernards Hotel PUB $$
(☎07-5545 1177; www.stbernardshotel.com; 101 Alpine Tce, Mt Tamborine; mains $22-39; ⊙10am-midnight) A woody old mountain pub with a large terrace and sweeping views. Offers reasonable pub grub such as fish and chips, and chicken parmigiana. The macadamia nut chicken tenderloins ($29.90) are a tasty local alternative.

Mason Winery Eden Restaurant MODERN AUSTRALIAN $$
(☎07-5545 2000; www.masonwines.com.au; 32 Hartley Rd, North Tamborine; mains $15-30; ⊙11am-3pm) One of Tamborine's more recent culinary additions, Mason Wines has free wine tastings daily. It's the place to go for a leisurely lunch – nab a seat under the covered verandah overlooking lush gardens. Although the meat and seafood platters are for two, solo diners also have great choices, such as the Gold Coast panko-crumbed whiting fillets and superfood salads using fresh, local produce. All dishes are beautifully presented.

Information

Tamborine Mountain Visitor Information Centre (☎07-5545 3200; www.tamborinemtncc.org.au; Doughty Park, Main Western Rd, North Tamborine; ⊙10am-4pm;) Plenty of info on Tamborine National Park.

Springbrook National Park

About a 40-minute drive west of Burleigh Heads, **Springbrook National Park** (www.nprsr.qld.gov.au/parks/springbrook) is a steep remnant of the huge Tweed Shield volcano that centred on nearby Mt Warning in NSW more than 20 million years ago. It's a wonderland for hikers, with excellent trails through cool-temperate, subtropical and eucalypt forests offering a mosaic of gorges, cliffs and waterfalls.

The park is divided into four sections. The 1000m-plus high **Springbrook Plateau** section houses the strung-out township of Springbrook along Springbrook Rd, and receives the most visitors: it's laced with waterfalls, trails and eye-popping lookouts. The scenic **Natural Bridge** section, off the Nerang–Murwillumbah road, has a 1km walking circuit leading to a huge rock arch spanning a water-formed cave – home to a luminous colony of glow-worms. The **Mt Cougal** section, accessed via Currumbin Creek Rd, has several waterfalls and swimming holes (watch out for submerged logs and slippery rocks); while the heavily forested **Numinbah** section to the north is the fourth section of the park.

Sights

Best of All Lookout VIEWPOINT
(Repeater Station Rd) True to its name, the Best of All Lookout offers phenomenal views from the southern edge of the Springbrook Plateau to the lowlands below. The 350m trail from the car park to the lookout takes you past a clump of gnarled Antarctic beech trees: you'll only find them around the Scenic Rim region.

Purling Brook Falls WATERFALL
(Forestry Rd) Just off Springbrook Rd, the feathery Purling Brook Falls drop a rather astonishing 109m into the rainforest: check them out from the vertigo-inducing lookout.

Canyon Lookout VIEWPOINT
(Canyon Pde) Canyon Lookout affords jagged views through the valley all the way to Surfers Paradise. This is also the start of a 4km circuit walk to **Twin Falls**, which is part of Springbrook's longest trail, the 17km **Warrie Circuit**.

Goomoolahra Falls WATERFALL
(Springbrook Rd) At the end of Springbrook Rd there's a superb lookout beside the 60m Goomoolahra Falls, with views across the plateau and all the way back to the coast. There's a creek-side picnic area here, too.

Sleeping & Eating

Settlement Campground CAMPGROUND $
(☎13 74 68; www.nprsr.qld.gov.au/parks/springbrook/camping.html; 52 Carricks Rd; per person/family $5.50/22) There are 11 grassy sites at this pretty, trim camping ground (the only one at Springbrook), which also has toilets and barbecues. Book ahead. The Gold Coast Hinterland Great Walk runs through here.

Dancing Waters Café CAFE $
(☎07-5533 5335; www.dancingwaterscafe.com; 33 Forestry Rd; dishes $6-13; ⊙10.30am-4.30pm) Next to the Purling Brook Falls car park, this affable cafe serves healthy salads and light meals (fab toasted chicken sandwiches and homemade scones). Open fire in winter; sunny deck in summer.

Information

Visitor Information Centre (Springbrook Rd; ⊙10am-2pm) You'll find maps, brochures, accommodation and information at this friendly spot.

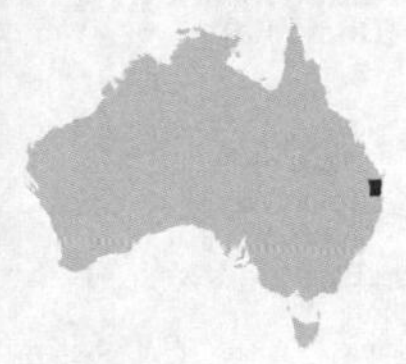

Noosa & the Sunshine Coast

Includes ➡

Best Places to Eat

- Little Humid (p330)
- Spice Bar (p335)
- Mooloolah River Fisheries (p335)

Best Places to Stay

- YHA Halse Lodge (p329)
- Glass House Mountains Ecolodge (p332)
- Boreen Point Camping Ground (p338)

Why Go?

The Sunshine Coast – the 100 golden kilometres stretching from the tip of Bribie Island to the Cooloola Coast – is aglow with glimmering coastlines, great surf spots and a laid-back, friendly populace for whom smiles are the norm. Stylish Noosa boasts a sophisticated dining and resort scene, while Mooloolaba, with its popular beach and outdoor cafes, is a favourite with holidaying Australian families.

Not to be outdone, the hinterland, too, has some gems. The ethereal Glass House Mountains, looming over the land- and seascapes, offer fabulous walks. For views, drivers can easily access the region's lookouts. Further north, the Blackall Range offers a change of scenery with thick forests, lush pastures and quaint villages. The hinterland boasts a growing cuisine scene; excellent sophisticated eateries abound. The area is also home to the iconic Australia Zoo.

When to Go

Noosa

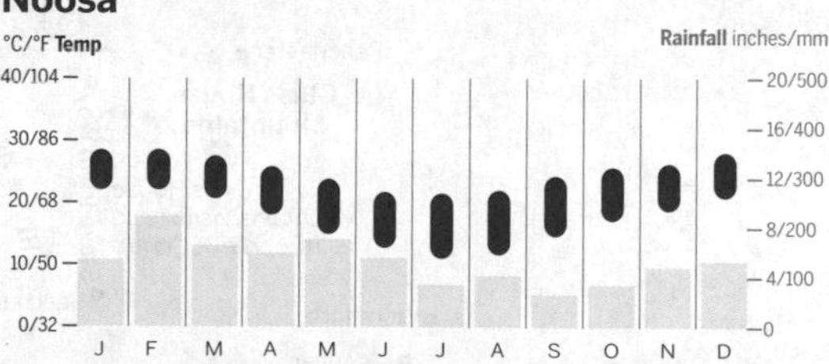

May Satisfy culinary cravings at the Noosa International Food & Wine Festival.

Aug Postholiday lull means fewer crowds, warm weather and solitary beach walks.

Sep Noosa's streets fill with music during the four-day Noosa Jazz Festival.

Noosa & the Sunshine Coast Highlights

1. Hiking the coastal track at **Noosa National Park** (p327).
2. Sampling gourmet beach fare in one of Noosa's swish **restaurants** (p330).
3. Lapping up the beach scene in **Mooloolaba** (p334).
4. Absorbing the vistas of (and from) the **Glass House Mountains** (p332).
5. Canoeing in the **Noosa Everglades** (p327) and exploring the **Great Sandy National Park** (Cooloola; p338).

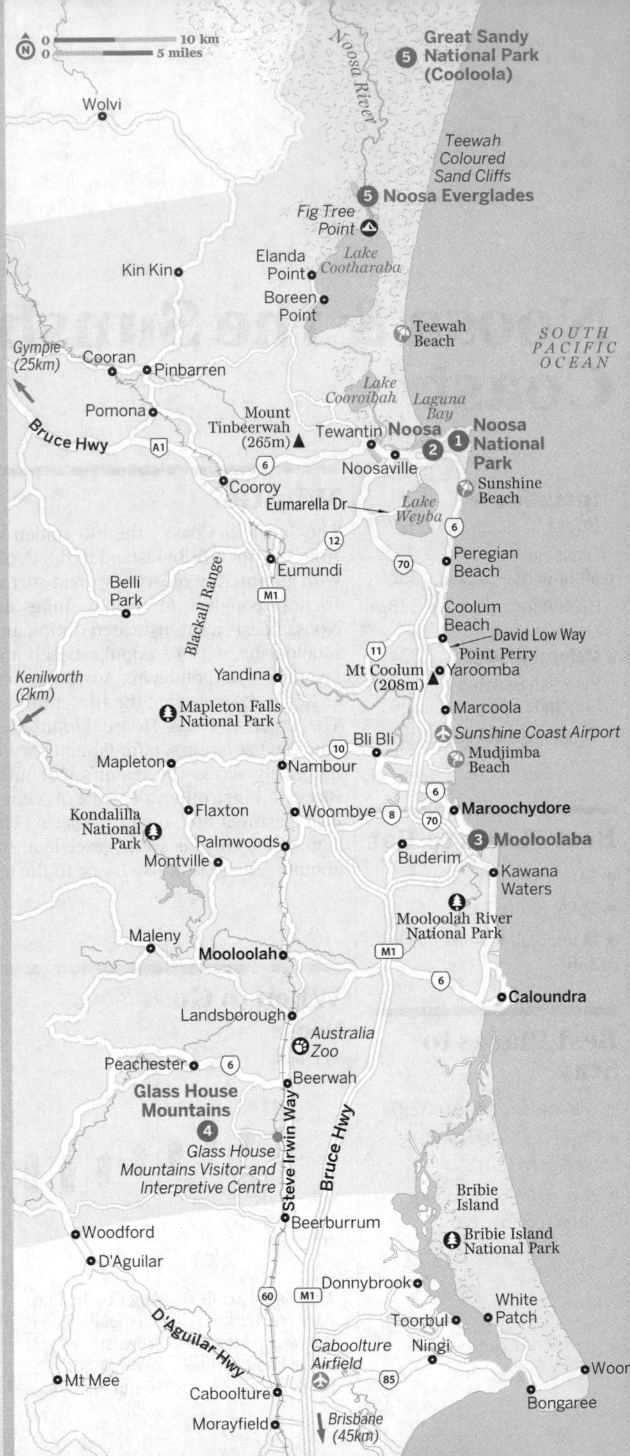

Getting There & Around

AIR

Sunshine Coast Airport (☎07-5453 1500; www.sunshinecoastairport.com; Friendship Ave, Marcoola) is at Marcoola, 10km north of Maroochydore and 26km south of Noosa. **Jetstar** (☎13 15 38; www.jetstar.com.au) and **Virgin Australia** (☎13 67 89; www.virginaustralia.com) have daily flights from Sydney and Melbourne.

BUS

Greyhound Australia (☎1300 473 946; www.greyhound.com.au) has several daily services from Brisbane to Caloundra (from $11, two hours), Maroochydore ($21, two hours) and Noosa ($28, 2½ hours). **Premier Motor Service** (☎13 34 10; www.premierms.com.au) also services Maroochydore ($23, 1½ hours) and Noosa ($23, 2½ hours) from Brisbane.

Several companies offer transfers from Sunshine Coast Airport and Brisbane to points along the coast. Fares from Brisbane cost $40 to $50 and from Sunshine Coast Airport around $25 to $35. (Fares are around half price for children).

Con-X-ion (☎07-5450 5933; www.con-x-ion.com) Does airport transfers from the Sunshine Coast and Brisbane Airports.

Henry's (☎07-5474 0199; www.henrys.com.au) Runs a door-to-door service from Sunshine Coast Airport to points north as far as Noosa Heads and Tewantin.

Sunbus (☎13 12 30; www.sunbus.com.au) This local TransLink-operated bus buzzes between Caloundra and Noosa, and from Noosa to the train station at Nambour ($10.50, one hour) via Eumundi.

Noosa

POP 14,000

Noosa is a swanky resort town with a stunning natural landscape of crystalline beaches and tropical rainforests. Designer boutiques and smart restaurants draw beach-elite sophisticates, but the beach and bush are still free, so fashionistas share the beat with thongs, board shorts and bronzed bikini bods.

On long weekends and school holidays, bustling Hastings St becomes a slow-moving file of traffic; the rest of the time, it's delightfully low(er) key.

Noosa encompasses three main zones: Noosa Heads (around Laguna Bay and Hastings St), Noosaville (along the Noosa River) and Noosa Junction (the administrative centre).

Sights

Noosa National Park NATIONAL PARK

(www.noosanationalpark.com) One of Noosa's best features, this lovely park covers the headland, and has fine walks, great coastal scenery and a string of bays with great surfing. The most scenic way to access the national park is to follow the boardwalk along the coast from town.

Koalas are often spotted in the trees near Tea Tree Bay, and dolphins are commonly seen from the rocky headlands around Alexandria Bay, an informal nudist beach on the eastern side. Pick up a walking-track map from the **Noosa National Park Information Centre** (☎07-5447 3522; ⊙9.15am-4.45pm) at the entrance to the park.

Laguna Lookout VIEWPOINT

For a panoramic view of Noosa's lovely national park, walk or drive up to Laguna Lookout from Viewland Dr in Noosa Junction.

Everglades NATIONAL PARK

The passage of the Noosa River that cuts into the Great Sandy National Park (p338) is poetically known as the 'river of mirrors' or the Everglades. It's a great place to launch a kayak and camp in one of the many national park campgrounds along the riverbank.

Activities

Surfing & Water Sports

With a string of breaks around an unspoiled national park, Noosa is a fine place to catch a wave. Generally the waves are best in December and January. Sunshine Corner, at the northern end of Sunshine Beach, has an excellent year-round break, although it has a brutal beach dump. The point breaks around the headland only perform during the summer, but when they do, expect wild conditions and good walls at Boiling Point and Tea Tree on the northern coast of the headland. There are also gentler breaks on Noosa Spit at the far end of Hastings St, where most of the surf schools do their training.

Kitesurfers will find conditions at the river mouth and Lake Weyba are best between October and January, and on windy days the Noosa River is a playground for serious daredevils.

Noosa Heads

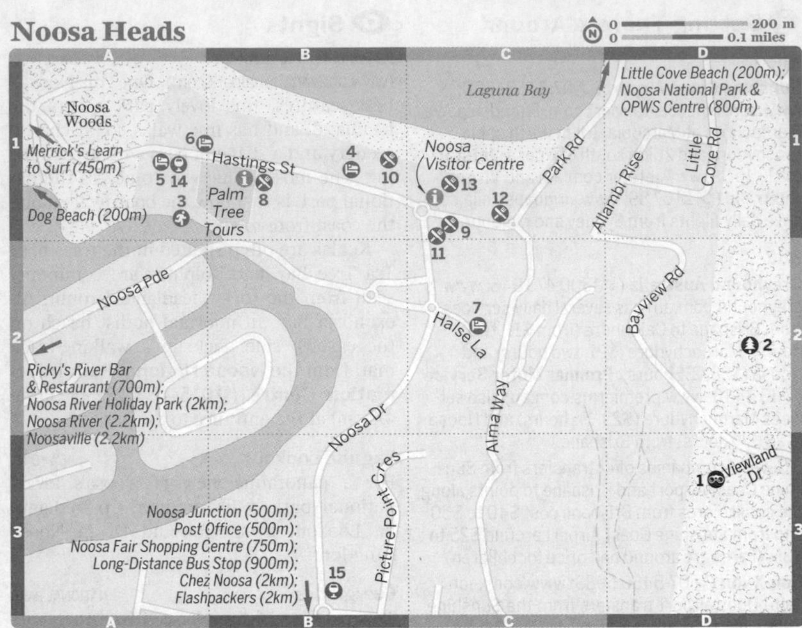

Noosa Heads

Sights
1 Laguna Lookout ... D3
2 Noosa National Park ... D2

Activities, Courses & Tours
3 Noosa Ferry ... A1

Sleeping
4 Accom Noosa ... B1
5 Hotel Laguna ... A1
6 Seahaven Noosa ... A1
7 YHA Halse Lodge ... C2

Eating
8 Bay Village Shopping Centre Food Court ... B1
9 Berardo's ... C1
10 Bistro C ... B1
11 Gaston ... C1
12 Massimo's ... C1
13 Noosa Heads SLSC ... C1

Drinking & Nightlife
14 Miss Moneypenny's ... A1
15 Reef Hotel ... B3

Merrick's Learn to Surf SURFING
(0418 787 577; www.learntosurf.com.au; Beach Access 14, Noosa Main Beach; 2hr lessons $60; 9am & 1.30pm) Holds one-, three- and five-day surfing programs.

Adventure Sports Noosa KITESURFING
(07-5455 6677; www.kitesurfaustralia.com.au; 203 Gympie Tce, Noosaville; kitesurfing 2½hr lessons $275) As well as kitesurfing lessons, Adventure Sports hires kayaks (half day $35), bikes (two hours $19, full day $25) and stand-up paddle boards (two hours $19, full day $25).

Noosa Stand Up Paddle WATER SPORTS
(0423 869 962; www.noosastanduppaddle.com.au; lessons $55; lessons 9am, 11am, 1pm, 3pm) For those who like to do it (paddle, that is) standing up.

Canoeing & Kayaking

The Noosa River is excellent for canoeing; it's possible to follow it up through Lakes Cooroibah and Cootharaba, and through the Cooloola Section of Great Sandy National Park.

Noosa Ocean Kayak Tours KAYAKING
(☎0418 787 577; www.noosakayaktours.com; 2hr tours $70, kayak hire per day $60) Tours around Noosa National Park and along the Noosa River.

Adventure Activities

Bike On Australia MOUNTAIN BIKING
(☎07-5474 3322; www.bikeon.com.au; tours from $80, bike hire per day $25) Hosts a variety of tours, including self-guided and adventurous eco-jaunts. The fun half-day 'off-the-top tour' – downhill on a mountain bike – costs $79. Also hires road bikes ($30 per day).

Cruises

Noosa Ferry CRUISE
(☎07-5449 8442; www.noosaferry.com) This excellent ferry service has informative 90-minute round-trip cruises ($20) that run between Tewantin and the Sheraton Jetty. It also has an eco-cruise (it's great for birdwatchers and includes a nature walk; per person $45), a dinner cruise, and a wonderful one-hour sunset cruise (you can BYO, 'bring your own' alcoholic drinks; per person $20).

Tours

Fraser Island Adventure Tours ADVENTURE TOUR
(☎07-5444 6957; www.fraserislandadventuretours.com.au; day tours from $145) Popular day trips to Eli Creek, the *Maheno* shipwreck and Lake McKenzie pack as much punch as a two-day tour.

Discovery Group DRIVING TOUR
(☎07-5449 0393; www.thediscoverygroup.com.au; Jetty 186, Gympie Tce, Noosaville; day tours adult/child $175/120) Visit Fraser Island on a wonderful 4WD truck tour. Also offers trips through the Everglades (p337).

Festivals & Events

Noosa International Food & Wine Festival FOOD, WINE
(www.noosafoodandwine.com.au) A three-day tribute to all manner of gastronomic delights, held each May.

Noosa Long Weekend FOOD, FASHION
(www.noosalongweekend.com) Ten-day festival of arts, culture, food and fashion in June/July.

Noosa Jazz Festival JAZZ
(www.noosajazz.com.au) Four-day event in early September with a range of jazz styles in venues around town.

Sleeping

Accommodation prices can rise between 50% and 100% in peak season. During these times most places require a minimum two- or three-night stay.

For an extensive list of short-term holiday rentals, try the Noosa Visitor Centre (p331) and the privately run **Accom Noosa** (☎07-5447 3444; www.accomnoosa.com.au; Shop 5/41 Hastings St, Noosa Heads).

★**YHA Halse Lodge** HOSTEL $
(☎07-5447 3377; www.halselodge.com.au; 2 Halse Lane, Noosa Heads; dm $32, d $96; @🛜) This splendid colonial-era timber Queenslander is a legendary stopover on the backpacker trail, and well worth the clamber up its steep drive. There are three- and six-bed dorms, doubles and a lovely wide verandah. The bar is a mix-and-meet bonanza and serves great meals ($10 to $15). Close to the Main Beach action.

Noosa River Holiday Park CARAVAN PARK $
(☎07-5449 7050; www.noosaholidayparks.com.au; 4 Russell St, Noosaville; unpowered/powered sites $36/44; 🛜) In a lovely spot on the banks of the Noosa River, this park has the closest camping facilities to Noosa. Keep in mind that they do so love their rules and regulations here.

Hotel Laguna APARTMENT $$
(www.hotellaguna.com.au; 6 Hastings St, Noosa Heads; studio/ste from $155/210; ❄🛜🏊) One of the area's best-value accommodation options in this price range, and neatly wedged between the river and Hastings St, La Laguna has self-contained apartments and smaller studios. Given that all apartments are privately owned, each is individually decorated, but all are clean and smart. The location is a plus: a roll-out-of-bed away from the beach, and a coffee whiff from great cafes.

Coral Beach Noosa Resort APARTMENT $$
(☎07-5449 7777; www.coralbeach.com.au; 12 Robert St, Noosaville; 2-bed apt from $185; P❄🛜🏊) One of Noosa's best-value options, these double-storey, spacious and airy apartments are individually furnished and feature their own patch of grass, plus small balconies. It's especially popular with families – think kids' swimming pool antics. Management is particularly helpful, and the resort has easy access to riverfront action, leafy surrounds and a choice of pools.

Noosa Sun Motel APARTMENT $$
(07-5474 0477; www.noosasunmotel.com.au; 131 Gympie Tce, Noosaville; r $115-240;) Uninspiring from the outside, but what lies within is most unexpected: modern, spacious and surprisingly stylish apartments replete with kitchenettes and free wi-fi. Some boast water views, while cheaper units overlook the garden. Within walking distance of loads of eateries and shops.

Seahaven Noosa APARTMENT $$$
(seahavennoosa.com.au; 15 Hastings St, Noosa Heads; studio from $199, apt from $490) This beachfront spot has the 'wow' factor: smart, contemporary interiors, electric blinds and smart kitchenettes. The beach-facing units are light and spacious and perfect for a 'swim-read-sleep-let's-do-it-all-again' cycle. The studios on Hastings St are a bit tight in size and, as such, expensive for what you get.

Eating

Noosa prides itself on being a foodie destination, with global and local flavours on offer everywhere from fine restaurants to beachside takeaways. In Noosa Heads, eateries clutter happening Hastings St; in Noosaville, head to the strip along Thomas St and Gympie Tce.

You can select from a range of cheaper takeaway or casual dining options at the **Bay Village Shopping Centre food court** (Hastings St, Noosa Heads; mains $12). Self-caterers can stock up at the **Noosa Fair Shopping Centre** (Lanyana Way, Noosa Junction) in Noosa Junction.

Burger Bar BURGERS $
(07-5474 4189; theburgerbar.com.au; 4 Thomas St, Noosaville; burgers $11-15; 11am-8pm;) This informal and quirky venue whips up hormone-free, vegetarian, and weird and wonderful between-bun delights; the lamb burgers (especially 'Top Bun', with brie cheese, lime slaw, and piccalilli sauce; $14) are particularly divine.

Massimo's GELATERIA $
(75 Hastings St, Noosa Heads; gelati $2-6; 10am-9.30pm) With a selection of flavours as tall as the Tower of Pisa, and loyal local clientele who appreciate the ice creams' natural ingredients, this is definitely one of the best *gelaterias* in Queensland.

★**Little Humid** MODERN AUSTRALIAN $$
(07-5449 9755; www.humid.com.au; 2/235 Gympie Tce, Noosaville; mains from $25; noon-2pm Wed-Sun & from 6pm Tue-Sun) Fine dining without pretensions. This extremely popular eatery is, according to locals, one of the best in town. It lives up to the hype, with toothsome treats including superb fillet steaks, sticky pork belly, and a large range of creative vegie options. Definitely book ahead.

★**Gaston** MODERN AUSTRALIAN $$
(facebook.com/gastonnoosa; 5/50 Hastings St, Noosa Heads; mains $25-36; 7am-late) Unpretentious, but with a menu that's up there with the best of them, Gaston is a (beautiful-) people-watching paradise. Gawk at the passing parade over superb-value lunch specials (main and a drink $20) or dinner deals (two mains and a bottle of wine $55), offered during quieter periods.

Bistro C MODERN AUSTRALIAN $$
(07-5447 2855; bistroc.com.au; Hastings St, On the Beach Resort, Noosa Heads; mains $19-40; 7.30am-11.30pm) This ever-attractive spot keeps long hours and the location, on the beach, is superb for a relaxing experience, from coffee to cocktail. Brunch offers the best value for money (try the corn-and-chive griddle cake, $22). In the evening, the locale's atmosphere wins over cuisine quality, but the bar is fun. Afternoon tapas is on offer, too.

Noosa Heads SLSC INTERNATIONAL $$
(07-5474 9788; www.noosasurfclub.com.au; 69 Hastings St, Noosa Heads; mains $16.50-31; 8am-late) Perfect beach views from the deck make for idyllic beer-sipping and reasonable (if erring towards the pricey) pub-food chomping. That is, everything from 'ironman' breakfasts (think eggs and bacon and a plateful of extras) to lunch- or dinner-time fish 'n' chips and burgers.

Berardo's MODERN AUSTRALIAN $$$
(07-5447 5666; berardos.com.au; 52 Hastings St, Noosa Heads; mains $30-42; from 6pm) Beautiful Berardo's is culinary utopia and one of Noosa's most famous restaurants. The elegance of its food matches the surrounds, an all-white affair with tinkling piano and sun-dappled chic. Ingredients are almost all locally sourced, with interesting little touches such as green mango and sugar-cane sauces.

WORTH A TRIP

FAMOUS EUMUNDI MARKETS

Sweet little Eumundi is a quaint highland village with a quirky New Age vibe that's greatly amplified during its famous market days. The historic streetscape is lined with fig trees and blends well with modern cafes, arty boutiques and crafty folk. Most people head here for the **Eumundi Markets** (www.eumundimarkets.com.au; 80 Memorial Dr; ⌚8am-1.30pm Wed, 7am-2pm Sat) and its 600-plus stalls that sell everything from hand-crafted furniture and jewellery to homemade clothes and alternative healing. After you've worn holes in your purse, grab a bite at **Bohemian Bungalow** (☎07-5442 8679; www.bohemianbungalow.com.au; 69 Memorial Dr; mains lunch $13-28, dinner $26-34; ⌚breakfast Wed, Sat & Sun, lunch Wed & Sun, dinner Thu-Sat), one of town's best eateries.

If you're hankering after a high-end, don't-miss kind of feed, the legendary **Spirit House** (☎07-5446 8977; www.spirithouse.com.au; 20 Nindery Rd, Yandina; share plates $12-53; ⌚lunch daily, dinner Wed-Sat) in Yandina, 11km further south of Eumundi, is the place to spend an afternoon – think amazing cuisine in subtropical, Southeast Asian setting.

Sunbus (☎13 12 30; www.sunbus.com.au) runs hourly from Noosa Heads ($4.50, 45 minutes) and Nambour ($5.90, 40 minutes). A number of tour operators visit the Eumundi markets on Wednesdays and Saturdays.

Ricky's River Bar & Restaurant MODERN AUSTRALIAN $$$
(☎07-5447 2455; rickys.com.au; Noosa Wharf, 2 Quamby Pl, Noosa Heads; mains $30-40; ⌚noon-late) In a perfect location on the Noosa River in Noosa Sound, this elegant restaurant is popular among the local businessfolk for looonnng lunches. It has as a simple, well-executed menu favouring local produce such as Noosa spanner-crab spaghettini. The tapas menu is equally tantalising, and there's an excellent wine list.

Drinking & Nightlife

Miss Moneypenny's BAR
(☎07-5474 9999; missmoneypennys.com.au; 6 Hastings St, Noosa Heads; ⌚7.30am-late) Miss Moneypenny touts herself as 'bringing Sydney to Noosa Heads' and indeed she sports smart city-style decor, sleek seating and dimmed lighting (unfortunately, no sign of 007). She offers every cocktail imaginable – from traditional (shaken, not stirred, of course) to the experimental – plus bar and à la carte menus.

Noosa Yacht Club BAR
(Gympie Tce, Noosaville; ⌚10am-late Mon-Sat, 8am-late Sun) Everything you'd expect from a yacht club: cheap grog, water views and sociable salts.

Reef Hotel PUB
(☎07-5430 7500; noosareef.com.au; 19 Noosa Dr, Noosa Junction; ⌚11am-midnight Sun-Thu, to 3am Fri & Sat) A little on the soulless side, decor-wise, but live music and cold bevvies make it all OK.

ℹ Information

Noosa visitor centre (☎07-5430 5000; www.visitnoosa.com.au; 61 Hastings St, Noosa Heads; ⌚9am-5pm) Helpful tourist office covering Noosa and surrounds.

Palm Tree Tours (☎07-5474 9166; www.palmtreetours.com.au; Bay Village Shopping Centre, Hastings St, Noosa Heads; ⌚9am-5pm) Very helpful, long-standing tour desk. Can book tours, accommodation and bus tickets.

Post office (91 Noosa Dr, Noosa Junction)

ℹ Getting There & Away

Long-distance bus services stop at the **Noosa Transit Centre** (Sunshine Beach Rd) in Noosa Junction. **Greyhound Australia** (☎1300 473 946; www.greyhound.com.au) has several daily bus connections with Brisbane ($28, 2½ hours), while **Premier Motor Service** (☎13 34 10; www.premierms.com.au) has one ($23, 2½ hours).

Most hostels have courtesy pick-ups.

Sunbus (Translink; ☎13 12 30; sunbus.com.au; ⌚8.30am-4.30pm) (TransLink) has frequent services to Maroochydore ($10.50, 1½ hours) and the Nambour train station ($11.20, one hour).

ℹ Getting Around

BICYCLE

Bike On Australia (p329) rents out bicycles from several locations in Noosa including the Flashpackers (p336) in Sunshine Beach. Alternatively, bikes can be delivered to and from your door ($35 or free if booking is more than $100).

DON'T MISS

CREATURE FEATURE: AUSTRALIA ZOO

Just north of Beerwah is one of Queensland's, if not Australia's, most famous tourist attractions. **Australia Zoo** (07-5436 2000; www.australiazoo.com.au; Steve Irwin Way, Beerwah; adult/child/family $59/35/172; 9am-5pm) is a fitting homage to its founder, zany wildlife enthusiast Steve Irwin. As well as all things slimy and scaly, the zoo has an amazing wildlife menagerie complete with a Cambodian-style Tiger Temple and the famous Crocoseum.

Various companies offer tours from Brisbane and the Sunshine Coast. The zoo operates a free bus to/from the Beerwah train station (bookings essential).

The zoo also has macaws, birds of prey, giant tortoises, snakes, otters, camels and more crocs and critters than you can poke a stick at. Plan to spend a full day at this amazing wildlife park.

BOAT

Noosa Ferry (p329) operates ferries between Noosa Heads and Tewantin every 30 minutes (all-day pass adult $20, child $6).

BUS

Sunbus (p331) has local services that link Noosa Heads, Noosaville, Noosa Junction and Tewantin.

CAR

All the big car-rental brands can be found in Noosa; rentals start at about $55 per day.

Noosa Car Rentals (0429 053 728; www.noosacarrentals.com.au) is a good local car-hire option; delivers to your accommodation.

Glass House Mountains

The volcanic plugs of the Glass House Mountains rise abruptly from the subtropical plains 20km northwest of Caboolture. In Dreaming legend, these rocky peaks belong to a family of mountain spirits. The explorer James Cook thought the shapes resembled the industrial conical (glass-making) furnaces of his native Yorkshire. It's worth diverting off the Bruce Hwy onto the slower Steve Irwin Way to snake your way through dense pine forests and green pastureland for a close-up view of these spectacular magma intrusions.

The **Glass House Mountains National Park** is broken into several sections (all within cooee of Beerwah), with picnic grounds and lookouts but no camping grounds. The peaks are reached by a series of sealed and unsealed roads that head inland from Steve Irwin Way.

For maps and directions, visit the extremely helpful **Glass House Mountains Visitor and Interpretive Centre** (07-5438 7220; www.visitsunshinecoast.com.au; cnr Bruce Pde & Reed St; 9am-4pm).

Sights & Activities

The easiest and best viewing point for peaks and distant beaches is the **Glasshouse Mountains Lookout** on Woodford Rd, 9km from the visitor information centre.

Hikers are spoilt for choice. A number of signposted walking tracks reach several of the peaks, but be prepared for some steep and rocky trails. A new track, the 6km **Soldier Settlers Walk**, has wonderful views and plants plus a crossing over a recently opened timber bridge. The moderate walk up **Ngungun** (253m) has sensational views while **Tibrogargan** (364m) offers a challenging scramble. The steepish **Beerburrum** (278m) is also open. Note – at the time of research, several summit walks were closed due to rock falls; check the **Queensland Parks and Wildlife Service** (07-5494 0150; www.nprsr.qld.gov.au; Bells Creek Rd, Beerwah) website for the condition and closure status.

Rock climbers can usually be seen scaling Tibrogargan and Ngungun. **Mt Coonowrin** (aka 'crook-neck'), the most dramatic of the volcanic plugs, is closed to the public.

Sleeping

★Glass House Mountains Ecolodge LODGE $$

(07-5493 0008; www.glasshouseecolodge.com; 198 Barrs Rd; r $120-220; P❄wifi) This novel retreat, overseen by a keen environmentalist, is close to Australia Zoo and offers a range of good-value, tranquil sleeping options, including cosy Orchard Rooms ($120), the converted Church Loft ($220), and converted railway carriages. Mt Tibrogargan can be seen from the gorgeous garden. Pick-ups available from Glass House Mountains station.

Caloundra

POP 10,000

Straddling a headland at the southern end of the Sunshine Coast, Caloundra is a strange mix of retirement village and seaside suburb. Excellent fishing and a number of pleasant surf beaches make it a popular holiday resort for families and water-sports fans.

A lovely coastal track starts in Caloundra and continues around the headland to Point Cartwright.

Sights & Activities

Queensland Air Museum MUSEUM
(07-5492 5930; www.qam.com.au; Caloundra Airport; adult/child/family $13/7/30; 10am-4pm) Plenty of planes to keep budding aviators happy for hours.

Caloundra Surf School SURFING
(0413 381 010; www.caloundrasurfschool.com; lessons from $45) The pick of the surf schools, with board hire also available.

Blue Water Kayak Tours KAYAKING
(07-5494 7789; www.bluewaterkayaktours.com; half-/full-day tours min 4 people $90/150, twilight tours $55) Energetic kayak tours across the channel to the northern tip of Bribie Island National Park.

Caloundra Cruise CRUISE
(07-5492 8280; www.caloundracruise.com; Maloja Jetty; adult/child/family $20/10/55; Sun, Tue, Wed, Fri) Various cruises into Pumicestone Passage on a 1930s-style boat.

Sunshine Coast Skydivers ADVENTURE SPORTS
(07-5437 0211; www.sunshinecoastskydivers.com.au; Caloundra Airport; tandem jumps from $279) Let your eyelids flap over stunning views of Caloundra from a brain-squeezing 15,000ft (or 7000ft, if you prefer).

Sleeping

There's often a minimum three- to five-night stay in high season.

Caloundra Backpackers HOSTEL $
(07-5499 7655; www.caloundrabackpackers.com.au; 84 Omrah Ave; dm/d $32/75;) Caloundra's only hostel, this is a no-nonsense budget option with a sociable courtyard, book exchange, and BBQ and pizza nights. Dorms aren't thrilling, but they're clean and peaceful.

Rumba Resort RESORT $$$
(07-5492 0555; www.rumbaresort.com.au; 10 Leeding Tce; r from $260) This sparkling, resort-white five-star playground is ultra trendy for Caloundra. Staff are positively buoyant and the rooms and pool area live up to the hype.

Eating

The Bulcock Beach esplanade is dotted with al fresco cafes and restaurants, all with perfect sea views.

Green House Cafe VEGETARIAN $
(07-5438 1647; www.greenhousecafe.com.au; 5/8 Orumuz Ave; mains $8-16; 7.30am-3pm;) A welcome addition to the coastal cafes, this lovely little spot, hidden up a small laneway, serves up some of the best bites around. Dishes are 100% vegetarian, organic and oh so tasty. The funky interiors comprise locally made lights and furniture.

Pocket Bar CAFE $
(www.facebook.com/thepocketespressobar; 8 Seaview Tce, Moffat Beach; 6am-2pm Mon-Wed, to 6pm Thu-Sun) Funk hits Caloundra. This gorgeous little pocket-sized coffee spot–cum-bar holds other surprises: its own ale and cider, good coffee blends and free-range ingredients. Go for the 'Gourmet Pocket of Joy' (a pie). It's the perfect spot to chill, or grab a snack and head to the beach, a short jaunt away.

Amici ITALIAN $$
(07-5491 9511; www.amicicafe.com.au; 2/80 Lower Gay Tce; mains $17-30; from 5pm Tue-Sun, 7am-3pm Sun) Despite it's off-beach location, this is the current 'hot' place in town for its quality Italian fare served in unfussy, modern surrounds. On Sundays only, panini and burgers are the thing for a postswim lunch, or opt in early for fabulous breakfasts, from fancy raisin toast to excellent egg dishes.

Information

Sunshine Coast visitor centre (07-5420 6240; 7 Caloundra Rd; 9am-3pm) On the roundabout at the town's entrance; there's also a kiosk on Bulcock St (07-5420 8718; 77 Bulcock St; 9am-5pm).

Getting There & Away

Greyhound (1300 473 946; www.greyhound.com.au) Buses from Brisbane (from $11, two hours) stop at the bus interchange in Cooma Tce, a block back from Bulcock Beach.

Sunbus (TransLink; 13 12 30; www.sunbus.com.au) Runs frequent services to Noosa

($12.20, 1½ hours) via Maroochydore ($6.70, 50 minutes).

Mooloolaba & Maroochydore

POP 11,000 & 15,000

Mooloolaba has seduced many with its sublime climate, golden beach and cruisy lifestyle. Eateries, boutiques and pockets of resorts and apartments have spread along the Esplanade, transforming this once-humble fishing village into one of Queensland's most popular holiday destinations.

Nearby Maroochydore takes care of the business end, though it, too, has several pretty spots and good eateries.

Sights & Activities

Mooloolaba's north-facing main beach is one of the region's most sheltered and safest beaches. There are good surf breaks along the strip – one of Queensland's best for longboarders is the **Bluff**, the prominent point at Alexandra Headland. **Pincushion** near the Maroochy River mouth can provide an excellent break in the winter offshore winds.

Diving to the wreck of the sunken warship, the **ex–HMAS Brisbane**, is also incredibly popular. Sunk in July 2005, the wreck lies in 28m of water; its funnels are only 4m below the surface.

Underwater World – Sea Life Mooloolaba AQUARIUM
(07-5458 6280; www.underwaterworld.com.au; Wharf, Mooloolaba; adult/child/family $38/23/104; 9am-5pm) At this popular tropical oceanarium you can marvel at the ocean life, including via an 80m-long transparent underwater tunnel. For an extra fee you can also swim with seals and dive with sharks. There's a touch tank, live shows and presentations to entertain both kids and adults. A 'behind the scenes' tour costs $10.

Robbie Sherwell's XL Surfing Academy SURFING
(07-5478 1337; www.xlsurfingacademy.com; 1hr lessons private/group $95/45) Dip a toe into Aussie surf culture at this long-established school.

Suncoast Kite & SUP Fun KITESURFING
(075-479 2131; www.sunshinecoastkitesurfingnsupfun.com) Based in Maroochydore, and offers both kitesurfing lessons ($150, 1½ hours) and stand-up paddle lessons ($50 per hour).

Sunreef DIVING
(07-5444 5656; www.sunreef.com.au; 110 Brisbane Rd, Mooloolaba; PADI Open Water Diver courses $495) Offers two dives ($175) on the wreck of the ex-HMAS *Brisbane*. Also runs night dives on the sunken warship.

Sunshine Coast Bike & Board Hire SURFING, BICYCLE RENTAL
(0439 706 206; www.adventurehire.com.au) Hires out bikes and surfboards as a package from $50 a day. Free delivery to local accommodation.

Swan Boat Hire BOATING
(07-5443 7225; www.swanboathire.com.au; 59 Bradman Ave, Maroochydore; half-/full-day hire from $190/285; 6am-6pm) On the Maroochy River. Also hires out kayaks (one hour/half day $30/95).

Tours

Whale One WHALE WATCHING
(1800 942 531; www.whaleone.com.au; Wharf, Mooloolaba; adult/child/family $119/79/320) Whale-watching cruises between June and November.

Canal Cruise BOAT TOUR
(07-5444 7477; www.mooloolabacanalcruise.com; Wharf, Mooloolaba; adult/child/family $20/8/50; 11am, 1pm & 2.30pm) These boat trips cruise past the McMansions preening beside the Mooloolah River.

Coastal Cruises BOAT TOUR
(0419 704 797; www.cruisemooloolaba.com.au; Wharf, Mooloolaba) Sunset ($25) and seafood lunch cruises ($35) through Mooloolaba Harbour, the river and canals.

Sleeping

During school holidays, rates can double and most places require a minimum two- or three-night stay.

Mooloolaba Beach Backpackers HOSTEL $
(07-5444 3399; www.mooloolababackpackers.com; 75 Brisbane Rd, Mooloolaba; dm/d $30/70; P) Some dorms have en suites, and although the rooms are a little drab, the number of freebies (bikes, surfboards, stand-up paddleboards and breakfast) more than compensates. Besides, it's only 500m from beachside activities and nightlife.

Cotton Tree Holiday Park CAMPING $
(07-5459 9070; www.sunshinecoastholidayparks.com.au; Cotton Tree Pde, Cotton Tree, Maroochydore;

powered sites $43, villas from $140) In a lovely location on the Maroochy River in Cotton Tree, a popular area of Maroochydore.

Mooloolaba Motel MOTEL $$
(07-5444 2988; www.mooloolabamotel.com.au; 46 Brisbane Rd, Mooloolaba; d/tr from $105/165; P ❄ 📶 🏊) You've gotta give it to the '70s: the design might be brown brick, but the rooms are spacious and airy, with floor-to-ceiling windows and clean, modern interiors. The motel's location, on a main road, isn't a problem given that you're a few hundred metres from the Mooloolaba shops, beach and action.

Maroochydore Beach Motel MOTEL $$
(07-5443 7355; www.maroochydorebeachmotel.com; 69 Sixth Ave, Maroochydore; s/d/f from $120/135/180; P ❄ @ 🏊) A snazzy, spotless theme hotel with 18 different rooms, including the Elvis Room (naturally), the Egyptian Room, and the Aussie Room (complete with toy wombat). Although on a main road, it's just 50m to the beach.

Eating

★**Mooloolah River Fisheries** SEAFOOD $
(Mooloolaba Fish Market; www.mooloolahfish.com.au; Lot 201, Parkyn Pde, The Spit, Mooloolaba; fish & chips from $12, seafood platters $60; 8am-7.30pm Mon-Thu, to 8pm Fri-Sun) This splashy, stinky and altogether atmospheric fish market–cum-shop sells the freshest of fresh seafood (what else?) in a variety of ways: order and eat on the upstairs Deck on Parkyn, buy fresh to take away and prepare yourself, or have the chefs cook your purchase so you can have a picnic in the park.

★**Spice Bar** ASIAN FUSION $$
(07-5444 2022; www.spicebar.com.au; 1st fl, 123 Mooloolaba Esplanade, Mooloolaba; mains $27-35; 6pm-late Tue-Sun, from noon Wed-Sun) In short: this is where the local foodie crowd comes to play. This attractive, modern eatery with a red and black decor serves up superb Asian fusion cuisine. Share plates are the go – the likes of Hervey Bay scallops and 'Numbing Chicken' – chilli pepper–covered poultry parts that leave you 'zinging' for more. Offers a fabulous degustation menu.

Boat Shed SEAFOOD $$
(07-5443 3808; www.boatshed.net.au; Esplanade, Cotton Tree, Maroochydore; mains $28-38; 9am-11.30pm Mon-Sat, from 5pm Sun) A shabby-chic gem on the banks of the Maroochy River, great for sunset drinks beneath the sprawling cotton tree. Seafood is the star of the Mod Oz menu; after dinner, roll back to the outdoor lounges for dessert and some seriously romantic stargazing. Or grab a riverside sofa seat for sunset drinks.

Drinking & Nightlife

Taps@Mooloolaba BAR
(www.tapsaustralia.com.au; cnr Esplanade & Brisbane Rd, Mooloolaba; noon-late) A beer lover's frothy dream: you get to pull your own brew. Seriously. This high-tech spot has iButtons for credit and beer selection. It may sound gimmicky, but it's serious business: there are around 20 craft and other brews to choose from. Plus there are burgers and bruschetta to help you soak it all up.

SolBar CLUB
(07-5443 9550; www.solbar.com.au; 19 Ocean St, Maroochydore; 7.30am-late Mon-Fri, from 10.30am Sat & Sun) SolBar is a godsend for city-starved indie fans. A constantly surprising line-up takes to the stages here, while punters enjoy an array of international beers and a less-surfy atmosphere than most other joints in town.

Information

The Mooloolaba Esplanade seamlessly morphs into Alexandra Pde along the beachfront at Alexandra Headland ('Alex' to the locals), then flows into Aerodrome Rd and the main CBD of Maroochydore. Cotton Tree is at the mouth of the Maroochy River.

Sunshine Coast visitor information centre (1300 847 481; www.visitsunshinecoast.com.au; cnr Brisbane Rd & First Ave, Mooloolaba; 9am-3pm) also has other branches throughout the region: Maroochydore (www.visitsunshinecoast.com.au; cnr Sixth Ave & Melrose St, Maroochydore; 9am-4pm); and Sunshine Coast Airport. (www.visitsunshinecoast.com.au; Marcoola; airport hours).

Getting There & Around

Long-distance buses stop in front of the Sunshine Coast visitor information centre in Maroochydore. **Greyhound Australia** (1300 473 946; www.greyhound.com.au; one way $21) and **Premier Motor Services** (13 34 10; www.premierms.com.au; one way $23) run to and from Brisbane (both two hours).

Sunbus (Translink; 13 12 30; www.sunbus.com.au) has frequent services between Mooloolaba and Maroochydore ($4.80, 15 minutes) and on to Noosa ($10.50, 1½ hours). The local bus interchange is at the Sunshine Plaza.

EXPLORING THE HINTERLAND

Inland from **Nambour**, the Blackall Range forms a stunning backdrop to the Sunshine Coast's beaches a short 50km away. A relaxed half- or full-day circuit drive from the coast follows a winding road along the razorback line of the escarpment, passing through quaint mountain villages, including **Kenilworth** and **Montville**, and offering spectacular views of the coastal lowlands. The villages suffer from an overdose of kitschy craft shops and Devonshire tearooms. While they are worth a visit the real attraction is the landscape, with its lush green pastures and softly folded valleys and ridges, plus the waterfalls, swimming holes, rainforests and walks in the national parks. Cosy cabins and B&Bs are popular weekend retreats, especially during winter.

If any village's vibe will hook you in, it's **Maleny**'s. This pretty village is an intriguing melange of creative souls, ageing hippies, younger escapees from the city and co-op ventures. Its bohemian edge underscores a thriving commercial township that hasn't yielded to the tacky ye olde tourist-trap developments of nearby mountain villages. The **Maleny visitor information centre** (07-5499 9033; www.malenycommunitycentre.org; Shop 2, 23 Maple St; 9.30am-4pm) is useful for information on what to see (there are some stunning gardens and a nature reserve) and where to stay.

A couple of tour companies head into the hinterland and will pick up from anywhere along the Sunshine Coast: **SunAir Bus Service** (www.sunair.com.au; adult/child $55/35) does touristy sojourns around the area; and **Off Beat Eco Tours** (0417 787 318; www.offbeattours.com.au; half-day tours per person $65; full day adult/child $195/135) heads into the rainforests and wilderness areas of the hinterland.

Peregian Beach & Sunshine Beach

POP 3500 & 2300

Fifteen kilometres of uncrowded, unobstructed beach stretch north from Coolum to Sunshine Beach and the rocky northeast headland of Noosa National Park.

Peregian is the place to indulge in long solitary beach walks, surf excellent breaks, and take in fresh air and plenty of sunshine; it's not uncommon to see whales breaking offshore.

A little further north, the laid-back latte ethos of **Sunshine Beach** attracts Noosa locals escaping the summer hordes. Beach walks morph into bush trails over the headland; a stroll through the **Noosa National Park** takes an hour to reach Alexandria Bay and two hours to Noosa's Laguna Bay. Road access to the park is from McAnally Dr or Parkedge Rd.

Sleeping

Flashpackers HOSTEL $
(07-5455 4088; www.flashpackersnoosa.com; 102 Pacific Ave, Sunshine Beach; dm from $33, girls' dm $38, d from $85;) Flashpackers challenges the notion of hostels as flea-bitten dives. Thoughtful touches to its neat dorms include mirrors, ample wall sockets and free surfboard use.

Chez Noosa MOTEL $$
(07-5447 2027; www.cheznoosa.com.au; 263 Edwards St, Sunshine Beach; standard/deluxe units from $120/130;) Right by Noosa National Park and set in aptly bushy gardens, the Chez is fantastic value for money. The self-contained units (for two) are basic but cute, and there's a heated pool and spa with BBQ areas.

Peregian Court Resort APARTMENT $$
(07-5448 1622; www.peregiancourt.com; 380 David Low Way, Peregian Beach; 1-bedroom apt $115-$160, 2-bedroom apt $145-180; P) It's just a minute's walk to the beach from these clean, airy and altogether comfy resort-style apartments. Each is uniquely furnished, and all have a fully equipped kitchen. The sea-breezy BBQ area encourages al fresco feasting. Two-night minimum stay.

Eating

Le Bon Delice CAFE $
(www.lebondelice.com.au; Shop 8, 224 David Low Way, Peregian Beach; cakes from $3, snacks $8-14; 7am-4pm Wed-Sat & Mon, to 2pm Sun) Run by a highly trained and hands-on French *pâtissier*, Jean Jacques, this little place, on the corner of the village square, is indeed as Gallic as a croissant. As you sink your teeth into a delectable eclair, macaron or quiche, you'll

swear Peregian Beach Sq has just morphed into the Champs-Élysées.

Fratellini ITALIAN $$
(☎07-5474 8080; www.fratellini.com.au; 36 Duke St, Sunshine Beach; mains $23-35; ⊙6.30am-late) This fun spot is no little *fratellino* ('little brother' in Italian) to the cafes on this Sunshine Beach cafe strip. The kitchen pumps out Big Mamma–quality Italian dishes including delicious homemade pasta and crispy-thin pizza. And, hurrah, the coffee is good, too.

Pitchfork MODERN AUSTRALIAN $$
(☎07-5471 3697; www.pitchforkrestaurant.com.au; 5/4 Kingfisher Dr, Peregian Beach; mains $25-35; ⊙noon-2pm & 5pm-late Tue-Sun) This smart eatery's award-winning chefs pump out a concise menu, with an emphasis on seafood dishes. The daily line-caught fish is usually the star pick. Allow time for a meal here: sip on a wine and soak up both the atmosphere and the action from within Pitchfork's delightful, contemporary setting on Peregian Beach Sq. Then, err, dig in and enjoy.

Cooloola Coast

Stretching for 50km between Noosa and Rainbow Beach, the Cooloola Coast is a remote strip of long sandy beach backed by the Cooloola Section of the **Great Sandy National Park**. Although it's undeveloped, the 4WD and tin-boat set flock here in droves, so it's not always as peaceful as you might imagine. If you head off on foot or by canoe along one of the many inlets or waterways, however, you'll soon escape the crowds.

From the end of Moorindil St in Tewantin, **Noosa North Shore Ferries** (☎07-5447 1321; www.noosanorthshoreferries.com.au; one way per pedestrian/car $1/7; ⊙5.30am-10.20pm Sun-Thu, to 12.20am Fri & Sat) shuttle across the river to Noosa North Shore. If you have a 4WD, you can drive along the beach to Rainbow Beach (and on up to Inskip Point to the Fraser Island ferry), but you'll need a **permit** (www.nprsr.qld.gov.au; per day/week/month $11.40/28.65/45.10). You can also buy a permit from the QPWS office (p338). Note: check the tide times!

On the way up the beach, you'll pass the **Teewah coloured sand cliffs**, estimated to be about 40,000 years old.

Lake Cooroibah

A couple of kilometres north of Tewantin, the Noosa River widens into Lake Cooroibah, which is surrounded by lush bushland. If you take the Noosa North Shore Ferry, you can drive up to the lake in a conventional vehicle and camp along sections of the beach.

Sleeping

Noosa North Shore Retreat RESORT $
(☎07-5447 1225; www.noosanorthshoreretreat.com.au; Beach Rd; unpowered/powered sites from $20/30, cabins/r from $80/145; ❄@≋) They've got everything here, from camping and vinyl 'village tents' to shiny motel rooms and cottages. Ditch your bags, then head out for a paddle around the lake, a bushwalk or a bounce on the jumping pillow. The retreat also houses the **Great Sandy Bar & Restaurant** (mains $15-30), open weekends for lunch and dinner.

Lake Cootharaba & Boreen Point

Cootharaba is the biggest lake in the Cooloola Section of Great Sandy National Park, measuring about 5km across and 10km in length. On the western shores of the lake and at the southern edge of the national park, **Boreen Point** is a relaxed little community with several places to stay and to eat. The lake is the gateway to the **Noosa Everglades**, offering bushwalking, canoeing and bush camping.

From Boreen Point, a road leads another 5km to **Elanda Point** (unsealed for half the way).

Tours

Kanu Kapers KAYAKING
(☎07-5485 3328; www.kanukapersaustralia.com; 11 Toolara St, Boreen Point; half-/full-day guided tours $155/185, 1-day self-guided tours $85) Paddle into the placid Everglades.

Discovery Group CANOEING
(☎07-5449 0393; www.thediscoverygroup.com.au; 1 day $125, 3-day/2-night self-guided canoe safaris $155) Wonderful full-day cruise and canoe down the Everglades to Fig Tree Point (morning tea and BBQ lunch provided). For those who want to go it alone, you can canoe and camp your way over three days. It also runs afternoon cruises ($79).

Sleeping & Eating

Boreen Point Camping Ground CAMPGROUND $
(07-5485 3244; www.noosaholidayparks.com.au; Esplanade, Boreen Point; unpowered/powered sites $23/29) On Lake Cootharaba, this stunning little campground, dominated by large gums, is crowd free and provides your own secluded patch of lake-front, native bush.

Lake Cootharaba Motel MOTEL $$
(07-5485 3127; www.cootharabamotel.com; 75 Laguna St, Boreen Point; r $105-140;) A quaint and tidy spot that's less motel than lakeside retreat, this is a great base for visiting the Everglades or simply splashing about on Cootharaba. There are only five rooms; be sure to book ahead.

Apollonian Hotel PUB $$
(07-5485 3100; www.apollonianhotel.com.au; 19 Laguna St, Boreen Point; mains $12-30; 10am-midnight) This is a gorgeous old pub with sturdy timber walls, shady verandahs and a beautifully preserved interior. The pub grub is tasty and popular. Book ahead for the famous Sunday spit-roast lunch ($25).

Great Sandy National Park: Cooloola Section

This 540-sq-km section of national park extends from Lake Cootharaba north to Rainbow Beach. It's a varied wilderness area with long sandy beaches, mangrove-lined waterways, forest and heathland, all featuring plentiful bird life, including rarities such as the red goshawk and the grass owl, and lots of wild flowers in spring.

The **Cooloola Way**, from Tewantin up to Rainbow Beach, is open to 4WD vehicles unless there's been heavy rain – check with the rangers before setting out. Most people prefer to bomb up the beach, though you're restricted to a few hours either side of low tide. You'll need a **permit** (www.nprsr.qld.gov.au; per day/week/month $11.40/28.65/45.10).

The best way to see Cooloola is by boat or canoe along the numerous tributaries of the Noosa River. Boats can be hired from Tewantin and Noosa (along Gympie Tce), Boreen Point and Elanda Point on Lake Cootharaba.

There are some fantastic walking trails starting from Elanda Point on the shore of Lake Cootharaba, including the 46km **Cooloola Wilderness Trail** to Rainbow Beach and a 7km trail to an unstaffed QPWS information centre at Kinaba.

The **QPWS Great Sandy Information Centre** (07-5449 7792; 240 Moorindil St, Tewantin; 8am-4pm) provides information on park access, tide times and fire bans within the park. The centre also issues car and camping permits for both Fraser Island and the Great Sandy National Park, but these are best booked online at www.nprsr.qld.gov.au.

The park has a number of **camping grounds** (13 74 68; www.nprsr.qld.gov.au; per person/family $5.75/23.15), many of them along the river. The most popular (and best-equipped) camping grounds are **Fig Tree Point** (at the northern end of Lake Cootharaba), **Harry's Hut** (about 4km upstream) and **Freshwater** (about 6km south of Double Island Point) on the coast. You can also camp at designated zones on the beach if you're driving up to Rainbow Beach. Apart from Harry's Hut, Freshwater and Teewah Beach, all sites are accessible by hiking or river only.

Fraser Island & the Fraser Coast

Includes ➜

Best Places to Eat

- ➜ Waterview Bistro (p346)
- ➜ Pop In (p347)
- ➜ Enzo's on the Beach (p344)
- ➜ Rosie Blu (p349)
- ➜ Arcobaleno on the Beach (p346)

Best Places to Stay

- ➜ Kingfisher Bay Resort (p353)
- ➜ Debbie's Place (p346)
- ➜ Beachfront Tourist Parks (p343)
- ➜ Colonial Lodge (p343)
- ➜ Inglebrae (p348)

Why Go?

Nature lovers, rejoice! World Heritage–listed Fraser Island is the world's largest sand island, a mystical, at times eerie, land of giant dunes, ancient rainforests, luminous lakes and wildlife including Australia's purest strain of dingo. It's truly unlike any other place on earth. Across the waters of the Great Sandy Strait, the mellow coastal community of Hervey Bay is the gateway to Fraser Island. From July to October, migrating humpback whales stream into the bay before continuing on to Antarctica. Further south, tiny Rainbow Beach is a laid-back seaside village and an alternative launching pad to Fraser. Fishing, swimming, boating and camping are hugely popular along this stretch of coastline.

Inland, agricultural fields surround old-fashioned country towns steeped in history. Bundaberg, the largest city in the region, overlooks the sea of cane fields that fuels its eponymous rum, a fiery spirit guaranteed to scramble a few brain cells.

When to Go

Bundaberg

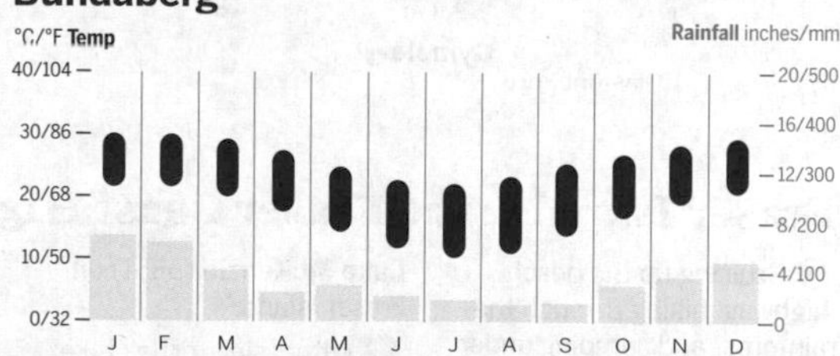

Jun & Jul Bring your brolly to Maryborough's Mary Poppins Festival.

Jul–Nov Look out for humpback whales – optimal sighting time is August to October.

Nov–Mar Spy on turtles laying eggs in the sand at Mon Repos.

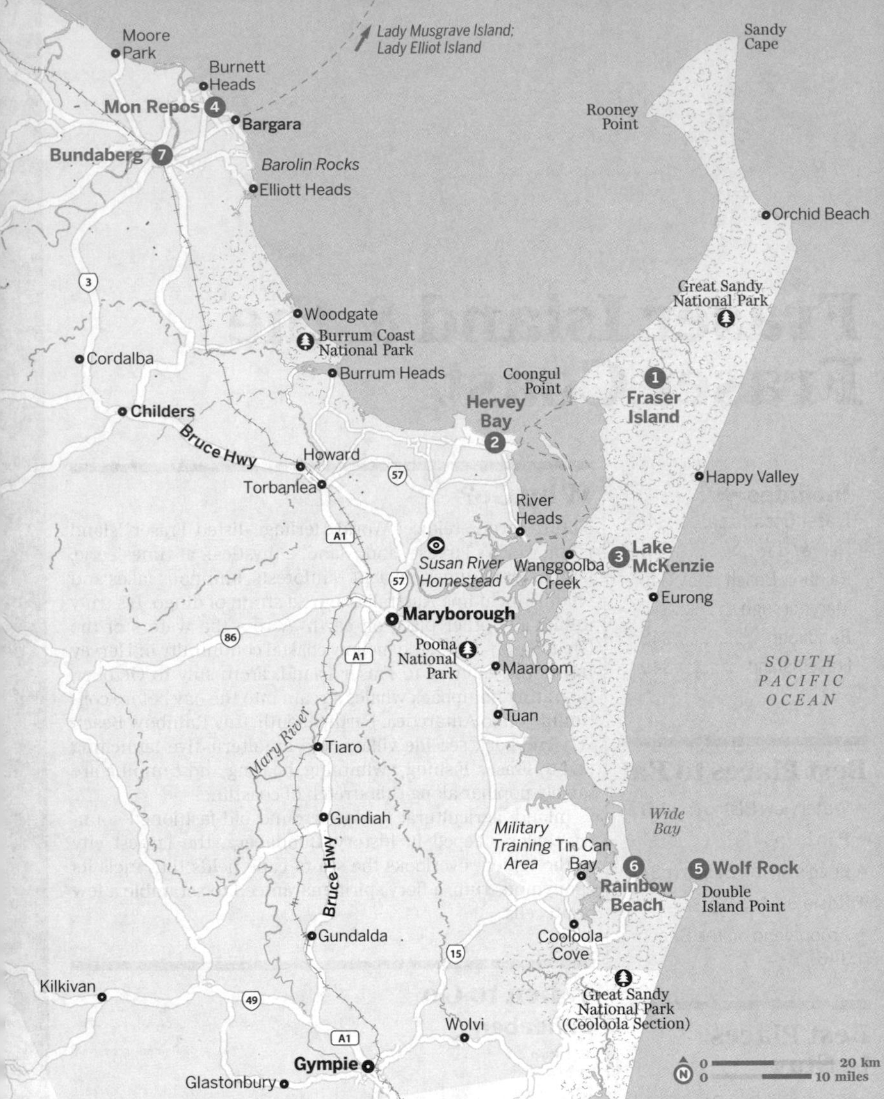

Fraser Island & the Fraser Coast Highlights

1. Cruising up the beach 'highway', hiking through the rainforest and camping under the stars on **Fraser Island** (p349).
2. Watching the whales play in **Hervey Bay** (p341).
3. Cooling off in the pristine, electric-blue water of the white-sand-fringed freshwater **Lake McKenzie** (p351) on Fraser Island.
4. Witnessing turtles take their first flipper-stumble down the beach at **Mon Repos** (p348).
5. Diving with sharks at **Wolf Rock** (p345) off Rainbow Beach.
6. Gazing over the rainbow cliffs from atop the Carlo Sandblow at **Rainbow Beach** (p345).
7. Sampling 'liquid gold' at the rum distillery in **Bundaberg** (p348).

Getting There & Away

AIR

Qantas (13 13 13; www.qantas.com.au) and **Virgin** (13 67 89; www.virginaustralia.com.au) fly to Bundaberg and Hervey Bay.

BUS

Greyhound (1300 473 946; www.greyhound.com.au) and **Premier Motor Service** (13 34 10; www.premierms.com.au) both have regular coach services along the Bruce Hwy (A1) with stops at all the major towns. They also detour off the highway to Hervey Bay and Rainbow Beach.

TRAIN

Queensland Rail (1800 872 467; www.queenslandrail.com.au) Has frequent services between Brisbane and Rockhampton passing through the region. Choose between the high-speed Tilt Train or the more sedate Sunlander.

FRASER COAST

The Fraser Coast runs the gamut from coastal beauty, beachfront national parks and tiny seaside villages to agricultural farms and sugar-cane fields surrounding old-fashioned country towns.

Hervey Bay

POP 76,403

Named after an English Casanova, it's no wonder that Hervey Bay's seductive charms are difficult to resist. Its warm subtropical climate, long sandy beaches, calm blue ocean, and a relaxed, unpretentious local community lure all sorts of travellers to its shores – from backpackers to families and retirees. Throw in the chance to see majestic humpback whales frolicking in the water and the town's convenient access to the World Heritage–listed Fraser Island, and it's easy to understand how Hervey Bay has become an unflashy, yet undeniably appealing, tourist hotspot.

Fraser Island shelters Hervey Bay from the ocean surf and the sea here is shallow and completely flat – perfect for kiddies and postcardy summer-holiday pics.

Sights

Reef World AQUARIUM

(07-4128 9828; Pulgul St, Urangan; adult/child $18/9, shark dives $50; 9.30am-4pm) A small aquarium stocked with some of the Great Barrier Reef's most colourful characters, including a giant 18-year-old groper. You can also take a dip with lemon, whaler and other nonpredatory sharks.

Fraser Coast Discovery Sphere MUSEUM

(07-4197 4207; www.frasercoastdiscoverysphere.com.au; 166 Old Maryborough Rd, Pialba; adult/child/family $7/5/20; 10am-4pm) Loads of educational activities inspired by the region. Ideal for kids and curious adults.

Wetside Water Education Park PARK

(www.widebaywater.qld.gov.au; The Esplanade, Scarness; 10am-6pm Wed-Sun, daily during school holidays) On hot days, this wet spot on the foreshore can't be beaten. There's plenty of shade, fountains, tipping buckets and a boardwalk with water infotainment. Opening hours vary so check the website for updates.

Activities

Hire paddle boards, kayaks, aqua trikes, jet skis and more with **Aquavue** (07-4125 5528; www.aquavue.com.au; The Esplanade, Torquay) or **Enzo's on the Beach** (07-4124 6375; www.enzosonthebeach.com.au; The Esplanade, Scarness). Rentals start around $20 per hour.

Whale Watching

Whale-watching tours operate out of Hervey Bay every day (weather permitting) during the annual migrations between late July and early November. Sightings are guaranteed from August to the end of October (with a free subsequent trip if the whales don't show). Out of season, many boats offer dolphin-spotting tours. Boats cruise from **Urangan Harbour** out to Platypus Bay and then zip around from pod to pod to find the most active whales. Most vessels offer half-day tours for around $120 for adults and $70 for children, and most include lunch and/or morning or afternoon tea. Tour bookings can be made through your accommodation or the information centres.

Spirit of Hervey Bay WHALE WATCHING

(1800 642 544; www.spiritofherveybay.com; Urangan Harbour; 8.30am & 1.30pm) The largest vessel with the greatest number of passengers.

MV Tasman Venture WHALE WATCHING

(1800 620 322; www.tasmanventure.com.au; Urangan Harbour; 8.30am & 1.30pm) One of the best, with underwater microphones and viewing windows. Sightings are guaranteed during the season; you get a free subsequent trip if the whales don't show.

Hervey Bay

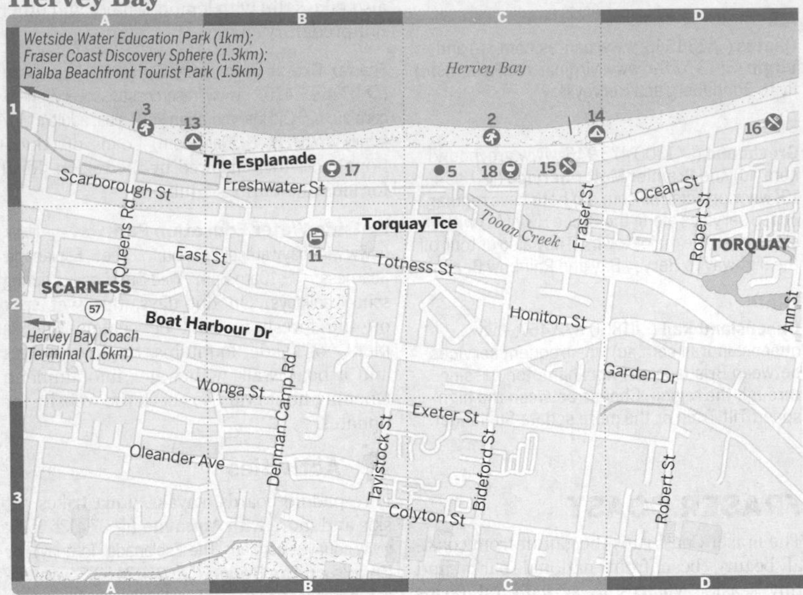

Hervey Bay

Sights
1 Reef World H2

Activities, Courses & Tours
2 Aquavue C1
Blue Dolphin Marine Tours .... (see 6)
3 Enzo's on the Beach A1
4 Krystal Klear H3
MV Tasman Venture .... (see 6)
5 Nomads C1
6 Spirit of Hervey Bay H2

Sleeping
7 Alexander Lakeside B&B E1
8 Bay B&B F1
9 Colonial Lodge E1
10 Colonial Village YHA G3
11 Flashpackers B2
12 Quarterdecks Harbour Retreat G3
13 Scarness Beachfront Tourist Park A1
14 Torquay Beachfront Tourist Park C1

Eating
15 Bayaroma Cafe C1
16 Coast D1
Enzo's on the Beach .... (see 3)

Drinking & Nightlife
17 Hoolihan's B1
18 Viper C1

Blue Dolphin Marine Tours WHALE WATCHING
(☎07-4124 9600; www.bluedolphintours.com.au; Urangan Harbour) Skipper Pete has almost 30 years of marine mammal experience, making him the ideal receptacle for the many questions this up-close whale-watching trip will throw up.

Other Activities

MV Fighting Whiting FISHING
(☎07-4124 3377; www.fightingwhiting.com.au; adult/child/family $70/35/175) Keep your catch on these calm-water tours. Sandwiches, bait and all fishing gear included.

MV Princess II FISHING
(☎07-4124 0400; adult/child $160/100) Wet your hook with an experienced crew who've been trolling these waters for more than two decades.

Krystal Klear CRUISE
(☎07-4124 0066; www.krystalkleer.com.au; Urangan Marina; 5hr tours adult/child $90/50) Cruise on a 12m glass-bottomed boat, the only one

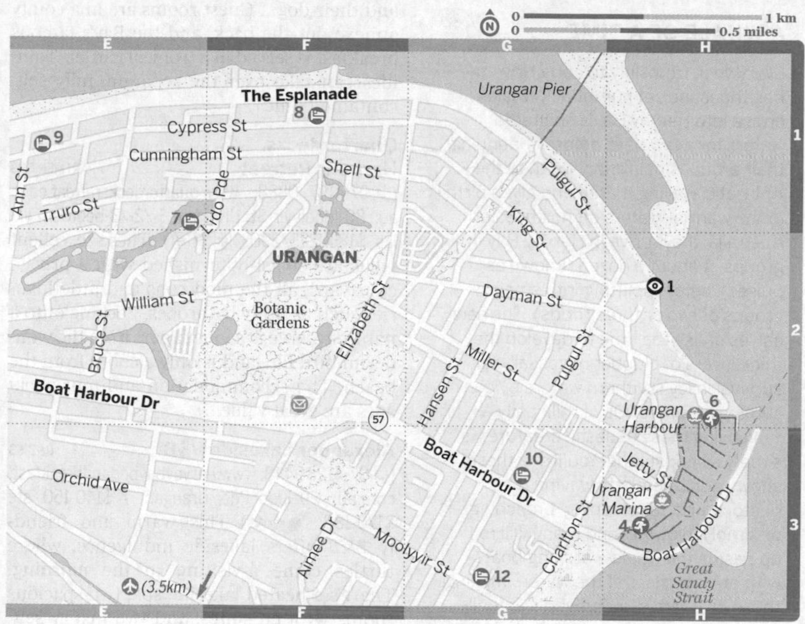

in Hervey Bay. Includes snorkelling, coral viewing and an island barbecue.

Fraser Coast Microlites SCENIC FLIGHTS
(☎1800 811 728; flights $125-250) Soar with your hair in the wind over islands and lakes on 20-, 30-, 45- and 70-minute flights. Book ahead.

Skydive Hervey Bay SKYDIVING
(☎0458 064 703; www.skydiveherveybay.com.au) Tandem skydives from $325 at 3660m, with up to 45 mouth-flapping seconds of free fall.

Susan River Homestead HORSE RIDING
(☎07-4121 6846; www.susanriver.com; Hervey Bay–Maryborough Rd) Horse-riding packages (adult/child $250/160) include accommodation, all meals and use of the on-site swimming pool and tennis courts. Day-trippers can canter off on two-hour horse rides (adult/child $85/75).

Festivals & Events

Hervey Bay Whale Festival CULTURAL
(www.herveybaywhalefestival.com.au;) Celebrates the return of the whales in August.

Sleeping

Hervey Bay has heaps of great hostels. A few are clustered in Scarness on Torquay Rd – a good hunting ground if you're showing up without a reservation.

★Colonial Lodge HOTEL $
(☎07-4125 1073; www.herveybaycoloniallodge.com.au; 94 Cypress St, Torquay; r $90-140;) Hacienda-style, immaculate and wonderfully friendly, these self-contained one- and two-bedroom units are a steal. Hang out by the pool or walk a block to the beach.

Torquay Beachfront Tourist Park CARAVAN PARK $
(☎07-4125 1578; www.beachfronttouristparks.com.au; The Esplanade, Torquay; unpowered/powered sites from $26/31;) Fronting Hervey Bay's exquisitely long sandy beach, all of Beachfront's three shady parks live up to their name, with fantastic ocean views. This Torquay site is in the heart of the action. Other branches are at **Pialba** (☎07-4128 1399; www.beachfronttouristparks.com.au; The Esplanade, Pialba; unpowered/powered sites from $26/31;) and **Scarness** (☎07-4128 1274; www.beachfronttouristparks.com.au; The

A WHALE OF A TIME

Every year, from July to early November, thousands of humpback whales cruise into Hervey Bay's sheltered waters for a few days before continuing their arduous migration south to the Antarctic. Having mated and given birth in the warmer waters off northeastern Australia, they arrive in Hervey Bay in groups of about a dozen (known as pulses), before splitting into smaller groups of two or three (pods). The new calves utilise the time to develop the thick layers of blubber necessary for survival in icy southern waters by consuming around 600L of milk daily.

Viewing these majestic creatures is simply awe-inspiring. You'll see these showy aqua-acrobats waving their pectoral fins, tail slapping, breaching or simply 'blowing', and many will roll up beside the whale-watching boats with one eye clear of the water...making those on board wonder who's actually watching whom.

Esplanade, Scarness; unpowered/powered sites from $26/31;)).

Colonial Village YHA HOSTEL $
(07-4125 1844; www.yha.com.au; 820 Boat Harbour Dr, Urangan; dm/d/cabins from $23/52/79;) This excellent YHA is set on 8 hectares of tranquil bushland, close to the marina and only 50m from the beach. It's a lovely spot, thick with ambience, possums and parrots. Facilities include a pool, tennis and basketball courts, and a sociable bar-restaurant.

Flashpackers HOSTEL $
(07-4124 1366; www.flashpackersherveybay.com; 195 Torquay Tce, Torquay; dm $25-30, d $70;) Comfortable, spacious dorm and en suite rooms, with reading lights, numerous power sockets, walk-in communal fridge, spotless communal areas and showers with power. Set a street back from the beach.

Bay B&B B&B $$
(07-4125 6919; www.baybedandbreakfast.com.au; 180 Cypress St, Urangan; s $100, d $125-140;) This great-value B&B is run by a friendly, well-travelled Frenchman, his wife and their dog... Guest rooms are in a comfy annexe out the back, and the Bay's famous breakfast is served in a tropical garden. Families can take over the separate, fully self-contained unit.

Quarterdecks Harbour Retreat APARTMENT $$
(07-4197 0888; www.quarterdecksretreat.com.au; 80 Moolyyir St, Urangan; 1-/2-/3-bedroom villas $185/225/290;) These excellent villas are stylishly furnished with a private courtyard, all the mod cons and little luxuries such as fluffy bathrobes. Backing onto a nature reserve, it's quiet apart from the wonderful bird life, and is only a cooee from the beach. The accommodation and tour packages are great value.

Alexander Lakeside B&B B&B $$
(07-4128 9448; www.herveybaybedandbreakfast.com.au; 29 Lido Pde, Urangan; r $140-150, ste $170-180;) This warm and friendly B&B offers lakeside indulgence, where turtles come a-visiting in the morning. There's a heated lakeside spa, two spacious rooms with en suites, and two luxury self-contained suites.

Eating

Enzo's on the Beach CAFE $
(www.enzosonthebeach.com.au; 351a The Esplanade, Scarness; mains $8-20; 6.30am-5pm) This shabby-chic beachside cafe is the place to fill up on sandwiches, wraps, salads and coffees before working it off on a hired kayak or during a kite-surfing lesson.

Bayaroma Cafe CAFE $
(07-4125 1515; 428 The Esplanade, Torquay; breakfast $10-22, mains $9.50-20; 6.30am-3.30pm) Famous for its coffee, all-day breakfasts and people-watching pole position, Bayorama has a jam-packed menu that truly has something for everyone (even vegetarians!). Attentive, chirpy service is an added bonus.

Coast FUSION $$
(07-4125 5454; 469 The Esplanade, Torquay; mains $21-60; 5pm-late Tue & Wed, 11.30am-late Thu-Sun) Gourmet grub for the discerning diner prepared to splurge. Fancy meat and seafood dishes get the Asian/Middle Eastern fusion touch; desserts such as the pumpkin cheesecake go beyond the realms of the superlative adjective.

Drinking & Nightlife

Hoolihan's PUB

(382 The Esplanade, Scarness; 11am-2am) Like all good Irish pubs, Hoolihan's is wildly popular, especially with the backpacker crowd.

Viper CLUB

(410 The Esplanade, Torquay; 10pm-3am Wed, Fri & Sat) This new club is a rough diamond with cranking music and an energetic crowd, especially during summer.

Information

Hervey Bay covers a string of beachside suburbs – Point Vernon, Pialba, Scarness, Torquay and Urangan – but behind the flawless beachfront and pockets of sedate suburbia, the outskirts of town dissolve into a sprawling industrial jungle.

Hervey Bay Visitor Information Centre (1800 811 728; www.visitfrasercoast.com; cnr Urraween & Maryborough Rds) Helpful and well-stocked with brochures and information. On the outskirts of town.

Getting There & Away

AIR

Hervey Bay Airport is on Don Adams Dr, just off Booral Rd. **Qantas** (13 13 13; www.qantas.com.au) and **Virgin** (13 67 89; www.virginaustralia.com.au) have daily flights to/from destinations around Australia.

BOAT

Boats to Fraser Island leave from River Heads, about 10km south of town, and from Urangan's Great Sandy Straits Marina. Most tours leave from Urangan Harbour.

BUS

Buses depart **Hervey Bay Coach Terminal** (07-4124 4000; Central Ave, Pialba). **Greyhound** (1300 473 946; www.greyhound.com.au) and **Premier Motor Service** (13 34 10; www.premierms.com.au) have several services daily to/from Brisbane ($71, 5½ hours), Maroochydore ($48, 3½ hours), Bundaberg ($25, 1½ hours) and Rockhampton ($88, six hours).

Tory's Tours (07-4128 6500; www.torystours.com.au) Has twice daily services to Brisbane airport ($75).

Wide Bay Transit (07-4121 3719; www.widebaytransit.com.au) Has hourly services from Urangan Marina (stopping along the Esplanade) to Maryborough ($8, one hour) every weekday, with fewer services on weekends.

Getting Around

CAR

Hervey Bay is the the best place to hire a 4WD for Fraser Island.

Aussie Trax (07-4124 4433; www.fraserisland4wd.com.au; 56 Boat Harbour Dr, Pialba)

Hervey Bay Rent A Car (07-4194 6626; www.herveybayrentacar.com.au; 5 Cunningham St, Torquay) Also rents out scooters ($30 per day).

Rainbow Beach

POP 1103

Gorgeous Rainbow Beach is a tiny town at the base of the Inskip Peninsula with spectacular multicoloured sand cliffs overlooking its rolling surf and white sandy beach. The town's friendly locals, relaxed vibe, and convenient access to Fraser Island (only 10 minutes by barge) and the Cooloola Section of the Great Sandy National Park makes it a mellow stop for outdoorsy types and beach lovers.

Sights

The town is named for the **coloured sand cliffs**, which trace a 2km walk along the beach. The cliffs arc their red-hued way around Wide Bay, offering a sweeping panorama from the lighthouse at Double Island Point to Fraser Island in the north.

A 600m track through forest at the southern end of Cooloola Dr leads to the **Carlo Sandblow**, a spectacular 120m-tall dune high up on a cliff. You can walk out onto the dune for amazing views over the colourful cliffs and beach – do heed the signs of where to go for the sake of your own safety, and for the preservation of the dune.

Activities

There's a good surf break at Double Island Point.

Wolf Rock Dive Centre DIVING

(07-5486 8004, 0438 740 811; www.wolfrockdive.com.au; 20 Karoonda Rd; double dive charters from $220) Wolf Rock, a congregation of volcanic pinnacles off Double Island Point, is regarded as one of Queensland's best scuba-diving sites. The endangered grey nurse shark is found here year-round.

Skydive Rainbow Beach SKYDIVING

(0418 218 358; www.skydiverainbowbeach.com; 2400/4570m dives $299/429) Soft landings on the beach.

Rainbow Paragliding PARAGLIDING
(☎07-5486 3048, 0418 754 157; www.paraglidingrainbow.com; glides $180) Exhilarating tandem flights over the colourful cliffs.

Epic Ocean Adventures SURFING
(☎0408 738 192; www.epicoceanadventures.com.au; 3hr surf lessons $60, 3hr kayak tours $70) Surf classes and dolphin-spotting sea kayak tours.

Bushwalking & Camping

The Cooloola Section of the Great Sandy National Park (p338) has a number of bushwalking tracks and camp sites, including a wonderful stretch of beach camping along Teewah Beach. Book camping and 4WD permits online.

Camping on the beach is one of the best ways to experience this part of the coast; if you don't have camping gear **Rainbow Beach Hire-a-Camp** (☎07-5486 8633; www.rainbow-beach-hire-a-camp.com.au; tent per night from $30, additional nights $10) can hire out equipment, set up your tent and camp site, organise camping permits and break camp for you when you're done.

Tours

Surf & Sand Safaris DRIVING TOUR
(☎07-5486 3131; www.surfandsandsafaris.com.au; adult/child $75/40) Half-day 4WD tours through the national park and along the beach to the coloured sands and lighthouse at Double Island Point.

Sleeping

There are a handful of hostel options in Rainbow Beach and all are pretty standard. Most of the hostels are clustered together on Spectrum St, so it's easy to look in and choose your favourite. Alternatively, consider camping in the great outdoors.

Pippies Beach House HOSTEL $
(☎07-5486 8503; www.pippiesbeachhouse.com.au; 22 Spectrum St; dm/d $24/65; ❄@📶🏊) With only 12 rooms, this small, relaxed hostel is the place to catch your breath between outdoor pursuits. Free breakfast, wi-fi and body boards, and lots of organised group activities, sweeten the stay.

Dingo's Backpacker's Resort HOSTEL $
(☎1800 111 126; www.dingosresort.com; 20 Spectrum St; dm $24; ❄@📶🏊) This party hostel with bar has live music, karaoke and face-painting nights, a chill-out gazebo, free pancake breakfasts and cheap meals nightly.

Rainbow Sands Holiday Units MOTEL $
(☎07-5486 3400; www.rainbowsands.com.au; 42-46 Rainbow Beach Rd; d $100, 1-bedroom apt from $115; ❄📶🏊) Perfectly pleasing low-rise, palm-fronted complex with standard motel rooms. There are also self-contained units with full laundries for comfortable longer stays.

Rainbow Beach Holiday Village CARAVAN PARK $
(☎07-5486 3222; www.rainbowbeachholidayvillage.com; 13 Rainbow Beach Rd; unpowered/powered sites from $38/47, villas from $145; ❄🏊) Popular but pricey beachfront park.

★**Debbie's Place** B&B $$
(☎07-5486 3506; www.rainbowbeachaccommodation.com.au; 30 Kurana St; d/ste from $119/140, 3-bedroom apt from $300; ❄📶🐾) Inside this beautiful timber Queenslander dripping with pot plants, the charming rooms are fully self-contained, with private entrances and verandahs. The effervescent Debbie is a mine of information and makes this a cosy home away from home.

Eating

Self-caterers will find a supermarket on Rainbow Beach Rd. There are a few cheap cafes along this same strip.

★**Waterview Bistro** MODERN AUSTRALIAN $$
(☎07-5486 8344; Cooloola Dr; mains $26-35; ⊙11.30am-11.30pm Wed-Sat, to 6pm Sun) Sunset drinks are a must at this swish restaurant with sensational views of Fraser Island from its hilltop perch. Get stuck into the signature seafood chowder, steaks and seafood, or have fun cooking your own meal over hot stones.

Arcobaleno on the Beach ITALIAN $$
(1 Rainbow Beach Rd; pizzas $15-25; ⊙9am-10pm) It's actually just near the beach, and has no beach views. But the Zen-tinged, plant-filled patio, couch-laden interior and friendly staff make this a relaxing hang-out for a meal (breakfast, lunch and dinner), a good coffee any time, or an excellent Italian-style pizza.

Rainbow Beach Hotel PUB FOOD $$
(1 Rainbow Beach Rd; mains $18-35; ⊙from 11.30am) The spruced-up pub brings to mind all things plantation, with ceiling fans, palm trees, timber floors and cane furnishings – plus the smell of beer. The restaurant serves up traditional pub grub. Scope the street scene from the upstairs balcony.

Information

Queensland Parks & Wildlife Service (QPWS, Rainbow Beach Rd; 8am-4pm)

Rainbow Beach Visitor Centre (07-5486 3227; www.rainbowbeachinfo.com.au; 8 Rainbow Beach Rd; 7am-5.30pm) Despite the posted hours, it's open sporadically.

Shell Tourist Centre (36 Rainbow Beach Rd; 6am-6pm) At the Shell service station; arranges tour bookings and barge tickets for Fraser Island.

Getting There & Around

Greyhound (1300 473 946; www.greyhound.com.au) has several daily services from Brisbane ($49, five hours), Noosa ($32, three hours) and Hervey Bay ($26, two hours). **Premier Motor Service** (13 34 10; www.premierms.com.au) has less-expensive services. **Cooloola Connections** (07-5481 1667; www.coolconnect.com.au) runs a shuttle bus to Rainbow Beach from Brisbane Airport ($135, three hours) and Sunshine Coast Airport ($95, two hours).

Most 4WD-hire companies will also arrange permits and barge costs (per vehicle $100 return), and hire out camping gear. Try **All Trax** (07-5486 8767; www.fraserisland4x4.com.au; Rainbow Beach Rd, Shell service station; per day from $165) or **Rainbow Beach Adventure Centre** (07-5486 3288; www.adventurecentre.com.au; 13 Spectrum Street, Rainbow Beach; per day from $180).

Maryborough

POP 21,777

Born in 1847, Maryborough is one of Queensland's oldest towns, and its port saw the first shaky step ashore for thousands of 19th-century free settlers looking for a better life in the new country. Heritage and history are Maryborough's specialities; the pace of yesteryear is reflected in its beautifully restored colonial-era buildings and gracious Queenslander homes.

This charming old country town is also the birthplace of Pamela Lyndon (PL) Travers, creator of the umbrella-wielding Mary Poppins. The award-winning film *Saving Mr Banks* tells Travers' story, with early-1900s Maryborough in a starring role. There's a life-sized **statue** of Ms Poppins on the corner of Richmond and Wharf Sts.

Stroll the historic area beside the Mary River known as **Portside** (101 Wharf St; 10am-4pm Mon-Fri, to 1pm Sat & Sun) and explore its 13 heritage-listed buildings, parkland and museum. On Thursdays the town is enlivened by the **Maryborough Heritage City Markets** (cnr Adelaide & Ellena Sts; 8am-1.30pm Thu) – don't miss the firing of the cannon at 1pm. **Guided walking tours** (9am Mon-Sat) FREE of town from the visitor centre at City Hall are good fun, but real Mary Poppins groupies should schedule their trips for the **Mary Poppins Festival** (www.marypoppinsfestival.com.au) in June/July.

Sleeping & Eating

Eco Queenslander BOUTIQUE HOTEL $$
(0438 195 443; www.ecoqueenslander.com; 15 Treasure St; per couple $140) You won't want to leave this lovely converted Queenslander with comfy lounge, full kitchen, laundry and a cast-iron bathtub. Sustainable features include solar power, rainwater tanks, energy-efficient lighting and bikes for you to use. Minimum two-night stay.

★**Pop In** CAFE $
(203 Bazaar St; sandwiches $8.50; 7am-3pm Mon-Fri, to 1pm Sat) A cheery, bright and friendly cafe that encourages lingering. On offer are great coffee, fresh juices, and homemade goodies from stuffed mushrooms to salads, full breakfasts and sandwiches.

Information

Maryborough/Fraser Island Visitor Centre (1800 214 789; www.visitfrasercoast.com; Kent St; 9am-5pm Mon-Fri, to 1pm Sat & Sun) This visitor centre in the 100-year-old City Hall is extremely helpful and has free leaflets detailing comprehensive self-guided walking tours. Speak with them about inclusive tickets to Portside's museums and attractions.

Getting There & Away

Both the Sunlander ($75, five hours) and the Tilt Train ($75, 3½ hours) connect Brisbane with Maryborough West station. The station is 7km west of the centre, and is connected via a shuttle bus.

Greyhound (1300 473 946; www.greyhound.com.au) and **Premier Motor Service** (13 34 10; www.premierms.com.au) have buses to Gympie ($30, one hour), Bundaberg ($40, three hours) and Brisbane ($64, 4½ hours).

Wide Bay Transit (07-4121 4070; www.widebaytransit.com.au) Has hourly services (fewer on weekends) between Maryborough and Hervey Bay ($8, one hour), departing from outside City Hall in Kent St.

Bundaberg

POP 69,805

Despite boasting a sublime climate, coral-fringed beaches and waving fields of sugar cane, 'Bundy' is still overlooked by most travellers. Hordes of backpackers flock here for fruit-picking and farm work; other visitors quickly pass through on their way to family summer holidays at the nearby seaside villages.

This is the birthplace of the famous Bundaberg Rum, a potent liquor bizarrely endorsed by a polar bear, and as iconically Australian as Tim Tams and Vegemite.

In many people's eyes, the beach hamlets around Bundaberg are more attractive than the town itself. Some 25km north of the centre is Moore Park with wide, flat beaches. To the south is the very popular Elliott Heads with a nice beach, rocky foreshore and good fishing.

Sights & Activities

★Bundaberg Rum Distillery — DISTILLERY

(☎07-4131 2999; www.bundabergrum.com.au; Avenue St; self-guided tours adult/child $15/8, guided tours $25/12; ⏱10am-3pm Mon-Fri, to 2pm Sat & Sun) Bundaberg's biggest claim to fame is the iconic Bundaberg Rum: you'll see the Bundy Rum polar bear on billboards and bumper stickers all over town. Choose from either a self-guided tour through the museum, or a guided tour of the distillery – tours depart on the hour. Both include a tasting for the over-18s. Wear closed shoes.

Bundaberg Barrel — BREWERY

(☎07-4154 5480; www.bundaberg.com; 147 Bargara Rd; adult/child $12/5; ⏱9am-4.30pm Mon-Sat, 10am-3pm Sun) Bundaberg's nonalcoholic ginger beer and other soft drinks aren't as famous as Bundy Rum, but they are very good. Visit the Barrel to take an audio tour of the small museum. Tastings are included and it's geared to families.

Hinkler Hall of Aviation — MUSEUM

(www.hinklerhallofaviation.com; Mt Perry Rd, Botanic Gardens; adult/child/family $18/10/38; ⏱9am-4pm) This modern museum has multimedia exhibits, a flight simulator and informative displays chronicling the life of Bundaberg's famous son Bert Hinkler, who made the first solo flight between England and Australia in 1928.

> **TURTLE TOTS**
>
> **Mon Repos**, 15km northeast of Bundaberg, is one of Australia's most accessible turtle rookeries. From November to late March, female loggerheads lumber laboriously up the beach to lay eggs in the sand. About eight weeks later, the hatchlings dig their way to the surface, and, under cover of darkness, emerge en masse to scurry as quickly as their little flippers allow down to the water.
>
> The Bundaberg Visitor Centre has information on turtle conservation and organises nightly tours (adult/child $11.25/6) from 7pm during the season. Bookings are mandatory and need to be made through the visitor centre or online at www.bookbundaberg region.com.au. The Bundaberg Visitor Centre also has reports of how many turtles have been seen through the season.

Bundaberg Aqua Scuba — DIVING

(☎07-4153 5761; www.aquascuba.com.au; 239 Bourbong St; diving courses from $349) Leads dives to nearby sites around Innes Park.

Burnett River Cruises — CRUISE

(☎0427 099 009; www.burnettrivercruises.com.au; School Lane, East Bundaberg; 2½hr tours adult/child $25/10) The *Bundy Belle*, an old-fashioned ferry, chugs at a pleasant pace to the mouth of the Burnett River. See website or call for tour times.

Sleeping & Eating

There are plenty of midrange motels on the Bundaberg–Childers Road into town. Bundaberg's handful of hostels caters to working backpackers, and most can arrange harvest work.

Bigfoot Backpackers — HOSTEL $

(☎07-4152 3659; www.footprintsadventures.com.au; 66 Targo St; dm from $24; P ❄) Comfortable and friendly central hostel that also runs fabulous turtle tours to Mon Repos. Fresh paint, happy staff and a relaxed vibe raise Bigfoot above its competitors. There are ample fruit-picking opportunities available.

★Inglebrae — B&B $$

(☎07-4154 4003; www.inglebrae.com; 17 Branyan St; r incl breakfast $120-150; ❄) For old-world

English charm in a glorious Queenslander, this delightful B&B is just the ticket. Polished timber and stained glass seep from the entrance into the rooms, which come with high beds and small antiques.

Rosie Blu DELI $
(☎07-4151 0957; 90a Bourbong St; mains $9-20; ⏲8am-4pm Mon, 8.30am-4pm Tue-Fri, 8am-1.30pm Sat) Locals congregate en masse at this cute little spot, which isn't shy with its portions of gourmet sandwiches, salads, vegie-friendly options and hot lunches dished up at lightning speed.

Indulge CAFE $
(80 Bourbong St; dishes $9-18; ⏲8.30am-4.30pm Mon-Fri, 7.30am-12.30pm Sat) Delicious pastries and a fancy menu built around local produce.

Information

Bundaberg Visitor Centre (☎07-4153 8888, 1300 722 099; www.bundabergregion.org; 271 Bourbong St; ⏲9am-5pm)

Getting There & Around

AIR

Bundaberg Airport (Airport Dr) About 6km southwest of the centre.

QantasLink (☎13 13 13; www.qantas.com.au) Has several daily flights to Brisbane.

BUS

The coach terminal is on Targo St. Both **Greyhound** (☎1300 473 946; www.greyhound.com.au) and **Premier Motor Service** (☎13 34 10; www.premierms.com.au) have daily services connecting Bundaberg with Brisbane ($89, seven hours), Hervey Bay ($25, 1½ hours) and Rockhampton ($51, four hours).

Duffy's Coaches (☎1300 383 397) Has numerous services every weekday to Bargara ($5, 35 minutes), leaving from the back of Target on Woongarra St.

TRAIN

Queensland Rail (☎1800 872 467; www.traveltrain.com.au) The Sunlander ($89, seven hours, three weekly) and Tilt Train ($89, five hours, Sunday to Friday) travel from Brisbane to Bundaberg on their respective routes to Cairns and Rockhampton.

FRASER ISLAND

The local Butchulla people call it K'Gari – paradise – and for good reason. Sculpted from wind, sand and surf, the striking blue freshwater lakes, crystalline creeks, giant dunes and lush rainforests of this gigantic sandbar form an enigmatic island paradise unlike anywhere else. Created over hundreds of thousands of years from sand drifting off the east coast of mainland Australia, Fraser Island is the largest sand island in the world (measuring 120km by 15km), and is the only known place where rainforest grows on sand.

Inland, the vegetation varies from dense tropical rainforest and wild heath to wetlands and wallum scrub, with sandblows (giant dunes over 200m high), mineral streams and freshwater lakes opening on to long

DEALING WITH DINGOES

Despite its many natural attractions and opportunities for adventure, there's nothing on Fraser Island that gives a thrill comparable to your first glimpse of a dingo. Believed to be among the most genetically pure in the world, the dingoes of Fraser are sleek, spry and utterly beautiful. They're also wild beasts that can become aggressive at the drop of a hat (or a strong-smelling food sack). While attacks are rare, there are precautions that must be taken by every visitor to the island.

- However skinny they appear, or whatever woebegone look they give you, never feed dingoes. Dingoes that are human-fed quickly lose their shyness and can become combative and competitive. Feeding dingoes is illegal and carries heavy fines.
- Don't leave any food scraps lying around, and don't take food to the lakes: eating on the shore puts your food at 'dingo level', an easy target for scrounging scavengers.
- Stay in groups, and keep any children within arm's reach at all times.
- Teasing dingoes is not only cruel, but dangerous. Leave them alone, and they'll do same.
- Dingoes are best observed at a distance. Pack a zoom lens and practise some silence, and you'll come away with some brilliant photographs…and all your limbs intact.

Fraser Island

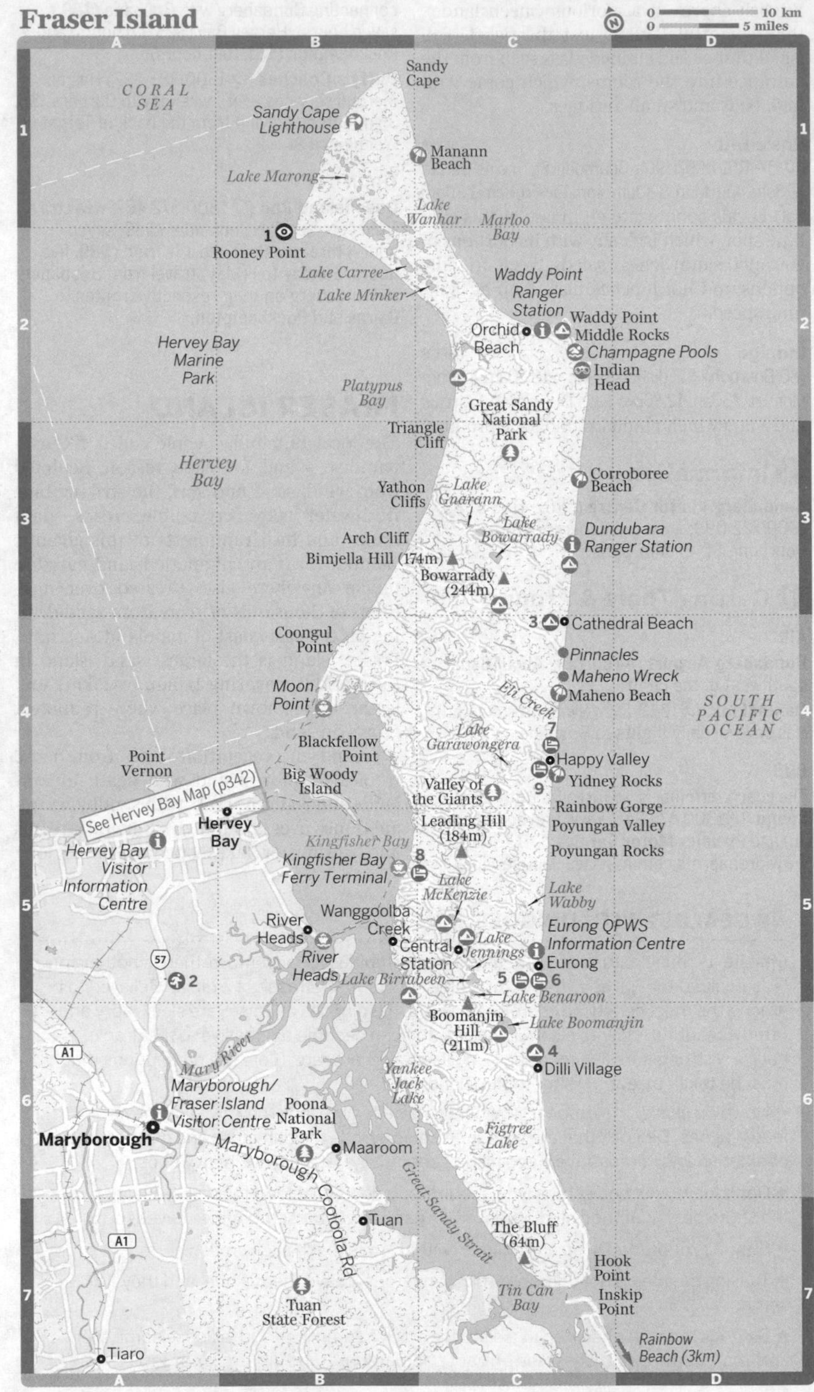

Fraser Island

Sights

1 Panama B2

Activities, Courses & Tours

2 Susan River Homestead A5

Sleeping

3 Cathedrals on Fraser C4
4 Dilli Village Fraser Island C6
5 Eurong Beach Resort C5
6 Fraser Island Beachhouses C5
7 Fraser Island Retreat C4
8 Kingfisher Bay Resort C5
9 Sailfish on Fraser C4

sandy beaches fringed with pounding surf. The island is home to a profusion of bird life and wildlife, including the famous dingo, while offshore waters teem with dugong, dolphins, manta rays, sharks and migrating humpback whales.

Once exploited for its natural resources, sand and timber, Fraser Island joined the World Heritage List in 1992. The majority of the island is protected as part of the **Great Sandy National Park**.

This island utopia, however, is marred by an ever-increasing volume of 4WD traffic tearing down the beach and along sandy inland tracks. With an average of 1000 people per day visiting the island, Fraser can sometimes feel like a giant sandpit with its own peak hour and congested beach highway.

In late October 2014 the native Butchulla won a native title land claim for Fraser Island – they had been trying to get their land rights recognised since the 1970s. This will allow the Butchulla to protect places of cultural significance as they see fit, and potentially to teach visitors more about the historical and spiritual attributes of the island.

Before crossing via ferry from either Rainbow Beach or Hervey Bay, ensure that your vehicle has suitably high clearance (if you're one of the few not visiting on a tour that is) and, if camping, that you have adequate food, water and fuel.

Sights & Activities

Starting at the island's southern tip, where the ferry leaves for Inskip Point on the mainland, a high-tide access track cuts inland, avoiding dangerous Hook Point, and leads to the entrance of the Eastern Beach's main thoroughfare. The first settlement is **Dilli Village**, the former sand-mining centre; **Eurong**, with shops, fuel and places to eat, is another 9km north. From here, an inland track crosses to Central Station and Wanggoolba Creek (for the ferry to River Heads).

Right in the middle of the island is the ranger centre at **Central Station**, the starting point for numerous walking trails. From here you can walk or drive to the beautiful **McKenzie**, **Jennings**, **Birrabeen** and **Boomanjin Lakes**. Lake McKenzie is spectacularly clear and ringed by white-sand beaches, making it a great place to swim; Lake Birrabeen sees fewer tour and backpacker groups.

About 4km north of Eurong along the beach, a signposted walking trail leads across sandblows to the beautiful **Lake Wabby**, the most accessible of Fraser's lakes. An easier route is from the Lake Wabby Lookout, off Cornwell's Break Rd from the inland side. Lake Wabby is surrounded on three sides by eucalyptus forest, while the fourth side is a massive sandblow that encroaches on the lake at a rate of about 3m a year. The lake is deceptively shallow and diving is very dangerous.

As you drive up the beach, during high tide you may have to detour inland to avoid **Poyungan** and **Yidney Rocks**, before reaching **Happy Valley**, which has places to stay, a shop and a bistro. About 10km further north is **Eli Creek**, a fast-moving, crystal-clear waterway that will carry you effortlessly downstream. About 2km from Eli Creek is the rotting hulk of the **Maheno**, a former passenger liner which was blown ashore by a cyclone in 1935 as it was being towed to a Japanese scrap yard.

Roughly 5km north of the *Maheno* you'll find the **Pinnacles**, an eroded section of coloured sand cliffs, and about 10km beyond, **Dundubara**, with a ranger station and excellent camping ground. Then there's a 20km stretch of beach before you come to the rock outcrop of **Indian Head**. Sharks, manta rays, dolphins and (during the migration season) whales can often be seen from the top of this headland.

Between Indian Head and Waddy Point, the trail branches inland, passing **Champagne Pools**, which offers the only safe saltwater swimming on the island. There are good camping areas at **Waddy Point** and **Orchid Beach**, the last settlement on the island. Many tracks north of here are closed for environmental protection.

SAND SAFARIS: EXPLORING FRASER ISLAND

The only way to explore Fraser Island (besides walking) is with a 4WD. For most travellers, there are three transport options: tag-along tours, organised tours or 4WD hire; the fourth option is to stay at one of the island's accommodations and take day tours from there.

This is a fragile environment; bear in mind that the greater the number of individual vehicles driving on the island, the greater the environmental damage.

Tag-Along Tours

Popular with backpackers, tag-along tours see groups of travellers pile into a 4WD convoy and follow a lead vehicle with an experienced guide and driver. Travellers take turns driving the other vehicles, which can be great fun, but has also led to accidents. Rates hover around $350 to $400; be sure to check if your tour includes food, fuel, alcohol etc. Accommodation is often in tents.

Advantages You can make new friends fast; driving the beaches is exhilarating.
Disadvantages If food isn't included you'll have to cook; groups can be even bigger than on bus tours.

Dropbear Adventures (☎1800 061 156; www.dropbearadventures.com.au) Lots of departures from Hervey Bay, Rainbow Beach and Noosa to Fraser Island; easy to get a spot.

Fraser's on Rainbow (☎07-5486 8885; www.frasersonrainbow.com) Departs from Rainbow Beach.

Fraser Dingo (☎0400 779 880; fraserislandtagalongtours.com; Unit 13/3 Southern Cross Circuit, Urangan; 2-day tours $304) Includes food and dorm accommodation.

Pippies Beach House (☎07-5486 8503; www.pippiesbeachhouse.com.au) Departs from Rainbow Beach; well-organised, small convoys with high safety standards.

Nomads (☎07-5447 3355; www.nomadsfraserisland.com) Departs from Noosa.

Organised Tours

Most organised tours cover Fraser's hotspots: rainforests, Eli Creek, Lakes McKenzie and Wabby, the coloured Pinnacles and the *Maheno* shipwreck.

Advantages Expert commentary; decent food and comfortable accommodation; often the most economical choice.
Disadvantages Day-tour buses often arrive en masse at the same place at the same time; less social.

Cool Dingo Tours (☎07-4120 3333; www.cooldingotour.com; 2-/3-day tours from $325/395) Overnight at lodges with the option to stay extra nights on the island. The party option.

Fraser Explorer Tours (☎07-4194 9222; www.fraserexplorertours.com.au; 1-/2-day tours $175/319) Very experienced drivers; lots of departures.

Fraser Experience (☎07-4124 4244; www.fraserexperience.com; 1-/2-day tours $180/327) Small-group tours offer greater freedom with the itinerary.

Remote Fraser (☎07-4124 3222; www.tasmanventure.com.au; tours $150) Day tours to the less-visited west coast.

4WD Hire

You can hire a 4WD from Hervey Bay, Rainbow Beach or on Fraser Island itself. All companies require a hefty bond, usually in the form of a credit-card imprint, which you *will* lose if you drive in salt water – don't even think about running the waves!

When planning your trip, reckon on covering 20km/h on the inland tracks and 40km/h on the eastern beach. Most companies will help arrange ferries, permits and camping gear. Rates for multiday rentals start at around $185 a day.

Advantages Complete freedom to roam the island and escape the crowds.
Disadvantages You may encounter beach and track conditions that even experienced drivers find challenging; expensive.

There are rental companies in **Hervey Bay** (p345) and **Rainbow Beach** (p347). On the island, **Aussie Trax** (☎07-4124 4433; www.fraserisland4wd.com.au) hires out 4WDs from $283 per person, per day.

Kingfisher Bay Resort (07-4194 9300; www.kingfisherbay.com) can organise scenic helicopter flights, and **Air Fraser Island** (07-4125 3600; www.airfraserisland.com.au) offer optional, 15-minute flights to many of the islands tours for $75.

Sleeping & Eating

★Kingfisher Bay Resort RESORT $$
(1800 072 555, 07-4194 9300; www.kingfisherbay.com; Kingfisher Bay; d $188, 2-bedroom villas $258;) This elegant eco-resort has hotel rooms with private balcony, and sophisticated two- and three-bedroom timber villas which are elevated to limit their environmental impact. There's a three-night minimum stay in high season. The resort has restaurants, bars and shops and operates daily ranger-guided, eco-accredited tours of the island (adult/child $160/110).

Fraser Island Beachhouses CABIN $$
(1800 626 230, 07-4127 9205; www.fraserislandbeachhouses.com.au; Eurong Second Valley; studios/houses from $150/275;) A top option for those wanting their own space without sand or tents. The sunny, self-contained units are kitted out with polished wood, cable TVs and ocean views; there are four categories of beach house, with prices varying by size and location. Minimum stays apply.

Eurong Beach Resort RESORT $$
(1800 111 808, 07-4120 1600; www.eurong.com.au; Eurong; r from $135, 2-bedroom apt $199;) Cheerful but basic Eurong is the main resort on the east coast, and a solid option for most budgets. Choose from simple motel rooms and comfortable, self-contained apartments. There's a **restaurant** (mains $18-40; breakfast, lunch & dinner;), a bar, a shop, two pools, tennis courts and a petrol station.

Fraser Island Retreat CABIN $$
(07-4127 9144; www.fraserisretreat.com.au; Happy Valley; cabins per 2 nights $360;) The retreat's nine timber cabins (each sleeping up to four people) offer some of the best-value accommodation on the island. The cabins are airy, nestled in native foliage and close to the beach. On-site are a camp kitchen, licensed restaurant and shop – which sells fuel.

Sailfish on Fraser APARTMENT $$$
(07-4127 9494; www.sailfishonfraser.com.au; Happy Valley; d $230-250, extra person $10;) Any notions of rugged wilderness will be forgotten quick smart at this plush, indulgent retreat. These two-bedroom apartments (which sleep up to six people) are cavernous and classy. There are spas, mod cons, an alluring pool and a 4WD washing area.

Camping

Supplies on the island are limited and costly. Stock up well before arriving, and be prepared for mosquitoes and March flies.

Camping permits are required in order to camp at Department of National Parks, Sport and Racing (NPRSR) camping grounds and any public areas (ie along the beach). The most developed **NPRSR camping grounds** (13 74 68; www.nprsr.qld.gov.au; per person/family $5.45/21.80), with coin-operated hot showers, toilets and BBQs, are at Waddy Point, Dundubara and Central Station. Campers with vehicles can also use the smaller camping grounds with fewer facilities at Lake Boomanjin, and at Ungowa and Wathumba on the western coast. Walkers' camps are set away from the main camping grounds, along the Fraser Island Great Walk trail. The trail map lists the camp sites and their facilities. Camping is permitted on designated stretches of the eastern beach, but there are no facilities. Fires are prohibited except in communal fire rings at Waddy Point and Dundubara – bring your own firewood in the form of untreated, milled timber.

Dilli Village Fraser Island CAMPGROUND $
(07-4127 9130; www.usc.edu.au; camp sites per person $10, bunkroom/cabins $50/120) Managed by the University of the Sunshine Coast, Dilli Village offers good sites on a softly sloping camping ground.

Cathedrals on Fraser CARAVAN PARK $
(07-4127 9177; www.cathedralsonfraser.com.au; Cathedral Beach; unpowered/powered sites $39/45, cabins with/without bathroom $220/180;) Spacious, privately run, dingo-fenced park with abundant, flat, grassy sites. It's a hit with families.

Information

Shops at Cathedral Beach, Eurong, Kingfisher Bay, Happy Valley and Orchid Beach have general supplies and public telephones; there are also phones at most camping grounds.

Eurong QPWS Information Centre (07-4127 9128) is the main ranger station. Others can be found at **Dundubara** (07-4127 9138) and **Waddy Point** (07-4127 9190). Offices are often unattended as the rangers are out on patrol.

FRASER ISLAND GREAT WALK

The Fraser Island Great Walk is a stunning way to experience this enigmatic island. The trail undulates through the island's interior for 90km from Dilli Village to Happy Valley. Broken up into seven sections of around 6km to 16km each, plus some side trails, it follows the pathways of Fraser Island's original inhabitants, the Butchulla people. En route, the walk passes underneath rainforest canopies, circles around some of the island's vivid lakes, and courses through shifting dunes.

It's imperative to visit www.nprsr.qld.gov.au for maps, detailed information and updates on the track, which can close when conditions are bad.

PERMITS

You must purchase permits from **NPRSR** (☎13 74 68; nprsr.qld.gov.au) for vehicles (per day/week/month $11/27.70/43.60) and to camp in the NPRSR camping grounds (per person/family $5.45/21.80) before you arrive. Permits aren't required for private camping grounds or resorts. Buy permits online or check with visitors centres for up-to-date lists of where to buy them.

Getting There & Away

AIR

Air Fraser Island (p353) charges from $135 for a return flight (30-minute round trip) to the island's eastern beach, departing Hervey Bay Airport.

BOAT

Vehicle ferries connect Fraser Island with River Heads, about 10km south of Hervey Bay, or further south at Inskip Point, near Rainbow Beach.

Fraser Venture Barge (☎1800 227 437, 07-4194 9300; www.fraserislandferry.com.au) Makes the crossing (vehicle and four passengers $165 return, 30 minutes) from River Heads to Wanggoolba Creek on the western coast of Fraser Island. It departs daily from River Heads at 8.30am, 10.15am and 4pm, and returns from the island at 9am, 3pm and 5pm.

Kingfisher Bay Ferry (☎1800 227 437, 07-4194 9300; www.fraserislandferry.com) Operates a daily vehicle and passenger ferry (pedestrian adult/child return $50/25, vehicle and four passengers return $165, 50 minutes) from River Heads to Kingfisher Bay, departing at 6.45am, 9am, 12.30pm, 3.30pm, 6.45pm and 9.30pm (Friday and Saturday only) and returning at 7.50am, 10.30am, 2pm, 5pm, 8.30pm and 11pm (Friday and Saturday only).

Manta Ray (☎07-5486 3935; mantarayfraserislandbarge.com.au) Coming from Rainbow Beach, Manta Ray has two ferries making the 15-minute crossing from Inskip Point to Hook Point on Fraser Island, continuously from about 6am to 5.30pm daily (vehicle return $110).

Getting Around

A 4WD is necessary if you're driving on Fraser Island; you'll need a permit (p354). Expensive fuel is available from stores at Cathedral Beach, Eurong, Kingfisher Bay, Happy Valley and Orchid Beach. If your vehicle breaks down, call the **tow-truck service** (☎0428 353 164, 07-4127 9449) in Eurong.

The 4WD **Fraser Island Taxi Service** (☎07-4127 9188; www.fraserservice.com.au) operates all over the island. Bookings are essential, as there's only one cab for the whole island!

Capricorn Coast & the Southern Reef Islands

Includes ➡

Best Places to Eat

- ➡ Ferns Hideaway Restaurant (p365)
- ➡ Getaway Garden Café (p358)
- ➡ Ginger Mule (p361)
- ➡ Great Western Hotel (p361)
- ➡ Megalomania (p363)

Best Places to Stay

- ➡ Svendsen's Beach (p364)
- ➡ LaLaLand Retreat (p358)
- ➡ Coral Inn Yeppoon (p363)
- ➡ Lady Elliot Island Resort (p359)
- ➡ Myella Farm Stay (p361)

Why Go?

The stretch of coastline that straddles the tropic of Capricorn is one of the quietest and most lovely lengths of the east coast. While local families flock to the main beaches during school holidays, the scene is uncrowded for most of the year, and even in high season you needn't travel far to find a deserted beach.

The stunning powdery white sand and turquoise waters of the Capricorn Coast fit the holiday-brochure image perfectly. The pristine islands of the southern Great Barrier Reef offer some of the best snorkelling and diving in Queensland, and opportunities for wildlife spotting – from turtle hatchlings to passing whales – are plentiful. Unspoiled beaches and windswept national parks can be found along the entire coastline.

Inland, you'll find bustling Rockhampton – Capricornia's economic hub and the capital of cattle country, with the steakhouses, rodeos and gigantic hats to prove it.

When to Go

Rockhampton

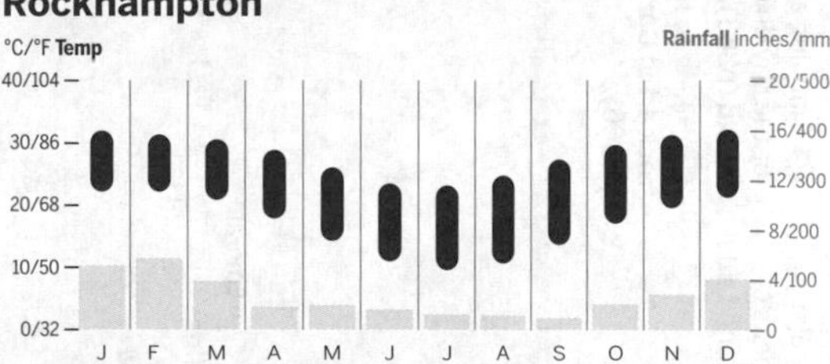

Feb The Agnes Blues & Roots Festival rocks the Discovery Coast.

May–Sep Warm winter temperatures are ideal for swimming and sunning.

Dec Nature puts on a stunning light show during the summer solstice at Capricorn Caves.

Capricorn Coast & the Southern Reef Islands Highlights

1. Diving the spectacular underwater coral gardens of **Heron Island** (p360) and **Lady Elliot Island** (p359).
2. Claiming a tropical beach for the day on **Great Keppel Island** (p363).
3. Hiking to find Aboriginal rock art in **Carnarvon Gorge** (p366).
4. Tucking into a huge steak in Australia's beef capital, **Rockhampton** (p360).
5. Crawling through black holes and tight tunnels in the **Capricorn Caves** (p362).
6. Digging and sifting in the hope of finding a fortune-changing sapphire in the **gem fields** (p365).
7. Surfing and chilling at Queensland's most northerly surf beach, **Agnes Water** (p357).

Agnes Water & Town of 1770

POP 1815

Surrounded by national parks and the Pacific Ocean, the twin coastal towns of Agnes Water and Town of 1770 are among Queensland's loveliest and least hectic seaside destinations. The tiny settlement of Agnes Water has the east coast's most northerly surf beach, while the even tinier Town of 1770 (little more than a marina!) marks Captain Cook's first landing in the state, and is great for kayaking and stand-up paddle boarding. The 'Discovery Coast' (as it's known) is also popular for boating, and fishing away from the crowds. To get here, turn east off the Bruce Hwy at Miriam Vale, 70km south of Gladstone. It's another 57km to Agnes Water and a further 6km to the Town of 1770.

Sights & Activities

Agnes Water is Queensland's northernmost **surf beach**. A surf life-saving club patrols the main beach and there are often good breaks along the coast. There's also good **fishing** and **mud-crabbing** upstream on Round Hill Creek. Charter boats are available for fishing, surfing, snorkelling and diving trips to the reef. You can rent a dinghy for fishing (half day $75, full day $110) at Town of 1770's small marina; ask for Poppy Bob. If you don't want to go it alone, **Hooked on 1770** (07-4974 9794; www.1770tours.com; half-/full-day tours $150/220) runs charter tours.

Deepwater National Park NATIONAL PARK
(www.nprsr.qld.gov.au/parks/deepwater) Eight kilometres south of Agnes Water you'll find an unspoiled coastal landscape with long sandy beaches, walking trails, freshwater creeks, good fishing spots and two camping grounds accessible only by 4WD. It's also a major breeding ground for loggerhead turtles, which lay eggs on the beaches between November and February; hatchlings emerge at night between January and April.

Reef 2 Beach Surf School SURFING
(07-4974 9072; www.reef2beachsurf.com; Agnes Water Shopping Centre, Agnes Water) Learn to surf on the gentle breaks of the main beach with this highly acclaimed surf school. A three-hour group lesson is $17 per person; surfboard hire is $20 for four hours.

1770 Liquid Adventures KAYAKING
(0428 956 630; www.1770liquidadventures.com.au) Paddle off on a spectacular twilight kayak tour. For $55 you ride the waves off 1770, before retiring to the beach for drinks and snacks as the sun sets – keep an eye out for dolphins. You can also rent kayaks (from $20 per hour).

1770 SUP WATER SPORTS
(0421 026 255; www.1770SUP.com.au; 1/2hr tours $35/50) Explore the calm waters and sandy banks of 1770 via peaceful stand-up paddle boarding. Tours include an intro lesson, or rent your own board for $20/30 for one/two hours. The roving SUP trailer can often be found on the 1770 waterfront across from Tree Bar.

Scooteroo MOTORCYCLING
(07-4974 7697; www.scooterrootours.com; 21 Bicentennial Dr, Agnes Water; 3hr rides $75) Straddle a chopper and vroom off on an irreverent and engaging 50km ride around the area. Anyone with a car licence can ride the gearless bikes. Wear long pants and closed shoes; Scooteroo will supply the tough-guy leather jackets (with flames, of course).

Tours

★**Lady Musgrave Cruises** CRUISE
(07-4974 9077; www.1770reefcruises.com; Captain Cook Dr, Town of 1770; adult/child $190/90; departs daily 8.30am) This family-owned company has excellent day trips to Lady Musgrave Island. Groups spend five hours at the island, and cruises include coral viewing in a semisubmersible, lunch, morning and afternoon tea, and snorkelling gear. For an extra cost you can go diving or reef fishing. Island camping transfers are also available for $450 per person.

ThunderCat 1770 ADVENTURE TOUR
(0411 078 810; tours from $70) Go wave-jumping on a surf-racing craft, slingshot over the waves on the Tube Rider Xpress or – best of all – bounce and spin through the water in a sumo suit. For those less in need of an adrenaline hit, explore calmer waterways on a Wilderness Explorer eco-tour.

1770 Larc Tours TOUR
(07-4974 9422; www.1770larctours.com.au; adult/child $155/95) Ride the world's most peculiar eco-tourism chariot (a hot pink amphibious military vehicle) on adventurous seven-hour tours around Bustard Head and Eurimbula National Park. It also runs hour-long afternoon tours (adult/child $38/17) and sandboarding safaris ($120).

Festivals

Agnes Blues & Roots Festival MUSIC
(www.agnesbluesandroots.com.au; SES Grounds, Agnes Water) Top names and up-and-coming Aussie acts crank it up in the last weekend of February.

Sleeping

Workmans Beach Camping Area CAMPGROUND $
(Workmans Beach, Springs Rd, Agnes Water; sites per person $6) Workmans Beach is a council-run camping ground with spacious sites in gorgeous beachside surrounds. Facilities include cold-water showers, drop toilets and gas BBQs. If you're really smitten, you can stay up to 44 days. You can't book sites; just turn up, and good-humoured council staff will knock on your van/tent at an ungodly hour of the morning to sort out payment.

Cool Bananas HOSTEL $
(07-4974 7660, 1800 227 660; www.coolbananas.net.au; 2 Springs Rd, Agnes Water; dm $28;) This young, busy, Balinese-themed backpackers has roomy six- and eight-bed dorms, and open and airy communal areas. It's only a five-minute walk to the beach and shops. Otherwise, you can laze the day away in a hammock in the tropical gardens.

1770 Southern Cross Tourist Retreat HOSTEL $
(07-4974 7225; www.1770southerncross.com; 2694 Round Hill Rd, Agnes Water; dm/d incl breakfast $25/85;) Chill out at this fun eucalyptus-forest retreat, with plenty of natural, open spaces, a swimming pool and even a little pond-side barbecue area with hammocks and a bonfire. Nights lean to partying but this is still the best hostel choice for a decent night's sleep. It's 2.5km out of town, and is connected by a courtesy bus.

1770 Camping Ground CARAVAN PARK $
(07-4974 9286; www.1770campingground.com.au; Captain Cook Dr, Town of 1770; unpowered/powered sites from $33/37) A large, peaceful park with sites right by the beach and plenty of shady trees.

★ **LaLaLand Retreat** GUESTHOUSE $$
(07-4974 9554; www.lalalandholiday.com.au; 61 Bicentennial Dr, Agnes Water; cottages $135-240;) The colourful cottages at this vibrant guesthouse on the road into town are set in attractive bushland scrub; each sleeps up to five people. There is an excellent lagoon-style pool, wheelchair access and a sense of being removed from civilisation. Call for deals on rates.

Agnes Water Beach Club APARTMENT $$
(07-4974 7355; www.agneswaterbeachclub.com.au; 3 Agnes St, Agnes Water; 1-/2-bedroom apt from $150/250;) Great-value luxury apartments for groups and families, with excellent facilities. In a prime location near the beach.

Eating

Agnes Water Bakery BAKERY $
(Endeavour Plaza, Agnes Water; pies $5; 6am-4pm Mon-Sat, to 2pm Sun) Do. Not. Miss. This. The pies here are above and beyond the offerings of most city bakeries, let alone those in a sleepy seaside village. Expect gourmet stuffings and even a vegetarian option (broccoli cheddar when we passed). Sweet treats are equally divine. It gets packed, so get in early.

★ **Getaway Garden Café** MODERN AUSTRALIAN $$
(07-4974 9232; 303 Bicentennial Dr, Agnes Water; breakfast $7-19, lunch $10-22, dinner $20-25; 8am-4pm Sun-Thu & 5.30-late Wed & Sun) An airy cafe with views of lily ponds, just a short walk from some deserted beaches. Everything is delectable, from the salmon Benedict breakfasts to burgers at lunch. The lamb spit roasts on Wednesday and Sunday nights that are very popular with locals (book ahead). Stop in for cake and coffee outside of main meal times.

Tree Bar MODERN AUSTRALIAN $$
(07-4974 7446; 576 Captain Cook Dr, Town of 1770; mains $16-34; breakfast, lunch & dinner) This little salt-encrusted waterfront diner and bar is simple, with plastic tables, but it marvellously catches sea views and breezes from the beach through the trees. Local seafood is a winner here, though breakfasts (from $8) are pretty damn fine as well.

Agnes Water Tavern PUB FOOD $$
(07-4974 9469; 1 Tavern Rd, Agnes Water; mains $15-30; from 11.30am) Pleasant multipurpose pub with plenty of outdoor seating. Lunch and dinner specials daily.

Shopping

1770 Markets MARKET
(SES Grounds, Town of 1770; 8am-noon Sun) Mellow markets with chatty stallholders flogging everything from edibles to antiques. Held the second and fourth Sunday of the month.

Information

Agnes Water Visitors Centre (☎07-4902 1533; 71 Springs Rd, Town of 1770; ⏲9am-5pm Mon-Fri, to 4pm Sat & Sun) Staffed by above-and-beyond volunteers who even leave out information and brochures when the centre's closed, just in case a lost soul blows into town.

Getting There & Away

A handful of **Greyhound** (☎1300 473 946; www.greyhound.com.au) buses detour off the Bruce Hwy to Agnes Water; daily services include Bundaberg ($26, 1½ hours) and Cairns ($224, 21 hours). **Premier Motor Service** (☎13 34 10; www.premierms.com.au) also goes in and out of town.

Southern Reef Islands

If you've ever had 'castaway' dreams of tiny coral atolls fringed with sugary white sand and turquoise-blue seas, you've found your island paradise in the southern Great Barrier Reef islands. From beautiful Lady Elliot Island, 80km northeast of Bundaberg, secluded and uninhabited coral reefs and atolls dot the ocean for about 140km up to Tryon Island.

Several cays in this part of the reef are excellent for snorkelling and diving – though reaching them is generally more expensive than reaching islands nearer the coast. Some of the islands are important breeding grounds for turtles and seabirds, and visitors should be aware of precautions to ensure the wildlife's protection, as outlined in the relevant Department of National Parks, Sport and Racing (NPRSR) information sheets.

Camping is allowed on Lady Musgrave, Masthead and North West national park islands; campers must be totally self-sufficient. Numbers are limited, so it's advisable to apply for a camping permit well in advance – contact **NPRSR** (☎13 74 68; www.nprsr.qld.gov.au; permits per person/family $5.45/21.80).

Access is from Town of 1770 and Gladstone.

Lady Elliot Island

On the southern frontier of the Great Barrier Reef, Lady Elliot is a 40-hectare vegetated coral cay populated with nesting sea turtles and an impressive number of seabirds. It's considered to have the best snorkelling in the southern Great Barrier Reef and the diving is good too: explore an ocean-bed of shipwrecks, coral gardens, bommies (coral pinnacles or outcroppings) and blowholes, and abundant marine life including barracuda, giant manta rays and harmless leopard sharks.

STINGERS

The potentially deadly chironex and irukandji box jellyfish, also known as sea wasps or marine stingers, occur in Queensland's coastal waters north of Agnes Water (and occasionally further south) from around October to April. Swimming near the coast is not advisable during these times. Fortunately, swimming and snorkelling are usually safe around the reef islands throughout the year; however, appearances of the rare and tiny (1cm to 2cm across) irukandji have been recorded on the outer reef and islands. Check locally or hire a full-body stinger suit.

Lady Elliot Island is not a national park, and camping is not allowed; your only option is the low-key **Lady Elliot Island Resort** (☎1800 072 200; www.ladyelliot.com.au; per person $147-350). Accommodation is in tent cabins, simple motel-style units or more expensive two-bedroom, self-contained suites. Rates include breakfast and dinner, snorkelling gear and some tours.

The only way to reach the island is in a light aircraft. Resort guests are flown in from Bundaberg, the Gold Coast and Hervey Bay. The resort also manages fantastic, great-value **day trips** for around $300, including a scenic flight, a snorkelling tour and lunch; see its website for more info. Flights and day trips can be booked through local travel booking agencies.

Lady Musgrave Island

Wannabe castaways look no further. This tiny, 15-hectare cay, 100km northeast of Bundaberg, sits on the western rim of a stunning, turquoise-blue reef lagoon renowned for its safe swimming, snorkelling and diving. A squeaky, white-sand beach fringes a dense canopy of pisonia forest brimming with roosting bird life, including terns, shearwaters and white-capped noddies. Birds nest from October to April while green turtles nest from November to February.

The uninhabited island is part of the Capricornia Cays National Park and there is a NPRSR camping ground on the island's west side; you must be totally self-sufficient and bring your own water. Numbers are limited to 40 at any one time, so apply well ahead for a permit with the **NPRSR**

(☎13 74 68; www.nprsr.qld.gov.au; per person/family $5.45/21.80). Bring a gas stove; fires are not permitted on the island.

Day trips ($190) to Lady Musgrave depart from the Town of 1770 marina.

Heron & Wilson Islands

With the underwater reef world accessible directly from the beach, Heron Island is famed for the best easily accessed scuba diving in the Southern Reef Islands, and also for great snorkelling, although you'll need a fair amount of cash to visit. A true coral cay, it is densely vegetated with pisonia trees and surrounded by 24 sq km of reef. There's a resort and research station on the north-eastern third of the island; the remainder is national park.

Sleeping

Heron Island Resort RESORT $$$
(☎1300 863 248; www.heronisland.com; d/f/beach houses from $434/798/3198) Comfortable accommodation suited to families and couples; the Point Suites have the best views. Great deals are often available on its website. Meal packages are extra, and guests will pay $50/25 (one way) per adult/child for launch transfer, $291 by seaplane, or $395 for helicopter transfer. All are from Gladstone.

Wilson Island RETREAT $$$
(☎1300 863 248; www.wilsonisland.com; d per person $463) Wilson Island, part of a national park, is an exclusive wilderness retreat with six permanent 'tents' and solar-heated showers. The only access is from Heron Island; to get here, you'll need to buy a combined Wilson-Heron package and spend at least two nights on Wilson Island. Transfers between Wilson and Heron are included in the tariff, as are meals and drinks.

The island has excellent beaches, superb snorkelling and, during the season, turtle watching.

Rockhampton

POP 61,724

Welcome to Rockhampton ('Rocky' to its mates), where the hats, boots and utes are big…but the bulls are even bigger. With over 2.5 million cattle within a 250km radius of Rockhampton, it's called Australia's Beef Capital for a reason. This sprawling country town is the administrative and commercial centre of central Queensland, its wide streets and fine Victorian-era buildings (take a stroll down Quay St) reflecting the region's prosperous 19th-century heyday of gold and copper mining and beef-cattle industry.

Straddling the tropic of Capricorn, Rocky can be aptly scorching. It's 40km inland and lacks coastal sea breezes; summers are often unbearably humid. The town has a smattering of attractions but is best seen as a gateway to the coastal gems of Yeppoon and Great Keppel Island.

Sights

★**Botanic Gardens** GARDENS
(☎07-4932 9000; Spencer St; ⏲6am-6pm) FREE Just south of town, these gardens are a beautiful oasis, with tropical and subtropical rainforest, landscaped gardens and lily-covered lagoons. The formal Japanese garden is a Zen-zone of tranquillity, there's a **cafe** (⏲8am-5pm), and the awesome **free zoo** (⏲8.30am-4.30pm) has koalas, wombats, dingoes, apes, a walk-through aviary and tons more.

Tropic of Capricorn LANDMARK
(Gladstone Rd) Attitude on the latitude! Straddle the Tropic of Capricorn at the visitor centre on Gladstone Rd; it's marked by a huge spire.

Dreamtime Cultural Centre CULTURAL CENTRE
(☎07-4936 1655; www.dreamtimecentre.com.au; Bruce Hwy; adult/child $14/6.50; ⏲10am-3.30pm Mon-Fri, tours 10.30am & 1pm) An easily accessible insight into Aboriginal and Torres Strait Islander heritage and history. The excellent 90-minute tours are hands on (throw your own boomerangs!) and appeal to all ages. About 7km north of the centre.

Tours

Little Johnny's Tours and Rentals TOUR
(☎0414 793 637; www.littlejohnnysrentals.com.au) Runs trips to many nearby attractions such as Byfield and the Capricorn Caves, and also does minibus runs between Rockhampton Airport and Yeppoon.

Sleeping

The northern and southern approach roads to Rocky are lined with numerous motels but if you want to stroll the elegant palm-lined streets overlooking the Fitzroy River, choose somewhere in the old town centre, south of the river.

RINGERS & COWBOYS: FARM STAYS

Kick up some red dust on a fair-dinkum Aussie outback cattle station and find out the difference between a jackeroo, a ringer, a stockman and a cowboy. On a farm stay, you'll be immersed in the daily activities of a working cattle station – riding horses and motorbikes, mustering cattle, fencing, and cooking damper and billy tea over a campfire.

Myella Farm Stay (07-4998 1290; www.myella.com; Baralaba Rd; 2/3 days $260/370, day trips $120;) Myella Farm Stay, 125km southwest of Rockhampton, gives you a taste of the outback on its 10.6-sq-km farm. The package includes bush explorations by horseback, motorcycle and 4WD, all meals, accommodation in a renovated homestead with polished timber floors and a wide verandah, farm clothes and free transfers from Rockhampton.

Kroombit Lochenbar Station (07-4992 2186; www.kroombit.com.au; 2-day & 1-night packages per person from $229;) Offers several farm-stay packages to choose from; you can pitch a tent or stay in bush-timber or upmarket cabins. While soaking up the Aussie experience you can learn to crack a whip, throw a boomerang or loop a lasso, and earn your spurs on a mechanical bucking bull. Rates include meals and pick-up from nearby Biloela.

Rockhampton Backpackers HOSTEL $
(07-4927 5288; www.rockhamptonbackpackers.com.au; 60 MacFarlane St; dm $28;) A Youth Hostelling Association (YHA) member, this unpretentious backpackers has an easy-to-mingle-in lounge and dining area. Dorms are basic and most have four beds. It's often busy with a mixed crowd including backpackers looking for work on cattle stations.

Southside Holiday Village CARAVAN PARK $
(07-4927 3013; www.sshv.com.au; Lower Dawson Rd; unpowered/powered sites $30/38, cabins $69-88, villas $98-120;) This is one of the city's best caravan parks, with neat, self-contained cabins and villas, large grassed camp sites and a good kitchen. Prices are for two people. It's about 3km south of the centre on a busy main road.

Criterion HOTEL $$
(07-4922 1225; www.thecriterion.com.au; 150 Quay St; pub r $60-85, motel r $130-160;) The Criterion is Rockhampton's grandest old pub, with an elegant foyer, a friendly bar and a well-respected steakhouse. Its top two stories have dozens of period rooms; rooms have showers, although the toilets are down the hall. It also has a number of 4½-star motel rooms.

Eating & Drinking

★Ginger Mule STEAK $
(07-4927 7255; 8 William St; mains from $10; 11.30am-midnight Wed & Thu, to 2am Fri, 4pm-2am Sat) Rocky's coolest eatery bills itself as a tapas bar, but everyone's here for one thing: steak! And bloody (or chargrilled) good steak it is too. It has regular late-week meals specials (including $10 steaks); pop down early or prepare to battle for a table. Morphs into a cocktail bar late in the evening.

★Great Western Hotel PUB
(07-4922 1862; www.greatwesternhotel.com.au; cnr Stanley & Denison Sts; 10am-2am) Yeehaw! Looking like a spaghetti-Western film set, this 1862 pub is home to Rocky's cowboys and 'gals. Out the back there's a rodeo arena where every Wednesday and Friday night you can watch brave cattlefolk being tossed in the air by bucking bulls and broncos. Touring bands occasionally rock here; you can get tickets online. The food is all about great steak.

Information

Tropic of Capricorn Visitor Centre (1800 676 701; Gladstone Rd; 9am-5pm) Helpful centre on the highway right beside the Tropic of Capricorn marker, 3km south of the centre.

Getting There & Away

AIR

Qantas (13 13 13; www.qantas.com.au) and **Virgin** (13 67 89; www.virginaustralia.com) connect Rockhampton with various cities. The airport is about 6km from the centre of town.

BUS

Greyhound (1300 473 946; www.greyhound.com.au) Has regular services from Rocky to Mackay ($62, four hours), Brisbane ($160, 11 hours) and Cairns ($200, 17 hours). All services stop at the Mobil Roadhouse (91 George St).

CAPRICORN CAVES

In the Berserker Range, 24km north of Rockhampton near the Caves township, the amazing **Capricorn Caves** (☎07-4934 2883; www.capricorncaves.com.au; 30 Olsens Caves Rd; adult/child $28/14.50; ⏰9am-4pm) are not to be missed. These ancient caves honeycomb a limestone ridge, and on a guided tour through the caverns and labyrinths you'll see cave coral, stalactites, dangling fig-tree roots and, less likely, little insectivorous bats.

The highlight of the one-hour 'cathedral tour' is the beautiful natural rock cathedral where a recording is played to demonstrate the cavern's incredible acoustics – it's a full body and mind experience. The cathedral has become a popular wedding spot, and there are also several concerts held there throughout the year. In December, around the summer solstice (1 December to 14 January), sunlight beams directly through a 14m vertical shaft into Belfry Cave, creating an electrifying light show. If you stand directly below the beam, reflected sunlight colours the whole cavern with whatever colour you're wearing.

Daring spelunkers can book a two-hour **adventure tour** ($75) – reserve a day or more in advance – which takes you through tight spots with names such as 'Fat Man's Misery'. You must be at least 16 years old for this tour.

The Capricorn Caves complex has barbecue areas, a pool, a kiosk, and **accommodation** (powered sites $35, cabins $140-170).

Premier Motor Service (☎13 34 10; www.premierms.com.au) Operates a Brisbane–Cairns service, stopping at Rockhampton.

Young's Bus Service (☎07-4922 3813; www.youngsbusservice.com.au; 171 Bolsover St) Travels to Yeppoon and Mt Morgan ($6.70 one way) Monday to Friday. Buses depart from Bolsover St, outside the police station.

TRAIN

Queensland Rail (☎1800 872 467; www.queenslandrailtravel.com.au) Connects Rockhampton with Brisbane, Cairns and Queensland's dusty interior including bush towns such as Longreach and Emerald. The train station is 450m southwest of the city centre.

Getting Around

Sunbus (www.sunbus.com.au) runs a reasonably comprehensive city bus network operating all day Monday to Friday, and Saturday morning; pick up a timetable at the visitor centre. Otherwise, there's always **Rocky Cabs** (☎13 10 08).

Yeppoon

POP 13,500

Pretty little Yeppoon is a small seaside town with a long beach, a calm ocean and an attractive hinterland of volcanic outcrops, pineapple patches and grazing lands. The handful of quiet streets, sleepy motels and beachside cafes attracts Rockhamptonites beating the heat, and tourists heading for Great Keppel Island, only 13km offshore.

Sights & Activities

Cruises and the ferry to Great Keppel Island depart from the Keppel Bay Marina at Rosslyn Bay, just south of Yeppoon.

Check out the flying foxes along Fig Tree Creek and in large trees around town. At sunset they often fill the sky in spectacular flight.

Cooberrie Park WILDLIFE RESERVE

(☎07-4939 7590; www.cooberriepark.com.au; Woodbury Rd; adult/child/family $30/15/70; ⏰10am-3pm, animal show 1pm) About 15km north of Yeppoon, Cooberrie Park is a small wildlife sanctuary on 10 hectares of bushland. You can see kangaroos, wallabies and peacocks wandering freely through the grounds. You can also feed the critters and, for an extra cost, hold a furry koala or some slithering reptiles.

Koorana Crocodile Farm WILDLIFE RESERVE

(☎07-4934 4749; www.koorana.com.au; Coowonga Rd; adult/child $28/13; ⏰tours 10.30am & 1pm) Fifteen kilometres along the Emu Park–Rockhampton road, the Koorana Crocodile Farm can only be explored via informative guided tours. After watching the man-eaters splash and dash around frighteningly, get your feeble human revenge by sampling croc kebabs, croc ribs or a croc pie at the restaurant.

Funtastic Cruises CRUISE

(☎0438 909 502; www.funtasticcruises.com; full-day cruises adult/child/family $98/80/350) Funtastic Cruises operates full-day snorkelling trips on board its 17m catamaran, with a two-hour stopover on Great Keppel Island, morning and afternoon tea, and all snorkelling equipment included. It can also organise camping drop-offs to islands en route.

Sail Capricornia CRUISE
(☎0402 102 373; www.sailcapricornia.com.au; full-day cruises incl lunch adult/child $115/75) Sail Capricornia offers snorkelling cruises on board the *Grace* catamaran, as well as sunset ($55) and three-day ($499) cruises.

Sleeping

There are beaches, caravan parks, motels and holiday units along the 19km coastline running south from Yeppoon to Emu Park.

A fairly complete listing of local accommodation can be found at www.yeppooninfo.com.au.

★Coral Inn Yeppoon HOSTEL $
(☎07-4939 2925; www.flashpackers.net.au; 14 Maple St; dm $29, d from $90;) Extremely friendly and helpful owners, reef-bright colours and vibrant communal spaces make Coral Inn a difficult place to leave. All rooms have en suites and are quite luxurious for the price. There's a great communal kitchen, a mini 'beach' area with hammocks and an inviting pool. There's only one six-bed dorm room. Note that there's absolutely no smoking here.

★Emu's Beach Resort & Backpackers HOSTEL $
(☎07-4939 6111; www.emusbeachresort.com; 92 Pattison St, Emu Park; dm $25-28, d/tr/q $80/95/105;) Across the road from Emu Beach, 19km south of Yeppoon, the central pool and barbecue at this great-value, friendly place are a major draw. Dorms (no bunks!) are self-contained and spacious.

Beachside Caravan Park CARAVAN PARK $
(☎07-4939 3738; Farnborough Rd; unpowered sites $28, powered sites $32-36) This basic, neat little camping ground north of the town centre commands a wonderful, totally beachfront location. It has good amenities and grassed sites with some shade, but no cabins or on-site vans. Rates are for two people.

Surfside Motel MOTEL $$
(☎07-4939 1272; 30 Anzac Pde; r from $129;) Across the road from the beach and close to town, this 1950s strip of lime-green motel units epitomises summer holidays at the beach. And it's terrific value – the rooms are spacious and unusually well equipped, complete with toaster, hair dryer and free wi-fi. Prices go down for three or more nights.

Eating

Flour CAFE $
(☎07-4925 0725; 9 Normanby St; pastries from $3.50, breakfast $9; ⊙8am-3pm Mon-Fri, to 2pm Sat) Adorable small-town cafe with big-city breakfasts and melt-in-the-mouth cakes. Loads of gluten-free options, and without a doubt the best coffee for miles.

Megalomania FUSION $$
(☎07-4939 2333; Arthur St; mains $22-36; ⊙noon-3pm & 5.30-9pm Tue-Sat, noon-3pm Sun) An urban-island feel permeates Yeppoon's best restaurant, which serves up Oz-Asian fusion cuisine with interesting takes on local seafood. Loll beneath the fig tree, or clink silverware in the indoor woodsy surrounds.

Information

Capricorn Coast Information Centre (☎1800 675 785; www.capricorncoast.com.au; Ross Creek Roundabout; ⊙9am-5pm) Has plenty of information on the Capricorn Coast and Great Keppel Island, and can book accommodation and tours.

Getting There & Away

Yeppoon is 43km northeast of Rockhampton. **Young's Bus Service** (☎07-4922 3813; www.youngsbusservice.com.au) runs frequent buses from Rockhampton ($6.70 one way) to Yeppoon and down to the Keppel Bay Marina.

Some ferry operators will transport you between your accommodation and Keppel Bay Marina. If you're driving, there's a free daytime car park at the marina. For longer, secure undercover parking, the **Great Keppel Island Security Car Park** (☎07-4933 6670; 422 Scenic Hwy; per day from $15) is on the Scenic Hwy south of Yeppoon, by the turn-off to the marina.

Great Keppel Island

Great Keppel Island is a ruggedly perfect island with rocky headlands, forested hills and a wide, dreamy fringe of powdery white sand lapped by clear azure waters. Numerous 'castaway' beaches ring the 14-sq-km island, while natural bushland covers 90% of the interior.

For now, there's just a string of huts and accommodation that sits behind the trees lining the main beach, and the island, only 13km from the mainland, is one of the best destinations near the Great Barrier Reef for serenity-seeking backpackers. But huge development is coming with approved plans for a 250-room hotel, some 700 villas, a ferry terminal and an 18-hole golf course, among many other things, so the calm will not last much longer.

The Rainbow Hut Shop, Great Keppel Island Hideaway and Great Keppel Island Holiday Village have a few essentials, but if you want to cook, bring your own supplies.

Sights

The beaches of Great Keppel rate among Queensland's best. There are several bushwalking tracks from **Fisherman's Beach** (the main beach); the longest and perhaps most difficult leads to the 2.5m 'lighthouse' near Bald Rock Point on the far side of the island (three hours return). A steep 45-minute walk via walking track, or 25-minutes south across the rocky headland, brings you to **Monkey Beach**, where there's very good snorkelling. A walking trail from the southern end of the airfield takes you to **Long Beach**, perhaps the best of the island's beaches.

Activities

Watersports Hut WATER SPORTS
(07-4925 0624; Putney Beach; Sat, Sun & school holidays) The Watersports Hut on the main beach hires out snorkelling equipment, kayaks and catamarans, and runs tube rides.

Sleeping

★ **Svendsen's Beach** CABIN **$$**
(07-4938 3717; www.svendsensbeach.com; d $105) This secluded boutique retreat has two luxury tent-bungalows on elevated timber decks, plus a colourful studio ($130) and house (from $200; sleeps up to four people), all on lovely Svendsen's Beach. It's an eco-friendly operation, run on solar and wind power; there's even a bush-bucket shower. It's the perfect place for snorkelling, bushwalking and romantic getaways. Minimum charge per stay is $315.

Transfers from the ferry drop-off on Fisherman's Beach are included in the tariff. Cash only.

Great Keppel Island Hideaway RESORT **$$**
(07-4939 2050; www.greatkeppelislandhideaway.com.au; tent cabins $60-100, r $100-160, cabins $160-200) Located at a sublime bend of Fisherman's Beach, this sprawling place is a fun and friendly work in progress. The beachfront **restaurant** (mains $12-25) and bar are in full swing with a good menu and an even better view. Lodging is scheduled for upgrading (everything was a bit scruffy when we passed) and there will hopefully be camp sites available in future too.

Look for great deal packages on the website.

Great Keppel Island Holiday Village HOSTEL, CABIN **$$**
(07-4939 8655; www.gkiholidayvillage.com.au; dm $35, s & d tents $90, cabins $150) The village offers various types of good budget accommodation (dorms, cabins, decked tents), as well as entire houses (from $230). It's a friendly, relaxed place with shared bathrooms, a decent communal kitchen and a barbecue area. Snorkelling gear is free and it runs motorised canoe trips to top snorkelling spots.

Getting There & Away

Freedom Fast Cats (07-4933 6888; www.freedomfastcats.com; return adult/child/family $55/35/160) Makes the trip from the Keppel Bay Marina in Rosslyn Bay (7km south of Yeppoon) to and from Great Keppel Island daily (check the website for exact times). The company also operates a few day packages that add on snorkelling trips, glass-bottom boat rides and/or meals from $78.

Capricorn Hinterland

The Central Highlands, west of Rockhampton, are home to two excellent national parks. Blackdown Tableland National Park is a brooding, powerful place, while visitors to Carnarvon National Park will be gobsmacked by the spectacular gorge.

At Emerald, 270km inland, try fossicking for gems in the heat and rubble – you'll be surrounded by the good people and vibe of the outback. Try to stick to the cooler months between April and November.

Blackdown Tableland National Park

Surprising, spectacular Blackdown Tableland is a 600m sandstone plateau that rises suddenly out of the flat plains of central Queensland. It's a bushwalker's heaven here, with unique wildlife and plant species, and a

WORTH A TRIP

BYFIELD

The staggeringly beautiful Byfield National Park is a diverse playground of mammoth sand dunes, thick semitropical rainforest, wetlands and rocky pinnacles. It's superb Sunday-arvo driving terrain, with enough hiking paths and isolated beaches to warrant a longer stay. There are five **camping grounds** (☎13 74 68; www.nprsr.qld.gov.au; per person/family $5.85/21.80) to choose from (prebook). Nine Mile Beach and Five Rocks are on the beach and you'll need a 4WD to access them. When conditions are right, there's decent surf at Nine Mile.

Nob Creek Pottery (☎07-4935 1161; www.nobcreekpottery.com.au; 216 Arnolds Rd; ⏲10am-4pm) FREE is a working pottery and gallery showcasing hand-blown glass, woodwork and jewellery; the handmade ceramics are outstanding.

Signposted just north of Byfield, **Ferns Hideaway** (☎07-4935 1235; www.fernshide-away.com; 67 Cahills Rd; unpowered site per person $15, cabins $150;) is a secluded bush oasis with cabins, a camping ground, canoeing and nature walks. Day trippers can visit the **restaurant** (☎07-4935 1235; www.fernshideaway.com; 67 Cahills Rd; mains $20-38; ⏲lunch Fri & Sun, lunch & dinner Sat) on weekends (it's popular with locals) and will find hearty, heart-warming meals, live music and general good times.

Byfield General Store (☎07-4935 1190; Byfield Rd; ⏲8am-6pm Wed-Mon) has fuel, surprisingly eclectic groceries and a simple courtyard cafe serving pies, sandwiches and highly recommended burgers and fresh juices.

The park is a 40km drive north from Yeppoon. North of Byfield, the Shoalwater Bay military training area borders the forest and park, and is strictly off limits.

strong Indigenous artistic and spiritual presence. The turn-off to Blackdown Tableland is 11km west of Dingo. The 23km gravel road, which begins at the base of the tableland, isn't suitable for caravans and can be unsafe in wet weather – the first 8km stretch is steep, winding and often slippery. At the top you'll come to the breathtaking **Horseshoe Lookout**, with picnic tables, barbecues and toilets. There's a walking trail to **Two Mile Creek** (1.8km) starting here.

Munall Camping Ground (☎13 74 68; www.qld.gov.au/camping; per person/family $5.45/21.80) is about 8km on from Horseshoe Lookout. It has pit toilets and fireplaces – you'll need water, firewood and/or a fuel stove. Reserve online. The not-to-be-missed **Goon Goon Dina circuit** is an easy 2.5km loop that takes you from the camping area to the Ghungalu cave painting site. Those looking for more exercise can drive a few kilometres past the camping grounds to the **Gudda Gumoo** trailhead; from here 240 stairs and 2km of steep slopes lead to the base of a **waterfall** in a deep gorge of green ferns.

Gem Fields

West of **Emerald** (named after Emerald Downs, emeralds are not actually found here) sit 640 sq km of gem fields. The fields draw heart-strong prospectors who eke out a living until a jackpot (or sunstroke) arrives. Fossickers descend in winter – in the hot summers the towns are nearly deserted. Sapphires are the main haul, but zircons are also found and, very rarely, rubies. Sixteen kilometres on from Emerald are Sapphire and then Rubyvale, the two main towns on the fields.

Sights

To go fossicking you need a licence; they can be found at a few places in the area – the **Central Highlands Visitors Centre** (www.centralhighlands.co.au; 3 Clermont St, Emerald; ⏲10am-4.30pm) in Emerald has a list – or online (www.dnrm.qld.gov.au; adult/family $7.25/10.45). If you just wish to dabble, you can buy a bucket of 'wash' (mine dirt in water) from one of the fossicking parks to hand-sieve and wash.

Miners Heritage Walk-in Mine MINE
(☎07-4985 4444; Heritage Rd, Rubyvale; adult/child $20/10; ⏲9am-5pm) Just beyond Rubyvale is this walk-in mine. Informative 30-minute underground tours, in which you descend into a maze of tunnels 18m beneath the surface, are available here throughout the day. Tours usually start at 15 minutes past the hour.

Sleeping & Eating

There are several caravan-camping parks at Anakie, Rubyvale and Sapphire.

Sapphire Caravan Park CAMPGROUND $
(07-4985 4281; www.sapphirecaravanpark.com.au; 57 Sunrise Rd, Sapphire; unpowered/powered sites $25/29, cottages $115) The superclean and friendly Sapphire Caravan Park, set on a hilly 1.6 hectares with sites and cabins tucked into the eucalyptus forest, is great for fossickers.

Pat's Gems HOTEL $
(07-4985 4544; 1056 Rubyvale Rd, Sapphire; cabins $85;) Pat's Gems has four clean cabins, which fill quickly with happy regulars and families. There's a camp barbecue, a kitchen area and an **on-site cafe** (8.30am-5pm).

Rubyvale Gem Gallery HOTEL $$
(www.rubyvalegemgallery.com; 3 Main St, Rubyvale; d from $125;) Huge, modern suites include living room, equipped kitchen and washer and drier. There's also a shop with the area's finest display of local gems, and a cafe serving urban-worthy espresso and light meals.

Carnarvon National Park

Carnarvon Gorge is a dramatic rendition of Australian natural beauty. Escaped convicts often took refuge here among ancient rock paintings. The area was made a national park in 1932 after defeated farmers forfeited their pastoral lease.

The 30km-long, 200m-high gorge was carved out over millions of years by Carnarvon Creek and its tributaries twisting through soft sedimentary rock. What was left behind is a lush, other-worldly oasis, where life flourishes, shielded from the stark terrain. You'll find giant cycads, king ferns, river oaks, flooded gums, cabbage palms, deep pools, and platypuses in the creek.

For most people, Carnarvon Gorge *is* the Carnarvon National Park, because the other sections – including Mt Moffatt (where Indigenous groups lived some 19,000 years ago), Ka Ka Mundi and Salvator Rosa – have long been difficult to access.

Coming from Rolleston the road is bitumen for 75km and unsealed for 20km. From Roma via Injune and Wyseby homestead, the road is good bitumen for about 215km, then unsealed and fairly rough for the last 30km. After heavy rain, both these roads can become impassable.

The entrance road leads to an **information centre** (07-4984 4505; 8-10am & 3-5pm) and scenic picnic ground. Limited camping is available by the entrance during school holidays. The main walking track also starts here, following Carnarvon Creek through the gorge, with detours to various points of interest. These include the **Moss Garden** (3.6km from the picnic area), **Ward's Canyon** (4.8km), the **Art Gallery** (5.6km) and **Cathedral Cave** (9.3km). Allow *at least* a whole day for a visit. Basic groceries and ice are available at Takarakka Bush Resort. Petrol is not available anywhere in the gorge – fill up at Rolleston or Injune.

You cannot drive from Carnarvon Gorge to other sections of the park, although you can reach beautiful Mt Moffatt via an unsealed road from Injune (4WD necessary).

Sunrover Expeditions (1800 353 717; www.sunrover.com.au; per person incl all meals $940) runs a five-day camping safari into Carnarvon Gorge between August and October.

Sleeping

For accommodation, book ahead before entering the park.

Big Bend Camping Ground CAMPGROUND $
(13 74 68; www.qld.gov.au/camping; sites per person/family $5.85/21.80) An isolated camping ground a 10km walk up the gorge.

Mt Moffatt Camping Ground CAMPGROUND $
(13 74 68; www.qld.gov.au/camping; sites per person/family $5.85/21.80) Campers here need to be self-sufficient and have a 4WD.

Takarakka Bush Resort CAMPGROUND $$
(07-4984 4535; www.takarakka.com.au; Wyseby Rd; unpowered/powered sites from $38/45, cabins $195-228) The recently refurbished Takarakka Bush Resort is very popular with families and bush whackers. Reception sells basic groceries, maps, booze, ice and fresh linen ($10). The resort is 5km from the entry to the gorge.

Carnarvon Gorge Wilderness Lodge LODGE $$$
(1800 644 150; www.carnarvon-gorge.com; Wyseby Rd; d from $220; closed Nov-Feb;) Outback chic is on offer at this attractive lodge, set deep in the bush. Excellent guided tours are available, plus a full-board package (from $155 to $300 per person).

Getting There & Away

There are no bus services to Carnarvon, so the best way to get here is to hire a car or take an overnight tour from the coast.

Whitsunday Coast

Includes ➡

Best Places to Eat

➡ Mr Bones (p376)

➡ Spice n Flavour (p371)

➡ Fish D'vine (p376)

➡ Jochheims Pies (p382)

➡ Bommie Restaurant (p381)

Best Places to Stay

➡ Qualia (p380)

➡ Whitehaven Campgrounds (p381)

➡ Platypus Bushcamp (p374)

➡ Kipara (p375)

➡ Stoney Creek Farmstay (p370)

Why Go?

Speckling the calm waters of the Coral Sea, the superlative Whitsunday Islands are one of Australia's best-known natural attractions. Opal-jade waters and pure-white beaches fringe the forested isles; around them, tropical fish swarm through the world's largest coral garden in the Great Barrier Reef Marine Park. The best way to visit the islands is by sailing boat; however you visit, this is not a budget destination. The gateway to the islands, Airlie Beach, is a backpacker hub with a parade of tanned faces zinging between boats, beaches and nightclubs. This is as close to the islands as some budget travellers will get.

South of Airlie, Mackay is a typical coastal Queensland town with palm-lined streets framed by a jumble of art deco buildings. It's a handy base for trips to Eungella National Park – a lush hinterland oasis where platypuses cavort in the wild.

When to Go

Mackay

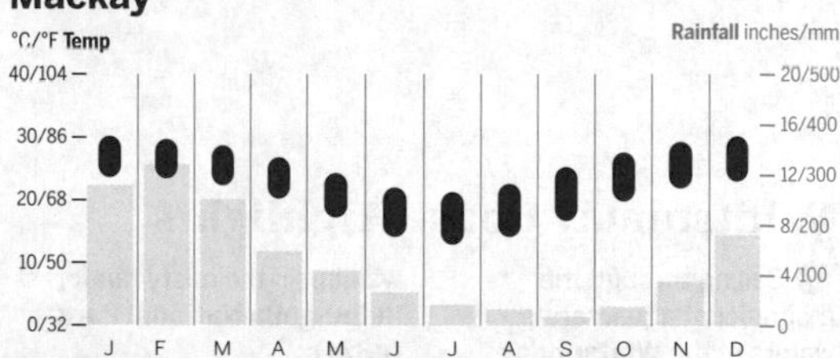

Jun–Oct The perfect time to enjoy sunny skies, calm days, mild weather and stinger-free seas.

Aug Sailing boats skim across the water and parties are held during Airlie Beach Race Week.

Sep & Oct Optimal conditions for kayaking around the islands.

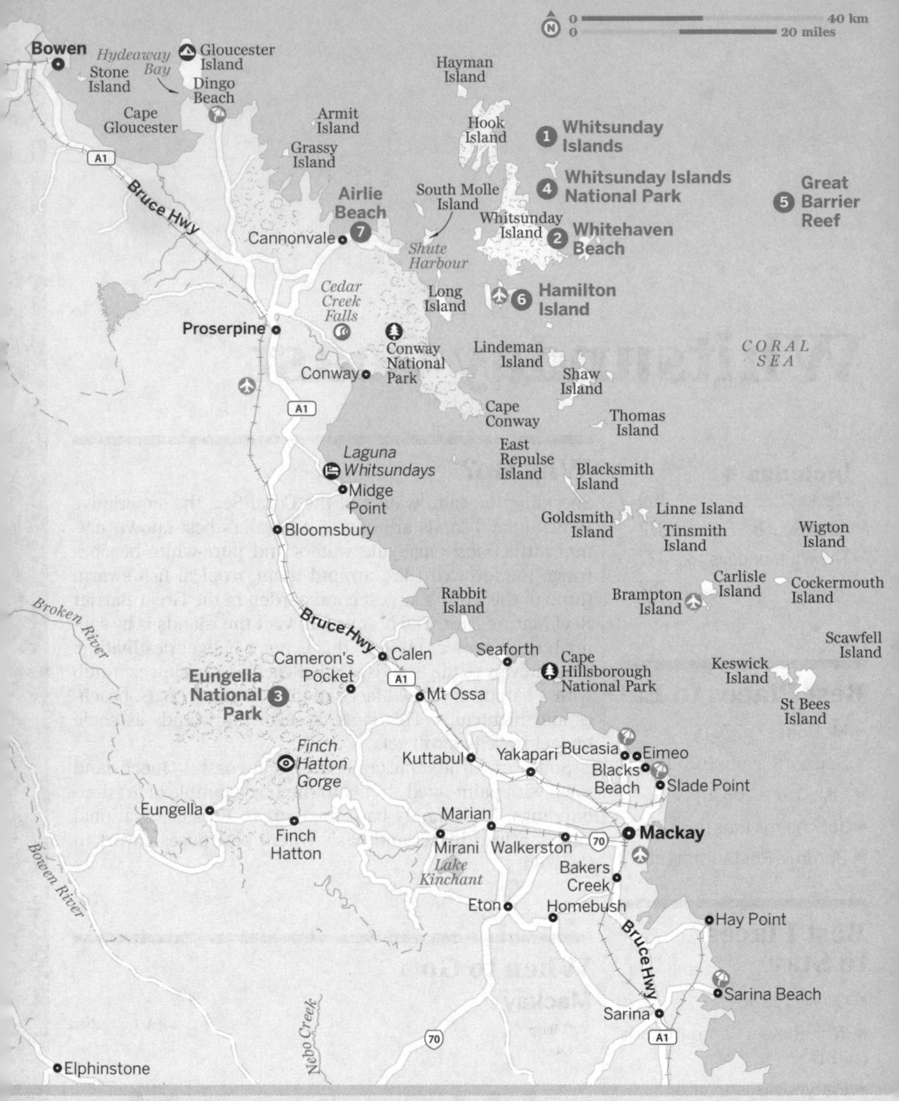

Whitsunday Coast Highlights

1. Sailing through the magnificent aquamarine waters of the **Whitsunday Islands** (p377).
2. Being dazzled by the bright-white silica sand at stunning **Whitehaven Beach** (p381).
3. Waiting patiently for a glimpse of a shy platypus and walking in the misty rainforest at **Eungella National Park** (p374).
4. Camping under the stars and making like an island castaway in the **Whitsunday Islands National Park** (p380).
5. Diving and snorkelling the fringing reefs of the outer **Great Barrier Reef** (p374).
6. Hiking the steep forest trails of **Hamilton Island** (p380).
7. Swilling beer and partying hard in fun-lovin' **Airlie Beach** (p372).

Getting There & Away

AIR

Mackay has a major domestic **airport** (www.mackayairport.com.au). **Jetstar** (13 15 38; www.jetstar.com.au), **Qantas** (13 13 13; www.qantas.com.au) and **Virgin** (13 67 89; www.virginaustralia.com) have regular flights to/from the major centres. **Tiger Airways** (02-8073 3421; www.tigerairways.com.au) flies to Mackay from Melbourne and Sydney.

Jetstar and Virgin have frequent flights to Hamilton Island, from where there are boat/air transfers to the other islands. They also fly into the Whitsunday Coast Airport on the mainland; from there you can take a charter flight to the islands or a bus to Airlie Beach or nearby Shute Harbour.

BOAT

Airlie Beach and Shute Harbour are the launching pads for boat trips to the Whitsundays.

BUS

Greyhound (1300 473 946; www.greyhound.com.au) and **Premier** (13 34 10; www.premierms.com.au) have coach services along the Bruce Hwy (A1) with stops at the major towns. They detour off the highway from Proserpine to Airlie Beach.

TRAIN

Queensland Rail (www.queenslandrailtravel.com.au) has services between Brisbane and Townsville/Cairns passing through the region.

Mackay

POP 85,399

Attractive tropical streets, art deco buildings, winding mangroves and welcoming populace aside, Mackay doesn't quite make the tourist hit list. Instead, this big country coastal town caters more to the surrounding agricultural and mining industries – but it's a refreshing stop if you've been to one too many resort towns. Although the redeveloped marina does entice with al fresco restaurants and outdoor cafes along its picturesque promenade, Mackay is more a convenient base for excursions out of town. It's only a 1½-hour drive to Airlie Beach and boats to the Whitsundays, and a scenic jaunt past the sugar-cane fields to Eungella National Park.

Sights

Mackay's impressive **art deco architecture** owes much to a devastating cyclone in 1918, which flattened many of the town's buildings. Enthusiasts should pick up a copy of *Art Deco in Mackay* from the Mackay visitor centre.

There are good views over the harbour from **Rotary Lookout** in North Mackay and over the beach at **Lampert's Lookout**.

Artspace Mackay GALLERY
(07-4961 9722; www.artspacemackay.com.au; Gordon St; 10am-5pm Tue-Sun) FREE Mackay's small regional art gallery showcases works from local and visiting artists. Chew over the masterpieces at on-site noshery **Foodspace** (www.artspacemackay.com.au; mains $16-26; 9am-3pm Tue-Sun).

Mackay Regional Botanical Gardens GARDENS
(Lagoon St) On 33 hectares, 3km south of the city centre, these gardens are a must-see for flora fans. Home to five themed gardens and the Lagoon cafe-restaurant (open from 9am to 4pm Wednesday to Sunday).

Bluewater Lagoon LAGOON
(9am-5.45pm;) FREE Mackay's pleasant artificial lagoon near Caneland Shopping Centre has water fountains, water slides, grassed picnic areas, free wi-fi and a cafe.

Mackay Marina HARBOUR
(Mackay Harbour) The lively marina is a pleasant place to wine and dine with a waterfront view, or to simply picnic in the park and stroll along the breakwater. Good fishing, too.

Beaches

Mackay has plenty of beaches, although not all are ideal for swimming.

The best option near town is **Harbour Beach**, 6km north of the centre and just south of the Mackay Marina. The beach here is patrolled and there's a foreshore reserve with picnic tables and barbecues.

Even better are the beaches about 16km north of Mackay. At long, flat, residence-encroached **Blacks Beach**, the beach extends for 6km. **Bucasia** is the most undeveloped and arguably the prettiest of this area's beaches. For easy access, stay at Blacks Beach Holiday Park (p371) or Bucasia Beachfront Caravan Resort (p371).

Tours

Farleigh Sugar Mill TOUR
(07-4959 8360; 2hr tours adult/child $25/13; 9.30am & 1pm May-Dec) In the cane-crushing season, you can see how sugar cane is

Mackay

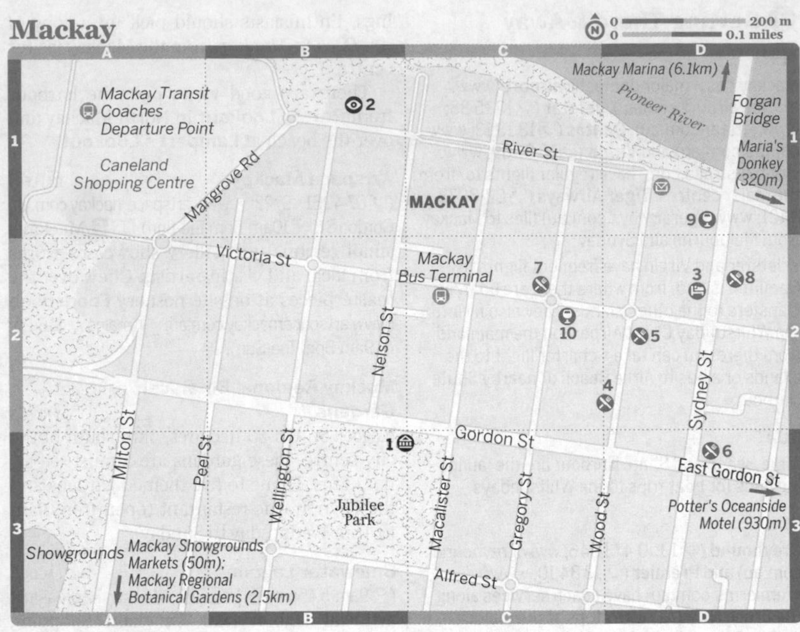

Mackay

Sights
1 Artspace Mackay ... B3
2 Bluewater Lagoon ... B1

Sleeping
3 Gecko's Rest ... D2

Eating
4 Burp Eat Drink ... D2
Foodspace ... (see 1)
5 Kevin's Place ... D2
6 Oscar's on Sydney ... D3
7 Spice n Flavour ... C2
8 Woodsman's Axe Coffee ... D2

Drinking & Nightlife
9 Ambassador Hotel ... D1
10 Tryst ... C2

turned into sweet crystals. Dress appropriately for a working mill: long sleeves, long pants, enclosed shoes. Morning/afternoon tea included.

Reeforest Adventure Tours CULTURAL TOUR
(☎1800 500 353; www.reeforest.com) Offers a wide range of junkets, including a platypus and rainforest eco-safari, two-day Eungella tours, and Paddock to Port tours for a fun look into the local sugar industry.

Heritage Walk WALKING TOUR
(☎07-4944 5888; ⏲9am Wed May-Sep) FREE Weekly wandering (1½ to two hours) that takes in the sights and secrets of ye olde Mackay. Leaves from the Old Town Hall, Sydney St.

Sleeping

There are plenty of motels strung along busy Nebo Rd, south of the centre. The budget options (from around $110 for a double) post their prices out front and tend to suffer from road noise.

★ **Stoney Creek Farmstay** FARM STAY $
(☎07-4954 1177; www.stoneycreekfarmstay.com; Peak Downs Hwy; dm/stables/cottages $25/130/175) This bush retreat (32km south of Mackay) is a down-and-dirty option in the best possible way. Stay in an endearingly ramshackle cottage, the rustic livery stable or the charismatic Dead Horse Hostel, and forget all about the mod-cons: this is dead-set bush livin'. Three-hour horse rides cost

$105 per person and lots of other activities are available.

Blacks Beach Holiday Park CARAVAN PARK $
(☎07-4954 9334; www.mackayblacksbeachholidaypark.com.au; 16 Bourke St, Blacks Beach; unpowered/powered sites $30/35, villas $140-180; P❄≋) This excellent park has tent sites overlooking a gloriously long stretch of Blacks Beach, about 16km north of Mackay.

Bucasia Beachfront Caravan Resort CARAVAN PARK $
(☎07-4954 6375; www.bucasiabeach.com.au; 2 The Esplanade; powered sites $30-45; ≋🐾) Recently upgraded, Bucasia resort has a selection of sites, some with absolute beachfront views. It's roughly 16km north of Mackay.

Mackay Marine Tourist Park CARAVAN PARK $
(☎07-4955 1496; www.mmtp.com.au; 379 Harbour Rd; unpowered/powered sites $32/35, villas $97-150; ❄@📶≋🐾) A step up from the usual caravan parks: all cabins and villas come with private patios and widescreen TVs, and you've gotta love anywhere with a giant jumping pillow.

Gecko's Rest HOSTEL $
(☎07-4944 1230; www.geckosrest.com.au; 34 Sydney St; dm/s/d $30/45/55; ❄@📶) Gecko's almost bursts at the seams with adventurous travellers and mine workers. It ain't the Ritz, but it's the only hostel in town and has a central location.

Potter's Oceanside Motel MOTEL $$
(☎07-5689 0388; www.pottersoceansidemotel.com.au; 2c East Gordon St; d $149-169, f $269; ❄📶≋) Opened in 2014, this well-run, friendly spot boasts big, modern rooms (some wheelchair accessible) a short stroll from Town Beach. Perfect for a dose of clean comfort if you've been taking the rough road too long.

Eating

Maria's Donkey TAPAS $
(☎07-4957 6055; 8 River St; tapas $8-15; ⏲noon-10pm Wed & Thu, to midnight Fri-Sun) Quirky, energetic riverfront joint dishing up tapas, jugs of sangria, occasional live music and general good times. Service is erratic, but somehow, that's part of the charm.

> **SUMMER STING: WHERE TO SWIM?**
>
> The presence of marine stingers means swimming in the sea isn't advisable between October and May unless you wear a stinger suit. In Airlie Beach, the gorgeous lagoon (p373) on the foreshore provides year-round safe swimming.

Woodsman's Axe Coffee CAFE $
(41 Sydney St; coffee from $4.30; ⏲6am-2pm Mon-Fri, 7am-2pm Sat & Sun) The best coffee in town paired with light eats, from wraps to quiches and muffins.

Oscar's on Sydney FUSION $
(☎07-4944 0173; cnr Sydney & Gordon Sts; mains $10-23; ⏲7am-5pm Mon-Fri, to 4pm Sat, 8am-4pm Sun) The delicious *poffertjes* (Dutch pancakes with traditional toppings) are still going strong at this very popular corner cafe, but don't be afraid to give the other dishes a go. Top spot for breakfast.

★ **Spice n Flavour** INDIAN $$
(☎07-4999 9639; 162 Victoria St; mains $15-25, banquets per person from $35; ⏲11.30am-2.30pm Mon-Fri, 5.30pm-late daily) Chilli lovers disappointed by what passes for 'hot' in other Indian restaurants will get their fill of mouth-burning here (by request). All the favourites plus some more exotic tastes are on the menu, and staff offer drink-pairing advice for the unsure. Come what may, you must try the mango beer.

Kevin's Place ASIAN $$
(☎07-4953 5835; 79 Victoria St; mains $16-27; ⏲11.30am-2pm & 5.30-8pm Mon-Fri, 5.30-8pm Sat) Sizzling, spicy Singaporean dishes and efficient, revved-up staff combine with outdoor seating for a wonderfully tropical experience. Lunch specials are a bargain from $12.

Burp Eat Drink MODERN AUSTRALIAN $$$
(☎07-4951 3546; www.burp.net.au; 86 Wood St; mains from $33; ⏲11.30am-3pm & 6pm-late Tue-Fri, 6pm-late Sat) A swish Melbourne-style restaurant in the tropics, Burp has a small but tantalising menu. Sophisticated selections include pork belly with scallops, Kaffir-lime-crusted soft-shell crab, plus some serious steaks.

Drinking & Nightlife

Ambassador Hotel BAR
(☎07-4953 3233; www.ambassadorhotel.net.au; 2 Sydney St; ⏰5pm-late Thu, 4pm-late Fri-Sun) Art deco outside, wild 'n' crazy inside. Multilevel carousing, including Mackay's only rooftop bar.

Tryst CLUB
(99 Victoria St; ⏰10pm-4am Thu-Sat) Frenetic dance club hosting a mix of resident and guest-star DJs.

Shopping

Mackay Showgrounds Markets MARKET
(Milton St; ⏰from 7.30am Sat) A farmers market with great baked goods.

Troppo Market MARKET
(Mt Pleasant Shopping Centre carpark; ⏰from 7.30am 2nd Sun of the month) Has a bit of everything, including plenty of entertainment, food and drink.

Information

The airport, botanic gardens and visitor centre are about 3km south of the city centre. Mackay Harbour, 6km northeast of the centre, is dominated by a massive sugar terminal, while the adjacent marina has a smattering of waterfront restaurants.

Mackay visitor centre (☎1300 130 001; www.mackayregion.com; 320 Nebo Rd; ⏰9am-5pm; @📶) About 3km south of the centre. Internet access and wi-fi.

Getting There & Away

AIR

The airport is about 3km south of the centre of Mackay.

Jetstar (☎13 15 38; www.jetstar.com.au), **Qantas** (☎13 13 13; www.qantas.com.au) and **Virgin** (☎13 67 89; www.virginaustralia.com) have flights to/from Brisbane. **Tiger Airways** (☎02-8073 3421; www.tigerairways.com.au) has direct flights between Mackay and Melbourne/Sydney.

BUS

Buses stop at the **Mackay Bus Terminal** (cnr Victoria & Macalister Sts), where tickets can also be booked. **Greyhound** (☎1300 473 946; www.greyhound.com.au) travels up and down the coast. Sample one-way adult fares and journey times: Airlie Beach ($31, two hours), Townsville ($69, 6½hours), Cairns ($117, 13 hours) and Brisbane ($218, 17 hours).

Premier (☎13 34 10; www.premierms.com.au) is less expensive than Greyhound but has fewer services.

TRAIN

Queensland Rail (☎1800 872 467; www.queenslandrail.com.au) Connects Mackay with Brisbane, Cairns and cities between. The train station is at Paget, 5km south of the city centre.

Getting Around

Major car-rental firms have desks at the Mackay Airport: see www.mackayairport.com.au/travel/car-hire for listings.

Mackay Taxis (☎13 10 08)

Mackay Transit Coaches (☎07-4957 3330; www.mackaytransit.com.au) Has several services around the city, and connects the city with the harbour and northern beaches; pick up a timetable at the visitor centre or look online.

Ocean Breeze Transfers (www.ocean-breeze-transfers.com.au) Runs between the city and airport: book in advance.

Airlie Beach

POP 7868

Aside from being the jump-off point for the dreamy Whitsunday Islands, Airlie Beach is a backpacker's good-time town of the highest order, with cavernous bar-hostels lining the bright main drag and a lawn-surrounded swimming lagoon just beyond for sleeping it all off. But the 2014 opening of the new, slick Port of Airlie marina, hotel and restaurant complex is an unmissable sign that the village is going more upscale; there are now more options than ever to attract older, more sophisticated travellers wanting a little of the wild life before lifting anchor for the serenity of the sparkling seas and jungle-clad isles in the distance. Those looking to avoid the party scene all together will have no trouble finding quieter lodgings near town.

The Port of Airlie, from where the Cruise Whitsundays ferries depart and where many of the cruising yachts are moored, is about 750m east along a pleasant boardwalk. Many other vessels leave from Abel Point Marina (1km west) or Shute Harbour (about 12km east); most cruise companies run courtesy buses into town.

Airlie Beach

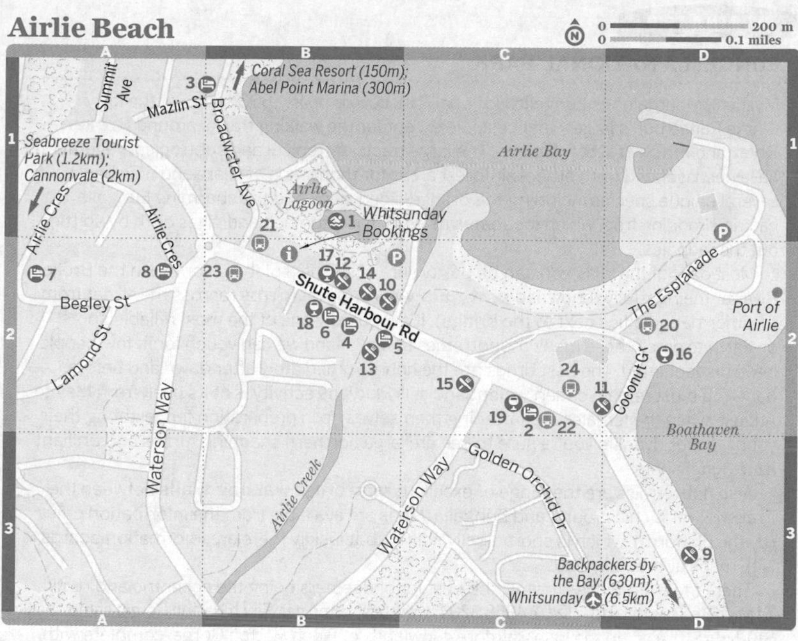

Airlie Beach

Activities, Courses & Tours
1 Lagoon B1

Sleeping
2 Airlie Beach YHA C2
3 Airlie Waterfront B&B B1
4 Beaches Backpackers B2
5 Magnums Backpackers C2
6 Nomads Backpackers B2
7 Sunlit Waters A2
8 Waterview A2

Eating
9 Denman Cellars Beer Cafe D3
10 Easy Cafe C2
11 Fish D'vine D2
12 Mr Bones B2
13 Village Cafe B2
14 Wisdom Health B2
15 Woolworths Supermarket C2

Drinking & Nightlife
16 Just Wine & Cheese D2
17 Mama Africa B2
18 Paddy's Shenanigans B2
19 Phoenix Bar C2

Transport
20 Long-Distance Bus Stop D2
21 Whitsunday Transit Bus Stop B2
22 Whitsunday Transit Bus Stop C2
23 Whitsunday Transit Bus Stop B2
24 Whitsunday Transit Bus Stop C2

Activities

There are seasonal operators in front of the Airlie Beach Hotel that hire out jet skis, catamarans, sailboards and paddle skis.

Lagoon SWIMMING
(Shute Harbour Rd) FREE Take a dip year-round in the stinger-croc-and-tropical-nasties-free lagoon in the centre of town.

Tandem Skydive Airlie Beach SKYDIVING
(☎07-4946 9115; www.skydiveairliebeach.com.au; from $199) Jump out of a plane from 6000, 8,000 or 14,000ft up.

Salty Dog Sea Kayaking KAYAKING
(☎07-4946 1388; www.saltydog.com.au; Shute Harbour; half-/full-day trips $80/130) Offers guided full-day tours and kayak rental ($50/80 per half-/full day), plus longer kayak/camping missions (the six-day challenge costs $1650).

WORTH A TRIP

EUNGELLA NATIONAL PARK

Mystical, mountainous Eungella National Park covers nearly 500 sq km of the lofty Clarke Range but is largely inaccessible except for the walking tracks around **Broken River** and **Finch Hatton Gorge**. The large tracts of tropical and subtropical vegetation have been isolated from other rainforest areas for thousands of years and now boast several unique species including the orange-sided skink and the charming Eungella gastric-brooding frog, which incubates its eggs in its stomach and gives birth by spitting out the tadpoles.

Most days of the year, you can be pretty sure of seeing a platypus or two in the Broken River at the rightfully renowned **platypus-viewing platforms** (across the street from the information office next to the bridge). It's reputedly one of the most reliable spots on earth to catch these meek monotremes at play – and we can vouch for it; few people leave disappointed. The best times are the hours immediately after dawn and before dark. You must remain patient, silent and still. Platypus activity is at its peak from May to August, when the females are fattening themselves up in preparation for gestating their young. Other river life you're sure to see are large northern snapping turtles and brilliant azure kingfishers.

Also not-to-miss are the range of excellent **rainforest walking trails** between the Broken River picnic ground and Eungella. Maps are available from the information office (by the platform), which is sporadically staffed, but luckily there are information boards with maps at the trail heads.

There are a few places to stay, the best for budgeteers being the eccentric and rustic **Platypus Bushcamp** (07-4958 3204; www.bushcamp.net; Finch Hatton Gorge; camp sites $10, huts $100), in the lush, rainforest lowlands of Finch Hatton Gorge, complete with its own platypus swimming hole. Those with a little more cash should head straight to the friendly and comfortable **Broken River Mountain Resort** (07-4958 4000; www.brokenrivermr.com.au; d $130-190;), right across from Broken River's platypus-viewing platform high up in the mountains. Find information on the handful of camping grounds at www.nprsr.qld.gov.au/parks/eungella/camping.html.

The park is 84km west of Mackay. There are no buses to Eungella or Finch Hatton, but Reeforest Adventure Tours (p370) runs day trips from Mackay and will drop off and pick up those who want to linger; however, tours don't run every day so your stay may wind up longer than intended.

It's a charming and healthy way to see the islands.

Diving

You'll notice a lack of dedicated dive shops in Airlie Beach and the Whitsundays. While the Great Barrier Reef may beckon, most dives in this area visit the fringing reefs around the Whitsundays (especially on their northern tips) because they are much easier to reach and often hold more abundant soft corals. Serious divers wanting to dive on the Great Barrier Reef proper will find many more options around Cairns, although this area around the Whitsundays does have some lovely sites if you're really hoping to blow some bubbles.

Costs for open-water courses with several ocean dives start at around $1000. **Whitsunday Diving Academy** (1300 348 464; www.whitsundaydivingacademy.com.au; 2579 Shute Harbour Rd, Jubilee Pocket) is a good place to start.

A number of **sailing cruises** include diving as an optional extra. Prices start from $85 for introductory or certified dives. Ferry operator Cruise Whitsundays (p377) offers dives (from $119) on day trips to its reef pontoon.

Most of the **island resorts** also have dive schools and free snorkelling gear.

Fishing

Grab a cheap hand-line and have a go at catching your own dinner. Popular spots in Airlie include the rock walls by the sailing club in Cannonvale and the fishing pontoon in Shute Harbour. Myriad tours (easily booked in Airlie Beach) cost around $120/210 for a half/full day.

Tours

Most day trips include activities such as snorkelling or boom-netting, with scuba diving as an optional extra. Most of the cruise operators run out of the Port of Airlie; those that run from Shute Harbour do coach pickups from Airlie Beach and Cannonvale. You can also take a public bus to Shute Harbour.

Day-trip bookings can generally be made at any Airlie Beach tour agent.

Cruise Whitsundays CRUISE
(☎07-4946 4662; www.cruisewhitsundays.com; Shingley Dr, Abel Point Marina; full-day cruises from $99) As well as operating a ferry to the Whitsunday Islands, Cruise Whitsundays offers trips to Hardy Reef, Whitehaven Beach and islands including Daydream and Long. Or grab a daily **Island Hopper pass** (adult/child $120/59) and make your own itinerary. It also operates a popular day trip aboard the *Camira* (p378).

Ecojet Safari TOUR
(☎07-4948 2653; www.ecojetsafari.com.au; per person $195) Explore the islands, mangroves and marine life of the northern Whitsundays on these three-hour, small-group jet-ski safaris (two people per jet ski).

Ocean Rafting BOAT TOUR
(☎07-4946 6848; www.oceanrafting.com.au; adult/child/family from $134/87/399) Visit the 'wild' side of the islands in a very fast, big yellow speedboat. Swim at Whitehaven Beach, regain your land legs with a guided national park walk, or snorkel the reef at Mantaray Bay and Border Island.

Big Fury BOAT TOUR
(☎07-4948 2201; adult/child/family $130/70/350) Speed out to Whitehaven Beach on an open-air sports boat, and follow up with lunch and snorkelling at a secluded reef nearby. Great value and bookable through Airlie Beach travel agencies.

Air Whitsunday SCENIC FLIGHTS
(☎07-4946 9111; www.airwhitsunday.com.au; Terminal 1, Whitsunday Airport) Offers a range of tours, including day trips to Whitehaven ($255) and scenic-flight-plus-snorkelling tours of the Great Barrier Reef ($375).

Whitsunday Crocodile Safari TOUR
(☎07-4948 3310; www.crocodilesafari.com.au; adult/child $120/60) Spy on wild crocs, explore secret estuaries and eat real bush tucker.

Festivals & Events

Airlie Beach Race Week SAILING
(www.airlieraceweek.com) Sailors from across the world descend on Airlie for the town's annual regatta, held in August.

Airlie Beach Music Festival MUSIC
(airliebeachfestivalofmusic.com.au) Started in 2012 and getting more popular by the year. Party to three days of live rock and folk music in November.

Sleeping

Airlie Beach is a backpacker haven, but with so many hostels, standards vary and bedbugs are a common problem.

Most of the resorts have package deals online and stand-by rates that are much cheaper than those advertised.

★**Kipara** RESORT $
(www.kipara.com.au; 2614 Shute Harbour Rd; r/cabins/villas from $65/100/105; ❄@📶🏊) Tucked away in lush, green environs, this budget resort makes it easy to forget you're only 2km from the frenzy of town. It's mega clean and outstanding value, with helpful staff, cooking facilities and regular wildlife visits – one of Airlie's best options. Rates go down if you stay two or more nights.

Nomads Backpackers HOSTEL $
(☎07-4999 6600; www.nomadsairliebeach.com; 354 Shute Harbour Rd; dm/d $25/88; ❄@📶🏊) Set on a 2.8-hectacre leafy lot with volleyball and a sparkling pool, Nomads feels a bit more 'resorty' than many of the other hostels in town. Accommodation is nothing special, though tent sites are nice and shady, and private rooms have TV, fridge and kitchenette.

Seabreeze Tourist Park CARAVAN PARK $
(☎07-4946 6379; www.theseabreezepark.com.au; 234 Shute Harbour Rd; unpowered/powered sites from $20/35, cabins/villas from $100/130; P❄@📶🏊🐾) Grassy and sprawling with fresh ocean views and a nice kicked-back feel. Camp sites are shady, while the new timber Bali villas offer an exoticism most caravan parks are decidedly lacking.

Beaches Backpackers HOSTEL $
(☎07-4946 6244; www.beaches.com.au; 356 Shute Harbour Rd; dm/d $22/85; ❄@📶🏊) You must at least enjoy a drink at the big open-air bar, even if you're not staying here. If you do choose to hang your hat, bring earplugs and your biggest party boots. Not one for the serenity set.

Backpackers by the Bay HOSTEL $
(☎07-4946 7267; www.backpackersbythebay.com; 12 Hermitage Dr; dm $26, d & tw $80;) A low-key alternative to the seething party-hostel cluster downtown, with tidy rooms, hammocks, a good pool and a distinct lack of skull-clanging tunes. It's about a 10-minute walk from Airlie's centre.

Magnums Backpackers HOSTEL $
(☎1800 624 634; www.magnums.com.au; 366 Shute Harbour Rd; camp sites/van sites $22/24, dm/d from $22/56;) A loud party bar, loads of alcohol and a bevy of pretty young things. Forget the tent sites close to the bar – you won't sleep unless you're comatose. Once you get past the hectic reception, you'll find simple dorms in a tropical garden setting.

Airlie Beach YHA HOSTEL $
(☎07-4946 6312; www.yha.com.au; 394 Shute Harbour Rd; dm $28.50, d $79;) Central and reasonably quiet with a sparkling pool and great kitchen facilities.

Waterview APARTMENT $$
(☎07-4948 1748; www.waterviewairliebeach.com.au; 42 Airlie Cres; studios/1-bedroom units from $140/155;) An excellent choice for location and comfort, this boutique accommodation overlooks the main street and has gorgeous views of the bay. The rooms are modern, airy and spacious, and have kitchenettes for self-caterers.

Coral Sea Resort RESORT $$
(☎1800 075 061; www.coralsearesort.com; 25 Ocean View Ave; d/2-bedroom apt from $175/330;) At the end of a low headland overlooking the water, just west of the town centre, Coral Sea Resort has one of the best positions around. Many rooms have stunning views.

Sunlit Waters APARTMENT $$
(☎07-4946 6352; www.sunlitwaters.com; 20 Airlie Cres; studios from $92, 1-bedroom apt $115;) These large studios have everything you could want, including a self-contained kitchenette and stunning views from the long balconies. They also go pretty easy on your wallet.

Airlie Waterfront B&B B&B $$$
(☎07-4946 7631; www.airliewaterfrontbnb.com.au; cnr Broadwater Ave & Mazlin St; 1/2-bedroom apt from $179/249;) Gorgeous views and immaculately presented from top to toe, this sumptuously furnished B&B oozes class and is a leisurely five-minute walk into town along the boardwalk. Some rooms have a spa.

Eating

There's a massive new **Woolworths Supermarket** (Shute Harbour Rd; 8am-9pm), conveniently located in the centre of town for self-caterers. The strip facing the port at the new Port of Airlie is a good hunting ground for sophisticated, upmarket dining options, while downtown Airlie Beach has a mishmash of everything from cheap take-away kebab shops to fancier restaurants with outdoor patios.

Wisdom Health CAFE $
(1b/275 Shute Harbour Dr; toasties from $4.95, juices from $6.45; 7.30am-3.30pm;) Mostly a takeaway place, this rightfully busy corner cafe does have a few indoor and outdoor tables. It serves healthy toasties, sandwiches (including lots of vegetarian options such as a tasty lentil burger), pizzas, and a huge array of fresh smoothies and juices.

Easy Cafe CAFE $
(Pavillion Arcade; mains $9.50-16; 7.30am-3pm Thu-Tue;) A hidden-away modern cafe-deli escape from Airlie's busy streets. Find the town's best salad selections, as well as lauded eggs Benedict on delicious fresh bread.

★**Mr Bones** PIZZA $$
(☎0416 011 615; Lagoon Plaza, 263 Shute Harbour Rd; shared plates $12-17, pizzas $15-23; 9am-9pm Tue-Sat) Mr Bones is the standard bearer in Airlie Beach for hip, affordable dining. It's rightfully gained a reputation for its perfect thin-based pizzas – try the prawn and harissa. The 'not pizzas' (appetisers including lip-licking blackened fish skewers with pineapple and mint salsa) are also spectacular.

Fish D'vine SEAFOOD $$
(☎07-4948 0088; 303 Shute Harbour Rd; mains $16-30; 5pm-late) Pirates were definitely onto something: this fish-and-rum bar is shiploads of fun, serving up all things nibbly from Neptune's realm and lashings and lashings of rum (over 200 kinds of the stuff). Yo-ho-ho!

Denman Cellars Beer Cafe TAPAS $$
(☎07-4948 1333; Shop 15, 33 Port Dr; tapas $10, mains $18-36; 11am-10pm Mon-Fri, 8am-11pm Sat & Sun) Solid Mod Oz food – including lamb meatballs, very small shared seafood tapas, and a stock breakfast menu – pales in comparison to the beer menu (over 700 brews!).

Village Cafe CAFE $$
(☎07-4946 5745; 366 Shute Harbour Rd; mains $20-30; 7.30am-9pm) Village Cafe is always

busy with hungover backpackers and those chasing good coffee. The breakfasts at this popular place are just the tonic to get the day started. Order a 'hot rock' and cook your protein of choice to perfection on a sizzling volcanic slab that's been heated for 12 hours.

Drinking & Nightlife

It's said that Airlie Beach is a drinking town with a sailing problem. The bars at Magnums and Beaches, the two big backpackers in the centre of town, are always crowded, and are popular places to kick off a ribald evening.

Phoenix Bar BAR
(390 Shute Harbour Rd; 7pm-3am) Dance and DJ hotspot with drink specials and free pizzas nightly (from 6pm to 8pm).

Paddy's Shenanigans IRISH PUB
(352 Shute Harbour Rd; 5pm-3am) As one would expect.

Just Wine & Cheese WINE BAR
(Shop 8, 33 Port Dr; wines by the glass $7-18; 3-10pm) Showing that Airlie Beach is going more upscale, this place serves fine examples of what it promises, with a view of the Port of Airlie marina.

Mama Africa CLUB
(263 Shute Harbour Rd; 10pm-5am) Just a stumble across the road from the main party bars, this African-style safari nightclub throbs with a beat that both hunter and prey find hard to resist.

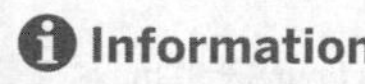

Information

The main drag is stacked with privately run tour agencies; we recommend **Whitsunday Bookings** (07-4948 2201; www.whitsundaybooking.com.au; 346 Shute Harbour Rd). Check out its noticeboards for stand-by rates on sailing tours and resort accommodation. Internet and wi-fi access is widely available.

Department of National Parks, Sport & Racing (NPRSR; 13 74 68; www.nprsr.qld.gov.au; cnr Shute Harbour & Mandalay Rds; 9am-4.30pm Mon-Fri) It's best to call or go online for camping permits and info.

Getting There & Away

AIR

The closest major airports are Whitsunday Coast (Proserpine) and Hamilton Island.

Whitsunday Airport (07-4946 9180) A small airfield 6km east of Airlie Beach, midway between Airlie Beach and Shute Harbour.

BOAT

Transfers between the **Port of Airlie** (www.portofairlie.com.au) and Hamilton, Daydream and Long Islands are provided by **Cruise Whitsundays** (07-4946 4662; www.cruisewhitsundays.com).

BUS

Greyhound (1300 473 946; www.greyhound.com.au) and **Premier Motor Service** (13 34 10; www.premierms.com.au) buses detour off the Bruce Hwy to Airlie Beach. There are buses between Airlie Beach and all the major centres along the coast, including Brisbane ($245, 19 hours), Mackay ($31, two hours), Townsville ($47, four hours) and Cairns ($85, nine hours).

Long-distance buses stop on the Esplanade, between the sailing club and the Airlie Beach Hotel.

Whitsunday Transit (07-4946 1800; www.whitsundaytransit.com.au) connects Proserpine (Whitsunday Airport), Cannonvale, Abel Point, Airlie Beach and Shute Harbour.

Getting Around

Airlie Beach is small enough to cover by foot. Most cruise boats have courtesy buses that will pick you up from wherever you're staying and take you to either Shute Harbour or Abel Point Marina. To book a taxi, call **Whitsunday Taxis** (13 10 08).

Most of the major car-rental agencies are represented here: offices line Shute Harbour Rd.

The Whitsundays

Spread majestically through the Coral Sea, the sandy fringes of these 74 islands disappear into beautiful shades of crystal, aqua, blue and indigo ocean. Sheltered by the Great Barrier Reef, there are no crashing waves or deadly undertows, and the waters are particularly perfect for sailing.

Of the numerous stunning beaches and secluded bays, Whitehaven Beach stands out for its pure white silica sand. It is undoubtedly the finest beach in the Whitsundays, and many claim, in the world. It's great for a day trip if your budget only allows for one splurge to the islands.

Airlie Beach, on the mainland, is the coastal hub and major gateway to the islands. Only seven of the islands have tourist resorts: choose from the basic accommodation at Hook Island to the exclusive luxury of Hayman Island. Most of the Whitsunday Islands are uninhabited, and several offer back-to-nature beach camping and bushwalking.

SAILING THE WHITSUNDAYS

The Whitsundays are *the* place to skim across fantasy-blue waters on a tropical breeze. If you're flexible with dates, last-minute stand-by rates can considerably reduce the price and you'll also have a better idea of weather conditions.

Most vessels offer snorkelling on the fringing reefs, where the colourful soft corals are often more abundant than on the outer reef. Diving and other activities nearly always cost extra. Once you've decided, book at one of the many booking agencies in Airlie Beach.

Day Trips

Other than the superfast *Camira*, sailing boats aren't able to make it all the way to destinations such as Whitehaven Beach on a day trip. Instead they usually go to the lovely Langford Reef and Hayman Island; check before booking.

Camira (www.cruisewhitsundays.com; day trips $195) One of the world's fastest commercial sailing catamarans is now a lilac-coloured Whitsunday icon. This good-value day trip includes Whitehaven Beach, snorkelling, morning and afternoon tea, a barbecue lunch and all refreshments (including wine and beer).

Derwent Hunter (www.tallshipadventures.com.au; day trips $179) A deservedly popular sailing safari on a beautiful timber gaff-rigged schooner. A good option for couples and those more keen on wildlife than the wild life.

SV Domino (www.aussieyachting.com; day trips $180) Takes a maximum of eight guests to Bali Hai Island, a little-visited 'secret' of the Whitsundays. Includes lunch and a good two-hour snorkel. The boat is also available for custom, private charters.

Illusions (☎0455 142 021; www.illusion.net.au; day tours $125) A 12m catamaran that offers the least expensive, yet consistently good, sailing tours to the islands.

Multiday Trips

Most overnight sailing packages are for three days and two nights, or two days and two nights.

Solway Lass (www.solwaylass.com; 3-day/3-night trips from $579) You get a full three days on this 28m tall ship – the only authentic tall ship in Airlie Beach. Popular with backpackers.

Prima Sailing (www.primasailing.com.au; 2-day/2-night tours from $390) Fun tours with a 12-person maximum. Ideal for couples chasing style and substance.

Atlantic Clipper (www.atlanticclipper.com.au; 2-day/2-night trips from $460) Young, beautiful and boozy crowd…and there's no escaping the antics. Snorkelling (or recovering) on Langford Island is a highlight.

Explore Whitsundays (www.explorewhitsundays.com; 2-day/1-night trips from $359) Inexpensive but well-run trips with a number of different options and ambiences offered on a few different vessels. Generally geared towards the backpacker set.

Bareboat Charters

Rent a boat without skipper, crew or provisions. You don't need formal qualifications, but you (or one of your party) have to prove that you can competently operate a vessel. Expect to pay between $500 to $1000 a day in high season (September to January) for a yacht sleeping four to six people, plus a booking deposit and a security bond (refunded when the boat is returned undamaged). Most companies have a minimum hire period of five days.

There are a number of bareboat charter companies around Airlie Beach:

Charter Yachts Australia (☎1800 639 520; www.cya.com.au; Abel Point Marina)

Cumberland Charter Yachts (☎1800 075 101; www.ccy.com.au; Abel Point Marina)

Queensland Yacht Charters (☎1800 075 013; www.yachtcharters.com.au; Abel Point Marina)

Whitsunday Escape (☎1800 075 145; www.whitsundayescape.com; Abel Point Marina)

Whitsunday Rent A Yacht (☎1800 075 000; www.rentayacht.com.au; 6 Bay Tce, Shute Harbour)

Crewing

In return for a free bunk, meals and a sailing adventure, crewing will get you hoisting the mainsail and cleaning the head. Your experience will depend on the vessel, skipper, other crew members (if any) and your own attitude. Be sure to let someone know where you're going, with whom and for how long.

Most organised tours and activities on the Whitsundays are based in Airlie Beach, although many of these same tours can be booked from individual islands.

Information

Airlie Beach is the mainland centre for the Whitsundays, and has a bewildering array of accommodation options, travel agents and tour operators. The Port of Airlie is the main port for day-trip cruises and island ferries, although some companies berth at Abel Point Marina about 1km west of Airlie Beach.

Whitsundays Region Information Centre (1300 717 407; www.whitsundaytourism.com; 10am-5pm) On the Bruce Hwy at the southern entry to Proserpine.

Getting There & Around

AIR

The two main airports for the Whitsundays are at Hamilton Island and Proserpine (Whitsunday Coast). Airlie Beach is home to the small Whitsunday Airport, about 6km from town.

BOAT

Cruise Whitsundays (07-4946 4662; www.cruisewhitsundays.com; one way adult/child from $36/24) Provides ferry transfers to Daydream, Long, South Molle and Hamilton Islands.

Long Island

Long Island has secluded, pretty white beaches, lots of adorable, wild rock wallabies and 13km of walking tracks. Some very good deals can be found online to stay at the **Break Free Long Island Resort** (1800 075 125; www.oceanhotels.com.au/longisland; d from $139;). It's an easy-going, remote place, great for splashing around in the pool with the kids, drinking beer on the gorgeous beach or swinging in a hammock in the shade of a palm tree. Several forest walking trails start at the resort. Kayaks and pedal boats are free, there's minigolf, and plenty of other water-sports equipment is available for hire.

Day trippers can also use the facilities at Break Free Long Island Resort, and there's a basic **camping ground** (www.nprsr.qld.gov.au; per person/family $5.75/23) on the island.

Getting There & Around

Cruise Whitsundays (07-4946 4662; www.cruisewhitsundays.com) Connects Long Island Resort to the Port of Airlie by frequent daily services. The direct trip takes about 20 minutes, and costs $48 each way.

Hook Island

The 53-sq-km Hook Island, second-largest of the Whitsundays, is predominantly national park and rises to 450m at Hook Peak. There are a number of good beaches dotted around the island, and some of the region's best diving and snorkelling locations.

There are national-park **camping grounds** (www.nprsr.qld.gov.au; per person/family $5.45/21.80) at Maureen Cove, Steen's Beach, Curlew Beach and Crayfish Beach. Although basic, they provide some wonderful back-to-nature opportunities.

Transfers are arranged when you book your accommodation. Otherwise, **Whitsunday Island Camping Connections – Scamper** (07-4946 6285; www.whitsundaycamping.com.au) can organise drop-offs to the camping grounds (minimum four people) for around $160 per person return.

South Molle Island

The largest of the Molle group of islands at 4 sq km, South Molle is virtually joined to Mid and North Molle Islands. Apart from the private residence area and golf course at Bauer Bay in the north, the island is all national park and is criss-crossed by 15km of walking tracks, with some superb lookout points.

There are national park **camping grounds** (13 74 68; www.nprsr.qld.gov.au; per person/family $5.45/21.80) at Sandy Bay in the south, and at Paddle Bay near the resort.

Day trippers and campers can get to South Molle with Whitsunday Island Camping Connections – Scamper ($65 return).

Daydream Island

Daydream Island, just over 1km long and 200m wide, would live up to its name a bit more if it wasn't quite so busy; one could be forgiven for mistaking it for a floating theme park. The closest resort to the mainland, it's a very popular day-trip destination and is suitable for everybody, especially busy families, swinging singles and couples looking for a romantic island wedding.

The large and delightfully kitsch **Daydream Island Resort & Spa** (1800 075 040; www.daydreamisland.com; d from $368;) is surrounded by beautifully landscaped tropical gardens, with a stingray-, shark- and fish-filled lagoon running through it. It has tennis courts, a gym, catamarans, sailboards, three swimming pools and an open-air cinema

OFF THE BEATEN TRACK

CAMPING THE WHITSUNDAYS

Department of National Parks, Sport & Racing (NPRSR; www.nprsr.qld.gov.au) manages the **Whitsunday Islands National Park** camping grounds on several islands for both independent campers as well as groups on commercial trips. Camping permits (per person/family $5.75/23) are available online or at the NPRSR booking office in Airlie Beach.

You must be self-sufficient and are advised to take 5L of water per person per day plus three days' extra supply in case you get stuck. You should also have a fuel stove as wood fires are banned on all islands.

If Cruise Whitsundays (p379) doesn't service the island it, get to your island with **Whitsunday Island Camping Connections – Scamper** (07-4946 6285; www.whitsundaycamping.com.au). It leaves from Shute Harbour and can drop you at South Molle, Denman or Planton Islands ($65 return); Whitsunday Island ($105 return); Whitehaven Beach ($155 return); and Hook Island ($160 return). Camping transfers include complimentary 5L water containers. You can also hire camp kits ($40 first night; $20 subsequent nights) which include a tent, gas stove, esky and more. The website is full of more details and helpful information.

all included in the tariff. There's also a club with constant activities to keep children occupied. The resort occupies the entire island; Daydream is not the place to head if you're seeking isolation.

Cruise Whitsundays (07-4946 4662; www.cruisewhitsundays.com; one way adult/child $36/24) connects Daydream Island to Abel Point Marina and Shute Harbour with frequent daily services.

Hamilton Island

POP 1209

Welcome to a little slice of resort paradise where the paved roads are plied by golf buggies, steep, rocky hills are criss-crossed by walking trails blessed with magnificent sea views, and the white beaches are buzzing with water-sports action. Though it's not everyone's idea of a perfect getaway, it's hard not to be impressed by the selection of high-end accommodation options, restaurants, bars and activities – if you've got the cash, there's something for everyone. Day trippers can use some resort facilities including tennis courts, a golf driving range and a minigolf course and enjoy the island on a relatively economical budget.

From **Catseye Beach**, in front of the resort area, you can hire stand-up paddle oards, kayaks, sailboards, catamarans, jet skis and other equipment, and go parasailing or waterskiing. Nonmotorised equipment costs around $12 for half-hour rental, $20 for an hour.

A few shops by the harbour organise dives and certificate courses, and just about everyone is ready to sign you up for a variety of cruises to other islands and the outer reef.

If you only have time for one walk, make it the clamber up to Passage Peak (239m) on the northeastern corner of the island.

Sleeping

Qualia RESORT $$$
(1300 780 959; www.qualia.com.au; d from $995;) Stunning, ultraluxe Qualia is set on 12 secluded hectares, with modern villas materialising like heavenly tree houses in the leafy hillside. The resort has a private beach, two restaurants, a spa and two pools.

Beach Club RESORT $$$
(www.hamiltonisland.com.au/BeachClub; d from $595;) Flanking the main resort complex, the Beach Club has terraced rooms with absolute beachfront positions. It's adults only, and the best choice on Catseye Beach for a romantic getaway.

Whitsunday Holiday Homes APARTMENT $$$
(13 73 33; www.hihh.com.au; from $288;) Private accommodation ranging from three-star apartments to family-friendly houses and five-star luxury digs. Rates include your own golf buggy for highbrow hooning. There's a four-night minimum stay in some properties.

Palm Bungalows CABIN $$$
(www.hamiltonisland.com.au/palm-bungalows; d from $350;) Set in shady, tropical gardens

walking distance up a little hill on Catseye Beach, these attractive individual units are packed closely together but are still private.

Eating

The main resort complex has a number of restaurants. The marina also offers plenty of choices including a good **bakery-deli** (Front St; sandwiches from $9; 7am-4pm), a **fish 'n' chip shop** (Front St; fish & chips $11.50; 10am-9pm Sun-Thu, 11.30am-9pm Fri & Sat), a **tavern** (07-4946 8839; Marina Village; mains from $17.50; 11am-midnight), and a supermarket/general store for self-caterers.

Bommie Restaurant MODERN AUSTRALIAN **$$$**
(07-4948 9433; mains $38-50; 6pm-midnight Tue-Sat) Upmarket Mod Oz cuisine with water views as exclusive as the prices. It's within the resort complex.

Romano's ITALIAN **$$$**
(07-4946 8212; Marina Village; mains $33-40; 6pm-midnight Thu-Mon) Popular Italian restaurant with a large enclosed deck jutting over the water.

Mariners Seafood Restaurant SEAFOOD **$$$**
(07-4946 8628; Marina Village; mains $38-48; 6pm-late Sat-Wed) While the emphasis is on seafood, grills are also available.

Getting There & Away

AIR

Hamilton Island Airport is the main arrival centre for the Whitsundays, and is serviced by **Qantas** (13 13 13; www.qantas.com.au), **Jetstar** (13 15 38; www.jetstar.com.au) and **Virgin** (13 67 89; www.virginaustralia.com.au).

BOAT

Cruise Whitsundays (07-4946 4662; www.cruisewhitsundays.com) Connects Hamilton Island Airport and the marina with the Port of Airlie in Airlie Beach ($48).

Getting Around

There's a free shuttle-bus service operating around the island from 7am to 11pm.

You can hire a golf buggy (per one/two/three/24 hours $45/55/60/85) on which to whiz around the island.

Hayman Island

The most northern of the Whitsunday group, little Hayman is just 4 sq km in area and rises to 250m above sea level. It has forested hills, valleys and beaches, and a luxury five-star resort.

An avenue of stately date palms leads to the main entrance of the gorgeous **One&Only Hayman Island Resort** (07-4940 1838; www.hayman.com.au; r incl breakfast $730-12,300;). It's one of the most gilded playgrounds on the Great Barrier Reef with a hectare of swimming pools, landscaped gardens and grounds, and exclusive boutiques.

Resort guests must first fly to Hamilton Island Airport before being escorted to Hayman's fleet of luxury cruisers for a pampered transfer to the resort.

Lindeman Island

Lovely little Lindeman was once home to a busy Club Med resort. These days, it's only nature photographers and hikers who provide any semblance of bustle, making independent treks for the varied island tree life and the sublime view from Mt Oldfield (210m). Lindeman is mostly national park, with empty bays and 20km of impressive walking trails. **Boat Port** is the best spot for camping.

Whitsunday Island

Whitehaven Beach, on Whitsunday Island, is a pristine 7km-long stretch of blinding sand (at 98% pure silica, said sand is some of the whitest in the world), bounded by lush tropical vegetation and a brilliant blue sea. From Hill Inlet at the northern end of the beach, the swirling pattern of dazzling sand through the turquoise and aquamarine water paints a magical picture. There's excellent snorkelling from its southern end. Whitehaven is one of Australia's most beautiful beaches.

There are national-park **camping grounds** (13 74 68; www.nprsr.qld.gov.au; adult/family $5.45/21.80) at Dugong, Nari's and Joe's Beaches in the west; at Chance Bay in the south; at the southern end of Whitehaven Beach; and Peter Bay in the north.

Whitsunday Island Camping Connections – Scamper can get you there from $105 return.

Other Whitsunday Islands

The northern islands are undeveloped and seldom visited by cruise boats or water taxis. Several of these – Gloucester, Saddleback and Armit Islands – have national-park camping grounds. The NPRSR (p377) office in Airlie Beach can issue camping permits and advise you on which islands to visit and how to get there.

Bowen

POP 10,260

Bowen is a typical, old-style, small Queensland coastal town: wide streets, low-rise buildings, wooden Queenslander houses and laid-back, friendly locals. What makes Bowen stand out from other similar towns is its 24 colourful murals, all depicting various events and facets of the region's history; grab a walking map and more info at the visitor centre or information booth.

The foreshore, with its landscaped esplanade, picnic tables and barbecues, is a focal point, and there are some truly stunning – and little-visited – beaches and bays northeast of the town centre.

Bowen gets busy during fruit-picking season (April to November). The famous Bowen mango unsurprisingly hails from here.

Keep an eye out for the 'Bowenwood' sign on the town's water tower; Baz Luhrmann's epic movie *Australia* was shot here in 2007 and the locals are still a little star-struck.

If you're looking for fruit-picking work, check with just-off-the-beach **Bowen Backpackers** (07-4786 3433; www.bowenbackpackers.net; Herbert St; dm per night/week from $40/180;); book a bed well in advance if you want to stay. Even if you're just passing through, stop in at **Jochheims Pies** (49 George St; pies $4.60; 5.30am-3.30pm Mon-Fri, to 12.30pm Sat) for a 'hunky beef' pie, so named because it was Hugh Jackman's favourite while filming *Australia*. Afterwards, stop by **Tourism Bowen** (07-4786 4222; www.tourismbowen.com.au; 8.30am-5pm Mon-Fri, 10.30am-5pm Sat & Sun), about 7km south of town on the Bruce Hwy, or at the **information booth** (Santa Barbara Pde; 10am-5pm Mon-Fri, hours vary Sat & Sun) at the beach end of Herbert St for a scoop of Bowen mango sorbet ($4).

Getting There & Away

BUS

Greyhound (1300 473 946; www.greyhound.com.au) and **Premier** (13 34 10; www.premierms.com.au) are two companies that have frequent bus services running to/from Airlie Beach ($24, 1½ hours) and Townsville ($27, four hours).

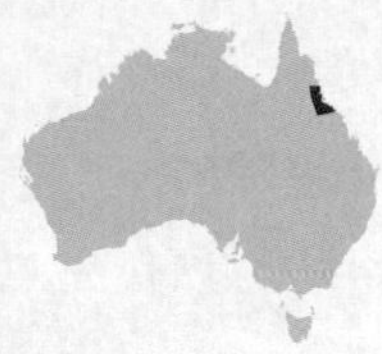

Townsville & Mission Beach

Includes ➡

Best Places to Eat

➡ Wayne & Adele's Garden of Eating (p388)
➡ Dunk Island kiosk (p400)
➡ Caffe Rustica (p399)
➡ Bingil Bay Cafe (p399)
➡ Marlin Bar (p394)

Best Places to Stay

➡ Shambhala Retreat (p393)
➡ Noorla Heritage Resort (p394)
➡ Jackaroo Hostel (p398)
➡ Bungalow Bay Koala Village (p393)
➡ Coral Lodge (p387)

Why Go?

Spread out between the tourist darlings of Cairns and the Whitsunday Islands, this lesser-known, rainforested stretch of quiet, palm-edged beaches is where giant endangered cassowary graze for seeds, and koalas nap in gum trees on turquoise encircled islands. Oft-overlooked Townsville is the urban centre and offers pleasant, wide, modern streets, a landscaped seaside promenade, gracious 19th-century architecture, and a host of cultural venues and sporting events. It's also the jumping-off point for Magnetic Island, a great budget alternative to the Whitsundays and with far more wildlife – hand feed wild wallabies, spot an incredible range of bird life on fantastic bushwalking trails, and look for koalas.

North of Townsville beautiful Mission Beach is a laid-back village that ironically attracts thrill seekers by the busload, all keen on skydiving over the reef and on to white-sand beaches, or on adrenaline-pumping white-water rafting on the Tully River.

When to Go

Townsville

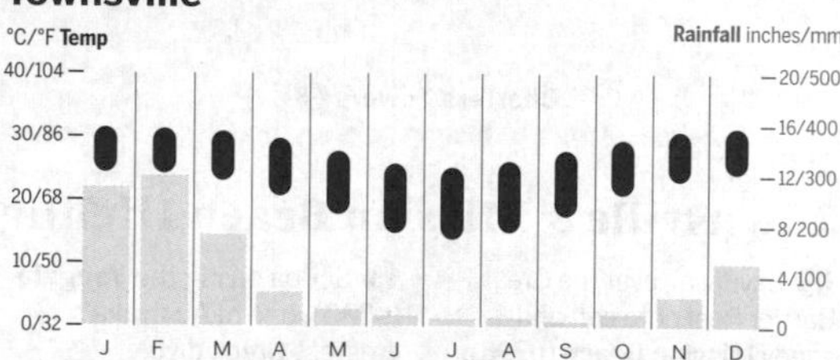

May–Oct Stinger-free seas make this the best time for water activities.

Aug Townsville shows off its cultural side during the Australian Festival of Chamber Music.

Oct Let your dreads down at Mission Beach's Mission Evolve Music Fest.

Wooroonooran National Park
Eubenangee Swamp National Park
0 50 km
0 25 miles
Innisfail
Flying Fish Point
Millaa Millaa
Ravenshoe
Mamu Rainforest Canopy Walk
Mourilyan
Silkwood
Kurrimine
El Arish
Bingil Bay
Tully Gorge National Park
CORAL SEA
1 Mission Beach
Wongaling Beach
Tully
Dunk Island
South Mission Beach
A1
2 Tully River
Herbert River
Murray Falls
Girringun National Park (Edmund Kennedy Section)
Goold Island
Great Barrier Reef
Cardwell
Girringun National Park
Hinchinbrook Island
Burdekin River
Lucinda
Pelorus Is (North Palm Island) (Yanooa Island)
Halifax
Orpheus Island (Goolboddi)
5 Wallaman Falls
Ingham
Forest Beach
Curacoa Island (Noogoo)
Great Palm Island
Fantome Island (Eumilli)
Jourama Falls
Mt Spec (1000m)
Havannah Island
Mt Fox (811m)
Paluma Range National Park
Lake Paluma
Mutarnee
Herald Island
Paluma
A1
Rattlesnake Island
Magnetic Island
3
Horseshoe Bay
Nelly Bay
63
Cape Cleveland
Australian Institute of Marine Science
6 Townsville
Thuringowa
Bowling Green Bay National Park
Nome
Yongala
Alva Beach 4
Giru
Mt Elliot National Park
A1
Ayr
Home Hill
A6
Burdekin River
Burdekin River
A7
Ravenswood
Charters Towers 7

Townsville & Mission Beach Highlights

1 Skydiving over the Great Barrier Reef onto soft and sandy **Mission Beach** (p396).

2 Veering wildly around white-water bends in a raft on the **Tully River** (p397).

3 Spotting a dozing koala or hand-feeding rock wallabies on paradisiacal **Magnetic Island** (p391).

4 Scuba diving the **Yongala** (p390), one of Australia's greatest wreck dives.

5 Admiring the view then schlepping down to the bottom of Australia's highest single-drop waterfall, **Wallaman Falls** (p395).

6 Cheering on the Cowboys, North Queensland's revered National Rugby League team, or its National Basketball League team, the Crocodiles, in **Townsville** (p385).

7 Watching a *Ghosts After Dark* outdoor film screening in the outback gold-rush town of **Charters Towers** (p391).

TOWNSVILLE & AROUND

North Queensland's largest city is an ideal base for coastal, inland and offshore day trips.

Townsville

POP 189,238

Sprawling between a brooding red hill and a sparking blue sea, Townsville is a tidy and relatively modern-feeling spot with a lot to offer: excellent museums, a huge aquarium, world-class diving, two major sporting teams, vibrant nightlife and an endless esplanade. It's a pedestrian-friendly city, and its grand, refurbished 19th-century buildings offer loads of landmarks – if you do get lost, the friendly locals will be only too happy to lend a hand…or shout you a beer. Townsville has a lively, young populace, with thousands of students and armed forces members intermingling with old-school locals, fly-in-fly-out mine workers, and summer-seekers lapping up the average 320 days of sunshine per year.

Townsville is only 350km from Cairns, but is much drier than its tropical rival: if 'Brownsville' is baking your bones, the splendid beaches of Magnetic Island are but a ferry jaunt away.

DANGER: STINGERS & CROCS

From around late October to May, swimming in coastal waters is inadvisable due to the presence of box jellyfish, irukandji and other marine stingers. Only swim where there is a patrolled stinger net.

Saltwater crocodiles inhabit the mangroves, estuaries and open water. Warning signs are posted around the waterways where crocodiles might be present. Pay heed, as these signs are not just quirky props for your holiday snaps: crocs are faster and more clever than you might think!

Ask at the tourist office or check with locals involved in sea sports for up-to-date information.

Sights & Activities

★ Reef HQ Aquarium AQUARIUM
(www.reefhq.com.au; Flinders St E; adult/child $28/14; ⌚9.30am-5pm) A staggering 2.5 million litres of water flow through the coral-reef tank here, home to 130 coral and 120 fish species. Kids will love seeing, feeding and touching turtles at the **turtle hospital**. Talks and tours (included with admission) throughout the day focus on different aspects of the reef and the aquarium.

Castle Hill VIEWPOINT
Hoof it up this striking 286m-high red hill (an isolated pink granite monolith) that dominates Townsville's skyline for stunning views of the city and Cleveland Bay. Walk up via the rough 'goat track' (2km one way) from Hillside Cres. Otherwise, drive via Gregory St up the narrow, winding 2.6km Castle Hill Rd. A signboard up top details short trails leading to various lookout points.

Museum of Tropical Queensland MUSEUM
(www.mtq.qm.qld.gov.au; 70-102 Flinders St E; adult/child $15/8.80; ⌚9.30am-5pm) Not your everyday museum, the Museum of Tropical Queensland reconstructs scenes using detailed models with interactive displays. At 11am and 2.30pm, you can load and fire a cannon, 1700s-style. Galleries include the kid-friendly MindZone science centre, and displays on North Queensland's history from the dinosaurs to the rainforest and reef.

Billabong Sanctuary WILDLIFE RESERVE
(www.billabongsanctuary.com.au; Bruce Hwy; adult/child $33/20; ⌚9am-5pm) Just 17km south of Townsville, this eco-certified wildlife park offers up-close-and-personal encounters with Australian wildlife – from dingoes to cassowaries – in their natural habitat. You could easily spend all day at the 11-hectare park, with feedings, shows and talks every half-hour or so.

Botanic Gardens GARDENS
(⌚sunrise-sunset) FREE Townsville's botanic gardens are spread across three locations: each has its own character, but all have tropical plants and are abundantly green. Closest to the centre, the formal, ornamental **Queens Gardens** (cnr Gregory & Paxton Sts; ⌚sunrise-sunset) are 1km northwest of town at the base of Castle Hill.

Cultural Centre CULTURAL CENTRE
(☎07-4772 7679; www.cctownsville.com.au; 2-68 Flinders St E; adult/child $5/2; ⌚9.30am-4.30pm) Showcases the history, traditions and customs of the local Wulgurukaba and Bindal peoples. Call for guided-tour times.

Perc Tucker Regional Gallery GALLERY
(www.townsville.qld.gov.au/facilities/galleries/perctucker; cnr Denham & Flinders Sts; ⌚10am-5pm

Townsville

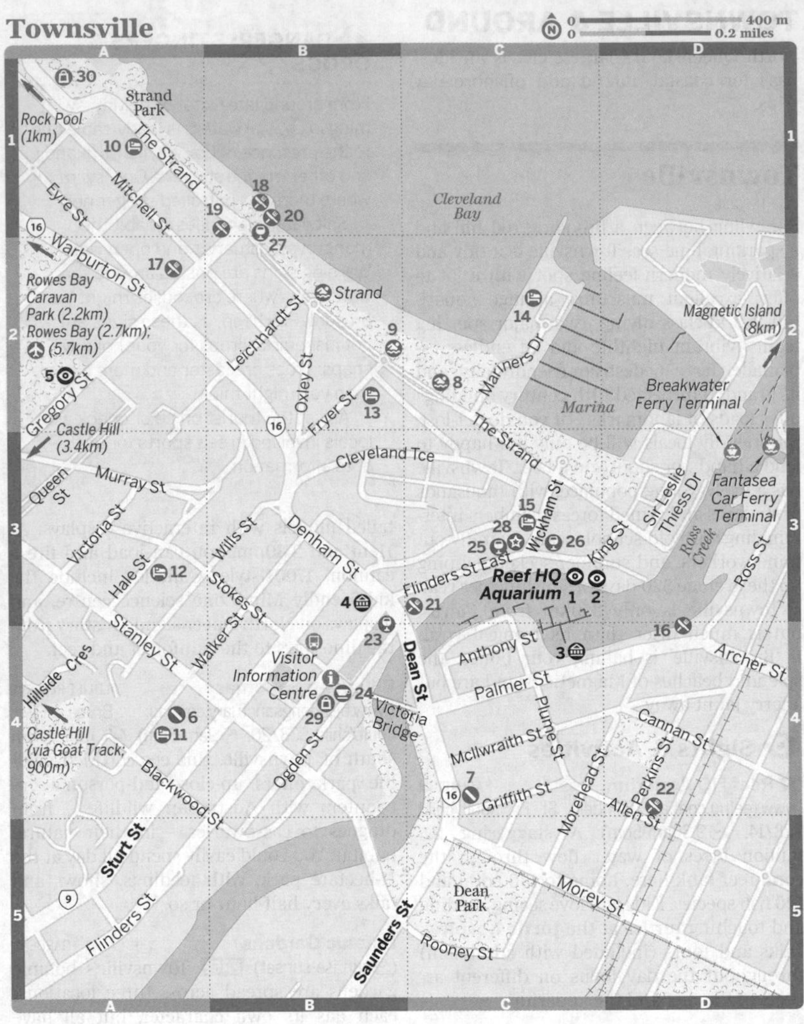

Mon-Fri, to 2pm Sat & Sun) FREE Contemporary art gallery in a stately 1885-built former bank. Exhibitions focus on North Queensland artists.

Maritime Museum of Townsville MUSEUM
(www.townsvillemaritimemuseum.org.au; 42-68 Palmer St; adult/child $6/3; ⏲10am-3pm Mon-Fri, noon-3pm Sat & Sun) One for the boat buffs, with a gallery dedicated to the wreck of the *Yongala* and exhibits on North Queensland's naval industries. Tours of decommissioned patrol boat HMAS *Townsville* are available.

Strand SWIMMING
Stretching 2.2km, Townsville's waterfront is interspersed with parks, pools, cafes and playgrounds – with hundreds of palm trees providing shade. Its golden-sand beach is patrolled and protected by two stinger enclosures.

At the northern tip is the **rock pool** (The Strand; ⏲24hr) FREE, an enormous artificial swimming pool surrounded by lawns and sandy beaches. Alternatively, head to the chlorinated safety of the heritage-listed, Olympic-sized swimming pool, **Tobruk Memorial Baths** (www.townsville.qld.gov.au;

Townsville

Top Sights
1 Reef HQ Aquarium ... C3

Sights
2 Cultural Centre ... C3
3 Maritime Museum of Townsville ... C4
Museum of Tropical Queensland ... (see 2)
4 Perc Tucker Regional Gallery ... B3
5 Queens (Botanic) Gardens ... A2

Activities, Courses & Tours
6 Adrenalin Dive ... A4
7 Remote Area Dive ... C4
8 Tobruk Memorial Baths ... C2
9 Water Playground ... B2

Sleeping
10 Aquarius on the Beach ... A1
11 Civic Guest House ... A4
12 Coral Lodge ... A3
13 Historic Yongala Lodge Motel ... B2
14 Mariners North ... C2
Orchid Guest House ... (see 12)
15 Reef Lodge ... C3

Eating
16 Brandy's ... D4
17 Cafe Bambini ... A2
18 Cbar ... B1
19 Harold's Seafood ... B1
20 Longboard Bar & Grill ... D1
Souvlaki Bar ... (see 19)
21 Summerie's Thai Cuisine ... C3
22 Wayne & Adele's Garden of Eating ... D4

Drinking & Nightlife
23 Brewery ... B4
24 Coffee Dominion ... B4
25 Heritage Bar ... C3
26 Molly Malones ... C3
27 Seaview Hotel ... B1

Entertainment
28 Flynns ... C3

Shopping
29 Cotters Market ... B4
30 Strand Night Market ... A1

The Strand; adult/child $5/3; ⏱5.30am-7pm Mon-Thu, to 6pm Fri, 7am-4pm Sat, 8am-5pm Sun). There's also a fantastic **water playground** (The Strand; ⏱10am-8pm Dec-Mar, to 6pm Sep-Nov, Apr & May, to 5pm Jun-Aug) FREE for the kids.

Skydive Townsville SKYDIVING
(☎07 4721 4721; www.skydivetownsville.com.au; tandem dives from $395) Hurl yourself from a perfectly good plane and land right on the Strand.

Festivals & Events

The city has a packed calendar of festivals and events, including home games of its cherished sporting teams, the **North Queensland Cowboys** (www.cowboys.com.au; season Mar-Sep) National Rugby League team and the **Crocodiles** (www.crocodiles.com.au; season mid-Oct–Apr) National Basketball League team. If you don't believe basketball is truly popular in Australia, you will when you see locals driving around with croc tails hanging out of their car boots.

Townsville 500 SPORTS
(www.v8supercars.com.au) V8 Supercars roar through a purpose-built street circuit each July during the V8 Supercar Championship.

Australian Festival of Chamber Music MUSIC
(www.afcm.com.au; ⏱Aug) Townsville gets cultural during this internationally renowned festival each August.

Sleeping

Townsville fills to capacity during festivals and events, so it's wise to book ahead. Mid-range motels and self-catering units stretch along the Strand, while international chains and backpacker places cluster in the city centre and around Palmer St.

Coral Lodge B&B $
(☎07-4771 5512; www.corallodge.com.au; 32 Hale St; s/d without bathroom $80/85, tr/q $110/135; ❄📶) If you're looking to stay in a charming, old-fashioned Aussie home (with a three-legged cat), this century-old property can't be beat. Upstairs self-contained units are like having your own apartment, while downstairs guest rooms share bathrooms. The welcoming owners will pick you up from the bus, train or ferry.

Reef Lodge HOSTEL $
(☎07-4721 1112; www.reeflodge.com.au; 4 Wickham St; dm $23-35, d with/without bathroom $80/62; ❄@📶) The cruisy atmosphere at Townsville's best – and most central – hostel extends from Buddhist sculptures and

hammocks strewn through the garden to a nerdishly compelling '80s video-game room.

Civic Guest House HOSTEL $
(07-4771 5381; www.civicguesthousetownsville.com.au; 262 Walker St; dm/d from $24/58;) A contender for cleanest hostel on earth, the charming, colonial-tinged Civic lives up to its name with friendly staff and a laid-back clientele. Free transport to/from the ferry or bus station.

Rowes Bay Caravan Park CARAVAN PARK $
(07-4771 3576; www.rowesbaycp.com.au; Heatley Pde; unpowered/powered sites $27/38, cabins with/without bathroom from $99/77;) Leafy park opposite Rowes Bay's beachfront. Brand-new villas are smaller than cabins, but spiffier.

Orchid Guest House GUESTHOUSE $
(07-4771 6683; www.orchidguesthouse.com.au; 34 Hale St; dm $28, d with/without bathroom $85/65;) Not one for the party set, but a godsend for those looking for somewhere cheap and cheerful to lay their head. Weekly rates available for working backpackers.

Historic Yongala Lodge Motel MOTEL $$
(07-4772 4633; www.historicyongala.com.au; 11 Fryer St; motel r $89-135, 1/2-bedroom apt $139/159;) Built in 1884 this lovely historic building with gingerbread balustrades is but a short stroll from the Strand and city centre. The rooms and apartments are small but good value. The excellent **restaurant** (closed for refurbishment when we passed) is long-loved by locals.

Aquarius on the Beach HOTEL $$
(1800 622 474; www.aquariusonthebeach.com.au; 75 The Strand; d $117-270;) The spectacular balcony views impress almost as much as the size of this place, the tallest building on the Strand. Don't be put off by the dated facade – this is one of the better places around, and the service is faultless.

Mariners North APARTMENT $$$
(07-4722 0777; www.marinersnorth.com.au; 7 Mariners Dr; r from $199, 2-/3-bedroom apt from $239/290;) Self-contained, absolute oceanfront apartments have generous living areas, big bathrooms and brilliant balconies overlooking Cleveland Bay and out to Magnetic Island. Free gym use; minimum two-night stay.

Eating

Perpendicular to the Strand, Gregory St has a clutch of cafes and takeaway joints. The Palmer St dining strip offers a diverse range of cuisines: wander along and take your pick. Many of Townsville's bars and pubs also serve food.

Cafe Bambini CAFE $
(46 Gregory St; mains $11-21; 5.30am-5pm Mon-Fri, 6.30am-4pm Sat & Sun;) With four locations strewn around town, this local success story cooks up some of the best (all-day!) breakfasts in Townsville, while lunches are fresh and filling.

Souvlaki Bar GREEK $
(Shops 3 & 4, 58 The Strand; meals $7.50-10.60; 10.30am-9pm Mon-Fri, to 10pm Sat & Sun) Big, filling takeaways include juicy gyros, meze galore, burgers and homemade honey puffs.

Harold's Seafood SEAFOOD $
(cnr The Strand & Gregory St; meals $4-10; 8am-9pm Mon-Thu, to 9.30pm Fri-Sun) This takeaway joint has fantastic-value eats from burgers to a $10 plate of barramundi and salad.

Wayne & Adele's Garden of Eating MODERN AUSTRALIAN $$
(07-4772 2984; 11 Allen St; mains from $19; 6.30-10pm Mon, to 11pm Thu-Sat, noon-3pm Sun) Those who like a side serving of quirky with their grub shouldn't miss mains such as 'Don't Lose Your Tempeh' (curried vegie tempeh fritter with Kaffir-lime gado-gado salad) or 'Goat in a Boat' (Moroccan goat pie on date dhal). The purple courtyard is as flamboyant as the menu.

Longboard Bar & Grill MODERN AUSTRALIAN $$
(07-4724 1234; The Strand, opposite Gregory St; mains $15-37; 11.30am-3pm & 5.30pm-late) This waterfront eatery plies a lively crowd with grill-house favourites such as sticky barbecue pork ribs, steaks and buffalo wings. Ignore the incongruous surf theme and be sure to pack a bib.

Brandy's CAFE $$
(30-34 Palmer St; breakfasts $14-20, pizzas $22-30; 5pm-late Mon-Fri, 6am-late Sat & Sun) Find one of Townsville's best breakfasts here on the weekends, and tasty wood-fired pizzas, tapas and pasta nightly. A bright, busy and convivial atmosphere.

Cbar CAFE $$
(The Strand, opposite Gregory St; mains $16-32; 7am-10pm;) Dependable and delicious, with an all-day dining menu that caters to the grazers (antipasto $18) and the gluttons (huge battered fish burgers $17).

BLOWIN' IN THE WIND

Queensland is the Sunshine State, known for its sultry climate and year-round holiday weather; an old slogan went as far as claiming it was 'Beautiful one day, perfect the next'. But up in the far north, between November and April each year, cyclones – known in the northern hemisphere as hurricanes – are a part of life in the tropics, with an average of four or five forming each season. While it's rare for these cyclones to escalate into full-blown destructive storms, big ones do come a'crashing: in February 2011, Cyclone Yasi smashed into the coast around Mission Beach with winds estimated at up to 300km/h, ripping through the towns of Tully and Cardwell and islands including Dunk, Bedarra and Hinchinbrook. Hundreds of homes along the coast between Innisfail and Ingham were severely damaged, banana plantations and cane fields flattened, and areas of national park rainforest pummelled. Amazingly, there were no deaths or serious injuries.

During the season, keep a sharp ear out for cyclone predictions and alerts. If a cyclone watch or warning is issued, stay tuned to local radio and monitor the **Bureau of Meteorology** (www.bom.gov.au) website for updates and advice. Locals tend to be complacent about cyclones, but will still buy out the bottle shop when a threat is imminent!

Summerie's Thai Cuisine THAI $$
(07-4420 1282; 232 Flinders St; lunch specials $12.50, dinner mains from $17; 11.30am-2.30pm & 5.30-10pm) Authentic Thai food that gets the thumbs up from coconut-curry-crazed locals. The name of speciality dish 'Heaven on Earth' (slow-cooked coconut prawns with crunchy greens) is definitely not false advertising.

Drinking & Entertainment

It must be the sunny climate, because Townsville sure loves a sip. Most nightlife concentrates on Flinders St East, while Palmer St and the Strand offer lower key spots. Check listings in Thursday's edition of the *Townsville Bulletin*. Opening hours vary according to the season and the crowds; nightclubs generally stay open until 5am.

Heritage Bar BAR
(www.heritagebar.com.au; 137 Flinders St E; bar snacks from $10.50; 5pm-2am Tue-Sat) A surprisingly chic craft bar. Suave 'mixologists' deliver creative cocktails to a cool crowd looking for something more than a beer-barn swillfest. Also has a sophisticated bar menu for meals (think BBQ bourbon pork, and scallop and chorizo gnocchi), as well as tipsy nibbles such as yummy coconut prawns.

Brewery BREWERY
(252 Flinders St; 11.30am-midnight Mon-Sat) Brews are made on-site at this hopping and stunningly restored 1880s former post office. Soak up a Townsville Bitter or Bandito Loco with a meal at its refined **restaurant** (mains $17-36).

Coffee Dominion CAFE
(cnr Stokes & Ogden Sts; 6am-5pm Mon-Fri, 7am-1pm Sat & Sun) An eco-conscious establishment roasting beans sourced from as nearby as the Atherton Tableland, and from as far away as Zambia. If you don't find a blend you like, invent your own and they'll grind it fresh.

Seaview Hotel PUB
(cnr The Strand & Gregory St; 10am-midnight) Renowned for its Sunday beer-garden sessions and prime position on the Strand, the Seaview serves ice-cold schooners and has live music and entertainment. Its immense **restaurant** (mains $21-44) serves steaks on a par with the size of the premises.

Molly Malones PUB, CLUB
(87 Flinders St E; 11.30am-1am Mon & Tue, to 2am Wed, to 3am Thu, to 5am Fri, 5pm-5am Sat, 5pm-1am Sun) This boisterous Irish pub stages live music on Friday and Saturday nights. Cheap and tasty food too.

Flynns LIVE MUSIC
(101 Flinders St E; 5pm-late Tue-Sun) A jolly Irish pub that doesn't try too hard to be Irish. Wildly popular for its live music every night except Wednesdays, when karaoke takes over.

Shopping

Cotters Market MARKET
(www.townsvillerotarymarkets.com.au; Flinders St Mall; 8.30am-1pm Sun) Around 200 craft and food stalls, as well as live entertainment.

Strand Night Market MARKET
(www.townsvillerotarymarkets.com.au; The Strand; 5-9.30pm 1st Fri of month May-Dec) Browse

the stalls on the Strand for curios, crafts and knick-knacks.

Information

Visitor information centre (07-4721 3660; www.townsvilleholidays.info; cnr Flinders & Stokes Sts; 9am-5pm) Extensive visitor information on Townsville, Magnetic Island and nearby national parks. There's another branch on the Bruce Hwy 10km south of the city.

Getting There & Away

AIR

From **Townsville Airport** (www.townsvilleairport.com.au), **Virgin** (13 67 89; www.virginaustralia.com), **Qantas** (13 13 13; www.qantas.com.au), **Air North** (1800 627 474; www.airnorth.com.au) and **Jetstar** (13 15 38; www.jetstar.com.au) fly to Cairns, Brisbane, the Gold Coast, Sydney, Melbourne, Mackay and Rockhampton, with connections to other major cities.

BUS

Greyhound (1300 473 946; www.greyhound.com.au) has three daily services to Brisbane ($272, 24 hours), Rockhampton ($124, 12 hours), Airlie Beach ($47, 4½ hours), Mission Beach ($42, 3¾ hours) and Cairns ($61, six hours). Buses pick up and drop off at the **Breakwater Ferry Terminal** (2/14 Sir Leslie Thiess Dr; lockers per day $4-6).

Premier Motor Service (13 34 10; www.premierms.com.au) has one service a day to/from Brisbane and Cairns, stopping in Townsville at the **Fantasea car ferry terminal** (Ross St, South Townsville).

CAR

Major car-rental agencies are represented in Townsville and at the airport.

TRAIN

Townsville's **train station** (Charters Towers Rd) is 1km south of the centre.

The Brisbane–Cairns *Spirit of Queensland* travels through Townsville five times a week. Journey time between Brisbane and Townsville is 25 hours (one way from $189); contact **Queensland Rail** (1800 872 467; www.queenslandrail.com.au).

Getting Around

TO/FROM THE AIRPORT

Townsville Airport is 5km northwest of the city centre in Garbutt. A taxi to the centre costs about $22.

Airport Shuttle (1300 266 946; www.con-x-ion.com; one way/return $10/18) Services all arrivals and departures, with pick-ups and drop-offs throughout the central business district (bookings essential).

GREAT BARRIER REEF TRIPS FROM TOWNSVILLE

The Great Barrier Reef lies further offshore from Townsville than it does from Cairns and Port Douglas; the extra fuel costs push up prices. On the upside, it's less crowded (and the reef suffers less from the effects of crowds). Trips from Townsville are generally dive-oriented; if you only want to snorkel, take a day trip that just goes to the reef – the *Yongala* wreck is for diving only. The *Yongala* is considerably closer to Alva Beach near Ayr than to Townsville, so if your main interest is wreck diving, you may want to consider a trip with Alva Beach–based **Yongala Dive** (07-4783 1519; www.yongaladive.com.au; 56 Narrah St, Alva Beach).

The visitor centre has a list of Townsville-based operators offering Professional Association of Diving Instructors (PADI)–certified learn-to-dive courses with two days' training in the pool, plus at least two days and one night living aboard the boat. Prices start at about $615, and you'll need to obtain a dive medical (around $60).

Adrenalin Dive (07-4724 0600; www.adrenalinedive.com.au; 252 Walker St) Day trips to the Yongala (from $220) and Wheeler Reef (from $280), both including two dives. Also offers snorkelling (from $180) on Wheeler Reef as well as live-aboard trips and dive-certification courses.

Remote Area Dive (RAD; 07-4721 4424; www.remoteareadive.com.au; 16 Dean St) Runs day trips (from $220) to Orpheus and Pelorus islands. Also live-aboard trips and dive courses.

Yongala Dive (07-4783 1519; www.yongaladive.com.au; 56 Narrah St) Does dive trips ($259 including gear) out to the *Yongala* wreck from Alva Beach, 17km northeast of Ayr. It only takes 30 minutes to get out to the wreck from here, instead of a 2½-hour boat trip from Townsville. Book ahead for backpacker-style accommodation at its onshore dive lodge, with free pickups from Ayr.

WORTH A TRIP

RAVENSWOOD & CHARTERS TOWERS

You don't have to venture too far inland for a taste of the dry, dusty Queensland outback – a stark contrast to the verdant coast. This detour is easily accessible on a day trip from Townsville, but it's worth staying overnight if you can, to get to know the friendly locals a bit more.

Along the Flinders Hwy a turn-off at Mingela, 88km southwest of Townsville, leads 40km south to the tiny gold-mining village of **Ravenswood** (population 350), with a couple of gorgeous turn-of-the-20th-century pubs with basic (shared-bathroom) accommodation.

A further 47km west along the Flinders Hwy from Mingela is the historic gold-rush town of **Charters Towers** (population 8234). The 'towers' are its surrounding tors (hills). William Skelton Ewbank Melbourne (WSEM) Charters was the gold commissioner during the rush, when the town was the second-largest, and wealthiest, in Queensland. With almost 100 mines, some 90 pubs and a stock exchange, it became known simply as 'the World'.

Today, a highlight of a visit to the Towers is strolling past its glorious facades recalling the grandeur of those heady days, and listening to locals' stories.

History oozes from the walls of the 1890 **Stock Exchange Arcade** (try the cafe), next door to the **Charters Towers visitor centre** (07-4761 5533; www.charterstowers.qld.gov.au; 74 Mosman St; 9am-5pm). The visitor centre has a free brochure outlining the **One Square Mile Trail** of the town centre's beautifully preserved 19th-century buildings. The centre books all tours in town, including those to the reputedly haunted **Venus Gold Battery**, where gold-bearing ore was crushed and processed from 1872 to 1973.

Come nightfall, panoramic **Towers Hill**, the site where gold was first discovered, is the atmospheric setting for an **open-air cinema** showing the 20-minute film *Ghosts After Dark* – check seasonal screening times and buy tickets ($10) at the visitor centre.

The in-town accommodation highlight is the extremely friendly, period-furniture-filled former pub, the **Royal Private Hotel** (07-4787 8688; www.royalprivate-hotel.com; 100 Mosman St; s/d without bathroom $65/75, d with bathroom from $114;). Three caravan parks sit at the town's outskirts.

Greyhound (1300 473 946; www.greyhound.com.au) has two weekly services between Townsville and Charters Towers ($29, 1¾ hours).

The **Queensland Rail** (1800 872 467; www.queenslandrail.com.au) Inlander train runs twice weekly between Townsville and Charters Towers ($21, three hours).

BUS

Sunbus (07-4771 9800; www.sunbus.com.au) Runs local bus services around Townsville. Route maps and timetables are available at the visitor information centre and online.

TAXI

Taxis congregate at ranks across town, or call **Townsville Taxis** (13 10 08; www.tsvtaxi.com.au).

Magnetic Island

POP 2500

It's hard not to love Maggie, as she's affectionately known, with her coastal, rocky walking trails, gum trees full of dozing koalas (you're likely to spot some), and surrounding bright turquoise seas. While she may rake in the tourists, there are also plenty of permanent residents who live and work here, making it feel more like a laid-back community than a holiday hotspot.

Over half of this mountainous, triangular-shaped island's 52 sq km is national park, with scenic walks and abundant wildlife, including a large (and adorable) rock wallaby population. Inviting beaches offer adrenalin-pumping water sports, and the chance to just bask in the sunshine. The granite boulders, hoop pines and eucalyptuses are a fresh change from the clichéd tropical-island paradise.

Sights & Activities

There's one main road across the island, which goes from Picnic Bay, past Nelly and Geoffrey Bays, to Horseshoe Bay. Local buses ply the route regularly. Walking trails through the bush also link the main towns.

Picnic Bay

Picnic Bay was once home to the ferry terminal (now at Nelly Bay), but now that's gone it's transformed into one of the most low-key spots on the island, dominated more by a community of friendly locals than anything else. There's a stinger net during the season (November to May) and the swimming is superb.

Nelly Bay

Your time on Maggie will begin and end here if you travel by ferry. There's a wide range of busy but relaxing eating and sleeping options and a decent beach. There's also a children's playground towards the northern end of the beach, and good snorkelling on the fringing coral reef.

Arcadia

Arcadia village is a fairly bland, midrange conglomerate of shops, eateries and accommodation. Its main beach, **Geoffrey Bay**, has a reef at its southern end (reef walking at low tide is discouraged). By far its prettiest beach is **Alma Bay cove**, with huge boulders tumbling into the sea. There's plenty of shade here, along with picnic tables and a children's playground.

If you head to the end of the road at **Bremner Point**, between Geoffrey Bay and Alma Bay, at around 5pm you can have wild rock wallabies – accustomed to being fed at the same time each day – literally eating out of your hand. For those that make it out here, this can be a trip highlight.

Radical Bay & the Forts

Townsville was a supply base for the Pacific during WWII, and the forts were designed to protect the town from naval attack. If you're going to do just one walk, then the **forts walk** (1½ hours return, 2.8km) is a must. It starts near the Radical Bay turn-off, passing lots of ex-military sites, gun emplacements and false 'rocks'. At the top of the walk is the observation tower and command post, which have spectacular coastal views, and you'll almost certainly spot **koalas** lazing about in the treetops. Return the same way or continue along the connecting paths, which deposit you at Horseshoe Bay (you can catch the bus back).

Nearby **Balding Bay** is Maggie's unofficial nudie beach.

Horseshoe Bay

Horseshoe Bay, on the north coast, is the best of Maggie's accessible beaches and attracts its share of young, hippie-ish nature lovers and older day trippers. You'll find water-sports gear for hire, a stinger net, a row of cafes and a fantastic pub.

Bungalow Bay Koala Village has a wildlife park, where you can cuddle crocs and koalas.

Pick up local arts and crafts at Horseshoe Bay's **market** (9am-2pm 2nd & last Sun of month), which sets up along the beachfront.

Tours

Pleasure Divers DIVING

(07-4778 5788; www.pleasuredivers.com.au; 10 Marine Pde, Arcadia; open-water courses per person $349) Three-day PADI open-water courses, as well as advanced courses and *Yongala* wreck dives. If you're an experienced diver wanting to dive the Great Barrier Reef, this is one of the best deals around with two-dive trips to little-visited Lodestone Reef for $226 ($196 for snorkellers).

Tropicana Tours DRIVING

(07-4758 1800; www.tropicanatours.com.au; full day adult/child $198/99) This full-day tour with guides takes in the island's best spots in its stretch 4WD. Price includes close encounters with wildlife, lunch at a local cafe and a sunset cocktail. Shorter tours are also available.

Horseshoe Bay Ranch HORSE RIDING

(07-4778 5109; www.horseshoebayranch.com.au; 38 Gifford St, Horseshoe Bay; 2hr rides $110) Gallop dramatically into the not-so-crashing surf on this popular bushland-to-beach two-hour tour. Pony rides for littlies are available too (20 minutes, $20).

Magnetic Island Sea Kayaks KAYAKING

(07-4778 5424; www.seakayak.com.au; 93 Horseshoe Bay Rd, Horseshoe Bay; tours from $60) Join an eco-certified morning or sunset tour, or go it alone on a rented kayak (single/double per day $75/150).

Providence V CRUISE

(0427 882 062; www.providencesailing.com.au) Snorkel, ride the boom-net, and simply indulge sailing-off-into-the-sunset fantasies on Maggie's only tall ship. Two-hour sails from $70 per person.

Sleeping

★**Bungalow Bay Koala Village** HOSTEL $
(☎1800 285 577, 07-4778 5577; www.bungalowbay.com.au; 40 Horseshoe Bay Rd, Horseshoe Bay; unpowered/powered sites per person $12.50/15, dm $28, d with/without bathroom $90/75; ❄@🛜≋) It's like summer camp for everyone here. Rooms, dorms and camp sites are spread over a nature wonderland with its own **wildlife park** (☎07-4778 5577, 1800 285 577; www.bungalowbay.com.au; 40 Horseshoe Bay Rd, Horseshoe Bay; adult/child $19/12; ⏲2hr tours 10am, noon & 2.30pm) where you can cuddle koalas. Cool off in the pool or at the breezy bar, walk five minutes to the beach, or tuck into pizza and beer at the on-site **bar/restaurant** (☎07-4778 5577, 1800 285 577; www.bungalowbay.com.au; 40 Horseshoe Bay Rd, Horseshoe Bay; mains $15.50-24; ⏲noon to late).

Base Backpackers HOSTEL $
(☎1800 242 273; www.stayatbase.com; 1 Nelly Bay Rd, Nelly Bay; camping per person $15, dm $28-33, d with/without bathroom from $125/105; @🛜≋) If sleep is a dirty word, then step right up. Base is famous for wild full-moon parties, but things can get raucous any time, thanks to the infamous on-site Island Bar. Sleep/food/transport package deals are available. It's in a fairly isolated but gorgeous beachfront spot between Nelly and Picnic Bays.

★**Shambhala Retreat** BUNGALOW $$
(☎0448 160 580; www.shambhala-retreat-magnetic-island.com.au; 11 Barton St, Nelly Bay; d from $105; ❄≋) Serenity now. This green-powered property consists of three tropical units complete with Buddhist wall hangings and tree-screened patios for spying on local wildlife. Two units have outdoor courtyard showers; all have fully equipped kitchens, large bathrooms and laundry facilities. Minimum stay is two nights.

Tropical Palms Inn MOTEL $$
(☎07-4778 5076; www.tropicalpalmsinn.com.au; 34 Picnic St, Picnic Bay; units from $120; ❄🛜≋) With a terrific little swimming pool right outside your front door and superbly friendly hosts, the simple, self-contained motel units here are bright and comfortable. Prices drop if you stay two or more nights, and you can also rent 4WDs here.

Arcadia Village Motel HOTEL $$
(☎07-4778 5481; www.arcadiavillage.com.au; 7 Marine Pde, Arcadia; r $100-155; ❄🛜≋) Friendly and unpretentious, this motel oozes a holiday vibe, and its on-site bistro and bar, the **Island Tavern** (☎07-4778 5481; www.arcadiavillage.com.au; 7 Marine Pde, Arcadia; mains $19.50-28; ⏲bistro 11am-8pm, bar noon-3am), keeps punters happy with cheap jugs, live music and cane-toad races every Wednesday night. There are two awesome pools, and a great beach a short stroll across the street.

Arcadia Beach Guest House GUESTHOUSE $$
(☎07-4778 5668; www.arcadiabeachguesthouse.com.au; 27 Marine Pde, Arcadia; dm from $58, safari tents $65, r without bathroom $69-89, r with bathroom $140-249; ❄🛜≋) So much to choose from! Will you stay in a bright, beachy room (named after Magnetic Island's bays), a safari tent or a dorm? Go turtle-spotting from the balcony, rent a canoe, a Moke or a 4WD... or all of the above? Free ferry pickups.

Eating & Drinking

Several hotels and hostels have restaurants and bars that are at least as popular with locals as they are with guests and visitors. Opening hours can fluctuate according to the season and the crowds. Nelly Bay and Horseshoe Bay have the most dining choices.

Seafood is, unsurprisingly, the chomp of choice on Maggie.

Noodies on the Beach MEXICAN $
(☎07-4778 5786; 2/6 Pacific Dr, Horseshoe Bay; from $10; ⏲10am-10pm Mon-Wed & Fri, 8am-10pm Sat, 8am-3pm Sun; P) You can't help but love a joint which hands out free sombreros with jugs of margarita. Noodies dishes up fine Mexican food, but is arguably more famous for its coffee – reputedly the best on Maggie – and it has a book exchange to boot.

Picnic Bay Hotel PUB FOOD $
(The Esplanade, Picnic Bay; mains $11-26; ⏲9.30am-10pm) Settle in for a drink, with Townsville's city lights sparkling across the bay. Its **R&R Cafe Bar** (⏲9am-late) has an all-day grazing menu and huge salads, including Cajun prawn.

Man Friday MEXICAN, INTERNATIONAL $
(☎07-4778 5658; 37 Warboy St, Nelly Bay; mains $14-39; ⏲from 6pm Wed-Mon; 🍷) Chow down on classy Mexican favourites in an incongruous but idyllic fairy-lit garden with occasional wildlife sauntering by. Does not cater to dietary restrictions, and if it's busy don't expect your food in a hurry, but otherwise great food.

Arcadia Night Market MARKET $
(RSL Hall, Hayles Ave, Arcadia; ⏲5-8pm Fri) Small but lively night market, with licensed bar and plenty of cheap eats to chow through.

Marlin Bar PUB FOOD $$
(3 Pacific Dr, Horseshoe Bay; mains $16-24; ⏲lunch & dinner) You can't leave Maggie without enjoying a cold one by the window as the sun sets across the bay at this popular seaside pub. The meals are on the large side and (surprise!) revolve around seafood.

Information

There's no official visitor information centre on Magnetic Island, but Townsville's visitor information centre (p390) has info and maps, and can help find accommodation. Maps are also available at both ferry terminals in Townsville and at the terminal at Nelly Bay.

Most business take Eftpos, and ATMs are scattered throughout the island, including one at the **post office** (Sooning St, Nelly Bay; ⏲9am-5pm Mon-Fri, to 11am Sat).

Getting There & Away

All ferries arrive and depart Maggie from the terminal at Nelly Bay. Both Townsville ferry terminals have car parking.

Fantasea (☎07-4796 9300; www.magnetic-islandferry.com.au; Ross St, South Townsville) Operates a car ferry crossing eight times daily (seven on weekends) from the south side of Ross Creek, taking 35 minutes. It costs $178 (return) for a car and up to three passengers, and $29/17 (adult/child return) for foot passengers only. Bookings are essential and bicycles are transported free.

Sealink (☎07-4726 0800; www.sealinkqld.com.au) Operates a frequent passenger ferry between Townsville and Magnetic Island (adult/child return $32/16), which takes around 20 minutes. Ferries depart Townsville from the Breakwater Terminal on Sir Leslie Thiess Dr.

Getting Around

Magnetic Island has a fantastic trail network that leads along coastal ridges, the interior, between towns and to remote beaches. Not-very-detailed, but sufficient, maps are available at the ferry terminal ticket desk.

BICYCLE

Magnetic Island is ideal for cycling although some of the hills can be hard going. Most places to stay rent bikes for around $20 per day, and many offer them free to guests.

BUS

Sunbus (www.sunbus.com.au/sit_magnetic_island) ploughs between Picnic and Horseshoe Bays, meeting all ferries and stopping at major accommodation places. A day pass covering all zones is $7.20. Be sure to talk to the bus drivers, who love chatting about everything Maggie.

CAR & SCOOTER

Moke ('topless' car) and scooter rental places abound. You'll need to be over 21, have a current driving licence and leave a credit-card deposit. Scooter hire starts at around $35 per day, Mokes about $75. Try **MI Wheels** (☎07-4758 1111; www.miwheels.com.au; 138 Sooning St, Nelly Bay) for a classic Moke, or **Roadrunner Scooter Hire** (☎07-4778 5222; 3/64 Kelly St, Nelly Bay) for scooters and trail bikes.

NORTH OF TOWNSVILLE

As you leave Townsville, you also leave the dry tropics. Heading north, the scorched-brown landscape slowly gives way to sugarcane plantations lining the highway and tropical rainforest shrouding the hillsides.

Waterfalls, national parks and small villages hide up in the hinterland, including **Paluma Range National Park** (part of the Wet Tropics World Heritage Area); visitor centres in the area have leaflets outlining walking trails, swimming holes and camping grounds.

The region north of Townsville was hardest hit by Cyclone Yasi in February 2011 (and by Cyclone Larry in 2006), with damage to the coastline, islands, national parks and farmland. Much of the damage has been cleaned up, though some areas are still recovering.

Ingham & Around

POP 4767

Ingham is the proud guardian of the 120-hectare **Tyto wetlands** (Tyto Wetlands Information Centre; ☎07-4776 4792; www.tyto.com.au; cnr Cooper St & Bruce Hwy; ⏲8.45am-5pm Mon-Fri, 9am-4pm Sat & Sun), which has 4km of walking trails and attracts around 230 species of birds, including far-flung guests from Siberia and Japan. The locals – hundreds of wallabies – love it too, converging at dawn and dusk. There's an art gallery and library on site. The poem which inspired the iconic Slim Dusty hit 'Pub With No Beer' (1957) was written in the **Lees Hotel** (☎07-4776 1577; www.leeshotel.com.au; 58 Lannercost St, Ingham; s/d from $64/84, meals from $12; ⏲lunch & dinner Mon-Sat; ❄📶) by Ingham cane-cutter Dan Sheahan, after American soldiers drank the place dry. You'll spot the pub – which today has rooms, meals and even beer – by the mounted horseman on the roof. **Noorla Heritage Resort** (☎07-4776 1100; www.hotelnoorla.com.au; 5-9 Warren St, Ingham; s $69-169, d $79-179; ❄📶🏊) was once the domain of Italian cane cutters. These days, Ingham's wonderful 1920s art deco guesthouse has magnificently restored high-ceilinged rooms, plus cheaper container-style rooms in the garden.

Ingham is the jumping-off point for the majestic, well-worth-the-trip **Wallaman Falls**; at 305m, it's the longest single-drop waterfall in Australia. Located in **Girringun National Park**, 51km west of the town (the road is sealed except for the last 10km), the falls look their best in the Wet, though they are spectacular at any time. A steep but very worthwhile walking track (2km) takes you to the bottom of the falls. The **camping ground** (www.nprsr.qld.gov.au; per person/family $5.75/23) has barbecues and showers, plus regular wildlife visits, including – for those who can sit quietly and still – the occasional bobbing platypus in the swimming hole. Pick up a leaflet from the Tyto Wetlands Information Centre.

Twenty-four kilometres south of Ingham and 91km north of Townsville is the easily accessible **Jourama Falls** (6km off the Bruce Hwy), a lovely spot for walking, wildlife watching (look out for mahogany gliders) and camping. Continuing on to 40km south of Ingham (61km north of Townsville), is **Mt Spec**, a misty Eden of rainforest and eucalyptus trees criss-crossed by a variety of walking tracks. Access the area via the north by taking Spiegelhaur Rd towards Big Crystal Creek (4km) off the Bruce Hwy or via the southern route from charming **Paluma Village**.

Mungalla Station (☎07-4777 8718; www.mungallaaboriginaltours.com.au; 2hr tours adult/child $52.50/30) , 15km east of Ingham, runs insightful Aboriginal-led tours, including boomerang throwing and stories from the local Nywaigi culture. It's worth the extra cash to experience the traditional Kupmurri lunch of meat and vegies wrapped in banana leaves and cooked underground in an earth 'oven' (adult/child including tour $102.50/60).

Greyhound (☎1300 473 946; www.greyhound.com.au; Townsville/Cairns $39/52) and **Premier** (☎13 34 10; www.premierms.com.au; Townsville/Cairns $26/34) buses stop in Ingham on their Cairns–Brisbane runs.

Ingham sits along the **Queensland Rail** (☎1800 872 467; www.queenslandrail.com.au) Brisbane–Cairns train line.

Cardwell & Around

POP 1250

Most of the Bruce Hwy runs several kilometres inland from the coast, so it comes as something of a shock to see the sea lapping right next to the road as you pull into the small town of Cardwell. Most travellers stop here for seasonal fruit picking (check at the backpackers if you're looking for work).

Activities

Cardwell Forest Drive OUTDOORS

From the town centre, this scenic 26km round trip through the national park is chock-a-block with lookouts, walking tracks and picnic areas signposted along the way. There are super swimming opportunities at **Attie Creek Falls**, as well as at the aptly named **Spa Pool**, where you can sit in a rock hollow as water gushes over you.

Cardwell's visitor centre has brochures detailing other walking trails and swimming holes in the park.

Sleeping

Cardwell Beachcomber Motel & Tourist Park CARAVAN PARK $

(☎07-4066 8550; www.cardwellbeachcomber.com.au; 43a Marine Pde; unpowered/powered sites $27/36, motel d $98-125, cabins & studios $95-115;) This large park took a thrashing from Cyclone Yasi in 2011, but is back in action with new poolside cabins, cute studios and modern ocean-view villas. A surprisingly swish **restaurant** dishes up seafood, steaks and whiz-bang pizzas.

Cardwell Central Backpackers HOSTEL $

(☎07-4066 8404; www.cardwellbackpackers.com.au; 6 Brasenose St; dm $22;) Friendly hostel catering mostly to seasonal workers (management can help find jobs), but it also accepts overnighters. Free internet and pool table.

Mudbrick Manor B&B $$

(☎07-4066 2299; www.mudbrickmanor.com.au; Lot 13, Stony Creek Rd; s/d $90/120;) As the name suggests, this family home is handbuilt from mud bricks (and timber and stone). Huge, beautifully appointed rooms congregate around a fountained courtyard. Rates include hot breakfast; book at least a few hours ahead for delicious three-course dinners (per person $30).

Information

Rainforest & Reef Centre (☎07-4066 8601; www.greatgreenwaytourism.com/rainforest-reef.html; 142 Victoria St; 8.30am-5pm Mon-Fri, 9am-1pm Sat & Sun) The Rainforest & Reef Centre, next to Cardwell's jetty, has a truly brilliant interactive rainforest display, and detailed info on Hinchinbrook Island and other nearby national parks.

Getting There & Away

Greyhound (☎1300 473 946; www.greyhound.com.au) and **Premier** (☎13 34 10; www.premier-ms.com.au) buses on the Brisbane–Cairns route stop at Cardwell. Fares to Cairns are $50, to Townsville $37.

Cardwell is on the Brisbane–Cairns train line; contact **Queensland Rail** (☎1800 872 467; www.queenslandrail.com.au) for details.

Boats depart for Hinchinbrook Island from Port Hinchinbrook Marina, 2km south of town.

Mission Beach

POP 4852

Less than 30km east of the Bruce Hwy's rolling sugar-cane and banana plantations, the hamlets that make up greater Mission Beach are hidden among World Heritage rainforest. The rainforest extends right to the Coral Sea, giving this 14km-long palm-fringed stretch of secluded inlets and wide beaches the castaway feel of a tropical island.

The frightfully powerful Cyclone Yasi made landfall at Mission Beach in 2011, stripping much of the rainforest and vegetation bare. The communities here are still recovering a little – for example at the time of research there was no scuba-diving operator, although there are hopes one will open in the near future.

Collectively referred to as Mission Beach, or just 'Mission', the area comprises a sequence of individual, very small and laid-back villages strung along the coast. **Bingil Bay** lies 4.8km north of **Mission Beach proper** (sometimes called North Mission). **Wongaling Beach** is 5km south; from here it's a further 5.5km south to **South Mission Beach**. Most amenities are in Mission proper and Wongaling Beach; South Mission Beach and Bingil Bay are mainly residential.

Mission is one of the closest access points to the Great Barrier Reef, and is the gateway to Dunk Island. There are plenty of opportunities for on-foot exploring here: walking tracks fan out around Mission Beach, with Australia's highest density of cassowaries (around 40) roaming the rainforest. While Mission's coastline seems to scream 'toe dip!', don't just fling yourself into the water any old where: stick to the swimming enclosures, lest you have a nasty encounter with a marine stinger…or croc.

Activities

Adrenalin junkies flock to Mission Beach for extreme and water-based sports, including white-water rafting on the nearby Tully River. If you've got your own board, Bingil Bay is one of the rare spots inside the reef where it's possible to surf, with small but consistent swells of around 1m.

Stinger enclosures at Mission Beach and South Mission Beach provide safe year-round swimming.

The visitor centre has heaps of information on the many superb walking tracks in the area.

OFF THE BEATEN TRACK

HINCHINBROOK ISLAND

Australia's largest island national park (399 sq km) is a holy grail for walkers, but it's not easy to get to and advance planning is essential. Granite mountains rise dramatically from the sea. The mainland side is dense with lush tropical vegetation, while long sandy beaches and tangles of mangrove curve around the eastern shore.

Hinchinbrook's highlight is the **Thorsborne Trail** (also known as the East Coast Trail), a very challenging 32km coastal track. **NPRSR camp sites** (☎13 74 68; www.nprsr.qld.gov.au; per person $5.45) are interspersed along the route. It's recommended that you take three nights to complete the trail; return walks of individual sections are also possible. Be prepared for hungry native beasts (including crocs), saber-toothed mosquitoes, and very rough patches. You'll have to draw your own water.

As only 40 walkers are allowed to traverse the trail at any one time, NPRSR recommends booking a year ahead for a place during the high season and six months ahead for other dates. Cancellations are not unheard of, so it's worth asking if you've arrived without a booking.

Hinchinbrook Island Cruises (☎07-4066 8601; www.hinchinbrookislandcruises.com.au) runs a service from Cardwell to Hinchinbrook (one way per person $90, 1½ hours). It also operates a five-hour day cruise to Hinchinbrook (per person $99, minimum four people), though the schedule is very erratic: book through Cardwell's Rainforest & Reef Centre (p395).

★ **Skydive Mission Beach** SKYDIVING
(☎1300 800 840; www.skydivemissionbeach.com.au; 1 Wongaling Rd, Wongaling Beach; 4267m tandem dives $334) Mission Beach is rightfully one of the most popular spots in Queensland for skydiving, with views over gorgeous islands and blue water, and a soft landing on a white-sand beach. Sky Dive Australia, known locally as Sky Dive Mission Beach, runs several flights per day.

Blokart Mission Beach ADVENTURE SPORTS
(☎07-4068 8310; www.missionbeachadventurehire.com; 71 Banfield Pde, Wongaling Beach) Blokarting is like sand sailing: wheeled, low-to-the-ground 'karts' have a sail that propels you along the beach. Otherwise, come here for all your rental needs, from kayaks to bicycles.

Big Mama Sailing SAILING
(☎0437 206 360; www.bigmamasailing.com; adult/child from $75/50) Hit the water on an 18m ketch with passionate boaties Stu, Lisa and Fletcher. Choose from a 2.5-hour sunset tour, a barbecue lunch cruise or a full day on the reef.

Coral Sea Kayaking KAYAKING
(☎07-4068 9154; www.coralseakayaking.com; half-/full-day tours $80/136) Knowledgeable full-day guided tours to Dunk Island; easy-going bob-arounds on the half-day option.

Fishin' Mission FISHING
(☎0427 323 469; www.fishinmission.com.au; half-/full-day trips $160/260) Chilled-out reef-fishing charters with local pros.

Mission Beach Tropical Fruit Safari FOOD TASTING
(☎07-4068 7099; www.missionbeachtourism.com; Mission Beach Visitor Centre, Porter Promenade, Mission Beach; adult/family $9.50/23.50; ⏲1-2pm Mon & Tue) Get to know (and taste) weird and wonderful local tropical fruits.

Festivals & Events

Mission Evolve Music Fest MUSIC
(www.missionevolve.com.au) Two days of live music in October featuring blues, roots, soul, funk and DJs from around Far North Queensland.

Sleeping

The visitor centre has a list of booking agents for holiday rentals.

Hostels have courtesy bus pick-ups.

DON'T MISS

TULLY RIVER RAFTING

The Tully River provides thrilling white water year-round thanks to Tully's trademark bucket-downs and the river's hydroelectric floodgates. Rafting trips are timed to coincide with the daily release of the gates, resulting in grade-four rapids foaming against a backdrop of stunning rainforest scenery.

Day trips with **Raging Thunder Adventures** (☎07-4030 7990; www.ragingthunder.com.au; standard/extreme trips $189/215) or **R'n'R White Water Rafting** (☎07-4041 9444; www.raft.com.au; from $179) include a barbecue lunch and transport from Tully or nearby Mission Beach. Transfers from Cairns are an extra $10.

South Mission Beach

Sea-S-Ta GUESTHOUSE $$$
(☎07-4088 6699; www.sea-s-ta.com.au; 38 Kennedy Esplanade; per night $375; 📶) Awkward name, amazing place. This self-contained holiday beach house is a great option for groups looking to stay and play in Mission. The bright, Mexico-inspired hacienda sleeps six, and comes with *mucho* extras, from juicers to his 'n' hers slippers. Two-night minimum stay; rates go down the longer you stay.

Wongaling Beach

Scotty's Mission Beach House HOSTEL $
(☎1800 665 567; www.scottysbeachhouse.com.au; 167 Reid Rd; dm $25-29, d $71; ❄@📶🏊) Clean, comfy rooms (including girls-only dorms with Barbie-pink sheets!) are grouped around Scotty's grassy, social pool area. Out front, **Scotty's Bar & Grill** (☎1800 665 567; 167 Reid Rd; mains $10-30; ⏲5pm-midnight), open to nonguests, has something happening virtually every night, from fire-twirling shows to pool comps and live music. Classic backpackery good times, ahoy!

Dunk Island View Caravan Park CARAVAN PARK $
(☎07-40688248; www.dunkislandviewcaravanpark; 21 Webb Rd; unpowered/powered sites $28/38, 1-/2-bedroom unit $98/128; ❄📶🏊🐾) Wake to fresh sea breezes at this clean and congenial spot just 50m from the beach. Everything you'd want from a caravan park, with the bonus of a new **on-site cafe** (fish & chips $8).

THE CASSOWARY: ENDANGERED NATIVE

Like something out of *Jurassic Park*, this flightless prehistoric bird struts through the rainforest. It's as tall as a grown man, has three razor-sharp, dagger-style clawed toes, a bright-blue head, red wattles (the lobes hanging from its neck), a helmetlike horn, and shaggy black feathers similar to an emu's. Meet the cassowary, an important link in the rainforest ecosystem. It's the only animal capable of dispersing the seeds of more than 70 species of trees whose fruit is too large for other rainforest animals to digest and pass (which acts as fertiliser). You're most likely to see cassowaries in the wild around Mission Beach, Etty Bay and the Cape Tribulation section of the Daintree National Park. They can be aggressive, particularly if they have chicks. Do not approach them; if one threatens you, don't run – give the bird right-of-way and try to keep something solid between you and it, preferably a tree.

It is estimated that there are 1000 or fewer cassowaries in the wild north of Queensland. An endangered species, the cassowary's biggest threat is loss of habitat, and most recently the cause has been natural. Tropical Cyclone Yasi stripped much of the rainforest around Mission Beach bare, threatening the struggling population with starvation. The cyclone also left the birds exposed to the elements, and more vulnerable to dog attacks and cars as they venture out in search of food.

Next to the Mission Beach visitor centre there are cassowary conservation displays at the **Wet Tropics Environment Centre** (07-4068 7197; www.wettropics.gov.au; Porter Promenade; 10am-4pm), staffed by volunteers from the **Community for Cassowary & Coastal Conservation** (www.cassowaryconservation.asn.au). Proceeds from gift-shop purchases go towards buying cassowary habitat. The website www.savethecassowary.org.au is also a good source of info.

★Licuala Lodge B&B **$$**
(07-4068 8194; www.licualalodge.com.au; 11 Mission Circle; s/d/t incl breakfast $99/135/185;) Chummy B&B with a guest kitchen, a wonderful verandah, a waterfall swimming pool and cassowary gatecrashers. Don't be alarmed by the teddy bears in your bedroom. It's 1.5km from the beach and pretty much anything else, making this a serene escape.

Hibiscus Lodge B&B B&B **$$**
(07-4068 9096; www.hibiscuslodge.com.au; 5 Kurrajong Cl; r from $135;) Wake to the sound of birds chirping and, more than likely, spot a cassowary or two during breakfast (an absolute must) on the rainforest-facing deck of this lovely B&B. With only three (very private) rooms, bookings are essential. No kids.

Mission Beach

Mission Beach Retreat HOSTEL **$**
(07-4088 6229; www.missionbeachretreat.com.au; 49 Porter Promenade; dm $22-25, d $56;) Bang in the centre of town with the bonus of being beachfront, this is an easy, breezy backpacker spot that's hard not to like.

Mission Beach Ecovillage CABIN **$$**
(07-4068 7534; www.ecovillage.com.au; Clump Point Rd; d $130-210;) With its own banana and lime trees scattered around its tropical gardens and a direct path through the rainforest to the beach, this 'ecovillage' makes the most of its environment. Bungalows cluster around a rocky pool, and deluxe cottages have private spas. There's a licensed **restaurant** (07-4068 7534; Clump Point Rd; mains $18.50; 7am-10pm Wed-Sat).

Bingil Bay

★Jackaroo Hostel HOSTEL **$**
(07-4068 7137; www.jackaroohostel.com; 13 Frizelle Rd; camp sites $15, dm/d incl breakfast $24/58;) This timber-pole-frame retreat high in the rainforest has it all, and then some. Jungly surrounds, airy rooms and the breezy terrace tempt you to linger longer; the jungle pool seals the deal.

★Sanctuary CABIN **$$**
(07-4088 6064, 1800 777 012; www.sanctuaryatmission.com; 72 Holt Rd; dm $35, s/d huts from $65/70, cabins $145/165; mid-Apr–mid-Dec;) Reached by a steep 600m-long rainforest walking track from the car park (4WD pick-up available), at Sanctuary you can sleep surrounded only by fly screen on a platform in a simple hut, or opt for an en suite cabin whose shower has floor-to-ceiling rainforest views.

Tramp the walking tracks, take a yoga class ($15), and indulge in a massage (per hour $80). Cook in the self-catering kitchen or dine on wholesome fare at the restaurant. Eco-initiatives include its own sewerage system, rainwater harvesting and biodegradable detergents. Not suitable for kids under 11.

Eating

The majority of bars and/or restaurants are clustered in Mission Beach proper along Porter Promenade and its adjoining spider's web of tiny walkways and arcades. There's a small supermarket here, and a huge Woolworths supermarket at Wongaling Beach (look for the giant cassowary). Wongaling also has a handful of eateries, bars and bottle shops.

Wongaling Beach

Millers Beach Bar & Grill PUB FOOD $

(07-4068 8177; 1 Banfield Pde; $10-38; 3pm-late Tue-Fri, noon-late Sat & Sun) So close to the beach you'll be picking sand out of your beer, Millers has a rockin' little courtyard custom-made for lazy loitering. Graze on $10 pizzas (4pm to 6pm daily), attack a giant steak, or just devour the view of Dunk Island over a cocktail. Gluten free options and a kids' menu too.

★**Caffe Rustica** ITALIAN $$

(07-4068 9111; 24 Wongaling Beach Rd; mains $13-25, pizzas $10-25; 5pm-late Wed-Sat, 10am-9pm Sun;) This contemporary corrugated-iron beach shack is home to some seriously delicious homemade pastas and crispy-crust pizzas; it also makes its own gelato and sorbet. Be sure to book ahead.

Mission Beach

Fish Bar SEAFOOD $

(07-4088 6419; Porter Promenade; mains $10-17; 10am-midnight) For socialising and scarfing, this place is tough to top. It's laid-back yet lively, with a zingy menu that includes lots of seafood.

Zenbah INTERNATIONAL $

(07-4088 6040; 39 Porter Promenade; mains $9-25; 10am-1.30am Fri & Sat, to midnight Sun-Thu) The colourful chairs on the pavement mark Zenbah as the vibrant little eatery/hang-out that it is. The food ranges from Middle Eastern to Asian all the way back to pizza, and you can digest it all against a backdrop of live tunes on Fridays and Saturdays.

Garage Bar & Grill MODERN AUSTRALIAN $$

(07-4088 6280; 41 Donkin Lane; meze plates $17; 9am-late;) This supersocial spot on Mission's 'Village Green' serves delicious 'sliders' (mini burgers), free-pour cocktails ($14), good coffee, cakes and tapas. Wash it all down with some toe-tappin' live music.

Bingil Bay

★**Bingil Bay Cafe** CAFE $$

(29 Bingil Bay Rd; mains $14-23; 6.30am-10pm;) Everything is groovy at this lavender landmark, from the eclectic menu to the mellow vibes emanating from the porch. Breakfast is a highlight, or just grab a coldie and immerse yourself in the art displays, live music and hey-dude buzz.

Shopping

Mission Beach Markets MARKET

(Porter Promenade, Mission Beach; 8am-1pm 1st & 3rd Sun of month) Local arts, crafts, jewellery, tropical fruit, homemade gourmet goods and more overflow from stalls at the Mission Beach Markets.

Mission Beach Rotary Monster Market MARKET

(Marcs Park, Cassowary Dr, Wongaling Beach; 8am-12.30pm last Sun of month Apr-Nov) Wonderful stuff, including handmade log furniture.

Information

Mission Beach Visitor Centre (07-4068 7099; www.missionbeachtourism.com; Porters Promenade, Mission Beach; 9am-4.45pm Mon-Sat, 10am-4pm Sun) Has reams of information in multiple languages.

Getting There & Away

Greyhound (1300 473 946; www.greyhound.com.au) and **Premier** (13 34 10; www.premierms.com.au) buses stop in Wongaling Beach next to the 'big cassowary'. Fares with Greyhound/Premier are $24/19 to Cairns, $42/46 to Townsville.

Sugarland Car Rentals (07-4068 8272; www.sugarland.com.au; 30 Wongaling Beach Rd, Wongaling Beach; 8am-5pm) Rents small cars from $35 per day.

Dunk Island

Dunk is known to the Djiru Aboriginal people as Coonanglebah (the island of peace and plenty). They're not wrong: this is pretty much your ideal tropical island, with jungle, white-sand beaches and impossibly blue water.

Walking trails criss-cross (and almost circumnavigate) Dunk: the circuit track (9.2km) is the best way to have a proper stickybeak at the island's interior and abundant wildlife. There's snorkelling over bommies at Muggy Muggy (although algae growth had covered most of the coral when we passed) and great swimming at truly beautiful Coconut Beach. On weekends there are often special events such as bongo lessons or a ukulele band – check with the Mission Beach Visitor Centre (p399).

The island's resort is currently closed due to cyclone damage, though **camping** (☎0417 873 390; per person $5.15) has reopened, with gorgeous sites on the beach, hot showers and a gas grill. Bring your own supplies. On Friday, Saturday and Sunday a **kiosk** (mains $10.50-30; ⊙open with taxi boat times) opens until the last taxi boat leaves and serves cold beer plus very good fresh prawns, fish and burgers.

Mission Beach Dunk Island Water Taxi (☎07-4068 8310; www.missionbeachwatertaxi.com; Banfield Pde, Wongaling Beach; adult/child return $35/18), departing from Wongaling Beach, makes the 20-minute trip to Dunk Island.

Mission Beach to Innisfail

The road north from Mission Beach rejoins the Bruce Hwy at **El Arish** (population 442), from where you can take the direct route north by continuing straight along the Bruce Hwy. Turn-offs lead to beach communities including exquisite **Etty Bay**, with its wandering cassowaries, rocky headlands, rainforest, large stinger enclosure and a simple but superbly sited caravan park.

Innisfail & Around

POP 10,143

Sitting pretty just 80km south of the Cairns tourism frenzy, Innisfail is a textbook example of a laid-back, Far North Queensland country town. Fisherfolk ply the wide Johnstone River, tractors trundle down the main street, and locals are equally proud of their art deco architecture (although it was severely damaged in 2006 by Cyclone Larry) and born-and-bred footy (rugby league) hero Billy Slater.

Relaxing, beachside Flying Fish Point is 8km northeast of Innisfail's town centre, while national parks, including the fun **Mamu Tropical Sky Walk** (www.mamutropical-skywalk.com.au; Palmerston Hwy; adult/child $20/10; ⊙9.30am-5.30pm, last entry 4.30pm) – a 2.5km, wheelchair accessible walking circuit through the canopy – are within a short drive.

Sleeping

Innisfail's hostels primarily cater to banana pickers who work the surrounding plantations (they are also the places you should inquire with if you're looking for work); weekly rates average about $185 (dorm). The friendly and helpful visitor information centre has a full list of accommodation options that can help with finding work.

Backpackers Shack HOSTEL $
(☎049 904 2446, 07-4061 7760; www.backpackersshack.com; 7 Ernest St; dm per week $195; P ❄ @) Central and friendly.

Codge Lodge HOSTEL $
(☎07-4061 8055; www.codgelodge.com; 63 Rankin St; dm per week $185; ❄ @ ≋) This cheerful hostel has plenty of farm workers bunking down for an extended stay, but it also welcomes overnight travellers.

Barrier Reef Motel MOTEL $$
(☎07-4061 4988; www.barrierreefmotel.com.au; Bruce Hwy; r from $120, units $160-180; ❄ @ ≋) The best place to stay in Innisfail, this motel has airy, tiled rooms with large bathrooms.

Eating

Innisfail Fish Depot SEAFOOD $
(51 Fitzgerald Esplanade; ⊙8am-6pm Mon-Fri, 9am-4pm Sat, 10am-4pm Sun) Fresh-as-it-gets fish to throw on the BBQ and organic cooked prawns by the bagful (per kg $18 to $20).

Flying Fish Point Cafe CAFE $$
(9 Elizabeth St, Flying Fish Point; mains $12-25; ⊙7.30am-8pm) Come hungry to finish the huge seafood baskets of battered and crumbed fish, barbecued calamari, wonton prawns, tempura scallops and more.

Oliveri's Continental Deli DELI $
(www.oliverisdeli.com.au; 41 Edith St; sandwiches $8.50-11; ⊙8.30am-5.15pm Mon-Fri, to 12.30pm Sat) An Innisfail institution offering goodies including 60-plus varieties of European cheese, ham and salami, and scrumptious sandwiches. Fantastic coffee.

Getting There & Away

Bus services operate once daily with **Premier** (☎13 34 10; www.premierms.com.au) and several times daily with **Greyhound** (☎1300 473 946; www.greyhound.com.au) between Innisfail and Townsville ($47, 4½ hours) and Cairns ($20, 1½ hours).

Innisfail is on the Cairns–Brisbane train line; contact **Queensland Rail** (☎1800 872 467; www.queenslandrail.com.au) for information.

Cairns & the Daintree Rainforest

Includes ➡

Best Places to Eat

- Vivo Bar & Grill (p422)
- Yorkeys Knob Boating Club (p419)
- Tokyo Dumpling (p414)
- Candy (p414)
- Chianti's (p420)

Best Places to Stay

- Bloomfield Lodge (p436)
- Peppers Beach Club (p433)
- Cape Trib Beach House (p437)
- Travellers Oasis (p413)
- Port O' Call Eco Lodge (p432)

Why Go?

Cairns means R & R – the Reef and Rainforest. Together, they make this far-flung city an East Coast essential. Endless bus- and boatloads of eager beavers shuttle between Cairns and these World Heritage wonders, although upmarket Port Douglas is closer to the outer Reef and the Daintree Rainforest. Sultry, carefree Cairns swings between backpacker samsara and family fun-land. Head to Palm Cove or Port Douglas for upscale retreats. Inland, lush Atherton Tableland's cooler climes, lakes and waterfalls offer welcome relief from Cairns' humidity and crowds.

Highways hug scenic sections of the shoreline to Port Douglas, before meeting the mighty Daintree River's vehicular ferry. From here, the protected rainforest stretches up to Cape Tribulation, tumbling onto seductive white-sand beaches where hidden perils – marine stingers (October to May) and saltwater crocodiles (year-round) – should be taken seriously.

True-blue adventure-seekers head onwards to Cooktown on the 4WD-only Bloomfield Track.

When to Go

Cairns

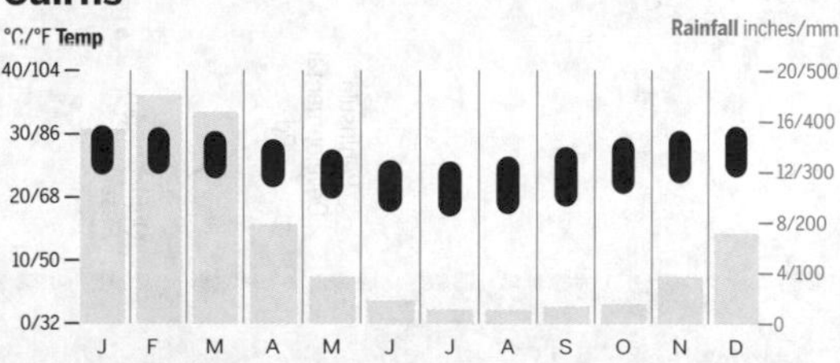

May Port Douglas pizzazz at Carnivale. Stinger season ends.

Jun Cooktown Discovery Festival's costumed reenactment of Cook's landing.

Nov Divers delight in the reef's annual coral spawning.

Cairns & the Daintree Rainforest Highlights

1. Diving, snorkelling and swimming among the fish, turtles and corals of the **Great Barrier Reef** (p407).
2. Taking the **Kuku-Yalanji Dreamtime Walk** (p434) alongside the clear waters of the **Mossman Gorge** (p434) section of the Daintree National Park.
3. Riding the **Skyrail** (p418) above the rainforest to the markets of Kuranda, returning by the **Kuranda Scenic Railway** (p418).
4. Indulging in life's finer pleasures in the romantic restaurants and resorts of pristine **Palm Cove** (p421).
5. Savouring a coldie at the iconic **Lion's Den Hotel** (p441) upon

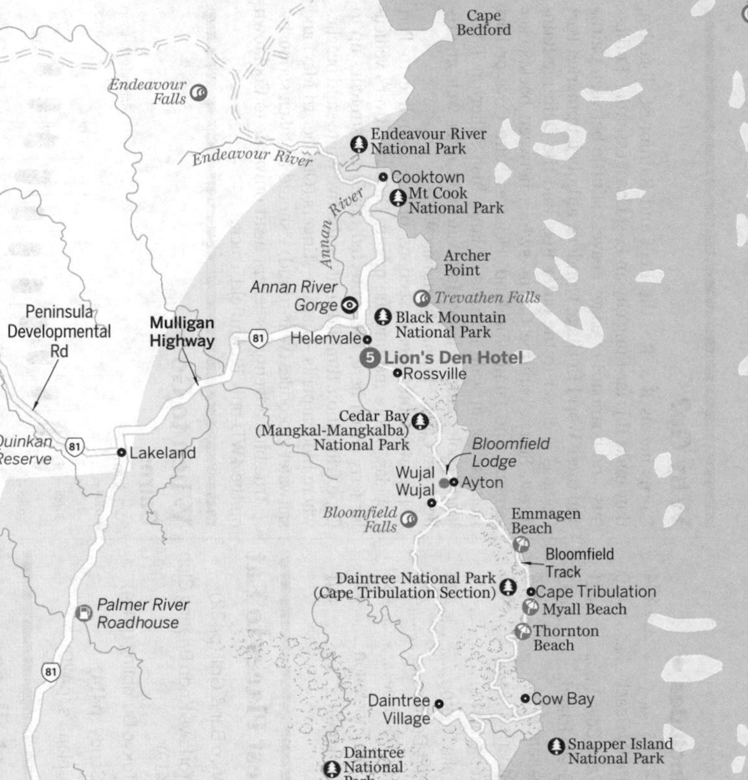

completion of the bone-shaking 4WD Bloomfield Track.

6 Getting educated about our ancient ancestors at **Hartley's Crocodile Adventures** (p423).

7 Fishing for barra on **Lake Tinaroo** (p428) then stopping for a coldie at Yungaburra's must-see pub.

8 Cooling down amid the lush scenery of the **Atherton Tablelands** (p426), stopping for a swim on the Millaa Millaa **Waterfalls Circuit** (p428).

9 Travelling back in time to **Historic Village Herberton** (p427), spending the night in gorgeous Yungaburra.

10 Contemplating determination, romance and tragedy at **Paronella Park** (p426).

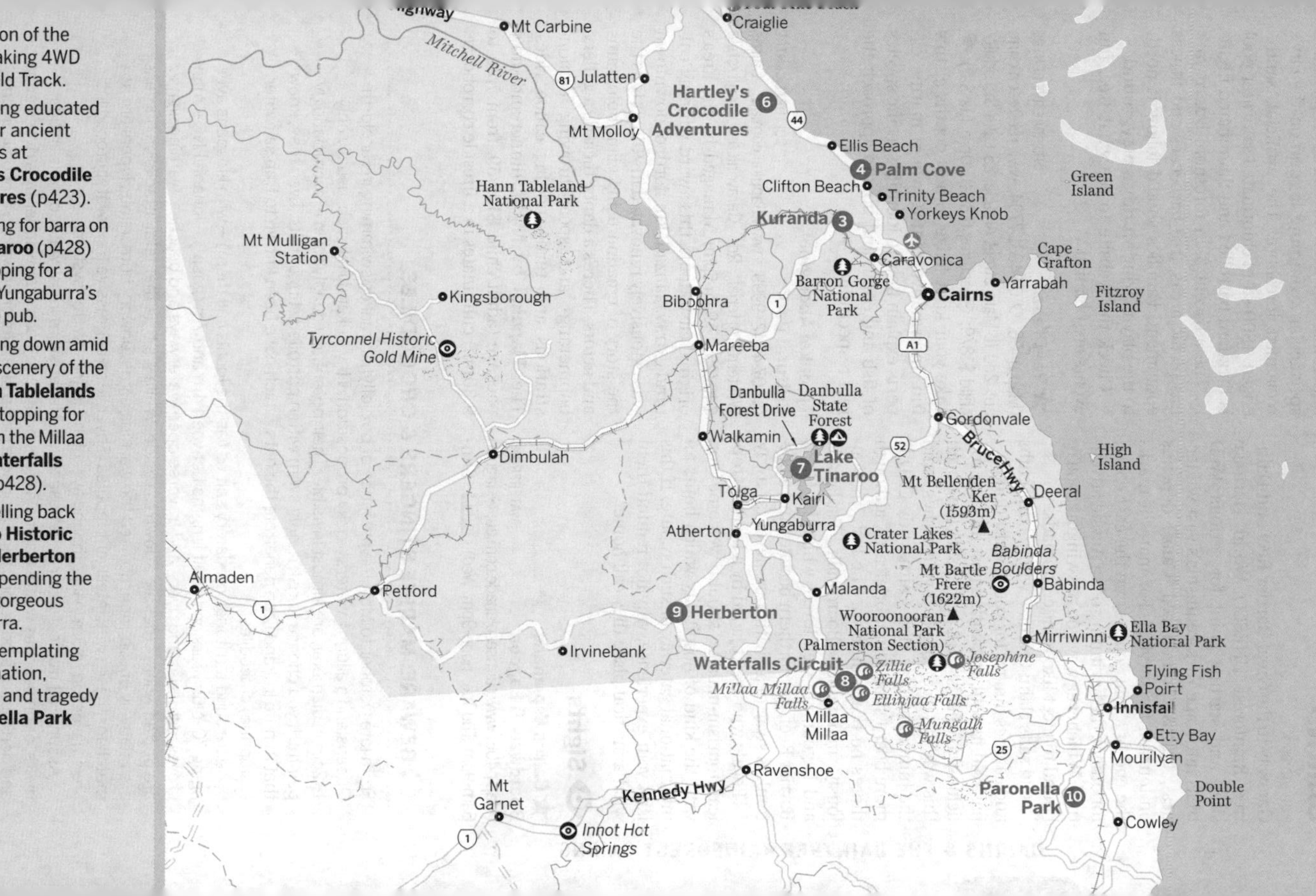

CAIRNS

POP 165,860

Gateway to the Great Barrier Reef and Daintree Rainforest UNESCO World Heritage sites, and starting point for serious 4WD treks into Cape York Peninsula's vast wilderness, Cairns (pronounced 'Cans') depends on tourism for survival. For many, it marks the end of a long journey up the east coast; for others, the beginning of an Aussie adventure. Whichever way you're swinging, you're bound to meet like-minded nomads.

Old salts claim Cairns – whose bars, clubs and eateries hunger for your tourist dollars – has sold its soul, but with a past life as a rollicking goldfields' port, perhaps it's long been this way. It's easy to spend your riches amid the humid, holiday vibe. Cairns' tidy CBD is more board shorts than briefcases, although there's no beach in town. The lush, meticulously maintained Boardwalk, Esplanade and Lagoon are well loved, while the Great Barrier Reef, the northern beaches and a bottomless swag of activities are never far away.

Locals who aren't jaded by a kind of tropical tourism-malaise should welcome you with the kind of hospitality which befits an international gateway of such repute. If this isn't your experience, why not remind them what a magical place they call home?

Sights

★Cairns Esplanade, Boardwalk & Lagoon — WATERFRONT

(Map p406; www.cairnsesplanade.com.au; lagoon 6am-9pm Thu-Tue, noon-9pm Wed) FREE Sun- and fun-lovers flock to Cairns' Esplanade's spectacular **swimming lagoon** on the city's reclaimed foreshore. The artificial, sandy-edged, 4800-sq-m chlorinated saltwater pool is lifeguard patrolled and illuminated nightly. The adjacent 3km foreshore **boardwalk** has picnic areas, free barbecues and fitness equipment. Families should follow it north to the play-mazing **Muddy's playground**.

Check the website to see what free, fun events are planned.

★Reef Teach — INTERPRETIVE CENTRE

(Map p406; 07-4031 7794; www.reefteach.com.au; 2nd fl, Main Street Arcade, 85 Lake St; adult/child $18/9; lectures 6.30-8.30pm Tue-Sat) Take your knowledge to new depths at this fun, informative centre, where marine experts explain how to identify specific species of fish and coral, and how to approach the reef respectfully.

Tjapukai Aboriginal Cultural Park — CULTURAL CENTRE

(07-4042 9999; www.tjapukai.com.au; Cairns Western Arterial Rd, Caravonica; adult/child $40/25; 9am-5pm) Managed by the area's original custodians, this award-winning cultural extravaganza 15km north of downtown was extensively renovated in 2015. It tells the story of creation using giant holograms and actors. There's a dance theatre, a gallery, boomerang- and spear-throwing demonstrations and turtle-spotting canoe rides. The **Tjapukai by Night** dinner-and-show package (adult/child $109/59, from 7pm to 9.30pm) culminates in a fireside corroboree.

BEWARE: MARINE STINGERS & CROCODILES

From late October to May, the presence of box jellyfish makes swimming in Far North Queensland's alluring waters a risky proposition. Tiny irukandji jellyfish, usually only 1–2cm in diameter, are almost invisible. Their potentially deadly toxin is excruciatingly painful. If you choose to risk it, *only* swim within patrolled stinger nets. Even then, know that minute irukandji can penetrate the nets, which have been known to trap saltwater (estuarine) crocodiles!

Year-round territorial, predatory salties (as the locals call them) – with lifespans averaging 70-plus years and adult lengths between 4m and 7m (gasp!) – inhabit FNQ's mangroves, estuaries and rivers, and traverse open waterways and beaches: warning signs are posted where crocs are known to reside. While it's true that fatal attacks on humans are relatively uncommon, do heed the warning signs: unwary human interlopers are no match for these swift, intelligent reptiles. Shyer, less-aggressive freshwater crocodiles are smaller (up to 3m in length) and live inland in freshwater systems.

Assume all tropical waterways pose a risk. Never swim in saltwater creeks, in tidal rivers, or on beaches where water clarity is poor. Don't camp or wander by a river's edge, and don't leave food scraps lying around a camp site. Never provoke a crocodile in *any* way. Search 'be croc wise' at www.ehp.qld.gov.au for more.

When in doubt, stick with that lovely resort pool...

OFF THE BEATEN TRACK

BABINDA BOULDERS & WOOROONOORAN NATIONAL PARK

On the Bruce Hwy, 60km south of Cairns, Babinda is a small working-class town that leads 7km inland to the **Babinda Boulders**, where a photogenic creek rushes between 4m-high granite rocks. It's croc-free, but here lurks an equal danger: highly treacherous waters. Dreaming stories say that a young woman threw herself into the then-still waters after being separated from her love; her anguish caused the creek to become the surging, swirling torrent it is today. Almost 20 visitors have lost their lives at the boulders. Swimming is permitted in calm, well-marked parts of the creek, but pay careful heed to all warning signs. Walking tracks give you safe access for obligatory gasps and photographs.

The free **Babinda Boulders Camping Ground** (two-night maximum) has toilets, cold showers and free barbecues. Nearby, you can kayak the clear waters of Babinda Creek with **Babinda Kayak Hire** (☎07-4067 2678; www.babindakayakhire.com.au; 330 Stager Rd; half/full day incl pickups $55/83).

Part of the Wet Tropics World Heritage Area, the rainforest of the Josephine Falls section of Wooroonooran National Park creeps to the peak of Queensland's highest mountain, Mt Bartle Frere (1622m), providing an exclusive environment for numerous plant and animal species. The car park for Josephine Falls – a spectacular series of waterfalls and pools – is signposted 6km off the Bruce Hwy, 10km south of Babinda. It's then a steep, paved, 600m walk through the forest to the falls, at the foot of the Bellenden Ker Range.

The Mt Bartle Frere Summit Track (15km, two days return) leads from the Josephine Falls car park to the summit. The ascent is for fit, well-equipped hikers only; rain and cloud can close in suddenly. Camping is permitted along the trail; book ahead with the **NPRSR** (☎13 74 68; www.nprsr.qld.gov.au), and drop into the **Babinda Information Centre** (☎07-4067 1008; www.babindainfocentre.com.au; cnr Munro St & Bruce Hwy; ⏱9am-4pm) for trail maps.

Flecker Botanic Gardens — GARDENS

(☎07-4032 6650; www.cairns.qld.gov.au; 64 Collins Ave; ⏱grounds 7.30am-5.30pm daily, visitor centre 9am-4.30pm Mon-Fri, 10am-2.30pm Sat & Sun) FREE The made-of-mirrors **visitor centre** can advise on free guided walks around these beautiful tropical gardens. Follow the **Rainforest Boardwalk** to Saltwater Creek and Centenary Lakes, a birdwatcher's delight. Uphill from the gardens, **Mt Whitfield Conservation Park** has walking tracks through rainforest climbing to viewpoints over the city.

Enquire for directions to the **Mangrove Boardwalk** and its two revelatory routes into the wetlands.

Crystal Cascades — WATERFALLS

(via Redlynch) About 14km from Cairns, the Crystal Cascades are a series of beautiful waterfalls and idyllic, croc-free swimming holes that locals would rather keep to themselves. The area is accessed by a 1.2km (30-minute) pathway. Crystal Cascades is linked to Lake Morris (the city's reservoir) by a *steep* rainforest **walking trail** (allow three hours return); it starts near the picnic area.

There is no public transport to the pools. Drive to the suburb of Redlynch, then follow the signs to Crystal Cascades.

Cairns Regional Gallery — GALLERY

(Map p406; ☎07-4046 4800; www.cairnsregionalgallery.com.au; cnr Abbott & Shields Sts; adult/child $5/free; ⏱9am-5pm Mon-Fri, 10am-5pm Sat, 10am-2pm Sun) The permanent collection of this acclaimed gallery, housed in the heritage-listed former State Government Insurance Office (1936), has an emphasis on local and Indigenous work. There's also usually a visiting exhibition.

Tanks Arts Centre — GALLERY

(☎07-4032 6600; www.tanksartscentre.com; 46 Collins Ave; admission varies; ⏱9.30am-4pm Mon-Fri) Three gigantic, ex-WWII fuel-storage tanks have been transformed into local galleries and an inspired performing-arts venue. Lively market days are held here on the last Sunday of the month (April to November).

Australian Armour & Artillery Museum — MUSEUM

(☎07-4038 1665; ausarmour.com; 1145 Kamerunga Rd, Smithfield; adult/child $25/15; ⏱9.30am-4.30pm) Military and history buffs will enjoy this, the largest display of armoured vehicles and artillery in the southern hemisphere, opened in September 2014.

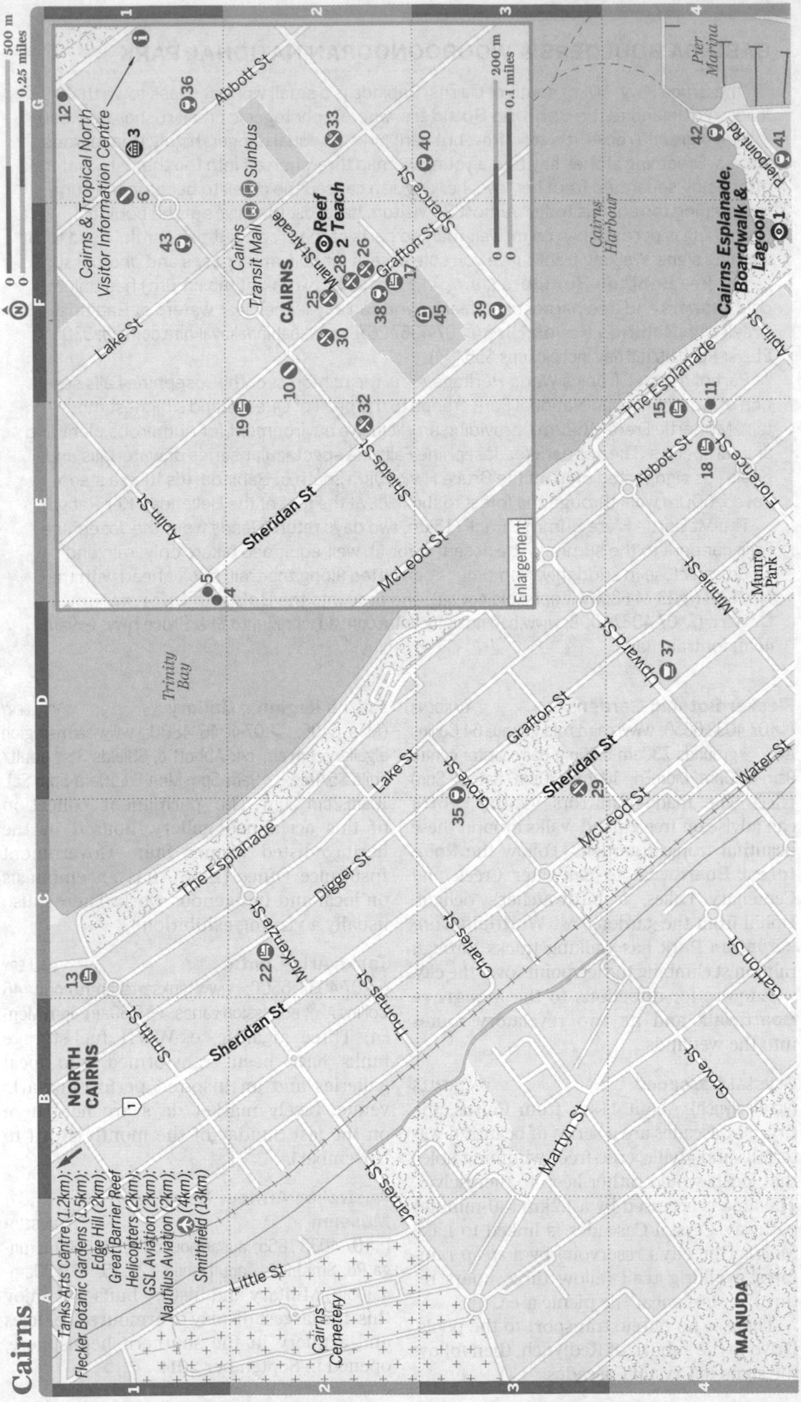

Cairns

0 500 m
0 0.25 miles

Tanks Arts Centre (1.2km); Flecker Botanic Gardens (1.5km); Edge Hill (2km); Great Barrier Reef Helicopters (2km); GSL Aviation (2km); Nautilus Aviation (2km); ✈ (4km); Smithfield (13km)

NORTH CAIRNS
13
Smith St
Sheridan St
22
McKenzie St
The Esplanade
Trinity Bay
Little St
Cairns Cemetery
James St
Thomas St
Digger St
Lake St
Charles St
35
Grove St
Martyn St
Sheridan St
29
Grafton St
McLeod St
Upward St
37
Abbott St
15
The Esplanade
18
11
Minnie St
Florence St
Munro Park
Aplin St
Water St
Grove St
Gatton St
MANUDA
Cairns Harbour
42
Pier Marina
Cairns Esplanade, Boardwalk & Lagoon
1
Pierpoint Rd
41

Enlargement
0 200 m
0 0.1 miles
12
Cairns & Tropical North Visitor Information Centre
6
3
Lake St
Aplin St
43
36
5
4
Sheridan St
19
Cairns Transit Mall
Sunbus
Abbott St
10
CAIRNS
Main St Arcade
25
Reef Teach
2
28
30
33
32
26
Shields St
38
17
Grafton St
McLeod St
45
Spence St
40
39

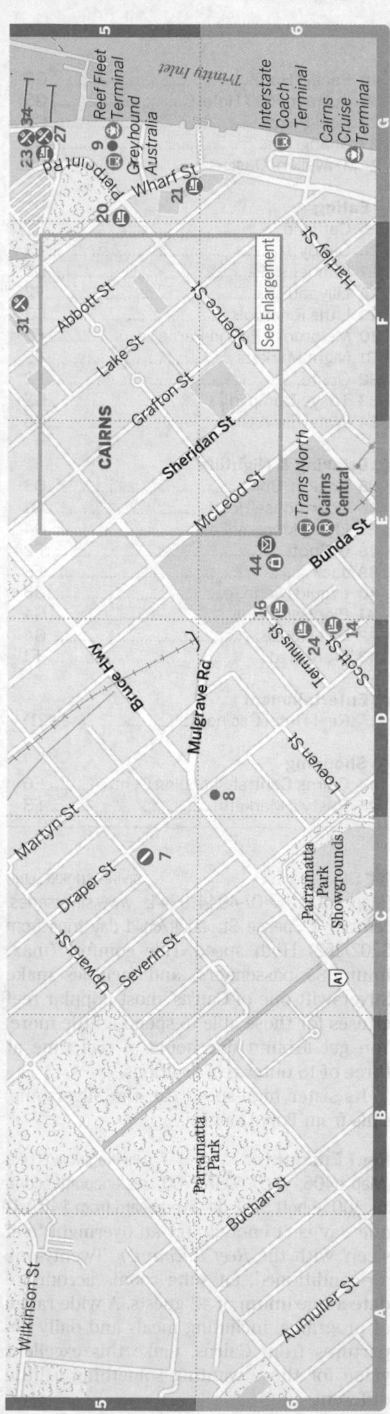

Activities

Innumerable tour operators run adventure-based activities from Cairns, most offering transfers to/from your accommodation.

AJ Hackett Bungee & Minjin ADVENTURE SPORTS
(☎1800 622 888; www.ajhackett.com; McGregor Rd, Smithfield; bungee $169, minjin $129, combos $249; ⏲10am-5pm) Bungee jump from the 50m tower or drop 45m and swing through the trees at 120km/h in the unique Minjin harness swing. Pricing includes return transfers from Cairns.

Fishing Cairns FISHING
(☎0448 563 586; www.fishingcairns.com.au; 60 Collinson St, Westcourt; half-day trips from $95) This experienced operator has a burley-bucket-load of half- to multiday fly, sports and game fishing tours and charters, on calm or open-water. Prices vary accordingly.

Cairns Wake Park WATER SPORTS
(☎07-4038 1304; www.cairnswakepark.com; Captain Cook Hwy, Smithfield; adult/child per hr $39/34, per day $74/69; ⏲10am-6pm) Learn to waterski, wakeboard or kneeboard without the boat at this water-sports park near the Skyrail. Pricing includes basic equipment and coaching.

Tours

An astounding 800+ tours drive, sail and fly out of Cairns daily, making the selection process almost overwhelming. We recommend operators with the benefit of years of experience, and who cover the bases of what visitors are generally looking for, and then some.

Cairns Discovery Tours GUIDED TOUR
(Map p406; ☎07-4028 3567; www.cairnsdiscoverytours.com; 36 Aplin St; adult/child $75/40; ⏲Mon-Sat) Half-day afternoon tours run by horticulturists; includes the botanic gardens and Palm Cove. Northern-beaches transfers are an extra $8 for adults, $4 for children.

Great Barrier Reef

Reef trips generally include transport, lunch, stinger-suits and snorkelling gear. When choosing a tour, consider the vessel type, its capacity, inclusions and destination: outer reefs are more pristine but further afield; inner reefs can be patchy and show signs of decay. Some prefer smaller, less-crowded vessels, while others go for the wide range of inclusions bigger boats promise.

Cairns

Top Sights
1 Cairns Esplanade, Boardwalk & Lagoon ... F4
2 Reef Teach ... F2

Sights
3 Cairns Regional Gallery ... G1

Activities, Courses & Tours
4 Adventure North Australia ... E1
5 Cairns Discovery Tours ... E1
6 Cairns Dive Centre ... G1
7 Deep Sea Divers Den ... C5
8 Down Under Cruise & Dive ... D6
Great Adventures ... (see 9)
Hot Air Cairns ... (see 9)
Ocean Free ... (see 9)
9 Passions of Paradise ... G5
10 Pro-Dive ... F2
Raging Thunder ... (see 9)
11 Reef Encounter ... E4
Reef Magic ... (see 9)
Silverswift ... (see 9)
Sunlover ... (see 9)
12 Tusa Dive ... G1

Sleeping
13 Cairns Plaza Hotel ... C1
14 Cairns Sharehouse ... D6
15 Doubletree by Hilton ... E4
16 Dreamtime Travellers Rest ... E6
17 Gilligan's Backpacker's Hotel & Resort ... F2
18 Hotel Cairns ... E4
19 Northern Greenhouse ... E2
20 Pacific Hotel ... G5
21 Pullman Reef Hotel Casino ... G5
22 Reef Palms ... C2
23 Shangri-La ... G5
24 Travellers Oasis ... D6

Eating
25 Caffiend ... F2
26 Candy ... F2
27 Dundees ... G5
28 Lillypad ... F2
29 Little Ricardo's ... D3
30 Meldrum's Pies in Paradise ... F2
31 Night Markets ... F5
32 Ochre ... E2
33 Tokyo Dumpling ... G2
34 Waterbar & Grill ... G5

Drinking & Nightlife
35 Cock 'n' Bull ... D3
36 Courthouse Hotel ... G1
37 Flying Monkey Cafe ... D4
38 G-Spot ... F2
39 Jack ... F3
40 Lyquid Nightlife ... G3
41 Pier Bar & Grill ... G4
42 Salt House ... G4
43 Woolshed ... F1

Entertainment
Reef Hotel Casino ... (see 21)

Shopping
44 Cairns Central Shopping Centre ... E6
45 Rusty's Markets ... F3

Vendors with their own pontoon offer all-round value; pontoons are a great way for families to experience the reef – those who aren't keen on getting in the water can enjoy the pontoon's facilities, or a trip in a glass-bottomed boat or semisubmersible.

Almost all boats depart from the Marlin Wharf (with check-in and booking facilities located inside the Reef Fleet Terminal) around 8am, returning around 6pm. Smaller operators may check-in boat-side at their berth on the wharf itself; check with your operator.

★ Tusa Dive DIVING, SNORKELLING
(Map p406; ☎07-4047 9100; www.tusadive.com; cnr Shields St & The Esplanade; adult/child day trips from $185/110) A maximum of 60 passengers aboard Cairns' newest, custom-designed reef vessel (the *T6*), a roving outer-reef permit and a high staff-to-passenger ratio make this operator an excellent choice for day trips.

★ Silverswift DIVING, SNORKELLING
(Map p406; ☎07-4044 9944; www.silverseries.com.au; 1 Spence St; adult/child day trips from $202/152) High speed, ride comfort (maximum 85 passengers) and facilities make Silverswift one of Cairns' most popular reef cruises for those able to spend a little more. You get around five hours of reef time at three of 16 outer reef locations.

Its sister high-speed cat, the Silversonic, sails from Port Douglas.

Reef Encounter DIVING, SNORKELLING
(Map p406; ☎07-4037 2700; reefencounter.com.au; 100 Abbott St; 2-day live-aboard from $410) If one day isn't enough, try an overnight 'reef sleep' with the *Reef Encounter*. Twenty-one air-conditioned, en suite rooms accommodate a maximum of 42 guests. A wide range of programs, including meals and daily departures from Cairns, make this excellent value for those wanting something a little different.

Passions of Paradise DIVING, SNORKELLING
(Map p406; ☎1800 111 346; www.passions.com.au; 1 Spence St; adult/child day trips from $159/109) This award-winning, high-speed catamaran takes you to Michaelmas Cay, where you can snorkel from a white sandy beach in the middle of the reef, and then to its exclusive mooring on Paradise Reef, away from the maddening crowds.

Great Adventures DIVING, SNORKELLING
(Map p406; ☎07-4044 9944; www.greatadventures.com.au; 1 Spence St; adult/child day trips from $218/112;) With a multilevel pontoon on the edge of the reef, Great Adventures offers fast catamaran reef day trips, and tours to Green Island. Diving add-ons, and glass-bottomed boat and semisubmersible tours are also available.

Reef Daytripper SAILING
(☎07-4036 0566; www.reefdaytripper.com.au; 1 Spence St; adult/child day trips from $139/100) Backpackers love these small-group sailing trips on an older-style catamaran to Upolu Reef on the outer Great Barrier Reef.

Down Under Cruise & Dive DIVING, SNORKELLING
(Map p406; ☎1800 079 099; www.downunderdive.com.au; 287 Draper St; adult/child day trips from $159/80) There's a fun Aussie feel to the great-value $159 basic outer reef snorkel package, with access to two reef sites and a swag of optional extras. PADI dive courses are also available.

Reef Magic DIVING, SNORKELLING
(Map p406; ☎07-4031 1588; www.reefmagiccruises.com; 1 Spence St; adult/child day trips from $195/95) Excellent for families, Reef Magic's high-speed cat sails to its all-weather Marineworld pontoon moored on the edge of the outer reef. If you're water shy, try a glass-bottomed boat ride, chat with the marine biologist or have a massage!

Sunlover DIVING, SNORKELLING
(Map p406; ☎07-4050 1333; www.sunlover.com.au; 1 Spence St; adult/child day trips from $195/90) This fast family-friendly catamaran glides to a pontoon on the outer Moore Reef. Options include semisubmersible trips and helmet diving.

Coral Princess CRUISE
(☎1800 079 545; www.coralprincess.com.au; 24 Redden St, Portsmith; d/tw per person from $1596) Luxury three- to seven-night cruises on the compact, refurbished *Coral Princess I* and *II* between Cairns, Pelorus Island and Lizard Island, including all meals.

☞ Atherton Tableland

Food Trail Tours TOUR
(☎07-4032 0322; www.foodtrailtours.com.au; Manoora, Cairns; adult/child from $175/115; ⊙Mon-Sat) Taste your way around the Tableland, visiting farms producing macadamias, tropical fruits, wine, cheese, chocolate and coffee.

DIVE COURSES & TRIPS

Cairns, scuba-dive capital of the Great Barrier Reef, is a popular place to attain Professional Association of Diving Instructors (PADI) open-water certification. A staggering number of courses (many multilingual) are available; check inclusions thoroughly. All operators require you to have a dive medical certificate, which they can arrange (around $60). Reef taxes ($20 to $80) may apply.

Keen, certified divers should look for specialised dive opportunities such as night diving, yearly coral spawning, and trips to Cod Hole, near Lizard Island, one of Australia's premier diving locations.

Pro-Dive (Map p406; ☎07-4031 5255; www.prodivecairns.com; cnr Grafton & Shields Sts; day trips adult/child from $185/110, PADI courses from $700) One of Cairns' most experienced operators, Pro-Dive has multilingual staff. The comprehensive PADI five-day learn-to-dive course is regarded as one of the best.

Cairns Dive Centre (Map p406; ☎1800 642 591; www.cairnsdive.com.au; 121 Abbott St; live-aboard 2/3 days from $540/680, day trips from $200) This popular, long-running operator's prices are cheaper due to its affiliation with Scuba Schools International (SSI) rather than PADI.

Deep Sea Divers Den (Map p406; ☎07-4046 7333; www.diversden.com.au; 319 Draper St; day trips from $160, PADI certification from $640) These passionate locals have been training divers since 1974.

Great Barrier Reef Gateways

There are numerous ways to approach this massive undersea wonder: head to a gateway town and join an organised tour; sign up for a multiday sailing or diving trip exploring the reefs less-travelled outer reaches; or fly out to a remote island, where you'll have the reef largely to yourself.

The Whitsundays

Fringed by turquoise waters, coral gardens and palm-backed beaches, the Whitsundays (p377) are a heaven-sent archipelago. Base yourself on an island and go sailing, or stay at Airlie Beach on the mainland and island-hop on day trips.

Cairns

The most popular gateway to the reef, Cairns (p404; often pronounced 'Cans' with a nasal twang) has dozens of boat operators offering snorkelling day trips and multiday reef explorations on live-aboard vessels. For the uninitiated, Cairns is also a good place to learn to scuba dive.

Port Douglas

An hour's drive north of Cairns, Port Douglas (p429) is an affluent, laid-back beach town. From here, diving and snorkelling boats head out to over a dozen sites, including pristine outer reefs like Agincourt Reef.

Townsville

Australia's largest tropical city (p385) is a fair hike from the outer reef (2½ hours by boat) but it has other virtues: access to Australia's best wreck dive, an excellent aquarium and marine-themed museums, plus several live-aboard dive boats embarking on multiday trips.

Southern Reef Islands

For an idyllic getaway off the tourist trail, book a trip to one of the remote islands (p359) on the southern edge of the Great Barrier Reef. Look forward to fantastic snorkelling and diving right off the beach.

1. Clownfish **2.** Airlie Beach (p372) **3.** Reef HQ Aquarium (p385), Townsville

2

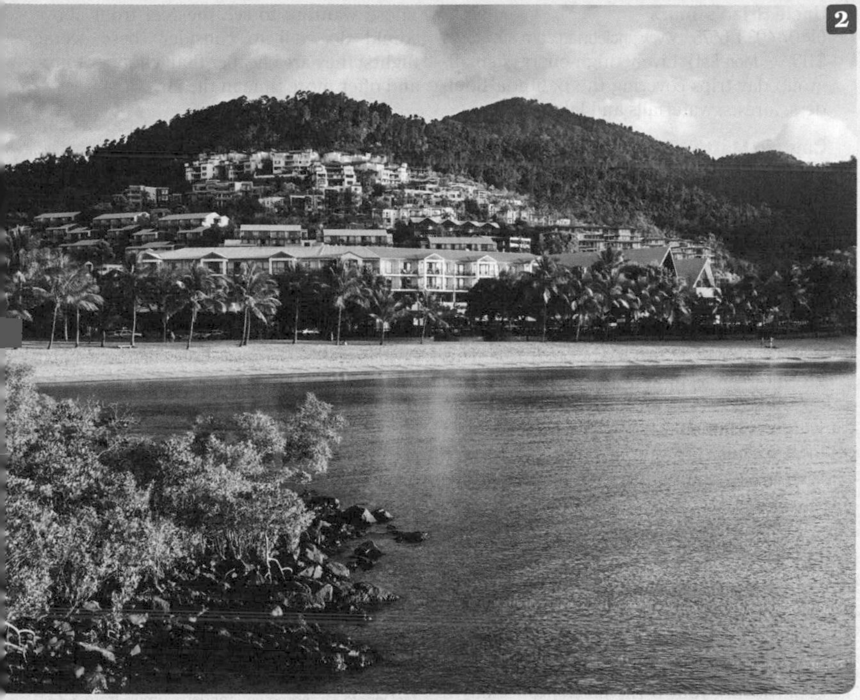

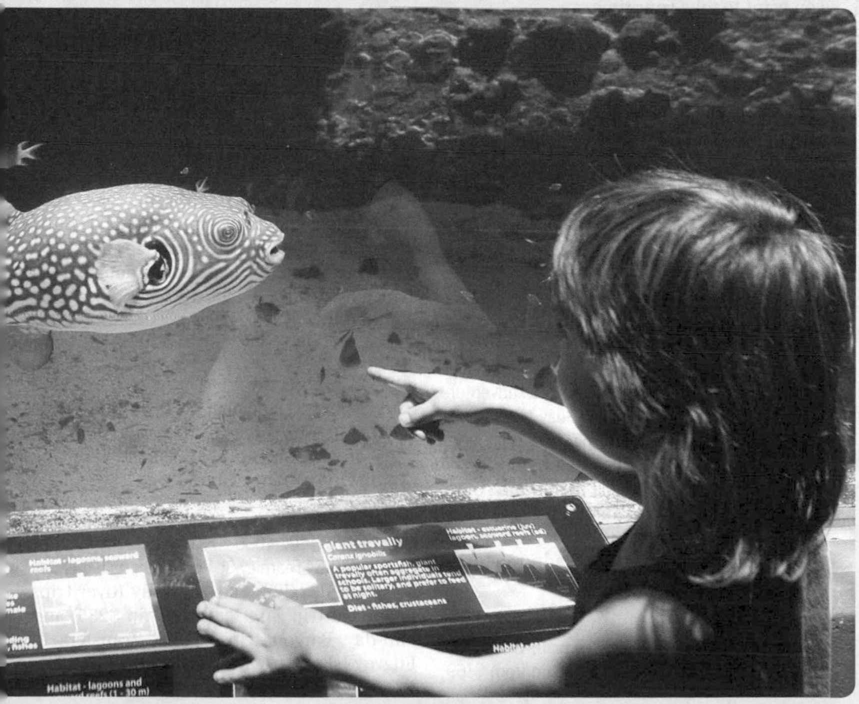

ULLA LOHMANN / LOOK-FOTO / GETTY IMAGES ©

Uncle Brian's Tours OUTDOORS
(☎07-4033 6575; www.unclebrian.com.au; tours $119; ⊙Mon-Sat) Lively, high-energy, small-group day trips covering the Babinda Boulders, forests, waterfalls and lakes.

Captain Matty's Barefoot Tours OUTDOORS
(☎07-4055 9082; www.barefoottours.com.au; adult $85) Backpackers love this fun, full-day jaunt around the Tableland, with swimming stops at waterfalls and a natural water slide. Unsuitable for kids.

Organic Experience TOUR
(☎0474-311 885; www.theorganicexperience.com.au; tours from $175; ⊙8.30am-5pm Fri) This green (green as in new and green as in eco) operator takes you on a journey into a world where sustainable living is a reality. Meet local organic growers and farmers to pick their brains and sample their wares.

Cape Tribulation & the Daintree

After the Great Barrier Reef, visits to Cape Tribulation are the region's next most-popular day trip. Access to the cape is via a well-signposted sealed road, so don't discount hiring your own vehicle, especially if you want to take your time.

Billy Tea Bush Safaris OUTDOORS
(☎07-4032 0077; www.billytea.com.au; day trips adult/child $205/155) This reliable operator offers exciting small-group day trips to Cape Trib in purpose-built 4WD vehicles.

Tropics Explorer OUTDOORS
(☎1800 801 540; www.tropicsexplorer.com.au; day tours from $110) Purhcase your own lunch on these fun Cape Trib trips; overnight tours also available.

Cooktown & Cape York

Adventure North Australia DRIVING TOUR
(Map p406; ☎07-4028 3376; www.adventurenorthaustralia.com; 36 Aplin St; 1-day tours adult/child $260/220) For a jam-packed day, consider these 4WD trips to Cooktown via the coastal route, returning via the inland route. A variety of other tours offer a more relaxed pace: there are two- or three-day tours, fly-drive tours, and Aboriginal cultural tours, including the Bama Way.

GSL Aviation SCENIC FLIGHTS
(☎1300 475 000; gslaviation.com.au; 3 Tom McDonald Dr, Aeroglen; flights per person from $169) Those wanting to see the reef from above would do well to consider these scenic flights; they are cheaper than chopper tours, and offer more time in the air.

Nautilus Aviation SCENIC FLIGHTS
(☎07-4034 9000; www.nautilusaviation.com.au; Bush Pilots Ave, Aeroglen; flights per person from $386) Cairns' newest operator in the luxe helicopter tour market offers a range of packaged 'experiences' and charter services.

Great Barrier Reef Helicopters SCENIC FLIGHTS
(☎07-4081 8888; www.gbrhelicopters.com.au; Bush Pilots Ave, Aeroglen; flights per person from $165) Offers a wide range of helicopter flights, from a 10-minute soar above Cairns city ($165) to an hour-long reef and rainforest trip ($699).

Hot Air Cairns BALLOONING
(Map p406; ☎07-4039 9900; www.hotair.com.au/cairns; 1 Spence St; 30-min flight adult/child from $235/160) Balloons take off from Mareeba to witness dawn over the Atherton Tablelands. Prices include return transfers from Cairns.

Skydive Cairns SKYDIVING
(☎1300 800 840; www.skydivecairns.com.au; Tom McDonald Dr, Aeroglen; tandem jumps from $334) See the reef from a whole new perspective with a drop zone encompassing a warm tropical climate, and spectacular views of the reef, World Heritage rainforest and Trinity Inlet.

White-Water Rafting

The thrill level of white-water rafting down the Barron, Russell and North Johnstone Rivers is hitched to the season: the wetter the weather, the whiter the water. The Tully River has rapids year-round. Trips are graded according to the degree of difficulty, from armchair rafting (Grade 1) to white-knuckle (Grade 5).

Foaming Fury RAFTING
(☎1800 801 540; www.foamingfury.com.au; 19-21 Barry St; half-day trip from $133) Full-day trips on the Russell River ($200), and half-day trips on the Barron ($133). Family rafting options are also available.

Raging Thunder RAFTING
(Map p406; ☎07-4030 7990; www.ragingthunder.com.au; 52-54 Fearnley St, Portsmith; half-/full-day trips from $133/199) Full-day Tully River trips (standard trip $199, 'xtreme' trip $235) and half-day Barron trips ($133). Transfers to Fitzroy Island are available ($74).

Festivals & Events

Cairns Festival FESTIVAL
(www.cairns.qld.gov.au/festival; ⏱end Aug–early Sep) The Cairns Festival takes over the city with a packed program of performing arts, visual arts, music and family events.

Sleeping

For a small city, Cairns has a huge volume of tourist traffic and a high turnover of seasonal staff. Room refurbishment is frequently undertaken in the wettest months (January to March). To avoid disappointment, be realistic: Cairns' hotel inventory does not compare to that of New York City or the Côte d'Azur.

Cairns is a backpacker hotspot: there are hostels a-plenty, ranging from intimate converted houses to rowdy resorts. Nondescript, drive-in motels line Sheridan St from Upward St towards the airport, offering a low-cost private alternative. Popular tourist-class hotels vie for the best spots along the Esplanade. Although there's a handful of high-end hotels in town, those seeking a luxurious retreat might consider heading straight to Palm Cove or Port Douglas.

Families and groups should check out **Cairns Holiday Homes** (☎07-4045 2143; www.cairnsholidayhomes.com.au). If you plan to stick around, **Cairns Sharehouse** (Map p406; ☎07-4041 1875; www.cairns-sharehouse.com; 17 Scott St; s/d per person, per week from $160/$125; ❄📶🏊) has around 200 long-stay rooms strewn across the city.

★ **Travellers Oasis** HOSTEL $
(Map p406; ☎1800 621 353; travellersoasis.com.au; 8 Scott St; dm/s/d per person from $27/49/33; ❄@📶🏊) Folks love this little hippy hostel, hidden away in a side street behind Cairns Central (p416). It's intimate, inviting and less party-centric than other offerings. A range of room types, from three-, four and six-bed dorms, to single, twin and deluxe double rooms, are available. Air conditioning is $1 for three hours.

Gilligan's Backpacker's Hotel & Resort HOSTEL $
(Map p406; ☎07-4041 6566; www.gilligansbackpackers.com.au; 57-89 Grafton St; dm/s/d per person from $22/129/65; ❄@📶🏊) There's nothing quite like Gilligan's: a loud, proud, party-hardy backpacker's oasis, where all rooms have en suites and most have balconies. Higher-priced rooms come with fridges and TVs. The mammoth bar and adjacent lounge-worthy lagoon pool is where to be seen. There's more nightly entertainment than you can poke a stick at. Pickup central.

Dreamtime Travellers Rest HOSTEL $
(Map p406; ☎1800 058 440; www.dreamtimehostel.com; cnr Bunda & Terminus Sts; dm/s/d per person from $24/45/29; @📶🏊) This hostel in a rambling old Queenslander on the city's fringe combines friendly staff with cosy rooms that are bright but not tacky. Cheap pizza, fire twirling and barbecue nights make your stay all the sweeter.

Northern Greenhouse HOSTEL $
(Map p406; ☎07-4047 7200; www.northerngreenhouse.com.au; 117 Grafton St; dm/d per person from $24/48; P❄@📶🏊) These friendly digs benefit from a relaxed attitude. Rooms range from dorms to neat studio-style apartments with kitchens and balconies. The central deck, pool and games room are great for socialising. Free breakfast and Sunday BBQ seal the deal.

★ **Cairns Plaza Hotel** HOTEL $$
(Map p406; ☎07-4051 4688; www.cairnsplaza.com.au; 145 The Esplanade; d from $129; P❄@📶🏊) One of Cairns' original high-rise hotels, the trimuphant Plaza is freshly refurbished and under new ownership. Rooms have crisp, clean decor, and functional kitchenettes and balconies; many enjoy stunning views over Trinity Bay. A guest laundry, friendly round-the-clock reception staff, quiet Esplanade location and great rates make it an excellent midrange choice.

Hotel Cairns HOTEL $$
(Map p406; ☎07-4051 6188; www.thehotelcairns.com; cnr Abbott & Florence Sts; d from $129; ❄📶🏊) There's a tropical charm to this boutique hotel, built in traditional Queenslander 'plantation' style, a block back from the Esplanade. Stylish, solid rooms, ageing gracefully, have an understated elegance. Suites offer luxury touches including private balconies. Those with a discerning eye will recognise the opportunity to snag a sizzling deal.

Doubletree by Hilton HOTEL $$
(Map p406; ☎07-4050 6070; doubletree3.hilton.com; 121-123 The Esplanade; d/ste from $160/296) An enviable location on the northern end of the Esplanade, 24-hoor room service and stylish, modern guestrooms with floor-to-ceiling windows define this well-presented chain hotel. Balcony rooms are available for a fee.

Pacific Hotel HOTEL $$
(Map p406; ☎07-4051 788; www.pacifichotelcairns.com; cnr The Esplanade & Spence St; d from $139)

In a prime location at the beginning of the Esplanade, this older hotel has been lovingly maintained and recently refurbished. There's a fun blend of original '70s features and woodwork, with fresh, modern amenities. All rooms have balconies. Friendly, helpful staff make this an excellent midrange choice.

Reef Palms APARTMENTS $$
(Map p406; ☎1800 815 421; www.reefpalms.com.au; 41-47 Digger St; apt from $130;) Couples and families love the excellent value and friendly service found in these squeaky-clean apartments with cooking facilities, though some might find the decor a little too gaudy. Larger apartments include a lounge area and spa.

Pullman Reef Hotel Casino HOTEL $$$
(Map p406; ☎07-4030 8888; www.reefcasino.com.au/hotel; 35-41 Wharf St; d/ste from $229/319) You'll find some of Cairns' finest rooms and best service in this five-star hotel atop the casino complex in the heart of the CBD. Offers a variety of room types, many with balcony and Jacuzzi, including plush suites.

Shangri-La HOTEL $$$
(Map p406; ☎07-4031 1411; www.shangri-la.com/cairns; 1 Pierpoint Rd; d/ste from $205/365;) At time of writing, five-star Shangri-La failed to knock our socks off, despite its prime position overlooking the marina, in close proximity to Cairns' finest dining. Ongoing refurbishment means airy, older rooms, with their exceptional outlook, can be nabbed at bargain rates, while freshly renovated rooms offer the opulence (and price) synonymous with this luxury brand.

Eating

With so many hungry tourists and so much choice, Cairns' culinary scene can be hit-and-miss, but there are some stunners to be found. Pubs are known for hearty, good-value grub. The Esplanade has an array of lively eateries, including the **Night Markets** (Map p406; The Esplanade; dishes $10-15; 5-11pm) buffet food court. The boardwalk adjacent to the marina has the fanciest atmosphere, but some of the better finds are back from the water, along Grafton St.

★ **Tokyo Dumpling** JAPANESE $
(Map p406; ☎07-4041 2848; 46 Lake St; dumplings from $7, bowls from $10.80; 11.30am-8.30pm) Come to this spotless little takeaway for the best *tantanmen* (a kind of spicy sesame ramen) outside Japan and some seriously drool-worthy gyoza (dumplings): the cheese and potato variety are to die for. We predict you won't be able to eat here just once.

Meldrum's Pies in Paradise BAKERY $
(Map p406; ☎07-4051 8333; 97 Grafton St; pies $4.70-5.90; 7am-4.30pm Mon-Fri, to 2.30pm Sat;) Multi-award-winning Meldrum's deserves the accolades bestowed upon its seemingly innumerable renditions of the humble Aussie pie since 1972. From chicken and avocado, to pumpkin gnocchi and tuna mornay. We loved the steak and mushroo-mmm in creamy pepper sauce!

★ **Candy** CAFE $$
(Map p406; ☎07-4031 8816; 70 Grafton St; 7am-2.30pm) This quirky, licensed cafe has some seriously sweet treats on it's more-than-tempting menu: eggs Benedict with light, fluffy hollandaise; caramelised French toast with poached pears and mascarpone; and the infamous Wagyu beef candy burger with egg, bacon, beetroot jam and vintage cheddar.

Lillypad CAFE $$
(Map p406; ☎07-4051 9565; 72 Grafton St; dishes $10-14; 7am-3pm;) With humongous feasts, from crepes to wraps and a truckload of vegetarian options, this is one of the best-value options in town. It's a little bit hippy, and a whole lot busy: you'll probably have to wait a while. Don't miss the fresh juices.

Caffiend CAFE $$
(Map p406; ☎07-4051 5522; www.caffiend.com.au; 5/78 Grafton St; dishes from $12; 7.30am-3pm Mon-Sat, 8am-2pm Sun;) Follow your nose down the Melbourne-esque graffitied alleyway to this cosy cafe for superb barista coffee, all-day breakfast, gourmet lunches, art, beer and the occasional live gig.

Little Ricardo's ITALIAN $$
(Map p406; ☎07-4051 5266; www.littlericardos.com; 191 Sheridan St; pizzas from $17, mains from $19; 5-10pm Mon-Sat) This romantic little old-school Italian joint serves up all your favourite pizzas, pastas and homestyle favourites, including calamari and veal every which way you can think of. Takeaway available.

★ **Waterbar & Grill** STEAKHOUSE $$$
(Map p406; ☎07-4031 1199; www.waterbarandgrill.com.au; Pier Shopping Centre, 1 Pierpoint Rd; mains $19-42; 11.30am-11pm Mon-Sat, to 9pm Sun) Cairns' award-winning steakhouse shouldn't fail to deliver on it's promise of succulent, juicy steaks, tender burgers and pricey sides.

In the unlikely event that you do leave a crabby carnivore, be sure to let them know so they can make it right. Save room for the homemade sticky date pudding…

Dundees SEAFOOD **$$$**
(Map p406; 07-4051 0399; www.dundees.com.au; Harbour Lights, 1 Marlin Pde; mains $25-79; 11.30am-9.30pm) This tried-and-true waterfront seafood restaurant comes up trumps for ambience, generous portions and friendly service. The varied menu of appealing appetizers begins with chunky seafood chowder, tempura soft-shell crab and lightly dusted calamari strips, while the main event features pasta, a full grill menu and enormous seafood platters.

Ochre MODERN AUSTRALIAN **$$$**
(Map p406; 07-4051 0100; www.ochrerestaurant.com.au; 43 Shields St; mains $19-38; 11.30-2.30pm Mon-Fri, 5.30-9.30pm Mon-Sun;) The menu at this innovative restaurant utilises native Aussie fauna (such as croc with native pepper, or roo with quandong-chilli glaze) and flora (try wattle-seed damper loaf or lemon-myrtle pannacotta). Can't decide? Try a tasting plate.

Drinking & Nightlife

Cairns is the undisputed party capital of the north. Most venues offer food, booze and some form of entertainment.

To find out what's going on in town, hit www.entertainmentcairns.com and the *Time Out* section in Thursday's *Cairns Post*. If you really want to get raucous, try **Ultimate Party** (07-4041 0332; www.ultimatepartycairns.com; per person $35; Wed & Sat nights), a wild-n-crazy pub crawl that takes in five suitably frenetic venues over six hours.

★ **Salt House** BAR
(Map p406; 07-4041 7733; www.salthouse.com.au; 6/2 Pierpoint Rd; 9am-2am Fri-Sun, noon-midnight Mon-Thu) By the yacht club, Cairns' coolest and classiest bar caters to a 20-to-30-something crowd. Killer cocktails are paired with occasional live music and DJs. The restaurant serves up excellent modern Australian food. Come with cash to burn.

★ **Jack** PUB
(Map p406; 07-4051 2490; www.thejack.com.au; cnr Spence & Sheridan Sts; 10am-late) The Jack is a kick-ass pub by any standards, housed in an unmissable heritage Queenslander with an enormous shaded beer garden. There are nightly events, including live music and DJs, killer pub grub, and an adjacent backpackers, for those who just can't tear themselves away.

Pier Bar & Grill BAR
(Map p406; 07-4031 4677; www.pierbar.com.au; Pier Shopping Centre, 1 Pierpoint Rd; 11.30am-late) Thoroughly refurbished in 2014, this local institution is loved for its killer waterfront location and daily happy hour (5pm to 7pm). The still-going-strong Sunday Sesh is the place to see and be seen, with live music, food and drink specials and an always happening crowd.

Courthouse Hotel PUB
(Map p406; 07-4081 7777; www.lanternhotels.com.au/courthouse-hotel; 38 Abbott St; 9am-late) Housed in Cairns' gleaming-white former courthouse (1921), this classy pub is now a buzzing watering hole with polished timber bar, heaps of outdoor nooks and live music every weekend. None too shabby.

Flying Monkey Cafe CAFE
(Map p406; 0411 084 176; 154 Sheridan St; coffee $4; 6.30am-3.30pm Mon-Fri, 7am-noon Sat) Fantastic coffee, ever-changing local art exhibitions, colourful buskers and a beyond-affable staff make the Monkey a must-do for caffeine-and-culture hounds.

Cock 'n' Bull PUB
(Map p406; 07-4031 1160; www.cocknbull.net.au; 6 Grove St; 10am-3am Mon-Sat, to midnight Sun) A local favourite near Cairns Hospital, there's something for everyone at this English tavern–themed pub, with a very un-English tropical beer garden. Huge, tasty pub meals are great value, as are regular drink specials at the lively bar.

G-Spot BAR, CLUB
(Map p406; 07-4040 2777; www.thegspotcairns.com; 57-89 Grafton St; 10pm-late) Home of Gilligan's nightclub and the Attic, G-Spot's weekly theme nights and special events go off. Expect a throng of randy backpackers and Cairns' most intense soundsystem.

Lyquid Nightlife CLUB
(Map p406; 07-4028 3773; www.lyquid.com.au; 33 Spence St; 9pm-3am) Cairns sexiest new venue promises to be the hottest ticket in town: dress to impress and party the night away.

Woolshed BAR, CLUB
(Map p406; 07-4031 6304; www.thewoolshed.com.au; 24 Shields St; 7pm-3am Sun-Thu, to 5am Fri & Sat) An eternal backpacker magnet/meat market, where dashing dudes, dive

instructors and nubile nomads get happily hammered and dance on tables.

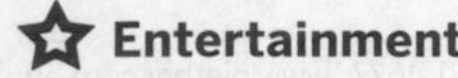

Entertainment

Reef Hotel Casino CASINO
(Map p406; ☎07-4030 8888; www.reefcasino.com.au; 35-41 Wharf St; ⏰9am-5am Fri & Sat, to 3am Sun-Thu) In addition to table games and pokies, Cairns' casino has four restaurants and four bars, including Vertigo Cocktail Bar & Lounge (with free live music and ticketed shows) and the enormous Casino Sports Arena bar.

Shopping

Cairns offers the gamut of shopping, from high-end boutiques to garish souvenir barns.

★**Rusty's Markets** MARKET
(Map p406; ☎07-4040 2705; www.rustysmarkets.com.au; 57 Grafton St; ⏰5am-6pm Fri & Sat, to 3pm Sun) No weekend in Cairns is complete without a visit to this fresh produce market where stall holders have mangoes, bananas, pineapples and all manner of tropical fruits piled high, plus farm-fresh honey, hot chips, curries and cold drinks.

Cairns Central Shopping Centre SHOPPING CENTRE
(Map p406; ☎07-4041 4111; www.cairnscentral.com.au; cnr McLeod & Spence Sts; ⏰9am-5.30pm Mon-Wed, Fri & Sat, to 9pm Thu, 10am-4.30pm Sun) Atop Cairns Central Railway Station (p418), you'll find the region's largest shopping mall. It boasts multiple supermarkets and a huge range of stores selling everything from books to bikinis and sunscreen to SIM cards.

TOO MUCH (TOURIST) INFORMATION?

Most of Cairns' thousands of tours and activities are bookable from your accommodation's 'tour desk' and from the myriad of purported 'tourist information' agencies around the city. Confused? So were we! Many of these so-called agencies (the ones with a white 'i' on a blue background) are offered incentives daily by affiliated operators to 'beef up' tours with poor booking numbers.

There's only one official, impartial tourist information agency in town, the Cairns & Tropical North Visitor Information Centre. It's the only one with a yellow 'i' on a blue background, and is found at the beginning of the Esplanade, before the lagoon. Friendly, expert staff (most are volunteers who love their city) will do their best to help match you to the right product for your needs.

Information

INTERNET ACCESS

Dedicated internet cafes are clustered along Abbott St between Shields and Aplin Sts.

POST

Post Office (Map p406; ☎13 13 18; www.auspost.com.au; Shop 112, Cairns Central Shopping Centre; ⏰9am-5.30pm Mon-Wed, Fri & Sat, to 9pm Thu, 10.30am-4pm Sun)

TOURIST INFORMATION

Cairns & Tropical North Visitor Information Centre (Map p406; ☎1800 093 300; www.cairns-greatbarrierreef.org.au; 51 The Esplanade; ⏰8.30am-6pm Mon-Fri, 10am-6pm Sat & Sun) There's only one government-run visitor information centre in town offering impartial advice. Hundreds of free brochures, maps and pamphlets are available. Friendly staff can help with booking accommodation and tours. Look for the yellow 'i' on the blue background.

Royal Automobile Club of Queensland (RACQ; ☎07-4042 3100; www.racq.com.au; 537 Mulgrave Rd, Earlville; ⏰9am-5pm Mon-Fri) Maps and information on road conditions state-wide, including Cape York. For a 24-hour, recorded road-report service, call ☎1300 130 595.

Getting There & Away

AIR

Qantas (☎13 13 13; www.qantas.com.au), **Virgin Australia** (☎13 67 89; www.virginaustralia.com) and **Jetstar** (☎13 15 38; www.jetstar.com.au) arrive and depart Cairns Airport (p1086), located approximately 6km from the CBD, with direct services to all capital cities except Canberra and Hobart, and to regional centres including Townsville, Weipa and Horn Island. Direct international connections include Bali, Shanghai, Guam, Tokyo and Port Moresby.

Hinterland Aviation (☎07-4040 1333; www.hinterlandaviation.com.au) has up to three flights daily (Monday to Saturday) to Cooktown (one way from $175, 40 minutes).

In January 2015 Skytrans, a regional airline which serviced remote communities such as Coen, Bamaga and Lockhart River, ceased operations after 25 years. At the time of writing, it was unknown whether alternative carriers would commence service to these areas.

BOAT

Almost all reef trips from Cairns depart the Marlin Wharf (sometimes called the Marlin Jetty), with booking and check-in facilities located

Around Cairns

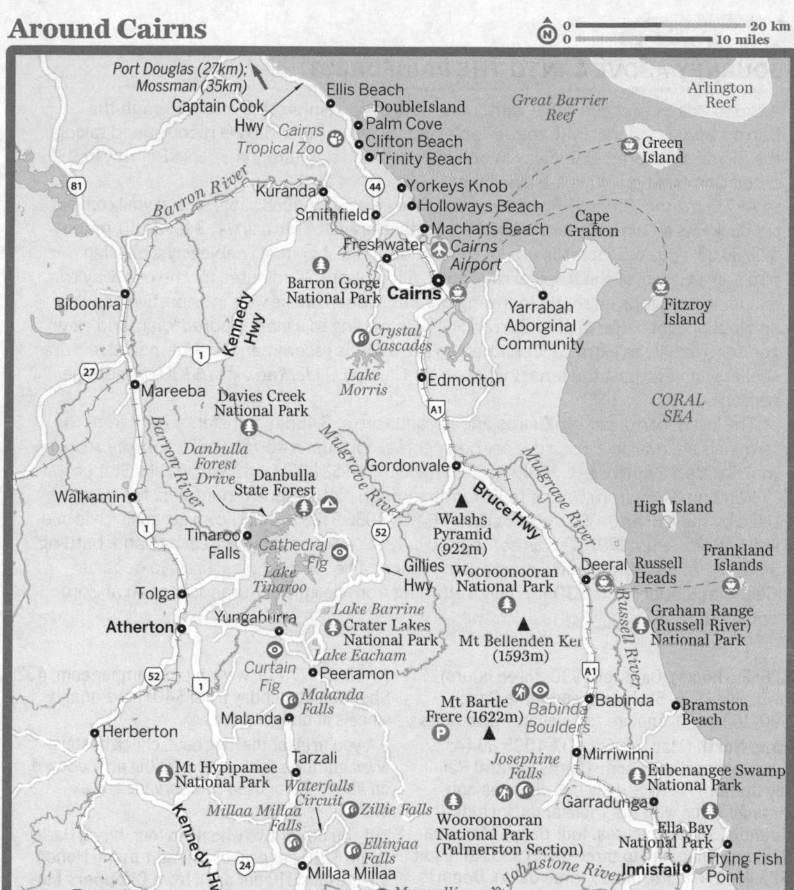

inside the **Reef Fleet Terminal** (Map p406). A handful of smaller operators may have their check-in facilities boat-side, on the wharf itself. Be sure to ask for the correct berth number.

International cruise ships and SeaSwift (p447) ferries to Seisia on Cape York dock at and depart from the **Cairns Cruise Terminal** (Map p406; ☎07-4052 3888; www.cairnscruiselinerterminal.com.au; cnr Wharf & Lake Sts).

BUS

Cairns Cooktown Express (☎07-4059 1423; www.cairnsbuscharters.com/services/cairns-cooktown-express) Cairns Bus Charters operate the daily Cairns Cooktown Express ($79, five hours) along the inland route to Cooktown.

Greyhound Australia (Map p406; ☎1300 473 946; www.greyhound.com.au) Departing the **Interstate Coach Terminal** (Map p406); (within the Reef Fleet Terminal), Greyhound has daily services down the coast to Townsville (from $55, six hours), Airlie Beach (from $85, 11 hours), Rockhampton ($201, 18 hours) and Brisbane ($311, 29 hours). Discount passes are available.

John's Kuranda Bus (☎0418 772 953) Runs a service ($5, 30 minutes) between Cairns (departs Lake St Transit Centre) and Kuranda, two to five times daily.

Premier Motor Service (☎13 34 10; www.premierms.com.au) Runs one daily service to Brisbane ($205, 29 hours) via Innisfail ($19, 1½ hours), Mission Beach ($19, two hours), Tully

DON'T MISS

JOURNEY ABOVE & INTO THE RAINFOREST

A trip to Cairns isn't complete without an obligatory rainforest journey through the Barron Gorge National Park to the Tableland village of Kuranda. We recommend taking the Skyrail Rainforest Cableway in one direction and the Kuranda Scenic Railway in the other. Combination deals are available.

At 7.5km long, **Skyrail Rainforest Cableway** (07-4038 5555; www.skyrail.com.au; cnr Cook Hwy & Cairns Western Arterial Rd, Smithfield; adult/child one way $49/24.50, return $73/36.50; 9am-5.15pm) is one of the world's longest gondola cableways, offering a bird's-eye view over the tropical rainforest. Allow about 90 minutes for the one-way trip, including two stops en route, featuring rainforest boardwalks with interpretive panels and lookouts over the mighty Barron Falls. Upgrading to a glass-floored 'diamond view' gondola (adults an extra $10, children an extra $5) is recommended, but real adventure seekers can't go past the amazing, open-air Canopy Glider (an extra $100 or more per person).

The last departures from Cairns and Kuranda are at 3.45pm; transfers to and from the terminals are available. For a deeper perspective, consider a 40-minute **Djabugay Aboriginal Guided Rainforest Walking Tour** (adult/child $24/12) from Barron Falls Station.

Winding 34km from Cairns to Kuranda through picturesque mountains, the track used by the **Kuranda Scenic Railway** (07-4036 9333; www.ksr.com.au; adult/child one way $49/25, return $79/37) was completed in 1891: workers dug tunnels by hand, battling sickness, steep terrain and venomous creatures. The 1¾-hour pleasure trip departs Cairns at 8.30am and 9.30am daily, returning from delightful Kuranda station at 2pm and 3.30pm.

($26, 2½ hours), Cardwell ($30, three hours), Townsville ($55, 5½ hours) and Airlie Beach ($90, 10 hours). Enquire for available discounts.

Trans North (Map p406; 07-4095 8644; www.transnorthbus.com; Cairns Central Railway Station) Has five daily bus services connecting Cairns with the Tablelands, including Kuranda ($8, 30 minutes, four daily), Mareeba ($18, one hour, one to three daily) and Atherton ($23.40, 1¾ hours, one to three daily). Departs from Cairns Central Railway Station; buy tickets when boarding.

Sun Palm (07-4087 2900; www.sunpalmtransport.com.au) Operates scheduled and charter services between Cairns CBD, the airport ($15, 20 minutes) and Port Douglas (from $40, 1½ hours) via Palm Cove and the northern beaches (from $20).

CAR & MOTORCYCLE

Major car-rental companies have downtown and airport branches. Daily rates start around $45 for a compact auto and $80 for a 4WD. **Cairns Older Car Hire** (07-4053 1066; www.cairnsoldercarhire.com; 410 Sheridan St; per day from $25) and **Rent-a-Bomb** (07-4031 4477; www.rentabomb.com.au; 144 Sheridan St; per day from $30) have cheap rates on older model vehicles. If you're looking for a cheap campervan, **Jucy** (1800 150 850; www.jucy.com.au; 55 Dutton St, Portsmith; per day from $40), **Spaceships** (1300 132 469; www.spaceshipsrentals.com.au; 3/52 Fearnley St, Portsmith; per day from $59) and **Hippie Camper Hire** (1800 777 779; www.hippiecamper.com; 432 Sheridan St; per day from $40) have quality wheels at budget prices.

If you're in for the long haul, check hostels, www.gumtree.com.au and the big noticeboard on Abbott St for used campervans and ex-backpackers' cars.

If you prefer two wheels to four, hire a Harley (from $210 per day) or a head-turning Honda VTR (from $110 per day), from **Choppers Motorcycle Tours & Hire** (1300 735 577; www.choppersmotorcycles.com.au; 150 Sheridan St). A swag of tours are also available.

TRAIN

New in 2015, **Queensland Rail's** (1800 872 467; www.traveltrain.com.au) scenic, state-of-the-art Spirit of Queensland train, offers Railbed class, reminiscent of business class on a plane, and standard Premium Economy class seats, with personal entertainment systems. Departs **Cairns Central Railway Station** (Bunda St) on Monday, Wednesday, Thursday, Friday and Sunday, for Brisbane (one way from $222, 24 hours).

The Kuranda Scenic Railway runs daily.

Getting Around

TO/FROM THE AIRPORT

The airport is about 6km north of central Cairns; many accommodation places offer courtesy pickup. Sun Palm meets all incoming flights and runs a shuttle bus (adult/child $15/7.50) to the CBD. The cheapest shuttle service (from $12 per person) is operated by **Cairns Airport Shuttle** (☎0432 488 783; www.cairnsairportshuttle.com.au; per person from $12): the more passengers, the cheaper the fare – online bookings recommended.

Taxis to the CBD are around $25.

BICYCLE & SCOOTER

Bike Man (☎07-4041 5566; www.bikeman.com.au; 99 Sheridan St; per day/week $15/60) Hire, sales and repairs.

Cairns Scooter & Bicycle Hire (☎07-4031 3444; www.cairnsbicyclehire.com.au; 47 Shields St; scooters/bikes per day from $95/35) Zip around on a nifty-fifty, or take it slow on a pushie. Also sells used scooters.

BUS

Sunbus (Map p406; ☎07-4057 7411; www.sunbus.com.au; rides from $2.20) runs regular services in and around Cairns from the **Cairns Transit Mall** (Map p406) on Lake St, where schedules are posted. Useful routes include: Flecker Botanic Gardens/Edge Hill (route 131), Holloways Beach and Yorkeys Knob (route 113), Trinity Beach (route 111) and Palm Cove via Clifton Beach (route 110). Most buses heading north go via Smithfield. All routes are served by the late-running night service (N). Heading south, Bus 140 runs as far south as Gordonvale. Single tickets cost from $2.20, day passes from $4.40.

TAXI

Cairns Taxis (☎13 10 08; www.cairnstaxis.com.au) Ranks are dotted throughout the city, including at Abbott St and Cairns Central Shopping Centre.

CAIRNS' NORTHERN BEACHES

Surprisingly, few visitors realise before arrival that Cairns' beaches are 15-minutes' drive from the CBD. A string of lovely beach communities known as the northern beaches, each with their own character, awaits. Yorkeys Knob is popular with sailors, Trinity is big with families, and Palm Cove is a swanky honeymoon haven in its own league entirely.

All beaches can be reached via well-marked turn-offs from the Cook Hwy.

Once you're there, **Northern Beaches Bike Hire** (☎0417 361 012; cairnsbeachesbikehire.com; 41 Iridescent Dr, Ellis Beach; per day from $20) can deliver rental bikes to most northern beaches accommodation options, and collect them when you're done!

Yorkeys Knob

Yorkeys Knob (giggle once, then move on) is a low-key settlement known for its Half Moon Bay and marina. A proposed mega-casino (aquiscasino.com) would change the town irrevocably and has many locals (who've already lost their apostrophe) up in arms. For now, it's business (or lack thereof) as usual.

Activities

Kite Rite WATER SPORTS
(☎07-4055 7918; www.kiterite.com.au; Shop 9, 471 Varley St; per hr $79) Offers kite- and windsurfing instruction, unique to Yorkeys, including gear hire, and a two-day certificate course ($499).

Sleeping & Eating

Villa Marine APARTMENT $$
(☎07-4055 7158; www.villamarine.com.au; 8 Rutherford St; apt from $99-189; ❄📶🏊) Friendly owner Peter makes you feel at home in his collection of retro, single-storey self-contained apartments arranged around a pool, just a short stroll from the beach.

York APARTMENTS $$
(☎07-4055 8733; www.yorkapartments.com.au; 61-63 Sims Esplanade; apt from $165) Directly opposite the beach you'll find these low-rise, airy apartments with high-quality furnishings, tiled floors, full kitchen facilities and balconies.

★ **Yorkeys Knob Boating Club** SEAFOOD $$
(☎07-4055 7711; www.ykbc.com.au; 25-29 Buckley St; mains from $16; ⏰noon-3pm & 6-9pm; 🖋) A diamond find for fresh seafood, and for delightful views of the marina's expensive floating toys from its expansive dining deck. You can't go past Lobster Fridays ($35 including bubbles) and Oyster Saturdays ($12 per dozen!), as well as the daily specials. Perfect for lunch, it's well worth the trip from Cairns.

Getting There & Away

If you don't have a car, Sunbus' route 113 will get you from Cairns to Yorkeys in about 40 minutes.

Trinity Beach

One of the region's better-kept secrets, Trinity Beach, with its gorgeous stretch of sheltered sand, pretty esplanade, and sensibly priced

LOCAL KNOWLEDGE

THE BAMA WAY

Running between Cairns and Cooktown, the Bama Way is a tourist route designed by the traditional custodians of the region, the Aboriginal nations of the Kuku Yalanji and Guugu Yimithirr people. The term Bama (pronounced Bumma) is widely used throughout tropical North Queensland, and means 'Aboriginal person'. For the Kuku Yalanji and Guugu Yimithirr, it means 'person' or 'all people'. A variety of guided tours are available for those seeking the most enlightening cultural experience. The **Walker family tours** (p441) of the Bloomfield Track and Willie Gordon's enlightening **Guurrbi Tours** (p442) in Cooktown are highly recommended. If you're interested in self-driving, pick up a Bama Way map from a visitor centre, or download it from the Bama Way homepage: www.bamaway.com.au.

dining and accommodation, has managed to stave off the tourism vibe, despite being a holiday hotspot and popular dining destination for Cairns locals in the know. There's not much to do here except eat, sleep and chill-out, but Trinity Beach's central position makes it easy to get out and about when you are feeling active.

Sleeping

A wealth of wonderful, affordable apartment-style accommodation makes Trinity an excellent alternative to sleeping in Cairns for families and those travelling in groups.

Comfort Inn & Suites Trinity Beach Club HOTEL $$
(☎07-4055 6776; www.choicehotels.com.au; 19-23 Trinity Beach Rd; apt from $195) This property offers hotel-style management and service. Its one- and two-bedroom, apartment-style accommodation has full kitchen facilities, and is just 200m from Trinity Beach.

Sea Change Beachfront Apartments APARTMENTS $$$
(☎07-4057 5822; www.seachange-beachfront-apartments.com; 31-35 Vasey Esplanade; apt from $290) These professionally managed luxury apartments benefit from a quiet position on the southern end of Trinity's spectacular beach. Apartments range in size from one to four bedrooms. Some offer swim-out pool access or a private roof deck. A high rate of repeat guests speaks for itself. Minimum three-night stay.

Eating

Trinity may seem top-heavy on Italian restaurants, but, when in Rome…

★**Chianti's** ITALIAN $$
(☎07-4057 5338; www.chianttis.com; 81 Vasey Esplanade; mains from $18; ⏰4-10pm) We love the unpretentious, old-school romance of this feisty, family-run business that's grown on word-of-mouth recommendations; don't expect silver service. Eat on the cosy verandah for the best views and vibe. Pizzas and pastas are homestyle and hearty, and the daily early-bird dinner special is great value.

Fratelli on Trinity ITALIAN $$
(☎07-4057 5775; www.fratelli.net.au; 47 Vasey Esplanade; mains from $20; ⏰7am-10pm Thu-Sun, from 5.30pm Mon-Wed) Don't let the easy-breezy beach shack vibe fool you into thinking the food here is anything less than top-class. Pastas are superb, and dishes like slow-cooked lamb shoulder and garlic-and-rosemary rolled pork-belly roast might even distract you from the million-dollar views.

Blue Moon Grill MODERN AUSTRALIAN $$$
(☎07-4057 8957; Shop 6, 22-24 Trinity Beach Rd; mains $26-39; ⏰7-11am & 4-10pm Fri-Sun, 4-10pm Mon-Thu) A slightly overwhelming menu of creative, original dishes are presented with passion at this cosy, family-run bistro two blocks back from the beach. Where else can you try crocodile popcorn?

L'Unico Trattoria ITALIAN $$$
(☎07-4057 8855; www.lunico.com.au; 75 Vasey Esplanade; mains from $22; ⏰noon-10pm; ✎) Opening to a wrap-around, beachfront deck, upscale L'Unico Trattoria serves stylish Italian cuisine. Items include bugs (crayfish) with garlic, chilli and white wine, homemade four-cheese gnocchi and wood-fired pizzas, paired with a stellar wine list.

Getting There & Around

Renting a car upon arrival into Cairns is highly recommended. Trinity Beach is about 20-minutes' drive from the airport, and 30 minutes from downtonwn Cairns. Otherwise, Sunbus (p419) route 111 services Trinity Beach.

Palm Cove

Best known of Cairns' northern beaches, Palm Cove has grown into a destination in its own right. More intimate than Port Douglas and more upmarket than its southern neighbours, Palm Cove is a cloistered coastal community with a beautiful promenade along the paperbark-lined Williams Esplanade. Its gorgeous stretch of white-sand beach and its sprinkling of fancy restaurants do their best to lure young lovers from their luxury resorts, and, inevitably, they succeed.

Unlike Port Douglas, you can walk everywhere. Unlike Cairns, you'll hardly notice the presence of other sun and reef seekers. If you can afford to stay here, you won't flinch at the extra expense of a rental car, which you'll need if you plan on leaving paradise for some thrill seeking.

Sights & Activities

Cairns Tropical Zoo ZOO
(07-4055 3669; www.cairnstropicalzoo.com.au; Captain Cook Hwy; adult/child $34/17; 8.30am-4pm) This zoo offers an up-close wildlife experience with crocodiles and snakes, koala photo sessions and kangaroo feeding. Its Cairns Night Zoo experience includes a barbecue dinner and entertainment (adults $105, children $52.50). Transfers are available for an additional cost.

Palm Cove Watersports KAYAKING
(0402 861 011; www.palmcovewatersports.com; kayak hire per hr from $20) Organises two-hour sunrise sea-kayaking trips ($55) and half-day paddles to offshore Double Island (adult/child $110/80). Gear hire is also available.

Beach Fun Co. WATER SPORTS
(0411-848 580; www.beachfunco.com; cnr Williams Esplanade & Harpa St) Hires catamarans ($50 per hour), jet skis (per 15 minutes single/double $60/80), paddle boats ($30) and SUP boards ($30). Also organises jet-ski tours around Double Island and Haycock – aka Scouts Hat – Island (30-minute single/double from $150/200). Advance phone bookings recommended.

Sleeping

There are over 30 places to stay in this small village – many require a minimum two-night stay. If you're lucky with the weather, you could snap up a real bargain during low-season.

Palm Cove Holiday Park CAMPGROUND $
(1800 736 640; www.palmcovehp.com.au; 149 Williams Esplanade; unpowered/powered sites from $20/28;) The only way to do Palm Cove on the cheap, this beachfront campground near the jetty has tent and van sites, a barbecue area, a laundry and wi-fi hotspots.

Reef Retreat APARTMENTS $$
(07-4059 1744; reefretreat.com.au; 10-14 Harpa St; apt from $145;) We're confident the new management of this delightful property will continue to uphold it's reputation for excellent service. In a peaceful forested setting around a shaded pool, the well-maintained one-, two- and three-bedroom apartments feature an east-meets-west theme with lots of rich timbers, durable high-quality furnishings and wide, airy balconies.

Silvester Palms APARTMENTS $$
(07-4055 3831; www.silvesterpalms.com.au; 32 Veivers Rd; apt from $125;) These bright, self-contained one-, two- and three-bedroom apartments are an affordable alternative to Palm Cove's city-sized resorts. Think family holiday over romantic resort retreat.

Sanctuary Palm Cove APARTMENTS $$$
(07-4059 2200; www.sanctuarypalmcove.com.au; 6 Cedar Rd; apt from $175;) At the northern end of the strip, just a hop, skip and jump from the beach, Sanctuary's enticing one-, two- and three-bedroom apartments turn heads. A host of delights await discerning guests: wide open spaces, tiled floors, plantation shutters, stylish high-end furnishings, balconies, Jacuzzis, and a beautiful 25m pool shaded by melaleucas and lush tropical gardens.

Peppers Beach Club & Spa HOTEL $$$
(07-4059 9200; www.peppers.com.au; 123 Williams Esplanade; d from $275; @) Step into a world of relaxation and retreat. You'll find it difficult to get out of the enormous sand-edged lagoon pool (with swim-up bar), unless you feel inspired to try the secluded leafy rainforest pool, play tennis or indulge in a spa treatment. All rooms have private balcony spas, and the penthouses (from $720) have individual rooftop lap pools.

Reef House Resort & Spa BOUTIQUE HOTEL $$$
(07-4080 2600; www.reefhouse.com.au; 99 Williams Esplanade; d from $239; @) Once the private residence of an army brigadier, Reef House is more intimate

LOCAL KNOWLEDGE

WHY ALL THE STAIRS?

Visitors to Palm Cove and Port Douglas are often shocked to find their accommodation is sans elevator. Strict height limits in Palm Cove and Port Douglas apply – buildings must be no higher than the tallest palm tree, generally three storeys – and it's costly and design-restrictive to incorporate elevators into low-rise complexes. Additionally, salty ocean air means elevators require regular, expensive maintenance. If mobility is a concern, confirm your accommodation has an elevator, or request a ground-floor room, when you book.

and understated than most of Palm Cove's resorts. The whitewashed walls, wicker furniture and big beds romantically draped in muslin all add to the air of refinement. The Brigadier's Bar works on an honesty system; complimentary punch is served by candlelight at twilight.

Eating

The cafes and restaurants lining the scenic Esplanade are generally pricey, but fabulous. Most resorts open their restaurants to nonguests. If your wallet is suffering, consider eating like the locals: **Clifton Village Shopping Centre** in neighboring Clifton Beach has some excellent casual dining options, and a supermarket for self-caterers. Otherwise, Trinity Beach is just 10 minutes' down the road.

Deli Adrift CAFE **$**
(☎07-4055 3354; 2 Veivers Rd; sandwiches from $9; ⏰7am-3.30pm) Friendly service and a relaxed, casual vibe make this a great little spot for coffee, breakfast or flavoursome, freshly made sandwiches. Devour on-site or carry to the beach for a picnic.

Chill Cafe CAFE **$$**
(☎0402 665 523; www.chillcafepalmcove.com.au; Shop 1, 41 Williams Esplanade; mains from $15; ⏰7am-4pm Sun-Thu, to 8pm Fri & Sat) The *el-primo* position on the corner of the waterfront Esplanade, combined with fun, friendly and attentive service, sexy tunes and a huge airy deck, are all great reasons to try the oversized, tasty bites (think fish tacos and chunky club sandwiches) of this hip cafe. You can also just chill in the sunshine with a juice or a beer.

A Taste of Italy PIZZA **$$**
(☎07-4059 2727; www.atasteofitaly.com.au; Clifton Village Shopping Centre, Clifton Beach; pizzas from $13; ⏰11am-9pm) If you just want to kick back and eat pizza in paradise, you can. Whizz over to neighbouring Clifton Beach to pickup, or dial-in for delivery: hundreds do (minimum order $20, delivery fee $5). And yes, the pizzas are gooooood.

★ **Vivo Bar & Grill** MODERN AUSTRALIAN **$$$**
(www.vivo.com.au; 49 Williams Esplanade; mains from $28; ⏰7.30am-9pm) The most beautiful restaurant on the Esplanade is also one of the finest. Menus (breakfast, lunch and dinner) are inventive and well executed using fresh local ingredients, service is second to none, and the outlook is superb. When you've got those three elements down pat, Palm Cove pricing is justified. Daily set menus are excellent value.

Beach Almond ASIAN, SEAFOOD **$$$**
(☎07-4059 1908; www.beachalmond.com; 145 Williams Esplanade; mains from $30; ⏰5.30-10pm Mon-Tue & Thu-Sat, 12-3pm & 5.30-10pm Sun) Awesome and unmissable – the rustic, ramshackle, beachhouse-on-sticks exterior belies the fine dining experience that awaits within. Black-pepper prawns, Singaporean mud crab and Balinese barra are among the fragrant innovations here, combining Asian flavours and spices.

Drinking & Nightlife

Surf Club Palm Cove BAR
(☎07-4059 1244; www.surfclubpalmcove.com.au; 135 Williams Esplanade; ⏰6pm-late) A great locale for a drink in the sunny garden bar, bargain-priced seafood and decent kids' meals.

Apres Beach Bar & Grill BAR
(☎07-4059 2000; www.apresbeachbar.com.au; 119 Williams Esplanade; ⏰7.30am-11pm) The most happening place in Palm Cove, with a zany interior of old motorcycles, racing cars, and a biplane hanging from the ceiling, plus regular live music. Big on steaks of all sorts, too.

Information

Commercially run tour-booking companies are strung along Williams Esplanade; the Cairns & Tropical North Visitor Information Centre (p416) in Cairns can help with bookings.

Palm Cove Shopping Village (113 Williams Esplanade; ⏲7am-10pm) has a post office (with internet access, $4 per hour), small supermarket and newsagent.

Getting There & Away

Palm Cove is ideally positioned halfway between Cairns and Port Douglas – about a 30 minute drive in either direction. Having your own wheels will open up a myriad of possibilities for exploration. It's possible to pick up a car at Cairns Airport and drive straight here, bypassing Cairns.

Otherwise, Sunbus (p419) route 110 services Clifton Beach and Palm Cove via Smithfield.

Ellis Beach

Little Ellis Beach is the last of Cairns' northern beaches and the closest to the highway, which runs right past it. The long sheltered bay is a stunner, with a palm-fringed, patrolled swimming beach, and a stinger net in summer.

Activities

★Hartley's Crocodile Adventures ANIMAL SANCTUARY
(☎07-4055 3576; www.crocodileadventures.com; Captain Cook Hwy, Wangetti Beach; adult/child $35/17.50; ⏲8.30am-5pm daily) North of Ellis Beach, towards Port Douglas, Hartley's Crocodile Adventures is stealing the limelight from a bunch of other attractions. Their daily range of exciting events includes tours of this croc farm, along with feedings, 'crocodile attack' shows and cruises. Rest assured, you will see crocodiles up close and personal. Not for the squeamish!

Sleeping & Eating

Ellis Beach Oceanfront Bungalows CARAVAN PARK $
(☎1800 637 036; www.ellisbeach.com; Captain Cook Hwy; unpowered sites $32, bungalows from $155; ❄@≋) This low-key, palm-shaded, beachfront slice of paradise, has camping, cabins and contemporary bungalows, all of which enjoy wide-screen ocean views in full high definition.

Ellis Beach Bar 'n' Grill PUB FOOD $$
(☎07-4055 3534; ellisbeachbarandgrill.com.au; Captain Cook Hwy; mains from $16; ⏲8am-8pm) Just try to drive past the Ellis Beach Bar 'n' Grill and not stop for a beer and a burger. Oh, and did we mention $1 oysters and live music on Sundays?

This is the only place in Ellis to get a meal.

ISLANDS OFF CAIRNS

Green Island

Showing some of the scars that come with fame and popularity, this pretty coral cay, only 45 minutes from Cairns, retains much of its beauty, though more spectacular coral can be viewed on outer reef excursions. The island has a rainforest interior with interpretive walks, a fringe of white-sand beach, and snorkelling just offshore: great for kids. You can walk around the island (which, along with its surrounding waters, is protected by national- and marine-park status) in about 30 minutes.

Sights & Activities

Great Adventures (p409) and **Big Cat** (☎07-4051 0444; www.greenisland.com.au; adult/child from $86/43) run day trips, with optional glass-bottomed boat and semisubmersible tours. Alternatively, hop aboard **Ocean Free** (Map p406; ☎07-4052 1111; www.oceanfree.com.au; 1 Spence St; adult/child from $195/110), and spend most of the day offshore at Pinnacle Reef, with a short stop on the island.

Marineland Melanesia AQUARIUM
(☎07-4051 4032; www.marinelandgreenisland.com.au; Green Island; adult/child $18.50/8.50) This family-owned, tropical-themed aquarium has plenty of fish, turtles, stingrays and crocodiles, including Cassius, the largest in captivity: he's thought to be over 100 years old and is 5.5m long! Crocs are fed at 10.30am and 1.30pm daily. There's also a collection of Melanesian artefacts. Your ticket entitles you to reentry throughout the day.

Sleeping

Green Island Resort RESORT $$$
(☎1800 673 366; www.greenislandresort.com.au; Green Island; ste from $670; ❄@≋) Luxurious Green Island Resort maintains a sense of privacy and exclusivity despite having some sections opened to the general public, including restaurants, bars, the ice-cream parlour and water-sports facilities. Spacious, refurbished, split-level suites feature tropical themes, timber furnishings, and inviting balconies. Room rates include breakfast, sunset drinks, guided walks, free nonmotorised water-sports equipment hire, and round-trip high-speed catamaran transfers from Cairns.

Fitzroy Island

A steep mountaintop rising from the sea, Fitzroy Island has coral-strewn beaches, woodlands and walking tracks, one of which ends at a now inactive lighthouse. The most popular snorkelling spot is around the rocks at Nudey Beach, which, despite its name, is not officially clothing optional. Unlike the rest of the island, Nudey actually has some sand on it.

The **Fitzroy Island Turtle Rehabilitation Centre** (www.saveourseaturtles.com.au; Fitzroy Island; adult/child $5.50/2.20; ⌚tours 2pm) looks after sick and injured sea turtles before releasing them back into the wild. Daily educational tours (maximum 15 guests) visit the new turtle hospital. Book through the **Fitzroy Island Resort** (☎07-4044 6700; www.fitzroyisland.com; Fitzroy Island; studios/cabins from $155/300, 1-/2-bedroom ste from $215/325;), where tropi-cool accommodation ranges from sleek studios and beachfront cabins through to luxurious self-contained apartments. The resort's restaurant, bar and kiosk are open to day trippers. It offers excellent value for a Reef Island stay. The resort also manages the **Fitzroy Island Camping Ground** (☎07-4044 6700; www.fitzroyisland.com; Fitzroy Island; camp sites $32): idyllic and isolated, with showers, toilets and barbecues. Advance bookings essential.

To get here, take the 45-minute **Fast Cat** (www.fitzroyisland.com/getting-here; adult/child return $72/36) departing Cairns Marlin Wharf (berth 20) at 8am, 11am and 1.30pm (bookings essential), or do a day trip with Raging Thunder (p412) and bounce off their ocean trampoline!

Frankland Islands

If the idea of hanging out on one of five uninhabited, coral-fringed islands with excellent snorkelling and stunning white-sand beaches appeals – how can it not? – cruise out to the Frankland Group National Park.

Camping is available on the rainforested High and Russell Islands; contact the **NPRSR** (☎13 74 68; www.nprsr.qld.gov.au; permits $5.45) for advance reservations and seasonal restrictions.

Frankland Islands Cruise & Dive (☎07-4031 6300; www.franklandislands.com.au; adult/child from $159/89) runs excellent day trips which include a cruise down the Mulgrave River, snorkelling gear, tuition and lunch. Guided snorkelling tours with a marine biologist and diving packages are also offered. Transfers for campers to/from Russell Island are available. Boats depart from Deeral, about 45km south of Cairns; transfers from Cairns and the northern beaches cost $16 per person.

You'll need to organise your own boat or charter to reach High Island.

ATHERTON TABLELAND

Climbing back from the coast between Innisfail and Cairns is the fertile food bowl of the far north, the Atherton Tableland. Quaint country towns, eco-wilderness lodges and luxurious B&Bs dot greener-than-green hills between patchwork fields, pockets of rainforest, spectacular lakes and waterfalls, and Queensland's highest mountains, Bartle Frere (1622m) and Bellenden Ker (1593m).

Four main roads lead in from the coast: the Palmerston Hwy from Innisfail, the Gillies Hwy from Gordonvale, the Kennedy Hwy from Cairns, and Rex Range Rd between Mossman and Port Douglas.

Getting There & Around

Trans North (p417) has regular bus services connecting Cairns with the Tableland, departing from Cairns Central Railway Station and running to Kuranda ($8, 30 minutes), Mareeba ($18, one hour) and Atherton ($23.40, 1¾ hours) at least once daily, and to Herberton ($31, two hours) and Ravenshoe ($36, 2½ hours) on Mondays, Wednesdays and Fridays.

That said, it's worth hiring your own wheels or doing a day tour from Cairns.

Kuranda

POP 2966

Nestled in the rainforest, arty Kuranda is one of Cairns' most popular day trips.

Sights

During the Wet, the mighty, must-see Barron Falls are in full thunder; they're a 3km walk down Barron Falls Rd.

Kuranda Original Rainforest Markets MARKET

(☎07-4093 9440; www.kurandaoriginalrainforestmarket.com.au; Therwine St; ⌚9.30am-3pm) Operating since 1978, these markets are the best place to see local artists at work and hippies at play. Pick up all manner of folksy arts and crafts, and sample local honey and fruit wines.

Kuranda

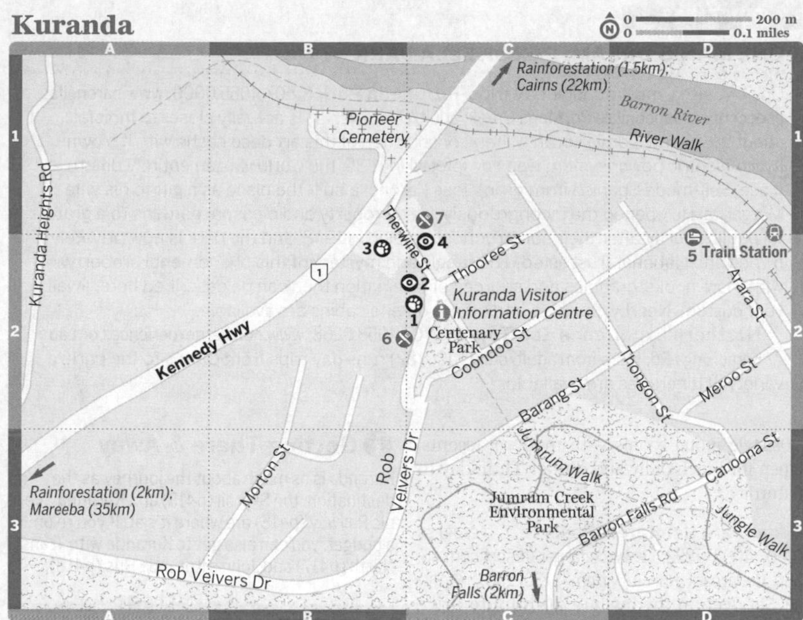

Heritage Markets MARKET
(☎07-4093 8060; www.kurandamarkets.com.au; Rob Veivers Dr; ⏲9.30am-3.30pm) These markets hawk Australiana souvenirs by the busload, and are home to a handful of wildlife sanctuaries. If they're feeling friendly, you can cuddle a koala (or pat wombats and wallabies) at the **Kuranda Koala Gardens** (☎07-4093 9953; www.koalagardens.com; Rob Veivers Dr; adult/child $17/8.50, koala photos extra; ⏲9.45am-4pm). The **Australian Butterfly Sanctuary** (☎07-4093 7575; www.australianbutterflies.com; Rob Veivers Dr; adult/child/family $19/9.50/47.50; ⏲9.45am-4pm) is Australia's largest butterfly aviary, with over 1500 tropical butterflies: half-hour tours are available. **Birdworld** (☎07-4093 9188; www.birdworldkuranda.com; Rob Veivers Dr; adult/child $17/8.50; ⏲9am-4pm) re-creates the habitats of over 80 species in its unique rainforest environment.

Combination Wildlife Experience tickets cost $46/23 (adult/child).

Rainforestation PARK
(☎07-4085 5008; www.rainforest.com.au; Kennedy Hwy; adult/child $44/23; ⏲9am-4pm) Kuranda's rainforest twitters, growls and snaps with all manner of creatures. To get a sense of it, take a shuttle bus (adults $10, children $5) to this enormous tourist park outside of town, with its wildlife section, rainforest/river tours and interactive Aboriginal experience.

Kuranda

Sights

1 Australian Butterfly Sanctuary C2
Birdworld ....(see 3)
2 Heritage Markets C2
3 Kuranda Koala Gardens B2
4 Kuranda Original Rainforest Markets C2

Sleeping

5 Kuranda Hotel Motel D2

Eating

6 Kuranda Cyber Cafe B2
7 Petit Cafe C1

Sleeping & Eating

There are endless eateries catering to the tourist dollar. Kuranda becomes a ghost town at night, once the last train and Skyrail have departed.

Kuranda Hotel Motel MOTEL $$
(☎07-4093 7206; www.kurandahotel.com.au; cnr Coondoo & Arara Sts; s/d $95/100; ❄☒) Locally known as the 'bottom pub', the back of the convenient Kuranda Hotel Motel has spacious

DON'T MISS

ONE MAN'S DREAM: PARONELLA PARK

One of Cairns' most popular day trips, **Paronella Park** (☎07-4065 0000; www.paronellapark.com.au; Japoonvale Rd, Mena Creek; adult/child $42/21) is actually closer to Innisfail, about 90-minutes drive south. When construction of this art deco castle with it's own hydro-electric power system was completed in 1935, the world was an entirely different place. Self-made Spanish immigrant José Paronella built the place as a gift to his wife Margarita. He opened the incongruously sited property and pleasure gardens to a grateful public shortly after their construction. He died in 1948, and the park is now privately owned and National Trust listed. The magic and mystery of this phenomenal property, with more nooks, crannies and sources of fascination then can be described here, await your custom. Nearby camping and quaint on-site cabins are available.

Northern Experience Eco Tours (☎07-4058 0268; www.northernexperience.com.au; 77 Kamerunga Rd; tours from adult/child $120/82) runs day trips from Cairns to the park; a variety of itineraries are available.

'70s-style motel rooms with modern accents. Open for lunch daily and dinner Thursday to Saturday.

Cedar Park Rainforest Resort RESORT **$$**
(☎07-4093 7892; www.cedarparkresort.com.au; 250 Cedarpark Rd; s/d from $130/150; @) Set deep in the bush (a 20-minute drive from Kuranda towards Mareeba), this unusual property is part Euro-castle, part Aussie-bush-retreat. In lieu of TV, visitors goggle at wallabies, peacocks and dozens of native birds; there are hammocks aplenty, creek access, a fireplace, and a gourmet restaurant with well-priced meals and free port wine.

Petit Cafe CREPERIE **$**
(www.petitcafekuranda.com; Shop 35, Kuranda Original Rainforest Markets; crepes $10-17; ⏲8am-3pm) Duck out the back of the original markets for a mouth-watering range of crepes with savoury or sweet fillings. Winning combinations such as macadamia pesto and feta cheese will entice *le* drool.

Kuranda Cyber Cafe CAFE **$**
(☎07-4093 7576; 8/12 Rob Veivers Dr; meals from $8; ⏲11am-9pm Tue-Sun, from 3pm Mon) Drop in to see the friendly kids at the Kuranda Cyber Cafe for cheap delicious pizzas, barra burgers and the best caramel milkshake we've had in a long time. One of the few eateries in town that remains open after dark.

Information

Kuranda Visitor Information Centre (☎07-4093 9311; www.kuranda.org; Centenary Park; ⏲10am-4pm) The knowledgeable staff at the unmissable, map-laden visitor centre in Centenary Park are happy to make recommendations.

Getting There & Away

Kuranda is as much about the journey as the destination: the Skyrail (p418) and Kuranda Scenic Railway (p418) are where it's at. If you're on a budget, you can also get to Kuranda with Trans North (p417) and John's Kuranda Bus (p418).

Atherton

POP 7288

The largest town of the same-named Tableland offers year-round picking jobs and a handful of attractions. Contact the **Atherton Visitor Information Centre** (☎07-4091 4222; www.itablelands.com.au; cnr Main & Silo Rds) for up-to-date work info and self-drive itineraries.

Sights & Activities

Serious mountain bikers rate the area's well-maintained trails. For details visit www.nprsr.qld.gov.au/parks/herberton-range/mountain-bike.html.

Hou Wang Miau TEMPLE
(☎07-4091 6945; www.houwang.org.au; 86 Herberton Rd; adult/child $10/5; ⏲11am-4pm Wed-Sun) Thousands of Chinese migrants came to the region in search of gold in the late 1800s. All that's left of Atherton's Chinatown now is this corrugated-iron temple museum, run by the National Trust. Admission includes a guided tour.

Crystal Caves MUSEUM
(☎07-4091 2365; www.crystalcaves.com.au; 69 Main St; adult/child $22.50/10; ⏲8.30am-5pm Mon-Fri, to 4pm Sat, 10am-4pm Sun, closed Feb) Crystal Caves is a gaudy mineralogical museum that houses the world's biggest amethyst geode (more than 3m high and weighing 2.7

tonnes). Crack a geode and take home your own glittery, gazillion-year-old souvenir.

Sleeping

Barron Valley Hotel HOTEL $
(07-4091 1222; www.bvhotel.com.au; 53 Main St; dm $40, s/d with bathroom $60/85;) This hotel is an art deco beauty, with tidy rooms and a **restaurant** (mains $18-35) serving hearty meals, including giant steaks.

Yungaburra

POP 1150

If you have limited time, head straight to lovable Yungaburra, Queensland's largest National Trust village. A local platypus colony, 19 heritage-listed sites and stunning surrounds make it a popular retreat for those in the know. Abundant, quality accommodation means it's the perfect place to lay one's head in the Tableland.

Sights & Activities

Curtain Fig NATURE
(07-4091 4222; Fig Tree Rd, East Barron) The sacred, 500-year-old Curtain Fig tree (signposted 3km out of town) is a spectacular example of a parasitic fig with a gigantic curtain of dangling roots.

Avenue of Honour MEMORIAL
(www.avenueofhonour.com.au; Tinaburra Dr) By Lake Tinaroo, this touching memorial to Australian soldiers lost in conflict in Afghanistan opened in 2013, and features a spectacular grove of Illawarra flame trees.

Yungaburra Markets MARKET
(www.yungaburramarkets.com; Gillies Hwy; 7.30am-12.30pm 4th Sat of the month) On the fourth Saturday of every month the town is besieged by day trippers hunting for crafts and local produce at these vibrant markets.

Platypus Viewing WILDLIFE WATCHING
(Gilles Hwy) FREE If you're very quiet, you might catch a glimpse of a timid monotreme at this platypus viewing platform on Peterson Creek. Dusk and dawn give you your best chance.

Festivals

Tablelands Folk Festival MUSIC
(www.tablelandsfolkfestival.org) This fabulous community event held each October in Yungaburra and neighbouring Herberton features music, workshops, performances and a market.

Sleeping

★ **On the Wallaby** HOSTEL $
(07-4095 2031; www.onthewallaby.com; 34 Eacham Rd; camping $10, dm/d with shared bathroom $24/55; @) This cosy hostel features handmade timber furniture and mosaics, spotless rooms and no TV! Nature-based tours ($40) include night canoeing; tour packages and transfers (one way $30) are available from Cairns.

Eden House Retreat BOUTIQUE HOTEL $$$
(07-4089 7000; www.edenhouse.com.au; 20 Gillies Hwy; d from $175; @) Set among gardens behind an historic homestead in the village centre are romantic cottages with large spa baths and raised beds, and family-oriented villas. An on-site restaurant serves dinner Tuesday through Saturday.

Eating & Drinking

Nick's Restaurant SWISS, ITALIAN $$
(07-4095 9330; www.nicksrestaurant.com.au; 33 Gillies Hwy; mains from $8.50; 11.30am-3pm Sat & Sun, 5.30-11pm Tue-Sun) Friendly and fun – think Swiss chalet with costumed staff, beer steins, a piano-accordion serenade and maybe some impromptu yodelling. Food spans schnitzels to smoked pork loin with sauerkraut, plus several vegetarian options.

OFF THE BEATEN TRACK

HISTORIC VILLAGE HERBERTON

Historic Village Herberton (07-4097 2002; www.herbertonhistoricvillage.com.au; 6 Broadway; adult/child $25/12; 9am-5pm, last entry 3.30pm) A must-see on any comprehensive Tablelands trip is this fascinating and unique village, comprised of over 50 heritage buildings, restored and relocated to their current location. Exhibits range from the school to the sawmill, the bank to the Bishop's house, the coach-house to the camera store and everything in between. Memorabilia includes working farm equipment, antique cars and a printing press. There's nothing quite like it anywhere else in Australia.

The village is 90-minutes' drive from Cairns in the sweet, sleepy Tablelands township of Herberton.

DON'T MISS

MALANDA & THE MILLAA MILLAA WATERFALLS CIRCUIT

If you need to escape the heat, the shady, croc-free Malanda Falls, about 75km southwest of Cairns, have been tamed into a kind of public swimming pool. **Guided rainforest walks** (per person $16; ⏲9.30am & 11.00am Sat & Sun, bookings essential), led by members of the Ngadjonji community, can be organised through the **Malanda Falls Visitor Centre** (☎07-4096 6957; www.malandafalls.com; Malanda-Atherton Rd; ⏲9.30am-4.30pm), opposite the falls. Enquire here for the low-down on the Millaa Millaa **Waterfalls Circuit** (www.millaamillaa.com.au), a picturesque loop 25km further south, near the dairy community of Millaa Millaa.

Take in four of the Tableland's picturesque waterfalls on a leisurely 15km circuit, beginning 1km east of Millaa Millaa off the Palmerston Hwy. You'll soon arrive at the 'most-photographed', 12m Millaa Millaa Falls, the best for swimming. Zillie Falls, 8km further on, are reached by a short trail leading to a lookout above the falls. Next, at Ellinjaa Falls a 200m walking trail leads down to a rocky swimming hole at the base of the falls. A further 5.5km down the Palmerston Hwy there's a turn-off to Mungalli Falls.

Hungry? Warm your bones by the fireplace at the **Falls Teahouse** (☎07-4097 2237; www.fallsteahouse.com.au; 6 Theresa Creek Rd; meals from $9; ⏲10am-5pm), or soak up rolling farmland views on the back verandah, as you hoe into dishes like pan-fried barra and local beef pies. Accommodation is available.

If you dig the serenity, midway between Malanda and Millaa Millaa you'll find the **Canopy Treehouses** (☎07-4096 5364; www.canopytreehouses.com.au; Hogan Rd, Tarzali, via Malanda; d from $199;) . These luxuriously appointed treehouses are nestled among 100 acres of old-growth rainforest, with abundant inquisitive wildlife to observe. Two-night minimum stay.

Lake Eacham Hotel PUB
(☎07-4095 3515; 6-8 Kehoe Pl; ⏲11am-11pm) Better known as the 'Yungaburra Pub', the downstairs dining room and swirling wooden staircase of this grand old dame are original and inspirational: we hope they don't change a thing. Cheap and cheery accommodation is available upstairs; enquire at the bar.

ℹ Information

Yungaburra Visitor Information Centre (☎07-4095 2416; www.yungaburra.com; 16 Cedar St) The utterly delightful volunteers at Yungaburra's immaculate Visitor Information Centre can help recommend accomodation. Be sure to pick up the *Old Town Loop* walking guide. If Syb's around, see if she'd be happy to have a yarn about the town through Indigenous eyes. Internet access is available.

ℹ Getting There & Away

You'll need your own wheels to get to Yungaburra, and two feet and a heartbeat once you're here. Access is via the steep and windy Gilles Hwy, heading south from Cairns, or on the Palmerston Hwy (via Kuranda, Mareeba and Atherton) from the north. Either way, it's about an hour's drive.

Lake Tinaroo

Lake Tinaroo was allegedly named when a prospector stumbled across a deposit of alluvial tin and, in a fit of excitement, shouted 'Tin! Hurroo!'. The excitement hasn't died down since, with locals fleeing the swelter of the coast for boating, waterskiing and shoreline lolling. **Barramundi fishing** is permitted year-round, though you'll need to pick up a permit. Or you might like to head out for a fish, a BBQ or a glass of wine during a sunset cruise aboard a super-comfy 'floating lounge room', skippered by **Lake Tinaroo Cruises** (☎0457 033 016; www.laketinaroocruises.com.au; 2/4hr boat charters $200/300).

The 28km **Danbulla Forest Drive** winds its way through rainforest and softwood plantations along the north side of the lake. There are five Queensland Parks campgrounds in the Danbulla State Forest. All have water, barbecues and toilets; contact **NPRSR** (☎13 74 68; www.nprsr.qld.gov.au; permits $5.45) for essential advance bookings. Otherwise, **Lake Tinaroo Holiday Park** (☎07-4095 8232; www.laketinarooholidaypark.com.au; 3 Tinaroo Falls Dam Rd, Tinaroo Falls; unpowered/powered sites $27/31, cabins from $89;) has mod-cons and rents out boats ($90 per half day) and canoes ($10 per hour).

Crater Lakes National Park

Part of the Wet Tropics World Heritage Area, the two mirrorlike, croc-free crater lakes of **Lake Eacham** and **Lake Barrine** are easily reached by sealed roads off the Gillies Hwy. Camping is not permitted.

Lake Barrine is the largest of the lakes, and is cloaked in thick old-growth rainforest; a 5km walking track around its edge takes about 1½ hours. Stop for Devonshire tea at the charming **Lake Barrine Rainforest Tea House**, (07-4095 3847; www.lakebarrine.com.au; Gillies Hwy; mains from $8; 9am-3pm) perched over the lakefront. Lake Eacham's clear waters are idyllic for swimming and turtle spotting; there are sheltered picnic areas, a pontoon and a boat ramp. The 3km lake-circuit track is an easy one-hour walk.

Each of the four individually themed **Crater Lakes Rainforest Cottages** (07-4095 2322; www.craterlakes.com.au; Lot 17, Eacham Close; d $240;) is a romantic hideaway in its own private patch of rainforest, replete with candles, fresh flowers, wood stoves, spa baths, full kitchens with breakfast hampers and fruit to feed the birds! For something more basic, the **Lake Eacham Tourist Park** (07-4095 3730; www.lakeeachamtouristpark.com; Lakes Dr; unpowered/powered sites $22/25, cabins $90-110; @) has shady camp sites and cute cabins.

PORT DOUGLAS

POP 3205

From its humble origins as a sleepy 1960s fishing village, Port Douglas has grown into a sophisticated alternative to Cairns' hectic tourist scene. With the outer Great Barrier Reef less than an hour offshore, the Daintree Rainforest practically in the backyard, and more resorts than you can poke a stick at, a growing number of flashpackers, cashed-up couples and fiscally flush families now choose Port Douglas as their base, leaving Cairns at the airport.

The town's main attraction is Four Mile Beach, a pristine strip of palm-fringed, white sand which begins at the eastern end of Macrossan St, the main drag for shopping, wining and dining. On the western end of Macrossan you'll find the picturesque Dickson Inlet and Reef Marina, where the rich and famous park their aquatic toys.

Sights

Trinity Bay Lookout VIEWPOINT

(Island Point Rd) Head to Trinity Bay Lookout for spectacular views of the Coral Sea and nearby coral cays.

St Mary's by the Sea CHURCH

(0418 456 880; 6 Dixie St) FREE Worth a peek inside (when it's not overflowing with wedding parties), this quaint, nondenominational, white timber church was built in 1911.

Wildlife Habitat Port Douglas ZOO

(07-4099 3235; www.wildlifehabitat.com.au; Port Douglas Rd; adult/child $33/16.50; 8am-5pm) This sanctuary endeavours to keep and showcase native animals in enclosures that mimic their natural environment, while allowing you to get up close to koalas, kangaroos, crocs, cassowaries and more. Tickets are valid for three days. It's 4km from town; head south along Davidson St.

Activities

Ballyhooley Steam Railway MINIATURE TRAIN

(07-4099 1839; www.ballyhooley.com.au; 44 Wharf St; adult/child day passes $10/5; Sun) Kids will get a kick out of this cute miniature steam train. Every Sunday (and some public holidays), it runs from the little station at Reef Marina to St Crispins Station. A round trip takes about one hour; discounts are available for shorter sections.

Port Douglas Yacht Club SAILING

(07-4099 4386; www.portdouglasyachtclub.com.au; 1 Spinnaker Cl; from 4pm Wed) Free sailing

YEEE-HAA: MAREEBA RODEO

Mareeba revels in a Wild West atmosphere, with local merchants selling leather saddles, handcrafted bush hats and the oversized belt buckle of your bronco-bustin' dreams. July's **Mareeba Rodeo** (www.mareebarodeo.com.au) is one of Australia's biggest and best, with bull riding, a 'beaut ute' muster and boot scootin' country music. The **Mareeba Heritage Museum & Tourist Information Centre** (07-4092 5674; www.mareebaheritagecentre.com.au; Centenary Park, 345 Byrnes St; 9am-5pm) FREE has info on the rodeo, the town's history, and it's handful of local attractions.

Port Douglas

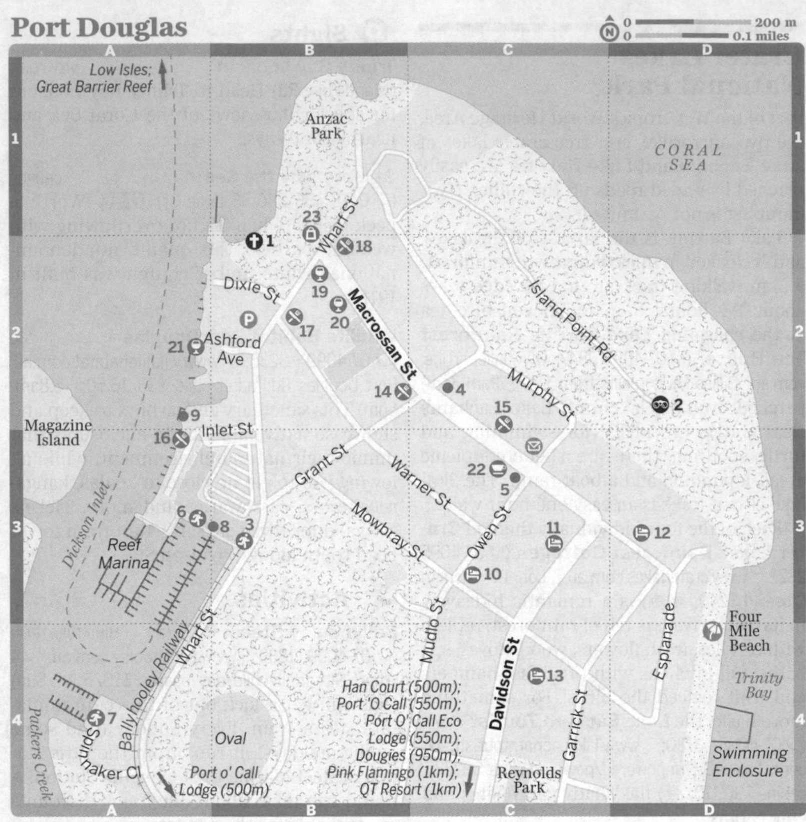

Port Douglas

Sights
1 St Mary's by the Sea B2
2 Trinity Bay Lookout D2

Activities, Courses & Tours
3 Ballyhooley Steam Railway B3
4 Blue Dive C2
5 BTS Tours C3
6 Port Douglas Boat Hire A3
7 Port Douglas Yacht Club A4
8 Quicksilver B3
9 Reef Sprinter A2

Sleeping
10 Hibiscus Gardens C3
11 Mantra Aqueous on Port C3
12 Martinique on Macrossan D3
13 Peppers Beach Club C4

Eating
14 Cafe Fresq B2
15 Little Larder C2
16 On the Inlet A3
17 Salsa Bar & Grill B2
18 Sassi Cucina e Bar B2

Drinking & Nightlife
19 Court House Hotel B2
20 Iron Bar B2
Port Douglas Yacht Club .... (see 7)
21 Tin Shed A2
22 Whileaway Bookshop Cafe C3

Shopping
23 Port Douglas Markets B1

with club members every Wednesday afternoon: sign on from 4pm. Those chosen to go sailing are expected to stay for dinner and drinks in the club postsailing.

Port Douglas Boat Hire BOATING
(☎07-4099 6277; www.pdboathire.com.au; Berth C1, Reef Marina; rentals from $33) Rents dinghies (per hour $33) and canopied, family-friendly pontoon boats (per hour $43), plus fishing gear.

Lady Douglas CRUISES
(☎07-4099 1603; www.ladydouglas.com.au; 1½hr cruises adult/child $30/20) Lovely paddle steamer running croc-spotting tours (including a sunset cruise) along the Dickson Inlet.

Bike N Hike CYCLING
(☎0477-774 443; www.bikenhiketours.com.au; bike adventures from $99) Mountain bike down the aptly named Bump Track on a cross-country bike tour, or take on a beserk night tour.

Fishing Port Douglas FISHING
(☎0409 610 869; www.fishingportdouglas.com.au; share/sole charters per half day from $90/320) Private and shared charters on the river and reef. Gear and bait included.

Tours

Port Douglas is a hub for tours. Many tours based out of Cairns, including some white-water rafting and hot-air ballooning trips, also offer pickups from Port Douglas, and vice versa.

Great Barrier Reef

The outer reef is closer to Port Douglas than it is to Cairns, and the unrelenting surge of visitors has had a similar impact on its condition here. You will still see colourful corals and marine life, but it is patchy in parts.

Most day tours depart from Reef Marina. Tour prices usually include reef tax, snorkelling, transfers from your accommodation, lunch and refreshments. An introductory, controlled scuba dive, with no certification or experience necessary, costs around $250, with additional dives around $50; certified divers will pay around $260 for two dives with all gear included.

Several operators visit the Low Isles, a small, idyllic group of islands surrounded by beautiful coral reef just 15km offshore; you've got a great chance of spotting turtles here.

★ **Quicksilver** CRUISE
(☎07-4087 2100; www.quicksilver-cruises.com; Reef Marina; adult/child $225/113) Major operator with fast cruises to its own pontoon on Agincourt Reef. Try an 'ocean walk' helmet dive ($158) on a submerged platform. Also offers 10-minute scenic helicopter flights ($165, minimum two passengers).

Poseidon SNORKELLING
(☎07-4087 2100; www.poseidon-cruises.com.au; Reef Marina; adult/child $226/158) Now part of the Quicksilver group, this luxury catamaran specialises in trips to the Agincourt Ribbon Reefs.

Blue Dive DIVING
(☎0427 983 907; www.bluedive.com.au; 32 Macrossan St; reef intro diving courses from $285) Port Douglas' most acclaimed dive operator offers a range of programs including liveaboard trips and PADI certification. Private, guided scuba dives of the reef are available.

Sailaway SAILING, SNORKELLING
(☎07-4099 4200; www.sailawayportdouglas.com; adult/child $225/155) Runs a popular sailing and snorkelling trip to the Low Isles that's great for families. Also offers 90-minute twilight sails ($60) off the coast of Port Douglas.

Sail Tallarook SAILING
(☎07-4099 4070; www.sailtallarook.com.au; adult/child half-day sails $120/100) Sunset cruises (from $60, Tuesday and Thursday), including cheese platters, on an historic 30m yacht.

Reef Sprinter SNORKELLING, BOATING
(☎07-4099 6127; www.reefsprinter.com.au; Shop 3, Reef Marina; adult/child $120/100) This 2¼-hour round trip gets to the Low Isles in just 15 minutes for one to 1½ hours in the water. Half-day outer reef trips are also available (from $200).

The Daintree & Around

There are 4WD tours from Cairns via Port Douglas to Cooktown and Cape York.

★ **Tony's Tropical Tours** OUTDOORS
(☎07-4099 3230; www.tropicaltours.com.au; Lot 2, Captain Cook Hwy; day tours from $185) This luxury, small-group (eight to 10 passengers) tour operator specialises in trips to out-of-the-way sections of the Mossman Gorge and Daintree Rainforest (Tour A, adult/child $185/155), and Bloomfield Falls and Cape Trib (Tour B, adults only $210 – good mobility required). Highly recommended.

COME TO CARNIVALE!

For 10 days at the end of May, Port Douglas comes alive to the tune of its own **Carnivale** (www.carnivale.com.au): there's a parade, live music, performances galore and lashings of good food and wine. Check the website for details and be sure to book in advance if your visit coincides with the festival. Rooms fill fast and rates go through the roof!

Daintree Discovery Tours OUTDOORS
(☎07-4098 2878; www.daintreediscoverytours.com.au; 12 Thooleer Close, Mossman; half-day tours adult/child from $90/70) Runs half- and full-day tours (adult/child $180/160) of Mossman Gorge, Cassowary Falls and Cape Trib, including waterfalls, river cruises and friendly, knowledgeable guides.

Back Country Bliss Adventures SNORKELLING
(☎07-4099 3677; www.backcountryblissadventures.com.au; trips $99) Go with the flow as you drift-snorkel down the Mossman River. Expect to see turtles and freshwater fish. Kid-friendly. A range of tours are available.

BTS Tours OUTDOORS
(☎07-4099 5665; www.btstours.com.au; 49 Macrossan St; adult/child from $83/52) Tours to the Daintree Rainforest and Cape Trib, including canoeing, swimming and rainforest walks.

Sleeping

Port Douglas' main drawback is that much of its accommodation is located off the 5km-long Port Douglas Rd, while almost all restaurants, bars, pubs and the marina are on the main drag, Macrossan St. Taxis aren't superfluous; walking home after a night on the tiles can be a real drag.

★ **Port O' Call Eco Lodge** HOSTEL $
(☎07-4099 5422; www.portocall.com.au; cnr Port St & Craven Close; 5-/4-bed dm from $25/30, d from $69; ❄@📶🏊) 🍃 Under friendly new management, this fabulous, chilled-out hostel has colourful spick-and-span dorms and private rooms, iPod docks, free tablets and wi-fi for guest use, a lovely pool and a kick-ass bar and bistro. All rooms have en suite bathrooms. Highly recommended.

Dougies HOSTEL $
(☎07-4099 6200; www.dougies.com.au; 111 Davidson St; camp sites per person $17, dm $26, d $68; ❄@📶🏊) It's easy to hang about Dougies' sprawling grounds in a hammock by day and move to the bar at night. If you can summon the energy, bikes and fishing gear are available for rent. Free pickup from Cairns on Monday, Wednesday and Saturday.

★ **Pink Flamingo** BOUTIQUE HOTEL $$
(☎07-4099 6622; www.pinkflamingo.com.au; 115 Davidson St; d from $135; ❄@📶🏊🐾) Flamboyantly painted rooms, private walled courtyards (with hammocks, outdoor baths and outdoor showers) and a groovy al fresco bar make the Pink Flamingo Port Douglas' hippest digs. Outdoor movie nights, gym and bike rental are also on offer.

Mantra Aqueous on Port APARTMENTS $$
(☎07-4099 0000; www.mantra.com.au; 3-5 Davidson St; d from $140; 🏊) You can't beat the location of this unique resort with four individual pools. All ground floor rooms have swim-up balconies, and all rooms have outdoor Jacuzzi tubs! Studio, one- and two-bedroom apartments are available. Great rates and a fresh new colour scheme in 2015 make this an excellent all-rounder and good for romancin'. Longer stays attract cheaper rates.

Martinique on Macrossan APARTMENTS $$
(☎07-4099 6222; www.martinique.com.au; 66 Macrossan St; r from $129; 📶🏊) This terracotta block contains lovely, tiled one-bedroom apartments, each with a small kitchen, a private balcony, colourful accents and plantation shutters. Wonderful hosts and an excellent main street location near the beach seal the deal. The pool has six coves and is supervised by a lavish elephant and dolphin shrine. Great value.

QT Resort RESORT $$
(☎07-4099 8900; www.qtportdouglas.com.au; 87-109 Port Douglas Rd; d from $159; ❄@📶🏊) Fresh, fun and funky, this one is aimed at a trendy, 20-to-30-something crowd. There's a lagoon pool and swim-up bar, retro-kitsch rooms with free wi-fi, all-round good-lookin' staff, and DJs spinning lounge beats in Estil-

TURTLE COVE BEACH RESORT

Turtle Cove Beach Resort (☎07-4059 1800; www.turtlecove.com; Captain Cook Hwy; d/ste from $157/279; P❄@🏊) Midway between Palm Cove and Port Douglas, this resort earns props for being the only gay venue in Tropical Far North Queensland: there's not even a gay bar in Cairns! Lucky locals are free to frequent this fun little resort with its own, stunning, private beach. There's a beautiful pool shaded by gum trees, lazy hammocks and a relaxed, welcoming vibe. Clothing is optional.

Rooms have been recently refurbished, and rates include continental breakfast. Of course, the on-site bar and bistro is open for lunch, dinner and pina coladas, darling! Stay longer, pay less.

io, the cocktail lounge. We rate the breakfast buffet as one of the best we've seen: you really have to see it…and eat it.

Hibiscus Gardens RESORT $$
(07-4099 5995; www.hibiscusportdouglas.com.au; 22 Owen St; d from $170;) Balinese influences such as teak furnishing and fixtures and plantation shutters – plus the occasional Buddha – give this stylish resort an exotic ambience. Their day spa is renowned as one of the best in town.

★ **Peppers Beach Club** RESORT $$$
(1300 987 600; www.peppers.com.au/beach-club; 20-22 Davidson St; d from $207;) A killer location and an exceptional, enormous, sandy lagoon-pool. Luxurious, airy apartments with high-end furnishings and amenities. Surround sound systems, Jacuzzis and swim-up access in some rooms. For all this plus a management team that doesn't miss a trick, Peppers earns our top choice in the hotly contested Port Douglas luxury resort category. Family friendly, but recommended for young romantics.

Eating

Port Douglas has some fittingly sophisticated dining: reservations are advised. Self-caterers will find a large supermarket in the **Port Village Shopping Centre** (Macrossan St).

★ **Port 'O Call** AUSTRALIAN $$
(07-4099 5422; www.portocall.com.au; cnr Port St & Craven Close; mains from $16; 6pm-9.30pm Tue-Sun) The kitchen of this equally regarded hostel turns out some seriously good grub at reasonable prices, in a cheery casual environment. Standard staples of fish, steak, pastas and salads are anything but ordinary, and the talented chef's daily specials (including Mexican nights!) are well worth a look-see. Fettuccine carbonara, which can so often be way too creamy, is just right.

Cafe Fresq CAFE $$
(07-4099 6111; 27 Macrossan St; breakfast from $10, mains from $15; 7.30am-3pm) Best for breakfast (though you'll likely have to wait for a table) this al fresco cafe on Macrossan serves up big helpings of deliciousness, killer coffee and kick-start-your-day fresh juices.

Little Larder CAFE $$
(07-4099 6450; Shop 2, 40 Macrossan St; breakfast from $6, sandwiches $12.50; 7.30am-3pm Wed-Mon) Brekky until 11.30am then serious sandwiches from noon: take your pick – we bet you'll be happy either way. The coffee is great and you can also try freshly brewed and super healthy kombucha tea.

Han Court CHINESE $$
(07-4099 5007; 85 Davidson St; mains from $16; noon-2pm & 5-10pm) If Port's fancy buzz-word-du-jour menus are wearing you out, head to Han for good old-fashioned comfort food. They've been in town forever, and dish up familiar – but very tasty – staples, such as honey chicken and black-bean beef, on a lovely candlelit deck. The dumplings are amazing.

★ **Flames of the Forest** MODERN AUSTRALIAN $$$
(07-4099 5983; www.flamesoftheforest.com.au; Mowbray River Rd; dinner with show, drinks & transfers from $182) This unique experience goes way beyond the traditional concept of 'dinner and a show', with diners escorted deep in to the rainforest for a truly immersive night of theatre, culture and gourmet cuisine. Bookings essential.

Salsa Bar & Grill MODERN AUSTRALIAN $$$
(07-4099 4922; www.salsaportdouglas.com.au; 26 Wharf St; mains from $22.50; noon-3.00pm & 5.30-9.30pm;) Salsa is a stayer on Port's fickle scene. For something a little different try the Creole jambalaya (rice with prawns, squid, crocodile and smoked chicken), or the roo with tamarillo marmalade. We think you'd like a cocktail with that.

On the Inlet SEAFOOD $$$
(07-4099 5255; www.portdouglasseafood.com; 3 Inlet St; mains from $24; noon-11.30pm) Jutting out over Dickson Inlet, tables here are spread out along a huge deck, where you can await the 5pm arrival of George the 250kg groper, who comes to feed most days. Take up the bucket-of-prawns-and-a-drink deal ($18 from 3.30pm to 5.30pm).

Sassi Cucina e Bar ITALIAN $$$
(07-4099 6744; www.sassi.com.au; cnr Wharf & Macrossan Sts; mains from $26; noon-10pm) You may have to scrimp and save to splurge on an authentic Italian feast at this legendary local eatery. It's the brainchild of owner-chef Tony Sassi, who hails from Abruzzo in the mother country. His spin on seafood is world renowned: the balanced flavours of each dish should linger longer than your Four Mile Beach tan.

WORTH A TRIP

MOSSMAN GORGE

Mossman, 20km north of Port Douglas, is an obligatory stop on a visit to **Mossman Gorge** (www.mossmangorge.com.au), and a good place to fill up and stock up if you're heading further north.

Just 5km west of town, in the southeast corner of Daintree National Park, Mossman Gorge forms part of the traditional lands of the Kuku Yalanji people. Carved by the Mossman River, the gorge is a boulder-strewn valley where sparkling water washes over ancient rocks. From the fantastic **Mossman Gorge Centre** (07-4099 7000; www.mossmangorge.com.au; Dreaming walk adult/child $50/25; 8am-6pm), which houses an art gallery and bush-tucker restaurant, walking tracks loop along the river to a refreshing swimming hole – take care, as the currents can be swift. There's a picnic area, but no camping. The complete circuit takes over an hour, or you can get a shuttle bus (every 15 minutes; adults $8.50, children $4.25) into the heart of the gorge. Bookings for the unforgettable 1½-hour Indigenous-guided **Kuku-Yalanji Dreamtime Walks** (adult/child $50/25; 9am, 11am & 3pm) can be made through the Mossman Gorge Centre.

Drinking & Nightlife

Tin Shed BAR

(07-4099 5553; www.thetinshed-portdouglas.com.au; 7 Ashford Ave; 10am-10pm) Port Douglas' Combined Services Club is a rare find: bargain dining on the waterfront. Even the drinks are cheap.

Iron Bar PUB

(07-4099 4776; www.ironbarportdouglas.com.au; 5 Macrossan St; 11am-3am) Wacky outback decor sets the scene for a wild night out. Nightly 8pm cane-toad races ($5) are a must.

Court House Hotel PUB

(07-4099 5181; courthousehotelportdouglas.com.au; cnr Macrossan & Wharf Sts; 11am-late) Elegant and unmissable, the old 'Courty' is a lively local, with bands on weekends. There's good pub grub, too.

Whileaway Bookshop Cafe CAFE

(07-4099 4066; whileaway.com.au; 2/43 Macrossan St; 7am-6pm) For smart coffees in literary surrounds.

Port Douglas Yacht Club BAR

(07-4099 4386; www.portdouglasyachtclub.com.au; 1 Spinnaker Close; 4-10pm Mon-Fri, noon-10pm Sat & Sun) There's a spirited nautical atmosphere at the PDYC. Inexpensive meals are served nightly.

Entertainment

Moonlight Cinema CINEMA

(www.moonlight.com.au/port-douglas; QT Resort, 87-109 Port Douglas Rd; adult/child $16/12; Jun-Oct) Bring a picnic or hire a bean bag for outdoor twilight movie screenings. Check website for details.

Shopping

Port Douglas Markets MARKET

(Anzac Park, Macrossan St; 8am-1pm Sun) These Sunday markets feature handmade crafts and jewellery, local tropical fruits and fresh produce.

Information

The *Port Douglas & Mossman Gazette* comes out every Thursday, and has heaps of local info, gig guides and more.

There's no impartial, government-accredited visitor information centre in Port Douglas.

Douglas Shire Historical Society (07-4098 1284; www.douglashistory.org.au; Wharf St, Port Douglas; admission $2; 10am-1pm Tue, Thu, Sat & Sun) Download DIY historical walks through Port Douglas, Mossman and Daintree, or chat with a local at the on-site Court House museum.

Post Office (07-4099 5210; 5 Owen St; 8.30am-5pm Mon-Fri, 9am-noon Sat)

Getting There & Away

About half of the 65km drive between Cairns and Port Douglas hugs the coast, affording magical vistas: drivers, keep your eyes on the road!

Port Douglas Bus (07-4099 5665; www.portdouglasbus.com.au; one way adult/child $34/20) Operates daily services ($34, 1½ hours) between Port Douglas and Cairns via Palm Cove and Cairns Airport.

Coral Reef Coaches (07-4098 2800; www.coralreefcoaches.com.au; adult from $44) Connects Port Douglas with Cairns ($44, 1¼ hours) via Palm Cove and Cairns Airport, and offers a local shuttle around town.

Sun Palm (07-4087 2900; www.sunpalmtransport.com.au; adult from $44) Has frequent daily services between Port Douglas and Cairns ($44, 1½ hours) via the northern beaches and the airport.

Getting Around

Major car-rental chains have branches here, or try **Paradise Wheels** (07-4099 6625; www.paradisewheels.com.au; 7 Warner St) and keep it local.

Port Douglas Bike Hire (07-4099 5799; www.portdouglasbikehire.com.au; cnr Wharf & Warner Sts; per day from $19) Has high-performance bikes for hire as well as tandems ($32 per day). Free delivery and pickup.

THE DAINTREE

The Daintree represents many things: World Heritage rainforest, a river, a reef, a village and the home of its traditional custodians, the Kuku Yalanji people. It encompasses the coastal lowland area between the Daintree and Bloomfield Rivers, where the rainforest meets the coast. It's a fragile, ancient ecosystem, once threatened by logging but now protected as a national park.

Daintree River to Cape Tribulation

Part of the Wet Tropics World Heritage Area, the spectacular region from the Daintree River north to Cape Tribulation features ancient rainforest, sandy beaches and rugged mountains. North of the Daintree River, electricity is supplied by generators or, increasingly, solar power. Shops and services are limited, and mobile-phone reception is largely nonexistent. The **Daintree River Ferry** (douglas.qld.gov.au/community/daintree-ferry; car/motorcycle $13.50/5, bicycle & pedestrian $1; 6am-midnight, no bookings) carries wanderers and their wheels across the river every 15 minutes or so.

Sights & Activities

On the steep, winding road between Cape Kimberley and Cow Bay the **Walu Wugirriga Lookout** offers sweeping views beyond the Daintree River inlet; it's especially breathtaking at sunset.

The white-sand **Cow Bay Beach**, at the end of Buchanan Creek Rd, rivals any coastal paradise.

Daintree Discovery Centre NATURE RESERVE
(07-4098 9171; www.discoverthedaintree.com; Tulip Oak Rd; adult/child/family $32/16/78; 8.30am-5pm) This award-winning attraction's **aerial walkway**, which includes a 23m tower used to study carbon levels, takes you high into the forest canopy. A theatre screens films on cassowaries, crocodiles, conservation and climate change. An excellent Aboriginal audio-guide tour is included in the admission fee; tickets are vaild for seven days.

Daintree Rainforest Tours TOUR
(07-4098 9126; www.daintreerainforest.net.au; Cape Tribulation Rd; guided walks $55-300) Book ahead for expert guided rainforest walks which include a dip in Cooper Creek. A variety of itineraries are available.

Cape Tribulation Wilderness Cruises CRUISE
(0457 731 000; www.capetribcruises.com; Cape Tribulation Rd; adult/child from $30/22) Join the only tour boat permitted in the Cape Trib section of the Daintree National Park for insightful mangrove and croc-spotting tours.

DAINTREE NATIONAL PARK: THEN & NOW

The greater Daintree Rainforest is protected as part of Daintree National Park, but this protection is not without controversy. In 1983, despite conservationist blockades, what's now the Bloomfield Track was bulldozed through lowland rainforest from Cape Tribulation to the Bloomfield River. Ensuing publicity led to the federal government nominating Queensland's wet tropical rainforests for World Heritage listing, generating state government and timber industry opposition. In 1988 the area was inscribed on the World Heritage List and commercial logging here was banned.

UNESCO World Heritage listing (whc.unesco.org) doesn't affect ownership rights or control. Since the 1990s the Queensland Government and conservation agencies have attempted to buy back and rehabilitate freehold properties in the area, adding them to the Daintree National Park. Sealing the road to Cape Tribulation in 2002 triggered the buy back of even more land, which, coupled with development controls, now bears the fruits of forest regeneration. Check out **Rainforest Rescue** (www.rainforestrescue.org.au) for more information.

OFF THE BEATEN TRACK

SOMETHING SPECIAL: BLOOMFIELD LODGE

Bloomfield Lodge (07-4035 9166; www.bloomfieldlodge.com.au; Weary Bay Rd, Cape Tribulation; d per person incl all meals from $350 ;) Backing on to the Daintree Rainforest, deliciously all-inclusive Bloomfield Lodge is one of FNQ's best-kept secrets. Friendly staff pull out all the stops to make you feel special, from your arrival greeting to a warm farewell as the boat pulls away from the dock. Rooms are airy and simple, with stunning views out to sea – some have Jacuzzis on the deck.

Mouthwatering meals are a communal affair and feature fresh local seafood, delicious salads and hearty breakfasts.

This is one for that special occasion, or for when you really need to get away from it all. Access is by water only, from tiny Ayton wharf.

Sleeping

Lync-Haven Rainforest Retreat CAMPGROUND $
(07-4098 9155; www.lynchaven.com.au; Lot 44, Cape Tribulation Rd; unpowered/powered sites $14/32, d from $99;) This family-friendly retreat is set on a 16-hectare property on the main road, about 5km north of Cow Bay, and has walking trails and hand-reared kangaroos. Its **restaurant** serves robust steaks, good pasta and fish.

Thornton Beach Bungalows BUNGALOW $$
(07-4098 9179; www.thorntonbeach.com; Cape Tribulation Rd; cabins/houses $95/250) Paradise found: two adorable teeny-weeny cabins with verandahs, and a modern house with an amazing tub and beds for four, just across the road from the beach. Two-night minimum.

Epiphyte B&B B&B $$
(07-4098 9039; www.rainforestbb.com; 22 Silkwood Rd; s/d/cabins from $80/110/150) This laid-back place is set on a lush 3.5-hectare property. Individually styled rooms are of varying sizes, but all have their own verandah. A spacious, private cabin features a patio, kitchenette and sunken bathroom.

Daintree Rainforest Bungalows BUNGALOW $$
(07-4098 9229; www.daintreerainforestbungalows.com; Lot 40, Spurwood Rd; bungalows from $105) Great value accommodation comprising simple, freestanding cabins with covered decks in a tropical orchard close to the beach, forest and swimming holes. Two-night minimum stay.

★ **Heritage Lodge** LODGE $$$
(07-4098 9321; www.heritagelodge.net.au; Lot 236/R96 Turpentine Rd, Diwan; cabins from $250;) The friendly, accommodating owners of this wonderful retreat in the forest will do their best to make sure you feel at home here. Their comfortable, tastefully renovated cabins have air conditioning and free wifi. The crystal clear waters of their Cooper Creek swimming hole are something to behold. On-site dining is superb.

Eating

South of Cooper Creek, **Rainforest Village** (07-4098 9015; www.rainforestvillage.com.au; Cape Tribulation Rd; 7am-7pm) sells groceries, ice and fuel.

Daintree Ice Cream Company ICE CREAM $
(07-4098 9114; Lot 100, Cape Tribulation Rd; ice creams $6; 11am-5pm) We dare you to drive past this all-natural ice-cream producer with a palette of flavours that changes daily.

Thornton Beach Kiosk KIOSK $
(07-4098 9118; Cape Tribulation Rd; mains $12-25; 9am-4pm) Grab a beer and a burger and enjoy the breathtaking views from the sprawling deck of this on-the-beach kiosk; better still, grab the $10 fish-and-chips special and eat 'em on the beach.

Cow Bay Hotel PUB FOOD $$
(07-4098 9011; Cape Tribulation Rd; mains from $14; 11am-9.30pm) If you're craving a decent counter meal, a coldie and that Aussie country pub atmosphere, the Cow Bay (adjacent to the turn-off to the beach) is your only option: thankfully, it delivers on expectations.

On the Turps MODERN AUSTRALIAN $$$
(07-4098 9321; Lot 236/R96 Turpentine Rd, Diwan; mains from $18; 12-2pm & 5.30-9pm) The restaurant of the Heritage Lodge serves up some of the Daintree's finest cuisine in a delightfully atmospheric indoor/outdoor setting by the babbling crystal waters of Cooper Creek. Inventive dishes include kangaroo fillet steak, crocodile dumplings and gourmet pies.

Cape Tribulation

This isolated piece of paradise retains a frontier quality, with road signs alerting drivers to cassowary crossings, and croc warnings that make beach strolls a little less relaxing.

The rainforest tumbles right down to magnificent Myall and Cape Tribulation beaches, which are separated by a knobby cape. The little village here marks the end of the road: beyond here, the strictly 4WD-only Bloomfield track continues to Cooktown.

There is no public transport to Cape Tribulation, nor airport shuttles to any accomodation beyond the Daintree River. To get here, rent your own wheels or join a day tour.

Sights

Bat House WILDLIFE CENTRE
(07-4098 0063; www.austrop.org.au; Cape Tribulation Rd; admission $5; 10.30am-3.30pm Tue-Sun) A nursery for injured or orphaned fruit bats (flying foxes), run by conservation organisation Austrop.

Mt Sorrow WALKING
Fit walkers should lace up early for the strenuous but rewarding Mt Sorrow Ridge walk (7km, five-to-six hours return, start no later than 10am). The marked trail begins about 150m north of the Kulki picnic area car park.

Tours & Activites

★**Ocean Safari** SNORKELLING
(07-4098 0006; www.oceansafari.com.au; Cape Tribulation Rd; adult/child $128/82) Ocean Safari leads small groups (25 people maximum) on snorkelling cruises to the Great Barrier Reef, just half an hour offshore.

Jungle Surfing OUTDOORS, HIKING
(07-4098 0043; www.junglesurfing.com.au; ziplines $90, night walks $40, combo $120; night walks 7.30pm) Get right up into the rainforest on an exhilarating flying fox (zipline) ride through the canopy. Guided night walks follow biologist-guides, who shed light on the dark jungle. Rates include pickup from Cape Trib accommodation (self-drive not allowed).

D'Arcy of the Daintree DRIVING TOUR
(07-4098 9180; www.darcyofdaintree.com.au; 116 Palm Rd, Diwan; tours adult/child from $129/77) Exciting, entertaining small-group 4WD trips up the Bloomfield Track to Wujal Wujal Falls and as far as Cooktown.

Paddle Trek Kayak Tours KAYAKING
(07-4098 0062; www.capetribpaddletrek.com.au; Lot 7, Rykers Rd; kayak hire per hr $16-55, trips $69-79) Guided sea-kayaking trips and kayak hire.

Cape Trib Horse Rides HORSE RIDING
(07-4098 0043; www.capetribhorserides.com.au; per person from $99; 8am & 2.30pm) Leisurely rides along the beach and into the forest.

Sleeping

★**Cape Trib Beach House** HOSTEL, RESORT $
(07-4098 0030; www.capetribbeach.com.au; 152 Rykers Rd; dm from $29, cabins from $150;) This is a great choice for everyone, from backpackers to couples and families. Expect friendly management and staff,

OFF THE BEATEN TRACK

DAINTREE VILLAGE

You may be racing to the beaches of Cape Trib, but for wildlife lovers it's worth taking the 20km each-way detour to tiny Daintree village. Croc-spotting cruises on the Daintree River are the main event. Try **Crocodile Express** (07-4098 6120; www.crocodileexpress.com; 1hr cruises adult/child $23/12; from 8.30am) or **Daintree River Wild Watch** (0447 734 933; www.daintreeriverwildwatch.com.au; 2hr cruises adult/child $60/35), which has informative sunrise birdwatching cruises and sunset photography nature cruises.

The 15 boutique banyans (treehouses) of **Daintree Eco Lodge & Spa** (07-4098 6100; www.daintree-ecolodge.com.au; 20 Daintree Rd; treehouses from $215;) sit high in the rainforest a few kilometres south of the village. Nonguests are welcome at its superb **Julaymba Restaurant** (07-4098 6100; www.daintree-ecolodge.com.au; 20 Daintree Rd; mains $26.50-40; breakfast, lunch & dinner), where the menu makes tasty use of local produce.

No fuel is available in Daintree village.

Cape Tribulation Area

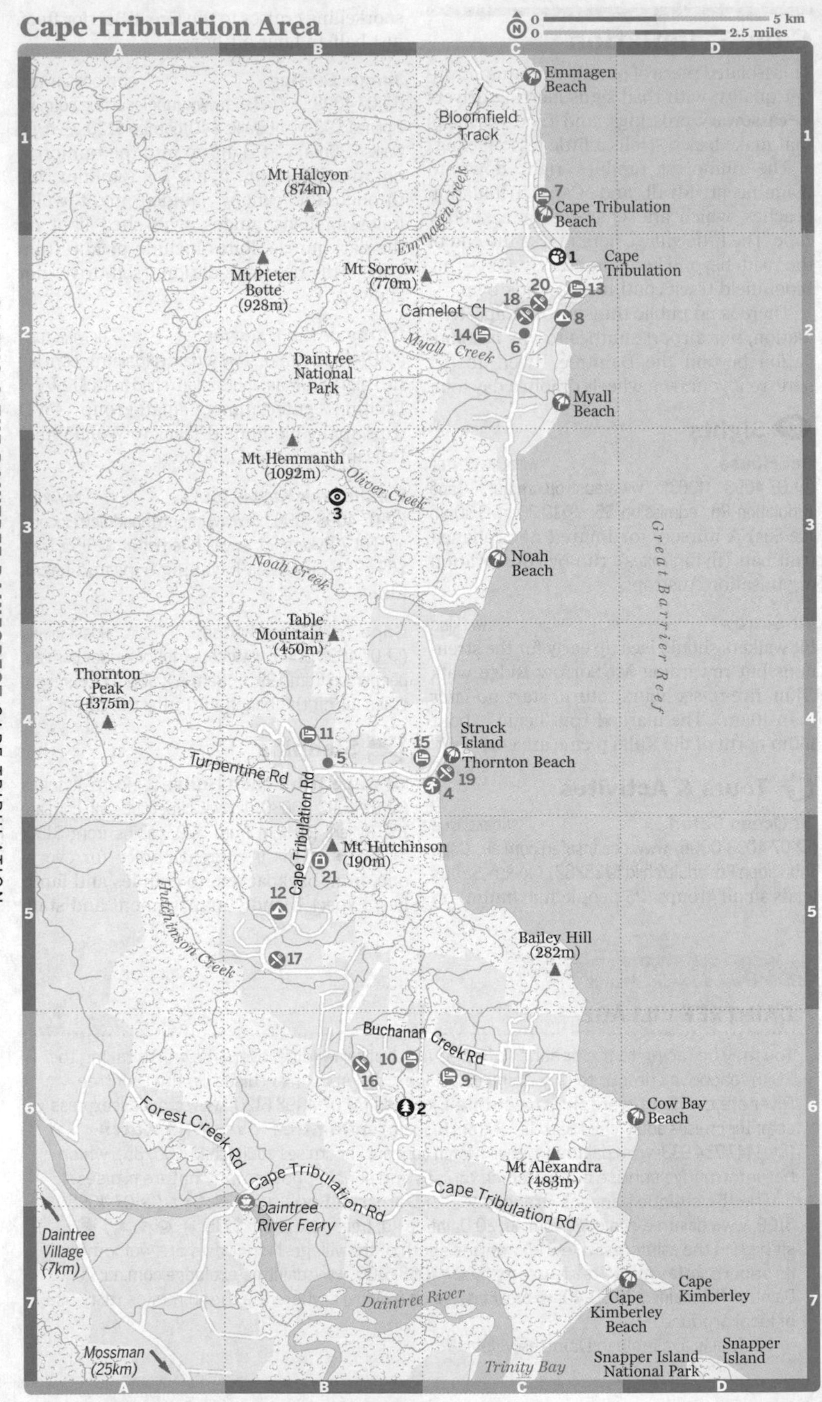

Cape Tribulation Area

and a wide range of accommodation options, from dorms to romantic almost-beachfront cabins. Highlights include a pristine private stretch of beach, a tidy communal kitchen, and a kick-ass open-deck licensed restaurant and bar.

PK's Jungle Village HOSTEL $
(07-4098 0040; www.pksjunglevillage.com; Cape Tribulation Rd; unpowered sites per person $15, dm from $25, d from $125;) You can reach Myall Beach by boardwalk from this longstanding backpackers' hub. The on-site Jungle Bar is Cape Trib's entertainment epicentre.

Rainforest Hideaway B&B $$
(07-4098 0108; www.rainforesthideaway.com; 19 Camelot Close; d from $129) This colourful B&B was single-handedly built by its owner, artist and sculptor 'Dutch Rob' – even the furniture and beds are handmade. A sculpture trail winds through the property.

Ferntree Rainforest Resort RESORT $$
(07-4098 0000; www.ferntreerainforestlodge.com.au; Camelot Close; dm from $28, d from $130;) Cape Trib's only resort-style accomodation could do with some TLC, but the key elements are all in place. There's a lovely pool area in the manicured grounds, free wi-fi in the lobby, and airy rooms and cabins with plantation shutters.

Eating

Whet AUSTRALIAN $$
(07-4098 0007; www.whet.net.au; 1 Cape Tribulation Rd; mains from $16.50; 11.30am-3pm & 5.30-9.30pm) Cape Trib's coolest address and undisputed best dining, offering trendy Mod-Oz cuisine and occasional themed nights and events.

Sandbar PIZZA $$
(07-4098 0077; Lot 11, Cape Tribulation Rd; pizzas from $14; 5-9pm Apr-Nov) The wood-fired pizzas and general good-vibes at **Cape Tribulation Camping** (07-4098 0077; www.capetribcamping.com.au; Lot 11, Cape Tribulation Rd; unpowered sites from $15; @) are turning heads. Refreshing beverages are available!

Mason's Store & Cafe CAFE $$
(07 4098 0016; 3781 Cape Tribulation Rd; mains from $15; 10am-4pm Sun-Thu, to 7pm Fri & Sat) This laid-back local does good fish and chips and huge steak sarnies. There's a small general and liquor store, a tourist information counter and, best of all, a crystal-clear, croc-free swimming hole (admission by gold coin donation) out the back.

Information

Mason's Store (07-4098 0070; Cape Tribulation Rd; 8am-6pm) Has regional info including Bloomfield Track conditions.

North to Cooktown

There are two routes to Cooktown from the south: the coastal route from Cape Tribulation via the 4WD-only Bloomfield Track, and the inland route, sealed all the way via the Mulligan Hwy.

Inland Route

The inland route skirts along the western side of the Great Dividing Range for 332km

IF YOU CAN AFFORD IT: LIZARD ISLAND

The five islands of the Lizard Island Group lie 33km off the coast about 100km north from Cooktown. Lizard – the main island – has rocky, mountainous terrain, glistening white beaches and spectacular fringing reefs for snorkelling and diving. Most of the island is national park, teeming with wildlife. Sumptuous accommodation and dining epitomise five-star luxury at the *ultra*-exclusive **Lizard Island Resort** (☎1300 863 248; www.lizardisland.com.au; Anchor Bay; d from $1699;), decimated by Cyclone Ita in April 2014 and exquisitely rebuilt and refurbished in 2015. There's limited bush camping at the island's **camp site** (☎13 74 68; www.nprsr.qld.gov.au/parks/lizard-island/camping.html; Watsons Bay; per person $5.75). There are no shops on the island. Book air transfers to/from Cairns (return $670, one hour) through the resort.

Daintree Air Services (☎1800 246 206; www.daintreeair.com.au; day tours from $750) offers spectacular full-day tours from Cairns including gourmet lunch, snorkelling gear, transfers and a local guide to take you to some of the most magnificent spots in this pristine ecosystem.

(about 4½ hours' drive) from Cairns to Cooktown.

If you're coming from Port Douglas, you'll pass through **Julatten**. This village is home to the romantic, sensationally designed and deliciously isolated, luxury, self-contained cabins of **Sweetwater Lodge** (☎07-4094 1594; www.sweetwaterlodge.com.au; 2472 Mossman-Mt Molloy Rd, Julatten; d from $225), where the rainforest meets the bush. Sweetwater is popular with birdwatchers and those seeking solace. Minimum two-night stay.

About 40km north of Mareeba, and 45km southwest of Port Douglas, **Mt Molloy** (population 274) marks the start of the **Mulligan Highway** and journeys north. Since its mining heyday, the township has shriveled to comprise a pub, bakery, post office and cafe serving allegedly world-famous burgers: they are certainly enormous. It's about 30km from here to don't-blink-or-you'll-miss-it **Mt Carbine**; if you turn off the Mulligan Hwy about 8km before that (when you see the signs), you'll find the purpose-built camp sites, restored tobacco-workers cottages and delightful B&B accommodation of **Bustard Downs Organic Farm** (☎07-4094 3094; www.bustarddowns.com.au; 61-03 East Mary Rd, Maryfarms; camping $12.50, cottages $220, B&B s/d $135/220).

If you have a high-clearance 4WD and are interested in exploring some fascinating ruins, the ghost town of **Maytown**, once the glorious centre of the Palmer River gold rush (1873–83), is about 80km inland from the highway. It's an extreme but rewarding drive, complete with river crossings, and not for the inexperienced. The turn-off is 17km south of the **Palmer River Roadhouse** (☎07-4060 2020; Peninsula Development Rd; unpowered sites $20, cabins $45-90), one of your last stops for tucker and fuel before things get rough. There's a nice campground and cheery cabins for those ready to bed-down. Check out the quaint local history museum inside and ask Andrew anything about journeys further north.

It's another 15km to **Lakeland**, where the Mulligan meets the legendary **Peninsula Developmental Rd**. Take it west and you're on your way to **Laura**. Beyond Laura, it's unsealed, seriously hard going, not-for-the-faint-hearted 4WD-ing to **Cape York**. Most folks stay on the Mulligan for another 80km to Cooktown: about 30km before you arrive, the eerie, awe-inspiring and other-worldly **Black Mountain National Park**, comprising thousands of black granite boulders formed 260 million years ago, marks the northern end of the Wet Tropics World Heritage Area. The sacred mountain is cloaked in mystery and legend: ask a local!

Coastal Route

The legendary 4WD-only Bloomfield Track connecting Cape Tribulation to Cooktown traverses creek crossings, diabolically steep climbs and patchy surfaces. It can be impassable for weeks on end during the Wet, and even in the Dry you should check road conditions, as creek crossings are affected by tide times. It's unsuitable for trailers. The track is a contentious one: bulldozed through pristine forest in the early '80s, it was the site of fierce battles between protestors and police. Unsubstantiated rumours abound that the track is soon to be sealed.

It's 8km from Cape Trib to **Emmagen Creek**, from where the road climbs and dips steeply, and turns sharp corners, then follows the broad Bloomfield River before crossing it 22km further in. Turn left immediately after the bridge to see the **Bloomfield Falls**. Crocs inhabit the river – the site is significant to the local Indigenous Wujal Wujal community. The half-hour **Walker Family Walking Tours** (07-4040 7500; www.bamaway.com.au; adult/child $25/12.50; by reservation) of the falls and surrounding forest are highly recommended.

About 5km north of Wujal Wujal, the **Bloomfield Track Takeaway & Middleshop** (07-4060 8174; dishes from $10; 8am-10pm Tue-Sat, to 8pm Sun & Mon) sells fast food, fuel, fishing tackle and groceries. North of Bloomfield, several walks begin from **Home Rule Rainforest Lodge** (07-4060 3925; www.home-rule.com.au; Rossville; unpowered sites per adult/child $10/5, r adult/child $35/20), at the end of a bumpy 3km driveway. Spotless facilities include shared cabins and a communal kitchen; meals and canoe hire are also available. Home Rule is ground zero for the weekend-long **Wallaby Creek Festival** (www.wallabycreekfestival.org.au; end Sep), a three-day, multicultural, family-friendly festival featuring roots, blues and Indigenous music.

Soldier on another 9km to the fun-tastic **Lion's Den Hotel** (07-4060 3911; www.lionsdenhotel.com.au; 398 Shiptons Flat Rd, Helenvale; unpowered/powered sites per person $12/28, s/d $45/65;): an iconic oasis with a tangible history dating back to 1875. You'll find fuel, ice-cold beer, strong coffee, awesome pizzas and pub grub. If you can, spend a night camping or in one of the pole-tent cabins. Don't miss a swim in the croc-free creek.

Explore the surrounding rainforest and waterfall of **Mungumby Lodge** (07-4060 3158; www.mungumby.com; Helenvale; s/d $260/279;) . En suite bungalows are scattered among the lawns and mango trees. Rates include breakfast. Nature tours available. About 4km further north, the Bloomfield Track meets the sealed Mulligan Hwy, from where it's 28km to Cooktown.

COOKTOWN

POP 2339

At the southeastern edge of Cape York Peninsula, Cooktown is a small place with a big history: for thousands of years, Waymbuurr was the place the local Guugu Yimithirr and Kuku Yalanji people used as a meeting ground, and it was here that on 17 June 1770, Lieutenant (later Captain) Cook beached the *Endeavour,* which had earlier struck a reef offshore from Cape Tribulation. Cook's crew spent 48 days here repairing the damage, making Cooktown Australia's first (albeit transient) non-Indigenous settlement.

Today, it's a hotspot for history hounds, work-hungry World Wide Opportunities on Organic Farm-ers (WWOOFers), and those for whom happiness is a fishing rod and an esky of coldies.

Sights & Activities

Cooktown's main street, Charlotte St, has some beautiful 19th-century buildings.

After-dark, the town centre can feel a little disconcerting, especially for single female travellers, and for everyone on Friday and Saturday nights. It's tough country up here; exercise reasonable caution.

Grassy Hill VIEWPOINT

Cook climbed this 162m-high hill looking for a passage through the reefs. At dusk and dawn the 360-degree views of the town, river and ocean are truly spectacular! Easy vehicular access is up a steep road from town. Walkers can ascend via bush trail from Cherry Tree Bay.

Nature's Powerhouse INTERPRETIVE CENTRE

(07-4069 6004; www.naturespowerhouse.com.au; off Walker St; admission by donation; 9am-5pm) Incorporating adjacent **Cooktown Botanical Gardens**, this fantastic environmental centre is home to two excellent galleries: the **Charlie Tanner Gallery**, with pickled and preserved creepy-crawlies, and the **Vera Scarth-Johnson Gallery**, displaying botanical illustrations of the region's native plants.

James Cook Museum MUSEUM

(07-4069 5386; www.nationaltrust.org.au/qld/JamesCookMuseum; cnr Helen & Furneaux Sts; adult/child $10/3; 9.30am-4pm) Cooktown's finest building (an 1899 convent) houses well-preserved relics including journal entries, the cannon and anchor from the *Endeavour*, and displays on local Indigenous culture.

Bicentennial Park PARK

Home to a much-photographed bronze **Captain Cook statue** and nearby **Milbi Wall** – a 12m-long mosaic depicting the history of the local Gungarde (Guugu Yimithirr) people, from creation stories through to attempts at reconciliation. Just out in the water there's a rock marking the spot where Cook ran aground.

Fishing Cooktown FISHING
(07-4069 5980; www.fishingcooktown.com; Lot 4 Wilkinson St; per person from $115) Fishing and heli-fishing trips plus croc-spotting, bird-watching, mud-crabbing and eco-tours.

Tours

There are no regular diving or snorkelling trips to the nearby reef. Water-based tours depart from the wharf. Many operators have reduced hours during the Wet.

★ **Guurrbi Tours** CULTURAL TOUR
(07-4034 5020; guurrbitours.blogspot.com.au; tours 2/4hr from $95/120, self-drive from $65/85; Mon-Sat) Nugal-warra family elder Willie Gordon runs revelatory tours using the physical landscape to describe the spiritual one, providing a powerful insight into Aboriginal culture and lore.

Maaramaka Walkabout Tours CULTURAL TOUR
(07-4045 6328; www.maaramaka.com.au; tours 1/2hr from $84/42) Aboriginal cultural stories, rainforest walks, bush tucker and home cooking in a gorgeous setting near Hopevale; call for arrangements.

Cooktown Tours TOUR
(1300 789 550; www.cooktowntours.com; tours from adult/child $60/35) Offers two-hour town tours, and half-day trips to Black Mountain National Park and the Lion's Den Hotel.

Festivals & Events

Cooktown Discovery Festival CULTURAL
(www.cooktowndiscoveryfestival.com) This festival in early June commemorates Cook's landing in 1770 with a costumed reenactment, fancy-dress grand parade and Indigenous events.

Sleeping & Eating

Pam's Place Hostel & Cooktown Motel HOSTEL, MOTEL $
(07-4069 5166; www.cooktownhostel.com; cnr Charlotte & Boundary Sts; dm $30, s & d $60, motel d from $95;) Cooktown's YHA-associated hostel offers the cheapest sleeps in town. Friendly managers can help find harvest work.

Seaview Motel MOTEL $$
(07-4069 5377; www.cooktownseaviewmotel.com.au; 178 Charlotte St; d from $95, townhouses $235;) A great location opposite the wharf, with tasteful, modern rooms (some with private balconies).

Sovereign Resort Hotel HOTEL $$$
(07-4043 0500; www.sovereign-resort.com.au; cnr Charlotte & Green Sts; d from $180;) Cooktown's swishest digs have tropical-style rooms, gorgeous gardens, the biggest pool in town and on-site wining and dining.

The Italian ITALIAN $$
(07-4069 6338; 95 Charlotte St; mains $13-22; 4-10pm Tue-Sat) Generous, satisfying portions of hearty Italian fare served in an inviting al fresco atmosphere with occasional live music and efficient service. There's even Chinese on the menu: go figure.

Cooktown Bowls Club BISTRO $$
(07-4069 5819; 129 Charlotte St; mains from $15; 11.30am-2.30pm Wed-Fri, 5.30-10pm daily;) Big bistro meals. Join the locals in social bowls Wednesday and Saturday afternoons.

Restaurant 1770 MODERN AUSTRALIAN $$$
(07-4069 5440; 3/7 Webber Esplanade; mains from $28; 7.30-9.30am, 11.30am-2pm & 6-9.30pm Tue-Sat;) Opening on to a romantic waterside deck, Restaurant 1770 gives fresh local fish top billing. Save space for mouth-watering desserts.

Information

Tourist Information Centre (07-4069 6004; www.naturespowerhouse.com.au; Walker St; 9am-5pm) In the Nature's Powerhouse complex, friendly staff dispense maps and advice. Ask for John!

Getting There & Around

Cooktown's airfield is 7.5km west of town along McIvor Rd. **Hinterland Aviation** (07-4040 1333; www.hinterlandaviation.com.au) has up to three flights daily (Monday to Saturday) to Cairns (one way from $175, 40 minutes).

Cairns Bus Charters operate the daily **Cairns Cooktown Express** (07-4059 1423; www.cairnsbuscharters.com/services/cairns-cooktown-express) along the inland route to Cairns ($79, five hours).

Cape York Peninsula

Includes ➡

Best Tours

- ➡ Cape York Day Tour (p446)
- ➡ Heritage Tours (p446)
- ➡ Aurukun Wetland Charters (p446)

Best Places to Stay

- ➡ Cape York Camping Punsand Bay (p450)
- ➡ Grand Hotel (p451)
- ➡ Laura Motel (p448)
- ➡ Eliot Falls Campground (p449)

Why Go?

Rugged, remote, Cape York Peninsula has one of the wildest tropical environments on the planet. The Great Dividing Range forms the spine of the Cape: tropical rainforests and palm-fringed beaches flank its eastern side; sweeping savannah woodlands, eucalyptus forests and coastal mangroves its west. This untamed landscape undergoes a spectacular transformation each year when the torrential rains of the monsoonal wet season set in: dry earth turns into rich, red, mud; quenched, the tinder-dry bush awakens in vibrant greens, and trickling creek-beds swell to raging rivers.

Generally impossible in the Wet, the overland pilgrimage to the Tip is an exhilarating 4WD trek into one of Australia's last great frontiers. Rough, corrugated roads numb your bum, and challenging croc-infested river crossings are par for the course, while fine dining and pillow-top mattresses are nonexistent. Adventure, abundant wildlife, the stunning, unexpected vistas of the Tip, true isolation and a deep sense of achievement (however far you get) are the rewards.

When to Go

Cape York Peninsula

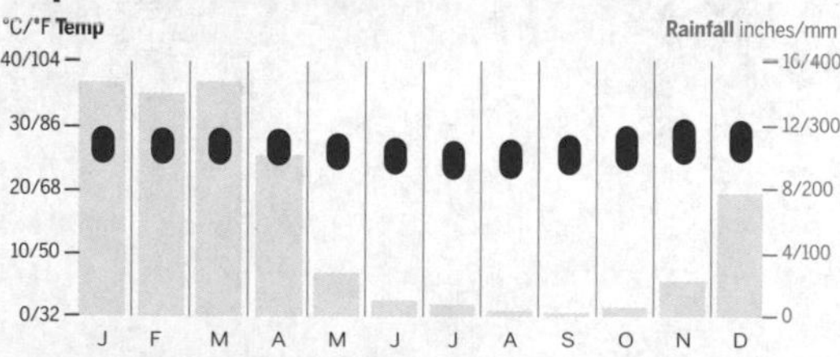

Jun–Aug Dry Season days are warm and evenings cool; Top End pilgrims ply the dusty 4WD tracks.

Sep & Oct Visitor numbers drop in anticipation of the Wet; go under the radar.

Nov–Apr Sail, fly or ferry-hop to experience the sheer lushness of Cape York in the Wet.

Cape York Peninsula Highlights

1. Marvelling at the ancient Aboriginal rock paintings of the **Split Rock Gallery** (p447), outside Laura.
2. Congratulating yourself for making it to the **Tip** (p450), the northernmost point of the Australian continent.
3. Exploring the unique history and culture of tiny **Thursday Island** (p451).
4. Being amazed by the region's rich military history at the Torres Strait Heritage Museum on **Horn Island** (p451).
5. Camping beneath a carpet of stars at the remote and atmospheric **Eliot Falls Campground** (p449).

6 Looking out for crocs as you fish for barramundi in **Weipa** (p449) or on the mighty **Jardine River** (p450).

7 Embracing your inner ornithologist amid the abundant bird life of **Rinyirru (Lakefield) National Park** (p448).

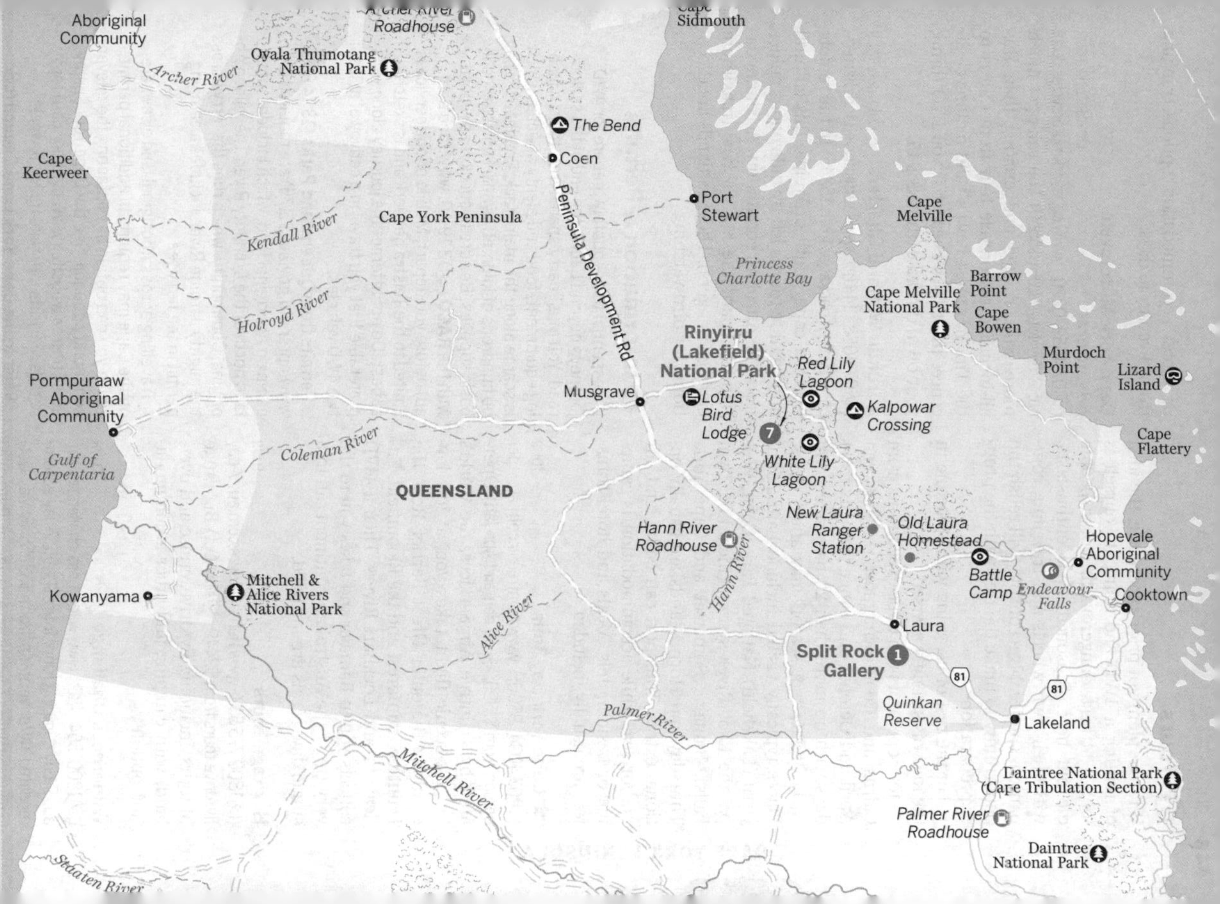

Tours

Without plenty of prior experience, the idea of renting a 4WD and doing it yourself is foolish at best, dangerous at worst: people die out here. Seasoned 4WD enthusiasts, with their own wheels and travelling companions (preferably a convoy), will relish the opportunity to make the trek with the proper preparations.

For the rest of us, going with someone in the know is strongly advised.

Tour operators run Cape expeditions from Cairns and Cooktown: most run between April and October and range from six to 14 days with no more than 20 passengers. An early or late wet season may affect dates. Places typically visited include Laura, Rinyirru (Lakefield) National Park, Coen, Weipa, the Eliot River system (including Twin Falls), Bamaga, Somerset and Cape York. Thursday and Horn Islands are usually optional extras. Transport can be by land, air and/or sea, while accommodation is camping or basic motels. Meals and hotel transfers are usually included.

★Cape York Day Tour TOUR
(07-4034 9300; www.daintreeair.com.au; per person from $1399; on demand Apr-Jan) Operated by Daintree Air Services, the world's longest scenic flight takes you, at low level, along the outer Great Barrier Reef, the Daintree Rainforest and the Bloomfield, Endeavour and Lockhart Rivers. Then a 4WD collects you in Bamaga and takes you to the very tip of the Australian continent: all in a single day! Meals are included.

Heritage Tours TOUR
(1800 775 533; www.heritagetours.com.au; 7-day fly/drive tours from $2449; May-Oct) Big range of tours, including fly/drive, cruise and overland, with camping and other accommodation options.

Wilderness Challenge TOUR
(1800 354 486; www.wilderness-challenge.com.au; 5-day camping tours from $2095, 7-day accommodated fly/drive tours from $3395; May-Oct) Informative guides host a range of fly/drive/cruise and accommodation options, ranging from five to 12 days.

Oz Tours Safaris TOUR
(1800 079 006; www.oztours.com.au; 10-day fly/drive camping tours from $3090, 16-day overland tours from $3790) Numerous tours, with air/sea/overland transport options, and camping or motel accommodation options, ranging from seven to 16 days.

Cape York Motorcycle Adventures MOTORCYCLE TOUR
(07-4059 0220; www.capeyorkmotorcycles.com.au; 8-day tours from $5550) You can't get much more wild, rugged and exciting than this all-inclusive motorcycle tour from Cairns to the Tip. You must have a valid motorcycle licence: the trip is cheaper if you BYO (bring your own) dirt bike (from $3945).

Aurukun Wetland Charters CULTURAL TOUR
(07-4058 1441; www.aurukunwetlandcharters.com; 6-night packages from $5845) In the remote western cape, south of Weipa, this cultural and wildlife tour is led by Indigenous guides from the Aurukun community. Accommodation is aboard the MV *Pikkuw* (maximum eight passengers). These wetlands are exceptional for birdwatching.

Information & Permits

It's essential to adequately prepare for 4WD journeys beyond Laura, the end of the sealed road. You must carry spare tyres, tools, winching equipment, food and plenty of water, which is scarce along the main track. Roadhouses can be hundreds of kilometres apart and stock only basic supplies. Be sure to check road reports with the **RACQ** (13 19 40; www.racq.com.au) before you depart. Mobile phone service is limited to the Telstra network and is sketchy at best. Do not attempt the journey alone – it's preferable that you travel in a convoy of at least two 4WD vehicles.

Permits from **Queensland Parks** (13 74 68; www.nprsr.qld.gov.au; $5.75) are required to camp on Aboriginal land, which includes most land north of the Dulhunty River. The Injinoo Aboriginal Community, which runs the ferry across the mighty Jardine River, includes a camping permit in the ferry fee.

Travelling across Aboriginal land elsewhere on the Cape may require an additional permit, which you can obtain by contacting the relevant community council. See the Cape York Sustainable Futures website (www.cysf.com.au) for details. Permits can take up to six weeks.

Refer to the **Cape York Land Council** (cylc.org.au) for a comprehensive overview of the historic native title claims that have seen up to 30% of Cape York's land handed back to its traditional owners in recent years.

ALCOHOL RESTRICTIONS

On the way up to the Cape you'll see signs warning of alcohol restrictions, which apply to all visitors. In some communities alcohol is banned completely and cannot be carried in. In the Northern Peninsula Area (north of the Jardine River) you can carry a maximum of 11.25L of beer (or 9L of premixed spirits) and 2L of wine per vehicle (not per person). Fines for breaking the restrictions are huge – up to $42,693 for first offenders. For up-to-date information see www.datsima.qld.gov.au/funding-grants/atsi/alcohol-limits/index.page?.

MAPS & BOOKS

The *HEMA Cape York Atlas & Guide* and the RACQ maps *Cairns/Cooktown/Townsville* and *Cape York Peninsula* are the best.

Ron and Viv Moon's *Cape York – an Adventurer's Guide* is regarded as the most comprehensive guide for 4WD and camping enthusiasts.

Getting There & Away

AIR

QantasLink (☎13 13 13; www.qantas.com.au) flies daily from Cairns to Weipa and Horn Island.

In January 2015, Skytrans, a regional airline which serviced remote communities such as Coen, Bamaga and Lockhart River, ceased operation after 25 years. At the time of writing, it was unknown whether alternative carriers would commence service to these areas.

BOAT

MV Trinity Bay (☎07-4035 1234; www.seaswift.com.au; one way from $670) Runs a weekly cargo ferry to Thursday Island and Seisia that takes up to 38 passengers. It departs from Cairns every Tuesday and returns from Seisia on Friday.

CAR & MOTORCYCLE

It is 925km from Cairns to the top of Cape York (known as 'the Tip') via the shortest and most challenging route. This journey should only ever be attempted in a high-clearance 4WD vehicle, or on a suitable trail bike.

The first 245km of the journey on the Mulligan Hwy to Lakeland, then on the Peninsula Developmental Rd (PDR) as far as Laura, is sealed.

The journey from Laura to Weipa on the PDR comprises just over 500km of wide, reasonably well-maintained but often corrugated unsealed road: prepare for a very bumpy ride. The road splits at the Weipa turn-off, the junction of the PDR and the Telegraph Rd. From here, the real adventure to Cape York begins: creek crossings become numerous and more challenging.

At Bramwell Junction, 120km from the Weipa turn-off, most drivers follow the Bamaga Rd (otherwise known as the bypass road) for 217km into Bamaga, but hard-core, experienced four-wheel drivers can opt to follow the 110km-long Old Telegraph Track (OTT), an extreme 4WD route north to the Jardine River – a full day's expert driving. The OTT reconnects with Bamaga Rd at the Jardine River crossing. The Telegraph and Bamaga Rds combined are often referred to as the Northern Peninsula Rd. Either way, you're in pure 4WD territory: not for the inexperienced or faint-hearted.

DON'T MISS

SPLIT ROCK ABORIGINAL ART GALLERY

About 50km north of Lakeland and 12km south of Laura, you'll find the turn-off to the **Split Rock Gallery** (Peninsula Development Rd; by donation), the only rock-art site open to the public without a guide. Entrance is by donation at the car park. The sandstone escarpments here are covered with paintings dating back 14,000 years! Depending on when you come, it can be quite a surreal experience to walk the path up the hillside in silence, solitude and isolation, before coming upon the various other-worldly 'galleries' in the rock faces.

There's a real sense of the sacred at Split Rock: it's both eerie and breathtaking. You'll find yourself wondering what the landscape looked like that many years ago and what life must have been like here then.

Lakeland

To travel from from Cooktown up the Cape, at Lakeland take the PDR as it leads northwest. It's paved as far as Laura, and then continues as a wide, well-maintained dirt road to Weipa. Lakeland has a general store with fuel, a small caravan park and the **Lakeland Hotel Motel** (☎07-4060 2142; Peninsula Development Rd; d from $90), the last watering-hole and meal stop before Laura, with very basic accommodation.

Leaving Lakeland you enter **Quinkan Country**, so named for the Aboriginal spirits depicted at the rock-art sites scattered throughout this area. Unesco lists Quinkan Country in the world's top 10 rock-art regions.

Laura

Since 2013, when the PDR was sealed as far as Laura, visitor numbers have been on the rise, but not much else has changed in this sleepy community. It's known for

OFF THE BEATEN TRACK

RINYIRRU (LAKEFIELD) NATIONAL PARK

Queensland's second-largest national park is renowned for its 537,000 hectares of vast river systems, spectacular wetlands and prolific bird life. This extensive river system drains into Princess Charlotte Bay on the park's northern perimeter. The **New Laura Ranger Station** (07-4060 3260) is located about 25km north of the junction with Battle Camp Rd. Book permits online via **Queensland Parks** (13 74 68; www.nprsr.qld.gov.au; permits $5.75) for the best camping facilities (with toilets and showers) at **Kalpowar Crossing**. The picturesque **Red Lily Lagoon**, with its red lotus lilies (best appreciated in the morning), and **White Lily Lagoon** attract masses of bird life.

its proximity to Quinkan Country rock-art sites and the three-day **Laura Aboriginal Dance Festival** (www.lauradancefestival.com), Australia's largest celebration of Indigenous dance and culture.

The **Quinkan & Regional Cultural Centre** (07-4060 3457; www.quinkancc.com.au; admission by donation; 8.30am-5pm Mon-Fri, 9am-3.30pm Sat & Sun) covers the history of the region. Insightful tours of Quinkan Country rock-art sites with an Indigenous guide (price on application) can be booked here.

You can camp at the basic **Quinkan Hotel** (07-4060 3393; Deighton Rd; unpowered/powered sites $25/32), which is where you'll be drinking and eating dinner if you stay at the new, spick-and-span **Laura Motel** (07-4060 3238; Deighton Rd; d from $120;), opposite.

You can fuel up at the **Laura Roadhouse** (07-4060 3440; Peninsular Development Rd; meals from $10), which does good breakfasts, or the **Laura Store & Post Office** (07-4060 3238; Terminus St). Both sell ice and basic groceries.

Laura to Musgrave

North of Laura, some of the creek crossings, such as at the Little Laura and Kennedy Rivers, are great places to camp. For a scenic alternative route to Musgrave, take the turn-off for Rinyirru (Lakefield) National Park, about 28km north of Laura.

Staying on the PDR brings you to a food-and-fuel (and beer) pit stop, the **Hann River Roadhouse** (07-4060 3242; Peninsula Developmental Rd), 76km north of Laura. From here on, the flat, treeless landscape stretches from horizon to horizon, its spectacular monotony broken only by sweeping grasslands and giant termite mounds.

Sleeping

Musgrave Roadhouse MOTEL, CAMPGROUND $
(07-4060 3229; www.musgraveroadhouse.com.au; camp sites $10, r $110) The Musgrave Roadhouse, 80km north of Hann River, was built in 1887. Originally a telegraph station, it's now a licensed cafe and roadhouse selling fuel, basic groceries and beer. Rooms are simple, while the camping area is green and grassy.

Lotus Bird Lodge LODGE $$$
(07-4060 3400; www.lotusbird.com.au; Marina Plains Rd; s/d incl meals $300/440; May-Nov only;) About 26km before Musgrave, Lotus Bird Lodge, a favourite with birdwatchers, has comfortable timber cabins overlooking a lagoon.

Musgrave to Archer River Roadhouse

Coen (pop 416), the 'capital' of the Cape, is a tiny township 108km north of Musgrave, with a bit of an outlaw vibe. Wash down the bulldust with a beer at the legendary **S'Exchange Hotel** (07-4060 1133; Regent St): after a boozy prank the 'S' became a permanent fixture. Nicer rooms are available next door at the **Homestead Guesthouse** (07-4060 1157; www.coenguesthouse.com.au; 37 Regent St; d from $90).

About 5km north of town, the **Bend** is a picturesque riverside camping ground. The turn-off to the remote **Oyala Thumotang National Park** (formerly known as the Mungkan Kandju National Park) is 25km north.

The **Archer River Roadhouse** (07-4060 3266; unpowered sites adult/child $10/5, r from $70; 7.30am-10pm;), 66km north of Coen, serves the best burgers on the Cape and is the last fuel stop before Bramwell Junction (170km north on Telegraph Rd) or Weipa (197km west on the PDR). Camp sites and basic rooms are available. Check out the memorial dedicated to Toots, a tough-talking female truckie and Cape York legend.

A working cattle station, **Merluna Station** (☎07-4060 3209; www.merlunastation.com.au; unpowered sites $13, s/d without bathroom $80/100; ❄), about 80km northwest of the Archer River Roadhouse, has accommodation in converted workers quarters.

Weipa

POP 3344

The largest town on the Cape, Weipa is the site of the world's largest bauxite mine (the ore from which aluminium is processed), set for further expansion. Most nonminers come to fish for barramundi.

Sleeping

Albatross Bay Resort RESORT **$$**
(☎1800 240 663; www.albatrossbayresort.com.au; Duyfken Cres; bungalows/r $130/$155; ❄) Near the waterfront, this glorified pub has the area's best meals and accommodation.

Weipa Caravan Park & Camping Ground CAMPGROUND **$$**
(☎07-4069 7871; www.campweipa.com; unpowered/powered sites $30/35, cabins with bathroom $120-140, lodge r $165-180; ❄@) This shady spot on the waterfront operates as the town's informal tourist office, organising mine and fishing tours. It offers a town and mine tour (adult/child $40/12) to see the mind-boggling extent of the mining operation – 22,000 tons of bauxite are mined every 24 hours and promptly sent onto waiting ships in the harbour.

Getting There & Away

Qantaslink (p447) has daily flights to/from Cairns.

Archer River to Bramwell Junction

Roughly 36km north of the Archer River Roadhouse, a turn-off leads 135km through the **Iron Range National Park** – comprising Australia's largest area of lowland rainforest, with animals found no further south in Australia – to the tiny coastal settlement of **Portland Roads**. Camp just south of here at **Chili Beach**, or savour a little comfort in **Portland House** (☎07-4060 7193; www.portlandhouse.com.au; per person from $95), a self-contained beachside cottage.

From Archer River, the PDR continues towards Weipa, but after 48km the **Telegraph Road** branches off north for a rough and bumpy 22km stretch to the **Wenlock River** crossing. Floodwaters can reach over 14m here! North of the Wenlock, **Moreton Telegraph Station** (☎07-4060 3360; www.moretonstation.com.au; unpowered sites per person $10, safari tents s/d $172/212), has a safari camp set-up, fuel, meals and beer.

The turn-off to **Bramwell Station** (☎07-4060 3300; www.bramwellstationcapeyork.com.au; camping per person $10), Australia's northernmost cattle station, with basic accommodation, camping and meals, is 15km before the **Bramwell Junction Roadhouse** (☎07-4060 3230; unpowered sites per person $12). The roadhouse marks the junction of the **Southern Bypass Road** and the **Old Telegraph Track**. The roadhouse has the last fuel and supplies before the Jardine River Ferry (crossings 8am to 5pm only).

Bramwell Junction to Jardine River

Bramwell Junction marks the intersection of the two routes north to the Jardine River Ferry. The longer route on the graded and regularly maintained Southern and Northern Bypass Rds is quicker, avoiding most of the difficult crossings between the Wenlock and Jardine Rivers.

The more direct but extreme 4WD route along the **Old Telegraph Track** (OTT) is for serious adventurers only, with deep corrugations, powdery sand and difficult creek crossings, especially the Palm Creek and Dulhunty River crossings. The OTT follows the remnants of the Overland Telegraph Line, constructed during the 1880s to allow communication between Cairns and the Cape.

Roughly halfway along its northern trajectory, the OTT reconnects with the Southern Bypass Rd for about 9km, until the Northern Bypass Rd heads west (then north) to the Jardine River Ferry crossing. Stay on the OTT for just a few kilometres and you'll reach the turn-off to **Fruit Bat Falls**. It's a further 7km from this turn-off to the **Eliot & Twin Falls'** turn-off. The falls and the deep, emerald green swimming holes are spectacular. It's worth a long sojourn at the extremely popular **Eliot Falls Campground** (☎13 74 68; www.nprsr.qld.gov.au; per person $5.75).

After Eliot Falls, between Sam Creek and Mistake Creek, a track heads west, rejoining the Northern Bypass Rd for about 45km to the Jardine River Ferry: the only means of getting further north.

If you're a die-hard four-wheel-driver and elect to stay on the OTT, prepare for a number of serious, risky creek crossings before reaching the end of the track where it meets the Jardine. Crossings are no longer permitted at this dangerous and croc-infested stretch of the river. From here, you must swing west and follow the track for about 15km to the ferry.

Queensland's largest perennial river, the croc-infested Jardine spills more freshwater into the sea than any other river in Australia. The **Jardine River Ferry** (07-4069 1369; with/without trailer $145/129; 8am-5pm), run by the Injinoo Community Council, operates during the dry season. The fee includes a permit for bush camping between the Dulhunty and Jardine Rivers, and in designated areas north of the Jardine. Food and fuel is available here.

Stretching east to the coast from the main track is the impenetrable country of **Jardine River National Park**, including the headwaters of the Jardine and Escape Rivers.

Northern Peninsula Area

Everything north of the Jardine River on the mainland is known as the Northern Peninsula Area (NPA to the locals).

Bamaga & Seisia

Bamaga (population 1046), 45km north of the Jardine River and the first settlement after the river crossing, is home to Cape York Peninsula's largest Torres Strait Islander community. Five kilometres northwest of Bamaga, coastal Seisia (population 204) overlooks the Torres Strait and is a great base from which to explore the Tip.

Activities

Cape York Adventures FISHING
(07-4069 3302; www.capeyorkadventures.com.au; boat charter per day from $800) Offers half- and full-day fishing trips and sunset cruises, as well as tours from Cairns up to Bamaga.

Sleeping

Seisia Holiday Park CAMPGROUND $
(07-4069 3243; www.seisiaholidaypark.com; unpowered/powered sites per person $12/20, s/d from $80/120;) Next to Seisia's wharf, this popular camping ground has good facilities and a restaurant (meals from $15). The park is also a booking agent for scenic flights, 4WD tours and the ferry to Thursday Island.

Loyalty Beach Campground & Fishing Lodge CAMPGROUND $
(07-4069 3372; www.loyaltybeach.com; unpowered/powered sites $12/32, s/d from $120/175) On the beachfront 3km from the wharf, this is a quieter option than the holiday park. Meals and tour bookings are available.

Getting There & Away

Peddells Ferry Service (07-4069 1551; www.peddellsferry.com.au; one way adult/child $58/29; 8am & 4pm Mon-Sat Jun-Sep, Mon, Wed & Fri Oct-May) runs regular ferries from Seisia jetty to Thursday Island.

The Tip

From Bamaga the road north passes Lockerbie Homestead. The **Croc Tent** (07-4069 3210; www.croctent.com.au; cnr Punsand Bay & Pajinka Rds; 7.30am-6pm), across the road, sells souvenirs and provides an unofficial tourist information service. From here, it's just a few kilometres to the welcoming oasis of **Cape York Camping Punsand Bay** (07-4069 1722; www.punsand.com.au; Punsand Bay Rd; unpowered/powered sites per person $15/20, d from $176;). Camping, beachfront cabins, helpful, welcoming staff, killer wood-fired pizzas and home-cooked meals served in the sociable, breezy Corrugation Bar reward you for making it this far. But don't stop yet...

The main road passes through **Lockerbie Scrub**, the northernmost rainforest in Australia, before reaching a Y-junction.

The track right leads to the pretty foreshore and camping ground at **Somerset**. The inviting lodge you see across the water on Pabaju (Albany) Island awaits you at the end of a serious day's fishing with the friendly folk at **CY Fishing Charters** (07-4069 2708; www.cyfishingcharters.com.au; Pabaju Island; day charters per person from $200, d per person from $150). Ask about the Pabaju Private Island Adventure if you just want to chill in paradise for a night or two.

The left track leads 10km down the road past the now-derelict Pajinka Wilderness Lodge to a car park, from where a 1km walk through the forest and along the beach (or over the headland) takes you to **Cape York**, the northernmost tip of Australia! You made it! Did you realise the vista would be quite so amazing?

Horn, Thursday & the Torres Strait Islands

Australia's most northern frontier consists of more than 100 islands stretching like stepping stones for 150km from the top of Cape York Peninsula to Papua New Guinea. The islands vary from the rocky, northern extensions of the Great Dividing Range to small coral cays and rainforested volcanic mountains.

Torres Strait Islanders came from Melanesia and Polynesia about 2000 years ago, establishing a unique culture, different from that of both Papua New Guinea and the Australian Aboriginal people.

An important strategic air base in WWII, Horn Island was once home to over 5000 troops. Today, with a population of 539, it's the air hub for the islands and the Cape, connected by regular ferries to nearby **Thursday Island (TI)**.

Although **Prince of Wales Island** is the largest of the group, tiny TI (only 3 sq km) is the administrative capital, 30km off the Cape. Although it lacks its own fresh-water supply, the island (population 2610) was selected for its deep harbour, sheltered port and proximity to major shipping channels. One of 17 inhabited islands in the strait, TI was once a major pearling centre, resulting in today's cultural mix of Southeast Asians, Europeans and Islanders.

Permission to visit outer islands may be required; contact the **Torres Strait Regional Council** (☎07-4048 6200; www.tsirc.qld.gov.au; 46 Victoria Pde).

Sights

★Torres Strait Heritage Museum MUSEUM
(☎07 4090 3333; www.torresstraitheritage.com; 24 Outie St, Horn Island; adult/child $7/3.50) Fascinating, educational day tours (adults from $45, children from $22.50) revealing the island's significant and all-but-forgotten military history, including fixed gun sites and aircraft wrecks, are run by the friendly folks at this wonderful local-history museum on Horn Island. Lunch packages available.

Gab Titui Cultural Centre GALLERY
(☎07-4090 2130; www.gabtitui.com.au; cnr Victoria Pde & Blackall St, Thursday Island; admission $6; ⏲9am-4.30pm Mon-Sat, by appointment Sun) On Thursday Island, the Gab Titui Cultural Centre houses a modern gallery displaying the cultural history of the Torres Strait, and hosts cultural events and exhibitions by local artists.

All Souls & St Bartholomew Memorial Church CHURCH
(Thursday Island) Built in 1893 in memory of the 134 lives that were lost when the *Quetta* struck an uncharted reef and sank within three minutes. Inside is memorabilia from a number of shipwrecks.

Tours

Peddells Tours BUS TOUR
(☎07-4069 1551; www.peddellsferry.com.au; adult/child from $32/16; ⏲8.30am-5pm) Ninety-minute bus tours of TI, taking in all the major tourist sites. Also runs Cape York 4WD day trips and Horn Island WWII tours.

LAX Tours CULTURAL TOUR
(☎0427 691 356; www.laxchartersandtours.com.au; Thursday Island; tours per person from $60) Friendly local Dirk is eager to show you around his island, including Green Hill Fort and the Japanese Pearl Divers Memorial, on personalised air-conditioned tours. Charter fishing trips are also available.

Sleeping & Eating

Gateway Torres Strait Resort RESORT $$$
(☎07-4069 2222; www.torresstrait.com.au; 24 Outie St, Horn Island; r from $180; ❄@≋) This tidy resort has basic rooms, self-contained units and a pool. It's a five-minute walk from the Horn Island wharf.

Wongai Beach Hotel HOTEL $$$
(☎07-4083 1100; www.wongaibeachresort.bigpondhosting.com; 2 Wees St, Horn Island; s/d $200/220; ≋) This pleasant hotel has Horn Island's nicest rooms, with fridge and microwave. There's a lovely pool and manicured gardens.

Grand Hotel HOTEL $$$
(☎07-4069 1557; www.grandhotelti.com.au; 6 Victoria Pde, Thursday Island; s $200-210, d $235-260; ❄@) On the hill behind TI wharf, the Grand has modern rooms with ocean and mountain views. Rates include breakfast.

Thursday Island Motel MOTEL $$$
(☎07-4069 1569; cnr Jardine & Douglas Sts, Thursday Island; s/d incl breakfast $200/215; ❄@) Comfortable motel units at the back of the Federal Hotel.

Torres Strait Hotel PUB $$
(☎07-4609 1141; cnr Normanby & Douglas Sts, Thursday Island; dishes from $14) Claim bragging rights by chowing down on a saucy crayfish pie at 'Australia's Northernmost Pub'.

Getting There & Around

McDonald Charter Boats (☎1300 664 875; www.tiferry.com.au; adult/child return $14/7) Runs ferries between TI and Horn Island during daylight hours and a water-taxi service between other Torres Strait Islands. A bus meeting flights to/from Horn Island airport is available (adult/child return $20/10).

Peddells Ferry Service (☎07-4069 1551; www.peddellsferry.com.au; Engineers Jetty) Runs regular ferries from Seisia jetty to Thursday Island.

QantasLink (☎13 13 13; www.qantas.com.au) Flies daily from Cairns to Horn Island.

West Wing Aviation (☎1300 937 894; www.westwing.com.au) Connects Horn Island to other islands.

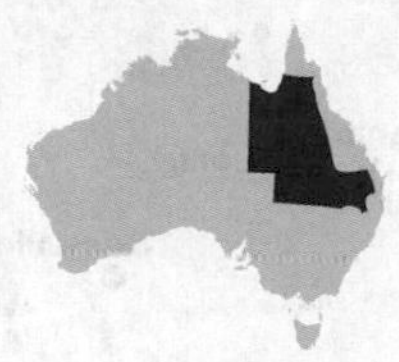

Outback Queensland & Gulf Savannah

Includes ➡

Best Festivals

- ➡ Birdsville Cup (p463)
- ➡ Mt Isa Rodeo (p456)
- ➡ Outback Festival (p459)
- ➡ Boulia Camel Races (p462)
- ➡ Undara Opera in the Outback (p464)

Best Places to Stay

- ➡ Undara Experience (p465)
- ➡ Adel's Grove (p468)
- ➡ North Gregory Hotel (p459)
- ➡ McKinnon & Co Outback Lodges (p460)
- ➡ Cobbold Gorge Village (p465)

Why Go?

If you've done the coast, why stop there? Queensland has some of the most accessible, big-sky, genuine outback Australian country you can experience.

Beyond the Great Dividing Range the sky opens up over tough country, both relentless and beautiful. Travellers come for the exotic and intimate Australian experience, their restlessness tamed by the sheer size of the place, its luminous colours and its silence.

This a region of rodeos and bush races, country pubs and characters, caravanning nomads and backpackers behind bars, barramundi fishing and burnt orange sunsets. In the dry season, endless blue skies hover over stony deserts, matched only by the brilliant velvety clarity of the Milky Way at night.

Queensland's Outback and Gulf Savannah is an eye-wateringly vast region, but it's surprisingly accessible, criss-crossed by sealed roads and peppered with towns small and slightly less small. It's a long way between drinks out here, but it's well worth the drive.

When to Go

Mt Isa

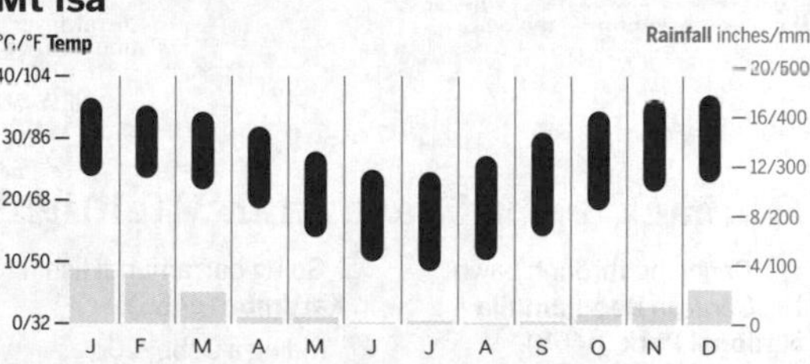

Jun-Aug Perfect winter weather – blue skies, warm days, Gulf fishing.

Mar-Apr & Sep-Oct Either side of peak season, weather still good but crowds and prices down.

Nov-Feb Summer off-season: too hot to travel most of the outback. Heavy rains can cut roads.

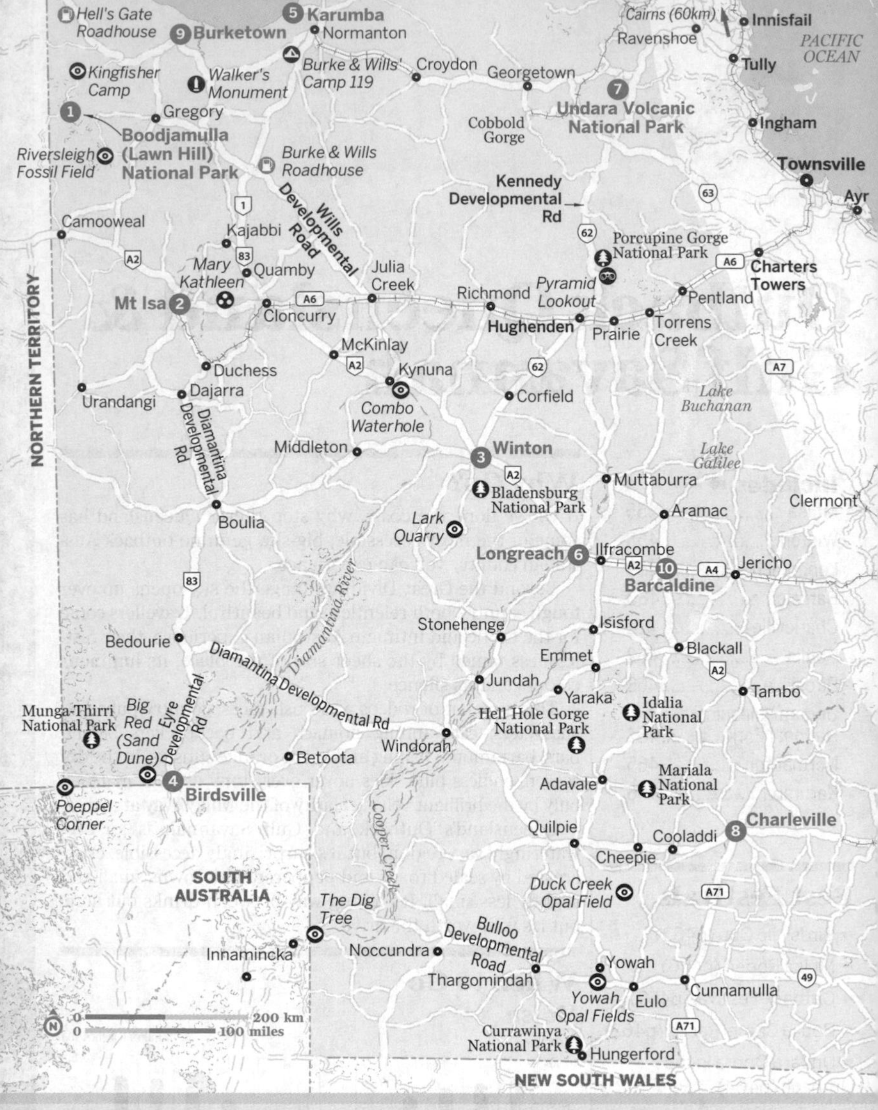

Outback & Gulf Savannah Highlights

1. Canoeing through Lawn Hill Gorge in **Boodjamulla National Park** (p468).
2. Heading underground in **Mt Isa** (p455).
3. Fossil-hunting on the Dinosaur Trail, **Winton** (p458).
4. Travelling out to remote **Birdsville** (p463).
5. Going barramundi fishing in **Karumba** (p466).
6. Riding a Cobb & Co stagecoach, wing-walking on a Boeing 747 and paying tribute to early explorers and stockmen at **Longreach** (p459).
7. Exploring ancient lava tubes at **Undara Volcanic National Park** (p464).
8. Gazing at the starry outback sky near **Charleville** (p461).
9. Chasing the cloud phenomenon known as Morning Glory (p467) at isolated **Burketown.**
10. Chilling in a classic outback timber pub such as those in **Barcaldine** (p461).

CHARTERS TOWERS TO MT ISA

The Flinders Hwy runs deep into the outback along 650km of mostly flat road from Charters Towers west to little Cloncurry, then the Barkly Hwy runs another 120km to Mt Isa. The highway was originally a Cobb & Co coach run, and along its length are small towns established as coach stopovers. The main ones out here are Prairie (200km west of Charters Towers and worth a stop for its supposedly haunted hotel), Hughenden, Richmond and Julia Creek.

Hughenden

The first stop on the dinosaur trail, Hughenden is well worth a look for its **Flinders Discovery Centre** (07-4741 2970; www.visithughenden.com.au; 37 Gray St; adult/child $5/2; 9am-5pm daily Apr-Oct, 9am-5pm Mon-Fri & reduced weekend hrs Nov-Mar), which houses a replica skeleton of the Muttaburrasaurus, a dinosaur found south of here in the 1960s.

FJ Holden's (07-4741 5121; cnr Brodie St & Flinders Hwy; meals $7-14; 8am-8pm Mon-Sat) is a retro cafe, and quite a find in outback Queensland. Expect '50s Americana decor and tip-top burgers and shakes.

The relatively lush **Porcupine Gorge National Park** (07-4741 1113; www.nprsr.qld.gov.au/parks/porcupine-gorge; camping per person/family $5.75/23) is an oasis in the dry country 70km north of Hughenden. Camp by a (usually) running creek at Pyramid Lookout, and hike into the gorge.

Richmond

Tiny Richmond is best known for **Kronosaurus Korner** (07-4741 3429; www.kronosaurus-korner.com.au; 91-93 Goldring St; adult/child/family $20/10/40; 8.30am-5pm Apr-Oct, 8.30pm-4pm Nov-Mar), which houses easily the best collection of marine fossils in Australia, most found by local landholders. Pride of place goes to an almost complete 4.25m pliosaur skeleton – one of Australia's best vertebrate fossils – and a partial skeleton of *Kronosaurus queenslandicus*, the largest known marine reptile to have ever lived in Australia.

There are two easily accessible fossil sites, where bones are still being uncovered, about 12km drive north of Richmond. Maps and tools are available from Kronosaurus Korner, and they also run two-hour guided digs ($20) on Thursday from May to September.

Cloncurry

POP 2313

The 'Curry' is renowned as the birthplace of the Royal Flying Doctor Service (RFDS) and it's the only town of any real size between Charters Towers and Mt Isa. In the 19th century Cloncurry was the largest producer of copper in the British Empire. Today it's a busy pastoral centre with a reinvigorated mining industry.

There's information and historical displays at **Cloncurry Unearthed** (07-4742 1361; www.cloncurry.qld.gov.au; Flinders Hwy; museum adult/child $10.50/5; 8.30am-4.30pm Mon-Fri, 9am-4pm Sat & Sun Apr-Sep, 8.30am-4.30pm Mon-Fri, 9am-1pm Sat & Sun Oct-May;) in the Mary Kathleen Memorial Park.

John Flynn Place (07-4742 4125; www.johnflynnplace.com.au; cnr Daintree & King Sts; adult/child $10.50/5; 8am-4.30pm Mon-Fri year round, 9am-3pm Sat & Sun May-Sep) is a must-see museum celebrating Dr John Flynn's work setting up the invaluable and groundbreaking Royal Flying Doctor Service, which gave hope and help to everyone in the remote outback. The museum's three levels include interactive displays on the RFDS and early pedal radio, Flynn's old Dodge and the Fred McKay art gallery.

Cloncurry has a good range of pubs, motels and caravan parks.

Wagon Wheel Motel (07-4742 1866; 54 Ramsay St; s/d $90/101, deluxe s/d $105/116;) is said to be the oldest licensed premises in northwest Queensland. At the back, the motel rooms are clean and comfortable with TV and fridge. It's worth paying the few extra dollars for the larger and newer deluxe rooms. The restaurant (mains $22 to $36) is one of the better places to eat in town and is open for breakfast and dinner.

MT ISA

POP 20,570

You can't miss the smokestacks as you drive into Mt Isa, one of the Queensland's longest-running mining towns and a travel and lifestyle hub for central Queensland. Whether you've come to work, to play or are just passing through, a night spent in one of Isa's clubs may cause you to forget you're in the remote outback.

At night the surrounding cliffs glow and zing with industry; the City Lookout's view

Mt Isa

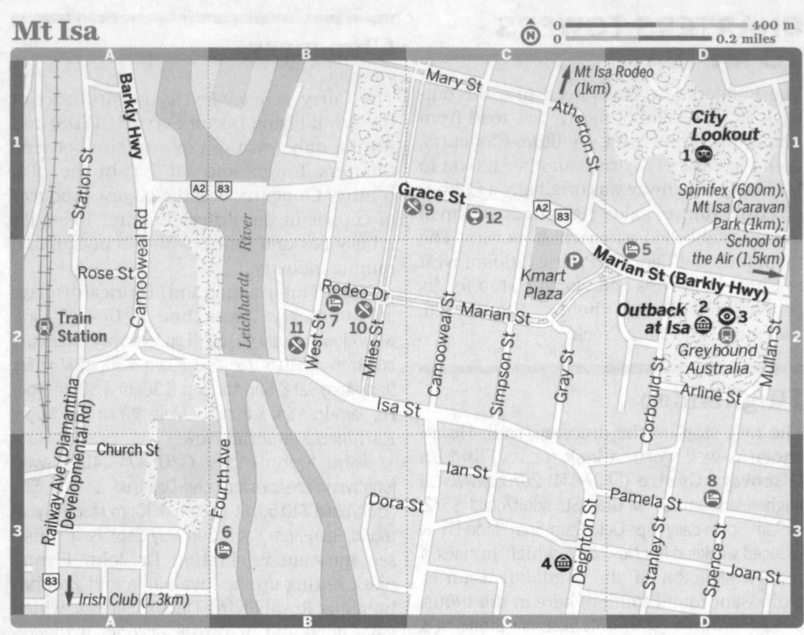

of the twinkling mine lights and silhouetted smokestacks is strangely pretty. The surrounding country has a stark red beauty, too. Strange rock formations – padded with olive-green spinifex – line the perimeter of town, and deep-blue sunsets eclipse all unnatural light.

Proud locals share life in the dusty heat and the geographic isolation – often over multiple beers – and the sense of community is palpable. Try to visit in mid-August for Australia's largest **rodeo** (www.isarodeo.com.au; ⏲2nd weekend in Aug).

Sights & Activities

★Outback at Isa MUSEUM
(☎1300 659 660; www.outbackatisa.com.au; 19 Marian St; ⏲8.30am-5pm) The award-winning Outback at Isa combines the visitor centre and booking office with three of Isa's major attractions, all under one roof. The **Hard Times Mine** (adult/child $49/30; ⏲daily) is an authentic underground trip to give you the full Isa mining experience. **Isa Experience & Outback Park** (adult/child $12/7.50; ⏲8.30am-5pm) is a hands-on museum providing a colourful and articulate overview of mining, pioneering and local history.

The fascinating **Riversleigh Fossil Centre** (adult/child $12/7.50; ⏲8.30am-5pm) recreates finds from the world-renowned fossil fields at Boodjamulla National Park. There are various combination packages, including the good-value two-day pass (adult/child $59/36), which includes admission to all of the attractions.

★City Lookout VIEWPOINT
FREE Everyone should make the short trip up to the city lookout for excellent 360-degree views of Mt Isa. The best time is sunset, when the smokestacks are silhouetted and the mine lights begin to twinkle.

School of the Air SCHOOL
(☎07-4744 8333; www.mtisasde.eq.edu.au; 137-143 Abel Smith Pde; tours $2; ⏲tours 10am Mon-Fri) The one-hour tours during school term demonstrate the outback's isolation and innovation in teaching its young '.uns.

Underground Hospital MUSEUM
(☎07-4743 3853; Joan St; guided tours adult/child $15/5; ⏲10am-2pm) With the threat of Japanese bombing raids in 1942, and a ready supply of miners and equipment, Mt Isa Hospital went underground. The bombs

Mt Isa

Top Sights

Sights

Sleeping

Eating

Drinking & Nightlife

never came but the underground hospital was preserved. You can also see an example of a tent house, once common in Mt Isa.

Sleeping

Travellers Haven HOSTEL $

(07-4743 0313; www.travellershaven.com.au; 75 Spence St; dm/s/d $35/60/70;) The rooms are fairly modest but this is the only genuine backpacker hostel in Isa – and most of outback Queensland – so it's a great meeting place. Polly, the British owner, will share her passion for the region. It's a short walk from Outback at Isa, or you can call ahead for pick up.

Mt Isa Caravan Park CARAVAN PARK $

(07-4743 3252; www.mtisacaravanpark.com.au; 112 Marian St; powered sites $28-35, on-site caravans $70, cabins $90-140;) The closest caravan park to the town centre is an impressive tourist village with a swag of sleeping options, including self-contained units. There's also a big pool and shady grassed areas.

Fourth Avenue Motor Inn MOTEL $$

(07-4743 3477; www.fourthavemotorinn.com; 14 Fourth Ave; d/f from $140/160;) This friendly, colourful motor inn, in a quiet residential zone, has a large saltwater pool in a neat outdoor area. Rooms are a touch above the town average.

Central Point Motel MOTEL $$

(07-4743 0666; www.centralpoint-motel.com; 6 Marian St; s/d from $135/140;) A short walk from town, the Central Point looks a bit dated, but it has a tropical atmosphere, and well-equipped kitchenettes in sunny rooms.

Red Earth Hotel HOTEL $$$

(1800 603 488; www.redearth-hotel.com.au; Rodeo Dr; d $189-229;) The boutique Red Earth is undoubtedly Mt Isa's top address, with elegant furniture and claw-foot bathtubs. It's worth paying the little extra for a private balcony, spa and huge TV. There's a cocktail bar, and an excellent but pricey restaurant in the lobby. In the same block, the Mt Isa Hotel is part of the same hotel complex, with cheaper rooms.

Eating & Drinking

Happy Box Noodles ASIAN $

(07-4743 0889; 32 Miles St; mains $12; 11.30am-9.30pm Sun-Wed, to 10pm Thu-Sat) Quick and tasty pan-Asian noodle and rice dishes, including sushi, laksa and chow mein.

Three Doors Coffee House CAFE $

(07-4743 3353; 13 West St; dishes $7.50-18; 6.30am-3pm Mon-Fri, 8.30am-3pm Sat, 8.30am-2pm Sun) For good coffee and a funky atmosphere, Three Doors is the best in Isa. Great spot for an early breakfast.

Rodeo Bar & Grill PUB FOOD $$

(07-4749 8888; cnr Miles St & Rodeo Dr; mains $15-40; 6.30am-11.30am, noon-3pm & 6-9pm) Booth seating brings a touch of intimacy to this cavernous bar-restaurant inside the renovated Isa Hotel. The menu offers something for everyone, from pizzas ($16) and tapas-style snacks to outback-sized steaks. Breakfast (from 6.30am) in a booth is surprisingly good, too.

Buffs Club BAR

(07-4743 2365; www.buffs.com.au; cnr Grace & Camooweal Sts; 10am-midnight Sun-Thu, to 2am Fri & Sat) The most central and enduringly popular of Isa's clubs, Buffs has the Billabong Bar with DJs from Wednesday to Saturday, a sports bar, a sun deck and live entertainment on weekends. You can eat well at the Frog & Toad Bar & Grill.

Irish Club BAR

(07-4743 2577; www.theirishclub.com.au; 1 19th Ave; 10am-2am, till 3am Fri & Sat) A couple of kilometres south of town, the Irish Club is one of Isa's multipurpose venues. There's a gaming room, the cavernous Blarney Bar, a karaoke bar, the slightly tacky but heaving Rish nightclub and a decent restaurant.

ℹ Getting There & Around

Rex (☎13 17 13; www.rex.com.au) flies direct from Mt Isa to Townsville daily.

Mt Isa is on the transnational bus route. **Greyhound Australia** (☎1300 473 946; www.greyhound.com.au) has daily services to Townsville ($174, 11½ hours), Longreach ($125, 8½ hours), Brisbane ($232, 26½ hours) and Alice Springs ($243, 14 hours). Conveniently, the depot is at Outback at Isa (p456).

The **Queensland Rail** (☎1800 872 467; www.queenslandrailtravel.com.au) Inlander train runs between Mt Isa and Townsville (economy seat/sleeper from $108/265, 21 hours) twice a week.

Avis (☎07-4743 3733; www.avis.com.au), **Hertz** (☎07-4743 4142; www.hertz.com.au) and **Thrifty** (☎07-4743 2911; www.thrifty.com.au) have car-hire desks at the airport. For a taxi to town ($30 to $35), call **Mt Isa Taxis** (☎07-4749 9999).

MT ISA TO CHARLEVILLE

Arguably the most popular road trip in central outback Queensland runs east along the Barkly Hwy then southeast on the Landsborough Hwy for almost 1200km. This is largely flat cattle country but it's also by turns dinosaur country, Waltzing Matilda country, Qantas country and even *Crocodile Dundee* country.

Greyhound Australia (p460) services this route, with daily buses from Brisbane (via Charleville) or Rockhampton via Longreach.

Winton

POP 954

It's pioneer days at 40 paces on main-street Winton, a cattle and sheep centre that does its best to make the most of its Waltzing Matilda connections. Banjo Paterson reputedly wrote the Aussie anthem after a visit here, and it was first performed at the North Gregory Hotel 120 years ago.

THE DINOSAUR TRAIL

Fossil fiends, amateur palaeontologists and those who are simply fans of *Jurassic Park* will love outback Queensland's triangular Dinosaur Trail. The northern points are **Richmond** (p455), home of Australia's richest collection of marine dinosaur fossils, and **Hughenden** (p455), home of the Muttaburrasaurus. But it's the Winton region that offers two of the best prehistoric attractions.

About 95 million years ago – give or take a few million – a herd of small dinosaurs got spooked by a predator and scattered. The resulting stampede left thousands of footprints in the stream bed, which nature remarkably conspired to fossilise and preserve. The **Lark Quarry Dinosaur Trackways** (☎1300 665 115; www.dinosaurtrackways.com.au; guided tours adult/child/family $12/7/30; ⏲tours 10am, noon & 2pm), 110km southwest of Winton, is outback Queensland's mini *Jurassic Park*, where you can see the remnants of the prehistoric stampede. Protected by a sheltered walkway, the site can only be visited by guided tour where guides will explain what scientists have deduced happened that day. There are no facilities to stay or eat, but it's a well-signposted drive on the partly unsealed Winton–Jundah road, suitable for 2WD vehicles in the Dry (allow 1½ hours).

The **Australian Age of Dinosaurs** (☎07-4657 0712; www.australianageofdinosaurs.com; Lot 1 Dinosaur Dr; adult/child/family $30/16/69; ⏲8.30am-5pm, guided tours hourly 9am-3pm), 15km east of Winton on the Landsborough Hwy, is a fascinating interactive research museum housed on a local cattle station atop a rugged plateau known as the Jump Up. There are two sides to the museum – the laboratory and the collection, the latter comprising the original dinosaur fossils found in the region that make up the incomplete skeletons of 'Matilda' and 'Banjo'. Each side is visited on a 30-minute tour with a half-hour break in between. Fossil enthusiasts can book in advance for a day ($65) or a week's worth of bone preparation, or book well in advance for one of the annual three-week digs ($3500 per week).

Matilda Country Tours (☎07-4657 1607; tours $30-75; ⏲daily) offers daily bus transport to both sites.

Ask at visitor centres in the region about the Dino Pass, which gives reduced admission to all attractions on the Dinosaur Trail.

Elderslie St is a colourful streetscape of old timber pubs and historic buildings, so there's plenty of photogenic period charm here. Winton is also the best base for diving into the Dinosaur Trail, with the two biggest dinosaur attractions in outback Queensland within easy reach.

The **Outback Festival** (☎07-4657 1558; www.outbackfestival.org) offers hilarious outback antics in mid-September.

Sights

Waltzing Matilda Centre MUSEUM
(☎1300 665 115; www.facebook.com/waltzingmatildacentre; 73 Elderslie St) This visitor centre, museum and gallery burned down in June 2015. The centre housed an indoor billabong scene and a huge range of Qantas artefacts. The town vows to rebuild - check the website for updates.

Royal Theatre THEATRE
(73 Elderslie St; adult/child $7/5; ⌚screenings 8pm Wed Apr-Sep) There's an old-movie-world charm in the canvas-slung chairs, corrugated tin walls and star-studded ceiling at this classic semioutdoor theatre, complete with the world's biggest deckchair. It has a small museum in the projection room and screens old classics. For a gold-coin donation you can usually wander through for a look.

Arno's Wall SCULPTURE
(Vindex St) Arno's Wall is one of Winton's quirky outback attractions – a 70m-long work-in-progress by artist Arno Grotjahn, featuring a huge range of industrial and household items, from TVs to motorcycles, ensnared in mortar.

Sleeping & Eating

Pelican Van Park CARAVAN PARK $
(☎07-4657 1478; 92 Elderslie St; unpowered/powered sites $25/30, cabins from $80; ❄) Basic but friendly van park, one of two right in the town centre – handy for walking to local pubs.

★**North Gregory Hotel** HOTEL $$
(☎07-4657 0647; www.northgregoryhotel.com; 67 Elderslie St; r $95-125; ❄) This historic art deco beauty has plenty of stories and is the best of the town's pubs for accommodation in pub-style or en-suite rooms. The lobby is like a glamorous film-noir set and the rooms are styled somewhere between the pub's heyday and 20th-century Brisbane. 'Waltzing Matilda' was allegedly first performed by its author, Banjo Paterson, in the hotel on 6 April 1895.

Musical Fence Cafe CAFE $
(☎07-4657 0647; 67 Elderslie St; mains $5-16; ⌚7am-2pm) This licensed cafe attached to the North Gregory Hotel is a great spot for breakfast or a light lunch of sandwiches, burgers or pizza.

Tattersalls Hotel PUB FOOD $$
(☎07-4657 1309; 78 Elderslie St; mains $12-28; ⌚11am-9pm) This friendly timber corner pub is an incongruous foodie destination with reasonably priced pub food best devoured on the wooden verandah facing the street. There are rooms upstairs and a van park across the street.

Longreach

POP 3200

A prosperous outback town, Longreach was the home of Qantas early last century, but these days it's equally famous for the Australian Stockman's Hall of Fame & Outback Heritage Centre, one of outback Queensland's best museums. The tropic of Capricorn passes through here – look for the marker near the visitor centre which points to the torrid (north) and temperate (south) zones.

Sights

★**Qantas Founders Outback Museum** MUSEUM
(☎07-4658 3737; www.qfom.com.au; Landsborough Hwy; adult/child/family $25/15/70; ⌚9am-5pm) Qantas Founders Outback Museum houses a life-size replica of an Avro 504K, the first aircraft owned by the fledgling airline. Interactive multimedia and working displays tell the history of Qantas. Next door, the original 1921 Qantas hangar houses a replica DH-61. Towering over everything outside is a bright and shiny retired 1979 **747-200B Jumbo** (☎07-4658 3737; www.qfom.com.au; Landsborough Hwy; museum & jet tour adult/child/family $60/40/175, wing walks adult/child $65/55; ⌚jet tours 9.30am, 11am, 1pm & 2.30pm; wing walks 11am, 12.30pm & 2.30pm). The tour of the jumbo and nearby Boeing 707 is fascinating, and you can do a wing-walk with safety harness (bookings essential).

★**Australian Stockman's Hall of Fame & Outback Heritage Centre** MUSEUM
(☎07-4658 2166; www.outbackheritage.com.au; Landsborough Hwy; adult/child/family $31/15.50/82; ⌚9am-5pm) In a beautifully conceived building with an impressive multiarched design, this is a fine museum, and also a

tribute to outback pioneers, early explorers, stockmen and Indigenous Australians. Five themed galleries, some featuring interactive touch-screen displays, cover: Aboriginal culture; European exploration (there's a nifty map showing the trails of Burke and Wills, Ludwig Leichhardt, Ernest Giles and co); pioneers and pastoralists; 'Life in the Outback'; and the stockmen's gallery. Look out for the Outback Stockman Show, a live storytelling show held at 11am Tuesday to Sunday (adult/child $20/10).

The museum complex also includes a cafe, garden and souvenir shops. Tickets are valid for two days.

Tours

Kinnon & Co Longreach TOUR
(07-4658 1776; www.kinnonandco.com.au; 115a Eagle St) The main tour operator in Longreach runs a sunset cruise on the Thomson River, followed by dinner under the stars and campfire entertainment (adult/child/family $89/50/250). The Cobb & Co 'Gallop thru the Scrub' (adult/child/family $89/59/266) is a highlight, combining stagecoaching with a theatre show, lunch and a film, or you can opt for a 45-minute stagecoach ride. Book ahead.

Outback Aussie Tours TOUR
(07-4658 3000; www.oat.net.au; Landsborough Hwy) Based at the train station, Outback offers the popular Drover's Sunset Cruise (adult/child $89/59) on the Thomson River, which includes dinner and a show, as well as a variety of day tours (Winton, Strathmore Station) and multiday tours as far as Cape York and Birdsville.

Sleeping & Eating

Eagle St is the hub, with motels, cafes, bakeries and pubs.

Longreach Tourist Park CARAVAN PARK $
(07-4658 1781; www.longreachtouristpark.com.au; 12 Thrush Rd; unpowered/powered sites $26/32, cabins $98;) This large, spacious park lacks grass but has a small area of spa pools and the Woolshed restaurant and bar.

Commercial Hotel PUB $
(07-4658 1677; 102 Eagle St; s/d with bathroom $85/100, without bathroom $36/50;) The Commercial has basic but comfy rooms, and its friendly, bougainvillea-filled beer garden is a good place to dine (mains $12.50 to $22.50).

★ **McKinnon & Co Outback Lodges** LODGE $$
(07-4658 3811; www.kinnonandco.com.au; 63-65 Ilfracombe St; self-contained cabins $120-135, slab huts $180;) The comfortable self-contained lodges here are excellent value – when we visited they were putting the finishes touches on new timber slab huts that offer a rustic outback feel with modern styling. There's a palm-shaded pool, native gardens and a large covered communal area. It's opposite the Qantas museum.

Longreach Motor Inn MOTEL $$
(07-4658 2322; 84 Galah St; r $124-134;) Huge rooms with corresponding balconies and professional staff are the features of this popular motel on the edge of the shopping strip. The gated pool and shady garden kill an afternoon with ease. The on-site restaurant, Harry's (mains $16 to $32), is among the best in Longreach.

Eagle's Nest Bar & Grill MODERN AUSTRALIAN $$
(07-4658 0144; 110 Eagle St; meals $15-34; 11.30am-midnight Wed-Fri, 7.45am-noon Sat & Sun) Popular licensed bistro serving up steaks and seafood. Great for breakfast on weekends.

Information

Longreach Visitor Information Centre (07-4658 3555; 99 Eagle St; 8am-4.45pm Mon-Fri, 9am-noon Sat & Sun) is at the north end of Eagle St.

Getting There & Away

Greyhound Australia (1300 473 946; www.greyhound.com.au) has a daily bus service to Brisbane ($173, 18 hours) via Charleville, and to Mt Isa ($125, 8½ hours) via Winton and Cloncurry. Buses stop behind the Commercial Hotel.

Queensland Rail (1800 872 467; www.queenslandrailtravel.com.au) operates the twice-weekly *Spirit of the Outback* service between Longreach and Brisbane via Rockhampton.

Barcaldine

POP 1500

Barcaldine (bar-*call*-din) is a colourful little pub town at the junction of the Landsborough and Capricorn Hwys (Rte 66), 108km east of Longreach.

The town gained a place in Australian history in 1891 when it became the headquarters of a major shearers' strike. The confrontation led to the formation of the Australian Workers' Party, forerunner of the Australian Labor Party. The organisers' meeting place was the Tree of Knowledge, a ghost gum planted near the train station that long stood as a monument to workers and their rights. It was mysterlously poisoned in 2006 but a radical new monument now raises plenty of political ire.

The original inhabitants of Barcaldine were the Inningai, who 'disappeared' soon after explorer Thomas Mitchell arrived in 1824.

Sights & Activities

★Tree of Knowledge Memorial MEMORIAL
(Oak St) This $5m contemporary art installation – labelled an 'upside-down milk crate' by one disgruntled local – is best seen at night when dappled light filters through the wooden wind chimes. Love it or not, it certainly makes art critics of the pubs' patrons across the road, but most locals claim it's grown on them.

Australian Workers Heritage Centre MUSEUM
(07-4651 1579; www.australianworkersheritagecentre.com.au; Ash St; adult/child/family $16/9/40; 9am-5pm Mon-Sat, 10am-4pm Sun) This centre is dedicated to Australian social, political and industrial movements, with a variety of permanent and changing exhibits celebrating working women, shearers, the formation of the Australian Workers Union and more.

Artesian Country Tours TOUR
(07-4651 2211; www.artesiancountrytours.com.au; adult/child $145/65; Mon, Wed & Sat) Runs a highly regarded historical tour to local Aboriginal rock-art sites, lava caves and cattle stations around Aramac and Gracevale.

Sleeping & Eating

Homestead Caravan Park CARAVAN PARK $
(07-4651 1308; www.homesteadcvpark.com.au; Landsborough Hwy; unpowered/powered site $18/27, cabins $55-90) This compact little caravan park with grassy sites is only a short walk to the town centre and pubs. The friendly management are at the local roadhouse.

Shakespeare Hotel PUB $
(07-4651 1111; 95 Oak St; s/d without bathroom $30/40, d units $60, mains $23-29) The big red pub opposite the Tree of Knowledge, Shakespeare Hotel has the pick of the pub rooms and good meals.

Barcaldine Country Motor Inn MOTEL $$
(07-4651 1488; www.barcaldinecountrymotorinn.com.au; 1 Box St; s/d $110/120;) The very cosy rooms here are well presented, cool and clean. It's just around the corner from the main street's iconic pubs.

Ironbark Inn MOTEL $$
(07-4651 2311; www.ironbarkmotel.com.au; 72 Box St; d cabins from $90, motel units $120-145) The Ironbark Inn is in a quiet location a few blocks south of the main street and has clean, comfortable motel-style rooms set in native gardens. The popular and rustic **3Ls Bar & Bistro** (mains $20-30) is also here.

Information

The **Visitor Information Centre** (07-4651 1724; Oak St; 8.15am-4.30pm daily Mar-Oct, 9am-2pm Sat & Sun Nov-Feb) is next to the train station.

CHARLEVILLE

POP 3300

Charleville is the grand old dame of central Queensland. It's the largest town in Mulga country, and the gateway to the outback from the south. Due largely to its prime locale on the Warrego River, the town was an important centre for early explorers – Cobb & Co had its largest coach-making factory here. The town has maintained its prosperity as a major Australian wool centre and has some interesting attractions for travellers.

The **visitor information centre** (07-4654 7771; Qantas Dr), at the Cosmos Centre south of town, can book tours in the region.

Sights & Activities

Cosmos Centre OBSERVATORY
(07-4654 7771; www.cosmoscentre.com; Qantas Dr; night observatory $28/19, sun viewing $12/9; 10am-4pm, observatory 7.30pm) See the outback night sky in all its glory at the Cosmos Centre via a high-powered telescope and an expert guide. The 90-minute sessions start at 7.30pm, soon after sunset. There's also a solar telescope here for daytime sun viewing. Both are dependent on cloudless skies, which are frequent out here.

Bilby Experience WILDLIFE
(07-4654 7771; www.savethebilbyfund.com; 1 Park St; $10; 6pm Mon, Wed, Fri, Sun Apr-Oct) A rare opportunity to see the native marsupial bilby. Volunteers explain the captive breeding and conservation program.

Sleeping & Eating

Evening Star FARMSTAY $
(Thurlby Station; 07-4654 2430; Adavale Rd; unpowered/powered sites $26/30, cabins $110; Apr-Oct) This welcoming station property, only 9km west of Charleville, has camping, a single ensuite cabin, a rustic bar and regular music around the campfire. Station tours ($40 per person) are run on Wednesday and Saturday.

Hotel Corones HOTEL $
(07-4654 1022; 33 Wills St; s/d basic rooms $50/70, s/d motel $89/99, s/d heritage rooms $95/115;) Majestic Hotel Corones is a classic country pub with basic rooms upstairs, resurrected heritage rooms featuring fireplaces and stained-glass windows, and motel rooms at the side. Eat in the grandiose dining room, beer garden or old-school public bar.

Moo Steakhouse STEAK $$
(07-4654 1002; 34 Wills St; mains $14-27; noon-3pm & 6-11pm) Describing itself as 'Charleville's worst vegetarian restaurant', Moo, at the Hotel Corones, brings juicy city-style steaks back to cattle country.

THE CHANNEL COUNTRY

You wanted outback? Well, here it is, mate – miles and bloody square miles of it! The Channel Country is an unforgiving, eerily empty region where red-sand hills, the odd wild flower and strange luminous phenomena run across prime beef-grazing land. The channels are formed by water rushing south from the summer monsoons to fill the Georgina, Hamilton and Diamantina Rivers and Cooper Creek. Avoid the summer months (October to April), unless you go for searing heat and dust.

Getting There & Around

There are no train or bus services in the Channel Country, and the closest car rental is in Mt Isa. Some roads from the east and north to the fringes of the Channel Country are sealed, but between October and May even these can be cut off when dirt roads become quagmires. Visiting this area requires a sturdy vehicle (a 4WD if you want to get off the beaten track) with decent clearance. Always carry plenty of drinking water and fuel.

The main road through this area is the Diamantina Developmental Rd, which is sealed from Mt Isa through Boulia to Bedourie, then unsealed east to Windorah. The roads in to Birdsville are unsealed from Bedourie and most of the way from Windorah. Conventional vehicles should be able to get through in the Dry, but check road conditions.

Boulia

POP 230

The unofficial capital of the Channel Country is a neat little outpost on the cusp of the great Simpson Desert. The world's longest mail run ends here, having travelled some 3000km from Port Augusta in South Australia. If you're here for the third weekend in July, the **Boulia Camel Races** is one of Australia's premier camel-racing events.

The most famous residents of Boulia are the mysterious min-min lights, a supposedly natural phenomenon that occurs when the temperature plummets after dark, and erratic lights appear on the unusually flat horizon. They're out there, perhaps, or at least there's sci-fi animatronic gadgetry and eerie lighting in an hourly 'alien' show at the **Min Min Encounter** (07-4746 3386; Herbert St; adult/child/family $18/15/45; 8.45am-5pm daily Apr-Sep, 8.45am-5pm Mon-Fri, 10am-2pm Sat & Sun). Doubling as the information centre, this is classic travel kitsch.

The **Stone House Museum** (cnr Pituri & Hamilton Sts; adult/child $5/3; 8.30am-5pm Mon-Fri, 8am-noon Sat & Sun) has sheds full of outback stuff, space junk, local history, Aboriginal artefacts and the preserved 1888 home of the pioneering Jones family (the Stone House).

There's a **caravan park** (07-4746 3320; Herbert St; swag sites $10, unpowered/powered sites $20/25, cabins $75-95) and **pub** (07-4746 3144; Herbert St; s/d $44/55, motel units $99;) in town, or try the **Desert Sands Motel** (07-4746 3000; www.desertsandsmotel.com.au; Herbert St; s/d $127/137;), with modern and spacious units.

The sealed Kennedy Developmental Rd (Rte 62) runs east from Boulia, 369km to Winton. The only stop along the way is **Middleton**, 175km from Boulia, where there's a **pub** (07-4657 3980; Kennedy Developmental Rd; mains $16-30, bar snacks from $10) and fuel.

Bedourie

POP 280

Bedourie is the administrative centre for the huge Diamantina Shire Council, and a friendly outback outpost. Coming from Boulia, it's 200km south on a recently sealed

OFF THE BEATEN TRACK

WINDORAH, QUILPIE & AROUND

The Birdsville Developmental Rd heads east from Birdsville, meeting the Diamantina Developmental Rd after 277km of rough gravel and sand. Motorists must carry enough fuel and water to cover the 395km to the nearest town of Windorah.

Just west of Cooper Creek, **Windorah** has a pub, a general store and a basic caravan park. The **Western Star Hotel** (☎07-4656 3166; www.westernstarhotel.com.au; 15 Albert St, Windorah; hotel s/d $80/90, motel s/d $130/140; ❄), originally built in 1878, is a terrific country pub. **Yabbie races** are staged here on the Wednesday before the **Birdsville Cup** (p463).

Quilpie is an opal-mining town and the railhead from which cattle are sent to the coast. South of Quilpie and west of Cunnamulla are the remote **Yowah Opal Fields** and the town of **Eulo**, which co-hosts the **World Lizard Racing Championships** with Cunnamulla in late August. **Thargomindah**, 130km west of Eulo, has a couple of motels and a guesthouse. **Noccundra**, another 145km further west, has just one hotel supplying basic accommodation, meals and fuel. If you have a 4WD you can continue west to Innamincka, in South Australia, on the rough and stony Strzelecki Track, via the site of the famous **Dig Tree**, where William Brahe buried provisions during the ill-fated Burke and Wills expedition of 1860–61.

road. A big attraction is the free public swimming pool and **artesian spa**.

The charming adobe-brick **Bedourie Hotel** (☎07-4746 1201; www.bedouriehotel.com; Herbert St; r from $88; ❄) was built in the 1880s and is a social hub for the region. There are cosy motel rooms out the back. Monstrous plates of steak and barramundi are served in the dining room.

There's also a caravan park and comfortable motel units at the **Simpson Desert Oasis** (☎07-4746 1291; www.simpsondesertoasis.com.au; 1 Herbert St; powered en-suite sites $35, s/d motel $149/150; ❄@), a roadhouse with fuel, a supermarket and a restaurant.

Birdsville

POP 120

Aspiring off-the-beaten-track travellers can't claim the title until they visit Birdsville, an iconic Australian settlement on the fringe of the Simpson Desert, and Queensland's most remote 'town'.

During the first weekend in September, the annual **Birdsville Cup** (www.birdsvilleraces.com) horse races draw up to 7000 fans from all over the country to drink, dance and gamble for three dusty days. Parking is free for all light aircraft.

Standing strong in sandstone since 1884 is the much-loved **Birdsville Hotel** (☎07-4656 3244; www.theoutback.com.au; Adelaide St; s/d $140/160; ❄). The motel-style units are tasteful and spacious, while the restaurant is surprisingly slick.

Birdsville Track

The 517km Birdsville Track stretches south of Birdsville to Maree in South Australia, taking a desolate course between the Simpson Desert to the west and Sturt Stony Desert to the east. The first stretch from Birdsville has two alternative routes, but only the longer, more easterly Outside Track is open these days.

Check in at the **Wirrarri Centre** (☎07-4656 3300) in Birdsville for more information.

Munga-Thirri National Park

The waterless Simpson Desert occupies a massive 200,000 sq km of central Australia and stretches across the Queensland, Northern Territory and South Australia (SA) borders. The Queensland section, in the state's far southwestern corner, is protected as the 10,000-sq-km Munga-Thirri National Park, and is a remote, arid landscape of high, red sand dunes, spinifex and cane grass.

While conventional vehicles can tackle the Birdsville Track in dry conditions, the Simpson crossing requires a 4WD and far more preparation. Crossings should only be undertaken by parties of at least two 4WD vehicles equipped with suitable communications (such as an EPIRB) to call for help if necessary. Alternatively, you can hire a satellite phone from **Birdsville police** (☎07-4656 3220; Birdsville) and return it to **Maree police** (☎08-8675 8346; Maree, SA) in SA.

Permits ($5.75/23 per person/family) are required to camp anywhere in the park and can be obtained online (www.nprsr.qld.gov.au), at the national parks offices in Birdsville or Longreach, and at Birdsville's service stations. You also need a separate permit to travel into the SA parks, and these are available through **National Parks South Australia** (☎1800 816 078; www.environment.sa.gov.au).

THE SAVANNAH WAY

The epic Savannah Way runs all the way from Cairns to Broome, skirting the top of the country. The Queensland section, linking the east coast with the Gulf of Carpentaria, from Cairns to Burketown, is one of the state's great road trips.

The world has a different tint out here: the east coast's green, cloud-tipped mountains and sugar-cane fields give way to a flat, red dust–coated landscape of sweeping grass plains, scrubby forest and mangroves engraved by an intricate network of seasonal rivers and croc-filled tidal creeks that drain into the Gulf of Carpentaria. The fishing here is legendary, particularly for barramundi (barra season runs from mid-January to the end of September).

With detours to Karumba and Boodjamulla (Lawn Hill) National Park, this is a real outback adventure, and you don't even need a 4WD to explore most of this route in the Dry.

Trans North (☎07-4096 8644; www.transnorthbus.com) runs a bus three times a week between Cairns and Karumba ($154, 11 hours), stopping at all towns, including Undara ($67, 4 ½ hours) and Normanton ($148, 10 hours). It departs Cairns Monday, Wednesday and Friday, and Karumba Tuesday, Thursday and Saturday.

No buses link Normanton with Mt Isa or Burketown.

Undara Volcanic National Park

About 190,000 years ago, the Undara shield volcano erupted, sending molten lava coursing through the surrounding landscape. While the surface of the lava cooled and hardened, hot lava continued to race through the centre of the flows, eventually leaving the world's longest continuous (though fragmented) lava tubes from a single vent.

All up there are over 160km of tubes, but only a fraction can be visited, and on guided tours only. Most are operated by **Undara Experience** (☎07-4097 1900, 1800 990 992; www.undara.com.au; 2-4hr tours adult/child/family from $55/27.50/165). There are four main daily tours leaving from the Undara Experience resort (p465), including the two-hour Archway Explorer and Active Explorer. A popular tour is Wildlife at Sunset (adult/child $60/30) where you'll see tiny microbats swarm out of a cave entrance and provide dinner for lightning-fast hanging tree snakes known as night tigers. **Bedrock Village Caravan Park & Tours** (☎07-4062 3193; www.bedrock-village.com.au; Mt Surprise; full day adult/child $128/65, half day $82/42) also has tours, departing from Mt Surprise.

A worthwhile detour is the signposted drive to **Kalkani Crater**. The crater rim walk is an easy 2.5km circuit from the day-use car park, with good views over the surrounding countryside.

Opera in the Outback, held at Undara Experience in October, is a unique performance of classical music under the stars.

Undara is 15km south of the Savannah Way on a sealed road.

HISTORIC GULF TRAINS

Two nostalgic train trips operate in the Gulf. The historic **Savannahlander** (☎1800 793 848, 07-4053 6848; www.savannahlander.com.au; one way/return $232/392), aka the 'Silver Bullet', chugs along a traditional mining route from Cairns to Forsayth and back, departing from Cairns on Wednesday at 6.30am and returning on Saturday at 6.40pm. A range of tours (including side trips to Chillagoe, Undara and Cobbold Gorge) and accommodation can be booked online.

The snub-nosed **Gulflander** (☎07-4745 1391; www.gulflander.com.au; adult one way/return $69/115, child $34.50/57.50) runs once weekly in each direction between Normanton and Croydon on the 1891 gold-to-port railway line alongside the Gulf Developmental Rd. It leaves Normanton on Wednesday at 8.30am, and leaves Croydon on Thursday at 8.30am.

Sleeping & Eating

★Undara Experience RESORT $$
(☎1800 990 992; www.undara.com.au; unpowered/powered sites per person $12.50/18, s/d railway carriages from $90/170;) Just outside the national park, Undara Experience has a great range of accommodation, from a shady campground to nifty little swag tents on raised platforms and modern en-suite rooms. Pride of place goes to the restored railway carriages, charmingly fitted out, some with en suite. Staying here puts you close to the caves and surrounding bushwalks, and there's a good restaurant, a bar and barbecue areas. There's a small shop on site and pricey fuel.

Undara to Croydon

About 32km west of Mt Surprise, the partly sealed **Explorers' Loop** (check road conditions) takes you on a 150km circuit through old gold-mining towns. At **Einasleigh**, have a drink at the only pub and check out the publican's amazing miniature doll's house collection before strolling across to the Copperfield gorge. Continue past **Forsayth** to the private spring-fed oasis of **Cobbold Gorge**, the main attraction out here and one of those unexpectedly beautiful outback finds. **Cobbold Gorge Village** (☎1800 669 922, 07-4062 5470; www.cobboldgorge.com.au; Cobbold Gorge; sites unpowered/powered/with bathroom $26/36/49, s/d from $89/99; Apr-Oct;) runs three-hour bushwalking **tours** (☎07-4062 5470, 1800 669 922; www.cobboldgorge.com.au; Cobbold Gorge; adult/child/family $79/39.50/205; 10am Apr-Oct, plus 1.30pm Jun-Aug) that culminate in a boat cruise through the stunning gorge. Look for crocs basking on the rocks. The infinity pool with a swim up bar at the village is a welcome find in the middle of the dry surroundings.

Georgetown (population 244) is the endpoint of the loop, back on the Savannah Way. The only real attraction here is the flash **Terrestrial Centre** (☎07-4062 1485; Low St; 8am-5pm May-Sep, 8.30am-4.30pm Mon-Fri Oct-Apr), home to a **visitor centre** and the **Ted Elliot Mineral Collection** (☎07-4062 1485; Low St; admission $8; 8am-5pm), a shimmering collection of more than 4500 minerals, gems and crystals from all over Australia.

Croydon

POP 312

Incredibly, little Croydon was once the biggest town in the Gulf thanks to a short but lucrative gold rush. Gold was discovered in Croydon in 1885, but by the end of WWI it had run out and the place became little more than a ghost town.

Croydon's **visitor information centre** (☎07-4748 7152; Samwell St; 9am-4.30pm daily Apr-Sep, 9am-4.30pm Mon-Fri Oct-Mar) has details of the historic precinct and shows a short (free) film about the gold-rush days. Lake Belmore, 4km north of the centre, is stocked with barramundi if you feel like fishing or swimming.

The **Club Hotel** (☎07-4745 6184; www.clubhotelcroydon.com.au; cnr Brown & Sircom Sts; d $80, units $115;), built in 1887, is the only pub left from the mining heyday when there were more than 30. It serves up huge meals, ice-cold beer, and sunset views from the verandah. Campers can pitch up at **Croydon Caravan Park** (☎07-4745 6238; www.croydon.qld.gov.au/croydon-caravan-park; cnr Brown & Alldridge Sts; unpowered/powered sites $20/30, d/f cabins $100/120;).

At the timber **Croydon General Store** (☎07-4745 6163; Sircom St; 7am-6.30pm Mon-Fri, 9am-7.30pm Sat & Sun) the sign declares this the 'oldest store in Australia, established 1894'. The interior is definitely a throwback to ye olde days: wooden floorboards and a small collection of historical curios worth checking out.

Normanton

POP 1469

The port for Croydon's gold rush, Normanton boasts a broad and rather long main street lined with with some colourful old buildings. These days it's a tourist junction for Karumba- and Burketown-bound travellers, and the terminus for the *Gulflander* train. The Norman River produces whopping barramundi; every Easter the **Barra Bash** lures big crowds, as do the **Normanton Rodeo & Show** (mid-June) and the **Normanton Races** (September).

In the historic Burns Philp building, Normanton's excellent **visitor information & heritage centre** (☎07-4745 8444; www.carpentaria.qld.gov.au; cnr Caroline & Landsborough Sts; 9am-4pm Mon-Fri, to noon Sat & Sun Apr-Sep, closed Sun Oct-Mar) has a library, historical displays and lots of regional information. If it's closed, you can get information at the Normanton Train Station.

Everyone stops to take a photo of **Krys the Crocodile** on Landsborough St. It's a supposedly life-sized statue of an 8.64m saltie shot by croc hunter Krystina Pawloski on the Norman River in 1958 – the largest recorded croc in the world.

Normanton Tourist Park (☎1800 193 469, 07-4745 1121; www.normantontouristpark.com.au; 14 Brown St; unpowered/powered sites $24/32, cabins with/without bathroom $105/100; ❄📶🏊), in a shady setting on the main street, has cabins and an artesian spa.

You can't miss the colourful timber **Purple Pub** (☎07-4745 1324; cnr Landsborough & Brown Sts; s/d $100/120, mains $15-25; ❄). There are motel style rooms out the back and good pub meals ($15 to $25).

Karumba

POP 587

Aaah, Karumba: fishing mecca and winter base of many a southern retiree. When the sun sinks into the Gulf of Carpentaria in a fiery ball of burnt ochre, this is a little piece of outback paradise. Even if you don't like fishing, Karumba is the only town accessible by sealed road on the entire Gulf coast, and it's a great place to kick back for a few days.

The actual town is on the Norman River, while Karumba Point – the better place to stay – is about 6km away by road on the beach. The two communities are also linked by a hot, exposed 3km walking path. Karumba's **visitor information centre** (☎07-4745 9582; www.carpentaria.qld.gov.au; Walker St, Karumba Town; ⏲9am-4.30pm Mon-Fri, to noon Sat & Sun Apr-Sep, closed Sun Oct-Mar; 📶) has details of fishing charters and cruises.

Sights & Activities

Barramundi Discovery Centre HATCHERY TOUR
(☎07-4745 9359; 148 Yappar St, Karumba Town; adult/child $15/7.50; ⏲tours 10.30am & 1.30pm Mon-Fri, 9.30am Sat & Sun, shop 9.30am-3.30pm Mon-Fri & 9am-noon Sat & Sun) Everything you ever wanted to know about the barramundi can be learned on the guided tours at this hatchery and breeding centre, where you can also hand-feed a barra. The gift shop stocks locally made bags and wallets fashioned from barramundi, crocodile and cane toad leather.

Ferryman CRUISE
(☎07-4745 9155; www.ferryman.net.au; cruises $45, croc-spotting $60) A sunset cruise on the Gulf is just about de rigueur in Karumba. Ferryman operates regular cruises in the Dry which include drinks and prawn, fruit and cheese platters. Ferryman also does fishing charters ($100/200 half/full day).

Croc & Crab Tours TOUR
(☎0428 496 026; www.crocandcrab.com.au; half-day tours adult/child $119/60, cruises adult/child $65/30) These excellent half-day tours include crab-catching and croc-spotting on the Norman River, and a lunch of mud crabs and local prawns. Also offers sunset cruises.

Sleeping & Eating

Prawning is still a big industry here and you can buy fresh (and frozen) local seafood from outlets around Karumba Town and Point – look out for signs. A 1kg bag of prawns costs $20.

★**Karumba Point Sunset Caravan Park** CARAVAN PARK $
(☎07-4745 9277; www.sunsetcp.com.au; 53 Palmer St, Karumba Point; unpowered/powered sites $34/41, cabins $105-125; ❄📶🏊) The best of the four caravan parks in Karumba region, Karumba Point Sunset Caravan Park has shady palm trees, spotless amenities and it's right next to the boat ramp and beach.

Ash's Holiday Units MOTEL $$
(☎07-4745 9132; www.ashsholidayunits.com.au; 21 Palmer St, Karumba Point; s/d $105/114; ❄@📶🏊) Self-contained motel-style cabins surround a small pool. The cafe ($8 to $22) serves great fish and chips, plus the barra burger ($9.50).

End of the Road Motel MOTEL $$
(☎07-4745 9599; www.endoftheroadmotel.com.au; 26 Palmer St, Karumba Point; d $165-210; ❄📶🏊) Karumba's best motel has a range of rooms, and sunset views from the garden. The best rooms have Gulf views, of course.

★**Sunset Tavern** PUB $$
(☎07-4745 9183; www.sunsettavern.com.au; The Esplanade, Karumba Point; mains $15-35; ⏲10am-10pm) This big open-sided place is the hub of Karumba Point at sunset. It's *the* place to watch the sun sink into the Gulf over a glass of wine and a seafood platter. The food is reasonably good but the view is better – arrive early for a seat at an outdoor table for the sweetest sunset experience.

Northwest Corner

The road from Normanton to Burketown is sealed for about 30km, then it's a well-maintained dirt road with concrete flood ways for about 120km to the Leichhardt River – usually passable to all vehicles in the Dry. The final 70km to Burketown is sealed. About 37km out of Normanton, turn-off at the signposted stop by eerie **Burke & Wills Camp 119**, the northernmost camp of the ill-equipped explorers' wretched 1861 expedition – they came within just 5km of reaching the Gulf.

The alternative route south from Normanton is the Burke Developmental Rd (also called the Matilda Hwy), which is sealed all the way to Cloncurry (380km), where it joins the Barkly and Flinders Highways. As you head south, the flat dry-grass country slowly morphs into small rises and forests of termite hills. Flood-way signs give you an idea of what it's like during the Wet: wet.

Everyone stops at the **Burke & Wills Roadhouse** (☎07-4742 5909; sites per person $10, s/d $70/80, mains $18-28; ⌚5.30am-midnight, restaurant to 9pm; ❄) to down a cold drink or refuel. From here the sealed Wills Developmental Rd shoots west to Gregory, from where you can continue north to Burketown or west to Boodjamulla National Park.

MORNING GLORY

Roughly between August and November, Burketown becomes the home of intrepid cloud-surfers, when 'morning glory' clouds frequently (but unpredictably) roll in. A rare meteorological phenomenon, these tubular clouds come in wave-like sets of up to eight. Each can be up to 1000km long by 2km high, and they travel at speeds of up to 60km per hour. As the sun rises, gliders head up in the hope of catching one; ask around and chances are someone will take you along for the ride. For a close-up look at the clouds aboard a light plane, contact Gulf-wide charter company **Savannah Aviation** (☎07-4745 5177; www.savannah-aviation.com; Burketown; per hr for up to 4 people $650).

Burketown

Sleeping & Eating

★ Burketown Pub — PUB $$

(☎07-4745 5104; www.burketownpub.com; cnr Musgrave & Beames St; s/d units $135/145, mains $17-38; ⌚Wed-Sat from 10am, Sun-Tue from 11am; ❄) The Burketown Pub is the heart and soul of the town. The original 140-year-old pub burnt down in 2012 and it was completely rebuilt and reopened in 2013. What it lost in old-time character it makes up for in shiny new facilities and a large bar where you can swap fishing stories with locals or travellers. Meals are generous and naturally include barramundi.

Burketown Caravan Park — CARAVAN PARK $

(☎07-4745 5118; www.burketowncaravanpark.net.au; Sloman St; powered sites $34, d cabins without bathroom $75-90; ❄) The local caravan park has a range of cabins (with private bathrooms costs a little more), spacious powered sites and a camp kitchen.

Morning Glory Restaurant — BISTRO $

(☎07-4745 5295; Beames St; mains $8.50-18.50; ⌚8am-8.30pm; 📶) This licensed restaurant and cafe across the road from the pub serves up a bit of everything, from takeaway barra burgers to steaks. Owner Rosita is planning to introduce Asian dishes to the menu.

Burketown to Boodjamulla National Park

The 120km road from Burketown to Gregory is sealed all the way so it's an easy drive and the most direct route to beautiful Boodjamulla (Lawn Hill) National Park. It's another 185km of rough dirt road south to the Barkly Hwy which can take you west to Camooweal or east to Mt Isa.

The entrance to Boodjamulla is 100km west of **Gregory** (population 40), a mere roadside stop on the pretty Gregory River. Fuel is available at the **Gregory Downs Hotel** (☎07-4748 5566; Gregory; s/d camp sites $10/12, d motel units $100; ❄), a laid-back spot to quench your thirst and tuck into decent pub meals (dinner Monday to Friday, a barbecue on Saturday night and lunch Sunday).

From Gregory, the sealed Wills Development Rd leads 147km east to join the Matilda Hwy at Burke & Wills Roadhouse.

TRAVELLING TO THE TERRITORY

If you're travelling from outback Queensland to the Northern Territory (NT) there are two main routes. The easy way is the sealed Barkly Hwy from Mt Isa to Three Ways (640km), from where you can head south to Alice Springs or north to Darwin on the sealed Stuart Hwy. The more adventurous route is the continuation of the Savannah Way west of Burketown. It's almost 500km of partly sealed but occasionally rough 4WD territory from Burketown to Borroloola (NT) and beyond. This road is usually impassable in the Wet. Along the way you'll pass the **Doomadgee Aboriginal Community** (07-4745 8188), where you're welcome to buy fuel and supplies; village access is subject to council permission, and alcohol is restricted. It's another 80km of melaleuca scrub to **Hell's Gate Roadhouse** (07-4745 8258; camping per person $10), 50km from the NT border. It has fuel, camping (no power) and snacks; cash only.

Boodjamulla (Lawn Hill) National Park

Boodjamulla is simply one of the most beautiful and pristine places in all of outback Queensland. A series of deep flame-red sandstone gorges tower above the spring-fed, luminous green Lawn Hill Creek. Lush vegetation, including cabbage-leaf palms, pandanus and turkey bush line the gorge, providing a haven for wildlife at this outback oasis. The Waanyi Aboriginal people have inhabited the area for some 30,000 years, leaving works of rock art.

Some 20km of walking tracks fan out around Lawn Hill Gorge, leading to some unforgettable lookouts. The emerald-green waters are idyllic for swimming, especially at Indarri Falls.

A special way to experience the gorge is paddling a canoe (double canoe $25 per hour). If you're reasonably fit it's worth the effort and time to get to the upper gorge. Alternatively, a guided cruise on a solar-powered eco-boat (adult/child $35/25) will give you a good insight into the park. Book both through Adel's Grove.

There's an excellent national parks **campground** (13 74 68; www.nprsr.qld.gov.au; per person/family $5.75/23) right next to Lawn Hill Gorge. No power but running water, showers, toilets and a ranger office.

In the southern part of the park is the World Heritage–listed **Riversleigh fossil field**, with a small **campground** (13 74 68; www.nprsr.qld.gov.au; per person/family $5.75/23; Mar-Oct), 4km south of the Riversleigh D site (the only part of the fossil field open to the public). This is thought to be the richest fossil mammal site in Australia with everything from giant snakes and carnivorous kangaroos to pocket-sized koalas. Campers must book ahead, and be totally self-sufficient.

The main hub for accommodation is **Adel's Grove** (07-4748 5502; www.adelsgrove.com.au; camping d/f $34/45, safari tents with dinner, bed & breakfast $220-290), 10km east of the park entrance. It's an excellent miniresort on the banks of Lawn Hill Creek with an on-site bar and **restaurant** (07-4748 5502; www.adelsgrove.com.au; breakfast $13, lunch mains $10-18, 2-course dinner $35) with a big open-air deck. There's a shady riverside camping area (no power) separated from the main accommodation area. Other options are safari tents on raised platforms (riverside ones are more expensive), simple air-con cabins and new en-suite cabins. Most of the accommodation (other than camping) is on a dinner, bed and breakfast basis, but you can ask about bed only if you prefer to self-cater. Fuel, food packs and basic groceries are available.

Tours from Adel's Grove include the fascinating Riversleigh fossil field tours ($75 for a half-day tour) and a tour of the Century 21 mine.

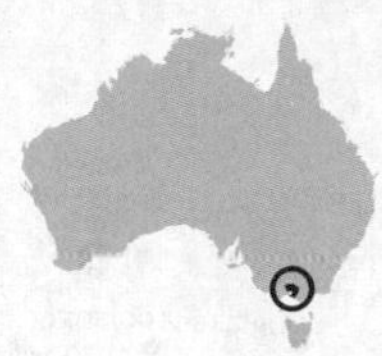

Melbourne & Around

Includes ➜

Best Places to Eat

➜ Vue de Monde (p499)
➜ MoVida (p497)
➜ Attica (p503)
➜ Charcoal Lane (p500)
➜ Supernormal (p497)

Best Places to Stay

➜ Art Series (Cullen; p496)
➜ Ovolo (p494)
➜ Adina Apartment Hotel (p494)
➜ Space Hotel (p493)
➜ Lake House (p519)

Why Go?

Regularly ranked among the world's most liveable cities, Melbourne has blossomed over the past decade. Where Sydney's appeal rests largely on its geography and name recognition, Melbourne has always had to work a little harder for plaudits. Stylish and arty, dynamic and cosmopolitan, this is a city that goes from strength to strength. It's home to Australia's most varied dining scene and lays claim to being the country's arts and sporting capital. Throw in stately gold-rush-era architecture, expansive parklands, lanes of street art, top museums and a thriving live-music tradition and there's not much that Melbourne doesn't do well. Beyond the city limits, you'll also encounter some worthwhile detours, including the penguins of Phillip Island, the hot springs of Hepburn Springs and the wines and wildlife of the Yarra Valley.

When to Go

Melbourne

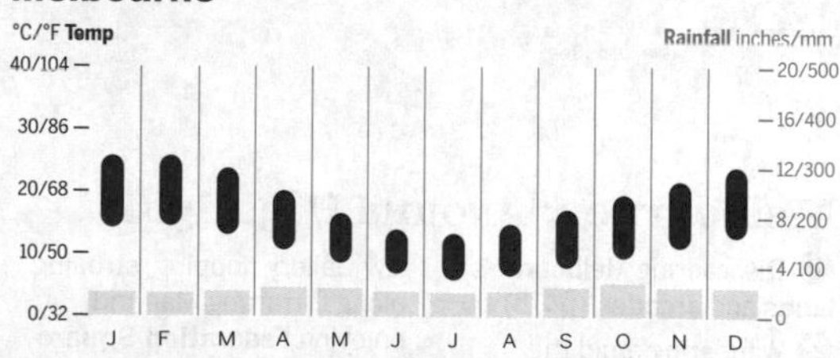

Mid-Dec–Mar Balmy nights, Grand Slam tennis and music festivals.

Apr–Sep Escape the cold with gallery hopping, boutique shopping and warm, inviting pubs.

Sep–Nov Footy finals fever hits, then the horses start cantering during the Spring Racing Carnival.

Melbourne & Around Highlights

1. Discovering Melbourne's **lanes** and **arcades** (p475).
2. Wandering amid the produce at historic **Queen Victoria Market** (p479).
3. Taking a **kayak tour** (p489) of the Yarra.
4. Joining Melbourne's dumpling craze at **HuTong Dumpling Bar** (p498).
5. Gallery hopping, strolling along Birrarung Mar and enjoying **Federation Square** (p471).
6. Quaffing coffee at industrial-chic **Auction Rooms** (p502).
7. Going on a tour of wineries and breweries in the **Yarra Valley** (p522).
8. Getting up close and personal with wildlife at **Healesville Sanctuary** (p522).
9. Watching the penguins come ashore at sunset at **Phillip Island** (p526).
10. Discovering one of Melbourne's favourite getaways at **Daylesford** (p519).

MELBOURNE

POP 4.25 MILLION

Melbourne is best experienced as a local would, because its character is largely reliant upon its collection of inner-city neighbourhoods. Dive into the city's lanes, or climb to an open-air bar atop a former industrial building, and you'll very quickly learn why Melbourne is Australia's most happening city.

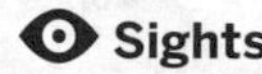

Sights

Central Melbourne

Melbourne's wide main streets and legion of lanes buzz day and night, seven days a week. Museums and art galleries are dotted throughout. City-centre living has boomed in the past decade with some 100,000 now claiming city apartments as their home. There are two big ends of town. Skyscrapers cluster on the east and west ends of the grid – these areas are mostly used by business. Southern Cross Station sits to the west, with Docklands Stadium and the regenerated Docklands beyond. Opposite the central Flinders Street Station, Federation Sq (better known as Fed Square) squats beside the Yarra River and has become a favourite Melbourne gathering place. To the east is the top end of town (locals call it the 'Paris end'), with its monumental gold-rush-era buildings and designer stores.

★Federation Square SQUARE

(Map p476; www.fedsquare.com.au; cnr Flinders & Swanston Sts; 🚋1, 3, 5, 6, 8, 16, 64, 67, 72, 🚆Flinders St) It took some time, but Melburnians have embraced Federation Sq, accepting it as the congregation place it was meant to be – somewhere to celebrate, protest, watch major sporting events or just hang out. Occupying a prominent city block, Fed Square is far from square: its undulating and patterned forecourt is paved with 460,000 hand-laid cobblestones from the Kimberley region, with sight lines to Melbourne's iconic landmarks; while its buildings are clad in a fractal-patterned reptilian skin.

At the square's street junction is the subterranean Melbourne Visitor Centre. (p517) Highly recommended free tours of Fed Square depart Monday to Saturday at 11am; spaces are limited, so get here 10 to 15 minutes early. The square has free wi-fi, and there's free daily tai chi from 7.30am and meditation at 12.30pm on Tuesday.

★Ian Potter Centre: NGV Australia GALLERY

(Map p476; ☎03-8620 2222; www.ngv.vic.gov.au; Federation Sq; exhibition costs vary; ⏰10am-5pm Tue-Sun; 🚋1, 3, 5, 6, 8, 16, 64, 67, 72, 🚆Flinders St) Hidden away in the basement of Federation Sq, the Ian Potter Centre is the second half of the National Gallery of Victoria (NGV), set up to showcase the gallery's impressive collection of Australian works. Set over three levels, it's a mix of permanent (free) and

MELBOURNE IN...

Two Days

Check out the **Ian Potter Centre: NGV Australia** (p471) and **ACMI** (p474) museums, then enjoy lunch at **MoVida** (p497). Join a walking tour to see Melbourne's **street art** then chill out at a **rooftop bar** (508) until it's time to join an evening **kayak tour** (p489) of the Yarra River. The next day, stroll along **Birrarung Marr** (p474) and into the **Royal Botanic Gardens** (p487), then shop your way through the **Queen Vic Market** (p479). Catch a tram to **St Kilda** (p487) and stroll along the beach, before catching a band and propping up a bar in lively Acland St for the evening.

One Week

Spend a couple of hours at the **Melbourne Museum** (p485) and then revive with a coffee at **DOC Espresso** (p502). Head to Fitzroy and Collingwood and shop along **Gertrude St** before feasting at **Cutler & Co** (p501). Back in the city centre, wander through **Chinatown** (p478) and check out the **State Library** (p478) before grabbing some dumplings for dinner. Spend the rest of the week **shopping** (p513), cafe hopping and people watching. In winter, catch a footy game at the **MCG** (p483) before drinks at one of the city's **laneway bars** (p504). Make sure to hit **Mamasita** (p498) for tacos and the **Tote** (p512) in Collingwood for live music.

Melbourne

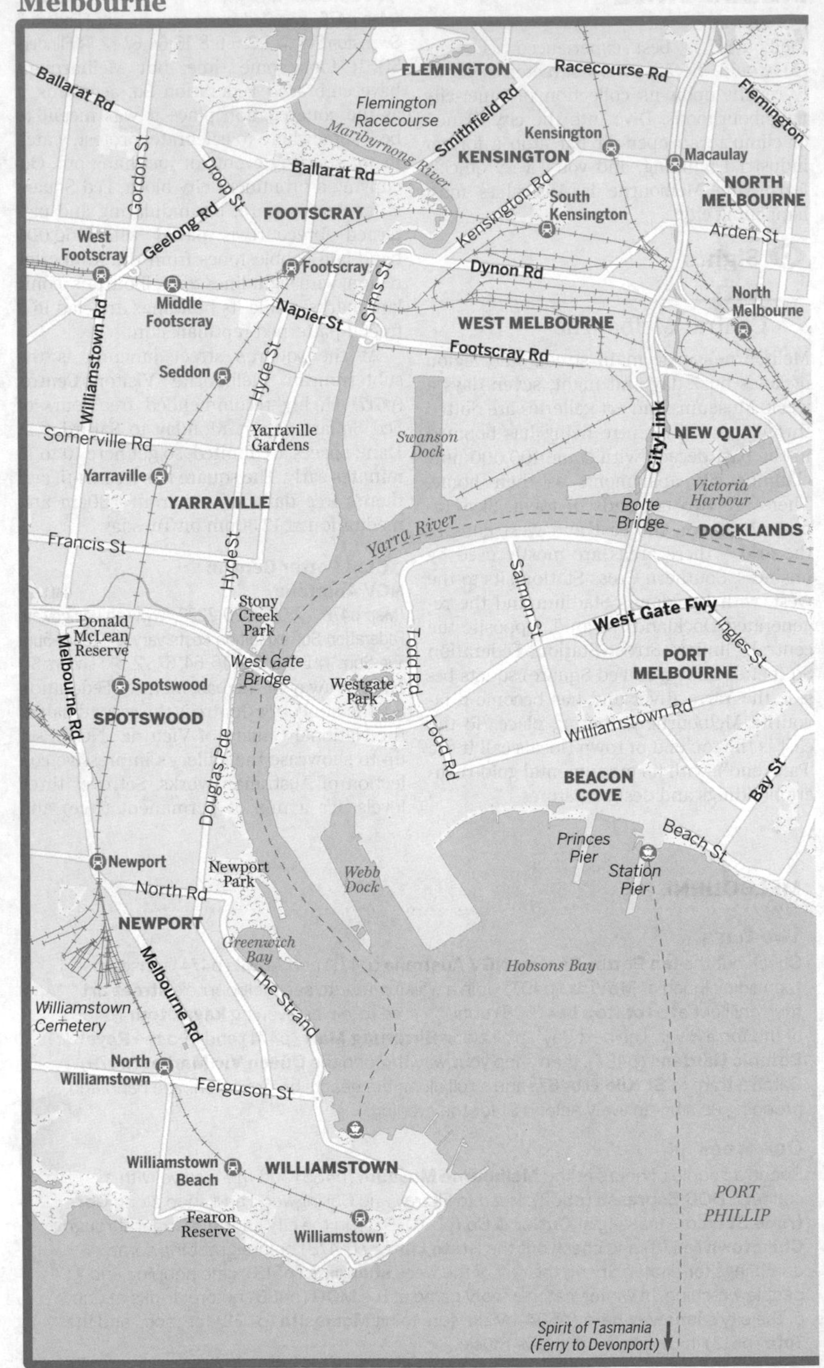

FLEMINGTON
Racecourse Rd
Ballarat Rd
Flemington
Racecourse
Flemington
Smithfield Rd
Kensington
Macaulay
Maribyrnong River
KENSINGTON
Gordon St
Droop St
Ballarat Rd
NORTH
MELBOURNE
Kensington Rd
South
Kensington
FOOTSCRAY
Geelong Rd
West
Footscray
Arden St
Footscray
Dynon Rd
Sims St
Middle
Footscray
North
Melbourne
Napier St
WEST MELBOURNE
Williamstown Rd
Footscray Rd
Seddon
Hyde St
CityLink
NEW QUAY
Somerville Rd
Yarraville
Gardens
Swanson
Dock
Yarraville
Victoria
Harbour
YARRAVILLE
Bolte
Bridge
Yarra River
DOCKLANDS
Francis St
Hyde St
Salmon St
Stony
Creek
Park
West Gate Fwy
Ingles St
Donald
McLean
Reserve
Todd Rd
Melbourne Rd
West Gate
Bridge
PORT
MELBOURNE
Spotswood
Westgate
Park
SPOTSWOOD
Williamstown Rd
Todd Rd
Douglas Pde
BEACON
COVE
Bay St
Beach St
Princes
Pier
Newport
Newport
Park
Station
Pier
Webb
Dock
North Rd
NEWPORT
Greenwich
Bay
Hobsons Bay
Melbourne Rd
The Strand
Williamstown
Cemetery
North
Williamstown
Ferguson St
Williamstown
Beach
WILLIAMSTOWN
PORT
PHILLIP
Fearon
Reserve
Williamstown
Spirit of Tasmania
(Ferry to Devonport)

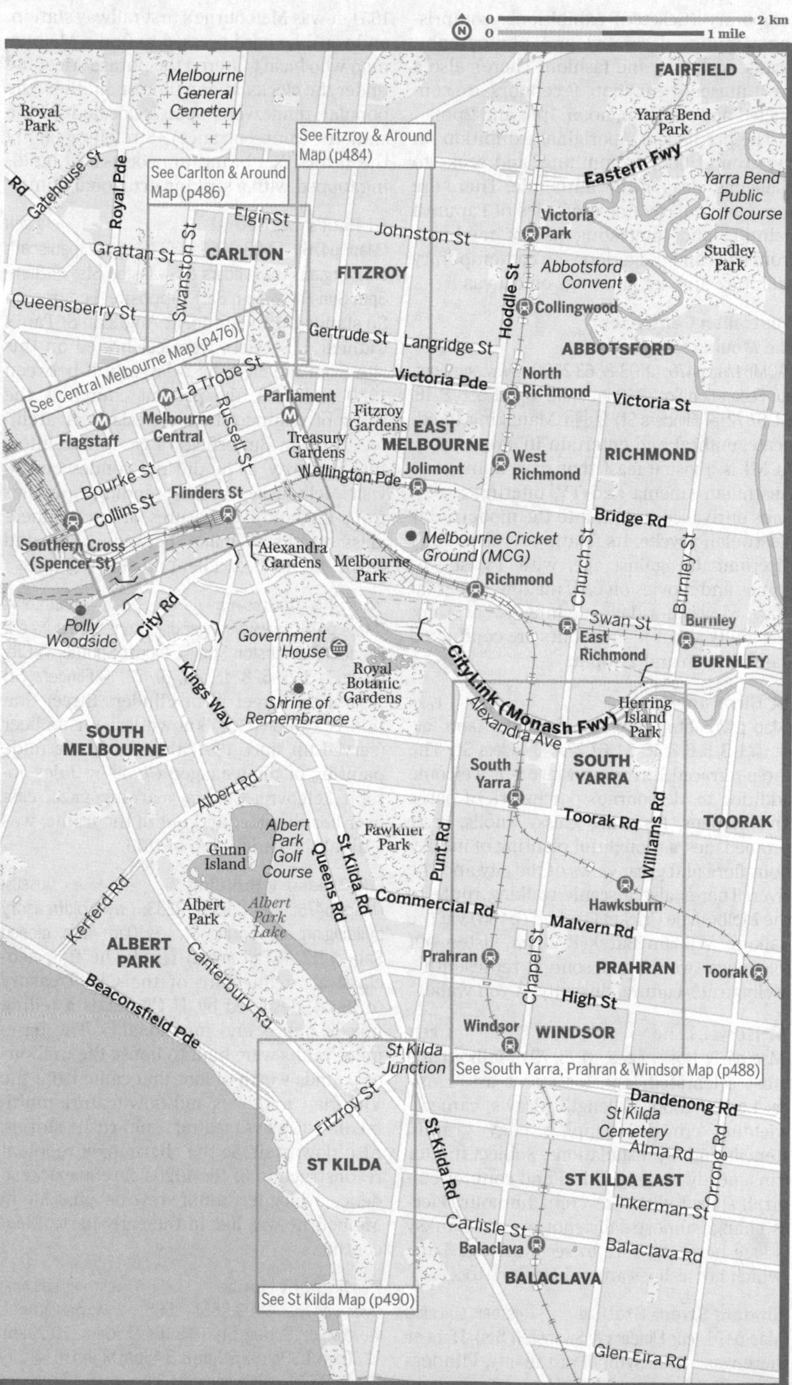
0 2 km
0 1 mile
Melbourne General Cemetery
Royal Park
FAIRFIELD
Yarra Bend Park
See Fitzroy & Around Map (p484)
See Carlton & Around Map (p486)
Eastern Fwy
Yarra Bend Public Golf Course
Gatehouse St
Royal Pde
Rd
Elgin St
Johnston St
Victoria Park
Grattan St
CARLTON
FITZROY
Studley Park
Abbotsford Convent
Swanston St
Hoddle St
Collingwood
Queensberry St
Gertrude St
Langridge St
ABBOTSFORD
See Central Melbourne Map (p476)
La Trobe St
Victoria Pde
North Richmond
Parliament
Russell St
Victoria St
Melbourne Central
Flagstaff
Fitzroy Gardens
EAST MELBOURNE
Treasury Gardens
West Richmond
RICHMOND
Bourke St
Wellington Pde
Jolimont
Collins St
Flinders St
Bridge Rd
Southern Cross (Spencer St)
Alexandra Gardens
Melbourne Cricket Ground (MCG)
Melbourne Park
Church St
Burnley St
Richmond
Swan St
Burnley
Polly Woodside
City Rd
Government House
East Richmond
BURNLEY
Kings Way
Royal Botanic Gardens
CityLink (Monash Fwy)
Shrine of Remembrance
Herring Island Park
Alexandra Ave
SOUTH MELBOURNE
South Yarra
SOUTH YARRA
Albert Rd
Toorak Rd
TOORAK
Albert Park Golf Course
Fawkner Park
Punt Rd
Williams Rd
Gunn Island
St Kilda Rd
Queens Rd
Commercial Rd
Hawksburn
Kerferd Rd
Albert Park
Albert Park Lake
Malvern Rd
ALBERT PARK
Chapel St
Prahran
PRAHRAN
Toorak
Canterbury Rd
Beaconsfield Pde
High St
Windsor
WINDSOR
St Kilda Junction
See South Yarra, Prahran & Windsor Map (p488)
Dandenong Rd
Fitzroy St
St Kilda Cemetery
Alma Rd
Orrong Rd
ST KILDA
St Kilda Rd
ST KILDA EAST
Inkerman St
Carlisle St
Balaclava
Balaclava Rd
BALACLAVA
See St Kilda Map (p490)
Glen Eira Rd

temporary (ticketed) exhibitions, comprising paintings, decorative arts, photography, prints, sculpture and fashion. There's also a great museum gift shop. Free tours are conducted daily at 11am, noon, 1pm and 2pm.

The permanent Aboriginal exhibition on the ground floor is stunning, and seeks to challenge ideas of the 'authentic'. There are some particularly fine examples of Papunya painting and interesting use of mediums from bark and didgeridoos to contemporary sculpture and dot paintings on canvas.

Australian Centre for the Moving Image MUSEUM

(ACMI; Map p476; ☎03-8663 2200; www.acmi.net.au; Federation Sq; ⏰10am-6pm; 🚋1, 3, 5, 6, 8, 16, 64, 67, 72, 🚉Flinders St) FREE Managing to educate, enthral and entertain in equal parts, ACMI is a visual feast that pays homage to Australian cinema and TV, offering a perhaps unrivalled insight into the modern-day Australian psyche. Its floating screens don't discriminate against age, with TV shows, games and movies on call, making it a great place to waste a day watching TV and not feel guilty about it. Free tours are conducted daily at 11am and 2.30pm.

★Birrarung Marr PARK

(Map p476; btwn Federation Sq & the Yarra River; 🚋1, 3, 5, 6, 8, 16, 64, 67, 72, 🚉Flinders St) The three-terraced Birrarung Marr is a welcome addition to Melbourne's patchwork of parks and gardens, featuring grassy knolls, river promenades, a thoughtful planting of indigenous flora and great views of the city and the river. There's also a scenic walking route to the Melbourne Cricket Ground (p483) via the 'talking' William Barak Bridge – listen out for songs, words and sounds representing Melbourne's cultural diversity as you walk.

★Hosier Lane STREET

(Map p476; Hosier Lane; 🚋75, 70) Melbourne's most celebrated lane for street art, Hosier Lane's cobbled length draws camera-wielding crowds snapping edgy graffiti, stencils and art installations. Subject matter runs mostly to the political and counter cultural, spiced with irreverent humour. Pieces change almost daily (not even a Banksy is safe here). Be sure to see Rutledge Lane (which horseshoes around Hosier), too.

Flinders Street Station HISTORIC BUILDING

(Map p476; cnr Flinders & Swanston Sts) If ever there was a true symbol of the city, Flinders Street Station would have to be it. Built in 1854, it was Melbourne's first railway station, and you'd be hard pressed to find a Melburnian who hasn't uttered the phrase 'Meet me under the clocks' at one time or another (the popular rendezvous spot is located at the station's front entrance). Stretching along the Yarra, it's a beautiful neoclassical building topped with a striking octagonal dome.

St Paul's Cathedral CHURCH

(Map p476; ☎03-9653 4333; www.stpaulscathedral.org.au; cnr Flinders & Swanston Sts; ⏰8am-6pm Sun-Fri, to 5pm Sat) Opposite Federation Sq stands the magnificent Anglican St Paul's Cathedral. Services were celebrated on this site from the city's first days. Built between 1880 and 1891, the present church is the work of distinguished ecclesiastical architect William Butterfield (a case of architecture by proxy, as he did not condescend to visit Melbourne, instead sending drawings from England). It features ornate stained-glass windows, made between 1887 and 1890, and holds excellent music programs.

Young & Jackson's HISTORIC BUILDING

(Map p476; www.youngandjacksons.com.au; cnr Flinders & Swanston Sts; 🚌Tourist Shuttle, 🚋City Circle, 1, 3, 5, 6, 8, 16, 64, 67, 72, 🚉Flinders St) Across the street from Flinders Street Station is a pub (p507) known less for its beer (served up since 1861) than its iconic nude painting of the teenaged *Chloe* by Jules Joseph Lefebvre. Chloe's yearning gaze, cast over her shoulder and out of the frame, was a hit at the Paris Salon of 1875.

Old Treasury Building MUSEUM

(Map p476; ☎03-9651 2233; www.oldtreasurybuilding.org.au; Spring St; ⏰10am-4pm, closed Sat; 🚋112, 🚉Parliament) FREE The fine neoclassical architecture of the Old Treasury (c 1862), designed by JJ Clarke, is a telling mix of hubris and functionality. The basement vaults were built to house the millions of pounds worth of loot that came from the Victorian goldfields and now feature multimedia displays telling gold-rush stories. Also downstairs is the charmingly redolent reconstruction of the 1920s caretaker's residence, which beautifully reveals what life in Melbourne was like in the early part of last century.

Parliament House HISTORIC BUILDING

(Map p476; ☎03-9651 8568; www.parliament.vic.gov.au; Spring St; ⏰tours 9.30am, 10.30am, 11.30am, 1.30pm, 2.30pm & 3.45pm Mon-Fri; 🚋City Circle, 86, 96, 🚉Parliament) The grand steps of

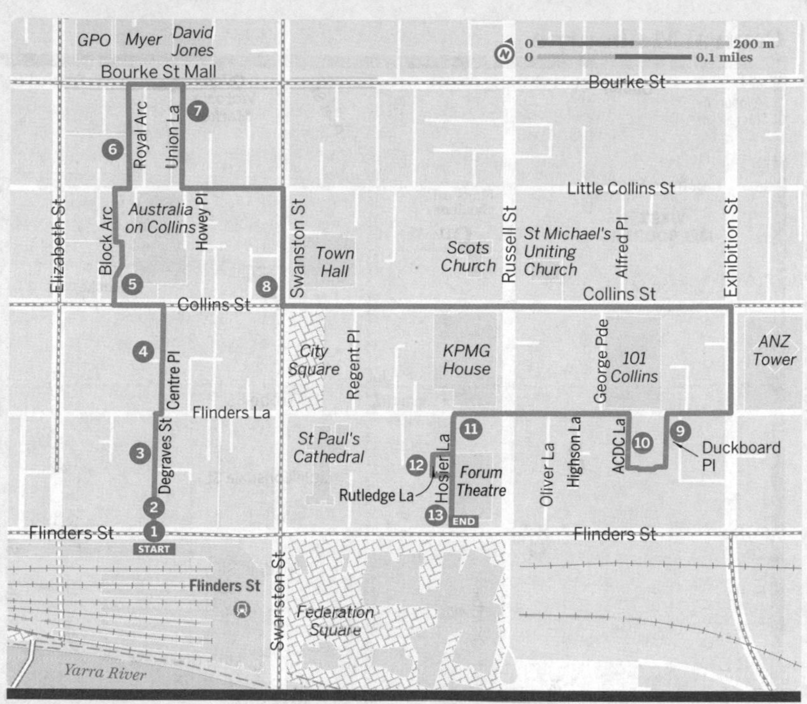

City Walk
Arcades & Lanes

START CAMPBELL ARCADE
FINISH MOVIDA
LENGTH 3KM, 2½ HOURS

Central Melbourne is a warren of 19th-century arcades and gritty-turned-hip cobbled bluestone lanes featuring street art, basement restaurants, boutiques and bars.

Start off underground at the art deco 1 **Campbell Arcade**, also known as Degraves Subway, built for the '56 Olympics and now home to indie stores. Head upstairs to 2 **Degraves St**, grab a coffee at 3 **Degraves Espresso** and then continue north, crossing over Flinders Lane to cafe-filled 4 **Centre Place**, a good place to start street-art spotting.

Cross over Collins St, turn left and enter the 5 **Block Arcade**. Built in 1891 and featuring etched-glass ceilings and mosaic floors, it's based on Milan's Galleria Vittorio Emanuele plaza. Ogle the window display at the Hopetoun Tea Rooms. Exit the other end of the arcade into Little Collins St and perhaps grab an afternoon cocktail at Chuckle Park.

Across Little Collins, head into 6 **Royal Arcade** for a potter. Wander through to Bourke St Mall, then turn right and walk until you find street-art-covered 7 **Union Lane** on the right.

Follow Union Lane out and turn left onto Little Collins St, then take a right on Swanston St and walk south to the 8 **Manchester Unity Arcade** (1932) on the corner of Collins St. Take a look in this beautiful arcade, then go back out to Swanston and head east, up the hill, to the 'Paris End' of Collins St.

Turn right into Exhibition St, then right into Flinders Lane and continue until you see 9 **Duckboard Place**. Head down the lane, taking time to soak up the street art before horseshoeing around into ACDC Lane, past rock 'n' roll dive bar 10 **Cherry** (p512).

Continue down Flinders Lane to the street-art meccas of 11 **Hosier Lane** (p474) and 12 **Rutledge Lane** before finishing with tapas and a hard-earned drink at 13 **MoVida** (p497).

Central Melbourne

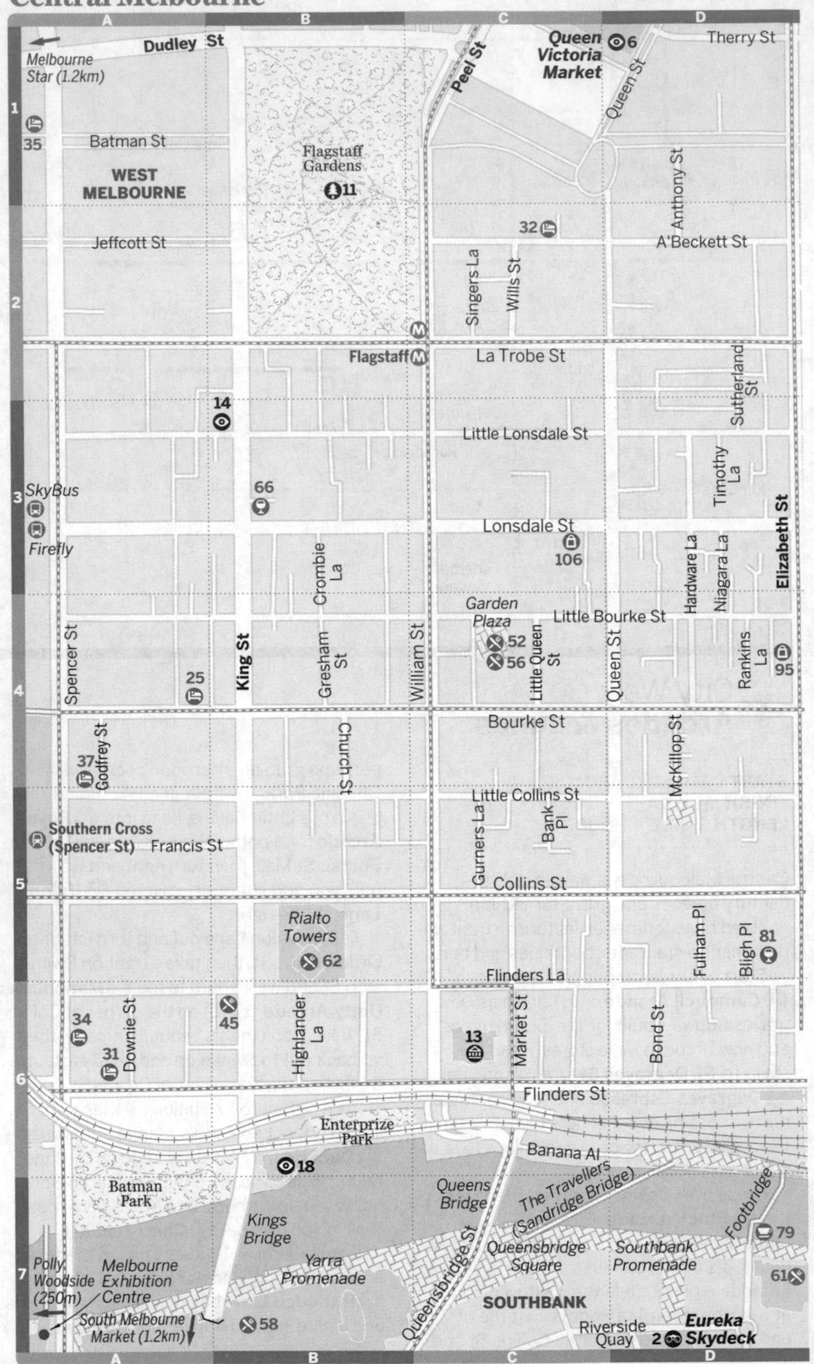

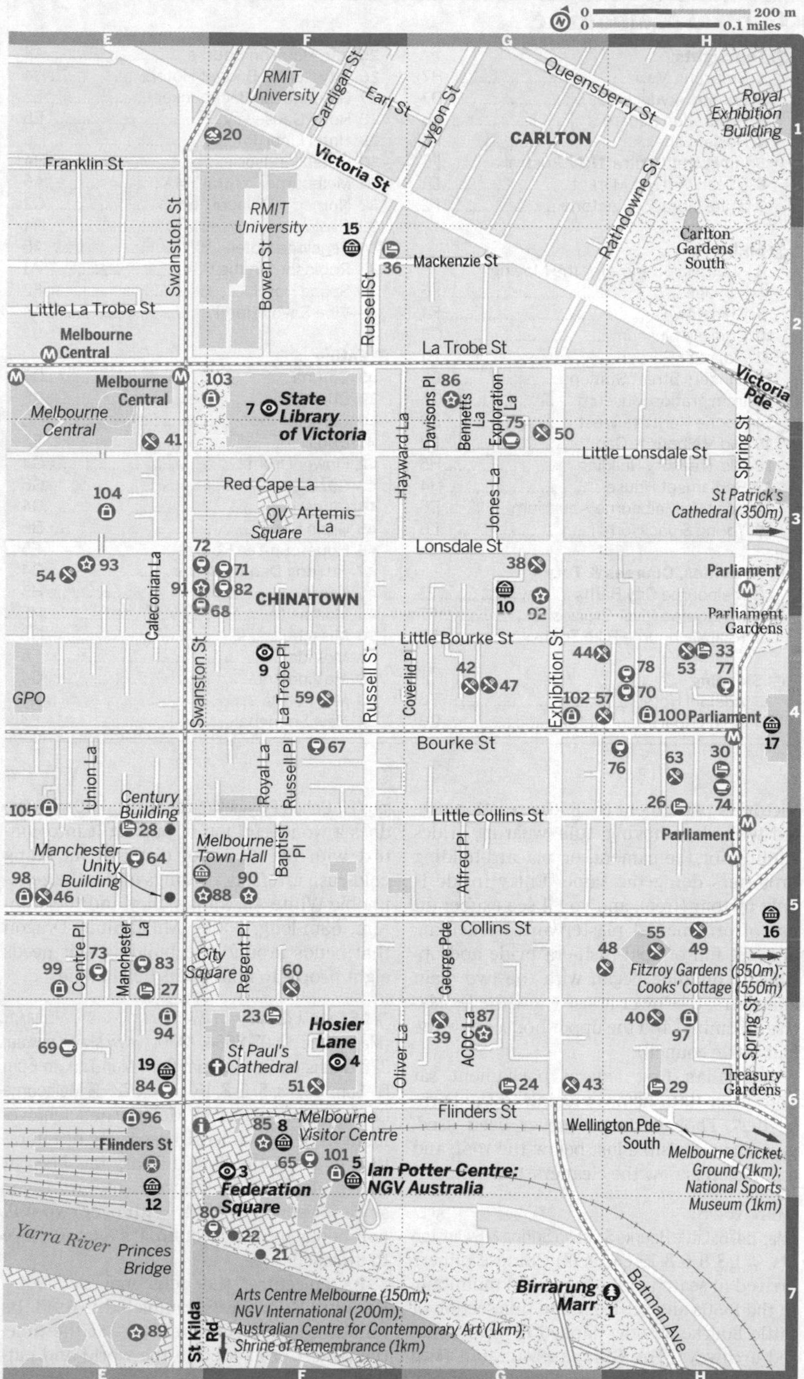

0 200 m
0 0.1 miles
RMIT University
Cardigan St
Earl St
Lygon St
Queensberry St
Royal Exhibition Building
CARLTON
Victoria St
Franklin St
Rathdowne St
Carlton Gardens South
Swanston St
Bowen St
Russell St
Mackenzie St
Little La Trobe St
Melbourne Central
La Trobe St
Victoria Pde
State Library of Victoria
Davisons Pl
Bennetts La
Exploration La
Hayward La
Little Lonsdale St
Spring St
Red Cape La
QV Square
Artemis La
Jones La
St Patrick's Cathedral (350m)
Lonsdale St
Parliament
Parliament Gardens
Caleconian La
CHINATOWN
Little Bourke St
Exhibition St
La Trobe Pl
Coverlid Pl
GPO
Bourke St
Union La
Royal La
Russell Pl
Century Building
Little Collins St
Melbourne Town Hall
Baptist Pl
Manchester Unity Building
Alfred Pl
Collins St
Centre Pl
Manchester La
City Square
Regent Pl
George Pde
Fitzroy Gardens (350m); Cooks' Cottage (550m)
Hosier Lane
St Paul's Cathedral
Oliver La
ACDC La
Treasury Gardens
Flinders St
Melbourne Visitor Centre
Wellington Pde South
Melbourne Cricket Ground (1km); National Sports Museum (1km)
Ian Potter Centre: NGV Australia
Federation Square
Yarra River
Princes Bridge
Arts Centre Melbourne (150m); NGV International (200m); Australian Centre for Contemporary Art (1km); Shrine of Remembrance (1km)
Birrarung Marr
Batman Ave
St Kilda Rd
MELBOURNE & AROUND

Central Melbourne

Top Sights
1 Birrarung Marr ... H7
2 Eureka Skydeck ... D7
3 Federation Square ... F6
4 Hosier Lane ... F6
5 Ian Potter Centre: NGV Australia ... F6
6 Queen Victoria Market ... D1
7 State Library of Victoria ... F2

Sights
8 Australian Centre for the Moving Image ... F6
9 Chinatown ... F4
10 Chinese Museum ... G3
11 Flagstaff Gardens ... B1
12 Flinders Street Station ... E6
13 Immigration Museum ... C6
14 Koorie Heritage Trust ... B3
15 Old Melbourne Gaol ... F2
16 Old Treasury Building ... H5
17 Parliament House ... H4
18 Sea Life Melbourne Aquarium ... B6
19 Young & Jackson's ... E6

Activities, Courses & Tours
20 Melbourne City Baths ... F1
21 Melbourne River Cruises ... F7
22 Real Melbourne Bike Tours ... F7

Sleeping
23 Adelphi Hotel ... F6
24 Adina Apartment Hotel ... G6
25 Alto Hotel on Bourke ... A4
26 City Centre Budget Hotel ... H4
27 Greenhouse Backpacker ... E5
28 Hotel Causeway ... E5
29 Hotel Lindrum ... H6
30 Hotel Windsor ... H4
31 Melbourne Central YHA ... A6
32 Nomad's Melbourne ... C2
33 Ovolo ... H4
34 Pensione Hotel ... A6
35 Robinsons in the City ... A1
36 Space Hotel ... F2
37 Vibe Savoy Hotel ... A4

Eating
38 Bomba ... G3
39 Chin Chin ... G6
40 Cumulus Inc ... H6
41 Don Don ... E3
42 Flower Drum ... G4
43 Gazi ... G6
44 Gingerboy ... G4
45 Grain Store ... B6
46 Hopetoun Tea Rooms ... E5
47 HuTong Dumpling Bar ... G4
48 Kenzan ... H5
49 Mamasita ... H5
50 Misschu ... G3
51 MoVida ... F6
52 MoVida Aqui ... C4
53 Mrs Parma's ... H4
54 New Shanghai ... E3

Victoria's parliament (c 1856) are often dotted with slow-moving, tulle-wearing brides smiling for the camera, or placard-holding protesters doing the same. Entry inside is only by tour (free), and you'll see exuberant use of ornamental plasterwork, stencilling and gilt full of gold-rush-era pride and optimism. Building began with the two main chambers: the lower house (now the legislative assembly) and the upper house (now the legislative council).

Australia's first federal parliament sat here from 1901, before moving to Canberra in 1927. Though they've never been used, gun slits are visible just below the roof, and a dungeon is now the cleaners' tearoom.

Chinatown AREA

(Map p476; Little Bourke St, btwn Spring & Swanston Sts; 1, 3, 5, 6, 8, 16, 64, 67, 72) Chinese miners arrived in search of the 'new gold mountain' in the 1850s and settled along this section of Little Bourke St, now flanked by traditional red archways. The **Chinese Museum** (Map p476; 03-9662 2888; www.chinesemuseum.com.au; 22 Cohen Pl; adult/child $8/6; 10am-5pm) does a wonderful job of putting it into context with five floors of displays, including gold-rush artefacts, dealings under the xenophobic White Australia policy and the stunning 63m-long, 200kg Millennium Dragon that bends around the building – it needs eight people to hold up its head alone.

★ **State Library of Victoria** LIBRARY

(Map p476; 03-8664 7000; www.slv.vic.gov.au; 328 Swanston St; 10am-9pm Mon-Thu, to 6pm Fri-Sun; 1, 3, 5, 6, 8, 16, 64, 67, 72, Melbourne Central) A big player in Melbourne's achievement of being named Unesco City of Literature in 2008, the State Library has been at the forefront of Melbourne's literary scene since it opened in 1854. With over two million books in its collection, it's a great place to browse.

Its epicentre, the octagonal **La Trobe Reading Room**, was completed in 1913. Its reinforced-concrete dome was, at the time, the largest of its kind in the world and natural light illuminates its ornate plasterwork and the studious Melbourne writers who come here to pen their works.

Another highlight is the collection of **Ned Kelly memorabilia**, including his suit of armour.

Old Melbourne Gaol HISTORIC BUILDING
(Map p476; ☎03-8663 7228; www.oldmelbournegaol.com.au; 337 Russell St; adult/child/family $25/13.50/55; ⊙9.30am-5pm; 🚊24, 30, City Circle) Built in 1841, this forbidding bluestone prison was in operation until 1929. It's now one of Melbourne's most popular museums, where you can tour the tiny, bleak cells. Around 135 people were hanged here, including Ned Kelly, Australia's most infamous bushranger, in 1880. One of his death masks is on display.

★ **Queen Victoria Market** MARKET
(Map p476; www.qvm.com.au; 513 Elizabeth St; ⊙6am-2pm Tue & Thu, to 5pm Fri, to 3pm Sat, 9am-4pm Sun; 🚌Tourist Shuttle, 🚊19, 55, 57, 59) With over 600 traders, the Vic Market is the largest open-air market in the southern hemisphere and attracts thousands of shoppers. It's where Melburnians sniff out fresh produce among the booming cries of spruiking fishmongers and fruit-and-veg vendors. The wonderful deli hall (with art deco features) is lined with everything from soft cheeses, wines and Polish sausages to Greek dips, truffle oil and kangaroo biltong.

Flagstaff Gardens PARK
(Map p476; William St, btwn La Trobe, Dudley & King Sts; 🚌Tourist Shuttle, 🚊24, 30, 55, City Circle, 🚉Flagstaff) Originally known as Burial Hill, these gardens were the site of Melbourne's first cemetery – eight of the city's early settlers were buried here. Today its pleasant, open lawns are popular with workers taking a lunchtime break. The gardens contain trees that are well over 100 years old, including Moreton Bay fig trees and a variety of eucalypts, including spotted gums, sugar gums and river red gums. There are plenty of possums about, but don't feed them.

THE PARIS END OF COLLINS STREET

The top end of Collins St (between Spring and Elizabeth Sts), aka the 'Paris End', is lined with plane trees, grand buildings and luxe boutiques (hence its moniker). You'll find ornate arcades leading off Collins St. The Block network, comprising Block Pl, Block Arcade and Block Ct, was named after the 19th-century pastime of 'doing the block', which referred to walking the city's fashionable area.

Koorie Heritage Trust CULTURAL CENTRE
(Map p476; ☎03-8622 2600; www.kooriehheritagetrust.com; 295 King St; admission by gold coin donation, tours $15; ⏲9am-5pm Mon-Fri; 🚊24,30, 🚆Flagstaff) Devoted to southeastern Aboriginal culture, this cultural centre displays interesting artefacts and oral history. Its gallery spaces show a variety of contemporary and traditional work, a model scar tree at the centre's heart, and a permanent chronological display of Victorian Koorie history. Behind the scenes, significant objects are carefully preserved – replicas that can be touched by visitors are used in the displays. The centre is in the process of relocating, so check the website for details.

It also runs highly recommended **tours** to Flagstaff Gardens and along the Yarra, which put the areas into context with irrevocable changes to both the people and the place. Its impact on all senses evokes memories that lie beneath the modern city. Tours are mainly for school groups, but it's normally OK to tag along; call ahead to enquire.

Another reason to visit is its shop, which sells books on Aboriginal culture, CDs, crafts and bush-food supplies.

Immigration Museum MUSEUM
(Map p476; ☎13 11 02; www.museumvictoria.com.au/immigrationmuseum; 400 Flinders St; adult/child $12/free; ⏲10am-5pm; 🚊70, 75) The Immigration Museum uses personal and community voices, images and memorabilia to tell the many stories of Australian immigration. Symbolically housed in the old Customs House, the restored building alone is worth the visit: the **Long Room** is a magnificent piece of Renaissance revival architecture.

Sea Life Melbourne Aquarium AQUARIUM
(Map p476; ☎03-9923 5999; www.melbourneaquarium.com.au; cnr Flinders & King Sts; adult/child/family $38/22/96; ⏲9.30am-6pm, last entry 5pm; 🚊70, 75) This aquarium is home to rays, gropers and sharks, all of which cruise around a 2.2-million-litre tank, watched closely by visitors in a see-through tunnel. See the penguins in icy 'Antarctica' or get up close to one of Australia's largest saltwater crocs in the crocodile lair. Divers are thrown to the sharks three times a day; for between $210 and $300 you can join them. Admission tickets are cheaper online.

St Patrick's Cathedral CHURCH
(☎03-9662 2233; www.stpatrickscathedral.org.au; cnr Gisborne St & Cathedral Pl; ⏲9am-5pm Mon-Fri; 🚊112) Head up McArthur St (the extension of Collins St) to see one of the world's largest and finest examples of Gothic Revival architecture. Designed by William Wardell, St Patrick's was named after the patron saint of Ireland, reflecting the local Catholic community's main origin. Construction began in 1863 and continued until the spires were added in 1939.

City Circle Trams TRAM
(Tram 35; ☎13 16 38; www.ptv.vic.gov.au; ⏲10am-6pm Sun-Wed, to 9pm Thu-Sat; 🚊35) FREE Designed primarily for tourists, this free tram service travels around the city centre, passing many sights along the way with an audio commentary. It runs every 10 minutes or so.

Southbank & Docklands

Southbank, once a gritty industrial site, sits directly across the Yarra from Flinders St. Behind it is the city's major arts precinct. Back down by the river, the promenade stretches to the **Crown Casino & Entertainment Complex**, a self-proclaimed 'world of entertainment', and further on to **South Wharf**, the newest development of bars and restaurants. To the city's west lies the Docklands, a mini-city of apartment buildings, offices, restaurants, plazas, public art and parkland. It's early days, but its manufactured sameness has yet to be overwritten with the organic cadences and colour of neighbourhood life.

★NGV International GALLERY
(☎03-8662 1555; www.ngv.vic.gov.au; 180 St Kilda Rd; exhibition costs vary; ⏲10am-5pm Wed-Mon; 🚆Tourist Shuttle, 🚊1, 3, 5, 6, 8, 16, 64,

67, 72) Beyond the water-wall facade you'll find an expansive collection set over three levels, covering international art that runs from the ancient to the contemporary. Key works include a Rembrandt, a Tiepolo and a Bonnard. You might also bump into a Monet, a Modigliani or a Bacon. It's also home to Picasso's *Weeping Woman*, which was the victim of an art heist in 1986. Free 45-minute tours run hourly from 11am to 2pm and alternate to different parts of the collection.

★ **Arts Centre Melbourne** ARTS CENTRE

(☎ bookings 1300 182 183; www.artscentremelbourne.com.au; 100 St Kilda Rd; ⊙ box office 9am-8.30pm Mon-Fri, 10am-5pm Sat; Tourist Shuttle, 1, 3, 5, 6, 8, 16, 64, 67, 72, Flinders St) The Arts Centre is made up of two separate buildings: **Hamer Hall** (the concert hall) and the **theatres building** (under the spire). They're linked by a series of landscaped walkways. The **George Adams Gallery** and **St Kilda Road Foyer Gallery** are free gallery spaces with changing exhibitions. In the foyer of the theatres building, pick up a self-guided booklet for a tour of art commissioned for the building, including works by Arthur Boyd, Sidney Nolan and Jeffrey Smart.

★ **Eureka Skydeck** VIEWPOINT

(Map p476; www.eurekaskydeck.com.au; 7 Riverside Quay; adult/child/family $19.50/11/44, The Edge extra $12/8/29; ⊙ 10am-10pm, last entry 9.30pm; Tourist Shuttle) Melbourne's tallest building, the 297m-high Eureka Tower, was built in 2006 and a wild elevator ride takes you to its 88th floor in less than 40 seconds (check out the photo on the elevator floor if there's time). **The Edge** – a slightly sadistic glass cube – cantilevers you out of the building; you've got no choice but to look down.

Australian Centre for Contemporary Art GALLERY

(ACCA; ☎ 03-9697 9999; www.accaonline.org.au; 111 Sturt St; ⊙ 10am-5pm Tue & Thu-Sun, to 8pm Wed; 1) FREE ACCA is one of Australia's most exciting and challenging contemporary galleries, showcasing a range of local and international artists. The building is, fittingly, sculptural, with a rusted exterior evoking the factories that once stood on the site, and a soaring interior designed to house often-massive installations. From Flinders St Station, walk across Princes Bridge and along St Kilda Rd. Turn right at Grant St, then left into Sturt St.

Polly Woodside MUSEUM

(☎ 03-9699 9760; www.pollywoodside.com.au; 2a Clarendon St; adult/child/family $16/9.50/43; ⊙ 10am-4pm Sat & Sun, daily during school holidays; 96, 109, 112) The *Polly Woodside* is a restored iron-hulled merchant ship (or 'tall ship'), dating from 1885, that now rests in a pen off the Yarra River. A glimpse of the rigging makes for a tiny reminder of what the Yarra, dense with ships at anchor, would have looked like in the 19th century.

Melbourne Star FERRIS WHEEL

(☎ 03-8688 9688; www.melbournestar.com; 101 Waterfront Way, Docklands; adult/child/family $32/19/82; ⊙ 10am-10pm; City Circle, 70, 86, Southern Cross) Originally erected in 2009, then disassembled due to structural problems before financial issues delayed it for several years more, the Melbourne Star Ferris wheel is finally turning. Joining the London Eye and Singapore Flyer, this giant observation wheel has glass cabins that take you up 120m for 360-degree views of the city, Port Philip Bay and further afield to Geelong and the Dandenongs. Rides last 30 minutes.

For an extra $8 you can head back for another ride at night to see the bright lights of the city.

East Melbourne & Richmond

East Melbourne's sedate, wide streets are lined with grand double-fronted Victorian terraces, Italianate mansions and art deco apartment blocks. Locals commute to the city on foot across the Fitzroy Gardens. During the footy season, or when a cricket match is played, the roar of the crowd shatters the calm – you're in lobbing distance of the MCG here.

MELBOURNE BIKE SHARE

Melbourne Bike Share (☎ 1300 711 590; www.melbournebikeshare.com.au) began in 2010 and has had a slow start, mainly blamed on Victoria's compulsory helmet laws. Subsidised safety helmets ($5 with a $3 refund on return) are now available at 7Eleven stores around the CBD. Each first half-hour of hire is free. Daily ($2.80) and weekly ($8) subscriptions require a credit card and $300 security deposit.

WORTH A TRIP

WILLIAMSTOWN & AROUND

Over the Westgate Bridge, the historic suburb of Williamstown is a yacht-filled gem with salty seafaring atmosphere. It has stunning views of Melbourne and a small beach on its south side if you're looking for somewhere to paddle. Historic markers around town allow for a self-directed walking tour through a bygone era.

Sights & Activities

Point Gellibrand was the site of Victoria's first white settlement, where Victoria's navy was established, and where the Timeball Tower, once used by ships to set their chronometers, was built by convict labour in 1840.

Scienceworks (☎13 11 02; www.museumvictoria.com.au/scienceworks; 2 Booker St, Spotswood; adult/child $10/free, Planetarium & Lightning Room additional adult/child $6/4.50; ⏰10am-4.30pm; 🚆Spotswood) Scienceworks will happily occupy kids' inquisitive minds for a full day with its interactive displays. It's set in three historic buildings and incorporates the **Melbourne Planetarium**. Unlock the mysteries of the universe (or your anatomy) by poking buttons, pulling levers, lifting flaps and learning all sorts of weird facts.

Seaworks (☎0417 292 021; www.seaworks.com.au; 82 Nelson Pl) The industrial Seaworks precinct comprises historic boat sheds, a maritime museum and exhibition space. It's also the headquarters for **Sea Shepherd Australia** (www.seashepherd.org.au), and on weekends you can tour its antipoaching vessels from noon to 4.30pm (when its ships are out to sea tackling Japanese whalers, it's still worth dropping by for displays and video about its antiwhaling campaign). Seaworks also has a shipbuilding yard, a pirate-themed tavern and Victoria's oldest morgue, which you can visit on a **ghost tour** (☎1300 390 119; www.lanternghosttours.com; adult/child $24/34).

Sleeping & Eating

Williamstown has plenty of historic pubs to explore, on and off the main streets.

Quest Williamstown (☎03-9393 5300; www.questwilliamstown.com.au; 1 Syme St; 1-bedroom apt from $199; 🅿📶) The excellent Quest Williamstown has self-contained apartments on the waterfront overlooking the marina. A great option if you're looking to stay somewhere outside the city centre.

Ragusa (☎03-9399 8500; www.ragusarestaurant.com.au; 139 Nelson Pl; mains $17-34; ⏰noon-3pm & 6pm-late) Ragusa is doing good things with its menu of modern Croatian in a beautful heritage building.

Jimmy Grants (www.jimmygrants.com.au; 28 Ferguson St, Williamstown; mains from $7.50) Jimmy Grants, much loved across Melbourne for its gourmet souvlakis, has recently opened a Wlliamstown outpost inside the public bar of the Hobsons Bay Hotel. It may sound like a strange mix but the beer-and-souvlaki combination is a proven winner.

Information

Hobsons Bay Visitor Information Centre (☎03-9932 4310; www.visithobsonsbay.com.au; cnr Syme St & Nelson Pl) Just back from the waterfront, the tourist office has information on local and statewide attractions.

Getting There & Away

The most popular and undoubtedly the most scenic way to get to Williamstown is by ferry – a fitting way to arrive, given the area's maritime ambience. **Williamstown Ferries** (☎03-9682 9555; www.williamstownferries.com.au; Williamstown-Southbank adult/child $18/9, return $28/14) plies Hobsons Bay daily, stopping at Southbank and visiting a number of sites along the way, including Scienceworks and Docklands. **Melbourne River Cruises** (☎03-8610 2600; www.melbcruises.com.au; Williamstown-city adult/child $22/11) also docks at Gem Pier.

Across perpetually clogged Punt Rd/ Hoddle St is the suburb of Richmond, which stretches all the way to the Yarra. Once a ragtag collection of workers' cottages inhabited by generations of labourers who toiled in the tanneries and the clothing and food-processing industries, it's now a rather genteel suburb, although it retains a fair swag of solid, regular pubs and is home to a thriving Vietnamese community along Victoria St. Running parallel with Victoria St are clothing-outlet-lined Bridge Rd and Swan St, a jumble of restaurants, shops and smart drinking holes. Richmond's main north–south thoroughfare is Church St.

★Melbourne Cricket Ground STADIUM
(MCG; ☎03-9657 8888; www.mcg.org.au; Brunton Ave; tour adult/child/family $20/10/50, with National Sports Museum $30/15/70; ⏲tours 10am-3pm; 🚌Tourist Shuttle, 🚋48, 70, 75, 🚆Jolimont or Richmond) With a capacity of 100,000 people, the 'G' is one of the world's great sporting venues, hosting cricket in the summer and AFL footy in the winter – for many Australians it's considered hallowed ground. Make it to a game if you can (highly recommended), but otherwise you can still make a pilgrimage on non-match-day **tours** that take you through the stands, media and coaches' areas, change rooms and out onto the ground (though unfortunately not beyond the boundary).

National Sports Museum MUSEUM
(☎03-9657 8856; www.nsm.org.au; MCG, Olympic Stand, Gate 3; adult/concession/family $20/10/50, with MCG tour $30/15/70; ⏲10am-5pm) Hidden away in the bowels of the Melbourne Cricket Ground, this sports museum features five permanent exhibitions focusing on Australia's favourite sports and celebrates historic sporting moments. Kids will love the interactive sports section where they can test their footy, cricket and netball (among other sports) skills.

Fitzroy Gardens PARK
(www.fitzroygardens.com; Wellington Pde, btwn Lansdowne & Albert Sts; 🚌Tourist Shuttle, 🚋75, 🚆Jolimont) The city drops away suddenly just east of Spring St, giving way to Melbourne's beautiful backyard, the Fitzroy Gardens. The stately avenues lined with English elms, flower beds, expansive lawns, strange fountains and a creek are a short stroll from town.

The highlight is **Cooks' Cottage** (☎03-9419 5766; adult/child/family $6/3/16.50; ⏲9am-5pm), shipped brick by brick from Yorkshire and reconstructed in 1934 (the cottage actually belonged to the navigator's parents). It's decorated in mid-18th-century style, with an exhibition about Captain James Cook's eventful, if controversial, voyages to the Southern Ocean.

Fitzroy & Around

Fitzroy, Melbourne's first suburb, long had a reputation for vice and squalor. Today, despite a long bout of gentrification, it's still where creative people meet up, though now it's more to 'do' lunch and blog about it before checking out the offerings at local one-off boutiques and vintage shops. It's also home to a bunch of art galleries.

Gertrude St, where once grannies feared to tread, is Melbourne's street of the moment. Smith St in Collingwood has some rough edges, though talk is more of its smart restaurants, cafes and boutiques rather than its down-and-out days of old.

Collingwood Children's Farm FARM
(www.farm.org.au; 18 St Heliers St, Abbotsford; adult/child/family $9/5/18; ⏲9.15am-4.30pm; 🚌200, 201, 207, 🚆Victoria Park) The inner city melts away at this rustic riverside retreat beloved not just by children. There's a range of frolicking farm animals that kids can help feed, as well as rambling gardens and grounds for picnicking on warm days. The farm cafe is open early and can be visited without entering the farm itself. The monthly **farmers market** (www.mfm.com.au; adult/child $2/free; ⏲8am-1pm 2nd Sat of the month), held by the river, is a local highlight, with everything from rabbits to roses to organic milk hoisted into baskets.

Carlton & United Breweries BREWERY
(☎03-9420 6800; www.carltonbrewhouse.com.au; cnr Nelson & Thompson Sts, Abbotsford; tours adult/concession $25/20; 🚋109) Foster's beer-brewing empire runs 1½-hour **tours** of its Abbotsford operations, where you'll encounter 30m-wide vats of beer and a super-fast bottling operation – and yes, samples are included in the price. Tours run Monday to Saturday; times vary so check the website. Visitors need to be aged over 18 and wearing closed-toed shoes. Bookings essential.

Centre for Contemporary Photography GALLERY
(CCP; Map p484; ☎03-9417 1549; www.ccp.org.au; 404 George St, Fitzroy; ⏲11am-6pm Wed-Fri, noon-5pm Sat & Sun; 🚋86) FREE This not-for-profit centre has a changing schedule of

Fitzroy & Around

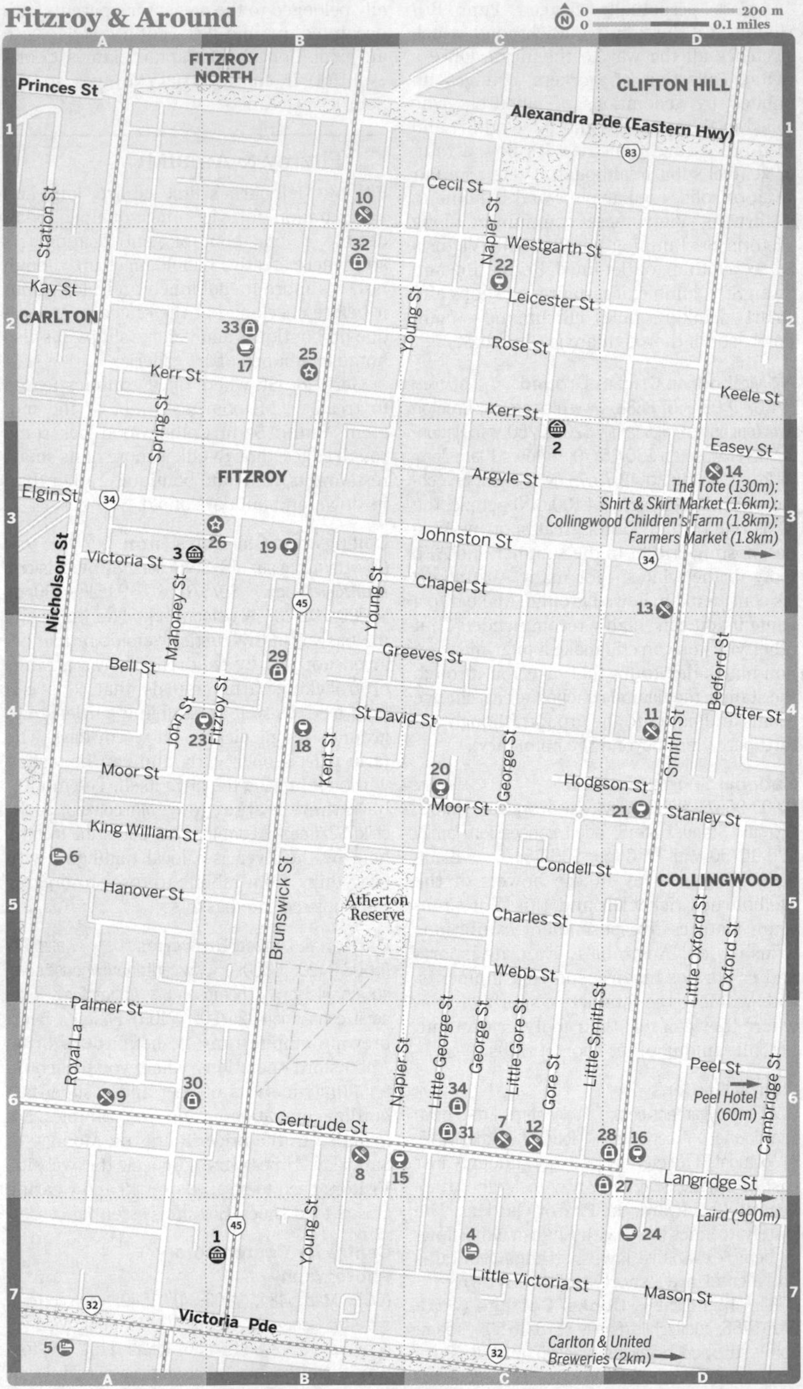

Fitzroy & Around

Sights
1 Alcaston Gallery B7
2 Centre for Contemporary Photography C3
3 Gallery Gabrielle Pizzi A3

Sleeping
4 Brooklyn Arts Hotel C7
5 Home@The Mansion A7
6 Nunnery A5

Eating
7 Añada C6
8 Charcoal Lane B6
9 Cutler & Co A6
10 Hammer & Tong 412 .... B1
11 Jimmy Grants D4
12 Moon Under Water C6
13 Po' Boy Quarter D3
14 Robert Burns Hotel D3

Drinking & Nightlife
15 Everleigh B6
16 Forester's Hall D6
17 Industry Beans B2
18 Little Creatures Dining Hall B4
19 Naked for Satan B3
20 Napier Hotel C4
21 Panama Dining Room D5
22 Rose C2
23 Standard A4
24 Storm in a Teacup D7

Entertainment
25 Evelyn Hotel B2
26 Old Bar B3

Shopping
27 Aesop D6
28 Crumpler D6
29 Gorman B4
30 Little Salon A6
31 Mud Australia C6
32 Poison City Records B2
33 Rose Street Artists' Market B2
34 Third Drawer Down C6

photography exhibitions across a couple of galleries. Shows traverse traditional technique and the highly conceptual. There's a particular fascination with work involving video projection, including a nightly after-hours screening in a window. Also offers photography courses.

Alcaston Gallery GALLERY
(Map p484; ☎03-9418 6444; www.alcastongallery.com.au; 11 Brunswick St, Fitzroy; ⏰10am-6pm Tue-Fri, 11am-5pm Sat; 🚋112) FREE Set in an imposing boom-style terrace, the Alcaston's focus is on living Indigenous Australian artists. The gallery works directly with Indigenous communities and is particularly attentive to cultural sensitivities. It shows a wide range of styles, from traditional to contemporary work. There's also a space dedicated to works on paper.

Gallery Gabrielle Pizzi GALLERY
(Map p484; ☎03-9416 4170; www.gabriellepizzi.com.au; 51 Victoria St, Fitzroy; ⏰10am-5pm Wed-Fri, noon-6pm Sat; 🚋11, 96, 112) FREE Gabrielle Pizzi, one of Australia's most respected dealers of Indigenous art, founded this gallery in the 1980s. Her daughter Samantha continues to show contemporary city-based artists, as well as traditional artists from the communities of Balgo Hills, Papunya, Maningrida and the Tiwi Islands.

Carlton & Around

Carlton is the traditional home of Melbourne's Italian community, so you'll see the *tricolori* unfurled with characteristic passion come soccer finals and the Formula One Grand Prix. The heady mix of intellectual activity, espresso and phenomenal food lured bohemians to the area in the 1950s. By the 1970s it was the centre of the city's burgeoning counterculture scene and has produced some of the city's most legendary theatre, music and literature.

★ **Melbourne Museum** MUSEUM
(Map p486; ☎13 11 02; www.museumvictoria.com.au; 11 Nicholson St, Carlton; adult $12, child & student free, exhibitions extra; ⏰10am-5pm; 🚋Tourist Shuttle, 🚋City Circle, 86, 96, 🚉Parliament) This museum provides a grand sweep of Victoria's natural and cultural histories, with exhibitions covering everything from dinosaur fossils and giant squid specimens to a taxidermy hall, a 3D volcano and an open-air forest atrium of Victorian flora. Become immersed in the legend of champion racehorse and national hero Phar Lap. The excellent **Bunjilaka**, on the ground floor, presents Indigenous Australian stories and history told through objects and Aboriginal voices with state-of-the-art technology. There's also an **IMAX cinema** on site.

Carlton & Around

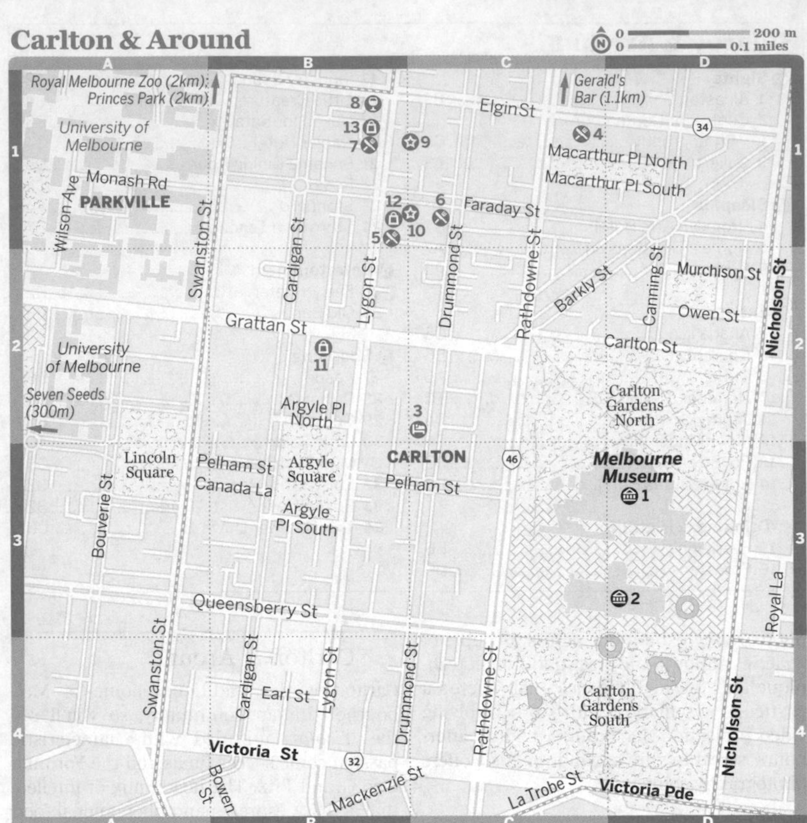

Royal Exhibition Building HISTORIC BUILDING (Map p486; ☎13 11 02; www.museumvictoria.com.au/reb; 9 Nicholson St, Carlton; tours adult/child $10/7; Tourist Shuttle, City Circle, 86, 96, Parliament) Built for the International Exhibition in 1880, and granted Unesco World Heritage status in 2004, this beautiful Victorian edifice symbolises the glory days of the Industrial Revolution, the British Empire and 19th-century Melbourne's economic supremacy. It was the first building to fly the Australian flag, and Australia's first parliament sat here in 1901. It now hosts everything from trade fairs to car shows. Tours of the building leave from the Melbourne Museum at 2pm.

Royal Melbourne Zoo ZOO (☎03-9285 9300; www.zoo.org.au; Elliott Ave, Parkville; adult/child $30/13.20, children free on weekends & holidays; 9am-5pm; 505, 55, Royal Park) Established in 1861, this is the oldest zoo in Australia and the third oldest in the world. Today it's one of the city's most popular attractions. Set in spacious, prettily landscaped gardens, the zoo's enclosures aim to simulate the animals' natural habitats. There's also a large collection of native animals in natural bush settings, a platypus aquarium, a fine butterfly house, fur seals, elephants, lions, tigers and plenty of reptiles.

South Yarra, Prahran & Windsor

These neighbourhoods have always been synonymous with glitz and glamour, with their elevated aspect and large allotments considered prestigious. Access from the city centre to South Yarra was by boat or punt – hence Punt Rd – before Princes Bridge was built in 1850.

Carlton & Around

Top Sights
1 Melbourne Museum D3

Sights
2 Royal Exhibition Building D3

Sleeping
3 169 Drummond C2

Eating
4 Abla's C1
5 D.O.C Delicatessen B1
D.O.C Espresso ....(see 5)
6 DOC Pizzeria C1
7 Tiamo B1

Drinking & Nightlife
8 Jimmy Watson's B1

Entertainment
9 Cinema Nova C1
10 La Mama C1

Shopping
11 Eastern Market B2
12 Gewürzhaus B1
13 Readings B1

★Royal Botanic Gardens GARDENS
(www.rbg.vic.gov.au; Birdwood Ave, South Yarra; 7.30am-sunset, Children's Garden open Wed-Sun, closed mid-Jul–mid-Sep; Tourist Shuttle, 1, 3, 5, 6, 8, 16, 64, 67, 72) FREE One of the world's finest botanic gardens, the Royal Botanical Gardens are one of Melbourne's most glorious attractions. Sprawling beside the Yarra River, the beautifully designed gardens feature a global selection of plantings and specifically endemic Australian flora. Mini-ecosystems, such as a cacti and succulents area, a herb garden and an indigenous rainforest, are set amid vast lawns. Take a book, picnic or Frisbee – but most importantly, take your time.

Shrine of Remembrance MONUMENT
(www.shrine.org.au; Birdwood Ave, South Yarra; 10am-5pm; Tourist Shuttle, 1, 3, 5, 6, 8, 16, 64, 67, 72) FREE Beside St Kilda Rd stands the massive Shrine of Remembrance, built as a memorial to Victorians killed in WWI. It was constructed between 1928 and 1934, much of it with Depression-relief, or 'susso', labour. Its bombastic classical design is partly based on the Mausoleum of Halicarnassus, one of the seven ancient wonders of the world. Visible from the other end of town, planning regulations continue to restrict any building that would obstruct the view of the shrine from Swanston St as far back as Lonsdale St.

St Kilda & Around

Come to St Kilda for the sea breezes, its seedy history and a bit of good ol' people watching. St Kilda was once a playground full of dance halls, a fun park, an ice-skating rink, theatres, sea baths and gardens. Now its art deco apartments fetch astronomical real estate prices. On weekends the volume is turned up, the traffic crawls and the street-party atmosphere sets in. It's still a neighbourhood of extreme, and often exhilarating, contrasts: backpacker hostels sit beside fine-dining restaurants, and souvlaki bars next to designer shops.

St Kilda Foreshore BEACH
(Map p490; Jacka Blvd; 16, 96) While there are palm-fringed promenades, a parkland strand and a long stretch of sand, St Kilda's seaside appeal is more Brighton, England, than *Baywatch,* despite 20-odd years of glitzy development. The kiosk at the end of **St Kilda Pier** (an exact replica of the original, which burnt down in 2003, a year short of its centenary) is as much about the journey as the destination.

Luna Park AMUSEMENT PARK
(Map p490; 03-9525 5033; www.lunapark.com.au; 18 Lower Esplanade, St Kilda; single ride adult/child $11/9, unlimited rides $49/39; 16, 96) It opened in 1912 and still retains the feel of an old-style amusement park, with creepy Mr Moon's gaping mouth swallowing you up as you enter. There's a heritage-listed scenic railway (the world's oldest operating roller coaster) and a beautifully baroque carousel with hand-painted horses, swans and chariots, as well as the full complement of gut-churning rides.

South Melbourne, Port Melbourne & Albert Park

There's something boastful about these suburbs, and it runs along the lines of being close to Melbourne's watery highlights: the bay, the beach and expansive Albert Park Lake. These are upmarket suburbs rejoicing in their peaceful environment (though come Grand Prix time, the noise is ramped up big time).

South Yarra, Prahran & Windsor

0 — 400 m
0 — 0.2 miles

Corner Hotel (1km)
Moonlight Cinema (850m); Royal Botanic Gardens (1km); Sidney Myer Music Bowl (1.4km)
The Tan (400m); Shrine of Remembrance (1.4km)
Art Series (The Blackman) (800m); Albert Park Lake (2km)

CREMORNE
RICHMOND
Herring Island Park
CityLink (Monash Fwy)
Yarra River
Como Park
SOUTH YARRA
TOORAK
PRAHRAN
WINDSOR
ST KILDA
Princes Gardens
Victoria Gardens

South Yarra
Hawksburn
Prahran
Windsor

Misschu
Exchange Bar
Art Series (The Cullen)
HuTong Dumpling Bar

Punt Rd
Cubitt St
Green St
Church St
Brighton St
Mary St
Caroline St
Williams Rd North
Verdant Ave
Alexandra Ave
Domain Rd
Avoca St
Murphy St
Darling St
Yarra St
Claremont St
Malcolm St
River St
Tivoli Rd
Rockley Rd
Kensington Rd
Como Ave
Lechlade Ave
Williams Rd
Bruce St
Washington St
Caroline St S
Powell St
Davis St
William St
Chambers St
Toorak Rd
Oxford St
Clara St
Alexandra St
Lang St
Arthur St
Palermo St
Hawksburn Rd
Fawkner St
Osborne St
Portland Pl
Phoenix St
Fitzgerald St
Garden St
Cassell St
Albion St
Moore St
Cliff St
Argo St
Hardy St
Balmoral St
Grosvenor St
Chapel St
Barry St
Surrey Rd
Cromwell Rd
Motherwell St
Joy St
Howitt St
McKillop St
May Rd
Commercial Rd
Malvern Rd
Little Chapel St
Essex St
Moss St
Porter St
Grattan St
Izett St
Greville St
Clarke St
Lorne Rd
Perth St
Charles St
King St
Mackay St
Murray St
Spring St
Wrights Tce
Clifton St
Mount St
Bangs St
York St
Lewisham Rd N
Pridham St
Bayview St
Aberdeen Rd
Andrew St
Raleigh St
High St
Upton Rd
Green St
Eastbourne St
Earl St
Duke St
Hornby St
The Avenue
Lewisham Rd
Newry St
Union St
Henry St
Peel St
Albert St
Dandenong Rd
Wellington St
Chomley St

South Melbourne Market MARKET
(www.southmelbournemarket.com.au; cnr Coventry & Cecil Sts, South Melbourne; 8am-4pm Wed, Sat & Sun, to 5pm Fri; 96) The market's labyrinthine interior is packed to overflowing with an eccentric collection of stalls ranging from old-school to boutique. It's been on this site since 1864 and is a neighbourhood institution, as are its famous dim sims (sold here since 1949). There are plenty of atmospheric eateries and a lively night market on Thursdays from mid-January to early March. There's a cooking school, too – see the website for details.

Albert Park Lake LAKE
(btwn Queens Rd, Fitzroy St, Aughtie Dr & Albert Rd; 96) Elegant black swans give their inimitable bottoms-up salute as you jog, cycle or walk the 5km perimeter of this constructed lake. Lakeside Dr was used as an international motor-racing circuit in the 1950s, and since 1996 the revamped track has been the venue for the **Australian Formula One Grand Prix** each March. Also on the periphery is the **Melbourne Sports & Aquatic Centre**, with an Olympic-size pool and child-delighting wave machine.

Activities

Kayak Melbourne KAYAKING
(0418 106 427; www.kayakmelbourne.com.au; tours $72-117; 11, 31, 48) Don't miss the chance to see the Yarra River by kayak. These two-hour tours take you past Melbourne's newest city developments and explain the history of the older ones. Moonlight tours are most evocative and include a dinner of fish and chips. Tours usually depart from Victoria Harbour, Docklands – check the website for directions.

Cycling

Cycling maps are available from the visitor centre in Federation Sq. The urban series includes the Main Yarra Trail (35km), off which runs the Merri Creek Trail (19km), the Outer Circle Trail (34km) and the Maribyrnong River Trail (22km). There are also paths taking you along Melbourne's beaches.

Humble Vintage BICYCLE RENTAL
(0432 032 450; www.thehumblevintage.com; 2hr/day/week $25/35/90) Get yourself a set of special wheels from this collection of retro racers, city bikes and ladies' bikes. Rates include a lock, helmet and a terrific map with plenty of ideas about what to do with your non-bike-riding hours. Check the website for pickup locations.

Running

The Tan RUNNING
(Royal Botanical Gardens, Birdwood Ave; Tourist Shuttle, 8) A 3.8km-long former horse-exercising track is now the city's most popular running spot. It surrounds the Royal Botanical Gardens and King's Domain.

Princes Park RUNNING
(Princes Park Dr, North Carlton; 19) Joggers and walkers pound the 3.2km gravel path around the perimeter of the park, while cricket and soccer games and dog walking fill up the centre. It's the former home of the Carlton Football Club (and its current training ground).

Swimming

In summer, do as most Melburnians do and hit the sand at one of the city's metropolitan beaches. St Kilda, Middle Park and Port Melbourne are popular patches, with suburban beaches at Brighton and Sandringham. Public pools are also well loved.

Melbourne City Baths SWIMMING
(Map p476; 03-9663 5888; www.melbourne.vic.gov.au/melbournecitybaths; 420 Swanston St, Melbourne; adult/child $6.10/3.60; 6am-10pm Mon-Thu, to 8pm Fri, 8am-6pm Sat & Sun; Melbourne Central) The City Baths were literally public baths when they first opened in 1860 and were intended to stop people bathing in and drinking from the seriously polluted Yarra River. They now boast the city centre's largest pool (30m), plus you can do your laps in a 1903 heritage-listed building.

Melbourne Sports & Aquatic Centre SWIMMING
(MSAC; 03-9926 1555; www.msac.com.au; Albert Rd, Albert Park; adult/child $7.40/5.20; 5.30am-10pm Mon-Fri, 7am-8pm Sat & Sun; 96, 112) Has a fantastic indoor 50m pool, wave pool, water slides, spa-sauna-steam room and spacious common areas, on the shore of Albert Park Lake.

Windsurfing, Kiteboarding & Stand-Up Paddle Boarding

Kiteboarding has a fast-emerging scene around St Kilda between November and April. Elwood, just south of St Kilda, is a popular sailboarding area.

St Kilda

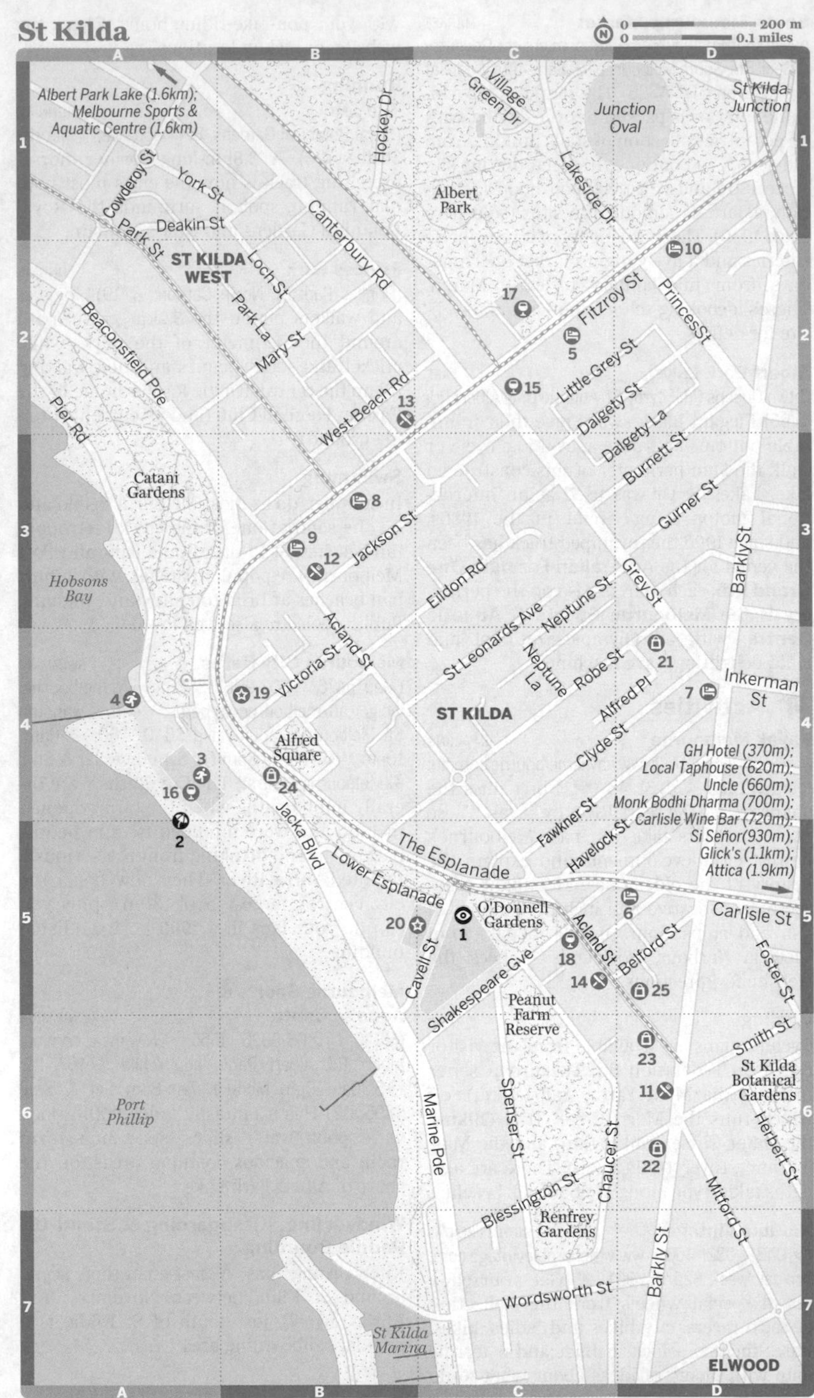

0 200 m
0 0.1 miles
Albert Park Lake (1.6km); Melbourne Sports & Aquatic Centre (1.6km)
St Kilda Junction
Junction Oval
Village Green Dr
Hockey Dr
Lakeside Dr
Albert Park
Cowderoy St
York St
Deakin St
Park St
ST KILDA WEST
Loch St
Canterbury Rd
Park La
Mary St
Beaconsfield Pde
Fitzroy St
Princes St
Little Grey St
Dalgety St
Dalgety La
Burnett St
Gurner St
West Beach Rd
Pier Rd
Catani Gardens
Jackson St
Eildon Rd
Hobsons Bay
Acland St
Victoria St
St Leonards Ave
Neptune St
Grey St
Barkly St
Neptune La
Robe St
Alfred Pl
Inkerman St
ST KILDA
Clyde St
Alfred Square
GH Hotel (370m); Local Taphouse (620m); Uncle (660m); Monk Bodhi Dharma (700m); Carlisle Wine Bar (720m); Si Señor (930m); Glick's (1.1km); Attica (1.9km)
Jacka Blvd
Fawkner St
Havelock St
The Esplanade
Lower Esplanade
O'Donnell Gardens
Carlisle St
Belford St
Foster St
Cavell St
Shakespeare Gve
Peanut Farm Reserve
Smith St
St Kilda Botanical Gardens
Port Phillip
Marine Pde
Spenser St
Chaucer St
Herbert St
Mitford St
Blessington St
Renfrey Gardens
Wordsworth St
St Kilda Marina
ELWOOD

St Kilda

Sights
1 Luna Park ... C5
2 St Kilda Foreshore ... A5

Activities, Courses & Tours
Aurora Spa Retreat ... (see 9)
3 Kite Republic ... A4
4 Stand Up Paddle HQ ... A4

Sleeping
5 Adina Apartment Hotel St Kilda ... C2
6 Base ... D5
7 Hotel Barkly ... D4
8 Hotel Urban ... B3
9 Prince ... B3
10 Ritz ... D2

Eating
11 Claypots ... D6
12 Lau's Family Kitchen ... B3
13 Mirka's at Tolarno ... B2
14 Monarch Cake Shop ... C5

Drinking & Nightlife
15 George Lane Bar ... C2
Hotel Barkly ... (see 7)
16 Republica ... A4
17 St Kilda Bowling Club ... C2
18 Vineyard ... C5

Entertainment
19 Esplanade Hotel ... B4
20 Palais Theatre ... C5
Prince Bandroom ... (see 9)

Shopping
21 Bookhouse ... D4
22 Dot Herbey ... D6
23 Eclectico ... D6
24 Esplanade Market ... B4
25 Readings ... D5

Stand Up Paddle HQ WATER SPORTS
(Map p490; ☎0416 184 994; www.supb.com.au; St Kilda Pier; hire per hr $30, 2hr tour $89; 🚋96) Arrange a lesson, hire SUP equipment, or join a Yarra River tour.

Kite Republic KITESURFING
(Map p490; ☎03-9537 0644; www.kiterepublic.com.au; St Kilda Seabaths, 4/10-18 Jacka Blvd; 1hr lesson $90; ⊙10am-7pm) Offers kiteboarding lessons, tours and equipment; also a good source of info. In winter it can arrange snow-kiting at Mt Hotham. Also rents SUPs and Street SUPs.

Tours

Melbourne By Foot WALKING TOUR
(☎0418 394 000; www.melbournebyfoot.com; tours $40; 🚉Flinders St) Take a few hours out and experience a mellow, informative 4km walking tour that covers lane art, politics, Melbourne's history and diversity. Tours include a refreshment break. There's also the enticing Beer Lovers' Guide to Melbourne. Highly recommended; book online.

Aboriginal Heritage Walk CULTURAL TOUR
(☎03-9252 2300; www.rbg.vic.gov.au; adult/child $25/10; ⊙11am Sun-Thu; 🚌Tourist Shuttle, 🚋8) The Royal Botanic Gardens are on a traditional camping and meeting place of the original Indigenous owners, and this tour takes you through their story – from songlines to plant lore, all in 90 fascinating minutes. The tour departs from the visitor centre.

Melbourne Street Art Tours WALKING TOUR
(☎03-9328 5556; www.melbournestreettours.com; tours $69; ⊙1.30pm Tue, Thu & Sat) Three-hour tours exploring the street-art side of Melbourne. The tour guides are street artists themselves, so you'll get a good insight into this art form.

St Kilda Music Walking Tours WALKING TOUR
(SKMWT; www.skmwt.com.au; tours $40; ⊙weekends) Take a walk on the wild side with this rock 'n' roll tour that takes in the infamous bars and landmarks that played starring roles in St Kilda's underground music scene. As you're led by St Kilda music icons, including Fred Negro and Fiona Lee Maynard, expect a hilarious and lewd behind-the-scenes tour of what makes St Kilda so great.

Real Melbourne Bike Tours BICYCLE TOUR
(Map p476; ☎0417 339 203; www.rentabike.net.au/biketours; Federation Sq; 4hr tour incl lunch adult/child $110/79; ⊙10am; 🚉Flinders St) These bike tours allow you to cover more ground on a well-thought-out itinerary that provides a local's insight to Melbourne, with a foodie focus. Rents bikes, too.

Hidden Secrets Tours WALKING TOUR
(☎03-9663 3358; www.hiddensecretstours.com; tours $29-150) Offers a variety of walking tours covering subjects such as lanes and arcades, wine, architecture, coffee and cafes, and vintage Melbourne.

Melbourne Visitor Shuttle BUS TOUR
(Tourist Shuttle; www.thatsmelbourne.com.au; daily ticket $5, children under 10 free; ⌚9.30am-4.30pm) This bus runs a 1½-hour round-trip route, with audio commentary and 13 stops that take passengers to all of Melbourne's main sights.

Melbourne River Cruises BOAT TOUR
(Map p476; ☎03-9681 3284; www.melbcruises.com.au; Federation Wharf; adult/child from $23/11) Take a one-hour cruise upstream or downstream along the Yarra River, or a 2½-hour return cruise, departing from a couple of locations – check for details. It also operates a ferry between Southgate and Gem Pier in Williamstown, sailing three to nine times daily, depending on the season.

Festivals & Events

Australian Open SPORTS
(www.australianopen.com; National Tennis Centre) The world's top tennis players and huge merry-making crowds descend for Australia's Grand Slam tennis championship in January.

Midsumma Festival GAY & LESBIAN
(www.midsumma.org.au) Melbourne's annual gay-and-lesbian arts festival features more than 100 events from mid-January to mid-February, with a Pride March finale.

Chinese New Year CULTURAL
(www.chinatownmelbourne.com.au; Little Bourke St) Melbourne has celebrated the lunar new year in February since Little Bourke St became Chinatown in the 1860s.

White Night CULTURAL
(whitenightmelbourne.com.au) Melbourne's annual all-night event, held in February, where the city is illuminated in colourful projections, forming a backdrop to free art, music and film.

MELBOURNE FOR CHILDREN

Collingwood Children's Farm (p483)
ACMI (p474)
Luna Park (p487)
Royal Melbourne Zoo (p486)
National Sports Museum (p483)
Melbourne Museum (p485)
Scienceworks (p482)

St Kilda Festival MUSIC
(www.stkildafestival.com.au; Acland & Fitzroy Sts) This week-long festival in February ends in a suburb-wide street party on the final Sunday.

Melbourne Food & Wine Festival FOOD
(www.melbournefoodandwine.com.au) Market tours, wine tastings, cooking classes and presentations by celeb chefs take place at venues across the city (and state) in March.

Moomba CULTURAL
(www.thatsmelbourne.com.au; Alexandra Gardens) A waterside festival famous locally for its wacky Birdman Rally, where competitors launch themselves into the Yarra in home-made flying machines. Held in March.

Australian Formula One Grand Prix SPORTS
(☎1800 100 030; www.grandprix.com.au; Albert Park; tickets from $55) The 5.3km street circuit around the normally tranquil Albert Park Lake is known for its smooth, fast surface. The buzz, both on the streets and in your ears, takes over Melbourne for four days of rev-head action in March.

Melbourne International Comedy Festival COMEDY
(www.comedyfestival.com.au; Melbourne Town Hall) An enormous range of local and international comic talent hits town in March/April with four weeks of laughs.

Melbourne Jazz JAZZ
(www.melbournejazz.com) International jazz cats head to town in May/June and join locals for gigs at Hamer Hall, the Regent Theatre and the Palms at Crown Casino.

Melbourne International Film Festival FILM
(MIFF; miff.com.au) Midwinter movie love-in in July and August brings out black-skivvy-wearing cinephiles in droves.

Melbourne Writers Festival LITERATURE
(www.mwf.com.au) Yes, Melbourne is a Unesco city of literature and it's proud of its writers and, indeed, readers. Beginning in the last week of August, the Writers Festival features forums and events at various venues.

AFL Grand Final SPORTS
(www.afl.com.au; MCG) It's easier to kick a goal from the boundary line than to pick up tickets to September's grand final, but it's not hard to get your share of finals fever anywhere in Melbourne (particularly at pubs).

Melbourne Fringe Festival ART
(www.melbournefringe.com.au) The Fringe showcases experimental theatre, music and visual arts from September to October.

Melbourne International Arts Festival ART
(www.melbournefestival.com.au) Held at various venues around the city in October, this festival features a thought-provoking program of Australian and international theatre, opera, dance, visual art and music.

Melbourne Cup SPORTS
(www.springracingcarnival.com.au) Culminating in the prestigious Melbourne Cup, the Spring Racing Carnival is as much a social event as a sporting one. The Cup, held on the first Tuesday in November, is a public holiday in Melbourne.

Boxing Day Test SPORTS
(www.mcg.org.au; MCG) Boxing Day is day one of Melbourne's annually scheduled international Test cricket match, drawing out the cricket fans. Expect some shenanigans from Bay 13.

INDIGENOUS MELBOURNE

Sights

Bunjilaka Aboriginal Cultural Centre (p485) At the Melbourne Museum

Koorie Heritage Trust (p480)

Aboriginal Heritage Walk (p491)

Birrarung Marr (p474)

Alcaston Gallery (p485)

Gallery Gabrielle Pizzi (p485)

Ian Potter Centre: NGV Australia (p471)

Eating

Charcoal Lane (p500)

Media

➡ Melbourne radio station 3KND (Kool n Deadly; 1503AM)

➡ NITV, a nationwide television station featuring all-Indigenous content.

Sleeping

Central Melbourne

There are a lot of places across all price ranges that will put you in the heart of the action, whether you've come to town to shop, party, catch a match or take in some culture.

★ **Space Hotel** HOSTEL, HOTEL $
(Map p476; ☎03-9662 3888; www.spacehotel.com.au; 380 Russell St; dm/s/d without bathroom from $29/77/93; ❄@📶; 🚊City Circle, 24, 30) One of Melbourne's few genuine flashpackers, this sleek, modern and immaculate hotel has something for all demographics, all at very reasonable prices. Rooms have iPod docks and flat-screen TVs, while dorms have thoughtful touches such as large lockers equipped with sensor lights and lockable adapters. A few doubles have en suites and balconies.

Melbourne Central YHA HOSTEL $
(Map p476; ☎03-9621 2523; www.yha.com.au; 562 Flinders St; dm/d $34/100; @📶; 🚊70) This heritage building has been totally transformed by the YHA gang with a recent overhaul making it even better. Expect a lively reception, handsome rooms, and kitchens and common areas on each of the four levels. Entertainment's high on the agenda, and there's a fab restaurant called Bertha Brown on the ground floor and a grand rooftop area.

Nomad's Melbourne HOSTEL $
(Map p476; ☎03-9328 4383; www.nomadshostels.com; 198 A'Beckett St; dm $20-45, d $100-145; P@📶; 🚊Flagstaff) Flashpacking hits Melbourne's city centre with this smart hostel boasting a mix of four- to 14-bed dorms (some with en suite) and spacious doubles. There's a rooftop area with BBQ, cinema lounge, bar and plenty of gloss (especially in the females-only wing).

City Centre Budget Hotel HOTEL $
(Map p476; ☎03-9654 5401; www.citycentrebudgethotel.com.au; 22 Little Collins St; d with shared/private bathroom from $79/94; @📶; 🚊Parliament) Intimate, independent and inconspicuous, this 38-room budget hotel is a find. It's located at the city's prettier end, up some stairs inside an unassuming building. Rooms are no-frills yet neat and tidy, staff are ultra-friendly and there's free wi-fi, a laundry and communal kitchen on the pebbled rooftop.

Greenhouse Backpacker HOSTEL $
(Map p476; ☎03-9639 6400; www.greenhousebackpacker.com.au; 6/228 Flinders Lane; dm/s/d incl breakfast from $37/80/90; ❄@📶; 🚊Flinders St) Greenhouse has a fun vibe

and is extremely well run – they know what keeps backpackers content. This includes free wi-fi, free rooftop BBQs, huge communal spaces, luggage storage and activities. There's also chatty, helpful staff and spic-and-span facilities. A five-minute walk from Flinders Street Station.

★Adina Apartment Hotel APARTMENT **$$**
(Map p476; ☎03-8663 0000; www.adinahotels.com.au; 88 Flinders St; apt from $141; P ❄ 📶; 🚊City Circle, 70, 75) Quintessential Melbourne, these designer, cool monochromatic warehouse-style loft apartments are extra large and luxurious. Ask for one at the front for amazing parkland views or get glimpses into Melbourne's lanes from the giant polished-floorboard studios, all with full kitchens. Also has apartments in **St Kilda** (Map p490; ☎03-9536 0000; 157 Fitzroy St, St Kilda; apt from $139) overlooking Albert Park.

Alto Hotel on Bourke HOTEL **$$**
(Map p476; ☎03-8608 5500; www.altohotel.com.au; 636 Bourke St; r from $166; P ❄ @ 📶; 🚊86, 96) 🍃 Environment-minded Alto has water-saving showers, energy-efficient lights and double-glazed windows, and in-room recycling is encouraged. Rooms are also well equipped, with good light and neutral decoration. Apartments (but not studios) have full kitchens and multiple LCD TVs, and some have spas. Freebies include organic espresso coffee, apples and access to a massage room. Guests can use an electric car for $17 per hour.

Pensione Hotel HOTEL **$$**
(Map p476; ☎03-9621 3333; www.pensione.com.au; 16 Spencer St; r from $114; P ❄ @ 📶; 🚊96, 109, 112) With refreshing honesty, the lovely, boutique Pensione Hotel names some rooms as 'shoebox' and 'matchbox' – but what you don't get in size is more than made up for in spot-on style, room extras and super-reasonable rates.

Hotel Causeway HOTEL **$$**
(Map p476; ☎03-9660 8888; www.causeway.com.au; 275 Little Collins St; r from $139; ❄ @ 📶; 🚊86, 96) With a discreet entrance in the Howey Place covered arcade, Causeway will appeal to those who've come to Melbourne to shop and bar hop. It's intimate in scale, so don't expect the facilities of a big hotel. Rooms are boutiquey and feature luxurious linen, robes and slippers.

Robinsons in the City BOUTIQUE HOTEL **$$**
(Map p476; ☎03-9329 2552; www.ritc.com.au; 405 Spencer St; r from $149; P ❄ 📶; 🚊75, 96) Robinsons is a gem, with six large rooms and warm service. The building is a former bakery, dating from 1850, but it's been given a modern, eclectic look. Bathrooms are not in the rooms; each room has its own in the hall. Service is warm and personal, and repeat visits are common.

Vibe Savoy Hotel HOTEL **$$**
(Map p476; ☎03-9622 8888; www.vibehotels.com.au; 630 Little Collins St; r from $101; ❄ @ 📶; 🚆Southern Cross) This lovely heritage building at Collins St's western end (opposite Southern Cross Station) has been given a bold makeover, though some rooms retain subtle period features. It's a concoction of traditional hotel comforts, bright colours and contemporary furnishings.

★Ovolo BOUTIQUE HOTEL **$$$**
(Map p476; ☎03-8692 0777; www.ovologroup.com; 19 Little Bourke St; r incl breakfast from $215; P ❄ @ 📶; 🚆Parliament) Melbourne's newest boutique hotel mixes hipster chic with a funky executive vibe. It's friendly, fun and loaded with goodies – there's a free minibar in each room, and free booze downstairs at the daily happy hour. Throw in a 'goodie bag' on arrival, Nespresso machine in the lobby and Le Patisserie breakfast pastries and you'll be wanting to move in permanently.

Adelphi Hotel HOTEL **$$$**
(Map p476; ☎03-8080 8888; www.adelphi.com.au; 187 Flinders Lane; r from $275; ❄ @ 📶 🏊; 🚊3, 5, 6, 16, 64, 67, 72) This discreet Flinders Lane property was one of Australia's first boutique hotels, and it's still rock 'n' roll. It's had a five-star makeover and its cosy rooms have a distinctly glam European feel with design touches throughout. Thankfully its iconic rooftop pool, which juts out over Flinders Lane, remains.

Hotel Lindrum BOUTIQUE HOTEL **$$$**
(Map p476; ☎03-9668 1111; www.hotellindrum.com.au; 26 Flinders St; r from $275; P ❄ 📶; 🚊70, 75) One of the city's most attractive hotels, this was once the snooker hall of the legendary and literally unbeatable Walter Lindrum. Expect rich tones, subtle lighting and tactile fabrics. Spring for a deluxe room and you'll snare either arch or bay windows and marvellous Melbourne views. And yes,

there's a billiard table – one of Lindrum's originals, no less.

Crown Metropol HOTEL $$$

(☎03-9292 6211; www.crownhotels.com.au; Crown Casino, 8 Whiteman St; r from $280; ❄@📶🏊; 🚋96, 109, 112) The most boutique of Crown's hotels, guests here have access to the most extraordinary infinity pool in Melbourne, with 270-degree views over the city to the Dandenongs in the distance. The beautifully appointed luxe twin rooms are the least expensive on offer and sleep four.

Hotel Windsor HOTEL $$$

(Map p476; ☎03-9633 6000; www.thehotelwindsor.com.au; 111 Spring St; r from $200; ❄@; 🚆Parliament) Sparkling chandeliers and a grand piano in the lobby set the scene for this opulent, heritage-listed 1883 building that's one of Australia's most famous and self-consciously grand hotels. It was still awaiting a controversial $260 million redevelopment at time of research. Adding to its English quaintness is high tea service (p506) and the historic Cricketers Bar, decked out in cricketing memorabilia.

East Melbourne & Fitzroy

East Melbourne takes you out of the action, yet is still walking distance from the city and offers ready access to the MCG. Vibrant Fitzroy hums with attractions day and night, and is a walk away from the city.

★**Nunnery** HOSTEL $

(Map p484; ☎03-9419 8637; www.nunnery.com.au; 116 Nicholson St, Fitzroy; dm/s/d incl breakfast from $32/90/120; @📶; 🚋96) Built in 1888, the Nunnery oozes atmosphere, with sweeping staircases and many original features – the walls are dripping with religious works of art and ornate stained-glass windows. You'll be giving thanks for the big comfortable lounges and communal areas. Next door to the main building is the Nunnery Guesthouse, which has larger rooms in a private setting (from $130). It's perennially popular, so book ahead.

Home@The Mansion HOSTEL $

(Map p484; ☎03-9663 4212; www.homehostels.com.au; 80 Victoria Pde, East Melbourne; dm $25-36, d $80-99; @📶; 🚋City Circle, 30, 96, 🚆Parliament) Located within a grand, heritage Salvation Army building, this is one of Melbourne's few hostels with genuine character.

WORTH A TRIP

HEIDE MUSEUM OF MODERN ART

The former home of notable locals John and Sunday Reed **Heide Museum of Modern Art** (☎03-9850 1500; www.heide.com.au; 7 Templestowe Rd, Bulleen; adult/child $16/free; ⏲10am-5pm Tue-Sun; 🚌903, 🚆Heidelberg) is a large public art gallery with wonderful grounds. It holds regularly changing exhibitions, many of which include works by the artists that called Heide home, including Sidney Nolan and Albert Tucker. There's an excellent on-site **cafe** or grab a lunch box or picnic hamper to dine by the Yarra. The free tours (2pm) are a great introduction to Melbourne's early painting scene.

It has 92 dorm beds and a couple of doubles, all of which are light and bright and have lovely high ceilings. There are two small TV areas with gaming console, a courtyard out the front and a sunny kitchen.

Brooklyn Arts Hotel BOUTIQUE HOTEL $$

(Map p484; ☎03-9419 9328; www.brooklynartshotel.com.au; 48-50 George St, Fitzroy; s/d incl breakfast from $115/155; 📶; 🚋86) There are seven very different rooms in this character-filled and very unique hotel. Owner Maggie has put the call out for artistic people and they've responded by staying, so expect lively conversation around the continental breakfast. Rooms vary in size, but all are clean, quirky, colourful and beautifully decorated; one even houses a piano. Spacious upstairs rooms with high ceilings and street views are the pick.

Knightsbridge Apartments APARTMENT $$

(☎03-9470 9100; www.knightsbridgeapartments.com.au; 101 George St, East Melbourne; apt from $119; P❄@📶; 🚋48, 75, 🚆Jolimont) Rejuvenated studio apartments over three floors each feature a well-equipped kitchen, plus furniture and accessories that suggest a higher price bracket. There's a chirpy welcome and the overall impression is one of 'nothing's too much trouble'. Opt for the upper floors for a better outlook and light (but note, there's no lift). Call ahead to arrange parking.

MELBOURNE FOR FREE

Royal Botanic Gardens (p487)
Birrarung Marr (p474)
City Circle tram (p480)
Australian Centre for Contemporary Art (p481)
Ian Potter Centre: NGV Australia (p471)
NGV International (p480)
Hosier Lane (p474)
Queen Victoria Market (p479)
Australian Centre for the Moving Image (ACMI; p474)
State Library of Victoria (p478)

South Yarra & Prahran

South of the river, South Yarra has some tremendous boutique and upmarket places set in pretty, tree-lined residential streets.

★ **Art Series (The Cullen)** BOUTIQUE HOTEL **$$$**

(Map p488; ☎03-9098 1555; www.artserieshotels.com.au/cullen; 164 Commercial Rd, Prahran; r from $215; ❄@📶; 🚊72, 78, 79, 🚆Prahran) The edgiest of the Art Series hotels, this one's decked out by the late grunge painter Adam Cullen, whose vibrant and often graphic works provide visions of Ned Kelly shooting you from the glam opaque room/bathroom dividers. Rooms are classic boutique – ultra-comfy but not big on space.

St Kilda

St Kilda is a budget-traveller enclave, but there are also some stylish options a short walk from the beach.

★ **Base** HOSTEL **$**

(Map p490; ☎03-8598 6200; www.stayatbase.com; 17 Carlisle St; dm $27-39, d $90-125; P❄@📶; 🚊3a, 16, 79, 96) Well-run Base has streamlined dorms (each with en suite) and slick doubles. There's a floor set aside for female travellers, complete with hair straighteners and champagne deals, and a bar and live music nights to keep the good-time vibe happening.

Ritz HOSTEL **$**

(Map p490; ☎03-9525 3501; www.ritzbackpackers.com; 169 Fitzroy St; dm/d incl breakfast from $23/65; ❄@📶; 🚊3a, 16, 79, 96, 112) Above an English pub renowned for hosting riotously popular *Neighbours* nights, the Ritz has an excellent location, opposite an inner-city lake and park, and a five-minute walk from St Kilda's heart. It has movie nights and a free BBQ on Fridays.

Hotel Barkly HOTEL **$**

(St Kilda Beach House; Map p490; ☎03-9525 3371; www.stkildabeachhouse.com; 109 Barkly St; dm/d incl breakfast from $28/99; ❄@📶; 🚊3, 67) Hotel Barkly is the party and you're on the guest list. Bright dorms are on the 1st floor, and moody, though not luxurious, private rooms, some with balconies and views, are on the 2nd and 3rd floors. Below is a heaving pub, above is a happy, house-cranking bar. Noisy? You bet. But if you're up for it, there's definitely fun to be had.

Hotel Urban HOTEL **$$**

(Map p490; ☎03-8530 8888; www.hotelurban.com.au/melbourne; 35-37 Fitzroy St; r from $149; P❄@📶🏊; 🚊3a, 16, 79, 96, 112) Rooms here use a lot of blonde wood and white to maximise space, and are simple, light and calming. All rooms are different: some have free-standing in-room spas while others are circular in shape. It also has a small gym.

Prince HOTEL **$$**

(Map p490; ☎03-9536 1111; www.theprince.com.au; 2 Acland St; r incl breakfast from $185; P❄@📶🏊; 🚊3a, 16, 79, 96, 112) Chic Prince has a dramatic lobby while rooms feature natural materials and a pared-back aesthetic. Onsite facilities take in some of the neighbourhood stars: **Aurora** (Map p490; ☎03-9536 1130; www.aurorasparetreat.com; 2 Acland St, St Kilda; 1hr from $120; ⊙8.30am-8pm Mon-Fri, to 6pm Sat, 10am-7pm Sun; 🚊3a, 16, 96, 112) day spa, **Circa** restaurant, bars and band room, and breakfast is provided by **Acland St Cantina** downstairs. Be prepared for seepage of nightclub noise if you're staying the weekend. Free wi-fi is a bonus.

Around St Kilda

Drop Bear Inn HOSTEL **$**

(☎03-9690 2220; www.dropbearinn.com.au; 115 Cecil St, South Melbourne; dm/d from $27/50; @📶; 🚊112) Named after Australia's legendary fearsome creature, this hostel has the advantage of being right opposite the South Melbourne Market, so it's great for fresh produce – particularly the bargains available at closing time. It's above a pub, so will suit those looking to party. Most rooms have good natural light and more charm than most hostels. Free wi-fi.

Art Series (The Blackman) BOUTIQUE HOTEL $$$
(1800 278 468, 03-9039 1444; www.artserieshotels.com.au/blackman; 452 St Kilda Rd, Melbourne; r from $220; 3, 5, 6, 8, 16, 64, 67, 72) While it may not have any original Charles Blackman paintings (though loads of prints and Blackman room decals), it does have superb views – aim for a corner suite for views of Albert Park Lake and the city skyline – and luxurious beds and blackout curtains for a sleep-in.

Eating

Central Melbourne

★ **ShanDong MaMa** ASIAN $
(Map p476; 03-9650 3818; shop 7, Mid City Arcade, 200 Bourke St; mains from $11; 11am-9pm) Melbourne's passion for dumplings finds its truest expression in this simple little place. Dumplings here are boiled, rather than steamed as they are elsewhere, and arrive any later than noon for lunch and you'll have to wait. Our favourite order for two is a plate of Little Rachaels and another of King Prawn dumplings. Bliss.

Miss Katie's Crab Shack AMERICAN $
(03-9329 9888; www.misskatiescrabshack.com; 238 Victoria St; dishes $8-25; 5-9pm Tue-Fri, noon-9pm Sat, noon-8pm Sun; 19, 57, 59) Set up inside the Public Bar, Miss Katie's shack puts a twist on pub food through her Southern home-style cooking, using fresh produce from the Vic Market across the road and homemade hot sauces. Thank her grandma from Virginia for the signature fried chicken, and her mum from Maryland for the Chesapeake Bay–style blue swimmer crab dishes.

Misschu SOUTHEAST ASIAN $
(Map p476; 03-9077 1097; www.misschu.com.au; 297 Exhibition St; mains $7-16; 11am-10pm; City Circle, 24, 30) The self-proclaimed 'queen of rice paper rolls', Misschu continues to expand her empire of hole-in-the-wall eateries serving cheap and tasty Laotian-Vietnamese hawker-style food and furnished in eclectic design, with wooden-crate seating and 1950s retro blinds. Fill out your order form for roast-duck-and-banana-flower rice paper rolls, or beef and oxtail pho. It's in **South Yarra** (Map p488; 03-9041 5848; 276 Toorak Rd, South Yarra; 11am-11pm; 8, 78, 79), too.

Don Don JAPANESE $
(Map p476; 198 Little Lonsdale St; mains $6-9; 11am-9pm Mon-Sat, to 8.30pm Sun; 3, 5, 6, 16, 64, 67, 72, Melbourne Central) Due to its popularity, Don Don had to move digs to a bigger space, yet it still fills up fast. Grab a big bowl or bento box full of Japanese goodness and wolf it down indoors, or join the masses eating it on the State Library's lawns.

★ **MoVida** SPANISH $$
(Map p476; 03-9663 3038; www.movida.com.au; 1 Hosier Lane; tapas $4-6, raciones $8-30; noon-late; 70, 75, Flinders St) MoVida sits in a cobbled lane emblazoned with one of the world's densest collections of street art – it doesn't get much more Melbourne than this. Line up along the bar, cluster around little window tables or, if you've booked, take a table in the dining area for fantastic Spanish tapas and *raciones*.

MoVida Next Door – yes, right next door – is the perfect place for a pre-show beer and tapas. Also brought to you by MoVida is **MoVida Aqui** (Map p476; 03-9663 3038; www.movida.com.au; 1st fl, 500 Bourke St; tapas from $4.50, raciones $22-30; noon-late Mon-Fri, 6pm-late Sat; 86, 96), a huge, open space with similar tapas menu and chargrilled cooking, while next door is its Mexican offering of **Paco's Tacos** (Map p476; 03-9663 3038; www.pacostacos.com.au; 1st fl, 500 Bourke St; tacos $6; noon-11pm; 86, 96). It's also recently opened **Bar Pulpo** (www.movida.com.au/airport; Terminal 2 (International), Melbourne Airport; breakfast $7.90-22.50, tapas from $4.90, raciones from $13.90; 8am-12.30am) at Melbourne Airport for pre-flight tapas and drinks.

★ **Supernormal** ASIAN $$
(Map p476; 03-9650 8688; www.supernormal.net.au; 180 Flinders Lane; mains $15-37; 11am-11pm Sun-Thu, to midnight Fri & Sat) Andrew McConnell can, it seems, do no wrong. Drawing on his years spent living and cooking in Shanghai and Hong Kong, McConnell presents a creative selection, from dumplings to raw seafood and mains such as slow-cooked Szechuan lamb.

Even if you don't dine in, stop by for his now-famous takeaway New England lobster roll – lobster in a small brioche...what's not to like? No dinner bookings for five or less people.

Mamasita MEXICAN $$
(Map p476; ☎03-9650 3821; www.mamasita.com.au; 1/11 Collins St; tacos from $5, shared plates from $19; ⊙noon-late Mon-Sat, from 1pm Sun; City Circle, 11, 31, 48, 112) The restaurant responsible for kicking off Melbourne's obsession with authentic Mexican street food, Mamasita is still one of the very best – as evidenced by the perpetual queues to get into the place. The chargrilled corn sprinkled with cheese and chipotle mayo is a legendary starter, and there's a fantastic range of corn-tortilla tacos and 180 types of tequilla. No reservations, so prepare to wait.

Cumulus Inc MODERN AUSTRALIAN $$
(Map p476; www.cumulusinc.com.au; 45 Flinders Lane; mains $19-39; ⊙7am-11pm Mon-Fri, from 8am Sat & Sun; City Circle, 48) One of Melbourne's best for any meal, giving you that wonderful Andrew McConnell–style along with reasonable prices. The focus is on beautiful produce and simple but artful cooking, from breakfasts of sardines and smoked tomato on toast at the marble bar, to suppers of freshly shucked *clair de lune* oysters tucked away on the leather banquettes.

No reservations, so queues are highly probable.

Chin Chin ASIAN $$
(Map p476; ☎03-8663 2000; www.chinchinrestaurant.com.au; 125 Flinders Lane; mains $19-33; ⊙11am-late; City Circle, 70, 75) Yet another great option on Flinders Lane, Chin Chin does delicious Southeast Asian hawker-style food designed as shared plates. It's inside a busied-up shell of an old building with a real New York feel, and while there are no bookings, **Go Go Bar** downstairs will have you till there's space.

Waiters Restaurant ITALIAN $$
(Map p476; ☎03-9650 1508; 1st fl, 20 Meyers Pl; mains $15-25; ⊙noon-2.30pm Mon-Fri, 6pm-late Mon-Sat; Parliament) Head down a lane and up some stairs to step into this restaurant – and into another era. Opened in 1947, it still bears 1950s drapes, wood panelling and Laminex tables. Once only for Italian and Spanish waiters to unwind after work over a game of *scopa* (a card game), now everyone is welcome for its delicious, hearty plates of red-sauce pasta.

BEST FOR YUM CHA & DUMPLINGS

ShanDong MaMa (p497)
HuTong Dumpling Bar
New Shanghai
Supernormal (p497)

HuTong Dumpling Bar CHINESE $$
(Map p476; www.hutong.com.au; 14-16 Market Lane; mains $15-25; ⊙11.30am-3pm & 5.30-10.30pm; 86, 96) HuTong's windows face out on famed Flower Drum (p499), and its reputation for divine *xiao long bao* (soupy dumplings) means getting a lunchtime seat anywhere in this three-level building isn't easy. Downstairs, watch chefs make the delicate dumplings, then hope they don't watch you making a mess eating them. There's also a branch in **Prahran** (Map p488; www.hutong.com.au; 162 Commercial Rd, Prahran; mains $15-25; 72, 78, 79).

New Shanghai CHINESE $$
(Map p476; ☎03-9994 9386; www.newshanghai.com.au; shop 323, level 3, Emporium, 287 Lonsdale St; mains $8-32; ⊙11am-7pm Sat-Wed, to 9pm Thu & Fri) According to local dumpling experts, New Shanghai, high in the new Emporium shopping complex, serves up Melbourne's best *xiao long bao*, the soup-filled dumplings. We're not quite ready to shift the crown from HuTong Dumpling Bar, but if you like the genre (and have a decent chopstick technique), why not try both?

Pellegrini's Espresso Bar ITALIAN $$
(Map p476; ☎03-9662 1885; 66 Bourke St; mains $15-18; ⊙8am-11.30pm Mon-Sat, noon-8pm Sun; Parliament) The iconic Italian equivalent of a classic '50s diner, Pellegrini's has remained genuinely unchanged for decades. Pick and mix from the variety of homemade pastas and sauces – from the table out the back you can watch it all being thrown together from enormous, ever-simmering pots. In summer, finish with a glass of watermelon granita.

Gazi GREEK $$
(Map p476; ☎03-9207 7444; www.gazirestaurant.com.au; 2 Exhibition St; shared plates from $11.50, mains $23; ⊙11.30am-11pm; 48, 70, 75) The lastest offering from George Calombaris of *MasterChef* fame, this rebadged side project to the fancier Press Club (next door) is set in a cavernous industrial space with a menu inspired by Greek street food. Select from authentic shared starters and gourmet mini souvlakis filled with prawn or duck to wood-fire spit mains.

Calombaris also owns the East Brunswick eatery **Hellenic Republic** (03-9381 1222; www.hellenicrepublic.com.au; 434 Lygon St, East Brunswick; mains $12-32; noon-4pm Fri, 11am-4pm Sat & Sun, 5.30pm-late Mon-Sun; ; 1, 8).

Bomba SPANISH, TAPAS $$
(Map p476; 03-9077 0451; http://bombabar.com.au; 103 Lonsdale St; tapas $3.50-8, dishes $15-32; noon-3pm Mon-Fri, 5pm-late daily; Parliament) Reminiscent of a buzzing Spanish bodega, Bomba offers up tasty authentic tapas, *raciones* for the hungrier and Catalan stew and paellas. The wine list is predominantly Spanish, and the vermouth flows freely, as does the cold Estrella – all perfect for enjoying on the rooftop terrace to the backdrop of the St Patrick's Cathedral spire.

Grain Store CAFE $$
(Map p476; 03-9972 6993; www.grainstore.com.au; 517 Flinders Lane; lunch mains $18-29, dinner mains $26-38; 7am-4pm Mon-Wed, 7am-4pm & 6-10pm Thu-Sat, 8am-4pm Sun) Inhabiting one of those post-industrial spaces that Melbourne does so well, the Grain Store adds a touch of class to the city centre's cafe scene. Dishes range from eight-hour-slow-cooked free-range Otway pork shoulder to cumin-roasted cauliflower. The weekend brunch offers a more varied menu than most breakfast places – the ricotta and passionfruit pancakes caught our eye.

Hopetoun Tea Rooms TEAHOUSE $$
(Map p476; 03-9650 2777; www.hopetountearooms.com.au; 282 Collins St; dishes $13-23; 8am-5pm Mon-Sat, 9am-5pm Sun) Since 1892 patrons have been nibbling pinwheel sandwiches here, taking tea (with pinkies raised) and delicately polishing off lamingtons. Hopetoun's venerable status has queues almost stretching out the entrance of Block Arcade. Salivate over the window display while you wait.

★ **Vue de Monde** MODERN AUSTRALIAN $$$
(Map p476; 03-9691 3888; www.vuedemonde.com.au; level 55, Rialto, 525 Collins St; set menus $150-250; reservations from noon-2pm Tue-Fri & Sun, 6-9.15pm Mon-Sat; 11, 31, 48, 109, 112, Southern Cross) Sitting pretty in the old observation deck of the Rialto, Melbourne's favoured spot for occasion dining has views to match its name. Visionary chef Shannon Bennett has moved away from its classic French style to a subtle Modern Australian theme that runs through everything from the decor to the menu.

★ **Kenzan** JAPANESE $$$
(Map p476; 03-9654 8933; www.kenzan.com.au; 56 Flinders Lane; mains $30-45, lunch/dinner set menu from $36/85; noon-2.30pm & 6-10pm) One of numerous candidates for the title of Melbourne's best Japanese restaurant, Kenzan inhabits an unpromising setting but serves up sublime sashimi and sushi, with the *nabe ryori* (which you cook at your table) another fine option. Can't choose? Lunch and dinner set menus are outstanding. Order the more expensive marbled beef when given the choice.

Flower Drum CHINESE $$$
(Map p476; 03-9662 3655; www.flower-drum.com; 17 Market Lane; mains $15-60; noon-3pm & 6-11pm Mon-Sat, 6-10.30pm Sun; ; 86, 96) The Flower Drum continues to be Melbourne's most celebrated Chinese restaurant. The finest, freshest produce prepared with absolute attention to detail keeps this Chinatown institution booked out weeks in advance. The sumptuous, but ostensibly simple, Cantonese food (from a menu that changes daily) is delivered with the slick service you'd expect in such elegant surrounds.

Gingerboy ASIAN $$$
(Map p476; 03-9662 4200; www.gingerboy.com.au; 27-29 Crossley St; shared dishes $32-52; noon-2.30pm & 5.30-10.30pm Mon-Fri, 5.30-10.30pm Sat; 86, 96) Brave the aggressively trendy surrounds and weekend party scene, as talented Teague Ezard does a fine turn in flash hawker cooking. Flavours pop in dishes such as scallops with green chilli jam or coconut kingfish with peanut and tamarind dressing. There are two dinner sittings; bookings are required. Upstairs, Gingerboy has a long, long cocktail bar.

No 35 at Sofitel MODERN AUSTRALIAN $$$
(Map p476; www.no35.com.au; level 35, Sofitel, 25 Collins St; mains $30-48; noon-2.30pm & 6pm-late; 11, 48, 109, 112, Parliament) Melbourne's equivalent to the *Lost in Translation* bar in Tokyo. The views of the city skyline are superb through this restaurant-bar's floor-to-ceiling windows (memorable views from its toilets, too). It's a great choice for a special occasion, and you can expect a menu of rich, delicious dishes, such as roasted sea trout and parmesan gnocchi with crab-caviar butter sauce and spinach cream.

Mrs Parma's MODERN AUSTRALIAN $$
(Map p476; www.mrsparmas.com.au; 25 Little Bourke St, Melbourne; chicken parma $21.50-27.50;

⏲11am-late Mon-Fri, noon-late Sat & Sun; 🚉Parliament) Aussies have long adopted the humble parma (chicken parmiagana) as their own, but Mrs Parma's takes things to a whole new level with 15 different types of parmas of the chicken, veal or eggplant variety, including some that are downright weird. Its huge selection of Victorian craft beers is another reason to visit.

Southgate, South Wharf & the Docklands

Tutto Bene ITALIAN $$

(Map p476; ☎03-9696 3334; www.tuttobene.com.au; midlevel, Southgate; mains $24-45; ⏲noon-3pm & 6-10pm; 🚉Flinders St) This Italian restaurant is especially known for its risotto dishes, which range from a simple Venetian *risi e bisi* (rice and peas) to some fabulously luxe options involving truffles, roast quail or aged balsamic. Don't miss its fine house-made gelato.

Rockpool Bar & Grill STEAK $$$

(Map p476; ☎03-8648 1900; www.rockpoolmelbourne.com; Crown Entertainment Complex; mains $24-110; ⏲noon-2.30pm Sun-Fri, 6-11pm daily; 🚋55, 🚉Flinders St) The Melbourne outpost of Neil Perry's empire offers his signature seafood raw bar, but it's really all about beef, from grass-fed to full-blood Wagyu. The darkly masculine space is simple and stylish, as is the menu. The bar offers the same level of food service, with the added bonus of a rather spectacular drinks menu.

Richmond

Known for its increasingly upscale foodie scene, Richmond can still be an earthy place to eat, especially in the cheap Vietnamese restaurants along Victoria St.

Richmond Hill Cafe & Larder CAFE $$

(☎03-9421 2808; www.rhcl.com.au; 48-50 Bridge Rd; lunch $12-30; ⏲8am-5pm; 🚋75, 🚉West Richmond) Once the domain of well-known cook Stephanie Alexander, it still boasts its lovely cheese room and simple, comforting foods such as cheesy toast. There are breakfast cocktails for the brave.

Fitzroy & Around

Smith St has developed an astounding array of great new eateries in the last couple of years, while Gertrude St also packs in some winning options. Brunswick St has a few long-established favourites, but the rest is a little hit-and-miss. Further along you'll hit Northcote's High St strip, which is turning into a great dining area.

Po' Boy Quarter AMERICAN $

(Map p484; ☎03-9419 2130; www.gumbokitchen.com.au; 295 Smith St, Fitzroy; rolls $10-14; ⏲11.30am-1am; 🚋86) The boys behind the Gumbo Kitchen truck have parked permanently on Smith St with this smart canteen-style eatery. Wolf down one of their rolls of pulled pork, shrimp with Louisiana hot sauce, or fried green tomatoes with Cajun slaw while people watching out front.

Jimmy Grants GREEK $

(Map p484; www.jimmygrants.com.au; 113 St David St, Fitzroy; souvlakis from $9; ⏲11am-10pm; 🚋86) Set up by celebrity chef George Calombaris, this is not your ordinary souva joint – these are gourmet souvlakis, which you don't need to be plastered at 3am to enjoy. Options may include a pita stuffed with lamb, mustard aioli and chips, or honey prawn and herbs.

★Charcoal Lane MODERN AUSTRALIAN $$

(Map p484; ☎03-9418 3400; www.charcoallane.com.au; 136 Gertrude St, Fitzroy; mains $19-31; ⏲noon-3pm & 6-9pm Tue-Sat; 🚋86) Housed in an old bluestone former bank, this training restaurant for Indigenous and disadvantaged young people is one of the best places to try native flora and fauna – menu items may include kangaroo burger with bush tomato chutney and wallaby tartare. Weekend bookings advised. It also holds cooking masterclasses using native ingredients; check the website for details.

Añada TAPAS $$

(Map p484; ☎03-9415 6101; www.anada.com.au; 197 Gertrude St, Fitzroy; tapas from $4, raciones $10-26; ⏲5pm-late Mon-Fri, noon-late Sat & Sun; 🚋86) Dishes in this lovely little restaurant are alive with hearty Spanish and Muslim-Mediterranean flavours. It has a great tapas selection, or go the nine-course banquet (chef's choice) for $50.

Hammer & Tong 412 CAFE $$

(Map p484; ☎03-9041 6033; www.hammerandtong.com.au; rear 412 Brunswick St, Fitzroy; mains $14-32; ⏲7am-late Tue-Sat, to 4pm Mon & Sun; 🚋112) Tucked down a Brunswick St side street, Hammer & Tong's forbidding facade may have you second-guessing what kind of place this is, but within is a popular cafe set up by owners of impeccable pedigree (courte-

MEALS ON WHEELS: MELBOURNE'S FOOD TRUCKS

Melbourne's long had an association with food vans – a game of suburban footy isn't complete without someone dishing out hot jam donuts, meat pies and hot chips to freezing fans over a truck counter (and what would a trip to the beach be without an ice-cream van playing its tune?). But getting quality food from a van is a different matter. Taking the cue from LA's food-truck revolution, fabulous food trucks have begun plying the streets of Melbourne in recent years. Each day the vendors post to let their Twitter and Facebook followers know where they'll be, and hungry folk dutifully respond by turning up street-side for a meal. Favourite Melbourne food trucks (and their Twitter handles) to chase down include the following.

Beatbox Kitchen (@BeatboxKitchen) Gourmet burgers and fries.

Cornutopia (@Cornutopia) Mexican street food.

GrumbleTumms (@GrumbleTumms) Bush tucker: croc or emu pies and roo burgers.

Gumbo Kitchen (@GumboKitchen) New Orleans–style po' boys.

Mr Burger (@MrBurgerTruck) As the name suggests.

Smokin' Barry's (@SmokinBarrys) Smoky BBQ meats.

Also check out www.wherethetruck.at for more food trucks around town.

sy of Vue du Monde and Jacques Reymond). Expect yabby-tail omelettes for breakfast and soft-shell-crab burgers for lunch and elaborate mains. Excellent coffee, too.

Robert Burns Hotel SPANISH **$$**
(Map p484; www.robertburnshotel.com.au; 376 Smith St, Collingwood; mains from $19; ⏲5pm-late Mon & Tue, noon-late Wed-Sun; 🚋86) Receiving a slick makeover meant the loss of its appealing dingy charm, but thankfully the authenticity of the Spanish flavours remain: its seafood paella is still one of Melbourne's best. The $12 lunch menu is great value.

Cutler & Co MODERN AUSTRALIAN **$$$**
(Map p484; ☎03-9419 4888; www.cutlerandco.com.au; 55 Gertrude St, Fitzroy; mains $36-49; ⏲noon-late Fri & Sun, 6pm-late Mon-Thu; 🚋86) Hyped for all the right reasons, this is another of Andrew McConnell's restaurants and though its decor might be a little over the top, its attentive, informed staff and joy-inducing dishes (roast suckling pig, Earl Grey ice cream and Moonlight Bay oysters, to name a few) have quickly made this one of Melbourne's best.

Moon Under Water MODERN AUSTRALIAN **$$$**
(Map p484; ☎03-9417 7700; www.buildersarmshotel.com.au; 211 Gertrude St, Fitzroy; 3-/4-/6-course set menu $65/75/95; ⏲6-10pm Wed-Sat, noon-3pm & 6-10pm Sun; 🚋86) Another string to Andrew McConnell's bow is this elegant dining room hidden in the back of the Builders Arms Hotel. The set menu changes weekly and wine pairing comes at $55 extra. Vegetarian menus available. If you prefer something more casual and à la carte, check out the adjoining bistro with its daily rotisserie menu (suckling pig) from 6pm.

Bookings advised at least two weeks in advance.

Estelle MODERN AUSTRALIAN **$$$**
(☎03-9489 4609; www.estellebarkitchen.com.au; 243 High St, Northcote; 5-/8-course tasting menu $80/120; ⏲6pm-late Tue-Thu, noon-late Fri-Sun; 🚋86, 🚆Northcote) Classy establishment where you can enjoy the elegant interior of gleaming tiled floors, or casual rear courtyard with your classic Northcote backyard feel. The menu spans rich French cuisine to Asian-inspired fish dishes. The five-course tasting menus, matched with wine, are popular and start from $70.

Carlton & Around

Since the arrival of Mediterranean immigrants in the 1950s, Lygon St has been synonymous with Italian cuisine, albeit it with a twist to suit the Australian palate. Avoid its spruikers and keep travelling north past Grattan St – some lovely cafes and restaurants lie here and beyond. The East Brunswick end of Lygon St is doing good things, too.

Sugardough Panificio & Patisserie BAKERY **$**
(☎03-9380 4060; www.sugardough.com.au; 163 Lygon St, East Brunswick; mains $8.60; ⏲7.30am-5pm Tue-Fri, to 4pm Sat & Sun; 🚋1, 8)

DON'T MISS

MIDDLE EAST UP NORTH

Sydney Rd in Brunswick is Melbourne's Middle Eastern hub. Its busy **A1 Lebanese Bakehouse** (www.a1lebanesebakery.com.au; 643-5 Sydney Rd, Brunswick; mains from $10; ⏲7am-7pm Sun-Wed, to 9pm Thu-Sat ; 🚊19, 🚉Anstey) and alcohol-free **Tiba's Restaurant** (www.tibasrestaurant.com.au; 504 Sydney Rd, Brunswick; mains from $11; ⏲11am-11pm Sun-Thu, to midnight Fri & Sat; 🚊19, 🚉Brunswick) are worth a trip in themselves, or check out Middle Eastern–influenced **Ray** (☎03-9380 8593; 332 Victoria St, Brunswick; meals $8-20; ⏲7.30am-4pm Mon-Fri, 8.30am-5pm Sat & Sun; 📶; 🚊19, 🚉Brunswick) for more of a cafe feel.

Sugardough does a roaring trade in home-made pies (including vegetarian ones), home-baked bread and pastries. Mismatched cutlery and cups and saucers make it rather like being at Grandma's on family reunion day.

D.O.C Espresso ITALIAN **$$**
(Map p486; ☎03-9347 8482; www.docgroup.net; 326 Lygon St, Carlton; mains $12-20; ⏲7.30am-9.30pm Mon-Sat, 8am-9pm Sun; 🚌205, 🚊1, 8, 96) Run by third-generation Italians, D.O.C is bringing authenticity, and breathing new life, back into Lygon St. The espresso bar features homemade pasta specials, Italian microbrewery beers and *aperitivo* time (4pm to 7pm), where you can enjoy a Negroni cocktail with complimentary nibble board while surrounded by dangling legs of meat and huge wheels of cheese behind glass shelves.

The **deli** (Map p486; ☎03-9347 8482; www.docgroup.net; 326 Lygon St, Carlton; mains from $12; ⏲9am-8pm) next door does great cheese boards and panini, while around the corner is D.O.C's original **pizzeria** (Map p486; ☎03-9347 2998; www.docgroup.net; 295 Drummond St, Carlton; pizzas around $13-18; ⏲5.30-10.30pm Mon-Wed, noon-10.30pm Fri-Sun; 🚌205, 🚊1, 8), with excellent thin-crust pizzas and a convivial atmosphere.

Rumi MIDDLE EASTERN **$$**
(☎03-9388 8255; www.rumirestaurant.com.au; 116 Lygon St, East Brunswick; mains $12-24; ⏲6-10pm; 🚊1, 8) A fabulously well-considered place that serves up a mix of traditional Lebanese cooking and contemporary interpretations of old Persian dishes. The *sigara boregi* (cheese and pine-nut pastries) are a local institution, and tasty mains such as meatballs are balanced with a large and interesting selection of vegetable dishes (the near-caramelised cauliflower and the broad beans are standouts).

Auction Rooms CAFE **$$**
(☎03-9326 7749; www.auctionroomscafe.com.au; 103-107 Errol St, North Melbourne; mains $14-22; ⏲7am-5pm Mon-Fri, from 7.30am Sat & Sun; 📶; 🚊57) This former auction house–turned–North Melbourne success story serves up some of Melbourne's best coffee, both espresso and filter, using ever-changing, house-roasted, single-origin beans. Then there's its food, with a highly seasonal menu of creative breakfasts and lunches. From Queen Vic Market, head west along Victoria St, then right at Errol St.

Bar Idda ITALIAN **$$**
(☎03-9380 5339; www.baridda.com.au; 132 Lygon St, East Brunswick; mains $15-20; ⏲6-10pm Tue-Sat; 🚊1, 8) The diner-style table coverings give little clue to the tasty morsels this Sicilian restaurant serves for dinner. Shared plates are the go and range from pistachio-crumbed lamb loin to vegetarian layered eggplant.

Tiamo ITALIAN **$$**
(Map p486; www.tiamo.com.au; 303 Lygon St, Carlton; mains $9-26; ⏲6.30am-11pm; 🚌Tourist Shuttle, 🚊1, 8) When you've had enough of pressed, siphoned, Slayer-machined, poured-over, filtered and plunged coffee, head here to one of Lygon St's original Italian cafe-restaurants. There's the laughter and relaxed joie de vivre that only a well-established restaurant can have. Great pastas and pizza, too. Also has the upmarket Tiamo 2 next door.

Abla's LEBANESE **$$**
(Map p486; ☎03-9347 0006; www.ablas.com.au; 109 Elgin St, Carlton; mains $27-30; ⏲noon-3pm Thu & Fri, 6-11pm Mon-Sat; 🚌205, 🚊1, 8, 96) The kitchen here is steered by Abla Amad, whose authentic, flavour-packed food has inspired a whole generation of local Lebanese chefs. Bring a bottle of your favourite plonk and settle in for the compulsory banquet ($70) on Friday and Saturday nights.

St Kilda & Around

Fitzroy St is a popular eating strip, and you'll find the good, the very good and the downright ugly along its length. Acland St also hums with dining options, as well as its famed cake shops. Over the Nepean Hwy, Carlisle St has more than its fair share of cute cafes and a couple of restaurants that keep the locals happy.

Monarch Cake Shop DESSERTS, EUROPEAN $

(Map p490; ☎03-9534 2972; www.monarchcakes.com.au; 103 Acland St, St Kilda; slice of cake from $5; ⏰8am-10pm; 🚋96) St Kilda's Eastern European cake shops have long drawn crowds that come to peer at the sweetly stocked windows. Monarch is a favourite – its *kugelhopf* (marble cake), plum cake and poppy-seed cheesecake can't be beaten. In business since 1934, and not much has changed with its wonderful buttery aromas and old-time atmosphere. Also does good coffee.

Si Señor MEXICAN $

(193 Carlisle St, Balaclava; tacos $5-8, tortas $13.50-16; ⏰11.30am-late; 📶; 🚋3, 16, 79) One of the latest additions to Melbourne's Mexican restaurant takeover, Si Señor is also one of the most authentic. Tasty spit-and-grilled meats are heaped onto soft corn tortillas under direction of its Mexican owner. If you've overdone the hot sauce, cool it down with an authentic *horchata*, a delicious rice milk and cinammon drink.

Glick's BAGELS $

(www.glicks.com.au; 330a Carlisle St, Balaclava; bagels $4-10; ⏰5.30am-8pm Mon-Fri & Sun, 30min after sunset–midnight Sat; 🚋3, 16, 79) No-frills bakery keeping the local Jewish community happy with bagels baked and boiled in-house and kosher options available. Stick with the classics and try the 'New Yorker' with cream cheese and egg salad.

Monk Bodhi Dharma CAFE $$

(☎03-9534 7250; www.monkbodhidharma.com; rear 202 Carlisle St, Balaclava; breakfast $9-20; ⏰7am-5pm Mon-Fri, 8am-5pm Sat & Sun; 🥕; 🚋3, 16, 79) Monk Bodhi Dharma's hidden location, down an alley off Carlisle St (next to Safeway), means it doesn't get much passing foot traffic, which is lucky given this cosy brick cafe has enough devotees as it is. A former 1920s bakehouse, these days it's all about transcendental vegetarian food, house-made Bircher muesli and house-roasted single-estate coffee.

Book ahead for Friday night dinners.

Uncle VIETNAMESE $$

(☎03-9041 2668; www.unclestkilda.com.au; 188 Carlisle St, St Kilda; mains $24-34; ⏰5pm-late Tue, noon-late Wed-Sun) With stellar Vietnamese cooking in a quintessentially St Kilda space (complete with rooftop dining area), Uncle is one of Melbourne's more exciting Asian openings in recent years. The drinks list includes Viet sangria, and mains might include lemongrass and coconut scotch fillet, while traditionalists will love the pho (Vietnamese noodle soup).

Mirka's at Tolarno INTERNATIONAL, ITALIAN $$

(Map p490; ☎03-9525 3088; www.mirkatolarnohotel.com; Tolarno Hotel, 42 Fitzroy St, St Kilda; mains $18-38; ⏰6pm-late; 🚋16, 96, 112) Beloved artist Mirka Mora's murals grace the walls in this dining room with a history (it's been delighting diners since the early '60s). Guy Grossi's Italian menu has some rustic classics like veal satimbocca mixed with interesting surprises such as walnut and pear gnocchi with gorgonzola. There's also a four-course sharing menu ($60).

Claypots SEAFOOD $$

(Map p490; ☎03-9534 1282; 213 Barkly St, St Kilda; mains $24-38; ⏰noon-3pm & 6pm-1am; 🚋96) A local favourite, Claypots serves up seafood in its namesake dish. Get in early to get a seat and ensure the good stuff is still available, as hot items go fast. It also has a spot in the South Melbourne Market (p489).

Lau's Family Kitchen CHINESE $$

(Map p490; ☎03-8598 9880; www.lauskitchen.com.au; 4 Acland St, St Kilda; mains $24-38; ⏰dinner sittings 6pm & 8pm; 🚋16, 96) The owner's family comes with flawless pedigree (father Gilbert Lau is the former owner of famed Flower Drum) and the restaurant is in a lovely leafy location. The mainly Cantonese menu is simple, and dishes are beautifully done (if not particularly exciting), with a few surprises thrown in for more adventurous diners.

Make a reservation for one of the two dinner sittings.

★ **Attica** MODERN AUSTRALIAN $$$

(☎03-9530 0111; www.attica.com.au; 74 Glen Eira Rd, Ripponlea; 8-course tasting menu $190; ⏰6.30pm-late Wed-Sat; 🚋67, 🚆Ripponlea) Consistent, award-winning Attica is a suburban restaurant that serves Ben Shewry's creative dishes degustation-style. Many dishes aren't complete on delivery; staff perform minor miracles on cue with a sprinkle of this or a drop of that. 'Trials' of Shewry's new ideas take place on Tuesday night's Chef's Table ($125 per head). Booking several months in advance is essential.

Follow Brighton Rd south to Glen Eira Rd.

South Melbourne, Port Melbourne & Albert Park

Andrew's Burgers BURGERS $

(03-9690 2126; www.andrewshamburgers.com.au; 144 Bridport St, Albert Park; burgers from $7.50; 11am-3pm & 4.30-9pm Mon-Sat; 1) Andrew's is a family-run burger institution that's been around since the '50s. Walls are still wood-panelled and now covered with photos of local celebs who, like many, drop in for a classic burger with the lot and a big bag of chips to takeaway. Veg option available.

St Ali CAFE $$

(03-9689 2990; www.stali.com.au; 12-18 Yarra Pl, South Melbourne; dishes $8-23; 7am-6pm; 112) A hideaway warehouse conversion where the coffee is carefully sourced and guaranteed to be good. If you can't decide between house blend, speciality, black or white, there's a tasting plate ($18). Awarded best food cafe in *The Age Good Cafe Guide 2013* – the corn fritters with poached eggs and haloumi are legendary.

Off Clarendon St, between Coventry and York Sts.

Albert Park Hotel Oyster Bar & Grill SEAFOOD, PUB $$

(03-9690 5459; www.thealbertpark.com.au; cnr Montague St & Dundas Pl, Albert Park; mains $15-30; 1, 96) With a focus on oysters and seafood as well as bar food, this incarnation of the Albert Park Hotel is filling seats with its promise of market-priced fish and wood-barbecued 'big fish' served in five different Mediterranean styles.

Drinking & Nightlife

Melbourne's bars are legendary, from lane hideaways to brassy corner establishments. The same goes for coffee. Out of the city centre, shopping strips are embedded with shopfront drinking holes: try Fitzroy, Collingwood, Northcote, Prahran and St Kilda. Many inner-city pubs have pushed out the barflies, pulled up the beer-stained carpet, polished the concrete and brought in talented chefs and mixologists, but don't dismiss the character-filled oldies that still exist.

Central Melbourne

★**Bar Americano** COCKTAIL BAR

(Map p476; 20 Pesgrave Pl, off Howey Pl; 8.30am-1am; 11, 31, 48, 109, 112) A hideaway bar in a city alleyway, Bar Americano is a standing-room-only affair with black-and-white chequered floors complemented with classic 'do not spit' subway tiled walls and the subtle air of a speakeasy. By day it serves excellent coffee, but after dark it's all about the cocktails; they don't come cheap but they do come superb.

Lui Bar COCKTAIL BAR

(Map p476; www.vuedemonde.com.au; level 55, Rialto, 525 Collins St; 5.30pm-midnight Mon, noon-midnight Tue-Fri, 5.30pm-late Sat, noon-evening Sun; 11, 31, 48, 109, 112, Southern Cross) One of the city's most sophisticated bars, Lui offers the chance to sample the views and excellent bar snacks (smoked ocean trout jerky!) without having to indulge in the whole Vue de Monde dining experience. Suits and jet-setters cram in most nights so get there early (nicely dressed), claim your table and order drinks from the pop-up-book menu.

Drinks include macadamia martinis – vacuum distilled at the bar.

Melbourne Supper Club BAR

(Map p476; 03-9654 6300; 1st fl, 161 Spring St; 5pm-4am Sun-Thu, to 6am Fri & Sat; 95, 96, Parliament) Melbourne's own Betty Ford's (the place you go when there's nowhere left to go), the Supper Club is open very late and is a favoured after-work spot for performers and hospitality types. It's entered through an unsigned wooden door, where you can leave your coat before cosying into a chesterfield.

Browse the encyclopedic wine menu and relax; the sommeliers will cater to any liquid desire.

Madame Brussels BAR

(Map p476; www.madamebrussels.com; level 3, 59-63 Bourke St; noon-1am; 86, 96) Head here if you've had it with Melbourne-moody and all that dark wood. Although named for a famous 19th-century brothel owner, it feels like a camp '60s rabbit hole, with much AstroTurfery and staff dressed à la country club. It's just the tonic to escape the city for a jug of Madame Brussels–style Pimms on its wonderful rooftop terrace.

GAY & LESBIAN MELBOURNE

Melbourne's gay and lesbian community is well integrated into the general populace, but clubs and bars are found in two distinct locations: Abbotsford and Collingwood, and Prahran and South Yarra. Commercial Rd, which separates Prahran and South Yarra, is home to a couple of gay clubs, cafes and businesses. It's more glamorous than the 'northside', which has a reputation as more down-to-earth and a little less pretentious.

For local info, pick up a copy of the free weekly newspaper *MCV (Melbourne Community Voice)*. GLBT-community radio station **JOY 94.9FM** (www.joy.org.au) is another important resource for visitors and locals.

Festivals & Events

Plenty of Melbourne venues get into the spirit during **Midsumma Festival** (p492). It has a diverse program of cultural, community and sporting events, including the popular Midsumma Carnival at Alexandra Gardens, St Kilda's Pride March and much more.

Melbourne Queer Film Festival (www.melbournequeerfilm.com.au) Australia's largest gay film festival, held in March, showcases everything from full-length features and animations to experimental works.

Sleeping

169 Drummond (Map p486; ☎03-9663 3081; www.169drummond.com.au; 169 Drummond St, Carlton; d incl breakfast $120-145; 📶; 🚋1, 8) A privately owned gay guesthouse in a renovated 19th-century terrace in the inner north, one block from vibrant Lygon St.

Drinking & Nightlife

Exchange Bar (Map p488; ☎03-9804 5771; www.exchangebar.com.au; 119 Commercial Rd, South Yarra; ⏲5pm late Wed-Sat; 🚋72) The former Exchange Hotel, this is one of the few remaining gay venues along Commerical Rd, with regular DJs and drag shows.

Laird (☎03-9417 2832; www.lairdhotel.com; 149 Gipps St, Collingwood; ⏲5pm-late; 🚆Collingwood) The Laird's been running its men-only gay hotel for over 30 years now. It's on the Abbotsford side of Gipps St, which runs off Collingwood's Wellington St.

DT's Hotel (☎03-9428 5724; www.dtshotel.com.au; 164 Church St, Richmond; 🚋78, 79) This small and intimate gay pub hosts some of Melbourne's best drag shows, retro nights and happy hours.

Peel Hotel (☎03-9419 4762; www.thepeel.com.au; 113 Wellington St, Collingwood; ⏲9pm-dawn Thu-Sat; 🚋86) The Peel is one of the best known and most popular gay venues in Melbourne. It's the last stop of a big night.

Commercial Hotel (☎03-9689 9354; www.hotelcommercial.com.au; 238 Whitehall St, Yarraville; ⏲Thu-Sat; 🚆Yarraville) A friendly, low-key pub in Melbourne's inner west that presents drag shows every Saturday night. From the city centre, follow Footscray Rd and turn left down Whitehall.

GH Hotel (Greyhound Hotel; ☎03-9534 4189; www.ghhotel.com.au; cnr Carlisle St & Brighton Rd, St Kilda; 🚋16, 67, 79) The old Greyhound's had a facelift – expect drag-filled evenings from Thursday to Saturday and a nightclub with a state-of-the-art sound system.

Double Happiness BAR
(Map p476; ☎03-9650 4488; www.double-happiness.org; 21 Liverpool St; ⏲4pm-1am Mon-Wed, to 3am Thu & Fri, 6pm-3am Sat, to 1am Sun; 🚋86, 96, 🚆Parliament) This stylish hole-in-the-wall is decked out in Chinese propaganda posters and Mao statues, with an excellent range of Asian-influenced chilli- or coriander-flavoured cocktails. Upstairs is the **New Gold Mountain** (Map p476; ☎03-9650 8859; www.newgoldmountain.org; level 1, 21 Liverpool St; ⏲6pm-late Tue-Thu, to 5am Fri & Sat; 🚋86, 96, 🚆Parliament) bar, run by the same owners, with table service.

Hell's Kitchen BAR
(Map p476; level 1, 20 Centre Pl; ⏲noon-10pm Mon & Tues, to late Wed-Sat, to 11pm Sun; 🚆Flinders St) Hidden lane bar located in the beautiful

Centre Place Arcade, Hell's is up a narrow flight of stairs where you can sip on classic cocktails (Negroni, whisky sour and martinis), beer or cider and people watch from the large windows. Attracts a young, hip crowd and also serves food.

Shebeen BAR

(Map p476; www.shebeen.com.au; 36 Manchester Lane; ⏲ noon-late Mon-Fri, 4pm-late Sat; 🚊 11, 31, 48, 109, 112) Corrugated-iron walls and awnings give this relaxed bar a canteen-shack feel. Shebeen (the name for illegal drinking bars in South Africa during apartheid) offers a place to have a tipple without feeling too guilty about it – 100% of all drink profits go towards a charity partner overseas.

At the time of research there were plans for live music and DJs.

Hotel Windsor TEAHOUSE

(Map p476; www.thehotelwindsor.com.au; 111 Spring St; afternoon tea Mon-Fri $69, Sat & Sun $89; ⏲ noon Mon & Tue, noon & 2.30pm Wed-Sun; 🚆 Parliament) This grand hotel has been serving afternoon tea since 1883. Indulge in the delights of its three-tier platters of finger sandwiches, scones, pastries and champagne, hosted in either its front dining room or the art nouveau ballroom.

BARS & BREWERIES FOR BEER SNOBS

The last few years in Melbourne have seen the emergence of numerous microbreweries and craft-beer bars – primed to meet the demands of beer geeks who treat their drinking seriously.

The two biggest events on the Melbourne beer calendar are **Good Beer Week** (www.goodbeerweek.com.au) and the **Great Australasian Beer SpecTAPular** (www.gabsfestival.com.au); both held in May, they showcase local, national and foreign craft beers.

Mountain Goat Brewery (www.goatbeer.com.au; cnr North & Clark Sts, Richmond; ⏲ 5pm-midnight Wed & Fri; 🚊 48, 75, 109, 🚆 Burnley) In the backstreets of industrial Richmond, this local microbrewery is set in a massive beer-producing warehouse. Enjoy its range of beers ($11 tasting paddles) while nibbling on pizza. There are free brewery tours on Wednesday. It's tricky to reach: head down Bridge Rd, turn left at Burnley and right at North St.

Temple Brewery (☎ 03-9380 8999; www.templebrewing.com.au; 122 Weston St, Brunswick East; ⏲ 5.30-11pm Mon-Thu, noon-11pm Fri & Sat, noon-9pm Sun; 🚊 1, 8) Try a seasonal craft brew at this classy brewery with a brasserie.

Matilda Bay Brewery (☎ 03-9673 4545; www.matildabay.com.au; 89 Bertie St, Port Melbourne ; ⏲ 11.30am-10pm Tue-Thu, to 11pm Fri & Sat; 🚊 109) Great selection of beers brewed on site that you can sample among its production equipment. Free tours on Saturday.

Local Taphouse (www.thelocal.com.au; 184 Carlisle St, St Kilda; ⏲ noon-late; 🚊 16, 78, 🚆 Balaclava) Reminiscent of an old-school Brooklyn bar. Prop up its dark-wood polished bar and decide which of its 19 craft beers on tap, or its impressive bottle list, to order. There's a beer garden upstairs, while downstairs has chesterfield couches, an open fire and indoor bocce pit. It's also known for its live comedy nights.

Alehouse Project (☎ 03-9387 1218; www.thealehouseproject.com.au; 98-100 Lygon St, East Brunswick; ⏲ 3pm-late Tue-Fri, noon-late Sat & Sun; 📶; 🚊 1, 8) Brunswick venue for beer snobs to convene and compare notes, or just rock up to get drunk from a great selection of 12 craft beers on tap. Has beer-hall-style seating, op-shop couches, a small courtyard and sports on the big telly.

Beer DeLuxe (Map p476; www.beerdeluxe.com.au; Federation Sq; ⏲ 11am-11pm Sun-Wed, to late Thu-Sat; 🚌 Tourist Shuttle, 🚊 City Circle, 🚆 Flinders St) In the heart of the city, you'll find a beer bible in place of a menu – select from 160 beers from around the world, including 12 on tap. There's an attractive beer-hall-style beer garden.

Forester's Hall (Map p484; www.forestershall.com.au; 64 Smith St, Collingwood; ⏲ 4pm-2am Mon-Thu, noon-4am Fri & Sat, noon-2am Sun) With 50 taps serving more than 30 craft and boutique beers from Australia and around the world, beer lovers will adore this pilgrimage out to Collingwood.

Cookie BAR
(Map p476; 03-9663 7660; www.cookie.net.au; level 1, Curtin House, 252 Swanston St; noon-1am Sun-Thu, to 3am Fri & Sat) Part swanky bar, part Thai restaurant, Cookie does both exceptionally well and is one of the more enduring rites of passage of the Melbourne night. The bar is unbelievably well stocked with fine whiskies and wines, with plenty of craft beers among the 200-plus brews on offer. It also knows how to make a serious cocktail.

Goldilocks BAR
(Map p476; 0401 174 962; www.goldliocksbar.com; level 4, 262 Swanston St; 2pm-3am) Fabulous cocktails (whisky with chilli anyone?) and a brilliant rooftop setting made this one of the stars of the Melbourne night and there's no reason to think the crowds will go elsewhere.

Section 8 BAR
(Map p476; www.section8.com.au; 27-29 Tattersalls Lane; 10am-11pm Mon-Wed, to 1am Thu & Fri, noon-1am Sat & Sun; 3, 5, 6, 16, 64, 67, 72) Enclosed within a cage full of shipping containers and wooden-pallet seating, Section 8 remains one of the city's hippest bars. It does great hot dogs, including vegan ones.

Ferdydurke BAR
(Map p476; 03-9639 3750; www.ferdydurke.com.au; levels 1 & 2, 31 Tattersalls Lane, cnr Lonsdale St; noon-1am; ; Melbourne Central) Run by same folk as Section 8 next door, this dive bar/art space is set over several levels. Within its gritty confines they play everything from electronic to live Polish jazz, while Wednesday nights they project computer games on the opposing giant brick wall. They also sell hot dogs.

Robot BAR
(Map p476; 03-9620 3646; www.robotsushi.com; 12 Bligh Pl; 5pm-late Mon-Fri, 8pm-late Sat; Flinders St) If neo-Tokyo is your thing, or you just have a sudden urge for a sushi handroll washed down with an Asahi, check out Robot. It has an all-welcome door policy, big windows that open to the laneway, a cute mezzanine level and attracts a laid-back young crowd.

Riverland BAR
(Map p476; 03-9662 1771; www.riverlandbar.com; Vaults 1-9 Federation Wharf, under Princes Bridge; 10am-late Mon-Fri, 9am-late Sat & Sun; Flinders St) Perched below Princes Bridge alongside the Yarra River, this bluestone beauty keeps things simple with good wine, beer on tap and bar snacks that hit the mark: charcuterie, cheese and BBQ sausages. Outside tables are a treat when the weather is kind. Be prepared for rowdiness pre- and post-footy matches at the nearby MCG.

Ponyfish Island CAFE, BAR
(Map p476; www.ponyfish.com.au; under Yarra Pedestrian Bridge; 8am-1am; Flinders St) Laneway bars have been done to death; now Melburnians are finding new creative spots to do their drinkin'. Where better than an open-air nook under a bridge arcing over the Yarra? From Flinders St Station underground passage, head over the pedestrian bridge towards Southgate, where you'll find steps down to people knocking back beers with toasted sangas or cheese plates.

Carlton Hotel BAR
(Map p476; www.thecarlton.com.au; 193 Bourke St; 4pm-late; 86, 96) Over-the-top Melbourne rococo gets another workout here and never fails to raise a smile. Check out the rooftop **Palmz** if you're looking for some Miami-flavoured vice, or just a great view.

Young & Jackson's PUB
(Map p476; www.youngandjacksons.com.au; cnr Flinders & Swanston Sts; 11am-late; Flinders St) Opposite Flinders St station, this historic pub has been serving up beer since 1861 and makes for a popular meeting spot. Lounge on chesterfields in Chloe's Bar, or head up to the rooftop cider bar, where nine Australian ciders are on tap, including the house-brewed speciality.

Alumbra CLUB
(03-8623 9666; www.alumbra.com.au; Shed 9, Central Pier, 161 Harbour Esplanade; 4pm-3am Fri & Sat, to 1am Sun; Tourist Shuttle, 70, City Circle) Great music and a stunning location will impress – even if the Bali-meets-Morocco follies of the decor don't. If you're going to do one megaclub in Melbourne (and like the idea of a glass dance floor), this is going to be your best bet. It's in one of the old sheds jutting out into Docklands' Victoria Harbour.

Brown Alley CLUB
(Colonial Hotel; Map p476; 03-9670 8599; www.brownalley.com; 585 Lonsdale St; 10pm-7am Thu-Sun; Flagstaff) This historic pub hides a fully fledged nightclub with a 24-hour licence. It's enormous, with distinct rooms over three levels that can fit up to 1000

people. Its sound equipment is the business and the rota of DJs includes spinners of breakbeat, psy-trance and deep house.

Fitzroy & Around

Possessing the highest density of pubs of any suburb in Melbourne, Fitzroy has a big drinking scene. Neighbouring Collingwood and Northcote, along High St, also see a lot of action.

Naked for Satan BAR

(Map p484; ☎03-9416 2238; www.nakedforsatan.com.au; 285 Brunswick St, Fitzroy; ⊙noon-midnight Sun-Thu, to 1am Fri & Sat; 🚊112) Vibrant, loud and reviving an apparent Brunswick St legend (a man nicknamed Satan who would get down and dirty, naked because of the heat, in an illegal vodka distillery under the shop), this place packs a punch both with its popular *pintxos* (Basque tapas; $2), huge range of cleverly named beverages and unbeatable roof terrace with wraparound decked balcony.

Everleigh COCKTAIL BAR

(Map p484; www.theeverleigh.com; 150-156 Gertrude St, Fitzroy; ⊙5.30pm-1am; 🚊86) Sophistication and bartending standards are off the charts at this upstairs hidden nook. Settle into a leather booth in the intimate setting with a few friends for conversation and oohing and ahhing over classic 'golden era' cocktails like you've never tasted before.

DRINKING UNDER THE STARS

Melbourne may be home to some of the coolest bars hidden down rotten-cabbage-leaf-strewn city alleyways, but when the summer sun beats down and the evenings are long and cool, it's time for some fresh air and natural light. Whether it's riding an elevator to a secret rooftop, or chugging jugs of ale at a beer garden, Melbourne has some top open-air drinking spots.

Rooftop Bars

Goldilocks (p507)

Naked for Satan (p508)

Madame Brussels (p504)

Palmz at the Carlton Hotel (p507)

Outdoor Bars & Beer Gardens

Ponyfish Island (p507)

The Standard (p509)

Riverland (p507)

Wesley Anne BAR

(☎03-9482 1333; www.wesleyanne.com.au; 250 High St, Northcote; ⊙noon-late; 🚊86, 🚆Northcote) This atmospheric pub set up shop in a church mission's house of assembly. What else can you expect when the demon drink wins out against the forces of temperance? Booze, yes, but also interesting food, live music, a big beer garden with space heaters and a cruisy crowd who often bring their kids along in daylight hours.

Panama Dining Room BAR

(Map p484; ☎03-9417 7663; www.thepanama.com.au; 3rd fl, 231 Smith St, Fitzroy; ⊙5-11pm Sun-Wed, to midnight Thu, to 1am Fri & Sat; 🚊86) Gawp at the ersatz Manhattan views in this large warehouse-style space while sipping serious cocktails and snacking on truffled polenta chips or falafel balls with tahini. The dining area gets packed around 9pm for its Mod European menu.

Industry Beans CAFE

(Map p484; www.industrybeans.com; cnr Fitzroy & Rose Sts, Fitzroy; ⊙7am-4pm Mon-Fri, 8am-5pm Sat & Sun; 📶; 🚊96, 112) It's all about coffee chemistry at this warehouse cafe tucked in a Fitzroy side street. The coffee guide takes you through the speciality styles on offer (roasted on site) and helpful staff take the pressure off deciding. Pair your brew with some latte coffee pearls or coffee toffee prepared in the 'lab'.

The food menu is ambitious, but doesn't always hit the mark.

Napier Hotel PUB

(Map p484; ☎03-9419 4240; www.thenapierhotel.com; 210 Napier St, Fitzroy; ⊙3-11pm Mon-Thu, 1pm-1am Fri & Sat, 1-11pm Sun; 🚊86, 112) The Napier has stood on this corner for over a century – many pots have been pulled as the face of the neighbourhood changed, as demonstrated by the memorabilia of the sadly departed Fitzroy footy team. Worm your way around the central bar to the boisterous dining room for an iconic Bogan Burger. Head upstairs to check out its gallery, too.

Rose PUB

(Map p484; 406 Napier St, Fitzroy; ⊙noon-midnight Sun-Wed, to 1am Thu-Sat; 🚊86, 112) A much-loved Fitzroy backstreet local, the Rose has remained true to its roots with cheap counter meals and a non-pretentious crowd here to watch the footy.

Little Creatures Dining Hall BEER HALL
(Map p484; ☎03-9417 5500; www.littlecreatures.com.au; 222 Brunswick St, Fitzroy; ⏰8am-late; 📶; 🚋112) This vast drinking hall is the perfect place to imbibe from one of Australia's most successful microbreweries and gorge on pizzas. Also has free use of community bikes with picnic baskets, so pick up one of its beery hampers.

Standard PUB
(Map p484; ☎03-9419 4793; 293 Fitzroy St, Fitzroy; ⏰3-11pm Mon & Tue, noon-11pm Wed-Sat, noon-9pm Sun; 🚋96, 112) Flaunting a great beer garden, the Standard is anything but its moniker. The Fitzroy backstreet local has down-to-earth bar staff and a truly eclectic crowd enhancing an atmosphere defined by live music, footy on the small screen and loud and enthusiastic chatter.

Storm in a Teacup CAFE
(Map p484; ☎03-9415 9593; www.storminateacup.com.au; 48a Smith St, Collingwood; ⏰10am-6pm Tue-Sun; 📶; 🚋86) With Melbourne's infatuation with fancy coffees, it's great to see a cafe with the same devotion to tea. There's a selection of 40 different types of cuppas on offer, with black, green and white teas from around the world, including several single-origin leaves. It also does food and tea-based cocktails.

Carlton & Around

Seven Seeds CAFE
(www.sevenseeds.com.au; 114 Berkeley St, Carlton; ⏰7am-5pm Mon-Sat, 8am-5pm Sun; 🚋19, 59) The most spacious of the Seven Seeds coffee empire – there's plenty of room to store your bike and sip a splendid coffee beside the other lucky people who've found this rather out-of-the-way warehouse cafe. Public cuppings (coffee tastings) are held Wednesday (9am) and Saturday (10am).

Jimmy Watson's WINE BAR
(Map p486; ☎03-9347 3985; www.jimmywatsons.com.au; 333 Lygon St, Carlton; ⏰11am-11pm; 🚋1, 8) Keep it tidy at Watson's wine bar with something nice by the glass, or go a bottle of dry and dry (vermouth and ginger ale) and settle in for the afternoon and evening. If this Robyn Boyd–designed stunning mid-century building had ears, there'd be a few generations of writers, students and academics in trouble.

BEST COFFEE IN MELBOURNE

Auction Rooms (p502)
Industry Beans (p508)
Seven Seeds
Brunswick East Project

Alderman WINE BAR
(134 Lygon St, East Brunswick; ⏰5pm-late Tue-Fri, 2pm-late Sat & Sun; 📶; 🚋1, 8) A classic East Brunswick local, the Alderman has an inviting, traditional, heavy wooden bar, open fireplace, good beer selection and cocktails by the jug. There's a small courtyard and you can order from restaurant Bar Idda (p502) next door.

Town Hall Hotel PUB
(☎03-9328 1983; www.townhallhotelnorthmelbourne.com.au; 33 Errol St, North Melbourne; ⏰4pm-1am Mon-Thu, noon-1am Fri & Sat, noon-11pm Sun; 🚋57) The Town Hall is an unfussy local with some fabulously incongruous religious iconography high on the walls. Live music is staged free in the front room from Thursday to Saturday, otherwise they'll be spinning some classic vinyl. There's a beer garden and pub meals, too. From the Queen Vic Market head west along Victoria St, then right at Errol St.

Gerald's Bar WINE BAR
(http://geraldsbar.com.au; 386 Rathdowne St, North Carlton; ⏰5-11pm Mon-Sat; 🚌253, 🚋1, 8) Wine by the glass is democratically selected at Gerald's, and they spin some fine vintage vinyl from behind the curved wooden bar. Gerald himself is out the back preparing to feed you whatever he feels like on the day: goat curry, seared calamari, meatballs, trifle.

Brunswick East Project CAFE
(☎03-9381 1881; www.padrecoffee.com.au; 438 Lygon St, East Brunswick; ⏰7am-4pm Mon-Sat, 8am-4pm Sun; 🚋1, 8) Another big player in Melbourne's coffee movement, this East Brunswick warehouse-style cafe is the original roaster for Padre Coffee and brews its premium single-origins and blends. Also has **League of Honest Coffee** (Map p476; 8 Exploration Lane; ⏰7am-5pm Mon-Fri; 🚋City Circle, 24, 30) and stalls at the **Queen Victoria Market**

(String Bean Alley, M Shed near Peel St; 7am-2pm Tue & Thu, to 4pm Fri-Sun; 55) and **South Melbourne Market** (www.padrecoffee.com.au; shop 33, South Melbourne Market; 7am-4pm Wed, Sat & Sun, to 5pm Fri; 96).

Retreat PUB

(03-9380 4090; www.retreathotelbrunswick.com.au; 280 Sydney Rd, Brunswick; noon-late; 19, Brunswick) This pub is so big as to be a tad overwhelming. Find your habitat – garden backyard, grungy band room or intimate front bar – and relax. Sundays are very popular with locals who like to laze on the (fake) grass, and there's live music on most nights.

Brunswick Green BAR

(313 Sydney Rd, Brunswick; 4pm-midnight Tue-Thu, 2pm-1am Fri & Sat, 2-11pm Sun; 19, Brunswick) A cool Brunswick local with bohemian front bar, comfy share-house-style lounge and backyard beer garden. Wednesday nights feature the popular Variety Collective performers.

South Melbourne

Clement CAFE

(www.clementcoffee.com; South Melbourne Market, 116-136 Cecil St, South Melbourne; 7am-5pm; 96) There's a buzz about this tiny cafe on the perimeter of the South Melbourne Market, not only for its expertly crafted brew but also for the homemade salted-caramel or jam-and-custard donuts. Grab a streetside stool or takeaway and wander the market.

Eve CLUB

(03-9696 7388; www.evebar.com.au; 334 City Rd, South Melbourne; dusk-late Thu-Sat; 112) Florence Broadhurst wallpaper, a black granite bar and Louis chairs set the tone, which gets rapidly lower as the night progresses. Footballers, glamour girls and the odd lost soul come for cocktails and commercial house. Expect to queue after 9pm.

St Kilda & Around

Carlisle Wine Bar WINE BAR

(03-9531 3222; www.carlislewinebar.com.au; 137 Carlisle St, Balaclava; 3pm-1am Mon-Fri, 11am-1am Sat & Sun; 3, 16, Balaclava) Locals love this often-rowdy, wine-worshiping former butcher's shop. The staff will treat you like a regular and find you a glass of something special, or effortlessly throw together a cocktail amid the weekend rush. The rustic Italian food is good, too. Carlisle St runs east off St Kilda Rd.

George Lane Bar BAR

(Map p490; www.georgelanebar.com.au; 1 George Lane, St Kilda; 7pm-1am Thu-Sun; 96, 16) Hidden behind the hulk of the George Hotel, tucked away off Grey St, this little bar is a good rabbit hole to dive into. Its pleasantly ad hoc decor is a relief from the inch-of-its-life design aesthetic elsewhere. There are DJs (and queues) on the weekends.

Republica BAR

(Map p490; www.republica.net.au; St Kilda Sea Baths, 10-18 Jacka Blvd, St Kilda; 11.30am-1am Mon-Fri, 9am-1am Sat & Sun; ; 3a, 16, 96) Opening right up to St Kilda beach, Republica is the closest you'll get to a beach bar in Melbourne. A great spot for a sunset beer or cocktail lounging in a hanging wicker chair, but you can also start the day here by the sea with breakfast and coffee.

St Kilda Bowling Club PUB

(Map p490; www.stkildasportsclub.com.au; 66 Fitzroy St, St Kilda; noon-11pm Sun-Thu, to 1am Fri & Sat; 16, 96, 112) This fabulously intact old clubhouse is tucked behind a trimmed hedge and a splendid bowling green. The long bar serves drinks at club prices (ie cheap) and you'll be joined by St Kilda's hippest on Sunday afternoons. Kick off your shoes, roll a few bowls, knock back beers and watch the sun go down along with your bowling accuracy.

Hotel Barkly PUB

(Map p490; 03-9525 3354; www.hotelbarkly.com; 109 Barkly St, St Kilda; 16, 67, 79) The street-level public bar is the place to go if you're up for sinking a few pints, wiggling to whatever comes on the jukebox and snogging a stranger before last drinks are called. The rooftop bar feigns a bit of class, but things get messy up there, too. Worth it for the spectacular sunset views across St Kilda, though.

Vineyard BAR

(Map p490; www.thevineyard.com.au; 71a Acland St, St Kilda; 10.30am-3.30am Mon-Fri, 10am-3.30am Sat & Sun; 3a, 16, 96) An old favourite, the Vineyard has the perfect corner position and a courtyard BBQ that attracts crowds of backpackers and scantily clad young locals enjoying themselves so much they drown out the neighbouring roller coaster. Sunday afternoon sessions are big here.

Entertainment

Australian Centre for the Moving Image CINEMA
(ACMI; Map p476; 03-9663 2583; www.acmi.net.au; Federation Sq; 1, 48, 70, 72, 75, Flinders St) ACMI's cinemas screen a diverse range of films. It programs regular events and festivals for film genres and audiences, as well as screening one-offs.

Cinema Nova CINEMA
(Map p486; 03-9347 5331; www.cinemanova.com.au; 380 Lygon St, Carlton; Tourist Shuttle, 1, 8) The latest in art house, docos and foreign films. Cheap Monday screenings.

Rooftop Cinema CINEMA
(Map p476; www.rooftopcinema.com.au; level 6, Curtin House, 252 Swanston St; Melbourne Central) This rooftop bar sits at dizzying heights on top of the happening Curtin House. In summer it transforms into an outdoor cinema with striped deckchairs and a calendar of new and classic flicks.

Moonlight Cinema CINEMA
(www.moonlight.com.au; Gate D, Birdwood Ave, Royal Botanic Gardens; 8) Melbourne's original outdoor cinema, with the option of 'Gold Grass' tickets that include a glass of wine and a reserved bean-bag bed.

La Mama THEATRE
(Map p486; 03-9347 6948; www.lamama.com.au; 205 Faraday St, Carlton; 1, 8) La Mama is historically significant in Melbourne's theatre scene. This tiny, intimate forum produces new Australian works and experimental theatre, and has a reputation for developing emerging playwrights. It's a ramshackle building with an open-air bar. Shows also run at its larger **Courthouse Theater** (349 Drummond St), so check tickets carefully for the correct location.

Malthouse Theatre THEATRE
(03-9685 5111; www.malthousetheatre.com.au; 113 Sturt St, Southbank; 1) The Malthouse Theatre Company often produces the most exciting theatre in Melbourne. Dedicated to promoting Australian works, the company has been housed in the atmospheric Malthouse Theatre since 1990 (when it was known as the Playbox). From Flinders St Station walk across Princes Bridge and along St Kilda Rd. Turn right at Grant St, then left into Sturt St.

TICKETS

Moshtix (www.moshtix.com.au) Tickets for concerts, theatre, comedy and other events.

Halftix Melbourne (Map p476; www.halftixmelbourne.com; Melbourne Town Hall, 90-120 Swanston St; 10am-2pm Mon, 11am-6pm Tue-Fri, 10am-4pm Sat; Flinders St) A good resource for tickets.

Ticketek (Map p476; http://premier.ticketek.com.au) Visit the outlet, or make phone or internet bookings for large sporting events and mainstream entertainment.

Ticketmaster (Map p476; www.ticketmaster.com.au) Main booking agency for theatre, concerts, sports and other events.

Melbourne Theatre Company THEATRE
(MTC; 03-8688 0800; www.mtc.com.au; 140 Southbank Blvd, Southbank; 1) Melbourne's major theatrical company stages around 15 productions each year, ranging from contemporary and modern (including many new Australian works) to Shakespearean and other classics. Performances take place in a brand-new, award-winning venue in Southbank.

Last Laugh at the Comedy Club COMEDY
(Map p476; 03-9650 1977; www.thecomedyclub.com.au; Athenaeum Theatre, 188 Collins St; show $25; Fri & Sat; 1, 72, 112, Flinders St) The Last Laugh is open Friday and Saturday night year-round, with additional evenings in summer. This is professional stand-up, featuring local and international artists. Dinner-show packages ($55) are available – bookings recommended. The club is also a venue for acts during the Comedy Festival.

Comic's Lounge COMEDY
(03-9348 9488; www.thecomicslounge.com.au; 26 Errol St, North Melbourne; 57) There is stand-up every night of the week here. Admission prices vary, but are usually between $15 and $25. Dinner-and-show nights are popular and feature Melbourne's best-known comedians (many of whom also host radio shows). Tuesday is a kind of open-mic night, where aspiring comics have their eight minutes of fame (or shame).

Live Music

Check daily papers and weekly street magazines **Beat** (www.beat.com.au) and **The Music** (www.themusic.com.au) for gig info. Radio station 3RRR (102.7FM) broadcasts a gig guide at 7pm each evening and puts it online at www.rrr.org.au.

Esplanade Hotel LIVE MUSIC
(The Espy; Map p490; ☎03-9534 0211; www.espy.com.au; 11 The Esplanade, St Kilda; ⊙noon-1am Sun-Wed, to 3am Thu-Sat; 🚊16, 96) Rock pigs rejoice. The Espy remains gloriously shabby and welcoming to all. A mix of local and international bands play nightly, everything from rock 'n' roll to hip hop, either in the legendary Gershwin Room, the front bar or down in the basement.

The Tote LIVE MUSIC
(☎03-9419 5320; www.thetotehotel.com; cnr Johnston & Wellington Sts, Collingwood; ⊙4pm-late Tue-Sun; 🚊86) One of Melbourne's most iconic live-music venues, not only does this divey Collingwood pub have a great roster of local and international underground bands, but one of the best jukeboxes in the universe. Its temporary closure in 2010 brought Melbourne to a stop, literally – people protested on the streets against the liquor licensing laws blamed for the closure.

Corner Hotel LIVE MUSIC
(☎03-9427 9198; www.cornerhotel.com; 57 Swan St, Richmond; ⊙4pm-late Tue & Wed, noon-late Thu-Sun; 🚊70, 🚆Richmond) The band room here is one of Melbourne's most popular midsized venues and has seen plenty of loud and live action over the years, from Dinosaur Jr to the Buzzcocks. If your ears need a break, there's a friendly front bar. The rooftop has city views, but gets super-packed, often with a different crowd from the music fans below.

Northcote Social Club LIVE MUSIC
(☎03-9489 3917; www.northcotesocialclub.com; 301 High St, Northcote; ⊙4pm-late Mon & Tue, noon-late Wed-Sun; 🚊86, 🚆Northcote) The stage at this inner-north local has seen plenty of international folk just one album out from star status. Its home-grown line-up is also notable. If you're just after a drink, the front bar buzzes every night of the week, and there's a large deck out back for lazy afternoons.

Cherry LIVE MUSIC
(Map p476; www.cherrybar.com.au; AC/DC Lane; ⊙6pm-3am Tue & Wed, 5pm-5am Thu-Sat, 2-6.30pm Sun; 🚊City Circle, 70, 75) Melbourne's legendary rock 'n' roll bar is still going strong. Located down AC/DC Lane (yep, named after the band, who are home-grown heroes), there's often a queue, but once inside, a welcoming, slightly anarchic spirit prevails. Live music and DJs play rock 'n' roll seven nights a week, and there's a long-standing soul night on Thursdays.

It's the choice of touring bands to hang out post-gig – the bar made headlines by knocking back Lady Gaga to honour a local band's booking.

Old Bar LIVE MUSIC
(Map p484; ☎03-9417 4155; www.theoldbar.com.au; 74-76 Johnston St, Fitzroy; 📶; 🚊96, 112) With live bands seven days a week and a license till 3am, the Old Bar's another reason why Melbourne is the rock 'n' roll capital of Australia. It gets great local bands and a few internationals playing in its grungy bandroom with a house-party vibe.

Bennetts Lane JAZZ
(Map p476; ☎03-9663 2856; www.bennettslane.com; 25 Bennetts Lane, Melbourne; ⊙9pm-late; 🚊City Circle, 24, 30) Bennetts Lane has long been the boiler room of Melbourne jazz. It attracts the cream of local and international talent and an audience that knows when it's time to applaud a solo. Beyond the cosy front bar, there's another space reserved for big gigs.

Prince Bandroom LIVE MUSIC
(Map p490; ☎03-9536 1168; www.princebandroom.com.au; 29 Fitzroy St, St Kilda; 🚊16, 96, 112) The Prince is a much-loved St Kilda venue, with quality international and local rock, indie, DJs and hip-hop bands having graced its stage. Its leafy balcony and raucous downstairs bar are added attractions. These days it leans more towards dance and electropop acts.

Evelyn Hotel LIVE MUSIC
(Map p484; ☎03-9419 5500; www.evelynhotel.com; 351 Brunswick St, Fitzroy; ⊙12.30pm-1.30am; 🚊112) Playing mostly local acts, the Evelyn also pulls the occasional international performer. The Ev doesn't discriminate by genre: if it's quality, it gets a look in here.

Palais Theatre CONCERT VENUE
(Map p490; ☎03-9525 3240, tickets 13 61 00; www.palaistheatre.net.au; Lower Esplanade, St Kilda; 🚊3a, 16, 79, 96) Standing gracefully next to Luna Park, the heritage-listed Palais (c 1927) is a St Kilda icon. Not only is the theatre a

beautiful old space, but it also stages some pretty special performances, from international bands to big-name comedians.

Sidney Myer Music Bowl CONCERT VENUE
(☎1300 182 183; www.artscentremelbourne.com.au; Linlithgow Ave, King Domain Gardens; 🚊1, 3, 5, 6, 8, 16, 64, 67, 72) This beautiful amphitheatre in the park is used for a variety of outdoor events, from the Tropfest film festival to Nick Cave and the Bad Seeds, Opera in the Bowl or the New Year's Day rave Summerdayze.

Dance, Classical Music & Opera

Australian Ballet BALLET
(☎1300 369 741; www.australianballet.com.au; 2 Kavanagh St; 🚊1) Based in Melbourne and now more than 40 years old, the Australian Ballet performs traditional and new works at the State Theatre in the Arts Centre. You can take an hour-long Australian Ballet Centre tour ($18, bookings essential) that includes a visit to the production and wardrobe departments as well as the studios of both the company and the school.

Hamer Hall CONCERT VENUE
(Melbourne Concert Hall; Map p476; ☎1300 182 183; www.artscentremelbourne.com.au; Arts Centre Melbourne, 100 St Kilda Rd; 🚊1, 3, 16, 64, 72, 🚉Flinders St) Having recently undergone a multimillion-dollar redevelopment, the concert hall is well known for its excellent acoustics, with a decor inspired by Australia's mineral and gemstone deposits.

Melbourne Symphony Orchestra ORCHESTRA
(MSO; Map p476; ☎03-9929 9600; www.mso.com.au) The MSO has a broad reach – while not afraid to be populist (it's done sell-out performances with both Burt Bacharach and the Whitlams), it can also do edgy – such as performing with Kiss – along with its performances of the great masterworks of symphony. It performs regularly at venues around the city, including Melbourne Town Hall, the Recital Centre and Hamer Hall. Also runs a summer series of free concerts at the Sidney Myer Music Bowl.

Opera Australia OPERA
(☎03-9685 3700; www.opera.org.au; cnr Fawkner & Fanning Sts, Southbank) The national opera company performs with some regularity at Melbourne's Victorian Arts Centre.

Sport

Melbourne is a sport-obsessed city. From March to October it's all about AFL footy, while rugby league, soccer and union are also very popular. In summer, cricket dominates.

Melbourne Cricket Ground SPECTATOR SPORT
(☎03-9657 8888; www.mcg.org.au) Melbourne's sporting mecca, the MCG (p483), or 'G', hosts cricket in the summer and AFL footy in the winter. Attendance is a rite of passage for many locals.

Melbourne Park SPECTATOR SPORT
(☎03-9286 1600; www.mopt.com.au; Batman Ave, Richmond; tours adult/child/family $15/7/35; 🚊48, 70, 75, 🚉Jolimont) Home to the **Australian Open Tennis** grand slam in January, Melbourne Park precinct has 34 courts, including its centrepiece **Rod Laver Arena**. You can take a tour to the dressing rooms, VIP areas and super-boxes. Its indoor-court hire ranges from $36 to $42, and outdoor courts cost between $28 and $36, plus racquet hire.

Flemington Racecourse HORSE RACING
(☎1300 727 575; www.vrc.net.au; 400 Epsom Rd, Flemington; 🚊57, 🚉Flemington Racecourse) Home of the Victoria Racing Club, Flemington has regular horse-race meets, climaxing with the Spring Racing Carnival (including the Melbourne Cup; p493) from October to November.

Shopping

Melbourne is a city of passionate, dedicated retailers catering to a broad range of tastes, whims and lifestyles. From boutique-filled city lanes to suburban shopping streets and malls, you'll find plenty of places to offload your cash and pick up something unique.

Central Melbourne

Melbourne's city centre has everything from boutiques hidden in lanes to large shopping complexes such as QV, Emporium and Melbourne Central with major international brands.

★Craft Victoria Shop CRAFTS
(Craft Victoria; Map p476; ☎03-9650 7775; www.craft.org.au; 31 Flinders Lane; ⏲11am-6pm Mon-Sat; 🚊City Circle, 70, 75) This retail arm of Craft Victoria showcases the best of handmade crafts, mainly from local Victorian artists. Its range of jewellery, textiles, accessories, glass and ceramics bridges the art/craft divide and makes for some wonderful mementos of Melbourne. There are also a

few galleries with changing exhibitions; admission is free.

Somewhere FASHION, ACCESSORIES
(Map p476; www.someplace.com.au; Royal Arcade, 2/314 Little Collins St; 10am-6pm Mon-Thu & Sat, to 8pm Fri, 11am-5pm Sun; 86, 96) Somewhere is an apt name for this hard-to-find treasure. It's located at the Little Collins St end of Royal Arcade (look for the Marais sign and take the stairs to level 2). The white-washed warehouse space stocks predominantly Scandinavian labels, as well as local designers, along with leather tote bags, Anne Black ceramic jewellery and a good range of denim.

Incu FASHION
(Map p476; 03-9663 9933; www.incuclothing.com; shop 6a, 274 Flinders Lane; 10am-6pm Mon-Thu & Sat, to 8pm Fri, 11am-5pm Sun; Flinders St) Sydney retailer Incu has set up store in Melbourne and stocks a range of contemporary designers for menswear, with crisp tailored shirts from Weathered, comfy chinos and great stuff from labels such as Vanishing Elephant and Kloke. Its women's store is in the QV Building.

Captains of Industry CLOTHING, ACCESSORIES
(Map p476; 03-9670 4405; www.captainsofindustry.com.au; level 1, 2 Somerset Pl; 9am-5pm; 19, 57, 59) Where can you get a haircut, a bespoke suit and a pair of shoes or a leather wallet made in the one place? Here. The hard-working folk at spacious and industrial Captains also offer homey breakfasts and lunches, and it turns into a low-key bar on Friday nights.

City Hatters ACCESSORIES
(Map p476; 03-9614 3294; www.cityhatters.com.au; 211 Flinders St; 9.30am-6pm Mon-Fri, 9am-5pm Sat, 10am-4pm Sun; Flinders St) Located beside the main entrance to Flinders St Station, this is the most convenient place to purchase an iconic Akubra hat, kangaroo-leather sun hat or something a little more unique.

QUEEN VIC NIGHT MARKET

On Wednesday evenings from mid-November to the end of February the Summer Night Market takes over the **Queen Victoria Market** (p479). It's a lively social event featuring hawker-style food stalls, bars and music and dance performances. There's also a winter night market each Wednesday evening in August.

Wunderkammer ANTIQUES
(Map p476; 03-9642 4694; www.wunderkammer.com.au; 439 Lonsdale St; 10am-6pm Mon-Sat, to 4pm Sun; 55) Surprises abound in this 'Wonder Chamber', the strangest of shops: taxidermy, bugs in jars, antique scientific tools, surgical equipment and carnivorous plants, to name a few.

RM Williams CLOTHING
(Map p476; 03-9663 7126; www.rmwilliams.com.au; Melbourne Central, Lonsdale St; 10am-6pm Mon-Thu & Sat, to 9pm Fri, to 5pm Sun) An Aussie icon, even for city slickers, this brand will kit you up with stylish essentials for working the land, including a pair of those famous boots.

Original & Authentic Aboriginal Art ARTS, CRAFTS
(Map p476; 03-9663 5133; www.originalandauthenticaboriginalart.com; 90 Bourke St; 11am-6pm; 86, 96) Open for 25 years this centrally located gallery has a good relationship with its Indigenous artists across Australia and offers stunning and affordable pieces, all with author profiles.

Alice Euphemia FASHION, JEWELLERY
(Map p476; shop 6, Cathedral Arcade, 37 Swanston St; 10am-6pm Mon-Thu & Sat, to 7pm Fri, noon-5pm Sun; Flinders St) Art-school cheek abounds in the Australian-made-and-designed labels sold here – Romance was Born, Karla Spetic and Kloke, to name a few. Jewellery sways between the shocking and exquisitely pretty, and its upstairs space hosts regular events and exhibitions.

NGV Shop at the Ian Potter Centre BOOKS, GIFTS
(Map p476; www.ngv.vic.gov.au; Federation Sq; Flinders St) This gallery shop has a wide range of international design magazines, a kids' section and the usual gallery standards. Also at NGV International (p480).

Melbournalia GIFTS, SOUVENIRS
(Map p476; www.melbournalia.com.au; shop 5, 50 Bourke St; 10am-6pm Mon-Thu, to 8pm Fri, 11am-5pm Sat & Sun; 86, 96) Pop-up store turned permanent, this is the place to stock up on interesting souvenirs by local designers – from tram tote bags and city-rooftop honey to prints of the city's icons and great books on Melbourne.

Fitzroy & Around

Gertrude St has become one of Melbourne's most interesting shopping strips. Smith St is decidedly vintage, with small boutique stores, though its northern end, beyond Johnston St, is jam-packed with clearance stores. Brunswick St is a mixed bag, but does have some good boutique designers from Johnston St to Gertrude St. Northcote's High St has an interesting collection of homewares, vintage and young designer shops, too.

★Third Drawer Down HOMEWARES
(Map p484; www.thirddrawerdown.com; 93 George St, Fitzroy; 11am-5pm Mon-Sat; 86) It all started with its signature tea-towel designs (now found in MOMA in New York) at this 'museum of art souvenirs'. Third Drawer Down makes life beautifully unusual by stocking absurdist pieces with a sense of humour, as well as high-end art by well-known designers.

Mud Australia CERAMICS
(Map p484; 03-9419 5161; www.mudaustralia.com; 181 Gertrude St, Fitzroy; 10am-6pm Mon-Fri, to 5pm Sat, noon-5pm Sun; 86) You'll find some of the most aesthetically beautiful – as well as functional – porcelain from Australian-designed Mud. Coffee mugs, milk pourers, salad bowls and serving plates come in muted pastel colours with a raw matt finish. Prices start from $20 per piece.

Crumpler ACCESSORIES
(Map p484; 03-9417 5338; www.crumpler.com; 87 Smith St, cnr Gertrude St, Fitzroy; 10am-6pm Mon-Sat, to 5pm Sun; 86) Crumpler's bike-courier bags, designed by two former couriers looking for a bag they could hold their beer in while cycling home, started it all. Its durable, practical designs now extend to bags for cameras, laptops and iPods, and can be found around the world.

Gorman CLOTHING, ACCESSORIES
(Map p484; www.gormanshop.com.au; 235 Brunswick St, Fitzroy; 10am-6pm Mon-Thu & Sat, to 7pm Fri, 11am-5pm Sun; 112) Lisa Gorman makes everyday clothes that are far from ordinary: boyish, but sexy, short shapes are cut from exquisite fabrics, and pretty cardigans are coupled with relaxed, organic tees. You can find other branches in the **GPO** (Map p476; 03-9663 0066; www.melbournesgpo.com; cnr Elizabeth St & Bourke St Mall; 10am-6pm Mon-Thu & Sat, to 8pm Fri, 11am-5pm Sun; 19, 57, 59, 86, 96) and elsewhere around town.

MELBOURNE'S BEST MARKETS

South Melbourne Market (p489)

Queen Victoria Night Market (p479)

Rose Street Artists' Market (Map p484; www.rosestmarket.com.au; 60 Rose St, Fitzroy; 11am-5pm Sat; 112) One of Melbourne's most popular art-and-craft markets showcases the best of local designers just a short stroll from Brunswick St. You'll find up to 70 stalls selling matt silver jewellery, clothing, milk-bottle ceramics, iconic Melbourne screen prints, wild fig candles and ugly-cute toys. **Humble Vintage** (p489) has bike hire from here.

Esplanade Market (Map p490; www.esplanademarket.com; btwn Cavell & Fitzroy Sts, St Kilda; 10am-4pm Sun May-Sep, to 5pm Oct-Apr; 96) Fancy a Sunday stroll shopping by the seaside? Well, here's the place, with 1km of trestle tables joined end to end carrying individually crafted products, from toys and organic soaps to large metal sculptures of fishy creatures.

Poison City Records MUSIC
(Map p484; www.poisoncityrecords.com; 400 Brunswick St, Fitzroy; 11am-6pm; 112) Independent record/skate shop with its own Poison City label releasing excellent indie, punk and fuzz-rock Melbourne bands, such as the Nation Blue, White Walls and Smith Street Band.

Aesop BEAUTY
(Map p484; 03-9419 8356; www.aesop.com; 242 Gertrude St, Fitzroy; 11am-5pm Mon & Sun, 10am-6pm Tue-Fri, 10am-5pm Sat; 86) This home-grown empire specialises in citrus-and-botanical-based aromatic balms, hair masques, scents, cleansers and oils in beautifully simple packaging for both men and women. There are plenty of branches around town (and plenty of opportunity to sample the products in most of Melbourne's cafe bathrooms).

Shirt & Skirt Market CLOTHING, CRAFTS
(www.shirtandskirtmarkets.com.au; Abbotsford Convent, 1 St Heliers St, Abbotsford; 10am-4pm 3rd Sun of the month; Collingwood) Buy limited-run clothes and accessories, for both adults and kids, from emerging designers. The Convent makes for leisurely outdoor browsing. Check the website for regular stallholder

MELBOURNE WEBSITES

Broadsheet Melbourne (www.broadsheet.com.au) Great source for reviews of the city's best eating, drinking and shopping spots.

That's Melbourne (www.thatsmelbourne.com.au) Downloadable maps, info and podcasts from the City of Melbourne.

Three Thousand (thethousands.com.au/melbourne) A weekly round-up of (cool) local goings on.

Visit Victoria (www.visitvictoria.com.au) Highlights events in Melbourne and Victoria.

Good Food (www.goodfood.com.au) Restaurant and foodie happenings around Melbourne.

details. To get here, head east down Johnson St, turn right at Clarke St, then left.

Little Salon CRAFT, FASHION
(Map p484; www.littlesalon.com.au; 71 Gertrude St, Fitzroy; ⏲10am-6pm Mon-Sat; 🚊86, 112) Cute little store that stocks wearable art pieces from local designers, as well as decorative items for your wall or shelf.

Carlton & Around

Readings BOOKS
(Map p486; www.readings.com.au; 309 Lygon St, Carlton; ⏲8am-11pm Mon-Fri, 9am-11pm Sat, 9am-9pm Sun; 🚌Tourist Shuttle, 🚊1, 8) A potter around this defiantly prospering indie bookshop can occupy an entire afternoon if you're so inclined. There's a dangerously loaded (and good-value) specials table, switched-on staff and everyone from Lacan to *Charlie & Lola* on the shelves. Its exterior housemate-wanted board is legendary. Also in **St Kilda** (Map p490; ☎03-9525 3852; www.readings.com.au; 112 Acland St; 🚊96) and the **city centre** (Map p476; State Library, cnr La Trobe & Swanston Sts; 🚉Melbourne Central).

Gewürzhaus FOOD
(Map p486; www.gewurzhaus.com.au; 342 Lygon St, Carlton; ⏲10am-6pm Mon-Sat, 11am-5pm Sun; 🚊1, 8) Set up by two enterprising young German girls, this store is a chef's dream with its displays of spices from around the world, including indigenous Australian blends, flavoured salts and sugars. It has high-quality cooking accessories and gifts, and cooking classes, too. There's a city store inside the **Block Arcade** (Map p476; 282 Collins St; 🚊19, 57, 59).

Eastern Market CLOTHING
(Map p486; ☎03-9348 0890; www.easternmarket.com.au; 107 Grattan St, Carlton; ⏲11am-6pm Mon-Sat; 🚊1, 8, 16) Fashion-maven territory with a deconstructed Euro-Tokyo edge. The space is itself an attraction: it's a 19th-century chapel with the owner's inimitable additions.

St Kilda

Dot Herbey FASHION, ACCESSORIES
(Map p490; www.dotandherbey.com; 229 Barkly St; ⏲10.30am-6.30pm Mon-Wed, to7pm Thu & Fri, 10am-6pm Sat & Sun; 🚊96) Grandma Dot and Grandpa Herb smile down upon this tiny corner boutique from a mural-sized photo, right at home among the vintage floral fabrics and retro style. This is definitely not somewhere to go if you're looking for chain-store same-same – it's also a colourful departure from the Melbourne-black dictate.

Eclectico CLOTHING
(Map p490; www.eclectico.com.au; 163a Acland St; ⏲10.30am-6.30pm Mon-Sat, 11am-6pm Sun; 🚊96) Your one-stop shop for all your St Kilda hippy apparel, beanies, tie-dye shirts, Indian jewellery etc. Otherwise pop in for a free chai and hang out on the rooftop patio at this funky upstairs Acland St shop. It has a good Afrobeat vinyl collection, too.

Bookhouse BOOKS
(Map p490; www.bookhousestkilda.com.au; 52 Robe St; ⏲10am-6pm Wed-Sun; 🚊3, 67) A much-loved local, Bookhouse recently relocated from Fitzroy St to this quiet backstreet shop, where you might find a quality copy of a Chomsky, Kerouac or beautiful coffee-table book on the shelves, as well as a great selection of Australiana and Melbourne-specific titles.

Information

DANGERS & ANNOYANCES

There are occasional reports of alcohol-fuelled violence in some parts of Melbourne's city centre late on weekend nights – King St in particular.

EMERGENCY

For police, ambulance or fire emergencies, dial ☎000.

Centre Against Sexual Assault (CASA; ☎1800 806 292)

Police (228 Flinders Lane) Centrally located police station.

Translating & Interpreting Service (☎13 14 50) Available 24 hours.

INTERNET ACCESS

Wi-fi is available free at central city spots such as Federation Sq, Flinders St Station, Crown Casino and the State Library. Most accommodation options have wi-fi and computer terminals, costing anything from nothing to $10 per hour.

MEDICAL SERVICES

Visitors from Belgium, Finland, Italy, Ireland, Malta, the Netherlands, Norway, New Zealand, Slovenia, Sweden and the UK have reciprocal health-care agreements with Australia and can access cheaper health services through **Medicare** (☎13 20 11; www.humanservices.gov.au/customer/dhs/medicare).

Chemist Warehouse (www.chemistwarehouse.com.au) Discount pharmacy chain with stores across Melbourne. See the website for locations.

Royal Children's Hospital (☎03-9345 5522; www.rch.org.au; 50 Flemington Rd, Parkville) Children's hospital with 24-hour emergency department.

Royal Melbourne Hospital (☎03-9342 7000; www.rmh.mh.org.au; cnr Grattan St & Royal Pde, Parkville; 🚊19, 59) Public hospital with an emergency department.

Travel Doctor (TVMC; ☎03-9935 8100; www.traveldoctor.com.au; level 2, 393 Little Bourke St; ⊙9am-5pm Mon, Wed, Fri, to 8.30pm Tue & Thu, to 1pm Sat; 🚊19, 57, 59) Specialises in vaccinations and health advice for overseas trips. Also at Southgate (☎03-9690 1433; 3 Southgate Ave, Southbank; ⊙8.30am-5.30pm Mon-Fri).

TOURIST INFORMATION

Melbourne Visitor Centre (MVC; Map p476; ☎03-9658 9658; www.melbourne.vic.gov.au/touristinformation; Federation Sq; ⊙9am-6pm; 📶; 🚉Flinders St) The centre has comprehensive tourist information on Melbourne and regional Victoria, including excellent resources for mobility-impaired travellers, and a travel desk for accommodation and tour bookings. There are power sockets for recharging phones, too. There's also a booth on the Bourke St Mall (mostly for shopping and basic enquirics).

ℹ Getting There & Away

AIR

Melbourne Airport (www.melbourneairport.com.au; Centre Rd, Tullamarine) Most major airlines have direct domestic and international flights to Melbourne Airport in Tullamarine, 22km northwest of the city centre. Domestic and international flights are offered by, among others, Qantas, Jetstar, Virgin Australia and Tiger Airways. Qantaslink, a Qantas subsidiary, flies to Mildura, Launceston, Devonport and Canberra.

Regional Express has flights to/from Mildura, Mt Gambier, King Island and Burnie.

Avalon Airport (AVV; ☎1800 282 566, 03-5227 9100; www.avalonairport.com.au) Jetstar flights to and from Sydney and Brisbane use Avalon Airport, around 55km southwest of Melbourne's city centre.

Essendon Airport (MEB; ☎03-9948 9300; www.essendonairport.com.au) Smaller airport with Sharp Airlines (☎1300 556 694; www.sharpairlines.com) services to Portland, Warrnambool and Flinders Island.

BOAT

Spirit of Tasmania (☎1800 634 906; www.spiritoftasmania.com.au; adult/car one way from $159/83) The *Spirit of Tasmania* crosses Bass Strait from Melbourne to Devonport, Tasmania, at least nightly. There are also day sailings during peak season. It takes 11 hours and departs from Station Pier, Port Melbourne.

MYKI CARD

Melbourne's buses, trams and trains use **myki** (www.myki.com.au), the controversial 'touch on, touch off' travel-pass system. It's not particularly convenient for short-term visitors, requiring you to purchase a $6 plastic myki card and then put credit on it before you travel. Cards can be purchased from machines at stations, 7-Eleven stores or newsagents, but some hostels also collect myki cards from travellers who leave Melbourne. Travellers are best advised to buy a myki Visitor Value Pack ($14), which gets you one day's travel and discounts on various sights. It's available only from the airport, Skybus terminal or the PTV Hub at Southern Cross Station.

The myki card can be topped up at 7-Eleven stores and myki machines at most train stations and some tram stops in the city centre. Frustratingly, online top-ups take at least 24 hours to process. For Zone 1, which is all that most travellers will need, the Myki Money costs $3.76 for two hours, or $7.52 for the day. Machines don't always issue change, so bring exact money. The fine for travelling without a valid myki card is $212 (or $75 if you pay on the spot) – ticket inspectors are vigilant and unforgiving.

FREE TRAMS

Changes to the public transport fare structure in 2015 mean that tram travel within Melbourne's city centre – between the Queen Victoria Market, Victoria Harbour in Docklands, Spring Street and Federation Square – is now free. No myki card is needed for journeys inside this area.

BUS & TRAIN

Southern Cross Station (www.southern crossstation.net.au; cnr Collins & Spencer Sts) The main terminal for interstate bus services.

Firefly (Map p476; ☎1300 730 740; www.fireflyexpress.com.au) Day and overnight buses from Melbourne to Adelaide (from $55, 11 hours) and Sydney (from $60, 14 hours).

Greyhound (☎1300 473 946; www.greyhound.com.au) Bus services across Australia.

V/Line (☎1800 800 007; www.vline.com.au) Bus and train services around Victoria.

Getting Around

TO/FROM THE AIRPORT

Tullamarine Airport

Inconveniently, there are no direct train or tram routes from Tullamarine airport to the city. The only option by public transport is to take **bus 901**, departing Terminal 1, to Broadmeadows railway station (not the best place to hang out at night), from where you can catch the train to the city. It'll cost around $10 (including myki card) and take around an hour. The last bus to/from from the airport is around 11pm.

The fare for a **taxi** to Melbourne's city centre will start from $50 but can go as high as $75 after midnight once you factor in surcharges and tolls.

Drivers need to be aware that part of the main route into Melbourne from Tullamarine Airport is a toll road run by **CityLink** (☎13 26 29; www.citylink.com.au). If you're travelling on toll roads (including CityLink and EastLink) for less than 30 days, you'll need to buy a Melbourne Pass ($5.50 start-up fee, plus tolls and a vehicle-matching fee). If you have more time than money, take the exit ramp at Bell St, then turn right onto Nicholson St and follow it all the way south to the city centre.

SkyBus (Map p476; ☎03-9335 2811; www.skybus.com.au; adult one way $18; Ⓡ Southern Cross Station) Skybus runs a 24-hour shuttle between the city centre and the airport, with city hotel drop offs. Depending on traffic, it takes around 25 minutes.

Avalon Airport

Sita Coaches (☎03-9689 7999; www.sitacoaches.com.au; adult/child $22/10) Sita Coaches meets all flights into and out of Avalon. It departs from Southern Cross Station (50 minutes). No bookings are required.

CAR & MOTORCYCLE

Car Rental

Avis (☎13 63 33; www.avis.com.au)

Budget (☎1300 362 848; www.budget.com.au)

Europcar (☎1300 131 390; www.europcar.com.au)

Hertz (☎13 30 39; www.hertz.com.au)

Rent a Bomb (☎13 15 53; www.rentabomb.com.au)

Thrifty (☎1300 367 227; www.thrifty.com.au)

Parking

Parking inspectors are particularly vigilant in the city centre. Most of the street parking is metered and it's more likely than not that you'll be fined (between $72 to $144) if you overstay your metered time. Also keep an eye out for 'clearway' zones (prohibited kerb-side parking indicated by signs), which can result in sizeable fines. Central city parking is around $6 per hour, and $3.50 per hour in the outer central areas. There are plenty of parking garages in the city; rates vary. Motorcyclists are allowed to park on the footpath.

Toll Roads

Drivers and motorcyclists will need to purchase a toll pass if they're planning on using one of the two toll roads: CityLink from Tullamarine Airport to the city and eastern suburbs; or **EastLink** (☎13 54 65; www.eastlink.com.au), which runs from Ringwood to Frankston. Pay online or via phone – but pay within three days of using the toll road to avoid a fine.

PUBLIC TRANSPORT

Flinders Street Station is the main metro **train** station connecting the city and suburbs. The City Loop runs under the city, linking the four corners of town.

An extensive network of **trams** covers every corner of the city, running north–south and east–west along most major roads. Trams run roughly every 10 minutes Monday to Friday, every 15 minutes on Saturday and every 20 minutes on Sunday. Tram travel is free within the city centre and Docklands area.

Bicycles cannot be taken on trams or buses, but can be taken on trains.

Public Transport Victoria (☎1800 800 007; www.ptv.vic.gov.au) Oversees the region's public transport - check the website for details.

TAXI

Melbourne's taxis are metered and require an estimated prepaid fare when hailed between 10pm and 5am. You may need to pay more, or get a refund, depending on the final fare. Toll charges are added to fares.

13 Cabs (☎13 22 27; www.13cabs.com.au)

Silver Top (☎131 008; www.silvertop.com.au)

AROUND MELBOURNE

Daylesford & Hepburn Springs

POP 3265

Set among the scenic hills, lakes and forests of the Central Highlands, Daylesford and Hepburn Springs form the 'spa centre of Victoria'. It's a fabulous year-round destination where you can soak away your troubles and sip wine by the fireplace. The region is one of Victoria's favourite boutique weekend getaways – even if you don't indulge in a spa treatment, there are plenty of great walks, well-preserved and restored buildings, a fabulous foodie scene and remnants of an arty, alternative vibe. During the week some businesses close, so it's best to visit Thursday to Sunday.

Sights & Activities

Daylesford sits above pretty, artificial **Lake Daylesford**, a popular fishing and picnicking area. **Jubilee Lake**, about 3km southeast of town, is another pretty picnic spot with canoe hire. Good local walks incorporating various mineral-spring pumps include **Sailors Falls**, **Tipperary Springs**, **Central Springs Reserve** and the **Hepburn Springs Reserve**; take a water bottle with you to taste test the pump water. The visitor centre has maps and walking guides.

Convent Gallery GALLERY
(03-5348 3211; www.theconvent.com.au; 7 Daly St, Daylesford; admission $5; 10am-4pm) This beautiful 19th-century convent on Wombat Hill has been brilliantly converted into an art gallery with soaring ceilings, grand archways and magnificent gardens. Head up the path in the gardens behind the convent for sweeping views over the town. There's also an atrium **cafe**, **bar** and penthouse **apartment**. It runs night **ghost tours** ($45, book ahead) for the brave.

★**Hepburn Bathhouse & Spa** SPA
(03-5321 6000; www.hepburnbathhouse.com; Mineral Springs Reserve Rd, Hepburn Springs; 2hr bathhouse entry from $27; 9am-6.30pm) Within the Hepburn Mineral Springs Reserve, the main bathhouse is a sleek, ultramodern building where you can gaze out on the bush setting while soaking in the public pool or lazing on spa couches. The spa offers various treatments, or a soak in a private mineral-springs pool in the original historic building.

Around the bathhouse are picnic areas, mineral-spring pumps and the historic **Pavilion** cafe.

Festivals & Events

ChillOut Festival GAY & LESBIAN
(www.chilloutfestival.com.au) Held over the Labour Day weekend in March, this gay and lesbian pride festival is Daylesford's biggest annual event, attracting thousands of people for street parades, music and dance parties.

Swiss Italian Festa CULTURAL
(www.swissitalianfesta.com) Held in late October, this festival draws on the region's European roots with literary events, music, food, wine and art.

Sleeping & Eating

Daylesford

2 Dukes GUESTHOUSE $$
(03-5348 4848; 2 Duke St, Daylesford; r from $99;) Flying the flag for affordable accommodation in Daylesford, this former doctor's surgery turned guesthouse is kitted out with vintage finds and original bright artworks. The five rooms each have their own personality and share a bathroom (one room has en suite). Light breakfast is included and there's free wi-fi rounding out the best offer in town.

Lake House BOUTIQUE HOTEL $$$
(03-5348 3329; www.lakehouse.com.au; King St, Daylesford; d incl half-board from $550;) Overlooking Lake Daylesford, the famous Lake House is set in rambling gardens with bridges and waterfalls. Its 35 rooms are split into spacious waterfront rooms with balcony decks, and lodge rooms with private courtyards. Rates include breakfast and three-course dinner at its famed

> **DAYLESFORD ACCOMMODATION BOOKING**
>
> **Daylesford Accommodation Escapes** (03-5348 1448; www.dabs.com.au; 94 Vincent St, Daylesford)
>
> **Daylesford Getaways** (03-5348 4422; www.dayget.com.au; 14 Vincent St, Daylesford)
>
> **Daylesford Cottage Directory** (03-5348 1255; www.cottagedirectory.com.au; 16 Hepburn Rd, Daylesford)

restaurant. Two-night minimum stay on weekends.

Farmers Arms PUB FOOD $$

(03-5348 2091; www.thefarmersarms.com.au; 1 East St, Daylesford; mains $25-40; noon-3pm & 6pm-late) Modern and rustic – both the surroundings and the food – meld tastefully in this classic country red-brick gastropub. There's a welcoming front bar and a beer garden for summer days.

★**Lake House** MODERN AUSTRALIAN $$$

(03-5348 3329; www.lakehouse.com.au; King St, Daylesford; 2-4 course meals from $80; noon-2.30pm & 6-9.30pm;) You can't talk about Daylesford without waxing on about the Lake House, long regarded as the town's top dining experience. It doesn't disappoint with stylish purple high-back furniture, picture windows showing off Lake Daylesford, a superb seasonal menu, an award-winning wine list and impressive service. Book well ahead for weekends.

Hepburn Springs

★**Hepburn Springs Chalet** HOTEL $$

(03-5348 2344; www.hepburnspringschalet.com.au; 78 Main Rd, Hepburn Springs; r midweek/weekend $120/180;) If Don Draper was in town, this is where he'd drop his briefcase. Originally a 1920s guesthouse, the owners have retained the original features, complementing them with retro charm such as deco mirrors and velvet lounges in the sitting areas and bar. Rooms are basic, but comfortable, and come with en suites.

Shizuka Ryokan GUESTHOUSE $$$

(03-5348 2030; www.shizuka.com.au; 7 Lakeside Dr, Hepburn Springs; d $280-380) Inspired by traditional places of renewal and rejuvenation in Japan, this traditional minimalist getaway has six rooms with private Japanese gardens, tatami matting and plenty of green tea. Not suitable for children.

Red Star Café CAFE $$

(03-5348 2297; 115 Main Rd, Hepburn Springs; mains $8-26; 8am-4pm) The weatherboard

BLACK SATURDAY

Victoria is no stranger to bushfires. In 1939, 71 people died in the Black Friday fires; in 1983 Ash Wednesday claimed 75 lives in Victoria and South Australia. But no one was prepared for the utter devastation of the 2009 bushfires that became known as Black Saturday.

On 7 February, Victoria recorded its hottest temperature on record, with Melbourne exceeding 46°C and some parts of the state topping 48°C. Strong winds and tinder-dry undergrowth from years of drought, combined with the record-high temperatures, created conditions in which the risk of bushfires was extreme. The first recorded fires began near Kilmore and strong winds from a southerly change fanned the flames towards the Yarra Ranges. Within a few devastating hours a ferocious firestorm engulfed the towns of Marysville, Kinglake, Strathewen, Flowerdale and Narbethong, while separate fires started at Horsham, Bendigo and an area southeast of Beechworth. The fires virtually razed the towns of Marysville and Kinglake and moved so quickly that many residents had no chance to escape. Many victims of the fires died in their homes or trapped in their cars, some blocked by trees that had fallen across the road.

Fires raged across the state for more than a month, with high temperatures, winds and practically no rainfall making it impossible for fire crews to contain the worst blazes. New fires began at Wilson's Promontory National Park (burning more than 50% of the park area), the Dandenong Ranges and in the Daylesford area.

The statistics tell a tragic tale: 173 people died, more than 2000 homes were destroyed, an estimated 7500 people were left homeless and more than 4500 sq km were burned. What followed from the shell-shocked state and nation was a huge outpouring of grief, humanitarian aid and charity. Strangers donated tonnes of clothing, toys, food, caravans and even houses to bushfire survivors, while an appeal set up by the Australian Red Cross raised more than $300 million.

Today the blackened forests around Kinglake and Marysville are regenerating, and the communities are rebuilding. Tourism remains a big part of the economy, and visiting the shops, cafes and hotels in the area continues to boost their recovery.

shopfront feels like someone's home, with loungy couches, bookshelves full of reading material, great music, a garden out the back and a funky local vibe. Great place for a morning coffee or lunch of focaccia, curry or steak sandwich.

Information

Daylesford Visitors Centre (1800 454 891, 03-5321 6123; www.visitdaylesford.com; 98 Vincent St, Daylesford; 9am-5pm) Within the old fire station, this excellent tourist centre has good information on the area and mineral springs. There's a history **museum** (03-5348 1453; www.daylesfordhistory.com.au; 100 Vincent St, Daylesford; adult/child $3/1; 1.30-4.30pm Sat & Sun) next door.

Getting There & Away

Daylesford is 115km from Melbourne, a 1½-hour drive via the Calder Hwy; take the Woodend turn off, from where it's a 35-minute drive.

Local buses operate the 3km journey between Daylesford (from Bridport St) and Hepburn Springs; it's a 15-minute journey.

V/Line (1800 800 007; www.vline.com.au) Daily V/Line services connect Melbourne by train to Woodend, Ballarat or Castlemaine then bus to Daylesford ($11.40, two hours). The buses run from Bridport St, opposite the fire station.

The Dandenongs

The low ranges of the verdant Dandenongs, just 35km from Melbourne, feel a world away from the city and make a fantastic day trip. Mt Dandenong (633m) is the tallest peak and the landscape is a patchwork of exotic and native flora with a lush understorey of tree ferns. Take care driving on the winding roads – apart from other traffic, you might see a lyrebird wandering across.

The consumption of tea and scones is de rigueur in the many cafes in the hills, or you can stop for lunch at some quality restaurants in towns such as Olinda, Sassafras and Emerald.

Sights & Activities

Dandenong Ranges National Park NATIONAL PARK
(www.parkweb.vic.gov.au; Upper Ferntree Gully, Belgrave) This national park contains the four largest areas of remaining forest in the Dandenongs. The Ferntree Gully Area has several short walks, including the popular **1000 Steps** up to **One Tree Hill Picnic Ground** (two hours return), part of the **Kokoda Memorial Track**, which commemorates Australian WWII servicemen who fought in New Guinea. Bring sturdy shoes as its steps get slippery.

Sherbrooke Forest, just north of Belgrave, has a towering cover of mountain ash trees and several walking trails. **Grants Picnic Ground**, at Kallista, attracts flocks of sulphur-crested cockatoos.

National Rhododendron Gardens GARDENS
(03-9751 1980; www.parkweb.vic.gov.au; Georgian Rd, Olinda; 10am-5pm) FREE Giant eucalypts tower over shady lawns and brilliant flower beds at these gardens with over 15,000 rhododendrons and 12,000 azaleas. The best time to see the rhododendrons is September to November.

SkyHigh Mt Dandenong VIEWPOINT
(03-9751 0443; www.skyhighmtdandenong.com.au; 26 Observatory Rd, Mt Dandenong; vehicle entry $5; 9am-10pm Mon-Thu, to 10.30pm Fri, 8am-11pm Sat & Sun; 688) Drive up to SkyHigh for amazing views over Melbourne and Port Phillip Bay from the highest point in the Dandenongs. The view of the city lights at dusk is spectacular. There's a cafe-restaurant, a garden, picnic areas and a maze (adult/child/family $6/4/16).

Puffing Billy TRAIN
(03-9757 0700; www.puffingbilly.com.au; Old Monbulk Rd, Belgrave; return adult/child/family $65/32.50/131; Belgrave) Holding fond childhood memories for many a Melburnian, Puffing Billy is an iconic restored steam

WORTH A TRIP

ST ANDREWS

Sleepily ensconced in the hills 35km north of Melbourne, this little town is best known for the weekly **St Andrews Community Market** (www.standrewsmarket.com.au; 8am-2pm Sat). Every Saturday morning the scent of eucalypt competes with incense as an alternative crowd comes to mingle and buy handmade crafts, enjoy a shiatsu massage, sip chai, have their chakra aligned, or just listen to the street musos. To get here, a shuttle bus departs from Hurstbridge train station.

Beyond, the winding road from St Andrews up to Kinglake is one of the region's great touring routes.

train that toots its way through the ferny hills from Belgrave to Emerald Lake Park and Gembrook. Kids love dangling their legs out the sides of the open-air compartments. You can hop on and hop off en route to enjoy a picnic or walk.

Puffing Billy train station is a short walk from Belgrave train station on Melbourne's suburban network.

Trees Adventure ADVENTURE SPORTS
(☎09752 5354; www.treesadventure.com.au; Old Monbulk Rd, Glen Harrow Gardens; 2hr session adult/child $40/25; ⏰11am-5pm Mon-Fri, 9am-5pm Sat & Sun; 🚆Belgrave) Reminiscent of the Ewok village from *Return of the Jedi*, Trees Adventure is a blast of tree climbs, flying foxes and obstacle courses in a stunning patch of old-growth forest boasting sequoia, mountain ash and Japanese oak trees.

The safety system on the course ensures you're always attached to a secure line and the beginner sections are suitable for kids as young as five.

Eating & Drinking

Pie in the Sky AUSTRALIAN $
(www.pieinthesky.net.au; 43 Olinda-Monbulk Rd, Olinda; pies from $5; ⏰10am-4.30pm Mon-Fri, 9.30am-5pm Sat & Sun) Try an Aussie *poi*, mate – go the award-winning classic Aussie or beef burgundy.

Miss Marple's Tearoom TEAHOUSE
(382 Mt Dandenong Tourist Rd, Sassafras; dishes $13-17, Devonshire scones two for $9; ⏰11am-4pm Mon-Fri, to 4.30pm Sat & Sun) This quaint English tearoom, inspired by an Agathie Christie character, comes with floral tablecloths, Devonshire scones and sticky toffee pudding, as well as lunch mains. It's wildly popular on weekends – two-hour waits aren't unusual.

Information

Dandenong Ranges & Knox Visitor Information Centre (☎03-9758 7522; www.dandenongrangestourism.com.au; 1211 Burwood Hwy, Upper Ferntree Gully; ⏰1-5pm Mon, 9am-5pm Tue-Sat, 10.30am-2.30pm Sun; 🚆Upper Ferntree Gully) Outside the Upper Ferntree Gully train station. Good for walking maps.

Getting There & Away

It's just under an hour's drive from Melbourne's city centre to Olinda, Sassafras or Belgrave. The quickest route is along the Eastern Fwy, exiting on Burwood Hwy or Boronia Rd. Suburban trains from Melbourne (Belgrave Line) head to Belgrave station.

Yarra Valley

The lush Yarra Valley is Victoria's premier wine region and weekend getaway – partly for its close proximity to Melbourne, but mainly for the 80-plus wineries, superb restaurants, national parks and wildlife. The valley covers a huge area, from the ruggedly beautiful Yarra Ranges National Park in the east to Kinglake National Park, a huge eucalypt forest on the slopes of the Great Dividing Range, in the west. In between is the vine-covered valley itself. Coldstream is considered the gateway to the Yarra Valley winery region and most of the wineries are found within a triangle bound by Coldstream, Healesville and Yarra Glen.

Healesville

Pretty little Healesville is the main town and base for exploring the triangular area of the Lower Yarra Valley. It's famous for its wildlife sanctuary, and perfectly located for easy access to some of the region's finest wineries – from here it's a scenic drive or cycle circuit to Yarra Glen and Coldstream.

Sights & Activities

★**Healesville Sanctuary** ZOO
(☎03-5957 2800; www.zoo.org.au/healesville; Badger Creek Rd, Healesville; adult/child/family $30.80/13.60/74.60; ⏰9am-5pm; 🚌685, 686) One of the best places in southern Australia to see native fauna, this wildlife park is full of kangaroos, dingoes, lyrebirds, Tasmanian devils, bats, koalas, eagles, snakes and lizards. The Platypus House displays the shy underwater creatures and there's a daily interactive show at 11.30am (plus 2pm weekends). The exciting Birds of Prey presentation (noon and 2.30pm daily) features huge wedge-tailed eagles and owls soaring through the air. Admission for kids is free on weekends.

Sleeping & Eating

A number of wineries offer luxury accommodation and there are lots of B&Bs, farmstays and guesthouses in the Yarra Valley – check out the accommodation booking service at www.visityarravalley.com.au.

YARRA VALLEY WINERIES

The Yarra Valley (www.wineyarravalley.com) has more than 80 wineries and 50 cellar doors scattered around its rolling, vine-cloaked hills, and is recognised as Victoria's oldest wine region – the first vines were planted at Yering Station in 1838. The region produces cool-climate, food-friendly drops such as chardonnay, pinot noir and pinot gris, as well as not-half-bad, full-bodied reds.

Domain Chandon (☎03-9738 9200; www.chandon.com; 727 Maroondah Hwy, Coldstream; ⏲10.30am-4.30pm) On the Maroondah Hwy, between Coldstream and Healesville, Domaine Chandon is an example of mass wine tourism done well. The winery – a subsidiary of Moët & Chandon – has a superbly designed reception area overlooking a stunning vista where visitors can sample and buy wines. Guided tours run at 11am, 1pm and 3pm and include a peek at the atmospheric riddling hall.

Oakridge (☎03-9738 9900; www.oakridgewines.com.au; 864 Maroondah Hwy, Coldstream; ⏲10am-5pm) Won *The Age* and *Sydney Morning Herald* winery of the year in 2012.

Rochford (☎03-5962 2119; www.rochfordwines.com.au; 878-880 Maroondah Hwy, cnr Hill Rd, Coldstream; ⏲9am-5pm) Large winery with restaurant and gallery, plus fine cabernet sauvignon and pinot noir. Best known for its huge winery concerts.

TarraWarra Estate (☎03-5957 3510; www.tarrawarra.com.au; 311 Healesville–Yarra Glen Rd, Healesville; tastings $4; ⏲11am-5pm) TarraWarra is a surprisingly striking and modern art gallery showing wonderful exhibitions. Refuel at the neighbouring bistro and cellar door.

Yering Station (☎03-9730 0100; www.yering.com; 38 Melba Hwy, Yering; ⏲10am-5pm Mon-Fri, to 6pm Sat & Sun) Taste wines in the original 1859 winery then take in the view from the upstairs cafe and buy up in the produce store. Walk through the lovely grounds to the modern fine-dining restaurant. The **Yarra Valley Farmers' Market** is held here every third Sunday.

Yarra Valley Winery Tours (☎1300 496 105; www.yarravalleywinerytours.com.au; tours from Yarra Valley/Melbourne $105/140) Daily tours taking in four or five wineries, plus lunch.

Healesville Hotel HOTEL **$$**
(☎03-5962 4002; www.yarravalleyharvest.com.au; 256 Maroondah Hwy, Healesville; d midweek/weekend from $110/130, Sat incl dinner $325; ❄📶) A Healesville landmark, this restored 1910 hotel offers boutique rooms upstairs with crisp white linen, pressed-metal ceilings and spotless shared bathrooms. Also has chic apartments behind the hotel in Furmston House (studio from $180).

Tuck Inn B&B **$$**
(☎03-5962 3600; www.tuckinn.com.au; 2 Church St, Healesville; d midweek/weekend from $150/180; ❄) This former Masonic lodge has been refitted in a contemporary style – a beautiful and stylish five-room guesthouse with friendly hosts. Full breakfast included.

★**Giant Steps & Innocent Bystander** TAPAS, PIZZA **$$**
(☎03-5962 6111; www.innocentbystander.com.au; 336 Maroondah Hwy, Healesville; mains $20-45; ⏲10am-10pm Mon-Fri, 8am-10pm Sat & Sun; 📶) The industrial-sized Giants Steps & Innocent Bystander is a buzzing restaurant and cellar door – a great place for delicious pizzas, tapas and cheese platters, or a lazy afternoon drink. Wine tasting is free at the bar, or tour its barrel hall to sample the vintages for $10 (redeemable upon wine purchase).

ℹ Information

Yarra Valley Visitor Centre (☎03-5962 2600; www.visityarravalley.com.au; Harker St, Healesville; ⏲9am-5pm) The main info centre for the Lower Yarra Valley, with loads of brochures as well as maps for sale.

ℹ Getting There & Away

Healesville is 65km north of Melbourne, an easy one-hour drive via the Eastern Fwy and Maroondah Hwy/B360. From Melbourne, suburban trains run to Lilydale, where there are regular buses to Healesville.

McKenzie's Bus Lines (☎03-5962 5088; www.mckenzies.com.au) Buses daily from Melbourne's Southern Cross Station to Healesville (1½ hours, $6.20) en route to Marysville and Eildon; check website for schedule.

YARRA VALLEY CIDER & ALE TRAIL

While it's wine that brings most visitors to the Yarra Valley, the **Cider & Ale Trail** (www.ciderandaletrail.com.au) will lead you on a fantastic route visiting local microbreweries and cider producers.

Buckley's Beer (☎0408 354 909; www.buckleysbeer.com.au; 30 Hunter Rd, Healesville; ⏲11am-5pm Sat & Sun) On a mission to 'save the world one brew at a time', Buckley's has been hand-crafting its traditional lagers and ales for over a decade. Tours and tastings on weekends only.

Kelly Brothers Cider Co (☎03-9722 1304; www.kellybrothers.com.au; Fulford Rd, Wonga Park; ⏲10am-5pm Mon-Sat, 11am-5pm Sun) In the business of making cider since the 1960s. Sample its goods made with local pears and apples.

Napoleone Cider (☎03-9739 0666; www.napoleonecider.com.au; 10 St Huberts Rd, Coldstream; ⏲10am-5pm) Produces a variety of pear and apple ciders crushed on site using fruit picked from its orchard. Also does a pale ale beer. Free tastings.

White Rabbit Brewery (☎03-5962 6516; www.whiterabbitbeer.com.au; 316 Maroondah Hwy, Healesville; ⏲11am-5pm Sat-Thu, to 9pm Fri) A must-visit for beer lovers, this microbrewery has an understated blokiness about it with a few retro couches and benches set up deadset in the middle of its production area so you can enjoy a few cold ones surrounded by huge vats and bottling machines. Expect a lot of clamour midweek. Also does great pizzas.

Aussie Brewery Tours (☎1300 787 039; www.aussiebrewerytours.com.au; tour incl transport, lunch and tastings $150) Melbourne-based Aussie Brewery Tours offers popular trips.

Mornington Peninsula

The Mornington Peninsula – the boot-shaped area of land between Port Phillip Bay and Western Port Bay – has been Melbourne's summer playground since the 1870s, when paddle steamers ran down to Portsea. Today, much of the interior farmland has been replaced by vineyards and orchards – foodies love the peninsula, where a winery lunch is a real highlight – but it still retains lovely stands of native bushland.

The calm front beaches are on the Port Phillip Bay side, where families holiday at bayside towns from Mornington to Sorrento. The rugged ocean back beaches face Bass Strait and are easily reached from Portsea, Sorrento and Rye – there are stunning walks along this coastal strip, which is part of the Mornington Peninsula National Park.

ℹ Information

Peninsula Visitor Information Centre (☎1800 804 009, 03-5987 3078; www.visitmorningtonpeninsula.org; 359b Nepean Hwy, Dromana; ⏲9am-5pm) The main information centre for the peninsula can book accommodation and tours. There are also visitor centres in Mornington (☎03-5975 1644; www.visitmorningtonpeninsula.org; 320 Main St, Mornington; ⏲9am-5pm) and Sorrento (☎03-5984 1478; cnr George St & Ocean Beach Rd).

ℹ Getting There & Away

Moorooduc Hwy and Point Nepean Rd both feed into the Mornington Peninsula Fwy, the main peninsula access. Alternately, exit the Moorooduc Hwy to Mornington and take the coast road around Port Phillip Bay.

Queenscliff–Sorrento Ferry (☎03-5258 3244; www.searoad.com.au; foot passenger one way adult/child $11/8, 2 adults & car one way/return $73/136; ⏲hourly 7am-6pm, until 7pm Jan & long weekends) Connects Sorrento with Queenscliff across Port Phillip Bay.

Sorrento & Portsea

Historic Sorrento is the standout town on the Mornington Peninsula for its beautiful limestone buildings, ocean and bay beaches and buzzing seaside summer atmosphere. This was the site of Victoria's first official European settlement, established by an expedition of convicts, marines, civil officers and free settlers who arrived from England in 1803.

Only 4km further west, tiny Portsea also has good back beaches, and diving and water-sports operators.

Sights & Activities

The calm bay beach is good for families and you can hire **paddle boards** on the foreshore. At low tide, the **rock pool** at the back beach is a safe spot for adults and children to swim and snorkel, and the surf beach is patrolled in summer.

★**Moonraker Charters** WILDLIFE WATCHING
(☎03-5984 4211; www.moonrakercharters.com.au; 7 George St, Sorrento; adult/child sightseeing $55/44, dolphin & seal swimming $129/115) Operates three-hour dolphin- and seal-swimming tours from Sorrento Pier.

★**Polperro Dolphin Swims** WILDLIFE WATCHING
(☎03-5988 8437; www.polperro.com.au; adult/child sightseeing $55/35, dolphin & seal swimming adult & child $135) Popular morning and afternoon dolphin- and seal-swimming tours from Sorrento Pier.

Sleeping & Eating

Carmel of Sorrento GUESTHOUSE $$
(☎03-5984 3512; www.carmelofsorrento.com.au; 142 Ocean Beach Rd, Sorrento; d $130-220) This lovely old limestone house, right in the centre of Sorrento, has been tastefully restored in period style and neatly marries the

WORTH A TRIP

LAKE MOUNTAIN & MARYSVILLE

Spread across a valley between Narbethong and Lake Mountain, Marysville was at the epicentre of the tragic 2009 bushfires (p520), during which most of the town's buildings were destroyed and 34 people lost their lives. The town's tight-knit community is steadily rebuilding and it's still the main base for the cross-country ski fields at Lake Mountain.

Part of the Yarra Ranges National Park, Lake Mountain (1433m) is the premier **cross-country skiing** resort in Australia, with 37km of trails and several toboggan runs. In summer there are marked **hiking** and **mountain-biking** trails. There's no on-mountain accommodation, but Marysville is only 10km away.

During the ski season the daily gate fee is $35 per car on weekends and holidays, and $25 midweek; trail fees costs from $11.90/5.90 per adult/child. Outside the season there's only a parking fee of $2.

Activities

Lake Mountain Alpine Resort (☎03-5957 7222; www.lakemountainresort.com.au; Snowy Rd; ⏲8am-4.30pm Mon-Fri Oct-May, to 6.30pm Jun-Sep) Has ski hire, a ski school, a cafe and undercover barbecue areas.

Marysville Ski Centre (www.marysvilleski.com.au; 27 Murchison St, Marysville; ⏲Jun-Sep) Hires skis, toboggans, clothing and car chains.

Sleeping

Crossways Historic Country Inn (☎03-5963 3290; www.crosswaysmarysville.com.au; 4 Woods Point Rd, Marysville; d $120, 2-bedroom cottage $195) Crossways has been around since the 1920s and, remarkably, survived the bushfires. Family-friendly accommodation includes individual log-cabin-style units and the River Cottage, a modern two-bedroom unit.

The Tower (☎03-5963 3225; www.towermotel.com.au; 33 Murchison St, Marysville; s/d/f $125/145/165; ❄📶) One of the few buildings on the main road to survive Black Saturday, the Tower embraces its 1970s motel facade, and recent renovations have jazzed it up to almost boutique levels. The owners are ultra friendly and it has an attractive courtyard and wine bar, while rooms come with minibars, cable TV and free wi-fi. Rates increase in ski season.

Getting There & Away

Lake Mountain Snow Bus (Country Touch Tours; ☎03-5963 3753; www.lakemountainsnowbus.com; 24 Murchison St, Marysville) The Lake Mountain Snow Bus operates a return service to Lake Mountain, including gate entry fee, from Marysville (departs 10.30am, adult/child $45/40) and Healesville (10am Saturday, adult/child $45/40). The bus returns from Lake Mountain at 3pm.

town's history with contemporary comfort. There are three Edwardian-style suites with bathrooms and continental breakfast, and two modern self-contained units.

Portsea Hotel HOTEL $$
(☎03-5984 2213; www.portseahotel.com.au; Point Nepean Rd, Portsea; s/d without bathroom from $75/105, s/d with bathroom from $135/175) Portsea's pulse is the sprawling, half-timber Portsea Hotel, an enormous pub with a great lawn and terrace area looking out over the bay. There's an excellent **bistro** (mains $24 to $39) and old-style accommodation (most rooms have shared bathroom) that increases in price based on sea views (weekend rates are higher).

Hotel Sorrento HOTEL $$$
(☎03-5984 2206; www.hotelsorrento.com.au; 5-15 Hotham Rd, Sorrento; motel r $195-280, apt $220-320) The legendary Hotel Sorrento trades on its famous name and has a swag of accommodation. 'Sorrento on the Park' offers standard and overpriced motel rooms, but the lovely 'On the Hill' double and family apartments have airy living spaces, spacious bathrooms and private balconies.

The Baths FISH & CHIPS $
(☎03-5984 1500; www.thebaths.com.au; 3278 Point Nepean Rd, Sorrento; fish & chips $10, restaurant mains $27-36; ⏰noon-8pm) The waterfront deck of the former sea baths is the perfect spot for lunch or a romantic sunset dinner overlooking the jetty and the Queenscliff ferry. The menu has some good seafood choices and there's a popular takeaway fish and chippery at the front.

Smokehouse ITALIAN $$
(☎03-5984 1246; 182 Ocean Beach Rd, Sorrento; mains $20-34; ⏰6-9pm) Gourmet pizzas and pastas are the speciality at this local family favourite. Innovative toppings and the aromas wafting from the wood-fired oven hint at the key to its success.

Phillip Island

POP 9406

Famous for the Penguin Parade and Motorcycle Grand Prix racing circuit, Phillip Island attracts a curious mix of surfers, petrolheads and international tourists making a beeline for those little penguins.

At its heart Phillip Island is still a farming community, but nature has conspired to turn it into one of Victoria's hottest tourist destinations. Apart from the nightly waddling of the penguins, there's a large seal colony, abundant bird life around the Rhyll wetlands and a koala colony. The rugged south coast has some fabulous surf beaches and the swell of tourists – the holiday population jumps to around 40,000 over summer – means there's a swag of family attractions, plenty of accommodation and a buzzing, if unexciting, cafe and restaurant scene in the island capital, Cowes. Visit in winter, though, and you'll find a very quiet place where the local population of farmers, surfers and hippies goes about its business.

Sights & Activities

Cowes **Main Beach** is calm and safe for swimming – head over to the long Cowes East Beach for a quieter time. The best surf beaches are along the southern coast. Spectacular **Cape Woolamai** is the most popular surf beach, but rips and currents make it suitable only for experienced surfers. Beginners and families head to **Smiths Beach**, which is often teeming with surf-school groups. Both are patrolled in summer. **Berrys Beach** is another beautiful spot and usually quieter than Woolamai or Smiths. Around the Nobbies, **Cat Bay** and **Flynns Reef** will often be calm when the wind is blowing onshore at the Woolamai and Smiths areas.

★**Penguin Parade** WILDLIFE RESERVE
(☎03-5951 2800; www.penguins.org.au; Summerland Beach; adult/child/family $23.80/11.90/59.50; ⏰10am-dusk, penguins arrive at sunset) The Penguin Parade attracts more than 500,000 visitors annually to see the little penguins *(Eudyptula minor)*, the world's smallest penguins, and probably the cutest of their kind. The penguin complex includes concrete amphitheatres that hold up to 3800 spectators who come to see the little fellas just after sunset as they waddle from the sea to their burrows.

Penguin numbers swell in summer, after breeding, but they're in residence year-round. After the parade, hang around the boardwalks for a closer view as the stragglers search for their burrows and mates. Bring warm clothing. There are a variety of specialised **tours** (www.penguins.org.au; adult $44-80), where you can be accompanied by rangers to explain the behaviour of penguins, or see the penguins from the vantage of a Skybox (an elevated platform). There's also a cafe and an interpretive centre at the complex.

Phillip Island

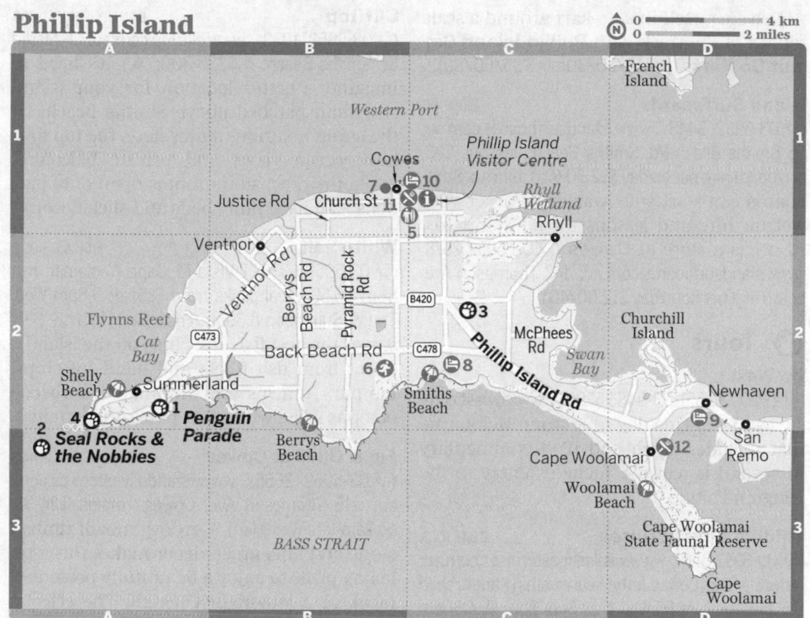

Koala Conservation Centre ZOO
(☎03-5951 2800; www.penguins.org.au; 1810 Phillip Island Rd, Cowes; adult/child/family $11.90/5.95/29.75; ⊙10am-5pm, extended hours in summer) From the boardwalks here you're certain to see koalas chewing on eucalyptus leaves or dozing away – they sleep about 20 hours a day!

★ **Seal Rocks & the Nobbies** WILDLIFE WATCHING
(⊙11am-5pm) The Nobbies are a couple of large, craggy, offshore rocks at the island's southwestern tip. Beyond them are Seal Rocks, which are inhabited by Australia's largest fur-seal colony. The **Nobbies Centre** (☎03-5951 2852; www.penguins.org.au; ⊙11am-1hr before sunset) FREE offers great views over the Nobbies and the 6000-or-so distant Australian fur seals that sun themselves there. You can view the seals from boardwalk binoculars or use the centre's underwater cameras ($5).

The centre also has some fascinating interactive exhibits, a kids' games room and a cafe.

★ **Phillip Island Grand Prix Circuit** ADVENTURE SPORTS
(☎03-5952 9400; Back Beach Rd) Even when the motorbikes aren't racing, petrolheads love the Grand Prix Motor Racing Circuit, which was souped up for the Australian

Phillip Island

Top Sights

1	Penguin Parade	A2
2	Seal Rocks & the Nobbies	A3

Sights

3	Koala Conservation Centre	C2
4	Nobbies Centre	A2

Activities, Courses & Tours

5	Island Surfboards	C1
6	Phillip Island Grand Prix Circuit	B2
7	Wildlife Coast Cruises	B1

Sleeping

8	Clifftop	C2
9	Island Accommodation YHA	D2
10	Waves Apartments	C1

Eating

11	Fig & Olive at Cowes	B1
12	White Salt	D3

Motorcycle Grand Prix in 1989. The visitor centre runs **guided circuit tours** (http://phillipislandcircuit.com.au; adult/child/family $22/13/57; ⊙tours 2pm), or check out the **History of Motorsport Museum** (adult/child/family $15/8/38). The more adventurous can cut laps of the track with a racing driver in hotted-up V8s ($330; bookings essential).

Drive yourself in a go-kart around a scale replica of the track with **Phillip Island Circuit Go Karts** (per 10/20/30min $35/60/80).

Island Surfboards SURFING
(☎03-5952 3443; www.islandsurfboards.com.au; 65 Smiths Beach Rd, Smiths Beach; lessons $65, surfboard hire per hr/day $12.50/40) Island Surfboards can start your waxhead career with wetsuit hire and lessons for all standards. Also has a store at **Cowes** (☎03-5952 2578; www.islandsurfboards.com.au; 147 Thompson Ave; board hire per hour/day $12.50/40).

Tours

Go West TOUR
(☎1300 736 551, 03-9485 5290; www.gowest.com.au; tour $135) One-day tour from Melbourne that includes lunch and iPod commentary in several languages. Includes entry to the Penguin Parade.

Wildlife Coast Cruises BOAT TOUR
(☎03-5952 3501; www.wildlifecoastcruises.com.au; Rotunda Bldg, Cowes Jetty; seal watching adult/child $72/49; ⏲2pm Fri-Wed May-Sep, 2pm & 4.30pm daily Oct-Apr) Runs a variety of cruises, including seal-watching, twilight and cape cruises. Also runs a two-hour cruise to French Island (adult/child $30/20) and a full-day cruise to Wilsons Promontory ($190/140).

Festivals & Events

Australian Motorcycle Grand Prix SPORTS
(www.motogp.com.au) The island's biggest event – three days of bike action in October.

Sleeping & Eating

Island Accommodation YHA HOSTEL $
(☎03-5956 6123; www.theislandaccommodation.com.au; 10-12 Phillip Island Rd, Newhaven; dm/d from $35/165; @☎) This large, purpose-built backpackers has huge identical living areas on each floor, complete with table-tennis tables and cosy fireplaces for winter. Its rooftop deck has terrific views and its eco-credentials are excellent. Cheapest dorms sleep 12 and doubles are motel standard.

Waves Apartments APARTMENT $$
(☎03-5952 1351; www.thewaves.com.au; 1 Esplanade, Cowes; d from $195; ❄☎) These slick apartments overlook Cowes Main Beach, so you can't beat the balcony views if you go for a beachfront unit. The modern, self-contained apartments come with spa, and balcony or patio.

Clifftop BOUTIQUE HOTEL $$$
(☎03-5952 1033; www.clifftop.com.au; 1 Marlin St, Smiths Beach; d $235-300; ❄) It's hard to imagine a better location for your island stay than perched above Smiths Beach. Of the seven luxurious suites here, the top four have ocean views and private balconies, while the downstairs rooms open onto gardens – all have fluffy beds and slick decor.

White Salt FISH & CHIPS $
(☎03-5956 6336; 7 Vista Pl, Cape Woolamai; fish from $6.50, meal packs from $15; ⏲5-8pm Wed, Thu & Sun, noon-8.30pm Fri & Sat) White Salt serves the best fish and chips on the island – select from fish fillets and hand-cut chips, tempura prawns and marinated barbecue octopus salad with corn, pesto and lemon.

Fig & Olive at Cowes MODERN AUSTRALIAN $$
(☎03-5952 2655; www.figandoliveatcowes.com.au; 115 Thompson Ave, Cowes; mains $24-38; ⏲9am-late Wed-Mon) A groovy mix of timber, stone and lime-green decor makes this a relaxing place to enjoy a beautifully presented meal, or a late-night cocktail. The eclectic menu is strong on seafood and moves from paella or pork belly to wood-fired Tasmanian salmon.

Information

Phillip Island Visitor Centre (☎1300 366 422; www.visitphillipisland.com; 895 Phillip Island Tourist Rd, Newhaven; ⏲9am-5pm, to 6pm school holidays) The main visitor centre for the island is on the main road at Newhaven, and there's a smaller centre at Cowes (cnr Thompson & Church Sts). Both sell the Three Parks Pass (adult/child/family $36/18/90), covering the Penguin Parade, Koala Conservation Centre and Churchill Island Heritage Farm, and the main centre has a free accommodation- and tour-booking service.

Getting There & Away

About 140km from Melbourne, Phillip Island can only be accessed by car across the bridge between San Remo and Newhaven. From Melbourne take the Monash Fwy and exit at Pakenham, joining the South Gippsland Hwy at Koo Wee Rup.

V/Line (☎1800 800 007; www.vline.com.au) V/Line has train/bus services from Melbourne's Southern Cross Station via Dandenong Station or Koo Wee Rup ($12.80, 2½ hours). There are no direct services.

Great Ocean Road

Includes ➡

Best Places to Eat

- Brae (p540)
- A La Grecque (p539)
- Merrijig Kitchen (p547)
- Chris's Beacon Point Restaurant (p542)

Best Places to Stay

- Bimbi Park (p542)
- Great Ocean Ecolodge (p542)
- Beacon Point Ocean View Villas (p541)
- Vue Grand (p535)
- Cimarron B&B (p538)

Why Go?

The Great Ocean Road (B100) is one of Australia's most famous road-touring routes. It takes travellers past world-class surfing breaks, through pockets of rainforest, calm seaside towns and under koala-filled tree canopies. It shows off sheer limestone cliffs, dairy farms and heathlands, and gets you up close and personal with the crashing waves of the Southern Ocean.

Hunt out the isolated beaches and lighthouses in between the towns, and the thick eucalypt forests in the Otway hinterlands to really escape the crowds. Rather than heading straight to the Great Ocean Road, a fork in the road in Geelong can take you the long, leisurely way there through the Bellarine Peninsula, which allows you to visit charming Queenscliff and wineries en route.

Day-tripping tourists from Melbourne rush in and out of the area in less than 12 hours but, in a perfect world, you'd spend at least a week here.

When to Go

Cape Otway

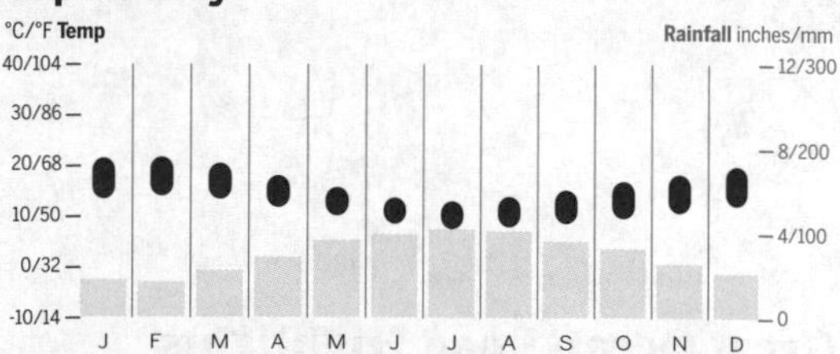

Mar Chill out to folk and roots tunes at the hugely popular Port Fairy Folk Festival.

Easter Head to Bells Beach during the Rip Curl Pro to witness spectacular surfing action.

Jul Visit coastal towns mid-winter for bright seascapes, cosy cafes and whale watching.

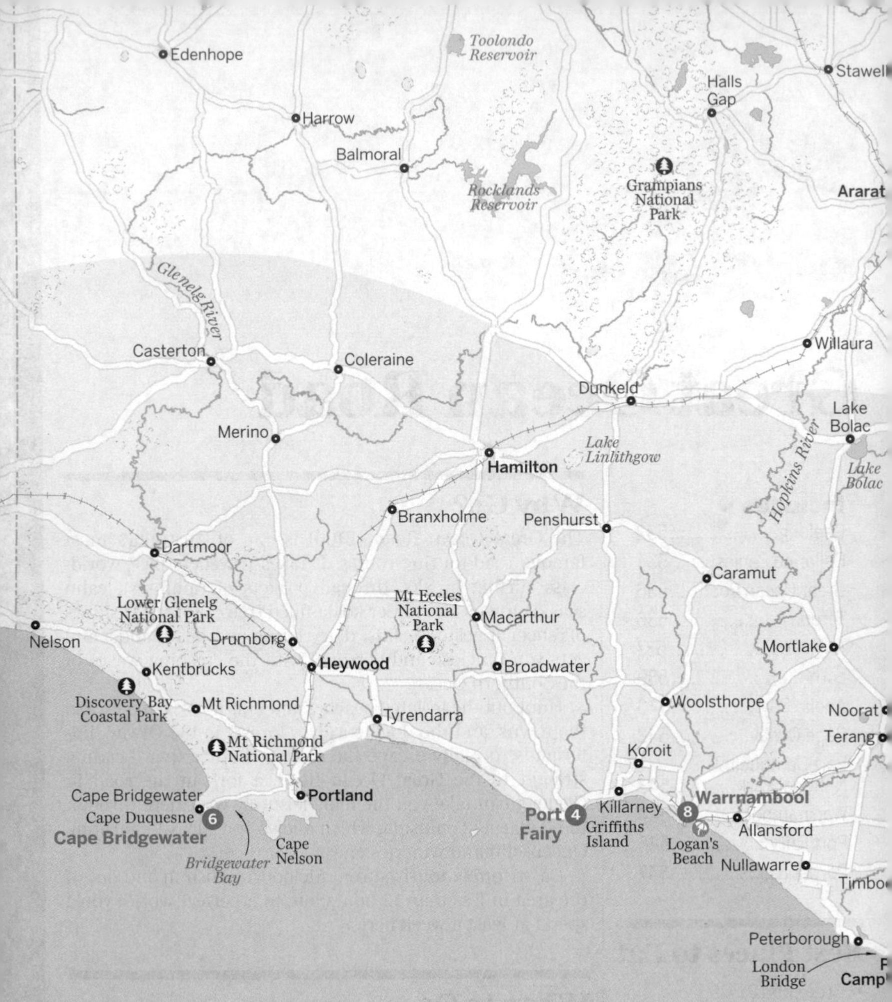

Great Ocean Road Highlights

1. Counting the upstanding **Twelve Apostles** (p543) near Port Campbell.
2. Camping by beaches abutting the lighthouse and watching for koalas at **Cape Otway** (p542).
3. Lapping up the resort-style living in tree-lined **Lorne** (p539).
4. Soaking up the best in coastal village life with a few nights in **Port Fairy** (p546).
5. Shopping for surf gear and then taking a surf lesson at **Torquay** (p536).

❻ Checking out the seals at isolated and beautiful **Cape Bridgewater** (p548).

❼ Discovering one of Melbourne's favourite weekend escapes at lovely **Queenscliff** (p534).

❽ Keeping a lookout for whales off the coast of **Warrnambool** (p544).

❾ Reliving the legend of lives lost at haunting **Loch Ard Gorge** (p543).

❿ Watching the waves roll in at **Bells Beach** (p538).

GEELONG & BELLARINE PENINSULA

Geelong

POP 143,921

Geelong is Victoria's second-largest centre, a proud, industrial town with an interesting history and pockets of charm. While Melburnians love to deride their city's little cousin as a boring backwater, and a new bypass means travellers can skip the city and head straight to the Great Ocean Road, the town is undergoing something of a makeover. It's centred around sparkling Corio Bay waterfront, and in its city centre heritage buildings from the boom days of the wool industry and the gold-rush era have now been converted into swanky restaurants and bars.

Sights & Activities

Geelong Waterfront WATERFRONT

Geelong's sparkling waterfront precinct is a great place to stroll, with plenty of restaurants set on scenic piers, plus historical landmarks, sculptures, swimming areas, playgrounds and grassy sections ideal for picnics. In summer you can cool off at popular **Eastern Beach**, which features a sandy beach and art deco bathing pavilion with classic European-style enclosed bay swimming, complete with diving boards, sunbathing area and toddler pool.

Geelong Art Gallery GALLERY

(www.geelonggallery.org.au; Little Malop St; 10am-5pm) FREE With over 4000 works in its collection, this excellent gallery has celebrated Australian paintings such as Eugene von Guérard's *View of Geelong* and Frederick McCubbin's 1890 *A Bush Burial*. Also exhibits contemporary works and has free tours on Saturday at 2pm.

National Wool Museum MUSEUM

(03-5272 4701; www.geelongaustralia.com.au/nwm; 26 Moorabool St; adult/child/family $8.25/4.50/25; 9.30am-5pm Mon-Fri, 10am-5pm Sat & Sun) More interesting than it may sound, this museum showcases the importance of the wool industry in shaping Geelong economically, socially and architecturally – many of the grand buildings in the area are former wool-store buildings, including the museum's 1872 bluestone building. There's a sock-making machine and a massive 1910 Axminster carpet loom that gets chugging on weekends.

Narana Creations CULTURAL CENTRE

(03-5241 5700; www.narana.com.au; 410 Torquay Rd, Grovedale; 9am-5pm Mon-Fri, 10am-4pm Sat) On the road to Torquay in Grovedale, on Geelong's far outskirts, this Aboriginal cultural centre has didgeridoo performances (or play it yourself), a boomerang-throwing gallery and a native garden. Daily tours are at 11am and 2pm, and its gift shop sells Indigenous books and music.

City Walking Tours WALKING TOUR

(03-5222 2900; 26 Moorabool St; tours $12) Volunteer-led city tours show Geelong's historic architecture and landmarks. Prices include a ride on the waterfront carousel, tea and cake and two-for-one admission to the National Wool Museum. Book one day in advance.

Sleeping

Irish Murphy's HOSTEL $

(03-5221 4335; www.irishmurphysgeelong.com.au; 30 Aberdeen St, Geelong West; dm/s/d $40/45/80; P 📶) Upstairs from an Irish pub, Geelong's only backpackers hostel is a family-owned affair with clean dorms, most of which only have two beds – a good deal. Guests also get 20% off pub meals downstairs. It's a short walk from the city, Pakington St and Geelong station.

Gatehouse on Ryrie GUESTHOUSE $$

(0417 545 196; www.gatehouseonryrie.com.au; 83 Yarra St; d incl breakfast $110-145; P @ 📶) Geelong's best midrange choice, this guesthouse was built in 1897 and has gorgeous timber floorboards throughout, spacious rooms (most with shared facilities) and a communal kitchen and lounge area. Breakfast is in the glorious front room.

Eating & Drinking

Geelong Boat House FISH & CHIPS $

(Geelong Waterfront; fish & chips from $8.50; 10am-8pm) Jutting out into the water, this fish-and-chip joint is built on top of a barge once used to dredge the Yarra River. Grab a chair on the deck or rooftop, or laze on one of its picnic blankets on the grassy banks. There's also a seafood restaurant in its attached boat shed.

★**Jack & Jill** MODERN AUSTRALIAN $$

(03-5229 9935; www.jackandjillrestaurant.com.au; 247 Moorabool St; tasting plates from $33.50; 6pm-late daily, noon-2.30pm Fri) Choose three small dishes from the menu of regional produce (perhaps local Barwon lamb and

Geelong

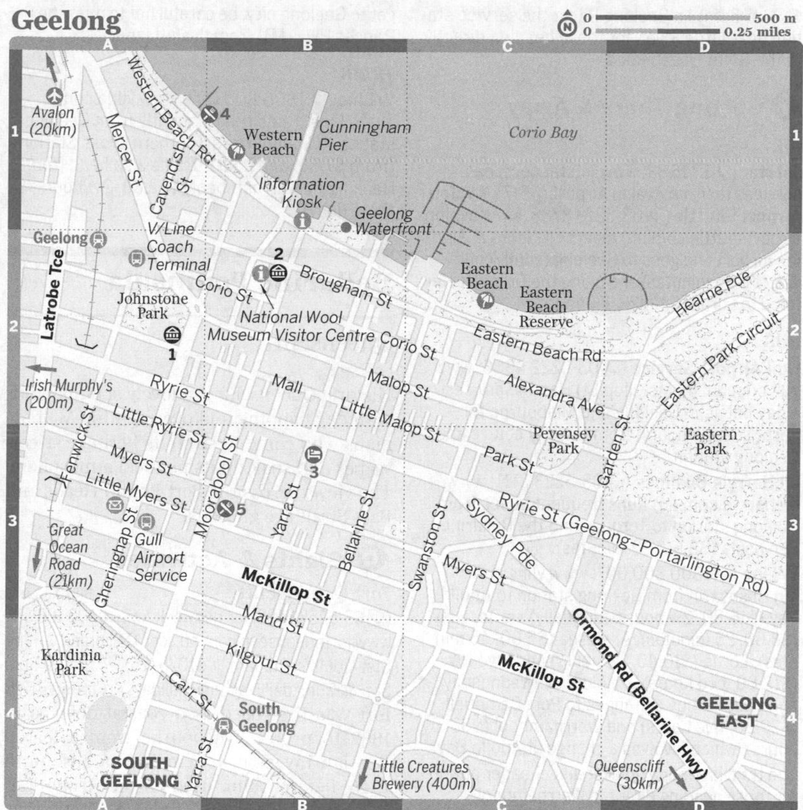

Geelong

Sights

1 Geelong Art Gallery A2
2 National Wool Museum B2

Activities, Courses & Tours

City Walking Tours .... (see 2)

Sleeping

3 Gatehouse on Ryrie B3

Eating

4 Geelong Boat House B1
5 Jack & Jill B3

couscous filo parcel with lemon yoghurt and pomegranate molasses) and they'll all be served to you on one plate. Upstairs has a rooftop beer garden with top craft beers. Roll the dice Fridays for free drinks between 5pm and 6.30pm. Also has regular live music.

★ **Little Creatures Brewery** BREWERY
(☎ 03-5202 4009; www.littlecreatures.com.au; cnr Fyans & Swanston Sts; ⏰ 11am-5pm Mon-Tue, 11am-9pm Wed-Fri, 8am-9pm Sat, 8am-5pm Sun; 📶) Geelong is the newest addition to the growing Little Creatures beer empire. Within an old wool mill and kitted out in an industrial-warehouse feel, this is a cracking place to sample its brews with a thin-crust pizza ($10 to $23) or seared kangaroo skewers.

Tours of the brewery operate a few times a day and include free tastings. Kids will love the sandboxes and room to run around.

Information

National Wool Museum Visitor Centre (www.visitgreatoceanroad.org.au; 26 Moorabool St; ⏰ 9am-5pm; 📶) Geelong's main tourist information office has brochures on Geelong, the Bellarine Peninsula and the Otways, as well as free wi-fi. There's also a visitor centre (www.visitgreatoceanroad.org.au; Princes Hwy;

9am-5pm) on Geelong Rd, at the service station near Little River, for those heading directly to the Great Ocean Road.

Getting There & Away

AIR

Jetstar (13 15 38; www.jetstar.com) has services to/from Avalon Airport (p517). **Avalon Airport Shuttle** (03-5278 8788; www.avalonairportshuttle.com.au) meets all flights at Avalon Airport and goes to Geelong (adult/child $18/14, 35 minutes) and along the Great Ocean Road to Lorne ($32/26, 1¾ hours).

BUS

Gull Airport Service (03-5222 4966; www.gull.com.au; 45 McKillop St) Has 14 services a day between Geelong and Melbourne Airport ($32, 1¼ hours) from the city centre and Geelong station.

McHarry's Buslines (03-5223 2111; www.mcharrys.com.au) Runs frequent buses from Geelong station to Torquay and the Bellarine Peninsula ($3.60, 20 minutes).

V/Line (1800 800 007; www.vline.com.au) Buses run from Geelong station to Apollo Bay ($16.80, 2½ hours, four daily) via Torquay ($3.60, 25 minutes), Anglesea ($5.60, 45 minutes), Lorne ($10.40, 1½ hours) and Wye River ($12.80, two hours). On Monday, Wednesday and Friday a bus continues to Port Campbell ($29.20, five hours) and Warrnambool ($33, 6½ hours), which involves a change at Apollo Bay.

The train is a much quicker and cheaper option for those heading direct to Warrnambool, though you'll miss out on the Great Ocean Road experience.

CAR

The 25km Geelong Ring Road runs from Corio to Waurn Ponds, bypassing Geelong entirely. To get to Geelong city, be careful not to miss the Princes Hwy (M1) from the left lanes.

TRAIN

V/Line (1800 800 007; www.vline.com.au) V/Line trains run frequently from Geelong station to Melbourne's Southern Cross Station (from $7.80, one hour). Trains also head from Geelong to Warrnambool ($22.80, 2½ hours, three daily).

Bellarine Peninsula

Queenscliff

POP 1418

Historic Queenscliff is a lovely spot, popular with day-tripping and overnighting Melburnians who come to stroll its heritage streetscapes and soak up its nautical atmosphere. The views across the Port Phillip Heads and Bass Strait are glorious.

Sights & Activities

Fort Queenscliff HISTORIC SITE

(03-5258 1488, for midweek tours 0403 193 311; www.fortqueenscliff.com.au; cnr Gellibrand & King Sts; adult/child/family $10/5/25; 1pm & 3pm Sat & Sun, daily school holidays) Queensliff's fort was first used as a coastal defence in 1882 to protect Melbourne from a feared Russian invasion. It remained a base until 1946, before being used as the Army Staff College until late 2012; today it functions as the defence archive centre. The 30-minute guided tours take in the military museum, magazine, cells and its twin lighthouses. Bring ID for entry.

GREAT OCEAN ROAD DISTANCES & TIMES

ROUTE	DISTANCE	TIME
Melbourne–Geelong	75km	1hr
Geelong–Torquay	21km	15-20min
Torquay–Anglesea	16km	15min
Anglesea–Aireys Inlet	10km	10min
Aireys Inlet–Lorne	19km	20min
Lorne–Apollo Bay	45km	1hr
Apollo Bay–Port Campbell	96km	1½hr
Port Campbell–Warrnambool	66km	1hr
Warrnambool–Port Fairy	28km	20min
Port Fairy–Portland	72km	1hr
Portland–Melbourne	via Great Ocean Road 440km/ via Hamilton Hwy 358km	6½hr/4¼hr

Bellarine Peninsula Railway TRAIN
(☎03-5258 2069; www.bellarinerailway.com.au; Queenscliff train station; Drysdale return adult/child/family $30/20/70, Lakers Siding $15/12/40; ⏲departs 11am & 2.45pm Sun, plus Tue & Thu during school holidays) Run by a group of cheerful volunteer steam-train tragics, the railway has beautiful heritage steam and diesel trains that ply the 1¾-hour return journey to Drysdale, with one daily trip to Lakers Siding (33 minutes return), leaving Queenscliff at 1.15pm.

Sea-All Dolphin Swims WILDLIFE WATCHING
(☎03-5258 3889; www.dolphinswims.com.au; Queenscliff Harbour; sightseeing adult/child $75/65, 3½hr snorkel $140/120; ⏲8am & 1pm Oct-Apr) Offers sightseeing tours and swims with seals and dolphins in Port Phillip Bay. Seal sightings are guaranteed; dolphins aren't always seen, but there's a good chance.

Tours

The visitor centre hands out the free *Queenscliff – A Living Heritage* booklet for self-guided tours around town.

Queenscliff Heritage Walk WALKING TOUR
(☎03-5258 4843; incl afternoon tea $12) The visitor centre runs the 1¼-hour guided Queenscliff Heritage Walk at 2pm each Saturday, or by appointment, taking in the town's historic buildings.

Festivals & Events

Queenscliff Music Festival MUSIC
(☎03-5258 4816; www.qmf.net.au) One of the coast's best festivals features big-name Australian musos with a folksy, bluesy bent. Held late November.

Blues Train MUSIC
(www.thebluestrain.com.au; tickets $97.70) Get your foot tapping with irregular train trips that feature rootsy music and meals. Check the website for dates and artists.

Sleeping

Athelstane House BOUTIQUE HOTEL $$
(☎03-5258 1024; www.athelstane.com.au; 4 Hobson St; r incl breakfast $160-270;) Athelstane House has comfortable rooms with some period touches and corner spa baths in a beautifully kept historic building. Its restaurant will keep you well fed and there's a lovely verandah for warmer nights.

WORTH A TRIP

BELLARINE FOODIE DETOUR

The Bellarine Peninsula has a growing reputation as a gourmet food region, with a particular focus on wines. With over 50 wineries in the Bellarine and-Geelong area, it's known for its cool-climate pinot, shiraz and chardonnay. You could easily spend a lazy couple of days exploring the region. For a list of wineries, check out www.winegeelong.com.au, while visitor centres across the region can help you with suggestions.

Bellarine Taste Trail (www.thebellarinetastetrail.com.au) Combine a winery hop with the Bellarine Taste Trail, which builds itineraries around mostly artisan gourmet-food producers, and you've got yourself a fantastic day out.

Queenscliff Hotel HOTEL $$
(☎03-5258 1066; www.queenscliffhotel.com.au; 16 Gellibrand St; d from $149;) Classified by the National Trust, this is a superb, authentically old-world luxury hotel. Small Victorian-style rooms have no telephones or TVs, and bathrooms are shared. You can relax in the comfortable guest lounges, or dine and drink at the wonderful restaurant and bar.

★**Vue Grand** HOTEL $$$
(☎03-5258 1544; www.vuegrand.com.au; 46 Hesse St; standard/turret r incl breakfast from $200/400) The Vue has everything from standard pub rooms to its modern turret suite (boasting 360-degree views) and bay-view rooms (with free-standing baths in the lounge). If you can't get the room, the turret-level deck is a fine spot for a beverage or two on a sunny day.

Eating & Drinking

Athelstane House MODERN AUSTRALIAN $$
(☎03-5258 1024; www.athelstane.com.au; 4 Hobson St; mains $28-34; ⏲6-9pm Mon-Fri, noon-2pm & 6-9pm Sat & Sun, 8am-9pm daily in summer) Eat inside this lovely heritage home, or on the pretty garden deck, and choose from a varied menu that ranges from Queensland tiger prawn linguine or roasted duck breast to lighter open sandwiches.

Café Gusto CAFE $$
(☎03-5258 3604; 25 Hesse St; mains $12-26; ⏲8.30am-4pm) A favourite Queenscliff eatery that's great for breakfast, with a spacious garden courtyard out the back. The service

can struggle a little when things get busy, but the food's good and the setting is worth the wait.

Vue Grand MODERN AUSTRALIAN $$$
(☎03-5258 1544; www.vuegrand.com.au; 46 Hesse St; 2-/3-course meal $59/79, 5-course Bellarine tasting menu without/with wine or beers $95/145; ⏲6-9pm Wed-Sat) The grande dame of Queenscliff dining, the stately Vue Grand serves up fabulous dishes such as lamb back strap with saffron, fennel, pomegranate and whipped feta, backed up by a splendid wine and beer menu. The Bellarine tasting menu is a fine journey around the peninsula, with local-produce-heavy dishes matched with local wine or beers. Tables can be hard to come by on weekends.

Information

Queenscliff Visitor Centre (☎03-5258 4843; www.queenscliffe.vic.gov.au; 55 Hesse St; ⏲9am-5pm) Plenty of brochures, with free internet access next door at the library.

Getting There & Away

From Melbourne, Queenscliff (and the rest of the Bellarine Peninsula) is easily accessible via the Princes Fwy (M1) to Geelong. Rather than taking the Geelong bypass, head through Geelong to the Bellarine Hwy (B110).

Queenscliff–Sorrento Ferry (☎03-5258 3244; www.searoad.com.au; one way foot passenger adult/child $11/8, 2 adults & car $73; ⏲hourly 7am-6pm) Ferries run between Queenscliff and Sorrento (40 minutes). They run until 7pm at peak times.

GREAT OCEAN ROAD

Torquay

POP 13,339

In the 1960s and '70s Torquay was just another sleepy seaside town. Back then, surfing in Australia was a decidedly counter-cultural pursuit, its devotees crusty hippy dropouts living in clapped-out Kombis, smoking pot and making off with your daughters. These days it's become unabashedly mainstream and the town's proximity to world-famous Bells Beach, and status as home of two iconic surf brands – Rip Curl and Quicksilver, both initially wetsuit makers – ensures Torquay's place as the undisputed capital of the Australian surf industry.

Sights & Activities

Torquay's beaches lure everyone from kids in floaties to backpacker surf-school pupils. **Fisherman's Beach**, protected from ocean swells, is the family favourite. Ringed by shady pines and sloping lawns, the **Front Beach** beckons lazy bums, while surf lifesavers patrol the frothing **Back Beach** during summer. Famous surf beaches include nearby Jan Juc, Winki Pop and, of course, Bells Beach.

Surf World Museum MUSEUM
(www.surfworld.com.au; Surf City Plaza; adult/child/family $12/8/30; ⏲9am-5pm) The perfect starting point for those embarking on a surfing safari, this well-curated museum pays homage to Australian surfing, from Simon Anderson's ground-breaking 1981 thruster to Mark Richard's board collection and, most notably, Australia's Surfing Hall of Fame. It's full of great memorabilia (including Duke Kahanamoku's wooden longboard), videos and displays on surfing culture through the 1960s to '80s.

Go Ride a Wave SURFING
(☎1300 132 441; www.gorideawave.com.au; 1/15 Bell St; 2hr lesson incl hire $65) Hires surfing gear, sells secondhand equipment and offers lessons (cheaper with advance booking).

Torquay Surfing Academy SURFING
(☎03-5261 2022; www.torquaysurf.com.au; 34a Bell St; 2hr group/private lessons $60/180) Serious surf school.

Westcoast Surf School SURFING
(☎03-5261 2241; www.westcoastsurfschool.com; 2hr lesson $60) Reputable Westcoast Surf School offers surf lessons and board hire.

Sleeping

Bells Beach Backpackers HOSTEL $
(☎03-5261 4029; www.bellsbeachbackpackers.com.au; 51-53 Surfcoast Hwy; dm/d from $26/80; @📶) On the main highway, this friendly backpackers does a great job of fitting into the fabric of this surf town, with board hire, daily surf reports and a good collection of surf videos. Its basic rooms are clean and in good nick.

Woolshed B&B B&B $$$
(☎0408 333 433; www.thewoolshedtorquay.com.au; 75 Aquarius Ave; apt incl breakfast $275; ❄🏊) Set on a gorgeous farm on Torquay's outskirts, this century-old woolshed has been converted into a gorgeous open and airy

space with two bedrooms. It sleeps up to six, and guests can use the pool and tennis court. Book well in advance.

Eating & Drinking

Cafe Moby CAFE $

(☎03 5261 2339; www.cafemoby.com; 41 Esplanade; mains $12-18; ⏲7am-4pm; 📶) This old weatherboard house on the Esplanade harks back to a time when Torquay was simple, which is not to say its meals aren't modern: fill up on a linguini or honey-roasted lamb souvlaki. There's a whopping great playground out the back for kids.

Bottle of Milk BURGERS, BAR $

(☎0456 748 617; www.thebottleofmilk.com; 24 Bell St; burgers from $10; ⏲10.30am-late) Trading off the success of its Lorne (p540) branch, Bottle of Milk's winning formula of burgers, beaches and beers makes it rightfully popular. There's a beer garden, too, and excellent coffee.

Shopping

A smorgasbord of surf shops lines Torquay's main thoroughfare, from big brands to local board shapers. For bargains head down Baines Cres alongside Surf City Plaza for discount surf seconds.

Information

Torquay Visitor Information Centre (www.greatoceanroad.org; Surf City Plaza, Beach Rd; ⏲9am-5pm) Torquay has a well-resourced tourist office next to Surf World Museum. There's free wi-fi and internet available at the library next door.

Getting There & Away

Torquay is 15 minutes' drive south of Geelong on the B100.

BUS

McHarry's Buslines (☎03-5223 2111; www.mcharrys.com.au) Runs buses hourly from 9am to 8pm (around 5pm weekends) from Geelong to Torquay ($3.60, 30 minutes).

V/Line (☎1800 800 007; www.vline.com.au) Buses run six times daily Monday to Friday (two on weekends) from Geelong to Torquay ($3.60, 25 minutes).

ORGANISED TOURS

Go West Tours (☎1300 736 551; www.gowest.com.au; tour $125) Full-day tours visit Bells Beach, koalas in the Otways and Port Campbell, returning back to Melbourne. Free wi-fi on bus.

Otway Discovery Tour (☎03-9629 5844; www.greatoceanroadtour.com.au; 1-/2-/3-day tour $99/249/355) Very affordable Great Ocean Road tours. The two-day tours include Phillip Island, while the three-day version takes in the Grampians.

Ride Tours (☎1800 605 120; www.ridetours.com.au; tour $210) Two-day, one-night trips along the Great Ocean Road.

Great Ocean Road Surf Tours (☎1800 787 353; www.gorsurftours.com.au; 106 Surf Coast Hwy) Multi-day surf trips down the coast from $309, including accommodation in Torquay.

Anglesea

POP 2454

Mix sheer orange cliffs falling into the ocean with hilly, tree-filled 'burbs and a population that booms in summer and you've got Anglesea, where sharing fish and chips with seagulls by the Anglesea River is a decades-long family tradition for many.

The new Geelong bypass has reduced the time it takes to drive from Melbourne to Anglesea to around 75 minutes.

Sights & Activities

Main Beach is the ideal spot to learn to surf, while sheltered **Point Roadknight Beach** is good for families.

Anglesea Golf Club GOLF

(☎03-5263 1582; www.angleseagolfclub.com.au; Noble St; 9 holes from $25; ⏲clubhouse 8am-midnight) You can watch kangaroos graze on the fairways from the big glass windows at the clubhouse here, or, even better, pair your sightings with a round of golf.

Go Ride a Wave SURFING

(☎1300 132 441; www.gorideawave.com.au; 143b Great Ocean Rd; 2hr lessons from $65, board hire from $25; ⏲9am-5pm) Long-established surf school that runs lessons and hires out boards, SUPs and kayaks.

Sleeping

Anglesea Backpackers HOSTEL $

(☎03-5263 2664; www.angleseabackpackers.com; 40 Noble St; dm from $35, d $95-115, f $150; @) While most hostels like to cram 'em in, this

DON'T MISS

BELLS BEACH & POINT ADDIS

The Great Ocean Road officially begins on the stretch between Torquay and Anglesea. A slight detour takes you to famous **Bells Beach**, the powerful point break that is part of international surfing folklore (it was here, in name only, that Keanu Reeves and Patrick Swayze had their ultimate showdown in the film *Point Break*). When the long right hander is working, it's one of the longest rides in the country.

Since 1973, Bells has hosted the **Rip Curl Pro** (www.aspworldtour.com) every Easter. The world championship ASP tour event draws thousands to watch the world's best surfers carve up the big autumn swells – waves have reached 5m during the contest! The Rip Curl Pro occasionally decamps to Johanna Beach, two hours west, when fickle Bells isn't working.

Nine kilometres southwest of Torquay is the turn-off to spectacular **Point Addis**, a vast sweep of pristine clothing-optional beach that attracts surfers, nudists, hang-gliders and swimmers. The signposted **Koorie Cultural Walk** is a 1km circuit trail to the beach through the **Ironbark Basin** nature reserve.

simple, homely backpackers has just two dorm rooms and one double/triple, and is clean, bright and welcoming. In winter the fire glows warmly in the cosy living room.

Anglesea Rivergums B&B **$$**
(☎03-5263 3066; www.anglesearivergums.com.au; 10 Bingley Pde; d $125-160; ❄) Tucked in by the river with tranquil views, these two spacious, tastefully furnished rooms (there's a self-contained bungalow and a room attached to the house) are excellent value.

Eating

★**Uber Mama** MODERN AUSTRALIAN **$$**
(☎03-5263 1717; www.ubermama.com.au; 113 Great Ocean Rd; mains $19-33; ⏲noon-3pm & 6-9pm Thu-Sat, 9am-3pm Sun) An example of the subtle revolution sweeping the kitchens of regional Australia, Uber Mama does modern Aussie cooking with Asian inflections that's creative without straying too far from local roots. Try the shared plates such as baked Otway brie or seared scallops with prosciutto, or classic fish and chips for a main.

Locanda Del Mare ITALIAN **$$**
(☎03-5263 2904; 5 Diggers Pde; mains $19.50-25; ⏲from 6pm Thu-Mon summer, from 6pm Thu-Sun winter) Don't be deceived by its ugly exterior; this authentic Italian restaurant, hidden behind Anglesea's petrol station, gets rave reviews, especially for its wonderful desserts.

Information

Anglesea Visitor Information Centre (Great Ocean Rd; ⏲9am-5pm) Located opposite Angahook Cafe, this new information centre sits beside an equally new BBQ area.

Aireys Inlet & Around

POP 1071

Aireys Inlet is midway between Anglesea and Lorne, and is home to glorious stretches of beach, including **Fairhaven** and **Moggs Creek**. Ask at the visitor centre for great coastal walks around here.

Sights & Activities

★**Split Point Lighthouse** LIGHTHOUSE
(☎03-5263 1133; www.splitpointlighthouse.com.au; 45min tours adult/child/family $14/8/40; ⏲tours hourly 11am-2pm, summer holidays 10am-4pm) Scale the 136 steps to the top of the beautiful 'White Queen' lighthouse for sensational 360-degree views. Built in 1891, the 34m-high lighthouse is still operational (though now fully automated). It's only accessible by booking a tour.

Blazing Saddles HORSE RIDING
(☎03-5289 7322; www.blazingsaddlestrailrides.com; Lot 1 Bimbadeen Dr; 1/2½hr rides $50/100) People come from around the world to hop on a Blazing Saddles horse and head along the stunning beach or into the bush.

Sleeping & Eating

★**Cimarron B&B** B&B **$$**
(☎03-5289 7044; www.cimarron.com.au; 105 Gilbert St; d $150-175; wifi) Built in 1979 from local timbers and using only wooden pegs and shiplap joins, Cimarron is an idyllic getaway with views over Point Roadknight. The large

lounge area has book-lined walls and a cosy fireplace, while upstairs are two unique, loft-style doubles with vaulted timber ceilings; otherwise there's a den-like apartment. Out back, it's all state park and wildlife.

Gay friendly, but no kids.

★ A La Grecque GREEK $$
(☎03-5289 6922; www.alagrecque.com.au; 60 Great Ocean Rd; mains $22-35; ⊙9-11.30am, 12.30-2.30pm & 6-10pm daily Dec-Mar, Wed-Sun Apr, May & Sep-Nov) Be whisked away to the Mediterranean at this outstanding modern Greek taverna. Mezze such as seared scallops or braised cuttlefish with apple, celery and a lime dressing, and mains such as grilled pork shoulder are sensational.

Aireys Pub PUB $$
(☎03-5289 6804; www.aireyspub.com.au; 45 Great Ocean Rd; mains $20-34; ⊙noon-late; 📶) Established in 1904, this pub is a survivor, twice burning to the ground before closing its doors in 2011, only to be saved by a bunch of locals chipping in to save it. Now it's better than ever, with a fantastic kitchen (try the kangaroo burger), roaring fire, sprawling beer garden, live music and its own Aireys draught beer.

Lorne

POP 1046

Lorne has an incredible natural beauty, something you see vividly as you drive into town from Aireys Inlet: tall old gum trees line its hilly streets, and Loutit Bay gleams irresistibly. It's this beauty that has attracted visitors for generations. It gets busy; in summer you'll be competing with day trippers for restaurant seats and lattes, but, thronged by tourists or not, it's a lovely place to hang out.

Sights & Activities

Kids will love the beachside swimming pool, trampolines and skate park. There's more than 50km of **bushwalking** tracks around Lorne, taking in lush forests and waterfalls – pick up the *Lorne Walks & Waterfalls* brochure from the visitor centre.

Erskine Falls WATERFALL
(Erskine Falls Access Rd) Head out of town to see this lovely waterfall. It's an easy walk to the viewing platform, or 250 (often slippery) steps down to its base, from where you can explore further or head back on up.

Southern Exposure WATER SPORTS
(☎03-5261 9170; www.southernexposure.com.au; 2hr surf lesson $75) Offers surfing lessons, and is big on kayaking and mountain biking.

Festivals & Events

Falls Festival MUSIC
(www.fallsfestival.com; 2-/3-/4-day tickets $320/390/433; ⊙28 Dec - 1 Jan) A four-day knees-up over New Year's on a farm just out of town, this stellar music festival attracts a top line-up of international rock and indie groups. Past headliners have included Iggy Pop, Spiderbait, Kings of Leon and the Black Keys. Sells out fast, and tickets include camping.

Pier to Pub Swim SPORTS
(www.lornesurfclub.com.au) This popular event in January inspires up to 4500 swimmers to splash 1.2km across Loutit Bay to the Lorne

WHERE TO SEE WILDLIFE

The Great Ocean Road is not just one of the world's best road trips. It's also one of the best places in Australia to see wildlife.

Kangaroos

Anglesea Golf Club (p537)

Tower Hill Reserve (15km west of Warrnambool). Also good for emus and koalas.

Platypus

Lake Elizabeth (7km from Forrest, which is a 30-minute drive from Apollo Bay). Contact **Otway Eco Tours** (☎0419 670 985; www.platypustours.net.au; adult/child $85/50).

Koalas

Kennett River (especially behind the caravan park)

Cape Otway (along the road between the main highway and the lighthouse)

Penguins

Twelve Apostles (p543)

London Bridge (p543)

Southern Right Whales

Warrnambool (May to September)

Portland (May to September)

Black Wallabies

Battery Hill (p546)

Port Fairy (p540)

Hotel. It's a photo opportunity for local politicians and celebrities.

Sleeping

Great Ocean Road Backpackers HOSTEL **$**
(☎03-5289 1070; http://greatoceanroadcottages.com; 10 Erskine Ave; dm/d $35/90;) Tucked away in the bush among the cockatoos, koalas and other wildlife, this two-storey timber lodge has dorms and good-value doubles. Unisex bathrooms take some getting used to. Also has pricier A-frame cottages that come with kitchens and en suite.

Grand Pacific Hotel HOTEL **$$**
(☎03-5289 1609; www.grandpacific.com.au; 268 Mountjoy Pde; d/apt from $130/180;) An iconic Lorne landmark, harking back to 1875, the Grand Pacific has been restored with a sleek modern decor that retains some classic period features. The best rooms have balconies and stunning sea views looking out to the pier. Plainer rooms are boxy, but still top value, and there are self-contained apartments, too.

Qdos RYOKAN **$$$**
(☎03-5289 1989; www.qdosarts.com; 35 Allenvale Rd; r incl breakfast from $250;) The perfect choice for those seeking a romantic getaway or forest retreat, Qdos' luxury Zen treehouses are fitted with tatami mats, rice-paper screens and no TV. Two-night minimum; no kids.

WORTH A TRIP

BRAE AT BIRREGURRA

Brae (☎03-5236 2226; www.braerestaurant.com; 4285 Cape Otway Rd, Birregurra; 8-course tasting plates per person $180, plus matched wines $120; ⏲noon-3pm Fri-Mon, from 6pm Thu-Sun) Given the success chef Dan Hunter had at the Royal Mail Hotel in Dunkeld, the Birregurra tourism guys must've been licking their lips for several reasons when they heard he was moving to their town to open his new restaurant. Brae takes over from the much-loved Sunnybrae, with its farmhouse getting a refit by renowned architects Six Degrees.

The restaurant uses whatever is growing in its 12 hectares of organic gardens. Reservations are essential, well in advance. Future plans include boutique accommodation on-site.

It's located in the small historic town of Birregurra, between Colac and Lorne.

Eating

Bottle of Milk BURGERS **$**
(☎03-5289 2005; www.thebottleofmilk.com; 52 Mountjoy Pde; burgers from $12; ⏲8am-3pm Mon-Fri, to 5pm Sat & Sun, 8am-9pm Nov-Feb) With a menu of 24 inventive burgers, all stacked with fresh ingredients, it's hard to go wrong at this popular hang-out on the main strip.

Lorne Beach Pavilion MODERN AUSTRALIAN **$$**
(☎03-5289 2882; www.lornebeachpavilion.com.au; 81 Mountjoy Pde; breakfast & lunch mains $9-20, dinner $25-37; ⏲8am-9pm) With its unbeatable spot on the foreshore, life here is literally a beach, especially with a cold beer in hand. Come at happy hour for 1kg of mussels for $10 and two-for-one cocktails. Cafe-style breakfasts and lunches are tasty, while a more upmarket Modern Australian menu is on for dinner.

Arab CAFE **$$**
(☎03-5289 1435; 94 Mountjoy Pde; mains $19-26; ⏲7am-8pm Mon-Fri, to 9.30pm Sat & Sun) Arab started as a beatnik coffee lounge in 1956, and single-handedly transformed Lorne from a daggy family-holiday destination into a place for groovers and shakers. It's been trading ever since, and still hits the spot for coffee and all-day breakfasts.

Information

Lorne Visitor Centre (☎1300 891 152; www.visitgreatoceanroad.org.au/lorne; 15 Mountjoy Pde; ⏲9am-5pm;) Stacks of information (including walking maps), helpful staff, fishing licences, bus tickets and accommodation booking service. Also has internet access and free wi-fi.

Getting There & Away

V/Line (www.vline.com.au) V/Line buses pass through daily from Geelong ($10.40, 1½ hours) en route to Apollo Bay ($4.40, one hour).

Apollo Bay

POP 1094

One of the larger towns along the Great Ocean Road, Apollo Bay has a tight-knit community of fisherfolk, artists, musicians and sea changers. Rolling hills provide a postcard backdrop to the town, while broad, white-sand beaches dominate the foreground. It's also an ideal base for exploring

DON'T MISS

WALKING THE GREAT OCEAN ROAD

The superb multiday **Great Ocean Walk** (www.visitgreatoceanroad.org.au/greatoceanwalk) starts at Apollo Bay and runs all the way to the Twelve Apostles. It takes you through changing landscapes along spectacular clifftops, deserted beaches and forested Otway National Park.

It's possible to start at one point and arrange a pick up at another (public transport options are few and far between). You can do shorter walks or the whole 104km trek over eight days. Designated camp sites are spread along the trail, catering for registered walkers only; bring cooking equipment and tents (no fires allowed). Check out the helpful FAQ page on the website for all info.

Walk 91 (03-5237 1189; www.walk91.com.au; 157-159 Great Ocean Rd, Apollo Bay) Walk 91 can arrange your itinerary, transport and equipment hire, and can shuttle your backpack to your destination.

GOR Shuttle (03-5237 9278, 0428 379 278) GOR Shuttle is a recommended shuttle service for luggage and walkers. It'll pick you up when your walking's done (costing anywhere from $35 to $85, depending on the distance).

magical Cape Otway (p542) and Otway National Park. It has some of the best restaurants along the coast and two lively pubs.

Activities

Mark's Walking Tours WALKING TOUR
(0417 983 985; www.greatoceanwalk.asn.au/markstours; 2-3hr tour adult/child $50/15) Take a walk around the area with local Mark Brack, son of the Cape Otway Lighthouse keeper. He knows this stretch of coast, its history and its ghosts better than anyone around. Daily tours include shipwreck tours, historical tours, glow-worm tours and Great Ocean Walk tours. Minimum two people – prices drop the more people on the tour.

Apollo Bay Surf & Kayak WATER SPORTS
(0405 495 909; www.apollobaysurfkayak.com.au; 157 Great Ocean Rd; 2hr kayak tours $65, 1½hr surf lessons $60) Head out to an Australian fur seal colony in a double kayak. Tours (with full instructions for beginners) depart from Marengo Beach (to the south of the town centre). Also offers surf lessons, plus boards, stand-up paddle boards and mountain bikes for hire.

Sleeping

YHA Eco Beach HOSTEL $
(03-5237 7899; www.yha.com.au; 5 Pascoe St; dm from $36.50, d/f $101.50/122; @) This $3-million, architect-designed hostel is an outstanding place to stay, with eco credentials, great lounge areas, kitchens, boules pit and rooftop terraces. Rooms are generic but spotless. It's a block behind the beach.

Surfside Backpacker HOSTEL $
(03-5237 7263; www.surfsidebackpacker.com; cnr Great Ocean Rd & Gambier St; dm from $28, d $75) Right across from the beach, this fantastic, sprawling, old-school 1940s beach house will appeal to those looking for budget accommodation with character (though possibly not to those seeking a sleek, modern hostel). Its homely lounge is full of couches, board games and huge windows looking out onto the ocean. It's a 15-minute walk from the bus stop.

★ **Beacon Point Ocean View Villas** VILLA $$
(03-5237 6196; www.beaconpoint.com.au; 270 Skenes Creek Rd; r from $165) With a commanding hill location among the trees, this wonderful collection of comfortable one- and two-bedroom villas is a luxurious yet affordable bush retreat. Most villas have sensational coast views, balcony and wood-fired heater.

Eating & Drinking

Bay Leaf Café CAFE $
(03-5237 6470; 131 Great Ocean Rd; mains $11-17; 8.30am-2.30pm) A local favourite for its innovative menu, good coffee, friendly atmosphere and boutique-beer selection.

Apollo Bay Hotel PUB $$
(03-5237 6250; www.apollobayhotel.com.au; 95 Great Ocean Rd; mains $18-36; 11am-11pm) This pub's enticing street-front beer garden is the place to be in summer. The bistro has good seafood options and there are live bands on weekends.

THE SHIPWRECK COAST

In the era of sailing ships, Victoria's beautiful and rugged southwest coastline was one of the most treacherous on Earth. Between the 1830s and 1930s, more than 200 ships were torn asunder along the so-called Shipwreck Coast between Cape Otway and Port Fairy. From the early 1850s to late 1880s, Victoria's gold rush and subsequent economic boom brought countless shiploads of prospectors and hopefuls from Europe, North America and China. After spending months at sea, many vessels (and lives) were lost on the 'home straight'.

The **lighthouses** along this coast – at Aireys Inlet, Cape Otway, Port Fairy and Warrnambool – are still operating and you'll find shipwreck museums, memorial plaques and anchors that tell the story of wrecks along this coast. The most famous is that of the iron-hulled clipper **Loch Ard**, which foundered off Mutton Bird Island (near Port Campbell) at 4am on the final night of its long voyage from England in 1878. Of 37 crew and 19 passengers on board, only two survived. Eva Carmichael, a non-swimmer, clung to wreckage and was washed into a gorge – since renamed **Loch Ard Gorge** (p543) – where apprentice officer Tom Pearce rescued her. Despite rumours of a romance, they never saw each other again and Eva soon returned to Ireland.

★Chris's Beacon Point Restaurant GREEK **$$$**
(☎03-5237 6411; www.chriss.com.au; 280 Skenes Creek Rd; mains from $38; ⏲8.30-10am & 6pm-late daily, plus noon-2pm Sat & Sun;) Feast on memorable ocean views, deliciously fresh seafood and Greek-influenced dishes at Chris' hilltop fine-dining sanctuary among the treetops. Reservations recommended. You can also stay in its wonderful stilted villas ($265 to $330). It's accessed via Skenes Creek.

Information

Great Ocean Road Visitor Centre (☎1300 689 297; 100 Great Ocean Rd; ⏲9am-5pm;) Modern and professional tourist office with a heap of info for the area, and an 'eco-centre' with displays. It has free wi-fi and can book bus tickets, too.

Cape Otway

Cape Otway is the second-most-southerly point of mainland Australia (after Wilsons Promontory) and one of the wettest parts of the state. This coastline is particularly beautiful, rugged and historically treacherous for passing ships. The turn-off for Lighthouse Rd, which leads 12km down to the lighthouse, is 21km from Apollo Bay.

Sights & Activities

Cape Otway Lightstation LIGHTHOUSE
(☎03-5237 9240; www.lightstation.com; Lighthouse Rd; adult/child/family $19.50/7.50/49.50; ⏲9am-5pm) Cape Otway lightstation is the oldest surviving lighthouse on mainland Australia and was built in 1848 by more than 40 stonemasons without mortar or cement. The **Telegraph Station** has fascinating displays on the 250km undersea telegraph cable link with Tasmania, laid in 1859. It's a sprawling complex with plenty to see, from Aboriginal cultural sites to WWII bunkers.

Sleeping

★Bimbi Park CARAVAN PARK **$**
(☎03-5237 9246; www.bimbipark.com.au; 90 Manna Gum Dr; unpowered/powered sites $20/30, dm $45, d cabins $60-185;) Down a dirt road 3km from the lighthouse is this character-filled caravan park with bush sites, cabins, dorms and old-school caravans. It's good for families, with plenty of wildlife, including koalas, horse rides ($45 per hour) and a rock-climbing wall. Good use of water-saving initiatives.

Cape Otway Lightstation B&B **$$$**
(Cape Otway lightstation; ☎03-5237 9240; www.lightstation.com; Lighthouse Rd; d from $255) There's a range of options at this windswept spot. You can book out the whole Head Lightkeeper's House (sleeps 16), or the smaller Manager's House (sleeps two). Prices are halved if you stay a second night. Vans are also permitted to stay for $25, but you'll need to pay the admission fee.

★Great Ocean Ecolodge LODGE **$$$**
(☎03-5237 9297; www.greatoceanecolodge.com; 635 Lighthouse Rd; r incl breakfast & activities

from $380; ⊜) Reminiscent of a luxury African safari lodge, this mud-brick homestead stands in pastoral surrounds with plenty of wildlife. It's all solar-powered and rates go towards the on-site **Centre for Conservation Ecology** (www.conservationecologycentre.org).

It also serves as an animal hospital for local fauna, and it has a captive tiger quoll breeding program, which you'll visit on its dusk wildlife walk with an ecologist.

Port Campbell National Park

The road levels out after leaving the Otways and enters narrow, flat scrubby escarpment lands that fall away to sheer, 70m-high cliffs along the coast between Princetown and Peterborough – a distinct change of scene. This is Port Campbell National Park, home to the Twelve Apostles, and the most famous and most photographed stretch of the Great Ocean Road.

None of the beaches along this stretch are suitable for swimming because of strong currents and undertows.

Sights & Activities

★Twelve Apostles LANDMARK

(Great Ocean Rd; ⊙visitor centre 9am-5pm) The most iconic sight and enduring image for most visitors to the Great Ocean Road, the Twelve Apostles provide a fitting climax to the journey. Jutting out from the ocean in spectacular fashion, these rocky stacks stand like they've been abandoned to the ocean by the retreating headland. Today only seven 'apostles' can be seen from a network of viewing platforms connected by timber boardwalks around the clifftops.

There's pedestrian access to the viewing platforms from the car park at the Twelve Apostles Visitor Centre (more a kiosk and toilets than an info centre) via a tunnel beneath the Great Ocean Road.

The best time to visit is sunset, not only for optimum photography opportunities and to beat the tour buses, but to see **little penguins** returning ashore. Sightings vary, but generally they arrive 20 to 40 minutes after sunset. You'll need binoculars, which can be borrowed from the Port Campbell Visitor Centre (p544).

Gibson Steps BEACH

These 86 steps, hacked by hand into the cliffs by 19th-century landowner Hugh Gibson (and more recently replaced by concrete steps), lead down to wild Gibson Beach. You can walk along the beach, but be careful not to be stranded by high tides.

Loch Ard Gorge BEACH

Close to the Twelve Apostles, Loch Ard Gorge is where the Shipwreck Coast's most famous and haunting tale unfolded when two young survivors of the wrecked iron clipper *Loch Ard* made it to shore. There are several walks in the area taking you down to the cave where they took shelter, plus a cemetery and rugged beach.

London Bridge LANDMARK

Just outside Port Campbell, en route to Peterborough, London Bridge has indeed fallen down. It was once a double-arched rock platform linked to the mainland, yet

HOW MANY APOSTLES?

The Twelve Apostles are not 12 in number and, from all records, never have been. From the viewing platform you can clearly count seven Apostles, but maybe some obscure others? We consulted widely with Parks Victoria officers, tourist-office staff and even the cleaner at the lookout, but it's still not clear. Locals tend to say 'It depends where you look from', which really is true.

The Apostles are called 'stacks' in geologic parlance, and the rock formations were originally called the 'Sow and Piglets'. Someone in the 1960s (nobody can recall who) thought they might attract some tourists with a more venerable name, so they were renamed 'the Apostles'. Since apostles tend to come by the dozen, the number 12 was added sometime later. The two stacks on the eastern (Otway) side of the viewing platform are not technically Apostles – they're Gog and Magog.

The soft limestone cliffs are dynamic and changeable, with constant erosion from the unceasing waves – one 70m-high stack collapsed into the sea in July 2005 and the Island Archway lost its archway in June 2009.

it remains a spectacular sight nevertheless. In January 1990 the bridge collapsed, leaving two terrified tourists marooned on the world's newest island – they were eventually rescued by helicopter.

Port Campbell

POP 260

This small, laid-back coastal town was named after Scottish Captain Alexander Campbell, a whaler who took refuge here on trading voyages between Tasmania and Port Fairy. It's a friendly spot with some great budget-accommodation options, which make for an ideal spot to debrief after visiting the Twelve Apostles. Its tiny bay has a lovely sandy beach, one of the few safe places for swimming along this tempestuous stretch of coast.

Tours

Port Campbell Touring Company TOUR
(03-5598 6424; www.portcampbelltouring.com.au; half-day tours from $100) Runs Apostle Coast tours and walking tours, including a Loch Ard evening walk ($65).

Sleeping

Port Campbell Guesthouse GUESTHOUSE $
(0407 696 559; www.portcampbellguesthouse.com; 54 Lord St; s/d incl breakfast from $40/68; @) It's great to find a home away from home, and this historic cottage close to town has four cosy rooms and a relaxed lounge and country kitchen. For added privacy there's a separate motel-style section up front with en suite rooms. Its ultra-relaxed owner, Mark, is knowledgeable about the area.

Port Bayou B&B $$
(03-5598 6009; www.portbayou.portcampbell.nu; 52 Lord St; d cottage from $185;) Choose from the cosy in-house B&B or a rustic self-contained cottage fitted with exposed ceiling beams and corrugated-tin walls (we'd go for the cottage).

Eating & Drinking

12 Rocks Cafe Bar CAFE $$
(19 Lord St; mains $21-37; 9.30am-11pm) Watch flotsam wash up on the beach from this busy eatery, which has perfect beachfront views. Try a local Otways beer with a pasta or seafood main, or just duck in for a coffee.

Port Campbell Hotel PUB
(40 Lord St; 11am-1am Mon-Sat, noon-11pm Sun) Head in for a beer and a feed with the locals. Kitchen closes at 8.30pm.

Information

Port Campbell Visitor Centre (1300 137 255; www.visit12apostles.com.au; 26 Morris St; 9am-5pm) Stacks of regional and accommodation information and interesting shipwreck displays – the anchor from the *Loch Ard* is out the front. Offers free use of binoculars and GPS equipment.

Getting There & Away

V/Line (13 61 96; www.vline.com.au) V/Line buses leave Geelong on Monday, Wednesday and Friday and travel through to Port Campbell ($29.20, five hours), with a possible stop in Apollo Bay, and onto Warrnambool ($6.80, one hour 20 minutes).

Warrnambool

POP 29,284

Warrnambool was originally a whaling and sealing station – now it's booming as a major regional commercial and whale-watching centre. Its historic buildings, waterways and tree-lined streets are attractive, and there's a large population of students.

Sights & Activities

Sheltered **Lady Bay**, with fortifications at the breakwater at its western end, is the main swimming beach. **Logan's Beach** has the best surf and there are breaks at **Levy's Beach** and **Second Bay**.

★Flagstaff Hill Maritime Village HISTORIC SITE
(03-5559 4600; www.flagstaffhill.com; 89 Merri St; adult/child/concession/family $16/6.50/12.50/39; 9am-5pm) The world-class Flagstaff Hill precinct is of equal interest for its shipwreck museum, heritage listed lighthouses and garrison as it is for its reproduction of a historical Victorian port town. It also has the nightly **Shipwrecked** (adult/child/family $26/14/67), an engaging 70-minute sound-and-laser show telling the story of the *Loch Ard's* plunge. The village is modelled on a pioneer-era Australian coastal port, with ye-olde shops such as blacksmiths, candlemakers and shipbuilders.

WHALES AT WARRNAMBOOL

In the 19th century Warrnambool's whale industry involved hunting them with harpoons, but these days they're a major tourist attraction, with crowds gathering to see them frolic offshore on their migration between May and September. Southern right whales (named due to being the 'right' whales to hunt) are the most common visitors, heading from Antarctica to these more temperate waters.

Although whales can be seen between Portland and Anglesea, undoubtedly the best place to see them is at Warrnambool's **Logan's Beach whale-watching platform** – they use the waters here as a nursery. Sightings aren't guaranteed, but you've got a very good chance of spotting them breaching and slapping their tails about as they nurse their bubs in the waters. Call ahead to the **visitor centre** (see below) to check if whales are about, or see www.visitwarrnambool.com.au for latest sightings.

Rundell's Mahogany Trail Rides HORSE RIDING
(0408 589 546; www.rundellshorseriding.com.au; 1½hr beach ride $65) Get to know some of Warrnambool's quiet beach spots on horseback.

Sleeping

Warrnambool Beach Backpackers HOSTEL $
(03-5562 4874; www.beachbackpackers.com.au; 17 Stanley St; dm/d from $26/80; @) A short stroll to the beach, this hostel has all backpackers' needs, with huge living area, kitchsy Aussie-themed bar, internet access, kitchen and free pick-up service. Its rooms are clean and good value, and it hires out surfboards and bikes. Vanpackers pay $12 per person to stay here.

Hotel Warrnambool PUB $$
(03-5562 2377; www.hotelwarrnambool.com.au; cnr Koroit & Kepler Sts; d incl breakfast without/with bathroom from $110/140) Renovations to this historic 1894 hotel have seen rooms upgraded to the more boutique end of the scale, while still keeping its classic pub-accommodation feel.

Lighthouse Lodge GUESTHOUSE $$
(www.lighthouselodge.com.au; Flagstaff Hill; d/house from $155/375) Once the former harbour master's residence, this charming weatherboard cottage can be rented as the entire house or separate rooms. It has a grassy area overlooking the Maritime Village and coastline. In the village there's also lodging in the **Garrison Camp** ($25 per person), a unique option for budget travellers within small wooden A-frame bunk cabins. BYO linen.

Eating

★**Kermond's Hamburgers** BURGERS $
(03-5562 4854; 151 Lava St; burgers $8; 9am-9.30pm) Likely not much has changed at this burger joint since it opened in 1949, with Laminex tables, wood-panelled walls and classic milkshakes served in stainless-steel tumblers. Its burgers are an institution.

Bojangles PIZZA $$
(03-5562 8751; www.bojanglespizza.com.au; 61 Liebig St; mains $16-31; 5-10pm) A step above your usual country pizza places, with seriously delicious thin-crust pizzas.

Hotel Warrnambool PUB FOOD $$
(www.hotelwarrnambool.com.au; cnr Koroit & Kepler Sts; lunch mains $12-27, dinner mains $28-34; noon-late) One of Victoria's best coastal pubs, Hotel Warrnambool mixes pub charm with bohemian character and serves wood-fired pizzas, among other gastropub fare.

Information

Warrnambool Visitor Centre (1800 637 725; www.visitwarrnambool.com.au; Merri St; 9am-5pm) For the latest on whale sightings, plus bike maps and several walking maps. Also has bicycle hire ($30 per day).

Getting There & Away

Warrnambool is an hour's drive west of Port Campbell on the B100.

V/Line (1800 800 007; www.vline.com.au; Merri St) V/Line trains run to Melbourne ($31.80, 3¼ hours, three or four daily) via Geelong ($22.80, 2½ hours).

There are also three V/Line buses a week from Geelong along the Great Ocean Road to Warrnambool ($33, 6½ hours), as well as three daily buses from Warrnambool to Port Fairy ($4.20, 35 minutes) and Portland ($11.40, 1½ hours).

WEST OF THE GREAT OCEAN ROAD

Port Fairy

POP 2835

Settled in 1833 as a whaling and sealing station, Port Fairy retains its historic 19th-century charm with a relaxed, salty feel, heritage bluestone and sandstone buildings, whitewashed cottages, colourful fishing boats and wide, tree-lined streets. In 2012 it was voted the world's most liveable community, and for most visitors it's not hard to see why.

Sights & Activities

Battery Hill HISTORIC SITE

Located across the bridge from the picturesque harbour, Battery Hill is worthy of exploration, with cannons and fortifications positioned here in 1887 to protect the town from foreign warships. You'll also encounter resident black wallabies. It was originally used as a flagstaff, so the views are good.

Self-Guided Walking Tours WALKING

Pick up a range of maps and brochures at the visitor centre that will guide you through various aspects of the town's heritage. It also has maps for the popular Maritime & Shipwreck Heritage Walk, while architecture buffs will want to buy a copy of *Historic Buildings of Port Fairy*.

PORT FAIRY ACCOMMODATION

Much of Port Fairy's holiday accommodation is managed by agents. The **visitor centre** (p547) offers a free booking service.

Port Fairy Accommodation Centre (☎03-5568 3150; www.portfairyaccom.com.au; 2/54 Sackville St) Local accommodation booking service.

Port Fairy Holiday Rentals (☎03-5568 1066; www.lockettrealestate.com.au; 62 Sackville St) A local clearing house for accommodation.

Go Surf SURFING

(☎0408 310 001; www.gosurf.com.au; 2hr lesson $40, board hire 2hr/1 day $25/50) Surf school and stand-up paddle board tours.

Festivals & Events

★**Port Fairy Folk Festival** MUSIC

(www.portfairyfolkfestival.com; tickets $75-290) Australia's premier folk-music festival is held on the Labour Day long weekend in March. It includes an excellent mix of international and national acts, while the streets are abuzz with buskers. Accommodation can book out a year in advance.

Sleeping

Port Fairy YHA HOSTEL $

(☎03-5568 2468; www.portfairyhostel.com.au; 8 Cox St; dm $26-30, s/tw/d from $41.50/70/75; @ Wi-Fi) In the rambling 1844 home of merchant William Rutledge, this friendly, well-run hostel has a large kitchen, a pool table, free cable TV and peaceful gardens.

★**Douglas on River** B&B $$

(www.douglasonriver.com.au; 85 Gipps St; r incl breakfast from $160; Wi-Fi) On the waterfront along the wharf, this 1852 heritage guesthouse lays claims to being the oldest in Port Fairy and is a great choice for those seeking boutique accommodation. The lovely front lawn and common area are both perfect for relaxing, and it does wonderful breakfasts using local produce.

Pelican Waters CABIN $$

(☎03-5568 1002; www.pelicanwatersportfairy.com.au; 34 Regent St; cabins from $100; A/C) Why stay in a hotel when you can sleep in a train? This beautifully presented farm property has cabins as well as rooms in converted old-school Melbourne suburban MET trains. Has alpacas and llamas, too.

Eating & Drinking

Pantry Door at Basalt CAFE $$

(☎03-5568 7442; 1131 Princes Hwy, Killarney; mains $12-26; ⏲7.30am-noon Mon, to 4.30pm Wed-Sun; Wi-Fi) Just outside Port Fairy, in the township of Killarney, this bluestone homestead cafe focuses on seasonal local produce and has an outdoor deck among fruit trees. Next door is **Basalt Wines** (☎0429 682 251; www.basaltwines.com; 1131 Princes Hwy, Killarney; ⏲11am-4.30pm Sat & Sun), a family-run biodynamic winery that does tastings in its shed.

Stump Hotel PUB $$
(☎03-5568 1044; www.caledonianinnportfairy.com.au; 41 Bank St; mains $16-22; ⏲noon-late) Victoria's oldest continuously licensed pub (1844), the Stump, aka Caledonian Inn, has a beer garden and pub grub. Also has no-frills motel rooms from $100.

★ **Merrijig Kitchen** MODERN AUSTRALIAN $$$
(☎03-5568 2324; www.merrijiginn.com; 1 Campbell St; mains $28-38; ⏲6-9pm Thu-Mon; 📶) One of coastal Victoria's most atmospheric restaurants; warm yourself by the open fire and enjoy superb dining with a menu that changes according to what's seasonal. Delectable food with great service.

Information

Port Fairy Visitor Centre (☎03-5568 2682; www.visitportfairy-moyneshire.com.au; Bank St; ⏲9am-5pm) Provides spot-on tourist information, walking tour brochures, V/Line tickets and bike hire (half/full day $15/25).

Getting There & Away

Port Fairy is 20 minutes' drive west of Warrnambool on the A1.

V/Line (☎1800 800 007; www.vline.com.au) Buses run three times daily on weekdays (twice on Saturday and once on Sunday) to Portland ($7.80, 55 minutes) and Warrnambool ($4.20, 35 minutes).

Portland

POP 9950

Portland's claim to fame is as Victoria's first European settlement, founded as a whaling and sealing base in the early 1800s. Despite its colonial history and architecture and its size, blue-collared Portland lacks a real drawcard, which sees it fall short of its potential. There are some good beaches and surf breaks outside town.

Sights & Activities

Whales often visit during winter; see www.whalemail.com.au for latest sightings.

Historic Waterfront WATERFRONT
(Cliff St) The grassy precinct overlooking the harbour has several heritage bluestone buildings. The **History House** (☎03-5522 2266; Cliff St; adult/child $3/2; ⏲10am-noon & 1-4pm), located in the former town hall (1863), has an interesting museum detailing Portland's colonial past. **Customs House** (1850) has a fascinating display of confiscated booty, including a stuffed black bear. Also here is the 1845 **courthouse**, the 1886 **Rocket Shed**, with a display of ship rescue equipment, and the 1889 **battery**, built as defence against feared Russian invasion.

Self-guided Walking Tours WALKING TOUR
The tourist office offers several self-guided walking-tour brochures, including a **heritage building** tour and one that traces the steps of **St Mary MacKillop's** time in Portland.

Sleeping

Annesley House BOUTIQUE HOTEL $$
(☎0429 852 235; www.annesleyhouse.com.au; 60 Julia St; d from $150; ❄📶) This recently restored former doctor's mansion (c 1878) has six very different self-contained rooms, some featuring claw-foot baths and lovely views. All have a unique sense of style.

Clifftop Accommodation GUESTHOUSE $$
(☎03-5523 1126; www.portlandaccommodation.com.au; 13 Clifton Ct; d from $140; ❄📶) The panoramic ocean views from the balconies here are incredible. Three self-contained rooms are huge, with big brass beds, telescopes and a modern maritime feel.

Eating

Deegan Seafoods FISH & CHIPS $
(106 Percy St; mains from $10; ⏲9am-6pm Mon-Fri) This fish-and-chip shop famously serves up the freshest fish in Victoria.

Cafe Bahloo CAFE $$
(85 Cliff St; mains $12-29; ⏲7.30am-3.30pm Tue-Sat) Housed in the original bluestone watchkeeper's house across from the harbour, Bahloo serves good breakfasts and coffee.

Information

Portland Visitor Centre (☎1800 035 567; www.visitportland.com.au; Lee Breakwater Rd; ⏲9am-5pm) In a modern building on the waterfront, this excellent information centre has a stack of suggestions of things to do and see.

Getting There & Away

Portland is a one-hour drive west of Port Fairy on the A1.

V/Line (☎1800 800 007; www.vline.com.au) V/Line buses connect Portland with Port Fairy ($7.80, 55 minutes) and Warrnambool ($11.40, 1½ hours) three times daily on weekdays, twice on Saturday and once on Sunday. Buses depart from Henty St.

Portland to South Australia

From Portland you can head northwest along the beautiful Portland–Nelson Rd. This road runs inland from the coast, but along the way there are turn-offs leading to beaches and national parks.

Cape Bridgewater is an essential 21km detour off the Portland–Nelson Rd. The stunning 4km arc of Bridgewater Bay is one of Australia's finest stretches of white-sand surf beach. The road continues on to **Cape Duquesne**, where walking tracks lead to a spectacular Blowhole and the eerie Petrified Forest (and wind farms) on the clifftop. A longer two-hour return walk takes you to a **seal colony**.

Tiny **Nelson**, 65km from Portland and 4km short of the South Australian border, is little more than a general store, a pub and a handful of accommodation places, but you can take boat and kayak tours from here up the Glenelg River.

Gippsland & Wilsons Promontory

Includes ➡

Best Places to Eat

➡ Koonwarra Food & Wine Store (p555)

➡ Metung Galley (p558)

➡ Ferryman's Seafood Cafe (p560)

➡ Lucy's (p562)

Best Places to Stay

➡ Walhalla Star Hotel (p553)

➡ Lighthouse Keepers' Cottages (p555)

➡ Wilderness Retreat (p556)

➡ Limosa Rise (p556)

➡ Adobe Mudbrick Flats (p561)

Why Go?

The Great Ocean Road may get the crowds, but Gippsland hides all the secrets. Gippsland is one region where it pays to avoid the cities – the towns along the Princes Hwy are barely worth a traveller's glance. Elsewhere are some of the state's most absorbing, unspoilt and beautiful wilderness areas and beaches.

Along the coast there's Wilsons Promontory National Park, a fabulous destination for hikers and sightseers alike. This is only the start when it comes to stirring beaches. Epic Ninety Mile Beach yields to Cape Conran Coastal Park and Croajingolong National Park. Put them together and it's one of the wildest, most beautiful coastlines on Earth.

Inland, Walhalla is an utterly beguiling village, while the national parks at Snowy River and Errinundra are as deeply forested, remote and pristine as any in the country.

When to Go

Point Hicks

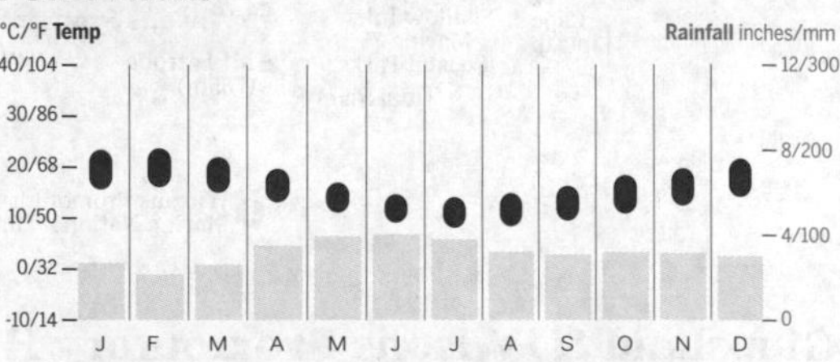

Feb–Mar For toe-tapping jazz festivals at Inverloch and Paynesville.

Sep–Nov Spring is the time for wild flowers and wildlife, as well as bushwalking.

Dec–Jan It gets busy, but there's no better time to hit the oceans and lakes than summer!

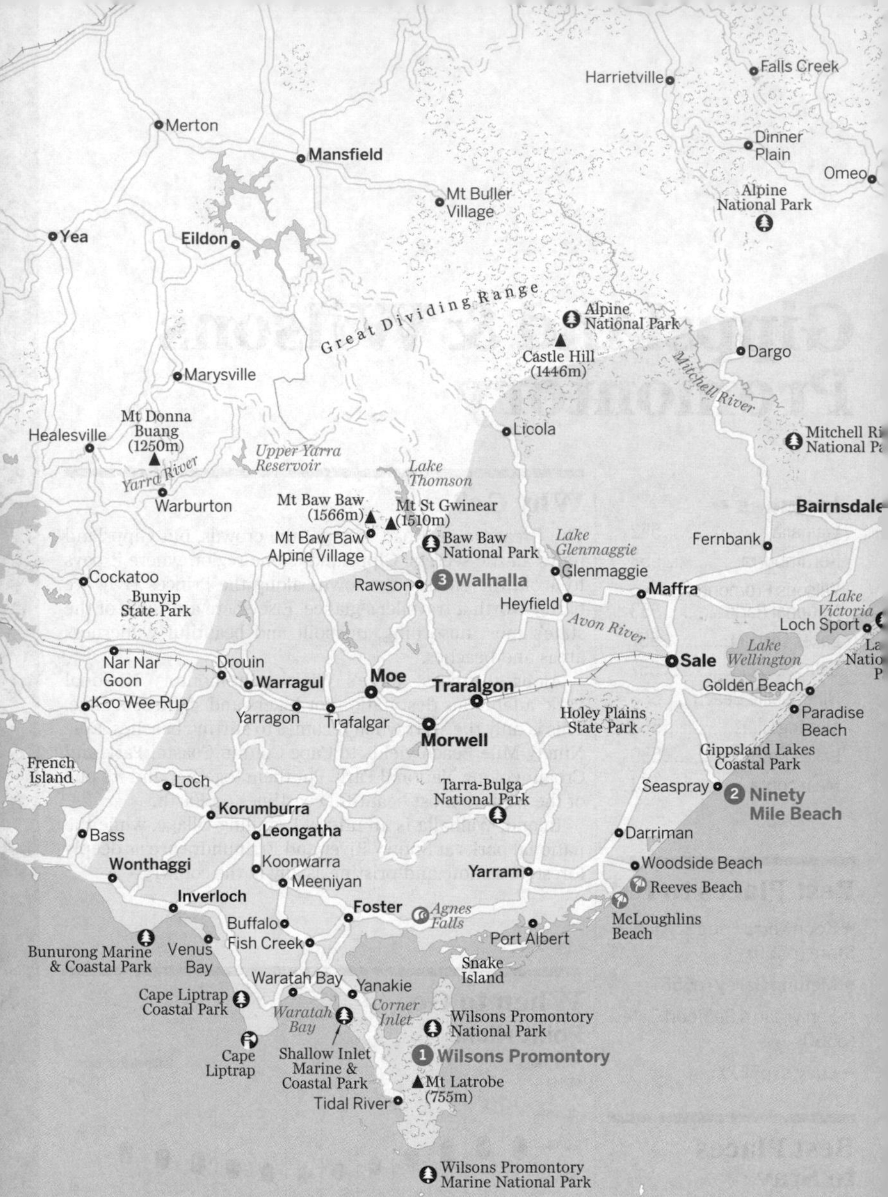

Gippsland & Wilsons Promontory Highlights

1. Hiking from Tidal River to Sealers Cove, or to a remote lighthouse, at spectacular **Wilsons Promontory** (p553).
2. Camping in the dunes and fish from the beach at legendary **Ninety Mile Beach** (p558).
3. Stepping back in time at **Walhalla** (p552), an authentic gold-mining village.
4. Hiking into the forest or driving the tracks of **Snowy River National Park** (p561).
5. Descending into ancient limestone caves and camping out at **Buchan** (p560).

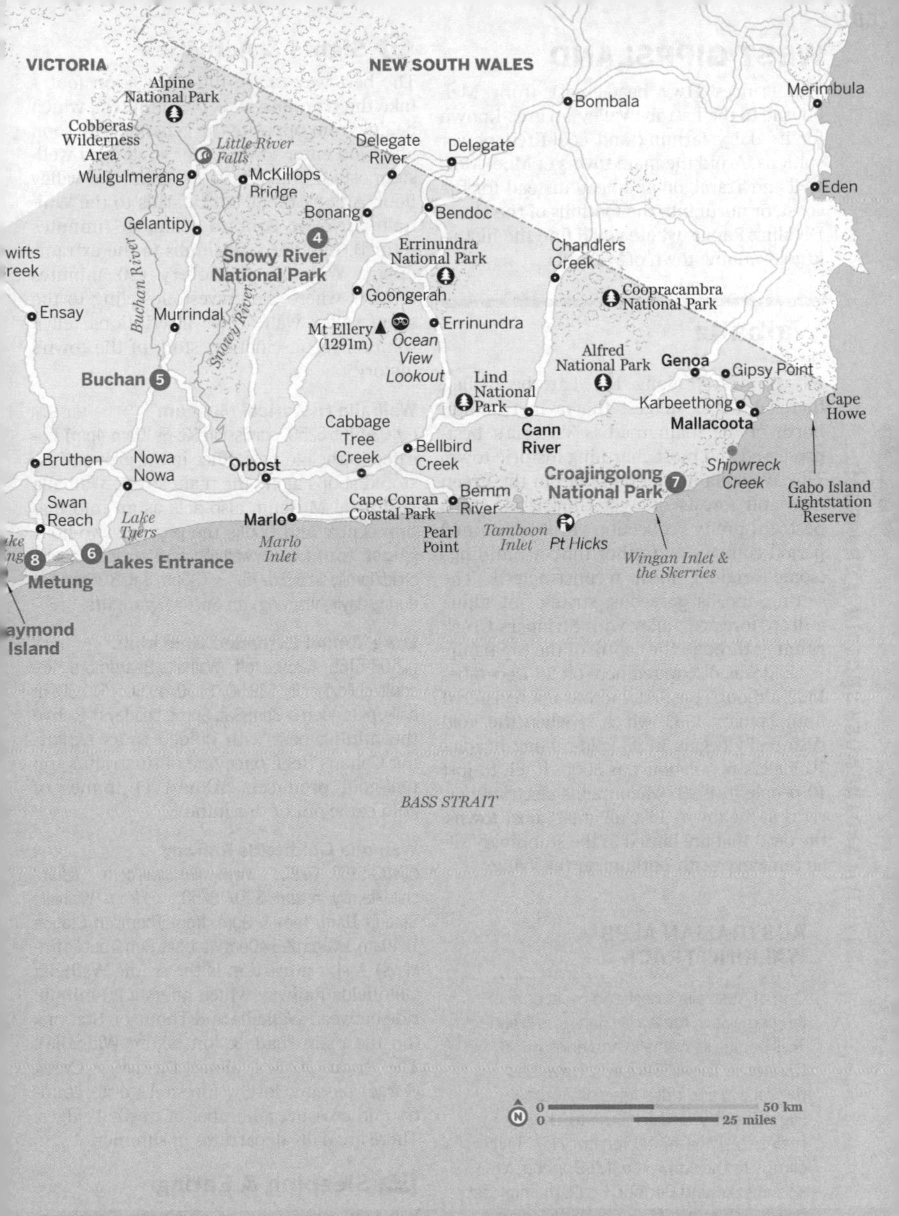

6 Taking an afternoon winery cruise then feasting on a seafood dinner at **Lakes Entrance** (p559).

7 Finding your quiet corner of the world in humbling **Croajingolong National Park** (p561).

8 Cruising the waters of the Lakes District from the tranquil marina village of **Metung** (p558).

9 Looking for koalas on little-known **Raymond Island** (p559).

WEST GIPPSLAND

The Princes Hwy heads east from Melbourne to the Latrobe Valley, an area known for its dairy farming and coal-fired power stations. Avoid the main towns of Moe, Morwell and Traralgon and head instead for the coast, or north into the foothills of the Great Dividing Range, where you'll find the historic gold-mining town of Walhalla.

Walhalla

POP 15

As you travel along the Latrobe Valley, there's little to suggest that a mere 35km north of the main road is Victoria's best-preserved and most charming historic town. Tiny Walhalla lies hidden high in the green hills and forests of west Gippsland. It's a postcard-pretty collection of sepia-toned period cottages and other timber buildings (some original, most reconstructed). The setting, too, is gorgeous, strung out along a deep, forested valley with Stringers Creek running through the centre of the township.

Gold was discovered here on 26 December 1862, although the first find was not registered until January 1863, which is when the gold rush really began. In its gold-mining heyday, Walhalla's population was 5000. It fell to just 10 people in 1998 (when mains electricity arrived in the town). Like all great ghost towns, the dead that are buried in the stunningly sited cemetery vastly outnumber the living.

AUSTRALIAN ALPS WALKING TRACK

One of Australia's best and most challenging walks, the Australian Alps Walking Trail begins in Walhalla and ends near Canberra. This 655km epic traverses the valleys and ridge lines of Victoria's High Country, and en route to Tharwa in the Australian Capital Territory (ACT) it climbs to the summit of Mt Bogong, Mt Kosciuszko and Bimberi Peak, the highest points in Victoria, New South Wales and the ACT respectively. Making the full trek is a serious undertaking that requires good navigational skills and high levels of fitness and self-sufficiency. If you're planning on doing the walk, which takes up to eight weeks to complete, track down a copy of *Australian Alps Walking Track* by John and Monica Chapman.

Sights & Activities

The best way to see the town is on foot – take the **tramline walk** (45 minutes), which begins from opposite the general store soon after you enter town. Other good (and well-signposted) walks lead up from the valley floor. Among them, a trail leads to the **Walhalla Cricket Ground** (2km, 45 minutes return). Another trail climbs to the extraordinary **Walhalla Cemetery** (20 minutes return), where the gravestones cling to the steep valley wall. Their inscriptions tell a sombre, yet fascinating, story of the town's history.

Walhalla Historical Museum MUSEUM
(03-5165 6250; admission $2; 10am-4pm) Located in the old post office in the group of restored shops along the main street, Walhalla Historical Museum also acts as an information centre and books the popular two-hour **ghost tours** (www.walhallaghosttour.info; adult/child/family $25/20/75; 7.30pm Sat, 8.30pm Sat during daylight saving) on Saturday nights.

Long Tunnel Extended Gold Mine MINE
(03-5165 6259; off Walhalla-Beardmore Rd; adult/child/family $19.50/13.50/49.50; 1.30pm daily, plus noon & 3pm Sat, Sun & holidays) Relive the mining past with guided tours exploring Cohens Reef, once one of Australia's top reef-gold producers. Almost 14 tonnes of gold came out of this mine.

Walhalla Goldfields Railway TRAIN
(03-5165 6280; www.walhallarail.com; adult/child/family return $20/15/50; from Walhalla Station 11am, 1pm & 3pm, from Thomson Station 11.40am, 1.40pm & 3.40pm Wed, Sat, Sun & public holidays) A star attraction is the scenic Walhalla Goldfields Railway, which offers a 20-minute ride between Walhalla and Thomson Stations (on the main road, 3.5km before Walhalla). The train snakes along Stringers Creek Gorge, passing lovely, forested gorge country and crossing a number of trestle bridges. There are daily departures in summer.

Sleeping & Eating

You can camp for free at **North Gardens**, a camp site with toilets and barbecues (but no showers) at the north end of the village.

Chinese Garden CAMPGROUND $
(www.walhallaboard.org.au; off Main St; per person $25) At the northern end of town, this recently opened camping ground has full toilet and shower facilities, a laundrette and a barbecue area.

WORTH A TRIP

BUNURONG MARINE & COASTAL PARK

This surprising little marine and coastal park offers some of Australia's best snorkelling and diving, and a stunning, cliff-hugging drive between Inverloch and Cape Paterson. It certainly surprised the archaeological world in the early 1990s when dinosaur remains dating back 120 million years were discovered here. Eagles Nest, Shack Bay, the Caves and Twin Reefs are great for **snorkelling**. The Oaks is the locals' favourite **surf beach**. The Caves is where the **dinosaur dig** action is at.

SEAL Diving Services (03-5174 3434; www.sealdivingservices.com.au; 7/27 Princes Hwy, Traralgon) SEAL offers PADI open-water dive courses in Inverloch in summer. Also available are one-day dives for beginners and experienced divers, kids programs and weekend trips for certified divers at Bunurong Marine and Coastal Park.

★ **Walhalla Star Hotel** HISTORIC HOTEL **$$**
(03-5165 6262; www.starhotel.com.au; Main St; d incl breakfast $189-249;) The rebuilt historic Star offers stylish boutique accommodation with king-sized beds and simple but sophisticated designer decor, making good use of local materials such as corrugated-iron water tanks. Guests can dine at the in-house restaurant; others need to reserve in advance. Or you can get good breakfasts, pies, coffee and cake at the attached **Greyhorse Café** (mains from $5; 10am-2pm).

Windsor House B&B **$$**
(03-5165 6237; www.windsorhouse.com.au; off Walhalla Rd; d $170, ste $175-215) The five rooms and suites in this beautifully restored two-storey 1878 home are fittingly old fashioned and ghost free. No children under 12.

Walhalla Lodge Hotel PUB FOOD **$$**
(03-5165 6226; Main St; mains $15-28; noon-2pm & 6-9pm Wed-Mon) The Wally Pub is a cosy, one-room pub decked out with prints of old Walhalla and serving good-value counter meals – think burgers, pasta, schnitzels and T-bone steaks.

Getting There & Away

Walhalla lies approximately 180km east of Melbourne. There's no public transport. By road, the town can be reached along a lovely, winding forest drive from Moe or Traralgon.

SOUTH GIPPSLAND

South Gippsland has plenty of gems along the coast between Melbourne and Wilsons Promontory – Venus Bay, Cape Liptrap Coastal Park and Waratah Bay are all worth exploring. Inland among the farming communities are some great drives through the Strzelecki Ranges and trendy villages such as Koonwarra.

Korumburra

POP 3350

The first sizeable town along the South Gippsland Hwy if you're coming from Melbourne, Korumburra is scenically situated on the edge of the Strzelecki Ranges. It makes a decent pause on your way to Wilsons Prom.

Sights

Coal Creek Village MUSEUM
(03-5655 1811; www.coalcreekvillage.com.au; 12 Silkstone Rd; 10am-4.30pm Thu-Mon, daily during school holidays) FREE Coal Creek Village is a re-creation of a 19th-century mining town. It's a little less polished and touristy than other similar places in Victoria, which may appeal to many.

Getting There & Away

V/Line (1800 800 007; www.vline.com.au) V/Line coaches from Melbourne's Southern Cross Station run to Korumburra ($12.80, 1¾ hours) up to seven times daily.

WILSONS PROMONTORY NATIONAL PARK

If you like wilderness bushwalking, stunning coastal scenery and secluded white-sand beaches, you'll absolutely love this place. The Prom, as it's affectionately known, is one of the most popular national parks in Australia. Hardly surprising, given its accessibility from Melbourne, its network of more than 80km of walking tracks, its swimming and surf beaches and the abundant wildlife. The southernmost part of mainland Australia, the Prom once formed part of a land bridge that allowed people to walk to Tasmania.

Wilsons Promontory National Park

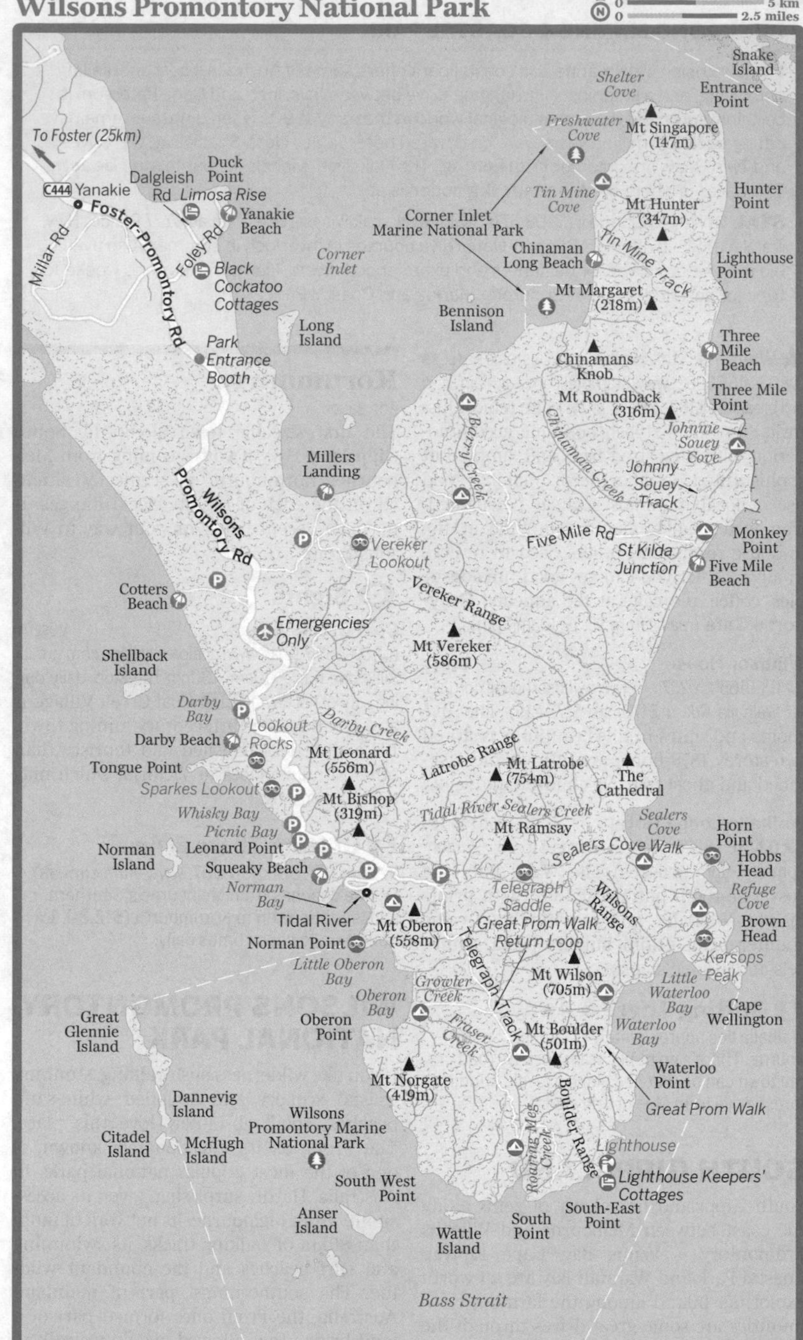

Tidal River, 30km from the park entrance, is the hub, although there's no fuel to be had here. It's home to the Parks Victoria office, a general store, cafe and accommodation. The wildlife around Tidal River is incredibly tame.

Activities

There's an extensive choice of marked **walking trails**, taking you through forests, marshes, valleys of tree ferns, low granite mountains and along beaches lined with sand dunes. The Parks Victoria office at Tidal River has brochures with details of walks, from 15-minute strolls to multi-day hikes. Even non-walkers can enjoy some of the park's beauty, with car-park access off the Tidal River road leading to gorgeous beaches and lookouts.

Swimming is safe at the gorgeous beaches at Norman Bay (Tidal River) and around the headland at Squeaky Beach – the ultra-fine quartz sand here really does squeak beneath your feet!

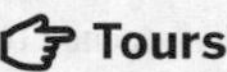

Tours

Bunyip Tours BUS TOUR
(☎1300 286 947; www.bunyiptours.com; tours from $120; ⊙Wed & Sun, plus Fri in summer) Proudly carbon-neutral, Bunyip Tours offers a one-day guided tour to the Prom from Melbourne, with the option of staying on another two days to explore by yourself.

First Track Adventures ADVENTURE TOUR
(☎03-5634 2761; www.firsttrack.com.au) This Yarragon-based company organises customised bushwalking, canoeing and abseiling trips to the Prom for individuals and groups. Prices vary with group size and activity.

Sleeping

Tidal River

★ **Lighthouse Keepers' Cottages** COTTAGE $$$
(☎Parks Victoria 13 19 63; www.parkweb.vic.gov.au; d cottage $334-371, 12-bed cottage per person from $133.80) These isolated, heritage-listed 1850s

WORTH A TRIP

KOONWARRA

Tucked away in rolling dairy country along the South Gippsland Hwy, this tiny township has built itself a reputation as something of a niche foodie destination, thanks to its cooking school and general store.

Koonwarra is served by buses running between Korumburra and Foster three times a day weekdays and up to six times daily on weekends. By road the town is 32km southwest of Korumburra and 21km northeast of Inverloch.

Farmers Market (☎0408 619 182; www.kfm.org.au; Memorial Park, Koala Dr; ⊙8am-1pm 1st Sat of month) Koonwarra hosts a Farmers Market at Memorial Park on the first Saturday of each month, with organic everything (fruit, vegetables, berries, coffee), plus hormone-free beef and chemical-free cheeses.

Milly & Romeo's Artisan Bakery & Cooking School (☎03-5664 2211; www.millyand-romeos.com.au; 1 Koala Dr; adult/child from $90/50 ; ⊙9.30am-4.30pm Thu & Fri, 8.30am-4.30pm Sat & Sun, longer hrs in summer) Victoria's first organic-certified cooking school offers short courses in making cakes, bread, traditional pastries, French classics and pasta, as well as running cooking classes for kids.

Lyre Bird Hill Winery & Guest House (☎03-5664 3204; www.lyrebirdhill.com.au; 370 Inverloch Rd; s/d $125/175; ⊙cellar door 10am-5pm Wed-Mon Oct, Nov & Feb-Apr, daily Dec & Jan, by appointment May-Sep; ❄) Stay among the vines 4km southwest of Koonwarra. The quaint, old-fashioned B&B has light-filled rooms overlooking the garden, while the self-contained country-style cottage is perfect for a family. The vineyard is right next door.

Koonwarra Food & Wine Store (☎03-5664 2285; www.koonwarrastore.com; cnr South Gippsland Hwy & Koala Dr; mains $12-26; ⊙8.30am-4pm) Local produce and wines are on sale in this renovated timber building. Inside is a renowned cafe that serves simple food with flair, priding itself on using organic, low-impact suppliers and products. Themed dinners occur twice monthly on Saturdays. Soak up the ambience in the wooden interior, or relax at a table in the shaded cottage gardens.

cottages with thick granite walls, attached to a working lightstation on a pimple of land that juts out into the wild ocean, are a real getaway. Kick back after the 19km hike from Tidal River and watch ships or whales passing by. The cottages have shared facilities, including a fully equipped kitchen.

★ Wilderness Retreat SAFARI TENT **$$$**
(www.wildernessretreats.com.au; d $312, extra person $25) Nestled in bushland at Tidal River, these luxury safari tents, each with their own deck, bathroom, queen-sized beds, heating and a communal tent kitchen, sleep up to four people and are pretty cool. It's like being on an African safari with a kookaburra soundtrack.

Yanakie & Foster

The tiny settlement of Yanakie offers the closest accommodation – from cabins and camping to luxury cottages – outside the park boundaries. Foster, the nearest main town, has a backpackers and several motels.

Prom Coast Backpackers HOSTEL **$**
(☎0427 875 735; www.promcoastyha.com.au; 40 Station Rd, Foster; dm/d from $35/70; @) The closest backpacker hostel to the park is this friendly YHA in Foster. The cosy renovated cottage sleeps only 10, so it's always intimate.

Black Cockatoo Cottages COTTAGE **$$**
(☎03-5687 1306; www.blackcockatoo.com; 60 Foley Rd, Yanakie; d $140-170, 6-person house $250) You can take in glorious views of the national park without leaving your very comfortable bed – or breaking the bank – in these private, stylish, black-timber cottages. There are three modern cottages and a three-bedroom house.

★ Limosa Rise COTTAGE **$$$**
(☎03-5687 1135; www.limosarise.com.au; 40 Dalgleish Rd, Yanakie; d $260-455; ❄) The views are stupendous from these luxury, self-contained cottages near the Prom entrance. The three tastefully appointed cottages (a studio, one bedroom and two bedroom) are fitted with full-length glass windows taking complete advantage of sweeping views across Corner Inlet and the Prom's mountains.

Eating

Tidal River General Store & Cafe CAFE **$**
(mains $5-24; ⏲9am-5pm Sun-Fri, to 6pm Sat) The Tidal River general store stocks grocery items and some camping equipment, but if you're hiking or staying a while it's cheaper

TOP PROM WALKS

From Christmas to the end of January a free shuttle bus operates between the Tidal River visitor car park and the Telegraph Saddle car park (a nice way to start the Great Prom Walk).

Great Prom Walk The most popular long-distance hike is a moderate 45km circuit across to Sealers Cove from Tidal River, down to Refuge Cove, Waterloo Bay and the lighthouse, returning to Tidal River via Oberon Bay. Allow three days and coordinate your walk with tide times, as creek crossings can be hazardous. It's possible to visit or stay at the **lighthouse** (p555) by prior arrangement with the Parks office.

Sealers Cove Walk The best overnight hike, this two-day walk starts at Telegraph Saddle and heads down Telegraph Track to stay overnight at beautiful Little Waterloo Bay (12km, 4½ hours). The next day, walk on to Sealers Cove via Refuge Cove and return to Telegraph Saddle (24km, 7½ hours).

Lilly Pilly Gully Nature Walk An easy 5km (two-hour) walk through heathland and eucalypt forests, with lots of wildlife.

Mt Oberon Summit Starting from the Mt Oberon car park, this moderate-to-hard 7km (2½-hour) walk is an ideal introduction to the Prom with panoramic views from the summit. The free Mt Oberon shuttle bus can take you to the Telegraph Saddle car park and back.

Little Oberon Bay An easy-to-moderate 8km (three-hour) walk over sand dunes covered in coastal tea trees with beautiful views over Little Oberon Bay.

Squeaky Beach Nature Walk Another easy 5km return stroll through coastal tea trees and banksias to a sensational white-sand beach.

PROM ACCOMMODATION

Nothing beats a night at the Prom. The main accommodation base is Tidal River, but there are 11 bush-camping (outstation) areas around the Prom, all with pit or compost toilets, but no other facilities; you need to carry in your own drinking water.

Unpowered/powered **camp sites** with a vehicle and up to eight people start at $54.90/$61.10 per site. There are also wooden **huts** with bunks and kitchenettes but no bathrooms (4/6-bed hut from $98.50/150), and spacious and private self-contained **cabins** sleeping up to six people ($229.60 to $313.80).

Tidal River has 484 camp sites, but only 20 powered sites. For the Christmas school holiday period there's a ballot for sites (apply online by 30 June through Parks Victoria).

Parks Victoria (03-5680 9555, 13 19 63; www.parkweb.vic.gov.au; 8.30am-4.30pm) The helpful visitor centre at Tidal River books all park accommodation, including permits for camping away from Tidal River.

Wilsons Prom & Surrounds Accommodation Service (www.promcountry.com.au) For bookings in the Prom's hinterland, try the Wilsons Prom & Surrounds Accommodation Service.

to stock up in Foster. The attached cafe serves takeaway food such as pies and sandwiches, as well as breakfasts, light lunches and bistro-style meals on weekends and holidays.

Getting There & Away

Tidal River lies approximately 224km southeast of Melbourne. There's no direct public transport between Melbourne and the Prom.

V/Line (1800 800 007; www.vline.com.au) Buses from Melbourne's Southern Cross Station travel to Foster ($20.40, three hours, four daily) via Dandenong and Koo Wee Rup.

Wilsons Promontory Bus Service (Moon's Bus Lines; 03-5687 1249) The Wilsons Promontory Bus Service operates from Foster to Tidal River (via Fish Creek) on Friday at 4.30pm, returning on Sunday at 4.30pm. This service connects with the V/Line bus from Melbourne at Fish Creek.

LAKES DISTRICT

The Gippsland Lakes form the largest inland waterway system in Australia, with the three main interconnecting lakes – Wellington, King and Victoria – stretching from Sale to beyond Lakes Entrance. The lakes are actually saltwater lagoons, separated from the ocean by the Gippsland Lakes Coastal Park and the narrow coastal strip of sand dunes known as Ninety Mile Beach. Apart from the beach and taking to the water, the highlights here involve hanging out at the pretty seaside communities.

Sale

POP 12,766

Gateway to the Lakes District, Sale is an important regional centre with little charm of its own – stay here only if you find yourself stuck on your way elsewhere.

Sights

Port of Sale PORT

The Port of Sale is a redeveloped marina area in the town centre with boardwalks, cafes and a canal leading out to the Gippsland Lakes.

Sleeping & Eating

Cambrai Hostel HOSTEL $

(03-5147 1600; www.maffra.net.au/hostel; 117 Johnson St; dm per night/week $28/160; @) In Maffra, 16km north of Sale, this relaxed hostel is a budget haven and one of the few true backpackers in Gippsland. In a 120-year-old building that was once a doctor's residence, it has a licensed bar, an open fire and a pool table in the cosy lounge, a tiny self-catering kitchen and clean, cheerful rooms.

The owners can sometimes arrange work in the region.

Quest Serviced Apartments APARTMENT $$

(03-5142 0900; www.questapartments.com.au; 180-184 York St; studio/1-bedroom/2-bedroom apt $120/205/285;) This reliable chain offers modern, self-contained apartments that feel more luxurious than you'd expect for these prices. As such it's streets ahead of most other motels around town.

WORTH A TRIP

BAW BAW NATIONAL PARK

Baw Baw National Park, an offshoot of the Great Dividing Range, is the southernmost region of Victoria's High Country. The Baw Baw Plateau and the forested valleys of the Thomson and Aberfeldy Rivers are wonderful places for bushwalking, with marked tracks through subalpine vegetation, ranging from open eucalypt stands to wet gullies and tall forests on the plateau. The highest points are Mt St Phillack (1566m) and Mt Baw Baw (1564m). The higher sections of the park are snow-covered in winter, when everyone heads for Baw Baw Village ski resort and the Mt St Gwinear cross-country skiing area. Quiet back roads (and the Australian Alps Walking Track) connect this region with Walhalla.

Mt Baw Baw Alpine Resort Management Board (☎03-5165 1136; www.mountbawbaw.com.au; ⏲8.30am-7.30pm Sat-Thu, to 9.30pm Fri ski season, 9am-5pm rest of year) In the centre of the village, this office provides general tourist information and an accommodation service.

Mister Raymond CAFE $$

(☎03-5144 4007; 268-270 Raymond St; mains $14-28; ⏲8am-4pm Tue-Thu, Sat & Sun, to 9pm Fri) Breakfast, brunch or lunch at Mister Raymond is Sale's best choice, with pulled-pork or soft-shell-crab tacos and other fresh tastes in a slick cafe environment. We prefer the indoor tables but you can also sit out on the footpath.

Information

Wellington Visitor Information Centre (☎03-5144 1108; www.tourismwellington.com.au; 8 Foster St; ⏲9am-5pm) Internet facilities and a free accommodation-booking service.

Getting There & Away

Sale lies along the Princes Hwy, 214km from Melbourne.

V/Line (☎1800 800 007; www.vline.com.au) Train and train-bus services between Melbourne and Sale ($25, three hours, four daily), sometimes with a change in Traralgon.

Ninety Mile Beach

To paraphrase the immortal words of Crocodile Dundee...that's not a beach, *this* is a beach. Isolated Ninety Mile Beach is a narrow strip of sand backed by dunes, featuring lagoons and stretching unbroken for more or less 90 miles (150km) from near McLoughlins Beach to the channel at Lakes Entrance. The area is great for surf fishing, camping and long beach walks, though the crashing surf can be dangerous for swimming, except where patrolled at Seaspray, Woodside Beach and Lakes Entrance.

The main access road to Ninety Mile Beach is the South Gippsland Hwy from Sale or Foster, turning off to Seaspray, Golden Beach and Loch Sport.

Metung

POP 1010

Curling around Bancroft Bay, little Metung is one of the prettiest towns in the Lakes District. Besotted locals call it the Gippsland Riviera, and with its absolute waterfront location and unhurried charm, it's hard to argue.

Activities

Riviera Nautic BOATING

(☎03-5156 2243; www.rivieranautic.com.au; 185 Metung Rd; yachts & cruisers for 3 days from $1056) Getting out on the water is easy enough: Riviera Nautic hires out boats and yachts for cruising, fishing and sailing on the Gippsland Lakes.

Sleeping & Eating

Metung Holiday Villas CABIN $$

(☎03-5156 2306; www.metungholidayvillas.com; cnr Mairburn & Stirling Rds; cabins $150-240; ❄🏊) Metung's former caravan park has reinvented itself as a mini village of semi-luxury cabins and is one of the best deals in town.

Moorings at Metung APARTMENT $$$

(☎03-5156 2750; www.themoorings.com.au; 44 Metung Rd; apt $150-390; ❄📶🏊) At the end of the road in Metung, and with water views to either Lake King or Bancroft Bay, this contemporary complex has a range of apartments from spacious studios to two-bedroom, split-level town houses. The complex has a tennis court, indoor and outdoor pools, spa and marina. Outside the peak season it's good value.

★**Metung Galley** CAFE $$

(☎03-5156 2330; www.themetunggalley.com.au; 50 Metung Rd; lunch mains $10-22, dinner mains

$19-35; 8am-4pm Tue, to late Wed-Fri, 7.30am-late Sat, 7.30am-4pm Sun) Felicity and Richard's city hospitality experience shines through in this friendly, innovative cafe. It serves up beautifully presented, quality food using local ingredients such as fresh seafood and Gippsland lamb (try the lamb 'cigars' with tzatziki).

Metung Hotel PUB FOOD **$$**
(03-5156 2206; www.metunghotel.com.au; 1 Kurnai Ave; mains $25-36; noon-2pm & 6-8pm) You can't beat the location overlooking Metung Wharf, and the big windows and outdoor timber decking make the most of the water views. The bistro serves top-notch pub food with a focus on fresh local seafood. The hotel also has the cheapest rooms in town ($85).

Information

Metung Visitor Centre (03-5156 2969; www.metungtourism.com.au; 3/50 Metung Rd; 9am-5pm) Accommodation-booking and boat-hire services.

Getting There & Away

Metung lies south of the Princes Hwy along the C606; the turn off is signposted at Swan Reach. The nearest major towns are Bairnsdale (28km) and Lakes Entrance (24km). The nearest inter-city rail services are at Bairnsdale.

Lakes Entrance

POP 5965

With the shallow Cunninghame Arm waterway separating the town from the crashing ocean beaches, Lakes Entrance basks in an undeniably pretty location, but in holiday season it's a packed-out tourist town with a graceless strip of motels, caravan parks, minigolf courses and souvenir shops lining the Esplanade. Still, the bobbing fishing boats, fresh seafood, endless beaches and cruises out to Metung and Wyanga Park Winery should win you over.

Sights & Activities

Lakes Entrance is all about the beach and boating. A long footbridge crosses the Cunninghame Arm inlet from the east of town to the ocean and **Ninety Mile Beach**. This is also where the **Eastern Beach Walking Track** (2.3km, 45 minutes) starts, taking you through coastal scrub to the entrance itself.

Surf Shack SURFING
(03-5155 4933; www.surfshack.com.au; 507 Esplanade; 2hr lesson $50) Surfing lessons (gear provided) are run by the Surf Shack at nearby Lake Tyers Beach, around 10km from Lakes Entrance.

Tours

Peels Lake Cruises CRUISE
(03-5155 1246, 0409 946 292; www.peelscruises.com.au; Post Office Jetty; 4hr Metung lunch cruise adult/child $60/18, 2½hr cruise $45; 11am Tue-Sun, 2pm Tue-Thu & Sat) This long-running operator has daily lunch cruises aboard the *Stormbird* to Metung and 2½-hour cruises on the *Thunderbird*.

Sea Safari CRUISE
(0458 511 438; www.lakes-explorer.com.au; Post Office Jetty; 1/2hr cruise $15/25) These safaris aboard the *Lakes Explorer* have a focus on research and ecology, identifying and counting seabirds, testing water for salinity levels and learning about marine life.

Sleeping

Eastern Beach Tourist Park CARAVAN PARK **$**
(03-5155 1581; www.easternbeach.com.au; 42 Eastern Beach Rd; unpowered/powered sites from $27/32, cabins $110-300;) Most caravan parks in Lakes pack 'em in, but this one has space, grassy sites and a great location away from the hubbub of town, in a bush setting back from Eastern Beach. A walking track takes you into town (30 minutes). New facilities are excellent, including a camp kitchen, barbecues and a kids' playground.

WORTH A TRIP

RAYMOND ISLAND

For one of the best places in Victoria to see koalas, drop down off the Princes Hwy to the relaxed lakeside town of Paynesville. Although agreeable in its own right, Paynesville is the port for a five-minute ferry crossing to Raymond Island. There's a large colony of koalas here, mostly relocated from Phillip Island in the 1950s. The flat-bottom car-and-passenger ferry operates every half-hour from 7am to 11pm and is free for pedestrians and cyclists. Cars and motorcycles cost $10.

Paynesville is 16km south of Bairnsdale along the C604.

Kalimna Woods COTTAGE **$$**

(03-5155 1957; www.kalimnawoods.com.au; Kalimna Jetty Rd; d $99-170;) Retreat 2km from the town centre to Kalimna Woods, set in a large rainforest-and-bush garden, complete with friendly resident possums and birds. These self-contained country-style cottages with either spa or wood-burning fireplace are spacious, private and cosy.

Bellevue on the Lakes HOTEL **$$**

(03-5155 3055; www.bellevuelakes.com; 201 Esplanade; d from $179, 2-bedroom apt from $284;) Right in the heart of the Esplanade, Bellevue brings a bit of style to the strip with neatly furnished rooms in earthy tones, most with water views. For extra luxury, go for the spacious spa suites or two-bedroom self-contained apartments.

Eating

Six Sisters & A Pigeon CAFE **$**

(03-5155 1144; 567 Esplanade; mains $9-19; 7am-3pm Tue-Sun;) The name alone should guide you to this quirky, licensed cafe on the Esplanade, opposite the footbridge. Good coffee, all-day breakfasts – Mexican eggs, French toast or Spanish omelettes – lunches of focaccias and baguettes, and light mains with an Asian-Italian influence.

★ **Ferryman's Seafood Cafe** SEAFOOD **$$**

(03-5155 3000; www.ferrymans.com.au; Middle Harbour, Esplanade; lunch mains $18-24, dinner $21-45; 10am-late;) It's hard to beat the ambience of dining on the deck of this floating cafe-restaurant, which will fill you to the gills with fish and seafood dishes, including good ol' fish and chips. The seafood platter is a great order. It's child friendly and downstairs you can buy fresh seafood, including prawns and crayfish (from 8.30am to 5pm).

Miriam's Restaurant STEAK, SEAFOOD **$$**

(03-5155 3999; www.miriamsrestaurant.com.au; cnr Esplanade & Bulmer St; mains $24-39; 6pm-late) The upstairs dining room at Miriam's overlooks the Esplanade, and the Gippsland steaks, local seafood dishes and casual cocktail-bar atmosphere are excellent. Try its epic 'Greek fisherman's plate' – 500g of local seafood for $55.

Information

Lakes Entrance Visitor Centre (1800 637 060, 03-5155 1966; www.discovereast-gippsland.com.au; cnr Princes Hwy & Marine Pde; 9am-5pm) Free accommodation- and tour-booking services. Also check out www.lakesentrance.com.

Getting There & Away

Lakes Entrance lies 314km from Melbourne along the Princes Hwy.

V/Line (1800 800 007; www.vline.com.au) Runs a train-bus service from Melbourne to Lakes Entrance via Bairnsdale ($35, 4½ hours, three daily).

EAST GIPPSLAND & THE WILDERNESS COAST

Beyond Lakes Entrance stretches a wilderness area of spectacular coastal national parks and old-growth forest. Much of this re-

WORTH A TRIP

BUCHAN

The sleepy town of Buchan, in the foothills of the Snowy Mountains, is famous for the spectacular and intricate limestone cave system at the Buchan Caves Reserve. Underground rivers cutting through ancient limestone rock formed the caves and caverns, and they provided shelter for Aboriginal people at least as far back as 18,000 years ago.

Camping is possible close to the caves (book with Parks Victoria), with further accommodation in Buchan.

Buchan is an easy drive 56km north of Lakes Entrance.

Buchan Caves (13 19 63; www.parks.vic.gov.au; tours adult/child/family $20.90/12.20/57.50, 2 caves $31.20/18.10/85.80; tours 10am, 11.15am, 1pm, 2.15pm & 3.30pm, hrs vary seasonally) Parks Victoria runs guided cave tours daily, alternating between **Royal** and **Fairy Caves**. They're both impressive: Royal has more colour, a higher chamber and extinct kangaroo remains; Fairy has more delicate decorations and potential fairy sightings. The rangers also offer hard-hat guided tours to the less-developed Federal Cave during the high season.

EAST GIPPSLAND NATIONAL PARKS

The far eastern reaches of Gippsland are home to some of Victoria's most appealing national parks, protecting rugged coastal wilderness to the deep forests of the interior. For information on camping grounds and walking tracks, visit www.parkweb.vic.gov.au.

Snowy River National Park Dominated by deep gorges carved through limestone and sandstone by the Snowy River on its route from the Snowy Mountains in New South Wales (NSW) to its mouth at Marlo. The entire park is a smorgasbord of unspoilt, superb bush and mountain scenery.

Errinundra National Park Contains Victoria's largest cool-temperate rainforest and is one of east Gippsland's most outstanding natural areas. Its three granite outcrops extend into the cloud, resulting in high rainfall, deep, fertile soils, abundant wildlife and a network of creeks and rivers that flow north, south and east. Bushfires in early 2014 left the park scarred and some tracks were closed at the time of research.

Croajingolong National Park One of Australia's finest coastal wilderness national parks, stretching for about 100km from the town of Bemm River to the NSW border. Magnificent, unspoilt beaches, inlets, estuaries and forests make it an ideal park for camping, walking, swimming and surfing. Point Hicks was the first part of Australia to be spotted by Captain Cook and the *Endeavour* crew in 1770.

Cape Conran Coastal Park This blissfully undeveloped part of the coast is one of Gippsland's most beautiful corners, with long stretches of remote white-sand beaches. The 19km coastal route from Marlo to Cape Conran is particularly pretty, bordered by banksia trees, grass plains, sand dunes and the ocean.

gion has never been cleared for agriculture and contains some of the most remote and pristine national parks in the state, making logging in these ancient forests a hot issue.

Mallacoota

POP 1031

One of Gippsland's, and indeed Victoria's, little gems, Mallacoota is the state's most easterly town, snuggled on the vast Mallacoota Inlet and surrounded by the tumbling hills and beachside dunes of beautiful Croajingolong National Park. Those prepared to come this far are treated to long, empty, ocean-surf beaches, tidal estuaries and swimming, fishing and boating on the inlet.

Sights & Activities

The calm estuarine waters of Mallacoota Inlet have more than 300km of shoreline – hiring a boat is the best way to explore, with plenty of great walks along the water's edge.

For good **surf**, head to Bastion Point or Tip Beach. There's swimmable surf and some sheltered water at Betka Beach, which is patrolled during Christmas school holidays. There are also good **swimming spots** along the beaches of the foreshore reserve, at Bastion Point and Quarry Beach.

Mallacoota Hire Boats BOATING
(☎03-5158 0704, 0438 447 558; Main Wharf, cnr Allan & Buckland Drs; motor boats per 2/4/6hr $60/100/140) Mallacoota Hire Boats is centrally located and hires out canoes and boats. No licence required; cash only.

Tours

MV Loch-Ard CRUISE
(☎03-5158 0764; Main Wharf; adult/child 2hr cruise $35/15) Runs several inlet cruises, including wildlife spotting and a twilight cruise.

Sleeping

Mallacoota Foreshore Holiday Park CARAVAN PARK $
(☎03-5158 0300; cnr Allan Dr & Maurice Ave; unpowered sites $21-30, powered $27-40; wi-fi) Curling around the waterfront, the grassy sites here morph into one of Victoria's most sociable and scenic caravan parks, with sublime views of the inlet and its resident population of black swans and pelicans. No cabins, but the best of Mallacoota's many parks for campers.

★ **Adobe Mudbrick Flats** APARTMENT $
(☎03-5158 0329, 0409 580 0329; www.adobeholidayflats.com.au; 17 Karbeethong Ave; d $80, q $95-180) A labour of love by Margaret and Peter Kurz, these unique mud-brick flats in Karbeethong are something special. With an

WORTH A TRIP

GABO ISLAND

On Gabo Island, 14km offshore from Mallacoota, the windswept 154-hectare Gabo Island Lightstation Reserve is home to seabirds and one of the world's largest colonies of little penguins – far outnumbering those at Phillip Island. Whales, dolphins and fur seals are regularly sighted offshore. The island has an operating lighthouse, built in 1862 and the tallest in the southern hemisphere.

Wilderness Coast Ocean Charters (03-5158 0701, 0417 398 068) Runs day trips to Gabo Island ($75, minimum eight people; $75 each way if you stay overnight) and may run trips down the coast to view the seal colony off Wingan Inlet if there's enough demand.

Gabo Island Lighthouse (03-5161 9500, Parks Victoria 13 19 63; www.parkweb.vic.gov.au; up to 8 people $315-350) For a truly wild experience head out to stay at this remote lighthouse. Accommodation is available in the three-bedroom assistant lighthouse keeper's residence. There's a two-night minimum stay and a ballot for use during the Christmas and Easter holidays.

emphasis on recycling and eco-friendliness, the flats have solar hot water and guests are encouraged to compost their kitchen scraps. The array of whimsical apartments are comfortable, well equipped and cheap.

Karbeethong Lodge GUESTHOUSE **$$**
(03-5158 0411; www.karbeethonglodge.com.au; 16 Schnapper Point Dr; d $110-220) It's hard not to be overcome by a sense of serenity as you rest on the broad verandahs of this early 1900s timber guesthouse, which gives uninterrupted views over Mallacoota Inlet. The large guest lounge and dining room have an open fire and period furnishings, there's a mammoth kitchen and the pastel-toned bedrooms are small but tastefully decorated.

Eating & Drinking

★**Lucy's** ASIAN **$$**
(03-5158 466; 64 Maurice Ave; mains $10-23; 8am-8pm) Lucy's is popular for delicious and great-value homemade rice noodles with chicken, prawn or abalone, as well as dumplings stuffed with ingredients from the garden. It's also good for breakfast.

Mallacoota Hotel PUB FOOD **$$**
(03-5158 0455; www.mallacootahotel.com.au; 51-55 Maurice Ave; mains $17-33; noon-2pm & 6-8pm) The local pub bistro serves hearty meals from its varied menu, with reliable favourites such as chicken Parmigiana and Gippsland steak. Bands play regularly in the summer.

Information

Mallacoota Visitor Centre (03-5158 0800; www.visitmallacoota.com.au; Main Wharf, cnr Allan & Buckland Dr; 10am-4pm) In a small shed on the main wharf and operated by friendly volunteers. Opening hours may vary.

Getting There & Away

Mallacoota is 23km southeast of Genoa (on the Princes Hwy), which is 492km from Melbourne. Take the train to Bairnsdale (3¾ hours), then the V/Line bus to Genoa ($45.20, 3½ hours, one daily). The Mallacoota–Genoa bus meets the V/Line coach on Monday, Thursday and Friday, plus Sunday during school holidays, and runs to Mallacoota ($4.70, 30 minutes).

Grampians & the Goldfields

Includes ➡

Best Places to Eat

- Royal Mail Hotel (p582)
- Public Inn (p576)
- Dispensary Enoteca (p573)
- Mr Carsisi (p574)
- Catfish (p569)

Best Places to Stay

- The Schaller Studio (p573)
- Maldon Miners Cottages (p577)
- D'Altons Resort (p581)
- Little Desert Nature Lodge (p581)
- Comfort Inn Sovereign Hill (p567)

Why Go?

History, nature and culture combine spectacularly in Victoria's regional heart. For a brief time in the mid-19th century, more than a third of the world's gold came out of Victoria and, today, the spoils of all that precious metal can be seen in the grand regional cities of Bendigo and Ballarat, and the charming towns of Castlemaine, Kyneton and Maldon. This is a fantastic region for touring, with a range of contrasting landscapes, from pretty countryside and green forests, red earth and granite country, to farmland, orchards and wineries.

Further west, there's a different type of history to experience at Grampians National Park, one of Victoria's great natural wonders. Some 80% of Victoria's Aboriginal rock-art sites are found here, and the majestic ranges are an adventurer's paradise, lording it over the idyllic Wartook Valley and the towns of Halls Gap and Dunkeld.

When to Go

Ballarat

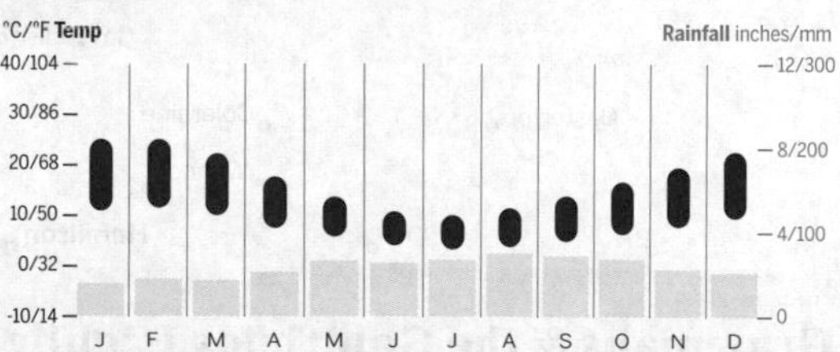

Easter Join the dragon procession at the Bendigo Easter Festival.

Mar–May Autumn colours, hiking and wine touring without the crowds.

Sep–Nov When the wild flowers bloom in Grampians National Park.

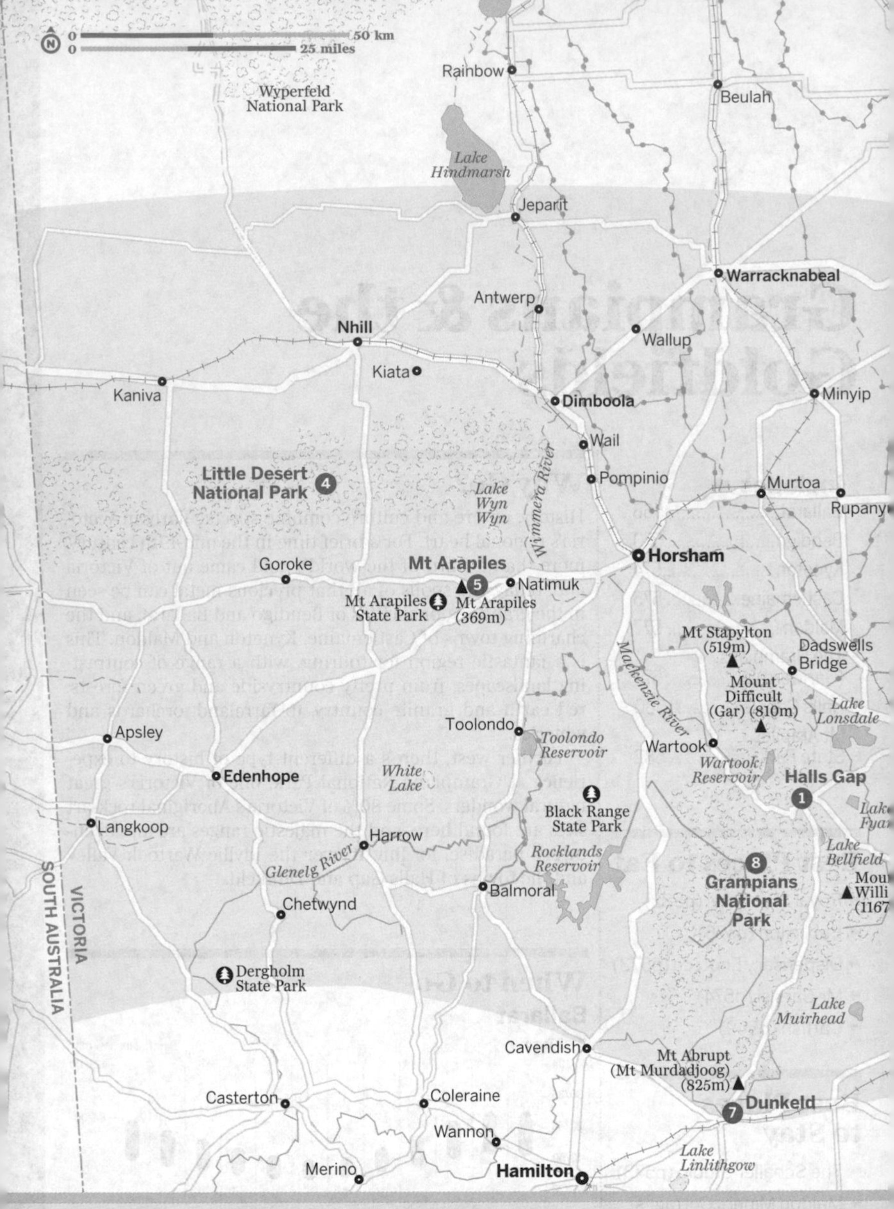

Grampians & the Goldfields Highlights

1. Discovering the traditional stories of Gariwerd at **Brambuk Cultural Centre** (p580) in Halls Gap.

2. Descending deep into a gold mine, riding the talking tram, then eating well in **Bendigo** (p570).

3. Riding the restored **steam train** (p575) from Maldon to Castlemaine.

4. Camping under the stars in **Little Desert National Park** (p581).

5. Scaling the heights at Victoria's best rock-climbing

destination, **Mt Arapiles** (p582).

❻ Experiencing the closest thing to a real gold-rush town at Ballarat's **Sovereign Hill** (p566).

❼ Climbing Mt Sturgeon, then wining and dining in style at the Royal Mail Hotel in **Dunkeld** (p582).

❽ Setting up camp and walking to waterfalls and stunning lookouts at **Grampians National Park** (p578).

❾ Revisiting the past along the postcard-pretty main street of **Maldon** (p577).

BALLARAT

POP 85,935

Ballarat was built on gold and it's easy to see the proceeds of those days in the grand Victorian-era architecture around the city centre. The single biggest attraction here is the fabulous, re-created gold-mining village at Sovereign Hill, but there's plenty more in this busy provincial city to keep you occupied, including grand gold-mining-era architecture and a stunning new museum dedicated to the Eureka Stockade. Rug up if you visit in the winter months – Ballarat is renowned for being chilly.

History

The area around here was known to the local Indigenous population as 'Ballaarat', meaning 'resting place'. When gold was discovered here in August 1851, giving irresistible momentum to the central Victorian gold rush that had begun two months earlier in Clunes, thousands of diggers flooded in, forming a shanty town of tents and huts. Ballarat's alluvial goldfields were the tip of the golden iceberg, and when deep shaft mines were sunk they struck incredibly rich quartz reefs. In 1854 the Eureka Rebellion pitted miners against the government and put Ballarat at the forefront of miners' rights.

Sights & Activities

Take the time to walk along **Lydiard St**, one of Australia's finest streetscapes for Victorian-era architecture. Impressive buildings include **Her Majesty's Theatre** (03-5333 5888; www.hermaj.com; 17 Lydiard St Sth), **Craig's Royal Hotel** (03-5331 1377; www.craigsroyal.com; 10 Lydiard St South; d $230-450), **George Hotel** (03-5333 4866; www.georgehotelballarat.com.au; 27 Lydiard St Nth; d/f/ste from $145/220/260;) and the **art gallery**. The main drag, impressive **Sturt St**, had to be three chains wide (60m) to allow for the turning circle of bullock wagons.

★ **Sovereign Hill** HISTORIC SITE

(03-5337 1100; www.sovereignhill.com.au; Bradshaw St; adult/child/student/family $49.50/22/39.60/122; 10am-5pm, to 5.30pm during daylight saving) You'll need to set aside at least half a day to visit this fascinating re-creation of an 1860s gold-mining township. The site was mined in the gold-rush era and much of the equipment is original, as is the mine shaft. Kids love panning for gold in the stream, watching the hourly gold pour and exploring the old-style lolly shop.

The main street here is a living history museum, with people performing their chores dressed in costumes of the time. Sovereign Hill opens again at night for the impressive sound-and-light show, **Blood on the Southern Cross** (03-5337 1199; adult/child/student/family $59/31.50/47.20/160, combined with Sovereign Hill ticket $107.50/53.50/86/282), a dramatic simulation of the Eureka Stockade battle. There are two shows nightly, but times vary so check in advance; bookings are essential.

Your ticket also gets you into the nearby **Gold Museum** (Bradshaw St; adult/child $11.20/5.90; 9.30am-5.30pm), which sits on a mullock heap from an old mine. There are imaginative displays and samples from all the old mining areas, as well as gold nuggets, coins and a display on the Eureka Rebellion.

★ **Museum of Australian Democracy at Eureka** MUSEUM

(MADE; 1800 287 113; www.made.org; cnr Eureka & Rodier Sts; adult/child/family $12/8/35; 10am-5pm) Standing on the site of the Eureka Rebellion, this fine museum opened in May 2013 and has already established itself as one of Ballarat's top attractions. Taking the Eureka Rebellion as its starting point – pride of place goes to the preserved remnants of the original Eureka flag and multimedia displays re-create the events of 1854 – the museum then broadens out to discuss democracy in Australia and beyond through a series of interactive exhibits.

★ **Art Gallery of Ballarat** GALLERY

(03-5320 5858; www.balgal.com; 40 Lydiard St Nth; 10am-5pm) FREE Established in 1884 and moved to its current location in 1890, the Art Gallery of Ballarat is the oldest provincial gallery in Australia. The architectural gem houses a wonderful collection of early colonial paintings, with works from noted Australian artists (including Tom Roberts, Sir Sidney Nolan, Russell Drysdale and Fred Williams) and contemporary works. Free iPod tours are available and there are free guided tours at 2pm Wednesday to Sunday.

Ballarat Wildlife Park ZOO

(03-5333 5933; www.wildlifepark.com.au; cnr York & Fussell Sts; adult/child/family $28/16/75; 9am-5.30pm, tour 11am) Ballarat's tranquil wildlife park is strong on native fauna, from the sweet little King Island wallabies to Tasmanian devils, emus, quokkas, snakes, eagles and crocs.

THE EUREKA STOCKADE

On 29 November, 1854, about 800 miners tossed their licences into a bonfire during a mass meeting then, led by Irishman Peter Lalor, built a stockade at Eureka, where they prepared to fight for their rights. A veteran of Italy's independence struggle named Raffaello Carboni called on the crowd, 'irrespective of nationality, religion and colour', to salute the Southern Cross as the 'refuge of all the oppressed from all the countries on Earth'.

On 3 December the government ordered troopers (the mounted colonial police) to attack the stockade. There were only 150 miners within the makeshift barricades and the fight lasted a short but devastating 20 minutes, leaving 25 miners and four troopers dead.

Though the rebellion was short-lived, the miners won the sympathy and support of many Victorians. The government deemed it wise to acquit the leaders of the charge of high treason. It's interesting to note that only four of the miners were Australian born; the others hailed from Ireland, Britain, Italy, Corsica, Greece, Germany, Russia, Holland, France, Switzerland, Spain, Portugal, Sweden, the US, Canada and the West Indies.

The licence fee was abolished and replaced by a Miners' Right, which cost one pound a year. This gave miners the right to search for gold; to fence in, cultivate and build a dwelling on a piece of land; and to vote for members of the Legislative Assembly. The rebel miner Peter Lalor became a member of parliament some years later. Eureka remains a powerful symbol in Australian culture, standing as it does for the treasured notions of workers' rights, democracy and 'a fair go for all'.

Goldfield brotherhood in 1854, sadly, had its limits. The 40,000 miners who arrived from southern China to try their luck on the 'new gold mountain' were often a target of individual violence and systemic prejudice. Still, the Chinese community persevered, and it has to this day been a strong and enduring presence in the city of Melbourne and throughout regional Victoria.

There's a daily guided tour, and weekend programs include a koala show, wombat show, snake show and crocodile feeding.

Kryal Castle CASTLE
(☎03-5334 7388; http://kryalcastle.com.au; 121 Forbes Rd, Leigh Creek; adult/child/family $31/19/89; ⏰10am-4pm Sat & Sun, & daily during school holidays) It may be kitsch but the kids will love a day out at this mock medieval castle and self-styled medieval adventure park. Knights and damsels in distress wander the grounds and there's everything from a Dragon's Labyrinth and Wizard's Workshop to jousting re-enactments and a torture dungeon. You can also sleep overnight in one of the semi-luxurious Castle Suites (r from $130).

Gold Shop GOLD PANNING
(☎03-5333 4242; www.thegoldshop.com.au; 8a Lydiard St North; ⏰10am-5pm Mon-Sat) Hopeful prospectors can pick up miners' rights and rent metal detectors at the Gold Shop in the historic Mining Exchange.

Tours

Eerie Tours TOUR
(☎1300 856 668; www.eerietours.com.au; adult/child/family $27.50/17.50/75; ⏰8pm or 9pm Wed-Sun) Relive the ghoulish parts of Ballarat's past with a night-time ghost tour or cemetery tour.

Festivals & Events

Begonia Festival STREET CARNIVAL
(www.ballaratbegoniafestival.com) This 100-year-old festival, held over the Labour Day weekend in early March, includes sensational floral displays, a street parade, fireworks, art shows and music.

Sleeping

Ballarat Backpackers Hostel HOSTEL $
(☎0427 440 661; www.ballaratbackpackers.com.au; 81 Humffray St Nth; dm/s/d $30/40/70) In the old Eastern Station Hotel (1862), this refurbished guesthouse is also a decent corner pub with occasional live music. Rooms are simple but fresh and good value.

★**Comfort Inn Sovereign Hill** HISTORIC HOTEL $$
(☎03-5337 1159; www.sovereignhill.com.au/comfort-inn-sovereign-hill; 39-41 Magpie St; r $175-195; ❄📶) Formerly known as Sovereign Hill Lodge, this excellent place has bright, modern rooms that are located a stone's throw from Sovereign Hill

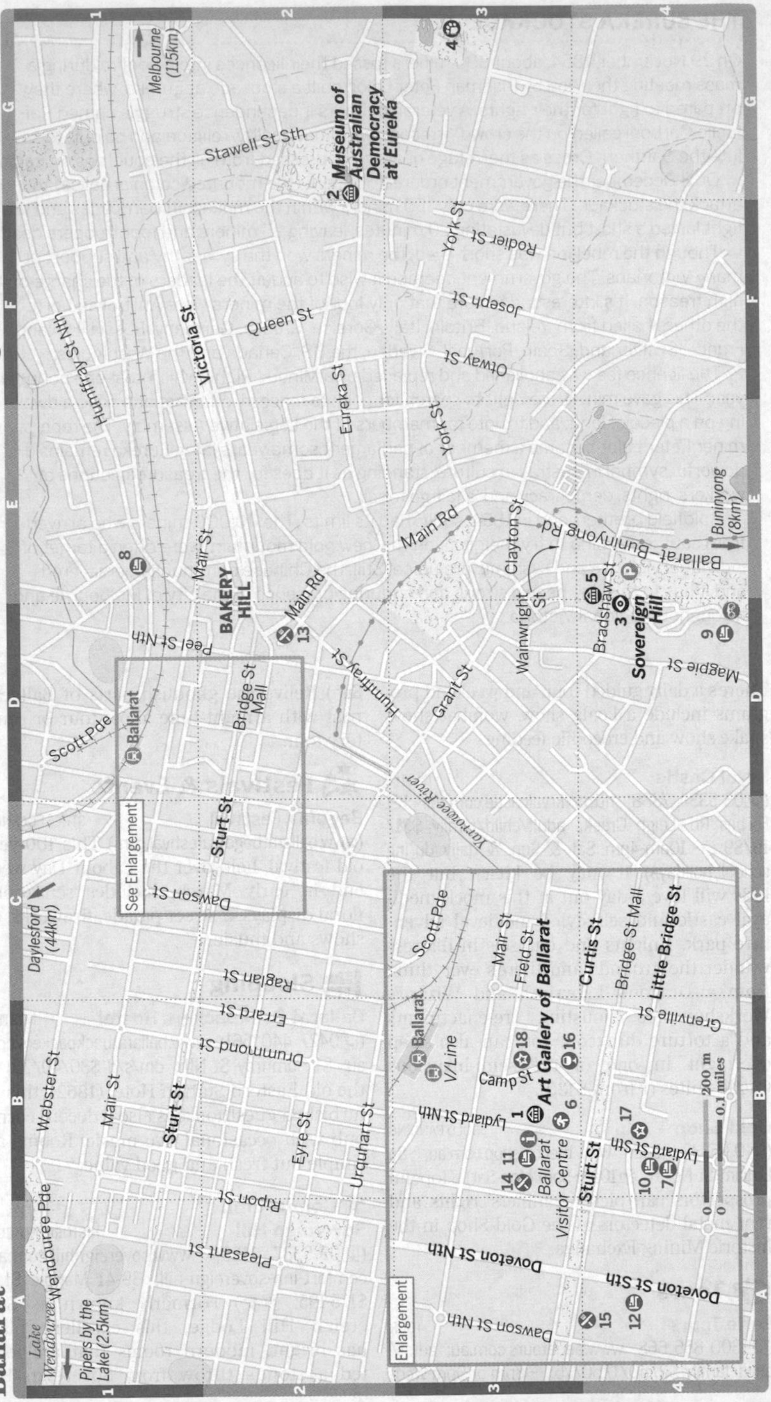

Ballarat

0 — 1 km
0 — 0.5 miles

A B C D E F G
1 2 3 4

Lake Wendouree
Wendouree Pde
Webster St
Pipers by the Lake (2.5km)
Mair St
Sturt St
Pleasant St
Ripon St
Drummond St
Errard St
Raglan St
Eyre St
Urquhart St
Daylesford (44km)
See Enlargement
Ballarat
Dawson St
Sturt St
Bridge St Mall
Scott Pde
Peel St Nth
8
Humffray St Nth
Melbourne (115km)
Mair St
Victoria St
BAKERY HILL
13
Main Rd
Queen St
Stawell St Sth
Eureka St
2 Museum of Australian Democracy at Eureka
Humffray St
Yarrowee River
Grant St
Main Rd
York St
Otway St
Joseph St
Rodier St
York St
4
Wainwright St
Clayton St
Ballarat–Buninyong Rd
5
Bradshaw St
3
Sovereign Hill
Magpie St
9
Buninyong (8km)

Enlargement
Dawson St Nth
Doveton St Nth
Lydiard St Nth
Ballarat
V/Line
Scott Pde
Camp St
Mair St
Field St
14 11
1
18
Ballarat Visitor Centre
Art Gallery of Ballarat
6
16
Sturt St
Curtis St
15
12
Lydiard St Sth
17
10
7
Bridge St Mall
Little Bridge St
Grenville St
Doveton St Sth
0 — 200 m
0 — 0.1 miles

Ballarat

Top Sights

Sights

Activities, Courses & Tours

Sleeping

Eating

Drinking & Nightlife

Entertainment

itself. Ask about its accommodation-and-entertainment packages.

Its 'Night in the Museum' package (single/double $425/695) lets you stay in the Steinfeld's building at the top of Main St within Sovereign Hill itself, where you'll be served by staff in period dress.

★Oscar's BOUTIQUE HOTEL $$

(☎03-5331 1451; www.oscarshotel.com.au; 18 Doveton St; d $150-200, spa room $225; ❄📶) The 13 rooms in this attractive art deco hotel have been tastefully refurbished to include double showers and spas (watch TV from your spa).

Ansonia on Lydiard B&B $$

(☎03-5332 4678; www.theansonianlydiard.com.au; 32 Lydiard St South; r $125-225; ❄📶) One of Lydiard St's great hotels, the Ansonia exudes calm with its minimalist design, polished floors, dark-wood furnishings and light-filled atrium. Stylish rooms have large-screen TVs and range from studio apartments for two to family suites.

Eating

L'Espresso ITALIAN $

(☎03-5333 1789; 417 Sturt St; mains $11-20; ⏲7.30am-6pm Sun-Thu, to 11pm Fri & Sat) A mainstay on Ballarat's cafe scene, this trendy Italian-style place doubles as a record shop – choose from the whopping jazz, blues and world-music selection while you wait for your espresso or Tuscan bean soup.

★Catfish THAI $$

(☎03-5331 5248; www.catfishthai.com.au; 42-44 Main Rd; mains $18-34; ⏲6pm-late Tue-Sat) Catfish is the kitchen of chef Damien Jones, who made the Lydiard Wine Bar such a treasured local secret. Thai cooking classes only add to what is an increasingly popular package.

Forge Pizzeria ITALIAN, PIZZA $$

(☎03-5337 6635; www.theforgepizzeria.com.au; 14 Armstrong St North; pizzas $15-25; ⏲noon-11pm) Could this be the start of Ballarat's Bendigo-style renaissance? This brick-walled dining area is the city's coolest eating ticket, with outstanding pizzas and Italian dishes and a fine charcuterie board of Italian cured meats.

Pipers by the Lake CAFE $$

(☎03-5334 1811; www.pipersbythelake.com.au; 403 Wendouree Pde; mains $19-33; ⏲9am-4pm Sat-Thu, 9am-4pm & 6-10pm Fri) The 1890 Lakeside Lodge was designed by WH Piper and today it's a lovely light-filled cafe with huge windows looking out over the lake and an al fresco courtyard. Dishes range from pulled-pork sandwiches to roasted pumpkin, feta and pine nut risotto.

Drinking & Entertainment

With its large student population, Ballarat has a lively nightlife. There are some fine old pubs around town but most of the entertainment is centred on Lydiard St and the nearby Camp St precinct.

Haida LOUNGE

(☎03-5331 5346; www.haidabar.com; 12 Camp St; ⏲5pm-late Wed-Sun) Haida is a loungy two-level bar where you can relax with a cocktail by the open fire or chill out to DJs and live music downstairs.

Karova Lounge LIVE MUSIC

(☎03-5332 9122; www.karovalounge.com; cnr Field & Camp Sts; ⏲9pm-late Wed-Sat) Ballarat's best original live-music venue showcases local and touring bands in a grungy, industrial style.

BALLARAT PASS

The **Ballarat Pass** (1800 446 633; www.visitballarat.com.au/things-to-do/ballarat-pass; adult 3/4-attraction pass $96/107, child $51/58, family $257/288), a three-attraction pass, covers entry to Sovereign Hill, Kryal Castle and Ballarat Wildlife Park. The four-attraction pass adds in the Museum of Australian Democracy at Eureka. Buying a pass will save you around 10% off the normal entry price. The pass can be bought over the phone or at the Ballarat visitor centre.

Shopping

Mill Markets MARKET
(03-5334 7877; www.millmarkets.com.au; 9367 Western Hwy; 10am-6pm) A little sister of the popular Mill Markets at Daylesford, this huge collection of antiques, retro furnishings and knick-knacks is in the old woolsheds.

Information

Ballarat Visitor Centre (1800 446 633, 03-5320 5741; www.visitballarat.com.au; 43 Lydiard St North; 9am-5pm) Opposite the art gallery.

Getting There & Away

Airport Shuttle Bus (03-5333 4181; www.airportshuttlebus.com.au) Goes direct from Melbourne Airport to Ballarat train station (adult/child $34/17, 1½ hours, nine Monday to Friday, seven on weekends).

Greyhound Australia (1300 473 946; www.greyhound.com.au) Greyhound Australia buses between Adelaide ($92, 8¾ hours, departs Adelaide 8.15pm) and Melbourne ($29, 1¾ hours) stop in Ballarat if you ask the driver.

V/Line (1800 800 007; www.vline.com.au) V/Line has frequent direct trains between Melbourne (Southern Cross Station) and Ballarat (from $12.75, 1½ hours, 18 daily) and at least three services via Geelong.

BENDIGO

POP 82,794

Bendigo is a city to watch, fast becoming one of the coolest places in the state. New hotels, a dynamic dining scene and a stunning reimagining of historic spaces (the one-time jail will soon be reborn as as a 1000-seat theatre) have joined an already formidable array of attractions that range from gold-rush-era architecture and a fine art gallery to the Chinese dragons that awaken for the Easter Festival. Sitting as it does in the heart of goldfield and wine-growing country, the only question is why Bendigo has taken so long to take off.

History

The fantastically rich Bendigo Diggings covered more than 360 sq km after gold was discovered in nearby Ravenswood in 1851, and later Bendigo Creek. It's said the maids at the Shamrock Hotel mopped the floor every night to collect the gold dust brought in on the drinkers' boots. The arrival of thousands of Chinese miners in 1854 had a lasting affect on the town, despite the racial tensions that surfaced.

In the 1860s the scene changed again as independent miners were outclassed by the powerful mining companies with their heavy machinery. The companies poured money into the town and some 35 quartz reefs were found. The ground underneath Bendigo is still honeycombed with mine shafts and the gold is still around – Bendigo Mining successfully resumed operations at the Kangaroo Flat mine in 2008.

Sights

The city's most impressive buildings are found in **Pall Mall**, while **View St** is a historic streetscape with some fine buildings, including the **Capital**, which houses the Bendigo Art Gallery.

★**Central Deborah Goldmine** HISTORIC SITE
(03-5443 8322; www.central-deborah.com; 76 Violet St; adult/child/family mine experience $30/16/83; 9.30am-5pm) For a very deep experience, descend into this 500m-deep mine with a geologist. The mine has been worked on 17 levels, and about 1 tonne of gold has been removed. After donning hard hats and lights, you're taken down the shaft to inspect the operations, complete with drilling demonstrations. There are five tours on weekdays and six on weekends and they last about 75 minutes.

Other tours include the 2½-hour **Underground Adventure** (adult/child/family $85/52.50/245) and, for the claustrophobes, a self-guided **surface tour** ($15/7.50/40).

★**Bendigo Talking Tram** TRAM
(03-5442 2821; www.bendigotramways.com; adult/child/family $17.50/11/51; 10am-5pm) For

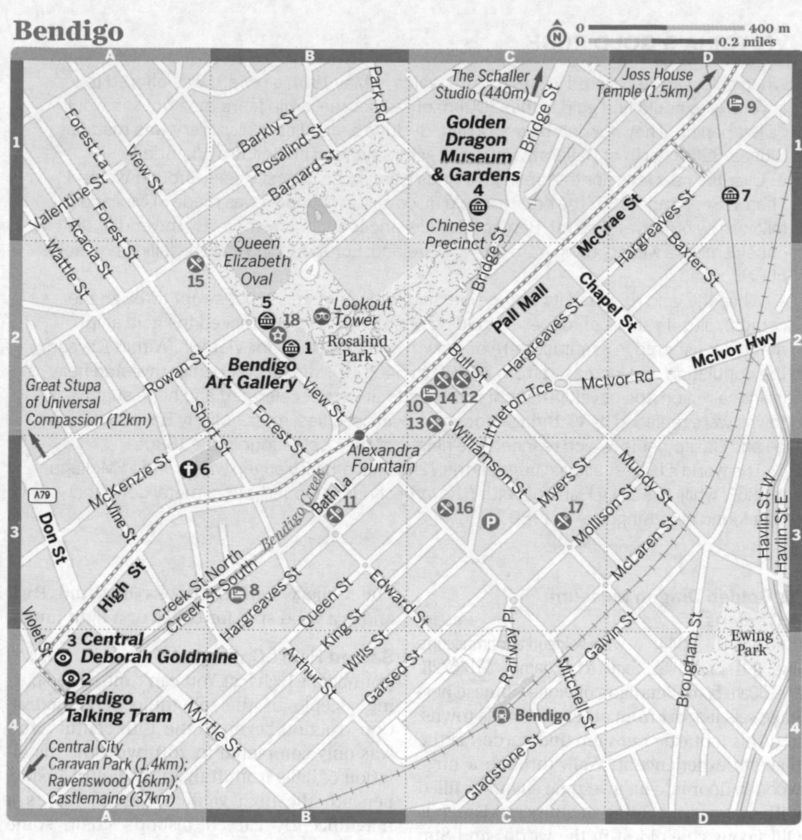

Bendigo

Top Sights
1 Bendigo Art Gallery B2
2 Bendigo Talking Tram A4
3 Central Deborah Goldmine A4
4 Golden Dragon Museum & Gardens C1

Sights
5 Dudley House B2
6 Sacred Heart Cathedral A3
7 Tramways Museum D1

Sleeping
8 Bendigo Backpackers B3
9 Quest Bendigo D1
10 Shamrock Hotel C2

Eating
11 Brewhouse Cafe B3
12 Dispensary Enoteca C2
13 Gillies Bendigo Original Pie Shop C2
14 GPO Bar & Grill C2
15 Malayan Orchid A2
16 Mason's of Bendigo C3
17 Woodhouse C3

Entertainment
18 Capital B2

an interesting tour of the city, hop aboard one of the restored vintage 'talking' trams. The hop-on, hop-off trip runs from the Central Deborah Goldmine to the **Tramways Museum** (1 Tramways Rd; admission free with tram ticket; ⏲10am-5pm) every half-hour, making half-a-dozen stops, including at the Golden Dragon Museum and Lake Weeroona.

VICTORIA'S GOLD RUSH

When gold was discovered in New South Wales in May 1851, a reward was offered to anyone who could find gold within 300km of Melbourne, amid fears that Victoria would be left behind. They needn't have worried. By June a significant discovery was made at Clunes, 32km north of Ballarat, and prospectors flooded into central Victoria.

Over the next few months, fresh gold finds were made almost weekly around Victoria. Then in September 1851 the greatest gold discovery ever known was made at Moliagul, followed by others at Ballarat, Bendigo, Mt Alexander and many more. By the end of 1851 hopeful miners were coming from England, Ireland, Europe, China and the failing goldfields of California.

While the gold rush had its tragic side (including epidemics that swept through the camps), plus its share of rogues (including bushrangers who attacked the gold shipments), it ushered in a fantastic era of growth and prosperity for Victoria. Within 12 years the population had increased from 77,000 to 540,000. Mining companies invested heavily in the region, the development of roads and railways accelerated and huge shanty towns were replaced by Victoria's modern provincial cities, most notably Ballarat, Bendigo and Castlemaine, which reached the height of their splendour in the 1880s.

The world's largest alluvial nugget, the 72kg Welcome Stranger, was found in Moliagul in 1869, while the 27kg Hand of Faith (the largest nugget found with a metal detector) was found near Kingower in 1980.

★Golden Dragon Museum & Gardens MUSEUM

(☎03-5441 5044; www.goldendragonmuseum.org; 1-11 Bridge St; adult/child/family $11/6/28; ⏲9.30am-5pm) Bendigo's obvious Chinese heritage sets it apart from other goldfields towns, and this fantastic museum and garden is the place to experience it. Walk through a huge wooden door into an awesome chamber filled with dragons, including the Imperial Dragons Old Loong (the oldest in the world) and Sun Loong (the longest in the world at over 100m).

The museum also displays amazing Chinese heritage items and costumes. The area outside the museum has been redeveloped as the Dai Gum San Chinese precinct, complete with a large lotus flower.

Joss House Temple TEMPLE

(☎03-5443 8255; www.bendigojosshouse.com; Finn St; adult/child/family $6/4/18; ⏲11am-4pm) Painted red, the traditional colour for strength, this is the only remaining practising joss house in central Victoria. It's 2km northwest of the centre.

★Bendigo Art Gallery GALLERY

(☎03-5434 6088; www.bendigoartgallery.com.au; 42 View St; admission by donation; ⏲10am-5pm, tours 2pm) One of Victoria's finest regional galleries, the permanent collection here includes outstanding colonial and contemporary Australian art. The annual temporary exhibitions are cutting edge and have been an important part of Bendigo's renaissance. The Gallery Café overlooks Rosalind Park and is a good spot for coffee or a light lunch.

Sacred Heart Cathedral CHURCH

(cnr Wattle & High Sts) You can't miss the soaring steeple of this magnificent cathedral. Construction began in the 19th century and was only completed in 2001 with the installation of bells from Italy in the belfry. Inside, beneath the high vaulted ceiling, there's a magnificently carved bishop's chair, some beautiful stained-glass windows, and wooden angels jutting out of the ceiling arches.

Great Stupa of Universal Compassion BUDDHIST

(☎03-5466-7568; www.stupa.org.au; 25 Sandhurst Town Rd, Myers Flat) In Myers Flat, just beyond Bendigo's city limits, this Buddhist stupa, surrounded by gum trees, promises to be the largest stupa in the Western world (with its 50m base and a height of 50m). When completed it will house a massive Buddha statue (also the world's largest) carved from jade. It can be visited, though it was still to be completed at the time of research.

Festivals & Events

Easter Festival CARNIVAL

Bendigo's major festival, held in March or April, attracts thousands with its carnival atmosphere and colourful and noisy procession of Chinese dragons, led by Sun Loong, the world's longest imperial dragon.

Sleeping

Bendigo Backpackers HOSTEL $

(03-5443 7680; www.bendigobackpackers.com.au; 33 Creek St South; dm/d/f $30/70/100;) This small, homey hostel is in a weatherboard cottage in a great central location. It has bright cheery rooms with all the usual amenities plus a few extras, including bike hire.

Central City Caravan Park CARAVAN PARK $

(1800 500 475, 03-5443 6937; www.centralcitycaravanpark.com.au; 362 High St, Golden Square; unpowered/powered sites from $30/37, cabins $89-190;) The closest caravan park to the city centre has shady sites, a camp kitchen and en suite cabins.

★**The Schaller Studio** BOUTIQUE HOTEL $$

(03-4433 6100; www.artserieshotels.com.au/schaller; cnr Bayne & Lucan Sts; d from $112;) At the forefront of Bendigo's style makeover, the Schaller Studio is part of the classy Art Series hotel chain that has won plaudits in Melbourne. The hotel takes as its inspiration the studio of Australian artist Mark Schaller, with his landscapes and still lifes in all their colourful glory.

Public areas are edgy and cool, while most of the rooms have an almost playful energy. Outrageously good value as well. There's even a garden filled with Schaller's sculptures.

★**Shamrock Hotel** HOTEL $$

(03-5443 0333; www.hotelshamrock.com.au; cnr Pall Mall & Williamson St; d $130-200, ste $250) One of Bendigo's historic icons, the Shamrock is a stunning Victorian building with stained glass, original paintings, fancy columns and a *Gone with the Wind*–style staircase. The refurbished upstairs rooms range from small standard rooms to spacious deluxe and spa suites.

Quest Bendigo APARTMENT $$

(03-5410 1300; www.questapartments.com.au; 228 McCrae St; studio $140, 1-/2-bed apt $165/240;) The Bendigo outpost of this excellent chain offers stylish, spacious and modern serviced apartments close to the city centre.

Eating

★**Gillies Bendigo Original Pie Shop** BAKERY $

(Hargreaves St Mall; pies from $5; 9am-5.30pm Sat-Thu, to 7pm Fri) The pie window on the corner of the mall is a Bendigo institution, and the pies are as good as you'll find.

★**Dispensary Enoteca** MODERN AUSTRALIAN $$

(03-5444 5885; www.thedispensaryenoteca.com; 9 Chancery Lane; mains $18-55; 11.30am-late Tue-Sat) Local produce, a hip eating space and a talented chef make this one of regional Victoria's more creative restaurants. The chargrilled jumbo quail could yield to the juniper cured and seared Aylesbury duck breast. The abundance of beer bottles and the lane location add to the sense of a designer-eating (and, later, drinking) den for people in the know.

★**Mason's of Bendigo** MODERN AUSTRALIAN $$

(03-5443 3877; www.masonsofbendigo.com.au; 25 Queen St; mains $18-49; 8.30am-9.30am Tue-Sat) Casual yet sophisticated, dominated by local produce yet influenced by cooking techniques from around the world, Mason's inhabits a former glass factory. It's an agreeable mix of fine food and great atmosphere at any time of day. Dishes might include beetroot gnocchi, roasted goat shoulder or quail and pistachio terrine. Great beer list, too.

Brewhouse Cafe CAFE $$

(03-5442 8224; www.brewhousecoffee.com.au; 402 Hargreaves St; mains $14-22; 7am-5pm Mon-Thu, to 9pm Fri, to 4pm Sat, 8am-4pm Sun) A Melbourne-like warehouse space and Bendigo's best coffee is a winning combination at the cafe of Brewhouse Coffee Roasters, which sources globally and roasts locally. Great breakfasts segue nicely into lunchtime pizzas, sandwiches and dishes such as Thai fish balls or Guinness-braised lamb shanks.

GPO Bar & Grill MEDITERRANEAN $$

(03-5443 4343; www.gpobendigo.com.au; 60-64 Pall Mall; tapas from $9, lunch mains $16-27, dinner mains $21-36; 11am-late;) The food and atmosphere here is superb and it's rated highly by locals. Slow-braised beef cheek or Harcourt pear and blue cheese salad are terrific lunch orders, or go for the innovative pizza, pasta or tapas plates. The bar is a chilled place for a drink from the impressive wine and cocktail list.

Malayan Orchid MALAYSIAN, AUSTRALIAN $$

(03-5442 4411; www.malayanorchid.com.au; 155 View St; mains $20-30; noon-2pm & 5pm-late Mon-Fri, 5pm-late Sat) This fine Malaysian restaurant does all the usual staples, but its seamless incorporation of emu, kangaroo and even camel into its Malay sauces is typical of how well Bendigo does cross-cultural fusion.

Woodhouse STEAK $$$

(☎03-5443 8671; www.thewoodhouse.com.au; 101 Williamson St; pizza $18-23, mains $33-59; ⏰noon-2.30pm & 5.30pm-late Tue-Fri, 5.30pm-late Mon & Sat) Some of the finest steaks you'll find anywhere in regional Victoria are why Bendigo has fallen in love with this warehouse-style space clad in warm brick tones. The Woodhouse Wagyu Tasting Plate ($58.90) is pricey but close to heaven for dedicated carnivores. Its $20 lunch special gets you pizza and a glass of wine and is altogether lighter.

Drinking & Entertainment

Bendigo has a lively nightlife – uni nights are Tuesday and Thursday. Although some clubs remain open as late as 5am, all have a 2am lockout. The main nightlife zone is Bull St and along Pall Mall. Many restaurants, including Wine Bank, the Dispensary Enoteca and Whirrawee, segue easily into classy wine bars after the kitchen closes.

Capital THEATRE

(☎03-5434 6100; www.bendigo.vic.gov.au; 50 View St) The beautifully restored Capital is the main venue for the performing arts, with hundreds of performances and exhibitions each year.

Information

Bendigo Visitor Centre (☎1800 813 153, 03-5434 6060; www.bendigotourism.com; 51-67 Pall Mall; ⏰9am-5pm) In the historic former post office; offers an accommodation booking service and the Post Office Gallery, an outpost of the Bendigo Art Gallery.

Getting There & Away

Bendigo Airport Service (☎03-5444 3939; www.bendigoairportservice.com.au; adult one way/return $42/78, child $20/40) Runs direct between Melbourne's Tullamarine Airport and Bendigo train station. Bookings essential.

V/Line (☎13 61 96; www.vline.com.au) V/Line has frequent trains between Melbourne (Southern Cross Station) and Bendigo (from $19.30, two hours, 12 to 18 daily) via Kyneton and Castlemaine.

GOLDFIELDS TOWNS

As splendid as Ballarat and Bendigo are, you need to get out and explore the country towns and former gold-mining relics that make up central Victoria to really appreciate this part of the world. Touring the likes of Castlemaine, Kyneton, Maryborough and Maldon will give you a good understanding of the incredible growth and inevitable decline of the gold towns, but you'll also pass through gorgeous countryside and an increasingly flourishing (and trendy) wine and food region. Head north of Melbourne along the Calder Hwy (M79 and A79) to start the journey.

Kyneton

POP 4460

Kyneton, established a year before gold was discovered, was the main coach stop between Melbourne and Bendigo, and the centre for the farmers who supplied the diggings with fresh produce. Today, Piper St is a historic precinct lined with bluestone buildings that have been transformed into cafes, antique shops, museums and restaurants.

Sights

Kyneton Historical Museum MUSEUM

(☎03-5422 1228; 67 Piper St; adult/child $6.50/3; ⏰11am-4pm Fri-Sun) The old bank building (1855) is now a museum housing a display of local history items – the upper floor is furnished in period style. The building itself is perhaps more interesting than the exhibits.

Festivals & Events

Kyneton Daffodil & Arts Festival CARNIVAL

(www.kynetondaffodilarts.org.au; ⏰Sep) Kyneton is renowned for its daffodils. The annual Kyneton Daffodil & Arts Festival has 10 days of gala evenings, markets, concerts, fairs and art and flower shows.

Budburst FOOD, WINE

(☎1800 244 711; www.macedonrangeswine.com.au/budburst-festival/; ⏰mid-Nov) Budburst is a wine and food festival hosted at wineries throughout the Macedon Ranges region over several days.

Sleeping & Eating

Kyneton's eat street is historic Piper St, with a fabulous cafe and restaurant scene.

Airleigh-Rose Cottage B&B $$$

(☎0402 783 489; www.airleighrosecottage.com.au; 10 Begg St; r 2 nights $490, min 2-night stay) Attractive wood-and-brick rooms in a Federation-era cottage.

★**Mr Carsisi** MIDDLE EASTERN $$$

(☎03-5422 3769; http://mrcarsisi.com; 37c Piper St; mains $29-39; ⏰11.30am-late Fri-Tue) Turkish tastes and Middle Eastern mezze dominate this well-regarded place, which does a faultless job of combining foreign flavours with local produce – the honey-and-cardamom Milawa duck breast is typical of the genre.

Annie Smithers Bistrot MODERN AUSTRALIAN **$$$**
(☎03-5422 2039; www.anniesmithers.com.au; 72 Piper St; mains $36-40; ⊙noon-2.30pm & 6-9pm Thu-Sat, noon-2.30pm Sun) One of central Victoria's most exciting new restaurants, this fine place has a menu that changes with the seasons and dish descriptions that read like a culinary short story about regional produce and carefully conceived taste combinations – such as hazelnut and fennel seed crumbed cutlet of pork, apple and fennel puree, spring 'slaw and pork and cider jus.

Information

Kyneton Visitor Centre (☎1800 244 711, 03-5422 6110; www.visitmacedonranges.com; 127 High St; ⊙9am-5pm) On the southeastern entry to town. Ask for the *Town Walks*, *Self Drive Tour* and *Campaspe River Walk* brochures.

Getting There & Away

Kyneton is just off the Calder Hwy about 90km northwest of Melbourne.

V/Line (www.vline.com.au) Regular V/Line trains on the Bendigo line run here from Melbourne (from $10.35, 1¼ hours). The train station is 1km south of the town centre.

Castlemaine

POP 9124

At the heart of the central Victorian goldfields, Castlemaine is a rewarding working-class town where a growing community of artists and tree-changers live amid some inspiring architecture and gardens. The main grid of streets is home to some stirring examples of late-19th-century architecture.

History

After gold was discovered at Specimen Gully in 1851, the Mt Alexander Diggings attracted some 30,000 diggers and Castlemaine became the thriving marketplace for the goldfields. The town's importance waned as the surface gold was exhausted by the 1860s but, fortunately, the centre of town was well established by then and remains relatively intact.

Even after the gold rush subsided, Castlemaine has always had a reputation for industry and innovation – this was the birthplace of the Castlemaine XXXX beer-brewing company (now based in Queensland) and Castlemaine Rock, a hard-boiled sweet lovingly produced by the Barnes family since 1853.

Sights & Activities

★**Castlemaine Art Gallery & Historical Museum** GALLERY, MUSEUM
(☎03-5472 2292; www.castlemainegallery.com; 14 Lyttleton St; adult/student/child $4/3/free; ⊙10am-5pm) A superb art deco building houses this gallery, which features colonial and contemporary Australian art, including works by well-known Australian artists such as Frederick McCubbin and Russell Drysdale. The museum, in the basement, provides an insight into local history, with costumes, china and gold-mining relics.

Castlemaine Botanical Gardens GARDENS
(Walker St) These majestic gardens, one of the oldest in Victoria (established 1860), strike a perfect balance between sculpture and wild bush among awe-inspiring National Trust-registered trees and the artificial Lake Joanna.

Burke & Wills Monument MONUMENT
(Wills St) For a good view over town, head up to the Burke and Wills Monument on Wills St (follow Lyttleton St east of the centre). Robert O'Hara Burke was a police superintendent in Castlemaine before his fateful trek.

Victorian Goldfields Railway TRAIN
(☎03-5470 6658; www.vgr.com.au; adult/child return $45/20) This historic steam train heads through the box-ironbark forests of Victoria's gold country, running between Castlemaine and Maldon up to three times a week.

Festivals & Events

Castlemaine State Festival ART
(www.castlemainefestival.com.au; ⊙Mar-Apr) One of Victoria's leading arts events, featuring theatre, music, art and dance. Held in March or April in odd-numbered years.

Festival of Gardens GARDEN
(www.festivalofgardens.org; ⊙Nov) More than 50 locals open their properties to the public. Held in even-numbered years.

Sleeping

Bookings are essential during festival times, so make use of the area's free **accommodation booking service** (☎1800 171 888; www.maldoncastlemaine.com).

WORTH A TRIP

MARYBOROUGH

Maryborough is part of central Victoria's 'Golden Triangle', where prospectors still turn up a nugget or two. The town's pride and joy is the magnificent railway station, and now that passenger trains are running here again from Melbourne, it's worth a day trip. Currently there's one direct train a day from Melbourne ($29, 2¼ hours), with others going via Geelong, Ballarat or Castlemaine by bus.

Maryborough Railway Station (☎03-5461 4683; 38 Victoria St; ⌚10am-5pm) The town boasts plenty of impressive Victorian-era buildings, but Maryborough Railway Station leaves them all for dead. Built in 1892, the inordinately large station, complete with clock tower, was described by Mark Twain as 'a train station with a town attached'. Today, it houses a mammoth antique emporium, a regional wine centre and a cafe.

Coiltek Gold Centre (☎03-5460 4700; www.marybroughgoldcentre.com.au; 6 Drive-in Ct; ⌚9am-5pm) If you're interested in finding your own gold nuggets, Coiltek Gold Centre offers full-day prospecting courses (one/two people $120/200) with state-of-the-art metal detectors. It also sells and hires out prospecting gear.

Central Goldfields Visitor Centre (☎1800 356 511, 03-5460 4511; www.visitmaryborough.com.au; cnr Alma & Nolan Sts; ⌚9am-5pm) Loads of helpful maps and friendly staff.

Castlemaine Gardens Caravan Park CARAVAN PARK $
(☎03-5472 1125; www.castlemaine-gardens-caravan-park.vic.big4.com.au; Doran Ave; unpowered/powered sites $32/37, cabins $85-155) Beautifully situated next to the botanical gardens and public swimming pool, this leafy park has a camp kitchen, barbecues and recreation hut.

★ Apple Annie's APARTMENTS $$
(☎03-5472 5311; www.appleannies.com.au; 31 Templeton St; apt $120-160) Beautifully appointed apartments with rustic wooden floorboards, pastel shades, open fireplaces and (in the front apartment) a lovely private patio.

Midland Private Hotel GUESTHOUSE $$
(☎0487 198 931; www.themidland.com.au; 2 Templeton St; d $150) Opposite the train station, this lace-decked 1879 hotel is mostly original, so the rooms are old fashioned, but it has plenty of charm, from the art deco entrance to the magnificent guest lounge and attached Maurocco Bar. No children.

Eating

Apple Annie's BAKERY, CAFE $
(☎03-5472 5311; www.appleannies.com.au; 31 Templeton St; mains $10-17; ⌚8am-4pm Wed-Sat, to 3pm Sun) For freshly baked bread, feta and zucchini fritters or filled baguettes, it's hard to beat this country-style cafe and bakery.

Good Table EUROPEAN $$
(☎03-5472 4400; www.thegoodtable.com.au; 233 Barker St; mains $26-32, 2-/3-course dinner set menu Mon-Thu $25/30; ⌚noon-2pm Thu-Sun, from 6pm daily) In a lovely corner hotel, the Good Table does it well with a thoughtful European-influenced menu that changes regularly in keeping with seasons and fresh market produce. A good wine list is another highlight.

★ Public Inn MODERN AUSTRALIAN $$$
(☎03-5472 3568; www.publicinn.com.au; 165 Barker St; 2-course lunch $39, mains $19-45; ⌚noon-late Fri-Sun, 4pm-late Mon-Thu) The former Criterion Hotel has been brilliantly transformed into a slick bar and restaurant that, with its plush tones and leather couches, wouldn't look out of place in Manhattan. Food is high-end 'gastropub'. Check out the 'barrel wall', where local wines are dispensed.

Entertainment

Bridge Hotel LIVE MUSIC
(☎03-5472 1161; http://bridgehotelcastlemaine.com; 21 Walker St; ⌚4-11pm Mon-Wed, to 1am Thu, noon-1pm Fri, noon-midnight Sat, noon-11pm Sun) It's always worth checking out what's on here at one of regional Victoria's best live-music venues. It's an unassuming place with a regular calendar of live acts, including indie gems and star performers, plus karaoke and trivia nights when things are quiet.

Theatre Royal CINEMA
(☎03-5472 1196; www.theatreroyal.info; 28 Hargreaves St; cinema tickets adult/child $15.50/12) A continually operating theatre since the 1850s, this is a fabulous entertainment venue – classic cinema (dine while watching a movie), touring live performers, a bar and a cafe. Check the program on the website.

Information

Castlemaine Visitor Centre (☎03-5471 1795; www.maldoncastlemaine.com; 44 Mostyn St; ⏲9am-5pm) In the magnificent old Castlemaine Market, a building fronted with a classical Roman-basilica facade, complete with a statue of Ceres, the Roman goddess of the harvest, on top.

Getting There & Away

V/Line (☎13 61 96; www.vline.com.au) V/Line trains run hourly between Melbourne and Castlemaine (from $14.15, 1½ hours) and continue on to Bendigo ($3.90).

Maldon

POP 1236

Like a pop-up folk museum, the whole of tiny Maldon is a well-preserved relic of the gold-rush era, with many fine buildings constructed from local stone. The population is significantly lower than the 20,000 who used to work the local goldfields, but this is still a living, working town – packed with tourists on weekends but reverting to its sleepy self during the week.

Sights & Activities

Old Post Office HISTORIC BUILDING

(95 High St) The Old Post Office, built in 1870, was the childhood home of local author Henry Handel Richardson. She (yes, she!) writes about it in her autobiography, *Myself When Young* (1948).

Carman's Tunnel HISTORIC SITE

(☎03-5475 2656; off Parkin's Reef Rd; adult/child $7.50/2.50; ⏲tours 1.30pm, 2.30pm & 3.30pm Sat & Sun, daily in school holidays) For a hands-on experience, Carman's Tunnel is a 570m-long mine tunnel that was excavated in the 1880s and took two years to dig, yet produced only $300 worth of gold. Now you can descend with a guide for a 45-minute candlelit tour.

Mt Tarrengower VIEWPOINT

Don't miss the 3km drive up to Mt Tarrengower for panoramic views from the poppet-head lookout.

Victorian Goldfields Railway TRAIN

(☎03-5470 6658; www.vgr.com.au; adult/child return $45/20) This beautifully restored steam train runs along the original line through the Muckleford forest to Castlemaine (and back) up to three times a week. For a little extra, go 1st class in an oak-lined viewing carriage. The Maldon train station dates from 1884.

Festivals & Events

Maldon Folk Festival MUSIC

(www.maldonfolkfestival.com; 2-day ticket $115; ⏲Oct-Nov) Maldon's main event, this four-day festival attracts dozens of performers, who provide a wide variety of world music at venues around town and at the main stage at Mt Tarrengower Reserve.

Sleeping & Eating

There are plenty of self-contained cottages and charming B&Bs in restored buildings around town. Try the accommodation booking service (p575).

★**Maldon Miners Cottages** COTTAGE $$

(☎0413 541 941; www.heritagecottages.com.au; 41 High St; cottages from $150) Books accommodation in Maldon's 19th-century heritage cottages – a great choice.

Gold Exchange Cafe CAFE $

(www.goldexchangecafe.com; 44 Main St; meals $7-15; ⏲9am-5pm Wed-Sun) This tiny licensed cafe is worth a visit for the yabby pies, made from locally farmed yabbies.

Information

Maldon Visitor Centre (☎03-5475 2569; www.maldoncastlemaine.com; 95 High St; ⏲9am-5pm) Has internet access. Pick up the *Information Guide* and the *Historic Town Walk* brochure, which guides you past some of the town's most historic buildings.

THE GRAMPIANS (GARIWERD)

Rising up from the western Victorian plains, and acting as a haven for bushwalkers, rock climbers and nature lovers, the Grampians are one of the state's most outstanding natural and cultural features. The rich diversity of wildlife and flora, unique rock formations, Aboriginal rock art, spectacular viewpoints and an extensive network of trails and bush camp sites offer something for everyone. The local Indigenous Jardwadjali people called the mountains Gariwerd – in the local language *'gari'* means 'pointed mountain', while *'werd'* means 'shoulder'. Explorer Major Thomas Mitchell named the ranges the Grampians after the mountains in Scotland.

Grampians National Park

The four greatest mountain ranges of the Grampians are the **Mt Difficult Range** in the north, **Mt William Range** in the east, **Serra Range** in the southeast and **Victoria Range** in the southwest. They spread from Ararat to the Wartook Valley and from Dunkeld almost to Horsham. **Halls Gap**, the main accommodation base and service town, lies in the Fyans Valley. The smaller **Wonderland Range**, close to Halls Gap, has some of the most splendid and accessible outlooks, scenic drives, picnic grounds and gum-scented walks, such as those that go to the **Pinnacles** or **Silverband Falls**.

There are more than 150km of well-marked **walking tracks**, ranging from half-hour strolls to overnight treks through difficult terrain, all starting from the various car parks, picnic grounds and camping areas. For longer walks, let someone know where you're going (preferably the Parks Victoria rangers).

One of the most popular sights is spectacular **MacKenzie Falls**. From the car park the steep 600m path leads to the base of the falls and a large plunge pool (no swimming). Other popular places include: **Boroka Lookout**, with excellent views over Halls Gap and Lake Bellfield; and **Reed Lookout** with its short walk to the **Balconies** and views over Lake Wartook. **Mt Stapylton** and **Hollow Mountain** in the north are renowned as abseiling and rock-climbing spots.

In mid-January 2014, a series of bushfires swept through the Grampians region. Embers rained down on Halls Gap but an earlier-than-expected wind change spared the town. The northern Grampians region was hardest hit with homes lost around Wartook and Brimpaen, while large swathes of forest turned to ash in the areas around Mt Difficult. In spite of the fires the Grampians remain very much open for business – check with the various visitors centres and Parks Victoria to see which, if any, trails are closed.

ROCK ART

Traditional Aboriginal owners have been occupying Gariwerd (the Grampians) for more than 20,000 years and this is the most accessible place in Victoria to see Indigenous rock art. Sites include **Bunjil's Shelter**, near Stawell, one of Victoria's most sacred Indigenous sites, best seen on a guided tour from the **Brambuk Cultural Centre** (☎03-5356 4452; www.brambuk.com.au; Grampians Rd/C216). Other rock-art sites in the west of the park are the **Manja Shelter**, reached from the Harrop Track car park, and the **Billimina Shelter**, near the Buandik camping ground. In the north is the **Ngamadjidj Shelter**, reached from the Stapylton camping ground.

These paintings, in protected rock overhangs, are mostly handprints, animal tracks and stick figures. They indicate the esteem in which these mountains are held by local Indigenous communities and should be treated with respect.

☞ Tours

Absolute Outdoors ADVENTURE TOUR
(☎03-5356 4556; www.absoluteoutdoors.com.au; 105 Main Rd, Halls Gap) Rock climbing, abseiling, mountain biking, canoeing and guided nature walks. Also offers equipment hire.

★ **Brambuk Cultural Centre** CULTURAL TOUR
(☎03-5356 4452; www.brambuk.com.au; Grampians Tourist Rd, Halls Gap; 3/5hr tours $70/140) Rangers lead cultural and rock-art tours with numerous fascinating insights into local Indigenous culture. Bookings essential.

Grampians Horseriding Adventures HORSE RIDING
(☎03-5383 9255; www.grampianshorseriding.com.au; 430 Schmidts Rd, Wartook Valley; 2½hr rides $100; ⏲10am & 2pm) Horse-riding adventures around a grand property with sweeping views, lakes and wandering bush tracks. Beginners are well looked after and there are pony rides ($30) for the kids.

Grampians Mountain Adventure Company ADVENTURE TOUR
(GMAC; ☎0427 747 047; www.grampiansadventure.com.au; half/full day from $95/145) Specialises in rock climbing and abseiling adventures and instruction from beginner to advanced.

Hangin' Out ROCK CLIMBING
(☎0407 684 831, 03-5356 4535; www.hanginout.com.au; 4hr/full-day rock climbing $115/160) Rock-climbing specialists here will get you started with a four-hour introductory session and private guiding. Experienced guide Earl will get you onto the cliff faces, giving you a lively interpretation of the surrounding country as you go. His full-day adventure walk includes rock climbs and abseils.

The Grampians (Gariwerd)

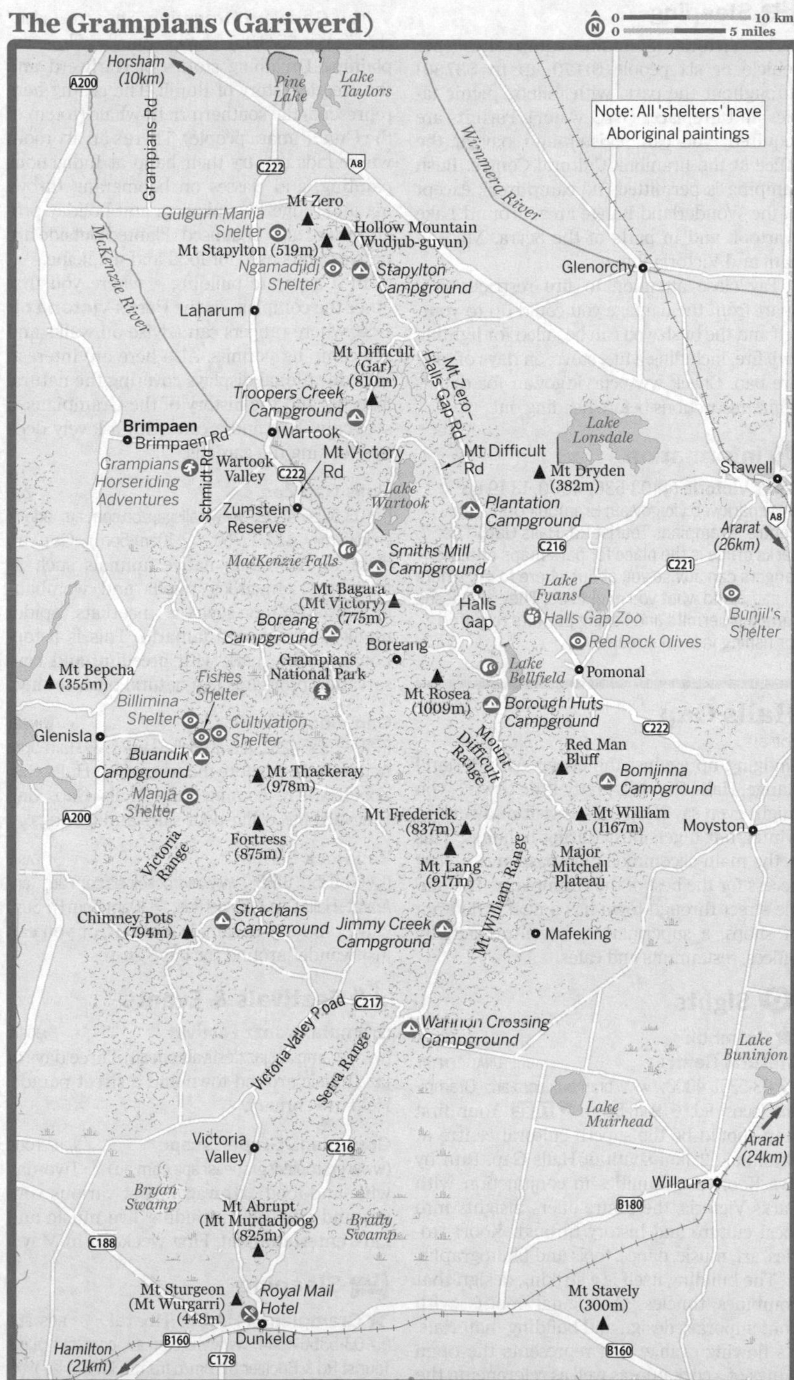

Sleeping

Parks Victoria maintains camp sites (per vehicle or six people $11.70 up to $37.80) throughout the park, with toilets, picnic tables and fireplaces (BYO water). Permits are required; you can register and pay at the office at the Brambuk Cultural Centre. Bush camping is permitted (no campfires), except in the Wonderland Range area, around Lake Wartook and in parts of the Serra, Mt William and Victoria Ranges.

Pay close attention to fire restrictions – apart from the damage you could do to yourself and the bush, you can be jailed for lighting *any* fire, including a fuel stove, on days of total fire ban. Check www.cfa.vic.gov.au for details of fire restrictions before heading out.

Information

Parks Victoria (☎03-5361 4000, 13 19 63; www.parkweb.vic.gov.au; Brambuk Cultural Centre, Grampians Tourist Rd, Halls Gap) The parks office is the place for park maps and the rangers can advise you about where to go, where to camp and what you might see. They also issue camping permits and fishing permits required for fishing in local streams.

Halls Gap

POP 613

Nudging up against the craggy Wonderland Range, Halls Gap is a pretty little town – you might even say sleepy if you visit midweek in winter, but it gets busy during holidays. This is the main accommodation base and easiest access for the best of the Grampians. The single street through town has a neat little knot of shops, a supermarket, adventure-activity offices, restaurants and cafes.

Sights

★Brambuk Cultural Centre CULTURAL CENTRE
(☎03-5361 4000; www.brambuk.com.au; Grampians Tourist Rd; ⏲9am-5pm) FREE Your first stop should be the superb cultural centre at Brambuk, 2.5km south of Halls Gap. Run by five Koori communities in conjunction with Parks Victoria, the centre offers insights into local culture and history through Koori stories, art, music, dance, tools and photographs.

The building itself is a striking design that combines timeless Aboriginal motifs with contemporary design and building materials. Its flowing orange roof represents the open wings of a cockatoo, as well as referencing the peaks of the Grampians.

The **Gariwerd Dreaming Theatre** (adult/child/family $5/3/15) shows hourly films explaining Dreaming stories of Gariwerd and the creation story of Bunjil. The ceiling here represents the southern right whale (totem of the Gunditjmara people). There's an art room where kids can try their hand at Indigenous painting, and classes on boomerang throwing and didgeridoo playing, and holiday programs are also organised. Planted outside are native plants used for food and medicine.

In a separate building – where you first enter the complex – is the **Parks Victoria office**, where rangers can advise on walks and sell camping permits. Also here are interesting educational displays covering the natural features and the history of the Grampians, a souvenir shop and a cafe with a lovely deck overlooking the gardens.

Halls Gap Zoo ZOO
(☎03-5356 4668; www.hallsgapzoo.com.au; adult/child/family $24/12/60; ⏲10am-5pm) Get up close to Australian native animals such as wallabies, kangaroos, quolls and wombats, but also critters such as meerkats, spider monkeys, bison and tamarin. This is a top-notch wildlife park with breeding and conservation programs in a natural bush setting.

Gap Vineyard WINERY
(☎03-5356 4252; Ararat–Halls Gap Rd; ⏲11am-5pm Wed-Mon) Just before the turn off to Halls Gap Zoo if you're coming from Halls Gap, Gap Vineyard has cellar-door sales and tastings.

Red Rock Olives FARM
(☎03-5356 6168; www.redrockolives.com.au; cnr Ararat–Halls Gap & Tunnel Rds; ⏲10am-5pm Fri-Sun) Olive products to sample and buy, or you can just wander around the olive groves.

Festivals & Events

Grampians Jazz Festival MUSIC
(www.grampiansjazzfestival.com.au) Three days of jazz music around town and a street parade. Held in February.

Grampians Grape Escape WINE, FOOD
(www.grampiansgrapeescape.com.au) Two-day wine-and-food extravaganza at various venues and wineries, including live music and kids' entertainment. First weekend in May.

Sleeping

★Grampians YHA Eco-Hostel HOSTEL $
(☎03-5356 4544; www.yha.com.au; cnr Grampians Tourist Rd & Buckler St; dm/d from $30/85; @) This architecturally designed and ecofriend-

WORTH A TRIP

LITTLE DESERT NATIONAL PARK

Don't expect rolling sand dunes, but this arid park covers a huge 1320 sq km and is rich in flora and fauna that thrive in the dry environment. There are over 670 indigenous plant species here, and in spring and early summer the landscape is transformed into a colourful wonderland of wild flowers. The best-known resident is the mallee fowl, an industrious bird that can be seen in an aviary at the Little Desert Nature Lodge.

The Nhill–Harrow Rd through the park is sealed and the road from Dimboola is gravel, but in the park the tracks are mostly sand and only suitable for 4WD vehicles or walking. Some are closed to 4WDs in the wet season (July to October).

Little Desert Nature Lodge (☎03-5391 5232; www.littledesertlodge.com.au; camp sites $25, bunkhouse d $44, B&B r $125; ❄) On the northern edge of the desert, 16km south of Nhill, this well-equipped bush retreat is a superb base for exploring the park. With a spacious camping ground, bunkhouse, comfortable en suite motel-style rooms and a restaurant, there's something for everyone. A key attraction here is the tour of the mallee fowl aviary ($15), where you can see these rare birds in a breeding program. Otherwise, take the mallee fowl sanctuary tour ($65) and a night spotlighting walk ($15).

Little Desert Park Office (☎13 19 63; www.parkweb.vic.gov.au; Nursery Rd) Information on camping inside the park. It's off the Western Hwy south of Dimboola.

ly hostel utilises solar power and rainwater tanks and makes the most of light and space. It's beautifully equipped with a spacious lounge, a *MasterChef*-quality kitchen and spotless rooms.

★D'Altons Resort COTTAGE $$
(☎03-5356 4666; www.daltonsresort.com.au; 48 Glen St; studio/deluxe/family cottages from $110/125/160; ❄📶🏊) These lovely cottages, with lounge chairs, cute verandahs and log fires, spread up the hill from the main road between the gums and kangaroos. They're immaculately kept and the friendly owners have loads of local information. There's even a tennis court and a saltwater pool.

Mountain Grand Guesthouse GUESTHOUSE $$
(☎03-5356 4232; www.mountaingrand.com.au; Grampians Tourist Rd; s/d incl breakfast $146/166; ❄📶) This gracious, old-fashioned timber guesthouse prides itself on being a traditional old-fashioned lodge where you can take a pre-dinner port in one of the lounge areas and mingle with other guests. The rooms are still quaint but with a bright, fresh feel. The Balconies Restaurant here is well regarded.

Aspect Villas VILLA $$$
(☎03-5356 4457; www.aspectvillas.com.au; off Mackey's Peak Rd; d $475; ❄) These two luxury villas are situated close to town, but seem a world away when you're reclining on your bed or by the log fire, taking in views of the Wonderland Range through floor-to-ceiling windows. They make the most of local building materials, and sit on a secluded property complete with its own lagoon. With a spa and king-size bed, it's a real couples' getaway.

Eating

Livefast Lifestyle Cafe CAFE $
(☎03-5356 4400; www.livefast.com.au; shop 5, Stony Creek Stores; mains $9-17; ⏰7am-4pm Mon-Fri, to 5pm Sat & Sun; 📶) Halls Gap's best coffee and a sunny atmosphere are the hallmarks of this cafe. The cooking is fresh and tasty with dishes such as the slow-cooked pulled-lamb salad or the beetroot and spinach felafel.

Kookaburra Restaurant MODERN AUSTRALIAN $$
(☎03-5356 4222; www.kookaburrabarbistro.com.au; 125-127 Grampians Rd; mains $19-35; ⏰6-9pm Tue-Fri, noon-3pm & 6-9pm Sat & Sun) This Halls Gap institution is famed for its excellent pub food, such as the sublime crispy-skin duck and Aussie dishes such as barramundi and kangaroo fillet (cooked rare or medium rare only, as it should be). The wine list features mostly Grampians area wines, and there's beer on tap at the convivial bar.

Halls Gap Hotel PUB FOOD $$
(☎03-5356 4566; www.hallsgaphotel.com.au; 2262 Grampians Rd; mains $18-30; ⏰noon-2pm Wed-Sun, from 6pm daily) For generous, no-nonsense bistro food, you can't beat the local pub, about 2km north of town, with views of the Grampians. Dishes include seafood risotto, roast of the day and warm Moroccan chicken salad. There are play areas for kids and it's a social place for a beer after a day's bushwalking.

Information

Halls Gap Visitor Centre (1800 065 599; www.grampianstravel.com.au; Grampians Rd; 9am-5pm) The staff here is helpful and can book tours, accommodation and activities.

The Southern Grampians

The southern point of access for the Grampians, Dunkeld is a sleepy little town with a very big-name restaurant. The setting is superb, with Mt Abrupt and Mt Sturgeon rising up to the north, while the Grampians Tourist Rd to Halls Gap gives you a glorious passage into the park, with the cliffs and sky opening up as you pass between the Serra and Mt William Ranges. Fit hikers can walk to the summit of **Mt Abrupt** (6.5km, three hours return) and **Mt Sturgeon** (7km, three hours return) for panoramic views of the ranges.

Eating

★ **Royal Mail Hotel** MODERN AUSTRALIAN $$$
(03-5577 2241; www.royalmail.com.au; Parker St, Dunkeld; bar meals $31-44, restaurant mains $39-55, 5/8-course set menu $110/150; bar & bistro noon-2.30pm & 6-9pm, restaurant from 6pm Wed-Sun) Dunkeld's main attraction is the restaurant at the Royal Mail Hotel. Continuously licensed since 1855, the Royal Mail is today one of Victoria's top restaurants. Chef Robin Wickens oversees the kitchens for the upmarket showpiece restaurant, but also the more affordable bistro. You need to book months ahead to dine in the main restaurant.

Information

Dunkeld Visitor Centre (03-5577 2558; www.visitsoutherngrampians.com.au; Parker St, Dunkeld) Has useful information about this small town south of the Grampians.

Wartook Valley & the Northern Grampians

Wartook Valley runs along the Grampians' western foothills, giving a completely different perspective of the mountains. Heading to or from Horsham, this is the scenic alternative to the Western Hwy (A8). From Wartook, the sealed Roses Gap Rd and Mt Victoria Rd pass through the park, and there are lots of unsealed roads passing little creeks, waterfalls and picnic spots. Most of the tourist infrastructure was spared during the 2014 fires, but much of the land has turned from green to black and will take some time to recover.

Sights

Mt Zero Olives FARM
(03-5383 8280; www.mountzeroolives.com; Mt Zero Rd; 10am-4pm) Planted in 1953, the olive grove at Mt Zero Olives produces olives, olive oils (including infused varieties), tapenades and other gourmet products in a picturesque setting. There are tastings and farm-gate sales daily, and an excellent cafe that opens on weekends and holidays.

NORTHWEST OF THE GRAMPIANS

Mt Arapiles State Park

Mt Arapiles is Australia's premier rock-climbing destination. Topping out at 369m, it's not the world's biggest mountain, but with more than 2000 routes to scale it attracts climbers from around the world. Popular climbs include the Bard Buttress, Tiger Wall and the Pharos. In the nearby town of Natimuk, a community of avid climbers has set up to service visitors, and the town has developed into something of a centre for artists.

Activities

Natimuk Climbing Company ROCK CLIMBING
(03-5387 1329; www.climbco.com.au; 6 Jory St, Natimuk) Offers climbing and abseiling instruction.

Arapiles Climbing Guides ROCK CLIMBING
(03-5384 0376; www.arapiles.com.au; Natimuk) Climbing instruction and guiding around Mt Arapiles.

Festivals & Events

Nati Frinj Festival PERFORMING ARTS
(http://actnatimuk.com/nati-frinj) The biennial Nati Frinj Festival, held in November in odd years, includes performances and a colourful street parade.

Sleeping

Pines Camping Ground CAMPGROUND $
(Centenary Park; camp sites $7) Most climbers head for this popular site at the base of the mountain.

Victorian High Country

Includes ➡

Best Places to Eat

- ➡ Simone's Restaurant (p598)
- ➡ Provenance (p592)
- ➡ Pepperleaf Bushtucker Restaurant (p598)
- ➡ Tuileries Restaurant & Cafe (p593)

Best Places to Stay

- ➡ Freeman on Ford (p592)
- ➡ Odd Frog (p597)
- ➡ Dreamers (p599)
- ➡ Eildon Houseboat Hire (p586)

Why Go?

With its enticing mix of history, adventure and culinary temptations, Victoria's High Country is a wonderful place to spend some time. The Great Dividing Range – Australia's eastern mountain spine – curls around eastern Victoria from the Snowy Mountains to the Grampians, peaking in the spectacular High Country. These are Victoria's Alps – a mountain playground attracting skiers and snowboarders in winter and bushwalkers and mountain bikers in summer. Here the mountain air is clear and invigorating, winter snowfalls at the resorts of Mt Buller, Mt Hotham and Falls Creek are fairly reliable, and the scenery is spectacular.

Away from the mountain tops, there are activities aplenty and Bright is one of the loveliest gateway towns in the state. Throw in historic towns such as Beechworth, the wineries of King Valley and Rutherglen, and the gourmet food offerings of Milawa and you'll find plenty of reasons to linger.

When to Go

Mt Hotham

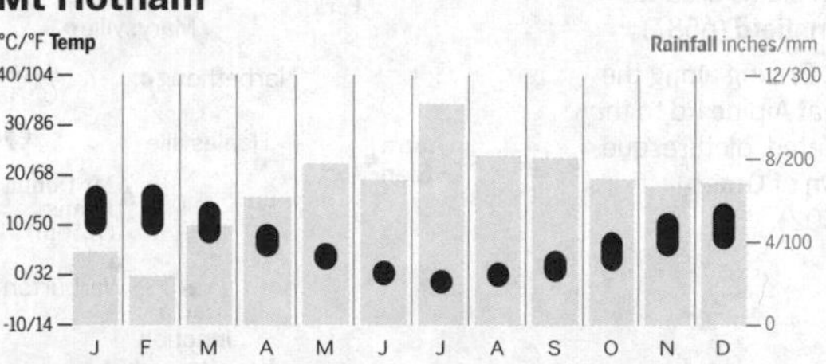

Apr–May Best time for glorious autumn colours around Bright and Omeo.

Jul–Aug Hit the snowy mountain slopes for the peak ski season.

Dec–Feb The green season for mountain biking, horse riding and wine touring.

Victorian High Country Highlights

1. Cycling the **Murray to Mountains Rail Trail** (p592), Victoria's second-longest bike path.
2. Visiting Ned Kelly's cell, then sampling the brews at Bridge Road Brewers in historic **Beechworth** (p591).
3. Hitting the gourmet trail, tasting wine, cheese, mustard and olives in **Milawa** (p590).
4. Skiing the pistes at fashionable **Falls Creek** (p600).
5. Enjoying the vibrant colours of the autumn and spring festivals in **Bright** (p596).
6. Spending a day or two sampling the reds in one of Victoria's best wine regions near **Rutherglen** (p592).
7. Making like *The Man from Snowy River* and going horse riding on the high plains around **Mansfield** (p587).
8. Driving along the Great Alpine Rd to the isolated, picturesque town of **Omeo** (p602).

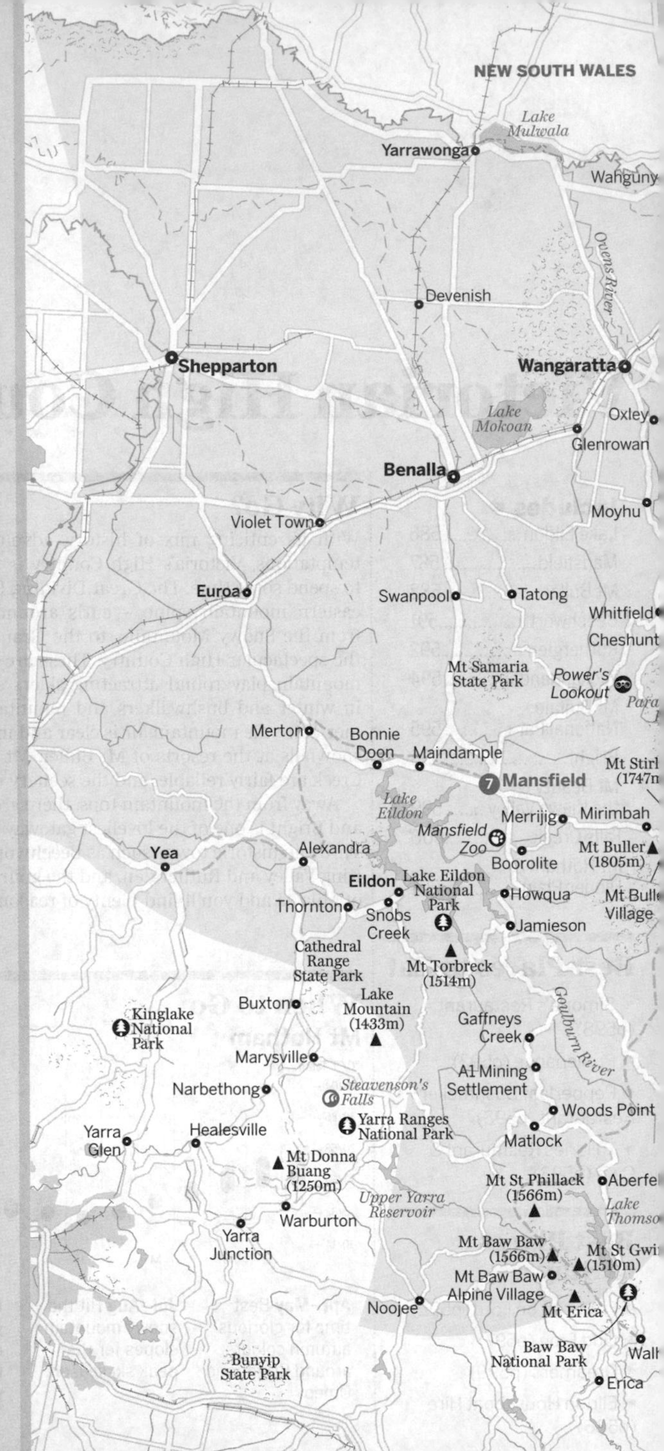

0
50 km
0
25 miles
Walwa
Pine
Mountain
(1062m)
Burrowa-Pine
Mountain
National Park
Tintaldra
Murray River
Albury
Rutherglen
Talgarno
Bellbridge
Granya
Chiltern
Wodonga
Mt Burrowa
(1300m)
Towong
Tallangatta
Bullioh
Stanley
State
Forest
Red Bluff
Corryong
Berringama
Colac Colac
Khancoban
Yackandandah
Beechworth
Stanley
Everton
Milawa
Whorouly
Gapsted
Tallandoon
Mitta Mitta River
Eskdale
Murray River
NEW SOUTH
WALES
Myrtleford
Ovens
Mitta Mitta
Dartmouth
Mt Buffalo National Park
Lake
Dartmouth
Murray to Mountains Rail Trail
Tawonga
Park Entrance
Station
Porepunkah
Mt Bogong
(1986m)
Dingo
Dell
Bright
Mt Beauty
The Horn
(1723m)
Cresta
Valley
Wandiligong
Bogong
Falls Creek
Harrietville
Mt Feathertop
(1922m)
Glen Valley
Mount
Hotham
Anglers
Rest
Benambra
Alpine
National
Park
Mt Hotham
(1868m)
Dinner
Plain
Mt Hotham
Airport
Omeo
Mt Howitt
(1742m)
Wonnangatta River
Road
Closed in
Winter
Victoria Falls
Camping Area
Alpine
National
Park
Swifts Creek
Buchan River
Dargo River
Ensay
Dargo
Buchan
Licola
Mitchell River
National Park
Bruthen
Nowa Nowa
Mitchell River
Bairnsdale
Lake
Tyers
Eagle Point
Metung
Lake Tyers
Paynesville
Raymond
Island
Lakes
Entrance
Heyfield
Maffra
Stratford

Lake Eildon

Surrounding most of its namesake lake, **Lake Eildon National Park** is the low-lying southern gateway to the High Country, covering over 270 sq km and providing superb opportunities for walking and camping.

Originally called Sugarloaf Reserve, Lake Eildon was created as a massive reservoir for irrigation and hydroelectric schemes. It was constructed between 1915 and 1929 and flooded the town of Darlingford and surrounding farm homesteads. After years of drought, recent rains have brought the lake back to near capacity. Behind the dam wall, the 'pondage' (outflow from the dam) spreads below Eildon township, a little one-pub town and a popular recreation and holiday base.

On the northern arm of the lake is **Bonnie Doon**, a popular weekend getaway, which reached icon status as the nondescript spot where the Kerrigan family enjoyed 'serenity' in the satirical 1997 Australian film *The Castle*.

Activities

Eildon Trout Farm FISHING
(☎03-5773 2377; www.eildontroutfarm.com.au; 460 Back Eildon Rd; entry/fishing $2.50/2.50; ⏲9am-5pm) Catching a trout or salmon is guaranteed at this farm located on the back road between Thornton and Eildon. There are five ponds to choose from and you can either bring your own gear or rent some ($2.50). Better still, you can keep what you catch and take it home for dinner (or barbecue it on the spot).

Rubicon Valley Horse Riding HORSE RIDING
(☎03-5773 2292; www.rubiconhorseriding.com.au; Rubicon Rd; rides introductory/2hr/half day/full day $55/80/120/210) This company caters for all levels, including children, and the setting is lovely.

Sleeping

Lake Eildon is a beautiful place for bush camping, with several lakeside national park sites. All **camp sites** (www.parkweb.vic.gov.au; per site $11.70-48.70) must be booked online.

There are a few places to stay in Eildon township and on the back road to Thornton.

Eildon Lake Motel MOTEL $$
(☎03-5774 2800; www.eildonlakemotel.com.au; 2 Gordwood Pde; s/d $90/100; P❄) A block back from the Goulburn River, this motel has spacious if fairly standard brick-walled rooms.

★**Eildon Houseboat Hire** HOUSEBOAT $$$
(☎0408 005 535; www.eildonhouseboathire.com.au; per week winter/summer $2400/3500) If the Murray River is too far, or you want more room to manoeuvre, Lake Eildon is the next-best place in Victoria to stay on a houseboat. Here you can hire a luxurious 10- or 12-berth houseboat (minimum hire per three-night weekend $1700). Book well ahead for holiday periods.

★**Lake Eildon Marina & Houseboat Hire** HOUSEBOAT $$$
(☎03-5774 2107; www.houseboatholidays.com.au; 190 Sugarloaf Rd; 10-bed houseboat high season per week $2500-3500) Ten- or 12-berth houseboats, but you'll need to book months in advance during high season.

Information

Eildon Visitor Information Centre (☎03-5774 2909; www.lakeeildon.com; Main St; ⏲10am-2pm) Friendly staff run this small office opposite the shopping centre.

Getting There & Away

Lake Eildon, 215km northeast of Melbourne, can be reached via the Hume Fwy (M31; take the turn-off at Seymour), or via the far prettier route through Healesville.

Jamieson

POP 384

From Eildon, a sealed and scenic back road skirts the southern edge of the national park to Jamieson, a charming little town where the Goulburn and Jamieson Rivers join Lake Eildon. Jamieson was established as a supply town for gold miners in the 1850s and a number of interesting historical buildings remain.

Sleeping & Eating

Twin River Cabins CABIN $
(☎03-5777 0582; www.twinrivercabins.com.au; 3 Chenery St; s/d $50/90) These rustic little cabins make a great budget retreat close to town. They sleep four to six people and have basic kitchen facilities and shared amenities. The owners rent mountain bikes for $20 a day.

Jamieson Brewery PUB FOOD $$
(☎03-5777 0515; www.jamiesonbrewery.com.au; Eildon-Jamieson Rd; mains $16-32; ⏰11am-10pm) An essential stop 3km from town, the Jamieson Brewery produces flavoursome beers on-site, including a raspberry ale and the knockout 'Beast'. Try a tasting plate of four beers and homemade pesto ($15) and take the free daily brewery tour at 12.30pm. There's even free tastings of homemade fudge. The bistro serves up good pub food.

Mansfield

POP 3067

Mansfield is the gateway to Victoria's largest snowfields at Mt Buller, but also an exciting all-seasons destination in its own right. There's plenty to do here in *The Man from Snowy River* country, with horse riding and mountain biking popular in summer, and a buzzing atmosphere in winter when the snow bunnies hit town.

Sights

Mansfield Cemetery CEMETERY
The three Mansfield police officers killed at Stringybark Creek by Ned Kelly and his gang in 1878 rest in Mansfield Cemetery.

Mansfield Zoo ZOO
(☎03-5777 3576; www.mansfieldzoo.com.au; 1064 Mansfield Woods Point Rd; adult/child/family $15/8/44; ⏰10am-5.30pm, to 6.30pm or sunset in summer) Mansfield Zoo is a surprisingly good wildlife park with lots of native fauna and some exotics, such as a pair of lions. If you're older than eight, you can sleep in the paddocks in a swag (adult/child $65/45, including zoo entry for two days) and wake to the dawn wildlife chorus.

Mansfield Farmers Market MARKET
(www.mansfieldfarmersmarket.com.au; 30 High St; ⏰8.30am-1pm 4th Sat of the month) On the fourth Saturday of each month, the farmers bring produce to town at the Mansfield Primary School.

Activities

All Terrain Cycles MOUNTAIN BIKING
(☎03-5775 2724; www.allterraincycles.com.au; 58 High St; mountain-bike hire per day $50-130) Hires out top-quality mountain bikes and safety equipment. Also runs guided tours and mountain-biking clinics.

High Country Horses HORSE RIDING
(☎03-5777 5590; www.highcountryhorses.com.au; Mt Buller Rd, Merrijig; 2hr/half-day rides $100/130, overnight from $590; ⏰Oct-May) Based at Merrijig on the way to Mt Buller, High Country Horses offers anything from a short trot to overnight treks to Craig's Hut, Howqua River and Mt Stirling.

McCormacks Mountain Valley Trail Rides HORSE RIDING
(☎03-5777 5542; www.mountainvalleytrailrides.com.au; 43 McCormack's Rd, Merrijig; 2hr/half-day ride $90/120; ⏰Oct-May) Experienced locals take you into the King Valley and High Country. Options include multiday adventures.

Festivals & Events

Upper Goulburn Wine Region Vintage Celebration WINE
(www.uppergoulburnwine.org.au) Local wines, musicians and chefs make for three fun days in April.

High Country Festival & Spring Arts ART
(www.highcountryfestival.com.au) A week of arts, bush markets and activities from late October, culminating in the Melbourne Cup day picnic races.

Sleeping

Mansfield Holiday Park CARAVAN PARK $
(☎03-5775 1383; www.mansfieldholidaypark.com.au; Mt Buller Rd; unpowered/powered sites from $25/30, d cabins $70-140; ❄) On the edge of town, this is a spacious caravan park with a pool, minigolf, camp kitchen and comfortable cabins.

Highton Manor B&B $$
(☎03-5775 2700; www.hightonmanor.com.au; 140 Highton Lane; d stable/tower incl breakfast $130/365; ❄) Built in 1896 for Francis Highett, who sang with Dame Nellie Melba, this stately two-storey manor has style and romance but doesn't take itself too seriously. There's group accommodation in the shared room, modern rooms in the converted stables and lavish period rooms in the main house. If you want the royal treatment, choose the tower room.

Wappan Station FARMSTAY $$
(☎03-5778 7786; www.wappanstation.com.au; Royal Town Rd; shearers' quarters for 20 people $450, cottages d from $200; ❄) Watch farm activities from your deck at this sheep-and-cattle property on the banks of Lake Eildon.

Eating & Drinking

★Mansfield Regional Produce Store CAFE $
(☎03-5779 1404; www.theproducestore.com.au; 68 High St; mains $12-19; ⏰9am-5pm Tue-Thu, Sat & Sun, to 9pm Fri; ✍) The best spot in town for coffee or a light lunch, this rustic store stocks an array of local produce, wine and freshly baked artisan breads. The ever-changing blackboard menu offers full breakfasts, baguettes and salads.

Mansfield Hotel PUB FOOD $$
(☎03-5775 2101; www.mansfieldhotel.com.au; 86 High St; mains $18-35; ⏰noon-2pm & 6-9pm) Newly renovated after a 2010 fire, the Mansfield has a huge dining room and an extensive bistro menu to go with it. Pull up a couch by the fireplace in winter, or eat out in the sunny beer terrace in summer.

Deck on High MODERN AUSTRALIAN $$
(☎03-5775 1144; www.thedeckonhigh.com.au; 13-15 High St; mains $12-37; ⏰11am-late Wed-Mon) A sophisticated but relaxed bar-restaurant serving up genuinely good contemporary Aussie cuisine such as tiger prawn fettucini and chargrilled swordfish. The upper deck is brilliant for a drink on a summer afternoon and the downstairs bar, with soft couches and sleek lines, is a cosy place to explore the extensive local wine list in winter.

Information

Mansfield & Mt Buller High Country Visitor Centre (☎1800 039 049; www.mansfieldmtbuller.com.au; 175 High St; ⏰9am-5pm) In a modern building next to the town's original railway station, the visitor centre books accommodation for the region and sells lift tickets.

Getting There & Away

Mansfield is 209km northeast of Melbourne, but allow at least 2½ hours if you're driving; take the Tallarook or Euroa exits from the Hume Fwy.

V/Line (☎1800 800 007; www.vline.com.au) coaches run between Melbourne's Southern Cross Station and Mansfield (three hours, $25) at least once daily, with more frequent departures during the ski season.

Mt Buller

ELEV 1805M

Victoria's largest and busiest ski resort is also the closest major resort to Melbourne, so it buzzes all winter long. It's also developing into a popular summer destination for mountain bikers and hikers, with a range of cross-country and downhill trails. The downhill-skiing area covers 180 hectares, with a vertical drop of 400m.

Sights & Activities

Buller is a well-developed resort with a vibrant village atmosphere in the white season and on summer weekends. In winter there's **night skiing** on Wednesday and Saturday, and for nonskiers there's tobogganing, snowtubing and excellent snowshoeing. The entrance fee to the Horse Hill day car park in winter is $35 per car (free in summer).

At least eight outlets spread across Mansfield and Mt Buller rent ski and other equipment; check out www.mtbuller.com.au for a full list of options.

Sleeping

Mt Buller Alpine Reservations ACCOMMODATION SERVICES
(☎03-5777 6633; www.mtbullerreservations.com.au) Mt Buller Alpine Reservations books accommodation. There's generally a two-night minimum stay on weekends.

High Country Reservations ACCOMMODATION SERVICES
(☎1800 039 049; www.mansfieldmtbuller.com.au) Can help with online accommodation bookings.

Buller Backpackers HOSTEL $
(www.bullerbackpackers.com.au; dm from $55) Run by Mt Buller Chalet, this buzzing backpackers is one of the best budget choices.

Mt Buller Chalet CHALET $$$
(☎03-5777 6566; www.mtbullerchalet.com.au; Summit Rd; d incl breakfast summer/winter from $250/325; 📶🏊) With a central location, the Chalet offers a sweet range of suites, a library with billiard table, well-regarded eateries, an impressive sports centre and a heated pool.

Eating & Drinking

You'll find plenty of great dining experiences here in winter, and a few places open year-round. There's a licensed and reasonably well-stocked **supermarket** in the village centre.

Cattleman's Café CAFE, BISTRO $
(☎03-5777 7970; Village Centre; mains $8-19; ⏰8am-2pm Oct-May, to 9pm Jun-Sep) At the base of the Blue Bullet chairlift and open

BIKING MT BULLER

Mt Buller has developed into one of the great summer mountain-biking destinations in Victoria, with a network of trails around the summit, and exhilarating downhill tracks. From 26 December to the end of January, the Horse Hill chairlift operates on weekends, lifting you and your bike up to the plateau (all-day lift and trails access $60). If you're not biking you can still ride the chairlift all day (adult/child $20/15).

From 26 December until the Easter weekend, a bus shuttle runs every weekend from the **Mirimbah Store** (03-5777 5529; www.mirimbah.com.au; per ride $15, daily $40; 8am-4pm Thu-Sun Sep-May, daily in winter) at the base of the mountain to the summit car park, from where you can ride all the way back down on a number of trails. The most popular trail is the **Delatite River Trail** (one to 1½ hours), partly following the Delatite River with 13 river crossings. More challenging is the new **Australian Alpine Epic** (four to five hours). The owners of the Mirimbah Store (which, incidentally, is also a fabulous cafe) are experienced riders and a mine of information on the trails.

You can hire quality mountain bikes from All Terrain Cycles (p587) in Mansfield. During the biking season it also has a hire service and store at Buller village.

year-round, this is the place for breakfast, coffee or a bistro meal of steak, burgers or fish and chips.

Black Cockatoo MODERN AUSTRALIAN $$$
(03-5777 6566; Summit Rd; mains $31-45, 2-/3-course menu $60/70; 7-11am & 6-9pm) At Mt Buller Chalet, this is year-round fine dining – the best on the mountain. In winter the **Après Bar & Cafe** has more casual dining.

Pension Grimus AUSTRIAN $$$
(03-5777 6396; www.pensiongrimus.com.au; Breathtaker Rd; mains $34-42; noon-2pm & 6-9pm Sat & Sun, 6-9pm Mon-Fri) One of Buller's originals, there's Austrian-style food at the Kaptan's Restaurant, impromptu music and a pumping bar that will give you a warm, fuzzy feeling after a day on the slopes.

Information

Mt Buller Resort Management Board (03-5777 6077; www.mtbuller.com.au; Community Centre, Summit Rd; 8.30am-5pm) Also runs an information office in the village square clock tower during winter.

Getting There & Around

Ski-season car parking is below the village. A 4WD taxi service transports people to their village accommodation.

Day trippers park in the Horse Hill car park and take the quad chairlift into the skiing area, or there's a free day-tripper shuttle-bus service between the day car park and the village. Ski hire and lift tickets are available at the base of the chairlift.

Mansfield–Mt Buller Buslines (03-5775 2606; www.mmbl.com.au) Runs a winter bus service from Mansfield (adult/child return $62/42).

V/Line (1800 800 007; www.vline.com.au) V/Line operates at least one daily bus between Melbourne and Mt Buller (adult/child return from $132/82).

King Valley

From Melbourne, turning east off the Hume Fwy near Wangaratta and onto the Snow Rd brings you to the King Valley, a prosperous cool-climate wine region and an important gourmet-food region. The valley extends south along the King River, through the tiny towns of Mohyu, Whitfield and Cheshunt, with a sprinkling of 20-or-so wineries noted for Italian varietals and cool-climate wines such as sangiovese, barbera, sparkling prosecco and pinot grigio. Check out www.winesofthekingvalley.com.au.

There's good camping along the King River and a few places to stay around Whitfield.

Sights

Dal Zotto Estate WINERY
(03-5729 8321; www.dalzotto.com.au; Main Rd, Whitfield; cellar door 10am-5pm, trattoria noon-3pm Thu, Sat & Sun, noon-3pm & 6-10pm Fri) Dal Zotto Estate is one of the best wineries in the area. It also has an excellent trattoria, serving north Italian cuisine.

Pizzini WINERY
(☎03-5729 8278; www.pizzini.com.au; 175 King Valley Rd, Whitfield; ⏰10am-5pm) Pizzini is one of the more respected wineries in the King Valley region. It also has a cooking school with a focus on Italian dishes.

Milawa Gourmet Region

The Milawa/Oxley gourmet region (www.milawagourmet.com) is the place to indulge your tastebuds. As well as wine tasting, you can sample cheese, olives, mustards and marinades, or dine in some of the region's best restaurants.

Sights & Activities

★ **Milawa Cheese Company** CHEESE
(☎03-5727 3589; www.milawacheese.com.au; Factory Rd, Milawa; ⏰9am-5pm, meals 9.30am-3pm) About 2km north of Milawa, Milawa Cheese Company is our favourite produce store. From humble origins, it now produces a mouth-watering array of cheeses to sample or buy. It excels at soft farmhouse brie (from goat or cow) and pungent washed-rind cheeses. There's a bakery here and an excellent restaurant where the speciality is a variety of pizzas using Milawa cheese. Also here is the cellar door for **Wood Park Wines** (☎03-5727 3500; www.woodparkwines.com.au; ⏰11am-4pm Fri-Wed).

★ **Brown Brothers** WINERY
(☎03-5720 5500; www.brownbrothers.com.au; Bobbinawarrah Rd, Milawa; ⏰9am-5pm) The region's best-known winery, Brown Brothers Vineyard's first vintage was in 1889 and it has remained in the hands of the same family ever since. As well as the tasting room, there's the superb **Epicurean Centre** restaurant, a gorgeous garden, kids' play equipment and picnic and barbecue facilities.

Gapsted Wines WINERY
(☎03-5751 1383; www.gapstedwines.com.au; Great Alpine Rd; ⏰10am-5pm, lunch daily) Where the Snow Rd meets the Great Alpine Rd (B500), Gapsted Wines is an outstanding winery where you can eat from the seasonal lunch menu in beautiful surroundings.

Sam Miranda WINERY
(☎03-5727 3888; www.sammiranda.com.au; 1019 Snow Rd, Oxley; ⏰cellar door 10am-5pm) The unmistakable Sam Miranda has an architecturally designed tasting room and a wide range of Italian-style wines.

Milawa Mustard MUSTARD
(☎03-5727 3202; www.milawamustards.com.au; The Cross Roads, Milawa; ⏰10am-5pm) Along the main street of Milawa, Milawa Mustard offers tastings of its handmade seeded mustards, herbed vinegars and preserves.

Olive Shop OLIVES
(☎03-5727 3887; www.theoliveshop.com.au; 1605 Snow Rd, Milawa; ⏰10am-5pm) The Olive Shop has locally produced olive oil for sale as well as delicious tapenades and exotic spices.

EV Olives Groves OLIVES
(☎03-5727 0209; www.evolives.com; 203 Everton Rd, Markwood; ⏰10am-5pm) On the road from Milawa to Everton, EV Olives Groves offers the fruity taste of oils, olives and tapenades.

Sleeping & Eating

Most people exploring the Milawa region stay in Bright, Wangaratta or Myrtleford. Most of the wineries have good restaurants.

Whorouly Hotel HOTEL $
(☎03-5727 1424; www.whoroulyhotel.com; 542 Whorouly Rd, Whorouly; d $50, mains $16-28; ⏰meals 6-9pm Fri & Sat) Simple pub rooms and no-nonsense pub food best enjoyed in the beer garden) are a refreshingly down-to-earth option in Whorouly.

2 Cooks Cafe CAFE $
(☎03-5783 6110; the2cookscafe.com.au; 577 Whorouly Rd, Whorouly; mains $12.50-17.50; ⏰9am-5pm Fri-Mon, 6-9pm Fri) Whorouly is home to the 2 Cooks Cafe, a sweet deli, food store and cafe serving everything from shepherds pie to coconut beef vindaloo curry.

Milawa Gourmet Hotel MODERN AUSTRALIAN $$
(☎03-5727 3208; www.milawagourmethotel.com.au; cnr Snow & Factory Rds, Milawa; mains $15-36; ⏰noon-2.30pm & 6-8.30pm) A traditional country pub serving meals with gourmet flair and an emphasis on local produce. Try the Milawa chicken stuffed with local camembert, wrapped in bacon and served with Milawa mustard.

Getting There & Away

Milawa lies along the Snow Rd, between Wangaratta and Myrtleford. There's no public transport through the region and a car is the best way to get around.

Beechworth

POP 3559

Beechworth's historic honey-coloured granite buildings and wonderful gourmet offerings make this one of northeast Victoria's most enjoyable towns. It's also listed by the National Trust as one of Victoria's two 'notable' towns (the other is Maldon), and you'll soon see why.

Sights & Activities

Beechworth's main attraction is the group of well-preserved, honey-tinged buildings that make up the Historic & Cultural Precinct. One of the best places to begin is the **town hall** (Ford St), where you'll find the visitors centre and the free *Echoes of History* audiovisual tour.

Beechworth Courthouse HISTORIC BUILDING
(adult/child/family $8/5/16; ⊙9.30am-5pm) The Beechworth Courthouse is notable for Ned Kelly's first court appearance. See the cell where Ned was held in the basement behind the Shire Hall. Behind the courthouse is the **Old Police Station Museum** (admission $2.50; ⊙10am-2pm Fri-Sun).

Telegraph Station MUSEUM
(Ford St; admission $2.50; ⊙10am-4pm) You can send a telegram to anywhere in the world from the Telegraph Station, the original Morse-code office.

Robert O'Hara Burke Museum MUSEUM
(☎03-5728 8067; adult/child/family $8/5/16; ⊙10am-5pm) Burke Museum is named after the explorer Robert O'Hara Burke, who was the police superintendent at Beechworth from 1854 to 1858. It shows gold-rush relics and an arcade of shopfronts preserved as they were over 140 years ago.

Beechworth Honey Experience HONEY
(☎03-5728 1432; www.beechworthhoney.com.au; cnr Ford & Church Sts; ⊙9am-5pm) FREE Beechworth Honey Experience takes you into the world of honey and bees with a self-guided audiovisual tour, a live hive and honey tastings. The shop sells locally made honey, beeswax candles, nougat and soaps.

★**Sticks & Stones Adventures** OUTDOORS
(☎02-6027 1483; www.sticksandstonesadventures.com.au) This company offers some of Victoria's more intriguing excursions, with a mix of bush survival skills (learning how to start fires without a match, or finding medicinal plants) and interesting bush experiences (panning for gold or cooking damper). Wildlife and local foods also feature high on its itineraries.

> **COMBINED TICKET**
>
> If you're going to visit more than a couple of Beechworth's museums, it's worth buying the combined 'Golden Ticket' (adult/child/family $25/15/50), which can be bought online or in person through the visitor centre (p592). It covers entry over four consecutive days to most of the major sights and includes two guided tours.

Tours

Daily guided **walking tours** (adult/child/family $10/7.50/25) leave from the visitor centre and feature lots of gossip and interesting details. The Gold Rush tour is at 10.15am; the Ned Kelly tour at 1.15pm.

Beechworth Ghost Tours TOUR
(☎1300 856 668, 0447 432 816; www.beechworthghosttours.com; adult/child/family $35/20/110; ⊙8pm) Beechworth's most popular after-dark outing is Beechworth Ghost Tours, which explore the town's former lunatic asylum by lamplight, with plenty of eerie tales of murder and mayhem. There are four tours on weekends, including a midnight walk. Not suitable for children under eight.

Sleeping

Beechworth is well endowed with cottages and heritage B&Bs; check out www.beechworthonline.com.au.

Lake Sambell Caravan Park CARAVAN PARK $
(☎03-5728 1421; www.caravanparkbeechworth.com.au; Peach Dr; unpowered/powered sites from $29/35, cabins $90-170;) This shady park next to beautiful Lake Sambell has great facilities, including a camp kitchen, playground and bike hire. The sunsets reflected in the lake are spectacular.

Old Priory GUESTHOUSE $$
(☎03-5728 1024; www.oldpriory.com.au; 8 Priory Lane; dm/s/d $50/70/100, cottages $150-170) This historic convent is a spooky but charming old place. It's often used by school groups, but it's the best budget choice in Beechworth, with lovely gardens and a range of rooms, including beautifully renovated miners' cottages.

★**Freeman on Ford** B&B $$$
(☎03-5728 2371; www.freemanonford.com.au; 97 Ford St; s/d incl breakfast from $255/275; ❄) In the 1876 Oriental Bank, this sumptuous but homely place offers Victorian luxury in six beautifully renovated rooms, right in the heart of town. The owner, Heidi, will make you feel very special.

Eating & Drinking

Beechworth Bakery BAKERY $
(☎1300 233 784; www.beechworthbakery.com.au; 27 Camp St; light meals $4.50-11; ⏰6am-7pm) This popular place is the original in a well-known, statewide bakery chain. It's great for pies and pastries, cakes and sandwiches.

★**Bridge Road Brewers** PIZZA $$
(☎03-5728 2703; www.bridgeroadbrewers.com.au; Old Coach House Brewers Lane, 50 Ford St; pizzas $12-23; ⏰11am-4pm Mon-Thu, to 11pm Fri-Sun) Hiding behind the imposing Tanswells Commercial Hotel, Beechworth's gem of a microbrewery produces some excellent beers (taste 10 for $15), with nine of them on tap, and serves freshly baked pretzels and super house-made pizzas.

MURRAY TO MOUNTAINS RAIL TRAIL

The **Murray to Mountains Rail Trail** (www.murraytomountains.com.au) is Victoria's second-longest bike path and one of the High Country's best walking/cycling trails for families or casual riders. It's sealed and relatively flat much of the way, and passes through spectacular rural scenery of farms, forest and vineyards, with views of the alpine ranges.

The 94km trail runs from Wangaratta to Bright via Myrtleford and Porepunkah. A newly completed section heads northwest from Wangaratta to Wahgunyah via Rutherglen, completing the true Murray to Mountains experience.

Aficionados say the 16km between Everton and Beechworth, which detours off the main trail, is the best part of the ride (despite a challenging uphill section), as you're cycling through bush. Bikes can be hired in Wangaratta and Bright, as well as towns in between.

★**Provenance** MODERN AUSTRALIAN $$$
(☎03-5728 1786; www.theprovenance.com.au; 86 Ford St; 2-/3-course meals $63/80, degustation menu without/with matching wines $100/155; ⏰6.30pm-late Wed-Sun) In an 1856 bank building, Provenance has elegant but contemporary fine dining. Under the guidance of acclaimed local chef Michael Ryan, the innovative menu features dishes such as Berkshire pork belly, tea-smoked duck breast and some inspiring vegetarian choices. If you can't decide, go for the degustation menu. Bookings essential.

Information

Beechworth Visitor Centre (☎1300 366 321; www.beechworthonline.com.au; 103 Ford St; ⏰9am-5pm) Information and an accommodation and activity booking service in the town hall.

Getting There & Away

Beechworth is just off the Great Alpine Rd, 36km east of Wangaratta and 280km northeast of Melbourne.

V/Line (☎1800 800 007; www.vline.com.au) runs a train/bus service between Melbourne and Beechworth ($31.80, 3½ hours, three daily), with a change at Seymour or Wangaratta. There are direct buses from Wangaratta ($4.40, 35 minutes, six daily) and Bright ($9.20, 50 minutes, two daily).

Rutherglen

POP 2125

Rutherglen combines some marvellous gold-rush-era buildings (gold was discovered here in 1860) with northern Victoria's most celebrated winemaking tradition. The town itself has all the essential ingredients that merit a stopover, among them a great pie shop, antique dealers and a labyrinthine secondhand bookshop. It all adds up to an engaging destination in its own right and a good base for exploring the Murray River's Victorian hinterland.

Sights & Activities

Rutherglen Wine Experience WINERY
(☎1800 622 871; www.rutherglenvic.com; 57 Main St; ⏰9am-5pm; Ⓟ) Rutherglen Wine Experience is the in-town centrepiece for the region's wine industry. Information on local wineries and wine tasting is what it's all about.

Sleeping

Rutherglen Caravan & Tourist Park CARAVAN PARK $
(02-6032 8577; www.rutherglentouristpark.com; 72 Murray St; unpowered/powered sites from $27/34, d cabins $95-145;) This friendly park with good facilities sits on the banks of Lake King, close to the golf course and swimming pool.

★ **Tuileries** BOUTIQUE HOTEL $$
(02-6032 9033; www.tuileriesrutherglen.com.au; 13 Drummond St; d incl breakfast $199, with dinner $299;) All rooms are individually decorated in bright contemporary tones at this luxurious place next to Jolimont Cellars. There's a guest lounge, tennis court, pool and an outstanding restaurant and cafe.

Carlyle House B&B $$
(02-6032 8444; www.carlylehouse.com.au; 147 High St; r incl breakfast $150-240;) The four traditional suites and modern garden apartments are beautifully presented in this lovingly restored home. The Tokay suite boasts a private lounge.

Eating

★ **Parker Pies** BAKERY $
(02-6032 9605; www.parkerpies.com.au; 86-88 Main St; pies $5-7.50; 8am-5pm Mon-Sat, 9am-4.30pm Sun) If you think a pie is a pie, this award-winning local institution might change your mind. Try the gourmet pastries – emu, venison, crocodile, buffalo or the lovely Jolly Jumbuck (a lamb pastry with rosemary and mint).

★ **Tuileries Restaurant & Cafe** MEDITERRANEAN $$
(02-6032 9033; www.tuileriesrutherglen.com.au; 13-35 Drummond St; lunch mains $13.50, dinner $30.50-38; noon-2pm & 6.30-9pm) The bright courtyard cafe is a fine place for lunch, and in the evening the fine-dining restaurant produces superb Mediterranean-influenced dishes with local produce such as gum-smoked kangaroo fillet or Murray Valley pork belly.

Taste @ Rutherglen MODERN AUSTRALIAN $$$
(03-5728 1480; www.taste-at-rutherglen.com; 121b Main St; dinner mains $28-34, set menu without/with wines $80/130; noon-2.30pm & 6-9pm) Hip cafe by day, sophisticated restaurant by night, this place is quietly winning plaudits for its dishes such as gnocchi with rabbit and duck or Persian feta souffle.

RUTHERGLEN REDS

Rutherglen's wineries produce superb fortifieds (port, muscat and tokay) and some potent durifs and shirazes – among the biggest, baddest and strongest reds. See www.winemakers.com.au for more information.

All Saints (02-6035 2222; www.allsaintswine.com.au; All Saints Rd, Wahgunyah; 9am-5.30pm Mon-Sat, 10am-5.30pm Sun) A fairy-tale castle, the Terrace restaurant and cheese tasting.

Buller Wines (03-9936 0200; www.buller.com.au; Three Chain Rd; 9am-5pm Mon-Fri, 10am-5pm Sat & Sun) Making fine shiraz since 1921.

Rutherglen Estates (02-6032 7999; www.rutherglenestates.com.au; Tuileries Complex, 13-35 Drummond St; 10am-5.30pm) Closest winery to town with shiraz, grenache and other table wines.

Stanton & Killeen Wines (02-6032 9457; www.stantonandkilleenwines.com.au; Jacks Rd; 9am-5pm Mon-Fri, 10am-5pm Sat & Sun) Table reds, muscats and vintage ports in this century-old winery.

Warrabilla Wines (02-6035 7242; www.warrabillawines.com.au; Murray Valley Hwy; 10am-5pm) Small winery producing quality shiraz and cabernet sauvignon varieties.

Festivals & Events

Tastes of Rutherglen WINE, FOOD
Two weekends of total indulgence, with food-and-wine packages at dozens of vineyards and restaurants in March.

Winery Walkabout Weekend WINE, MUSIC
Australia's original wine festival, held in June – there's music, barrel racing and probably some wine.

Rutherglen Wine Show WINE
(www.rutherglenwineshow.com.au) Don't miss this late-September, early-October show with gourmet dinners and public tastings.

Information

Rutherglen Visitor Information Centre (1800 622 871; 57 Main St; 9am-5pm) is in the same complex as the Rutherglen Wine Experience.

WORTH A TRIP

CHILTERN

Like an old-time movie set, tiny Chiltern is one of Victoria's most historic and charming colonial townships. Its two main streets are lined with 19th-century buildings, antique shops and a couple of pubs – authentic enough that the town has been used as a set for period films, including the early Walt Disney classic *Ride a Wild Pony*. Originally called Black Dog Creek, it was established in 1851 and prospered when gold was discovered here in 1859. Pick up a copy of the *Chiltern Touring Guide* from the **Chiltern visitor centre** (☎03-5726 1611; www.chilternvic.com; 30 Main St; ⊙10am-4pm); it guides you around 20 historic sites scattered around the town.

At the rear of Chiltern's historic post office, 1950s **Linesman's Cottage** (☎03-5726 1300; www.linesmanscottage.com.au; 56 Main St; 1-/2-/3-night stay $120/220/300; ❄) retains its historic facade, but has been beautifully renovated within. With a kitchen, courtyard garden, a queen-sized bed and sofa bed, it's ideal for a family.

Chiltern is 290km northeast of Melbourne and lies just off the Hume Fwy (M31). Up to three bus or train V/Line services run here from Melbourne's Southern Cross Station ($31.80, 3¼ hours).

Getting There & Away

Rutherglen is 295km northeast of Melbourne. To get there by car, take the Hume Fwy (M31) and turn off at Chiltern.

V/Line (☎1800 800 007; www.vline.com.au) has a train and coach service between Melbourne and Rutherglen, with a change at Wangaratta ($31.80, 3½ hours, eight weekly). During festivals, bus transport to wineries can be organised through the visitor centre.

Yackandandah

POP 950

An old gold-mining town nestled in beautiful hills and valleys east of Beechworth, 'Yack', as it's universally known, is original enough to be classified by the National Trust. You might even recognise it as the setting for the 2004 film *Strange Bedfellows,* starring Paul Hogan and Michael Caton.

Sights

A stroll along the historic main street is the town's highlight. Before setting out, pick up the free *A Walk in High Street* brochure from the visitor centre.

Karrs Reef Goldmine MINE
(☎0408 975 991; adult/child $25/20; ⊙10am, 1pm & 4pm Sat & Sun) Karrs Reef Goldmine dates from 1857. On the 1½-hour guided tour you don a hard hat and descend into the original tunnels to learn a bit about the mine's history. Bookings can be made through the visitor centre.

Schmidt's Strawberry Winery WINERY
(☎02-6027 1454; 932 Osborne's Flat Rd, Allans Flat; ⊙9am-5pm Mon-Sat, 10am-4pm Sun) Fresh strawberries are on sale here from mid-October to mid-January, but what makes this place stand out are its strawberry wines. They won't be to everyone's taste, but they're unlike anything you'll try elsewhere. It's around 5km northeast of Yackandandah along the road to Baranduda.

Festivals & Events

Yackandandah Folk Festival MUSIC
(http://folkfestival.yackandandah.com) The biggest event of the year: three days of music, parades, workshops and fun in mid- to late March.

Sleeping & Eating

Yackandandah Holiday Park CARAVAN PARK $
(☎02-6027 1380; www.yhp.com.au; Taymac Dr; powered sites $32-43, cabins $105-170) Beside pretty Yackandandah Creek, but close to town, this well-equipped park is a little oasis of greenery and autumn colours.

Star Hotel PUB $$
(☎02-6027 1493; 30 High St; mains $17-21; ⊙noon-late Fri-Sun, 3pm-late Mon-Thu) This 1863 hotel, known locally as the 'Top Pub', has good bistro meals that range from a mixed grill or steak sandwich to vegetarian lasagne or red chicken curry.

Shopping

Many of the historic shops in the main street contain galleries, antiques and curios.

Kirby's Flat Pottery CERAMICS
(☎02-6027 1416; www.johndermer.com.au; 225 Kirby's Flat Rd; ⏰10.30am-5.30pm Sat & Sun) This studio-cum-gallery-cum-shop is 4km south of Yackandandah. Even if you're not interested in buying, the gallery contains a stunning collcction.

Information

Yackandandah Visitor Centre (☎02-6027 1988; www.uniqueyackandandah.com.au; 27 High St; ⏰9am-5pm) In the grand 1878 Athenaeum building.

Getting There & Away

Yackandandah is 307km northeast of Melbourne; take the Hume Fwy to the Great Alpine Rd exit north of Wangaratta then follow the signs to Beechworth. From here it's a further 22km into Yackandandah.

Myrtleford

POP 2707

Along the Great Alpine Rd, near the foothills of Mt Buffalo, Myrtleford is a 'Gateway to the Alps' and a worthwhile stop if you're heading to the snowfields or exploring the gourmet region.

Sights & Activities

Myrtleford Butter Factory BUTTER
(☎03-5752 2300; www.thebutterfactory.com.au; Great Alpine Rd; ⏰10am-4pm Mon-Fri, 9am-5pm Sat & Sun) This butter factory and produce store is in an old butter factory, and you can still see butter being churned here. There are 45-minute guided tours of the factory at 11am on Thursday ($8). The produce store stocks a wide range of local products, including more uses for butter than you could ever have imagined.

Myrtleford Cycle Centre BICYCLE RENTAL
(☎03-5752 1511; www.myrtlefordcycle.com; 59 Clyde St; per day/weekend $25/45; ⏰9am-5.30pm Tue-Sat, 10am-2pm Sun) Rents bikes and helmets.

Sleeping

Myrtleford Caravan Park CARAVAN PARK $
(☎03-5752 1598; www.myrtlefordholidaypark.com.au; Lewis Ave; unpowered/powered sites from $26/28, dm $29, cabins $86-138; ❄) Grassy sites, well-maintained cabins, kids playground and a 40-bed bunkhouse for groups or backpackers.

Motel on Alpine MOTEL $$
(☎03-5752 1438; www.motelonalpine.com; 258 Great Alpine Rd; d/f incl breakfast from $130/195; ❄📶🏊) Quality motel close to the town centre with a pool and spa, manicured garden and a highly regarded restaurant.

Information

Myrtleford Visitor Centre (☎03-5755 0514; www.visitmyrtleford.com; 38 Myrtle St; ⏰9am-5pm) Information and a booking service for the nearby ski fields. Ask for the *Myrtleford Discovery Trail Guide*, which outlines historical sites around town.

Getting There & Away

Myrtleford lies 296km northeast of Melbourne. The easiest access road is the Great Alpine Rd (B500) between Wangaratta (46km) and Bright (30km).

Mt Buffalo National Park

Beautiful Mt Buffalo is an easily accessible year-round destination: in winter it's a tiny, family-friendly ski resort with gentle runs, and in summer it's a great spot for bushwalking, mountain biking and rock climbing.

It was named in 1824 by the explorers Hume and Hovell on their trek from Sydney to Port Phillip – they thought its bulky shape resembled a buffalo – and declared a national park in 1898.

Sights & Activities

You'll find granite outcrops, lookouts, streams, waterfalls, wild flowers and wildlife here. The **Big Walk**, an 11km, five-hour ascent of the mountain, starts from Eurobin Creek picnic area, north of Porepunkah, and finishes at the Gorge day visitor area. A road leads to just below the summit of the Horn (1723m), the highest point on the massif. Nearby **Lake Catani** is good for swimming, canoeing and camping. There are 14km of groomed **cross-country ski trails** starting out from the Cresta Valley car park, as well as a **tobogganing area**. In summer Mt Buffalo is a **hang-gliding** paradise, and the near-vertical walls of the Gorge provide some of Australia's most challenging **rock climbing**.

Mt Buffalo Olives OLIVES
(☎03-5756 2143; www.mtbuffaloolives.com.au; 307 Mt Buffalo Rd, Porepunkah; ⏰11am-5pm

Fri-Mon & daily during school holidays) On the road up to Mt Buffalo from Porepunkah, this working olive grove has tastings and sales of olives, olive oils and other locally farmed products. It also has a lovely place to stay ($180 a night Sunday to Thursday, $220 Friday and Saturday, two-night minimum stay).

Adventure Guides Australia OUTDOORS
(☎0419 280 614; www.visitmountbuffalo.com.au) This established operator offers abseiling (from $90), rock climbing (from $88) and caving with glow-worms through an underground river system (from $120). It also runs a cross-country ski school in winter.

Sleeping

Lake Catani Campground CAMPGROUND $
(per site from $46.30; ⊙Nov-Apr) A summer camping ground with toilets and showers. Book through **Parks Victoria** (☎13 19 63; www.parkweb.vic.gov.au).

Getting There & Away

The main access road is out of Porepunkah, between Myrtleford and Bright.

Bright

POP 2165

Famous for its glorious autumn colours, Bright is a popular year-round destination in the foothills of the alps and a gateway to Mt Hotham and Falls Creek. Skiers make a beeline through Bright in winter, but it's a lovely base for exploring the Alpine National Park, paragliding, fishing and kayaking on local rivers, bushwalking and exploring the region's wineries. Plentiful accommodation and some sophisticated restaurants and cafes complete the rather-appealing picture.

Activities

Bright is a base for all sorts of adventure activities, including paragliding – enthusiasts catch the thermals from nearby Mystic Mountain.

Murray to Mountains Rail Trail CYCLING
(www.murraytomountains.com.au) The Murray to Mountains Rail Trail between Bright and Wangaratta starts (or ends) behind the old train station. Bikes, tandems and baby trailers can be rented from **Cyclepath** (☎03-5750 1442; www.cyclepath.com.au; 74 Gavan St; per hour/half day/full day from $20/24/32, per day mountain/road bikes $44/60; ⊙9am-5.30pm Mon-Fri, 9.30am-4pm Sat & Sun).

Active Flight ADVENTURE SPORTS
(☎0428 854 455; www.activeflight.com.au) Introductory paragliding course (from $265) or tandem flights (from $150).

Alpine Paragliding ADVENTURE SPORTS
(☎0428 352 048; www.alpineparagliding.com; ⊙Oct-Jun) Tandem flights from Mystic Mountain ($130) and two-day courses ($500).

Alpine Gravity MOUNTAIN BIKING
(☎03-5758 3393; www.alpinegravity.net; 100 Gavan St; half-/full-day tours $60/75) This experienced operator runs a mountain-biking festival in mid-November and spends the rest of the year taking people out onto the trails on half-, full- and multi-day tours.

Courses

★**Patrizia Simone Country Cooking School** COOKING COURSE
(☎03-5755 2266; www.simonesbright.com.au; 98 Gavan St; per person $180) One of northeastern Victoria's most celebrated chefs, Patrizia Simone runs fabulous four-hour cooking classes centred around Italian (especially Umbrian) cooking techniques using local ingredients. Her signature class is 'Umbrian Experience', which touches on some of the recipes from Patrizia's cookbook, *My Umbrian Kitchen*.

Festivals & Events

Bright Autumn Festival STREET CARNIVAL
(www.brightautumnfestival.org.au) Open gardens, scenic convoy tours and a popular gala day; held April or May.

Bright Spring Festival STREET CARNIVAL
(www.brightspringfestival.com.au) Celebrate all things Bright and beautiful over the Melbourne Cup weekend and beyond in late October/early November.

Sleeping

There's an abundance of accommodation here, but rooms are scarce during the holiday seasons. If you're stuck, check out **Bright Escapes** (☎1300 551 117; www.brightescapes.com.au; 76a Gavan St) or **Bright Holiday Accommodation** (www.brightholidays.com.au).

NED KELLY

Bushranger and outlaw he may have been, but Ned Kelly is probably Australia's greatest folk hero. His life and death have been embraced as part of the national culture – from Sidney Nolan's famous paintings to Peter Carey's Man Booker Prize–winning novel *True History of the Kelly Gang* – and a symbol of the Australian rebel character.

Born in 1855, Ned was first arrested in Benalla when he was 14 and spent the next 10 years in and out of jails. In 1878 a warrant was issued for his arrest for stealing horses, so he and his brother Dan went into hiding. Their mother and two friends were arrested, sentenced and imprisoned for aiding and abetting. The Kelly family had long felt persecuted by the authorities, and the jailing of Mrs Kelly was the last straw.

Ned and Dan were joined in their hideout in the Wombat Ranges, near Mansfield, by Steve Hart and Joe Byrne. Four policemen (Kennedy, Lonigan, Scanlon and McIntyre) came looking for them and, in a shootout at Stringybark Creek, Ned killed Kennedy, Lonigan and Scanlon. McIntyre escaped to Mansfield and raised the alarm.

The government put up a £500 reward for any of the gang members, dead or alive. In December 1878 the gang held up the National Bank at Euroa, and got away with £2000. Then in February 1879, they took over the police station at Jerilderie, locked the two policemen in the cells and robbed the Bank of New South Wales wearing the policemen's uniforms. By this time the reward was £2000 a head.

On 27 June 1880 the gang held 60 people captive in a hotel at Glenrowan. A trainload of police and trackers was sent from Melbourne. Ned's plan to destroy the train was foiled when a schoolteacher warned the police. Surrounded, the gang holed up in the hotel and returned fire for hours, wearing heavy armour made from ploughshares. Ned was shot in the legs and captured, and Dan Kelly, Joe Byrne and Steve Hart, along with several of their hostages, were killed.

Ned Kelly was brought to Melbourne and tried, and then hanged on 11 November 1880. He met his end bravely; his last words are famously quoted as, 'Such is life'. His death mask, armour and the gallows on which he died are on display in the Old Melbourne Gaol (p479).

Of all the towns associated with Ned Kelly, it's **Glenrowan**, a short detour off the Hume Fwy, that makes the most of it. For a start, you can't drive through Glenrowan without being confronted by the legend, including a 2m-high, armour-clad statue. The main sites of the capture are signposted, so pick up a walking map and follow the trail.

Ned Kelly Museum & Homestead (☎03-5766 2448; 35 Gladstone St, Glenrowan; adult/child $6/1; ⏲9am-5.30pm) Behind Kate's Cottage with the same owners, you'll find this museum displaying Kelly memorabilia and artefacts gathered from all over the district, plus a replica of the Kelly home. An undercover picnic area makes it a welcome stop just off the Hume.

Ned Kelly's Last Stand (☎03-5766 2367; www.glenrowantouristcentre.com.au; 41 Gladstone St, Glenrowan; adult/child/family $27/20/90; ⏲9.30am-4.30pm, shows every 30min) At the Glenrowan Tourist Centre, Ned Kelly's Last Stand is an over-the-top animated performance where Ned's story is told in a series of rooms by a cast of surprisingly lifelike animatronic characters and culminating in a smoky shootout and the hanging (it may be too scary for young children).

You can browse the shop and small exhibition of memorabilia and paintings for free. You can also pick up a map here detailing the important sites leading up to the shootout.

Bright Holiday Park CARAVAN PARK $

(☎03-5755 1141; www.brightholidaypark.com.au; Cherry Lane; unpowered/powered sites from $32/37, cabins $115-240; 📶) Straddling pretty Morses Creek, this lovely park is five minutes' walk to the shops. The riverside spa cabins are very nice.

★**Odd Frog** BOUTIQUE HOTEL $$

(☎0418 362 791; www.theoddfrog.com; 3 McFadyens Lane; d $150-195, q $250) 🌿These contemporary, ecofriendly studios feature light, breezy spaces and fabulous outdoor decks with a telescope for stargazing. The design features clever use of the hilly site

WORTH A TRIP

CORRYONG & THE MAN FROM SNOWY RIVER

You've seen the film and probably read Banjo Paterson's famous poem, but out at Corryong, close to the source of the Murray River, they live the legend. Corryong is a pretty township ringed by mountains – a natural playground for trout fishing, canoeing, cycling and bushwalking.

Man From Snowy River Museum (☎03-6076 2600; www.manfromsnowyrivermuseum.com; 103 Hanson St, Corryong; adult/child $5/1; ⊙10am-4pm Sep-May, 11am-3pm Jun-Aug) The Man From Snowy River Museum tells the story of Jack Riley, a stockman who lived and worked near Corryong and might have been Paterson's inspiration. It's also a local-history museum, featuring a set of snow skis from 1870 and the Jarvis Homestead, a 19th-century slab-timber hut.

Jack Riley's Grave (Corryong Cemetery) Jack Riley's grave, in the town cemetery, is inscribed with the words, 'In memory of the Man from Snowy River, Jack Riley, buried here 16th July 1914'.

Man From Snowy River Bush Festival (☎02-6076 1992; www.manfromsnowyriverbushfestival.com.au; ⊙Mar-Apr) It looked like so much fun in the film the locals just had to try it – mountain horse racing where 'the hills are twice as steep and twice as rough'. Yes, it's the Country Wide Challenge, Australia's ultimate test of horse-riding prowess! The race is a feature of this festival – four days of whip-cracking and yarn-spinning fun.

Corryong Visitor Centre (☎03-6076 2277; 50 Hanson St, Corryong; ⊙9am-5pm) Has info on the region.

with sculptural steel-frame foundations and flying balconies.

Coach House Inn MOTEL **$$**
(☎1800 813 992; www.coachhousebright.com.au; 100 Gavan St; s/d from $85/105, apt $125-205; ❄≋) This central place has simple but super-value rooms and self-contained units for two to six people. In winter there's a ski-hire shop with discounts for guests, and the popular **Lawlers Hut Restaurant** is next door. High-season surcharge is a flat $22 per unit.

Aalborg APARTMENT **$$$**
(☎0401 357 329; www.aalborgbright.com.au; 6 Orchard Ct; r $220-250; 📶) Clean-lined Scandinavian design with plenty of pine-and-white furnishings dominate this gorgeous place. Every fitting is perfectly chosen and abundant glass opens out onto sweeping bush views. There's a minimum two-night stay.

Eating & Drinking

Blackbird Café & Food Store CAFE **$**
(☎03-5750 1838; www.blackbirdfood.com.au; 95 Gavan St; mains $8-21; ⊙8am-4pm) Newspapers spread across couches and coffee tables, while locals mingle with tourists in this light-filled corner cafe that captures the essence of laid-back, food-loving Bright. The baked Harrietville trout caught our eye.

★**Pepperleaf Bushtucker Restaurant** MODERN AUSTRALIAN **$$**
(☎03-5755 1537; 2a Anderson St; 1/10 tapas $8/70, mains $18-30; ⊙noon-2pm & 6pm-late Fri-Tue, breakfast weekends) This place doesn't look fancy but the philosophy and flavours – using native ingredients such as wattleseed, quandong, wild limes and lemon myrtle – are something of a taste revelation. Mains range from salt-and-pepper crocodile to wallaby and chorizo.

★**Simone's Restaurant** ITALIAN **$$$**
(☎03-5755 2266; www.simonesbright.com.au; 98 Gavan St; mains $37-40, vegetarian/nonvegetarian tasting menu $85/95; ⊙6.30-10pm Tue-Sat) For 20 years owner-chef Patrizia Simone has been serving outstanding Italian food, with a focus on local ingredients and seasonal produce, in the rustic dining room of this heritage-listed house. This is one of regional Victoria's great restaurants and well worth the splurge. Bookings are essential.

★**Bright Brewery** BREWERY
(☎03-5755 1301; www.brightbrewery.com.au; 121 Gavan St; ⊙noon-10pm; 📶) This small boutique brewery produces a quality range of beers (sample six for $12) and beer-friendly food such as pizzas, kranskys and nachos. There's a guided tour and tasting on Monday, Friday and Saturday at 3pm ($18) and

live blues on Sunday, or you can learn to be a brewer for a day ($360).

Information

Alpine Visitor Information Centre (☎1800 111 885, 03-5755 0584; www.brightvictoria.com.au; 119 Gavan St; ⊙9am-5pm) Has a busy accommodation booking service, Parks Victoria information and cafe.

Getting There & Away

Bright is 310km northeast of Melbourne.

Snowball Express (☎1300 656 546; www.snowballexpress.com.au) During the ski season the Snowball Express operates from Bright to Mt Hotham (adult/child return $50/40, 1½ hours).

V/Line (☎1800 800 007; www.vline.com.au) V/Line runs train/coach services from Melbourne ($33, 4½ hours, two daily) with a change at Wangaratta.

Mt Beauty & the Kiewa Valley

POP 1654

Huddled at the foot of Victoria's highest mountain, Mt Bogong (1986m), on the Kiewa River, Mt Beauty and its twin villages of Tawonga and Tawonga South are the gateways to Falls Creek ski resort. It's reached by a steep and winding road from Bright, with some lovely alpine views.

Sights & Activities

Annapurna Estate WINERY
(☎03-5754 4517; www.annapurnaestate.com.au; 217 Simmonds Creek Rd, Tawonga South; ⊙11am-4pm Fri-Sun) Annapurna Estate, about 3km from Mt Beauty, is a stunning vineyard with cellar-door sales and a **restaurant** where you can dine on the lovely deck.

Rocky Valley Bikes BICYCLE RENTAL
(☎03-5754 1118; www.rockyvalley.com.au; Kiewa Valley Hwy; bicycle hire per hour $20, cross-country bicycle per half/full day $35/50) Rocky Valley Bikes hires mountain and cross-country bikes in summer and snow-sports equipment in the white season.

Bogong Horseback Adventures HORSE RIDING
(☎03-5754 4849; www.bogonghorse.com.au; Mountain Creek Rd, Tawonga; 2/3hr ride $90/110, full day with lunch $220) Horse riders can experience this beautiful area on horseback with Bogong Horseback Adventures. It's 12km northwest of Tawonga.

Festivals & Events

Mt Beauty Music Festival MUSIC
(www.musicmuster.org.au) The Mt Beauty Music Festival in April brings together folk, blues and country musicians.

Sleeping

Mt Beauty Holiday Centre CARAVAN PARK $
(☎03-5754 4396; www.holidaycentre.com.au; Kiewa Valley Hwy; unpowered/powered sites $30/35, cabins & yurts $80-150; ❄📶) This family caravan park close to Mt Beauty town centre has river frontage, games and an interesting range of cabins, including hexagonal 'yurts'.

★ **Dreamers** APARTMENT $$$
(☎03-5754 1222; www.dreamersmtbeauty.com.au; Kiewa Valley Hwy, Mt Beauty; d $200-490; 📶) 🍃 Each of Dreamer's stunning self-contained eco apartments offers something special and architecturally unique. Sunken lounges, open fireplaces, loft bedrooms and balcony spas are just some of the highlights. Great views and a pretty lagoon complete a dreamily romantic five-star experience.

Eating

★ **A Skafferi** SWEDISH $$
(☎03-5754 4544; www.svarmisk.com.au; 84 Bogong High Plains Rd, Mt Beauty; mains $12-21; ⊙8am-4pm Thu-Mon) This cool Swedish pantry and food store is a fabulous place to stop. Try the grilled Milawa cheese sandwiches for breakfast and the Swedish meatballs or the sampler of herring and *knackebrod* for lunch. It sells a range of local and Scandinavian produce, and has some excellent **apartments** (1-/2-/3-bedroom apt $295/365/515), too.

Roi's Diner Restaurant ITALIAN $$
(☎03-5754 4495; 177 Kiewa Valley Hwy; mains $27-34; ⊙6.30-9.30pm Thu-Sun) It's hard to believe this unassuming timber shack on the highway 5km from Mt Beauty is an award-winning restaurant, specialising in exceptional modern-Italian cuisine. Great risotto, eye-fillet carpaccio or the surprising roasted pork chop.

Information

Mt Beauty Visitor Centre (☎1800 111 885, 03-5755 0596; www.visitmountbeauty.com.au; 31 Bogong High Plains Rd; ⊙9am-5pm) Has an accommodation booking service, displays on the history and nature of the region and advice on local walks.

Getting There & Away

In winter **Falls Creek Coach Service** (☎03-5754 4024; www.fallscreekcoachservice.com.au) operates direct buses to Mt Beauty from Melbourne on Wednesday, Friday, Saturday and Sunday (one way/return $85/134), and from Albury from Thursday to Sunday ($34/53), both continuing on to Falls Creek.

V/Line (☎1800 800 007; www.vline.com.au) operates a train/bus/taxi service from Melbourne to Mt Beauty ($37.20, 5½ hours), via Wangaratta and Bright.

Falls Creek

ELEV 1780M

Victoria's glitzy, fashion-conscious resort, Falls Creek combines a picturesque alpine setting with impressive skiing and infamous après-ski entertainment.

Activities

Skiing at Falls Creek is spread over two areas – the **Village Bowl** and **Sun Valley** – with 19 lifts, a vertical drop of 267m and Australia's longest beginner's run at **Wombat's Ramble**. Falls is also the free-ride snowboard capital, with four parks. **Night skiing** in the Village Bowl operates several times a week. For information on other winter activities, call the **activities hotline** (☎1800 204 424).

The **Summit chairlift** operates during the summer school holidays (per ride/day $15/25). **Mountain biking** is popular here in the green season with downhill trails, three lift-accessed trails, spur fire trails, aqueduct trails, road circuits and bike rental (from $55 per day).

The best local **hiking trails** include the walk to **Wallace Hut**, built in 1889, and said to be the oldest cattleman's hut in the High Country; and **Rocky Valley Lake**.

FALLS CREEK ACCOMMODATION

Falls Creek Central Reservations (☎1800 033 079; www.fallscreek.com.au/centralreservations) Accommodation bookings.

Falls Creek Reservation Centre (☎1800 453 525; www.fallscreek.com.au/ResCentre) A clearing house for Falls Creek accommodation.

Packers High Country Horse Riding HORSE RIDING
(☎03-5159 7241; www.horsetreks.com; Anglers Rest; 1½ hr/half-/full-day ride $80/150/250) Packers High Country Horse Riding, based at Anglers Rest on the road to Omeo, offers true High Country riding through river valleys and snowgum forests.

Festivals & Events

Mile High Dragon Boat Festival CULTURAL
(www.fallscreek.com.au/dragonboats) Gorgeous, glorious dragon boats race on Rocky Valley Lake. Held from 26 to 27 January.

Easter Festival FOOD
(www.fallscreek.com.au/easterfestival) A giant Easter egg hunt.

Sleeping

Most lodges in Falls Creek have a minimum two-night stay, particularly on weekends.

Alpha Lodge LODGE $
(☎03-5758 3488; www.alphaskilodge.com.au; dm summer/winter from $61/159) A spacious, affordable lodge with a sauna, a large lounge with panoramic views and a communal kitchen.

Frueauf Village APARTMENT $$$
(☎1300 300 709; www.fvfallscreek.com.au; 4 Schuss St; d 2 nights from $400; wi-fi) These luxurious, architect-designed apartments have everything, including private outdoor hot tubs and the funky **Milch Cafe Wine Bar**.

Eating & Drinking

Three Blue Ducks CAFE $$
(☎03-5758 3863; www.huski.com.au; 3 Sitzmark St; mains $12-16; ⏲7.30am-11pm Jun-Sep) Chic store and cafe with great casual dining, coffee and High Country produce.

The Gully by Three Blue Ducks MODERN AUSTRALIAN $$
(☎03-5758 3863; www.thegully.com.au; 3 Sitzmark St; lunch mains $14-25, dinner $35; ⏲7.30am-9.30pm) At Huski Luxury Apartments, this fine restaurant takes the same fresh approach to cooking as its sister cafe, Three Blue Ducks. Highlights when we passed through included beetroot risotto and salt-roasted local rainbow trout.

Man Hotel PUB
(☎03-5758 3362; www.themanfallscreek.com; 20 Slalom St; ⏲4pm-late) 'The Man' has been around forever, is open all year and is the heart of Falls' nightlife. In winter it fires up as a club, cocktail bar and live-music venue featuring popular Aussie bands. Good pub dinners and pizzas are available.

Information

Ski season daily resort entry is $20 to $45 per car. One-day lift tickets per adult/child cost $113/57. Combined adult lift-and-lesson packages cost $178. Lift tickets also cover Mt Hotham.

Falls Creek Resort Management (☎03-5758 1202; www.fallscreek.com.au; 1 Slalom St; ⏲8.30am-5pm daily winter, 9am-5pm Mon-Fri, 10am-3pm Sat & Sun summer) Has informative pamphlets, including *Crosscountry* (about ski trails that are also good for summer walking).

Getting There & Around

Falls Creek is 375km – a 4½-hour drive – from Melbourne.

Falls Creek Coach Service (☎03-5754 4024; www.fallscreekcoachservice.com.au) operates four times a week between Falls Creek and Melbourne (one way/return $80/140) during winter and also runs services to and from Albury ($60/95) and Mt Beauty ($37/58). There's a reduced service in summer.

An over-snow taxi service ($40 return) operates between the car parks and the lodges from 7am to midnight daily (to 2am Friday night, to 1am Saturday and Sunday). Car parking for day visitors is at the base of the village, next to the ski lifts.

Mt Hotham & Dinner Plain

ELEV 1868M

Serious hikers, skiers and snowboarders make tracks for Mt Hotham, which has some of the best and most challenging downhill runs in the country.

Activities

Mt Hotham is home to 320 hectares of downhill runs, with a vertical drop of 428m. About 80% of the ski trails are intermediate or advanced black-diamond runs. Beginners hit the Big D, which is open for **night skiing** every Wednesday and Saturday in winter.

Over at Dinner Plain, 10km from Hotham village and linked by a free shuttle, there are excellent **cross-country trails** around the village, including the Hotham–Dinner Plain Ski Trail. At least six operators offer ski and other equipment hire; the visitor centres have full lists of outlets, or visit www.mthotham.com.au. From November to May, Hotham and Dinner Plain boast some stunning alpine trails for **hiking** and **mountain biking**.

> **MT HOTHAM BOOKING AGENCIES**
>
> **Mt Hotham Accommodation Service** (☎1800 032 061; www.mthotham accommodation.com.au) Books mountain accommodation during the ski season.
>
> **Dinner Plain Accommodation** (☎1800 444 066, 03-5159 6696; www.accommdinnerplain.com.au; Big Muster Dr, Dinner Plain) Booking agency for Dinner Plain.
>
> **Dinner Plain Central Reservations** (☎1800 670 019; www.dinnerplain.com; Big Muster Dr, Dinner Plain) Accommodation booking service for Dinner Plain.

Festivals

Cool Summer Festival MUSIC
(www.coolsummerfestival.com) Three days of music in the middle of nowhere. Held in January or February.

Sleeping

Ski-season accommodation generally requires a minimum two-night stay.

Leeton Lodge LODGE $
(☎03-5759 3283; www.leetonlodge.com; Dargo Ct, Mt Hotham; dm summer $45, winter $65-85) Classic family ski-club lodge with 30 beds, cooking facilities and good views. Open year-round.

General Lodge LODGE $$$
(☎03-5759 3523; www.thegeneral.com.au; Great Alpine Rd, Mt Hotham; 1- & 2-bedroom apt from $350) Behind the General pub are these brand-new, fully self-contained apartments with lounge and kitchen and views.

Arlberg Resort APARTMENT $$$
(☎03-5986 8200; www.arlberghotham.com.au; Mt Hotham; d 2 nights from $430-870; 📶🏊) The largest resort on the mountain, the Arlberg has a large range of apartments and motel-style rooms, plus restaurants, bars, ski hire and a heated pool. Ski season only.

Eating

In winter there are plenty of great eating choices at Mt Hotham. In summer a couple of places serve meals and the small supermarket at the General is open.

General PUB FOOD **$$**
(03-5759 3523; Great Alpine Rd, Mt Hotham; meals $12-32; noon-2pm & 6-8.30pm) The ever-reliable 'Gen' is open all year and is a popular watering hole, with a menu of pizzas and good bistro meals.

Dinner Plain Hotel PUB FOOD **$$**
(03-5159 6462; www.dinnerplainhotel.com.au; Dinner Plain; mains $10-29; noon-2pm & 6-9pm) This pub is the social hub of Dinner Plain and is a friendly place to hang out, with a bistro serving good pub grub and pizzas.

★**Graze** MODERN AUSTRALIAN **$$$**
(03-5159 6422; www.rundells.com.au; 12 Big Muster Dr, Dinner Plain; mains $35-45, 5-course tasting menu without/with wine $89/134; 12.30-2.30pm & 6-8.30pm Jun-Sep, 6-8.30pm Tue-Sat Mar-May) Easily the best restaurant in the area, Graze chef Leigh Irish uses local produce: dishes might include braised Milawa duck or Ovens Valley cured venison carpaccio.

Information

The ski-season admission fee is $40 per car per day, and $15 for bus passengers (this may be included in your fare). Lift tickets (peak) per adult/student/child cost $120/100/58. Passes are cheaper in September and there are packages that include gear hire and lessons. Lift tickets also cover Falls Creek.

Dinner Plain Visitor Centre (1300 734 365; www.visitdinnerplain.com) In the village centre.

Mt Hotham Alpine Resort Management Board (03-5759 3550; www.mthotham.com.au) At the village administration centre. Collect a range of brochures with maps for short, eco, heritage and village walks.

Getting There & Around

Mt Hotham is 360km northeast of Melbourne. By car take the Hume Fwy to Wangaratta, then follow the Great Alpine Rd to Mt Hotham.

Mt Hotham Airport (03-5159 6777) Mt Hotham Airport services Mt Hotham and Dinner Plain, but it's currently only served in winter by **QantasLink** (www.qantas.com.au) from Sydney and by charter flights.

Snowball Express (03-9370 9055, 1800 659 009; www.snowballexpress.com.au) During the ski season Snowball Express has daily buses from Melbourne to Mt Hotham ($164 return, six hours) via Wangaratta, Myrtleford, Bright and Harrietville.

A free shuttle runs frequently around the Mt Hotham resort from 7am to 3am. A separate shuttle service also operates to Dinner Plain.

Omeo

POP 487

High in the hills, historic Omeo is a pretty town reached after the winding drive up from the coast or down from the mountains. This is the southern access route to Mt Hotham and Falls Creek and the main town on the eastern section of the Great Alpine Rd. The road can be snowbound in winter, so always check conditions before leaving.

Sleeping & Eating

Omeo Caravan Park CARAVAN PARK **$**
(03-5159 1351; www.omeocaravanpark.com.au; Old Omeo Hwy; unpowered/powered sites $30/35, d cabins from $100) In a pretty valley alongside the Livingstone Creek about 2km from town, this park has spacious, grassy sites. This is also the base for **Howling Husky Sled Dog Tours** (www.howlinghuskys.com.au), which offers short local rides and longer weekend packages at Mt Baw Baw.

Golden Age Hotel HOTEL **$**
(03-5159 1344; www.goldenageomeo.com.au; Day Ave; s/d from $50/80, d with spa $160) This beautiful art deco corner pub dominates Omeo's main street. Upstairs are simple but elegant pub rooms, some with en suite and spa. The welcoming **restaurant** (mains $15-25) serves plates piled high with steaks, salads and gourmet pizzas.

Information

Omeo Visitor Information Centre (03-5159 1455; www.omeoregion.com.au; 179 Day Ave; 8.30am-5pm Mon-Fri, 10am-2pm Sat & Sun) Friendly visitor centre in the library.

Getting There & Away

Omeo is 400km from Melbourne.

O'Connell's Bus Lines (0428 591 377; www.omeobus.com.au) Operates a daily summer 'Alps Link' service between Omeo and Bright ($11) via Mt Hotham ($5.40) and Dinner Plain ($4.40). A winter service to Dinner Plain and Mt Hotham operates on Sunday, Wednesday and Friday.

Omeo Bus Lines (0427 017 732) Runs one bus on weekdays between Omeo and Bairnsdale ($22, two hours).

Northwest Victoria

Includes ➡

Best Places to Eat

- Jim McDougall in Stefano's Cellar (p609)
- Spoons Riverside Café (p611)
- Shebani's (p615)
- Fish in a Flash (p615)

Best Places to Stay

- Houseboat in Echuca (p615)
- Quality Hotel Mildura Grand (p608)
- Adelphi Boutique Apartments (p615)
- Indulge Apartments (p608)

Why Go?

The mighty Murray River is Australia's longest and most important inland waterway, and arrayed along its banks are some of Victoria's most captivating towns. It's a stirring place of wineries and orchards, bush camping, balmy weather and river red gum forests. The Murray changes character constantly along its 2400km route. Here, history looms large in towns such as Echuca, food and wine dominate proceedings around Mildura, and national parks enclose soulful desert expanses in the far northwest. It's a world of picturesque river beaches, of paddle steamers that were once the lifeblood of Victoria's inland settlements, and of unending horizons that serve as a precursor to the true outback not far away. It's an intriguing, if relatively far-flung mix, one that enables you to follow in the footsteps of some of Australia's earliest explorers who travelled along the river.

When to Go

Mildura

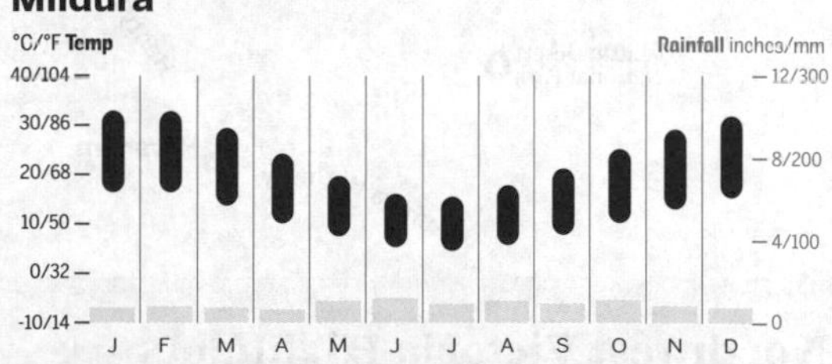

Anytime The Murray region, especially Mildura, enjoys year-round sunshine.

Sep–Nov Spring sees some of the best local festivals, without the heat.

Feb–Mar A good time for camping by the river after the holiday crowds have left.

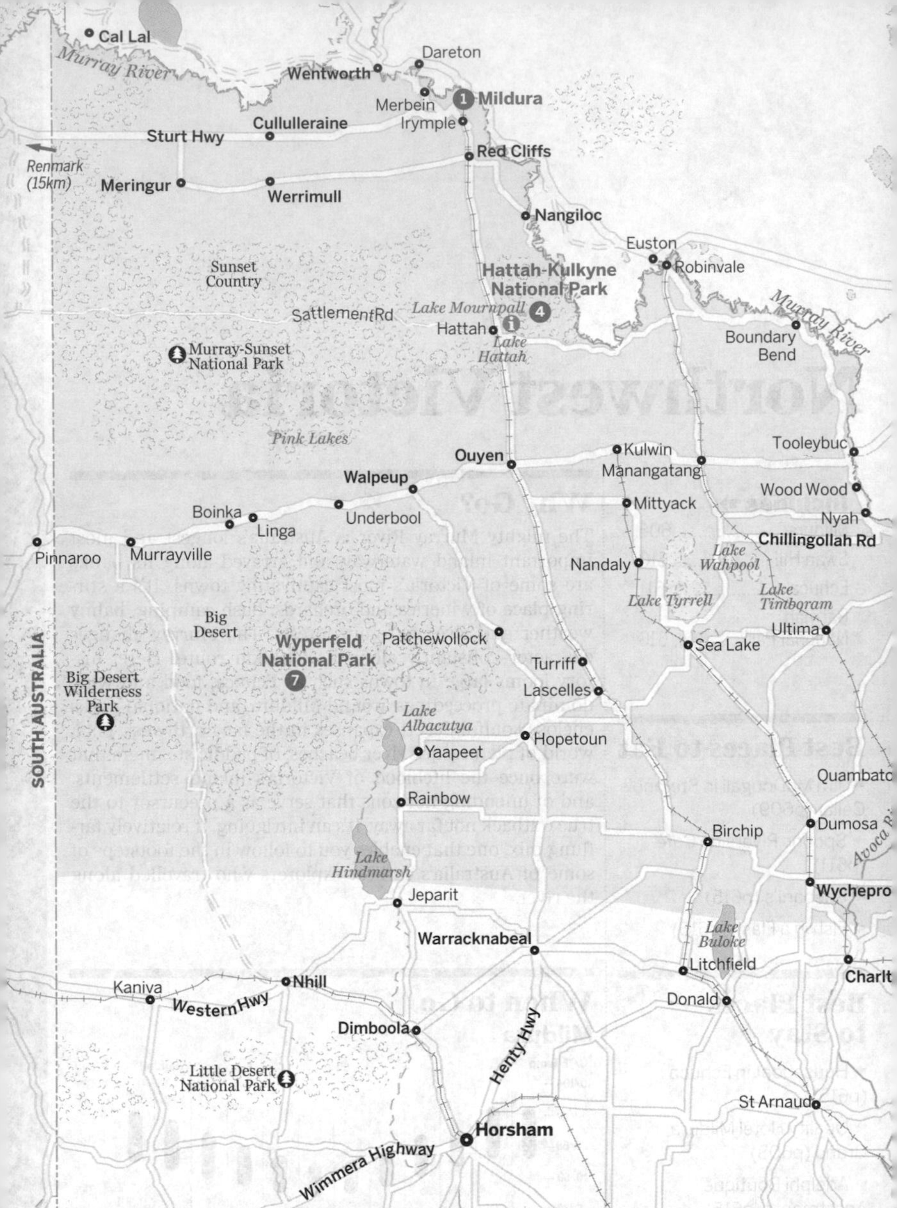

Northwest Victoria Highlights

1. Relaxing on a houseboat and dining out on 'Feast Street' in sunny **Mildura** (p606).

2. Riding a paddle steamer down the Murray for lunch at a winery in **Echuca** (p611).

3. Exploring Echuca's past in the new **discovery centre** (p612), old wharf area and historic Murray Esplanade in the Port of Echuca.

4. Spotting the many species of waterbirds at beautiful **Hattah-Kulkyne National Park** (p610).

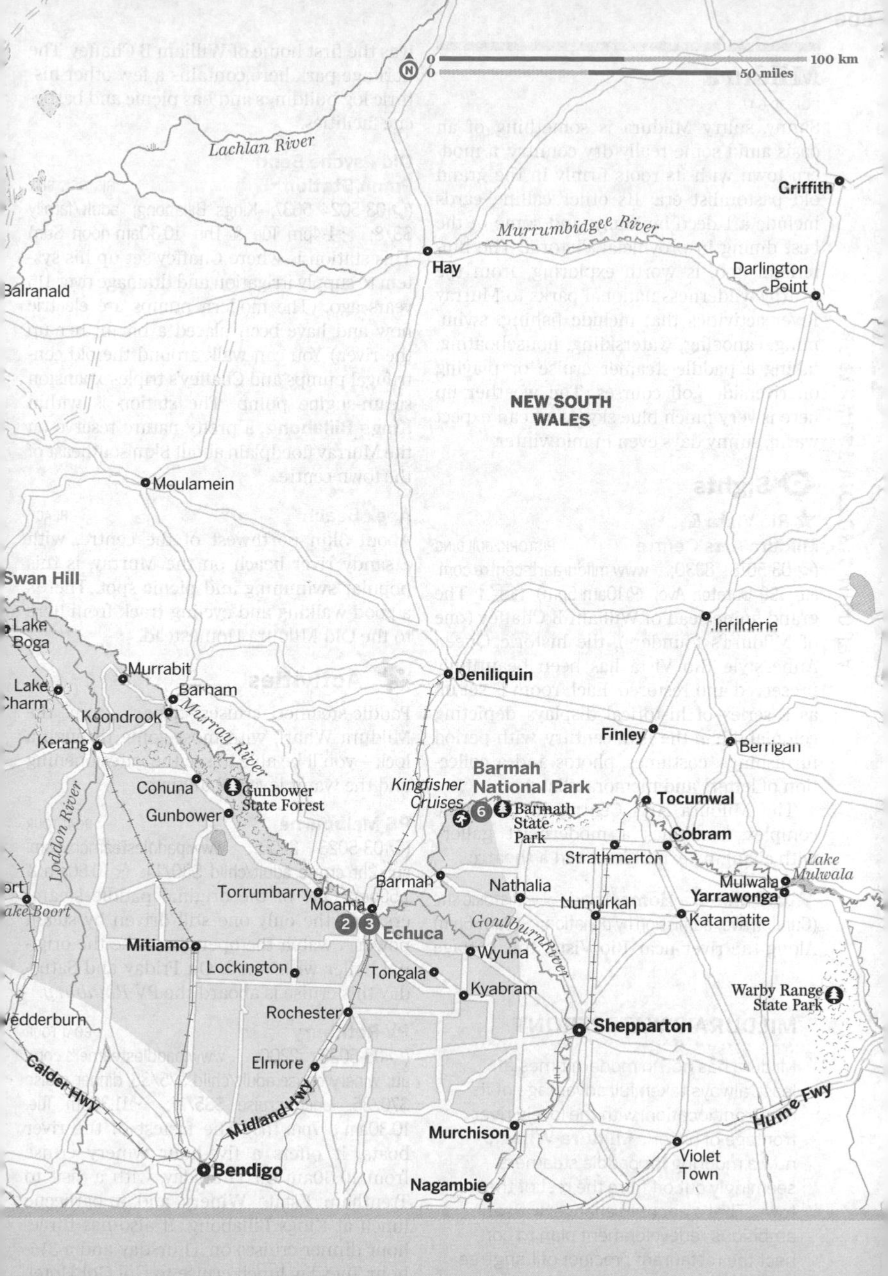

5 Taking the kids on a trip back in time at the **Pioneer Settlement** (p611) in Swan Hill.

6 Taking a boat ride amid the river red gums of **Barmah National Park** (p616).

7 Disappearing in remote **Wyperfeld National Park** (p610) and discovering the vastness of the Mallee.

Mildura

POP 30,647

Sunny, sultry Mildura is something of an oasis amid some really dry country, a modern town with its roots firmly in the grand old pastoralist era. Its other calling cards include art deco buildings and some of the best dining in provincial Victoria. The hinterland, too, is worth exploring, from the nearby wilderness national parks to Murray River activities that include fishing, swimming, canoeing, waterskiing, houseboating, taking a paddle-steamer cruise or playing on riverside golf courses. The weather up here is very much blue sky – you can expect warm, sunny days even in midwinter.

Sights

★Rio Vista & Mildura Arts Centre HISTORIC BUILDING
(☎03-5018 8330; www.milduraartscentre.com.au; 199 Cureton Ave; ⏲10am-5pm) FREE The grand homestead of William B Chaffey (one of Mildura's founders), the historic Queen Anne–style Rio Vista has been beautifully preserved and restored. Each room is set up as a series of historical displays depicting colonial life in the 19th century, with period furnishings, costumes, photos and a collection of letters and memorabilia.

The Mildura Arts Centre, in the same complex, combines a modern-art gallery with changing exhibitions and a theatre.

★Old Mildura Homestead HISTORIC SITE
(Cureton Ave; admission by donation; ⏲9am-6pm) Along the river near Rio Vista, this cottage was the first home of William B Chaffey. The heritage park here contains a few other historic log buildings and has picnic and barbecue facilities.

Old Psyche Bend Pump Station HISTORIC SITE
(☎03-5024 5637; Kings Billabong; adult/family $3/8; ⏲1-4pm Tue & Thu, 10.30am-noon Sun) This station is where Chaffey set up his system to supply irrigation and drainage over 115 years ago. (The modern pumps are electric now and have been placed a bit further up the river.) You can walk around the old centrifugal pumps and Chaffey's triple-expansion steam-engine pump. The station is within **Kings Billabong**, a pretty nature reserve on the Murray floodplain about 8km southeast of the town centre.

Apex Beach BEACH
About 3km northwest of the centre, with a sandy river beach on the Murray, is this popular swimming and picnic spot. There's a good walking and cycling track from here to the Old Mildura Homestead.

MILDURA'S WATERFRONT

Mildura has not, in modern times at least, always taken full advantage of its riverfront location, with the lovely river frontage of historic **Mildura Wharf**, now a mooring for paddle steamers, seemingly cut off from the rest of the town. That's about to change, with an ambitious redevelopment plan to connect the restaurant precinct of Langtree Ave with the waterfront using parkland and walking trails. There are also plans to relocate the visitor information centre to this waterfront area, although it may not happen before 2016 at the earliest.

Activities

Paddle-steamer cruises depart from the Mildura Wharf, with most going through a lock – you'll be able to see the gates opening and the water levels changing.

PS Melbourne BOAT TOUR
(☎03-5023 2200; www.paddlesteamers.com.au; 2hr cruise adult/child $30/14; ⏲10.50am & 1.50pm) One of the original paddle steamers, and the only one still driven by steam power – watch the operator stoke the original boiler with wood. On Friday and Saturday this cruise is aboard the PV *Rothbury.*

PV Rothbury BOAT TOUR
(☎03-5023 2200; www.paddlesteamers.com.au; winery cruise adult/child $75/35, dinner cruise $70/35, lunch cruise $35/17; ⏲11.30am Tue, 10.30am & 7pm Thu) The fastest of the river boats, it offers a five-hour winery cruise from 10.30am on Thursday, with a visit to Trentham Estate Winery and a barbecue lunch at Kings Billabong. It also has three-hour dinner cruises on Thursday and a 3½-hour Tuesday lunch cruise to Gol Gol Hotel, where you buy your own meal.

Tours

A standout is the extraordinary and ancient natural formations of Mungo National Park (in NSW). Several operators run tours out

Mildura

Mildura

Top Sights
1 Rio Vista & Mildura Arts Centre C1

Activities, Courses & Tours
2 PS Melbourne D2
PV Rothbury .... (see 2)

Sleeping
3 Acacia Houseboats D2
4 Indulge Apartments B3
5 Mildura Houseboats D1
6 Pied-à-Terre B2
7 Quality Hotel Mildura Grand B3

Eating
Jim McDougall in Stefano's Cellar .... (see 7)
Pizza Café at the Grand .... (see 9)
8 Restaurant Rendezvous A3
9 Spanish Bar & Grill A2

Drinking & Nightlife
10 Dom's Nightclub A3
11 Mildura Brewery A2

Entertainment
12 Sandbar A3

Shopping
13 Sunraysia Cellar Door B2

there, focusing on its culture, its 45,000 years of history and its wildlife.

★Harry Nanya Tours CULTURAL TOUR
(☎03-5027 2076; www.harrynanyatours.com.au; tours adult/child $180/110, tag along in your own car $90/45) Indigenous guide Graham Clarke keeps you enchanted with Dreaming stories and his deep knowledge and understanding of the Mungo region. In summer (November to March) there's a spectacular sunset tour.

Mungo National Park Tours TOUR
(☎0408 147 330, 1800 797 530; www.murraytrek.com.au; day/sunset tour $145/175) Small-group day and sunset tours to Mungo led by the experienced Trevor Hancock.

Discover Mildura Tours TOUR
(☎03-5024 7448; www.discovermildura.com.au; tours per person $150-165) The guided tours here cover wine tasting, Mungo National Park or farm visits.

Moontongue Eco-Adventures KAYAKING
(☎0427 898 317; www.moontongue.com.au; kayak tours $35-65) A sunset kayaking trip is a great way to see the river and its wildlife. Local guide Ian will tell you about the landscape and bird life as you work those muscles in the magnificent, peaceful surroundings of Gol Gol Creek and the Murray.

Wild Side Outdoors ADVENTURE TOUR
(☎0428 242 852, 03-5024 3721; www.wildsideoutdoors.com.au) Wild Side is an ecofriendly outfit offering a range of activities, including a sunset kayaking tour at Kings Billabong (adult/child $35/15) and a six-hour 4WD tour into Hattah-Kulkyne National Park (adult/child $85/30). It also has canoe/kayak/mountain-bike hire for $30/20/20 per hour.

Festivals & Events

Mildura Wentworth Arts Festival ART
(www.artsmildura.com.au) Magical concerts by the river, in the sandhills and all around. Held in February to March.

Mildura Country Music Festival MUSIC
(www.milduracountrymusic.com.au) Ten days of free concerts in late September and/or early October.

Mildura Jazz, Food & Wine Festival MUSIC
(www.artsmildura.com.au/jazz) Traditional bands, great food, good wine. Held in October or November.

MILDURA HOUSEBOATS

Staying on a houseboat is bliss. The Mildura region has over a dozen companies that hire houseboats, ranging from two- to 12-berth boats and from modest to luxurious. Most have a minimum hire of three days, and prices increase dramatically in summer and during school holidays. Most operators are located just across from Mildura Wharf in Buronga.

Acacia Houseboats (☎1800 085 500, 03-5022 1510; www.murrayriver.com.au/acacia-houseboats-949/fleet; 3 nights $525-1800) Has five houseboats, ranging from four to 12 berths, with everything supplied, except food and drink.

Mildura Houseboats (☎1800 800 842, 03-5024 7770; www.mildurahouseboats.com.au; 3 nights $990-3700) Willandra has six houseboats sleeping two to 12 people. Offers gourmet and golf packages.

Sleeping

Apex RiverBeach Holiday Park CARAVAN PARK $
(☎03-5023 6879; www.apexriverbeach.com.au; Cureton Ave; unpowered/powered sites $34/39, cabins $75-125;) Thanks to a fantastic location on sandy Apex Beach, just outside town, this bush park is always popular – prices are 25% higher during school holidays. There are campfires, a bush kitchen, barbecue area, boat ramp, good swimming and a cafe.

Oasis Backpackers HOSTEL $
(☎03-5022 8200, 0401 344 251; www.milduraoasisbackpackers.com.au; 230-232 Deakin Ave; dm/d per week $160/340;) Mildura is a big destination for travellers looking for fruit-picking work, so most of the city's half-dozen hostels are set up with them in mind. Oasis is Mildura's best-equipped backpacker hostel, with a great pool and patio bar area, ultramodern kitchen and free internet. The owners can organise plenty of seasonal work. Minimum one-week stay.

★ **Quality Hotel Mildura Grand** HOTEL $$
(☎03-5023 0511, 1800 034 228; www.qualityhotelmilduragrand.com.au; Seventh St; s/d incl breakfast from $85/130;) The standard rooms at the Grand aren't the most luxurious in town, but staying at this landmark hotel – Mildura's top address – gives you the feeling of being part of something special. Although cheaper rooms in the original wing are comfortable, go for one of the stylish suites with private spa.

Many rooms open onto a delightful courtyard garden, and there's a gym, pool and spa.

★ **Indulge Apartments** APARTMENT $$
(☎1300 539 559, 03-5018 4900; www.indulgeapartments.com.au; 150 Langtree Ave; studio $149, 1-/2-bedroom apt $175/265;) These stunning contemporary apartments in the centre of town could be Mildura's best, with polished floors, plenty of floor space and excellent facilities. It has a couple of other locations around town if the Langtree Ave property is full.

Pied-à-Terre B&B $$
(☎03-5022 9883; www.piedaterre.com.au; 97 Chaffey Ave; d $175, per night extra adult/child $25/15;) It's French for 'a home away from home', but we doubt home ever looked this good! Five stylish and luxurious bedrooms sleep up to 10 people, with all amenities including free wi-fi, boat and car parking and a barbecue area.

Eating

Mildura's cafe and restaurant precinct runs along Langtree Ave (otherwise known as 'Feast Street') and around the block dominated by the Grand hotel. Italian raconteur Stefano de Pieri perhaps single-handedly stamped the town on the foodie map, but others are jumping on board.

Pizza Café at the Grand PIZZA **$**
(☎03-5022 2223; www.pizzacafe.com.au; 18 Langtree Ave; pizza & pasta $15-21; ⊙11am-11pm Mon-Sat, 11.30am-11pm Sun) For simple and inexpensive (but stylish) family dining, with all the atmosphere of the Grand Hotel dining strip, Pizza Café is perfect. The wood-fired pizzas hit the spot and there's a supporting cast of salads, pastas and chicken dishes.

Spanish Bar & Grill STEAK **$$**
(☎03-5021 2377; www.spanishgrill.com.au; cnr Langtree Ave & Seventh St; mains $26-48; ⊙6-10pm Tue-Sat) In the Grand hotel, this place keeps it simple, with top-quality steaks and barbecue food, including kangaroo. No tapas, but it is a carnivore's heaven.

Restaurant Rendezvous FRENCH **$$**
(☎03-5023 1571; www.rendezvousmildura.com.au; 34 Langtree Ave; mains $17-39; ⊙noon-4pm & 6pm-late Mon-Fri, 6pm-late Sat) The warm, casual atmosphere of this long-running place that's almost swallowed up by the Grand hotel complements the perfectly prepared, Mediterranean-style seafood, grills, pastas, crepes and unusual specials.

★Jim McDougall in Stefano's Cellar ITALIAN **$$$**
(☎03-5023 0511; www.jimmcdougall.com.au; Quality Hotel Mildura Grand, Seventh St; 2-/3-course lunch set menu $55/62, dinner set menu $130-175; ⊙7-11pm Tue-Thu, noon-3pm & 7-11pm Fri & Sat) Stefano de Pieri may no longer run the kitchen but his protege, Jim McDougall, is a fine heir to the throne. The food has broadened beyond Stefano's Italian roots to a fresh, contemporary menu that sources most of its produce locally. The menu changes with the seasons, but expect kangaroo, yabbies, Murray cod and local fruits to feature.

It's an intimate, candlelit experience and very popular – book well in advance.

Drinking

★Mildura Brewery BREWERY
(☎03-5022 2988; www.mildurabrewery.com.au; 20 Langtree Ave; ⊙noon-late) Set in the former Astor cinema, in the same block as the Grand hotel, this is Mildura's trendiest drinking hole. Shiny stainless-steel vats, pipes and brewing equipment make a great backdrop to the stylish lounge, and the beers brewed here – Honey Wheat and Mallee Bull among them – are superb. Good food, too.

The interior retains many of the sleek art deco features from the original theatre.

Dom's Nightclub CLUB
(☎03-5021 3822; www.doms.com.au; 28 Langtree Ave; ⊙9pm-late Sat) The upstairs club at Dom's, in the heart of Feast Street, attracts the after-pub crowd on a Saturday night.

Entertainment

Sandbar LIVE MUSIC
(☎03-5021 2181; www.thesandbar.com.au; cnr Langtree Ave & Eighth St; ⊙noon-late Tue-Sun) On a balmy evening locals flock to the fabulous beer garden at the back of this lounge bar in a classic art deco building. Local, national, original and mainstream bands play in the front bar nightly from Thursday to Sunday.

WORTH A TRIP

WINERIES AROUND MILDURA

Mildura is one of Australia's most prolific wine-producing areas. If you plan on touring the region's wineries, pick up a copy of the *Mildura Wines* brochure from the visitor information centre, or visit www.milduravines.com.au.

If you can't make it out to the wineries themselves, the in-town **Sunraysia Cellar Door** (☎03-5021 0794; www.sunraysiacellardoor.com.au; 125 Lime Ave; ⊙9am-5pm Mon-Fri, 11am-5pm Sat & Sun) has tastings and sales for around 250 local wines from 22 different wineries, as well as a handful of local craft beers.

Chateau Mildura (☎03-5024 5901; www.chateaumildura.com.au; 191 Belar Ave; adult/child $5/free; ⊙10am-4pm) Established in 1888 and still producing table wines, Chateau Mildura is part vineyard and part museum, with wine tastings and historical displays.

Nursery Ridge Estate Wines (☎03-5024 3311; www.nrewines.com.au; 8514 Calder Hwy, Red Cliffs; ⊙10am-4.30pm Thu-Sun) A full range of reds and whites, around 20km south of central Mildura.

WORTH A TRIP

NATIONAL PARKS OF NORTHWESTERN VICTORIA

Occupying the relatively vast northwestern corner of Victoria, the Mallee appears as a flat horizon and endless, undulating, twisted mallee scrub and desert. The attractions – other than the sheer solitude – are the semi-arid wilderness areas, which are particularly notable for their abundance of native plants, spring wild flowers and birds. This is 'Sunset Country', the one genuinely empty part of the state. Nature lovers might delight in it, but much of it is inaccessible to all but experienced 4WD enthusiasts. Like most outback areas, visiting here is best avoided in the hot summer months.

The following are the main national parks in the area. For more information, contact **Parks Victoria** (☎13 19 63; www.parkweb.vic.gov.au).

Hattah-Kulkyne National Park The most accessible of the Mallee parks, with more than 20 lakes, Murray River frontage lined with red gum, black box, wattle and bottlebrush, and dry, sandy mallee-scrub country. There are nature drives, cycling tracks and camp sites. The main access road is from Hattah, 70km south of Mildura on the Calder Hwy. The **Hattah-Kulkyne National Park visitor cente** (☎03-5029 3253) is at the park entrance.

Wyperfeld National Park Vast but accessible park of river red gum, mallee scrub, dry lake beds, sand plains, a carpet of native wild flowers in spring, over 200 bird species, two camping grounds and a network of walking and cycling tracks. Access is from Patchewollock, Hopetoun, Underbool or Rainbow.

Big Desert Wilderness Park West of Wyperfeld, along the South Australian border, it has no roads, facilities or water. Walking and camping are permitted, but only for the experienced and totally self-sufficient.

Murray-Sunset National Park Stunning 6330 sq km of mallee woodland and pink lakes, reaching from the river red gums of Lindsay Island down to Underbool. Most of the park is remote 4WD-only territory and the easiest access is from Underbool.

Information

Mildura Visitor Centre (☎1800 039 043, 03-5018 8380; www.visitmildura.com.au; cnr Deakin Ave & 12th St; ⏲9am-5.30pm Mon-Fri, to 5pm Sat & Sun) There's a free service for booking accommodation, interesting displays, local produce, a cafe, library, swimming centre and very helpful staff who book tours and activities.

Getting There & Away

Mildura is 542km northwest of Melbourne along the Calder Highway (A79).

AIR

Mildura Airport (MQL; ☎03-5055 0500; www.milduraairport.com.au) Victoria's busiest regional airport, Mildura airport is about 10km west of the town centre, off the Sturt Hwy.

Qantas (☎13 13 13; www.qantas.com.au) Connects Mildura with Melbourne.

Regional Express Airlines (Rex; ☎13 17 13; www.regionalexpress.com.au) Flies between Mildura and Melbourne, Sydney, Adelaide and Broken Hill.

Virgin Australia (☎13 67 89; www.virgin-australia.com) Flies between Melbourne and Mildura.

BUS & TRAIN

Long-distance buses operate from the **V/Line bus depot** at the train station on Seventh St, but there are currently no direct passenger trains to or from Mildura.

Greyhound (☎1300 473 946; www.greyhound.com.au) has services from Mildura to Adelaide from $40 per person.

V/Line (☎1800 800 007; www.vline.com.au) has a train-bus service to/from Melbourne ($45.50, 7½ hours, four daily) via Bendigo or Swan Hill. V/Line's Murraylink is a daily bus service connecting Mildura with towns along the Murray: Swan Hill ($27.20, three hours, three daily), Echuca ($37.20, six hours, one daily) and Albury-Wodonga ($46.40, 11 hours, one daily).

Swan Hill

POP 9894

Swan Hill is a sleepy river town without the tourist hype of Mildura and Echuca, but with some appeal nonetheless. The riverside Pioneer Settlement is one of the best open-air museums in Victoria and the town has some good places to eat. While you wouldn't cross the state to come here, it makes an ideal stopover as you meander along the Murray.

Sights & Activities

The **Burke & Wills Tree**, an enormous Moreton Bay fig tree planted to commemorate the explorers as they passed through Swan Hill on their ill-fated journey, is located on Curlewis St.

Pioneer Settlement MUSEUM
(☎03-5036 2410; www.pioneersettlement.com.au; Monash Dr, Horseshoe Bend; adult/child/family $28/20.50/76.50; ⌚9.30am-4pm) Swan Hill's main tourist attraction is a fun re-creation of a riverside port town of the paddle-steamer era. The settlement's displays include the restored PS *Gem,* one of Australia's largest riverboats, a great collection of old carriages and buggies, an old-time photographic parlour, an Aboriginal keeping place, a lolly shop, a school classroom and the fascinating Kaiser Stereoscope. The paddle steamer **PS Pyap** (adult/child/family $22/15/59; ⌚cruises 2.30pm daily, also 10.30am on weekends & school holidays) makes short cruises along the Murray.

Every night at dusk the 45-minute **sound-and-light show** (adult/child/family $22/15/59) entails a dramatic journey through the settlement in an open-air transporter. A combined package for cruise and show reduces the cost.

Swan Hill Regional Art Gallery GALLERY
(☎03-5036 2430; www.swanhillart.com; Monash Dr, Horseshoe Bend; admission by donation; ⌚10am-5pm Tue-Sun) Opposite Pioneer Settlement, this gallery has a permanent collection of more than 300 pieces, focusing on the works of contemporary and local artists.

Festivals & Events

Swan Hill Food & Wine Festival FOOD, WINE
(www.swanhillfoodandwine.com.au) Foodies will love this early March festival, which celebrates local producers. The quality is high.

Sleeping & Eating

Riverside Caravan Park CARAVAN PARK $
(☎03-5032 1494, 1800 101 012; www.big4.com.au; 1 Monash Dr; unpowered/powered sites from $31/35, cabins $105-170) On the banks of the Murray, close to Pioneer Settlement, this park enjoys a fabulous central location. There's a good range of cabins, but prices soar by more than 50% in holiday periods.

Travellers Rest Motor Inn MOTEL $$
(☎03-5032 9644; www.bestwestern.com.au/travellersrest; 110 Curlewis St; d from $133; ❄📶🏊) Sitting in the shade of the Burke and Wills Tree, rooms here are spacious and comfortable, with the usual motel accompaniments. There's a heated spa and outdoor pool.

★ **Spoons Riverside Café** MODERN AUSTRALIAN $$
(☎03-5032 2601; www.spoonsriverside.com.au; 125 Monash Dr, Horseshoe Bend; lunch mains $9.50-25, dinner $26-35; ⌚8am-5pm Sun-Wed, to 11pm Thu-Sat) The riverside location alone is enough to lure you to this licensed cafe, which offers a big timber deck overlooking the Marraboor River and Pioneer Settlement. As well as light lunches and innovative dinners (in which fresh local ingredients take centre stage), there's a providore selling fresh produce and gourmet hampers.

Java Spice THAI $$
(☎03-5033 0511; www.javaspice.com.au; 17 Beveridge St; mains $21-32; ⌚noon-2pm & 6pm-late Fri & Sun, 6pm-late Tue-Thu & Sat; 🖉) Dining under open-sided thatched and teak-wood huts in a tropical garden, you'll think you've been transported to Southeast Asia. The authentic cuisine is predominantly Thai, with some Malaysian and Indonesian influences mixed in. There's a takeaway version in the **town centre** (☎03-5033 0015; 24 McRae St).

Information

Swan Hill Region Information Centre (☎1800 625 373, 03-5032 3033; www.swanhillonline.com; cnr McCrae & Curlewis Sts; ⌚9am-5pm) Helpful maps and brochures on the region.

Getting There & Away

Swan Hill is 338km northwest of Melbourne, travelling via Bendigo and Kerang. It sits on the Murray Valley Hwy (B400), 218km from Mildura and 156km from Echuca.

V/Line (☎1800 800 007; www.vline.com.au) Runs trains between Melbourne and Swan Hill ($36.60, four hours, three to four daily) and some train and coach services with a change at Bendigo. There are daily V/line coaches to Mildura ($27.20, three hours) and Echuca ($16.80, two hours).

Echuca

POP 12,613

One of the loveliest towns in rural Victoria, Echuca is the state's paddle-steamer capital and a classic Murray River town, bursting with history, nostalgia and, of course, riverboats. The Aboriginal name translates as 'meeting of the waters', as it's here that three great rivers meet – the Goulburn, Campaspe

Echuca

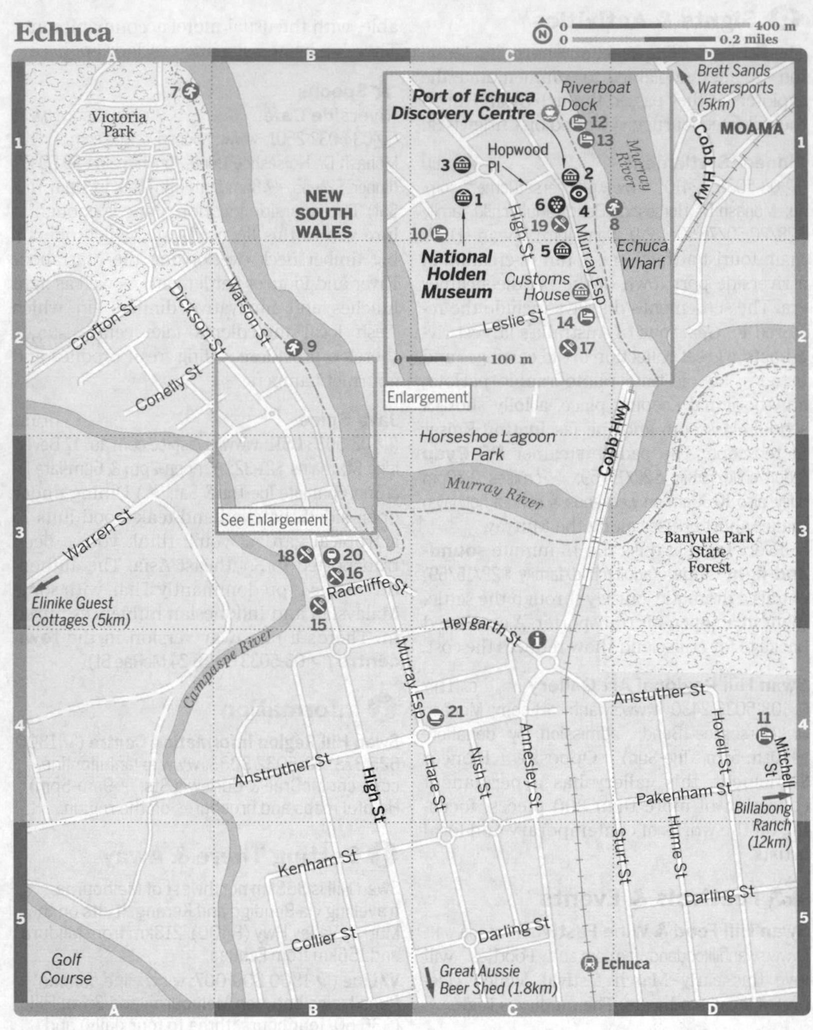

and Murray. The highlight is unquestionably the historic port area and the rivers themselves, best enjoyed on a riverboat cruise or a sunset stroll as cockatoos and corellas screech overhead.

Sights

Ask at Echuca Visitors Centre for the *Heritage Walk Echuca* brochure, which outlines a self-guided walking itinerary taking in the town centre's historic buildings.

Echuca's star attraction is the historic Port of Echuca. Everything is original – you're exploring living history as you walk along the pedestrian-only Murray Esplanade, which you can wander for free.

★Port of Echuca Discovery Centre — MUSEUM

(☎03-5481 0500; www.portofechuca.org.au; 74 Murray Esplanade; adult/child $11/8; ⏲9am-5pm) At the northern end of Murray Esplanade, the stunning new Port of Echuca Discovery Centre is your gateway to the Echuca Wharf area, with excellent displays (some of them interactive) on the port's history, the paddle steamers and the riverboat trade. Guided tours set out from the discovery centre twice daily.

Echuca

The wharf was built with three tiers because of the changing river levels; there are gauges marking the highest points. Original features include the sawmill and a selection of old paddle steamer rudders.

Red Gum Works HISTORIC SITE
(Murray Esplanade; admission free; ⏲9am-4pm) FREE At Red Gum Works you can watch woodturners and blacksmiths at work with traditional equipment, and purchase red-gum products.

Sharp's Magic Movie House & Penny Arcade HISTORIC BUILDING
(☎03-5482 2361; 43 Murray Esplanade; adult/child/family $15/10/45; ⏲9am-5pm) This place has authentic penny-arcade machines and free fudge tasting. The movie house shows old movies such as Buster Keaton or Laurel and Hardy classics.

St Anne's WINERY
(☎03-5480 6955; www.stanneswinery.com.au; 53 Murray Esplanade; ⏲10am-6pm) There are free tastings of local wines at St Anne's. Taste the range of ports, aged in bourbon and rum barrels.

★ **National Holden Museum** MUSEUM
(☎03-5480 2033; www.holdenmuseum.com.au; 7 Warren St; adult/child/family $7/3/16; ⏲9am-5pm) Car buffs should check out this museum dedicated to Australia's four-wheeled icon, with more than 40 beautifully restored Holdens, from FJ to Monaro, as well as racing footage and memorabilia.

Great Aussie Beer Shed MUSEUM
(☎03-5480 6904; www.greataussiebeershed.com.au; 377 Mary Ann Rd; adult/child/family $12/5/25; ⏲9.30am-5pm Sat, Sun & holidays) This is a wall-to-wall shrine of over 17,000 beer cans in a huge shed. It's the result of 30 years of collecting – one dates back to Federation. Guided tours will take you through the history of beer. Very Aussie.

Activities

A paddle-steamer cruise here is almost obligatory. There are five operating – wood-fired, steam-driven and with interesting commentary – at one time or another. Buy tickets from the Port of Echuca Discovery Centre, Echuca visitor centre (p616) or at sales points along Murray Esplanade. Check the timetables for lunch, dinner, twilight and sunset cruises.

PS Alexander Arbuthnot CRUISE
(☎03-5482 4248; www.echucapaddlesteamers.net.au; 1hr cruise adult/child/family $24/10/62.50) One-hour cruises aboard this 1923-built steamer, with less regular two-hour twilight trips, or 2½-hour dinner cruises.

PS Canberra CRUISE
(☎03-5482 5244; www.emmylou.com.au; adult/child/family $24/10/65) One-hour cruises aboard this lovely old steamer that was built in 1912 and restored in 2003.

PS Emmylou CRUISE
(☎03-5482 5244; www.emmylou.com.au; 1hr cruise adult/child/family $27.50/13/75, 2hr cruise $35/16/87.50) One of the most impressive

boats in Echuca, fully restored and driven by an original engine. Offers two one-hour cruises and one two-hour cruise daily, plus lunch, dinner and overnight cruises. The three-hour dinner cruise costs $130/55 per adult/child.

PS Pevensey CRUISE
(☎1300 942 737, 03-5482 4248; www.echucapaddlesteamers.net.au; adult/child/family $24/10/62.50) Star of the TV miniseries *All the Rivers Run* and one of the oldest paddle steamers (1911) still running, the PS *Pevensey* offers one-hour cruises up to five times daily.

PS Pride of the Murray CRUISE
(☎03-5482 5244; www.murraypaddlesteamers.com.au; adult/child/family $24/10/65) One-hour cruises.

Billabong Ranch HORSE RIDING
(☎03-5483 5122; www.billabongranch.com.au; 1/2/3hr ride $55/100/145) This ranch offers rides through the bush and along the Murray and Goulburn Rivers from its base, 12km east of Echuca. It also has minigolf, pedal boats, an animal nursery, tenpin bowling, a playground, cafe, bar and pony rides.

Echuca Boat & Canoe Hire BOATING
(☎03-5480 6208; www.echucaboatcanoehire.com; Victoria Park Boat Ramp) Hires out motor boats (one/two hours $40/60), 'barbie boats' with on-board BBQs (10 people from $100/150), kayaks ($16/26) and canoes ($20/30). Multiday, self-guided 'campanoeing' trips, where you can arrange to be dropped upstream and canoe back, are also available.

River Country Adventours CANOEING
(☎0428 585 227; www.adventours.com.au; half-/full-/2-day safaris $55/88/245) For organised canoe safaris on the Goulburn River, this Kyabram-based team is the expert in this part of the world. It has canoe and camping safaris around the Barmah and Goulburn regions, as well as on the Murray.

Tours

Echuca Moama Wine Tours WINERY
(☎1300 798 822; www.echucamoamawinetours.com.au; tours from $95; ⏲Tue-Sun) Tours include the historic port, a cruise along the Murray and local wineries.

Festivals & Events

Check the online event calendar at www.echucamoama.com.

Riverboats Music Festival MUSIC
(www.riverboatsmusic.com.au) Music, food and wine by the Murray. Held in late February. Recent performers include Tim Finn, Archie Roach and Colin Hay.

Echuca-Moama Winter Blues Festival MUSIC
(www.winterblues.com.au) Blues and folk musos play in the streets and at venues around town at this weekend festival in late July.

Sleeping

About 5km east of town, **Christies Beach** is a free camping area on the banks of the Murray. There are pit toilets, but bring water and firewood.

COMBINATION TICKETS

Echuca's attractions can be grouped together in a series of combination tickets that can save you both time and money.

Heritage Package (adult/concession/child/family $50/44/23/120) Includes admission to the Port of Echucha Discovery Centre (p612), the National Holden Museum (p613), the Great Aussie Beer Shed (p613), the **Echuca Historical Museum** (☎03-5480 1325; www.echucahistoricalsociety.org.au; 1 Dickson St; adult/child $5/1; ⏲11am-3pm) and a one-hour paddle-steamer cruise.

Discovery Centre & One-Hour Cruise Package (adult/concession/child/family $34.50/28.50/16/96) Includes all-day access to the historic port area (guided tours offered at 11.30am and 1.30pm) and a one-hour cruise aboard any of the paddle steamers, except the *PS Emmylou*.

Riverboat Discovery Package (adult/child/family $38/19/108.50) A 1½-hour cruise aboard the *PS Emmylou*, plus all-day entry to the Port of Echuca Discovery Centre.

Wharf to Winery Package (per person $69.50) Paddle-steamer cruise to Morrisons Winery, two-course lunch and wine tasting.

For the contact details of five B&B options, pick up a copy of *Echuca Moama - Traditional Bed & Breakfasts* from the tourist office, or visit www.echucabandbs.com.

Echuca Gardens HOSTEL, GUESTHOUSE $

(☎0419 881 054, 03-5480 6522; www.echucagardens.com; 103 Mitchell St; dm $30, wagon $80-160, guesthouse $110-200;) Run by inveterate traveller Kym, this enjoyable place is part YHA hostel and part guesthouse, all set in beautiful gardens with ponds, statues, chickens and fruit trees. The 140-year-old workers cottage has bunk beds, smart bathrooms, a country kitchen and a TV room. The cute 'gypsy wagons' in the garden offer unique accommodation, complete with en suite and kitchenette.

Steampacket B&B B&B $$

(☎03-5482 3411; www.steampacketinn.com.au; cnr Murray Esplanade & Leslie St; d $135-200;) Staying in the old port area is all part of the Echuca experience. This 19th-century National Trust–classified B&B offers genteel rooms with all the old-fashioned charm, linen, lace and brass bedstead you could want (but with air-con and flat-screen TVs, too). Ask for the large corner rooms for a view of the wharf.

The lounge room is cosy and breakfast is served on fine china.

Elinike Guest Cottages COTTAGE $$

(☎03-5480 6311; www.elinike.com.au; 209 Latham Rd; d incl breakfast $160-195) These romantic little self-contained cottages are set in rambling gardens on the Murray River around 5km out of town. They blend old-world style with modern conveniences such as double spas. The lilac cottage has a glass-roofed garden room.

★Adelphi Boutique Apartments APARTMENT $$$

(☎03-5482 5575; www.adelphiapartments.com.au; 25 Campaspe St; 1-/2-bedroom apt from $175/360;) The semi-luxurious riverside accommodation here, a block back from the main street, is a good choice, especially if you're willing to pay a little more for the ones with a terrace overlooking the Campaspe River.

Eating

★Fish in a Flash FISH & CHIPS $

(☎03-5480 0824; 602 High St; fish & chips from $8.90; ⏲11am-8pm) Consistently ranked among the best fish-and-chip places in Victoria, Fish in a Flash does occasional river fish as well as the usual suspects, all dipped in the owner's secret batter. Great for a riverside picnic.

HIRE A HOUSEBOAT

Echuca is a great place to hire a houseboat. The Echuca visitor centre has brochures and information about houseboat operators.

Murray River Houseboats (☎03-5480 2343; www.murrayriverhouseboats.com.au; Riverboat Dock; 2-7 bed houseboat per week $1550-2720) Five houseboats in the fleet, including the stunning four-bedroom *Indulgence*.

Rich River Houseboats (☎03-5480 2444; www.richriverhouseboats.com.au; Riverboat Dock; 8-bed houseboat per week $3850-6800) The six beautiful boats here include a budget six-berth and a couple of floating palaces.

Beechworth Bakery BAKERY $

(☎1300 233 784; www.beechworthbakery.com.au; 513 High St; mains $5-12; ⏲6am-6pm) In a magnificent old building with wraparound balcony and deck overlooking the Campaspe River, this cheerful bakery prepares breads, pies, cakes and sandwiches.

★Shebani's MEDITERRANEAN $$

(☎03-5480 7075; 535 High St; mains $12-22; ⏲8am-4pm) This wonderful addition to Echuca's eating scene is like taking a culinary tour of the Mediterranean – Greek, Lebanese, even North African all get a run with subtle flavours. The decor effortlessly brings together Mediterranean tile work, Moroccan lamps and a fresh Aussie-cafe style.

Ceres EUROPEAN $$

(☎03-5482 5599; www.ceresechuca.com.au; 554 High St; lunch $14-27, dinner $26-38; ⏲10am-late Mon-Fri, 9am-late Sat & Sun) In a beautifully converted 1881 brick flour mill, Ceres oozes style with its high-back leather chairs, starched tablecloths and occasional couches. It's actually a relaxed place for lunch, with all-day coffee and tapas, but there's an atmospheric fine-dining evening restaurant with an innovative menu of Italian-influenced pastas, steaks and roast duckling.

Star Hotel BISTRO $$

(☎03-5480 1181; www.starhotelechuca.com.au; 45 Murray Esplanade; mains $13-26, pizzas $19-23; ⏲8am-2pm & 6pm-late Wed-Sun) The historic

'Star Bar' is one of the liveliest places in town for a meal or drink, especially on weekends when there's live music. Full cooked breakfasts and a reasonably priced lunch of calamari or chicken parma can be enjoyed right beside the port, but its wood-fired pizzas are easily the best in town.

Drinking

Bordello Wine Bar WINE BAR
(☎03-5480 6902; www.rivergalleryinn.com.au; 578 High St; ⏲5-11pm Thu-Sun) Ideal for fine local wines, a fabulous range of 65 world beers, comfy armchairs and Saturday-night live music. It's Echuca's most intimate venue.

Office 3564 CAFE, WINE BAR
(☎03-5482 3564; 252 Hare St; ⏲7am-midnight) Inhabiting the old Echuca post office, this smart contemporary cafe does fabulous coffee, light lunches, sweets and excellent wines, most of them local.

Information

Echuca Visitor Centre (☎1800 804 446; www.echucamoama.com; 2 Heygarth St; ⏲9am-5pm) In the old pump station, the visitor centre has helpful staff and steamboat- and accommodation-booking services.

Getting There & Away

Echuca lies 222km north of Melbourne. Take the Hume Fwy (M31) then the well-signposted turn off to the B75, which passes through Heathcote and Rochester en route to Echuca.

V/Line (☎13 61 96; www.vline.com.au) Direct Melbourne–Echuca trains on Fridays and weekends and train/bus services (return $50, 3½ hours) on weekdays, the latter with changes at Bendigo, Murchison or Shepparton.

Barmah National Park

About 40km northeast of Echuca, via the Cobb Hwy in NSW, Barmah is a significant wetlands area of the Murray River floodplain. It's the largest remaining red-gum forest in Australia and the swampy understorey usually floods, creating a wonderful breeding area for many species of fish and birds – it's one of few places in Victoria to see the superb parrot.

You can camp for free in the park, or at the **Barmah Lakes camping area**, which has tables, barbecue areas and pit toilets. The park entry is about 6km north of the tiny town of Barmah (turn at the pub).

Activities

Kingfisher Cruises CRUISE
(☎03-5855 2855; www.kingfishercruises.com.au; 1hr cruise adult/child/family $32/17/80, 2hr cruise $37/21/100; ⏲10.30am Mon, Wed, Thu, Sat & Sun) From the day-use area, Kingfisher Cruises takes you out in a flat-bottom boat for an informative cruise. Your captain points out bird and mammal species along the way. Call ahead for departure times and bookings.

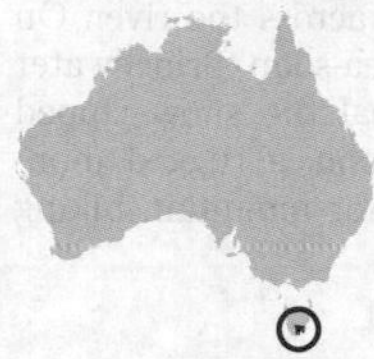

Hobart & Southeast Tasmania

Includes ➡

Best Places to Eat

- Pilgrim Coffee (p630)
- Jackman & McRoss (p632)
- Lotus Eaters Cafe (p643)
- Summer Kitchen Bakery (p643)

Best Places to Stay

- Henry Jones Art Hotel (p628)
- Alabama Hotel (p627)
- Duffy's Country Accommodation (p639)
- Huon Bush Retreats (p643)
- Jetty House (p645)

Why Go?

Australia's second-oldest city, Hobart, dapples the foothills of Mt Wellington. The town's rich cache of colonial architecture and natural charms are complemented by hip festivals, happening markets and top-notch food and drink. Don't miss MONA, Hobart's dizzyingly good Museum of Old & New Art, which has vehemently stamped Tasmania onto the global cultural map.

Heading southeast, the fruity hillsides of the Huon Valley give way to the sparkling inlets of the D'Entrecasteaux Channel, with Bruny Island awaiting enticingly offshore. The apple-producing heartland of the Apple Isle, this area now also produces cherries, apricots, Atlantic salmon, wines, mushrooms and cheeses.

Also a short hop from Hobart are the staggering coastal landscapes and historic sites of the Tasman Peninsula. Bushwalking, surfing and sea-kayaking opportunities abound. Waiting portentously is World Heritage–listed Port Arthur, the infamous penal colony.

When to Go

Hobart

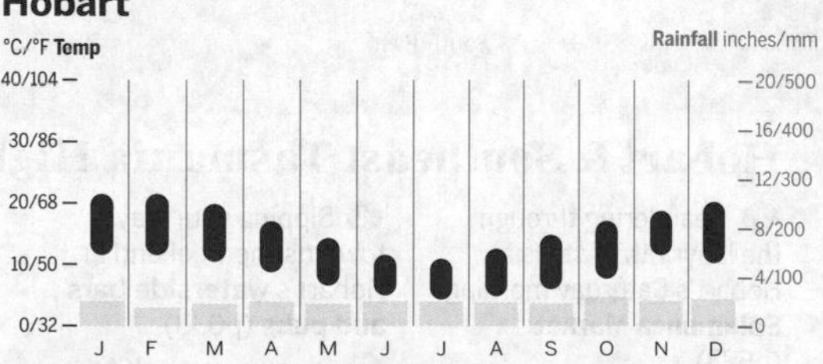

New Year's Eve Around NYE, Hobart heaves with sailors, travellers, food festivals and concerts.

Jan–Mar Long summer days: eating, drinking, bushwalking, cricket and maybe even a swim.

Jun–Aug Snow on Mt Wellington, AFL football and affordable waterfront accommodation in Hobart.

HOBART

POP 218,000

No doubt about it, Hobart's future is looking rosy. Tourism is booming and the old town is treading confidently onto the world stage. Plan on staying a while – you'll need at least a few days to savour the full range of beers flowing from the city's pubs.

On summer afternoons the sea breeze blows and yachts tack across the river. On winter mornings the pea-soup 'Bridgewater Jerry' fog lifts to reveal the snow-capped summit of Mt Wellington, a rugged monolith seemingly made for mountain biking and bushwalking.

Hobart & Southeast Tasmania Highlights

1. Meandering through the labyrinth of stalls at Hobart's Saturday morning **Salamanca Market** (p623).
2. Being inspired, turned on, appalled, educated and amused at **MONA** (p622).
3. Careering down from the summit of **Mt Wellington** (p623) on a mountain bike.
4. Sipping your way towards the weekend in Hobart's **waterside bars and pubs** (p633).
5. Bracing yourself for a cold-water spray at **Russell Falls** (p638) in Mt Field National Park.
6. Dropping out of mobile-phone reception on **Bruny Island** (p639) for a couple of days.
7. Paying your respects to the past, both distant and recent, at the **Port Arthur Historic Site** (p649).
8. **Sea kayaking** (p646) around the Tasman Peninsula's wild, broken coastline.

Down on the waterfront, the cafes, bars and restaurants along Salamanca Pl and in nearby Battery Point showcase the best of Tassie produce. There's more great eating and boozing in cashed-up Sandy Bay and along Elizabeth St in bohemian North Hobart. Further north, savvy MONA (the Museum of Old and New Art) has bolstered the city's international rep.

History

The semi-nomadic Mouheneer people were the original inhabitants of the area. Risdon Cove, on the Derwent River's eastern shore, was the first European settlement in 1803, but just a year later the settlers decamped to the site of present-day Hobart.

Britain's jails were overflowing with criminals in the 1820s, and so tens of thousands of convicts were chained together into rotting hulks and transported to Hobart Town to serve their sentences in vile conditions. By the 1850s Hobart was rife with sailors, soldiers, whalers, ratbags and prostitutes shamelessly boozing, brawling and bonking in and around countless harbourside taverns.

It could be argued that the city has only ever partially sobered up – the day Hobart's waterfront is no longer the place to go for a beer will be a sad day indeed – but today's convicts are more likely to be white-collared than bad company at the bar. Skeletons rattle in Hobart's closet – Indigenous Tasmanians and thousands of convicts suffered here – but the old town's shimmering beauty and relaxed vibe scare away the ghosts of the past.

Sights

City Centre

★Farm Gate Market MARKET

(Map p624; www.farmgatemarket.com.au; Bathurst St, btwn Elizabeth & Murray Sts; ⏲9am-1pm Sun) Salamanca Market on the waterfront has been a success for decades, but this hyperactive new foodie street-mart might just give it a run for its money. Trading commences with the ding of a big brass bell at 9am. Elbow your way in for the best buys, or take your time to browse the fruit, veg, honey, wine, baked goods, beer, smoked meats, coffee, nuts, oils, cut flowers and jams… Terrific!

Penitentiary Chapel Historic Site HISTORIC SITE

(Map p620; ☎03-6231 0911; www.penitentiarychapel.com; cnr Brisbane & Campbell Sts; tours adult/child/family $12/5/25; ⏲tours 10am, 11.30am, 1pm & 2.30pm Sun-Fri, 1pm & 2.30pm Sat) Ruminating over the courtrooms, cells and gallows here, writer TG Ford mused: 'As the Devil was going through Hobart Gaol, he saw a solitary cell; and the Devil was pleased for it gave him a hint, for improving the prisons in hell'. Take the excellent National Trust–run tour here, or the one-hour **Penitentiary Chapel Ghost Tour** (Map p620; ☎03-6231 0911; www.hobartghosts.com; adult/child/family $15/10/50; ⏲8.30pm Mon & Fri) held twice weekly (bookings essential).

Maritime Museum of Tasmania MUSEUM

(Map p624; ☎03-6234 1427; www.maritimetas.org; 16 Argyle St; adult/child/family $9/5/18; ⏲9am-5pm) Highlighting shipwrecks, boat building, whaling and Hobart's unbreakable bond with the sea, the Maritime Museum of Tasmania has an interesting (if a little static) collection of photos, paintings, models and relics (try to resist ringing the huge brass bell from the *Rhexenor*). Upstairs is council-run **Carnegie Gallery** (Map p624; ⏲10am-5pm) FREE, exhibiting contemporary Tasmanian art, craft, design and photography.

Parliament House HISTORIC BUILDING

(Map p624; ☎03-6212 2248; www.parliament.tas.gov.au; Salamanca Pl; ⏲tours 10am & 2pm Mon-Fri on nonsitting days) FREE Presiding over an oak-studded park adjacent to Salamanca Pl, Tasmania's sandstone Parliament House (1840) was originally a customs house. There's a tunnel under Murray St from Parliament House to the Customs House pub opposite: the official line is that no one knows what it was used for, but we'd hazard a guess… Public 45-minute tours run when parliament isn't sitting.

Theatre Royal HISTORIC BUILDING

(Map p624; www.theatreroyal.com.au; 29 Campbell St; 1hr tour adult/child $12/10; ⏲tours 11am Mon, Wed & Fri) Take a backstage tour of Hobart's prestigious Theatre Royal. Host to bombastic thespians since 1834, and despite a major fire in 1984, it remains Australia's oldest continuously operating theatre.

Waterfront & Salamanca Place

Salamanca Place HISTORIC SITE

(Map p624; www.salamanca.com.au) This picturesque row of four-storey sandstone warehouses is a classic example of Australian colonial architecture. Dating back to the whaling days of the 1830s, Salamanca was

Hobart

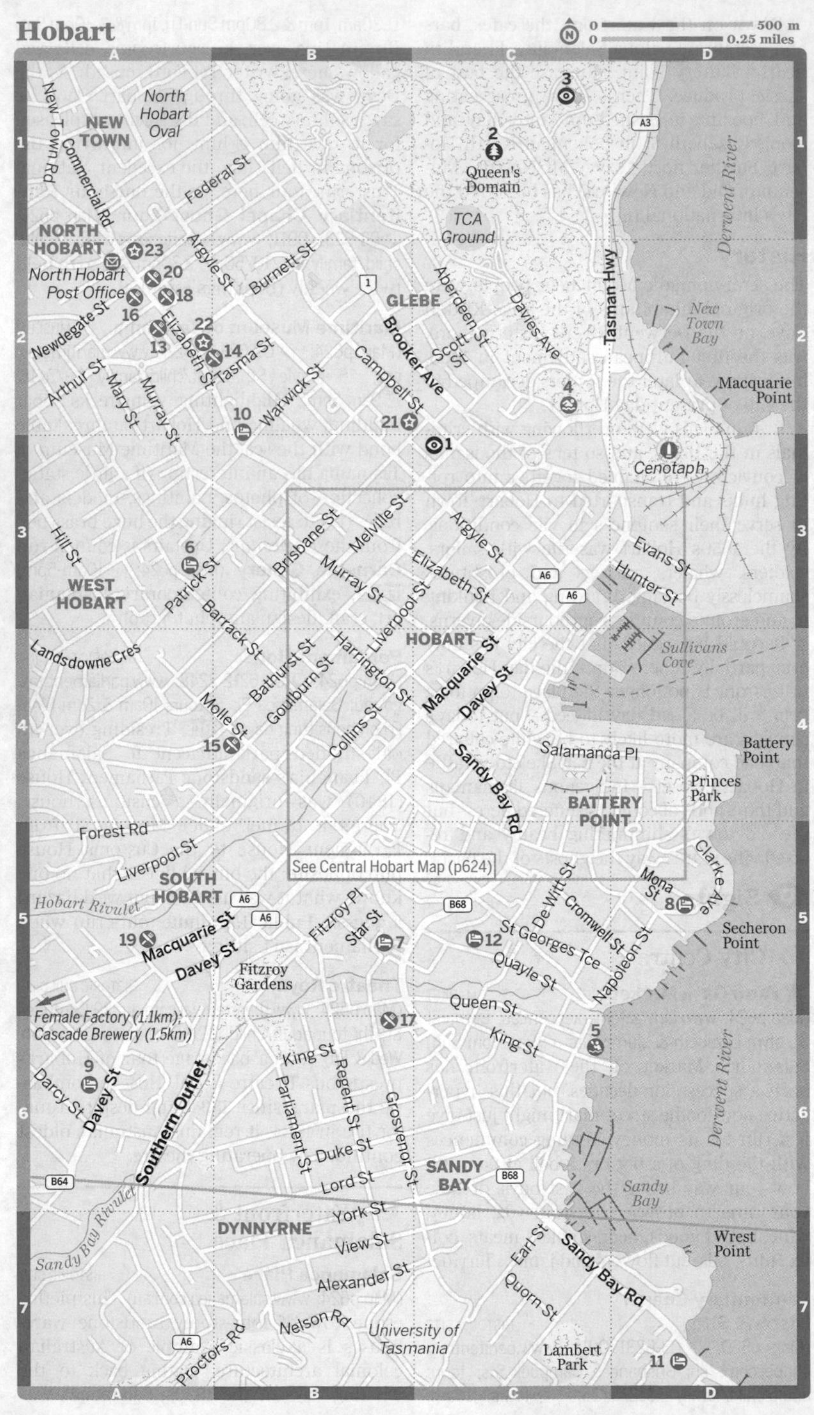

0 500 m
0 0.25 miles
North Hobart Oval
NEW TOWN
New Town Rd
Commercial Rd
Federal St
NORTH HOBART
North Hobart Post Office
Newdegate St
Argyle St
Burnett St
Elizabeth St
Tasma St
Arthur St
Mary St
Murray St
Warwick St
GLEBE
Brooker Ave
Campbell St
Aberdeen St
Scott St
Davies Ave
Queen's Domain
TCA Ground
Tasman Hwy
Derwent River
New Town Bay
Macquarie Point
Cenotaph
Hill St
WEST HOBART
Patrick St
Brisbane St
Melville St
Murray St
Argyle St
Elizabeth St
Liverpool St
Evans St
Hunter St
Barrack St
Landsdowne Cres
Bathurst St
Goulburn St
Harrington St
HOBART
Macquarie St
Davey St
Sullivans Cove
Molle St
Collins St
Sandy Bay Rd
Salamanca Pl
Battery Point
Princes Park
BATTERY POINT
Forest Rd
Liverpool St
SOUTH HOBART
Hobart Rivulet
See Central Hobart Map (p624)
Fitzroy Pl
Star St
De Witt St
Cromwell St
Mona St
Clarke Ave
Secheron Point
Macquarie St
Davey St
Fitzroy Gardens
St Georges Tce
Quayle St
Napoleon St
Queen St
Female Factory (1.1km); Cascade Brewery (1.5km)
King St
Darcy St
Davey St
Southern Outlet
King St
Regent St
Parliament St
Grosvenor St
Duke St
Lord St
SANDY BAY
Sandy Bay
Sandy Bay Rivulet
DYNNYRNE
York St
View St
Earl St
Sandy Bay Rd
Wrest Point
Alexander St
Quorn St
Nelson Rd
Proctors Rd
University of Tasmania
Lambert Park
A1
A3
A6
B64
B68

Hobart

Sights

Activities, Courses & Tours

Sleeping

Eating

Entertainment

the hub of Hobart's trade and commerce. By the mid-20th century many of the warehouses had fallen into ruin, before restorations began in the 1970s. These days Salamanca hosts myriad restaurants, cafes, bars and shops, and the unmissable Saturday morning Salamanca Market (p623).

Waterfront HISTORIC SITE

(Map p624) Hobartians flock to the city's waterfront like seagulls to chips. Centred around **Victoria Dock** (a working fishing harbour) and **Constitution Dock** (chock-full of floating takeaway-seafood punts), it's a brilliant place to explore. The obligatory Hobart experience is to sit in the sun, munch some fish and chips and watch the harbour hubbub. If you'd prefer something with a knife and fork, there are some superb restaurants here, too – head for **Elizabeth Street Pier**.

★ Mawson's Huts Replica Museum MUSEUM

(Map p624; www.mawsons-huts-replica.org.au; cnr Morrison & Argyle Sts; adult/child/family $12/4/26; ⌚9am-6pm Oct-Apr, 10am-5pm May-Sep) This excellent new waterfront installation is an exact model of the hut in which Sir Douglas Mawson hunkered down on his 1911–14 Australasian Antarctic Expedition, which set sail from Hobart. Inside it is 100% authentic, right down to the matches, the stove and the bunks. A knowledgeable guide sits at a rustic table, ready to answer your Antarctic enquiries. Entry fees go towards the upkeep of the original hut at Cape Denison in the Antarctic.

Tasmanian Museum & Art Gallery MUSEUM

(Map p624; www.tmag.tas.gov.au; Dunn Pl; ⌚10am-4pm Tue-Sun) FREE Incorporating Hobart's oldest building, the Commissariat Store (1808), this revamped museum features colonial relics and excellent Aboriginal and wildlife displays. The gallery curates a collection of Tasmanian colonial art. There are free guided tours at 1pm and 2pm from Wednesday to Sunday (hordes of school kids might be a little less interested in proceedings than you are), plus tours of a historic cottage within the museum grounds at 11am on Wednesdays. There's a cool cafe, too.

Battery Point, Sandy Bay & South Hobart

Battery Point HISTORIC SITE

(Map p624; www.batterypoint.net; Battery Point) An empty rum bottle's throw from the waterfront, the old maritime village of **Battery Point** is a tight nest of lanes and 19th-century cottages, packed together like shanghaied landlubbers in a ship's belly. Spend an afternoon exploring: stumble up **Kelly's Steps** from Salamanca Pl and dogleg into **South Street**, where the red lights once burned night and day. Spin around picturesque **Arthur Circus**, refuel in the cafes on **Hampden Road**, then ogle **St George's Anglican Church** on Cromwell St.

Cascade Brewery BREWERY

(☎03-6224 1117; www.cascadebrewery.com.au; 140 Cascade Rd, South Hobart; brewery tours adult/family $25/65, heritage tours adult/family $15/37; ⌚brewery tours 11am & 12.30pm daily, heritage tours

12.30pm Mon, Wed & Fri) Standing in startling, gothic isolation next to the clean-running Hobart Rivulet, Cascade is Australia's oldest brewery (1832) and is still pumping out superb beers. Tours involve plenty of history, with tastings at the end. Note that under-16s aren't permitted on the main brewery tour (take the family-friendly Heritage Tour instead), and that brewery machinery doesn't operate on weekends (brewers have weekends, too). Bookings essential. To get here, take bus 44, 46, 47 or 49.

Mt Wellington MOUNTAIN

(Kunanyi; www.wellingtonpark.org.au; Pinnacle Rd, via Fern Tree) Cloaked in winter snow, Mt Wellington (1270m) towers over Hobart like a benevolent overlord. The citizens find reassurance in its constant, solid presence, while outdoorsy types find the space to hike and bike on its leafy flanks. And the view from the top is unbelievable! You can drive all the way to the summit on a sealed road; alternatively, the **Hobart Shuttle Bus Company** (☎0408 341 804; www.hobartshuttlebus.com; tours per adult/child $30/20, transfers per person $20) runs daily two-hour tours to the summit, plus one-way transfers for walkers.

Female Factory HISTORIC SITE

(☎03-6233 6656; www.femalefactory.org.au; 16 Degraves St, South Hobart; adult/child/family $5/5/15, tour adult/child/family $15/10/40, 'Her Story' dramatisation adult/child/family $20/12.50/60; ⏰9.30am-4pm, tours hourly 10am-3pm, 'Her Story' dramatisation 11am) Finally being recognised as an important historic site (one in four convicts transported to Van Diemen's Land was a woman), this was where Hobart's female convicts were incarcerated. Explore the site under your own steam, or book a guided tour or 'Her Story' dramatisation. It's not far from the Cascade Brewery – combining the two makes an engaging afternoon. To get here by public transport, take bus 44, 46, 47 or 49 and jump off at stop 13.

Northern Suburbs

★MONA MUSEUM, GALLERY

(Museum of Old & New Art; ☎03-6277 9900; www.mona.net.au; 655 Main Rd, Berriedale; adult/child $20/free, Tasmanian residents free; ⏰10am-6pm Wed-Mon Dec & Feb-Apr, 10am-6pm daily Jan, 10am-5pm Wed-Mon May-Nov) Twelve kilometres north of Hobart's city centre, MONA occupies a saucepan-shaped peninsula jutting into the Derwent River. Arrayed across three underground levels, abutting a sheer rock face, the $75-million museum has been described by philanthropist owner David Walsh as 'a subversive adult Disneyland'. Ancient antiquities are showcased next to contemporary works: sexy, provocative, disturbing and deeply engaging. Don't miss it!

To get here catch the MONA Roma ferry or shuttle bus from Hobart's Brooke St Pier ($20 return). Book everything online.

Royal Tasmanian Botanical Gardens GARDENS

(Map p620; ☎03-6236 3057; www.rtbg.tas.gov.au; Lower Domain Rd, Queen's Domain; ⏰8am-6.30pm Oct-Mar, to 5.30pm Apr & Sep, to 5pm May-Aug) FREE On the eastern side of the Queen's Domain, these small but beguiling gardens hark back to 1818 and feature more than 6000 exotic and native plant species. Picnic on the lawns, check out the Subantarctic Plant House or grab a bite at the **Botanical Restaurant**, which also houses a gift shop

HOBART IN...

Two Days

Get your head into history mode with an amble around **Battery Point** (p621) – coffee and cake at **Jackman & McRoss** (p632) is mandatory. Afterwards, wander down Kelly's Steps to **Salamanca Place** (p619), where you can check out the craft shops and galleries or chug a few cool Cascades at **Knopwood's Retreat** (p633), the quintessential Hobart pub. Bone up on Hobart's Antarctic heritage at the **Mawson's Hut Replica Museum** (p621) before a promenade along the Sullivans Cove waterfront with fish and chips for dinner from **Flippers** (p631).

On day two recuperate over a big breakfast at **Retro Café** (p631) on Salamanca Pl (if it's a Saturday, **Salamanca Market** (p623) will be pumping) then catch the ferry out to **MONA** (p622) for an afternoon of saucy, subversive, mindful distraction. Come down to earth with dinner and drinks in North Hobart then some live music at **Republic Bar & Café** (p634).

DON'T MISS

SALAMANCA MARKET

Every Saturday morning since 1972, the open-air **Salamanca Market** (Map p624; www.salamanca.com.au; ⌚8am-3pm Sat) has lured hippies and craft merchants from the foothills to fill the tree-lined expanses of Salamanca Pl with their stalls. Fresh organic produce, secondhand clothes and books, tacky tourist souvenirs, ceramics and woodwork, cheap sunglasses, antiques, exuberant buskers, quality food and drink... It's all here, but people watching is the real name of the game. Rain or shine – don't miss it!

and kiosk. Across from the main entrance is the site of the former **Beaumaris Zoo**, where the last captive Tasmanian tiger died in 1936.

Eastern Shore

Tasmanian Cricket Museum MUSEUM
(☎03-6282 0433; www.crickettas.com.au/blundstone-arena/museum-library; cnr Church & Derwent Sts, Bellerive; adult/child $2/1, tours $10/2; ⌚10am-3pm Tue-Thu, to noon Fri) Cricket fans should steer a well-directed cover drive towards Blundstone Arena. There's a beaut cricket museum and library here, plus oval tours (call for times and bookings). Don't miss the corner of the museum dedicated to the achievements of Tasmanian legend Ricky 'Punter' Ponting. There's still no commemoration of David Boon's 52 cans of beer quaffed on a Sydney-to-London flight in 1989 though. Bus 608 from the city runs past the oval.

Activities

Cycling

★ **Mt Wellington Descent** CYCLING
(☎1800 064 726; www.underdownunder.com.au; adult/child $75/65; ⌚10am & 1pm daily year-round, plus 4pm Jan & Feb) Take a van ride to the summit of Mt Wellington (1270m), and follow with 22km of downhill cruising on a mountain bike. It's terrific fun, with minimal energy output and maximum views! Tours start and end at Brooke St Pier on the Hobart waterfront.

Artbikes BICYCLE RENTAL
(Map p624; ☎03-6165 6666; www.artbikes.com.au; 146 Elizabeth St; ⌚9am-4.30pm Mon-Fri) More than 140cm tall? You qualify for free city-bike hire from Artbikes. Just bring a credit card and some photo ID, and off you go. If you want to keep the bike overnight it's $22; for a weekend it's $44.

Hobart Bike Hire BICYCLE RENTAL
(Map p624; ☎0447 556 189; www.hobartbikehire.com.au; 35 Hunter St; bike hire per day/overnight from $25/35; ⌚9am-5.30pm) Centrally located on Hobart's waterfront, and has lots of ideas for self-guided tours around the city or along the Derwent River to MONA. Electric bikes and tandems also available, and maps and helmets included.

Sea Kayaking

Roaring 40s Kayaking KAYAKING
(Map p620; ☎0455 949 777; www.roaring40skayaking.com.au; adult/child $90/50; ⌚10am daily year-round, plus 4pm Nov-Apr) Hobart is perhaps at its prettiest when viewed from the water. Take a safe, steady, 2½-hour guided paddle with Roaring 40s, named after the prevailing winds at these latitudes. You'll cruise from Sandy Bay past Battery Point and into the Hobart docks for some fish and chips while you float, before returning to Sandy Bay.

Swimming & Surfing

For a safe, clean swim, head south of town to **Kingston** or **Blackmans Bay**. The most reliable local surfing spots are **Clifton Beach** and **Goats Beach**, en route to South Arm.

Hobart Aquatic Centre SWIMMING
(Map p620; ☎03-6222 6999; www.hobartcity.com.au/recreation/the_hobart_aquatic_centre; 1 Davies Ave, Queen's Domain; adult/child/family $7.50/5/20; ⌚6am-9pm Mon-Fri, 8am-6pm Sat & Sun) The Hobart Aquatic Centre offers recreational moisture, even when it's raining. Inside are leisure pools, lap-swimming pools, a spa, a sauna, a steam room, aqua aerobics, and regulation aerobics for landlubbers.

Sailing

Lady Nelson SAILING
(Map p624; ☎03-6234 3348; www.ladynelson.org.au; Elizabeth St Pier; adult/child $30/10; ⌚11am, 1pm & 3pm Sat & Sun Oct-Mar, 11am & 1pm Apr-Sep) Sail around the harbour for 90 minutes on a replica of the surprisingly compact brig, *Lady Nelson*, one of the first colonial ships to sail to Tasmania. Longer trips are occasionally on offer: check the website.

Central Hobart

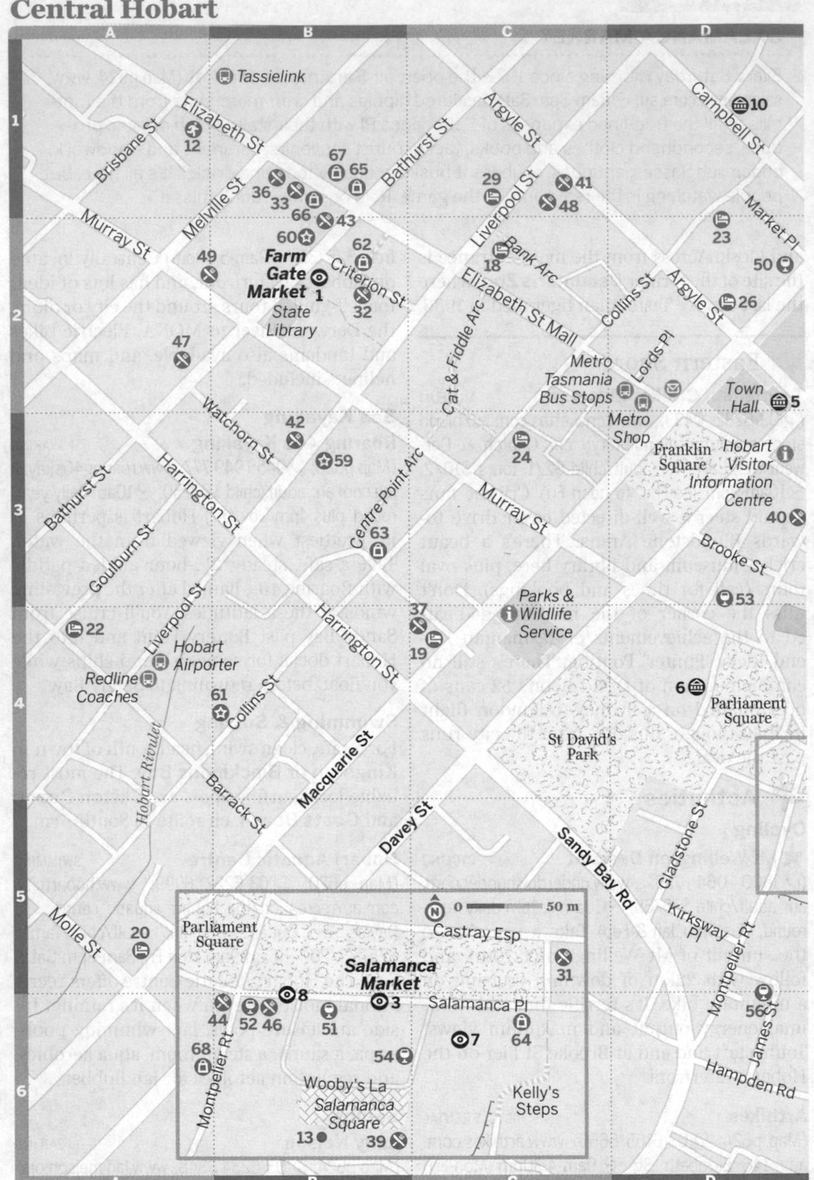

☞ Tours

Hobart Historic Tours WALKING TOUR

(☎ 03-6238 4222, 03-6231 4214; www.hobarthistorictours.com.au; tours adult/child/family $30/14/75) Informative, entertaining 90-minute walking tours of Hobart (3pm Thursday to Saturday and 9.30am Sunday) and historic Battery Point (5pm Wednesday and 1pm Saturday). There's also an Old Hobart Pub Tour (5pm Thursday to Saturday), which sluices through some waterfront watering holes. Reduced winter schedule, and bookings essential.

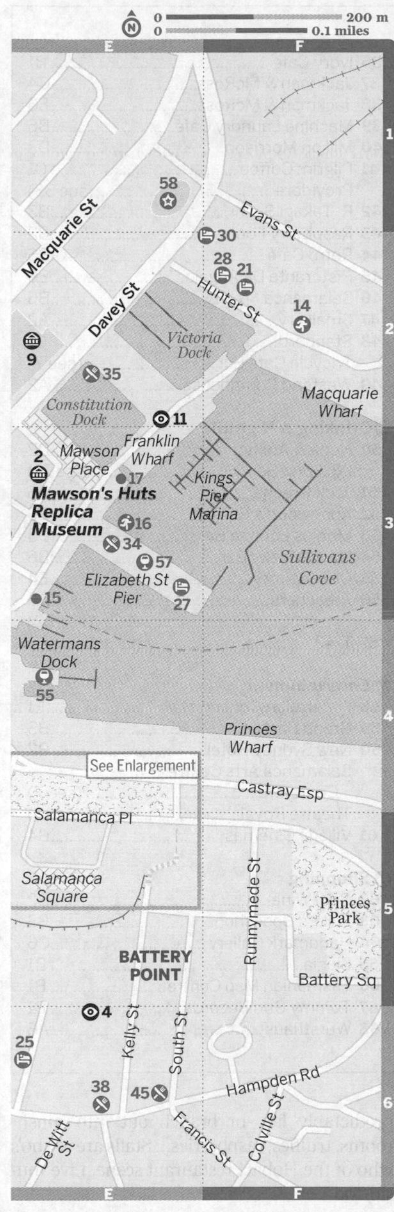

Gourmania FOOD TOUR
(☎0419 180 113; www.gourmaniafoodtours.com.au; per person from $95) Flavour-filled walking tours around Salamanca Pl and central Hobart, with plenty of opportunities to try local foods and chat to restaurant, cafe and shop owners. A tour of Hobart's best cafes was also mooted at the time of writing.

Louisa's Walk WALKING TOUR
(☎03-6229 8959, 0437 276 417; www.livehistoryhobart.com.au; 2hr tour adult/family $35/90) Engaging tours of Hobart's female convict heritage at the Female Factory (p622), interpreted through 'strolling theatre' with live actors. Tours depart Cascade Brewery at 2pm.

Hobart Historic Cruises BOAT TOUR
(Map p624; ☎03-6223 5893; www.hobarthistoriccruises.com.au; 6 Franklin Wharf; 1hr cruises adult/child/family $20/15/60; ⊙daily) Chug up or down the Derwent River from Hobart's waterfront on cute old ferries. Also runs longer lunch (adult/child/family $30/25/100) and dinner ($49/45/150) cruises travelling both up and down the river. Call for times and bookings.

Red Decker BUS TOUR
(☎03-6236 9116; www.reddecker.com.au; 20-stop pass adult/child/family $30/15/80) Commentated sightseeing on an old London double-decker bus. Buy a 20-stop, hop-on-hop-off pass (vaild for three days), or do the tour as a 90-minute loop. Pay a bit more and add a Cascade Brewery tour (adult/child/family $55/30/140) or Mt Wellington tour ($55/30/130) to the deal.

Jump Tours BUS TOUR
(☎0422 130 630; www.jumptours.com) Youth- and backpacker-oriented three- and five-day Tassie tours.

Under Down Under BUS TOUR
(☎1800 064 726; www.underdownunder.com.au) Offers pro-green, nature-based, backpacker-friendly trips. There are tours from three to nine days.

Tasmanian Whisky Tours DISTILLERY TOUR
(☎0412 099 933; www.tasmanianwhiskytours.com.au; per person $185; ⊙9am Wed, Fri & Sun) Tasmanian whisky has been getting plenty of press since Sullivans Cove Whisky won the coveted 'Best Single Malt' gong at the World Whisky Awards in 2014. Take a day tour with this passionate outfit, visiting three or four distilleries and tasting up to 10 top Tassie single malts. Minimum four passengers.

Ghost Tours of Hobart & Battery Point WALKING TOUR
(Map p624; ☎0439 335 696, 03-3933 5696; www.ghosttoursofhobart.com.au; adult/child $25/15)

Central Hobart

Top Sights
1 Farm Gate Market ... B2
2 Mawson's Huts Replica Museum ... E3
3 Salamanca Market ... B6

Sights
4 Battery Point ... E6
Carnegie Gallery ... (see 5)
5 Maritime Museum of Tasmania ... D2
6 Parliament House ... D4
7 Salamanca Arts Centre ... C6
8 Salamanca Place ... B6
9 Tasmanian Museum & Art Gallery ... E2
10 Theatre Royal ... D1
11 Waterfront ... E2

Activities, Courses & Tours
12 Artbikes ... A1
13 Ghost Tours of Hobart & Battery Point ... B6
14 Hobart Bike Hire ... F2
15 Hobart Historic Cruises ... E3
16 Lady Nelson ... E3
17 Tasman Island Cruises ... E3

Sleeping
18 Alabama Hotel ... C2
19 Astor Private Hotel ... C4
20 Edinburgh Gallery B&B ... A5
21 Henry Jones Art Hotel ... F2
22 Hobart Hostel ... A4
23 Hotel Collins ... D2
24 Imperial Hotel Backpackers ... C3
25 Montacute ... E6
26 Montgomery's Private Hotel & YHA ... D2
27 Somerset on the Pier ... E3
28 Sullivans Cove Apartments ... F2
29 Tassie Backpackers ... C1
30 Zero Davey ... F2

Eating
31 Blue Eye ... C5
32 Criterion Street Café ... B2
33 Ethos ... B1
34 Fish Frenzy ... E3
35 Flippers ... E2
36 Ivory Cafe ... B1
37 Jackman & McRoss ... C4
38 Jackman & McRoss ... E6
39 Machine Laundry Café ... B6
40 Mill on Morrison ... D3
41 Pilgrim Coffee ... C1
Providore ... (see 33)
42 R. Takagi Sushi ... B3
43 Raspberry Fool ... B2
44 Retro Café ... B6
45 Ristorante Da Angelo ... E6
46 Salamanca Fresh ... B6
47 Small Fry ... A2
48 Standard ... C1
Tricycle Café Bar ... (see 7)
49 Westend Pumphouse ... A2

Drinking & Nightlife
50 Hope & Anchor ... D2
IXL Long Bar ... (see 21)
51 Jack Greene ... B6
52 Knopwood's Retreat ... B6
53 Mobius Lounge Bar ... D3
54 Nant Whisky Bar ... B6
55 Observatory ... E4
56 Preachers ... D6
Syrup ... (see 52)
57 T-42° ... E3

Entertainment
58 Federation Concert Hall ... E1
59 Grand Poobah ... B3
60 New Sydney Hotel ... B2
Salamanca Arts Centre Courtyard ... (see 7)
Theatre Royal ... (see 10)
61 Village Cinemas ... B4

Shopping
62 Cool Wine ... B2
63 Fullers Bookshop ... B3
64 Handmark Gallery ... C6
65 Skigia ... B1
66 Tasmanian Map Centre ... B1
67 Tommy Gun Records ... B1
68 Wursthaus ... A6

Walking tours oozing ectoplasmic tall tales, departing the Bakehouse in Salamanca Sq at dusk most nights. Bookings essential, and no kids under eight.

Festivals & Events

★Taste of Tasmania FOOD, WINE

(www.thetasteoftasmania.com.au) On either side of New Year's Eve, this week-long harbourside event is a celebration of Tassie's gastronomic prowess. The seafood, wines and cheeses are predictably fab, or branch out into mushrooms, truffles, raspberries… Stalls are a who's who of the Hobart restaurant scene. Live music, too.

MONA FOMA MUSIC, ART

(MOFO; www.mofo.net.au; Jan) Acronyms ahoy! On the grounds of MONA, January's wonderfully eclectic Festival of Music & Arts features a high-profile 'Eminent Artist in Residence' (EAR) every year. Previous EARs have included John Cale and Nick Cave. Stirring stuff.

Australian Wooden Boat Festival CULTURAL
(www.australianwoodenboatfestival.com.au) Biennial event (odd-numbered years) in mid-February to coincide with the Royal Hobart Regatta. The festival showcases Tasmania's boat-building heritage and maritime traditions. You can almost smell the Huon pine!

Ten Days on the Island CULTURAL, ART
(www.tendaysontheisland.com) Tasmania's premier cultural festival is a biennial event (odd-numbered years, usually late March to early April) celebrating Tasmanian arts, music and culture at statewide venues. Expect concerts, exhibitions, dance, film, theatre and workshops.

Dark MOFO MUSIC, ART
(www.darkmofo.net.au) The sinister sister of MONA FOMA, Dark MOFO broods in the half-light of June's winter solstice. Expect live music, installations, readings, film noir and midnight feasts, all tapping into Tasmania's edgy gothic undercurrents.

Tasmanian Beerfest BEER
(www.tasmanianbeerfest.com.au) More than 200 brews from around Australia and the world, with brewing classes and lots of opportunities for waterfront snacking, foot tapping and imbibing. Held in November.

Sydney to Hobart Yacht Race SPORTS
(www.rolexsydneyhobart.com) Maxi-yachts competing in this gruelling annual open-ocean race start arriving in Hobart around 29 December – just in time for New Year's Eve! (Yachties sure can party...)

Falls Festival MUSIC
(www.fallsfestival.com.au) The Tasmanian version of the Victorian rock festival is a winner! Three nights and four days of live Oz and international tunes (eg Paul Kelly, Dan Sultan, Cold War Kids, Alt J) at Marion Bay, an hour east of Hobart from 29 December to 1 January.

Sleeping

The pumping-est areas to stay in Hobart are the waterfront and Salamanca Pl, though prices here are usually sky-high and vacancy rates low. If you're visiting in January, book as far in advance as humanly possible. The CBD has less atmosphere, but most of the backpacker hostels, pubs with accommodation and midrange hotels are here.

To the north of the city centre are suburban North Hobart and New Town, with apartments and B&Bs within walking distance of the North Hobart restaurants. To the south, accommodation in Sandy Bay is surprisingly well priced.

City Centre

★ **Alabama Hotel** HOTEL $
(Map p624; ☎0499 987 698; www.alabamahobart.com.au; level 1, 72 Liverpool St; d/tw from $85/90; wifi) Sweet home Alabama! This old art-deco boozer – once a grim, sticky-carpet lush magnet – has been reborn as a boutique budget hotel. None of the 17 rooms has a bathroom, but the shared facilities are immaculate and plentiful. Decor is funky and colourful with retro-deco flourishes, and there's an all-day bar with a sunny balcony over the street. Cool!

Tassie Backpackers HOSTEL $
(Brunswick Hotel; Map p624; ☎03-6234 4981; www.tassiebackpackers.com; 67 Liverpool St; dm $20-30, d/tr with bathroom from $79/85; wifi) While we struggle with the hokey overuse of 'Tassie' nomenclature around the state, it's hard to deny this hostel's merits (Hobart's cheapest beds?). The venerable old Brunswick Hotel (some of the sandstone walls here date back to 1816) now offers plenty of shared spaces, a kitchen and a laundry in a central location. Energetic management also runs the bar downstairs.

Hobart Hostel HOSTEL $
(Map p624; ☎1300 252 192, 03-6234 6122; www.hobarthostel.com; cnr Goulburn & Barrack Sts; dm $26-30, s/d without bathroom $65/73, d & tw with bathroom $85-95; @wifi) In a former pub (the ever-rockin' Doghouse), Hobart Hostel

SYDNEY TO HOBART YACHT RACE

Arguably the world's greatest and most treacherous open-ocean yacht race, the **Sydney to Hobart Yacht Race** winds up at Hobart's Constitution Dock every New Year's Eve. As the storm-battered maxis limp across the finish line, champagne corks pop and weary sailors turn the town upside down. On New Year's Day, find a sunny spot by the harbour, munch some lunch from the **Taste of Tasmania** (p626) food festival and count spinnakers on the river. New Year's resolutions? What New Year's resolutions?

HOBART FOR CHILDREN

Parents won't break the bank keeping the troops entertained in Hobart. The free **Friday-night music** (p635) in the courtyard at the Salamanca Arts Centre is a family-friendly affair, while the street performers, buskers and visual smorgasbord of Saturday's **Salamanca Market** (p623) captivate kids of all ages. There's always something going on around the **waterfront** (p621): fishing boats chugging in and out of Victoria Dock, yachts tacking in Sullivans Cove…and you can feed the tribe on a budget at the floating fish punts on Constitution Dock.

Rainy-day attractions to satisfy your child (or inner child) include the **Tasmanian Museum & Art Gallery** (p621), the **Maritime Museum of Tasmania** (p619) and the excellent new **Mawson's Hut Replica Museum** (p621).

If you're in need of a romantic dinner for two, contact the **Mobile Nanny Service** (☎03-6273 3773, 0437 504 064; www.mobilenannyservice.com.au).

offers clean, recently redecorated dorms, with good-value en suite twins and doubles upstairs. Downstairs there are huge red sofas, and well-behaved backpackers going about their business (party somewhere else).

Imperial Hotel Backpackers HOSTEL $
(Map p624; ☎03-6223 5215; www.backpackersimperialhobart.com.au; 138 Collins St; dm/s/tw/d from $24/59/82/90; 📶) Right in the middle of the city, in one of Hobart's original hotels (1870), this maze-like hostel has loads of communal space, an upgraded kitchen, high ceilings and friendly staff, plus extras such as baggage storage and a tour desk. Ask for a sunny north-facing room over Collins St.

Montgomery's Private Hotel & YHA HOSTEL $
(Map p624; ☎03-6231 2660; www.montgomerys.com.au; 9 Argyle St; dm from $29, d & tw with/without bathroom from $140/120, f from $118; @) Attached to a historic pub (lately called the Fluke & Bruce), this simple but clean YHA offers bright, secure accommodation right in the middle of town. Spread over three maze-like levels are dorms of all sizes, including nifty en suite rooms and family-sized rooms. No parking, but you're walking distance from everything here.

★ **Astor Private Hotel** HOTEL $$
(Map p624; ☎03-6234 6611; www.astorprivatehotel.com.au; 157 Macquarie St; s $79-89, d $93-140, all incl breakfast; 📶) A rambling downtown 1920s charmer, the Astor retains much of its character: stained-glass windows, old furniture, lofty celings (with ceiling roses) and the irrepressible Tildy at the helm. Older-style rooms have shared facilities, which are plentiful, while newer en suite rooms top the price range. Strict 'No Bogans' policy!

Edinburgh Gallery B&B B&B $$
(Map p624; ☎03-6224 9229; www.artaccom.com.au; 211 Macquarie St; r incl breakfast $90-230; P@📶) This funky, art-filled boutique hotel puts an eclectic stamp on a 1909 Federation house, just to the west of the CBD. Some rooms share immaculate bathrooms, and all have DVD players and quirky, artsy decor (try for a verandah suite). Continental breakfast (farm honey and jam, yoghurt, cereals and chocolate-chip cookies!) centres around the lovely communal kitchen.

Hotel Collins HOTEL $$
(Map p624; ☎03-6226 1111; www.hotelcollins.com.au; 58 Collins St; d $180-275, apt from $385; ❄@📶) One of Hobart's newest hotels effortlessly shows up other places around town as a little old and weary. A youthful energy at reception flows through all 10 floors of spacious rooms and apartments, some with super views of Mt Wellington's gargantuan bulk. There's also a relaxed cafe-bar downstairs. No parking is the only bummer.

Waterfront & Salamanca Place

Zero Davey APARTMENT $$
(Map p624; ☎03-6270 1444, 1300 733 422; www.escapesresorts.com.au; 15 Hunter St; 1-/2-/3-bedroom apt from $185/329/429; P❄📶) These modern, funky apartments on the edge of Hobart's kinetic waterfront precinct don't garner much external architectural kudos, but inside they're great and the location is primo. Nab one with a balcony for views over Hobart's raffish fishing fleet. Good discounts online.

★ **Henry Jones Art Hotel** BOUTIQUE HOTEL $$$
(Map p624; ☎03-6210 7700; www.thehenryjones.com; 25 Hunter St; d from $310; P❄@📶)

Super-swish HJs is a beacon of sophistication. In the restored waterfront Henry Jones IXL jam factory, with remnant bits of jam-making machinery and huge timber beams, it oozes class but is far from snooty (this is Hobart, not Sydney). Modern art enlivens the walls, while facilities and distractions (bar, restaurant, cafe) are world class. Just brilliant.

Sullivans Cove Apartments APARTMENT $$$
(Map p624; ☎03-6234 5063; www.sullivanscove apartments.com.au; 5/19a Hunter St; 1-/2-/3-bedroom d apt from $260/320/520, extra person $45; P❄📶) Exclusive, boutique, luxury, private... All apply to these sassy apartments, dotted around the Hobart waterfront in five locations (check-in for all is at 5/19a Hunter St). Our faves are the hip new architect-designed units inside the charismatic old Gibson's Flour Mill on Morrison St, where the mill's original timber and steel structures are highlighted in the interior design.

Somerset on the Pier HOTEL $$$
(Map p624; ☎03-6220 6600, 1800 766 377; www.somerset.com; Elizabeth St Pier; 1-2-bedroom apt from $295/395; P❄@📶) In a definitively Hobart location, on the upper level of the Elizabeth Pier, this cool complex offers luxe apartments with beaut harbour views and breezy, contemporary design. You'll pay more for a balcony, but with these views you won't need to do any other sightseeing! Limited free parking.

Battery Point, Sandy Bay & South Hobart

★ **Montacute** HOSTEL $
(Map p624; ☎03-6212 0474; www.montacute.com.au; 1 Stowell Ave, Battery Point; dm/tw/d from $35/90/100; P📶) Getting rave reviews, this new 'boutique bunkhouse' occupies a renovated house in Battery Point. Many Hobart hostels are cheap remodellings of old pubs, but Montacute sets the bar a mile higher, with immaculate rooms and shared bathrooms, nice art, quality linen and mattresses, and proximity to cafes – all just a 10-minute walk from the city and Salamanca. Nice one!

★ **Quayle Terrace** RENTAL HOUSE $$
(Map p620; ☎0418 395 543; www.quayleterrace.com.au; 51 Quayle St, Battery Point; d $180-250, extra person $20; P❄) Tracing the boundary between Battery Point and Sandy Bay, Quayle St features a long run of photogenic terrace houses (ignore the power lines and this could be 1890). Quayle Terrace is one such edifice – a two-storey, two-bedroom, tastefully renovated house with a cosy gas fire and mountain views from the shower (any snow this morning?). Free street parking.

Tree Tops Cascades RENTAL HOUSE $$
(☎03-6223 2839, 0408 323 839; www.treetops cascades.com.au; 165 Strickland Ave, South Hobart; d/q from $150/250, extra person $25; P📶) Book ahead for this lovely three-bedroom house (sleeps five) in an idyllic bush setting, 6km from town near Cascade Brewery and several Mt Wellington walks. Built on 2 hectares, there's a zoo-full of wildlife about: possums, wallabies, bandicoots and tame kookaburras (which you can feed on the barbecue deck). Buses 44, 46, 47 and 49 run here from the city.

Apartments on Star APARTMENT $$
(Map p620; ☎03-6225 4799, 0400 414 656; www.apartmentsonstar.com.au; 22 Star St, Sandy Bay; 1-/2-/3-bedroom apt from $190/230/300; P📶) This old brick house at the bottom of Star St (the lower floor of which was once home to a Lonely Planet author who shan't be named) now comprises two hip apartments, bolstered by a new adjacent building housing a further two slick units. Cool kitchens, big TVs and quality furnishings...and Sandy Bay's buzzing restaurant scene is metres away.

Motel 429 MOTEL $$
(Map p620; ☎03-6225 2511; www.motel429.com.au; 429 Sandy Bay Rd, Sandy Bay; d $130-200; P❄@📶) This motel's ongoing facelift has given most rooms (all but six of 33) a sleek designer sheen. The staff are friendly, everything's clean and shipshape and the restaurants of Sandy Bay are a short drive away. The deluxe rooms are super comfortable, and Wrest Point Casino is across the road if you're feeling lucky.

Grand Vue Private Hotel B&B $$$
(Map p620; ☎03-6223 8216; www.grande-vue-hotel.com; 8 Mona St, Battery Point; d $225-285; P📶) 'Vues' from the best rooms at this lovingly restored 1906 mansion take in a broad sweep of Sandy Bay and the Derwent River, or Mt Wellington in the other direction. Sleek new bathrooms and super-friendly service lift Grande Vue above similar B&Bs nearby. Breakfast ($12.50) includes still-warm baked goodies from Jackman & McRoss.

North & West Hobart

Hobart Cabins & Cottages CARAVAN PARK $
(03-6272 7115; www.hobartcabinscottages.com.au; 19 Goodwood Rd, Glenorchy; powered sites $35, cabins d & f from $110, 3-bedroom house $200;) An unflattering 8km north of the city in Glenorchy, but offers a range of tidy cottages and cabins and a three-bedroom house sleeping up to 10 bods.

Lodge on Elizabeth B&B $$
(Map p620; 03-6231 3830; www.thelodge.com.au; 249 Elizabeth St; r incl breakfast $165-230;) Built in 1829 this old-timer has been a schoolhouse, a boarding house and a halfway house, but now opens its doors as a value-for-money guesthouse. Rooms are dotted with antiques (not for the modernists) and all have en suites. The self-contained cottage overlooks the tulip-dappled courtyard out the back. Two-night minimum stay.

Bay View Villas MOTEL, APARTMENT $$
(1800 061 505, 03-6234 7611; www.bayviewvillas.com; 34 Poets Rd, West Hobart; d $149-219, extra person $20;) A few kilometres up the steep West Hobart slopes from the city, this family-focused option offers a games room and an indoor pool (follow the scent of chlorine from reception). There's a rank of tarted-up motel units out the front, and 12 stylish one-bedroom units behind with magical river views.

Islington BOUTIQUE HOTEL $$$
(Map p620; 03-6220 2123; www.islingtonhotel.com; 321 Davey St, South Hobart; d from $395;) At the top of Hobart's accommodation tree, the classy Islington effortlessly merges heritage architecture with antique furniture, contemporary art and a glorious garden. Service is attentive but understated, with breakfast served in an expansive conservatory. In the evening, wind down with a wine in the guest library, study/music room or drawing room. Exquisite private dinners are also available. Superb.

Altamont House APARTMENT $$$
(Map p620; 0409 145 844, 0437 344 932; www.altamonthouse.com.au; 109 Patrick St, West Hobart; d $200, extra adult/child $60/30;) Are there rules about how steep a street can be? The town planners weren't paying attention when they laid out Patrick St...but the views are great! Occupying the ground floor of a gorgeous old stone-and-slate house, Altamont offers a plush double suite with an extra room that can be opened up as required. No sign of the Rolling Stones...

Eating

Downtown Hobart proffers some classy brunch and lunch venues, but when the sun sinks behind the mountain, there's not much going on here. Instead, head for Salamanca Pl and the waterfront, the epicentre of the city's culinary scene, with quality seafood everywhere you look.

Battery Point's Hampden Rd restaurants are always worth a look, while Elizabeth St in North Hobart (aka 'NoHo') has evolved into a diverse collection of cosmopolitan eateries.

For Hobart's best pub grub, head to the New Sydney Hotel (p634) or the Republic Bar & Café (p634).

City Centre

★ **Pilgrim Coffee** CAFE $
(Map p624; 03-6234 1999; 48 Argyle St; mains $11-20; 7am-5pm Mon-Fri) With exposed bricks, timber beams and distressed walls, L-shaped Pilgrim is Hobart's hippest cafe. Expect wraps, panini and interesting mains (Peruvian spiced alpaca with quinoa and beetroot!), plus expertly prepared coffee. Fall into conversation with the locals at big shared tables. Down a laneway around the back is the **Standard** (Map p624; 03-6234 1999; Hudsons Lane; burgers $7-12; 11am-10pm daily), a fab burger bar run by the same hipsters.

Small Fry CAFE $
(Map p624; 03-6231 1338; www.small-fryhobart.com.au; 129 Bathurst St; mains $6-25; 7.30am-3.30pm Mon-Thu, to 9pm Fri, 8.30am-9pm Sat) Hip Small Fry is now one of Hobart's best cafe-bars in its own right. Conversation comes naturally at the shared steel counter: sip a glass of wine, some soup or a coffee; talk, listen, laugh, crunch a salad... It's a flexible vibe designed to 'avoid labels'. Love the wooden menu cubes!

Raspberry Fool CAFE $
(Map p624; 03-6231 1274; 85 Bathurst St; mains $9-17; 7.30am-4pm Mon-Fri, to 2.30pm Sat & Sun) The all-day menu here features dressed-up comfort food with a chef's spin. Try the cheesy leeks on toast with bacon and a fried egg, or the baked eggs with caramelised onion, ham and Gruyère. It gets as busy as a woodpecker when the Farm Gate Mar-

ket (p619) is happening outside on Sunday mornings. Great coffee, too.

Criterion Street Café CAFE $
(Map p624; ☎03-6234 5858; www.criterionstcafe.com; 10 Criterion St; mains $6-15; ⊙7am-4pm Mon-Fri, 8am-3pm Sat & Sun) It's a short menu on a short street, but Criterion Street Café effortlessly meets the criteria for keeping both breakfast and lunch fans sated, and caffeine fiends buzzing through the day. Try the Spanish omelette or the haloumi salad with brown rice and baby spinach. Beers and wines, too.

R. Takagi Sushi JAPANESE $
(Map p624; ☎03-6234 8524; 155 Liverpool St; sushi from $3; ⊙10.30am-5.50pm Mon-Fri, to 4pm Sat, 11.30am-3pm Sun) Hobart's best sushi spot makes the most of Tasmania's great seafood. Udon noodles and miso also make an appearance at this sleek, compact eatery – a favourite of Hobart desk jockeys.

Providore CAFE, DELI $
(Map p624; ☎03-6231 1165; 100 Elizabeth St; mains $3-12; ⊙10am-4pm Mon-Sat) A daytime business adjunct to night-time restaurant Ethos, funky Providore conducts trade with moral fortitude, sourcing ethically produced local ingredients. Super salads and awesome sandwiches are the main thrust, plus shelves full of artisan breads, oils, pestos, pastes, honey and cookbooks. There's a great **yoghurt and juice bar** next door, too.

Westend Pumphouse CAFE $$
(Map p624; ☎03-6234 7339; www.pumphouse.com.au; 105 Murray St; mains $19-38; ⊙8.30am-late) An excellent wine list, good coffee and craft beers on tap feature at the versatile, industrial Pumphouse. Smash your first coffee of the morning, then come back later in the day with some friends for shared plates (try the lamb shoulder, cabbage and mustard salad) and a few ales. Check out the milk-container wall!

Ivory Cafe THAI $$
(Map p624; ☎03-6231 6808; 112 Elizabeth St; mains $12-20; ⊙11.30am-3pm Mon-Sat, 5-9pm Tue-Sat) Hobart's most popular Thai restaurant is a modest, slender affair, with a long bench seat along one wall and three stools in the front window, which are perfect if you're dining solo. Order the excellent green chicken curry and peer out at Elizabeth St's occasional bustle.

Ethos MODERN AUSTRALIAN $$$
(Map p624; ☎03-6231 1165; www.ethoseatdrink.com; 100 Elizabeth St; 6-/8-course menu $75/90; ⊙6pm-late Tue-Sat) Hidden in a courtyard down a flagstone alley off Elizabeth St, Ethos rigorously supports local farmers and ethically produced Tasmanian food. The menu is very seasonal, with artisan-produced ingredients showcasing whatever's fresh. Servings are on the small side, but the flavours are innovative and delicious. Bookings essential. There's also a moody new **wine bar** downstairs.

Waterfront & Salamanca Place

★**Retro Café** CAFE $
(Map p624; ☎03-6223 3073; 31 Salamanca Pl; mains $10-18; ⊙7am-5pm) So popular it hurts, funky Retro is ground zero for Saturday brunch among the market stalls (or any day, really). Masterful breakfasts, bagels, salads and burgers interweave with laughing staff, chilled-out jazz and the whirr and bang of the coffee machine. A classic Hobart cafe.

Flippers SEAFOOD $
(Map p624; www.flippersfishandchips.com.au; Constitution Dock; meals $10-24; ⊙9.30am-8.30pm) With its voluptuous fish-shaped profile and alluring sea-blue paint job, floating Flippers is a Hobart institution. Not to mention the awesome fish and chips! Fillets of flathead and curls of calamari – straight from the deep blue sea and into the deep fryer. The local seagulls will adore you.

Machine Laundry Café CAFE $
(Map p624; ☎03-6224 9922; 12 Salamanca Sq; mains $7-17; ⊙7.30am-5pm Mon-Sat, 8.30am-5pm Sun) Hypnotise yourself watching the tumble dryers spin at this bright retro cafe, where you can wash your dirty clothes ($5) while discreetly adding fresh juice, soup or coffee stains to your clean ones. Don't miss the chilli-infused roti wrap for breakfast.

Tricycle Café Bar CAFE $
(Map p624; ☎03-6223 7228; www.salarts.org.au/portfolio/tricycle; 71 Salamanca Pl; mains $8-15; ⊙8.30am-4pm Mon-Sat) This cosy red-painted nook inside the **Salamanca Arts Centre** (Map p624; ☎03-6234 8414; www.salarts.org.au; 77 Salamanca Pl; ⊙shops & galleries 9am-5pm) serves up a range of cafe classics (BLTs, toasties, free-range scrambled eggs, salads, house-brewed chai and Fair Trade coffee), plus awesome daily specials (braised Wagyu

rice bowl with jalapeño cream – wow!). Wines by the glass from the bar.

Salamanca Fresh SUPERMARKET $
(Map p624; ☎03-6223 2700; www.salamancafresh.com.au; 41 Salamanca Pl; ⏰7am-7pm) Gourmet self-caterers alert: don't miss the fruit, veg, meats and groceries here, plus a suite of Tasmanian wines.

Fish Frenzy SEAFOOD $$
(Map p624; ☎03-6231 2134; www.fishfrenzy.com.au; Elizabeth St Pier; mains $14-35; ⏰11am-9pm) A casual, waterside fish nook, overflowing with fish fiends and brimming with fish and chips, fishy salads (spicy calamari, smoked salmon and brie) and fish burgers. The eponymous 'Fish Frenzy' ($18) delivers a little bit of everything. Quality can be inconsistent, but good staff and buzzy harbourside vibes compensate. No bookings.

Mill on Morrison SPANISH, MODERN AUSTRALIAN $$
(Map p624; ☎03-6234 3490; www.themillonmorrison.com.au; 11 Morrison St; tapas $4-16; ⏰noon-2pm Mon-Fri, 5.30pm-late Mon-Sat) Inside the gorgeously renovated Gibson's City Mill (cast-iron columns, exposed timber celings, dark-wood tables and chairs) is this sharp but relaxed tapas restaurant: a bit Spanish, a bit Mexican, a bit Mod Oz. Don't overlook the chargrilled calamari or the cheese and arancini balls. Terrific wines by the glass, from the Coal River Valley to Catalonia.

Blue Eye SEAFOOD $$$
(Map p624; ☎03-6223 5297; www.blueeye.net.au; 1 Castray Esplanade; mains $29-45; ⏰5-9pm Mon, 11am-9pm Tue-Sat) Ignore the slightly clinical decor and dive into some of Hobart's best seafood. Standouts include scallop and prawn linguini, curried seafood chowder and a terrific seafood pie with dill-and-spinach cream. Moo Brew ale on tap and a Tasmanian-skewed wine list complete a very zesty picture.

Battery Point, Sandy Bay & South Hobart

★Jackman & McRoss BAKERY $
(Map p624; ☎03-6223 3186; 57-59 Hampden Rd, Battery Point; meals $8-13; ⏰7am-6pm Mon-Fri, to 5pm Sat & Sun) Don't bypass this conversational, neighbourhood bakery-cafe, even if it's just to gawk at the display cabinet full of delectable pies, tarts, baguettes and pastries. Early morning cake and coffee may evolve into a quiche for lunch, or perhaps a blackberry-and-wallaby pie. Staff stay cheery despite being run off their feet. The city **branch** (Map p624; ☎03-6231 0601; 4 Victoria St; ⏰7am-4.30pm Mon-Fri) has parallel prices.

Ginger Brown CAFE $
(☎03-6223 3531; 464 Macquarie St, South Hobart; mains $10-20; ⏰7.30am-4pm Tue-Fri, 8.30am-4pm Sat & Sun; 👪) When a food business is this well run, the mood infects the entire room: happy staff, happy customers and happy vibes. Try the slow-cooked lamb panini with cornichons and hummus. Very kid- and cyclist-friendly. Last orders 3pm.

Ristorante Da Angelo ITALIAN $$
(Map p624; ☎03-6223 7011; www.daangelo.com; 47 Hampden Rd, Battery Point; mains $18-32; ⏰5pm-late) An enduring (and endearing) Italian *ristorante,* Da Angelo presents an impressively long menu of homemade pastas, veal and chicken dishes, calzone and pizzas with 20 different toppings. Colosseum and Carlton Football Club team photos add authenticity. Takeaway, BYO and open late.

Solo Pasta & Pizza ITALIAN $$
(Map p620; ☎03-6234 9898; www.solopastaandpizza.com.au; 50b King St, Sandy Bay; mains $12-26; ⏰5-10pm Tue-Sun) The brilliant pastas, pizzas, risottos and calzones at Solo have been drawing hungry hordes for decades. Not that you'd know its age from looking at it: the snazzy glass-fronted room backed by racks of wine is almost futuristic.

North & West Hobart

★Burger Haus BURGERS $
(Map p620; ☎03-6234 9507; 364a Elizabeth St, North Hobart; mains $10-14; ⏰11.30am-9.30pm Mon-Fri, 11am-9.45pm Sat & Sun) Blaring 1980s rock, big beefy burgers and a little terrace on which to sit, chew and contemplate the moody hues of Mt Wellington...this place has got it all! The Haus Burger (with bacon, onion rings, caramelised pineapple and mustard mayo) reigns supreme.

Pigeon Hole CAFE $
(Map p620; ☎03-6236 9306; www.pigeonholecafe.com.au; 93 Goulburn St, West Hobart; mains $10-13; ⏰8am-4.30pm Tue-Sat) This funky, friendly cafe is the kind of place every inner-city neighbourhood should have. A serious coffee attitude comes together with cafe food that's definitely a cut above. The freshly baked panini are the best you'll have, while

the baked eggs *en cocotte* (casserole) with serrano ham is an absolute knockout.

Sweet Envy CAFE $

(Map p620; ☎03-6234 8805; www.sweetenvy.com; 341 Elizabeth St, North Hobart; items $5-10; ⏰8.30am-6pm Tue-Fri, to 5pm Sat) A delicate diversion along North Hobart's restaurant strip, Sweet Envy conjures up gossamer-light macarons, madeleines and cupcakes. Gourmet pies and sausage rolls (try the pork and fennel version) and fantastic ice creams and sorbets, all made on the premises. Grab a scoop of bad-ass black-sesame ice cream and hit the streets.

Elizabeth St Food + Wine MODERN AUSTRALIAN, DELI $$

(Map p620; ☎03-6231 2626; 285 Elizabeth St, North Hobart; mains $10-20; ⏰8am-6pm Sun-Thu, to 8pm Fri, to 4pm Sat) Cafe, providore, wine room – take your pick at this vibrant North Hobart foodie space. Expect excellent breakfasts, big salads and classy mains (try the spicy beef cheek with potato and peperonata), all paired with local wines (except the breakfasts...). Communal tables and shelves crammed with 100% seasonal and sustainable Tasmanian produce.

Raincheck Lounge CAFE $$

(Map p620; ☎03-6234 5975; www.raincheck lounge.com.au; 392 Elizabeth St, North Hobart; tapas $6-17, mains $9-22; ⏰7am-late Mon-Fri, 8am-late Sat, 8.30am-late Sun) A slice of urban cool, Raincheck's bohemian, quasi-Moroccan room and streetside tables see punters sipping coffee, reconstituting over big breakfasts, and conversing over generous tapas such as broccolini with anchovy crumb and chorizo in peperonata. Great wine list and sassy staff to boot. Perfect before or after a movie at the State Cinema (p634). Nice one.

Vanidol's ASIAN $$

(Map p620; ☎03-6234 9307; www.vanidols-north-hobart.com; 353 Elizabeth St, North Hobart; mains $18-30; ⏰5.30-9pm daily; ✎) A pioneering North Hobart restaurant, Vanidol's has a diverse menu that travels effortlessly around Asia with dishes including spicy Thai beef salad, Nepalese lamb curry and Balinese chicken. Expect a well-thumbed passport full of vegetarian dishes, too. Also in **South Hobart** (Map p620; ☎03-6224 5986; www.vanidol south.com; 361a Macquarie St, South Hobart; mains $20-25; ⏰11am-2pm & 5.30-9pm Tue-Sat).

Drinking & Nightlife

Hobart's younger drinkers are 10,000 leagues removed from the rum-addled whalers of the past, but the general intentions remain the same – drink a little, relax a lot and maybe get lucky and take someone home. Salamanca Pl and the waterfront host a slew of pubs and bars with outdoor imbibing on summer evenings and open fires in winter. North Hobart is another solid (or rather, liquid) option.

★Knopwood's Retreat PUB

(Map p624; www.knopwoods.com; 39 Salamanca Pl; ⏰10am-late) Adhere to the 'when in Rome...' dictum and head for 'Knoppies', Hobart's best pub, which has been serving ales to sea-going types since the convict era. For most of the week it's a cosy watering hole with an open fire. On Friday nights, city workers swarm and the crowd spills across the street.

Preachers BAR

(Map p624; 5 Knopwood St, Battery Point; ⏰noon-late) Grab a retro sofa seat inside, or adjourn to the ramshackle garden bar – in which an old Hobart bus is now full of beer booths – with the hipsters. Lots of Tasmanian craft beers on tap, plus cool staff and a resident ghost. A steady flow of $15 burgers and $12 tapas keeps the beer in check.

Jack Greene BAR

(Map p624; www.jackgreene.com.au; 47-48 Salamanca Pl; ⏰11am-late) The gourmet burgers here cost up to $20 but atmospheric Jack Greene (a European hunting lodge on the run?) is worthwhile if you're a wandering beer fan. Glowing racks of bottled brews fill the fridges, and there are at least 16 beers on tap from around Australia and New Zealand. Occasional acoustic troubadors perch next to the stairs.

IXL Long Bar BAR

(Map p624; www.thehenryjones.com; 25 Hunter St; ⏰5-10.30pm Mon-Fri, 3pm-late Sat & Sun) Prop yourself at the glowing bar at the Henry Jones Art Hotel (p628) and check out Hobart's fashionistas over a whisky sour. If there are no spare stools at the not-so-long bar, flop onto the leather couches in the lobby. Moo Brew on tap, and live jazz Friday to Sunday.

T-42° BAR

(Map p624; www.tav42.com.au; Elizabeth St Pier; ⏰7.30am-late Mon-Fri, from 8.30am Sat & Sun) Waterfront T-42° makes a big splash with its food (mains from $13 to $30), but also draws late-week barflies with its minimalist interior, spinnaker-shaped bar and ambient tunes. If you stay out late enough, it also does breakfast.

Nant Whisky Bar BAR

(Map p624; www.nant.com.au; 63 Woobys Lane; ⏲noon-midnight Sun-Fri, 10am to midnight Sat) Prop yourself at the bar in this compact, heritage-hued room off Salamanca Pl and see how whisky from the **Nant Distillery** (☎1800 746 453, 03-6259 5790; www.nant.com.au; 254 Nant Lane; tastings & tours $15; ⏲10am-4.45pm, tours 11am & 3pm) in Tasmania's central highlands stacks up next to other peaty drops from around the globe.

Hope & Anchor PUB

(Map p624; www.hopeandanchor.com.au; 65 Macquarie St; ⏲11am-late) Depending on who you believe (don't listen to the barman at the Fortune of War in Sydney), this is the oldest pub in Australia (1807). The woody interior is lined with nautical knick-knacks. Not a bad spot for a cold Cascade.

Syrup CLUB

(Map p624; 39 Salamanca Pl; ⏲9pm-5am Fri & Sat) Over two floors above Knopwood's Retreat, this is an ace place for late-night drinks and DJs playing to the techno-house crowd. Vale Round Midnight, the blues bar that used to be on the top floor.

Mobius Lounge Bar CLUB, BAR

(Map p624; 7 Despard St; ⏲9pm-4am Wed, 10.30pm-4.30am Fri, 10pm-5am Sat) A pumping, clubby dungeon meets cool lounge bar, tucked in behind the main waterfront area. Occasional name DJs.

Observatory CLUB

(Map p624; www.observatorybar.com.au; level 1, Murray St Pier; ⏲9pm-late Wed, Fri & Sat) Sip a 'Big O' cocktail as you swan between the moody nooks at Observatory. Commercial dance in the main room, urban funk in the lounge. Don't dress down (the bouncers can be picky).

☆ Entertainment

State Cinema CINEMA

(Map p620; ☎03-6234 6318; www.statecinema.com.au; 375 Elizabeth St, North Hobart; tickets adult/child $18/14; ⏲10am-late) Saved from the wrecking ball in the 1990s, the multiscreen State shows independent and art-house flicks from both local and international film-makers. There's a great cafe and bar on-site, a browse-worthy bookshop and the foodie temptations of North Hobart's restaurants right outside.

Republic Bar & Café LIVE MUSIC

(Map p620; ☎03-6234 6954; www.republicbar.com; 299 Elizabeth St, North Hobart; ⏲11am-late) The Republic is a raucous art-deco pub hosting live music every night (often free entry). It's the number-one live-music pub around town, with an always-interesting line-up, including international acts. Loads of different beers and excellent food – just the kind of place you'd love to call your local.

Brisbane Hotel LIVE MUSIC

(Map p620; 3 Brisbane St; ⏲noon-late Tue-Sat, 3pm-late Sun) The bad old Brisbane has dragged itself up from the pit of old-man, sticky-carpet alcoholism to be reinvented as a progressive live-music venue. This is where anyone doing anything original, offbeat or uncommercial gets a gig: punk, metal, hip hop and singer-songwriters.

New Sydney Hotel LIVE MUSIC

(Map p624; www.newsydneyhotel.com.au; 87 Bathurst St; ⏲noon-midnight) Low-key folk, jazz, blues and comedy play to a mature crowd Tuesday to Sunday nights (usually free): see the website for gig listings. Great pub food and a terrific beer selection, including an ever-changing array of island microbrews. Irish jam session 2pm Saturdays.

Theatre Royal THEATRE

(Map p624; ☎03-6233 2299, 1800 650 277; www.theatreroyal.com.au; 29 Campbell St; shows $20-60; ⏲box office 9am-5pm Mon-Fri) This venerable old stager is Australia's oldest continuously operating theatre, with actors first cracking the boards here back in 1834. Expect a range of music, ballet, theatre, opera and university revues.

Grand Poobah LIVE MUSIC

(Map p624; 142 Liverpool St; ⏲8pm-1am Wed, 9pm-4.30am Fri & Sat) This versatile bohemian bar doubles as a music venue with everything from live bands to DJs, dance and comedy.

Federation Concert Hall CLASSICAL MUSIC

(Map p624; ☎1800 001 190; www.tso.com.au; 1 Davey St; ⏲box office 9am-5pm Mon-Fri) Welded to the Hotel Grand Chancellor, this concert hall resembles a huge aluminium can leaking insulation from gaps in the panelling. Inside, the Tasmanian Symphony Orchestra does what it does best.

Village Cinemas CINEMA
(Map p624; ☎1300 555 400; www.villagecinemas.com.au; 181 Collins St; tickets adult/child $17.50/13, Gold Class from $30; ⏲10am-late) An inner-city multiplex screening mainstream releases. Cheap-arse Tuesday tickets $12.

Shopping

Fullers Bookshop BOOKS
(Map p624; www.fullersbookshop.com.au; 131 Collins St; ⏲8.30am-6pm Mon-Fri, 9am-5pm Sat, 10am-4pm Sun) Hobart's best bookshop has a great range of literature and travel guides, plus regular launches and readings, and a cool cafe in the corner.

Cool Wine WINE
(Map p624; www.coolwine.com.au; shop 8, MidCity Arcade, Criterion St; ⏲9.30am-6.30pm Mon-Sat, 10am-2pm Sun) Excellent selection of Tasmanian wine and global craft beers.

Tommy Gun Records MUSIC, CLOTHING
(Map p624; 127 Elizabeth St; ⏲10am-5pm Mon-Fri, to 3pm Sat) For all your vinyl, studded-leather wristband and black rock T-shirt requirements.

Wursthaus FOOD
(Map p624; www.wursthaus.com.au; 1 Montpelier Retreat; ⏲8am-6pm Mon-Fri, to 5pm Sat, 9am-5pm Sun) Fine-food showcase just off Salamanca Pl selling speciality smallgoods, cheeses, cakes, breads, wines and pre-prepared meals.

Handmark Gallery ARTS
(Map p624; www.handmark.com.au; 77 Salamanca Pl; ⏲10am-5pm) Handmark has been here for 30 years, displaying unique ceramics, glass, woodwork and jewellery, plus paintings and sculpture – 100% Tasmanian.

Tasmanian Map Centre MAPS
(Map p624; www.map-centre.com.au; 110 Elizabeth St; ⏲9.30am-5.30pm Mon-Fri, 10.30am-2.30pm Sat) Bushwalking maps, GPS units and travel guides.

Information

EMERGENCY

Hobart Police Station (☎03-6230 2111, non-emergency assistance 13 14 44; www.police.tas.gov.au; 43 Liverpool St; ⏲24hr) Hobart's main cop shop.

Police, Fire & Ambulance (☎000) Emergencies.

INTERNET ACCESS

Ruffcut Records (www.ruffcut-records.com; 35a Elizabeth St; ⏲8.30am-6pm Mon-Fri, 10am-5pm Sat) Internet terminals and offbeat vinyl.

State Library (www.linc.tas.gov.au; 91 Murray St; ⏲9.30am-6pm Mon-Thu, to 8pm Fri, to 2pm Sat) Free one-hour internet access.

INTERNET RESOURCES

Hobart City Council (www.hobartcity.com.au) City-council website: parks, transport and recreation.

Welcome to Hobart (www.welcometohobart.com.au) Official visitors guide.

MEDIA

Hobart's long-running newspaper, the *Mercury* (www.themercury.com.au; aka 'the Mockery'), is handy for discovering what's on where. The Thursday edition lists entertainment options. For gig listings, pick up a copy of the free street-press *Warp* (www.warpmagazine.com.au) or see **The Dwarf** (www.thedwarf.com.au).

MEDICAL SERVICES

City Doctors & Travel Clinic (☎03-6231 3003; www.citydoctors.com.au; 188 Collins St; ⏲9am-5pm Mon-Fri) General medical appointments and travel immunisations.

My Chemist Salamanca (☎03-6235 0257; www.mychemist.com.au; 6 Montpelier Retreat, Battery Point; ⏲8.30am-6.30pm Mon-Fri, to 5pm Sat, 10am-4pm Sun) Handy chemist just off Salamanca Pl.

Royal Hobart Hospital (☎03-6222 8423; www.dhhs.tas.gov.au; 48 Liverpool St; ⏲24hr) Emergency entry on Liverpool St.

MONEY

The major banks all have branches and ATMs around Elizabeth St Mall. There are also ATMs around Salamanca Pl.

DON'T MISS

FRIDAY NIGHT FANDANGO

Some of Hobart's best live tunes get an airing every Friday night at the **Salamanca Arts Centre Courtyard** (Map p624; www.salarts.org.au/portfolio/rektango; 77 Salamanca Pl; ⏲5.30-7.30pm), just off Wooby's Lane. It's a free community event with the adopted name 'Rektango', borrowed from a band that sometimes graces the stage. Acts vary month to month – expect anything from African beats to rockabilly, folk and gypsy-Latino. Drinks essential (sangria in summer, mulled wine in winter); dancing near-essential.

POST

General Post Office (GPO; Map p624; www.auspost.com.au; cnr Elizabeth & Macquarie Sts; ⌚8.30am-5.30pm Mon-Fri) Forget about the mail...check out the heritage architecture!

TOURIST INFORMATION

Hobart Visitor Information Centre (Map p624; ☎03-6238 4222; www.hobarttravelcentre.com.au; cnr Davey & Elizabeth Sts; ⌚9am-5pm daily, extended hours in summer) Information, maps and state-wide tour, transport and accommodation bookings.

Parks & Wildlife Service (Map p624; ☎1300 827 727, 1300 135 513; www.parks.tas.gov.au; 134 Macquarie St; ⌚9am-5pm Mon-Fri) Information, maps, passes and fact sheets for bushwalking in national parks. Inside the Service Tasmania office.

Getting There & Away

AIR

There are no direct international flights to/from Tasmania. The following airlines fly between Tasmania and mainland Australia.

Jetstar (☎13 15 38; www.jetstar.com.au) Qantas' low-cost airline. Direct flights from Melbourne and Sydney to Hobart and Launceston.

Qantas (☎13 13 13; www.qantas.com.au) Direct flights from Sydney, Brisbane and Melbourne to Hobart and Launceston. QantasLink (the regional subsidiary) offers flights between Melbourne and Devonport.

Tiger Airways (☎03-9999 2888; www.tigerairways.com.au) Flies from Melbourne to Hobart.

Virgin Australia (☎13 67 89; www.virginaustralia.com.au) Direct flights from Melbourne, Sydney, Brisbane and Canberra to Hobart, and from Melbourne, Brisbane and Sydney to Launceston.

BUS

There are two main intrastate bus companies operating to/from Hobart. Check online for timetable/fare information, or ask at the Hobart Visitor Information Centre (p636).

Redline Coaches (Map p624; ☎1300 360 000; www.redlinecoaches.com.au; 230 Liverpool St) Buses leave from outside the Liverpool St shopfront.

Tassielink (Map p624; ☎1300 300 520; www.tassielink.com.au; 64 Brisbane St) Until a new bus terminal can be found/built (the lease is up on the old one), Tassielink buses will run from Brisbane St as well as a temporary stop on Elizabeth St, across the road from the Hobart Visitor Information Centre. Call or check online for location updates.

Getting Around

TO/FROM THE AIRPORT

Hobart Airport (☎03-6216 1600; www.hobartairport.com.au; Strachan St, Cambridge) is at Cambridge, 19km east of the city. A taxi into the city will cost around $42 between 6am and 8pm weekdays, and around $50 at other times.

Hobart Airporter (Map p624; ☎1300 385 511; www.airporterhobart.com.au; one way/return $18/32) Hotel-door-to-airport services (and the other way around), connecting with all flights. Bookings essential.

BICYCLE

There are a number of bike-hire options (p623) around the city.

BUS

Metro Tasmania (☎13 22 01; www.metrotas.com.au) operates the local bus network, which is reliable but infrequent outside of business hours. The **Metro Shop** (Map p624; 22 Elizabeth St; ⌚8am-6pm Mon-Fri) handles ticketing and enquiries: most buses depart from this section of Elizabeth St, or from nearby Franklin Sq.

One-way fares vary with distances ('sections') travelled (from $3 to $6.20). For $5.30 you can buy an unlimited-travel **Day Rover** ticket, valid after 9am Monday to Friday and all weekend. Buy one-way tickets from the Metro Shop or driver (exact change required) or ticket agents (newsagents and post offices). Drivers don't sell Day Rover tickets.

CAR, CAMPERVAN & MOTORCYCLE

AAA Car Rentals (☎0437 313 314, 03-6231 3313; www.aaacarrentals.com.au; 73 Warwick St; ⌚9am-5pm Mon-Fri, 10am-2pm Sat & Sun)

AutoRent-Hertz (☎03-6237 1111, 1300 067 222; www.autorent.com.au; cnr Bathurst & Harrington Sts; ⌚8am-5pm)

Avis (☎03-6214 1711; www.avis.com.au; 2/4 Market Pl; ⌚8am-5.30pm Mon-Fri, to 4pm Sat & Sun)

Bargain Car Rentals (☎1300 729 230; www.bargaincarrentals.com.au; 173 Harrington St; ⌚8am-5pm Mon-Fri, 9am-3pm Sat & Sun)

Britz (☎1300 738 087; www.britz.com.au)

Budget (☎03-6234 5222, 1300 362 848; www.budget.com.au; 96 Harrington St; ⌚7.30am-5.30pm Mon-Fri, to 4.30pm Sat, 9am-2pm Sun)

Europcar (☎03-6231 1077, 1300 131 390; www.europcar.com.au; 112 Harrington St; ⌚8am-5.30pm Mon-Fri, to 4pm Sat, 8am-2pm Sun)

Tasmanian Campervan Hire (☎1800 807 119; www.tascamper.com) Specialises in two-berth vans.

Tasmanian Motorcycle Hire (☎0418 365 210; www.tasmotorcyclehire.com.au)

TAXI

131008 Hobart (☎13 10 08; www.131008hobart.com) Standard taxis.

Maxi-Taxi Services (☎13 32 22; www.hobartmaxitaxi.com.au) Wheelchair-accessible vehicles and taxis for groups.

AROUND HOBART

Riverside communities, historic towns, pretty pastureland and stands of native bush are all just a few minutes' drive beyond the Hobart city limits. The ghosts of Tasmania's convict past drag their leg irons around historic Richmond, while the wilderness, wildlife, waterfalls and short walks at Mt Field National Park make a terrific day trip.

Richmond

POP 750

Straddling the Coal River, 27km northeast of Hobart, historic Richmond was once a strategic military post and convict station on the road to Port Arthur. Riddled with 19th-century buildings, it's arguably Tasmania's premier historic town, but like the Rocks in Sydney and Hahndorf in Adelaide, it's in danger of becoming a parody of itself, with the passing tourist trade picking over the bones of the colonial past. That said, Richmond is undeniably picturesque and kids love chasing the ducks around the riverbanks.

See www.richmondvillage.com.au for more information.

Sights & Activities

Richmond Bridge BRIDGE

(Wellington St) This chunky but not inelegant bridge still funnels traffic across the Coal River and is the town's proud centrepiece. Built by convicts in 1823 (making it the oldest road bridge in Australia), it's purportedly haunted by the 'Flagellator of Richmond', George Grover, who died here in 1832.

Bonorong Wildlife Centre WILDLIFE RESERVE

(☎03-6268 1184; www.bonorong.com.au; 593 Briggs Rd, Brighton; adult/child/family $25/11/65; ⏲9am-5pm) This impressive operation is about 17km west of Richmond (or alternatively, signposted off Hwy 1 at Brighton). From Richmond, take Middle Tea Tree Rd, and turn left into Tea Tree Rd after 11km. 'Bonorong' derives from an Aboriginal word meaning 'native companion' – look forward to Tasmanian devils, koalas, wombats, echidnas and quolls. The emphasis here is on conservation, education and the rehabilitation of injured animals.

ZooDoo Wildlife Park WILDLIFE RESERVE

(☎03 6260 2444; www.zoodoo.com.au; 620 Middle Tea Tree Rd; adult/child $25/13; ⏲9am-5pm) Six kilometres west of Richmond on the road to Brighton (Middle Tea Tree Rd), ZooDoo has 'safari bus' rides, playgrounds, picnic areas and half of Dr Dolittle's appointment book, including tigers, llamas, Tasmanian devils and wallabies. Hungry white lions chow down at regularly scheduled intervals.

Richmond Gaol Historic Site HISTORIC BUILDING

(☎03-6260 2127; www.richmondgaol.com.au; 37 Bathurst St; adult/child/family $9/4/22; ⏲9am-5pm) The northern wing of the remarkably well-preserved jail was built in 1825, five years before the penitentiary at Port Arthur, making it Australia's oldest jail. And like Port Arthur, fascinating historic insights abound, but the mood is pretty sombre.

Old Hobart Town Historical Model Village HISTORIC SITE

(☎03-6260 2502; www.oldhobarttown.com; 21a Bridge St; adult/family $14/35; ⏲9am-5pm) A painstaking re-creation of Hobart Town in the 1820s, built from the city's original plans – the kids will love it. Admission is a bit steep, but it's actually pretty amazing, with some solid historical insights.

Richmond Park Boat House BOATING

(☎0401 233 652, 03-6260 1099; www.richmondparkboathouse.com.au; 56 Bridge St; rowboats per 30min $25, bikes per hr $25; ⏲10am-4pm Wed-Sun) Hire a bike and wheel yourself around the town, or jump in a little rowboat down on the river and dodge the local ducks.

Sleeping & Eating

Barilla Holiday Park CARAVAN PARK $

(☎03-6248 5453, 1800 465 453; www.barilla.com.au; 75 Richmond Rd, Cambridge; unpowered/powered sites $34/40, cabins & units $80-150;) A decent option for those with wheels, Barilla is midway between Hobart (14km) and Richmond (14km). It's close to the airport, the Coal River Valley wineries and a couple of good wildlife parks. The grounds are dotted with well-kept cabins, plus there's minigolf (oh, how quaint) and an on-site restaurant serving wood-fired pizzas.

WORTH A TRIP

COAL RIVER VALLEY WINE REGION

Richmond and nearby Cambridge are at the centre of Tasmania's fastest-growing wine region, the Coal River Valley. Some operations here are sophisticated affairs with gourmet restaurants; others are small, family-owned vineyards with cellar doors open by appointment. See www.winesouth.com.au for more info. Here are a couple of spots to get you started.

Puddleduck Vineyard (☎03-6260 2301; www.puddleduck.com.au; 992 Richmond Rd, Richmond; ⏲10am-5pm) Small, family-run vineyard producing just 1200 cases per year: shoot for the riesling, pinot noir and 'Bubbleduck' sparkling white. Snaffle a cheese platter ($20), or fire up the barbecues (BYO meat) for lunch by the lake with Lucky the duck.

Frogmore Creek (☎03-6274 5844; www.frogmorecreek.com.au; 699 Richmond Rd, Cambridge; 4-/5-/6-course menu $80/95/125, with wine $100/125/160; ⏲10am-5pm, restaurant noon-4pm) Overlooking the Mt Pleasant Observatory, 9km southwest of Richmond, corporate Frogmore Creek has a flashy restaurant serving lunch, along with excellent chardonnay, pinot noir and sticky botrytis riesling. Don't miss *Flawed History*, an in-floor jigsaw by local artist Tom Samek. Restaurant bookings recommended (no kids).

★**Daisy Bank Cottages** B&B **$$**
(☎03-6260 2390; www.daisybankcottages.com.au; 78 Middle Tea Tree Rd; d $150-190) This place is a rural delight: two spotless, stylish self-contained units (one with spa) in a converted 1840s sandstone barn on a working sheep farm. There are loft bedrooms, views of the Richmond rooftops and plenty of bucolic distractions for the kids. The surrounding farmland has interpretative walks and soaring birds of prey. Breakfast provisions daily. Hard to beat.

Number 3 Henry Street COTTAGE **$$$**
(☎03-6260 2847; www.numberthree.com.au; 3 Henry St; d $350, extra person $75; ❄📶) This lovely old house has had its innards extended, reorganised and modernised – it still looks quaint from the street, but out the back things are utterly contemporary. Expect muted hues, plush linen, flash bathrooms (plural) and a private flagstone-paved courtyard. Sleeps four in two bedooms (the upstairs one is built into the roof space – fabulously angular!).

Richmond Bakery BAKERY **$**
(☎03-6260 2628; 50 Bridge St, off Edward St; items $3-8; ⏲7.30am-6pm) Pies, pastries, sandwiches, croissants, muffins and cakes – takeaway or munch in the courtyard. If the main street is empty, chances are everyone is in here.

ℹ Getting There & Away

Tassielink (☎1300 653 633; www.tassielink.com.au) runs multiple buses to Richmond every day (just two on Saturday, one on Sunday). The one-way fare is $7.60 (45 minutes).

Richmond Tourist Bus (☎0408 341 804; www.hobartshuttlebus.com/richmond-village.html; adult/child return $30/20; ⏲9am Sun-Fri, 12.15pm daily) runs daily services from Hobart, allowing three hours to explore Richmond (unguided) before returning. Call for bookings and pick-up locations.

Mt Field National Park

Mt Field, 80km northwest of Hobart, was declared a national park in 1916 and is famed for its alpine moorlands, lakes, rainforest, waterfalls, walks, skiing and rampant wildlife. It's an accessible day trip from Hobart, or you can bunk down overnight.

👁 Sights & Activities

Russell Falls WATERFALL
Don't miss the magnificently tiered, 45m-high Russell Falls, an easy 20-minute return amble from behind the visitor information centre. The path is suitable for prams and wheelchairs. There are also easy walks to **Lady Barron Falls** and **Horseshoe Falls**, and longer bushwalks.

Mt Mawson SKIING
(www.mtmawson.info; skiing full day adult/child $30/15, half day $20/10, ski tow deposit $10; ⏲10am-4pm Sat & Sun mid-Jul–mid-Sep) Skiing at Mt Mawson is sometimes an option, when nature sees fit to deposit snow (infrequently in recent years). Snow reports are available online at www.ski.com.au.

Sleeping

Mt Field National Park Campground CAMPGROUND $
(☎03-6288 1149; www.parks.tas.gov.au; off Lake Dobson Rd; unpowered/powered sites per 2 adults $16/20, extra adult $7/9, extra child $3/4) Run by the park administration, this self-registration campground is a few hundred metres past the visitor information centre and has adequate facilities (toilets, showers, laundry and free barbecues). No bookings. Site prices are additional to national park entry fees.

Lake Dobson Cabins CABIN $
(☎03-6288 1149; www.parks.tas.gov.au; Lake Dobson Rd; cabins up to 6 people $45) Get back to your rootsy mountaintop essence at these three simple, six-bed cabins 16km inside Mt Field National Park. All are equipped with mattresses, cold water, wood stove and firewood (there's no power), with a communal outdoor toilet block. BYO gas lamps, cookers, utensils and bedding. Book via the visitor centre (p639) or online.

★**Duffy's Country Accommodation** COTTAGE $$
(☎03-6288 1373; www.duffyscountry.com; 49 Clark's Rd, Westerway; d $130-145, extra adult/child $25/15; wifi) Overlooking a field of raspberry canes are two immaculate self-contained cottages, one a studio-style cabin for couples, the other a two-bedroom relocated rangers' hut from Mt Field National Park for families. There are also a couple of cute two-bed bunkhouses (one next to each cottage) where you can file the teenagers. Breakfast provisions available. Wallabies a distinct possibility.

Information

Mt Field National Park Visitor Centre (☎03-6288 1149; www.parks.tas.gov.au; 66 Lake Dobson Rd; ⊙8.30am-5pm Nov-Apr, 9am-4pm May-Oct)

Getting There & Away

The drive to Mt Field through the Derwent Valley and Bushy Park is an absolute stunner, with river rapids, hop fields, old oast houses, rows of poplars and hawthorn hedgerows. There's no public transport to the park, but some Hobart-based tour operators offer Mt Field day trips.

THE SOUTHEAST

The Southeast offers rolling hills and valleys, apple orchards, riverside towns and whisper-still harbours and inlets. It's a gentle, rather English-feeling collection of agrarian communities, with Bruny Island and Hartz Mountains National Park within easy reach.

Online, see www.huontrail.org.au.

Getting There & Around

Metro Tasmania (☎13 22 01; www.metrotas.com.au) buses 94–97 run regularly from Hobart to Kettering ($8, 50 minutes), the access point for Bruny Island. Bus 98 rocks in/out of Cygnet from Hobart ($10.50, 80 minutes) once daily (Monday to Friday only) each way.

Tassielink (☎1300 300 520; www.tassielink.com.au) buses service the Huon Hwy from Hobart through Huonville ($10.50, 45 minutes) several times a day, with some continuing to Cygnet ($12.50, 1¼ hours), Geeveston ($14, 1¼ hours) and Dover ($21, 1¾ hours).

Bruny Island

POP 600

Bruny Island is almost two islands joined by a narrow, sandy isthmus called the Neck. Famous for its wildlife (little penguins, echidnas, mutton birds, wallabies), it's a sparsely populated and undeveloped retreat, soaked in ocean rain in the south, and dry and scrubby in the north. It was named after French explorer Bruni D'Entrecasteaux.

You need a few days to appreciate Bruny's isolated coastal communities, swimming and surf beaches, forests and walking tracks – don't try to cram it into a day trip, especially on holiday weekends when there are long waits for the ferry.

Accommodation is largely in self-contained cottages and guesthouses. A car or bicycle is essential for getting around. Supplies are available at the well-stocked Adventure Bay general store and a small shop at Alonnah. Note that some island roads are unsealed: not all car-rental companies are cool with this concept.

Sights & Activities

Bruny Island Neck NATURE RESERVE, VIEWPOINT
(www.brunyisland.org.au/about-bruny-island/the-neck) Park halfway across the isthmus – aka the Neck – between North and South Bruny and climb the 279 steps (correct?) to the **Truganini Memorial** for broad views of both ends of the island. Another timber

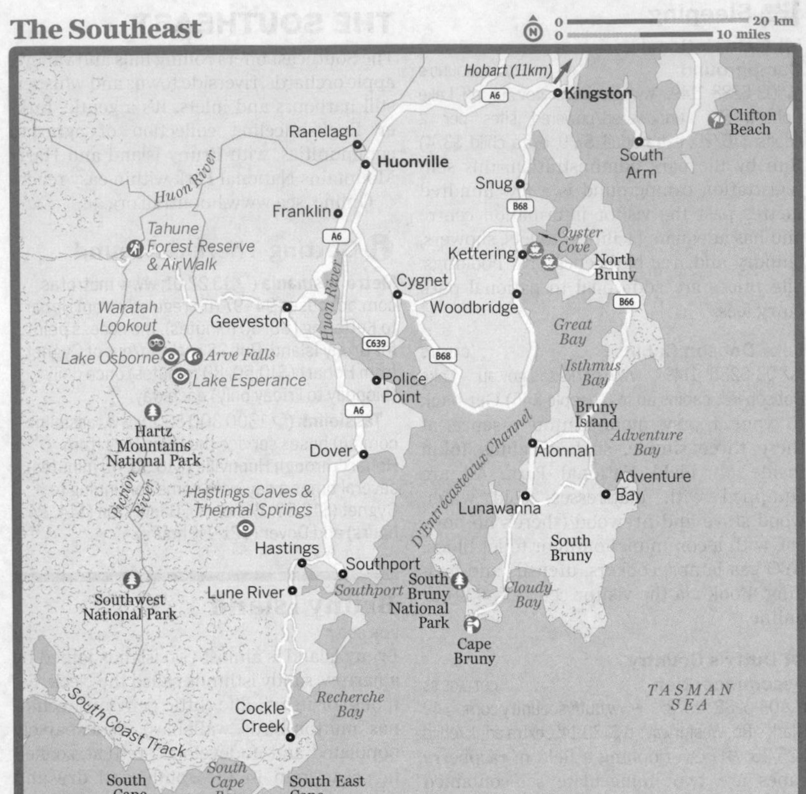

walkway crosses the Neck to the beach on the other side. Keep to the boardwalk in this area: mutton birds and little (fairy) penguins nest here. Your best chance of seeing the penguins is at dusk in the warmer months.

South Bruny National Park NATIONAL PARK
(☎03-6293 1419; www.parks.tas.gov.au; car/person per day $24/12) There's terrific bushwalking here. At **Fluted Cape**, east of Adventure Bay, an easy trail winds out to the old whaling station at **Grass Point** (1½ hours return). From here follow the shore to **Penguin Island**, accessible at low tide, or complete the more difficult **cape circuit** (2½ hours return).

The park's southwestern portion comprises the **Labillardiere Peninsula**, featuring jagged coastal scenery and a lighthouse. Walks here range from leisurely beach meanderings to a seven-hour circuit of the entire peninsula.

Bligh Museum of Pacific Exploration MUSEUM
(☎03-6293 1117; www.southcom.com.au/~jontan/index.html; 876 Main Rd, Adventure Bay; adult/child/family $4/2/10; ⏲10am-4pm) This curio-crammed museum details the local exploits of explorers Bligh, Cook, Furneaux, Baudin and, of course, Bruni d'Entrecasteaux. The engaging collection includes maps, charts and manuscripts, many of them originals or first editions.

Tours

Bruny Island Cruises BOAT TOUR
(Pennicott Wilderness Journeys; ☎03-6234 4270; www.brunycruises.com.au; adult/child/family $125/75/390) This highly recommended three-hour tour of the island's awesome southeast coastline takes in rookeries, seal colonies, bays, caves and towering sea cliffs. Trips depart Adventure Bay jetty at 11am daily, with an extra 2pm cruise in summer.

You can also take the tour as a full-day trip from Hobart (adult/child $195/140, including lunch) or from Kettering (adult/child $140/90).

Bruny Island Traveller TOUR
(Pennicott Wilderness Journeys; ☎03 6234 4270; www.brunyislandtraveller.com.au; adult/child $195/170) Operated by the same folks who run Bruny Island Cruises, this is a full-day tour ex-Hobart for landlubbers who don't fancy the idea of too much time in a boat. The itinerary includes beaches, wildlife, Bruny Island Cheese Co, Cape Bruny Lighthouse and lunch at Bruny Island Premium Wines. Prices include transfers, ferry crossings, lunch and national park fees.

Bruny Island Safaris TOUR
(☎0437 499 795; www.brunyislandsafaris.com.au; per person $149) Full-day tours departing Hobart, focusing on Bruny's history and landscapes. Look forward to opportunities to sample the island's culinary bounty, including oysters, salmon, cheese, wine and berries, and a look inside the old Cape Bruny Lighthouse.

Sleeping

The **Bruny d'Entrecasteaux Visitor Information Centre** (☎03-6267 4494; www.brunyisland.org.au; 81 Ferry Rd, Kettering; ⏲9am-5pm) in Kettering is a good starting point for accommodation bookings. Online, see www. brunyisland.net.au and www.brunyisland.com.

Captain Cook Caravan Park CARAVAN PARK $
(☎03-6293 1128; www.captaincookpark.com; 786 Main Rd, Adventure Bay; unpowered/powered sites $25/30, on-site vans/cabins d $70/140; ❄) Across the road from the beach in Adventure Bay, this park could do with a few trees but has decent facilities, including some swish new one-bedroom cabins with little decks out the front. The new owners are tidying things up.

★ **43 Degrees** APARTMENT $$
(☎03-6293 1018; www.43degrees.com.au; 948 Adventure Bay Rd, Adventure Bay; d/apt $190/240, extra person $40) At 43 degrees south latitude, the accommodation here neatly bookends Adventure Bay beach: there are three nifty, roll-roofed studios (sleeping two) at the western end; and two similarly styled apartments (sleeping four) at the eastern end near the jetty. Double-glazing keeps the heat out/in, depending on the season. Ask about package deals with Bruny Island Cruises (p640).

Morella Island Retreats RENTAL HOUSE $$
(☎03-6293 1131; www.morella-island.com; 46 Adventure Bay Rd, Adventure Bay; d $180-250, extra person $25) These unique, arty cottages are 6km north of Adventure Bay. There are a couple of retreats for couples (we love 'the Cockpit') and a family-sized holiday house. All are self-contained, with design and decor best described as 'classic castaway'. Prices drop by $30 for stays longer than one night. The **Hothouse Cafe** (☎03-6293 1131; www.morella-island.com/hothouse.htm; 46 Adventure Bay Rd, Adventure Bay; mains $11-18; ⏲9am-5pm; ✍) is here, too.

Satellite Island RENTAL HOUSE $$$
(☎0400 336 444; www.satelliteisland.com.au; Satellite Island, via Alonnah or Middleton; d/extra person from $950/450) An island, off an island, off an island... Adrift in the D'Entrecasteaux Channel, this amazing private-island lodge (boatshed-chic) offers self-contained accommodation for up to 15 castaways. Kayaks and fishing rods for distraction; walking trails and oyster-clad rocks for exploring. Private-boat access from Alonnah on Bruny Island or Middleton on the Tasmanian 'mainland'. Two-night minimum (though you'll want to stay longer).

All Angels Church House RENTAL HOUSE $$$
(☎03-6293 1271; www.brunyisland.com/accommodation; 4561 Main Rd, Lunawanna; d from $235) Your prayers have been answered with this restored 1912 church near Daniels Bay, now rental accommodation with three bedrooms and a soaring-ceiling open-plan lounge. Fire up the BBQ in the sheltered garden, eat alfresco on the picnic table or dine inside at the huge shared table. Sleeps five.

Eating

Penguin Cafe CAFE $
(☎03-6293 1352; 710 Main Rd, Adventure Bay; mains $5-12; ⏲9am-3pm, extended summer hours) Next to the Adventure Bay store, the eccentric little Penguin Cafe serves up simple homemade burgers, fish and chips, egg-and-bacon rolls, amazing curried scallop pies and muffins baked inside coffee cups.

Jetty Cafe CAFE $$
(☎03-6260 6245; www.jettycafebrunyisland.com; 18 Main Rd, Dennes Point; lunch $15-20, dinner $28-30; ⏲10am-9pm Thu-Sun) Part cafe-restaurant, part providore, part local art gallery – the stylish Jetty Cafe (designed by ace architect John Wardle) is a great addition to Bruny's

BRUNY ISLAND ON A PLATE

Bruny Island has a growing rep for top-quality food and wine. Here's a rundown of the best Bruny foodie experiences to get you started.

Get Shucked Oyster Farm (☎0428 606 250; www.getshucked.com.au; 1735 Main Rd, Great Bay; 12 oysters from $12; ⏲9.30am-6.30pm, reduced winter hours) Get Shucked cultivates the 'fuel for love' in chilly Great Bay. Visit the tasting room and wolf down a briny dozen with lemon juice and Tabasco and a cold flute of Jansz bubbles. Shucking brilliant.

Bruny Island Smokehouse & Whisky Bar (☎03-6260 6344; 360 Lennon Rd, North Bruny; mains from $30; ⏲9.30am-5.30pm Sep-May, to 4.30pm Jun-Aug) The old Bruny Island Smokehouse has expanded its repertoire and is now a tasting room for every whisky distillery in the state. Gourmet platters, smoked meats and seafood chowder are also on offer. Don't blame us if you miss the last ferry back to Kettering…

Bruny Island Cheese Co (☎03-6260 6353; www.brunyislandcheese.com.au; 1087 Main Rd, Great Bay; meals $10-24; ⏲10am-5pm) Hankering for a quivering sliver of cheese? Head to the Bruny Island Cheese Co, where Kiwi cheesemaker Nick Haddow draws inspiration from time spent working and travelling in France, Spain, Italy and the UK. Artisan bread, wood-fired pizzas, zippy coffee and local wines also available.

Bruny Island Premium Wines (☎03-6293 1008, 0409 973 033; www.brunyislandwine.com; 4391 Main Rd, Lunawanna; ⏲11am-4pm) If you're working up a thirst, swing into the cellar door at Australia's most southerly vineyard. Pinot noir and chardonnay rule the roost; burgers, platters and meaty mains also available.

dining scene. Duck in for a coffee, or book for lunch or Friday-night fish and chips – seasonal menus showcase local produce. Phone ahead as opening hours tend to sway in the sea breeze.

ℹ Information

Bruny d'Entrecasteaux Visitor Information Centre (☎03-6267 4494; www.brunyisland.org.au; 81 Ferry Rd; ⏲9am-5pm) The local visitor centre is at the ferry terminal – it's the best place for info on accommodation and services on Bruny Island, including walking maps and driving advice. There's a cafe here, too.

ℹ Getting There & Away

Bruny Island Ferry (☎03-6273 6725; www.brunyislandferry.com.au; Ferry Rd, Kettering; car return $30-35, motorcycle/bike/foot passenger $5/5/free) The double-decker *Mirambeena* shuttles cars and passengers from Kettering to Roberts Point on North Bruny. There are at least 10 services daily each way (a 20-minute trip). The first ferry leaves Kettering at 6.35am (7.45am Sunday); the last one leaves at 6.30pm (7.30pm Friday). The first ferry from Bruny sails at 7am (8.25am Sunday); the last one leaves at 7pm (7.50pm Friday).

Cygnet

POP 1460

Groovy Cygnet was originally named Port de Cygne Noir (Port of the Black Swan) by Bruni d'Entrecasteaux, after the big noir birds that cruise around the bay. Youthfully reincarnated as Cygnet (a baby swan), the town has evolved into a dreadlocked, artsy enclave, while still functioning as a major fruit-producing centre. Weathered farmers and banjo-carrying hippies chat amiably in the main street and prop up the bars of the town's pubs.

The ever-popular **Cygnet Folk Festival** (www.cygnetfolkfestival.org; tickets per day/weekend from $70/130) is three days of words, music and dance in January.

🛏 Sleeping & Eating

Commercial Hotel PUB $
(☎03-6295 1296; 2 Mary St; s/d without bathroom $65/85; 📶) Upstairs at the rambling 1884 Commercial Hotel (aka 'the bottom pub') are decent pub rooms, recently dolled up and with little TVs, fridges and new beds. Downstairs, a laconic crew of locals drink at the bar and hit the bistro for robust steak dinners (mains $10 to $28, serving noon to 2pm and 6pm to 8pm).

★Cherryview COTTAGE $$
(☎03-6295 0569; www.cherryview.com.au; 90 Supplices Rd; d $130-160) Backed by a tall stand of eucalypts on 10 quiet hectares, this self-contained studio is a beauty. It's a simple, stylish affair, overlooking a valley with the Hartz Mountains beyond. Love the antique-door bedhead! Your GPS might freak out: is it Supplice Rd or Supplices Rd? Either way, it's 4km north of Cygnet's bright lights.

★Lotus Eaters Cafe CAFE $
(☎03-6295 1996; www.thelotuseaterscafe.com.au; 10 Mary St; mains $10-25; ⏰9am-4pm Thu-Mon; 🌶) This mighty-fine hippie cafe has rustic decor that belies real culinary savvy: expect terrific eggy breakfasts, curries and soups, with a rigorous focus on the seasonal, the organic, the free-range and the local. Superlative homemade cakes, almond croissants and coffee.

Huonville & Around

POP 2540

The biggest town in the southeast, agrarian Huonville flanks the Huon River 35km south of Hobart. Having made its name as Tasmania's apple-growing powerhouse, it remains a functional, working town – low on charm but with all the services you need. Just down the road, pretty riverside **Franklin** (population 1110) has some good eateries.

Sights & Activities

Apple Shed MUSEUM
(☎03-6266 4345; www.williesmiths.com.au; 2064 Main Rd, Grove; gold coin donation; ⏰10am-6pm) At Grove, 6km north of Huonville, this revamped cafe/providore/museum is home to Willie Smith's Organic Apple Cider, at the fore of the cider wave that's been sweeping Australia's pubs and bars of late. Swing by for a coffee, a cheese plate, meals (mains $7 to $24), a cider tasting paddle ($12), or a more purposeful 1.89L 'growler' of Willie Smith's Bone Dry. The museum zooms in on Huonville's appley heritage, with old cider presses and an amazing wall of different apple varieties.

Wooden Boat Centre MUSEUM
(☎03-6266 3586; www.woodenboatcentre.com; 3341 Huon Hwy, Franklin; adult/child/family $9/3/20; ⏰9am-5pm) This engaging, sea-centric spot incorporates the School of Wooden Boatbuilding, a unique institution running accredited courses (from one to seven weeks) in traditional boat building, using Tasmanian timbers. Stick your head in the door to learn all about it, watch boats being cobbled together and catch a whiff of Huon pine.

Huon Jet BOATING
(☎03-6264 1838; www.huonjet.com; Esplanade, Huonville; adult/child $80/58; ⏰9am-5pm Oct-Apr, 10am-4pm May-Sep) Jet boating? That's so '80s... Still, these frenetic, 35-minute rides are a great way to see the river up close. Bookings recommended.

Sleeping & Eating

Huon Valley Caravan Park CARAVAN PARK $
(☎0438 304 383; www.huonvalleycaravanpark.com.au; 177 Wilmot Rd, Huonville; unpowered/powered sites $30/34) At the junction of the Huon and Mountain Rivers is this grassy patch, filling a budget-shaped gap in the local accommodation market. There are no cabins here (yet), but there's a brand-new camp kitchen with a pizza oven and tidy amenities.

★Huon Bush Retreats CABIN $$
(☎03 6264 2233; www.huonbushretreats.com; 300 Browns Rd, Ranelagh; unpowered sites $30, tepees/cabins d $145/295) 🍃 This private, wildlife-friendly retreat dapples the flanks of not-miserable Mt Misery. On-site are five modern, self-contained cabins, luxury tepees, tent and campervan sites, plus 5km of walking tracks and a fantastic BBQ camp kitchen. Superb blue wrens flit through the branches. Check the website for directions – it's 12km from Huonville (beware: steep dirt road!).

★Summer Kitchen Bakery BAKERY, CAFE $
(☎03-6264 3388; 1 Marguerite St, Ranelagh; items $4-7; ⏰7.30am-4pm Tue-Fri, 8am-4pm Sat) Locals come from miles around just for a loaf of bread from this excellent little bakery, on a street corner in Ranelagh a few kilometres out of Huonville. Organic wood-fired sourdough, sprouted-rye sourdough, organic beef-and-wallaby pies, pastries and the best coffee in the Huon. Nice one.

Petty Sessions CAFE $$
(☎03-6266 3488; www.pettysessions.com.au; 3445 Huon Hwy, Franklin; mains $19-32; ⏰9am-4pm & 5.30-8pm Mon-Fri, 9am-8pm Sat & Sun) A picket fence and garden blooms encircle this likeable cafe, inside an 1860 courthouse. Head for the deck and order classic cafe fare (salads, BLTs, grilled Huon River salmon and seafood fettuccine) – or try the house special: abalone chowder.

Information

Huon Valley Visitor Information Centre (03-6264 0326; www.huontrail.org.au; 2273 Huon Hwy, Huonville; 9am-5pm) Southeast tourist information on the way into town from Hobart.

Geeveston & Around

POP 1430

A rugged timber town, Geeveston is 31km south of Huonville. It's a utiltarian sort of place without much of a tourist angle, but offers accommodation close to the Hartz Mountains and Tahune Forest AirWalk.

Activities

Tahune Forest AirWalk WALKING

(1300 720 507; www.adventureforests.com.au; Tahune Forest Reserve, Arve Rd; adult/child/family $26/13/52; 9am-5pm Oct-Mar, 10am-4pm Apr-Sep) Tahune Forest has 600m of wheelchair-accessible steel walkways suspended 20m above the forest floor. One 24m cantilevered section is designed to sway disconcertingly with approaching footsteps. Vertigo? Ground-level walks include a 20-minute riverside stroll through stands of young Huon pine. There's also a **cafe** (mains $10 to $30) and lodge **accommodation** (dorm/double/family $47/95/115).

Eagle Hang Glider ADVENTURE TOUR

(1300 720 507; www.tahuneairwalk.com.au; Tahune Forest Reserve, Arve Rd; adult/child $15/13.50; 9am-5pm Nov-Mar, 10am-4pm Sep-Apr) Near the AirWalk, wannabe birds of prey are strapped into a hang-glider, which in turn is latched to a 250m-long cable 50m above the Huon River and forest. Fly my pretties! Minimum/maximum weight 25/100kg.

Sleeping & Eating

Cambridge House B&B $$

(03-6297 1561; www.cambridgehouse.com.au; 2 School Rd; d with/without bathroom incl breakfast $140/115) This photogenic 1870s B&B – cottagey but not kitsch – offers three bedrooms upstairs with shared facilities (good for families), and two downstairs en suite rooms. The timber staircase and Baltic pine ceilings are wonders. If you're quiet you might spy a platypus in the creek at the bottom of the garden. Cooked breakfast.

Masaaki's Sushi JAPANESE $

(0408 712 340; 20b Church St; sushi $8-20; 11.30am-6.30pm Fri &Sat) What a surprise! Tasmania's best sushi – including fresh Tasmanian wasabi – is in sleepy Geeveston. Opening hours are disappointingly limited, but you'll also find Masaaki and his outstanding sushi at Hobart's Sunday morning Farm Gate Market (p619).

Hartz Mountains National Park

The 65-sq-km **Hartz Mountains National Park** (03-6264 8460; www.parks.tas.gov.au; vehicle/person per day $24/12) is renowned for its jagged peaks, glacial tarns, gorges and bleak alpine moorlands, hunkering down in the cold, misty airs. Rapid weather changes bluster through: even day walkers should bring waterproofs and warm clothing.

There are some great hikes and isolated, sit-and-ponder-your-existence viewpoints in the park. **Waratah Lookout**, 24km from Geeveston, is an easy five-minute shuffle from the road. Other well-surfaced short walks include **Arve Falls** (20 minutes return) and **Lake Osborne** (40 minutes return). The steeper **Lake Esperance** walk (1½ hours return) takes you through sublime high country.

There's no camping within the park – just basic day facilities. See the website for details. Access is via the Arve Rd from Geeveston: the last 10.5km is unsealed and sometimes snowed under.

Dover & Around

POP 770

Dover is a chilled-out base for exploring the deep south. In the 19th century Dover was a timber-milling town, but nowadays fish farms harvest Atlantic salmon for export throughout Asia. Travellers heading south can stock up on fuel and supplies here. About 28km further south is **Southport** (population 280), another low-key former timber town on the coast.

Online see www.farsouthtasmania.com.

Sleeping & Eating

Dover Beachside Tourist Park CARVAN PARK $

(03-6298 1301; www.dovercaravanpark.com.au; 27 Kent Beach Rd; unpowered/powered sites $22.50/35, cabins from $95;) Opposite the sandy shore and new kids' playground, this decent southern set-up features grassy expanses, trim cabins and a chatty cockatoo in reception (don't take any of his lip).

★Jetty House B&B $$
(☎03-6298 3139; www.southportjettyhouse.com; 8848 Huon Hwy; s/d incl breakfast $120/170, extra person $30; 📶) Perfect for your post-South Coast Track recovery, this family-run guesthouse near the wharf is a rustic, verandah-encircled homestead built in 1875 for the sawmill boss. Rates include full cooked breakfast and afternoon tea. Open fires, intersting art, a total absence of doilies and the friendly feline attentions of Pushkin complete the package. Dinner by arrangement; cheaper rates for longer stays.

Ashdowns of Dover B&B $$
(☎0417 746 437; www.ashdownsofdover.com.au; 6957 Huon Hwy; d $140, extra person $25; 📶) Forget about the white cliffs; Ashdowns of Dover is a far more welcoming prospect. Three cosy en suite rooms in this 1950 timber house come with Asian and African thematic touches, full cooked breakfasts and a field full of sheep to observe out the back. The kids can collect eggs from the resident chooks.

★Post>Office 6985 SEAFOOD, PIZZA $$
(☎03-6298 1905; 6985 Huon Hwy; mains $15-30; ⏲noon-2.30pm Wed-Sun & 6-8pm Thu-Sun Sep-May, 4-8pm Thu-Sat Jun-Aug) Leonard Cohen and alt-country on the stereo, cool decor, foodie magazines... And that's before you get to the menu, which features local seafood and wood-fired pizzas (try the scallop, caramelised onion and pancetta version). An evening here will probably have you asking your accommodation if you can stay an extra night. Sterling beer and wine list, too.

Cockle Creek

Australia's most southerly drive is a 19km corrugated-gravel stretch from **Ida Bay** – don't miss the super-scenic 14km **Ida Bay Railway** (☎0428 383 262, 03-6298 3110; www.idabayrailway.com.au; 328 Lune River Rd; adult/child/family $30/15/75; ⏲9am-5pm) en route – past the soft-lulling waves of **Recherche Bay** to Cockle Creek. A grand grid of streets was once planned for Cockle Creek, but dwindling coal seams and whale numbers poured cold water on that idea.

This is epic country, studded with craggy, clouded mountains, sigh-inducing beaches and (best of all) hardly any people. The challenging **South Coast Track** starts (or ends) here, taking you through to Melaleuca in the **Southwest National Park** (www.parks.tas.gov.au; vehicle/person per day $24/12). Combined with the **Port Davey Track** you can walk all the way to Lake Pedder. Shorter walks from Cockle Creek include ambles along the shoreline to the lighthouse at **Fishers Point** (two hours return), and a section of the South Coast Track to **South Cape Bay** (four hours return). National park entry fees apply; self-register at Cockle Creek.

There are some brilliant free, very basic **campgrounds** along Recherche Bay, including at Gilhams Beach, just before Catamaran. You can also camp for free at Cockle Creek itself, but national park fees apply as soon as you cross the bridge.

Contact **Evans Coaches** (☎03-6297 1335; www.evanscoaches.com.au) to see if it's running the Geeveston–Cockle Creek route when you want it to be. Otherwise, BYO wheels.

DON'T MISS

HASTINGS CAVES & THERMAL SPRINGS

Signposted 5km inland from the Huon Hwy, about 15km south of Dover (just past the Southport turn-off), is the entrance to the amazing **Hastings Caves and Thermal Springs** (☎03-6298 3209; www.parks.tas.gov.au/reserves/hastings; 754 Hastings Caves Rd, Hastings; caves & pool adult/child/family $21/15/60, pool only $5/2/12; ⏲9am-5pm Jan, 10am-4pm Feb-Apr, 10.30am-3.30pm May-Sep, 10am-3.30pm Oct-Dec). The only way to explore the caves (which are within the Hastings Caves State Reserve) is on a guided tour. Buy tickets at the visitor centre. Tours leave roughly hourly, but times vary through the year: call or check the website for specifics.

Admission includes a 45-minute tour of the amazing dolomite **Newdegate Cave**, plus entry to the **thermal swimming pool** behind the visitor centre, filled with 28°C water from thermal springs.

From the visitor centre the cave entrance is a further 5km drive. No public transport runs out this way.

TASMAN PENINSULA

The amazing, austere Port Arthur Historic Site is the Tasman Peninsula's centre of activity, but the area also offers 300m-high sea cliffs, empty surf beaches and brilliant bushwalks through thickly wooded forests and along isolated coastlines. Much of the area constitutes **Tasman National Park** (www.parks.tas.gov.au).

Online, see www.tasmanregion.com.au and www.portarthur.org.au.

Tours

Tasman Island Cruises BOAT TOUR
(Map p624; ☎03-6234 4270; www.tasmancruises.com.au; Franklin Wharf; full-day tour adult/child $225/155; ⏲7.45am) Take a bus to Port Arthur for a three-hour eco-cruise around Tasman Island – checking out the astonishing sea cliffs at Cape Pillar, the highest in the southern hemisphere – then exploring the Port Arthur Historic Site and bussing it back to town. Includes morning tea, lunch and Port Arthur admission.

Roaring 40s Kayaking KAYAKING
(☎0455 949 777; www.roaring40skayaking.com.au; day tour $200; ⏲Nov-Apr) Roaring 40s conducts epic sea-kayaking day tours around the Tasman Peninsula, paddling past the monumental coastline of Cape Hauy. Prices include equipment, lunch and transfers from Hobart.

Under Down Under TOUR
(☎1800 444 442; www.underdownunder.com.au; per person $110) Guided backpacker-style day trips to Port Arthur, including accommodation pick-up, admission fees, a guided walk and a harbour cruise. There's also a quick look at Richmond en route.

Tours Tasmania TOUR
(☎1800 777 103; www.tourstas.com.au; full-day tour $120; ⏲Sun-Fri) Good-value, small-group day tours to Port Arthur (including admission fees, walking tour and harbour cruise) via Richmond, Devil's Kitchen and Tasman Arch. Backpacker focused.

Navigators CRUISE
(☎03-6223 1914; www.navigators.net.au; Brooke St Pier, Hobart; full-day tour adult/child $229/204; ⏲Oct-Apr) Cruises from Hobart to Port Arthur, returning on a coach. Includes entrance to the historic site, morning tea, lunch, a walking tour and a tour of the Isle of the Dead. Omit the meals and the Isle of the Dead and the price drops (adult/child $159/128).

Gray Line BUS TOUR
(☎1300 858 687; www.grayline.com.au; full-day tour adult/child $139/70) Cushy coach tours ex-Hobart, including a harbour cruise around the Isle of the Dead, Port Arthur admission and guided tour, and pit stops at Tasman Arch and the Devil's Kitchen.

Getting There & Around

Tassielink (☎1300 300 520; www.tassielink.com.au) Services the Tasman Peninsula from Hobart, stopping at Eaglehawk Neck ($21, 1½ hours) and Port Arthur ($25, 2¼ hours).

Eaglehawk Neck to Port Arthur

The historical importance of Eaglehawk Neck (population 340) harks back to convict days, when the 100m-wide isthmus here had a row of ornery dogs – the infamous Dogline – chained across it to prevent escape. To discourage swimming, rumours were circulated that the waters were shark infested. Remarkably, despite these efforts, several convicts made successful bids for freedom.

On the way to Eaglehawk Neck, at Sorell, stop by the pick-your-own **Sorell Fruit Farm** (☎03-6265 2744; www.sorellfruitfarm.com; 174 Pawleena Rd; containers from $8.50; ⏲8.30am-5pm Oct-May) to see what's in season.

Sights & Activities

Eaglehawk Neck Historic Site HISTORIC SITE, MUSEUM
(☎03-6214 8100; www.parks.tas.gov.au; Arthur Hwy; ⏲24hr, museum 9am-3.30pm) FREE Down on the isthmus, the only remaining structure from the convict days is the **Officers Quarters Museum** (1832) – the oldest wooden military building in Australia. Inside is a series of rooms loaded with historical info, covering the Dogline, escapee prisoners and the erudite bushranger Martin Cash.

Blowhole, Tasman Arch & Devil's Kitchen LANDMARK
(off Blowhole Rd) For a close-up look at the spectacular coastline south of the Neck, follow the signs to the **Blowhole**, **Tasman Arch** (a cavern-like natural bridge) and **Devil's Kitchen** (a rugged 60m-deep cleft). Watch out for sporadic bursts at the Blow-

Tasman Peninsula

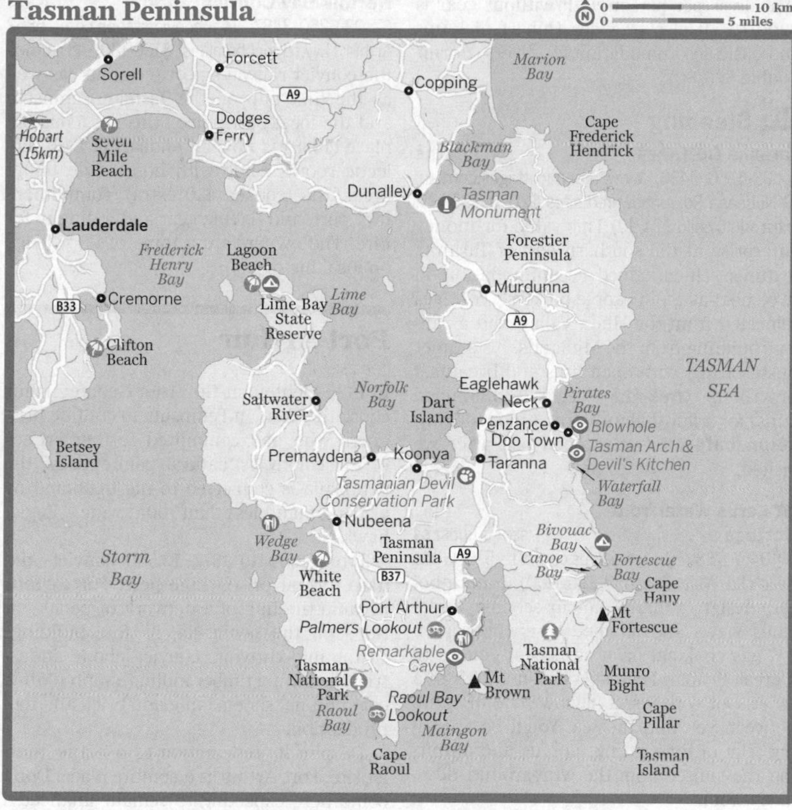

hole, and keep behind the fences at the other sites – the cliff edges do decay. On the road to the Blowhole, look for the signposted 4km gravel road leading to **Waterfall Bay**, which has further camera-conducive views.

Tasmanian Devil Conservation Park WILDLIFE RESERVE
(☎1800 641 641; www.tasmaniandevilpark.com; 5990 Arthur Hwy; adult/child/family $33/18/79; ⏲9am-5pm) Taranna's main attraction is this wildlife reserve, in the process of rebranding itself as the **Tasmanian Devil Unzoo** when we visited. The native habitat here is rampant with wildlife – native hens, wallabies, quolls, eagles, wattlebirds, pademelons and, of course, Tasmanian devils, which you can see being fed every hour. Walking trails extend to 2.5km. See the website for updates.

Tasman Coastal Trail WALKING
(www.parks.tas.gov.au/recreation/tracknotes/tasman.html; off Blowhole Rd) Waterfall Bay is the gateway to this trail that heads into Tasman National Park. The track climbs over Tatnells Hill (two hours) then follows the coast to Bivouac Bay (six hours) and Fortescue Bay (eight hours), then extends out to Cape Hauy and on to Cape Pillar. Allow five to six days for the full return trip.

At the time of writing, parts of the track were being upgraded to form the epic new **Three Capes Track**, encompassing Cape Raoul, Cape Pillar and Cape Hauy. Check the website for updates.

Eaglehawk Dive Centre DIVING
(☎03-6250 3566; www.eaglehawkdive.com.au; 178 Pirates Bay Dr) Runs underwater explorations (sea caves, giant kelp forests, a sea-lion colony and shipwrecks) and a range of PADI courses. A one-day introduction to diving costs $310 (no experience necessary). Two

boat dives per person with/without gear is $200/115. It also provides Hobart pick-ups and basic accommodation for divers (dorm/double $25/80).

Sleeping

Taranna Cottages CABIN $
(☎03-6250 3436; www.tarannacottages.com.au; 19 Nubeena Rd; unpowered sites $20, d $95-125, extra adult/child $24/12) This value-for-money enterprise at the southern end of Taranna features self-contained accommodation in two neat-as-a-pin apple-pickers' cottages relocated from the Huon Valley, and a railway building from the Midlands. It's a quiet bush setting, with open fires and breakfast provisions (free-range eggs, homemade jams) for a few dollars extra. A pioneer **museum/cafe** was set to open just after we visited.

★ **Larus Waterfront Cottage** RENTAL HOUSE $$
(☎0457 758 711; www.larus.com.au; 576 White Beach Rd, White Beach; d $145-200) Contemporary design, a marine colour scheme, audacious views and all mod cons (big-screen TV, gas cooking, flash barbecue) equate to a great Tasman Peninsula bolt-hole. It's in a quiet spot with just a narrow strip of scrub between you and the sea. You'll be spending a lot of time sitting, sipping and admiring the sunset from the wraparound deck. Sleeps four.

Norfolk Bay Convict Station B&B $$
(☎03-6250 3487; www.convictstation.com; 5862 Arthur Hwy; d incl breakfast $160-180; 📶) Once the convict railway's port terminus (as well as the first pub on the Tasman Peninsula and the local post office), this gorgeous old place (1838) is now an endearing B&B. Eclectic rooms come with homemade buffet breakfasts (cooked $10 extra), complimentary port, and fishing gear and a dinghy for hire. The owners are a mine of knowledge on local history.

Port Arthur

POP 250

In 1830 Lieutenant-Governor George Arthur chose the Tasman Peninsula to confine prisoners who had committed further crimes in the colony. A 'natural penitentiary', the peninsula is connected to the mainland by a strip of land less than 100m wide – Eaglehawk Neck.

From 1830 to 1877, 12,500 convicts did hard, brutal prison time here. Port Arthur became the hub of a network of penal stations on the peninsula, its fine buildings sustaining thriving convict-labour industries, including timber milling, shipbuilding, coal mining, shoemaking and brick and nail production.

Despite its redemption as a major tourist site, Port Arthur is a sombre place. Don't come here expecting to remain unaffected by what you see. There's a sadness that's

TIGERS & DEVILS

There are two endings to the story of the Tasmanian tiger (*Thylacinus cynocephalus*, or thylacine) – a striped, nocturnal, dog-like predator once widespread in Tasmania and mainland Australia. Conventional wisdom says it was hunted to extinction in the early 20th century, with the last-known specimen dying in Hobart Zoo in 1936. Despite hundreds of alleged sightings since, no specimen, living or dead, has been confirmed. The second version of the story is that shy, elusive tigers still exist in the Tasmania wilderness. Scientists scoff at such suggestions, but Tasmanian folklore seems reluctant to let go of this tantalising possibility. David Owen's *Thylacine* and Col Bailey's *Shadow of the Thylacine* examine this phenomenon, while in the 2011 film *The Hunter*, grumpy Willem Dafoe stars as a man searching for Tasmania's last thylacine.

The rambunctious Tasmanian devil *(Sarcophilus harrisii)* is definitely still alive, but devil facial tumour disease (DFTD, a communicable cancer) infects up to 75% of the wild population (the real beast looks nothing like the Warner Bros cartoon). Quarantined populations have been established around the state, but efforts to find a cure have been depressingly fruitless. In the meantime you can check them out at wildlife parks around the state and get up-to-date information on ongoing efforts to control the impact of DFTD.

WORTH A TRIP

REMARKABLE CAVE

About 5km south of Port Arthur is Remarkable Cave, a long tunnel eroded from the base of a collapsed gully, under a cliff and out to sea. Waves surge through the tunnel and fill the gully with sea spray. A boardwalk and stairs provide access to a metal viewing platform above the gully, a few minutes' amble from the car park. Believe it or not, hard-core surfers brave the cave, paddling out through the opening to surf the offshore reefs beyond.

undeniable, and a Gothic pall of woe that can cloud your senses on the sunniest of days. Compounding this, in April 1996 a young gunman fired bullets indiscriminately at the community, murdering 35 people and injuring 37 more. After burning down a guesthouse, he was finally captured and remains imprisoned north of Hobart. The incident precipitated Australia's strict gun-control laws.

Sights & Activities

Port Arthur Historic Site HISTORIC SITE
(☎03-6251 2310; www.portarthur.org.au; Arthur Hwy; adult/child/family from $37/17/90; ⊙tours & buildings 9am-5pm, grounds 9am-dusk) This amazing World Heritage convict site is one of Tasmania's big-ticket tourist attractions. There are dozens of structures here, best interpreted via a guided tour. The **museum** was originally an asylum, and the **Separate Prison** was built to punish prisoners through isolation and sensory deprivation. The 1836 **church** burned down in 1884, and the **penitentiary** was originally a granary. The shell of the Broad Arrow Café, scene of many of the 1996 shootings, has been preserved with a **memorial garden** around it.

Inside the main visitor centre is a cafe, Felons Bistro (p650) and a gift shop (which stocks some interesting convict-focused publications). Downstairs is an interpretative gallery where you can follow the convicts' journey from England to Tasmania. Buggy transport around the site can be arranged for people with restricted mobility – ask at the information counter. The ferry plying the harbour is also wheelchair accessible.

Sleeping

Port Arthur Holiday Park CARAVAN PARK $
(☎1800 620 708, 03-6250 2340; www.portarthurhp.com.au; Garden Point Rd; dm $25, unpowered/powered/en suite sites $28/33/43; cabins from $120; ❄📶) Spacious and with plenty of greenery and sing-song bird life, this park is 2km before Port Arthur, not far from a sheltered beach. Facilities are abundant, including a camp kitchen, wood BBQs, petrol pump and shop. The best (and only) budget option around these latitudes.

Sea Change Safety Cove B&B $$
(☎0438 502 719, 03-6250 2719; www.safetycove.com; 425 Safety Cove Rd, Safety Cove; d $180-240, extra adult/child $40/20; 📶) Whichever way you look from this guesthouse, 4km south of Port Arthur, there are fantastic views – misty cliffs, sea-wracked Safety Cove Beach or scrubby bushland. There are a couple of B&B rooms inside the house plus a self-contained unit downstairs that sleeps five. Outside, camellia-filled gardens roll down to a beaut deck overlooking the beach (G&Ts anyone?).

Stewarts Bay Lodge RESORT $$
(☎03-6250 2888; www.stewartsbaylodge.com.au; 6955 Arthur Hwy; cabins/units d from $159/219, 2-bedroom $260/319, 3-bedroom cabin $360; ❄📶) Arrayed around a gorgeous hidden cove – seemingly made for swimming and kayaking – Stewarts Bay Lodge combines older, rustic log cabins with newer deluxe units, some with private spa baths. Modern kitchens are great for making the most of good local produce, but you'll probably spend more time in the sleek Gabriel's on the Bay restaurant.

Eating

Gabriel's on the Bay MODERN AUSTRALIAN $$
(☎03-6250 2771; www.stewartsbaylodge.com.au; Stewarts Bay Lodge, 6955 Arthur Hwy; mains lunch $18-35, dinner $28-35; ⊙8-10am & noon-2pm daily, 5.30-8.30pm Thu-Mon; 📶) Housed in a modern glass-and-wood pavilion with water views, Gabe's showcases local produce with Eaglehawk Neck oysters, Tasman Peninsula salmon burgers and Tasmanian scotch fillet with sweet-potato mash,

braised leeks and red wine jus. Definitely worth a detour if you're overnighting anywhere nearby. Bookings recommended.

Felons Bistro MODERN AUSTRALIAN $$
(☎1800 659 101; www.portarthur.org.au; Port Arthur Historic Site; mains $23-32; ⏰5pm-late) Swing into a wing of the visitor centre at the historic site and shackle dinner at Felons onto the nocturnal ghost tour. Upmarket, creative dinners with a seafood bias reinforce Felons' catchy slogan, 'dine with conviction'. Hungry carnivores should try Cape Grim braised beef cheek or the grilled Doo Town venison with Tasmanian ginseng. Reservations advised.

Launceston & Eastern Tasmania

Includes ➡

Best Places to Eat

- ➡ Stillwater (p671)
- ➡ Freycinet Marine Farm (p661)
- ➡ Moresco Restaurant (p665)
- ➡ River Cafe (p674)

Best Places to Stay

- ➡ Two Four Two (p669)
- ➡ Fresh on Charles (p668)
- ➡ Red Feather Inn (p677)
- ➡ The View (p674)
- ➡ Piermont (p659)

Why Go?

Trucking north from Hobart to Launceston, Tasmania's agricultural Midlands have a distinctly English feel, with baked, straw-coloured fields, stands of poplar trees, hedgerows and well-preserved Georgian villages.

Heading east, Tasmania's east coast is sea-salty and rejuvenating – a land of quiet bays punctuated by granite headlands splashed with flaming orange lichen. You'll find plenty of opportunities to hike, cycle, kayak, surf, dive and fish.

In the state's north, it's hard to imagine a pocket-sized city more appealing than Launceston. Well, maybe Wellington or Bergen...but Lonnie, as the locals call it, is certainly large enough for some urban buzz, while small enough for country congeniality.

Just outside Launceston are the vine-covered hillsides of the gently beautiful Tamar Valley. The historic towns to the south and west of the city offer stately homes, heritage streetscapes and buckets of small-town charm.

When to Go

Launceston

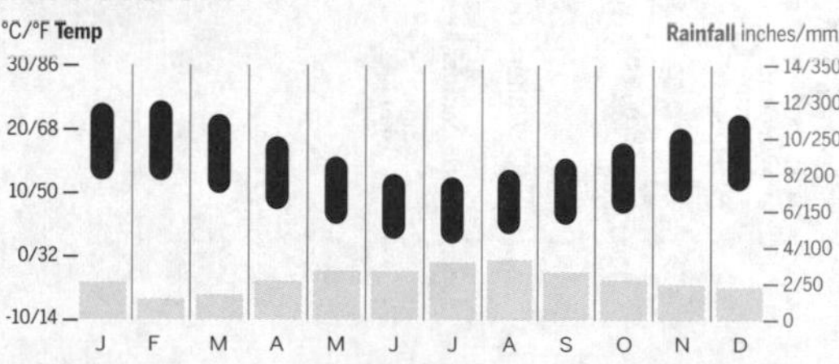

Dec–Feb Launceston gets giddy with summer festivals and long, still riverside evenings.

Mar–Apr Vintage time in the Tamar Valley, while the east-coast sea is at its warmest.

Jun–Aug Snow on Ben Lomond and clear, still Midlands days. Accommodation deals abound.

Launceston & Eastern Tasmania Highlights

1. Walking, swimming, eating or just chilling out at Launceston's **Cataract Gorge** (p666).
2. Checking out Launceston from the water with **Tamar River Cruises** (p667).
3. Wobbling between cellar doors in the **Pipers River Wine Region** (p676).
4. Sweating it out on the track to picture-perfect **Wineglass Bay** (p660) on the east coast.
5. Bumping into wombats and wallabies at **Maria Island National Park** (p656), just off the east coast.

6 Dunking your head under the waves at **Binalong Bay** (665) in the northeast.

7 Swooping down the ski slopes at lofty **Ben Lomond National Park** (p678).

8 Cheering on the speeding cyclists in the National Penny Farthing Championships in **Evandale** (p677).

THE MIDLANDS

Getting There & Around

Redline (☎1300 360 000; www.tasredline.com.au) buses power along the Midland Hwy several times daily. One way from Hobart/Launceston to Oatlands costs $22/25; to Ross or Campbell Town it's $31/14.

Oatlands

POP 860

Established as a garrison town in 1832, Oatlands serves a thriving tourist trade, but remains stately and restrained about it. The little town contains Australia's largest collection of Georgian architecture – on the impressive main street alone there are 87 historic buildings, some now housing galleries and craft stores.

Sights

Callington Mill HISTORIC BUILDING

(☎03-6254 1212; www.callingtonmill.com.au; 1 Mill Lane; tours adult/child/family $15/8/40; ⊙9am-5pm) Spinning above the Oatlands rooftops, the Callington Mill was built in 1837 and ground flour until 1891. After decades of neglect, with the innards collecting pigeon poo and the stonework crumbling, it's been fully restored and is once again producing high-grade organic flour. It's an amazing piece of engineering, fully explained on guided tours leaving hourly from 10am to 3pm. The town's visitor information centre is here, too.

Sleeping & Eating

Blossom's Cottage B&B $$

(☎03-6254 1516; www.blossomscottageoatlands.com.au; 116 High St; d incl breakfast $110;) In a self-contained garden studio, Blossom's is bright and cheerful, with a cast-iron bed, blackwood timber floors, leadlight windows, a small kitchenette and a couple of easy chairs under a silver birch. Great value. Full-some breakfast basket provided.

Woodfired Bakery Cafe BAKERY, CAFE $

(☎0418 551 546; www.naturespath.com.au; 106 High St; mains $10-16; ⊙10am-4pm Wed-Mon) The newest eatery in town (they were still putting the signs up when we visited), this upbeat outfit splits its attention between selling natural olive-oil soaps and quality cafe fare, such as breakfast burritos, soups, toasted panini and buttermilk pancakes. Saturday-night pizzas were also looking like a distinct possibility.

Information

Oatlands Visitor Information Centre (☎03-6254 1212; www.heritagehighwaytasmania.com.au; Callington Mill, 1 Mill Lane; ⊙9am-5pm) Proffers general info and handles accommodation bookings. Pick up the free handouts: *Welcome to Oatlands*, which includes self-guided town-tour directions; *Lake Dulverton Walkway Guide*, for explorations around the lake; and guides to the town's old military and supreme court precincts.

Ross

POP 420

Another tidy (nay, immaculate) Midlands town is Ross, 120km north of Hobart. Established in 1812 as a garrison town to protect Hobart–Launceston travellers from bushrangers, it quickly became an important coach staging post. Tree-lined streets are wrapped in colonial charm and history.

The **crossroads** in the middle of town leads you in one of four directions: temptation (the Man O'Ross Hotel), salvation (the Catholic church), recreation (the town hall) or damnation (the old jail).

Sights

Ross Bridge BRIDGE

(Bridge St) The oft-photographed 1836 Ross Bridge is the third-oldest bridge in Australia. Its graceful arches were designed by colonial architect John Lee Archer, and it was built by two convict stonemasons, Messrs Colbeck and Herbert, who were granted pardons for their efforts. Herbert chiselled the 186 intricate carvings decorating the arches, including Celtic symbols, animals and the faces of notable people (including Governor Arthur and Anglo-Danish convict Jorgen Jorgenson, the farcical ex-king of Iceland). At night the bridge is lit up – the carvings shimmer with spooky shadows.

Ross Female Factory MUSEUM

(www.parks.tas.gov.au; cnr Bond & Portugal Sts; ⊙site 9am-5pm, cottage 9.30am-4.30pm Mon-Fri & 1-4pm Sat & Sun) FREE This barren site was one of Tasmania's two female convict prisons (the other was in Hobart; p622). Only one cottage remains, full of interesting historical info, but archaeological excavations among the sunburnt stubble are under way. Descriptive panels provide insight into the hard lives these women led. Pick up the *Ross Female Factory* brochure from the visitor centre, then walk along the track from the top of Church St to get here.

Sleeping & Eating

Ross Caravan Park CARAVAN PARK $
(☎03-6381 5224; www.rossmotel.com.au; Bridge St; unpowered/powered sites $24/32, cabins s/d $50/70;) An appealing patch of green near Ross Bridge on the banks of the fish-filled Macquarie River. Utilitarian, sandstone, barracks-style cabins sleep two to four people (with cooking facilities) and are the cheapest accommodation in town. Bathrooms are shared; BYO linen. Reception is at the Ross Motel.

Stone Cottage RENTAL HOUSE $$
(☎03-6381 5444; www.stonecottageross.com.au; 4 Church St; d $120, extra adult/child $20/10;) One of the town's best options for families is indeed made of stone (amazingly detailed!), with a truckload of kids' toys and DVDs and an expansive garden with established fruit trees. The country kitchen with a long wooden table is perfect for lazy lunches and dinners. Sleeps seven.

Ross Motel MOTEL $$
(☎03-6381 5224; www.rossmotel.com.au; 2 High St; d/f incl breakfast from $135/195;) The independently owned Ross Motel offers spick-and-span Georgian-style cottage units (reasonably inoffensive reproductions), each with microwave, fridge and TV. Family units sleep four. Quiet and central, with breakfast provisions included for your first morning.

Ross Village Bakery BAKERY $
(☎03-6381 5246; www.rossbakery.com.au; 15 Church St; items $3-20; 8.30am-4.30pm) Overdose on savoury carbs, pies, astonishingly tall vanilla slices and Saturday-night wood-fired pizzas in summer, plus virtuous soups and salads of all kinds. The owners get up at 4am every day to light the 1860 wood oven.

Man O'Ross Hotel PUB FOOD $$
(☎03-6381 5445; www.manoross.com; 35 Church St; mains $19-30; noon-2pm & 6-8pm;) Dinner options in Ross are scant, but the town's heritage pub offers an old-school pub menu, including beer-battered east-coast flathead, homemade rissoles with chips and veg, chicken Kiev and roast o' the day. There's a beaut beer garden out the back that's all raised decks and brollies.

Information

Ross Visitor Information Centre (☎03-6381 5466; www.visitross.com.au; 48 Church St; 9am-5pm) Inside the Tasmanian Wool Centre. If you've got a group of eight or more, the centre runs guided town tours (per person $5, bookings essential).

Campbell Town

POP 990

Campbell Town, 12km north of Ross, is another former garrison and convict settlement. Unlike in Oatlands and Ross, the Midlands Hwy still trucks right on through town, making it a handy pitstop. Rows of **red bricks** set into the High St footpath detail the crimes, sentences and arrival dates of convicts such as Ephram Brain and English Corney, sent to Van Diemen's Land for crimes as various as stealing potatoes, bigamy and murder.

See www.campbelltowntasmania.com.

Sights

Campbell Town Museum MUSEUM
(☎03-6381 1503; Town Hall, 75 High St; 10am-3pm Mon-Fri) FREE The curio-strewn, volunteer-run museum features histories of characters such as John Batman and Martin Cash (a local bushranger) and sundry old artefacts such as an amazing 1930s film projector, once used by the Bye brothers, who screened Saturday-night movies here in the 1930s.

Red Bridge BRIDGE
(High St) The convict-built bridge across the Elizabeth River here was completed in 1838, making it almost as venerable as the Ross Bridge. Locals call it the Red Bridge because it was built from more than 1.5 million red bricks, baked on site.

Eating

Red Bridge Cafe & Providore CAFE $
(☎03-6381 1169; 137 High St; items $4-13; 7.30am-4pm Mon, Wed & Thu, to 5pm Fri, 8am-5pm Sat & Sun;) At the southern end of town, near the Red Bridge, a former brewery has been transformed into a funky dining room with shared wooden tables and a providore packed with beaut Tasmanian food, wine and beer. Fab cakes, quiches, tarts and gourmet pies make this an essential stop, whether you're heading north or south.

Information

Campbell Town Visitor Information Centre (☎03-6381 1353; www.campbelltowntasmania.com; Town Hall, 75 High St; 10am-3pm

Mon-Sat) Local info, plus the Campbell Town Museum (p655). The centre is volunteer run so hours may vary. Pick up the *Campbell Town – Historic Heart of Tasmania* brochure which plots sundry historic edifices on a map.

EAST COAST

Tasmania's laid-back east coast is drop-dead gorgeous. The west coast cops all the rain – by the time the clouds make it out here they're empty! No surprise, then, that this is prime holiday terrain for Tasmanians. Wineglass Bay and the pink granite peaks of Freycinet National Park are justifiably world famous. Online see www.eastcoasttasmania.com.

Getting There & Around

BICYCLE

The Tasman Hwy along the east coast is Tasmania's most popular cycle-touring route, with seaside towns, forests and plenty of places to swim. Traffic is usually light, and the hills aren't too steep.

BUS

Tassielink (☎1300 300 520; www.tassielink.com.au) provides east-coast services from Hobart to Triabunna ($21, 1¾ hours), Swansea ($30, 2¼ hours), the Coles Bay turn off ($34, three hours) and Bicheno ($38, three to four hours).

Bicheno Coach Service (☎03-6257 0293, 0419 570 293; www.freycinetconnections.com.au) runs between Bicheno, Coles Bay and Freycinet National Park, connecting with east-coast Tassielink coaches at the Coles Bay turn off.

North of Bicheno, **Calow's Coaches** (☎0400 570 036, 03-6376 2161; www.calowscoaches.com.au) runs to St Helens ($14, two hours) and Launceston ($36, three to four hours).

Maria Island National Park

Heading up the coast from Hobart, about 8km north of Orford, is **Triabunna** (population 900), the departure point for ferries to **Maria Island National Park** (www.parks.tas.gov.au; 24hr per person $12), just a few kilometres offshore. Book and buy ferry tickets and national park passes at the **Triabunna visitor information centre** (☎03-6257 4772; cnr Charles St & The Esplanade; 9am-5pm, closed for lunch 12.30-1.30pm).

Car-free, care-free Maria (pronounced 'ma-*rye*-ah') was declared a national park in 1972. Its mixed history provides some interesting convict and industrial ruins among exquisite natural features: forests, fern gullies, craggy peaks, fossil-studded cliffs and empty beaches. Maria is popular with bushwalkers and mountain bikers (BYO or hire one from the ferry company), while snorkellers and divers are in for a treat. National park fees apply, and island info is available at the reception area in the old commissariat store near the ferry pier.

Sights & Activities

Darlington HISTORIC SITE

The township of Darlington is where you'll start your time on the island. Close to the ferry jetty are some amazing old **silos** (good for some monastic chanting inside) and the historic **commissariat store**, now the national park visitor centre. Through an avenue of gnarled macrocarpa trees, lies the **penitentiary**, which once housed convicts (now bunkhouse-style accommodation) as well as the restored **Coffee Palace** and **mess hall**.

Painted Cliffs LANDMARK

From Darlington it's a one-hour return walk to the Painted Cliffs, at the southern end of Hopground Beach. From the beach you can clamber along the sculpted sandstone cliffs, stained with iron oxide in a kaleidoscope of colours. We suggest a visit in the late afternoon when the sun paints the cliffs a fiery orange.

Fossil Cliffs, Bishop and Clerk & Mt Maria WALKING

From Darlington, there's a two-hour loop walk to the Fossil Cliffs and the old brickworks. If you have more time (four hours return from Darlington), climb **Bishop and Clerk** (620m) for a bird's-eye view while you eat your packed lunch on the exposed, rocky summit. **Mt Maria** (711m) is the island's highest point; it's a seven-hour return hike through the eucalypt forests from Darlington, with brilliant views over the island's isthmus from the top.

Maria Island Walk WALKING

(☎03-6234 2999; www.mariaislandwalk.com.au; per person $2350) Blisters, soggy tents and two-minute noodles? Redefine your concept of bushwalking on this luxury guided four-day hike through Maria's best bits. The first two nights are spent at secluded bush camps, with the third at the historic former

East Coast

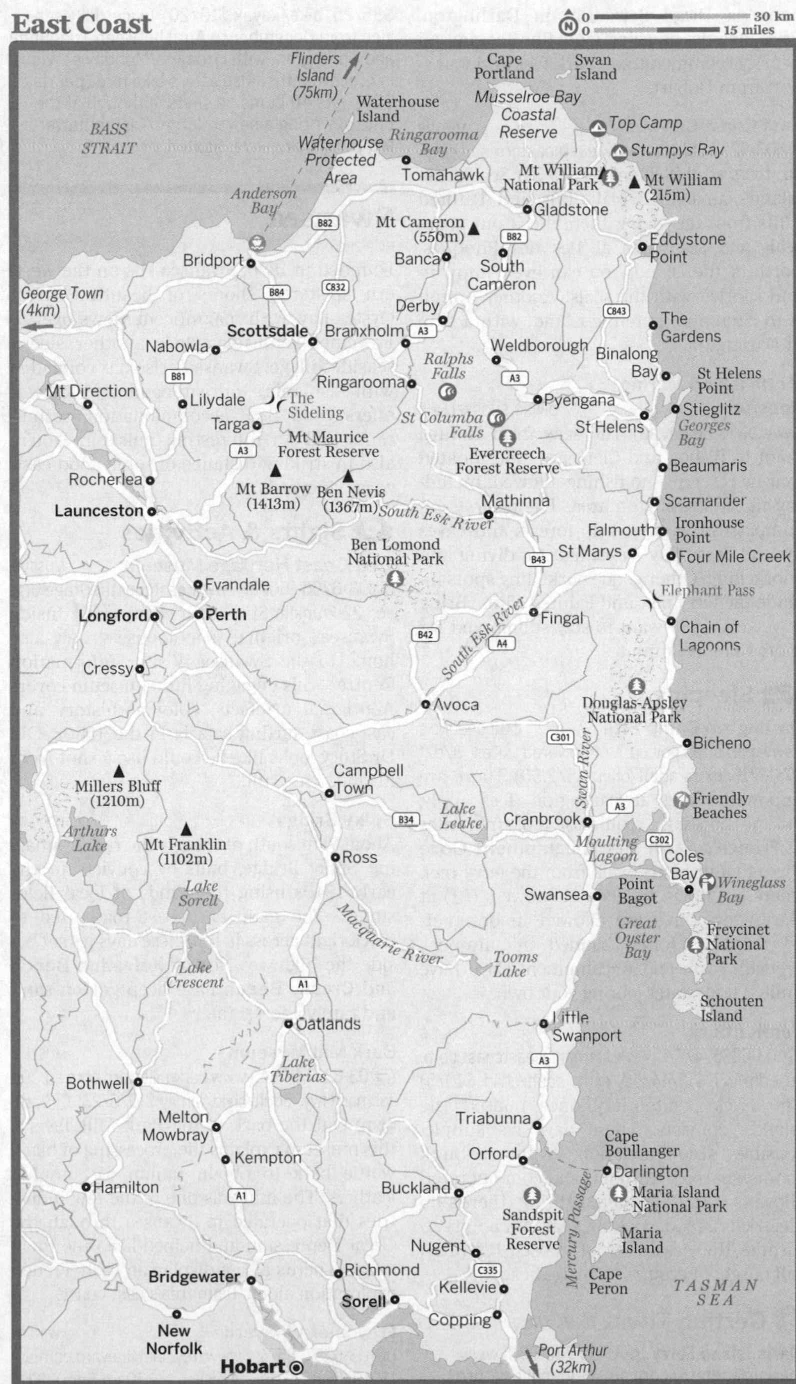
0 30 km
0 15 miles
Flinders Island (75km)
Cape Portland
Swan Island
BASS STRAIT
Waterhouse Island
Musselroe Bay Coastal Reserve
Top Camp
Waterhouse Protected Area
Ringarooma Bay
Stumpys Bay
Tomahawk
Mt William National Park
Mt William (215m)
Anderson Bay
Gladstone
Mt Cameron (550m)
B82
Eddystone Point
Bridport
Banca
South Cameron
George Town (4km)
B84
C832
Derby
C843
The Gardens
Scottsdale
Branxholm
A3
Nabowla
Weldborough
Binalong Bay
St Helens Point
Ralphs Falls
B81
Ringarooma
Mt Direction
Lilydale
The Sideling
Pyengana
Stieglitz
St Columba Falls
St Helens
Georges Bay
Targa
Mt Maurice Forest Reserve
Evercreech Forest Reserve
Beaumaris
Rocherlea
Mt Barrow (1413m)
Ben Nevis (1367m)
South Esk River
Mathinna
Scamander
Launceston
Ironhouse Point
Falmouth
Ben Lomond National Park
St Marys
Four Mile Creek
B43
Evandale
Elephant Pass
Longford
Perth
Fingal
Chain of Lagoons
B42
A4
Cressy
Avoca
Douglas-Apsley National Park
C301
Bicheno
Swan River
Millers Bluff (1210m)
Campbell Town
Friendly Beaches
Arthurs Lake
Lake Leake
B34
Cranbrook
Mt Franklin (1102m)
Moulting Lagoon
C302
Ross
Coles Bay
Wineglass Bay
Lake Sorell
Swansea
Point Bagot
Great Oyster Bay
Macquarie River
Freycinet National Park
Tooms Lake
Lake Crescent
A1
Schouten Island
Oatlands
Little Swanport
Lake Tiberias
Bothwell
Triabunna
Melton Mowbray
Cape Boullanger
Kempton
Orford
Darlington
Hamilton
Buckland
Maria Island National Park
Sandspit Forest Reserve
Mercury Passage
Maria Island
Nugent
Bridgewater
Richmond
C335
Cape Peron
Kellevie
TASMAN SEA
Sorell
Copping
New Norfolk
Port Arthur (32km)
Hobart

home of Diego Bernacchi in Darlington. Price includes amazing food, fine Tasmanian wines, accommodation, park fees and transport from Hobart.

East Coast Cruises BOAT TOUR
(☎03-6257 1300; www.eastcoastcruises.com.au; tours adult/child from $175/65) See Maria Island's amazing Fossil Cliffs and Painted Cliffs from the water, then check out some seals and sea caves at Iles des Phoques, north of the island. You can even jump in and snorkel with the seals! Another option is to circumnavigate the island, with a stop at Darlington.

Maria Island Marine Reserve DIVING, SNORKELLING
(www.parks.tas.gov.au) The seas from Return Point to Bishop and Clerk are a designated marine reserve – no fishing allowed, including in the Darlington area. The reserve encompasses the giant kelp forests and caves around Fossil Bay – excellent for diving and snorkelling. Other good snorkelling spots include the ferry pier and Painted Cliffs. Bring a wetsuit if you want to stay submerged for more than five minutes!

Sleeping

Darlington Camp Site CAMPGROUND $
(www.parks.tas.gov.au; unpowered sites s/d/f $7/13/16, extra adult/child $5/2.50) There are unpowered sites at Darlington (fees apply, but no bookings required), plus free sites at **French's Farm** and **Encampment Cove** three to four hours' walk from the ferry pier. There are BBQs, toilets and showers ($1) at Darlington. Fires are allowed in designated fireplaces (often banned in summer). French's Farm and Encampment Cove have limited tank water – bring your own.

Penitentiary LODGE $
(☎03-6256 4772; www.tasmaniaseastcoast.com.au; dm/d/f $15/44/50, extra adult/child $10/5) The brick penitentiary once housed the island's convicts. These days it's simple, sensible accommodation, with six-bunk rooms, shared bathrooms and coin-operated showers ($1). BYO linen, lighting (there's no electricity), food, cooking gear and ability to dismiss the possibility of ghosts. It's often full of school groups, so plan ahead.

Getting There & Away

Maria Island Ferry (☎0419 746 668; www.mariaislandferry.com.au; adult/child return $35/25, bike/kayak $10/20) Twice-daily service from December to April between Triabunna and Darlington, with Friday-to-Monday services in other months. Also offers bike hire (per day $20). Fits 40 bums on seats, although at the time of writing a newer/larger/faster/better ferry was being investigated.

Swansea

POP 780

Founded in 1820, Swansea sits on the western sheltered shores of beautiful Great Oyster Bay, with magnificent views over to Freycinet Peninsula. Once another sleepy seaside village, Swansea's rise has coincided with Tasmania's tourism boom and today it offers good B&B accommodation, restaurants and an interesting museum. You're also in striking distance of some good east-coast vineyards.

Sights & Activities

East Coast Heritage Museum MUSEUM
(☎03-6256 5072; www.eastcoastheritage.org.au; 22 Franklin St; ⏲10am-4pm) FREE Inside Swansea's original schoolhouse – now also home to the Swansea Visitor Information Centre – this engaging little museum covers Aboriginal artefacts, colonial history and east-coast surfing safaris in the 1960s. Old Dr Story looks like he could use a shot from his medicine still…

Spiky Bridge LANDMARK
About 7km south of town is the rather amazing Spiky Bridge, built by convicts in the early 1840s using thousands of local fieldstones. The main east-coast road used to truck right across it, but these days it's set beside the highway. Nearby **Kelvedon Beach** and **Cressy Beach** have deep golden sand and rarely a footprint.

Bark Mill Museum MUSEUM
(☎03-6257 8094; www.barkmilltavern.com.au; 96 Tasman Hwy; adult/child/family $10/6/23; ⏲9am-4pm) Out the back of the Bark Mill Tavern, this museum explains the processing of black wattle bark to obtain tannin for tanning leathers. The mill was one of the few industries that operated in Swansea through the Great Depression and helped keep the town afloat. There's also a display on early French exploration along Tasmania's east coast.

Freycinet Vineyard WINERY
(☎03-6257 8574; www.freycinetvineyard.com.au; 15919 Tasman Hwy, Apslawn; ⏲10am-5pm) The

Bull family has been growing grapes 'neath the east-coast sun since 1980 – it was the first vineyard on the coast. The vibe at the cellar door is agricultural, not flashy – we like it! Super sauvignon blanc.

Devil's Corner WINERY
(03-6257 8881; www.brownbrothers.com.au; Sherbourne Rd, Apslawn; 10am-5pm) Just past the Great Oyster Bay lookout, Devil's Corner is one of Tasmania's largest vineyards, run by the estimable Brown Brothers company. The mod cellar door here overlooks Moulting Lagoon, beyond which is Freycinet Peninsula.

Loontitetermairrelehoiner Walk WALKING
(Foreshore) This trail skirts the headland between Waterloo Beach and the Esplanade, passing a mutton bird (short-tailed shearwater) rookery. During breeding season (September to April) the adult birds return at dusk after feeding at sea. Allow 30 to 50 minutes to loop around the trail (you'll need at least that long to figure out how to pronounce it – it's named after the Aboriginal community that lived in the area).

Sleeping

Swansea Backpackers HOSTEL $
(03-6257 8650; www.swanseabackpackers.com.au; 98 Tasman Hwy; unpowered & powered sites $18, dm/d/tr/q from $31/81/81/87;) This hip backpackers, next door to the Bark Mill, was purpose-built a few years ago, and is still looking sharp. Inside are smart, spacious public areas and a shiny stainless-steel kitchen. Rooms surround a shady deck and are clean and shipshape. The bar is right next door.

★ **Schouten House** B&B $$
(03-6257 8564; www.schoutenhouse.com.au; 1 Waterloo Rd; d incl breakfast $160-200) This brick-and-sandstone 1844 mansion was built by convicts, and was the centre of 'Great Swanport' before the action shifted a little to the north. Decorated in simple, masculine Georgian style (no frills), its huge rooms now house antique beds and bathrooms. The history-buff owners do a mean pancake breakfast, and have perfected the art of making shortbread.

Swansea Beach Chalets CABIN $$
(03-6257 8177; www.swanseachalets.com.au; 27 Shaw St; d $180-240, extra adult/child $20/10;) These 20 chic, self-contained, grey-and-blue chalets are just steps from Jubilee Beach. The best ones have amazing 180-degree water vistas – high, wide and handsome. There's also a BBQ pavilion, a games room and an outdoor pool if the beach doesn't do it for you.

★ **Piermont** CABIN $$$
(03-6257 8131; www.piermont.com.au; 12990 Tasman Hwy; d $235-355;) Down a hawthorn-hedged driveway, 10km south of Swansea, these 21 stylish stone cabins array out from an old farmhouse close to the sea. Each unit has a fireplace and a spa. There's also a pool, tennis court, bikes for hire, sea kayaks and an eponymous **restaurant** (03-6257 8131; www.piermont.com.au; 12990 Tasman Hwy; mains $32-38, degustation with/without wine $150/120; 6-8pm, closed Aug) that's been getting positive press. Big on weddings (book ahead).

Eating

Kate's Berry Farm CAFE $
(www.katesberryfarm.com; 12 Addison St; meals $10-14; 9.30am-4.30pm) Sit under the wisteria-draped pergola at Kate's (3km south of Swansea) and decide which handmade berry incarnation suits your mood: berry ice creams, jams, sauces, chocolates, waffles, pancakes or pies (go for anything with raspberries involved). Great coffee and 'potted' pies (think beef and burgundy or pork and chorizo), too. Look for the signs off the Tasman Hwy.

Ugly Duck Out CAFE, MODERN AUSTRALIAN $$
(03-6257 8850; www.theuglyduckout.com.au; 2 Franklin St; mains $12-32; 8.30am-8pm) The meaning of the name seems lost on everybody, but this little shore-side diner is one of the best places to eat around here. Burgers, salads, curries, pastas, grills, rolls...locally sourced, homemade, biodegradable and sustainable all the way. Try the wallaby sausage sandwich. The owner loves a chat.

Saltshaker CAFE, MODERN AUSTRALIAN $$
(03-6257 8488; www.saltshakerrestaurant.com.au; 11a Franklin St; mains lunch $18-27, dinner $20-39; noon-2pm & 5.30pm-late, cafe 8.30am-9pm, to 4pm Jun-Aug) Ebullient Saltshaker gets the urban vote in Swansea. This bright, chic, waterfront dining room, serves fresh lunches and classy dinners that are big on local seafood (try the crab pasta with spinach, red pepper and white-wine-and-dill sauce). There's a wine list as long as your afternoon, and a takeaway cafe (mains $6 to $12) next door.

Information

Swansea Visitor Information Centre (☎03-6256 5072; www.tasmaniaseastcoast.com.au; 22 Franklin St; ⏲9am-5pm; 📶) In the old school building on the corner of Noyes St (sharing space with the East Coast Heritage Museum).

Coles Bay & Freycinet National Park

POP 310

Coles Bay township sits on a sweep of sand looking across the bay to the dramatic pink-granite peaks of the Hazards. It's a laid-back holiday town with plenty of accommodation (though book well ahead in summer) and some active tour options. The sublime Freycinet National Park, a wild domain of sugar-white beaches and gin-clear water, is the reason everyone is here. The park's big-ticket sight is the gorgeous goblet of Wineglass Bay. Online see www.freycinetcolesbay.com.

Sights & Activities

Cape Tourville LANDMARK

There's an easy 20-minute circuit here for eye-popping panoramas of the peninsula's eastern coastline. You can even get a wheelchair or a pram along here. Also here is **Cape Tourville Lighthouse**, which is totally spectacular when the sun cracks a smile over the horizon at dawn.

★**Wineglass Bay Walk** WALKING

This route is deservedly one of the most popular walks in Tasmania. You can make the steep climb to the **Wineglass Bay Lookout** (1½ hours return) for a super view over the bay and peninsula, but if you want to hear the beach squeak beneath your feet, you're in for a longer walk. The steep descent from the lookout to the bay takes another 30 minutes, making the out-and-back trip from the car park 2½ to three hours.

Tours

Freycinet Experience Walk WALKING

(☎03-6223 7565, 1800 506 003; www.freycinet.com.au; adult/child $2350/2000; ⏲Nov-Apr) For those who like their wilderness more mild, less wild, Freycinet Experience Walk offers a four-day, fully catered exploration of the peninsula. Walkers return each evening to the secluded, environmentally attuned Friendly Beaches Lodge for superb meals, local wine, hot showers and comfortable beds. The walk covers around 37km.

Freycinet Adventures KAYAKING

(☎03-6257 0500; www.freycinetadventures.com.au; 2 Freycinet Dr, Coles Bay; tour per person $95; ⏲tours 8.30am Oct-Apr, 9am May-Sep) Get an eyeful of the peninsula from the sheltered waters around Coles Bay on these terrific three-hour paddles. There are also daily twilight tours, setting off three hours before sunset. No experience necessary. Kayak hire is also available ($55 per person per day, including safety gear).

Wineglass Bay Cruises BOAT TOUR

(☎03-6257 0355; www.wineglassbaycruises.com; Jetty Rd, Coles Bay; adult/child $130/85; ⏲tours 10am Sep-May) Sedate, four-hour cruises from Coles Bay to Wineglass Bay, including champagne, oysters and nibbles. The boat chugs around the southern end of the peninsula, passing Hazards Beach and Schouten Island en route. You're likely to see dolphins, sea eagles, seals, penguins and perhaps even migrating whales in the right season. Book ahead.

Wineglass Bay Day Tour BUS TOUR

(☎0407 778 308, 03-6265 7722; www.wineglassbaytours.com.au; adult/child $105/60) Full-day minibus tours to the gorgeous goblet, departing Hobart at 7.45am and getting back around 7pm. You'll walk into Wineglass Bay, and also see Spiky Bridge, Cape Tourville and Honeymoon Bay.

All4Adventure ADVENTURE SPORTS

(☎03-6257 0018; www.all4adventure.com.au; 1 Reserve Rd, Coles Bay; adult/child 2hr $139/89, half day $239/129) Get OTBT (off the beaten track) into parts of the national park few others access on these quad-bike tours. Tours depart at 1pm daily (with 30 minutes' training beforehand), plus 4.30pm November to March. Half-day tours to the Friendly Beaches area depart 8am daily. Bring your driver's licence.

Sleeping

Richardsons Beach CAMPGROUND $

(☎03-6256 7000; www.parks.tas.gov.au; unpowered/powered sites from $13/16) Tucked behind Richardsons Beach, these camp sites are seriously popular. From late December to mid-February and at Easter, site allocation is via a ballot system: download the application form and submit it by 31 July. Outside the ballot period, book via the Freycinet National Park Visitor Information Centre (p662). National park entry fees apply.

BIG4 Iluka on Freycinet Holiday Park CARAVAN PARK, HOSTEL $
(☎1800 786 512, 03-6257 0115; www.big4.com.au; end of Reserve Rd; unpowered sites $30, powered sites $36-40, hostel dm/d $30/78, cabins & units d $100-185;) Iluka is a big, rambling park that's been here forever and is an unfaltering favourite with local holidaymakers – book well ahead. The backpackers section is managed by YHA; there are six four-bed dorms, a double and a predictably decent kitchen. The local shop, bakery and tavern are a short stroll down the hill.

Freycinet Rentals RENTAL HOUSE $$
(☎03-6257 0320; www.freycinetrentals.com; 5 East Esplanade; cottages $170-250) This is your hub for renting (mostly older-style, affordable) holiday houses and beach 'shacks' in and around Coles Bay. Prices swing wildly between summer and winter, and minimum stays apply for long weekends and Christmas holidays. One option, **81 On Freycinet**, has heaps of charm – the stone-and-timber house has three bedrooms, a spiral staircase and Hazards views (double $180).

★**Eagle Peaks** APARTMENT $$$
(☎03-6257 0444, 0419 101 847; www.eaglepeaks.com.au; 11-13 Oyster Bay Ct; d $275-425, beach house $295-445, extra person $50;) These two beautiful Tasmanian-oak and rammed-earth studios are 4km north of Coles Bay. Each unit has its own kitchenette, timber deck and comfortable king-size bed. The immaculate Beach House is here, too, sleeping four. All guests have access to BBQs; eat outside as wattlebirds dart in and out of the foliage. The property is a five-minute walk to Sandpiper Beach.

Saffire Freycinet RESORT $$$
(☎1800 723 347, 03-6256 7888; www.saffire-freycinet.com.au; 2352 Coles Bay Rd; d incl meals from $1800;) Saffire is an architectural, gastronomic and wallet-slimming marvel that sets the bar for top-notch Tasmanian hospitality. There are 20 luxe suites here, 'where the cerulean sky collides with the azure ocean'. The curvilicious main building houses a swanky restaurant, self-serve bar, library, art gallery and spa. There's also a menu of activity options, many included in the price.

Edge of the Bay RESORT $$$
(☎03-6257 0102; www.edgeofthebay.com.au; 2308 Main Rd; d $218-360, extra person $30;) Away from the main holiday hubbub, right on the beach about 4km north of Coles Bay, this small resort dances to the beat of its own drum. It has keenly decorated waterside suites, great staff and cottages sleeping five. Once you've woken up, there are mountain bikes, dinghies and tennis courts for guests to serve-and-volley on. There's also an excellent **restaurant** (☎03-6257 0102; www.edgeofthebay.com.au; 2308 Main Rd, Edge of the Bay; mains $25-39; ⏲6-8pm).

DON'T MISS

WINEGLASS BAY

You've no doubt seen the photos of Wineglass Bay, its perfect arc fringed with clear waters and talc-white sand – it's a regular on lists of 'World's Top 10 Beaches'. But visiting Wineglass is no lazy day at the beach. To reach the bay on foot is at least a half-day expedition, with 800 steep steps each way.

If you only climb to the viewpoint over the bay, your Wineglass Bay wineglass will likely be overflowing with a horde of other camera clickers (some of the 250,000 who come here annually). To beat the crowds, visit early and trudge right down to the bay on the other side of the viewpoint. Take water, food and sun protection – and have a swim!

Eating

Freycinet Cafe & Bakery BAKERY, CAFE $
(☎03-6257 0272; 2 Esplanade; items $6-15; ⏲8am-4pm;) This bakery has fuelled many a Freycinet walking epic. Pick up pies, cakes and sandwiches, or lurch into an all-day breakfast after a night at the tavern next door. Unexpected interlopers such as Thai beef salad and freshly squeezed juices also make an appearance.

★**Freycinet Marine Farm** SEAFOOD $$
(☎03-6257 0140; www.freycinetmarinefarm.com; 1784 Coles Bay Rd; plates $15-25; ⏲9am-5pm Sep-May, 10am-4pm Jun, 11am-4pm Jul & Aug) Super-popular Freycinet Marine Farm grows huge, succulent oysters ($15 a dozen) in the tidal waters of Moulting Lagoon. Also for your consideration are mussels, rock lobsters, scallops and abalone. Sit on the deck, sip some chardonnay and dig into your seafood picnic, as fresh as Freycinet.

Tombolo Freycinet CAFE, PIZZA $$
(☎03-6257 0124; 6 Garnet Ave; mains $16-24; ⏲8.30am-4pm Mon & Tue, to 8.30pm Wed-Sun)

Local wines and seafood, wood-fired pizzas and the best coffee in town (Villino, roasted in Hobart), all served on a trim little deck overlooking the main street. Ooh look – poached pear and frangipani tarts!

Information

Freycinet National Park Visitor Information Centre (☎ 03-6256 7000; www.parks.tas.gov.au; Freycinet Dr; ⏲ 8am-5pm Nov-Apr, 9am-4pm May-Oct) At the park entrance; get your parks passes here. Ask about free ranger-led activities December to February.

Getting There & Away

Bicheno Coach Service (p656) runs buses from Bicheno to Coles Bay ($11.50, 45 minutes) then on to the national park walking tracks ($14.50, 50 minutes). These buses connect with Tassielink east-coast buses from Hobart ($34, three hours) at the Coles Bay turn off. From the turn off to Coles Bay, it's $9 (30 minutes).

Bicheno

POP 750

Unlike upmarket Swansea and Coles Bay, Bicheno (pronounced '*bish*-uh-no') is still a functioning fishing port. With brilliant ocean views and lovely beaches, it's madly popular with holidaymakers, but has never sold its soul to the tourism devil and remains rough-edged and unwashed. Food and accommodation prices here will seem realistic if you're heading north from Freycinet.

Sights & Activities

★Bicheno Motorcycle Museum MUSEUM
(☎ 03-6375 1485; www.bichenomotorcycle-museum.com; 33 Burgess St; adult/child $9/free; ⏲ 9am-5pm, closed Sun Jun-Aug) Andrew Quin got his first Honda at four years of age, and since then he's been hooked on motorbikes. You don't have to be an aficionado, though, to visit his wonderful little museum out the back of his bike-repair shop. It's all shiny chrome and enamel under the bright lights here, with 60 immaculately restored bikes on display, including the unique Noriel 4 Café Racer – the only one of its kind in the world.

Diamond Island ISLAND
(Redbill Beach, off Gordon St) Off the northern end of Redbill Beach is this photogenic granite outcrop, connected to the mainland via a short, semi-submerged, sandy isthmus, which you can wade across. Time your expedition with low tide – otherwise you might end up chest-deep in the waves trying to get back!

East Coast Natureworld ZOO
(☎ 03-6375 1311; www.natureworld.com.au; 18356 Tasman Hwy; adult/child/family $22/10.50/56; ⏲ 9am-5pm) About 7km north of Bicheno, this wildlife park is overrun with native and non-native wildlife, including Tasmanian devils, wallabies, quolls, snakes, wombats and enormous roos. There are devil feedings daily at 10am, 12.30pm and 3.30pm, and a devil house where you can see these little demons up close. There's a cafe here, too.

Douglas-Apsley National Park NATIONAL PARK
(☎ 03-6359 2217; www.parks.tas.gov.au; person/vehicle per day $12/24) Four kilometres north of Bicheno is the turn-off to Douglas-Apsley National Park, protecting undisturbed dry eucalypt forest, waterfalls, gorges and an abundance of birds and animals. Walk to the swimming hole at **Apsley Gorge** (two to three hours return) or to the **Apsley River Waterhole** (15 minutes return). There's basic, walk-in bush camping here, too (free, but national park fees apply).

Foreshore Footway WALKING
This 3km seaside stroll extends from **Redbill Beach** to the **Blowhole** via **Waubedebar's Grave** and the **Gulch**. When the sea is angry (or just a bit annoyed), huge columns of foamy seawater spurt spectacularly into the air at the Blowhole. Don't get too close: even on calm days you can be unexpectedly drenched. Return along the path up **Whalers Hill**, which offers broad views over town. In whaling days, passing sea giants were spotted from here.

Tours

Bicheno Penguin Tours BIRDWATCHING
(☎ 03-6375 1333; www.bichenopenguintours.com.au; Tasman Hwy; adult/child $30/15; ⏲ dusk nightly) Bicheno is one of the top spots in Tasmania to see penguins. Spy them on these one-hour dusk tours as they waddle back to their burrows. Expect a sincere, pure nature experience: no cafes or souvenirs (and no photography allowed). Departure times vary year-round, depending on when dusk falls. Bookings essential.

Bicheno's Glass Bottom Boat BOAT TOUR
(☎ 03-6375 1294, 0407 812 217; bichenoglassbottomboat@activ8.net.au; Esplanade, the Gulch;

adult/child $20/5; ⌚10am, noon & 2pm) This 40-minute trip will give you a watery perspective on Bicheno's submarine wonders. Tours run October to May from the Gulch, weather permitting (bookings advised in January).

Sleeping

Bicheno Backpackers HOSTEL $
(☎03-6375 1651; www.bichenobackpackers.com; 11 Morrison St; dm $28-31, d $75-95; 📶) This congenial backpackers has dorms spread across two mural-painted buildings, plus the **Shack**, a 12-berth house a block away on Foster St (set up as six doubles). The communal kitchen is the place to be. There's also free luggage storage, and the friendly owners can help with bookings.

Bicheno East Coast Holiday Park CARAVAN PARK $
(☎03-6375 1999; www.bichenoholidaypark.com.au; 4 Champ St; unpowered/powered sites $25/33, units/cabins from $95/138, extra person $25; 📶) This neat, decent park with plenty of grass (not many trees) is right in the middle of town and has BBQs, a camp kitchen, laundry facilities and a kids' playground. Cabins sleep up to seven. If you're slumming it in the back of a campervan, showers are available for non-stayers ($5).

Bicheno Hideaway CABIN $$
(☎03-6375 1312; www.bichenohideaway.com; 179 Harveys Farm Rd; d from $155, extra person $25) A scatter of architecturally interesting chalets in wildlife-rich bushland a few kilometres south of town, close to the sea and with show-stopping views. Tune your ears into the raucous bird life (including a peacock wandering around), or browse the herb garden for edibles. Minimum stays apply, depending on the cabin and the season.

Diamond Island Resort RESORT $$$
(☎03-6375 0100; www.diamondisland.com.au; 69 Tasman Hwy; d $250-510; 📶🏊) About 2km north of Bicheno, this complex of 27 sun-soaked apartments is surrounded by lawns and has winning views north along the coast. There's private beach access, or a swimming pool if you'd rather have chlorine than salt in your hair. Wander over to namesake Diamond Island itself when the tide is low. On-site **Facets** (☎03-6375 0100; www.diamondisland.com.au; 69 Tasman Hwy; mains from $24; ⌚5.30-8.30pm) restaurant, and free penguin tours for guests.

Eating

Sir Loin Breier DELI $
(☎03-6375 1182; 57 Burgess St; items $5-20; ⌚8.30am-5.30pm Mon-Fri, 9am-4pm Sat) This superior butcher's shop has an amazing range of deli items, so stock up for picnics. The shop brims with cooked local crayfish, smoked trout, oysters, gourmet pies, cheeses, dips, terrines, soups, east-coast beer and wine and awesome smoked-quail sausages. Divine...but we can't decode the name – any ideas? Open Sundays in January.

★ **Pasini's** CAFE $$
(☎03-6375 1076; 70 Burgess St; mains $10-17; ⌚9am-8pm Tue-Sat, 9am-3pm Sun) This impressive outfit does Italian staples such as antipasto plates, wood-fired pizzas and lasagne – but oh, *so much* better than most. The breakfasts border on artisanal, the pastas and gnocchi are homemade and the coffees ('Ooomph' brand, roasted in Hobart) are richly delicious. Takeaways, east-coast beers and wines and sumptuous sandwiches also make the cut. What a winner!

Information

Bicheno Visitor Information Centre (☎03-6256 5072; www.tasmaniaseastcoast.com.au; 41b Foster St; ⌚9am-5pm Oct-Apr, 10am-4pm May-Sep) Assists with local information and accommodation bookings.

THE NORTHEAST

The northeast gets relatively few travellers, giving the region a more undeveloped and wild feeling than the rest of the east coast. Pretty, seaside St Helens is the main centre and a good base for exploring the wildlife-rich Mt William National Park, waterfalls and miles of empty coastline. Fishing opportunities abound, with a corresponding array of good seafood eateries. Online see www.northeasttasmania.com.au.

Getting There & Around

Calow's Coaches (☎03-6372 5166; www.calowscoaches.com.au) services link Bicheno and St Helens ($14, two hours) and St Helens and Launceston ($33, three hours via St Marys). Some buses connect with Tassielink on the Midlands Hwy for southward travel to Hobart.

St Helens

POP 2180

Wrapping around picturesque Georges Bay, raffish St Helens was established as a whaling town in 1830 and soon after 'swanners' came to harvest the downy under-feathers of the bay's black swans. It's long been an important fishing port and today is home to Tasmania's largest fishing fleet.

About 26km west of St Helens, turn off to tiny **Pyengana** and the feathery, 90m-high **St Columba Falls**, the state's highest. Further on is **Weldborough** (population 50), home to the outstanding **Weldborough Hotel** (☎03-6354 2223; www.weldborough.com.au; 12 Main Rd; unpowered/powered sites $15/30, s/tw/d/f $70/82/98/125; ⏲reception 11.30am-late Tue-Sun); and **Derby**, an old tin-mining town now home to the **Tin Dragon Interpretation Centre & Cafe** (Tin Centre; ☎03-6354 1062; www.trailofthetindragon.com.au/derby; Main St; adult/child/family $12/6/30; ⏲9am-5pm, reduced winter hours). The centre tells the fascinating story of Derby's past as a mining hub – thousands of Chinese miners lived and worked here in the late 1800s.

Sights & Activities

There are good swimming beaches at **Binalong Bay** (11km north on Binalong Bay Rd), **Jeanneret Beach** and **Sloop Rock** (15km north; take Binalong Bay Rd then The Gardens turn off for both), **Stieglitz** (7km east on St Helens Point), **St Helens Point** and **Humbug Point**.

Gone Fishing Charters FISHING
(☎0419 353 041, 03-6376 1553; www.breamfishing.com.au) Hook a bream or two on a close-to-shore fishing trip with a local guide.

East Lines WATER SPORTS
(☎03-6376 1720; https://.eastlines.wordpress.com; 28 Cecilia St; ⏲9am-5pm Mon-Fri, 10am-2pm Sat & Sun Dec-Feb) Hires surfboards, wetsuits, snorkelling gear, fishing rods and bicycles. For diving, contact Bay of Fires Dive (☎03-6376 8335; www.bayoffiresdive.com.au) at Binalong Bay.

Sleeping

BIG4 St Helens Holiday Park CARAVAN PARK $
(☎03-6376 1290; www.sthelenscp.com.au; 2 Penelope St; unpowered/powered sites from $35/37, cabins & villas d $95-225, extra person $22;) This park rolls itself across a green hillside 1.5km south of town and has plenty of family-centric amenities (games room, jumping pillow, playground, swimming pool). Shoot for one of the smart row of blue-and-cream villas running up the hill. Decent camp kitchen.

St Helens Backpackers HOSTEL $
(☎03-6376 2017; www.sthelensbackpackers.com.au; 9 Cecilia St; dm $27-30, d with/without bathroom $80/65;) Spick and span, laid-back and spacious – this main-street hostel has a 'flashpacker' section upstairs (good for families) and a couple of dorms out the back with super-chunky handmade timber bunks. Hang out on the deck or ponder the amazing wall of beer-bottle labels (not that this is a party place – keep it down after dark).

Bed in the Treetops B&B B&B $$$
(☎03-6376 1318; www.bedinthetreetops.com.au; 701 Binalong Bay Rd; s $220-310, d $250-310, extra person $70, all incl breakfast;) Some 7km out of St Helens en route to Binalong Bay, take the (steep!) drive up and up through the trees to reach this secluded, stylish timber home. There are two plush apartments, tastefully furnished and with private decks, spas and verdant views. Rates include afternoon tea or pre-dinner drinks, and a cooked breakfast.

Eating

Lifebuoy Cafe CAFE $
(☎0439 761 371; 29 Quail St; mains $8-14; ⏲7.30am-4pm Mon-Sat) This secretive, bookish little coffee joint is tucked in behind an eccentric antiques shop off the main drag. Reliable coffee and homemade soups are what you're here for, plus salmon burgers, waffles, eggs Benedict and good ol' country scones.

Mohr & Smith CAFE, MODERN AUSTRALIAN $$
(☎03-6376 2039; 55/59 Cecilia St; mains breakfast & lunch $10-22, dinner mains $22-30; ⏲8am-4.30pm Sun-Wed, to 8pm Thu-Sat) Oh look! A classy urban nook! With a sunny front terrace, snug open-fire lounge area, chilled tunes and sexy staff, M&S would feel right at home on Salamanca Pl in Hobart. Order a pulled-pork quesadilla or some baked eggs with avocado, cheese and chorizo for breakfast and see what the day brings. Good for an evening drink, too.

Blue Shed Restaurant SEAFOOD $$
(☎03-6376 1170; www.blueshedrestaurant.com.au; 1 Marina Pde; mains $29-30, takeaways $10-18; ⏲restaurant noon-2pm & 6-8pm, takeaways 10am-7.30pm Mon-Fri, from 11.30am Sat & Sun)

This classy harbourside eatery does wonders with seafood. Start with a spicy oyster shooter then move on to the signature crispy squid, or maybe the grilled rock lobster with herb and mascarpone butter. Pork, chicken and beef dishes for the non-piscatorial. There's a takeaway outlet on the side called **Captain's Catch**, with the same winning menu since 1994.

Information

St Helens Visitor Information Centre (03-6376 1744; www.tasmaniaseastcoast.com.au; 61 Cecilia St; 9am-5pm) Just off the main street behind the library. Sells national parks passes. The town's history is recorded through memorabilia and photographs.

Bay of Fires

The Bay of Fires is exquisite – powder-white sands and cerulean-blue water backed by scrubby bush and lagoons. Despite the proliferation of signature bright-orange lichen on the rocky points and headlands, the early explorers named the bay after seeing Aboriginal fires along the shore.

Binalong Bay (population 210) is the only permanent community at the Bay of Fires and has a beaut swimming beach. To get to the Bay of Fires proper, follow the road towards the ramshackle shack town of **The Gardens**. The Bay of Fires' northern end is reached via the C843, the road to the Ansons Bay settlement and Mt William National Park.

Activities

Bay of Fires Lodge Walk WALKING
(03-6392 2211; www.bayoffires.com.au; tour from $2250; Oct-May) A four-day, three-night guided adventure through this glorious wave-washed domain. A maximum of 10 guests beachcomb the coastline, led by knowledgeable guides. The first night is spent at a secluded tented beach camp, with the next two at the sublime Bay of Fires Lodge. Based here for day three, you can kayak on Ansons River or just laze around in the sun, working up an appetite for dinner. Fine food and wine included. Magic!

Sleeping & Eating

There are wonderful free **camping** spots along the bay, with good options immediately north of Binalong Bay, accessed by road from St Helens (take the turn off to The Gardens). In the northern reaches, there are beachfront sites at Policemans Point, reached by a turn off before Ansons Bay. BYO everything.

Bay of Fires Character Cottages RENTAL HOUSE $$
(03-6376 8262; www.bayoffirescottages.com.au; 66-74 Main Rd; d $180-230;) These five well-kitted-out cottages have a million-dollar location overlooking the bay. Interspersed with native scrub, all have mesmerising views in which you can lose yourself as you prod the BBQ on your deck. There are full kitchen and laundry facilities in each unit.

Arthouse Tasmania RENTAL HOUSE $$$
(0457 750 035; www.arthousetasmania.com.au; 61 Lyall Rd; 4 people from $500;) Lasso some like-minded amigos and book this architect-designed beach house, with polished floorboards, granite benchtops and a wide curvy deck backed by a phalanx of sliding doors. About 50m away is a classic Bay of Fires scene: white sand, rocks studded with orange lichen, and gently rolling waves. Sleeps four; no kids under 12.

★ **Moresco Restaurant** CAFE, MODERN AUSTRALIAN $$
(03-6376 8131; www.morescorestaurant.com.au; 64 Main Rd; mains breakfast $11-24, lunch & dinner $22-39; 7.30am-9pm daily, closed Mon Jun-Aug) Binalong Bay's only business means business: a fantastic food room overlooking the water, serving top-flight meals all day. Roll in for some Huon Valley mushrooms on toast with Tasmanian truffle oil for breakfast, hit the surf, then come back for Moulting Bay oysters and Bass Strait calamari with spicy tomato relish for dinner. Great coffee and even greater wine list.

Mt William National Park

The isolated **Mt William National Park** (03-6376 1550; www.parks.tas.gov.au; person/vehicle per day $12/24, camping s/d/f $13/13/16, extra adult/child $5/2.50) features long sandy beaches, low ridges and coastal heathlands. Visit during spring or early summer for blooming wild flowers. The highest point, **Mt William** (1½-hour return walk), stands only 216m tall, but offers great views. The area was declared a national park in 1973, primarily to protect Tasmania's remaining Forester (eastern grey) kangaroos, which were nearly wiped out by disease in the 1950s and '60s.

At Eddystone Point is the impressive **Eddystone Lighthouse**, built from granite blocks in the 1890s. A small picnic spot here overlooks a beach with red granite outcrops. You can also camp at **Stumpys Bay** and **Musselroe Top Camp**.

The park is well off the main roads, and is accessible from the north or south. The northern end is 17km from Gladstone; the southern end around 60km from St Helens. Watch out for wildlife if driving at night.

LAUNCESTON

POP 106,200

Tasmania's second city has forever been locked in rivalry with big-smoke Hobart to the south. Launcestonians argue their architecture is more elegant, their parks more beautiful, their surrounding hills more verdant – and even their food scene just downright zestier. And on some of these points it's hard to argue.

Launceston's beginnings, however, were anything but impressive. When the Reverend Horton visited in 1822, he wrote to his superiors: 'The wickedness of the people of Launceston exceeds all description. If you could witness the ignorance, blasphemy, drunkenness, adultery and vice of every description, you would use every effort to send them more missionaries.' Launceston is still buffing off some rough edges, but is transforming itself into a hedonistic historic town with a glam all its own.

Online see www.visitlauncestontamar.com.au.

Sights

★Cataract Gorge PARK

(Map p668; ☎03-6331 5915; www.launcestoncataractgorge.com.au; via Cataract Walk, Trevallyn; chairlift one way adult/child $12/8, return $15/10; ⏱24hr) A 10-minute wander west of the city centre is magnificent Cataract Gorge. The bushland, cliffs and ice-cold South Esk River here feel a million miles from town. At First Basin there's a free outdoor **swimming pool** (November to March), the world's longest single-span **chairlift** (9am to 5.30pm), summer concerts, huge European trees and sociable peacocks. Eating options include a cafe, kiosk and the sassy **Gorge Restaurant** (Map p668; ☎03-6331 3330; www.launcestoncataractgorge.com.au/gorgerestaurant.html; Cataract Gorge; mains lunch from $22, dinner $30-39; ⏱noon-2.30pm daily, 6.30pm-late Tue-Sat). The whole shebang is impressively floodlit at night.

★Queen Victoria Museum & Art Gallery MUSEUM, GALLERY

(QVMAG; Map p670; ☎03-6323 3777; www.qvmag.tas.gov.au; 2 Wellington St; ⏱10am-4pm) FREE Launceston's brilliant QVMAG spreads itself over two locations: the meticulously restored **art gallery** (colonial painting and decorative arts) on the edge of Royal Park; and the natural, social and technology-focused collections at the **museum** at the **Inveresk Railyards** (QVMAG; Map p670; 2 Invermay Rd, Invermay; ⏱10am-4pm, planetarium shows noon & 2pm Tue-Fri, 2pm & 3pm Sat). The buildings themselves are half the attraction, particularly the Inveresk site, which was Launceston's rail hub until not-so-long ago. Learn about black holes at the **planetarium** (adult/child/family $6/4/16), or fill a stomach hole at the **cafe**.

Boag's Brewery BREWERY

(Map p670; ☎03-6332 6300; www.boags.com.au; 39 William St; tours adult/child $30/15; ⏱tours 11am, 1pm & 3pm) James Boag's beer has been brewed on William St since 1881. See the amber alchemy in action on 90-minute tours with tastings afterwards. The free on-site museum sheds further light on brewing history (old TV ads, beer labels and photographs aplenty). Tour bookings essential. Extra tours December to March.

City Park PARK

(Map p670; www.launceston.tas.gov.au; cnr Tamar & Cimitiere Sts; ⏱daylight hours) Expansive City Park has enormous oak and plane trees, an elegant fountain, a glass conservatory, a Victorian bandstand and a playground and mini-train for kids. Peer into your gene pool at the glass-walled **Japanese macaque enclosure** (8am to 4pm April to September, to 4.30pm October to March), a gift from Japanese sister-city Ikeda.

National Automobile Museum of Tasmania MUSEUM

(Map p670; ☎03-6334 8888; www.namt.com.au; 86 Cimitiere St; adult/child/family $13/7/32.50; ⏱9am-5pm Sep-May, 10am-4pm Jun-Aug) Revheads get all revved up over the displays here – one of Australia's slickest presentations of classic and historic cars and motorbikes, all privately owned. The saucy 1969 Corvette Stingray will burn tyre tracks into your retinas.

Activities

Mountain Bike Tasmania MOUNTAIN BIKING
(☎0447 712 638; www.mountainbiketasmania.com.au) Runs guided rides along the North Esk River ($100), through the Trevallyn State Recreation Area ($120) and down the slopes of Ben Lomond ($225) – a downhill rush shedding 1050m in altitude as fast as you can say 'Marzocchi shocks'.

Tasmanian Expeditions ROCK CLIMBING
(☎1300 666 856, 03-6331 9000; www.tasmanianexpeditions.com.au) Rock-climbing adventures on the dolerite cliffs of Cataract Gorge. It offers half-day ($250 per person, $150 per person for two or more climbers) and full-day ($400 per person, $225 for two or more) climbs. No experience necessary for half-day trips (but you'll need it for a full day). All gear included.

Tours

Tamar River Cruises BOAT TOUR
(Map p670; ☎03-6334 9900; www.tamarrivercruises.com.au; Home Point Pde) To check out Launceston from the water, hop aboard the 1890s-style *Lady Launceston* for a 50-minute exploration of Cataract Gorge and the riverfront (adult/child/family $29/12/70). Longer morning and afternoon cruises (2½ hours, adult/child/family $79/35/179) on the *Tamar Odyssey* take you downstream to Rosevears and back.

Launceston Historic Walks WALKING TOUR
(Map p670; ☎03-6331 2213; www.1842.com.au/launceston-historic-walks; per person $15; ⏱4pm Mon, 10am Tue-Sat) Get your historical bearings with a 1½-hour walking journey through the Georgian, Victorian and modern architecture of the city. Walks depart from the '1842' building, on the corner of St John and Cimitiere Sts.

Valleybrook Wine Tours WINERY
(☎0400 037 250, 03-6334 0586; www.valleybrook.com.au; half-/full-day tours from $100/150) Full-day vino tours visiting six Tamar Valley cellar doors. Morning/afternoon tours visiting four wineries also available. Pick-up/drop-off at your accommodation.

Launceston City Ghost Tours WALKING TOUR
(Map p670; ☎0421 819 373; www.launcestoncityghosttours.com; adult/child/family $25/15/55; ⏱dusk) Just after sunset, get spooked on a 90-minute wander around the city's back alleys. Tours depart at dusk from the **Royal Oak Hotel** (☎6331 5346; 14 Brisbane St) – where Cyril is the resident ghost. Bookings essential, and departure time varies throughout the year. Not for little kids.

Festivals & Events

Festivale FOOD, ART
(www.festivale.com.au) Three festive days in City Park in February, with eating, drinking, arts and live bands (usually of the washed-up-but-still-touring variety). Tasmanian food and wine get an appropriate airing.

Junction Arts Festival ART
(www.junctionartsfestival.com.au) Five days of offbeat and interesting arts performances, installations, gigs and nocturnal brouhahas, held in September.

Tasmanian Breath of Fresh Air Film Festival FILM
(BOFA; www.bofa.com.au) At Inveresk Park in November screens flicker with the art house, the independent, the innovative – films to inspire thought and change. What a BOFA!

Sleeping

Arthouse Backpacker Hostel HOSTEL $
(Map p670; ☎03-6333 0222, 1800 041 135; www.arthousehostel.com.au; 20 Lindsay St, Invermay; dm $23-27, s/d $57/67; @📶) 🍃 In the old Esplanade Hotel (1881), Arthouse is our favourite Launceston hostel: airy dorms (love the attic rooms); a welcoming sitting room with huge TV, a handsome upstairs balcony (and bell tower) for shooting the breeze, and a BBQ courtyard out the back. It's also Australia's first carbon-neutral backpackers (recycling, tree planting and worm farms ahoy!). Bike and camping-gear hire available.

Sportsmans Hall Hotel PUB $
(Map p670; ☎03-6331 3968; www.sportieshotel.com.au; cnr Charles & Balfour Sts; s $55, d with/without bathroom $80/70; P📶) On hip Charles St, Sporties is a bit of a local institution. It's been done up recently and the rooms are pretty good: three have bathrooms and others have their own private bathrooms down the hallway. Ask for a room away from the bar on a Friday or Saturday night (live bands).

Launceston Backpackers HOSTEL $
(Map p670; ☎03-6334 2327; www.launcestonbackpackers.com.au; 103 Canning St; dm/s/tw/tr $24/52/56/75, d with/without bathroom $67/58; P📶) This large Federation house has been gutted to make way for a cavernous backpackers. It's in a leafy spot looking over Brickfields Reserve, but it's not the most

Launceston

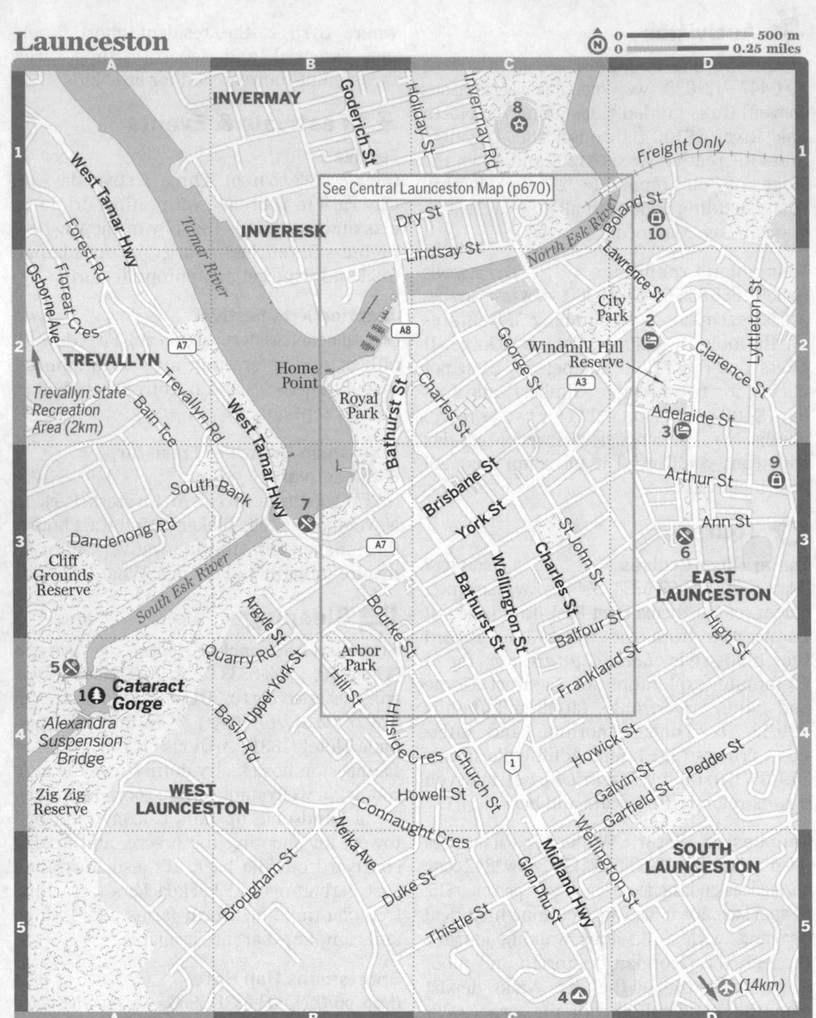

inspiring hostel in which you'll ever stay. Still, there are hardly any hostels in Launceston these days, so take what you can get. Rooms are clean and bright.

Treasure Island Caravan Park CARAVAN PARK **$**
(Map p668; ☎03-6344 2600; www.treasureisland tasmania.com.au; 94 Glen Dhu St, South Launceston; unpowered/powered sites $27/32, on-site caravans $60, cabins $90-100; P) The closest camping to the city centre – about 2.5km to the south – but it's right on the highway and pretty noisy. OK as a last resort. The business was rebranding when we visited, so it might be called something else when you arrive.

★ **Fresh on Charles** APARTMENT **$$**
(Map p670; ☎03-6331 4299; www.freshoncharles.com.au; 178 Charles St; d $120-150;) Take the stairs up from **Fresh on Charles** (Map p670; ☎03-6331 4299; www.freshoncharles.com.au; 178 Charles St; mains $10-22, shared plates $35-65; ⏲8.30am-3pm Sat-Thu, 8.30am-late Fri;) vegetarian cafe to these two excellent self-contained apartments with polished concrete floors. They're retro, minimal, brilliantly central and great value for money.

Launceston

Top Sights

1 Cataract Gorge........A4

Sleeping

2 Hi George........D2
3 Kurrajong House........D2
4 Treasure Island Caravan Park........C5

Eating

5 Gorge Restaurant........A4
6 Le Café........D3
7 Stillwater........B3

Entertainment

8 Aurora Stadium........C1

Shopping

9 Alps & Amici........D3
10 Autobarn........D1
Mill Providore & Gallery........(see 7)

The pricier unit faces off with the boughs of Princes Sq across the road. Free street parking out the front after dark.

Hi George B&B $$

(Map p668; ☎03-6331 2144; www.higeorge.com.au; 64 York St; d incl breakfast from $130; P Wi-Fi) Somewhat confusingly, Hi George isn't on George St. You'll have to wander up York St if you want to say hello. And if you do, you'll find six simple, tasteful en-suite rooms in an appealing 1880 brick house, with no fiddly bits to collect dust. Cooked breakfast included. Nice one!

Quest Launceston Serviced Apartments APARTMENT $$

(Map p670; ☎03-6333 3555; www.questlaunceston.com.au; 16 Paterson St; d from $159, 2-bedroom apt from $249; P ❄ @ Wi-Fi) Occupying the beautifully restored Murray Building in the heart of town, these 43 apartments are everything you could want in an upmarket home away from home: spacious, comfortable, fully self-contained and decorated with pizzazz. The architects have retained sections of exposed brickwork here and there as well as the original steel columns, all appearing in unexpected locations throughout.

Auldington BOUTIQUE HOTEL $$

(Map p670; ☎03-6331 2050; www.auldington.com.au; 110 Frederick St; d from $129, 2-bedroom apt from $252; P Wi-Fi) This small boutique hotel has an historic exterior – all earnest brown brick with lacy wrought-iron balconies – that belies the funky internal fit-out. Right in the middle of town yet convent-quiet, it has great city views and the kind of amiable service you just don't get in the larger hotels.

Kurrajong House B&B $$

(Map p668; ☎03-6331 6655; www.kurrajonghouse.com.au; cnr High & Adelaide Sts; d/cottage from $155/175; P Wi-Fi) Angling for a mature clientele (over 21s only), this quiet 1887 B&B has a just-like-home-but-much-smarter vibe. Outside are blooming roses and a self-contained cottage set up for longer stays. The mile-a-minute Scottish host serves impressive cooked breakfasts in the bright conservatory.

★ **Two Four Two** APARTMENT $$$

(Map p670; ☎03-6331 9242; www.twofourtwo.com.au; 242 Charles St; d incl breakfast from $250; Wi-Fi) Now *this* is a cool renovation! Furniture maker Alan has channelled his craft into four self-contained town houses, each with blackwood, myrtle or Tasmanian-oak detailing. Stainless-steel kitchens, coffee machines, private courtyards and spa baths complete the experience. The Charles St restaurants are on tap.

Hotel Charles HOTEL $$$

(Map p670; ☎03-6337 4100; www.hotelcharles.com.au; 287 Charles St; d from $220; P ❄ @ Wi-Fi) Launceston's hippest hotel was once a dreary hospital. The entrance ramps and sliding doors still feel like you should be arriving in an ambulance, but inside the Charles is all light and bright, with snappy decor, intelligent service and a stylish **restaurant**. Cheaper rooms are a squeeze; pay a bit more for a studio. All rooms have kitchenettes.

Eating

★ **Sweetbrew** CAFE $

(Map p670; ☎03-6333 0443; 93a George St; mains $4-10; ⏲7am-5pm Mon-Fri, 8am-3pm Sat, 9am-2pm Sun) 'Melbourne is just a suburb of Launceston,' says the barista at this new cafe. If his coffee is anything to go by, he's not wrong because the sweet brew here is definitely Melbourne-worthy, as are the pastries, baguettes, quiches and classy tarts on the counter. Dig the little booth room out the back!

Le Café CAFE $

(Map p668; ☎03-6334 8887; 39 Ann St, East Launceston; mains $8-16; ⏲8.30am-5pm Mon-Fri, to 4pm Sat) Crowded with conversations, this Frenchy little number faces onto St George's Sq on top of the hill in East Launceston. Beyond the beautiful old shopfront (stained

Central Launceston

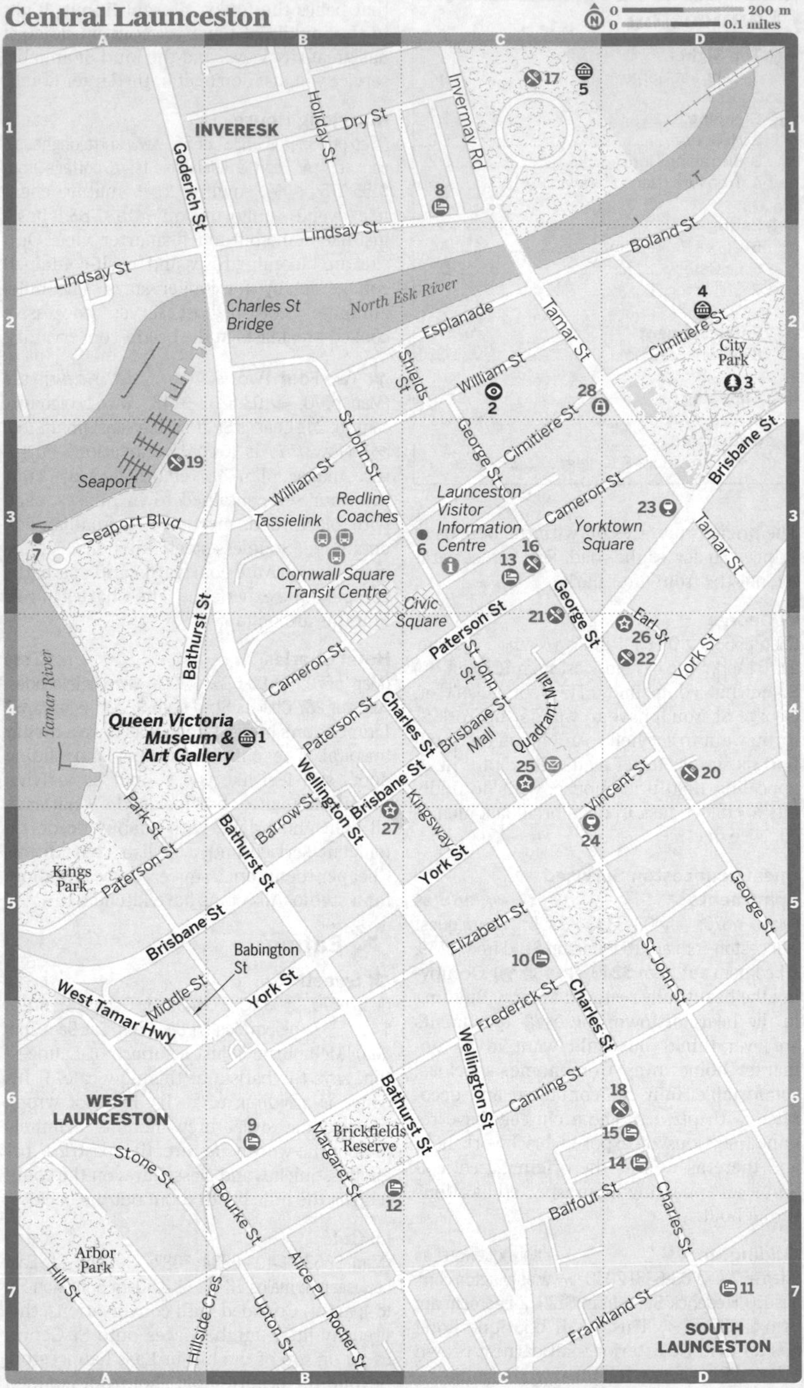
0 200 m
0 0.1 miles
INVERESK
Goderich St
Holiday St
Dry St
Invermay Rd
17
5
8
Lindsay St
Lindsay St
Boland St
North Esk River
Charles St Bridge
Esplanade
Tamar St
4
Cimitiere St
City Park
3
Shields St
William St
2
28
George St
Cimitiere St
Brisbane St
19
Seaport
St John St
William St
Redline Coaches
Tassielink
Launceston Visitor Information Centre
Cameron St
Yorktown Square
23
Seaport Blvd
7
6
16
13
Tamar St
Cornwall Square Transit Centre
Civic Square
Paterson St
George St
21
Earl St
26
22
York St
Bathurst St
Tamar River
Cameron St
St John St
Queen Victoria Museum & Art Gallery
1
Paterson St
Charles St
Brisbane St Mall
Quadrant Mall
25
Vincent St
20
Park St
Wellington St
Brisbane St
Kingsway
Barrow St
27
24
Bathurst St
Kings Park
Paterson St
York St
George St
Brisbane St
Elizabeth St
Babington St
10
St John St
Middle St
York St
West Tamar Hwy
Frederick St
Charles St
Wellington St
Bathurst St
Canning St
18
WEST LAUNCESTON
9
Brickfields Reserve
15
Stone St
Margaret St
14
12
Balfour St
Charles St
Bourke St
Arbor Park
Alice Pl
Hill St
11
Frankland St
Hillside Cres
Upton St
Rocher St
SOUTH LAUNCESTON

Central Launceston

glass, art-deco tiles) you'll find fresh juices, cakes, tarts, chicken-and-pumpkin pie, happy staff and kickin' coffee. *Très bon.*

★ Stillwater MODERN AUSTRALIAN $$

(Map p668; ☎03-6331 4153; www.stillwater.net.au; 2 Bridge Rd, Ritchie's Mill; breakfast $12-23, lunch & dinner mains $29-35; ⊙8.30am-3.30pm daily, 6pm-late Tue-Sat;) Still waters run deep here – deep into the realm of outstanding service and excellent Mod Oz, that is. Beside the Tamar, in the renovated Ritchie's Flour Mill (parts of which date back to 1832), Stillwater does laid-back breakfasts and relaxed lunches...then puts on the ritz for dinner. The best restaurant in Launceston, hands down. The wine cellar also runs deep.

Blue Café Bar CAFE $$

(Map p670; ☎03-6334 3133; www.bluecafebar.com.au; Inveresk Railyards, Invermay; mains $15-30; ⊙8am-4pm Sun-Thu, til late Fri & Sat, closed evenings Jul & Aug) In a converted chunky-concrete power station next to the Tasmanian College of the Arts, this cool cafe serves awesome coffee and creative local, organic dishes to architecture students on the run from the books. Go for the Reuben pizza, with Wagyu, pastrami, Gruyère, sauerkraut and horseradish.

Elaia CAFE $$

(Map p670; ☎03-6331 3307; www.elaia.com.au; 240 Charles St; mains $11-30; ⊙7.30am-8pm Mon-Sat, to 3.30pm Sun;) Elaia – Charles St's pioneering cafe. Here's a list of everything you need to know: pizzas, pastas, risottos, salads, all-day breakfasts, alt-country tunes, hip tattooed staff, wrap-around bench seats, live music Friday nights and colourful footpath tables. Hard to beat.

Pickled Evenings INDIAN $$

(Map p670; ☎03-6331 0110; www.pickledevenings.com.au; 135 George St; mains $17-22; ⊙5.30-9.30pm Tue-Sun;) Pickled evenings and holidays go hand in hand, but a visit to this excellent Indian restaurant will not (necessarily) involve excessive drinking. What you're here for are the curries, which are generous, spicy and sublime. Good vegetarian options, and takeaways available.

Pierre's FRENCH $$

(Map p670; ☎03-6331 6835; www.pierres.net.au; 88 George St; mains lunch $18-29, dinner $28-38; ⊙11am-late Tue-Fri, 8am-late Sat) Pierre's is a Launceston institution (since 1956). Coolly dressed in dark leather with subdued lighting, it offers a tight menu of long-time classics (steak tartare with dijon mustard, cognac and fries) and – some say – the best coffee in Launceston. Dishes are expertly paired with local wines. *Oui, oui!*

Black Cow Bistro STEAKHOUSE $$$

(Map p670; 03-6331 9333; www.blackcowbistro.com.au; 70 George St; dinner mains $35-47; noon-2.30pm Fri, 5.30pm-late daily) This high-class bistro/steakhouse specialises in Tasmanian free-range, grass-fed, artificial-hormone-free beef. It offers six different cuts and claims to be the best steakhouse in Tassie, which, judging by the restaurant's runaway success, can't be too far wrong. Go the Cape Grim eye fillet with truffled Béarnaise sauce. Worth every cent.

Mud MODERN AUSTRALIAN $$$

(Map p670; 03-6334 5066; www.mudbar.com.au; 28 Seaport Blvd; mains lunch $24-29, dinner $35-48; 11am-late) This hip bar-restaurant is the pick of the eateries in the moneyed Seaport enclave. Hang out with a beer at the bar then migrate to your table for superior Asian-inspired fare (Vietnamese sugar-cooked pork belly, soy-roasted duck, ginger-rubbed salmon). Views of the crews from the North Esk Rowing Club gliding past.

Drinking & Entertainment

★Royal Oak Hotel PUB

(Map p670; 03-6331 5346; 14 Brisbane St; noon-late) Launceston's best pub. We really don't need to expand on this fact, but it's hard not to – brilliant beers on tap, open-mic nights (last Wednesday of the month), live music Wednesday to Sunday and ballsy 1970s rock on the stereo. If you're too old to be a hipster, but still feel culturally valid, this is the place for you.

★Saint John BAR

(Map p670; 0424 175 147; 133 St John St; noon-midnight Tue-Sun) Hipsters rejoice! Bearded barmen pour craft beers from the taps here, the huge beer menu behind them listing your options in exhaustive detail. Out the back is an unexpected little food van, plating up Philly cheese steaks and lamb burgers that you can eat in the bar. The perfect symbiosis!

Princess Theatre THEATRE

(Map p670; 03-6323 3666; www.theatrenorth.com.au; 57 Brisbane St; box office 9am-5pm Mon-Fri, 10am-1pm Sat) Built in 1911 and incorporating the smaller Earl Arts Centre out the back, the old Princess stages an eclectic schedule of drama, dance and comedy, drawing acts from across Tasmania and the mainland.

Aurora Stadium SPECTATOR SPORT

(Map p668; 03-6323 3383; www.aurorastadiumlaunceston.com.au; Invermay Rd, Invermay; tickets adult/child from $25/15) If you're in town during football season (April to August), see the big men fly – Melbourne-based AFL team Hawthorn plays a handful of home games each season at Aurora Stadium. 'BAAAAAALL!!!'

Hotel New York LIVE MUSIC

(Map p670; www.hotelnewyork.net.au; 122 York St; 4pm-late Wed, Fri & Sat) This clubby pub with international pretensions hosts a steady stream of DJs and local and interstate rock acts (not too many from NYC). Cover charges (from $10) usually apply.

Village Cinemas CINEMA

(Map p670; 1300 866 843; www.villagecinemas.com.au; 163 Brisbane St; tickets adult/child $17.50/13) Escape your present reality with Hollywood blockbusters and the saliva-stirring aroma of popcorn.

Shopping

Harvest MARKET

(Map p670; 0417 352 780; www.harvestmarket.org.au; Cimitiere St car park; 8.30am-12.30pm Sat) Excellent weekly gathering of organic producers and sustainable suppliers from around northern and western Tasmania. Craft beer, artisan baked goods, cheese and salmon all feature heavily, beneath little green tents.

Mill Providore & Gallery FOOD

(Map p668; 03-6331 0777; www.millprovidore.com.au; 2 Bridge Rd; 9.30am-5.30pm Mon-Fri, 9am-5.30pm Sat, to 4pm Sun) Above Stillwater restaurant at Ritchie's Flour Mill you'll find this most excellent treasure trove of good things for the home, kitchen, stomach and soul. There are shelves full of books, food and wine (and books about food and wine), a brilliant deli section for picnic fodder and a browse-worthy community gallery area.

Alps & Amici FOOD

(Map p668; 03-6331 1777; www.alpsandamici.com; 52 Abbott St, East Launceston; 7.30am-6.30pm Mon-Fri, 8am-2pm Sun) Super-chef Daniel Alps has set up this smart providore where you can buy his restaurant-quality meals to take home and adore. Classy cakes, cheeses, meats and seafood, the freshest fruit and veg, and Tasmanian beer and wine also available. Good coffee, too.

Information

Banks and ATMs are located on St John and Brisbane Sts near the mall.

Launceston General Hospital (03-6348 7111; www.dhhs.tas.gov.au; 287-289 Charles St; 24hr) 24-hour accident and emergency.

Launceston Visitor Information Centre (Map p670; 03-6336 3133, 1800 651 827; www.visitlaunceston tamar.com.au; 68-72 Cameron St; 9am-5pm Mon-Fri, to 1pm Sat & Sun) Everything you ever wanted to know about Launceston, but were afraid to ask.

Main Post Office (GPO; Map p670; 13 13 18; 68-72 Cameron St; 8.30am-5.30pm Mon-Fri, 9am-12.30pm Sat) Inside a fab 1880s red-brick building.

Getting There & Away

AIR

Jetstar (www.jetstar.com) Flights to Brisbane, Sydney and Melbourne.

Qantas (www.qantas.com.au) Direct flights to Melbourne, Sydney and Brisbane.

Virgin Australia (www.virginaustralia.com) Direct flights to Melbourne and Sydney.

BUS

The depot for most services is the **Cornwall Square Transit Centre** (Map p670; 200 Cimitiere St). Check online for the latest fares and timetables.

Redline Coaches (Map p670; 1300 360 000; www.tasredline.com.au) From Launceston west to Westbury, Deloraine, Devonport, Burnie and Stanley, and south to Hobart. Plenty of stops in between.

Tassielink (Map p670; 1300 300 520; www.tassielink.com.au) West coast buses via Devonport and Cradle Mountain, and an express service from the Devonport ferry terminal to Hobart via Launceston. Also runs from Launceston to Evandale and Longford.

Getting Around

TO/FROM THE AIRPORT

Launceston Airport (03-6391 6222; www.launcestonairport.com.au; 201 Evandale Rd, Western Junction) is 15km south of the city on the road to Evandale. **Launceston Airporter** (1300 38 55 22; www.airporterlaunceston.com.au; adult/child $18/14) is a shuttle bus running door-to-door services. A taxi into the city costs about $35.

BICYCLE

Arthouse Backpacker Hostel (p667) rents out bikes for $15 per day.

Artbikes (03-6331 5506; www.artbikes.com.au; Design Centre Tasmania, cnr Brisbane & Tamar Sts; 9.30am-5.30pm Mon-Fri, 10am-4pm Sat & Sun) City-bike hire from the Design Centre Tasmania. Bring a credit card and photo ID. Overnight hire costs $22; for a weekend it's $44.

BUS

Metro Tasmania (13 22 01; www.metrotas.com.au) Runs Launceston's suburban bus network. One-way fares vary with distances ('sections') travelled (from $3 to $6.20). A Day Rover pass ($5.30) allows unlimited travel after 9am. Buses depart from the two blocks of St John St between Paterson and York Sts. Many routes don't operate in the evenings or on Sundays.

Free Tiger Bus (03-6323 3000; www.launceston.tas.gov.au) Runs from Inveresk to Princes Park, Windmill Hill and back to Inveresk every 30 minutes between 10am and 3.30pm Monday to Friday.

CAR

The big-name rental companies have either Launceston Airport or city offices. Smaller operators have cars from around $40 per day:

Rent For Less (03-6391 9182, 1300 883 739; www.rentforless.com.au; 153 St John St; 8am-5pm Mon-Fri, 8.30am-5pm Sat, 9am-1pm Sun)

AROUND LAUNCESTON

Tamar Valley

The broad Tamar River funnels north 64km from Launceston and empties into Bass Strait. Along its flanks are orchards, forests, pastures and vineyards aplenty. This is Tasmania's key wine-producing area: the premium wines created here have achieved international recognition. See www.tamarvalleywineroute.com.au for wine-touring info.

The **Tamar Visitor Information Centre** (1800 637 989, 03-6394 4454; www.tamarvalley.com.au; Main Rd, Exeter; 8.30am-5pm) is in Exeter in the West Tamar Valley.

Getting There & Around

Manlons' Coaches (☎03-6383 1221; www.manionscoaches.com.au) services the West Tamar Valley from Launceston; **Lee's Coaches** (☎03-6334 7979; www.leescoaches.com) services the East Tamar Valley from Launceston.

Rosevears & Around

POP 310

This pretty little riverside hamlet is on a side road off the West Tamar Hwy. With some super wineries in the area, it's wine-buff heaven. Three of the best are **Ninth Island Vineyard** (☎03-6330 2388; www.kreglingerwineestates.com; 95 Rosevears Dr, Rosevears; ⏲10am-5pm), which does a mean pinot noir; the sizeable **Tamar Ridge** (☎03-6330 0300; www.tamarridge.com.au; 1a Waldhorn Dr, Rosevears; ⏲10am-5pm), with its sunny terrace; and **Velo Wines** (☎03-6330 3677; www.velowines.com.au; 755 West Tamar Hwy, Legana; ⏲cellar door 10am-5pm Wed-Sun, restaurant 12.30-3.30pm Wed-Sun & 6pm-late Fri & Sat), run by former Olympic cyclist Michael Wilson. Velo's cafe is super-popular.

Sleeping & Eating

★View APARTMENT, B&B **$$**
(☎0434 200 300; 279 Gravelly Beach Rd, Gravelly Beach; d $120-140) The View is a hip B&B studio next to a mechanic's workshop, sleeping two. The breakfast hamper is stuffed with fruit, eggs, bread, jams, cereals and coffee, which you can cobble together in the little kitchen in the corner. And indeed, the view is awesome!

Rosevears Waterfront Tavern PUB FOOD **$$**
(☎03-6394 4074; www.rosevearstavern.com.au; 215 Rosevears Dr, Rosevears; mains $25-29; ⏲noon-3pm daily, 6-9pm Wed-Sat) Built in 1831 Rosevears Waterfront Tavern offers pub-grub faves (burgers, chicken parmigiana) and more up-tempo fare such as lamb-leg rogan josh and grilled tiger prawn pizza. The river views are wild, and the beer terrace is pumping. Live music most Sunday afternoons.

> **WORTH A TRIP**
>
> **BRIDESTOWE LAVENDER ESTATE**
>
> Near Nabowla, 52km northeast of Launceston, is the turn off to the largest lavender farm in the southern hemisphere – **Bridestowe Lavender Estate** (☎03-6352 8182; www.bridestowelavender.com.au; 296 Gillespies Rd, Nabowla; ⏲9am-5pm) FREE – producing lavender oil for the perfume industry. The purple fields in flowering season (mid-December to late January) are unforgettable. There's also a **cafe** and **gift shop** that sells all things lavender: drawer scenters, fudge, ice cream and 'Bobbie Bears' – lavender-stuffed toys that (inexplicably) sell by the thousands.

Beauty Point & Around

POP 1210

On the pier at beauteous Beauty Point is the coo-inducing **Seahorse World** (☎03-6383 4111; www.seahorseworld.com.au; 200 Flinders St, Inspection Head Wharf, Beauty Point; adult/child/family $22/9/54; ⏲9.30am-4pm Dec-Apr, 10am-3pm May-Nov), where sea horses are hatched and raised to supply aquariums worldwide. Next door is **Platypus House** (☎03-6383 4884; www.platypushouse.com.au; 200 Flinders St, Inspection Head Wharf, Beauty Point; adult/child/family $23/9/55; ⏲9.30am-3.30pm), a wildlife centre with platypuses and echidnas.

South of Beauty Point is **Beaconsfield** (population 1200), a gold-mining town that made world news during a mine rescue in 2006. The **Beaconsfield Mine & Heritage Centre** (☎03-6383 1473; www.beaconsfieldheritage.com.au; West St, Beaconsfield; adult/child/family $12/4/30; ⏲9.30am-4.30pm) details mining history through interactive exhibits.

Visit all of the above attractions with a **Triple Pass** (adult/family $50/136) from the Tamar Visitor Information Centre (p673) in Exeter.

Sleeping & Eating

★Tamar Cove MOTEL **$$**
(☎03-6383 4375; www.tamarcove.com; 4421 Main Rd; d $119-150, 2-bedroom apt $149; 📶🏊) What a winning little hillside enclave! Nine stylishly done-up motel rooms front well-manicured gardens with a solar-heated pool. The **restaurant** (mains $15 to $30, serving 8am until late) gets rave reviews, too – don't go past the house-special seafood chowder. Free wi-fi. Good one!

★River Cafe CAFE, MODERN AUSTRALIAN **$$**
(☎03-6383 4099; www.therivercafe.com.au; 225 Flinders St; mains $8-30; ⏲11am-late; 📶) On

Around Launceston

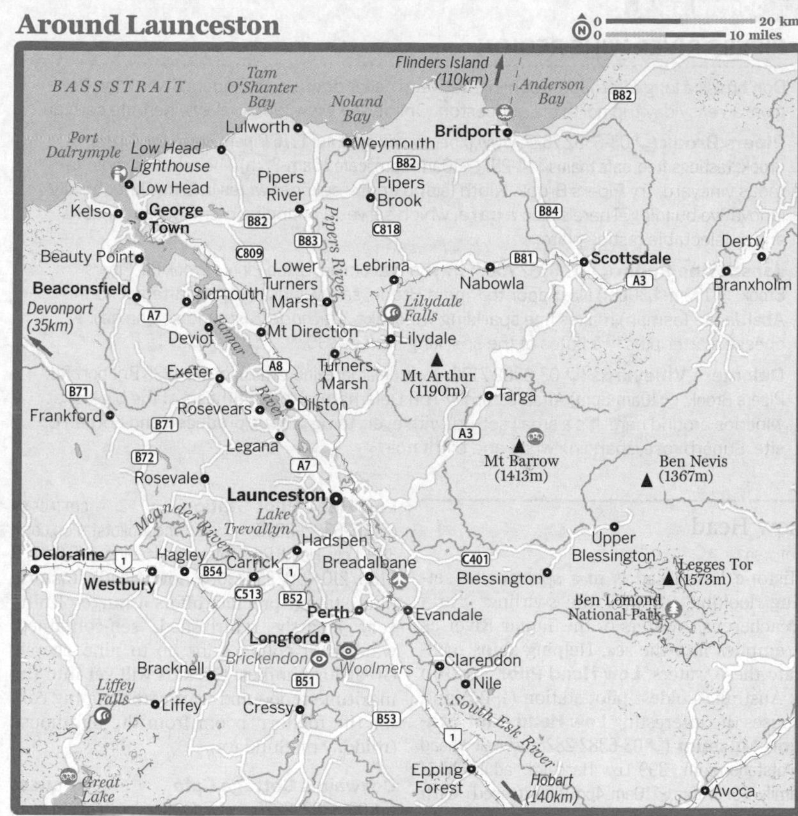

sunny days at the River Cafe the windows fold right back and the water feels so close you could touch it. The menu tempts with fresh local fare – the Tasmanian eye fillet is sublime – and the coffee is just about perfect, too. Takeaway pizzas, free wi-fi and Tamar Valley wines all the way.

George Town

POP 4310

Historic George Town, on the eastern lip of the Tamar River mouth, is Australia's third-oldest white settlement (after Sydney and Hobart). George Town was established in 1804 by Lieutenant Colonel Paterson to guard against the French who were reconnoitring the area. Sadly, little remains of the original township.

The **George Town Visitor Information Centre** (☎03-6382 1700; www.provincialtamar.com.au; 92-96 Main Rd; ⏰9am-5pm) rents bicycles for two-wheeled explorations. Ask for directions to the **Bass & Flinders Centre** (☎03-6382 3792; www.bassandflinders.org.au; 8 Elizabeth St, George Town; adult/child/family $10/4/24; ⏰9am-4pm), an excellent museum with a replica of the *Norfolk*, the compact craft that Bass and Flinders used for their 1897 circumnavigation of Van Diemen's Land.

Sleeping & Eating

Pier Hotel Motel HOTEL, MOTEL **$$**
(☎03-6382 1300; www.pierhotel.com.au; 5 Elizabeth St; d $110-260; 📶) There's a wing of quiet motel rooms out the back and renovated pub rooms upstairs here, but the star attraction is the **bistro** (mains $14-33; ⏰noon-2pm & 6-8pm), which serves excellent pizzas, porterhouse steaks, salads and surf 'n' turf with an awesome sweet-chilli béchamel sauce. Fold-back doors open towards the water in warm weather.

DON'T MISS

PIPERS RIVER WINE REGION

Don't miss a long afternoon wobbling between cellar doors in the Pipers River Wine Region, an easy day trip north of Launceston. Online see www.tamarvalleywineroute.com.au.

Pipers Brook (☎03-6382 7527; www.pipersbrook.com.au; 1216 Pipers Brook Rd, Pipers Brook; tastings free, cafe mains $14-25; ⊙10am-5pm, cafe 10am-3pm) The region's most famous vineyard. Try Pipers Brook, Ninth Island and Kreglinger wines in an architecturally innovative building. There's also a **cafe**, which serves a changing menu of light snacks and a delectable tasting plate.

Jansz Wine Room (☎03-6382 7066; www.jansz.com.au; 1216b Pipers Brook Rd, Pipers Brook; ⊙10am-4.30pm) Next door to Pipers Brook, savvy Jansz (named after explorer Abel Jansz Tasman) makes fine sparkling wine, aka *'Méthode Tasmanoise'* (ha ha). A cheese platter plus two flutes of the sparking stuff is $30.

Delamere Vineyards (☎03-6382 7190; www.delamerevineyards.com.au; 4238 Bridport Rd, Pipers Brook; ⊙10am-5pm) Affable, family-run Delamere is the antithesis of the big-ticket wineries around here. It's a small set-up, with everything grown, produced and bottled on site. Superb rosé, sparkling white and pinot noir.

Low Head

POP 450

Historic Low Head is in a spectacular setting, looking out over the swirling – and treacherous – waters of the Tamar River as it empties into the sea. Helping ships navigate these waters, **Low Head Pilot Station** is Australia's oldest pilot station (1805) and houses the interesting **Low Head Pilot Station Museum** (☎03-6382 2826; www.lowheadpilotstation.com; 399 Low Head Rd; adult/child/family $5/3/15; ⊙10am-4pm), cluttered with historical items and displays.

On Low Head itself, the view from the 1888 **lighthouse** is a winner. Penguins return to their burrows here every night: check them out with **Low Head Penguin Tours** (☎0418 361 860; http://penguintours.lowhead.com; end of Low Head Rd; adult/child $18/10; ⊙dusk). There's good surf at **East Beach** on Bass Strait, and safe swimming in the river.

Sleeping & Eating

Low Head Tourist Park CARAVAN PARK **$**
(☎03-6382 1573; www.lowheadtouristpark.com.au; 136 Low Head Rd; unpowered sites $15-20, powered sites $24-30, en-suite sites $34-40, dm $28, on-site caravans $60-80, cabins $95-115, cottages $120-140) There are two sections – old and new – to this strangely treeless riverside park. Price ranges reflect the variations between the two. Dorm beds are in a converted caravan with an annex. Book one of the new timber-lined cabins and settle in for a sunset spectacular.

Low Head Pilot Station COTTAGE **$$**
(☎03-6382 2826; www.lowheadpilotstation.com; 399 Low Head Rd; cottages sleeping 2/5/6/8/9 $180/210/210/250/300) Low Head's historic pilot station precinct offers a range of nine very smartly refurbished, self-contained, waterfront cottages for up to nine people. Great for families; the kids will get into the maritime mood and wait with flapping ears for the foghorn boom from the lighthouse (midday on Sundays).

Coxwain's Cottage Café CAFE **$$**
(☎03-6382 2826; www.lowheadpilotstation.com; 399 Low Head Rd, Low Head Pilot Station; mains $6-20; ⊙10am-5pm Jun-Nov, 9am-5pm Dec-May) The best (only) place to eat in Low Head is this excellent cafe in an 1847 cottage at the Low Head Pilot Station. Offerings include homemade pies (try the lamb-and-vegie version), quiches, toasted sandwiches and hearty soups in winter – plus Pipers River wines and fine espresso.

Longford & Around

Longford (population 3760), a National Trust–classified town 27km south of Launceston, hosted the 1965 Australian Grand Prix. The town is also noted for its most famous son, author Richard Flanagan, who won the 2014 Man Booker Prize for his novel *The Narrow Road to the Deep North.*

Also nearby are some fabulous historic estates. Unesco World Heritage–listed **Woolmers** (☎03-6391 2230; www.woolmers.com.au; Woolmers Lane, Longford; admission $14/5, tours adult/child/family from $20/7/45; ⏲10am-4pm, tours 11.15am, 12.30pm & 2pm) was built in 1819 and features a 2-hectare rose garden and buildings full of antiques. Nearby is **Brickendon** (☎03-6391 1383; www.brickendon.com.au; Woolmers Lane; adult/child/family $12.50/5/38; ⏲9.30am-5pm Oct-May, to 4pm Jun-Sep), a more modest estate dating from 1824, with heritage gardens and a still-functioning farm village. Both Woolmers and Brickendon offer self-contained **accommodation** (doubles from $145) in restored colonial-era cottages.

Grand, government-owned 1819 **Entally Estate** (www.entally.com.au; Old Bass Hwy, Hadspen; adult/child $10/8; ⏲10am-4pm), set in beautiful grounds, is the highlight of **Hadspen** (population 2070), 15km north of Longford.

Online see www.longfordtasmania.com.

Sleeping & Eating

★Red Feather Inn BOUTIQUE HOTEL $$$
(☎03-6393 6506; www.redfeatherinn.com.au; 42 Main St, Hadspen; d/q incl breakfast from $250/450; ❄) The unreservedly gorgeous 1852 Red Feather Inn is a magical boutique hotel and cooking school, lifted from the pages of a chic magazine. Rooms range from attic doubles to a cottage sleeping 10. Full-day **cooking classes** (from $195) happen in the country kitchen, which also services the **restaurant** (three courses from $90), open to the public on Friday and Saturday nights.

★Home of the Artisan CAFE $$
(☎03-6391 2042; 15 Wellington St, Longford; mains lunch $18-22, dinner $38-45; ⏲9am-4.30pm Mon-Wed & Fri, to 8pm Thu) Longford's best cafe is an earthy, value-for-money eatery in an 1860 shopfront (a former pharmacy). Fresh herbs and vegetables from the garden out the back find their way into terrifc salads, plus there are super homemade cakes, muffins and great coffee. Thursday-night dinners feature rustic country mains. Providore shelves, affordable wines and takeaway sauces and chutneys, too.

Getting There & Away

Metro Tasmania (☎13 22 01; www.metrotas.com.au) Bus 78 runs from Launceston to Hadspen ($4.50, 30 minutes). Monday to Saturday only. No Carrick service.

Tassielink (☎1300 300 520; www.tassielink.com.au) Monday to Saturday buses between Launceston and Longford ($7.50, 50 minutes) via Evandale.

Evandale

POP POP 1410

National Trust–listed Evandale is a ridiculously photogenic place: a few hours wandering the quiet, historic streets, browsing the galleries and hanging out the cafes is time well spent.

The highlight of the year here is February's **National Penny Farthing Championships** (www.evandalevillagefair.com), when two-wheel warriors race around the town's streets at alarming velocities.

Sights

Clarendon HISTORIC BUILDING
(☎03-6398 6220; www.nationaltrust.org.au/tas/clarendon; 234 Clarendon Station Rd; adult/child $15/free; ⏲10am-4pm Sep-Jun) South of town via Nile Rd is stately, two-storey Clarendon. Built in 1838 in neoclassical style, it looks like it's stepped straight out of *Gone with the Wind;* it was long the grandest house in the colony. Take a self-guided tour of the home, which is graced with antiques, and the seven park-like hectares of gardens on the South Esk River. Also here is the Australian Fly Fishing Museum.

Evandale Market MARKET
(☎03-6391 9191; Falls Park, Logan Rd; ⏲8am-1.30pm Sun) An exuberant mix of happy locals selling fresh fruit and veg, kids' pony rides (and occasionally a mini train), food vans and stalls selling crafts and bric-a-brac.

Australian Fly Fishing Museum MUSEUM
(☎03-6398 6220; www.affm.net.au; 234 Clarendon Station Rd, Clarendon; admission $5; ⏲10am-4pm Mon-Sat, noon-4pm Sun) 'Tis a noble art, fly fishing. Not to mention actually tying the flies so they look like something a trout might want to eat. This new museum has a beaut collection of rods, reels and flies. Think of it as a value-added experience when you're visiting Clarendon.

Sleeping & Eating

Wesleyan Chapel COTTAGE $$
(☎03-6331 9337; www.windmillhilllodge.com.au; 28 Russell St; d incl breakfast from $150) Built in 1836, this tiny brick chapel has since been used variously as a druids hall, an RSL hall and a scout hall. Now it's stylish, self-contained accommodation for two, right on the main street. Check out the old steel tie rods running through the lofty ceiling space, holding the external walls together.

Grandma's House COTTAGE $$
(☎0408 295 387; www.grandmashouse.com.au; 10 Rodgers Lane; d $130-170, extra person $50; 📶) This four-bedroom house (sleeps five) occupies the leafy gardens of historic Marlborough House in the centre of town. There's a wisteria-draped verandah with a BBQ out the back, and you have the run of the extensive gardens. Reduced rates for longer stays. Check out the photos of the cottage before the renovations – an inconceivable transformation!

Vitalogy CAFE $
(☎0437 840 035; 1/14 Russell St; mains $9-25; ⊙9.30am-4pm Wed-Fri, 10am-4pm Sat, 9am-4pm Sun) One for the Pearl Jam fans (what a great album that was...), this cool little eatery does delicious cafe fare using plenty of fresh local produce. Order the pumpkin soup with cornbread, the triple-cheese-and-herb omelette, or a brick of deluxe beef lasagne. The best coffee in town, too.

Information

Evandale Visitor Information Centre (☎03-6391 8128; www.evandaletasmania.com; 18 High St; ⊙9.30am-4.30pm) Local info and accommodation bookings. Stocks the *Evandale Heritage Walk* pamphlet ($3), detailing the town's historic riches. The **history room** here has displays on local painter John Glover and decorated WWI soldier Harry Murray. Both are commemorated with statues on Russell St: Glover, 18 stone and club footed; Murray, hurling a grenade.

Getting There & Away

Tassielink (☎1300 300 520; www.tassielink.com.au) Monday to Saturday buses between Launceston and Evandale ($6.50, 30 minutes) continue to Longford.

Ben Lomond National Park

Tassie's most reliable snow sports centre is the 181-sq-km **Ben Lomond National Park** (☎03-6336 5312; www.parks.tas.gov.au; vehicle/person per day $24/12), 55km southeast of Launceston. Bushwalkers traipse through when the snow melts, swooning over alpine wild flowers during spring and summer.

Full-day ski-lift passes cost $55/30 per adult/child; half-day passes cost $38/20. For snow reports and cams see www.ski.com.au/reports/australia/tas/benlomond.

Ben Lomond Snow Sports (☎03-6390 6185; www.skibenlomond.com.au; Ben Lomond Rd, Ben Lomond National Park; ⊙9am-4.30pm in season) runs a kiosk selling takeaway fare and a shop doing ski, snowboard and toboggan rental, and associated gear. Skis, boots, poles and a lesson cost $85/70 per adult/child; just skis, boots and poles costs $55/40. National park entry fees apply to access the ski fields.

Sleeping & Eating

Ben Lomond Alpine Hotel LODGE $$
(☎03-6390 6199; www.northerntasmania.com.au/accommodation/ben-lomond-alpine-hotel; Alpine Village, Ben Lomond Rd; d $150-250) There's accommodation year-round here at Tasmania's highest pub. There are cosily heated en-suite rooms and – snow permitting – you can ski right to the door. There's also a **restaurant** (mains $16 to $32) where you can replenish your skiing or hiking energies.

Getting There & Away

There's no public transport to the mountain, so driving is your only option. The track up to the plateau is unsealed and traverses Jacob's Ladder, a ludicrously steep climb with six white-knuckle hairpin bends and no safety barriers. During the snow season, chains are standard issue: hire them from **Skigia** (Map p624; www.skigia.com.au; 123 Elizabeth St, Hobart; ⊙9.30am-6pm Mon-Fri, to 4pm Sat) in Hobart or **Autobarn** (Map p668; ☎03-6334 5601; www.autobarn.com.au/stores/launceston; 6 Innes St, Launceston; ⊙8am-5.30pm Mon-Fri, 9am-5pm Sat, 9am-4pm Sun) in Launceston (around $40 per day, plus $60 deposit).

Ben Lomond Snow Sports runs a shuttle bus ($15 per person each way) from the rangers' station 1km from the national park entry booth: call for pick ups.

North & Western Tasmania

Includes ➡

Why Go?

If you imagined Tasmania as a land of soaring alpine peaks and dreamy, untouched wilderness, then you've imagined this part of the state. This is one of Australia's most pristine corners, a land of forested wilderness and remote rivers, from the dense and ancient rainforests of the Tarkine wilderness to remote beaches swept by the cleanest air on Earth. The northern coast consists of dramatic beaches and historic towns such as movie-set Stanley and Penguin, where little penguins come ashore from mid-September to March or April. In the hinterland are some of the best places in Australia to see platypuses, while you can sleep the night in charming towns where the past sits lightly. Best of all, the sense of exploring one of the world's last unspoiled corners will linger long after you leave.

Best Places to Eat

- ➡ Mrs Jones (p683)
- ➡ Linda Valley Cafe (p696)
- ➡ Renaessance (p684)
- ➡ Xanders (p693)

Best Places to Stay

- ➡ @VDL (p693)
- ➡ Corinna Wilderness Experience (p694)
- ➡ Cradle Mountain Lodge (p702)
- ➡ Franklin Manor (p698)

When to Go

Devonport

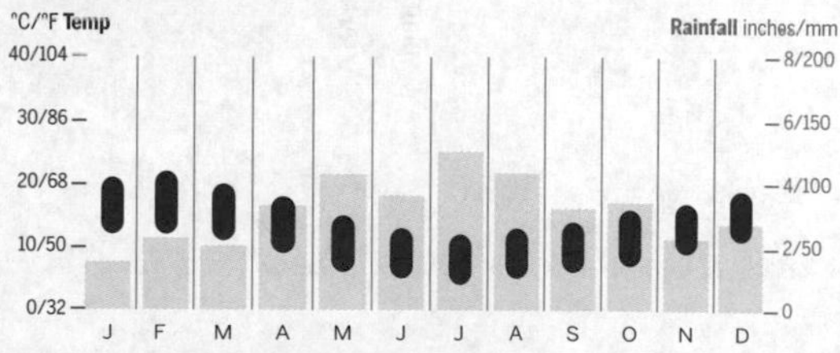

Jan–Mar This whole region buzzes and the long days give you more time in the outdoors.

Jun–Aug Experience the power of the Roaring Forties lashing the area.

Oct–Dec The northwest blooms, plus there's fresh crayfish and penguin watching.

North & Western Tasmania Highlights

1 Exploring Tasmania's alpine heart as you search for wombats, then climb **Cradle Mountain** (p699).

2 Getting a bird's-eye view of World Heritage wilderness, then landing on the **Gordon River** (p699).

3 Going beyond the paved road, deep into the Tarkine rainforest at **Corinna** (p694).

4 Watching the true tale of convict escape in **Strahan**'s hilarious **The Ship That Never Was** (p697).

5 Travelling through deep rainforest on the **West Coast Wilderness Railway** (p695) from Strahan.

6 Experiencing wilderness on water

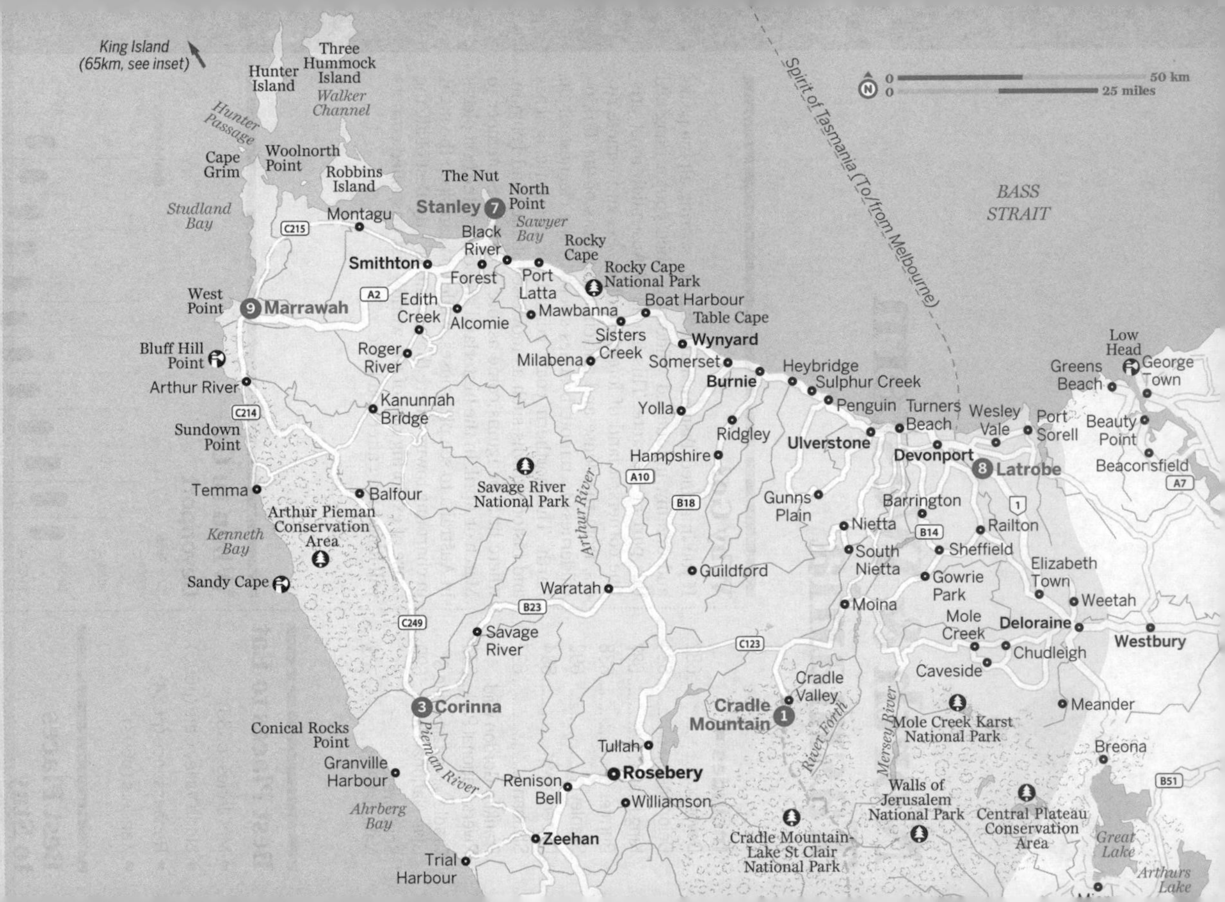

King Island (65km, see inset)
Hunter Island
Three Hummock Island
Walker Channel
Hunter Passage
Cape Grim
Woolnorth Point
Robbins Island
Studland Bay
Montagu
The Nut
Stanley 7
North Point
Sawyer Bay
Black River
Rocky Cape
Rocky Cape National Park
Smithton
Forest
Port Latta
West Point
9 Marrawah
Edith Creek
Alcomie
Mawbanna
Boat Harbour
Table Cape
Wynyard
Sisters Creek
Milabena
Somerset
Burnie
Bluff Hill Point
Roger River
Arthur River
Kanunnah Bridge
Yolla
Heybridge
Sulphur Creek
Penguin
Turners Beach
Wesley Vale
Port Sorell
Greens Beach
Low Head
George Town
Beauty Point
Beaconsfield
Ridgley
Ulverstone
Devonport
8 Latrobe
Sundown Point
Hampshire
Savage River National Park
Arthur River
Temma
Balfour
Arthur Pieman Conservation Area
Kenneth Bay
Gunns Plain
Barrington
Nietta
Railton
South Nietta
Sheffield
Elizabeth Town
Weetah
Gowrie Park
Guildford
Sandy Cape
Waratah
Moina
Mole Creek
Deloraine
Westbury
Chudleigh
Caveside
Savage River
Cradle Valley
Cradle Mountain 1
River Forth
Mersey River
Mole Creek Karst National Park
Meander
3 Corinna
Conical Rocks Point
Pieman River
Tullah
Breona
Granville Harbour
Renison Bell
Rosebery
Williamson
Walls of Jerusalem National Park
Central Plateau Conservation Area
Ahrberg Bay
Cradle Mountain-Lake St Clair National Park
Great Lake
Zeehan
Trial Harbour
Arthurs Lake
BASS STRAIT
Spirit of Tasmania (To/from Melbourne)
0 50 km
0 25 miles
C215
A2
C214
C249
B23
A10
B18
B14
C123
1
A7
B51

on a rafting journey down the **Franklin River** (p699).

7 Walking a heritage trail, then climbing the Nut for fabulous views in **Stanley** (p692).

8 Searching for a platypus in the Mersey River south of **Latrobe** (p683).

9 Looking out into eternity, or catching a Roaring Forties wave, at **Marrawah** (p693).

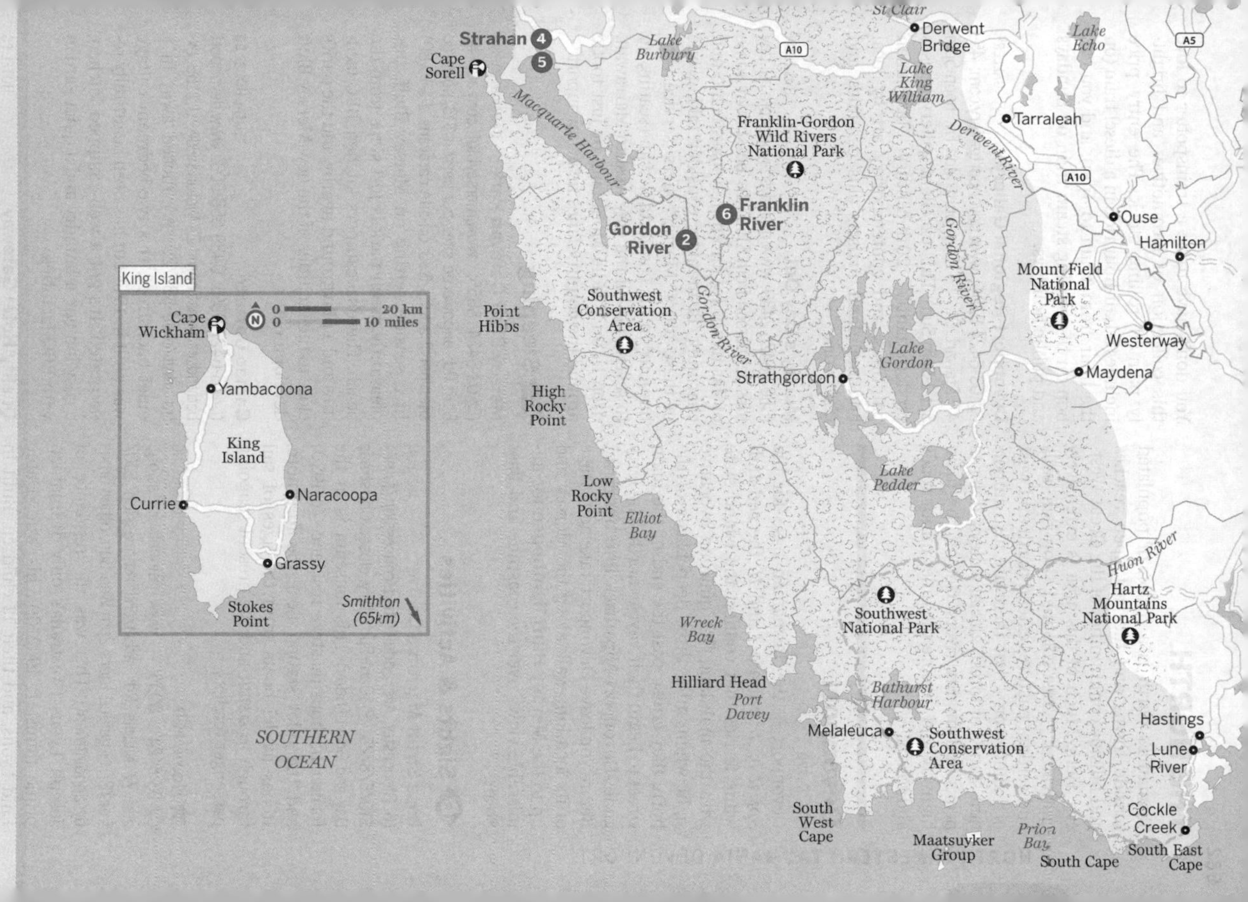

St Clair
Strahan 4
5
Cape Sorell
Lake Burbury
A10
Derwent Bridge
Lake King William
Lake Echo
A5
Macquarie Harbour
Franklin-Gordon Wild Rivers National Park
Tarraleah
Derwent River
A10
6 Franklin River
Gordon River 2
Ouse
Hamilton
Mount Field National Park
Gordon River
Westerway
Maydena
Point Hibbs
Southwest Conservation Area
Gordon River
Lake Gordon
Strathgordon
High Rocky Point
Lake Pedder
Low Rocky Point
Elliot Bay
Huon River
Hartz Mountains National Park
Southwest National Park
Wreck Bay
Hilliard Head
Port Davey
Bathurst Harbour
Melaleuca
Southwest Conservation Area
Hastings
Lune River
South West Cape
Maatsuyker Group
Prion Bay
South Cape
Cockle Creek
South East Cape

King Island
0 20 km
0 10 miles
Cape Wickham
Yambacoona
King Island
Currie
Naracoopa
Grassy
Stokes Point
Smithton (65km)
SOUTHERN OCEAN

THE NORTH

Tasmania's north is a region of populated seaside towns and the vast open reaches and hillside communities of the Great Western Tiers. Much of this area is extensively cultivated – rust-coloured, iron-rich soils and verdant pastures extend north and west of Launceston – but there are also important stands of forest, glacial valleys, dolerite peaks and mighty rivers. Get off the main highway and explore the quiet minor roads and towns.

Devonport

POP 22,770

Devonport is the Tasmanian base for the *Spirit of Tasmania I* and *II*, the red-and-white ferries that connect the island state with the mainland. It's quite an evocative sight when, after three deep blasts of the horn, they cruise past the end of the main street to begin their voyage north. The ferry gone, Devonport slips back into obscurity. Before you leave Devonport, take advantage of its location: walk along the Mersey and up to the **Mersey Bluff lighthouse** for unmissable views over the coastline and Bass Strait.

Sights & Activities

Bass Strait Maritime Centre MUSEUM
(6 Gloucester Ave; adult/child/concession/family $10/5/8/25; 10am-5pm daily, closed Christmas Day and Good Friday) This museum is in the former harbour-master's residence (c 1920) and the pilot station near the foreshore. It has model boats from the ages of sail through to steam and the present seagoing passenger ferries.

★**Home Hill** HISTORIC BUILDING
(03-6424 8055; www.nationaltrusttas.org.au; 77 Middle Rd; adult/child/concession $10/free/8; guided tours 2pm Wed-Sun, other times by appointment) This was the residence of Joseph Lyons (Australia's only Tasmanian prime minister; 1932–39), his wife, Dame Enid Lyons, and their 12 children. Built in 1916, the handsome white home contains some fascinating personal family effects, many of which touch on the couple's active public life.

Don River Railway MUSEUM
(03-6424 6335; www.donriverrailway.com.au; Forth Main Rd; adult/child/family $18/13/40; 9am-5pm) You don't have to be a trainspotter to love this collection of locomotives and brightly painted rolling stock. The entry price includes a half-hour ride in a diesel train (on the hour from 10am to 4pm), and you can hop on the puffing steam train on Sundays and public holidays.

Devonport Regional Gallery GALLERY
(03-6424 8296; www.devonportgallery.com; 45-47 Stewart St; 10am-5pm Mon-Fri, noon-5pm Sat, 1-5pm Sun) This excellent gallery houses predominantly 20th-century Tasmanian paintings, and contemporary art by local and mainland artists, plus ceramics and glasswork.

Murray's Day Out BUS TOUR
(03-6425 2439; www.murraysdayout.com.au; day trips per person from $150) To be shown some of Tasmania by an entirely passionate and charming Tasmanian, consider taking one of these tours. Murray offers 'service with humour' in his comfortable van (seating up to seven). Go all the way west to Marrawah, drop in on Cradle Mountain, or just tootle around the country lanes near Devonport.

Sleeping

Mersey Bluff Caravan Park CARAVAN PARK $
(03-6424 8655; www.merseybluff.com.au; 41 Bluff Rd; unpowered sites per person $13, powered sites per 2 adults $33, on-site caravans d $40-80) In a seaside setting on Mersey Bluff, this pleasantly green park is just steps from the beach. There's a campers' kitchen, BBQ facilities and a playground nearby, and the park's close to the facilities of the new Mersey Bluff development.

Cameo Cottage RENTAL HOUSE $$
(03-6427 0991, 0439 658 503; www.devonportbedandbreakfast.com; 27 Victoria Pde; d $165, extra adult/child $35/25; P) Tucked away in a quiet backstreet, this two-bedroom cottage was built in 1914 but has been beautifully redecorated. It's got a well-equipped kitchen, a cosy lounge, a laundry and a quiet garden with BBQ facilities.

Quality Hotel Gateway HOTEL $$
(03-6424 4922; www.gatewayinn.com.au; 16 Fenton St; d from $136; P ✻ @ ☎) Contemporary rooms, recently renovated, catch the eye here, three short blocks back from the waterfront. It lacks the personal touch of a B&B, but the quality is excellent. It has an on-site **restaurant** as well.

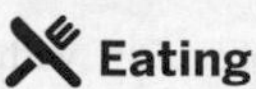

Eating

★Drift Cafe Restaurant CAFE $$
(☎03-6424 4695; www.driftdevonport.com; 41 Bluff Rd; mains $22-28, burgers $8-16; ⏱10am-late Wed-Sun, to 4pm Mon & Tue) Part of the new surf-club complex out on the Mersey Bluff road, this place segues effortlessly from classy to casual. Tasmanian craft beers, gourmet burgers and a sea breeze – what more could you ask for? There's also a fine menu of everything from Tassie salmon to sweet-potato-and-chickpea curry, plus occasional Greek and Thai inflections. It opens later in summer.

★Laneway CAFE $$
(www.lane-way.com.au; 2/38 Steele St; mains $11-20; ⏱7.30am-4pm) Filling a former bakery, we reckon Laneway is one of Tassie's best cafes. Hip waitstaff deliver robust brekkies, including smashed avocado with poached eggs and pancetta, and the sunny, heritage space also functions as a deli showcasing local beer, wine and artisan produce. Evening events with special dinner menus are sometimes scheduled, so pop by to see what's on.

★Mrs Jones MODERN AUSTRALIAN $$$
(☎03-6423 3881; www.mrsjonesrbl.com.au; 41 Bluff Rd; mains $29-40; ⏱noon-late) When the owners closed the much-loved Wild Cafe along the coast in Penguin to open Mrs Jones, it was definitely Penguin's loss and Devonport's gain. Upstairs in the swish new surf-club development, Mrs Jones has stunning decor (Tasmanian oak tables and leather sofas, plus an open kitchen) and exceptional food, with a commitment to local produce.

Menus change with the seasons, but the slow-braised lamb shoulder in cinnamon and all-spice, and the aromatic coconut duck curry, both caught our eye when we passed through.

Drinking

Central at the Formby BAR
(82 Formby Rd; ⏱2pm-late) Locals regard this as Devonport's best bar. It's decked out with leather sofas and laid-back cool, and the concertina windows open onto the river on warm nights. There are live bands Friday and Saturday, while Sunday afternoon sees acoustic sessions and a more sophisticated crowd.

Information

Devonport Visitor Information Centre (☎1800 649 514, 03-6424 4466; www.devonporttasmania.travel; 92 Formby Rd; ⏱7.30am-5pm) Across the river from the ferry terminal, the info centre opens to meet ferry arrivals. Free baggage storage available.

> **WORTH A TRIP**
>
> ### PLATYPUSES AT LATROBE
>
> Latrobe markets itself – with as much justification as hyperbole, it must be said – as the 'Platypus Capital of the World'. There are several good platypus-related visitor opportunities.
>
> ➡ Platypus Interpretation Centre, **Australian Axeman's Hall of Fame** (☎03-6426 2099; www.axemanscomplex.com.au; 1 Bells Pde; ⏱9am-5pm) FREE
>
> ➡ **Warrawee Forest Reserve** (⏱9am-dusk)
>
> ➡ **Platypus-Spotting Tours** (☎03-6426 1774, 03-6421 4699; adult/child $10/free; ⏱8am & 4pm)

Getting There & Away

AIR

QantasLink (☎13 13 13; www.qantas.com.au) Regular flights to Melbourne.

BOAT

Spirit of Tasmania (☎1800 634 906; www.spiritoftasmania.com.au; ⏱customer contact centre 8am-8.30pm Mon-Sat, 9am-8pm Sun) Ferries sail between Station Pier in Melbourne and the ferry terminal on the Esplanade in East Devonport.

BUS

Redline Coaches (☎1300 360 000; www.tasredline.com.au) Redline Coaches stop at 9 Edward St and the *Spirit of Tasmania* terminal in Devonport. There's a Launceston to Devonport ($25.40, 2½ hours) service, via Deloraine and Latrobe. Other services include Ulverstone ($6.50, 25 minutes), Penguin ($8.50, 40 minutes) and Burnie ($11.20, one hour).

Tassielink (☎1300 300 520; www.tassielink.com.au) Tassielink buses stop at the visitor centre and at the *Spirit of Tasmania* terminal. Services from Devonport include Launceston ($25.50, 70 minutes), Sheffield ($5.60, 40 minutes), Gowrie Park ($10.20, 55 minutes), Cradle Mountain ($42.40, two hours), Queenstown ($56.20, four hours) and Strahan ($66.80, five hours).

Getting Around

Devonport Airport & Spirit Shuttle (☎1300 659 878)

Penguin

POP 3159

Penguin feels like one of those pretty little English seaside towns where it's all ice cream, buckets and spades, and the occasional sneaky breeze as you brave it out on the beach. But there's one very un-English thing about this place: penguins! The world's smallest penguin *(Eudyptula minor)* comes ashore here during its breeding season, and even if you don't see any of them in the feather, you can get acquainted with model penguins around town.

Sleeping & Eating

Happy Backpacker PUB $

(Neptune Grand Hotel; ☎03-6437 2406; www.thehappybackpacker.com.au; 84 Main Rd; dm/d without bathroom from $25/65; P 📶) This friendly pub has basic but fairly modern accommodation. Rooms have sinks, but toilets and showers are shared. The dining room serves cheap staples such as chicken parmigiana as well as a few Thai and seafood dishes.

Madsen BOUTIQUE HOTEL $$$

(☎0438 373 456, 03-6437 2588; www.themadsen.com; 64 Main St; d $165-300, f $220; @ 📶) This boutique hotel is housed in a grand former bank building across the road from the water. Some of the rooms have great views of Bass Strait. Decorated in good taste, with a touch of the antique and a good measure of contemporary cool, this is a particularly pleasurable place to stay. Book the new penthouse suite for the ultimate luxury.

★ **Renaessance** CAFE $$

(☎0409 723 771; 95 Main Rd; mains $12-25; ⏲9am-5pm Mon-Thu & Sat, to 6pm Fri, 10am-4pm Sun) A slice of sophistication along the main street, Renaessance does salads, sandwiches, dips and great coffee. The back terrace, with its Bass Strait views, is arguably the best place to nurse a coffee or glass of wine in town.

WHERE TO SEE PENGUINS

True to its name, Penguin is a base for the little (or fairy) penguins that nightly come ashore along this stretch of coast between mid-September or October and March or April. There are three places to see them:

- The largest breeding colony arrives around sunset at **Lalico Beach**, 22km east of Penguin. There's a viewing platform here and, on most nights in season, there's a park ranger in residence to answer any questions. Contact the **Parks & Wildlife Office** (☎03-6464 3018; parks.tas.gov.au; Short St, Ulverstone) or Penguin's **visitor information centre** for more details.
- A smaller colony comes ashore at **Sulphur Creek** (4km west of Penguin).
- **West Beach** in Burnie (19km west of Penguin), behind the Makers' Workshop.

Information

Penguin Visitor Information Centre (☎03-6437 1421; 78 Main Rd; ⏲9am-4pm Mon-Fri & 9am-3.30pm Sat & Sun Oct-Mar, 9.30am-3.30pm Mon-Fri, 9am-12.30pm Sat & 9am-3.30pm Sun Apr-Sep) Staffed by volunteers, the friendly Penguin visitor centre has information about finding penguins and other local attractions.

Getting There & Away

Redline (www.tasredline.com.au) Redline buses go from Penguin to Burnie ($6.50, 15 minutes) and Devonport ($8.50, 40 minutes) as part of their northwest-coast runs.

Deloraine

POP 2333

At the foot of the Great Western Tiers, Deloraine has wonderful views at every turn. In the town itself, Georgian and Victorian buildings, ornate with wrought-iron tracery, crowd the main street, which leads to green parkland on the banks of the Meander River. The town has an artsy, vibrant feel, with several cool little eateries, some bohemian boutiques and secondhand shops.

Sights & Activities

Deloraine Museum MUSEUM

(YARNS: Artwork in Silk; ☎03-6362 3471; www.yarnsartworkinsilk.com; 98-100 Emu Bay Rd; adult/child/family $8/2/18; ⏲9am-5pm) The centrepiece of this museum is an exquisite four-panel, quilted and appliquéd depiction of the Meander Valley through a year of seasonal change. It's an astoundingly detailed piece of work that was a labour of love for 300 creative local men and women. Each of the four panels entailed 2500 hours of labour, and the whole project took three years to complete. It's now housed in

WORTH A TRIP

MOLE CREEK KARST NATIONAL PARK

Welcome to one of Tasmania's more unusual national parks. The clue to the appeal of **Mole Creek Karst National Park** (☎ tour bookings 03-6363 5182; www.parks.tas.gov.au) lies in the name – the word 'karst' refers to the scenery characteristic of a limestone region, including caves and underground streams. The Mole Creek area contains over 300 known caves and sinkholes, including public caves, which you can tour, and wild caves, which are strictly for experienced cavers.

Marakoopa Cave The name Marakoopa derives from an Aboriginal word meaning 'handsome' – which this cave surely is, with its delicate stalactites and stalagmites, glowworms, sparkling crystals and reflective pools. Two tours are available here. The easy **Underground Rivers and Glowworms Tour** (adult/child $19/9.50; ⏲10am, noon, 2pm & 4pm Oct-May, no 4pm tour Jun-Sep) is for all ages. The **Great Cathedral and Glowworms Tour** (adult/child $19/9.50; ⏲11am, 1pm & 3pm) is more challenging, with a stairway ascent to the vast cavern known as Great Cathedral.

King Solomons Cave (adult/child $19/9.50; ⏲hourly departures 10.30am-4.30pm Dec-Apr, 11.30am-3.30pm May-Nov) Tours of this compact cave will show you lavish colours and formations. Entry to King Solomons Cave is payable only by credit card or Eftpos – no cash. If you don't have a card, cash payments for entry to both caves can be made at the ticket office near the Marakoopa Cave, 11km away.

Mole Creek Caves Ticket Office (☎03-6363 5182; www.molecreek.info; 330 Mayberry Rd, Mayberry) Tour tickets are available at the Mole Creek Caves ticket office, close to the Marakoopa Cave entrance.

a purpose-built auditorium, where you can witness a presentation explaining the work.

41° South Tasmania FARM
(☎03-6362 4130; www.41southtasmania.com; 323 Montana Rd; ⏲9am-5pm Nov-Mar, to 4pm Apr-Oct) FREE At this interesting farm, salmon are reared in raised tanks and a wetland is used as a natural biofilter. This no-waste, no-chemical method of fish farming is the cleanest way of raising fish – and also makes for superb smoked salmon, which you can taste (free) and buy in the tasting room, or lunch on in the **cafe**. Optional self-guided **walks** (adult/child/family $10/5/25) take you through the wetlands.

Sleeping & Eating

Deloraine Hotel PUB $
(☎03-6362 2022; www.delorainehotel.com.au; Emu Bay Rd; s without bathroom $40, d with bathroom $80-120) This 1848 pub is veritably draped in wrought-iron lace, and its once-pubbish interior recently had a cool, contemporary makeover. The simple rooms upstairs have also been given a stylish, if unpretentious, overhaul.

★**Bluestone Grainstore** B&B $$
(☎03-6362 4722; www.bluestonegrainstore.com.au; 14 Parsonage St; d incl breakfast $165-180; 📶) A 150-year-old warehouse has been renovated with great style here: think whitewashed stone walls, crisp linen, leather bedheads, deep oval bathtubs...and a few funky touches such as origami flowers. There's even a mini-cinema and films to choose from. Breakfasts draw on local produce – organic where possible.

★**Forest Walks Lodge** LODGE $$
(☎03-6369 5150; www.forestwalkslodge.com; Jackeys Marsh; s/d/f incl breakfast from $140/160/170) Set in a lovely rural area, this fabulous place gets consistently good reviews. The rooms are spacious, filled with warm colours, sprinkled lightly with tasteful local crafts and artwork, and yet are smart and contemporary in the quality of the furnishings.

Make a reservation for a fine three-course evening meal, then take a guided walk through the forests of the Great Western Tiers. Bliss.

Deloraine Deli DELI, CAFE $$
(☎03-6362 2127; 81 Emu Bay Rd; mains $11-21; ⏲8.30am-5pm Mon-Fri, to 2.30pm Sat) A fine place for late-morning baguettes, bagels and focaccias, with a variety of tasty fillings. Its coffee is superb, and it does dairy- and gluten-free meals, too.

Getting There & Away

Redline Coaches (03-6336 1446, 1300 360 000; www.redlinecoaches.com.au) Buses to Launceston ($14.30, 45 minutes).

Tassielink (03-6230 8900, 1300 300 520; www.tassielink.com.au) Buses to Cradle Mountain ($61.50, three hours) and Strahan (with transfer in Queenstown; $85.40, 6½ hours).

Walls of Jerusalem National Park

The **Walls of Jerusalem National Park** (www.parks.tas.gov.au; per person/vehicle per day $12/24) is one of Tasmania's most beautiful parks. It's a glacier-scoured landscape of spectacularly craggy dolerite peaks, alpine tarns and forests of ancient pines. The park adjoins the lake-spangled wilderness of the Central Plateau and is part of the Tasmanian Wilderness World Heritage Area. Several walking tracks lead through it, and also join the park with hikes in Cradle Mountain-Lake St Clair National Park.

Activities

The most popular walk here is the full-day trek to the 'Walls' themselves. A steep path leads up from the car park on Mersey Forest Rd to **Trappers Hut** (two hours return), **Solomon's Jewels** (four hours return) and through **Herod's Gate** to **Lake Salome** (six to eight hours return) and **Damascus Gate** (nine hours return). If you plan to visit historic **Dixon's Kingdom Hut** and the hauntingly beautiful pencil-pine forests that surround it (10 hours return from the car park), or climb to the top of **Mt Jerusalem** (12 hours return), it's better to camp overnight. There are tent platforms and a composting toilet at **Wild Dog Creek**.

You'll need to be prepared for harsh weather conditions: it snows a substantial amount here, and not only in winter. Walks across the park are described in *Cradle Mountain Lake St Clair and Walls of Jerusalem National Parks* by John Chapman and John Siseman, and in Lonely Planet's *Walking in Australia*.

Tasmanian Expeditions WALKING
(03-6331 9000, 1300 666 856; www.tasmanian-expeditions.com.au) Tasmanian Expeditions conducts a six-day Walls of Jerusalem trip ($1695), taking in the park's highlights as well as some of the more out-of-the-way spots.

Getting There & Away

The park is reached from Mole Creek by taking Mersey Forest Rd to Lake Rowallan. The last 11km is on well-maintained gravel roads.

Sheffield & Around

POP 1108

In the 1980s Sheffield was a typical small Tasmanian town in the doldrums of rural decline. That was until some astute townsfolk came up with an idea that had been applied to the small town of Chemainus in Canada, with some surprisingly wonderful results. The plan was to paint large murals on walls around town, depicting scenes from the district's pioneer days. Sheffield is now a veritable outdoor art gallery, with over 50 fantastic large-scale murals and an annual painting festival to produce more.

Tours

★ **Mural Audio Tours** WALKING
Grab a headset ($9) from the visitor centre and take a thoroughly informative audio tour of Sheffield's outdoor art. The tour takes about 90 minutes (though you can keep the headset all day) and guides you past about 20 of the town's best murals. It also leads you through the **Working Art Space** (www.traksheffield.blogspot.com.au; 2 Albert St; 11am-3pm, reduced winter hours), where you can see local artists at work.

Festivals & Events

Muralfest ART
(www.muralfest.com.au) Sheffield's celebration of outdoor art is held each year in late March/early April. It's a massive paint-off – a theme is set and artists from all over Australia descend upon the town to compete for a cash prize, with another nine murals added to the town's walls. Book accommodation well ahead.

Sleeping & Eating

Sheffield Cabins CABIN $$
(03-6491 2176; www.sheffieldcabins.com.au; 1 Pioneer Cres; d $100-105, extra adult/child $15/10) These are simple, clean, self-contained cabins, close to the visitor centre: you can't beat what you get for the price. They're pet friendly, too.

Glencoe Rural Retreat B&B $$
(03-6492 3267; www.glencoeruralretreat.com.au; 1468 Sheffield Rd, Barrington; d $175-210;) Just north of Sheffield, on the B14 at

Barrington, this gorgeous property, owned by celebrated French chef Remi Bancal, is making a great name for itself. You can stay in its romantic and eminently stylish rooms (no kids under 12) and you mustn't miss the superb three-course dinners ($65), available by prior arrangement.

★ Blacksmith Gallery Cafe CAFE $
(☎03-6491 1887; www.fridaynitemusic.org; 63 Main St; mains $9-18; ⊙8.30am-5pm) This friendly, arty cafe boasts of having the best coffee in Sheffield – and it may just be right. With its retro decor, funky music and roaring wood stove on cold days, it's a great place to hang out, have a slap-up breakfast, lazy lunch (the quiche is excellent), or coffee and cake in between. There's a rollicking folk-singing night the last Friday of every month.

Getting There & Away

Tassielink (www.tassielink.com.au) Tassielink buses stop directly outside the visitor centre. Services to/from Sheffield include Launceston ($31.20, two hours), Devonport ($5.60, 40 minutes), Cradle Mountain ($27.60, 70 minutes) and Strahan ($60.30, five hours).

King Island

King Island is the kind of place where the only traffic control is a leisurely wave of the hand from a local as you pass by. A skinny sliver of land 64km long and 27km wide, King Island (or 'KI', as locals call it) is a laid-back place where everyone knows everyone and life is mighty relaxed. The island's green pastures famously produce a rich dairy bounty and its surrounding seas supply fabulously fresh seafood (and fine surfing).

Sights

King Island Dairy DAIRY
(☎1800 677 852, 03-6462 0947; www.kidairy.com.au; 869 North Rd; ⊙noon-4pm Sun-Fri) Low-key but top-quality, King Island Dairy's Fromagerie is 8km north of Currie (just beyond the airport). Taste its award-winning bries, cheddars and feisty blues, and then stock up in its shop on cheeses that are budget priced – only here – to fuel your King Island exploring. Its cream is sinfully delicious.

Cape Wickham HISTORIC SITE
You can drive right up to the tallest **lighthouse** in the southern hemisphere at Cape Wickham, on KI's northern tip. This 48m-high tower was built in 1861 after several ships had been wrecked on the island's treacherous coastline. Most famous of all King Island shipwrecks is the *Cataraqui* (1845), Australia's worst civil maritime disaster, with the loss of 400 lives.

King Island Museum MUSEUM
(Lighthouse St, Currie; adult/child $5/1; ⊙2-4pm, closed Jul & Aug) There's information on lightkeeping, shipwrecks and monuments here and also in the *King Island Maritime Trail: Shipwrecks & Safe Havens* booklet, which you can pick up wherever visitor information is available.

Activities

King Island is one of Australia's premier **surfing** destinations – *Surfing Life* magazine has voted the break at Martha Lavinia as one of the top 10 waves in the world.

You can **swim** at many of the island's unpopulated beaches (beware rips and currents) and freshwater lagoons.

For **hiking**, pick up a map from King Island Tourism and go independently, or take a guided walk with **King Island Wilderness Walks** (☎0400 858 339; Lighthouse St, Currie).

You don't even need to get out on foot for **wildlife spotting** on KI: it's just about everywhere you look. There are rufous and Bennett's wallabies, pademelons, snakes, echidnas and platypuses, and you may even glimpse seals. The island has 78 bird species and, on summer evenings, little penguins come ashore around the Grassy breakwater.

Sleeping & Eating

KI is foodie heaven. Must tries include KI cheese and dairy products, but also crayfish in season (November to August),

> WORTH A TRIP
>
> **TROWUNNA WILDLIFE PARK**
>
> About 5km east of Mole Creek on the B12 road, and 2km west of Chudleigh, is the first-rate **Trowunna Wildlife Park** (☎03-6363 6162; www.trowunna.com.au; adult/child/family $22/12/60; ⊙9am-5pm, guided tours 11am, 1pm & 3pm) , which specialises in Tasmanian devils, wombats and koalas, as well as birds. There's an informative tour, during which you get to pat, feed or even hold some of the wildlife. While there, don't miss the interactive **Devil Education and Research Centre**.

oysters, crabs, grass-fed beef, free-range pork and game. Don't forget to find some Cloud Juice, KI's pure bottled rainwater. There are two supermarkets in Currie and a store in Grassy.

Bass Cabins & Campground CAMPGROUND $
(☎03-6462 1260; 5 Fraser Rd, Currie; camp site per person $14, d cabin from $85) There are a few camp spots here, with bathroom facilities adjacent, and two two-bedroom cabins. The campground is 1.5km from the centre of Currie.

Portside Links APARTMENT, B&B $$
(☎03-6461 1134; www.portsidelinks.com.au; Grassy Harbour Rd, Grassy; d apt $170) This fantastic accommodation is the best place to stay on KI. There are two stylish and well-equipped self-catering apartments here as well as a B&B room in the owners' home. It's a short stroll to pretty Grassy Harbour and Sand Blow Beach. Penguins nest nearby. There's a minimum two-night stay, but prices drop the longer you stay.

Boomerang by the Sea MODERN AUSTRALIAN $$$
(☎03-6462 1288; www.boomerangbythesea.com.au; Golf Club Rd, Currie; mains $29-42; ⏲6-9pm Mon-Sat) Arguably the best place to eat on the island, this has wraparound views and a fine menu that's big on seafood.

ℹ Information

King Island Tourism (☎03-6462 1355, 1800 645 014; www.kingisland.org.au; 5 George St, Currie) Ask about the *King Island Grazing Trails* map, which details historical, natural and cultural walks around the island. King Island Tourism's website is an excellent pre-trip planning resource.

ℹ Getting There & Away

King Island Airlines (☎03-9580 3777; www.kingislandair.com.au) Melbourne Moorabbin to King Island twice daily.

Regional Express (☎13 17 13; www.regional-express.com.au) Melbourne Tullamarine to King Island.

Sharp Airlines (☎1300 556 694; www.sharpairlines.com) Launceston–King Island (one way from $261).

ℹ Getting Around

King Island Car Rental (☎03-6462 1282, 1800 777 282; kicars2@bigpond.com; 2 Meech St, Currie) Per day from around $73.

P&A Car Rental (☎03-6462 1603; 1 Netherby Rd, Currie) Per day from around $80.

THE NORTHWEST

Tassie's northwest is lashed by Roaring Forties winds and in excess of 2m of rain each year, and boasts coastal heathlands, wetlands and dense temperate rainforests unchanged from Gondwana times. Communities here are either isolated rural outposts or tricked-up tourist traps. The further west you get, the fewer fellow travellers you'll encounter until you reach the woolly wilds of Tasmania's northwest tip, a region of writhing ocean beaches and tiny communities, facing an ocean with no landfall until South America.

Burnie

POP 19,819

Long dismissed as Tasmania's ugly duckling, once-industrial Burnie is busily reinventing itself as a 'City of Makers', referring both to its heavy manufacturing past and its present creative flair. The amazing new Makers' Workshop is Burnie's showcase tourist attraction and should be your first stop when you visit. Watch also for penguins coming ashore from September or October until February.

Sights & Activities

Burnie has some impressive civic and domestic architecture that you can view on two **Federation walking trails**. The city is also renowned for its art deco buildings, and you can see these on the **Art Deco Trail**. Ask at the visitor information counter in the Makers' Workshop for interpretative maps of all three walks.

★**Makers' Workshop** MUSEUM
(☎03-6430 5831; www.discoverburnie.net; 2 Bass Hwy; ⏲9am-5pm) Part museum, part arts centre, this dramatic new structure dominates the western end of Burnie's main beach. It's a fabulous place to get acquainted with this city's creative heart. You'll notice the life-size **paper people** in odd corners of the workshop's cavernous contemporary interior. These are the work of **Creative Paper** (☎03-6430 5830; tours adult/child $15/8; ⏲tours 9.15am-4.30pm), Burnie's handmade-paper producers. Its tours take you through the production process of making paper from such unusual raw materials as kangaroo poo, apple pulp and rainforest leaves.

WORTH A TRIP

BOAT HARBOUR BEACH

Were it not for the weather, this could be paradise. Picture-perfect Boat Harbour has the kind of blonde-sand beach and sapphire-blue waters that make you feel like you've taken a wrong turn off the Bass Hwy and ended up somewhere in the Caribbean. The usually calm seas are perfect for kids and it's a low-key, family-friendly place.

The daily Redline bus service from Burnie will drop you at the turn off to Boat Harbour (3km) or Sisters Beach (8km) for $6.50. If driving from Wynyard, the best route is to follow the C234 northwest – there are some great views of the cliffs and rocky coast along this road.

Azzure Holiday Houses (0430 066 312, 03-6445 1155; www.azzurebeachhouses.com.au; 263 Port Rd; 4/6-bed house from $280/410;) It's all contemporary style at the beach houses in this complex. There's every convenience you could imagine: DVD-CD players, wi-fi, air-conditioning, and swanky kitchens, and walls are hung with contemporary art. There's an on-site health spa in the pipeline, too.

Harbourside B&B (0400 595 036, 0400 595 066; www.harboursidebnb.com.au; 237 Port Rd; d incl breakfast from $195) This cute B&B is more a contemporary private apartment with great water views. There are sensational vistas right from your bed, plus a spa and private decks.

Burnie Regional Art Gallery GALLERY
(03-6430 5875; www.burniearts.net; Burnie Arts & Function Centre, 77-79 Wilmot St; 10am-4.30pm Mon-Fri, 1.30-4.30pm Sat & Sun) FREE This art gallery has excellent exhibitions of contemporary Tasmanian artworks, including fine prints by some of Australia's most prominent artists such as Sidney Nolan and Brett Whiteley.

★ **Burnie Penguin Centre** BIRDWATCHING
(0437 436 803) FREE A boardwalk on Burnie's foreshore leads from Hilder Pde to the western end of West Beach, close to the Makers' Workshop, where there's a spot for watching penguins. From October to March you can take a free **Penguin Interpretation Tour**, about one hour after dusk as the penguins emerge from the sea and waddle back to their burrows. Volunteer wildlife guides are present to talk about the penguins and their habits.

Sleeping

Burnie Oceanview CARAVAN PARK $
(03-6431 1925; www.burniebeachaccommodation.com.au; 253 Bass Hwy; unpowered/powered sites d $24/30, dm $25, on-site caravans d $55, cabins & units d $95-139;) Located 4km west of the city centre, this park has backpacker rooms, some grassy camp sites at the property's rear, caravans with kitchenettes and a range of cabins. The indoor heated pool is the best attraction.

★ **Ikon Hotel** BOUTIQUE HOTEL $$
(03-6432 4566; www.ikonhotel.com.au; 22 Mount St; d $185-220;) Boutique hotel chic comes to Burnie at the centrally located Ikon Hotel. The building's heritage exterior is complemented by sleek and (extremely) spacious modern suites with leather furniture and compact kitchenettes. Interesting modern and retro art adorns the walls; the bathrooms are huge; and the rooms are bright and airy.

Seabreeze Cottages RENTAL HOUSE $$
(0439 353 491; www.seabreezecottages.com.au; s $160-185, d $175-185) These cottages just west of the city centre may just be Burnie's best. There's the cool, contemporary Beach House (243 Bass Hwy, Cooee), just a stroll across the road from the beach; West Park (14 Paraka St); and cute Number Six (6 Mollison St), the latter two an easy 10-minute walk to town. All are kitted out with modern, chic decor – Number Six has a jukebox and all. We love them!

Eating

Another Mother CAFE $
(03-6431 8000; 14 Cattley St; mains $9-16; 8am-3pm Mon-Fri;) A cute, vibrant eatery with bright red walls, eclectic furniture and local photography for decoration, Another Mother offers wholesome, predominantly vegetarian (and some meaty) dishes crafted from local produce – organic where possible. It serves an exceptional pumpkin-and-cashew burger with yoghurt

The Northwest

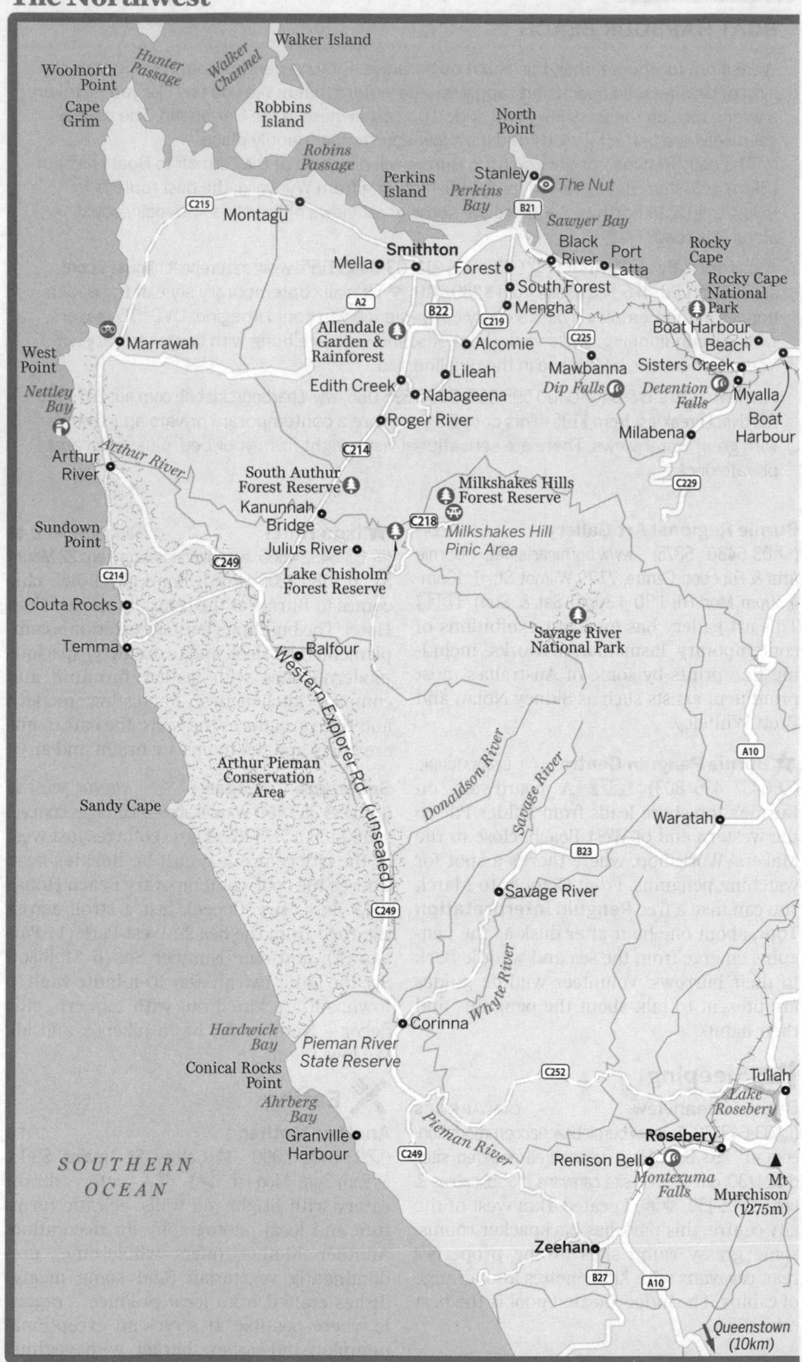

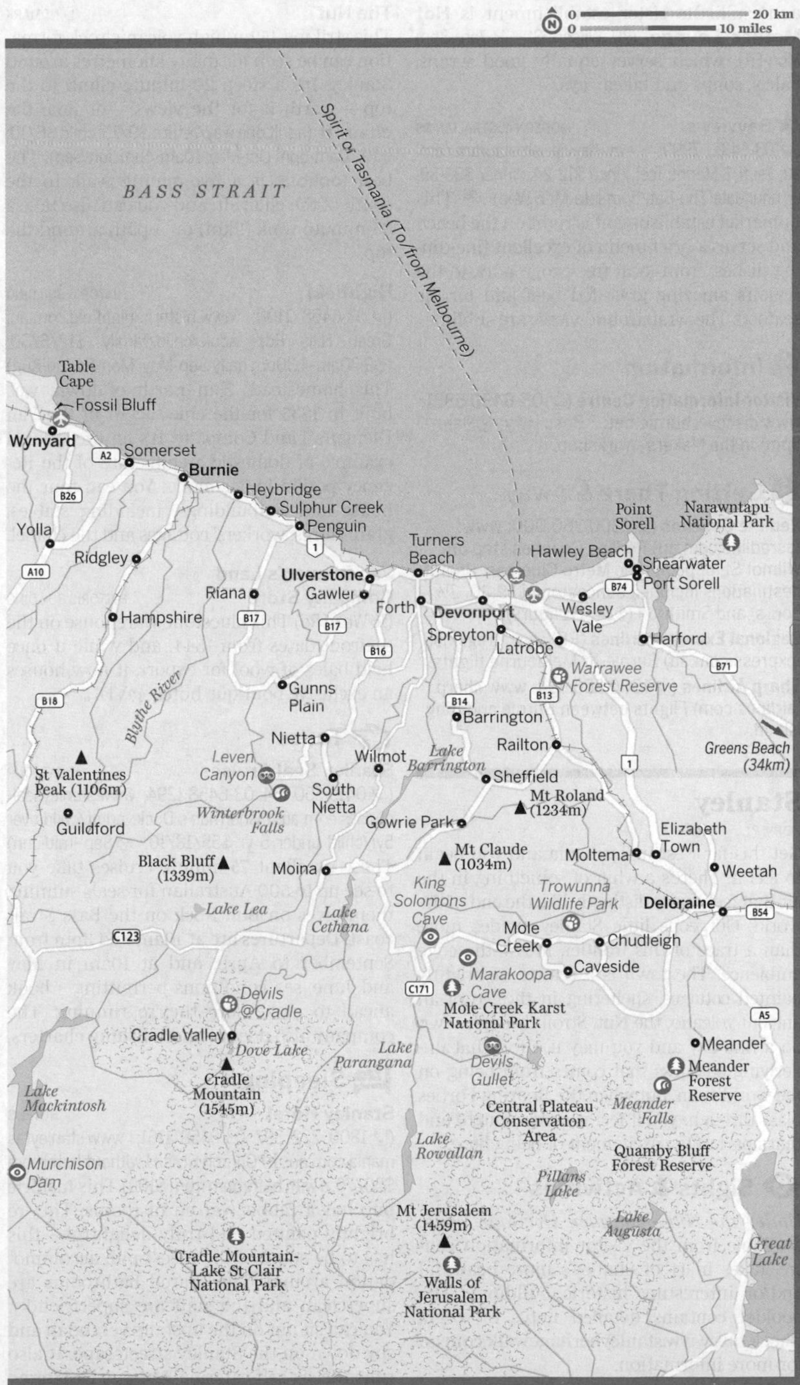
0 20 km
0 10 miles
BASS STRAIT
Spirit of Tasmania (To/from Melbourne)
Table Cape
Fossil Bluff
Wynyard
Somerset
Burnie
Heybridge
Sulphur Creek
Penguin
Yolla
Ridgley
Ulverstone
Gawler
Riana
Hampshire
Turners Beach
Forth
Devonport
Spreyton
Latrobe
Point Sorell
Narawntapu National Park
Hawley Beach
Shearwater
Port Sorell
Wesley Vale
Harford
Warrawee Forest Reserve
Gunns Plain
Barrington
Railton
Greens Beach (34km)
Blythe River
Nietta
St Valentines Peak (1106m)
Guildford
Leven Canyon
Winterbrook Falls
Wilmot
Lake Barrington
South Nietta
Sheffield
Mt Roland (1234m)
Gowrie Park
Elizabeth Town
Moltema
Weetah
Black Bluff (1339m)
Moina
Mt Claude (1034m)
King Solomons Cave
Trowunna Wildlife Park
Deloraine
Lake Lea
Lake Cethana
Mole Creek
Chudleigh
Caveside
Marakoopa Cave
Devils @Cradle
Mole Creek Karst National Park
Cradle Valley
Dove Lake
Cradle Mountain (1545m)
Lake Parangana
Devils Gullet
Meander
Meander Forest Reserve
Meander Falls
Lake Mackintosh
Central Plateau Conservation Area
Lake Rowallan
Murchison Dam
Quamby Bluff Forest Reserve
Pillans Lake
Lake Augusta
Mt Jerusalem (1459m)
Great Lake
Cradle Mountain-Lake St Clair National Park
Walls of Jerusalem National Park
A2
B26
A10
B17
B16
B18
B74
B71
B13
B14
B54
C123
C171
A5
1

and chilli. Its sister establishment is **Hot Mother Lounge** (70 Wilson St; ⏲7am-3pm Mon-Fri), which serves equally good wraps, bakes, soups and takeaways.

★ **Bayviews** MODERN AUSTRALIAN **$$**
(☎03-6431 7999; www.bayviewsrestaurant.com.au; 1st fl, 2 Marine Tce; lunch $12-24, dinner $33-39; ⏲noon-late Thu-Sat, 5pm-late Mon-Wed) This upmarket establishment is right on the beach and serves a brief menu of excellent fine-dining dishes, from local free-range pork to the region's amazing grass-fed beef and terrific seafood. The wraparound views are sublime.

Information

Visitor Information Centre (☎03-6430 5831; www.discoverburnie.net; 2 Bass Hwy; ⏲9am-5pm) In the Makers' Workshop.

Getting There & Away

Redline Coaches (☎1300 360 000; www.tasredline.com.au) Redline Coaches stop on Wilmot St, opposite the Metro Cinemas. Useful destinations include Launceston ($39.30, 2½ hours) and Smithton ($24, 1½ hours).

Regional Express Airlines (REX; www.regional-express.com.au) Burnie-to-Melbourne flights.

Sharp Airlines (☎1300 556 694; www.sharp-airlines.com) Flights between Burnie and King Island.

Stanley

POP 481

Get this far west in Tasmania and you begin to feel it. There's a whiff of something in the air that feels quite distinctly like the end of the world. Gorgeous little Stanley exudes more than a trace of this frontier, life-on-the edge ambience. The town is a scatter of brightly painted cottages, sheltering in the lee of an ancient volcano, the Nut. Stroll through town on a fine day and you may not feel that underlying edginess that comes from being on the world's rim, but when the Roaring Forties blast through, you'll feel it sure enough, and that's part of the excitement of being here.

Sights & Activities

Under the Nut – Stanley Heritage Walk, available from the visitor information centre, takes in 14 of Stanley's more beautiful and/or interesting historic buildings. The booklet contains detailed notes on each. Check out www.stanleyheritagewalk.com.au for more information.

The Nut LANDMARK
This striking 152m-high volcanic rock formation can be seen for many kilometres around Stanley. It's a steep 20-minute climb to the top – worth it for the views – or take the **chairlift** (adult one way/return $9/15, child $6/10; ⏲9.30am-5pm Oct-May, 10am-4pm Jun-Sep). The best **lookout** is a five-minute walk to the south of the chairlift, and you can also take a 35-minute walk (2km) on a path around the top.

Highfield HISTORIC BUILDING
(☎03-6458 1100; www.historic-highfield.com.au; Green Hills Rd; adult/child/family $12/6/30; ⏲9.30am-4.30pm daily Sep-May, Mon-Fri Jun-Aug) This homestead, 2km north of town, was built in 1835 for the chief agent of the Van Diemen's Land Company. It's an exceptional example of domestic architecture of the Regency period in Tasmania. You can tour the house and outbuildings, including stables, grain stores, workers' cottages and the chapel.

Van Diemen's Land Company Store HISTORIC BUILDING
(16 Wharf Rd) This bluestone warehouse on the seafront dates from 1844, and while it once held bales of wool for export, it now houses an exclusive boutique hotel, @VDL.

Tours

Stanley Seal Cruises BOAT TOUR
(☎0419 550 134, 03-6458 1294; www.stanleysealcruises.com.au; Fisherman's Dock; adult/child over 5yr/child under 5 yr $55/18/10; ⏲Sep–mid-Jun) These excellent 75-minute cruises take you to see up to 500 Australian fur seals sunning themselves on Bull Rock on the Bass Strait coast. Departures are at 10am and 3pm from September to April, and at 10am in May and June, sea conditions permitting – book ahead to make sure they're running. The company also does offshore fishing charters.

Sleeping

Stanley Hotel HOTEL **$**
(☎1800 222 397, 03-6458 1161; www.stanleytasmania.com.au; 19 Church St; s/d without bathroom $50/70, d with bathroom from $109) This historic pub has a rabbit warren of rooms. They're brightly painted and truly delightful – this has to be some of the nicest pub accommodation around. The shared bathrooms are superclean and the staff are superfriendly. You can sit out on the upstairs verandah and spy down on the Stanley streetscape. It also runs the six self-catering **Abbeys Cottages**

(☎1800 222 397; www.stanleytasmania.com.au; d incl breakfast $135-240).

★Ark Stanley BOUTIQUE HOTEL **$$**

(☎0421 695 224; www.thearkstanley.com.au; 18 Wharf Rd; d $140-300) Polished wooden floors, wrought-iron furnishings, luxury linens, goose-down duvets…this place, with its individually styled rooms, takes attention to detail to a whole new level. Fine views are to be had from some of the rooms and the service is discreet but attentive.

★@VDL BOUTIQUE HOTEL **$$$**

(☎0437 070 222, 03-6458 2032; www.atvdlstanley.com.au; 16 Wharf Rd; d $175-255;) What's been done within the bluestone walls of this 1840s warehouse is quite incredible. This ultra-hip boutique hotel has two suites and a self-contained loft apartment, which are, frankly, the coolest of the cool. Everything's top class, from the bedding to the artworks on the walls. The same people run a sister property, **@The Base** (32 Alexander Tce; d $115-140), which is a heritage house divided into two similarly stylish suites.

Eating

Moby Dicks Breakfast Bar CAFE **$**

(☎03-6458 1414; 5 Church St; mains $8-16; 7am-noon) Tuck into an enormous breakfast here before you go out and battle the wild west winds – try a cooked-egg breakfast with the lot or waffles with maple syrup…yum.

★Xanders MODERN AUSTRALIAN **$$$**

(☎03-6458 1111; 25 Church St; mains $28-42; 6-9pm Wed-Sun) Stanley's best fine-dining restaurant is set in an old house on the main street with views back and front. The menu has an accent on fish and seafood, but Xanders also serves the area's excellent beef and specials such as duck and tandoori-rubbed rack of lamb. There's a good kids' menu, too.

Stanley's on the Bay MODERN AUSTRALIAN **$$$**

(☎03-6458 1404; 15 Wharf Rd; mains $23-41; 6-9pm Mon-Sat Sep-Jun) Set inside the historic Ford's Store, this fine-dining establishment specialises in steak and seafood. The wonderful seafood platter for two ($100) overflows with local scallops, oysters, fish, octopus and salmon.

Information

Stanley Visitor Information Centre (☎03-6458 1330, 1300 138 229; www.stanley.com.au; 45 Main Rd; 9.30am-5pm Oct-May, 10am-4pm Jun-Sep) A mine of information on Stanley and surrounding areas. Pick up the *Take on the Edge* brochure for extensive coverage of the far northwest.

Getting There & Away

Redline Coaches (www.tasredline.com.au) Buses stop at the visitor centre en route to/from Burnie ($21.10, 75 minutes) and Smithton ($6.10, 25 minutes)

Marrawah

POP 371

Untamed, unspoilt Marrawah is a domain of vast ocean beaches, mind-blowing sunsets and green, rural hills. The power of the ocean here is astounding, and the wild beaches, rocky coves and headlands have changed little since they were the homeland of Tasmania's first people. This coast is abundant with signs of Aboriginal Tasmania – and somehow there's a feeling of lonely emptiness, as if these original custodians have only just left the land.

It's huge ocean waves that Marrawah is best known for today. Sometimes the Southern Ocean throws up the remains of long-forgotten shipwrecks here – things tumble in on waves that sometimes reach over 10m in length. Experienced surfers and windsurfers also come here for the challenging breaks.

The **general store** (800 Comeback Rd; 7.30am-7pm Mon-Fri, 8am-7.30pm Sat & Sun) sells supplies and petrol and is an agent for Australia Post and Commonwealth Bank. Fill up on fuel here if you're planning to take the Western Explorer to Corinna as there's no other petrol outlet until Zeehan or Waratah, about 200km away.

Sleeping & Eating

Ann Bay Cabins CABIN **$$**

(☎03-6457 1361, 0428 548 760; 99 Green Point Rd; d from $150) These two cosy wooden cabins are just the place to hang out and get away from it all. You can sit on the deck and admire the views, or luxuriate in the deep spa bath, with bathing essentials and choccies supplied.

Marrawah Beach House RENTAL HOUSE **$$**

(☎03-6457 1285; www.marrawahbeachhouse.com.au; d from $160) This place is secluded, view-filled and brightly decorated with starfish and seashells. The friendly owners set it up with treats such as fresh flowers and sometimes local honey before you arrive. Sleeps up to four. It's just up the hill from Green Point Beach, and the views have few rivals in Tasmania.

Marrawah Tavern TAVERN $$
(☎03-6457 1102; Comeback Rd; mains $15-33; ⊙noon-10pm Mon-Wed, to midnight Thu-Sat, to 9pm Sun) You can get a good meal and a drink at this casual country pub. Choices include steak sandwiches, prawns, roasts, beef 'n' reef and whole local flounders.

THE WEST

Primeval, tempestuous and elemental – this region of Tasmania is unlike anywhere else in Australia. Towering, jagged mountain ranges, buttongrass-covered alpine plateaus, raging tannin-stained rivers, dense impenetrable rainforest and unyielding rain. Humans never tamed this western wilderness and today much of the region comprises Tasmania's Wilderness World Heritage Area. Tourist-centric Strahan aside, the few towns and settlements here are rough and primitive, weathered and hardened by wilderness.

Corinna

In rip-roaring gold-rush days Corinna was a humming town with two hotels, a post office, plenty of shops and a population that numbered 2500 souls. That's hard to believe now when you pull up on the forested edge of the Pieman River, turn off your car's engine and absorb the unbelievable forest peace.

Less than a decade ago, the owners of what remains transformed Corinna into a deep-forest wilderness experience that offers a sense of adventure and immersion in the rainforest without forsaking too many comforts. That said, there's no mobile-phone reception and no TVs – the most prevalent sound is birdsong. Wallabies, pademelons, wombats and other wildlife are commonly sighted here.

Activities

Pieman River Cruises BOAT TOUR
(☎03-6446 1170; adult/child $90/51; ⊙10am) While in Corinna you can't miss the Pieman River Cruise, a pleasingly rustic alternative to the crowded Gordon River cruises out of Strahan. The tour on the historic MV *Arcadia II* lasts 4½ hours and heads downstream to where the Pieman River meets the Southern Ocean. A packed lunch is included and you've time to walk out to the remote beach before returning to Corinna. Book well ahead.

Sleeping

★**Corinna Wilderness Experience** COTTAGE $$$
(☎03-6446 1170; www.corinna.com.au; camp sites per 2 people $20, cottages d $200-250, f $250) Corinna has a collection of new self-contained timber eco-cottages, as well as some older-style houses. The newer cottages are modern and rather lovely inside, and the rainforest starts right at your back door.

The pub has a well-stocked bar while the **restaurant** (mains $14 to $38, serving noon to 2pm and 6pm to 8pm) serves up dishes such as steak sandwiches for lunch, and two or three excellent mains (such as steak or salmon) for dinner. Picnic hampers and BBQ packs are also available for order.

Getting There & Away

You can approach Corinna from Somerset, just west of Burnie, via the Murchison Hwy through magnificent Hellyer Gorge (perfect for picnic stops). After Waratah, the C247 is sealed as far as Savage River, from where it's 26km of unsealed, but well-maintained, gravel that's almost always passable in a 2WD. If you're taking the C249 Western Explorer Rd, it's 109 unsealed kilometres from Arthur River.

Fatman Vehicle Barge (☎03-6446 1170; motorbike/car/caravan $10/20/25; ⊙9am-5pm Apr-Sep, to 7pm Oct-Mar) The cable-driven Fatman vehicle barge plying the Pieman River at Corinna allows you to travel from Corinna down to Zeehan and Strahan. There's a 9m-long, 6.5-tonne limit on vehicles.

Queenstown

POP 1975

Most of western Tasmania is green. Queenstown is orange or red. The winding descent into Queenstown from the Lyell Hwy is unforgettable for its moonscape of bare, dusty hills and eroded gullies, where once there was rainforest. The area is the clearest testimony anywhere to the scarification of the west coast's environment by mining. Copper was discovered here in the 1890s and mining has continued ever since.

The town itself retains its authentic, rough-and-ready pioneer feel. When we last visited, the mine had closed, numerous businesses across the town were boarded up and apocalyptic rumours of permanent de-

DON'T MISS

WEST COAST WILDERNESS RAILWAY

Love the romance of the days of steam? The old wood-lined carriages with shiny brass trimmings, the breathy puffing of steam engines and the evocative, echoing train whistle? Then hop on board and make the breathtaking 35km rainforest rail journey aboard the **West Coast Wilderness Railway** (☎ 03-6471 0100; www.wcwr.com.au) between Strahan and Queenstown.

When it was first built in 1896, this train and its route through torturously remote country was a marvel of engineering. It clings to the steep-sided gorge of the (once-polluted, now-recovering) King River, passing through dense myrtle rainforest over 40 bridges and on gradients that few other rolling stock could handle. The railway was the lifeblood of the Mt Lyell Mining and Railway Co in Queenstown, connecting it for ore and passenger haulage to the port of Teepookana on the King River, and later with Strahan. The original railway closed in 1963.

Since it was reopened as a tourist railway, it's had a chequered run and only reopened in 2014 after a period of closure thanks to the prohibitive cost of keeping the line open through such difficult country.

Ride options on offer (expect reduced services in winter months):

Rack & Gorge Trip that departs Queenstown at 9am Wednesday to Sunday, loops through the King River Gorge and returns at 1pm (adult/child/family $89/30/195).

River & Rainforest Departs Strahan at 2pm Wednesday to Friday, skirts the harbour, enters the rainforest and then returns to Strahan at 5.30pm after crossing many of the route's spectacular bridges (adult/child/family $89/30/195).

Queenstown Explorer Departs Strahan at 9am on Monday and Tuesday, running the railway's full length through gorge and rainforest to Queenstown (where there's a one-hour stop), before returning to Strahan at 5.30pm (adult/child/family $95/40/220).

cline were on the rise. That said, they're a hardy lot out here, Queenstown's tourism star is on the rise and the optimists among the locals were convinced the mine would reopen. Whatever happens, this is a town like no other in Tasmania.

Sights

★Iron Blow — VIEWPOINT

On top of Gormanston Hill on the Lyell Hwy, just before the final descent along hairpin bends into Queenstown, is a sealed side road leading to an utterly spectacular lookout over the geological wound of Iron Blow. This decommissioned open-cut mine, where Queenstown's illustrious mining career began, is awesomely deep and is now filled with emerald water. You can get an eagle's-eye view from the new 'springboard' walkway projecting out into thin air above the mine pit.

★LARQ Gallery — GALLERY

(☎ 0407 527 330; www.landscapeartresearch queenstown.wordpress.com; 8 Hunter St; ⊙ 2-6pm Tue-Sat mid-Jan–mid-Jun) FREE Run by internationally renowned Tasmanian artist Raymond Arnold, Landscape Art Research Queenstown is a wonderful gallery that runs exhibitions by local and visiting artists, and community workshops in printmaking and painting. Its mission is to nurture a breed of art that's inspired by the powerful natural landscapes of the west coast. It's an excellent institution and definitely worth visiting. If it's not open, ask at the tourist office for access.

Spion Kop Lookout — VIEWPOINT

Follow Hunter St uphill, turn left onto Bowes St, then do a sharp left onto Latrobe St to a small car park, from where a short, steep track leads to the summit of Spion Kop (named by returned soldiers after a battle in the Boer War). The rhododendron-lined track features a rail adit near the car park, and the top of the hill has a pithead on it.

Tours

★Queenstown Heritage Tours — MINE TOUR

(Mt Lyell Mine Tours; ☎ 0407 049 612; www.queens-townheritagetours.com) The 'Lake Margaret Historic Hydropower' tour (adult/child $45/30) takes you into an early 20th-century hydroelectric power plant, and the 'Mt Lyell Underground Mine Tour' (adult $80) takes you inside the copper mine. But the

WORTH A TRIP

LINDA VALLEY CAFE

In mining boom days, hundreds of people lived in the hills just west of Queenstown. Today there are just four residents in Linda Valley...and one unexpected gem. About 5km west of Queenstown is the much-lauded **Linda Valley Cafe** (03-6471 3082; 1 Lyell Hwy, Linda Valley, Gormanston; mains $32-38; 10am-8pm Oct-Apr, reduced hours May-Sep) , which locals swear serves some of the best food on the west coast.

The cafe offers contemporary, delicious dining in unpretentious surrounds. Expect dishes such as slow-roasted pork belly and lemon pepper squid, as well as special liqueur coffees and beautiful homemade cakes. There's free camping for tents and RVs out the back.

real charmer is 'Lost Mines, Ancient Pines' (adult/child $80/40), which takes in some old copper and gold mines, a commercial sawmill and a stand of rainforest.

Sleeping

Empire Hotel PUB $
(03-6471 1699; www.empirehotel.net.au; 2 Orr St; s with shared bathroom $45, d with shared/private bathroom $70/90) The rooms here aren't as magnificent as the imposing blackwood staircase, which is a National Trust-listed treasure, but they've a certain jaded pub charm and are generally kept clean.

Mt Lyell Anchorage B&B $$
(03-6471 1900; www.mtlyellanchorage.com; 17 Cutten St; d incl breakfast $160-170; P) Though you wouldn't guess from the outside, this 1890s weatherboard home has been completely transformed into a wonderful little guesthouse with quality beds, linen and luxuriously deep carpets. Two of the spacious rooms have smart bathrooms (the others have private facilities across the hall), there's a shared kitchen, and a comfortable lounge with wood fire.

Penghana B&B $$
(03-6471 2560; www.penghana.com.au; 32 Esplanade; s $135-150, d $150-175, all incl breakfast; P) This National Trust–listed mansion was built in 1898 for the first general manager of the Mt Lyell Mining & Railway Co and, as befits its managerial stature, is located on a hill above town amid a beautiful garden with a rare number of trees. There's comfortably old-fashioned B&B accommodation here.

Eating

Café Serenade CAFE $$
(40 Orr St; mains $11-18; 8.30am-4pm;) This is the best cafe in Queenstown. The food is deliciously homemade from scratch with yummy soups, sourdough toasted sandwiches, salads and good vegetarian options, as well as hearty roasts and curries. The curried scallop pies are the speciality. It also does gluten-free and dairy-free sweet treats, and the coffee is excellent.

Empire Hotel MODERN AUSTRALIAN $$
(03-6471 1699; www.empirehotel.net.au; 2 Orr St; mains lunch $12, dinner $17-30; bar 11am-10pm, lunch noon-2pm, dinner 5.30-8pm) This old miners' pub has survived the ages and includes an atmospheric heritage dining room serving a changing menu of hearty pub standards, including roasts, pastas and fine steaks and ribs. Try the apple and pork rissoles or the Beef Tower, a grilled steak piled high with vegies.

Entertainment

Paragon Theatre CINEMA
(www.theparagon.com.au; 1 McNamara St) This amazingly refurbished art deco theatre shows some Hollywood and art-house films, as well as a revolving program of short films about the west coast and Queenstown. You can take your coffee or a glass of vino (and popcorn, of course) into the theatre, where seating is in deep leather couches.

Information

Queenstown Visitor Centre (03-6471 1483; 1-7 Driffield St; 9.30am-5.30pm Mon-Fri, 12.30-5pm Sat & Sun Oct-Apr, reduced winter hours) In the Eric Thomas Galley Museum and run by volunteers, so opening hours can vary.

Getting There & Away

Tassielink (www.tassielink.com.au) Buses arrive at, and depart from, the milk bar at 65 Orr St. The two main routes go to Hobart ($67.60, six hours) and Launceston ($74.80, 5½ hours); the latter goes via Strahan ($10.60, 45 minutes).

Strahan

POP 660

The *Chicago Tribune* newspaper once dubbed Strahan 'the best little town in the world' and we know what it meant. With its perfect location, nestled between the waters of Macquarie Harbour and the rainforest, it has faultless natural assets. Add to that the restored pioneer buildings – the cutesy shops, hotels and cottages crowding up the slope from the compact waterfront – and you've got a scene that could work as a Disney film set. These days it's more sugary sweet than wild west, but it works as a gateway town because of the unbelievable beauty that surrounds it.

Sights & Activities

West Coast Reflections MUSEUM

(Esplanade; 10am-6pm summer, noon-5pm winter) FREE This is the museum section of the Strahan visitor centre. It's a creative and thought-provoking display on the history of the west coast, with a refreshingly blunt appraisal of the region's environmental disappointments and achievements, including the Franklin River Blockade.

Ocean Beach BEACH

Six kilometres from town is Ocean Beach, awesome as much for its 33km length as for the strength of the surf that pounds it. This stretch of sand and sea runs uninterrupted from Trial Harbour in the north to Macquarie Heads in the south – and is *the* place to watch the orange orb of the sun melt into the sea. The water is treacherous: don't swim.

★ **The Ship That Never Was** THEATRE

(Esplanade; adult/child $20/10; 5.30pm Sep-May, box office opens at 5pm) This unmissable play tells the story of convicts who escaped from Sarah Island in 1834 by hijacking a ship they were building. It's highly entertaining fun (with crowd participation) for all age groups.

Tours

A Gordon River cruise is what most visitors come to do, and the dense rainforest that lines the riverbank, and the sense of peace in these trackless wilds are things you'll never forget.

You can cruise the Gordon on a large, fancy catamaran in the company of a crowd of fellow river admirers (with plenty of comforts laid on), or be a bit more adventurous and visit with a small group by sailing boat. All cruises cross vast Macquarie Harbour before entering the mouth of the Gordon and proceeding to Heritage Landing for a rainforest walk. Most cruises visit Sarah Island – site of Van Diemen's Land's most infamously cruel penal colony – as well as Macquarie Heads and Hells Gates – the narrow harbour entrance. If you visit under sail, you can sneak a little further up the river than other cruise vessels are allowed to go, to beautiful Sir John Falls.

★ **World Heritage Cruises** BOAT TOUR

(03-6471 7174; www.worldheritagecruises.com.au; Esplanade; adult $105-150, child $50-80, family $260-340; 9am mid-Aug–mid-Jul) This business is run by the Grining family, who have been taking visitors to the Gordon since 1896 and are Strahan's true river experts. You can join the Grinings aboard their new low-wash, environmentally sensitive catamaran, the *Eagle,* for a cruise through Macquarie Harbour out through Hells Gates, to Sarah Island and up the Gordon River.

Prices vary depending on whether you take a window seat (premium, or gold if on the upper deck) or one in the centre of the boat (standard). All prices include a buffet meal. If you're travelling as a family, World Heritage Cruises is the best choice as the kids can go up and visit the captain at no extra cost. There may be an additional afternoon departure in the height of summer, or no service at all in the depths of winter.

Gordon River Cruises BOAT TOUR

(03-6471 4300; www.gordonrivercruises.com.au; Esplanade; adult $105-220, child $52-220, f $260-334) Run by the Royal Automobile Club of Tasmania (which seems to own half of Strahan), the *Lady Jane Franklin II* departs Strahan at 8.30am and returns at 2.15pm, en route exploring Macquarie Harbour, Sarah Island and the Gordon River as far as Heritage Landing.

Prices vary depending on where you are on the boat – the upper deck is an exclusive wine-and-dine experience.

★ **West Coast Yacht Charters** BOAT TOUR

(03-6471 7422; www.westcoastyachtcharters.com.au; Esplanade; Oct-Apr) If you'd like your Gordon River experience with a little adventure (and fewer people), then sailing on *Stormbreaker* is the way to go. There's a 2½ to three-hour kayaking and fishing cruise that departs on demand most days at noon and/or 5pm (adult/child $90/50). There's also an overnight trip up the Gordon River (adult/child $380/190), with a visit to Sarah Island and meals included.

Strahan Seaplanes & Helicopters SCENIC FLIGHTS
(☎03-6471 7718; www.adventureflights.com.au; ⏲Mid-Sep–May) Seaplane and helicopter flights over the region. Seaplane options include 80-minute flights over Frenchmans Cap, the Franklin and Gordon Rivers, and Sarah Island (per adult/child $199/110), and 65-minute flights over the Cradle Mountain region ($210/95). A 60-minute helicopter flight over the Teepookana Forest Reserve costs $199/120, and a quick 15 minutes over Hells Gates and Macquarie Harbour costs $110/70.

Sleeping

Strahan Backpackers HOSTEL $
(☎03-6471 7255; www.strahanbackpackers.com.au; 43 Harvey St; unpowered sites per two people $20, dm $27-30, d from $65, cabins from $75; P@📶) In an attractive bush setting 15 minutes' walk from the town centre, with plain bunks and doubles, and cute A-frame cabins. There's a kitchen block, a laundry and a games room.

★**Gordon Gateway** APARTMENT $$
(☎03-6471 7165, 1300 134 425; www.gordongateway.com.au; Grining St; d $79-140) On the hillside on the way to Regatta Point, this place has motel-like studio units and larger A-frame chalets, most with sweeping water and township views.

Crays COTTAGE $$
(☎0419 300 994, 03-6471 7422; www.thecrays-accommodation.com; 11 Innes St; d $130-220; P📶) The Crays has two self-contained units on Innes St and six new bright, roomy cottages at 59 Esplanade, opposite Risby Cove. Only some have views. Guests who stay three nights are rewarded with a succulent Tasmanian crayfish on the house, and there are reduced prices for cruises with West Coast Yacht Charters (p697).

★**Franklin Manor** BOUTIQUE HOTEL $$$
(☎03-6471 7311; www.franklinmanor.com.au; Esplanade; d $175-250; P📶) This beautiful historic home is the top spot to stay in Strahan. Set in well-tended gardens just back from the waterfront, it's now an elegant boutique guesthouse with refined rooms, fine dining and equally fine service. There's a legendary wine cellar and now also a Tasmanian produce room where you can taste and buy local delicacies.

Eating

Risby Cove MODERN AUSTRALIAN $$
(☎03-6471 7572; www.risbycove.com.au; Esplanade; mains $22-38; ⏲6-9pm) People come from all over to dine at the Cove, a quietly sophisticated place just across the water from the town centre. The menu features fancy dishes such as roast Tamar Valley duck, and there's always fresh Macquarie Harbour ocean trout. There's a good kids' menu, too. The views over the water are sensational.

Hamer's Hotel PUB FOOD $$
(☎03-6471 4335; Esplanade; mains lunch $12-23, dinner $19-32; ⏲noon-2.30pm & 6-10pm) This done-up historic pub is where most tourists go to eat in Strahan. It serves a varied menu of excellent pub fare – try the Macquarie Harbour ocean trout or the huge eye-fillet steaks. It's often packed in summer, and it doesn't take bookings, so get here early for meals.

Regatta Point Tavern PUB FOOD $$
(Esplanade; mains $16-29; ⏲bar noon-10pm, meals noon-2pm & 6-8pm) If you want to eat with the locals, away from the glitz, make your way to this down-to-earth pub near the railway terminus 2km around the bay from Strahan's centre. There are the usual steaks and burgers, as well as good fresh fish. Check out the crayfish mornay – in season – if you're after something fancy.

Information

Parks & Wildlife Service (☎03-6471 7122; www.parks.tas.gov.au; Esplanade; ⏲9am-5pm Mon-Fri) In the old Customs House – also houses the post office, online access centre and an ATM.

West Coast Visitor Information Centre (☎03-6472 6800; www.westcoast.tas.gov.au; Esplanade; ⏲10am-6.30pm Dec-Mar, to 6pm Apr-Nov) Includes the West Coast Reflections museum.

Getting There & Away

Tassielink (☎1300 300 520; www.tassie-link.com.au) Services arrive at, and depart from, the visitor centre. Destinations include Launceston ($85.40, seven hours), Hobart ($78.20, 7½ hours) and Queenstown ($10.60, 45 minutes).

Franklin-Gordon Wild Rivers National Park

Saved from hydroelectric immersion in the 1980s, this World Heritage-listed **national park** (www.parks.tas.gov.au) embraces the catchment areas of the Franklin and Olga Rivers and part of the Gordon River – all exceptional rafting, bushwalking and climbing areas. The park's snow-capped summit is **Frenchmans Cap** (1443m; a challenging three- to five-day walk). The park also boasts a number of unique plant species and the major Indigenous Australian archaeological site at **Kutikina Cave**.

Much of the park consists of deep river gorges and impenetrable rainforest, but the Lyell Hwy traverses its northern end. There are a handful of short walks starting from the highway, including hikes to **Nelson Falls** (20 minutes return) and **Donaghys Hill** (40 minutes return), from where you can see the Franklin River and the sky-high white quartzite dome of Frenchmans Cap.

Cradle Mountain-Lake St Clair National Park

Cradle Mountain – that perfect new-moon curve of rock that photographers love to capture reflected in mirror-still waters – has become something of a symbol of Tasmania. It's perhaps the best-known feature on the island and is regarded as the crowning glory of the 1262-sq-km Cradle Mountain-Lake St Clair National Park. The park's glacier-sculpted mountain peaks, river gorges, lakes, tarns and wild alpine moorlands extend from the Great Western Tiers in the north to Derwent Bridge in the south.

The legendary adventure within the park is the celebrated Overland Track, a week-long hike that's become something of a

RAFTING THE FRANKLIN

Rafting the Franklin River is about as wild and thrilling a journey as it's possible to make in Tasmania. This is extreme adventure and a world-class rafting experience. Experienced rafters can tackle it independently if they're fully equipped and prepared, but for anyone who's less than completely river savvy (and that's about 90% of all Franklin rafters), there are tour companies offering complete rafting packages. If you go with an independent group you must contact the park rangers at the **Queenstown Parks and Wildlife Service** (03-6471 2511; Penghana Rd, Queenstown) for current information on permits, regulations and environmental considerations. You should also check out the Franklin rafting notes at www.parks.tas.gov.au. All expeditions should register at the booth at the point where the Lyell Hwy crosses the Collingwood River, 49km west of Derwent Bridge.

The trip down the Franklin, starting at Collingwood River and ending at Sir John Falls, takes between eight and 14 days, depending on river conditions. Shorter trips on certain sections of the river are also possible. From the exit point at Sir John Falls, you can be picked up by a **Strahan Seaplanes & Helicopters** (03-6471 7718; www.strahanseaplanesandhelicopters.com.au; Strahan Wharf; 8.30am-5pm Sep-May) seaplane, or by **Stormbreaker** (p697) for the trip back to Strahan.

The upper Franklin, from Collingwood River to the Fincham Track, passes through the bewitchingly beautiful Irenabyss Gorge, from where you can scale Frenchmans Cap as a side trip. The lower Franklin, from the Fincham Track to Sir John Falls, passes through the wild Great Ravine.

Tasmanian Expeditions (1300 666 856; www.tasmanianexpeditions.com.au; 9-day trip $2695) Classic Franklin River trip, with a boat back to Strahan.

Franklin River Rafting (0422 642 190; www.franklinriverrafting.com; 70 Dillons Hill Rd, Glaziers Bay; 8/10-day trip $2695/2995) Excellent eight- and 10-day trips from Collingwood Bridge, with trips on the *Stormbreaker* back to Strahan. The longer trip includes the chance to climb Frenchmans Cap.

Water By Nature (0408 242 941, 1800 111 142; www.franklinrivertasmania.com; 5/7/10-day trips $1980/2440/2980) This outfit provides five, seven and 10-day trips and you get to fly out of the Gordon River in a seaplane. Also offers climbs of Frenchmans Cap.

holy grail for bushwalkers. The 65km track, stretching from Cradle Mountain to Lake St Clair (Leeawuleena or 'sleeping water' to Tasmania's Indigenous people), is an unforgettable journey through Tasmania's alpine heart.

Less known is that Cradle Mountain is a fabulous wildlife-watching destination as well – sightings of wombats, Bennett's wallabies and pademelons are almost guaranteed, with Tassie devils and platypuses also possible.

Sights

Devils@Cradle WILDLIFE RESERVE

(☎03-6492 1491; www.devilsatcradle.com; 3950 Cradle Mountain Rd; adult/child $18/10, family $45-60, night feeding tours adult/child $27.50/15, family $70-90; ⏰10am-4pm, tours 10.30am, 1pm & 3pm, night tours 5.30pm) This excellent wildlife park is filled with Tasmanian devils, a wombat or two, and elusive eastern and spotted-tail quolls. Here you can learn about the facial tumour disease that's threatening the devils' survival. You can visit on your own at any time, but try getting here at tour times to really get the most from your visit. The mainly nocturnal animals are observed most spectacularly at feeding time (5.30pm); there's an additional night feeding time at 8.30pm during daylight saving.

Wilderness Gallery GALLERY

(☎03-6492 1404; www.wildernessgallery.com.au; Cradle Mountain Rd; admission $7, free for Cradle Mountain Hotel guests; ⏰10am-5pm) At the Cradle Mountain Hotel complex, on the road into Cradle Mountain, this impressive gallery showcases incredible environmental photography. It also has a fascinating **Tasmanian Tiger Exhibition**, complete with the only thylacine-skin rug in existence.

THE OVERLAND TRACK

This is Tasmania's iconic alpine journey, a 65km, six- to eight-day odyssey with backpack through incredible World Heritage–listed mountainscapes from Ronny Creek, near Cradle Mountain, to Lake St Clair. The track ends on the northern shore of Lake St Clair – from here you can catch the **ferry** (p703), or walk the 15km Lakeside Track back to civilisation. If you have experience of camping and multi-day hikes, good fitness and are well prepared for Tasmania's erratic weather, it's a very achievable independent adventure. Inexperienced walkers should consider going with a guided group.

Most hikers walk the Overland Track during summer when alpine plants are fragrantly in flower, daylight hours are long and you can work up enough heat to swim in one of the frigid alpine tarns. The track is very busy at this time and is subject to a crowd-limiting permit system. The track is quiet and icily beautiful for experienced walkers in winter. Spring and autumn have their own charms, and fewer walkers than in summer (though the permit system still applies).

Apart from the permit season, when a north-south walking regulation is enforced, the track can be walked in either direction. The trail is well marked for its entire length. Side trips lead to features such as **Mt Ossa**, and some fantastic **waterfalls** – so it's worth budgeting time for some of these. Apart from in the dead of winter, you can expect to meet many walkers each day.

There are unattended huts with bare wooden bunks and gas heaters spaced a day's walking distance apart along the track, but don't count on any room inside in summer – carry a tent. Campfires are banned and you must carry a fuel stove for cooking.

The walk itself is extremely varied, negotiating high alpine moors, rocky scree, gorges and tall forest. A detailed description of the walk and major side trips is given in Lonely Planet's *Walking in Australia*. For further notes on the tracks in the park, read *Cradle Mountain–Lake St Clair and Walls of Jerusalem National Parks* by John Chapman and John Siseman. A handy pocket-sized reference for the walk is the P&WS's *The Overland Track: One Walk, Many Journeys,* which has notes on ecology and history plus illustrations of flora and fauna you may see along the way. You can get all the latest on the track and walk planning at www.parks.tas.gov.au. The reference map for the track and surrounds is the 1:100,000 *Cradle Mountain–Lake St Clair* map published by Tasmap.

The permit system (adult/child $200/160) is in place from 1 October to 31 May, with a maximum of 34 independent walkers setting out each day. Permits can be obtained at www.parks.tas.gov.au – bookings for each season open on 1 July.

Activities

Cradle Valley Walks

Cradle Valley has some of the most accessible trailheads in the park. The following is by no means an exhaustive list.

Knyvet Falls (25 minutes return) Begins opposite Cradle Mountain Lodge.

Crater Lake (two hours return) Climb up to this lake-filled crater from the Ronny Creek car park.

Cradle Valley Walk (two hours one way) An easy 8.5km walk from the interpretation centre to Dove Lake. It's boardwalked as far as Ronny Creek (5.5km); the rest of the track to Dove Lake can get quite muddy and is sometimes closed after heavy rain.

Dove Lake Circuit (two- to three-hour loop) Go all the way around the lake from Dove Lake car park, with near-constant Cradle Mountain views.

Cradle Mountain Summit (six to eight hours return) A tough but spectacular climb with incredible views in fine weather. Not recommended in bad visibility or when it's snowy and icy in winter. Can begin at either Dove Lake car park or Ronny Creek.

Cynthia Bay Walks

If you're at the southern, Lake St Clair end of the national park, these are our pick of the day hikes on offer.

Larmairremener tabelti (one hour return) Aboriginal cultural-interpretative walk that winds through the traditional lands of the Larmairremener, the Indigenous people of the region. It starts at the visitor centre and loops through the lakeside forest before leading along the shoreline back to the centre.

Platypus Bay Circuit (30 minutes return) From Watersmeet, near the visitor centre.

Shadow Lake Circuit (four to five hours return)

Mt Rufus Circuit (seven to eight hours return)

Lake St Clair Lakeside Walk Catch the ferry to Echo Point (three to four hours walk back to Cynthia Bay) or Narcissus Hut (five to seven hours back to Cynthia Bay) and walk back along the lakeshore.

Family Walks

Although it depends on the age of your kids, many of the walks in Cradle Valley are suitable for children of reasonable fitness. If your kids are *really* young, the following might appeal.

Rainforest Walk & Pencil Pine Falls (10 minutes return) Begins at the interpretation centre. It's easy and boardwalked, but quite spectacular.

Enchanted Nature Walk (25 minutes return) Begins near Cradle Mountain Lodge and runs alongside Pencil Pine Creek. Accessible for prams and wheelchairs for most of the way.

Weindorfers Forest Walk (20 minutes return) Begins next to Waldheim Cabins and climbs up through the forest. Not pram or wheelchair accessible.

Ronny Creek (20 to 25 minutes return) The boardwalks that mark the start of the Overland Track are ideal for families, with wombats in abundance.

Tours

Tasmanian Expeditions WALKING
(☎1300 666 856; www.tasmanianexpeditions.com.au; ⊙Oct–early May) Tasmanian Expeditions does a six-day Overland Track trek (from $1995), plus a range of other hikes through the national park and beyond.

Cradle Mountain Huts WALKING
(☎03-6392 2211; www.cradlehuts.com.au; from $2850; ⊙Oct-May) A six-day/five-night, guided walk along the Overland Track staying in private huts with others carrying your pack.

PARK ACCESS

Traffic is strictly controlled within the park and once the vehicle quota (or parking capacity) is reached on the Cradle Valley road, the boom gates won't open to let vehicles in until enough vehicles have left. This can be a particular problem in the morning.

To keep traffic out of the park, most access is now by **shuttle bus**. Buses run every 10 to 20 minutes between about 8am and 8pm in summer (reduced hours in winter) from the **Cradle Mountain Transit Centre** (by the visitor centre) where you park your car. The fare is included in a valid parks pass. Buses stop at the ranger station interpretation centre, Snake Hill, Ronny Creek and Dove Lake.

Sleeping & Eating

Cradle Valley

Discovery Holiday Parks Cradle Mountain CARAVAN PARK $
(☎03-6492 1395; www.discoveryholidayparks.com.au; Cradle Mountain Rd; unpowered/powered sites per 2 people $36/46, dm $32, cabins from $144, cottages from $159; P@) This bushland complex is 2.5km from the national park. It has well-separated sites, a YHA-affiliated hostel, a camp kitchen and a laundry, and self-contained cabins.

★ **Cradle Mountain Highlanders Cottages** COTTAGE $$
(☎03-6492 1116; www.cradlehighlander.com.au; Cradle Mountain Rd; d $125-285; P) This is the best-kept secret at Cradle Mountain! The genuinely hospitable hosts have a charming collection of immaculately kept self-contained timber cottages. All have wood or gas fires, queen-sized beds, electric blankets and continental-breakfast provisions. Three cabins include a spa, and all are serviced daily.

Cradle Mountain Hotel HOTEL $$
(☎03-6492 1404, 1800 420 155; www.cradlemountainhotel.com.au; Cradle Mountain Rd; d from $169; P@) This large complex is the first you come to on the way into Cradle Valley, and heralds its presence with a grand porticoed gate. Though the public areas are pleasantly timbered and log-fire-warmed, the rooms are, frankly, rather motel-ish. Get one on the front side to ensure a rainforest view.

There's a decent **buffet restaurant** (adult/child $38/19), or the more refined **Grey Gum à la carte restaurant** (mains from $28).

★ **Cradle Mountain Lodge** LODGE $$$
(☎1300 806 192, 03-6492 2103; www.cradlemountainlodge.com.au; Cradle Mountain Rd; d $189-870; P❄@) When this mountain resort of wooden cabins emerges from the swirling mist on a winter's day, you can't help but be charmed by its ambience. Most rooms wear a contemporary feel and some have open fires, the lodge puts on dozens of activities and guided walks, and the Waldheim Alpine Spa offers relaxing massages and beauty treatments.

Tavern Bar & Bistro BISTRO $$
(☎03-6492 2100; www.cradlemountainlodge.com.au; mains $16-29; ⊙noon-8.30pm) Hearty mountain fare and a roaring open fire give this unpretentious place at Cradle Mountain Lodge its charm. It's all about pasta, burgers, steaks and salmon, and it has a good kids' menu. There's also live music some Wednesdays at 8.30pm.

Cynthia Bay & Derwent Bridge

Lake St Clair Lodge LODGE $$
(☎03-6289 1137; www.lakestclairlodge.com.au; unpowered/powered sites per 2 people $25/30, dm/d $40/110, cottages $185-550; P@) Unpowered bush-camping sites on the lakeshore, and powered caravan spots. The backpackers lodge has two- to four-bunk rooms and kitchen facilities. There are also upmarket self-contained cottages. In the main building opposite the Lake St Clair visitor centre there's a cafe, serving a hearty menu to fill you up before or after a bushwalk. Last orders at 6.30pm.

Hungry Wombat Café CAFE $
(Lyell Hwy; mains $6-16; ⊙8am-6pm summer, 9am-5pm winter) Part of the service station, this friendly cafe serves breakfasts that'll

WATCHING WILDLIFE

Cradle Mountain is one of the easiest places in Australia to see wildlife in abundance. In addition to the following, it's possible to see Tasmanian devils, echidnas, spotted-tailed quolls and eastern quolls.

Common wombat Seen regularly throughout the park, but best found along the Ronny Creek valley before dusk.

Tasmanian pademelon This small, plump, wallaby-like creature is commonly seen throughout the park, especially around accommodation such as Cradle Mountain Hotel.

Bennett's wallaby Not as common as the pademelon, but still seen regularly, including around Ronny Creek.

Platypus Present in most of the park's rivers, but try Ronny Creek close to dawn or dusk.

keep you going all day. For lunch there are soups, sandwiches, fish and chips, pies, wraps and burgers, and there's a range of all-day snacks, coffees and cakes. Everything's homemade and jolly good. There's a small grocery section, too, and it gives tourist info.

Information

Cradle Mountain Visitor Information Centre (03-6492 1110; www.parks.tas.gov.au; 4057 Cradle Mountain Rd; 8am-5pm, reduced winter hours) Cradle Mountain visitor centre is just outside the park boundary. Here you can buy your park passes, get detailed bushwalking information and maps, weather condition updates and advice on bushwalking gear, bush safety and bush etiquette. The centre has toilets, a small shop-cafe (03-6492 1024; Cradle Mountain Rd; mains $8-11; 8am-9pm Dec-Mar, 9am-5pm Apr-Nov) and Eftpos (cash out may be available). It also accepts credit-card payment. There are no ATMs.

Ranger Station Interpretation Centre (8.30am-5pm during daylight saving, to 4pm in winter) Just inside the park boundary at Cradle Valley is the ranger station interpretation centre. At the time of writing, it was building an auditorium for video presentations on the natural history of Cradle Mountain and the tracks in the area. There are also Aboriginal cultural displays.

Lake St Clair Visitor Information Centre (03-6289 1172; www.parks.tas.gov.au; Cynthia Bay; 8am-5pm) Cynthia Bay, on the southern boundary of the park, has the Lake St Clair visitor centre. It provides park and walking information and has displays on the area's geology, flora, fauna and Aboriginal heritage. If you've forgotten your rain gear you can pick up some waterproof attire in the shop here.

Getting There & Away

Tassielink (1300 300 520; www.tassielink.com.au) Services to Cradle Mountain Transit Centre from Launceston via Devonport – pick-up at the ferry terminal can be arranged. Destinations from Cradle include Launceston ($61.50, 3¼ hours), Devonport ($42.40, two hours) and Strahan ($42.40, three to four hours). It also has a Hobart–Lake St Clair service ($53.60, 2½ hours).

Getting Around

Lake St Clair Ferry (03-6289 1137; www.lakestclairlodge.com.au; one way adult/child $40/20) Lake St Clair Lodge operates bushwalkers' ferry trips to and from Narcissus Hut at Lake St Clair's northern end. The boat departs Cynthia Bay three times daily (9am, noon and 3pm) year-round (or on demand, minimum six people), reaching Narcissus Hut about 30 minutes later. Winter departures may be reduced, so always ring ahead.

If you're using the ferry service at the end of your Overland Track hike, for which bookings are essential, you must radio the ferry operator when you arrive at Narcissus to reconfirm your booking. You can also ride the ferry from Cynthia Bay to Echo Point (adult/child $35/17), and then walk back to Cynthia Bay (two to three hours).

DON'T MISS

WALL IN THE WILDERNESS

On your journey between Derwent Bridge and Bronte Park, don't miss the **Wall in the Wilderness** (03-6289 1134; www.thewalltasmania.com; adult/child $10/6; 9am-5pm Sep-Apr, to 4pm May-Aug). This amazing creation is a work of art in progress. Wood sculptor Greg Duncan is carving a panorama in wood panels depicting the history of the Tasmanian highlands. The scale is incredible – when it's finished, which will take an estimated 10 years, the scene will be 100m long.

Though the tableau is large-scale, it's carved with breathtaking skill and detail – from the veins in the workers' hands, to the creases in their shirts, to the hair of their beards. The Wall is 2km east of Derwent Bridge, and is definitely worth making time to check out.

THE SOUTHWEST

Southwest National Park

The state's largest national park is made up of remote, wild country – forest, mountain, grassy plains and seascapes. Here grows the Huon pine, which lives for 3000 years, and the swamp gum, the world's tallest flowering plant. About 300 species of lichen, moss and fern – some very rare – festoon the rainforests, and the alpine meadows are picture-perfect with wild flowers and flowering shrubs. Through it all run wild rivers, their rapids tearing through deep gorges and their waterfalls plunging over cliffs.

Activities

Bushwalking

The most-trodden walks in the park are the 70km **Port Davey Track** between Scotts

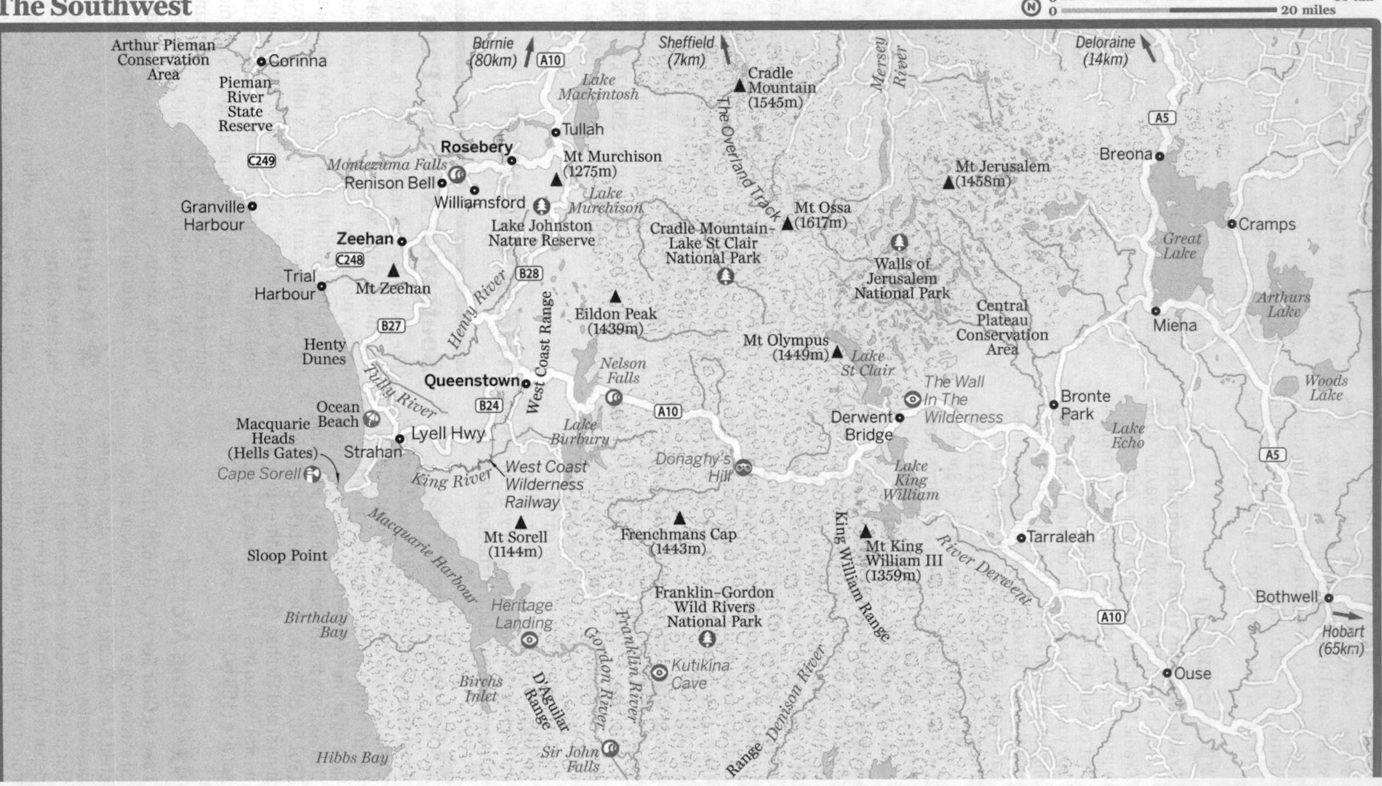
The Southwest
0
0
40 km
20 miles
Arthur Pieman Conservation Area
Corinna
Burnie (80km)
A10
Sheffield (7km)
Cradle Mountain (1545m)
Mersey River
Deloraine (14km)
Pieman River State Reserve
Lake Mackintosh
The Overland Track
A5
Tullah
Rosebery
C249
Montezuma Falls
Renison Bell
Williamsford
Mt Murchison (1275m)
Lake Murchison
Mt Jerusalem (1458m)
Breona
Granville Harbour
Lake Johnston Nature Reserve
Cradle Mountain-Lake St Clair National Park
Mt Ossa (1617m)
Walls of Jerusalem National Park
Great Lake
Cramps
Zeehan
C248
Trial Harbour
Mt Zeehan
B28
Henty River
West Coast Range
Eildon Peak (1439m)
Central Plateau Conservation Area
Arthurs Lake
Miena
B27
Henty Dunes
Mt Olympus (1449m)
Lake St Clair
Tully River
Queenstown
Nelson Falls
The Wall In The Wilderness
Bronte Park
Woods Lake
Ocean Beach
B24
A10
Derwent Bridge
Lake Echo
Macquarie Heads (Hells Gates)
Lyell Hwy
Strahan
Lake Burbury
Donaghy's Hill
A5
Cape Sorell
King River
West Coast Wilderness Railway
Lake King William
Macquarie Harbour
Mt Sorell (1144m)
Frenchmans Cap (1443m)
King William Range
Mt King William III (1359m)
Tarraleah
River Derwent
Sloop Point
Heritage Landing
Franklin-Gordon Wild Rivers National Park
Bothwell
A10
Hobart (65km)
Birthday Bay
Gordon River
Franklin River
Kutikina Cave
Denison River
Ouse
Birchs Inlet
D'Aguilar Range
Hibbs Bay
Sir John Falls
Range

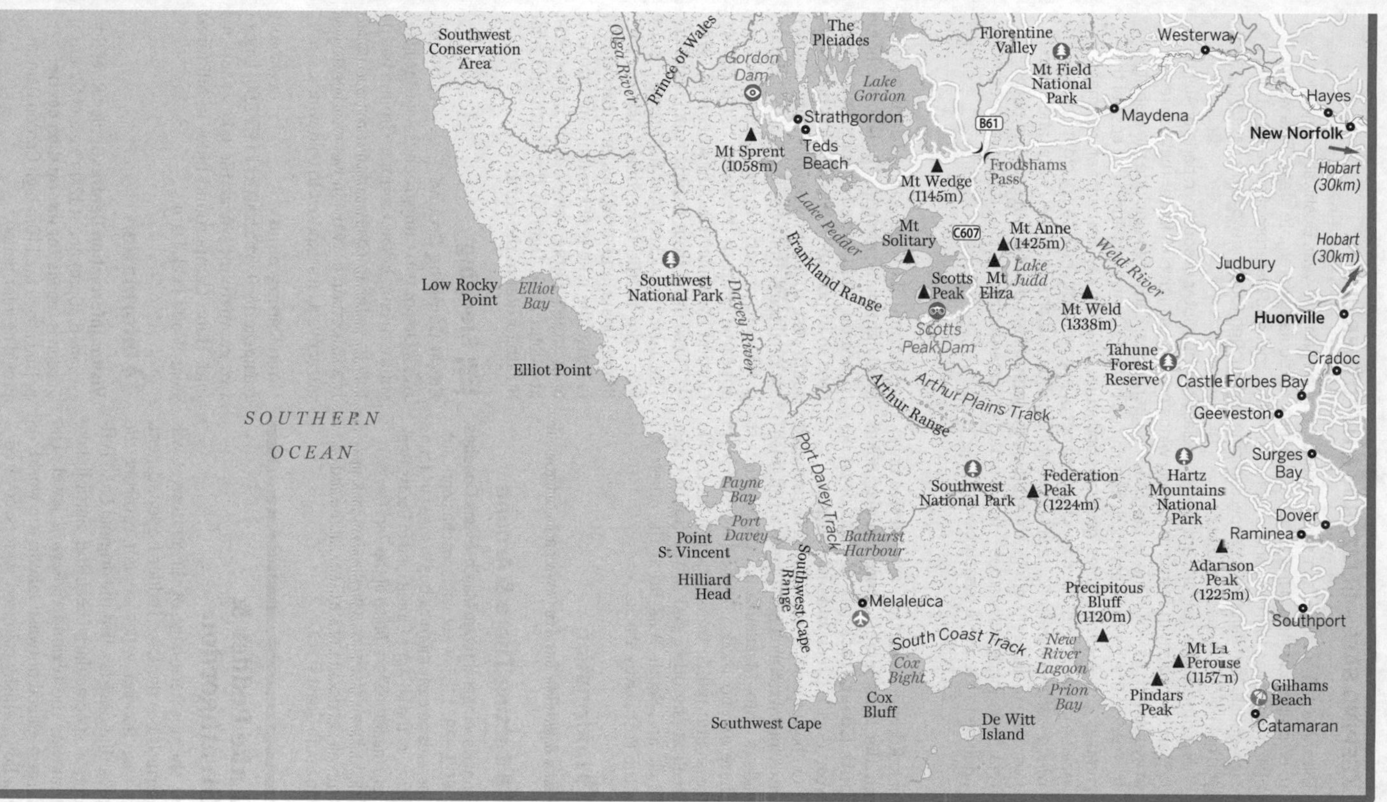
Southwest Conservation Area
Olga River
Prince of Wales
The Pleiades
Gordon Dam
Lake Gordon
Strathgordon
Teds Beach
Mt Sprent (1058m)
Florentine Valley
Mt Field National Park
Westerway
Maydena
Hayes
New Norfolk
Hobart (30km)
B61
Frodshams Pass
Mt Wedge (1145m)
Lake Pedder
Mt Solitary
C607
Mt Anne (1425m)
Lake Judd
Mt Eliza
Scotts Peak
Scotts Peak Dam
Frankland Range
Weld River
Mt Weld (1338m)
Judbury
Hobart (30km)
Huonville
Cradoc
Tahune Forest Reserve
Castle Forbes Bay
Geeveston
Low Rocky Point
Elliot Bay
Southwest National Park
Davey River
Elliot Point
Arthur Plains Track
Arthur Range
SOUTHERN OCEAN
Port Davey Track
Southwest National Park
Federation Peak (1224m)
Hartz Mountains National Park
Surges Bay
Dover
Raminea
Payne Bay
Port Davey
Point St Vincent
Bathurst Harbour
Southwest Cape Range
Hilliard Head
Melaleuca
Adamson Peak (1225m)
Precipitous Bluff (1120m)
Southport
South Coast Track
New River Lagoon
Cox Bight
Cox Bluff
Mt La Perouse (1157m)
Pindars Peak
Prion Bay
Gilhams Beach
Catamaran
De Witt Island
Southwest Cape

KEEPING SAFE – BLIZZARDS & HYPOTHERMIA

Blizzards can occur in Tasmania's mountains at any time of year. Bushwalkers need to be prepared for such freezing eventualities, particularly in remote areas. Take warm clothing such as thermals and jackets, plus windproof and waterproof garments. Carry a high-quality tent suitable for snow camping and enough food for two extra days, in case you get held up by bad weather.

Hypothermia is a significant risk, especially during winter in southern parts of Australia – and especially in Tasmania. Strong winds produce a high chill factor that can result in hypothermia even in moderately cool temperatures. Early signs include the inability to perform fine movements (such as doing up buttons), shivering and a bad case of the 'umbles' (fumbles, mumbles, grumbles and stumbles). The key elements of treatment include moving out of the cold, changing out of any wet clothing into dry clothes with windproof and waterproof layers, adding insulation and providing fuel (water and carbohydrates) to allow shivering, which builds the internal temperature. In severe hypothermia, shivering actually stops – this is a medical emergency requiring rapid evacuation in addition to the above measures.

Peak Rd and Melaleuca (around five days), and the considerably more popular 85km **South Coast Track** (six to eight days) between Cockle Creek and Melaleuca.

On both tracks, hikers should be prepared for vicious weather. Light planes airlift bushwalkers into Melaleuca in the southwest (there are no roads), while there's vehicle access and public transport to/from Cockle Creek at the other end of the South Coast Track, and Scotts Peak Rd at the other end of the Port Davey Track.

Information

Parks & Wildlife Service (www.parks.tas.gov.au)

Getting There & Around

From November through March, **Evans Coaches** (☎ 03-6297 1335; www.evanscoaches.com.au) operates an early morning bus to the start (and finish) of the Mt Anne Circuit, and to Scotts Peak Dam (near the start/finish of the Port Davey Track). Evans also runs a bushwalker pick-up/drop-off service at Cockle Creek, at the end of the South Coast Track.

Lake Pedder & Strathgordon

At the northern edge of the southwest wilderness lies the Lake Pedder Impoundment, a vast flooded valley system covering the area that once cradled the original Lake Pedder, a spectacularly beautiful natural lake that was the region's ecological jewel. The largest glacial outwash lake in the world, its shallow, whisky-coloured waters covered 3 sq km and its wide, sandy beach made an ideal light-plane airstrip. The lake was home to several endangered species and considered so important it was the first part of the southwest to be protected within its own national park. But even this status ultimately failed to preserve it and Lake Pedder disappeared beneath the waters of the Pedder/Gordon hydroelectric dam scheme in 1972.

These days, trout fishing is popular here. The lake is stocked and fish caught range from 1kg to the occasional 20kg monster. Small boats and dinghies are discouraged because the lake is 55km long and prone to dangerously large waves. Boat ramps exist at Scotts Peak Dam in the south and near Strathgordon in the north.

Sleeping

Edgar Camping Ground CAMPGROUND

FREE One of two campgrounds near the lake's southern end, Edgar Camping Ground has pit toilets, water, fine views of the area and usually a fisherman or two – in wet weather it's less attractive as it's exposed to cold winds.

Huon Campground CAMPGROUND

(camp site d $10, extra adult/child $5/2.50) One of two campgrounds near the lake's southern end, Huon Campground hides in tall forest near Scotts Peak Dam.

Information

Visitor Information Centre (Gordon River Rd; ⌚ 9am-6.30pm) About 12km west of Strathgordon is the **visitor information centre**, poised above the 140m-high Gordon Dam and providing information.

Adelaide & Around

Includes ➡

Best Places to Eat

- Peel Street (p725)
- Gin Long Canteen (p726)
- Star of Greece (p740)
- Flying Fish Cafe (p743)
- Dudley Cellar Door (p750)

Best Places to Stay

- Adabco Boutique Hotel (p721)
- Port Elliot Beach House YHA (p743)
- Stirling Hotel (p736)
- Largs Pier Hotel (p724)
- Australasian (p745)

Why Go?

Escape the frenzy of Australia's east coast with a few days in gracious, relaxed Adelaide. Capital of the driest state on the driest inhabited continent, Adelaide beats the heat by celebrating life's finer things: fine landscapes, fine festivals, fine food, and (...OK, forget the other three) fine wine.

Just down the tram tracks is beachy Glenelg, Adelaide with its guard down and board shorts up. Nearby, Port Adelaide is slowly gentrifying but remains a raffish harbour 'hood with buckets of soul. Inland, Adelaide's winking plains rise to the Adelaide Hills, just 12 minutes up the freeway. The Hills' gorgeous valley folds, old-fangled towns and cool-climate vineyards are all close at hand.

A day trip away, the Fleurieu Peninsula is Adelaide's weekend playground, with surf and safe-swimming beaches, historic towns and the fabulous McLaren Vale wine region (love that shiraz...). Further afield, Kangaroo Island's wildlife, forests and seafood await just offshore.

When to Go

Adelaide

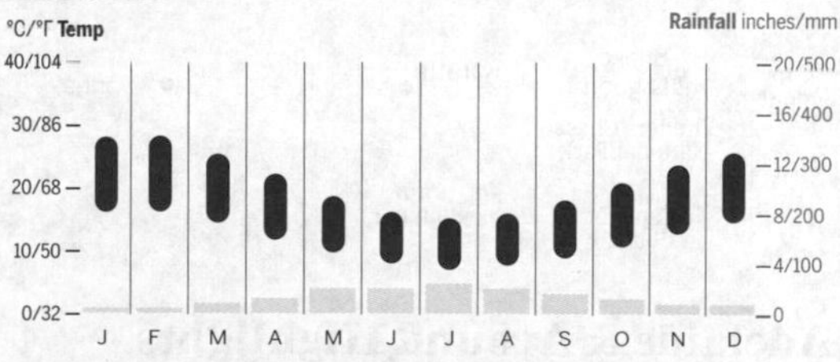

Feb–Mar Adelaide's festival season hits its straps: Fringe and WOMADelaide are highlights.

Mar–May Beat the summer city heat in shoulder season (also September to November).

Sep Football finals time: yell yourself silly in the stands, beer and pie in hand(s).

0 40 km
0 20 miles
Spencer Gulf
Corny Point
Corny Point
Minlaton
Port Vincent
Yorke Peninsula
Stansbu
Warooka
Yorketown
Yorke Peninsula
Edithburgh
Troubridge Point
West Cape
Innes National Park
Marion Bay
Cape Spencer
Investigator Strait
Cape Cassini
Emu Bay
Point Marsden
Emu Bay
Stokes Bay
Kingscote
Cygnet River
Nepean Bay
Cape Forbin
Western River Conservation Park
Cygnet River
American River
Cape Borda
Parndana
Timber Creek
4 Kangaroo Island
Rocky River
Cape Bedout
Snake Lagoon
Karatta
Vivonne Bay
Cape Gantheaume Conservation Park
Flinders Chase National Park
Cape Bouguer
Cape du Couedic
Cape Gantheaume

Adelaide & Around Highlights

1 Sniffing out the ripest cheese, fullest fruit and strongest coffee at Adelaide's **Central Market** (p710).

2 Swirling, nosing and quaffing your way through **McLaren Vale** (p737), our favourite SA wine region.

3 Day tripping through the **Adelaide Hills** (p733), checking out cellar doors, markets and historic towns.

4 Listening to the seals snort on **Kangaroo Island** (p745).

5 Joining the after-work booze hounds on Adelaide's **Peel St** (p727) or at the **Exeter Hotel** (p727).

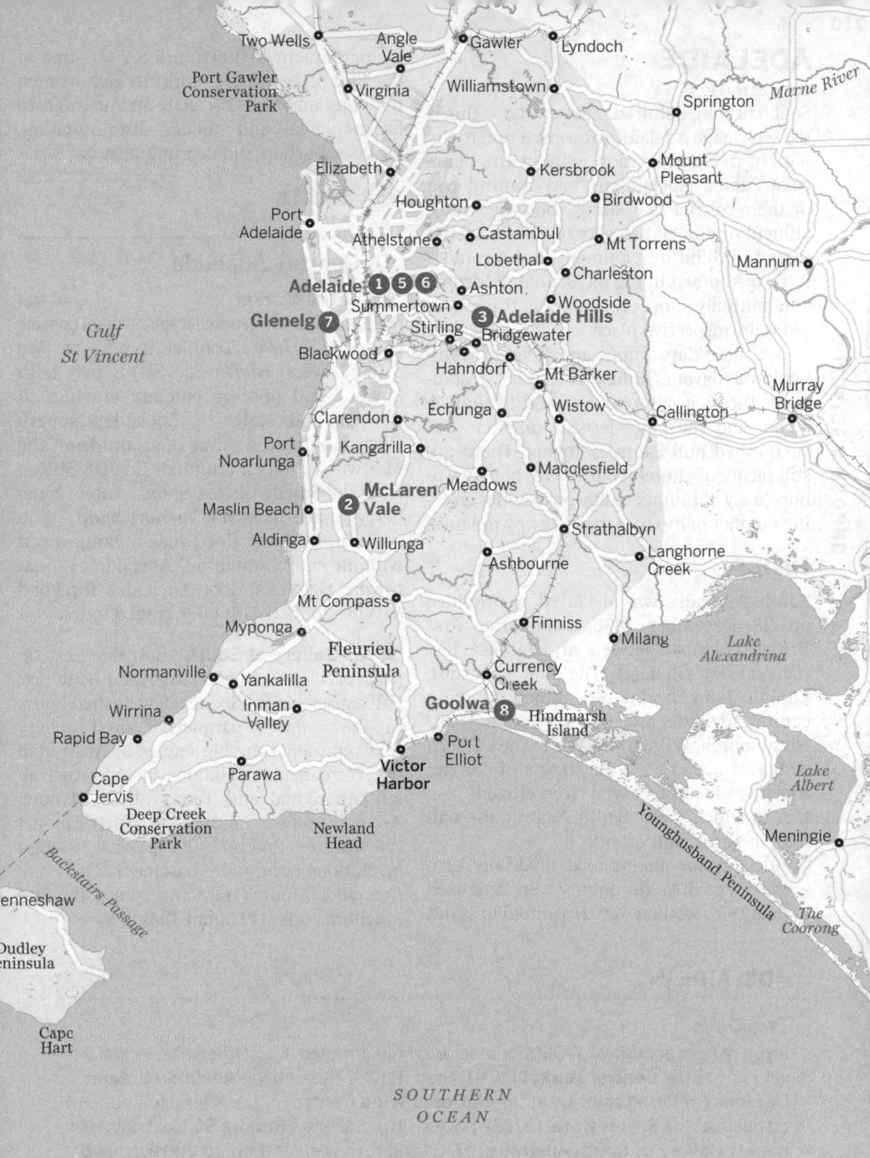

6 Catching a cricket match or some AFL football at the revamped **Adelaide Oval** (p712).

7 Riding the tram to **Glenelg** (p715) for a swim and some sunset fish and chips by the sea.

8 Cycling along the Encounter Bikeway from Victor Harbor to **Goolwa** (p743), keeping an eye out for passing whales.

ADELAIDE

POP 1.29 MILLION

Sophisticated, cultured, neat-casual – this is the self-image Adelaide projects, a nod to the days of free colonisation without the penal colony taint. Adelaidians may remind you of their convict-free status, but the stuffy, affluent origins of the 'City of Churches' did more to inhibit development than promote it. Bogged down in the old-school doldrums and painfully short on charisma, this was a pious, introspective place.

But these days things are different. Multicultural flavours infuse Adelaide's restaurants; there's a pumping arts and live-music scene; and the city's festival calendar has vanquished dull Saturday nights. There are still plenty of church spires here, but they're hopelessly outnumbered by pubs and a growing number of hip bars tucked away in lanes.

History

South Australia was declared a province on 28 December 1836, when the first British colonists landed at Holdfast Bay (current-day Glenelg). The first governor, Captain John Hindmarsh, named the state capital Adelaide, after the wife of the British monarch, William IV. While the eastern states struggled with the stigma of convict society, Adelaidians were free citizens – a fact to which many South Australians will happily draw your attention.

Adelaide has maintained a socially progressive creed: trade unions were legalised here in 1876; women were permitted to stand for parliament in 1894; and SA was one of the first places in the world to give women the vote, and the first state in Australia to outlaw racial and gender discrimination, legalise abortion and decriminalise gay sex.

Sights

Central Adelaide

★Central Market MARKET

(Map p714; www.adelaidecentralmarket.com.au; Gouger St; 7am-5.30pm Tue, 9am-5.30pm Wed & Thu, 7am-9pm Fri, 7am-3pm Sat) Satisfy both obvious and obscure culinary cravings at the 250-odd stalls in Adelaide's superb Central Market. A sliver of salami from the Mettwurst Shop, a crumb of English Stilton from the Smelly Cheese Shop, a tub of blueberry yogurt from the Yoghurt Shop – you name it, it's here. Good luck making it out without eating anything. Adelaide's Chinatown is right next door. Adelaide's Top Food & Wine Tours (p718) offer guided tours.

★Art Gallery of South Australia GALLERY

(Map p714; www.artgallery.sa.gov.au; North Tce; 10am-5pm) FREE Spend a few hushed hours in the vaulted, parquetry-floored gallery that represents the big names in Australian art. Permanent exhibitions include Australian, Aboriginal and Torres Strait Islander, Asian, European and North American art (20 bronze Rodins!). Progressive visiting exhibitions occupy the basement. There are free guided tours (11am and 2pm daily) and lunchtime talks (12.30pm Tuesdays).

ADELAIDE IN...

Two Days

If you're here at Festival, WOMADelaide or Fringe time, lap it up. Otherwise, kick-start your day at the **Central Market** (p710) then wander through the **Adelaide Botanic Gardens** (p711), finishing up at the **National Wine Centre** (p711). After a few bohemian beers at the **Exeter Hotel** (p727), have a ritzy dinner on **Rundle St**. Next day, visit the **Art Gallery of South Australia** (p710) and then wander down to the revamped Adelaide Oval to check out the **Bradman Collection** (p713). Grab a cab out to **Coopers Brewery** (p714) for a beer-tinged tour, then ride the tram to **Glenelg** (p715) for an evening swim and fish and chips on the sand.

Four Days

Follow the two-day itinerary – perhaps slotting in the **South Australian Museum** (p711) and **Jam Factory Contemporary Craft & Design Centre** (p711) – then pack a picnic basket of Central Market produce and take a day trip to the nearby **Adelaide Hills**, **McLaren Vale** or **Barossa Valley** wine regions. Next day, truck out to the museums and historic pubs of **Port Adelaide**, then catch a live band at the **Grace Emily Hotel** (p727) back in the city, before dinner on **Gouger St** (p724).

National Wine Centre of Australia WINERY
(Map p714; www.wineaustralia.com.au; cnr Botanic & Hackney Rds; 8am-9pm Mon-Fri, 9am-9pm Sat, 9am-7am Sun, tours & tastings 10am-5pm) FREE Check out the free self-guided, interactive *Wine Discovery Journey* exhibition, paired with tastings of Australian wines (from $10), at this very sexy wine centre (actually a research facility for the University of Adelaide, rather than a visitor centre per se). You will gain an insight into the issues winemakers contend with, and can even have your own virtual vintage rated. Friday-evening 'uncorked' drinks happen at 4.30pm, and there's a cool cafe here, too.

South Australian Museum MUSEUM
(Map p714; www.samuseum.sa.gov.au; North Tce; 10am-5pm) FREE Dig into Australia's natural history with the museum's special exhibits on whales and Antarctic explorer Sir Douglas Mawson. An Aboriginal Cultures Gallery displays artefacts of the Ngarrindjeri people of the Coorong and lower Murray. The giant squid and the lion with the twitchy tail are definite highlights. Free tours depart 11am weekdays and 2pm and 3pm weekends. The cafe here is a good spot for lunch.

Adelaide Zoo ZOO
(Map p720; www.zoossa.com.au/adelaide-zoo; Frome Rd; adult/child/family $32.50/18/85; 9.30am-5pm) Around 1800 exotic and native mammals, birds and reptiles roar, growl and screech at Adelaide's wonderful zoo, dating from 1883. There are free walking tours half-hourly (plus a slew of longer and overnight tours), feeding sessions and a children's zoo. Wang Wang and Funi are Australia's only giant pandas – they arrived in 2009 (pandemonium!) and always draw a crowd. Other highlights include the nocturnal and reptile houses. You can take a river cruise to the zoo on *Popeye* (p722).

Adelaide Botanic Gardens GARDENS
(Map p714; www.botanicgardens.sa.gov.au; North Tce; 7.15am-sunset Mon-Fri, from 9am Sat & Sun) FREE Chew through your trashy airport novel or go jogging in these lush gardens. Highlights include a restored 1877 palm house, the waterlily pavilion (housing the gigantic *Victoria amazonica*), the new First Creek wetlands, the engrossing **Museum of Economic Botany** and the fabulous steel-and-glass arc of the **Bicentennial Conservatory** (open 10am to 4pm), which recreates a tropical rainforest. Free 1½-hour guided walks depart the Schomburgk Pavilion at 10.30am daily.

Migration Museum MUSEUM
(Map p714; www.migrationmuseum.com.au; 82 Kintore Ave; 10am-5pm Mon-Fri, 1-5pm Sat & Sun) FREE This engaging social-history museum tells the story of the many migrants who have made SA their home. The museum has info on 100-plus nationalities (as opposed to individuals) in its database, along with some poignant personal stories. Occupies the site of a former Aboriginal boarding school and destitute asylum.

West Terrace Cemetery CEMETERY
(Map p714; 08-8139 7400; www.aca.sa.gov.au; West Tce; 6.30am-6pm Nov-Apr to 8.30pm May-Oct) FREE Driven-by and overlooked by most Adelaidians, this amazing old cemetery (established in 1837, and now with 150,000 residents) makes a serene and fascinating detour. The 2km self-guided **Heritage Highlights Interpretive Trail** meanders past 29 key sites; pick up a brochure at the West Tce entrance. Guided tours run at 10.30am Tuesday and Sunday ($10 per person); call for bookings.

Tandanya National Aboriginal Cultural Institute GALLERY
(Map p714; 08-8224 3200; www.tandanya.com.au; 253 Grenfell St; 9am-4pm Mon-Sat) FREE Tandanya offers an insight into the culture of the local Kaurna people, whose territory extends south to Cape Jervis and north to Port Wakefield. Inside are interactive visual-arts gallery spaces, plus a gift shop and a cafe. Call for info on regular didgeridoo or Torres Strait Islander cultural performances and prebooked group tours.

Adelaide Park Lands GARDENS
FREE The city centre and ritzy North Adelaide are surrounded by a broad band of parkland. Colonel William Light, Adelaide's controversial planner, came up with the concept, which has been both a blessing and a curse for the city. Pros: heaps of green space, clean air and playgrounds for the kids. Cons: bone dry in summer, loitering perverts and a sense that the city is cut off from its suburbs.

Don't miss the **playgrounds** and **Adelaide-Himeji Garden** (Map p714) on South Tce, and the **statue of Colonel William Light** (Map p720) overlooking the Adelaide Oval and city office towers from Montefiore Hill.

Jam Factory Contemporary Craft & Design Centre ART GALLERY
(Map p714; 08-8410 0727; www.jamfactory.com.au; 19 Morphett St; 10am-5pm Mon-Sat)

Adelaide

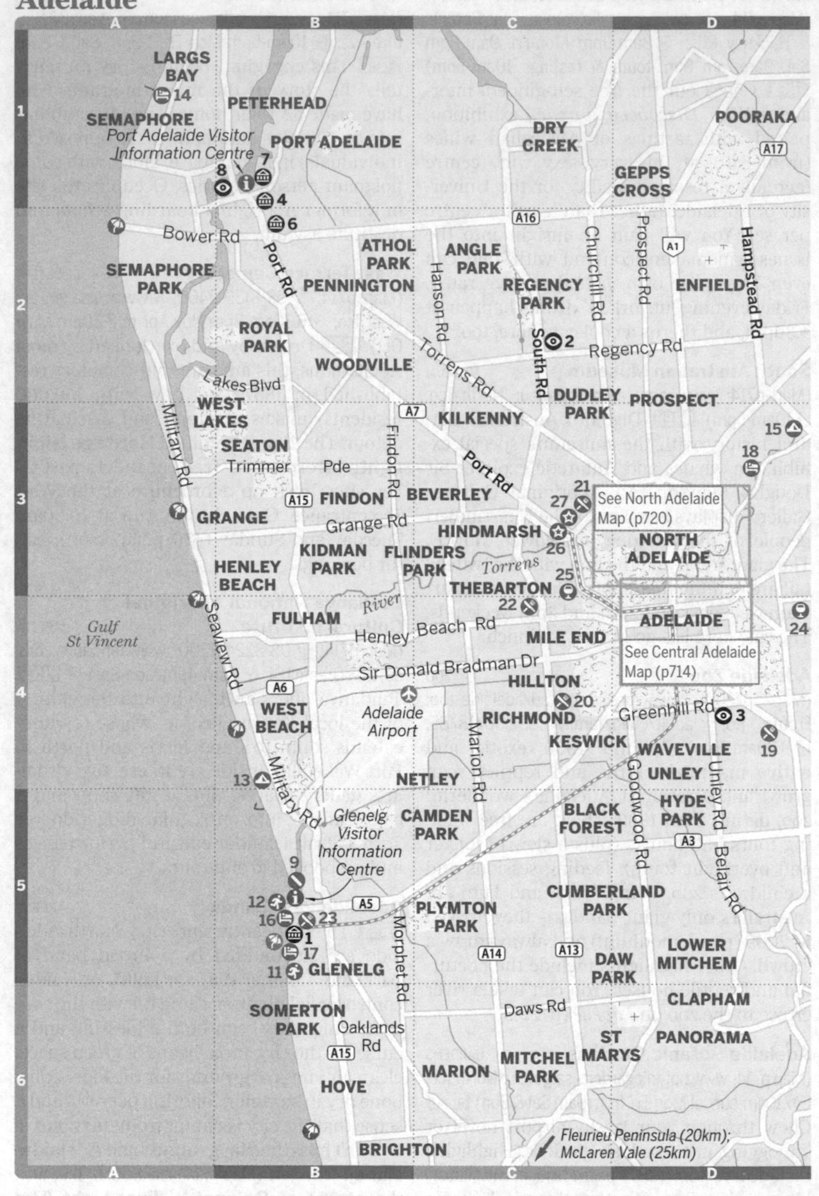

FREE Quality contemporary local arts and crafts, plus workshops and a hellishly hot glass-blowing studio (watch from the balcony above) turning out gorgeous glass. Group tours (six or more people) by arrangement.

North Adelaide

★ Adelaide Oval LANDMARK
(Map p720; 08-8205 4700; www.adelaideoval.com.au; King William Rd, North Adelaide; tours adult/child $20/10; tours 11am & 2pm Mon-Fri

Adelaide

Sights

1 Bay Discovery Centre B5
City of Adelaide .... (see 7)
2 Coopers Brewery C2
3 Haigh's Chocolates Visitor Centre D4
4 National Railway Museum B1
5 Penfolds Magill Estate Winery F3
6 South Australian Aviation Museum B2
7 South Australian Maritime Museum B1
8 Wild at Hart Fresh Food Market B1

Activities, Courses & Tours

9 Adelaide Scuba B5
Dolphin Explorer Cruises .... (see 7)
10 Eagle Mountain Bike Park F5
11 Glenelg Bicycle Hire B5
12 Temptation Sailing B5

Sleeping

13 BIG4 Adelaide Shores B4
Glenelg Beach Hostel .... (see 1)
14 Largs Pier Hotel A1
15 Levi Park Caravan Park D3
16 Oaks Plaza Pier B5
Port Adelaide Backpackers .... (see 4)
17 Seawall Apartments B5
18 Watson D3

Eating

19 Bar 9 .... D4
20 Café de Vili's C4
Good Life .... (see 1)
21 Jarmer's Kitchen C3
22 Parwana Afghan Kitchen C4
23 Zest Cafe Gallery B5
Zucca Greek Mezze .... (see 12)

Drinking & Nightlife

24 Colonist D4
Pier Bar .... (see 12)
25 Wheatsheaf C3

Entertainment

26 Adelaide Entertainment Centre C3
27 Governor Hindmarsh Hotel C3

nongame days) Hailed as the world's prettiest cricket ground, the Adelaide Oval hosts interstate and international cricket matches in summer, plus national AFL football and state football games in winter. A wholesale redevelopment has boosted seating capacity to 50,000 – when they're all yelling, it's a serious home-town advantage! Guided tours depart from the Riverbank Stand, off War Memorial Dr: call for bookings.

Also here is the **Bradman Collection** (Map p720; Riverbank Stand; 10am-4pm Mon-Fri) FREE, where devotees of Don Bradman, cricket's greatest batsman, can pore over the minutiae of his legend. Check out the bronze statue of the Don cracking a cover drive out the front of the stadium.

Central Adelaide

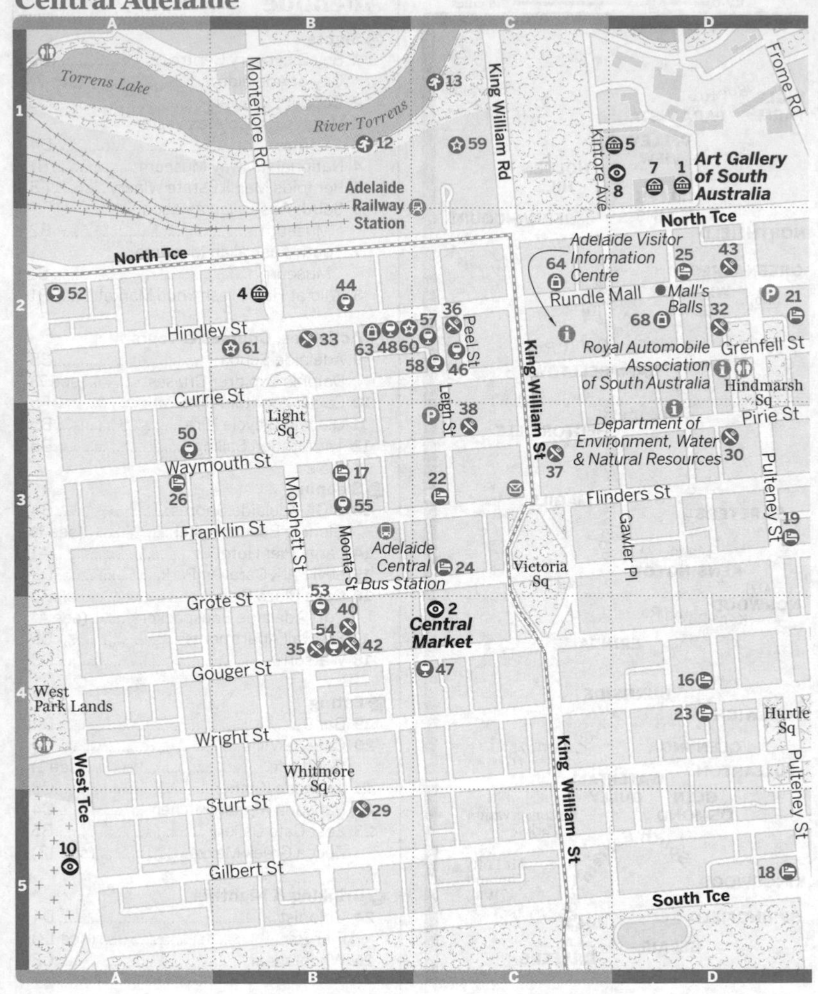

Inner Suburbs

Coopers Brewery BREWERY

(Map p712; ☎08-8440 1800; www.coopers.com.au; 461 South Rd, Regency Park; 1hr tours per person $22; ⏰tours 1pm Tue-Fri) You can't possibly come to Adelaide without entertaining thoughts of touring Coopers Brewery. Tours take you through the brewhouse, bottling hall and history museum, where you can get stuck into samples of stouts, ales and lagers. Bookings required; minimum age 18. The brewery is in the northern suburbs – grab a cab, or walk 1km from Islington train station.

Penfolds Magill Estate Winery WINERY

(Map p712; ☎08-8301 5569; www.penfolds.com; 78 Penfolds Rd, Magill; tastings free-$50; ⏰10am-5pm) This 100-year-old winery is home to Australia's best-known wine – the legendary Grange. Taste the product at the cellar door; dine at the restaurant; take the Heritage Tour ($15); or steel your wallet for the Great Grange Tour ($150). Tour bookings are essential.

Haigh's Chocolates Visitor Centre CHOCOLATE

(Map p712; ☎08-8372 7070; www.haighschocolates.com; 154 Greenhill Rd, Parkside; ⏰8.30am-5.30pm Mon-Fri, 9am-5pm Sat) FREE If you've got a chocolate problem, get guilty at this iconic factory.

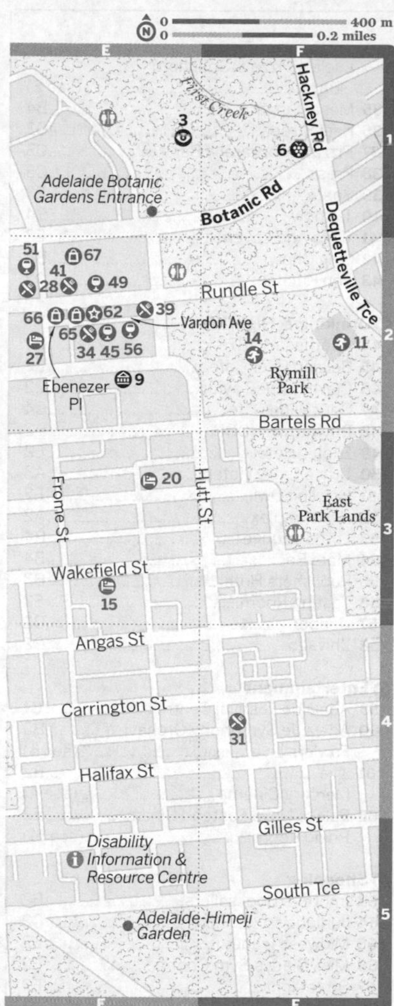

Free 20-minute tours take you through the chocolate life cycle from cacao bean to hand-dipped truffle (with samples if you're good). Call for tour times and bookings.

Glenelg

Glenelg, or 'the Bay' – the site of SA's colonial landing – is Adelaide at its most LA. Glenelg's **beach** faces towards the west, and as the sun sinks into the sea, the pubs and bars burgeon with surfies, backpackers and sun-damaged sexagenarians. The tram rumbles in from the city, past the **Jetty Rd** shopping strip to the al fresco cafes around **Moseley Sq**.

The **Glenelg Visitor Information Centre** (Map p712; 08-8294 5833; www.glenelgsa.com.au; Shop 22, Marina Pier, Holdfast Shores, Glenelg; 9am-4.30pm Mon-Fri, 10am-2pm Sat & Sun) has the local low-down, including information on **diving** and **sailing** opportunities.

From the city, take the tram or bus 167, 168 or 190 to get to Glenelg.

Bay Discovery Centre MUSEUM

(Map p712; www.glenelgsa.com.au/baydiscover; Moseley Sq, Town Hall; admission by donation; 10am-5pm Oct-Mar, to 4pm Apr-Sep) This low-key museum in Glenelg's 1887 Town Hall building depicts the social history of Glenelg from colonisation to today, and addresses the plight of the local Kaurna people, who lost both their land and voice. Don't miss the relics dredged up from the original pier, and the spooky old sideshow machines.

Port Adelaide

Mired in the economic doldrums for decades, Port Adelaide – 15km northwest of the city – is slowly gentrifying, morphing its warehouses into art spaces and museums, and its brawl-house pubs into boutique beer emporia. There's even an organic food market here now: things are on the up!

The helpful **Port Adelaide Visitor Information Centre** (Map p712; 08-8405 6560, 1800 629 888; www.portenf.sa.gov.au; 66 Commercial Rd, Port Adelaide; 9am-5pm;) stocks brochures on self-guided history, heritage-pub and dolphin-spotting walks and drives, plus the enticements of neighbouring Semaphore, a very bohemian beach 'burb. Activities include dolphin cruises and kayaking.

Adelaide's solitary tram line is rumoured to be extending to Port Adelaide at some stage. Until then, bus 150 will get you here from North Tce, or take the train.

South Australian Maritime Museum MUSEUM

(Map p712; www.samaritimemuseum.com.au; 126 Lipson St, Port Adelaide; adult/child/family $10/5/25; 10am-5pm daily, lighthouse 10am-3pm Sun-Fri) This salty cache is the oldest of its kind in Australia. Highlights include the iconic **Port Adelaide Lighthouse** ($1 on its own, or included in museum admission), busty figureheads made everywhere from Londonderry to Quebec, shipwreck and explorer displays, and a computer register of early migrants.

Central Adelaide

Top Sights
1 Art Gallery of South Australia D1
2 Central Market C4

Sights
3 Adelaide Botanic Gardens E1
4 Jam Factory Contemporary Craft & Design Centre B2
5 Migration Museum D1
6 National Wine Centre of Australia F1
7 South Australian Museum D1
8 State Library of South Australia D1
9 Tandanya National Aboriginal Cultural Institute E2
10 West Terrace Cemetery A5

Activities, Courses & Tours
11 Adelaide Bowling Club F2
12 Captain Jolley's Paddle Boats B1
13 Popeye C1
14 Rymill Park Rowboats F2

Sleeping
15 Adabco Boutique Hotel E3
16 Adelaide Backpackers Inn D4
17 Adelaide Central YHA B3
18 Adelaide City Park Motel D5
19 Backpack Oz D3
20 Clarion Hotel Soho E3
21 Crowne Plaza Adelaide D2
22 Franklin Central Apartments C3
23 Hostel 109 .... D4
24 Hotel Metropolitan C3
25 Hotel Richmond D2
26 My Place A3
27 Roof Garden Hotel E2

Eating
28 Amalfi Pizzeria Ristorante E2
29 Café Troppo B5
Central Market .... (see 2)
30 Earth's Kitchen D3
31 Good Life F4
32 Jasmin Indian Restaurant D2
33 Jerusalem Sheshkabab House B2
34 Kutchi Deli Parwana E2
Lucia's Pizza & Spaghetti Bar .... (see 2)
35 Mesa Lunga B4
36 Peel Street C2
37 Pizza e Mozzarella Bar C3
38 Press C3
39 Sosta E2
40 T-Chow B4
41 Vego And Loven' It E2
42 Ying Chow B4
43 Zen Kitchen D2

Drinking & Nightlife
44 Apothecary 1878 .... B2
45 Belgian Beer Café E2
46 Clever Little Taylor C2
47 Cork Wine Cafe C4
48 Downtown HDCB B2
49 Exeter Hotel E2
50 Grace Emily Hotel A3
51 Howling Owl E2
52 HQ Complex A2
53 Lotus Lounge B4
54 Mars Bar B4
55 Publishers Hotel B3
56 Tasting Room E2
57 Udaberri C2
58 Zhivago C2

Entertainment
59 Adelaide Festival Centre C1
60 Adelaide Symphony Orchestra B2
Fowlers Live .... (see 4)
61 Jive B2
Mercury Cinema .... (see 4)
62 Palace Nova Eastend Cinemas E2
Rhino Room .... (see 51)

Shopping
63 Imprints Booksellers B2
64 Jurlique C2
65 Midwest Trader E2
66 Miss Gladys Sym Choon E2
67 Streetlight E2
68 Tarts D2
Urban Cow Studio .... (see 51)

Wild at Hart Fresh Food Market MARKET
(Map p712; www.wildathart.com.au; Mundy St, Port Adelaide; ⌚9am-1pm Sun) Skip the trashy mainstream market on the wharf: this one is a much better bet, with organic produce, buskers, home-cooked meals, baked goods, coffee and a great vibe. Love the old Hart's Mill buildings, too.

National Railway Museum MUSEUM
(Map p712; www.natrailmuseum.org.au; 76 Lipson St, Port Adelaide; adult/child/family $12/6/32; ⌚10am-5pm) Trainspotters rejoice! A delightfully nerdy museum crammed with railway memorabilia. The bookshop stocks as much *Thomas the Tank Engine* merchandise as you can handle.

City of Adelaide SHIP
(Map p712; www.cityofadelaide.org.au; Divett St, Port Adelaide; ⌚24hr) FREE Wander down to the end of Divett St for a look (through the fence) at the oldest clipper ship in the world (1864).

The high-and-dry hulk of the *City of Adelaide* was transported here from Scotland in 2013.

Activities

Adelaide is a flat town – perfect for cycling and walking (if it's not too hot!). You can take your bike on trains any time, but not on buses. **Trails SA** (www.southaustraliantrails.com) offers loads of cycling- and hiking-trail info: pick up its *40 Great South Australian Short Walks* brochure.

There are free guided walks in the Adelaide Botanic Gardens (p711). The riverside **Linear Park Trail** is a 40km walking/cycling path running from Glenelg to the foot of the Adelaide Hills, mainly along the River Torrens. Another popular hiking trail is the steep **Waterfall Gully Track** (three hours return) up to Mt Lofty Summit and back.

For a free **Adelaide City Bike** for a day, contact Bicycle SA (p733).

Eagle Mountain Bike Park MOUNTAIN BIKING
(Map p712; www.bikesa.asn.au; Mt Barker Rd, Leawood Gardens; ⏲dawn-dusk) FREE Mountain bikers should check out the this bike park in the Adelaide Hills, which has 21km of trails. Check the website for directions.

Escapegoat DICYCLE TOURS
(☎0422 916 289, 08-8121 8112; www.escapegoat.com.au) Ride from the 710m Mt Lofty Summit down to Adelaide ($99), or take a day trip through McLaren Vale by bike ($129). Flinders Ranges bike trips also available.

Adelaide Bowling Club BOWLING
(Map p714; ☎08-8223 5516; www.adelaidebowlingclub.com.au; 58 Dequetteville Tce; per person $15; ⏲2pm-late Sun Oct-Mar) Trundle down a few lawn bowls on Sunday Superbowlz sessions at this old club, just east of the CBD. Take a break with dinner and drinks in the clubhouse.

Bikeabout MOUNTAIN BIKING
(☎0413 525 733; www.bikeabout.com.au) Barnstorming one-day 'Radelaide' mountain-bike sessions in the Adelaide Hills (from $130), plus mountain-bike hire (from $65 per 24 hours) and tours through the Barossa Valley, McLaren Vale and Clare Valley wine regions.

Glenelg Bicycle Hire BICYCLE RENTAL
(Map p712; ☎08-8376 1934; www.glenelgbicyclehire.com.au; 71 Broadway, Norfolk Motor Inn, Glenelg South; per 4hr/day $25/50, tandems $40/60) Down at the beach, hire a bike from Glenelg Bicycle Hire.

Water Activities

Adelaide gets *reeeeally* hot in summer. Hit the beach at Glenelg, or try any other activity that gets you out on the water. For more options, check out *Popeye* (p722) river cruises and Captain Jolley's Paddle Boats (p722).

Adelaide Aquatic Centre SWIMMING
(Map p720; www.adelaideaquaticcentre.com.au; Jeffcott Rd, North Adelaide; adult/child/family $7.50/6/21; ⏲6am-9pm Mon-Fri, 7am-7pm Sat & Sun) The closest pool to the city, with indoor swimming and diving pools, and the usual gym, sauna and spa stuff.

Adventure Kayaking SA KAYAKING
(☎08-8295 8812; www.adventurekayak.com.au; tours adult/child from $50/25, kayak hire per 3hr 1/2/3 seater $40/60/80) Family-friendly guided kayak tours around the Port River estuary (dolphins, mangroves, shipwrecks). Also offers kayak hire.

Rymill Park Rowboats BOATING
(Map p714; ☎08-8232 2814; www.rymillparkkiosk.com.au; Rymill Park, East Tce; boats per hr $8; ⏲9am-4.30pm Sat & Sun) Hire a dinky little dinghy and row the kids around the duck-filled lake in Rymill Park, just east of the city centre.

Temptation Sailing BOATING
(Map p712; ☎0412 811 838; www.dolphinboat.com.au; Holdfast Shores Marina, Glenelg; 3½hr dolphin watch/swim per adult $68/98, child $58/88)

TAKE THE LONG WAY HOME

South Australia has three epic long-distance trails for hiking and cycling, all running through or past Adelaide.

Heysen Trail (www.heysentrail.asn.au) Australia's longest walking trail: 1200km between Cape Jervis on the Fleurieu Peninsula and Parachilna Gorge in the Flinders Ranges. Access points along the way make it ideal for half- and full-day walks. Note that due to fire restrictions, some sections of the trail are closed between December and April.

Kidman Trail (www.kidmantrail.org.au) A 10-section cycling and walking trail between Willunga on the Fleurieu Peninsula and Kapunda, north of the Barossa Valley.

Mawson Trail (www.southaustraliantrails.com) A 900km bike trail between Adelaide and Blinman in the Flinders Ranges, via the Adelaide Hills and Clare Valley.

Eco-accredited catamaran cruises to watch or swim with dolphins. There are twilight and 1½-hour day cruises too (adult/child $24/16).

Earth Adventure KAYAKING
(☎08-8165 2024; www.earthadventure.com.au; 3hr kayaking per person from $75) Earth Adventure offers morning kayaking trips exploring the mangroves and shipwrecks around the Port River near Port Adelaide. Trips are more expensive per person for groups smaller than five people. Longer paddles around the Murray River, Kangaroo Island and Coffin Bay are also available.

Dolphin Explorer Cruises BOATING, CRUISE
(Map p712; ☎08-8447 2366; www.dolphinexplorer.com.au; Commercial Rd, Port Adelaide; 2hr cruises from adult/child $10/6; ⊙daily) Cruises departing Port Adelaide's Fishermen's Wharf to ogle bottlenose dolphins in the Port River. Lots of cruise-and-dine options also available.

Adelaide Scuba DIVING
(Map p712; ☎08-8294 7744; www.adelaidescuba.com.au; Patawalonga Frontage, Glenelg North; ⊙9am-5.30pm Mon-Fri, 8am-5pm Sat & Sun) Hires out snorkelling gear (per day $30) and runs local dives (single/double dive $65/130). There are also two-weekend learn-to-dive courses for $450.

Tours

A great way to see Adelaide is to circle around the main sights on the free city buses (p733). Beyond the city, day tours cover the Adelaide Hills, Fleurieu Peninsula, Barossa Valley and Clare Valley. One-day trips to the Flinders Ranges and Kangaroo Island tend to be rushed and not great value for money.

Adelaide's Top Food & Wine Tours TOUR
(☎08-8386 0888; www.topfoodandwinetours.com.au) Uncovers SA's gastronomic soul with dawn ($70 including breakfast) and morning ($55) tours of the buzzing Central Market where stallholders introduce their produce. Adelaide Hills, McLaren Vale, Barossa and Clare Valley wine tours are also available.

Bookabee Tours CULTURAL TOUR
(☎08-8235 9954; www.bookabee.com.au) Indigenous-run half-/full-day city tours ($180/255) focusing on bush foods in the Adelaide Botanic Gardens, Tandanya National Aboriginal Cultural Institute and the South Australian Museum. A great insight into Kaurna culture. Longer Flinders Ranges tours also available.

Bums on Seats GUIDED TOUR
(☎0438 808 253; www.bumsonseats.com.au; per person $55, combo $85) One of the few tours which runs through Port Adelaide. See the Port on it's own, or do a combo tour with Adelaide's main sights and landmarks.

Adelaide Sightseeing GUIDED TOUR
(☎1300 769 762; www.adelaidesightseeing.com.au) Runs a city highlights tour ($64) including North Tce, Glenelg, Haigh's Chocolates and the Adelaide Oval (among other sights). Central Market, Barossa Valley, McLaren Vale, Adelaide Hills and Kangaroo Island tours also available.

Haunted Horizons GUIDED TOUR
(☎0407 715 866; www.adelaidehauntedhorizons.com.au; per adult $30) Get spooked on these two-hour, adults-only nocturnal walking tours, digging up the dirt on Adelaide's macabre, murderous and mysterious past.

Integrity Tours GUIDED TOUR
(☎08-8382 9755; www.integritytoursandcharter.com.au) Adelaide city-lights evening tours ($59), plus half-/full-day tours to the Adelaide Hills (from $69/99) and full-day McLaren Vale/Fleurieu Peninsula trips (from $99).

Festivals & Events

Tour Down Under SPORTS
(www.tourdownunder.com.au) The world's best cyclists sweating in their lycra: six races through SA towns, with the grand finale in Adelaide in January.

Adelaide Fringe ARTS
(www.adelaidefringe.com.au) This annual independent arts festival in February and March is second only to the Edinburgh Fringe. Funky, unpredictable and downright hilarious.

Adelaide Festival ARTS
(www.adelaidefestival.com.au) Top-flight international and Australian dance, drama, opera, literature and theatre performances in March. Don't miss the Northern Lights along North Tce – old sandstone buildings ablaze with lights – and Lola's Pergola late-night club.

Clipsal 500 SPORTS
(www.clipsal500.com.au) Rev-heads flail their mullets as Adelaide's streets become a four-day Holden versus Ford racing track in March.

WOMADelaide MUSIC
(www.womadelaide.com.au) One of the world's best live-music events, with more than 300 musicians and performers from around the globe. In March.

LOCAL KNOWLEDGE

ADELAIDE ARTS & FESTIVALS

Emma Fey, Adelaide arts doyen and former Development Manager at the Art Gallery of South Australia, filled us in on some highlights of Adelaide's festival calendar and arts scene.

Festival Season

The Adelaide Festival, the Fringe Festival, Adelaide Writers' Week and the Clipsal 500 (V8 race) all happen around February/March. Energy breeds energy: everyone is out and about and the weather's good. I can't think of anywhere else where you can see alternative Fringe-dwellers next to racing enthusiasts. The people-watching is great!

Art in the City

The Art Gallery of South Australia is in the middle of the North Tce precinct (next to the museum and the university, between the city and the river). The gallery has refurbished and rehung its Elder and Melrose wings, and is engaging a wider audience – especially young people and children with a new dedicated art-making space called the Studio. There are also contemporary art spaces popping up in little lanes around the precinct.

Best Free Events

All sorts of amazing free events appear around the city, especially during the Adelaide Festival. Guerilla street art teamed with pop-up dining experiences, the sensational Adelaide Festival late-night club Lola's Pergola, and the Art Gallery of SA's free daily programs.

Tasting Australia FOOD, WINE
(www.tastingaustralia.com.au) SA foodie experiences around the city, categorised as either 'Eat', Drink', 'Share' or 'Think'. Classes, demonstrations and lots to put in your mouth. Held in late April.

Adelaide Cabaret Festival PERFORMING ARTS
(www.adelaidecabaretfestival.com) The only one of its kind in the country. Held in June.

Adelaide Guitar Festival MUSIC
(www.adelaideguitarfestival.com.au) Annual axe-fest with a whole lotta rock, classical, country, blues and jazz. In July.

South Australian Living Artists Festival ART
(SALA; www.salafestival.com.au) Progressive exhibitions and displays across town in August (expired artists not allowed).

City to Bay SPORTS
(www.city-bay.org.au) In September there's an annual 12km fun run from the city to Glenelg: much sweat and cardiac duress.

Royal Adelaide Show CULTURAL
(www.theshow.com.au) The agricultural, the horticultural and plenty of carnies and show bags. In September.

OzAsia Festival CULTURAL
(www.ozasiafestival.com.au) Food, arts, conversation, music and the mesmerising Moon Lantern Festival. September.

SANFL Grand Final SPORTS
(www.sanfl.com.au) September is the zenith of the local Aussie Rules football season. Watch it at the Adelaide Oval, watch it at the pub, watch it on TV – just watch it!

Christmas Pageant CULTURAL
(www.cupageant.com.au) An Adelaide institution for 70-plus years – kitschy floats, bands and marching troupes occupy city streets for a day in (oddly) November.

Feast Festival GAY & LESBIAN
(www.feast.org.au) Adelaide's big-ticket gay-and-lesbian festival happens over two weeks in November, with a carnival, theatre, dialogue and dance.

Sleeping

Most of Adelaide's budget accommodation is in the city centre, but in a town this easy to navigate, staying outside the CBD is viable. North Adelaide is under the flight path, but is low-key. For beachside accommodation, try Glenelg. 'Motel Alley' is along Glen Osmond Rd, the main southeast city access road.

See www.bandbfsa.com.au for B&B listings.

Central Adelaide

My Place HOSTEL $
(Map p714; ☎1800 221 529, 08-8221 5299; www.adelaidehostel.com.au; 257 Waymouth St; dm/tw/d incl breakfast from $26/72/72; P ❄ wi-fi) The antithesis of the big formal operations, My Place has a welcoming, personal vibe and is just a

North Adelaide

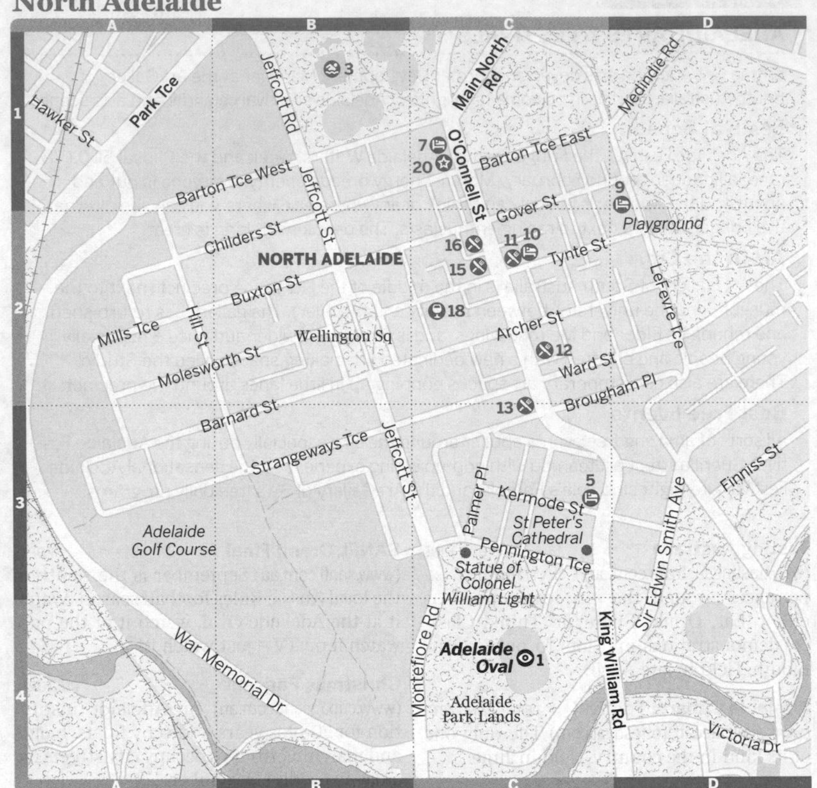

stumble from the Grace Emily, arguably Adelaide's best pub! There's a cosy TV room, a barbecue terrace above the street, free bikes and wi-fi, hiking trips and regular pizza and pub nights – great for solo travellers.

Adelaide Central YHA HOSTEL $
(Map p714; ☎08-8414 3010; www.yha.com.au; 135 Waymouth St; dm from $32, d with/without bathroom from $105/90, f from $130; P ❄ @ 📶) The YHA isn't known for its gregariousness – you'll get plenty of sleep in the spacious and comfortable rooms here. This is a seriously schmick hostel with great security, a roomy kitchen and lounge area, and immaculate bathrooms. A real step up from the average backpackers around town. Parking from $10 per day.

Backpack Oz HOSTEL $
(Map p714; ☎1800 633 307, 08-8223 3551; www.backpackoz.com.au; cnr Wakefield & Pulteney Sts; dm/s/d/tw/tr $26/65/70/75/105; ❄ @ 📶) It doesn't look like much externally, but this converted pub (the old Orient Hotel) strikes the right balance between party and placid. There are spacious dorms and an additional no-frills guesthouse over the road (good for couples). Get a coldie and shoot some pool in the bar. Lots of free stuff, too: breakfast, wi-fi, bikes, linen and Wednesday night BBQ.

Hostel 109 HOSTEL $
(Map p714; ☎1800 099 318, 08-8223 1771; www.hostel109.com; 109 Carrington St; dm/s/tw/d/tr $30/65/75/90/105; ❄ @ 📶) A small, well-managed hostel in a quiet corner of town, with a couple of little balconies over the street and a cosy kitchen/communal area. Spotlessly clean and super-friendly, with lockers, good security and gas cooking. The only negative: rooms open onto light wells rather than the outside world. Free on-street parking after 5pm.

Hotel Metropolitan PUB $
(Map p714; ☎08-8231 5471; www.hotelmetro.com.au; 46 Grote St; s/tw/d/f from $55/90/90/180; 📶) The 1883 Metropolitan pub has 26 rooms upstairs, with stripy linen, high ceilings, little

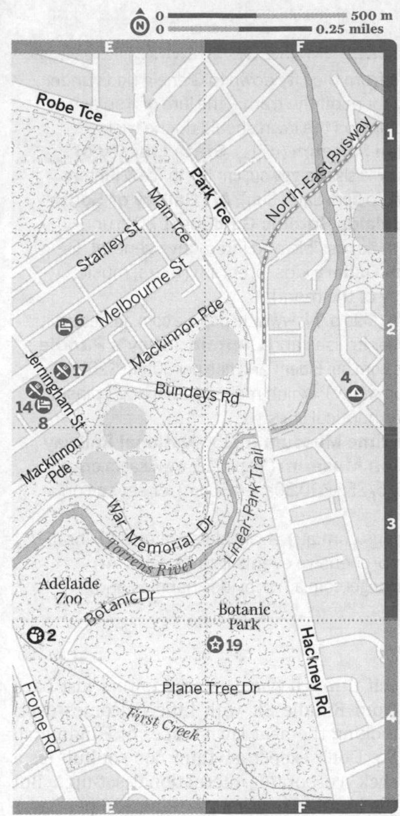

North Adelaide

flat-screen TVs and various bedding configurations. 'It used to be quite an experience staying here...' says the barman, raising his eyebrows. We're not sure what he meant, but these days you can expect a decent budget sleep in a beaut location. Shared bathrooms.

Adelaide Backpackers Inn HOSTEL $
(Map p714; 1800 099 318, 08-8223 6635; www.abpi.com.au; 112 Carrington St; dm from $27;) A relaxed, decent hostel filling out an 1841 pub (the ol' Horse & Jockey) that's had a recent facelift; new bathrooms, fridges, carpets, washing machines, snappy paint colours etc. Handy to Hutt and Rundle Sts. There are cars and mopeds for rent, and free bikes to borrow. Free on-street parking after 5pm.

★ **Adabco Boutique Hotel** BOUTIQUE HOTEL $$
(Map p714; 08-8100 7500; www.adabcohotel.com.au; 223 Wakefield St; d from $139;) This excellent, stone-clad boutique hotel – built in 1894 in high Venetian Gothic style – has at various times been an Aboriginal education facility, a rollerskating rink and an abseiling venue! These days you can expect three levels of lovely rooms with interesting art and quality linen, plus complimentary breakfast, free wi-fi and smiling staff. A top choice.

Hotel Richmond HOTEL $$
(Map p714; 08-8215 4444; www.hotelrichmond.com.au; 128 Rundle Mall; d from $140;) This opulent hotel in a grand 1920s building in the middle of Rundle Mall has mod-minimalist rooms with king-sized beds, marble bathrooms, and American oak and Italian furnishings. Oh, and that hotel rarity – opening windows. Rates include movies and newspapers. Parking from $20 per day.

Clarion Hotel Soho HOTEL $$
(Map p714; 08-8412 5600; www.clarionhotelsoho.com.au; 264 Flinders St; d from $145;) Attempting to conjure up the vibe of London's Soho district, these plush suites in Adelaide's East End (some with spas, most with balconies) are complemented

ADELAIDE FOR CHILDREN

There are few kids who won't love the **tram ride** from the city down to Glenelg (kids under five ride for free!). You may have trouble getting them off the tram – the lure of a splash in the shallows at the **beach** then some fish and chips on the lawn should do the trick.

During school holidays, the **South Australian Museum** (p711), **State Library of South Australia** (Map p714; 08-8207 7250; www.slsa.sa.gov.au; cnr North Tce & Kintore Ave, 1st fl; 10am-8pm Mon-Wed, to 6pm Thu & Fri, to 5pm Sat & Sun), **Art Gallery of South Australia** (p710), **Adelaide Zoo** (p711) and **Adelaide Botanic Gardens** (p711) run inspired kid- and family-oriented programs with accessible and interactive general displays. The Art Gallery also runs a **START at the Gallery** kids' program (tours, music, activities) from noon to 3pm on the first Sunday of the month.

Down on the River Torrens there are **Popeye** (Map p714; www.thepopeye.com.au; return adult/child $12/6, one way $4/2; 10am-4pm) river cruises and **Captain Jolley's Paddle Boats** (Map p714; www.captainjolleyspaddleboats.com.au; Elder Park; hire per 30min $20; 9.30am-6pm daily summer, 10am-4pm Sat & Sun winter), which make a satisfying splash. **Rymill Park Rowboats** (p717) are along similar nautical lines.

In Port Adelaide, you can check out the **Maritime Museum** (p715), **National Railway Museum** (p716) or **South Australian Aviation Museum** (Map p712; www.saam.org.au; 66 Lipson St, Port Adelaide; adult/child/family $10/5/25; 10.30am-4.30pm), or set sail on a **dolphin-spotting cruise**.

The free monthly paper **Child** (www.childmags.com.au), available at cafes and libraries, is largely advertorial, but does contain comprehensive events listings. **Dial-An-Angel** (1300 721 111, 08-8267 3700; www.dialanangel.com.au) provides nannies and babysitters to all areas.

by sumptuous linen, 24-hour room service, Italian marble bathrooms, jet pool and a fab restaurant. Rates take a tumble midweek. Parking from $20; free wi-fi.

Franklin Central Apartments APARTMENTS $$
(Map p714; 1300 662 288, 08-8221 7050; www.franklinapartments.com.au; 36 Franklin St; 1-/2-/3-bedroom apt from $148/199/298; P ❄ ᯤ) This old red-brick office building has heaps of charm, and now houses five levels of good-value downtown apartments with smart interiors. The marketing angle sways towards corporate, but the location and rates spell 'h-o-l-i-d-a-y'. Parking $15 per day.

Adelaide City Park Motel MOTEL $$
(Map p714; 08-8223 1444; www.citypark.com.au; 471 Pulteney St; d with/without bathroom from $110/88, f from $210; P ❄ ᯤ) One of the better motels around town (there are surprisingly few that pass muster), with immaculate bathrooms, leather lounges and winsome French prints. An easy walk to the Hutt St restaurants, and well-placed for the freeway to the Adelaide Hills and Melbourne. Free parking, DVDs and wi-fi, too.

Crowne Plaza Adelaide HOTEL $$
(Map p714; 08-8206 8888; www.crowneplaza.com/adelaide; 16 Hindmarsh Sq; d from $180; P ❄ @ ᯤ) The Crowne Plaza spreads itself through two 14-storey towers just back from Rundle St, with little balconies overlooking the neat lawn-scapes of Hindmarsh Sq. Don't exepct anything too soulful: it's a slick, corporate, international set-up... But the location is primo. Parking $36 per day.

Roof Garden Hotel HOTEL $$$
(Map p714; 1800 008 499, 08-8100 4400; www.majestichotels.com.au; 55 Frome St; d from $200; P ❄ @ ᯤ) Everything looks new in this central, Japanese-themed place. Book a room facing Frome St for a balcony and the best views, or take a bottle of wine up to the namesake rooftop garden to watch the sunset. Free wif-fi and good walk-in and last-minute rates. Parking from $20 per day.

North Adelaide

Princes Lodge Motel MOTEL $
(Map p720; 08-8267 5566; www.princeslodge.com.au; 73 LeFevre Tce, North Adelaide; s/d/f incl breakfast from $65/85/145; P ❄ ᯤ) In a grand 1913 house overlooking the parklands, this friendly, eclectic lodge has high ceilings, new TVs and a faded grandeur. Close to the chichi North Adelaide restaurants and within walking distance of the city, this is a great value motel with heaps of character. The budget rooms in the old coachhouse out the back are a steal.

Minima Hotel HOTEL **$$**
(Map p720; ☎08-8334 7766; www.majestichotels.com.au; 146 Melbourne St, North Adelaide; d from $100; P❄@wi-fi) A spaceship has landed in ye olde North Adelaide! The Minima offers compact but stylish rooms, each decorated by a different SA artist, in a winning Melbourne St location. Check-in is DIY – use the touch screen in the lobby. Limited parking from $10 per night.

Greenways Apartments APARTMENTS **$$**
(Map p720; ☎08-8267 5903; www.greenwaysapartments.com.au; 41-45 King William Rd, North Adelaide; 1-/2-/3-bedroom apt $127/168/220; P❄wi-fi) These 1938 apartments ain't flash, but if you have a pathological hatred of slick, 21st-century open-plan 'lifestyles', then Greenways is for you! And where else can you stay in clean, perfectly operational apartments so close to town at these rates? It's a must for cricket fans, as the Adelaide Oval is a lofted hook shot away – book early for Test matches.

O'Connell Inn MOTEL **$$**
(Map p720; ☎08-8239 0766; www.oconnellinn.com.au; 197 O'Connell St, North Adelaide; d/f from $155/185; P❄wi-fi) It's absurdly difficult to find a decent motel in Adelaide (most are mired in the '90s), but this one makes a reasonable fist of the new century. It's smallish, friendly, affordable and in a beaut location – handy for forays north to the Barossa, Clare, Flinders etc.

Tynte Street Apartments APARTMENTS **$$**
(Map p720; ☎1800 779 919, 08-8334 7783; www.majestichotels.com.au; 82 Tynte St, North Adelaide; d & 1-bedroom apt from $140; P❄wi-fi) A complex of 24 postmodern, red-brick, self-contained apartments on a tree-lined street near the O'Connell St cafes and pubs, sleeping three. Check-in is 1km away at the affiliated **Old Lion Apartments** (Map p720; ☎1800 779 919, 08-8334 7799; 9 Jerningham St, North Adelaide; d from $145, 1-/2-/3-bedroom apt from $155/205/305; P❄wi-fi). Free parking and wi-fi to boot.

Inner Suburbs

Levi Park Caravan Park CARAVAN PARK **$**
(Map p712; ☎08-8344 2209; www.levipark.com.au; 1a Harris Rd, Vale Park; unpowered/powered sites from $36/38, cabins/apt from $105/145; P❄@wi-fi) This leafy, grassy park is 4km from town and loaded with facilities, including tennis courts and a palm-fringed cricket oval. Apartments are in the restored Vale House, purportedly Adelaide's oldest residence!

Adelaide Caravan Park CARAVAN PARK **$**
(Map p720; ☎08-8363 1566; www.adelaidecaravanpark.com.au; 46 Richmond St, Hackney; powered sites $35-40, cabins & units from $129; P❄wi-fi pool) A compact, no-frills park on the River Torrens, rather surprisingly slotted in on a quiet street 2km northeast of the city centre. Clean and well run, with a bit of green grass if it's not too far into summer.

Watson BOUTIQUE HOTEL **$$**
(Map p712; ☎1800 278 468, 08-7087 9666; www.artserieshotels.com.au/watson; 33 Warwick St, Walkerville; d from $155, B&B from $205; P❄wi-fi pool) Brand new in 2014, the Watson (named after Indigenous artist Tommy Watson, whose works dazzle here) is a sassy, multilevel 24-unit complex 4km north of the CBD in Walkerville (an easy commute). There's a gym, a lap pool, 24-hour concierge, bike-hire…but the simple fact that it's a new boutique hotel in unchanging Adelaide was enough to grab our attention! Nice one.

Glenelg, Port Adelaide & Around

Glenelg Holiday & Corporate Letting (☎08-8376 1934; www.glenelgholiday.com.au; ❄) and **Glenelg Letting Agency** (☎08-8294 9666; www.baybeachfront.com.au; ❄) offer self-contained beachside apartments in Glenelg from around $140 per night.

Glenelg Beach Hostel HOSTEL **$**
(Map p712; ☎1800 359 181, 08-8376 0007; www.glenelgbeachhostel.com.au; 1-7 Moseley St, Glenelg; dm/s/d/f from $25/60/70/110; @wi-fi) A couple of streets back from the beach, this beaut old terrace (1879) is Adelaide's budget golden child. Fan-cooled rooms maintain period details and are mostly bunk-free. There's cold Coopers in the basement bar (live music on weekends), open fireplaces, lofty ceilings, girls-only dorms and a courtyard garden. Book *waaay* in advance in summer.

Port Adelaide Backpackers HOSTEL **$**
(Map p712; ☎08-8447 6267; www.portadelaidebackpackers.com.au; 24 Nile St, Port Adelaide; dm/s/d from $19/60/65; ❄wi-fi) We're unashamed fans of Port Adelaide, and it gladdens the heart to see a new backpackers here. Still a work-in-progress when we visited – abuzz with painting, tiling, and general upgrading – we have high hopes for this re-imagined, bricky seaman's lodge in the Port's historic hub. Tell us how things are shaping up! Free wi-fi and on-street parking.

BIG4 Adelaide Shores CARAVAN PARK $

(Map p712; ☎1800 444 567, 08-8355 7320; www.adelaideshores.com.au; 1 Military Rd, West Beach; powered sites $38-53, eco-tents $92, 1-/2-/3-bed cabins from $105/141/245; P ❄ @ 🛜 🏊) Hunkered-down behind the West Beach dunes, with a walking/cycling track extending to Glenelg (3.4km) in one direction and Henley Beach (3.5km) in the other, this is a choice spot in summer. There are lush sites, permanent eco-tents, glistening amenities and passing dolphins.

★ **Largs Pier Hotel** HOTEL $$

(Map p712; ☎08-8449 5666; www.largspierhotel.com.au; 198 Esplanade, Largs Bay; d/f/apt from $164/184/199; P ❄ 🛜) What a surprise! In the snoozy beach 'burb of Largs Bay, 5km north of Port Adelaide, is this gorgeous, 130-year-old, three-storey wedding-cake hotel. After extensive renovations, it's looking great: sky-high ceilings, big beds, taupe-and-chocolate colours and beach views. There's also a low-slung wing of motel rooms off to one side, and some apartments across the street.

Oaks Plaza Pier HOTEL, APARTMENTS $$

(Map p712; ☎1300 551 111, 08-8350 6688; www.oakshotelsresorts.com; 16 Holdfast Promenade, Glenelg; d from $185, 1-/2-/3-bedroom apt from $210/299/499; P ❄ 🛜) The pick of the multi-level apartment buildings along the Glenelg foreshore, the eight-storey Oaks Plaza Pier offers flashy corporate-style rooms, free wi-fi, sea-view balconies, bars and restaurants (but no pier). Parking $20.

Seawall Apartments APARTMENTS $$$

(Map p712; ☎08-8295 1197; www.seawallapartments.com.au; 21-25 South Esplanade, Glenelg; 1-/2-/3-/4-bed apts from $200/329/499/599; P ❄ 🛜) This renovated row of old houses is a five-minute wander along the sea wall from Moseley Sq in Glenelg. They really didn't need a gimmick – the location seals the deal – but the facades are festooned with kitsch nautical paraphernalia (anchors, boats, oars, shark jaws...). Inside the apartments are roomy, contemporary and immaculate.

Eating

Foodies flock to West End hotspots such as Gouger St (pronounced 'goo-jer'), Chinatown and the food-filled Central Market. There are some great pubs here too. Arty/alternative Hindley St – Adelaide's dirty little secret – has a smattering of good eateries. In the East End, Rundle St and Hutt St offer al fresco cafes and people-watching. North Adelaide's Melbourne and O'Connell Sts have a healthy spread of bistros, cafes and pubs.

Central Adelaide

Central Market MARKET $

(Map p714; www.adelaidecentralmarket.com.au; Gouger St; ⏲7am-5.30pm Tue, 9am-5.30pm Wed & Thu, 7am-9pm Fri, 7am-3pm Sat) This place is an exercise in sensory bombardment: a barrage of smells, colours and yodelling stallholders selling fresh vegetables, breads, cheeses, seafood and gourmet produce. Cafes, hectic food courts, a supermarket and Adelaide's Chinatown are here, too.

Zen Kitchen VIETNAMESE $

(Map p714; ☎08-8232 3542; www.facebook.com/zenkitchenadelaide; Unit 7, Tenancy 2, Renaissance Arc; mains $5-11; ⏲10.30am-4.30pm Mon-Thu, 10.30am-8pm Fri, 11am-3pm Sat) Superb, freshly constructed cold rolls, *pho* soups and super-crunchy barbecue-pork bread rolls, eat-in or take away. Wash it all down with a cold coconut milk or a teeth-grindingly strong Vietnamese coffee with sugary condensed milk. Authentic, affordable and delicious.

Café Troppo CAFE $

(Map p714; ☎08-8211 8812; www.cafetroppoadelaide.com; 42 Whitmore Sq; mains $9-16; ⏲7.30am-4pm Tue-Fri, 9am-4pm Sat & Sun; 🛜) 🍃 Breathing new vigour into Whitmore Sq, the least utilised of central Adelaide's five squares, corner-cafe Troppo has jaunty exposed timberwork and a sustainable outlook (local ingredients, recycling, organic milk, ecofriendly cleaning products etc). The coffee is fab, and so are their marinated kangaroo and haloumi sandwiches, and baked eggs with spinach and local Swiss-style cheese.

Lucia's Pizza & Spaghetti Bar ITALIAN $

(Map p714; ☎08-8231 2260; www.lucias.com.au; 2 Western Mall, Central Market; meals $8-14; ⏲7am-4pm Mon-Thu & Sat, to 9pm Fri) This little slice of Italy has been around since Lucia was a lot younger. All her pasta, sauces and pizzas are authentically homemade. If you like what you're eating, you can buy fresh pasta next door at Lucia's Fine Foods.

Vego And Loven' It VEGETARIAN $

(Map p714; www.vegoandlovenit.webs.com; Level 1, 240 Rundle St; meals $7-14; ⏲10am-4pm Mon-Fri; 🖉) Get your weekly vitamins disguised in a scrumptious vegie burger, wrap or focaccia at this arty upstairs kitchen. Dreadlocked urban renegades order 'extra alfalfa but no hummus'. Look for the mosaic sign and take the skinny stairs.

Jerusalem Sheshkabab House MIDDLE EASTERN $
(Map p714; ☎08-8212 6185; 131b Hindley St; mains $10-15; ⊙noon-2pm & 5.30-10pm Tue-Sun; ✎) A skinny Hindley St room that's been here forever, serving magnificent Middle Eastern and Lebanese delights: falafels, hummus, tabouleh, tahini and (of course) sheshkababs. The plastic furniture and draped tent material are appropriately tacky.

★**Peel Street** MODERN AUSTRALIA, ASIAN $$
(Map p714; ☎08-8231 8887; www.peelst.com.au; 9 Peel St; mains $20-30, tasting menu $68; ⊙7.30am-3pm Mon-Fri, 6.30pm-late Thu-Sat) A long-neglected service lane in Adelaide's West End, Peel St has spawned a slew of new bar-eateries recently, the first (and still best) of which is Peel Street itself, a supercool cafe-bistro–wine bar that just keeps packing 'em in. Glam city girls sit at window seats nibbling parmesan-crumbed parsnips and turkey meatballs with preserved lemon. Killer wine list.

Pizza e Mozzarella Bar ITALIAN $$
(Map p714; ☎08-8164 1003; www.pizzaemozzarellabar.com.au; 33 Pirie St; pizzas $19-23, mains $20-36; ⊙11.30am-3pm Mon-Thu, 1.30-9.30pm Fri, 5.30-9.30pm Sat) Everything at this split-level, rustic Italian eatery – adorned with bread baskets and terracotta; beautified by Italian staff and leadlight – is cooked in the wood oven you see when you walk in the door. Pizzas are thin-based (Roma style); mozzarella plates come with wood-oven bread and meats (octopus, tuna, salumi). Super Italian/SA wine and beer list. Just super!

Jasmin Indian Restaurant INDIAN $$
(Map p714; ☎08-8223 7837; www.jasmin.com.au; basement, 31 Hindmarsh Sq; mains $17-29; ⊙noon-2.30pm Thu & Fri, 5.30-9pm Tue-Sat) Magical North Indian curries and consummately professional staff (they might remember your name from when you ate here in 2011). There's nothing too surprising about the menu, but it's done to absolute perfection. Bookings essential.

Earth's Kitchen VEGETARIAN $$
(Map p714; ☎08-8215 0458; www.kitchensonearthcommunities.com.au; 131 Pirie St; mains $17-21; ⊙7am-4pm Mon-Thu, 7am-9pm Fri, 9.30am-2.30pm Sat; ✎) An alternative to the myriad glass-and-granite lunch spots around town, this hippie cafe – all terracotta, hessian sacks and racks of organic produce – serves beaut salads, dips and pizzas. It's almost all vegetarian, but we couldn't go past the spicy braised kangaroo pizza with roast capsicum and mozzarella.

DON'T MISS

SA WINE REGIONS

Let's cut to the chase: we all know why you're here. South Australian wines are arguably the best in the world, and there's no shortage of wine regions – both established and emerging – in which to taste them. Most of them are but a day trip away from Adelaide.

Adelaide Hills (p733) Impressive cool-climate wines in Adelaide's back yard.

Barossa Valley (p758) Old-school estates and famous reds.

Clare Valley (p763) Niche riesling vintages and cosy weekend retreats.

Coonawarra (p778) Lip-smacking cabernet sauvignon on the Limestone Coast plains.

McLaren Vale (p737) Awesome shiraz and vine-covered hillsides rolling down to the sea.

Mesa Lunga MEDITERRANEAN $$
(Map p714; ☎08 8410 7617; www.mesalunga.com; cnr Gouger & Morphett Sts; tapas $4-19, mains $18-31; ⊙noon-3pm Fri, noon-late Sun, 6pm-late Tue-Sat) In a fishbowl corner room with a dark-wood wine wall, sassy Mesa Lunga serves tapas and quality pizzas. Order some *gamba* (black-salted prawn and chorizo in pastry) and Manzanillo olives stuffed with anchovies, washed down with some sparkling sangria. Magic.

Ying Chow CHINESE $$
(Map p714; ☎08-8211 7998; 114 Gouger St; mains $11-24; ⊙noon-2.45pm Fri, 5pm-midnight daily) This fluoro-lit, bossy-staffed eatery is a culinary gem; serving cuisine styled from the Guangzhou region, such as 'BBC' (bean curd, broad beans and Chinese chutney) and steamed duck with salty sauce. It gets packed – with queues out the door (no bookings) – but it's worth the wait.

Amalfi Pizzeria Ristorante ITALIAN $$
(Map p714; ☎08-8223 1948; 29 Frome St; mains $17-32; ⊙noon-2.30pm Mon-Fri, 5.30-10.30pm Mon-Sat) This classic old joint has been around since the days when Adelaide phone numbers only had seven digits. Authentic pizza and pasta with bentwood chairs, terrazzo floors, specials scribbled on a chalkboard, sleep-defeating coffee and imagined Mafioso mutterings in the back room.

T-Chow CHINESE $$
(Map p714; ☎08-8410 1413; www.tchow.eatout-adelaide.com.au; 68 Moonta St; mains $13-25; ⏲11am-3pm & 5-11pm; ✍) Big, bright and brassy: quick-fire Chinese on the main Chinatown strip, with an impressive menu ranging from the predictable (braised beef hotpot, steamed garlic prawns) to the fearless (pork intestines with salted cabbage, tender duck with 'most fats drained'). Yum-cha daily 11am to 3pm.

★ **Press** MODERN AUSTRALIAN $$$
(Map p714; ☎08-8211 8048; www.pressfoodandwine.com.au; 40 Waymouth St; mains $16-48; ⏲noon-late Mon-Sat) The best of an emerging strip of restaurants on office-heavy Waymouth St. Super-stylish (brick, glass, lemon-coloured chairs) and not afraid of offal (pan-fried lamb's brains, grilled calf's tongue) or things raw (beef carpaccio, gravlax salmon) and confit (duck leg, onion, olives). Tasting menu $68 per person. Book for upstairs seating only; otherwise they'll fit you downstairs near the bar.

Sosta ARGENTINE $$$
(Map p714; ☎08-8232 6799; www.sostaargentiniankitchen.com.au; 291 Rundle St; tapas $16-26, mains $33-45; ⏲noon-2.30pm Mon-Fri, 6pm-late daily) Beef, lamb, pork, chicken, fish... vegetarians run for the hills! Sosta's aged 1kg T-bone steaks are legendary. With crisp white tablecloths and blood-brown floorboards, it's an elegant place to launch your nocturnal East End foray.

North Adelaide

O'Connell St General SUPERMARKET, DELI $
(Map p720; www.foodland.net.au; 113 O'Connell St, North Adelaide; ⏲8am-10pm) A Foodland supermarket with a nifty deli/butcher counter out the front.

★ **Gin Long Canteen** ASIAN $$
(Map p720; ☎08-7120 2897; www.ginlongcanteen.com.au; 42 O'Connell St, North Adelaide; small plates $5-13, mains $18-24; ⏲noon-2.30pm Tue-Fri, 5.30pm-late Tue-Sat) This energetic food room is a winner. Chipper staff allocate you a space at the communal tables (no bookings) and take your order pronto. The food arrives just as fast: fab curries, slow-braised Thai beef and pork, netted spring rolls, Malay curry puffs... It's a pan-Asian vibe, bolstered by jumbo bottles of Vietnamese beer and smiles all round.

Store CAFE, BISTRO $$
(Map p720; ☎08-8361 6999; www.thestore.com.au; 157 Melbourne St, North Adelaide; breakfast $10-20, mains $15-28; ⏲7am-3pm Mon, 7am-10pm Tue-Fri, 8am-10pm Sat, 8am-3pm Sun; ✍) Store is an enticing combo of casual Parisian bistro and jazzy cafe. The vibe is retro-kitsch (art nouveau posters, stag horns, Tretchikoff prints), while on your plate you can expect rapid-fire pastas, risottos, burgers and classy fish, chicken and beef dishes, none of which will break the bank. Impressive wine list, too.

Royal Oak PUB FOOD $$
(Map p720; ☎08-8267 2488; www.royaloakhotel.com.au; 123 O'Connell St, North Adelaide; mains $18-29; ⏲8am-noon Sat & Sun, noon-3pm & 6-9pm daily) Winning pub grub at this enduring (and endearing) local: steak sangers (sandwiches), vegie lasagne, lamb-shank pie, pulled-pork buns and French toast with maple syrup (not all at once). There's a quirky retro vibe, and live jazz/indie-rock Tuesday, Wednesday, Friday and Sunday.

Amarin Thai THAI $$
(Map p720; ☎08-8239 0026; www.theamarinthai.com.au; 108 Tynte St, North Adelaide; mains $13-27; ⏲noon-2.30pm Wed-Fri, 6-9.30pm daily) Unpretentious and reliable neighbourhood Thai just off the main North Adelaide strip. The scatter of mustard-coloured chairs on the footpath is the place to be on a warm night.

Lion Hotel PUB FOOD $$$
(Map p720; ☎08-8367 0222; www.thelionhotel.com; 161 Melbourne St, North Adelaide; mains $38-43; ⏲noon-3pm Mon-Fri & Sun, 6-10pm Mon-Sat) Off to one side of this upmarket boozer (all big screens, beer terraces and business types) is a sassy restaurant with a cool retro interior and romantic vibes. Hot off the menu are luscious Coorong Angus steaks, market fish and chilli prawn fettuccine, served with very unpubby professionalism. Breakfast is available next door in the bar (mains $10 to $21) from 8am to noon Monday to Friday, and 8am to 3pm on weekends.

Inner Suburbs

Bar 9 CAFE $
(Map p712; ☎08-8373 1108; www.bar9.com.au; 96 Glen Osmond Rd, Parkside; mains $9-18; ⏲7.30am-4pm Mon-Fri, 8.30am-2pm Sat & Sun) If you're serious about coffee, this bean barn – a short hop southeast of the city centre – is for you. Food is almost secondary here: the hipster, cardigan-wearing customers are too busy

discussing the coffee-specials board to eat. But if you are hungry, they do a mean bacon and eggs, vanilla bircher muesli, or truffled mushrooms on toast.

Café de Vili's FAST FOOD $
(Map p712; www.vilis.com; 2 14 Manchester St, Mile End Sth; meals $4-14; 24hr) Vili's pies are a South Australian institution. Next to its factory, just west of the CBD, is this all-night diner, serving equally iconic pie floaters (a meat pie floating in pea soup, topped with mashed potato, gravy and sauce – outstanding!), plus sausage rolls, pasties, burgers, pancakes, cooked breakfasts, custard tarts, donuts...

Parwana Afghan Kitchen AFGHAN $$
(Map p712; 08-8443 9001; www.parwana.com.au; 124b Henley Beach Rd, Torrensville; mains $14-25; 6-10pm Tue-Thu & Sun, 6-10.30pm Fri & Sat) Nutty, spicy, slippery and a little bit funky: Afghan food is unique, and this authentic restaurant, west of the CBD across the parklands, is a great place to try it. The signature *banjaan borani* eggplant dish is a knockout. There's also a lunchtime branch just off Rundle St in the city called **Kutchi Deli Parwana** (Map p714; 08-7225 8586; 7 Ebenezer Pl; 11.30am-4pm Mon-Fri). BYO; cash only.

Jarmer's Kitchen CAFE, MODERN AUSTRALIAN $$
(Map p712; 08-8340 1055; www.jarmerskitchen.com.au; 18 Park Tce, Bowden; mains $11-33; 7.30am-4pm Mon, 7.30am-10pm Tue-Fri, 8am-10pm Sat, 8am-4pm Sun) This flagship eatery heralds the newly redeveloped Bowden, a city-edge suburb once an industrial wasteland, now home to hundreds of hip new town houses and the hip urbanites who live in them. Jarmer's is a fancy day/night cafe in an old pub building, serving savvy sandwiches, pastas, burgers and substantial mains: try the pork-and-fennel sausages. Terrific wine list, too.

Glenelg

Zest Cafe Gallery CAFE $
(Map p712; 08-8295 3599; www.zestcafegallery.com.au; 2a Sussex St, Glenelg; meals $9-17; 7.30am-5pm Mon-Sat, 8am-5pm Sun;) Little sidestreet Zest has a laid-back vibe and brilliant breakfasts – more than enough compensation for any shortcomings in size. Baguettes and bagels are crammed with creative combos, or you can banish your hangover with some 'Hell's Eggs': baked in a ramekin with rosemary, tomato salsa, cheese and Tabasco sauce. Great coffee, arty staff, and vegetarian specials, too.

Good Life PIZZA $$
(Map p712; 08-8376 5900; www.goodlifepizza.com; Level 1, cnr Jetty Rd & Moseley St, Glenelg; pizzas $14-35; noon-2.30pm Tue-Fri & Sun, 6pm-late daily;) At this brilliant organic pizzeria above the Jetty Rd tram-scape, thin crusts are stacked with tasty toppings like free-range roast duck, Spencer Gulf prawns and spicy Hahndorf salami. *Ahhh,* life is good... Also has branches in the **city** (Map p714; 08-8223 2618; 170 Hutt St; pizzas $14-35; noon-2.30pm Mon-Fri, 6pm-late daily;) and **North Adelaide** (Map p720; 08-8267 3431; Shop 5, 11 O'Connell St, North Adelaide; pizzas $14-35; noon-2.30pm Tue-Thu, 6pm-late Tue-Sun;) .

Zucca Greek Mezze GREEK $$
(Map p712; 08-8376 8222; www.zucca.com.au; Shop 5, Marina Pier, Holdfast Shores, Glenelg; mezze $5-24, mains $17-48; noon-3pm & 6pm-late) Spartan linen, marina views, super service and a contemporary menu of tapas-style mezze plates – you'd struggle to find anything this classy on Santorini. The grilled Hindmarsh Valley haloumi with spiced raisins and the seared scallops with feta and pistachio are sublime.

Drinking & Nightlife

Rundle St has a few iconic pubs, while in the West End, Hindley St's red-light sleaze collides with the hip bars on Leigh and Peel Sts. Cover charges at clubs can be anything from free to $15, depending on the night. Most clubs close Monday to Thursday.

Central Adelaide

★**Exeter Hotel** PUB
(Map p714; 08-8223 2623; www.facebook.com; 246 Rundle St; 8am-late) Adelaide's best pub, this legendary boozer attracts an eclectic mix of postwork, punk and uni drinkers, shaking the day off their backs. Pull up a stool at the bar, or a table in the grungy beer garden, and settle in for the evening. Original music nightly (indie, electronica, acoustic); no pokies. Book for curry nights in the upstairs restaurant (usually Wednesdays).

★**Grace Emily Hotel** PUB
(Map p714; www.graceemilyhotel.com.au; 232 Waymouth St; 4pm-late) Duking it out with the Exeter Hotel for the title of 'Adelaide's Best Pub' (it pains us to separate the two) the Gracie has live music most nights (alt-rock,

country, acoustic, open-mic nights), kooky '50s-meets-voodoo decor, open fires and great beers. Regular cult cinema; no pokies. Are the Bastard Sons of Ruination playing tonight?

Downtown HDCB BAR

(Map p714; ☎08-8212 7334; www.facebook.com/DowntownHDCB; 99 Hindley St; ⏰noon-midnight Wed-Fri, 6pm-2am Sat) HDCB equals Hot Dogs, Cold Beer. You'll find plenty of each inside this slender Hindley St bar, plus walls spangled with vintage music posters and tattooed DJs playing rock and hip hop. It's something different for Hindley St – a beacon of grit and substance amidst the strip clubs, fluoro-lit convenience stores, sex shops and mainstream beer barns.

Cork Wine Cafe WINE BAR

(Map p714; www.corkwinecafe.com.au; 61a Gouger St; ⏰4pm-midnight Mon-Thu, 3pm-1am Fri & Sat) A down-sized, Frenchie hole-in-the-wall wine bar, unexpected among the fluoro-lit Chinese restaurants along this stretch of Gouger St. Well-worn floorboards, Bentwood chairs, absinthe posters…perfect for a quick vino before dinner (see fluoro-lit Chinese restaurants, above).

Udaberri BAR

(Map p714; www.udaberri.com.au; 11-13 Leigh St; ⏰4pm-late Tue-Thu, 3pm-late Fri, 6pm-late Sat) Taking a leaf out of the Melbourne book on laneside boozing, nouveau-industrial Udaberri is a compact bar on Leigh St, serving Spanish wines by the glass, good beers on tap and *pintxos* (Basque bar snacks) like oysters, cheeses, *jamon* and tortillas. The crowd is cashed-up and city-centric.

Howling Owl BAR, CAFE

(Map p714; www.thehowlingowl.com.au; 13 Frome St; ⏰8.30am-6pm Mon & Tue, 8.30am-late Wed-Fri, noon-late Sat) Gin, anyone? This cafe/bar keeps the caffeine coming by day, then slows the pace by night with a devastatingly good selection of 'mother's ruin', infused with everything from coriander to cardamom. SA beers and wines too, plus quirky tunes, a brilliant booth seat at the back and offbeat urban drinkers. Another gin, anyone?

Clever Little Taylor BAR

(Map p714; www.cleverlittletailor.com.au; 19 Peel St; ⏰4pm-late) CLT was one of the vanguard which ushered in a new brigade of small bars in Adelaide's lanes. Good liquor is the thrust here, along with fine SA wines and a hip brick-and-stone renovation (no prizes for guessing what this space used to be). Zippy bar food, too.

Apothecary 1878 WINE BAR

(Map p714; www.theapothecary1878.com.au; 118 Hindley St; ⏰5pm-late) Classy coffee and wine at this gorgeous chemist-turned-bar, dating from (you guessed it) 1878. Dark-timber medicine cabinets and Parisian marble-topped tables: perfect first-date territory.

Tasting Room WINE BAR

(Map p714; www.eastendcellars.com.au; 25 Vardon Ave; ⏰9am-7pm Mon & Tue, 9am-9pm Wed & Thu, 9am-10pm Fri, 10am-10pm Sat, noon-7pm Sun) A commercial offshoot of East End Cellars, Adelaide's best bottle shop, this classy new wine room gives you the chance to try before you buy. The range is vast: prop yourself on a window seat, watch beautiful East Enders sashay past, and work your way through it.

Publishers Hotel BAR

(Map p714; www.publishershotel.com.au; cnr Cannon & Franklin Sts; ⏰11am-late Tue-Sat, 3pm-late Sun) 'Established 1914' says the signage. By our reckoning it was closer to 2014… Either way, the Publishers of today is an upmarket bar with white-jacketed bartenders, interesting wines and craft beers (love the Lobethal Bierhaus pilsner from the Adelaide Hills). Weekend DJs spin everything from old soul to Dire Straits (the vibe is very over-30s).

Belgian Beer Café BAR

(Map p714; www.oostende.com.au; 27-29 Ebenezer Pl; ⏰11am-midnight Sun-Thu, to 2am Fri & Sat) There's shiny brass, sexy staff, much presluicing of glasses, and somewhere upwards of 26 imported Belgian superbrews (we lost count…). Order some *moules-frites* to go with your *weiss* beer. Off Rundle St.

Zhivago CLUB

(Map p714; www.zhivago.com.au; 54 Currie St; ⏰9pm-late Fri-Sun) The pick of the West End clubs (there are quite a few of 'em around Light Sq – some are a bit moron-prone), Zhivago's DJs pump out everything from reggae and dub to quality house. Popular with the 18 to 25 dawn patrol.

Lotus Lounge CLUB

(Map p714; www.lotuslounge.net.au; 268 Morphett St; ⏰6pm-late Wed-Sat) We like the signage here – a very minimal fluoro martini glass with a flashing olive. Inside it's a glam lounge with cocktails, quality beers and Adelaide dolls cuttin' the rug. Expect queues around the corner on Saturday nights.

HQ Complex CLUB
(Map p714; www.hqcomplex.com.au; 1 North Tce; ⏲8pm-late Wed, Fri & Sat) Adelaide's biggest club fills five big rooms with shimmering sound and light. Night-time is the right time on Saturdays – the biggest (and trashiest) club night in town. Retro Wednesdays; live acts Fridays.

Mars Bar CLUB
(Map p714; www.themarsbar.com.au; 120 Gouger St; ⏲9pm-late Fri & Sat) The lynchpin of Adelaide's nocturnal gay and lesbian scene, always-busy Mars Bar features glitzy decor, flashy clientele and OTT drag shows.

North Adelaide

Daniel O'Connell PUB
(Map p720; www.danieloconnell.com.au; 165 Tynte St, North Adelaide; ⏲11am-late) An 1881 Irish pub with just enough of a whiff of Celtic kitsch. Great Guinness, open fires, 170-plus SA wines, acoustic music, contemporary menu (mains $12 to $26) and a house-sized pepper tree in the beer garden (168 years old and counting).

Inner Suburbs

★**Wheatsheaf** PUB
(Map p712; www.wheatsheafhotel.com.au; 39 George St, Thebarton; ⏲11am-midnight Mon-Fri, noon-midnight Sat, noon-9pm Sun; 📶) A hidden gem under the flight path in industrial Thebarton, with an arty crowd of students, jazz musos, lesbians, punks and rockers. Tidy beer garden, live music (acoustic, blues, country), open fires and rumours of a new kitchen opening soon. Kick-ass craft beers.

Colonist PUB
(Map p712; www.colonist.com.au; 44 The Parade, Norwood; ⏲9am late) Funky countercultural boozing on Norwood's otherwise mainstream Parade. Wonderfully well-worn, with crafty beers and Gustav Klimt–esque murals. Packed after Norwood FC (Aussie Rules football) games empty out from the ground across the road.

Glenelg

Pier Bar BAR
(Map p712; www.glenelgpier.com.au; 18 Holdfast Promenade, Glenelg; ⏲noon-late Mon-Fri, 11am-late Sat & Sun) A cavernous mainstream sports bar with voyeuristic beach views and fold-back windows for when the sea breeze drops. Has as many screens as staff (there's a lot of each) and raucous Sunday sessions.

☆ Entertainment

Arty Adelaide has a rich cultural life that stacks up favourably with much larger cities.

For listings and reviews see **Adelaide Now** (www.adelaidenow.com.au) and **Adelaide Review** (www.adelaidereview.com.au).

There are a few agencies for big-ticket event bookings:

BASS (☎13 12 46; www.bass.net.au)

Moshtix (☎1300 438 849; www.moshtix.com.au)

Venue Tix (☎08-8225 8888; www.venuetix.com.au)

Live Music

Adelaide knows how to kick out the jams! Top pub venues around town include the Wheatsheaf, Grace Emily (p727) and Exeter Hotel (p727).

The free street-press papers *Rip It Up* (www.ripitup.com.au) and *dB* (www.dbmagazine.com.au) have band and DJ listings and reviews. For gig listings see **Music SA** (www.musicsa.com.au) and **Jazz Adelaide** (www.jazz.adelaide.onau.net).

★**Governor Hindmarsh Hotel** LIVE MUSIC
(Map p712; www.thegov.com.au; 59 Port Rd, Hindmarsh; ⏲11am-late) Ground Zero for live music in Adelaide, The Gov hosts some legendary local and international acts. The odd Irish band fiddles around in the bar, while the main venue features rock, folk, jazz, blues, salsa, reggae and dance. A huge place with an inexplicably personal vibe. Good food, too.

Jive LIVE MUSIC
(Map p714; www.jivevenue.com; 181 Hindley St; ⏲hours vary) In a converted theatre, Jive caters to an off-beat crowd of student types who like their tunes funky, left-field and removed from the mainstream. A sunken dance floor = great views from the bar!

Fowlers Live LIVE MUSIC
(Map p714; www.fowlerslive.com.au; 68 North Tce; ⏲hours vary) Inside the former Fowler Flour Factory, this 500-capacity venue is a devilish temple of hard rock, punk and metal.

Adelaide Entertainment Centre CONCERT VENUE
(Map p712; www.theaec.net; 98 Port Rd, Hindmarsh; ⏲box office 8.30am-5pm Mon-Fri) Around 12,000 bums on seats for everyone from the Wiggles to Stevie Wonder.

Adelaide Symphony Orchestra CLASSICAL
(Map p714; www.aso.com.au; 91 Hindley St; box office 9am-4.30pm Mon-Fri) The estimable ASO: check the website for perfomance info.

Cinema

See www.my247.com.au/adelaide/cinemas for movie listings.

Palace Nova Eastend Cinemas CINEMA
(Map p714; 08-8232 3434; www.palacecinemas.com.au; 250 & 251 Rundle St; tickets adult/child $19.50/15.50; 10am-late) Facing-off across Rundle St, both these cinema complexes screen 'sophisticated cinema': new-release art-house, foreign-language and independent films as well as some mainstream flicks. Fully licensed, too.

Mercury Cinema CINEMA
(Map p714; 08-8410 0979; www.mercurycinema.org.au; 13 Morphett St, Lion Arts Centre; tickets adult/concession $17/13; hours vary) The not-for-profit Mercury screens art-house releases, and is home to the Adelaide Cinémathèque (classic, cult and experimental flicks). Check the website for screen times.

Moonlight Cinema CINEMA
(Map p720; 1300 551 908; www.moonlight.com.au; Botanic Park; tickets adult/child $18/14; 7pm daily mid-Nov–Feb) In summer, pack a picnic and mosquito repellent, and spread out on the lawn to watch old and new classics under the stars. 'Gold Grass' tickets, which cost a little more, secure you a prime-viewing beanbag.

Piccadilly Cinema CINEMA
(Map p720; 08-8267 1500; www.wallis.com.au; 181 O'Connell St, North Adelaide; tickets adult/child $18.50/14; 10am-late) A beaut old art deco cinema on the main North Adelaide strip, with a sexily curved street frontage and chevron-shaped windows spangled across the facade. Mostly mainstream releases.

Theatre & Comedy

See **Adelaide Theatre Guide** (www.theatreguide.com.au) for booking details, venues and reviews for comedy, drama and musicals.

Adelaide Festival Centre PERFORMING ARTS
(Map p714; www.adelaidefestivalcentre.com.au; King William Rd; box office 9am-6pm Mon-Fri) The hub of performing arts in SA, this crystalline white Festival Centre opened in June 1973, four proud months before the Sydney Opera House! The **State Theatre Company** (www.statetheatrecompany.com.au) is based here.

Rhino Room COMEDY
(Map p714; www.rhinoroom.com.au; 13 Frome St; tickets $20-25; 6.30pm-late Mon, Fri & Sat) Live stand-up acts from around Australia and overseas on Friday and Saturday nights, plus open-mic comedy on Mondays.

Sport

As most Australian cities do, Adelaide hangs its hat on the successes of its sporting teams. In the **Australian Football League** (www.afl.com.au), the Adelaide Crows and Port Adelaide Power have sporadic success and play at the Adelaide Oval. Suburban Adelaide teams compete in the confusingly named **South Australian National Football League** (www.sanfl.com.au). The football season runs from March to September.

In the **National Basketball League** (www.nbl.com.au), the Adelaide 36ers have been a force for decades. In netball, the Adelaide Thunderbirds play in the **ANZ Championship** (www.anz-championship.com) with regular success. In soccer's **A League** (www.a-league.com.au), Adelaide United are usually competitive. In summer, under the auspices of **Cricket SA** (www.cricketsa.com.au), the Redbacks play one-day and multiday state matches at the Adelaide Oval. The Redbacks rebrand as the Adelaide Strikers in the national **T20 Big Bash** (www.bigbash.com.au) competition.

Shopping

Shops and department stores line Rundle Mall. The beautiful old arcades between the mall and Grenfell St retain their original splendour and house eclectic little shops. Rundle St and the adjunct Ebenezer Pl are home to boutique and retro clothing shops.

★ **Streetlight** BOOKS, MUSIC
(Map p714; www.facebook.com/streetlightadelaide; 2/15 Vaughan Pl; 10am-6pm Mon-Thu & Sat, 10am-9pm Fri, 11am-5pm Sun) Lefty, arty and subversive in the best possible way, Streetlight is the place to find that elusive Miles Davis disc or Charles Bukowski poetry compilation.

Midwest Trader CLOTHING, ACCESSORIES
(Map p714; www.facebook.com; Shop 1 & 2 Ebenezer Pl; 10am-6pm Mon-Thu & Sat, 10am-9pm Fri, noon-5pm Sun) Stocks a snarling range of punk, skate, vintage, biker and rockabilly gear, plus second-hand cowboy boots. Rock on!

Imprints Booksellers BOOKS
(Map p714; www.imprints.com.au; 107 Hindley St; 9am-6pm Mon-Wed, 9am-9pm Thu & Fri, 9am-5pm Sat, 11am-5pm Sun) The best bookshop

in Adelaide in the worst location (in the thick of the Hindley St strip-club fray)? Jazz, floorboards, Persian rugs and occasional live readings and book launches.

Urban Cow Studio DESIGN
(Map p714; www.urbancow.com.au; 11 Frome St; ⏲10am-6pm Mon-Thu, 10am-9pm Fri, 10am-5pm Sat, noon-5pm Sun) The catch cry here is 'Handmade in Adelaide' – a brilliant assortment of paintings, jewellery, glassware, ceramics and textiles, plus a gallery upstairs. Their 'Heaps Good' T-shirts are appropriately pro-SA on a hot summer's day.

Miss Gladys Sym Choon FASHION
(Map p714; www.missgladyssymchoon.com.au; 235a Rundle St; ⏲9.30am-6.15pm Mon-Thu, 9.30am-9.30pm Fri, 10am-6pm Sat, 10.45am-5.30pm Sun) Named after a famed Rundle St trader from the 1920s, this hip shop is the place for fab frocks, rockin' boots, street-beating sneakers, jewellery, watches and hats.

Jurlique COSMETICS
(Map p714; www.jurlique.com.au; Shop 2Ga, 50 Rundle Mall Plaza; ⏲9am-6pm Mon-Thu, 9am-9pm Fri, 9am-5pm Sat, 11am-5pm Sun) An international success story, SA's own Jurlique sells fragrant skincare products (some Rosewater Balancing Mist, anyone?) that are pricey but worth every cent.

Tarts DESIGN
(Map p714; www.tartscollective.com.au; 10g Gays Arcade, Adelaide Arcade, Rundle Mall; ⏲10am-5pm Mon-Sat) Textiles, jewellery, bags, cards and canvasses from a 35-member local arts co-op. Meet the artists in-store.

Information

EMERGENCY

Ambulance, Fire, Police (☎000) Adelaide's main police station is at 60 Wakefield St.

RAA Emergency Roadside Assistance (☎13 11 11; www.raa.com.au) Car break-down assistance.

INTERNET ACCESS

Arena Internet Café (Level 1, 264 Rundle St; ⏲11am-midnight Mon-Thu, 10am-late Fri-Sun)

Wireless Cafe (53 Hindley St; ⏲7am-7.30am Mon-Fri, 8am-6pm Sat) Hindley St hotspot.

MEDIA

Adelaide's daily tabloid is the parochial *Advertiser*, though the *Age*, *Australian* and *Financial Review* are also widely available.

Adelaide Review (www.adelaidereview.com.au) Highbrow articles, culture and arts. Free monthly.

> **PINT OF COOPERS PLEASE!**
>
> Things can get confusing at the bar in Adelaide. Aside from the 200ml (7oz) 'butchers' – the choice of old men in dim, sticky-carpet pubs – there are three main beer sizes: 285ml (10oz) 'schooners' (pots or middies elsewhere in Australia), 425ml (15oz) 'pints' (schooners elsewhere) and 568ml (20oz) 'imperial pints' (traditional English pints). Now go forth and order with confidence!

Blaze (www.gaynewsnetwork.com.au) Gay-and-lesbian street press; free fortnightly.

dB (www.dbmagazine.com.au) Local street press; loaded with music info.

Rip it Up (www.ripitup.com.au) Rival street press to dB; buckets of music info plus eating and drinking reviews.

MEDICAL SERVICES

Emergency Dental Service (☎08-8222 8222; www.sadental.sa.gov.au) Sore tooth?

Midnight Pharmacy (☎08-8231 6333; 13 West Tce; ⏲7am-midnight Mon-Sat, 9am-midnight Sun) Late-night subscriptions.

Royal Adelaide Hospital (☎08-8222 4000; www.rah.sa.gov.au; 275 North Tce; ⏲24hr) Emergency department (not for blisters!) and STD clinic.

Women's & Children's Hospital (☎08-8161 7000; www.cywhs.sa.gov.au; 72 King William Rd, North Adelaide; ⏲24hr) Emergency and sexual-assault services.

MONEY

American Express (www.americanexpress.com; 147 Rundle Mall, Citi Centre Arcade; ⏲9am-5pm Mon-Fri, to noon Sat) Foreign currency exchange.

Travelex (www.travelex.com.au; HSBC, 55 Grenfell St; ⏲9.30am-4pm Mon-Thu, to 5pm Fri) Foreign currency exchange in the HSBC building.

POST

Adelaide General Post Office (GPO; Map p714; www.auspost.com.au; 141 King William St; ⏲9am-5.30pm Mon-Fri) Adelaide's main (and rather stately) post office.

TOURIST INFORMATION

Adelaide Visitor Information Centre (Map p714; ☎1300 588 140; www.adelaidecitycouncil.com; 9 James Pl, off Rundle Mall; ⏲9am-5pm Mon-Fri, 10am-4pm Sat & Sun, 11am-3pm public holidays) Adelaide-specific information, plus abundant info on SA including fab regional booklets.

Department of Environment, Water & Natural Resources (DEWNR; Map p714; ☎08-8204 1910; www.environment.sa.gov.au; Level 1, 100 Pirie St; ⏰9am-5pm Mon-Fri) National parks information and bookings.

Disability Information & Resource Centre (DIRC; Map p714; ☎1300 305 558, 08-8236 0555; www.dircsa.org.au; 195 Gilles St; ⏰10am-4pm Mon-Fri) Info on accommodation, venues and travel for people with disabilities.

Getting There & Away

AIR

International, interstate and regional flights via a number of airlines service **Adelaide Airport** (ADL; Map p712; ☎08-8308 9211; www.adelaideairport.com.au; 1 James Schofield Dr, Adelaide Airport), 7km west of the city centre.

Jetstar (www.jetstar.com.au) Direct flights between Adelaide and Perth, Darwin, Cairns, Brisbane, Gold Coast, Sydney and Melbourne.

Qantas (www.qantas.com.au) Direct flights between Adelaide and Perth, Alice Springs, Darwin, Cairns, Brisbane, Sydney, Canberra and Melbourne.

Regional Express (Rex; www.regionalexpress.com.au) Flies from Adelaide to regional centres around SA – Kingscote, Coober Pedy, Ceduna, Mount Gambier, Port Lincoln and Whyalla – plus Broken Hill in NSW and Mildura in Victoria.

Tiger Airways (www.tigerairways.com.au) Direct flights between Adelaide and Melbourne, Sydney and Brisbane.

Virgin Australia (www.virginaustralia.com.au) Direct flights between Adelaide and Perth, Brisbane, Gold Coast, Sydney, Canberra and Melbourne.

BUS

Adelaide Central Bus Station (Map p714; ☎08-8221 5080; www.adelaidemetro.com.au/bussa; 85 Franklin St; ⏰6am-9.30pm) is the hub for all major interstate and statewide bus services; see the website for route and timetable info. Note: there is no Adelaide–Perth bus service.

Firefly Express (www.fireflyexpress.com.au) Runs between Sydney, Canberra, Melbourne and Adelaide.

Greyhound Australia (☎1300 473 946; www.greyhound.com.au) Australia's main long-distance player, with services between Adelaide and Melbourne, Canberra, Sydney, Alice Springs and Darwin.

Premier Stateliner (☎1300 851 345; www.premierstateliner.com.au) State-wide bus services.

V/Line (☎1800 800 007; www.vline.com.au) Bus and bus/train services between Adelaide and Melbourne.

CAR & MOTORCYCLE

The major international car-rental companies have offices at Adelaide Airport and in the city. There are also a handful of local operators. Note that some companies don't allow vehicles to be taken to Kangaroo Island.

Acacia Car Rentals (☎08-8234 0911; www.acaciacarrentals.com.au; 91 Sir Donald Bradman Dr, Hilton; ⏰8am-5pm Mon-Fri, to noon Sat) Cheap rentals for travel within a 100km radius of Adelaide; scooter hire available.

Access Rent-a-Car (☎08-8340 0400, 1800 812 580; www.accessrentacar.com; 464 Port Rd, West Hindmarsh; ⏰8am-6pm Mon-Fri, to noon Sat & Sun) Kangaroo Island travel permitted; 4WDs available.

Cut Price Car & Truck Rentals (☎08-8443 7788; www.cutprice.com.au; cnr Sir Donald Bradman Dr & South Rd, Mile End; ⏰7.30am-5pm Mon-Fri, 8am-3pm Sat & Sun) 4WDs available.

Smile Rent-a-Car (☎08-8234 0655; www.smilerentacar.com.au; 315 Sir Donald Bradman Dr, Brooklyn Park; ⏰8am-6pm) 'Service with a smile!'.

TRAIN

Interstate trains run by **Great Southern Rail** (☎08-8213 4401, 1800 703 357; www.greatsouthernrail.com.au) grind into the **Adelaide Parklands Terminal** (Railway Tce, Keswick; ⏰6am-5pm Mon & Fri, 6.30am-5.30pm Tue, 9am-5pm Wed, 9am-7pm Thu, 8.30am-1pm Sun), 1km southwest of the city centre. The following trains depart Adelaide regularly; backpacker discounts apply:

The Ghan To Alice Springs (seat/sleeper $449/1089, 19 hours)

The Ghan To Darwin ($889/2099, 47 hours)

The Indian Pacific To Perth ($569/1599, 39 hours)

The Indian Pacific To Sydney ($389/779, 25 hours)

The Overland To Melbourne (from $129, 11 hours)

Getting Around

TO/FROM THE AIRPORT & TRAIN STATION

Prebooked private **Adelaide Airport Flyer** (☎08-8353 5233, 1300 856 444; www.adelaideairportflyer.com) minibuses run door-to-door between the airport and anywhere around Adelaide; get a quote and book online (into the city from the airport for one person costs $35). Public Adelaide Metro **JetBuses** (www.adelaidemetro.com.au/routes/J1; tickets $3.20-5.10; ⏰6.30am-11.15pm Mon-Fri, 8am-11.15pm Sat & Sun) connect the airport with Glenelg and the CBD.

Taxis charge around $30 into the city from the airport (15 minutes); or about $15 from Adelaide

Parklands Terminal (10 minutes). Many hostels will pick you up and drop you off if you're staying with them. Adelaide Transport also offers transfers.

BICYCLE

Adelaide is pancake-flat: great for cycling! With a valid passport or driver's licence you can borrow a free **Adelaide City Bike** from **Bicycle SA** (☎08-8168 9999; www.bikesa.asn.au/bikehire; 111 Franklin St; ⏰9am-5pm); helmet and lock provided. There are 18 other locations around town: you can collect a bike at any of them, provided you return it to the same place.

Down at the beach, hire a bike from Glenelg Bicycle Hire (p717).

PUBLIC TRANSPORT

Adelaide Metro (☎1300 311 108; www.adelaidemetro.com.au; cnr King William & Currie Sts; ⏰8am-6pm Mon-Fri, 9am-5pm Sat, 11am-4pm Sun) runs Adelaide's decent and integrated bus, train and tram network.

Tickets can also be purchased on board, at staffed train stations and in delis and newsagents. Ticket types include day trip ($9.70), two-hour peak ($5.10) and two-hour off-peak ($3.20) tickets. Peak travel time is before 9am and after 3pm. Kids under five ride free! There's also a new three-day, unlimited-travel visitor pass ($25).

Bus

Adelaide's buses are clean and reliable. Most services start around 6am and run until midnight.

99C & 99A City Loop Buses (www.adelaidemetro.com.au; ⏰9am-7.30pm Mon-Fri) Adelaide Metro's free 99C and 99A City Loop buses run clockwise and anticlockwise respectively around the CBD fringe, passing Adelaide Station, North Tce and the Central Market en route. Every 20 minutes. The 98C and 98A buses ply the same route, but they extend into North Adelaide and run on weekends too.

After Midnight Buses (www.adelaidemetro.com.au; ⏰midnight-5am Sat) Adelaide Metro's After Midnight buses run select standard routes but have an 'N' preceding the route number on their displays. Standard ticket prices apply.

Train

Adelaide's hokey old diesel trains depart from **Adelaide Station** (www.railmaps.com.au/adelaide.htm; North Tce), plying five suburban routes (Belair, Gawler, Grange, Noarlunga and Outer Harbour). Trains generally run between 6am and midnight (some services start at 4.30am).

Tram

Adelaide state-of-the-art trams rumble to/from Moseley Sq in Glenelg, through Victoria Sq in the city and along North Tce to the Adelaide Entertainment Centre. Trams run approximately every seven or eight minutes on weekdays (every 15 minutes on weekends) from 6am to midnight daily. Standard ticket prices apply, but the section between South Tce and the Adelaide Entertainment Centre is free.

TAXI

Adelaide Independent Taxis (☎13 22 11, wheelchair-access cabs 1300 360 940; www.aitaxis.com.au) Regular and wheelchair-access cabs.

Adelaide Transport (☎08-8212 1861; www.adelaidetransport.com.au) Minibus taxis for four or more people, plus airport-to-city transfers.

Yellow Cabs (☎13 22 27; www.yellowcabgroup.com.au) Regular cabs (most of which are white!).

ADELAIDE HILLS

When the Adelaide plains are desert-hot in the summer months, the Adelaide Hills (technically the Mt Lofty Ranges) are always a few degrees cooler, with crisp air, woodland shade and labyrinthine valleys. Early colonists built stately summer houses around Stirling and Aldgate, and German settlers escaping religious persecution also arrived, infusing towns like Hahndorf and Lobethal with European values and architecture.

The Hills make a brilliant day trip from Adelaide: hop from town to town (all with at least one pub), passing carts of fresh produce for sale, stone cottages, olive groves and wineries along the way.

☞ Tours

In addition to the local offerings, there are a number of day-tour options (p718) departing ex-Adelaide.

Adelaide Hills Ambler GUIDED TOUR
(☎0414 447 134; www.ambler.net.au; half-/full-day tours per person $70/100) See the Hills in style with these personalised, locally run tours starting in Hahndorf. Plenty of wine, cheese, chocolate and arts.

Tour Adelaide Hills GUIDED TOUR
(☎08-8563 1000, 1300 136 970; www.touradelaidehills.com; full-day tours per person $145) Full-day tours through the Hills with pick-up locally, or from Adelaide or the Barossa Valley. Views, vines and fine food.

Adelaide Hills

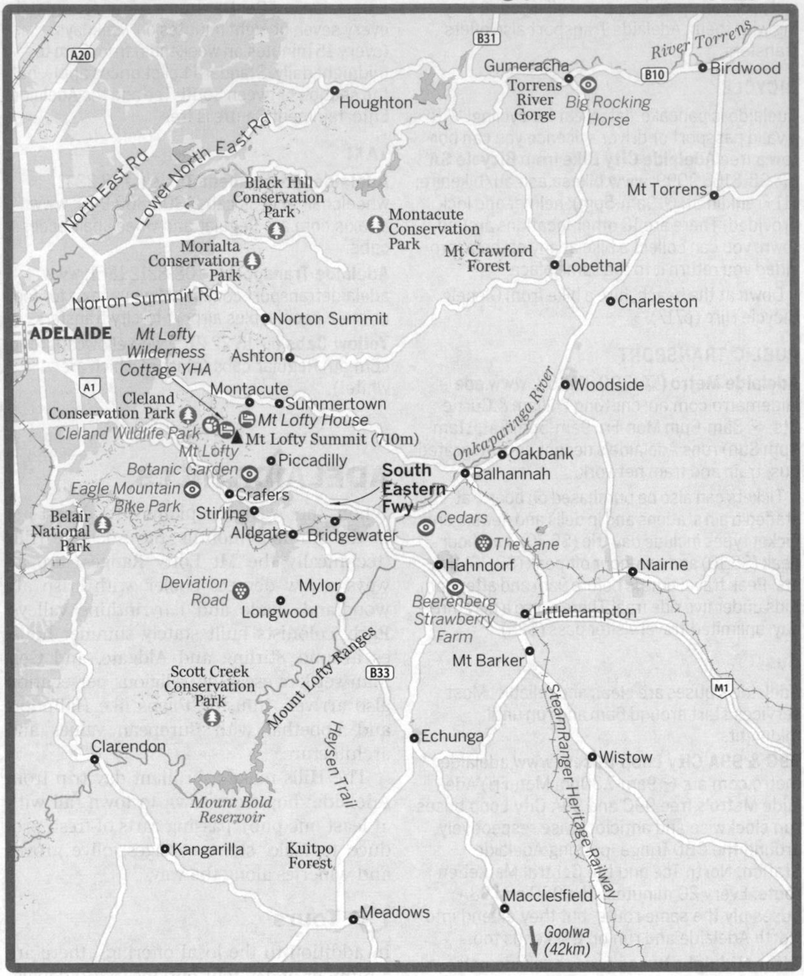

Getting There & Around

To best explore the Hills, BYO wheels. Alternatively, **Adelaide Metro** (www.adelaidemetro.com.au) runs buses between the city and most Hills towns. The 864 and 864F city–Mt Barker buses stop at Stirling, Aldgate and Hahndorf. The 823 runs from Crafers to Mt Lofty Summit and Cleland Wildlife Park; the 830F runs from the city to Oakbank, Woodside and Lobethal on weekdays.

Hahndorf

POP 1810

Like the Rocks in Sydney, and Richmond near Hobart, Hahndorf is a 'ye olde worlde' colonial enclave that trades ruthlessly on its history: it's something of a kitsch parody of itself.

That said, Hahndorf is undeniably pretty, with Teutonic sandstone architecture, European trees, and flowers overflowing from half wine barrels. And it *is* interesting: Australia's oldest surviving German settlement (1839), founded by 50 Lutheran families fleeing religious persecution in Prussia. Hahndorf was placed under martial law during WWI, and its name changed to 'Ambleside' (renamed Hahndorf in 1935). It's also slowly becoming less kitsch, more cool: there are a few good cafes here now, and on a sunny day the main street is positively lively.

Sights & Activities

Hahndorf Academy MUSEUM

(www.hahndorfacademy.org.au; 68 Main St, Hahndorf; 10am-5pm) FREE This 1857 building houses an **art gallery** with rotating exhibitions and original sketches by Sir Hans Heysen, the famed landscape artist and Hahndorf homeboy (ask about tours of his nearby former studio, **The Cedars**). The **museum** depicts the lives of early German settlers, with churchy paraphernalia, dour dresses and farm equipment. The Adelaide Hills Visitor Information Centre is here, too.

Beerenberg Strawberry Farm FARM

(08-8388 7272; www.beerenberg.com.au; Mount Barker Rd, Hahndorf; strawberry picking per adult/child $4/free, strawberries per kg from $9.50; 9am-5pm) Pick your own strawberries between November and May from this famous, family-run farm, also big-noted for its myriad jams, chutneys and sauces. Last entry for picking 4.15pm; open til 8.30pm Fridays in December and January.

Lane WINERY

(08-8388 1250; www.thelane.com.au; Ravenswood Lane, Hahndorf; 10am-4pm) Wow! What a cool building, and what a setting! Camera-conducive views and contemporary varietals (viognier, pinot grigio, pinot gris), plus an outstanding restaurant (book for lunch). Tasting fee refundable if you buy a bottle.

Hahndorf Walking Tours WALKING TOUR

(0477 288 011; www.facebook.com/hahndorfwalkingtours; 45/90min tours per person $18/25; 45min tour noon & 1pm Sat & Sun, 90min tour 2pm Sat & Sat plus 6pm daily Oct-Mar) Short on distance but big on insight, these history-soaked walks are a great way to get a feel for the old town. Bookings essential.

Sleeping & Eating

Hit the **German Arms Hotel** (08-8388 7013; www.germanarmshotel.com.au; 69 Main St; mains $16-30; 8.30am-10pm) or **Hahndorf Inn** (08-8388 7063; www.hahndorfinn.com.au; 35 Main St; mains $17-32; 8.30am-9pm) for German-style bratwursts, schnitzels and strudels. The Lane also offers meals.

Manna MOTEL, APARTMENTS $$

(08-8388 1000; www.themanna.com.au; 25 & 35a Main St; d with/without spa from $225/150, 1-/2-bedroom apt from $159/318;) The Manna is a stylish, contemporary maze of motel suites on the main street, spread over several buildings. The older (more affordable) units occupy a refurbished, exposed-brick motel complex set back from the street. Free wi-fi.

Thiele House Retreat APARTMENT $$$

(0421 983 291; www.stayz.com.au; 102 Main St; per 6 people from $570, extra person $50;) Behind Rockbare cellar door is this renovated former restaurant – brilliant value for groups. Sleeping six comfortably (and up to eight in total), the stone-walled apartment has two bathrooms and an industrial kitchen, and is all decked out in chic urbane colours with exposed timbers and abstract art. Partial-rental arrangements possible for couples.

Udder Delights CAFE $

(www.udderdelights.com.au; 91a Main St; meals $12-25; 9am-5pm;) This udderly delightful cheese cellar/cafe serves salads, tarts, pies, soups, cakes, generous cheese platters, funky fondue and the best coffee this side of Stirling. Free cheese tastings, too.

Seasonal Garden Cafe CAFE $

(08-8388 7714; www.facebook.com/theseasonalgardencafe; 79 Main St; mains $8-20; 8am-5pm;) Swimming against Hahndorf's mainstream currents, this earthy, zero-waste cafe is adorned with bags of oranges, pots of spices, piles of pumpkins by the counter and bowls of chubby chillies. Food-wise it's good coffee, grass-green smoothies and lots of local, seasonal and organic ingredients (try the potted baked eggs with house made beans).

Haus CAFE $$

(08-8388 7555; www.haushahndorf.com.au; 38 Main St; breakfast mains $8-22, lunch & dinner $20-55; 7.30am-11pm) Haus brings some urban hip to the Hills. Rustic-style pizzas are laden with local smallgoods, and the wine list is huge (lots of Hills drops). Also on offer are baguettes, pasta, burgers, salads and quiches. Good coffee, too.

Information

Adelaide Hills Visitor Information Centre

(1800 353 323, 08-8388 1185; www.visitadelaidehills.com.au; 68 Main St; 9am-5pm Mon-Fri, 10am-4pm Sat & Sun) The usual barrage of brochures, plus accommodation bookings.

Stirling Area

The photogenic little villages of old-school **Stirling** (population 2870) and one-horse **Aldgate** (population 3350) are famed for their bedazzling autumn colours, thanks to the deciduous trees the early residents saw fit to seed. Oddly, Aldgate has also been home to both Bon Scott and Mel Gibson over the years.

Sights

Cleland Wildlife Park WILDLIFE RESERVE
(☎07-8339 2444; www.clelandwildlifepark.sa.gov.au; 365 Mt Lofty Summit Rd, Crafers; adult/child/family $22/11/50; ⏰9.30am-5pm, last entry 4.30pm) Within the steep **Cleland Conservation Park** (www.environment.sa.gov.au/parks; ⏰24hr), this place lets you interact with all kinds of Australian beasts. There are keeper talks and feeding sessions throughout the day, plus occasional NightWalks (adult/child $45/35) and you can have your mugshot taken with a koala ($30, 2pm to 3.15pm daily and 11am to 11.45am Sundays). There's a **cafe**, here too. From the city, take bus 864 or 864F from Grenfell St to Crafers for connecting bus 823 to the park.

Mt Lofty Summit VIEWPOINT
(www.environment.sa.gov.au/parks; Mt Lofty Summit Rd, Crafers; ⏰24hr) From Cleland Wildlife Park you can bushwalk (2km) or drive up to Mt Lofty Summit (a surprising 710m), which has eye-popping views across Adelaide. **Mt Lofty Summit Visitor Information Centre** (☎08-8370 1054; www.mtloftysummit.com; ⏰9am-5pm) has info on local attractions and **walking tracks**, including the steep Waterfall Gully Track (8km return, 2½ hours) and Mt Lofty Botanic Gardens Loop Trail (7km loop, two hours). The video of the Ash Wednesday bushfires of 16 February 1983 is harrowing. There's a snazzy **cafe-restaurant** here, too.

Deviation Road WINERY
(www.deviationroad.com; 214 Scott Creek Rd, Longwood; ⏰10am-5pm) Nothing deviant about the wines here: sublime pinot noir, substantial shiraz, zingy pinot gris and a very decent bubbly, too. Grab a cheese platter and wind down in the afternoon in the sun.

Mt Lofty Botanic Garden GARDENS
(www.botanicgardens.sa.gov.au; gates on Mawson Dr & Lampert Rd, Crafers; ⏰8.30am-4pm Mon-Fri, 10am-5pm Sat & Sun) FREE From Mt Lofty, truck south 1.5km to the cool-climate slopes of the botanic garden. Nature trails wind past a lake, exotic temperate plants, native stringybark forest and bodacious rhododendron blooms. Free guided walks depart the Lampert Rd car park at 10.30am on Thursdays from September to October and March to May.

Stirling Markets MARKET
(www.stirlingmarket.com.au; Druids Ave, Stirling; ⏰10am-4pm 4th Sun of the month, 3rd Sun in Dec) This lively market takes over oak-lined Druids Ave in Stirling: much plant-life, busking, pies, cakes and Hills knick-knackery (not many druids...).

Sleeping & Eating

Mt Lofty Wilderness Cottage YHA CABIN $$
(☎08-8414 3000; www.yha.com.au; Mt Lofty Summit Rd, Crafers; per night from $110) A short detour off the road on the steep flanks of Mt Lofty, this 1880 stone cottage was originally a shepherd's hut. Today it's a basic, self-contained, two-bedroom cabin sleeping eight, with peek-a-boo views of Adelaide through the eucalyptuses. Minimum two-night stay.

Mt Lofty House HISTORIC HOTEL $$$
(☎08-8339 6777; www.mtloftyhouse.com.au; 74 Summit Rd, Crafers; d from $242; ❄📶🏊) Proprietorially poised above Mt Lofty Botanic Garden (*awesome* views), this 1850s stone baronial mansion has lavish heritage rooms and garden suites, plus an upmarket restaurant (also with killer views). The perfect honeymooner/dirty weekender. See also www.mtloftycottages.com.au for classy cottage accommodation on-site.

Organic Market & Café CAFE $
(www.organicmarket.com.au; 5 Druids Ave, Stirling; meals $6-16; ⏰8.30am-5pm; ✍) 🍃 Rejecting Stirling's pompous tendencies, hirsute Hills types flock to this vibrant, hippie eatery. It's the busiest cafe in town – and rightly so; the food's delicious and everything's made with love. Gorge on bruschetta, plump savoury muffins, great coffee and wicked Portuguese custard tarts.

★ **Stirling Hotel** PUB FOOD $$
(☎08-8339 2345; www.stirlinghotel.com.au; 52 Mt Barker Rd, Stirling; mains $16-32; ⏰noon-3pm & 6-9pm Mon-Fri, 8am-9pm Sat & Sun) The owners spent so much money tarting up this gorgeous old dame, it's a wonder they can pay the staff. A runaway success, the free-flowing bistro (classy pub grub and pizzas) and romantic restaurant (upmarket regional cuisine) are always packed.

Upstairs are five elegant, contemporary suites (doubles from $280), three of which have open fireplaces (for winter) and breezy balconies (for summer). All have flat-screen TVs, quality linen and luxe bathrooms you'll actually want to spend time in.

Oakbank & Woodside

Strung-out **Oakbank** (population 450) lives for the annual **Oakbank Easter Racing Carnival** (www.oakbankracingclub.com.au), said to be the greatest picnic horse race meeting in the world. It's a two-day festival of equine splendour, risqué dresses and 18-year-olds who can't hold their liquor.

Agricultural **Woodside** (population 1830) has a few enticements for galloping gourmands. **Woodside Cheese Wrights** (www.woodsidecheese.com.au; 22 Henry St, Woodside; tastings free, cheeses from $5; ⏲10am-4pm) is a passionate and unpretentious gem producing classic, artisan and experimental cheeses (soft styles a speciality) from locally grazing sheep and cows. Stock up on rocky road, scorched almonds and appallingly realistic chocolate cow pats at **Melba's Chocolate & Confectionery Factory** (www.melbaschocolates.com; 22 Henry St, Woodside; tastings free, chocolates from $2; ⏲9am-4.30pm).

Gumeracha, Birdwood & Lobethal

A scenic drive from Adelaide to Birdwood leads through the **Torrens River Gorge** to **Gumeracha** (population 400), a hardy hillside town with a pub at the bottom (making it hard to roll home). The main lure here is climbing the 18.3m-high **Big Rocking Horse** (www.thetoyfactory.com.au; Birdwood Rd, Gumeracha; admission $2; ⏲9am-5pm), which doesn't actually rock, but is unusually tasteful as far as Australia's 'big' tourist attractions go.

Behind an impressive 1852 flour mill in **Birdwood** (population 1130), the **National Motor Museum** (☎08-8568 4000; www.motorhistorysa.com.au; Shannon St, Birdwood; adult/child/family $12/5/30; ⏲10am-5pm) has a collection of immaculate vintage and classic cars (check out the DeLorean!) and motorcycles. The museum marks the finishing line for September's **Bay to Birdwood** (www.baytobirdwood.com.au): a convoy of classic cars chugging up from the city.

Nearby is **Lobethal** (population 1660), established by Lutheran Pastor Fritzsche and his followers in 1842. Like Hahndorf, Lobethal was renamed during WWI – 'Tweedale' was the unfortunate choice. The town hits its straps during December's **Lights of Lobethal** (www.lightsoflobethal.com.au) Christmas lights festival. Repair to the **Lobethal Bierhaus** (☎08-8389 5570; www.bierhaus.com.au; 3a Main St, Lobethal; ⏲noon-10pm Fri & Sat, to 6pm Sun) for some serious microbrewed concoctions (try the Red Truck Porter).

FLEURIEU PENINSULA

Patterned with vineyards, olive groves and almond plantations running down to the sea, the Fleurieu (pronounced *floo*-ree-oh) is Adelaide's weekend playground. The McLaren Vale Wine Region is booming, producing gutsy reds (salubrious shiraz) to rival those from the Barossa Valley (actually, we think McLaren Vale wins hands down). Further east, the Fleurieu's Encounter Coast is an engaging mix of surf beaches, historic towns and whales cavorting offshore.

McLaren Vale

POP 3870

Flanked by the wheat-coloured Willunga Scarp and encircled by vines, McLaren Vale is just 40 minutes south of Adelaide. Servicing the wine industry, it's an energetic, utilitarian town that's not much to look at – but it has some great eateries and offers easy access to some excellent winery cellar doors.

Sights & Activities

Most people come to McLaren Vale to cruise the 60-plus **wineries** here: you could spend days doing nothing else! Pick up a winery map at the visitor information centre (p739).

It seems like most of Adelaide gets tizzied up and buses down to the annual **Sea & Vines Festival** (www.mclarenvaleseaandvines.com.au) over the June long weekend. Local wineries cook up seafood, splash wine around and host live bands.

Goodieson Brewery BREWERY
(www.goodiesonbrewery.com.au; 194 Sand Rd; tastings $5; ⏲11am-5.30pm) There sure are a lot of wineries around here... Anyone for a beer? This family-run outfit brews a pale ale, pilsner, wheat beer and brown ale, plus brilliant seasonal beers. Sip a few on the sunny terrace.

Shiraz Trail CYCLING
Get the McLaren Vale vibe on this 8km walking/cycling track, along an old railway

Fleurieu Peninsula

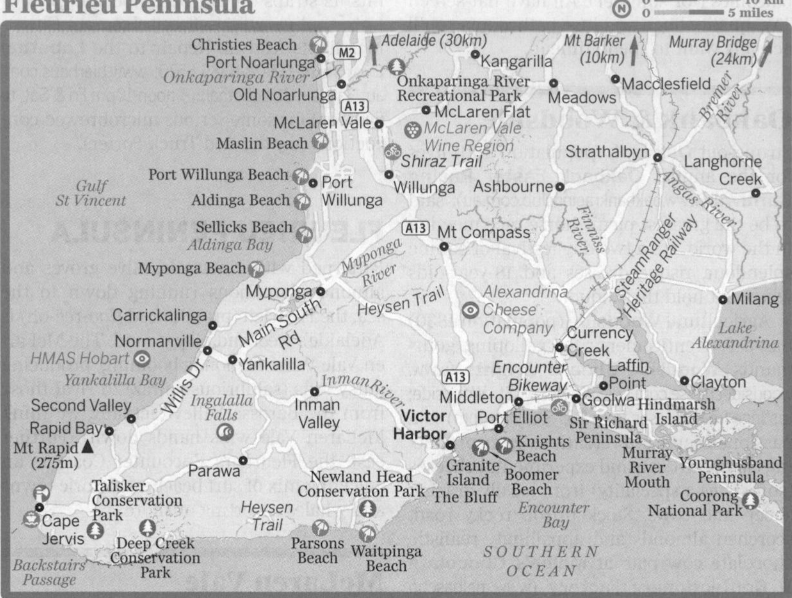

line between McLaren Vale and Willunga. If you're up for it, the trail continues another 29km to Marino Rocks as the **Coast to Vines Rail Trail**. Hire a bike from **Oxygen Cycles** (☎08-8323 7345; www.oxygencycles.com; 143 Main Rd; bike hire per half/full day/overnight $15/25/40; ⊙10am-6pm Tue-Fri, 9am-5pm Sat, plus Sun & Mon Dec-Feb); ask the visitor information centre for a map.

Tours

Most tours can be taken from Adelaide, or, for a few dollars less, from McLaren Vale itself.

Chook's Little Winery Tours GUIDED TOUR
(☎0414 922 200; www.chookslittlewinerytours.com.au; per person from $90) Small-group tours visiting some of the lesser-known boutique McLaren Vale wineries, ex-Adelaide.

McLaren Vale Wine Tours GUIDED TOUR
(☎0414 784 666; www.mclarenvaletours.com.au) Customised, locally run group tours around McLaren Vale and the Fleurieu; call for prices. Ex-Adelaide.

Off Piste 4WD Tours GUIDED TOUR
(☎0423 725 409; www.offpistetours.com.au; half-/full-day tours $129/225) Full- or half-day 4WD adventure tours around the Fleurieu for two to 10 folks, with lots of wilderness, wine, beer and beaches.

Sacred Earth Safaris GUIDED TOUR
(☎08-8555 3838; www.sacredearthsafaris.com.au) Two-day 4WD Fleurieu tours from Adelaide ($595), and McLaren Vale day tours from Victor Harbor ($99).

Sleeping & Eating

In addition to options in town, you can eat at many of McLaren Vale's cellar doors.

McLaren Vale Lakeside Caravan Park CARAVAN PARK $
(☎08-8323 9255; www.mclarenvale.net; 48 Field St; unpowered/powered/en-suite sites from $28/33/43, cabins $110-155; ❄ 🏊) A short walk from town, this grassy park by an artificial lake (any water this summer?) occupies the affordable end of McLaren Vale's accommodation scale. There's a camp kitchen, pool, spa, tennis court and trashy book exchange. Good winter rates. The Shiraz Trail (p737) runs right past.

McLaren Vale Backpackers HOSTEL $
(☎08-8323 0916; www.mclarenvalebackpackers.com.au; 106 Main Rd; dm/s/d from $27/75/80; ❄ @ 📶 🏊) In the final stages of construction when we visited, this new backpackers fills an old heath club on the main street, with winery workers' beds in the old squash courts and regular dorms and private rooms out the front. Plus there's a sauna, spa and

plunge pool! Drop us a line and tell us about the finished product (we're optimistic).

Red Poles B&B $$
(☎08-8323 8994; www.redpoles.com.au; 190 McMurtrie Rd; d with/without bathroom $125/115; ❄📶) Bushy, eccentric Red Poles is a great place to stay (and eat!). Aim for the rustic en suite room (bigger than its two counterparts). Order some gnocchi with goats curd (mains from $14, serving 9am to 4.30pm), and check out some local artwork while you wait. Live music Sunday afternoons, and tastings of McLaren Vale Beer Company (www.mvbeer.com) ales.

McLaren Vale Studio Apartments APARTMENTS $$$
(☎08-8323 9536; www.mvsa.com.au; 222 Main Rd; d from $225, extra person $50; ❄) A tightly arranged crop of six fancy units on the main road (each sleeping six), with snappy contemporary furnishings, full kitchens, BBQs and architectural appeal. Walking distance to cafes, eateries and the pub.

★Blessed Cheese CAFE $
(www.blessedcheese.com.au; 150 Main Rd; mains breakfast $6-16, lunch $11-28; ⏲8am-4.30pm Mon-Thu, to 5pm Fri-Sun) The cute staff at this blessed cafe crank out great coffee, croissants, wraps, salads, tarts, burgers, cheese platters, murderous cakes and funky sausage rolls. The menu changes every couple of days, always with an emphasis on local produce. The aromas emanating from the cheese counter are deliciously stinky.

Salopian Inn MODERN AUSTRALIAN $$
(☎08-8323 8769; www.salopian.com.au; cnr Main & McMurtrie Rds; mains $28-58; ⏲noon-3.30pm daily, 6pm-late Thu-Sat) This old vine-covered inn has been here since 1851. Its latest incarnation features super Mod Oz offerings with an Asian twist: launch into the Berkshire pork buns or blue swimmer crab and prawn dumplings, with a bottle of something local which you can hand-select from the cellar. And there are 170 gins with which to construct your G&T!

ℹ Information

McLaren Vale & Fleurieu Visitor Information Centre (☎1800 628 410, 08-8323 9944; www.mclarenvale.info; 796 Main Rd; ⏲9am-5pm Mon-Fri, 10am-4pm Sat & Sun) At the northern end of McLaren Vale. Winery info, plus

DON'T MISS

MCLAREN VALE WINERIES

If the Barossa Valley is SA wine's old school, then McLaren Vale is the upstart teenager smoking cigarettes behind the shed and stealing nips from dad's port bottle. The gorgeous vineyards around here have a Tuscan haze in summer, rippling down to a calm coastline that's similarly Ligurian. This is shiraz country – solid, punchy and seriously good.

Alpha Box & Dice (www.alphaboxdice.com; Lot 8 Olivers Rd; ⏲11am-4pm Mon-Thu, 10am-5pm Fri-Sun) One out of the box, this refreshing little gambler wins top billing for interesting blends, funky retro furnishings, quirky labels and laid-back staff.

Coriole (www.coriole.com; Chaffeys Rd; ⏲10am-5pm Mon-Fri, 11am-5pm Sat & Sun) Take your regional tasting platter out into the garden of this beautiful cottage cellar door (1860) to share kalamata olives, homemade breads and Adelaide Hills' Woodside cheeses, made lovelier by a swill of the Redstone shiraz or the flagship chenin blanc.

d'Arenberg (☎08-8329 4888; www.darenberg.com.au; Osborn Rd; ⏲10am-5pm) 'd'Arry's' relaxes atop a hillside with mighty fine views. The wine labels are part of the character of this place: the Dead Arm shiraz and the Broken Fishplate sauvignon blanc are our faves. Book for lunch.

Samuel's Gorge (☎08-8323 8651; www.gorge.com.au; Chaffeys Rd; ⏲11am-5pm) On a hill behind McLaren Vale township is this understated winner, inside an 1853 stone barn and with valley views that are bordering on English. Great grenache; BYO picnic.

Wirra Wirra (www.wirrawirra.com; McMurtrie Rd; ⏲10am-5pm Mon-Sat, 11am-5pm Sun) Fancy some pétanque with your plonk? This barnlike, 1894 cellar door has a grassy picnic area, and there's a roaring fire inside in winter. Sample reasonably priced stickies (dessert wines) and the super-popular Church Block blend. Whites include a citrusy viognier and an aromatic riesling.

accommodation assistance and Sealink bus/ferry bookings for Kangaroo Island.

Getting There & Away

Regular **Adelaide Metro** (www.adelaidemetro.com.au) suburban trains run between Adelaide and Noarlunga (one hour). From here, buses 751 and 753 run to McLaren Vale and Willunga (45 minutes). Regular Adelaide Metro ticket prices apply.

Willunga

POP 2420

A one-horse town with three pubs (a winning combo!), arty Willunga took off in 1840 when high-quality slate was discovered nearby and exported across Australia. Today, the town's early buildings along sloping High St are occupied by some terrific eateries, B&B accommodation and galleries. The Kidman Trail (p717) kicks off here.

Sights

Willunga Farmers Market MARKET
(www.willungafarmersmarket.com; Willunga Town Sq; 8am-12.30pm Sat) Heavy on the organic, the bespoke and the locally sourced, Willunga Farmers Market happens every Saturday morning, on the corner of High St and Main Rd.

Willunga Slate Museum MUSEUM
(www.nationaltrust.org.au/sa/willunga-slate-museum; 61 High St; adult/child $5/1; 1-4pm Tue, Sat & Sun) At the top end of Willunga's ascending high street is this cluster of old stone buildings, which at various times have housed a police station, a courthouse, a prison and a boys' school. These days the emphasis is on Willunga's slate-mining history and the Cornish miners who did all the dirty work.

Sleeping & Eating

Willunga House B&B B&B $$$
(08-8556 2467; www.willungahouse.com.au; 1 St Peters Tce; d incl breakfast $210-280;) If you're looking for a real treat, this graceful, two-storey 1850 mansion off the main street is for you: Baltic-pine floorboards, Italian cherrywood beds, open fires, Indigenous art and a swimming pool. Breakfast is a feast of organic muesli, fruit salad and poached pears, followed by cooked delights.

Fino MODERN AUSTRALIAN $$
(08-8556 4488; www.fino.net.au; 8 Hill St; mains $28-33; noon-3pm Tue-Sun, 6.30-9pm Fri & Sat) A regular on 'Australia's Top 100 Restaurants' lists and with a cabinet full of regional awards for both food and wine, Fino is fine indeed. It's a low-key conversion of a slate-floored stone cottage, with a small, simple menu of small, simple dishes, sourced locally as much as possible. The Coorong Angus rib with mustard leaves is a winner.

Russell's Pizza PIZZA $$
(08-8556 2571; www.facebook.com; 13 High St; pizzas from $24; 6-11.30pm Fri & Sat) It may look like a ramshackle chicken coop, but Russell's is the place to be on weekends for sensational wood-fired pizza. No one minds the wait for a meal (which could be an hour) – it's all about the atmosphere. It's super popular, so book way ahead.

Gulf St Vincent Beaches

The stretch of coast from Adelaide's southern suburbs down to Cape Jervis is prime territory for a beachy day trip from the city. The area also makes a handy overnight stop on the way to Kangaroo Island, or for some seaside time-out from the McLaren Vale vines.

There are some ace swimming beaches (but no surf) along the Gulf St Vincent coastline from suburban **Christies Beach** onto **Maslin Beach**, the southern end of which is a nudist and gay hang-out. Maslin is 45 minutes from Adelaide by car – just far enough to escape the sprawling shopping centres and new housing developments trickling south from the city.

Port Willunga is home to the eternally busy, cliff-top seafood shack the **Star of Greece** (08-8557 7420; www.starofgreececafe.com.au; 1 The Esplanade, Port Willunga; mains $29-35; noon-3pm Wed-Sun, 6pm-late Fri & Sat), named after a shipwreck. Expect funky decor, great staff and a sunny outdoor patio. We asked the waiter where the whiting was caught: he looked out across the bay and said, 'See that boat out there?' There's a takeaway kiosk, too (snacks $4 to $8, open 10am to 3pm October to May).

On the highway above **Sellicks Beach** is a classily renovated 1858 pub, the **Victory Hotel** (08-8556 3083; www.victoryhotel.com.au; Main South Rd, Sellicks Beach; mains $17-35; noon-2.30pm & 6-8.30pm). There are awesome views of the silvery gulf, a cheery, laid-back vibe and a beaut beer garden. Factor in inspired meals, an impressive cellar and wines by the glass and you'll be feeling victorious. Three B&B cabins, too (doubles from $150).

Keep trucking south to cute little **Yankalilla**, which has the regional **Yankalilla Bay Visitor Information Centre** (☎1300 965 842, 08-8558 0240; www.yankalilla.sa.gov.au; 163 Main South Rd, Yankalilla; ⌚9am-5pm Mon-Fri, 10am-4pm Sat & Sun; 📶). There's a small local history **museum** (www.yankalilla.sa.gov.au; 169 Main South Rd, Yankalilla; admission $5; ⌚9am-5pm Mon-Fri, 10am-4pm Sat & Sun) out the back (look for the radar antenna from the scuttled **HMAS Hobart** (www.exhmashobart.com.au), now a nearby dive site offshore. Also in 'Yank' is quirky **Lilla's Cafe** (☎08-8558 2525; www.lillascafe.com.au; 117 Main South Rd, Yankalilla; mains breakfast $7-20, lunch & dinner $15-32; ⌚8.30am-4pm Sun-Tue & Thu, to 11pm Fri & Sat) – perfect for coffee and cake, or generous wood-fired pizzas on Friday and Saturday nights.

About 60km south of Adelaide is **Carrickalinga**, which has a gorgeous arc of white sandy beach: it's a very chilled spot with no shops. For supplies and accommodation, head to neighbouring **Normanville**, which has a rambling pub, a supermarket and a couple of caravan parks. Also here is **One Little Sister** (☎08-8558 3759; www.onelittlesister.com.au; 4/48 Main Rd, Normanville; mains $10-18, pizzas $19-23; ⌚8am-4pm Sun-Thu, to 8.30pm Fri & Sat), a hip, city-style cafe doing a roaring trade in coffee, big breakfasts and pizzas. About 10km out of Normanville along Hay Flat Rd are the picturesque little **Ingalalla Falls** (follow the signs from the Yankalilla side of town). Along similar lines, the **Hindmarsh Falls** are off Hindmarsh Tiers Rd, inland from Myponga.

There's not much at **Cape Jervis**, 107km from Adelaide, other than the Kangaroo Island ferry terminal, and the start point for the Heysen Trail (p717). Nearby, **Deep Creek Conservation Park** (www.environment.sa.gov.au; per car $10) has sweeping coastal views, a wicked waterfall, man-size yakkas *(Xanthorrhoea semiplana tateana)*, sandy beaches, kangaroos, kookaburras and bush camping areas (per car from $13).

Off the road to Deep Creek Conservation Park you'll find the curved roofs of **Ridgetop Retreats** (☎08-8598 4169; www.southernoceanretreats.com.au; Tapanappa Rd; d $245), three superb, corrugated-iron-clad, self-contained luxury units in the bush, with wood heaters, leather lounges and stainless-steel benchtops. See Ridgetop's website for more-affordable local options.

Victor Harbor

POP 13,850

The biggest town on the Encounter Coast is Victor Harbor (yes, that's the correct spelling: blame one of SA's poorly schooled early Surveyor Generals). It's a raggedy, brawling holiday destination with three huge pubs, and migrating whales offshore. In November the grassy foreshore runs rampant with teenage school-leavers blowing off hormones at the **Schoolies Festival** (www.schooliesfestival.com.au).

Sights & Activities

South Australian Whale Centre MUSEUM
(☎08-8551 0750; www.sawhalecentre.com; 2 Railway Tce; adult/child/family $9/4.50/24; ⌚10.30am-5pm) Victor Harbor is on the migratory path of southern right whales (May to October). The multilevel South Australian Whale Centre has impressive whale displays (including a big stinky skull) and can give you the low-down on where to see them. Not whale season? Check out the big mammals in their new 3D-cinema. For whale sightings info, call the **Whale Information Hotline** (☎1900 942 537).

Alexandrina Cheese Company CHEESE
(www.alexandrinacheese.com.au; Sneyd Rd, Mt Jagged; tastings free, cheese platters $10-13; ⌚noon-5pm Mon-Fri, 10am-4.30pm Sat & Sun) On the road to Mt Compass, 18km north of Victor Harbor, this Fleurieu success story opens its doors to cheese fans and milkshake mavens. Taste the gouda, the edam and the feta, then buy a block of the powerful vintage cheddar to go.

Horse-Drawn Tram TRAM
(☎08-8551 0720; www.horsedrawntram.com.au; Foreshore; return adult/child/family $9/7/25; ⌚hourly 10.30am-3.30pm) Just offshore is the boulder-strewn **Granite Island**, connected to the mainland by a 632m causeway built in 1875. You can walk to the island, but it's more fun to take the 1894 double-decker tram pulled by a big Clydesdale. Tickets are available from the driver or visitor information centre.

Encounter Bikeway CYCLING
(www.fleurieupeninsula.com.au/pdfs/bikeway_brochure09.pdf) FREE The much-wheeled

Encounter Bikeway extends 30km from Victor Harbor to Laffin Point beyond Goolwa. The visitors centre stocks maps; hire a bike from **Victor Harbor Cycle Skate Bay Rubber** (☎08-8552 1417; www.victorharborcycles.com; 73 Victoria St; bike hire per 4/8hrs $30/40; ⏲9am-5pm Mon-Fri, 10am-3pm Sat & Sun).

Big Duck BOAT TOUR
(☎0405 125 312; www.thebigduck.com.au; 30min tours adult/child/family $35/25/110, 1hr tours $60/50/195) Do a lap of Granite Island and check out seals, dolphins and whales (in season) on the rigid inflatable Big Duck boat. Call or go online for times and bookings.

Sleeping & Eating

Anchorage GUESTHOUSE $
(☎08-8552 5970; www.anchorageseafronthotel.com; 21 Flinders Pde; s/d/tr/q/apt from $55/80/110/160/240;) This grand old seafront guesthouse is the pick of the local crop. Immaculately maintained, great-value rooms open off long corridors. Most rooms face the beach, and some have a balcony (you'd pay through the nose for this in Sydney!). The cheapest rooms are view-free and share bathrooms. The cafe-bar downstairs is a winner. Free wi-fi (patchy in some rooms).

Victor Harbor Holiday & Cabin Park CARAVAN PARK $
(☎08-8552 1949; www.victorharborholiday.com.au; 19 Bay Rd; unpowered/powered sites $32/39, cabins/units/villas $114/114/174;) The friendliest caravan park in town (there are a few – none of them particularly contemporary in their approach), with tidy facilities, free barbecues and wi-fi and a rambling grassed area to pitch your tent on.

Nino's CAFE, ITALIAN $$
(☎08-8552 3501; www.ninoscafe.com.au; 17 Albert Pl; mains $18-29; ⏲10am-10pm Mon-Thu, to midnight Fri-Sun) Nino's cafe has been here since 1974, but it manages to put a contemporary sheen on downtown VH. Hip young staff and a mod interior set the scene for gourmet pizzas, pasta, salads, risottos and meaty Italian mains. Good coffee, cakes and takeaways, too.

Anchorage Cafe MODERN AUSTRALIAN $$
(☎08-8552 5970; www.anchorageseafronthotel.com; 21 Flinders Pde; tapas $4-17, mains $16-34; ⏲8-11am, noon-2.30pm & 5.30-8.30pm) This salty sea cave at the Anchorage hotel has an old whaling boat for a bar and a Med/Mod Oz menu (baguettes, pizzas, souvlaki) peppered with plenty of seafood. There's great coffee, tapas and cakes, plus Euro beers and a breezy terrace on which to drink too many of them.

Information

Victor Harbor Visitor Information Centre (☎08-8551 0777; www.tourismvictorharbor.com.au; Foreshore; ⏲9am-5pm) handles tour and accommodation bookings. Stocks the *Beaches on the South Coast* brochure for when you feel like a swim, and the *Old Port Victor* history walk brochure.

Getting There & Away

BUS

Premier Stateliner (www.premierstateliner.com.au) runs buses to Victor Harbor from Adelaide ($24, 1¾ hours, one to three daily), continuing on to Goolwa.

TRAIN

On the first and third Sundays from June to November inclusive, **SteamRanger Heritage Railway** (☎1300 655 991; www.steamranger.org.au) operates the *Southern Encounter* (adult/child return $71/37) tourist train from Mt Barker in the Adelaide Hills to Victor Harbor via Strathalbyn, Goolwa and Port Elliot. The Cockle Train (adult/child return $29/15) runs along the Encounter Coast between Victor Harbor and Goolwa via Port Elliot every Sunday and Wednesday, and daily during school holidays.

Port Elliot

POP 3100

About 8km east of Victor Harbor, historic (and today, rather affluent) Port Elliot is set back from **Horseshoe Bay**, an orange-sand arc with gentle surf and good swimming. Norfolk Island pines reach for the sky, and there are whale-spotting updates posted on the pub wall. If there are whales around, wander out to **Freemans Knob** lookout at the end of the Strand and peer through the free telescope.

Activities

History buffs should look for the *Walk Into History at Port Elliot* pamphlet (try Goolwa Visitor Information Centre, p745) detailing a couple of history walks around town.

Port Elliot Bike & Leisure Hire BIKE HIRE
(☎0448 370 007; www.portelliotbikeleisurehire.myob.net; 85-87 Hill St; per day from $40; ⏲9am-5pm Mon-Sat, from 10.30am Sun) Pick

up a mountain bike and hit the Encounter Bikeway (p741), running through Port Elliot to Goolwa (15km east) and Victor Harbor (7km west).

Surfing

Commodore Point, at the eastern end of Horseshoe Bay, and nearby **Boomer Beach** and **Knights Beach**, have reliable waves for experienced surfers, with swells often holding around 2m. The beach at otherwise missable **Middleton**, the next town towards Goolwa, also has solid breaks. Further afield, try wild **Waitpinga Beach** and **Parsons Beach**, 12km southwest of Victor Harbor.

The best surfing season is March to June, when the northerlies doth blow. See www.southaustralia.com for info, and www.surfsouthoz.com for surf reports. There are a few good surfing schools in Middleton.

South Coast Surf Academy SURFING
(☎0414 341 545; www.danosurf.com.au; Surfers Pde, Middleton) Learn to surf for around $50 for a two-hour lesson, including gear.

Surf & Sun SURFING
(☎1800 786 386; www.surfandsun.com.au; 44 Victor Harbor Rd, Middleton) Offers board/wetsuit hire (per half day $20/10), and surfing lessons (around $50 for a two-hour lesson, including gear).

Big Surf Australia SURFING
(☎08-8554 2399; www.bigsurfaustralia.com.au; 24 Goolwa Rd, Middleton; surfboards/bodyboards/wetsuits per day $20/15/15; ⏱9am-5pm) For surf-gear hire try Big Surf Australia in Middleton.

Sleeping & Eating

★Port Elliot Beach House YHA HOSTEL $
(☎08-8554 1885; www.yha.com.au; 13 The Strand; dm/tw/d/f from $28/90/90/125; ❄@📶) Built in 1910 (as the old Arcadia Hotel), this sandstone beauty has sweeping views across the Port Elliot coastline. If you can drag your eyes away from the scenery, you'll find polished floorboards, nice linen and contemporary colours splashed around: literally a million-dollar fit-out. Surf lessons are almost mandatory, and the Flying Fish Cafe – home of the southern Fleurieu's best fish and chips – is 200m away.

Port Elliot Holiday Park CARAVAN PARK $
(☎08-8554 2134; www.portelliotholidaypark.com.au; Port Elliot Rd; powered sites/cabins/units/cottages from $34/90/115/145; ❄@📶) In an unbeatable position behind the Horseshoe Bay dunes (it can be a touch windy), this grassy, 5-hectare park has all the requisite facilities, including a shiny camp kitchen and all-weather barbecue area. Lush grass and healthy-looking trees. Prices plummet in winter.

Royal Family Hotel PUB $
(☎08-8554 2219; www.royalfamilyhotel.com.au; 32 North Tce; tw/s/tr/d $40/50/60/65) It's doubtful that Prince Chuck has ever stayed here, but if he did he'd find surprisingly decent pub rooms with clean shared bathrooms, a TV lounge and a balcony over the main street. Downstairs there's Bon Jovi on the jukebox and counter meals fit for a king (mains $13 to $25, serving noon to 2pm and 6pm to 8pm).

Jetty Food Store CAFE, DELI $
(☎0448 147 097; www.jettyfoodstore.com; 42 North Tce; meals $8-16; ⏱9am-6pm Mon-Fri, 8.30am-4pm Sat, 9am-3pm Sun) The motto here is 'Coastal food hunted and gathered for you'. Grab an organic coffee, a dozen Kangaroo Island oysters, some local organic wine, or raid the fridge for gourmet cheeses, dips and olives. Zingy juices, too.

★Flying Fish Cafe MODERN AUSTRALIAN, FISH & CHIPS $$
(☎08-8554 3504; www.flyingfishcafe.com.au; 1 The Foreshore; mains cafe $5-18, restaurant $19-34; ⏱cafe 9am-4pm daily, restaurant noon-3pm daily & 6-8pm Fri & Sat) Sit down for a cafe breakfast and you'll be here all day – the views of Horseshoe Bay are sublime. Otherwise, grab some takeaway Coopers-battered flathead and chips and head for the sand. At night things get classy, with à la carte mains focusing on independent SA producers.

Getting There & Away

Premier Stateliner (www.premierstateliner.com.au) has daily bus services between Adelaide and Port Elliot ($24, two hours, one to three daily), via Victor Harbor and continuing to Goolwa.

Goolwa

POP 6500

Much more low-key and elegant than kissing cousin Victor Harbor, Goolwa is an unassuming town where the rejuvenated Murray River empties into the sea. Beyond

WORTH A TRIP

CURRENCY CREEK & LANGHORNE CREEK WINERIES

Once slated as the capital of SA, **Currency Creek**, 10km north of Goolwa, is now content with producing award-winning wines (www.currencycreekwineregion.com.au). **Currency Creek Winery** (08-8555 4069; www.currencycreekwinery.com.au; Winery Rd, Currency Creek; 10am-5pm) has 160 acres under vine (brilliant cabernet sauvignon) plus a fab restaurant (mains $26 to $30, open noon to 3pm Wednesday to Sunday and 6pm to 9pm Friday and Saturday). Bookings advised.

Further north, 16km east of Strathalbyn, **Langhorne Creek** is one of Australia's oldest wine-growing regions (www.langhornecreek.com). It's home to 20-plus wineries, producing shiraz, cabernet sauvignon and chardonnay. **Bleasdale Winery** (www.bleasdale.com.au; Wellington Rd, Langhorne Creek; 10am-5pm) was the district's first, and has a large range, historic cellars and an old red-gum lever press. Run by two sisters, **Bremerton** (www.bremerton.com.au; Strathalbyn Rd, Langhorne Creek; 10am-5pm) is an innovative operator in an old-school region. Top chardonnay and shiraz.

the dunes is a fantastic beach with ranks of breakers rolling in from the ocean, same as it ever was... The **South Australian Wooden Boat Festival** (www.woodenboatfestival.com.au) happens here in February in odd-numbered years.

Sights & Activities

At **Goolwa Beach** there's a little cafe and a boardwalk traversing the dunes, looking out at the barrelling surf: learn to carve it up with **Ocean Living Surf School** (0487 921 232; www.olsurfschool.com.au; 2/4hr lessons $35/65).

The coastal **Encounter Bikeway** (www.fleurieupeninsula.com.au/pdfs/bikeway_brochure09.pdf) runs for 30km between Goolwa and Victor Harbor (maps available at the Goolwa visitor centre).

Steam Exchange Brewery BREWERY
(08-8555 3406; www.steamexchange.com.au; Goolwa Wharf; tastings $3.20; 10am-5pm Wed-Sun) Down on the wharf, the Steam Exchange Brewery is a locally run brewery, turning out stouts and ales. Sip a Southerly Buster Dark Ale and look out over the rippling river. And SA's only single malt whiskey distillery is here! Small tasting fee; group tours by arrangement.

Canoe the Coorong CANOEING
(0424 826 008; www.canoethecoorong.com; adult/child $135/85) Full-day paddles around the Coorong and Murray River mouth departing Goolwa. Includes lunch and a bush-tucker walk through the dunes. Longer tours also available.

Spirit of the Coorong CRUISE
(08-8555 2203, 1800 442 203; www.coorongcruises.com.au; Goolwa Wharf) Spirit of the Coorong runs eco-cruises on the Murray and into the Coorong National Park, including lunch and guided walks. The four-hour Coorong Discovery Cruise (adult/child $90/66) runs on Thursdays all year, plus Mondays from October to May. The six-hour Coorong Adventure Cruise ($105/72) runs on Sundays all year, plus Wednesdays from October to May. Bookings essential.

There's also a two-hour Murray Mouth Cruise ($38/19) on Saturdays from October to April.

Goolwa Riverboat Centre CRUISE
(1300 466 592, 08-8555 2108; www.oscar-w.info; Goolwa Wharf; adult/child/family $20/8/48; 10am-3pm, call for cruise times) Check out the Murray River on a one-hour paddle-steamer ride aboard the 130-year-old *Oscar W*. It's hard to imagine now, but in 1875 there were 127 riverboats plying the river between here and NSW! Call for times and bookings.

Sleeping

Holiday rentals in and around Goolwa are managed by **LJ Hooker** (08-8555 1785; www.ljh.com.au/goolwa; 25 Cadell St) and the **Professionals** (08-8555 2122; www.goolwaprofessionals.com.au; 1 Cadell St), both of whom have houses for as little as $80 per night (though most are around $130) with good weekly rates.

Jackling Cottage B&B B&B $$
(08-8555 3489; www.goolwaheritagecottages.com; 18 Oliver St; d 2 nights incl breakfast from $340;) A lovely old 1860s cottage on a

nondescript Goolwa backstreet (just ignore the petrol station across the road), surrounded by rambling roses and limestone walls. There are two bedrooms, sleeping four – good for families or a couple of couples looking for a low-key weekend by the sea. It's a short stroll to the main drag. Two night minimum.

Also available as a holiday rental (no breakfast).

★ **Australasian** BOUTIQUE HOTEL **$$$**
(08-8555 1088; www.australasian1858.com; 1 Porter St; d incl breakfast from $395;) This gorgeous 1858 stone hotel at the head of Goolwa's main street has been reborn as a sassy B&B, with a sequence of Japanese-inspired decks and glazed extensions, and an upmarket dining room. The five plush suites all have views, and the breakfast will make you want to wake up here again. Two-night minimum.

Eating

Café Lime CAFE **$**
(1/11 Goolwa Tce; meals $9-20; 9am-4pm daily, to 8pm Fri & Sat Dec-Feb) Pick up heat-and-eat gourmet dinners or a takeaway cone of salt-and-pepper squid with lime-salted fries. If you feel like lingering, nab a table for beer-battered Coorong mullet (not a description of a haircut at the pub), baguettes, curries, soups and pasta. Espresso perfecto.

Hector's CAFE, MODERN AUSTRALIAN **$$**
(08-8555 5885; www.hectorsonthewharf.com; Goolwa Wharf; mains $15-30; 9am-5pm daily, 6pm-late Fri & Sat Dec-Feb) Right on the Murray under the span of the Hindmarsh Island Bridge, eating at Hector's (festooned with fishing rods) is like hanging out in your mate's boathouse. Seafood chowder, crumbed scallops and spinach-and-feta pie are sweetly complemented by jazzy tunes and local wines. Good coffee, too.

Information

Goolwa Visitor Information Centre (1300 466 592; www.visitalexandrina.com; 4 Goolwa Tce; 9am-5pm Mon-Fri, 10am-4pm Sat & Sun) Inside an 1857 post office, with detailed local info (including accommodation).

Getting There & Away

Premier Stateliner (www.premierstateliner.com.au) runs buses daily between Adelaide and Goolwa ($24, two hours, one to three daily).

KANGAROO ISLAND

From Cape Jervis, car ferries chug across the swells of the Backstairs Passage to Kangaroo Island (KI). Long devoid of tourist trappings, the island these days is a booming destination for wilderness and wildlife fans – it's a veritable zoo of seals, birds, dolphins, echidnas and (of course) kangaroos. Still, the island remains rurally paced and underdeveloped – the kind of place where kids ride bikes to school and farmers advertise for wives on noticeboards. Island produce is a highlight.

History

Many KI place names are French, attributable to Gallic explorer Nicholas Baudin who surveyed the coast in 1802 and 1803. Baudin's English rival, Matthew Flinders, named the island in 1802 after his crew feasted on kangaroo meat here. By this stage the island was uninhabited, but archaeologists think Indigenous Australians lived here as recently as 2000 years ago. Why they deserted KI is a matter of conjecture, though the answer is hinted at in the Indigenous name for KI: Karta (Land of the Dead). In the early 1800s an Indigenous presence (albeit a tragically displaced one)

ALL CREATURES GREAT & SMALL

You bump into a lot of wildlife on KI (sometimes literally). Kangaroos, wallabies, bandicoots and possums come out at night, especially in wilderness areas such as Flinders Chase National Park. Koalas and platypuses were introduced to Flinders Chase in the 1920s when it was feared they would become extinct on the mainland. Echidnas mooch around in the undergrowth, while goannas and tiger snakes keep KI suitably scaly.

Of the island's 267 bird species, several are rare or endangered. One notable species – the dwarf emu – has gone the way of the dodo. Glossy black cockatoos may soon follow it out the door due to habitat depletion.

Offshore, dolphins and southern right whales are often seen cavorting, and there are colonies of little penguins, New Zealand fur seals and Australian sea lions here, too.

Kangaroo Island

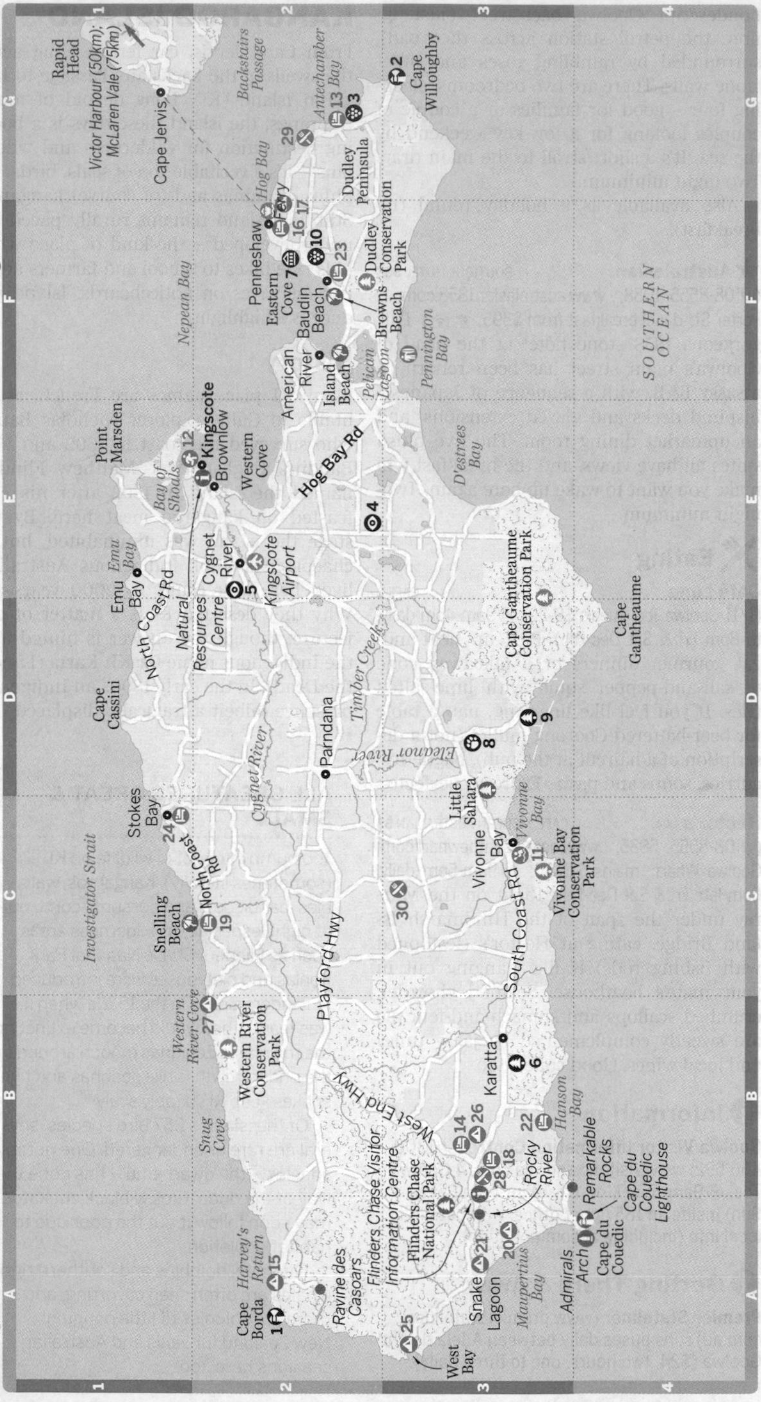

0 20 km
0 10 miles

Investigator Strait
Rapid Head
Victor Harbour (50km); McLaren Vale (75km)
Cape Jervis
Backstairs Passage
Nepean Bay
Point Marsden
Emu Bay
Cape Cassini
North Coast Rd
Stokes Bay
Snelling Beach
Western River Cove
Snug Cove
Western River Conservation Park
Cape Borda
Harvey's Return
Bay of Shoals
Natural Resources Centre
Kingscote
Brownlow
Cygnet River
Kingscote Airport
Western Cove
Cygnet River
Parndana
Playford Hwy
West End Hwy
Hog Bay Rd
Timber Creek
Eleanor River
Penneshaw
Hog Bay
Ferry
Eastern Cove
American River
Baudin Beach
Island Beach
Pelican Lagoon
Browns Beach
Dudley Conservation Park
Dudley Peninsula
Antechamber Bay
Cape Willoughby
Pennington Bay
D'estrees Bay
Ravine des Casoars
Flinders Chase Visitor Information Centre
Flinders Chase National Park
West Bay
Snake Lagoon
Maupertius Bay
Rocky River
Hanson Bay
Admirals Arch
Cape du Couedic
Remarkable Rocks
Cape du Couedic Lighthouse
Karatta
South Coast Rd
Vivonne Bay
Little Sahara
Vivonne Bay Conservation Park
Cape Gantheaume Conservation Park
Cape Gantheaume
SOUTHERN OCEAN

1 2 3 4 5 6 7 8 9 10 11 12 13 14 15 16 17 18 19 20 21 22 23 24 25 26 27 28 29 30

Kangaroo Island

Sights

1 Cape Borda Lightstation A2
2 Cape Willoughby Lightstation G3
3 Chapman River Wines G2
4 Clifford's Honey Farm E2
5 Island Pure Sheep Dairy E2
6 Kelly Hill Conservation Park B3
7 Penneshaw Maritime & Folk Museum F2
8 Raptor Domain D3
9 Seal Bay Conservation Park D3
10 Sunset Winery F2

Activities, Courses & Tours

11 Kangaroo Island Outdoor Action C3
12 Pelican Feeding E1

Sleeping

13 Antechamber Bay Ecocabins G2
14 Flinders Chase Farm B3
Gateway Visitor Information Centre .... (see 16)
15 Harvey's Return A2
16 Kangaroo Island Backpackers F2
17 Kangaroo Island Shores F2
18 Kangaroo Island Wilderness Retreat B3
19 Lifetime Private Rentals C2
20 Rocky River A3
21 Snake Lagoon A3
22 Southern Ocean Lodge B3
23 Wallaby Beach House F2
24 Waves & Wildlife C1
25 West Bay A3
26 Western KI Caravan Park B3
27 Western River Cove Campsite B2

Eating

28 Chase Cafe B3
29 Dudley Cellar Door G2
Isola Pizza .... (see 16)
30 Marron Café C3

Information

Gateway Visitor Information Centre .... (see 16)

was re-established on KI when whalers and sealers abducted Aboriginal women from Tasmania and brought them here.

Activities

The safest **swimming** is along the north coast, where the water is warmer and there are fewer rips than down south. Try Emu Bay, Stokes Bay, Snelling Beach or Western River Cove.

For **surfing**, hit the uncrowded swells along the south coast. Pennington Bay has strong, reliable breaks; Vivonne Bay and Hanson Bay in the southwest also serve up some tasty waves. Pick up the *Kangaroo Island Surfing Guide* brochure from visitor information centres, or download it from www.tourkangarooisland.com.au.

There's plenty to see under your own steam on KI. Check out www.tourkangarooisland.com.au/wildlife for info on **bushwalks** from 1km to 18km long.

The waters around KI are home to 230 species of fish, plus coral and around 60 shipwrecks – great **snorkelling** and **diving**! **Kangaroo Island Dive & Adventures** (08-8553 3196; www.kangarooislanddiveandadventures.com.au) runs diving trips (boat dives start from $320) and offers gear and kayak hire (snorkelling equipment hire from $35, and kayak full-day hire $70).

Skidding down the dunes at **Little Sahara** is great fun. **Kangaroo Island Outdoor Action** (08-8559 4296; www.kioutdooraction.com.au; 188 Jetty Rd, Vivonne Bay) rents out sandboards/toboggans ($29/39 per day), plus single/double kayaks ($39/69 for four hours).

There's plenty of good **fishing** around the island, including jetties at Kingscote, Penneshaw, Emu Bay and Vivonne Bay. Fishing charter tours (half/full day per person from $150/250) include tackle and refreshments, and you keep what you catch. Try **Kangaroo Island Fishing Adventures** (08-8559 3232; www.kangarooislandadventures.com.au).

Tours

Stay at least one night on the island if you can (one-day tours are hectic).

Adventures Beyond ADVENTURE TOUR
(1300 736 014; www.adventuresbeyond.com.au; 1-/2-day tours $258/415) All-inclusive, two-day island wildlife tours (small backpacker groups), departing Adelaide, with lots of activities (sandboarding, snorkelling, hiking…). One-day tours also available.

Cruising Kangaroo Island KAYAKING
(0418 767 667; www.cruisingkangarooisland.com; tours per person from $80) Two-hour guided kayak paddles around choice KI

KANGAROO ISLAND TOUR PASS

If you plan on seeing most of the main sights, you'll save cash with a **Kangaroo Island Tour Pass** (www.environment.sa.gov.au; adult/child/family $68/42/185), which covers all park and conservation area entry fees, and ranger-guided tours at Seal Bay, Kelly Hill Caves, Cape Borda and Cape Willoughby. The pass is available online, at visitor centres or at most sights.

coastal spots ex-Browns Beach. Ask about sunset paddles.

Groovy Grape TOUR
(☎08-8440 1640, 1800 661 177; www.groovygrape.com.au) Two-day, all-incusive, small-group wildlife safaris ($415) ex-Adelaide, with sandboarding, campfires and all the main sights.

Kangaroo Island Ocean Safari ADVENTURE TOUR
(☎0419 772 175; www.kangarooislandoceansafari.com.au; tours adult/child $77/55) Hop aboard this bouyant 12-seater for a 75-minute nautical tour ex-Penneshaw, spying seals, dolphins, birds and (sometimes) whales.

Kangaroo Island Adventure Tours GUIDED TOUR
(☎08-8202 8678; www.kiadventuretours.com.au) Two-day, all-inclusive tours ex-Adelaide (from $436 with dorm accommodation; more for private rooms) with a backpacker bent and plenty of activities.

Kangaroo Island Marine Adventures TOUR
(☎08-8553 3227; www.kimarineadventures.com) One-hour North Coast boat tours ($60) and longer half-day jaunts ($190) which include swimming with dolphins, visiting seal colonies and access to remote areas of KI.

Sleeping

KI accommodation is expensive, adding insult to your wallet's injury after the pricey ferry ride. Self-contained cottages, B&Bs and beach houses start at around $160 per night per double (usually with a two-night minimum stay). There are some great camp sites around the island though, plus a few midrange motels. Quality caravan parks and hostels are scarce.

There are a few agencies which can help book accommodation on the island.

Gateway Visitor Information Centre ACCOMMODATION SERVICES
(☎1800 811 080; www.tourkangarooisland.com.au/accommodation)

Kangaroo Island Holiday Accommodation ACCOMMODATION SERVICES
(☎08-8553 9007; www.kangarooislandholidayaccommodation.com.au)

Sealink ACCOMMODATION SERVICES
(☎13 13 01; www.sealink.com.au/kangaroo-island-accommodation)

Information

The main Gateway Visitor Information Centre (p750) is in Penneshaw. **Kangaroo Island Hospital** (☎08-8553 4200; www.countryhealthsa.sa.gov.au; The Esplanade, Kingscote; 24hr) is in Kingscote. There are ATMs in Kingscote and Penneshaw. Island mobile phone reception can be patchy outside the main towns (reception is best with Telstra). There are supermarkets at Penneshaw and Kingscote, and a general store at American River.

Online, see www.tourkangarooisland.com.au.

Getting There & Away

AIR

Regional Express (Rex; www.regionalexpress.com.au) flies daily between Adelaide and Kingscote (return from $240).

BUS

Sealink operates a morning and afternoon bus service between Adelaide Central Bus Station and Cape Jervis (return adult/child $52/28, 2¼ hours one way).

FERRY

Sealink (☎13 13 01; www.sealink.com.au) operates a car ferry between Cape Jervis and Penneshaw on KI, with at least three ferries each way daily (return adult/child from $98/50, bicycles/motorcycles/cars $22/64/286, 45 minutes one way). One driver is included with the vehicle price (cars only, not bikes).

Getting Around

There's no public transport on the island: take a tour or bring or hire some wheels. The island's main roads are sealed, but the rest are gravel, including those to Cape Willoughby, Cape Borda and the North Coast Rd (take it slowly, especially at night). There's petrol at Kingscote, Penneshaw, American River, Parndana and Vivonne Bay.

TO/FROM THE AIRPORT

Kingscote Airport (www.kangarooisland.sa.gov.au/airport) is 14km from Kingscote. **Kangaroo Island Transfers** (☎08-8553 3133, 0427 887 575; www.kitransfers.com.au) connects the airport with Kingscote (per person $20, minimum two people), American River ($30) and Penneshaw ($45). Solo travellers pay double (eg Kingscote $40). Bookings are essential. Sealink offers a similar service.

TO/FROM THE FERRY

Sealink runs daily shuttles between Penneshaw and American River (adult/child $15/8, 30 minutes) and Kingscote ($18/10, one hour). Bookings essential.

CAR HIRE

Not all Adelaide car-rental companies will let you take their cars onto KI. **Budget** (www.budget.com.au) and **Hertz** (www.hertz.com.au) supply cars to Penneshaw, Kingscote and Kingscote Airport.

Penneshaw & Dudley Peninsula

Looking across Backstairs Passage to the Fleurieu Peninsula, **Penneshaw** (population 300), on the north shore of the **Dudley Peninsula**, is the ferry arrival point. The passing tourist trade lends a certain transience to the businesses here, but the pub, hostel and general store remain authentically grounded. En route to American River, **Pennington Bay** has consistent surf.

Sights

Chapman River Wines WINERY
(www.chapmanriverwines.com.au; off Cape Willoughby Rd, Antechamber Bay; ⌚11am-4.30pm Thu-Mon Sep-Jun) Occupying a converted aircraft hangar, this eccentric winery makes a mean shiraz. The interior is festooned with art and quirky bits of salvage from churches, pubs and homesteads from around SA. Good coffee, too.

Kangaroo Island Farmers Market MARKET
(www.goodfoodkangarooisland.com; Lloyd Collins Reserve, Frenchmans Tce, Penneshaw; ⌚9am-1pm 1st Sun of the month) Baked goods, chutneys, seafood, olive oil, honey, eggs, cheese, yogurt...and of course buskers and wine! Sealink (p748) offers dedicated passenger-only return tickets from the mainland if you'd just like to visit the market for the day.

Cape Willoughby Lightstation LIGHTHOUSE
(☎accommodation 08-8553 4410; www.environment.sa.gov.au; Cape Willoughby Rd; self-guided tours grounds only per person $3, guided incl lighthouse adult/child/family $15/9/39; ⌚guided tours 11.30am, 12.30pm & 2pm) About 28km southeast of Penneshaw (unsealed road), this lighthouse first shone in 1852 and is now used as a weather station. Lots of shipwreck info, plus basic cottage accommodation (doubles from $170, extra person $28). Extra tours at 3pm and 4pm during school holidays.

Sunset Winery WINERY
(www.sunset-wines.com.au; 4564 Hog Bay Rd, Penneshaw; ⌚11am-5pm) Wow, what a view! If you can't make it up the steep driveway, there's another access around the back. Either way, expect brilliant sauvignon blanc and sparkling shiraz. Sunset also serves savoury platters to go with the panorama.

Penneshaw Maritime & Folk Museum MUSEUM
(www.nationaltrustsa.org.au; 52 Howard Dr, Penneshaw; adult/child/family $4/2/7; ⌚3-5pm Wed-Sun Sep-May) Displays artefacts from local shipwrecks and early settlement (check out those girthsome millstones!), plus endearingly geeky models of Flinders' *Investigator* and Baudin's *Geographe*.

Sleeping & Eating

Kangaroo Island YHA HOSTEL $
(☎08-8553 1344; www.yha.com.au; 33 Middle Tce, Penneshaw; dm $35, d with/without bathroom $110/75, f $160; @ wifi) Occupying an old '60s motel with faux-brick cladding close to downtown Penneshaw, the island YHA has neat, spacious rooms, mostly with en suite bathrooms. There's a sunny communal kitchen, little lounge, laundry and handsome hammock.

Kangaroo Island Backpackers HOSTEL $
(☎0439 750 727; www.kangarooislandbackpackers.com; 43 North Tce, Penneshaw; dm/s/tw/d/f from $28/38/58/80/120) A tidy, affable independent hostel a short wander from both the pub and the ferry dock. It's a simple setup and there's no wi-fi, but hey, you're on holiday on an island – who needs interior design and social media? Dangle a line off the jetty instead.

Kangaroo Island Shores CARAVAN PARK $
(☎08-8553 1028; www.seafront.com.au; Lot 501, Talinga Tce, Penneshaw; unpowered/powered sites $25/30) The closest camping to the ferry, a short wander around the foreshore from the Penneshaw jetty. Not the most wild or interesting of settings, but certainly clean and convenient.

Antechamber Bay Ecocabins CABINS $$
(☎08-8553 1557; www.kiecocabins.com; 142 Creek Bay Rd, Antechamber Bay; d from $130, extra adult/child $20/free, unpowered sites adult/child $20/free) Off Cape Willoughby Rd, these two eight-bed cabins are on 22-hectares behind the dunes: rudimentary but perfectly comfortable, with roofless showers, self-composting toilets, and solar power and hot water. Or you can pitch a tent and use the quirky camp kitchen. Kayaks and fishing gear available (there's bream in the river).

Wallaby Beach House RENTAL HOUSE $$
(☎08-8362 5293; www.wallabybeachhouse.com.au; Browns Beach; d from $180, extra person $25) A secluded, self-contained three-bedroom beach house, 13km west of Penneshaw on unpeopled Browns Beach. Simple but stylish decor, with broad sunset views and passing seals, dolphins and penguins to keep you company. Sleeps six.

Fish SEAFOOD $
(☎0439 803 843; www.2birds1squid.com; 43 North Tce, Penneshaw; mains $13-18; ⏲4.30-8pm mid-Oct–Apr) Takeaway fish and chips like you ain't never had before – grilled, beer-battered or crumbed whiting and garfish – plus giant KI scallops, marron, lobster medallions, prawns and oysters. Dunk them in an array of excellent homemade sauces. Hours can vary – call in advance.

★**Dudley Cellar Door** CAFE $$
(☎08-8553 1333; www.dudleywines.com.au; 1153 Cape Willoughby Rd, Cuttlefish Bay; mains $25-28; ⏲10am-5pm) KI's pioneering winery has a superb cellar door, 12km east of Penneshaw. It's a fancy corrugated-iron shed, with astonishing views back to the mainland and serving superb pizzas (try the King George whiting version), oysters and buckets of prawns – perfect with a bottle of chardonnay on the deck.

Isola Pizza PIZZA $$
(☎08-8553 1227; www.facebook.com/isolapizzakangarooisland; 43 North Tce, Penneshaw; mains $15-30; ⏲5-8pm; 📶) Sun going down, waiting for the ferry, getting hungry and eaten all your supplies? Duck into Isola (Spanish for 'island') and snare a fab pizza for dinner. The Greek lamb version takes the cake.

Information

Gateway Visitor Information Centre (☎1800 811 080, 08-8553 1185; www.tourkangarooisland.com.au; Lot 3 Howard Dr, Penneshaw; ⏲9am-5pm Mon-Fri, 10am-4pm Sat & Sun; 📶) Just outside Penneshaw on the road to Kingscote, this centre is stocked with brochures and maps. Also books accommodation, and sells park entry tickets and the Kangaroo Island Tour Pass.

American River

POP 230

Between Penneshaw and Kingscote, on the way to nowhere in particular, American River squats redundantly by the glassy **Pelican Lagoon**. The town was named after a crew of American sealers who built a trading schooner here in 1804. There's no such industriousness here today, just a general store and a gaggle of pelicans.

From the end of Scenic Dr, a **coastal walk** (2km one way) passes through natural scrub, sugar gums and she-oak en route to some old fish-cannery ruins.

Sleeping & Eating

American River Camping Ground CAMPGROUND $
(☎08-8553 4500; www.kangarooisland.sa.gov.au; Tangara Dr, American River; unpowered/powered sites per 2 people $15/25, extra person $5) Shady, council-run camping by the lagoon, with fire pits, showers, toilets and a nifty BBQ hut. Pay via self-registration.

Mercure Kangaroo Island Lodge MOTEL $$
(☎1800 355 581, 08-8553 7053; www.kilodge.com.au; Lot 2, Scenic Dr, American River; d incl breakfast from $180; ❄@📶🏊) Up-to-scratch motel suites overlooking either the pool or lagoon (the rammed-earth wing has the best rooms). The restaurant plates up buffet breakfasts and dinners featuring lots of local seafood (mains $20 to $30, serving 7.30am to 9am and 6pm to 8.30pm).

Island Coastal Units MOTEL, CABINS $$
(☎08-8553 7010; www.kangarooislandcoastalunits.com.au; Tangara Dr, American River; units/cabins from $100/120, extra person $20) A low row of basic one- and two-bedroom motel-

style units among trees opposite the foreshore, plus four beautiful self-contained cabins with solar hot water, gas cooktops and air-con (pay the extra $20!). Minimum two-night stay.

Oyster Farm Shop SEAFOOD $
(☎08-8553 7122; www.goodfoodkangarooisland.com/food/kio_shop.asp; 486 Tangara Dr, American River; meals $9-21; ⊙11am-4.30pm Mon-Fri, kitchen to 2.30pm) Run by a local oyster farm, this little shack acts as an outlet for sustainable seafood producers from all over KI. Oysters, marron, abalone, King George whiting… even barramundi, cooked into meals or takeaway uncooked. Get change from $10 for a dozen fresh unshucked oysters.

Kingscote

POP 1700

Snoozy seaside Kingscote (pronounced 'kings-coat') is the main settlement on KI, and the hub of island life. It's a photogenic town with swaying Norfolk Island pines, a couple of pubs and some decent eateries.

Sights & Activities

Kangaroo Island Spirits DISTILLERY
(KIS; www.kispirits.com.au; 856 Playford Hwy, Cygnet River; tastings free, bottles from $42; ⊙11am-5pm Wed-Mon, daily during school holidays) This fiesty little moonshiner makes small-batch gin with KI native juniper berries, plus vodka, brandy and liqueurs (pray the organic honey-and-walnut version hasn't sold out).

Island Beehive APIARY
(www.island-beehive.com.au; 59 Playford Hwy, Kingscote; tours adult/child/family $4.50/3/13; ⊙9am-5pm, tours every 30min 9.30am-3.30pm) Runs factory tours where you can study up on passive, hard-working Ligurian bees and beekeeping, then stock up on by-products (bee-products?) including delicious organic honey and honeycomb ice cream. Tours for groups available.

Island Pure Sheep Dairy DAIRY
(www.islandpure.com.au; 127 Gum Creek Rd, Cygnet River; tours adult/child/family $6.50/5.50/22; ⊙noon-4pm) Near Cygnet River, 12km from Kingscote, this dairy features 1500 sheep lining up to be milked (from 2pm daily). Take a tour of the factory, which includes yogurt and cheese tastings (the haloumi is magic).

Pelican Feeding BIRDWATCHING
(☎08-8553 3112; Kingscote Wharf, Kingscote; adult/child $5/3; ⊙5pm) Pull up a pew and watch the daily feeding frenzy of 20-something ravenous pelicans at Kingscote Wharf. The host is well protected – hatted, gloved and booted – and mic'd-up so you can hear the spiel above the voraciously snapping beaks.

Kingscote Tidal Pool SWIMMING
(www.kangarooisland.sa.gov.au/page.aspx?u=572&c=8272; Chapman Tce, Kingscote; ⊙daylight hours) FREE Kingscote beaches are lousy for swimming: locals usually head 18km northwest to **Emu Bay**, or to this 50m tidal swimming pool, which has a couple of pontoons and grassy banks on which to sun yourself on.

Sleeping & Eating

Kangaroo Island Central Backpackers HOSTEL $
(☎08-8553 2787; www.kicentralbackpackers.com; 19 Murray St, Kingscote; dm/d from $25/60; ❄📶) Just a couple of blocks from Kingscote's main strip, this small, innocuous hostel is clean and affordable, and has a cosy lounge, lush lawns and a beaut en suite double cabin out the back. It feels like staying at someone's house – good or bad, depending on how sociable you're feeling.

Kingscote Nepean Bay Tourist Park CARAVAN PARK $
(☎08-8553 2394; www.kingscotetouristpark.com.au; cnr First & Third Sts, Brownlow; unpowered/powered sites $34/40, cabins/units from $90/135; ❄📶) You'll find the standard gamut of caravan park delights behind the dunes in Brownlow, 3km southwest of Kingscote. You can walk back to Kingscote via a coastal walking trail. Better for camping than cabins.

Aurora Ozone Hotel HOTEL $$
(☎08-8553 2011, 1800 083 133; www.aurorare sorts.com.au; cnr Commercial St & Kingscote Tce, Kingscote; d pub/motel from $162/248, 1-/2-/3-bed apt from $270/482/543; ❄@📶🏊) Opposite the foreshore with killer views, the 100-year-old Ozone pub has quality pub rooms upstairs, motel rooms, and stylish deluxe apartments in a new wing across the street. The eternally busy bistro (mains $20 to $48) serves meaty grills and seafood, and you can pickle yourself on KI wines at the bar.

Seaview Motel MOTEL, GUESTHOUSE $$
(☎08-8553 2030; www.seaview.net.au; 51 Chapman Tce, Kingscote; guesthouse s/d $90/100, motel s/d $146/156, extra adult/child $25/15;) It seems like this place is always full – a good sign! Choose from older-style 1929 guesthouse rooms with shared facilities (no air-con), or refurbished 1980s motel rooms. Family-owned, and affordable by KI standards.

Kangaroo Island Fresh Seafoods SEAFOOD $
(www.goodfoodkangarooisland.com/eatingout/kifreshseafood.asp; 26 Telegraph Rd, Kingscote; meals $8-16; 8am-8pm Mon-Sat) This unassuming place attached to a petrol station has some of the best seafood you're ever likely to taste. Fat oysters go for around a dollar each, then there are all manner of cooked and fresh KI seafood packs and combos. Superb!

Bella ITALIAN $$
(☎08-8553 0400; www.goodfoodkangarooisland.com/eatingout/bella.asp; 54 Dauncey St, Kingscote; pizzas $15-39, mains $26-32; 10am-late) Sit inside or on the pavement, al fresco, at Bella, a cheery Italian cafe-restaurant–pizza bar. Pizzas start around lunchtime (eat in or takeaway); dinner is à la carte, featuring American River oysters, Spencer Gulf king prawns, local roo and whiting.

Information

Natural Resources Centre (☎08-8553 4444; www.naturalresources.sa.gov.au/kangarooisland; 37 Dauncey St, Kingscote; 9am-5pm Mon-Fri) Sells the Kangaroo Island Tour Pass and has info on national parks.

North Coast Road

Exquisite beaches (calmer than the south coast), bushland and undulating pastures dapple the North Coast Rd, running from Kingscote along the coast to the Playford Hwy 85km west (the bitumen expires at Emu Bay). There's not a whole lot to do here other than swan around on the beach – sounds good!

About 18km from Kingscote, **Emu Bay** is a holiday hamlet with a 5km-long, white-sand beach flanked by dunes – one of KI's best swimming spots. Around 36km further west, **Stokes Bay** has a penguin rookery and broad rock pool, accessible by scrambling through a 20m tunnel in the cliffs at the bay's eastern end (mind your head!). Beware the rip outside the pool.

The view as you look back over **Snelling Beach** from atop Constitution Hill is awesome! Continue 7km west and you'll hit the turn-off to **Western River Cove**, where a small beach is crowded in by sombre basalt cliffs. The ridge-top road in is utterly scenic (and steep).

Sleeping & Eating

Western River Cove Campsite CAMPGROUND $
(☎08-8553 4500; www.kangarooisland.sa.gov.au; unpowered sites per 2 people $15, extra person $5) It's a steep drive into this self-registration camp site, just a short walk from the beach and with a footbridge over the river (so tempting to dangle a line). There's a toilet block and a barbecue hut but no showers.

Emu Bay Holiday Homes CABINS, RENTAL HOUSE $
(☎08-8553 5241; www.emubaysuperviews.com.au; 21 Bayview Rd, Emu Bay; cabins $96, holiday homes $122-152, extra person $22;) Great-value (if a little frilly) cabins and holiday homes in a large flower-filled garden on the hill above Emu Bay beach (great views!). The self-contained cabins (caravan-park cabins with a facelift, sans air-con) sleep four or six; the holiday homes sleep six or 10.

Waves & Wildlife COTTAGES $$
(☎08-8559 2232; www.wavesandwildlife.com.au; North Coast Rd, Stokes Bay; 1-/3-bedroom per 2 people from $125/145, extra person $20) This phalanx of trim, tidy, newish cottages (built 2006) marches down a grassy hillside above Stokes Bay (love the tunnel and the rock pool!). There are one- and three-bedroom configurations, with full kitchens, sweeping views and kangaroos hopping around at dusk. Linen charges and minimum stays apply, but it's still good bang for your buck.

Lifetime Private Rentals RENTAL HOUSES $$$
(www.life-time.com.au; North Coast Rd, Snelling Beach; d from $490;) Pricey but worth every penny, these four gorgeous self-contained stone-and-timber houses dot the hillsides above beautiful Snelling Beach (...actually, they're not that pricey if there's a few of you: from $510 for six people in three bedrooms). Expect decks, big windows, quirky artworks and knock-out views.

Rockpool Café CAFE $$
(☎08-8559 2277; www.facebook.com/therockpoolcafe; North Coast Rd, Stokes Bay; mains $15-28; 11am-5pm) Don't worry about sandy

feet at this casual, al fresco joint in Stokes Bay. 'What's the house special?', we asked. 'Whatever I feel like doin'!', said the chef (usually seafood, washed down with local wines and decent espresso).

South Coast Road

The south coast is rough and wave swept, compared with the north.

Sights & Activities

Seal Bay Conservation Park NATURE RESERVE

(08-8553 4460; www.sealbay.sa.gov.au; Seal Bay Rd; guided tours adult/child/family $32/18/80; tours 9am-4pm year-round, extra tours Dec-Feb, twilight tours Oct-Mar) 'Observation, not interaction' is the mentality here. Guided tours stroll along the beach (or boardwalk on self-guided tours; adult $15, child $9, family $40) to a colony of (mostly sleeping) Australian sea lions. Twilight tours December and January (adult $60, child $38, family $165). Bookings advised.

Clifford's Honey Farm FARM

(www.cliffordshoney.com.au; 1157 Elsegood Rd, Haines; 9am-5pm) It's almost worth swimming the Backstairs Passage for the honey ice cream (sourced from a colony of rare Ligurian bees) at this charming, uncommercial farm. A bit off the tourist radar (again, charming).

Kelly Hill Conservation Park NATURE RESERVE

(08-8553 4464; www.environment.sa.gov.au; South Coast Rd; tours adult/child/family $18/10/45, adventure caving adult/child $70/40; 10.15am-4.30pm) This series of dry limestone caves was 'discovered' in the 1880s by a horse named Kelly, who fell into them through a hole. Take the standard show cave tour (10.30am, then hourly 11am to 4pm), or add on an adventure caving tour (2.15pm; bookings essential). The **Hanson Bay Walk** (9km one way) runs from the caves past freshwater wetlands. There are extra show cave tours during school holidays.

Raptor Domain ZOO

(www.kangarooislandbirdsofprey.com.au; cnr South Coast & Seal Bay Rds; birds of prey adult/child/family $16.50/12/50, reptiles $12/10/35; 10.30am-4pm) Check out some KI wedge-tailed eagles, barn owls and kookaburras at a one-hour birds-of-prey display (11.30am and 2.30pm), or go scaly at a one-hour lizards and snakes show (1pm).

SOUTHERN OCEAN LODGE

Millionaires, start your engines! The shining star in the SA tourism galaxy is **Southern Ocean Lodge** (08-8559 7347; www.southernoceanlodge.com.au; Hanson Bay Rd; d per night from $1050;), a sexy, low-profile snake tracing the Hanson Bay cliff-top – a real exercise in exclusivity. There's a two-night minimum stay; you get airport transfers, all meals and drinks, and guided tours of KI.

If you want a stickybeak, don't expect to see anything from the road: all you'll find is a steely set of gates and an unreceptive intercom: privacy is what guests are paying for here (Hey, wasn't that Teri Hatcher in that 4WD?). But you can catch a sneaky glimpse from Hanson Bay beach.

Sleeping & Eating

Western KI Caravan Park CAMPGROUND $

(08-8559 7201; www.westernki.com.au; 7928 South Coast Rd, Flinders Chase; unpowered/powered sites $25/30, cabins $110-190;) A few minutes' drive east of Flinders Chase National Park, this friendly park has shady gums and resident roos. Check out the koala and lagoon walks, and the phone booth inside an old bakery truck. The shop sells groceries, homemade heat-and-eats and (for guests only) beer and wine.

Flinders Chase Farm HOSTEL, CABINS $$

(08-8559 7223; www.flinderschasefarm.com.au; 1561 West End Hwy, Karatta; dm/cabins $25/70, d/f with bathroom from $110/120) A working farm with charm, a short drive from Flinders Chase National Park. Accommodation includes tidy dorms, a couple of cosy cabins and en-suite rooms in a lodge. There's also a terrific camp kitchen, fire pits and 'tropical' outdoor showers.

Kangaroo Island Wilderness Retreat HOTEL, RESORT $$

(08-8559 7275; www.kiwr.com; Lot 1, South Coast Rd, Flinders Chase; d/apt/ste from $175/182/256;) A low-key, log cabin–style resort on the Flinders Chase doorstep, with resident grazing wallabies. Accommodation ranges from basic motel-style rooms to flashy spa suites. There's also a petrol pump and a bar, and a **restaurant** (breakfast $15-25, dinner $24-36; 7.30-9.30am & 6-8.30pm).

Marron Café MODERN AUSTRALIAN $$
(08-8559 4114; www.andermel.com.au; 804 Harriet Rd, Central Kangaroo Island; mains $16-38; 11am-4.30pm Sep-Apr, noon-3.30pm May-Aug) Around 15km north of Vivonne Bay you can check out marron in breeding tanks, then eat some! It's a subtle taste, not necessarily enhanced by the heavy sauces issued by the kitchen. There are steak and chicken dishes, too, for the crustacean-shy. Last orders 30 minutes before closing.

Flinders Chase National Park

Occupying the western end of the island, Flinders Chase National Park is one of SA's top national parks. Much of the park is mallee scrub, and there are also some beautiful, tall sugar-gum forests, particularly around Rocky River and the Ravine des Casoars, 5km south of Cape Borda. Pay your park entry fees at the Flinders Chase Visitor Information Centre.

Sights & Activities

Once a farm, **Rocky River** is now a rampant hotbed of wildlife, with kangaroos, wallabies and Cape Barren geese competing for your affections. A slew of good walks launch from behind the visitors centre, including the **Rocky River Hike**, on which you might spy a platypus (9km loop, three hours).

From Rocky River, a road runs south to a remote 1906 **lighthouse** atop wild Cape du Couedic (pronounced 'coo-dick'). A boardwalk weaves down to **Admirals Arch**, a huge archway ground out by heavy seas, and passes a colony of New Zealand fur seals (sweet smelling they ain't...).

At Kirkpatrick Point, a few kilometres east of Cape du Couedic, the much-photographed **Remarkable Rocks** are a cluster of hefty, weather-gouged granite boulders atop a rocky dome that arcs 75m down to the sea. Remarkable!

On the northwestern corner of the island, the 1858 **Cape Borda Lightstation** (08-8559 3257; www.environment.sa.gov.au/parks; admission free, tours adult/child/family $14.50/9/38; 9am-5pm, tours 11am, 12.30pm & 2pm) stands tall above the rippling iron surface of the Southern Ocean. There are walks here from 1.5km to 9km, and extra tours at 3.15pm and 4pm during summer holidays.

At nearby Harvey's Return a **cemetery** speaks poignant volumes about the reality of isolation in the early days. From here you can drive to **Ravine des Casoars** (literally 'Ravine of the Cassowaries', referring to the now-extinct dwarf emus seen here by Baudin's expedition). The challenging **Ravine des Casoars Hike** (8km return, four hours) tracks through the ravine to the coast.

Sleeping & Eating

There are campgrounds at **Rocky River** (per person/car $10/28), **Snake Lagoon** (per person/car $7/13), **West Bay** (per person/car $7/13) and **Harvey's Return** (per person/car $7/13); book through the **Department of Environment, Water & Natural Resources** (DEWNR; 08-8553 4490; flinderschase@sa.gov.au).

There's also refurbished cottage accommodation at Rocky River – the budget **Postmans Cottage** (d $72) and family-friendly **Mays Homestead** (d $171) – and lightkeepers' cottages at **Cape du Couedic** and **Cape Borda** (d $48-219). Book online, by email or by phone through the **Department of Environment, Water & Natural Resources** (08-8553 4410; www.environment.sa.gov.au).

On the food front, if you're not self-catering the only option here is the **Chase Cafe** (08-8559 7339; www.thechasecafe.com.au; Flinders Chase Visitor Information Centre; meals $7-28; 9am-3.30pm) at the visitors centre, serving burgers, wraps, soup, coffee, and wines by the glass.

Information

Flinders Chase Visitor Information Centre (08-8559 7235; www.environment.sa.gov.au/parks; South Coast Rd, Flinders Chase; park entry adult/child/family $10/6/27; 9am-5pm) Info, maps and camping/accommodation bookings, plus a cafe and displays on island ecology.

Barossa Valley & Southeastern SA

Includes ➡

Best Places to Eat

➡ Skillogalee (p766)

➡ Terroir (p764)

➡ Banrock Station Wine & Wetland Centre (p769)

➡ Pipers of Penola (p778)

➡ Ferment Asian (p760)

Best Places to Stay

➡ Reilly's (p765)

➡ Waikerie Hotel Motel (p768)

➡ Dalton on the Lake (p773)

➡ Bompas (p775)

➡ BIG4 Renmark Riverfront Holiday Park (p771)

Why Go?

From legendary wine regions north of Adelaide, around the lugubrious bends of the Murray River and down along the Limestone Coast, this vast swathe of South Australia demands your undivided attention.

You can tackle the Barossa and Clare Valleys as day trips from Adelaide, but when the wine and food are this good, why rush? Spend a few days in each, exploring old-fangled towns, cycling between cellar doors, eating and revelling in general hedonism. These compact corners of SA are custom-built holiday haunts.

Conversely, the Murray River is vast, curling across the entire state. Towns here are utilitarian, with country sensibility at the helm. Silently sliding by, the river is undeniable in its beauty and grace.

Heading southeast, trace the Limestone Coast through the sea-salty Coorong, past beachy holiday towns to Mount Gambier, SA's second city. And, if you haven't already OD'd on wine, the Coonawarra Wine Region awaits.

When to Go

Tanunda

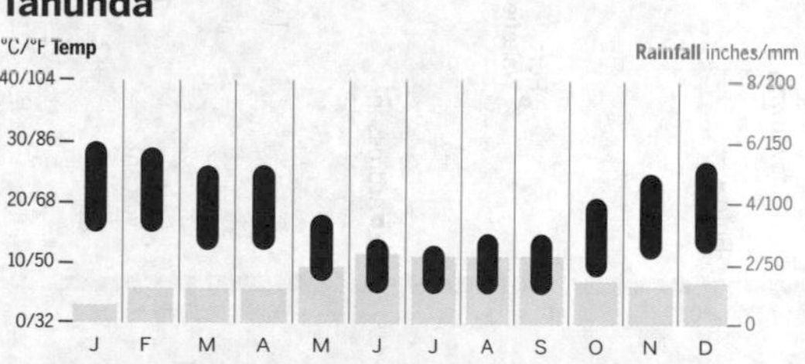

Mar–May Low autumn sunsets and russet-red grapevines: harvest is in the air.

Oct & Nov Springtime on the Murray River, before the jet skis arrive en masse.

Dec–Feb Summer's here and the time is right for snoozing on the beach.

Barossa Valley & Southeastern SA Highlights

1. Cycling between cellar doors along the **Riesling Trail** (p763) in the Clare Valley.
2. Eating some sauerkraut and schnitzels in the **Barossa Valley** (p758), washed down with fine wine.
3. Hiring a houseboat and chug around the bends of the **Murray River** (p766).
4. Losing a few hours (or days) exploring the quiet corners of the **Coorong National Park** (p772).
5. Assessing the colour of the Blue Lake in **Mount Gambier** (p775).
6. Going underground at the World Heritage–listed **Naracoorte**

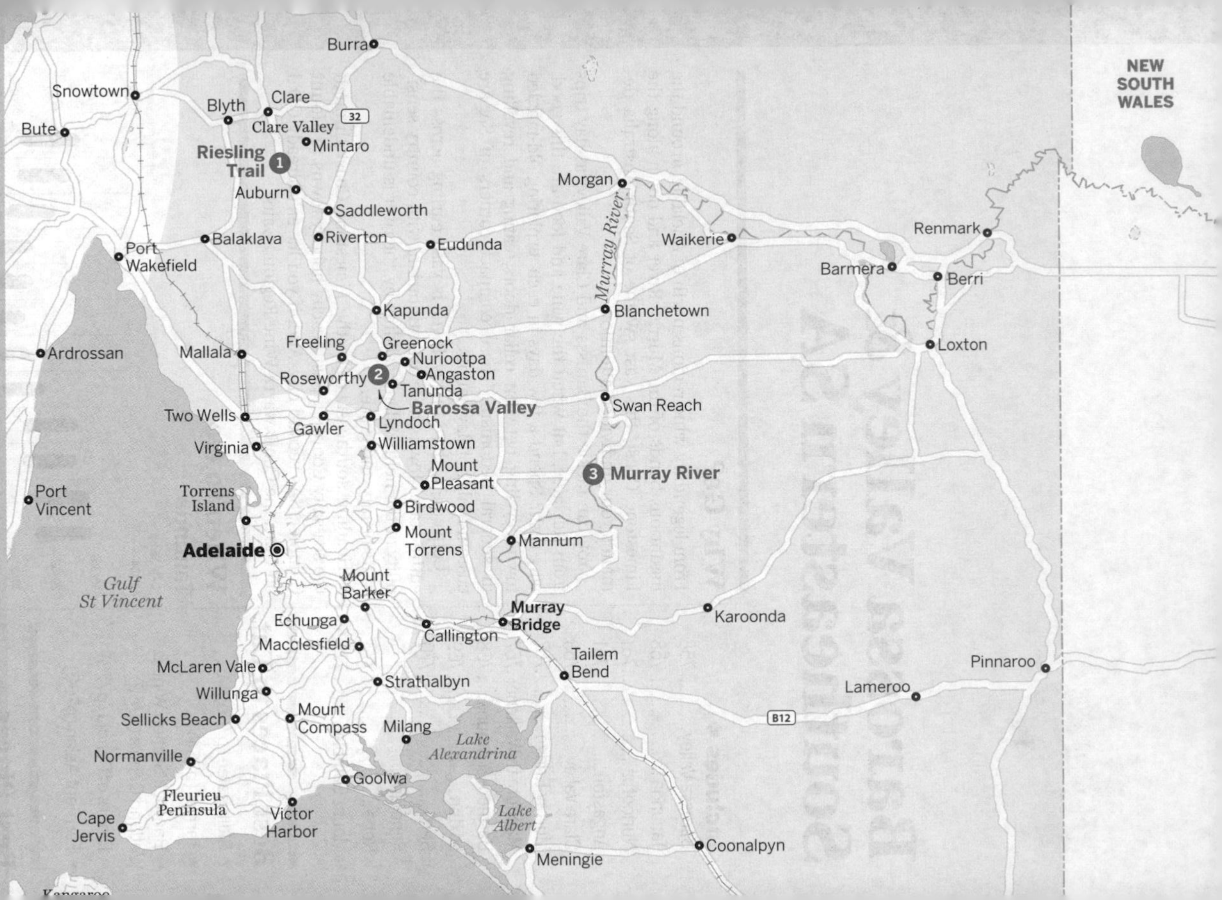

Caves National Park (p778).

7 Learning to tell your cab sav from your shiraz in the **Coonawarra Wine Region** (p777).

8 Chilling-out on the beach in **Robe** (p773) after a hard day in the surf.

BAROSSA VALLEY

With hot, dry summers and cool, moderate winters, the Barossa is one of the world's great wine regions – an absolute must for anyone with even the slightest interest in a good drop. It's a compact valley – just 25km long – yet it manages to produce 21% of Australia's wine, and it makes a no-fuss day trip from Adelaide, 65km to the southwest.

The local towns have a distinctly German heritage, dating back to 1842. Fleeing religious persecution in Prussia and Silesia, settlers (bringing their vine cuttings with them) created a Lutheran heartland where German traditions persist today. The physical remnants of colonisation – Gothic church steeples and stone cottages – are everywhere. Cultural legacies of the early days include a dubious passion for oom-pah bands, and an appetite for wurst, pretzels and sauerkraut.

Tours

Wine-flavoured day tours departing Adelaide or locally are bountiful; the Barossa Visitor Information Centre (p761) makes bookings.

Balloon Adventures BALLOONING
(☎08-8562 3111; www.balloonadventures.com.au; flights adult/child $300/195) Fly the Barossa sky in a hot-air balloon. One-hour flights depart Tanunda and include a champagne breakfast.

Barossa Wine Lovers Tours TOUR
(☎08-8270 5500; www.wineloverstours.com.au; tours incl lunch from $75) Minibus tours to wineries, lookouts, shops and heritage buildings...a good blend. Good for groups; minimum numbers apply.

Groovy Grape TOUR
(☎1800 661 177; www.groovygrape.com.au; full-day tours $90) Backpacker-centric day tours ex-Adelaide with a BBQ lunch: good value, good fun. November to April only.

Taste the Barossa TOUR
(☎08-8357 1594; www.winetoursbarossa.com; full-day tours $99) Great-value minibus tours ex-Adelaide visiting a fistful of top wineries, with lunch at Peter Lehmann.

Uber Cycle Adventures CYCLING
(☎08-8563 1148; www.ubercycle.com.au; 2hr/half-/full-day tours $95/145/195) Get on your bike and see the Barossa on two wheels, with lots of native flora and fauna en route (oh, and some wine!).

Festivals & Events

Barossa Vintage Festival FOOD, WINE
(www.barossavintagefestival.com.au) A week-long festival with music, maypole dancing, tug-of-war contests etc; around Easter in odd-numbered years.

Barossa Gourmet Weekend FOOD, WINE
(www.barossagourmet.com) Fab food matched with winning wines at select wineries; happens in late winter or early spring.

A Day on the Green MUSIC
(www.adayonthegreen.com.au) Mature-age mosh-pit at Peter Lehmann Wines, with mature-age acts (Jimmy Barnes, Cheap Trick, Dragon). Held in December.

Getting There & Around

BICYCLE

The 27km Jack Brobridge Track runs from Gawler to Tanunda, with a 13km rail trail continuing through Nuriootpa to Angaston, passing plenty of wineries.

Based in Nuriootpa, **Barossa Bike Hire** (☎0412 380 651; www.barossabikehire.com.au; 5 South Tce, Nuriootpa) rents out quality cycles/tandems from $35/70 per day. **Angaston Hardware** (☎08-8564 2055; www.facebook.com/angastonhardware; 5 Sturt St; ⏰8.30am-5.30pm Mon-Fri, 9am-4pm Sat, 10am-4pm Sun) also rents out bikes for $25/40 per half/full day. Pick up the *Barossa by Bike* brochure at the Barossa Visitor Information Centre (p761) in Tanunda.

BUS & TRAIN

Adelaide Metro (www.adelaidemetro.com.au) runs regular daily trains to Gawler ($5.10, one hour), from where **LinkSA** (www.linksa.com.au) buses run to Tanunda ($9.60, 45 minutes), Nuriootpa ($12.20, one hour) and Angaston ($14.80, 1¼ hours).

TAXI

Barossa Taxis (☎0411 150 850; www.barossataxis.com.au; ⏰24hr) Taxis for up to nine people.

Tanunda

POP 4680

At the centre of the valley both geographically and socially, Tanunda is the Barossa's main tourist town. Tanunda manages to morph the practicality of Nuriootpa with the charm of Angaston without a sniff of self-importance. The wineries are what you're here for – sip, sip, sip!

DON'T MISS

BAROSSA VALLEY WINERIES

The Barossa is best known for shiraz, with riesling the dominant white. There are around 80 vineyards here and 60 cellar doors, ranging from boutique wine rooms to monstrous complexes. The long-established 'Barossa Barons' hold sway – big, ballsy and brassy – while spritely young boutique wineries are harder to sniff out.

Henschke (www.henschke.com.au; Henschke Rd, Keyneton; ⏲9am-4.30pm Mon-Fri, to noon Sat) About 10km southeast of Angaston in the Eden Valley, old-school Henschke is known for its iconic Hill of Grace red, but most of the wines here are classics.

Penfolds (www.penfolds.com.au; 30 Tanunda Rd, Nuriootpa; ⏲10am-5pm) You know the name: Penfolds is a Barossa institution. Book ahead for the 'Make Your Own Blend' tour ($65), or the 'Taste of Grange' tour ($150), which allows you to slide some Grange Hermitage across your lips.

Peter Lehmann Wines (www.peterlehmannwines.com.au; Para Rd, Tanunda; ⏲9.30am-5pm Mon-Fri, 10.30am-4.30pm Sat & Sun) The shiraz and riesling vintages here (oh, and semillon) are probably the most consistent, affordable and widely distributed wines in the Barossa. Peter Lehmann passed away in 2013: pay your respects with a cellar door visit.

St Hallett (www.sthallett.com.au; St Hallett Rd, Tanunda; ⏲10am-5pm) Using only Barossa grapes, improving St Hallet produces reasonably priced but consistently good whites (try the Poacher's Blend) and the excellent Old Block Shiraz. Unpretentious and great value for money.

Rockford Wines (www.rockfordwines.com.au; Krondorf Rd, Tanunda; ⏲11am-5pm) One of our favourite boutique Barossa wineries, this 1850s cellar door sells traditionally made, small range wines, including sparkling reds. The Black Shiraz is a sparkling, spicy killer.

Sights

Mengler Hill Lookout VIEWPOINT
(Mengler Hill Rd; ⏲24hr) FREE From Tanunda, take the scenic route to Angaston via Bethany for hazy valley views (just ignore the naff sculptures in the foreground). The road tracks through beautiful rural country, studded with huge eucalyptuses.

Barossa Museum MUSEUM
(www.community.history.sa.gov.au/barossa-museum; 47 Murray St; adult/child $2/1; ⏲10am-5.30pm Tue-Fri, 9am-12.30pm Sat) Inside this 1856 post office building (access via the bike repair shop out the front) are displays of bone-handled cutlery, butter-making gear, photos of top-hatted locals, a re-created colonial bedroom and an amazing map of Germany pinpointing the homelands of Barossa settlers. The Indigenous coverage could use a little help.

Keg Factory FACTORY
(www.thekegfactory.com.au; 25 St Hallett Rd; ⏲10am-4pm) FREE Watch honest-to-goodness coopers make and repair wine barrels, 4km south of town. Amazing!

Goat Square HISTORIC SITE
(cnr John & Maria Sts) FREE Tanunda is flush with historic buildings, including the cottages around this square, on John St. This was the *ziegenmarkt,* a meeting and market place, laid out in 1842 as Tanunda's original town centre.

Barossa Regional Gallery GALLERY
(www.freewebs.com/barossagallery; 3 Basedow Rd, Soldiers Memorial Hall; ⏲11am-4pm Wed-Mon) FREE Has an eclectic collection of paintings, crafts and touring exhibitions, plus an impressive set of organ pipes at the back of the room.

Sleeping

Barossa Backpackers HOSTEL $
(☎08-8563 0198; www.barossabackpackers.com.au; 9 Basedow Rd; dm/s/d from $27/80/80; @ 📶) Occupying a converted, U-shaped winery office building 500m from Tanunda's main street, this newish backpackers is a clean, secure and shipshape affair, with good weekly rates. Management can help you find picking/pruning work. Bike hire $20 per day.

Tanunda Hotel PUB $
(☎08-8563 2030; www.tanundahotel.com.au; 51 Murray St; d with/without bathroom $80/70, apt from $200; ❄ 📶) This boisterous ol' 1846 pub in the town centre is a real community hub. Pub rooms upstairs are good value and clean; out the back are nine ritzy mauve-coloured

OFF THE BEATEN TRACK

BAROSSA REGIONAL PARKS

For a little grape-free time away from the vines, you can't beat the Barossa's regional parks, with walking tracks for everyone from Sunday strollers to hardcore bushwalkers. The Barossa Visitor Information Centre can help with maps and directions.

Kaiserstuhl Conservation Park (08-8280 7048; www.environment.sa.gov.au; Tanunda Creek Rd, Angaston; daylight hours) Known for excellent walks, 390-hectare Kaiserstuhl is en route from Mengler Hill to Angaston. The Stringybark Hike (2km loop) and Wallowa Hike (4.7km one way) start at the entrance, with fantastic views from atop the Barossa Ranges. Look for Nankeen kestrels and western grey roos.

Para Wirra Recreation Park (08-8280 7048; www.environment.sa.gov.au; Humbug Scrub Rd, One Tree Hill; per person/car $4/10; 8am-sunset) In the northern Mt Lofty Ranges, a 45km hook south of Tanunda, Parra Wirra offers 1417 hectares of walking tracks, scenic drives, barbecues and tennis courts. Emus search hopefully around picnic areas; western grey roos graze in the dusk.

Warren Conservation Park (08-8280 7048; www.environment.sa.gov.au; Watts Gully Rd, Kersbrook; daylight hours) Explore 363 tranquil hectares of wattles, banksias and spring heaths, plus pink, blue and statuesque river red gums. Steep tracks for experienced hikers.

apartments. Downstairs, Duran Duran wails on the jukebox and schnitzels fall off the edges of plates (mains $18 to $37, serving noon to 2pm and 6pm to 8pm).

Discovery Holiday Parks Barossa Valley CARAVAN PARK $
(1800 991 590, 08-8563 2784; www.discoveryholidayparks.com.au; Barossa Valley Way; unpowered/powered sites from $33/36, cabins with/without bathroom from $115/99, villas from $285;) This spacious park just south of town is dotted with mature trees offering a little shade to ease your hangover. Facilities include a playground, barbecues, a laundry and bike hire for guests (per day $35). The flashy villas sleep up to six and have a two-night minimum stay.

Stonewell Cottages B&B $$$
(0417 848 977; www.stonewellcottages.com.au; Stonewell Rd; d cottages incl breakfast from $335;) These romantic, waterfront spa retreats and cottages are surrounded by vines and offer unbeatable privacy, comfort and serenity. Pet ducks waddle around rusty old ploughs as waterbirds splash down in the reservoir. Pricey, but worth it (good online specials; cheaper for multinight stays).

Eating

Die Barossa Wurst Haus Bakery BAKERY $
(86a Murray St; meals $4-26; 7am-4pm) 'Give people what they want' is the creed at this German bakery, serving *mettwurst* (Bavarian sausage) rolls, cheeses, pies, cakes, strudel and all-day breakfasts. It's hard to go past a trad German roll with kransky sausage, sauerkraut, cheese and mustard. An emasculating display of phallic wursts dangles above the counter.

Cafe Pod CAFE $
(58 Murray St; mains $10-19; 9am-3pm Mon-Fri, 9am-4pm Sat, 8.30am-4pm Sun;) A casual slice of hippie life on main-street Tanunda, with plenty of GF and vegetarian options, and open fires and macramé rugs for chilly winter mornings. Falafels, Asian fish cakes, sandwiches, vegie burgers, nachos, herbal teas...centre your karma then head back out to the wineries.

★ **Ferment Asian** SOUTHEAST ASIAN $$
(08-8563 0765; www.fermentasian.com.au; 90 Murray St; mains $23-33; noon-2pm Thu-Sun, 6pm-8.30pm Wed-Sat) In a lovely old stone villa facing Tanunda's main street at a jaunty angle, Ferment always does things a little differently. What sounds exotic is actually refreshingly simple: *cari rau* = yellow vegetable curry; *vit voi hoa chuoi* = duck breast salad. Chef Tuoi Do really knows how to put it all together.

1918 Bistro & Grill MODERN AUSTRALIAN $$
(08-8563 0405; www.1918.com.au; 94 Murray St; mains $29-40; noon-2.30pm daily, 6.30-9pm Mon-Sat, to 8pm Sun) This enduring restaurant occupies a lovely old villa, set back from the street beneath a massive Norfolk Island pine. It's a sassy affair serving adventurous mains such as Szechuan-spiced roast duck with mandarin caramel. Book a verandah table.

Information

Barossa Visitor Information Centre (☎1300 852 982, 08-8563 0600; www.barossa.com; 66-68 Murray St, Tanunda; ⏲9am-5pm Mon-Fri, 10am-4pm Sat & Sun; 📶) The low-down on the valley, plus internet access, and accommodation and tour bookings. Stocks the *A Town Walk of Tanunda* brochure.

Nuriootpa

POP 5705

Along an endless main street at the northern end of the valley, Nuriootpa is the Barossa's commercial centre. It's not as endearing as Tanunda or Angaston, but has a certain agrarian appeal. Lutheran spirit runs deep in Nuri: a sign says, 'God has invested in you – are you showing any interest?'

Don't miss a drive along **Seppeltsfield Road** (www.seppeltsfieldroad.com), an incongruous avenue of huge palm trees meandering through the vineyards behind Nuri. Beyond Marananga the palm rows veer off the roadside and track up a hill to the **Seppelt Family Mausoleum** – a Grecian shrine fronted by chunky Doric columns.

Sleeping & Eating

Barossa Valley Tourist Park CARAVAN PARK **$**
(☎08-8562 1404; www.barossatouristpark.com.au; Penrice Rd; unpowered/powered sites from $30/35, cabins from $78; ❄@📶) There are at least six different kinds of cabin at this shady park lined with pine trees, next to the Nuriootpa football oval (go Tigers!). All cabins have TVs, fridges and cooking facilities (not all come with with linen). Check out the 1930 Dodge 'House on Wheels' out the front – the seminal caravan?

Whistler Farm B&B **$$$**
(☎0415 139 758; www.whistlerfarm.com.au; 616 Samuel Rd; d incl breakfast $250; ❄📶) Surrounded by vineyards and native shrubs, this farmhouse B&B has a private guest wing with exposed timber beams, separate guest entry and two country-style rooms. Snooze on the wide verandah and contemplate a day's successful (or imminent) wine touring.

Barossa Old Garage B&B B&B **$$$**
(☎0407 203 016; www.barossaoldgaragebnb.com.au; Lot 15 Saleyards Rd; d from $265, extra person $75; ❄📶) Until a few years ago this quirky, retro place was actually a garage: now it's a bright B&B crammed full of amazing '50s and '60s memorabilia – everything from an old petrol pump to Coca-Cola glassware and chrome-and-red-vinyl barstools. Sleeps six in two bedrooms (no kids, sadly).

Maggie Beer's Farm Shop DELI **$**
(www.maggiebeer.com.au; 50 Pheasant Farm Rd; items $5-20, picnic baskets from $16; ⏲10.30am-5pm) Celebrity SA gourmet Maggie Beer has been hugely successful with her range of condiments, preserves and pâtés (and TV appearances!). The vibe here isn't as relaxed as it used to be, but stop by for some gourmet tastings, an ice cream, a cooking demo or a takeaway hamper of delicious bites. Off Samuel Rd.

Barossa Indian Cuisine INDIAN **$$**
(☎08-8562 4005; www.barossa-indian-cuisine.com.au; 15 Murray St; mains $13-19; ⏲noon-3pm Wed-Sun, 6-9pm Tue-Sun; 🖉) Spice up your Barossa experience with a visit to this converted red-brick bank (love the old brass vault!), now the backdrop for select Indian offerings such as ginger and garlic prawns, vegetable korma and a 'ridiculously tasty' chicken vindaloo.

Angaston

POP 1910

Photo-worthy Angaston was named after George Fife Angas, a pioneering Barossa pastoralist. An agricultural vibe persists, as there are relatively few wineries on the town doorstep: cows graze in paddocks at end of the town's streets, and there's a vague whiff of fertiliser in the air. Along the main drag are two pubs, some terrific eateries and a few B&Bs in old stone cottages (check for double glazing and ghosts – we had a sleepless night!).

Sights

Barossa Valley Cheese Company CHEESE WRIGHT
(www.barossacheese.com.au; 67b Murray St; ⏲10am-5pm Mon-Fri, 10am-4pm Sat, 11am-3pm Sun) The Barossa Valley Cheese Company is a fabulously stinky room, selling handmade cheeses from local cows and goats. Tastings are free, but it's unlikely you'll leave without buying a wedge of the Washington Washed Rind.

Barossa Farmers Market MARKET
(www.barossafarmersmarket.com; cnr Stockwell & Nuriootpa Rds; ⏲7.30-11.30am Sat) Happens in the big farm shed behind Vintners Bar & Grill every Saturday. Expect hearty Germanic

Barossa Valley

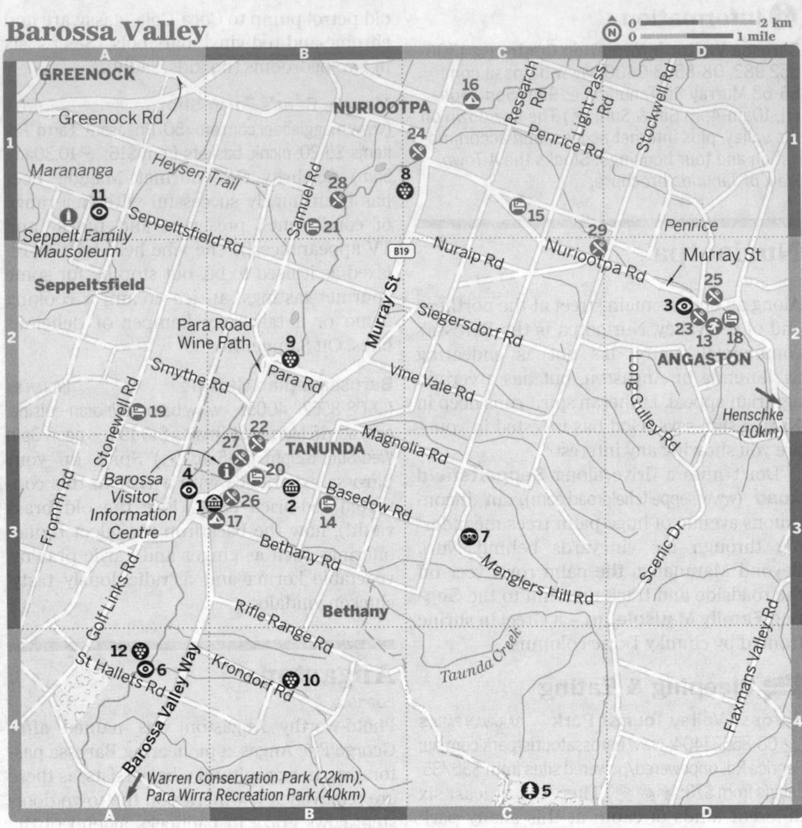

Barossa Valley

Sights

- Barossa Farmers Market .... (see 29)
- 1 Barossa Museum B3
- 2 Barossa Regional Gallery B3
- 3 Barossa Valley Cheese Company D2
- 4 Goat Square A3
- 5 Kaiserstuhl Conservation Park C4
- 6 Keg Factory A4
- 7 Mengler Hill Lookout C3
- 8 Penfolds C1
- 9 Peter Lehmann Wines B2
- 10 Rockford Wines B4
- 11 Seppeltsfield Road A1
- 12 St Hallett A4

Activities, Courses & Tours

- 13 Angaston Hardware D2

Sleeping

- 14 Barossa Backpackers B3
- 15 Barossa Old Garage B&B C1
- 16 Barossa Valley Tourist Park C1
- 17 Discovery Holiday Parks Barossa Valley B3
- 18 Marble Lodge D2
- 19 Stonewell Cottages A2
- 20 Tanunda Hotel B3
- 21 Whistler Farm B1

Eating

- 22 1918 Bistro & Grill B3
- 23 Angaston Hotel D2
- 24 Barossa Indian Cuisine C1
- 25 Blond Coffee D2
- 26 Cafe Pod B3
- Die Barossa Wurst Haus Bakery .... (see 27)
- 27 Ferment Asian B3
- 28 Maggie Beer's Farm Shop B1
- 29 Vintners Bar & Grill C2

offerings, coffee, flowers, lots of local produce and questionable buskers.

Sleeping & Eating

Marble Lodge B&B $$$

(08-8564 2478; www.marblelodge.com.au; 21 Dean St; d $225;) A grandiose 1915 Federation-style villa on the hill behind the town, built from local pink and white granite. Accommodation in two plush suites behind the house (high-colonial or high-kitsch, depending on your world view). Breakfast is served in the main house.

Blond Coffee CAFE $

(www.blondcoffee.com.au; 60 Murray St; mains $6-18; 7.30am-4pm Mon-Fri, 8.30am-3pm Sat, 9am-3pm Sun) An elegant, breezy room with huge windows facing the main street, Blond serves nutty coffee and all-day cafe fare, including awesome pumpkin, capsicum and feta muffins, plus blackboard specials (beef and shiraz pie!). Fake-blonde, botoxed tourists share the window seats with down-to-earth regulars.

Angaston Hotel PUB FOOD $$

(08-8564 2428; www.angastonhotel.com.au; 59 Murray St; mains $16-30; noon-2.30pm & 6 8.30pm) The better looking of the town's two pubs, the friendly 1846 Angaston serves Barossa wines and the cheapest steaks this side of Argentina. Just try to ignore the *Triumph of Silenus* mural on the dining room wall ('Oh, it's hideous!' says the barmaid). There's basic shared-bathroom pub accommodation upstairs (singles and doubles $70).

Vintners Bar & Grill MODERN AUSTRALIAN $$$

(08-8564 2488; www.vintners.com.au; cnr Stockwell & Nuriootpa Rds; mains lunch $16-36, dinner $34-39; noon-2.30pm daily, 6.30-9pm Mon-Sat) One of the Barossa's landmark restaurants, Vintners stresses simple elegance in both food and atmosphere. The dining room has an open fire, vineyard views and bolts of crisp white linen; menus concentrate on local produce (pray the cider-baked pork belly is on the menu when you visit).

CLARE VALLEY

At the centre of the fertile midnorth agricultural district, two hours north of Adelaide, this skinny valley produces world-class rieslings and reds. This is gorgeous countryside, with open skies, rounded hills, stands of large gums and wind rippling over wheat fields. Towns here date from the 1840s; many were built to service the Burra copper mines.

Tours

Adelaide's Top Food & Wine Tours WINE

(08-8386 0888, 0412 268 829; www.topfoodandwinetours.com.au; tours per person incl lunch from $200) Full-day, small group 'Clare Valley Explorer' tours ex-Adelaide, with a heavy/heady wine focus and some interesting small-town sights en route.

Clare Valley Experiences TOUR

(08-8842 1880; www.clarevalleyexperiences.com; tours per 2 people incl lunch $430) Small-group winery tours ex-Clare Valley, including a winery lunch. Cheaper per person if you're with a group (eg $115 per person for five people). Tours with a half day of cycling incorporated also available.

Grape Valley Tours TOUR

(0418 881 075; www.grapevalleytours.com.au; per person incl lunch from $265) Full-day, small group tours (two to seven people) ex-Adelaide or the Clare Valley, taking in plenty of wineries and with lunch included (angle the driver towards Skillogalee winery).

Swagabout Tours TOUR

(0408 845 3780, 08-8266 1879; www.swagabouttours.com.au; tours from $190) Dependable, informative, small-group, full-day Clare Valley day trips, ex-Adelaide. Low on the 'wine ponce' factor.

THE RIESLING TRAIL

Following the course of a disused railway line between Auburn and Barinia, north of Clare, the fabulous Riesling Trail is 33km of wines, wheels and wonderment. It's primarily a **cycling** trail, but the gentle gradient means you can walk or push a pram along it just as easily. It's a two-hour dash end to end on a bike, but why hurry? There are three loop track detours and extensions to explore, and dozens of cellar doors to tempt you along the way. The **Rattler Trail** continues for another 19km south of Auburn to Riverton.

For bike hire, check out **Clare Valley Cycle Hire** (p765) or **Riesling Trail Bike Hire** (p765) in Clare, or **Cogwebs** (p764) in Auburn.

Festivals & Events

A Day on the Green MUSIC
(www.adayonthegreen.com.au) The Barossa's favourite festival comes to Annie's Lane winery in the Clare Valley in February. Jimmy Barnes, Crowded House, Daryl Braithwaite...

Clare Valley Gourmet Weekend FOOD, WINE
(www.clarevalley.com.au) A frenzy of wine, food and music in May.

Clare Show FAIR
(www.sacountryshows.com) The largest one-day show in SA, held in October.

Getting There & Around

BICYCLE

In Auburn and Clare you can hire a bike to pelt around the wineries. Rates are around $25/40 per half/full day.

BUS

Yorke Peninsula Coaches (08-8821 2755; www.ypcoaches.com.au) Runs Adelaide to Auburn ($32, 2¼ hours) and Clare ($40, 2¾ hours) Tuesday to Friday and Sunday. Extends to Burra ($40, 3¼ hours) on Thursday.

TAXI

Clare Valley Taxis (08-8842 1400; www.131008.com) Drop-off/pick-up anywhere along the Riesling Trail.

Auburn

POP 320

Sleepy Auburn (1849) – the Clare Valley's southernmost village – is a leave-the-back-door-open-and-the-keys-in-the-ignition kinda town, with a time-warp vibe that makes you feel like you're in an old black-and-white photograph. The streets are defined by beautifully preserved, hand-built stone buildings; cottage gardens overflow with untidy blooms. Pick up a copy of the *Walk with History at Auburn* brochure from the Clare Valley Visitor Information Centre.

Now on the main route to the valley's wineries, Auburn initially serviced bullockies and South American muleteers whose wagons – up to 100 a day – trundled between Burra's copper mines and Port Wakefield.

The brilliant 33km **Riesling Trail** starts (or ends) at the restored Auburn Train Station. **Cogwebs** (08-8849 2380, 0400 290 687; www.cogwebs.com.au; 30 Main North Rd; bike hire per half/full day $25/40, tandems $35/60; 8.30am-6pm, reduced winter hours;) has bike hire (and internet access).

Sleeping & Eating

Auburn Shiraz Motel MOTEL $
(08-8849 2125; www.auburnshirazmotel.com.au; Main North Rd; s/d/tr from $85/95/125;) This small motel on the Adelaide side of town has been proudly renovated with shiraz-coloured render and cabernet-coloured doors. There are nine bright units and friendly hosts. Bike hire $40 per day.

Rising Sun Hotel PUB FOOD $$
(08-8849 2015; www.therisingsunhotel.com.au; 19 Main North Rd; mains $18-30; noon-2pm & 6-8pm;) This classic 1850 pub has a huge rep for its atmosphere, food and accommodation. The pub food is inventive with plenty of local wines to try. Accommodation takes the form of en suite pub rooms and cottage mews rooms out the back (doubles including breakfast from $80 and $125, respectively).

★ **Terroir** MODERN AUSTRALIAN $$$
(08-8849 2509; www.facebook.com/terroirauburn; Main North Rd; mains breakfast $17-20, lunch $18-25, dinner $35-40; noon-2pm & 6-8pm Thu-Sat, 8.30-11am & noon-2pm Sun;) 'Terroir' – a word often associated with the wine trade – defines the nature of a place: its altitude, its soil, its climate, its vibe. At this excellent restaurant it applies to ingredients, sourced seasonally from within 100 miles, and cooked with contemporary savvy. The menu changes weekly (pray for the house halloumi). Love the Mintaro slate floor!

Mintaro

POP 230

Heritage-listed Mintaro (founded 1849; pronounced 'min-*tair*-oh') is a lovely stone village that could have been lifted out of the Cotswolds and plonked into the Australian bush. There are very few architectural intrusions from the 1900s – the whole place seems to have been largely left to its own devices. A fact for your next trivia night: Mintaro slate is used internationally in the manufacture of billiard tables. Pick up the *Historic Mintaro* pamphlet around the valley.

Sights & Activities

★ **Martindale Hall** HISTORIC BUILDING
(08-8843 9088; www.martindalehall.com; 1 Manoora Rd; adult/child $10/2.50; 11am-4pm Mon-Fri, noon-4pm Sat & Sun) Martindale Hall is an astonishing 1880 manor 3km from Mintaro. Built for young pastoralist Edmund Bow-

man Jnr, who subsequently partied away the family fortune (OK, so drought and plummeting wool prices played a part…but it was mostly the partying), the manor features original furnishings, a magnificent blackwood staircase, Mintaro-slate billiard table and an opulent, museumlike smoking room. The hall starred as Appleyard College in the 1975 film *Picnic at Hanging Rock,* directed by Peter Weir. *Mirandaaa…*

B&B, and dinner plus B&B, packages allow you to spend a spooky night here ($130 and $260, respectively).

Mintaro Maze MAZE
(www.mintaromaze.com; Jacka Rd; adult/child $12/8; ⏲10am-4pm Thu-Mon, daily school holidays, closed Feb) Hedge your bets at Mintaro Maze as you try to find your way into the middle and back out again. There's a cafe here, too.

Eating

★Reilly's MODERN AUSTRALIAN $$
(☎08-8843 9013; www.reillyswines.com.au; cnr Hill St & Leasingham Rd; mains $18-30; ⏲10am-4pm) Reilly's started life as a cobbler's shop in 1856. An organic vegie garden out the back supplies the current restaurant, which is decorated with local art and serves creative, seasonal Mod Oz food (antipasto, rabbit terrine, spanikopita) and Reilly's wines. The owners also rent out four gorgeous old stone cottages on Hill St (doubles from $145).

Magpie & Stump Hotel PUB FOOD $$
(☎08-8843 9014; www.mintaro.com.au/attractions/eateries; Burra St; mains $18-40; ⏲noon-2pm Fri-Sun, 6-8pm Wed-Sat) The old Magpie & Stump was first licensed in 1851, and was a vital rehydration point for the copper carriers travelling between Burra and Port Wakefield. Schnitzels and steaks, log fires, a pool table, Mintaro-slate floors and a sunny beer garden out the front – the perfect pub?

Clare

POP 3280

Named after County Clare in Ireland, this town was founded in 1842 and is the biggest in the valley – it's more practical than charming. All the requisite services are here (post, supermarket, fuel etc), but you'll have a more interesting Clare Valley experience sleeping out of town.

Sights & Activities

Old Police Station Museum MUSEUM
(☎08-8842 2376; www.nationaltrustsa.org.au; cnr Victoria & Neagles Rock Rd; adult/child $2/0.50; ⏲10am-noon & 2-4pm Sat & Sun) The 1850 cop shop and courthouse is now the Old Police Station Museum, displaying Victorian clothing, old photos, furniture and domestic bits and pieces.

Riesling Trail Bike Hire BICYCLE RENTAL
(☎0418 777 318; www.rieslingtrailbikehire.com.au; 10 Warenda Rd; bike hire per half/full day $25/40, tandems $40/60; ⏲8am-6pm) Quality two-wheelers (including two-seaters) right on the Riesling Trail itself.

Clare Valley Cycle Hire BICYCLE RENTAL
(☎08-8842 2782, 0418 802 077; www.clarevalleycyclehire.com.au; 32 Victoria Rd; bike hire per half/full day $17/25; ⏲9am-5pm) Also has baby seats and pull-along buggies for the little 'uns.

Sleeping

Bungaree Station B&B $
(☎08-8842 2677; www.bungareestation.com.au; Main North Rd; per person per night $59-99; 🏊) About 12km north of Clare this beautiful, 170-year-old homestead – once with 50 staff members, a church and a school – is still a 3000-acre working farm. Accommodation is in simple, renovated heritage buildings, sleeping two-to-10, some with shared bathrooms. You can also feed farm animals, walk a history trail (per person $15) or have a dip in the pool.

Clare Caravan Park CARAVAN PARK $
(☎08-8842 2724; www.clarecaravanpark.com.au; Lot 136, Main North Rd; unpowered/powered sites from $20/35, cabins from $89; ❄📶🏊) This efficiently-run park 4km south of town towards Auburn has secluded sites, all en suite cabins, a creek, and giant gum trees. There's also an in-ground pool for cooling off post-cycling.

Battunga B&B B&B $$
(☎08-8843 0120; www.battunga.com.au; Upper Skilly Rd, Watervale; d/q incl breakfast $195/315, extra person $60; ❄) On an 80-hectare farm over the hills 2km west of Watervale (it's a little hard to find – ask for directions), Batunga has four apartments in two stone cottages with Mintaro-slate floors, barbecues, kitchenettes and wood fires. This is beautiful country – undulating farmland studded with huge eucalyptuses.

DON'T MISS

CLARE VALLEY WINERIES

The Clare Valley's cool microclimates (around rivers, creeks and gullies) noticeably affect the local wines, enabling whites to be laid down for long periods and still be brilliant. The valley produces some of the world's best riesling, plus grand semillon and shiraz.

Hop & Vine (www.clarevalleybrewing.com.au; 20 Main North Rd, Auburn; ⌚10am-5pm) This charismatic Auburn shopfront is an outlet for the Clare Valley Brewing Co – try their excellent red ale, Australian pale ale and grape cider. It's also the cellar door for three valley vineyards: Jeanneret, County Clare and Good Catholic Girl. Good bang for your buck!

Knappstein (www.knappstein.com.au; 2 Pioneer Ave, Clare; ⌚9am-5pm Mon-Fri, 11am-5pm Sat, 11am-4pm Sun) Taking a minimal-intervention approach to wine making, Knappstein has built quite a name for itself. Shiraz and riesling steal the show, but they also make a mighty fine semillon–sauvignon blanc blend (and beer!).

Pikes (www.pikeswines.com.au; Polish Hill River Rd, Sevenhill; ⌚10am-4pm) The industrious Pike family set up shop in 1984, and have been producing show-stopping riesling ever since (and shiraz, sangiovese, pinot grigio, viognier...). It also bottles up the zingy 'Oakbank Pilsener', if you're parched.

Sevenhill Cellars (☎08-8843 4222; www.sevenhill.com.au; College Rd, Sevenhill; ⌚10am-5pm) Want some religion with your drink? This place was established by Jesuits in 1851, making it the oldest winery in the Clare Valley (check out the incredible 1866 St Aloysius Church). Oh, and the wine is fine, too!

Skillogalee (☎08-8843 4311; www.skillogalee.com.au; 23 Trevarrick Rd, Sevenhill; ⌚10am-5pm) Skillogalee is a small family outfit known for its spicy shiraz, fabulous food and top-notch riesling (a glass of which is like kissing a pretty girl on a summer afternoon). Kick back with a long, lazy lunch on the verandah (mains $20 to $35; book ahead).

Riesling Trail & Clare Valley Cottages B&B $$
(☎0427 842 232; www.rtcvcottages.com.au; 9 Warenda Rd; d incl breakfast from $150, extra person $50; ❄) A well-managed outfit offering seven contemporary cottages, encircled by country gardens and right on the Riesling Trail (Riesling Trail Bike Hire (p765) is across the street). The biggest cottage sleeps six; there are good deals on multinight stays.

Eating

Wild Saffron CAFE $
(☎08-8842 4255; www.wildsaffron.com.au; 288 Main North Rd; mains $7-18; ⌚8.30am-5.30pm Mon-Fri, 8.30am-12.30pm Sat, 9am-12.30pm Sun) We're not sure how much wild saffron grows in the Clare Valley (most of it seems to be 'under vine', as they say), but this cafe is hugely popular, regardless. No surprises on the menu (focaccias, steak sandwiches, soup, homemade cakes), but it's simple stuff done well.

Artisans Table MODERN AUSTRALIAN $$
(☎08-8842 1796; www.artisanstable.com.au; Lot 3, Wendouree Rd; mains $28-32; ⌚noon-3pm Sat & Sun, 6-9pm Wed-Sat) This mod, airy, hillside bar-restaurant has a broad, sunny balcony – perfect for a bottle of local riesling and some internationally inspired culinary offerings: a bit of Thai, a bit of Indian, a bit of Brazilian... Lots of seasonal and local produce.

Information

Clare Valley Visitor Information Centre (☎1800 242 131, 08-8842 2131; www.clarevalley.com.au; 33 Old North Rd; ⌚10am-6pm Mon-Fri, to 2pm Sat & Sun; 📶) Local info, internet access, valley-wide accommodation bookings and the *Clare History Walk* brochure. Located inside the Clare Library.

MURRAY RIVER

On the lowest gradient of any Australian river, the slow-flowing Murray hooks through 650 South Australian kilometres. Tamed by weirs and locks, the Murray irrigates the fruit trees and vines of the sandy **Riverland** district to the north, and winds through the dairy country of the **Murraylands** district to the south. Flocks of white corellas and pink galahs launch from cliffs and river red gums, darting across lush vineyards and orchards.

Prior to European colonisation, the Murray was home to Meru communities. Then came shallow-draught paddle steamers, carrying wool, wheat and supplies from Murray Bridge as far as central Queensland along the Darling River. With the advent of railways, river transport declined. These days, waterskiers, jet skis and houseboats crowd out the river, especially during summer. If your concept of riverine serenity doesn't include the roar of V8 inboards, then avoid the major towns and caravan parks during holidays and weekends.

Getting There & Away

LinkSA (www.linksa.com.au) runs several daily bus services between Adelaide and Murray Bridge ($22, 1¼ hours) sometimes via a bus change at Mt Barker in the Adelaide Hills; plus Murray Bridge to Mannum ($8, 30 minutes) from Monday to Friday.

Premier Stateliner (www.premierstateliner.com.au) runs daily Riverland buses from Adelaide, stopping in Waikerie ($45, 2½ hours), Barmera ($56, 3¼ hours), Berri ($56, 3½ hours) and Renmark ($56, four hours). Buses stop at Loxton ($56, 3¾ hours) daily, except Saturday.

Murray Bridge

POP 16,710

SA's largest river town is a rambling regional hub (the fifth-biggest town in SA) with lots of old pubs, an underutilised riverfront, a huge prison and charms more subtle than obvious.

Sights & Activities

Murray Bridge Regional Gallery GALLERY
(www.murraybridgegallery.com.au; 27 Sixth St; 10am-4pm Tue-Sat, 11am-4pm Sun) FREE This is the town's cultural epicentre, a great space housing touring and local exhibitions: paintings, ceramics, glassware, jewellery and prints. A terrific diversion on a rainy afternoon.

Monarto Zoo ZOO
(www.monartozoo.com.au; Princes Hwy, Monarto; adult/child/family $32.50/18/85; 9.30am-5pm, last entry 3pm) About 14km west of Murray Bridge, this excellent open-range zoo is home to Australian and African beasts including cheetahs, rhino, zebras and giraffe (and the photogenic offspring thereof). A hop-on/hop-off bus tour is included in the price; keeper talks happen throughout the day.

Riverglen Marina Kayak Hire KAYAKING
(08-8532 1986; www.riverglen.com.au; Jervois Rd; per hr kayaks/lifejackets $10/2.50) Hire a two-person kayak for a DIY river exploration.

Captain Proud Paddle Boat Cruises CRUISE
(0466 304 092; www.captainproud.com.au; Wharf Rd; 3hr cruises lunch/dinner $59/79) Mainstream river cruises with lunch or dinner to boot. Call for times and bookings.

Sleeping & Eating

Houseboating on the Murray is a popular option. See p1074 for more details.

Balcony on Sixth LODGE $$
(08-8531 1411; www.balconyonsixth.com.au; 6 Sixth Ave; s/d without bathroom $109/159, d/f with bathroom $189/259;) Upstairs in this reimagined 1918 corner building are 10 surprisingly mod motel-style rooms. Very central, and with a long balcony above the street on which to sit, sip and survey. Two- and three-bedroom apartments also available (from $259).

Murray Bridge Hotel PUB $$
(08-8532 2024; www.murraybridgehotel.com.au; 20 Sixth St; mains $16-31; noon-2pm & 6-8pm;) There are plenty of rambling old pubs around town, but the stately Murray Bridge Hotel is your best bet for a feed, with roasts, sticky BBQ beef ribs and more seafood than steaks. Savvy wine list, too.

Information

Murray Bridge Visitor Information Centre (08-8339 1142, 1800 442 784; www.murraybridge.sa.gov.au; 3 South Tce; 9am-5pm Mon-Fri, 10am-4pm Sat & Sun) Stocks the Murray Bridge *Accommodation Guide* and *Dining Guide* brochures, and history walk and drive pamphlets. Also has information on river-cruise operators.

Mannum to Waikerie

Clinging to a narrow strip of riverbank 84km east of Adelaide, improbably cute **Mannum** (population 2170) is the unofficial houseboat capital of the world! The *Mary Ann*, Australia's first riverboat, was knocked together here in 1853 and made the first paddle-steamer trip up the Murray. The Mannum Visitor Information Centre (p768) incorporates the **Mannum Dock Museum of River History** (08-8569 1303, 1300 626 686; www.psmarion.com; 6 Randell St; adult/child $7.50/3.50; 9am-5pm Mon-Fri, 10am-4pm Sat & Sun), featuring info on local Ngarrindjeri Aboriginal communities, an 1876 dry dock and the restored 1897 paddle steamer *PS Marion*, on which you can occasionally chug around the river.

Breeze Holiday Hire (0439 829 964; www.murrayriver.com.au/breeze-holiday-hire-1052)

hires out canoes and kayaks (per day $75), dinghies with outboards (per day $95) and fishing gear (per day $15); they can get you waterskiing, too.

From Mannum to Swan Reach, the eastern riverside road often tracks a fair way east of the river, but various lookouts en route help you scan the scene. Around 9km south of Swan Reach, the Murray takes a tight meander called **Big Bend**, a sweeping river curve with pock-marked, ochre-coloured cliffs.

Sedentary old **Swan Reach** (population 850), 70km southwest of Waikerie, is a bit of a misnomer: there's an old pub, a museum and plenty of pelicans, but not many swans.

A citrus-growing centre oddly festooned with TV antennas, **Waikerie** (population 4630) takes its name from the Aboriginal phrase for 'anything that flies'. There's plenty of bird life around here, with 180 species recorded at **Gluepot Reserve** (☎08-8892 8600, Shell service station 08-8541 2621; www.gluepot.org; Gluepot Rd; cars per day/overnight $5/10; ⏰8am-6pm), a mallee scrub area 64km north of Waikerie (off Lunn Rd) that's part of Unesco's Riverland Biosphere Reserve. Before you head off, check with Waikerie's Shell service station on Peake Tce to see if you'll need a gate key.

Also in Waiklerie is **Nippy's** (www.nippys.com.au; 2 Ian Oliver Dr, Waikerie; ⏰8am-4pm Mon-Fri), a local fruit-juice company with factory-front sales.

Tours

Proud Mary CRUISE
(☎08-8406 4444; www.proudmary.com.au; 1½hr tours adult/child $60/42.50) Lunch cruises on a big boat on the big river, departing Mannum on Mondays. Brush up on your Creedence Clearwater Revival lyrics.

Jester Cruises CRUISE
(☎0419 909 116; www.jestercruises.com.au; 1/2hr tours per person $16/36, 2hr tours incl lunch $44) Cruise up and down the river from Mannum on the 40-seat *Jester*, running most days. Minimum numbers apply.

Sleeping & Eating

Mannum Caravan Park CARAVAN PARK $
(☎08-8569 1402; www.mannumcaravanpark.com.au; Purnong Rd, Mannum; unpowered/powered sites from $29/32, cabins/villas from $64/132; ❄@📶) A clean-cut caravan park right on the river next to the Mannum ferry crossing. Ducks and water hens patrol the lawns, and there's a pool table in the games room for when it rains. Lots of shade-giving gums.

Murray River Queen HOSTEL $
(☎0410 416 655; www.murrayriverqueen.com; Leonard Norman Dr, Waikerie; dm $30, d with/without bathroom from $90/55; ❄📶) This 1974 paddle boat is done with chugging up and down the river: these days it's a floating backpackers on the Waikerie riverfront, with basic bunkrooms – low-ceilinged and a tad dim, but undeniably novel. Also onboard are a bar, pool table, sundeck and Thai cafe (mains $14 to $20). Popular with the fruit-picking set.

★ **Waikerie Hotel Motel** HOTEL, MOTEL $$
(☎08-8541 2999; www.waikeriehotel.com; 2 McCoy St, Waikerie; d $99-149; ❄📶) Much of this pub burnt down in 2012, two days shy of its 100th birthday! The 19 rebuilt en suite pub rooms upstairs are awesome: fancy linen, bar fridges and big TVs, with leather and granite everywhere. The bistro does pub-grub classics (mains $16 to $35). Slightly cheaper are the updated motel rooms out the back.

River Shack Rentals ACCOMMODATION SERVICES $$
(☎0447 263 549; www.rivershackrentals.com.au; d from $100) Offers a raft of riverside properties to rent from Mannum heading upstream, sleeping two to 20 bods. Most of them are right on the water: 36 River Lane is a solid Mannum-centric option with room for 10 (from $450). Houseboats also available.

Pretoria Hotel PUB FOOD $$
(☎08-8569 1109; www.pretoriahotel.com.au; 50 Randell St, Mannum; mains $18-32; ⏰11.30am-2.30pm & 5.30-8.30pm) The family-friendly Pretoria (built 1900) has a vast bistro and deck fronting the river, and plates up big steaks, roo medallions, parmas and good seafood. When the 1956 flood swamped the town they kept pouring beer from the 1st-floor balcony!

Information

Mannum Visitor Information Centre (☎1300 626 686, 08-8569 1303; www.psmarion.com; 6 Randell St; ⏰9am-5pm Mon-Fri, 10am-4pm Sat & Sun) Cruise and houseboat bookings, *Mannum Historic Walks* brochures and the Mannum Dock Museum of River History (p767).

Barmera & Around

On the shallow shores of Lake Bonney (upon which world land-speed record holder Donald Campbell unsuccessfully attempted to break his water-speed record in 1964), snoozy **Barmera** (population 3020) was once a key town on the overland stock route from NSW. These days the local passion for both kinds of music (country *and* western) lends a simple optimism to proceedings. **Kingston-On-Murray** (population 260; aka Kingston OM) is a tiny town en route to Waikerie.

Sights & Activities

The once ephemeral **Lake Bonney** has been transformed into a permanent lake ringed by large, drowned red gums, whose stark branches are often festooned with birds. If you're feeling uninhibited, you might like to know that there's a nudist beach at **Pelican Point Holiday Park** (www.riverland.net.au/pelicanpoint) on the lake's western shore.

There are wildlife reserves with walking trails and camping (per person/car $6/10) at **Moorook** on the road to Loxton, and **Loch Luna** across the river from Kingston-On-Murray. Loch Luna backs onto the Overland Corner Hotel. Both reserves have nature trails and are prime spots for birdwatching and canoeing. Self-register camping permits are available at reserve entrances.

There are also **walking trails** at the Overland Corner Hotel.

★ Banrock Station Wine & Wetland Centre WINERY
(08-8583 0299; www.banrockstation.com.au; Holmes Rd, Kingston OM; tastings free, wetland walks by gold-coin donation; 9am-4pm Mon-Fri, to 5pm Sat & Sun) Overlooking regenerated, feral-proofed wetlands off the Sturt Hwy at Kingston OM, carbon-neutral Banrock Station Wine & Wetland Centre is a stylish, rammed-earth wine-tasting centre (love the tempranillo). Ther jazzy lunchtime restaurant (mains $20 to $30 – try the Banrock pizza) uses ingredients sourced locally. There are three **wetland walks** here too: 2.5km, 4.5km and 8km.

Rocky's Hall of Fame Pioneers Museum MUSEUM
(www.murrayriver.com.au/barmera/rockys-hall-of-fame-pioneers-museum; 4 Pascoe Tce, Barmera; admission $2; 9am-noon Mon, Wed & Thu, 8.30am-noon Fri) Country music is a big deal in Barmera, with the **South Australian Country Music Festival & Awards** (www.riverlandcountrymusic.com) happening here in June, and Rocky's Museum blaring sincere rural twangings down the main street from outdoor speakers. Don't miss the 35m Botanical Garden Guitar out the back, inlaid with the handprints of 160 country musos: Slim Dusty to Kasey Chambers and everyone in-between.

Sleeping & Eating

Discovery Holiday Parks Lake Bonney CARAVAN PARK $
(08-8588 2234; www.discoveryholidayparks.com.au; Lakeside Ave, Barmera; unpowered/powered sites from $22/31, cabins from $94;) This keenly managed, facility-rich lakeside park has small beaches (safe swimming), electric barbecues, a camp kitchen, a laundry and plenty of room for kids to run amok. Lots of trees and waterfront camp sites too, plus tandems, canoes and paddleboats for hire.

Barmera Lake Resort Motel MOTEL $
(08-8588 2555; www.barmeralakeresortmotel.com.au; Lakeside Dr, Barmera; d $80-135, f from $195;) Right across the road from the lake, this tidy, good-value motel has a pool, in case the lake is looking a bit soupy. Rooms are compact and nothing flash, but they're immaculate and many have lake views.

Overland Corner Hotel PUB FOOD $$
(08-8588 7021; www.overlandcornerhotel.com.au; 205 Old Coach Rd; mains $16-28; noon-2pm Tue-Sun, 6-8pm Fri & Sat) About 19km northwest of Barmera, this moody 1859 boozer is named after a Murray River bend where drovers used to camp. The pub walls ooze character and the meals are drover sized, plus there's a museum, resident ghosts, a beaut beer garden and four walking trails leading down to the river (pick up the *Historic Overland Corner* brochure in Barmera).

Information

Barmera Visitor Information Centre (08-8588 2289; www.barmeratourism.com.au; Barwell Ave, Barmera; 9am-4pm Mon-Fri, 10am-1pm Sat & Sun) Can help with transport and accommodation bookings. Pick up the *Historic Overland Corner* and *Heritage Walk Barmera* walking trail brochures.

Loxton

POP 3780

Sitting above a broad loop of the slow-roaming Murray, Loxton proclaims itself the 'Garden City of the Riverland'. The vibe here is low-key, agricultural and untouristy, with more tyre distributors, hardware shops and irrigation supply outlets than anything else.

Sights & Activities

From Loxton you can canoe across to **Katarapko Creek** in the **Murray River National Park** (www.environment.sa.gov.au); hire canoes from Loxton Riverfront Caravan Park.

Tree of Knowledge LANDMARK
(Grant Schubert Dr) Down by the river near the caravan park, the Tree of Knowledge is marked with flood levels from previous years. The bumper flows of 1931, '73, '74, '75, and 2011 were totally outclassed by the flood-to-end-all-floods of 1956, marked about 4m up the trunk.

Loxton Historic Village MUSEUM
(www.thevillageloxton.com.au; Allen Hosking Dr; adult/child/family $12.50/6.50/32; 10am-4pm) Down by the river, the mildly kitsch (but nonetheless interesting) Loxton Historic Village is a re-created time warp of 45 dusty, rusty old buildings and old country curios.

Sleeping

Loxton Riverfront Caravan Park CARAVAN PARK $
(1800 887 733, 08-8584 7862; www.lrcp.com.au; 1 Sophie Edington Dr; unpowered/powered sites from $27/32, cabins with/without bathroom from $115/85;) On the gum-studded Habels Bend, 2km from town, this affable riverside park bills itself as 'The Quiet One'. You can hire a canoe (per hour $15), and there's a free nine-hole golf course (usually sandy, occasionally flooded). Free wi-fi.

Loxton Hotel HOTEL, MOTEL $$
(1800 656 686, 08-8584 7266; www.loxtonhotel.com.au; 45 East Tce; hotel s/d from $90/115, motel from $135/150;) With all profits siphoned back into the Loxton community, this large complex offers immaculate rooms with tasty weekend packages. The original pub dates from 1908, and it has been relentlessly extended. Bistro meals available for breakfast, lunch and dinner (mains $18 to $32). Free wi-fi, too.

Information

Loxton Visitor Information Centre (1300 869 990, 08-8584 8071; www.loxtontourism.com.au; Bookpurnong Tce, Loxton Roundabout; 9am-5pm Mon-Fri, 9am-4pm Sat, 10am-4pm Sun) A friendly place for accommodation, transport and national-park info, plus there's an art gallery and local dried fruits for sale. Look for the *History Walk of Loxton* brochure.

Berri

POP 4110

The name Berri derives from the Aboriginal term *berri berri,* meaning 'big bend in the river', and it was once a busy refuelling stop for wood-burning paddle steamers. These days Berri is an affluent regional hub for both state government and agricultural casual-labour agencies; it's one of the best places to chase down casual harvest jobs.

Sights & Activities

Road access to the scenic **Katarapko Creek** section of the **Murray River National Park** (www.environment.sa.gov.au) is off the Stuart Hwy between Berri and Barmera. This is a beaut spot for bush camping (per car/person $10/6), canoeing and birdwatching.

Riverland Farmers Market MARKET
(www.riverlandfarmersmarket.org.au; Crawford Tce, Senior Citizens Hall; 7.30-11.30am Sat) All the good stuff that grows around here in one place. A bacon-and-egg roll and some freshly squeezed orange juice will right your rudder.

A Special Place for Jimmy James GARDENS
(Riverview Dr; 24hr) A short amble from the visitor centre, this living riverbank memorial honours an Aboriginal tracker who could 'read the bush like a newspaper'. Whimsical tracks and traces are scattered around granite boulders.

River Lands Gallery GALLERY
(www.countryarts.org.au; 23 Wilson St; 10am-4pm Mon-Fri, to 1pm Sat) As the murals and totem poles around the base of Berri Bridge attest, Berri is an arty kinda town. This gallery displays local, Indigenous and travelling painting, sculpture, weaving and digital media exhibitions.

Canoe Adventures CANOEING
(0421 167 645; www.canoeadventure.com.au; canoe hire per half/full day $55/65, tours per adult/child half day $75/50, full day $120/80) Canoe hire, guided canoe trips and camping expeditions, ahoy! This outfit conducts all of the above from its Berri base, and can also deliver to most Riverland towns.

BMS Tours CRUISE
(0408 282 300; www.houseboatadventure.com.au; tours from $70) Murray tours from Berri on an Everglades-style airboat called *Elka*. Call for bookings, times and minimum numbers.

Sleeping & Eating

Berri Backpackers HOSTEL $
(08-8582 3144; www.berribackpackers.com.au; 1081 Old Sturt Hwy; dm per night/week $35/160;) This eclectic hostel is destination *numero uno* for work seeking travellers, who chill out in quirky New Age surrounds after a hard day's manual toil. Rooms range from messy dorms to doubles, share houses, a tepee and a yurt – all for the same price. The managers can hook you up with harvest work (call in advance).

Berri Hotel HOTEL, MOTEL $$
(1800 088 226, 08-8582 1411; www.berrihotel.com; Riverview Dr; hotel s/d $77/145, motel d/f $155/175;) This mustard-and-maroon monolith near the river has hotel rooms (shared bathrooms) and a wing of spacious en suite motel rooms. The cavernous bistro serves upmarket pub grub (mains $19 to $33, open for dinner), or there's a cafe for lighter breakfasts and lunches. A slick operation, albeit a bit Vegas. Free wi-fi.

Sprouts Café CAFE $
(08-8582 1228; www.sproutscafe.com.au; 28 Wilson St; mains $7-14; 8.30am-4pm Mon-Fri, 9.30am-1pm Sat) A cheery new cafe on the hill a few blocks back from the river, with a natty lime-green colour scheme. Serves soups, quiches, burgers, curries, wraps and good coffee. Homemade cakes, scones and chocolate pecan pudding, too.

Information

Berri Visitor Information Centre (08-8582 5511, 1300 768 582; www.berribarmera.sa.gov.au; Riverview Dr; 9am-5pm Mon-Fri, 9am-2pm Sat, 10am-2pm Sun) Right by the river, with brochures, internet, maps, waterproof canoeing guides ($10) and clued-up staff.

Renmark

POP 7500

Renmark is the first major river town across from the Victorian border, and is about 254km from Adelaide. It's not a pumping tourist destination by any means; it has a relaxed vibe and a grassy waterfront, where you can pick up a houseboat. This is the hub of the Riverland wine region: lurid signs on the roads into town scream 'Buy 6 Get 1 Free!' and 'Bulk port $5/litre!' On the other side of the river, 4km upstream, is Renmark's low-key satellite town, Paringa.

RIVERLAND FRUIT PICKING

The fruit- and grape-growing centres of Berri, Barmera, Waikerie, Loxton and Renmark are always seeking harvest workers. Work is seasonal but there's usually something that needs picking (stone fruit, oranges, grapes, apples…), except for mid-September to mid-October and mid-April to mid-May when things get a bit quiet. If you have a valid working visa and don't mind sweating it out in the fields (for around $100 a day once you get the hang of it), ask the local backpacker hostels about work. Also try the **MADEC Labour Hire** (08-8586 1900; www.madec.edu.au; 8 Ral Ral Ave, Renmark) office in Renmark and the **National Harvest Information Service** (1800 062 332; www.jobsearch.gov.au/harvesttrail).

Sights & Activities

Chowilla Regional Reserve NATURE RESERVE
(www.environment.sa.gov.au) Upstream from town, Chowilla is great for bush camping (per person/car $6/10), canoeing and bushwalking. Access is along the north bank from Renmark or along the south bank from Paringa. For more info, contact the **Department of Environment, Water & Natural Resources** (DEWNR; 08-8595 2111; 28 Vaughan Tce, Berri) in Berri.

Riverland Leisure Canoe Tours CANOEING
(08-8595 5399; www.riverlandcanoes.com.au; half-/full-day tours $75/120) Slow-paced guided canoe tours on the Murray, departing Paringa, across the river from Renmark. Canoe/kayak hire (per day $65/55) and evening and moonlight tours also available.

Sleeping & Eating

BIG4 Renmark Riverfront Holiday Park CARAVAN PARK $
(1300 664 612, 08-8586 6315; www.big4renmark.com.au; Sturt Hwy; unpowered/powered sites from $30/42, cabins with/without bathroom from $104/80;) Highlights of this spiffy riverfront park, 1km east of town, include a camp kitchen, canoe and paddleboat hire, and absolute waterfront cabins and powered sites. The newish corrugated-iron cabins are top notch, and look a little 'Riviera' surrounded by scraggy palms. The waterskiing fraternity swarms here during holidays.

Renmark Hotel HOTEL, MOTEL $$
(☎1800 736 627, 08-8586 6755; www.renmarkhotel.com.au; Murray Ave; hotel/motel d from $90/110; ❄📶🏊) What a beauty! The sexy art deco curves of Renmark's huge pub are looking good. Choose from older-style hotel rooms and upmarket motel rooms. On a sultry evening it's hard to beat a cold beer and some grilled barramundi on the balcony at Nanya Bistro (mains $18 to $37, serving noon to 2.30pm and 5.30pm to 9pm). Free wi-fi.

Renmark Club PUB FOOD $$
(☎08-8586 6611; www.renmarkclub.com.au; Murray Ave; mains $13-35; ⏰noon-2.30pm & 6-8.30pm) Right on the river, this old pub/club has been reborn as a shiny mod bistro, serving upmarket pub food (rustic shank pie, brandy-braised beef cheeks) with unbeatable water views. The club also runs the slick new taupe-and-timber **Renmark Holiday Apartments** (☎1300 855 563; www.renmarkholidayapartments.com.au; 161 Murray Ave; 1-/2-bedroom apt from $195/235; ❄), across the road.

Information

Renmark Paringa Visitor Information Centre (☎1300 661 704, 08-8586 6704; www.visitrenmark.com; 84 Murray Ave; ⏰9am-5pm Mon-Fri, 10am-4pm Sat & Sun) Has the usual local info, brochures and contacts for backpacker accommodation around town, plus an interpretive centre and bike hire (per half-/full-day $25/40). The recommissioned 1911 paddle steamer *PS Industry* goes for a 90-minute chug every Sunday (adult/child $20/10).

LIMESTONE COAST

The Limestone Coast – strung-out along southeastern SA between the flat, olive span of the lower Murray River and the Victorian border – is a curiously engaging place. On the highways you can blow across these flatlands in under a day, no sweat, but around here the delight is in the detail. Detour off-road to check out the area's lagoons, surf beaches and sequestered bays. Also on offer are wine regions, photogenic fishing ports and snoozy agricultural towns. And what's *below* the road is even more amazing: a bizarre subterranean landscape of limestone caves, sinkholes and bottomless crater lakes – a broad, formerly volcanic area that's known as the **Kanawinka Geopark** (www.kanawinkageopark.org.au).

Getting There & Away

The Dukes Hwy (Rte A8) is the most direct route between Adelaide and Melbourne (729km), but the coastal Princes Hwy (Rte B1; about 900km) adjacent to the Coorong National Park, is definitely more scenic.

AIR

Regional Express (Rex; www.regionalexpress.com.au) flies daily between Adelaide and Mount Gambier (one way from $170).

BUS

Premier Stateliner (www.premierstateliner.com.au) runs two bus routes – coastal and inland – between Adelaide and Mount Gambier ($80, six hours). From Adelaide along the coast (Monday, Wednesday, Friday and Sunday) via the Coorong you can stop at Meningie ($39, two hours), Robe ($70, 4½ hours) and Beachport ($74, five hours). The inland bus runs daily via Naracoorte ($74, five hours) and Penola ($76, 5¾ hours).

Coorong National Park

The amazing **Coorong National Park** (www.environment.sa.gov.au) is a fecund lagoon landscape curving along the coast for 145km from Lake Alexandrina towards Kingston SE. A complex series of soaks and salt pans, it's separated from the sea by the chunky dunes of the **Younghusband Peninsula**. More than 200 species of waterbirds live here. *Storm Boy,* an endearing film about a young boy's friendship with a pelican (based on the novel by Colin Thiele), was filmed here.

In the 1800s the bountiful resources of the Coorong supported a large Ngarrindjeri population. The Ngarrindjeri are still connected to the Coorong, and many still live here.

At the edge of the Coorong on **Lake Albert** (a large arm of Lake Alexandrina), **Meningie** (population 900) was established as a minor port in 1866. These 'lower lakes' have returned to life recently in the wake of the 2011 Murray River floods. A momentary reprive from climate change? Time will tell…

The Princes Hwy scuttles through the park, but you can't see much from the road. Instead, take the 13km, unsealed **Coorong Scenic Drive**. Signed as Seven Mile Rd, it starts 10km southwest of Meningie off the Narrung Rd, and takes you right into the landscape, with its stinky lagoons, sea mists, fishing shanties, pelicans, black swans and wild emus. The road rejoins the Princes Hwy 10km south of Meningie.

With a 4WD you can access **Ninety Mile Beach**, a well-known surf-fishing spot. The easiest ocean access point is 3km off the Princes Hwy at 42 Mile Crossing, 19km south of Salt Creek – a worthy dirt-road detour.

On the southern fringe of the Coorong is Kingston SE (population 2200; www.kingstonse.com.au). The town is a hotbed of crayfishing: try some nearby at the **Cape Jaffa Seafood & Wine Festival** (www.capejaffafest.com.au) in January. One of Australia's 'big' tourist attractions, the anatomically correct **Larry the Lobster**, is a famed resident.

For a watery perspective, try Spirit of the Coorong (p744) cruises or Canoe the Coorong (p744), both based in Goolwa on the Fleurieu Peninsula.

Sleeping & Eating

There are 11 bush **camp sites** (www.environment.sa.gov.au; per person/car $7/13) in the park; book online via the DEWNR website (www.environment.sa.gov.au/parks). There are also 'honesty boxes' at most of the campgrounds.

Lake Albert Caravan Park CARAVAN PARK $
(☎08-8575 1411; www.lakealbertcaravanpark.com.au; 25 Narrung Rd, Meningie; unpowered/powered sites from $20/30, cabins with/without bathroom from $110/75;) A breezy park with a beaut aspect overlooking pelican-prone Lake Albert (the best camp sites are right on the lakefront). The four deluxe two-bedroom cabins ($155) are the pick of the cabins.

★**Dalton on the Lake** B&B $$
(☎0428 737 161; admason@lm.net.au; 30 Narrung Rd, Meningie; d from $145;) Generous in spirit and unfailingly clean, this lakeside B&B goes to great lengths to ensure your stay is comfortable. There'll be fresh bread baking when you arrive, jars of homemade biscuits, and bountiful bacon and eggs for breakfast. There's a modern self-contained studio off to one side, and a renovated stone cottage – book either, or both.

Cheese Factory Restaurant PUB FOOD $$
(☎08-8575 1914; www.meningie.com.au; 3 Fiebig Rd, Meningie; mains $15-33; ⏲10.30am-3pm Tue-Sun, 5.30pm-late Wed-Sat) Lean on the front bar with the locals, or munch into steaks, schnitzels, Coorong mullet or a Coorong wrap (with mullet!) in the cavernous dining room of this converted cheese factory (you might have guessed!). The very lo-fi **Meningie Cheese Factory Museum** (☎08-8575 1914; www.meningiecheesefactorymuseum.com; admission $5; ⏲8.30am-5pm) is here too (butter churns, old typewriters, domestic knick-knackery).

Information

Meningie Visitor Information Centre (Coorong Cottage Industries; ☎08-8575 1770; www.meningie.com.au; 14 Princes Hwy; ⏲10am-4.30pm) Coorong camping permits and local info.

Robe

POP 1020

Robe is a cherubic little fishing port that's become a holiday hotspot for Adelaidians and Melburnians alike. The sign saying 'Drain L Outlet' as you roll into town doesn't promise much, but along the main street you'll find quality eateries and boundless accommodation, and there are some magic beaches and lakes around town. Over Christmas and Easter, Robe is packed to the heavens – book *waaay* in advance.

Sights & Activities

Heritage-listed buildings dating from the late 1840s to the 1870s litter the streets of Robe, including the upstanding little 1863 **Customs House** (www.nationaltrustsa.org.au; Royal Circus; adult/child $2/0.50; ⏲2-4pm Tue & Sat Feb-Dec, 2-4pm Mon-Sat Jan), now a nautical museum.

Little Dip Conservation Park (www.environment.sa.gov.au) FREE runs along the coast for about 13km south of town. It features a variety of habitats including lakes, wetlands and dunes, and some beaut beaches, Aboriginal middens, walks and camping spots (per person/car $7/13). Access is via Nora Creina Rd.

Robe's small town beach has safe swimming, while **Long Beach** (2km from town), is good for surfing, sailboarding and lazy days (safe swimming in some sections – ask at the visitors centre). **Steve's Place** (☎08-8768 2094; stevesplace66@internode.on.net; 26 Victoria St; ⏲9.30am-5pm Mon-Fri, 9.30am-1pm Sat, 10am-1pm Sun) rents out boards (per day $40), bodyboards ($20) and wetsuits ($20). It's also the place for info on surfing lessons and the annual **Robe Easter Classic** in April, SA's longest-running surf comp (since 1968).

Sleeping

Local rental agents with properties from as low as $80 per night in the off season include **Happyshack** (☎08-8768 2341, 0403 578

382; www.happyshack.com.au), **SAL Real Estate** (☎08-8768 2737; www.salrealestate.com.au; 25 Victoria St) and **Robe Lifestyle** (☎1300 760 629; www.robelifestyle.com.au).

Caledonian Inn HOTEL $
(☎08-8768 2029; www.caledonian.net.au; 1 Victoria St; d from $75;) This historic inn (1859) has a half-dozen bright and cosy upstairs pub rooms with shared bathrooms – great value. The pub grub is good, too (mains $17 to $40, serving noon to 2pm and 6pm to 8.30pm).

Lakeside Tourist Park CARAVAN PARK $
(☎08-8768 2193; www.lakesiderobe.com.au; 24 Main Rd; unpowered/powered sites from $34/35, cabins/villas from $70/105;) Right on Lake Fellmongery (a 'fellmonger' is a wool washer, don't you know), this abstractly laid out, rather boutique park has heritage-listed pine trees and reception building (130-year-old former stables), plenty of grass, basic cabins and flashy villas.

Robe Harbour View Motel MOTEL $$
(☎08-8768 2155; www.robeharbourview.com.au; 2 Sturt St; d/f from $120/155;) At the quiet end of town (and a five-minute walk from the action), this tidy, well-run motel has namesake harbour views from the best half-dozen rooms at the front. The standard rooms out the back don't have views but are perfectly decent (who needs views when you're asleep?). Expect nice linen, subtle colours and vamped-up bathrooms.

Robe Lakeview Motel & Apartments MOTEL $$
(☎08-8768 2100; www.robelakeviewmotel.com.au; 2 Lakeside Tce; d/2-bedroom apt from $125/240, extra person $15;) Overlooking the water-skiing mecca Lake Fellmongery, Lakeview is one of Robe's better motels. The decor is on the improve (slowly banishing the late-'90s), the rooms are roomy and immaculately clean, and the barbecue area pumps during summer. Free wi-fi.

Grey Masts B&B $$$
(☎0419 571 003; www.greymasts.com.au; cnr Victoria & Smillie Sts; house incl breakfast from $200) A lovely, low-ceilinged 1850s stone cottage behind the local bookshop. The two bedrooms sleep four, and there's a compact kitchen, welcoming lounge and flower-filled garden. The Savage family (Mr and Mrs Savage and their 12 sons!) once lived here. Minimum stay of three nights during summer.

Eating

Union Cafe CAFE $
(☎08-8768 2627; 4/17-19 Victoria St; mains $7-16; ⏲8am-4pm;) Always busy, this curiously angled corner cafe has polished-glass fragments in the floor and surf art on the walls. Unionise your hangover with an EBT (egg and bacon on Turkish bread with cheese and house-made tomato sauce), plus good coffee, pancakes, curries, salads and wraps.

Polly's Fish 'n' Chips FISH & CHIPS $
(☎08-8768 2712; www.pollysfishnchips.com.au; Lot 1, Lipson Tce; meals $5-16; ⏲10am-8pm Sun-Wed, to 9pm Thu-Sat) Down on Robe's harbour is this beaut little fish 'n' chipper, cooking up today's catch, straight off the fishing boats. It's not always the fastest of fast food, but quality takes time: sit and study the boats while you wait.

Mahalia Coffee CAFE $
(☎08-8768 2778; www.mahaliacoffee.com.au; 2 Flint St; items $5-9; ⏲8.30am-5pm) Everywhere you go on the Limestone Coast you'll see Mahalia Coffee signs: a marketing success story! Visit the roasting rooms in Robe's industrial back blocks for a double-shot flat white, a croissant, or a white-chocolate and macadamia muffin.

Sails MODERN AUSTRALIAN $$$
(☎08-8768 1954; www.sailsatrobe.com.au; 21 Victoria St; mains $31-38; ⏲6pm-late) Sails is Robe's classiest restaurant, and comes with a big rep for seafood. Not in an undersea mood? Try the kangaroo fillets with beetroot fritters and horseradish, or the lentil empanadas with goats cheese, cauliflower and sweet onion. Lovely ambience; smooth service.

ℹ Information

Robe Visitor Information Centre (☎1300 367 144, 08-8768 2465; www.robe.com.au; Mundy Tce, Public Library; ⏲9am-5pm Mon-Fri, 10am-1pm Sat & Sun) History displays, brochures and free internet. Look for the *Scenic Drive*, *Heritage Drive* and *A Walk Through History* pamphlets.

Beachport

POP 890

'See and be seen: headlights 24 hours!' say signs around this stretch of the Limestone Coast. Is Beachport desperate to be noticed? A plaintive cry for attention? We like it the way it is: low-key and beachy, with aquamarine surf, the famous 772m-long jetty, staunch stone buildings and rows of Norfolk Island pines. Forget about being seen – your time here will be perfectly anonymous.

Sights & Activities

Old Wool & Grain Store Museum MUSEUM
(☎08-8735 8029; www.nationaltrust.org.au/sa; 5 Railway Tce; adult/child/family $5/2/10; ⊙10am-4pm) In a stately National Trust building on the main street you'll find relics from Beachport's whaling and shipping days, rooms decked out in 1870s style, and a display on the local Buandi people.

Beachport Conservation Park NATURE RESERVE
(www.environment.sa.gov.au) FREE There are some great walking tracks in this 710-hectare park, sandwiched between the coast and Lake George 2km north of town. Aboriginal middens, sheltered coves, lagoons and bush camping (per person/car $7/13).

Pool of Siloam SWIMMING
(Bowman Scenic Dr) FREE In the dunes on the western outskirts of town, the pool is great for swimming (and floating: the water is seven times saltier than the sea!). Ask at the vistor information centre for directions.

Sleeping

Southern Ocean Tourist Park CARAVAN PARK $
(☎08-8735 8153; www.southernoceantouristpark.com.au; Somerville St; unpowered/powered sites from $25/28, cabins $95-160; ❄📶) A well-pruned, shady park nooked into the base of a hill in the town centre; new management has really lifted it off the canvas. Facilities include a laundry, covered barbecues, crayfish cookers and a great little playground. The kitchen cabins on the hilltop are lovely.

Bompas HOTEL $$
(☎08-8735 8333; www.bompas.com.au; 3 Railway Tce; d with/without bathroom from $125/100; 📶) In what was Beachport's first pub (1873), Bompas is an all-in-one small hotel and licensed restaurant-cafe. Rooms upstairs are generously sized and strewn with modern art (room No 3 has million-dollar views). Menu offerings downstairs (mains $13 to $32, serving noon to 2pm and 6pm to 8pm) include Chinese stir-fries, lamb shanks and steaks, plus there are quiz nights and decent beers.

Information

Beachport Visitor Information Centre
(☎08-8735 8029; www.wattlerange.sa.gov.au; Millicent Rd; ⊙9am-5pm Mon-Fri, 10am-4pm Sat & Sun) An info-packed centre on the road into town. Look for the *Beachport's Bowman Scenic Drive* and *Beachport's Historic Buildings Drive* brochures.

Mount Gambier

POP 25,200

Strung out along the flatlands below an extinct volcano, Mount Gambier is the Limestone Coast's major town and service hub. 'The Mount' sometimes seems a little short on urban virtues, but it's not what's above the streets that makes Mount Gambier special – it's the deep Blue Lake and the caves that worm their way though the limestone beneath the town. Amazing!

Sights

Blue Lake LAKE
(www.mountgambierpoint.com.au/attractions/blue-lake; John Watson Dr; ⊙24hr) FREE Mount Gambier's big-ticket item is the luminous, 75m-deep lake, which turns an insane hue of blue during summer. Perplexed scientists think it has to do with calcite crystals suspended in the water, which form at a faster rate during the warmer months. Consequently, if you visit between April and November, the lake will look much like any other – a steely grey. **Acquifer Tours** (☎08-8723 1199; www.aquifertours.com; cnr Bay Rd & John Watson Dr; adult/child/family $9/4/25; ⊙tours hourly 9am-5pm Nov-Jan, 9am-2pm Feb-May & Sep-Oct, 9am-noon Jun-Aug) runs hourly tours, taking you down near the lake shore in a glass-panelled lift.

Riddoch Art Gallery GALLERY
(☎08-8723 9566; www.riddochartgallery.org.au; 1 Bay Rd; ⊙10am-5pm Mon & Wed-Fri, 11am-3pm Sat & Sun) FREE If Mount Gambier's famed Blue Lake isn't blue, don't feel blue – cheer yourself up at one of Australia's best regional galleries. There are three galleries housing touring and permanent exhibitions, contemporary installations, community displays. In the same 'Main Corner' complex are heritage exhibits and a cinema screening local history flicks. Free tours 11am Thursday.

Cave Gardens CAVE
(www.mountgambierpoint.com.au/attractions/cave-gardens; cnr Bay Rd & Watson Tce; ⊙24hr) FREE A 50m-deep sinkhole right in the

middle of town, with the odd suicidal shopping trolley at the bottom. You can walk down into it, and watch the nightly Sound & Light Show (from 8.30pm) telling local Aboriginal Dreaming stories.

Engelbrecht Cave CAVE
(08-8723 5552; www.engelbrechtcave.com.au; Jubilee Hwy W, off Chute St; tours adult/child/family $12.50/8/35; tours hourly 10am-3pm Thu-Tue) A rubbish dump prior to 1979, this meandering cave system runs beneath Jubilee Hwy and 19 local houses! Tours last 45 minutes and take you down to an underground lake (call for cave-diving info). There's a cafe here, too. Reduced winter hours.

Sleeping

Old Mount Gambier Gaol HOSTEL $
(08-8723 0032; www.theoldmountgambiergaol.com.au; 25 Margaret St; dm/tw/d/f from $26/60/80/150;) If you can forget that this place was a prison until 1995 (either that or embrace the fact), these refurbished old buildings make for an atmospheric and comfortable stay. There's a backpacker dorm in one building, or you can up the spooky stakes and sleep in a former cell. There's a bar with occasional live bands, too. Free wi-fi.

Blue Lake Holiday Park CARAVAN PARK $
(1800 676 028, 08-8725 9856; www.bluelake.com.au; Bay Rd; unpowered/powered sites $34/39, cabins/units/bungalows from $99/127/156;) Adjacent to the Blue Lake, a golf course and walking and cycling tracks, this amiable park has some natty grey-and-white cabins and well-weeded lawns. There are also spiffy contemporary, self-contained 'retreats' (from $192) that sleep four.

Colhurst House B&B $$
(08-8723 1309; www.colhursthouse.com.au; 3 Colhurst Pl; d from $170;) Most locals don't know about Colhurst – it's up a laneway off a side street (Wyatt St), and you can't really see it from downtown Mt G. It's an 1878 mansion built by Welsh migrants, and manages to be old-fashioned without being overly twee. There's a gorgeous wrap-around balcony upstairs with great views over the rooftops. Cooked breakfast.

Park Hotel PUB $$
(08-8725 2430; www.parkhotel.net.au; 163 Commercial St W; d/f from $140/190;) In Mount Gambier's western wastelands, this old corner pub has spent a fortune renovating its three upstairs rooms. Polished timber floors, double glazing, marble bathrooms and coffee-and-cream colour schemes – a really slick product. Shared kitchen for cooking breakfast (provisions provided).

Barn APARTMENTS, MOTEL $$
(08-8726 9999; www.barn.com.au; 747 Glenelg River Rd; d/apt/house from $135/190/280;) A 7km drive out of town on the road to Nelson, the Barn is a complex of fancy new motel-style accommodation options – from doubles to two-bedroom apartments and four-bedroom houses – plus a fab steak restaurant, plating up local beef (mains $33 to $38, serving dinner nightly).

Eating

★ **Metro Bakery & Cafe** CAFE $
(08-8723 3179; www.metrobakeryandcafe.com.au; 13 Commercial St E; mains $8-23; 8.30am-5pm Mon-Wed, to late Thu-Sat) Ask a local where they go for coffee: chances are they'll say 'Metro'. Right in the thick of things on the main drag, it's an efficient cafe with natty black-and-white decor, serving omelettes, focaccias, sandwiches, pastries and meatier mains (try the cider-braised pork belly). There's a wine bar here, too, brimming with Coonawarra cabernets. Book for dinner.

Yoeys CAFE, DELI $
(www.yoeys.com.au; 32 James St; items $5-15; 8.30am-5.30pm Mon-Fri, to 1.30pm Sat) This gourmet cafe-providore has shelves full of cakes, muffins, breads, chocolates, pasta and gourmet foodie hampers; a fabulous cheese fridge; and good coffee. Soups, pies and salads, too. Nice one!

Wild Ginger THAI $$
(08-8723 6264; www.wildginger.com.au; 17 Commercial St W; mains $16-24; 11.30am-2pm Tue-Fri, 5.30pm-late Tue-Sun) Locals recommend this authentic, gilt-fringed Thai nook on the main street, plating-up the likes of citrus-rich larp chicken salad and menacingly good red beef curry. It's a classy operation, with a lot of attention to detail (food presentation, interiors, staff attire etc). Good stuff.

Jens Town Hall Hotel PUB FOOD $$
(08-8725 1671; www.jenshotel.com; 40 Commercial St E; mains $18-32; noon-2pm & 6-8pm) The most palatable place for a beer in the Mount (there are a lot of rambling old pubs here), the 1884 Jens has a vast dining room plating up equally large steaks, pastas, seafood and damn fine minted lamb chops. The lunch specials are winning value ($6 to $12).

Information

Mount Gambier Visitor Information Centre (☎1800 087 187, 08-8724 9750; www.mountgambiertourism.com.au; 35 Jubilee Hwy E; ⏲9am-5pm Mon-Fri, 10am-4pm Sat & Sun) Has details on local sights, activities, transport and accommodation, plus *Heritage Walk* and *Historic Hotels* pamphlets and a town history movie. The **Lady Nelson Discovery Centre** (adult/child/family $4/2/10) is here too, featuring a replica of the historic brig *Lady Nelson* (which named 192m-high Mount Gambier as it sailed past in 1800) and displays on geology, wetlands and Indigenous history.

Penola & the Coonawarra Wine Region

A rural town on the way up (what a rarity!), **Penola** (population 1710) is the kind of place where you walk down the main street and three people say 'Hello!' to you before you reach the pub. The town is famous for two things: first, for its association with the Sisters of St Joseph of the Sacred Heart, co-founded in 1867 by Australia's first saint, Mary MacKillop; and secondly, for being smack bang in the middle of the **Coonawarra Wine Region**.

Sights

Mary MacKillop Interpretive Centre MUSEUM
(www.mackilloppenola.org.au; cnr Portland St & Petticoat Lane; adult/child $5/free; ⏲10am-4pm) The centre occupies a jaunty building with a gregarious entrance pergola (perhaps not as modest as Saint Mary might have liked!). There's oodles of info on Australia's first saint here, plus the Woods MacKillop Schoolhouse, the first school in Australia for children from lower socioeconomic backgrounds.

John Riddoch Centre MUSEUM
(www.wattlerange.sa.gov.au/tourism; 27 Arthur St; ⏲9am-5pm Mon-Fri, 10am-4pm Sat & Sun) FREE In the visitor centre building, this museum casts a web over local history back to the 1850s, covering the local Pinejunga people and original Penola pastoralist Riddoch, who 'never gave in to misfortune' and was 'steady and persistent'.

Petticoat Lane STREET
(⏲24hr) FREE One of Penola's first streets. Most of the original buildings have been razed, but there are still a few old timber-slab houses, red-gum kerbs and gnarly trees to see.

Sleeping & Eating

See www.coonawarradiscovery.com for B&B listings. Many local wineries also have restaurants.

Penola Backpackers HOSTEL $
(☎08-8736 6170, 0428 866 700; www.penolabackpackers.com.au; 59 Church St; dm/s/d/f from $35/45/95/140; ❄📶) In a Spanish Mission–style house on the main street, this five-bedroom backpackers is a timely addition to the Limestone Coast accommodation scene. There's a tidy and clean kitchen, roses and daffodils out the front and a BBQ terrace out the back. Air-con in some rooms. Ask about their beach house in Southend.

Heyward's Royal Oak Hotel PUB $
(☎08-8737 2322; www.heywardshotel.com.au; 31 Church St; s $66, d & tw $99) This lace-trimmed megalith (1872) is Penola's community hub. The rooms upstairs are nothing flash and share bathrooms, but they're decent bang for your buck. Downstairs is a huge tartan-carpeted dining room (mains $15 to $23, serving 11.30am to 2pm and 6pm to 8pm) serving contemporary pub food and schnitzels as big as your head.

Must@Coonawarra MOTEL $$
(☎08-8737 3444; www.mustatcoonawarra.com.au; 126 Church St; r from $160; ❄📶) 🍃 Plush Must has roof curves reminiscent of a certain opera venue in Sydney. Accommodation ranges from studios to apartments, with sustainable features aplenty: rainwater showers, double glazing and insulation, solar hot water, natural cleaning products etc. Bike hire is $20 per day.

Georgie's Cottage B&B $$$
(☎08-8737 3540; www.georgiescottage.com; 1 Riddoch St; d from $200; ❄) Feeling romantic? A short stroll from town on the road to Millicent, Georgie's is a cute little stone cottage fronted by blooming roses and hollyhocks. Gourmet provisions include chocolates and sparkling wine, which you may or may not feel like cracking into for breakfast.

diVine CAFE, DELI $
(☎08-8737 2122; www.penola.org/listing/divine-cafe; 39 Church St; mains $9-19; ⏲9am-4.30pm Mon & Tue, 8am-4.30pm Wed-Sun) A bright, mod cafe serving baguettes, all-day breakfasts, great coffee and internationally inspired lunches (try the Chinese pork-and-prawn rice paper rolls). Nattering Penolans chew muffins and local cheeses, discussing the nuances of various vintages.

DON'T MISS

COONAWARRA WINERIES

When it comes to spicy cabernet sauvignon, it's just plain foolish to dispute the virtues of the Coonawarra Wine Region (www.coonawarra.org). The *terra rossa* (red earth) soils here also produce irresistible shiraz and chardonnay.

Balnaves of Coonawarra (www.balnaves.com.au; Riddoch Hwy; ⏲9am-5pm Mon-Fri, noon-5pm Sat & Sun) The tasting notes here ooze florid wine speak (dark seaweed, anyone?), but even if your nosing skills aren't that subtle, you'll enjoy the cab sav and chardonnay.

Majella Wines (www.majellawines.com.au; Lynn Rd; ⏲10am-4.30pm) The family that runs Majella are fourth-generation Coonawarrans, so they know a thing or two about gutsy reds (love 'The Musician' shiraz cabernet).

Rymill Coonawarra (www.rymill.com.au; Riddoch Hwy; ⏲10am-5pm) Rymill rocks the local boat by turning out some of the best sauvignon blanc you'll ever taste. The cellar door is fronted by a statue of two duelling steeds – appropriately rebellious.

Wynns Coonawarra Estate (www.wynns.com.au; 1 Memorial Dr; ⏲10am-5pm) The oldest Coonawarra winery, Wynns' cellar door dates from 1896 and was built by Penola pioneer John Riddoch. Top-quality shiraz, riesling and golden chardonnay are the mainstays.

Zema Estate (www.zema.com.au; Riddoch Hwy; ⏲9am-5pm Mon-Fri, 10am-4pm Sat & Sun) A steadfast, traditional winery started by the Zema family in the early '80s. It's a low-key affair with a handmade vibe infusing the shiraz and cab sav.

★**Pipers of Penola** MODERN AUSTRALIAN **$$$**
(☎08-8737 3999; www.pipersofpenola.com.au; 58 Riddoch St; mains $30-37; ⏲6-9pm Tue-Sat) A classy, intimate dining room tastefully constructed inside an old Methodist church, with friendly staff and seasonal fare. The menu is studded with ingredients like truffled parsnip, date couscous and mustard 'liaison' – serious gourmet indicators! The prices are going up, but so is the quality. Superb wine list with lots of locals (…the beer list could be craftier).

ℹ Information

Penola Visitor Information Centre (☎1300 045 373, 08-8737 2855; www.wattlerange.sa.gov.au/tourism; 27 Arthur St; ⏲9am-5pm Mon-Fri, 10am-4pm Sat & Sun) Services the Coonawarra region, with info about local cycling routes and winery tours. The John Riddoch Centre is also here. Pick up the *Walk With History* brochures.

Naracoorte Caves National Park

About 10km southeast of Naracoorte township, off the Penola road, is the only World Heritage–listed site in SA. The discovery of an ancient fossilised marsupial in these limestone caves raised palaeontological eyebrows around the world, and featured in the BBC's David Attenborough series *Life on Earth*.

The park visitor centre doubles as the impressive **Wonambi Fossil Centre** (☎08-8762 2340; www.environment.sa.gov.au/naracoorte; 89 Wonambi Rd; adult/child/family $13/8/36; ⏲9am-5pm) – a re-creation of the rainforest that covered this area 200,000 years ago. Follow a ramp down past grunting, life-sized reconstructions of extinct animals, including a marsupial lion, a giant echidna, *Diprotodon australis* (koala meets grizzly bear), and *Megalania prisca* – 500kg of bad-ass goanna.

The 26 limestone caves here, including **Alexandra Cave**, **Cathedral Cave** and **Victoria Fossil Cave**, have bizarre formations of stalactites and stalagmites. Prospective Bruce Waynes should check out the **Bat Cave**, from which thousands of endangered southern bentwing bats exit en masse at dusk during summer. You can see the **Wet Cave** by self-guided tour (adult/child/family $9/5.50/25), but the others require ranger-guided tours. Single-cave tours start at $20/12/55 per adult/child/family; adventure caving starts at $60/35 per adult/child. There's also budget accommodation available at **Wirreanda Bunkhouse** (☎08-87622340; www.environment.sa.gov.au/naracoorte; unpowered/powered sites from $27.50/30, dm/f from $22/75), which is often full of school kids but can be booked by travellers.

For more local info and tips on places to stay, contact **Naracoorte Visitor Information Centre** (☎1800 244 421, 08-8762 1399; www.naracoortelucindale.com; 36 MacDonnell St; ⏲9am-5pm Mon-Fri, 10am-4pm Sat & Sun) in Naracoorte.

Yorke Peninsula & Western SA

Includes ➡

Why Go?

A couple of hours west of Adelaide, boot-shaped Yorke Peninsula (aka 'Yorkes') bills itself as 'Agriculturally Rich – Naturally Beautiful'. And indeed, while Yorkes is thin on urban hubbub, it does have a certain agrarian beauty – deep azure summer skies and yellow barley fields spread across hazy, gently rolling hills. The coastline here is gorgeous, with great surf, roaming emus, kangaroos and ospreys, plus whales and dolphins cruising by.

Further west, the vast, straw-coloured triangle of Eyre Peninsula is Australia's big-sky country, and is the promised land for seafood fans. Meals out here rarely transpire without the option of trying the local oysters, tuna and whiting. Sublime national parks punctuate the coast along with world-class surf breaks and low-key holiday towns, thinning out as you head west towards the Great Australian Bight, the Nullarbor Plain and Western Australia (WA).

Best Places to Eat

- Fresh Fish Place (p787)
- Dragon Well (p781)
- Mocean (p789)
- Ceduna Oyster Bar (p789)

Best Places to Stay

- Point Turton Caravan Park (p783)
- Tanonga (p787)
- Port Lincoln YHA (p786)
- Dawes Point Cottage (p788)

When to Go

Ceduna

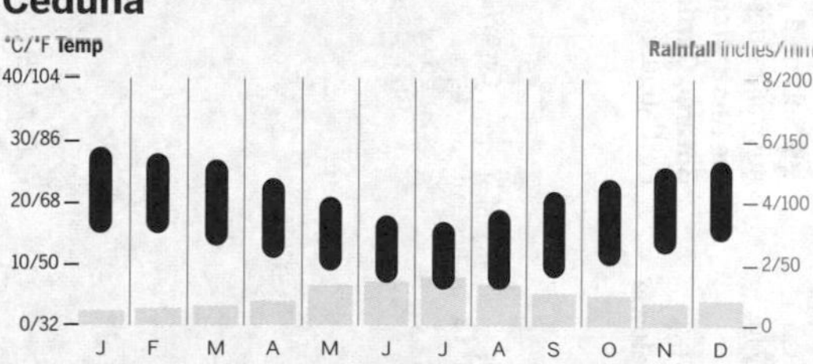

Nov–Dec The tourist season hits its straps and it's warm enough to swim.

Mar–May Warm autumn days and cool nights: perfect beach and oyster-slurping weather.

Aug–Oct Spring is in the air, the wheat fields are green and the roads are empty.

Yorke Peninsula & Western SA Highlights

1. Digging into Cornish copper-mining history in **Moonta** (p782).
2. Paddling out into the surf at isolated **Pondalowie Bay** (p783).
3. Getting a feel for Australia's desert heart at the **Australian Arid Lands Botanic Garden** (p785) in Port Augusta.
4. Seeing some seafood (or better still, eating some) in **Port Lincoln** (p786), the tuna capital of Australia.
5. Staring mortality in the eye on a **shark-cage dive** (p786) off Port Lincoln.
6. Exploring bays, dunes and remote walking tracks in **Coffin Bay National Park** (p787).
7. Slurping down a dozen briny oysters au naturel in **Ceduna** (p789).
8. Scanning the sea for migrating southern right whales at **Head of Bight** (p790).

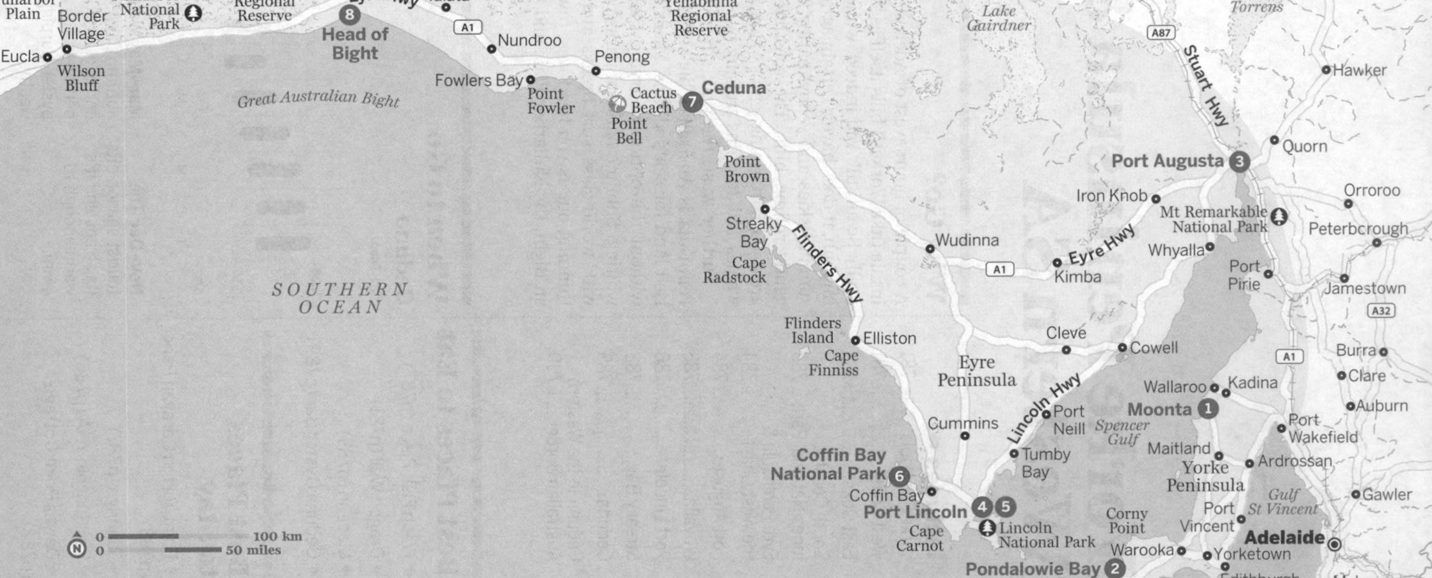

YORKE PENINSULA

For history buffs, the northwestern end of 'Yorkes' has a trio of towns called the Copper Triangle: Moonta (the mine), Wallaroo (the smelter) and Kadina (the service town). Settled by Cornish miners, this area drove the regional economy following a copper boom in the early 1860s. To the east and south, things are much more agricultural and laid-back, with sleepy holiday towns, isolated Innes National Park, remote surf breaks and empty coastline.

Tours

Aboriginal Cultural Tours South Australia CULTURAL
(☎0429 367 121; www.aboriginalsa.com.au; half-/1-/2-/3-day tours $85/150/350/495) Highly regarded Indigenous cultural tours of the peninsula, exploring the incredibly long Narungga Aboriginal association with this country. Lots of culture, wilderness and camping. Tours ex-Adelaide.

Heading Bush WILDERNESS
(☎1800 639 933, 08-8356 5501; www.headingbush.com; 3-day tours from $695) Explore Yorkes – wildlife, cliffs, beaches, Aboriginal culture and even a winery – on a three-day tour ex-Adelaide. Price includes dorm accommodation; single, double or twin accommodation is available at extra cost.

Sleeping

There are 15 council-run **camp sites** (☎08-8832 0000; www.yorke.sa.gov.au; per night $10) around the peninsula.

For holiday-house rentals from as little as $100 per night, try **Accommodation on Yorkes** (☎08-8852 2000; www.accommodationonyorkes.com.au) or **Country Getaways** (☎08-8832 2623; www.countrygetaways.info).

Getting There & Around

BUS

Yorke Peninsula Coaches (☎08-8821 2755; www.ypcoaches.com.au) Daily buses from Adelaide to Kadina ($36, 2¼ hours), Wallaroo ($36, 2½ hours) and Moonta ($36, three hours), travelling as far south as Edithburgh and Yorketown ($52, four hours, daily except Wednesday).

FERRY

SEASA (☎08-8823 0777; www.seasa.com.au; one way adult/child/car $35/10/140) Daily vehicle ferry between Wallaroo (Yorke Peninsula) and Lucky Bay (Eyre Peninsula) – a shortcut which shaves 350km and several hours off the drive via Port Augusta. The voyage takes around 1¾ hours one way.

West Coast

Fronting Spencer Gulf, the west coast has a string of shallow swimming beaches, plus the Copper Triangle towns, all a short drive from each other. **Kernewek Lowender** (www.kernewek.org), aka the Copper Coast Cornish Festival, happens around here in May of odd-numbered years.

Kadina

POP 4470

Baking-hot, inland Kadina (ka-*dee*-na) has some impressive copper-era civic buildings and a slew of massive old pubs, car yards and petrol stations. The **Copper Coast Visitor Information Centre** (☎08-8821 2333, 1800 654 991; www.yorkepeninsula.com.au; 50 Moonta Rd; ⏲9am-5pm Mon-Fri, 10am-4pm Sat & Sun) is here – it's the peninsula's main visitor centre. Behind it is an amazing collection of old farming, mining and domestic bits and pieces at the **Farm Shed Museum** (www.nationaltrust.org.au/sa; 50 Moonta Rd; adult/child/family $8/3/20; ⏲9am-5pm Mon-Fri, 10am-3.30pm Sat & Sun).

Sleeping & Eating

Kadina Gateway Motor Inn MOTEL $$
(☎1800 665 005, 08-8821 2777; www.kadinagatewaymotorinn.com.au; 4754 Copper Coast Hwy; d/f from $110/155;) If you're just after a basic, clean place to rest your head, try this well-run motel on the Adelaide side of town, with a bistro for dinner and a pool for those hot Yorkes afternoons.

Dragon Well CAFE $
(cnr Graves & Digby Sts; items $3-6; ⏲7am-5pm Mon-Fri, to noon Sat & Sun) What a surprise! A grungy little graffiti-spangled coffee bunker in downtown Kadina, with kooky retro furniture, a tattooed barista and walls covered with old record sleeves: straight outta Redfern! Super coffee, plus biscuits and cake.

Wallaroo

POP 3050

Still a major wheat port, Wallaroo is a town on the way up: the Eyre Peninsula ferry is running, there are plenty of pubs and the pubs are full of folks. There's a huge new subdivision north of town, and the shiny new **Copper Cove Marina** (www.coppercoastproperty.com.au/marina) is full of expensive boats.

Eyre Peninsula & Yorke Peninsula

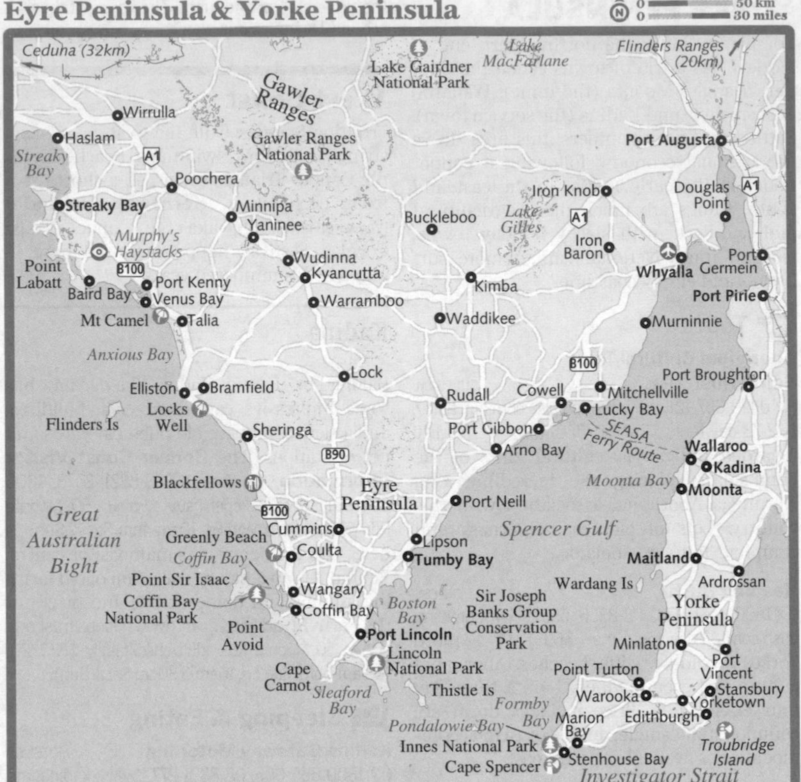

Down by the water, a stoic 1865 post office now houses the **Heritage & Nautical Museum** (www.nationaltrust.org.au; cnr Jetty Rd & Emu St; adult/child $6/3; ⏲10am-4pm), with tales of square-rigged English ships and George the pickled giant squid. For more on local history, pick up the *Discovering Historic Wallaroo* walk/drive brochures from the Copper Coast Visitor Information Centre (p781).

Sleeping

Sonbern Lodge Motel HOTEL, MOTEL **$**
(☎08-8823 2291; www.sonbernlodgemotel.com.au; 18 John Tce; s/d/f from $80/95/125; ❄) A 100-year-old grand temperance hotel, Sonbern is an old-fashioned charmer, right down to the old wooden balcony and antique wind-up phone. There are basic pub-style rooms in the main building (with bathrooms), and newish motel units out the back. Breakfast available.

Wallaroo Marina Apartments HOTEL, APARTMENT **$$**
(☎08-8823 4068; www.wallarooapartments.com.au; 11 Heritage Dr; d/apt from $144/184; ❄ 📶) The new multistorey Wallaroo Marina Apartments, at the marina on the northern edge of town, has spiffy suites, plus cold Coopers Pale Ale, bistro meals (mixed grills, local seafood), seductive marina views and regular live bands downstairs in the **Coopers Alehouse** (☎08-8823 2488; www.wallaroomarinahotel.com; mains $17-30; ⏲noon-2.30pm & 6-8.30pm).

Moonta

POP 3350

In the late 19th century, the Moonta copper mine was the richest in Australia. These days the town, which calls itself 'Australia's Little Cornwall', maintains a faded glory and a couple of decent pubs. Shallow Moonta Bay is 1km west of the town centre, with good fishing from the jetty and a netted swimming area.

Moonta Visitor Information Centre (☎08-8825 1891; www.moontatourism.org.au; Old Railway Station, Blanche Tce; ⏲9am-5pm) has a smattering of history pamphlets, and details on the **Moonta Heritage Site** 1.5km east of town. The site includes the excellent **Moonta Mines Museum** (www.nationaltrust.org.au/sa; Verran Tce; adult/child $8/4; ⏲1-4pm), once a grand school with 1100 pupils; the **Old Sweet Shop** (Verran Tce; ⏲10am-4pm) across the road (built 1846); and a fully restored **Miner's Cottage** (Verco St; adult/child $4/2; ⏲1.30-4pm Wed, Sat & Sun, daily during school holidays).

Sleeping & Eating

Moonta Bay Caravan Park CARAVAN PARK $
(☎08-8825 2406; www.moontabaycaravanpark.com.au; 5 Tossell St, Moonta Bay; unpowered/powered sites from $32/34, cabins without/with spa from $112/150; ❄📶) Handy to the beach and jetty, this caravan park has a decent crop of cabins with spas and little decks. The grassy camping areas are almost on the beach (wi-fi reception can be patchy down here...but the sunsets are awesome!).

Cottage by Cornwall B&B $$
(☎0438 313 952; www.cottagebycornwall.com.au; 24 Ryan St; d incl breakfast from $160, extra adult/child $20/free; ❄) The classiest accommodation in Moonta by a country mile, this tizzied-up 1863 cottage has three bedrooms (sleeping six), plus fancy bedding, mod furnishings and a claw-foot bath. It's just a short stroll to the pub and the Cornish Kitchen. Two-night minimum stay.

Cornish Kitchen FAST FOOD $
(10-12 Ellen St; items $4-11; ⏲9am-3pm Mon-Fri, to 2pm Sat) After a hard day's copper mining, swing your shovel into the Cornish Kitchen for the ultimate Cornish pastie.

Point Turton

Heading south on the west coast, Point Turton (population 250) is a laid-back beach town with a lot of new building going on. You can learn to surf near here with **Neptunes Surf Coaching** (☎0417 839 142; www.neptunes.net.au; 2hr lessons from $50).

Sleeping & Eating

Point Turton Caravan Park CARAVAN PARK $
(☎08-8854 5222; www.pointturtoncp.com.au; Bayview Rd; unpowered/powered sites from $22/27, cabins $55-150; ❄📶) Down on the shore, this superfriendly caravan park has grassy sites and cabins overlooking the sea.

Tavern on Turton PUB FOOD $$
(☎08-8854 5063; www.tavernonturton.com; 154 Bayview Rd; mains $17-35; ⏲9am-2pm & 6-8pm) Fab water views and seafood salads.

Inland Sea SEAFOOD $$
(☎08-8854 5499; www.inlandsea.com.au; 12918 Yorke Hwy, Warooka; mains $19-34; ⏲noon-2pm & 6-8pm Wed-Sat) A few kilometres inland from Point Turton, Inland Sea is a seafood diner that's close enough to the coast for the catch of the day to still be wriggling.

East Coast

The east-coast road along Gulf St Vincent traces the coast within 1km or 2km of the water. En route, roads dart east to sandy beaches and holiday towns. Like the suburban Adelaide beaches across the gulf, this is prime **crab fishing** territory.

Most of the coastal towns have a tavern, a jetty and a caravan park or camping ground, including unpretentious **Port Vincent** (population 480). Continuing south, **Stansbury** (population 550) has a couple of motels and the beaut waterside **Dalrymple Hotel** (☎08-8852 4202; www.facebook.com/thedalrymplehotel; 1 Anzac Pde; mains $16-33; ⏲noon-2pm & 6-8pm) – sit on the deck and chew some calamari.

Further south again, **Edithburgh** (population 400) is roughly aligned with Adelaide's latitude, and has a **tidal swimming pool** in a small cove. From the clifftops, views extend offshore to sandy **Troubridge Island Conservation Park** (www.environment.sa.gov.au). You can stay the night at the **Troubridge Island Lighthouse** (☎08-8852 6290; www.environment.sa.gov.au; per adult/child incl transfers $90/45, min charge $360). It sleeps 10; BYO food and linen.

Back on the mainland, the surprisingly hip **Tipper's B&B** (☎08-8852 6181; www.tippersedithburgh.com.au; 35 Blanche St; d/q incl breakfast from $150/210; ❄) is on Edithburgh's main street, with two suites occupying an ochre-coloured former blacksmiths (1890s). Two-night minimum stay.

South Coast & Innes National Park

The peninsula's south coast is largely sheltered from the Southern Ocean's fury by Kangaroo Island, so there are some great **swimming** beaches along here. The surf finds its way through around Troubridge Point and Cape Spencer.

THE PENINSULA FINGER

Something strange happens below a certain latitude on both the Yorke and Eyre Peninsulas: drivers in oncoming vehicles begin raising their index fingers off their steering wheels in cheery acknowledgement of your passing. It's a country courtesy, as if to say, 'Hello! Good to see you driving along this same sunny road today!' Stew in your cityside cynicism and ignore them, or respond in kind and see who can deliver the Peninsula Finger first!

Cape Spencer is part of **Innes National Park** (☎08-8854 3200; www.environment.sa.gov.au; Stenhouse Bay Rd, Stenhouse Bay; per car $10; ⏲visitor centre 10.30am-3pm Wed-Sun), where sheer cliffs plunge into indigo waters and rocky offshore islands hide small coves and sandy beaches. **Marion Bay** (www.marionbay.com.au), just outside the park, and **Stenhouse Bay** and **Pondalowie Bay**, both within the park, are the main local settlements. Pondalowie Bay has a bobbing lobster-fishing fleet and a gnarly surf beach.

The rusty ribs of the 711-tonne steel barque *Ethel*, which foundered in 1904, arc forlornly from the sands just south of Pondalowie Bay. Follow the sign past the Cape Spencer turn-off to the ghost-town of **Inneston**, a gypsum-mining community abandoned in 1930.

Sleeping

Innes National Park CAMPGROUND, LODGE $

(☎08-8854 3200; www.environment.sa.gov.au; camping per car $10, lodges $108-160) Innes National Park has seven bushy camp sites. Our favourite spot is Pondalowie, or try Cable Bay for beach access, Surfers for surfing or Browns Beach for fishing. Alternatively, the heritage lodges at Inneston sleep four to 10 people and have showers and cooking facilities. Book camp sites and lodges online, or with a credit card at the park visitor centre; BYO drinking water in summer.

★**Marion Bay Motel & Tavern** MOTEL $$

(☎08-8854 4044; www.marionbaymotel.com.au; Jetty Rd, Marion Bay; s/d/tr $120/140/160; ❄📶) The highlight of tiny Marion Bay is this wing of five spiffy motel rooms (white walls, new TVs, nice linen). The glass-fronted tavern next door (mains $17 to $38; serving noon to 2pm and 6pm to 8pm) surveys the bay, with a pizza oven in a corrugated-iron water tank and Asian-influenced pub standards (try the Vietnamese chicken salad).

EYRE PENINSULA & THE WEST COAST

Eyre Peninsula's photogenic wild western flank is an important breeding ground for southern right whales, Australian sea lions and great white sharks (the scariest scenes of *Jaws* were shot here). There are some memorable opportunities to encounter these submariners along the way.

Tours

Goin' Off Safaris GUIDED TOUR

(☎0427 755 065; www.goinoffsafaris.com.au; tours from $150) Check the big-ticket items off your Eyre Peninsula 'to-do' list – sharks, tuna, sea lions and seafood – with local guides. Day trips around Port Lincoln and Coffin Bay, plus overnight jaunts, seafood-focused trips and fishing expeditions.

Getting There & Away

A handy car ferry (p781) runs between the Yorke Peninsula and the Eyre Peninsula.

AIR

Regional Express (Rex; www.regionalexpress.com.au) Daily flights from Adelaide to Whyalla (one way from $154), Port Lincoln (from $115) and Ceduna (from $190).

BUS

Premier Stateliner (www.premierstateliner.com.au) Daily buses from Adelaide to Port Augusta ($60, 4¼ hours), Whyalla ($68, 5½ hours), Port Lincoln ($119, 9¾ hours), Streaky Bay ($122, 10 hours) and Ceduna ($135, 11¼ hours).

TRAIN

The famous Ghan train connects Adelaide with Darwin via Port Augusta, and the Indian Pacific (between Perth and Sydney) connects with the Ghan at Port Augusta. **Pichi Richi Railway** (☎1800 440 101; www.prr.org.au; Port Augusta Train Station, Stirling Rd; one way adult/child/family $52/19/122) runs between Port Augusta and Quorn (two hours) on Saturdays.

Port Augusta

POP 13,900

From utilitarian Port Augusta – the 'Crossroads of Australia' – highways and railways roll west across the Nullarbor into WA, north to the Flinders Ranges or Darwin, south to Adelaide or Port Lincoln, and east to Sydney. Not a bad position! The old town centre has considerable appeal, with some elegant old buildings and a revitalised waterfront: locals cast lines into the blue as Indigenous kids backflip off jetties.

Sights & Activities

Australian Arid Lands Botanic Garden GARDENS
(www.aalbg.sa.gov.au; Stuart Hwy; tour charges apply; gardens 7.30am-dusk, visitor centre 9am-5pm Mon-Fri, 10am-4pm Sat & Sun) FREE Just north of town, the excellent (and free!) botanic garden has 250 hectares of sand hills, clay flats and desert flora and fauna. Explore on your own, or take a guided tour (10am Monday to Friday). There's a cafe here too.

Port Augusta Aquatic & Outdoor Adventure Centre OUTDOORS
(08-8642 2699, 0427 722 450; www.augustaoutdoors.com.au; 4 El Alamein Rd; 9am-4pm Mon-Fri) Offers lessons and gear rental for kayaking, windsurfing, rock climbing, abseiling, snorkelling, bushwalking, sailing... Bike hire $20 per hour.

Sleeping & Eating

Shoreline Caravan Park CARAVAN PARK $
(08-8642 2965; www.shorelinecaravanpark.com.au; Gardiner Ave; unpowered/powered sites $30/33, dm $40, cabins $60-130;) It's a dusty site and a fair walk from town (and from the shoreline when the tide is out), but the cabins here are decent and there are simple four-bed dorm units for backpackers. The cheapest beds in town for those who don't fancy sleeping above a pub.

Oasis Apartments APARTMENT $$
(08-8648 9000, 1800 008 648; www.majestichotels.com.au; Marryatt St; apt $153-219;) Catering largely to conventioneers, this group of 75 luxury units (from studios to two bedrooms) with jaunty designs is right by the water. All rooms have washing machines, dryers, TVs, fridges, microwaves, fortresslike security and flashy interior design. Free wi-fi too.

Crossroads Ecomotel MOTEL $$
(08-8642 2540; www.ecomotel.com.au; 45 Eyre Hwy; d from $120;) Brand new when we visited, this is one cool motel (literally). Built using rammed earth, double glazing and structural insulated panels (SIPs), the aim is to provide a thermally stable environment for guests, plus 100% more architectural style than anything else in Port Augusta. Desert hues, nice linen and free wi-fi seal the deal. A pool is on the cards.

Standpipe INDIAN $$
(08-8642 4033; www.standpipe.com.au; cnr Stuart Hwy & Hwy 1; mains $18-39; 6-9pm) The sprawling Standpipe motel attracts government delegates and business types with its pool, adjacent golf course and 85 reasonably hip units (doubles/two-bedroom apartments from $128/233), but the main lure is the awesome (and very unexpected) Indian restaurant here. Unbelievable!

Information

Port Augusta Visitor Information Centre
(08-8641 9193, 1800 633 060; www.portaugusta.sa.gov.au; Wadlata Outback Centre, 41 Flinders Tce; 9am-5.30pm Mon-Fri, 10am-4pm Sat & Sun) This is the major information outlet for the Eyre Peninsula, Flinders Ranges and outback. It's part of the **Wadlata Outback Centre** (www.wadlata.sa.gov.au; 41 Flinders Tce; adult/child/family $19.50/11/42; 9am-5.30pm Mon-Fri, 10am-4pm Sat & Sun), where the 'Tunnel of Time' traces Aboriginal and European histories using audiovisual displays, interactive exhibits and a distressingly big snake.

Whyalla

POP 21,130

An hour's drive south of Port Augusta is Whyalla – the third-biggest city in South Australia (SA) – with a deep-water port sustaining steel mills, oil and gas refineries and a morass of chugging chimneys, port facilities and industrial estates. Ugly, yes, but the old town has some good pubs, well-preserved domestic architecture and migrating giant Australian cuttlefish in the waters offshore (May to August).

Whyalla Visitor Information Centre (1800 088 589, 08-8645 7900; www.whyalla.com; Lincoln Hwy; 9am-5pm Mon-Fri, 10am-4pm Sat & Sun) can help with cuttlefish info, tour bookings for the One Steel facility and accommodation listings. Next to the visitor centre is the **Whyalla Maritime Museum** (08-8645 8900; www.whyallamaritimemuseum.com.au; Lincoln Hwy; adult/child/family $12/7/31; 10am-3pm, ship tours hourly 11am-2pm), which includes the HMAS *Whyalla,* allegedly the largest landlocked ship in Australia (...who keeps track of these things?). The utilitarian **Foreshore Motor Inn** (08-8645 8877; www.whyallaforeshore.com.au; Watson Tce; d/f from $145/165;) is down by the white sandy expanse of Whyalla's foreshore.

Port Lincoln

POP 15,000

Prosperous Port Lincoln, the 'Tuna Capital of the World', overlooks broad Boston Bay on the southern end of Eyre Peninsula. It's still a fishing town a long way from anywhere, but the vibe here is energetic (dare we say progressive!). The grassy foreshore is a busy promenade, and there are some good pubs, eateries and aquatic activities here to keep you out of trouble.

If not for a lack of fresh water, Port Lincoln might have become the South Australian capital. These days it's saltwater (and the tuna therein) that keeps the town ticking. A guaranteed friend-maker here is to slip Dean Lukin's name into every conversation. Straight off the tuna boats, Big Dean won the Super Heavyweight weightlifting gold medal at the 1984 Olympics in LA – what a champ!

The annual **Tunarama Festival** (www.tunarama.net) on the Australia Day weekend in January celebrates every finny facet of the tuna-fishing industry.

Sights & Activities

There's good beginner/intermediate surfing at Fisheries Bay, Lone Pine and Wreck Beach. For info visit **Lincoln Surf** (08-8682 4428; www.facebook.com/lincolnsurfsa; 7-11 Lewis St; 9am-5.30pm Mon-Fri, to 1pm Sat).

If you'd rather be on the water than in it, you're in luck; the local fishing is outstanding. Ask **Spot On Fishing Tackle** (www.spotonfishing.com.au; 39 Tasman Tce; 8.30am-5.30pm Mon-Fri, 8am-4pm Sat, 9am-2pm Sun) about what's biting where.

Boston Bay Wines WINERY
(08-8684 3600; www.bostonbaywines.com.au; Lincoln Hwy; noon-4pm) Seems like everywhere you go in SA these days there's a winery cellar door (…well, except the desert). Port Lincoln is no exception. On the northern outskirts of town, Boston Bay Wines does a mean merlot and a 'Great White' sauvignon blanc, in keeping with the local aquatic fauna.

Adventure Bay Charters ADVENTURE TOUR
(08-8682 2979; www.adventurebaycharters.com.au) Carbon-neutral Adventure Bay Charters takes you swimming with sea lions (adult/child $195/135) and cage diving with Great White sharks ($345/245). Multiday ocean safaris are also available, plus more laid-back 90-minute cruises around the Port Lincoln marina ($45/25).

Calypso Star Charters ADVENTURE TOUR
(08-8682 3939, 1300 788 378; www.sharkcagediving.com.au; 1-day dive adult/child $495/345) Runs shark cage dives with Great White sharks around the Neptune Islands. Book in advance; it's cheaper if you're just watching nervously from the boat. Also runs four-hour swimming with sea lion trips (adult/child $150/105).

Swim with the Tuna ADVENTURE TOUR
(1300 788 378, 08-8682 6010; www.swimwiththetuna.com.au; adult/child $90/60) Three-hour boat tours out to a floating tuna enclosure, where you can check out the big fish from an underwater observatory or jump into the brine with them.

Port Lincoln Walk & Talk History Tours GUIDED TOUR
(0474 222 020; www.facebook.com/portlincolnwalkandtalktours; adult/child $12/10) Tag along on a 90-minute walk along the Port Lincoln foreshore with a fifth-generation local who knows the town backwards.

Sleeping & Eating

★**Port Lincoln YHA** HOSTEL $
(08-8682 3605; www.yha.com.au; 26 London St; dm/tw/d/f from $33/80/100/200;) Run by a high-energy couple who have spent a fortune renovating the place, this impressive 84-bed hostel occupies a former squash-court complex. Thoughtful bonuses include chunky sprung mattresses, reading lights, a cafe/bar and power outlets in lockers (for phones!). Outrageously clean, and with 300 movies for a rainy day (including *Jaws*). Staff can help with activities bookings too.

Pier Hotel PUB $
(08-8682 1322; www.portlincolnpier.com.au; 33 Tasman Tce; d/tw/2-bedroom apt from $80/80/130;) The old Pier has had a facelift, including the dozen en suite rooms upstairs – they're now bright and clean with polished floorboards and TVs. The **bistro** (mains $18-34; noon-2pm & 6-8pm) downstairs is big on local seafood: oysters, calamari and scallops reign supreme.

Port Lincoln Tourist Park CARAVAN PARK $
(08-8621 4444; www.portlincolntouristpark.com.au; 11 Hindmarsh St; unpowered/powered sites $25/32, cabins & units $70-155;) This breezy waterside operation is Port Lincoln's best caravan park, with some beaut executive cabins by the water and plenty of elbow room. Fish from the jetty and swim at the private beach. BYO linen in the basic cabins.

Port Lincoln Hotel HOTEL $$
(☎1300 766 100, 08-8621 2000; www.portlincolnhotel.com.au; 1 Lincoln Hwy; d $145-250;) Bankrolled by a couple of Adelaide Crows Australian Football League (AFL) footballers, this ritzy seven-storey hotel lifts Port Lincoln above the fray. It's a classy, contemporary affair with switched-on staff. Good on-site bars and eateries too, open all day (mains $25 to $42).

★**Tanonga** B&B $$$
(☎0427 812 013; www.tanonga.com.au; Charlton Gully; d incl breakfast from $310, minimum 2-night stay;) Two plush, solar-powered, architect-designed ecolodges in the hills behind Port Lincoln. They're both superprivate and surrounded by native bush, bird life and walking trails. Roll into town for dinner, or take advantage of the DIY packs of local produce available.

★**Fresh Fish Place** SEAFOOD $
(☎08-8682 2166; www.portlincolnseafood.com.au; 20 Proper Bay Rd; meals $10-14; 8.30am-5.30pm Mon-Fri, to 12.30pm Sat) Check the fish of the day on the blackboard out the front of this fabulous seafood shack. Inside you can buy fresh local seafood straight off the boats (King George whiting, tuna, kingfish, flathead etc), plus Coffin Bay oysters for $12 a dozen and superb fish and chips. Seafood-tasting tours and cooking classes also available.

GLO CAFE $
(Good Living Organics; ☎08-8682 6655; www.goodlivingorganics.net; 23 Liverpool St; items $6-12; 8.30am-5.30pm Mon-Fri, 9am-noon Sat;) A local hang-out a block away from the beach (and thus not on many tourist radars), GLO serves wholesome organic quiches, wraps, salads, falafels, cous-cous and Port Lincoln's best coffee. What's the soup of the day?

Del Giorno's ITALIAN $$
(☎08-8683 0577; www.delgiornos.com.au; 80 Tasman Tce; mains $17-33; 7.30am-9pm Mon-Sat, 8.30am-9pm Sun) The busiest eatery in town, and with good reason: there's good coffee, big breakfasts and excellent local produce (especially seafood) at prices lower than at the pubs. Fab pizzas, pastas and pots of Kinkawooka mussels with tomato, chilli and white wine.

Information

Port Lincoln Visitor Information Centre
(☎1300 788 378, 08-8683 3544; www.visitportlincoln.net; 3 Adelaide Pl; 9am-5pm Mon-Fri, 10am-4pm Sat & Sun) Books accommodation, has national parks' information and passes, and stocks the *Port Lincoln & District Cycling Guide*. Ask about the interesting local railway, maritime and heritage museums.

Port Lincoln to Streaky Bay

Around Port Lincoln

About 50km north of Port Lincoln, **Tumby Bay** (www.tumbybay.com.au) is a quiet little town with a beach, jetty, pub, caravan park and motel – serious holiday territory!

About 15km south of Port Lincoln is **Lincoln National Park** (www.environment.sa.gov.au; per car $11), with roaming emus, roos and brush-tailed bettongs, safe swimming coves and pounding surf beaches. Entry is via self-registration on the way in. If you want to stay the night, the two-bedroom, self-contained **Donnington Cottage** (per night $93) at Spalding Cove, built in 1899, sleeps six and has photo-worthy views. Book through Port Lincoln visitor information centre; BYO linen and food. The visitor centre can also advise on **bush camping** (per car $10) in the park, including sites at Fisherman's Point, Memory Cove, September Beach and Surfleet Cove.

The Port Lincoln visitor information centre also sells permits to **Whalers Way** (24hr pass per car incl 1 night camping $30), a scenic 14km coastal drive 32km southwest of Port Lincoln.

Coffin Bay

POP 650

Oyster lovers rejoice! Deathly sounding Coffin Bay (named by Matthew Flinders after his buddy Sir Isaac Coffin) is a snoozy fishing village basking languidly in the warm sun... until a 4000-strong holiday horde arrives every January. Slippery, salty **oysters** from the nearby beds are exported worldwide, but you shouldn't pay more than $1 per oyster around town. Online, see www.coffinbay.net.

Along the ocean side of Coffin Bay there's some wild coastal scenery, most of which is part of **Coffin Bay National Park** (www.environment.sa.gov.au; per car $10), overrun with roos, emus and fat goannas. Access for conventional vehicles is limited: you can get to picturesque **Point Avoid** (coastal lookouts, rocky cliffs, good surf and whales passing between May and October) and **Yangie Bay** (arid-looking rocky landscapes and walking trails), but otherwise you'll need a 4WD. There are some isolated **camp sites** (per car $10) within the park, generally with dirt-road access.

Coffin Bay Explorer (☎0428 880 621; www.coffinbayexplorer.com; adult/child $85/45) runs half-day wildlife and seafood tours with plenty of dolphins and oysters, or you can go kayaking with Earth Adventure (p718).

Sleeping & Eating

For holiday shacks from $50 to $300 per night try **Coffin Bay Holiday Rentals** (☎0427 844 568; www.coffinbayholidayrentals.com.au) or **Coffin Bay Holiday Homes** (☎0447 658 288; www.coffinbayholidayhomes.com.au).

Coffin Bay Caravan Park CARAVAN PARK $
(☎08-8685 4170; www.coffinbaycaravanpark.com.au; 91 Esplanade; unpowered/powered sites $24/33, cabins with/without bathroom from $100/85, villas $120; ❄) Resident cockatoos, galahs and parrots squawk around the she-oak shaded sites here, and the cabins offer reasonable bang for your buck (BYO linen). Lovely two-bedroom family villas, too.

★**Dawes Point Cottage** RENTAL HOUSE $$
(☎0427 844 568; www.coffinbayholidayrentals.com.au/2_DawesPoint.htm; 5 Heron Ct; per night $140-200; ❄) This old-fashioned fishing shack (Aussie author Tim Winton would call it 'fish deco') was won by the present owners in a card game! Now a million-dollar property, it maintains its modesty despite sitting right on the water.

Coffin Bay Pizza & Homemade Food PIZZA $
(☎0458 248 725; www.coffinbaypizza.com.au; 4/61 Esplanade; meals $7-17; ⏲10am-2pm Mon, 11am-9.30pm Wed-Sun) An unassuming little takeaway that's been here forever, serving decent pizzas, basic pastas, and fish and chips, plus homemade pies, pasties and sausage rolls. Gotta try the oyster pie! Open daily during school holidays.

Coffin Bay to Streaky Bay

There's reliable surf at **Greenly Beach** just south of **Coulta**, 40km north of Coffin Bay. There's also good salmon fishing along this wild stretch of coast, notably at **Locks Well**, where a long, steep stairway called the **Staircase to Heaven** (283 steps? Count 'em...) leads from the car park down to an awesome surf beach, the deep orange sand strewn with seashells.

About 15km further north, tiny **Elliston** (population 380) is a small fishing town on soporific Waterloo Bay, with a beautiful swimming beach and a fishing jetty (hope the whiting are biting). Waterside **Waterloo Bay Tourist Park** (☎08-8687 9076; www.visitelliston.net; 10 Beach Tce; unpowered/powered sites $25/30, cabins $65-130; ❄📶) is a smallish operation with decent cabins (aim for one on top of the dunes) and fishing gear for sale. Check out the old council-chambers building out the front.

Elliston Visitor Information Centre (☎08-8687 9200; www.elliston.com.au; Beach Tce; ⏲9am-5pm Mon-Fri, 10am-1pm Sat & Sun) can direct you towards the **Great Ocean Tourist Drive** just north of town – a 10km detour to **Anxious Bay** via some anxiety-relieving ocean scenery. En route you'll pass **Blackfellows**, which boasts some of the west coast's best surf. From here you can eyeball the 36-sq-km **Flinders Island** 35km offshore, where there's a sheep station and the self-contained, nine-bed **Flinders Island Getaway** (☎0428 261 132; www.flindersgetaway.com; per person from $90). To get here you have to charter a plane from Port Lincoln or a boat from Elliston (additional to accommodation costs); ask for details when you book.

At **Venus Bay** there are sheltered beaches (and the not-so-sheltered Mount Camel Beach), a squadron of pelicans, a small caravan park and the obligatory fishing jetty.

If you feel like taking a plunge and swimming with sea lions and dolphins, stop by Baird Bay and organise a tour with **Baird Bay Ocean Eco Experience** (☎08-8626 5017; www.bairdbay.com; 4hr tours adult/child $150/75; ⏲Sep-May) 🍃. Accommodation is also available.

If you'd rather stay high and dry, the road to **Point Labatt**, 43km south of Streaky Bay, takes you to one of the few permanent sea-lion colonies on the Australian mainland; ogle them from the clifftops (with binoculars).

A few kilometres down the Point Labatt road are the globular **Murphy's Haystacks** (www.streakybay.sa.gov.au; per person/family $2/5), an improbable congregation of inselbergs (colourful, weather-sculpted granite outcrops which are millions of years old).

Streaky Bay

POP 1150

This endearing little seasider (actually on Blanche Port) takes its name from the streaks of seaweed Matt Flinders spied in the bay as he sailed by. Visible at low tide, the seagrass attracts ocean critters and the bigger critters that eat them – first-class fishing.

Sights

The **Streaky Bay Museum** (www.nationaltrust.org.au/sa; 42 Montgomery Tce; adult/child $6.50/1; ⏲1.30-4pm Tue & Fri) is inside a 1901 schoolhouse, and features a fully furnished pug-and-pine hut, an old iron lung and plenty of pioneering history. More recently (1990), a 5m-long, 1.5-tonne **White Pointer shark** was reeled in off Streaky Bay: check out the unnerving replica inside **Stewarts Roadhouse** (☎08-8626 1222; 15 Alfred Tce; ⏲7am-9pm).

Sleeping & Eating

Foreshore Tourist Park CARAVAN PARK $
(☎08-8626 1666; www.streakybayftpark.com.au; 82 Wells St; unpowered/powered sites from $23/29, cabins & units $87-133; ❄) Right on Doctors Beach just east of town, this sandy park is overrun with cavorting families in summer and caravanning grey nomads in winter. Plenty of space and sea-based things to do.

Streaky Bay Hotel/Motel HOTEL, MOTEL $
(☎08-8626 1008; www.streakybayhotel.com.au; 33 Alfred Tce; hotel d & tw $50-135, motel d $110; all incl breakfast; ❄) The upstairs rooms at this 1866 beauty have rip-snorting views and a balcony from which to snort them! The downstairs rooms don't have views, bathrooms, TV or air-con but are decent. Motel rooms are unglamorous but more private. Meals happen in the **bistro** (mains $16-35, ⏲7-9am, noon-2pm & 6-8.30pm).

Streaky Bay Motel & Villas MOTEL $$
(☎08-8626 1126; www.streakybaymotelandvillas.com.au; 11-13 Alfred Tce; motel d $130, villa d/f $160/220; ❄📶🏊) A tidy row of bricky, older-style motel units (with a facelift), plus a crop of new family-size villas that are much more 'now' (spiky pot plants, mushroom-hued render, lime-coloured outdoor furniture). Cheaper off-season rates and three-bedroom houses also available.

★**Mocean** CAFE $$
(☎08-8626 1775; www.moceancafe.com.au; 34b Alfred Tce; mains $17-35; ⏲10am-3pm Tue, Wed & Sun, 10am-late Thu-Sat; 🖊) It looks like a big shipping container from the street, but this jaunty corrugated-iron-clad cafe is the town's social pacemaker, with murals, Moroccan lanterns and water views from the wrap-around balcony. Dishes focus on scrumptious Eyre Peninsula seafood; try the chilli-and-lime squid or the abalone. Super coffee and takeaways, too. Closed in August.

Information

Streaky Bay Visitor Information Centre (☎08-8626 7033; www.streakybay.com.au; 21 Bay Rd; ⏲9am-12.30pm & 1.30-5pm Mon-Fri) For the local low-down, swing by the visitor info centre.

Ceduna

POP 2290

Despite the locals' best intentions, Ceduna remains a raggedy fishing town that just can't shake its tag as a blow-through pit stop en route to WA (there are *five* caravan parks here). But the local oysters love it! **Oysterfest** (www.ceduna.sa.gov.au/oysterfest) in early October is the undisputed king of Australian oyster parties. And if you're heading west in whale season (May to October), Ceduna is the place for updates on sightings at Head of Bight.

Sights

Ceduna School House Museum MUSEUM
(www.nationaltrust.org.au/sa; 2 Park Tce; adult/child/family $4/2.50/9; ⏲10am-noon Mon, Tue & Thu-Sat, 2-4pm Wed & Thu) This little museum has pioneer exhibits, Indigenous artefacts and a display on the tragic British nuclear tests at Maralinga.

Sleeping & Eating

Ceduna Foreshore Hotel/Motel MOTEL $$
(☎08-8625 2008; www.cedunahotel.com.au; 32 O'Loughlin Tce; d $125-195, f $160-180; ❄📶) The renovated 54-room Foreshore is the most luxurious option in town, with water views and a **bistro** (mains $17-38, ⏲6.30-9am, noon-2pm & 6-8.30pm) focused on west-coast seafood. The view from the outdoor terrace extends through Norfolk Island pines and out across the bay.

★**Ceduna Oyster Bar** SEAFOOD $$
(☎08-8626 9086; www.facebook.com/oysterbarceduna; Eyre Hwy; 12 oysters $12, meals $14-22; ⏲9.30am-7.30pm) Pick up a box of freshly shucked molluscs and head for the foreshore, or sit up on the rooftop here (are the renovations finished yet?) and watch the road trains rumble in from WA. Fresh as can be.

Information

Ceduna Visitor Information Centre (☎1800 639 413, 08-8625 2780; www.cedunatourism.com.au; 58 Poynton St; ⏲9am-5.30pm Mon-Fri, to 5pm Sat & Sun) The Ceduna Visitor Information Centre can help with local info.

Ceduna to the Western Australian Border

It's 480km from Ceduna to the WA border. Along the stretch you can get a bed and a beer at Penong (72km from Ceduna), Fowlers Bay (141km), Nundroo (151km), the Nullarbor Roadhouse (295km) near Head of Bight, and at Border Village on the border itself.

Wheat and sheep paddocks line the road to Nundroo, after which you're in mallee scrub for another 100km. Around 20km later, the trees thin to low bluebush as you enter the true Nullarbor (Latin for 'no trees'). Road trains, caravans and cyclists of questionable sanity are your only companions as you put your foot down and careen towards the setting sun.

Turn off the highway at **Penong** (population 200), and follow the 21km dirt road to Point Sinclair and **Cactus Beach**, which has three of Australia's most famous surf breaks. Caves is a wicked right-hand break for experienced surfers (locals don't take too kindly to tourists dropping in). There's **bush camping** (www.youcamp.com/properties/51; unpowered sites $13) on private property close to the breaks; BYO drinking water.

The viewing platforms at **Head of Bight** (☎0407 832 297; www.yalata.org; adult $20, child under/over 15 free/$15; ⏲8am-5pm) overlook a major southern-right-whale breeding ground. Whales migrate here from Antarctica, and you can see them cavorting from May to October. The breeding area is protected by the **Great Australian Bight Commonwealth Marine Reserve** (www.environment.gov.au), the world's second-largest marine park after the Great Barrier Reef.

Head of Bight is a part of the Yalata Indigenous Protected Area. Pay your entry fee and get the latest whale information from the **White Well Ranger Station** on the way in to the viewing area. The signposted turn-off is 14km east of the Nullarbor Roadhouse.

While you're in the Head of Bight area, you can also check out **Murrawijinie Cave**, a large overhang behind the Nullarbor Roadhouse, and have a look at the signposted coastal lookouts along the top of the 80m-high **Bunda Cliffs**.

If you're continuing west into WA, dump all fruit, vegetables, cheese and plants at Border Village (as per quarantine regulations), and watch out for animals if you're driving at night. Note that if you're driving east rather than west, SA's quarantine checkpoint isn't until Ceduna.

Sleeping

Penong Caravan Park CARAVAN PARK $
(☎08-8625 1111; www.nullarbornet.com.au/towns/penong.html; 3 Stiggants Rd, Penong; unpowered/powered sites from $22/25, on-site vans/cabins from $45/75; ❄) A short hop from Ceduna, this well-kept park is rated by some travellers as the best on the Nullarbor. The cabins are in good shape, and the camping area has a laundry and barbecues. Extra charge for linen.

Fowlers Bay Eco Park CARAVAN PARK $
(☎08-8625 6143; www.fowlerseco.com; Esplanade, Fowlers Bay; powered sites per 2 people $28, extra person $8) 🍃 You'll find powered sites, a kiosk and sophisticated solar systems at this cheery caravan park. Nearby are heritage buildings, good fishing, passing whales and rambling dunes. Ask about whale-watching tours (May to October). The Fowlers Bay turn-off is 106km from Ceduna.

Fowlers Bay Holiday Flats APARTMENT $$
(☎08-8625 6179; www.fowlersbay.com; Fowlers Bay; d from $100; ❄) Basic motel-style units sleeping four, with full kitchens. It's a short walk from the town jetty (bring your fishing rod).

Nundroo Hotel Motel MOTEL $
(☎08-8625 6120; www.nundrooaccommodation.com; Eyre Hwy, Nundroo; unpowered/powered sites $8/20, d $99; ❄📶) If you're heading west, Nundroo has this decent hotel/motel and the last mechanic until Norseman, WA, 1038km away. Expect worn but comfy motel rooms with updated bathrooms. There's also a **bar-restaurant** (meals $15-35; ⏲11am-late) on-site.

Nullarbor Roadhouse MOTEL $
(☎08-8625 6271; www.nullarbornet.com.au/towns/nullarbor.html; Eyre Hwy, Nullarbor; unpowered/powered sites $20/25, budget rooms s/d/tr $47/57/67, motel s/d/tr from $125/145/165; ❄) Close to the Head of Bight whale-watching area, this roadhouse is a real oasis for weary road warriors. Also has an on-site **bar-restaurant** (meals $15-30; ⏲7am-10pm).

Border Village Motel MOTEL $
(☎08-9039 3474; www.nullarbornet.com.au/towns/bordervillage.html; Eyre Hwy, Border Village; unpowered/powered sites $15/20, budget s/d/tr $40/60/70, motel s/d/f from $95/110/120; ❄@🏊) Just 50m from the WA border, this rebuilt motel has a variety of modern rooms and cabins, plus a licensed restaurant (meals $15 to $28; open noon to 2pm and 6pm to 8pm).

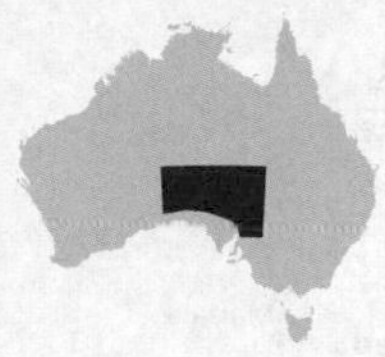

Flinders Ranges & Outback SA

Includes ➡

Best Places to Eat

- Rawnsley Park Station (p797)
- Prairie Hotel (p799)
- John's Pizza Bar & Restaurant (p804)
- Quorn Cafe (p797)

Best Places to Stay

- North Star Hotel (p796)
- Quorn Caravan Park (p796)
- Wilpena Pound Resort (p798)
- Down to Erth B&B (p803)

Why Go?

If you want to experience the Outback (the loose geographic zone comprising 70% of mainland Australia) wheeling into the Flinders Ranges is a great way to start.

Approaching the Ranges from the south, the wheat fields and wineries of South Australia's midnorth district give way to arid cattle stations beneath ochre-coloured peaks. This is ancient country, imbued with the Dreaming stories of the Adnyamathanha people. Emus wander across roads; yellow-footed rock wallabies bound from boulder to boulder.

Further north on the Stuart Hwy and along the legendary Oodnadatta and Strzelecki Tracks, eccentric outback towns such as Woomera, William Creek, Innamincka and Coober Pedy emerge from the heat haze. This is no country for the faint-hearted: it's waterless, flyblown and dizzyingly hot. No wonder the opal miners in Coober Pedy live underground!

When to Go

Quorn

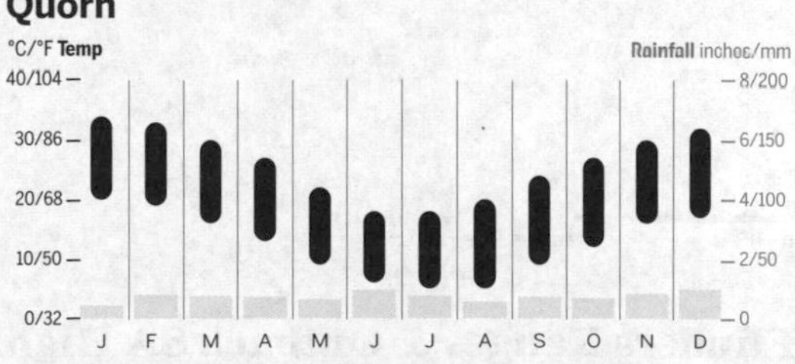

May Sunbaked desert colours shimmer as the Outback cools at the end of autumn.

Jun–Aug Winter is peak season in the Outback: mild temperatures, clear skies and Grey Nomads.

Sep Last chance to hit the Outback without 35-degree days. Spring flowers in the Flinders Ranges.

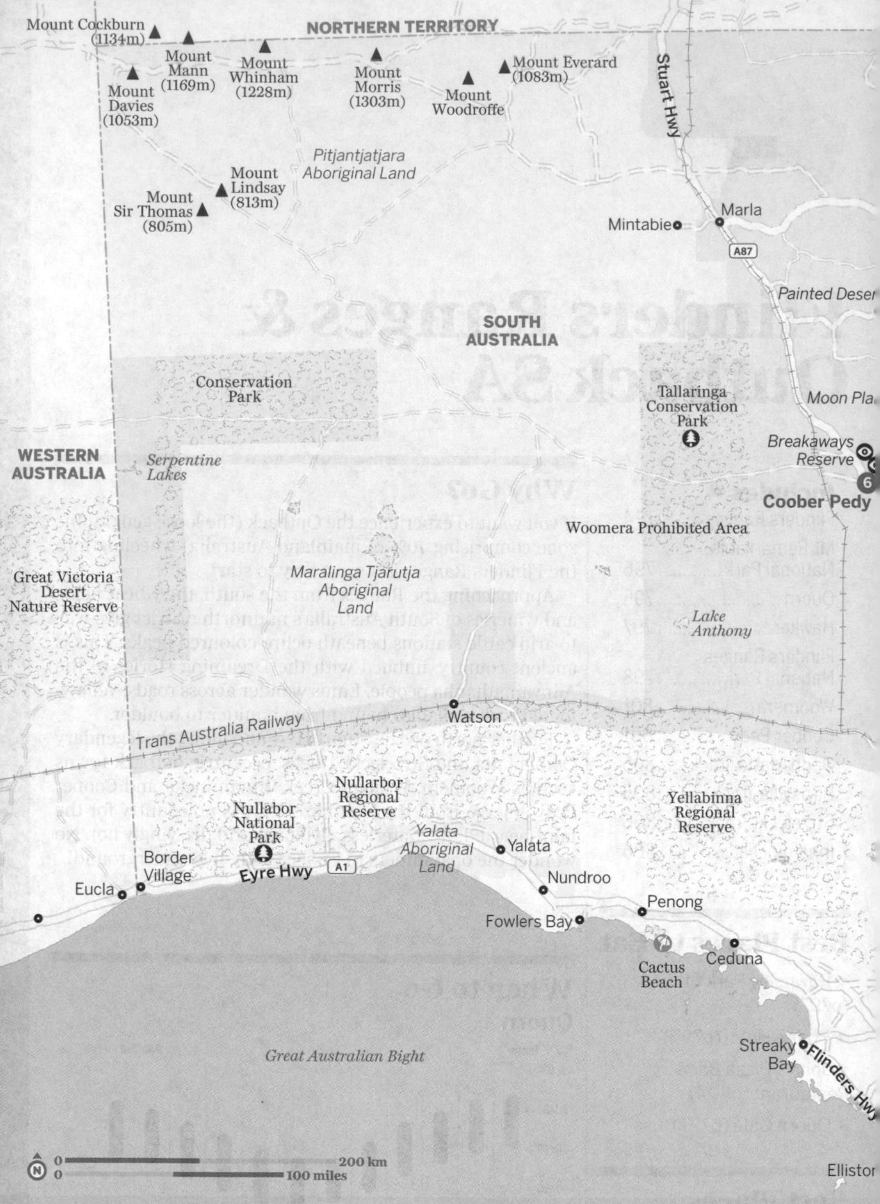

Flinders Ranges & Outback SA Highlights

1. Exploring the gorges and scenic slopes of **Mt Remarkable National Park** (p796).
2. Kicking back with a cold beer at the **North Star Hotel** (p796) in Melrose.
3. Checking out the old buildings and Wild West vibes in **Quorn** (p796).
4. Hiking up to Wangarra Lookout at **Ikara** (Wilpena Pound; p798).
5. Jumping in a 4WD and truck along the **Oodnadatta Track** (p805), a great Australian adventure.

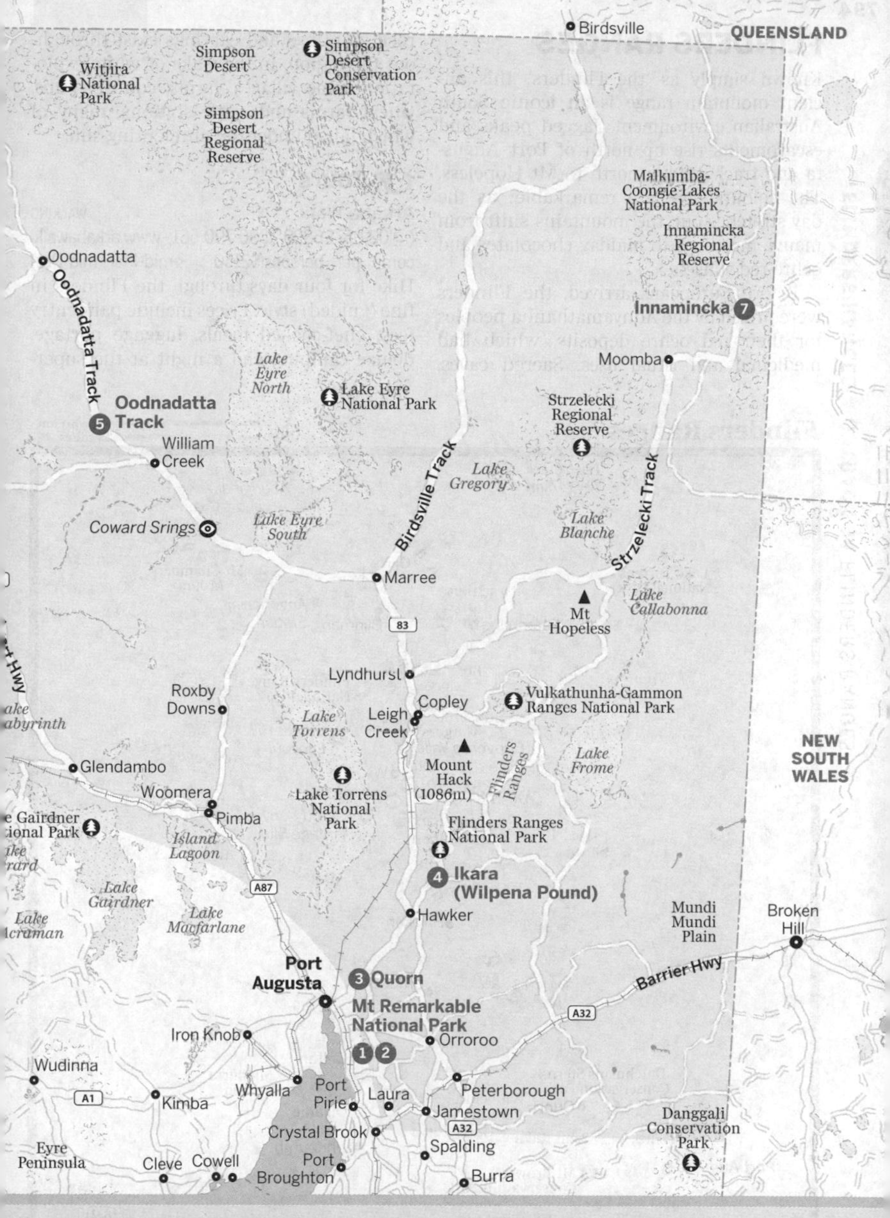

6 Noodling for opals in **Coober Pedy** (p801), then bunking down underground.

7 Camping under the stars along Cooper Creek at **Innamincka** (p806).

FLINDERS RANGES

Known simply as 'the Flinders', this ancient mountain range is an iconic South Australian environment. Jagged peaks and escarpments rise up north of Port Augusta and track 400km north to Mt Hopeless. The colours here are remarkable: as the day stretches out, the mountains shift from mauve mornings to midday chocolates and ochre-red sunsets.

Before Europeans arrived, the Flinders were prized by the Adnyamathanha peoples for their red ochre deposits, which had medicinal and ritual uses. Sacred caves, rock paintings and carvings exist throughout the region. In the wake of white exploration came villages, farms, country pubs, wheat farms and cattle stations, many of which failed under the unrelenting sun.

Tours

Arkaba Walk WALKING
(02-9571 6399, 1300 790 561; www.arkabawalk.com; per person $2150; mid-Mar–mid-Oct) Hike for four days through the Flinders in fine (guided) style. Prices include park entry fees, chef-cooked meals, luggage portage, deluxe camping and a night at the super-

Flinders Ranges

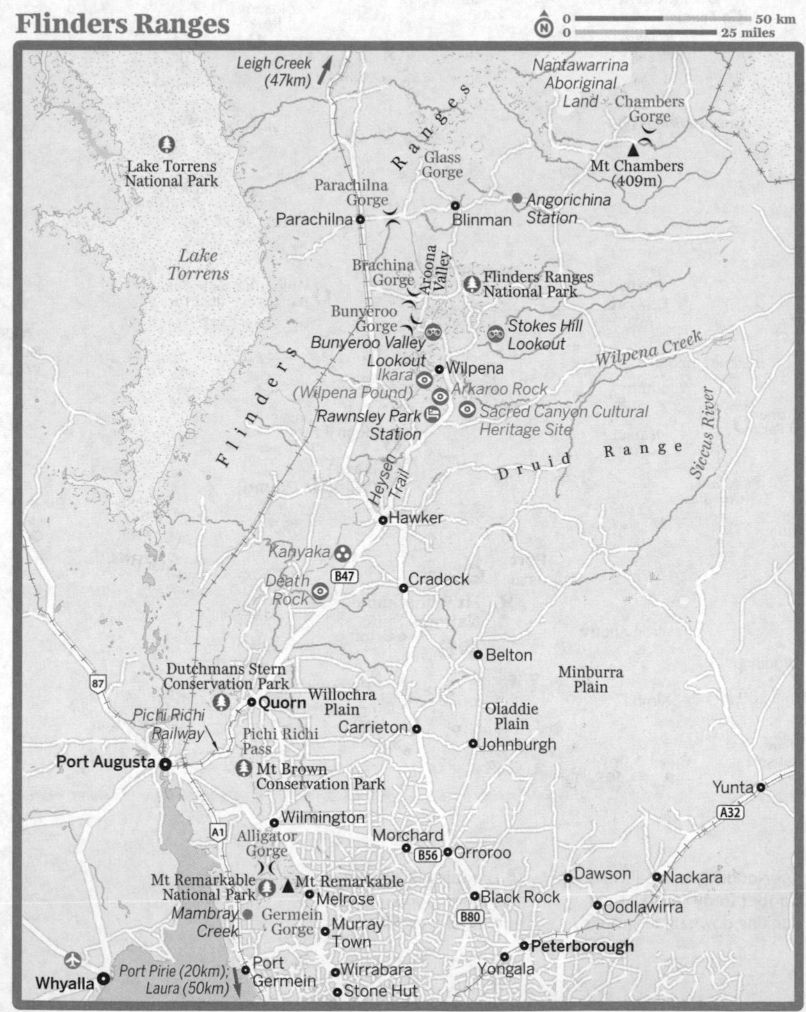

plush Arkaba Station (p798). A once-in-a-lifetime treat!

Groovy Grape OUTDOORS
(☎1800 661 177, 08-8440 1640; www.groovygrape.com.au) Small-group tours including: four days, Adelaide to Coober Pedy return via the Flinders Ranges ($495); and seven days, Adelaide to Alice Springs via the Flinders Ranges, Coober Pedy and Uluru ($975). Meals, camping and national park entry fees are included.

Heading Bush OUTDOORS
(☎08-8356 5501, 1800 639 933; www.headingbush.com) Rugged, small-group, 10-day Adelaide to Alice Springs expeditions are $2495 all-inclusive, and run via the Flinders Ranges, Coober Pedy, the Simpson Desert, Aboriginal communities, Uluru and the West MacDonnell Ranges. Three-day Flinders Ranges camping tours are $695, or from $1250 with cabin accommodation.

Flinders Ranges By Bike MOUNTAIN BIKING
(☎08-8648 0048; www.flindersrangesbybike.com.au; per person 1/2/3/4 days $35/40/45/50) Pedal your way along a 200km circuit through the best bits of the Flinders Ranges, starting (and ending) at Rawnsley Park Station (p797), south of Wilpena. Fees cover park entry and access to private properties en route; book your own accommodation. Luggage transfers also available.

Wallaby Tracks Adventure Tours OUTDOORS
(☎08-8648 6655, 0428 486 655; www.wallabytracks.com; 1-/4-day tours $250/1200) Small-group, backpacker-savvy 4WD tours around the Ranges and Ikara (Wilpena Pound). One-day tours ex-Port Augusta; four-day tours ex-Adelaide. Lake Eyre and Arkaroola tours are also available.

Getting There & Away

Exploring the Flinders on a tour or under your own steam is the only way to go. From Port Augusta, **Pichi Richi Railway** (☎1800 440 1011800 440 101; www.prr.org.au; one way $52) runs trains to Quorn (two hours) on Saturdays.

Southern Ranges Towns

Port Pirie (population 13,830) is a big lead- and zinc-smelting town on the edge of the Southern Flinders Ranges; the Nyrstar smelter dominates the skyline. It's a good spot to stock up on supplies before heading north. The **Port Pirie Regional Tourism & Arts Centre** (☎1800 000 424, 08-8633 8700; www.pirie.sa.gov.au; 3 Mary Elie St; ⏲9am-5pm Mon-Fri, 9am-4pm Sat, 10am-4pm Sun) has local info.

You enter the Southern Ranges proper near **Laura** (population 550), which emerges from the wheat fields like Superman's Smallville (all civic pride and 1950s prosperity). The long, geranium-adorned main street has a supermarket, chemist, bakery, bank, post office...even a shoe shop!

The oldest town in the Flinders (1853) is **Melrose** (population 200), snug in the elbow of the 960m Mt Remarkable. It has the perfect mix of well-preserved architecture, a cracking-good pub, quality accommodation and parks with *actual grass*. Don't miss the decaying multistorey ruins of **Jacka's Brewery** (1878) on Mount St, which once employed 40 staff. Mountain biking is big here: **Over The Edge** (☎08-8666 2222; www.otesports.com.au; 6 Stuart St, Melrose; ⏲9am-5pm Wed-Mon) has spares, repairs and a cafe.

ADNYAMATHANHA DREAMING

Land and nature are integral to the culture of the traditional owners of the Flinders Ranges. The people collectively called Adnyamathanha (Hill People) are actually a collection of the Wailpi, Kuyani, Jadliaura, Piladappa and Pangkala tribes, who exchanged and elaborated on stories to explain their spectacular local geography.

The walls of Ikara (Wilpena Pound), for example, are the bodies of two *akurra* (giant snakes), who coiled around Ikara during an initiation ceremony, eating most of the participants. The snakes were so full after their feast they couldn't move and willed themselves to die, creating the landmark.

Sleeping

Melrose Caravan Park CARAVAN PARK $
(☎08-8666 2060; www.parks-sa.com.au/caravan_park/250; Joe's Rd, Melrose; dm $20, unpowered/powered sites $20/25, cabins $60-120; ❄) Bounded by 5 acres of bush camp sites, this small, tidy park has self-contained cabins salvaged from the 2000 Sydney Olympics (all with TVs and cooking facilities – the cheaper ones are sans bathrooms). The 12km return hike up **Mt Remarkable** starts on the back doorstep. Next door is a converted agricultural shed with basic dorm facilities.

★ **North Star Hotel** PUB $$
(08-8666 2110; www.northstarhotel.com.au; 43 Nott St, Melrose; d/trucks from $125/160;) As welcome as summer rain: the North Star is a fab 1854 pub renovated in city-meets-woolshed style. Sit under spinning ceiling fans at the bistro (mains $16 to $30, serving noon to 2pm Wednesday to Sunday and 6pm to 8pm Thursday to Sunday) for a fresh menu, great coffee and cold beer. Accommodation ranges from plush suites upstairs, to Bundaleer Cottage next door (sleeps 16) and quirky cabins built on two old trucks.

Mt Remarkable National Park

Bush boffins rave about the steep, jagged **Mt Remarkable National Park** (08-8634 7068; www.environment.sa.gov.au; per person/car $4/10), which straddles the Southern Flinders. Pay park entry fees via self-registration at Mambray Creek, off Hwy 1 about 21km north of Port Germein; or at Alligator Gorge on the inland route (Main North Rd between Melrose and Wilmington). Wildlife and bushwalking are the main lures, with various tracks (including part of the **Heysen Trail**) meandering through isolated gorges.

From the car park at **Alligator Gorge** take the short, steep walk (2km, two hours) down into the craggy gorge (no sign of any 'gators), the ring route (9km, four hours), or the walk to **Hidden Gorge** (18km, seven hours) or **Mambray Creek** (13km, seven hours). Or you can sweat up the track to the 960m-high summit of **Mt Remarkable** (12km, five hours); the trail starts behind Melrose Caravan Park (p795).

If you want to stay the night, there's plenty of **bush camping** (per adult/child $18/free) and two lodges, at **Mambray Creek** (per night from $57) and **Alligator Gorge** (per night from $160). Both are solar powered; Alligator Gorge has better cooking facilities and showers. Book camp sites and lodges online; with cash at the Port Pirie, Port Augusta or Quorn visitor information centres; or at Over The Edge (p795) bike shop in Melrose.

Quorn

POP 1210

Is Quorn a film set after the crew has gone home? With more jeering crows than people, it's a cinematographic little outback town. Wheat farming took off here in 1875, and the town prospered with the arrival of the Great Northern Railway from Port Augusta. Quorn (pronounced 'corn') remained an important railroad junction until trains into the Flinders were cut in 1970.

Sights & Activities

Quorn's streetscapes, especially **Railway Terrace**, are a real history lesson, and have featured in iconic Australian films such as *Gallipoli* and *Sunday Too Far Away*. Out of town, derelict ruins litter the Quorn–Hawker road, the most impressive of which is **Kanyaka**, a once-thriving sheep station founded in 1851. From the ruins (41km from Quorn) it's a 20-minute walk to a waterhole loomed over by the massive **Death Rock**. The story goes that local Aboriginal people once placed their dying kinfolk here to see out their last hours.

Tours

Four Winds Cultural Guiding CULTURAL
(08-8648 6993; www.southaustralia.com; tours per person from $35) Guided one-hour bushwalking tours with Adnyamathanha guides, covering either local culture and Dreaming stories, or bush tucker, tracking and hunting.

Sleeping & Eating

★ **Quorn Caravan Park** CARAVAN PARK $
(08-8648 6206; www.quorncaravanpark.com.au; 8 Silo Rd; unpowered/powered sites $26/32, dm $40, van s/d $60/70, cabins $90-135;) Fully clued-in to climate change, this passionately run park on Pinkerton Creek is hell bent on reducing emissions and restoring native habitat. Features include spotless cabins, a backpacker cabin (sleeps eight), a camp kitchen made from recycled timbers, shady sites, rainwater tanks everywhere and a few lazy roos lounging about under the red gums.

Austral Inn HOTEL, MOTEL $
(08-8648 6017; www.australinn.info; 16 Railway Tce; motel s/d $70/90, pub s/d $110/115;) There's always a few locals here giving the jukebox a workout. The pub rooms are renovated – simple and clean with new linen (nicer than the five motel rooms out the back). Try a kangaroo schnitzel in the bistro (mains $16 to $24, serving noon to 2pm and 6pm to 8pm).

Savings Bank of South Australia RENTAL HOUSE $$
(☎ 0448 727 622; www.stayz.com.au/131032; 39 First St; d from $180; ❄) Bank on a good night's sleep at Quorn's lovely old red-brick bank, a two-storey, two-bathroom, three-bedroom conversion of this 1906 charmer. It's a terrific base for exploring the Flinders. Sleeps six; two-night minimum stay (good weekly rates).

★**Quorn Cafe** CAFE $
(☎ 08-8648 6368; www.quorncafe.com.au; 43 First St; mains $9-17; ⏲ 9am-5pm; ✎) The menu board at this unexpected hippie cafe is an old door hung on the wall, covered with brown-paper sandwich bags. Each bag has a menu item scribbled on it: lamb burger, chicken and smoked salmon salad, egg and bacon sandwich... Everything is homemade and generous. Try the goat curry ('a little bit bony, but delicious'). Quorn's best coffee, too.

Information

Flinders Ranges Visitor Information Centre
(☎ 08-8620 0510; www.flindersranges.com; Railway Tce, Quorn Railway Station; ⏲ 9am-5pm Mar-Oct, 10am-4pm Nov-Feb) Maps, brochures, internet access and advice.

Hawker

POP 300

Hawker is the last outpost of civilisation before Ikara (Wilpena Pound), 55km to the north. Much like Quorn, Hawker has seen better days, most of which were when the old Ghan train stopped here. These days Hawker is a pancake-flat, pit-stop town with an ATM, a general store, a pub and the world's most helpful petrol station.

Sights & Activities

It's not so much what's in Hawker that's interesting – it's more what's around it – but for those who like their great outdoors inside (and a little bit eccentric), the Wilpena Panorama at the **Jeff Morgan Gallery** (☎ 08-8648 4071; www.wilpenapanorama.com; cnr Wilpena & Cradock Rds; adult/child/family $8/5.50/20; ⏲ 9am-5pm Mon-Fri, to noon Sat, closed Jan & Feb) is a large circular room with a painting of Ikara (Wilpena Pound) surrounding you on all sides.

Around 40km north of Hawker towards Wilpena, **Arkaroo Rock** is a sacred Aboriginal site. The rock art here features reptile and human figures in charcoal, bird-lime, and yellow and red ochre. It's a short(ish) return walk from the car park (2km, one hour).

Tours

Derek's 4WD Tours DRIVING TOUR
(☎ 0417 475 770; www.dereks4wdtours.com; half-/full-day tours from $160/220) These are 4WD trips with an environmental bent, including visits to Bunyeroo and Brachina Gorges.

Bush Pilots Australia SCENIC FLIGHTS
(☎ 08-8648 4444; www.bushpilots.com.au; 60 Elder Tce; 30min flights per person $180) Get up and above the Flinders with these scenic flights, operating out of Hawker. Longer outback jaunts are also available.

Sleeping

BIG4 Hawker Flinders Ranges Holiday Park CARAVAN PARK $
(☎ 08-8648 4006; www.big4hawker.com.au; 44 Chace View Tce; unpowered/powered sites $28/32, en suite sites $42-50, cabins $96-162; ❄@☎≋) At the Wilpena end of town, this upbeat, fastidiously maintained acreage has generous gravelly sites and a range of cabins. And there's a pool! It runs an additional overflow site at 12 Carpenter Rd from April to October (no pool here...).

★**Rawnsley Park Station** RESORT $$
(☎ caravan park 08-8648 0008, reception 08-8648 0030; www.rawnsleypark.com.au; Wilpena Rd, via Hawker; unpowered/powered sites $25/35, hostel per adult/child $38/28, cabins/units/villas from $98/150/410; ❄@☎≋) This rangy homestead 35km from Hawker offers everything from tent sites to luxe eco-villas, plus caravan-park cabins set up as **YHA** (www.yha.com.au) dorms. Outback activities include mountain-bike hire (per hour $15), bushwalks (30 minutes to four hours), 4WD tours and scenic flights. The excellent **Woolshed Restaurant** (☎ 08-8648 0126; www.rawnsleypark.com.au; Wilpena Rd, via Hawker; mains $27-36; ⏲ noon-2pm Wed-Sun, 5-8.30pm daily) does bang-up bush tucker, plus curries, seafood and pizzas.

Outback Motel & Chapmanton Holiday Units MOTEL $$
(☎ 08-8648 4100; www.outbackmotel.com.au; 1 Wilpena Rd; s/d motel $120/125, s/d units $130/150; ❄) Like a transplanted vision from the Utah desert, this orange-brick, drive-up

motel offers the best rooms in downtown Hawker. The two-bedroom units are good value for families: the biggest one sleeps six (extra person $15).

Arkaba Station BOUTIQUE HOTEL **$$$**
(☎02-9571 6399, 1300 790 561; www.arkabastation.com; Wilpena Rd via Hawker; d from $1632) Flashy outback station accommodation in an 1850s homestead. 'Wild bush luxury' is the marketing pitch.

Information

Hawker Motors (☎08-8648 4014, 1800 777 880; www.hawkermotors.com.au; cnr Wilpena & Cradock Rds; ⏱7.30am-6pm) The town's petrol station (fill up if you're heading north) doubles as the visitor information centre.

Flinders Ranges National Park

One of SA's most treasured parks, **Flinders Ranges National Park** (www.environment.sa.gov.au; per car $10) is laced with craggy gorges, sawtoothed ranges, abandoned homesteads, Aboriginal sites, native wildlife and, after it rains, carpets of wild flowers. The park's big-ticket drawcard is the 80-sq-km natural basin **Ikara (Wilpena Pound)** – a sunken elliptical valley ringed by gnarled ridges (don't let anyone tell you it's a meteorite crater!).

The only vehicular access to the Pound is via the Wilpena Pound Resort's **shuttle bus** (return adult/child/family $5/3/10), which drops you about 1km from the old **Hills Homestead**, from where you can walk to **Wangarra Lookout** (another 300m). The shuttle runs at 9am, 11am, 1pm and 3pm. Otherwise it's a three-hour, 8km return walk between the resort and lookout.

The 20km **Brachina Gorge Geological Trail** features an amazing layering of exposed sedimentary rock, covering 120 million years of the earth's history. Grab a brochure from the visitors centre.

The **Bunyeroo–Brachina–Aroona Scenic Drive** is a 110km round trip, passing by Bunyeroo Valley, Brachina Gorge, Aroona Valley and **Stokes Hill Lookout**. The drive starts north of Wilpena off the road to Blinman.

Sights & Activities

Bushwalking in the Flinders is unforgettable. Before you make happy trails, ensure you've got enough water, sunscreen and a massive hat, and tell someone where you're going. Pick up the *Bushwalking in Flinders Ranges National Park* brochure from the visitor information centre. Many walks kick off at Wilpena Pound Resort.

For a really good look at Ikara, the walk up to **Tanderra Saddle** (return 15km, six hours) on the ridge of **St Mary Peak** is brilliant, though it's a thigh-pounding scramble at times. The Adnyamathanha people request that you restrict your climbing to the ridge and don't climb St Mary Peak itself, due to its traditional significance to them.

The quick, tough track up to **Mt Ohlssen Bagge** (return 6.5km, four hours) rewards the sweaty hiker with a stunning panorama. Good short walks include the stroll to **Hills Homestead** (return 6.5km, two hours), or the dash up to the **Wilpena Solar Power Station** (return 500m, 30 minutes).

Just beyond the park's southeast corner, a one-hour, 1km return walk leads to the **Sacred Canyon Cultural Heritage Site**, with Aboriginal rock-art galleries featuring animal tracks and designs.

Tours

Four-wheel-drive park tours are run by both Wilpena Pound Resort (half/full day from $189/295) and Rawnsley Park Station (half/full day from $160/245). There are also tour companies operating from Hawker.

Air Wilpena Scenic Flight Tours SCENIC FLIGHTS
(☎08-8648 0048; www.airwilpena.com.au; flights 20min/30min/1hr $169/199/299) Scenic flights from Wilpena Pound Resort.

Sleeping

Permits for **bush camping** (per person/car $7/13) within the national park (ie outside the Wilpena Pound Resort) are available from the visitor information centre, and via self-registration stations at camp sites.

★ **Wilpena Pound Resort** RESORT **$$$**
(☎1800 805 802, 08-8648 0004; www.wilpenapound.com.au; Wilpena Rd via Hawker; unpowered/powered sites $23/34, safari tent $180-230, d $236-300;) Accommodation at this excellent resort includes motel-style rooms, more upmarket self-contained suites, and a great (although hugely popular) camp site with plush safari tents. Book way in advance over winter (high season). Don't miss a swim in the pool, happy hour at the bar (5pm to

6.30pm) and dinner at the bistro (mains $19 to $32 – try the roo!).

Information

Wilpena Pound Visitor Information Centre (1800 805 802, 08-8648 0048; www.wilpenapound.com.au; Wilpena Pound Resort; 8am-5pm) At the resort's info centre you'll find a shop, petrol, park and bushwalking info, internet access and bike hire (per half/full day $35/65). Also handles bookings for scenic flights and 4WD tours. Pay your park entry fees here.

Blinman & Parachilna

About an hour north of Ikara (Wilpena Pound) on a sealed road, ubercute Blinman (population 30), owes its existence to the copper ore discovered here in 1859 and the smelter built in 1903. But the boom went bust and 1500 folks left town. Today Blinman's main claim to fame is as SA's highest town (610m above sea level).

Much of the old **Heritage Blinman Mine** (08-8648 4782; www.heritageblinmanmine.com.au; Main St, Blinman; tours adult/child/family $28/11/65; 9am-4pm, reduced hours Dec-Mar) has been redeveloped with lookouts, audiovisual interpretation and information boards. One-hour tours run at 10am, noon and 2pm.

Chunky slate floors, old-time photographs and colonial-style rooms collide at the renovated 1869 **North Blinman Hotel** (08-8648 4867; www.blinmanhotel.com; Main St, Blinman; unpowered/powered sites $10/20, d motel/hotel $90/155;), which has raggedy tent sites out the back (...D'oh! They filled in the pool!). The bistro (mains $20 to $30; serving noon to 2pm and 6pm to 8pm) plates up pubby delights. En route to Arkaroola, **Angorichina Station** (08-8648 4863; www.angorichina.com.au; Blinman-Arkaroola Rd; unpowered sites $20, shearers quarters per 5 people $200, cottages per 4 people $200;) offers shearers-quarters beds, camping and a lovely self-contained cottage.

The road between Blinman and Parachilna tracks through gorgeous **Parachilna Gorge**, where you'll find free creekside camping and chill-out spots. The northern end of the **Heysen Trail** starts/finishes here. Halfway between Blinman and Parachilna the **Blinman Pools Walk** (12km return, five hours) kicks off, following a creek past abandoned dugouts and river gums.

NATIONAL PARKS HOLIDAY PASS

Around 22% of South Australia's land area is under some form of official conservation management, including national parks, recreation parks, conservation parks and wildlife reserves. The **Department of Environment, Water & Natural Resources** (www.environment.sa.gov.au/parks) manages the state's conservation areas and sells park passes and camping permits. A two-month 'Holiday Pass' ($40 per vehicle; $80 including camping) covers entry to most of SA's parks, excluding the desert parks and Flinders Chase on Kangaroo Island. Purchase online or at park offices.

On the Hawker–Leigh Creek road, Parachilna (population somewhere between four and seven) is an essential Flinders Ranges destination. The drawcard here is the legendary **Prairie Hotel** (1800 331 473, 08-8648 4895; www.prairiehotel.com.au; cnr High St & West Tce, Parachilna; powered sites $35, budget cabins s/d $65/80, hotel s/d/tr from $195/225/320;), a world-class stay with slick suites, plus camping and workers' cabins across the street. Don't miss a meal in the bar (mains $18 to $35; serving 11.30am to 3pm and 6pm to 8.30pm) – try the feral mixed grill (camel sausage, kangaroo fillet and emu). We arrived at 10.42am: 'Too early for a beer!? Whose rules are those?' said the barman.

Leigh Creek & Copley

In the early 1980s, the previously nonexistent town of Leigh Creek (population 700) was built by the state government – it's a coal-mining town, supplying the Port Augusta power stations. The **Leigh Creek Tavern** (08-8675 2025; leighcreektavern@alintaenergy.com.au; Black Oak Dr, Leigh Creek; motel s/d $115/140, cabins s/d/f $100/110/150;) offers jaunty '90s-style motel rooms, basic cabins and miner-sized bistro meals (mains $18 to $30; serving noon to 2pm and 6pm to 8pm).The **Leigh Creek Visitor Information Centre** (08-8675 2315; www.loccleighcreek.com.au; Shop 2, Black Oak Dr, Leigh Creek; 8.30am-5.30pm Mon-Fri, to 2pm Sat) is at Liz's Open Cut Cafe.

About 6km north of Leigh Creek is the sweet meaninglessness of little Copley (population 80). **Copley Caravan Park** (☎08-8675 2288; www.copleycaravan.com.au; Lot 100 Railway Tce W, Copley; unpowered/powered sites $25/30, cabins d $80-150, f $150; ❄) is a small, immaculate park. At reception is the **Quandong Cafe** (Lot 100 Railway Tce W, Copley; items $5-7; ⌚8am-5pm), serving delicious quandong pies (a quandong is a kind of native cherry).

Iga Warta (☎08-8648 3737; www.igawarta.com; Arkaroola Rd; unpowered sites $22, dm & tents per person $36, cabins/safari tents d $104/150), 57km east of Copley on the way into Vulkathunha-Gammon Ranges National Park, is an Indigenous-run establishment offering Adnyamathanha cultural experiences ($25 to $84) as well as 4WD and bushwalking tours ($138).

Vulkathunha-Gammon Ranges National Park

Blanketing 1282 sq km of desert, the remote **Vulkathunha-Gammon Ranges National Park** (www.environment.sa.gov.au) has deep gorges, rugged ranges, yellow-footed rock wallabies and gum-lined creeks. Most of the park is difficult to access (4WDs are near compulsory) and has limited facilities. The rangers hang out at the **Balcanoona Park Headquarters** (☎08-8204 1910, 08-8648 5300), 99km from Copley.

The park has five bush camping (per person/car $10/6) areas: pick up camping permits at park HQ. There are also a couple of huts here: **Grindells Hut** (up to 8 people $155) and **Balcanoona Shearers' Quarters** (d/tr $44/65, exclusive use up to 19 people $285); book through the park HQ.

Arkaroola

A privately operated wildlife reserve-resort 129km east of Copley on unsealed roads, **Arkaroola Wilderness Sanctuary** (☎08-8648 4848; www.arkaroola.com.au) occupies a far-flung and utterly spectacular part of the Flinders Ranges. The **visitor centre** (⌚9am-5pm) has natural-history displays, including a scientific explanation of the tremors that often shake things up hereabouts.

The Arkaroola must-do is the four-hour 4WD **Ridgetop Tour** (☎08-8648 4848; www.arkaroola.com.au; adult/child $145/55) through wild mountain country, complete with white-knuckle climbs and descents towards the freakish Sillers Lookout. You can also book guided or tag-along **tours** (drives and walks) through the area.

The **resort** (Arkaroola Rd Camp; unpowered/powered sites $22/29, cottages f $130-175, motel d $149-179; ❄❄) includes a motel complex, caravan park, bar-restaurant (mains $20 to $30, serving noon to 2pm and 6pm to 8pm), supermarket and service station.

OUTBACK

The area north of the Eyre Peninsula and the Flinders Ranges stretches into the vast, empty spaces of SA's outback. If you're prepared, travelling through this sparsely populated and harsh country is utterly rewarding.

Heading into the red heart of Australia on the Stuart Hwy, Woomera is the first pit stop, with its dark legacy of nuclear tests and shiny collection of leftover rockets. Further north, the opal-mining town of Coober Pedy is an absolute one-off: a desolate human anomaly amid the blistering, arid plains. If you're feeling gung-ho, tackle a section of the iconic Oodnadatta Track, a rugged outback alternative to the Stuart Hwy tarmac.

Tours

In addition to dedicated Outback tours, tours of the Flinders Ranges sometimes extend further north into the Outback. There are also scenic flights departing from Coober Pedy (p803), William Creek (p805) and Marree (p805).

Arabunna Tours CULTURAL TOUR
(☎08-8675 8351; www.arabunnatours.com.au; 7-day tours ex-Adelaide from $1800) Aboriginal-owned company offering cultural tours from Adelaide to the Flinders Ranges, Marree, Oodnadatta Track and Lake Eyre.

Sacred Earth Safaris ADVENTURE TOUR
(tours per adult/child $4900/4700) Epic 10-day Outback 4WD tours trundling along the big three desert tracks – Oodnadatta, Strzelecki and Birdsville – plus Coober Pedy and the Flinders Ranges.

Getting There & Around

AIR

Regional Express (Rex; www.regionalexpress.com.au) Flies most days between Adelaide and Coober Pedy (from $247, two hours).

BUS

Greyhound Australia (www.greyhound.com.au) Daily coaches from Adelaide to Alice Springs ($244, 20½ hours), stopping at Pimba ($82, seven hours), Glendambo ($95, 8¼ hours) and Coober Pedy ($147, 11¼ hours).

CAR

The Stuart Hwy tracks from Port Augusta to Darwin. In SA, fuel and accommodation are available at Pimba (171km from Port Augusta), Glendambo (285km), Coober Pedy (535km), Cadney Homestead (689km) and Marla (771km). Pimba, Coober Pedy and Marla have 24-hour fuel sales.

The Oodnadatta, Birdsville and Strzelecki Tracks are subject to closure after heavy rains; check conditions with the **Royal Automobile Association** (RAA; Map p714; ☎08-8202 4600; www.raa.com.au; 41 Hindmarsh Sq; ⊙8.30am-5pm Mon-Fri, 9am-4pm Sat) in Adelaide, or online at www.dpti.sa.gov.au/OutbackRoads.

TRAIN

Operated by Great Southern Rail (p732), the Ghan train runs through Outback SA between Adelaide and Alice Springs. Different services stop at (or near) Coober Pedy and Marla; see the website for details.

Woomera

POP 200

A 6km detour off the Stuart Hwy from **Pimba** (population 50), Woomera began in 1947 as HQ for experimental British rocket and nuclear tests at notorious sites like Maralinga. Local Indigenous tribes suffered greatly from the resulting nuclear fallout. These days Woomera is an eerie artificial town that's still an active Department of Defence test site.

Rocket into the **Woomera Heritage & Visitor Information Centre** (☎08-8673 7042; www.southaustralia.com; Dewrang Ave; museum adult/child $6/3; ⊙9am-5pm Mar-Nov, 10am-2pm Dec-Feb), with its displays on Woomera's past and present (plus a bowling alley!). Just across the car park is the **Lions Club Aircraft & Missile Park**, studded with jets and rocket remnants.

Built to house rocket scientists, the **Eldo Hotel** (☎08-8673 7867; eldohotel@transfieldservices.com; Kotara Ave; d from $110; ❄) has comfortable motel-style rooms and serves meals in an urbane bistro (mains $19 to $32, serving 7am to 9am, noon to 2pm and 6pm to 8.30pm). Try the meaty game plate.

ℹ DESERT PARKS PASS

Explore the outback environment with a **Desert Parks Pass** (☎08-8648 5328, 1800 816 078; www.environment.sa.gov.au; per vehicle $150); this allows access to seven outback parks (including camping), and comes with a map and handbook. Pick one up from the Royal Automobile Association in Adelaide, order one online and have it mailed to you (Australia only), or see www.environment.sa.gov.au for regional pass agents in the Flinders Ranges and Outback South Australia.

Continue north past Woomera for 90km (sealed road) and you'll hit **Roxby Downs** (www.roxbydowns.com), population 4500, a bizarrely affluent desert town built to service the massive Olympic Dam Mine, which digs up untold amounts of copper, silver, gold and uranium.

Woomera to Coober Pedy

Around 115km northwest of Pimba and 245km shy of Coober Pedy, middle-of-nowhere **Glendambo** (population 30) was established in 1982 as a Stuart Hwy service centre. This is the last fuel stop before Coober Pedy.

You can bunk down at the oasislike **Glendambo Hotel-Motel** (☎08-86721030; manager@glendambo.com.au; Stuart Hwy; unpowered/powered sites $23/27, s/d/f from $94/99/140; ❄🗷), which has bars, a restaurant and a bunch of decent motel units. Outside are dusty camp sites; inside are meaty mains at the bistro ($16 to $30, serving noon to 2pm and 6pm to 8pm).

North of Glendambo the Stuart Hwy enters the government-owned **Woomera Prohibited Area** – the highway itself is unrestricted, but don't go a-wanderin' now, y'hear?

Coober Pedy

POP 3500

Coming into cosmopolitan Coober Pedy (there are 44 nationalities represented here!) the dry, barren desert suddenly becomes riddled with holes and adjunct piles of dirt – reputedly more than a million around the township. The reason for

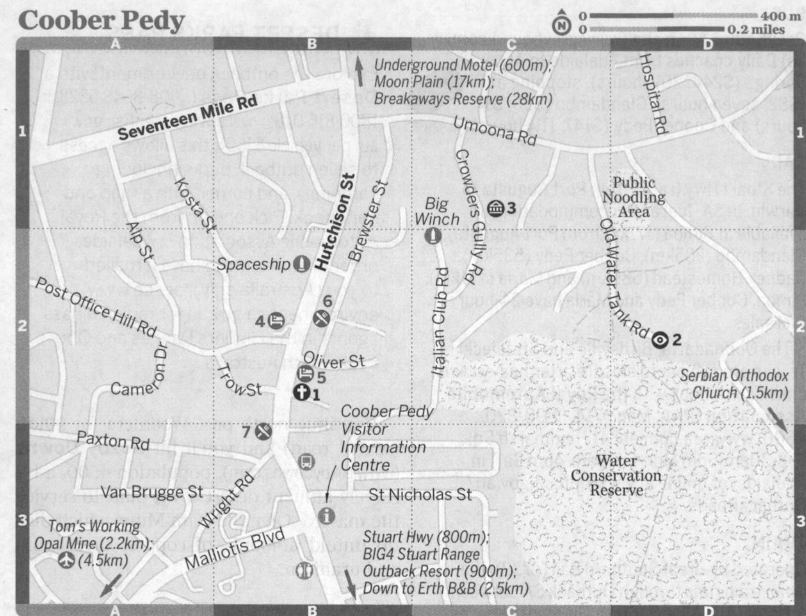

Coober Pedy

Sights

1 Catholic Church of St Peter & St Paul B2
2 Faye's Underground Home D2
3 Old Timers Mine C1

Sleeping

4 Desert Cave Hotel B2
5 Radeka Downunder B2

Eating

6 John's Pizza Bar & Restaurant B2
7 Tom & Mary's Greek Taverna B3
Umberto's ....(see 4)

all this rabid digging is opals. Discovered here 100 years ago, these gemstones have made this small town a mining mecca. This isn't to say it's also a tourist mecca – with swarms of flies, no trees, 50°C summer days, cave-dwelling locals and rusty car wrecks in front yards, you might think you've arrived in a postapocalyptic wasteland – but it sure is interesting! The name derives from local Aboriginal words *kupa* (white man) and *piti* (hole).

The surrounding desert is jaw-droppingly desolate, a fact not overlooked by international film-makers who've come here to shoot end-of-the-world epics like *Mad Max III, Red Planet, Ground Zero, Pitch Black* and the slightly more believable *Priscilla, Queen of the Desert*.

Sights

Big Winch SCULPTURE, VIEWPOINT

You can't miss the Big Winch, from which there are sweeping views over Coober Pedy. An optimistic 'if' painted on the side of the big bucket sums up the town's spirit.

Spaceship SCULPTURE

Check out this amazing leftover prop from the film *Pitch Black,* which has crash-landed on Hutchison St.

Tom's Working Opal Mine MINE

(www.tomsworkingopalmine.com; Lot 1993, Stuart Hwy; tours adult/child/family $25/10/55; 8am-5pm) The best place to check out a working excavation is Tom's, 2km southwest of town: miners continue their search for the big vein; visitors noodle for small fortunes. Self-guided tours run from 8am to 5pm and cost $10 per adult, $5 per child.

Old Timers Mine MUSEUM

(www.oldtimersmine.com; 1 Crowders Gully Rd; self-guided tours adult/child/family $15/5/40; 9am-5.30pm) This interesting warren of tunnels was mined in 1916, and then hidden by the miners. The mine was rediscovered when excavations for a dugout home punched through into the labyrinth of tunnels. As well as the great self-guided tunnel tours, there's a museum, a re-created 1920s underground home, and free mining-equipment demos daily (9.30am, 1.30pm and 3.30pm).

Dugout Homes & Churches

Even when it's face-meltingly hot here in summer, subterranean temperatures never exceed 23°C – no air-con required for underground houses! The same goes for churches (miners are big on faith and hope).

Faye's Underground Home UNDERGROUND
(08-8672 5029; www.cooberpedy.sa.gov.au; Old Water Tank Rd; adult/child $5/1.50; 8am-5pm Mon-Sat Mar-Oct) Faye's was hand dug by three women in the 1960s. It's a little flowery, but the living-room swimming pool is a winner!

Serbian Orthodox Church CHURCH
(08-8672 3048; Saint Elijah Dr, off Flinders St; admission $5; 24hr) This is the town's largest and most impressive underground church, with intricate rock-wall carvings and a gorgeous vaulted ceiling. It's about 3km south of town.

Catholic Church of St Peter & St Paul CHURCH
(cnr Halliday Pl & Hutchison St; 10am-4pm daily, Mass 10am Sun) FREE Coober Pedy's first church still has a sweet appeal, with statue-filled nooks and hushed classical music.

Tours

Arid Areas Tours DRIVING TOUR
(08-8672 3008; www.aridareastours.com; 2-/4-/6hr tours per 2 people from $120/240/420) Offers 4WD tours around town, extending to the Painted Desert and the Breakaways.

Desert Cave Tours TOUR
(1800 088 521, 08-8672 5688; www.desertcave.com.au; 4hr tours per adult/child $98/49) A convenient highlight tour taking in the town, the Dog Fence, the Breakaways and Moon Plain. Also on offer are four-hour 'Down 'N' Dirty' opal-digging tours (adult/child $110/55).

Mail Run Tour DRIVING TOUR
(08-8672 5226, 1800 069 911; www.mailruntour.com; tours per person $195) Coober Pedy–based full-day mail-run tours through the desert and along the Oodnadatta Track to Oodnadatta and William Creek return.

Opal Air SCENIC FLIGHTS
(08-8670 7997; www.opalair.com.au; flights per person from $470) Half-day scenic flights from Coober Pedy winging over Lake Eyre, William Creek and the Painted Desert.

Sleeping

Riba's CAMPGROUND $
(08-8672 5614; www.camp-underground.com.au; Lot 1811 William Creek Rd; underground sites $30, above-ground unpowered/powered sites $20/28, s & d $66;) Around 5km from town, Riba's offers the unique option of underground camping! Extras include an underground TV lounge, cell-like underground budget rooms and a nightly opal-mine tour (adult $24; free for underground and unpowered-site campers, discounted for other guests).

BIG4 Stuart Range Outback Resort CARAVAN PARK $
(08-8672 5179; www.stuartrangeoutbackresort.com.au; Yanikas Dr; unpowered/powered sites $27/34, d from $99, 1-/2-bedroom apt $170/255;) Spending up big on renovating their units and extensive landscaping (oh look – olive trees!), Stuart Range is probably the best traditional (ie above ground!) caravan park around town. The pool was being renovated when we visited: make sure it's full before you dive in. Tours also available.

Radeka Downunder HOSTEL $
(08-8672 5223; www.radekadownunder.com.au; 1 Oliver St; dm/d/tr/q $35/85/120/155, motel units d/tr/f $130/165/200; @) The owners started excavating this place in 1960: they haven't found much opal, but they sure have an interesting backpackers! On multiple levels extending 6.5m underground are budget beds, plus passable individual rooms and motel units. There's also a shared kitchen/bar, barbecue, laundry, tours and airport transfers. Getting some mixed reviews of late.

★Down to Erth B&B B&B $$
(08-8672 5762; www.downtoerth.com.au; Lot 1785 Monument Rd; d incl breakfast $165, extra person $25;) A real dugout gem about 3km from town: your own subterranean two-bedroom bunker (sleeps five – perfect for a family) with a kitchen-lounge area, a shady plunge pool for cooling off after a day

exploring the Earth, wood-fuelled BBQ and complimentary chocolates.

Desert Cave Hotel HOTEL $$
(08-8672 5688; www.desertcave.com.au; Lot 1 Hutchison St; d/tr from $170/200, extra person $35;) Top of the CP price tree, the Desert Cave brings a much-needed shot of desert luxury – plus a beaut pool, a daytime cafe, airport transfers and the excellent **Umberto's** (08-8672 5688; www.desertcave.com.au; Lot 1 Hutchison St; mains $28-38; 6-9pm) restaurant. Staff are supercourteous and there are tours on offer. Above-ground rooms also available (huge, but there are more soulful places to stay in town).

Underground Motel MOTEL $$
(08-8672 5324; www.theundergroundmotel.com.au; Catacomb Rd; standard s/d/f $110/125/157, ste $125/135/182;) Choose between standard rooms and suites (with separate lounge and kitchen) at this serviceable spot with a broad Breakaways panorama. It's a fair walk from town, but friendly and affordable. One of a few decent motel options on Catacomb Rd.

Eating

★ **John's Pizza Bar & Restaurant** ITALIAN $$
(08-8672 5561; www.johnspizzabarandrestaurant.com.au; Shop 24, 1 Hutchison St; mains $13-32; 10am-10pm) You can't go past John's, where staff serve up table-sized pizzas, hearty pastas and heat-beating gelato. Grills, salads, burgers, yiros, and fish and chips also available. Sit inside, order some takeaways, or pull up a seat with the bedraggled pot plants by the street.

Tom & Mary's Greek Taverna GREEK $$
(08-8672 5622; Shop 4/2 Hutchison St; mains $17-32; 6-9pm Mon-Sat) This busy Greek diner does everything from a superb moussaka to yiros, seafood, Greek salads and pastas with Hellenic zing. Sit back with a cold retsina as the red sun sets on another dusty day in Coober Pedy.

Information

24-hour Water Dispenser (Hutchison St; per 30L $0.20) Fill your canteens next to the visitor information centre.

Coober Pedy Visitor Information Centre (1800 637 076, 08-8672 4617; www.opalcapitaloftheworld.com.au; Council Offices, Lot 773 Hutchison St; 8.30am-5pm Mon-Fri, 10am-1pm Sat & Sun) Free 30-minute internet access (prebooked), history displays and comprehensive tour and accommodation info.

Coober Pedy Hospital (08-8672 5009; www.sahealth.sa.gov.au; Lot 89 Hospital Rd; 24hr) Accident and emergency.

Getting There & Around

Note that the closest Ghan train stop is 42km northeast at Manguri: you'll need to arrange transport into town.

Budget (08-8672 5333; www.budget.com.au; Coober Pedy Airport) Cars, 4WDs and camping vehicles from around $80 per day.

Coober Pedy to Marla

The **Breakaways Reserve** is a stark but colourful area of arid hills and scarps 33km north from Coober Pedy along a rough road; turn off the highway 22km west of town. Entry permits (per adult/child $2.20/free) are available at the Coober Pedy Visitor Information Centre (note that Indigenous land owners may change this process at some stage in the future).

An interesting 70km loop on mainly unsealed road from Coober Pedy takes in the Breakaways, the **Dog Fence** (built to keep dingos out of southeastern Australia) and the tablelike **Moon Plain** on the Coober Pedy–Oodnadatta Rd. If it's been raining, you'll need a 4WD.

If you're heading for Oodnadatta, turning off the Stuart Hwy at Cadney Homestead (151km north of Coober Pedy) gives you a shorter run on dirt roads than the routes via Marla or Coober Pedy. En route you pass through the aptly named **Painted Desert** (bring your camera).

Cadney Homestead (08-8670 7994; cadney@bigpond.com; Stuart Hwy; unpowered/powered sites from $16/25, d cabin/motel $85/125;) itself has caravan and tent sites, serviceable motel rooms and basic cabins (BYO towel to use the shared caravan-park facilities), plus petrol, puncture repairs, takeaways, cold beer, an ATM, a swimming pool...

In mulga scrub about 82km from Cadney Homestead, Marla (population 245) replaced Oodnadatta as the official regional centre when the Ghan railway line was rerouted in 1980. **Marla Travellers Rest** (08-8670 7001; www.marla.com.au; Stuart Hwy; unpowered/powered sites $20/30, cabins $40, d from $120;) has fuel, motel rooms, camp sites, a pool, a cafe and a supermarket.

Frontier-style **Mintabie** (population 250) is an opal-field settlement on Aboriginal land

35km west of Marla; there's a general store, restaurant and basic caravan park here.

From Marla the Northern Territory (NT) border is another 180km, with a fuel stop 20km beyond that in Kulgera.

Oodnadatta Track

The legendary, lonesome Oodnadatta Track is an unsealed, 615km road between Marla on the Stuart Hwy and Marree in the northern Flinders Ranges. The track traces the route of the old Overland Telegraph Line and the defunct Great Northern Railway. **Lake Eyre** (Kati Thanda; www.environment.sa.gov.au), the world's sixth-largest lake (usually dry), is just off the road. Bring a 4WD – the track is often passable in a regular car, but it gets bumpy, muddy, dusty and potholed.

Information

Before you hit the Oodnadatta, check track conditions (and for closure after rains) with the Coober Pedy visitor information centre, the Royal Automobile Association (p801) in Adelaide, or online at www.dpti.sa.gov.au/OutbackRoads.

Fuel, accommodation and meals are available at Marla, Oodnadatta, William Creek and Marree.

For track info, download the *Oodnadatta Track – String of Springs* brochure from www.southaustralia.com. Also see the sketchy-but-useful 'mud maps' on the Pink Roadhouse website.

Oodnadatta to William Creek

Around 209km from Marla, Oodnadatta (population 170) is where the main road and the old railway line diverged. Here you'll find the **Pink Roadhouse** (☎1800 802 074, 08-8670 7822; www.pinkroadhouse.com.au; unpowered/powered sites from $22/32, cabins d from $120), a solid source of track info (it's big on maintaining correct tyre pressure) and meals (try the 'Oodnaburger'). The roadhouse also has an attached caravan park; options run from basic camping through to self-contained cabins.

In another 201km you'll hit William Creek (population six), best enjoyed in the weather-beaten **William Creek Hotel** (☎08-8670 7880; www.gdaypubs.com.au; William Creek; unpowered/powered sites $24/30, d cabin/hotel $90/150; ❄), an iconic 1887 pub festooned with photos, business cards, old licence plates and money stapled to the walls. There's a dusty camping ground, and modest cabins and motel rooms. Also on offer are fuel, cold beer, basic provisions, all-day meals (mains $16 to $32) and spare tyres.

William Creek is also a base for **Wrightsair** (☎08-8670 7962; www.wrightsair.com.au; William Creek; flights per person from $285), which runs scenic flights over Lake Eyre (two-passenger minimum).

Coward Springs to Marree

Some 130km shy of Marree, **Coward Springs Campground** (☎08-8675 8336; www.cowardsprings.com.au; unpowered sites adult/child $12.50/6.25) is the first stop at the old Coward Springs railway siding. You can soak yourself silly in a **natural hot-spring tub** (per adult/child $2/1) made from old rail sleepers, or take a six-day **camel trek** (per person $1760) to Lake Eyre from here.

Next stop is the lookout over **Lake Eyre South**, which is 12m below sea level. For a Lake Eyre water-level report, see www.lakeeyreyc.com. About 60km from Marree is the **Mutonia Sculpture Park** (⏲24hr) FREE, featuring several planes welded together with their tails buried in the ground to form 'Planehenge'.

Marree (population 100) was once a vital hub for Afghan camel teams and the Great Northern Railway, and is the end (or start) of both the Oodnadatta and Birdsville Tracks. The big, stone 1883 **Marree Hotel** (☎08-8675 8344; www.marreehotel.com.au; Railway Tce S; unpowered sites free, d hotel/cabin $120/140; ❄📶🏊) has decent pub rooms (shared bathrooms), smart en suite cabins and free camp sites! Marree is also a good place to organise scenic flights: try **Aus Air Services** (☎08-8675 8212; www.ausairservices.com.au; 2hr flights per person from $280).

From the air you'll get a good look at **Marree Man**, a 4.2km-long outline of a Pitjantjatjara Aboriginal warrior etched into the desert near Lake Eyre. It was only discovered in 1988, and no one seems to know who created it. It's eroding rapidly these days.

From Marree it's 80km south to Lyndhurst, where the bitumen kicks back in, then 33km down to Copley at the northern end of the Flinders Ranges.

Birdsville Track

This old droving trail runs 517km from Marree in SA to Birdsville (p463), just across the border in Queensland, passing between the Simpson Desert to the east and Sturt Stony Desert to the west. It's one of Australia's classic outback routes. For road conditions see www.dpti.sa.gov.au/OutbackRoads (...a 4WD is the only way to go, regardless).

Strzelecki Track

Meandering through the sand hills of the **Strzelecki Regional Reserve** (www.environment.sa.gov.au), the Strzelecki Track spans 460km from Lyndhurst, 80km south of Marree, to the tiny outpost of Innamincka. The discovery of oil and gas at Moomba (closed to travellers) saw the upgrading of the road from a camel track to a decent dirt road, though heavy transport travelling along it has created bone-rattling corrugations. The newer Moomba–Strzelecki Track is better kept, but longer and less interesting than the old track, which follows Strzelecki Creek. Accommodation, provisions and fuel are available at Lyndhurst and Innamincka, but there's nothing in between.

Innamincka

POP 12

On Cooper Creek at the northern end of the Strzelecki Track, Innamincka is near where Burke and Wills' ill-fated 1860 expedition expired. The famous **Dig Tree** marks the expedition's base camp, and although the word 'dig' is no longer visible you can still see the expedition's camp number.

Part of the **Innamincka Regional Reserve** (www.environment.sa.gov.au/parks; per vehicle $10; ⏲24hr), Cooper Creek has deep, permanent waterholes. There are also semi-permanent lakes in **Malkumba-Coongie Lakes National Park** (www.environment.sa.gov.au; per vehicle $10; ⏲24hr). Prior to European settlement this area had a large Aboriginal population; relics such as middens and grinding stones can still be seen.

The **Innamincka Trading Post** (☎08-8675 9900; www.innaminckatp.com.au; South Tce; ⏲8am-5pm) sells fuel, Desert Parks passes, camping permits and provisions, including fresh bread and rolls. There's accommodation here too in air-conditioned en suite cabins (doubles from $150). The old-fashioned **Innamincka Hotel** (☎08-8675 9901; www.theoutback.com.au/innaminckahotel; 2 South Tce; s/d $130/155; ❄) also offers accommodation (decent motel-style rooms, a family-friendly bunkhouse and single cabins), cold beer (Innamincka Pale Ale!) and hefty counter meals (mains $20 to $30, serving noon to 2pm and 6pm to 8pm).

There are plenty of shady **bush camping sites** (☎08-8648 5328; per vehicle $18) along Cooper Creek; Innamincka Trading Post sells permits, or you can use a Desert Parks Pass. There's a hot shower ($2) and toilet outside the Trading Post.

Darwin & Around

Includes ➡

Best Places to Eat

- ➡ Laneway Speciality Coffee (p823)
- ➡ Exotic North Indian Cuisine (p823)
- ➡ Darwin Ski Club (p823)
- ➡ Moorish Café (p822)
- ➡ Stokes Hill Wharf (p822)

Best Places to Stay

- ➡ Melaleuca on Mitchell (p820)
- ➡ Darwin Central Hotel (p821)
- ➡ Wildman Wilderness Lodge (p831)
- ➡ Pine Creek Railway Resort (p834)
- ➡ Anbinik (Lakeview) Resort (p839)

Why Go?

The Top End is frontier country. It feels wild out here; time spent exploring the region's outer reaches will calibrate your senses away from urban grit. The wildness comes in many forms – from remote Arnhem Land to backpackers letting loose on Darwin's Mitchell St.

You will find unparalleled opportunities to experience timeless Indigenous culture, and the legacy left behind from tens of thousands of years of occupation. Indigenous rock art has left an extraordinary mark on the landscape – an ancient diary of human existence, seemingly oblivious to years of climatic onslaught.

The cosmopolitan capital of Darwin is Australia's doorway to Asia and celebrates its multicultural mix with delicious fusion cuisine and a relaxed tropical vibe. Darwin feels more like a big town than a city, and the dreamy coastline around its outer reaches rakes at the heart when a blood red sun is dipping over the horizon.

When to Go

Darwin

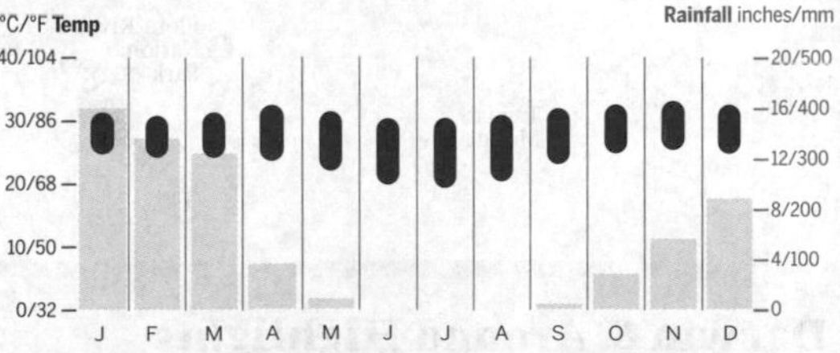

Apr-Aug Peak season with lower humidity in the north.

Jun & Jul Darwin is alight with the sounds, sights and cultural blitz of the Fringe Festival.

Sep-Mar Barramundi fishing heats up as the Wet turns the Top End into a watery wonderland.

Darwin & Around Highlights

1. Seeing glinting crocodile eyes peering from the watery wonderland of **Kakadu National Park** (p834).
2. Sampling a satay and other exotic fare at Darwin's **Mindil Beach Sunset Market** (p825).
3. Plunging into a, crystal-clear rock pool at **Litchfield National Park** (p832).
4. Hooking up a barra on the **Daly or Mary rivers** (p830); some of Australia's best **barramundi fishing** (p811).

5 Touring remote and hypnotically beautiful **Arnhem Land** (p841) and experiencing some Indigenous culture.

6 Experiencing the unique Indigenous culture of the **Tiwi Islands** (p828), and picking up some excellent local souvenirs.

7 Marvelling at Australia's unique critters in the **Territory Wildlife Park** (p831).

History

Early European attempts to settle the Top End were mainly due to British fears that the French or Dutch might get a foothold in Australia. The Brits established three forts between 1824 and 1838, but all were short-lived. Then the desire for more grazing land and trade routes spurred speculators from Queensland and South Australia (SA) to explore the vast untamed north. With an eye to development, SA governors annexed the Northern Territory (NT) in 1863 (it became self-governing only in 1978).

From the mid-1860s to 1895 hundreds of thousands of sheep, cattle and horses were overlanded to immense pastoral settlements. Dislocation and hardship were bedfellows of the industry, with Aboriginal Australians forced from their lands and pastoralists confronted by a swath of difficulties. Some Indigenous people took employment as stockmen or domestic servants on cattle stations, while others moved on in an attempt to maintain their traditional lifestyle.

In the early 1870s, during digging to establish the Overland Telegraph (from Adelaide to Darwin), gold was discovered. A minor rush ensued, with an influx of Chinese prospectors. Though the gold finds were relatively insignificant, the searches for it unearthed a wealth of natural resources that would lead to mining becoming a major economic presence.

WWII had a significant impact on the NT. Just weeks after the Japanese levelled Darwin, causing 243 deaths, the entire NT north of Alice Springs was placed under military control, with 32,000 soldiers stationed in the Top End.

On Christmas morning 1974, Darwin was flattened again by Cyclone Tracy, which killed 71 people.

Indigenous Northern Territory

Aboriginal Australians have occupied parts of the NT for around 60,000 years, although the central regions were not inhabited until about 24,000 years ago. The first significant contact with outsiders occurred in the 17th century when Macassan traders from modern-day Sulawesi in Indonesia came to the Top End to collect trepang (sea cucumber).

While the process of white settlement in the NT was slower than elsewhere in Australia, it had an equally troubled and violent effect. By the early 20th century, most Aboriginal people were confined to government reserves or Christian missions. During the 1960s Aboriginal people began to demand more rights.

In 1966 a group of Aboriginal stockmen, led by Vincent Lingiari, went on strike on Wave Hill Station, to protest over the low wages and poor conditions that they received compared with white stockmen. The Wave Hill walk-off gave rise to the Aboriginal land-rights movement.

In 1976 the *Aboriginal Land Rights (Northern Territory) Act* was passed in Canberra. It handed over all reserves and mission lands in the NT to Aboriginal people and allowed Aboriginal groups to claim vacant government land if they could prove continuous occupation – provided the land wasn't already leased, in a town or set aside for some other special purpose.

Today, Aboriginal people own about half of the land in the NT, including Kakadu and Uluru-Kata Tjuta National Parks, which are leased back to the federal government. Minerals on Aboriginal land are still government property, though the landowners' permission is usually required for exploration and mining, and landowners are remunerated.

Around 30% of the NT's 200,000 people are Aboriginal Australians. While non-Aboriginal Australia's awareness of the need for reconciliation with the Indigenous community has increased in recent years, there are still huge gulfs between the cultures. Entrenched disadvantage and substance abuse are causing enormous social problems within some Indigenous communities.

It's often difficult for short-term visitors to make meaningful contact with Indigenous people, as they generally prefer to be left to themselves. The impressions given by some Aboriginal people on the streets of Alice Springs, Katherine and Darwin, where social problems and substance abuse among a few people can present an unpleasant picture, are not indicative of Aboriginal communities as a whole.

Tours to Aboriginal lands (most operated by the communities themselves) and visits to arts centres are gradually becoming more widely available, as communities feel more inclined to share their culture. Benefits are numerous: financial gain through self-determined endeavour, and educating non-Aboriginal people about traditional culture and customs, which helps to alleviate the problems caused by the ignorance and misunderstandings of the past.

National Parks

Aside from Darwin, the Top End is all about its national parks; it has some of the largest and most famous natural areas in Australia, including Kakadu and Litchfield. **Parks Australia** (www.environment.gov.au/parks) manages Kakadu, while the Parks & Wildlife Commission of the Northern Territory manages the other parks and produces fact sheets, available online or from its various offices.

Activities

Bushwalking

The Territory's national parks offer well-maintained tracks of different lengths and degrees of difficulty, which introduce walkers to various environments and wildlife habitats. Carry plenty of water, take rubbish out with you and stick to the tracks. Top bushwalks include the Barrk Sandstone Bushwalk in Kakadu National Park.

Fishing

No permit is required to fish the Territory's waterways, though there are limits on the minimum size and number of fish per person. Travel NT publishes some info online (www.travelnt.com). The Amateur Fishermen's Association of the Northern Territory (www.afant.com.au) also has online info.

The feisty barramundi lures most fisherfolk to the Top End, particularly to Borroloola (p854), Daly River (p833) and Mary River (p830). Increasingly, the recreational-fishing fraternity encourages catch and release to maintain sustainable fish levels. Loads of tours offer transport and gear and start at $275 per person.

Swimming

The cool waterfalls, waterholes and rejuvenating thermal pools throughout the Top End are perfect spots to soak. Litchfield National Park is particularly rewarding.

Saltwater crocodiles inhabit both salt and fresh waters in the Top End, though there are quite a few safe, natural swimming holes. Before taking the plunge, be sure to obey the signs and seek local advice. If in doubt, don't risk it.

Box jellyfish seasonally infest the sea around Darwin; swimming at the city's beaches is safest from May to September.

Wildlife Watching

The best place for guaranteed wildlife sightings, from bilbies to emus, is at excellent Territory Wildlife Park (p831) outside Darwin.

If you prefer to see wildlife in the wild, there are few guarantees; many of the region's critters are nocturnal. One exception is at Kakadu, where you'll certainly see crocodiles at Cahill's Crossing or Yellow Waters, and numerous species of bird at its wealth of wetlands.

Information

RESOURCES

Parks & Wildlife Commission of the Northern Territory (☎08-8999 4555; www.parksandwildlife.nt.gov.au) Details on NT parks and reserves, including fact sheets.

Road Report (☎1800 246 199; www.roadreport.nt.gov.au) NT road conditions.

Tourism Top End (www.tourismtopend.com.au) Darwin-based tourism body.

Travel NT (www.travelnt.com) Official tourism site.

ABORIGINAL LAND PERMITS

Permits may be required to enter Aboriginal land, unless you are using recognised public roads that cross Aboriginal territory. Permits can take four to six weeks to be processed, although for the Injalak Arts Centre at Gunbalanya (Oenpelli) they are generally issued on the spot in **Jabiru** (☎08-8938 3000; Flinders St, Jabiru; ⏲8am-4.30pm Mon-Fri).

Northern Land Council (www.nlc.org.au) Responsible for land north of a line drawn between Kununurra (Western Australia) and Mt Isa (Queensland). Branch in Katherine (Map p848; ☎08-8971 9802; 5 Katherine Tce).

Tiwi Land Council (Map p814; ☎08-8970 9373; www.tiwilandcouncil.com) Permits for the Tiwi Islands.

Getting There & Around

AIR

International and domestic flights arrive at and depart from **Darwin International Airport** (Map p814; www.darwinairport.com.au; Henry Wrigley Dr, Marrara) There are also flights between Darwin, Alice Springs and Uluru.

Airnorth (www.airnorth.com.au) To/from East Timor, and to Arnhem Land, Broome, Perth, Kununurra and the Gold Coast.

Jetstar (www.jetstar.com.au) Services most major Australian cities and several Southeast Asian cities.

Qantas (www.qantas.com.au) To/from Asia and Europe, and servicing all major Australian cities.

Virgin Australia (www.virginaustralia.com) Direct flights between Darwin and Brisbane, Melbourne, Perth and Sydney.

BUS

Greyhound Australia (www.greyhound.com.au) regularly services the main road routes throughout the NT, including side trips to Kakadu.

Alternatively, there are tour-bus companies such as AAT Kings, and backpacker buses that cover vast distances while savouring the sights along the way.

CAR

To truly explore the Top End by car, you'll need a well-prepared 4WD vehicle and some outback nous. The **Automobile Association of the Northern Territory** (AANT; ☎08-8925 5901; www.aant.com.au; 2/14 Knuckey St, Darwin; ⊙9am-5pm Mon-Fri, to 12.30pm Sat) can advise on preparation and additional resources; members of automobile associations in other Australian states have reciprocal rights.

Many roads are open to conventional cars and campervans, which can be hired in Darwin and Alice Springs, and can work out to be quite economical when split by a group.

Some driving conditions are particular to the NT. While traffic may be light and roads dead straight, distances between places are long. Watch out for the four great NT road hazards: speed (maximum speed on the open highway is 130km/h), driver fatigue, road trains and animals (driving at night is particularly dangerous). Note that some roads are regularly closed during the Wet due to flooding; head to www.ntlis.nt.gov.au/roadreport/ for information.

TRAIN

The famous interstate Ghan train is run by **Great Southern Rail** (www.gsr.com.au), grinding between Darwin and Adelaide via Katherine and Alice Springs. The Ghan is met in Port Augusta (SA) by the Indian Pacific, which travels between Sydney and Perth; and in Adelaide by the Overland, which travels to/from Melbourne.

The Ghan has three levels of sleeper berths plus a chair class.

DARWIN

☎08 / POP 127,500

Australia's only tropical capital city, Darwin gazes out confidently across the Timor Sea. It's closer to Bali than Bondi and can certainly feel removed from the rest of the country.

Darwin has plenty to offer the traveller. Chairs and tables spill out of streetside restaurants and bars, innovative museums celebrate the city's past, and galleries showcase the region's rich Indigenous art. Darwin's cosmopolitan mix – more than 50 nationalities are seamlessly represented here – is typified by the wonderful markets held throughout the dry season.

Nature is well and truly part of Darwin's backyard; the famous national parks of Kakadu and Litchfield are only a few hours' drive away, and the unique Tiwi Islands are a boat ride away. For locals the perfect weekend is going fishing for barra in a tinny (small boat) with an esky full of cold beer.

History

The Larrakia Aboriginal people lived for thousands of years in Darwin, hunting, fishing and foraging. In 1869 a permanent white settlement was established and the grid for a new town laid out. Originally called Palmerston, and renamed Darwin in 1911, the new town developed rapidly, transforming the physical and social landscape.

The discovery of gold at nearby Pine Creek brought an influx of Chinese, who soon settled into other industries. Asians and Islanders came to work in the pearling industry and on the railway line and wharf.

DARWIN IN...

Two Days

Start with breakfast at **Four Birds** (Map p816; ☎0408 729 708; 32 Smith St Mall, Shop 2, Star Village; items $6-12; ⊙7am-3pm Mon-Fri, 8am-2pm Sat) or **Roma Bar** (p822), flipping through the *Northern Territory News*. Take a stroll downtown and through **Bicentennial Park** (Map p816; www.darwin.nt.gov.au; ⊙24hr). Don't miss the high-tide action at **Aquascene** (Map p816; ☎08-8981 7837; www.aquascene.com.au; 28 Doctors Gully Rd; adult/child $15/10; ⊙high tide, check website) and as the day warms up, head down to the **waterfront precinct** (p813), stopping for lunch at **Curve** (p822) and a dip in the Wave Lagoon. As the sun sets, make your way to **Mindil Beach Sunset Market** (p825), packed with food outlets, buskers and souvenirs.

On day two, hire a bike and head out to the **Museum & Art Gallery of the Northern Territory** (p814), then lunch at the adjacent **Cornucopia Cafe** (p823). Continue your coastal jaunt with visits to the **East Point Reserve** (p818) and the **Defence of Darwin Experience** (p815). At night, hit the bars along **Mitchell St** (p824), or find a quiet waterfront restaurant at Cullen Bay and catch a movie under the stars at the **Deckchair Cinema** (p824).

More recently, neighbouring East Timorese and Papuans have sought asylum in Darwin.

During WWII, Darwin was the frontline for the Allied action against the Japanese in the Pacific. It was the only Australian city ever bombed, and official reports of the time downplayed the damage – to buoy Australians' morale. Though the city wasn't destroyed by the attacks, the impact of full-scale military occupation on Darwin was enormous.

More physically damaging was Cyclone Tracy, which hit Darwin at around midnight on Christmas Eve 1974. By Christmas morning, Darwin effectively ceased to exist as a city, with only 400 of its 11,200 homes left standing and 71 people killed. The town was rebuilt to a new, stringent building code and has steadily expanded outwards and upwards.

Sights

Central Darwin

★Crocosaurus Cove ZOO

(Map p816; ☎08-8981 7522; www.crocosauruscove.com; 58 Mitchell St; adult/child $32/20; ⏲9am-6pm, last admission 5pm) If the tourists won't go out to see the crocs, then bring the crocs to the tourists. Right in the middle of Mitchell St, Crocosaurus Cove is as close as you'll ever want to get to these amazing creatures. Six of the largest crocs in captivity can be seen in state-of-the-art aquariums and pools. Other aquariums feature barramundi, turtles and stingrays, plus there's an enormous reptile house (allegedly displaying the greatest variety of reptiles in the country).

You can be lowered right into a pool with the crocs in the transparent Cage of Death (one/two people $160/240). If that's too scary, there's another pool where you can swim with a clear tank wall separating you from some mildly less menacing baby crocs.

George Brown Botanic Gardens GARDENS

(Map p816; http://www.parksandwildlife.nt.gov.au/botanic; Geranium St, Stuart Park; ⏲7am-7pm, information centre 8am-4pm) FREE Named after the gardens' curator from 1971 to 1990, these 42-hectare gardens showcase plants from the Top End and around the world – monsoon vine forest, the mangroves and coastal plants habitat, boabs, and a magnificent collection of native and exotic palms and cycads.

The gardens are an easy 2km bicycle ride out from Darwin, along Gilruth Ave and Gardens Rd, or there's another entrance off Geranium St, which runs off the Stuart Hwy in Stuart Park. Alternatively, bus 7 from the city stops near the Stuart Hwy/Geranium St corner.

Many of the plants here were traditionally used by the local Aboriginal people, and self-guiding Aboriginal plant-use trails have been set up; pick up a brochure at the gardens' information centre near the Geranium St entry. You'll also find birdwatching brochures and garden maps here.

Myilly Point Heritage Precinct HISTORIC SITE

(Map p816) At the far northern end of Smith St is this small but important precinct of four houses built from 1930 to 1939 (which means they survived both the WWII bombings and Cyclone Tracy!). They're now managed by the National Trust. One of them, **Burnett House** (Map p816; www.nationaltrustnt.org.au; admission by donation; ⏲10am-1pm Mon-Sat, 2.30-5pm Sun), operates as a museum. There's a tantalising **colonial high tea** ($10) in the gardens on Sunday afternoon from 3pm between April and October.

Darwin Waterfront Precinct

The bold redevelopment of the old **Darwin Waterfront Precinct** (www.waterfront.nt.gov.au) has transformed the city. The multimillion-dollar redevelopment features a cruise-ship terminal, luxury hotels, boutique restaurants and shopping, the Sky Bridge, an elevated walkway and elevator at the south end of Smith St, and a Wave Lagoon.

Wave & Recreation Lagoons WATER PARK

(Map p816; ☎08-8985 6588; www.waterfront.nt.gov.au; Wave Lagoon adult/child $7/5; ⏲Wave Lagoon 10am-6pm) The hugely popular **Wave Lagoon** is a hit with locals and travellers alike. There are 10 different wave patterns produced (20 minutes on with a 10-minute rest in between) and there are lifeguards, a kiosk and a strip of lawn to bask on. Adjacent is the **Recreation Lagoon** with a sandy beach, lifeguards and stinger-filtered seawater (although the nets and filters are not guaranteed to be 100% effective).

WWII Oil-Storage Tunnels TUNNEL

(Map p816; ☎08-8985 6322; www.darwintours.com.au/ww2tunnels; self-guided tour per person $7; ⏲9am-4pm May-Sep, to 1pm Oct-Apr) You can escape from the heat of the day and relive your Hitchcockian fantasies by walking through the WWII oil-storage tunnels. They were built in 1942 to store the navy's oil supplies (but never used); now they exhibit wartime photos.

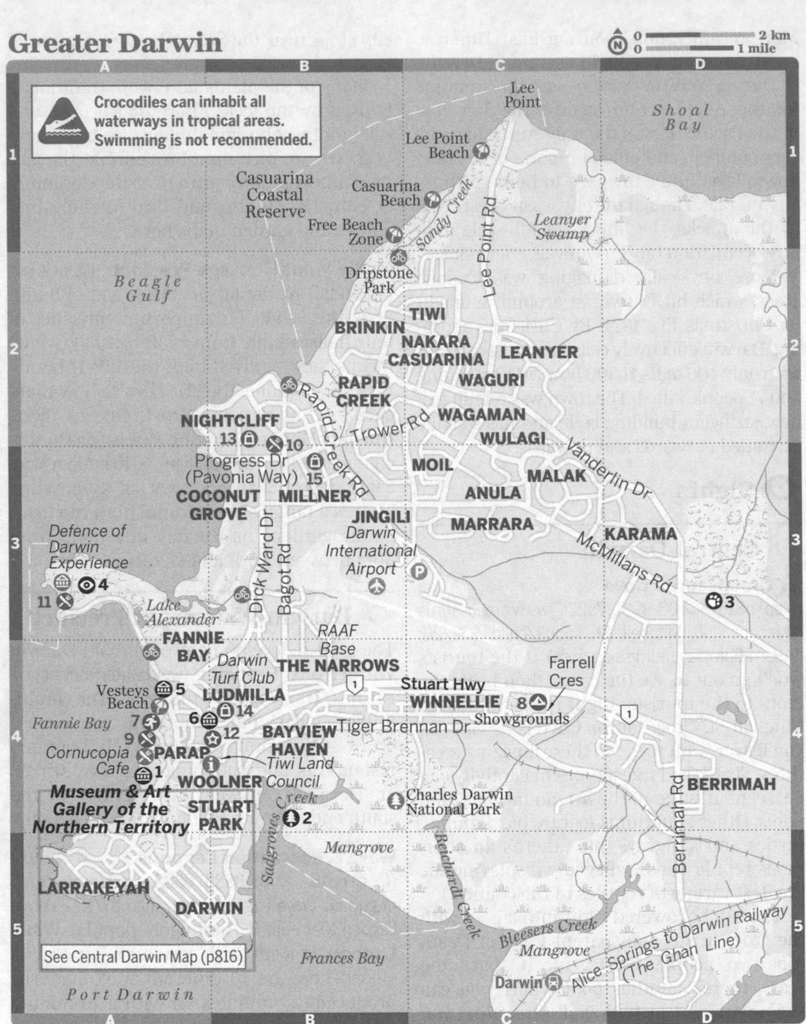

Indo-Pacific Marine Exhibition AQUARIUM (Map p816; ☎08-8981 1294; www.indopacificmarine.com.au; 29 Stokes Hill Rd; adult/child $24/10; ⏲10am-4pm Apr-Oct, call Nov-Mar) This excellent marine aquarium at the Waterfront Precinct gives you a close encounter with the denizens at the bottom of Darwin Harbour. Each small tank is a complete ecosystem, with only the occasional extra fish introduced as food for some of the predators, such as stonefish or the bizarre angler fish.

Also recommended here is the **Coral Reef by Night** (Map p816; ☎08-8981 1294; www.indopacificmarine.com.au; 29 Stokes Hill Rd; adult/child $120/60; ⏲6.30pm Wed, Fri & Sun), which consists of a tour of the aquarium, seafood dinner (on biodegradable plates, no less!) and an impressive show of fluorescing animals.

Fannie Bay

★Museum & Art Gallery of the Northern Territory MUSEUM (MAGNT; Map p814; ☎08-8999 8264; www.magnt.net.au; 19 Conacher St, Fannie Bay; ⏲9am-5pm Mon-Fri, 10am-5pm Sat & Sun) FREE This superb museum and gallery boasts beautifully presented galleries of Top End–centric exhibits. The **Aboriginal art collection** is a highlight, with carvings from the Tiwi Islands, bark paintings from

Greater Darwin

Top Sights
1 Museum & Art Gallery of the Northern Territory A4

Sights
2 Charles Darwin National Park B4
3 Crocodylus Park D3
4 East Point Reserve A3
5 Fannie Bay Gaol Museum A4
6 Northern Centre for Contemporary Art B4

Activities, Courses & Tours
7 Darwin Sailing Club A4

Sleeping
8 Discovery Holiday Park – Darwin C4

Eating
Cyclone Cafe ..... (see 14)
9 Darwin Ski Club A4
Laneway Speciality Coffee ..... (see 6)
Parap Fine Foods ..... (see 14)
10 Pavonia Place B2
11 Pee Wee's at the Point A3

Drinking & Nightlife
Bogarts ..... (see 6)
Darwin Ski Club ..... (see 9)

Entertainment
12 Darwin Railway Club B4

Shopping
13 Nightcliff Market B2
14 Parap Village Market B4
15 Rapid Creek Market B3
Tiwi Art Network ..... (see 14)

Arnhem Land and dot paintings from the desert. An entire room is devoted to **Cyclone Tracy**, in a display that graphically illustrates life before and after the disaster. You can stand in a darkened room and listen to the whirring sound of Tracy at full throttle – a sound you won't forget in a hurry.

The cavernous **Maritime Gallery** houses an assortment of weird and wonderful crafts from the nearby islands and Indonesia, as well as a pearling lugger and a Vietnamese refugee boat.

Pride of place among the stuffed animals undoubtedly goes to Sweetheart: a 5m-long, 780kg saltwater crocodile. It became a Top End personality after attacking several fishing dinghies on the Finniss River, south of Darwin.

The museum has a good bookshop, and the Cornucopia Cafe (p823) is a great lunch spot with views over the sea.

Fannie Bay Gaol Museum MUSEUM
(Map p814; ☎08-8999 8290; http://artsandmuseums.nt.gov.au/museums/moretosee/gaolitage/visit/gaol; cnr East Point Rd & Ross Smith Ave; admission by donation; ⏲10am-3pm) This interesting (if slightly grim) museum represents almost 100 years of solitude. Serving as Darwin's main jail from 1883 to 1979, the solid cells contain information panels that provide a window into the region's unique social history. Lepers, refugees and juveniles were among the groups of people confined here. You can still see the old cells, and the gallows constructed for two hangings in 1952.

Defence of Darwin Experience MUSEUM
(Map p814; ☎08-8981 9702; www.defenceofdarwin.nt.gov.au; adult/child/family $14/5.50/35; ⏲9.30am-5pm) At this innovative, multimedia experience, you can hear personal accounts of those affected by, or those who actively participated in, Australia's defence during WWII. Darwin and the Top End is the focus – the area was bombed 64 times, with 188 aircraft attacking the city on 19 February 1942. A small theatre runs a 20-minute show bringing it all to life. On East Point's northern side is a series of WWII gun emplacements and the **Darwin Military Museum**.

Northern Centre for Contemporary Art GALLERY
(NCCA; Map p814; ☎08-8981 5368; http://nccart.com.au; Vimy Lane, Parap Shopping Village; ⏲10am-4pm Wed-Fri, to 2pm Sat) FREE The NCCA is a really small space but has some changing and challenging exhibitions. It's worth checking out while doing the Parap Market.

Outer East

Crocodylus Park ZOO
(Map p814; www.crocodyluspark.com.au; 815 McMillans Rd, Berrimah; adult/child $40/20; ⏲9am-5pm) Crocodylus Park showcases hundreds of crocs and a minizoo comprising lions, tigers and other big cats, spider monkeys, marmosets, cassowaries and large birds. Allow about two hours to look around the whole park, and you should time your visit with a **tour** (10am, noon, 2pm & 3.30pm), which includes a feeding demonstration. Croc-meat BBQ packs for sale!

Central Darwin

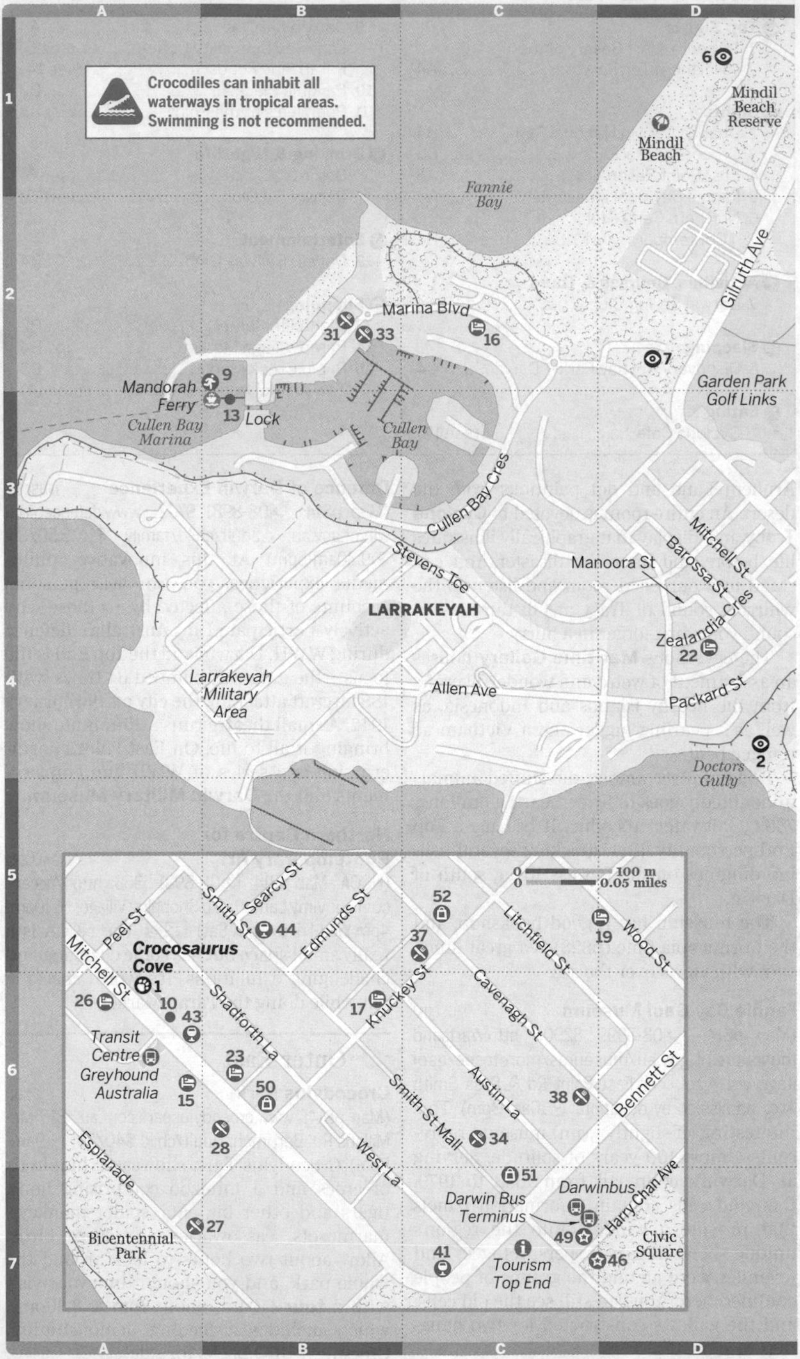

Crocodiles can inhabit all waterways in tropical areas. Swimming is not recommended.

A B C D

1 2 3 4 5 6 7

Fannie Bay
Mindil Beach
Mindil Beach Reserve
6
Gilruth Ave
Marina Blvd
31
33
16
7
Garden Park Golf Links
Mandorah Ferry
9
13
Lock
Cullen Bay Marina
Cullen Bay
Cullen Bay Cres
Stevens Tce
Mitchell St
Barossa St
Manoora St
Zealandia Cres
22
LARRAKEYAH
Larrakeyah Military Area
Allen Ave
Packard St
2
Doctors Gully

0 100 m
0 0.05 miles

Peel St
Mitchell St
Smith St
Searcy St
44
Edmunds St
52
37
Litchfield St
19
Wood St
Crocosaurus Cove
1
26
10
43
Shadforth La
17
Knuckey St
Cavenagh St
Transit Centre
Greyhound Australia
15
23
50
Smith St Mall
Austin La
38
Bennett St
28
West La
34
Esplanade
51
Darwin Bus Terminus
Darwinbus
Harry Chan Ave
27
49
Civic Square
Bicentennial Park
41
Tourism Top End
46

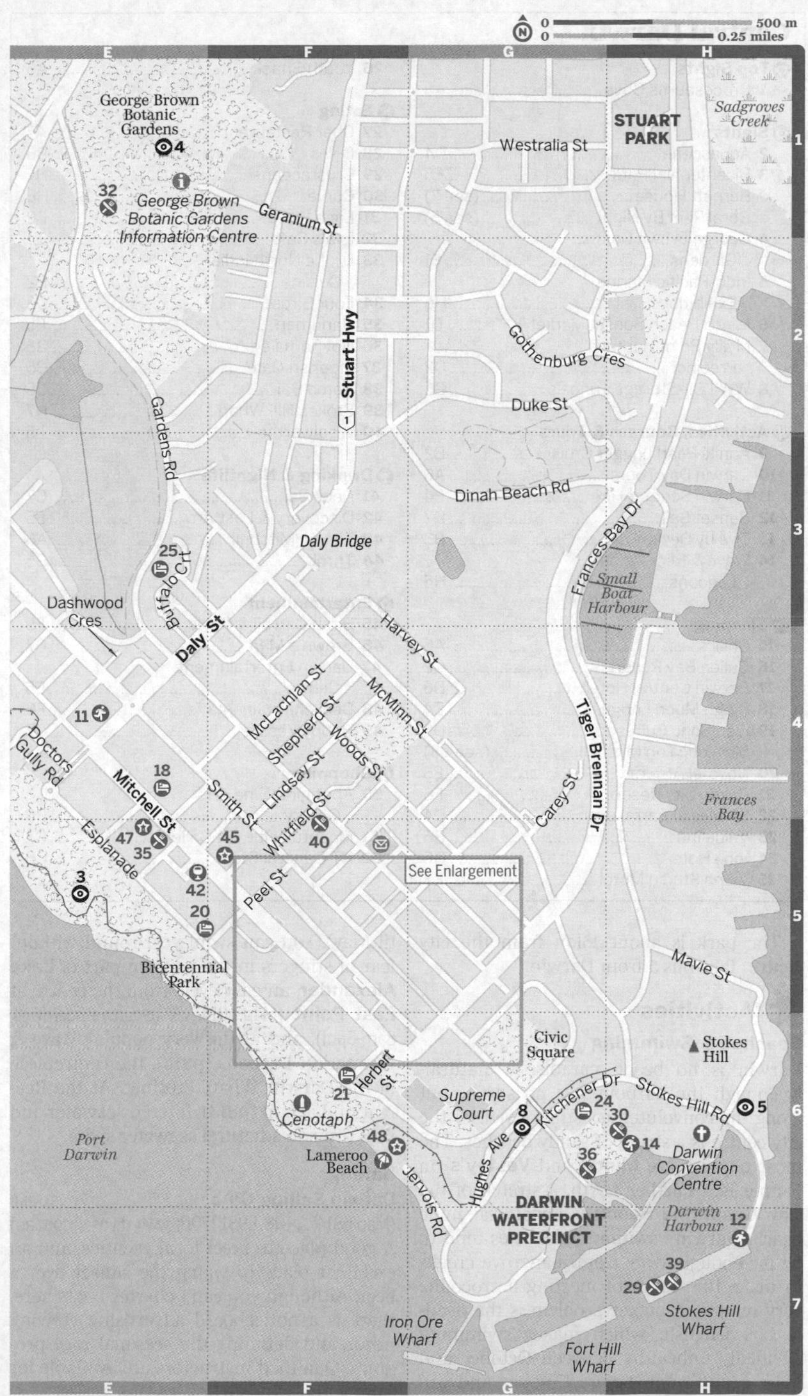

0 500 m
0 0.25 miles
George Brown Botanic Gardens
4
George Brown Botanic Gardens Information Centre
32
Geranium St
Stuart Hwy
1
STUART PARK
Westralia St
Sadgroves Creek
Gothenburg Cres
Duke St
Gardens Rd
Dinah Beach Rd
Daly Bridge
Frances Bay Dr
Small Boat Harbour
25
Buffalo Crt
Dashwood Cres
Daly St
Harvey St
McLachlan St
McMinn St
Shepherd St
Woods St
Tiger Brennan Dr
11
Doctors Gully Rd
Mitchell St
18
Lindsay St
Smith St
Whitfield St
Carey St
Frances Bay
47
35
45
40
Esplanade
3
42
20
Peel St
See Enlargement
Mavie St
Bicentennial Park
Civic Square
Stokes Hill
21
Herbert St
Supreme Court
Kitchener Dr
24
Stokes Hill Rd
5
Cenotaph
8
30
14
Port Darwin
48
Lameroo Beach
Hughes Ave
36
Darwin Convention Centre
Jervois Rd
DARWIN WATERFRONT PRECINCT
Darwin Harbour
12
39
29
Stokes Hill Wharf
Iron Ore Wharf
Fort Hill Wharf
DARWIN & AROUND

Central Darwin

Top Sights
1 Crocosaurus Cove A6

Sights
2 Aquascene D4
3 Bicentennial Park E5
Burnett House .... (see 7)
Coral Reef By Night .... (see 5)
4 George Brown Botanic Gardens E1
5 Indo-Pacific Marine Exhibition H6
6 Mindil Beach Sunset Market D1
7 Myilly Point Heritage Precinct D2
8 WWII Oil-Storage Tunnels G6

Activities, Courses & Tours
9 Anniki Pearl Lugger Cruises B2
10 Darwin Day Tours A6
11 Darwin Scooter Hire E4
12 Sunset Sail H7
13 Tiwi by Design B3
14 Wave & Recreation Lagoons H6

Sleeping
15 Chilli's A6
16 Cullen Bay Resorts C2
17 Darwin Central Hotel B6
18 Dingo Moon Lodge E4
19 Elan Soho Suites D5
Melaleuca on Mitchell .... (see 23)
20 Novotel Atrium E5
21 Palms City Resort F6
22 Steeles at Larrakeyah D4
23 Value Inn B6
24 Vibe Hotel G6
25 Vitina Studio Motel E3
26 Youth Shack A6

Eating
27 Char Restaurant A7
28 Coles B6
29 Crustaceans H7
30 Curve H6
31 Eat a Pizza B2
32 Eva's Cafe E1
33 Exotic North Indian Cuisine B2
34 Four Birds C6
35 Hanuman E5
36 Hot Tamale G6
37 Moorish Café C5
38 Roma Bar C6
39 Stokes Hill Wharf H7
40 Woolworths F5

Drinking & Nightlife
41 Deck Bar C7
42 Discovery & Lost Arc E5
43 Tap on Mitchell A6
44 Throb B5

Entertainment
45 Birch Carroll & Coyle F5
46 Brown's Mart C7
47 Darwin Entertainment Centre E5
48 Deckchair Cinema F6
49 Happy Yess C7

Shopping
50 Aboriginal Fine Arts Gallery B6
51 Mbantua Fine Art Gallery C7
52 NT General Store C5

The park is about 15km from the city centre. Take bus 5 from Darwin.

Activities

Beaches & Swimming

Darwin is no beach paradise – naturally enough the harbour has no surf – but along the convoluted coastline north of the city centre is a string of sandy beaches. The most popular are **Mindil** and **Vestey's** on Fannie Bay. Further north, a stretch of the 7km **Casuarina Beach** is an official nude beach. Darwin's swimming beaches tend to be far enough away from mangrove creeks to make the threat of meeting a crocodile very remote. A bigger problem is the deadly box jellyfish, which makes swimming decidedly unhealthy between October and March (and often before October and until May). You can swim year-round without fear of stingers in the western part of **Lake Alexander**, an easy cycle from the centre at **East Point** (Map p814; mangrove boardwalk 8am-6pm), and at the very popular Wave & Recreation Lagoons (p813), the centrepiece of the Darwin Wharf Precinct. At the Recreation Lagoon (p813), filtered seawater and nets provide a natural seawater swim.

Sailing

Darwin Sailing Club SAILING
(Map p814; 08-8981 1700; www.dwnsail.com.au)
A good place to meet local yachties, and an excellent place to watch the sunset over a beer. Although you can't charter boats here, there is a noticeboard advertising crewing needs and detailing the seasonal race program. Qualified instructors are available for sailing and windsurfing lessons.

Cycling

Darwin is great for cycling (in winter!). Traffic is light and a series of **bike tracks** covers most of the city, with the main one running from the northern end of Cavenagh St to Fannie Bay, Coconut Grove, Nightcliff and Casuarina. At Fannie Bay, a side track heads out to the **East Point Reserve.** Consider heading for **Charles Darwin National Park** (Map p814; www.parksandwildlife.nt.gov.au/parks/find/charlesdarwin#; ⊙8am-7pm), 5km southeast of the city, with a few kilometres of path around the park's wetlands, woodlands and WWII bunkers. Some hostels hire out bicycles for $15 to $25 per day for a mountain bike, or try:

Darwin Scooter Hire CYCLING
(Map p816; ☎08-8941 2434; www.thescootershop.com.au; 9 Daly St; ⊙8am-5pm Mon-Fri, 9am-3pm Sat) Mountain bikes for $20 a day ($100 deposit required).

Skydiving

Top End Tandems ADVENTURE SPORTS
(☎0417 190 140; www.topendtandems.com.au; tandem jumps from $380) Tandem skydives starting at Darwin Airport and landing at Lee Point Reserve.

Tours

There are dozens of tours in and around Darwin, and lots of combinations covering Kakadu, Arnhem Land, Litchfield and further afield.

Batji Indigenous Waterfront Walking Tour CULTURAL TOUR
(☎0416 731 353; www.batjitours.com.au; adult/child $70/free; ⊙10am Wed & Fri) An excellent two-hour walking tour along the Esplanade run by the Larrakia people of Darwin. You will learn about the local wildlife, discover Lameroo beach and gain insight into places of cultural significance to the Larrakia people.

Darwin Explorer BUS TOUR
(☎0416 140 903; http://theaustralianexplorer.com.au/darwin-explorer.html; 24hr ticket adult/child $35/20) Open-top bus tours that explore Darwin's major sights; hop on/hop off with either a 24-hour or 48-hour ticket. Departs every 30 minutes from the tourist information centre.

Tour Tub BUS TOUR
(☎08-8985 6322; www.tourtub.com.au; adult/child $100/60) Offering five-hour guided, minibus tours around Darwin's big-ticket sights; price includes admission charges to attractions such as Defence of Darwin Experience.

Sea Darwin ECOTOUR
(☎1300 065 022; www.seadarwin.com; tours adult/child from $35/20) One-, two-, or three-hour eco tours around the city and Darwin Harbour, checking out mangroves, a crocodile trap, a shipwreck and (if you're lucky) dugongs and dolphins.

Darwin Day Tours TOUR
(Map p816; ☎1300 721 365; www.darwindaytours.com.au; afternoon city tours adult/child $75/38) Runs an afternoon city tour that takes in all the major attractions, including Stokes Hill Wharf, the Museum & Art Gallery and East Point Reserve. Can be linked with a 'sunset fish 'n' chips harbour cruise' ($55/40).

Tiwi Tours CULTURAL TOUR
(☎1300 721 365; www.aussieadventures.com.au; adult/child inc flights $550/410) Small-group cultural tours out to the nearby Tiwi Islands with Indigenous guides (adult/child including flights $550/410). Kakadu and Litchfield tours also available through the company's other brands: Darwin Day Tours and Aussie Adventure.

Northern Territory Indigenous Tours CULTURAL TOUR
(☎1300 921 188; www.ntitours.com.au; adult/child $249/124) Upmarket Indigenous tours to Litchfield National Park.

Sacred Earth Safaris OUTDOORS
(☎08-8555 3838; www.sacredearthsafaris.com.au) Multiday, small-group 4WD camping tours around Kakadu, Katherine and the Kimberley. Two-day Kakadu tour starts at $850; the five-day Top End National Parks Safari is $2600.

Kakadu Dreams TOUR
(☎1800 813 266; www.kakadudreams.com.au) Backpacker day tours to Litchfield ($119), and boisterous two/three-day trips to Kakadu ($400/535).

Wallaroo Tours TOUR
(☎08-8981 6670; www.wallarootours.com; tours $160) Small-group tours to Litchfield National Park.

Harbour Cruises

Between April and October there are plenty of boats based at the Cullen Bay Marina and Stokes Hill Wharf to take you on a cruise of the harbour.

Anniki Pearl Lugger Cruises SAILING
(Map p816; ☎0428 414 000; www.australianharbourcruises.com.au; tours adult/child $70/50)

Three-hour sunset cruises on this historical pearling lugger depart from Cullen Bay Marina and include sparkling wine and nibbles. You might recognise the ship from the film *Australia*.

Sunset Sail SAILING
(Map p816; ☎0408 795 567; www.sailnt.com.au; tours adult/child $70/45) This three-hour afternoon cruise aboard the catamaran *Daymirri 2* departs from Stokes Hill Wharf. Refreshments are included but BYO alcohol.

Festivals & Events

WordStorm LITERATURE
(www.wordstorm.org.au) The biannual NT Writers' Festival event in May (even-numbered years), includes song, storytelling, visual-art collaboration, theatre, performance poetry, history, biography, poetry and fiction.

Darwin Blues Festival MUSIC
In late June the Darwin Botanic Gardens charge up with electrifying live blues. Much beer and bending of guitar strings.

Beer Can Regatta CULTURAL
(www.beercanregatta.org.au) An utterly insane and typically Territorian festival that features races for boats made out of beer cans. It takes place at Mindil Beach in July and is a good, fun day.

Darwin Aboriginal Art Fair ART
(www.darwinaboriginalartfair.com.au) Held at the Darwin Convention Centre, this three-day August festival showcases Indigenous art from communities throughout the Territory.

Darwin Festival ART
(www.darwinfestival.org.au) This mainly outdoor arts and culture festival celebrates music, theatre, visual art, dance and cabaret and runs for 18 days in August. Festivities are centred in the large park next to Civic Sq, off Harry Chan Ave.

Sleeping

Darwin has a good range of accommodation, most of it handy to the CBD, but finding a bed in the peak May to September period can be difficult at short notice – book ahead, at least for the first night. Accommodation prices vary greatly with the season and demand; expect big discounts between November and March, especially for midrange and top-end accommodation.

Backpacker hostels fluctuate the least, and prices differ little between places – concentrated as they are in a small stretch of bar-heavy Mitchell St. If you want a quieter stay, choose somewhere a bit further out – they're usually still within walking distance of the action. Hostel facilities generally include communal kitchen, pool and laundry facilities, and they all have tour-booking desks. Some offer airport, bus or train-station pick-ups with advance bookings, and most give YHA/VIP discounts.

City Centre

Melaleuca on Mitchell HOSTEL $
(Map p816; ☎1300 723 437; www.momdarwin.com.au; 52 Mitchell St; dm $32, d with/without bathroom $115/95; ❄@📶🏊) If you stay here take note – 24-hour check-in and it's plonked right in the action on Mitchell Street. So, sleeping...maybe not. Partying? Oh yes! The highlight is the rooftop island bar and pool area overlooking Mitchell St – complete with waterfall spa and big-screen TV. Party heaven! This modern hostel is immaculate with great facilities and it's very secure. The 3rd floor is female only.

Dingo Moon Lodge HOSTEL $
(Map p816; ☎08-8941 3444; www.dingomoonlodge.com; 88 Mitchell St; incl breakfast dm $32-38, d & tw $105; ❄@📶🏊) Howl at the moon at the Dingo. This fun, laid-back hostel is slightly removed from the party scene, although everything is still at your doorstep. It's a two-building affair with 65 beds – big enough to be sociable but not rowdy. Cleanliness and service tend to fluctuate. A highlight is the pool, sparkling underneath a massive frangipani tree.

Chilli's HOSTEL $
(Map p816; ☎1800 351 313, 08-8980 5800; www.chillis.com.au; 69a Mitchell St; dm $34, tw & d without bathroom $100; ❄@📶) Friendly Chilli's is a funky place with a small sun deck and spa (use the pool next door). There's also a pool table and a breezy kitchen/meals terrace overlooking Mitchell St. Rooms are compact but clean. There are nice touches to this place, such as pots with scented herbs hanging from the roof of the balcony.

Youth Shack HOSTEL $
(Map p816; ☎1300 793 302; www.youthshack.com.au; 69 Mitchell St; dm $34, tw & d without bathroom $90; 🏊) At one end of the Transit Centre, this popular hostel has a large open kitchen and meals area overlooking a pool big enough to actually swim in. The bar here is very popular and at times raucous. Rooms are a little

tired but clean, and the staff are consistently praised for being friendly and helpful. The tour desk here has a great reputation.

Darwin Central Hotel HOTEL $$

(Map p816; ☎08-8944 9000, 1300 364 263; www.darwincentral.com.au; 21 Knuckey St; d from $180; P ❄ @ 📶 🏊 🐾; 🚌4, 5, 8, 10) Right in the centre of town, this plush independent hotel oozes contemporary style and impeccable facilities. There are a range of stylish rooms with excellent accessibility for disabled travellers. Rack rates are steep, but internet, weekend and three-night-stay discounts make it great value. The excellent breakfast caps things off nicely.

Value Inn HOTEL $$

(Map p816; ☎08-8981 4733; www.valueinn.com.au; 50 Mitchell St; d from $140; P ❄ 🏊) A great option right in the thick of the Mitchell St action but (mostly) quiet and comfortable. Value Inn lives up to its name, especially out of season. En-suite rooms are small but sleep up to three and have fridge and TV.

Palms City Resort RESORT $$

(Map p816; ☎1800 829 211, 08-8982 9200; http://palmscityresort.com; 64 The Esplanade; d motel/villas $230/280; P ❄ 📶 🏊) Consistently receiving the thumbs up from travellers, this centrally located resort is fringed by palm-filled gardens. If you covet a microwave and have space cravings, the superior motel rooms are worth a bit extra, while the Asian-influenced, hexagonal villas with outdoor spas are utterly indulgent. Butterflies and dragonflies drift between bougainvillea in the knockout gardens.

Vibe Hotel HOTEL $$$

(Map p816; ☎08-8982 9998; www.tfehotels.com/brands/vibe-hotels/vibe-hotel-darwin-waterfront; 7 Kitchener Dr; r $260-310; P ❄ @ 📶 🏊) You're in for an upmarket stay at this professional set-up with friendly staff and a great location at the Darwin Waterfront Precinct. Room prices creep upwards with more bed space and water views. The Wave Lagoon is right next door if the shady swimming pool is too placid for you.

Elan Soho Suites HOTEL, APARTMENTS $$$

(Map p816; ☎08-8981 0888; www.elansohosuites.com; 31 Woods St; r $220, 1-/2-bed apt $270/310; P ❄ 📶 🏊) This innovative newcomer was still in the midst of major renovations when we dropped in, but had just started to accept guests. Room prices (at least initially, while the place gets established) promise to be great value. Views are stunning, facilities first-rate; you can even check-in online, and unlock your room door via your mobile phone. Its restaurant 'Seoul Food' brings Korean cooking to Darwin.

Novotel Atrium HOTEL $$$

(Map p816; ☎08-8941 0755; www.novotel.com; 100 The Esplanade; d from $350, 2-bedroom apt from $470; P ❄ @ 📶 🏊) Yes, it's a chain hotel, but this one, with to-die-for ocean views, stands out from the crowd. Stylistic standards are above the norm: subtle lighting, fresh flowers and interesting Indigenous art. Breathe the sea air on your balcony or descend into the kidney-shaped swimming pool, one of the best-looking puddles in Darwin. Breakfasts are a highlight.

City Fringe & Suburbs

Discovery Holiday Park – Darwin CARAVAN PARK $

(Map p814; ☎1800 662 253, 08-8984 3330; www.discoveryholidayparks.com.au/nt/darwin/darwin; cnr Farrell Cres & Stuart Hwy, Winnellie; camp sites $34, cabins $104-184; ❄ 🏊) Caravan park with immaculate facilities, a camp kitchen, a licensed shop, a covered outdoor saltwater pool and friendly staff. Public bus 8 rolls into downtown Darwin from the corner of the street.

FreeSpirit Resort Darwin CARAVAN PARK $

(Map p828; ☎08-8935 0888; www.darwinfreespiritresort.com.au; 901 Stuart Hwy, Berrimah; camp sites $50, cabins & units $140-300; ❄ @ 📶 🏊) An impressive highway-side park about a 10-minute drive from the city, with loads of facilities (including three pools). With a jumping cushion, a kidz corner, a bar and live music in the Dry, adults and kids are easily entertained.

Vitina Studio Motel MOTEL $$

(Map p816; ☎08-8981 1544; www.vitinastudiomotel.com.au; 38 Gardens Rd; d/ste $175/250; P ❄ @ 📶 🏊) We like this place: value-for-money rooms, friendly and efficient service, and a convenient Darwin location. It's a deal. Contemporary motel rooms and larger studios with kitchenettes are on offer. It's right on the city fringe, convenient to the Gardens Park golf course, the Botanic Gardens and Mindil Beach. Keep an eye on its website for discounts.

Steeles at Larrakeyah B&B $$

(Darwin City B&B; Map p816; ☎08-8941 3636; www.darwinbnb.com.au; 4 Zealandia Cres, Larrakeyah; d from $225, 1 & 2-bedroom apts $285-410; ❄ 🏊) Some B&Bs are businesslike and others feel like you're staying with friends; Steeles is one of the latter. There are three rooms in this pleasant Spanish Mission–style home, equipped with fridges, flat-screen TVs and private entrances. The owners also run apartments nearby which have excellent facilities and Indigenous art adorning the walls.

Cullen Bay Resorts APARTMENTS **$$$**
(Map p816; 1800 625 533, 08-8981 7999; www.cullenbayresortsdarwin.com.au; 26-32 Marina Blvd; 1-bed apt with standard/sea views $310/330;) This pair of twin apartment towers boasts a million-dollar outlook over Cullen Bay marina and harbour. It's worth shelling out extra for the water views. There are restaurants a short stroll away, as is the ferry to Mandorah. You should get at least 10% off these rates if it's not busy.

Eating

Darwin is the glistening pearl in the Territory's dining scene. Eateries make the most of the tropical ambience with alfresco seating, and the quality and diversity of produce top anywhere else in the Territory.

City Centre

There are two large supermarkets in downtown Darwin: **Coles** (Map p816; 55-59 Mitchell St, Mitchell Centre; 24hr) and **Woolworths** (Map p816; cnr Cavenagh & Whitfield Sts; 6am-10pm).

Roma Bar CAFE **$**
(Map p816; 8981 6729; www.romabar.com.au; 9-11 Cavenagh St; mains $8-15; 7am-4pm Mon-Fri, 8am-2pm Sat, 8am-1pm Sun;) Roma is a local institution and the most reliable place for quality coffee in Darwin. It's a meeting place for lefties, literati and travellers. It's well away from the craziness of Mitchell St, with free wi-fi and fresh juices, and you can get anything from muesli and eggs Benedict for breakfast to excellent toasted focaccia and even fish curry for lunch.

Stokes Hill Wharf SEAFOOD, FAST FOOD **$$**
(Map p816; Stokes Hill Wharf; mains $10-20; from 11am) Squatting on the end of Stokes Hill Wharf is a hectic food centre with a dozen food counters and outdoor tables lined up along the pier. It's a pumping place for some fish and chips, oysters, a stir-fry, a laksa or just a cold sunset beer.

Crustaceans SEAFOOD **$$**
(Map p816; 08-8981 8658; www.crustaceans.net.au; Stokes Hill Wharf; mains $18-40; from 5.30pm;) This casual, licensed restaurant features fresh fish, bugs, lobster, oysters, even crocodile, as well as succulent steaks. It's all about the location, perched right at the end of Stokes Hill Wharf with sunset views over Francis Bay. The cold beer and a first-rate wine list seal the deal.

Hot Tamale MEXICAN **$$**
(Map p816; 08-8981 5471; www.hottamale.net.au; Bldg 3, 19 Kitchener Dr; mains $20-25; noon-9pm) With drink specials aplenty and a fun, laid-back attitude, this place is recommended as much for the atmosphere and brilliant waterfront location as for the delicious Mexican food. Tacos, burritos and nachos galore.

Curve CAFE **$$**
(Map p816; 08-8982 9709; 7 Kitchener Dr; mains $22-35; 6am-9pm;) Spacious and clean inside and with comfy seating out the front to catch the breeze, this all-rounder is good for a bite any time of the day. Lunch is a good deal: a burger or panini with a beer or glass of wine is $18. In the evening tuck into pan-seared Cajun tuna. It's opposite the wave lagoon – handy for families needing extra shade or something to fuel up on.

Moorish Café MIDDLE EASTERN **$$$**
(Map p816; 08-8981 0010; www.moorishcafe.com.au; 37 Knuckey St; tapas $7-11, mains $33; 9am-2.30pm & 6-10pm Tue-Fri, 9am-10pm Sat) Seductive aromas emanate from this divine terracotta-tiled cafe fusing North African, Mediterranean and Middle Eastern delights. The tapas can be a bit hit-and-miss but dishes such as the pork belly with chilli-chocolate sauce and Berber spiced kangaroo are tasty and reliable. It's a lovely dining experience, especially with a table overlooking the street.

Hanuman INDIAN, THAI **$$$**
(Map p816; 08-8941 3500; www.hanuman.com.au; 93 Mitchell St; mains $19-38; noon-2.30pm, dinner from 6pm;) Ask most locals about fine dining in Darwin and they'll usually mention Hanuman. It's sophisticated but not stuffy. Enticing aromas of innovative Indian and Thai Nonya dishes waft from the kitchen to the stylish open dining room and deck. The menu is broad, with exotic vegetarian choices and banquets also available.

Char Restaurant STEAK **$$$**
(Map p816; 08-8981 4544; www.charrestaurant.com.au; cnr The Esplanade & Knuckey St; mains $30-60; noon-3pm Wed-Fri, 6-11pm daily) Housed in the grounds of the historic Admiralty House is Char, a carnivore's paradise. The speciality here is chargrilled steaks –

aged, grain-fed and cooked to perfection – but there's also a range of clever seafood creations such as banana prawn and crab tian, with avocado purée and *tobiko* caviar.

City Fringe & Suburbs

Laneway Speciality Coffee CAFE **$**
(Map p814; ☎08-8941 4511; 4/1 Vickers St, Parap; mains $12-18; ⏲8am-3pm Mon-Sat) The pared-back, industrial interior, corner location and powerhouse coffee here have locals wondering if they could be in Melbourne. Getting rave reviews, this place is fast becoming popular. Its well-prepared dishes use local and organic ingredients; the almost artistic bacon and egg roll is worth the trip here alone. For lunch the Wagyu beef burger beckons.

Cyclone Cafe CAFE **$**
(Map p814; www.parapvillage.com.au; 8 Urquhart St, Parap; meals $12-18; ⏲7.30am-3pm Mon-Fri, 8.30am-noon Sat) Cyclone's decor is all rusty corrugated iron, although it's surprisingly cosy inside, with local art on the walls, upbeat staff and strong, aromatic coffee (try the triple-shot 'Hypercino'). The menu is diverse offering breakfast goodies such as Middle Eastern eggs, spinach, feta, lemon rind and dukkah on a muffin. Yummy. Lunch is salads, burgers and melts.

Eva's Cafe CAFE **$**
(Map p816; George Brown Botanic Gardens; mains $8-14; ⏲7am-3pm) Brought to Darwin by ship in 1897, this lovely Methodist church building provides an atmospheric respite in Darwin's botanic gardens. The outdoor areas, including shaded deck in the rear, means it's favoured by parents and kids. Breakfast is short and sweet – think muesli and toasties – while sandwiches and salads feature at lunchtime.

★Exotic North Indian Cuisine INDIAN **$$**
(Map p816; ☎08-8941 3396; http://exoticnorthindiancuisine.com.au; Cullen Bay Marina; mains $15-20; ⏲from 5pm; 👪) Offering outstanding value for quality Indian cuisine, this place has taken over the mantle of Darwin's best Indian restaurant. It's positioned right on the waterfront at Cullen Bay, making for extremely pleasant waterside dining in the evening. The service is attentive, there are high chairs for young 'uns and, unusually for Darwin, you can BYO wine.

★Darwin Ski Club MODERN AUSTRALIAN **$$**
(Map p814; ☎08-8981 6630; www.darwinskiclub.com.au; Conacher St, Fannie Bay; mains $18-24; ⏲1-9pm) This place just keeps getting better. Already Darwin's finest location for a sunset beer, it now does seriously good tucker too. The dishes are well prepared, and the menu is thoughtful and enticing. We had the pork belly and were astonished with the quality of the dish, while the chorizo and barramundi linguine also gets the thumbs up. Highly recommended by locals.

LOCAL KNOWLEDGE

PARAP VILLAGE MARKET

Parap Village is a foodie's heaven with several good restaurants, bars and cafes as well as the highly recommended deli **Parap Fine Foods** (Map p814; ☎08-8981 8597; www.parapfinefoods.com; 40 Parap Rd, Parap; ⏲8am-6.30pm Mon-Fri, to 6pm Sat, 9am-1pm Sun). However, it's the Saturday morning **markets** (p825) that attract locals like bees to honey. It's got a relaxed vibe as breakfast merges into brunch and then lunch. Between visits to the takeaway food stalls (most serving spicy Southeast Asian snacks) shoppers stock up on tropical fruit and vegetables – all you need to make your own laksa or rendang. The produce is local so you know it's fresh.

Cornucopia Cafe CAFE **$$**
(Map p814; ☎08-8941 9009; Bullocky Point, Conacher St, Fannie Bay; mains $20-30; ⏲9am-5pm Mon-Sat & 5.30-8.30pm Wed-Sat) Appended to the museum and gallery, this cafe makes for a good stop while you're in the 'hood. The outdoor eating area is breezy and scenic, overlooking the water. The menu is varied and has great salads including Thai grilled beef or octopus. For something more filling, local barra and wagyu rump round out the options.

Eat a Pizza PIZZA **$$**
(Map p816; ☎08-8941 0963; 1/57 Marina Blvd, Cullen Bay; large pizzas $22, pasta $18; ⏲5-10pm Tue-Sun) A long-time family-owned business just across the road from the waterfront at Cullen Bay. The large, shaded, outdoor dining area is often buzzing with contented diners tucking into scrumptious homemade pizza and pasta dishes.

Pavonia Place MODERN AUSTRALIAN **$$**
(Map p814; ☎08-8948 1515; www.pavoniaplace.com.au; 2 Pavonia Place, Nightcliff; mains $26-36; ⏲5.30pm-late Tue-Sat) A hidden gem in the backstreets of Nightcliff. Pavonia has a great take on modern Australian fusion cuisine; the oven-baked eggplant filled with

broccoli, creamy goat's cheese, garlic cloves, mushroom and cherry tomatoes goes down a treat. It uses fresh local ingredients and the dining area is spacious but also intimate.

Pee Wee's at the Point MODERN AUSTRALIAN **$$$**
(Map p814; ☎08-8981 6868; www.peewees.com.au; Alec Fong Lim Dr, East Point Reserve; mains $40-50; ⊙from 6.30pm) With lobster tail kicking in at $70 a serve, this is indeed a place for a treat. One of Darwin's finest restaurants, it is well worth shelling out for the experience. Enjoy your lemongrass, ginger and duck-stock-braised pork belly among tropical palms at East Point Reserve, right on the waterfront.

Drinking & Nightlife

Drinking is big business in tropical Darwin (cold beer and humidity have a symbiotic relationship), and the city has dozens of pubs and terrace bars that make the most of balmy evenings. Virtually all bars double as restaurants, especially along Mitchell St – a frenzied row of booze rooms full of travellers, all within stumbling distance of one another.

★**Darwin Ski Club** PUB
(Map p814; ☎080-8981 6630; www.darwinskiclub.com.au; Conacher St, Fannie Bay) Leave Mitchell St behind and head for a sublime sunset at this laid-back water-ski club on Vestey's Beach. The view through the palm trees from the beer garden is a winner, and there are often live bands. Hands down best venue for a sunset beer in Darwin.

Bogarts BAR
(Map p814; ☎08-8981 3561; 52 Gregory St, Parap; ⊙4pm-late Tue-Sat) Bogarts is one of Darwin's best bars and well worth the trek out into the suburbs. The decor is old movie posters, cane furniture and animal-print lounges in a mishmash that, strangely enough, works beautifully. It has a low-key ambience and is a local favourite for the over-30s crowd.

Tap on Mitchell BAR
(Map p816; www.thetap.com.au; 51 Mitchell St) One of the busiest and best of the Mitchell St terrace bars, the Tap is always buzzing and there are inexpensive meals (nachos, burgers, calamari) to complement a great range of beer and wine.

Beachfront Hotel PUB
(☎08-8985 3000; 342 Casuarina Dr, Rapid Creek) Close to the border of Nightcliff, this rollicking pub attracts a local crowd and often has bands. A spot out on the breezy front deck with a cold drink is ideal.

Deck Bar BAR
(Map p816; www.thedeckbar.com.au; 22 Mitchell St) At the nonpartying parliamentary end of Mitchell St, the Deck Bar still manages to get lively with happy hours, pub trivia and regular live music. Blurring the line between indoors and outdoors brilliantly, the namesake deck is perfect for people-watching.

Discovery & Lost Arc CLUB
(Map p816; www.discoverydarwin.com.au; 89 Mitchell St) Discovery is Darwin's biggest nightclub and dance venue, with three levels featuring hip hop, techno and house, bars, private booths, karaoke, an elevated dance floor and plenty of partygoers. The Lost Arc is the classy chill-out bar opening on to Mitchell St, which starts to thaw after about 10pm.

✩ Entertainment

Darwin's balmy nights invite a bit of late-night exploration and while there are only a handful of nightclubs, you'll find something on every night of the week. There's also a thriving arts and entertainment scene: theatre, film and concerts.

Off the Leash (www.offtheleash.net.au) magazine lists events happening around town, as does **Darwin Community Arts** (www.darwincommunityarts.org.au). Keep an eye out for bills posted on noticeboards and telegraph poles that advertise dance and full-moon parties.

Just about every pub/bar in town puts on some form of live music, mostly on Friday and Saturday nights, and sometimes filling the midweek void with karaoke and DJs.

Throb CLUB
(Map p816; 64 Smith St; ⊙11pm-4am Fri & Sat) Darwin's premier gay- and lesbian-friendly nightclub and cocktail bar, Throb attracts partygoers of all genders and persuasions for its hot DJs and cool atmosphere. Hosts drag shows and touring live acts. Don't miss the Batman & Throbbin' show on Friday.

★**Deckchair Cinema** CINEMA
(Map p816; ☎08-8981 0700; www.deckchaircinema.com; Jervois Rd, Waterfront Precinct; adult/child $16/8; ⊙box office from 6.30pm Apr-Nov) During the Dry, the Darwin Film Society runs this fabulous outdoor cinema below the southern end of the Esplanade. Watch a movie under the stars while reclining in a deckchair. There's a licensed bar serving food or you can bring a picnic (no BYO alcohol). There are usually double features on Friday and Saturday nights (adult/child $24/12).

Birch Carroll & Coyle CINEMA
(Map p816; ☎08-8981 5999; www.eventcinemas.com.au; 76 Mitchell St; adult/child $19/14.50) Darwin's mainstream cinema complex, screening latest-release films across five theatres. Head down on Tropical Tuesday for $12.50 entry.

Darwin Entertainment Centre ARTS CENTRE
(Map p816; ☎08-8980 3333; www.darwinentertainment.com.au; 93 Mitchell St; ⌚box office 10am-5.30pm Mon-Fri & 1hr prior to shows) Darwin's main community arts venue houses the Playhouse and Studio Theatres, and hosts events from fashion-award nights to plays, rock operas, comedies and concerts.

Brown's Mart PERFORMING ARTS
(Map p816; ☎08-8981 5522; www.brownsmart.com.au; 12 Smith St) This historic venue (a former mining exchange) features live theatre performances, music and short films.

Happy Yess LIVE MUSIC
(Map p816; happyyess.tumblr.com; 12 Smith St, Browns Mart) This venue is Darwin's leading place for live music. It's run by musicians so you won't hear cover bands in here. Original, sometimes weird, always fun.

Darwin Railway Club LIVE MUSIC
(Map p814; ☎08 8981 4171; www.darwinrailwayclub.com; 17 Somerville Gardens, Parap) Big supporters of Darwin's live-music scene, this place pulls in some class acts.

Shopping

You don't have to walk far along the Smith St Mall to find a souvenir shop selling lousy NT souvenirs: tea towels, T-shirts, stubbie holders and cane-toad coin purses (most of it made in China). Also in oversupply are outlets selling Aboriginal arts and crafts (be informed about reliable operators; see p826). Darwin's fabulous markets sell unique handcrafted items such as seed-pod hats, shell jewellery, kites, clothing and original photos.

NT General Store OUTDOOR EQUIPMENT
(Map p816; ☎08-8981 8242; www.thentgeneralstore.com.au; 42 Cavenagh St; ⌚8.30am-5.30pm Mon-Wed, to 6pm Thu & Fri, to 1pm Sat) This casual, corrugated-iron warehouse has shelves piled high with camping and bushwalking gear, as well as a range of maps.

Aboriginal Fine Arts Gallery ARTS
(Map p816; www.aaia.com.au; 1st fl, cnr Mitchell & Knuckey Sts; ⌚9am-5pm) Displays and sells art from Arnhem Land and the central desert region.

DARWIN'S MAGICAL MARKETS

Mindil Beach Sunset Market (Map p816; www.mindil.com.au; off Gilruth Ave; ⌚5-10pm Thu, 4-9pm Sun May-Oct) Food is the main attraction here – from Thai, Sri Lankan, Indian, Chinese and Malaysian to Brazilian, Greek, Portuguese and more – all at around $6 to $12 a serve. But that's only half the fun – arts and crafts stalls bulge with handmade jewellery, fabulous rainbow tie-dyed clothes, Aboriginal artefacts, and wares from Indonesia and Thailand. Mindil Beach is about 2km from Darwin's city centre; an easy walk or hop on buses 4 or 6 which go past the market area.

As the sun heads towards the horizon, half of Darwin descends on the market, with tables, chairs, rugs, grog and kids in tow. Peruse and promenade, stop for a pummelling massage or to listen to rhythmic live music. Don't miss a flaming satay stick from Bobby's brazier. Top it off with fresh fruit salad, decadent cakes or luscious crêpes.

Similar stalls (you'll recognise many of the stallholders) can be found at various suburban markets from Friday to Sunday.

Parap Village Market (Map p814; www.parapvillage.com.au; Parap Shopping Village, Parap Rd, Parap; ⌚8am-2pm Sat) This compact, crowded food-focused market is a local favourite. There's the full gamut of Southeast Asian cuisine, as well as plenty of ingredients to cook up your own tropical storm.

Rapid Creek Market (Map p814; www.rapidcreekshoppingcentre.com.au; 48 Trower Rd, Rapid Creek; ⌚6.30am-1.30pm Sun) Darwin's oldest market is an Asian marketplace, with a tremendous range of tropical fruit and vegetables mingled with a heady mixture of spices and swirling satay smoke.

Nightcliff Market (Map p814; www.nightcliffmarkets.com.au; Pavonia Way, Nightcliff; ⌚6am-2pm Sun) A popular community market north of the city in the Nightcliff Shopping Centre. You'll will find lots of secondhand goods and designer clothing.

BUYING ABORIGINAL ART

Taking home a piece of Aboriginal art can create an enduring connection with Australia. For Aboriginal artists, painting is an important cultural and economic enterprise. To ensure you're not perpetuating non-Indigenous cash-in on Aboriginal art's popularity, avoid buying cheap imported fridge magnets, stubbie holders, boomerangs or didgeridoos. Make sure you're buying from an authentic dealer selling original art, and if the gallery doesn't pay their artists upfront, ask exactly how much of your money will make it back to the artist or community.

A good test is to request some biographical info on the artists – if the vendor can't produce it, keep walking. An authentic piece will come with a certificate indicating the artist's name, language group and community, and the work's title, its story and when it was made.

You may also check that the selling gallery is associated with a regulatory body, such as the **Australian Commercial Galleries Association** (www.acga.com.au). Where possible, buy direct from Aboriginal arts centres or their city outlets (see www.ankaaa.org.au or www.aboriginalart.org); this is generally cheaper and ensures authenticity. You also get to view the works in the context in which they were created.

Mbantua Fine Art Gallery ARTS
(Map p816; ☎08-8941 6611; www.mbantua.com.au; 2/30 Smith St Mall; ⏲9am-5pm Mon-Sat) Vivid Utopian designs painted on everything from canvases to ceramics.

Tiwi Art Network ARTS
(Map p814; ☎08-8941 3593; www.tiwiart.com; 3/3 Vickers St, Parap; ⏲10am-5pm Wed-Fri, to 2pm Sat) The office and showroom for three arts communities on the Tiwi Islands.

Information

EMERGENCY

AANT Roadside Assistance (☎13 11 11; www.aant.com.au) Roadside assistance.

Ambulance (☎000) For emergencies.

Fire (☎000; www.nt.gov.au/pfes)

Poisons Information Centre (☎13 11 26; ⏲24hr) Advice on poisons, bites and stings.

Police (☎000; www.nt.gov.au/pfes) For local police service.

INTERNET ACCESS

Most accommodation in Darwin provides some form of internet access, and there is free wi-fi available in Smith Street Mall.

Northern Territory Library (☎1800 019 155; www.ntl.nt.gov.au; Parliament House, Mitchell St; ⏲10am-5pm Mon-Fri, 1-5pm Sat & Sun; wi-fi) Book ahead for free access. Wi-fi also available.

MEDICAL SERVICES

Royal Darwin Hospital (☎08-8920 6011; www.health.nt.gov.au; Rocklands Dr, Tiwi; ⏲24hr) Accident and emergency.

MONEY

There are 24-hour ATMs dotted around the city centre, and exchange bureaux on Mitchell St.

POST

General Post Office (Map p816; ☎13 13 18; www.auspost.com.au; 48 Cavenagh St; ⏲9am-5pm Mon-Fri, to 12.30pm Sat) Efficient poste restante.

TOURIST INFORMATION

Tourism Top End (Map p816; ☎1300 138 886, 08-8980 6000; www.tourismtopend.com.au; cnr Smith & Bennett Sts; ⏲8.30am-5pm Mon-Fri, 9am-3pm Sat & Sun) is a helpful office with hundreds of brochures; books tours and accommodation.

Getting There & Away

AIR

Apart from the following major carriers arriving at Darwin International Airport (p811), smaller routes are flown by local operators; ask a travel agent.

Airnorth (☎1800 627 474; www.airnorth.com.au) To/from East Timor, Broome, Perth, Kununurra and the Gold Coast.

Jetstar (www.jetstar.com) Direct flights to the eastern coast capitals and major hubs, as well as several Southeast Asian cities.

Qantas (www.qantas.com.au) Direct flights to Perth, Adelaide, Canberra, Sydney, Brisbane, Alice Springs and Cairns.

Virgin Australia (www.virginaustralia.com) Direct flights between Darwin and Brisbane, Broome, Melbourne, Sydney and Perth.

BUS

Greyhound Australia (Map p816; www.greyhound.com.au) operates long-distance bus services from the **Transit Centre** (Map p816; www.enjoy-darwin.com/transit-bus.html; 69 Mitchell St). There's at least one service per day up and down the Stuart Hwy, stopping at Pine Creek (three hours), Katherine (4½ hours),

Mataranka (seven hours), Tennant Creek (14½ hours) and Alice Springs (22 hours).

For Kakadu, there's a daily return service from Darwin to Jabiru ($66, 3½ hours).

Backpacker buses can also get you to out-of-the-way places.

Adventure Tours (☎1300 654 604; www.adventuretours.com.au; 52 Mitchell St) Has a good reputation.

Oz Experience (www.ozexperience.com) Makes backpacking to Alice Springs easy.

CAR & CAMPERVAN

For driving around Darwin, conventional vehicles are cheap enough, but most companies offer only 100km per day free, which won't get you very far out of town. Rates start at around $40 per day for a small car with 100km per day.

There are also plenty of 4WD vehicles available in Darwin, but you usually have to book ahead and fees/deposits are higher than for 2WD vehicles. Larger companies offer one-way rentals plus better mileage deals for more-expensive vehicles. Campervans are a great option for touring around the Territory and you generally get unlimited kilometres even for short rentals. Prices start at around $60 a day for a basic camper or $100 to $120 for a three-berth hi-top camper, to $220-plus for the bigger mobile homes or 4WD bushcampers. Additional insurance cover or excess reduction costs extra.

Most rental companies are open every day and have agencies in the city centre. Avis, Budget, Hertz and Thrifty all have offices at the airport.

Britz Australia (www.britz.com.au; 17 Bombing Rd, Winnellie) Britz is a reliable outfit with a big range of campervans and motorhomes, including 4WD bushcampers.

JJ's Car Hire (www.jjscarhire.com.au; 7 Goyder Rd, Parap) Good local operator.

Mighty Cars & Campervans (www.mightycampers.com.au; 17 Bombing Rd, Winnellie) At the same depot as Britz, this is a budget outfit with small campers and hi-tops at reasonable rates.

Travellers Autobarn (www.travellers-autobarn.com.au; 13 Daly St) Campervan specialist.

TRAIN

The legendary Ghan train, operated by **Great Southern Rail** (www.gsr.com.au), runs weekly (twice weekly May to July) between Adelaide and Darwin via Alice Springs. The Darwin terminus is on Berrimah Rd, 15km/20 minutes from the city centre. A taxi fare into the centre is about $30, though there is a shuttle service to/from the Transit Centre.

ℹ Getting Around

TO/FROM THE AIRPORT

Darwin International Airport (p811) is 12km north of the city centre, and handles both international and domestic flights. **Darwin Airport Shuttle** (☎08-8981 5066; www.darwinairportshuttle.com.au) will pick up or drop off almost anywhere in the centre for $16. When leaving Darwin book a day before departure. A taxi fare into the centre is about $35.

PUBLIC TRANSPORT

Darwinbus (Map p816; www.nt.gov.au/transport) runs a comprehensive bus network that departs from the **Darwin Bus Terminus** (Map p816; Harry Chan Ave), opposite Brown's Mart.

A $3 adult ticket gives unlimited travel on the bus network for three hours (validate your ticket when you first get on). Daily ($7) and weekly ($20) travel cards are also available from bus interchanges, newsagencies and the visitor information centre. Bus 4 (to Fannie Bay, Nightcliff, Rapid Creek and Casuarina) and bus 6 (Fannie Bay, Parap and Stuart Park) are useful for getting to Aquascene, the Botanic Gardens, Mindil Beach, the Museum & Art Gallery, Fannie Bay Gaol Museum, East Point Reserve and the markets.

SCOOTER

Darwin Scooter Hire (☎08-8941 2434; www.thescootershop.com.au; 9 Daly St) Rents out mountain bikes/50cc scooters/motorbikes for $20/60/180 per day.

TAXI

Taxis wait along Knuckey St, diagonally opposite the north end of Smith St Mall, and are usually easy to flag down. Call **Darwin Radio Taxis** (☎13 10 08; www.131008.com).

AROUND DARWIN

Mandorah

Mandorah is a low-key, relaxed residential **beach suburb** looking out across the harbour to Darwin. It sits on the tip of Cox Peninsula, 128km by road from Darwin but only 6km across the harbour by regular ferry. The main reason to visit is for the ferry ride across the harbour and to throw in a fishing line off the jetty here. The nearby Wagait Aboriginal community numbers around 400 residents. Sadly, the Mandorah Beach Hotel has now closed.

The **Mandorah Ferry** (Map p816; www.sealinknt.com.au; adult/child return $25/12.50) operates about a dozen daily services (adult/child return $25/12.50), with the first departure from the Cullen Bay Marina in Darwin at 5.45am and the last at 11pm (midnight on Friday and Saturday). The last ferry from Mandorah is at 11.20pm (12.20am Friday and Saturday). Bookings not required.

Around Darwin

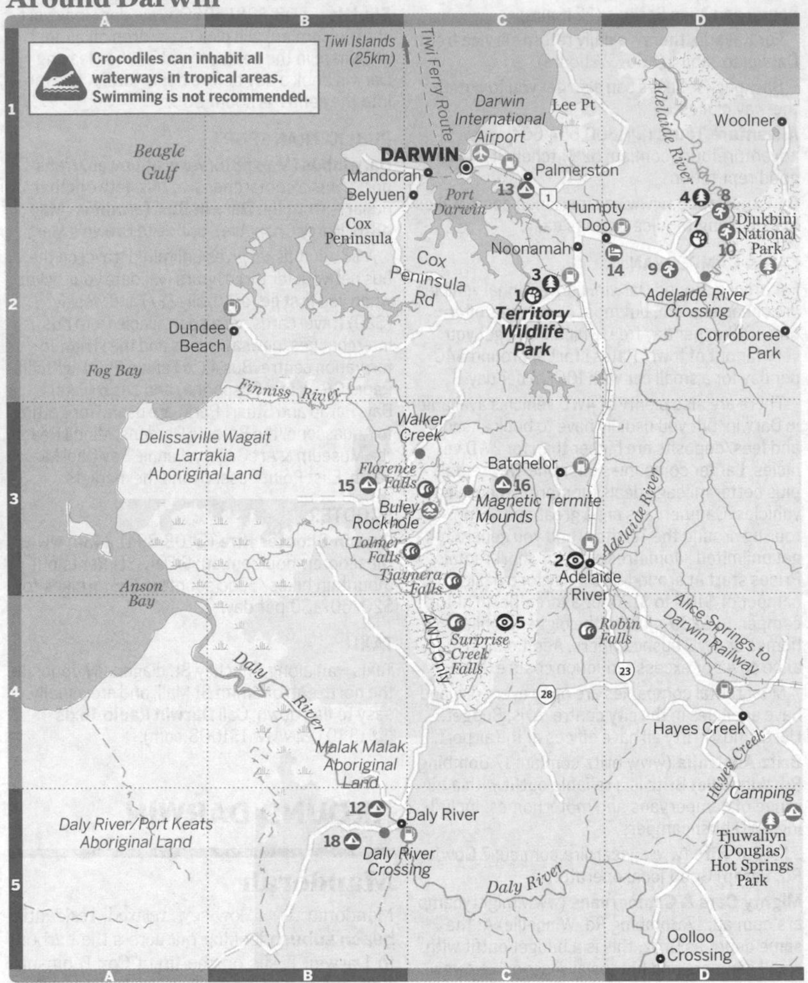

Tiwi Islands

The Tiwi Islands – **Bathurst Island** and **Melville Island** – lie about 80km north of Darwin, and are home to the Tiwi Aboriginal people. The Tiwis ('We People') have a distinct culture and today are well known for producing vibrant art and the occasional champion Aussie Rules football player.

Tourism is restricted on the islands and for most tourists the only way to visit is on one of the daily organised tours from Darwin.

The Tiwis' island homes kept them fairly isolated from mainland developments until the 20th century, and their culture has retained several unique features. Perhaps the best known are the pukumani (burial poles), carved and painted with symbolic and mythological figures, which are erected around graves. More recently the Tiwis have turned their hand to art for sale: carving, painting, textile screen-printing, batik and pottery using traditional designs and motifs. The Bima Wear textile factory was set up in 1969 to employ Tiwi women, and today makes many bright fabrics in distinctive designs.

The main settlement on the islands is **Nguiu** in the southeast of Bathurst Island, which was founded in 1911 as a Catholic mis-

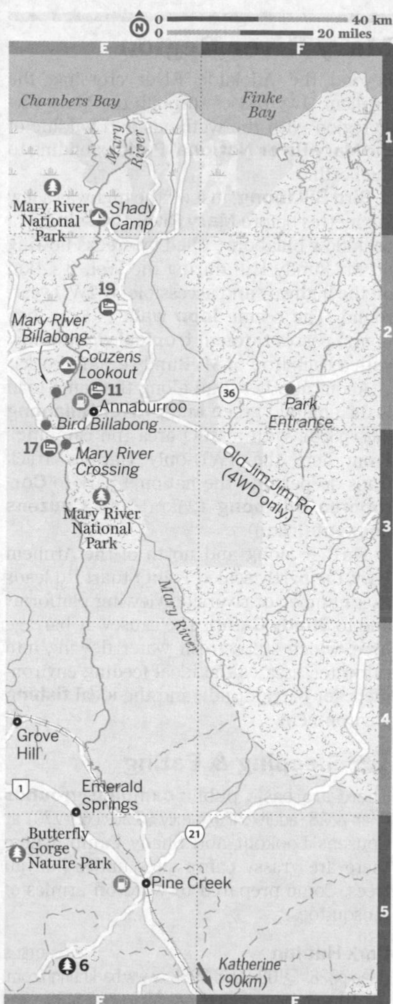

Around Darwin

sion. On Melville Island the settlements are **Pirlangimpi** and **Milikapiti**.

Most of the 2700 Tiwi Islanders live on Bathurst Island (there are about 900 people on Melville Island). Most follow a mainly nontraditional lifestyle, but they still hunt dugong and gather turtle eggs, and hunting and gathering usually supplements the mainland diet a couple of times a week. Tiwis also go back to their traditional lands on Melville Island for a few weeks each year to teach and to learn traditional culture. Descendants of the Japanese pearl divers who regularly visited here early last century also live on Melville Island.

Aussie Rules football is a passion among the islanders and one of the biggest events of the year (and the only time it's possible to visit without a permit or on a tour) is the **Tiwi football grand-final** day in late March. Huge numbers of people come across from the mainland for the event – book your tour/ferry well in advance.

Tours

There's no public transport on the islands, so the best way to see them is on a tour. You can catch the **Tiwi Ferry** over to Nguiu and have a look around the town without taking a tour or buying a permit, but if you want to explore further you'll need a permit from the Tiwi Land Council (p811).

Tiwi Tours Aboriginal Cultural Experience CULTURAL

(☎1300 228 546; www.aatkings.com/tours/tiwi-tours-aboriginal-cultural-experience) Runs fascinating day trips to the Tiwis, although interaction with the local community tends to be limited to your guides and the local workshops and showrooms. The tour is available by ferry (adult/child $250/125, two and a half hours each way Thursday and Friday) or air (adult/child $275/138, 20 minutes each way, Monday to Wednesday)

The tour includes permit, welcome ceremony, craft workshops, and visits to the early Catholic-mission buildings, the Patakijiyali Museum and a pukumani burial site.

Tiwi by Design CULTURAL TOUR
(Map p816; ☎1300 130 679; www.sealinknt.com.au; adult $319) Leaving from Cullen Bay ferry terminal at 7.30am on Thursday and Friday, this tour includes permits, lunch and a welcome ceremony, as well as visits to a local museum, church and art workshop, where you get to create your own design. It's run by Sealink, the ferry operator.

Ferry only prices to get to the island are adult/child $80/40.

Arnhem Highway

The Arnhem Hwy (Rte 36) branches off towards Kakadu 34km southeast of Darwin. About 10km along the road, in the small agricultural hub of Humpty Doo, the self-proclaimed 'world famous' **Humpty Doo Hotel** (Map p828; ☎08-8988 1372; www.humptydoohotel.net; Arnhem Hwy; d/cabins $130/150;) is a brawling kinda roadhouse, serving big meals (mains $20 to $30, lunch and dinner). There are unremarkable motel rooms and cabins out the back.

About 15km beyond Humpty Doo is the turn-off to the fecund green carpet of **Fogg Dam Conservation Reserve** (Map p828; www.foggdamfriends.org). Bring your binoculars – there are ludicrous numbers of waterbirds living here. The dam walls are closed to walkers (crocs), but there are a couple of nature walks (2.2km and 3.6km) through the forest and woodlands. Bird numbers are highest between December and July.

Three kilometres past the Fogg Dam turn-off, is the dashing-looking **Window on the Wetlands Visitor Centre** (Map p828; www.nretas.nt.gov.au/national-parks-and-reserves/parks/windowwetlands; Arnhem Hwy; 8am-5.30pm) FREE full of displays (static and interactive) explaining the wetland ecosystem, as well as the history of the local Limilgnan-Wulna Aboriginal people. There are great views over the Adelaide River floodplain from the observation deck, and binoculars for studying the waterbirds on Lake Beatrice.

A further 8km beyond the Window on the Wetlands Visitor Centre is **Adelaide River Crossing**. It's from the murky waters of this river that large crocs are tempted to jump for camera-wielding tourists.

Mary River Region

Beyond the Adelaide River crossing, the Arnhem Hwy passes through the Mary River region with the wetlands and wildlife of the **Mary River National Park** extending to the north.

Bird Billabong, just off the highway a few kilometres before **Mary River Crossing**, is a back-flow billabong, filled by creeks flowing off Mt Bundy Hill during the Wet. It's 4km off the highway and accessible by 2WD year-round. The scenic **loop walk** (4.5km, two hours) passes through **tropical woodlands**, with a backdrop of Mt Bundy granite rocks.

About another 2km along the same road is the emerald green **Mary River Billabong** (Map p828), with a BBQ area (no camping). From here the 4WD-only Hardies Track leads deeper into the national park to **Corroboree Billabong** (25km) and **Couzens Lookout** (37km).

Further along and north of the Arnhem Hwy, the partly sealed Point Stuart Rd leads to a number of riverside viewing platforms and to **Shady Camp**. The causeway barrage here, which stops fresh water flowing into saltwater, creates the ideal feeding environment for barramundi, and the ideal **fishing** environment.

Sleeping & Eating

There are basic public **camping grounds** (Map p828; adult/child/family $3.30/1.65/7.70) at Couzens Lookout and Shady Camp, where there are grassy camp sites under banyan trees. Come prepared to ward off armies of mosquitoes.

Bark Hut Inn HOTEL $
(Map p828; ☎08-8978 8988; www.barkhutinn.com.au; Arnhem Hwy; budget s/d $50/65, d $130, villas $200) The Bark Hut is a big barn of a place with beefy bistro meals (mains $15 to $26) and some interesting buffalo-farming history on display. The art gallery is really an opportunity to flog souvenirs, but it's worth dropping in to see Franklin, the yellow-faced turtle.

Mary River Wilderness Retreat RESORT $$
(Map p828; ☎08-8978 8877; www.maryriverpark.com.au; Arnhem Hwy, Mary River Crossing; unpowered/powered sites $24/33, cabins $130-220;) Boasting 3km of Mary River frontage, this bush retreat has excellent poolside and bush cabins with decks surrounded by trees. Pool cabins are the pick of the bunch with high ceilings, walk-in showers and more space to knock around in; both sleep

up to three people. Camping on the grassy slopes here is delightful.

Go on a croc cruise ($50), hire a fishing boat, or ask about fishing charters; bookings essential.

Wildman Wilderness Lodge RESORT **$$$**
(Map p828; ☎08-8978 8955; www.wildmanwildernesslodge.com.au; Point Stuart Rd; safari tents/cabins $550/700;) Wildman Wilderness Lodge is out-and-out an upmarket safari lodge with an exceptional program of optional tours and activities. There are just 10 air-conditioned stylish cabins and 15 fan-cooled luxury tents. The daily tariff includes a three-course dinner and breakfast.

Stuart Highway to Litchfield National Park

Territory Wildlife Park & Berry Springs Nature Park

The turn-off to the Territory Wildlife Park and Berry Springs is 48km down the Stuart Hwy from Darwin; it's then about 10km to the park.

Sights & Activities

★**Territory Wildlife Park** ZOO
(Map p828; ☎08-8988 7200; www.territorywildlifepark.com.au; 960 Cox Peninsula Rd; adult/child/family $26/13/45.50; 8.30am-6pm, last admission 4pm) This excellent park showcases the best of Aussie wildlife. Pride of place must go to the aquarium, where a clear walk-through tunnel puts you among giant barramundi, stingrays, sawfish and saratogas, while a separate tank holds a 3.8m saltwater crocodile. To see everything you can either walk around the 4km perimeter road, or hop on and off the shuttle trains that run every 15 to 30 minutes and stop at all the exhibits.

Highlights include the Flight Deck, where birds of prey display their dexterity (free-flying demonstrations at 11am and 2.30pm daily); the nocturnal house, where you can observe nocturnal fauna such as bilbies and bats; 11 different habitat aviaries; and a huge walk-through aviary, representing a monsoon rainforest.

Berry Springs Nature Park NATURE RESERVE
(Map p828; www.parksandwildlife.nt.gov.au/parks/find/berrysprings; 8am-6.30pm) This wonderful waterhole is the closest to Darwin and very popular with locals. It's a beautiful series of spring-fed swimming holes shaded by paperbarks and pandanus palms and serenaded by abundant birds. Facilities include a kiosk, a picnic area with BBQs, toilets, changing sheds and showers. And there are large grassed areas to lounge around on in between swims.

The turn-off to Berry Springs is 48km down the Stuart Hwy from Darwin; it's then about 10km to the park.

Batchelor

POP 538

The government once gave Batchelor's blocks of land away to encourage settlement in the little town. That was before uranium was discovered and the nearby **Rum Jungle mine** developed (it closed in 1971 after operating for almost 20 years). These days, Batchelor exists as a gateway and service centre for neighbouring Litchfield National Park (p832).

Sleeping & Eating

Litchfield Tourist Park CARAVAN PARK **$**
(Map p828; ☎08-8976 0070; www.litchfieldtouristpark.com.au; 2916 Litchfield Park Rd; camp sites $35, bunkhouse $75, ensuite cabins $150-240;) Just 4km from Litchfield, there's a great range of accommodation here and it's the closest option to the park. There's also a breezy, open-sided bar/restaurant (all-day food $10 to $18, open breakfast and dinner) where you can get a beer, a burger or a real coffee.

Pandanus AUSTRALIAN **$**
(☎08-8976 0242; www.pandanuslitchfield.com.au; 275 Litchfield Park Rd; budget r $50, cabin $115, mains $10-15) This handy little place has some great value accommodation but the real reason to stay, or at least stop in, is the food. The restaurant here specialises in Australian indigenous ingredients and puts an Aussie twist on most dishes. Wattleseed damper anyone? The menu uses the language of the local Koongurrukun people. It's a real gem and great value too. Pandanus is 2.5km past the Litchfield Park Road turn-off.

Batchelor Butterfly Farm RESORT **$$**
(☎08-8976 0199; 8 Meneling Rd; d $120-170;) This compact retreat divides itself between a low-key tourist attraction and friendly tropical-style resort. The kids will love the butterfly farm (adult/child $10/5) and mini zoo, which is free for staying guests. There are ensuite cabins, a large homestay

and a busy all-day cafe/restaurant (mains $20 to $30) featuring Asian-inspired dishes. It's all a bit Zen with Buddha statues, chill music and wicker chairs on the shaded deck.

Litchfield National Park

It may not be as well known as Kakadu, but many Territory locals rate Litchfield even higher. In fact, there's a local saying that goes: 'Litchfield-do, Kaka-don't'. We don't entirely agree – we think Kaka-do-too – but this is certainly one of the best places in the Top End for **bushwalking**, **camping** and especially **swimming**, with waterfalls plunging into gorgeous, safe swimming holes.

The 1500-sq-km national park encloses much of the spectacular Tabletop Range, a wide sandstone plateau mostly surrounded by cliffs. The **waterfalls** that pour off the edge of this plateau are a highlight of the park, feeding crystal-clear cascades and croc-free plunge pools.

The two routes to Litchfield (115km south of Darwin) from the Stuart Hwy join up and loop through the park. The southern access road via Batchelor is all sealed, while the northern access route, off the Cox Peninsula Rd, is partly unsealed, corrugated and often closed in the Wet.

About 17km after entering the park from Batchelor you come to what look like tombstones. But only the very tip of these **magnetic termite mounds** is used to bury the dead; at the bottom are the king and queen, with workers in between. They're perfectly aligned to regulate temperature, catching the morning sun, then allowing the residents to dodge the midday heat. Nearby are some giant mounds made by the aptly named cathedral termites.

Another 6km further along is the turn-off to **Buley Rockhole** (2km), where water cascades through a series of rock pools big enough to lodge your bod in. This turn-off also takes you to **Florence Falls** (5km), accessed by a 15-minute, 135-step descent to a deep, beautiful pool surrounded by monsoon forest. Alternatively, you can see the falls from a lookout, 120m from the car park. There's a walking track (1.7km, 45 minutes) between the two places that follows Florence Creek.

About 18km beyond the turn-off to Florence Falls is the turn-off to the spectacular **Tolmer Falls**, which are for looking at only. A 1.6km loop track (45 minutes) offers beautiful views of the valley.

It's a further 7km along the main road to the turn-off for Litchfield's big-ticket attraction, **Wangi Falls** (pronounced *Wong*-guy), 1.6km up a side road. The falls flow year-round, spilling either side of a huge orange-rock outcrop and filling an enormous swimming hole bordered by rainforest. Bring swimming goggles to spot local fish. It's immensely popular during the Dry (when there's a portable refreshment kiosk here; and, in a Territory first, free public

JUMPING CROCS

Few people seem to be able to resist the sight of a 3m-long saltwater crocodile launching itself out of the water towards a hunk of meat. Like a well-trained circus act, these wild crocs know where to get a free feed – and down on the Adelaide River, a croc-jumping show is guaranteed.

Jumping out of the water to grab prey is actually natural behaviour for crocs, usually to take surprised birds or animals from overhanging branches. They use their powerful tails to propel themselves up from a stationary start just below the surface, from where they can see their prey.

There are three operators at different locations along the Adelaide River.

Adelaide River Cruises (Map p828; ☎08-8983 3224; www.adelaiderivercruises.com.au; tours adult/child $35/20; ⏲9am, 11am, 1pm & 3pm May-Oct) See the jumping crocodiles on a private stretch of river past the Fogg Dam turn-off. Also runs small-group full-day wildlife cruises.

Adelaide River Queen (Map p828; ☎08-8988 8144; www.jumpingcrocodilecruises.com.au; tours adult/child $35/25; ⏲9am, 11am, 1pm & 3pm Mar-Oct, for times Nov-Feb see website) Well-established jumping-crocodile operator on the highway just before Adelaide River Crossing.

Spectacular Jumping Crocodile Cruise (Map p828; ☎08-8978 9077; www.jumpingcrocodile.com.au; tours adult/child $35/20; ⏲9am, 11am, 1pm & 3pm) Along the Window on the Wetlands access road, this outfit runs one-hour tours. Ask about trips ex-Darwin.

wi-fi), but water levels in the Wet can make it unsafe; look for signposted warnings.

The park offers plenty of bushwalking, including the **Tabletop Track** (39km), a circuit of the park that takes three to five days to complete depending on how many side tracks you follow. You can access the track at Florence Falls, Wangi Falls and Walker Creek. You must carry a topographic map of the area, available from tourist and retail outlets in Batchelor. The track is closed late September to March.

Sleeping

There is excellent public **camping** (adult/child $6.60/3.30) within the park. Grounds with toilets and fireplaces are located at Florence Falls, Florence Creek, Buley Rockhole, Wangi Falls (better for vans than tents) and Tjaynera Falls (Sandy Creek; 4WD required). There are more-basic camp sites at Surprise Creek Falls (4WD required) and Walker Creek. Walker Creek has its own swimming hole, and camping here involves bushwalking to a series of sublime, isolated riverside sites.

Litchfield Safari Camp CAMPGROUND $
(Map p828; ☎08-8978 2185; www.litchfieldsafaricamp.com.au; Litchfield Park Rd; unpowered/powered sites $25/35, dm $30, d safari tents $150, extra person $10; 🏊) Shady grassed sites make this a good alternative to Litchfield's bush camping sites, especially if you want power. The safari tents are great value as they comfortably sleep up to four folks. There's also a ramshackle camp kitchen, a kiosk and a pint-sized pool.

Adelaide River to Katherine

Adelaide River

POP 238

Blink and you'll miss this tiny highway town, 111km south of Darwin. The **Adelaide River War Cemetery** (Map p828; Memorial Tce) is an important legacy: a sea of little brass plaques commemorating those killed in the 1942–43 air raids on northern Australia.

Daly River

POP 512

The Daly River is considered some of the best **barramundi fishing** country in the Territory and the hub is this small community 117km southwest of Hayes Creek, reached by a narrow sealed road off the Dorat Rd (Old Stuart Hwy; Rte 23). There's a shop and fuel here and visitors are welcome without a permit, but note that this is a dry community (no alcohol).

Other than fishing, the main attraction here is **Merrepen Arts** (☎08-8978 2533; www.merrepenarts.com.au; ⏰9am-5pm Mon-Fri, Sat Jun-Sep) FREE, a gallery displaying locally made arts and crafts including etchings, screen prints, acrylic paintings, carvings, weaving and textiles.

The **Merrepen Arts Festival** (www.merrepenfestival.com.au; adult/child $20/10) celebrates arts and music from communities around the district, including Nauiyu, Wadeye and Peppimenarti, with displays, art auctions, workshops and dancing. The festival is held in Nauiyu, about 5km northwest of Daly River.

The camping ground at **Daly River Mango Farm** (Map p828; ☎08-8978 2464; www.mangofarm.com.au; unpowered/powered sites $30/35, d $130-200; ❄🏊), on the Daly River 9km from the crossing, is shaded by a magnificent grove of near-century-old mango trees. Other accommodation includes budget and self-contained cabins. Guided fishing trips and boat hire available.

Perry's (Map p828; ☎08-8978 2452; www.dalyriver.com; Mayo Park; unpowered/powered sites $28/38, fisherman's hut $95; 🏊) is a very peaceful campground with 2km of river frontage and gardens where orphaned wallabies bound around. Dick Perry, a well-known fishing expert, operates guided trips, and boat hire is available. The fisherman's hut has no air-con and is pretty basic with queen bed and bunks. Note, the boat ramp was not operating at the time of writing so you can't launch your own boat.

Pine Creek

POP 381

A short detour off the Stuart Hwy, Pine Creek is a small, dusty settlement which was once the scene of a frantic gold rush. The Kakadu Hwy (Rte 21) branches off the Stuart Hwy here, connecting it to Cooinda and Jabiru, making Pine Creek a useful base for exploring the region.

Sights & Activities

Railway Museum & Steam Train MUSEUM
(Railway Tce; ⏰10am-2pm Mon-Fri May-Sep) FREE
Dating from 1889, the Railway Museum

has a display on the Darwin-to-Pine Creek railway which ran from 1889 to 1976. The lovingly restored steam engine, built in Manchester in 1877, sits in its own enclosure next to the museum.

Umbrawarra Gorge Nature Park NATURE RESERVE
(Map p828; www.parksandwildlife.nt.gov.au/parks/find/umbrawarragorge) About 3km south of Pine Creek on the Stuart Hwy is the turn-off to pretty Umbrawarra Gorge, with a safe swimming hole, a little beach and a basic **campground** (campground adult/child $3.30/1.65). It's 22km southwest on a rugged dirt road (just OK for 2WDs in the Dry; often impassable in the Wet). Bring plenty of water and mozzie repellent.

Sleeping & Eating

Lazy Lizard Caravan Park & Tavern CAMPGROUND $
(☎08-8976 1019; www.lazylizardpinecreek.com.au; 299 Millar Tce; unpowered/powered sites $17/30;) The small, well-grassed camping area at the Lazy Lizard is really only secondary to the pulsing pub next door. The open-sided bar supported by carved ironwood pillars is a busy local watering hole with a pool table and old saddles slung across the rafters. The kitchen serves top-notch pub food (mains $18 to $35, open lunch and dinner), featuring big steaks and barra dishes.

Pine Creek Railway Resort BOUTIQUE HOTEL $$
(☎08-8976 1001; www.pinecreekrailwayresort.com.au; s/d $90/130, cabins $150-170;) This charming hotel uses raw iron, steel and wood in its stylish and modern rooms with options for singles, doubles and families. The dining area has been designed with romantic rail journeys of yore in mind; it's a scene-stealer with pressed-tin ceilings and elaborate chandeliers. The menu (mains $22 to $30) is, however, modern, with steaks, pasta, ribs and risotto on offer.

KAKADU & ARNHEM LAND

Kakadu and neighbouring Arnhem Land epitomise the remarkable landscape and cultural heritage of the Top End. Each is a treasure house of natural history and Aboriginal art, and both are significant homelands of contemporary Indigenous culture.

Kakadu National Park

Kakadu is a whole lot more than a national park. It's also a vibrant, living acknowledgement of the elemental link between the Aboriginal custodians and the country they have nurtured, endured and respected for thousands of generations. Encompassing almost 20,000 sq km (about 200km north–south and 100km east–west), it holds a spectacular ecosystem and a mind-blowing concentration of ancient **rock art**. The landscape is an ever-changing tapestry – periodically scorched and flooded, apparently desolate or obviously abundant depending on the season.

In just a few days you can cruise on billabongs bursting with **wildlife**, examine 25,000-year-old rock paintings with the help of an Indigenous guide, swim in pools at the foot of tumbling **waterfalls** and hike through ancient sandstone escarpment country.

If Kakadu has a downside it's that it's very popular – in the Dry at least. Resorts, camping grounds and rock-art sites can be very crowded, but this is a vast park and with a little adventurous spirit you can easily get off the beaten track and be alone with nature.

The Arnhem and Kakadu Hwys traverse the park; both are sealed and accessible year-round. The 4WD-only Old Jim Jim Rd is an alternative access from the Arnhem Hwy, joining the Kakadu Hwy 7km south of Cooinda.

Geography

The circuitous Arnhem Land escarpment, a dramatic 30m- to 200m-high sandstone cliff line, forms the natural boundary between Kakadu and Arnhem Land and winds 500km through eastern and southeastern Kakadu.

Creeks cut across the rocky plateau and, in the wet season, tumble off it as thundering waterfalls. They then flow across the lowlands to swamp Kakadu's vast northern flood plains. From west to east, the rivers are the Wildman, West Alligator, South Alligator and East Alligator (the latter forming the eastern boundary of the park). The coastal zone has long stretches of mangrove swamp, important for halting erosion and as a breeding ground for bird and marine life. The southern part of the park is dry lowlands with open grassland and eucalyptuses. Pockets of monsoon rainforest crop up throughout the park.

More than 80% of Kakadu is savannah woodland. It has more than 1000 plant species, many still used by Aboriginal people for food and medicinal purposes.

Kakadu National Park

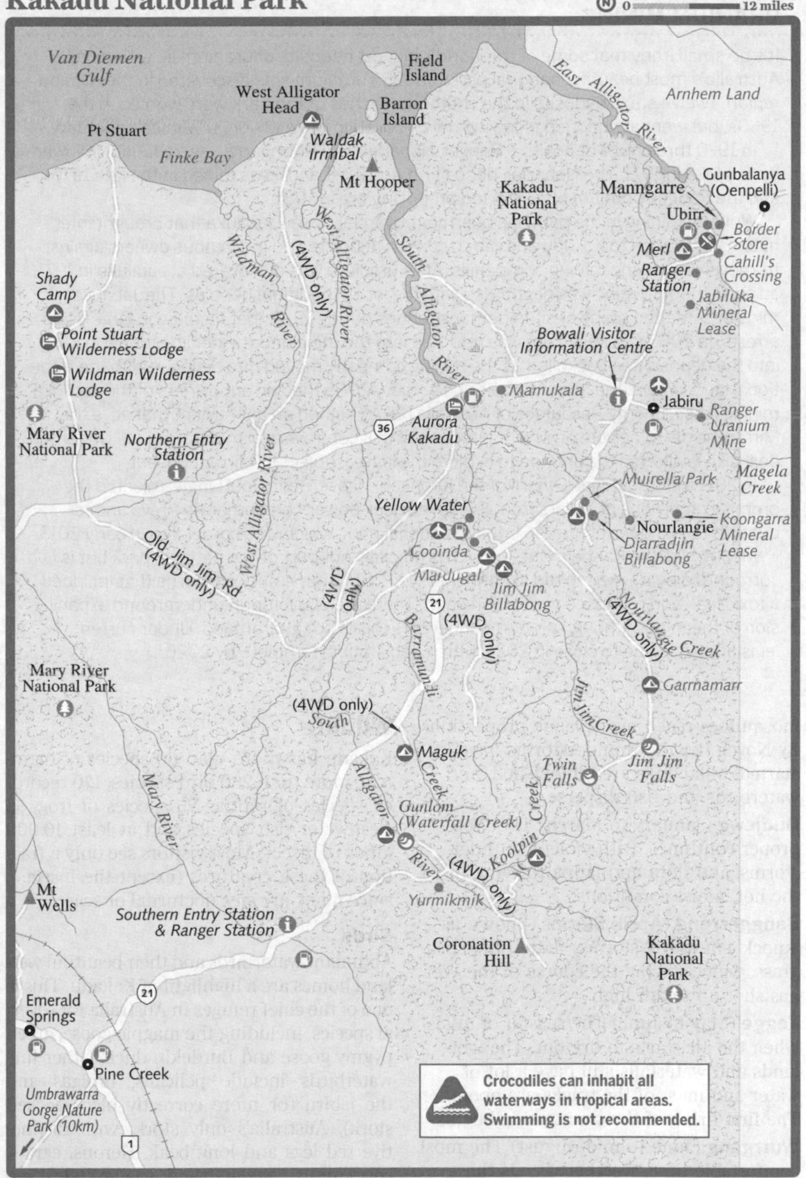

Climate

The average maximum temperature in Kakadu is 34°C, year-round. The Dry is roughly April to September, and the Wet, when most of Kakadu's average rainfall of 1500mm falls, is from October to March. As wetlands and waterfalls swell, unsealed roads become impassable, cutting off some highlights such as Jim Jim Falls.

Local Aboriginal people recognise six seasons in the annual cycle:

Gunumeleng (October to December) The build-up to the Wet. Humidity increases, the temperature rises to 35°C or more and

URANIUM MINING

It's no small irony that some of the world's biggest deposits of uranium lie within one of Australia's most beautiful national parks. In 1953 uranium was discovered in the Kakadu region. Twelve small deposits in the southern reaches of the park were worked in the 1960s, but were abandoned following the declaration of Woolwonga Wildlife Sanctuary.

In 1970 three huge deposits – Ranger, Nabarlek and Koongarra – were found, followed by Jabiluka in 1971. The Nabarlek deposit (in Arnhem Land) was mined in the late 1970s, and the Ranger Uranium Mine started producing ore in 1981.

While all mining in the park has been controversial, it was Jabiluka that brought international attention to Kakadu and pitted conservationists and Indigenous owners against the government and mining companies. After uranium was discovered at Jabiluka in 1971, an agreement to mine was negotiated with the local Aboriginal peoples. The Jabiluka mine became the scene of sit-in demonstrations during 1998 that resulted in large-scale arrests. In 2003 stockpiled ore was returned into the mine and the decline tunnel leading into the deposit was backfilled as the mining company moved into dialogue with the traditional landowners, the Mirrar people. In February 2005 the current owners of the Jabiluka mining lease, Energy Resources of Australia (ERA), signed an agreement that gave the Mirrar the deciding vote on any resumption of this controversial mining project. Under the deal ERA is allowed to continue to explore the lease, subject to Mirrar consent.

In 2011 the traditional owners of the Koongarra lease, near Nourlangie, rejected the promise of millions of dollars from French nuclear-power conglomerate Areva and requested the land be integrated into the national park, which was completed in early 2013.

Meanwhile, the Ranger mine – which is officially not part of the national park but is surrounded by it – was mired in controversy in 2014 after safety concerns that included a toxic leak and collapsed ventilation shaft. There are plans for an underground expansion of the mine, although given recent events this is not guaranteed. Under current legislation it is due to close in 2021, with rehabilitation complete by 2026.

mosquitoes reach near-plague proportions. By November the thunderstorms have started, billabongs are replenished, and waterbirds and fish disperse.

Gudjewg (January to March) The Wet proper continues, with violent thunderstorms, and flora and fauna thriving in the hot, moist conditions.

Banggerreng (April) Storms (known as 'knock 'em down' storms) flatten the spear grass, which during the course of the Wet has shot up to 2m high.

Yegge (May to June) The season of mists, when the air starts to dry out. The wetlands and waterfalls still have a lot of water and most of the tracks are open. The first firing of the countryside begins.

Wurrgeng (June to mid-August) The most comfortable time, weatherwise, is the late Dry, beginning in July. This is when animals, especially birds, gather in large numbers around shrinking billabongs, and when most tourists visit.

Gurrung (mid-August to September) The end of the Dry and the beginning of another cycle.

Wildlife

Kakadu has more than 60 species of mammal, more than 280 bird species, 120 recorded species of reptile, 25 species of frog, 55 freshwater fish species and at least 10,000 kinds of insect. Most visitors see only a fraction of these creatures (except the insects), since many are shy, nocturnal or scarce.

Birds

Abundant waterbirds and their beautiful wetland homes are a highlight of Kakadu. This is one of the chief refuges in Australia for several species, including the magpie goose, green pygmy goose and Burdekin duck. Other fine waterbirds include pelicans, brolgas and the jabiru (or more correctly black-necked stork), Australia's only stork, with distinctive red legs and long beak. Herons, egrets, cormorants, wedge-tailed eagles, whistling kites and black kites are common. The open woodlands harbour rainbow bee-eaters, kingfishers and the endangered bustard. Majestic white-breasted sea eagles are seen near inland waterways. At night, you might hear barking owls calling – they sound just like dogs – or the plaintive wail of the bush stone curlew. The raucous call of the spectacular red-tailed black cockatoo is often considered the signature sound of Kakadu.

At **Mamukala**, 8km east of the South Alligator River on the Arnhem Hwy, is a wonderful observation building, plus bird-watching hides and a 3km walking track.

Fish

You can't miss the silver barramundi, which creates a distinctive swirl near the water's surface. A renowned sportfish, it can grow to more than 1m in length and changes sex from male to female at the age of five or six years.

Mammals

Several types of kangaroo and wallaby inhabit the park; the shy black wallaroo is unique to Kakadu and Arnhem Land; look for them at Nourlangie Rock, where individuals rest under rocky overhangs. At Ubirr, short-eared rock wallabies can be spotted in the early morning. You may see a sugar glider or a shy dingo in wooded areas in the daytime. Kakadu has 26 bat species, four of them endangered.

Reptiles

Twin Falls and Jim Jim Falls have freshwater crocodiles, which have narrow snouts and rarely exceed 3m, while the dangerous saltwater variety is found throughout the park.

Kakadu's other reptiles include the frilled lizard, 11 species of goanna, and five freshwater turtle species, of which the most common is the northern snake-necked turtle. Kakadu has many snakes, though most are nocturnal and rarely encountered. The striking Oenpelli python was first recorded by non-Aboriginal people in 1976. The odd-looking file snake lives in billabongs and is much sought after as bush tucker. They have square heads, tiny eyes and saggy skin covered in tiny rough scales (hence 'file'). They move very slowly (and not at all on land), eating only once a month and breeding once every decade.

Rock Art

Kakadu is one of Australia's richest, most accessible repositories of rock art. There are more than 5000 sites, which date from 20,000 years to 10 years ago. The vast majority of these sites are off limits or inaccessible, but two of the finest collections are the easily visited galleries at Ubirr and Nourlangie.

Rock paintings have been classified into three roughly defined periods: Pre-estuarine, which is from the earliest paintings up to around 6000 years ago; Estuarine, which covers the period from 6000 to around 2000 years ago, when rising sea levels brought the coast to its present level; and Freshwater, from 2000 years ago until the present day.

For local Aboriginal people, these rock-art sites are a major source of traditional knowledge and represent their archives. Aboriginal people rarely paint on rocks anymore, as they no longer live in rock shelters and there are fewer people with the requisite knowledge. Some older paintings are believed by many Aboriginal people to have been painted by mimi spirits, connecting people with creation legends and the development of lore.

As the paintings are all rendered with natural, water-soluble ochres, they are very susceptible to water damage. Drip lines of clear silicon rubber have been laid on the rocks above the paintings to divert rain. As the most accessible sites receive up to 4000 visitors a week, boardwalks have been erected to keep the dust down and to keep people at a suitable distance from the paintings.

Tours

There are dozens of Kakadu tours on offer; book at least a day ahead if possible. There are plenty of tours departing Darwin. Operators generally collect you from your accommodation. Keep an eye out for excellent, short ranger-led tours and activities throughout the park.

Kakadu Animal Tracks CULTURAL TOUR
(0409 350 842; www.animaltracks.com.au; adult/child $205/135) Based at Cooinda, this outfit runs seven-hour tours with an Indigenous guide combining a wildlife safari and Aboriginal cultural tour. You'll see thousands of birds, get to hunt, gather, prepare and consume bush tucker, and crunch on some green ants.

Arnhemlander Cultural & Heritage Tour CULTURAL TOUR
(08-8979 2548; www.kakadutours.com.au; adult/child $258/205) Aboriginal-owned and -operated tour into northern Kakadu and Arnhem Land. See ancient rock art, learn bush skills and meet local artists at Injalak Arts Centre in Oenpelli.

Top End Explorer Tours OUTDOORS
(08-8979 3615; www.kakadutours.net.au; adult/child $230/170) Small-group 4WD tours to Jim Jim and Twin Falls from Jabiru and Cooinda.

Ayal Aboriginal Tours CULTURAL TOUR
(0429 470 384; www.ayalkakadu.com.au; adult/child $220/99) Full-day Indigenous-run tours around Kakadu, with former ranger and local Victor Cooper, shining a light on art, culture and wildlife.

Kakadu Air SCENIC FLIGHTS
(1800 089 113, 08-8941 9611; www.kakaduair.com.au) Offers 30-minute/one-hour fixed-wing flights for $150/250 per adult. Helicopter tours, though more expensive, give a more dynamic aerial perspective. They cost from $230 (20 minutes) to $650 (one hour) per person. Note that flights are only available over Jim Jim Falls in the wet season – traditional owners request that the 'skies are rested' in the Dry.

Yellow Water Cruises CRUISE
(1800 500 401; www.gagudju-dreaming.com) Cruise the South Alligator River and Yellow Water Billabong spotting wildlife. Purchase tickets from Gagudju Lodge, Cooinda; a shuttle bus will take you from here to the tour's departure point. Two-hour cruises ($99/70 per adult/child) depart at 6.45am, 9am and 4.30pm; 1½-hour cruises ($72/50) leave at 11.30am, 1.15pm and 2.45pm.

Guluyambi Cultural Cruise CULTURAL TOUR
(www.aptouring.com.au/KCT; adult/child $72/48; 9am, 11am, 1pm & 3pm May-Nov) Launch into an Aboriginal-led river cruise from the upstream boat ramp on the East Alligator River near Cahill's Crossing. Highly recommended by Darwin locals.

Information

About 200,000 people visit Kakadu between April and October, so expect some tour-bus action at sites such as Ubirr and Yellow Water. Consider spending some time bushwalking and camping in the south of the park – it's less visited but inimitably impressive.

Admission to the park is via a 14-day Park Pass (adult $25, child free). Pick up a pass, along with the excellent *Visitor Guide* booklet, from Bowali Visitor Information Centre, Tourism Top End (p826) in Darwin, Gagudju Lodge Cooinda (p840) or Katherine Visitor Information Centre (p847). Carry it with you at all times, as rangers conduct spot checks – penalties apply for nonpayment. Fuel is available at Kakadu Resort, Cooinda and Jabiru.

Accommodation prices in Kakadu vary tremendously depending on the season – resort rates can drop by as much as 50% during the Wet.

The excellent **Bowali Visitor Information Centre** (08-8938 1121; www.kakadunationalparkaustralia.com/bowali_visitors_center.htm; Kakadu Hwy, Jabiru; 8am-5pm) has walk-through displays that sweep you across the land, explaining Kakadu's ecology from Aboriginal and non-Aboriginal perspectives. The centre is about 2.5km south of the Arnhem Hwy intersection; a 1km walking track connects it with Jabiru.

A great online site is **Kakadu National Park** (www.kakadu.au), which has a visitors guide, what's on listings and suggested itineraries to download.

The Northern Land Council (p811) issues permits (adult/child $18/free) to visit Gunbalanya (Oenpelli), across the East Alligator River.

Getting There & Around

Many people choose to access Kakadu on a tour, which shuffles them around the major sights with the minimum of hassle. But it's just as easy with your own wheels, if you know what kinds of road conditions your trusty steed can handle (Jim Jim and Twin Falls, for example, are 4WD-access only).

Greyhound Australia (www.greyhound.com.au) runs a return coach service from Darwin to Jabiru ($66, 3½ hours).

Ubirr & Around

It'll take a lot more than the busloads of visitors to disturb the inherent majesty and grace of **Ubirr** (8.30am-sunset Apr-Nov, from 2pm Dec-Mar). Layers of **rock-art paintings**, in various styles and from various centuries, command a mesmerising stillness. Part of the main gallery reads like a menu, with images of kangaroos, tortoises and fish painted in x-ray, which became the dominant style about 8000 years ago. Predating these are the paintings of mimi spirits: cheeky, dynamic figures who, it's believed, were the first of the Creation Ancestors to paint on rock (...given the lack of cherry pickers in 6000 BC, you have to wonder who else but a spirit could have painted at that height and angle). Look out for the yam-head figures, where the head is depicted as a yam on the body of a human or animal; these date back around 15,000 years.

The magnificent **Nardab Lookout** is a 250m scramble from the main gallery. Surveying the billiard-table-green floodplain and watching the sun set and the moon rise, like they're on an invisible set of scales, is glorious, to say the least. Ubirr is 39km north of the Arnhem Hwy via a sealed road.

On the way you'll pass the turn-off to **Merl** (adult/child $10/free) camping ground, which is only open in the Dry and has an amenities block and BBQs, and the **Border Store** (08-8979 2474; mains $20-28; 8.30am-8pm Apr-Nov), selling groceries, real coffee, and delicious Thai food (no fuel).

Activities

Bardedjilidji Sandstone Walk WALKING
Starting from the upstream picnic-area car park, this walk (2.5km, 90 minutes, easy) takes in wetland areas of the East Alligator

River and some eroded sandstone outliers of the Arnhem Land escarpment. Informative track notes point out features on the walk.

Manngarre Monsoon Forest Walk WALKING
Mainly sticking to a boardwalk, this walk (1.5km return, 30 minutes, easy) starts by the boat ramp near the Border Store and winds through shaded vegetation, palms and vines.

Sandstone & River Rock Holes WALKING
This extension (6.5km, three hours, medium) of the Bardedjilidji Walk features sandstone outcrops, paperbark swamps and riverbanks. Closed in the Wet.

Jabiru

POP 1129

It may seem surprising to find a town of Jabiru's size and structure in the midst of a wilderness national park, but it exists solely because of the nearby Ranger uranium mine. It's Kakadu's major service centre, with a bank, newsagent, medical centre, supermarket, bakery and service station. You can even play a round of golf here.

Festivals & Events

Mahbilil Festival CULTURAL
(mahbililfestival.com) A one-day celebration in early September of Indigenous culture in Jabiru. There are exhibitions showcasing local art as well as craft demonstrations, including weaving and painting. Also on offer are competitions in spear throwing, didgeridoo blowing and magpie goose cooking. In the evening the focus is on Indigenous music and dance.

Sleeping & Eating

★**Anbinik (Lakeview) Resort** CABINS $$
(08-8979 3144; www.lakeviewkakadu.com.au; 27 Lakeside Dr; ensuite powered sites $40, bungalows/d/cabins $130/140/245;) This Aboriginal-owned park is one of Kakadu's best with a range of tropical-design bungalows set in lush gardens. The doubles share a communal kitchen, bathroom and lounge, and also come equipped with their own TV and fridge. The 'bush bungalows' are stylish, elevated safari designs (no air-con) with private external bathroom. Bungalows sleep up to four. By far the best value in Jabiru.

Aurora Kakadu Lodge & Caravan Park RESORT $$
(08-8979 2422, 1800 811 154; www.aurorareso rts.com.au; Jabiru Dr; unpowered/powered sites $28/40, cabins from $250;) One of the best places to camp in town with lots of grass, trees and natural barriers between camping areas, creating a sense of privacy. This impeccable resort/caravan park also has a lagoon-style swimming pool. Self-contained cabins sleep up to five people. The restaurant is a lovely outdoor place for meals overlooking the pool. The menu is limited but dishes such as buffalo sausages are well prepared.

Mercure Kakadu (Crocodile Hotel) HOTEL $$$
(08-8979 9000; www.accorhotels.com; 1 Flinders St; d from $310;) Known locally as 'the Croc', this hotel is designed in the shape of a crocodile, which, of course, is only obvious when viewed from the air or Google Earth. The rooms are clean and comfortable if a little pedestrian for the price (check its website for great deals). Try for one on the ground floor opening out to the central pool.

Kakadu Bakery BAKERY $
(Gregory Pl; meals $6-15; 6am-3pm Mon-Fri, 8am-3.30pm Sat, 8am-4pm Sun) Superb made-to-order sandwiches on home-baked bread. There are also mean burgers, slices, breakfast fry-ups, pizzas, cakes and basic salads.

Jabiru Sports & Social Club PUB FOOD $$
(08-8979 2326; Lakeside Dr; mains $16-35; noon-2pm Thu-Sun, 6-8.30pm Tue-Sat) Along with the golf club, this low-slung hangar is the place to meet locals over a beer or glass of wine. The bistro meals, such as steak, chicken parma or fish and chips, are honest, and there's an outdoor deck overlooking the lake, a kids playground, and sport on TV.

Nourlangie

The sight of this looming outlier of the Arnhem Land escarpment makes it easy to understand its ancient importance to Aboriginal people. Its long red-sandstone bulk, striped in places with orange, white and black, slopes up from surrounding woodland to fall away at one end in stepped cliffs. Below is Kakadu's best-known collection of **rock art**.

The name Nourlangie is a corruption of *nawulandja*, an Aboriginal word that refers to an area bigger than the rock itself. The 2km looped walking track (open 8am to sunset) takes you first to the **Anbangbang Shelter**, used for 20,000 years as a refuge and canvas. Next is the **Anbangbang Gallery**, featuring Dreaming characters repainted in the 1960s. Look for Nabulwinjbulwinj, a dangerous spirit who likes to eat females after banging them on the head with a yam. From here it's a short walk to **Gunwarddehwarde Lookout**, with views of the Arnhem Land escarpment.

Nourlangie is at the end of a 12km sealed road that turns east off Kakadu Hwy. About 7km south is the turn-off to **Muirella Park** (adult/child $10/free) camping ground at **Djarradjin Billabong**, with BBQs, excellent amenities and the 5km-return **Bubba Wetland Walk**.

Activities

Nawurlandja Lookout WALKING
This is a short walk (600m return, 30 minutes, medium) up a gradual slope, but it gives excellent views of the Nourlangie rock area and is a good place to catch the sunset.

Anbangbang Billabong Walk WALKING
This picturesque billabong lies close to Nourlangie, and the picnic tables dotted around its edge make it a popular lunch spot. The track (2.5km loop, 45 minutes, easy) circles the billabong and passes through paperbark swamp.

Barrk Walk WALKING
This long day walk (12km loop, five to six hours, difficult) will take you away from the crowds on a circuit of the Nourlangie area. Barrk is the male black wallaroo and you might see this elusive marsupial if you set out early. Pick up a brochure from the Bowali Visitor Information Centre.

Starting at the Nourlangie car park, this demanding walk passes through the Anbangbang galleries before a steep climb to the top of Nourlangie Rock. Cross the flat top of the rock weaving through sandstone pillars before descending along a wet-season watercourse. The track then follows the rock's base past the Nanguluwur Gallery and western cliffs before re-emerging at the car park.

Nanguluwur Gallery WALKING
This outstanding rock-art gallery sees far fewer visitors than Nourlangie simply because it's further to walk (3.5km return, 1½ hours, easy) and has a gravel access road. Here the paintings cover most of the styles found in the park, including very early dynamic style work, x-ray work and a good example of 'contact art', a painting of a two-masted sailing ship towing a dinghy.

Jim Jim Falls & Twin Falls

Remote and spectacular, these two falls epitomise the rugged Top End. **Jim Jim Falls**, a sheer 215m drop, is awesome after rain (when it can only be seen from the air), but its waters shrink to a trickle by about June. **Twin Falls** flows year-round (no swimming), but half the fun is getting here, involving a little **boat trip** (adult/child $12.50/free, running 7.30am to 5pm, last boat 4pm) and an over-the-water boardwalk.

These two waterfalls are reached via a 4WD track that turns south off the Kakadu Hwy between the Nourlangie and Cooinda turn-offs. Jim Jim Falls is about 56km from the turn-off (the last 1km on foot), and it's a further five corrugated kilometres to Twin Falls. The track is open in the Dry only and can still be closed into late May; it's off limits to most rental vehicles (check the fine print). A couple of tour companies make trips here in the Dry and there's a camping area, **Garnamarr** (adult/child $10/free) near Jim Jim Falls.

Cooinda & Yellow Water

Cooinda is best known for the cruises (p838) on the wetland area known as Yellow Water, and has developed into a slick resort. About 1km from the resort, the **Warradjan Aboriginal Cultural Centre** (www.gagudju-dreaming.com; Yellow Water Area; ⏲9am-5pm) depicts Creation stories and has a great permanent exhibition that includes clap sticks, sugarbag holders and rock-art samples. You'll be introduced to the moiety system (the law of interpersonal relationships), languages and skin names, and there's a minitheatre with a huge selection of films to choose from. A mesmeric soundtrack of chants and didgeridoos plays in the background.

Gagudju Lodge & Camping Cooinda (☎1800 500 401; www.gagudju-dreaming.com; Cooinda; unpowered/powered sites $38/50, budget/lodge r from $75/310; ❄@🏊) is the most popular accommodation resort in the park. It's a modern oasis but, even with 380 camp sites, facilities can get very stretched. The budget air-con units share camping-ground facilities and are compact and comfy enough. The lodge rooms are spacious and more comfortable, sleeping up to four people. There's also a grocery shop, tour desk, fuel pump and the excellent open-air **Barra Bar & Bistro** (☎1800 500 401; www.gagudju-dreaming.com; Cooinda; mains $15-36; ⏲all day) here.

The turn-off to the Cooinda accommodation complex and Yellow Water wetlands is 47km down the Kakadu Hwy from the Arnhem Hwy intersection. Just off the Kakadu Hwy, 2km south of the Cooinda turn-off, is the scrubby **Mardugal camping ground** (adult/child $10/free), an excellent year-round camping area with shower and toilets.

Cooinda to Pine Creek

This southern section of the park sees far fewer tour buses. Though it's unlikely you'll have dreamy **Maguk** (Barramundi Gorge; 45km south of Cooinda and 10km along a corrugated 4WD track) to yourself, you might time it right to have the glorious natural pool and falls between just a few of you. Forty-odd kilometres further south is the turn-off to **Gunlom** (Waterfall Creek), another superb escarpment waterfall, plunge pool and camping area. It's located 37km along an unsealed road, again 4WD recommended. Take the steep Waterfall Walk (1km, one hour) here, which affords incredible views.

Arnhem Land

Arnhem Land is a vast, overwhelming and mysterious corner of the Northern Territory. About the size of the state of Victoria and with a population of only around 17,000, mostly Yolngu people, this Aboriginal reserve is one of Australia's last great untouched wilderness areas. Most people live on outstations, combining traditional practices with modern Western ones, so they might go out for a hunt and be back in time to watch the 6pm news. Outside commercial interests and visits are highly regulated through a permit system, designed to protect the environment, the rock art and ceremonial grounds. *Balanda* (white people) are unaware of the locations of burial grounds and ceremonial lands. Basically, you need a specific purpose for entering, usually to visit an arts centre, in order to be granted a permit. If you're travelling far enough to warrant an overnight stay, you'll need to organise accommodation (which is in short supply). It's easy to visit Gunbalanya (Oenpelli) and its arts centre, just over the border, either on a tour or independently. Elsewhere, it's best to travel with a tour, which will include the necessary permit(s) to enter Aboriginal lands.

Tours

Arnhemlander Cultural & Heritage Tour TOUR
(☎1800 665 220; www.aptouring.com.au/KCT; adult/child $258/205) Four-wheel-drive tours to ancient rock-art sites, Inkiyu Billabong and Injalak art centre at Gunbalanya (Oenpelli).

Davidson's Arnhemland Safaris TOUR
(☎08-8979 0413; www.arnhemland-safaris.com) Experienced operator taking tours to Mt Borradaile, north of Oenpelli. Meals, guided tours, fishing and safari-camp accommodation are included in the daily price (from $750); transfers from Darwin can be arranged.

Venture North Australia TOUR
(☎08-8927 5500; venturenorth.com.au; 4-/5-day tours $2590/2890) Four-wheel drive tours to remote areas; features expert guidance on rock art. Also has a safari camp near Smith Point on the Cobourg Peninsula.

Lord's Kakadu & Arnhemland Safaris TOUR
(☎08-8948 2200; www.lords-safaris.com; adult/child $225/180) One-day trip into Arnhem Land (Gunbalanya) from Jabiru (or Darwin adult/child $255/195), visiting Oenpelli with an Aboriginal-guided walk around Injalak Hill rock-art site.

Nomad Tours TOUR
(☎08-8987 8085; www.banubanu.com; half-/full-day per person $250/380) Luxury small-group tours including fishing charters, 4WD and cultural tours. Transfers and guided activities are available for an extra fee.

Gove Diving & Fishing Charters FISHING
(☎08-8987 3445; www.govefish.com.au) Variety of fishing, diving and snorkelling, and wilderness trips from Nhulunbuy. Half-/full-day fishing trips cost $225/325.

Gunbalanya (Oenpelli)

POP 1121

Gunbalanya is a small Aboriginal community 17km into Arnhem Land across the East Alligator River from the Border Store in Kakadu. The drive in itself is worth the trip, with brilliant green wetlands and spectacular escarpments all around. Road access is only possible between May and October: check the tides at Cahill's Crossing on the East Alligator River before setting out so you don't get stuck on the other side.

A permit is required to visit the town, usually issued for visits to the **Injalak Arts & Crafts Centre** (☎08-8979 0190; www.injalak.com; ⌚8am-5pm Mon-Fri, 9am-2pm Sat). At this centre, artists and craftspeople display traditional paintings on bark and paper, plus didgeridoos, pandanus weavings and baskets, and screen-printed fabrics. Artworks are produced either at the arts centre itself or on remote outstations throughout Arnhem Land.

As you walk around the verandah of the arts centre to see the artists at work (morning only), peer out over the wetland at the rear to the escarpment and **Injalak Hill** (Long Tom Dreaming). Knowledgeable local guides lead tours to see the fine rock-art galleries here.

The three-hour tours cost $110/33 per adult/child. Although it may be possible to join a tour as a walk-in, it's generally best to book a tour from Jabiru or Darwin.

The **Stone Country Festival** is an open day and cultural festival held in August. It has traditional music, dancing, and arts and crafts demonstrations, and is the only day you can visit Gunbalanya without a permit. Camping allowed; no alcohol. Check dates online.

The **Northern Land Council** (☎1800 645 299, 08-8938 3000; www.nlc.org.au; 3 Government Bldg, Flinders St, Jabiru; ⊙8am-4.30pm Mon-Fri) issues permits (adult/child $16.50/free) to visit Injalak, usually on the spot. It also provides tide times for the East Alligator River, which is impassable at high tide.

Cobourg Peninsula

The entire wilderness of this remote peninsula forms the **Garig Gunak Barlu National Park** (www.parksandwildlife.nt.gov.au/parks/find/gariggunak), which includes the surrounding sea. In the turquoise water you'll likely see dolphins and turtles, and – what most people come for – a threadfin salmon thrashing on the end of your line. On the shores of **Port Essington** are the stone ruins and headstones of Victoria settlement – Britain's 1838 attempt to establish a military outpost here.

At **Algarlarlgarl** (Black Point) there's a **ranger station** (☎08-8979 0244) with a visitor information and cultural centre, and the **Garig Store** (☎08-8979 0455; ⊙4-6pm Mon-Sat), which sells basic provisions, ice and camping gas.

Two permits are required to visit the Cobourg Peninsula: for a transit pass ($12.10 per vehicle) to drive through Aboriginal land contact the Northern Land Council (p811); for permission to stay overnight in the national park contact the **Cobourg Peninsula Sanctuary & Marine Park Board** (☎08-8999 4814; www.parksandwildlife.nt.gov.au/parks/find/gariggunak). The overnight fee is $232.10 per vehicle, which covers up to five people for seven days and includes a camping and transit pass.

There are two camping grounds in the park with shower, toilet, BBQs and limited bore water; generators are allowed in one area. Camping fees (per person per day $16.50) are covered by your vehicle permit, but if you fly in you'll have to pay them. Other accommodation is available in pricey fishing resorts.

Getting There & Away

The quickest route here is by private charter flight, which can be arranged by accommodation providers. The track to Cobourg starts at Gunbalanya (Oenpelli) and is accessible by 4WD vehicles only from May to October. The 270km drive to Black Point from the East Alligator River takes about four hours.

Eastern Arnhem Land

The wildly beautiful coast and country of **Eastern Arnhem Land** (www.ealta.org) is really off the beaten track. About 4000 people live in the region's main settlement, Nhulunbuy, built to service the bauxite mine here. The 1963 plans to establish a manganese mine were hotly protested by the traditional owners, the Yolngu people; though mining proceeded, the case became an important step in establishing land rights. Some of the country's most respected art comes out of this region too, including bark paintings, carved mimi figures, *yidaki* (didgeridoos), woven baskets and mats, and jewellery.

Buku Larrnggay Mulka Art Centre & Museum (www.yirrkala.com; Yirrkala; admission by donation; ⊙8am-4.30pm Mon-Fri, 9am-noon Sat), 20km southeast of Nhulunbuy in Yirrkala, is one of Arnhem Land's best. No permit is required to visit from Nhulunbuy or Gove airport.

In August, the **Garma Festival** (www.yyf.com.au) is a four-day celebration in north-eastern Arnhem Land. It's one of the most significant regional festivals, a celebration of Yolngu culture that includes ceremonial performances, bushcraft lessons, a *yidaki* (didgeridoo) master class and an academic forum. Serious planning is required to attend, so start early.

Overland travel through Arnhem Land from Katherine requires a permit (free) from the Northern Land Council (p811). The **Dhimurru Land Management Aboriginal Corporation** (☎08-8987 3992; www.dhimurru.com.au; Arnhem Rd, Nhulunbuy) issues recreation permits ($35/45 for seven days/two months) for visits to particular recreational areas in Eastern Arnhem Land.

Getting There & Away

Airnorth (☎1800 627 474; www.airnorth.com.au) and Qantaslink (p826) fly from Darwin to Gove Airport (for Nhulunbuy) daily from $355 one way. Overland, it's a 10-hour 4WD trip and only possible in the Dry. The Central Arnhem Hwy to Gove leaves the Stuart Hwy (Rte 87) 52km south of Katherine. At the time of writing **Sea Swift** (☎08-8935 2400, 1800 424 422; www.seaswift.com.au) was launching a cruise service aboard a working cargo boat from Darwin to Gove.

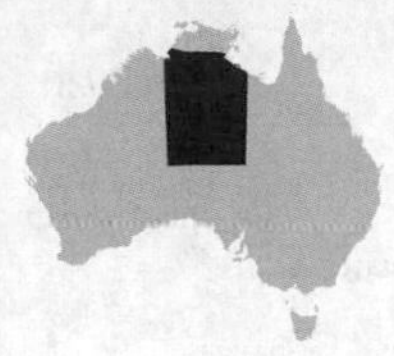

Uluru & Outback NT

Includes ➡

Best Places to Eat

➡ Savannah Bar & Restaurant (p847)

➡ Epilogue Lounge (p864)

➡ Hanuman Restaurant (p864)

➡ Piccolo's (p864)

Best Places to Stay

➡ Nitmiluk National Park Campground (p851)

➡ Territory Manor Motel & Caravan Park (p853)

➡ Alice in the Territory (p863)

➡ Elkira Court Motel (p863)

Why Go?

The remote and largely untamed chunk of the Northern Territory (NT) from Darwin to Uluru is where dreams end and adventure begins. If you enjoy off-road driving, meeting real characters of the Australian outback and contortions of an ancient land sliced into escapments, canyons, gorges, and pockets of verdant bush, then you've come to the right place.

The Stuart Hwy from Katherine to Alice Springs is still referred to as 'The Track' – it has been since WWII, when it was literally a dirt track connecting the Territory's two main towns, roughly following the Overland Telegraph Line. It's dead straight most of the way. The Red Centre is Australia's heartland boasting the iconic attractions of Uluru and Kata Tjuta, plus an enigmatic central desert culture that continues to produce extraordinary abstract art. And delighting travellers with its eccentric offerings, pioneering spirit and weathered mountain setting, Alice Springs is the city at the centre of a continent.

When to Go

Alice Springs

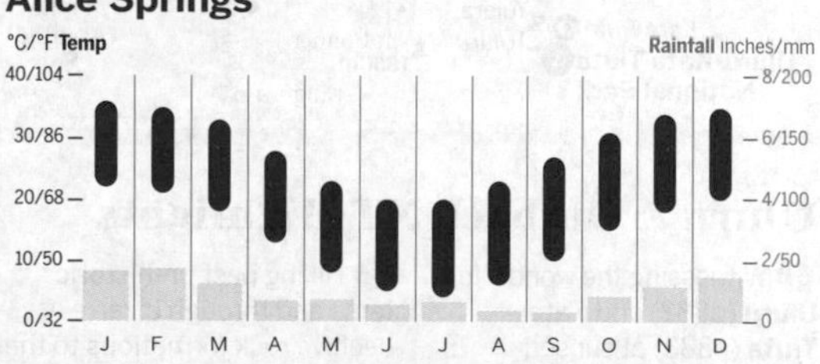

Apr–Aug Peak season with cooler temperatures in the Red Centre.

Jun & Jul Festival season – Beanie Festival and Camel Cup in Alice Springs.

Sep–Mar It's hot, hot, hot around Alice Springs; storms bring relief in Katherine.

Uluru & Outback NT Highlights

1. Witnessing the wonderful **Uluru** (p882) and **Kata Tjuta** (p883) at sunset; discovering the spiritual side of these awesome rocks from local Anangu guides.

2. Paddling a canoe beneath soaring sandstone ramparts in **Nitmiluk (Katherine Gorge) National Park** (p849).

3. Hiking past prehistoric ferns and through bizarre beehive rock formations to the dramatic cliff face of **Kings Canyon** (p875).

4. Soaking away the cobwebs in a steamy thermal spring at **Mataranka** (p853).

5. Gazing at ghost gums, budgerigars and wallabies among the gaps, gorges and waterholes of **West MacDonnell National Park** (p873).

6. Wandering among precarious balancing boulders at the **Devil's Marbles** (p856).

7. Exploring **Alice Springs** (p857), and some of central Australia's best Indigenous art.

History

See the History section at the beginning of the Darwin & Around chapter for historical information relevant to the whole Northern Territory.

Indigenous Northern Territory

See the Indigenous Northern Territory section at the beginning of the Darwin & Around chapter for historical information on the region's Indigenous people, relevant to the whole Northern Territory.

National Parks

The Northern Territory's outback has some of the most famous natural areas in Australia, including Uluru-Kata Tjuta National Park and the West MacDonnell National Park.

Parks Australia manages Uluru-Kata Tjuta, while the Parks & Wildlife Commission of the Northern Territory manages the other parks and produces fact sheets, available online or from its various offices.

Activities

Bushwalking

The Territory's national parks offer well-maintained tracks of different lengths and degrees of difficulty, which introduce walkers to various environments and wildlife habitats. Carry plenty of water, take rubbish out with you and stick to the tracks.

Top bushwalks include the Jatbula Trail in Nitmiluk (Katherine Gorge) National Park, Ormiston Pound in the West MacDonnell Ranges, Trephina Gorge in the East MacDonnell Ranges, and the Valley of the Winds at Kata Tjuta.

Wildlife Watching

The best place for guaranteed wildlife sightings, from bilbies to emus, is at the excellent Alice Springs Desert Park.

If you prefer to see wildlife in the wild, there are few guarantees; many of the region's critters are nocturnal. In the arid Centre you may see wallabies, reptiles and eagles. Good places to keep an eye out include the West MacDonnell Ranges and Watarrka (Kings Canyon) National Park.

Information

RESOURCES

Parks & Wildlife Commission of the Northern Territory (☎08-8999 4555; www.parksandwildlife.nt.gov.au) Details on NT parks and reserves, including fact sheets.

Travel NT (www.travelnt.com) Official tourism site.

ABORIGINAL LAND PERMITS

Permits may be required to enter Aboriginal land, unless you are using recognised public roads that cross Aboriginal territory.

Central Land Council (www.clc.org.au) Deals with all land south of a line drawn between Kununurra (Western Australia) and Mt Isa (Queensland). Offices in Alice Springs (p866) and Tennant Creek (☎08-8962 2343; www.clc.org.au; 63 Paterson St, Tennant Creek).

Northern Land Council (www.nlc.org.au) Responsible for land north of a line drawn between Kununurra (Western Australia) and Mt Isa (Queensland). Branch in Katherine (Map p848; ☎08-8971 9802; 5 Katherine Tce).

Getting There & Around

AIR

Domestic flights arrive at and depart from **Alice Springs Airport** (☎08-8951 1211; www.alicespringsairport.com.au; Santa Teresa Rd). There are also flights between Darwin, Alice Springs and Ayers Rock airport near Uluru.

Qantas (☎13 13 13, 08-8950 5211; www.qantas.com.au) Qantas flies regularly between Alice Springs and Sydney, Melbourne, Adelaide, Perth, Darwin, Cairns and Brisbane. It also flies out to Uluru.

Virgin Australia (☎13 67 89; www.virginaustralia.com) Virgin flies between Sydney and Uluru, and Alice Springs, Darwin and Adelaide.

Jetstar (www.jetstar.com) Flies from Uluru to Melbourne and Sydney, including direct flights.

BUS

Greyhound Australia (p866) regularly services the main road routes throughout the Territory, stopping at Katherine, Tenant Creek and Alice Springs.

An alternative is tour-bus companies such as AAT Kings, and backpacker buses that cover vast distances while savouring the sights along the way.

CAR

See the corresponding Car section under the Darwin & Around chapter, which gives information about driving around the NT.

TRAIN

See the corresponding Train section under the Darwin & Around chapter, which gives information about catching the Ghan between Adelaide and Darwin.

KATHERINE

POP 9187

Katherine is considered a big town in this part of the world and you'll certainly feel like you've arrived somewhere if you've just made the long trip up the highway from Alice Springs. Its namesake river is the first permanent running water on the road north of Alice Springs. Katherine is probably best known for the Nitmiluk (Katherine Gorge) National Park to the east, and the town makes an obvious base, with plenty of accommodation.

Sights & Activities

Godinymayin Yijard Rivers Arts & Culture Centre — GALLERY

(☎08-8972 3751; www.gyracc.org.au; Stuart Hwy, Katherine East; ⏰10am-5pm Tue-Fri, to 3pm Sat) This stunning new arts and culture centre in Katherine is housed in a beautiful, contemporary building that is a real landmark for the town. The centre is designed to be a meeting place for Indigenous and non-Indigenous people, and a chance to share cultures – you can listen to locals share their stories on multimedia screens. Don't miss this place when you're in town. It's 1km south of Katherine, just after the public swimming pool.

The centre houses a beautiful gallery space hosting Territory artworks, and a performing arts venue seating up to 400 people.

Top Didj Cultural Experience & Art Gallery — GALLERY

(☎08-8971 2751; www.topdidj.com; cnr Gorge & Jaensch Rds; cultural experience adult/child/family $65/45/200; ⏰cultural experience 9.30am & 2.30pm Sun-Fri, 9.30am & 1.30pm Sat) Run by the owners of the Katherine Art Gallery, Top Didj is a good place to see Aboriginal artists at work. The cultural experience is hands-on with fire sticks, spear throwing, painting and basket weaving.

Katherine Museum — MUSEUM

(Map p848; ☎08-8972 3945; www.katherinemuseum.com; Gorge Rd; adult/child $10/4; ⏰9am-4pm) The museum is in the old airport terminal, about 3km from town on the road to the gorge. The original Gypsy Moth biplane flown by Dr Clyde Fenton, the first Flying Doctor, is housed here, along with plenty of interesting old rusty trucks. There's a good selection of historical photos, including a display on the 1998 flood.

Tours

Gecko Canoeing & Trekking — OUTDOORS

(☎1800 634 319, 0427 067 154; www.geckocanoeing.com.au) Exhilarating guided canoe trips on the more remote stretches of the Katherine River. Trips include three days ($860) on the Katherine River and six days ($1600) on the Daly and Katherine Rivers. A five-day hike along the Jatbula Trail in Nitmiluk National Park costs $1600. Gecko can also shuttle Jatbula Trail hikers from Leliyn back to Katherine or Nitmiluk National Park HQ. Minimum numbers apply.

Crocodile Night Adventure — CRUISE

(☎1800 089 103; www.travelnorth.com.au; adult/child $75/49; ⏰6.30pm May-Oct) At Springvale Homestead, this evening cruise seeks out crocs and other nocturnal wildlife on the Katherine River. Includes BBQ dinner and drinks.

Travel North — SIGHTSEEING

(Map p848; ☎08-8971 9999, 1800 089 103; www.travelnorth.com.au; 6 Katherine Tce, Transit Centre) Katherine-based tour operator with a range of tours to Kakadu, Arnhem Land and Litchfield, and full-day Katherine town tours. Also booking agent for the Ghan and Greyhound.

Festivals & Events

Katherine Country Music Muster — MUSIC

(www.kcmm.com.au; adult/child $35/free) 'We like both kinds of music: country *and* western.' Plenty of live music in the pubs and entertainment at the Tick Market Lindsay St Complex on a weekend in May or June. Check the website for actual dates.

Sleeping

Coco's Backpackers — HOSTEL $

(Map p848; ☎08-8971 2889; coco@21firstst.com.au; 21 First St; camping per person $20, dm $35) Travellers love this place, with Indigenous art on the walls and didgeridoos in the tin shed next door helping to provide an authentic Katherine experience. Coco's is a converted home where the owner chats with the guests and has great knowledge about the town and local area. Aboriginal artists are often here painting didgeridoos.

Katherine Low Level Caravan Park — CARAVAN PARK $

(☎08-8972 3962; http://katherine-low-level-caravan-park.nt.big4.com.au; Shadforth Rd; unpowered/powered sites $37/40, safari tent $90;

❄📶🏊) A well-manicured park with plenty of shady sites, a great swimming pool adjoining a bar and an excellent bistro (mains $22 to $27) that is sheltered by a magnificent fig tree. The amenities are first rate, making it the pick of the town's several caravan parks. It's about 5km along the Victoria Hwy from town and across the Low Level bridge.

Knott's Crossing Resort MOTEL $$
(Map p848; ☎08-8972 2511; www.knottscrossing.com.au; cnr Cameron & Giles Sts; unpowered/powered sites $27/43, cabin/motel d from $110/160; ❄@📶🏊🐾) Probably the pick of Katherine's accommodation options. There is variety to suit most budgets; a fantastic restaurant; and the whole place is very professionally run. Everything is packed pretty tightly into the tropical gardens at Knott's, but it's easy to find your own little nook. It's also on the way to Katherine Gorge, giving you a head start if you want to get there early.

Katherine River Lodge Motel MOTEL $$
(Map p848; ☎08-8971 0266; http://katherineriverlodge.com.au; 50 Giles St; d/f from $120/180; ❄@🏊) The rooms here recently underwent a facelift. While the service could do with a facelift too, the rooms are secure, have a modern touch and are well kept. This large complex (three three-storey blocks) in a tropical garden is particularly recommended for families, as there are interconnecting rooms available. The attached restaurant serves up excellent tucker.

St Andrews Apartments APARTMENTS $$$
(Map p848; ☎1800 686 106, 08-8971 2288; www.standrewsapts.com.au; 27 First St; apt $230-285; ❄📶🏊) In the heart of town, these serviced apartments are great for families and those pining for a few home comforts. The two-bedroom apartments sleep four (six if you use the sofa bed), and come with fully equipped kitchen and lounge/dining area. Nifty little BBQ decks are attached to the ground-floor units.

Eating

Coffee Club CAFE $
(Map p848; www.coffeeclub.com.au; cnr Katherine Tce & Warburton St; meals $12-20; ⏲6.30am-5pm Mon-Fri, 7am-4pm Sat & Sun) This is the best place in town for breakfast, as well as being a good bet at lunchtime. Dining is in a light-filled contemporary space. On offer is decent coffee, healthy breakfast options including fruit and muesli, plus burgers, sandwiches, wraps and salads all day.

★Escarpment Restaurant MODERN AUSTRALIAN $$
(Map p848; ☎08-8971 1600; 50 Giles St; lunch $12, dinner $25; ⏲11.30am-2.30pm & 5-10pm Mon-Sat) The exceedingly nice outdoor area, apart from its view of the car park, makes outdoor dining here very tempting. Happily the food backs the aesthetics. Lunches consist of burgers, wraps, salads and seafood dishes, with food preparation and presentation a step above most other places in town.

Savannah Bar & Restaurant MODERN AUSTRALIAN $$
(Map p848; ☎08-8972 2511; www.knottscrossing.com.au/restaurant; cnr Giles & Cameron Sts, Knott's Crossing Resort; mains $25-35; ⏲6.30-9am & 6-9pm) Undoubtedly one of the best dining choices in Katherine. It's predominantly an outdoors garden restaurant, with a cool breeze often wafting through the tropical vegetation. The menu includes steak, barramundi and Venus Bay prawn dishes. There's even a suckling pig you can tuck into. Service is fast and friendly, and the whole place is very well run.

Information

Katherine Hospital (☎08-8973 9211; www.health.nt.gov.au; Giles St) About 3km north of town, with an emergency department.

Katherine Visitor Information Centre (Map p848; ☎1800 653 142; www.visitkatherine.com.au; cnr Lindsay St & Stuart Hwy; ⏲8.30am-5pm daily in the Dry, 8.30am-5pm Mon-Fri, 10am-2pm Sat & Sun in the Wet) Modern, air-con information centre stocking information on all areas of the Northern Territory. Pick up the handy *Katherine Region Visitor Guide*.

Parks & Wildlife (Map p848; ☎08-8973 8888; www.parksandwildlife.nt.gov.au; 32 Giles St; ⏲8am-4.20pm) National park information and notes.

Getting There & Around

Katherine is a major road junction: from here the Stuart Hwy tracks north and south, and the Victoria Hwy heads west to Kununurra in WA.

Greyhound Australia (www.greyhound.com.au) has regular services between Darwin and Alice Springs, Queensland or WA. Buses stop at **Katherine Transit Centre** (Map p848; ☎08-8971 9999; 6 Katherine Tce). One-way fares from Katherine include: Darwin ($105, four hours), Alice Springs ($335, 16 hours), Tennant Creek ($220, 8½ hours) and Kununurra ($158, 4½ hours).

Katherine

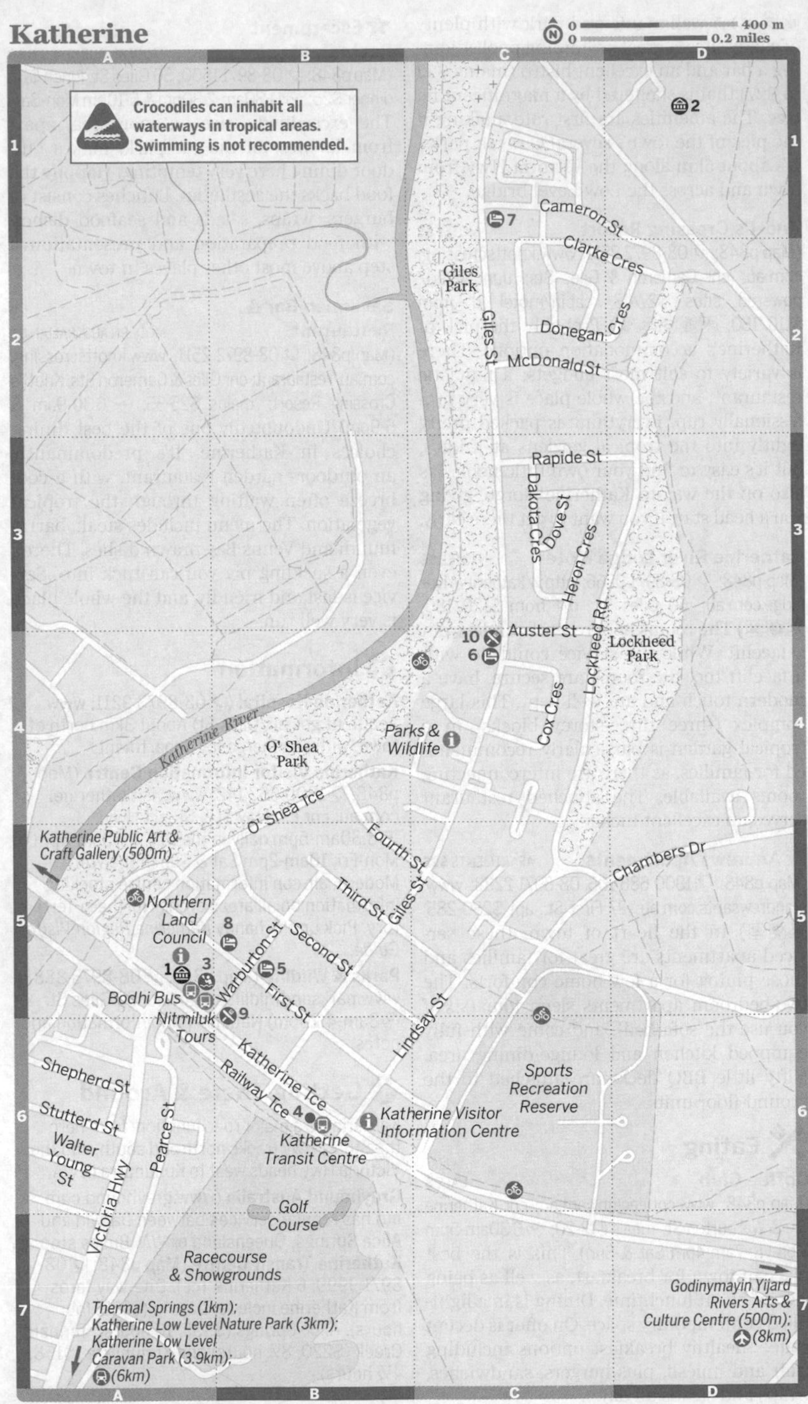

0 400 m
0 0.2 miles
Crocodiles can inhabit all waterways in tropical areas. Swimming is not recommended.
Cameron St
Clarke Cres
Giles Park
Donegan Cres
Giles St
McDonald St
Rapide St
Dakota Cres
Dove St
Heron Cres
Auster St
Lockheed Rd
Lockheed Park
Cox Cres
Katherine River
O' Shea Park
Parks & Wildlife
O' Shea Tce
Fourth St
Chambers Dr
Katherine Public Art & Craft Gallery (500m)
Northern Land Council
Third St
Giles St
Second St
Warburton St
First St
Bodhi Bus
Nitmiluk Tours
Lindsay St
Katherine Tce
Railway Tce
Shepherd St
Stutterd St
Walter Young St
Pearce St
Victoria Hwy
Sports Recreation Reserve
Katherine Visitor Information Centre
Katherine Transit Centre
Golf Course
Racecourse & Showgrounds
Thermal Springs (1km); Katherine Low Level Nature Park (3km); Katherine Low Level Caravan Park (3.9km); (6km)
Godinymayin Yijard Rivers Arts & Culture Centre (500m); (8km)

Katherine

Sights

1 Djilpin Arts A5
2 Katherine Museum D1

Activities, Courses & Tours

3 Nitmiluk Tours A5
4 Travel North B6

Sleeping

5 Coco's Backpackers B5
6 Katherine River Lodge Motel C4
7 Knott's Crossing Resort C1
8 St Andrews Apartments B5

Eating

9 Coffee Club B5
10 Escarpment Restaurant C4
Savannah Bar & Restaurant .... (see 7)

An alternative is the **Bodhi Bus** (Map p848; http://thebodhibus.com.au), which travels to remote communities and also services the Katherine-Darwin route ($60 one way, Monday, Thursday and Saturday), dropping off passengers at the Palmerston bus exchange or Darwin airport.

The Ghan train, operated by **Great Southern Rail** (www.gsr.com.au), travels between Adelaide and Darwin twice a week, stopping at Katherine for four hours – enough for a whistlestop tour to Katherine Gorge! **Nitmiluk Tours** (Map p848; ☎1300 146 743; www.nitmiluktours.com.au; Katherine Tce; ⏲9am-5pm Mon-Sat) runs shuttles between the station and town.

AROUND KATHERINE

Cutta Cutta Caves Nature Park

About 30km south of Katherine, turn your back on the searing sun and dip down 15m below terra firma into this mazelike limestone cave system. The 1499-hectare **Cutta Cutta Caves Nature Park** (☎08-8972 1940; www.parksandwildlife.nt.gov.au/parks/find/cuttacuttacaves; tours adult/child $20/10; ⏲8.30am-4.30pm, guided tours 9am, 10am, 11am, 1pm, 2pm & 3pm) has a unique ecology and you'll be sharing the space with brown tree snakes and pythons, plus the endangered ghost bats and orange horseshoe bats that they feed on. Cutta Cutta is a Jawoyn name meaning many stars; it was taboo for Aboriginal people to enter the cave, which they believed was where the stars were kept during the day. Admission by tour only.

Nitmiluk (Katherine Gorge) National Park

Spectacular **Katherine Gorge** forms the backbone of the 2920-sq-km **Nitmiluk (Katherine Gorge) National Park** (www.parksandwildlife.nt.gov.au/parks/find/nitmiluk), about 30km from Katherine. A series of 13 deep sandstone **gorges** have been carved out by the **Katherine River** on its journey from Arnhem Land to the Timor Sea. It is a hauntingly beautiful place – though it can get crowded in peak season – and a must-do from Katherine. In the Dry the tranquil river is perfect for a paddle, but in the Wet the deep, still waters and dividing rapids are engulfed by an awesome torrent that churns through the gorge. Plan to spend at least a full day canoeing or cruising on the river and bushwalking.

The traditional owners are the Jawoyn Aboriginal people who jointly manage Nitmiluk with Parks & Wildlife. Nitmiluk Tours manages accommodation, cruises and activities within the park.

Sights

Leliyn (Edith Falls) NATURE RESERVE

Reached off the Stuart Hwy 40km north of Katherine and a further 20km along a sealed road, Leliyn is an idyllic, safe haven for swimming and hiking. The moderate **Leliyn Trail** (2.6km loop, 1½ hours) climbs into escarpment country through grevillea and spinifex and past scenic lookouts (Bemang is best in the afternoon) to the Upper Pool, where the moderate **Sweetwater Pool Trail** (8.6km return, three to five hours) branches off. The peaceful Sweetwater Pool has a small **camping ground** (per person $3.30, plus deposit $50); overnight permits are available at the kiosk.

The main **Lower Pool** – a gorgeous, mirror-flat swimming lagoon – is a quick 150m dash from the car park. The Parks & Wildlife **camping ground** (☎08-8975 4869; adult/child $12/6) next to the car park has grassy sites, lots of shade, toilets, showers, a laundry and facilities for the disabled. Fees are paid at the **kiosk** (⏲8am-6pm May-Oct, 9.30am-3pm Nov-Apr), which sells snacks and basic supplies. Nearby is a picnic area with BBQs and tables.

Activities

Bushwalking

The park has around 120km of marked walking tracks, ranging from 2km stretches to 66km multinight hikes. Overnight hikers must register at the Nitmiluk Centre. There's a $50 refundable deposit for any overnight walk and a camping fee of $3.30 per person per night. The Nitmiluk Centre has maps and info on the full range of walks.

Barrawei (Lookout) Loop BUSHWALKING
Starting with a short, steep climb this walk (3.7km loop, two hours, moderate difficulty) provides good views over the Katherine River.

Butterfly Gorge BUSHWALKING
A challenging, shady walk (12km return, 4½ hours) through a pocket of monsoon rainforest, often with butterflies, leads to midway along the second gorge and a deep-water swimming spot.

Jawoyn Valley BUSHWALKING
A difficult (40km loop, overnight) wilderness trail leading off the Eighth Gorge Walk into a valley with rock outcrops and rock-art galleries.

Jatbula Trail BUSHWALKING
This renowned walk (66km one way, five days, difficult) to Leliyn (Edith Falls) climbs the Arnhem Land escarpment, passing the swamp-fed Biddlecombe Cascades, Crystal Falls, the Amphitheatre and the Sweetwater Pool. This walk can only be done one way (ie you can't walk from Leliyn to Katherine Gorge), is closed from October to April, and requires a minimum of two walkers.

A ferry service takes you across the gorge to kick things off.

Canoeing

Nothing beats exploring the gorges in your own boat, and lots of travellers canoe at least as far as the first or second gorge. Bear in mind the intensity of the sun and heat, and the fact that you may have to carry your canoe over the rock bars and rapids that separate the gorges. Pick up the *Canoeing Guide* at the Nitmiluk Centre. If you want to use your own canoe you need to pay a registration fee of $5.50 per person, plus a refundable $50 deposit.

Nitmiluk Tours CANOEING
(Map p848; ☎08-8972 1253, 1300 146 743; www.nitmiluktours.com.au) From April to November, Nitmiluk Tours hires out single/double canoes for a half day ($53/76 plus $50 deposit, departing 8am and 12.30pm) or full day ($66/98, departing 8am), including the use of a splash-proof drum for cameras and other gear (it's not fully waterproof), a map and a life jacket. The canoe shed is at the boat ramp by the main car park, about 500m beyond the Nitmiluk Centre.

The half-day hire only allows you to paddle up the first gorge; with the full day you can get up as far as the third gorge depending on your level of fitness – start early. You can also be a little more adventurous and take the canoes out overnight for $126/140 a single/double, plus $3.30 for a camping permit – there are camp sites at the fifth, sixth, eighth and ninth gorges. Bookings are essential as overnight permits are limited and there is a $60 deposit. Don't take this trip lightly though.

Tours

Nitmiluk Tours CRUISES
(☎08-8972 1253, 1300 146 743; www.nitmiluktours.com.au) An easy way to see far into the gorge is on a cruise. Bookings on some cruises can be tight in the peak season; make your reservation at least a day in advance.

The two-hour cruise goes to the second gorge and visits a rock-art gallery (including an 800m walk). Departures are at 9am, 11am, 1pm and 3pm daily year-round depending on river level. There's wheelchair access to the top of the first gorge only. The four-hour cruise goes to the third gorge and includes refreshments and a chance to swim. This cruise leaves at 9am daily from April to November, plus at 11am and 1pm May to August.

There's also a more leisurely two-hour breakfast cruise, leaving at 7am April to November, and a sunset cruise, sailing at 4.30pm, nightly from May to October, with a candlelit buffet dinner and champagne.

Nitmiluk Tours SCENIC FLIGHTS
(☎1300 146 743; www.nitmiluktours.com.au) Nitmiluk Tours offers a variety of flights ranging from an eight-minute buzz over the first gorge (per person $99) to a 20-minute flight over all 13 gorges ($235). There are broader tours that take in Aboriginal rock-art sites and Kakadu National Park. Book at the Nitmiluk Centre.

Sleeping

There are bush-camping sites for overnight walkers throughout the park, and perma-

GHUNMARN CULTURAL CENTRE

If you're interested in seeing genuine Aboriginal art produced by local communities, it's worth detouring off the Stuart Hwy to the remote cultural centre of Beswick.

The small community, reached via the sealed Central Arnhem Hwy, is 56km east of the Stuart Hwy on the southern fringes of Arnhem Land. Here you'll find the **Ghunmarn Culture Centre** (☎08-8977 4250; www.djilpinarts.org.au; Beswick; ⏲9.30am-4pm Mon-Fri Apr-Nov), opened in 2007, and displaying local artworks, prints, carvings, weavings and didgeridoos from western Arnhem Land. The centre also features the Blanasi Collection, a permanent exhibition of works by elders from the western Arnhem Land region. Visitors are welcome to visit the centre without a permit – call ahead to check that it's open. If you can't get out here, drop in to **Djilpin Arts** (Map p848; ☎08-8971 1770; www.djilpinarts.org.au; 27 Katherine Tce; ⏲9am-4pm Mon-Fri) in Katherine instead.

A very special festival at Beswick is **Walking With Spirits** (www.djilpinarts.org.au/visit-us/walking-with-spirits); magical performances of traditional corroborees staged in conjunction with the Australian Shakespeare Company. It's held in July. Camping is possible at Beswick Falls over this weekend but advance bookings are essential.

nent camping grounds near the Nitmiluk Visitor Centre and at Leliyn (Edith Falls).

Nitmiluk National Park Campground CAMPGROUND $
(☎1300 146 743, 08-8972 1253; www.nitmiluktours.com.au; unpowered/powered sites $38/44, safari tents $130; 📶🏊) Plenty of grass and shade, hot showers, toilets, BBQs, a laundry and a kiosk by the good-lookin' swimming pool. Wallabies and goannas are frequent visitors. There's a 'tent village' here with permanent safari tents sleeping two people. Book at the Nitmiluk Centre.

Nitmiluk Chalets CABINS $$$
(☎1300 146 743, 08-8972 1253; www.nitmiluktours.com.au; 1-/2-bedroom cabins $205/255; ❄📶🏊) Next door to the caravan park, these cabins are a serviceable choice if you'd rather have a solid roof over your head (and a flat-screen TV). Access to all the caravan park facilities (pool, BBQs, kiosk etc).

Cicada Lodge BOUTIQUE HOTEL $$$
(☎08-8974 3100, 1800 242 232; www.cicadalodge.com.au; Nitmiluk National Park; d incl breakfast $700; ❄@📶🏊) This luxury lodge has been architecturally designed to meld modern sophistication and traditional Jawoyn themes. It has just 18 luxury rooms overlooking the Katherine River. Decor is tasteful and stylish, and features include full-length louvred doors that open onto private balconies. Indigenous artworks decorate the walls. The outdoor deck overlooking the swimming pool, itself looking into bushland, is all class. If you're after a treat, this could be the place.

ℹ Information

The **Nitmiluk Centre** (☎1300 146 743, 08-8972 1253; www.nitmiluktours.com.au; ⏲6.30am-5.30pm) has excellent displays and information on the park's geology, wildlife, the traditional owners (the Jawoyn) and European history. There's also a restaurant here (snacks and meals $7 to $25), and a desk for Parks & Wildlife, which has information sheets on a wide range of marked walking tracks that start here and traverse the picturesque country south of the gorge. Registration for overnight walks and camping permits ($3.30 per night) is from 8am to 1pm; canoeing permits are also issued.

ℹ Getting There & Away

It's 30km by sealed road from Katherine to the Nitmiluk Centre, and a few hundred metres further to the car park, where the gorge begins and the cruises start.

Daily transfers between Katherine and the gorge are run by **Nitmiluk Tours** (Map p848; ☎1300 146 743, 08-8972 1253; www.nitmiluktours.com.au; 27 Katherine Tce, Shop 2, Katherine; adult/child return $27/19), departing the Nitmiluk Town Booking Office and also picking up at local accommodation places on request. Buses leave Katherine three times daily.

KATHERINE TO WESTERN AUSTRALIA

The sealed Victoria Hwy – part of the Savannah Way – stretches 513km from Katherine to Kununurra in WA. A 4WD will get you into a few out-of-the-way national parks accessed off the Victoria Hwy, or you can meander through semiarid desert and sandstone outcrops until bloated boab trees herald your imminent arrival in WA. All fruits, vegetables, nuts and honey must be left at the quarantine inspection post on the border.

Giwining/Flora River Nature Park

The dams were created as the mineral-rich Flora River deposited calcium carbonate onto roots and fallen branches, creating limestone tufa dams; the effect is a series of pretty cascades. Within **Giwining/Flora River Nature Park** (www.parksandwildlife.nt.gov.au/parks/find/florariver) there's a **camping ground** (www.parksandwildlife.nt.gov.au/parks/find/florariver; adult/child $6.60/3.30) at Djarrung with an amenities block. The Flora River has crocs, so there's no swimming.

The park turn-off is 90km southwest of Katherine; the park entrance is a further 32km along a passable dirt road (OK for 2WD cars in the Dry).

Victoria River Crossing

The red sandstone cliffs surrounding the spot where the highway crosses the Victoria River (194km west of Katherine) create a dramatic setting. Much of this area forms the eastern section of Judbarra (Gregory National Park). The **Victoria River Roadhouse Caravan Park** (fax 08-8975 0744; Victoria Hwy; unpowered/powered sites $20/25, d $135), west of the bridge, has a shop, a bar and meals ($14 to $32).

Timber Creek

POP 231

Tiny Timber Creek is the only town between Katherine and Kununurra. It has a pretty big history for such a small place, with an early European exploration aboard the *Tom Tough* requiring repairs to be carried out with local timber (hence the town's name). The expedition's leader, AC Gregory, inscribed his arrival date into a boab; it is still discernable (and is explained in detail through interpretive panels) at **Gregory's Tree**, 15km northwest of town. The Tree is off the Victoria Hwy down a 3km unsealed road, which can become corrugated.

A highlight of Timber Creek is the **Victoria River Cruise** (☎0427 750 731; www.victoriarivercruise.com; sunset cruises adult/child $95/50, wildlife cruises adult/child $60/30; ⌚daily Apr-Sep), which takes you 40km downriver spotting wildlife and returning in time for a fiery sunset.

The town is dominated by the roadside **Timber Creek Hotel & Circle F Caravan Park** (☎08-8975 0722; www.timbercreekhotel.com.au; Victoria Hwy; unpowered/powered sites $27/30, d $100; ❄️🏊). Enormous trees shade parts of the camping area, which is next to a small creek where there's croc feeding every evening (5pm). The complex includes the Timber Creek Hotel and Fogarty's Store.

Judbarra/Gregory National Park

The remote and rugged wilderness of the little-visited **Judbarra/Gregory National Park** (www.parksandwildlife.nt.gov.au/parks/find/gregory) will swallow you up. Covering 12,860 sq km, it sits at the transitional zone between the tropical and semiarid regions. The park consists of old cattle country and is made up of two separate sections: the eastern (Victoria River) section and the much larger Bullita section in the west.

Parks & Wildlife (☎08-8975 0888; www.parksandwildlife.nt.gov.au; Timber Creek; ⌚7am-4.30pm) in Timber Creek has park and 4WD notes. It can also provide a map featuring the various walks, camping spots, tracks and the historic homestead and ruggedly romantic original stockyards – a must before heading in. This is croc country; swimming isn't safe.

Keep River National Park

The remote **Keep River National Park** (www.nretas.nt.gov.au/national-parks-and-reserves/parks/find/keepriver) is noted for its stunning sandstone formations, beautiful desolation and rock art. Pamphlets detailing walks are available at the start of the excellent trails. Don't miss the **rock-art walk** (5.5km return, two hours) near Jarnem, and the **gorge walk** (3km return, two hours) at Jinumum.

The park entrance is just 3km from the WA border. You can reach the park's main points by conventional vehicle during the Dry. A **rangers station** (☎08-9167 8827) lies 3km into the park from the main road, and there are basic, sandstone-surrounded **camping grounds** (adult/child $3.30/1.65) at Gurrandalng (18km into the park) and Jarnem (32km). Tank water is available at Jarnem.

MATARANKA & ELSEY NATIONAL PARK

POP 244

With soothing, warm thermal springs set in pockets of palms and tropical vegetation, you'd be mad not to pull into Mataranka for at least a few hours to soak off the road dust. The small settlement regularly swells with towel-toting visitors shuffling to the thermal pool or the spring-fed Elsey National Park.

Sights & Activities

Mataranka's crystal-clear **thermal pool**, shrouded in rainforest, is 10km from town beside the Mataranka Homestead Resort. The warm, clear water, dappled by light filtered through overhanging palms, rejuvenates a lot of bodies on any given day; it's reached via a boardwalk from the resort and can get mighty crowded. About 200m away (keep following the boardwalk) is the **Waterhouse River**, where you can rent canoes for $12 per hour. **Stevie's Hole**, a natural swimming hole in the cooler Waterhouse River, about 1.5km from the homestead, is rarely crowded.

Elsey National Park NATIONAL PARK
(www.parksandwildlife.nt.gov.au/parks/find/elsey) The national park adjoins the thermal-pool reserve and offers peaceful **camping**, **fishing** and **walking** along the Waterhouse and Roper Rivers. **Bitter Springs** is a serene palm-fringed thermal pool within the national park, 3km from Mataranka along the sealed Martin Rd. The almost unnatural blue-green colour of the 34°C water is due to dissolved limestone particles.

Sleeping & Eating

Mataranka Homestead Resort CAMPGROUND $
(☎08-8975 4544; www.matarankahomestead.com.au; Homestead Rd; unpowered/powered sites $24/29, dm/d/cabins $25/90/115;) Only metres from the main thermal pool and with a range of budget accommodation, this is a *very* popular option. The large camping ground is dusty but has a few shady areas and decent amenities. The fan-cooled hostel rooms are very basic (linen provided). The air-con motel rooms (also rudimentary) have fridge, TV and bathroom, while the cabins have a kitchenette and sleep up to six people. Book ahead.

Mataranka Cabins CABINS $$
(☎08-8975 4838; www.matarankacabins.com.au; 4705 Martin Rd, Bitter Springs; unpowered/powered sites $25/30, cabins $120;) On the banks of the Little Roper River, only a few hundred metres from Bitter Springs thermal pool, this quiet bush setting has some amazing termite mounds adorning the front paddock. The TV-equipped, open-plan cabins have a balcony with bush views. Pets welcome.

★**Territory Manor Motel & Caravan Park** MOTEL $$
(☎08-8975 4516; www.matarankamotel.com; Martin Rd; unpowered/powered sites $26/30, s/d $105/120;) Mataranka's best caravan park is well positioned and a class act – no surprise it's also popular. Smallish motel rooms are well decked out and have good-size bathrooms, and the grounds are well shaded for camping. Pet barramundi are hand fed in spectacular fashion twice a day. Their cousins are served up in the licensed bistro (mains $20 to $35) along with steaks, salad etc.

BARKLY TABLELAND & GULF COUNTRY

East of the Stuart Hwy lies some of the Territory's most remote cattle country, but parts are accessible by sealed road and the rivers and inshore waters of the Gulf coast are regarded as some of the best **fishing** locales in the country.

Roper Highway

Not far south of Mataranka on the Stuart Hwy, the mostly sealed single-lane Roper Hwy strikes 175km eastwards to **Roper Bar**, crossing the paperbark- and pandanus-lined Roper River, where freshwater meets saltwater. It's passable only in the Dry. Keen fisherfolk stop here, with accommodation, fuel and supplies available at the **Roper Bar Store** (☎08-8975 4636; www.roperbar.com.au; unpowered site $20, s/d $115/135). Roper Bar is an access point to Borroloola. Head south along the rough-going Nathan River Rd through **Limmen National Park** (www.parksandwildlife.nt.gov.au/parks/find/limmen) – high-clearance with two spares required – and into southeastern Arnhem Land.

Continuing east along the highway for 45km from Roper Bar leads to the Aboriginal community of **Ngukurr**, home to about 1000 people from nine different language groups and cultures. This cultural diversity informs the unique works on show and available to buy from the **Ngukurr Arts Centre** (☎08-8975 4260; http://ngukurrarts.net.au/Ngukurr_Art/About_art_center.html; ⊙10am-4pm Mon-Fri); no permit is required to visit the centre.

Carpentaria & Tablelands Highways

Just south of Daly Waters, the sealed Carpentaria Hwy (Hwy 1) heads 378km east to Borroloola near the Gulf of Carpentaria – one of the NT's top barramundi fishing spots. After 267km the Carpentaria Hwy meets the sealed Tablelands Hwy at Cape Crawford. At this intersection is the famous **Heartbreak Hotel** (☎08-8975 9928; www.heartbreakhotel.com.au; cnr Carpentaria & Tablelands Hwys, Cape Crawford; unpowered/powered sites $20/28, s/d $75/90; ❄). Pitch the tent on the shaded grassy lawn and park yourself on the wide verandah with a cold beer. Breakfast, lunch and dinner (meals $16 to $28) are available.

From here it's a desolate 374km south across the Barkly Tableland to the Barkly Hwy (Rte 66) and the **Barkly Homestead Roadhouse** (☎08-8964 4549; www.barklyhomestead.com.au; unpowered/powered sites $25/32, cabins & motel d $150; ❄≋), a surprisingly upbeat roadhouse. From here it's 210km west to Tennant Creek and 252km east to the Queensland border.

Borroloola

POP 927

On the **McArthur River** close to the bountiful waters of the Gulf, Borroloola is big news for **fishing** fans, but unless you're keen on baiting a hook (the barramundi season peaks from February to April) or driving the remote (preferably 4WD) **Savannah Way** to Queensland, it's a long way to go for not much reward.

The **Savannah Way Motel** (☎08-8975 8883; www.savannahwaymotel.com.au; Robinson Rd; r $80-130, cabins $130; ❄≋), on the main road through town, is clean and comfortable, with cabins, lodge rooms and tropical gardens.

MATARANKA TO TENNANT CREEK

Larrimah

POP 18

Once upon a time the railway line from Darwin came as far as Birdum, 8km south of tiny Larrimah, which itself is 185km south of Katherine. Originally a WWII officers' mess, **Pink Panther (Larrimah) Hotel** (☎08-8975 9931; unpowered/powered sites $20/25, d $70-90; ❄≋) is a cheerfully rustic and quirky pub offering basic rooms, meals (mains $12 to $32) and a menagerie of animals. **Fran's Devonshire Teahouse** (Stuart Hwy; meals $6-20; ⊙8am-4pm) makes a great lunchtime pit stop. Try a legendary camel or buffalo pie, or just a Devonshire tea (a long way from Exeter) or fresh coffee.

Daly Waters

POP 25

About 3km off the highway and 160km south of Mataranka is Daly Waters, an important staging post in the early days of aviation – Amy Johnson landed here on her epic flight from England to Australia in 1930. Just about everyone stops at the famous **Daly Waters Pub** (☎08-8975 9927; www.dalywaterspub.com; unpowered/powered sites $16/28, d $70-110, cabins $135-175; ❄≋). Decorated with business cards, bras, banknotes and memorabilia from passing travellers, the pub claims to be the oldest in the Territory (its liquor licence has been valid since 1893). It has become a bit of a legend along the Track, although it may be a bit too popular for its own good. Every evening from April to September there's an Australiana show with host Chilli, often supported by local musicians. Hearty meals (mains $12 to $30, open lunch and dinner), including the filling barra burger, are served. Beside the pub is a dustbowl camping ground with a bit of shade – book ahead or arrive early to secure a powered site. Accommodation ranges from basic dongas (small, transportable buildings) to spacious self-contained cabins.

Daly Waters to Three Ways

Heading south from Daly Waters, you encounter the fascinating ghost town of **Newcastle Waters**, 3km west of the highway. Its atmospheric, historic buildings include the Junction Hotel, cobbled together from abandoned windmills in 1932. South of the cattle town of **Elliott**, the land gets drier and drier and the vegetation sparser. The mesmerising sameness breaks at **Renner Springs**, generally accepted as the dividing line between the seasonally wet Top End and the dry Centre; there's a decent roadhouse here.

Banka Banka (☎08-8964 4511; adult/child $10/5) is a historic cattle station 100km north of Tennant Creek, with a grassy camping area (no power), marked walking tracks (one leading to a tranquil waterhole), a mud-brick bar, and a small kiosk selling basic refreshments.

Three Ways, 537km north of Alice, is the junction of the Stuart and Barkly Hwys, from where you can head south to Alice, north to Darwin (988km) or east to Mt Isa in Queensland (643km). **Threeways Roadhouse** (☎08-8962 2744; www.threewaysroadhouse.com.au; Stuart Hwy; unpowered/powered sites $24/32, d $100-115; ❄@≋) is a potential stopover with a bar and restaurant, but Tennant Creek is only 26km further south.

TENNANT CREEK

POP 3061

Tennant Creek is the only town of any size between Katherine, 680km to the north, and Alice Springs, 511km to the south. It's a good place to break up a long drive and check out the town's few attractions. Tennant Creek is known as Jurnkurakurr to the local Warumungu people and almost half of the population is of Aboriginal descent.

Sights & Activities

Nyinkka Nyunyu GALLERY

(☎08-8962 2699; www.nyinkkanyunyu.com.au; Paterson St; tour guide $15; ⌚9am-5pm Mon-Fri, 10am-2pm Sat & Sun Oct-Apr, 8am-6pm Mon-Sat, 10am-2pm Sun May-Sep) This innovative museum and gallery highlights the dynamic art and culture of the local Warumungu people. The absorbing displays focus on contemporary art, traditional objects (many returned from interstate museums), bush medicine and regional history. The diorama series, or bush TVs as they became known within the community, are particularly special.

Nyinkka Nyunyu is located beside a sacred site of the spiky tailed goanna. Learn about bush tucker and Dreaming stories with your personal guide. There's also a gallery store and the lovely Jajjikari Café, which serves espresso coffee and light meals.

Battery Hill Mining Centre MINE

(☎08-8962 1281; www.barklytourism.com.au; Peko Rd; adult/child $25/15; ⌚9am-5pm) Experience life in Tennant Creek's 1930s gold rush at this mining centre, which doubles as the Visitor Information Centre, 2km east of town. There are **underground mine tours** and audio tours of the 10-head **battery**. In addition there is a superb **Minerals Museum** and you can try your hand at gold panning. The admission price gives access to all of the above, or you can choose to visit the Minerals and Social History Museums only (adult/family $7/15), or just go panning (per person $2).

While you're here, ask for the key ($20 refundable deposit) to the old Telegraph Station, which is just off the highway about 12km north of town. This is one of only four of the original 11 stations remaining in the Territory. Just north of the Telegraph Station is the turn-off west to Kundjarra (The Pebbles), a formation of granite boulders like a miniature version of the better-known Devil's Marbles found 100km south. It's a sacred women's Dreaming site of the Warumungu.

Sleeping & Eating

Tourist's Rest Youth Hostel HOSTEL $

(☎08-8962 2719; www.touristrest.com.au; cnr Leichhardt & Windley Sts; dm/d $30/65; ❄@≋) This small, friendly and slightly ramshackle hostel has bright clean rooms, free breakfast and VIP discounts. The hostel can organise tours of the gold mines and Devil's Marbles, plus pick-up from the bus stop.

Outback Caravan Park CAMPGROUND $

(☎08-8962 2459; Peko Rd; unpowered/powered sites $15/36, cabins $70-150; ❄≋) In a town that often feels parched, it's nice to be in the shade of this grassy caravan park about 1km east of the centre. There's a well-stocked kiosk, camp kitchen and fuel. You may even be treated to some bush poetry and bush tucker, courtesy of yarn spinner Jimmy Hooker, at 7.30pm ($5). Decent outdoor bar area, but be quick, as it closes early.

Safari Lodge Motel MOTEL $$

(☎08-8962 2207; http://safari.budgetmotelchain.com.au; Davidson St; s/d $110/130; ❄@🛜)

You should book ahead to stay at this family-run motel. Safari Lodge is centrally located next to the best restaurant in town and has clean, fairly standard rooms with phone, fridge and TV.

Top of the Town Cafe CAFE **$**
(☎08-8962 1311; 163 Paterson St; breakfast $7-14; ⏲7am-3pm Mon-Fri, to 1pm Sat) Home of pinkmolly cupcakes, this little gem is slightly twee. It's cute, quirky and a little cramped inside, but there are tables and chairs on the footpath too. There are a range of toasties and bacon-and-egg options for brekky, making it the best place in town for breakfast.

Woks Up CHINESE **$$**
(☎08-8962 3888; 108 Paterson St; mains $14-24; ⏲5pm-late) The clean, modern dining room, backed by delicious, tasty food with clean flavours, makes Woks Up one of the Territory's best Chinese diners. Generous portions of stir-fry in satay, Mongolian or black-bean sauce.

Information

Leading Edge Computers (☎08-8962 3907; 145 Paterson St; per 20min $2; ⏲9am-5.30pm Mon-Wed & Fri, to 7pm Thu, to noon Sat; 📶) Internet access.

Police Station (☎08-8962 4444; Paterson St) The town police station.

Tennant Creek Hospital (☎08-8962 4399; Schmidt St) For medical emergencies.

Visitor Information Centre (☎1800 500 879; www.barklytourism.com.au; Peko Rd; ⏲9am-5pm Mon-Fri, to 1pm Sat) Located 2km east of town at Battery Hill.

Getting There & Away

All long-distance buses stop at the **Transit Centre** (☎08-8962 2727; 151 Paterson St; 9am-5pm Mon-Fri, 8.30-11.30am Sat), where you can purchase tickets. **Greyhound Australia** (☎1300 473 946; www.greyhound.com.au) has regular buses from Tennant Creek to Alice Springs ($205, six hours), Katherine ($215, 8½ hours), Darwin ($290, 14 hours) and Mount Isa ($170, eight hours).

The weekly Ghan rail link between Alice Springs and Darwin can drop off passengers in Tennant Creek, although cars can't be loaded or offloaded. The train station is about 6km south of town so you will need a **taxi** (☎08-8962 3626).

Car hire is available from **Thrifty** (☎08-8962 2207; Davidson St, Safari Lodge Motel).

TENNANT CREEK TO ALICE SPRINGS

The gigantic boulders in precarious piles beside the Stuart Hwy, 105km south of Tennant Creek, are called the **Devil's Marbles**. Karlu Karlu is their Warumungu name, and this registered sacred site has great cultural importance. The rocks are believed to be the eggs of the Rainbow Serpent.

A 15-minute walk loops around the main site. This geological phenomenon is particularly beautiful at sunrise and sunset, when these oddballs glow warmly. The **camping ground** (adult/child $3.30/1.65) has remarkably hard ground, pit toilets and fireplaces (BYO firewood).

At Wauchope (*war*-kup), 10km south of the Devil's Marbles, you will find the **Wauchope Hotel** (☎08-8964 1963; www.wauchopehotel.com.au; Stuart Hwy; unpowered/powered sites $14/20, budget s/d $60/100; ❄🏊). Budget rooms are dongas; the costlier rooms are more spacious, with bathrooms. Meals from the **restaurant** (☎08-8964 1963; www.wauchopehotel.com.au; Stuart Hwy; mains $18-33) are more than satisfactory.

At the kooky **Wycliffe Well Roadhouse & Holiday Park** (☎08-8964 1966, 1800 222 195; www.wycliffe.com.au; unpowered/powered sites $35/36, budget s/d from $60/70, s/d cabins with bathroom $120/140; ⏲6.30am-9pm; ❄@🏊), 17km south of Wauchope, you can fill up with fuel and food (mains $15 to $25) or stay and spot UFOs that apparently fly over with astonishing regularity. The place is decorated with alien figures and UFO newspaper clippings. The park has a grassy campground, an indoor pool, a kids' playground, a cafe and a range of international beer.

Heading south, you reach the rustic **Barrow Creek Hotel** (☎08-8956 9753; Stuart Hwy; powered camp sites $20, s/d $60/75), one of the highway's eccentric outback pubs. In the tradition of shearers who'd write their name on a banknote and pin it to the wall to ensure they could afford a drink when next they passed through, travellers continue to leave notes and photos. Food and fuel are available and next door is one of the original **Telegraph Stations** on the Overland Telegraph Line.

In the grand Australian tradition of building very big things by the side of the road to entice drivers to pull up, **Aileron**, 135km north of Alice, has Naked Charlie Quartpot, the 12m Anmatjere (Anmatyerre) man.

Charlie cuts a fine figure at the back of the local roadhouse, along with his larger-than-life family. The **Homestead Art Gallery** (☎08-8956 9111; Stuart Hwy) sells inexpensive paintings by the local Anmatjere community, as well as works from the Warlpiri community of Yuendumu.

About 70km north of Alice, the Plenty Hwy heads off to the east towards the **Harts Range**. The main reason to detour is to fossick in the gem fields about 78km east of the Stuart Hwy, which are well known for garnets and zircons. You're guaranteed to get lucky at the popular **Gemtree Caravan Park** (☎08-8956 9855; www.gemtree.com.au; Gemtree; unpowered/powered sites $22/30, cabins $85). For a taste of desert life, time your visit with the annual **Harts Range Races** (in August), one of the Territory's best outback rodeos.

THE TANAMI ROAD

Synonymous with isolated outback driving, the 1000km Tanami Rd connects Alice Springs with Halls Creek in WA and is essentially a short cut between central Australia and the Kimberley. In dry conditions it's possible to make it through the unsealed dust and corrugations in a well-prepared 2WD. Stay alert, as rollovers are common, and stock up with fuel, tyres, food and water.

The NT section is wide and usually well graded, and starts 20km north of Alice Springs. The road is sealed to **Tilmouth Well** (☎08-8956 8777; www.tilmouthwell.com; unpowered/powered sites $30/40, cabins without bathroom $80; ❄@≋) on the edge of Napperby Station which bills itself as an oasis in the desert with a sparkling pool and lush, sprawling lawns.

The next fuel stop is at **Yuendumu**, the largest remote community in the region and home to the Warlpiri people who were made famous in *Bush Mechanics* (www.bushmechanics.com). It's worth popping in to the **Warlukurlangu Art Centre** (☎08-8956 4133; www.warlu.com; ⊙9am-4pm Mon-Fri), a locally owned venture specialising in acrylic paintings.

From here there is no fuel for another 600km until you cross the WA border and hit the community of **Billiluna** (08-9168 8076, www.billiluna.org.au). Note, Rabbit Flat Roadhouse has closed permanently. Another 170km will have you resting your weary bones in Halls Creek.

ALICE SPRINGS

POP 25,186

Alice Springs tends to evoke contradiction and polarises travellers – some love it and some hate it. But either way, you'll undoubtedly end up here at some point if you tour the Red Centre. The town has a lot to offer visitors including a wide range of accommodation, excellent dining options and travel connections. For many travellers, Alice Springs is their first encounter with contemporary Indigenous Australia – with its enchanting art, mesmerising culture and present-day challenges.

This ruggedly beautiful town is shaped by its mythical landscapes, vibrant Aboriginal culture (where else can you hear six uniquely Australian languages in the main street?) and tough pioneering past. The town is a natural base for exploring central Australia, with Uluru-Kata Tjuta National Park a relatively short four-hour drive away. The mesmerising MacDonnell Ranges stretch east and west from the town centre, and you don't have to venture far to find yourself among ochre-red gorges, pastel-hued hills and ghostly white gum trees.

Sights

Alice Springs Desert Park WILDLIFE PARK
(☎08-8951 8788; www.alicespringsdesertpark.com.au; Larapinta Dr; adult/child $25/12.50; ⊙7.30am-6pm, last entry 4.30pm) If you haven't managed to glimpse a spangled grunter or marbled velvet gecko on your travels, head to the Desert Park where the creatures of central Australia are all on display in one place. The predominantly open-air exhibits faithfully recreate the animals' natural environments in a series of habitats: inland river, sand country and woodland.

It's an easy 2.5km cycle to the park. Alternatively, **Desert Park Transfers** (☎08-8952 1731; www.tailormadetours.com.au; adult/child $40/22) runs from Alice Springs five times daily. The cost includes park entry and pick-up/drop-off at your accommodation.

Try to time your visit with the terrific birds of prey show, featuring free-flying Australian kestrels, kites and awesome wedge-tailed eagles. To catch some of the park's rare and elusive animals, such as the bilby, visit the excellent nocturnal house. If you like what you see, come back at night and spotlight endangered species on the guided nocturnal tour (bookings essential).

Alice Springs

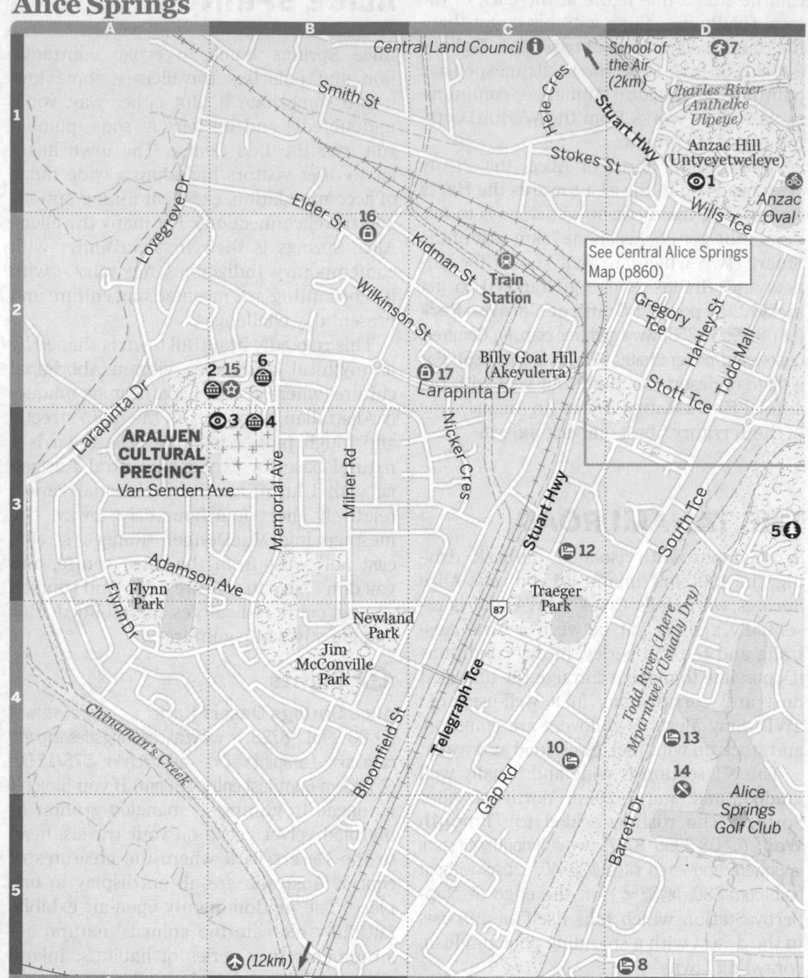

To get the most out of the park pick up a free audioguide (available in various languages) or join one of the free ranger-led talks held throughout the day.

Araluen Cultural Precinct CULTURAL CENTRE
(Map p858; ☎08-8951 1122; http://artsandmuseums.nt.gov.au/araluen-cultural-precinct; cnr Larapinta Dr & Memorial Ave; precinct pass adult/child $15/10) The Araluen Cultural Precinct is Alice Springs' cultural hub; leave at least an afternoon aside for exploration of its excellent sights. You can wander around freely outside, accessing the cemetery and grounds, but the 'precinct pass' provides entry to the exhibitions and displays for two days (with 14 days to use the pass).

➡ **Araluen Arts Centre**

(Map p858) For a small town, Alice Springs has a thriving arts scene, and the Araluen Arts Centre is at its heart. There is a 500-seat theatre (p865), and four galleries with a focus on art from the central desert region.

The Albert Namatjira Gallery features works by the artist, who began painting watercolours in the 1930s at Hermannsburg. The exhibition draws comparisons between Namatjira and his initial mentor,

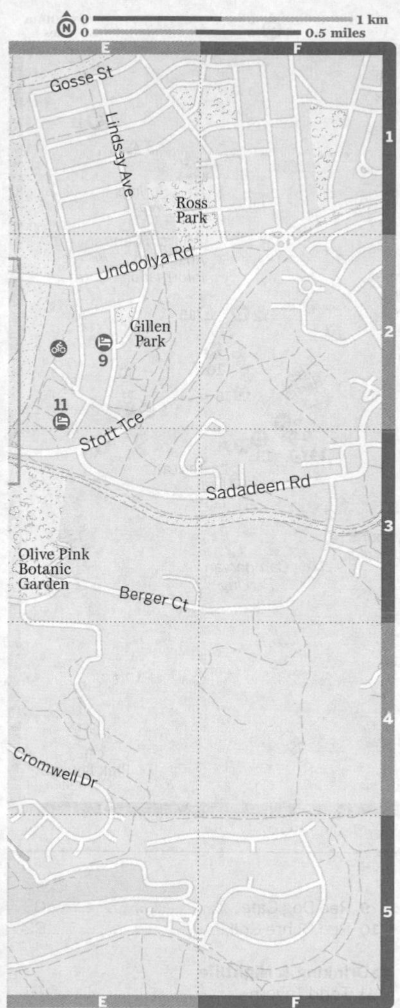

Alice Springs

Sights

1 Anzac Hill D1
2 Araluen Arts Centre B2
3 Araluen Cultural Precinct B3
4 Central Australia Aviation Museum B3
Museum of Central Australia .... (see 6)
5 Olive Pink Botanic Garden D3
6 Strehlow Research Centre B2

Activities, Courses & Tours

7 Outback Cycling D1

Sleeping

8 Alice in the Territory D5
9 Alice Lodge Backpackers E2
10 Alice on Todd C4
11 Alice's Secret Traveller's Inn E2
12 Annie's Place C3
13 Desert Palms Resort D4

Eating

Bean Tree Cafe .... (see 5)
14 Hanuman Restaurant D4

Drinking & Nightlife

Annie's Place .... (see 12)

Entertainment

15 Araluen Arts Centre B2

Shopping

16 Desert Dwellers B2
17 Tjanpi Desert Weavers C2

Rex Battarbee, and other Hermannsburg School artists. It also features 14 early acrylic works from the Papunya Community School Collection.

Other galleries showcase local artists, travelling exhibitions and newer works from Indigenous community art centres.

Museum of Central Australia

(Map p858; 10am-5pm Mon-Fri) The natural history collection at this compact museum recalls the days of megafauna – when hippo-sized wombats and 3m-tall flightless birds roamed the land. Among the geological displays are meteorite fragments and fossils. There's a free audio tour, narrated by a palaeontologist, which helps bring the exhibition to life.

There's also a display on the work of Professor TGH Strehlow, a linguist and anthropologist born at the Hermannsburg Mission among the Arrernte people. During his lifetime he gathered one of the world's most documented collections of Australian Aboriginal artefacts, songs, genealogies, film and sound recordings. It's upstairs in the **Strehlow Research Centre** (Map p858), which has a library open to the public.

Central Australia Aviation Museum

(Map p858; www.centralaustralianaviationmuseum.com; Memorial Ave; 10am-4pm Mon-Fri, 11am-4pm Sat & Sun) FREE Housed in the Connellan Airways Hangar are displays on pioneer aviation in the Territory including Royal Flying Doctor Service (RFDS) planes.

Central Alice Springs

Sights
1 Royal Flying Doctor Service Base A4

Activities, Courses & Tours
2 Emu Run Tours C3

Sleeping
3 Aurora Alice Springs D2
4 Elkira Court Motel B3

Eating
5 Epilogue Lounge C2
6 Overlanders Steakhouse B3
7 Page 27 Cafe C3
8 Piccolo's D1
9 Red Dog Cafe C3
10 Red Ochre Grill C2

Drinking & Nightlife
11 Todd Tavern D1

Entertainment
Alice Springs Cinema .... (see 8)
12 Sounds of Starlight Theatre C2

Shopping
13 Aboriginal Art World C3
14 Mbantua Gallery C3
15 Talapi C2
16 Todd Mall Market C2

Easily the most interesting exhibit is the wreck of the *Kookaburra,* a tiny plane that crashed in the Tanami Desert in 1929 while searching for Charles Kingsford Smith and his co-pilot Charles Ulm, who had gone down in their plane, the *Southern Cross.* The *Kookaburra* pilots, Keith Anderson and Bob Hitchcock, perished in the desert, while Kingsford Smith and Ulm were rescued.

Royal Flying Doctor Service Base MUSEUM
(RFDS; Map p860; ☎08-8958 8411; www.flyingdoctor.org.au; Stuart Tce; adult/child $12/6; ⏰9am-5pm Mon-Sat, 1-5pm Sun, cafe 8.30am-4.30pm Mon-Sat) A $3 million facelift, which includes interactive information portals, has given this excellent museum a new lease of life. It is the home of the Royal Flying Doctor Service, whose dedicated health workers provide 24-hour emergency retrievals across an area of around 1.25 million sq km. State-of-the-art facilities include a video presentation and a look at the operational control room, as well as some ancient medical gear and a flight simulator.

School of the Air MUSEUM
(☎08-8951-6834; www.assoa.nt.edu.au; 80 Head St; adult/child $7.50/5; ⏰8.30am-4.30pm Mon-Sat, 1-4.30pm Sun) Started in 1951, this was the first school of its type in Australia, broadcasting lessons to children over an area of 1.3 million sq km. While transmissions were originally all done over high-frequency radio, satellite broadband internet and web-cams now mean students can study in a virtual classroom. The guided tour of the centre includes a video. The school is about 3km north of the town centre.

Alice Springs Transport Heritage Centre MUSEUM
(www.roadtransporthall.com) At the MacDonnell siding, 10km south of Alice and 1km west of the Stuart Hwy, are a couple of museums dedicated to big trucks and old trains. The **Old Ghan Heritage Railway Museum** (☎08-8952 7161; 1 Norris Bell Dr; adult/child $10/6; ⏰9am-5pm) has a collection of restored Ghan locos, tea rooms, and a collection of railway memorabilia in the lovely Stuart railway station. For a truckin' good time, head to the **National Road Transport Hall of Fame** (www.roadtransporthall.com; 2 Norris Bell Ave; adult/child $15/8; ⏰9am-5pm) which has a fabulous collection of big rigs, including a few ancient road trains.

The transport hall of fame has more than 100 restored trucks and vintage cars, including many of the outback's pioneering vehicles. Admission includes entry to the Kenworth Dealer Truck Museum.

Olive Pink Botanic Garden NATURE RESERVE
(Map p858; ☎08-8952 2154; www.opbg.com.au; Tuncks Rd; admission by donation; ⏰8am-6pm) A network of meandering trails leads through this lovely arid zone botanic garden, which was founded by the prominent anthropologist Olive Pink. The garden has more than 500 central Australian plant species and grows bush foods and medicinal plants like native lemon grass, quandong and bush passionfruit.

There's a gentle climb up Meyers Hill with fine views over Alice and Ntyarlkarle Tyaneme, one of the first sites created by the caterpillar ancestors.

The small visitor centre has various exhibitions during the year, and the excellent **Bean Tree Cafe** (Map p858; ☎08-8952 0190; www.opbg.com.au/bean-tree-cafe; Tuncks Rd, Olive Pink Botanic Garden; mains $12-20; ⏰8am-4pm) alone is worth a trip to the gardens.

Anzac Hill LANDMARK
(Map p858) For a tremendous view, particularly at sunrise and sunset, take a hike (use Lions Walk from Wills Tce) or a drive up to the top of Anzac Hill, known as Untyeyetweleye in Arrernte. From the war memorial there is a 365-degree view over the town down to Heavitree Gap and the Ranges.

 Activities

Bushwalking

Experience the bush around Alice with several easy walks radiating from the Olive Pink Botanic Garden and the Telegraph Station, which marks the start of the first stage of the Larapinta Trail.

Central Australian Bushwalkers BUSHWALKING
(http://centralaustralianbushwalkers.com; walks $5) A group of local bushwalkers that schedules a wide variety of walks in the area, particularly the West MacDonnell Ranges, from March to November.

Camel Riding

Camels played an integral part in pioneering central Australia before roads and railways, and travellers can relive some of that adventure.

Pyndan Camel Tracks CAMEL TOURS
(☎0416 170 1640; www.cameltracks.com; Jane Rd; 1hr rides adult/child $60/30) Local cameleer Marcus Williams offers one-hour rides, as well as half-day jaunts (per person $110).

Cycling & Mountain-Bike Riding

Bikes are the perfect way to get around Alice Springs. There are cycle paths along the Todd River to the Telegraph Station, west to the Alice Springs Desert Park and further out to Simpsons Gap. For a map of cycling and walking paths go to the visitor information centre (p866).

Mountain bike trails are easily accessed from town or meet up for a **social sunset ride** (☎08-8952 5800; centralaustralianroughriders.asn.au; rides $5) with the Central Australian Rough Riders' Club.

Outback Cycling BICYCLE RENTAL
(Map p858; ☎08-8952 3993; http://outbackcycling.com/alice-springs/bicycle-hire; Alice Springs Telegraph Station; day/week $30/140) Bike hire with urban and mountain bikes available, as well as baskets, kids' bikes and baby seats.

Tours

Around Alice & MacDonnell Ranges

Dreamtime Tours CULTURAL TOUR
(☎08-8953 3739; www.rstours.com.au; adult/child $85/42, self-drive $66/33; ⏲8.30-11.30am) Runs the three-hour Dreamtime & Bushtucker Tour, where you meet Warlpiri Aboriginal people and learn a little about their traditions. As it caters for large bus groups it can be impersonal, but you can tag along with your own vehicle.

Foot Falcon WALKING TOUR
(☎0427 569 531; http://footfalcon.wordpress.com; tours $30; ⏲4pm Mon-Fri, 3pm Sun) Local historian, author and teacher Linda Wells leads two-hour walks around town with insights into Alice's Indigenous and pioneering history.

Rainbow Valley Cultural Tours CULTURAL TOUR
(☎08-8956 0661; www.rainbowvalleyculturaltours.com; afternoon walking tours adult/child $80/50) Tour beautiful Rainbow Valley with a traditional owner and visit rock-art sites not open to the general public. Tours can include overnight camping and dinner for an extra $20.

RT Tours TOUR
(☎08-8952 0327; www.rttoursaustralia.com; tours $160) Chef and Arrernte guide Bob Taylor runs a popular lunch and dinner tour at Simpsons Gap and the Telegraph Station Historical Reserve, where he whips up a bush-inspired meal. Other tours available.

Trek Larapinta WALKING
(☎1300 133 278; www.treklarapinta.com.au; from 3/6 days $1195/2195) Guided multiday walks along sections of the Larapinta Trail. Also runs volunteer projects involving trail maintenance, and bush regeneration on Aboriginal outstations.

Uluru, Kings Canyon & Palm Valley

Emu Run Tours OUTDOORS
(Map p860; ☎1800 687 220; www.emurun.com.au; 72 Todd St) Operates day tours to Uluru ($220) and two-day tours to Uluru and Kings Canyon ($520). Prices include park entry fees, meals and accommodation. There are also recommended small-group day tours through the West MacDonnell Ranges ($125), and an Aboriginal cultural day tour ($195).

Wayoutback Desert Safaris 4WD TOUR
(☎1300 551 510, 08-8952 4324; www.wayoutback.com) Small group 4WD safari tours including the chance for remote desert camping near Uluru on the overnight Red Centre safari ($325). There are also three-day safaris that traverse 4WD tracks to Uluru and Kings Canyon for $695, and five-day safaris that top it up with the West MacDonnells for $1045.

Festivals & Events

Alice Springs Cup Carnival HORSE RACING
(www.alicespringsturfclub.org.au) On the first Monday in May, don a hat and gallop down to the Pioneer Park Racecourse for the main event of this five-day carnival.

Finke Desert Race MOTOCROSS
(www.finkedesertrace.com.au) Motorcyclists and buggy drivers vie to take out the title of this crazy June race 240km from Alice along the Old South Rd to Finke; the following day they race back again. Spectators camp along the road to cheer them on.

Alice Springs Beanie Festival ARTS
(www.beaniefest.org) This four-day festival in June/July, held at the Araluen Art Centre, celebrates the humble beanie (knitted woollen hat) – handmade by women throughout the central desert.

Camel Cup CAMEL RACING
(www.camelcup.com.au) A carnival atmosphere prevails during the running of the Camel Cup at Blatherskite Park in mid-July.

Alice Springs Rodeo RODEO
Bareback bull riding, steer wrestling and ladies' barrel races are on the bill at Blatherskite Park in August.

Old Timers Fete FETE
Stock up on doilies and tea towels at this ode to granny arts, held on the second Saturday in August at the Old Timers Village.

Alice Desert Festival ART
(www.alicedesertfestival.com.au) A cracker of a festival, including a circus program, music, film and comedy. A colourful parade down Todd Mall marks the beginning of the festival. It's held in September.

Henley-on-Todd Regatta REGATTA
(www.henleyontodd.com.au) These boat races in September on the dry bed of the Todd River are a typically Australian light-hearted denial of reality. The boats are bottomless; the crews' legs stick through and they run down the course.

Sleeping

If you are travelling in peak season (June to September) make sure you book ahead, but if you're trying your luck, check the internet for last-minute rates, which often bring top-end places into midrange reach.

Alice Lodge Backpackers HOSTEL $
(Map p858; ☎1800 351 925, 08-8953 1975; www.alicelodge.com.au; 4 Mueller St; dm $24-26, d/tr $68/80;) Alice Lodge gets great feedback from travellers, particularly for the friendly and helpful management. An easy 10-minute walk from town, this is a small, highly recommended, low-key hostel. Friendly staff are as accommodating as the variety of room options, which include mixed and female, three-, four- and six-bed dorms, as well as comfortable doubles and twins built around a central pool.

Alice's Secret Traveller's Inn HOSTEL $
(Map p858; ☎08-8952 8686; www.asecret.com.au; 6 Khalick St; dm $23-26, s/d/tr $60/70/90;) Get the best accommodation deals here by booking your tour to Uluru through the inn. One of our favourite hostels in Alice, just across the Todd River from town, this place gets a big thumbs up for cleanliness and the helpful, friendly owner. Relax around the pool, puff on a didgeridoo, or lie in a hammock in the garden.

Rooms in the dongas are a bit of a squeeze, and those in the house are simple, comfortable and well kept.

Annie's Place HOSTEL $
(Map p858; ☎08-8952 1545, 1800 359 089; www.anniesplace.com.au; 4 Traeger Ave; dm $22-25, d & tw $60-75;) With its leafy beer garden – madly popular with travellers and locals alike – and great poolside area, Annie's is a lively place to hang out any night of the week. This is only a problem if you actually enjoy sleeping. The converted motel rooms (all with bathroom and some with a fridge) are a bit small, but they're cosy, and breakfast is included.

MacDonnell Range Holiday Park CARAVAN PARK $
(☎1800 808 373, 08-8952 6111; www.macrange.com.au; Palm Pl; unpowered/powered sites $41/47, cabins d $100-230;) Probably Alice's biggest and best kept, this caravan park has grassy sites and spotless amenities. Accommodation ranges from simple cabins with shared bathroom to self-contained two-bedroom villas. Kids can cavort in the adventure playground, on the BMX track and in the basketball court. Three new pools open in 2015.

Heavitree Gap Outback Lodge CARAVAN PARK $
(☎1800 896 119, 08-8950 4444; www.auroraresorts.com.au; Palm Circuit; unpowered/powered sites $26/34, d $100 180;) At the foot of the MacDonnell Ranges and dotted with eucalyptuses and bounding rock wallabies, Heavitree makes a shady place to pitch or park. There are rooms: a four-bed dorm, and a lodge with very basic kitchenette rooms that sleep six. The lodge offers a free shuttle into the town centre, which is about 4km north.

The neighbouring tavern has live country music most nights of the week.

Elkira Court Motel MOTEL $$
(Map p860; ☎08-8952 1222; www.bestwestern.com.au/alice-springs/hotels/best-western-elkira-court-motel/; 65 Bath St; r $80-150;) Elkira is a great midrange option, handily positioned close to the centre of the action. There's budget, queen and king rooms, which all represent good value. Try nabbing an upstairs room so you get a small, sun-drenched balcony.

★ **Alice in the Territory** RESORT $$
(Map p858; ☎08-8952 6100; www.alicent.com.au; 46 Stephens Rd; dm $25-35, s & d $110-150;) One of the Alice's best-value accommodation options. Sure, it's a large sprawling resort, and the rooms are pretty straight up and down – doubles or four-bed dorms, with tiny bathrooms. But rooms are bright, spotless and comfortable.

There's a great bar and a multicuisine restaurant, and the big pool sits at the foot of the MacDonnell Ranges.

Alice on Todd APARTMENTS $$
(Map p858; ☎08-8953 8033; www.aliceontodd.com; cnr Strehlow St & South Tce; studio/1-bed apt $135/158;) This place has a great set-up, with friendly and helpful staff. It's an attractive and secure apartment complex on the banks of the Todd River offering one- and two- bedroom self-contained units with kitchen and lounge. There are also studios. The balconied units sleep up to six so they're a great option for families. The landscaped grounds enclose a BBQ area, playground and games room.

Desert Palms Resort HOTEL $$
(Map p858; ☎08-8952 5977, 1800 678 037; www.desertpalms.com.au; 74 Barrett Dr; villas $140;) This hotel has a relaxed island vibe with shady palms, cascading bougainvillea and Indonesian-style villas. Rooms have cathedral ceilings, kitchenette, tiny bathroom, TV and private balcony – rather dated but comfy. The island swimming pool is a big hit with kids.

Aurora Alice Springs HOTEL $$
(Map p860; ☎1800 089 644, 08-8950 6666; www.auroraresorts.com.au; 11 Leichhardt Tce; standard/deluxe/executive d $110/150/180;) Grab an executive room in the refurbished wing if you can; they have private balconies overlooking Todd River. Right in the town centre – the 'back' door opens out onto Todd Mall – this modern hotel has a relaxed atmosphere and a great restaurant, the Red Ochre Grill (p864). Standard rooms are comfortable and well appointed with fridge, phone and free in-house movies.

Eating

★Piccolo's CAFE $
(Map p860; ☎08-8953 1936; Shop 1, Cinema Complex 11, Todd Mall; breakfast $10-18; ⏲7.30am-3pm Mon-Fri, to 2pm Sat, 8am-1.30pm Sun) This modern, stylish cafe is popular with locals for its excellent food and probably Alice's best coffee. It wouldn't be out of place in Melbourne except service is faster and friendlier. The BRAT is recommended.

Page 27 Cafe CAFE $
(Map p860; ☎08-8952 0191; Fan Lane; mains $9-15; ⏲7.30am-2.30pm Tue-Fri, 8am-2pm Sat & Sun;) Alice's locals duck down this arcade for great coffee or fresh juice. There are wholesome home-style breakfasts (eggs any style, pancakes), pita wraps and fancy salads such as chicken fattoush, herbed quinoa, rocket and baba ganoush. Excellent vegetarian menu.

Epilogue Lounge TAPAS $$
(Map p860; ☎08-8953 4206; 58 Todd Mall; tapas/mains $15/25; ⏲8am-11.30pm Wed-Mon) This urban, retro delight is definitely the coolest place to hang in town. With a decent wine list, food served all day, and service with a smile, it is a real Alice Springs standout. They hadn't quite honed some of their tapas dishes when we last visited – but a revamped menu was a work in progress.

Red Dog Cafe CAFE $$
(Map p860; ☎08-8953 1353; 64 Todd Mall; breakfast $12.50, lunch $16.50) There is no better place to people watch than here at one of the table and chairs strewn out over Todd Mall. Breakfasts are hearty, coffee is fresh and well brewed. Lunch is all about burgers, with a few vegie options thrown in.

★Hanuman Restaurant THAI $$
(Map p858; ☎08-8953 7188; www.hanuman.com.au/alice-springs; 82 Barrett Dr, Doubletree by Hilton; mains $25-36; ⏲12.30-2.30pm Mon-Fri, from 6.30pm daily;) You won't believe you're in the outback when you try the incredible Thai- and Indian-influenced cuisine at this stylish restaurant. The delicate Thai entrees are a real triumph as are the seafood dishes, particularly the Hanuman prawns. Although the menu is ostensibly Thai, there are enough Indian dishes to satisfy a curry craving. There are several vegetarian offerings and a good wine list.

Red Ochre Grill MODERN AUSTRALIAN $$$
(Map p860; ☎08-8952 9614; www.redochrealice.com.au; Todd Mall; lunch mains $15-18, dinner mains $30-37; ⏲10am-9pm) Offering innovative fusion dishes with a focus on outback cuisine, the menu here usually features traditional meats plus locally bred proteins, such as kangaroo and emu, matched with native herbs: lemon myrtle, pepperberries and bush tomatoes. There are lots of special deals such as tapas with a bottle of wine for $49, or 20% off for an early-bird dinner.

Overlanders Steakhouse STEAK $$$
(Map p860; ☎08-8952 2159; 72 Hartley St; mains $30-50; ⏲6pm-late) The place for steaks, big succulent cuts of beef (and crocodile, camel, kangaroo or emu). Amid the cattle station decor (saddles, branding irons and the like)

you can try Stuart's Tucker Bag: a half sausage of croc, kangaroo, emu and camel.

Drinking

Annie's Place BAR
(Map p858; 4 Traeger Ave; ⏲5pm-late) Bustling backpackers bar. Decent music (sometimes live), leafy beer garden, cheap jugs and poolside drinking.

Todd Tavern PUB
(Map p860; www.toddtavern.com.au; 1 Todd Mall; ⏲10am-midnight) This enduring, classically Aussie pub has a lively bar, pokies, decent pub grub and occasional live music on the weekend.

☆ Entertainment

The gig guide in the entertainment section of the *Centralian Advocate* (published every Tuesday and Friday) lists what's on in and around town. Check out the Epilogue Lounge (p864) for some of Alice Spring's best live music on the weekend.

Araluen Arts Centre ARTS CENTRE
(Map p858; ☎08-8951 1122; http://artsandmuseums.nt.gov.au/araluen-cultural-precinct; Larapinta Dr) In the cultural heart of Alice, the 500-seat Araluen Theatre hosts a diverse range of performers, from dance troupes to comedians, while the Art House Cinema screens films every Sunday evening at 7pm (adult/child $15/12). The website has an events calendar.

Sounds of Starlight Theatre LIVE MUSIC
(Map p860; ☎08-8953 0826; www.soundsofstarlight.com; 40 Todd Mall; adult/concession/family $30/25/90; ⏲8pm Tue, Fri & Sat) This atmospheric 1½-hour musical performance evoking the spirit of the outback with didgeridoo, drums and keyboards, plus wonderful photography and lighting, is an Alice institution. Musician Andrew Langford also runs free didgeridoo lessons (11am Monday to Friday).

Alice Springs Cinema CINEMA
(Map p860; ☎08-8953 2888; www.alicespringscinema.com.au; 11 Todd Mall; adult/child $17.50/13.50, Tue all tickets $12.50) The place to go for the latest-release Hollywood blockbusters.

Shopping

Alice is the centre for Aboriginal arts from all over central Australia. The places owned and run by community art centres ensure that a better slice of the proceeds goes to the artist and artist's community. Look for the black over red Indigenous Art Code (www.indigenousartcode.org) displayed by dealers dedicated to fair and transparent dealings with artists.

Talapi ARTS
(Map p860; ☎08-8953 6389; http://talapi.com.au; 45 Todd Mall) One of Alice Spring's newest galleries, Talapi is a beautiful space in the heart of town, exhibiting and promoting central desert Indigenous art. It sources its artworks directly from Aboriginal-owned art centres and is a member of the Indigenous Art Code. Drop in to ask about upcoming exhibitions.

Aboriginal Art World ARTS
(Map p860; ☎08-8952 7788; www.aboriginalartworld.com.au; 89 Todd Mall) Specialises in art from artists living in the central desert region around Alice Springs, particularly Pitjantjatjara lands. You can buy a completed work or commission your own piece.

Desert Dwellers OUTDOOR EQUIPMENT
(Map p858; ☎08-8953 2240; www.desertdwellers.com.au; 38 Elder St; ⏲9am-5pm Mon-Fri, to 2pm Sat) For camping and hiking gear, head to this shop, which has just about everything you need to equip yourself for an outback jaunt – maps, swags, tents, portable fridges, stoves and more.

Mbantua Gallery ARTS
(Map p860; ☎08-8952 5571; www.mbantua.com.au; 64 Todd Mall; ⏲9am-6pm Mon-Fri, to 1pm Sat, 10am-1pm Sun) This privately owned gallery includes extensive exhibits of works from the renowned Utopia region, as well as watercolour landscapes from the Namatjira school. There is a superb cultural exhibition space here with panels explaining Aboriginal mythology and customs.

Tjanpi Desert Weavers ARTS
(Map p858; ☎08-8958 2377; www.tjanpi.com.au; 3 Wilkinson St; ⏲10am-4pm Mon-Fri) This small enterprise employs and supports central desert weavers from 18 remote communities. Their store is well worth a visit to see the magnificent woven baskets and quirky sculptures created from locally collected grasses.

Todd Mall Market MARKET
(Map p860; ww.toddmallmarkets.com.au; ⏲9am-1pm or 2pm) Buskers, craft stalls, sizzling woks, smoky satay stands, Aboriginal art,

jewellery and knick-knacks make for a relaxed stroll. The market runs two to three times monthly – check the website for dates.

Information

DANGERS & ANNOYANCES

Avoid walking alone at night anywhere in town. Catch a taxi back to your accommodation if you're out late.

EMERGENCY

Ambulance (000) For emergencies.

Internet Access

Travel Bug (19 Todd Mall; 24min $2) Internet access.

MEDICAL SERVICES

Alice Springs Hospital (08-8951 7777; www.health.nt.gov.au/hospitals/alice_springs_hospital; Gap Rd) For medical care.

MONEY

Major banks with ATMs, such as ANZ, Commonwealth, National Australia and Westpac, are located in and around Todd Mall in the town centre.

POST

Main Post Office (Map p860; 13 13 18; 31-33 Hartley St; 8.15am-5pm Mon-Fri) All the usual services are available here.

TOURIST INFORMATION

Central Land Council (Map p858; 08-8951 6211; www.clc.org.au; PO Box 3321, 27 Stuart Hwy, Alice Springs; 8.30am-noon & 2-4pm) For Aboriginal land permits and transit permits.

Tourism Central Australia Visitor Information Centre (Map p860; 1800 645 199, 08-8952 5199; www.discovercentralaustralia.com; cnr Todd Mall & Parsons St; 8.30am-5pm Mon-Fri, 9.30am-4pm Sat & Sun;) This helpful centre can load you up with stacks of brochures and the free visitors guide. Weather forecasts and road conditions are posted on the wall. National parks information is also available. Ask about their unlimited kilometre deals if you are thinking of renting a car.

Getting There & Away

AIR

Alice Springs is well connected, with Qantas and Virgin Australia (p845) operating daily flights to/from capital cities. Airline representatives are based at Alice Springs airport. Check the airline websites for latest timetables and fare offers.

BUS

Greyhound Australia (Map p860; 1300 473 946; www.greyhound.com.au; 113 Todd St, shop 3) has regular services from Alice Springs (check website for timetables and discounted fares). Buses arrive at, and depart from, the Greyhound office in Todd St. The following are Flexi Fares:

DESTINATION	ONE-WAY FARE ($)	DURATION (HR)
Adelaide	244	20
Coober Pedy	127	8
Darwin	244	22
Katherine	222	16½
Tennant Creek	134	6½

Emu Run (p862) runs cheap daily connections between Alice Springs and Yulara (one way adult/child $135/80). **Gray Line** (Map p860; 1300 858 687; www.grayline.com; Capricornia Centre 9, Gregory Tce) also runs between Alice Springs and Yulara (one way adult/child $170/120).

Backpacker buses roam to and from Alice providing a party atmosphere and a chance to see some of the sights along the way. **Groovy Grape Getaways Australia** (1800 661 177; www.groovygrape.com.au) plies the route from Alice to Adelaide on a seven-day, backpacker camping jaunt for $975.

CAR & MOTORCYCLE

Alice Springs is a long way from everywhere. It's 1180km to Mt Isa in Queensland, 1490km to Darwin and 441km (4½ hours) to Yulara (for Uluru). Although the roads to the north and south are sealed and in good condition, these are still outback roads, and it's wise to have your vehicle well prepared, particularly as you won't get a mobile phone signal outside Alice or Yulara. Carry plenty of drinking water and emergency food at all times.

All the major car-hire companies have offices in Alice Springs, and many have counters at the airport. Prices drop by about 20% between November and April, but rentals don't come cheap, as most firms offer only 100km free per day, which won't get you far. Talk to the Tourism Central Australia Visitor Information Centre about its unlimited kilometres deal before you book. A conventional (2WD) vehicle will get you to most sights in the MacDonnell Ranges and out to Uluru and Kings Canyon via sealed roads. If you want to go further afield, say to Chambers Pillar, Finke Gorge or even the Mereenie Loop Rd, a 4WD is essential.

Alice Camp 'n' Drive (☎08-8952 0098; www.alicecampndrive.com; 76 Hartley St) Provides vehicles fully equipped for camping with swags (or tents), sleeping bags, cooking gear, chairs etc. Rates include unlimited kilometres and vehicles can be dropped off at your accommodation.

Britz (☎08-8952 8814; www.britz.com.au; cnr Stuart Hwy & Power St) Campervans and cars; also at the airport. This is also the base for Maui (☎1800 670 232; www.maui.com.au) and Mighty (☎1800 670 232; www.mightycampers.com.au) campervans.

Budget (☎13 27 27, 08-8952 8899; www.budget.com.au; 113 Todd St; ⏲9am-5pm Mon-Fri, to noon Sat) Reliable car rental operator; also has a branch at the airport.

Central Car Rentals (☎08-8952 0098; www.centralcarrentals.com.au; 76 Hartley St) A local operator (associated with Alice Camp 'n' Drive) with 2WD and 4WD vehicles which can be equipped with camping gear. Unlimited kilometre rates are available.

Territory Thrifty Car Rental (☎08-8952 9999; www.rentacar.com.au; cnr Stott Tce & Hartley St) Reliable car rental operator.

TRAIN

A classic way to enter or leave the Territory is by the Ghan, which can be booked through **Great Southern Rail** (☎13 21 47; www.greatsouthernrail.com.au). Discounted fares are sometimes offered, especially in the low season (February to June). Bookings are essential.

The train station is at the end of George Cres off Larapinta Dr.

ℹ Getting Around

Alice Springs is compact enough to get to most parts of town on foot, and you can reach quite a few of the closer attractions by bicycle.

TO/FROM THE AIRPORT

Alice Springs airport is 15km south of the town. It's about $45 by taxi. The **airport shuttle** (☎08-8952 2111; Gregory Tce; one way $16) meets all flights and drops off passengers at city accommodation. Book a day in advance for pick-up from accommodation.

BUS

The public bus service, **Asbus** (☎08-8944 2444), departs from outside the Yeperenye Shopping Centre. Buses run about every 1½ hours Monday to Friday, and Saturday morning. There are three routes of interest to travellers: 400/401 has a detour to the cultural precinct, 100/101 passes the School of the Air, and 300/301 passes many southern hotels and caravan parks along Gap Rd and Palm Circuit. The visitor information centre (p866) has timetables.

TAXI

Taxis congregate near the visitor information centre. To book one, call ☎13 10 08 or 08-8952 1877.

MACDONNELL RANGES

The beautiful, weather-beaten MacDonnell Ranges, stretching 400km across the desert, are a hidden world of spectacular gorges, rare wildlife and poignant Aboriginal heritage all within a day from Alice. There's no public transport to either the East or West MacDonnell Ranges; there are plenty of tours from Alice.

East MacDonnell Ranges

Although overshadowed by the more popular West Macs, the East MacDonnell Ranges are no less picturesque and, with fewer visitors, can be a more enjoyable outback experience. The sealed Ross Hwy runs 100km along the Ranges, which are intersected by a series of scenic gaps and gorges. The gold-mining ghost town of Arltunga is 33km off the Ross Hwy along an unsealed road that is usually OK for 2WD vehicles; however, access to John Hayes Rockhole (in Trephina Gorge Nature Park), N'Dhala Gorge and Ruby Gap is by 4WD only.

Emily & Jessie Gaps Nature Park

Both of these gaps are associated with the Eastern Arrernte Caterpillar Dreaming trail. **Emily Gap**, 16km out of town, has stylised rock paintings and a fairly deep waterhole in the narrow gorge. Known to the Arrernte as Anthwerrke, this is one of the most important Aboriginal sites in the Alice Springs area; it was from here that the caterpillar ancestral beings of Mparntwe originated before crawling across the landscape to create the topographical features that exist today. The gap is a sacred site with some well-preserved paintings on the eastern wall. **Jessie Gap**, 8km further on, is equally scenic and usually much quieter. Both sites have toilets, but camping is not permitted. And both attract flocks of birds looking for a drink. An 8km unmarked bushwalk leads around the ridge between the two gaps.

(Continued on page 872)

1

2

1. Kata Tjuta (the Olgas; p883) 2. Watarrka (Kings Canyon; p875) 3. Standley Chasm (p873), West MacDonnell Ranges

Ultimate Outback

'Outback' means different things to different people and in different parts of Australia – deserts, tropical savannah, wetlands... But what's consistent is the idea that it's far from the comforts of home. The outback is 'beyond the black stump' and holds many surprises.

Uluru (Ayers Rock)

Uluru-Kata Tjuta National Park (p880) is the undisputed highlight of Central Australia. There's not much that hasn't been said about Uluru, and not many parts of it that haven't been explored, photographed and documented. Still, nothing can prepare you for its almighty bulk, spiritual stories, remarkable textures and camera-worthy colours.

Kata Tjuta (The Olgas)

The tallest dome of Kata Tjuta (p883) is taller than Uluru (546m versus 348m), and some say exploring these 36 mounded monoliths is a more intimate, moving experience. Trails weave in amongst the red rocks, leading to pockets of silent beauty and spiritual gravitas.

Watarrka (Kings Canyon)

In Watarrka National Park (p875), about 300km north of Uluru by road, Kings Canyon is the inverse of Uluru – as if someone had grabbed the big rock and pushed it into the desert sand. Here, 270m-high cliffs drop away to a palm-lined valley floor, home to 600 plant species and delighted-to-be-here native animals. The 6km canyon rim walk is four hours well spent.

MacDonnell Ranges

The 'Macs' (p867) stretch east and west of Alice Springs. In their ancient folds are hidden worlds where rock wallabies and colourful birds can find water even on the hottest days.

Indigenous Art & Culture

The intricate and mesmerising art, stories and dances of Australia's Aboriginal peoples resonate with a deep association with the land itself. The outback is the best place to engage with Aboriginal cuture: take a cultural tour, hear spoken stories of the Dreaming, see galleries of ancient rock art or check out some contemporary canvasses in modern acrylics.

Cultural Tours

There's a proliferation of Indigenous-owned and -operated cultural tours across outback Australia – a chance to learn about the outback from the people who know it best. Sign up for a cultural tour in Darwin, Kakadu National Park and Arnhem Land in the tropical north; and Alice Springs and Uluru-Kata Tjuta National Park in the red centre.

Rock Art

Evidence of Australia's ancient Indigenous culture can be found at the outdoor rock-art sites scattered across the outback. Highlights include the 5000-plus sites in Kakadu National Park that document a timeline of spirits from the Dreaming, extinct fauna, and remarkable 'contact art', portraying the interaction between Indigenous Australians, Macassan fishermen and early European settlers. Standout Kakadu sites include Ubirr and Nourlangie. More rock art can easily be seen at Nitmiluk and Keep River national parks, the MacDonnell Ranges near Alice, and Uluru.

1

Contemporary Indigenous Art

Contemporary Australian Indigenous art – the lion's share of which is produced in outback communities – has soared to global heights of late. Traditional methods and spiritual significance are fastidiously maintained, but often finding a counterpart in Western materials – the results can be wildly original interpretations of traditional stories and ceremonial designs. Dot paintings (acrylic on canvas) are the most recognisable form, but you may also see synthetic polymer paintings, weavings, barks, weapons, boomerangs and sculptures.

Indigenous Festivals

For an unforgettable Aboriginal cultural experience, time your outback visit to coincide with a traditional Indigenous festival. These celebrations offer visitors a look at Aboriginal culture in action. Witnessing a timeless dance and feeling the primal beats is a journey beyond time and place. The Northern Territory plays host to several Indigenous festivals and events, including the popular Walking With Spirits in Beswick, Barunga Festival near Katherine, Merrepen Arts Festival at Daly River, and Arnhem Land's Stone Country Festival.

OLIVER STREWE / GETTY IMAGES ©

LEANNE WALKER / GETTY IMAGES ©

1. Dot painting, Northern Territory **2.** Barunga Festival dancing, near Katherine (p846)

(Continued from page 867)

Corroboree Rock Conservation Reserve

Past Jessie Gap you drive over eroded flats before entering a valley between red ridges. **Corroboree Rock**, 51km from Alice Springs, is one of many strangely shaped dolomite outcrops scattered over the valley floor. Despite the name, it's doubtful the rock was ever used as a corroboree area, but it is associated with the Perentie Dreaming trail. The perentie lizard grows in excess of 2.5m, and takes refuge within the area's rock falls. There's a short walking track (15 minutes) around the rock.

Trephina Gorge Nature Park

If you only have time for a couple of stops in the East MacDonnell Ranges, make Trephina Gorge Nature Park (75km from Alice) one of them. The play between the pale sandy river beds, the red and purple gorge walls, the white tree trunks, the eucalyptus-green foliage and the blue sky is spectacular. You'll also find deep swimming holes and abundant wildlife. The Trephina Gorge Walk (45 minutes, 2km) loops around the gorge's rim. The Ridgetop Walk (five hours, 10km one way) traverses the ridges from the gorge to John Hayes Rockhole; the 8km return along the road takes about two hours.

The delightful **John Hayes Rockhole**, 9km from the Trephina Gorge turn-off (the last 4km is 4WD only) has three basic **camping sites** (John Hayes Rockhole, Trephina Gorge Nature Park; adult/child $3.30/1.65). From here, the gorgeous Chain of Ponds Walk (1½ hours, 4km loop) leads past rock pools and up to a lookout above the gorge.

There's a **rangers station** (☎08-8956 9765) and **camping grounds** (Trephina Gorge Nature Park; adult/child $3.30/1.65) with BBQs, water and toilets at Trephina Gorge and the Bluff.

N'Dhala Gorge Nature Park

Just southwest of the Ross River Resort, a strictly 4WD-only track leads 11km south to **N'Dhala Gorge**. More than 5900 ancient Aboriginal rock carvings and some rare endemic plants decorate a deep, narrow gorge, although the art isn't easy to spot. There's a small, exposed **camping ground** (N'Dhala Gorge; adult/child $3.30/1.65) without reliable water.

Ross River

Secluded **Ross River Resort** (☎08-8956 9711; www.rossriverresort.com.au; Ross Hwy; unpowered & powered sites $38, bunkhouse $30, d/f cabin $130/160; ❄☒) is built around a historic stone homestead, with basic timber cabins encircling a swimming pool. The stunning campground is grassy and studded with gums. There's a store with fuel, and it's worth grabbing lunch (mains $17 to $25) or a beer in the Stockman's Bar. Coming from Alice Springs, the resort is about 9km past the Arltunga turn-off.

Arltunga Historical Reserve

Situated at the eastern end of the MacDonnell Ranges, 110km east of Alice Springs, is the old gold-mining ghost town of **Arltunga** (40km on unsealed road from the Ross Hwy). Its history, from the discovery of alluvial (surface) gold in 1887 until mining activity petered out in 1912, is fascinating. **Old buildings**, a couple of **cemeteries** and the many deserted **mine sites** in this parched landscape give visitors an idea of what life was like for the miners. There are walking tracks and old mines (with bats!) to explore, so bring a torch.

The unstaffed **visitor information centre** has old photographs of the gold-extracting process, plus a slide show on the area's history, and drinking water and toilets. There's no camping in the reserve itself.

From Arltunga it's possible to loop back to Alice along the Arltunga Tourist Dr, which pops out at the Stuart Hwy about 50km north of town. The road runs past the gracious **Old Ambalindum Homestead** (☎08-8956 9993; www.oldambalindumhomestead.com.au; unpowered/powered sites $30/35, dm $80; ❄☒) which offers self-catered accommodation for up to 12 people in the homestead and in the bunkhouse on a working cattle station. Bookings are essential and you need to bring your own food.

West MacDonnell Ranges

With their stunning beauty and rich diversity of plants and animals, the West MacDonnell Ranges are not to be missed. Their easy access by conventional vehicle makes them especially popular with day-trippers. Heading west from Alice, Namatjira Dr turns northwest off Larapinta Dr 6km beyond

Standley Chasm and is sealed all the way to Tylers Pass.

Most sites in the West MacDonnell Ranges lie within the **West MacDonnell National Park**, except for Standley Chasm, which is privately owned. There are ranger stations at Simpsons Gap and Ormiston Gorge.

Larapinta Trail

The 230km Larapinta Trail extends along the backbone of the West MacDonnell Ranges and is one of Australia's great long-distance walks. The track is split into 12 stages of varying difficulty, stretching from the Telegraph Station in Alice Springs to the craggy 1380m summit of Mt Sonder. Each section takes one to two days to navigate and the trail passes many of the attractions in the West MacDonnells.

Section 1 Alice Springs Telegraph Station to Simpsons Gap (23.8km)

Section 2 Simpsons Gap to Jay Creek (24.5km)

Section 3 Jay Creek to Standley Chasm (13.6km)

Section 4 Standley Chasm to Birthday Waterhole (17.7km)

Section 5 Birthday Waterhole to Hugh Gorge (16km)

Section 6 Hugh Gorge to Ellery Creek (31.2km)

Section 7 Ellery Creek to Serpentine Gorge (13.8km)

Section 8 Serpentine Gorge to Serpentine Chalet Dam (13.4km)

Section 9 Serpentine Chalet Dam to Ormiston Gorge (28.6km)

Section 10 Ormiston Gorge to Finke River (9.9km)

Section 11 Finke River to Redbank Gorge (25.2km)

Section 12 Redbank Gorge to Mt Sonder (15.8km return)

Trail notes and maps are available from **Parks & Wildlife** (☎08-8951 8250; www.parksandwildlife.nt.gov.au/parks/walks/larapinta). Walking groups of eight or more should contact Parks & Wildlife with a trip plan.

There's no public transport out to this area, but transfers can be arranged through the **Alice Wanderer** (☎1800 722 111, 08-8952 2111; www.alicewanderer.com.au); see the website for the various costs. For guided walks, including transport from Alice Springs, go through Trek Larapinta (p862).

Simpsons Gap

Westbound from Alice Springs on Larapinta Dr you come to the grave of **John Flynn**, the founder of the Royal Flying Doctor Service, which is topped by a boulder donated by the Arrernte people (the original was a since-returned Devil's Marble). Opposite the car park is the start of the sealed **cycling track** to Simpsons Gap, a recommended three- to four-hour return ride.

By road, **Simpsons Gap** is 22km from Alice Springs and 8km off Larapinta Dr. It's a popular picnic spot and has some excellent short walks. Early morning and late afternoon are the best times to glimpse black-footed rock wallabies. The visitor information centre is 1km from the park entrance.

Standley Chasm (Angkerle)

About 50km west of Alice Springs is the spectacular **Standley Chasm** (☎08-8956 7440; adult/concession $10/8; ⏲8am-5pm, last chasm entry 4.30pm) which is owned and run by the nearby community of Iwupataka. This narrow corridor slices neatly through the rocky range and in places the smooth walls rise to 80m. The rocky path into the gorge (20 minutes, 1.2km) follows a creek bed lined with ghost gums and cycads. You can continue to a second chasm (one hour return) or head up Larapinta Hill (45 minutes return) for a fine view. There's a cafe, picnic facilities and toilets near the car park.

Namatjira Drive

Namatjira Dr takes you to a whole series of gorges and gaps in the West MacDonnell Ranges. Not far beyond Standley Chasm you can choose the northwesterly Namatjira Dr (which loops down to connect with Larapinta Dr west of Hermannsburg), or you can continue along Larapinta Dr.

If you choose Namatjira Dr, one of your first stops might be **Ellery Creek Big Hole**, 91km from Alice Springs, and with a large permanent waterhole – a popular place for a swim on a hot day (the water is usually freezing). About 11km further, a rough gravel track leads to narrow, ochre-red **Serpentine Gorge**, which has a lovely waterhole blocking the entrance and a lookout at the end of a short, steep track (30 minutes, return), where you can view ancient cycads.

The **Ochre Pits** line a dry creek bed 11km west of Serpentine and were a source of pigment for Aboriginal people. The various coloured ochres – mainly yellow, white and red-brown – are weathered limestone, with iron-oxide creating the colours.

The car park for the majestic **Ormiston Gorge** is 25km beyond the Ochre Pits. It's the most impressive chasm in the West MacDonnells. There's a waterhole shaded with ghost gums, and the gorge curls around to the enclosed **Ormiston Pound**. It is a haven for wildlife and you can expect to see some critters among the spinifex slopes and mulga woodland. There are **walking tracks**, including the **Ghost Gum Lookout** (20 minutes), which affords brilliant views down the gorge, and the excellent, circuitous **Pound Walk** (three hours, 7.5km). There's a **visitor centre** (08-8956 7799; 10am-4pm) and a **kiosk**.

About 2km further is the turn-off to **Glen Helen Gorge**, where the Finke River cuts through the MacDonnells. Only 1km past Glen Helen is a good **lookout** over Mt Sonder; sunrise and sunset here are particularly impressive.

If you continue northwest for 25km you'll reach the turn-off (4WD only) to multihued, cathedral-like **Redbank Gorge**. This permanent waterhole runs for kilometres through the labyrinthine gorge, and makes for an incredible swimming and scrambling adventure on a hot day. Namatjira Dr then heads south and is sealed as far as **Tylers Pass Lookout**, which provides a dramatic view of **Tnorala** (Grosse Bluff), the legacy of an earth-shattering comet impact.

Sleeping & Eating

There are basic **camping grounds** (adult/child $5/1.50) at Ellery Creek Big Hole, Redbank Gorge and 6km west of Serpentine Gorge at Serpentine Chalet (a 4WD or high-clearance 2WD vehicle is recommended to reach the chalet ruins). The ritzy **camping area** (Ormiston Gorge; adult/child $10/5) at Ormiston Gorge has showers, toilets, gas barbecues and picnic tables.

Glen Helen Resort HOTEL $
(08-8956 7489; www.glenhelen.com.au; Namatjira Dr; unpowered/powered sites $24/35, dm/r $35/170;) At the edge of the West MacDonnell National Park is the popular Glen Helen Resort, which has an idyllic back verandah slammed up against the red ochre cliffs of the spectacular gorge. There's a busy restaurant-pub serving hearty meals and live music on the weekend. There are also 4WD tours available and helicopter flights.

There's a good chance you'll spot flocks of colourful budgerigars here while enjoying a cold drink in the evening. Pitching a tent on a grassy patch with your own campfire is a delight.

RED CENTRE WAY (MEREENIE LOOP)

The Red Centre Way is the 'back road' from Alice to the Rock. It incorporates an 'inner loop' comprising Namatjira and Larapinta Drs, plus the rugged Mereenie Loop Rd, the short cut to Kings Canyon. This dusty, heavily corrugated road is not to be taken lightly, and hire car companies won't permit their 2WDs to be driven on it.

Larapinta Drive

South of Standley Chasm, Larapinta Dr crosses the intersection with Namatjira Dr and the Hugh River before reaching the turn-off to the Western Arrernte community of **Wallace Rockhole**, 18km off the main road and 109km from Alice Springs.

You'll be virtually guaranteed seclusion at the **Wallace Rockhole Tourist Park** (08-8956 7993; www.wallacerockholetours.com.au; unpowered/powered sites $20/24, cabins $130;), which has a camping area with good facilities. Tours must be booked in advance and can include a 1½-hour rock-art and bush medicine tour (adult/child $15/13) with billy tea and damper.

About 26km from the Wallace Rockhole turn-off, continuing along Larapinta Dr, you will pass the lonely **Namatjira Monument**, which is about 8km from Hermannsburg.

Hermannsburg

POP 625

The Aboriginal community of Hermannsburg (Ntaria), about 125km from Alice Springs, is famous as the one-time home of artist Albert Namatjira and as the site of the Hermannsburg Mission.

In the Hermannsburg Historic Precinct, the whitewashed walls of the **mission** (☎08-8956 7402; www.hermannsburg.com.au; adult/child $10/5; ⏰9am-5pm Mon-Sat, 10.30am-5pm Sun) are shaded by majestic river gums and date palms. This fascinating monument to the Territory's early Lutheran missionaries includes a school building, a church and various outbuildings. The 'Manse' houses an art gallery and a history of the life and times of Albert Namatjira, as well as works of 39 Hermannsburg artists.

The **Kata-Anga Tea Room** (meals $8-14; ⏰9am-4pm), in the old missionary house, serves yummy treats. Distinctive paintings and pottery by the locals is also on display here and is for sale.

Just west of Hermannsburg is **Namatjira's House**.

Finke Gorge National Park

With its primordial landscape, the Finke Gorge National Park, south of Hermannsburg, is one of central Australia's premier wilderness reserves. The top attraction is **Palm Valley**, famous for its red cabbage palms, which exist nowhere else in the world. These relics from prehistoric times give the valley the feel of a picture-book oasis.

Tracks include the **Arankaia Walk** (2km loop, one hour), which traverses the valley, returning via the sandstone plateau; the **Mpulungkinya Track** (5km loop, two hours), heading down the gorge before joining the Arankaia Walk; and the **Mpaara Track** (5km loop, two hours), taking in the Finke River, Palm Bend and a rugged natural amphitheatre (a semicircle of sandstone formations sculpted by a now-extinct meander of Palm Creek). There's a popular **camping ground** (Finke Gorge National Park; adult/child $6.60/3.30).

Access to the park follows the sandy bed of the Finke River and rocky tracks, and so a high-clearance 4WD is essential. If you don't have one, several tour operators go to Palm Valley from Alice Springs. The turn-off to Palm Valley starts about 1km west of the Hermannsburg turn-off on Larapinta Dr.

If you are well prepared there's a challenging route through the national park along the sandy bed of the Finke River. This is a remote and scenic drive to the Ernest Giles Rd, from where you can continue west to Kings Canyon (or Uluru), or east back to the Stuart Hwy. It pays to travel in a convoy (getting bogged is part of the adventure) and get a copy of the *Finke River 4WD Route* notes (www.parksandwildlife.nt.gov.au).

Mereenie Loop Road

From Hermannsburg you can head west to the turn-off to Areyonga (no visitors) and then take the Mereenie Loop Rd to Kings Canyon. This is an alternative route from Alice to Kings Canyon. There can be deep sandy patches and countless corrugations, depending on the time of year and how recently it's been graded. It's best travelled in a high-clearance vehicle, preferably a 4WD. Be aware that 2WD hire vehicles will not be covered by insurance on this road.

To travel along this route, which passes through Aboriginal land, you need a Mereenie Tour Pass ($5), which is valid for one day and includes a booklet with details about the local Aboriginal culture and a route map. The pass is issued on the spot (usually only on the day of travel) at the visitor information centre in Alice Springs, Glen Helen Resort, Kings Canyon Resort and Hermannsburg service station.

Kings Canyon & Watarrka National Park

The yawning chasm of Kings Canyon in Watarrka National Park is one of the most spectacular sights in central Australia, and one of the main attractions of the Mereenie Loop. The other ways to get here include the unsealed Ernest Giles Rd, which heads west off the Stuart Hwy 140km south of Alice Springs, and the sealed Luritja Rd which detours off the Lasseter Hwy on the way to Uluru. The latter is the longest route but easily the most popular and comfortable.

Whichever way you get here you will want to spend some time shaking off the road miles and taking in the scenery. Walkers are rewarded with awesome views on the **Kings Canyon Rim Walk** (6km loop, four hours; you must begin before 9am on hot days), which many travellers rate as a highlight of their trip to the Centre. After a short but steep climb (the only 'difficult' part of the trail), the walk skirts the canyon's rim before descending down wooden stairs to the **Garden of Eden**: a lush pocket of ferns and prehistoric cycads around a tranquil pool. The next section of the trail winds through

Kings Canyon

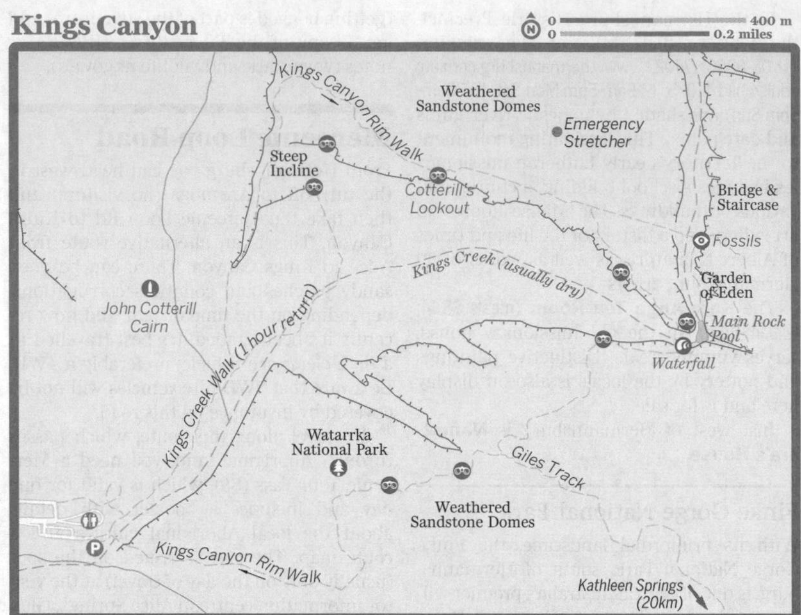

a swarm of giant beehive domes: weathered sandstone outcrops, which to the Luritja represent the men of the Kuniya Dreaming.

The **Kings Creek Walk** (2km return) is a short stroll along the rocky creek bed to a raised platform with views of the towering canyon rim.

About 10km east of the car park, the **Kathleen Springs Walk** (one hour, 2.6km return) is a pleasant wheelchair-accessible track leading to a waterhole at the head of a gorge.

The **Giles Track** (22km one way, overnight) is a marked track that meanders along the George Gill Range between Kathleen Springs and the canyon; fill out the logbook at Reedy Creek rangers office so that in the event of an emergency, rangers can more easily locate you.

Tours

Several tour companies depart Alice and stop here on the way to/from Uluru.

Kings Creek Helicopters SCENIC FLIGHT
(☎08-8956 7474; www.kingscreekstation.com.au; flights per person $70-480) Flies from Kings Creek Station, including a breathtaking 30-minute canyon flight.

Professional Helicopter Services SCENIC FLIGHT
(PHS; ☎08-8956 2003; www.phs.com.au; flights per person $95-275) Picking up from Kings Canyon Resort, PHS buzzes the canyon for eight/15 minutes ($95/145).

Sleeping & Eating

Kings Creek Station CAMPING $$
(☎08-8956 7474; www.kingscreekstation.com.au; Luritja Rd; unpowered/powered sites for 2 people $40/44, safari cabins s/d incl breakfast $105/170; @) Located 35km before the canyon, this family-run station offers a bush camping experience among the desert oaks. The cosy safari-style cabins (small canvas tents on solid floors) share amenities and a kitchen-BBQ area. You can tear around the desert on a quad bike (one-hour ride $93) or enjoy the more sedate thrills of a sunset camel ride (one-hour ride $65).

Fuel, ice, beer, wine, BBQ packs and meals are available at the shop (open 7am to 7pm). Ask about Conways' Kids (www.conwayskids.org.au), a charitable trust set up by the owners to send local Indigenous children to school in Adelaide.

Kings Canyon Resort RESORT **$$$**
(☎08-8956 7442, 1300 863 248; www.kingscanyonresort.com.au; Luritja Rd; unpowered/powered sites $39/45, dm $35, d $285/469;) Only 10km from the canyon, this well-designed resort boasts a wide range of accommodation, from a grassy camping area with its own pool and bar to deluxe rooms looking out onto native bushland. Eating and drinking options are as varied, with a bistro, the Thirsty Dingo bar and an outback BBQ for big steaks and live entertainment. There's a general store with fuel and an ATM at reception.

Kings Canyon Wilderness Lodge RESORT **$$$**
(☎1300 336 932; www.aptouring.com.au; Luritja Rd; tented cabins $640;) In a secret pocket of Kings Creek Station is this luxury retreat with 10 stylish tents offering private en suite facilities and decks with relaxing bush views. It's run by APT, so independent travellers may find themselves squeezed in among tour groups. Tariff includes breakfast and dinner.

SOUTH OF ALICE SPRINGS

Old South Road

The Old South Road, which runs close to the old Ghan railway line, is pretty rough and really requires a 4WD. It's only 39km from Alice Springs to **Ewaninga**, where prehistoric Aboriginal petroglyphs are carved into sandstone. The rock carvings found here and at N'Dhala Gorge are thought to have been made by Aboriginal people who lived here before those currently in the region, between 1000 and 5000 years ago.

The eerie, sandstone **Chambers Pillar**, southwest of Maryvale Station, towers 50m above the surrounding plain and is carved with the names and visit dates of early explorers – and, unfortunately, some much less worthy modern-day graffiti. To the Aboriginal people of the area, Chambers Pillar is the remains of Itirkawara, a powerful gecko ancestor. Most photogenic at sunset and sunrise, it's best to stay overnight at the **camping ground** (Chambers Pillar; adult/child $3.30/1.65). It's 160km from Alice Springs, and a 4WD is required for the last 44km from the turn-off at Maryvale Station.

Back on the main track south, you eventually arrive at **Finke** (Aputula), a small Aboriginal community 230km from Alice Springs. When the old Ghan was running, Finke was a thriving town; these days it seems to have drifted into a permanent torpor, except when the **Finke Desert Race** is staged. Fuel is sold at the **Aputula Store** (☎08-8956 0968; 9am-noon & 2-4pm Mon-Fri, 9am-noon Sat).

From Finke, you can turn west along the Goyder Stock Route to join the Stuart Hwy at Kulgera (150km), or east to Old Andado station on the edge of the Simpson Desert (120km). Just 21km west of Finke, and 12km north of the road along a signposted track, is the **Lambert Centre**. The point marks Australia's geographical centre and features a 5m-high version of the flagpole found on top of Parliament House in Canberra.

Rainbow Valley Conservation Reserve

This series of free-standing sandstone bluffs and cliffs, in shades ranging from cream to red, is one of central Australia's more extraordinary sights. A marked walking trail takes you past claypans and in between the multihued outcrops to the aptly named Mushroom Rock. Rainbow Valley is most striking in the early morning or at sunset, but the area's silence will overwhelm you whatever time of day you are here.

The park lies 24km off the Stuart Hwy along a 4WD track that's 77km south of Alice Springs. It has a pretty exposed **camping ground** (Rainbow Valley Conservation Reserve; adult/child $3.30/1.65) but the setting is perfectly positioned for sunset viewing.

Ernest Giles Road

The Ernest Giles Rd heads off to the west of the Stuart Hwy about 140km south of Alice and is a shorter but much rougher route to Kings Canyon only recommended for 4WD vehicles.

Henbury Meteorite Craters

About 11km west of the Stuart Hwy, a corrugated track leads 5km off Ernest Giles Rd to this cluster of 12 small craters, formed after

South of Alice Springs

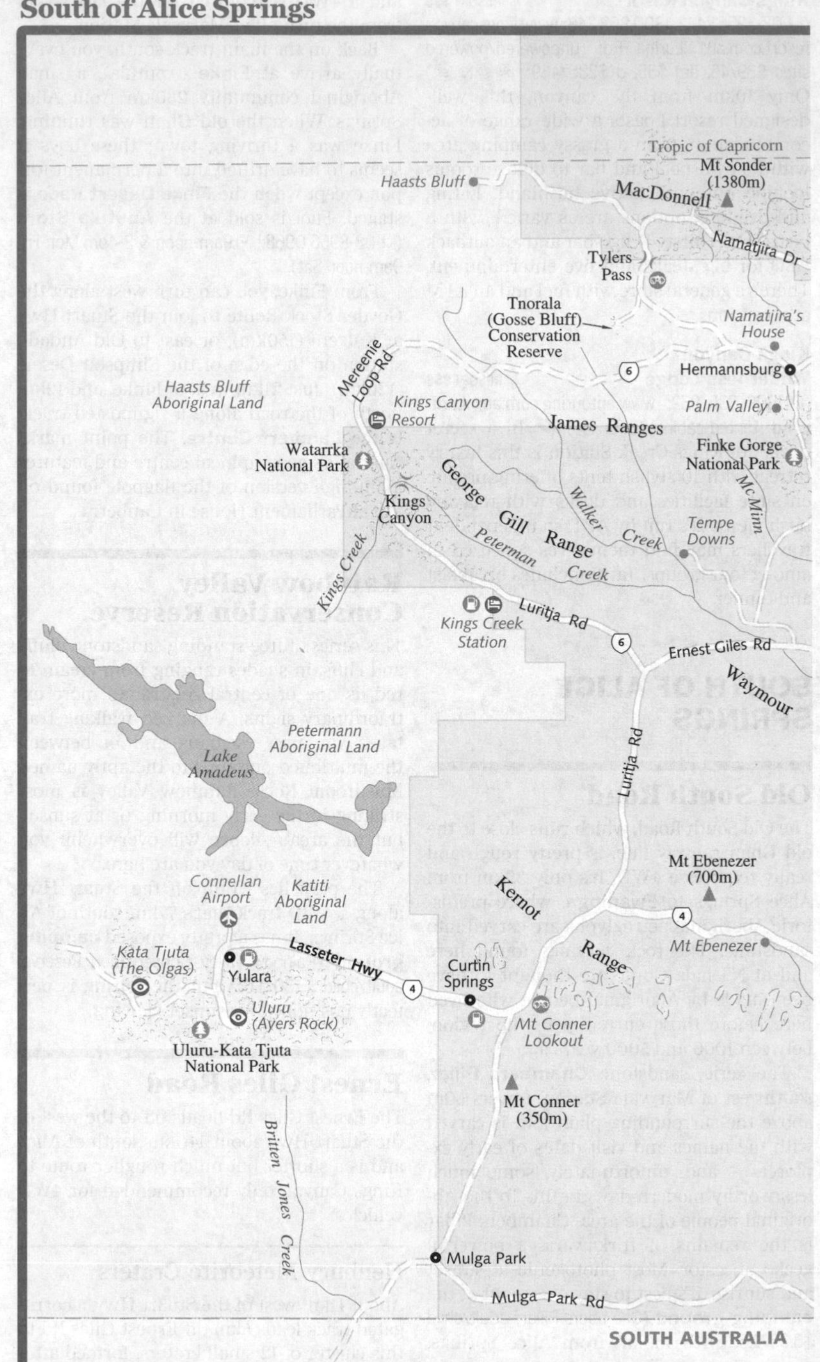

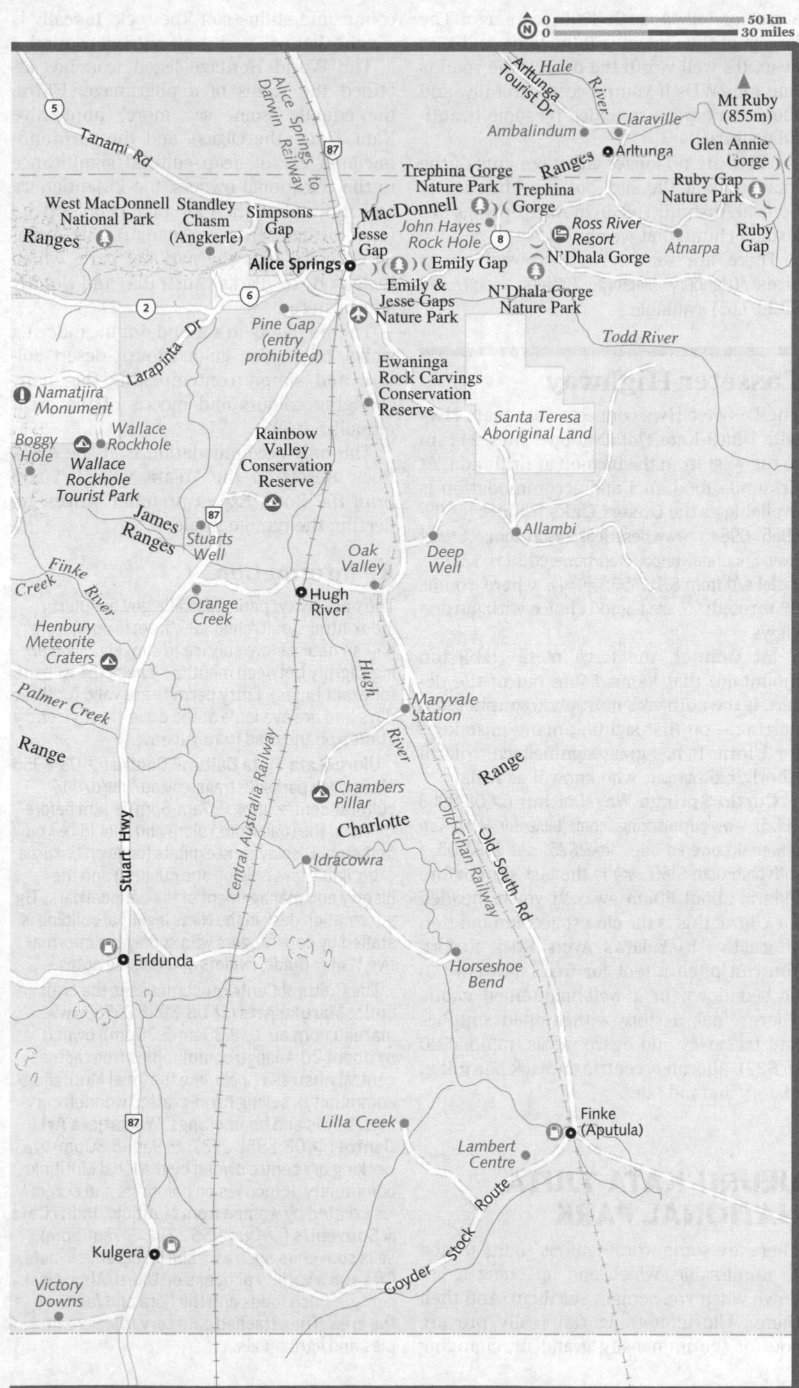

0 50 km
0 30 miles
Hale River
Arltunga Tourist Dr
Mt Ruby (855m)
Claraville
Ambalindum
Arltunga
Glen Annie Gorge
Alice Springs to Darwin Railway
Tanami Rd
Trephina Gorge Nature Park
Ranges
Trephina Gorge
Ruby Gap Nature Park
West MacDonnell National Park
Standley Chasm (Angkerle)
Simpsons Gap
MacDonnell
John Hayes Rock Hole
Ross River Resort
Ruby Gap
Ranges
Jesse Gap
Atnarpa
Alice Springs
Emily Gap
N'Dhala Gorge
Emily & Jesse Gaps Nature Park
N'Dhala Gorge Nature Park
Larapinta Dr
Pine Gap (entry prohibited)
Todd River
Ewaninga Rock Carvings Conservation Reserve
Namatjira Monument
Santa Teresa Aboriginal Land
Wallace Rockhole
Boggy Hole
Rainbow Valley Conservation Reserve
Wallace Rockhole Tourist Park
James Ranges
Stuarts Well
Allambi
Deep Well
Oak Valley
Finke River
Creek
Hugh River
Orange Creek
Henbury Meteorite Craters
Hugh River
Palmer Creek
Maryvale Station
Range
Range
Chambers Pillar
Central Australia Railway
Charlotte
Old South Rd
Old Ghan Railway
Stuart Hwy
Idracowra
Erldunda
Horseshoe Bend
Finke (Aputula)
Lilla Creek
Lambert Centre
Goyder Stock Route
Kulgera
Victory Downs

a meteor fell to earth 4700 years ago. The largest of the craters is 180m wide and 15m deep. It's well worth the detour, the road is fine for 2WDs if you proceed carefully, and the craters are surrounded by some beautiful country.

There are no longer any fragments of the meteorites at the site, but the Museum of Central Australia (p859) in Alice Springs has a small chunk that weighs 46.5kg.

There are some pretty exposed **camp sites** (Henbury Meteorite Craters; adult/child $3.30/1.65) available.

Lasseter Highway

The Lasseter Hwy connects the Stuart Hwy with Uluru-Kata Tjuta National Park, 244km to the west from the turn-off at Erldunda. At Erldunda food, fuel and accommodation is available at the **Desert Oaks Resort** (08-8956 0984; www.desertoaksresort.com; Stuart Hwy, Erldunda; unpowered/powered sites $22/32, motel s/d from $115/150;), where rooms 23 through 27 are a good choice with garden views.

Mt Conner, the large mesa (table-top mountain) that looms 350m out of the desert, is the outback's most photographed red herring – on first sighting many mistake it for Uluru. It has great significance to local Aboriginal people, who know it as Atila.

Curtin Springs Wayside Inn (08-8956 2906; www.curtinsprings.com; Lasseter Hwy; unpowered/powered sites free/$25, s/d $75/105, r with bathroom $160;) is the last stop before Yulara, about 80km away. If you're headed for Uluru, this is the closest accommodation alternative to Yulara's Ayers Rock Resort. You can pitch a tent for free (showers $3) or bed down in a well-maintained cabin. There's fuel, a store with limited supplies and takeaway and bistro meals (mains $20 to $32), plus an eccentric outback bar full of history and tall tales.

ULURU-KATA TJUTA NATIONAL PARK

There are some world-famous sights touted as unmissable, which end up being a letdown when you actually see them. And then there's Uluru: nothing can really prepare you for the immensity, grandeur, changing colour and stillness of 'the rock'. It really is a sight that will sear itself onto your mind.

The World Heritage–listed icon has attained the status of a pilgrimage. Uluru, the equally (some say more) impressive Kata Tjuta (the Olgas), and the surrounding area are of deep cultural significance to the traditional owners, the Pitjantjatjara and Yankuntjatjara Aboriginal peoples (who refer to themselves as Anangu). The Anangu officially own the national park, which is leased to Parks Australia and jointly administered.

There's plenty to see and do: meandering walks, bike rides, guided tours, desert culture and simply contemplating the many changing colours and moods of the great monolith itself.

The only accommodation is at the Ayers Rock Resort in the Yulara village, 20km from the Rock. Expect premium prices, reflecting the remote locale.

Information

The **park** (www.parksaustralia.gov.au/uluru/index.html; adult/child $25/free) is open from half an hour before sunrise to sunset daily (varying slightly between months – check the website for exact times). Entry permits are valid for three days and are available at the drive-through entry station on the road from Yulara.

Uluru-Kata Tjuta Cultural Centre (08-8956 1128; www.parksaustralia.gov.au/uluru/do/cultural-centre.html; 7am-6pm) is 1km before Uluru on the road from Yulara and should be your first stop. Displays and exhibits focus on *tjukurpa* (Aboriginal law, religion and custom) and the history and management of the national park. The information desk in the Nintiringkupai building is staffed by park rangers who supply the informative *Visitor Guide*, leaflets and walking notes.

The Cultural Centre encompasses the craft outlet **Maruku Arts** (08-8956 2558; www.maruku.com.au; 8.30am-5.30pm), owned by about 20 Anangu communities from across central Australia (including the local Mutitjulu community), selling hand-crafted wooden carvings, bowls and boomerangs. **Walkatjara Art Centre** (08-8956 2537; 9am-5.30pm) is a working art centre owned by the local Mutitjulu community. It focuses on paintings and ceramics created by women from Mutitjulu. **Ininti Cafe & Souvenirs** (08-8956 2214; 7am-5pm) sells souvenirs such as T-shirts, ceramics, hats, CDs and a variety of books on Uluru, Aboriginal culture, bush foods and the flora and fauna of the area. The attached cafe serves ice cream, pies and light meals.

SUNSET WITH SOLITUDE

Uluru at sunset is a mesmerising experience but it can be hard to escape the crowds and their cameras. Here park rangers share their secrets for a sunset with solitude.

Talinguru Nyakunytjaku Wildly popular at dawn, but at sunset you'll have both Uluru and Kata Tjuta, in silhouette, in the same shot, all to yourself.

Kantju Gorge Head to the end of the Mala Walk in time for a dazzling sunset on the walls of the Rock.

Kata Tjuta Sunset Viewing Take a seat in a private area and watch the colours change to the deepest red.

Mutitjulu Waterhole For profound peace follow the Kuniya Walk to this glorious waterhole.

Tours

Seit Outback Australia BUS TOUR
(☎08-8956 3156; www.seitoutbackaustralia.com.au) This small group-tour operator has numerous options including a sunset tour around Uluru (adult/child $149/121), and a sunrise tour at Kata Tjuta for the same price including breakfast and a walk into Walpa Gorge.

AAT Kings BUS TOUR
(☎08-8956 2171; www.aatkings.com) Operating the largest range of coach tours to Uluru, AAT offers a range of half- and full-day tours from Yulara. Check the website or enquire at the Tour & Information Centre (p886) in Yulara.

Uluru Camel Tours CAMEL TOUR
(☎08-8956 3333; www.ulurucameltours.com.au) View Uluru and Kata Tjuta from a distance atop a camel ($80, 1½ hours) or take the popular Camel to Sunrise and Sunset tours ($125, 2½ hours).

★**Uluru Aboriginal Tours** CULTURAL TOUR
(☎0447 878 851; www.uluruaboriginaltours.com.au; guided tours from $99) Owned and operated by Anangu from the Mutitjulu community, this company offers a range of trips to give you an insight into the significance of the Rock through the eyes of the traditional owners. Tours operate and depart from the cultural centre (p880), as well as from Yulara Ayers Rock Resort (through AAT Kings) and from Alice Springs.

There are a range of tours including the Rising Sun & Sacred Walk tour, which includes bush skills demonstrations, such as spear throwing, a hot buffet breakfast around a campfire, and unparalleled insights into the area's traditional lore and legend from your local guide. Call or email for the latest offerings of self-drive tours and packages.

Desert Tracks CULTURAL TOUR
(☎0439 500 419; www.deserttracks.com.au; adult/child $249/199) This Pitjantjatjara-run company offers a full-day 4WD journey into the remote Pitjantjatjara Lands to meet the traditional owners of Cave Hill and view some spectacular rock art depicting the Seven Sisters story.

Sounds of Silence DINING
(☎08-8957 7448; www.ayersrockresort.com.au/sounds-of-silence; adult/child $195/96) Waiters serve champagne and canapés on a desert dune with stunning sunset views of Uluru and Kata Tjuta. Then it's a buffet dinner (with emu, croc and roo) beneath the southern sky, which, after dinner, is dissected and explained with the help of a telescope. If you're more of a morning person, try the similarly styled **Desert Awakenings 4WD Tour** (www.ayersrockresort.com.au/desert-awakenings; adult/child $168/130). Neither tour is suitable for children under 10 years.

Motorcycle Tours

Sunrise and sunset tours to Uluru and Kata Tjuta can be had on the back of a Harley Davidson.

Uluru Motorcycle Tours TOUR
(☎08-8956 2019; www.ulurucycles.com; rides $99-429) Motors out to Uluru at sunset ($199, 1½ hours).

Scenic Flights

Prices are quoted per person and include airport transfers from Ayers Rock Resort.

Ayers Rock Helicopters SCENIC FLIGHTS
(☎08-8956 2077; www.helicoptergroup.com/arh-index) A 15-minute buzz of Uluru costs $150; to include Kata Tjuta costs $285.

Uluru (Ayers Rock)

The first sight of Uluru on the horizon will astound even the most jaded traveller. Uluru is 3.6km long and rises a towering 348m from the surrounding sandy scrubland (867m above sea level). If that's not impressive enough, it's believed that two-thirds of the rock lies beneath the sand. Closer inspection reveals a wondrous contoured surface concealing numerous sacred sites of particular significance to the Anangu. If your first sight of Uluru is during the afternoon, it appears as an ochre-brown colour, scored and pitted by dark shadows. As the sun sets, it illuminates the rock in burnished orange, then a series of deeper reds before it fades into charcoal. A performance in reverse, with marginally fewer spectators, is given at dawn.

Activities

There are walking tracks around Uluru, and ranger-led walks explain the area's plants, wildlife, geology and cultural significance. All the trails are flat and suitable for wheelchairs. Several areas of spiritual significance are off limits to visitors; these are marked with fences and signs. The Anangu ask you not to photograph these sites.

The excellent *Visitor Guide & Maps* brochure, which can be picked up at the Cultural Centre, gives details on a few self-guided walks.

Base Walk WALKING
This track (10.6km, three to four hours) circumnavigates the rock, passing caves, paintings, sandstone folds and geological abrasions along the way.

Liru Walk WALKING
Links the Cultural Centre with the start of the Mala Walk and climb, and winds through strands of mulga before opening up near Uluru (4km return, 1½ hours).

Mala Walk WALKING
From the base of the climbing point (2km return, one hour), interpretive signs explain the tjukurpa of the Mala (hare-wallaby people), which is significant to the Anangu,

Uluru (Ayers Rock)

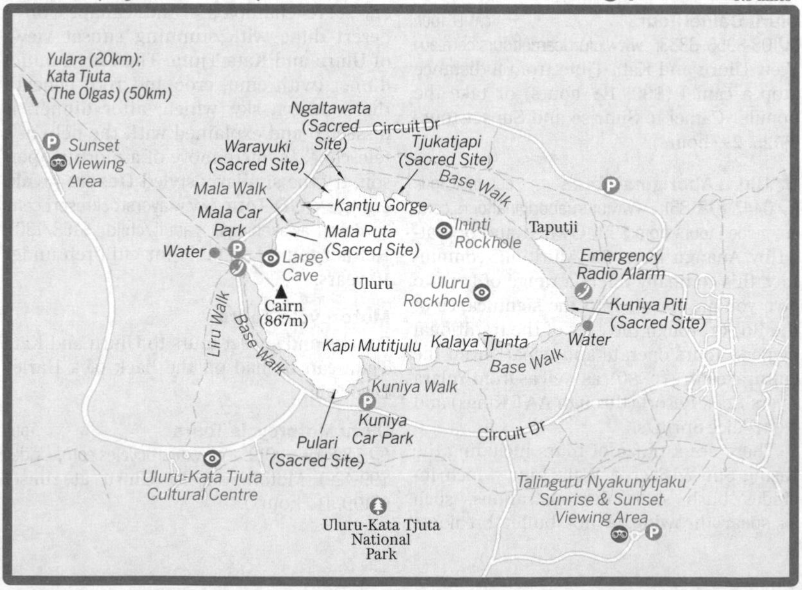

A QUESTION OF CLIMBING

Many visitors consider climbing Uluru to be a highlight of a trip to the Centre, and even a rite of passage. But for the traditional owners, the Anangu, Uluru is a sacred place. The path up the side of the Rock is part of the route taken by the Mala ancestors on their arrival at Uluru and has great spiritual significance – and is not to be trampled by human feet. When you arrive at Uluru you'll see a sign from the Anangu saying 'We don't climb', and a request that you don't climb either.

The Anangu are the custodians of Uluru and take responsibility for the safety of visitors. Any injuries or deaths that occur are a source of distress and sadness to them. For similar reasons of public safety, Parks Australia would prefer that people didn't climb. It's a very steep ascent, not to be taken lightly, and each year there are several air rescues, mostly of people suffering heart attacks. Furthermore, Parks Australia must constantly monitor the climb and close it on days where the temperature is forecast to reach 36°C or over, and when strong winds are expected.

So if the Anangu and Parks Australia don't want people to climb Uluru, why does the climb remain open? The answer is tourism. The tourism industry believes visitor numbers would drop significantly – at least initially – if the climb was closed, particularly among those who think there is nothing else to do at Uluru.

A commitment has been made to close the climb for good, but only when there are adequate new visitor experiences in place or when the proportion of visitors climbing falls below 20%. Until then, it remains a personal decision and a question of respect. Before deciding, visit the **Cultural Centre** (p880) and perhaps take an **Anangu guided tour** (p881).

as well as fine examples of rock art. A ranger-guided walk (free) along this route departs at 10am (8am from October to April) from the car park.

Kuniya Walk WALKING

A short walk (1km return, 45 minutes) from the car park on the southern side leads to the most permanent waterhole, Mutitjulu, home of the ancestral watersnake. Great birdwatching and some excellent rock art are highlights of this walk.

Uluru Climb WALKING

The Anangu ask that visitors respect Aboriginal law by not climbing Uluru. The steep and demanding path (1.6km return, two hours) follows the traditional route taken by ancestral Mala men. The climb is often closed (sometimes at short notice) due to weather and Anangu business.

Sunset & Sunrise Viewing Areas

About halfway between Yulara and Uluru, the **sunset viewing area** has plenty of car and coach parking for that familiar postcard view. The **Talnguru Nyakunytjaku sunrise viewing area** is perched on a sand dune and captures both the Rock and Kata Tjuta in all their glory. It also has two great interpretive walks (1.5km) about women's and men's business. There's a shaded viewing area, toilets and a place to picnic.

Kata Tjuta (The Olgas)

No journey to Uluru is complete without a visit to Kata Tjuta (the Olgas), a striking group of domed rocks huddled together about 35km west of the Rock. There are 36 boulders shoulder to shoulder forming deep valleys and steep-sided gorges. Many visitors find them even more captivating than their prominent neighbour. The tallest rock, **Mt Olga** (546m, 1066m above sea level) is approximately 200m higher than Uluru. Kata Tjuta means 'many heads' and is of great tjukurpa significance, particularly for men, so stick to the tracks.

The 7.4km **Valley of the Winds** loop (two to four hours) is one of the most challenging and rewarding bushwalks in the park. It winds through the gorges, giving excellent views of the surreal domes and traversing varied terrain. It's not particularly arduous, but wear sturdy shoes, and take plenty of water. Starting this walk at first light often rewards you with solitude, enabling you to appreciate the sounds of the wind and bird calls carried up the valley.

Kata Tjuta (The Olgas)

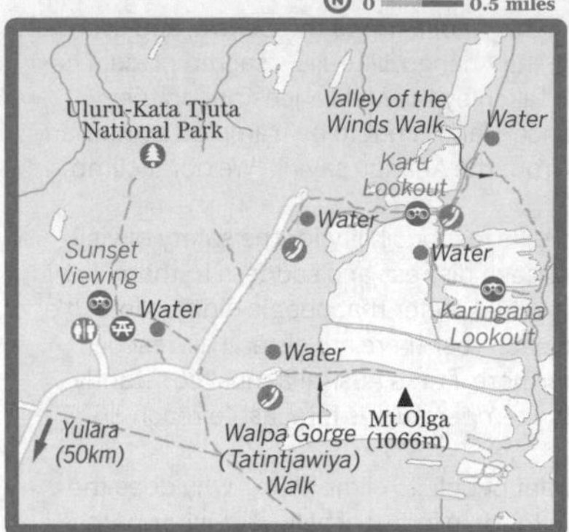

The short signposted track beneath towering rock walls into pretty **Walpa Gorge** (2.6km return, 45 minutes) is especially beautiful in the afternoon, when sunlight floods the gorge.

There's a picnic and sunset-viewing area with toilet facilities just off the access road a few kilometres west of the base of Kata Tjuta. Like Uluru, Kata Tjuta is at its glorious, blood-red best at sunset.

Heading West

A lonely sign at the western end of Kata Tjuta points in the direction of WA. If suitably equipped you can travel the 181km to Kaltukatjara (Docker River), an Aboriginal settlement to the west, and then about 1500km on to Kalgoorlie in WA. You need a permit from the Central Land Council for this trip.

Yulara (Ayers Rock Resort)

POP 887

Yulara is the service village for the Uluru-Kata Tjuta National Park, and has effectively turned one of the world's least hospitable regions into a comfortable place to stay. Lying just outside the national park, 20km from Uluru and 53km from Kata Tjuta, the complex is the closest base for exploring the park.

Sights & Activities

The Ayers Rock Resort conducts numerous free activities throughout the day: from spear, boomerang and dij classes to dance programs. Pick up a program at your accommodation.

Sleeping

All of the accommodation in Yulara, including the camping ground and hostel, is owned by the Ayers Rock Resort. Even though there are almost 5000 beds, it's wise to make a reservation, especially during school holidays. Substantial discounts are usually offered if you book for more than two or three nights.

Ayers Rock Resort Campground CAMPGROUND $
(☎08-8957 7001; www.ayersrockresort.com.au/arrcamp; unpowered/powered sites $38/48, cabins $165;) A saviour for the budget conscious, this sprawling campground is set among native gardens. There are good facilities including a kiosk, free BBQs, a camp kitchen and a pool. During the peak season it's very busy, and the inevitable predawn convoy heading for Uluru can provide an unwanted wake-up call. The cramped cabins (shared facilities) sleep six people and are only really suitable for a family.

Outback Pioneer Hotel & Lodge HOSTEL $
(☎1300 134 044 www.ayersrockresort.com.au/outback; dm $38-46, d $240-310;) With a lively bar, barbecue restaurant and musical entertainment, this is the budget choice for noncampers. The cheapest options are the 20-bed YHA unisex dorms, and squashy four-bed budget cabins with fridge, TV and shared bathroom. There are also more spacious motel-style rooms that sleep up to four people. Children under 12 stay free, though anyone over 12 is an extra $50 a night.

Emu Walk Apartments APARTMENTS $$$
(☎1300 134 044; www.ayersrockresort.com.au/emu; 1-/2-bedroom apt from $400/500;) The pick of the bunch for families looking for self-contained accommodation, Emu Walk has comfortable, modern apartments, each with a lounge room (with TV) and a well-equipped kitchen with washer and dryer. The one-bedroom apartments accommodate four people, while the two-bedroom version sleeps six.

Desert Gardens Hotel HOTEL $$$
(☎1300 134 044; r $410-530;) One of Yulara's original hotels, and showing its age. This place gets very busy over school holiday periods, which can overwhelm cleaning

Yulara (Ayers Rock Resort)

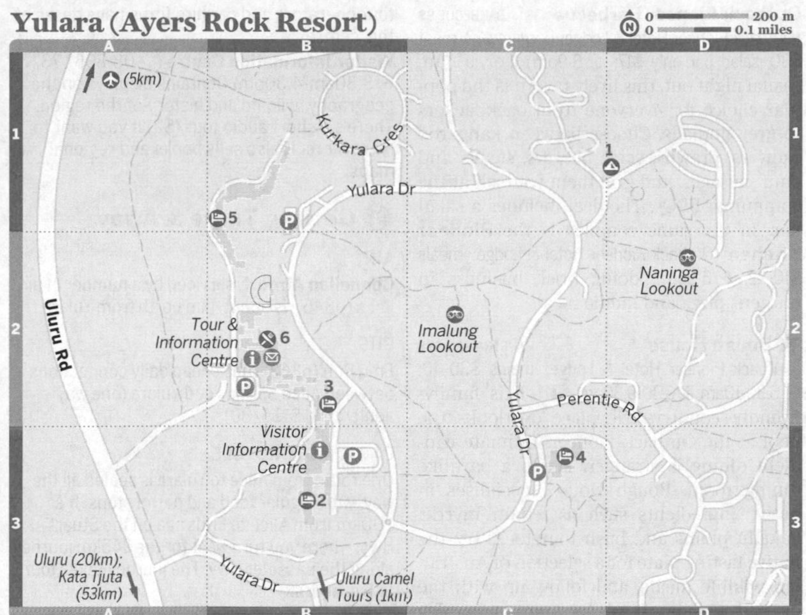

staff, but generally service is friendly and efficient. The spacious deluxe rooms are the best option, featuring balconies with desert or Uluru views. A big buffet breakfast is served in the restaurant and there's a pleasant pool area shaded with gums.

Sails in the Desert HOTEL **$$$**
(1300 134 044; http://www.ayersrockresort.com.au/sails; superior d $540, ste $1000;) The rooms still seem overpriced at the resort's flagship hotel. There's a lovely pool and surrounding lawn shaded by sails and trees. There are also tennis courts, a health spa, several restaurants and a piano bar. The best rooms have balcony views of the rock – request one when you make a booking.

Eating

Walpa Lobby Bar MODERN AUSTRALIAN **$$**
(Sails in the Desert; mains $30; 11am-10pm) If you want to treat yourself, this is the place to try. With a recent makeover, and the feel of a Hilton Hotel bar, the excellent food and friendly service make up for for the slight sterility. Hot and cold seafood platters are a treat, and most dishes feature Australian bush ingredients. Salads and antipasto also available. 'Walpa' is the Pitjantjatjara name for wind.

Yulara (Ayers Rock Resort)

Sleeping

1	Ayers Rock Resort Campground	D1
2	Desert Gardens Hotel	B3
3	Emu Walk Apartments	B2
4	Outback Pioneer Hotel & Lodge	C3
5	Sails in the Desert	B1

Eating

	Bough House	(see 4)
6	Geckos Cafe	B2
	Outback Pioneer Barbecue	(see 4)
	Pioneer Kitchen	(see 4)
	Walpa Lobby Bar	(see 5)

Geckos Cafe MEDITERRANEAN **$$**
(Resort Shopping Centre; mains $20-30; 11am-9pm;) For great value, a warm atmosphere and tasty food head to this buzzing licensed cafe. The wood-fired pizzas, pastas, burgers and fish and chips go well with a carafe of sangria, and the courtyard tables are a great place to enjoy the desert night air. There are several vegie and gluten-free options, plus meals can be made to takeaway.

Outback Pioneer Barbecue BARBECUE **$$**
(Outback Pioneer Hotel & Lodge; burgers $18, meat $30, salad bar only $17; ⏲6-9pm) For a fun, casual night out, this lively tavern is the popular choice for everyone from backpackers to grey nomads. Choose between kangaroo skewers, prawns, vegie burgers, steaks and emu sausages, and grill them yourself at the communal BBQs. The deal includes a salad bar. In the same complex is the **Pioneer Kitchen** (Outback Pioneer Hotel & Lodge; meals $10-22; ⏲6-9pm), doing brisk business in burgers, pizza and kiddie meals.

★**Bough House** AUSTRALIAN **$$$**
(Outback Pioneer Hotel & Lodge; mains $30-40; ⏲6.30-10am & 6.30-9.30pm; 👪) This family-friendly, country-style place overlooks the pool at the Outback Pioneer. Intimate candlelit dining is strangely set in a barnlike dining room. Bough House specialises in native ingredients such as lemon myrtle, kakadu plums and bush tomatoes. Try the native tasting plate for a selection of Australian wildlife meats, and follow up with the braised wallaby shank for your main. The dessert buffet is free with your main course.

Information

ANZ bank (☎08-8956 2070) Currency exchange and 24-hour ATMs.

Emergency (☎ambulance 0420 101 403, police 08-8956 2166)

Internet Cafe (Outback Pioneer Hotel & Lodge; ⏲5am-11pm; 📶) In the backpacker common room.

Post Office (☎08-8956 2288; Resort Shopping Centre; ⏲9am-6pm Mon-Fri, 10am-2pm Sat & Sun) An agent for the Commonwealth and NAB banks. Pay phones are outside.

Royal Flying Doctor Service Medical Centre (☎08-8956 2286; ⏲9am-noon & 2-5pm Mon-Fri, 10-11am Sat & Sun) The resort's medical centre and ambulance service.

Tour & Information Centre (☎08-8957 7324; Resort Shopping Centre; ⏲8am-8pm) Most tour operators and car-hire firms have desks at this centre.

Visitor Information Centre (☎08-8957 7377; ⏲8.30am-4.30pm) Contains displays on the geography, wildlife and history of the region. There's a short audio tour ($2) if you want to learn more. It also sells books and regional maps.

Getting There & Away

AIR

Connellan Airport, serviced by a number of airlines (p845), is about 4km north from Yulara.

BUS

Emu Run (p862) runs cheap daily connections between Alice Springs and Yulara (one way adult/child $135/80).

CAR & MOTORCYCLE

One route from Alice to Yulara is sealed all the way, with regular food and petrol stops. It's 200km from Alice to Erldunda on the Stuart Hwy, where you turn west for the 245km journey along the Lasseter Hwy. The journey takes four to five hours.

Renting a car in Alice Springs to go to Uluru and back is a reasonably priced option if you make the trip in a group.

Getting Around

A free shuttle bus meets all flights and drops off at all accommodation points around the resort; pick-up is 90 minutes before your flight. Another free shuttle bus loops through the resort – stopping at all accommodation points and the shopping centre – every 15 minutes from 10.30am to 6pm and from 6.30pm to 12.30am daily.

Uluru Express (☎08-8956 2152; www.uluruexpress.com.au) falls somewhere between a shuttle-bus service and an organised tour. It provides return transport from the resort to Uluru and Kata Tjuta – see website for details.

Hiring a car will give you the flexibility to visit the Rock and the Olgas whenever you want. Car rental offices are at the Tour & Information Centre and Connellan Airport.

Perth & Fremantle

Includes ➡

Best Places to Eat

- Duende (p906)
- Brika (p904)
- Restaurant Amusé (p904)
- Pleased to Meet You (p905)
- Bread in Common (p917)

Best Places to Stay

- Durack House (p902)
- Above Bored (p902)
- Witch's Hat (p902)
- Alex Hotel (p902)
- Hougoumont Hotel (p916)

Why Go?

Planted by a river and beneath an almost permanent canopy of blue sky, the city of Perth is a modern-day boom town, stoking Australia's economy from its glitzy central business district. Yet it remains as relaxed as the sleepy Swan River – black swans bobbing atop – which winds past the skyscrapers and out to the Indian Ocean.

Even in its boardrooms, Perth's heart is down at the beach, tossing around in clear ocean surf and stretching out on the sand. The city's beaches trace the western edge of Australia for some 40km, and you can have one to yourself on any given day – for a city this size, Perth is sparsely populated.

Perth has sprawled to enfold Fremantle within its suburbs, yet the port city maintains its own distinct personality, proud of its nautical ties, working-class roots, bohemian reputation and, especially, its football team.

When to Go

Perth

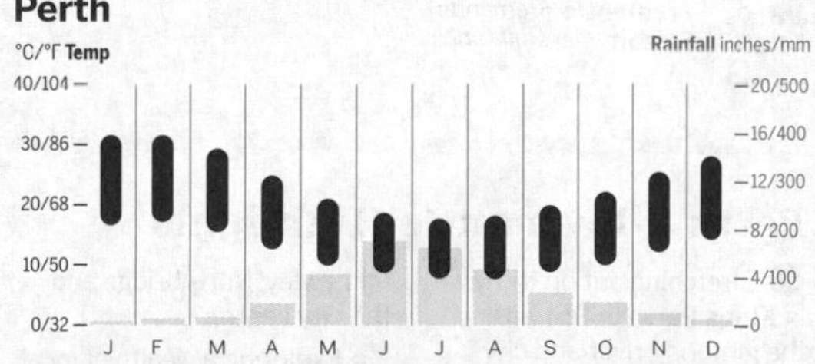

Feb Perth's Arts Festival is on and school starts, so the beaches are less crowded.

Mar Warm and dry, so great weather for the beach, and not as swelteringly hot.

Sep Kings Park wild flowers, the Perth Royal Show and the Listen Out festival.

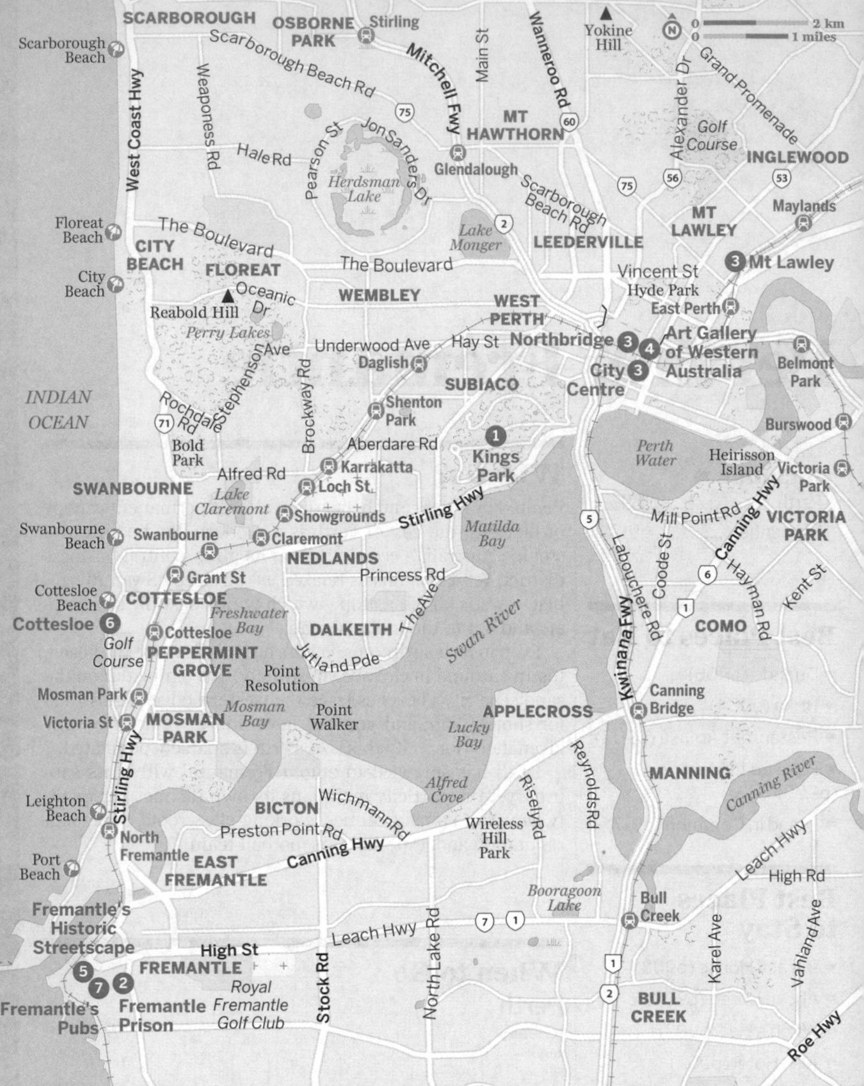

Perth & Fremantle Highlights

1 Stretching out on the lawn in **Kings Park** (p895) with the glittering river and city spread out below you.

2 Doing time with the ghosts of convicts past in World Heritage–listed **Fremantle Prison** (p912).

3 Experiencing Perth's bustling **eateries** (p904) of Mt Lawley, Northbridge and the city centre.

4 Exploring a wealth of local art, Indigenous and otherwise, at the **Art Gallery of Western Australia** (p896).

5 Soaking up the decaying gold-rush grandeur of **Fremantle's historic streetscape** (p912).

6 Enjoying the sunset with a sundowner in hand after a hard day's beaching at **Cottesloe** (p897).

7 Hitting **Fremantle's pubs** (p918) and letting the bands of Bon Scott's home town shake you all night long.

History

Archaeological records suggest Aboriginal people entered Australia in the northwest, and were trading with Indonesian fishermen from the 17th century. Dutchman Dirk Hartog landed here in 1616, and countryman Abel Tasman charted parts of the coastline in 1644. Competition with French explorers tempted British authorities to found the first settlement at Albany in 1826.

When transportation was concluding in other parts of Australia, over 10,000 convicts were sent to slow-growing Western Australia (WA). Postsentence, they established local businesses and were a sizeable, stable wave of settlers.

Late in the 19th century, gold was discovered, further creating a viable population. Prosperity and proud isolation led to a 1933 referendum on secession: Western Australians voted two to one in favour of leaving the Commonwealth. It didn't eventuate, but WA locals still have a strong independent streak that's reinforced when they feel slighted by the eastern states or the federal government.

Thanks to its mining industry, WA has been Australia's strongest economic performer over recent years. Family incomes are higher, and the population is growing faster than elsewhere.

Indigenous Western Australia

Paintings, etchings and stone tools confirm that Indigenous Australians lived as far south as present-day Perth around 40,000 years ago. Despite their resistance, dispossession and poor treatment, the Aboriginal story in WA is ultimately a story of survival.

With around 72,000 people, WA has one of the largest Indigenous communities in Australia today, particularly around the Pilbara and Kimberley regions.

Colonisation irrevocably changed Indigenous ways of life. Across the state, confrontations led to massacres or jail. Forced off traditional lands, some communities were decimated by European diseases. The *Aborigines Act 1905* (WA) allowed authorities to remove children, control employment and restrict movement.

After WWII many Indigenous people protested against their appalling treatment on cattle stations, their first public displays of political action since the early resistance fighters were defeated. Today, native-title claims are being made across WA, but Aboriginal people remain the state's most disadvantaged group. Many live in deplorable conditions, outbreaks of preventable diseases are common, and infant-mortality rates are higher than in many developing countries.

In 1993 the federal government recognised that Indigenous Australians with an ongoing association with their traditional lands were the rightful owners, unless those lands had been sold to someone else. Despite this recognition, relations between the authorities and certain Indigenous and non-Indigenous communities can be fraught, and some travellers may find this confronting. A willingness to understand the (almost always) local issues will go a long way.

National Parks

WA has 96 national parks managed by the Department of Parks & Wildlife. Thirty of these charge vehicle entry fees (per car/motorcycle $12/6). If you plan to visit more than three chargeable parks, purchase a four-week Holiday Pass ($44). If you've already paid a day-entry fee in the last week (and have the voucher), you can subtract it from the cost.

Wine Regions

Known for Bordeaux-style wines, Margaret River is one of Australia's most acclaimed wine regions. The vast cool-climate Great Southern wine region includes Denmark, Mt Barker and Porongurup. Less lauded is the Swan Valley near Perth.

Seasonal Work

Opportunities for travellers include:

TIME	INDUSTRY	REGION(S)
Feb-Mar	grapes	Denmark, Margaret River, Mt Barker, Manjimup
Feb-Apr	apples/pears	Donnybrook, Manjimup
Mar-Jun	prawn trawlers	Carnarvon
Apr-Dec	bananas	Kununurra
year-round	bananas	Carnarvon
May-Nov	vegetables	Kununurra, Carnarvon
May-Dec	tourism	Kununurra
Sep-Nov	flowers	Midlands
Nov-May	lobsters	Esperance

Greater Perth

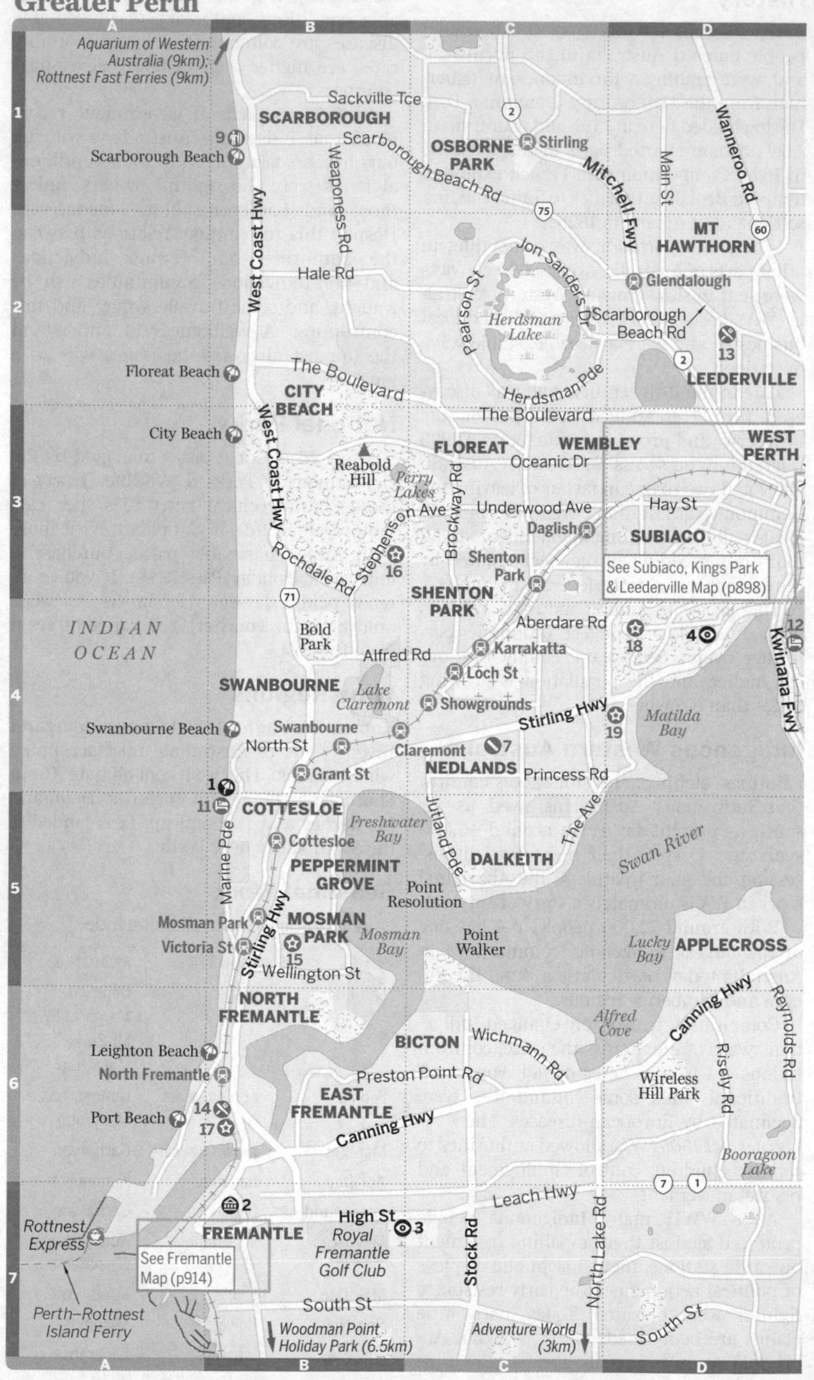

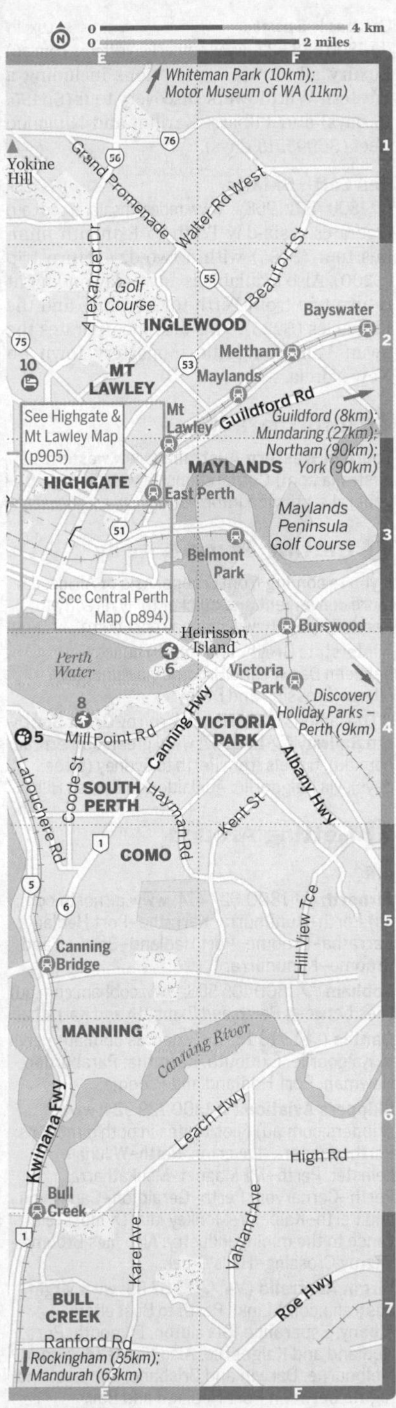

Greater Perth

Sights

1 Cottesloe Beach........B4
2 Fremantle Arts Centre........B7
3 Fremantle Cemetery........B7
4 Lotterywest Federation Walkway........D4
5 Perth Zoo........E4

Activities, Courses & Tours

6 About Bike Hire........E4
7 Australasian Diving Academy........C4
8 Funcats........E4
9 Surfschool........B1

Sleeping

10 Above Bored........E2
11 Ocean Beach Backpackers........B5
12 Peninsula........D4

Eating

Canvas........(see 2)
13 Divido........D2
14 Flipside........B6

Drinking & Nightlife

Mrs Browns........(see 14)

Entertainment

15 Camelot Outdoor Cinema........B5
16 HBF Stadium........B3
17 Mojo's........B6
18 Moonlight Cinema........D4
19 Somerville Auditorium........D4

Shopping

Found........(see 2)

Activities

Camping

From the southwest's cool, fertile forests to the rugged, tropical Kimberley in the far north, WA has wonderful bushwalking terrain. The **Bibbulmun Track** (www.bibbulmuntrack.org.au) is a 963km walking trail south from Kalamunda near Perth, through natural environment around Walpole, and along the coast to Albany. Camp sites and shelters are spaced at regular intervals. The track's best time is from late winter to spring (August to October).

Camping

WA has plenty of opportunity to get back to basics, especially in the national parks.

Cycling

Perth has many bike paths, and the southwest is good for cycle touring. For mountain bikers, the **Munda Biddi Trail** (www.mundabiddi.org.au) heads 1000km from Mundaring near Perth through the southwest forests to Albany.

Diving & Snorkelling

Shipwrecks and marine life can be found off the beaches of Rottnest Island; other areas good for diving and snorkelling include Shoalwater Islands Marine Park and Geographe Bay. In the Ningaloo Marine Park, there's excellent diving and snorkelling just 100m offshore.

Surfing & Windsurfing

WA gets huge swells (often over 3m), so it's critical to align where you surf with your ability. Look out for strong currents, sharks and occasionally territorial local surfers.

In the southwest, head to the beaches from Yallingup to Margaret River. Heading north, best-known spots include Jake's Point near Kalbarri; Gnaraloo Station, 150km north of Carnarvon; and Surfers Beach at Exmouth.

For windsurfers and kitesurfers, WA offers excellent flat-water and wave sailing. The premier location is Lancelin, north of Perth.

Whale Watching

From June, upwards of 30,000 southern right and humpback whales make their annual pilgrimage from Antarctica to the warm, tropical waters of WA's northwest coast. In early summer they then slowly migrate back south down the coast. Mothers with calves populate King George Sound in Albany from July to October.

Wild Flower Spotting

From August to October the WA bush is ablaze with vibrant wild flowers. It's a colourful time on the Bibbulmun Track and in the Stirling Range and Lesueur National Parks.

Tours

Perth's WA visitor centre can recommend tours across the state, including 4WD safaris accessing challenging and remote areas.

AAT Kings Australian Tours 4WD TOUR
(☎1300 228 456; www.aatkings.com.au) A long-established and professional outfit offering a wide range of fully escorted bus trips and 4WD adventures. Tours in WA range from a six-day Perth to Monkey Mia trip to a 11-day Untamed Kimberley adventure.

Adventure Tours 4WD TOUR
(☎1300 654 604; www.adventuretours.com.au) WA trips up to 14 days, often with a focus on adventure and Indigenous culture. Accommodation may include hostels and camping, and tour options include Perth to Broome ($1995, 14 days).

Outback Spirit LUXURY
(☎1800 688 222; www.outbackspirittours.com.au) Luxury all-terrain explorations including a Western Wildflowers Discovery tour ($6495, 15 days) and Pilbara, Karijini and Ningaloo Reef ($6995, 13 days).

Red Earth Safaris BUS TOUR
(☎1800 501 968; www.redearthsafaris.com.au) Operates a six-day Perth to Exmouth minibus tour ($785) with a two-day return trip ($200). Also available is a two-day/one-night return trip from Perth to Cervantes and the Pinnacles ($225). This also incorporates the Swan Valley and the monastery town on New Norcia.

Information

Tourism Western Australia (www.westernaustralia.com) Comprehensive website for general statewide information.

Getting There & Away

If you're coming from Europe, Asia or Africa, it's more convenient and quicker to fly directly to **Perth Airport** (www.perthairport.com).

Interstate Greyhound (p893) buses run between Darwin and Broome via Kununurra, Fitzroy Crossing and Derby.

The famous Indian Pacific, run by **Great Southern Railway** (☎13 21 47; www.greatsouthernrail.com.au), travels from Perth to Sydney (three days), via Kalgoorlie, Adelaide and Broken Hill.

Getting Around

AIR

Airnorth (☎1800 627 474; www.airnorth.com.au) Perth–Kununurra, Karratha–Port Hedland, Karratha–Broome, Port Hedland–Broome and Broome–Kununurra.

Cobham (☎1800 105 503; www.cobham.com.au) Flies between Perth and Exmouth and Karratha.

Qantas (☎13 13 13; www.qantas.com.au) Perth to Kalgoorlie, Exmouth, Karratha, Paraburdoo, Newman, Port Hedland and Broome.

Skippers Aviation (☎1300 729 924; www.skippers.com.au) Flies routes in both directions: Perth–Leonora–Laverton, Perth–Wiluna–Leinster, Perth–Mt Magnet–Meekatharra, Perth–Carnarvon, Perth–Geraldton–Carnarvon and Perth–Kalbarri–Monkey Mia. Of most relevance to the mining industry. Also flies Broome–Fitzroy Crossing–Halls Creek.

Virgin Australia (VA; ☎13 67 89; www.virginaustralia.com) Links Perth to Busselton, Albany, Esperance, Geraldton, Exmouth, Port Hedland and Kalgoorlie. Also flights to Sydney, Melbourne, Darwin and Brisbane, and weekend flights between Port Hedland and Bali.

BUS

Greyhound (☎1300 473 946; www.greyhound.com.au) Service between Darwin and Broome via Kununurra, Fitzroy Crossing and Derby.

Integrity Coach Lines (☎1800 226 339; www.integritycoachlines.com.au) Buses between Perth and Port Hedland via the Great Northern Hwy, and also from Perth to Lancelin, Cervantes, Geraldton, Exmouth, Karratha and Broome. Hop-on/hop-off tickets valid for 12 months with unlimited stops are available (Perth–Exmouth $245, Perth–Broome $365). This includes connecting shuttle services west to the coast for Kalbarri and Shark Bay. Also runs handy services linking Exmouth and Karijini.

South West Coach Lines (☎08-9261 7600; www.transdevsw.com.au) From Perth to all the major towns in the southwest – your best choice for Margaret River.

Transwa (Map p894; ☎1300 662 205; www.transwa.wa.gov.au) Perth–Augusta, Perth–Pemberton, Perth–Albany (three routes), Perth–Esperance (two routes), Albany–Esperance, Kalgoorlie–Esperance, Perth–Geraldton (three routes) and Geraldton–Meekathara.

CAR

WA is not only enormous but also sparsely populated, so plan safely for significant journeys with extra water and fuel. A 4WD is recommended for many places such as the spectacular Kimberley.

Department of Aboriginal Affairs (DAA; ☎1300 651 077; www.daa.wa.gov.au; 151 Royal St, East Perth) To travel through Aboriginal land in WA you need a permit. Applications can be lodged on the internet.

Mainroads (☎13 81 38; www.mainroads.wa.gov.au) Provides statewide road-condition reports, updated daily (and more frequently if necessary).

TRAIN

Transwa services are limited to the *Prospector* (Perth–Kalgoorlie), *AvonLink* (Perth–Northam) and *Australind* (Perth–Bunbury). Transperth's local train network reaches as far south as Mandurah.

PERTH

POP 1.8 MILLION

Far away from the machinations of national affairs in Sydney, Melbourne and Canberra, Perth is a confident and bold urban statement on Australia's far western shores. Built around the broad expanse of the Swan River and fringing the cobalt waters of the Indian Ocean, one of the world's most remote state capitals effortlessly combines big-city sophistication with a relaxed and easygoing lifestyle.

About as close to Southeast Asia as to Australia's eastern state capitals, Perth offers an appealing lifestyle for locals and a variety of things to do for visitors. It's a cosmopolitan city with myriad bars, restaurants and cultural activities all vying for attention. Recent urban development is boldly making over the CBD, but the city's lucky residents know relaxation and escape on 40km of arcing beaches is always close at hand.

History

Modern Perth was founded in 1829 when Captain James Stirling established the Swan River colony on the lands of the Wadjuk, a subgroup of the Noongar people. The discovery of stone implements near the Swan River suggests that the area had already been occupied for around 40,000 years.

Relations were friendly at first, the Noongar believing the British to be the returned spirits of their dead, but competition for resources led to conflict. By 1843 the Wadjuk had been dispossessed of all their lands around the new city and were forced to camp near the swamps and lakes to the north.

The early settlement grew very slowly until 1850, when convicts alleviated the labour shortage and boosted the population. Convict labour was also responsible for

PERTH IN...

Two Days

Have a leisurely dinner in **Highgate** or **Mt Lawley** (p904) and then spend your first morning in the art galleries and museum of the **Perth Cultural Centre** (p896). Grab lunch in **Subiaco** or **Leederville** (p906) before exploring view-friendly **Kings Park** (p895). For your second day, catch the train to **Fremantle**, prioritising the world-heritage prison, maritime museum and Shipwreck Galleries. Dine in **South Fremantle**, before heading to a pub to catch a band or drink Western Australian (WA) craft beer.

Four Days

Take the two-day itinerary but stretch it to a comfortable pace. Head to **Rottnest Island** (p922) for a day trip and spend any time left over on Perth's **beaches**. Allocate a night each to **Northbridge** (p907) and the city centre's best new bars and restaurants.

Central Perth

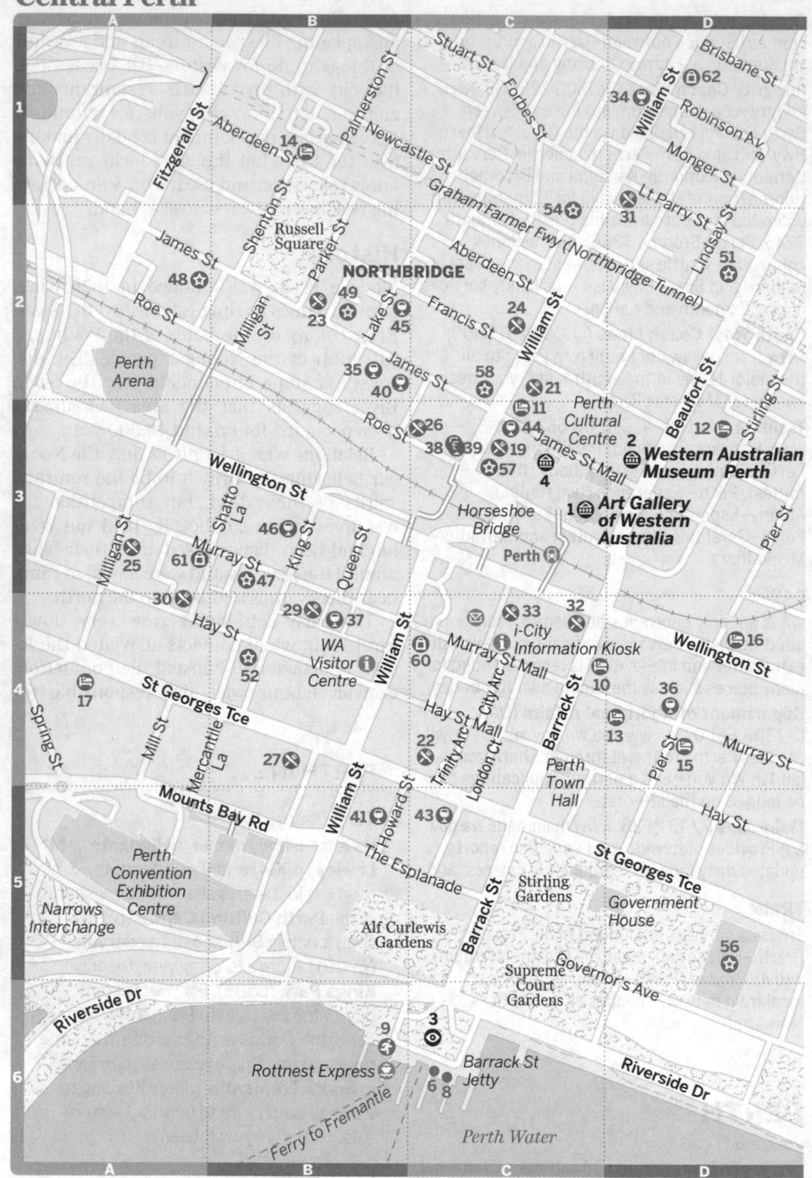

constructing the city's substantial buildings, such as Government House and the town hall. The discovery of gold inland in the 1890s increased Perth's population fourfold in a decade and initiated a building bonanza, mirrored in the current mining and economic boom.

Although there has been a relative slowdown in WA's resources boom recently, Perth remains a vibrant city being transformed by major urban construction projects, and the revitalisation of the CBD and inner suburbs like Northbridge.

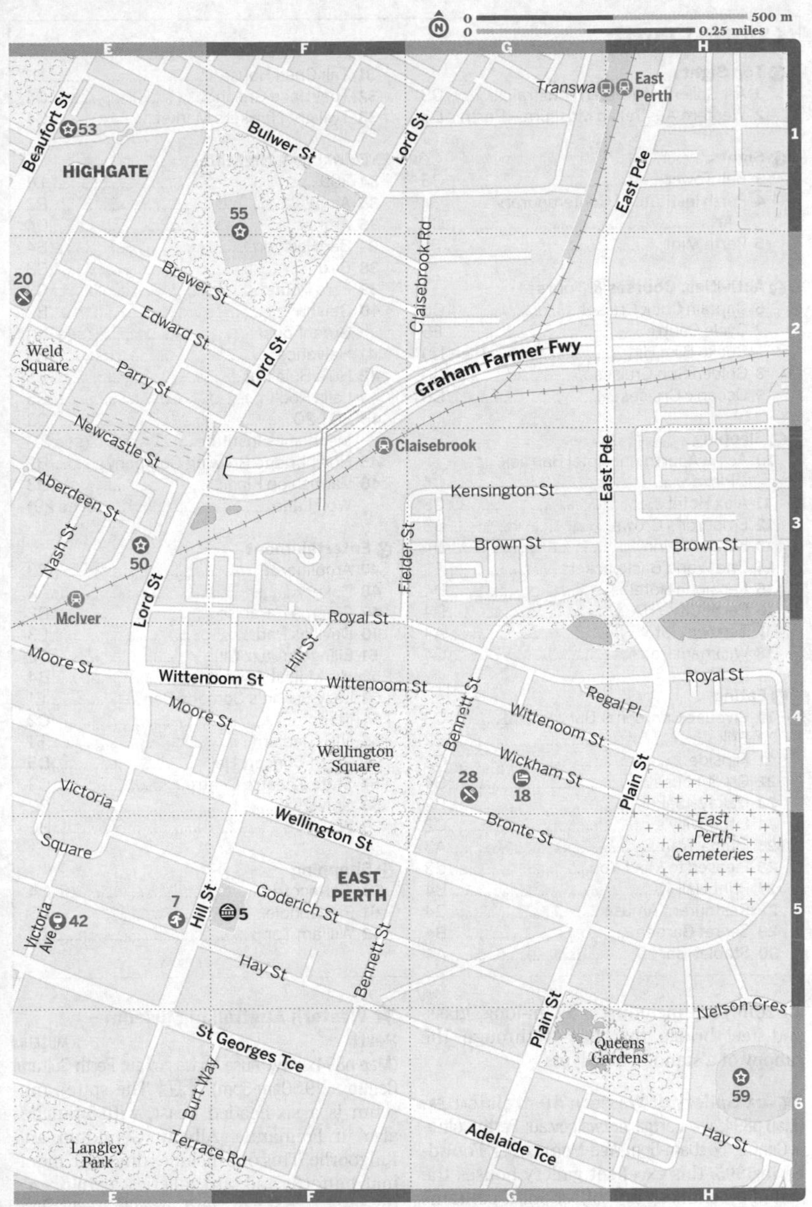

Sights

★Kings Park & Botanic Garden PARK

(Map p898; www.bgpa.wa.gov.au; guided walks 10am, noon & 2pm) FREE Rising above the Swan River on the city's western flank, the 400-hectare bush-filled expanse of Kings Park is Perth's pride and joy. At the park's heart is the 17-hectare Botanic Garden, containing over 2000 plant species indigenous to WA. In spring there's an impressive display of the state's famed wild flowers. A year-round highlight is the **Lotterywest Federation Walkway** (Map p890; 9am-5pm),

Central Perth

Top Sights
1 Art Gallery of Western Australia........... C3
2 Western Australian Museum – Perth .. D3

Sights
3 Bell Tower... C6
4 Perth Institute of Contemporary Arts... C3
5 Perth Mint...F5

Activities, Courses & Tours
6 Captain Cook Cruises........................... C6
7 Cycle Centre..E5
Gecko Bike Hire............................(see 12)
8 Golden Sun Cruises.............................. C6
9 Oceanic Cruises..................................... B6

Sleeping
10 Adina Apartment Hotel Barrack Plaza... C4
11 Alex Hotel... C3
12 Emperor's Crown.................................. D3
13 Kangaroo Inn.. D4
14 One World Backpackers B1
15 Pensione Hotel..................................... D4
16 Perth City YHA D4
17 Terrace Hotel.. A4
18 Wickham Retreat.................................. G4

Eating
19 Bivouac Canteen & Bar......................... C3
20 Brika E2
21 Flipside C2
22 Greenhouse C4
23 Izakaya Sakura...................................... B2
24 Little Willy's... C2
25 Mama Tran A3
26 Pleased to Meet You............................. C3
27 Print Hall B4
28 Restaurant Amusé................................ G4
29 Secret Garden....................................... B4
30 Stables Bar A4
31 Tak Chee House D1
32 Toastface Grillah C4
33 Twilight Hawkers Market......................C4

Drinking & Nightlife
34 399 .... D1
35 Air B2
36 Ambar D4
37 Bar Halcyon...B4
38 Bird C3
39 Ezra Pound..C3
40 Geisha B2
Greenhouse.......................................(see 22)
41 Helvetica..B5
42 Hula Bula Bar E5
43 Lalla Rookh..C5
44 LOT 20 ....C3
Mechanics Institute.......................(see 21)
45 Northbridge Brewing Company B2
46 Varnish on King.....................................B3
Wolf Lane..(see 29)

Entertainment
47 Amplifier B3
48 Bakery..A2
49 Cinema Paradiso B2
50 Devilles Pad E3
51 Ellington Jazz Club D2
52 His Majesty's Theatre............................B4
53 Lazy Susan's Comedy Den E1
54 Moon C2
55 NIB Stadium...F1
56 Perth Concert Hall.................................D5
57 State Theatre Centre.............................C3
58 Universal..C2
59 WACA... H6

Shopping
60 78 Records C4
61 Pigeonhole...A3
62 William Topp D1

a 620m path including a 222m-long, glass-and-steel bridge that passes through the canopy of a stand of eucalypts.

★ Art Gallery of Western Australia GALLERY
(Map p894; www.artgallery.wa.gov.au; Perth Cultural Centre; 10am-5pm Wed-Mon) FREE Founded in 1895, this excellent gallery houses the state's preeminent art collection. It contains important post-WWII works by Australian luminaries such as Arthur Boyd, Albert Tucker, Grace Cossington Smith, Russell Drysdale, Arthur Streeton and Sidney Nolan. Check the website for a changing array of free tours run most days at 11am and 1pm. The gallery's Indigenous galleries are also very well regarded.

★ Western Australian Museum – Perth MUSEUM
(Map p894; www.museum.wa.gov.au; Perth Cultural Centre; 9.30am-5pm) FREE The state's museum is a six-headed beast, with branches also in Fremantle, Albany, Geraldton and Kalgoorlie. This one includes dinosaur, mammal, butterfly and bird galleries, a **children's discovery centre**, and excellent displays covering Indigenous and colonial history.

Aquarium of Western Australia AQUARIUM
(AQWA; 08-9447 7500; www.aqwa.com.au; Hillarys Boat Harbour; adult/child $29/17; 10am-5pm) Dividing WA's vast coastline into five distinct zones (Far North, Coral Coast, Shipwreck Coast, Perth and Great Southern),

AQWA features a 98m underwater tunnel showcasing stingrays, turtles, fish and sharks. On weekdays, take the Joondalup train to Warwick station and then transfer to bus 423. By car, take the Mitchell Fwy north and exit at Hepburn Ave. The daring can snorkel or dive with the sharks with the aquarium's in-house dive master.

Perth Institute of Contemporary Arts GALLERY
(PICA; Map p894; www.pica.org.au; Perth Cultural Centre; ⏲10am-5pm) FREE PICA (pee-kah) may look traditional – it's housed in an elegant 1896 red-brick former school – but inside it's one of Australia's principal platforms for contemporary art including installations, performance, sculpture and video. PICA actively promotes new and experimental art, and exhibits graduate works annually. From 10am from Tuesday to Sunday, the PICA Bar is a top spot for a coffee or cocktail, and has occasional live music.

Bell Tower LANDMARK
(Map p894; www.thebelltower.com.au; adult/child $14/9; ⏲10am-4pm, ringing noon-1pm Sat-Mon & Thu) This glass spire fronted by copper sails contains the royal bells of London's St Martin's-in-the-Fields, the oldest of which dates to 1550. They were given to WA by the British government in 1988, and are the only set known to have left England. Clamber to the top for 360-degree views of Perth.

Perth Mint HISTORIC BUILDING
(Map p894; www.perthmint.com.au; 310 Hay St; adult/child $25/8; ⏲9am-5pm) Dating from 1899, the compelling Mint displays a collection of coins, nuggets and gold bars. You can fondle a bar worth over $200,000, mint your own coins and watch gold pours (on the half-hour, from 9.30am to 3.30pm). The Mint's Gold Exhibition features a massive one-tonne gold coin worth a staggering $50 million.

Perth Zoo ZOO
(Map p890; www.perthzoo.wa.gov.au; 20 Labouchere Rd; adult/child $27/13; ⏲9am-5pm) Part of the fun of a day at the zoo is getting there – taking the ferry across the Swan River from Barrack St Jetty to Mends St Jetty (every half-hour) and walking up the hill. Zones include Reptile Encounter, African Savannah (rhinos, cheetahs, zebras, giraffes and lions), Asian Rainforest (elephants, tigers, sun bears, orangutans) and Australian Bushwalk (kangaroos, emus, koalas, dingoes). Another transport option is bus 30 or 31 from the Wellington St bus station or Esplanade train station.

Swan Valley WINERY, BEER
(www.swanvalley.com.au) Perthites love to swan around this semirural valley on the city's eastern fringe to partake in the finer things in life: booze, nosh and the great outdoors. Perhaps in a tacit acknowledgement that its wines will never compete with the state's more prestigious regions (it doesn't really have the ideal climate), the Swan Valley compensates with galleries, breweries, providores and restaurants.

The gateway is National Trust–classified **Guildford**, established in 1829. A clutch of interesting old buildings, one housing the **visitor centre** (☎08-9379 9400; www.swanvalley.com.au; Old Courthouse, cnr Swan & Meadow Sts, Guildford; ⏲9am-4pm), make it the logical starting place for day trippers. Guildford is only 12km from central Perth and well served by suburban trains.

Cottesloe Beach BEACH
(Map p890) The safest swimming beach, Cottesloe has cafes, pubs, pine trees and fantastic sunsets. From Cottesloe train station (on the Fremantle line) it's 1km to the beach. Bus 102 from Wellington St station goes straight to the beach.

Activities

Mills Charters WHALE WATCHING
(☎08-9246 5334; www.millscharters.com.au; adult/child $80/65; ⏲9am daily, 1.30pm Sat & Sun mid-Sep–Nov) Informative three- to four-hour trips departing from Hillarys Boat Harbour.

Surf Sail Australia WINDSURFING, KITESURFING
(Map p898; ☎1800 686 089; www.surfsailaustralia.com.au; 260 Railway Pde, Trial; ⏲10am-5pm Mon-Sat) When the afternoon sea breeze blusters in, windsurfers take to the Swan River, Leighton and beaches north of Perth. This is where you can hire or buy your gear.

Oceanic Cruises WHALE WATCHING
(Map p894; ☎08-9325 1191; www.oceaniccruises.com.au; adult/child $77/34) Departs Perth's Barrack St Jetty or Fremantle's B Shed.

Australasian Diving Academy DIVING
(Map p890; ☎08-9389 5018; www.ausdiving.com.au; 142 Stirling Hwy) Hires diving gear (full set per day/week $75/200) and offers diving courses (four-day open-water course $495). There are a variety of sites in the vicinity, including several around Rottnest Island, and four wrecks.

Subiaco, Kings Park & Leederville

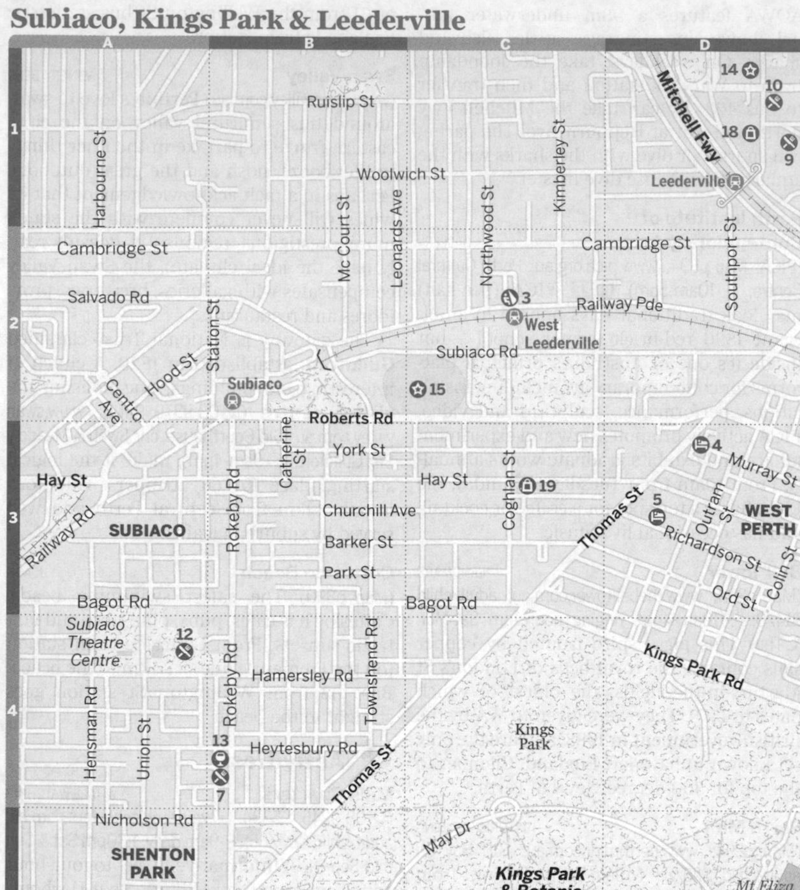

Funcats SAILING

(Map p890; ☎0408 926 003; www.funcats.com.au; Coode St Jetty; per hour $40; ⊙10am-6pm Oct-Apr) These easy-to-sail catamarans are for hire on the South Perth foreshore. Each boat holds up to three people.

Surfschool SURFING

(Map p890; ☎08-9447 5637; www.surfschool.com; Scarborough Beach; adult/child $60/55; ⊙Oct-May) Two-hour lessons at Scarborough Beach (at the end of Manning St), including boards and wetsuits. Bookings essential.

WA Skydiving Academy ADVENTURE SPORTS

(☎1300 137 855; www.waskydiving.com.au) Tandem jumps from 6000/8000/10,000/12,000ft from $260/300/340/380. Drop zone options include Perth, Mandurah and Pinjarra.

Cycling

Kings Park has good bike tracks, and there are cycling routes along the Swan River to Fremantle and the coast. Bikes can be taken free of charge on ferries any time, and on trains outside weekday peak hours (7am to 9am and 4pm to 6.30pm). For route maps, see www.transport.wa.gov.au/cycling.

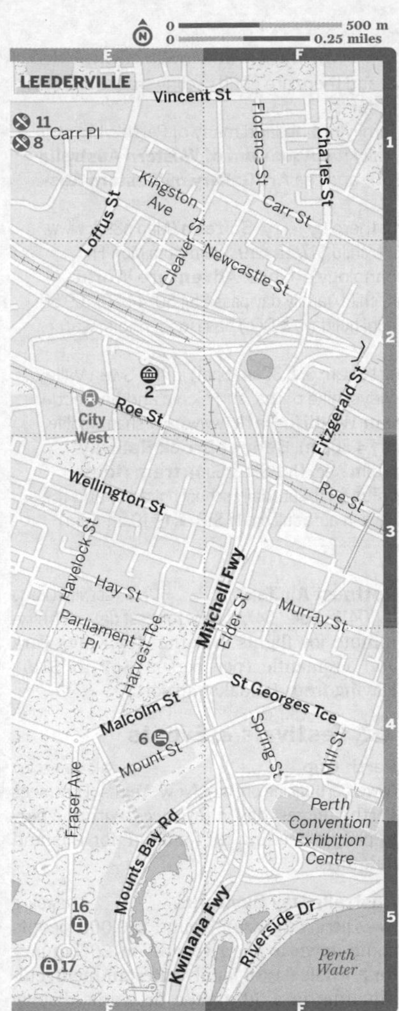

Subiaco, Kings Park & Leederville

Top Sights

1 Kings Park & Botanic Garden..............C5

Sights

2 Scitech..............E2

Activities, Courses & Tours

3 Surf Sail Australia..............C2

Sleeping

4 Murray Hotel..............D3
5 Richardson..............D3
6 Riverview 42 Mt St Hotel..............E4

Eating

7 Boucla..............B4
8 Duende..............E1
9 Leederville Farmers Market..............D1
10 Low Key Chow House..............D1
11 Sayers..............E1
12 Subiaco Farmers Market..............A4

Drinking & Nightlife

13 Juanita's..............B4

Entertainment

14 Luna..............D1
15 Patersons Stadium..............C2

Shopping

16 Aboriginal Art & Craft Gallery..............E5
17 Aspects of Kings Park..............E5
18 Atlas Divine..............D1
19 Indigenart..............C3

Cycle Centre BICYCLE RENTAL
(Map p894; ☎08-9325 1176; www.cyclecentre.com.au; 326 Hay St; per day/week $25/65; ⏲9am-5.30pm Mon-Fri, 9am-4pm Sat, 1-4pm Sun) See the website for recommended rides.

About Bike Hire BICYCLE RENTAL
(Map p890; ☎08-9221 2665; www.aboutbikehire.com.au; 1-7 Riverside Dr, Causeway Car Park; per hour/day/week from $10/36/80; ⏲9am-5pm) Also hires kayaks (per hour/four hours $16/45).

Gecko Bike Hire BICYCLE RENTAL
(Map p894; www.geckobikehire.com.au; 85 Stirling St; per four hours/day $22/33) Four locations around Perth, and further south in Bunbury and Busselton. See the website for route maps. The Stirling St branch is inside Emperor's Crown hostel.

Tours

Indigenous Tours WA CULTURAL TOUR
(www.indigenouswa.com) See Perth through the eyes of the local Wadjuk people. Options include the **Indigenous Heritage Tour** (☎0405 630 606; adult/child $50/15; ⏲1.30pm & 3.30pm Mon-Fri) – a 90-minute guided walk around Kings Park – and an Indigenous-themed stroll (p916) around Fremantle.

Beer Nuts BREWERY
(☎08-9295 0605; www.beernuts.com.au; per person from $60; ⏲Wed-Sun) Visits Swan Valley microbreweries and a rum distillery.

City Sightseeing Perth Tour BUS TOUR
(☎08-9203 8882; www.citysightseeingperth.com; adult/child from $30/12) Hop-on, hop-off double-decker bus tour, with loop routes taking in the central city, Kings Park and the

PERTH FOR CHILDREN

Kings Park has playgrounds and walking tracks, and there are good cycling tracks along the Swan River. Of the beaches, Cottesloe is the safest.

The **Perth Royal Show** (p901) is a popular family outing, and many of Perth's big attractions cater well for young audiences, especially the **Aquarium of Western Australia** (p896), the **Western Australian Museum** (p896) and the **Art Gallery of Western Australia** (p896).

Part of the fun of **Perth Zoo** (p897) is getting there by ferry. **Scitech** (Map p898; www.scitech.org.au; Sutherland St, City West Centre; adult/child $17/11; ⏲9.30am-4pm Mon-Fri, 10am-5pm Sat & Sun) has over 160 hands-on technology exhibits. **Adventure World** (www.adventureworld.net.au; 179 Progress Dr; adult/child/family day pass $54.50/44.50/169.50; ⏲10am-5pm Thu-Mon late Sep-early May, daily school holidays & Dec) has rides, pools, waterslides and a castle.

Whiteman Park (www.whitemanpark.com; West Swan; ⏲8.30am-6pm) in the Swan Valley (enter from Lord St or Beechboro Rd) has walkways, bike paths, and picnic and barbecue spots. Within its ordered grounds are **Caversham Wildlife Park** (www.cavershamwildlife.com.au; adult/child $25/11; ⏲9am-5.30pm, last entry 4.30pm), **Bennet Brook Railway** (www.whitemanpark.com; adult/child $8/4; ⏲11am-1pm Wed, Thu, Sat & Sun), **tram rides** (www.pets.org.au; adult/child $5/2.50; ⏲noon-2pm Tue & Fri-Sun, daily school holidays) and the **Motor Museum of WA** (www.motormuseumofwa.asn.au; adult/child $10/7; ⏲10am-4pm).

Burswood Entertainment Complex. Tickets are valid for up to two days.

Captain Cook Cruises CRUISE
(Map p894; ☎08-9325 3341; www.captaincookcruises.com.au; adult/child from $38/21) Cruises to the Swan Valley or Fremantle, with an array of add-ons such as meals, wine tastings and tram rides.

Golden Sun Cruises CRUISE
(Map p894; ☎08-9325 9916; www.goldensuncruises.com.au; tours from $22) Well-priced cruises and a good option to get to Fremantle.

Out & About WINE
(☎08-9377 3376; www.outandabouttours.com.au; per person from $85) Wine-focused tours of the Swan Valley and historic Guildford. Some include river cruises, breweries, cheese and chocolate stops. Day trips also to Margaret River.

Swan Valley Tours FOOD, WINE
(☎08-9274 1199; www.svtours.com.au; per person from $65) Food- and wine-driven tours that cruise up to and/or drive through the Swan Valley.

Two Feet & A Heartbeat WALKING TOUR
(☎1800 459 388; www.twofeet.com.au; per person $40-50) Daytime walking tours of Perth, and a popular after-dark 'Small Bar Tour'. Note 'Tight Arse Tuesdays' are just $20 for the Perth tour.

Rottnest Air Taxi SCENIC FLIGHTS
(☎0411 264 547; www.rottnest.de) Thirty-minute joy flights over the city, Kings Park and Fremantle (per person $67 to $115), leaving from Jandakot airport.

Festivals & Events

Perth Cup HORSE RACING
(www.perthracing.org.au) New Year's Day sees Perth's biggest day at the races, with the party people heading to 'Tentland' for DJs and daiquiris.

Australia Day Skyworks FIREWORKS
(www.perth.wa.gov.au) Around 250,000 people come down to the riverside on 26 January for a whole day of family entertainment, culminating in a 30-minute fireworks display at 8pm.

Perth International Arts Festival ARTS
(www.perthfestival.com.au) Artists such as Laurie Anderson, Dead Can Dance and Philip Glass perform alongside top local talent. Held over 25 days from mid-February to early March, it spans theatre, classical music, jazz, visual arts, dance, film and literature. Worth scheduling a trip around, especially for nocturnal types.

Kings Park Festival CULTURAL
(www.kingsparkfestival.com.au) Held throughout September to coincide with the wildflower displays, it includes live music every Sunday, guided walks and talks.

Perth Royal Show FAIR
(www.perthroyalshow.com.au; Claremont Showground) A week of fun-fair rides, spun sugar and showbags full of plastic junk. Oh, and farm animals. Held late September to early October.

Listen Out MUSIC
(www.listen-out.com.au; cnr Adelaide Tce & Riverside Dr, Ozone Reserve) A one-day festival of international and local purveyors of danceable beats. Late September.

Sleeping

The CBD and Northbridge are close to public transport, making hopping out to inner-city suburbs such as Leederville and Mt Lawley straightforward.

Perth is an expensive town for accommodation. Book as early as you can and note many hotels are cheaper from Friday to Sunday. B&Bs are usually good value and another option is to base yourself in better-value Fremantle.

City Centre

Kangaroo Inn HOSTEL $
(Map p894; 08-9325 3508; www.kangarooinn.com.au; 123 Murray St; dm $45-50, s/d $109/119;) Centrally located and near excellent cheap Asian food options, Kangaroo Inn is a very well-run recently opened addition to Perth's array of backpackers hostels. Private rooms and dorms are clean and modern, shared bathrooms are spotless and there's a great rooftop chill-out area that's perfect for meeting other travellers.

Wickham Retreat HOSTEL $
(Map p894; 08-9325 6398; www.wickhamretreat.com; 25-27 Wickham St; dm $34-38, d $80;) Located in a residential neighbourhood east of the city centre, Wickham Retreat has a quieter vibe than other hostels around town. Most of the guests are international travellers, drawn by the colourful rooms and dorms, and a funky Astroturf garden. Free food – including rice, fresh bread and vegies – stretches travel budgets eroded by Perth's high prices.

Perth City YHA HOSTEL $
(Map p894; 08-9287 3333; www.yha.com.au; 300 Wellington St; dm $37-40, r with/without bathroom $125/100;) Occupying an impressive 1940s art deco building by the train tracks, the centrally located YHA has a slight boarding-school feel in the corridors, but the rooms are clean and there are good facilities including a gym and a bar. Like many Perth hostels, it's popular with 'fly-in, fly-out' (FIFO) mine workers, so the traditional YHA's travellers' vibe has been diminished.

Riverview 42 Mt St Hotel APARTMENT $$
(Map p898; 08-9321 8963; www.riverviewperth.com.au; 42 Mount St; apt from $140;) There's a lot of brash new money up here on Mount St, but character-filled Riverview stands out as the best personality on the block. Its refurbished 1960s bachelor pads sit neatly atop a modern foyer and a relaxed cafe. Rooms are sunny and simple; the front ones have river views, while the back ones are quieter.

Pensione Hotel BOUTIQUE HOTEL $$
(Map p894; 08-9325 2133; www.pensione.com.au; 70 Pier St; d from $189;) Formerly the budget-oriented Aarons, this central-city 98-room property now features a shiny boutique sheen as the Pensione Hotel. The standard rooms definitely veer to cosy and (very) compact, but classy decor and a good location arc two definite pluses in an expensive city.

Adina Apartment Hotel Barrack Plaza APARTMENT $$$
(Map p894; 08-9267 0000; www.tfehotels.com/brands/adina-apartment-hotels; 138 Barrack St; apt from $289;) The Adina's meticulously decorated apartment-sized hotel rooms are minimalist yet welcoming. All one-bedrooms have balconies, and rooms on Barrack St tend to have more natural light.

Terrace Hotel BOUTIQUE HOTEL $$$
(Map p894; 08-9214 4444; www.terracehotelperth.com.au; 237 St Georges Tce; d from $432;) Opened in late 2012, the Terrace Hotel fills a heritage-listed terrace house in Perth's historic West End. There are just 15 deluxe rooms and suites, all with a clubby and luxurious ambience. Modern accoutrements include huge flat-screen TVs, Apple TV and iPads, and king-size four-poster beds with Egyptian-cotton linen.

Northbridge, Highgate & Mt Lawley

Most of Perth's hostels are in Northbridge, and it's possible to walk around and inspect rooms before putting your money down. It can be noisy on weekends.

Witch's Hat HOSTEL $

(Map p905; ☎08-9228 4228; www.witchs-hat.com; 148 Palmerston St; dm/tw/d $36/88/99;) Witch's Hat is like something out of a fairy tale. The 1897 building itself could be mistaken for a gingerbread house, and the witch's hat (an Edwardian turret) stands proudly out the front, beckoning the curious to step inside. Dorms are light and uncommonly spacious, and there's a red-brick barbecue area out the back.

Emperor's Crown HOSTEL $

(Map p894; ☎08-9227 1400; www.emperorscrown.com.au; 85 Stirling St; dm $30-34, r with/without bathroom from $109/99;) One of Perth's best hostels has a great position (close to the Northbridge scene without being in the thick of it), friendly staff and high housekeeping standards. Granted, it's a bit pricier than most, but it's worth it.

One World Backpackers HOSTEL $

(Map p894; ☎08-9228 8206; www.oneworldbackpackers.com.au; 162 Aberdeen St; dm $31-33, d $82;) Polished floorboards beam brightly in all the rooms of this nicely restored old house, and the dorms are big and sunny. The kitchen is large and functional, with everything provided, and there's a spacious lounge to relax in and plan your travels.

Alex Hotel BOUTIQUE HOTEL $$

(Map p894; ☎08-6430 4000; www.alexhotel.com.au; 50 James St; d from $190) The new Alex Hotel is more stylish evidence of the reinvention of Northbridge as a happening neighbourhood. Classy and compact rooms are decked out in neutral colours, stacked with fine linen and electronic gear, and the roof terrace has great city views. Relaxed shared spaces include a cafe and bar, and the Alex' streetfront restaurant channels a retro European bistro.

Durack House B&B $$

(Map p905; ☎08-9370 4305; www.durackhouse.com.au; 7 Almondbury Rd; r $195-215;) It's hard to avoid words like 'delightful' when describing this cottage, set on a peaceful suburban street behind a rose-adorned white picket fence. The three rooms have plenty of old-world charm, paired with thoroughly modern bathrooms. It's only 250m from Mt Lawley station; turn left onto Railway Pde and then take the first right onto Almondbury Rd.

Above Bored B&B $$

(Map p890; ☎08-9444 5455; www.abovebored.com.au; 14 Norham St; d $190-200;) In a quiet residential neighbourhood, this 1927 Federation house is owned by a friendly TV scriptwriter. The two themed rooms in the main house have eclectic decor, and in the garden there's a cosy self-contained cottage with a kitchenette. In an expensive town for accommodation, Above Bored is great value. Northbridge and Mt Lawley are a short drive away.

Pension of Perth B&B $$

(Map p905; ☎08-9228 9049; www.pensionperth.com.au; 3 Throssell St; s/d from $150/165;) Pension of Perth's French belle époque style lays luxury on thick: chaise longues, rich floral rugs, heavy brocade curtains, open fireplaces and gold-framed mirrors. Two doubles with bay windows (and small bathrooms) look out onto the park, and there are two rooms with spa baths. Location wise, it's just across the road from gorgeous Hyde Park.

Subiaco & Kings Park

Murray Hotel HOTEL $$

(Map p898; ☎08-9321 7441; www.themurrayhotel.com; 718 Murray St; d $149-199;) Handily located near Kings Park, the Murray is an older hotel that's recently had a 21st-century makeover. Decor is sharp and modern, and although the hotel's 1970s provenance is not completely concealed, it's still good value in an expensive city. The pool is a cooling addition in a sultry WA summer, and Perth's free CAT bus service stops outside.

Richardson HOTEL $$$

(Map p898; ☎08-9217 8888; www.therichardson.com.au; 32 Richardson St; r from $530;) Ship-shaped and shipshape, the Richardson offers luxurious, thoughtfully designed rooms – some with sliding doors to open them up into larger suites. The whole complex has a breezy, summery feel, with pale marble tiles, creamy walls and interesting art. There's an in-house spa centre if you require additional pampering.

Beaches

Ocean Beach Backpackers HOSTEL $

(Map p890; ☎08-9384 5111; www.oceanbeachbackpackers.com.au; 1 Eric St, Cottesloe; dm/s/d $29/75/84;) Offering (some) ocean views, this big, bright hostel in the heart of Cottesloe is just a short skip from the sand. Rooms are basic, but all have private bathrooms, and you'll probably just be here to sleep given the great location. Hire a bike to get around locally, or take advantage of the hostel's free bodyboards and surfboards.

Trigg Retreat B&B **$$**
(☎08-9447 6726; www.triggretreat.com; 59 Kitchener St, Trigg Beach; r incl breakfast $180-200; ❄@📶) Quietly classy, this three-room B&B offers attractive and supremely comfortable queen bedrooms in a modern house a short drive from Trigg Beach. Each has fridge, TV, DVD player and tea- and coffee-making facilities. Full cooked breakfast.

Other Areas

Discovery Holiday Parks – Perth CAMPGROUND **$**
(☎08-9453 6877; www.discoveryholidayparks.com.au; 186 Hale Rd; powered sites for 2 people $42-50, units $159-179; ❄@📶🏊) This well-kept holiday park, 15km out of the city, has a wide range of cabins and smart-looking units, many with deck, TV and DVD player.

Peninsula APARTMENT **$$**
(Map p890; ☎08-9368 6688; www.thepeninsula.net; 53 South Perth Esplanade; apt from $219; ❄@📶) While only the front few apartments have full-on views, the Peninsula's waterfront location lends itself to lazy ferry rides and sunset strolls along the river. It's a sprawling, older-style complex, but it's kept in good nick. The apartments all have kitchenettes and there's a communal laundry room.

Eating

Perth can be an expensive city to eat in, but it's still possible to eat cheaply, especially in the Little Asia section of William St, Northbridge. Many restaurants are BYO (bring your own wine; check first).

Cafes are good places to go for a midrange meal, and there are good ethnic food halls in most CBD shopping malls. Some establishments listed under Drinking & Nightlife offer good dining as well.

City Centre

Twilight Hawkers Market STREET FOOD **$**
(Map p894; www.twilighthawkersmarket.com; Forrest Chase; snacks & mains $10; ⏲4.30-9pm Fri mid-Oct–mid-Apr) Ethnic food stalls bring the flavours and aromas of the world to central Perth on Friday nights in spring and summer. Look forward to combining your Turkish *gözleme* (savoury crepe) or Colombian empanadas (deep-fried pastries) with regular live music from local Perth bands.

Toastface Grillah CAFE **$**
(Map p894; www.toastfacegrillah.com; Grand Lane; sandwiches $7-9; ⏲7am-4pm Mon-Fri, 9am-4pm Sat) Vibrant street art, excellent coffee and a sneaky laneway location combine with interesting toasted sandwiches such as the 'Pear Grillz' with blue cheese, pear and lime chutney. All this and a not-so-subtle Wu-Tang Clan reference too.

Mama Tran VIETNAMESE **$**
(Map p894; www.mamatran.com.au; 36-40 Milligan St; snacks & mains $8-14; ⏲7.30am-4pm Mon-Fri, 5.30pm-9pm Thu & Fri) Now you don't have to truck across to Northbridge for a hearty bowl of *pho* (Vietnamese noodle soup). The hip Mama Tran also serves excellent coffee, fresh rice-paper rolls and Asian salads. Grab a spot on one of the big shared tables and order up a storm including plump *banh mi ga* (Vietnamese chicken baguettes).

Secret Garden CAFE **$**
(Map p894; www.secretgardencafe.com.au; Murray Mews; mains $10-19; ⏲7am-3pm Mon-Fri; 📶) Tucked away down a boho laneway off Murray St, Secret Garden has good coffee, enticing counter food and all-day breakfasts for hangovers. Free wi-fi is the perfect partner to a robust espresso.

Greenhouse TAPAS **$$**
(Map p894; ☎08-9481 8333; www.greenhouseperth.com; 100 St Georges Tce; breakfast $10-20, shared plates $12-32; ⏲7am-late Mon-Fri, from 9am Sun) 🍃 Ground-breaking design – straw bales, plywood, corrugated iron and exterior walls covered with 5000 pot plants – combines with excellent food at this tapas-style eatery. Middle Eastern and Asian influences inform a sustainably sourced menu including lamb tagine with kalamata olives and harissa, or prawns with coriander and Vietnamese-style *nuoc cham* sauce. At night, Greenhouse morphs into a good bar.

Stables Bar BISTRO **$$**
(Map p894; www.thestablesbar.com.au; 888 Hay St; tapas $12-16, mains $25; ⏲11am-late Mon-Sat) Concealed down a heritage arcade, Stables Bar manages to be both an energetic and bustling bar, and a worthwhile destination for interesting food. On weekend nights, craft beers, cocktails and a rowdier bar persona definitely take over, but at quieter times it is worth popping in for well-priced tapas and mains including crab linguine and lamb with baba ganoush and dukkah.

Print Hall ASIAN, MODERN AUSTRALIAN $$$
(Map p894; www.printhall.com.au; 125 St Georges Tce; shared plates $14-36, mains $25-36; ⏲11.30am-midnight Mon-Fri, 4pm-midnight Sat) This sprawling complex in the Brookfield Place precinct includes The Apple Daily, featuring Southeast Asian–style street food, and the expansive Print Hall Dining Room, with an oyster bar and grilled WA meat and seafood. Don't miss having a drink and Spanish tapas in the rooftop Bob's Bar, named after Australia's larrikin former prime minister, Bob Hawke.

★ **Restaurant Amusé** MODERN AUSTRALIAN $$$
(Map p894; ☎08-9325 4900; www.restaurantamuse.com.au; 64 Bronte St; degustation without/with wine pairing $130/210; ⏲6.30pm-late Tue-Sat) The critics have certainly been amused by this degustation-only establishment, regularly rated as one of Australia's finest. Ongoing accolades include being dubbed WA's number-one eatery by *Gourmet Traveller* magazine every year since 2010. Book well ahead and come prepared for a culinary adventure. Look forward to a stellar WA-focused wine list, too.

Northbridge, Highgate & Mt Lawley

Veggie Mama VEGETARIAN $
(Map p905; www.veggiemama.com.au; cnr Beaufort & Vincent Sts; mains $10-20; ⏲8am-7pm Mon & Tue, 8am-9pm Wed-Fri, 9am-5pm Sat & Sun;) Loads of vegan and gluten-free options shine at this cute corner cafe where flavour is definitely not compromised. The menu includes delicious salads, smoothies, vegie curries and burgers; weekend breakfasts are very popular.

Little Willy's CAFE $
(Map p894; www.facebook.com/LittleWillys; 267 William St; mains $8-16; ⏲6am-6pm Mon-Fri, 8am-4pm Sat & Sun) It's tiny and it's on William St, and it's a go-to spot to grab a sidewalk table and tuck into robust treats such as the city's best breakfast burrito and Bircher museli. It's also a preferred coffee haunt for the hip Northbridge indie set. BYO skinny jeans.

Tak Chee House MALAYSIAN $
(Map p894; 1/364 William St; mains $11-17; ⏲11am-3pm & 5-9pm Tue-Sun) With Malaysian students crammed in for a taste of home, Tak Chee is our pick for one of the best Asian cheapies along William St. If you don't have a taste for satay, Hainan chicken or *char kway teo* (fried noodles), Thai, Vietnamese, Lao and Chinese flavours are all just footsteps away. Cash only; BYO wine or beer.

Flipside BURGERS $
(Map p894; www.flipsideburgerbar.com.au; 222 William St; burgers $11.50-15.50; ⏲11.30am-9.30pm Tue-Sun) Gourmet burgers with the option of take away to the bar upstairs, Mechanics Institute (p907).

★ **Brika** GREEK $$
(Map p894; www.brika.com.au; 3/177 Stirling St; meze & mains $9-27; ⏲noon-late Wed-Sun) Presenting a stylish spin on traditional Greek cuisine, Brika is our favourite new Perth restaurant. The whitewashed interior is enlivened by colourful traditional fabrics, and menu highlights include creamy zucchini fritters, slow-cooked lamb, and chargrilled swordfish skewers. Definitely leave room for dessert of *ravani* (semolina cake), and consider a $12 lunchtime souvlaki if time or money are tight.

Pleased to Meet You BISTRO, BAR $$
(Map p894; www.pleasedtomeetyou.com.au; 38 Roe St; shared plates $9-20; ⏲5pm-late Mon-Thu, noon-late Fri-Sun) Ticking all the hipster culinary boxes with its dedication to Asian and South American street food, Pleased to Meet You presents bold flavours in a menu that's perfect for sharing over a few cocktails, WA wines or craft beers. Grab a spot at the shared tables and tuck into flavour hits such as coconut ceviche, duck tacos and grilled garlic oysters.

El Público MEXICAN $$
(Map p905; ☎0418 187 708; www.elpublico.com.au; 511 Beaufort St; snacks & shared plates $9-18; ⏲5pm-midnight Mon-Fri, from 4pm Sat & Sun) Look forward to interesting and authentic spins on Mexican street food, all served as small plates that are perfect for sharing. Menu stand outs include cuttlefish soft-shell tacos and salmon ceviche, and peanut butter *dulce de leche* praline for dessert. Bring along a few friends and groove to the occasional DJs.

Cantina 663 MEDITERRANEAN $$
(Map p905; ☎08-9370 4883; www.cantina663.com; 663 Beaufort St; mains $15-33; ⏲7.30am-late Mon-Sat, to 3pm Sun) It's a mini culinary World Cup, featuring Spain, Portugal and Italy, at this cool but casual cantina with tables spilling into the arcade. Service can be a bit too cool for school, but it's worth waiting for dishes such as truffle risotto with chestnuts and artichoke, or seared cuttlefish with pickled carrot, cucumber, radish and white wine.

Highgate & Mt Lawley

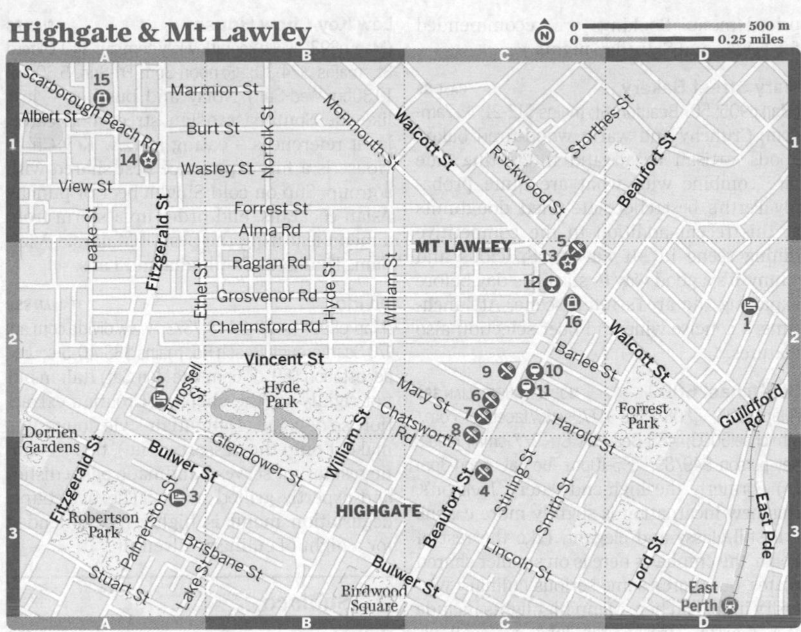

Highgate & Mt Lawley

Sleeping

1 Durack House ... D2
2 Pension of Perth ... A2
3 Witch's Hat ... A3

Eating

4 Ace Pizza ... C3
5 Cantina 663 ... C2
6 El Público ... C2
7 Mary Street Bakery ... C2
8 St Michael 6003 ... C2
9 Veggie Mama ... C2

Drinking & Nightlife

10 Clarence's ... C2
11 Five Bar ... C2
12 Flying Scotsman ... C2

Entertainment

13 Astor ... C2
14 Rosemount Hotel ... A1

Shopping

15 Future Shelter ... A1
16 Planet ... C2

Ace Pizza PIZZA **$$**
(Map p905; www.acepizza.com.au; 448 Beaufort St; snacks $8-16, mains & pizza $18-26; 5.30pm-late) Cosy banquette seating fills this dark and dramatic retreat serving Perth's best thin-crust pizza. The menu stretches to other Italian-inspired wood-fired goodies, but most punters are here for the crispy, garlicky and smoky combinations of runny cheese, fresh herbs, and prosciutto or seafood. A concise selection of bar snacks makes it good for a relaxed beer or wine too.

Bivouac Canteen & Bar CAFE **$$**
(Map p894; www.bivouac.com.au; 198 William St; shared plates $10-28, pizzas $23-25; noon-late Tue-Sat) Mediterranean-style cuisine partners with a good wine list, and gourmet pizzas go well with boutique beers and artisan ciders. The coffee is excellent, and Bivouac's utilitarian decor is softened with a rotating roster of work from local artists.

Izakaya Sakura JAPANESE **$$**
(Map p894; 08-9328 2525; www.izakayasakura.com.au; 2/182 James St; shared plates $10-15, mains $13-18) Small plates made for sharing feature at this stylish retreat from the occasional rough and tumble of Northbridge. The sushi and sashimi are superfresh, and other stand-out dishes include delicate tempura prawns and *takoyaki* (deep-fried octopus snacks). Come with a thirst for sake or cold beer, and work through the sensibly

priced menu. Bookings are recommended for Friday and Saturday nights.

Mary Street Bakery CAFE **$$**
(Map p905; 507 Beaufort St; mains $12-21; ⊙7am-4pm) Crunchy and warm wood-fired baked goods, artisan bread and interesting cafe fare combine with what are quite probably Perth's best chocolate-filled doughnuts at this recent addition to the competitive dining scene in Mt Lawley. Spacious and sunny, it's a good way to start the day before exploring the area's retail scene. At lunchtime, a concise wine and beer selection also features.

St Michael 6003 MODERN AUSTRALIAN **$$$**
(Map p905; ☎08-9328 1177; www.facebook.com/stmichael6003; 483 Beaufort St; 3/7 small plates per person $49/89; ⊙5-10pm Tue-Sat, noon-3pm Fri) Formerly the high-end eatery Jackson's, this new incarnation is slightly more casual, but still classy and elegant. Like the rest of Perth, the emphasis here is on smaller shared plates, but there's some serious culinary wizardry in the kitchen. Menu highlights include WA marron (freshwater lobster), scallops, quail and trout. Sign up for the seven-course menu for a leisurely treat.

Mt Hawthorn & Leederville

Leederville Farmers Market MARKET **$**
(Map p898; www.leedervillefarmers.com.au; Newcastle St, car park; ⊙8am-noon Sun) Every Sunday morning.

★**Duende** TAPAS **$$**
(Map p898; ☎08-9228 0123; www.duende.com.au; 662 Newcastle St; tapas & mains $15-32; ⊙7.30am-late) Sleek Duende occupies a corner site amid the comings and goings of Leederville. Stellar modern-accented tapas are served, so make a meal of it or call in for a late-night glass of dessert wine and *churros*. We're partial to starting the day with an espresso and Duende's ham and Manchego cheese croquettes.

Sayers CAFE **$$**
(Map p898; www.sayersfood.com.au; 224 Carr Pl; mains $12-28; ⊙7am-3pm) This classy cafe has a counter groaning under the weight of an alluring cake selection. The breakfast menu includes smoked salmon with scrambled eggs and asparagus, while lunch highlights include a chermoula-spiced chicken salad with quinoa, pistachio and a lemon yoghurt dressing. Welcome to one of Perth's best cafes.

Low Key Chow House ASIAN **$$**
(Map p898; www.keepitlowkey.com.au; 140 Oxford St; mains $24-30; ⊙noon-3pm Fri-Sun, 5.30pm-10.30pm Wed-Sun) Noisy and bustling – just like the Southeast Asian street-food eateries it references – eating at Low Key Chow House is a fun experience best shared with a group. Sup on cold Singha beer or punchy Asian cocktails, and order up a storm from a menu featuring the best of Malaysia, Vietnam, Thailand, Cambodia and Laos.

Divido ITALIAN **$$$**
(Map p890; ☎08-9443 7373; www.divido.com.au; 170 Scarborough Beach Rd; mains $38-40, 5-course degustation $89; ⊙6pm-late Mon-Sat) Italian but not rigidly so (the chef's of Croatian extraction, so delicious Dalmatian-style doughnuts make it onto the dessert menu), this romantic restaurant serves handmade pasta dishes and expertly grilled mains. The five-course degustation menu is highly recommended for a night of culinary adventure.

Subiaco

Boucla CAFE **$**
(Map p898; www.boucla.com; 349 Rokeby Rd; mains $11-24; ⊙7am-5pm Mon-Fri, 7am-3.30pm Sat) A locals' secret, this Greek- and Levantine-infused haven is pleasingly isolated from the thick of the Rokeby Rd action. Baklava and cakes tempt you from the corner, and huge tarts filled with blue-vein cheese and roast vegetables spill off plates. The salads are great too.

Subiaco Farmers Market MARKET **$**
(Map p898; www.subifarmersmarket.com.au; Subiaco Primary School, 271 Bagot Rd; ⊙8am-noon Sat) Every Saturday morning.

Drinking & Nightlife

A recent wave of quirky small bars has emerged in the formerly deserted-after-dark central city, and Northbridge also has more idiosyncratic drinking establishments.

WA's mining boom has seen the rise of young men with plenty of cash to splash on muscle cars, beer and drugs, and a spate of fights and glassings in bars caused many venues to step up security, particularly around Northbridge.

Most pubs now have lockouts, so you'll need to be in before midnight to gain entry. You may need to present photo ID, and you should keep your wits about you in pubs and on the streets after dark.

City Centre

Greenhouse COCKTAIL BAR
(Map p894; www.greenhouseperth.com; 100 St Georges Tce; ⏲7am-midnight Mon-Fri, from 9am Sat) In a city so in love with the great outdoors, a rooftop bar in the central city makes perfect sense. Hip, eco-conscious Greenhouse mixes up a storm amid the greenery with great cocktails and an interesting beer and wine list. Good food is also available.

Lalla Rookh WINE BAR
(Map p894; www.lallarookh.com.au; Lower Ground Fl, 77 St Georges Tce; pizzas $16-26, shared plates $14-21, 6 plates for $58; ⏲11.30am-midnight Mon-Fri, from 5pm Sat) Escape downstairs from the CBD to this cosy bar specialising in wine, craft beer and Italian food. Cocktails also come with a whisper of the Mediterranean, and the all-day menu encourages relaxed grazing over shared dishes. Our favourite combo is the chilli and king prawn pizza partnered with a zesty Feral Hop Hog Pale Ale from the nearby Swan Valley.

Helvetica BAR
(Map p894; www.helveticabar.com.au; rear 101 St Georges Tce; ⏲3pm-midnight Tue-Thu, noon-1am Fri, 6pm-1am Sat) Clever artsy types tap their toes to delicious alternative pop in this bar named after a typeface and specialising in whisky and cocktails. The concealed entry is off Howard St: look for the chandelier in the laneway.

Wolf Lane COCKTAIL BAR
(Map p894; www.wolflane.com.au; Wolfe Lane; ⏲4pm-midnight Fri & Sat) Exposed bricks, classic retro furniture and high ceilings create a pretty decent WA approximation of a New York loft. A serious approach to cocktails and wine combines with an eclectic beer selection, and bar snacks include share plates of Turkish bread and chorizo.

Bar Halcyon COCKTAIL BAR
(Map p894; www.bardehalcyon.com.au; Wolfe Lane; ⏲11.30am-late Tue-Fri, 4pm-late Sat) Concealed in the funky laneway that is Wolfe Lane, Bar Halcyon channels a Spanish vibe with sangria, tapas and *pinxtos* (savoury bar snacks), and a decent selection of cocktails and beer. DJs kick in most weekend nights, but it's also a top spot for a daytime coffee.

Hula Bula Bar COCKTAIL BAR
(Map p894; www.hulabulabar.com; 12 Victoria Ave; ⏲4pm-midnight Wed-Fri, 6pm-1am Sat, 4-10pm Sun; 📶) You'll feel like you're on *Gilligan's Island* in this tiny Polynesian-themed bar, decked out in bamboo, palm leaves and tikis. A cool but relaxed crowd jams in here on weekends to sip ostentatious cocktails out of ceramic monkey's heads.

Varnish on King WHISKY
(Map p894, www.varnishonking.com; 75 King St; ⏲11.30am-midnight Mon-Fri, 4pm-midnight Sat) With interesting shopping and new cafes and bars, lower King St is emerging as a Perth hotspot. Amid the hipster barber shops and single-origin coffee, our favourite new opening is a brick-lined homage to American whisky. More than 40 types are available, and a decent beer and wine list is partnered by grown-up party food such as moreish fried chicken wings.

Air CLUB
(Map p894; www.airclub.com.au; 139 James St; ⏲from 9pm Fri & Sat) Nonstop house, techno and trance.

Ambar CLUB
(Map p894; www.boomtick.com.au/ambar; 104 Murray St; ⏲10pm-5am Fri & Sat) Perth's premier club for breakbeat, drum and bass, and visiting international DJs.

Geisha CLUB
(Map p894; www.geishabar.com.au; 135a James St; ⏲11pm-6am Fri & Sat) A small and pumping, DJ-driven, gay-friendly club.

Northbridge, Highgate & Mt Lawley

Northbridge is the rough-edged hub of Perth's nightlife, with dozens of pubs and clubs clustered mainly around William and James Sts. Mt Lawley also has decent pubs and bars.

Northbridge Brewing Company MICROBREWERY
(Map p894; www.northbridgebrewingco.com.au; 44 Lake St; ⏲8am-10pm Sun-Tue, to midnight Wed-Sat) The four beers brewed here are decent enough, but the real attractions are the occasional guest beers on tap from around Australia. The outdoor bar adjoining the grassy expanse of Northbridge Plaza is relaxed and easygoing, and various big screens dotted around the multilevel industrial space make it a good spot to watch live sport. Go the Dockers!

Mechanics Institute BAR
(Map p894; www.mechanicsinstitutebar.com.au; 222 William St; ⏲noon-midnight Tue-Sat, to 10pm Sun)

Negotiate the laneway entrance around the corner on James St to discover one of Perth's most down-to-earth small bars. Share one of the big tables on the deck or nab a stool by the bar. Craft beers are on tap, and you can even order in a gourmet burger from Flipside (p904) downstairs.

LOT 20 BAR
(Map p894; www.lot20.co; 198-206 William St, entrance on James St; ⏲10am-midnight Mon-Sat, to 10pm Sun) LOT 20 is more evidence of the ongoing transformation of rough-and-ready Northbridge into the home of more intimate and sophisticated small bars. The brick-lined courtyard is perfect on a warm WA evening, and on cooler nights the cosy interior is best experienced with a few bar snacks – try the Asian-style 'Son in Law Eggs' – and wine or craft beer.

Clarence's COCKTAIL BAR
(Map p905; www.clarences.com.au; 506 Beaufort St, Mt Lawley; ⏲4pm-late Mon-Fri, noon-late Sat, noon-10pm Sun) Clarence's energetic collage of small bar buzz and intimate bistro dining is a dependable spot for good times along Mt Lawley's Beaufort St after-dark strip. Menu highlights include crab tacos, and sweetcorn and saffron arancini.

Five Bar BEER
(Map p905; www.fivebar.com.au; 560 Beaufort St, Mt Lawley; ⏲noon-midnight Mon-Sat, to 10pm Sun) International and Australian craft beers – including seasonal and one-off brews from WA's best – make Mt Lawley's Five Bar worth seeking out by the discerning drinker. Wine lovers are also well catered for, and the menu leans towards classy comfort food.

Ezra Pound BAR
(Map p894; www.epbar.com.au; 189 William St; ⏲1pm-midnight Tue-Sat, to 10pm Sun) Down a much-graffitied lane leading off William St, Ezra Pound is favoured by Northbridge's bohemian set. It's the kind of place where you can settle into a red velvet chair and sip a Tom Collins out of a jam jar. Earnest conversations about Kerouac and Kafka are strictly optional.

399 BAR
(Map p894; www.399bar.com; 399 William St; ⏲4pm-midnight Mon-Sat, to 10pm Sun; 📶) This friendly neighbourhood bar has booths along one side and a long bar down the other, making it easy to interact with the engaging bar staff. Cocktails are artfully crafted, and there's a serious approach to beer and wine. Nearby are lots of good, cheap Asian restaurants.

Bird BAR
(Map p894; www.williamstreetbird.com; 181 William St; ⏲noon-midnight Mon-Sat, to 10pm Sun) Cool indie bar with local bands, performers and DJs. Upstairs there's a brick-lined deck with city views.

Flying Scotsman PUB
(Map p905; www.facebook.com/scottoscottoscotto; 639 Beaufort St, Mt Lawley; ⏲11am-midnight) Old-style pub that attracts the Beaufort St indie crowd. A good spot for a drink before a gig up the road at the Astor (p909).

Subiaco

Juanita's BAR, CAFE
(Map p898; www.juanitas.com.au; 341 Rokeby Rd; ⏲9am-11pm Mon-Fri, 10am-1am Sat, noon-1am Sun) Welcome to Perth's most eclectic small (and we do mean small) bar. Tapas, shared platters and a concise selection of beer and wine partner with rescued 1960s furniture, walls trimmed with bric-a-brac, and a few outside tables. It's all thoroughly local, very charming, and a refreshing antidote to the flash, renovated pubs elsewhere in Subiaco.

☆ Entertainment

Live Music

Ellington Jazz Club JAZZ
(Map p894; www.ellingtonjazz.com.au; 191 Beaufort St; ⏲6.30pm-1am Mon-Thu, to 3am Fri & Sat, 5pm-midnight Sun) There's live jazz nightly in this handsome, intimate venue. Standing-only admission is $10, or you can book a table (per person $15 to $20) for tapas and pizza.

Bakery LIVE MUSIC
(Map p894; www.nowbaking.com.au; 233 James St; ⏲7pm-late) Run by Artrage, Perth's contemporary arts festival body, the Bakery draws an arty crowd. Popular indie gigs are held almost every weekend.

Amplifier LIVE MUSIC
(Map p894; www.amplifiercapitol.com.au; rear 383 Murray St) The good old Amplifier is one of the best places for live (mainly indie) bands. Part of the same complex is Capitol, used mainly for DJ gigs.

Moon LIVE MUSIC
(Map p894; www.themoon.com.au; 323 William St; ⏲6pm-late Mon & Tue, 11am-late Wed-Sun) Low-key, late-night cafe with singer-songwriters

on Wednesday nights, jazz on Thursdays, and poetry slams on Saturday afternoons from 2pm.

Universal LIVE MUSIC
(Map p894; www.universalbar.com.au; 221 William St; ⏱3pm-late Wed-Sun) The unpretentious Universal is one of Perth's oldest bars and much-loved by soul, R&B and blues enthusiasts.

Rosemount Hotel LIVE MUSIC
(Map p905; www.rosemounthotel.com.au; cnr Angove & Fitzgerald Sts; ⏱noon-late) Local and international bands play regularly in this spacious art deco pub with a laid-back beer garden.

Astor CONCERT VENUE
(Map p905; www.liveattheastor.com.au; 659 Beaufort St) The beautiful art deco Astor still screens the odd film but is mainly used for concerts these days.

Cabaret & Comedy

Lazy Susan's Comedy Den COMEDY
(Map p894; www.lazysusans.com.au; Brisbane Hotel, 292 Beaufort St; ⏱8.30pm Tue, Fri & Sat) Shapiro Tuesday offers a mix of first-timers, seasoned amateurs and pros trying out new shtick (for a very reasonable $5). Friday is for more grown-up stand-ups, including some interstaters. Saturday is the Big Hoo-haa – a team-based comedy wrassle. The Den is at the Brisbane Hotel.

Theatre & Classical Music

Check the *West Australian* newspaper for listings. Book through www.ticketek.com.au or www.ticketmaster.com.au.

State Theatre Centre THEATRE
(Map p894; www.statetheatrecentrewa.com.au; 174 William St) This complex includes the 575-seat Heath Ledger Theatre and the 234-seat Studio Underground. It's home to the Black Swan State Theatre Company and Perth Theatre Company.

His Majesty's Theatre THEATRE
(Map p894; www.hismajestystheatre.com.au; 825 Hay St) The majestic home to the **West Australian Ballet** (www.waballet.com.au) and **West Australian Opera** (www.waopera.asn.au), as well as lots of theatre, comedy and cabaret.

Perth Concert Hall CONCERT VENUE
(Map p894; www.perthconcerthall.com.au; 5 St Georges Tce) Home to the **Western Australian Symphony Orchestra** (WASO; www.waso.com.au).

Cinema

Somerville Auditorium CINEMA
(Map p890; www.perthfestival.com.au; 35 Stirling Hwy; ⏱Dec-Mar) A quintessential Perth experience, the Perth Festival's film program is held here on the University of WA's beautiful grounds surrounded by pines. Picnicking before the film is a must.

Luna CINEMA
(Map p898; www.lunapalace.com.au; 155 Oxford St) Art-house cinema in Leederville with Monday double features and a bar. Cheap tickets on Wednesdays.

Cinema Paradiso CINEMA
(Map p894; www.lunapalace.com.au; 164 James St) Art-house cinema in Northbridge. Cheap tickets on Tuesdays.

Moonlight Cinema CINEMA
(Map p890; www.moonlight.com.au; Synergy Parklands, Kings Park; ⏱Dec-Easter) Bring a picnic and blanket and enjoy a romantic moonlit movie; summer only.

Camelot Outdoor Cinema CINEMA
(Map p890; www.lunapalace.com.au; Memorial Hall, 16 Lochee St; ⏱Dec-Easter) Seated open-air cinema in Mosman Park.

Sport

In WA 'football' means Aussie Rules and during the Australian Football League (AFL) season it's hard to get locals to talk about anything but the two local teams – the **West Coast Eagles** (www.westcoasteagles.com.au) and the **Fremantle Dockers** (www.fremantlefc.com.au).

Patersons Stadium STADIUM
(Subiaco Oval; Map p898; ☎08-9381 2187; www.patersonsstadium.com.au; 250 Roberts Rd) The home of Aussie Rules and big concerts.

WACA STADIUM
(Western Australian Cricket Association; Map p894; ☎08-9265 7222; www.waca.com.au; Nelson Cres) Main venue for interstate and international cricket.

NIB Stadium STADIUM
(Perth Oval; Map p894; www.nibstadium.com.au; Lord St) Home to **Perth Glory** (www.perthglory.com.au) soccer (football) and **Western Force** (www.westernforce.com.au) rugby.

HBF Stadium STADIUM
(Map p890; www.hbfstadium.com.au; Stephenson Ave, Mt Claremont) Home to **West Coast Fever** (www.westcoastfever.com.au) netball.

Shopping

Murray St and Hay St Malls are the city's shopping heartland, while Leederville and Mt Lawley feature more eclectic shops. If you're after vintage or retro style, head to Northbridge, and lower King St near Wellington St in the CBD is developing as a hub for independent retail stores and designers.

City Centre

78 Records MUSIC
(Map p894; www.78records.com.au; upstairs, 255 Murray St Mall; 9am-5pm Mon-Sat, from 11am Sun) Independent record shop. Also good for vinyl and tickets to rock and indie gigs.

Pigeonhole CLOTHING, ACCESSORIES
(Map p894; www.pigeonhole.com; 9 Shafto Lane; 10am-6pm Mon-Sat, to 9pm Fri) Hip local and international clothing, and stylish retro accessories and gifts.

Northbridge, Highgate & Mt Lawley

William Topp DESIGN
(Map p894; www.williamtopp.com; 452 William St; 11am-6pm Tue-Fri, to 5pm Sat, to 4pm Sun) Cool designer knick-knacks.

Future Shelter HOMEWARES
(Map p905; www.futureshelter.com; 56 Angove St, North Perth; 10am-5pm Mon-Sat) Quirky clothing, gifts and homewares designed and manufactured locally. Surrounding Angove St is an emerging hip North Perth neighbourhood.

Planet BOOKS, MUSIC
(Map p905; www.planetvideo.com.au; 636-638 Beaufort St; 10am-late) Books, CDs and obscure DVDs.

Leederville

Leederville's Oxford St is the place for boutiques, eclectic music and bookshops.

Atlas Divine CLOTHING
(Map p898; 121 Oxford St; 9am-9pm) Hip women's and men's clobber: jeans, quirky tees, dresses etc.

Subiaco & Kings Park

Rokeby Rd and Hay St boast fashion, art and classy gifts.

Indigenart ARTS
(Map p898; www.mossensongalleries.com.au; 115 Hay St; 11am-4pm Wed-Sat) Indigenous art from around Australia, but with a focus on WA artists. Works include weavings, paintings on canvas, bark and paper, and sculpture.

Aboriginal Art & Craft Gallery ARTS
(Map p898; www.aboriginalgallery.com.au; Fraser Ave; 10.30am-4.30pm Mon-Fri, 11am-4pm Sat & Sun) Work from around WA; more populist than high-end or collectable.

Aspects of Kings Park ARTS, SOUVENIRS
(Map p898; www.aspectsofkingspark.com.au; Fraser Ave; 9am-5pm) Australian art, craft and books.

Information

EMERGENCY

Police station (13 14 44; www.police.wa.gov.au; 2 Fitzgerald St)

Sexual Assault Resource Centre (08-9340 1828, freecall 1800 199 888; www.kemh.health.wa.gov.au/services/sarc; 24hr) Twenty-four-hour emergency service.

INTERNET ACCESS

State Library of WA (www.slwa.wa.gov.au; Perth Cultural Centre; 9am-8pm Mon-Thu, 10am-5.30pm Fri-Sun;) Free wi-fi and internet access.

MEDIA

Drum Media (www.facebook.com/drumperth) Music, film and culture listings.

Go West (www.gowesternaustralia.com.au) Backpacker magazine with information on seasonal work opportunities.

Urban Walkabout (www.urbanwalkabout.com) Eating, drinking and shopping highlights in key inner-Perth neighbourhoods and Fremantle.

West Australian (www.thewest.com.au) Local newspaper with entertainment and cinema listings.

X-Press Magazine (www.xpressmag.com.au) A good online source of live-music information. Also available as an app.

MEDICAL SERVICES

Lifecare Dental (08-9221 2777; www.dentistsinperth.com.au; 419 Wellington St; 8am-8pm) In Forrest Chase.

Royal Perth Hospital (08-9224 2244; www.rph.wa.gov.au; Victoria Sq) In central Perth.

Travel Medicine Centre (08-9321 7888; www.travelmed.com.au; 5 Mill St; 8am-5pm Mon-Fri) Travel-specific advice and vaccinations.

POST

The **Main Post Office** (GPO; Map p894; 13 13 18; 3 Forrest Pl; 8.30am-5pm Mon-Fri, 9am-12.30pm Sat) is in a central location near the bus and train station.

TOURIST INFORMATION

i-City Information Kiosk (Map p894; Murray St Mall; ⏲9.30am-4.30pm Mon-Thu & Sat, to 8pm Fri, 11am-3.30pm Sun) Volunteers answer questions and run walking tours.

WA Visitor Centre (Map p894; ☎1800 812 808, 08-9483 1111; www.bestofwa.com.au; 55 William St; ⏲9am-5.30pm Mon-Fri, 9.30am-4.30pm Sat, 11am-4.30pm Sun) Excellent resource for information across WA.

USEFUL WEBSITES

Heatseeker (www.heatseeker.com.au) Gig guide and ticketing.

PerthNow (www.perthnow.com.au) Perth and WA news and restaurant reviews.

Scoop (www.scoop.com.au) Entertainment and dining information.

What's On (www.whatson.com.au) Events and travel information.

Getting There & Away

AIR

For details on flights to Perth from international, interstate and other Western Australian destinations, see the Transport chapter.

TRAIN

Transwa (☎1300 662 205; www.transwa.wa.gov.au) runs the following train services:

Australind (twice daily) Perth to Pinjarra ($17, 1¼ hours) and Bunbury ($31, 2½ hours).

AvonLink (daily) East Perth to Toodyay ($17, 1¼ hours) and Northam ($20, 1½ hours).

Prospector (daily) East Perth to Kalgoorlie-Boulder ($82, seven hours).

Getting Around

TO/FROM THE AIRPORT

The domestic and international terminals of Perth's airport are 10km and 13km east of Perth respectively, near Guildford. Taxi fares to the city are around $40 from the domestic and international terminals, and about $60 to Fremantle.

Connect (☎1300 666 806; www.perthairportconnect.com.au) runs shuttles to and from central accommodation and transport options in the city centre (one way/return $15/30, every 50 minutes). Bookings are recommended for groups.

Transperth buses 36, 37 and 40 travel to the domestic airport from St Georges Tce (stop 10121), near William St ($4.40, 40 minutes, every 10 to 30 minutes, hourly after 7pm). A free transfer bus links the domestic and international terminals.

CAR & MOTORCYCLE

Driving in the city takes a bit of practice, as some streets are one way and many aren't signed. There are plenty of car-parking buildings in the central city but no free parks. For unmetered street parking you'll need to look well away from the main commercial strips and check the signs carefully.

Some local Perth-based hire companies:

Backpacker Car Rentals (☎08-9430 8869; www.backpackercarrentals.com.au; 235 Hampton Rd, South Fremantle) Good-value local agency.

Bayswater Car Rental (☎08-9325 1000; www.bayswatercarrental.com.au) Local company with four branches in Perth and Fremantle.

Britz Rentals (☎1800 331 454; www.britz.com.au) Hires fully equipped 4WDs fitted out as campervans, popular on the roads of northern WA. Britz has offices in all the state capitals, as well as Perth and Broome, so one-way rentals are possible.

Campabout Oz (☎08-9301 2765; www.campaboutoz.com.au) Campervans, 4WDs and motorbikes.

Scootamoré (☎08-9380 6580; www.scootamore.com.au; 356a Rokeby Rd, Subiaco; day/3 days/week/month $45/111/200/400) Hires 50cc scooters with helmets (compulsory) and insurance included (for over 21 year olds).

PUBLIC TRANSPORT

Transperth (☎13 62 13; www.transperth.wa.gov.au) operates Perth's public buses, trains and ferries. There are Transperth information offices at Perth station (Wellington St), Wellington St bus station, Perth underground station (off Murray St) and the Esplanade Busport (Mounts Bay Rd). There's a good online journey planner.

From the central city, the following fares apply for all public transport:

Free Transit Zone (FTZ) Covers the central commercial area, bounded (roughly) by Fraser Ave, Kings Park Rd, Thomas St, Newcastle St, Parry St, Lord St and the river (including the City West and Claisebrook train stations, to the west and east respectively).

Zone 1 Includes the city centre and the inner suburbs ($2.90).

Zone 2 Fremantle, Guildford and the beaches as far north as Sorrento ($4.40).

Zone 3 Hillarys Boat Harbour (AQWA), the Swan Valley and Kalamunda ($5.30).

Zone 5 Rockingham ($7.80).

Zone 7 Mandurah ($10.30).

DayRider Unlimited travel after 9am weekdays and all day on the weekend in any zone ($12.10).

FamilyRider Lets two adults and up to five children travel for a total of $12.10 on weekends, after 6pm weekdays and after 9am on weekdays during school holidays.

If you're in Perth for a while, consider buying a SmartRider card, covering bus, train and ferry travel. It's $10 to purchase, then you add value to your card. The technology deducts the fare as you go, as long as you tap in and tap out (touch your card to the electronic reader) every time you travel, including within the FTZ. The SmartRider works out 15% cheaper than buying single tickets and automatically caps itself at the DayRider rate if you're avoiding the morning rush hour.

Bus

As well as regular buses the FTZ is well covered during the day by the three free Central Area Transit (CAT) services. The Yellow and Red CATs operate east–west routes, Yellow sticking mainly to Wellington St, and Red looping roughly east on Murray St and west on Hay St. The Blue Cat does a figure eight through Northbridge and the south end of the city; this is the only one to run late – until 1am on Friday and Saturday nights only. Pick up a copy of the free timetable (widely available on buses and elsewhere) for the exact routes and stops. They run every five to eight minutes during weekdays and every 15 minutes on weekends. Digital displays at the stops advise when the next bus is due.

The metropolitan area is serviced by a wide network of Transperth buses. Pick up timetables from any of the Transperth information centres or use the online journey planner.

Ferry

The only ferry runs every 20 to 30 minutes between Barrack St Jetty and Mends St Jetty in South Perth; use it to get to the zoo or for a bargain from-the-river glimpse of the Perth skyline.

Train

Transperth operates five train lines from around 5.20am to midnight weekdays and until about 2am Saturday and Sunday. Your rail ticket can also be used on Transperth buses and ferries within the ticket's zone. You're free to take your bike on the train during nonpeak times. The lines and useful stops are as follows:

Armadale Thornlie line Perth, Burswood

Fremantle line Perth, City West, West Leederville, Subiaco, Shenton Park, Swanbourne, Cottesloe, North Fremantle, Fremantle.

Joondalup line Esplanade, Perth Underground, Leederville.

Mandurah line Perth Underground, Esplanade, Rockingham, Mandurah.

Midland line Perth, East Perth, Mt Lawley, Guildford, Midland.

TAXI

Perth has a decent system of metered taxis, though the distances in the city make frequent use costly and on busy nights you may have trouble flagging a taxi down on the street. There are ranks throughout the city. The two main companies are **Swan Taxis** (☎13 13 30; www.swantaxis.com.au) and **Black & White** (☎13 10 08; www.bwtaxi.com.au), both of which have wheelchair-accessible cabs.

FREMANTLE

POP 28,100

The hippest city in Australia? Ride the train 20km south of Perth and find out. Defined by a classic cache of Victorian and Edwardian architecture, 'Freo' is a raffish harbour town with sea-salty soul to burn. It's an isolated place – closer to Singapore than Sydney. But like any port, the world washes in on the tide and washes out again, leaving the locals buzzing with global Zeitgeist.

Fremantle thrums with live-music rooms, hipster bars, boutique hotels, left-field bookshops, craft-beer breweries, Indian Ocean seafood shacks, buskers, beaches and students on the run from the books. It's an engaging place to base yourself for a few days (...especially if the local AFL team, the Fremantle Dockers, have been winning).

History

This was an important area for the Wadjuk Noongar people, as it was a hub of trading paths. It was occupied mainly in summer, when the Wadjuk would base themselves here to fish. In winter they would head further inland, avoiding seasonal flooding.

Fremantle's European history began when the HMS *Challenger* landed in 1829. Like Perth, the settlement made little progress until convict labour was used. The port blossomed during the gold rush and many of its distinctive buildings date from this period. It wasn't until 1987, when Fremantle hosted the America's Cup, that it transformed itself from a sleepy port town into today's vibrant, artsy city.

Sights

★Fremantle Prison HISTORIC BUILDING

(☎08-9336 9200; www.fremantleprison.com.au; 1 The Terrace; single day tour adult/child $20/11, combined day tours $28/19, Torchlight Tour $26/16, Tunnels Tour adult/child over 12 $60/40; ⏲9am-5.30pm) With its foreboding 5m-high walls, the old convict-era prison still dominates Fremantle. Daytime tour options include the Doing Time Tour taking in the kitchens, men's cells and solitary-confinement cells.

The Great Escapes Tour recounts famous inmates and takes in the women's prison. Book ahead for the Torchlight Tour focusing on macabre aspects of the prison's history, and the 2½-hour Tunnels Tour which includes an underground boat ride and subterranean tunnels built by prisoners.

★Western Australian Museum – Maritime MUSEUM
(www.museum.wa.gov.au; Victoria Quay; adult/child museum $10/3, submarine $10/3, museum & submarine $16/5; ⏲9.30am-5pm) Housed in an intriguing sail-shaped building on the harbour, just west of the city centre, the Maritime museum is a fascinating exploration of WA's relationship with the ocean. Well-presented displays range from yacht racing to Aboriginal fish traps and the sandalwood trade. If you're not claustrophobic, take an hour-long tour of the submarine HMAS *Ovens*. The vessel was part of the Australian Navy's fleet from 1969 to 1997. Tours leave every half-hour from 10am to 3.30pm.

★Western Australian Museum – Shipwreck Galleries MUSEUM
(www.museum.wa.gov.au; Cliff St; admission by donation; ⏲9.30am-5pm) Located within an 1852 commissarial store, the Shipwreck Galleries are considered the finest display of maritime archaeology in the southern hemisphere. The highlight is the **Batavia Gallery**, where a section of the hull of Dutch merchant ship *Batavia*, wrecked in 1629, is displayed. Nearby is a large stone gate, intended as an entrance to Batavia Castle, which was being carried when it sank.

Round House HISTORIC BUILDING
(☎08-9336 6897; www.fremantleroundhouse.com.au; Captains Lane; admission by donation; ⏲10.30am-3.30pm) Built from 1830 to 1831, this 12-sided stone prison is WA's oldest surviving building. It was the site of the colony's first hangings, and was later used for holding Aboriginal people before they were taken to Rottnest Island. On the hilltop outside is the Signal Station, where at 1pm daily a time ball and cannon blast were used to alert seamen to the correct time. The ceremony is reenacted daily; book ahead if you want to fire the cannon.

Fremantle Arts Centre GALLERY
(Map p890; www.fac.org.au; 1 Finnerty St; ⏲10am-5pm) FREE An impressive neo-Gothic building surrounded by lovely elm-shaded gardens, the Fremantle Arts Centre was constructed by convict labourers as a lunatic asylum in the 1860s. Saved from demolition in the 1960s, it houses interesting exhibitions and the excellent Canvas (p917) cafe. During summer there are concerts, courses and workshops.

Fremantle Markets MARKET
(www.fremantlemarkets.com.au; cnr South Tce & Henderson St; ⏲8am-8pm Fri, to 6pm Sat & Sun) FREE Originally opened in 1897, these colourful markets were reopened in 1975 and today draw slow-moving crowds, combing over souvenirs such as plastic boomerangs and swan-shaped magnets. The fresh-produce section is a good place to stock up on snacks.

Gold Rush Buildings
Fremantle boomed during the WA gold rush in the late 19th century, and many wonderful buildings remain that were constructed during, or shortly before, this period. High St, particularly around the bottom end, has some excellent examples including several old hotels.

Public Sculptures
Also in Fishing Boat Harbour is **To The Fishermen**, a cluster of bronze figures, unloading and carrying their catch up from the wharf. There's a lively statue of former member for Fremantle and wartime Labor prime minister **John Curtin** (1885–1945) in Kings Sq, outside the Town Hall. Nearby is a Greg James sculpture of fellow sculptor **Pietro Porcelli** (1872–1943), in the act of making a bust.

The most popular of Fremantle's public sculptures is Greg James' **statue of Bon Scott** (1946–80), strutting on a Marshall amplifier in Fishing Boat Harbour. The AC/DC singer moved to Fremantle with his family in 1956 and his ashes are interred in **Fremantle Cemetery** (Map p890; Carrington St). Enter the cemetery at the entrance near the corner of High and Carrington Sts. Bon's plaque is on the left around 15m along the path.

Beaches & Parks
Green spaces around Fremantle include **Esplanade Reserve** (Marine Tce), shaded by Norfolk Island pines and dividing the city from Fishing Boat Harbour. During summer, nearby **Bathers Beach** hosts a Saturday night market with music and food from 5pm to 9pm. A new waterfront restaurant also opened there in late 2014. **South Beach** is sheltered, swimmable, only 1.5km from the

Fremantle

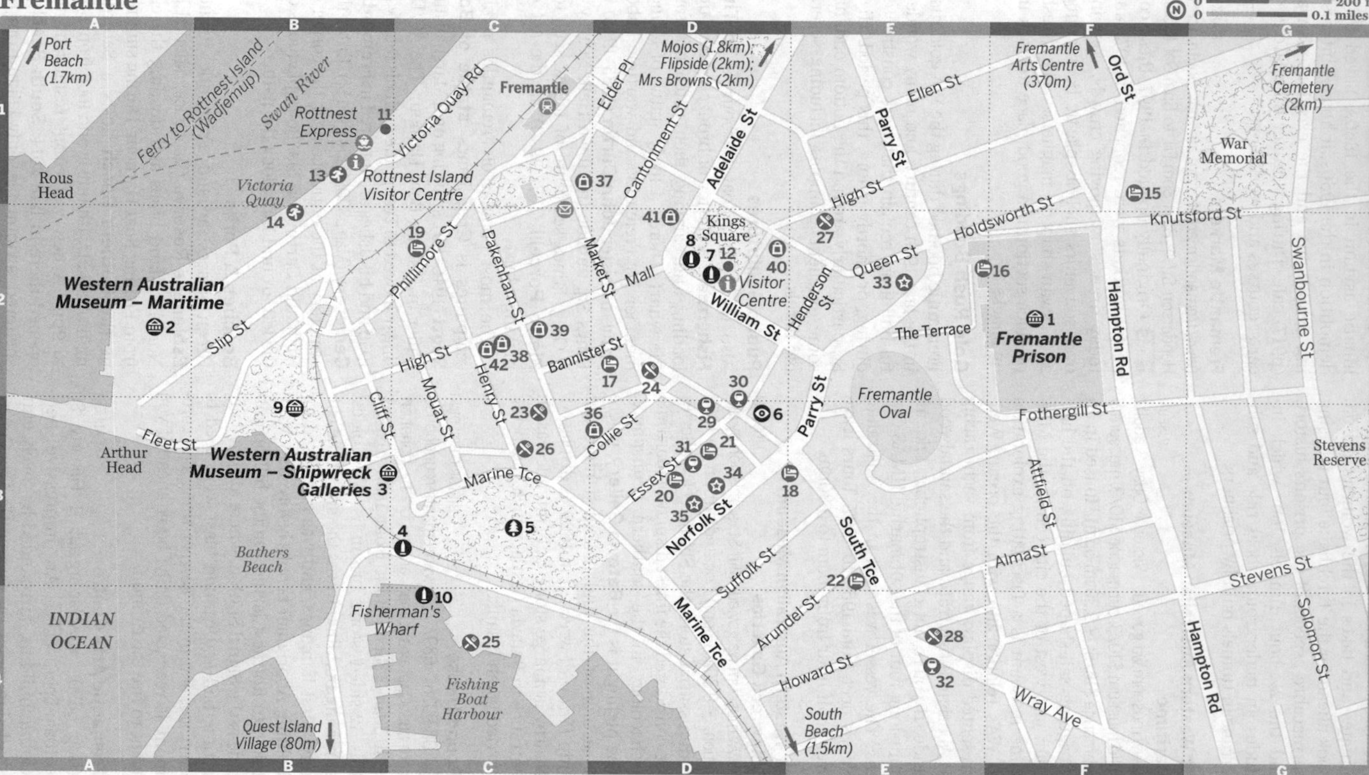
Port Beach (1.7km)
Ferry to Rottnest Island (Wadjemup)
Swan River
Rottnest Express
11
Victoria Quay Rd
Fremantle
Elder Pl
Mojos (1.8km); Flipside (2km); Mrs Browns (2km)
Ellen St
Fremantle Arts Centre (370m)
Ord St
Fremantle Cemetery (2km)
War Memorial
Rous Head
Victoria Quay
13
14
Rottnest Island Visitor Centre
37
Cantonment St
Adelaide St
Parry St
High St
15
Knutsford St
Holdsworth St
41
Kings Square
8
7
12
40
Visitor Centre
27
Queen St
33
16
Swanbourne St
19
Phillimore St
Pakenham St
Market St
Mall
William St
Henderson St
Western Australian Museum – Maritime
2
Slip St
39
High St
42
38
Bannister St
17
24
The Terrace
1
Fremantle Prison
Hampton Rd
Cliff St
Mouat St
Henry St
30
9
23
36
29
6
Fremantle Oval
Fothergill St
Fleet St
Arthur Head
Western Australian Museum – Shipwreck Galleries
3
26
Collie St
31
21
Essex St
34
20
35
18
Marine Tce
Norfolk St
South Tce
Attfield St
Stevens Reserve
4
5
Bathers Beach
Suffolk St
AlmaSt
Stevens St
10
Fisherman's Wharf
22
Arundel St
INDIAN OCEAN
25
28
Solomon St
Howard St
32
Wray Ave
Fishing Boat Harbour
Quest Island Village (80m)
South Beach (1.5km)
200 m
0.1 miles

Fremantle

Top Sights
1 Fremantle Prison F2
2 Western Australian Museum – Maritime A2
3 Western Australian Museum – Shipwreck Galleries B3

Sights
4 Bon Scott Statue C3
5 Esplanade Reserve C3
6 Fremantle Markets D3
7 John Curtin Statue D2
8 Pietro Porcelli Statue D2
9 Round House B3
10 To the Fishermen C4

Activities, Courses & Tours
11 Captain Cook Cruises B1
12 Fremantle Tram Tours D2
13 Oceanic Cruises B1
14 STS Leeuwin II B2

Sleeping
15 Fothergills of Fremantle F1
16 Fremantle Prison YHA Hostel E2
17 Hougoumont Hotel D2
18 Norfolk Hotel E3
19 Old Firestation Backpackers C2
20 Pirates D3
21 Port Mill B&B D3
22 Terrace Central B&B Hotel E3

Eating
23 Bread in Common C3
24 Gino's D2
25 Little Creatures C4
26 Moore & Moore C3
27 Raw Kitchen E2
28 Wild Poppy E4

Drinking & Nightlife
Little Creatures .... (see 25)
29 Monk D3
Norfolk Hotel .... (see 18)
30 Sail & Anchor D2
31 Whisper D3
32 Who's Your Mumma E4

Entertainment
33 Fly by Night Musicians Club E2
34 Luna on SX D3
35 X-Wray Cafe D3

Shopping
36 Chart & Map Shop D3
37 Didgeridoo Breath C1
38 Japingka C2
39 Love in Tokyo C2
40 MANY6160 .... D2
41 Mills Records D2
42 New Edition C2

city centre and on the free CAT bus route. The next major beach is Coogee Beach, 6km further south.

Activities

Fremantle Trails WALKING
(www.visitfremantle.com.au) Pick up trailcards from the visitor centre for 11 self-guided walking tours: Art and Culture, Convict, CY O'Connor (a pioneering civil engineer), Discovery (a Fremantle once-over), Fishing Boat Harbour, Hotels and Breweries, Maritime Heritage, Manjaree Heritage (Indigenous), Retail & Fashion, Waterfront and Writers.

Oceanic Cruises WHALE WATCHING
(08-9325 1191; www.oceaniccruises.com.au; adult/child $69/29; mid-Sep–early Dec) Departs B Shed, Victoria Quay, at 10.15am for a two-hour tour. Days of operation vary by month, so check the website.

STS Leeuwin II SAILING
(08-9430 4105; www.sailleeuwin.com; Berth B; adult/child $99/69; Nov–mid-Apr) Take a three-hour trip on a 55m, three-masted tall ship; see the website for details of morning, afternoon or twilight sails. Sails from Friday to Sunday.

Tours

Fremantle Tram Tours TOUR
(08-9433 6674; www.fremantletrams.com.au; ghostly tour adult/child $80/60, lunch & tram adult/child $89/54, triple tour adult/child $80/30, tram & prison adult/child $45/14) Looking like a heritage tram, this bus departs from the Town Hall on an all-day hop-on, hop-off circuit around the city (adult/child $26/5). The Ghostly Tour runs from 6.45pm to 10.30pm Friday and visits the prison, Round House and Fremantle Arts Centre (former asylum) by torchlight. Combos include Lunch & Tram (tram plus a lunch cruise on river), Triple Tour (tram, river cruise and Perth sightseeing bus), and Tram & Prison (incorporating the tram and Fremantle prison).

Captain Cook Cruises CRUISE
(08-9325 3341; www.captaincookcruises.com.au; C Shed; adult/child $28/16) Cruises between Fremantle and Perth (adult/child $28/16) departing Fremantle at 11.05am, 12.45pm and 3.30pm (the last is one way only). A three-hour lunch cruise departs at 12.45pm (adult/child $69/46).

Fremantle Indigenous Heritage Tours WALKING TOUR
(☎0405 630 606; www.indigenouswa.com; adult/child $50/15; ⊙1.30pm Sat) Highly regarded tour covering the history of Fremantle and the Nyoongar and Wadjuk people. Book through the Fremantle visitors centre.

Two Feet & A Heartbeat WALKING TOUR
(☎1800 459 388; www.twofeet.com.au; per person $20-40; ⊙10am daily) Operated by a younger, energetic crew, tours focus on Fremantle's often rambunctious history. 'Tight Arse Tuesdays' are good value.

Festivals & Events

Laneway MUSIC
(www.fremantle.lanewayfestival.com) WA's skinny-jean hipsters party to the planet's up-and-coming indie acts. The ubercool festival takes place around Fremantle's West End and Esplanade Reserve in early February.

West Coast Blues 'n' Roots Festival MUSIC
(www.westcoastbluesnroots.com.au) Interpreting its remit widely, recent festivals have featured Steve Earle, Grace Jones, Elvis Costello and My Morning Jacket. Held late March to mid-April.

Blessing of the Fleet RELIGIOUS
(www.fremantleseafoodfestival.com.au; Esplanade Reserve, Fishing Boat Harbour) An October tradition since 1948, brought to Fremantle by immigrants from Molfetta, Italy. It includes the procession of the Molfettese *Our Lady of Martyrs* statue (carried by men) and the Sicilian *Madonna di Capo d'Orlando* (carried by women), from St Patrick's Basilica (47 Adelaide St) to Fishing Boat Harbour, where the blessing takes place. An associated seafood festival also takes place nearby.

Fremantle Festival CULTURAL
(www.fremantle.wa.gov.au/festivals) In spring the city's streets and concert venues come alive with parades and performances in Australia's longest-running festival.

Sleeping

Fremantle Prison YHA Hostel HOSTEL $
(☎08-9433 4305; www.yha.com.au/hostels/wa/perth-surrounds/fremantle-prison-yha/; 6a The Terrace, 6160; dm from $36-40, private room $156; ❄📶) Newly opened in early 2015, Fremantle's iconic prison has a hostel wing with a mix of dorm-style accommodation and private rooms. Slightly more upmarket options include a private bathroom.

Pirates HOSTEL $
(☎08-9335 6635; www.piratesbackpackers.com.au; 11 Essex St; dm $31-33, r $80; @📶) Attracting a diverse international crew, this sun- and fun-filled hostel in the thick of the Freo action is a top spot to socialise. Rooms are small and reasonably basic, but the bathrooms are fresh and clean. The kitchen area is well equipped, there's a shady courtyard, and eye-catching marine murals remind you that an ocean swim is minutes away.

Old Firestation Backpackers HOSTEL $
(☎08-9430 5454; www.old-firestation.net; 18 Phillimore St; dm $28-32, d $75-80; @📶) There's entertainment aplenty in this converted fire station: free internet, foosball, movies and a sunny courtyard. Dorms have natural light and afternoon sea breezes, and there's a female-only section. The hippy vibe culminates in late-night guitar-led singalongs; bring earplugs if you value sleep.

Woodman Point Holiday Park CAMPGROUND $
(☎08-9434 1433; www.aspenparks.com.au; 132 Cockburn Rd; sites for 2 people $47-49, d $120-215; ❄@📶🏊) A particularly pleasant spot, 10km south of Fremantle. It's usually quiet, and its location makes it feel more summer beach holiday than outer-Freo staging post.

★**Hougoumont Hotel** BOUTIQUE HOTEL $$
(☎08-6160 6800; www.hougoumonthotel.com.au; 15 Bannister St; d $200-255) Standard 'cabin' rooms are definitely compact, but very stylish and efficiently designed, and you can't beat the central location of this recently opened boutique hotel. Top-end toiletries, a hip, breezy ambience, and complimentary late-afternoon wine and snacks for guests reinforce the Hougoumont's refreshingly different approach to accommodation. Service from the multinational team is relaxed but professional.

Fothergills of Fremantle B&B $$
(☎08-9335 6784; www.fothergills.net.au; 18-22 Ord St; r $195-245; ❄📶) Naked bronze women sprout from the front garden, while a life-size floral cow shelters on the verandah of these neighbouring mansions on the hill. Inside, the decor is in keeping with their venerable age (built in 1892), aside from the contemporary art scattered about – including some wonderful Aboriginal pieces. Breakfast is served in a sunny conservatory.

Terrace Central B&B Hotel B&B $$
(☎08-9335 6600; www.terracecentral.com.au; 79-85 South Tce; d $180-220; ❄@📶) Terrace Central may be a character-filled B&B at

heart, but its larger size gives it the feel of a boutique hotel. The main section is created from an 1888 bakery and an adjoined row of terrace houses, and there are modern one- and two-bedroom apartments out the back. You'll find ample off-street parking.

Port Mill B&B B&B $$
(08-9433 3832; www.portmillbb.com.au; 3/17 Essex St; r $199-299;) One of the most luxurious B&Bs in town, Port Mill is clearly the love child of Paris and Freo. Crafted from local limestone (it was built in 1862 as a mill), inside it's all modern Parisian style, with gleaming taps, contemporary French furniture and wrought-iron balconies. French doors open out to the sun-filled decks, where you can tinkle the china on your breakfast platter.

Norfolk Hotel HOTEL $$
(08-9335 5405; www.norfolkhotel.com.au; 47 South Tce; s/d without bathroom $90/120, d with bathroom $150;) While eucalypts and elms stand quietly in the sun-streaked beer garden, the old limestone Norfolk harbours a secret upstairs: its rooms. Far above your standard pub digs, they've all been tastefully decorated in muted tones and crisp white linen, and there's a communal sitting room. It can be noisy on weekends, but the bar closes at midnight.

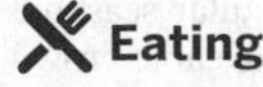

Eating

City Centre & South Fremantle

★ **Bread in Common** BISTRO, BAKERY $$
(www.breadincommon.com.au; 43 Pakenham St; shared platters $12-14, mains $21-26; 10am-10pm Mon-Fri, 9am-10pm Sat & Sun) Be initially lured by the comforting aroma of the in-house bakery, before staying on for cheese and charcuterie platters, or larger dishes such as chargrilled chicken with corn, ginger and coriander. There's an equal focus on comfort food and culinary flair, while big shared tables and a laid-back warehouse ambience encourage conversation over WA wines and Aussie craft beers and ciders.

Moore & Moore CAFE $$
(www.mooreandmoorecafe.com; 46 Henry St; mains $11-20; 7am-4pm;) An urban-chic cafe that spills into the adjoining art gallery and overflows into a flagstoned courtyard. With great coffee, good cooked breakfasts, pastries, wraps and free wi-fi, it's a great place to linger. Look forward to the company of a few Freo hipsters, and the international crew of students studying at Fremantle's University of Notre Dame.

Public & Co BISTRO, TAPAS $$
(www.publicandco.com.au; 25 Duoro St; shared plates $15-24, mains & pizzas $15-28; 6pm-10pm Wed-Fri, to 4pm & 6-10pm Sat, 8am-3pm Sun) Around 2.5km from central Fremantle, Public & Co is worth the journey for a relaxed meal in this spacious and airy corner bungalow. Shared plates (most with a Med or Asian spin) wood-fired pizza and top-notch burgers all reinforce a laid-back, WA-style approach to living. It also has one of the best craft-beer selections in Perth.

Canvas CAFE $$
(Map p890; www.canvasatfremantleartscentre.com; Fremantle Arts Centre; mains $12-25; 8am-3pm Mon-Fri, 8am-4pm Sat & Sun;) Freo's best cafe is in the shaded courtyard of the Fremantle Arts Centre with a menu channelling Middle Eastern, Spanish and North African influences. Breakfast highlights include baked-egg dishes – try the Israeli-style Red Shakshuka – and lunch presents everything from jerk chicken wraps to bouillabaisse and Tasmanian salmon. The concise drinks list includes craft beer, ciders and wine.

Wild Poppy CAFE $$
(2 Wray Ave; breakfast $10-18, lunch $16-22; 7am-4pm;) Lace doilies, kitschy furniture and a stupendous collection of retro portaits and landscapes make this hip cafe in South Freo worth seeking out. Soup and salad specials team with good coffee, beer and cider, and the chilli eggs are a great way to start the day. For lunch ask if the prawn laksa is available.

Raw Kitchen VEGETARIAN $$
(www.therawkitchen.com.au; 181a High St; mains $18-24; 11am-4pm Mon-Thu, to 9pm Fri-Sun;) Vegan, organic and sustainable, and therefore *very* Freo. Reset your chakra and boost your energy levels with the super-healthy but still very tasty food in this funky, brick-lined warehouse. A lot (but not all) of the menu showcases raw ingredients, but there's no trade-off for taste. Gluten-free beer and sustainably produced wine mean you don't have to be *too* virtuous.

Gino's CAFE $$
(www.ginoscafe.com.au; 1 South Tce; mains $17-31; 6am-late;) Old-school Gino's is Freo's most famous cafe, and while it's become a

tourist attraction in its own right, the locals still treat it as their second living room, only with better coffee. You'll need to order and pay, then collect your own coffee.

Fishing Boat Harbour

Little Creatures PUB FOOD $$
(www.littlecreatures.com.au; 40 Mews Rd; shared plates $8-24, pizzas $19-24; 10am-midnight Mon-Fri, from 9am Sat & Sun;) Little Creatures is classic Freo: harbour views, fantastic brews (made on the premises) and excellent food. In a cavernous converted boatshed overlooking the harbour, it can get chaotic at times, but a signature Pale Ale with a wood-fired pizza will be worth the wait. More substantial shared plates include kangaroo with tomato chutney and grilled prawn skewers. No bookings.

North Fremantle

Flipside BURGERS $
(Map p890; www.flipsideburgers.com.au; 239 Queen Victoria St; burgers $11.50-15.50; 5.30-9pm Tue-Thu, noon-2.30pm Thu, noon-9pm Fri-Sun) Gourmet burgers with the option of dining in next door at Mrs Browns (p918).

Drinking & Entertainment

Most of Fremantle's big pubs are lined up along South Tce and High St. They've long been incubators for rock kids, turning out WA bands like the John Butler Trio, San Cisco and Tame Impala.

Sail & Anchor PUB
(www.sailandanchor.com.au; 64 South Tce; 11am-midnight Mon-Sat, to 10pm Sun) Welcome to the best destination for the travelling beer geek in Western Australia. Built in 1854, this Fremantle landmark has been impressively restored to recall much of its former glory. Downstairs is big and beer focused, with 27 taps delivering an ever-changing range of local and international craft beers. Occasional live music and decent bar food complete the picture.

Little Creatures BREWERY
(www.littlecreatures.com.au; 40 Mews Rd, Fishing Boat Harbour; 10am-midnight Mon-Fri, from 9am Sat & Sun) Try the Little Creatures Pale Ale and Pilsner, and other beers and ciders under the White Rabbit and Pipsqueak labels. Keep an eye out also for one-off Shift Brewers' Stash beers. Creatures NextDoor is an adjacent lounge bar with regular live entertainment and DJs. Live jazz kicks off at 4.30pm on Sundays, and there's live comedy ($30) on Saturday nights from 8pm.

Who's Your Mumma BAR
(www.facebook.com/whosyourmummabar; cnr Wray Ave & South Tce; 4pm-midnight Mon-Sat, noon-10pm Sun) Industrial-chic lightbulbs and polished-concrete floors are softened by recycled timber at the laid-back Who's Your Mumma. An eclectic crew of South Freo locals crowd in for excellent cocktails, WA craft beer and moreish bar snacks including fluffy pork buns. Taco Thursdays are definitely good value with a Mexican accent.

Norfolk Hotel PUB
(www.norfolkhotel.com.au; 47 South Tce; 11am-midnight Mon-Sat, to 10pm Sun) Slow down to Freo pace at this 1887 pub. Interesting guest beers create havoc for the indecisive drinker, and the pub food and pizzas are very good. We love the heritage limestone courtyard, especially when sunlight peeks through the elms and eucalypts. Downstairs, The Odd Fellow channels a bohemian small-bar vibe, and hosts live gigs from Tuesday to Saturday.

Monk CRAFT BEER
(www.themonk.com.au; 33 South Tce; 11.30am-late Mon-Fri, 8.30am-late Sat & Sun) Park yourself on the spacious front terrace or in the chic interior, partly fashioned from recycled railway sleepers, and enjoy The Monk's own brews (kolsch, mild, wheat, porter, rauch, pale ale). The bar snacks and pizzas are also good, and guest beers and regular seasonal brews always draw a knowledgeable crowd of local craft-beer nerds.

Mrs Browns BAR
(Map p890; www.mrsbrownbar.com.au; 241 Queen Victoria St, North Fremantle; 4.30pm-midnight Tue-Thu, noon-midnight Fri-Sun) Exposed bricks and a copper bar combine with retro and antique furniture to create North Fremantle's most atmospheric bar. The music could include all those cult bands you thought were *your* personal secret, and an eclectic menu of beer, wine and tapas targets the more discerning, slightly older bar hound. And you can order in burgers from Flipside next door.

Whisper WINE BAR
(www.whisperwinebar.com.au; 1/15 Essex St; noon-late Wed-Sun) In a lovely heritage building, this classy French-themed wine bar also does shared plates of charcuterie and cheese.

Fly by Night Musicians Club LIVE MUSIC
(www.flybynight.org; Parry St) Variety is the key at Fly by Night, a not-for-profit club that's been run by musos for musos for years. All kinds perform here, and many local bands

made a start here. It's opposite the car park below the old Fremantle Prison.

X-Wray Cafe LIVE MUSIC

(www.facebook.com/xwray.fremantle; 3-13 Essex St; ⏲7am-midnight Mon-Sat, to 10pm Sun) There's something on every night (live jazz, rock, open piano) at this hipster hang-out, comprising a smallish indoor area and a large canvas-covered terrace. Light meals are available, kicking off with breakfasts.

Mojo's LIVE MUSIC

(Map p890; www.mojosbar.com.au; 237 Queen Victoria St, North Fremantle; ⏲7pm-late) Local and national bands (mainly Aussie rock and indie) and DJs play at this small place, and there's a sociable beer garden out the back. First Friday of the month is reggae night; every Monday is open-mic night.

Luna on SX CINEMA

(www.lunapalace.com.au; Essex St) Art-house cinema between Essex and Norfolk Sts. Cheaper Wednesday tickets.

Shopping

The bottom end of High St is the place for interesting and quirky shopping. Fashion stores run along Market St, towards the train station. Queen Victoria St in North Fremantle is the place to go for antiques.

Japingka ARTS

(www.japingka.com.au; 47 High St; ⏲10am-5.30pm Mon-Fri, noon-5pm Sat & Sun) Specialising in Aboriginal fine art from WA and beyond. Purchases come complete with extensive notes about the works and the artists who painted them.

Found ARTS, CRAFTS

(Map p890; www.fac.org.au; 1 Finnerty St; ⏲10am-5pm) The Fremantle Arts Centre shop stocks an inspiring range of WA art and craft.

Love in Tokyo CLOTHING

(www.loveintokyo.com.au; 61-63 High St; ⏲10am-5pm Mon-Sat, noon-4pm Sun) Local designer turning out gorgeously fashioned fabrics for women.

New Edition BOOKS

(www.newedition.com.au; cnr High & Henry Sts; ⏲9am-6pm) Recently relocated to a sunny corner location, and still a bookworm's dream with comfy armchairs for browsing.

Didgeridoo Breath ARTS, CRAFTS

(www.diggeridoobreath.com; 6 Market St; ⏲10.30am-5pm) The planet's biggest selection of didgeridoos, Indigenous Australian books and CDs, and how-to-play lessons ranging from one hour to four weeks. You'll probably hear the shop before you see it.

MANY6160 ARTS, CRAFTS

(www.many6160.com; 2 Newman Ct; ⏲10am-5pm Fri-Sun) A boho mash-up of local artists' studios and pop-up galleries and shops fills the spacious ground floor of the former Myer department store.

Mills Records MUSIC

(www.mills.com.au; 22 Adelaide St; ⏲9am-5.30pm Mon-Sat, noon-5pm Sun) Music (some rarities) and concert tickets. Check out the 'Local's Board' for recordings by Freo and WA acts.

Chart & Map Shop MAPS

(www.chartandmapshop.com.au; 14 Collie St; ⏲10am-5pm) Maps and travel guides.

Information

Fremantle City Library (☎08-9432 9766; www.frelibrary.wordpress.com; Kings Sq, Town Hall; ⏲9.30am-5.30pm Mon, Fri & Sat, to 8pm Tue-Thu; 📶) Free wi-fi and internet terminals.

Fremantle Hospital (☎08-9431 3333; www.fhhs.health.wa.gov.au; Alma St) At the edge of central Fremantle.

Post office (☎13 13 18; 1/13 Market St; ⏲9am-5pm Mon-Fri) Centrally located.

Visitor centre (☎08-9431 7878; www.visitfremantle.com.au; Kings Sq, Town Hall; ⏲9am-5pm Mon-Fri, 9am-4pm Sat, 10am-4pm Sun) Bookings for accommodation, tours and hire cars.

Getting There & Around

Fremantle sits within Zone 2 of the Perth public-transport system, **Transperth** (☎13 62 13; www.transperth.wa.gov.au), and is only 30 minutes away by train. There are numerous buses between Perth's city centre and Fremantle, including routes 103, 106, 107, 111 and 158. There is also a Connect (p911) airport shuttle.

Another very pleasant way to get here from Perth is by the 1¼-hour river cruise run by Captain Cook Cruises (p915).

There are numerous one-way streets and parking meters in Freo. It's easy enough to travel by foot or on the free CAT bus service, which takes in all the major sites on a continuous loop every 10 minutes from 7.30am to 6.30pm on weekdays, until 9pm on Fridays, and from 10am to 6.30pm on the weekend.

Bicycles (Fremantle Visitor Centre, Kings Sq; ⏲9.30am-4.30pm Mon-Fri, to 3.30pm Sat, 10.30am-3.30pm Sun) can be rented for free at the visitor centre, an ideal way to get around Freo's storied streets. A refundable bond of $200 applies.

Around Perth

Includes ➡

Best Places to Eat

- Hotel Rottnest (p925)
- New Norcia Hotel (p932)
- Taste & Graze (p928)
- Lobster Shack (p931)
- Beach Bistro (p932)

Best Places to Stay

- Cervantes Lodge & Pinnacles Beach Backpackers (p931)
- Amble Inn (p931)
- Rottnest Island Authority Cottages (p923)
- Lancelin Lodge YHA (p930)

Why Go?

Although Western Australia (WA) is huge, you don't have to travel too far from Perth to treat yourself to a tantalising taste of what the state has to offer. A day trip could see you frolicking with wild dolphins, snorkelling with sea lions, scooping up brilliant-blue crabs or spotting bilbies in the bush. Active types can find themselves canoeing, rafting, surfing, windsurfing, sandboarding, diving, skydiving and mountain biking.

Get up early to experience the Pinnacles in Nambung National Park at dawn, and return at dusk for a spectacular end to the day. Explore historic towns classified by the National Trust, or experience the monastic ambience of fascinating New Norcia.

We've designed this chapter so that the main headings can be tackled as day trips, or better still, overnighters. If you're embarking on a longer trip, whether north, south or east, you'll find your first stop within these pages.

When to Go

Mandurah

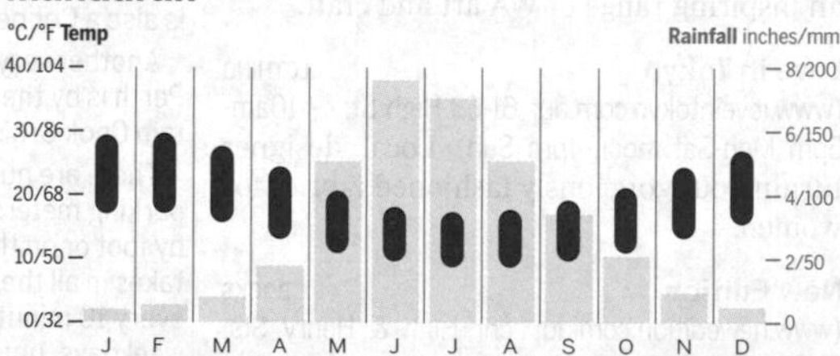

Mar Good beach weather and a fine time to spot thrombolites in Lake Clifton.

Jun Food and wine excellence at the Avon Valley Gourmet Food & Wine Festival in Northam.

Aug Wild flowers start to bloom, and brave/crazy paddlers take part in Northam's Avon River Festival.

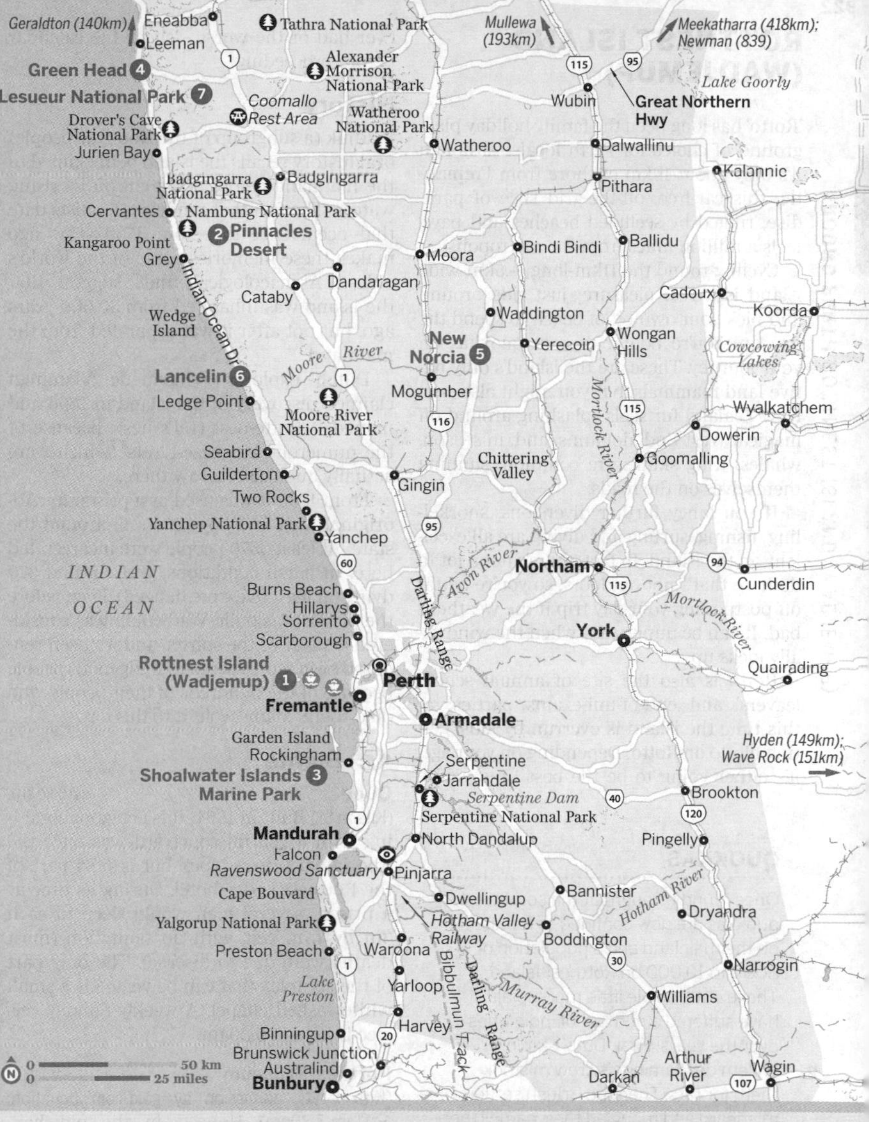

Around Perth Highlights

1 Cycling your way to a slice of coastal paradise on **Rottnest Island** (Wadjemup; p922), then spending the afternoon swimming, sunning and snorkelling.

2 Enjoying a sublime sunset over the other-worldly **Pinnacles Desert** (p930).

3 Getting chipper with Flipper while palling about with scores of wild dolphins in **Shoalwater Islands Marine Park** (p927), off Rockingham.

4 Splashing about with sea lions at **Green Head** (p932).

5 Exploring the intriguing monastery town of **New Norcia** (p932).

6 Learning the fine arts of windsurfing, kiteboarding and sandboarding in sleepy seaside **Lancelin** (p930).

7 Immersing yourself in the wonderful wild flowers of the **Lesueur National Park** (p930).

ROTTNEST ISLAND (WADJEMUP)

POP 475

'Rotto' has long been the family holiday playground of choice for Perth locals. Although it's only about 19km offshore from Fremantle, this car-free, off-the-grid slice of paradise, ringed by secluded beaches and bays, feels a million miles from the metropolis.

Cycling round the 11km-long, 4.5km-wide island is a real pleasure; just ride around and pick your own bit of beach to spend the day on. You're bound to spot quokkas on your journey. These are the island's only native land mammals, but you might also spot New Zealand fur seals splashing around off magical West End, dolphins, and, in season, whales. King skinks are common, sunning themselves on the roads.

If you fancy further diversions, snorkelling, fishing, surfing and diving are all excellent on the island. In fact, there's not a lot to do here that's not outdoors, so you're better off postponing your day trip if the weather's bad. It can be unpleasant when the wind really kicks up.

Rotto is also the site of annual school leavers' and end-of-uni-exams parties; at this time the island is overrun by kids 'getting blotto on Rotto'. Depending on your age, it's either going to be the best time you've ever had or the worst – check the calendar before proceeding.

History

Wadjuk (a subgroup of the Noongar people) oral history recalls the island being joined to the mainland before being cut off by rising waters. The fact that modern scientists date that occurrence to before 6500 years ago makes these memories some of the world's oldest. Archaeological finds suggest that the island was inhabited from 30,000 years ago, but not after it was separated from the mainland.

Dutch explorer Willem de Vlamingh claimed discovery of the island in 1696 and named it Rotte-nest (rat's nest) because of the numerous king-sized 'rats' (which were actually quokkas) he saw there.

From 1838 it was used as a prison for Aboriginal men and boys from all around the state. At least 3670 people were incarcerated here, in harsh conditions, with around 370 dying (at least five were hanged). Even before the prison was built, Wadjemup was considered a 'place of the spirits', and it's been rendered even more sacred to Indigenous people because of the hundreds of their people who died there. Many avoid it to this day.

QUOKKAS

Once found throughout the southwest, quokkas are now confined to forest on the mainland and a population of 8000 to 10,000 on Rottnest Island. These cute, docile little marsupials have suffered a number of indignities over the years. First, Dutch explorer Willem de Vlamingh's crew mistook them for rats. Then the British settlers misheard and mangled their name (the Noongar word was probably *quak-a* or *gwaga*). But worst of all, a cruel trend for 'quokka soccer' by sadistic louts in the 1990s saw many kicked to death before a $10,000 fine was imposed. On a more positive note, the phenomenon of 'quokka selfies' briefly illuminated the internet in 2015 with various Rottnest marsupials achieving minor global fame on Instagram. Google 'Rottnest quokka selfies' to see the best of #quokkaselfie.

Sights

Quod HISTORIC SITE

(Kitson St) Built in 1864, this octagonal building with a central courtyard was once the Aboriginal prison block but is now part of the Rottnest Lodge hotel. During its time as a prison, several men would sleep in each 3m by 1.7m cell, with no sanitation (most deaths were due to disease). The only part of the complex that can be visited is a small whitewashed chapel. A weekly Sunday service is held at 9.30am.

Rottnest Museum MUSEUM

(Kitson St; admission by gold-coin donation; 11am-3.30pm) Housed in the old haystore building, this little museum tells the island's natural and human history, warts and all, including dark tales of shipwrecks and incarceration.

Salt Store HISTORIC BUILDING

(Colebatch Ave) FREE A photographic exhibition in this 19th-century building looks at a different chapter of local history: when the island's salt lakes provided all of WA's salt (between 1838 and 1950). It's also the meeting point for walking tours.

Activities

Excellent visibility in the temperate waters, coral reefs and shipwrecks make Rottnest a top spot for **scuba diving** and **snorkelling**. There are snorkel trails with underwater plaques at **Little Salmon Bay** and **Parker Point**.

Over a dozen boats have come a cropper on Rottnest's reefs. Marker plaques around the island tell the sad tales of how and when the ships sank. The only wreck that is accessible to snorkellers without a boat is at **Thomson Bay**.

The best **surfing** breaks are at **Strickland**, **Salmon** and **Stark Bays**, at the west end of the island.

Rottnest Island Bike Hire BICYCLE RENTAL
(☎08-9292 5105; www.rottnestisland.com; cnr Bedford Ave & Welch Way; ⌚8.30am-4pm, to 5.30pm summer) Rents masks, snorkels and fins and surfboards.

Tours

Rottnest Voluntary Guides WALKING TOUR
(☎08-9372 9757; www.rvga.asn.au) Free, themed walks leave from the central Salt Store daily: History; Reefs, Wrecks & Daring Sailors; Vlamingh Lookout & Salt Lakes; and the Quokka Walk. They also run tours of Wadjemup Lighthouse (adult/child $9/4) and Oliver Hill Gun & Tunnels (adult/child $9/4); you'll need to make your own way there for the last two.

Oliver Hill Train & Tour TRAIN RIDES
(www.rottnestisland.com; adult/child $29/16.50) The Oliver Hill gun battery was built in the 1930s and played a major role in the defence of the WA coastline and Fremantle harbour. This trip takes you by train to Oliver Hill (departing from the train station at 1.30pm) and includes the Gun & Tunnels tour run by Rottnest Voluntary Guides.

Rottnest Adventure Tour CRUISE
(www.rottnestexpress.com.au; adult/child $55/27; ⌚mid-Sep–late Apr) Ninety-minute cruises around the coast with a special emphasis on spotting wildlife. Packages are also available ex Perth (adult/child $152/78 and Fremantle ($132/68). Check the website for other options including the Discover Rottnest coach tour and the Eco-Express snorkelling tour. From mid-September to late November two-hour whale-watching tours (adult/child ex Perth $77/34) are on offer.

Rottnest Air Taxi SCENIC FLIGHTS
(☎0411 264 547, 1800 500 006; www.rottnest.de) Ten-minute flights over the island ($45).

Sleeping & Eating

Rotto is wildly popular in summer and school holidays, when accommodation is booked out months in advance.

Most visitors to Rotto self-cater. The general store is like a small supermarket (and also stocks liquor), but if you're staying a while, it's better to bring supplies with you. You can also preorder supplies from www.rottnestgeneralstore.com.au.

Allison Tentland CAMPGROUND $
(☎08-9432 9111; www.rottnestisland.com; Thomson Bay; sites $36) Camping on the island is restricted to this leafy camping ground with barbecues. Be vigilant about your belongings, especially your food – cheeky quokkas have been known to help themselves.

Kingstown Barracks Youth Hostel HOSTEL $
(☎08-9432 9111; www.rottnestisland.com; dm/f $51/111) This hostel is located in old army barracks that still have a rather institutional feel, and few facilities. Check in at the visitor centre before you make the 1.8km walk, bike or bus trip to Kingstown.

★**Rottnest Island Authority Cottages** COTTAGE $$
(☎08-9432 9111; www.rottnestisland.com; cottages $114-256) There are more than 250 villas and cottages for rent around the island. Some have magnificent beachfront positions and are palatial; others are more like beach shacks. Prices rise by around $60 for Friday and Saturday nights, and they shoot up by up to $120 in peak season (late September to April). Check online for the labyrinthine pricing schedule.

Rottnest Lodge HOTEL $$
(☎08-9292 5161; www.rottnestlodge.com.au; Kitson St; r $210-320; ❄) It's claimed there are ghosts in this comfortable complex, which is based around the former Quod and boys' reformatory school. If that worries you, ask for a room in the new section, looking onto a salt lake. The lodge's Riva restaurant channels Italian flavours amid the island's vaguely Mediterranean ambience, especially when the sun is shining.

Hotel Rottnest HOTEL $$$
(☎08-9292 5011; www.hotelrottnest.com.au; 1 Bedford Ave; r $270-320; ❄) Based around the former

Rottnest Island

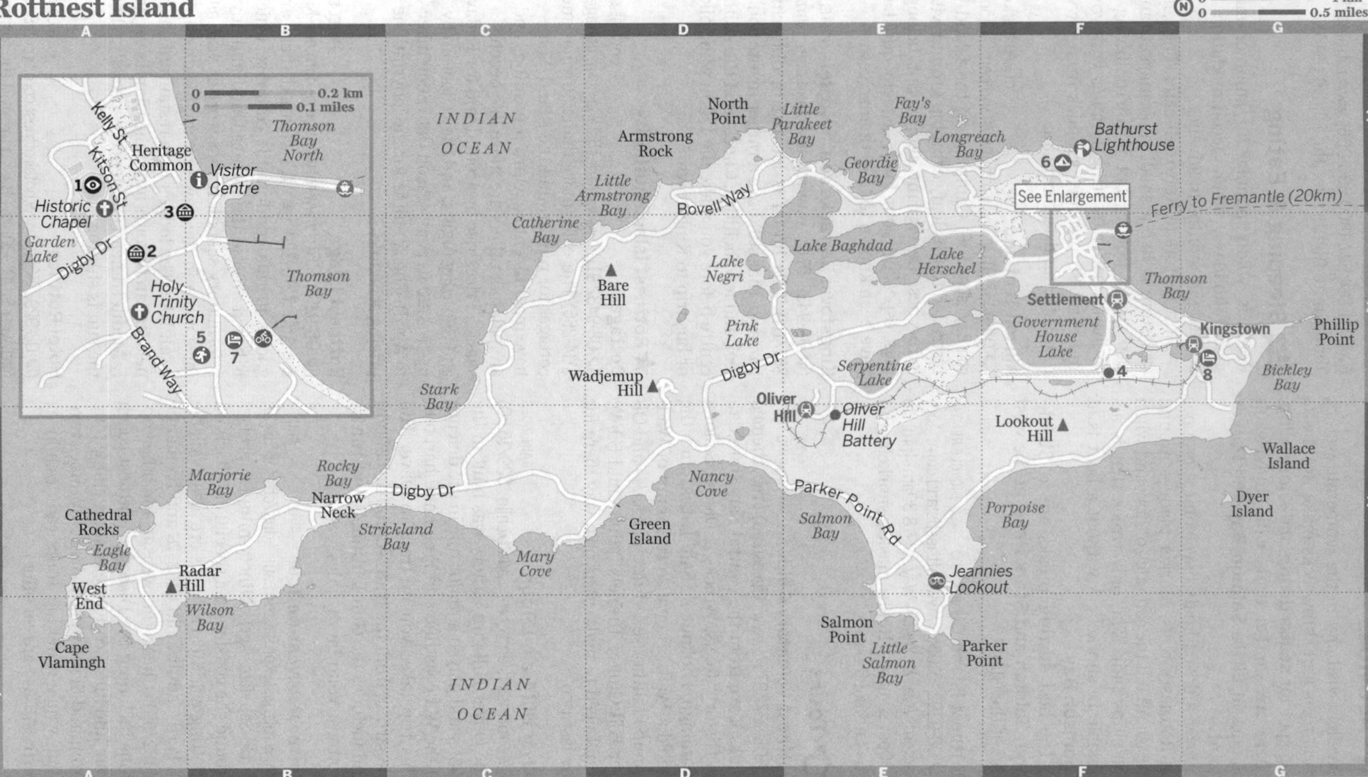

Rottnest Island

Sights	
1 Quod	A1
2 Rottnest Museum	A2
3 Salt Store	A1
Activities, Courses & Tours	
4 Rottnest Air Taxi	F2
5 Rottnest Island Bike Hire	B2
Rottnest Voluntary Guides	(see 3)
Sleeping	
6 Allison Tentland	F1
7 Hotel Rottnest	B2
8 Kingstown Barracks Youth Hostel	G2
Rottnest Lodge	(see 1)
Eating	
Hotel Rottnest	(see 7)
Riva	(see 1)

summer-holiday pad for the state's governors (built in 1864), the former Quokka Arms has been completely transformed by a stylish renovation. The whiter-than-white rooms in an adjoining building are smart and modern, if a tad pricey. Some have beautiful sea views.

Riva SEAFOOD $$
(Rottnest Lodge, Kitson St; lunch $18-20, dinner $24-38; ⌚noon-late) Classy Italian restaurant with a strong focus on grills and seafood. Prawns and salmon both receive an elegant touch of the Med, and there are also wood-fired pizzas and interesting spins on chicken and lamb.

★ **Hotel Rottnest** PUB FOOD $$
(www.hotelrottnest.com.au; 1 Bedford Ave; pizzas $20-26, mains $25-38; ⌚11am-late) It's hard to imagine a more inviting place for a sunset pint of Little Creatures than the Astroturf 'lawn' of this chic waterfront hotel. A big glass pavilion creates an open and inviting space, and bistro-style food and pizzas are reasonably priced given the location and ambience. Bands and DJs regularly boost the laid-back island mood during summer.

Information

Near the main jetty there's a shopping area with an ATM.

Ranger (☎08-9372 9788) For fishing and boating information.

Visitor centre (☎08-9372 9732; www.rottnestisland.com; Thomson Bay; ⌚7.30am-5pm Sat-Thu, to 7pm Fri, extended hours in summer) Handles check-ins for all of the island authority's accommodation. There's a bookings counter at the Fremantle office (Map p914; ☎08-9432 9300; www.rottnestisland.com; E Shed, Victoria Quay), near where the ferry departs.

Getting There & Away

AIR

Rottnest Air-Taxi (☎0411 264 547; www.rottnest.de) Flies from Jandakot airport in four-seater (one way/same-day return/extended return $260/360/460) or six-seater planes (one way/same-day return/extended return $380/480/580). Prices include up to three passengers in the four-seater and five passengers in the six-seater.

BOAT

Rottnest Express (☎1300 467 688; www.rottnestexpress.com.au) Has offices in Fremantle (Map p914; B Shed, Victoria Quay; adult/child $83.50/47), Northport (Map p890; 1 Emma Pl, Northport, Rous Head; adult/child $83.50/47) and Perth (Map p894; Pier 2, Barrack St Jetty; adult/child $103.50/57). Prices listed are for return day trips and include the island admission fee. Ferry schedules are seasonal, though those listed here are roughly the minimum: Perth (1¾ hours, once daily), Fremantle (30 minutes, five times daily) and North Fremantle (30 minutes, three times daily). Packages including bike hire, snorkelling equipment, meals, accommodation and tours are all available.

Rottnest Fast Ferries (☎08-9246 1039; www.rottnestfastferries.com.au; adult/child $85/48.50) Departs from Hillarys Boat Harbour (40 minutes; three times daily). Packages also available. Hillarys Boat Harbour is around 40 minutes' drive north of Perth. See www.hillarysboatharbour.com.au for public transport details. An additional 6pm ferry departs on Friday nights over summer.

Getting Around

Bikes can be booked in advance online or on arrival from **Rottnest Island Bike Hire** (☎08-9292 5105; www.rottnestisland.com; cnr Bedford Ave & Welch Way; per hour $13, 1/2/3/4/5 days $32/45/56/67/79; ⌚8.30am-4pm, to 5.30pm summer). Rottnest Express and the visitor centre also hire bikes.

A free shuttle runs between Thomson Bay and the main accommodation areas. The **Island Explorer** (www.rottnestisland.com; adult/child $20/12; ⌚departs every 1¼hr 8.45am-3pm) is a handy hop-on, hop-off coach service stopping at 18 locations around the island. It includes a commentary and is a great way to get your bearings when you first arrive.

THE AVON VALLEY

The lush green Avon Valley was 'discovered' by European settlers in early 1830 after food shortages forced Governor Stirling to dispatch Ensign Dale to search the Darling Range for arable land. What he found was the upper reaches of the Swan River, but he presumed it was a separate river – which is why its name changes from the Swan to the Avon in Walyunga National Park. Many historic stone buildings still stand proudly in the area's towns and countryside.

Highlights are sleepy York and Toodyay, and excellent annual festivals around **Northam** include the **Avon Valley Gourmet Food & Wine Festival** (www.avonvalleywa.com.au) in early June and the exciting **Avon River Festival** (www.avondescent.com.au) in early August.

York

Only 97km from Perth, York is the oldest inland town in WA, and was first settled in 1830, just two years after the Swan River colony. The settlers here saw similarities between the Avon Valley and their native Yorkshire, so Governor Stirling bestowed the name York. The entire town has been classified by the National Trust.

Sights

Avon Tce is lined with significant buildings including the **town hall**, **Castle Hotel**, **police station**, **Old Gaol & Courthouse** and **Settlers House**. The **suspension bridge** across the Avon was built in 1906.

Holy Trinity Church CHURCH
(Pool St) By the Avon River, this church was completed in 1854 and features stained-glass windows designed by WA artist Robert Juniper, as well as a rare pipe organ.

Motor Museum MUSEUM
(www.yorkwa.com.au/Motor.Museum; 116 Avon Tce; adult/child $9/4; ⌚9.30am-3pm) A must for vintage-car enthusiasts.

Residency Museum MUSEUM
(www.yorksoc.org.au; Brook St; adult/child $4/2; ⌚1-3pm Tue, Wed & Thu, 11am-3.30pm Sat & Sun) Built in 1858, this museum houses some intriguing historic exhibits and poignant old black-and-white photos of York.

Eating

Jules Cafe CAFE $
(121 Avon Tce; snacks & mains $10-18; ⌚8am-4pm Mon-Sat;) Putting a colourful spin on heritage York since 1990, Jules Cafe channels a Lebanese vibe for top-notch kebabs, falafel and Middle Eastern sweets. A funky new-age accent is introduced with organic, vegie and gluten-free options.

Getting There & Away

Transwa (☎1300 662 205; www.transwa.wa.gov.au) coach routes linking to York include East Perth ($17, 1½ hours), Mt Barker ($56, 5¼ hours, four weekly) and Albany ($61, six hours, four weekly).

Toodyay

Historic Toodyay, only 85km northeast of Perth, is a popular weekend destination for browsing the bric-a-brac shops or having a beer on the verandah of an old pub. Also classified by the National Trust, it has plenty of charming heritage buildings. Originally known by the name Newcastle, Toodyay (pronounced '2J') came from the Aboriginal word *duidgee* (place of plenty); the name was adopted around 1910.

Sights

Connor's Mill MUSEUM
(Stirling Tce; admission $3; ⌚9am-4pm) Start at the top of this aged flour mill (1870) and descend through three floors of chugging machinery and explanatory displays that cover the milling process, along with local history. Entry is through the neighbouring visitor centre. **St Stephen's Church** (1862), directly across the road, is also worth a look.

Newcastle Gaol MUSEUM
(17 Clinton St; admission $3; ⌚10am-4pm) Built in the 1860s using convict labour, the gaol includes a courtroom, cells and stables. A gallery tells the story of bushranger Moondyne Joe.

Coorinja WINERY
(Toodyay Rd; ⌚10am-5pm Mon-Sat) Operating continuously since the 1870s, this winery specialises in fortified wines including port, sherry, muscat and Marsala. It's 6km out of town, on the road to Perth.

Getting There & Away

Toodyay is a stop on the **Transwa** (☎1300 662 205; www.transwa.wa.gov.au) AvonLink and Prospector lines, with trains to East Perth ($17,

1¼ hours, seven weekly), Northam ($8, 20 minutes, 12 weekly) and Kalgoorlie ($78, 5½ hours, four weekly).

ROCKINGHAM & THE PEEL DISTRICT

Taking in swaths of jarrah forest and coastal resorts, this area can easily be tackled as a day trip from Perth or as the first stopping point of a southwest expedition. Entering the Peel District, you're passing out of Wadjuk country and into that of their fellow Noongar neighbours, the Pinjarup.

Rockingham

POP 100,000

Around 46km south of Perth, this seaside city has some nice beaches, and the **Shoalwater Islands Marine Park** (www.marineparks.wa.gov.au; ⊙closed for nesting Jun–mid-Sep) where you can observe dolphins, sea lions and penguins in the wild.

Just a few minutes' paddle, swim or **ferry ride** (Mersey Point Jetty; per person $12; ⊙hourly 9am-3pm Sep-May) from the mainland is **Penguin Island**, home to about 600 breeding pairs of penguins and several thousand ground-nesting silver gulls. Apart from birdwatching, you can swim and snorkel in the crystal-clear waters, and there are sunny opportunities for dining along Rockingham's esplanade.

Activities

Rockingham Wild Encounters WILDLIFE TOUR
(☎08-9591 1333; www.rockinghamwildencounters.com.au; cnr Arcadia Dr & Penguin Rd) The only operator licensed to take people to Penguin Island near Rockingham, and also run other low-impact tours. Most popular is the **dolphin swim tour** (departs Val St Jetty; per person $205-225; ⊙8am Sep-May), which lets you interact with some of the 200 wild bottlenose dolphins in the marine park. If you don't fancy getting wet, there are two-hour **dolphin-watch tours** (departs Mersey St Jetty, Shoalwater; adult/child $85/50; ⊙10.45am Sep-May). There's also a 45-minute penguin and sea lion cruise, in a glass-bottomed boat. Pickups can also be arranged from Perth hotels.

West Coast Dive Park DIVING
(www.westcoastdivepark.com.au; permits per day/week $25/50) Diving within the marine park became even more interesting after the sinking of the *Saxon Ranger*, a supposedly jinxed 400-tonne fishing vessel. Permits to dive at this site are available from the visitor centre. Contact the Australasian Diving Academy (p897) about expeditions to this and the wrecks of three other boats, two planes and various reefs in the vicinity.

> **WORTH A TRIP**
>
> **YALGORUP NATIONAL PARK**
>
> Fifty kilometres south of Mandurah is this beautiful 12,000-hectare coastal park, consisting of 10 tranquil lakes and surrounding woodlands and sand dunes. The park is a wetland of international significance for seasonally migrating water birds. Visit the distinctive **thrombolites** of Lake Clifton, descendants of the earliest living organisms on earth. These rocklike structures are most easily seen when the water is low, particularly in March and April. There's a viewing platform on Mt John Rd, off Old Coast Rd.

Information

Visitor centre (☎08-9592 3464; www.rockinghamvisitorcentre.com.au; 19 Kent St; ⊙9am-5pm) Accommodation listings if you want to overnight.

Getting There & Around

Rockingham has regular **Transperth** (☎13 62 13; www.transperth.wa.gov.au) trains via the Mandurah line to Perth Underground/Esplanade ($7.70, 34 minutes) and Mandurah ($5.20, 18 minutes).

Rockingham station is around 4km southeast of Rockingham Beach and around 6km east of Mersey Point, where the Penguin Island ferries depart; catch bus 551 or 555 to the beach, or stay on the 551 to Mersey Point.

Mandurah

POP 68,300

Shrugging off its fusty retirement-haven image, Mandurah has made concerted efforts to reinvent itself as an upmarket beach resort.

The town spans the Mandurah Estuary, which sits between the ocean and the large body of water known as the Peel Inlet. It's one of the best places in the region for fishing, crabbing, prawning (March to April) and dolphin-spotting.

Activities

Mandurah Cruises CRUISE
(☎08-9581 1242; www.mandurahcruises.com.au; Boardwalk) Take a one-hour Dolphin & Scenic Canal Cruise, a half-day Murray River Lunch Cruise and, through December, a one-hour Christmas Lights Canal Cruise, which gawps at millionaires' mansions under the pretence of admiring their festive displays. Other cruise options incorporate catching and cooking Mandurah's famous blue manna crabs, and a heritage cruise highlighting the region's history.

Mandurah Boat & Bike Hire BOATING, CYCLING
(☎08-9535 5877; www.mandurahboatandbikehire.com.au; Boardwalk) Chase the fish on a four-seat dinghy or six-seat pontoon (per hour/day from $50/320).

Eating

★Taste & Graze CAFE $$
(www.tasteandgraze.com.au; Shop 3/4 16 Mandurah Tce; shared plates & mains $14-32; ⊙8am-4pm Sun-Wed, 5pm-late Thu-Sat) Back in town in 'old' Mandurah, and perfectly located to catch the afternoon sun. Outdoor seating and a versatile Modern Australian menu covering breakfast, lunch and shared smaller plates make it a cosmopolitan slice of cafe cool.

Information

Visitor centre (☎08-9550 3999; www.visitmandurah.com; 75 Mandurah Tce; ⊙9am-5pm) On the estuary boardwalk.

Getting There & Away

Transwa (☎1300 662 205; www.transwa.wa.gov.au) and **South West Coach Lines** (☎08-9261 7600; www.transdevsw.com.au) buses stop here.

There are direct trains to Perth Underground/Esplanade ($10.20, 50 minutes) and Rockingham ($7.70, 18 minutes).

Dwellingup

POP 550

Dwellingup is a small, forest-shrouded township with character, 100km south of Perth. Its reputation as an activity hub has only been enhanced by the hardy long-distance walkers and cyclists passing through on the Bibbulmun Track and the Munda Biddi Trail, respectively.

Sights & Activities

Forest Heritage Centre NATURE RESERVE
(www.forestheritagecentre.com.au; 1 Acacia St; adult/child $5.50/2.20; ⊙10am-3pm) Set within the jarrah forest, this interesting rammed-earth building takes the shape of three interlinked gum leaves. Inside are displays about the forest's flora and fauna, and a shop that sells beautiful pieces crafted by the resident woodwork artists. Short marked trails lead into the forest, including an 11m-high canopy walk.

Hotham Valley Railway HISTORIC TRAIN
(☎08-6278 1111; www.hothamvalleyrailway.com.au; Forest Train adult/child $24/12, Restaurant Train $79, Steam Ranger adult/child $34/17; ⊙Forest Train departs 10.30am & 2pm Sat & Sun, Restaurant Train departs 7.45pm Sat, Steam Ranger departs 10.30am & 2pm Sun May-Oct) On weekends (and Tuesday and Thursday during school holidays), the Dwellingup **Forest Train** chugs along 8km of forest track on a 90-minute return trip. Every Saturday night and some Fridays, the **Restaurant Train** follows the same route, serving up a five-course meal in a 1919 dining car. A third option is the **Steam Ranger**, travelling 14km via Western Australia's steepest rail incline to Isandra Siding. Steam Ranger trains only run on Sunday from May to October.

Dwellingup Adventures ADVENTURE SPORTS
(☎08-9538 1127; www.dwellingupadventures.com.au; cnr Marrinup & Newton St; 1-person kayaks & 2-person canoes per three hours $30; ⊙8.30am-5pm) Don't miss the opportunity to get out on the beautiful Murray River. Hire camping gear, bikes, kayaks and canoes, or take an assisted, self-guided paddling (full day, per one-person kayak $107) or cycling tour (full day, per one/two/three people $107/140/198). White-water rafting tours are available from June to October (per person $150).

Information

Visitor centre (☎08-9538 1108; www.murraytourism.com.au; Marrinup St; ⊙9am-3pm) Interesting displays about the 1961 bushfires that wiped out the town, destroying 75 houses but taking no lives.

DRYANDRA TO HYDEN

A beautiful forest, rare marsupials, stunning, ancient granite-rock formations, salt lakes, interesting back roads and the unique Wave Rock are the scattered highlights of this widespread farming region.

WORTH A TRIP

DRYANDRA WOODLAND

With small populations of threatened numbats, woylies and tammar wallabies, this isolated remnant of eucalypt forest 164km southeast of Perth hints at what the wheat belt was like before large-scale land clearing and feral predators wreaked havoc on local ecosystems. With numerous walking trails, it makes a great getaway from Perth.

The excellent **Barna Mia Animal Sanctuary**, home to endangered bilbies, boodies, woylies and marla, conducts 90-minute after-dark torchlight tours, providing a rare opportunity to see these creatures up close. Book through **Parks & Wildlife** (☎08-9881 9222; www.parks.dpaw.wa.gov.au; 7 Wald St, Narrogin; adult/child/family $14/7.50/37.50; ⊙8.30am-4pm) for postsunset tours on Monday, Wednesday, Friday and Saturday, and book early for peak periods.

While you can hoist your tent at the **Congelin Camp Ground** (☎08-9881 9200; adult/child $7.50/2.20), Dryandra is one place you should splurge. The **Lions Dryandra Village** (☎08-9884 5231; www.dryandravillage.org.au; adult/child $30/15, 2-/4-person cabins $70/90, 8- to 12-person cabins $130) is a 1920s forestry camp offering self-contained, renovated woodcutters' cabins complete with fridge, stove, fireplace, en suite and nearby grazing wallabies. Narrogin, serviced by Transwa buses, is 22km southeast.

Hyden & Wave Rock

Large granite outcrops dot the central and southern wheat belts, and the most famous is the multicoloured cresting swell of Wave Rock, 350km from Perth. Formed some 60 million years ago by weathering and water erosion, Wave Rock is streaked with colours created by run-off from local mineral springs.

To get the most out of Wave Rock, obtain the *Walk Trails at Wave Rock and the Humps* brochure from the **visitor centre** (☎08-9880 5182; www.waverock.com.au; Wave Rock; ⊙9am-5pm). Park at Hippos Yawn (no fee) and follow the shady track back along the rock base to Wave Rock (1km).

Accommodation can fill quickly, so phone ahead for a spot amid the gum trees at **Wave Rock Cabins & Caravan Park** (☎08-9880 5022; www.waverock.com.au; unpowered/powered sites from $28/35, cabins/cottages from $140/$160; ❄🏊).

In Hyden (population 190), 4km east of the rock, the '70s brick **Wave Rock Motel** (☎08-9880 5052; www.waverock.com.au; 2 Lynch St, Hyden; s/d from $105/150; ❄🏊) has an indoor bush bistro.

Transwa runs a bus from Perth to Hyden ($51, five hours) and on to Esperance ($53, five hours) every Tuesday, returning on Thursday. See the WA Visitor Centre (p911) for tours visiting Wave Rock. Note it is a long day trip.

If heading to/from the Nullarbor, take the unsealed direct Hyden–Norseman Road, which will save 100km or so. Look for the brochure *The Granite and Woodlands Discovery Trail* at the Norseman or Wave Rock visitor centres.

SUNSET & TURQUOISE COASTS

The Indian Ocean Drive connects Perth to a succession of beautiful beaches, sleepy fishing villages, extraordinary geological formations, rugged national parks and incredibly diverse flora.

ℹ Getting There & Away

Integrity (☎1800 226 339; www.integritycoachlines.com.au) runs three times a week along the coast between Perth and Geraldton and on to Exmouth and Broome.

Transwa (☎1300 662 205; www.transwa.wa.gov.au) has 2pm Friday and Sunday departures heading to Cervantes and Green Head. The Friday bus continues to Geraldton.

Yanchep National Park

The woodlands and wetlands of **Yanchep National Park** (www.parks.dpaw.wa.gov.au; Wanneroo Rd; per car $12; ⊙visitor centre 9.15am-4.30pm) are home to fauna and flora including koalas, kangaroos, emus and cockatoos. Caves can be viewed on 45-minute tours (adult/child $10/5; five per day). On weekends at 2pm and 3pm, local Noongar guides run excellent **tours** on Indigenous history, lifestyle and culture (adult/child $10/5), and give didgeridoo and **dance performances** (adult/child $10/5).

Guilderton

POP 150

Some 43km north of Yanchep, Guilderton is a popular family holiday spot. Children paddle safely near the mouth of the Moore River, while adults enjoy the excellent fishing, surfing and sunbathing on the white sands of the ocean beach. The **Guilderton Caravan Park** (☎08-9577 1021; www.guildertoncaravanpark.com.au; 2 Dewar St; unpowered/powered sites $30/45, chalets $165) is the holidaymakers' hub, with self-contained chalets, a cafe and a general store, and there's a volunteer-run visitor centre (erratic hours).

Lancelin

POP 670

Afternoon winds and shallows protected by an outlying reef make this sleepy beach perfect for windsurfing and kitesurfing, attracting action seekers from around the world for the **Lancelin Ocean Classic** (www.lancelinoceanclassic.com.au) every January. It's also a great snorkelling spot.

Activities

Makanikai Kiteboarding KITEBOARDING
(☎0406 807 309; www.makanikaikiteboarding.com; lessons from $200) Lessons and tuition in the fine art of kiteboarding, and gear rental; accommodation packages are also available.

Sleeping & Eating

★**Lancelin Lodge YHA** HOSTEL $
(☎08-9655 2020; www.lancelinlodge.com.au; 10 Hopkins St; dm/d/f $30/85/105; @☎≋) This laid-back hostel is well equipped and welcoming, with wide verandahs and lots of communal spaces to hang about in. The excellent facilities include big kitchen, barbecue, wood-fire pizza oven, swimming pool, ping-pong table, volleyball court and free use of bikes and boogie boards.

Endeavour Tavern PUB FOOD $$
(58 Gingin Rd; mains $18-38) A classic beachfront Aussie pub with a beer garden overlooking the ocean. The casual eatery serves decent seafood, pub-grub classics and tasty wood-fired pizzas.

Cervantes & Pinnacles Desert

POP 480

The laid-back crayfishing town of Cervantes, 198km north of Perth, makes a pleasant base for exploring the Pinnacles Desert and the Kwongan, the wild flower-rich inland heathland of Lesueur and Badgingarra National Parks. There are also some lovely beaches to while away the time.

Sights & Activities

★**Nambung National Park** NATIONAL PARK
(per car $12) Situated 19km from Cervantes, Nambung is home to the spectacular **Pinnacles Desert**, a vast, alienlike plain studded with thousands of limestone pillars. Rising eerily from the desert floor, the pillars are remnants of compacted seashells that once covered the plain and, over millenniums, subsequently eroded. A loop road runs through the formations, but it's more fun to wander on foot, especially at sunset, full moon or dawn, when the light is sublime and the crowds evaporate.

Lesueur National Park NATIONAL PARK
(per car $12) This botanical paradise, 50km north of Cervantes, contains a staggering 820 plant species, many of them rare and endemic, such as the pine banksia *(Banksia tricupsis)* and Mt Lesueur grevillea *(Grevillea batrachioides)*. Late winter sees the heath erupt into a mass of colour, and the park is also home to the endangered Carnaby's cockatoo. An 18km circuit drive is dotted with lookouts and picnic areas. Flat-topped **Mt Lesueur** (4km return walk) has panoramic coastal views.

Tours

Many Perth-based companies offer day trips to the Pinnacles.

Turquoise Coast Enviro Tours SIGHTSEEING TOUR
(☎08-9652 7047; www.thepinnacles.com.au; 59 Seville St, Cervantes; full-day Kwongan tours $170) Cervantes local and ex-ranger Mike Newton runs a full-day Kwongan tour, including Lesueur National Park and the coast up to Leeman.

WORTH A TRIP

KWONGAN WILD FLOWERS

Take any road inland from the Turquoise Coast and you'll soon enter the Kwongan heathlands, where, depending on the season, the roadside verges burst with native wild flowers. Consider the following options.

Badgingarra National Park Three and a half kilometres of walking trails, kangaroo paw, banksia, grass tree, feather flower and a rare mallee (eucalyptus). The back road linking Badgingarra to Lesueur is particularly rich in flora. Obtain details from the Badgingarra Roadhouse.

Alexander Morrison National Park Named after Western Australia's first botanist. There are no trails, but you can drive through slowly on the Coorow Green Head Rd, which has loads of flora along its verge all the way from Lesueur. Expect to see dryandra, banksia, grevillea, smokebush, leschenaultia and honey myrtle.

Tathra National Park Tathra has similar flora to Alexander Morrison National Park and the drive between the two is rich with banksia, kangaroo paw and grevillea.

Coomallo Rest Area Orchids, feather flowers, black kangaroo paws, wandoo and river red gums can be found upstream and on the slopes of the small hill.

Brand Highway (Route 1) The route's not exactly conducive to slow meandering, but the highway verges are surprisingly rich in wild flowers, especially either side of Eneabba.

If you're overwhelmed and frustrated by not being able to identify all these strange new plants, consider staying at **Western Flora Caravan Park** (☎08-9955 2030; wfloracp@activ8.net.au; Brand Hwy, North Encabba; unpowered/powered siles $24/26, d $65, on-site vans $75, chalets $120), where the enthusiastic owners run free two-hour wild flower walks across their 65-hectare property every day at 4.30pm.

Sleeping & Eating

Prices surge during school holidays.

★Cervantes Lodge & Pinnacles Beach Backpackers HOSTEL $
(☎1800 245 232; www.cervanteslodge.com.au; 91 Seville St, www.pinnaclesholidaypark.com.au; dm $33, d with/without bathroom $130/90; @) In a great location behind the dunes, this relaxing hostel has a wide verandah, small and tidy dorms, a nice communal kitchen and a cosy lounge area. Bright, spacious en suite rooms, some with views, are next door in the lodge.

Pinnacles Holiday Park CARAVAN PARK $
(☎08-9652 7060; www.pinnaclesholidaypark.com.au; 35 Aragon St, Cervantes; unpowered & powered sites $25-49, cabins $90-105; 📶) Fantastic location right behind the dunes with plenty of shady, grassy sites and on-site cafe.

★Amble Inn B&B $$
(☎0429 652 401; 2150 Cadda Rd, Hill River; d from $170; ❄) High up on the heathland, about 25km east of Cervantes, this hidden gem of a B&B has beautiful thick stone walls, cool, wide verandahs and superbly styled rooms. Watch the sunset over the coast from the nearby hill with a glass of your complimentary wine.

★Lobster Shack SEAFOOD $$
(☎08-9652 7010; www.lobstershack.com.au; 11 Madrid St, Cervantes; ⊙shop 9am-5pm, lunch 11.30am-2.30pm, tours 12.30-2pm) Craving crayfish? They don't come much fresher than at this lobster factory-turned-lunch spot, where a delicious grilled cray, chips and salad will set you back $40. Lobster rolls are good value at $18. Tours (adult/child $15/7.50) and takeaway frozen seafood are also available.

Information

Cervantes' combined **post office and visitor centre** (☎08-9652 7700, 1800 610 660; www.visitpinnaclescountry.com.au; Cadiz St; ⊙9am-5.30pm Mon-Fri, to 5pm Sat & Sun) books accommodation and has touring information.

Getting There & Away

Integrity (www.integritycoachlines.com.au) runs three times a week to Perth ($44, three hours), Dongara ($34, two hours), Geraldton ($42, three hours) and Exmouth ($183, 14 hours). **Transwa** (www.transwa.wa.gov.au) runs twice weekly to Perth ($34, three hours), Dongara ($22, two hours) and Geraldton ($40, three hours).

Jurien Bay, Green Head & Leeman

Heading north from Cervantes, sprawling Jurien Bay (population 1500) is home to a large fishing fleet and pleasant seaside walks. Holiday houses and apartments can be booked via local **real estate agents** (08-9652 2055; www.jurienbayholidays.com; Shop 1a, 34 Bashford St), while **Jurien Bay Tourist Park** (08-9652 1595; www.jurienbaytouristpark.com.au; Roberts St; sites $38, chalets $140-170) has comfortable chalets right behind the beach.

Next door, the **Jetty Cafe** (08-9652 1999; meals $10-17; 7.30am-5pm) has decent brekkie and lunches, and the nearby **Beach Bistro** (2/1 Roberts St; lunch $15-22, dinner $21-36; noon-9pm Wed-Mon) is good for dinner. To see the coastline from the air and land on the beach, contact **Skydive Jurien Bay** (1300 293 766, 08-9652 1320; www.skydivejurienbay.com; 65 Bashford St; 8000/10,000/14,000ft jumps $300/350/450).

Tiny Green Head (population 280) has several beautiful bays great for swimming, and nearby Leeman (population 400) is popular with windsurfers.

Green Head has **Centrebreak Beach Stay** (08-9953 1896; www.centrebreakbeachstay.com.au; Lot 402, Ocean View Dr, Green Head; dm/d/f $35/150/190;), complete with a licensed **cafe** (meals $15-40), and the relaxed and shady **Green Head Caravan Park** (08-9953 1131; www.greenheadcaravanpark.com.au; 9 Green Head Rd, Green Head; unpowered/powered sites $20/28, on-site vans from $75).

Sea Lion Charters (0427 931 012; sealioncharters88@gmail.com; 24 Bryant St, Green Head; morning tours adult/child $150/75) offers trips where you can interact in shallow water with playful sea lions.

NEW NORCIA

The monastery settlement of New Norcia, 132km from Perth, consists of ornate, Spanish-style buildings set incongruously in the Australian bush. Founded in 1846 by Spanish Benedictine monks as an Aboriginal mission, the working monastery today holds prayers and retreats, alongside a business producing artisan baked goods. Bakeries licensed to produce New Norcia bread are in the Perth suburbs of Mt Hawthorn and Subiaco.

Sights & Activities

New Norcia Museum & Art Gallery MUSEUM, GALLERY
(08-9654 8056; www.newnorcia.wa.edu.au; Great Northern Hwy; combined museum & town tours adult/family $25/60; 10am-4.30pm) New Norcia Museum & Art Gallery traces the history of the monastery and houses impressive art, including contemporary exhibitions and one of the country's largest collections of post-Renaissance religious art. The gift shop sells souvenirs, honey, preserves and bread baked in the monks' wood-fired oven.

Abbey Church CHURCH
Inside the abbey church, try to spot the native wildlife in the sgraffito artworks that depict the Stations of the Cross. Look hard, as there's also an astronaut.

Town Tours TOUR
(www.newnorcia.wa.edu.au; adult/child $15/10; 11am & 1.30pm) Guided two-hour town tours offer a look at the abbey church and the frescoed college chapels; purchase tickets from the museum.

Sleeping

New Norcia Hotel HOTEL $
(08-9654 8034; www.newnorcia.wa.edu.au; Great Northern Hwy; s/d $75/95) New Norcia Hotel harks back to a more genteel time, with sweeping staircases, high ceilings, understated rooms (with shared bathrooms) and wide verandahs. An international menu (mains $15 to $36) is available at the bar or in the elegant dining room. Our pick is the ploughman's lunch served with New Norcia's own wood-fired sourdough bread.

Sit outside on the terrace and sample the delicious but deadly New Norcia Abbey Ale, a golden Belgian-style ale brewed especially for the abbey. Sunday is a good day to visit, either for a leisurely breakfast, or for popular wood-fired pizzas.

Monastery Guesthouse GUESTHOUSE $
(08-9654 8002; www.newnorcia.wa.edu.au; full board suggested donation $80) The abbey offers lodging in the Monastery Guesthouse within the walls of the southern cloister. Guests can join in prayers with the monks (and males can dine with them).

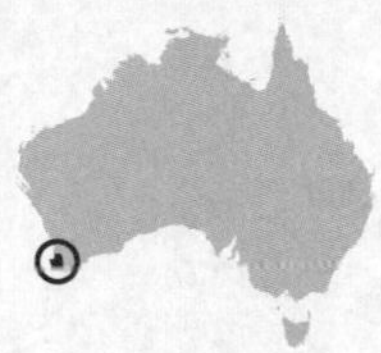

Margaret River & the Southwest Coast

Includes ➡

Best Places to Eat

- ➡ Laundry 43 (p937)
- ➡ Piari & Co (p938)
- ➡ Eagle Bay Brewing Co (p939)
- ➡ Vasse Felix (p942)
- ➡ Miki's Open Kitchen (p944)

Best Places to Stay

- ➡ Wildwood Valley Cottages (p941)
- ➡ Wharncliffe Mill Bush Retreat (p942)
- ➡ Acacia Chalets (p945)
- ➡ Burnside Organic Farm (p942)
- ➡ Foragers (p948)

Why Go?

The farmland, forests, rivers and coast of the lush, green southwestern corner of Western Australia (WA) contrast vividly with the stark, sunburnt terrain of much of the rest of the state. On land, world-class wineries and craft breweries beckon, and tall trees provide shade for walking trails and scenic drives. Offshore, bottlenose dolphins and whales frolic, and devoted surfers search for – and often find – their perfect break.

Unusually for WA, distances between the many attractions are short, and driving time is mercifully limited, making it a fantastic area to explore for a few days – you will get much more out of your stay here if you have your own wheels. Summer brings hordes of visitors, but in the wintry months from July to September the cosy pot-bellied stove rules and visitors are scarce, and while opening hours can be somewhat erratic, prices are much more reasonable.

When to Go

Margaret River

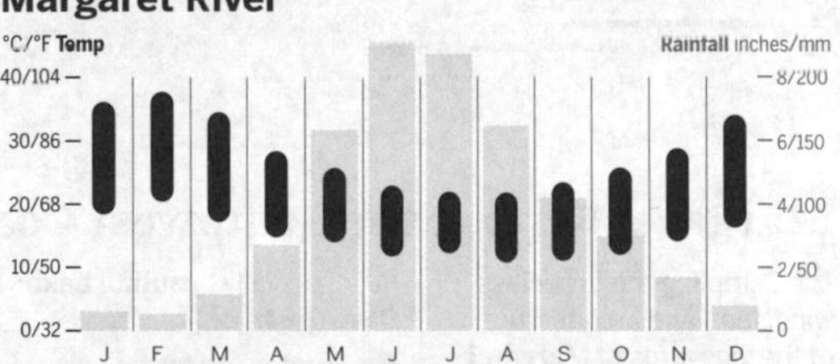

Jan Follow the party crowds from the Southbound festival to the beach.

Mar & Apr Catch the surf competition in Margaret River, and the Nannup Music Festival.

Aug Head to empty beaches, Margaret River wineries and Busselton's film festival.

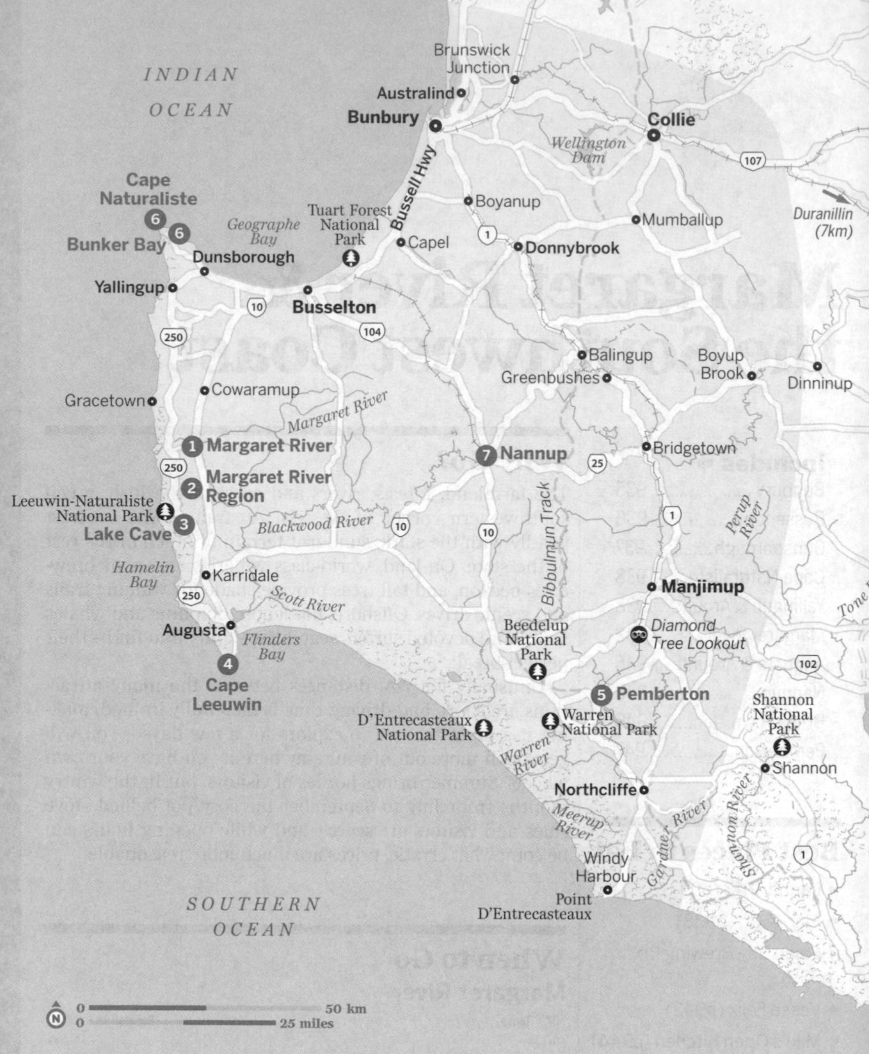

Margaret River & the Southwest Coast Highlights

1. Sampling the first-class wine, food and architecture of the vineyards of **Margaret River** (p942).
2. Getting active amid the dramatic seascapes and landscapes of the **Margaret River region** (p938).
3. Exploring the labyrinthine limestone caverns along Caves Rd, especially beautiful **Lake Cave** (p944).
4. Fronting up to the impressive coastline at Augusta's **Cape Leeuwin Lighthouse** (p945), at the confluence of the Indian and Southern Oceans.
5. Sinking into the dappled depths of the karri forests surrounding **Pemberton** (p947).
6. Revelling in the wild beauty of **Cape Naturaliste** and **Bunker Bay** (p938).
7. Canoeing from the forest to the sea along the Blackwood River, starting at **Nannup** (p946).

GEOGRAPHE BAY

Turquoise waters and white sands are the defining features of this gorgeous bay, lined with 30km of excellent swimming beaches. Positioned between the Indian Ocean and a sea of wine, the beachside towns of Busselton and Dunsborough attract hordes of holidaymakers wanting to spend their vacations with sand between their toes and a glass between their lips.

Bunbury

POP 66,100

The southwest's only city is remaking its image from that of an industrial port into a seaside holiday destination. Located 170km from Perth, Bunbury has good eateries and interesting attractions worthy of a stop.

Sights & Activities

Dolphin Discovery Centre WILDLIFE RESERVE
(08-9791 3088; www.dolphindiscovery.com.au; Koombana Beach; adult/child $10/5; 9am-2pm Jun-Sep, 8am-4pm Oct-May) Around 60 bottlenose dolphins live in the bay year-round, their numbers increasing to 260 in summer. This centre has a beachside zone where dolphins regularly come to interact with people in the shallows and you can wade in alongside them, under the supervision of trained volunteers.

If you want to up your chances, there are 1½-hour **Eco Cruises** (1½hr cruise adult/child $49/35; 11am daily Oct-May, 11am Sat & Sun Jun-Sep) and three-hour **Swim Encounter Cruises** (3hr cruises $149; 7.30am mid-Oct–mid-Dec & Feb-Apr, 7.30am & 11.30am mid-Dec–Jan).

Bunbury Wildlife Park ZOO
(www.bunburywildlifepark.com.au; Prince Philip Dr; adult/child $9/5; 10am-5pm) Parrots, kangaroos, wallabies, possums, owls and emus all feature. Across the road, the **Big Swamp** has good wetlands walking tracks and stops for birdwatching. Head south on Ocean Dr, turn left at Hayward St and continue through the roundabout to Prince Philip Dr.

Bunbury Regional Art Galleries GALLERY
(www.brag.org.au; 64 Wittenoom St; 10am-4pm) FREE Housed in a restored pink-painted convent (1897), this excellent gallery has a collection that includes works by Australian art luminaries Arthur Boyd and Sir Sidney Nolan.

Sleeping

Dolphin Retreat YHA HOSTEL $
(08-9792 4690; www.dolphinretreatbunbury.com.au; 14 Wellington St; dm/s/d $32/57/82;) Around the corner from the beach, this small hostel is in a labyrinthine old house with hammocks and a barbecue on the back verandah.

Clifton MOTEL $$
(08-9721 4300; www.theclifton.com.au; 2 Molloy St; r $150-275;) For luxurious heritage accommodation, go for the top-of-the-range rooms in the Clifton's historic Grittleton Lodge (1885). Good-value motel rooms are also available.

Mantra APARTMENT $$$
(08-9721 0100; www.mantra.com.au; 1 Holman St; apt from $204;) The Mantra has sculpted a set of modern studios and apartments around four grain silos by the harbour. Deluxe rooms have spa baths and full kitchens.

Eating & Drinking

Kokoro JAPANESE $
(30 Victoria St; mains $10-18; 11am-2.30pm & 6pm-late) Head to the cosy Kokoro and dine *izakaya* style on Japanese tapas. Moreish highlights include creamy crab croquettes and tempura prawns, and the broader menu includes sushi and sashimi, and more robust teriyaki salmon and beef dishes. Lunch specials from $9.50 are good value.

Happy Wife CAFE $$
(www.thehappywife.com.au; 98 Stirling St; mains $11-24; 6.30am-3.30pm Mon-Fri, 7.30am-2.30pm Sat) Grab a spot in the garden of this Cape Cod–style cottage just a short drive from the centre of town. Excellent home-style baking and regular lunch specials make it worth seeking out. Try the Asian-style sticky pork salad with nashi pear, cabbage salad and toasted peanuts.

Café 140 CAFE $$
(www.cafe140.com.au; 140 Victoria St; mains $12-21; 7.30am-4.30pm Mon-Fri, 8am-2pm Sat & Sun) Hip, onto-it staff make the funky Café 140 a top spot for a leisurely Bunbury breakfast. With one of WA's best salmon omelettes, good coffee, and lots of magazines and newspapers, you can kiss goodbye to at least an hour of your travel schedule. Later in the day, gourmet burgers and grilled Turkish sandwiches are among the lunchtime stars.

Mash CRAFT BEER
(www.mashbrewing.com.au; 2/11 Bonnefoi Blvd; 11am-3pm Mon & Tue, to 9pm Wed-Sun) This waterfront microbrewery turns out seven regular beers, plus always interesting seasonal concoctions. Try the Copycat AIPA, champion brew at the Australian International Beer Awards in 2014. The food (mains $18 to $38) is decent pub grub, but service can be hit and miss.

Information

Visitor centre (08-9792 7205; www.visitbunbury.com.au; Carmody Pl; 9am-5pm Mon-Sat, 10am-2pm Sun) Located in the historic train station (1904).

Getting There & Around

BUS

Coaches stop at the **central bus station** (08-9722 7800; Carmody Pl), next to the visitor centre, or at the **train station** (Picton Rd, Woolaston).

Transwa routes include the following:

SW1 (12 weekly) To East Perth ($31, 3¼ hours), Mandurah ($17, two hours), Busselton ($9.55, 43 minutes), Margaret River ($17, two hours) and Augusta ($25, 2½ hours).

SW2 (three weekly) To Balingup ($14, 53 minutes), Bridgetown ($17, 1¼ hours) and Pemberton ($28, 2¼ hours).

GS3 (daily) To Walpole ($45, 4½ hours), Denmark ($51, 5½ hours) and Albany ($58, six hours).

TRAIN

Bunbury is the terminus of the **Transwa** (1300 662 205; www.transwa.wa.gov.au) Australind train line, with two daily services to Perth ($31, 2½ hours) and Pinjarra ($17, 1¼ hours).

Busselton

POP 15,400

Unpretentious, uncomplicated and with a slightly faded charm, family-friendly Busselton is surrounded by calm waters and white-sand beaches. During school holidays it really bustles – the population increases fourfold and accommodation prices soar.

Sights & Activities

Busselton Jetty JETTY
(08-9754 0900; www.busseltonjetty.com.au; adult/child $2.50/free, return train adult/child $11/6, Interpretive Centre admission free; Interpretive Centre 9am-5pm) Busselton's 1865 timber-piled jetty – the longest in the southern hemisphere (1841m) – reopened in 2011 following a $27-million refurbishment. A little **train** chugs along to the **Underwater Observatory** (adult/child incl train $29.50/14; 9am-4.25pm), where tours take place 8m below the surface; bookings are essential. There's also an **Interpretive Centre**, an attractive building in the style of 1930s bathing sheds, about 50m along the jetty.

Dive Shed DIVING
(08-9754 1615; www.diveshed.com.au; 21 Queen St) Runs regular dive charters along the jetty, to Four Mile Reef (a 40km limestone ledge about 6.5km off the coast) and to the scuttled navy vessel HMAS *Swan* (off Dunsborough).

Festivals & Events

Southbound MUSIC
(www.southboundfestival.com.au) Start off the New Year with three days of alternative music and camping.

CinéfestOZ CINEMA
(www.cinefestoz.com) Busselton briefly morphs into St-Tropez in Late August with this oddly glamorous festival of French and Australian cinema, including lots of Australian premieres and the odd Aussie starlet.

Sleeping

Busselton is packed in the holidays and pretty much deserted in the low season. Accommodation sprawls along the beach for several kilometres either side of the town, so make sure you check the location if you don't have your own wheels.

Beachlands Holiday Park CARAVAN PARK $
(1800 622 107; www.beachlands.net; 10 Earnshaw Rd, West Busselton; sites per 2 people $45, chalets from $142;) This excellent family-friendly park offers a wide range of accommodation amid shady trees, palms and flax bushes. Deluxe spa villas ($185) have corner spas, huge TVs, DVD players and full kitchens.

Blue Bay Apartments APARTMENT $$
(08-9751 1796; www.bluebayapartments.com; 66 Adelaide St; apt from $140;) Close to the beach, these good-value self-contained apartments are bright and cheery, each with private courtyard and barbecue.

Eating

★Laundry 43 CAFE $$

(www.laundry43.com.au; 43 Prince St; shared plates $14-29; ⏲9am-late Tue-Sat) Brick walls and a honey-coloured jarrah bar form the backdrop for Margaret River beers and wines, great cocktails, and classy shared plates and bigger dishes. Definitely get ready to linger longer than you planned. Wednesday nights offer live music from 7.30pm.

Goose BISTRO $$

(www.thegoose.com.au; Geographe Bay Rd; breakfast $10-21, shared plates & mains $11-34; ⏲7am-late; 📶) Near the jetty, this stylish cafe has been reborn as a cool and classy bar and bistro. The drinks list bubbles away with WA craft beer and wine, and a versatile menu kicks off with eggy breakfasts, before graduating to shared plates including Vietnamese pulled pork sliders, and larger dishes like steamed mussels and seafood chowder.

Information

Visitor centre (☎08-9752 5800; www.geographebay.com; end of Queen St, Busselton Foreshore; ⏲9am 5pm Mon-Fri, 9am-4.30pm Sat & Sun) Underneath the lighthouse near the pier.

Getting There & Around

South West Coach Lines (☎08-9753 7700; www.transdevsw.com.au; 39 Albert St) Runs services to/from Perth's Esplanade Busport ($39, 3¾ hours, three daily), Bunbury ($11.50, one hour, three daily), Dunsborough ($11.50, 30 minutes, three daily) and Margaret River ($11.50, 50 minutes, three daily).

Transwa (☎1300 662 205; www.transwa.wa.gov.au) Coach SW1 (12 weekly) stops on Peel Tce, heading to/from East Perth ($37, 4¼ hours), Bunbury ($9.55, 43 minutes), Dunsborough ($8, 28 minutes), Margaret River ($14, 1½ hours) and Augusta ($17, 1¾ hours).

Dunsborough

POP 3400

Dunsborough is a relaxed, beach-worshipping town that goes bonkers towards the end of November when 7000 schoolies (school-leavers) descend. When it's not inundated with drunken, squealing teenagers, it's a thoroughly pleasant place to be. The beaches are better than Busselton's, but accommodation is more limited.

SURFING THE SOUTHWEST

The beaches between Capes Naturaliste and Leeuwin offer powerful reef breaks, mainly left-handers.

Around Dunsborough, the better locations are between Eagle and Bunker Bays. Near Yallingup there's Three Bears, Rabbits (a beach break north of Yallingup Beach), Yallingup, Injidup Car Park and Injidup Point. You'll need a 4WD to access Guillotine/Gallows, north of Gracetown. Also around Gracetown are Huzza's, South Point and Lefthanders.

The annual **Drug Aware Pro** (www.aspworldtour.com; ⏲Apr) surfing competition is held around Margaret River Mouth and Southside (aka 'Suicides').

Activities

Cape Dive DIVING

(☎08-9756 8778; www.capedive.com; 222 Naturaliste Tce) There is excellent diving in Geographe Bay, especially since the decommissioned Navy destroyer HMAS *Swan* was purposely scuttled in 1997 for use as a dive wreck. Marine life has colonised the ship, which lies at a depth of 30m, 2.5km offshore.

Naturaliste Charters WHALE WATCHING

(☎08-9750 5500; www.whales-australia.com; adult/child $80/50; ⏲10am & 2pm Sep–mid-Dec) Two-hour whale-watching cruises from September to mid-December. From January to March the emphasis switches to an **Eco Wilderness Tour** showcasing beaches, limestone caves with Indigenous art, and wildlife including dolphins and New Zealand fur seals. Tours also run out of Augusta from mid-May to September.

Sleeping

There are many options for self-contained rentals in town depending on the season; the visitor centre has current listings.

Dunsborough Beachouse YHA HOSTEL $

(☎08-9755 3107; www.dunsboroughbeachouse.com.au; 205 Geographe Bay Rd; dm $34-36, s/d $58/88; @📶) On the Quindalup beachfront, this friendly hostel has lawns stretching languidly to the water's edge; it's an easy 2km cycle from the town centre.

Dunsborough Central Motel MOTEL **$$**
(☎08-9756 7711; www.dunsboroughmotel.com.au; 50 Dunn Bay Rd; r $130-175;) Centrally located in Dunsborough town, this well-run motel is good value, especially if you can snare an online midweek discount. That means more of your travel budget to enjoy nearby wineries and breweries.

Eating & Drinking

Pourhouse BISTRO, PUB **$$**
(www.pourhouse.com.au; 26 Dunn Bay Rd; mains $19-31; ⏲4pm-late Mon-Sat, from 2pm Sun) Hip but not pretentious, with comfy couches, regular live bands, and an upstairs terrace for summer. The pizzas are excellent, and top-notch burgers come in a locally baked sour dough bun. A considered approach to beer includes rotating taps from the best of WA's craft breweries and lots of bottled surprises.

Samudra CAFE **$$**
(www.samudra.com.au; 226 Naturaliste Tce; mains $14-23; ⏲7am-3pm Thu-Tue, to 10pm Wed;) This funky garden cafe is one of WA's best vegetarian restaurants. Tasty wood-fired pizzas underpin a super healthy menu of salads, wraps and smoothies, and there are plenty of shady places to sit and read or write. Samudra also offers relaxing and reinvigorating yoga classes, and surfing and spa retreats.

★**Piari & Co** BISTRO, BAR **$$$**
(☎08-9756 7977; www.piariandco.com.au; 5/54 Dunn Bay Rd; small plates $17-20, mains $35-38; ⏲10am-5pm Tue, 10am-11pm Wed-Fri, 5-11pm Sat) This relaxed and stylish bistro has a strong emphasis on local and seasonal produce. Small plates include Esperance scallops with crispy duck, and a subtle combination of citrus-cured salmon and mandarin gel. Mains such as pork belly and roast apple go well with a drinks list proudly showcasing Margaret River wines and craft beer. Bookings recommended.

Information

Visitor centre (☎08-9752 5800; www.geographebay.com; 1/31 Dunn Bay Rd; ⏲9am-5pm Mon-Fri, 9.30am-4.30pm Sat & Sun) Information and bookings.

Getting There & Away

South West Coach Lines (☎08-9753 7700; www.transdevsw.com.au) Services to/from Perth's Esplanade Busport ($43.50, 4½ hours, daily), Bunbury ($18.50, 1¾ hours, daily) and Busselton ($11.50, 30 minutes, three daily).

Transwa (☎1300 662 205; www.transwa.wa.gov.au) Coach SW1 (12 weekly) stops at the visitor centre, heading to/from East Perth ($40, 4½ hours), Bunbury ($14, 1¼ hours), Busselton ($8, 28 minutes), Margaret River ($9.55, 49 minutes) and Augusta ($17, 1¼ hours).

Cape Naturaliste

Northwest of Dunsborough, Cape Naturaliste Rd leads to the excellent beaches of **Meelup**, **Eagle Bay** and **Bunker Bay**, and on to Cape Naturaliste. Bunker Bay is also home to **Bunkers Beach Cafe** (www.bunkersbeachcafe.com.au; Farm Break Lane; breakfast $14-25, lunch $16-34; ⏲8.30am-4pm), which serves an adventurous menu from a spot only metres from the sand.

The **Cape Naturaliste lighthouse** (adult/child $14/7; ⏲tours every 30min 9.30am-4pm), built in 1903, can be visited, and 'Above and Below' packages (adult/child $30/15) incorporate entry to Ngilgi Cave near Yallingup.

MARGARET RIVER WINE REGION

With its blissful country roads, crashing surf beaches, and excellent chardonnays and Bordeaux-style reds, Margaret River is a highlight of any trip to WA. And where there's fine wine, there are vineyard restaurants, cheese shops, craft breweries, art galleries and craft stores.

Many tour companies operate in Margaret River; options include visiting wineries and breweries. More active alternatives to wine tasting include mountain biking, abseiling, rock climbing, sea kayaking and caving.

Yallingup & Around

POP 1070

Beachside Yallingup is as much a mecca for salty-skinned surfers as it is for wine aficionados. You're permitted to let a 'wow' escape when the surf-battered coastline first comes into view. Romantics may be encouraged to know that the name Yallingup means 'place of love'.

GETTING CRAFTY IN MARGARET RIVER

The Margaret River region's wine credentials are impeccable, but the area is also a destination for craft beer fans. All of the following serve bar snacks and lunch.

Eagle Bay Brewing Co (www.eaglebaybrewing.com.au; Eagle Bay Rd, Dunsborough; ⏲11am-5pm) A lovely rural outlook, interesting beers and wines served in modern, spacious surroundings, and excellent food including crisp wood-fired pizzas ($20 to $24). Keep an eye out for Eagle Bay's Single Batch Specials.

Colonial Brewing Co (www.colonialbrewingco.com.au; Osmington Rd, Margaret River; ⏲11am-6pm) This modern microbrewery has great rural views, and an excellent range of authentic beers including a *witbier* (wheat beer) with coriander and mandarin, and a hop-fuelled India Pale Ale. Our favourite is the refreshing German-style kölsch.

Bush Shack Brewery (www.bushshackbrewery.com.au; Hemsley Rd, Yallingup; ⏲10am-5pm) A small-scale brewery in a great bush setting. A healthy addition of innovation results in interesting brews such as a chilli beer, a lemon-infused lager and a strawberry pale ale.

Bootleg Brewery (www.bootlegbrewery.com.au; off Yelverton Rd, Wilyabrup; ⏲11am-6pm) More rustic than some of the area's flasher breweries, but lots of fun with a pint in the sun – especially with live bands on Saturday. Try the award-winning Raging Bull Porter or the US West Coast–style Speakeasy IPA.

Cheeky Monkey Brewery (www.cheekymonkeybrewery.com.au; 4259 Caves Rd, Margaret River; ⏲10am-6pm) Set on the edge of a pretty lake, Cheeky Monkey has an expansive restaurant and lots of room for the kids to run around. Try the Hatseller pilsner with bold New Zealand hops or the Belgian-style Hagenbeck Pale Ale. Decent food and apple and pear ciders means you'll make a day of it.

Cowaramup Brewing Company (www.cowaramupbrewing.com.au; North Treeton Rd, Cowaramup; ⏲11am-5pm) Modern microbrewey with an award-winning pilsner and a moreish English-style Special Pale Ale. Four other beers and occasional seasonal brews also feature.

Sights & Activities

Wardan Aboriginal Centre CULTURAL EXPERIENCE, GALLERY

(Map p940; ☎08-9756 6566; www.wardan.com.au; Injidup Springs Rd, Yallingup; experiences adult/child $20/10; ⏲10am-4pm daily mid-Oct–mid-Mar, 10am-4pm Mon, Wed-Fri & Sun mid-Mar–mid-Jun & mid-Aug–mid-Oct, experiences Sun, Mon, Wed & Fri) Offers a window into the lives of the local Wardandi people. There's a gallery (free admission), an interpretive display on the six seasons that govern the Wardandi calendar (adult/child $8/3), and the opportunity to take part in various experiences including stone tool making, boomerang and spear throwing. A guided bushwalk explores Wardandi spirituality and the uses of various plants for food, medicine and shelter.

Ngilgi Cave CAVE

(Map p940; ☎08-9755 2152; www.geographebay.com; Yallingup Caves Rd; adult/child $22/12; ⏲9am-5pm) Between Dunsborough and Yallingup, this 500,000-year-old cave is associated in Wardandi spirituality with the victory of the good spirit Ngilgi over the evil spirit Wolgine. To the Wardandi people it became a kind of honeymoon location. A European man first stumbled upon it in 1899 while looking for his horse. Formations include the white **Mother of Pearl Shawl** and the equally beautiful **Arab's Tent** and **Oriental Shawl**. Tours depart every half hour. Check online for other options.

Koomal Dreaming GUIDED TOUR

(☎0413 843 426; www.koomaldreaming.com.au; adult/child from $50/25) Yallingup local and Wardandi man Josh Whiteland runs tours showcasing Indigenous food, culture and music, usually also including bushwalking and exploration of the Ngilgi Cave.

Sleeping & Eating

Yallingup Beach Holiday Park CARAVAN PARK $

(Map p940; ☎08-9755 2164; www.yallingupbeach.com.au; Valley Rd; sites per 2 people $38, cabins $115-165;) You'll sleep to the sound of the surf here, with the beach just across the road.

Margaret River Wine Region

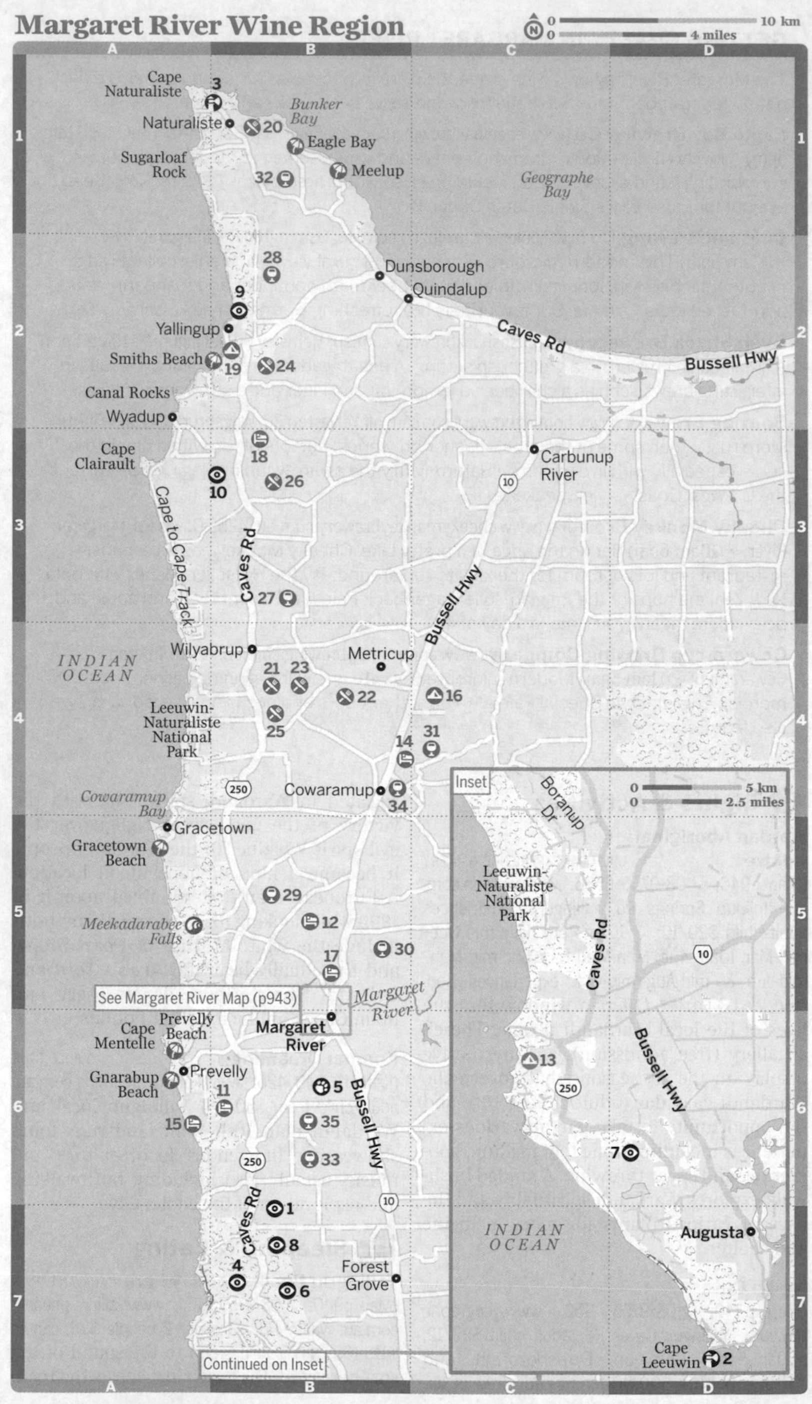

Margaret River Wine Region

Sights
1 Calgardup Cave....B7
2 Cape Leeuwin Lighthouse....D7
3 Cape Naturaliste Lighthouse....B1
4 CaveWorks & Lake Cave....B7
5 Eagles Heritage....B6
6 Giants Cave....B7
7 Jewel Cave....D6
8 Mammoth Cave....B7
9 Ngilgi Cave....B2
10 Wardan Aboriginal Centre....B3

Sleeping
11 Acacia Chalets....B6
12 Burnside Organic Farm....B5
13 Hamelin Bay Holiday Park....C6
14 Noble Grape Guesthouse....B4
15 Surfpoint....A6
16 Taunton Farm Holiday Park....C4
17 Wharncliffe Mill Bush Retreat....B5
18 Wildwood Valley Cottages & Cooking School....B3
19 Yallingup Beach Holiday Park....B2

Eating
20 Bunkers Beach Cafe....B1
21 Cullen Wines....B4
22 Margaret River Chocolate Company....B1
23 Providore....B4
24 Studio Bistro....B2
25 Vasse Felix....B4
26 Wills Domain....B3

Drinking & Nightlife
27 Bootleg Brewery....B3
28 Bush Shack Brewery....B2
29 Cheeky Monkey Brewery....B5
30 Colonial Brewing Co....B5
31 Cowaramup Brewing Company....C4
32 Eagle Bay Brewing Co....B1
33 Leeuwin Estate....B6
34 Margaret River Regional Wine Centre....B4
35 Voyager Estate....B6

Wildwood Valley Cottages & Cooking School COTTAGE $$$
(Map p940; 08-9755 2120; www.wildwoodvalley.com.au; 1481 Wildwood Rd; cottages from $250;) Luxury cottages trimmed by native bush are arrayed across 49 hectares, and the property's main house also hosts the **Mad About Food Cooking School** with Sioban and Carlo Baldini. Sioban's CV includes cooking at Longrain and living in Tuscany, so the culinary emphasis is Thai or Italian. Cooking classes are $135 per person and usually run on a Wednesday.

★**Studio Bistro** MODERN AUSTRALIAN $$$
(Map p940; 08-9756 6164; www.thestudiobistro.com.au; 7 Marrinup Dr; small plates $15-20, mains $28-39, degustation menu with/without wine matches $135/95; 10am-5pm Thu-Mon, 6pm-late Fri & Sat;) Studio Bistro's gallery focuses on Australian artists, while the garden restaurant showcases subtle dishes such as pan-fried fish with cauliflower cream, radicchio, peas and crab meat. Five-course degustation menus are offered on Friday and Saturday nights. Bookings recommended.

Wills Domain WINERY $$$
(Map p940; www.willsdomain.com.au; cnr Brash & Abbey Farm Rds; mains $29-40, charcuterie platters $38; tastings 10am-5pm, lunch noon-3pm) Restaurant, gallery and wonderful hilltop views over vines. An innovative seven-course tasting menu (with/without wine match $139/99) is also available.

Cowaramup & Wilyabrup

POP 990

Cowaramup is little more than a couple of blocks of shops lining Bussell Hwy. Nearby vineyards and gourmet food producers reinforce its tasty position at the heart of the wine region. The rustic area to the northwest known as Wilyabrup is where the Margaret River wine industry kicked off in the 1960s.

Sleeping

Taunton Farm Holiday Park CARAVAN PARK $
(Map p940; 1800 248 777; www.tauntonfarm.com.au; Bussell Hwy, Cowaramup; sites $42, cottages $115-175;) There are plenty of farm animals for the kids to meet at one of Margaret River's best family-oriented camping grounds. For caravan and tenting buffs, the amenities blocks are spotless, and also scattered about are farmstyle self-contained cottages.

Noble Grape Guesthouse B&B $$
(Map p940; 08-9755 5538; www.noblegrape.com.au; 29 Bussell Hwy, Cowaramup; s $140-160, d $145-190;) Noble Grape is more like an upmarket motel than a traditional B&B. Rooms offer a sense of privacy and each has a verdant little garden courtyard.

Eating & Drinking

Providore DELI $

(Map p940; www.providore.com.au; 448 Tom Cullity Dr, Wilyabrup; 9am-5pm) Voted one of Australia's Top 100 Gourmet Experiences by *Australian Traveller* magazine – and, given its amazing range of artisan produce including organic olive oil, tapenades and preserved fruits, we can only agree. Look forward to loads of free samples.

Margaret River Chocolate Company CHOCOLATES $

(Map p940; www.chocolatefactory.com.au; Harman's Mill Rd; 9am-5pm) Watch truffles being made and sample chocolate buttons.

Vasse Felix WINERY RESTAURANT $$$

(Map p940; 08-9756 5050; www.vassefelix.com.au; cnr Caves Rd & Harmans Rd S, Cowaramup; mains $32-39, 3-course menu $65, mains $32-39; cellar door 10am-5pm, restaurant 10am-3pm) Vasse Felix winery is considered by many to have the finest restaurant in the region, the big wooden dining room reminiscent of an extremely flash barn. The grounds are peppered with sculptures, while the gallery displaying works from the Holmes à Court collection is worth a trip in itself.

Cullen Wines WINERY RESTAURANT $$$

(Map p940; 08-9755 5277; www.cullenwines.com.au; 4323 Caves Rd, Cowaramup; mains $25-38; 10am-4pm) Grapes were first planted here in 1966 and Cullen has an ongoing commitment to organic and biodynamic principles in both food and wine. Celebrating a relaxed ambience, Cullen's food is excellent, with many of the fruit and vegetables from its own gardens.

Margaret River Regional Wine Centre WINE

(Map p940; www.mrwines.com; 9 Bussell Hwy, Cowaramup; 10am-7pm) A one-stop shop for Margaret River wine.

Margaret River

POP 4500

Although tourists might outnumber locals much of the time, Margaret River still feels like a country town. The advantage of basing yourself here is that after 5pm, once the surrounding wineries shut up shop, it's one of the few places with any vital signs.

Festivals & Events

Margaret River Gourmet Escape FOOD & WINE

(www.gourmetescape.com.au) From Rick Stein and Heston Blumenthal to Masterchef's George Calombaris, the Gourmet Escape food and wine festival attracts the big names in global and Australian cuisine. Look forward to three days of food workshops, tastings, vineyard events and demonstrations. An inaugural added attraction in 2014 was a vineyard concert at Sandalford Estate featuring Kiwi music icon Neil Finn. Held in late November.

Sleeping

★Wharncliffe Mill Bush Retreat ECO RETREAT $

(Map p940; 08-9758 8227; www.wharncliffemill.com.au; McQueen Rd, Bramley National Park; unpowered/powered sites $28/32, dm $25-30, safari tents & cabins $85-170;) Set amid shaded forests and around a former timber mill, Wharncliffe has accommodation ranging from simple shared dorms to safari tents and cosy wooden cabins. Solar power and sustainable environmental practices are encouraged, and there's plenty of excellent advice on local opportunities for bushwalking and mountain biking. Margaret River township is just 2km away, and mountain bikes can be hired (half/full day $15/25).

Margaret River Lodge HOSTEL $

(Map p943; 08-9757 9532; www.margaretriverbackpackers.com.au; 220 Railway Tce; dm $30-32, r with/without bathroom $87/76;) About 1.5km southwest of the town centre, this clean, well-run hostel has a pool, volleyball court and football field. Dorms share a big communal kitchen, and a quieter area with private rooms has its own kitchen and lounge.

Edge of the Forest MOTEL $$

(Map p943; 08-9757 2351; www.edgeoftheforest.com.au; 25 Bussell Hwy; r $160;) Just a pleasant stroll from Margaret River township, the rooms here have all been recenty renovated with new bathrooms and a chic Asian theme. Friendly owners have lots of local recommendations, and the leafy shared garden is perfect for an end-of-day barbecue.

★Burnside Organic Farm BUNGALOWS $$$

(Map p940; 08-9757 2139; www.burnsideorganicfarm.com.au; 287 Burnside Rd; d $280-325;) Rammed-earth and limestone bungalows

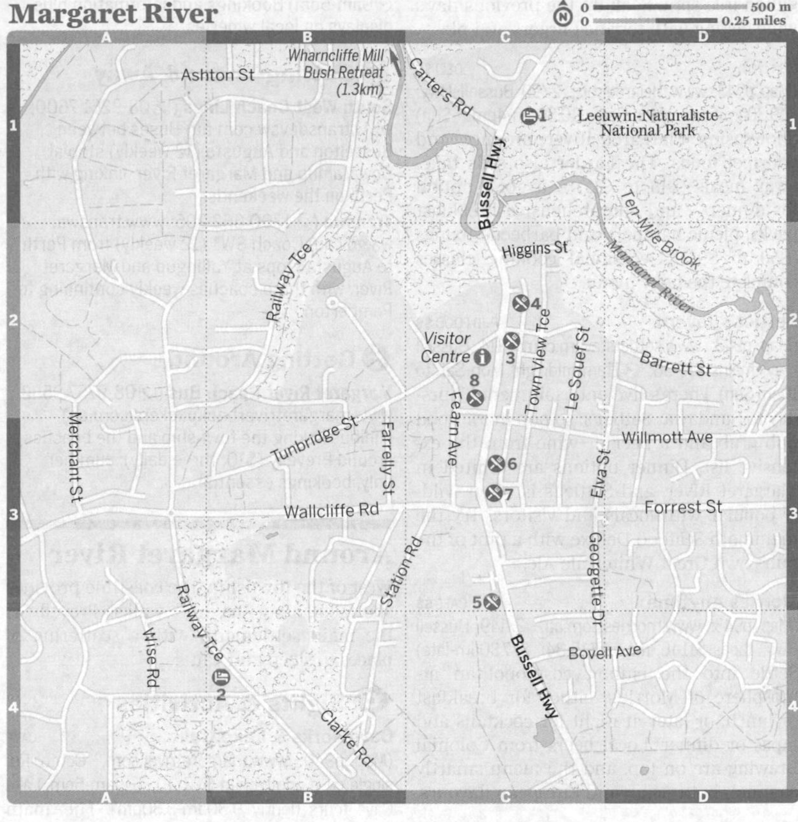

Margaret River

Sleeping
1 Edge of the Forest C1
2 Margaret River Lodge B4

Eating
3 Larder C2
4 Margaret River Bakery C2
5 Margaret River Farmers Market C3
6 Miki's Open Kitchen C3
7 Morries Anytime C3
8 Settler's Tavern C2

Shopping
Tunbridge Gallery .... (see 3)

have spacious decks and designer kitchens, and the surrounding farm hosts a menagerie of animals and organic orchards. Guests can also pick vegetables from the garden. Welcome to the perfect private retreat after a day cruising the region's wine, beer and food highlights. Minimum two-night stay.

Eating & Drinking

Margaret River Farmers Market MARKET $
(Map p943; www.margaretriverfarmersmarket.com.au; Lot 272 Bussell Hwy, Margaret River Education Campus; 8am-noon Sat) The region's organic and sustainable artisan producers come to town every Saturday. It's a top spot for breakfast. Check the website for your own foodie hit list.

Margaret River Bakery CAFE $
(Map p943; 89 Bussell Hwy; mains $10-18; 7am-4pm Mon-Sat;) Elvis on the stereo, retro furniture, and kitsch needlework art – the MRB has a rustic, playful interior. It's the perfect backdrop to the bakery's honest home-style baking, often with a veg or

gluten-free spin. Soak up the previous day's wine tasting with terrific burgers and pies.

Larder DELI $$

(Map p943; www.thelarder.biz; 2/99 Bussell Hwy; 9.30am-6pm Mon-Sat, 10.30am-4pm Sun) Showcasing Margaret River produce and gourmet foods, The Larder also sells takeaway meals ($15 to $17) – a good option for dinner – and comprehensive breakfast packs, picnic hampers and barbecue fixings ($50 to $95). Occasional cooking classes complete the tasty menu.

Settler's Tavern PUB FOOD $$

(Map p943; www.settlerstavern.com; 114 Bussell Hwy; mains $16-36; 11am-midnight Mon-Sat, to 10pm Sun) There's live entertainment Thursday to Sunday at Settler's, so pop in for good pub grub and a beer or wine from the extensive list. Dinner options are limited in Margaret River, and Settler's is often wildly popular with locals and visitors. Try the mammoth Seafood Deluxe with a pint of the pub's own Great White Pale Ale.

Morries Anytime CAFE $$

(Map p943; www.morries.com.au; 2/149 Bussell Hwy; tapas $11-16, mains $15-34; 7.30am-late) Settle into the clubby, cosmopolitan atmosphere of Morrie's, either for breakfast or lunch, or later at night for cocktails and tapas or dinner. Local beers from Colonial Brewing are on tap, and the menu smartly channels both Asian and European flavours.

★**Miki's Open Kitchen** JAPANESE $$$

(Map p943; 08-9758 7673; www.facebook.com/mikisopenkitchen; 131 Bussell Hwy; small plates $12-16, large plates $28-37; 6pm-late Tue-Sat) Secure a spot around the open kitchen and enjoy the irresistible theatre of the Miki's team creating innovative Japanese spins on the best of WA seafood and produce. Combine a Margaret River wine with the $55 multicourse tasting menu for the most diverse experience, and settle in to watch the chefs work their tempura magic. Bookings recommended.

Shopping

Tunbridge Gallery ARTS

(Map p943; www.tunbridgegallery.com.au; 101 Bussell Hwy; 10am-5pm Mon-Sat, to 3pm Sun) Excellent Aboriginal art gallery featuring WA works.

Information

Visitor centre (Map p943; 08-9780 5911; www.margaretriver.com; 100 Bussell Hwy; 9am-5pm) Bookings and information plus displays on local wineries.

Getting There & Away

South West Coach Lines (08-9261 7600; www.transdevsw.com.au) Buses between Busselton and Augusta (12 weekly) stop at Cowaramup and Margaret River, linking with Perth on the weekends.

Transwa (1300 662 205; www.transwa.wa.gov.au) Coach SW1 (12 weekly) from Perth to Augusta stops at Yallingup and Margaret River, with three coaches weekly continuing to Pemberton.

Getting Around

Margaret River Beach Bus (08-9757 9532; www.margaretriverbackpackers.com.au) Minibus linking the township and the beaches around Prevelly ($10, three daily); summer only, bookings essential.

Around Margaret River

West of the township, the coastline provides spectacular surfing and walks. Prevelly is the main settlement, with a scattering of places to sleep and eat.

Sights & Activities

CaveWorks & Lake Cave CAVE

(Map p940; www.margaretriver.com; Conto Rd; single cave adult/child $22/10; 9am-5pm, Lake Cave tours hourly 9.30am-3.30pm) The main ticket office for Lake, Mammoth and Jewel Caves, CaveWorks also has excellent displays about caves, cave conservation and local fossil discoveries. There's also an authentic model cave and a 'cave crawl' experience. Single cave tickets include entry to CaveWorks. The **Grand Tour Pass** (adult/child $55/24), covering CaveWorks and all three caves, is valid for seven days, while the **Ultimate Pass** (adult/child $70/30) also includes Cape Leeuwin lighthouse. CaveWorks is 20km south of Margaret River, off Caves Rd.

Mammoth Cave CAVE

(Map p940; www.margaretriver.com; Caves Rd; adult/child $22/10; 9am-5pm) Mammoth Cave boasts a fossilised jawbone of *Zygomaturus trilobus*, a giant wombatlike creature, as well as other fossil remains and the impressive Mammoth Shawl formation. Visits are self-guided; an MP3 audio player is provided.

Calgardup & Giants Caves CAVES
(www.parks.dpaw.wa.gov.au) These two self-guided caves are managed by the Department of Environment and Conservation (DEC), which provides helmets and torches. **Calgardup Cave** (Map p940; Caves Rd; adult/child $15/8; ⏲9am-4.15pm) has a seasonal underground lake and is an attractive illustration of the role of the caves in the ecosystem – a stream transports nutrients to the creatures living in the cave, while tree roots hang overhead. **Giants Cave** (Map p940; Caves Rd; adult/child $15/8; ⏲9.30am-3.30pm school & public holidays only), further south, is deeper and longer and has some steep ladders and scrambles.

Eagles Heritage WILDLIFE RESERVE
(Map p940; ☎08-9757 2960; www.eaglesheritage.com.au; adult/child $17/10; ⏲10am-4.15pm Sat-Thu) Housing Australia's largest collection of raptors, this centre, 5km south of Margaret River, rehabilitates many birds of prey each year. There are free-flight displays at 11am and 1.30pm.

Boranup Drive SCENIC DRIVE
This 14km diversion runs along an unsealed road through Leeuwin-Naturaliste National Park's beautiful karri forest. Near the southern end there's a lookout offering sea views.

Sleeping

Surfpoint GUESTHOUSE $
(Map p940; ☎08-9757 1777; www.surfpoint.com.au; Reidle Dr, Gnarabup; s/d from $70/110; @📶🏊) This light and airy place offers the beach on a budget. The rooms are clean and well presented, and there's a very enticing little pool. Private rooms with bathroom are good value.

★ **Acacia Chalets** CHALET $$$
(Map p940; ☎08-9757 2718; www.acaciachalets.com.au; 113 Yates Rd; d $250-280; ❄) Private bushland – complete with marsupial locals – conceals three luxury chalets that are well located to explore the region's vineyards, caves and rugged nearby coastline. Limestone walls and honey-coloured jarrah floors combine for some of the area's best self-contained accommodation. Spacious decks are equipped with gas barbecues.

Eating & Drinking

Voyager Estate WINERY
(Map p940; ☎08-9757 6354; www.voyagerestate.com.au; Stevens Rd; ⏲10am-5pm, tours 11am Tue, Thu, Sat & Sun) The formal gardens and Cape Dutch–style buildings delight at Voyager Estate, the grandest of Margaret River's wineries. Tours are available ($25 to $75 including tastings and lunch).

Leeuwin Estate WINERY
(Map p940; ☎08-9759 0000; www.leeuwinestate.com.au; Stevens Rd; mains $31 39; ⏲10am-5pm daily, dinner Sat) Another impressive estate, with tall trees and lawns gently rolling down to the bush. Its Art Series Chardonnay is one of the best in the country. Behind-the-scenes wine tours and tastings take place at 11am (adult/child $12.50/4). Big open-air concerts are regularly held here.

Augusta & Around

POP 1700

Augusta is positioned at the mouth of the Blackwood River, 5km north of Cape Leeuwin. There are a few vineyards scattered around, but the vibe here is less epicurean, more languid.

Sights & Activities

Cape Leeuwin Lighthouse LIGHTHOUSE
(Map p940; www.margaretriver.com; adult/child $8/5; ⏲9am-4.30pm) Wild and windy Cape Leeuwin, where the Indian and Southern Oceans meet, is the most southwesterly point in Australia. It takes its name from a Dutch ship that passed here in 1622. The lighthouse (1896), WA's tallest, offers magnificent views of the coastline. **Tours** (adult/child $20/13) leave every 40 minutes from 9am to 4.20pm – expect a short wait during the holiday season. The **Ultimate Pass** (adult/child $70/30) incorporates admission to the lighthouse with Jewel, Lake and Mammoth Caves.

Jewel Cave CAVE
(Map p940; www.margaretriver.com; Caves Rd; adult/child $22/10; ⏲tours hourly 9.30am-3.30pm) The most spectacular of the region's caves, Jewel Cave has an impressive 5.9m straw stalactite, so far the longest seen in a tourist cave. Fossil remains of a Tasmanian tiger (thylacine), believed to be 3500 years old, were discovered here. It's located near the south end of Caves Rd, 8km northwest of Augusta. **The Grand Tour Pass** (adult/child $55/24) incorporates admission to the Jewel, Lake and Mammoth Caves.

Absolutely Eco River Cruises CRUISE
(☎08-9758 4003; cdragon@westnet.com.au; adult/child $30/15; ⏲Oct-May) Blackwood River; October to May.

Miss Flinders CRUISE
(☎0409 377 809; adult/child $30/15; ⊙Oct-May) Blackwood River; October to May.

Sleeping & Eating

Hamelin Bay Holiday Park CARAVAN PARK $
(Map p940; ☎08-9758 5540; www.hamelinbayholidaypark.com.au; Hamelin Bay West Rd; 2-person sites $28-45, cabins $90-220) Absolute beachfront, northwest of Augusta, this secluded place gets very busy during holiday times.

Baywatch Manor YHA HOSTEL $
(☎08-9758 1290; www.baywatchmanor.com.au; 9 Heppingstone View, Augusta; dm $29, d with/without bathroom $93/73; @📶) Clean, modern rooms with creamy brick walls and pieces of antique furniture. There is a bay view from the deck and, in winter, a roaring fire in the communal lounge. Some doubles have compact balconies.

Deckchair Gourmet CAFE $
(Blackwood Ave, Augusta; mains $10-25; ⊙8am-3pm Mon-Sat, to noon Sun; 📶) Excellent coffee and good food. Try the bacon and egg wrap for breakfast.

Information

Visitor centre (☎08-9758 0166; www.margaretriver.com; cnr Blackwood Ave & Ellis St, Augusta; ⊙9am-5pm) Information and bookings.

SOUTHERN FORESTS

The tall forests of WA's southwest are simply magnificent, with towering gums (karri, jarrah, marri) sheltering cool undergrowth. Between the forests, small towns bear witness to the region's history of logging and mining. Many have redefined themselves as small-scale tourist centres where you can take walks, wine tours, canoe trips and trout- and marron-fishing expeditions.

Nannup

POP 500

Nannup's historic weatherboard buildings and cottage gardens have an idyllic bush setting on the Blackwood River. The Noongar-derived name means 'a place to stop and rest', which indeed it still is, although it's also a good base for bushwalkers and canoeists. **Blackwood River Canoeing** (☎08-9756 1209; www.blackwoodrivercanoeing.com; hire per day from $25) provides equipment, basic instruction and transfers for paddle-powered excursions.

Sporadic but persistent stories of sightings of a striped wolflike animal, dubbed the Nannup tiger, have led to hopes that a thylacine (Tasmanian tiger) may have survived in the surrounding bush (the last known one died at Hobart Zoo in 1936). Keep your camera handy and your eyes peeled!

The **Nannup Music Festival** (www.nannup-musicfestival.org) is held in early March, focusing on folk and world music.

Sleeping & Eating

Caravan Park CARAVAN PARK $
(☎08-9756 1211; www.nannupcaravanparks.com.au; sites $27-32) This riverside caravan park has overflow camping at two other nearby sites.

Holberry House B&B $$
(☎08-9756 1276; www.holberryhouse.com; 14 Grange Rd; r $140-190; 📶🏊) The decor might lean towards granny-chic, but this large house on the hill has charming hosts and comfortable rooms. It's surrounded by large gardens dotted with quirky sculptures (open to nonguests for $4).

Pickle & O CAFE $
(16 Warren Rd; snacks $7-12; ⊙10am-4pm; 🥗) 🍃 Good coffee, huge slabs of cheesecake, and smoked trout kebab wraps are all tasty reasons to stop in at this quirky combination of health food store and organic and sustainable cafe.

Information

Visitor Centre (☎08-9756 1211; www.nannup-wa.com; 4 Brockman St; ⊙9am-5pm Mon-Fri, 10am-3pm Sat, 10am-1pm Sun) Administers the neighbouring caravan park.

Bridgetown

POP 2400

Spread around the Blackwood River and surrounded by karri forests and farmland, Bridgetown is one of the loveliest little towns in the southwest. Despite being busy most weekends, and overrun with visitors on the second weekend of November during its annual **Blues at Bridgetown Festival** (www.bluesatbridgetown.com.au), it retains a community feel.

Sleeping & Eating

Bridgetown Riverside Chalets CHALET $$
(08-9761 1040; www.bridgetownchalets.com.au; 1338 Brockman Hwy; chalets from $140) On a rural riverside property, 5km up the road to Nannup, these four stand alone wooden chalets (complete with pot-bellied stoves and washing machines) sleep up to six in two bedrooms.

Barking Cow CAFE $$
(88 Hampton St; breakfast $11-18, lunch $13-21; 8am-2.30pm Mon-Sat) Colourful, cosy, and serving the best coffee in town, the Barking Cow is also worth stopping at for daily vegetarian specials and world-famous-in-Bridgetown gourmet burgers.

Cidery CAFE $$
(www.thecidery.com.au; 43 Gifford Rd; mains $10-25; 11am-4pm Sat-Thu, to 8pm Fri) Craft beer, cider and light lunches on outdoor tables by the river. On Friday nights from 5.30pm there's live music.

Information

Visitor centre (08-9761 1740; www.bridgetown.com.au; 154 Hampton St; 9am-5pm Mon-Fri, 10am-3pm Sat, 10am-1pm Sun) Includes apple-harvesting memorabilia.

Pemberton

POP 760

Hidden deep in the karri forests, drowsy Pemberton has taken an epicurean turn, producing excellent wine that rivals Margaret River's for quality if not scale. Wine tourism isn't as developed here, with some of the better names only offering tastings by appointment; grab a free map listing opening hours from the visitor centre.

The national parks circling Pemberton are impressive. Aim to spend a day or two driving the Karri Forest Explorer, walking the trails and picnicking in the green depths.

Activities

Salitage WINERY
(08-9776 1195; www.salitage.com.au; Vasse Hwy; 10am-4pm Fri-Tue) Sailtage's pinot noir has been rated the state's best, while its chardonnay and sauvignon blanc are also very highly regarded. Hour-long vineyard tours leave at 11am; call ahead.

WORTH A TRIP

MANJIMUP

To learn more about how the world's most expensive produce is harvested, follow your snout to the **Truffle & Wine Co** (08-9777 2474; www.truffleandwine.com.au; Seven Day Rd, Manjimup; 10am-4pm, lunch noon-3pm). Join a 2½-hour truffle hunt with the clever clogs truffle-hunting Labradors on Saturday or Sunday from June to August (adult/child $60/30; book ahead). A three-course truffle-infused lunch ($65) is optional afterwards. Throughout the year, there's plenty of truffle products to sample, and the attached provedore and cafe serves up cheese and charcuterie platters, and coffee and cake. Manjimup is en route from Bridgetown to Pemberton; the turn-off to the Truffle & Wine Co is about 3km south of town.

Pemberton Tramway TRAM RIDES
(08-9776 1322; www.pemtram.com.au; adult/child $24/12; 10.45am & 2pm) Built between 1929 and 1933, the route travels through lush karri and marri forests to Warren River. A commentary is provided and it's a fun – if noisy – 1¾-hour return trip.

Pemberton Wine Centre WINERY
(www.marima.com.au; 388 Old Vasse Rd; noon-4pm Mon-Fri) At the very heart of Warren National Park, this centre offers tastings of local wines and can compile a mixed case of your favourites.

Tours

Pemberton Hiking & Canoeing HIKING, CANOEING
(08-9776 1559; www.hikingandcanoeing.com.au; half/full day $50/100) Environmentally sound tours in Warren and D'Entrecasteaux National Parks and to the Yeagarup sand dunes. Specialist tours (wild flowers, frogs, rare fauna) are also available, as are night canoeing trips ($50) to spot nocturnal wildlife.

Pemberton Discovery Tours DRIVING, MOUNTAIN BIKING
(08-9776 0484; www.pembertondiscoverytours.com.au; 12 Brockman St; adult/child $105/50) Half-day 4WD tours to the Yeagarup sand dunes and the Warren River mouth. Other tours focus on local vineyards, breweries and cideries, and the wild coastal scenery of

WORTH A TRIP

KARRI FOREST EXPLORER

Punctuated by glorious walks, magnificent individual trees, picnic areas and lots of interpretive signage, this tourist drive wends its way along 86km of scenic (partly unsealed) roads through three national parks (vehicle entry $12).

Attractions include the **Gloucester Tree**; if you're feeling fit and fearless, make the 58m climb to the top. The **Dave Evans Bicentennial Tree**, tallest of the 'climbing trees' at 68m, is in Warren National Park, 11km south of Pemberton. The Bicentennial Tree one-way loop via **Maiden Bush** to the **Heartbreak Trail** passes through 250-year-old karri stands.

North of Pemberton, **Big Brook Arboretum** features big trees from all over the world.

The track loops on and off the main roads, so you can drive short sections at a time. Pick up a brochure from Pemberton's visitor centre.

D'Entrecasteaux National Park. Visit their central Pemberton location for local information and mountain-bike hire including details of nearby tracks and recommended rides.

Donnelly River Cruises BOAT TOUR
(08-9777 1018; www.donnellyrivercruises.com.au; adult/child $65/35) Cruises through 12km of D'Entrecasteaux National Park to the cliffs of the Southern Ocean.

Sleeping & Eating

Local culinary specialities are trout and marron.

Pemberton Backpackers YHA HOSTEL $
(08-9776 1105; www.yha.com.au; 7 Brockman St; dm/s/d $33/70/77;) The main hostel is given over to seasonal workers, but you'll need to check in here for a room in the separate cottage (8 Dean St) that's set aside for travellers. It's cute and cosy, but book ahead as it only has three rooms, one of which is a six-person dorm.

Old Picture Theatre Holiday Apartments APARTMENT $$
(08-9776 1513; www.oldpicturetheatre.com.au; cnr Ellis & Guppy Sts; apt $160-210;) The town's old cinema has been revamped into well-appointed, self-contained, spacious apartments with lots of jarrah detail and black-and-white movie photos. It offers good value for money and includes an on-site spa.

★ **Foragers** COTTAGES $$$
(08-9776 1580; www.foragers.com.au; cnr Roberts & Northcliffe Rds; cottages $225-270;) Choose between very nice, simple karri cottages, or leap to the top of the ladder with the luxury eco-chalets. The latter are light and airy, with elegant, contemporary decor, eco-conscious waste-water systems and a solar-passive design. You're also right on hand to enjoy culinary treats at the adjacent Foragers Field Kitchen.

Marima Cottages COTTAGE $$$
(08-9776 1211; www.marima.com.au; 388 Old Vasse Rd; cottages $249-269) Right in the middle of Warren National Park, these four country-style rammed-earth-and-cedar cottages with pot-bellied stoves and lots of privacy are luxurious getaways. Look forward to marsupial company at dusk.

Holy Smoke CAFE, SELF-CATERING $
(www.holysmoke.com.au; Dickinson St; snacks $5-15; 10am-4pm Mon-Fri, from 9am Sat & Sun) Good coffee and tasty cakes and toasted sandwiches adjacent to the excellent **Pemberton Fine Woodcraft Gallery**. Especially good are the tasting platters of Holy Smoke's smoked meats, fish and pâtés.

Foragers Field Kitchen INTERNATIONAL $$$
(08-9776 1503; www.foragers.com.au; cnr Roberts & Northcliffe Rds; dinner $55-75) Join renowned chef Sophie Zalokar at one of her regular Friday or Saturday set dinners – options could include wood-fired Italian dishes or seasonal four-course menus – or sign up for one of her **cooking classes** (usually on a Wednesday night). Check the website's events calendar for dates. Booking at least 48 hours ahead is preferred.

Information

Department of Parks & Wildlife (08-9776 1207; www.dpaw.wa.gov.au; Kennedy St; 8am-4.30pm) Information on local parks and bushwalks.

Visitor centre (08-9776 1133; www.pembertonvisitor.com.au; Brockman St; 9am-4pm) Includes a pioneer museum and karri-forest discovery centre.

Southern WA

Includes ➡

Best Places to Eat

- ➡ York Street Cafe (p956)
- ➡ Mrs Jones (p953)
- ➡ Maleeya's Thai Cafe (p959)
- ➡ Pepper & Salt (p953)
- ➡ Boston Brewery (p953)

Best Places to Stay

- ➡ Cape Howe Cottages (p953)
- ➡ Beach House at Bayside (p956)
- ➡ Esperance B&B by the Sea (p963)
- ➡ The Lily (p960)

Why Go?

Standing above the waves and cliffs of the rugged South Coast is an exhilarating experience. And on calm days, when the sea is aquamarine and white-sand beaches lie pristine and welcoming, it's an altogether different type of magnificent. Even busy summer holiday periods down here in the Great Southern are relaxed. It's just that bit too far from Perth for the holiday hordes.

Winter months bring pods of migrating whales, while the spectacular tingle trees of Walpole's Valley of the Giants are more super-sized evidence of nature's wonder.

For a change from the great outdoors, Albany – the state's earliest European settlement – has colonial and Anzac history, and Denmark has excellent wine, craft beer and good food.

From Esperance, strike out north to begin a compelling cross-country adventure across the Nullarbor Plain from Norseman, or continue on to the gold-mining past, present and future of rambunctious Kalgoorlie.

When to Go

Esperance

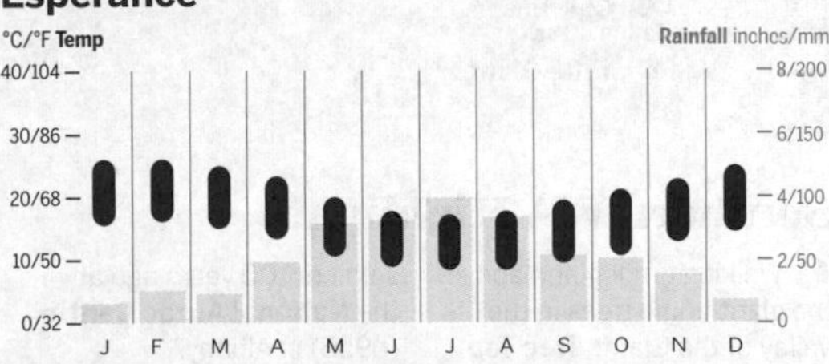

Jan The best beach weather – and it's not as hot or crowded as the west coast.

Sep Go wild for wild flowers and whales.

Dec Perfect weather for the Stirling Range and Porongurup National Parks.

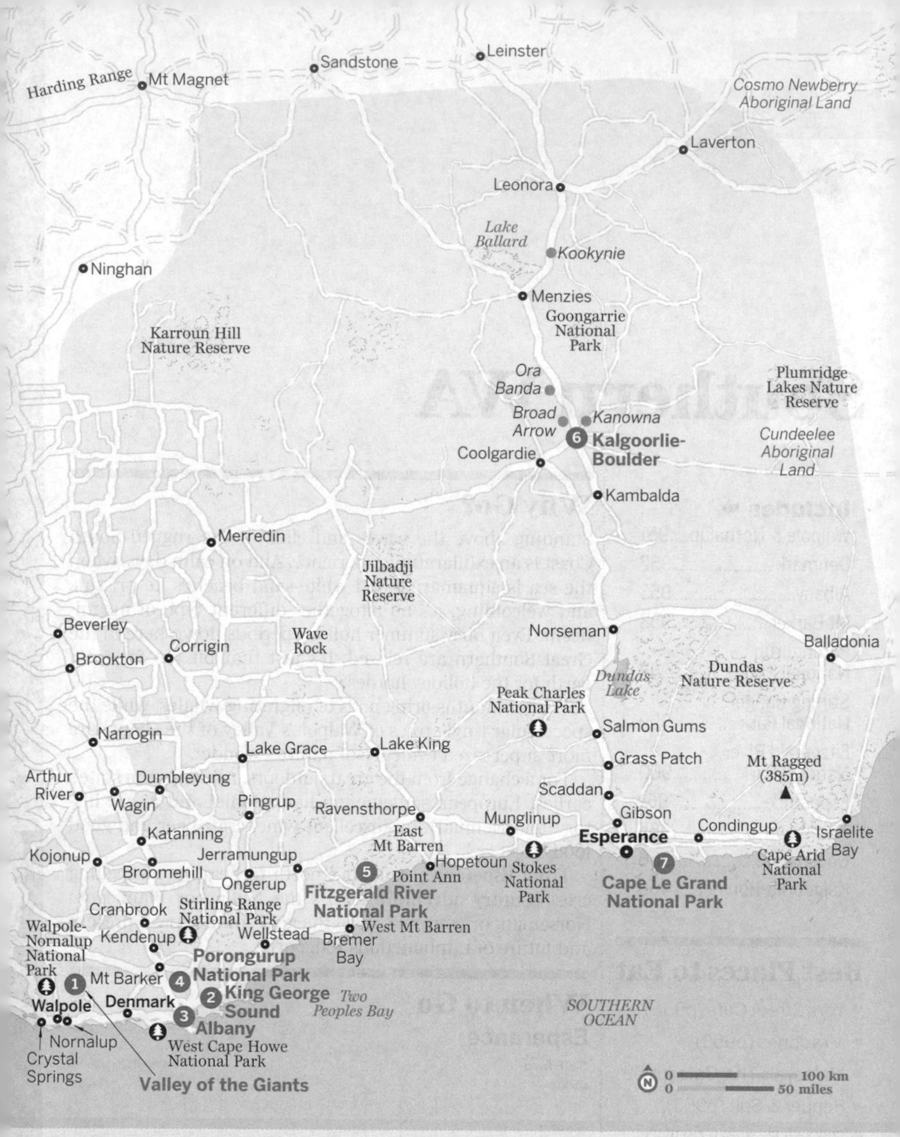

Harding Range
Mt Magnet
Sandstone
Leinster
Cosmo Newberry Aboriginal Land
Laverton
Leonora
Lake Ballard
Kookynie
Ninghan
Menzies
Goongarrie National Park
Karroun Hill Nature Reserve
Ora Banda
Broad Arrow
Kanowna
Plumridge Lakes Nature Reserve
Cundeelee Aboriginal Land
6 Kalgoorlie-Boulder
Coolgardie
Kambalda
Merredin
Jilbadji Nature Reserve
Beverley
Wave Rock
Corrigin
Brookton
Norseman
Balladonia
Dundas Lake
Dundas Nature Reserve
Peak Charles National Park
Salmon Gums
Narrogin
Lake Grace
Lake King
Grass Patch
Mt Ragged (385m)
Arthur River
Dumbleyung
Wagin
Pingrup
Scaddan
Ravensthorpe
Munglinup
Gibson
Katanning
East Mt Barren
Esperance
Condingup
Israelite Bay
Kojonup
Jerramungup
Broomehill
Ongerup
5 Point Ann
Hopetoun
Stokes National Park
7 Cape Le Grand National Park
Cape Arid National Park
Fitzgerald River National Park
Cranbrook
Stirling Range National Park
West Mt Barren
Walpole-Nornalup National Park
Kendenup
Wellstead
Bremer Bay
Porongurup National Park
1 Mt Barker
4
2 King George Sound
Two Peoples Bay
Walpole
Denmark
3 Albany
SOUTHERN OCEAN
Nornalup
Crystal Springs
West Cape Howe National Park
Valley of the Giants
0 100 km
0 50 miles

Southern WA Highlights

1. Walking among and above the giant tingle trees in the Valley of the Giants **Tree Top Walk** (p951).
2. Competing to see who can spot the most whales in Albany's **King George Sound** (p956).
3. Understanding the sacrifices made by brave soldiers 100 years ago at the **National Anzac Centre** (p955) in Albany.
4. Hiking among the tall trees and granite outcrops of **Porongurup National Park** (p958).
5. Wandering through wild flowers along the walking tracks of **Fitzgerald River National Park** (p960).
6. Feeling dwarfed in the depths of the spectacular Super Pit in **Kalgoorlie** (p966).
7. Swimming, surfing and soaking up the sun at the beaches of **Cape Le Grand National Park** (p964).

Walpole & Nornalup

The peaceful twin inlets of Walpole (pop 320) and Nornalup (pop 50) make good bases for exploring the heavily forested Walpole Wilderness Area – an immense wilderness incorporating a rugged coastline, several national parks, marine parks, nature reserves and forest conservation areas – covering a whopping 3630 sq km. Walpole is the bigger settlement, and it's here that the South Western Hwy (Rte 1) becomes the South Coast Hwy.

Sights & Activities

Walpole-Nornalup National Park NATURE RESERVE
(www.parks.dpaw.wa.gov.au) Giant trees include red, yellow and Rates tingle trees (all types of eucalypt, or gum, trees). Good walking tracks include a section of the Bibbulmun Track, which passes through Walpole to Coalmine Beach. Scenic drives include the Knoll Drive, 3km east of Walpole; the Valley of the Giants Road; and through pastoral country to Mt Frankland, 29km north of Walpole. Here you can climb to the summit for panoramic views or walk around the trail at its base. Opposite Knoll Drive, Hilltop Rd leads to a giant tingle tree; this road continues to the Circular Pool on the Frankland River, a popular canoeing spot. You can hire canoes from Nornalup Riverside Chalets.

Valley of the Giants NATURE RESERVE
(www.valleyofthegiants.com.au; Tree Top Walk adult/child $15/7.50; 9am-5pm, free guided tours 10.15am, 11.30am & 2pm) In the Valley of the Giants is the spectacular **Tree Top Walk.** A 600m-long ramp rises from the valley, allowing visitors access high into the canopy of the giant tingle trees. At its highest point, the ramp is 40m above the ground. It's on a gentle incline so it's easy to walk and is accessible by assisted wheelchair. At ground level, the Ancient Empire boardwalk (admission free) meanders through veteran red tingles, up to 16m in circumference and 46m high.

Conspicuous Cliffs LANDMARK
Midway between Nornalup and Peaceful Bay, Conspicuous Cliffs is a good spot for whale watching from July to November. There's a hilltop lookout and a steepish 800m walk to the beach.

Tours

WOW Wilderness Ecocruises CRUISE
(08-9840 1036; www.wowwilderness.com.au; adult/child $45/15) The magnificent landscape and its ecology are brought to life with anecdotes about Aboriginal settlement, salmon fishers and shipwrecked pirates. The 2½-hour cruise through the inlets and river systems leaves at 10am daily; book at the visitor centre.

Naturally Walpole Eco Tours ECOTOUR
(08-9840 1019; www.naturallywalpole.com.au) Half-day tours exploring the Walpole Wilderness (adult/child $95/55) and the Tree Top Walk (adult/child $105/60). Also customised winery and wild flower tours.

Sleeping

There are bush camping sites in the Walpole Wilderness Area, including at Crystal Springs and Fernhook Falls.

Walpole Lodge HOSTEL $
(08-9840 1244; www.walpolelodge.com.au; Pier St, Walpole; dm/s $27/45, d $65-90; @) This popular place is basic, open plan and informal, with great info boards and casual, cheery owners. En-suite rooms are excellent value.

Tingle All Over YHA HOSTEL $
(08-9840 1041; www.yha.com.au; 60 Nockolds St, Walpole; dm/s/d $31/54/74; @) Help yourself to lemons and chillies from the garden of this clean, basic option near the highway. Lots of advice on local walks is on offer.

Rest Point Holiday Village CARAVAN PARK $
(08-9840 1032; www.restpoint.com.au; Rest Point; 2-person sites $26, cabins $80-125) Set on wide lawns with direct water frontage, this spacious holiday park has shade for campers and a range of self-contained accommodation.

Riverside Retreat CHALETS $$
(08-9840 1255; www.riversideretreat.com.au; South Coast Hwy, Nornalup; chalets $150-210) On the banks of the beautiful Frankland River, these well-equipped chalets are great value, with pot-bellied stoves for cosy winter warmth, and tennis and canoeing as outdoor pursuits. Expect frequent visits from the local wildlife.

Nornalup Riverside Chalets CHALETS $$
(08-9840 1107; www.walpole.org.au/nornalupriversidechalets; Riverside Dr, Nornalup; chalets $110-180) Stay a night in sleepy Nornalup in

> **THE ROAD TO MANDALAY**
>
> About 13km west of Walpole, at Crystal Springs, is an 8km gravel road to **Mandalay Beach**, where the *Mandalay*, a Norwegian barque, was wrecked in 1911. The wreck eerily appears every 10 years or so after storms. See the photos at Walpole visitor centre. The beach is glorious, often deserted, and accessed by a boardwalk across sand dunes and cliffs. It's part of D'Entrecasteaux National Park.

these comfortable, colourful self-contained chalets, just a rod's throw from the fish in the Frankland River. The chalets are well spaced out, giving a feeling of privacy.

Eating

Thurlby Herb Farm CAFE $$
(www.thurlbyherb.com.au; 3 Gardiner Rd; mains $15-20; ⏲9am-5pm Mon-Fri) Thurlby offers light lunches and cakes accompanied by fresh-picked teas, as well as other herb-based products including soap and aromatherapy treatments. It's north of Walpole on the way to Mt Frankland National Park.

Top Deck Cafe CAFE $$
(25 Nockolds St, Walpole; mains $15-27; ⏲9am-2pm & 5.30-9pm) Tucked away in Walpole's main road, Top Deck kicks off with breakfast, and graduates to dinner options including spinach-and-feta pie and a daily curry special.

Information

The **Visitor Centre** (☎08-9840 1111; www.walpole.com.au; South Coast Hwy, Walpole; ⏲9am-5pm; @) is located in Pioneer Cottage.

Getting There & Away

Departing from the visitor centre, **Transwa** (☎1300 662 205; www.transwa.wa.gov.au) bus GS3 heads daily to/from Bunbury ($45, 4½ hours), Bridgetown ($26, 3¼ hours), Pemberton ($20, 1¾ hours), Denmark ($14, 42 minutes) and Albany ($22, 1½ hours).

Denmark

POP 2800

Denmark's beaches and coastline, river and sheltered inlet, forested backdrop and hinterland have attracted a varied, creative and environmentally aware community. Farmers, ferals, fishers and families all mingle during the town's four market days each year.

Denmark was established to supply timber to the early goldfields. Known by the Minang Noongar people as Koorabup (place of the black swan), there's evidence of early Aboriginal settlement in the 3000-year-old fish traps found in Wilson Inlet.

Sights & Activities

Denmark is located in the cool-climate Great Southern wine region and notable wineries include **Howard Park** (www.burchfamilywines.com.au; Scotsdale Rd; ⏲10am-4pm) and **Forest Hill** (www.foresthillwines.com.au; cnr South Coast Hwy & Myers Rd; ⏲10am-4pm). The latter features the excellent Pepper & Salt (p953) restaurant.

Surfing & Fishing

Surfers and anglers should head to ruggedly beautiful **Ocean Beach**. Accredited local instructor Mike Neunuebel gives **surfing lessons** (☎0401 349 8540; www.southcoastsurfinglessons.com.au; 2hr lessons incl equipment from $60).

Walking

To get your bearings, walk the **Mokare Heritage Trail** (a 3km circuit along the Denmark River), or the **Wilson Inlet Trail** (12km return, starting at the river mouth), which forms part of the longer **Nornalup Trail**. The **Mt Shadforth Lookout** has fine coastal views, and lush **Mt Shadforth Rd**, running from town to the South Coast Hwy west of town, makes a great scenic drive. A longer pastoral loop is via **Scotsdale Rd**. Attractions include alpaca farms, wineries, dairy farms, and arts and craft galleries.

Swimming

William Bay National Park, about 20km west of town, offers sheltered swimming in gorgeous **Greens Pool** and **Elephant Rocks**, and has good walking tracks. Swing by **Bartholomews Meadery** (www.honeywine.com.au; 2620 South Coast Hwy; ⏲9.30am-4.30pm) for a post-beach treat of mead (honey wine) or delicious home-made honey-rose-almond ice cream ($5).

Tours

Out of Sight! OUTDOORS
(☎08-9848 2814; www.outofsighttours.com; 5hr tour adult/child $150/75) 4WD nature trips exploring West Cape Howe National Park.

Denmark Wine Lovers Tour BUS TOUR
(☎0410 423 262; www.denmarkwinelovers.com.au) Full-day tours taking in Denmark wineries or heading further afield to Porongurup or Mt Barker.

Festivals & Events

Market Days MARKET
(www.denmarkarts.com.au) Four times a year (mid-December, early and late January and Easter) Denmark hosts riverside market days with craft stalls, music and food.

Festival of Voice MUSIC
(www.denmarkfestivalofvoice.com.au) Performances and workshops on the early June long weekend.

Sleeping

Blue Wren Travellers' Rest YHA HOSTEL $
(☎08-9848 3300; www.denmarkbluewren.com.au; 17 Price St; dm/d/f $28/80/120) Great info panels cover the walls and it's small enough (just 20 beds) to have a homey feel. Bikes can also be rented – $20 per day – and the friendly owner, Graham, is a whiz at bike repairs.

Denmark Rivermouth Caravan Park CARAVAN PARK $
(☎08-98481262; www.denmarkrivermouthcaravanpark.com.au; Inlet Dr; 2-person sites $30, cabins & chalets $135-210) Ideally located for nautical pursuits, this caravan park sits along Wilson Inlet beside the boat ramp. Some of the units are properly flash, although they are quite tightly arranged. There's also a kids playground and kayaks for hire.

31 on the Terrace BOUTIQUE HOTEL $$
(☎08-9848 1700; www.denmarkaccommodation.com.au; 31 Strickland St; r $115-155; ❄) Good-value, stylish en-suite rooms – some with balconies – fill this renovated corner pub in the centre of town. Compact apartments sleep up to five people.

★**Cape Howe Cottages** COTTAGE $$$
(☎08-9845 1295; www.capehowe.com.au; 322 Tennessee Rd S; cottages $180-290; ❄) For a remote getaway, these five cottages in bushland southeast of Denmark really make the grade. They're all different, but the best is only 1.5km from dolphin-favoured Lowlands Beach and is properly plush – with a BBQ on the deck, a dishwasher in the kitchen and laundry facilities.

Celestine Retreat CHALETS $$$
(☎08-9848 3000; www.celestineretreat.com; 413 Mt Shadforth Rd; d $239-289; ❄) With just four spa chalets scattered over 13 hectares, there are stunning ocean and valley views at this luxury retreat. Romance is also on the agenda, with private spas, fluffy bathrobes and high-end bathroom goodies. Renovation aplenty was happening when we last dropped by.

Eating & Drinking

★**Mrs Jones** CAFE $$
(☎0467 481 878; www.mrsjonescafe.com; 12 Mt Shadforth Rd; mains $9-18; ⏰7am-4pm) Denmark's best coffee is at this spacious spot. Settle in with locals and tourists for interesting cafe fare, often with an Asian or Mediterranean spin. The mixed platter ($42) with prawns, squid and salmon makes a great lunch for two.

★**Pepper & Salt** MODERN AUSTRALIAN, ASIAN $$$
(☎08-9848 3053; www.pepperandsalt.com.au; 1564 South Coast Hwy, Forest Hill Vineyard; mains $38-42; ⏰noon-3pm Thu-Sun, from 6pm Fri) With his Fijian-Indian heritage, chef Silas Masih's knowledge of spices and herbs is wonderfully showcased in his fresh and vibrant food. Highlights include king prawns with chilli popcorn and lime mayonnaise, or the excellent tapas platter ($62), which effortlessly detours from Asia to the Middle East. Bookings essential.

Boston Brewery BREWERY
(www.willoughbypark.com.au; Willoughby Park Winery, South Coast Hwy; pizzas $17-18, mains $25-38; ⏰10am-7pm Mon-Thu, to 10pm Fri & Sat, to 9pm Sun) The industrial chic of the brewery gives way to an absolute edge-of-vineyard location, where wood-fired pizzas, meals and bar snacks go well with Boston's hoppy portfolio of four beers. The Willoughby Park Winery is also on site, and there's live music from 4pm to 8pm every second Saturday.

Information

The **Visitor Centre** (☎08-9848 2055; www.denmark.com.au; 73 South Coast Hwy; ⏰9am-5pm) has information, accommodation bookings, and a display on the local wine scene.

Getting There & Away

Transwa (☎1300 662 205; www.transwa.wa.gov.au) bus service GS3 heads daily to/from Bunbury ($51, 5½ hours), Bridgetown ($34, 4¾ hours), Pemberton ($28, 2¾ hours), Walpole ($14, 42 minutes) and Albany ($10, 42 minutes).

Albany

POP 25,200

Established shortly before Perth in 1826, the oldest European settlement in the state is now the bustling commercial centre of the southern region. Albany is a mixed bag comprising a stately and genteel decaying colonial quarter, a waterfront in the midst of sophisticated redevelopment and a hectic sprawl of malls and fast-food joints. Less ambivalent is its spectacular coastline, from Torndirrup National Park's surf-pummelled cliffs to Middleton Beach's white sands, and the calm waters of King George Sound.

The town is in an area that's seen the violence of weather and whaling. Whales are still a part of the Albany experience, but these days are hunted through a camera lens.

The **Bibbulmun Track** (www.bibbulmuntrack.org.au) ends (or starts) here, just outside the visitor centre.

History

The Minang Noongar people called this place Kinjarling (the place of rain) and be-

Albany

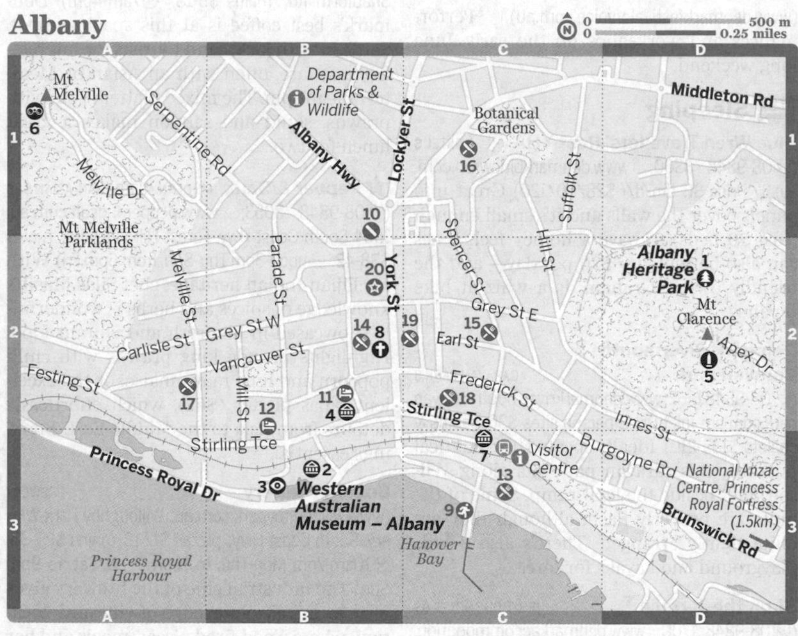

Albany

Top Sights
1 Albany Heritage Park D2
2 Western Australian Museum – Albany B3

Sights
3 Brig Amity B3
4 Courthouse B2
5 Desert Mounted Corps Memorial D2
6 Mt Melville Lookout Tower A1
7 Old Post Office C3
8 St John's Anglican Church B2

Activities, Courses & Tours
9 Albany Whale Tours C3
10 Southcoast Diving Supplies B1

Sleeping
11 1849 Backpackers B2
12 Albany Harbourside B2

Eating
13 Albany Boatshed Markets C3
14 Albany Farmers Market B2
15 Earl of Spencer C2
16 Lime 303 .... C1
17 Vancouver Cafe & Store A2
18 White Star Hotel C2
19 York Street Cafe C2

Entertainment
20 Town Hall B2

lieved that fighting Wargals (mystical giant serpents) created the fractured landscape.

Initial contacts with Europeans were friendly, with over 60 ships visiting between 1622 and 1826. The establishment of a British settlement was welcomed as it regulated the behaviour of sealers and whalers, who had been kidnapping, raping and murdering Minang people. Yet by the end of the 19th century, every shop in Albany refused entry to Aborigines, and control over every aspect of their lives (including the right to bring up their own children) had been lost.

For the British, Albany's raison d'être was its sheltered harbour, which made it a whaling port right up to 1978. During WWI it was the mustering point for transport ships for over 40,000 Australian and New Zealand Army Corps (Anzac) troops heading for Egypt and the Gallipoli campaign.

Sights

★ Albany Heritage Park — PARK

Inaugurated in 2014, the Albany Heritage Park incorporates the National Anzac Centre, Princess Royal Fortress, Padre White Lookout, Desert Mounted Corps Memorial and the Ataturk Memorial.

➡ National Anzac Centre

(www.nationalanzaccentre.com.au; Forts Rd, Princess Royal Fortress; adult/child $24/12; ⏲9am-4pm) Opened for Albany's Anzac centenary commemorations in late 2014, this new museum remembers the men and women who left by convoy from Albany to fight in WWI. Excellent multimedia installations provide realism and depth to the exhibitions, and there is a profound melancholy in the museum's location overlooking the same body of water the troop ships left from.

Visitors are assigned one of 32 photographs remembering actual soldiers and nurses upon entry – including a German soldier and a Turkish soldier – and they can then follow their life story on interactive installations. The exact fate of each of the people in the 32 photographs is poignantly not revealed until the final stages of the museum.

➡ Princess Royal Fortress

(Forts Rd; included with entry to the National Anzac Centre; ⏲9am-5pm) As a strategic port, Albany was historically regarded as being vulnerable to attack. Built in 1893 on Mt Adelaide, this fort was initially constructed as a defence against potential attacks from the Russians and French, and the restored buildings, gun emplacements and views are very interesting.

➡ Mt Melville & Mt Clarence

There are fine views over the coast and inland from Mt Clarence and **Mt Melville**. On top of Mt Clarence is the **Desert Mounted Corps Memorial**, originally erected in Port Said, Egypt as a WWI memorial. It was irreparably damaged during the Suez crisis in 1956, and this copy was made from masonry salvaged from the original. Mt Clarence sits atop Albany Heritage Park.

★ Western Australian Museum – Albany — MUSEUM

(www.museum.wa.gov.au; Residency Rd; admission by donation; ⏲10am-4.30pm) This branch of the state museum is split between two buildings. The newer Eclipse building has a kids' discovery section and a lighthouse exhibition. The restored 1850s home of the resident magistrate illuminates Minang Noongar history, local natural history and seafaring stories.

Brig Amity — SHIP

(adult/child $5/2; ⏲10am-4.30pm) This full-scale replica of the brig that carried Albany's first British settlers from Sydney in 1826 was completed for the city's 150th anniversary. Around the brig is a heritage area worth exploring.

Great Southern Distillery — DISTILLERY

(☎08-9842 5363; www.distillery.com.au; 252 Frenchman Bay Rd; tours $15; ⏲cellar door 10am-5pm, tours 1pm) Limeburners Single Malt whisky is the star at this waterfront distillery, but brandy, gin, absinthe and grappe also feature. Tours include tastings and there's a cafe offering tapas and snacks.

Historic Buildings

Near the foreshore is Albany's historic precinct. Take a stroll down Stirling Tce – noted for its Victorian shopfronts, **Courthouse** and **Old Post Office** – and up York St to **St John's Anglican Church** and Albany's **Town Hall** (www.albanytownhall.com.au; 217 York St). A guided walking-tour brochure is available from the visitor centre.

Beaches

East of the town centre, the beautiful Middleton and Emu Beaches face King George Sound and share one long stretch of family-friendly sand. In winter, you'll often see pods of mother whales and their calves here. Head around Emu Point to Oyster Harbour for swimming pontoons and even calmer waters.

A clifftop walking track hugs much of the waterfront between the town centre and Middleton Beach. Boardwalks continue along Emu Beach.

Activities

Whale Watching

After whaling ended in 1978, whales slowly began returning to the waters of Albany. Now southern right and humpback whales gather near the bays and coves of King George Sound from July to mid-October. You can sometimes spot them from the beach. Both **Albany Ocean Adventures** (0428 429 876; www.whales.com.au; adult/child $88/50; Jun-Oct) and **Albany Whale Tours** (08-9845 1068; www.albanywhaletours.com.au; Albany Waterfront Marina, cnr Princess Royal Dr & Toll Pl; adult/child $90/55; Jun-Oct) run whale-watching trips in season.

Diving

Albany's appeal as a top-class diving destination grew after the 2001 scuttling of the warship HMAS *Perth* to create an artificial reef for divers; visit www.hmasperth.com.au. **Southcoast Diving Supplies** (08-9841 7176; www.divealbany.com.au; 84b Serpentine Rd) can show you the underwater world.

Tours

Kalgan Queen BOAT TOUR
(08-9844 3166; www.albanyaustralia.com; Emu Point; adult/child $85/50; 9am Sep-Jun) Four-hour cruises up the Kalgan River in a glass-bottomed boat explain the history and wildlife of the area.

Sleeping

★1849 Backpackers HOSTEL $
(08-9842 1554; www.albanybackpackersaccommodation.com.au; 45 Peels Pl; dm $33, r $77;) Flags from many nations provide a colourful international welcome at this well-run hostel. A huge, modern kitchen, sunny rooms and a laid-back ambience make this one of WA's best stays for budget travellers. Make sure you book in for the free barbecue on Sunday night.

Albany Discovery Inn GUESTHOUSE $
(08-9842 5535; www.discoveryinn.com.au; 9 Middleton Rd, Middleton Beach; s $65, d $90-100;) Located close to the beach, Albany Discovery Inn features a cosy atmosphere with colourful rooms. Their cafe offers three-course evening meals for $20 and is also open for breakfast and lunch (mains $10 to $15). Outside dinner guests are welcome, but book ahead.

Emu Beach Holiday Park CARAVAN PARK $
(08-9844 1147; www.emubeach.com; 8 Medcalf Pde, Emu Point; sites $40, chalets $125-200;) Families love the Emu Beach area, and this friendly holiday park includes a BBQ area and a kids playground. Recently constructed motel units are spacious and modern.

Albany Harbourside APARTMENT $$
(08-9842 1769; www.albanyharbourside.com.au; 8 Festing St; d $159-219;) Albany Harbourside's portfolio includes spacious and spotless apartments on Festing St, and three other self-contained options arrayed around central Albany. Decor is modern and colourful, and some apartments have ocean views.

★Beach House at Bayside BOUTIQUE HOTEL $$$
(08-9844 8844; www.thebeachhouseatbayside.com.au; 33 Barry Ct, Collingwood Park; r $280-375;) Positioned right by the beach and the golf course in a quiet cul-de-sac, midway between Middleton Beach and Emu Point, this modern accommodation offers wonderful service. Rates include breakfast, afternoon tea, and evening port and chocolates.

Eating & Drinking

Albany Farmers Market FARMERS MARKET $
(www.albanyfarmermarket.com.au; Collie St; 8am-noon Sat) Weekly market with gourmet food and local artisan produce.

Albany Boatshed Markets MARKET $
(www.albanyboatshedmarkets.com; Princess Royal Dr, The Boatshed; 10am-1pm Sun) Local produce, arts and crafts, and wines from around the Great Southern area.

★York Street Cafe CAFE $$
(www.184york.com; 184 York St; breakfast & lunch $13-23, dinner $24-27; 7.30am-3pm Sun-Tue, 7.30am-late Wed-Sat;) The food is excellent at this cosmopolitan and versatile cafe on the main strip. Lunch includes Asian-style pork belly with spiced apple chutney on Turkish bread, while at dinner the attention turns to bistro items such as prosciutto-wrapped chicken on couscous. BYO wine.

Vancouver Cafe & Store CAFE $$
(☎08-9841 2475; 65 Vancouver St; mains $12-24, platters $32; ⏰8am-3.30pm) This heritage cafe features balcony views and delicious home baking. Toasted Turkish sandwiches combine with bigger dishes such as Moroccan lamb balls with pilaf and honey yoghurt, and good-value platters are a relaxed way to recharge over lunch.

White Star Hotel PUB FOOD $$
(72 Stirling Tce; mains $16-34; ⏰11am-late) With good beers on tap, excellent pub grub, a beer garden and lots of live music, this old pub gets a gold star. Sunday-night folk and blues gigs are a good opportunity to share a pint with Albany's laid-back locals.

Earl of Spencer PUB FOOD $$
(cnr Earl & Spencer Sts; mains $20-34; ⏰11.30am-late) Locals crowd in for the Earl's famous pie and pint deal or hearty lamb shanks. Live bands are regular visitors on weekends, often with a jaunty Irish brogue.

Lime 303 MODERN AUSTRALIAN $$$
(☎08-9845 7298; www.dogrockmotel.com.au; 303 Middleton Rd; mains $36-43; ⏰dinner 6pm-late, tapas 4.30-9pm) Pretty flash for regional WA, Lime 303 showcases local produce in dishes such as a creamy seafood moussaka with fish, scallops and prawns, and a confit duck and cabbage roll. More informal bar tapas are available from 4.30pm.

Information

Department of Parks & Wildlife (☎08-9842 4500; www.parks.dpaw.wa.gov.au; 120 Albany Hwy; ⏰8am-4.30pm Mon-Fri) For national park information.

Visitor Centre (☎08-9841 9290; www.amazingalbany.com; Proudlove Pde; ⏰9am-5pm) In the old train station.

Getting There & Away

Albany Airport (Albany Hwy) is 11km northwest of the city centre. **Skywest** (☎1300 660 088; www.skywest.com.au) has 18 flights a week to and from Perth (70 minutes).

Transwa (☎1300 662 205; www.transwa.wa.gov.au) services stop at the visitor centre. These include:

- GS1 to/from Perth ($61, six hours) and Mt Barker ($9.55, 39 minutes) daily.
- GS2 to/from Perth ($58, eight hours), Northam ($66, 6½ hours), York ($61, six hours) and Mt Barker ($9, 41 minutes) four times a week.
- GS3 to/from Bunbury ($58, six hours), Bridgetown ($45, 4¾ hours), Pemberton ($37, 3½ hours), Walpole ($22, 1½ hours) and Denmark ($9, 42 minutes) daily.

ALBANY TO ESPERANCE ALTERNATIVES

The rural 480km of South Coast Hwy (Rte 1) between Albany and Esperance is a relatively unpopulated stretch. Break up the first leg by taking the Albany Hwy (Rte 30) to Mt Barker, and then head east to Porongurup. Then travel north through the Stirling Ranges, and turn east again through Ongerup, and rejoin the highway at Jerramungup. This route adds 57km to the trip.

At Ongerup, the **Yongergnow Malleefowl Centre** (☎08-9828 2325; www.yongergnow.com.au; adult/child $8/4; ⏰10am-4pm Sat-Mon, Wed & Thu) is devoted to the conservation of a curious endangered bird that creates huge mounds to incubate its chicks.

Near Jerramungup is **Fitzgerald River National Park** – base yourself at Hopetoun or Bremer Bay. Note that Bremer Bay is best reached by taking the South Coast Hwy from Albany.

Getting Around

Loves (☎08-9841 1211) runs local bus services. The visitor centre has information on getting to Emu Point and Middleton Beach.

Around Albany

Discovery Bay MUSEUM
(☎08-9844 4021; www.discoverybay.com.au; Frenchman Bay Rd; adult/child $29/12; ⏰9am-5pm) When the Cheynes Beach Whaling Station ceased operations in November 1978, few could have guessed that the formerly gore-covered decks would eventually be covered in tourists discovering the area's bleakly fascinating story. An attached museum screens films about sharks and whales, and displays giant skeletons, harpoons, whaleboat models and scrimshaw (etchings on whalebone). Outside there's the rusting *Cheynes IV* whale chaser and station equipment to inspect. Free guided tours depart on the hour from 10am to 3pm. Part of the wider Discovery Bay complex is a new Australian wildlife park and botanic garden (adult/child $15/8) with plants endemic to the area. There are good ocean views from

the elevated sight, but the fledgeling gardens need a few years to develop more, and the animals – including koalas, pademelons and wallaroos – are cared for in fairly compact areas.

Torndirrup National Park NATIONAL PARK
(Frenchman Bay Rd) FREE Covering much of the peninsula enclosing the southern reaches of Princess Royal Harbour and King George Sound, this national park features windswept, ocean-bashed cliffs. **The Gap** is a natural cleft in the rock, channelling surf through walls of granite. Close by is the **Natural Bridge**. Further east, the **Blowholes** are spectacular. Rocky coves such as **Jimmy Newells Harbour** and **Salmon Holes** are popular with surfers. Better for swimmers are **Misery Beach** or **Frenchman Bay** on the peninsula's more sheltered side.

There's a challenging 10km-return bushwalk (five hours plus) over Isthmus Hill to Bald Heads.

Two Peoples Bay NATURE RESERVE
(Two Peoples Bay Rd) Around 20km east of Albany, Two Peoples Bay is a scenic 46-sq-km nature reserve with a good swimming beach.

Waychinicup National Park NATIONAL PARK
(Cheyne Beach Rd; park admission free, camp site adult/child $7.50/2.20) In a beautiful spot by the Waychinicup River, Gilbert's potoroos and scrub birds are often seen.

Mt Barker

POP 1770

Mt Barker (50km north of Albany) is the gateway to the Porongurup and Stirling Range National Parks. It's also the hub for the local wine industry. Pick up the *Mt Barker Wineries* map from the town's visitor centre and see www.mountbarkerwine.com.au.

Sights & Activities

Around 5km south of town, **Mt Barker** has excellent views. Southwest of Mt Barker, on the rolling grounds of the Egerton-Warburton estate, is the photogenic **St Werburgh's Chapel** (1872).

West Cape Howe Wines WINERY
(www.westcapehowewines.com.au; 14923 Muirs Hwy; ⏲cellar door 10am-5pm) In lovely grounds around 10km west of Mt Barker, West Cape Howe Wines are regular award winners for their riesling, merlot and cabernet sauvignon.

Plantagenet Wines WINE TASTING
(www.plantagenetwines.com; Albany Hwy; ⏲10am-4.30pm) Plantagenet Wines' cellar door is conveniently situated in the middle of town.

Mt Barker Police Station Museum MUSEUM
(Albany Hwy; adult/child $5/free; ⏲10am-3pm Sat & Sun) Mt Barker has been settled since the 1830s and the convict-built 1868 police station and gaol have been preserved as a museum.

Banksia Farm GARDENS
(☎08-9851 1770; www.banksiafarm.com.au; Pearce Rd; guided tours $20; ⏲tours 10am Mon-Fri mid Mar-mid Jun, daily mid Aug-mid Nov) See all 78 types and 24 subtypes of Australia's banksia plant at the Banksia Farm. There's also a cafe and B&B accommodation (singles/doubles from $95/150). From mid-August to mid-November 'Orchid Hunt' tours ($25) leave daily at 2pm.

Sleeping

Nomads Guest House GUESTHOUSE
(☎08-9851 2131; www.nomadsguesthousewa.com.au; 12 Morpeth St; s/d/yurts/chalets $70/90/100/110) A surprising sight is the authentic Mongolian yurt (felt tent) and gallery of Mongolian and Chinese art in the grounds of Nomads Guest House. The owners frequently rescue orphaned joeys (baby kangaroos), so don't be surprised to see a few temporary marsupial visitors in the main house.

Porongurup National Park

The 24-sq-km, 12km-long **Porongurup National Park** (entry per car $12) has 1100-million-year-old granite outcrops, panoramic views, beautiful scenery, large karri trees and some excellent bushwalks.

Bushwalks range from the 100m **Tree-in-the-Rock** stroll to the harder **Hayward and Nancy Peaks** (5.5km loop). The **Devil's Slide** (5km return) passes through karri forest to the stumpy vegetation of the granite zone. These walks start from the main day-use area (Bolganup Rd). **Castle Rock Trail to Balancing Rock** (3km return) starts further east, signposted off the Mt Barker–Porongurup Rd. The **Castle Rock Granite Skywalk Trail** (4.4km return, two hours) negotiates a steep and spectacular path up the rock. The final 200m ascent to the summit

Porongurup National Park

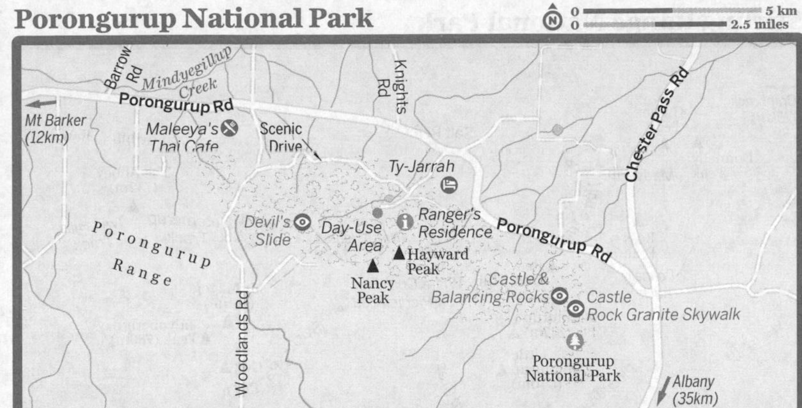

incorporates a steep rocky scramble and a vertical 7m ladder.

Porongurup is also part of the Great Southern wine region and there are 11 wineries in the vicinity. See www.porongurup.com.

Sleeping & Eating

There is no accommodation within the national park, but Ty-Jarrah is close by. Eating options are very limited.

Ty-Jarrah CHALET $$
(☎08-9853 1255; www.tyjarrah.com; 3 Bolganup Rd; ste/chalets $135/150) Located in a shady forest setting, these self-contained A-frame chalets are cosy and comfortable.

★ **Maleeya's Thai Cafe** THAI $$
(☎08-9853 1123; www.maleeya.com.au; 1376 Porongurup Rd; mains $25-33; ⏲11.30am-3pm & 6-9pm Fri-Sun) Foodies and chefs venture to Porongorup for some of WA's most authentic Thai food. Curries, soups and stir-fries all come punctuated with fresh herbs straight from Maleeya's garden, and other ingredients are organic and free range. Bookings recommended.

Stirling Range National Park

Rising abruptly from the surrounding flat and sandy plains, the Stirling Range's propensity to change colour through blues, reds and purples captivates photographers during the spectacular wild flower season from late August to early December. It's also recognised by the Noongar people as a place of special significance – a place where the spirits of the dead return. Every summit has an ancestral being associated with it, so it's appropriate to show proper respect when visiting.

This 1156-sq-km national park consists of a single chain of peaks pushed up by plate tectonics to form a range 10km wide and 65km long. Running most of its length are isolated summits, some knobbly and some perfect pyramids, towering above broad valleys covered in shrubs and heath. Bluff Knoll (Bular Mai), at 1095m, is the highest point in the southwest.

Park fees are charged at the start of Bluff Knoll Rd (entry per car/motorcycle $12/6).

Activities

The Stirlings are renowned for serious **bushwalking**. Keen walkers can choose from **Toolbrunup** (for views and a good climb; 1052m, 4km return) and **Bluff Knoll** (a well-graded tourist track; 1095m, 6km return). **Mt Hassell** (848m, 3km return) and **Talyuberlup** (783m, 2.6km return) are popular half-day walks.

Challenging walks cross the eastern sector include those from **Bluff Knoll to Ellen Peak** (three days), or the shorter traverse from **The Arrows to Ellen Peak** (two days).

Sleeping & Eating

Stock up on food in Mt Barker.

Stirling Range Retreat CARAVAN PARK $
(☎08-9827 9229; www.stirlingrange.com.au; 8639 Chester Pass Rd; unpowered/powered 2-person sites $32/34, cabins $55-95, units $145-185;

Stirling Range National Park

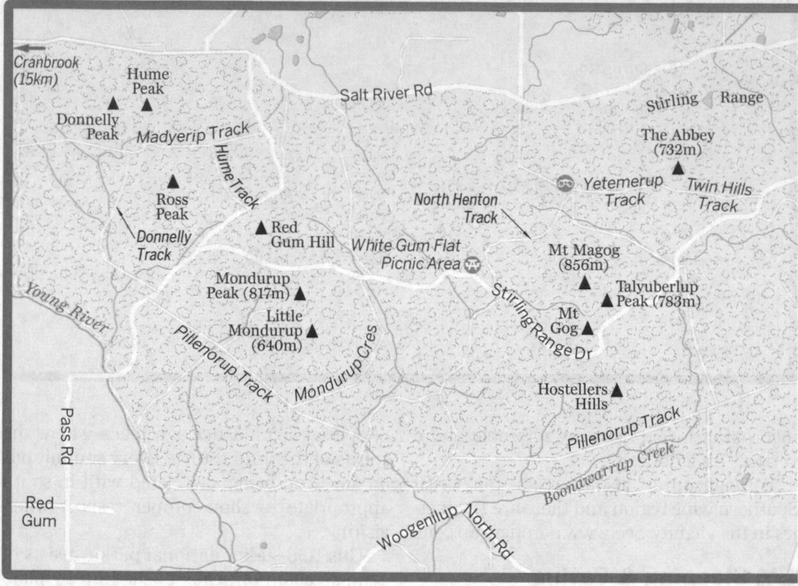

❄@≋) On the park's northern boundary, this shaded area offers camp sites, cabins and vans, and self-contained, rammed-earth units. Wild flower and orchid bus tours and walkabouts (three hours, per person $49) are conducted from mid-August to the end of October. The swimming pool only opens from November to April.

Mount Trio Bush Camping & Caravan Park CARAVAN PARK **$**
(☎08-9827 9270; www.mttrio.com.au; Salt River Rd; unpowered/powered sites per person $13/15) Rustic bush campground on a farm property close to the walking tracks, north of the centre of the park. It has hot showers, a kitchen, free gas BBQs and a campfire pit. Guided walks from 90 minutes to one day are on offer.

★**The Lily** COTTAGES **$$**
(☎08-9827 9205; www.thelily.com.au; Chester Pass Rd; cottages $149-179) These cottages 12km north of the park are grouped around a working windmill. Accommodation is self-contained, and meals are available for guests at the neighbouring restaurant. Call to enquire which nights the restaurant is open to the public and to arrange mill tours ($50, minimum of four people). There's also private accommodation in a restored 1944 Dakota aircraft.

Fitzgerald River National Park

Midway between Albany and Esperance, this gem of a park (entry per car/motorcycle $12/6) has been declared a Unesco Biosphere Reserve. Its 3300 sq km contain half of the orchid species in WA (more than 80, 70 of which occur nowhere else), 22 mammal species, 200 species of bird and 1700 species of plant (20% of WA's described flora species).

Walkers will discover beautiful coastline, sand plains, rugged coastal hills (known as 'the Barrens') and deep, wide river valleys. In season, you'll almost certainly see whales and their calves from the shore at **Point Ann**, where there's a lookout and a heritage walk that follows a short stretch of the 1164km **No 2 rabbit-proof fence**.

The three main 2WD entry points to the park are from the South Coast Hwy (Quiss Rd and Pabelup Dr), Hopetoun (Hamersley Dr) and Bremer Bay (along Swamp and Murray Rds). All roads are gravel, and likely to be impassable after rain, so check locally before you set out.

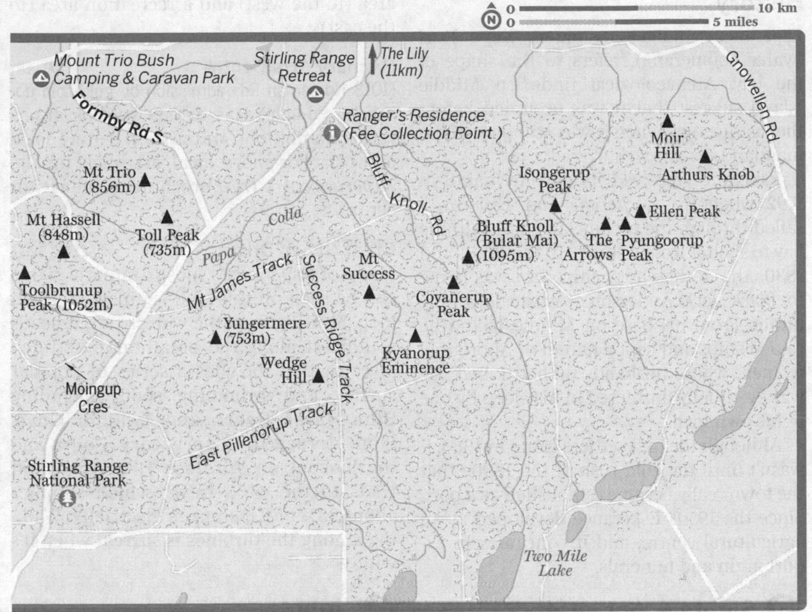

Bookending the park are the sleepy coastal settlements of **Bremer Bay** and **Hopetoun**, both with white sand and shimmering waters. To the east of Hopetoun is the scenic but often rough **Southern Ocean East Drive**, heading to beach camping sites at **Mason Bay** and **Starvation Bay**. If you're in a 2WD vehicle, don't head to Esperance this way.

Sleeping

Quaalup Homestead CAMPGROUND $
(08-9837 4124; www.whalesandwildflowers.com.au; Quaalup Rd; sites per person from $12, cabins $100-125) This 1858 homestead is secluded deep within the park's southern reaches. Electricity is solar generated, and forget about mobile-phone coverage. Accommodation includes a bush camp site with gas BBQs and cosy units and chalets. Quaalup Rd is reached from Pabelup Dr.

Parks & Wildlife Camp sites CAMPGROUND $
(www.parks.dpaw.wa.gov.au; sites per adult/child $10/2.20) Camp sites at St Mary Inlet (near Point Ann) and Four Mile Beach can be reached by 2WD. Others at Hamersley Inlet, Whale Bone Beach, Quoin Head and Fitzgerald Inlet are acccessible by 4WD or on foot.

Hopetoun Motel & Chalet Village MOTEL $$
(08-9838 3219; www.hopetounmotel.com.au; 458 Veal St, Hopetoun; r $140-200;) Rammed-earth complex with comfy beds and quality linen.

Information

Deck Treasures (www.decktreasures.com.au; Veal St, Hopetoun; 9am-12.30pm Nov-Apr; @), in Hopetoun, has information on local wildlife and recommended driving routes.

Esperance

POP 9600

Framed by aquamarine waters and pristine white beaches, Esperance sits in solitary splendour on the Bay of Isles. But despite its isolation, families still travel from Perth or Kalgoorlie just to plug into the easygoing vibe and great beach life. For travellers taking the coastal route across the continent, it's the last sizeable town before the Nullarbor.

Picture-perfect beaches dot the even more remote national parks to the town's southeast, and the pristine environment of the 105 islands of the offshore Recherche Archipelago are home to fur seals, penguins and sea birds.

History

Esperance's Indigenous name, Kepa Kurl (water boomerang), refers to the shape of the bay. Archaeological finds on Middle Island suggest that it was occupied before the last Ice Age, when it was still part of the mainland.

Esperance received its current name in 1792 when the *Recherche* and *Espérance* sailed through the archipelago and into the bay to shelter from a storm. In the 1820s and 1830s the Recherche Archipelago was home to Black Jack Anderson – Australia's only pirate. From his base on Middle Island he raided ships and kept a harem of Aboriginal women, whose husbands he had killed. He was eventually murdered in his sleep by one of his own men.

Although the first settlers came in 1863, it wasn't until the gold rush of the 1890s that the town really became established as a port. Since the 1950s Esperance developed as an agricultural centre, and it continues to export grain and minerals.

Sights & Activities

Esperance Museum MUSEUM
(cnr James & Dempster Sts; adult/child $6/2; 1.30-4.30pm) Glass cabinets are crammed with quirky collections of sea shells, frog ornaments, tennis rackets and bed pans. Bigger items include boats, a train carriage and the remains of the USA's spacecraft *Skylab,* which made its fiery re-entry at Balladonia, east of Esperance, in 1979.

Museum Village HISTORIC BUILDING
The museum consists of galleries and cafes occupying various restored heritage buildings; markets are held here every second Sunday morning. Aboriginal-run **Kepa Kurl Art Gallery** (www.kepakurl.com.au; cnr Dempster & Kemp Sts; 10am-4pm Mon-Fri, market Sun) has reasonably priced works by local and Central Desert artists.

Lake Warden Wetland System WETLANDS
Esperance is surrounded by extensive wetlands, which include seven large lakes and over 90 smaller ones. The 7.2km-return **Kepwari Wetland Trail** (off Fisheries Rd) takes in **Lake Wheatfield** and **Woody Lake**, with boardwalks, interpretive displays and good birdwatching. **Lake Monjimup**, 14km to the northwest along the South Coast Hwy, is divided by Telegraph Rd into a conservation area (to the west) and a recreation area (to the east).

Cannery Arts Centre GALLERY
(1018 Norseman Rd; admission by gold-coin donation; 1-4pm) Has artists studios, interesting exhibitions and a shop selling local artwork. For more local art, pick up the *Esperance Art Trail* brochure at the visitor centre.

Great Ocean Drive SCENIC DRIVE
Many of Esperance's most dramatic sights can be seen on this well-signposted 40km loop. Starting from the waterfront, it heads southwest along the breathtaking stretch of coast that includes a series of popular surfing and swimming spots, including **Blue Haven Beach** and **Twilight Cove**. Stop at rugged **Observatory Point** and the lookout on **Wireless Hill**. A turn-off leads to the **wind farm**, which supplies about 23% of Esperance's electricity. Walking among the turbines is surreal when it's windy.

Tours

Esperance Island Cruises BOAT TOUR
(08-9071 5757; www.woodyisland.com.au; 72 The Esplanade) Tours include Esperance Bay and Woody Island in a power catamaran (half/full day $120/185), getting close to fur seals, sea lions, Cape Barren geese and (with luck) dolphins. In January, there's a ferry to Woody Island (adult/child return $60/30).

Kepa Kurl Eco Cultural Discovery Tours CULTURAL TOUR
(08-9072 1688; www.kepakurl.com.au; Museum Village; adult/child $105/90, min 2 people) Explore the country from an Aboriginal perspective: visit rock art and waterholes, sample bush food and hear ancient stories.

Eco-Discovery Tours DRIVING TOUR
(0407 737 261; www.esperancetours.com.au) Runs 4WD tours along the sand to Cape Le Grand National Park (half/full day $105/195, minimum of two/four people) and two-hour circuits of Great Ocean Dr (adult/child $60/45).

Aussie Bight Expeditions 4WD TOUR
(0427 536 674; www.aussiebight.com; half/full day $90/160; Aug & Sep) Specialist wild flower tours from late August to September.

Esperance Diving & Fishing DIVING, FISHING
(☎08-9071 5111; www.esperancedivingandfishing.com.au; 72 The Esplanade) Takes you wreck diving on the *Sanko Harvest* (two-tank dive including all gear $260) or charter fishing throughout the archipelago.

Sleeping

Woody Island Eco-Stays CAMPGROUND $
(☎08-9071 5757; www.woodyisland.com.au; sites per person $25, on-site tents $41-61, huts $140-165; ⏲mid Dec-Jan, mid Apr-early May; ❄) It's not every day you get to stay in an A-class nature reserve. Choose between leafy camp sites (very close together) or canvas-sided bush huts, a few of which have a private deck and their own lighting. Power is mostly solar, and rainwater supplies the island – both are highly valued. Count on adding on a $60 return ferry transfer as well.

Blue Waters Lodge YHA HOSTEL $
(☎08-9071 1040; www.yha.com.au; 299 Goldfields Rd; dm/d/tr $28/74/95) On the beachfront about 1.5km from the town centre, this rambling place feels a little institutional, but management are friendly and it looks out over a tidy lawn to the water. Hire bikes to cycle the waterfront.

★**Esperance B&B by the Sea** B&B $$
(☎08-9071 5640; www.esperancebb.com; 34 Stewart St; s/d $125/180; ❄) This great-value beachhouse has a private guest wing and the views from the deck overlooking Blue Haven Beach are breathtaking, especially at sunset. It's just a stroll from the ocean and a five-minute drive from central Esperance.

Clearwater Motel Apartments MOTEL $$
(☎08-9071 3587; www.clearwatermotel.com.au; 1a William St; s $110, d $140-195; ❄) The bright and spacious rooms and apartments here have balconies and are fully self-contained, and there's a well-equipped shared barbecue area. It's just a short walk from both the waterfront and town.

Driftwood Apartments APARTMENT $$
(☎0428 716 677; www.driftwoodapartments.com.au; 69 The Esplanade; apt $165-220; ❄) Each of these seven smart blue-and-yellow apartments, right across from the waterfront, has its own BBQ and outdoor table setting. The two-storey, two-bedroom units have decks and a bit more privacy.

Eating & Drinking

Taylor's Beach Bar & Cafe CAFE $$
(www.taylorsbeachbar.com.au; Taylor St Jetty; breakfast $13-24, lunch & dinner $20-30; ⏲10am-late Mon-Fri, 7am-late Sat & Sun; 📶) This sprawling cafe by the jetty serves cafe fare, burgers, seafood and salads. Locals hang out at the tables on the grass or read on the terrace. Focaccia sandwiches ($11 to $14) are good value if you're heading for the beach, and it's good for a glass of wine or chilled pint of Little Creatures beer. Ask about occasional live music.

Ocean Blues CAFE $$
(19 The Esplanade; mains $11-35; ⏲8am-8.30pm Tue-Sat, 8am-4pm Sun) Wander in sandy-footed and order a simple lunch (burgers, salads, sandwiches) from this unpretentious eatery. Dinners are more adventurous, representing good value for the price.

Pier Hotel PUB FOOD $$
(www.pierhotelesperance.net.au; 47 The Esplanade; mains $20-35; ⏲11.30am-late) Lots of beers on tap, wood-fired pizzas and good-value bistro meals conspire to make the local pub a firm favourite with both locals and visitors.

Coffee Cat CAFE
(⏲7am-2pm Mon-Fri) WA's hippest mobile coffee caravan also serves up yummy home-baked cakes and muffins. Grab an early-morning java to fuel you for a stroll along Esperance's flash new esplanade. Look for the caravan along the waterfront.

S'Juice JUICES
(juices & smoothies $7-9; ⏲9am-4pm Mon-Fri, to 3pm Sat & Sun) Colourful caravan with excellent juices and smoothies, and a few warming soups in cooler months. Usually located in the car park opposite the Pier Hotel.

Information

Parks & Wildlife (☎08-9083 2100; www.parks.dpaw.wa.gov.au; 92 Dempster St) National parks information.

Visitor Centre (☎08-9083 1555; www.visitesperance.com; cnr Kemp & Dempster Sts; ⏲9am-5pm Mon-Fri, to 2pm Sat, to noon Sun) In the museum village.

Getting There & Away

Esperance Airport (Coolgardie-Esperance Hwy) is 18km north of the town centre. **Virgin Australia** (☎1300 660 088; www.virginaustralia.com) has around three flights per day to and from Perth (1¾ hours). **Transwa** (☎1300 662 205; www.transwa.wa.gov.au) services stop at the visitor centre:

➡ GE1 to/from Perth ($91, 10¼ hours, thrice weekly)

➡ GE2 to/from Perth ($91, 10 hours), Mundaring ($90, 9¼ hours), York ($82, 8½ hours) and Hyden ($56, five hours) thrice weekly

➡ GE3 to/from Kalgoorlie ($58, five hours, thrice weekly), Coolgardie ($56, 4¾ hours, weekly) and Norseman ($31, 2¼ hours, thrice weekly)

Around Esperance

Cape Le Grand National Park NATIONAL PARK
(entry per car/motorcycle $12/6, sites adult/child $10/2.20) Starting 60km east of Esperance, Cape Le Grand National Park boasts spectacular coastal scenery, dazzling beaches and excellent walking tracks. There's good fishing, swimming and camping at **Lucky Bay** and **Le Grand Beach**, and day-use facilities at gorgeous **Hellfire Bay**. Make the effort to climb **Frenchman Peak** (a steep 3km return, allow two hours), as the views from the top and through the rocky 'eye', especially during the late afternoon, are superb. The 15km Le Grand Coastal Trail links the bay, or you can do shorter stretches between beaches.

Cape Arid National Park NATIONAL PARK
(entry per car/motorcycle $12/6, sites adult/child $10/2.20) On the Great Australian Bight and edging the Nullarbor Plain, rugged and isolated Cape Arid National Park has good bushwalking, great beaches and crazy squeaky sand. Whales (in season), seals and Cape Barren geese are seen regularly here. Most of the park is 4WD-accessible only, although the Thomas River Rd leading to the shire camp site suits all vehicles.

There's a challenging walk to the top of Tower Peak on Mt Ragged (3km return, three hours).

SOUTHERN OUTBACK

The southern outback is an iconic Australian experience. Almost-empty roads run relentlessly towards South Australia (SA) via the Nullarbor Plain, and up to the Northern Territory (NT). This was (and is) gold-rush country, with the city of Kalgoorlie-Boulder as its hub, while less-sustainable gold towns now lie sunstruck, isolated and deserted. Aboriginal people have lived for an age in this region, which early colonists found unforgiving until the allure of gold made it worthwhile to stay.

History

Gold was discovered at Southern Cross in 1888, inspiring one of the world's last great gold rushes. Around 50 towns quickly sprouted, but enthusiasm and greed often outweighed common sense, and typhoid, inadequate water, housing and food led to many fatalities in the mining camps.

The area's population dwindled along with the gold, and today Kalgoorlie-Boulder is the only real survivor. Explore other diminished towns and prodigious mining structures along the 965km Golden Quest Discovery Trail (www.goldenquesttrail.com).

Stretching 560km from the Perth foothills, the 1903 Golden Pipeline brought water to the goldfields. It was a lifeline for the towns it passed through and filled Kalgoorlie with the sense of a future, with or without gold. The present-day Great Eastern Hwy follows the pipeline's route, incorporating heritage pumping stations and information signs.

ℹ Getting There & Away

AIR

Qantas (☎13 13 13; www.qantas.com.au) Kalgoorlie to Perth and Adelaide.

NOT NULLAR-BORING AT ALL

'Crossing the Nullarbor' is an iconic Australian trip. It's absolutely about the journey as much as the destination, so relax and enjoy the big skies and forever horizons.

All roadhouses sell food and fuel and have accommodation ranging from often barren camp sites to basic budget rooms and motels. There's free roadside camping with toilets and tables about every 250km.

Ensure your vehicle is up to the distance and carry more drinking water than you think you'll need. Fuel prices are high and there's a distance between fuel stops of about 200km.

See www.nullarbornet.com.au for touring information.

Skippers Aviation (1300 729 924; www.skippers.com.au) Perth–Leonora–Laverton and Perth–Wiluna–Meekathara routes.

Virgin Australia (13 67 89; www.virgin-australia.com) Kalgoorlie to Perth, Melbourne, Sydney and Brisbane.

BUS

Transwa (1300 662 205; www.transwa.wa.gov.au) Kalgoorlie to Esperance ($58.20, five hours) via Coolgardie and Norseman.

Goldrush Tours (1800 620 440; www.goldrushtours.com.au) Weekly service from Kalgoorlie to Laverton ($82, 4½ hours) via Menzies and Leonora, departing Thursday and returning Friday.

TRAIN

Transwa runs the *Prospector* service from East Perth to Kalgoorlie ($86, seven hours, daily).

Norseman

POP 860

From the crossroads township of Norseman head south to Esperance, north to Kalgoorlie, westwards to Hyden and Wave Rock, or east across the Nullarbor. Note the 300km road from Hyden and Wave Rock to Norseman is unsealed, but is suitable for 2WD vehicles in dry conditions. Check at Norseman or Hyden before setting out.

Stretch your legs at the **Beacon Hill Mararoa Lookout**, where there's a walking trail, and stop at the **Historical Museum** (Battery Rd; adult/child $3/1; 10am-1pm Mon-Sat). Pick up the **Dundas Coach Road Heritage Trail** brochure, for a 50km loop drive with interpretive panels.

Sleeping

Great Western Motel MOTEL $

(08-9039 1633; www.norsemangreatwesternmotel.com.au; Prinsep St; r $120;) 'Budget' and 'lodge' rooms in an older block are perfectly adequate, but the rammed-earth 'motel' rooms are much nicer. There's a cafe-restaurant on site.

Gateway Caravan Park CARAVAN PARK $

(08-9039 1500; www.acclaimparks.com.au; 23 Prinsep St; sites $35-40, cabins $132-158;) Decent cabins and a bushy atmosphere.

Information

Visitor Centre (08-9039 1071; www.norseman.info; 68 Roberts St; 9am-5pm Mon-Fri, 9.30am-4pm Sat & Sun) Lots of Nullarbor information.

Eyre Highway (the Nullarbor)

The 2700km Eyre Hwy crosses the southern edge of the vast **Nullarbor Plain**, parallel with the **Trans-Australia Railway** to the north.

John Eyre was the first European to cross this unforgiving stretch of country in 1841. After the 1877 telegraph line was laid, miners trekked to the goldfields under blistering sun and through freezing winters. By 1941 a rough-and-ready road carried a handful of vehicles, and in 1969 the road was sealed to the SA border. In 1976, the last coastal stretch was surfaced, with the Nullarbor region ending at the cliffs of the Great Australian Bight.

From Norseman it's 725km to the SA border, and a further 480km to Ceduna. From Ceduna, it's still another 793km to Adelaide.

Norseman to Eucla

Around the 100km mark from Norseman is **Fraser Range Station** (08-9039 3210; www.fraserrangestation.com.au; unpowered/powered sites $22/30, budget s/tw/d/f $55/95/95/120, cottage r $155) with heritage buildings and a camping ground. Next is **Balladonia** (193km), where the **Balladonia Hotel Motel** (08-9039 3453; www.balladoniahotelmotel.com.au; unpowered/powered sites $19/28, dm $50, r from $130;) has a small museum including debris from *Skylab*'s 1979 return to earth nearby.

Balladonia to Cocklebiddy is around 210km. The first 160km to **Caiguna** includes Australia's longest stretch of straight road (145km), ending at Caiguna's **John Eyre Motel** (08-9039 3459; caigunarh@bigpond.com; unpowered/powered sites $20/25, d $85-120, tr/q $130/140;).

Birds Australia's **Eyre Bird Observatory** (08-9039 3450; www.birdlife.org.au/visit-us/observatories/eyre; full board adult/child $90/45) is in the isolated 1897 former Eyre Telegraph Station, 50km south of Cocklebiddy. Book ahead for accommodation. Day visitors are welcome ($10 per vehicle), but the last 10km are soft sand and 4WD accessible only; 2WD travellers who want to stay can arrange pick-up with the wardens. There's no camping.

At **Madura**, 91km east of Cocklebiddy and near the Hampton Tablelands, the **Madura Pass Oasis Inn** (08-9039 3464; maduraoasis@

THE WORLD'S LONGEST GOLF COURSE

Stretching 1362km from Kalgoorlie, south to Norseman and across the desolate Nullarbor Plain to Ceduna, the **Nullarbor Links** (www.nullarborlinks.com; 18 holes $50) is a unique 18-hole, par-72 course.

Purchase your scorecard from the Kalgoorlie, Norseman or Ceduna visitor centres, and follow the directions along the route. Clubs are available for hire at each rocky and sandy hole ($5).

bigpond.com; unpowered/powered sites $15/25, r $105-125; ❄☒) has a very welcome pool.

In **Mundrabilla**, 116km further east, the **Mundrabilla Motel Hotel** (☎08-9039 3465; mundrabilla@bigpond.com.au; unpowered/powered sites $20/25, r $80-110; ❄) has cheaper fuel prices than roadhouses further west.

Just before the SA border is **Eucla**, surrounded by stunning sand dunes and pristine beaches. Visit the atmospheric ruins of the 1877 **telegraph station**, 5km south of town and gradually being engulfed by the dunes; the remains of the old jetty are a 15-minute walk beyond. The **Eucla Motor Hotel** (☎08-9039 3468; euclamotel@bigpond.com; unpowered/powered sites $10/20, r $45-110; ❄) has good camping and spacious rooms.

Coolgardie

POP 800

In 1898 sleepy Coolgardie was the third-biggest town in WA, with a population of 15,000, six newspapers, two stock exchanges, more than 20 hotels and three breweries. It all took off just hours after Arthur Bayley rode into Southern Cross in 1892 and dumped 554oz of Coolgardie gold on the mining warden's counter. The only echoes that remain are stately historic buildings lining the uncharacteristically wide main road.

Sights & Activities

Goldfields Museum & Visitor Centre MUSEUM
(☎08-9026 6090; www.coolgardie.wa.gov.au; Bayley St, Warden's Court; adult/child $4/2; ⌚8.30am-4.20pm Mon-Fri, 10am-3pm Sat & Sun) Goldfields memorabilia including information about former US president Herbert Hoover's days on the goldfields in Gwalia, as well as the fascinating story of Modesto Varischetti, the 'Entombed Miner'.

Warden Finnerty's Residence HISTORIC BUILDING
(www.nationaltrust.org.au; 2 McKenzie St; adult/child $4/2; ⌚11am-4pm Thu-Tue) Built in 1895 for Coolgardie's first mining warden and magistrate.

Sleeping & Eating

Coolgardie Goldrush Motel MOTEL $
(☎08-9026 6080; www.coolgardiemotels.com.au; 49-53 Bayley St; r $125-150; ❄☒☒) With bright linen, spotless bathrooms and flat-screen televisions, the Goldrush's compact but colourful rooms are very comfortable. The attached restaurant serves excellent home-made pies.

Kalgoorlie-Boulder

POP 28,300

With well-preserved historic buildings, Kalgoorlie-Boulder is an outback success story, and is still the centre for mining in this part of the state.

Historically, mine workers would come straight to town to spend up at Kalgoorlie's infamous brothels, or at pubs staffed by skimpies (scantily clad female bar staff). Today 'Kal' is definitely more family-friendly – mine workers must reside in town and cannot be transient 'fly-in, fly-out' labour.

It still feels a bit like the Wild West though, and the heritage pubs and skimpy bar staff are reminders of a more rambunctious past.

There are historical and modern mining sites to discover, and Kalgoorlie is a good base from which to explore the ghost towns in the surrounding area.

History

Long-time prospector Paddy Hannan set out from Coolgardie in search of another gold strike. He stumbled across the surface gold that sparked the 1893 gold rush, and inadvertently chose the site of Kalgoorlie for a township.

When surface sparkles subsided, the miners dug deeper, extracting the precious metal from the rocks by costly and complex processes. Kalgoorlie quickly prospered, and the town's magnificent public buildings, constructed at the end of the 19th century, are evidence of its fabulous wealth.

Despite its slow decline after WWI, Kal is still the largest producer of gold in Australia. What was a Golden Mile of small mining operators' head frames and corrugated-iron shacks is now the overwhelmingly huge Super Pit.

Sights & Activities

The city's main drag, Hannan St has retained many of its original gold rush–era buildings, including several grand hotels and the imposing town hall. Outside is a drinking fountain in the form of a statue of Paddy Hannan holding a water bag.

Super Pit LOOKOUT
(www.superpit.com.au; Outram St; 7am-7pm) The view is staggering here, with building-sized trucks zig-zagging up and down the huge hole and looking like kids' toys. Take a fascinating tour with Kalgoorlie Tours & Charters.

Western Australian Museum – Kalgoorlie-Boulder MUSEUM
(www.museum.wa.gov.au; 17 Hannan St; suggested donation $5; 10am-4.30pm) The impressive Ivanhoe-mine head frame marks this excellent museum's entrance; take the lift to look over the city. An underground vault displays giant nuggets and gold bars, and there's also a fantastic collection of trade union banners.

School of Mines Mineral Museum MUSEUM
(cnr Egan & Cassidy Sts; 9am-noon Mon-Fri, closed school holidays) FREE Geology displays including replicas of big nuggets discovered locally.

Royal Flying Doctor Service Visitor Centre TOUR
(08-9093 7595; www.flyingdoctor.net; Kalgoorlie-Boulder Airport; admission by donation; 10am-3pm Mon-Fri, tours 10.15am year-round, additional tour 2pm May-Oct) See how the Flying Doctors look after the people of the outback.

Tours

Kalgoorlie Tours & Charters BUS TOUR
(08-9021 2211; www.kalgoorlietours.com.au; 250 Hannan St; adult/child $70/45; 9.30am & 1.30pm Mon-Sat) Explore the Super Pit on 2½ hour tours. Shorter 90-minute tours (adult/child $45/25) run on demand during school holidays. All participants must wear long trousers and enclosed shoes.

Goldrush Tours BUS TOUR
(1800 620 440; www.goldrushtours.com.au; adult/child $150/75) Heritage jaunts around Kalgoorlie Boulder and day tours to Lake Ballard's sculptures.

Questa Casa HISTORICAL TOUR
(08-9021 4897; www.questacasa.com; 133 Hay St; tours $25; tours 3pm) Still operational, this is the last of the gold rush–era brothels that once lined Hay St. Tours conducted at 3pm for curious visitors (18 and older only).

Festivals & Events

Kalgoorlie Market MARKET
(Hannan St, St Barbara's Sq) First Sunday of the month.

Boulder Market Day MARKET
(Burt St) Held at Loopline Reserve Railway Park on the third Sunday of the month.

Kalgoorlie-Boulder Racing Round RACING
(www.kbrc.com.au) Locals and a huge influx of visitors dress up to watch horses race in September. Accommodation can be difficult to secure.

Sleeping

Most accommodation targets the mining industry. Smarter places tend to be overpriced, and hostels and pubs are often full of long-stayers.

Kalgoorlie Backpackers HOSTEL $
(08-9091 1482; www.kalgoorliebackpackers.com.au; 166 Hay St; dm/s/d $33/60/85;) Partly located in a former brothel, this hostel is in a central location, and is a good place to find out about work opportunities.

Discovery Holiday Parks CARAVAN PARK $
(www.discoveryholidayparks.com.au; sites $21-51, r $60, units $119-179;) **Kalgoorlie** (08-9039 4800; 286 Burt St, Kalgoorlie); **Boulder** (08-9093 1266; 201 Lane St, Boulder) Sister complexes with sizeable and well-fitted-out A-frame chalets and cabins, grassy tent sites, playgrounds and pools.

Rydges Kalgoorlie HOTEL $$
(08-9080 0800; www.rydges.com; 21 Davidson St; r from $209;) Kalgoorlie's best accommodation is located in a residential area between Kalgoorlie and Boulder. In an oasis

of lush native bush, the rooms are spacious and very comfortable.

Railway Motel MOTEL $$
(☎08-9088 0000; www.railwaymotel.com.au; 51 Forrest St; r from $135; ❄📶) Opposite the train station with bright, spruced-up rooms. Adjacent two-bedroom apartments are spacious and comfortable.

Langtrees BOUTIQUE HOTEL $$$
(☎08-9026 2181; www.langtreeshotel.com; 181 Hay St; d $300) Formerly a famous brothel, Langtrees has 10 themed rooms including an Afghan boudoir or the Holden-On room that's perfect for recovering petrolheads. Less ostentatious rooms are also available.

Eating

Relish CAFE $
(162 Hannan St; breakfast $8-16, lunch $10-14; ⏲6am-3pm Mon-Fri, 7am-2pm Sat & Sun) 🌿 The best coffee in town along with interesting food such as lamb-and-feta frittata, vegetarian wraps and sweet-potato-and-chorizo tart. Check out local art in the adjacent whitewashed laneway.

Hoover's Cafe PUB FOOD $$
(www.palacehotelkalgoorlie.com/hoovers-cafe/; 137 Hannan St; mains $11-26; ⏲8am-5pm; 📶) At the Palace Hotel, this pub dining room serves good-value, tasty food. Upstairs is the flash **Balcony Bar & Restaurant** (mains $36-47; ⏲from 5pm) serving steak and seafood.

Lemongrass THAI $$
(5/84-90 Brockman St; mains $18-22; ⏲11.30am-2.30pm Mon-Sat, 4.30-9pm daily) A healthy, lighter option in a town better known for robust pub grub.

Paddy's Ale House PUB FOOD $$
(135 Hannan St, Exchange Hotel; mains $17-30; ⏲11am-late) Classic counter meals including steaks and bangers-and-mash and lots of live TV sport.

Drinking & Entertainment

The gold rush–era pubs of Hannan St are full of hard-drinking blokes and female bar staff clad in underwear, suspenders and high heels. Pick your pub carefully if you prefer your bar staff not in skimpy uniform.

Palace Hotel PUB
(www.palacehotelkalgoorlie.com.au; 137 Hannan St) Watch the street life from the relatively demure balcony bar or descend to the Gold Bar for live bands, DJs and skimpies.

ℹ Information

Department of Parks & Wildlife (☎08-9080 5555; www.parks.dpaw.wa.gov.au; 32 Brockman St; ⏲8am-5pm Mon-Fri) Information on the Goldfields Woodlands National Park.

Visitor Centre (☎08-9021 1966; www.kalgoorlietourism.com; Town Hall, cnr Hannan & Wilson Sts; ⏲8.30am-5pm Mon-Fri, 9am-2pm Sat & Sun) Accommodation bookings and information.

CANNING STOCK ROUTE & GUNBARREL HIGHWAY

Wiluna, 300km north of Leonora, is the start or finish point for two of Australia's most extreme 4WD adventures – the Canning Stock Route and the Gunbarrel Hwy. These rough, remote routes head through unforgiving wilderness for thousands of kilometres. They can only be safely traversed from April to September. Don't attempt them at all without checking with visitor centres and Parks & Wildlife offices first as they're completely weather-dependent. HEMA Maps' detailed *Great Desert Tracks – North West Sheet* is essential.

The **Canning Stock Route** (www.exploroz.com/TrekNotes/WDeserts/Canning_Stock_Route.aspx) runs 2006km northeast to Halls Creek, crossing the Great Sandy and Gibson Deserts, and is a route to be taken very seriously. If you're starting from Wiluna, pick up road and safety information from the **shire office** (☎08-9981 8000; www.wiluna.wa.gov.au; Scotia St). You'll need a permit to cross the Birrilburru native-title area.

Taking the old **Gunbarrel Highway** (www.exploroz.com/TrekNotes/WDeserts/Gunbarrel_Highway.aspx) from Wiluna to Warakurna near the NT border (where it joins the Outback Way) is a long, rough, heavily corrugated trip through sand dunes. Like the Canning, it's strongly recommended you drive this in a convoy with other vehicles, and you carry all supplies – including fuel and water – for the duration of your trip with you. Let the police posts at either end of both tracks know your movements.

North of Kalgoorlie-Boulder

Heading north from Kalgoorlie-Boulder, the Goldfields Hwy is surfaced to Wiluna (580km north), the starting point for the 4WD Canning Stock Route and Gunbarrel Hwy. Branching east, the road from Leonora is sealed to Laverton (367km northeast of Kalgoorlie), the starting point for the unsealed Great Central Rd (Outback Way).

Many gravel roads are fine for regular cars, but rain can quickly close them. All the (non-ghost) towns have pub accommodation, caravan parks with cabins, fuel stops and grocery stores.

Kanowna, Broad Arrow & Ora Banda

Easy day trips north from Kalgoorlie include the gold ghost towns of Kanowna (18km northeast), Broad Arrow (38km north) and Ora Banda (65km northwest). Little remains of Kanowna apart from the foundations of its 16 hotels (!), but its pioneer cemetery is interesting. Broad Arrow was featured in *The Nickel Queen* (1971), the first full-length feature film made in WA. At the beginning of the 20th century it had a population of 2400. Now there's just one pub, popular with Kal locals at weekends. The 1911 **Ora Banda Historical Inn** (08-9024 2444; www.orabanda.com.au; sites per 2 people $20-30, r $75-120) has a beer garden, simple accommodation and dusty camping.

Menzies & Lake Ballard

The once thriving but now tiny township of Menzies, 132km from Kalgoorlie, is best known as the turn-off for the stunning **Antony Gormley sculptures** on **Lake Ballard**, an eye-dazzling salt lake 51km northwest of town. Camp here for free. There are toilets and a barbecue area.

The **Menzies visitor centre** (08-9024 2702; www.menzies.wa.gov.au; Shenton St; 9am-4.30pm Mon-Fri, 9am-1pm Sat & Sun; @) has information on visiting the sculptures and other local sites, and runs the neighbouring **caravan park** (08 9024 2702, after hours 0448 242 041; sites per 2 people $22-30). It also houses the **Spinifex Art Gallery**, exhibiting works from the Tjuntjuntjarra community, located 750km to the east.

PERMITS, PLEASE

The Canning Stock Route and Outback Way traverse various pockets of Aboriginal land and travellers must obtain a permit from the Department of Aboriginal Affairs (DAA; www.daa.wa.gov.au) to cross them. It's usually a quick online process, but if you're planning to stay and camp rather than merely pass through, additional approvals are required from the affected community; allow up to two weeks.

Kookynie

Midway between Menzies and Leonora, a good dirt road leads 25km to Kookynie, another interesting ghost town, where the **Kookynie Grand Hotel** (08-9031 3010; puseymin@bigpond.com; s/d $80/100) pulls pints and offers beds. Quiet **Niagara Dam**, 10km from Kookynie, has bush camping.

Leonora

North of Kookynie (237km from Kalgoorlie), Leonora is the area's service centre for mining exploration and farming. Old public buildings and pubs line the main street near the **visitor centre** (08-9037 7016; www.leonora.wa.gov.au; Tower St; 9am-4pm Mon-Fri). Just 4km southwest of town, **Gwalia Historic Site** was occupied in 1896 and deserted in 1963, after the pit closed. With houses and household goods disintegrating intact, it's a strangely fascinating ghost town. The **museum** (www.gwalia.org.au; adult/child $10/5; 9am-4pm) is full of wonderful curios, and there's a good audio tour ($2). **Hoover House** (08-9037 7122; www.gwalia.org.au; s $120-150, d $130-160;), the 1898 mine manager's house, is named for Gwalia's first mine manager, Herbert Hoover, who later became the 31st president of the United States. It's beautifully restored, and you can stay overnight in one of the antique-strewn bedrooms.

Laverton

Laverton crouches on the edge of the Great Victoria Desert. The **visitor centre** (08-9031 1361; www.laverton.wa.gov.au; Augusta St; 9.30am-4.30pm Mon-Fri, 9am-1pm Sat & Sun) is combined with the **Great Beyond – Explorers' Hall of Fame** (adult/child $10/5), which uses technology to tell pioneer stories. The not-for-profit **Laverton Outback Gallery** (www.laverton-outback-gallery.com.au; 4 Euro St; ⌚9am-5pm) is a great place to purchase paintings, necklaces, woomeras and boomerangs – 80% of the price goes straight to the Aboriginal artist.

Laverton marks the start of the Outback Way. Expect to overnight and/or stock up on supplies of fuel and water here, and *definitely* check at the visitor centre for current road conditions.

Outback Way (Great Central Road)

The unsealed **Outback Way** (www.outbackway.org.au) links Laverton with Winton in central Queensland, via the red centre of the Northern Territory. From Laverton it is a mere 1098km to Yulara, 1541km to Alice Springs and 2720km to Winton!

The road is sandy and corrugated in places, but it's wide and suitable for all vehicles. It can be closed for several days after rain. Fuel is available at roughly 300km intervals on the WA side.

Coming from Laverton, three WA roadhouses (www.ngaanyatjarraku.wa.gov.au) all provide food, fuel and limited mechanical services – **Tjukayirla** (☎08-9037 1108; tjukayirla roadhouse@bigpond.com; unpowered/powered sites $20/30, s $75, units $120-160; ⌚9am-5pm Mon-Fri, 9am-2pm Sat & Sun) at 315km, **Warburton** (☎08-8956 7656) at 567km and **Warakurna** (☎08-8956 7344; warakurnaroad house@bigpond.com) at 798km. All offer camping (around $25 per person), budget rooms (around $70) and self-contained units (around $160). Book ahead as rooms are limited. The Tjukayirla roadhouse offers tours to caves with 5000-year-old rock art.

At Warburton visit the **Tjulyuru Cultural & Civic Centre** (☎08-8956 7966; www.tjulyuru.com; ⌚8.30am-4.30pm Mon-Fri) containing an extensive collection of Ngaanyatjarra Aboriginal paintings.

Warakurna, Warburton and Giles run on NT time, 1½ hours ahead of WA time.

Monkey Mia & the Central West

Includes ➡

Best Places for Sunset

- Steep Point (p984)
- Fishermens Lookout (p973)
- Red Bluff (p979)
- Shark Bay Hotel (p984)
- Horrocks (p982)

Best Places to Stay

- Gnaraloo Station (p988)
- Ospreys Beach Chalet (p976)
- Dongara Breeze Inn (p973)
- Bentwood Olive Grove (p974)
- Hamelin Station (p982)

Why Go?

The pristine coastline and sheltered turquoise waters of Malgana country draw tourists and marine life from around the world. Aside from the dolphins of Monkey Mia, the submerged sea-grass meadows of World Heritage–listed Shark Bay host dugongs, rays, sharks and turtles. On land, rare marsupials take refuge in remote national parks, and limestone cliffs, red sand and salt lakes litter a stark interior.

Further south in the land of the Nhanda people, the gorges of Kalbarri invite adventurers to explore their depths, while wild flowers carpet the plains, and ospreys wheel away from battered Indian Ocean cliffs as humpback whales migrate slowly southwards.

Vegies are ripening in Carnarvon as anglers and board riders check the tides, and windsurfers are waiting for the 'Doctor' (strong afternoon sea breeze) to blow. In Geraldton, good cafes, weekend markets and an excellent museum combine with Indian Ocean views along the city's foreshore.

When to Go

Monkey Mia

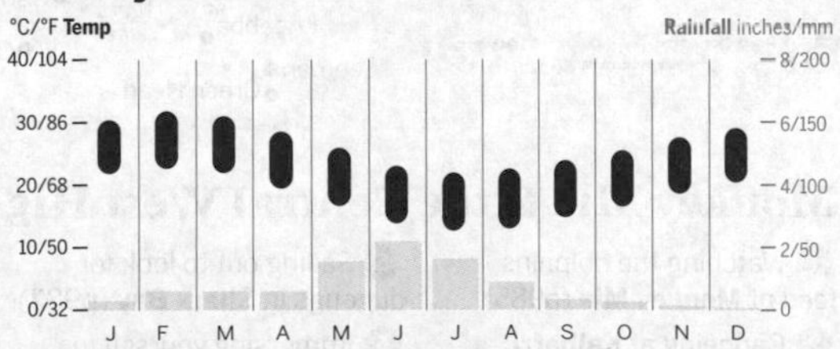

Jun–Aug The winter swells pump the breaks off Gnaraloo and Quobba.

Aug & Sep Kalbarri erupts in wild flowers.

Nov–Feb Windsurfers clutch their sails from Geraldton to Carnarvon.

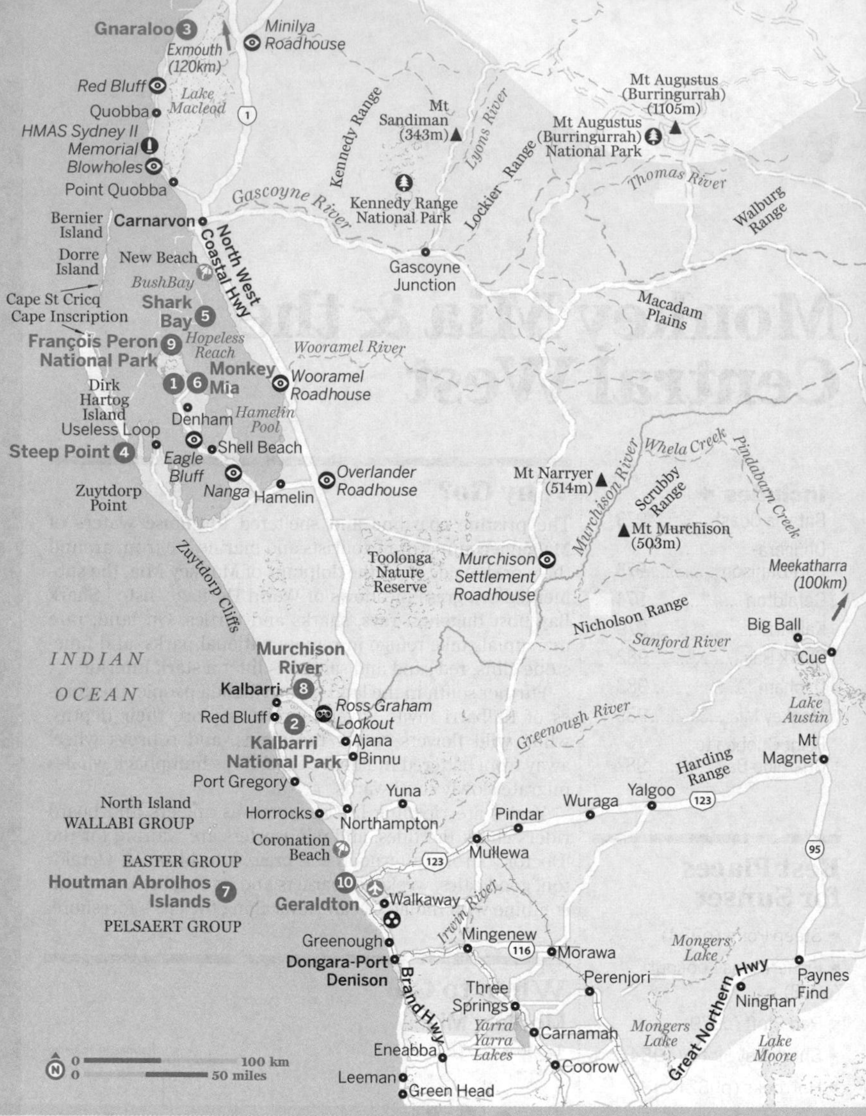

Monkey Mia & the Central West Highlights

1. Watching the dolphins feed at **Monkey Mia** (p985).
2. Canoeing at **Kalbarri National Park** (p979).
3. Surfing the Tombstones break at **Gnaraloo** (p988).
4. Driving out to the mainland's most westerly tip, **Steep Point** (p984).
5. Sailing out to look for dugongs in **Shark Bay** (p982).
6. Immersing yourself in Malgana culture on a **Wula Guda Nyinda** (p985) tour at Monkey Mia.
7. Diving on ancient shipwrecks at the **Houtman Abrolhos Islands** (p978).
8. Horse riding along the **Murchison River** (p979).
9. Spotting marine life from a coastal walk in the **François Peron National Park** (p985).
10. Soaking up some coffee and culture in **Geraldton's** (p974) museums, galleries and cafes.

Getting There & Around

AIR

Virgin Australia (13 67 89; www.virginaustralia.com) Perth to Geraldton.

Skippers (1300 729 924; www.skippers.com.au) Perth to Geraldton, Shark Bay and Carnarvon.

Qantas (13 13 13; www.qantas.com.au) Perth to Geraldton.

BUS

Integrity (1800 226 339; www.integritycoachlines.com.au) Sunday, Tuesday and Thursday evening departures from Perth to Broome stopping at Geraldton, Kalbarri and Carnarvon.

Transwa (1300 662 205; www.transwa.wa.gov.au) Buses between Perth and Kalbarri, Geraldton and Dongara along the Brand Hwy (Rte 1).

BATAVIA COAST

From tranquil Dongara-Port Denison to the remote, wind-scoured Zutydorp Cliffs stretches a dramatic coastline steeped in history, littered with shipwrecks and abounding in marine life. While the region proved the undoing of many early European sailors, today modern fleets make the most of a lucrative crayfish industry.

Dongara-Port Denison

POP 3100

Pretty little Dongara and Port Denison, twin seaside towns 359km from Perth, make an idyllic spot to break up a long drive. Surrounded by beautiful beaches, walking trails and historic buildings, the towns have a laid-back atmosphere. Port Denison has good beaches and accommodation, while Dongara's main street, shaded by century-old figs, offers the best eating.

Sights & Activities

The 12 itineraries in the free *Walk Dongara Denison* brochure include the **Irwin River Nature Trail**, where you might spot black swans, pelicans or cormorants. The **Heritage Trail** booklet ($2) details a 1.6km route linking buildings including 1860s **Russ Cottage** (Point Leander Dr), with a kitchen floor made from compacted anthills. The cells in the old police station hold the **Irwin District Museum** (08-9927 1404; admission $2.50; 10am-noon Mon-Sat), showcasing historical displays.

Denison Beach Marina brims with crayfish boats while sunsets are dazzling from nearby **Fishermens Lookout**.

Sleeping

Note that accommodation is more expensive during public and school holidays.

★ **Dongara Breeze Inn** GUESTHOUSE $
(08-9927 1332; www.dongarabackpackers.com.au; 32 Waldeck St, Dongara; dm/s/d $30/80/85) The cheapest beds in town look onto a leafy garden at this popular lodging, which has stylish doubles with a chic Asian ambience, rustic dorms (in a vintage railway carriage) and free bike use for guests. The shared spaces arrayed around the garden are very appealing.

Dongara Tourist Park CARAVAN PARK $
(08-9927 1210; www.dongaratouristpark.com.au; 8 George St, Port Denison; unpowered/powered sites $26/37, 1-/2-bedroom cabins $110/150;) The best camping option has shaded, spacious sites behind South Beach. The two-bed cabins on the hill have great views, and there's a lush pergola for dining outdoors.

Dongara Old Mill Motel MOTEL $
(08-9927 1200; www.dongaraoldmillmotel.com.au; 58 Waldeck St, Dongara; s/d 105/110;) Good-value renovated rooms, friendly owners and a palm-trimmed swimming pool make this place worthy of an overnight stay. Good eating and drinking in central Dongara is a pleasant stroll away.

Port Denison Holiday Units APARTMENT $
(08-9927 1104; www.dongaraaccommodation.com.au; 14 Carnarvon St, Port Denison; d $125-135;) These spotless, spacious, self-catering units, some with views, are just a block from the beach.

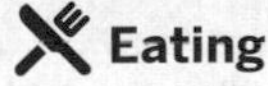

Eating

Starfish Cafe CAFE $
(0448 344 215; White Tops Rd, Port Denison; mains $10-30; 8am-2pm Wed-Sun) Hidden away in the South Beach car park, this casual snack shack offers coffee, jaffles, winter soups and summer salads.

Priory Hotel PUB, BISTRO $$
(08-9927 1090; www.prioryhotel.com.au; 11 St Dominics Rd, Dongara; mains $15-42;) There's a touch of *Picnic at Hanging Rock* about this leafy former nunnery and ladies college with its period furniture, polished floorboards, black-and-white photos and wide

verandahs. Sundays bring roasts and wood-fired pizza, several nights offer live music and steaks are available every evening.

Dongara Hotel Motel RESTAURANT **$$**
(☎08-9927 1023; www.dongaramotel.com.au; 12 Moreton Tce, Dongara; d $145, mains $22-42; ⏰7am-10pm; 📶) Locals love the Dongara's legendary servings of fresh seafood, steaks and 'Asian Corner' curries, *mie goreng* and *pad thai*. The motel rooms, popular with corporates, are surprisingly stylish.

Information

Telecentre (CRC; ☎08-9927 2111; 11 Moreton Tce, Dongara; internet $5 per hr; ⏰8.30am-4.30pm Mon-Fri; @) Internet access.

Visitor Centre (☎08-9927 1404; www.irwin.wa.gov.au; 9 Waldeck St, Dongara; ⏰9am-5pm Mon-Fri, to noon Sat) In Dongara's old post office.

Getting There & Around

Dongara-Port Denison is accessible via the Brand Hwy, Indian Ocean Dr or Midlands Rd (Rte 116). **Transwa** buses run daily to Perth ($56, five hours) and Geraldton ($14, one hour). **Integrity** runs three times a week to Perth ($56, five hours) and Geraldton ($34, one hour), and to Exmouth ($172, 13 hours). Buses arrive and depart from the visitor centre.

For a taxi, call ☎08-9927 1555.

Geraldton

POP 39,000

Capital of the midwest, sun-drenched 'Gero' is surrounded by excellent beaches offering myriad aquatic opportunities – swimming, snorkelling, surfing and, in particular, wind- and kitesurfing. The largest town between Perth and Darwin has huge wheat-handling and fishing industries that make it independent of the fickle tourist dollar, and seasonal workers flood the town during crayfish season. Still a work in progress, Gero blends big-city sophistication with small-town friendliness, offering a strong arts culture, a blossoming foodie scene and some great local music.

Sights

★Western Australian Museum – Geraldton MUSEUM
(☎08-9921 5080; www.museum.wa.gov.au; 1 Museum Pl; admission by donation; ⏰9.30am-4pm) At one of the state's best museums, intelligent multimedia displays relate the area's natural, cultural and Indigenous history. The Shipwreck Gallery documents the tragic story of the *Batavia*, while video footage reveals the sunken HMAS *Sydney II*. Enquire about sailing open days held on the longboat moored behind the museum.

Cathedral of St Francis Xavier Church CHURCH
(☎08-9921 3221; www.geraldtondiocese.org.au; Cathedral Ave; ⏰tours 10am Mon & Fri, 4pm Wed) Arguably the finest example of the architectural achievements of the multi-skilled Monsignor John Hawes. The cathedral's striking features include imposing twin towers with arched openings, a central dome, Romanesque columns and boldly striped walls.

Geraldton Regional Art Gallery GALLERY
(☎08-9964 7170; www.artgallery.cgg.wa.gov.au; 24 Chapman Rd; ⏰10am-5pm Tue-Sun) FREE With an excellent permanent collection, including paintings by Norman Lindsay and Elizabeth Durack, this gallery also presents

GREENOUGH

Located 24km south of Geraldton, the rural area of historic Greenough makes a pleasant overnight stay. Sights such as the **Central Greenough Historical Settlement** (☎08-9926 1084; www.centralgreenough.com; Brand Hwy; adult/child $6/3, cafe meals $10-28; ⏰9am-4pm, from 10am Nov-Dec & Feb-Mar), with its handful of 19th-century buildings, and the **Pioneer Museum** (www.greenoughmuseum.com; Phillips Rd; adult/child $5/free; ⏰9.30am-3.30pm) detail early settler life and offer a chance to stretch the legs, although the area's main attractions are its excellent food and lodgings. Around 2km north of Central Greenough, look out for the quirky **Leaning Trees**, twisted into idiosyncratic shapes by incessant Indian Ocean gusts.

Bentwood Olive Grove (☎08-9926 1196; www.bentwood.com.au; Brand Hwy; d $130-160; ❄) has a long connection to gourmet food, though its focus is now on accommodation, with a beautiful stone cottage sleeping up to six. The Transwa daily service to Geraldton will drop you on the Brand Hwy entrance.

THE WILD FLOWER WAY

Inland east from Geraldton, Rte 123 leads to wheat silos, wild flowers and little one-pub towns that are a hive of activity between August and September as minibuses full of senior travellers zoom around hunting blossoms. Accommodation includes caravan parks, pubs and motels, and there are regular transport links with Transwa. In wild flower season, local visitor centres sometimes run minibuses to the best sites.

Morawa, Mingenew & Mullewa

The 'three Ms' form a triangle that buzzes during wild flower season but offers limited appeal to travellers outside this time. Morawa and Mullewa both have distinctive churches designed by Monsignor John Hawes.

Coalseam Conservation Park (www.parks.dpaw.wa.gov.au/park/coalseam; camping per person $7), 34km northeast of Mingenew on the Irwin River, has everlastings (paper daisies), a short loop walk, and ancient fossil shells embedded in the cliffs.

Mullewa is famous for its wreath flower, *Lechenaultia macrantha.* The town holds an annual wild flower show at the end of August. In season, the roads heading northeast to Yalgoo are normally carpeted in everlastings.

Perenjori

Perenjori, 360km from Perth, is a pretty town surrounded by abundant wildlife and, from July to November, stunning wild flowers. The **visitor centre** (☎08-9973 1105; www.perenjori.wa.gov.au; Fowler St; ⏲9am-4pm Mon-Fri Jul-Oct), also home to the **pioneer museum** (adult/child $2/0.50), has self-drive brochures including *The Way of the Wildflowers* and *Monsignor Hawes Heritage Trail.* They can provide access to the beautiful **St Joseph's Church**, designed by the prolific Hawes.

provocative contemporary work and regular touring exhibitions.

Old Geraldton Gaol Craft Centre HISTORIC BUILDING
(☎08-9921 1614; Bill Sewell Complex, Chapman Rd; ⏲10am-3.30pm Mon-Sat) The crafts are secondary to the gloomy cells that housed prisoners from 1858 to 1986, and the historic documents that detail their grim circumstances.

HMAS Sydney II Memorial MONUMENT
(www.hmassydneymemorial.com.au; Mt Scott; ⏲tours 10.30am) FREE Commanding the hill overlooking Geraldton is this memorial commemorating the 1941 loss of the *Sydney* and its 645 men after a skirmish with the German raider *Kormoran*.

Activities

Most activities are water-based, but there is also an excellent network of bike paths, including the 10km-long coastal route from **Tarcoola Beach to Chapman River**. Grab the *Local Travelsmart Guide* from the visitor centre. Bikes can be hired from **Revolutions** (☎08-9964 1399; www.revolutions-geraldton.com.au; 2c Jensen St; bike hire per day $20; ⏲9am-5.30pm Mon-Fri, to noon Sat).

G-Spot Xtreme WINDSURFING
(☎08-9965 5577; www.gspotxtreme.com.au; 241a Lester Ave; hire per day windsurfers from $100, kayaks 2/4 hours from $30/45; ⏲10am-4pm Tue-Fri, 10am-1pm Sat) Hire or buy windsurfing and kiteboarding equipment and kayaks.

Batavia Coast Dive Academy DIVING
(☎08-9921 4229; www.facebook.com/bataviacoastdive; 118 Northwest Coastal Hwy; local dives with/without equipment $140/100; ⏲9am-5pm Mon-Fri, 8am-1pm Sat, 10am-noon Sun) Offers open-water courses (full PADI $630) and a range of diving trips, including chartered trips to the Houtman Abrolhos Islands (from $300 per person per day).

Midwest Surf School SURFING
(☎0419 988 756; http://surf2skool.com; lessons from $60, board hire $30) Courses for absolute beginners through to advanced at Geraldton's back beach.

KiteWest KITEBOARDING
(☎0449 021 7840449 021 784; www.kitewest.com.au; coaching per hr from $50) Kiteboarding courses, surfing lessons and paddleboarding tuition. Also 4WD camping tours and fishing, scenic and wild flower daytrips (per person from $95).

Geraldton

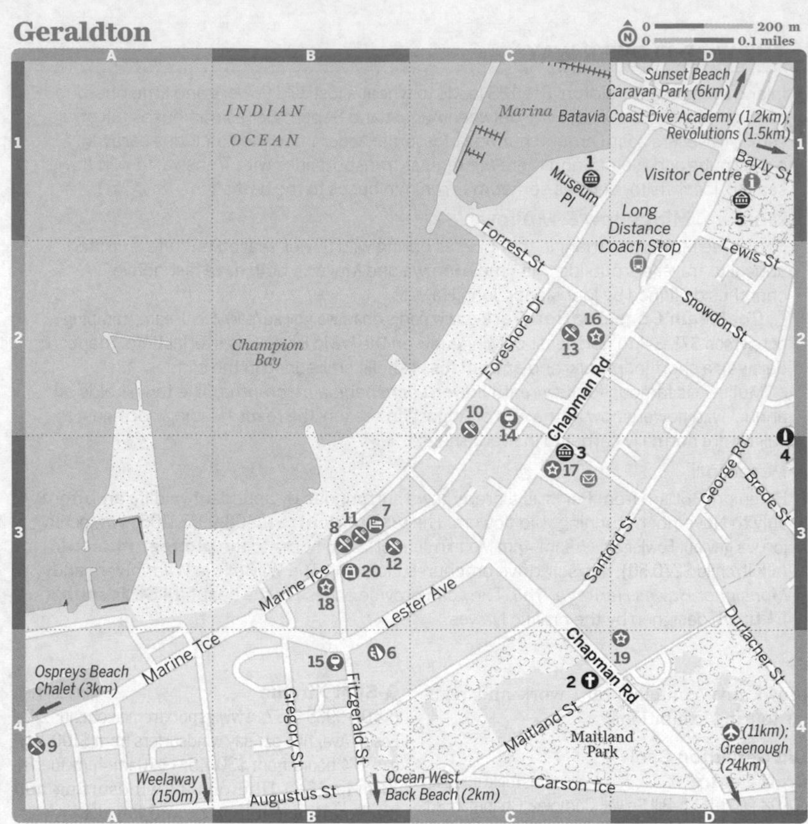

Sleeping

Expect price hikes for school and public holidays.

Foreshore Backpackers HOSTEL $
(08-9921 3275; www.foreshorebackpackers.com.au; 172 Marine Tce; dm/s/d $30/50/70; @) This rambling central hostel is full of hidden nooks, sunny balconies and world-weary travellers. It's very close to good bars and cafes, and a good place to find a job, lift or travel buddy.

Sunset Beach Holiday Park CARAVAN PARK $
(1800 353 389; www.sunsetbeachpark.com.au; Bosley St; powered sites $38, cabins $110-145) About 6km north of the CBD, Sunset Beach has roomy, shaded sites just a few steps from a lovely beach, and an ultramodern camp kitchen with the biggest plasma TV on the entire coast.

★**Ospreys Beach Chalet** COTTAGE $$
(0447 647 994; enerhkalm@gmail.com; 40 Bosuns Cr, Point Moore; 2 persons from $155) Both ospreys and beach are nearby this sustainably restored cottage, which began life as a proof-of-concept project. Rainwater tanks and solar panels complement recycled materials in a restoration that doesn't skimp on comfort. There are plenty of outdoor areas and the rear native garden is a gem.

Ocean West APARTMENT $$
(08-9921 1047; www.oceanwest.com.au; 1 Hadda Way; 1-/3-bedroom apt from $133/213;) Don't let the '60s brick put you off; these fully self-contained units have all been tastefully renovated, making them one of the better deals in town. The wildly beautiful back beach is just across the road.

Weelaway B&B $$
(08-9965 5232; www.weelaway.com.au; 104 Gregory St; r $100-135, 2-bedroom cottages from

Geraldton

$165;) Weelaway offers rooms in a heritage-listed house dating from 1862. There are formal lounge rooms, shady verandahs, and a well-stocked library, and it's all within walking distance of the centre of town.

Eating

Free barbecues and picnic tables dot the foreshore.

Jaffle Shack CAFE $

(www.facebook.com/TheJaffleShack; 188 Marine Tce; snacks $6-12; 7.30am-4pm Mon-Fri, to 3pm Sat, to 1pm Sun) The humble jaffle (toasted sandwich) is showcased at this rustic cafe. Fillings range from classic Aussie combos such as Vegemite and cheese, to butter chicken and raita, or Vietnamese-style pulled pork. Leave room for a Nutella one for dessert, and pop back later in the day for Gero's best ice-cream milkshakes. Damn fine coffee, too.

Geraldton Fish Market SEAFOOD $

(365 Marine Tce; 8.30am-5.30pm Mon-Fri, to noon Sat) Secure briny fresh fish and seafood for your next ad-hoc, al-fresco Aussie feast, or stock up on tasty treats including smoked fish and pickled octopus. Delicious ready-made seafood curries are good value at $14.95.

Go Health Lunch Bar CAFE $

(08-9965 5200; 122 Marine Tce; light meals around $11; 8.30am-3pm Mon-Sat;) Vegetarians can rejoice at the choice of fresh juices and smoothies, excellent espresso, healthy burritos, lentil burgers, focaccias and other light meals from this popular lunch bar in the middle of the mall.

Culinary HQ CAFE $

(08-9964 8308; www.culinaryhq.com.au; 202 Marine Tce; lunch $14.50; 7am-4pm Mon-Fri, 8am-1pm Sat) An eclectic gourmet menu changes weekly at this bustling providore and includes soups, baguettes and cooked meals that are also available for take-away – perfect for that hostel or campervan reheat.

★**Saltdish** CAFE $$

(08-9964 6030; 35 Marine Tce; breakfast $8-20, lunch $16-32; 7.30am-4pm Mon-Fri;) The hippest cafe in town serves innovative, contemporary brekkies, light lunches and industrial-strength coffee, and screens films in its courtyard on summer evenings. Try the sweetcorn and coriander fritters. BYO wine or beer.

Provincial MODERN AUSTRALIAN $$

(08-9964 1887; www.theprovincial.com.au; 167 Marine Tce; tapas $8-20, pizza $14-20, mains $20-30; 4.30pm-late Tue-Sat) Stencil art adorns this atmospheric wine bar serving up tapas, wood-fired pizzas and more robust main courses. Try the zesty coconut prawn curry with a pint of zingy White Rabbit Belgian Pale Ale. Service can be slightly haphazard, but The Provincial has a coolly cosmopolitan vibe. Live music most Friday and Saturday nights.

OFF THE BEATEN TRACK

HOUTMAN ABROLHOS ISLANDS

Better known as 'the Abrolhos', this archipelago of 122 coral islands, 60km off the coast of Geraldton, is home to amazing wildlife including sea lions, green turtles, carpet pythons, over 90 seabird species and the Tammar wallaby. Much of the flora is rare, endemic and protected, and the surrounding reefs offer great diving thanks to the warm Leeuwin Current, which allows tropical species such as *Acropora* (staghorn) coral to flourish further south than normal.

These gnarly reefs have claimed many ships over the years, including the ill-fated *Batavia* (1629), and *Hadda* (1877), and you can dive on the wreck sites, as well as follow a number of self-guided dive trails (see the WA Fisheries *Abrolhos Islands Information Guide* for details). Because the general public can't stay overnight, divers (and surfers) normally need a multi-day boat charter. If you're content with a day trip where you can bushwalk, picnic, snorkel or fish, then flying in is your best bet.

Batavia Coast Dive Academy (p975) Can help get a boat together.

Shine Aviation Services (☎08-9923 3600; www.shineaviation.com.au; 90min/full-day tours $175/240) Full-day tours include a landing on the Abrolhos Islands and snorkelling.

Geraldton Air Charter (☎08-9923 3434; www.geraldtonaircharter.com.au; Brierly Terminal, Geraldton Airport; half-/full-day tours $240/550) Some trips include the Pinnacles to the south.

Drinking

Freemasons Hotel PUB
(☎08-9964 3457; www.thefreemasonshotel.wix.com/home; cnr Marine Tce & Durlacher St; meals $18-33; ⏰11am-late) The heritage-listed Freo has been serving beer to thirsty travellers since the 1800s. Nowadays it's a popular hang-out, with live music, DJs and open-mic and trivia nights complemented by a good range of bar meals.

Entertainment

Live-music and clubbing options include **Vibe** (☎08-9921 3700; 38-42 Fitzgerald St; ⏰from 11pm Thu-Sun), **Breakers** (☎08-9921 8924; www.facebook.com/breakersgeraldton; 41 Chapman Rd; ⏰from 9pm), **Camel Bar** (☎08-9965 5500; 20 Chapman Rd), the Provincial (p977) and the Freemasons Hotel. There is also a **cinema** (☎08-9965 0568; www.orana-cinemas.com.au; cnr Marine Tce & Fitzgerald St) and **theatre** (☎08-9956 6662; www.queensparktheatre.com.au; cnr Cathedral Ave & Maitland St).

Shopping

Yamaji Art ARTS
(☎0487 420 237, 08-9965 3440; www.yamajiart.com; 205 Marine Tce; ⏰varied, call first) A good opportunity to purchase Yamaji arts, bowls, didgeridoo and music. Opening hours can be flexible, so phone ahead.

Information

There's free wi-fi at the **library** (☎08-9956 6659; www.library.cgg.wa.gov.au; 37 Marine Tce; wi-fi 1st hr free; ⏰from 9am Tue-Sat, from 1pm Sun & Mon; @ 📶) and across central Geraldton.

Sun City Books & Internet Corner (☎08-9964 7258; 49 Marine Tce; ⏰9am-5pm Mon-Fri, to 1pm Sat; @) Internet access and second-hand books.

Visitor Centre (☎08-9921 3999; www.geraldtontourist.com.au; Bill Sewell Complex, Chapman Rd; ⏰9am-5pm Mon-Fri, 10am-4pm Sat & Sun) Accommodation, tours and transport bookings.

Getting There & Around

AIR

Virgin Australia and Qantas both fly daily between Perth and Geraldton. Skippers flies direct to/from Carnarvon a few times weekly. The airport is 12km from Marine Tce.

BUS

Integrity runs three bus services per week linking Geraldton to Perth ($63, six hours), Carnarvon ($115, six hours) and Exmouth ($156, 11 hours). Transwa has daily inland services to Perth ($68, six hours) and thrice weekly services to Kalbarri ($28, two hours). There's also a twice-weekly service to Meekatharra ($76, seven hours). All long-distance buses leave from the **old railway station**, where there is also a Transwa booking office.

TAXI

Call ☎131 008.

Kalbarri

POP 2000

Magnificent red-sandstone cliffs terminate at the Indian Ocean. The beautiful Murchison River snakes through tall, steep gorges before ending treacherously at Gantheaume Bay. Wild flowers line paths frequented by kangaroos, emus and thorny devils, while whales breach just offshore, and rare orchids struggle in the rocky ground. To the north, the towering line of the limestone Zuytdorp Cliffs remains aloof, pristine and remote.

Kalbarri is surrounded by stunning nature, and there's great surfing, swimming, fishing, bushwalking, horse riding and canoeing both in town and in Kalbarri National Park. While the vibe is mostly low key, school holidays see Kalbarri stretched to the limit.

Sights & Activities

Kalbarri has cycle paths along the foreshore, and you can ride out to **Blue Holes** for snorkelling, **Jakes Point** for surfing and fishing, and **Red Bluff Beach**, 5.5km away.

Lookouts along the coast are perfect for watching the sunset. Look for wild flowers along Siles Rd, River Rd and near the airport. The visitor centre publishes wild flower updates in season.

Ask at the visitor centre about other activities including quad biking, skydiving and fishing.

★Kalbarri National Park NATIONAL PARK
(per car $12) With its magnificent river red gums and Tumblagooda sandstone, the rugged Kalbarri National Park contains almost 2000 sq km of wild bushland, stunning river gorges and savagely eroded coastal cliffs. There's abundant wildlife, including 200 species of birds, and spectacular wild flowers between July and November.

A string of lookouts dot the impressive coast south of town and the easy **Bigurda Trail** (8km one way) follows the cliff tops between **Natural Bridge** and **Eagle Gorge**; from July to November you may spot migrating whales. Closer to town are **Pot Alley**, **Rainbow Valley**, **Mushroom Rock** and **Red Bluff**, the latter accessible via a walking trail from Kalbarri (5.5km one way).

The river gorges are east of Kalbarri, 11km down Ajana Kalbarri Rd to the turn-off, and then 20km unsealed to a T-intersection. Turn left for lookouts over **The Loop** and the superb **Nature's Window** (1km return). Bring lots of water for the unshaded **Loop Trail** (8km return). Turning right at the T leads to **Z-Bend** with a breathtaking lookout (1.2km return) or you can continue steeply down to the gorge bottom (2.6km return). Head back to Ajana Kalbarri Rd and travel a further 24km before turning off to **Hawk's Head**, where there are great views and picnic tables, and **Ross Graham lookout**, where you can access the river. It's possible to **hike** 38km from Ross Graham to The Loop in a demanding four-day epic, but be warned: there are no marked trails and several river crossings.

Pelican Feeding WILDLIFE WATCHING
(☎08-9937 1104; ⏲8.45am) FREE Kalbarri's most popular attraction takes place on the waterfront. Look for the compact wooden viewing area and wait for the hungry birds to rock up.

Kalbarri Boat Hire CANOEING
(☎08-99371245; www.kalbarriboathire.com; Grey St; kayak/canoe/surf cat/powerboat per hr $15/15/45/50) Also runs four-hour breakfast and lunch canoe trips down the Murchison (adult/child $70/50).

Kalbarri Abseil CANYONING
(☎08-9937 1618; www.abseilaustralia.com.au; half-day abseiling $80, full-day canyoning $135; ⏲abseiling year round, canyoning Apr-Nov) Abseil into the sheer gorges of Kalbarri National Park, then float along the bottom on inner tubes. Canyoning includes a fairly strenuous 12km hike.

Kalbarri Sandboarding SANDBOARDING
(☎08-9937 2377; www.sandboardingaustralia.com.au; adult/child $80/70) Muck around on sand dunes, then go for a snorkel on these fun half-day tours.

Kalbarri Adventure Tours CANOEING
(☎08-9937 1677; www.kalbarritours.com.au; adult/child from $75/55) Combine canoeing, bushwalking and swimming around the national park's Z-Bend/Loop area. Full- and half-day tours available.

Big River Ranch HORSE RIDING
(☎08-9937 1214; www.bigriverranch.net; off Ajana Kalbarri Rd.; 90min trail rides $85) Track through the beautiful Murchison River floodplain on horseback. All experience levels are catered for. Camping (per person $15) and rustic bunkhouse rooms (per person $25) available.

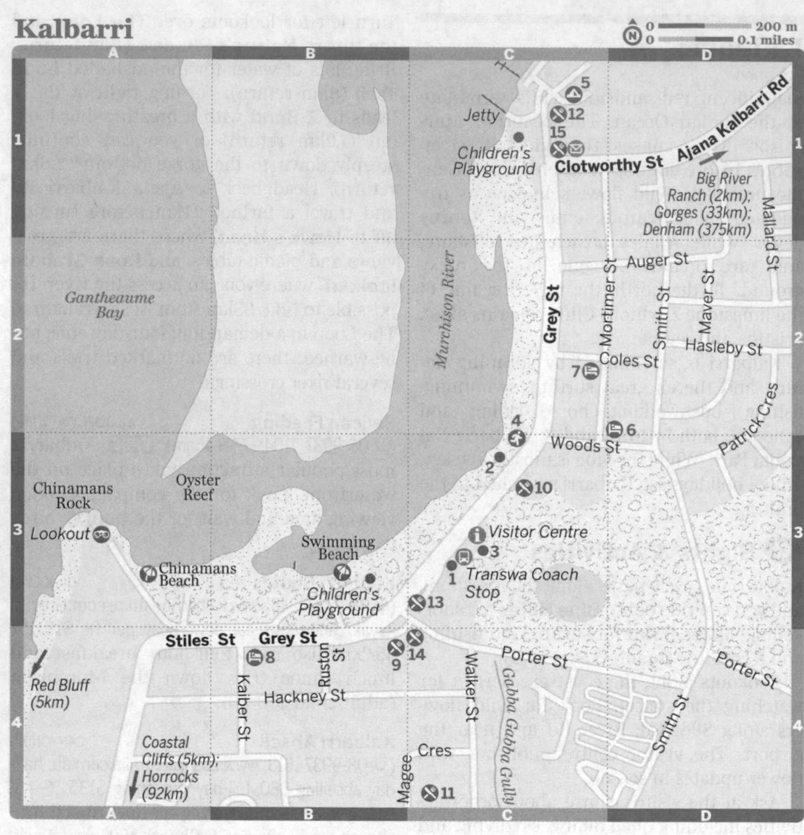

Kalbarri

Activities, Courses & Tours

1 Kalbarri Air Charter C3
2 Kalbarri Boat Hire C3
3 Kalbarri Wilderness Cruises C3
4 Pelican Feeding C3

Sleeping

5 Anchorage Caravan Park C1
6 Kalbarri Backpackers D2
7 Kalbarri Reef Villas C2
8 Pelican Shore Villas B4
Pelican's Nest .... (see 6)

Eating

9 Angies Cafe B4
10 Black Rock Cafe C3
11 Finlay's Fresh Fish BBQ C4
12 Gorges Café C1
13 Kalbarri Motor Hotel C3
14 Restaurant Upstairs C4
15 The Jetty Seafood Shack C1

Tours

The visitor centre can arrange all tour bookings.

Kalbarri Air Charter SCENIC FLIGHT
(☎08-9390 0999; www.kalbarriaircharter.com.au; 62 Grey St; flights $69-315) Offers 20-minute scenic flights over the coastal cliffs, and longer flights over gorges, the Zuytdorp Cliffs, Monkey Mia and the Abrolhos Islands. The River Gorges & Coastal Cliffs tour (45 minutes, $132) is a spectacular combo.

Kalbarri Wilderness Cruises CRUISE
(☎08-9937 1601; www.kalbarricruises.com; adult/child $46/25) Informative two-hour nature cruises along the Murchison.

Reefwalker Adventure Tours WHALE WATCHING
(☎0417 931 091; www.reefwalker.com.au; adult/child $85/55) Spot migrating humpbacks (from July to November). Also runs ocean fishing and sightseeing tours.

Sleeping

Try and avoid school holidays when prices sky rocket.

Kalbarri Backpackers HOSTEL $
(☎08-9937 1430; www.yha.com.au; cnr Woods & Mortimer Sts; dm/d $29/77, bike hire $20; @ 🏊) This nice, shady hostel with a decent pool and barbecue is one block back from the beach. Bikes are available for hire.

Anchorage Caravan Park CARAVAN PARK $
(☎08-9937 1181; www.kalbarrianchorage.com.au; cnr Anchorage Lane & Grey St; powered sites $37, cabins with/without bathroom $100/80; 🏊) The best option for campers, Anchorage has roomy, nicely shaded sites that overlook the river mouth.

Pelican Shore Villas APARTMENT $$
(☎08-9937 1708; www.pelicanshorevillas.com.au; cnr Grey & Kaiber Sts; villas $136-188; ❄ 📶 🏊) These modern and stylish town houses have the best view in town.

Pelican's Nest MOTEL $$
(☎08-9937 1598; www.pelicansnestkalbarri.com.au; 45-47 Mortimer St; d $120-180; ❄ @ 🏊) In a quiet location a short walk from the beach, the Nest has a selection of neat motel-style rooms and good facilities.

Kalbarri Reef Villas APARTMENT $$
(☎08-9937 1165; www.reefvillas.com.au; cnr Coles & Mortimer Sts; units $141-195; ❄ 📶 🏊) One block behind the foreshore, these fully self-contained, two-storey, two-bedroom apartments face onto a palm-filled garden.

Eating & Drinking

There are supermarkets at the two shopping centres.

Angies Cafe CAFE $
(☎08-9937 1738; Shop 6, 46 Grey St; meals $8-22; ⏲7am-4pm) Great little cafe serving fresh, tasty meals with a good selection of salads.

The Jetty Seafood Shack FISH & CHIPS $
(opposite the Marina; meals $11-25, burgers $9-13; ⏲4.30-8.30pm Mon-Sat) Excellent fish and chips, gourmet burgers, and take-away salads (to make you feel at least slightly healthy). Pop across the road and dine at one of the outdoor picnic tables.

★ **Gorges Café** CAFE $$
(☎08-9937 1200; Marina Complex, Grey St; meals $8-25; ⏲7am-3pm Mon-Fri, to 2pm Sat & Sun) Just opposite the jetty with excellent breakfasts and lunches, and friendly service. Try the breakfast wrap or the lemon pepper squid. Look forward to the best coffee in town.

Black Rock Cafe CAFE $$
(80 Grey St; mains $15-40; ⏲7am-10pm Tue-Sun) Friendly service, versatile opening hours, very good seafood, and a contender for Kalbarri's best place to watch an Indian Ocean sunset.

Finlay's Fresh Fish BBQ SEAFOOD $$
(☎08-9937 1260; 24 Magee Cres; mains $15-40; ⏲5pm-late Tue-Sun) Simple barbecue seafood dinners at this Kalbarri institution come with piles of chips and lashings of mayonnaise-packed salads. Don't miss the walls packed with a few decades' strata of kitsch Australiana and Oz popular culture. BYO drinks.

Kalbarri Motor Hotel PUB $$
(☎08-9937 1400; 50 Grey St; pizzas $22, mains $22-37) The garden bar's our favourite spot for a sunset beer. Occasional live bands on Friday and Saturday nights.

Restaurant Upstairs MODERN AUSTRALIAN $$$
(☎08-9937 1033; 2 Porter St, upstairs; mains $25-44; ⏲6pm-late Wed-Mon) The specials board sometimes confuses culinary ambition with talent, but stick to the core menu of seafood and Asian-influenced mains, and you'll be satisfied at the classiest dining spot in town. Book ahead and ask for a spot on the verandah. Good service and a decent wine list seal the deal.

Information

There are ATMs at the shopping centres on Grey and Porter Sts.

Visitor Centre (☎1800 639 468; www.kalbarri.org.au; Grey St; ⏲9am-5pm Mon-Sat, 10am-2pm Sun) Book accommodation and tours. There's internet at the adjacent library.

Getting There & Around

Getting to/from Perth ($80, nine hours) and Geraldton ($28, two hours) by bus is easiest with **Transwa**, which departs from the visitor centre. Heading to/from points further north, the only option is with **Integrity**, which has three

WORTH A TRIP

HORROCKS & PORT GREGORY

The tiny seaside villages of Horrocks and Port Gregory, 92km and 68km south of Kalbarri, respectively, are as quiet as they come. Horrocks, the smaller and prettier of the two, has the dune-side **Horrocks Beach Caravan Park** (☎08-9934 3039; www.horrocksbeachcaravanpark.com.au; sites $24-33, cabins $75-100; 📶) and good-value **Beachside Cottages** (☎08-9934 3031; www.horrocksbeachsidecottages.com; 5 Glance St, Horrocks; d $85-95). Port Gregory, on the far side of the mysterious Pink Lakes, and with a fringing reef, is great for fishing and snorkelling. **Port Gregory Caravan Park** (☎08-9935 1052; www.portgregorycaravanpark.com.au; powered sites $32, cabins $100-125) is your best choice.

departures per week heading to Exmouth ($146, 10 hours) and on to Broome. To link with these services, catch a shuttle linking Kalbarri to/from the Ajana-Kalbarri turn-off. Shuttles should be pre-booked with Integrity or via Kalbarri Backpackers (p981).

Kalbarri Auto Centre (☎08-9937 1290) rents 4WDs and sedans from around $60 per day. Bikes are available from Kalbarri Backpackers and the **entertainment centre** (☎08-9937 1105; www.kalbarripirate.com; 15 Magee Cres; per half/full day $10/20; ⏲9am-5pm Fri-Mon & Wed).

For a taxi, call ☎0419 371 888.

SHARK BAY

The World Heritage–listed area of Shark Bay, stretching from Kalbarri to Carnarvon, consists of more than 1500km of spectacular coastline, containing turquoise lagoons, barren finger-like peninsulas, hidden bays, white-sand beaches, towering limestone cliffs and numerous islands. It's the westernmost part of the Australian mainland, and one of WA's most biologically rich habitats, with an array of plant and animal life found nowhere else on earth. Lush beds of sea-grass and sheltered bays nourish dugongs, sea turtles, humpback whales, dolphins, stingrays, sharks and other aquatic life. On land, Shark Bay's biodiversity has benefited from Project Eden, an ambitious ecosystem-regeneration program that has sought to eradicate feral animals and reintroduce endemic species. Shark Bay is also home to the amazing stromatolites of Hamelin Pool.

The Malgana, Nhanda and Inggarda peoples originally inhabited the area, and visitors can take Indigenous cultural tours to learn about Country. Shark Bay played host to early European explorers and many geographical names display this legacy. In 1616, Dutch explorer Dirk Hartog nailed a pewter dinner plate (now in Amsterdam's Rijksmuseum) to a post on the island (WA's largest) that now bears his name.

ℹ Getting There & Away

Shark Bay airport is located between Denham and Monkey Mia. **Skippers Aviation** flies to/from Perth six times weekly.

The closest **Integrity** approach for buses is the Overlander Roadhouse, 128km away on the North West Coastal Hwy. **Shark Bay Car Hire** (☎08-9948 3032, 0427 483 032; www.carhire.net.au/shuttle-service/; 65 Knight Tce, Denham; shuttle $70, car/4WD hire per day $95/185) runs a connecting shuttle (book at least 24 hours ahead).

Overlander Roadhouse to Denham

Twenty-nine kilometres along Shark Bay Rd from the Overlander Roadhouse is the turn-off for **Hamelin Pool**, a marine reserve with the world's best-known colony of **stromatolites**. These coral-like formations consist of cyanobacteria almost identical to organisms that existed 3.5 billion years ago, and through their use of photosynthesis, are considered largely responsible for creating our current atmosphere, paving the way for more complex life. There's an excellent boardwalk with information panels, best seen at low tide.

The nearby 1884 **Telegraph Office** (admission $5.50; ⏲check at shop) houses a museum containing possibly the only living stromatolites in captivity. The **Postmasters Residence** has a cafe and is the office for the tiny **Hamelin Pool Caravan Park** (☎08-9942 5905; www.hamelinpoolcaravanpark.com; Hamelin Pool; unpowered/powered sites $22/27, units $90; 🏊).

Along the road you pass the turn-off for **Hamelin Station** (☎08-9948 5145; www.hamelinstationstay.com.au; sites per person $12, s/d/f $70/100/110, unit $150), which has lovely rooms in converted shearers' quarters, top-class amenities and somewhat arid camp sites. There's great bird life at the nearby waterhole.

As Shark Bay Rd swings north, you'll pass the turn-off for **Useless Loop** (a closed salt-mining town), **Edel Land** and **Steep Point**, the Australian mainland's most westerly tip.

The dusty former sheep station of **Nanga Bay Resort** (☎08-9948 3992; www.nangabayresort.com.au; Nanga Bay; unpowered/powered sites $25/30, dongas/motel r/huts/villas $50/165/180/250; ❄🌊) has a range of accommodation. Some accommodation options need a spruce-up, but there's a decent on-site restaurant and access to a sparkling, arcing beach.

Inside the vermin-proof fence, and 55km from the Hamelin turn-off, is the road to deserted **Shell Beach**, where tiny cockle shells, densely compacted over time, were once quarried as building material for places such as the Old Pearler Restaurant in Denham.

You'll pass turn-offs to bush camp sites before reaching **Eagle Bluff**, which has clifftop views overlooking an azure lagoon. You may spot turtles, sharks or manta rays.

Denham

POP 1500

Beautiful, laid-back Denham, with its aquamarine sea and palm-fringed beachfront, makes a great base for trips to the surrounding Shark Bay Marine Park, nearby François Peron and Dirk Hartog Island National Parks, and Monkey Mia, 26km away.

Australia's westernmost town originated as a pearling base, and the streets were once paved with pearl shell.

There's a pub, a supermarket, a bakery, cafes and take aways on Knight Tce.

Sights & Activities

Shark Bay World Heritage Discovery Centre MUSEUM
(☎08-9948 1590; www.sharkbayvisit.com; 53 Knight Tce; adult/child $11/6; ⏲9am-6pm) Informative and evocative displays of Shark Bay's ecosystems, marine and animal life, Indigenous culture, early explorers, settlers and shipwrecks.

Little Lagoon PICNIC SPOT
Little Lagoon, 4km from town, has picnic tables and barbecues. Don't be surprised if an emu wanders by.

Ocean Park AQUARIUM
(☎08-9948 1765; www.oceanpark.com.au; Shark Bay Rd; adult/child $20/15; ⏲9am-4pm) On a spectacular headland just before town, this family-run aquaculture farm features an artificial lagoon where you can observe feeding sharks, turtles, stingrays and fish on a 60-minute guided tour. Also on offer are full-day 4WD tours to François Peron National Park ($180) and Steep Point ($350) with bushwalks and snorkelling. A new half-day tour focuses on South Peron ($75).

Tours

Shark Bay Scenic Flights SCENIC FLIGHT
(☎0417 919 059; www.sharkbayair.com.au) Flights include 15-minute Monkey Mia fly overs ($59) and a sensational 40-minute trip over Steep Point and the Zuytdorp Cliffs ($195).

Shark Bay Coaches & Tours BUS TOUR
(☎08-9948 1081; www.sharkbaycoaches.com.au; tours $150) Half-day bus tours and transfers to Monkey Mia from Denham (per person $12, minimum $60).

Sleeping

Expect surcharges for accommodation during school holidays.

Bay Lodge HOSTEL $
(☎08-9948 1278; www.baylodge.info; 113 Knight Tce; dm/d from $34/100; ❄@🌊) Every room at this YHA-associated hostel has its own en suite, kitchenette and TV/DVD. Ideally located across from the beach, it also has a great pool, a larger common kitchen, and a free shuttle bus to Monkey Mia for guests.

SEASIDE BUSH CAMPING

Shark Bay shire offers a choice of four coastal bush camp sites – **Goulet Bluff**, **Whalebone**, **Fowlers Camp** and **Eagle Bluff** – all 20km to 40km south of Denham in the area known as South Peron. To camp here, you must first obtain a permit ($10 per vehicle) from the **Shark Bay visitor centre** (p985). While this is easily arranged via phone (if yours has any reception), in practice it's better to scope the sites first, then get the permit. There are no facilities and a one-night limit applies to the whole area.

OFF THE BEATEN TRACK

WAY OUT WEST IN EDEL LAND

The Australian mainland's westernmost tip is **Steep Point**, just below **Dirk Hartog Island**. It's a wild, wind-scarred, barren clifftop with a beauty born of desolation and remoteness. The **Zuytdorp Cliffs** stretch away to the south, the limestone peppered with blowholes, while leeward, bays with white sandy beaches provide sheltered camp sites. The entire area is known as **Edel Land**, and is a proposed national park. Anglers catch game fish from the towering cliffs, but few tourists make the 140km rough drive down a dead-end road to reach the point.

Access is via Useless Loop Rd, and is controlled by the **Department of Parks & Wildlife** (www.parks.dpaw.wa.gov.au; entry permit per vehicle $12, sites per person $19). There is a ranger station at **Shelter Bay**, with camping nearby; at Steep Point (rocky and exposed); and at **False Entrance** to the south. Sites are limited and must be booked in advance. There is also accommodation at the **Dirk Hartog Island Eco Lodge** (08-9948 1211; www.dirkhartogisland.com; full board per person $290-350, min 2-night stay; Mar-Oct;). Rates include excellent gourmet seafood meals.

You'll need a high-clearance 4WD as the road deteriorates past the Useless Loop turn-off (approximately 100km from Shark Bay Rd). Tyres should be deflated to 20psi. Ensure you bring ample water and enough fuel to return to the Overlander Roadhouse (185km) or Denham (230km). During winter, a barge runs from Shelter Bay to Dirk Hartog Island (bookings essential). See www.sharkbay.org.au for details and downloadable permits. Hire-car companies will not insure for this road, though tours can be arranged from Denham. Steep Point is definitely more easily reached by boat, but that's not the Point, is it?

Beachfront units ($130) have great ocean views.

Denham Seaside Tourist Village CARAVAN PARK $
(08-9948 1242; www.sharkbayfun.com; Knight Tce; unpowered/powered sites $36/43, units $95-160;) This lovely, shady park on the water's edge is the best in town, though you will need to borrow the drill for your tent pegs. Cover up at night against the insects and ring first if arriving after 6pm.

Oceanside Village CABIN $$
(08-9948 3003; www.oceanside.com.au; 117 Knight Tce; cabins $160-200;) These neat self-catering cottages with sunny balconies are perfectly located directly opposite the beach.

Tradewinds APARTMENT $$
(1800 816 160; www.tradewindsdenham.com.au; Knight Tce; units $145-165;) Spacious, fully self-contained, modern units right across from the beach.

Eating & Drinking

★**Ocean Restaurant** CAFE $$
(www.oceanpark.com.au; Shark Bay Rd; mains $26-32; 9am-5pm;) The most refined lunch in Shark Bay also comes with the best view. Inside Ocean Park, overlooking turquoise waters, you can partner beer and wine with tapas, all-day brekkies and local seafood. The platter for two people ($42) is excellent value. Fully licensed.

Old Pearler Restaurant SEAFOOD $$$
(08-9948 1373; 71 Knight Tce; meals $30-53; from 5pm Mon-Sat) Built from shell bricks, this atmospheric nautical haven serves fantastic seafood. The exceptional platter features local snapper, whiting, cray, oysters, prawns and squid – all grilled, not fried. BYO drinks; bookings recommended.

Shark Bay Hotel PUB
(08-9948 1203; www.sharkbayhotelwa.com.au; 43 Knight Tce; dinner $22-38; 10am-late) Sunsets are dynamite from the front beer garden of Australia's most westerly pub.

Information

For information, interactive maps and downloadable permits., check out www.sharkbay.org.au.

There are ATMs at Heritage Resort and Shark Bay Hotel, and internet access at the **Community Resource Centre** (CRC; 08-9948 1787; 67 Knight Tce;).

Department of Parks & Wildlife (08-9948 2226; www.parks.dpaw.wa.gov.au; 61-63 Knight Tce; 8am-5pm Mon-Fri) Park passes and information.

Shark Bay Visitor Centre (08-9948 1590; www.sharkbayvisit.com; 53 Knight Tce; 9am-6pm) Accommodation, tour bookings and bush-camping permits for South Peron.

François Peron National Park

François Peron National Park NATIONAL PARK
(per vehicle $12) Covering the whole peninsula north of Denham is an area of low scrub, salt lakes and red sandy dunes, home to the rare bilby, mallee fowl and woma python. There's a scattering of rough camp sites alongside brilliant white beaches, all accessible via 4WD (deflate tyres to 20psi). Don't miss the fantastic **Wanamalu Trail** (3km return), which follows the clifftop between Cape Peron and Skipjack Point. Spot marine life in the crystal waters below.

Note that 2WD vehicles can enter only as far as the old **Peron Homestead**, where there's a walk around the shearing sheds, and an artesian-bore hot tub. Tours to the park start at around $180 per person from Denham or Monkey Mia. Groups should consider hiring a 4WD from Denham for the same price.

Monkey Mia

Watching the wild dolphins turn up for a feed each morning in the shallow waters of **Monkey Mia** (adult/child/family $8.50/3.20/17), 26km northeast of Denham, is a highlight of every traveller's trip to the region. Watch the way they herd fish upside down, trying to trap them against the surface. The pier makes a good vantage point. The first feed is around 7.45am, but you'll see them arrive earlier. Stay around after the session, as the dolphins commonly come a second or third time.

Note that visitors are restricted to the edge of the water, and only a lucky three people per session are selected to wade in and help feed the dolphins.

Monkey Mia Visitors Centre (08-9948 1366; 8am-4pm) has information and tours.

You can volunteer to work full time with the dolphins for between four and 14 days – it's popular, so apply several months in advance and specify availability dates, though sometimes there are last-minute openings. Contact the **volunteer coordinator** (08-9948 1366; monkeymiavolunteers@westnet.com.au).

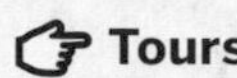

Tours

Wula Guda Nyinda Aboriginal Cultural Tours CULTURAL TOUR
(0429 708 847; www.wulaguda.com.au; 90min tours adult/child from $60/30) Learn 'how to let Country talk to you' on these excellent bushwalks led by local Aboriginal guide Darren 'Capes' Capewell. You'll pick up some local Malgana language and identify bush tucker and Indigenous medicine. The sunset 'Maru Maru Dreaming' tours (adult/child $60/30) are magical. There are also snorkelling and kayak tours (adult half/full day $140/185) and exciting 4WD adventures ($185).

Aristocat II CRUISES
(1800 030 427; www.monkey-mia.net; 1-/2½hr tours $50/86) Cruise in comfort on this large catamaran, and you might see dugongs, dolphins and loggerhead turtles. You'll also stop off at the Blue Lagoon Pearl Farm.

Wildsights ADVENTURE TOUR
(1800 241 481; www.monkeymiawildsights.com.au) On the small *Shotover* catamaran you're close to the action; 2½-hour wildlife cruises start from $89. There are also 1½-hour sunset cruises ($39) and full-day 4WD trips to François Peron National Park ($195); discounts are available for multiple trips.

Sleeping & Eating

Monkey Mia Dolphin Resort RESORT $$
(1800 653 611; www.monkeymia.com.au; tent sites per person $16, van sites from $44, dm/d $30/109, garden units $229, beachfront villas $329;) With a stunning location the only accommodation option in Monkey Mia caters to campers, backpackers, package and top-end tourists. The staff are friendly, and the backpacker 'shared en suites' are good value, but the top-end rooms are expensive. It can also get very crowded. The restaurant has sensational water views but meals are overpriced, while the backpacker bar has cheaper food and excitable backpackers.

Getting There & Away

There is no public transport to Monkey Mia from Denham. If you stay at Bay Lodge (p983) in Denham, you can use its shuttle but it only runs alternate days. Other options are hiring a car or bicycle, or using the shuttle from Shark Bay Coaches (p983).

GASCOYNE COAST

This wild, rugged, largely unpopulated coastline stretches from Shark Bay to Ningaloo, with excellent fishing and waves that attract surfers from around the world. Subtropical Carnarvon, the region's hub, is an important fruit- and vegetable-growing district, and farms are always looking for seasonal workers. The 760km Gascoyne River, WA's longest, is responsible for all that lushness, though it flows underground for most of the year. Inland, the distances are huge and the temperatures high; here you'll find the ancient eroded rocks of the Kennedy Range.

Carnarvon

POP 9000

On Yinggarda country at the mouth of the Gascoyne River, fertile Carnarvon, with its fruit and vegetable plantations and thriving fishing industry, makes a pleasant stopover between Denham and Exmouth. This friendly, vibrant town has quirky attractions, a range of decent accommodation, well-stocked supermarkets and great local produce. The tree-lined CBD exudes a tropical feel, and the palm-fringed waterfront is a relaxing place to amble. The long picking season from March to January ensures plenty of seasonal work.

The last weekend of October sees the town taken over by desert drivers and riders competing in the gruelling 511km **Gascoyne Dash** (Gassy Dash; www.gasdash.com).

Sights & Activities

Carnarvon's luxuriant plantations along North and South River Rds provide a large proportion of WA's fruit and veg; grab the *Gascoyne Food Trail* (www.gascoynefood.com.au) brochure from the visitor centre.

You can walk or ride 2.5km along the old tramway to the **Heritage Precinct** on Babbage Island (www.carnarvonheritage.com.au), once the city's port. **One Mile Jetty** (adult/child $5/free; 9am-4.30pm) provides great fishing and views; walk or take the quirky **Coffee Pot Train** (adult/child $10/5) to the end. The nearby **Lighthouse Keepers Cottage** (Heritage Precinct; 10am-1pm) FREE has been painstakingly restored; don't miss the view from the top of the creaky water tower in the **Railway Station Museum** (9am-5pm) FREE.

The palm-lined **walking path** along the side of the Fascine (the body of water at the end of Robinson St) is a pleasant place for a sunset wander.

OTC Dish LANDMARK
(Mahony Ave) Established jointly with NASA in 1966, the OTC Dish at the edge of town tracked the *Gemini* and *Apollo* space missions, as well as Halley's Comet before closing in 1987. The fascinating **Carnarvon Space and Technology Museum** (www.carnarvonmuseum.org.au; Mahony Ave; adult/child $7/5; 10am-2pm, shorter hrs outside tourist season) is nearby, expanded in late 2014 with an interactive mock-up of a *Saturn V* command module.

Gwoonwardu Mia GALLERY
(08-9941 1989; wwww.gahcc.com.au; 146 Robinson St; 10am-3pm Mon-Fri) Gwoonwardu Mia, built to depict a cyclone, represents the five local Aboriginal language groups and houses a cultural centre and art gallery. Highlights include the poignant oral testimonies from Aboriginal elders in the award-winning Burlganjya Wanggaya (Old People Talking) exhibition.

Bumbak's FARM TOUR
(08-9941 8006; 449 North River Rd; 1hr tours $8.80; shop 9am-4pm Mon-Fri, tours 10am Mon, Wed & Fri Apr-Oct) Bumbak's, a working banana and mango plantation, offers tours of the plantation and sells a variety of fresh and dried fruit, preserves and yummy homemade ice cream.

Sleeping

Most accommodation is spread out along the 5km feeder road from the highway. Try to arrive before 6pm.

Fish & Whistle HOSTEL $
(08-9941 1704; Beardaj@highway1.com.au; 35 Robinson St; s/d/tw $50/60/60, motel r $120;) Travellers love this big, breezy backpackers with its wide verandahs, bunk-free rooms and excellent kitchen. There are air-con motel rooms out the back and the **Port Hotel** serving decent beer downstairs. The owners can help guests find seasonal jobs and provide transport to orchards and farms.

Coral Coast Tourist Park CARAVAN PARK $
(08-9941 1438; www.coralcoasttouristpark.com.au; 108 Robinson St; powered sites $35-45, cabins & units $75-205;) This pleasant, shady park, with tropical pool and grassy sites, is

the closest to the town centre. There's a variety of well-appointed cabins, a decent camp kitchen, and bicycles for hire.

Carnarvon Central Apartments APARTMENT $
(☎08-9941 1317; www.carnarvonholidays.com; 120 Robinson St; 2-bedroom apt $140; ❄) These neat, fully self-contained apartments are popular with business travellers.

Hospitality Inn MOTEL $$
(Best Western; ☎08-9941 1600; www.carnarvon.wa.hospitalityinns.com.au; 6 West St; d $159-179) The best of the motels in town. Rooms are clean and quiet and there's a nice on-site restaurant (meals $19 to $42).

Eating

A good option to enjoy the local seafood is to cook your own on the free barbecues along the Fascine and at Baxter Park. There's also good dining at Carnarvon's handful of pubs.

Self-caterers should check out the delicious produce at the **Gascoyne Arts, Crafts & Growers Market** (www.gascoynefood.com.au/growers-market; Civic Centre car park; ⏲8-11.30am Sat May-Oct). The market is proudly plastic-free, so BYO bag.

River Gums Cafe CAFE $
(Margaret Row, off Robinson St; burgers & salads $7-10; ⏲10am-3pm Wed-Sun May-Oct) Legendary choc-topped banana smoothies, top-notch burgers and home baking are served at this rustic garden cafe in the middle of a fruit plantation.

Morel's Orchard MARKET $
(☎08-9941 8368; 486 Robinson St; ⏲8.30am-5.30pm mid Apr-mid Oct) Local fresh fruit and vegetables, as well as natural fruit ice creams. Our favourite are the frozen chocolate-dipped strawberries.

The Crab Shack SEAFOOD $$
(☎08-9941 4078; Small Boat Harbour; ⏲9am-5pm Mon-Sat Mar-Dec) Fill your esky with freshly steamed crabs, prawns, mussels, shucked oysters and fish fillets. Tasty crab cakes and prawn burgers are also available.

Gwoonwardu Mia Community Café CAFE $$
(☎08-9941 3127; 146 Robinson St; snacks $12.50, juices & smoothies $7; ⏲8am-3pm Mon-Fri) Located in the Gwoonwardu Mia complex, this training centre for Indigenous youth serves tasty snacks – try the breakfast wrap with eggs and chorizo – and the best fruit juices in town.

Information

ATMs are on Robinson St.

The **Visitor Centre** (☎08-9941 1146; www.carnarvon.org.au; Civic Centre, 21 Robinson St; ⏲9am-5pm Mon-Fri, to noon Sat; @) has information, maps and produce.

Getting There & Around

Skippers flies daily to Perth and weekly to Geraldton.

Integrity runs three times a week to Exmouth ($92, four hours), Geraldton ($115, six hours) and Perth ($167, 12 hours). Buses depart from the visitor centre.

Bikes can be hired from Coral Coast Tourist Park (p986).

For a taxi, call ☎131 008.

Point Quobba to Gnaraloo Bay

While the North West Coastal Hwy heads inland, the coast north of Carnarvon is wild, windswept and desolate, a favourite haunt of surfers and fisherfolk. Not many make it this far, but those who do are rewarded by huge winter swells, high summer temperatures, relentless winds, amazing marine life, breath-taking scenery and some truly magical experiences.

Turn down Blowholes Rd, 12km after the Gascoyne bridge, then proceed 49km along the sealed road to the coast. The **blowholes** (waves spraying out of limestone chimneys during a big swell) are just left of the T-intersection. **Point Quobba**, 1km further south, has beach shacks, excellent fishing, some gritty **camp sites** (sites per person $11), and not much else.

Heading right from the T onto dirt, after 8km you'll come across a lonely little cairn staring out to sea, commemorating HMAS *Sydney II*. Two kilometres further is **Quobba Station** (☎08-9948 5098; www.quobba.com.au; unpowered/powered sites per person $13/15, cabins & cottages per person $35-60), with plenty of rustic accommodation, a small store and legendary fishing.

Still on Quobba, 60km north of the homestead, **Red Bluff** (☎08-9948 5001; www.quobba.com.au; unpowered sites per person $15, shacks per person $20, bungalows/safari retreats $180/$200) is a spectacular headland with a wicked surf break and excellent fishing, and is the southern boundary of Ningaloo Marine Park. Accommodation comes in all forms, from exposed camp sites and palm shelters, to exclusive upmarket tents with balconies and superb views. Red Bluff's first shark attack happened in 2012.

The jewel, however, is at the end of the road around 150km from Carnarvon: **Gnaraloo Station** (☎08-9942 5927; www.gnaraloo.com; unpowered sites per person $20-25, cabins d $120-180; 📶) 🍃. Surfers from around the world come every winter to ride the notorious **Tombstones**, while summer brings turtle monitoring (☎08-9315 4809; www.gnaraloo.com/conservation/gnaraloo-turtle-conservation-program; ⏲Oct-Apr) and windsurfers trying to catch the strong afternoon sea breeze, the Carnarvon Doctor. There's excellent snorkelling close to shore and the coastline north from **Gnaraloo Bay** is eye-burningly pristine. You can stay in rough camp sites next to the beach at **3-Mile**, or there's a range of options up at the homestead, the nicest being stone cabins with uninterrupted ocean views – great for spotting migrating whales (June to November) and sea eagles. Gnaraloo is dedicated to sustainability and has implemented a number of visionary environmental programs. The station is always looking for willing workers. Just be aware this is a working station in the Australian outback, not a luxury resort.

Coral Coast & the Pilbara

Includes ➜

Best Places to Eat

- ➜ Whalers Restaurant (p996)
- ➜ Karijini Eco Retreat (p1006)
- ➜ Bills on the Ningaloo Reef (p993)
- ➜ The BBqFather (p997)
- ➜ Silver Star (p1008)

Best Places to Swim

- ➜ Turquoise Bay (p1000)
- ➜ Coral Bay (p992)
- ➜ Hamersley Gorge (p1005)
- ➜ Fern Pool (p1004)
- ➜ Deep Reach Pool (p1004)

Why Go?

Lapping languidly on the edge of the Indian Ocean, the shallow, turquoise waters of the Coral Coast nurture a unique marine paradise. Lonely bays, deserted beaches and crystal-clear lagoons offer superb snorkelling and diving among myriad sea life, including humpback whales, manta rays and loggerhead turtles. World Heritage Ningaloo Reef is one of the very few places you can swim with the world's largest fish, the gentle whale shark. Development is low-key, towns few and far between, and seafood and sunsets legendary.

Inland, miners swarm like ants over the high, eroded ranges of the Pilbara, while ore trains snake down to a string of busy ports stretching from Dampier to Port Hedland. But hidden in the hills are two beautiful gems – Karijini and Millstream Chichester National Parks, home to spectacular gorges, remote peaks, deep tranquil pools and abundant wildlife.

When to Go

Exmouth

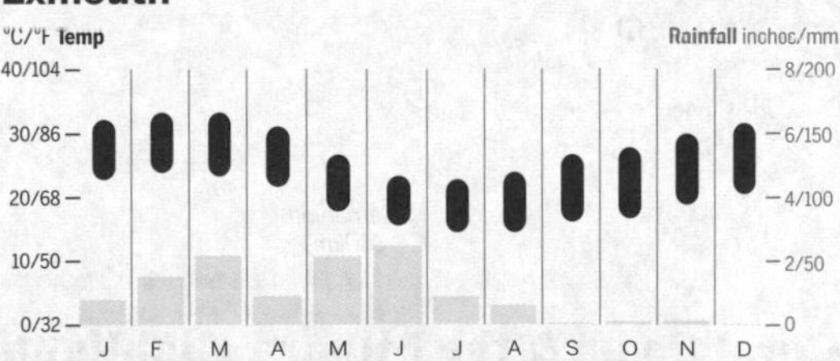

Apr–Jul Whale shark season – don't miss the swim of a lifetime.

Sep & Oct Karijini's gorges warm up and wild flowers blanket the ranges.

Nov–Mar Ningaloo is full of turtle love, eggs and hatchlings.

Coral Coast & the Pilbara Highlights

1. Swimming with 'gentle giant' whale sharks in **Ningaloo Marine Park** (p999).
2. Snorkelling over marine life at **Turquoise Bay** (p1000) in Ningaloo Marine Park.
3. Descending into the 'centre of the earth' on an adventure tour through the gorges of **Karijini National Park** (p1004).
4. Scuba diving off the **Navy Pier** (p999) at Point Murat, one of the world's finest shore dives.
5. Watching the annual humpback-whale migration from the lighthouse at **North West Cape** (p999).

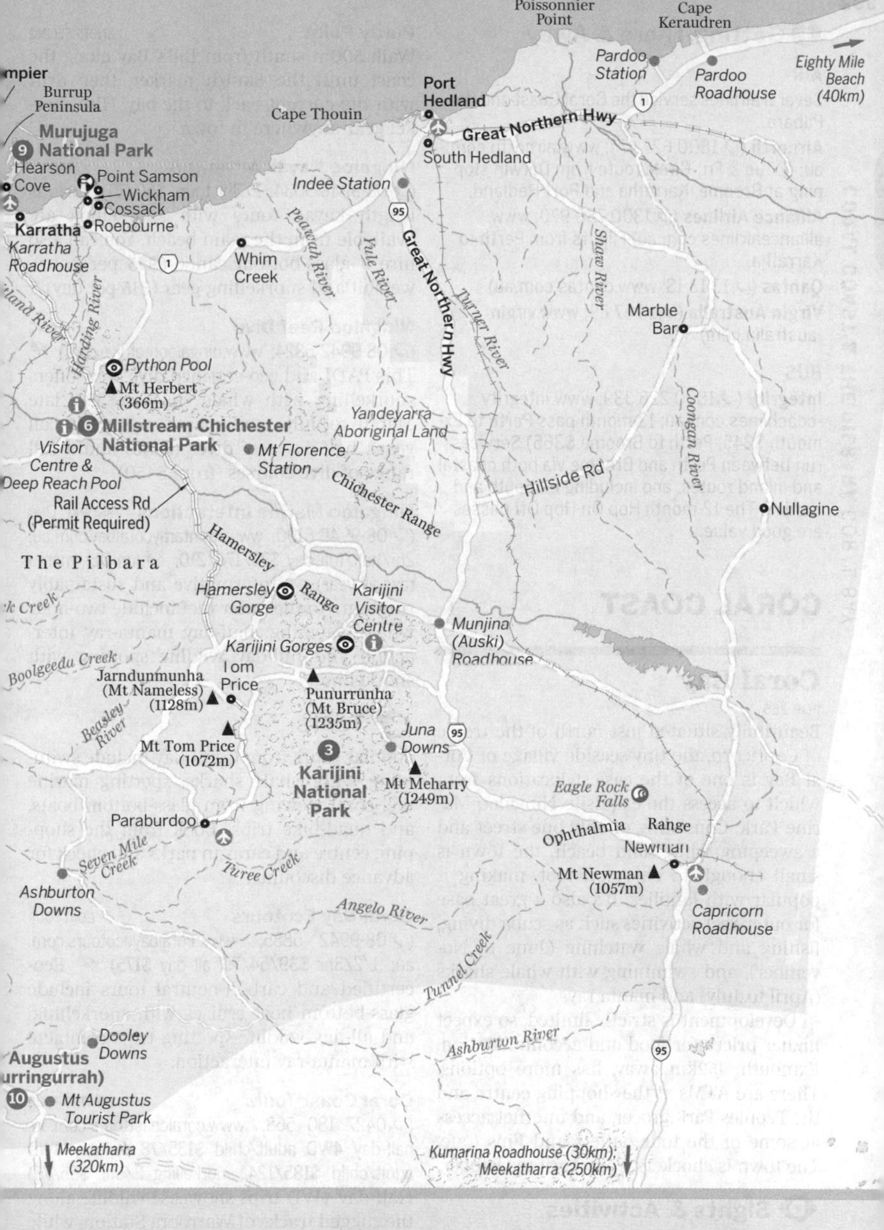

6 Cooling off in an idyllic waterhole at **Millstream Chichester National Park** (p1004).

7 Tracking turtles on remote beaches with the **Ningaloo Turtle Program** (p996).

8 Spotting rare black-flanked rock wallabies on a cruise into stunning **Yardie Creek Gorge** (p1001).

9 Being welcomed to Country on an **Indigenous cultural tour** (p1002) to Murujuga National Park.

10 Scaling the country's biggest, most remote monolith, **Mt Augustus** (p1003).

Getting There & Away

AIR

Several airlines service the Coral Coast and the Pilbara.

Airnorth (1800 627 474; www.airnorth.com.au; Tue & Fri) Circle route from Darwin stopping at Broome, Karratha and Port Hedland.

Alliance Airlines (1300 780 970; www.allianceairlines.com.au) Flights from Perth to Karratha.

Qantas (13 13 13; www.qantas.com.au)

Virgin Australia (13 67 89; www.virgin-australia.com)

BUS

Integrity (1800 226 339; www.integrity-coachlines.com.au; 12-month pass Perth to Exmouth $245, Perth to Broome $365) Services run between Perth and Broome via both coastal and inland routes, and including Exmouth and Karijini. The 12-month Hop On Hop Off passes are good value.

CORAL COAST

Coral Bay

POP 255

Beautifully situated just north of the tropic of Capricorn, the tiny seaside village of Coral Bay is one of the easiest locations from which to access the exquisite Ningaloo Marine Park. Consisting of only one street and a sweeping white-sand beach, the town is small enough to enjoy on foot, making it popular with families. It's also a great base for outer-reef activities such as scuba diving, fishing and whale watching (June to November), and swimming with whale sharks (April to July) and manta rays.

Development is strictly limited, so expect higher prices for food and accommodation. Exmouth, 152km away, has more options. There are ATMs at the shopping centre and the Peoples Park grocer, and internet access at some of the tour outlets and Fins Cafe. The town is chockers from April to October.

Sights & Activities

Fish feeding occurs on the beach at 3.30pm most days. Sunsets are sublime from the lookout above the beach car park.

Bill's Bay BEACH

(P) Keep to the southern end when snorkelling; the northern end (Skeleton Bay) is a breeding ground for reef sharks.

Purdy Point SNORKELLING

Walk 500m south from Bill's Bay along the coast until the 8km/h marker, then drift with the current back to the bay. Hire snorkel gear anywhere in town.

Ningaloo Kayak Adventures KAYAKING

(08-9948 5034; 2/3hr tours $50/70) Various length kayak tours with snorkelling are available from the main beach. You can also hire a glass-bottom canoe ($25 per hour), wetsuit and snorkelling gear ($15 per day).

Ningaloo Reef Dive DIVING

(08-9942 5824; www.ningalooreefdive.com) This PADI and eco-certified dive crew offers snorkelling with whale sharks ($390, late March to July) and manta rays ($140, all year), half-day reef dives ($180) and a full range of dive courses (from $450).

Ningaloo Marine Interactions SNORKELLING

(08-9948 5190; www.mantaraycoralbay.com.au; 2hr/half/full day $75/170/210; Jun-Oct, manta rays all year) Informative and sustainably run tours to the outer reef include two-hour whale watching, half-day manta-ray interaction and full-day wildlife spotting with snorkelling.

Tours

Popular tours from Coral Bay include swimming with whale sharks, spotting marine life, coral viewing from glass-bottom boats, and quad-bike trips. Book from the shopping centre and caravan parks and check for advance discounts.

Coral Bay Ecotours BOAT TOUR

(08-9942 5885; www.coralbayecotours.com.au; 1/2/3hr $39/54/75, all day $175) Eco-certified and carbon-neutral tours include glass-bottom boat cruises with snorkelling, and all-day wildlife-spotting trips complete with manta-ray interaction.

Coral Coast Tours DRIVING TOUR

(0427 180 568; www.coralcoasttours.com.au; half-day 4WD adult/child $135/78, full-day 4WD adult/child $185/124, snorkelling 2/3hr $55/75) Half-day 4WD trips showcase wildlife along the rugged tracks of Warroora Station, while full-day trips follow the coastal track to Yardie Creek and the Cape. There are also reef tours, and airport transfers ($88) continuing on to Exmouth ($110).

Coastal Adventure Tours ADVENTURE TOUR

(08-9948 5190; www.coralbaytours.com.au; 2/2.5hr quad bike $110/130, sailing from $75)

STATION STAYS

If you're sick of cramped caravan parks and want somewhere a little more relaxed and off the beaten track, consider a station stay. Scattered around the Coral Coast are a number of pastoral stations offering a range of rustic accommodation – be it an exquisite slice of empty coast, dusty home paddock, basic shearers' digs or fully self-contained, air-conditioned cottages. Don't expect top-notch facilities; most sites don't have any at all. Power and water are limited; the more self-sufficient you are, the more enjoyable the stay – remember, you're getting away from it all. You will find loads of wildlife, previously unseen stars, oodles of space, and some fair-dinkum outback.

Some stations offer wilderness camping away from the homestead (usually by the coast) and you'll need a 4WD and chemical toilet. These places tend to cater for fisher-types with boats and grey nomads who stay by the week.

Certain stations only offer accommodation during the peak season (April to October).

Giralia (☎08-9942 5937; www.giraliastation.com.au; Burkett Rd, 110km north of Coral Bay; camping per person $10, donga $70, cottage $160, homestead s/d $220/300; ❄ ≋) Popular with fishermen and well set-up for travellers, there's a bush camping area with amenities, dongas, a family cottage and air-conditioned homestead rooms with breakfast and dinner included. The coast is 40 minutes away by 4WD. Meals and liquor available.

Bullara (☎08-9942 5938; www.bullara-station.com.au; Burkett Rd, 70km north of Coral Bay; camping $13, tw/d/cottage $110/140/200; ⏲Apr-Oct) Near the Minilya road junction and 2WD accessible, there's several rooms in the renovated shearers' quarters, a three-bedroom cottage and unpowered camping with amenities.

Warroora (☎08-9942 5920; www.warroora.com; Minilya Exmouth Rd, 47km north of Minilya; camping per day/week $10/50, r per person $30, cottages $150) Offers wilderness camp sites along the coast (some 2WD accessible) and cheap rooms in the shearers' quarters as well as a self-contained cottage and homestead. Chemical toilets for hire (per day $15).

Ningaloo Station (☎08-9942 5936; www.ningaloostation.com.au; Minilya Rd, 85km north of Coral Bay; sites per week $35, bond $100) Not to be confused with the marine park, the original station offers limited, totally self-sufficient bush sites on pristine coastline.

More a booking service than an individual operator, the combined quad bike and snorkelling trips get rave reviews. You can also book sailing excursions, glass-bottom boat tours and manta-ray interaction.

Sleeping & Eating

Avoid school holidays and book well ahead for peak season (April to October). Consider self-catering, as eating out is expensive.

Peoples Park Caravan Village CARAVAN PARK $
(☎08-9942 5933; www.peoplesparkcoralbay.com; sites unpowered/powered $41/47, 1-/2-bedroom cabins $250/270, hilltop villas $295; ❄) This excellent park offers grassy, shaded sites and a variety of fully self-contained cabins. Friendly staff keep the modern amenities and spacious camp kitchen spotless, and it's the only place with freshwater showers. The hilltop villas have superb views, there are plenty of BBQs scattered around, and internet access is available at nearby Fins Cafe.

Ningaloo Club HOSTEL $
(☎08-9948 5100; www.ningalooclub.com; Robinson St; dm $28-32, d with/without bathroom $120/95; ❄@≋) Popular with the party crowd, this hostel is a great place to meet people, and boasts a central pool, a well-equipped kitchen and onsite bar. The rooms could be cleaner, and forget about sleeping before the bar closes. It also sells bus tickets (coach stop outside) and discounted tours.

★Bills on the Ningaloo Reef MODERN AUSTRALIAN $$
(☎08-9385 6655; Robinson St; lunch $16-24, dinner $18-28; ⏲11am-late) This new gastropub immediately ups the ante for fine dining in a location where the other food offerings look decidedly tired. Try the fabulous fish curry, a selection of tapas or wash down the 'bucket of prawns' with a refreshing boutique ale.

Fins Cafe INTERNATIONAL $$
(☎08-9942 5900; Peoples Park; dinner mains $24-46; ⏲breakfast, lunch & dinner; @) Casual,

outdoor BYO with ever-changing blackboard menu showcasing local seafood, curries and safe classics.

Getting There & Around

Coral Bay is 1144km north of Perth and 152km south of Exmouth. The closest airport (p997) is Learmonth, 118km to the north. Groups should consider hiring a car.

Integrity (1800 226 339; www.integrity coachlines.com.au; outside Ningaloo Club) Coaches run three times a week to Perth ($203, 16 hours) and Exmouth ($47, 90 minutes), and once a week to Karijini ($177, 12 hours).

Coral Coast Tours (0427 180 568; www.coralcoasttours.com.au; adult/child $88/44) Airport shuttle between Coral Bay and Learmonth

Exmouth

POP 2500

Once a WWII submarine base, Exmouth didn't flourish until the 1960s brought the Very Low Frequency (VLF) communications facility to North West Cape. Simultaneously, fishing (especially prawns) and resources exploration commenced, both still thriving today (gas flares are visible from Vlamingh Head at night).

With World Heritage protection of Ningaloo Reef, tourism provides the bulk of visitors, many coming to see the magnificent and enigmatic whale sharks (April to July). Peak season (April to October) sees this laid-back town stretched to epic proportions, but don't be put off, it's still the perfect base to explore nearby Ningaloo Marine and Cape Range National Parks. Alternatively, just relax, wash away the road dust and enjoy the local wildlife; emus wandering the footpaths, roos lounging in the shade, goannas ambling across the highway and corellas, galahs and ringnecks screeching and swooping through the trees.

Sights & Activities

Exmouth is flat, hot and sprawling, with most of the attractions located outside town and no public transport. Most activities are water based. Turtle volunteering (p996) is popular from November to January.

Snorkellers and divers head to Ningaloo Marine Park (p999) or the Muiron Islands (p1001). Try to find the informative Parks & Wildlife (DPaW) book *Dive and Snorkel Sites in Western Australia*. Several dive shops in town offer PADI courses.

A set of cycle paths ring Exmouth and continue north to Harold E Holt Naval Base (HEH), where the road continues to Bundegi Beach; watch out for dingos! Ask around for bike hire.

Town Beach BEACH

(1km east of Murat Rd; P) An easy walk from town, this beach is popular with kiteboarders when an easterly is blowing.

Sewerage Works BIRDWATCHING

(Willersdorf Rd) Good water-bird viewing here and at the golf course next door.

Exmouth Cape Horses HORSE RIDING

(0400 886 576; www.exmouthcapehorses.com.au; 1hr ride $70) These short, beautiful beach rides along Exmouth Gulf are suitable for all skill levels and ages.

Tours & Courses

Swim with whale sharks, spot wildlife, dive, snorkel, kayak, surf and fish to your heart's content – the visitor centre (p997) has the full list of tours available. Some are seasonal.

Outside whale-shark season, marine tours focus on manta rays. You need to be a capable snorkeller. Be wary of snorkelling on what may essentially be a dive tour – the action may be too deep. It's normally 30% cheaper if you stay on the boat. Most ocean tours depart from **Tantabiddi** on the western cape and include free transfers from Exmouth. Check conditions carefully regarding 'no sighting' policies and cancellations.

Kings Ningaloo Reef Tours WILDLIFE TOUR

(08-9949 1764; www.kingsningalooreeftours.com.au; snorkeller/observer $385/285) Long-time player Kings gets rave reviews for its whale shark tours. It's renowned for staying out longer than everyone else, and has a 'next available tour' no-sighting policy.

Ningaloo Ecology Cruises BOAT TOUR

(1800 554 062; www.ningalootreasures.com.au; 1/2½hr $50/70) Has one-hour glass-bottom boat trips (April to October), and longer 2½-hour trips (all year) including snorkelling.

Birds Eye View SCENIC FLIGHTS

(0427 996 833; www.ningaloomicrolights.com.au; Exmouth Aerodrome; 30-/60-/90-min flight $199/299/399) Don't want to get your feet wet but still after adrenalin? Get some altitude on these incredible microlight flights over the Cape and (longer flights only) Ningaloo Reef.

Exmouth

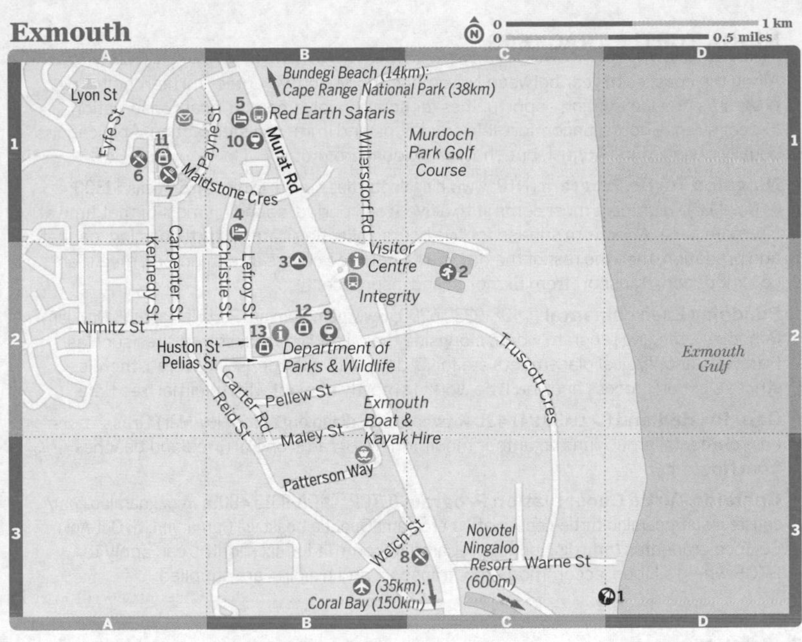

Exmouth

Sights
1 Town Beach D3

Activities, Courses & Tours
2 Sewerage Works C2

Sleeping
3 Exmouth Ningaloo Caravan & Holiday Resort B2
4 Ningaloo Lodge B1
5 Potshot Hotel Resort B1

Eating
6 5 Kennedy St A1
BBqFather .... (see 3)
7 See Salt A1
8 Whalers Restaurant C3

Drinking & Nightlife
9 Grace's Tavern B2
10 Potshot Hotel B1

Shopping
11 Exmouth Shopping Centre A1
12 Ningaloo Kite & Board B2
13 Reef Beef B2

Montebello Island Safaris CRUISE
(☎0419 091 670; www.montebello.com.au; ⊙Apr-Nov) Has a permanent houseboat moored at the Montebello Islands for maximum marine love on a six-night tour (per person $3000).

Capricorn Kayak Tours KAYAKING
(☎0427 485 123; www.capricornseakayaking.com.au; half-/1-/2-/5-day tour $99/179/665/1650) Capricorn offers single- and multi-day kayaking and snorkelling tours along the lagoons of Ningaloo Reef.

Ningaloo Whaleshark-N-Dive DIVING
(☎1800 224 060; www.ningaloowhalesharkndive.com.au) Offers daily dives to Lighthouse Bay ($185) and the Muiron Islands ($210) as well as longer live-aboard tours to the Muiron and Montebello Islands. Dive courses also available from intro ($255) to full PADI ($620).

Sleeping

Accommodation is limited so book ahead, especially for the peak season (April to October).

NINGA TURTLE TRACKERS

Along the coast each year between November and March, volunteer turtle-monitoring programs provide exciting opportunities for active involvement in local conservation. Expect strange hours, uncomfortable conditions and immense satisfaction. Applications usually open around August, but check individual programs.

Ningaloo Turtle Program (NTP; www.ningalooturtles.org.au; Exmouth; 5 weeks $1300; ⏲Nov-Mar) Volunteers must commit to a five-week period, spending most of that time at a remote base. Work from sunrise for five hours collecting data on turtle nesting, habitat and predation, then the rest of the day is free. Your fee covers all equipment, meals, accommodation, transport from Exmouth and insurance.

Pendoley Environmental (☎08-9330 6200; www.penv.com.au; Port Hedland; ⏲Nov-Jan) Pendoley's tagging program works alongside the oil and gas industry at sites such as Barrow Island. Typical placements are for 17 days with all expenses covered, there's a strict selection process and you'll be working mostly at night with minimal free time.

Care for Hedland (☎0439 941 431; www.careforhedland.org.au; ⏲Nov-Mar) Grass-roots environmental group runs volunteer monitoring programs on Port Hedland beaches from November.

Gnaraloo Turtle Conservation Program (GTCP; ☎08-9315 4809; www.gnaraloo.com/conservation/gnaraloo-turtle-conservation-program; Quobba Coast via Carnarvon; ⏲Oct-Apr) Science graduates (any discipline) prepared to commit for six months can apply to GTCP where all food, accommodation, transport and training are supplied.

Exmouth Ningaloo Caravan & Holiday Resort CARAVAN PARK $
(☎08-9949 2377; www.exmouthresort.com; Murat Rd; unpowered/powered sites $38/49, dm/d $39/80, chalets from $205; P❄📶🏊) Across from the visitor centre, this friendly, spacious park has grassy sites, self-contained chalets, four-bed dorms, an on-site restaurant and even a pet section. If you're camping, this is your best bet.

Potshot Hotel Resort RESORT $
(Excape Backpackers YHA; ☎08-9949 1200; www.potshotresort.com; Murat Rd; dm/d $30/72, motel d $145, studios $245, apt from $270; P❄@📶🏊) A town within a town, this bustling resort has 10-bed dorms, standard motel rooms, luxury Osprey apartments, several bars and a disco. The backpacker rooms can be noisy, but the apartments are good value for a group.

Ningaloo Lodge GUESTHOUSE $$
(☎1800 880 949; www.ningaloolodge.com.au; Lefroy St; d $150; P❄📶🏊) These clean, tastefully appointed motel rooms are one of the better deals in town, with a modern communal kitchen, barbecue, shady pool and free wi-fi.

Eating & Drinking

Some popular haunts have relocated or been renamed. There is a supermarket, bakery and several take aways at Exmouth Shopping Centre (p997).

Grace's Tavern (☎08-9949 1000; Murat Rd; ⏲noon-11pm) and **Potshot Hotel** (☎08-9949 1200; Murat Rd; ⏲10am-late) are your drinking options and both serve decent pub meals.

★ **Whalers Restaurant** SEAFOOD $$
(☎08-9949 2416; whalersrestaurant.com.au; 27 Murat Rd, inside Exmouth Escape; mains $29-40; ⏲6pm-late) Recently relocated, this Exmouth institution is famous for its delicious Creole-influenced seafood. Don't miss the signature New Orleans gumbo, complemented by a seafood tasting starter of soft-shell crab, local prawns and oyster shooters. Die-hard bug aficionados need look no further than the towering seafood medley.

See Salt CAFE $$
(☎08-9949 1400; www.seesalt.com.au; 1 Thew St, Shopping Centre; meals $8-22 ; ⏲6.30am-3.30pm daily, 6pm-8.30pm Thu-Sun) Repackaged and relocated Ningaloo Health retains the same wholesome daylight menu while expanding to dinners later in the week. Kick start your morning with chilli eggs or a bowl of Vietnamese *pho* (beef and rice-noodle soup). The more timid can dive into a berry pancake stack, Bircher muesli or a detox juice.

See Salt also offers light lunches, salads, smoothies, take-away picnic hampers (great for a day trip to Cape Range National Park) and excellent coffee.

★BBqFather BARBECUE, ITALIAN **$$**
(Pinocchio; ☎08-9949 4905; www.thebbqfather.com.au; Murat Rd, Exmouth Ningaloo Caravan Park & Resort; mains $18-40; ⊙6-9pm Mon-Sat Feb-Oct) This popular, licensed alfresco *ristorante* has changed its name and gone BBQ crazy, serving up huge, succulent, smoky slabs of beef, pork and veal ribs. After receiving a reality check from the locals, their much loved pizzas and home-made pastas are also back on the menu. The servings are as legendary as ever.

5 Kennedy St MODERN AUSTRALIAN **$$$**
(☎08-9949 4507; www.5kennedyst.com.au; 5 Kennedy St; mains from $30; ⊙noon-late Tue-Thu, 9am-late Fri-Sun) On the old Whalers site, Exmouth's newest restaurant offers sophisticated dishes using the best of local and sustainable ingredients. The menu is divided by dish size and ranges from bite-size snacks to 1kg slabs of meat and bone.

Shopping

Exmouth Shopping Centre SHOPPING CENTRE
(Maidstone Cres) The shopping centre includes a dive shop, gift shop, surf and camping stores, and two supermarkets. A Sunday craft market runs from April to October.

Ningaloo Kite & Board OUTDOOR EQUIPMENT
(Exmouth Camper Hire; ☎08-9949 4050; www.exmouthcamperhire.com.au; 16 Nimitz St; ⊙call first) New and second-hand kites, full beginners' kits and lots of local info from these experts who also rent out fully-stocked camper vans.

Reef Beef FOOD
(☎0408 951 775; 11 Pelias St; ⊙9am-5pm Mon-Fri, 9am-noon Sat) Their blurb says it all – delicious beef jerky. Best road-trip snack ever.

Information

For information on environmental projects around the cape, check out the Cape Conservation Group's website (www.ccg.org.au).

Internet access is available at the **library** (☎08-9949 1462; 22 Maidstone Cres; ⊙8.30am-4pm Mon-Thu, 8.30am-noon Sat; @) and at Potshot Hotel (p996).

Department of Parks & Wildlife (DPaW; ☎08-9947 8000; www.dpaw.wa.gov.au; 20 Nimitz St; ⊙8am-5pm Mon-Fri) Supplies maps, brochures and permits for Ningaloo, Cape Range and Muiron Islands, including excellent wildlife guides. Can advise on turtle volunteering.

Tours N Travel Ningaloo (Europcar; ☎0437 106 183; cnr Pellew St & Murat Rd; internet per hr $5; ⊙8.30am-7pm; @) Internet access, second-hand books and the local Europcar agent.

Visitor Centre (☎08-9949 1176; www.visit-ningaloo.com.au; Murat Rd; ⊙9am-5pm) Tour bookings, bus tickets, accommodation service, Yardie Creek boat tickets and parks information.

Getting There & Away

Exmouth's Learmonth Airport is 37km south of town.

Qantas (☎13 13 13; www.qantas.com.au) Daily flights between Perth and Learmonth.

Airport Shuttle Bus (☎08-9949 4623; $25) Meets all flights; reservations are required when heading to the airport.

Integrity (☎1800 226 339; www.integrity-coachlines.com.au) Coaches run from the visitors centre to Perth ($240, 17 hours), Coral Bay ($47, 90 minutes) and Broome ($240, 18 hours) three times a week; there are weekly services to Karijini ($167, 10 hours).

Red Earth Safaris (☎1800 501 968; www.redearthsafaris.com.au; $200) Weekly Perth express departing Exmouth from the Potshot Resort at 7am on Sunday ($200, 30 hours). Includes meals and an overnight stop.

Getting Around

Budget, Avis and Europcar have agents around town, with car hire starting at $80 per day.

Allens (☎08-9949 2403; rear 24 Nimitz St; per day from $60) Older cars with 150 free kilometres.

Exmouth Boat & Kayak Hire (☎0438 230 269; www.exmouthboathire.com; 7 Patterson Way; kayaks per day $50) Tinnies (small dinghies) or something larger (including a skipper!) can be hired from $100 per day.

Exmouth Camper Hire (☎08-9949 4050; www.exmouthcamperhire.com.au; 16 Nimitz St; 4 days from $660) Camper vans with everything you need to spend time in Cape Range National Park, including solar panels.

Scooters2go (☎08-9949 4488; www.facebook.com/pages/Exmouth-Scooters2go/1550679805188747; cnr Murat Rd & Pellew St; per day/week $80/$175) You only need a car licence for these 50 & 125cc scooters, which are much cheaper by the week. Best to ring first.

Around Exmouth

Head north past **Harold E Holt Naval Base** (HEH) to an intersection before the VLF antenna array. Continue straight on for Bundegi Beach or turn left onto Yardie Creek Rd for the magnificent beaches and bays of the western cape and Ningaloo Reef.

The Cape Range National Park entrance station is at the 40km mark and the road south is navigable by all vehicles as far as **Yardie Creek**. Experienced 4WD-ers can attempt crossing the sandy creek at low tide, before continuing along a rough coastal track all the way to Coral Bay (p992). Check road conditions first at Milyering visitor centre (p999).

Sights & Activities

Bundegi Beach BEACH

(P) In the shadow of the VLF antenna array, and within cycling range of Exmouth (it's 14km north), the calm, sheltered waters of Bundegi Beach and accompanying reef provide pleasant swimming, snorkelling, diving, kayaking and fishing.

North West Cape

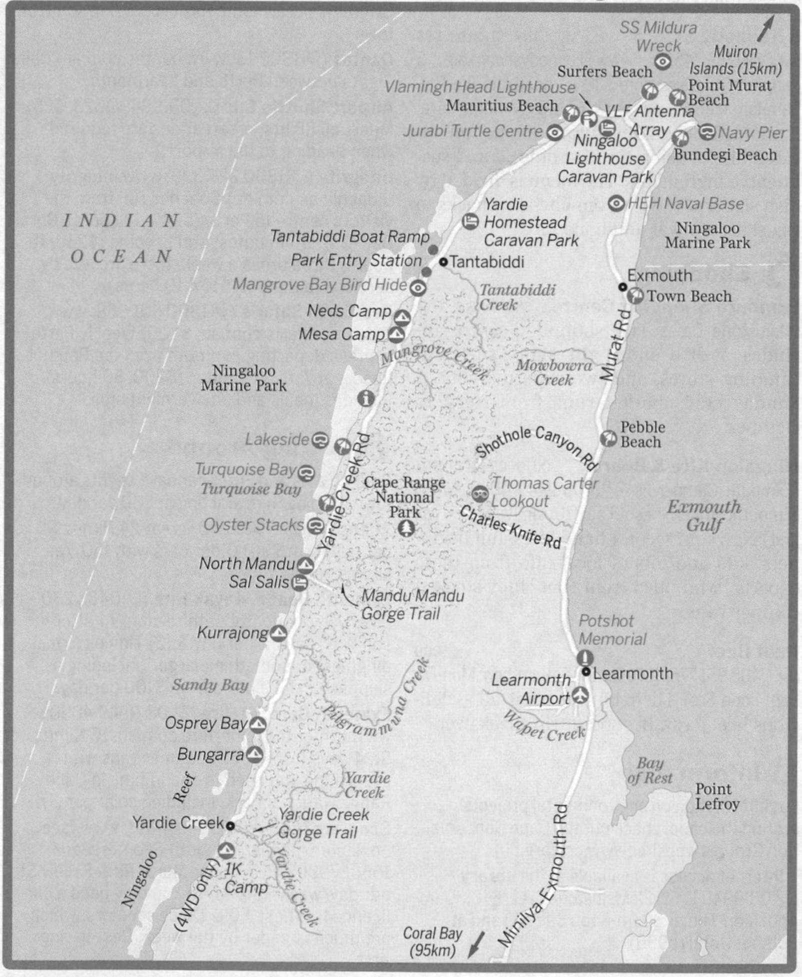

SS Mildura Wreck SHIPWRECK
(Mildura Wreck Rd) Follow the signpost from Yardie Creek Rd to find the 1907 cattle ship that ran aground on the reef.

Vlamingh Head Lighthouse LIGHTHOUSE
It's hard to miss this hilltop lighthouse built in 1912. Spectacular views of the entire cape make it a great place for watching whales and sunsets.

Mauritius Beach BEACH
(Yardie Ck Rd, 21km NW; P) Clothing-optional beach near Vlamingh Head Lighthouse.

★ **Navy Pier** DIVING
(Point Murat; dives $155) Point Murat, named after Napoleon's brother-in-law, is home to one of the world's best shore dives, under the Navy Pier. There's a fantastic array of marine life including nudibranchs, scorpion fish, moray eels and reef sharks. As it's on Defence territory, you'll need to join a tour and the exclusive licence rotates regularly among Exmouth dive shops.

Jurabi Turtle Centre WILDLIFE INTERACTION
(JTC; 08-9947 8000; Yardie Creek Rd; 2hr night tour adult/child $20/10; open 24hr; night tours from 6.30pm Nov-Mar) FREE Visit by day (free entry) to study turtle life cycles, and obtain the DPaW pamphlet *Marine Turtles in Ningaloo Marine Park*. Return at night to observe nesting turtles and hatchlings (November to March), remembering to keep the correct distance and never to shine a light or camera flash directly at any animal.

The best and ecologically safest way to encounter nesting turtles is on a DPaW guided night tour. Book at Exmouth Visitors Centre.

Exmouth Kite Centre KITESURFING
(0467 906 091; www.exmouthkitecentre.com.au; Lot 2 Yardie Creek Rd, Ningaloo Lighthouse Caravan Park; 1/3hr lessons $100/270) Learn to kitesurf with this fun crew based out at Vlamingh Head.

Sleeping

Ningaloo Lighthouse Caravan Park CARAVAN PARK $
(08-9949 1478; www.ningaloolighthouse.com; Yardie Creek Rd; unpowered/powered sites $33/41, cabins $115, bungalows $135, lighthouse/lookout chalets $155/245;) Superbly located on the western cape under Vlamingh lighthouse near Surfers Beach, the clifftop chalets have fantastic views. There's plenty of shady tent sites for lesser mortals and a cafe during peak season (May to September).

Yardie Homestead Caravan Park CARAVAN PARK $
(08-9949 1389; www.yardie.com.au; Yardie Creek Rd; unpowered/powered sites $32/38, cabins $130, chalets $180; P) Located just outside Cape Range National Park, this former sheep station caters mainly for anglers, though travellers are also welcome and there are some nice grassy tent sites. There's a range of cabins (most require a security bond) plus a pool, shop and camp kitchen.

Information

Milyering Visitor Centre (08-9949 2808; Yardie Creek Rd; snorkelling gear day/overnight $10/15; 9am-3.45pm) Serving both Ningaloo Marine Park and Cape Range National Park, this centre has informative natural and cultural displays, maps, tide charts, camp site photos and publications. Check here for road and water conditions. It's 53km from Exmouth.

Ningaloo Marine Park

World Heritage–listed Ningaloo Marine Park protects the full 300km length of exquisite Ningaloo Reef, from Bundegi Reef on the eastern tip of the peninsula to Red Bluff on Quobba Station far to the south. Home to a staggering array of marine life – sharks, manta rays, humpback whales, turtles, dugongs, dolphins and more than 500 species of fish – Australia's largest fringing reef is also easily accessible, in places only 100m offshore.

When to Go

Year-round marine awesomeness includes:

November to March Turtles – three endangered species nest and hatch in the dunes.

March Coral spawning – an amazing event occurring seven days after the full moon.

Mid-March to July Whale sharks – the biggest fish on the planet arrive for the coral spawning.

May to November Manta rays – present year round; their numbers increase dramatically over winter and spring.

June to November Humpback whales – breed in the warm tropics then head back south to feed in the Antarctic.

Wildlife

Over 220 species of hard coral have been recorded in Ningaloo, ranging from bulbous brain corals found on bommies, to delicate branching staghorns and the slow-growing massive coral. While less colourful than soft corals (which are normally found in deeper water on the outer reef), the hard corals have incredible formations. Spawning, where branches of hermaphroditic coral simultaneously eject eggs and sperm into the water, occurs after full and new moons between February and May, but the peak action is usually six to 10 days after the March full moon.

It's this spawning that attracts the park's biggest drawcard, the solitary speckled whale shark *(Rhiniodon typus)*. Ningaloo is one of the few places in the world where these gentle giants arrive like clockwork each year to feed on plankton and small fish, making it a mecca for marine biologists and visitors alike. The largest fish in the world, the whale shark can weigh up to 21 tonnes, although most weigh between 13 and 15 tonnes, and reach up to 18m long. They can live for 70 years.

Upload your amazing whale-shark pics to Ecocean (www.whaleshark.org), which will identify and track your whale shark, or geotag your other critters with Coastal Walkabout (www.coastalwalkabout.org). To learn more about Ningaloo's denizens, grab a copy of DPaW's *The Marine Life of Ningaloo Marine Park & Coral Bay*.

Activities

Most travellers visit Ningaloo Marine Park to **snorkel**. ALWAYS stop first at Milyering visitor centre (p999) for maps and info on the best spots and conditions. Check the tide chart and know your limits, as currents can be dangerous, the area is remote, and there's no phone coverage or lifeguards. While not common, unseasonal conditions can bring dangerous smacks of irukandji jellyfish. The park office also rents snorkelling equipment.

★Turquoise Bay SNORKELLING

(Yardie Creek Rd, 65km from Exmouth) The **Bay Snorkel Area** is suitable for all skill levels with myriad fish and corals just off the beach to the right of the Bay car park. The **Drift** attracts stronger swimmers where the current carries you over coral bommies. Don't miss the exit point or you'll be carried out through the gap in the reef.

The Drift Snorkel Area is 300m south along the beach from the Drift car park; swim out for about 40m then float face down in the current. Get out before the sandy point where the current strengthens, then run back along the beach and start all over!

Lakeside SNORKELLING

(Yardie Creek Rd, 54km from Exmouth) Walk 500m south along the beach from the car park then snorkel out with the current before returning close to your original point.

Oyster Stacks SNORKELLING

(Yardie Creek Rd, 69km from Exmouth) These spectacular bommies are just metres offshore, but you need a tide of at least 1.2m and sharp rocks make entry/exit difficult. If you tire, don't stand on the bommies; look for some sand.

★Ningaloo Kayak Trail KAYAKING

Still in its infancy, this fantastic new Parks & Wildlife initiative will see a string of specialist kayak-only moorings stretch from Bundegi Beach to Coral Bay, interspersed with designated remote beach camp sites. The moorings allow kayakers to tether their craft while snorkelling, and the camp sites allow for extended trips. Contact DPaW (p997) in Exmouth for more information, or enter Ningaloo Marine Park Kayak Moorings into your internet search engine for a downloadable brochure outlining the trail.

Lighthouse Bay DIVING

(Yardie Creek Rd) There's great scuba diving at Lighthouse Bay at sites such as the Labyrinth, Blizzard Ridge and Mandu Wall. Check out the DPaW book *Dive and Snorkel Sites in Western Australia* for other ideas.

Reef Search VOLUNTEERING

(Reef Check; www.reefcheckaustralia.org) Add a new dimension to your snorkelling or diving by collecting marine data in your own time, or volunteering for reef monitoring (courses available).

Cape Range National Park

The jagged limestone peaks and gorges of rugged 510-sq-km **Cape Range National Park** (per car $12) offer relief from the otherwise flat, arid expanse of North West Cape, and are rich in wildlife, including the rare black-flanked rock wallaby, five types of

SURFING THE CAPE

The big swells arrive on North West Cape between July and October and there's plenty of breaks and lots of rocks.

Surfers Beach (Dunes; Mildura Wreck Rd, 17km northwest of Exmouth) Ruggedly beautiful, surfers flock to the western cape during winter, while in the summer months windsurfing and kiteboarding are popular. The first car park provides the best access to the reef break.

Lighthouse Bombie (Yardie Creek Rd, 19km northwest of Exmouth) Off Vlamingh Head, the bombie is a big paddle out. Only for more experienced surfers.

Wobiri Access (Yardie Creek Rd, 23km northwest of Exmouth) On the western cape some 23km from Exmouth, gentle waves are suitable for beginners and surf classes are sometimes held.

Muiron Islands Serious surfers should grab a few mates and charter a boat to the Muiron Islands, just off Point Murat, where there are countless breaks and no one to ride them. You can camp on South Muiron with a permit from Exmouth DPaW (p997). There's also excellent snorkelling and diving. Your charter fee should include all meals, accommodation (onboard or camping) and fishing and snorkelling gear. Charters may be arranged from the Exmouth visitor centre (p997).

bat and over 200 species of bird. Spectacular deep canyons cut dramatically into the range, before emptying out onto the wind-blown coastal dunes and turquoise waters of Ningaloo Reef.

The main park access is via Yardie Creek Rd. Several areas in the east are accessible from unsealed roads off Minilya–Exmouth Rd, south of Exmouth. The park was hit by bad floods in 2014 and several camp sites and attractions are now closed: some permanently, others are being redeveloped. Check Parkstay (http://parkstay.dpaw.wa.gov.au) for the latest update.

Sights & Activities

Charles Knife Canyon GORGE

(Charles Knife Rd, Eastern Cape, 23km south of Exmouth) On the east coast, an incredibly scenic and at times dramatic road ascends a knife-edge ridge via rickety corners, necessitating frequent stops to make the most of the breathtaking views. A rough track continues to **Thomas Carter lookout**, where (in the cooler months) you can walk the 8km **Badjirrajirra loop trail** through spinifex and rocky gullies; there's no shade or water. Under no circumstances attempt this during summer.

Mangrove Bay Bird Hide BIRD SANCTUARY

(Western Cape, 8km from Cape Range National Park entrance station; P) FREE Spot migratory birds among the mangroves, or just wander out along the tidal flats.

Mandu Mandu Gorge GORGE

(20km south of Milyering; P) A pleasant but dry 3km return walk onto the gorge rim.

Yardie Creek Gorge GORGE

(36km south of Milyering; P) Excellent views above a water-filled gorge on this easy 2km return walk.

Yardie Creek Boat Tours BOAT TOUR

(08-9949 2920; www.yardiecreekboattours.com.au; adult/child/family $35/15/80; 11am & 12.30pm seasonally, closed Feb) A relaxing one-hour cruise up the short, sheer Yardie Creek Gorge where you might spot rare black-flanked rock wallabies.

Sleeping

Cape Range Camp Sites CAMPGROUND $

(per person $10) A string of sandy camp sites line the coast within the Cape Range National Park. Facilities and shade are minimal, though most have toilets and some shelter from prevailing winds. Some can be booked online using Parkstay (http://parkstay.dpaw.wa.gov.au), others are allocated on arrival at the park entrance station (not the visitor centre!). If you like quiet, ask for 'generator free'.

Most camps have resident caretakers during peak season. The two furthest sites are the other side of Yardie Creek, you'll need a high-clearance 4WD to access them.

Sal Salis LUXURY CAMPGROUND $$$
(1300 790 561; www.salsalis.com; wilderness tent s/d 2 nights from $1126/1500; Mar-Dec) Want to watch that flaming crimson Indian Ocean sunset from between 500-threadcount pure cotton sheets? Pass the chablis! For those who want their camp without the cramp, there's a minimum two-night stay, three gourmet meals a day, a free bar (!) and the same things to do as the couple over the dune in the pop-up camper.

THE PILBARA

Dampier to Roebourne

Most travellers skip the mining-services section of the coast from Dampier to Roebourn as there's little to see, unless you like huge industrial facilities. However, there are several interesting sights, good transport, well-stocked supermarkets and useful repair shops.

Tours

Ngurrangga Tours CULTURAL TOUR
(0423 424 093; www.facebook.com/Ngurrangga Tours; adult/child from $110/55; Feb-Nov) Ngarluma man, Clinton Walker's cultural tours are gathering rave reviews from travellers across the Pilbara. His half-day Murujuga National Park tour explores rock art petroglyphs on the Burrup Peninsula near Dampier, while longer day tours explore the culturally significant areas of Gregory's Gorge (adult $220, child $110) and Millstream (adult $220, child $110), the latter also available as an overnight option (adult $440, child $220).

Festivals

Red Earth Arts Festival ARTS
(www.reaf.com.au) An annual celebration of music, theatre and visual arts spread across the Pilbara coast in September.

Dampier

Dampier, spread around King Bay, is the region's main port and is home to heavy industry. Offshore, the coral waters and pristine island reserves of the **Dampier Archipelago** support a wealth of marine life and endangered marsupials.

Hearson Cove (P) has a pleasant beach providing Staircase to the Moon (p1029) viewing and access to Murujuga rock art.

Murujuga National Park FREE is home to the world's largest concentration of petroglyphs, stretched out along the unwanted rocky hills of the heavily industrialized Burrup Peninsula. The most accessible are at Deep Gorge, near Hearson Cove and devastatingly, some sites have been vandalised. You'll need a 4WD to explore north of Withnell Bay.

Karratha

Most travellers in Karratha bank, restock, repair stuff and get out of town before their wallet ignites.

If you have time, the **Jaburara Heritage Trail** (Yaburara) leaves from behind the visitor centre. This series of trails (the longest of which is 3.5km one way) winds through significant traditional sites, detailing the displacement and eventual extinction of the Jaburara people. Bring plenty of water and start early.

Sleeping & Eating

Accommodation prospects, previously dire, are gradually improving. Search online for last-minute deals or try the visitor centre. Weekends are usually cheaper than midweek. Point Samson and Millstream are nicer alternatives.

The shopping centre has most things you'll need, including ATMs, take-away food and supermarkets.

Pilbara Holiday Park CARAVAN PARK $
(08-9185 1855; www.aspenparks.com.au; Rosemary Rd; powered sites $42, motel/studio d $190/200;) This park is neat and well run with good facilities.

Soul CAFE $$
(0422 667 649; Warambie Rd, Pelago Centre; 6am-4pm) City-style sophisticated breakfasts and quick lunches.

Information

Karratha Visitor Centre (08-9144 4600; www.karrathavisitorcentre.com.au; Karratha Rd; 8.30am-5pm Mon-Fri, 9am-2pm Sat & Sun, shorter hrs Oct-Mar; @) has good local info, supplies Rail Access road permits, books tours (including to mining infrastructure) and may find you a room.

OFF THE BEATEN TRACK

MT AUGUSTUS (BURRINGURRAH) NATIONAL PARK

Mt Augustus (Burringurrah), in Wajarri country, is a huge monocline (1105m), twice as large as Uluru and a good deal more remote, which rises 717m above the surrounding plains. There are a number of walking trails and Aboriginal rock-art sites to explore, including the superb summit trail (12km return, six hours).

In a 2WD it's a rough 450km from Carnarvon via Gascoyne Junction or 350km from Meekatharra. With a 4WD there are at least three other routes including a handy back door to Karijini via Dooley Downs and Tom Price. All of these routes see little traffic, so be prepared for the worst. There's no camping in the park.

At the closest accommodation to Mt Augustus, **Mt Augustus Tourist Park** (08-9943 0527; www.mtaugustustouristpark.com; unpowered/powered sites $22/33, donga d $88, units $176; P ❄), dusty camp sites, wallabies and tumbleweeds are all you'll see here.

Getting There & Away

Karratha is well connected. Virgin (p992), Qantas (p992) and Alliance (p992) all fly daily to Perth. Airnorth (p992) flies to Broome, Darwin and Port Hedland twice weekly.

Integrity (1800 226 339; www.integrity-coachlines.com.au) Departs from the visitor centre for Perth ($282, 24 hours), Port Hedland ($89, three hours) and Broome ($187, 10 hours) twice a week.

Roebourne

Sitting on Ngaluma country, 40km east of Karratha, Roebourne is the oldest (1866) Pilbara town still functioning. It's home to a large Aboriginal community; Yindjibarndi is the dominant language group. There are some beautiful old buildings and a thriving Indigenous art scene (www.roebourneart.com.au). The **Yinjaa-Barni** (08-9182 1959; www.yinjaa-barni.com.au; Lot 3 Roe St; vary) Indigenous-run gallery showcases gifted Millstream artists.

Housed in the old gaol, the **visitor centre** (Old Gaol; 08-9182 1060; www.roebourne.org.au; Queen St; 9am-4pm Mon-Fri, 9am-3pm Sat & Sun, shorter hrs Nov-Apr) has an interesting museum, a courtyard minerals display and a guide to Roebourne's significant buildings.

Cossack

The scenic ghost town of Cossack, at the mouth of the Harding River, was previously the district's main port but was usurped by Point Samson and then eventually abandoned. Many of the historic bluestone buildings date from the late 1800s.

The small, self-guided **Social History Museum** (adult/child $2/1; 9am-4pm) in Cossack's old courthouse celebrates the town's halcyon days, while the Japanese section of the tiny **Pioneer Cemetery** bears witness to Cossack's pearling past.

At the road-end, **Reader Head Lookout** (P) has great views over the river mouth, beach and Staircase to the Moon (p1029). Usually empty, **Settlers Beach** is great for a dip.

The informative (and shadeless!) 6km **Cossack Heritage Trail** links all the major sites (grab the brochure from Roebourne visitor centre (p1003)).

There are five basic rooms at **Cossack Budget Accommodation** (08-9182 1190; www.karratha.wa.gov.au/cossack; d without/with air-con $100/120; ❄), housed in the atmospheric old police barracks. BYO food.

Point Samson

Point Samson is a small, industrial-free seaside village that's home to great seafood and clean beaches, making it the nicest place to stay in the area. There's good **snorkelling** off Point Samson, and the picturesque curved beach of Honeymoon Cove.

The tiny **Samson Beach Caravan Park** (08-9187 1414; Samson Rd; powered sites $42) is set in lovely, leafy surrounds, close to the water and tavern. Bookings are essential during school holidays. Over at **Cove** (08-9187 0199; www.thecoveholidayvillage.com.au; Macleod St; sites $49, 1-/2-bedroom units $240/310) it's a bit 'van city', but the modern, clean facilities complement a great location and it's an easy walk to all the attractions.

Samson Beach Chalets (08-9187 0202; www.samsonbeach.com.au; Samson Rd; chalets $280-650; P ❄) offers beautifully appointed self-contained chalets (various sizes) just a short walk from the beach. There's a shady pool, free wi-fi and in-house movies. While **Samson Beach Bistro** (☎08-9187 1435; mains $11-44; ⏰11am-3pm & 5-8.30pm), underneath the pub, serves great seafood on a shady deck overlooking the ocean.

Millstream Chichester National Park

Amongst the arid, spinifex-covered plateaus and basalt ranges between Karijini and the coast, the tranquil **Millstream Chichester National Park** (per vehicle $12) waterholes of the Fortescue River form cool, lush oases. In the park's north are the stunning breakaways and eroded mesas of the Chichester Range. A lifeline for local flora and fauna, the park is one of the most important Indigenous sites in WA. Once the station homestead, the unstaffed **visitor centre** houses historical, ecological and cultural displays.

Sights & Activities

Jirndarwurrunha Pool CULTURAL SITE
(Millstream) A short stroll from the Millstream Chichester National Park visitor centre, beautiful lily and palm-fringed Jirndarwurrunha is strongly significant to the traditional Yindjibarndi owners. Swimming is not permitted.

Deep Reach Pool SWIMMING HOLE
(Nhangganggunha; Millstream; Ⓟ) Shady picnic tables and barbecues back onto a perfect swimming hole believed to be the resting place of the Warlu (creation serpent).

Mt Herbert LOOKOUT
(Roebourne-Wittenoom Rd, Chichester Range; Ⓟ) A 10-minute climb from the car park on the road to Roebourne reveals a fantastic view of the ragged Chichester Range.

Python Pool SWIMMING HOLE
(Chichester Range; Ⓟ) This plunge pool is normally fine for swimming, though check for algal bloom before sliding in.

Murlamunyjunha Trail WALKING
This palm-lined 7km walking trail (two hours return) featuring interpretive plaques by the traditional Yindjibarndi owners, links Crossing Pool and Milliyanha Campground.

Chichester Range Camel Trail HIKING
Fit hikers might attempt the 8km Camel Trail linking Mt Herbert and Python Pool via McKenzie Spring. Allow three hours one way.

Sleeping

Milliyanha Campground CAMPGROUND
(Millstream; sites per person $10; Ⓟ) A nicely shaded, circular camp site near the visitors centre with a kitchen in the middle. If full, try the sparse Stargazers camp site.

Karijini National Park

The narrow, breathtaking gorges, hidden pools and spectacular waterfalls of Karijini National Park (per car $12) form one of WA's most impressive attractions. Adventurers and nature lovers flock to the rocky, red ranges and deep, dark chasms, home to abundant wildlife and over 800 different plant species.

Kangaroos, snappy gums and wild flowers dot the spinifex plains, rock wallabies cling to sheer cliffs and endangered olive pythons lurk in giant figs above quiet pools. The park also contains WA's three highest peaks: Mt Meharry, Mt Bruce and Mt Frederick.

Banyjima Dr, the park's main thoroughfare, connects with Karijini Dr at two entrance stations. The **eastern** access is closest to the visitor centre and Dales Gorge. Take extra care driving as tourist roll overs are common. Avoid driving at night.

Choose walks wisely, dress appropriately and never enter a restricted area without a certified guide. Avoid the gorges during and after rain, as flash flooding does occur.

Sights & Activities

Exploring Karijini's gorges is a magical experience, but obey all signs and keep out of restricted areas.

Dales Gorge GORGE
(19km from the East Entrance; Ⓟ) A short, sharp descent from near Dales Campground leads to **Fortescue Falls**, behind which a leafy stroll upstream reveals beautiful **Fern Pool** (Jubura); head 1km downstream from Fortescue Falls to picturesque **Circular Pool**; ascend to **Three Ways Lookout** and return along the cliff top.

Karijini National Park

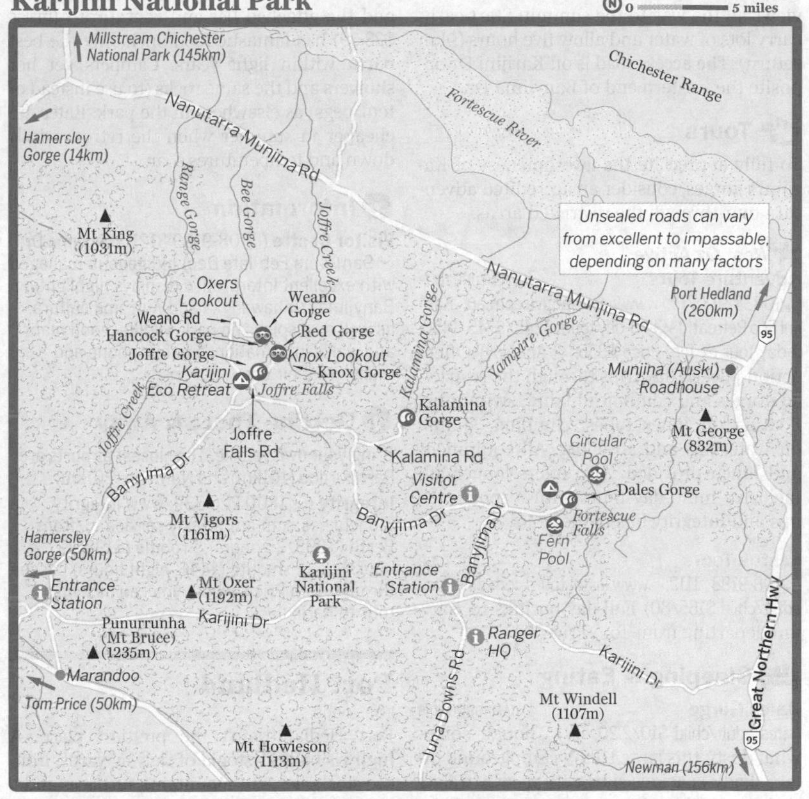

Kalamina Gorge GORGE
(Kalamina Gorge Rd; P) Wide, easy gorge with a small, tranquil pool and falls.

Joffre Gorge GORGE
(Joffre Falls Rd; P) **Joffre Falls** (when not trickling) are spectacular but the frigid pools below are perennially shaded. There's a walking track to the falls from the Karijini Eco Retreat (p1006).

Knox Gorge GORGE
(Joffre Falls Rd) Descend from **Knox Lookout** to several nice, sunny swimming holes, fringed by native figs.

Weano Gorge GORGE
(Weano Rd; P) The upper gorge is dry, but the steep track winding down from the car park to the lower gorge narrows until you reach the perfect, surreal bowl of **Handrail Pool**.

Oxers Lookout LOOKOUT
(Weano Rd; P) The final 13km to the breathtaking Oxers Lookout can be rough, but it's worth it for the magnificent views of the junction of the Red, Weano, Joffre and Hancock Gorges some 130m below.

Hancock Gorge GORGE
(Weano Rd; P) A steep descent (partly on ladders) brings you to the sunny **Amphitheatre.** Follow the slippery **Spider Walk** to sublime **Kermits Pool.**

Hamersley Gorge GORGE
(off Nanutarra-Wittenoom Rd; P) Away in Karijini's northwest corner, this idyllic swimming hole and waterfall makes a pleasant stopover if you're heading north towards the coast or Millstream.

Punurrunha WALKING
(Mt Bruce) Gorged out? Go and grab some altitude on WA's second-highest mountain

(1235m), a superb ridge walk with fantastic views all the way to the summit. Start early, carry lots of water and allow five hours (9km return). The access road is off Karijini Dr opposite the western end of Banyjima Dr.

Tours

To fully appreciate the awesomeness of Karijini's gorges, consider an accredited adventure tour through the restricted areas.

★West Oz Active Adventure Tours ADVENTURE TOUR
(☎0438 913 713; www.westozactive.com.au; Karijini Eco Retreat; 1-/3-/5-day tours $245/$745/1450, 3-day tour ex Tom Price $335; ⊙Apr-Nov) Offers action-packed day trips through the restricted gorges and combines hiking, swimming, floating on inner tubes, climbing, sliding off waterfalls and abseiling. All equipment and lunch provided. Also offers longer all-inclusive multi-day tours with airport pick ups and Integrity bus rendezvous.

Lestok Tours BUS TOUR
(☎08-9188 1112; www.lestoktours.com.au; day adult/child $165/80) Full-day outings to Karijini departing from Tom Price.

Sleeping & Eating

Dales Gorge CAMPGROUND $
(sites adult/child $10/2.20; P) Though somewhat dusty, this large DPaW campground offers shady, spacious sites with nearby toilets and picnic tables. Forget tent pegs – you'll be using rocks as anchors.

★Karijini Eco Retreat RESORT $$$
(☎08-9425 5591; www.karijiniecoretreat.com.au; Weano Rd; sites $40, tent d low/high season $190/315; P) This 100% Indigenous-owned retreat is a model for sustainable tourism, and the attached bar and **restaurant** (mains $28-39) has fantastic food, including the best barra within light years. Campers get hot showers and the same rocks (to use instead of tent pegs) as elsewhere in the park. Rates are cheaper in summer when the retreat winds down and temperatures soar.

Information

Visitor Centre (☎08-9189 8121; Banyjima Dr; ⊙9am-4pm Feb-late Dec) Indigenous-managed with excellent interpretive displays highlighting Banyjima, Yinhawangka and Kurrama culture, as well as displays on park wildlife, good maps and walks information, a public phone and really great air-con.

Getting There & Away

Bring your own vehicle. The closest airports are Paraburdoo (101km) and Newman (201km).

Integrity (☎1800 226 339; www.integrity-coachlines.com.au) Weekly service to/from Perth ($293, 25 hours), Broome ($198, 12 hours) and Exmouth ($146, eight hours) passes through Tom Price, where you can pick up a tour to Karijini.

Port Hedland

POP 14,000

Port Hedland ain't the prettiest place. A high-visibility dystopia of railway yards, iron-ore stockpiles, salt mountains, furnaces and a massive deep-water port confront the passing traveller. Yet under that red-dust lurks a colourful 130-year history of mining booms and busts, cyclones, pearling and WWII action. Several pleasant hours may be spent exploring Hedland's thriving art and cafe (real coffee!) scene, historic CBD and scenic foreshore.

TOM PRICE & NEWMAN

Bookending Karijini National Park are the neat, company-built mining towns of **Tom Price** and **Newman**. Newman, to the east on the Great Northern Hwy, is larger though more distant, with better transport and accommodation. Both have good (ie air-conditioned) supermarkets, petrol stations and visitor centres, where you can book mine tours if huge holes are your thing. The local libraries have internet access, and Newman's caravan parks are OK for a tent.

Newman Visitor Centre (☎08-9175 2888; www.newman.org.au; Fortescue Ave; mine tour adult/child $30/15; ⊙8am-5pm Mar-Oct, shorter hrs Nov-Feb) Has a mud map of local sights and six short-term chalets ($150) to stay in.

Tom Price Visitor Centre (☎08-9188 5488; www.tomprice.org.au; Central Rd; mine tour adult/child $30/15; ⊙8.30am-5pm Mon-Fri, 8.30am-12.30pm Sat & Sun, shorter hrs Nov-Apr) Can supply Rail Access Rd permits and book tours.

OFF THE BEATEN TRACK

MARBLE BAR

Marble Bar, a long way off everybody's beaten track, burnt itself into the Australian psyche as the country's hottest town when, back in 1921, the mercury didn't dip below 37.8°C (100°F) for 161 consecutive days. The town is (mistakenly) named after a bar of jasper beside a pool on the Coongan River, 5km southwest.

Most days there's not much to do. You can pore over the minerals at the **Comet Gold Mine** (☎08-9176 1015; Hillside Rd; admission $3; ⏲9am-4pm; P), 8km out of town on the Hillside Rd, or you can prop at the bar and have a yarn with Foxie at the **Ironclad Hotel** (☎08-9176 1066; 15 Francis St; ⏲vary). This classic outback pub offers comfy motel rooms, decent meals and a welcome to budget travellers.

But come the first weekend in July, the town swells to 10 times its normal size for a weekend of drinking, gambling, fashion crime, country music, nudie runs and horse racing known as the **Marble Bar Cup**. The **caravan park** (☎08-9176 1569; 64 Contest St; sites unpowered/powered $20/30) overflows and the Ironclad is besieged as punters from far and wide come for a bit of an outback knees-up.

The **shire office** (☎08-9176 1008) runs a weekly bus service to Port Hedland and Newman (via Nullagine) and provides tourist information. If you're heading south, the easiest route back to bitumen is the lonely but beautiful Hillside Rd.

Sights & Activities

Collect the excellent *Port Hedland, A Discoverer's Journal* from the visitor centre and take a self-guided tour around the CBD and foreshore.

Between November and February flat-back turtles nest on nearby beaches. Check at the visitor centre for volunteer options.

Goode St, near Pretty Pool, is handy to observe Port Hedland's Staircase to the Moon.

★Courthouse Gallery GALLERY
(☎08-9173 1064; www.courthousegallery.com.au; 16 Edgar St; ⏲9am-4.30pm Mon-Fri, 9am-2pm Sat & Sun) More than a gallery, this leafy arts HQ is the centre of all goodness in Hedland. Inside are stunning local contemporary and Indigenous exhibitions, while the shady surrounds host sporadic craft markets. If something is happening, these folks will know about it.

Spinifex Hill Studios GALLERY
(☎0457 422 875; www.spinifexhillstudio.com.au; 18 Hedditch St, South Hedland; ⏲9am-5pm Mon-Fri) Great new initiative showcasing Indigenous artists from Hedland and across the Pilbara. Call before visiting.

Marapikurrinya Park PARK
(end of Wedge St) Watch ridiculously large tankers pass by. After dark, nearby **Finucane Lookout** provides a smouldering view into BHP Billiton's Hot Briquetted Iron plant.

Pretty Pool FISHING
A popular fishing and picnicking spot (beware of stonefish and backpackers), 7km east of the town centre.

Tours

BHP Billiton GUIDED TOUR
(adult/child $45/30; ⏲vary) Popular iron-ore plant tour departing from the visitor centre.

Local History BUS TOUR
(90min $25; ⏲Apr-Sep) Run by a local historian these informative tours delve into Hedland's chequered past. Book at the visitor centre.

Sleeping & Eating

Finding a room in Hedland isn't easy or cheap. Try the visitor centre, otherwise head for 80 Mile Beach or Point Samson.

There are supermarkets, cafes and takeaways at both the **Boulevard** (cnr Wilson & McGregor Sts) and **South Hedland** (Throssell Rd) shopping centres.

Cooke Point Caravan Park CARAVAN PARK $$
(☎08-9173 1271; www.aspenparks.com.au; cnr Athol & Taylor Sts; powered sites $54, d without bathroom $130, unit d from $204; ❄📶🏊) You might be able to snag a dusty van or tent site here, but the other options are usually full. There's a nice view over the mangroves and the amenities are well maintained.

★ **Silver Star** CAFE $$

(☎0411 143 663; Edgar St; breakfast $10-20, lunch $18-24; ⊙7am-3pm) Possibly the coolest cafe in the Pilbara, this 1930s American Silver Star railcar serves up decent coffee, brekkies and sophisticated lunches in the original observation lounge and outside on a shady deck.

Information

There are ATMs along Wedge St and in the Boulevard shopping centre (p1007). The **library** (☎08-9158 9378; Dempster St; ⊙9am-5pm Mon-Fri, 10am-1pm Sat; @) has internet access.

Visitor Centre (☎08-9173 1711; www.visitporthedland.com; 13 Wedge St; ⊙9am-5pm Mon-Fri, 9am-2pm Sat-Sun; @ wi-fi) This amazing centre sells travel books, publishes shipping times, arranges iron-ore plant tours, and helps with accommodation and turtle monitoring (November to February).

Seafarers Centre (☎08-9173 1315; www.phseafarers.org; cnr Wedge & Wilson Sts; ⊙9am-11pm; @ wi-fi) High speed wi-fi and internet. Also sells Integrity bus tickets, Aboriginal artefacts and currency exchange.

Getting There & Around

Virgin and **Qantas** both fly to Perth daily, and on Tuesday Qantas also flies direct to Brisbane and Melbourne. Virgin has handy weekend flights to Bali and Broome. Airnorth (p992) heads to Broome (Tuesday and Friday) with a Darwin connection.

The airport is 13km from town; a **taxi** (☎08-9172 1010) will cost around $40.

Integrity (☎1800 226 339; www.integrity-coachlines.com.au) has coaches for Perth ($293, 28 to 31 hours) and Broome ($129, six hours) three times weekly. There's also a quicker inland route to Perth ($274, 22 hours) via Newman each week. Departs from the visitor centre and South Hedland shopping centre.

Broome & the Kimberley

Includes ➡

Best Cafes

- ➡ Whale Song Cafe (p1033)
- ➡ Jila Gallery (p1013)
- ➡ Wild Mango (p1022)
- ➡ Rusty Shed (p1020)
- ➡ Cygnet Bay Pearl Farm (p1034)

Best Off-the-Beaten-Track Locations

- ➡ Middle Lagoon (p1033)
- ➡ Mornington Wilderness Camp (p1016)
- ➡ Mitchell Falls National Park (p1015)
- ➡ Duncan Road (p1018)
- ➡ Kalumburu (p1017)

Why Go?

Australia's last frontier is a wild land of remote, spectacular scenery spread over huge distances, with a severe climate, a sparse population and minimal infrastructure. Larger than 75% of the world's countries, the Kimberley is hemmed by impenetrable coastline and unforgiving deserts. In between lie vast boab-studded spinifex plains, palm-fringed gorges, desolate mountains and magnificent waterfalls. Travelling here is a true adventure, and each dry season a steady flow of explorers search for the real outback along the legendary Gibb River Road.

Aboriginal culture runs deep across the region, from the Dampier Peninsula, where neat communities welcome travellers to Country, to distant Mitchell Plateau, where ancient Wandjina and Gwion Gwion stand vigil over sacred waterholes.

Swashbuckling Broome and practical Kununurra bookend the region. Both are great places to unwind, find a job and meet other travellers.

When to Go

Broome

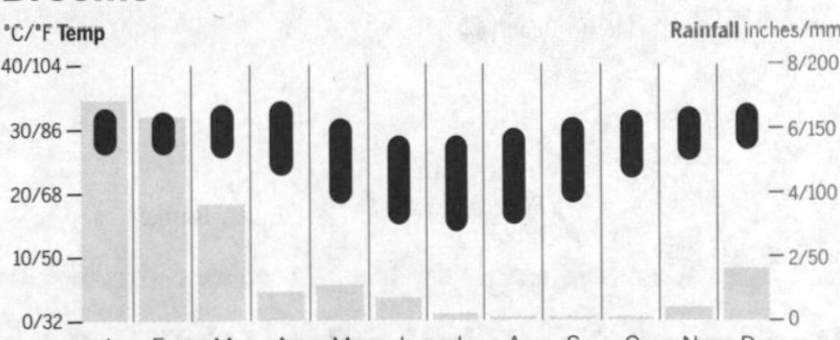

Apr Fly over thundering Mitchell and King George Falls.

May Broome's at its greenest right before the tourist tide.

Sep & Oct Hit Purnululu and the Gibb River Road as the season winds down.

Broome & the Kimberley Highlights

1. Taking a camel ride at sunset along Broome's **Cable Beach** (p1025).

2. Learning about traditional culture with Aboriginal communities on the pristine **Dampier Peninsula** (p1032).

3. Tackling the notorious **Gibb River Road** (p1014) in a 4WD adventure.

4. Flying over the stunning **Mitchell and King George Falls** (p1020) after the Wet.

5. Riding the wild **Horizontal Waterfalls** (p1013).

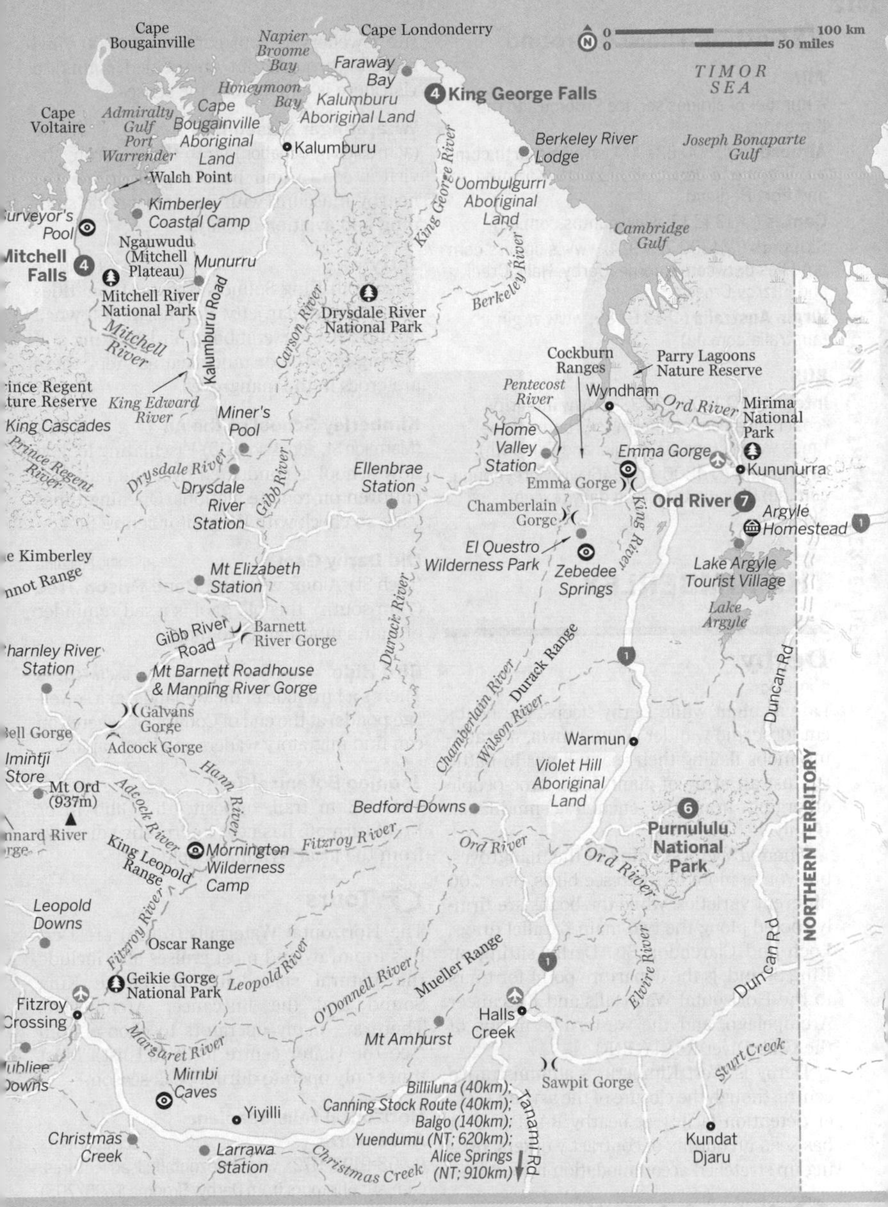

6 Losing yourself among the ancient domes of **Purnululu National Park** (p1022).

7 Canoeing the mighty **Ord River** (p1020) in a three-day self-guided epic.

8 Immersing yourself in Indigenous art at **Aboriginal art cooperatives** (p1021).

9 Trekking through the bowels of the earth at **Tunnel Creek National Park** (p1017).

10 Following the **Lurujarri Dreaming Trail** (p1029) to James Price Point and beyond.

Getting There & Around

AIR

A number of airlines service Broome and the Kimberley.

Airnorth (1800 627 474; www.airnorth.com.au) Broome to Darwin, Kununurra, Karratha and Port Hedland.

Qantas (13 13 13; www.qantas.com.au)

Skippers (1300 729 924; www.skippers.com.au) Flies between Broome, Derby, Halls Creek and Fitzroy Crossing.

Virgin Australia (13 67 89; www.virgin-australia.com.au)

BUS

Integrity (1300 226 339; www.integrity-coachlines.com.au) Perth to Broome three times weekly (one via Karijini and Exmouth).

Greyhound (1300 473 946; www.greyhound.com.au) Broome to Darwin daily (except Sunday).

THE KIMBERLEY

Derby

POP 3300

Late at night while Derby sleeps, the boabs cut loose and wander around town, marauding mobs flailing their many limbs in battle against an army of giant, killer croc-people emerging from the encircling mudflats... If only.

There *are* crocs hiding in the mangroves, but you're more likely to see birds, over 200 different varieties, while the boabs are firmly rooted along the two main parallel drags, Loch and Clarendon Sts. Derby, sitting on King Sound, is the departure point for tours to the Horizontal Waterfalls and Buccaneer Archipelago, and the western terminus of the Gibb River Road (GRR).

Derby is West Kimberley's administrative centre, though the closure of the asylum seeker detention facility at nearby RAAF Curtin has seen an outflux of contract workers, freeing up stretched accommodation resources.

Sights & Activities

The visitor centre's excellent town map lists every conceivable attraction.

★Norval Gallery GALLERY

(Loch St; vary) Kimberley art legends Mark and Mary Norval have set up an exciting gallery-cafe in an old tin shed on the edge of town. Featuring striking artwork, exquisite jewellery, decent coffee and 5000 vinyl records (brought out on themed nights), a visit here is a delight to the senses.

Wharefinger Museum MUSEUM

(admission by donation) Grab the key from the visitor centre and have a peek inside the nearby museum, with its atmospheric shipping and aviation displays.

Jetty LANDMARK

Check out King Sound's colossal 11.5m tides from the circular jetty, 1km north of town, a popular fishing, crabbing, bird-spotting and staring-into-the-distance haunt. Yep, there are crocs in the mangroves.

Kimberley School of the Air SCHOOL

(Marmion St; admission $10) Fascinating look at how school is conducted over the radio for children on remote stations. Opening times vary, so check with the visitor centre first.

Old Derby Gaol HISTORIC BUILDING

(Loch St) Along with the **Boab Prison Tree** (7km south), this old gaol is a sad reminder of man's inhumanity to man.

Bird Hide BIRDWATCHING

There's a bird hide in the wetlands (aka sewerage ponds) at the end of Conway St, where you can find migratory waders and local raptors.

Joonjoo Botanical Trail WALKING

This 2.3km trail, opposite the Gibb River Road turn off, has neat interpretive displays from the local Nyikina people.

Tours

The Horizontal Waterfalls (p1013) are Derby's top draw and most cruises also include the natural splendours of remote King Sound and the Buccaneer Archipelago. There are many operators to choose from (see the visitor centre for a full list). Most tours only operate during peak season.

Horizontal Falls Seaplane Adventures SCENIC FLIGHTS

(08-9192 1172; www.horizontalfallsadventures.com.au; 6hr tours from Derby/Broome $695/795) Flights to Horizontal Falls include a speedboat ride through the falls. There's also an overnight-stay option (ex-Derby) for $845.

North West Bush Pilots SCENIC FLIGHTS

(08-9193 2680; www.northwestbushpilots.com.au; flights from $352) Horizontal Waterfalls, Buccaneer Archipelago and Walcott Inlet – you can look but not touch.

Windjana Tours CULTURAL TOUR
(☎08-9193 1550; www.windjanatours.com.au; $195; ⏰Tue, Thu & Sun May-Aug) Bunuba man, Dillon Andrews, leads informative full-day cultural tours to Windjana Gorge and Tunnel Creek National Parks.

Uptuyu CULTURAL TOUR
(☎0400 878 898; www.uptuyu.com.au; Oongkalkada Wilderness Camp, Udialla Springs, 50km from Great Northern Hwy; per day from $450) Down in Nyikina country on the Fitzroy River, Neville and Jo run 'designer' cultural tours taking in wetlands, rock art, fishing and Indigenous communities along the Fitzroy and further afield.

Festivals & Events

Boab Festival MUSIC, CULTURE
(www.derbyboabfestival.org.au) Derby goes off in July with concerts, mud footy, horse and mud-crab races, poetry readings, art exhibitions and street parades. Try to catch the Long Table dinner out on the mudflats.

Sleeping & Eating

With the closure of the Curtin Detention Centre, accommodation is now easier to find. Try the visitor centre, but if you're heading to/from the Gibb River Road, consider Birdwood Downs Station (p1015) instead.

There are several takeaways and cafes along Loch and Clarendon Sts.

Kimberley Entrance Caravan Park CARAVAN PARK $
(☎08-9193 1055; www.kimberleyentrancecaravanpark.com; 2 Rowan St; unpowered/powered sites $32/38) Not all sites are shaded, though there's always room. Expect lots of insects this close to the mudflats.

Derby Lodge MOTEL $$
(☎08-9193 2924; www.derbylodge.com.au; 15-19 Clarendon St; r/apt $160/210; P❄@📶) Choose between neat, clean motel rooms or self-contained apartments with cooking facilities.

Spinifex Hotel RESORT $$
(☎08-9191 1233; www.spinifexhotel.com.au; 6 Clarendon St; dongas/motel r $160/250, mains $24-39; ❄@) Rising phoenix-like from the ashes of the old Spini, this sleek new resort has corporate-class rooms (some with kitchenettes) and an on-site restaurant. Peak season brings outdoor live music.

Sampey Meats BUTCHER $
(☎08-9193 2444; 59 Rowan St; ⏰7am-5pm Mon-Fri, to noon Sat) Homemade jerkies, biltong and vacuum-sealed roasts, all ready for the Gibb.

★ **Jila Gallery** ITALIAN $$
(☎08-9193 2560; www.facebook.com/Jilagallery; 18 Clarendon St; pizzas $20-28, mains $24-34; ⏰10.30am-2pm & 6pm-late Tue-Fri, 6pm-late Sat) Easily the best food in Derby with great wood-fired pizzas, perfect seafood risotto, wonderful cakes and shady, alfresco dining.

Information

The supermarkets and ATMs are on Loch and Clarendon Sts.

Derby Visitor Centre (☎08-9191 1426; www.derbytourism.com.au; 30 Loch St; ⏰8.30am-5pm Mon-Fri, 9am-3pm Sat & Sun dry season) is a helpful centre with the low-down on road conditions, accommodation, transport and tour bookings.

Getting There & Away

Derby has two airports. Flights for Perth arrive and depart from Curtin Airport (DCN), 40km

HORIZONTAL WATERFALLS

One of the most intriguing features of the Kimberley coastline is the phenomenon known as 'horizontal waterfalls'. Despite the name, the falls are simply tides gushing through narrow coastal gorges in the Buccaneer Archipelago, north of Derby. What creates such a spectacle are the huge tides, often varying up to 11m. The water flow reaches an astonishing 30 knots as it's forced through two narrow gaps 20m and 10m wide – resulting in a 'waterfall' reaching 4m in height.

Many tours leave Derby (and some Broome) each Dry, by air, sea or a combination of both. It's become de rigueur to 'ride' the tide change through the gorge on a high-powered speedboat, but this is risky at best, and accidents have occurred. Scenic flights are the quickest and cheapest option, and some seaplanes will land and transfer passengers to a waiting speedboat for the adrenalin hit. If you prefer to be stirred, not shaken, then consider seeing the falls as part of a longer cruise through the archipelago. Book tours at the Derby and Broome visitor centres.

away. A **shuttle** (☎08-9193 2568; per person $35) runs to/from Curtin into town; book the day before. Charter and sightseeing flights use the closer Derby Aerodrome (DRB), just past the Gibb turn-off.

All buses depart from the visitor centre.

Derby Bus Service (☎08-9193 1550; www.derbybus.com.au; one way/return $50/90; ⏲Mon, Wed & Fri) Leaves early for Broome (2½ hours), stopping at Willare Roadhouse (and basically anywhere else you ask them to along the way), returning the same day.

Greyhound (☎1300 473 946; www.greyhound.com.au) Broome ($52, 2½ hours), Darwin ($241, 23 hours) and Kununurra ($123, 11 hours) daily (except Sundays).

Skippers (☎1300 729 924; www.skippers.com.au) Flights to Broome, Fitzroy Crossing and Halls Creek several times weekly.

Virgin Australia (☎13 67 89; www.virgin-australia.com) Five flights to Perth from Curtin Airport weekly.

Getting Around

Taxi (☎13 10 08)

Gibb River Road

Cutting a brown swath through the scorched heart of the Kimberley, the legendary **Gibb River Road** ('the Gibb' or GRR) provides one of Australia's wildest outback experiences. Stretching some 660km between **Derby** and **Kununurra**, the largely unpaved Gibb River Road is an endless sea of red dirt, big open skies and dramatic terrain. Rough, sometimes deeply corrugated side roads lead to remote gorges, shady pools, distant waterfalls and million-acre cattle stations. Rain can close the road any time, and it's closed during the Wet. This is true wilderness with minimal services, so good planning and self-sufficiency are vital.

Several pastoral stations offer overnight accommodation from mid-April to late October; advance bookings are essential during the peak period of June to August. Hema Maps' *Kimberley Atlas & Guide* provides the best coverage, while visitor centres sell *The Gibb River & Kalumburu Road Guide* ($5).

A high-clearance 4WD (eg Toyota Land Cruiser) is mandatory, with two spare tyres, tools, emergency water (20L minimum) and several days' food in case of breakdown. Britz (p1032) in Broome is a reputable hire outfit. Fuel is limited and expensive, most mobile phones won't work, and temperatures can be life-threatening. Broome and Kununurra are best for supplies.

For just a sniff of outback adventure, try the 'tourist loop' along the Gibb from Derby onto Fairfield–Leopold Downs Rd to Windjana Gorge (p1017) and Tunnel Creek (p1017) National Parks, then exit onto the Great Northern Hwy near **Fitzroy Crossing**.

Tours

Adventure Tours 4WD TOUR
(☎03-8102 7800; www.adventuretours.com.au; from $1950) Nine-day Gibb River Road camping tours catering for a younger crowd.

Kimberley Wild Expeditions 4WD TOUR
(☎1300 738 870; www.kimberleywild.com.au) Consistent award winner. Tours from Broome range from one ($229) to 14 days ($3995) on the Gibb River Road.

Kimberley Adventure Tours 4WD TOUR
(☎1800 083 368; www.kimberleyadventures.com.au; 3-/9-day tour $550/$1995) Small group camping tours from Broome up the Gibb, with the nine-day tour continuing to Purnululu and Darwin.

Wundargoodie Aboriginal Safaris CULTURAL TOURS
(☎08-9161 1145; www.wundargoodie.com.au; tag-along per vehicle $250, women-only 11-day tour $3500; ⏲Apr-Sep) These insightful Indigenous-run 4WD tagalong tours (ie, you bring your own vehicle) showcase local culture and rock art in the remote West Kimberley. The women-only tour is all-inclusive, camping at special sites and sharing experiences with Aboriginal women from various communities.

Information

Online, check out www.gibbriverroad.net and www.kimberleyaustralia.com or visit the **Derby** and **Kununurra** visitor centre websites.

For maps, take Hema's *Kimberley Atlas & Guide* ($40) or *Regional Map – The Kimberley* ($15).

Mainroads Western Australia (MRWA; ☎13 81 38; www.mainroads.wa.gov.au; ⏲24hr) Highway and Gibb River Road conditions.

Parks & Wildlife (DPaW; www.dpaw.wa.gov.au) Park permits, camping fees and information. A Holiday Pass ($44) works out cheaper if you will be visiting more than three parks in one month.

Shire of Derby/West Kimberley (☎08-9191 0999; www.sdwk.wa.gov.au) Side-road conditions.

Shire of Wyndham/East Kimberley (☎08-9168 4100; www.swek.wa.gov.au) Kalumburu/Mitchell Falls road conditions.

WORTH A TRIP

MITCHELL FALLS & DRYSDALE RIVER

Drysdale River

In the Dry, Kalumburu Rd is normally navigable as far as **Drysdale River Station** (☎08-9161 4326; www.drysdaleriver.com.au; sites $10-15, d $170-250; ⏰8am-5pm Apr-Dec), 59km from the Gibb River Road, where there's fuel, meals and accommodation, and you can check ongoing road conditions. Scenic flights to Mitchell Falls operate from April to September (from $200 per person).

Mitchell Falls National Park

The **Ngauwudu** (Mitchell Plateau) turn off is 160km from the Gibb River Road, and within 6km a deep, rocky ford crosses the **King Edward River**, formidable early in the season.

On the shady banks of the King Edward river, many people prefer to camp at **Munurru Campground** (adult/child $10/2.20) rather than in Mitchell River National Park and then visit Mitchell Falls as a day trip. There's excellent Aboriginal rock art nearby.

From the Kalumburu Rd it's a rough 87km, past lookouts and forests of *livistona* palms to the dusty campground of **Mitchell River National Park** (entry per vehicle $12, camping adult/child $10/2.20). Leave early if walking to **Punamii-unpuu** (Mitchell Falls; 8.6km return). The easy trail meanders through spinifex, woodlands and gorge country, dotted with Wandjina and Gwion Gwion rock-art sites, secluded waterholes, lizards, wallabies and brolga.

The falls are stunning, whether trickling in the Dry, or raging in the Wet (when only visible from the air). You can swim in the long pool above the falls, but swimming in the lower pools is strictly forbidden because of their cultural importance to the Wunambal people. Most people will complete the walk in three hours.

Derby to Fairfield-Leopold Downs Rd Junction

The first 100-odd kilometres of the Gibb River Road are now sealed.

Mowanjum Art & Culture Centre GALLERY
(☎08-9191 1008; www.mowanjumarts.com; Gibb River Rd, Derby; ⏰9am-5pm daily during dry season, closed Sat & Sun during wet season, closed Jan; P) Just 4km along the Gibb River Road from Derby, Mowanjum artists recreate Wandjina and Gwion Gwion images in this incredible gallery shaped like their artwork.

Birdwood Downs Station PASTORAL STATION
(☎08-9191 1275; www.birdwooddowns.com; camping $14, savannah huts per person with/without meals $139/81) About 20km from Derby, 2000-hectare Birdwood Downs offers rustic savannah huts, butterflies and dusty camping. WWOOFers are welcome and it's also the home of the **Kimberley School of Horsemanship**, with lessons, riding camps and trail rides (90-minute sunset ride $99).

May River CAMPGROUND $
Forty kilometres from Derby, a rough track heads left 12km to several bush camp sites on the May River.

King Leopold Ranges

Continuing along the Gibb River Road from Derby, the **Windjana Gorge** turn off at 119km is your last chance to head back to the Great Northern Hwy. The scenery improves after crossing the Lennard River into Napier Downs Station as the **King Leopold** ranges loom straight ahead. Just after **Inglis Gap** is the Mt Hart turn off and another 7km brings the narrow **Lennard River Gorge** (P).

Mt Hart Homestead CAMPGROUND
(☎08-9191 4645; sites per person $18, r per person incl dinner & breakfast $210; ⏰dry season; ✖) Below Inglis Gap a rough 50km track leads to the remote Mt Hart Homestead with grassy camp sites, pleasant gorges, and swimming and fishing holes.

Imintji to Galvans Gorge

Despite its name **March Fly Glen**, 204km from Derby, is a pleasant, shady picnic area ringed by pandanus. Don't miss stunning **Bell Gorge** (per car $12; P), 29km down a rough track, with a picturesque waterfall and popular plunge pool. Refuel (diesel only), grab an ice cream and check your email at

Imintji Store (08-9191 7471; 8am-5pm dry season, shorter hrs wet season;).

Silent Grove CAMPGROUND
(adult/child $12/2.20; P) 19km from the Gibb, this sheltered, somewhat dusty Department of Parks & Wildlife campground in the King Leopold Ranges is popular with groups.

★ **Mornington Wilderness Camp** WILDLIFE RESERVE
(08-9191 7406; www.awc.org.au; entry fee per vehicle $25; dry season) Part of the Australian Wildlife Conservancy, the superb Mornington Wilderness Camp is as remote as it gets, lying on the Fitzroy River an incredibly scenic 95km drive across the savannah from the Gibb's 247km mark. Nearly 400,000 hectares are devoted to conserving the Kimberley's endangered fauna and there's excellent canoeing, birdwatching and bush walking. Choose from shady camp sites (per adult $18.50, child $8) or spacious raised tents with verandahs (including full board single $320, double $570). The bar and restaurant offer full dinner ($60), BBQ packs ($19) and the best cheese platter ($25) this side of Margaret River.

Charnley River Station CAMPGROUND $
(08-9191 4646; www.awc.org.au; sites per person $20, day visit $20) Now under the management of the Australian Wildlife Conservancy, this historic station, 44km north of the Gibb, offers shady, grassy camp sites. Check out beautiful Grevillea and Dillie gorges, and Donkey Pool. There's also incredible rock art and bird life.

Over the Range Repairs MECHANIC
(08-9191 7887; 8am-5pm dry season) Between Adcock and Galvans gorges, Nev and Leonie are your best – if not only – hope of mechanical salvation on the whole Gibb.

Galvans Gorge GORGE
(P) A waterfall, lovely swimming hole, rock wallabies and Wandjina art all less than 1km easy stroll from the road.

Mt Barnett to Mt Elizabeth

Fuel up at **Mt Barnett Roadhouse** (08-9191 7007; 8am-5pm), 300km from Derby, and get your camping permit if choosing to stay at nearby Manning River Gorge.

Manning River Gorge CAMPGROUND $
(7km behind Mt Barnett Roadhouse; per person $20;) This dusty campground is often full of travellers waiting for fuel, but at least there's a good swimming hole and even hot showers.

Barnett River Gorge CAMPGROUND
(29km east of Mt Barnett Roadhouse) FREE Bush camp sites several kilometres off the Gibb down a sandy track.

Mt Elizabeth Station PASTORAL STATION
(08-9191 4644; www.mountelizabethstation.com; sites per person $20, s/d incl breakfast & dinner $185/370; Dry) Further up the Gibb (around 338km from Derby) is the turn off to Mt Elizabeth Station, one of the few remaining private leaseholders in the Kimberley. Peter Lacy's 200,000-hectare property is a good base for exploration to nearby gorges, waterfalls and Indigenous rock art. Wallabies frequent the camp site, and the home-style, three-course dinners ($45) hit the spot.

Kalumburu Rd to Home Valley

At 406km from Derby you reach the **Kalumburu** turn off. Head right on the Gibb River Road, and continue through spectacular country, crossing the mighty Durack River then climbing though the **Pentecost Ranges** to 579km where there's panoramic views of the Cockburn Ranges, Cambridge Gulf and Pentecost River.

Ellenbrae Station PASTORAL STATION $
(08-9161 4325; www.ellenbraestation.com.au; 70km east Kalumburu turn off; sites per person $15, bungalow d $155) Atmospheric Ellenbrae Station serves up fresh scones, rather dusty camp sites and quirky bungalows.

★ **Home Valley Station** PASTORAL STATION $
(08-9161 4322; www.homevalley.com.au; sites adult/child $17/5, eco-tents sleeping 4 $190, homestead d from $250; P) The privations of the Gibb are left behind after pulling into amazing Home Valley Station, an Indigenous hospitality training resort with a superb range of luxurious accommodation. There are excellent grassy camp sites and motel-style rooms, a fantastic open bistro, tyre repairs and activities including trail rides, fishing and cattle mustering.

Pentecost River to Wyndham/Kununurra

At 589km from Derby you'll cross the infamous **Pentecost River** – take care as water levels are unpredictable and saltwater crocs lurk nearby. The last section of the Gibb Riv-

OFF THE BEATEN TRACK

KALUMBURU

Kalumburu is a picturesque mission nestled beneath giant mango trees and coconut palms with two shops and **fuel** (7am-11am & 1.30-4pm Mon-Fri, 8am-noon Sat). There's some interesting rock art nearby, and the odd WWII bomber wreck. You can stay at the **Kalumburu Mission** (08-9161 4333; kalumburumission@bigpond.com; sites per person $20, donga s/d $125/175), which has a small **museum** (admission $10; 11am-1pm), or obtain a permit from the KAC office to camp at **Honeymoon Bay** (08-9161 4378; sites $20) or **McGowan Island** (08-9161 4748; www.mcgowanisland.com.au; sites $20), 20km further out on the coast – the end of the road.

The road to Kalumburu deteriorates quickly after the Mitchell Plateau turn off and eventually becomes very rocky. You'll need a permit from the **DAA** (1300 651 077; www.daa.wa.gov.au) to visit Kalumburu and a visitors pass (valid for seven days) on entry from the **Kalumburu Aboriginal Community** (KAC; 08-9161 4300; www.kalumburu.org; visitors pass per car $50). Alcohol is banned at Kalumburu.

er Road is sealed. The Emma Gorge turn off is 10km past El Questro; 630km from Derby you cross King River and at 647km you finally hit the highway – turn left for Wyndham (48km) and right to Kununurra (53km).

El Questro Wilderness Park RESORT $
(08-9169 1777; www.elquestro.com.au; permit adult per day/week $12/20; dry season;) This vast 400,000-hectare former cattle station turned international resort incorporates scenic gorges (Amelia, El Questro) and Zebedee thermal springs (mornings only). **Boat tours** (adult/child $63/32; 3pm) explore **Chamberlain Gorge** or you can hire your own ($100). There are shady camp sites and air-con bungalows at **El Questro Station Township** (sites per person $20-28, bungalows d from $329;) and also an outdoor bar and upmarket **steakhouse** (mains $32 to $45). There are a million activities to choose from, but you'll pay for most of them.

Emma Gorge GORGE
(40min walk from the resort car park; P) Emma Gorge features a sublime plunge pool and waterfall, one of the prettiest in the whole Kimberley. The attached **resort** (safari cabin d from $289; Dry;) has an open-air bistro and expensive, stuffy cabins.

Devonian Reef National Parks

Three national parks with three stunning gorges were once part of a western 'great barrier reef' in the Devonian era, 350 million years ago. Windjana Gorge and Tunnel Creek National Parks are accessed via Fairfield–Leopold Downs Rd (linking the Great Northern Hwy with the Gibb River Road), while Geikie Gorge National Park is 22km northeast of Fitzroy Crossing.

Windjana Gorge NATIONAL PARK
(entry per car $12, camping adult/child $12/2.20; Dry; P) The walls of the gorge soar 100m above the Lennard River, which surges in the Wet but is a series of pools in the Dry. Scores of freshwater crocodiles lurk along the banks. Bring plenty of water for the 7km return walk from the campground.

★**Tunnel Creek** NATIONAL PARK
(per car $12, no camping; Dry; P) Sick of the sun? Then cool down underground at Tunnel Creek, which cuts through a spur of the Napier Range for almost 1km. It was the hideout of Jandamarra, an Indigenous guerilla fighter, in the 1800s. In the Dry, the full length is walkable by wading partly through knee-deep water; watch out for bats and bring good footwear and a strong torch.

Geikie Gorge NATIONAL PARK
(Darngku; Apr-Dec; P) Don't miss this magnificent gorge near Fitzroy Crossing. The self-guided trails are sandy and hot, so take one of the informative boat cruises run by either **Department of Parks & Wildlife** (08-9191 5121; 1hr tour adult/child $30/7.50; cruises from 8am May-Oct) or local Bunuba guides.

Tours

Bungoolee Tours CULTURAL TOUR
(08-9191 5355; www.bungoolee.com.au; 2hr tour adult/child $60/15; 9am & 2pm Mon, Wed & Fri during dry season) Bunuba lawman Dillon Andrews runs informative two-hour Tunnel Creek tours explaining the story of Jandamarra, as well as tag-along 4WD tours

on Leopold Downs Station. Overnighting is possible at simple Biridu camp site. Book through Fitzroy Crossing visitors centre.

Darngku Heritage Tours CRUISES
(☎0417 907 609; www.darngku.com.au; adult/child 2hr tour $70/60, 3hr tour $90/75, half-day tour $175/$138; ⊙Apr-Dec) Local Bunuba guides introduce Indigenous culture and bush tucker on these amazingly informative cruises through Geikie (Darngku) Gorge. A shorter one-hour cruise operates during the shoulder season (April and October to December).

Fitzroy Crossing to Halls Creek

Fitzroy Crossing

Gooniyandi, Bunuba, Walmatjarri and Wangkajungka people populate the small settlement of Fitzroy Crossing where the Great Northern Hwy crosses the mighty **Fitzroy River**. There's little reason to stay other than it's a good access point for the Devonian Reef national parks. Check out **Mangkaja Arts** (☎08-9191 5833; www.mangkaja.com; 8 Bell Rd, Fitzroy Crossing; ⊙noon-4pm Mon-Fri) with its unique acrylics, and the exquisite glass and ceramics at **Dr Sawfish** (☎0419 908 586; www.drsawfish.com; ⊙8am-4pm Mon-Fri, shorter hrs Sat & Sun), which is next to the tyre guy, whom you'll probably need. Camping and rooms are available at the atmospheric **Crossing Inn** (☎08-9191 5080; www.crossinginn.com.au; Skuthorpe Rd; unpowered/powered sites $30/38, r from $195; ❄@) and across the river at the upmarket **Fitzroy River Lodge** (☎08-9191 5141; www.fitzroyriverlodge.com.au; Great Northern Hwy; camping per person $15, tent d $160, motel d $220; ❄@🛜≋), which also offers decent counter meals ($22 to $36). There's a new, well-stocked supermarket, and the **visitor centre** (☎08-9191 5355; www.sdwk.wa.gov.au; ⊙8.30am-4pm Mon-Fri) and coach stop is just off the highway.

Mimbi Caves

★Mimbi Caves CAVES
(Mt Pierre Station) One of the Kimberley's best-kept secrets, this vast subterranean labyrinth, 90km south-east of Fitzroy Crossing, on Gooniyandi land, houses a significant collection of Aboriginal rock art and some of the most impressive fish fossils in the southern hemisphere. Indigenous-owned **Girloorloo Tours** (www.mimbicaves.com.au; 3hr tour adult/child $80/40; ⊙10am Tue-Sat Apr-Sep) runs trips including an introduction to local Dreaming stories, bush tucker and traditional medicines. Book through Fitzroy Crossing or Halls Creek visitor centres.

Larrawa Station

Larrawa Station CAMPGROUND $
(☎08-9191 7025; www.larrawabushcamp.com; Great Northern Hwy; sites $20, s with/without meals $120/70; @) Halfway between Fitzroy Crossing and Halls Creek, Larrawa makes a good overnight stop, with hot showers, basic camsites, a couple of shearers rooms,

OFF THE BEATEN TRACK

DUNCAN ROAD

Snaking its way east from Halls Creek before eventually turning north and playing hide and seek with the NT border, Duncan Rd is the Kimberley's 'other' great outback driving experience. Unsealed for its entire length (445km), it receives only a trickle of the travellers the Gibb River Road does, but those who make the effort are rewarded with stunning scenery, beautiful gorges, tranquil billabongs and breathtakingly lonely camp sites.

Technically no harder than the Gibb, all creek crossings are concrete lined and croc free. It also makes a nice loop if you've come down the Great Northern Hwy to Purnululu and want to return to Kununurra and/or NT. There are no services on the entire Duncan, so carry fuel for at least 500km. Enquire at Halls Creek or Kununurra visitor centres about road conditions.

The only accommodation on Duncan Rd is **Zebra Rock Mine** (Wetland Safaris; ☎0400 767 650; ruth.a.duncan@gmail.com; Duncan Rd, NT; sites per adult $10, sunset tour $90; ⊙Apr-Sep), which is 10km from the Victoria Hwy, and technically in NT. Travellers love the rustic vibe, and the sunset birdwatching tour is not to be missed. There's also a small cafe and gift shop.

WORTH A TRIP

PARRY LAGOONS NATURE RESERVE

This beautiful RAMSAR-listed wetland, 25km from Wyndham, teems in the Wet with migratory birds arriving from as far away as Siberia. There's a bird hide and boardwalk at **Marlgu Billabong** and an excellent view from **Telegraph Hill**.

The tranquil **Parry Creek Farm** (08-9161 1139; www.parrycreekfarm.com.au; Parry Creek Rd; unpowered/powered sites $34/37, r $125, cabins $230;), 25km from Wyndham and surrounded by Parry Lagoons Nature Reserve, has grassy camp sites that attract hordes of wildlife. Comfy rooms and air-con cabins are connected by a raised boardwalk overlooking a billabong for easy bird spotting. The licensed cafe serves excellent baked barramundi, wood-fired pizzas and other gourmet delights.

The Grotto (Great Northern Hwy) Just off the highway, 33km from Wyndham, steep steps lead down to a deep, peaceful pool in a small gorge, perfect for a quiet dip.

and meals (when available). There's also a three-room cottage.

Yiyilli

Laarri Gallery GALLERY

(08-9191 7195; www.laarrigallery.com; Yiyilli; 8am-4pm school days) This tiny not-for-profit gallery in the back of the community school has interesting contemporary-style art detailing local history. It's 120km west of Halls Creek and 5km from the Great Northern Hwy. Phone ahead.

Halls Creek

On the edge of the Great Sandy Desert, Halls Creek is a small town with communities of Kija, Jaru and Gooniyandi people. The excellent **visitor centre** (08-9168 6262; www.hallscreektourism.com.au; Great Northern Hwy; 7am-5pm) can book tours to the Bungles and tickets for Mimbi Caves. Check your email next door at the **Community Resource Centre** (inside the library, Shire Building; internet per hr $5; 8am-4pm Mon-Fri; @). Across the highway, **Yarliyil Gallery** (08-9168 6723; www.yarliyil.com.au; Great Northern Hwy; 9am-5pm Mon-Fri) is definitely worth a look.

Kimberley Hotel (08-9168 6101; www.kimberleyhotel.com.au; Roberta Ave; r from $172, restaurant mains $22-46;) is your best lunch option and you can find a bed there or at **Best Western** (08-9168 9600; www.bestwestern.com.au; d $260;). There's a caravan park, but you're better off heading out of town.

Skippers (p1012) flies from Fitzroy Crossing and Halls Creek to Broome and Greyhound (p1012) passes through daily.

Wyndham

POP 900

A gold-rush town that has fallen on leaner times, Wyndham is scenically nestled between rugged hills and Cambridge Gulf, some 100km northwest of Kununurra. Sunsets are superb from the spectacular **Five Rivers Lookout** on Mt Bastion (325m) overlooking the King, Pentecost, Durack, Forrest and Ord Rivers entering Cambridge Gulf.

A giant 20m croc greets visitors entering town. The historic port precinct is 5km further and contains a small **museum** (08-9161 1857; Old Courthouse, Port Precinct; 10am-3pm daily during dry season) and pioneer graveyard.

Greyhound (p1012) drops passengers 56km away at the Victoria Hwy junction; you'll need to arrange a pick up or **taxi** (0408 898 638) into town prior to arrival. Internet is available at the **Community Resource Centre** (CRC; 08-9161 1002; www.wyndham.crc.net.au; 990 Koojarra Rd; per hr $5; 8am-4pm Mon-Fri; @).

Sleeping & Eating

Wyndham Caravan Park CARAVAN PARK $

(08-9161 1064; Baker St; unpowered/powered sites $25/35, donga d $70;) Laid-back park with shady, grassy camp sites.

Rusty Wheelbarrow B&B $$

(0408 902 887; www.facebook.com/pages/The-Rusty-Wheelbarrow-Bed-Breakfast; 1293 Great Northern Hwy; d $160;) Wyndham's newest accommodation is set on a 10-acre block 5km from town. Beautiful, elevated rooms, all with en suites, open onto a common airy 'breezeway'. Both continental and cooked breakfasts are available, there's plenty of fresh fruit and you can even purchase a 'BBQ pack' should you feel like dining in.

★ Rusty Shed CAFE $

(☎08-9161 2427; www.facebook.com/TheRustyShedCafe; O'Donnell St, Port Precinct; mains $7-17; ⏰8am-3pm Tue-Sun, dinner from 5.30pm Sun during dry season) This local favourite has great coffee, sophisticated breakfasts and delicious cakes and pastries. Opens for roast dinners on selected Sundays, sometimes with guest musicians.

Five Rivers Cafe CAFE $

(☎08-9161 2271; www.facebook.com/FiveRivers-Cafe; 12 Great Northern Hwy; meals $6-16; ⏰7.30am-2pm Mon-Fri, 8am-1pm Sat, 8am-1pm & 5-8pm Sun) Enjoy an honest barra burger under the mango tree at this early opener. Excellent coffee, smoothies and breakfasts, as well as pizza on Sunday nights.

Kununurra

POP 6000

Kununurra, on Miriwoong country, is a relaxed town set in an oasis of lush farmland and tropical fruit and sandalwood plantations, thanks to the Ord River irrigation scheme. With good transport and communications, excellent services and well-stocked supermarkets, it's every traveller's favourite slice of civilisation between Broome and Darwin.

Kununurra is also the departure point for most of the tours in the East Kimberley, and with all that fruit, there's plenty of seasonal work. Note the Northern Territory is in the Australian Central time zone, which is 90 minutes ahead of Australian Western Standard Time.

Sights & Activities

Across the highway from the township, **Lily Creek Lagoon** is a mini-wetlands with amazing bird-life, boating and freshwater crocs. **Lake Kununurra** (Diversion Dam) has pleasant picnic spots and great fishing. Groups could consider hiring their own 'barbie' boat from **Kununurra Self Drive Hire Boats** (☎0409 291 959; Casuarina Way, near Lakeside Resort; from $174).

Don't miss the excellent **Waringarri Aboriginal Arts Centre** (☎08-9168 2212; www.waringarriarts.com.au; 16 Speargrass Rd; ⏰8.30am-4.30pm Mon-Fri, 10am-2pm Sat dry season, weekdays only wet season; Ⓟ), opposite the road to **Kelly's Knob**, a popular sunset viewpoint.

Mirima National Park NATIONAL PARK

(per car $12; Ⓟ) Like a mini-Bungle Bungles, the eroded gorges of Hidden Valley are home to brittle red peaks, spinifex, boab trees and abundant wildlife. Several walking trails lead to lookouts, and early morning or dusk are the best times for sighting fauna.

Kununurra Historical Society Museum MUSEUM

(www.kununurra.org.au/khs/museum; Coolibah Dr; admission by gold-coin donation; ⏰10am-3pm) Old photographs and newspaper articles document Kununurra's history, including the story of a wartime Wirraway aircraft crash and the subsequent recovery mission. The museum is opposite the country club exit.

Go Wild ADVENTURE SPORTS

(☎1300 663 369; www.gowild.com.au; 3-day canoe trips $220) Self-guided multi-day canoe trips from Lake Argyle along the Ord River, overnighting at riverside camp sites. Canoes, camping equipment and transport are provided; BYO food and sleeping bag. They also run group caving ($220), abseiling (from $150) and bushwalking (from $40) trips.

Tours

North West Airboats ADVENTURE TOUR

(☎0419 805 2780; www.northwestairboats.com; 45min trip $100) Possibly the biggest adrenalin hit you'll get in Kununurra: tie a huge fan to the back of a boat, connect it to a V8 and let it rip. Tours explore the rarely glimpsed lower Ord where salties frolic.

Kimberley Sunset Cruises CRUISE

(☎08-9169 1995; www.kimberleysunsetcruises.com.au; adult/child $85/35) Popular sunset 'BBQ Dinner' cruises on Lily Creek Lagoon and the Ord River. BYO drinks.

Triple J Tours CRUISE

(☎08-9168 2682; www.triplejtours.com.au; adult/child $180/140) Triple J cruises the 55km Ord River between Kununurra and Lake Argyle Dam.

Kingfisher Tours SCENIC FLIGHTS

(☎08-9168 1333; www.kingfishertours.net; per person from $290) Various flights around the Bungles, Cambridge Gulf, Kalumburu and majestic Mitchell and King George Falls.

THE KIMBERLEY'S ART SCENE

The Indigenous art of the Kimberley is unique. Encompassing powerful and strongly guarded Wandjina, prolific and puzzling Gwion Gwion (Bradshaws), bright tropical coastal x-rays, subtle and sombre bush ochres and topographical dots of the western desert, every work sings a story about Country.

To experience it firsthand, visit some of these Aboriginal-owned cooperatives; most are accessible by 2WD.

Mowanjum Art & Culture Centre (p1015) This incredible gallery, shaped like a Wandjina image, features work by Mowanjum artists.

Waringarri Aboriginal Arts Centre (p1020) This excellent Kununurra gallery-studio hosts local artists working with ochres in a unique abstract style. It also represents artists from Kalumburu.

Warmun Arts (☎08-9168 7496; www.warmunart.com; Great Northern Hwy, Warmun; ⏲9am-4pm Mon-Fri) Between Kununurra and Halls Creek, Warmun artists create beautiful works using ochres to explore Gija identity. Phone first from Warmun Roadhouse for a verbal permit.

Laarri Gallery (p1019) This tiny not-for-profit gallery, located in the back of the Yiyilli community school, depicts local history through interesting contemporary-style art. It's 120km west of Halls Creek and 5km from the Great Northern Hwy.

Mangkaja Arts (p1018) A Fitzroy Crossing gallery where desert and river tribes interact, producing unique acrylics, prints and baskets.

Yaruman Artists Centre (☎08-9168 8208; Kundat Djaru) Sitting on the edge of the Tanami, 162km from Halls Creek, Yaruman has acrylic works featuring the many local soaks (waterholes). The weekly mail run from Kununurra stops here (Ringer Soak).

Yarliyil Gallery (p1019) Great Halls Creek gallery showcasing talented local artists as well as some of the Ringer Soak mob.

Warlayirti Artists Centre (☎08-9168 8960; www.balgoart.org.au; Balgo; ⏲9am-5pm Mon-Fri) This centre, 255km down the Tanami Track, is a conduit for artists around the area and features bright acrylic dot-style works as well as lithographs and glass. Phone first to arrange an entry permit.

Festivals & Events

Ord Valley Muster CULTURAL
(www.ordvalleymuster.com; ⏲May) For 10 days each May, Kununurra hits overdrive with a collection of sporting, charity and cultural events culminating in a large outdoor concert under the full moon on the banks of the Ord River.

Sleeping

There's a great variety of accommodation to choose from, and the more it costs, the more of a discount you'll get in the Wet. Watch out for mozzies if you're camping near the lake.

★**Wunan House** B&B $
(☎08-9168 2436; www.wunanhouse.com; 167 Coolibah Dr; r from $90; P❄📶) Indigenous owned and run, this immaculate B&B offers light, airy rooms, all with en suites and TVs. There's free wi-fi, off-street parking and an ample Continental breakfast.

Hidden Valley Tourist Park CARAVAN PARK $
(☎08-9168 1790; www.hiddenvalleytouristpark.com; 110 Weaber Plains Rd; unpowered/powered sites $28/38, cabin d $125; @📶🏊) Under the looming crags of Mirima National Park, this excellent little park has nice grassy sites and is popular with seasonal workers. The self-contained cabins are good value.

Kimberley Croc Backpackers HOSTEL $
(☎1300 136 702; www.kimberleycroc.com.au; 120 Konkerberry Dr; dm $27-33, d $89-125; ❄@📶🏊) This slick, modern YHA close to the action has a large pool, barbecue area and excellent kitchen facilities. It also runs the nearby **Kimberley Croc Lodge** (☎08-9168 1411; www.kimberleycroclodge.com.au; 2 River Fig

Ave; dm per week $160; P❄📶🏊) for seasonal workers.

Freshwater APARTMENT **$$**
(☎08-9169 2010; www.freshwaterapartments.net.au; 19 Victoria Hwy; studio/1-/2-/3-bedroom apts $224/249/329/399; P❄📶🏊) Exquisite, fully self-contained units with exotic open-roofed showers.

Eating

The big resorts all have restaurants offering similar fare. There are two well-stocked supermarkets and several take aways. Most places keep shorter hours during the Wet, and you'll struggle to find lunch after 2pm.

★ **Wild Mango** CAFE **$**
(☎08-9169 2810; 20 Messmate Way; breakfasts $9-23, lunches $6-13; ⏱7.30am-4pm Mon-Fri, 8am-1pm Sat & Sun) The hippest, healthiest feed in town with curry wraps, mouth-watering pancakes, chai smoothies, real coffee and homemade gelato. The entrance is in Konkerberry Dr.

Ivanhoe Cafe CAFE **$$**
(☎0427 692 775; Ivanhoe Rd; mains $12.50-24; ⏱8am-4pm Apr-Sep) Grab a table under the leafy mango trees and tuck into tasty wraps, salads and burgers, all made from fresh, local produce. Don't miss their signature mango smoothie.

★ **PumpHouse** MODERN AUSTRALIAN **$$$**
(☎08-9169 3222; www.thepumphouserestaurant.com; Lakeview Dr; lunches $19-36, dinners $32-45; ⏱4.30pm-late Tue-Thu, 11.30am-late Fri, 8am-late Sat & Sun; 📶) Idyllically situated on Lake Kununurra, the PumpHouse creates succulent dishes featuring quality local ingredients. Watch the catfish swarm should a morsel slip off the verandah. Or just have a beer and watch the sunset. There's an excellent wine list and free wi-fi.

Shopping

Artlandish ARTS
(☎08-9168 1881; www.artlandish.com; cnr Papuana St & Konkerberry Dr; ⏱9am-4.30pm Mon-Fri, 9am-1pm Sat) Stunning collection of Kimberley ochres and Western Desert acrylics to suit all price ranges.

Bush Camp Surplus OUTDOOR EQUIPMENT
(☎08-9168 1476; cnr Papuana St & Konkerberry Dr; ⏱8.30am-5pm Mon-Fri, 8.30am-noon Sat) The biggest range of camping gear between Broome and Darwin.

Information

ATMs are near the supermarkets. Most cafes don't offer free wi-fi.

Community Resource Centre (CRC; ☎08-9169 1868; Banksia St; per hr $6; ⏱9am-4pm Mon-Fri; @📶) Internet, printing and after hours self-service wi-fi.

Parks & Wildlife Office (☎08-9168 4200; Lot 248 Ivanhoe Rd; ⏱8am-4.30pm Mon-Fri) Parks information and permits.

Visitor Centre (☎1800 586 868; www.visitkununurra.com; Coolibah Dr; ⏱8am-4.30pm daily, shorter hr Oct-Mar) Check here for accommodation, tours, seasonal work and road conditions.

Getting There & Away

Airnorth (TL; ☎1800 627 474; www.airnorth.com.au) Flights to Broome and Darwin daily; Perth on Saturday.

Greyhound (☎1300 473 946; www.greyhound.com.au) Greyhound buses stop at the BP Roadhouse. There are six weekly services to Broome ($146, 13 hours) via Halls Creek ($91, four hours), Fitzroy Crossing ($106, seven hours) and Derby ($125, 10 hours), and six weekly services to Darwin ($128, 11 hours) via Katherine ($95, six hours).

Virgin Australia (☎13 67 89; www.virgin-australia.com.au) Flights to Perth several times weekly.

Getting Around

Avis (☎08-9168 1999), **Budget** (☎08-9168 2033) and **Thrifty** (☎1800 626 515) all have offices at the airport.

BP Roadhouse (Messmate Way) Petrol, long-distance bus stop, and 24hr laundromat.

Ordco (Weaber Plain Rd; ⏱24hr) Local co-op selling the cheapest diesel in Kununurra.

Taxi (☎13 10 08)

Purnululu National Park & Bungle Bungle Range

Looking like a packet of half-melted Jaffas, World Heritage **Purnululu National Park** (per car $12; ⏱Apr-Nov) is home to the incredible ochre and black striped 'beehive' domes of the Bungle Bungle Range.

The distinctive rounded rock towers are made of sandstone and conglomerates moulded by rainfall over millions of years. Their stripes are the result of oxidised iron compounds and algae. To the local Kidja people, *purnululu* means sandstone, with

Purnululu National Park

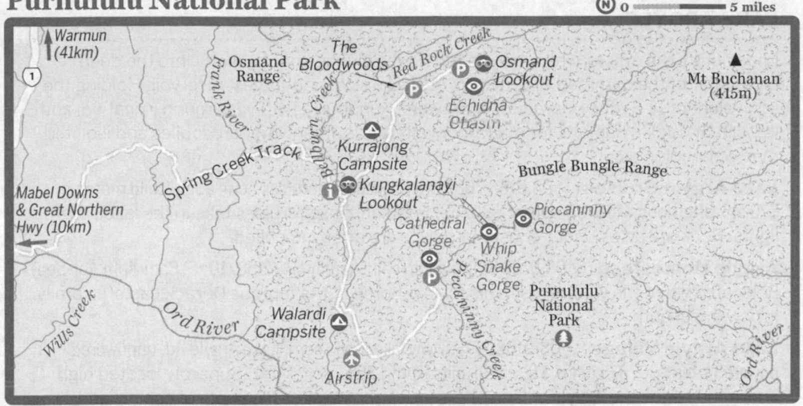

Bungle Bungle possibly a corruption of 'bundle bundle', a common grass.

Over 3000 sq km of ancient country contains a wide array of wildlife, including over 130 bird species. Whitefellas only 'discovered' the range during the mid-1980s. Rangers are based here from April to November and the park is closed outside this time.

You'll need a high clearance 4WD for the 52km twisting, rough road from the highway to the visitor centre near Three Ways junction; allow 2½ hours. There are five deep creek crossings, and the turn off is 53km south of Warmun. **Kurrajong** (sites per person $12; ⏲May-Sep) and **Walardi** (sites per person $12; ⏲Apr-Nov) camps have fresh water and toilets. Book camp sites online via **DPAW** (http://parkstay.dpaw.wa.gov.au/).

Sights & Activities

Kungkalanayi Lookout LOOKOUT
Sunsets are spectacular from this hill near Three Ways.

Echidna Chasm GORGE
(⏲return 2km, 1hr) Look for tiny bats high on the walls above this palm-fringed, narrow gorge in the northern park. The trail leaves from the Echidna Chasm car park and is marked on the park map available from the rangers office.

Cathedral Gorge GORGE
Aptly named, this immense and inspiring circular cavern is an easy 2km (return) stroll from the southern car park .

Whip Snake Gorge GORGE
(⏲return 10km, 4hrs) An energetic half-day outing from the southern car park to a shady gorge filled with ferns, figs and brittle gums. There's a small terminal pool.

Piccaninny Gorge GORGE
(⏲return 30km, 2-3 days) A 30km return overnight trek from the southern car park to a remote and pristine gorge, best suited for experienced hikers.

Tours

Most Kimberley tour operators include Purnululu in multi-day tours. You can also pick up tours at Warmun Roadhouse, Halls Creek and Mabel Downs. Helicopters will get you closer than fixed-wing flights.

East Kimberley SCENIC FLIGHTS
(☎08-9168 2213; www.eastkimberleytours.com.au; 1-/2-/3-day tours $720/1593/1831, safari tents from $225) Several fly/drive tours of the Bungle Bungles departing Kununurra. Also offers accommodation inside the park.

Helispirit HELICOPTER
(☎1800 180 085; www.helispirit.com.au; 18/30/48min flights $225/299/495) Scenic chopper flights over the Bungles from Bellbird and Warmun. They also have flights over Mitchell Falls, Kununurra and Lake Argyle.

Bungle Bungle Expeditions BUS, HELICOPTER
(☎08-9169 1995; www.bunglebungleexpeditions.com.au; bus day/overnight $285/695, helicopter from $290) Various bus, helicopter and fixed-wing tours of the Bungles from the caravan park on Mabel Downs, near the highway.

WORTH A TRIP

LAKE ARGYLE

Enormous Lake Argyle, where barren red ridges plunge spectacularly into the deep blue water of the dammed Ord River, is Australia's second-largest reservoir. Holding the equivalent of 18 Sydney Harbours, it provides Kununurra with year-round irrigation, and important wildlife habitats for migratory waterbirds, freshwater crocodiles and isolated marsupial colonies.

Lake Argyle Cruises (☎08-9168 7687; www.lakeargylecruises.com; adult/child morning $70/45, afternoon $155/90, sunset $90/55) Popular sunset cruises take in the lake's highlights. Book ahead as under-subscribed trips are often cancelled.

Argyle Homestead (☎08-9167 8088; adult/child/family $4/2.50/10; ⊙8am-4pm Apr-Sep) Relocated when the waters rose, this former home of the famous Durack pastoral family is now a museum.

Lake Argyle Village (☎08-9168 7777; www.lakeargyle.com; Lake Argyle Rd; unpowered/powered sites $30/37, cabins $125-219, units from $359; ❄@🛜🏊) Superbly located high above the lake, Lake Argyle Village offers grassy camp sites, a variety of cabins, and hearty meals from its licensed bistro. Don't miss a swim in the stunning infinity pool.

Sleeping

Mabel Downs CAMPGROUND
(Bungle Bungle Caravan Park; ☎08-9168 7220; www.bunglebunglecaravanpark.com.au; tent sites/powered sites $35/50, safari tents with/without enste $225/120, dinner $25; 🛜) Situated just 1km from the highway (outside Purnululu), don't expect much privacy. Tents are jammed between choppers and ridiculously long trailers. Various tours are available.

PORT HEDLAND TO BROOME

The Big Empty stretches from Port Hedland to Broome, as the Great Northern Highway skirts the Great Sandy Desert. It's 609km of willy-willies and dust and not much else. There are only two roadhouses, Pardoo (148km) and Sandfire (288km), so keep the tank full. The coast, wild and unspoilt, is never far away.

Sleeping

Places along the Great Northern Highway can be packed from May to September.

Eighty Mile Beach Caravan Park CARAVAN PARK $
(☎08-9176 5941; www.eightymilebeach.com.au; unpowered/powered sites $35/41, cabins $190; 🛜) Popular with fishermen, this shady, laid-back park 250km from Port Hedland backs onto a beautiful white-sand beach. Turtles nest from November to March.

Port Smith Caravan Park CARAVAN PARK $
(☎08-9192 4983; www.portsmithcaravanpark.com.au; unpowered/powered sites $30/40, dongas d $80, cabins $180) There's loads of wildlife at this park on a tidal lagoon, 487km from Port Hedland.

Barn Hill Station PASTORAL STATION $
(☎08-9192 4975; www.barnhill.com.au; unpowered sites $22, powered sites $27-35, cabins from $100) Barn Hill, 490km from Port Hedland, is a working cattle station with its own 'mini-Pinnacles'. It's especially popular among adventurous grey nomads (but all are welcome!).

Eco Beach RESORT $$$
(☎08-9193 8015; www.ecobeach.com.au; Great Northern Hwy, Thangoo Station; safari tent from $225, villa d from $345; ❄🏊) 🍃 This award-winning luxury eco-resort is set on secluded coastline 120km southwest of Broome. There's a choice of safari tents (no air-con) or villas, a top-notch restaurant and a host of tours and activities. From Broome, you can reach the resort by light aircraft ($60), helicopter ($270) or your own vehicle.

BROOME

POP 16,000

Like a paste jewel set in a tiara of natural splendours, Broome clings to a narrow strip of red pindan on the Kimberley's far-western edge, at the base of the pristine Dampier Peninsula. Surrounded by the aquamarine waters of the Indian Ocean and the creeks, mangroves and mudflats of Roebuck Bay, this Yawuru country is a good 2000km from the nearest capital city.

The history of Broome is centred around its pearling industry and Broome's cemeteries are a stark reminder of this heritage, which claimed the lives of many Japanese, Chinese, Malay and Aboriginal divers. Broome's pearls, now produced on modern sea farms, are still exported around the world.

Cable Beach, with its luxury resorts, hauls in the tourists during high (dry) season (April to October), with romantic notions of camels, surf and sunsets. Magnificent, sure, but there's a lot more to Broome than postcards, and tourists are sometimes surprised when they scratch the surface and find pindan just below.

Broome's centre is Chinatown, on the shores of Roebuck Bay, while Cable Beach and its resorts are 6km west on the Indian Ocean. The airport stretches between the two; the port and Gantheaume Point are 7km south.

High season is a great time to find casual work in hospitality or out on the pearl farms. In low (wet) season, it feels like you're swimming in a warm, moist glove, and while many places close or restrict their hours, others offer amazingly good deals as prices plummet.

Each evening, the whole town pauses, collective drinks in mid-air, while the sun slips slowly seawards.

Sights & Activities

Cable Beach Area

★Cable Beach BEACH

(Map p1028) Western Australia's most famous landmark offers turquoise waters and beautiful white sand curving away to the sunset. Clothing is optional north of the rocks, while south, walking trails lead through the red dunes of **Minyirr Park**, a spiritual place for the Yawuru people. Cable Beach is synonymous with camels, and an evening ride along the sand is a highlight for many visitors. Locals in their 4WDs swarm north of the rocks for sunset drinks.

Gantheaume Point & Dinosaur Prints LOOKOUT

FREE Beautiful at dawn or sunset when the pindan cliffs turn scarlet, this peaceful lookout holds a 135-million-year-old secret. Nearby lies one of the world's most varied collections of **dinosaur footprints**, impossible to find except at very low tides. (Hint: head off to the right of the cliffs but beware: rocks can be slippery.)

Reddell Beach BEACH

For a blistering sunset without tourists, camels or 4WDs, pull into any of the turnoffs along Kavite Rd between Gantheaume Point and the port and watch the pindan cliffs turn into molten lava.

Chinatown

Sun Pictures HISTORIC BUILDING

(Map p1026; ☎08-9192 1077; www.sunpictures.com.au; 27 Carnarvon St; adult/child $17/12) Sink back in a canvas deck chair in the world's oldest operating picture gardens. Opened in 1916 to entertain the ever increasing local community (with few means of 'clean' entertainment), the cinema started showing silent movies, then progressed to reels with sound. These days, it still shows evening movies. The history of the Sun building is the history of Broome itself – different racial groups were assigned to different seats, floods were frequent and, planes flew

DON'T MISS

WWII FLYING BOAT WRECKS

On a very low tide it's possible to walk out across the mudflats from Town Beach to the **wrecks** (Map p1026) of Catalina and Dornier flying boats attacked by Japanese 'Zeroes' during WWII. The planes had been evacuating refugees from Java and many still had passengers aboard. Over 60 people and 15 flying boats (mostly Dutch and British) were lost. Only six wrecks are visible, with the rest in deep water.

Start walking an hour before low tide, and head roughly southeast for 1.5km (about 30 minutes). Wear appropriate footwear – the mud is sticky and can hide sharp objects, not all of them inanimate. Watch out for marine hazards such as jellyfish and check with the visitor centre for tide times. The **museum** (p1027) also has a handy brochure. Or just take the **hovercraft** (☎08-9193 5025; www.broomehovercraft.com.au; 1hr adult/child $119/85, sunset/flying boat $172/109).

Broome

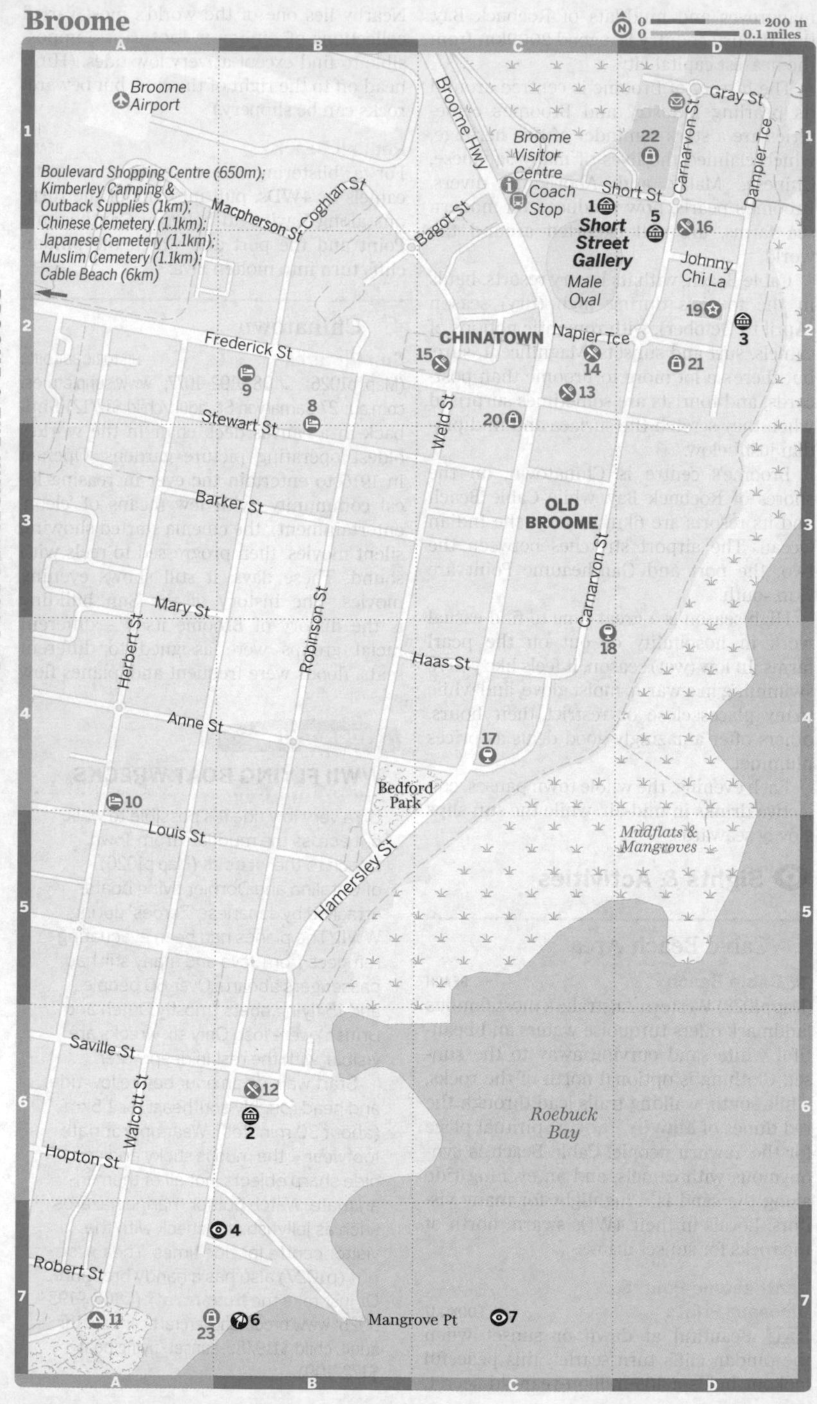

0 200 m
0 0.1 miles
A
B
C
D
1
2
3
4
5
6
7
Broome Airport
Boulevard Shopping Centre (650m); Kimberley Camping & Outback Supplies (1km); Chinese Cemetery (1.1km); Japanese Cemetery (1.1km); Muslim Cemetery (1.1km); Cable Beach (6km)
Broome Hwy
Broome Visitor Centre
Coach Stop
Macpherson St
Coghlan St
Bagot St
Gray St
Carnarvon St
Dampier Tce
Short St
Short Street Gallery
Johnny Chi La
Male Oval
Frederick St
CHINATOWN
Napier Tce
Stewart St
Weld St
Barker St
OLD BROOME
Mary St
Herbert St
Robinson St
Haas St
Anne St
Bedford Park
Louis St
Hamersley St
Mudflats & Mangroves
Saville St
Walcott St
Hopton St
Robert St
Roebuck Bay
Mangrove Pt
1
2
3
4
5
6
7
8
9
10
11
12
13
14
15
16
17
18
19
20
21
22
23

Broome

Top Sights
1 Short Street Gallery C1

Sights
2 Broome Museum B6
3 Pearl Luggers D2
4 Pioneer Cemetery B7
5 Sun Pictures D2
6 Town Beach B7
7 WWII Flying Boat Wrecks C7

Sleeping
8 Broome Town B&B B2
9 Kimberley Klub B2
10 McAlpine House A4
11 Roebuck Bay Caravan Park A7

Eating
12 18 Degrees B6
13 Aarli C2
14 Azuki C2
15 Good Cartel C2
16 Yuen Wing D1

Drinking & Nightlife
17 Matso's Broome Brewery C4
18 Tides Garden Bar C4

Entertainment
19 Roebuck Bay Hotel D2

Shopping
20 Courthouse Markets C2
21 Kimberley Bookshop D2
22 Paspaley Shopping Centre D1
23 Town Beach Markets A7

directly overhead (as they do today; the cinema is located under the approach flight path). To hear about this and more, don't miss the evocative 15-minute **audio history** (1pm daily from April to October; $5).

★ Short Street Gallery GALLERY

(Map p1026; ☎08-9192 6118; www.shortstgallery.com.au; 7 Short St; ⏰10am-3pm Mon-Fri, 11am-3pm Sat) This original building houses back-to-back exhibitions of contemporary Indigenous artworks. The stock room studio at 3 Hopton St, Old Broome holds a stunning collection of canvasses of all sizes (and some sculptures) by Indigenous artists. It's an agent for Yulparija artists plus art centres in the Kimberley and beyond.

Pearl Luggers MUSEUM

(Map p1026; ☎08-9192 0000; www.pearlluggers.com.au; 31 Dampier Tce; admission free, 1hr tour adult/child/family $25/12.50/60; ⏰tours 11.30am & 3.30pm) FREE The compact museum has some 'pearls' indeed, and provides an interesting talk on Broome's tragic pearling past, evoking the diver experience with genuine artefacts. You can also wander over two of the last surviving (and restored) luggers, named *Sam Male* and *DMcD*.

Old Broome

Broome Museum MUSEUM

(Map p1026; ☎08-9192 2075; www.broomemuseum.org.au; 67 Robinson St; adult/child $5/1; ⏰10am-4pm Mon-Fri, to 1pm Sat & Sun Jun-Sep, to 1pm daily Oct-May) Discover Cable Beach and Chinatown's origins through exhibits devoted to the area's pearling history and WWII bombing in this quirky museum, occupying the former Customs House.

Cemeteries

A number of cemeteries testify to Broome's multicultural past. The most striking is the **Japanese Cemetery** with 919 graves (mostly pearl divers). Next to this, the **Chinese burial ground** (Frederick St) has over 90 graves and monuments. The small **Muslim Cemetery** (Frederick St) honours Malay pearl-divers and Afghan camelteers.

A couple of kilometres southeast, the small **Pioneer Cemetery** (Map p1026) overlooks Roebuck Bay at Town Beach.

Tours

Camel Tours

It's a feisty business, but at last count there were three camel-tour operators running at Cable Beach offering similar trips.

Broome Camel Safaris CAMEL TOUR

(Map p1028; ☎0419 916 101; www.broomecamelsafaris.com.au; Cable Beach; 30min afternoon rides $25, 1hr sunset rides adult/child $70/55) Run by Alison, known as 'the Camel Lady', Broome Camel Safaris offers afternoon and sunset rides along Cable Beach.

Red Sun Camels CAMEL TOUR

(Map p1028; ☎1800 184 488; www.redsuncamels.com.au; Cable Beach; adult/child 40min morning rides $55/35, 1hr sunset rides $75/55) As well as morning and sunset rides, Red Sun offers a 30-minute trip at 4pm ($30).

Cable Beach

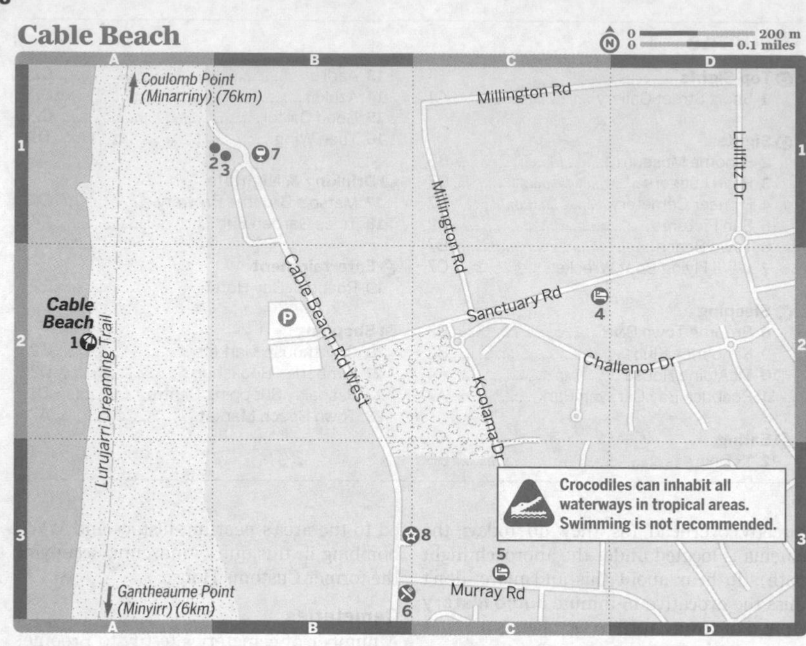

Cable Beach

Top Sights
1 Cable Beach A2

Activities, Courses & Tours
2 Broome Camel Safaris B1
3 Red Sun Camels B1

Sleeping
4 Beaches of Broome C2
5 Broome Beach Resort C3

Eating
6 Cable Beach General Store & Cafe B3

Drinking & Nightlife
7 Sunset Bar & Grill B1

Entertainment
8 Diver's Tavern B3

Sundowner Camel Tours CAMEL TOUR
(☎08-9195 2200; www.sundownercameltours.com.au; Cable Beach; adult/child 40min morning rides $55/45, 30min afternoon rides $40/25, 1hr sunset rides $75/55) In addition to morning, afternoon and sunset rides, Sundowner also has a 'lapsitters' for the little 'uns ($10).

Not Camels
There's seemingly a million tours to choose from, from walking tours of Broome to scenic flights; visit the visitor centre for the full selection.

Broome Adventure Company KAYAKING
(☎0419 895 367; www.broomeadventure.com.au; 3hr trip adult/child $75/60) Glide past turtles on these eco-certified coastal kayaking trips.

Astro Tours ASTRONOMY TOUR
(☎0417 949 958; www.astrotours.net; adult/child $80/50) Fascinating after-dark two-hour stargazing tours with big telescopes and great commentary, held just outside Broome. Self-drive and save $15.

Kimberley Birdwatching BIRDWATCHING
(☎08-9192 1246; www.kimberleybirdwatching.com.au; 3/6/10/12hr tours $90/150/250/300) Join ornithologist George Swann on his informative Broome nature tours. Overnight trips are also available.

Broome Historical Walking Tours WALKING TOUR
(☎0408 541 102; www.broomehistoricalwalkingtours.com; adult/child $35/20) This fabulous 1½ hour walking tour examines the Broome

of yesteryear through site visits and photographs – from WWII back to the pearling days – with raconteur Wil telling some fabulous stories.

Lurujarri Dreaming Trail GUIDED TOUR
(☎Frans 0423 817 925; www.goolarabooloo.org.au; ⊙changing dates) This 82km song cycle follows the coast north from Gantheaume Point (Minyirr) to Coulomb Point (Minarriny). The Goolarabooloo organise a yearly guided nine-day trip (adult/student $1600/900), staying at traditional camp sites.

Festivals & Events

Broome hosts many festivals, the timing of which may vary from year to year. Check with the visitor centre (p1031) or see www.visitbroome.com.au.

Broome Race Round SPORTS
(www.broometurfclub.com.au) Locals and tourists frock up and party hard for the Kimberley Cup, Ladies Day and Broome Cup horse races in July/August.

Shinju Matsuri Festival of the Pearl CULTURAL
(www.shinjumatsuri.com.au) Broome's homage to the pearl includes a week of parades, food, art, concerts, fireworks and dragon-boat races. Held August or September.

A Taste of Broome FOOD
(www.goolarri.com) Indigenous and multicultural flavours feature at this ticket-only event held monthly during high season. Alongside cuisine there are also music and dance events.

Sleeping

Accommodation is plentiful, but either book ahead or be flexible. Prices rocket during the high season and plummet in low season. If you're travelling in a group, consider renting an apartment.

Beaches of Broome HOSTEL $
(Map p1028; ☎1300 881 031; www.beachesofbroome.com.au; 4 Sanctuary Rd, Cable Beach; dm $32-45, motel d without/with bathroom $140/180; ❄@📶🏊) Beaches of Broome wins the hostel vote for clean, air-conditioned rooms, shady common areas, poolside bar and self-catering kitchen. Dorms come in a variety of sizes, while its motel-style rooms are well appointed. Scooter and bike hire available, and continental breakfast is included.

Kimberley Klub HOSTEL $
(Map p1026; ☎08-9192 3233; www.kimberleyklub.com; 62 Frederick St; dm $25-33, d $99-120; ❄@📶🏊) Handy to the airport, this popular, laid-back and slightly worn backpackers is a great place to meet other travellers.

Roebuck Bay Caravan Park CARAVAN PARK $
(Map p1026; ☎08-9192 1366; www.roebuckbaycp.com.au; 91 Walcott St; unpowered sites $32, powered sites $37-50, on-site van d $90) Right next to Town Beach, this shady, popular park by the waterside has several camp site options.

★**McAlpine House** B&B $$$
(Map p1026; ☎08-9192 0588; www.pinctada.com.au; 55 Herbert St; d $185-420; P❄📶🏊) A former pearl master's cottage (built in 1910), Lord McAlpine made this stunning house his Broome residence during the eighties, renovating it to its former glory. Rooms vary in size (some are squeezy), but a library, airy eating patio, pool and verandahs add to its charm. A canopy of trees, from mangos to frangipanis, provide cool relief from the heat.

Broome Town B&B B&B $$$
(Map p1026; ☎08-9192 2006; www.broometown.com.au; 15 Stewart St, Old Broome; r $285; P❄📶🏊) This delightful, boutique-style B&B has four spacious rooms with jarrah floors and lots of tropical charm. It epitomises Broome-style

STAIRCASE TO THE MOON

The reflections of a rising full moon rippling over exposed mudflats at low tide create the optical illusion of a **golden stairway** (⊙Mar-Oct) leading to the moon. Between March and October Broome buzzes around the full moon, with everyone eager to see the spectacle. At **Town Beach** (Map p1026) there's a lively **evening market** (Map p1026) with food stalls, and people bring fold-up chairs, although the small headland at the end of Hamersley St has a better view. While Roebuck Bay parties like nowhere else, this phenomenon happens across the Kimberley and Pilbara coasts – anywhere with some east-facing mudflats. Other good viewing spots are One Arm Point at Cape Leveque, Cooke Point in Port Hedland, Sunrise Beach at Onslow, Hearson Cove near Dampier and the lookout at Cossack. Most visitor centres publish the dates on their websites.

architecture: high-pitched roofs and wooden louvres. Continental breakfast is served the communal pool area.

Broome Beach Resort APARTMENT $$$
(Map p1028; ☎08-9158 3300; www.broomebeach-resort.com; 4 Murray Rd, Cable Beach; 1-/2-/3-bedroom apt $295/325/365;) Great for families and groups, these large, modest apartments surround a central pool and are within easy walking distance of Cable Beach.

Eating

Be prepared for 'Broome prices' (exorbitant), 'Broome time' (when it should be open but it's closed) and surcharges: credit cards, public holidays, bad karma. Service can fluctuate wildly – some excellent, others appalling – as most staff are just passing through. Most places close in low season.

You'll find cafes along Carnarvon St in Chinatown, while many resorts have in-house restaurants, though often you're just paying for the view.

Supermarkets are housed in several major shopping centres, including **Broome Boulevard** (106 Frederick St) and the central **Paspaley Shopping Centre** (Map p1026; Carnarvon St & Short St). **Yuen Wing** (Map p1026; ☎08-9192 1267; 19 Carnarvon St; 8.30am-5.30pm Mon-Fri, to 2pm Sat & Sun) grocery your best bet for spices, noodles and all things Asian.

Good Cartel CAFE $
(Map p1026; ☎0406 353 942; 3 Weld St; snacks $7-15; 5.30am-2pm Mon-Fri, 6.30am-2pm Sat, 7am-2pm Sun) What started as a pop-up cafe is now *the* place in town to grab a great coffee, plus Mexican-themed snacks. Its popcorn tin seats pay homage to its location – behind the (new) Sun Pictures Cinema.

Cable Beach General Store & Cafe CAFE $
(Map p1028; ☎08-9192 5572; www.cablebeachstore.com.au; cnr Cable Beach & Murray Rds; snacks $10-20; 6am-8.30pm daily;) Cable Beach unplugged – a typical Aussie corner shop with egg breakfasts, barra burgers, pies, internet and no hidden charges. You can even play a round of minigolf.

Azuki JAPANESE $$
(Map p1026; ☎08-9193 7211; 1/15 Napier Tce; sushi $13.50-15, mains $22.50-38; 11am-2.30pm & 5.30-8.30pm Mon-Fri) Enjoy the exquisite subtlety of authentic Japanese cuisine at this tiny BYO restaurant, from the fresh sushi rolls to the wonderfully tasty bento boxes. The downside: it's closed on weekends.

Aarli TAPAS $$
(Map p1026; ☎08-9192 5529; www.theaarli.com.au; 2/6 Hamersley St, cnr Frederick St; mains $24-38; 8am-late) 'Consistent' is how locals describe Aarli. Indeed, it cooks up some of the most inventive and tasty titbits in Broome, using local produce where possible. The Med-Asian fusion tapas are excellent, and the breakfasts are good, too. Depending on who makes it, coffee isn't bad either.

18 Degrees INTERNATIONAL $$
(Map p1026; ☎08-9192 7915; www.18degrees.com.au; Shop 4, 63 Robinson St, Seaview Centre; mains $20-33) Broome's new and very contemporary spot whips up some great share plates, delicious mains (for example, barramundi parcels and lamb tenderloin) and boasts a wine and cocktail list as large as a crocodile smile.

Wharf Restaurant SEAFOOD $$$
(☎08-9192 5800; 401 Port Dr; mains $25.50-55; 11am-11pm) Settle back for a long, lazy seafood lunch with waterside ambience and the chance of a whale sighting. OK, it's pricey, but the wine's cold, the sea stunning and the chilli blue swimmer crab sensational. Just wait until after 2pm before ordering oysters (then they're half price!)

Drinking & Entertainment

Avoid wandering around late at night, alone and off your dial; it's not as safe as it may seem.

Tides Garden Bar BAR
(Map p1026; ☎08-9192 1303; www.mangrove-hotel.com.au; 47 Carnarvon St; 11am-10pm) The Mangrove Resort's casual outdoor bar is perfect for a few early bevvies while contemplating Roebuck Bay. Decent bistro meals ($35 to $39) and live music (Wednesday to Sunday) complement excellent Staircase to the Moon viewing.

Sunset Bar & Grill BAR
(Map p1028; ☎08-9192 0470; www.cablebeachclub.com; Cable Beach Club Resort, Cable Beach Rd; breakfast 5-10.30am, bar 4-9pm, dinner 5.30-9pm) Arrive around 4.45pm, grab a front-row seat, order a drink and watch the show – backpackers, package tourists, locals, camels and a searing Indian Ocean sunset shaded by imported coconut palms.

Matso's Broome Brewery PUB

(Map p1026; ☎08-9193 5811; www.matsos.com.au; 60 Hamersley St; ⏰7am-midnight) Get a Pearler's Pale ale (or another home brew) into you at this popular spot; grab a bite (mains $20 to $42) and kick back to live music on the verandah.

Roebuck Bay Hotel LIVE MUSIC

(Map p1026; ☎08-91921221; www.roebuckbayhotel.com.au; 45 Dampier Tce; ⏰11am-late) Party central, where Broome's 'old timers' come to play, the Roey's labyrinthine bars offer sports, live music, DJs, cocktails and – love it or hate it – wet T-shirts.

Diver's Tavern LIVE MUSIC

(Map p1028; ☎08-9193 6066; www.diverstavern.com.au; Cable Beach Rd; ⏰11am-midnight) Diver's pumps most nights. Locals bands sometimes jam on Wednesday, but always on Sunday.

Shopping

The old tin shanties of Short St and Dampier Tce are chock-full of Indigenous art, jewellery (including pearl items, of course) and cheap, tacky souvenirs.

Kimberley Bookshop BOOKS

(Map p1026; ☎08-9192 1944; www.kimberleybookshop.com.au; 4 Napier Tce; ⏰10am-5pm Mon-Fri, 10am-2pm Sat) Extensive range of books on Broome and the Kimberley.

Kimberley Camping & Outback Supplies OUTDOOR EQUIPMENT

(☎08-9193 5909; www.kimberleycamping.com.au; cnr Frederick St & Cable Beach Rd) Camp ovens and everything else you need for a successful expedition.

Courthouse Markets MARKET

(Map p1026; Hamersley St; ⏰Sat morning year round, Sat & Sun Apr-Oct) Local arts, crafts, music and general hippie gear.

Information

The Broome Tourism website (www.visitbroome.com.au) has a good gig guide and what's on page. Environs Kimberley (www.environskimberley.org.au) covers the latest environmental issues as well as projects across the Kimberley.

INTERNET ACCESS

Broome Community Resource Centre (CRC; ☎08-9193 7153; 40 Dampier Tce; per hr $5; ⏰8.30am-4.30pm Mon-Fri; @📶) Cheap printing, wi-fi and internet ($3 per hour).

Galactica DMZ Internet Café (☎08-9192 5897; 4/2 Hamersley St; per hr $5; ⏰9am-6pm Mon-Thu, 9am-8pm Fri & Sat; @📶) The usual geek stuff; behind McDonalds.

TOURIST INFORMATION

Broome Visitor Centre (Map p1026; ☎08-9195 2200; www.visitbroome.com.au; Male Oval, Hamersley St; ⏰8.30am-5pm Mon-Fri, to 4.30pm Sat & Sun, shorter hrs during low season) Books accommodation and tours. Great for info on road conditions, Staircase to the Moon viewing, dinosaur footprints, WWII wrecks and tide times. Also sells books published by Indigenous publishing company Magabala Books. It's on the roundabout entering town.

Getting There & Away

If you're not on a long-haul road trip, by far the quickest and most convenient way to reach Broome is to fly in direct. Broome International Airport is located close to the centre (though in most instances, you'll need to grab a taxi from there.)

Bus services run between Perth and Derby. Many tours, especially to the Dampier Peninsula, run out of Broome.

AIR

Virgin Airlines (☎13 67 89; www.virgin-australia.com) Flies daily to Perth.

Qantas (☎13 13 13; www.qantas.com.au) Qantas has seasonal direct flights to and from eastern capital cities.

Airnorth (☎08-8920 4001; www.airnorth.com.au) Airnorth flies daily to Darwin (except Tuesday) and Kununurra, and to Karratha and Port Hedland twice weekly.

Skippers (☎1300 729 924; www.skippers.com.au) Flies to Fitzroy Crossing, Halls Creek and Port Hedland three times weekly.

BUS

Derby Bus Service (p1014).

Integrity (☎08-9274 7464; www.integrity-coachlines.com.au; one way/return $340/646) Integrity Busline runs twice weekly between Broome and Perth and vice-versa.

Getting Around

Broome is a very spread out town and distances can be deceiving. If you're staying in Old Broome or Chinatown, the local bus is a handy way to get to beaches and attractions. Those staying in Cable Beach or wanting to explore the surrounding areas are best served by having their own set of wheels.

Town Bus Service (☎08-9193 6585; www.broomebus.com.au; adult $4, day pass $10)

The town bus links Chinatown with Cable Beach every hour (from 7.10am to 7.10pm mid-October to April, 8.40am to 6.40pm from May to mid-October). Under 16s ride free with an adult; unders 16s riding independently are charged $2.

Broome Cycles (☎08-9192 1871; www.broomecycles.com.au; 2 Hamersley St; per day/week $24/84, deposit $50; ⊙8.30am-5pm Mon-Fri, to 2pm Sat) Located in Chinatown with an additional branch at Cable Beach (☎0409 192 289; Old Crocodile Park car park, Cable Beach; ⊙9am-noon May-Oct) operating during the high season.

Broome Broome (☎08-9192 2210; www.broomebroome.com.au; 3/15 Napier Tce; per day cars/4WDs/scooters from $65/155/35) Local operator Broome Broome offers an unlimited kilometre option plus alternative insurance conditions to nationwide companies.

Britz (☎08-9192 2647; www.britz.com; 10 Livingston St) Britz hires campervans (per day from $50 to $300) and rugged 4WDs (per day $160 to $280), the latter essential for Gibb River Road.

Broome Taxis (☎13 10 08) One of several taxi services in town.

Chinatown Taxis (☎1800 811 772) Reliable service about town.

AROUND BROOME

Malcolm Douglas Wilderness Park WILDLIFE RESERVE
(☎08-9193 6580; www.malcolmdouglas.com.au; Broome Hwy; adult/child/family $35/20/90; ⊙2-5pm daily) Visitors enter through the jaws of a giant crocodile at this 30-hectare animal refuge 16km northeast of Broome. The park is home to dozens of crocs (there are feedings and informative talks at 3pm), as well as kangaroos, cassowaries, emus, dingos, jabirus and numerous other birds.

Broome Bird Observatory NATURE RESERVE
(☎08-9193 5600; www.broomebirdobservatory.com; Crab Creek Rd; admission by donation, camping per person $15, unit with shared bathroom s/d/f $50/85/100, chalets $165; ⊙8am-4pm Mar-Nov) On Roebuck Bay, this amazing bird observatory in a beautiful bush setting near an accessible beach 25km from Broome is a vital staging post for thousands of migratory birds (around 40 species), some travelling over 12,000km. Tours range from one-hour introductory 'walk and talks' ($20) or 2½-hour driving tours ($70) to a five-day all-inclusive course ($1290). You can even stay here in a unit or a self-contained chalet.

Dampier Peninsula

Stretching north from Broome, the red pindan of the Dampier Peninsula ends abruptly above deserted beaches, secluded mangrove bays and cliffs burnished crimson by the setting sun. This remote and stunning country is home to thriving Indigenous settlements of the Ngumbarl, Jabirr Jabirr, Nyul Nyul, Nimanburu, Bardi Jawi and Goolarabooloo peoples. Access is by 4WD, along the largely unsealed 215km-long Cape Leveque Rd.

On Cape Leveque Rd, turn left after 14km onto Manari Rd, and head north along the spectacular coast. There are bush camping sites (no facilities) at Barred Creek, Quandong Point, James Price Point and Coulomb Point, where there is a nature reserve.

If you wish to visit Aboriginal communities, accessed from Cape Leveque Rd, you must *always* book ahead (directly with your community hosts or through the Broome Visitor Centre); check if permits and/or payments are required. Look for the excellent booklet *Ardi – Dampier Peninsula Travellers Guide* ($5). You should be self-sufficient, though limited supplies are available. Many communities (or outstations) offer accommodation – formal or camping – plus fishing, kayaking and crabbing opportunities.

☞ Tours

★**Chomley's Tours** GUIDED TOUR
(☎08-9192 6195; www.chomleystours.com.au; 1-/2-day tours $280/520) Chomley's offers several excellent day and overnight tours of the Peninsula (including mudcrabbing and other activities), plus one-way transfers. Reduced rates for children.

Beagle Bay

Beagle Bay Church CHURCH
(☎08-9192 4913; admission by donation) Around 110km from Broome, Beagle Bay is notable for the extraordinarily beautiful mother-of-pearl altar at Beagle Bay church, built by Pallottine monks in 1918. There's no accommodation, but fuel is available (weekdays only). Book ahead and proceed directly to the church.

Middle Lagoon & Around

Middle Lagoon COMMUNITY

(☎08-9192 4002; www.middlelagoon.com.au; unpowered/powered sites $30/40, beach shelter d $50, cabins d $140-240) Middle Lagoon, 180km from Broome and surrounded by empty beaches, is superb for swimming, snorkelling, fishing and well, doing nothing. There's plenty of shade and bird life, and the cabins are great value.

Mercedes Cove CABINS $$$

(☎08-91924687; www.mercedescove.com.au; Pender Bay; eco tents/air-con cabins $150/300) Near Middle Lagoon and with its own secluded beach, Mercedes Cove offers isolation, with several appealing meshed huts ('eco tents') and air-con cabins with gorgeous views. It's very well-run (read attention to detail) and you can almost roll into the sea from your camp site – it's a 20m stroll down down a gently sloping sandy path.

Gnylmarung Retreat CAMPGROUND $

(☎0429 411 241; www.gnylmarung.org.au; sites per person $20, bungalows from $90) This small, low-key community near Middle Lagoon offers a limited number of secluded camp sites and basic bungalows, and is popular with fishers.

Pender Bay

★ **Whale Song Cafe** CAFE $$

(☎08-9192 4000; Munget; light meals $7-25; ⏲9am-3pm Jun-Aug) This exquisitely located eco-cafe overlooking Pender Bay serves fabulous organic mango smoothies, homemade gourmet pizzas and the best coffee on the peninsula. There's a tiny bush campground (camp sites per person $20) with stunning views, funky outdoor shower and not a caravan in sight. Telstra mobile reception available.

Goombaragin CAMPGROUND $$

(☎0429 505 347; www.goombaragin.com.au; Pender Bay; camp site per person $18, nature tent with shared bathroom $75, eco tent with bathroom $175, bungalow with bathroom $220; 📶) This friendly spot has a couple of secluded camp sites, plus slightly worn safari tents, a fixed 'nature' tent (BYO food) and a comfortable bungalow. The location is superb – set on a bluff overlooking scarlet-hued (pindan) cliffs and the beach below.

Lombadina & Around

Lombadina COMMUNITY

(☎08-9192 4936; www.lombadina.com; entry per car $10, r with shared bathroom $170; ⏲office 8am-noon, 1-4pm Mon-Fri, weekends by prior arrangement) Between Middle Lagoon and Cape Leveque, Lombadina is located 200km from Broome. This beautiful tree-fringed village offers various tours (minimum of three people required) including fishing, whale watching, 4WD, mudcrabbing, kayaking and walking, which can be booked through the office. Accommodation is in backpacker-style rooms and self-contained cabins ($220 to $240), but there's no camping. Fuel is available on weekdays and there are lovely articles for sale at the Arts Centre (open weekdays).

Chile Creek COMMUNITY $$

(☎08-9192 4141; www.chilecreek.com; sites per adult/child $16.50/10, bush bungalows with shared bathroom $95, 4-person safari tents $185) Tiny Chile Creek, 10km from Lombadina down a very sandy track, offers basic bush camp sites and en-suite safari tents (minimum two-night stay), all just a short stroll to the creek, or 2km from the Indian Ocean. Good for birders.

Cape Leveque & Around

Cape Leveque (Kooljaman) CAMPGROUND

Cape Leveque is spectacular, with gorgeous white beaches and stunning red cliffs. Eco-tourism award-winner **Kooljaman** (☎08-9192 4970; www.kooljaman.com.au; entry per adult $5, unpowered/powered sites d $38/43, dome tents $65, cabins with/without bathroom d $170/145, safari tents d $275; 📶) offers grassy camp sites, driftwood beach shelters, hilltop safari tents, and budget tents. There's a minimum two-night stay, and the place is packed from June to October. The BYO **restaurant** (☎08-9192 4970; mains $29-38, BBQ packs $22-26; ⏲8am-4pm & 6pm-10pm, Apr-Oct, lunch Nov-Mar) opens for lunch and dinner, or you can order a BBQ pack.

Brian Lee Tagalong Tours GUIDED TOUR

(☎08-9192 4970; www.brianleetagalong.com.au; Kooljaman; adult/child ½ day from $75/35, full day $125/75) Be sure to hook up with one of Kimberley's characters, Brian, whose trips are considered tops for fishing lovers and keen crabbers. Own car required.

Bundy's Tours CULTURAL TOUR

(☎08-9192 4970; www.bundysculturaltours.com.au; Kooljaman; adult $45-75, child $25-35) Bardi custodian Bundy offers a tour through local eyes, providing a wonderful insight into traditional customs, including bush tucker, fish poisoning and spear making.

★**Cygnet Bay Pearl Farm** PEARL FARM

(☎08-9192 4283; www.cygnetbaypearls.com.au; Cygnet Bay) Overlooking stunning Cygnet Bay, this pearl farm-cum-tourist venture provides fascinating explanations of the pearling process (adult/child $27/10) and is home to the region's best restaurant (mains $17 to $50). Accommodation choices include camping ($90 per double), safari tents ($230 per double) or more luxurious pearlers' shacks (from $290 per double). Boat trips to the giant tides cost $155.

Ardyaloon (One Arm Point) COMMUNITY

(per person $10; ⏲8.30am-4.30pm Mon-Fri) The community of Ardyaloon (One Arm Point) has a well-stocked store, fuel, great fishing and swimming with views of the Buccaneer Archipelago. Entry to the community (which includes hatchery visit) is payable at the trochus hatchery. Note: there's no camping in Ardyaloon.

Gambanan CAMPGROUND $

(☎0427 786 345; near One Arm Point; per adult $20, under 12 free; ⏲end May-Sep) Offers little bling but this small outstation on the water, between Cape Leveque and Ardyaloon, has unpowered sites, a remote location and plenty of bush tucker trees.

Understand Australia

Australia Today

Australia's cultural and geographic identity has been forged by 45 million years of isolation. The country's harsh but beautiful landscape continues to survive bushfires, droughts and floods – a resilience that has rubbed off on the Australian people. Hiding behind larrikin wit and amicable informality, Australians have an innate optimism that helped steer their economy through the Global Financial Crisis (GFC). But can the good times last? If the political landscape and real estate market are any indication, the future is far from clear.

Best on Film

Lantana (director Ray Lawrence; 2001) Mystery for grown-ups: a meditation on love, truth and grief.
Gallipoli (director Peter Weir; 1981) Nationhood in the crucible of WWI.
Mad Max (director George Miller; 1979) Mel Gibson gets angry.
The Hunter (director Daniel Nettheim; 2011) Grumpy Willem Dafoe goes hunting for the last Tasmanian Tiger.
Ten Canoes (directors Rolf de Heer and Peter Djigirr; 2006) The first Australian film scripted entirely in Aboriginal language.

Best in Print

The Narrow Road to the Deep North (Richard Flangan; 2014) From Hobart to the Thai–Burma Death Railway. Man Booker Prize winner.
Dirt Music (Tim Winton; 2002) Guitar-strung Western Australian page-turner.
Oscar & Lucinda (Peter Carey; 1988) Man Booker Prize winner. How to relocate a glass church.
The Bodysurfers (Robert Drewe; 1983) Moody stories from Sydney's Northern Beaches.
The Secret River (Kate Grenville; 2005) Convict life in the 19th-century around Sydney.

Politics

Mimmicking global warming, the Australian political climate has been overheated and irritable of late. In 2013, the left-wing Labor Party was ousted from federal government by the conservative Liberal-National Party Coalition. In the lead-up to the election, Labor was destabilised by an extraordinary period of divisive infighting and factional power plays. Australia's first female prime minister, Julia Gillard, lost the top job to Kevin Rudd in early 2013, whom she herself had ousted as PM in 2010.

Sitting back and rubbing their eyes in disbelief, the conservatives watched the prime-ministerial circus play out. They then easily won the 2013 election, surfing into office on a wave of public dismay over Labor's leadership soap opera. New prime minister Tony Abbott had the look of a man standing on the threshold of a future he wasn't quite anticipating.

Then, in 2015, things started to go awry for Abbott. His popularity flagging, he made the bizarre choice of bestowing a knighthood on Prince Philip (husband of the British Queen) on Australia Day – a move lambasted by the media and hailed as un-Australian by the public. A leadership spill was mooted, with PM-in-waiting and former leader of the Liberal Party Malcolm Turnbull the favoured candidate. But the leadership vote didn't happen: Abbott dodged a bullet, but by the time you read this, there may be a different PM ruling the roost.

Real Estate Addiction

Australians love real estate. They love talking about it, building it, buying it, looking at it on TV and (most of all) making money selling it. When the GFC bit everybody in 2008, economists and bankers across the Western world very sensibly said, 'Whoops! We've been lending people money they can't afford to pay back, and they've been blowing it on home loans that are too expensive' – and real estate prices tumbled.

But not in Australia. There was a glorious mining boom in motion: nobody worried about ridiculous real estate prices when there was always another chunk of Western Australia waiting to be exhumed and sold to China. Australians just kept on buying pricey houses, driving the market skywards. Now – having reached a tipping point where the median house price is more than five times the median annual household income – Australian real estate prices are among the least affordable on the planet.

What happens next? The Chinese economy has slowed and Australian mining exports are flagging. Fears of a property bubble about to burst are rife in the media. But as long as interest rates remain low and the perception endures that Australia is the 'lucky country' and is somehow immune to global strife, the national real estate addiction will be hard to break.

City Scenes

Australia is an urbanised country: around 90% of Australians live in cities and towns. Cities here are in a constant state of growth, reinvention and flux, absorbing fresh influences from far corners of the globe. The sense that the local is inferior to the foreign – a phenomenon known as 'cultural cringe' – is less prevalent today than it was 30 years ago. National pride is on the up, manifest in urban arts and culinary scenes. Multiculturalism prevails and cities here remain distinct: Sydney is a luscious tart, Melbourne an arty glamour puss, Brisbane a blithe playmate, Adelaide a gracious dame and Perth a free spirit. Not to mention bookish Hobart, hedonistic Darwin and museum-fixated Canberra. Aussie cities are charmers: spend some time getting to know one of them and it'll be hard for you to leave!

POPULATION: **23.75 MILLION**

AREA: **7.7 MILLION SQ KM**

GDP: **US$1.53 TRILLION**

GDP GROWTH: **3.5%**

INFLATION: **1.7%**

UNEMPLOYMENT: **6.4%**

if Australia were 100 people

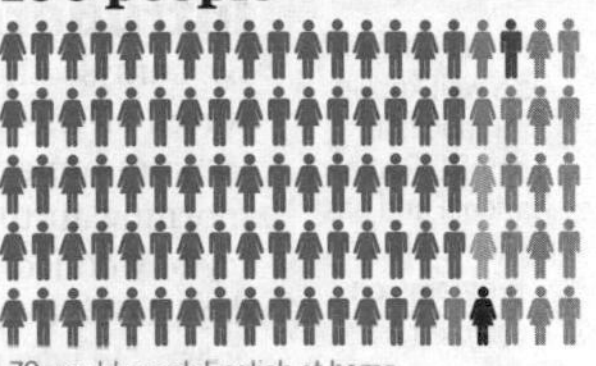

79 would speak English at home
3 would speak Chinese at home
2 would speak Italian at home
1 would speak Vietnamese at home
1 would speak Greek at home
14 would speak another language at home

belief systems

(% of population)

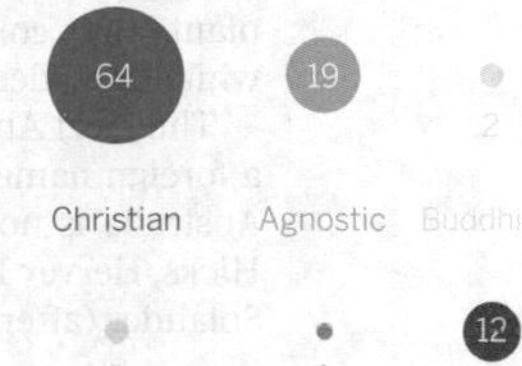

population per sq km

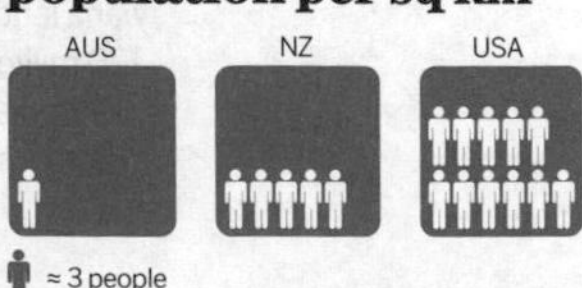

History

by Michael Cathcart

Australia is an ancient continent – its Indigenous peoples have been here more than 50,000 years. Given this backdrop, 'history' as we describe it can seem somewhat fleeting...but it sure makes an interesting read! From the days of struggling convict colonies to independence from Great Britain, the new nation found its feet. Wars, the Depression and cultural evolution defined the 20th century, when the impact of modern Australia on the country's ancient landscape and Indigenous peoples was thrown into stark relief.

Michael Cathcart is a well known broadcaster on ABC Radio National and has presented history programs on ABC TV.

Intruders Arrive

By sunrise the storm had passed. Zachary Hicks was keeping sleepy watch on the British ship *Endeavour* when suddenly he was wide awake. He summoned his commander, James Cook, who climbed into the brisk morning air to a miraculous sight. Ahead of them lay an uncharted country of wooded hills and gentle valleys. It was 19 April 1770. In the coming days Cook began to draw the first European map of Australia's eastern coast. He was mapping the end of Aboriginal supremacy.

Two weeks later Cook led a party of men onto a narrow beach. As they waded ashore, two Aboriginal men stepped onto the sand and challenged the intruders with spears. Cook drove the men off with musket fire. For the rest of that week, the Aboriginal people and the intruders watched each other warily.

Cook's ship *Endeavour* was a floating annexe of London's leading scientific organisation, the Royal Society. The ship's gentlemen passengers included technical artists, scientists, an astronomer and a wealthy botanist named Joseph Banks. As Banks and his colleagues strode about the Indigenous Australians' territory, they were delighted by the mass of new plants they collected. (The showy banksia flowers, which look like red, white or golden bottlebrushes, are named after Banks.)

The local Aboriginal people called the place Kurnell, but Cook gave it a foreign name: he called it 'Botany Bay'. The fertile eastern coastline of Australia is now festooned with Cook's place names – including Point Hicks, Hervey Bay (after an English admiral), Endeavour River and Point Solander (after one of the *Endeavour*'s scientists).

TIMELINE

80 million years ago

After separating from the prehistoric Gondwana landmass about 120 million years ago, Australia breaks free from Antarctica and heads north.

50,000 years ago

The earliest record of Aboriginal people inhabiting the land. The country is home to lush forests, teeming lakes and giant marsupials including a wombat the size of a rhinoceros.

1616

The Dutch trading route across the Indian Ocean to Indonesia utilises winds called 'the Roaring Forties'. These winds bring Captain Dirk Hartog to the Western Australian coast.

When the *Endeavour* reached the northern tip of Cape York, blue ocean opened up to the west. Cook and his men could smell the sea-route home. And on a small, hilly island (Possession Island), Cook raised the Union Jack. Amid volleys of gunfire, he claimed the eastern half of the continent for King George III.

Cook's intention was not to steal land from the Indigenous Australians. In fact he rather idealised them. 'They are far more happier than we Europeans,' he wrote. 'They think themselves provided with all the necessaries of Life and that they have no superfluities.' At most, his patriotic ceremony was intended to contain the territorial ambitions of the French, and of the Dutch, who had visited and mapped much of the western and southern coast over the previous two centuries. Indeed, Cook knew the western half of Australia as 'New Holland'.

Tasmania's Aboriginal peoples were separated from mainland Australia when sea levels rose after the last Ice Age – they subsequently developed their own utterly distinct languages and cultures.

Convict Beginnings

In 1788, 18 years after Cook's arrival, the English were back to stay. They arrived in a fleet of 11 ships, packed with supplies including weapons, tools, building materials and livestock. The ships also contained 751 convicts and around 250 soldiers, officials and their wives. This motley 'First Fleet' was under the command of a humane and diligent naval captain, Arthur Phillip. As his orders dictated, Phillip dropped anchor at Botany Bay. But the paradise that had so delighted Joseph Banks filled Phillip with dismay. The country was marshy; there was little healthy water; and the anchorage was exposed to wind and storm. So Phillip left his floating prison and embarked in a small boat to search for a better location. Just a short way up the coast his heart leapt as he sailed into the finest harbour in the world. There, in a small cove, in the idyllic lands of the Eora people, he established a British penal settlement. He renamed the place after the British Home Secretary, Lord Sydney.

The intruders set about clearing trees and building shelters and were soon trying to grow crops. Phillip's official instructions urged him to colonise the land without doing violence to local inhabitants, but Aboriginal peoples around Sydney were shattered by loss of their lands. Hundreds died of smallpox, and many succumbed to alcoholism and despair.

In 1803 English officers established a second convict settlement in Van Diemen's Land (later called Tasmania). Soon, re-offenders filled the grim prison at Port Arthur on the beautiful and wild coast near Hobart. In time, others would endure the senseless agonies of Norfolk Island prison in the remote Pacific Ocean.

So miserable were these convict beginnings, that Australians long regarded them as a period of shame. But things have changed: today most white Australians are inclined to brag a little if they find a convict in their family tree. Indeed, Australians annually celebrate the arrival of

In remote parts of Australia, and in centres such as Alice Springs and Darwin, many Aboriginal people still speak their traditional languages rather than English. Many people are multilingual – there were once more than 300 Aboriginal language groups on mainland Australia.

1770
Captain James Cook is the first European to map Australia's east coast, which he names 'New South Wales'. He returns to England having found an ideal place for settlement at 'Botany Bay'.

1788
The First Fleet brings British convicts and officials to the lands of the Eora people, where Governor Arthur Phillip establishes a penal settlement. He calls it 'Sydney'.

1789
An epidemic of smallpox devastates the Aboriginal groups around Sydney. British officers report that Indigenous Australians' bodies are rotting in every bay of the harbour.

1804
In Van Diemen's Land (now called Tasmania), David Collins moves the fledgling convict colony from Risdon Cove to the site of modern Hobart.

BENNELONG

Among the Indigenous Australians Governor Philip used as intermediaries was an influential Eora man named Bennelong, who adopted many white customs and manners. After his initial capture, Bennelong learnt to speak and write English and became an interlocutor between his people and the British, both in Australia and on a trip to the United Kingdom in 1792. His 1796 letter to Mr and Mrs Philips is the first known text in English by an Indigenous Australian.

For many years after his return to Sydney, Bennelong lived in a hut built for him on the finger of land now known as Bennelong Point, today the site of the Sydney Opera House. He led a clan of 100 people and advised then Governor Hunter. Although accounts suggest he was courageous, intelligent, feisty, funny and 'tender with children', in his later years Bennelong's health and temper were affected by alcohol. He was buried in the orchard of his friend, brewer James Squire, in 1813.

the First Fleet at Sydney Cove on 26 January 1788 as 'Australia Day'. It's no surprise that Indigenous Australians refer to the day as 'Invasion Day'.

From Shackles to Freedom

At first, Sydney and the smaller colonies depended on supplies brought in by ship. Anxious to develop productive farms, the government granted land to soldiers, officers and settlers. After 30 years of trial and error, farms began to flourish. The most irascible and ruthless of the new landholders was John Macarthur. Along with his spirited wife Elizabeth, Macarthur pioneered the breeding of merino sheep on his property near Sydney.

Macarthur was also a leading member of the 'Rum Corps', a clique of powerful officers who bullied successive governors (including William Bligh of *Bounty* fame) and grew rich by controlling much of Sydney's trade, notably rum. But the Corps' racketeering was ended in 1810 by a tough new governor named Lachlan Macquarie. Macquarie laid out the major roads of modern-day Sydney, built some fine public buildings (many of which were designed by talented convict-architect Francis Greenway) and helped to lay the foundations for a more civil society.

By now, word was reaching England that Australia offered cheap land and plenty of work, and adventurous migrants took to the oceans in search of their fortunes. At the same time the British government continued to transport prisoners.

In 1825 a party of soldiers and convicts established a penal settlement in the territory of the Yuggera people, close to modern-day Brisbane. Before long this warm, fertile region was attracting free settlers, who were soon busy farming, grazing, logging and mining.

Convict History Hotspots

Port Arthur Historic Site, Tasmania

Parramatta, Sydney

Rottnest Island, Western Australia

Hyde Park Barracks, Sydney

1820s

In Van Diemen's Land, Aboriginal people and settlers clash in the Black Wars. The bloody conflict devastates the Aboriginal population. Only a few survive.

1829

Captain James Stirling heads a private company that founds the settlement of Perth on Australia's west coast. The surrounding land is arid, retarding development of the colony.

1835

John Batman sails from Van Diemen's Land to Port Phillip and negotiates a land deal with elders of the Kulin Nation. The settlement of Melbourne follows that same year.

1836

Colonel William Light chooses the site for Adelaide on the banks of the Torrens River in the lands of the Kaurna people. Unlike Sydney and Hobart, settlers here are free, willing immigrants.

Two New Settlements: Melbourne & Adelaide

In the cooler grasslands of Tasmania, the sheep farmers were also thriving. In the 1820s they waged a bloody war against the island's Aboriginal peoples, driving them to the brink of extinction. Now these settlers were hungry for more land. In 1835 an ambitious young man named John Batman sailed to Port Phillip Bay on the mainland. On the banks of the Yarra River, he chose the location for Melbourne, famously announcing 'This is the place for a village.' Batman persuaded local Indigenous Australians to 'sell' him their traditional lands (a whopping 250,000 hectares) for a crate of blankets, knives and knick-knacks.

At the same time, a private British company settled Adelaide in South Australia (SA). Proud to have no links with convicts, these God-fearing folks instituted a scheme under which their company sold land to well-heeled settlers, and used the revenue to assist poor British labourers to emigrate. When these worthies earned enough to buy land from the company, that revenue would in turn pay the fare of another shipload of labourers. This charming theory collapsed in a welter of land speculation and bankruptcy, and in 1842 the South Australian Company yielded to government administration. By then miners had found rich deposits of silver, lead and copper at Burra, Kapunda and the Mt Lofty Ranges, and the settlement began to pay its way.

Acclimatisation societies of the 19th century tried to replace the 'inferior' Australian plants and animals with 'superior' European ones. Such cute 'blessings' as rabbits and foxes date from this time.

The Search for Land Continues

Each year, settlers pushed deeper into Aboriginal territories in search of pasture and water for their stock. These men became known as squatters (because they 'squatted' on Aboriginal lands) and many held this territory with a gun. To bring order and regulation to the frontier, from the 1830s the governments permitted the squatters to stay on these 'Crown lands' for payment of a nominal rent. Aboriginal stories tell of white men slaughtering groups of Aboriginal people in reprisal for the killing of sheep or settlers. Later, across the country, people would also tell stories of black resistance leaders, including Yagan of Swan River, Pemulwuy of Sydney, and Jandamarra, the outlaw-hero of the Kimberley.

In time, many of the squatters reached a compromise with local tribes. Indigenous Australians took low-paid jobs on sheep and cattle stations as drovers and domestics. In return they remained on their traditional lands, adapting their cultures to their changing circumstances. This arrangement continued in outback pastoral regions until after WWII.

The newcomers had fantasised about the wonders waiting to be discovered from the moment they arrived. Before explorers crossed the Blue Mountains west of Sydney in 1813, some credulous souls imagined that

A brilliant biography of Cook is JC Beaglehole's *The Life of Captain James Cook* (1974). Beaglehole also edited Cook's journals. There are several biographies online, including the excellent www.wikipedia.org/wiki/james_cook.

1851

Prospectors find gold in central Victoria, triggering a great rush of youthful prospectors from across the world. At the same time, the eastern colonies exchange the governor's rule for democracy.

1854

Angered by the hefty cost of licences, gold miners stage a protest at the Eureka Stockade near Ballarat. Several rebels are killed; others are charged with treason. Public opinion supports the rebels.

1861

The explorers Burke and Wills become the first Europeans to cross the continent from south to north. Their expedition is an expensive debacle that claims several lives, including their own.

1872

Engineer Charles Todd builds a telegraph line from Adelaide to Darwin. It joins an undersea cable to Java, linking Australia to Europe. The age of electronic information is born.

China lay on the other side. Then explorers, surveyors and scientists began trading theories about inland Australia. Most spoke of an Australian Mississippi. Others predicted desert. An obsessive explorer named Charles Sturt (there's a fine statue of him looking lost in Adelaide's Victoria Sq) believed in an almost mystical inland sea.

The explorers' expeditions inland were mostly journeys into disappointment. But Australians made heroes of explorers who died in the wilderness (Ludwig Leichhardt, and the duo of Burke and Wills, are the most striking examples). It was as though the Victorian era believed that a nation could not be born until its men had shed their blood in battle – even if that battle was with the land itself.

David Unaipon (Ngarrindjeri; 1872–1967), the 'Australian Leonardo da Vinci', is remembered as an advocate for Indigenous culture, a writer and an inventor. He took out 19 provisional patents, including drawings for a pre-WWI, boomerang-inspired helicopter. His portrait is on the Australian $50 note.

Gold & Rebellion

Transportation of convicts to eastern Australia ceased in the 1840s. This was just as well: in 1851 prospectors discovered gold in New South Wales (NSW) and central Victoria. The news hit the colonies with the force of a cyclone. Young men and some adventurous women from every social class headed for the diggings. Soon they were caught up in a great rush of prospectors, entertainers, publicans, sly-groggers (illicit liquor-sellers), prostitutes and quacks from overseas. In Victoria, the British governor was alarmed – both by the way the Victorian class system had been thrown into disarray, and by the need to finance law and order on the goldfields. His solution was to compel all miners to buy an expensive monthly licence, partly in the hope that the lower orders would return to their duties in town.

But the lure of gold was too great. In the reckless excitement of the goldfields, the miners initially endured the thuggish troopers who enforced the government licence. After three years, however, the easy gold at Ballarat was gone, and miners were toiling in deep, water-sodden shafts. They were now infuriated by a corrupt and brutal system of law which held them in contempt. Under the leadership of a charismatic Irishman named Peter Lalor, they raised their own flag, the Southern Cross, and swore to defend their rights and liberties. They armed themselves and gathered inside a rough stockade at Eureka, where they waited for the government to make its move.

In the pre-dawn of Sunday 3 December 1854, a force of troopers attacked the stockade. It was all over in 15 terrifying minutes. The brutal and one-sided battle claimed the lives of 30 miners and five soldiers. But democracy was in the air and public opinion sided with the miners. When 13 of the rebels were tried for their lives, Melbourne juries set them free. Many Australians have found a kind of splendour in these events: the story of the Eureka Stockade is often told as a battle for nationhood and democracy – again illustrating the notion that any 'true' nation must

1880

Police capture the notorious bushranger Ned Kelly at the Victorian town of Glenrowan. Kelly is hanged as a criminal – and remembered by the people as a folk hero.

1895

Publication of AB 'Banjo' Paterson's ballad *The Man from Snowy River*. Paterson and his rival Henry Lawson lead the literary movement that creates the legend of the Australian bush.

1901

The Australian colonies form a federation of states. The federal parliament sits in Melbourne, where it passes the *Immigration Restriction Act* – aka the White Australia policy.

1915

On 25 April the Australian and New Zealand Army Corps (the Anzacs) joins an ambitious British attempt to invade Turkey. The ensuing military disaster at Gallipoli spawns a nationalist legend.

be born out of blood. But these killings were tragically unnecessary. The eastern colonies were already in the process of establishing democratic parliaments, with the full support of the British authorities. In the 1880s Peter Lalor himself became speaker of the Victorian parliament.

The gold rush had also attracted boatloads of prospectors from China. These Asians sometimes endured serious hostility from whites, and were the victims of ugly race riots on the goldfields at Lambing Flat (now called Young) in NSW in 1860–61. Chinese precincts soon developed in the backstreets of Sydney and Melbourne, and popular literature indulged in tales of Chinese opium dens, dingy gambling parlours and brothels. But many Chinese went on to establish themselves in business and, particularly, in market gardening. Today the busy Chinatowns of the capital cities and the presence of Chinese restaurants in towns across the country are reminders of the vigorous role of the Chinese in Australia since the 1850s.

Gold and wool brought immense investment and gusto to Melbourne and Sydney. By the 1880s they were stylish modern cities, with gaslights in the streets, railways, electricity and that great new invention, the telegraph. In fact, the southern capital became known as 'Marvellous Melbourne', so opulent were its theatres, hotels, galleries and fashions. But the economy was overheating. Many politicians and speculators were engaged in corrupt land deals, while investors poured money into wild and fanciful ventures. It could not last.

Best History Museums

Rocks Discovery Museum, Sydney

Mawson's Huts Replica Museum, Hobart

Museum of Sydney

Commissariat Store, Brisbane

Meanwhile, in the West...

Western Australia (WA) lagged behind the eastern colonies by about 50 years. Though Perth was settled by genteel colonists back in 1829, their material progress was handicapped by isolation, Aboriginal resistance and the arid climate. It was not until the 1880s that the discovery of remote goldfields promised to gild the fortunes of the isolated colony. At the time, the west was just entering its own period of self-government, and its first premier was a forceful, weather-beaten explorer named John Forrest. He saw that the mining industry would fail if the government did not provide a first-class harbour, efficient railways and reliable water supplies. Ignoring the threats of private contractors, he appointed the brilliant engineer CY O'Connor to design and build each of these as government projects.

The hard-fought biennial 'Ashes' Test cricket series between Australia and England has been played since 1882. Despite long periods of dominance by both sides, at the time of writing the ledger stands at 32 series wins to Australia, 31 to England.

Growing Nationalism

By the end of the 19th century, Australian nationalists tended to idealise 'the bush' and its people. The great forum for this 'bush nationalism' was the massively popular *Bulletin* magazine. Its politics were egalitarian, democratic and republican, and its pages were filled with humour and

1919

Australian aviators Ross and Keith Smith become national heroes after they fly their Vickers Vimy biplane from England to Australia. Both receive knighthoods for their efforts.

1929

America's Great Depression spreads to Australia, where many working-class families are thrown into poverty. The violence and suffering of this period imprint themselves on the public memory.

1932

NSW firebrand premier Jack Lang is upstaged when a right-wing activist named Francis de Groot, wearing military uniform and riding a horse, cuts the ribbon to open the Sydney Harbour Bridge.

1936

The last captive thylacine (aka Tasmanian tiger) dies in a Hobart zoo. It's possible thylacines survived in the wild for subsequent decades, but extensive searches have failed to deliver credible evidence.

sentiment about daily life, written by a swag of writers, most notably Henry Lawson and AB 'Banjo' Paterson.

The 1890s were also a time of great trauma. As the speculative boom came crashing down, unemployment and hunger dealt cruelly with working-class families in the eastern colonies. However, Australian workers had developed a fierce sense that they were entitled to share in the country's prosperity. As the depression deepened, trade unions became more militant in their defence of workers' rights. At the same time, activists intent on winning legal reform established the Australian Labor Party (ALP).

Two very different, intelligent introductions to Australian history are Stuart Macintyre's *A Concise History of Australia* and Geoffrey Blainey's *A Shorter History of Australia*.

Nationhood

On 1 January 1901 Australia became a federation. When the bewhiskered members of the new national parliament met in Melbourne, their first aim was to protect the identity and values of a European Australia from an influx of Asians and Pacific Islanders. Their solution was a law which became known as the White Australia policy. It became a racial tenet of faith in Australia for the next 70 years.

For whites who lived inside the charmed circle of citizenship, this was to be a model society, nestled in the skirts of the British Empire. Just one year later, white women won the right to vote in federal elections. In a series of radical innovations, the government introduced a broad social welfare scheme and it protected Australian wage levels with import tariffs. Its radical mixture of capitalist dynamism and socialist compassion became known as the 'Australian settlement'.

Meanwhile, most Australians lived on the coastal 'edge' of the continent. So forbidding was the arid, desolate inland that they called the great dry Lake Eyre 'the Dead Heart' of the country. It was a grim image – as if the heart muscle, which should pump the water of life through inland Australia, was dead. But one prime minister in particular, the dapper Alfred Deakin, dismissed such talk. He led the 'boosters' who were determined to triumph over this tyranny of the climate. Even before Federation, in the 1880s, Deakin championed irrigated farming on the Murray River at Mildura. Soon the district was green with grapevines and orchards.

Members of the Palawa Aboriginal community in Tasmania are attempting to piece together a generic Tasmanian Aboriginal language called 'palawa kani', based on records of Indigenous languages on the island. The last native speaker of original Tasmanian language died in 1905.

Entering the World Stage

Living on the edge of a dry and forbidding land, and isolated from the rest of the world, most Australians took comfort in the knowledge that they were a dominion of the British Empire. When war broke out in Europe in 1914, thousands of Australian men rallied to the Empire's call. They had their first taste of death on 25 April 1915, when the Australian and New Zealand Army Corps (the Anzacs) joined thousands of other

1939

Prime Minister Robert Menzies announces that Britain has gone to war with Hitler's Germany and that 'as a result, Australia is also at war'.

1941

The Japanese attack Pearl Harbor and sweep through Southeast Asia. Australia discovers that it has been abandoned by traditional ally Britain. Instead, it welcomes US forces, based in Australia.

1945

WWII ends. Australia adopts a new slogan, 'Populate or Perish'. Over the next 30 years more than two million immigrants arrive. One-third are British.

1948

Cricketer Don Bradman retires with an unsurpassed test average of 99.94 runs. South African batsman Graeme Pollock is next in line, having retired in 1970 with a relatively paltry average of 60.97.

British and French troops in an assault on the Gallipoli Peninsula in Turkey. It was eight months before the British commanders acknowledged that the tactic had failed. By then 8141 young Australians were dead. Before long the Australian Imperial Force was fighting in the killing fields of Europe. By the time the war ended, 60,000 Australian men had died. Ever since, on 25 April, Australians have gathered at war memorials around the country for the sad and solemn services of Anzac Day.

The most accessible version of the Anzac legend is Peter Weir's Australian epic film *Gallipoli* (1981), with a cast that includes a fresh-faced Mel Gibson.

In the 1920s Australia embarked on a decade of chaotic change. Cars began to rival horses on the highway. In the new cinemas, young Australians enjoyed American movies. In an atmosphere of sexual freedom not equalled until the 1960s, young people partied and danced to American jazz. At the same time, popular enthusiasm for the British Empire grew more intense – as if imperial fervour were an antidote to grief. As radicals and reactionaries clashed, Australia careered wildly through the 1920s until it collapsed into the abyss of the Great Depression in 1929. World prices for wheat and wool plunged. Unemployment brought its shame and misery to one in three households. Once again working people experienced the cruelty of a system which treated them as expendable. For those who were wealthy – or who had jobs – the Depression was hardly noticed. In fact, the extreme deflation of the economy actually meant that the purchasing power of their wages was enhanced.

The year 1932 saw accusations of treachery on the cricket field. The English team, under their captain Douglas Jardine, employed a violent new bowling tactic known as 'bodyline'. The aim was to unnerve Australia's star batsman, the devastatingly efficient Donald Bradman. The bitterness of the tour provoked a diplomatic crisis with Britain, and became part of Australian legend. And Bradman batted on. When he retired in 1948 he had an unsurpassed career average of 99.94 runs.

The massive Murray River spans three states (New South Wales, Victoria and South Australia) and is navigable for 1986 of its 2756km: for half a century from 1853 it acted as a watery highway into inland Australia.

War with Japan

After 1933, the economy began to recover. The whirl of daily life was hardly dampened when Hitler hurled Europe into a new war in 1939. Though Australians had long feared Japan, they took it for granted that the British navy would keep them safe. In December 1941 Japan bombed the US Fleet at Pearl Harbor. Weeks later, the 'impregnable' British naval base in Singapore crumbled, and before long thousands of Australians and other Allied troops were enduring the savagery of Japanese prisoner-of-war camps.

As the Japanese swept through Southeast Asia and into Papua New Guinea, the British announced that they could not spare any resources to defend Australia. But the legendary US commander General Douglas MacArthur saw that Australia was the perfect base for American

1956

The Olympic Games are held in Melbourne. The Olympic flame is lit by running champion Ron Clarke, and Australia finishes third on the medal tally with an impressive 13 golds.

1965

Prime Minister Menzies commits Australian troops to the American war in Vietnam, and divides the nation. A total of 426 Australians were killed in action, with a further 2940 wounded.

1967

White Australians vote to grant citizenship to Indigenous Australians. The words 'other than the Aboriginal race in any State' are removed from citizenship qualifications in the Australian Constitution.

1973

After a conflict-ridden construction which included the sacking of Danish architect Jørn Utzon, the Sydney Opera House opens for business. This iconic building was granted World Heritage status in 2007.

PHAR LAP'S LAST LAP

In the midst of the Depression-era hardship, sport brought escape to Australians in love with games and gambling. A powerful chestnut horse called Phar Lap won race after race, culminating in an effortless and graceful victory in the 1930 Melbourne Cup (this annual event is still known as 'the race that stops a nation'). In 1932 the great horse travelled to the racetracks of America, where he mysteriously died. In Australia, the gossips insisted that the horse had been poisoned by envious Americans. And the legend grew of a sporting hero cut down in his prime. Phar Lap was stuffed and is a revered exhibit at the Melbourne Museum; his skeleton has been returned to his birthplace, New Zealand.

operations in the Pacific. In a series of fierce battles on sea and land, Allied forces gradually turned back the Japanese advance. Importantly, it was the USA, not the British Empire, that saved Australia. The days of the alliance with Britain alone were numbered.

Visionary Peace

When WWII ended, a new slogan rang through the land: 'Populate or Perish!' The Australian government embarked on an ambitious scheme to attract thousands of immigrants. With government assistance, people flocked from Britain and from non-English-speaking countries. They included Greeks, Italians, Slavs, Serbs, Croatians, Dutch and Poles, followed by Turks, Lebanese and many others. These 'new Australians' were expected to assimilate into a suburban stereotype known as the 'Australian way of life'.

A wonderful novel set in wartime Brisbane is *Johnno* (1975), the first novel by David Malouf, one of Australia's most acclaimed writers.

Many migrants found jobs in the growing manufacturing sector, in which companies such as General Motors and Ford operated with generous tariff support. In addition, the government embarked on audacious public works schemes, notably the mighty Snowy Mountains Hydro-Electric Scheme in the mountains near Canberra. Today, environmentalists point out the devastation caused by this huge network of tunnels, dams and power stations. But the Snowy scheme was an expression of a new-found optimism and testifies to the cooperation among the men of many nations who laboured on the project.

This era of growth and prosperity was dominated by Robert Menzies, the founder of the modern Liberal Party and Australia's longest-serving prime minister. Menzies was steeped in British history and tradition, and liked to play the part of a sentimental monarchist. He was also a vigilant opponent of communism. As Asia succumbed to the chill of the Cold War, Australia and New Zealand entered a formal military alliance with the USA – the 1951 Anzus security pact. When the USA hurled its

1975

Against a background of radical reform and uncontrolled inflation, Governor-General Sir John Kerr sacks Labor's Whitlam government and orders a federal election, which the conservatives win.

1979

Despite heated protests from environmental groups, the federal government grants authorisation for the Ranger consortium to mine uranium in the Northern Territory.

1979

After a federal government inquiry in 1978, whaling is banned in Australian waters, the last legally killed whale meeting its maker in November 1979.

1983

Tasmanian government plans for a hydroelectric dam on the wild Franklin River dominate a federal election campaign. Supporting a 'No Dams' policy, Labor's Bob Hawke becomes prime minister.

righteous fury into a civil war in Vietnam, Menzies committed Australian forces to the battle, introducing conscription for military service overseas. The following year Menzies retired, leaving his successors a bitter legacy. The antiwar movement split Australia.

There was a feeling too among many artists, intellectuals and the young that Menzies' Australia had become a rather dull, complacent country, more in love with American and British culture than with its own talents and stories. In an atmosphere of youthful rebellion and newfound nationalism, the Labor Party was elected to power in 1972 under the leadership of a brilliant, idealistic lawyer named Gough Whitlam. In just four short years his government transformed the country. He ended conscription and abolished all university fees. He introduced a free universal health scheme, no-fault divorce, the principle of Aboriginal land rights and equal pay for women. The White Australia policy had been gradually falling into disuse; under Whitlam it was finally abandoned altogether. By now, around one million migrants had arrived from non-English-speaking countries, and they had filled Australia with new languages, cultures, foods and ideas. Under Whitlam this achievement was embraced as 'multiculturalism'.

By 1975 the Whitlam government was rocked by a tempest of inflation and scandal. At the end of 1975 his government was controversially dismissed from office by the governor-general. But the general thrust of Whitlam's social reforms was continued by his successors. The principle of Aboriginal land rights was expanded. From the 1970s Asian immigration increased, and multiculturalism became a new Australian orthodoxy. China and Japan far outstripped Europe as major trading partners – Australia's economic future lay in Asia.

During WWII, Darwin in the Northern Territory was comprehensively bombed in 64 Japanese air raids (1942–43). Contrary to reports of 17 deaths, 243 people were killed, hundreds were injured and half the population fled to Adelaide River. Darwin was also flattened by Cyclone Tracy on Christmas morning, 1974.

British scientists detonated seven nuclear bombs at Maralinga in remote South Australia in the 1950s and early 1960s, with devastating effects on the local Maralinga Tjarutja people. Lesser-known are the three nuclear tests carried out in the Montebello Islands in Western Australia in the 1950s: a good read on the subject is Robert Drewe's *Montebello* (2012).

Contemporary Challenges

Today Australia faces new challenges. In the 1970s the country began dismantling its protectionist scaffolding. New efficiency brought new prosperity. At the same time, wages and working conditions, which were once protected by an independent tribunal, became more vulnerable as egalitarianism gave way to competition. And after two centuries of development, the strains on the environment were starting to show – on water supplies, forests, soils, air quality and the oceans.

Under the conservative John Howard, Australia's second-longest-serving prime minister (1996–2007), the country grew closer than ever to the USA, joining the Americans in their war in Iraq. The government's harsh treatment of asylum seekers, its refusal to acknowledge the reality of climate change, its anti-union reforms and the prime minister's lack of empathy with Indigenous Australians dismayed more liberal-minded Australians. But Howard presided over a period of economic growth that

1992

Directly overturning the established principle of 'terra nullius', the High Court of Australia recognises the principle of native title in the Mabo decision.

2000

The Sydney Olympic Games are a triumph of spectacle and good will. Aboriginal running champ Cathy Freeman lights the flame at the opening ceremony and wins gold in the 400m event.

2007

Kevin Rudd is elected Australian prime minister. Marking a change of direction from his conservative predecessor, Rudd says 'sorry' to Indigenous Australians and ratifies the Kyoto Protocol on climate change.

2009

On 7 February Australia experiences its worst loss of life in a natural disaster when 400 bushfires kill 173 people in country Victoria. The day is known thereafter as 'Black Saturday'.

In Melbourne you can learn about others who have come to Australia at the excellent Chinese and Immigration Museums (www.chinesemuseum.com.au and www.museumvictoria.com.au/immigrationmuseum).

emphasised the values of self-reliance and won him continuing support in middle Australia.

In 2007 Howard was defeated by the Labor Party's Kevin Rudd, an ex-diplomat who immediately issued a formal apology to Indigenous Australians for the injustices they had suffered over the past two centuries. Though it promised sweeping reforms in environment and education, the Rudd government found itself faced with a crisis when the world economy crashed in 2008; by 2010 it had cost Rudd his position. Incoming Prime Minister Julia Gillard, along with other world leaders, now faced three related challenges – climate change, a diminishing oil supply and a shrinking economy. This difficult landscape, shrinking popularity and ongoing agitations to return Rudd to the top job saw Gillard toppled and Rudd reinstated in 2013. Rudd then lost government in late 2013 to Tony Abbott's conservative Liberal-National Party Coalition.

2010

Australia's first female prime minister, Julia Gillard, is sworn in. Born in Wales, Gillard and her family emigrated to Australia's warmer climate due to her poor health as a child.

2011

Category 5 Tropical Cyclone Yasi makes landfall at Mission Beach on the north Queensland coast, causing mass devastation to property, infrastructure and crops.

2013

After widespread flooding in 2011, Queensland is again inundated as ex–Tropical Cyclone Oswald passed through; Bundaberg is particularly badly affected. The total damage bill is estimated at $2.4 billion.

2014

New conservative Prime Minister Tony Abbott commits RAAF combat aircraft and army special forces advisers to a multinational military operation against Islamic extremists in Iraq.

Aboriginal Australia

by Cathy Craigie

No visit to Australia would be complete without experiencing the rich cultures of Aboriginal and Torres Strait Islander people. Here is an opportunity to learn from the oldest continuous cultures in the world and share a way of life that has existed for more than 50,000 years. From the cities to the bush, there are opportunities to get up close with Australia's Indigenous people. Visit an art gallery or museum, or book a tour of Aboriginal lands. There is so much on offer for a truly unique Australian experience.

Cathy Craigie is a Gamilaori/Anaiwon woman from northern New South Wales. She is a freelance writer and cultural consultant and has extensive experience in Aboriginal Affairs.

Aboriginal Culture

Aboriginal cultures have evolved over thousands of years with strong links to the spiritual, economic and social lives of the people. This heritage has been kept alive through an oral tradition, with knowledge and skills passed on from one generation to the next through rituals, art, cultural material and language. Language has played an important part in preserving Aboriginal cultures.

Today there is a national movement to revive Aboriginal languages and a strong Aboriginal art sector. Traditional knowledge is being used in science, natural resource management and government programs. Aboriginal culture has never been static, and continues to evolve with the changing times and environment. New technologies and media are now used to tell Aboriginal stories, and cultural tourism ventures, through which visitors can experience an Aboriginal perspective, have been established. You can learn about ancestral beings at particular natural landmarks, look at rock art that is thousands of years old, taste traditional foods or attend an Aboriginal festival or performance.

Government support for cultural programs is sporadic and depends on the political climate at the time. However, Aboriginal people are determined to maintain their links with the past and to also use their cultural knowledge to shape a better future.

The Land

Aboriginal culture views humans as part of the ecology, not separate from it. Everything is connected, a whole environment that sustains the spiritual, economic and cultural lives of the people. In turn, Aboriginal people have sustained the land over thousands of years, through knowledge passed on in ceremonies, rituals, songs and stories. For Aboriginal people land is intrinsically connected to identity and spirituality. All land in Australia is reflected in Aboriginal lore but particular places may be significant for religious and cultural beliefs. Some well-known sites are the Three Sisters in the Blue Mountains, and Warreen Cave in Tasmania with artefacts dated around 40,000 years old.

Sacred sites can be parts of rocks, hills, trees or water and are associated with an ancestral being or an event that occurred. Often these sites are part of a Dreaming story and link people across areas. The ranges around Alice Springs are part of the caterpillar Dreaming with many

TORRES STRAIT ISLANDERS

Aboriginal society is a diverse group of several hundred sovereign nations. Torres Strait Islanders are a Melanesian people with a separate culture from that of Aboriginal Australians, though they have a shared history. Together, these two groups form Australia's Indigenous peoples. While this chapter touches on broader Indigenous issues relating to both groups, it focuses primarily on mainland Australia, which is Aboriginal land.

sites including Akeyulerre (Billy Goat Hill), Atnelkentyarliweke (Anzac Hill) and rock paintings at Emily Gap. The most well known are Uluru (Ayers Rock) and Kata Tjuta (The Olgas); the latter is the home of the snake Wanambi. His breath is the wind that blows through the gorge. Pirla Warna Warna, a significant site in the Tanami Desert for Warlpiri people, is 435 km northwest of Alice and is where several Walpiri Dreaming stories meet.

Aboriginal art is not just dot painting, dancing and didgeridoo, but a living and dynamic culture. It is the perfect vehicle through which to engage with Aboriginal people. Koori Heritage Trust (www.koorieheritagetrust.com) is a one-stop shop for Victorian Aboriginal culture.

Cultural tours to Aboriginal sites provide opportunities to learn about plants and animals, hunting and fishing, bush food or dance.

Please note that many Aboriginal sites are protected by law and are not to be disturbed in any way.

The Arts

Aboriginal art has impacted the Australian cultural landscape and is now showcased at national and international events and celebrated as a significant part of Australian culture. It still retains the role of passing on knowledge but today it is also important for economic, educational and political reasons. Art has been used to raise awareness of issues such as health and has been a primary tool for the reconciliation process in Australia. In many communities art has become a major source of employment and income.

Visual Arts

It is difficult to define Aboriginal art as one style because form and practice vary from one area to another. From the traditional forms of rock art, carving and body decoration, a dynamic contemporary art industry has grown into one of the success stories of Aboriginal Australia.

Rock Art

Rock art is the oldest form of human art, and Aboriginal rock art stretches back thousands of years. It is found in every state of Australia. For Aboriginal people, rock art is a direct link with life before Europeans. The art and the process of making it are part of songs, stories and customs that connect the people to the land. There are a number of different styles of rock art across Australia. These include engravings in sandstone, and stencils, prints and drawings in rock shelters. Aboriginal people carried out rock art for several reasons, including as part of a ritual or ceremony and to record events.

The Cairns Indigenous Art Fair (www.ciaf.com.au) has more than 300 Aboriginal artists showcasing work over three days. Held in August, the fair attracts thousands of visitors and is a great opportunity to see and purchase some of the best art in the country.

Some of the oldest examples of engravings can be found in the Pilbara in Western Australia (WA) and in Olary in South Australia (SA) where there is an engraving of a crocodile. This is quite amazing as crocodiles are not found in this part of Australia. The Kimberley rock art centres on the Wandjina, the ancestral creation spirits. All national parks surrounding Sydney have rock engravings and can be easily accessed and viewed. At Gariwerd (the Grampians) in Victoria there are hand prints and hand stencils. Aboriginal-owned tour company Guurrbi Tours (p442) guide visitors to the Wangaar-Wuri painted rock art sites near Cooktown in Queensland.

In the Northern Territory (NT) many of the rock-art sites have patterns and symbols that appear in paintings, carvings and other cultural material. Kakadu National Park has over 5000 recorded sites but many more are thought to exist. Some of these sites are 20,000 years old. Kakadu is World Heritage listed and is internationally recognised for its cultural significance.

In central Australia rock paintings still have religious significance. Here, people still retouch the art as part of ritual and to connect them to the stories. In most other areas people no longer paint rock images but instead work on bark, paper and canvas.

If you visit rock art sites, please do not touch or damage the art, and respect the sites and the surrounding areas.

Contemporary Art

The contemporary art industry started in a tiny community called Papunya in central Australia. It was occupied by residents from several language groups who had been displaced from their traditional lands. In 1971 an art teacher at Papunya school encouraged painting and some senior men took interest. This started the process of transferring sand and body drawings onto modern media and the 'dot and circle' style of contemporary painting began. The emergence of 'dot' paintings has been described as the greatest art movement of the 20th century and Papunya Tula artists became a model for other Aboriginal communities.

The National Gallery of Australia in Canberra has a fantastic collection, but contemporary Aboriginal art can also be viewed at any public art gallery or in one of the many independent galleries dealing in Aboriginal work. Contemporary artists work in all media and Aboriginal art has appeared on unconventional surfaces such as a BMW car and a Qantas plane. The central desert area is still a hub for Aboriginal art and Alice Springs is one of the best places to see and buy art. Cairns is another hotspot for innovative Aboriginal art.

If you are buying art make sure that provenance of the work is included. This tells the artist's name, their community/language group and the story of the work. If it is an authentic work, all proceeds go back to the artist. Australia has a resale royalty scheme.

Music

Music has always been a vital part of Aboriginal culture. Songs were important for teaching and passing on knowledge and musical instruments were often used in healing, ceremonies and rituals. The most well known instrument is the *yidaki* or didgeridoo, which was traditionally only played by men in northern Australia. Other instruments included clapsticks, rattles and boomerangs; in southern Australia animal skins were stretched across the lap to make a drumming sound.

This rich musical heritage continues today with a strong contemporary music industry. Like other art forms, Aboriginal music has developed into a fusion of new ideas and styles mixed with strong cultural identity.

KEY EVENTS

1928

Anthony Martin Fernando, the first Aboriginal activist to campaign internationally against racial discrimination in Australia, is arrested for protesting outside Australia House in London.

26 January 1938

To mark the 150th anniversary of the arrival of the British, the Aborigines Progressive Association holds a meeting in Australia Hall in Sydney, called 'A Day of Mourning and Protest'.

15 August 1963

A bark petition is presented to the House of Representatives from the people of Yirrikala in the Northern Territory, objecting to mining on their land, which the federal government had approved without consultation.

27 May 1967

A federal referendum allows the Commonwealth to make laws on Aboriginal issues and include them in the national census. They will now have the same citizen rights as other Australians.

12 July 1971

The Aboriginal flag first flies on National Aborigines Day in Adelaide. Designed by central Australian man Harold Thomas, the flag has become a unifying symbol of identity for Aboriginal people.

26 January 1972

The Aboriginal Tent Embassy is set up on the lawns of Parliament House in Canberra to oppose the treatment of Aboriginal people and the government's recent rejection of a proposal for Aboriginal Land Rights.

THE IMPORTANCE OF STORYTELLING

Aboriginal people had an oral culture so storytelling was an important way to learn. Stories gave meaning to life and were used to teach the messages of the spirit ancestors. Although beliefs and cultural practices vary according to region and language groups, there is a common world-view that these ancestors created the land, the sea and all living things. This is often referred to as the Dreaming. Through stories, the knowledge and beliefs are passed on from one generation to another and set out the social mores. They also recall events from the past. Today artists have continued this tradition but are using new media such as film and writing. The first Aboriginal writer to be published was David Unaipon, a Ngarrindjeri man from South Australia (SA) who was a writer, scientist and advocate for his people. Born in 1872, he published *Aboriginal Legends* (1927) and *Native Legends* (1929).

Other early published writers were Oodgeroo Noonuccal, Kevin Gilbert and Jack Davis. Contemporary writers of note include Alexis Wright, Kim Scott, Anita Heiss and Ali Cobby Eckerman. Award-winning novels to read are Kim Scott's *Deadman Dancing* (Picador Australia) and *Benang* (Fremantle Press), Alexis Wright's *Carpentaria* (Giramando) and Ali Cobby Eckerman's *Little Bit Long Time* (Picaro Press) and *Ruby Moonlight* (Magabala Books).

Contemporary artists such as Dan Sultan and Jessica Mauboy have crossed over successfully into the mainstream and have won major music awards and can be seen regularly on popular programs and at major music festivals. Aboriginal radio is the best and most accessible way to hear Aboriginal music.

Described by *Rolling Stone* magazine as 'Australia's Most Important Voice', blind singer Geoffrey Gurrumul Yunupingu (www.gurrumul.com) sings in the Yolngu language from Arnhem Land. His angelic voice tells of identity, connecting with land and ancestral beings. Gurrumul has entranced Australian and overseas audiences and reached platinum with his two albums.

Performing Arts

Dance and theatre are a vital part of Aboriginal culture. Traditional styles varied from one nation to the next; imitation of animals, birds and the elements was common across all nations, but arm, leg and body movements differed greatly. Ceremonial or ritual dances, often telling stories to pass on knowledge, were highly structured and were distinct from the social dancing at corroborees (festive events). Like other art forms, dance has adapted to the modern world, with contemporary dance groups bringing a modern interpretation to traditional forms. The most well-known dance company is the internationally acclaimed Bangarra Dance Theatre (p128).

Theatre also draws on the storytelling tradition, where drama and dance came together in ceremonies or corroborees, and this still occurs in many contemporary productions. Today, Australia has a thriving Aboriginal theatre industry and many Aboriginal actors and writers work in or collaborate with mainstream productions. There are two major Aboriginal theatre companies, Ilbijerri (www.ilbijerri.com.au) in Melbourne and Yirra Yakin (www.yirrayaakin.com.au) in Perth, as well as several mainstream companies specialising in Aboriginal stories who have had successful productions in Australia and overseas.

TV, Radio & Film

Aboriginal people have quickly adapted to electronic broadcasting and have developed an extensive media network of radio, print and television services. There are more than 120 Aboriginal radio stations and programs operating across Australia – in cities, rural areas and remote communities. Program formats differ from location to location. Some broadcast only in Aboriginal languages or cater to specific music tastes.

Aboriginal radio is the best and most accessible way to hear Aboriginal music. From its base in Brisbane, The National Indigenous Radio

Service (NIRS; www.nirs.org.au) broadcasts four radio channels of Aboriginal content via satellite and over the internet.

There is a thriving Aboriginal film industry and in recent years feature films such as *The Sapphires*, *Bran Nue Day* and *Samson and Delilah* have had mainstream success. Since the first Aboriginal television channel, NITV, was launched in 2007, there has been a growth in the number of film-makers wanting to tell their stories.

History of Aboriginal Australia

Before the coming of Europeans, culture was the common link for Aboriginal people across Australia. There were many aspects that were common to all the Aboriginal nations and it was through these commonalities that Aboriginal people were able to interact with each other. In postcolonial Australia it is also the shared history that binds Aboriginal people.

First Australians

Many academics believe Aboriginal people came here from somewhere else, with scientific evidence placing Aboriginal people on the continent at least 40,000 to 50,000 years ago. However, Aboriginal people believe they have always inhabited the land.

At the time of European contact the Aboriginal population was grouped into 300 or more different nations with distinct languages and land boundaries. Most Aboriginal people did not have permanent shelters but moved within their territory and followed seasonal patterns of animal migration and plant availability. The diversity of landscapes in Australia meant that each nation varied in their lifestyles. Although these nations were distinct cultural groups, there were also many common elements. Each nation had several clans or family groups who were responsible for looking after specific areas. For thousands of years Aboriginal people lived within a complex kinship system that tied them to the natural environment. From the desert to the sea Aboriginal people shaped their lives according to their environments and developed different skills and a wide body of knowledge on their territory.

Colonised

The effects of colonisation started immediately after the Europeans arrived. It began with the appropriation of land and water resources and an epidemic of diseases. Smallpox killed around half of the Sydney Harbour natives. A period of resistance occurred as Aboriginal people fought back to retain their land and way of life. As violence and massacres swept the country, many Aboriginal people were pushed away from their traditional lands. Over a century, the Aboriginal population was decimated by 90%.

By the late 1800s most of the fertile land had been taken and most Aboriginal people were living in poverty on the fringes of settlements or on land unsuitable for settlement. Aboriginal people had to adapt to the

10 August 1987

A Royal Commission investigates the high number of Aboriginal deaths in custody. Aboriginal people continue to be over-represented in the criminal system today.

3 June 1992

The previous legal concept of terra nullius is overturned by the Australian High Court, declaring Australia was occupied before the British settlement.

26 January 1988

On Australia's bicentenary, more than 40,000 Aboriginal people and their supporters march in Sydney to mark the 200-year anniversary of invasion.

28 May 2000

More than 300,000 people walk across Sydney Harbour Bridge to highlight the need for reconciliation between Aboriginal people and other Australians.

21 June 2007

The federal government suspends the Racial Discrimination Act to implement a large-scale intervention addressing child abuse in NT Aboriginal communities.

13 February 2008

The Prime Minister of Australia makes a national apology to Aboriginal people for the forced removal of their children and the injustices that occurred.

10 July 2010

Aboriginal leader Yagan is put to rest in a Perth park bearing his name. Murdered in 1833, his head had been sent to England.

22 January 2015

A Barngarla native title claim over a vast section of South Australia's Eyre Peninsula is upheld in the Federal Court.

THE STOLEN GENERATIONS

When Australia became a Federation in 1901, a government policy known as the 'White Australia policy' was put in place. It was implemented to restrict non-white immigration to Australia but the policy also impacted on Aboriginal Australia. Assimilation into the broader society was 'encouraged' by all sectors of government with the intent to eventually fade out the Aboriginal race. A policy of forcibly removing Aboriginal and Torres Strait Islander children from their families was official from 1909 to 1969, although the practice was happening before and after those years. Although accurate numbers will never be known, it is estimated that around 100,000 Aboriginal children were taken from their families (or one in three children).

A government agency, the Aborigines Protection Board, was set up to manage the policy and had the power to remove children without consent from families or without a court order. Many children never saw their families again and those that did manage to find their way home often found it difficult to maintain relationships. The generations of children who were taken from their families became known as the Stolen Generations.

In the 1990s the Australian Human Rights Commission held an inquiry into the practice of removing Aboriginal children. The 'Bring Them Home' report was tabled in parliament in May 1997 and told of the devastating impact that these polices had on the children and their families. Governments, churches and welfare bodies all took part in the forced removal. Sexual and physical abuse and cruelty was common in many of the institutions where children were placed. Today many of the Stolen Generations still suffer trauma associated with their early lives.

On 13 February 2008 Kevin Rudd, the then prime minister of Australia, offered a national apology to the Stolen Generations. For many Aboriginal people it was the start of a national healing process and today there are many organisations working with the Stolen Generations.

new culture but had few to no rights. Employment opportunities were scarce and most worked as labourers or domestic staff. This disadvantage has continued and even though successive government policies and programs have been implemented to assist Aboriginal people, most have had little effect on improving lives.

For an insight into the early days of British settlement and interaction with Aboriginal Australians, check the notebooks of William Dawes, officer of the First Fleet 1787–88. These diaries are accessible online (www.williamdawes.org) and contain words and phrases from the local Aboriginal language and aspects of traditional life. The principal informant was an Aboriginal girl, Patyegarang.

Rights & Reconciliation

The relationship between Aboriginal people and other Australians hasn't always been an easy one. Over the years several systematic policies have been put in place, but these have often had an underlying purpose including control over the land, decimating the population, protection, assimilation, self-determination and self-management.

The history of forced resettlement, removal of children, and the loss of land and culture can't be erased even with governments addressing some of the issues. Current policies focus on 'closing the gap' and centre on better delivery of essential services to improve lives, but there is still great disparity between Aboriginal people and other Australians, including lower standards of education, employment, health and living conditions, high incarceration and suicide rates, and a lower life expectancy.

Throughout all of this, Aboriginal people have managed to maintain their identity and link to Country and culture. Although there is a growing recognition and acceptance of Aboriginal people's place in this country, there is still a long way to go. Aboriginal people have no real political or economic wealth, but their struggle for legal and cultural rights continues today and is always at the forefront of politics. Any gains for Aboriginal people have been hard won and initiated by Aboriginal people themselves.

Environment

by Tim Flannery

Australia's plants and animals are just about the closest things to alien life on Earth. That's because Australia has been isolated from the other continents for a very long time – around 80 million years. Unlike those on other habitable continents that have been linked by land bridges, Australia's birds, mammals, reptiles and plants have taken their own separate and very different evolutionary journey and the result today is the world's most distinct – and one of the most diverse – natural realms.

A Unique Environment

The first naturalists to investigate Australia were astonished by what they found. Here the swans were black – to Europeans this was a metaphor for the impossible – and mammals such as the platypus and echidna were discovered to lay eggs. It really was an upside-down world, where many of the larger animals hopped and where each year the trees shed their bark rather than their leaves.

If you are visiting Australia for a short time, you might need to go out of your way to experience some of the richness of the environment. That's because Australia is a subtle place, and some of the natural environment – especially around the cities – has been damaged or replaced by trees and creatures from Europe. Places such as Sydney, however, have preserved extraordinary fragments of their original environment that are relatively easy to access. Before you enjoy them though, it's worthwhile understanding the basics about how nature operates in Australia. This is important because there's nowhere like Australia, and once you have an insight into its origins and natural rhythms, you will appreciate the place so much more.

There are two important factors that go a long way towards explaining nature in Australia: its soils and its climate. Both are unique.

Tim Flannery is a scientist, explorer, writer and the chief councillor of the independent Climate Council. He was a professor of science at Macquarie University in Sydney until 2013 and was named Australian of the Year in 2007. He has written several award-winning books including *The Future Eaters*, *Throwim Way Leg* (an account of his work as a biologist in New Guinea) and *The Weather Makers*.

Climate

Australia's misfortune in respect to soils is echoed in its climate. In most parts of the world outside the wet tropics, life responds to the rhythm of the seasons – summer to winter, or wet to dry. Most of Australia experiences seasons – sometimes severe ones – yet life does not respond solely to them. This can clearly be seen by the fact that although there's plenty of snow and cold country in Australia, there are almost no trees that shed their leaves in winter, nor do many Australian animals hibernate. Instead there is a far more potent climatic force that Australian life must obey: El Niño.

El Niño is a complex climatic pattern that can cause major weather shifts around the South Pacific. The cycle of flood and drought that El Niño brings to Australia is profound. Our rivers – even the mighty Murray River, the nation's largest, which runs through the southeast – can be miles wide one year, yet you can literally step over its flow the next. This is the power of El Niño, and its effect, when combined with Australia's poor soils, manifests itself compellingly.

ENVIRONMENT & CONSERVATION GROUPS

- The **Australian Conservation Foundation** (www.actonline.org.au) is Australia's largest nongovernment organisation involved in protecting the environment.
- **Bush Heritage Australia** (www.bushheritage.org.au) and **Australian Wildlife Conservancy** (AWC; www.australianwildlife.org) allow people to donate funds and time to conserving native species.
- **Conservation Volunteers Australia** (conservationvolunteers.com.au) is a nonprofit organisation focusing on practical conservation projects such as tree planting, walking-track construction, and flora and fauna surveys.
- **Ecotourism Australia** (www.ecotourism.org.au) has an accreditation system for environmentally friendly and sustainable tourism in Australia, and lists ecofriendly tours, accommodation and attractions by state.
- **Wilderness Society** (wilderness.org.au) focuses on protecting wilderness and forests.

Fauna & Flora

Australia's wildlife and plant species are as diverse as they are perfectly adapted to the country's soils and climate.

Mammals

Kangaroos

Australia is, of course, famous as the home of the kangaroo (roo) and other marsupials. Unless you visit a wildlife park, such creatures are not easy to see as most are nocturnal. Their lifestyles, however, are exquisitely attuned to Australia's harsh conditions. Have you ever wondered why kangaroos, alone among the world's larger mammals, hop? It turns out it's the most efficient way to get about at medium speeds. This is because the energy of the bounce is stored in the tendons of the legs – much like in a pogo stick – while the intestines bounce up and down like a piston, emptying and filling the lungs without needing to activate the chest muscles. When you travel long distances to find meagre feed, such efficiency is a must.

The website of the Australian Museum (www.australianmuseum.net.au) holds a wealth of info on Australia's animal life from the Cretaceous period until now. Kids can get stuck into online games, fact files and movies.

Koalas

Marsupials are so energy-efficient that they need to eat one-fifth less food than equivalent-sized placental mammals (everything from bats to rats, whales and ourselves). But some marsupials have taken energy efficiency much further. If you visit a wildlife park or zoo you might notice that faraway look in a koala's eyes. It seems as if nobody is home – and this in fact is near the truth. Several years ago biologists announced that koalas are the only living creatures that have brains that don't fit their skulls. Instead they have a shrivelled walnut of a brain that rattles around in a fluid-filled cranium. Other researchers have contested this finding, however, pointing out that the brains of the koalas examined for the study may have shrunk because these organs are so soft. Whether soft-brained or empty-headed, there is no doubt that the koala is not the Einstein of the animal world, and we now believe that it has sacrificed its brain to energy efficiency. Brains cost a lot to run. Koalas eat gum leaves, which are so toxic that they use 20% of their energy just detoxifying this food. This leaves little energy for the brain; fortunately, living in the treetops where there are so few predators means that they can get by with few wits at all.

Wombats

The peculiar constraints of the Australian environment have not made everything dumb. The koala's nearest relative, the wombat (of which there are three species), has a large brain for a marsupial. These creatures live in complex burrows and can weigh up to 35kg, making them the largest herbivorous burrowers on earth. Because their burrows are effectively air-conditioned, they have the neat trick of turning down their metabolic activity when they are in residence. One physiologist, who studied their thyroid hormones, found that biological activity ceased to such an extent in sleeping wombats that, from a hormonal point of view, they appeared to be dead! Wombats can remain underground for a week at a time, and can get by on just one-third of the food needed by a sheep of equivalent size. One day, perhaps, efficiency-minded farmers will keep wombats instead of sheep. At the moment, however, that isn't possible; the largest of the wombat species, the northern hairy-nose, is one of the world's rarest creatures, with only around 160 surviving in a remote nature reserve in central Queensland.

R Strahan's *The Mammals of Australia* is a comprehensive survey of Australia's somewhat cryptic mammals. Every species is illustrated, with descriptions penned by the nation's experts.

Other Mammals

Among the more common marsupials you might catch a glimpse of in the national parks around Australia's major cities are the species of antechinus. These nocturnal, rat-sized creatures lead an extraordinary life. The males live for just 11 months, the first 10 of which consist of a concentrated burst of eating and growing. The day comes when their minds turn to sex, and in the antechinus this becomes an obsession. As they embark on their quest for females they forget to eat and sleep. By the end of August – just two weeks after they reach 'puberty' – every male is dead, exhausted by sex and by carrying around swollen testes.

Two unique monotremes (egg-laying mammals) live in Australia: the bumbling echidna, something akin to a hedgehog; and the platypus, a bit like an otter, with webbed feet and a ducklike bill. Echidnas are common along bushland trails, but platypuses are elusive, seen at dawn and dusk in quiet rivers and streams.

If you are very lucky, you might see a honey possum. This tiny marsupial is an enigma. Somehow it gets all of its dietary requirements from nectar and pollen, and in the southwest there are always enough flowers around for it to survive. But no one knows why the males need sperm larger even than those of the blue whale, or why their testes are so massive. Were humans as well endowed, men would be walking around with the equivalent of a 4kg bag of potatoes between their legs!

Reptiles

One thing you will see lots of in Australia are reptiles. Snakes are abundant, and they include some of the most venomous species known. Where the opportunities to feed are few and far between, it's best not to give your prey a second chance, hence the potent venom. Snakes will usually leave you alone if you don't fool with them. Observe, back quietly away and don't panic, and most of the time you'll be OK.

BIRDS IN BED

Relatively few of Australia's birds are seasonal breeders, and few migrate. Instead, they breed when the rain comes and a large percentage are nomads, following the rain across the breadth of the continent.

So challenging are conditions in Australia that its birds have developed some extraordinary habits. Kookaburras, magpies and blue wrens – to name just a few – have developed a breeding system called 'helpers at the nest'. The helpers are the young adult birds of previous breedings, which stay with their parents to help bring up the new chicks. Just why they should do this was a mystery, until it was realised that conditions in Australia can be so harsh that more than two adult birds are needed to feed the nestlings. This pattern of breeding is very rare in places such as Asia, Europe and North America, but it is common among many Australian birds.

Some visitors mistake lizards for snakes, and indeed some Australian lizards look bizarre. One of the more abundant is the sleepy lizard. These creatures, which are found in the southern arid region, look like animated pine cones. They are the Australian equivalent of tortoises, and are harmless. Other lizards are much larger. Unless you visit the Indonesian island of Komodo you will not see a larger lizard than the desert-dwelling perentie. These creatures, with their leopardlike blotches, can grow to more than 2m long, and are efficient predators of introduced rabbits, feral cats and the like.

If you're interested in Australian reptiles (or exist in a state of mortal fear), H Cogger's *Reptiles and Amphibians of Australia* is a cold-blooded bible. This hefty volume will allow you to identify sundry species (or you can wield it as a defensive weapon if necessary!).

Feeling right at home in Kakadu National Park, the saltwater crocodile is the world's largest living reptile – old males can reach 6m long.

Flora

Australia's plants can be irresistibly fascinating. If you happen to be in the Perth area in spring it's well worth taking a wild flower tour. The best flowers grow on the arid and monotonous sand plains, and the blaze of colour produced by the kangaroo paws, banksias and similar native plants can be dizzying. The sheer variety of flowers is amazing, with 4000 species crowded into the southwestern corner of the continent. This diversity of prolific flowering plants has long puzzled botanists. Again, Australia's poor soils seem to be the cause. The sand plain is about the poorest soil in Australia – it's almost pure quartz. This prevents any single fast-growing species from dominating. Instead, thousands of specialist plant species have learned to find a narrow niche and so coexist. Some live at the foot of the metre-high sand dunes, some on top, some on an east-facing slope, some on the west and so on. Their flowers need to be striking in order to attract pollinators, for nutrients are so lacking in this sandy world that even insects such as bees are rare.

If you do get to walk the wild flower regions of the southwest, keep your eyes open for the sundews. Australia is the centre of diversity for these beautiful, carnivorous plants. They've given up on the soil supplying their nutritional needs and have turned instead to trapping insects with the sweet globs of moisture on their leaves, and digesting them to obtain nitrogen and phosphorus.

Environmental Challenges

The European colonisation of Australia, commencing in 1788, heralded a period of catastrophic environmental upheaval. The result today is that Australians are struggling with some of the most severe environmental problems to be found anywhere in the world. It may seem strange that a population of just 23 million, living in a continent the size of the USA minus Alaska, could inflict such damage on its environment, but Aus-

A WHALE OF A TIME

A driving economic force across much of southern Australia from the time of colonisation, whaling, was finally banned in Australia in 1979. The main species on the end of the harpoon were humpback, blue, southern right and sperm whales, which were culled in huge numbers in traditional breeding grounds such as Sydney Harbour, the Western Australia coast around Albany and Hobart's Derwent River estuary. The industry remained profitable until the mid-1800s, before drastically depleted whale numbers, the lure of inland gold rushes and the emergence of petrol as an alternative fuel started to have an impact.

Over recent years (and much to locals' delight), whales have made cautious returns to both Sydney Harbour and the Derwent River. Ironically, whale watching has emerged as a lucrative tourist activity in migratory hotspots such as Head of Bight in South Australia, Warrnambool in Victoria, Hervey Bay in Queensland and out on the ocean beyond Sydney Harbour.

SHARKY

Shark-o-phobia ruining your trip to the beach? Despite media hype spurred by five deaths in 2014, Australia has averaged just one shark-attack fatality per year since 1791. There are about 370 shark species in the world's oceans – around 160 of these swim through Australian waters. Of those, only a few pose any threat to humans: the usual suspects are oceanic white tip, great white, tiger and bull sharks.

It follows that where there are more people, there are more shark attacks. New South Wales, and Sydney in particular, has a bad rep. Attacks here peaked between 1920 and 1940, but since shark-net installation began in 1937 there's only been one fatality (1963), and dorsal-fin sightings are rare enough to make the nightly news. Realistically, you're more likely to get hit by a bus – so get wet and enjoy yourself!

tralia's long isolation, its fragile soils and difficult climate have made it particularly vulnerable to human-induced change.

Environmental damage has been inflicted in several ways, the most important including the introduction of pest species, destruction of forests, overstocking range lands and interference with water flows.

Beginning with the escape of domestic cats into the Australian bush shortly after 1788, a plethora of vermin – from foxes to wild camels and cane toads – have run wild in Australia, causing extinctions in the native fauna. One out of every 10 native mammals living in Australia prior to European colonisation is now extinct, and many more are highly endangered. Extinctions have also affected native plants, birds and amphibians.

The destruction of forests has also had an effect on the environment. Most of Australia's rainforests have suffered clearing, while conservationists fight with loggers over the fate of the last unprotected stands of 'old growth'.

Many Australian range lands have been chronically overstocked for more than a century, the result being the extreme vulnerability of both soils and rural economies to Australia's drought and flood cycle, as well as the extinction of many native species. The development of agriculture has involved land clearance and the provision of irrigation; again the effect has been profound. Clearing of the diverse and spectacular plant communities of the Western Australia wheat belt began just a century ago, yet today up to one-third of that country is degraded by salination of the soils.

Just 1.5% of Australia's land surface provides over 95% of its agricultural yield, and much of this land lies in the irrigated regions of the Murray-Darling Basin. This is Australia's agricultural heartland, yet it too is under severe threat from salting of soils and rivers. Irrigation water penetrates into the sediments laid down in an ancient sea, carrying salt into the catchments and fields. The Snowy River in New South Wales and Victoria also faces a battle for survival.

Despite the enormity of the biological crisis engulfing Australia, governments and the community have been slow to respond. It was in the 1980s that coordinated action began to take place, but not until the '90s that major steps were taken. The establishment of **Landcare** (www.landcareaustralia.com.au), an organisation enabling people to effectively address local environmental issues, and the expenditure of over $2 billion through the federal government initiative 'Caring for our Country' have been important national initiatives. Yet so difficult are some of the issues the nation faces that, as yet, little has been achieved in terms of halting the destructive processes.

So severe are Australia's environmental problems that it will take a revolution before they can be overcome, for sustainable practices need to be implemented in every arena of life – from farms to suburbs and city

Offical Floral Emblems

Common Heath (Victoria)

Cooktown Orchid (Queensland)

Red and Green Kangaroo Paw (WA)

Royal Bluebell (ACT)

Tasmanian Blue Gum (Tasmania)

Sturt's Desert Pea (SA)

Sturt's Desert Rose (NT)

Waratah (NSW)

centres. Renewable energy, sustainable agriculture and water use lie at the heart of these changes, and Australians are only now developing the road map to sustainability that they so desperately need if they are to have a long-term future on the continent.

Current Environmental Issues

Australia has seen some devastating bushfires in recent times: the 'Black Saturday' fires in Victoria in 2009 claimed 173 lives, while in 2013 fires in Tasmania killed a firefighter and destroyed hundreds of buildings. The 2015 Adelaide Hills fires burned 125 sq km and dozens of houses and outbuildings.

Headlining the environmental issues facing Australia's fragile landscape at present are climate change, water scarcity, nuclear energy and uranium mining. All are interconnected. For Australia, the warmer temperatures resulting from climate change spell disaster to an already fragile landscape. A 2°C climb in average temperatures on the globe's driest continent will result in an even drier southern half of the country and greater water scarcity. Scientists also agree that hotter and drier conditions will exacerbate bushfire conditions and increase cyclone intensity.

Australia is a heavy greenhouse-gas emitter because it relies on coal and other fossil fuels for its energy supplies. The most prominent and also contentious alternative energy source is nuclear power, which creates less greenhouse gases and relies on uranium, in which Australia is rich. But the radioactive waste created by nuclear power stations can take thousands of years to become harmless. Moreover, uranium is a finite energy source (as opposed to yet-cleaner and renewable energy sources such as solar and wind power), and even if Australia were to establish sufficient nuclear power stations now to make a real reduction in coal-dependency, it would be years before the environmental and economic benefits were realised.

Uranium mining also produces polarised opinions. Because countries around the world are also looking to nuclear energy, Australia finds itself in a position to increase exports of one of its top-dollar resources. But uranium mining in Australia has been met with fierce opposition, not only because the product is a core ingredient of nuclear weapons, but also because much of Australia's uranium supplies sit beneath sacred Indigenous land. Supporters of increased uranium mining and export suggest that the best way to police the use of uranium is to manage its entire life cycle; that is to sell the raw product to international buyers, and then charge a fee to accept the waste and dispose of it. Both major political parties consider an expansion of Australia's uranium export industry to be inevitable for economic reasons.

National & State Parks

World Heritage Wonders

- *Great Barrier Reef, Queensland*
- *Southwest Wilderness, Tasmania*
- *Uluru-Kata Tjuta National Park, NT*
- *Kakadu National Park, NT*

Australia has more than 500 national parks – nonurban protected wilderness areas of environmental or natural importance. Each state defines and runs its own national parks, but the principle is the same throughout Australia. National parks include rainforests, vast tracts of empty outback, strips of coastal dune land and rugged mountain ranges.

Public access is encouraged as long as safety and conservation regulations are observed. In all parks you're asked to do nothing to damage or alter the natural environment. Camping grounds (often with toilets and showers), walking tracks and information centres are often provided for visitors. In most national parks there are restrictions on bringing in pets.

State parks and state forests are owned by state governments and have fewer regulations. Although state forests can be logged, they are often recreational areas with camping grounds, walking trails and signposted forest drives. Some permit horses and dogs.

Watching Wildlife

Some regions of Australia offer unique opportunities to see wildlife, and one of the most fruitful is Tasmania. The island is jam-packed with wallabies, wombats and possums, principally because foxes, which have

MALAISE OF THE MURRAY-DARLING

The Murray-Darling Basin is Australia's largest river system, flowing through Queensland, New South Wales, the Australian Capital Territory, Victoria then South Australia, covering an area of 1.05 million sq km – roughly 14% of Australia. Aside from quenching around a third of the country's agricultural and urban thirsts, it also irrigates precious rainforests, wetlands, subtropical areas and scorched arid lands.

But drought, irrigation and climate change have depleted Murray-Darling flows. Wetland areas around the Darling River that used to flood every five years are now likely to do so every 25 years, and prolific species are threatened with extinction. That the entire system will become too salty and unusable is a very real danger.

Rains and widespread flooding across eastern Australia since 2010 (especially 2011) have increased flows, but finding the delicate balance between agricultural and environmental water allocations continues to cause political and social turmoil across five states and territories.

decimated marsupial populations on the mainland, were slow to reach the island state (the first fox was found in Tasmania only as recently as 2001!). It is also home to the Tasmanian devil. These marsupials are common on the island, and in some national parks you can watch them tear apart road-killed wombats. Their squabbling is fearsome, their shrieks ear-splitting. It's the nearest thing Australia can offer to experiencing a lion kill on the Masai Mara. Unfortunately, Tassie devil populations are being decimated by the devil facial tumour disease.

For those intrigued by the diversity of tropical rainforests, Queensland's World Heritage Sites are well worth visiting. Birds of paradise, cassowaries and a variety of other birds can be seen by day, while at night you can search for tree kangaroos (yes, some kinds of kangaroo do live in the treetops). In your nocturnal wanderings you are highly likely to see curious possums, some of which look like skunks, and other marsupials that are restricted to a small area of northeast Queensland.

Australia's deserts are a real hit-and-miss affair as far as wildlife is concerned. If you're visiting in a drought year, all you might see are dusty plains, the odd mob of kangaroos and emus, and a few struggling trees. Return after big rains, however, and you'll encounter something close to a Garden of Eden. Fields of white and gold daisies stretch endlessly into the distance. The salt lakes fill with fresh water, and millions of water birds can be seen feeding on the superabundant fish and insect life of the waters. It all seems like a mirage, and like a mirage it will vanish as the land dries out, only to spring to life again in a few years or a decade's time. For a more reliable birdwatching spectacular, Kakadu is worth a look, especially towards the end of the dry season around November.

The Coastal Studies Unit at the University of Sydney has deemed there to be an astonishing 10,685 beaches in Australia (their definition of a beach being a stretch of sand more than 20m long which remains dry at high tide).

The largest creatures found in the Australian region are marine mammals such as whales and seals, and there is no better place to see them than South Australia. During springtime southern right whales crowd into the head of the Great Australian Bight. You can readily observe them near the remote Aboriginal community of Yalata as they mate, frolic and suckle their young. Kangaroo Island, south of Adelaide, is a fantastic place to see seals and sea lions. There are well-developed visitor centres to facilitate the viewing of wildlife, and nightly penguin parades occur at some places where the adult blue penguins make their nest burrows. Kangaroo Island's beaches are magical places, where you're able to stroll among fabulous shells, whale bones and even jewel-like leafy sea dragons amid the sea wrack.

The fantastic diversity of Queensland's Great Barrier Reef is legendary, and a boat trip out to the reef from Cairns or Port Douglas is unforgettable. Just as extraordinary but less well known is the diversity of Australia's southern waters; the Great Australian Bight is home to more kinds of marine creatures than anywhere else on earth.

Food & Drink

In a decade not so long ago, Australians proudly survived on a diet of 'meat and three veg'. Fine fare was a Sunday roast, and lasagne was considered exotic. Fortunately the country's cuisine has evolved, and these days Australian gastronomy is keen to break rules, backed up by world-beating wines, kick-ass coffee and a booming craft beer scene.

Modern Australian (Mod Oz)

The phrase Modern Australian (Mod Oz) has been coined to classify contemporary Australian cuisine: a melange of East and West; a swirl of Atlantic and Pacific Rim; a flourish of authentic French and Italian.

Immigration has been the key to this culinary concoction. An influx of immigrants since WWII, from Europe, Asia, the Middle East and Africa, introduced new ingredients and new ways to use staples. Vietnamese, Japanese, Fijian – no matter where it's from, there are expat communities and interested locals keen to cook and eat it. You'll find Jamaicans using Scotch bonnet peppers and Tunisians making tajine.

As the Australian appetite for diversity and invention grows, so does the food culture surrounding it. Cookbooks and foodie magazines are bestsellers and Australian celebrity chefs – highly sought overseas – reflect Australia's multiculturalism in their backgrounds and dishes. Cooking TV shows – both competitions and foodie travel documentaries – have become mandatory nightly viewing.

If all this sounds overwhelming, never fear. The range of food in Australia is a true asset. You'll find that dishes are characterised by bold and interesting flavours and fresh ingredients. All palates are catered for: the chilli-metre spans gentle to extreme, seafood is plentiful, meats are full-flavoured, and vegetarian needs are considered (especially in the cities).

Fab Food Festivals

Taste of Tasmania, Hobart, Tasmania.

Melbourne Food & Wine Festival, Melbourne, Victoria.

Clare Valley Gourmet Weekend, Clare Valley, South Australia.

Margaret River Gourmet Escape, Western Australia.

Fresh Local Food

Australia is huge (similar in size to continental USA), and it varies so much in climate, from the tropical north to the temperate south, that at any time of the year there's an enormous array of produce on offer. Fruit is a fine example. In summer, kitchen bowls overflow with nectarines, peaches and cherries, and mangoes are so plentiful that Queenslanders get sick of them. The Murray River gives rise to orchards of citrus fruits, grapes and melons. Tasmania's cold climate means its strawberries and stone fruits are sublime. The tomatoes and olives of South Australia (SA) are the nation's best. Local supermarkets stock the pick of the bunch.

Seafood is always freshest close to the source; on this big island it's plentiful. Oysters are popular: connoisseurs prize Sydney rock oysters, a species that actually lives right along the New South Wales (NSW) coast; excellent oysters are grown in seven different regions in SA; and Tasmania is known for its Pacific oysters. Australia's southernmost state is also celebrated for its trout, salmon and abalone.

Australians consume more than 206,000 tonnes of seafood per year. Along the coast, fish-and-chip shops often get their seafood straight from the local fishing boats: ask the cook what's frozen (ie from elsewhere) and what's not.

An odd-sounding delicacy from these waters is bugs – shovel-nosed lobsters without a lobster's price tag (try the Balmain and Moreton Bay varieties). Marron are prehistoric-looking freshwater crayfish from Western Australia (WA), with a subtle taste that's not always enhanced by the

BUSH TUCKER: AUSTRALIAN NATIVE FOODS

There are around 350 food plants that are native to the Australian bush. Bush foods provide a real taste of the Australian landscape. There are the dried fruits and lean meats of the desert; shellfish and fish of the coast; alpine berries and mountain peppers of the high country; and citrus flavours, fruits and herbs of the rainforests.

This cuisine is based on Indigenous Australians' expert understanding of the environment, founded in cultural knowledge handed down over generations. Years of trial and error have ensured a rich appreciation of these foods and mastery of their preparation.

The harvesting of bush foods for commercial return has been occurring for about 30 years. In central Australia it is mainly carried out by middle-aged and senior Aboriginal women. Here and in other regions, bush meats such as kangaroo, emu and crocodile, fish such as barramundi, and bush fruits including desert raisins, quandongs, riberries, and Kakadu plums are seasonally hunted and gathered for personal enjoyment, as well as to supply local, national and international markets.

Janelle White is an applied anthropologist, currently completing a PhD on Aboriginal people's involvement in a variety of desert-based bush produce industries – including bush foods, bush medicines and bush jewellery. She splits her time between Adelaide, and the land 200km northwest of Alice Springs.

heavy dressings that seem popular. Prawns in Australia are incredible, particularly sweet school prawns or the eastern king (Yamba) prawns found along the northern NSW coast. You can sample countless wild fish species, including prized barramundi from the Northern Territory (NT), but even fish that are considered run-of-the-mill (such as snapper, trevally and whiting) taste fabulous simply barbecued.

There's a growing boutique cheese movement across the country's dairy regions; Tasmania alone now produces 50 cheese varieties.

Restaurant Dining

A restaurant meal in Australia is a relaxed affair. You'll probably order within 15 minutes and see the first course (entrée) 20 minutes later. The main course will arrive about half an hour after that. Even at the finest restaurants a jacket is not required (but certainly isn't frowned upon).

If a restaurant is BYO, you can bring your own alcohol. If it also sells alcohol, you can usually only bring your own bottled wine (no beer, no cask wine) and a corkage charge is added to your bill. The cost is either per person or per bottle, and can be up to $20 per bottle in fine-dining places (do the sums: you'll often be better off buying from the restaurant).

Tipping is not mandatory in Australia, but is appreciated if the food is great and service comes with a smile. Around 10% is the norm.

Quick Eats

In the big cities, street vending is on the rise – coffee carts have been joined by vans selling tacos, burritos, baked potatoes, burgers... Elsewhere around the cities you'll find fast-food chains, gourmet sandwich bars, food courts in shopping centres and market halls, bakeries, and sushi, noodle and salad bars. Beyond the big smoke the options are more limited and traditional, such as milk bars (known as delis in SA and WA). These corner stores often serve old-fashioned hamburgers (with bacon, egg, pineapple and beetroot!) and other takeaway foods.

There are almost a million Aussies with Italian heritage: it follows that pizza is (arguably) the most popular Australian fast food. Most home-delivered pizzas are of the American style (thick and with lots of toppings) rather than Italian style. However, wood-fired, thin, Neapolitan-style pizza can still be found, even in country towns.

Fish and chips are still hugely popular, the fish most often a form of shark (often called flake; don't worry, it's delicious), either grilled or dipped in batter and fried.

If you're at a rugby league or Aussie rules football match, a beer and a meat pie are as compulsory as wearing your team's colours and yelling loudly from the stands.

Eating with the Locals

Etiquette hint: if you're invited to someone's house for dinner, always take a gift (even if the host dissuades you): a bottle of wine, a six-pack of beer, some flowers or a box of chocolates.

Most Aussies eat cereal, toast and/or fruit for breakfast, often extending to bacon and eggs on weekends, washed down with tea and coffee. They devour sandwiches, salads and sushi for lunch, and then eat anything and everything in the evening.

The iconic Australian barbecue (BBQ or barbie) is a near-mandatory cultural experience. In summer locals invite their mates around at dinnertime and fire-up the barbie, grilling burgers, sausages (snags), steaks, seafood, and vegie, meat or seafood skewers. If you're invited to a BBQ, bring some meat and cold beer. Year-round the BBQ is wheeled out at weekends for quick-fire lunches. There are plenty of free electric or gas BBQs in parks around the country – a terrific traveller-friendly option.

Cafes & Coffee

Cafes in Australia generally serve good-value food: you can get a decent meal for around $15. Kids are usually more than welcome.

Coffee has become an Australian addiction. There are Italian-style espresso machines in virtually every cafe, boutique roasters are all the rage and, in urban areas, the qualified barista is ever-present (there are even barista-manned cafes attached to petrol stations). Sydney and Melbourne have given rise to a whole generation of coffee snobs, the two cities duking it out for bragging rights as Australia's coffee capital. The cafe scene in Melbourne's city laneways is particularly artsy. You'll also find decent places in the other big cities and towns, and there's now a sporting chance of good coffee in many rural areas.

Pubs & Drinking

You're in the right country if you're in need of a drink. Long recognised as some of the finest in the world, Australian wines are one of the nation's top exports. As the public develops a more sophisticated palate, local craft beers are rising to the occasion. There's a growing wealth of microbrewed flavours and varieties on offer, challenging the nation's entrenched predilection for mass-produced lager. If you're into whisky, head to Tasmania: there are a dozen distillers there now, bottling-up superb single malts and racking up international awards.

Most Australian beers have an alcohol content between 3.5% and 5.5%, less than European beers but more than most in North America.

FOOD: WHEN, WHERE & HOW

- Budget eating venues usually offer main courses for under $15, midrange places are generally between $15 and $32, with top-end venues charging over $32.
- Cafes serve breakfasts from around 8am on weekends – a bit earlier on weekdays – and close around 5pm.
- Pubs and bars usually open around lunchtime and continue till at least 10pm – later from Thursday to Saturday. Pubs usually serve food from noon to 2pm and 6pm to 8pm.
- Restaurants generally open around noon for lunch, 6pm for dinner. Australians usually eat lunch shortly after noon; dinner bookings are usually made between 7pm and 8pm, though in big cities some restaurants stay open past 10pm.
- Vegetarian eateries and vegetarian selections in nonveg places (including menu choices for vegans and for coeliac sufferers) are common in large cities. Rural Australia continues its dedication to meat.
- Smoking is banned in cafes, restaurants, clubs, pubs and an many city malls.

WINE REGIONS

All Australian states and mainland territories (except the tropical/desert Northern Territory) sustain wine industries, some almost 200 years old. Many wineries have tastings for free or a small fee, often redeemable if you buy a bottle. Although plenty of good wine comes from big wineries with economies of scale on their side, the most interesting wines are often made by small producers. The following rundown should give you a head start.

South Australia

South Australia's wine industry is a global giant, as a visit to the National Wine Centre in Adelaide will attest. Cabernet sauvignon from Coonawarra, riesling from the Clare Valley, sauvignon blanc from the Adelaide Hills and shiraz from the Barossa Valley and McLaren Vale are bliss in a bottle.

New South Wales & the Australian Capital Territory

Dating from the 1820s, the Hunter Valley is Australia's oldest wine region. The Lower Hunter is known for shiraz and unwooded semillon. Upper Hunter wineries specialise in cabernet sauvignon and shiraz, with forays into verdelho and chardonnay. Further inland are award-winning wineries at Griffith, Mudgee and Orange. In the ACT, Canberra's surrounds also have a growing number of excellent wineries.

Western Australia

Margaret River is synonymous with superb cabernets and chardonnays. Among old-growth forest, Pemberton wineries produce cabernet sauvignon, merlot, pinot noir, sauvignon blanc and shiraz. The south coast's Mt Barker is another budding wine region.

Victoria

Victoria has more than 500 wineries. A day-trip from Melbourne, the Yarra Valley produces excellent chardonnay and pinot noir, as does the Mornington Peninsula. Wineries around Rutherglen produce champion fortified wines as well as shiraz and durif.

Tasmania

Try the Pipers River Region and the Tamar Valley in the north, and explore the burgeoning wine industry in the Coal River Valley around Richmond near Hobart. Cool-climate drops are the name of the game here: especially pinot noir, sauvignon blanc and sparking whites (our favourite is made by Jansz – 'Méthode Tasmanoise', ha-ha...).

Queensland

High-altitude Stanthorpe and Ballandean in the southeast are the centres of the Queensland wine industry, though you'll find a few cellar doors at Tamborine Mountain in the Gold Coast hinterland.

Light beers contain under 3% alcohol and are a good choice if you have to drive (as long as you don't drink twice as much).

The terminology used to order beer varies state by state. In NSW you ask for a schooner (425mL) if you're thirsty and a middy (285mL) if you're not quite so dry. In Victoria the 285mL measure is called a pot; in Tasmania it's called a 10oz. Pints can either be 425mL or 568mL, depending on where you are. Mostly you can just ask for a beer and see what turns up.

'Shouting' is a revered custom where people take turns to pay for a round of drinks. At a toast, everyone should touch glasses and look each other in the eye as they clink – failure to do so is purported to result in seven years' bad sex (...which is better than seven years of no sex, but why not make eye-contact and hope for the best).

Pub meals (counter meals) are usually hefty and good value; standards such as sausages and mash or schnitzel and salad go for $15 to $25.

A competitively priced place to eat is at a club – Returned and Services League (RSL) or Surf Life Saving clubs are solid bets. You order at the kitchen take a number and wait until it's called out over the counter or intercom. You pick up the meal yourself, saving the restaurant on staffing costs and you on your total bill.

Vegemite: you'll either love it or hate it. For reference, Barack Obama diplomatically called it 'horrible'. It's certainly an acquired taste, but Australians consume more than 22 million jars of the stuff every year.

Sport

Whether they're filling stadiums, glued to the big screen at the pub or on the couch in front of the TV, Australians invest heavily in sport – both fiscally and emotionally. The federal government kicks in more than $300 million every year – enough cash for the nation to hold its own against formidable international sporting opponents. Despite slipping to 10th spot on the 2012 London Olympics medal tally, Australia is looking forward to redemption at the 2016 Rio Olympics.

'Footy' in Australia can mean a number of things. In NSW and Queensland it's rugby league; everywhere else it's Australian Rules football. Just to confuse you, 'football' can also mean soccer!

Australian Rules Football

Australia's most attended sport, and one of the two most watched, is Australian Rules football (Aussie rules). While traditionally embedded in Victorian state culture and identity, the Australian Football League (AFL; www.afl.com.au) has gradually expanded its popularity into all states, including rugby-dominated New South Wales and Queensland. Long kicks, high marks and brutal collisions whip crowds into frenzies: the roar of 50,000-plus fans yelling *'Baaall!!!'* upsets dogs in suburban backyards for miles around.

Rugby

The National Rugby League (NRL; www.nrl.com.au) is the most popular football code north of the Murray River, the season highlight being the annual State of Origin series between NSW and Queensland. To witness an NRL game is to appreciate all of Newton's laws of motion – bone-crunching!

The national rugby union team, the Wallabies, won the Rugby World Cup in 1991 and 1999 and was runner-up in 2003, but hasn't made the final since (let us know what happens in 2015!). Australia, New Zealand and South Africa compete in the superpopular Super 15s (www.superxv.com) competition, which includes five Australian teams: the Waratahs (Sydney), the Reds (Brisbane), the Brumbies (Australian Capital Territory, aka ACT), the Force (Perth) and the Rebels (Melbourne). The Waratahs beat New Zealand's Canterbury Crusaders by a point on the 2014 final – go 'tahs! The competition will expand to 18 teams from 2016, including teams from Argentina and Japan.

Soccer

Australia's national soccer team, the Socceroos, qualified for the 2006, 2010 and 2014 FIFA World Cups after a long history of almost-but-not-quite getting there. Results were mixed, but pride in the national team is sky-high (and actually reached the stratosphere when the Socceroos won the Asian Cup in 2015).

The national A-League (www.a-league.com.au) comp has enjoyed increased popularity in recent years, successfully luring a few big-name international players to bolster the home-grown talent pool.

Cricket

The Aussies dominated both test and one-day cricket for much of the noughties, holding the No 1 world ranking for most of the decade. But the subsequent retirement of once-in-a-lifetime players such as Shane Warne, Adam Gilchrist and Ricky Ponting sent the team into an extended rebuilding phase. Only now is the team returning to a level of success to which the viewing public has become accustomed.

The pinnacle of Australian cricket is the biennial test series played between Australia and England, known as 'The Ashes'. The unofficial Ashes trophy is a tiny terracotta urn containing the ashen remnants of an 1882 cricket bail (the perfect Australian BBQ conversation opener: ask a local what a 'bail' is). Series losses in 2009, 2011 and 2013 to the arch-enemy caused nationwide misery. Redemption came in 2014, when Australia won back the Ashes 5-0, only the third clean-sweep in Ashes history. (The 2014 series was due to be played in 2015, but was bumped forward a year to avoid a clash with the 2015 one-day World Cup.)

Despite the Australian cricket team's bad rep for sledging (verbally dressing down one's opponent on the field), cricket is still a gentleman's game. Take the time to watch a match if you never have – such tactical cut-and-thrust, such nuance, such grace.

Australia's T20 Big Bash League (www.bigbash.com.au), the 20-over form of cricket, is gaining ground on the traditional five-day and one-day formats. Fast, flashy and laced with pyrotechnics, it's thin on erudition but makes for a fun night out.

Tennis

Every January in Melbourne, the Australian Open (p492) attracts more people to Australia than any other sporting event. The men's competition was last won by an Australian, Mark Edmondson, back in 1976 – and while Lleyton Hewitt has been Australia's great hope for many years, the former world No 1's best playing days are behind him (but he looks set for a career as a commentator). Young gun Nick Kyrgios looks set to take up the mantle (or at least impress with his haircuts). In the women's game, Australian Sam Stosur won the US Open in 2011 and has been hovering around the top-10 player rankings ever since.

Swimming

Australia: girt by sea and pock-marked with pools; its population can swim. Australia's greatest female swimmer, Dawn Fraser, known simply as 'our Dawn', won the 100m freestyle gold at three successive Olympics (1956–64), plus the 4 x 100m freestyle relay in 1956. Australia's greatest male swimmer, Ian Thorpe (known as Thorpie or the Thorpedo), retired in 2006 aged 24 with five Olympic golds swinging from his neck. In early 2011, Thorpe announced his comeback, his eye fixed on the 2012 London Olympics – but he failed to make the team in the selection trials, and left

SURF'S UP!

Australia has been synonymous with surfing ever since the Beach Boys effused about 'Australia's Narrabeen', one of Sydney's northern beaches, in 'Surfin' USA'. Other surfing hotspots such as Bells Beach, Margaret River, the Pass at Byron Bay, the heavy-breaking Shipstern Bluff in Tasmania and Burleigh Heads on the Gold Coast also resonate with international wave addicts. Iron Man and Surf Lifesaving competitions are also held on beaches around the country, attracting dedicated fans to the sand.

More than a few Australian surfers have attained 'World Champion' status. In the men's comp, legendary surfers include Mark Richards, Tom Carroll, Joel Parkinson and 2013 champ Mick Fanning. In the women's competition, iconic Aussie surfers include Wendy Botha, seven-time champion Layne Beachley and 2014 champ (and six-time winner) Stephanie Gilmore.

the pool again to finish his autobiography. Speedy upstart James Magnussen hasn't won Olympic gold, but at the time of writing was the 100m freestyle world champ.

Horse Racing

Australians love to bet on the 'nags' – in fact, betting on horse racing is so mainstream and accessible that it's almost the national hobby! There are racecourses all around the country and local holidays for racing carnivals in Victoria, Tasmania and South Australia.

Australia's biggest race – the 'race that stops a nation' – is the Melbourne Cup (p493), which occurs on the first Tuesday in November. The most famous Melbourne Cup winner was the New Zealand–born Phar Lap, who won in 1930 before dying of a mystery illness (suspected arsenic poisoning) in the USA. Phar Lap is now a prize exhibit in the Melbourne Museum. The British-bred (but Australian-trained) Makybe Diva is a more recent star, winning three cups in a row before retiring in 2005.

Survival Guide

Deadly & Dangerous

If you're the pessimistic type, you might choose to focus on the things that can bite, sting, burn, freeze, drown or rob you in Australia. But chances are the worst you'll encounter are a few pesky flies and mosquitoes. Splash on some insect repellent and boldly venture forth!

See also p1077.

Where the Wild Things Are

Australia's profusion of dangerous creatures is legendary: snakes, spiders, sharks, crocodiles, jellyfish... Travellers needn't be alarmed, though – you're unlikely to see many of these creatures in the wild, much less be attacked by one.

Crocodiles

Around the northern Australian coastline, saltwater crocodiles (salties) are a real danger. They also inhabit estuaries, creeks and rivers, sometimes a long way inland. Observe safety signs or ask locals whether that inviting-looking waterhole or river is croc free before plunging in.

Jellyfish

With venomous tentacles up to 3m long, box jellyfish (aka sea wasps or stingers) inhabit Australia's tropical waters. They're most common during the wet season (October to March) when you should stay out of the sea in many places. Stinger nets are in place at some beaches, but never swim unless you've checked. 'Stinger suits' (full-body Lycra swimsuits) prevent stinging, as do wetsuits. If you are stung, wash the skin with vinegar then get to a hospital.

The box jellyfish also has a tiny, lethal relative called an irukandji, though to date, only two north-coast deaths have been directly attributed to it.

Sharks

Despite extensive media coverage, the risk of shark attack in Australia is no greater than in other countries with extensive coastlines. Check with surf life-saving groups about local risks.

Snakes

Australia has plenty of venomous snakes. Most common are brown and tiger snakes, but few species are aggressive. Unless you're poking a stick at or accidentally standing on one, it's extremely unlikely that you'll get bitten. If you are bitten, prevent the spread of venom by applying pressure to the wound and immobilising the area with a splint or sling. Stay put and get someone else to go for help.

Spiders

Australia has several poisonous spiders, bites from which are usually treatable with antivenenes. The deadly funnel-web spider lives in New South Wales (NSW; including Sydney); bites are treated as per snake bites (pressure and immobilisation before transferring to a hospital). Redback spiders live throughout Australia; bites cause pain, sweating and nausea. Apply ice or cold packs, then transfer to hospital. White-tailed-spider bites may cause an ulcer that's slow and difficult to heal. Clean the wound and

MAINTAINING PERSPECTIVE

There's approximately one fatal crocodile attack per year in Australia, and, despite five deaths in 2014, one fatal shark attack. Blue-ringed-octopus deaths are rarer – only two in the last century. Jellyfish do better – about two deaths annually – but you're still more than 100 times more likely to drown. Spiders haven't killed anyone in the last 20 years. Snake bites kill one or two people per year, as do bee stings, but you're about a thousand times more likely to perish on the nation's roads.

seek medical assistance. The disturbingly large huntsman spider is harmless, though seeing one can affect your blood pressure and/or underpants.

Out & About

At the Beach

Check surf conditions and be aware of your own expertise and limitations before entering the waves. Patrolled, safe-swimming areas are indicated by red-and-yellow flags – swim between them. Undertows (rips) are a problem: if you find yourself being carried out to sea, swim parallel to the shore until you're out of the rip, then head for the beach.

Several people are paralysed every year by diving into shallow waves and hitting sand bars: look before you leap.

Always use SPF30+ sunscreen; apply it 30 minutes before going into the sun and repeat applications regularly.

Bushfires

Bushfires happen yearly across Australia. In hot, dry and windy weather, and on total-fire-ban days, be extremely careful with naked flames (including cigarette butts) and don't use camping stoves, campfires or BBQs. Bushwalkers should delay trips until things cool down. If you're out in the bush and you see smoke, take it seriously: find the nearest open space (downhill if possible). Forested ridges are dangerous places to be.

Cold Weather

More bushwalkers in Australia die of cold than in bushfires. Even in summer, particularly in highland Tasmania, Victoria and NSW, conditions can change quickly, with temperatures dropping below freezing and blizzards blowing in. Hypothermia is a real risk. Early signs include the inability to perform fine movements (eg doing up buttons), shivering and a bad case of the 'umbles' (fumbles, mumbles, grumbles, stumbles). Get out of the cold, change out of wet clothing and into dry stuff, and eat and drink to warm up.

Heat Exhaustion

Symptoms of heat exhaustion include dizziness, fainting, fatigue, nausea or vomiting. Skin becomes pale, cool and clammy. Treatment consists of rest in a cool, shady place and fluid replacement with water or diluted sports drinks.

Heatstroke is a severe form of heat illness and is a true medical emergency, with heating of the brain leading to disorientation, hallucinations and seizures. Prevent heatstroke by maintaining adequate fluid intake, especially during physical exertion.

Crime

Australia is a relatively safe place to visit, but you should still take reasonable precautions. Avoid walking around alone at night, don't leave hotel rooms or cars unlocked, and don't leave valuables visible through car windows.

Some pubs in Sydney and other big cities post warnings about drugged or 'spiked' drinks: play it safe if someone offers you a drink in a bar.

Diseases & Discomforts

You'll be unlucky to pick any of these up in your travels, but the following diseases do crop up around Australia.

For protection against insect-borne illnesses (dengue fever, Ross River fever, tick typhus, viral encephalitis), wear loose-fitting, long-sleeved clothing, and apply 30% DEET to exposed skin.

Dengue Fever

Dengue fever occurs in northern Queensland, particularly during the wet season. Causing severe muscular aches, it's a viral disease spread by a day-feeding species of mosquito. Most people recover in a few days, but more severe forms of the disease can occur.

Giardiasis

Giardia is widespread in Australian waterways. Drinking untreated water from streams and lakes is not recommended. Use water filters, and boil or treat this water with iodine to help prevent giardiasis. Symptoms consist of intermittent diarrhoea, abdominal bloating and wind. Effective treatment is available (tinidazole or metronidazole).

Ross River Fever

The Ross River virus is widespread in Australia, transmitted by marsh-dwelling mosquitoes. In addition to fever, it causes headache, joint and muscular pain, and a rash that resolves after five to seven days.

Tick Typhus

Predominantly occurring in Queensland and NSW, tick typhus involves a dark area forming around a tick bite, followed by a rash, fever, headache and lymph-node inflammation. The disease is treatable with antibiotics (doxycycline).

Viral Encephalitis

This mosquito-borne disease is most common in northern Australia (especially during the wet season), but poses minimal risk to travellers. Symptoms include headache, muscle pain and sensitivity to light. Residual neurological damage can occur and no specific treatment is available.

Directory A–Z

Accommodation

Australia offers everything from the tent-pegged confines of camp sites and the communal space of hostels, to gourmet breakfasts in guesthouses, chaperoned farmstays and indulgent resorts, plus the full gamut of hotel and motel lodgings.

During the summer high season (December to February) and at other peak times, particularly school holidays and Easter, prices are usually at their highest. Outside these times you'll find useful discounts and lower walk-in rates. Notable exceptions include central Australia, the Top End and Australia's ski resorts, where summer is the low season and prices drop substantially.

B&Bs

Australian bed-and-breakfast options include restored miners' cottages, converted barns, rambling old houses, upmarket country manors and beachside bungalows. Tariffs are typically in the midrange bracket, but can be higher. In areas that attract weekenders – historic towns, wine regions, accessible forest regions such as the Blue Mountains in New South Wales (NSW) and the Dandenongs in Victoria – B&Bs are often upmarket, charging small fortunes for weekend stays in high season.

Some places advertised as B&Bs are actually self-contained cottages with breakfast provisions supplied. Only in the cheaper B&Bs will bathroom facilities be shared. Some B&B hosts may also cook dinner for guests (usually 24 hours' notice is required).

Online resources:

Beautiful Accommodation (www.beautifulaccommodation.com). A select crop of luxury B&Bs and self-contained houses.

Hosted Accommodation Australia (www.australianbedandbreakfast.com.au). Listings for B&Bs, farmstays, cottages and homesteads.

OZ Bed and Breakfast (www.ozbedandbreakfast.com). Nationwide website.

Camping & Caravanning

The nightly camping cost for two people is usually between $20 and $30, slightly more for a powered site. Camping in the bush is a highlight of travelling in Australia: in the outback and northern Australia you often won't even need a tent, and nights spent around a campfire under the stars are unforgettable.

Seasons To avoid extremes of hot and cold weather, camping is best done during winter (the dry season) across the north of Australia, and during summer in the south.

Costs Unless otherwise stated, prices for camp sites are for two people. Staying at designated camp sites in national parks normally costs between $7 and $15 per person.

Facilities Almost all caravan and holiday parks are equipped with hot showers, flushing toilets and laundry facilities, and frequently a pool. Most have cabins, powered caravan sites and tent sites. Cabin sizes and facilities vary, but expect to pay $70 to $80 for a small cabin with a kitchenette and up to $170 for a two- or three-bedroom cabin with a fully equipped kitchen, lounge room, TV and beds for up to six people.

Locations Note that most city camping grounds usually lie several kilometres from the town centre – only convenient if you have wheels. Caravan parks are popular in coastal areas: book well in advance during summer and Easter.

Resources Get your hands on *Camps Australia Wide* (www.

BOOK YOUR STAY ONLINE

For more accommodation reviews by Lonely Planet authors, check out http://lonelyplanet.com/australia/hotels. You'll find independent reviews, as well as recommendations on the best places to stay. Best of all, you can book online.

campsaustraliawide.com), a handy publication (and app) containing maps and information about camp sites across Australia.

Permits Applications for national-park camping permits are often handled online by state departments (eg in Queensland it's via the Department of National Parks, Recreation, Sport & Racing website, www.nprsr.qld.gov.au; in WA it's via the government Park Stay WA website, http://parkstay.dpaw.wa.gov.au). Regional sleeping listings in this book contain this booking info.

Major Chains If you're doing a lot of caravanning/camping, consider joining one of the chain organisations, which offer member discounts:

Big 4 Holiday Parks (www.big4.com.au)

Discovery Holiday Parks (www.discoveryholidayparks.com.au)

Top Tourist Parks (www.toptouristparks.com.au)

Holiday Apartments

Costs For a two-bedroom flat, you're looking at anywhere from $140 to $200 per night, but you will pay much more in high season and for serviced apartments in major cities.

Facilities Self-contained holiday apartments range from simple, studio-like rooms with small kitchenettes, to two-bedroom apartments with full laundries and state-of-the-art entertainment systems: great value for multinight stays. Sometimes they come in small, single-storey blocks, but in tourist hotspots such as the Gold Coast expect a sea of high-rises.

Hostels

Backpacker hostels are exceedingly popular in Australian cities and along the coast, but in the outback and rural areas you'll be hard-pressed to find one. Highly social affairs, they're generally overflowing with 18- to 30-year-olds, but some have reinvented themselves to attract other travellers who simply want to sleep for cheap.

SLEEPING PRICE RANGES

The following price ranges refer to a double room with bathroom in high season (summer):

$ less than $100

$$ $100 to $200

$$$ more than $200

Expect to pay $20 to $50 more in expensive areas – notably Sydney, Perth and parts of northern Western Australia. Some upmarket Australian hostels charge upwards of $100 for a double room, but in this book we still classify them as '$' for their budget dorm beds.

Costs Typically a dorm bed costs $25 to $35 per night, and a double (usually without bathroom) $70 to $90.

Facilities Hostels provide varying levels of accommodation, from the austere simplicity of wilderness hostels to city-centre buildings with a cafe-bar and en suite rooms. Most of the accommodation is in dormitories (bunk rooms), usually ranging in size from four to 12 beds. Many hostels also provide twin rooms and doubles. Hostels generally have cooking facilities, a communal area with a TV, laundry facilities and sometimes travel offices and job centres.

Bed linen Often provided; sleeping bags are not welcome due to hygiene concerns.

HOSTEL ORGANISATIONS & CHAINS

The **Youth Hostels Association** (YHA; www.yha.com.au) has around 60 Australian hostels, offering dorms, twin and double rooms, and cooking and laundry facilities: the vibe is generally less 'party' than in independent hostels.

Nightly charges start at $25 for members; hostels also take non-YHA members for an extra $3. Australian residents can become YHA members for $42 for one year ($32 if you're aged between 18 and 25). Join online or at any YHA hostel. Families can also join: just pay the adult price, then kids under 18 can join for free.

The YHA is part of **Hostelling International** (www.hihostels.com). If you already have HI membership in your own country, you're entitled to YHA rates in Australia. Preferably, visitors to Australia should purchase an HI card in their country of residence, but once you're in Australia you can also buy memberships online, at state offices or major YHA hostels.

Following are other international organisations with Australian hostels:

Base Backpackers (www.stayatbase.com)

Nomads (www.nomadsworld.com)

VIP Backpackers (www.vipbackpackers.com)

Hotels

Hotels in Australian cities and well-touristed places are generally of the business or luxury chain variety (midrange to top end): comfortable, anonymous, mod-con-filled rooms in multistorey blocks. For these hotels we quote 'rack rates' (official advertised rates, usually upwards of $160 a night), though significant discounts can be offered when business is quiet.

Motels

Drive-up motels offer comfortable midrange accommodation and are found all over Australia, often on the edges of urban centres. They rarely offer a cheaper rate for

PRACTICALITIES

- **DVDs** Australian DVDs are encoded for Region 4, which includes Mexico, South America, Central America, New Zealand, the Pacific and the Caribbean.
- **Newspapers** Leaf through the daily *Sydney Morning Herald*, Melbourne's *Age* or the national *Australian* broadsheet newspaper.
- **Radio** Tune in to ABC radio; check out www.abc.net.au/radio.
- **Smoking** Banned on public transport, in pubs, bars and eateries, and in some public outdoor spaces.
- **TV** The main free-to-air TV channels are the government-sponsored ABC, multicultural SBS and the three commercial networks – Seven, Nine and Ten. Numerous free spin-off and local channels enrich the viewing brew.
- **Weights & Measures** Australia uses the metric system.

singles, so are better value for couples or groups of three. You'll mostly pay between $120 and $160 for a simple room with a kettle, fridge, TV, air-con and bathroom.

Pubs

Many Australian pubs (from the term 'public house') were built during boom times, so they're often among the largest, most extravagant buildings in town. Some have been restored, but generally rooms remain small and weathered, with a long amble down the hall to the bathroom. They're usually central and cheap; singles/doubles with shared facilities from $60/90, more if you want a private bathroom. If you're a light sleeper, avoid booking a room above the bar and check whether a band is cranking out the rock downstairs that night.

Rental & Long-Term Accommodation

If you're in Australia for a while (visas permitting), then a rental property or room in a shared flat or house will be an economical option. Delve into the classified advertisement sections of the daily newspapers; Wednesday and Saturday are usually the best days. Noticeboards in universities, hostels, bookshops and cafes are also useful. Properties listed through a real-estate agent usually necessitate at least a six-month lease, plus a bond and first month's rent up front.

City Hobo (www.cityhobo.com) Matches your personality with your ideal big-city suburb.

Couch Surfing (www.couchsurfing.com) Connects spare couches with new friends.

Flatmate Finders (www.flatmatefinders.com.au) Long-term share-accommodation listings.

Gumtree (www.gumtree.com.au) Classified site with jobs, accommodation and items for sale.

Stayz (www.stayz.com.au) Holiday rentals.

Other Accommodation

There are lots of less-conventional and, in some cases, uniquely Australian accommodation possibilities scattered across the country.

HOUSEBOATING

Houseboating is big business on the Murray River. Meandering along the river is great fun; you just need to be over 18 with a current driving licence. Boats depart most riverside towns in northwest Victoria and South Australia (SA); book ahead, especially between October and April.

- The **Houseboat Hirers Association** (☎1300 665 122, 08-8231 8466; www.houseboatbookings.com) Has pictures of each boat and can make bookings on your behalf.
- SA Tourism's *Houseboat Holidays* booklet contains detailed houseboat listings.
- For houseboating in Mildura, see p608.
- For houseboats in Echuca, see p615.

COUNTRY FARMS

Country farms sometimes offer a bed for a night, while some remote outback stations allow you to stay in homestead rooms or shearers' quarters and try activities such as horse riding. Check out **Hosted Accommodation Australia** (www.australianbedandbreakfast.com.au) and **Farmstay Camping Australia** (www.farmstaycampingaustralia.com.au) for options. State tourist offices can also help.

UNIVERSITIES

Back within city limits, it's sometimes possible to stay in the hostels and halls of residence normally occupied by university students, though you'll need to time your stay to coincide with the longer university-holiday periods.

Children

If you can survive the long distances between cities, travelling around Australia with the kids can be a real delight. There's oodles of interesting stuff to see and do, both indoors and outdoors.

Lonely Planet's *Travel with Children* contains plenty of useful information.

Practicalities

Accommodation Many motels and the better-equipped caravan parks have playgrounds and swimming pools, and can supply cots and baby baths; motels may also have in-house children's videos and child-minding services. Top-end hotels and many (but not all) midrange hotels are well versed in the needs of guests with children. B&Bs, on the other hand, often market themselves as kid free.

Change rooms and breastfeeding All cities and most major towns have centrally located public rooms where parents can go to nurse their baby or change a nappy; check with the local tourist office or city council for details. Most Australians have a relaxed attitude about breastfeeding and nappy changing in public.

Child care Australia's numerous licensed child-care agencies offer babysitting services. Check under 'Baby Sitters' and 'Child Care Centres' in the *Yellow Pages* telephone directory, or phone the local council for a list. Licensed centres are subject to government regulations and usually adhere to high standards; avoid unlicensed operators.

Child safety seats Major hire-car companies will supply and fit child safety seats, charging a one-off fee of around $25. Call taxi companies in advance to organise child safety seats. The rules for travelling in taxis with kids vary from state to state: in most places safety seats aren't legally required but must be used if available.

Concessions Child concessions (and family rates) often apply to accommodation, tours, admission fees and transport, with some discounts as high as 50% of the adult rate. However, the definition of 'child' varies from under 12 to under 18 years. Accommodation concessions generally apply to children under 12 years sharing the same room as adults.

Eating out Many cafes and restaurants offer kids' meals, or will provide small serves from the main menu. Some also supply high chairs.

Health care Australia has high-standard medical services and facilities, and items such as baby formula and disposable nappies are widely available.

Customs Regulations

For detailed information on customs and quarantine regulations, contact the **Australian Customs & Border Protection Service** (☎1300 363 263, 02-6275 6666; www.customs.gov.au).

When entering Australia you can bring most articles in free of duty provided that customs is satisfied they are for personal use and that you'll be taking them with you when you leave. Duty-free quotas per person (note the unusually low figure for cigarettes):

Alcohol 2.25L (over the age of 18)

Cigarettes 50 cigarettes (over the age of 18)

Dutiable goods Up to the value of $900 ($450 for people under 18)

Narcotics, of course, are illegal, and customs inspectors and their highly trained hounds are diligent in sniffing them out. Quarantine regulations are strict, so you *must* declare all goods of animal or vegetable origin – wooden spoons, straw hats, the lot. Fresh food (meat, cheese, fruit, vegetables etc) and flowers are prohibited. There are disposal bins located in airports where you can dump any questionable items if you don't want to bother with an inspection. You must declare currency in excess of $10,000 (including foreign currency).

Discount Cards

Travellers over 60 with some form of identification (eg a state-issued seniors card or overseas equivalent) are sometimes eligible for concession prices for public transport.

The internationally recognised **International Student Identity Card** (ISIC; www.isic.org) is available to full-time students aged 12 and over. The card gives the bearer discounts on accommodation, transport and admission to various attractions. The same organisation also produces the International Youth Travel Card (IYTC), issued to people under 26 years of age and not full-time students, and has benefits equivalent to the ISIC; also similar is the International Teacher Identity Card (ITIC), available to teaching professionals. All three cards are available online (from the ISIC website) and from student travel companies ($30).

INTERSTATE QUARANTINE

When travelling within Australia, whether by land or air, you'll come across signs (mainly in airports and interstate train stations and at state borders) warning of the possible dangers of carrying fruit, vegetables and plants from one area to another. Certain pests and diseases (fruit fly, cucurbit thrips, grape phylloxera...) are prevalent in some areas but not in others: authorities would like to limit them spreading.

There are quarantine inspection posts on some state borders and occasionally elsewhere. While quarantine control often relies on honesty, many posts are staffed and officers are entitled to search your car for undeclared items. Generally they will confiscate all fresh fruit and vegetables, so it's best to leave shopping for these items until the first town past the inspection point.

Electricity

Embassies & Consulates

The main diplomatic representations are in Canberra. There are also consulates in other major cities, particularly for countries with a strong link to Australia, such as the USA, the UK and New Zealand, or in cities with important connections, such as Darwin, which has an Indonesian consulate.

Canadian Embassy Canberra (☎02-6270 4000; www.australia.gc.ca; Commonwealth Ave, Canberra, ACT); Sydney (☎02-9364 3000; www.australia.gc.ca; Level 5, 111 Harrington St, Sydney, NSW; 🚆Circular Quay)

Chinese Embassy (☎02-6228 3999; http://au.china-embassy.org/eng; 15 Coronation Dr, Yarralumla, ACT)

Dutch Embassy Canberra (☎02-6220 9400; www.netherlands.org.au; 120 Empire Circuit, Yarralumla, ACT); Sydney (☎02-9387 6644; http://australia.nlembassy.org; L23, 101 Grafton St, Bondi Junction, NSW; ⏲10am-1pm Mon-Fri; 🚆Bondi Junction)

French Embassy Canberra (☎02-6216 0100; www.ambafrance-au.org; 6 Perth Ave, Yarralumla, ACT); Sydney (☎02-9268 2400; www.ambafrance-au.org; Level 26, St Martins Tower, 31 Market St, Sydney, NSW; 🚆Town Hall)

German Embassy Canberra (☎02-6270 1911; www.canberra.diplo.de; 119 Empire Circuit, Yarralumla, ACT); Sydney (☎02-9328 7733; www.australien.diplo.de; 13 Trelawney St, Woollahra, NSW; 🚆Edgecliff)

Irish Embassy (☎02-6214 0000; www.embassyofireland.au.com; 20 Arkana St, Yarralumla, ACT)

Japanese Embassy Canberra (☎02-6273 3244; www.au.emb-japan.go.jp; 112 Empire Circuit, Yarralumla, ACT); Sydney (☎02-9250 1000; www.sydney.au.emb-japan.go.jp; Level 12, 1 O'Connell St, Sydney, NSW; 🚆Circular Quay)

Malaysian Embassy (☎02-6120 0300; www.malaysia.org.au; 7 Perth Ave, Yarralumla, ACT)

New Zealand Embassy Canberra (☎08-6270 4211; www.nzembassy.com; Commonwealth Ave, Canberra, ACT); Sydney (☎02-8256 2000; www.nzembassy.com; Level 10, 55 Hunter St, Sydney, NSW; 🚆Martin Place)

Singaporean Embassy (☎02-6271-2000; www.mfa.gov.sg/canberra; 17 Forster Cres, Yarralumla, ACT)

South African Embassy (☎02-6272 7300; www.sahc.org.au; cnr Rhodes Pl & State Circle, Yarralumla, ACT)

Thai Embassy (☎02-6206 0100; http://canberra.thaiembassy.org; 111 Empire Circuit, Yarralumla, ACT)

UK Embassy Canberra (☎02-6270 6666; www.ukinaustralia.fco.gov.uk; Commonwealth Ave, Yarralumla, ACT); Melbourne (☎03-9652 1600; www.gov.uk; Level 17, 90 Collins St, Melbourne, VIC); Sydney (☎02-9247 7521; www.gov.uk; Level 16, Gateway Bldg, 1 Macquarie Pl, Sydney, NSW; 🚆Circular Quay)

US Embassy Canberra (☎02-6214 5600; http://canberra.usembassy.gov; 1 Moonah Pl, Yarralumla, ACT); Melbourne (☎03-9526 5900; http://melbourne.usconsulate.gov; Level 6, 553 St Kilda Rd, Melbourne, VIC); Sydney (☎02-8278 1420; http://sydney.usconsulate.gov; Level 10, MLC Centre, 19-29 Martin Pl, Sydney, NSW)

Food

See the Food & Drink chapter, p1062.

In our reviews, we use the following price ranges to refer to a standard main course:

$ less than $15

$$ $15 to $32

$$$ more than $32

Gay & Lesbian Travellers

Australia is a popular destination for gay and lesbian travellers, with the so-called 'pink tourism' appeal of Sydney especially big, thanks largely to the city's annual, high-profile and spectacular Sydney Gay & Lesbian Mardi Gras. In general, Australians are open-minded about homosexuality, but the further from the cities you get, the more likely you are to run into overt homophobia.

Throughout the country, but particularly on the east coast, there are tour operators, travel agents and accommodation places that make a point of welcoming gay and lesbian guests.

Same-sex acts are legal in all states but the age of consent varies.

Major Gay & Lesbian Events

Midsumma Festival (www.midsumma.org.au) Melbourne's annual gay-and-lesbian arts fest features more than 100 events mid-January to mid-February, with a Pride March finale.

Sydney Gay & Lesbian Mardi Gras (www.mardigras.org.au) A two-week festival culminating in the world-famous massive parade and party on the first Saturday in March.

Brisbane Pride Festival (www.brisbanepridefestival.com.au) Brisbane's annual gay and lesbian celebration is held over four weeks in September (some events in June, including the fab Queen's Ball).

Pridefest (www.pridewa.com.au) In November in Perth.

Feast Festival (www.feast.org.au) Adelaide's big-ticket gay-and-lesbian festival happens over two weeks in November, with a carnival, theatre, dialogue and dance.

Resources

Gay newspapers are found in clubs, cafes, venues and newsagents in major cities. Gay and lesbian lifestyle magazines include *DNA, Lesbians on the Loose (LOTL)* and Sydney-based *SX*. In Melbourne look for *MCV;* in Queensland look for *Queensland Pride*. Perth has the free *OutinPerth* and Adelaide has *Blaze*.

Gay & Lesbian Tourism Australia (Galta; www.galta.com.au). General info.

Same Same (www.samesame.com.au) News, events and lifestyle features.

Health

Healthwise, Australia is a remarkably safe country in which to travel, considering that such a large portion of it lies in the tropics. Few travellers to Australia will experience anything worse than an upset stomach or a bad hangover and, if you do fall ill, the standard of hospitals and health care is high.

See also the Deadly & Dangerous chapter, p1070.

Vaccinations

Visit a physician four to eight weeks before departure. Ask your doctor for an International Certificate of Vaccination (aka the 'yellow booklet'), which will list the vaccinations you've received.

Upon entering Australia, you'll be required to fill out a 'travel history card' detailing any visits to Ebola-affected regions within the last 21 days.

If you're entering Australia within six days of having stayed overnight or longer in a yellow-fever-infected country, you'll need proof of yellow-fever vaccination. For a full list of these countries visit **Centers for Disease Control & Prevention** (www.cdc.gov/travel).

The **World Health Organization** (www.who.int) recommends that all travellers should be covered for diphtheria, tetanus, measles, mumps, rubella, chicken pox and polio, as well as hepatitis B, regardless of their destination. While Australia has high levels of childhood vaccination coverage, outbreaks of these diseases do occur.

Health Insurance

Health insurance is essential for all travellers; see p1078.

Internet Resources

There's a wealth of travel health advice on the internet: **Lonely Planet** (www.lonelyplanet.com) is a good place to start. The **World Health Organization** (www.who.int/ith) publishes *International Travel and Health,* revised annually and available free online. **MD Travel Health** (www.mdtravelhealth.com) provides complete travel health recommendations for every country, updated daily. Government travel health websites include the following:

Australia (www.smartraveller.gov.au)

Canada (www.hc-sc.gc.ca)

UK (www.nhs.uk/livewell/travelhealth)

USA (www.cdc.gov/travel)

Availability & Cost of Health Care

Facilities Australia has an excellent health-care system. It's a mixture of privately run medical clinics and hospitals alongside a system of public hospitals funded by the Australian government. There are also excellent specialised public-health facilities for women and children in major centres.

Medicare The Medicare system covers Australian residents for some health-care costs. Visitors from countries with which Australia has a reciprocal health-care agreement – New Zealand, the Republic of Ireland, Sweden, the Netherlands, Finland, Italy, Belgium, Malta, Slovenia, Norway and the UK – are eligible for benefits specified under the Medicare program. See www.humanservices.gov.au/customer/dhs/medicare.

Medications Painkillers, antihistamines for allergies, and skincare products are widely available at chemists throughout Australia. You may find that medications readily available over the counter in some countries are only available in Australia by prescription. These include the oral contraceptive pill, some medications for asthma and all antibiotics.

Health Care in Remote Areas

In Australia's remote locations, it is possible there'll be a significant delay in emergency services reaching you in the event of serious accident or illness. Do not underestimate the vast distances between most major outback towns; an increased level of self-reliance and preparation is essential. The **Royal Flying Doctor Service** (www.flyingdoctor.org.au) provides an important backup for remote communities.

Consider taking a wilderness first-aid course, such as those offered by **Wilderness First Aid Consultants** (www.wfac.com.au). Take a comprehensive first-aid kit that is appropriate for the activities planned.

Ensure that you have adequate means of communication. Australia has extensive mobile-phone coverage, but additional radio communication (such as a satellite phone) is important for remote areas.

Medical Checklist

- acetaminophen (paracetamol) or aspirin
- antibiotics
- antidiarrhoeal drugs (eg loperamide)
- antihistamines (for hayfever and allergic reactions)
- anti-inflammatory drugs (eg ibuprofen)
- antibacterial ointment in case of cuts or abrasions
- steroid cream or cortisone (for allergic rashes)
- bandages, gauze, gauze rolls
- adhesive or paper tape
- scissors, safety pins, tweezers
- thermometer
- pocket knife
- DEET-containing insect repellent for the skin
- permethrin-containing insect spray for clothing, tents and bed nets
- sunscreen
- oral rehydration salts
- iodine tablets or water filter (for water purification)

Insurance

Worldwide travel insurance is available at www.lonelyplanet.com/travel_services. You can buy, extend and claim online anytime – even if you're already on the road.

Level of Cover A good travel-insurance policy covering theft, loss and medical problems is essential. Some policies specifically exclude designated 'dangerous activities' such as scuba diving, skiing and even bushwalking. Make sure the policy you choose fully covers you for your activity of choice.

Car See p1093 for information on vehicle insurance.

Health You may prefer a policy that pays doctors or hospitals directly rather than requiring you to pay on the spot and claim later. If you have to claim later, make sure you keep all documentation. Check that the policy covers ambulances and emergency medical evacuations by air.

Internet Access

Access

There are fewer internet cafes around these days than there were five years ago (thanks to the advent of iPhones/iPads and wi-fi) but you'll still find them in most sizeable towns. Hourly costs range from $6 to $10. Most accommodation is phasing out internet terminals and kiosks in favour of wi-fi.

Most public libraries have internet access, but generally it's provided for research needs, not for travellers to check Facebook – so book ahead or find an internet cafe.

BYO

ISPS

If you're bringing your palmtop or laptop, check with your Internet Service Provider (ISP) for access numbers you can dial into in Australia. Some major Australian ISPs:

Australia On Line (☎1300 650 661; www.ozonline.com.au)

Dodo (☎13 36 36; www.dodo.com)

iinet (☎13 19 17; www.iinet.net.au)

iPrimus (☎13 17 89; www.iprimus.com.au)

Optus (☎1800 780 219; www.optus.com.au)

Telstra (☎13 76 63; www.telstra.com.au)

MODEM

Keep in mind that your PC-card modem may not work in Australia. The safest option is to buy a reputable 'global' modem before you leave home or buy a local PC-card modem once you get to Australia.

Wi-Fi

It's still rare in remote Australia, but wireless internet access is increasingly the norm in urban Australian accommodation (often free for guests). Cafes, bars and even some public gardens and town squares also provide wi-fi access. For locations, visit www.freewifi.com.au.

Legal Matters

Most travellers will have no contact with Australia's police or legal system; if they do, it's most likely to be while driving.

Driving There's a significant police presence on central Australian roads, and police have the power to stop your car, see your licence (you're required to carry it), check your vehicle for roadworthiness, and insist that you take a breath test for alcohol (and sometimes illicit drugs).

Drugs First-time offenders caught with small amounts of illegal drugs are likely to receive a fine rather than go to jail, but the recording of a conviction against you may affect your visa status.

Visas If you remain in Australia beyond the life of your visa, you'll officially be an 'overstayer' and could face detention and then be prevented from returning to Australia for up to three years.

Arrested? It's your right to telephone a friend, lawyer or relative before questioning begins. Legal aid is available only in serious cases; for Legal Aid office info see www.nationallegalaid.org. However, many solicitors do not charge for an initial consultation.

Money

The Australian dollar comprises 100 cents. There are 5c, 10c, 20c, 50c, $1 and $2 coins, and $5, $10, $20, $50 and $100 notes. Prices in shops are often marked in single cents then rounded to the nearest 5c when you come to pay.

In this book, prices refer to the Australian dollar.

ATMs & Eftpos

ATMs Australia's 'big four' banks – ANZ, Commonwealth, National Australia Bank and Westpac – and affiliated banks have branches all over Australia, plus a slew of 24-hour automated teller machines (ATMs). But don't expect to find ATMs *everywhere*, certainly not off the beaten track or in small towns. Most ATMs accept cards issued by other banks (for a fee) and are linked to international networks.

Eftpos Most service stations, supermarkets, restaurants, cafes and shops have Electronic Funds Transfer at Point of Sale (Eftpos) facilities these days, allowing you to make purchases and even draw out cash with your credit or debit card.

Fees Bear in mind that withdrawing cash via ATMs or Eftpos may attract significant fees; check the associated costs with your bank first.

Opening a Bank Account

Within six weeks If you're planning on staying in Australia a while (on a Working Holiday visa for instance), it makes sense to open a local bank account. This is easy enough for overseas visitors provided it's done within six weeks of arrival. Simply present your passport and provide the bank with a postal address and they'll open the account and send you an ATM card.

After six weeks ...it becomes much more complicated. A points system operates and you need to score a minimum of 100 points before you can have the privilege of letting the bank take your money. Passports or birth certificates are worth 70 points; an international driving licence with photo earns you 40 points; and minor IDs, such as credit cards, get you 25 points. You must have at least one ID with a photograph. Once the account is open, you should be able to have money transferred from your home account (for a fee, of course).

Before you arrive It's possible to set up an Australian bank account before you embark on your international trip and applications can be made online; check bank websites for details:

ANZ (www.anz.com.au)

Commonwealth Bank (www.commbank.com.au)

National Australia Bank (NAB; www.nab.com.au)

Westpac (www.westpac.com.au)

Credit Cards

Credit cards such as Visa and MasterCard are widely accepted for everything from a hostel bed or a restaurant meal to an adventure tour, and are pretty much essential (in lieu of a large deposit) for hiring a car. They can also be used to get cash advances over the counter at banks and from many ATMs, depending on the card, though these transactions incur immediate interest. Diners Club and American Express (Amex) are not as widely accepted.

Lost credit-card contact numbers:

American Express (☎1300 132 639; www.americanexpress.com.au)

Diners Club (☎1300 360 060; www.dinersclub.com.au)

MasterCard (☎1800 120 113; www.mastercard.com.au)

Visa (☎1800 450 346; www.visa.com.au)

Debit Cards

A debit card allows you to draw money directly from your home bank account using ATMs, banks or Eftpos machines. Any card connected to the international banking network – Cirrus, Maestro, Plus and Eurocard – should work with your PIN. Expect substantial fees.

Companies such as Travelex offer debit cards with set withdrawal fees and a balance you can top up from your personal bank account while on the road.

Exchanging Money

Changing foreign currency (or travellers cheques, if you're still using them) is usually no problem at banks throughout Australia, or at licensed money changers such as Travelex or Amex in cities and major towns.

Taxes & Refunds

Goods & Services Tax (GST) The GST is a flat 10% tax on all goods and services: accommodation, eating out, transport, electrical and other goods, books, furniture, clothing etc. There are exceptions, however, such as basic foods (milk, bread, fruit and vegetables etc). By law the tax is included in the quoted or shelf price, so all prices are GST-inclusive. International air and sea travel to/from Australia is GST-free, as is domestic air travel when purchased outside Australia by nonresidents.

Refund of GST If you purchase goods with a total minimum value of $300 from any one supplier no more than 30 days before you leave Australia, you are entitled under the Tourist Refund Scheme (TRS) to a refund of any GST paid. The scheme only applies to goods you take with you as hand luggage or wear onto the plane or ship. Also note that the refund is valid for goods bought from more than one supplier, but only if at least $300 is spent in each. For more info, see the website of the **Australian Customs & Border Protection Service** (☎1300 363 263, 02-6275 6666; www.customs.gov.au).

Income Tax Visitors entitled to work pay tax on earnings made within Australia, and must lodge a tax return with the Australian Taxation Office (ATO). If too much tax was withheld from your pay, you will receive a refund. See the **Australian Taxation Office** (www.ato.gov.au) website for details.

Travellers Cheques

➡ The ubiquity and convenience of internationally linked credit- and debit-card facilities in Australia means that travellers cheques are virtually redundant.

➡ Amex and Travelex will exchange their associated travellers cheques, and major banks will change travellers cheques also.

➡ In all instances you'll need to present your passport for identification when cashing them.

Opening Hours

Business hours vary from state to state, but use the following as a guide. Note that nearly all attractions across Australia are closed on Christmas Day; many also close on New Years Day and Good Friday.

Banks 9.30am to 4pm Monday to Thursday; until 5pm on Friday. Some large city branches open 8am to 6pm weekdays; a few also till 9pm Friday.

Cafes All-day affairs opening from around 7am until around 5pm, or continuing their business into the night.

Petrol stations and roadhouses Usually open 8am to 10pm. Some urban service stations open 24 hours.

Post offices 9am to 5pm Monday to Friday; some from 9am to noon on Saturday. You can also buy stamps from newsagents and some delis.

Pubs Usually serve food from noon to 2pm and from 6pm to 8pm. Pubs and bars often open for drinking at lunchtime and continue well into the evening, particularly from Thursday to Saturday.

Restaurants Open around noon for lunch and from 6pm for dinner, typically serving until at least 2pm and 9pm respectively, often later. Big-city eateries keep longer hours.

Shops and businesses 9am to 5pm or 6pm Monday to Friday, until either noon or 5pm on Saturday. Sunday trading operates in major cities, urban areas and tourist towns. There is late-night shopping till 9pm in major towns (usually Thursday or Friday night).

Supermarkets Generally open from 7am until at least 8pm; some open 24 hours. Delis (general stores) also open late.

Photography

Availability and printing If you're not happily snapping away with your smartphone, digital cameras, memory sticks and batteries are sold prolifically in cities and urban centres. Try electronics stores (Dick Smith, Tandy) or the larger department stores. Many internet cafes, camera stores and large stationers (Officeworks, Harvey Norman) have printing facilities.

Books Check out Lonely Planet's *Travel Photography* guide.

Etiquette As in any country, politeness goes a long way when taking photographs; ask before taking pictures of people. Particularly bear in mind that for Indigenous Australians, photography can be highly intrusive: photographing cultural places, practices and images, sites of significance and ceremonies may also be a sensitive matter. Always ask first.

Post

Australia Post (www.auspost.com.au) runs very reliable national and worldwide postal services; see the website for info on international delivery zones and rates. All post offices will hold mail for visitors: you need to provide some form of identification (such as a passport or driver's licence) to collect mail.

Public Holidays

Timing of public holidays can vary from state to state: check locally for precise dates. Some holidays are only observed locally within a state; where this is the case, the relevant town, city or region is also listed.

National

New Year's Day 1 January

Australia Day 26 January

Easter (Good Friday to Easter Monday inclusive) late March/early April

Anzac Day 25 April

Queen's Birthday (except WA) Second Monday in June

Queen's Birthday (WA) Last Monday in September

Christmas Day 25 December

Boxing Day 26 December

Australian Capital Territory

Canberra Day Second Monday in March

Bank Holiday First Monday in August

Labour Day First Monday in October

New South Wales

Bank Holiday First Monday in August

Labour Day First Monday in October

Northern Territory

May Day First Monday in May

Show Day First Friday in July (Alice Springs); second Friday in July (Tennant Creek); third Friday in July (Katherine); fourth Friday in July (Darwin)

Picnic Day First Monday in August

Queensland

Labour Day First Monday in May

Royal Queensland Show Day Second or third Wednesday in August (Brisbane)

South Australia

Adelaide Cup Day Third Monday in May

Labour Day First Monday in October

Proclamation Day Last Monday or Tuesday in December

Tasmania

Regatta Day 14 February (Hobart)

Launceston Cup Day Last Wednesday in February

Eight Hours Day First Monday in March

Bank Holiday Tuesday following Easter Monday

King Island Show First Tuesday in March

Launceston Show Day Thursday preceding second Saturday in October

Hobart Show Day Thursday preceding fourth Saturday in October

Recreation Day First Monday in November (Northern Tasmania)

Victoria

Labour Day Second Monday in March

Melbourne Cup Day First Tuesday in November

Western Australia

Labour Day First Monday in March

Foundation Day First Monday in June

School Holidays

➡ The Christmas/summer school-holiday season runs from mid-December to late January.

➡ Three shorter school-holiday periods occur during the year, varying by a week or two from state to state. They fall roughly from early to mid-April (usually including Easter), late June to mid-July, and late September to early October.

Safe Travel

Australia is a relatively safe place to travel by world standards – in terms of crime and war, at any rate – but natural disasters regularly wreak havoc. Bushfires, floods and cyclones decimate parts of most states and territories, but if you pay attention to warnings from local authorities and don't venture into affected areas, you should be fine.

GOVERNMENT TRAVEL ADVICE

The following government websites offer travel advisories and information on current hotspots.

Australian Department of Foreign Affairs & Trade (www.smarttraveller.gov.au)

British Foreign & Commonwealth Office (www.gov.uk/fco)

Government of Canada (www.travel.gc.ca)

US State Department (www.travel.state.gov)

Telephone

Australia's main telecommunication companies:

Telstra (☎13 22 00; www.telstra.com.au)

Optus (☎1800 780 219; www.optus.com.au)

Vodafone (☎1300 650 410; www.vodafone.com.au)

Virgin (☎1300 555 100; www.virginmobile.com.au)

Toll-Free & Information Calls

➡ Many businesses have either a toll-free ☎1800 number, dialled from anywhere within Australia for free, or a ☎13 or ☎1300 number, charged at a local call rate. None of these numbers can be dialled from outside Australia (and often can't be dialled from mobile phones within Australia).

➡ To make a reverse-charge (collect) call from any public or private phone, dial ☎1800 738 3773 or ☎12 550.

➡ Numbers starting with 190 are usually recorded information services, charged at anything from 35c to $5 or more per minute (more from mobiles and payphones).

International Calls

From payphones Most payphones allow International Subscriber Dialling (ISD) calls, the cost and international dialling code of which will vary depending on which international phonecard provider you are using. International phonecards are readily available from internet cafes and convenience stores.

From landlines International calls from landlines in Australia are also relatively cheap and often subject to special deals; rates vary with providers.

Codes When calling overseas you will need to dial the international access code from Australia (☎0011 or ☎0018), the country code and then the area code (without the initial ☎0). So for a London telephone number you'll need to dial ☎0011-44-20, then the number. In addition, certain operators will have you dial a special code to access their service. If dialling Australia from overseas, the country code is ☎61 and you need to drop the ☎0 in state/territory area codes. Other country codes:

COUNTRY	CODE
France	33
Germany	49
Ireland	353
Japan	81
Netherlands	31
New Zealand	64
UK	44
USA & Canada	1

Local Calls

Local calls from private phones cost up to 30c, depending on the provider; local calls from public phones cost 50c. Calls to mobile phones attract higher rates and are timed.

Long-Distance Calls & Area Codes

Long-distance calls (over around 50km) are timed. Australia uses four Subscriber Trunk Dialling (STD) area codes. These STD calls can be made from any public phone and are cheaper during off-peak hours (generally between 7pm and 7am, and on weekends). Broadly, the main area codes are as follows.

STATE/ TERRITORY	AREA CODE
ACT	02
NSW	02
NT	08
QLD	07
SA	08
TAS	03
VIC	03
WA	08

Area-code boundaries don't necessarily coincide with state borders; for example some parts of NSW use the neighbouring states' codes.

Mobile (Cell) Phones

Numbers Numbers with the prefix 04xx belong to mobile phones.

Networks Australia's digital network is compatible with GSM 900 and 1800 (used in Europe), but generally not with the systems used in the USA or Japan.

Reception Australia's mobile networks service more than 90% of the population but leave vast tracts of the country uncovered.

Prioviders It's easy enough to get connected short-term: the main service providers (Telstra, Optus, Virgin and Vodafone) all have prepaid mobile systems. Buy a starter kit, which may include a phone or, if you have your own phone, a SIM card and a prepaid charge card. Shop around for the best offer.

Phonecards & Public Phones

Phonecards A variety of phonecards can be bought at newsagents, hostels and post offices for a fixed dollar value (usually $10, $20 etc) and can be used with any public or private phone by dialling a toll-free access number and then the PIN number on the card. Shop around.

Public Phones Most public phones use phonecards; some also accept credit cards. Old-fashioned coin-operated public phones are becoming increasingly rare (and if you do find one, chances are the coin slot will be gummed up or vandalised beyond function).

Time

Zones Australia is divided into three time zones: Western Standard Time (GMT/UTC plus eight hours), covering WA; Central Standard Time (plus 9½ hours), covering SA and the NT; and Eastern Standard Time (plus 10 hours), covering Tasmania, Victoria, NSW, the ACT and Queensland. There are minor exceptions – Broken Hill (NSW), for instance, is on Central Standard Time. For international times, see www.timeanddate.com/worldclock.

Daylight saving Clocks are put forward an hour. This system operates in some states during the warmer months (October to early April), but things can get pretty confusing. Queensland, WA and the NT stay on standard time, while in Tasmania daylight saving starts a month earlier than in SA, Victoria, ACT and NSW.

Toilets

➡ Toilets in Australia are sit-down Western-style (though you mightn't find this prospect too appealing in some remote outback pit stops).

➡ See www.toiletmap.gov.au for public-toilet locations, including diabled-access toilets.

Tourist Information

The **Australian Tourist Commission** (www.australia.com) is the national government tourist body, and has a good website for pretrip research. The website also lists reliable travel agents in countries around the world to help you plan your trip, plus visa, work and customs information.

Within Australia, tourist information is disseminated by various regional and local offices. Almost every major town in Australia has a tourist office of some type and they can be super-helpful, with chatty staff (often retiree volunteers) providing local info not readily available from the state offices. If booking accommodation or tours from local offices, bear in mind that they often only promote businesses that are paying members of the local tourist association.

Travellers with Disabilities

➡ Disability awareness in Australia is high and getting higher.

➡ Legislation requires that new accommodation meets accessibility standards for mobility-impaired travellers, and discrimination by tourism operators is illegal.

➡ Many of Australia's key attractions, including many national parks, provide access for those with limited mobility and a number of sites also address the needs of visitors with visual or aural impairments. Contact attractions in advance to confirm the facilities.

- Tour operators with vehicles catering to mobility-impaired travellers operate from most capital cities.
- Facilities for wheelchairs are improving in accommodation, but there are still many older establishments where the necessary upgrades haven't been done.

Resources

Deaf Australia (www.deafau.org.au)

e-Bility (www.ebility.com)

Lonely Planet's Accessible Melbourne (www.lonelyplanet.com/accessible-melbourne)

National Information Communication & Awareness Network (Nican; ☎02-6241 1220, TTY 1800 806 769; www.nican.com.au)

Spinal Cord Injuries Australia (SCIA; ☎1800 819 775; www.spinalcordinjuries.com.au)

Vision Australia (☎1300 847 466; www.visionaustralia.org)

Air Travel

Qantas (www.qantas.com.au) entitles a disabled person with high-support needs and the carer travelling with them to a discount on full economy fares; contact Nican for eligibility info and an application form. Guide dogs travel for free on **Qantas**, **Jetstar** (www.jetstar.com.au), **Virgin Australia** (www.virginaustralia.com.au) and their affiliated carriers. All of Australia's major airports have dedicated parking spaces, wheelchair access to terminals, accessible toilets, and skychairs to convey passengers onto planes via airbridges.

Train Travel

In NSW, CountryLink's XPT trains have at least one carriage (usually the buffet car) with a seat removed for a wheelchair, and an accessible toilet. Queensland Rail's Tilt Train from Brisbane to Cairns has a wheelchair-accessible carriage.

Melbourne's suburban rail network is accessible and guide dogs and hearing dogs are permitted on all public transport in Victoria. **Metlink** (☎1800 800 007; www.ptv.vic.gov.au) offers a free travel pass to visually impaired people and wheelchair users for transport around Melbourne.

Visas

All visitors to Australia need a visa (only New Zealand nationals are exempt, and even they receive a 'special category' visa on arrival). Application forms for the several types of visa are available from Australian diplomatic missions overseas, travel agents or the website of the **Department of Immigration & Citizenship** (www.immi.gov.au). Visa types are as follows.

eVisitor (651)

- Many European passport holders are eligible for a free eVisitor visa, allowing stays in Australia for up to three months within a 12-month period.
- eVisitor visas must be applied for online (www.immi.gov.au/e_visa/evisitor.htm). They are electronically stored and linked to individual passport numbers, so no stamp in your passport is required.
- It's advisable to apply at least 14 days prior to the proposed date of travel to Australia.

Electronic Travel Authority (ETA; 601)

- Passport holders from eight countries which aren't part of the eVisitor scheme – Brunei, Canada, Hong Kong, Japan, Malaysia, Singapore, South Korea and the USA – can apply for either a visitor or business ETA.
- ETAs are valid for 12 months, with stays of up to three months on each visit.
- You can apply for an ETA online (www.eta.immi.gov.au), which attracts a nonrefundable service charge of $20.

Visitor (600)

- Short-term Visitor visas have largely been replaced by the eVisitor and ETA. However, if you are from a country not covered by either, or you want to stay longer than three months, you'll need to apply for a Visitor visa.
- Standard Visitor visas allow one entry for a stay of up to three, six or 12 months, and are valid for use within 12 months of issue.
- Apply online at www.immi.gov.au; costs range from $130 to $335.

Visa Extensions

If you want to stay in Australia for longer than your visa allows, you'll need to apply for a new visa (usually a $335 Visitor visa 600) via www.immi.gov.au. Apply at least two or three weeks before your visa expires.

Working Holiday (417)

- Young visitors (aged 18 to 30) from Belgium, Canada, Cyprus, Denmark, Estonia, Finland, France, Germany, Hong Kong, Ireland, Italy, Japan, South Korea, Malta, Netherlands, Norway, Sweden, Taiwan and the UK are eligible for a Working Holiday visa, which allows you to visit for up to 12 months and gain casual employment.
- Holders can leave and re-enter Australia any number of times within that 12 months.
- Holders can only work for any one employer for a maximum of six months.
- Apply prior to entry to Australia (up to a year in advance) – you can't change from another tourist visa to a Working Holiday visa once you're in Australia.

➡ Conditions include having a return air ticket or sufficient funds ($5000) for a return or onward fare. Application fee $420.

➡ Second Working Holiday visas can be applied for once you're in Australia, subject to certain conditions: see www.immi.gov.au/visas/pages/417.aspx. Application fee $420.

Work & Holiday (462)

➡ Nationals from Argentina, Bangladesh, Chile, Indonesia, Malaysia, Poland, Portugal, Spain, Thailand, Turkey, the USA and Uruguay aged between the ages of 18 and 30 can apply for a Work & Holiday visa prior to entry to Australia.

➡ Once granted, this visa allows the holder to enter Australia within three months of issue, stay for up to 12 months, leave and re-enter Australia any number of times within that 12 months, undertake temporary employment to supplement a trip, and study for up to four months.

➡ For details see www.immi.gov.au/visas/pages/462.aspx. Application fee $420.

Volunteering

Lonely Planet's *Volunteer: A Traveller's Guide to Making a Difference Around the World* provides useful information about volunteering.

See also the following websites:

Australian Volunteers International (www.australianvolunteers.com) Places skilled volunteers into Indigenous communities in northern and central Australia (mostly long-term placements). Occasional short-term unskilled opportunities too, helping out at community-run roadhouses.

Conservation Volunteers Australia (www.conservationvolunteers.com.au) Nonprofit organisation involved in tree planting, walking-track construction, and flora and fauna surveys.

Earthwatch Institute Australia (www.earthwatch.org) Volunteer expeditions that focus on conservation and wildlife.

GoVolunteer (www.govolunteer.com.au) Thousands of volunteering opportunities around the country.

i to i Volunteering (www.i-to-i.com) Conservation-based volunteer holidays in Australia.

Responsible Travel (www.responsibletravel.com) Travel to Australia and take up a fixed-term volunteering position when you arrive.

STA (www.statravel.com.au) Volunteer holiday opportunities in Australia; click on 'Planning' on the website then the volunteering link.

Volunteering Australia (www.volunteeringaustralia.org) State-by-state listings of volunteering opportunities around Australia.

Willing Workers on Organic Farms (WWOOF; www.wwoof.com.au) WWOOFing is where you do a few hours work each day on a farm in return for bed and board. Most hosts are concerned to some extent with alternative lifestyles, and have a minimum stay of two nights. Join online for $70. You'll get a membership number and a booklet listing participating enterprises ($5 overseas postage).

Women Travellers

Australia is generally a safe place for women travellers, although the usual sensible precautions apply.

Night-time Avoid walking alone late at night in any of the major cities and towns – keep enough money aside for a taxi back to your accommodation.

Pubs Be wary of staying in basic pub accommodation unless it looks safe and well managed.

Sexual harassment Rare, though some macho Aussie males still slip – particularly when they've been drinking.

Rural areas Stereotypically, the further you get from the big cities, the less enlightened your average Aussie male is probably going to be about women's issues. Having said that, many women travellers say that they have met the friendliest, most down-to-earth blokes in outback pubs and remote roadhouse stops.

Hitchhiking Hitching is not recommended for anyone. Even when travelling in pairs, exercise caution at all times.

Drugged drinks Some pubs in Sydney and other big cities post warnings about drugged or 'spiked' drinks: probably not cause for paranoia, but play it safe if someone offers you a drink in a bar.

Work

If you come to Australia on a tourist visa then you're not allowed to work for pay: you'll need a Working Holiday (417) or Work and Holiday (462) visa – visit www.immi.gov.au for details.

Backpacker magazines, newspapers and hostel noticeboards are good places to find local work opportunities. Casual work can often be found during peak season at the major tourist centres: places such as Alice Springs, Cairns and resort towns along the Queensland coast, and the ski fields of Victoria and NSW are all good prospects during holiday season. Other possibilities for casual employment include factory work, labouring, bar work, waiting tables, domestic chores at outback roadhouses, nanny work, working as a station hand and collecting for charities. People with computer, secretarial, nursing and teaching skills can find work temping in the major cities by registering with a relevant agency.

See also the following websites, good for opportunities in metropoliotan areas:

Adzuna (www.adzuna.com.au)

Career One (www.careerone.com.au)

Gumtree (www.gumtree.com.au)

Seek (www.seek.com.au)

TAW (www.taw.com.au)

Seasonal Work

Seasonal fruit picking (harvesting) relies on casual labour – there's always something that needs to be picked, pruned or farmed somewhere in Australia all year round. It's definitely hard work, involving early-morning starts, and you're usually paid by how much you pick (per bin, bucket, kilo etc). Expect to earn about $50 to $60 a day to start with; more when your skills and speed improve. Some work, such as pruning or sorting, is paid at around $15 per hour. Call the **National Harvest Telephone Information Service** (☎1800 062 332) for more information about when and where you're likely to pick up this sort of work.

Note that due to the complexities of visa situations, many local visitor information centres and backpacker hostels are stepping away from assisting travellers in finding work. To avoid disappointment, never put a deposit down to reserve a fruit-picking job, and never pay for fruit-picking accommodation in advance.

Additional resources:

Harvest Trail (www.jobsearch.gov.au/harvesttrail) Harvest job specialists.

QITE (www.qite.com) Nonprofit Queensland employment agency operating around Cairns, Innisfail and the Atherton Tablelands.

Viterra (www.viterra.com.au) Seasonal grain-harvest jobs in Victoria and SA (October to January).

Workabout Australia (www.workaboutaustralia.com.au) Gives a state-by-state breakdown of seasonal work opportunities.

Seasonal Work Hotspots

NSW The NSW ski fields have seasonal work during the ski season, particularly around Thredbo. There's also harvest work around Narrabri and Moree, and grape picking in the Hunter Valley. Fruit picking happens near Tenterfield, Orange and Young.

NT The majority of working-holiday opportunities in the NT for backpackers are in fruit picking, station handing, labouring and hospitality.

Queensland Queensland has vast tracts of farmland and orchards: there's fruit picking work to be found around Stanthorpe, Childers, Bundaberg and Cairns. Those looking for sturdier (and much better-paying) work should keep an eye on mining opportunities in mining towns such as Weipa and Cloncurry.

SA Good seasonal-work opportunities can be found on the Fleurieu Peninsula, in the Coonawarra region and Barossa Valley (wineries), and along the Murray River around Berri (fruit picking).

Tasmania The apple orchards in the south, especially around Cygnet and Huonville, are your best bet for work in Tassie.

Victoria Harvest work in Mildura and Shepparton.

WA In Perth, plenty of temporary work is available in tourism and hospitality, administration, IT, nursing, child care, factories and labouring. Outside of Perth, travellers can easily get jobs in tourism and hospitality, plus a variety of seasonal work. For grape-picking work, head for the vineyards around Margaret River.

Tax

TAX FILE NUMBER

If you're working in Australia, you should apply for a Tax File Number (TFN). Without it, tax will be deducted at the maximum rate from any wages you receive. Apply for a TFN online via the **Australian Taxation Office** (www.ato.gov.au); it takes up to four weeks to be issued.

PAYING TAX & TAX REFUNDS

Even with a TFN, nonresidents (including Working Holiday visa holders) pay a considerably higher rate of tax than most Australian residents. For a start, there's no tax-free threshold – you pay tax on every dollar you earn.

Because you have been paid wages in Australia, you must lodge a tax return with the ATO: see the website for info on how to do this, including getting a Payment Summary (an official summary of your earnings and tax payments) from your employer, timing/dates for lodging your tax return, and how to receive your Notice of Assessment.

Bear in mind that you're not entitled to a refund for the tax you paid – you will only receive a refund if too much tax was withheld from your pay. If you didn't pay enough while you were working then you will have to pay more. You are, however, entitled to any superannuation that you have accumulated.

Transport

GETTING THERE & AWAY

Australia is a long way from just about everywhere – getting there usually means a long-haul flight. If you're short on time on the ground, consider internal flights – they're affordable (compared with petrol and car-hire costs), can usually be carbon offset, and will save you some *looong* days in the saddle. Flights, tours and rail tickets can be booked online at www.lonelyplanet.com/bookings.

Entering the Country

Arrival in Australia is usually straightforward and efficient, with the usual customs declarations. There are no restrictions for citizens of any particular foreign countries entering Australia – if you have a current passport and visa, you should be fine.

Air

High season (with the highest prices) for flights into Australia is roughly over the country's summer (December to February); low season generally tallies with the winter months (June to August), though this is actually peak season in central Australia and the Top End. Australia's international carrier is **Qantas** (www.qantas.com.au).

International Airports

Australia has numerous international gateways, with Sydney and Melbourne being the busiest.

Adelaide Airport (www.adelaideairport.com.au)

Brisbane Airport (www.bne.com.au)

Cairns Airport (www.cairnsairport.com)

Darwin International Airport (www.darwinairport.com.au)

Gold Coast Airport (www.goldcoastairport.com.au)

Melbourne Airport (www.melbourneairport.com.au)

Perth Airport (www.perthairport.com)

Sydney Airport (www.sydneyairport.com.au).

Sea

It's possible (though by no means easy or safe) to make your way between Australia and countries such as Papua New Guinea, Indonesia, New Zealand and the Pacific islands by hitching rides or crewing on yachts; usually you have to at least contribute towards food. Ask around at marinas and sailing clubs in places like Coffs Harbour, Great Keppel Island, Airlie Beach, the Whitsundays, Darwin and Cairns. April is a good time to look for a berth in the Sydney area.

Alternatively, **P&O Cruises** (www.pocruises.com.au) operates holiday cruises

CLIMATE CHANGE & TRAVEL

Every form of transport that relies on carbon-based fuel generates CO_2, the main cause of human-induced climate change. Modern travel is dependent on aeroplanes, which might use less fuel per kilometre per person than most cars but travel much greater distances. The altitude at which aircraft emit gases (including CO_2) and particles also contributes to their climate change impact. Many websites offer 'carbon calculators' that allow people to estimate the carbon emissions generated by their journey and, for those who wish to do so, to offset the impact of the greenhouse gases emitted with contributions to portfolios of climate-friendly initiatives throughout the world. Lonely Planet offsets the carbon footprint of all staff and author travel.

between Brisbane, Melbourne or Sydney and destinations in New Zealand and the Pacific. Even more alternatively, some freighter ships allow passengers to travel on-board as they ship cargo to/from Australia; check out websites such as www.freighterexpeditions.com.au and www.freightercruises.com for options.

GETTING AROUND

Air

Airlines in Australia

Australia's main domestic airlines are **Qantas** (www.qantas.com.au) and **Virgin Australia** (www.virginaustralia.com.au), servicing all the main centres with regular flights. **Jetstar** (www.jetstar.com.au), a subsidiary of Qantas, and **Tiger Airways** (www.tigerair.com), a subsidiary of Singapore Airlines, are generally a bit cheaper and fly between most Australian capital cities. See regional chapters for info on airlines operating locally within Australia's states and territories.

Air Passes

Qantas offers a discount-fare Walkabout Air Pass for passengers flying into Australia across the Pacific with Qantas or American Airlines. The pass allows you to link up around 60 domestic Australian destinations for less than you'd pay booking flights individually. See www.qantas.com.au/travel/airlines/air-pass/us/en for details.

Bicycle

Australia has much to offer cyclists, from bike paths winding through most major cities to thousands of kilometres of good country roads. There's lots of flat countryside and gently rolling hills to explore and, although Australia is not as mountainous as, say, Switzerland or France, mountain bikers can find plenty of forest trails and high country. If you're really keen, outback cycling might also be an option.

Hire Bike hire in cities is easy.

Legalities Bike helmets are compulsory in all states and territories, as are white front-lights and red rear-lights for riding at night.

Maps You can get by with standard road maps, but to avoid low-grade unsealed roads, the government series is best. The 1:250,000 scale is suitable, though you'll need lots of maps if you're going far. The next scale up is 1:1,000,000.

Transport If you're bringing in your own bike, check with your airline for costs and the degree of dismantling or packing required. Within Australia, bus companies require you to dismantle your bike and it may not travel on the same bus as you.

Weather In summer carry plenty of water. Wear a helmet with a peak (or a cap under your helmet), use sunscreen and avoid cycling in the middle of the day. Beware summer northerly winds that can make a northbound cyclist's life hell. Southeasterly trade winds blow in April, when you can have (theoretically) tail winds all the way to Darwin. It can get very cold in Victoria, Tasmania, southern South Australia (SA) and the New South Wales (NSW) mountains.

Information

The national cycling body is the **Bicycle Federation of Australia** (www.bfa.asn.au). Each state and territory has a touring organisation that can also help with cycling information and put you in touch with touring clubs. **Bicycles Network Australia** (www.bicycles.net.au) offers information, news and links.

Bicycle Network Tasmania (www.biketas.org.au)

Bicycle Network Victoria (www.bicyclenetwork.com.au)

Bicycle NSW (www.bicyclensw.org.au)

Bicycle Queensland (www.bq.org.au)

Bicycle Transportation Alliance (www.btawa.org.au) In WA.

Bike SA (www.bikesa.asn.au)

Cycling Northern Territory (www.nt.cycling.org.au)

Pedal Power ACT (www.pedalpower.org.au)

Buying a Bike

If you want to buy a reliable, new road or mountain bike, your bottom-level starting price will be around $600. Throw in all the requisite on-the-road equipment (panniers, helmet etc), and your starting point becomes around $1600. Secondhand bikes are worth checking out in the cities, as are the post-Christmas sales and mid-year stocktakes, when newish cycles can be heavily discounted.

To sell your bike (or buy a secondhand one), try hostel noticeboards or online at **Trading Post** (www.tradingpost.com.au) or **Gumtree** (www.gumtree.com.au).

Boat

There's a hell of a lot of water around Australia, but unless you're fortunate/skilled/well-connected enough to land a position crewing a yacht, it's not really a feasible way of getting around. Other than short-hop regional ferries (eg to Kangaroo Island in SA, Rottnest Island in Western Australia (WA), Bruny Island in Tasmania, North Stradbroke Island in Queensland), the only long-range passenger services are the two high-speed, vehicle-carrying **Spirit of Tasmania** (☎1800 634 906; www.spiritoftasmania.com.au; ⊙customer contact centre 8am-8.30pm Mon-Sat, 9am-8pm Sun) boats between Melbourne and Devonport on Tasmania's northwest coast.

Bus

Australia's extensive bus network is a reliable way to get around, though bus travel

Principal Bus Routes & Railways

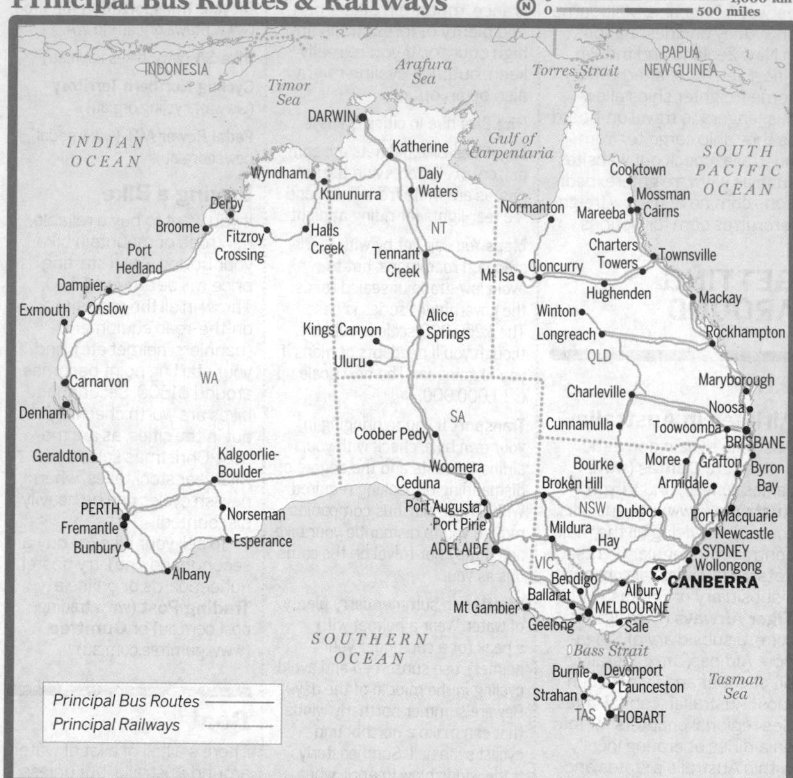

isn't always cheaper than flying and it can be tedious over huge distances. Most buses are equipped with air-con, toilets and videos; all are smoke free. There are no class divisions on Australian buses and the vehicles of the different companies all look pretty similar.

Small towns eschew formal bus terminals for a single drop-off/pick-up point (post office, newsagent etc).

Greyhound Australia (www.greyhound.com.au) runs a national network (notably not across the Nullarbor Plain between Adelaide and Perth, nor Perth to Broome). Book online for the cheapest fares.

Other operators:

Firefly Express (www.fireflyexpress.com.au) Runs between Sydney, Canberra, Melbourne and Adelaide.

Integrity Coach Lines (www.integritycoachlines.com.au) The main operator between Perth and Broome in WA.

Premier Motor Service (www.premierms.com.au) Greyhound's main competitor along the east coast.

V/Line (www.vline.com.au) Connects Victoria with NSW, SA and the Australian Capital Territory (ACT).

Greyhound Bus Passes

Greyhound offers a slew of passes geared towards various types and routes of travel: see www.greyhound.com.au/passes for details. Greyhound also offers a discount of up to 10% for members of YHA, VIP, ISIC and other approved organisations.

KILOMETRE PASS

These are the simplest passes, giving you specified amounts of travel starting at 1000km ($189), ascending in increments to a maximum of 25,000km ($2675). A 5000km pass costs $785; 10,000km is $1435. Passes are valid for 12 months, and you can travel where and in whatever direction you please, stopping as many times as you like. Use the online kilometre calculator to figure out which pass suits you. Book at least a day ahead to secure your seat.

HOP-ON, HOP-OFF & SHORT HOP PASSES

These passes allow you to traverse popular routes,

mostly along the east coast but also between Cairns and Alice Springs and Adelaide and Darwin via Alice Springs. Travel is in one direction, and you can jump on and off buses as many times as you like. Passes are valid for three months once travel begins, with six months in which to get started. Typical prices:

- Adelaide to Alice Springs $209
- Alice Springs to Darwin $199
- Cairns to Alice Springs $369
- Melbourne to Cairns $509
- Sydney to Cairns $419

See also **Oz Experience** (☎1300 300 028; www.ozexperience.com), a backpacker travel option utilising Greyhound services.

Costs

Following are the average one-way bus fares along some well-travelled routes, booked online:

ROUTE	ADULT/ CHILD
Adelaide–Darwin	$490/420
Adelaide–Melbourne	$105/85
Brisbane–Cairns	$310/270
Cairns–Sydney	$500/430
Sydney–Brisbane	$190/160
Sydney–Melbourne	$135/115

Car & Motorcycle

Driving Licence

To drive in Australia you'll need to hold a current driving licence issued in English from your home country. If the licence isn't in English, you'll also need to carry an International Driving Permit, issued in your home country.

Choosing a Vehicle

2WD Depending on where you want to travel, a regulation 2WD vehicle might suffice. They're cheaper to hire, buy and run than 4WDs and are more readily available. Most are fuel efficient, and easy to repair and sell. Downsides: no off-road capability and no room to sleep!

4WD Four-wheel drives are good for outback travel as they can access almost any track you get a hankering for. And there might even be space to sleep in the back. Downsides: poor fuel economy, awkward to park and more expensive to hire/buy.

Campervan Creature comforts at your fingertips: sink, fridge, cupboards, beds, kitchen and space to relax. Downsides: slow and often not fuel-efficient, not great on dirt roads and too big for nipping around the city.

Motorcycle The Australian climate is great for riding, and bikes are handy in city traffic. Downsides: Australia isn't particularly bike friendly in terms of driver awareness, there's limited luggage capacity, and exposure to the elements.

Ride-Sharing

Ride-sharing is a good way to split costs and environmental impact with other travellers. Noticeboards are good places to find ads; also check the online classifieds following:

Catch a Lift (www.catchalift.com)

Coseats (www.coseats.com)

Need a Ride (www.needaride.com.au)

Buying a Vehicle

Buying your own vehicle to travel around in gives you the freedom to go where and when the mood takes you, and may work out cheaper than renting in the long run. Downsides include dealing with confusing and expensive registration, roadworthy certificates and insurance; forking out for maintenance and repairs; and selling the vehicle, which may be more difficult than expected.

If you're buying a secondhand vehicle, keep in mind the hidden costs: stamp duty, registration, transfer fee, insurance and maintenance.

WHAT TO LOOK FOR

It's prudent to have a car checked by an independent expert: auto clubs offer vehicle checks, and road transport authorities have lists of licensed garages.

ONLINE

Private and dealer car sales are listed online on websites such as **Car Sales** (www.carsales.com.au), the **Trading Post** (www.tradingpost.com.au) and **Gumtree** (www.gumtree.com.au).

PRIVATE ADS

Buying privately can be time-consuming, and you'll have to travel around to assess your options. But you should expect a lower price than that charged by a licensed dealer. The seller should provide you with a roadworthy certificate (if required in the state you're in), but you won't get a cooling-off period or a statutory warranty.

It's your responsibility to ensure the car isn't stolen and that there's no money owing on it: check the car's details with the **Personal Property Securities Register** (☎1300 007 777; www.ppsr.gov.au).

Hostel noticeboards and the Thorn Tree travel forum at www.lonelyplanet.com are good places to find vehicles for sale. Tour desks also often have noticeboards.

DEALERS

Licenced car dealers are obliged to guarantee that no money is owing on the car. Depending on the age of the car and the kilometres travelled, you may also receive a statutory warranty. You will need to sign an agreement for sale; make sure you understand what it says before you sign. Some dealers will sell you a car with an undertaking to buy it back at an agreed price, but don't accept verbal guarantees – get it in writing.

Sydney to Melbourne via the Princes Hwy

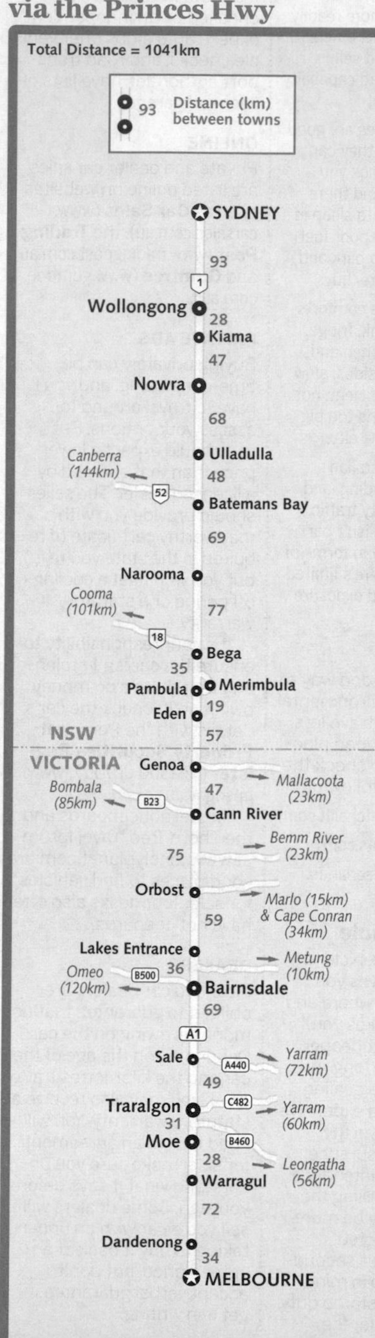

TRAVELLERS' MARKETS

Cairns, Sydney, Darwin and Perth (cities where travellers commonly begin or finish their travels) are the best places to buy or sell a vehicle, especially Cairns. It's possible these cars have been around Australia several times, so it can be a risky option.

Sydney Travellers Car Market (☎02-9331 4361; www.sydneytravellerscarmarket.com.au; Level 2, Kings Cross Car Park, Ward Ave, Kings Cross; ⏰10am-4.30pm Mon-Sun; 🚉Kings Cross)

PAPERWORK

Registration When you buy a vehicle in Australia, you need to transfer the registration into your own name within 14 days. Each state has slightly different requirements and different organisations that do this. Similarly, when selling a vehicle you need to advise the state or territory road-transport authority of the sale and change of name. In NSW, Northern Territory (NT), Queensland, Tasmania, Victoria and WA, the buyer and seller need to complete and sign a Transfer of Registration form. In the ACT and SA there is no form, but the buyer and seller need to complete and sign the reverse of the registration certificate.

Roadworthy certificate If the vehicle you're considering doesn't have a roadworthy certificate, it's worth having a roadworthiness check done before you buy it. This can cost upwards of $100 but can save you money on hidden costs. Road-transport authorities have lists of licensed vehicle testers. Sellers are required to provide a roadworthy certificate when transferring registration in the following situations:

- ACT – once the vehicle is six years old
- NSW – once the vehicle is five years old
- NT – once the vehicle is three years old
- Queensland – Safety Certificate required for all vehicles
- Victoria – Certificate of Roadworthiness required for all vehicles
- WA, SA and Tasmania – no inspections/certificates required in most circumstances

Gas certificate In Queensland, if a vehicle runs on gas, a gas certificate must be provided by the seller in order to transfer the registration. In the ACT, vehicles running on gas require an annual inspection.

Immobiliser fitting In WA it's compulsory to have an approved immobiliser fitted to most vehicles (not motorcycles) before transfer of registration; this is the buyer's responsibility.

Changing state of registration Note that registering a vehicle in a different state to the one it was previously registered in can be difficult, time-consuming and expensive.

Renewing registration Registration is paid annually Australia-wide, but most states/territories also give you the option of renewing it for six and sometimes three months.

ROAD TRANSPORT AUTHORITIES

For more information about processes and costs:

Department of Planning, Transport & Infrastructure (☎1300 872 677; www.dpti.sa.gov.au) SA.

Department of State Growth – Transport (☎1300 851 225; www.transport.tas.gov.au) Tasmania.

Department of Transport (☎1300 654 628; www.transport.nt.gov.au) NT.

Department of Transport (☎13 11 56; www.transport.wa.gov.au) WA.

Department of Transport & Main Roads (☎13 23 80; www.tmr.qld.gov.au) Queensland.

Roads & Maritime Services (☎13 22 13; www.rta.nsw.gov.au) NSW.

Road Transport Authority (☎13 22 81; www.rego.act.gov) ACT.

VicRoads (☎13 11 71; www.vicroads.vic.gov.au) Victoria.

Renting a Vehicle

Larger car-rental companies have drop-offs in major cities and towns. Most companies require drivers to be over the age of 21, though in some cases it's 18 and in others 25.

Suggestions to assist in the process:

➡ Read the contract cover to cover.

➡ Bond: some companies may require a signed credit-card slip, others may actually charge your credit card; if this is the case, find out when you'll get a refund.

➡ Ask if unlimited kilometres are included and, if not, what the extra charge per kilometre is.

➡ Find out what excess you'll have to pay if you have a crash, and if it can be lowered by an extra charge per day (this option will usually be offered to you whether you ask or not). Check if your personal travel insurance covers you for vehicle accidents and excess.

➡ Check for exclusions (hitting a kangaroo, damage on unsealed roads etc) and whether you're covered on unavoidable unsealed roads (eg accessing camp sites). Some companies also exclude parts of the car from cover, such as the underbelly, tyres and windscreen.

➡ At pick-up inspect the vehicle for any damage. Make a note of anything on the contract before you sign.

➡ Ask about breakdown and accident procedures.

➡ If you can, return the vehicle during business hours and insist on an inspection in your presence.

Sydney to Brisbane via the Pacific Hwy

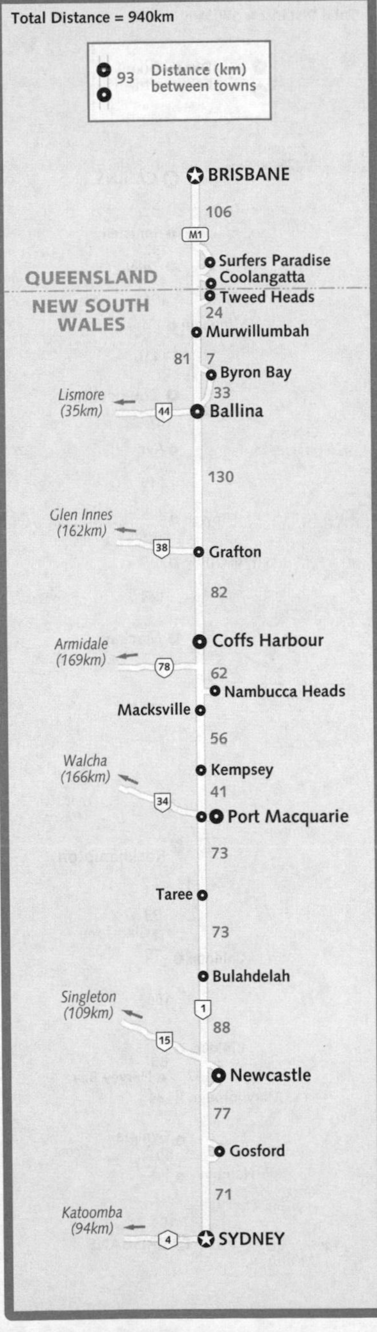

Brisbane to Cairns via the Bruce Hwy

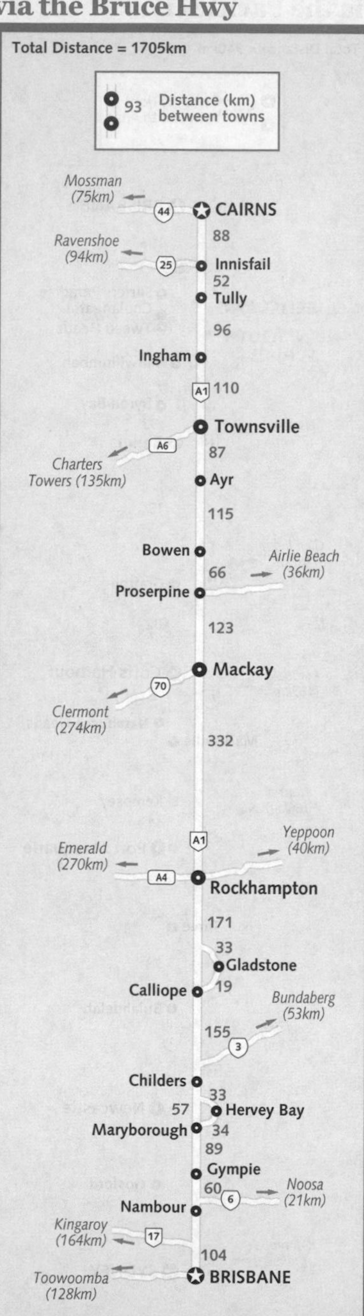

The usual big international companies all operate in Australia (Avis, Budget, Europcar, Hertz, Thrifty). The following websites offer last-minute discounts and give you the opportunity to compare rates between the big operators:

Carehire (www.carhire.com.au)

Drive Now (www.drivenow.com.au)

Webjet (www.webjet.com.au)

4WDS

Having a 4WD is essential for off-the-beaten-track driving into the outback. The major car-hire companies have 4WDs.

Renting a 4WD is affordable if a few people get together: something like a Nissan X-Trail (which can get you through most, but not all, tracks) costs around $100 to $150 per day; for a Toyota Landcruiser you're looking at around $150 up to $200, which should include unlimited kilometres.

Check the insurance conditions, especially the excess (which can be up to $5000), as they can be onerous and policies might not cover damage caused when travelling off-road. A refundable bond is also often required – this can be as much as $7500.

CAMPERVANS

Companies for campervan hire – with rates from around $90 (two berths) or $150 (four berths) per day, usually with minimum five-day hire and unlimited kilometres – include the following:

Apollo (☎1800 777 779; www.apollocamper.com, www.hippiecamper.com) Also has a backpacker-focused brand called Hippie Camper.

Britz (☎1300 738 087; www.britz.com.au)

Jucy Rentals (☎1800 150 850; www.jucy.com.au)

Maui (1300 363 800; www.maui.com.au)

Mighty Cars & Campers (☎1800 670 232; www.mightycampers.com)

Spaceships Campervans (☎1300 132 469; www.spaceshipsrentals.com.au)

Travelwheels (☎1800 289 222; www.travelwheels.com.au)

ONE-WAY RELOCATIONS

Relocations are usually cheap deals, although they don't allow much time flexibility. Most of the large hire companies offer deals, or try the following operators. See also www.hippiecamper.com and www.drivenow.com.au.

imoova (☎1300 789 059; www.imoova.com)

Relocations2Go (☎1800 735 627; www.relocations2go.com)

Transfercar (☎02-8011 1870; www.transfercar.com.au)

ROAD DISTANCES (KM)

	Adelaide	Albany	Alice Springs	Birdsville	Brisbane	Broome	Cairns	Canberra	Cape York	Darwin	Kalgoorlie	Melbourne	Perth	Sydney	Townsville
Albany	2649														
Alice Springs	1512	3573													
Birdsville	1183	3244	1176												
Brisbane	1942	4178	1849	1573											
Broome	4043	2865	2571	3564	5065										
Cairns	3079	5601	2396	1919	1705	4111									
Canberra	1372	4021	2725	2038	1287	5296	2923								
Cape York	4444	6566	3361	2884	2601	5076	965	3888							
Darwin	3006	5067	1494	2273	3774	1844	2820	3948	3785						
Kalgoorlie	2168	885	3092	2763	3697	3052	5234	3540	6199	4896					
Melbourne	728	3377	2240	1911	1860	4811	3496	637	4461	3734	2896				
Perth	2624	411	3548	3219	4153	2454	6565	3996	7530	4298	598	3352			
Sydney	1597	4246	3109	2007	940	5208	2634	289	3599	3917	3765	862	3869		
Townsville	3237	5374	2055	1578	1295	3770	341	2582	1306	2479	4893	3155	5349	2293	
Uluru	1559	3620	441	1617	2290	3012	2837	2931	3802	1935	3139	2287	3595	2804	2496

	Bicheno	Cradle Mountain	Devonport	Hobart	Launceston
Cradle Mountain	383				
Devonport	283	100			
Hobart	186	296	334		
Launceston	178	205	105	209	
Queenstown	443	69	168	257	273

These are the shortest distances by road; other routes may be considerably longer. For distances by coach, check the companies' leaflets.

Insurance

Third-party insurance With the exception of NSW and Queensland, third-party personal-injury insurance is included in the vehicle-registration cost, ensuring that every registered vehicle carries at least minimum insurance (if registering in NSW or Queensland you'll need to arrange this privately). We recommend extending that minimum to at least third-party property insurance – minor collisions can be amazingly expensive.

Rental vehicles When it comes to hire cars, understand your liability in the event of an accident. Rather than risk paying out thousands of dollars, consider taking out comprehensive car insurance or paying an additional daily amount to the rental company for excess reduction (this reduces the excess payable in the event of an accident from between $2000 and $5000 to a few hundred dollars).

Exclusions Be aware that if travelling on dirt roads you usually will not be covered by insurance unless you have a 4WD (read the fine print). Also, many companies' insurance won't cover the cost of damage to glass (including the windscreen) or tyres.

Auto Clubs

Under the auspices of the **Australian Automobile Association** (☎02-6247 7311; www.aaa.asn.au) are automobile clubs in each state, handy when it comes to insurance, regulations, maps and roadside assistance. Club membership (around $100 to $150) can save you a lot of trouble if things go wrong mechanically. If you're a member of an auto club in your home country, check if reciprocal rights are offered in Australia. The major Australian auto clubs generally offer reciprocal rights in other states and territories.

AANT (Automobile Association of the Northern Territory; ☎13 11 11; www.aant.com.au) NT.

NRMA (National Roads & Motorists' Association; ☎13 11 22; www.mynrma.com.au) NSW and the ACT.

RAC (Royal Automobile Club of Western Australia; ☎13 17 03; www.rac.com.au) WA.

RACQ (Royal Automobile Club of Queensland; ☎13 19 05; www.racq.com.au) Queensland.

RACT (Royal Automobile Club of Tasmania; ☎13 27 22; www.ract.com.au) Tasmania.

RACV (Royal Automobile Club of Victoria; ☎13 72 28; www.racv.com.au) Victoria.

Road Rules

Australians drive on the left-hand side of the road and all cars are right-hand drive.

Give way An important road rule is 'give way to the right' – if an intersection is unmarked (unusual) and at roundabouts, you must give way to vehicles entering the intersection from your right.

Speed limits The general speed limit in built-up and residential areas is 50km/h. Near schools, the limit is usually 25km/h (sometimes 40km/h) in the morning and afternoon. On the highway it's usually 100km/h or 110km/h; in the NT it's either 110km/h or 130km/h. Police have speed radar guns and cameras and are fond of using them in strategic locations.

Seatbelts and car seats It's the law to wear seatbelts in the front and back seats; you're likely to get a fine if you don't. Small children must be belted into an approved safety seat.

Drink-driving Random breath-tests are common. If you're caught with a blood-alcohol level of more than 0.05%, expect a fine and the loss of your licence. Police can randomly pull any driver over for a breathalyser or drug test.

Mobile phones Using a mobile phone while driving is illegal in Australia (excluding hands-free technology).

Hazards & Precautions

BEHIND THE WHEEL

Fatigue Be wary of driver fatigue; driving long distances (particularly in hot weather) can be utterly exhausting. Falling asleep at the wheel is not uncommon. On a long haul, stop and rest every two hours or so; do some exercise, change drivers or have a coffee.

Road trains Be careful overtaking road trains (trucks with two or three trailers stretching for as long as 50m); you'll need distance and plenty of speed. On single-lane roads get right off the road when one approaches.

Unsealed roads Unsealed road conditions vary wildly and cars perform differently when braking and turning on dirt. Don't exceed 80km/h on dirt roads; if you go faster you won't have time to respond to a sharp turn, stock on the road or an unmarked gate or cattle grid.

ANIMAL HAZARDS

➡ Roadkill is a huge problem in Australia, particularly in the NT, Queensland, NSW, SA and Tasmania. Many Australians avoid travelling once the sun drops because of the risks posed by nocturnal animals on the roads.

➡ Kangaroos are common on country roads, as are cows and sheep in the unfenced outback. Kangaroos are most active around dawn and dusk and often travel in groups: if you see one hopping across the road, slow right down, as its friends may be just behind it.

➡ If you hit and kill an animal while driving, pull it off the road, preventing the next car from having a potential accident. If the animal is only injured and is small, perhaps an orphaned joey (baby kangaroo), wrap it in a towel or blanket and call the relevant wildlife rescue line:

Department of Environment & Heritage Protection (☎1300 264 625; www.ehp.qld.gov.au) Queensland.

Department of Parks & Wildlife (Wildcare Helpline ☎08-9474 9055; www.parks.dpaw.wa.gov.au) WA.

Fauna Rescue of South Australia (☎08-7226 0017; www.faunarescue.org.au)

NSW Wildlife Information, Rescue & Education Service (WIRES; ☎1300 094 737; www.wires.org.au)

Parks & Wildlife Service (☎01300 827 727, after hours ☎03-6165 4305; www.parks.tas.gov.au) Tasmania.

Wildcare Inc NT (☎0408 885 341, 08-8988 6121; www.wildcarent.org.au)

Wildlife Victoria (☎1300 094 535; www.wildlifevictoria.org.au)

Fuel

Fuel types Unleaded and diesel fuel is available from service stations sporting well-known international brand names. LPG (liquefied petroleum gas) is not always stocked at more remote roadhouses; if you're on gas it's safer to have dual-fuel capacity.

Costs Prices vary from place to place, but at the time of writing unleaded was hovering between $1.20 and $1.50 in the cities. Out in the country, prices soar – in outback NT, SA, WA and Queensland you can pay as much as $2.20 per litre.

Availability In cities and towns petrol stations proliferate, but distances between fill-ups can be long in the outback. That said, there are only a handful of tracks where you'll require a long-range fuel tank. On main roads there'll be a small town or roadhouse roughly every 150km to 200km. Many petrol stations, but not all, are open 24 hours.

Resources

Australian Bureau of Meteorology (www.bom.gov.au) Weather information.

Department of Planning, Transport & Infrastructure (☎1300 361 033; www.transport.sa.gov.au) SA road conditions.

Green Vehicle Guide (www.greenvehicleguide.gov.au) Rates Australian vehicles based on greenhouse and air-pollution emissions.

Live Traffic NSW (☎1300 131 122; www.livetraffic.com) NSW road conditions.

Main Roads Western Australia (☎13 81 38; www.mainroads.wa.gov.au) WA road conditions.

Motorcycle Council of NSW (☎1300 679 622; www.mccofnsw.org.au) One of many such organisations around Australia.

Road Report (☎1800 246 199; www.roadreport.nt.gov.au) NT road conditions.

Traffic & Travel Information (☎13 19 40; www.transport.sa.gov.au) Queensland road conditions.

Hitching

Hitching is never entirely safe in any country in the world, and we don't recommend it. Travellers who decide to hitch should understand that they are taking a small but potentially serious risk. People who do choose to hitch will be safer if they travel in pairs and let someone know where they are planning to go.

Local Transport

All of Australia's major towns have reliable, affordable public bus networks, and there are suburban train lines in Sydney, Melbourne, Brisbane, Adelaide and Perth. Melbourne also has trams (Adelaide has one!), and Sydney has harbour ferries and a light-rail line. Taxis operate Australia-wide.

See regional chapters for detailed info.

Tours

Backpacker-style and more formal bus tours offer a convenient way to get from A to B and see the sights on the way. Following are some multistate operators; see regional chapters for smaller companies operating within individual states and territories.

AAT Kings (☎1300 228 546; www.aatkings.com) Big coach company (popular with the older set) with myriad tours all around Australia.

Adventure Tours Australia (☎1300 654 604; www.adventuretours.com.au) Affordable, young-at-heart tours in all states.

Autopia Tours (☎03-9397 7758; www.autopiatours.com.au) One- to three-day trips from Melbourne, Adelaide and Sydney.

Groovy Grape Tours (☎1800 661 177; www.groovygrape.com.au) Small-group, SA-based operator running one-day to one-week tours ex-Adelaide, Melbourne and Alice Springs.

Nullarbor Traveller (☎1800 816 858; www.thetraveller.net.au) Small company running relaxed minibus trips across the Nullarbor Plain between SA and WA.

Oz Experience (☎1300 300 028; www.ozexperience.com) Backpacker tour covering central, northern and eastern Australia in a U-shaped route – Cairns, Brisbane, Sydney, Melbourne, Adelaide, Alice Springs and Darwin – utilising Greyhound bus services.

Train

Long-distance rail travel in Australia is something you do because you really want to – not because it's cheap, convenient or fast. That said, trains are more comfortable than buses, and there is a certain long-distance 'romance of the rails' that's alive and kicking. Shorter-distance rail services within most states are run by state rail bodies, either government or private.

The three major interstate services in Australia are operated by **Great Southern Rail** (☎13 21 47; www.greatsouthernrail.com.au), namely the Indian Pacific between Sydney and Perth, the Overland between Melbourne and Adelaide, and the Ghan between Adelaide and Darwin via Alice Springs. There's also the new high-speed Spirit of Queensland service between Brisbane and Cairns, operated by **Queensland Rail** (☎13 16 17; www.queenslandrail.com.au). Trains from Sydney to Brisbane, Melbourne and Canberra are operated by **NSW TrainLink** (☎13 22 32; www.nswtrainlink.info). Within Victoria, **V/Line** (www.vline.com.au) runs trains, linking up with buses for connections into NSW, SA and the ACT.

Costs

Following are standard online one-way fares booked in advance. Backpacker discounts are also available.

Adelaide–Darwin Adult/child seated from $929/433; cabin from $1709/1489.

Adelaide–Melbourne Adult/child seated from $139/71.

Adelaide–Perth Adult/child seated from $589/273; cabin from $1349/1161.

Brisbane–Cairns Adult/child seated from $269/135; cabin from $519/311.

Sydney–Canberra Adult/child seated from $57/28.

Sydney–Brisbane Adult/child seated from $91/65; cabin from $216/179.

Sydney–Melbourne Adult/child seated from $91/65; cabin from $216/179.

Sydney–Perth Adult/child seated from $939/438, cabin from $1929/1689.

Train Passes

Queensland Rail offers the **Queensland Coastal Pass** allowing unlimited stopovers one way between Cairns and Brisbane in either direction. A one-month Coastal Pass costs $209; two months is $289. The **Queensland Explorer Pass** is similar but extends over the entire state rail network. A one-month Explorer Pass costs $299; two months is $389.

Great Southern Rail offers international visitors the **Rail Explorer Pass**, costing $545/655 per person for three/six months. Travel is on the Ghan, the Overland and the Indian Pacific (seated, not in cabins).

NSW TrainLink has the **Discovery Pass** for both international visitors and Australians, allowing unlimited one-way economy travel around NSW, plus connections to Brisbane, the Gold Coast, Melbourne and Canberra. A 14-day/one-/three-/six-month pass costs $232/275/298/420; premium-class upgrades are available.

Behind the Scenes

SEND US YOUR FEEDBACK

We love to hear from travellers – your comments keep us on our toes and help make our books better. Our well-travelled team reads every word on what you loved or loathed about this book. Although we cannot reply individually to your submissions, we always guarantee that your feedback goes straight to the appropriate authors, in time for the next edition. Each person who sends us information is thanked in the next edition – the most useful submissions are rewarded with a selection of digital PDF chapters.

Visit **lonelyplanet.com/contact** to submit your updates and suggestions or to ask for help. Our award-winning website also features inspirational travel stories, news and discussions.

Note: We may edit, reproduce and incorporate your comments in Lonely Planet products such as guidebooks, websites and digital products, so let us know if you don't want your comments reproduced or your name acknowledged. For a copy of our privacy policy visit lonelyplanet.com/privacy.

OUR READERS

Many thanks to the travellers who used the last edition and wrote to us with helpful hints, useful advice and interesting anecdotes: Candace Milner, Daniel Koschyk, Fiona Grech, Gabrielle Jameson, Gordon Liddle, Inèz Deckers, Jaap Prins, Jeff Rothman, Jeroen Loopstra, Jildau van den Berg, Julia Pursche, Karen Gibb, Kate Broadhurst, Knut Olawsky, Lara Dilger, Lise Gausset, Mick Pope, Olivia Hefford, Paul & Nicola Bilsby, Rebekah Boynton, Ross Hartley, Sain Alizada, ShyhPoh Teo, Theresa Philbrick, Tony Foster, Ute Zeitler, Viveca Gardiner, Zuzana Betkova

AUTHOR THANKS

Charles Rawlings-Way

Huge thanks to Tasmin for the gig, and to our crew of highway-addled co-authors. Thanks also to the all-star in-house LP production staff, and the friends who helped us out (or held our hands) on the road: Christian, Lauren, Rachel, Brett and all the kids in Brisbane; Mark, Cath, Fred, Lucy and the kids in Hobart; Georgie, Luke and the kids on KI (kids everywhere!); and Helen in Launceston. Special thanks as always to Meg, my road-trippin' sweetheart, and our daughters, Ione and Remy, who provided countless laughs, unscheduled pit-stops and ground-level perspectives along the way.

Meg Worby

A big thank you to Tasmin. Kudos to the in-house team at Lonely Planet for turning many weeks of exploration into this most reliable of handheld devices. Huge thanks to all our interstate friends for great company and insider tips. Love to the small and unflappable travellers, Ione and Remy, who saw snow for the first time on this trip. Thank you, as ever, to Charles: a pro.

Kate Armstrong

Thanks to Tasmin Waby for the opportunity to explore and write about my own country; in Broome, Robyn Maher, Liz Jack and the Chomley family; Neville Poelina for sharing his traditional and age-old wisdom; fellow authors Brett Atkinson and Steve Waters (WA). In Queensland: Jon and Chris Bowie for their early-morning swim meets, laughs and Noosa goss; Susan Ewington and Emily Comer; Mary and Ron for a genuine local take.

Brett Atkinson

Thanks to the helpful folk at visitor information centres and national parks offices throughout WA, NSW and Canberra. Special thanks to Jayde and Michelle in Perth, and *ahoj* and *děkuji* to Greg and Francie in Mathoura for the coffee and scones after an 'interesting' morning. At LP, cheers to Tasmin Waby, my fellow scribes, and the hardworking editors and cartographers. Final thanks to Carol for holding the fort across the ditch in New Zealand so we could escape to Burma.

Carolyn Bain

Big thanks to Tasmin Waby for the fun gig, Nick Smales for sorting out a decent car for me, and all the warm friendly locals who answered my questions and entertained me with stories. Much gratitude to octogenarian ex-miners in Broken Hill up for a yarn, to Lightning Ridge opal miners up for a yarn, and to chatty winemakers, museum volunteers and fellow travellers all over the state – you make this job a joy.

Celeste Brash

Thanks mostly to my husband and kids for supporting my crazy job. In Australia, big thanks to Tamara Sheward and family, Shawn Low, all the good folks at visitors centres along the coast, Peter and Eileen in Rubyvale, Whitsunday Bookings, koalas, wallabies, platypuses and all the unwitting travellers who became my spies. Special thanks to Tasmin Waby for sending me to OZ and for all the encouragement along the way.

Peter Dragicevich

I owe a great debt of thanks to all my Sydney support crew, particularly David Mills, Barry Sawtell, Tony Dragicevich, Debbie Debono, Tim Moyes and Michael Woodhouse. Thanks for sacrificing your stomachs and livers so enthusiastically for this book.

Anthony Ham

Heartfelt thanks to Tasmin Waby and to countless locals who shared their passion and expertise for this wonderful corner of the earth. To Marina, Carlota and Valentina – *os quiero*.

Paul Harding

Thanks to all the travellers and Queenslanders who, perhaps unknowingly, helped along the way. Thanks to Tasmin Waby for getting me on board and to all the team at LP. But mostly, thanks to Hannah and Layla for everything.

Alan Murphy

I would like to dedicate my work on this book to Maggie. There were so many people who helped with research on this update, a huge thanks to all I met on the road. A special thanks goes to Andy and Ellie in Darwin for their tips on the city and their hospitality. Lastly, thanks to my wife Alison, who is my strength and my home.

Miriam Raphael

Thank you Tasmin Waby for getting in touch, Di Schallmeiner and Lauren Wellicome for your insanely quick responses to my Christo crises (real and imagined), and the editing team for their flexibility around the birth of baby-Raph. Cheers to all the north coast locals who so happily shared their secrets. A huge thanks to Ken's red pen (let that ink never run out) and my wing-peeps Marcel and Pearl.

Benedict Walker

A massive shout out to Tasmin Waby for giving me a chance, for my Mum and travel buddy who never stops believing in me, my beloved wife-of-sorts, Sarah Sabell, for keeping me smiling on the road – as well as the ever-amazing Katie Avis, to Olivia at Leah Jay and my mystery landlord for helping me find the perfect writer's pad (let me stay forever!), to Rog at Punsand Bay for being the best 4WD tour guide anyone could hope for, to the Walkers and the Cowies for always putting me up and putting up with me and to Lonely Planet for truly allowing me to live my dreams as a traveller and writer: we live on an amazing planet. Thanks also to my Facebook friends for spurring me on and to all the amazing Queenslanders I met along the way. Buckets of gratitude all round!

Steve Waters

Thanks to the hire-car folks at Broome airport, the CP people for the late checkout in Exmouth, the tyre repair guys at Drysdale and Paraburdoo, Leonie and Nev for beer and sunsets, Trace & Heath, Brodie, Abbidene, Meika and Kaeghan for Wedge Love, Honest Ed's Steak & Car Cleaning Service, Roz and Megan for caretaking, Hamish for putting up with the same playlist forever and Seb and Tasmin for guiding me through the twittersphere.

ACKNOWLEDGEMENTS

Climate map data adapted from Peel MC, Finlayson BL & McMahon TA (2007) 'Updated World Map of the Köppen-Geiger Climate Classification', *Hydrology and Earth System Sciences*, 11, 1633–44.

Cover photograph: Hikers on the base walk at Uluru (Ayers Rock), Andrew Watson/AWL.

Page 14 photograph, bottom right: Image courtesy of MONA Museum of Old and New Art, Hobart, Tasmania, Australia.

THIS BOOK

This 18th edition of Lonely Planet's *Australia* was researched and written by 13 fabulous Lonely Planet writers. To see who did what, see Our Writers on page 1112. We'd also like to thank the following people for their contributions to this guide: Dr Michael Cathcart, Cathy Craigie and Dr Tim Flannery. Andrew Tudor wrote the Where to Surf section in the Australia Outdoors chapter. This guidebook was produced by the following:

Destination Editor Tasmin Waby

Product Editors Kate Chapman, Katie O'Connell

Senior Cartographer Julie Sheridan

Book Designer Wibowo Rusli

Assisting Editors Andrew Bain, Judith Bamber, Imogen Bannister, Michelle Bennett, Sarah Billington, Melanie Dankel, Kate Evans, Kate James, Jodie Martire, Anne Mulvaney, Jenna Myers, Lauren O'Connell, Charlotte Orr, Susan Paterson, Martine Power, Victoria Smith

Cartographers Hunor Csutoros, Rachel Imeson

Cover Researcher Naomi Parker

Thanks to Carolyn Boicos, Jo Cooke, Mark Griffiths, Anna Harris, Kate Kiely, Anne Mason, Kate Mathews, Claire Naylor, Karyn Noble, Diana Saengkham, Dianne Schallmeiner, Ellie Simpson, Angela Tinson, Samantha Tyson, Lauren Wellicome, Amanda Williamson

Index

A

Map Pages **000**
Photo Pages **000**

B

Map Pages **000**
Photo Pages **000**

H

N

Map Pages **000**
Photo Pages **000**

Q

R

S

Map Pages **000**
Photo Pages **000**

Y

Z

Map Pages **000**
Photo Pages **000**

Map Legend

Sights

- Beach
- Bird Sanctuary
- Buddhist
- Castle/Palace
- Christian
- Confucian
- Hindu
- Islamic
- Jain
- Jewish
- Monument
- Museum/Gallery/Historic Building
- Ruin
- Shinto
- Sikh
- Taoist
- Winery/Vineyard
- Zoo/Wildlife Sanctuary
- Other Sight

Activities, Courses & Tours

- Bodysurfing
- Diving
- Canoeing/Kayaking
- Course/Tour
- Sento Hot Baths/Onsen
- Skiing
- Snorkelling
- Surfing
- Swimming/Pool
- Walking
- Windsurfing
- Other Activity

Sleeping

- Sleeping
- Camping

Eating

- Eating

Drinking & Nightlife

- Drinking & Nightlife
- Cafe

Entertainment

- Entertainment

Shopping

- Shopping

Information

- Bank
- Embassy/Consulate
- Hospital/Medical
- Internet
- Police
- Post Office
- Telephone
- Toilet
- Tourist Information
- Other Information

Geographic

- Beach
- Hut/Shelter
- Lighthouse
- Lookout
- Mountain/Volcano
- Oasis
- Park
- Pass
- Picnic Area
- Waterfall

Population

- Capital (National)
- Capital (State/Province)
- City/Large Town
- Town/Village

Transport

- Airport
- Border crossing
- Bus
- Cable car/Funicular
- Cycling
- Ferry
- Metro station
- Monorail
- Parking
- Petrol station
- Subway station
- Taxi
- Train station/Railway
- Tram
- Underground station
- Other Transport

Note: Not all symbols displayed above appear on the maps in this book

Routes

- Tollway
- Freeway
- Primary
- Secondary
- Tertiary
- Lane
- Unsealed road
- Road under construction
- Plaza/Mall
- Steps
- Tunnel
- Pedestrian overpass
- Walking Tour
- Walking Tour detour
- Path/Walking Trail

Boundaries

- International
- State/Province
- Disputed
- Regional/Suburb
- Marine Park
- Cliff
- Wall

Hydrography

- River, Creek
- Intermittent River
- Canal
- Water
- Dry/Salt/Intermittent Lake
- Reef

Areas

- Airport/Runway
- Beach/Desert
- Cemetery (Christian)
- Cemetery (Other)
- Glacier
- Mudflat
- Park/Forest
- Sight (Building)
- Sportsground
- Swamp/Mangrove

Miriam Raphael

NSW Central Coast, Byron Bay & Northern NSW Miriam has authored over a dozen books for Lonely Planet, racking up thousands of kilometres driving across Australia's wide brown lands in pursuit of the greatest hidden beaches, outback pub meals and curious characters. She regularly enthuses on all things travel for a range of Australian and international publications, while blogging about intrepid journeys with kids at SevenSuitcases.com. After many years living in Australia's extraordinary Northern Territory she has recently returned to her hometown of Sydney.

Benedict Walker

Cairns & the Daintree Rainforest, Cape York Peninsula Currently hanging by the beach near his Mum, in hometown Newcastle, Ben's plan of 'livin' the dream', spending his days between his three great loves, Australia, North America and Japan, seems to be coming to fruition: it's not greedy – it's just sharing the love! Ben has also co-written LP's *Japan*, *Canada*, and *Florida* guidebooks, written and directed a play, toured Australia managing travel for rockstars and is an avid photographer toying with his original craft of film-making. He's an advocate of following your dreams – they can come true. For updates, see www.wordsandjourneys.com.

Steve Waters

Coral Coast & the Pilbara, The Kimberley This was Steve's sixth trip to the north of WA and while some things hadn't changed (huge distances, heat, blowing a tyre on the Kalumburu Rd), others were totally different (Cape Range NP after the floods, volunteering for the Mornington Bird Census, trying to find the same restaurant in Exmouth). Then there was the added novelty of coming to grips with social media :) Steve's written online articles on WA and co-authored previous editions of *Australia*, *Indonesia*, *Great Adventures* and *Best in Travel* and come the next Dry, will probably be heading north once again.

Carolyn Bain

Central & Outback NSW Every summer of her childhood, Carolyn's family whizzed through regional NSW (twice) on the 3500km return journey from their home near Melbourne to the beaches of the Gold Coast. On this research trip Carolyn had considerably more time to explore, and covered 6500km of glorious NSW scenery under big blue skies, from the scorching sands of Mungo to the vineyards of Mudgee. The outback's 40°C temps made a change from her usual travel-writing stomping grounds of Iceland and Denmark. Read more at carolynbain.com.au.

Celeste Brash

Fraser Island & the Fraser Coast, Capricorn Coast & the Southern Reef Islands, Whitsunday Coast, Townsville & Mission Beach Celeste has the great fortune to specialize in destinations involving islands, beaches and coral cays so the Queensland Coast was a match made in heaven. She's contributed to around 50 Lonely Planet guidebooks and her award winning writing has appeared in publications from BBC Travel to National Geographic's Intelligent Traveller. After 15 years in the South Pacific she now lives with her husband and two children in Portland, Oregon.

Peter Dragicevich

Sydney & Around After a decade of frequent flights between his native New Zealand and Sydney, the lure of the bright lights and endless beach days drew Peter across the Tasman on a more permanent basis. For the best part of the next decade he would call Sydney's inner suburbs home, while serving as general manager for various newspaper and magazine titles. More recently he's co-authored dozens of titles for Lonely Planet, including the East Coast Australia and Sydney guidebooks.

Read more about Peter at:
http://auth.lonelyplanet.com/profiles/peterdragicevich

Anthony Ham

Melbourne & Around, Great Ocean Road, Gippsland & Wilsons Promontory, Grampians & the Goldfields, Victorian High Country, Northwest Victoria, North & Western Tasmania Anthony (anthonyham.com) was born in Melbourne, grew up in Sydney and spent much of his adult life travelling the world. He recently returned to Australia after ten years living in Madrid and brings to this guide more than fifteen years' experience as a travel writer. As a recently returned expat, Anthony is loving the opportunity to rediscover his country and indulge his passion for wilderness. He brings to the book the unique perspective of knowing the land intimately and yet seeing it anew as if through the eyes of an outsider.

Paul Harding

Outback Queensland & Gulf Savannah Though born and raised down south in Victoria, Paul has an enduring passion for the great Australian outback – and for a great road trip – so it was an easy decision to take on the vast Queensland Outback and Gulf Savannah for this edition. After clocking up almost 6000km, two dozen outback pubs, countless cattle, a variety of roaming wildlife, a few fossils and some great Aussie characters, he's very glad he did. A travel writer and photographer, and backpacker at heart, Paul has contributed to almost 40 Lonely Planet guides, including numerous Australia titles. He still lives in Melbourne.

Alan Murphy

Darwin & Around, Uluru & Outback NT Alan has travelled extensively across Australia and worked on several Australian guidebook titles for Lonely Planet. The Northern Territory, with its ancient landscapes, outback characters and Indigenous culture holds a special place in his heart. For this update he criss-crossed the enormous expanse of the Territory and loved discovering new places. Alan has also written several online articles on the NT's Indigenous Australians and feels privileged to have had the opportunity of learning more about their culture on this trip.

OUR STORY

A beat-up old car, a few dollars in the pocket and a sense of adventure. In 1972 that's all Tony and Maureen Wheeler needed for the trip of a lifetime – across Europe and Asia overland to Australia. It took several months, and at the end – broke but inspired – they sat at their kitchen table writing and stapling together their first travel guide, *Across Asia on the Cheap*. Within a week they'd sold 1500 copies. Lonely Planet was born.

Today, Lonely Planet has offices in Franklin, London, Melbourne, Oakland, Beijing and Delhi, with more than 600 staff and writers. We share Tony's belief that 'a great guidebook should do three things: inform, educate and amuse'.

OUR WRITERS

Charles Rawlings-Way

Brisbane & Around, Hobart & Southeast Tasmania, Launceston & Eastern Tasmania, Adelaide & Around, Barossa Valley & Southeastern SA, Yorke Peninsula & Western SA, Flinders Ranges & Outback SA As a likely lad, Charles suffered in shorts through Tasmanian winters, and in summer counted the days til he visited his grandparents in Adelaide. With desert-hot days, cool swimming pools and *four* TV stations, this flat city held paradisiacal status. Little did he know that Brisbane was just as alluring – a fact confirmed by more recent encounters with the city's bookshops, bars and band rooms. Returning to Tasmania, he was thrilled to discover that Hobart has good coffee now and there's still snow on the mountain. Charles has penned 20-something Lonely Planet guidebooks. Charles also wrote the Australia Today, Food & Drink, Sport, Planning and Survival Guide chapters.

Meg Worby

Brisbane & Around, Hobart & Southeast Tasmania, Launceston & Eastern Tasmania, Adelaide & Around, Barossa Valley & Southeastern SA, Yorke Peninsula & Western SA, Flinders Ranges & Outback SA Let's do this by the numbers: this was Meg's fourth trip to ever-beautiful Tasmania, her seventh trip to temperate Queensland and her 780th re-entry into her most habitable home state of South Australia. She is a former member of Lonely Planet's languages, editorial, web and publishing teams in Melbourne and London. This is her eighth Lonely Planet guidebook as an author. Meg also wrote the Australia Today, Food & Drink, Sport, Planning and Survival Guide chapters.

Kate Armstrong

Surfers Paradise & the Gold Coast, Noosa & the Sunshine Coast, Broome Kate is a Victorian, but for years has enjoyed migrating northwards for the warmth and laid back attitudes of sunny Queensland. Having recently ditched her surfboard, for this edition, she bodysurfed at 6am daily. She also loved hitting the regions' foodie scenes and was thrilled to visit the Dampier Peninsula for the first time. With over 30 overseas LP titles to her name, Kate also finally enjoyed getting her car dirty in her own backyard. See more adventures at www.katearmstrong.com.au and @nomaditis.

Brett Atkinson

Canberra & NSW South Coast, Southern NSW, Perth & Fremantle, Around Perth, Margaret River & the Southwest Coast, Southern WA, Monkey Mia & the Central West For this edition, Brett flew across the gorges of WA's Karijini National Park, explored the galleries, museums and emerging urban vibe of Canberra, and uncovered even more excellent Australian craft breweries on both the west and east coasts of the country. Brett is based in Auckland, New Zealand and has covered around 50 countries as a guidebook author and travel and food writer. See www.brett-atkinson.net for his most recent work and upcoming travels.

OVER PAGE MORE WRITERS

Published by Lonely Planet Publications Pty Ltd
ABN 36 005 607 983
18th edition – Nov 2015
ISBN 978 1 74321 3889

10 9 8 7 6 5 4 3 2 1
Printed in Singapore